THE WORKS OF GEOFFREY CHAUCER

THE WORKS OF

Geoffrey Chaucer

A FACSIMILE OF THE WILLIAM MORRIS

Kelmscott Chaucer

WITH THE ORIGINAL 87 ILLUSTRATIONS BY EDWARD BURNE-JONES

TOGETHER WITH AN INTRODUCTION BY

John T. Winterich

AND A GLOSSARY FOR THE MODERN READER

THE WORLD PUBLISHING COMPANY

CLEVELAND AND NEW YORK

Introduction BY JOHN T. WINTERICH

GEOFFREY CHAUCER'S is the earliest voice in English poetry that still sounds a clear and universal note. He had forerunners, but today they are studied rather than read. During the five and a half centuries that have passed since Chaucer's death, his audience has come to circle the world. In America alone, twelve editions of *The Canterbury Tales* are available, one of them a forty-five-cent paperback.

The most memorable and beautiful edition of Chaucer's works was published in England in 1896. It was conceived, planned, designed, and seen through the press by William Morris, who had dedicated his life to poetry and the decorative arts, but who did not manifest an active interest in the production of fine books until he was in his fifty-fifth year. He died eight years later, but in that brief fragment of eternity he had established a validity and a prestige that still make him the most powerful and pervasive influence in book design in the English-speaking, English-reading world.

Today, endowed with the infallibility of hindsight, we can see how inevitable it was that these two great Englishmen, Geoffrey Chaucer and William Morris, living half a millennium apart, must one day meet on common ground, and that the later of them would build a great and durable monument to the earlier. It is fitting to discuss their careers and achievements briefly before moving on to the grand conjunction.

Geoffrey Chaucer was born in London between 1340 and 1345, the son of a prosperous wine importer who could afford to give him a good education, and undoubtedly did. That much is indicated by the extent of Chaucer's reading as revealed in his writing. In 1357, when he was no older than seventeen, he became a page in a noble household, and thereafter his nonliterary life was devoted to what we would now call the public service but was then called the king's business — and Chaucer lived under three kings: Edward III, Richard II, and Henry IV. He was charged with numerous important overseas missions, journeying often to France and occasionally to Italy. In addition he held various appointive offices at home. In 1394 Richard II awarded him a pension, and in 1399 Henry IV increased it. Chaucer died the following year, aged between fifty-five and sixty.

So much for his public career reduced to its bare bones — the sort of summary Chaucer himself might have prepared (with dates inserted) for a contemporary *Who's Who*. That same *Who's Who*, of course, would have included the important detail that in 1374 or earlier he married a lady of the court named Philippa Roet (as she was Flemish by birth, she probably pronounced it *root*); she died in 1386. Three Chaucers of the following generation — Elizabeth, Lewis, and Thomas — were presumably their children.

Chaucer wrote voluminously — *The Canterbury Tales* and much else: *The Book of the Duchesse, The Romaunt of the Rose* (in part), *The Hous of Fame, The Parlement of Foules* (birds), *Troilus and Cressida, The Legend of Goode Wimmen,* a translation of Boethius, *A Treatise on the Astrolabe,* and assorted odds and ends; some of the things that have been ascribed to him probably were not his work, others certainly were not.

v

If Chaucer had not written *The Canterbury Tales,* interest in his work would today be confined largely to the realm of scholarship. Fortunately for all of us, he did write them. *The Canterbury Tales* is a collection of stories told by a group of pilgrims who are riding to Canterbury, sixty miles from London, to pay homage to the memory of the martyred St. Thomas à Becket. There is about the expedition something of the air of a family picnic (if you can imagine a family picnic with horses and without children — and without a family, for that matter). The assembly point is the Tabard Inn, on the south bank of the Thames. On the eve of their departure, the company numbered thirty, including the landlord of the Tabard, who was going along too, and the over-all narrator, the "I" of the Prologue, Chaucer himself, under the thin disguise of plain "Geoffrey." It was as diverse a gathering of men and women (twenty-seven men and three women) as one could want; in drawing up his cast of characters, Chaucer was obviously aiming at a cross section of contemporary English society, and he scored a bull's-eye. The gentry are represented by a knight and his grown-up son, a prioress, a franklin (or country gentleman), a physician, and a well-to-do widow who has shed five husbands; at the other end of the social scale are a cook, a plowman, and a miller. In between are some of the most appealing and likable of Chaucer's people — the country parson and the Oxford student, for example. His descriptions (which read like condensed *New Yorker* profiles) are highly detailed; they tell what Chaucer's characters wore, what they ate and how they ate it, where they had traveled, what they talked like, how they earned their livings (and sometimes how much they earned), their manners or lack of them, their physical peculiarities, what made them tick.

The stories they tell are as varied in matter and manner as the tellers themselves. Chaucer's was a day (as was Shakespeare's) in which an author borrowed a plot as he might borrow a shilling, except that if he was an honest author he would pay back the shilling. Story-borrowing was wholly respectable — it was, in fact, a universal convention. Chaucer picked up two or three ideas from Boccaccio and improved them so extensively that Boccaccio's shade should have been grateful. He drew on his fellow countryman John Gower, on the Frenchman Jean de Meung, on the Italian Francesco Petrarca. He evolved a plot or two himself — a sensational innovation for his time. But wherever he got his material, he made it his own; he clothed it with life, endowed his characters with personality and soul. Some of his stories are as seemly as the most strait-laced headmistress of a young ladies' boarding school could ask; two are as rowdy and bawdy as anything ever written in English.

And many of them are fragments, for the vast edifice of *The Canterbury Tales* was never carried to completion. Chaucer's master plan called for two stories by each pilgrim on the road to Canterbury and two more on the ride back to London. That would have meant a grand total of one hundred and twenty stories. Actually there are only twenty-one. Some are complete, some are so nearly complete that they may be described as complete (and the little points that betray their incompleteness add immeasurably to their charm), still others had far to go. *The Canterbury Tales,* therefore, is an unfinished cathedral, but it towers above the sprawl of medieval England with magnificent authority, a superlative monument in which are enshrined a surpassing understanding of the hearts of men and a keen awareness of, and a kindly tolerance for, their failings.

Chaucer is as modern as Ogden Nash, but the language he wrote in was not. That language was Middle English, although Chaucer did not call it that, any more than he would have referred to the time in which he lived as the Middle Ages. Middle English had been preceded by Old English and was to be followed by Modern English. Old English was spoken and written from 700 to 1100, and Middle English from 1100 to 1450. These are the dates assigned by Professor John M. Clark of the University of Minnesota in *Early English: An Introduction to Old and Middle English;* Professor Clark is careful to explain that they are only approximate — that everybody did not suddenly switch from Old English to Middle English on New Year's Day of 1101.

If they had, it would have been a violent switch indeed — so violent that folks on one side of the linguistic fence would not have had the slightest idea what folks on the other side were talking about. Old English (or Anglo-Saxon) was a language in its own right, and a pretty rugged one. You can still study it, but if you prefer something simple, try Latin or Greek — they are infinitely easier, and French, Spanish, Italian, and German are easier still. Here is a sample of Old English from an account of the creation attributed to the poet Cædmon, who died toward the end of the seventh century:

Nu we sceolan herian	Now we shall praise
heofon-rices weard,	the guardian of heaven,
metodes mihte,	the might of the creator,
and his mod-ge-thonc,	and his counsel,
wera wuldor fæder!	the glory father of men!
swa he wundra ge-hwæs,	how he of all wonders,
ece dryhten,	the eternal lord,
oord onstealde.	formed the beginning.

Chaucer's English is much closer to the English of 1959 than it was to the English of 959. It contains a large infusion of French adoptions (this process began well before the Norman invasion of 1066), and these give it a pleasant air of up-to-dateness. The French adoptions really sound French, too, because in Middle English the continental pronunciation system was used, and it should be used by anyone reading Chaucer today. *Slepe* (disregard the terminal *e* for now; it will be discussed in a moment) is not *sleep* but *slape; seke* is not *seek* but *sake; lyf* is *leaf, ryde* is *reed. Night* is pronounced like its German cognate *nicht;* the *k* in *knight* is pronounced.

Make no mistake about it — Chaucer is not so easy to read as Shakespeare or Milton or Tennyson or Whitman or Robert Frost. And the very fact that he is so down-to-earth, so broadly and deeply and intimately concerned with the minutiae of everyday life in the Prologue to *The Canterbury Tales* and in many of the stories, adds to the difficulty. You can confront the same sort of difficulty with the language of the everyday life of our own time. An English motor mechanic (and if there had been motor mechanics in Chaucer's day he would have had one make the trip to Canterbury, and there would have been filling stations along the road) would call your battery an accumulator, your spark plugs sparking plugs, your windshield a windscreen, your hood a bonnet, your fender a mudguard; you would recognize his rendering of *tire,* but he would write it with a *y,* and he would put two *t*'s in *carburetor;* he would make adjustments not with a wrench but with a spanner, and he would fill your tank, of course, with petrol; he would call a traffic circle a round-about, a sedan a saloon car, and if your saloon car were brand new, he could caution you to drive it slowly not while you were breaking it in, but while you were running it in. You would need a glossary to understand him, and you will need a glossary to understand much of Chaucer. A glossary has been duly provided in the present volume.

Chaucer, in his multitudinous works, used a variety of meters, but *The Canterbury Tales* is written mainly in iambic pentameter — the noble measure of most of Shakespeare, of *Paradise Lost*, of *Idylls of the King*. The reader must continually bear in mind, however, that Chaucer, like the Greek and Roman poets before him, employs elision — the classical tradition was still strong. When a word ends in *e*, the *e* is pronounced (like the *a* in comma); *roote, soote, yonge, eye, ende,* for example, are dissyllables, not monosyllables. But when an *e* ending occurs immediately before a word beginning with a vowel or with *h*, the *e* is elided — simply dropped. (Elision is never carried over into the following line, however.)

As skillful a poetic craftsman as John Dryden was unaware of Chaucer's metrical precision (which was just as precise as Dryden's). "The verse of Chaucer, I confess," Dryden wrote in 1700, "is not harmonious to us." He could not agree with Thomas Speght, whose edition of Chaucer had appeared in 1597, and who "would make us believe the fault is in our ears, and that there were really ten syllables in a verse where we find but nine. It were an easy matter to produce some thousands of his verses which are lame for want of half a foot, and sometimes a whole one, and which no pronunciation can make otherwise." Yet Dryden himself, despite this completely erroneous criticism, left us one of the finest and most often quoted evaluations of Chaucer's greatness: "As he is the father of English poetry, so I hold him in the same degree of veneration as the Grecians held Homer, or the Romans Virgil. He is a perpetual fountain of good sense, learned in all sciences, and therefore speaks properly on all subjects. As he knew what to say, so he knows also when to leave off, a continence which is practised by few writers."

To accustom yourself to the music of Chaucer's prosody, approach his verse as you did your first dancing or piano lesson. Don't be afraid to count, or to mumble *de-dum, de-dum, de-dum*. Overstress the stresses until they begin to fall readily into place.

> And gládly wólde he lérne, and gládly téche.

(And remember those elisions.)

Like Geoffrey Chaucer, William Morris had the good sense to pick a prosperous father, and to choose London (or at least suburban London) for his birthplace. He was born at Walthamstow, Essex, March 24, 1834. William Morris, Sr., was a stockbroker, and did not have to extend himself to enroll his namesake in Exeter College, Oxford, in 1853. One of the first acquaintances Morris made at Oxford was a Birmingham youth named Edward Burne-Jones. Their friendship quickly developed into an intellectual and aesthetic partnership that was to endure until dissolved by death.

On leaving Oxford, Morris turned his attention to architecture at about the same time that Burne-Jones began to study drawing under Dante Gabriel Rossetti, leader of the Pre-Raphaelite movement, which sought to free art from the bondage of classical dogmatism. On the side, Morris took to writing poetry, and in 1858 he published a small collection called *The Defence of Guenevere*, but nobody paid much attention to it.

In 1861 Morris organized the firm of Morris, Marshall, Faulkner & Co. (Marshall was an authority on church decoration, and Faulkner an old Oxford associate), "Fine Art Workmen in Painting, Carving, Furniture, and the Metals"—the whole gamut of decoration, including jewelry, leather, stained glass, table glass, painted tile, pottery, embroidery, altar cloths, carpets, tapestries, candlesticks, wallpaper. It could be said of Morris, as Dr. Johnson said of Oliver Goldsmith, that he touched nothing that he did not adorn. In all this frenzy of artistic and administrative activity, Morris still found time to write *The Life and Death of Jason,* which was published in 1867, and *The Earthly Paradise* (three volumes), published in 1868-70. Both of these long narrative poems were highly successful —and each, significantly, contains a long tribute to Chaucer, and in each of these tributes Morris addresses Chaucer three times as his Master—with a capital M.

It was inevitable that Morris would one day turn his head, his heart, and his hand to the production of fine books—fine alike for their contents and for their investiture. The wonder is that the spark was so long in being struck. Not until twenty-seven years after the establishment of his decorating firm, not until he was midway of his fifty-fifth year, did Morris begin, and complete, his apprenticeship to the calling with which, ever since, his fame has been most closely associated, even to the exclusion of his still readable, still stirring verse. (He even wrote a sort of novel, *News from Nowhere,* an account of imagined existence in an ideal, decorative world; the book reflects his enthusiasm for his own specialized brand of aesthetic socialism.)

Morris had a neighbor named Emery Walker, a commercial printer who was both a skilled craftsman and a typographical connoisseur. In 1888, when a new book of Morris's, *The House of the Wolfings,* was in the making, Walker gave him some helpful suggestions that quickened Morris's consciousness of the physical book. From his school days on, Morris had shown a strong layman's interest in the niceties of typography and book design; he himself had a fine library, particularly of sixteenth-century books, with a good scattering of fifteenth—the first century of printing. Along with these treasures were books in manuscript dating back to the pre-printing era.

Morris had begun working out details for an Arts and Crafts Society exhibition, and he invited Walker to give an illustrated talk on printing. They worked together on the plan for this talk, examined material, selected slides. Morris's interest was sharply aroused by the enlarged details of type letters in the blueprint stage, and when Morris was aroused by an idea, that idea was going to go to work, and soon. Morris quickly came to envisage nothing less than a rebirth of the printing art, specifically of the art of the book—a return to the good taste and good sense and high dedication that had characterized the work of the earliest printers. What he envisaged was a sort of typographical Pre-Raphaelite movement.

He could not have picked a more propitious moment. The 1880's had inherited from the 1870's a quality (or lack of quality) called elegance which afflicted virtually every artifact—buildings of every sort and size, vehicles, dress, furniture, utensils that permitted any sort of ornamentation (and what utensil does not?), sculpture, wood carving. But on no area of human enterprise had the catastrophic hand of elegance descended more heavily or more blightingly than on books. Their outsides were prettied up with filigree, scrollwork, curlicues, scrimshaw, doodads; they were drowned in gilt, or attired, like Joseph, in coats of many colors. The insides were of a piece with the outsides. They looked, most of them, like the very devil, but to most people they seemed altogether wonderful and beyond words beautiful.

Setting out to implement his new program, Morris, characteristically, began at the the beginning. He designed a font of type. Type designing calls for much the same sort of facility with T square and compass and tracing paper as does house designing—Morris's drudgery in the architect's office stood him in good stead. By the end of 1890 the new type was ready—Morris christened it "Golden." The first book in which it was used was Morris's own *Story of the Glittering Plain;* the choice was dictated not by vanity, but by the fact that *The Glittering Plain* would make a small book, and a small book was desirable for experimentation.

Thus was the Kelmscott Press born (Kelmscott after Morris's country house in Gloucestershire). The press was not intended to be a commercial venture and it never became one — to break even was enough. But word of Morris's plans got out and requests for copies of the book came in, and the edition of two hundred copies was taken up before it was printed.

Between May 8, 1891, and March 24, 1898, the Kelmscott Press issued an over-all total of fifty-three units. Many of these units consisted of more than one volume — Keats was in two volumes, Shelley in three. Other authors represented by Kelmscott titles included Ruskin, Shakespeare (the poems only), Sir Thomas More, Tennyson, Rossetti, Swinburne. Five of the units were works which William Caxton, the first English printer and the first printer of Chaucer, had translated and printed. (In 1954, a single leaf of Caxton's *Chaucer* of 1478 sold at auction for $170.)

A majority of the Kelmscott Press books were printed in Golden type. Morris designed two other faces, which he christened "Troy" and "Chaucer." Golden was never used in combination with any other letter; Troy and Chaucer were frequently used together; Troy, in fact, was employed by itself in only one instance, Chaucer by itself in fourteen.

The Works of Geoffrey Chaucer was by long odds the most ambitious, the most massive, the most triumphant venture undertaken by the Kelmscott Press. Sheer physical bulk alone made its manufacture as much a problem in engineering as an act of artistic creation. Work on the *Chaucer* began on August 1, 1894. Only a single press was used at the start; a second was brought in six months later.

For the text, Morris chose Chaucer type. He could hardly have done otherwise, but it is a mistake to assert, as some authorities do, that the Chaucer type was designed especially for the *Chaucer;* the type had previously been used in fourteen Kelmscott books. Troy type was selected for the headings. There were eighty-seven woodcuts by Edward (now Sir Edward) Burne-Jones; these were engraved by W. H. Hooper (each engraving took him a week). Morris himself drew the borders, decorations, initials. The frames around the Burne-Jones woodcuts (there are fourteen different frame designs) were by Morris. He designed the title page — it took him two weeks. The over-all design of the book was also his, and he exercised general supervision over the entire production. The all-linen paper was especially made for the *Chaucer* by Joseph Batchelor at his mill near Ashford, Kent; the watermark was a perch with a spray in its mouth.

Morris took special care with the text. More than sixty fifteenth-century Chaucer manuscripts, some of them fragmentary, had become available to scholars over the centuries. The most trustworthy of these, in the opinion of the Chaucer Society, was that belonging to the Earl of Ellesmere. Walter William Skeat, the greatest living English philologist (he was professor of Anglo-Saxon at Cambridge University from 1878 until his death in 1912), and a ranking authority on fourteenth-century English literature, was using the Ellesmere manuscript as the basis for a seven-volume unexpurgated edition of

Chaucer which the Clarendon Press at Oxford began issuing in 1894. This was the text which Morris used.

Despite the magnitude of the enterprise (and of the book itself), its progress to completion was relatively uneventful. The one thing needful was to keep everlastingly at it. The *Chaucer* was the fortieth among the fifty-three Kelmscott books; most of the difficulties it might have encountered (paper, ink, presswork, vellum) had already been ironed out in processing the earlier volumes, which could have been regarded as dry runs for the *Chaucer*. The big job was simply more book. It was finished May 8, 1896 — one year, ten months, and seven days after the start. Publication date was June 26, 1896. The entire edition had been oversubscribed months earlier. It consisted of four hundred and twenty-five copies on paper at £20 each; forty-eight of the paper copies were bound in full white pigskin by Thomas J. Cobden-Sanderson of the Doves Bindery (who later established the Doves Press). The binding design was by Morris. The stamping of each binding, which was done by hand, required six days. These pigskin copies were priced at £33. There were thirteen copies on vellum, price 120 guineas each. Morris had originally planned for only three hundred and twenty-five paper copies, but orders streamed in so copiously that he added the extra hundred, with the express consent of all of the earlier subscribers.

The Kelmscott *Chaucer* was an expensive book to make; it was an expensive book to own. It still is. A good proportion of the edition was immediately absorbed into institutional collections and forever removed from the market; during the intervening years many other copies have found their way into other permanent repositories. But a copy still occasionally reaches the auction room or the rare-bookseller's shelves. Today a paper copy would probably be priced at from $800 to $1,200, a pigskin copy at around $1,750, a vellum copy at perhaps $15,000.

William Morris died on October 3, 1896, less than four months after the publication of the *Chaucer*. He was in his sixty-third year. He was buried at Kelmscott Manor, and his wife Jane and their daughters, Jane Alice and May, were at the grave.

The Kelmscott Press died with Morris, but its soul goes marching on. Forty-two books had already been published; eleven were still to appear, but they were books already in production, books to which the press was committed, or books by Morris which were published as a capstone to his writings and as a swan song to his great printing adventure. Nothing new was undertaken. Morris had toyed with the idea of publishing Shakespeare's plays in three volumes but had abandoned it; a suggestion for a reissue of the King James Bible of 1611 was in his pending file but might have stayed there indefinitely. But if he had lived, he would almost certainly have published a Froissart's *Chronicles* and a Malory's *Morte d'Arthur;* these and the *Chaucer* would have been the Big Three of the Kelmscott Press. The Malory was to have been illustrated with "at least" one hundred woodcuts by Sir Edward Burne-Jones. But Burne-Jones died in the spring of 1898, less than two years after Morris, and would probably have been unable to complete so formidable a task.

There is only one titan among the Kelmscotts: the *Chaucer*.

The final Kelmscott imprint was *A Note by William Morris on His Aims in Founding the Kelmscott Press.* "I began printing books," he wrote in this famous declaration of aesthetic faith, "with the hope of producing some which would have a definite claim to beauty, while at the same time they should be easy to read and should not dazzle the eye, or trouble the intellect of the reader by eccentricity of form in the letters."

The Kelmscott *Chaucer* has been described as a book for the lectern rather than for the lap. Its page measures 11 3/8 by 16 5/8 inches (almost the size of the Bruce Rogers World Bible, which is 13 1/2 by 18 3/4 inches — and which *is* a book for the lectern). A white pigskin copy of the *Chaucer* weighs 13 1/2 pounds. It is doubtful if anyone except the proofreader ever read a Kelmscott *Chaucer* clear through, all 553 pages of it (*The Canterbury Tales,* by the way, takes up less than half — 222 pages — of that total). The present edition, in which the page size has been slightly reduced, may legitimately be described as the first Kelmscott *Chaucer* ever published that is *designed for reading.*

But however little it may have been read, the Kelmscott *Chaucer,* and all the Kelmscott books, have been studied, examined, dissected by all succeeding generations of printing craftsmen. The Kelmscott was not the first private press (a private press may be defined, a shade too offhandedly, as one that subordinates profits to appearance), but it was far and away the most important private press in the history of printing measured by the influence it has exerted and continues to exert. It was directly responsible for the establishment of the host of private presses which followed it, especially in England and America. But the entire output of all these presses, as Douglas McMurtrie has pointed out, represents only "an infinitesimally small proportion" of all printing. Morris's influence extended much further than to a handful of books produced in small editions and sold (as they had to sell) for high prices. Today's novel or biography, today's dictionary and encyclopedia, today's school textbook, today's telephone book and checkbook are all likely to be better examples of good taste, good typography, and good craftsmanship because, toward the close of the nineteenth century, William Morris built the Kelmscott *Chaucer.*

Glossary

This glossary, based on Skeat's annotations, is designed to help the reader understand Chaucer's works in the original without undue difficulty. It is by no means a complete vocabulary, however, and serious students of the text are referred to the scholarly glossaries that may be found in modern editions of Chaucer's complete works. It has not been possible to list the many verb forms or varieties of spelling that occur in the text, and words not listed under one spelling may often be found under another. This is especially true for words containing *ay, ey, oy, aw, ew, ow, i,* which are sometimes entered as if spelled with *ai, ei, oi, au, eu, ou, y* respectively. The reader's attention is also called to the explanatory comments under *I-, M-, N-, T-, To-, Y-,* which may assist him in finding words not listed under their prefixes. The abbreviations *n., v., adj., adv.* refer to noun, verb, adjective, and adverb respectively; they have been used only where clarification is necessary.

A

abaissen, to be dismayed, disconcerted
abaved, confounded, disconcerted
abite, dress
abood, delay
abreyde, awake
abydinge, expectation
accesse, feverish attack
accidie, sloth
achatours, buyers
achoken, choke, stifle
acused, blamed
adawe, recover
adjeccioun, addition
afered, afraid
affiance, trust
affyle, make smooth
after, according to (as)
agaste, terrify
ageyn, against
agilten, do wrong
agregge, aggravate
agroted, surfeited, cloyed
agrysen, shudder, tremble
aknowe, conscious
al, *conj.* although; *adv.* quite
alaunts, mastiff-like dogs
alder-, of all
ale stake, ale-house pole to support a garland or sign
algates, in every way; nevertheless
aliene, alienate
allegged, allayed
alliaunce, kindred
alose, commend
amayed, dismayed
ambages, ambiguous words
amblere, ambling nag
amenuse, diminish
amerciments, fines
ameved, changed; perturbed
amonesteth, admonishes; recommends
amorettes, love knots
amorwe, on the morrow
amphibologyes, ambiguities
amy, friend
ancille, handmaiden
anhange, to hang
anientissed, brought to naught
anlas, two-edged knife or dagger

annueleer, a chaplain
anvelt, anvil
apalled, vapid; weakened; pale; languid
apaye, satisfy
apert, *adj.* manifest; *adv.* openly
apeyren, injure, impair
appropred, appropriated
approwours, informers
apyked, trimmed
arace, eradicate
arbitre, will, choice
archaungel, titmouse
archewyves, ruling wives
arede, explain; counsel
aretten, impute
arten, urge
arwe, arrow
ascaunce, as if; in such a way that; even as
asp, aspen
aspre, sharp
assoilen, pay; absolve
assure, feel secure, trust
asterte, escape
astonie, astonish
aswown, in a swoon
atake, overtake
atrede, surpass in counsel
atwinne, apart
auntre, risk
Austyn, St. Augustine
auter, altar
avale, fall down; take off
avaunt, boast
avenaunt, comely
aventure, chance; peril; misfortune
avouterye, adultery
avys, consideration
awen, own
aweyward, away, backward
awhape, amaze
awreke, avenge
ay, ever

B

ba, kiss
bachelere, aspirant to knighthood
bagge, look askance
balke, beam

bane, death; destruction; slayer
barbre, barbarian
batailled, notched with indentations
bathe, both
bauderye, bawdry; mirth
bawdryk, belt worn over one shoulder and across the chest
bedrede, bedridden
beme, trumpet
ben, been, be
bent, grassy slope
berd, beard; **make his berd,** fool him
bet, better
beth, are
bibbe, imbibe
bicched bones, dice
bidde, ask; request; command
biheste, promise; command
bihovely, helpful; needful
bijape, trick
biknowe, acknowledge
bilinne, cease
bille, petition; letter
bisemare, contemptuous conduct
bisette, employ; bestow
bismotered, marked with spots of rust
bisy, besy, industrious; active
bitake, commend; commit; resign
biware, spend
biwreye, reveal; betray
blake, ink
blandishe, fawn
blankmanger, creamed fowl or other meat, stewed with eggs, rice, almonds, and sugar
blende, blind; deceive
blinne, cease
blyve, soon
bobance, boast
boef, beef
boes, (it) behooves
bokeler, small round shield
bolle, bowl
bolt-upright, on (her) back
bord, table; board; meals
borel, coarse woolen clothes
borwe, *n.* pledge; *v.* borrow
bote, benefit; profit; help
bouk, trunk of the body
bour, bed-chamber; inner room
boydekin, dagger

bracer, guard for the arm in archery
breme, furious, furiously
brenne, burn
breste, burst
bretful, brimful
breyde, awake; start
brigge, bridge
brike, trap, dilemma
brinne, burn
brocage, mediation
brode, plainly; far and wide
brotel, frail; fickle; insecure
brouded, embroidered
brouke, enjoy, use
bulte, sift
burdoun, bass accompaniment of a song
burgeys, citizen
buriels, burial places
busk, bush
but-if, unless
byte, bite; cut deeply; burn

C

caas, cases
cacche, catch; lay hold of; come by
calle, net used to confine women's hair
camuse, low and concave
can, know
cantel, portion
capel, horse, nag
cappe, cap; set (someone's) cappe, make a fool of (someone)
careful, full of trouble; sorrowful
carl, man; countryman
carpe, talk, discourse
carrik, barge
cas, accident, chance; occasion
caste, cast (accounts); throw
catel, property, wealth, possessions
ceriously, with full details
ceruce, white lead ointment
ceynt, cincture
chaffare, bargaining; trade; merchandise
chalons, blankets or coverlets for a bed
chamberere, maidservant, lady's maid
champartye, equality, participation in power
chanon, canon
chapman, trader, merchant
chaunterie, endowment for payment of a priest to sing mass
chees, choose
cheeste, wrangling
chepe, bargain
chere, face, countenance; mirth; entertainment; appearance
chese, choose
chevyssaunce, borrowing; dealing for profit
chinche, miser
chirchehawe, churchyard
chivachie, military expedition
chukketh, clucks
circumscryve, enclose, comprehend
citole, a stringed instrument
clappe, clap; chatter, prattle
clarree, wine mixed with honey and spices and strained
clennesse, purity
clepen, call, name
clergeon, chorister boy
clergial, clerkly, learned
clerk, student
cliket, latchkey
clippe, embrace; cut hair
cloisterer, resident in a cloister
clom, sh!, mum!

cod, bag; stomach
coillons, testicles
cokenay, effeminate creature
collacioun, conference
colpons, shreds, bundles; billets
combust, burnt
commeveth, moves, induces
compasment, plotting, contrivance
complexioun, complexion; temperament
composicioun, agreement
condys, conduits
confiture, composition
confounde, destroy; put to confusion, overwhelm
congeyen, tell (us) to depart
conning, skill; knowledge; experience
constable, governor
contek, strife, contest
contemplaunce, contemplation
contubernial, familiar, at home with
conversacioun, manner of life
converte, change
cony, rabbit
cop, top; tip
corage, heart, spirit, mind, mood, inclination; courage; will, desire
cordewane, Cordovan leather
cornemuse, bagpipe
corniculere, registrar, secretary
correccioun, fine
corrumpeth, becomes corrupt
costage, cost, expense
costlewe, costly
cote, cot; dungeon; coat, jacket
couche, lay down, place; cower
countour, accountant
coupable, culpable, blameworthy
courtepy, short coat
couthe, *adv.* in a known way, manifestly; *v.* could; knew
coveityse, covetousness; bodily craving; lust
coverchief, kerchief
coverture, disguise
covyne, deceitfulness, deceitful agreement
craketh, utters boldly; sings in a grating tone
Cristen, Christian
croslet, crucible
crouche, mark with the cross
crouke, pitcher, jug
crul, curly
cryke, creek
culpe, guilt, blame
curacioun, cure, healing
curat, parish priest, vicar
curiositee, curious workmanship; intricacy
curious, careful, skillful
cursednesse, abominable sin; shrewishness; malice
curteis, courteous, compassionate

D

dagon, small piece
dampnacioun, condemnation, curse
dan, daun, lord, sir
darreyne, decide one's right to; decide
daunger, disdain; liability; power, control
daungerous, forbidding; hard to please; reluctant
dawes, days
dayerye, dairy
debaat, strife; war; mental conflict
deceivable, deceitful
deduyt, pleasure

deedly, mortal; dying; deathlike
deer, animals
defende, defend; forbid
degysinge, elaborate ornamentation
dekne, deacon
delen, have dealing with
delicacye, amusement, wantonness
delivernesse, activity
delyvere, quick, active
dere, injure, harm
derk, dark; inauspicious
derne, secret
desclaundred, slandered
desesperaunce, hopelessness
deshonestee, unseemliness
desirous, ambitious; ardent
deslavee, foul; inordinate, unrestrained
despence, expenditure, money for expenses
despitous, spiteful; angry; jealous; merciless
desponeth, disposes
desport, diversion, merriment
destreyne, distress; constrain, force
dette, debt
devoir, duty
devyse, relate, describe; recommend; suggest
dextrer, courser, war horse
deye, dairywoman
deynous, scornful
deyntee, worth, value
deys, dais, high table in a dining hall
dighte, prepare; serve; hasten
digne, worthy; noble; suitable
dilatacioun, diffuseness
disavaunce, defeat
disclaundre, reproach, slander
disese, discomfort, grief, misery; disease
disjoynt, failure; difficult position
dispence, expenditure, expense
dispitously, angrily; spitefully; cruelly
dispone, dispose
dispreisen, disparage
dissever, part, separate
disteyne, stain, bedim, dull
distreyne, constrain; get into his grasp, clutch
divisioun, distinction; difference
divynailes, divinations
divyninge, opinion
doke, duck
domesman, judge
doom, dome, judgment; decision
doon, do, execute; cause
dormant, permanent
dorste, durst, might venture
doseyn, dozen
d'outremere, foreign
drasty, filthy, worthless
drecche, be tedious; vex
drede, dread, doubt
drenchen, drown
dreye, dry
drogges, drugs
droghte, drought
dronkelewe, addicted to drink
drouped, were draggled
druerye, affection
durring, daring, bravery
dyke, dig ditches
dys, dice

E

ecclesiaste, minister
ech, each
eek, also, eke, moreover
eem, uncle

eftsone, soon after; immediately afterwards
eggement, instigation, incitement
egre, sharp, sour
eleccioun, choice; election (in astrology)
elenge, miserable
embrouded, embroidered, adorned
embusshements, ambuscades
empryse, enterprise, undertaking
enbibing, absorption
enchesoun, occasion, reason; cause
encorporing, incorporation
ende, end; purpose; point
endite, write, dictate; relate
enfamyned, starved
engreggen, burden
enhauncen, raise; exalt
enoynt, anointed
entaile, cutting, intaglio work
entende, attend; give attention to; apply oneself
entente, intention; design; wish; meaning
entremette, interfere
entreteden, discussed
envyned, stored with wine
er, before
erbe, herb
erchedeken, archdeacon
ere, n. ear; v. plow
erme, feel sad, grieve
ers, buttocks
erst, first, at first
eschaufinge, heating
ese, ease; relieve; entertain
especes, kinds, varieties
espiaille, sets of spies
estaat, state, condition; rank; position
estatlich, stately, dignified
estres, inward parts, recesses (of a building)
esy, moderate
Etik, the Ethics of Aristotle
evene-cristene, fellow Christian
everich, each; every; each one
everychon, every one; each one
everydeel, every whit; altogether
excusascioun, false excuse; plea
expoune, explain
ey, egg
eyle, ail

F

facounde, eloquence, fluency
facultee, capacity, authority; disposition; branch of study
fader, father
falding, a coarse cloth
fallen, occur; light; suit; prosper
falwes, fallow ground
fare, behavior, conduct; condition; business; company
faren, behave; go, travel
farsed, stuffed
faucon, falcon
fawe, glad
fayerye, troop of fairies; enchantment
fecchen, fetch
feendly, fiendlike, devilish
fel, dreadful
felaweshipe, partnership; company
felon, angry
fer, far
fere, companion; mate; wife
ferforthly, thoroughly
ferly, strange
fermerere, friar in charge of an infirmary
fern, long ago

ferne, distant, remote
ferre, farther
ferthyng, farthing; very small portion
festeth, feasts
festlich, fond of feasts; festive
festne, to fasten
fetis, neat, well-made, handsome; splendid; graceful
fetisly, elegantly; neatly, trimly
fey, faith; fidelity
finding, provision
fithele, fiddle
flatour, flatterer
flemen, banish
flete, float, bathe
flokmele, in a flock, in a great number
flour, flower; flour
floutours, flute players
floytinge, playing on the flute
fneseth, breathes heavily, puffs, snorts
folily, foolishly
fonde, endeavor; attempt; try to persuade
fonge, receive
foot-hot, instantly, on the spot
forblak, extremely black
forbrused, badly bruised
forcracchen, scratch excessively
forcutteth, cuts to pieces
fordwyned, shrunken
fore, path
forlaft, abandoned
forleten, abandon, give up
forme-fader, forefather, first father
forncast, premeditated
forneys, furnace
forpyned, wasted away
forshright, exhausted with shrieking
forster, forester
forthy, therefore, on that account
fortroden, trodden under foot
fortunen, to give (good or bad) fortune to
forwaked, tired out with watching
forwiting, foreknowledge
forward, agreement, covenant
foryetelnesse, forgetfulness
foryeten, forget
foryeve, forgive
foryifnesse, forgiveness
fother, load, a cartload; great quantity
fowles, birds
foyne, thrust
foyson, abundance, plenty
franchyse, liberality; nobleness; privilege
frankeleyn, franklin, freeholder
frayneth, prays, beseeches
freend, friend
freletee, frailty
frere, friar
freten, eat; devour; consume
freyne, ask, question
frounced, wrinkled
fumositee, fumes arising from drunkenness
furial, tormenting, furious
fyn, end; death; result; aim
fyr of seint Antony, erysipelas

G

gabbe, boast, prate; lie
gadereth, gathers
gale, sing, cry out
galianes, medicines
galingale, an aromatic spice (sweet cyperus root)
galwes, gallows

gamed, (it) pleased
gargat, throat
garnisoun, garrison
gat tothed, having the teeth far apart
gaure, stare; gaze
gere, gear, armor, apparel; changeful manner
gerner, granary
geste, story, romance
gif, if
gipoun, short cassock or doublet
gipser, pouch
girles, young people (male or female)
giterne, cithern
glede, burning coal, glowing coal or ashes
gleyre, white (of an egg)
glose, explain; cajole
godsib, baptismal sponsor
goldes, marigolds
goldless, moneyless
goliardeys, buffoon
gon, go, proceed; walk; move
gonge, privy
goodly, patiently; well
goon, go, move, proceed
governaille, mastery; rule
grame, anger, grief, harm
graythe, clothe, dress
gree, favor; good will; degree, rank
grenehede, wantonness
gretter, greater
greve, grove; boughs, sprays
greythen, prepare, get ready; adorn, clothe
grintinge, gnashing (of teeth)
grope, test
grot, particle, atom
ground, texture
groyn, n. (a swine's) snout; v. murmur
gruf, on their faces, grovelingly
gye, guide; conduct; rule
gylour, beguiler, trickster
gunglen, jingle
gyte, dress

H

haberdassher, hat-seller
habergeoun, hauberk or coat of mail
halke, corner; hiding place; nook
hals, neck
halse, conjure
halwes, saints; apostles; shrines of saints
hap, chance; luck, success
hardily, boldly; surely
hardinesse, boldness; insolence
harlot, person of low birth, servant lad; rascal (used of both sexes)
harneys, armor; gear
harre, hinge
harrow, help!
harwed, harried, despoiled
hasard, dicing
haunt, skill; abode
hauteyn, proud, stately; loud
heed, head; source; beginning
heele, health; recovery; prosperity
heep, heap, crowd, host
heeste, commandment
hele, conceal
hem, them
hemself, themselves
hende, courteous, polite
hente, catch; seize; acquire
her, their
herber, garden; arbor
herberwe or herberw, harbor; inn; lodging

herde, herder
here, her
herne, corner
herneys, armor
herte, heart; dear one; courage
heryinge, praising; praise; glory
heste, command, behest; promise
hete, promise, vow
heterly, fiercely
heyne, wretch
heyre, hair shirt
highte, was called
hir, to her; her; of them; their
hoker, scorn, frowardness
holde, keep, preserve; continue, go
    on with; think, consider
holour, lecher
holt, grove
holwe, hollow
honge, hang
hool, whole; unwounded; restored
    to health
hoomlinesse, domesticity; familiarity
hoost, army
hoot, hot; fervent
hoppesteres, dancers; dancing
hord, avarice
hostiler, innkeeper; servant at an inn
hote, command, promise; be called
hove, hover, dwell
humanitee, kindness
humblesse, meekness
hyne, servant

I

i-, *common prefix of past participles;*
    see Y-
icched, itched
il, evil
il-hayl, bad luck (to you)
ilke, same, very
impertinent, irrelevant
importable, insufferable
induracioun, hardening
infect, of no effect; dimmed
infere, together
inplitable, intricate, impracticable
inspired, quickened
inwith, within, in
ipocrite, hypocrite
irous, angry

J

jane, small coin of Genoa
janglere, storyteller, babbler
jet, fashion
jo, take effect, come about
jogelour, juggler
jolif, joyful, merry; in good spirits;
    pretty
jolitee, amusement, mirth; comfort;
    excellence
jolyer, handsomer
jordanes, chamber pots
jossa, down here
jouken, slumber
journee, day's work; day's march;
    journey
juggen, judge; deem
jupartye, jeopardy, peril, hazard
juste, joust, tourney

K

karf, carved
kechil, small cake
keep, heed; **take keep**, have regard for
kembe, to comb
kepe, take care (of); keep, preserve

kerve, carve, cut
kinges note, name of a tune
kitte, cut
knarre, thickset fellow
knobbes, large pimples
knowing, knowledge; consciousness
konning, cunning, skill
kyken, peep; gaze
kyn, cows
kythe, show, display

L

labbing, blabbing, babbling
lacche, snare, springe
lachesse, laziness
lakken, find fault with, disparage
lappe, fold, edge of garment
las, laas, lace, string; snare
lasse, less; lesser; smaller
lathe, barn
latoun, a zinc-copper compound
launcegay, kind of lance
launde, grassy clearing
lavender, laundress
lavours, basins
lay, song, lay; law, belief, faith
lazar, leper
leche, physician
lechour, lecher
lede, lead; carry; govern
ledene, language, talk
lees, deceit, fraud
lemes, flames
lemman, lover, sweetheart
lendes, loins
lene, lend, give
leos, people
lepart, leopard
lepe, run; leap
lered, instructed, learned
lerne, learn
lese, lose
lesing, falsehood
lest, *n.* pleasure; delight; desire;
    v. (it) pleases
lete, leave, forsake; let
lette, hinder; prevent
lettrure, learning
letuarie, remedy, electuary
leve, leave; let alone; believe; allow
leveful, permissible
levene, flash of lightning
lever, liefer, rather
lewed, ignorant; unlearned; foolish;
    wanton
leyser, leisure; deliberation;
    opportunity
libel, written declaration
licentiat, one licensed by pope to
    hear confessions
liche-wake, the watch over a corpse
licour, moisture; liquor; juice
liggen, lie
likerous, lecherous; wanton;
    gluttonous
linage, lineage; family
lissen, alleviate, soothe
list, *n.* pleasure; will; ear;
    v. (it) pleases
litarge, white lead
lite, little
lodemenage, pilotage
lodesterre, polestar
loke, lock up
loken, look; behold
lokkes, locks of hair
lond, land; country
lone, loan; gift, grace
longes, lungs

looth, odious
lore, teaching; learning; doctrine
lorel, worthless man, abandoned
    wretch
losengerie, flattery
lotinge, lurking
loute, bow, do obeisance
lovedayes, days for settling
    disputes by arbitration
loves, loaves
lovyere, lover
luce, pike
lussheburghes, spurious coin
lust, desire; amusement; delight
lusteth, (it) pleases
luxurie, lechery
lyard, gray
lyflode, means of living
lyknesse, parable
lymaille, filings of any metal
lymytour, friar licensed to beg for
    alms within certain limit
lystes, enclosed place for tournaments
lyte, little

M

m-, *sometimes put for* me *(before a*
    vowel); as in masterte *for* me
    asterte
maheym, maiming
maille, mail, ringed armor
maistrie, mastery, great skill;
    superiority
make, mate; equal, match
makeless, peerless
male, bag, wallet; male
malison, curse; cursing
mandement, summons
maner, manor, place to dwell in
mansuete, courteous
mareys, marsh
marybones, marrowbones
mased, bewildered; stunned with
    grief
mat, dejected; exhausted; dead
maugre, maugree, in spite of
Maumetrye, Mohammedanism, *thus*
    idolatry *(Moslems were held to be*
    idolators in Chaucer's time)
maunciple, steward of a college
may, maiden
mede, mead (drink); mead
    (meadow); reward
medewe, meadow
medlee, motley
meed, reward
meeth, mead
mele, meal (flour)
melle, mill
mendinants, mendicant friars
menen, say; signify; intend
mere, mare
meritorie, meritorious
merveille, marvel
meschief, misfirtune; trouble
mesel, leper
messuage, dwelling house
mester, service, office, occupation
mesurable, moderate
mesure, moderation; measure
mete, *adj.* meet, befitting, fit;
    n. equal; meat, food; *v.* meet;
    find; dream
meve, move, stir
mewe, coop
meynee, household; retainers;
    menials
minde, remembrance; memory
misaunter, misadventure, misfortune

xvi

misavyse, act unadvisedly
misboden, offered (to do) evil
misdeparteth, parts or divides amiss
misdooth, ill-treats
misgoon, gone astray
misgyed, misconducted
mister, trade; need
misterye, profession
mixen, dunghill
mo, *adj.* more; besides; others; another; *adv.* more, any longer
moder, mother
moiste, supple
mood, anger; thought
moon, moan, lamentation, complaint
moot, mot, mote, must, shall
mordre, murder
mormal, ulcerous sore
mortreux, thick soups
morwe, morning, morrow
morwetyde, morning hour
mottelee, motley array
moulen, grow moldy
mountance, amount, value, quantity
mowen, be able
moyste, fresh, new
muche, great
muchel, *adj.* much, great; *adv.* greatly
mullok, heap of refuse; confused heap of materials
murye, merry

N

n-, *for* ne, not; *as in* nacheveth *for* ne acheveth, *and the like*
na mo, no more, none else
naddre, adder
nakers, kettledrums
nale, ale, alehouse
nam, am not
narwe, small; close
nas, was not
natheless, nevertheless
nayte, deny
nedely, of necessity, necessarily
nedescost, of necessity
neet, cattle
neigh, *adj.* near, nigh; *adv.* nearly
nempnen, name
nere, was not
nevene, mention, name
neveradel, not a bit
newefangel, fond of novelty
nil, will not
niste, knew not
noble, a gold coin of England
nokked, notched
nolde, would not, did not want
nomen, taken; put
nones, for the, for the occasion; for now; on the spur of the moment
noot, know not
nortelrye, education
norture, instruction, good manners
nose thirles, nostrils
notemuge, nutmeg
not heed, head with hair cropped short
nouchis, nowches, jeweled ornaments, clasps
nyce, foolish; ignorant; weak; scrupulous
nyfles, mockeries, pretences
nyghtertale, nighttime

O

o, one
obeising, yielding

observaunce, respect; homage; ceremony
observe, favor; take heed
occasioun, cause
office, use; property
of-showve, repel
oliveres, olive trees
omelies, homilies
onde, envy
oneden, unite
open-ers, medlar
open-heeded, with head uncovered
ordinaat, orderly
ore, grace
orfrays, gold embroidery, braid
orisonte, horizon
orisoun, prayer
orloge, clock
ost, host, army
ostlements, furniture, household goods
ouche, clasp
oules, spiked irons in torture
ounces, small clusters
ounded, wavy
outen, put out, utter, exhibit
outhees, outcry, hue and cry, alarm
outraye, lose temper
outrely, utterly; entirely; decidedly
outridere, the monk who rode to inspect granges, etc.
outstraughte, stretched out
out-taken, excepted
overest, outer
overlad, put upon
oversloppe, upper garment
overthwart, across; opposite
owen, owe, own, possess
oynon, onions

P

paas, pace, step
pace, pass, go
palestral, pertaining to wrestling
palled, pale, languid
pan, cranium
panade, kind of knife
papejay, popinjay
parage, kindred, birth; rank
paraments, mantles, splendid clothing
pardoner, one licensed to sell indulgences
paregal, fully equal
parentele, kinship
parfit, perfect
parfourne, perform; fulfill
parisshens, parishioners
parten, share
parvys, church porch (of St. Paul's, London, where lawyers conferred)
pas, pace; step; distance
passen, surpass, exceed, conquer
payen, pagan
payndemayn, bread of a peculiar whiteness
pees, peace
penaunt, one who does penance
pencel, pencil, brush; small banner, sleeve worn as token
penible, painstaking; careful to please
pere, peer, equal
peregryn, peregrine
perejonette, a kind of early pear
perree, jewelry
pers, light blue
persoun, parson
peyne, *n.* pain of torture; care; toil; penalty; *v.* take pains, endeavor
peynture, painting

peytrel, breastplate of a horse in armor
physik, medicine
pigges-nye, a dear little thing
pile, pillage; rob
piled, very thin; bald
pilours, robbers, pillagers
pilwe-beer, pillowcase
piment, sweetened wine
pinche, find fault (with), pick a hole (in)
pissemyre, ant
pith, strength
plages, regions; quarters of the compass
plat, flat, certain
pleasaunce, pleasure; delight; pleasant thing; kindness
pleyn, *adj.* full, complete; plain, clear; honest; *adv.* full, entirely; plainly, openly
pleyne, complain, lament; whinny
plighte, plucked; pledged
plye, ply, mold; bend
policye, public business
pollax, poleax
polyve, pulley
pomely, dappled
popelote, poppet, darling
popper, small dagger
poraille, poor people
port, carriage, behavior; mien; haven
porthors, breviary
pose, head cold
potente, crutch; staff
potestat, potentate
poudre-marchant, a powdered spice
pounsoninge, punching of holes in garments
povre, poor
poynaunt, pungent
precious, valuable; over-refined
predicacioun, preaching, sermon
preef, proof, assertion; experience; text
prees, press, crowd
prest, priest
preve, *n.* proof; experimental proof; *v.* prove; succeed when tested
prikasour, hard rider
priken, incite, urge; excite
prikyng, hard riding
pris, prize
privetee, privacy; secrecy; secret
proheme, prologue
prolle, prowl about, search widely
propre, own; especial; peculiar
proprely, fitly; literally; naturally
propretee, pecularity; characteristic
prospectyves, perspective glasses, lenses
proyneth, trims, makes neat
pryme, prime (of day), usually 9 a.m.
prymerole, primrose
purchas, proceeds, gifts acquired; gain
pured, pure; very fine
purfiled, ornamented at the edge, trimmed
purtreye, draw
purveyaunce, providence; foresight; provision
purveyen, provide; foresee
puterie, prostitution
putours, pimps, procurers
putten, put, lay; suppose
pye, magpie; pie, pasty
pykepurs, pickpurse
pyled, peeled, bare, bald
pyne, torture
pyrie, pear tree

Q

quaad, evil; bad
quakke, state of hoarseness
qualm, pestilence; evil, plague; foreboding of death
quelle, kill; strike
questemongeres, jurymen
queynte, pudendum
queyntise, finery; art; ornament
quik, alive; lively; ready
quinible, shrill treble
quirboilly, boiled leather
quoniam, pudendum
quyte, requite, reward, give in return

R

rage, romp, toy wantonly
ragerye, wantonness; passion
rakelnesse, rashness
rakestele, handle of a rake
ram, ram
rammish, ramlike, strong-scented
rathe, soon; early
raughte, proceeded
raunson, ransom
real, royal, regal
rebekke, old woman
recche, reck, care, heed; interpret, expound
recchelees, careless, reckless; regardless
reche, reach, give, hand over
reconciled, reconsecrated
rede, read; advise; interpret
rede, red (i.e. gold); the blood; red wine
redoutinge, reverence
redy, ready; dressed
reed, n. counsel, plan; adviser; profit, help; adj. red
rees, great haste
refreyden, grow cold
refreyne, bridle, curb
registre, narrative
regne, kingdom, dominion; rule
rehersaille, enumeration
relente, melt
reme, realm
ren, run
renably, reasonably
reneye, deny, renounce, abjure
renne, run; be current; approach quickly
rente, revenue, income; payment, tribute
repleccioun, repletion
replicacioun, reply
reprevable, reprehensible
repreve, n. reproof; shame; v. reproach; reprove
rescous, a rescue, help
rese, shake
resonable, talkative
resoun, reason, right; argument, speech, sentence
rethor, orator
reule, rule
reve, n. reeve, steward, bailiff; v. to rob (from)
revelous, fond of revelry
rewe, n. row, line; v. have pity; be sorry; do penance for
rewelboon, ivory from whale's teeth
rewme, realm
reysed, gone on a military expedition
ribible, lute with two strings
ribybe, term of reproach for old woman

rightwisnesse, righteousness; justice
risshe, rush
roche, rock
rodebeem, rood beam (beam across entrance to church choir, supporting a rood or cross)
rody, ruddy
rombled, fumbled, groped about; buzzed, muttered
romen, roam, wander
roost, roast meat
roote, rote, root
rote, type of fiddle of Celtic origin
roten, rotten; corrupt, filthy
rouketh, cowers, crouches, is huddled up
roumer, larger
rouncy, hackney, nag
roune, whisper
route, n. company, group; v. roar, murmur; assemble
routing, snoring; whizzing noise
royne, roughness
roynous, rough
rudeliche, rudely
ruggy, rough

S

sad, stable, firm; staid; sober; constant
salewe, salute
saluing, salutation
salwes, osiers
sangwin, blood-red
sarge, serge
sarsinesshe, Saracenic
sauf, adj. safe, safely kept; prep. save, except
saule, soul
sauns, without
sautrye, psaltery
saveren, mind, care for
sawcefleem, covered with pimples
saylours, dancers
scabbe, scab; mange
scalled, scabby, scurfy
scarmyche, skirmish
scars, parsimonious
scathe, a pity
sclaundre, slander; disgrace
sclendre, slender, slight; thin; poor
scochouns, escutcheons
scoler, scholar
scoleye, study
scrippe, scrip, bag
secree, adj. secret, trusty; able to keep a secret; n. secret
seculer, layman
see, sea; seat; seat of empire
seek, seeke, sick, ill
seel, bliss; seal
seigh, saw
seistow, sayest thou
selde, adj. few; adv. seldom
selinesse, happiness
selle, boarding
sely, happy; kind; good; pitiable; hapless
semicope, short cope
semisoun, suppressed sound
semyly, becomingly
senatorie, senatorial rank
sencer, censer
sendal, a thin silk
senge, singe; broil
sengle, single, unmarried
sentence, meaning; subject; opinion; decision; theme

septemtrioun, north
serie, process, argument
sermoning, argument; talk
servage, servitude, thralldom
seur, adj. sure; adv. surely
sewe, follow, ensue
sewes, juices, gravies; seasoned dishes
shaar, plowshare
shadwe, shadow
shal, owe (to); shall; must
shamfast, modest, shy; ashamed
shap, shape; privy member
shapen, plan, devise; find means (to do)
shaply, fit; likely
shawe, wood, trees
sheld, shield; French crown (coin)
shende, disgrace; render contemptible; ruin, destroy
shendshipe, shame
shene, bright; beautiful
shepe, hire
shepne, stable, shed
sheten, shoot
shette, shut, enclose
shifte, provide, distribute, ordain
shilde, defend; shield; forbid
shine, shin
shipe, hire, pay, reward
shipnes, stables, sheds
shiten, defiled, dirty
shitting, shutting
sho, shoe
shode, parting of the hair; temple of the head
shrewe, scoundrel, accursed wretch; shrew
shrewednesse, wickedness, evil
shrifte-fadres, father confessors
shrighte, shrieked
significavit, writ of excommunication
sik, sick, ill
siker, adj. sure; safe; certain; adv. uninterruptedly; surely
sikerly, certainly, surely, truly
simphonye, kind of small drum
sin, since
sis cink, i.e. six-five, a throw with two dice
sith, since
skile, reason, cause
skilful, reasonable, discerning
slee, slay
sleere, slayer
sleight, sly, artful
slewthe, sloth
slogardye, sluggishness, sloth
slombry, sleepy
sloppes, loose garments
slyk, sleek; such
smerte, n. pain; anguish; adv. smartly, sharply; sorely; v. (it) pained
smitted, sullied with dishonor
smoterliche, smirched in reputation
snewed, abounded
snibben, reprove, chide
soden, sodden, boiled
soken, toll
sokingly, gradually
solempne, festive; importance; public
solempnitee, pomp; outward show
somdel, somewhat; in some measure
somnour, summoner
somonce, summons
sompne, summon
sond, sand

sonde, message; gifts; visitation; trial
sondry, various
sone, *n.* son; *adv.* soon; speedily
sonne, sun
soor, wounded, grieved; sore
soote, sweet
soothly, truly
soper, supper
sophyme, sophism; deceit
sorwe, sorrow, grief; mourning;
   compassion
soster, sister
sothe, truth
sotil, subtle; subtly woven; thin
souded, confirmed
souke, suck; embezzle
sounde, heal, make sound
soune, sound; tend (to)
souter, cobbler
soutiltee, device
sowdan, sultan
sowne, play upon, sound
space, room; space of time; course
sparhauk, sparrow hawk
sparth, battle-ax
sparwe, sparrow
spaynel, spaniel
spede, succeed; prosper
speedful, advantageous
speere, sphere
spelle, story
spence, pantry
spille, spill; destroy, ruin
springers, sources, origins
spyced, scrupulous
squames, scales
squire, carpenter's square
stamin, a coarse harsh cloth, tammy
stank, lake, tank, pool
stapen, advanced
stemed, shone, glowed
stenten, stay; cease, leave off
stepe, glittering, bright
stere, helm; guide
sterlinges, sterling coins
sterre, star
sterte, start, go quickly
sterve, die; die of famine
stevene, voice, language; rumor;
   time, esp. of an appointment
stewe, fishpond; small room, closet;
   brothel
stif, strong; bold
stinte, leave off; cease; cause to cease
stith, anvil
stonde, stand; be placed;
   be understood, be fixed
stoor, stock, store; value
storial, historical
stot, stallion; heifer (term of abuse)
stounde, hour, time, while
stree, straw
streen, stock, progeny, race
streit, narrow; scanty; strict
strepen, strip
strike, hank (of flax)
stronde, shore
strong, difficult; severe
strouted, stuck out
sturdy, cruel, hard, harsh, stern
styves, stews
styward, steward
subjeccion, suggestion; subjection,
   obedience
suffraunce, long-suffering; patience
suggestioun, criminal charge; hint
sukkenye, tunic
surement, pledge
surquidrie, presumption, arrogance

sursanure, wound healed outwardly,
   but not inwardly
suspect, suspicious, ominous of evil
suster, sister
swalwe, swallow
swappe, strike
swelte, die; languish, faint
swerd, sword
swete, *adj.* sweet; *v.* sweat
sweven, dream
swich, such
swink, labor
swogh, groan; swoon
swote, sweet
swoune, swowne, swoon, faint
swynes-heed, pig's head
   (term of abuse)
swynke, toil
swythe, quickly
swyve, lie with
syk, *adj.* sick, ill; *n.* sigh
syketh, sighs
sys, six
sythe, time; scythe

T

t-, *for* to, *frequently prefixed to*
   verbs; as tabyde, tamende, *etc.*
tabard, herald's coat of arms; the
   same, as an inn sign; a
   plowman's frock
taillages, taxes
taille, credit, account tallied upon
   notched sticks
takel, tackle, gear, arrows
talen, tell tales
talent, inclination, wish, desire
tapicer, upholsterer, maker of carpets
tappestere, female tapster, barmaid
targe, target, shield
tarien, tarry, delay
tas, heap
temple, lawyer's office
tene, vexation; sorrow, grief
tentifly, attentively, carefully
testers, headpieces (of armor)
testes, vessels for assaying metals
testif, heady, headstrong
tete, teat
thanne, then; than; next
thar, (it) is necessary, is needful
thedom, success
thee, thrive, prosper
theefly, like a thief
thenche, imagine
theras, there where, where; whereas
thewes, habits, natural qualities;
   virtues; customs
thider, thither
thikke-herd, thick-haired
thilke, that; such; that same;
   that sort of
thing, fact; property, wealth;
   deed, legal document
thinke, seem
tho, those; then, at that time
thoght, anxiety
thonderdint, stroke of lightning;
   thunderclap
thral, *n.* thrall, slave, subject;
   adj. enthralled
thridde, third
thries, thrice
thrift, success, welfare; profit
thrittene, thirteen
thritty, thirty
throp, thorp, small village
throtebolle, Adam's apple

throwe, short space of time,
   while, period
thrustel, thrush
thurgh, through
thurgh-girt, pierced through
thurrok, sink, the lowest internal
   part of ship's hull
thwitel, large knife
tikel, unstable
tiptoon, tiptoes
titleless, without a title, usurping
to-, *intensive prefix* in twain, asunder;
   as tocleve, cleave in twain
tobreke, break in pieces
tobreste, burst in twain
toght, taut
tollen, take toll; entice
tonne, cask
tord, piece of dung
torets, small rings on dog collar
toty, dizzy
toun, town; farm; neighborhood
touret, turret
toute, buttocks, backside
toverbyde, survive
toyeere, this year
trappures, trappings for horses
traunce, tramp about
trave, wooden frame for holding
   unruly horses
tree, wood
trentals, (sets of) thirty masses
   for the dead
tretable, tractable, docile
tretys, well-proportioned, long;
   graceful
trewe love, truelove (probably leaf
   of herb Paris or some aromatic
   confection)
treye, three
triacle, a sovereign remedy
trille, turn, twirl
trip, small piece
tronchoun, broken shaft of a spear
trone, throne; throne (of God),
   heaven
trouthe, truth; fidelity; promise, troth
trowen, believe, imagine
trufles, trifles
tryce, pull, drag away
trye, choice, excellent
tryne compas, the threefold world
   of earth, sea, and heaven
tulle, entice, allure
turtel, turtledove
turves, turf patches
tuwel, hole
tweye, two
twinne, sever, part
twinninge, separation
twyes, twice
typet, tippet, cape; hood
tytled, dedicated

U

unconvenable, unsuitable
uncouth, curious; strange
undergrowe, of short stature
undermeles, *perhaps* afternoons
undern, a particular time in the
   morning, about 9 a.m. or
   somewhat later
underpyghte, stuffed, filled
   underneath
underspore, thrust under,
   push beneath
unhele, misfortune, sickness
unleveful, not permissible

unlykly, unpleasing
unnethe, scarcely, hardly, with difficulty
unordred, not belonging to a religious order
unsad, unsettled
unset, unappointed
unshette, unlocked; not shut
unslekked, unslacked
unthank, want of thanks; a curse
unwemmed, unspotted, spotless
uphaf, uplifted
upplight, plucked up, pulled up
upright, lying on one's back (mostly of people dead or asleep)
up-so-doun, upside down
upyaf, yielded up, gave
usaunt, addicted; accustomed
usen, accustom

V

vassalage, prowess
vavasour, subvassal, next in dignity to baron
venerian, devoted to Venus
venerie, hunting
ventusinge, cupping (in surgery)
vernicle, copy of St. Veronica's handkerchief with impression of the Saviour's face
verray, very, true
versiflour, poet
vertu, virtue; quickening power, valor
vese, rush
veyne, vein
viage, voyage, travel, journey; expedition, attempt
vileins, vileyns, villainous, sinful, rude
vileinye, rudeness
vinolent, full of wine
violes, vials
viritoot, brisk movement
viritrate, hag
vitaille, provisions

W

waat, knows
wacche, sentinel
wachet, light blue color
wafereres, makers of wafer cakes, confectioners
wake-pleyes, funeral games
walwe, wallow, roll about
wanges, molar teeth
wanhope, despair
wanie, wane
wantrust, distrust
war, prudent; aware
wardecors, bodyguard
warderere, look out behind
wardrobe, privy
wariangles, shrikes
warien, curse
warisshe, cure; recover, be cured
warne, reject, refuse
warnestore, fortify, defend
waryce, heal, cure
wastel breed, cake-bread, bread of highest quality
wawe, wave
waymentinge, lamenting, lamentation
webbe, weaver
wede, weed, robe, garment

weeldinge, power, control
weet, wet
weex, waxed, grew
welden, have control over, move with ease
wele, happiness, success, prosperity
wem, blemish
wemmelees, stainless
wene, supposition, doubt
wenen, ween, suppose, imagine, consider
werbul, tune
werche, work, perform
werken, act
werkes, ache
werne, forbid; refuse
werre, war; trouble
werreye, make war, war against
werte, wart
wex, wax
wexen, wax, grow, become
weyen, weigh
weymentinge, lamenting; lament
weyven, turn aside; waive, forsake
whan, when
whelkes, pimples
whenne, whence
whennes, whence
whilk, which
whilom, once
whyler, formerly
wight, n. person, creature, man, living being; whit, short while; adj. active
wike, week
wikke, wikked, evil, bad, wicked
wilnen, desire
windas, windlass
wirche, work; provide; give relief
wis, wisly, certainly, truly, verily
wisse, instruct; inform; show, tell
wist, knew
witen, know
withouten, as well as
withseye, contradict, gainsay; refuse; renounce
witing, knowledge, cognizance
wlatsom, disgusting; heinous
wo, unhappy; sad, grieved
wode, made
wodewale, green woodpecker
wol, will; desire; be ready to
wone, v. dwell, inhabit; n. custom
wones, places of retreat, range of buildings
wonger, pillow
woning, dwelling
wood, mad
woodnesse, madness, rage
woon, resource; abundance; retreat, secure place
word and ende, beginning and end
wort, unfermented beer
wortes, herbs
worthen, be, dwell; become
wouke, week
wounde, wound; plague
wraw, angry; peevish; fretful
wreche, vengeance
wreke, wreak, avenge
wrenches, frauds, stratagems, tricks
wreye, bewray, reveal
wrooth, angry
wroteth, tears with the snout, pokes about
wrye, hide; cover

wydewhere, far and wide, everywhere
wydwe, widow
wyf, woman; wife; mistress of household
wyke, week
wympul, wimple, covering for the head
wyte, blame, reproach

Y

y-, prefix used especially with the past participle. For most entries see under the forms of the infinitive mood; e.g., for the meaning of ybrend see brenne
yaf, gave
yare, ready
yate, gate
yblent, blinded; deceived
yboren, born; borne, carried
ychaped, capped with metal (at the end of the sheath)
ycleped, called; invoked; summoned
ycorven, cut
ydel, idle, empty, vain
ydolastre, idolater
ye, eye
yeddinges, songs
yede, walked, went
yeftes, gifts
yelden, yield up; yield to, pay
yeldhalle, guildhall
yelpe, boast; prate
yelwe, yellow
yeman, yeoman
yerde, rod, stick; switch
yerne, adj. eager, brisk; adv. eagerly, soon
yeve, give
yexeth, hiccups
yfere, together
ygrave, cut; dug out; engraved
yherd, covered with hair
yholde, esteemed to be; celebrated; considered
yive, give
ylad, carried (in a cart)
ylissed, eased
ylogged, lodged
ylyk, like; alike
ypocras, Hippocrates; hence, a kind of cordial
yren, iron
yronne, run; continued; interlaced; clustered
ysene, visible; manifest
yshapen, shaped, prepared; provided; contrived
yshent, put to shame, severely blamed
yspreynd, sprinkled
ystiked, stuck; stabbed
ystint, stopped
ystorve, dead
yvel, ill, evil
ywroght, made; shaped, depicted; ornamented
ywryen, hidden; covered
y-yeve, given

Z

zeles, zeal
Zephirus, Zephyrus (or Zephyr), the west wind

THE CONTENTS OF THIS BOOK ❧ ❧ ❧

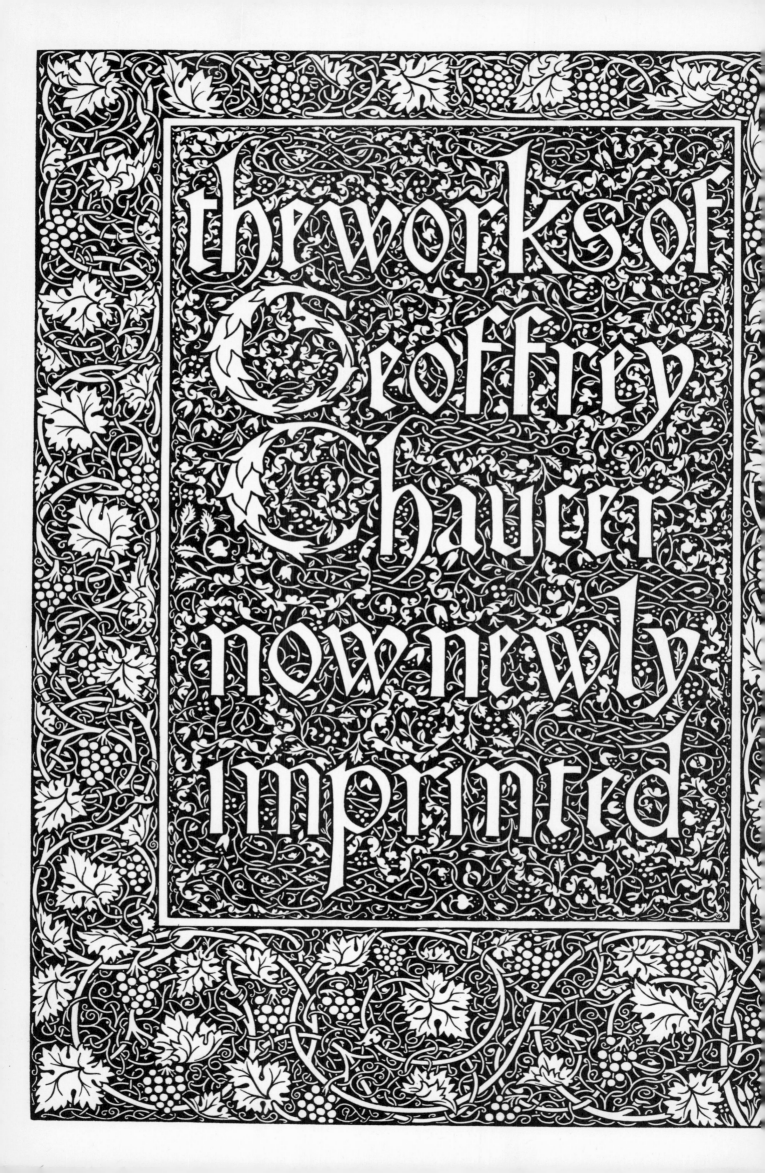

the works of Geoffrey Chaucer now newly imprinted

HERE BEGINNETH THE TALES OF CANTERBURY AND FIRST THE PROLOGUE THEREOF

WHAN

THAT Aprille with his shoures soote
The droghte of March hath perced to the roote,
And bathed every veyne in swich licour,
Of which vertu engendred is the flour;
Whan Zephirus eek with his swete breeth
Inspired hath in every holt and heeth

The tendre croppes, and the yonge sonne
Hath in the Ram his halfe cours yronne,
And smale foweles maken melodye,
That slepen al the nyght with open eye,
So priketh hem nature in hir corages;
Thanne longen folk to goon on pilgrimages,
And palmeres for to seken straunge strondes,
To ferne halwes, kowthe in sondry londes;
And specially, from every shires ende
Of Engelond, to Caunterbury they wende,
The hooly blisful martir for to seke,
That hem hath holpen whan that they were
seeke.

Bifil that in that seson on a day,
In Southwerk at the Tabard as
I lay,
Redy to wenden on my pilgrym-
age
To Caunterbury with ful devout
corage,
At nyght were come into that hostelrye
Wel nyne and twenty in a compaignye,
Of sondry folk, by aventure yfalle
In felaweshipe, and pilgrimes were they alle,
That toward Caunterbury wolden ryde.

The chambres and the stables weren wyde
And wel we weren esed atte beste.
And shortly, whan the sonne was to reste,
So hadde I spoken with hem everychon,
That I was of hir felaweshipe anon,
And made forward erly for to ryse
To take oure wey, ther as I yow devyse.
But nathelees, whil I have tyme and space,
Er that I ferther in this tale pace,
Me thynketh it acordaunt to resoun,
To telle yow al the condicioun
Of ech of hem, so as it semed me,
And whiche they weren, and of what degree,
And eek in what array that they were inne;
And at a Knyght than wol I first bigynne.

The Knyght

A KNYGHT ther was & that a worthy man,
That fro the tyme that he first bigan
To riden out, he loved chivalrie,
Trouthe and honour, fredom and curteisie.
Ful worthy was he in his lordes werre,
And therto hadde he riden, no man ferre,
As wel in cristendom as in hethenesse,
And evere honoured for his worthynesse.
At Alisaundre he was, whan it was wonne;
Ful ofte tyme he hadde the bord bigonne
Aboven alle nacions in Pruce.
In Lettow hadde he reysed and in Ruce,
No cristen man so ofte of his degree.
In Gernade at the seege eek hadde he be
Of Algezir, and riden in Belmarye.
At Lyeys was he, and at Satalye,
Whan they were wonne; and in the Grete See
At many a noble army hadde he be.
At mortal batailles hadde he been fiftene,
And foughten for oure feith at Tramyssene
In lystes thries, and ay slayn his foo.
This ilke worthy knyght hadde been also
Somtyme with the lord of Palatye
Agayn another hethen in Turkye;
And everemoore he hadde a sovereyn prys.
And though that he were worthy, he was wys,
And of his port as meeke as is a mayde.
He nevere yet no vileynye ne sayde
In al his lyf unto no maner wight;
He was a verray parfit gentil knyght.
But for to tellen yow of his array,
His hors were goode, but he was nat gay;
Of fustian he wered a gypoun
Al bismotered with his habergeoun;
For he was late ycome from his viage,
And wente for to doon his pilgrymage.

The Squier

WITH hym ther was his sone, a yong Squier,
A lovyere and a lusty bacheler,
With lokkes crulle as they were leyd in presse;
Of twenty yeer of age he was, I gesse.
Of his stature he was of evene lengthe,
And wonderly delyvere and of greet strengthe,
And he hadde been somtyme in chyvachie,
In Flaundres, in Artoys and Pycardie,
And born hym weel, as of so litel space,

2

In hope to stonden in his lady grace.
Embrouded was he, as it were a meede
Al ful of fresshe floures whyte and reede;
Syngynge he was, or floytynge, al the day;
He was as fressh as is the monthe of May.
Short was his gowne, with sleves longe and wyde;
Wel koude he sitte on hors and faire ryde;
He koude songes make and wel endite,
Juste, & eek daunce, and weel purtreye and write.
So hoote he lovede, that by nyghtertale
He slepte namoore than dooth a nyghtyngale;
Curteis he was, lowely and servysable,
And carf biforn his fader at the table.

The Yeman

A YEMAN hadde he, & servants namo
At that tyme, for him liste ride soo;
And he was clad in cote and hood of grene:
A sheef of pecok arwes bright and kene
Under his belt he bar ful thriftily,
Wel koude he dresse his takel yemanly;
His arwes drouped noght with fetheres lowe,
And in his hand he baar a myghty bowe.
A not heed hadde he, with a broun visage;
Of woodecraft wel koude he al the usage.
Upon his arm he bar a gay bracer,
And by his syde a swerd and a bokeler,
And on that oother syde a gay daggere,
Harneised wel and sharpe as point of spere;
A Cristophre on his brest of silver sheene.
An horn he bar, the bawdryk was of grene;
A forster was he, soothly, as I gesse.

The Nonne

THER was also a Nonne, a Prioresse,
That of hir smylyng was ful symple and coy;
Hire gretteste ooth was but by sëint Loy,
And she was cleped madame Eglentyne.
Ful weel she soong the service dyvyne
Entuned in hir nose ful semeely;
And Frenssh she spak ful faire and fetisly
After the scole of Stratford atte Bowe,
For frenssh of Parys was to hir unknowe.
At mete wel ytaught was she withalle,
She leet no morsel from hir lippes falle,
Ne wette hir fyngres in hir sauce depe.
Wel koude she carie a morsel and wel kepe,
That no drope ne fille upon hire brist;
In curteisie was set ful muchel hir list.
Hire over lippe wyped she so clene,
That in hir coppe ther was no ferthyng sene
Of grece, whan she dronken hadde hir draughte;
Ful semely after hir mete she raughte.
And sikerly she was of greet desport,
And ful plesaunt and amyable of port,
And peyned hire to countrefete cheere
Of court, and to been estatlich of manere,
And to ben holden digne of reverence.
But for to speken of hire conscience,
She was so charitable and so pitous,
She wolde wepe if that she saugh a mous
Kaught in a trappe, if it were deed or bledde.
Of smale houndes hadde she that she fedde

With rosted flessh, or milk and wastel breed;
But soore wepte she if oon of hem were deed,
Or if men smoot it with a yerde smerte,
And al was conscience and tendre herte.
Ful semyly hir wympul pynched was;
Hire nose tretys, hir eyen greye as glas,
Hir mouth ful smal, and therto softe and reed;
But sikerly she hadde a fair forheed,
It was almoost a spanne brood I trowe;
For hardily, she was nat undergrowe.
Ful fetys was hir cloke, as I was war;
Of smal coral aboute hire arm she bar
A peire of bedes, gauded al with grene,
And theron heng a brooch of gold ful sheene,
On which ther was first write a crowned A,
And after, Amor vincit omnia.
Another Nonne with hire hadde she,
That was hir Chapeleyne, and preestes thre.

A MONK ther was, a fair for the mais-
trie,
An out-ridere that lovede venerie;
A manly man, to been an abbot able.
Ful many a deyntee hors hadde he in
stable,
And whan he rood men myghte his brydel heere
Gynglen in a whistlynge wynd als cleere,
And eek as loude, as dooth the chapel belle.
Theras this lord was kepere of the celle,
The reule of seint Maure or of seint Beneit,
Bycause that it was old and somdel streit,
This ilke monk leet olde thynges pace,
And heeld after the newe world the space.
He yaf nat of that text a pulled hen,
That seith that hunters beth nat hooly men,
Ne that a monk whan he is recchelees
Is likned til a fissh that is waterlees;
This is to seyn, a monk out of his cloystre;
But thilke text heeld he nat worth an oystre;
And I seyde his opinioun was good.
What, sholde he studie & make himselven wood
Upon a book in cloystre alwey to poure,
Or swynken with his handes, and laboure,
As Austyn bit? How shal the world be served?
Lat Austyn have his swink to him reserved.
Therfore he was a prikasour aright;
Grehoundes he hadde, as swift as fowel in flight.
Of prikyng and of huntyng for the hare
Was al his lust, for no cost wolde he spare.
I seigh his sleves ypurfiled at the hond
With grys, and that the fyneste of a lond;
And for to festne his hood under his chyn
He hadde of gold ywrought a curious pyn,
A loveknotte in the gretter end ther was.
His heed was balled, that shoon as any glas,
And eek his face, as it hadde been enoynt;
He was a lord full fat and in good poynt.
Hise eyen stepe, and rollynge in his heed,
That stemed as a forneys of a leed;
His bootes souple, his hors in greet estaat.
Now certeinly he was a fair prelaat.
He was nat pale, as a forpyned goost;
A fat swan loved he best of any roost;
His palfrey was as broun as is a berye.

A FRERE ther was, a wantowne and a
merye,
A lymytour, a ful solempne man,
In alle the ordres foure is noon that
kan
So muchel of daliaunce & fair langage;
He hadde maad ful many a mariage
Of yonge wommen at his owene cost:
Unto his ordre he was a noble post.
And wel biloved and famulier was he
With frankeleyns over al in his contree;
And eek with worthy wommen of the toun:
For he hadde power of confessioun,
As seyde hymself, moore than a curat,
For of his ordre he was licenciat.
Ful swetely herde he confessioun,
And plesaunt was his absolucioun.
He was an esy man to yeve penaunce,
Theras he wiste to have a good pitaunce;
For unto a povre ordre for to yive
Is signe that a man is wel yshryve;
For if he yaf, he dorste make avaunt,
He wiste that a man was repentaunt:
For many a man so harde is of his herte,
He may nat wepe althogh hym soore smerte,
Therfore, in stede of wepynge and preyeres,
Men moote yeve silver to the povre freres.
His typet was ay farsed ful of knyves
And pynnes, for to yeven yonge wyves;
And certeinly he hadde a murye note,
Wel koude he synge and pleyen on a rote;
Of yeddynges he baar outrely the pris.
His nekke whit was as the flour-de-lys,
Therto he strong was as a champioun.
He knew the tavernes wel in al the toun,
And everich hostiler and tappestere
Bet than a lazar or a beggestere;
For unto swich a worthy man as he
Acorded nat, as by his facultee,
To have with sike lazars aqueyntaunce;
It is nat honeste, it may nat avaunce
For to deelen with no swich poraille,
But al with riche and selleres of vitaille.
And overal, ther as profit sholde arise,
Curteis he was, and lowely of servyse.
Ther nas no man nowher so vertuous;
He was the beste beggere in his hous;
For thogh a wydwe hadde noght a sho,
So plesaunt was his In principio,
Yet wolde he have a ferthyng er he wente.
His purchas was wel bettre than his rente;
And rage he koude as it were right a whelpe.
In love dayes ther koude he muchel helpe,
For there he was nat lyk a cloysterer
With a thredbare cope, as is a povre scoler,
But he was lyk a maister or a pope.
Of double worstede was his semycope,
That rounded as a belle out of the presse.
Somwhat he lipsed for his wantownesse,
To make his Englissh sweete upon his tonge,
And in his harpyng, whan that he hadde songe,
Hise eyen twynkled in his heed aryght,
As doon the sterres in the frosty nyght.
This worthy lymytour was cleped Huberd.

A MARCHANT was ther with a
forked berd,
In mottelee, and hye on horse he sat;
Upon his heed a flaundryssh bevere
hat;
His bootes clasped faire & fetisly.
His resons he spak ful solempnely,
Sownynge alway thencrees of his wynnyng.
He wolde the see were kept for any thing
Bitwixe Middelburgh and Orewelle.
Wel koude he in eschaunge sheeldes selle.
This worthy man ful wel his wit bisette,
Ther wiste no wight that he was in dette,
So estatly was he of his governaunce,
With his bargaynes and with his chevyssaunce.
For sothe he was a worthy man withalle,
But sooth to seyn, I noot how men hym calle.

A CLERK ther was of Oxenford also,
That unto logyk hadde longe ygo.
And leene was his hors as is a rake,
And he nas nat right fat, I under-
take,
But looked holwe, and therto
sobrely;
Ful thredbare was his overeste courtepy,
For he hadde geten hym yet no benefice,
Ne was so worldly for to have office.
For hym was levere have at his beddes heed
A twenty bookes, clad in blak or reed,
Of Aristotle and his philosophie,
Than robes riche, or fithele or gay sautrie:
But al be that he was a philosophre,
Yet hadde he but litel gold in cofre;
But al that he myghte of his freendes hente,
On bookes and his lernynge he it spente,
And bisily gan for the soules preye
Of hem that yaf hym wherwith to scoleye.
Of studie took he moost cure and moost heede,
Noght o word spak he moore than was neede,
And that was seyd in forme and reverence,
And short and quyk and ful of hy sentence.
Sownynge in moral vertu was his speche,
And gladly wolde he lerne and gladly teche.

A SERGEANT of the Lawe, war
and wys,
That often hadde been at the parvys,
Ther was also, ful riche of excellence.
Discreet he was, & of greet reverence;
He semed swich, hise wordes weren
so wise.
Justice he was ful often in assise,
By patente and by pleyn commissioun;
For his science, and for his heigh renoun
Of fees and robes hadde he many oon;
So greet a purchasour was nowher noon:
Al was fee symple to hym in effect,
His purchasyng myghte nat been infect.
Nowher so bisy a man as he ther nas,
And yet he semed bisier than he was.
In termes hadde he caas and doomes alle
That from the tyme of Kyng William were falle;
Therto he koude endite, and make a thyng,
Ther koude no wight pynchen at his writyng;
And every statut koude he pleyn by rote.

4

He rood but hoomly in a medlee cote
Girt with a ceint of silk, with barres smale;
Of his array telle I no lenger tale.

A FRANKELEYN was in his com-
paignye.
Whit was his heed as is a dayesye,
Of his complexioun he was sang-
wyn.
Wel loved he by the morwe a sope
in wyn;
To lyven in delit was evere his wone,
For he was Epicurus owene sone,
That heeld opinioun that pleyn delit
Was verraily felicitee parfit.
An housholdere, and that a greet, was he;
Seint Julian was he in his contree;
His breed, his ale, was alweys after oon;
A bettre envyned man was nevere noon.
Withoute bake mete was nevere his hous,
Of fissh and flessh, and that so plentevous,
It snewed in his hous of mete and drynke,
Of alle deyntees that men koude thynke:
After the sondry sesons of the yeer,
So chaunged he his mete and his soper.
Ful many a fat partrich hadde he in muwe
And many a breem and many a luce in stuwe.
Wo was his cook but if his sauce were
Poynaunt and sharpe, and redy al his geere.
His table dormant in his halle alway
Stood redy covered al the longe day.
At sessiouns ther was he lord and sire;
Ful ofte tyme he was knyght of the shire.
An anlaas, and a gipser al of silk,
Heeng at his girdel whit as morne milk.
A shirreve hadde he been and a countour:
Was nowher such a worthy vavasour.

AN Haberdasshere, and a Carpenter,
A Webbe, a Dyere, and a Tapycer,
And they were clothed alle in o lyveree
Of a solempne & a greet fraternitee;
Ful fressh and newe hir geere apiked
was;
Hir knyves were ychaped noght with bras,
But al with silver wroght ful clene and weel,
Hire girdles and hir pouches everydeel.
Wel semed ech of hem a fair burgeys
To sitten in a yeldehalle on a deys.
Everich, for the wisdom that he kan,
Was shaply for to been an alderman;
For catel hadde they ynogh, and rente,
And eek hir wyves wolde it wel assente;
And elles certeyn were they to blame.
It is ful fair to been ycleped Madame,
And goon to vigilies al bifore,
And have a mantel roialliche ybore.

A COOK they hadde with hem for the
nones,
To boille the chicknes with the
marybones
And poudre-marchant tart, and
galyngale;
Wel koude he knowe a draughte of London ale.
He koude rooste, and sethe, and broille, and frye,
Maken mortreux, and wel bake a pye;

But greet harm was it, as it thoughte me,
That on his shyne a mormal hadde he;
for blankmanger, that made he with the beste.

SHIPMAN was ther, wonynge fer
by weste;
for aught I woot, he was of Derte-
mouthe.
He rood upon a rouncy as he kouthe,
In a gowne of faldyng to the knee.
A daggere hangynge on a laas hadde he
Aboute his nekke under his arm adoun.
The hoote somer hadde maad his hewe al broun,
And certeinly he was a good felawe.
ful many a draughte of wyn had he ydrawe
fro Burdeuxward whil that the chapman sleepe;
Of nyce conscience took he no keepe;
If that he faught, and hadde the hyer hond,
By water he sente hem hoom to every lond.
But of his craft to rekene wel his tydes,
His stremes and his daungers hym bisides,
His herberwe and his moone, his lodemenage,
Ther nas noon swich from Hulle to Cartage.
Hardy he was, and wys to undertake;
With many a tempest hadde his berd been shake.
He knew alle the havenes as they were
from Gootlond to the Cape of fynystere,
And every cryke in Britaigne and in Spayne;
His barge ycleped was the Maudelayne.

ITH us ther was a Doctour of Phi-
sik;
In al this world ne was ther noon
hym lik
To speke of phisik and of surgerye;
for he was grounded in astronomye;
He kepte his pacient a ful greet deel
In houres by his magyk natureel.
Wel koude he fortunen the ascendent
Of his ymages for his pacient.
He knew the cause of everich maladye,
Were it of hoot, or cold, or moyste, or drye,
And where engendred and of what humour;
He was a verray parfit praktisour.
The cause yknowe, and of his harm the roote,
Anon he yaf the sike man his boote.
ful redy hadde he his apothecaries,
To sende him drogges and his letuaries,
for ech of hem made oother for to wynne,
Hir frendshipe nas nat newe to bigynne.
Wel knew he the olde Esculapius,
And Deyscorides, and eek Rufus,
Olde Ypocras, Haly, and Galyen,
Serapion, Razis, and Avycen,
Averrois, Damascien, and Constantyn,
Bernard, and Gatesden, and Gilbertyn.
Of his diete mesurable was he,
for it was of no superfluitee,
But of greet norrissyng and digestible;
His studie was but litel on the Bible.
In sangwyn and in pers he clad was al,
Lyned with taffata and with sendal;
And yet he was but esy of dispence,
He kepte that he wan in pestilence.
for gold in phisik is a cordial,
Therfore he lovede gold in special.

GOOD wif was ther of biside Bathe,
But she was somdel deef and that
was scathe.
Of clooth makyng she hadde swich
an haunt,
She passed hem of Ypres & of Gaunt.

In al the parisshe, wif ne was ther noon
That to the offrynge bifore hire sholde goon,
And if ther dide, certeyn so wrooth was she,
That she was out of alle charitee.
Hir coverchiefs ful fyne weren of ground,
I dorste swere they weyeden ten pound,
That on a Sonday weren upon hir heed.
Hir hosen weren of fyn scarlet reed,
ful streite yteyd, and shoes ful moyste & newe;
Boold was hir face, and fair, and reed of hewe.
She was a worthy womman al hir lyve,
Housbondes at chirche dore she hadde fyve,
Withouten oother compaignye in youthe,
But therof nedeth nat to speke as nowthe;
And thries hadde she been at Jerusalem;
She hadde passed many a straunge strem;
At Rome she hadde been, and at Boloigne,
In Galice at Seint Jame, and at Coloigne,
She koude muchel of wandrynge by the weye.
Gat tothed was she, soothly for to seye.
Upon an amblere esily she sat,
Ywympled wel, and on her heed an hat
As brood as is a bokeler or a targe;
A foot mantel aboute hir hipes large,
And on hire feet a paire of spores sharpe.
In felaweshipe wel koude she laughe and carpe
Of remedies of love she knew perchaunce,
for she koude of that art the olde daunce.

GOOD man was ther of religioun,
And was a povre Persoun of a toun;
But riche he was of hooly thoght
and werk.
He was also a lerned man, a clerk
That Cristes Gospel trewely wolde

preche;
His parisshens devoutly wolde he teche.
Benygne he was, and wonder diligent,
And in adversitee ful pacient;
And swich he was ypreved ofte sithes.
ful looth were hym to cursen for his tithes,
But rather wolde he yeven, out of doute,
Unto his povre parisshens aboute
Of his offryng, and eek of his substaunce:
He koude in litel thyng have suffisaunce.
Wyd was hys parisshe, and houses fer asonder,
But he ne lafte nat for reyn ne thonder,
In siknesse nor in meschief to visite
The ferreste in his parisshe, muche and lite,
Upon his feet, and in his hand a staf.
This noble ensample to his sheepe he yaf
That first he wroghte, and afterward he taughte;
Out of the gospel he tho wordes caughte;
And this figure he added eek therto,
That if gold ruste, what shal iren doo?
for if a preest be foul, on whom we truste,
No wonder is a lewed man to ruste;
And shame it is, if a prest take keepe,
A shiten shepherde and a clene sheepe.

Wel oghte a preest ensample for to yive,
By his clennesse, how that his sheepe sholde lyve.
He sette nat his benefice to hyre,
And leet his sheepe encombred in the myre,
And ran to London, unto sëint Poules,
To seken hym a chaunterie for soules;
Or with a bretherhed to been withholde,
But dwelte at hoom, and kepte wel his folde,
So that the wolf ne made it nat myscarie;
He was a shepherde, and noght a mercenarie:
And though he hooly were, and vertuous,
He was to synful man nat despitous,
Ne of his speche daungerous ne digne,
But in his techyng discreet and benygne,
To drawen folk to hevene by fairnesse,
By good ensample, this was his bisynesse.
But it were any persone obstinat,
What so he were, of heigh or lough estat,
Hym wolde he snybben sharply for the nonys;
A bettre preest I trowe that nowher noon ys.
He waited after no pompe and reverence,
Ne maked him a spiced conscience,
But Cristes loore, and his apostles twelve,
He taughte, but first he folwed it hymselve.

The Plowman

ITH hym ther was a Plowman, was
his brother,
That hadde ylad of dong ful many
a fother,
A trewe swynkere & a good was he,
Lyvynge in pees & parfit charitee.
God loved he best, with al his hoole herte
At alle tymes, thogh he gamed or smerte,
And thanne his neighebore right as himselve.
He wolde thresshe, and therto dyke and delve
For Cristes sake for every povre wight,
Withouten hire, if it lay in his myght.
His tithes payde he ful faire and wel,
Bothe of his propre swynk and his catel.
In a tabard he rood upon a mere.

The Reve
The Millere
The Somnour
The Pardoner
The Maunciple
Geoffrey Chaucer

HER was also a Reve and a Millere,
A Somnour and a Pardoner also,
A Maunciple, and myself; ther were
namo.
The Millere was a stout carl for the
nones,
Ful byg he was of brawn, and eek of bones;
That proved wel, for over al ther he cam,
At wrastlynge he wolde have alwey the ram.
He was short sholdred, brood, a thikke knarre,
Ther nas no dore that he ne wolde heve of harre,
Or breke it at a rennyng with his heed.
His berd as any sowe or fox was reed,
And therto brood, as though it were a spade.
Upon the cope right of his nose he hade
A werte, and theron stood a toft of herys,
Reed as the brustles of a sowes erys;
His nosethirles blake were and wyde,
A swerd and bokeler bar he by his syde;
His mouth as greet was as a greet forneys,
He was a janglere and a goliardeys,
And that was moost of synne and harlotries.
Wel koude he stelen corn, and tollen thries;
And yet he hadde a thombe of gold, pardee.
A whit cote and a blew hood wered he,
6

A baggepipe wel koude he blowe and sowne,
And therwithal he broghte us out of towne.

The
Ma

GENTIL Maunciple was ther of a
temple,
Of which achatours myghte take
exemple
for to be wise in byynge of vitaille;
for wheither that he payde, or took
by taille,
Algate he wayted so in his achaat,
That he was ay biforn and in good staat.
Now is nat that of God a ful fair grace,
That swich a lewed mannes wit shal pace
The wisdom of an heepe of lerned men?
Of maistres hadde he mo than thries ten,
That weren of lawe expert and curious,
Of whiche ther weren a duszeyne in that hous,
Worthy to been stywardes of rente and lond
Of any lord that is in Engelond,
To maken hym lyve by his propre good
In honour dettelees, but if he were wood,
Or lyve as scarsly as hym list desire,
And able for to helpen al a shire
In any caas that myghte falle or happe,
And yet this Maunciple sette hir alle cappe.

The

HE Reve was a sclendre colerik man,
His berd was shave as ny as ever he
kan;
His heer was by his erys ful round
yshorn,
His tope was doked lyk a preest
biforn.
Ful longe were his legges and ful lene,
Ylyk a staf, ther was no calf ysene.
Wel koude he kepe a gerner and a bynne,
Ther was noon auditour koude on him wynne.
Wel wiste he, by the droghte and by the reyn,
The yeldynge of his seed and of his greyn.
His lordes sheepe, his neet, his dayerye,
His swyn, his hors, his stoor, and his pultrye,
Was hoolly in this reves governyng,
And by his covenant yaf the rekenyng
Syn that his lord was twenty yeer of age;
Ther koude no man brynge hym in arrerage.
Ther nas baillif, ne hierde, nor oother hyne,
That he ne knew his sleighte and his covyne;
They were adrad of hym as of the deeth.
His wonyng was ful faire upon an heeth,
With grene trees yshadwed was his place.
He koude bettre than his lord purchace.
Ful riche he was astored pryvely,
His lord wel koude he plesen subtilly,
To yeve and lene him of his owene good,
And have a thank, and yet a gowne and hood.
In youthe he hadde lerned a good myster,
He was a wel good wrighte, a carpenter.
This Reve sat upon a ful good stot,
That was al pomely grey, and highte Scot.
A long surcote of pers upon he hade,
And by his syde he baar a rusty blade.
Of Northfolk was this Reve of which I telle,
Biside a toun men clepen Baldeswelle.
Tukked he was, as is a frere, aboute,
And evere he rood the hyndreste of oure route.

SOMONOUR was ther with us in that place,
That hadde a fyr reed cherubynnes face,
for sawcefleem he was, with eyen narwe;
As hoot he was, and lecherous as a sparwe,
With scaled browes blake, and piled berd,
Of his visage children were aferd.
Ther nas quyksilver, lytarge, ne brymstoon,
Boras, ceruce, ne oille of tartre noon,
Ne oynement that wolde clense and byte,
That hym myghte helpen of the whelkes white,
Nor of the knobbes sittynge on his chekes.
Wel loved he garleek, oynons, and eek lekes,
And for to drynken strong wyn, reed as blood,
Thanne wolde he speke and crie as he were wood;
And whan that he wel dronken hadde the wyn
Than wolde he speke no word but Latyn.
A fewe termes hadde he, two or thre,
That he had lerned out of som decree;
No wonder is, he herde it al the day;
And eek ye knowen wel, how that a jay
Kan clepen Watte, as wel as kan the pope.
But whoso koude in oother thyng hym grope,
Thanne hadde he spent al his philosophie;
Ay, Questio quid juris, wolde he crie.
He was a gentil harlot and a kynde;
A bettre felawe sholde men noght fynde.
He wolde suffre for a quart of wyn
A good felawe to have his concubyn
A twelf month, and excuse hym atte fulle;
And prively a fynch eek koude he pulle;
And if he foond owher a good felawe,
He wolde techen him to have noon awe,
In swich caas, of the Ercedekenes curs,
But if a mannes soule were in his purs;
for in his purs he sholde ypunysshed be:
Purs is the Ercedekenes helle, seyde he.
But wel I woot he lyed right in dede,
Of cursyng oghte ech gilty man to drede,
for curs wol slee right as assoillyng savith;
And also war him of a Significavit.
In daunger hadde he at his owene gise
The yonge girles of the diocise,
And knew hir conseil, and was al hir reed.
A gerland hadde he set upon his heed,
As greet as it were for an ale stake,
A bokeleer hadde he maad him of a cake.

WITH hym ther rood a gentil Pardoner
Of Rouncivale, his freend and his compeer,
That streight was comen fro the court of Rome.
ful loude he soong Com hider love to me.
This Somonour bar to hym a stif burdoun,
Was nevere trompe of half so greet a soun.
This Pardoner hadde heer as yelow as wex,
But smothe it heeng as dooth a strike of flex;
By ounces henge his lokkes that he hadde,
And therwith he his shuldres overspradde;
But thynne it lay by colpons oon and oon;
But hood, for jolitee, ne wered he noon,

for it was trussed up in his walet.
Hym thoughte he rood al of the newe jet,
Dischevelee, save his cappe, he rood al bare.
Swiche glarynge eyen hadde he as an hare,
A vernycle hadde he sowed upon his cappe;
His walet lay biforn hym in his lappe,
Bretful of pardon, comen from Rome al hoot.
A voys he hadde as smal as hath a goot;
No berd hadde he, ne nevere sholde have,
As smothe it was as it were late yshave;
I trowe he were a geldyng or a mare.
But of his craft, fro Berwyk in to Ware,
Ne was ther swich another pardoner;
for in his male he hadde a pilwe beer,
Which that he seyde was oure lady veyl.
He seyde he hadde a gobet of the seyl
That Seint Peter hadde whan that he wente
Upon the see, til Jhesu Crist hym hente.
He hadde a croys of latoun, ful of stones,
And in a glas he hadde pigges bones.
But with thise relikes, whan that he fond
A povre person dwellynge upon lond,
Upon a day he gat hym moore moneye
Than that the person gat in monthes tweye.
And thus with feyned flaterye and japes,
He made the person and the peple his apes.
But trewely to tellen, atte laste,
He was in chirche a noble ecclesiaste;
Wel koude he rede a lessoun or a storie,
But alderbest he song an offertorie;
for wel he wiste, whan that song was songe,
He moste preche, and wel affile his tonge
To wynne silver, as he ful wel koude;
Therefore he song the murierly and loude.

NOW have I toold you shortly, in a clause,
The staat, tharray, the nombre, and eek the cause
Why that assembled was this compaignye
In Southwerk, at this gentil hostelrye,
That highte the Tabard, faste by the Belle.
But now is tyme to yow for to telle
How that we baren us that ilke nyght,
Whan we were in that hostelrie alyght;
And after wol I telle of our viage,
And al the remenaunt of oure pilgrimage.

AT first, I pray yow of youre curteisye,
That ye narette it nat my vileynye,
Thogh that I pleynly speke in this mateere,
To telle yow hir wordes & hir cheere,
Ne thogh I speke hir wordes proprely:
for this ye knowen also wel as I,
Whoso shal telle a tale after a man,
He moote reherce, as ny as evere he kan,
Everich a word, if it be in his charge,
Al speke he never so rudeliche or large;
Or ellis he moot telle his tale untrewe,
Or feyne thyng, or fynde wordes newe.
He may nat spare, althogh he were his brother,
He moot as wel seye o word as another.
Crist spak himself ful brode in hooly writ,

And wel ye woot no vileynye is it.
Eek Plato seith, whoso that kan hym rede,
The wordes moote be cosyn to the dede.
Also I prey yow to foryeve it me,
Al have I nat set folk in hir degree
Heere in this tale, as that they sholde stonde;
My wit is short, ye may wel understonde.

GREET chiere made oure hoost us everichon,
And to the soper sette he us anon,
And served us with vitaille at the beste.
Strong was the wyn, & wel to drynke us leste.

A SEMELY man oure Hooste was withalle
For to han been a marchal in an halle.
A large man he was with eyen stepe,
A fairer burgeys was ther noon in Chepe;
Boold of his speche, and wys and well ytaught,
And of manhod hym lakkede right naught.
Eek therto he was right a myrie man,
And after soper pleyen he bigan,
And spak of myrthe amonges othere thynges,
Whan that we hadde maad our rekenynges;
And seyde thus ⁊ Now lordynges, trewely,
Ye been to me right welcome hertely;
For by my trouthe, if that I shal nat lye,
I saugh nat this yeer so myrie a compaignye
Atones in this herberwe as is now;
Fayn wolde I doon yow myrthe, wiste I how.
And of a myrthe I am right now bythoght,
To doon yow ese, and it shal coste noght.
Ye goon to Canterbury, God yow speede,
The blisful martir quite yow youre meede.
And wel I woot as ye goon by the weye
Ye shapen yow to talen and to pleye;
For trewely, confort ne myrthe is noon
To ride by the weye doumb as the stoon;
And therfore wol I maken yow disport,
As I seyde erst, and doon yow som confort.
And if yow liketh alle, by oon assent,
How for to stonden at my juggement,
And for to werken as I shal yow seye,
Tomorwe, whan ye riden by the weye,
Now by my fader soule that is deed,
But ye be myrie, I wol yeve yow myn heed.
Hoold up youre hond, withouten moore speche.
⁊ Oure conseil was nat longe for to seche;
Us thoughte it was noght worth to make it wys,
And graunted hym withouten moore avys,
And bad him seye his voirdit as hym leste.
Lordynges, quod he, now herkneth for the beste,
But taak it nought, I prey yow, in desdeyn;
This is the poynt, to speken short and pleyn,
That eche of yow, to shorte with oure weye,
In this viage shal telle tales tweye,
To Caunterburyward, I mene it so,
And homward he shal tellen othere two,
Of aventures that whilom han bifalle.
And which of yow that bereth hym best of alle,
That is to seyn, that telleth in this caas
Tales of best sentence and moost solaas,

8

Shal have a soper at oure aller cost
Heere in this place, sittynge by this post,
Whan that we come agayn fro Caunterbury.
And for to make yow the moore mury,
I wol myselfe goodly with yow ryde
Right at myn owene cost, and be youre gyde,
And whoso wole my juggement withseye,
Shal paye al that we spenden by the weye.
And if ye vouchesauf that it be so,
Tel me anon, withouten wordes mo,
And I wol erly shape me therfore.
This thyng was graunted, and oure othes swore
With ful glad herte, and preyden hym also
That he would vouchesauf for to do so,
And that he wolde been oure governour,
And of our tales juge and reportour,
And sette a soper at a certeyn pris;
And we wol reuled been at his devys
In heigh and lough; and thus by oon assent,
We been acorded to his juggement.
And therupon the wyn was fet anon;
We dronken, and to reste wente echon
Withouten any lenger taryynge.

A MORWE, whan that day gan for to sprynge,
Up roos oure hoost and was oure aller cok,
And gadrede us togidre alle in a flok,
And forth we riden, a litel moore than paas,
Unto the wateryng of Seint Thomas;
And there oure hoost bigan his hors areste,
And seyde ⁊ Lordynges, herkneth if yow leste:
Ye woot youre forward, and I it yow recorde.
If evensong and morwesong accorde,
Lat se now who shal telle the firste tale.
As evere mote I drynke wyn or ale,
Whoso be rebel to my juggement
Shal paye for al that by the wey is spent.
Now draweth cut, er that we ferrer twynne;
He which that hath the shorteste shal bigynne.
Sire Knyght, quod he, my mayster and my lord,
Now draweth cut, for that is myn accord.
Cometh neer, quod he, my lady Prioresse,
And ye, sire Clerk, lat be your shamefastnesse,
Ne studieth noght; ley hond to, every man.
⁊ Anon to drawen every wight bigan,
And shortly for to tellen as it was,
Were it by aventure, or sort, or cas,
The sothe is this, the cut fil to the knyght,
Of which ful blithe and glad was every wyght:
And telle he moste his tale as was resoun,
By forward and by composicioun,
As ye han herd; what nedeth wordes mo?
And whan this goode man saugh it was so,
As he that wys was and obedient
To kepe his forward by his free assent,
He seyde ⁊ Syn I shal bigynne the game,
What, welcome be the cut, a Goddes name!
Now lat us ryde, and herkneth what I seye.
And with that word we ryden forth oure weye;
And he bigan with right a myrie cheere
His tale anon, and seyde in this manere.
Heere endith the prolog of this book.

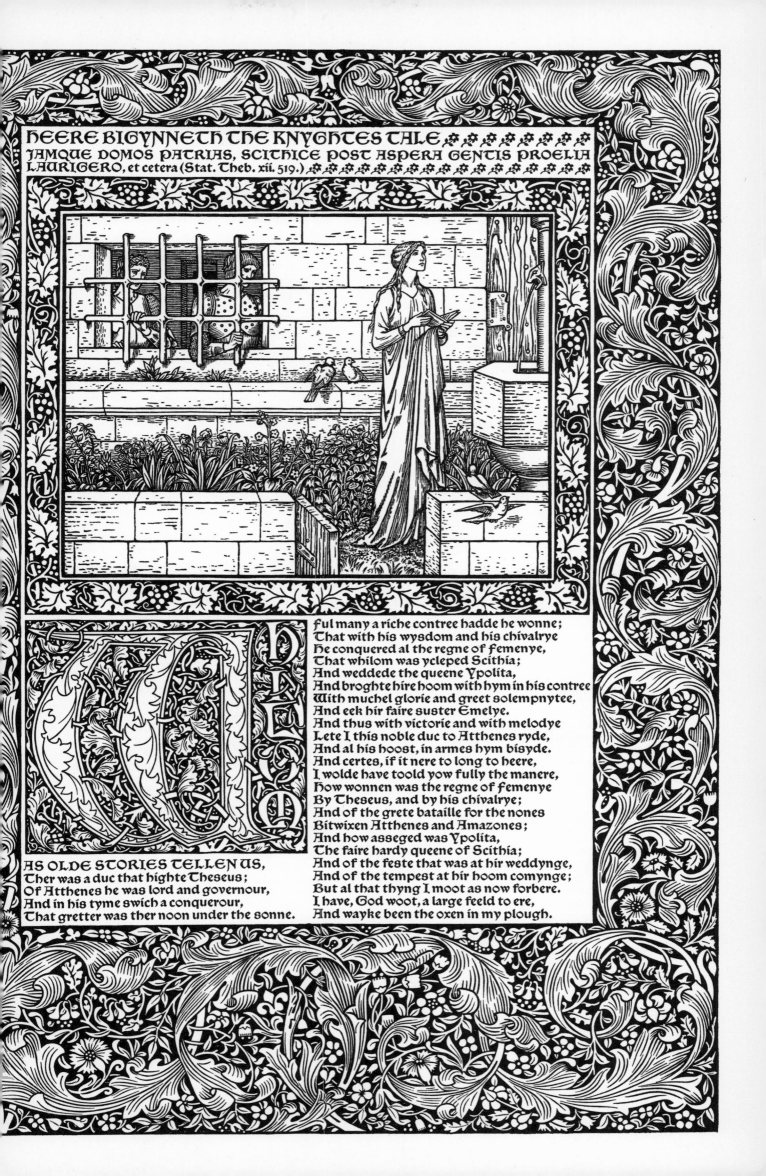

HEERE BIGYNNETH THE KNYGHTES TALE
IAMQUE DOMOS PATRIAS, SCITHICE POST ASPERA GENTIS PROELIA
LAURIGERO, et cetera (Stat. Theb. xii. 519.)

AS OLDE STORIES TELLEN US,
Ther was a duc that highte Theseus;
Of Atthenes he was lord and governour,
And in his tyme swich a conquerour,
That gretter was ther noon under the sonne.

Ful many a riche contree hadde he wonne;
That with his wysdom and his chivalrye
He conquered al the regne of Femenye,
That whilom was ycleped Scithia;
And weddede the queene Ypolita,
And broghte hire hoom with hym in his contree
With muchel glorie and greet solempnytee,
And eek hir faire suster Emelye.
And thus with victorie and with melodye
Lete I this noble duc to Atthenes ryde,
And al his hoost, in armes hym bisyde.
And certes, if it nere to long to heere,
I wolde have toold yow fully the manere,
How wonnen was the regne of Femenye
By Theseus, and by his chivalrye;
And of the grete bataille for the nones
Bitwixen Atthenes and Amazones;
And how asseged was Ypolita,
The faire hardy queene of Scithia;
And of the feste that was at hir weddynge,
And of the tempest at hir hoom comynge;
But al that thyng I moot as now forbere.
I have, God woot, a large feeld to ere,
And wayke been the oxen in my plough.

The remenant of the tale is long ynough:
I wol nat letten eek noon of this route;
Lat every felawe telle his tale aboute,
And lat se now who shal the soper wynne,
And ther I lefte, I wol ageyne bigynne.
THIS duc, of whom I make mencioun,
Whan he was come almoost unto the toun,
In al his wele, and in his mooste pride,
He was war, as he caste his eye aside,
Where that ther kneled in the hye weye
A compaignye of ladyes, tweye and tweye,
Ech after oother clad in clothes blake;
But swich a cry and swich a wo they make,
That in this world nys creature lyvynge,
That herde swich another waymentynge:
And of this cry they nolde nevere stenten,
Til they the reynes of his brydel henten.
🙚 What folk been ye, that at myn hom comynge
Perturben so my feste with criynge?
Quod Theseus: Have ye so greet envye
Of myn honour, that thus compleyne and crye?
Or who hath yow mysboden or offended?
And telleth me if it may been amended;
And why that ye been clothed thus in blak?
🙚 The eldest lady of hem alle spak
Whan she hadde swowned with a deedly cheere,
That it was routhe for to seen and heere,
And seyde 🙚 Lord, to whom Fortune hath yyven
Victorie, and as a conqueror to lyven,
Nat greveth us youre glorie and youre honour,
But we biseken mercy and socour.
Have mercy on oure wo and oure distresse;
Some drope of pitee, thurgh thy gentillesse,
Upon us wrecched wommen lat thou falle;
For certes, lord, there is noon of us alle
That she nath been a duchesse or a queene;
Now be we caytyves, as it is wel seene:
Thanked be Fortune, and hire false wheel,
That noon estat assureth to be weel.
And certes, lord, to abyden youre presence,
Heere in the temple of the goddesse Clemence
We han ben waitynge al this fourtenyght;
Now help us, lord, sith it is in thy myght.
I wrecche, which that wepe and waille thus,
Was whilom wyf to kyng Cappaneus,
That starf at Thebes, cursed be that day;
And alle we that been in this array,
And maken al this lamentacioun,
We losten alle oure housbondes at that toun,
Whil that the seege theraboute lay.
And yet the olde Creon, weylaway!
That lord is now of Thebes the citee,
Fulfild of ire and of iniquitee,
He, for despit, and for his tirannye,
To do the dede bodyes vileynye,
Of alle oure lordes, whiche that been slawe,
Hath alle the bodyes on an heepe ydrawe,
And wol nat suffren hem, by noon assent,
Neither to been yburyed nor ybrent,
But maketh houndes ete hem in despit.
🙚 And with that word, withouten moore respit,
They fillen gruf, and criden pitously,
Have on us wrecched wommen som mercy,
10

And lat oure sorwe synken in thyn herte.
🙚 This gentil duc doun from his courser sterte
With herte pitous, whan he herde hem speke.
Hym thoughte that his herte wolde breke,
Whan he saugh hem so pitous and so maat,
That whilom weren of so greet estaat;
And in his armes he hem alle up hente,
And hem conforteth in ful good entente;
And swoor his ooth, as he was trewe knyght,
He wolde doon so ferforthly his myght
Upon the tiraunt Creon hem to wreke,
That al the peple of Grece sholde speke
How Creon was of Theseus yserved,
As he that hadde his deeth ful wel deserved.
AND right anoon, withouten moore abood,
His baner he desplayeth, and forth rood
To Thebesward, and al his hoost biside;
No neer Atthenes wolde he go ne ride,
Ne take his ese fully half a day,
But onward on his wey that nyght he lay;
And sente anon Ypolita the queene,
And Emelye hir yonge suster sheene,
Unto the toun of Atthenes to dwelle,
And forth he rit; ther is namoore to telle.
🙚 The rede statue of Mars with spere and targe
So shyneth in his white baner large,
That alle the feeldes glyteren up and doun;
And by his baner born is his penoun
Of gold ful riche, in which ther was ybete
The Mynotaur, which that he slough in Crete.
THUS rit this duc, thus rit this conquerour,
And in his hoost of chivalrie the flour,
Til that he cam to Thebes, and alighte
Faire in a feeld, ther as he thoughte fighte.
But shortly for to speken of this thyng
With Creon, which that was of Thebes kyng,
He faught, and slough hym manly as a knyght
In pleyn bataille, and putte the folk to flyght;
And by assaut he wan the citee after,
And rente adoun bothe wall, and sparre, & rafter;
And to the ladyes he restored agayn
The bones of hir housbondes that were slayn,
To doon obsequies, as was tho the gyse.
BUT it were al to long for to devyse
The grete clamour and the waymentynge
Which that the ladyes made at the brennynge
Of the bodyes, and the grete honour
That Theseus, the noble conquerour,
Dooth to the ladyes whan they from hym wente.
But shortly for to telle is myn entente;
Whan that this worthy duc, this Theseus,
Hath Creon slayn, and wonne Thebes thus,
Stille in that feeld he took al nyght his reste,
And dide with al the contree as hym leste.
TO ransake in the taas of bodyes dede,
Hem for to strepe of harneys and of wede,
The pilours diden bisynesse and cure,
After the bataille and disconfiture.
And so bifel that in the taas they founde,
Thurghgirt with many a grevous blody wounde,
Two yonge knyghtes, liggynge by and by,
Bothe in oon armes, wroght ful richely,
Of whiche two, Arcita highte that oon,

And that oother knyght highte Palamon.
Nat fully quyke, ne fully dede they were,
But by here cote armures, and by hir gere,
The heraudes knewe hem best in special,
As they that weren of the blood roial
Of Thebes, and of sustren two yborn.
Out of the taas the pilours han hem torn,
And han hem caried softe unto the tente
Of Theseus, and ful soone he hem sente
To Atthenes, to dwellen in prisoun
Perpetuelly; he nolde no raunsoun.
And whan this worthy duc hath thus ydon,
He took his hoost, and hoom he rood anon,
With laurer crowned as a conquerour;
And ther he lyveth in joye and in honour
Terme of his lyve; what nedeth wordes mo?
And in a tour, in angwissh and in wo,
This Palamon, and his felawe Arcite,
For everemoore, ther may no gold hem quite.
THIS passeth yeer by yeer, and day by day,
Till it fil ones, in a morwe of May,
That Emelye, that fairer was to sene
Than is the lylie upon his stalke grene,
And fressher than the May with floures newe,
For with the rose colour stroof hire hewe,
I noot which was the fyner of hem two,
Er it were day, as was hir wone to do,
She was arisen, and al redy dight;
For May wole have no slogardrie anyght,
The sesoun priketh every gentil herte,
And maketh hym out of his slepe to sterte,
And seith Arys, and do thyn observaunce.
This maked Emelye have remembraunce
To doon honour to May, and for to ryse.
Yclothed was she fresshe, for to devyse;
Hir yelow heer was broyded in a tresse
Bihynde hir bak a yerde long, I gesse.
And in the gardyn at the sonne upriste,
She walketh up and doun, and as hire liste
She gadereth floures, party white and rede,
To make a subtil gerland for hire hede,
And as an aungel, hevenysshly she soong.
THE grete tour that was so thikke & stroong,
Which of the castel was the chief dongeoun,
Theras the knyghtes weren in prisoun,
Of whiche I tolde yow, and tellen shal,
Was evene joynant to the gardyn wal,
Theras this Emelye hadde hir pleyynge.
BRIGHT was the sonne, and cleer that
morwenynge,
And Palamon, this woful prisoner,
As was his wone, bi leve of his gayler,
Was risen, and romed in a chambre an heigh,
In which he al the noble citee seigh,
And eek the gardyn ful of braunches grene,
Theras this fresshe Emelye the sheene
Was in hire walk, and romed up and doun.
This sorweful prisoner, this Palamoun,
Goth in the chambre, romynge to and fro,
And to hymself compleynynge of his wo;
That he was born, ful ofte he seyde, allas!
And so bifel, by aventure or cas,
That thurgh a wyndow, thikke of many a barre

Of iren, greet and square as any sparre,
He cast his eye upon Emelya,
And therwithal he bleynte and cryed, A!
As though he stongen were unto the herte.
And with that cry Arcite anon upsterte,
And seyde, Cosyn myn, what eyleth thee,
That art so pale and deedly on to see?
Why cridestow? Who hath thee doon offence?
For Goddes love, taak al in pacience
Oure prisoun, for it may noon oother be;
Fortune hath yeven us this adversitee.
Somme wikke aspect or disposicioun
Of Saturne, by sum constellacioun,
Hath yeven us this, although we hadde it sworn,
So stood the hevene whan that we were born;
We moste endure: this is the short and playn.
This Palamon answerde, and seyde agayn,
Cosyn, for sothe, of this opinioun
Thow hast a veyn ymaginacioun;
This prison caused me nat for to crye,
But I was hurt right now thurghout myn eye
Into myn herte, that wol my bane be.
The fairnesse of that lady that I see
Yond in the gardyn romen to and fro,
Is cause of al my crying and my wo.
I noot wher she be womman or goddesse;
But Venus is it, soothly, as I gesse.
And therwithal on knees doun he fil,
And seyde, Venus, if it be thy wil
Yow in this gardyn thus to transfigure
Bifore me, sorweful wrecche creature,
Out of this prisoun helpe that we may scapen.
And if so be my destynee be shapen
By eterne word, to dyen in prisoun,
Of our lynage have som compassioun,
That is so lowe ybroght by tirannye.
And with that word Arcite gan espye
Wheras this lady romed to and fro;
And with that sighte hir beautee hurte hym so,
That if that Palamon was wounded sore,
Arcite is hurt as moche as he, or moore;
And with a sigh he seyde pitously:
The fresshe beautee sleeth me sodeynly
Of hire that rometh in the yonder place,
And but I have hir mercy and hir grace
That I may seen hire atte leeste weye
I nam but deed; ther is namoore to seye.
THIS Palamon, whan he tho wordes herde,
Dispitously he looked and answerde,
Wheither seistow this in ernest or in pley?
Nay, quod Arcite, in ernest, by my fey!
God helpe me so, me list ful yvele pleye.
This Palamon gan knytte his browes tweye,
It nere, quod he, to thee no greet honour,
For to be fals, ne for to be traitour
To me, that am thy cosyn and thy brother
Ysworn ful depe, and ech of us til oother,
That nevere for to dyene in the peyne,
Till that the deeth departe shal us tweyne,
Neither of us in love to hyndre oother
Ne in noon oother cas, my leeve brother,
But that thou sholdest trewely forthren me
In every cas, as I shal forthren thee.

11

This was thyn ooth, and myn also certeyn;
I woot right wel thou darst it nat withseyn.
Thus artow of my conseil, out of doute:
And now thow woldest falsly been aboute
To love my lady, whom I love and serve,
And evere shal, til that myn herte sterve.
Nay, certes, false Arcite, thow shalt nat so;
I loved hire first, and tolde thee my wo
As to my conseil, and my brother sworn
To forthre me, as I have toold biforn.
For which thou art ybounden as a knyght
To helpen me, if it lay in thy myght,
Or elles artow fals, I dar wel seyn.
THIS Arcite ful proudly spak ageyn;
Thow shalt, quod he, be rather fals than I,
And thou art fals, I telle thee, outrely,
For par amour I loved hire first er thow.
What wiltow seyn? thou wistest nat yet now
Wheither she be a womman or goddesse.
Thyn is affeccioun of hoolynesse,
And myn is love as to a creature,
For which I told thee myn aventure
As to my cosyn and my brother sworn.
I pose that thow lovedest hire biforn,
Wostow nat wel the olde clerkes sawe,
That who shal yeve a lovere any lawe?
Love is a gretter lawe, by my pan,
Than may be yeve of any erthely man?
And therfore positif lawe and swich decree
Is broken al day for love in ech degree.
A man moot nedes love maugree his heed;
He may nat flee it, thogh he sholde be deed,
Al be she mayde, or wydwe, or elles wyf;
And eek it is nat likly al thy lyf
To stonden in hir grace, namoore shal I;
For wel thou woost, thyselven verraily,
That thou and I be dampned to prisoun
Perpetuelly; us gayneth no raunsoun.
We stryven as dide the houndes for the boon,
They foughte al day, and yet hir part was noon;
Ther cam a kyte, whil they weren so wrothe,
And baar awey the boon bitwixe hem bothe;
And therfore, at the kynges court, my brother,
Ech man for hymself, ther is noon oother.
Love, if thee list, for I love and ay shal,
And soothly, leeve brother, this is al.
Heere in this prisoun moote we endure
And everich of us take his aventure.
GREET was the strif, and long, bitwix hem
tweye,
If that I hadde leyser for to seye;
But to theffect. It happed on a day,
To telle it yow as shortly as I may,
A worthy duc, that highte Perotheus,
That felawe was unto duc Theseus,
Syn thilke day that they were children lite,
Was come to Atthenes, his felawe to visite,
And for to pleye, as he was wont to do;
For in this world he loved no man so,
And he loved hym als tendrely agayn.
So wel they lovede, as old bookes sayn,
That whan that oon was deed, soothly to telle,
His felawe wente and soughte hym doun in helle;

12

But of that storie list me nat to write.
Duc Perotheus loved wel Arcite,
And hadde hym knowe at Thebes yeer by yere;
And finally, at request and preyere
Of Perotheus, withoute any raunsoun,
Duc Theseus hym leet out of prisoun
Frely to goon wher that hym liste over al,
In swich a gyse as I you tellen shal.
This was the forward, pleynly for tendite,
Bitwixen Theseus and hym Arcite;
That if so were that Arcite were yfounde,
Evere in his lif, by day or nyght, o stounde,
In any contree of this Theseus,
And he were caught, it was acorded thus,
That with a swerd he sholde lese his heed:
Ther nas noon oother remedie, ne reed,
But taketh his leve and homward he him spedde:
Lat hym be war, his nekke lith to wedde.
How greet a sorwe suffreth now Arcite!
The deeth he feeleth thurgh his herte smyte;
He wepeth, wayleth, crieth pitously;
To sleen hymself he waiteth prively.
He seyde, Allas that day that I was born!
Now is my prisoun worse than biforn;
Now is me shape eternally to dwelle,
Nat in my purgatorie, but in helle.
Allas that evere knew I Perotheus!
For elles hadde I dwelled with Theseus
Yfetered in his prisoun everemo.
Thanne hadde I been in blisse, and nat in wo,
Oonly the sighte of hire whom that I serve,
Though that I nevere hir grace may deserve,
Wolde han suffised right ynough for me.
O deere cosyn Palamon, quod he,
Thyn is the victorie of this aventure
Ful blisfully in prison maistow dure,
In prisoun? certes nay, but paradys!
Wel hath fortune yturned thee the dys,
That hast the sighte of hire and I thabsence.
For possible is, syn thou hast hire presence,
And art a knyght, a worthy and an able,
That by som cas, syn fortune is chaungeable,
Thow maist to thy desir some tyme atteyne,
But I, that am exiled and bareyne
Of alle grace, and in so greet dispeir,
That ther nys erthe, water, fyr, ne eir,
Ne creature, that of hem maked is,
That may me heele, or doon confort in this.
Wel oughte I sterve in wanhope and distresse;
Farwel, my lif, my lust and my gladnesse.
Allas, why pleynen folk so in commune
Of purveiaunce of God, or of Fortune,
That yeveth hem ful ofte in many a gyse
Wel bettre than they kan hemself devyse?
Som man desireth for to han richesse,
That cause is of his mordre, or greet siknesse;
And som man wolde out of his prisoun fayn,
That in his hous is of his meynee slayn.
Infinite harmes been in this mateere.
We witen nat what thing we preyen heere.
We faren as he that dronke is as a mous.
A dronke man woot wel he hath an hous,
But he noot which the righte wey is thider,

And to a dronke man the wey is slider;
And certes in this world so faren we,
We seken faste after felicitee,
But we goon wrong ful often trewely.
Thus may we seyen alle, and namely I,
That wende and hadde a greet opinioun
That if I myghte escapen from prisoun,
Thanne hadde I been in joye and perfit heele,
That now I am exiled fro my wele.
Syn that I may nat seen you, Emelye,
I nam but deed, there nys no remedye.
UPON that oother syde, Palamon,
Whan that he wiste Arcite was agon,
Swich sorwe he maketh that the grete tour
Resouned of his youlyng and clamour;
The pure fettres on his shynes grete
Weren of his bittre, salte teeres wete.
Allas! quod he, Arcite, cosyn myn,
Of al our strif, God woot, the fruyt is thyn;
Thow walkest now in Thebes at thy large,
And of my wo thow yevest litel charge.
Thou mayst, syn thou hast wysdom & man hede,
Assemblen alle the folk of oure kynrede,
And make a werre so sharpe on this citee,
That by som aventure, or som tretee,
Thow mayst have hire to lady and to wyf
For whom that I mot nedes lese my lyf.
For as by wey of possibilitee,
Sith thou art at thy large, of prisoun free,
And art a lord, greet is thyn avauntage,
Moore than is myn that sterve here in a cage;
For I moot wepe and wayle whil I lyve,
With al the wo that prison may me yeve,
And eek with peyne that love me yeveth also,
That doubleth al my torment and my wo.
Therwith the fyr of jalousie up sterte
Withinne his brest, and hente him by the herte
So woodly, that he lyk was to biholde
The boxtree, or the asshen, dede and colde.
Thanne seyde he, O cruel goddes that governe
This world with byndyng of youre word eterne
And writen in the table of atthamaunt
Youre parlement and youre eterne graunt,
What is mankynde moore unto you holde
Than is the sheepe that rouketh in the folde?
For slayn is man, right as another beest,
And dwelleth eek in prison and arreest,
And hath siknesse and greet adversitee,
And ofte tymes giltelees pardee.
What governance is in this prescience,
That giltelees tormenteth innocence?
And yet encresseth this al my penaunce,
That man is bounden to his observaunce
For Goddes sake to letten of his wille,
Ther as a beest may all his lust fulfille;
And whan a beest is deed he hath no peyne,
But after his deeth man moot wepe and pleyne,
Though in this world he have care and wo,
Withouten doute may it stonden so.
The answer of this lete I to dyvynys,
But well I woot that in this world greet pyne ys.
Allas! I se a serpent or a theef,
That many a trewe man hath doon mescheef,

Goon at his large, and where hym list may turne;
But I moot been in prisoun thurgh Saturne,
And eek thurgh Juno, jalous and eek wood,
That hath destroyed wel ny al the blood
Of Thebes with his waste walles wyde;
And Venus sleeth me on that oother syde
For jalousie and fere of hym Arcite.
NOW wol I stynte of Palamon a lite
And lete hym in his prisoun stille dwelle,
And of Arcite forth I wol yow telle.
The somer passeth, and the nyghtes longe
Encressen double wise the peynes stronge
Bothe of the lovere and the prisoner.
I noot which hath the wofuller mester;
For shortly for to seyn, this Palamoun
Perpetuelly is dampned to prisoun
In cheynes and in fettres to been deed,
And Arcite is exiled upon his heed
For evere mo as out of that contree,
Ne nevere mo he shal his lady see.
Yow loveres, axe I now this questioun,
Who hath the worse, Arcite or Palamoun?
That oon may seen his lady day by day,
But in prisoun he moot dwellen alway;
That oother, wher hym list may ride or go,
But seen his lady shal he nevere mo.
Now demeth as yow liste, ye that kan,
For I wol telle forth as I bigan.
Explicit pars prima. Sequitur pars secunda
WHAN that Arcite to The-
bes comen was,
Ful ofte a day he swelte
and seyde, Allas!
For seen his lady shal he
nevere mo.
And, shortly to conclud-
en al his wo,
So muche sorwe had
nevere creature
That is or shal, whil that the world may dure.
His slepe, his mete, his drynke, is hym biraft,
That lene he wexe and drye as is a shaft;
His eyen holwe, and grisly to biholde,
His hewe falow and pale as asshen colde,
And solitarie he was and evere allone,
And waillynge al the nyght, makynge his mone:
And if he herde song or instrument
Thanne wolde he wepe, he myghte nat be stent;
So feble eek were his spirits and so lowe,
And chaunged so that no man koude knowe
His speche nor his voys, though men it herde
And in his geere for al the world he ferde,
Nat oonly like the loveris maladye
Of Hereos, but rather lyk manye
Engendred of humour malencolik
Biforn his owene celle fantastik.
And shortly turned was al up so doun
Bothe habit and eek disposicioun
Of hym, this woful lovere daun Arcite.
WHAT sholde I al day of his wo endite?
Whan he endured hadde a yeer or two
This cruel torment and this peyne & woo,
At Thebes, in his contree, as I seyde,

13

Upon a nyght in sleepe as he hym leyde,
Hym thoughte how that the wynged god Mercurie
Biforn hym stood and bad hym to be murie;
His slepy yerde in hond he bar uprighte,
An hat he werede upon hise heris brighte.
Arrayed was this god, as he took keepe,
As he was whan that Argus took his sleepe,
And seyde hym thus, To Atthenes shaltou wende,
Ther is thee shapen of thy wo an ende.
And with that word Arcite wook and sterte,
Now trewely how soore that me smerte,
Quod he, To Atthenes right now wol I fare,
Ne for the drede of deeth shal I nat spare
To se my lady that I love and serve;
In hir presence I recche nat to sterve.
And with that word he caughte a greet mirrour
And saugh that chaunged was al his colour
And saugh his visage al in another kynde;
And right anon it ran hym in his mynde,
That sith his face was so disfigured
Of maladye, the which he hadde endured,
He myghte wel, if that he bar hym lowe,
Lyve in Atthenes everemore unknowe,
And seen his lady wel ny day by day.
And right anon he chaunged his array,
And cladde hym as a povre laborer,
And al allone, save oonly a squier
That knew his privetee and al his cas,
Which was disgised povrely as he was,
To Atthenes is he goon the nexte way.
And to the court he wente upon a day,
And at the gate he profreth his servyse
To drugge and drawe, what so men wol devyse.
And shortly of this matere for to seyn,
He fil in office with a chamberleyn,
The which that dwellynge was with Emelye,
For he was wys, and koude soone espye
Of every servaunt which that serveth here.
Wel koude he hewen wode, and water bere,
For he was yong and myghty for the nones,
And therto he was long and big of bones
To doon that any wight kan hym devyse.
A YEER or two he was in this servyse,
Page of the chambre of Emelye the brighte,
And Philostrate he seyde that he highte.
But half so wel biloved a man as he
Ne was ther nevere in court of his degree;
He was so gentil of condicioun
That thurghout al the court was his renoun.
They seyden that it were a charitee
That Theseus wolde enhauncen his degree,
And putten hym in worshipful servyse,
Theras he myghte his vertu excercise.
And thus withinne a while his name is spronge,
Bothe of his dedes and his goode tonge,
That Theseus hath taken hym so neer,
That of his chambre he made hym a squier,
And yaf him gold to mayntene his degree;
And eek men broghte hym out of his contree,
From yeer to yeer, ful pryvely, his rente,
But honestly and slyly he it spente,
That no man wondred how that he it hadde.
And thre yeer in this wise his lif he ladde

14

And bar hym so in pees, and eek in werre,
Ther was no man that Theseus hath derre.
AND in this blisse lete I now Arcite
And speke I wole of Palamon a lite.
In derknesse horrible, and strong prison
Thise seven yeer hath seten Palamon.
Forpyned, what for wo and for distresse;
Who feeleth double soor and hevynesse
But Palamon? that love destreyneth so,
That wood out of his wit he goth for wo;
And eek therto he is a prisoner
Perpetuelly, noght oonly for a yer.
Who koude ryme in Englyssh properly
His martirdom? forsothe it am nat I;
Therfore I passe as lightly as I may.
IT fel that in the seventhe yer in May,
The thridde nyght, as olde bookes seyn
That al this storie tellen moore pleyn,
Were it by aventure or destynee,
As whan a thyng is shapen it shal be,
That soone after the mydnyght, Palamoun,
By helpyng of a freend brak his prisoun
And fleeth the citee faste as he may go,
For he hade yeve his gayler drynke so
Of a clarree, maad of a certeyn wyn,
Of nercotikes, and opie of Thebes fyn,
That al that nyght, thogh that men wolde him
shake,
The gayler sleepe, he myghte nat awake.
And thus he fleeth, as faste as evere he may.
The nyght was short, and faste by the day,
That nedes cost he moot hymselven hyde,
And til a grove faste ther bisyde,
With dredeful foot than stalketh Palamoun.
For shortly, this was his opinioun,
That in that grove he wolde hym hyde al day,
And in the nyght thanne wolde he take his way
To Thebesward, his freendes for to preye
On Theseus to helpe him to werreye;
And shortly, outher he wolde lese his lif
Or wynnen Emelye unto his wyf.
This is theffect, and his entente pleyn.
NOW wol I turne to Arcite ageyn,
That litel wiste how ny that was his care,
Til that fortune had broght him in the snare.
The bisy larke, messager of day,
Saluteth in hir song the morwe gray,
And firy Phebus riseth up so brighte
That al the orient laugheth of the lighte,
And with his stremes dryeth in the greves
The silver dropes, hangynge on the leves.
And Arcite that is in the court roial,
With Theseus, his squier principal,
Is risen, and looketh on the myrie day;
And for to doon his observaunce to May,
Remembrynge on the poynt of his desir,
He on a courser, startlynge as the fir,
Is riden in to the feeldes hym to pleye,
Out of the court, were it a myle or tweye;
And to the grove of which that I yow tolde,
By aventure, his wey he gan to holde,
To maken hym a gerland of the greves,
Were it of wodebynde, or hawethorn leves,

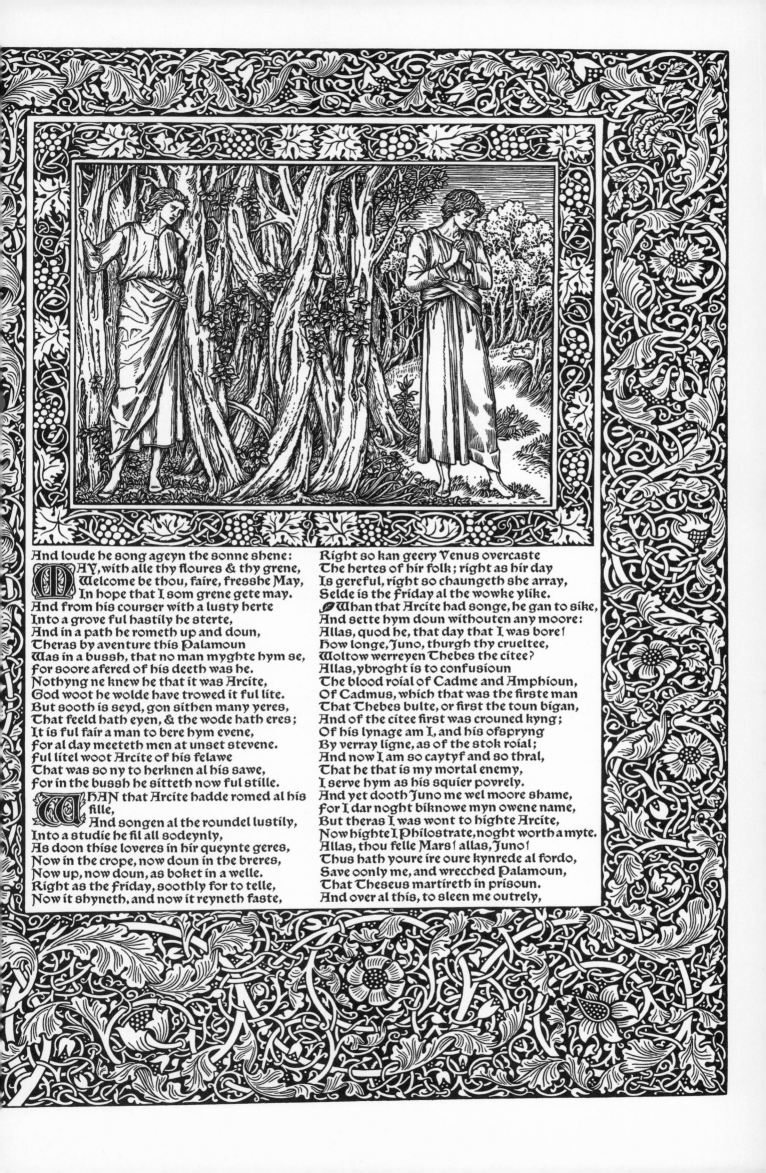

And loude he song ageyn the sonne shene:
MAY, with alle thy floures & thy grene,
Welcome be thou, faire, fresshe May,
In hope that I som grene gete may.
And from his courser with a lusty herte
Into a grove ful hastily he sterte,
And in a path he rometh up and doun,
Theras by aventure this Palamoun
Was in a bussh, that no man myghte hym se,
for soore afered of his deeth was he.
Nothyng ne knew he that it was Arcite,
God woot he wolde have trowed it ful lite.
But sooth is seyd, gon sithen many yeres,
That feeld hath eyen, & the wode hath eres;
It is ful fair a man to bere hym evene,
for al day meeteth men at unset stevene.
ful litel woot Arcite of his felawe
That was so ny to herknen al his sawe,
for in the bussh he sitteth now ful stille.
WHAN that Arcite hadde romed al his
fille,
And songen al the roundel lustily,
Into a studie he fil all sodeynly,
As doon thise loveres in hir queynte geres,
Now in the crope, now doun in the breres,
Now up, now doun, as boket in a welle.
Right as the friday, soothly for to telle,
Now it shyneth, and now it reyneth faste,

Right so kan geery Venus overcaste
The hertes of hir folk; right as hir day
Is gereful, right so chaungeth she array,
Selde is the friday al the wowke ylike.
Whan that Arcite had songe, he gan to sike,
And sette hym doun withouten any moore:
Allas, quod he, that day that I was bore!
How longe, Juno, thurgh thy crueltee,
Woltow werreyen Thebes the citee?
Allas, ybroght is to confusioun
The blood roial of Cadme and Amphioun,
Of Cadmus, which that was the firste man
That Thebes bulte, or first the toun bigan,
And of the citee first was crouned kyng;
Of his lynage am I, and his ofspryng
By verray ligne, as of the stok roial;
And now I am so caytyf and so thral,
That he that is my mortal enemy,
I serve hym as his squier povrely.
And yet dooth Juno me wel moore shame,
for I dar noght biknowe myn owene name,
But theras I was wont to highte Arcite,
Now highte I Philostrate, noght worth a myte.
Allas, thou felle Mars! allas, Juno!
Thus hath youre ire oure kynrede al fordo,
Save oonly me, and wrecched Palamoun,
That Theseus martireth in prisoun.
And over al this, to sleen me outrely,

Love hath his firy dart so brennyngly
Ystiked thurgh my trewe, careful herte,
That shapen was my deeth erst than my sherte.
Ye sleen me with youre eyen, Emelye;
Ye been the cause wherfore that I dye.
Of al the remenant of myn oother care
Ne sette I nat the montance of a tare,
So that I koude doon aught to youre plesaunce.
AND with that word he fil doun in a traunce
A longe tyme, and after he upsterte.
This Palamoun, that thoughte that
thurgh his herte
He felte a coold swerd sodeynliche glyde,
For ire he quook, no lenger wolde he byde.
And whan that he had herd Arcites tale,
As he were wood, with face deed and pale,
He stirte hym up out of the buskes thikke,
And seide, Arcite, false traytour wikke!
Now artow hent, that lovest my lady so,
For whom that I have al this peyne and wo,
And art my blood and to my conseil sworn,
As I ful ofte have seyd thee heer biforn,
And hast byjaped heere duc Theseus,
And falsly chaunged hast thy name thus;
I wol be deed, or elles thou shalt dye;
Thou shalt nat love my lady Emelye,
But I wol love hire oonly, and namo,
For I am Palamon, thy mortal foo;
And though that I no wepne have in this place,
But out of prison am astert by grace,
I drede noght, that outher thow shalt dye,
Or thow ne shalt nat loven Emelye.
Chees which thou wolt or thou shalt nat asterte!
THIS Arcite, with ful despitous herte,
Whan he hym knew, and hadde his tale herd,
As fiers as leoun pulled out his swerd,
And seyde thus By God that sit above,
Nere it that thou art sik and wood for love,
And eek that thow no wepne hast in this place,
Thou sholdest nevere out of this grove pace,
That thou ne sholdest dyen of myn hond;
For I defye the seurete and the bond
Which that thou seist that I have maad to thee.
What, verray fool, thynk wel that love is fre,
And I wol love hire mawgree al thy myght.
But for as muche thou art a worthy knyght,
And wilnest to darreyne hire by bataille,
Have heer my trouthe, tomorwe I wol nat faile,
Withoute wityng of any oother wight,
That heere I wol be founden as a knyght,
And bryngen harneys right ynough for thee
And chese the beste and leve the worste for me;
And mete and drynke this nyght wol I brynge
Ynough for thee, and clothes for thy beddynge;
And if so be that thou my lady wynne
And sle me in this wode ther I am inne,
Thou mayst wel have thy lady as for me.
This Palamon answerde, I graunte it thee.
And thus they been departed til amorwe,
Whan ech of hem had leyd his feith to borwe.
O CUPIDE, out of alle charitee!
O regne, that wolt no felawe have with thee!
Ful sooth is seyd that love ne lordshipe
16

Wol noght, hir thankes, have no felaweshipe.
Wel fynden that Arcite and Palamoun.
Arcite is riden anon unto the toun,
And on the morwe, er it were dayes light,
Ful prively two harneys hath he dight,
Bothe suffisaunt and mete to darreyne
The bataille in the feeld bitwix hem tweyne;
And on his hors, allone as he was born,
He carieth al the harneys hym biforn,
And in the grove, at tyme and place yset,
This Arcite and this Palamon ben met.
To chaungen gan the colour in hir face,
Right as the hunter in the regne of Trace,
That stondeth at the gappe with a spere,
Whan hunted is the leoun or the bere,
And hereth hym come russhyng in the greves,
And breketh bothe bowes and the leves,
And thynketh: Heere cometh my mortal enemy,
Withoute faile he moot be deed or I;
For outher I moot sleen hym at the gappe,
Or he moot sleen me if that me myshappe.
So ferden they in chaungyng of hir hewe,
As fer as everich of hem oother knewe.
Ther nas no Good day, ne no saluyng,
But streight withouten word or rehersyng
Everich of hem heelpe for to armen oother,
As frendly as he were his owene brother;
And after that, with sharpe speres stronge,
They foynen ech at oother wonder longe.
Thou myghtest wene that this Palamoun,
In his fightyng were as a wood leoun,
And as a cruel tigre was Arcite:
As wilde bores gonne they to smyte,
That frothen whit as foom for ire wood,
Up to the anclee foghte they in hir blood.
And in this wise I lete hem fightyng dwelle,
And forth I wole of Theseus yow telle.
THE Destinee, ministre general,
That executeth in the world over al
The purveiaunce that God hath seyn biforn;
So strong it is that though the world had sworn
The contrarie of a thyng by ye or nay,
Yet sometyme it shal fallen on a day
That falleth nat eft withinne a thousand yeere.
For certeinly oure appetites heere,
Be it of werre, or pees, or hate, or love,
Al is this reuled by the sighte above.
This mene I now by myghty Theseus,
That for to hunten is so desirus,
And namely at the grete hert in May,
That in his bed ther daweth hym no day
That he nys clad, and redy for to ryde
With hunte and horne, and houndes hym bisyde.
For in his huntyng hath he swich delit,
That it is al his joye and appetit
To been hymself the grete hertes bane,
For after Mars he serveth now Dyane.
CLEER was the day, as I have toold er this,
And Theseus, with alle joye and blis,
With his Ypolita, the faire quene,
And Emelye, clothed al in grene,
On huntyng be they riden roially;
And to the grove that stood ful faste by,

In which ther was an hert, as men hym tolde,
Duc Theseus the streighte wey hath holde.
And to the launde he rideth hym ful right,
For thider was the hert wont have his flight,
And over a brook, and so forth in his weye.
This duc wol han a cours at hym or tweye
With houndes, swiche as that hym list comaunde.
And whan this duc was come unto the launde,
Under the sonne he looketh, and anon,
He was war of Arcite and Palamon,
That foughten breme, as it were bores two.
The brighte swerdes wenten to and fro
So hidously, that with the leeste strook
It semed as it wolde felle an ook;
But what they were, nothyng he ne woot.
This duc his courser with his spores smoot,
And at a stert he was bitwix hem two,
And pulled out a swerd, and cride, Hoo!
Namoore, up peyne of lesynge of youre heed.
By myghty Mars, he shal anon be deed
That smyteth any strook, that I may seen!
But telleth me what myster men ye been,
That been so hardy for to fighten heere
Withouten juge or oother officere,
As it were in a lystes roially?
This Palamon answerde hastily
And seyde, Sire, what nedeth wordes mo?
We have the deeth disserved bothe two.
Two woful wrecches been we, two caytyves,
That been encombred of oure owene lyves;
And as thou art a rightful lord and juge,
Ne yeve us neither mercy ne refuge,
But sle me first, for seinte charitee,
And sle my felawe eek as wel as me;
Or sle hym first; for, though thow knowest it lite,
This is thy mortal foo, this is Arcite,
That fro thy lond is banysshed on his heed,
For which he hath deserved to be deed;
For this is he that cam unto thy gate
And seyde that he highte Philostrate.
Thus hath he japed thee ful many a yer,
And thou hast maked hym thy chief squier;
And this is he that loveth Emelye;
For sith the day is come that I shal dye,
I make pleynly my confessioun,
That I am thilke woful Palamoun,
That hath thy prisoun broken wikkedly.
I am thy mortal foo, and it am I
That loveth so hoote Emelye the brighte,
That I wol dye present in hir sighte.
Therfore I axe deeth and my juwise;
But sle my felawe in the same wise,
For bothe han we deserved to be slayn.
THIS worthy duc answerde anon agayn,
And seyde, This is a short conclusioun:
Youre owene mouth, by youre confessioun,
Hath dampned yow, and I wol it recorde,
It nedeth noght to pyne yow with the corde,
Ye shal be deed by myghty Mars the rede!
The queene anon, for verray wommanhede,
Gan for to wepe, and so dide Emelye,
And alle the ladyes in the compaignye.
Greet pitee was it, as it thoughte hem alle,

That evere swich a chaunce sholde falle;
For gentil men they were, of greet estaat,
And nothyng but for love was this debaat,
And saugh hir blody woundes wyde and soore;
And alle crieden, bothe lasse and moore,
Have mercy, lord, upon us wommen alle!
And on hir bare knees adoun they falle,
And wolde have kist his feet ther as he stood,
Til at the laste aslaked was his mood;
For pitee renneth soone in gentil herte.
And though he first for ire quook and sterte,
He hath considered shortly in a clause
The trespas of hem bothe, and eek the cause;
And although that his ire hir gilt accused,
Yet in his resoun he hem bothe excused,
And thus he thoghte wel, that every man
Wol helpe hymself in love if that he kan,
And eek delivere hymself out of prisoun;
And eek his herte hadde compassioun
Of wommen, for they wepen evere in oon;
And in his gentil herte he thoughte anon,
And soft unto hymself he seyde, Fy
Upon a lord that wol have no mercy,
But been a leoun bothe in word and dede
To hem that been in repentaunce and drede,
As wel as to a proud despitous man
That wol maynteyne that he first bigan.
That lord hath litel of discrecioun,
That in swich cas kan no divisioun,
But weyeth pride and humblesse after oon.
And shortly, whan his ire is thus agoon,
He gan to looken up with eyen lighte,
And spak thise same wordes, al on highte.
THE god of love, a! benedicite,
How myghty and how greet a lord is he!
Ayeyns his myght ther gayneth none
obstacles,
He may be cleped a god for his myracles,
For he kan maken, at his owene gyse,
Of everich herte as that hym list divyse.
Lo heere this Arcite, and this Palamoun,
That quitly weren out of my prisoun,
And myghte han lyved in Thebes roially,
And witen I am hir mortal enemy,
And that hir deth lith in my myght also,
And yet hath love, maugree hir eyen two,
Ybroght hem hyder, bothe for to dye.
Now looketh, is nat that an heigh folye?
Who may nat been a fole, but if he love?
Bihoold, for Goddes sake that sit above,
Se how they blede! be they noght wel arrayed?
Thus hath hir lord, the god of love, ypayed
Hir wages and hir fees for hir servyse:
And yet they wenen for to been ful wyse
That serven love, for aught that may bifalle.
But this is yet the beste game of alle,
That she, for whom they han this jolitee,
Kan hem therfore as muche thank as me.
She woot namoore of al this hoote fare,
By God, than woot a cokkow of an hare.
But all moot ben assayed, hoot and coold;
A man moot ben a fool, or yong or oold,
I woot it by myself ful yore agon,

C 1

17

for in my tyme a servant was I oon.
And therfore, syn I knowe of loves peyne,
And woot how soore it kan a man distreyne,
As he that hath ben caught ofte in his laas,
I yow foryeve al hoolly this trespas,
At requeste of the queene, that kneleth heere,
And eek of Emelye, my suster deere.
And ye shul bothe anon unto me swere,
That nevere mo ye shal my contree dere,
Ne make werre upon me, nyght ne day,
But been my freendes in al that ye may;
I yow foryeve this trespas every deel.
And they him sworen his axyng, faire and weel,
And hym of lordshipe and of mercy preyde,
And he hem graunteth grace, and thus he seyde:
To speke of roial lynage and richesse,
Though that she were a queene or a princesse,
Ech of you bothe is worthy, doutelees,
To wedden whan tyme is, but nathelees,
I speke as for my suster Emelye,
For whom ye have this strif and jalousye,
Ye woot yourself she may nat wedden two
Atones, though ye fighten everemo:
That oon of you, al be hym looth or lief,
He moot go pipen in an yvy leef:
This is to seyn, she may nat now han bothe,
Al be ye nevere so jalouse ne so wrothe;
And forthy, I yow putte in this degree,
That ech of yow shal have his destynee
As hym is shape, and herkneth in what wyse;
Lo heere your ende of that I shal devyse:
My wyl is this, for plat conclusioun
Withouten any repplicacioun,
If that you liketh, take it for the beste,
That everich of you shal goon where hym leste
Frely withouten raunson or daunger;
And this day fifty wykes, fer ne ner,
Everich of you shal brynge an hundred knyghtes,
Armed for lystes up at alle rightes,
Al redy to darreyne hire by bataille.
And this bihote I yow withouten faille
Upon my trouthe, and as I am a knyght,
That wheither of yow bothe that hath myght,
This is to seyn, that wheither he or thow
May with his hundred, as I spak of now,
Sleen his contrarie, or out of lystes dryve,
Thanne shal I yeve Emelye to wyve
To whom that fortune yeveth so fair a grace.
Tho lystes shal I maken in this place,
And God so wisly on my soule rewe
As I shal evene juge been and trewe.
Ye shul noon oother ende with me maken
That oon of yow ne shal be deed or taken.
And if yow thynketh this is weel ysayd,
Seyeth youre avys, and holdeth you apayd;
This is youre ende and youre conclusioun.
WHO looketh lightly now but Palamoun?
Who spryngeth up for joye but Arcite?
Who kouthe telle, or who kouthe it endite,
The joye that is maked in the place
Whan Theseus hath doon so fair a grace?
But doun on knees wente every maner wight
And thonken hym with al hir herte and myght;

18

And namely the Thebans often sithe.
And thus with good hope and with herte blithe
They take hir leve, and homward goone they ride
To Thebes with his olde walles wyde.
Explicit pars secunda. Sequitur pars tercia.
I TROWE men wolde deme
it necligence,
If I foryete to tellen the
dispence
Of Theseus, that gooth so
bisily
To maken up the lystes
roially;
That swich a noble theatre
as it was,
I dar wel seyn that in this world there nas.
The circuit a myle was aboute,
Walled of stoon and dyched al withoute.
Round was the shape in manere of compaas,
Ful of degrees, the heighte of sixty paas,
That whan a man was set on o degree,
He lette nat his felawe for to see.
Estward ther stood a gate of marbul whit,
Westward, right swich another in the opposit.
And shortly to concluden, swich a place
Was noon in erthe, as in so litel space;
For in the lond ther was no crafty man
That geometrie or arsmetrik kan,
Ne portreitour, ne kervere of ymages,
That Theseus ne yaf him mete and wages,
The theatre for to maken and devyse.
And for to doon his ryte and sacrifise,
He estward hath upon the gate above,
In worshipe of Venus, goddesse of love,
Doon make an auter and an oratorie;
And westward, in the mind and in memorie
Of Mars, he maked hath right swich another,
That coste largely of gold a fother.
And northward, in a touret on the wal,
Of alabastre whit and reed coral,
An oratorie riche for to see,
In worshipe of Dyane of chastitee,
Hath Theseus doon wroght in noble wyse.
But yet hadde I foryeten to devyse
The noble kervyng and the portreitures,
The shape, the contenaunce, and the figures,
That weren in thise oratories thre.
FIRST, in the temple of Venus mays-
tow se,
Wroght on the wal, ful pitous to
biholde,
The broken slepes, and the sikes
colde,
The sacred teeris, and the waymentynge,
The firy strokes of the desirynge,
That loves servaunts in this lyf enduren;
The othes that hir covenants assuren.
Plesaunce and Hope, Desir, foolhardynesse,
Beautee and Youthe, Bauderie, Richesse,
Charmes and Force, Lesynges, Flaterye,
Dispense, Bisynesse, and Jalousye
That wered of yelewe gooldes a gerland,
And a cokkow sittynge on hir hand;

festes, instruments, caroles, daunces,
Lust and array, and alle the circumstaunces
Of love, whiche that I reken and rekne shal,
By ordre weren peynted on the wal,
And mo than I kan make of mencioun;
For soothly al the mount of Citheroun,
Ther Venus hath hir principal dwellynge,
Was shewed on the wal in portreyynge,
With al the gardyn and the lustynesse.
Nat was foryeten the porter Ydelnesse,
Ne Narcisus the faire of yore agon,
Ne yet the folye of kyng Salamon,
And eek the grete strengthe of Ercules,
Thenchauntements of Medea and Circes,
Ne of Turnus with the hardy fiers corage,
The riche Cresus, kaytyf in servage.
THUS may ye seen that Wysdom ne Richesse,
Beautee ne Sleighte, Strengthe, ne Hardy-
nesse,
Ne may with Venus holde champartye,
For as hir list the world than may she gye.
Lo, alle thise folk so caught were in hir las,
Til they for wo ful ofte seyde, Allas!
Suffiseth heere ensamples oon or two,
And though I koude rekene a thousand mo.
THE statue of Venus, glorious for to see,
Was naked, fletynge in the large see,
And fro the navele doun al covered was
With wawes grene, and brighte as any glas.
A citole in hir right hand hadde she,
And on hir heed, ful semely for to see,
A rose gerland, fressh and wel smellynge,
Above hir heed hir dowves flikerynge.
Biforn hire stood hire sone Cupido,
Upon his shuldres wynges hadde he two,
And blynd he was, as it is often seene.
A bowe he bar and arwes brighte and kene.
WHY sholde I noght as wel eek telle
yow al
The portreiture that was upon the
wal
Withinne the temple of myghty
Mars the rede?
Al peynted was the wal, in lengthe and brede,
Lyk to the estres of the grisly place
That highte the grete temple of Mars in Trace,
In thilke colde frosty regioun,
Ther as Mars hath his sovereyn mansioun.
FIRST, on the wal was peynted a forest
In which ther dwelleth neither man ne best,
With knotty, knarry, bareyne trees olde
Of stubbes sharpe and hidouse to biholde,
In which ther ran a rumbel and a swough,
As though a storm sholde bresten every bough;
And dounward from an hille, under a bente,
Ther stood the temple of Mars armypotente,
Wroght al of burned steel, of which thentree
Was long and streit, and gastly for to see;
And therout cam a rage, and such a veze,
That it made all the gates for to rese.
The northren lyght in at the dores shoon,
For wyndowe on the wal ne was ther noon
Thurgh which men myghten any light discerne.

c 2

The dores were al of adamant eterne,
Yclenched overthwart and endelong
With iren tough; and for to make it strong,
Every pyler, the temple to sustene,
Was tonne greet, of iren bright and shene.
Ther saugh I first the derke ymagynyng
Of felonye, and al the compassyng;
The cruel ire, reed as any gleede;
The pykepurs, and eek the pale drede;
The smylere with the knyfe under the cloke;
The shepne brennynge with the blake smoke;
The tresoun of the mordrynge in the bedde;
The open werre, with woundes al bibledde;
Contek, with blody knyf and sharpe manace;
Al ful of chirkyng was that sory place.
The sleere of hymself yet saugh I ther,
His herte-blood hath bathed al his heer;
The nayl ydryven in the shode anyght;
The colde deeth, with mouth gapyng upright.
Amyddes of the temple sat Meschaunce,
With disconfort and sory contenaunce.
YET saugh I Woodnesse, laughynge in his
rage,
Armed compleint, outhees, & fiers outrage,
The careyne in the busk, with throte ycorve;
A thousand slayn, and not of qualm ystorve;
The tiraunt with the pray by force yraft;
The toun destroyed, ther was nothyng laft.
Yet saugh I brent the shippes hoppesteres;
The hunte strangled with the wilde beres;
The sowe freten the child right in the cradel;
The cook yscalded for al his longe ladel.
NOGHT was foryeten by thinfortune of
Marte;
The cartere overryden with his carte,
Under the wheel ful lowe he lay adoun.
Ther were also of Martes divisioun,
The barbour, and the bocher; and the smyth
That forgeth sharpe swerdes on his styth.
And al above, depeynted in a tour,
Saugh I Conquest sittynge in greet honour
With the sharpe swerde over his heed
Hangynge by a soutil twynes threed.
DEPEYNTED was the slaughtre of Julius,
Of grete Nero, and of Antonius;
Al be that thilke tyme they were unborn,
Yet was hir deeth depeynted therbiforn
By manasynge of Mars, right by figure;
So was it shewed in that portreiture
As is depeynted in the sterres above,
Who shal be sleyn or elles deed for love.
Suffiseth oon ensample in stories olde,
I may nat rekene hem alle, though I wolde.
THE statue of Mars upon a carte stood,
Armed, and looked grym as he were wood;
And over his heed ther shynen two figures
Of sterres, that been cleped in scriptures,
That oon Puella, that oother Rubeus.
This god of armes was arrayed thus:
A wolf ther stood biforn hym at his feet
With eyen rede, and of a man he eet.
With soutil pencel was depeynt this storie,
In redoutynge of Mars and of his glorie.

19

NOW to the temple of Dyane the chaste
As shortly as I kan I wol me haste,
To telle yow al the descripcioun.
Depeynted been the walles up & doun
Of huntyng and of shamefast chas-
titee.
℘ Ther saugh I how woful Calistopee,
Whan that Diane agreved was with here,
Was turned from a womman to a bere,
And after was she maad the loodesterre;
Thus was it peynt, I kan sey yow no ferre;
Hir sone is eek a sterre, as men may see.
℘ There saugh I Dane, yturned til a tree,
I mene nat the goddesse Diane,
But Penneus doughter, which that highte Dane.
Ther saugh I Attheon an hert ymaked,
for vengeaunce that he saugh Diane al naked;
I saugh how that his houndes have hym caught,
And freeten hym, for that they knewe hym naught.
℘ Yet peynted was a litel forthermoor
How Atthalante hunted the wilde boor,
And Meleagre, and many another mo,
for which Dyane wroghte hym care and wo.
Ther saugh I many another wonder storie,
The whiche me list nat drawen to memorie.
THIS goddesse on an hert ful hye seet,
With smale houndes al aboute hir feet,
And undernethe hir feet she hadde a
moone,
Wexynge it was, and sholde wanye soone.
In gaude grene hir statue clothed was,
With bowe in honde, and arwes in a cas.
Hir eyen caste she ful lowe adoun
Ther Pluto hath his derke regioun.
℘ A womman travaillynge was hire biforn,
But, for hir child so longe was unborn,
ful pitously Lucyna gan she calle,
And seyde, Help, for thou mayst best of alle.
Wel koude he peynten lifly, that it wroghte,
With many a floryn he the hewes boghte.
NOW been thise lystes maad, and
Theseus,
That at his grete cost arrayed thus
The temples & the theatre every deel,
Whan it was doon, hym lyked wonder
weel;
But stynte I wole of Theseus a lite,
And speke of Palamon and of Arcite.
℘ The day approcheth of hir retournynge,
That everich sholde an hundred knyghtes brynge,
The bataille to darreyne, as I yow tolde,
And til Atthenes, hir covenants for to holde,
Hath everich of hem broght an hundred knyghtes
Wel armed for the werre at alle rightes.
And sikerly ther trowed many a man
That nevere sithen that the world bigan,
As for to speke of knyghthod of hir hond,
As fer as God hath maked see or lond,
Nas, of so fewe, so noble a compaignye.
for every wight that lovede chivalrye,
And wolde, his thankes, han a passant name,
Hath preyed that he myghte been of that game;
And wel was hym that therto chosen was;

for if ther fille tomorwe swich a caas,
Ye knowen wel, that every lusty knyght
That loveth paramours, and hath his myght,
Were it in Engelond, or elleswhere,
They wolde, hir thankes, wilnen to be there.
To fighte for a lady; benedicite!
It were a lusty sighte for to see.
AND right so ferden they with Palamon.
With hym ther wenten knyghtes many oon;
Som wol ben armed in an haubergeoun,
And in brestplate and in a light gypoun;
And somme woln have a paire plates large;
And somme woln have a Pruce sheeld or a targe;
Somme woln ben armed on hir legges weel,
And have an ax, and somme a mace of steel;
Ther is no newe gyse, that it nas old.
Armed were they, as I have yow told
Everych after his opinioun.
THER maistow seen comynge with Palamoun
Lygurge hymself, the grete kyng of Trace;
Blak was his berd, and manly was his face;
The cercles of his eyen in his heed,
They gloweden bitwyxe yelow and reed,
And lik a grifphon looked he aboute,
With kempe heeris on his browes stoute;
His lymes grete, his brawnes harde and stronge,
His shuldres brode, his armes rounde and longe;
And, as the gyse was in his contree,
ful hye upon a chaar of gold stood he
With foure white boles in the trays.
Instede of cote armure over his harnays,
With nayles yelewe, and brighte as any gold,
He hadde a beres skyn, colblak, forold.
His longe heer was kembd bihynde his bak,
As any ravenes fethere it shoon forblak.
A wrethe of gold, armgreet, of huge wighte,
Upon his heed, set ful of stones brighte,
Of fyne rubyes and of dyamaunts;
Aboute his chaar ther wenten white alaunts,
Twenty and mo, as grete as any steer,
To hunten at the leoun or the deer;
And folwed hym with mosel faste ybounde,
Colered of gold and tourettes fyled rounde.
An hundred lordes hadde he in his route,
Armed ful wel, with hertes stierne and stoute.
WITH Arcite in stories as men fynde
The grete Emetreus, the kyng of Inde,
Upon a steede bay, trapped in steel,
Covered in clooth of gold, dyapred weel,
Cam ridynge lyk the god of armes, Mars.
His cote armure was of clooth of Tars
Couched with perles white and rounde and grete;
His sadel was of brend gold, newe ybete;
A mantelet upon his shulder hangynge,
Bretful of rubyes rede, as fyr sparklynge;
His crispe heer, lyk rynges was yronne,
And that was yelow, and glytered as the sonne.
His nose was heigh, his eyen bright citryn,
His lippes rounde, his colour was sangwyn,
A fewe frakenes in his face yspreynd,
Betwixen yelow and somdel blak ymeynd,
And as a leoun he his lookyng caste.
Of fyve and twenty yeer his age I caste.

20

His berd was wel bigonne for to sprynge;
His voys was as a trompe thonderynge;
Upon his heed he wered, of laurer grene,
A gerland fressh and lusty for to sene.
Upon his hand he bar, for his deduyt,
An egle tame, as any lilye whyt.
AN hundred lordes hadde he with hym there,
Al armed, save hir heddes, in al hir gere,
Ful richely in alle maner thynges;
For trusteth wel, that dukes, erles, kynges,
Were gadered in this noble compaignye,
For love, and for encrees of chivalrye.
Aboute this kyng ther ran on every part
Ful many a tame leoun and lepart.
AND in this wise thise lordes, all and some,
Been on the Sonday to the citee come
Aboute pryme, and in the toun alight.
THIS Theseus, this duc, this worthy knyght,
Whan he had broght hem into his citee
And inned hem, everich in his degree,
He festeth hem, and dooth so greet labour
To esen hem, and doon hem al honour,
That yet men weneth that no mannes wit
Of noon estaat ne koude amenden it.
The mynstralcye, the service at the feeste,
The grete yiftes to the meeste and leeste,
The riche array of Theseus paleys,
Ne who sat first ne last upon the deys,
What ladyes fairest been, or best daunsynge,
Or which of hem kan dauncen best and synge,
Ne who moost felyngly speketh of love;
What haukes sitten on the perche above,
What houndes liggen in the floor adoun;
Of al this make I now no mencioun;
But al theffect; that thynketh me the beste;
Now cometh the point, and herkneth if yow leste.
THE Sonday nyght, er day bigan to sprynge,
Whan Palamon the larke herde synge,
Al though it nere nat day by houres two,
Yet song the larke, and Palamon also.
With hooly herte and with an heigh corage,
He roos, to wenden on his pilgrymage
Unto the blisful Citherea benigne,
I mene Venus, honurable and digne:
And in hir houre he walketh forth a paas
Unto the lystes, ther hire temple was,
And doun he kneleth with ful humble chere
And herte soor, and seyde in this manere:
FAIRESTE of faire, o lady myn, Venus,
Doughter to Jove, and spouse of Vulcanus,
Thow gladere of the mount of Citheron,
For thilke love thow haddest to Adoon,
Have pitee of my bittre teeris smerte,
And taak myn humble preyere at thyn herte.
Allas! I ne have no langage to telle
Theffectes ne the torments of myn helle;
Myn herte may myne harmes nat biwreye;

I am so confus, that I kan noght seye.
But mercy, lady bright, that knowest weele
My thought, and seest what harmes that I feele,
Considere al this, and rewe upon my soore,
As wisly as I shal for everemoore,
Emforth my myght, thy trewe servant be,
And holden werre alwey with chastitee,
That make I myn avow, so ye me helpe,
I kepe noght of armes for to yelpe,
Ne I ne axe nat tomorwe to have victorie,
Ne renoun in this cas, ne veyne glorie
Of pris of armes blowen up and doun,
But I wolde have fully possessioun
Of Emelye, and dye in thy servyse;
Fynd thow the manere how, and in what wyse.
I recche nat but it may bettre be
To have victorie of hem, or they of me,
So that I have my lady in myne armes;
For though so be that Mars is god of armes,
Youre vertu is so greet in hevene above,
That if yow list, I shal wel have my love.
Thy temple wol I worshipe everemo,
And on thyn auter, wher I ride or go,
I wol doon sacrifice and fires beete;
And if ye wol nat so, my lady sweete,
Thanne preye I thee, tomorwe with a spere
That Arcite me thurgh the herte bere;
Thanne rekke I noght whan I have lost my lyf
Though that Arcite wynne hire to his wyf:
This is theffect and ende of my preyere,
Yif me my love, thow blisful lady deere.
WHAN thorison was doon of Palamon,
His sacrifice he dide, and that anon
Ful pitously, with alle circumstaunce,
Al telle I noght as now his observaunce;
But atte laste the statue of Venus shook
And made a signe, wherby that he took
That his preyere accepted was that day;
For thogh the signe shewed a delay,
Yet wiste he wel that graunted was his boone,
And with glad herte he wente hym hoom ful soone.
THE thridde houre inequal that Palamon
Bigan to Venus temple for to gon,
Up roos the sonne, and up roos Emelye,
And to the temple of Dyane gan hye.
Hir maydens that she thider with hire ladde
Ful redily with hem the fyr they hadde,
Thencens, the clothes, and the remenant al
That to the sacrifice longen shal;
The hornes fulle of meeth, as was the gyse;
Ther lakked noght to doon hir sacrifise.
Smokynge the temple, ful of clothes faire,
This Emelye, with herte debonaire,
Hir body wessh with water of a welle;
But how she dide her ryte, I dar nat telle,
But it be any thing in general,
And yet it were a game to heeren al;
To hym that meneth wel it were no charge,
But it is good a man been at his large.
HIR brighte heer was kempd, untressed al,
A coroune of a grene ook cerial
Upon hir heed was set ful fair and meete.

Two fyres on the auter gan she beete,
And dide hir thynges, as men may biholde
In Stace of Thebes, and thise bookes olde.
Whan kyndled was the fyr, with pitous cheere,
Unto Dyane she spak, as ye may heere.

CHASTE goddesse of the wodes grene,
To whom bothe hevene and erthe & see is sene,
Queene of the regne of Pluto derk and lowe,
Goddesse of maydens, that myn herte hast knowe
ful many a yeer, and woost what I desire,
As keepe me fro thy vengeaunce and thyn ire,
That Attheon aboughte cruelly.
Chaste goddesse, wel wostow that I
Desire to ben a mayden al my lyf,
Ne nevere wol I be no love, ne wyf.
I am, thow woost, yet of thy compaignye
A mayde, and love huntynge and venerye,
And for to walken in the wodes wilde,
And noght to ben a wyf and be with childe;
Noght wol I knowe the compaignye of man.
Now helpe me, lady, sith ye may and kan,
for tho thre formes that thou hast in thee.

And Palamon, that hast swich love to me,
And eek Arcite, that loveth me so soore,
This grace I preye thee withoute moore,
As sende love and pees bitwixe hem two,
And fro me turne awey hir hertes so,
That al hire hoote love and hir desir,
And al hir bisy torment and hir fir,
Be queynt, or turned in another place.
And if so be thou wolt do me no grace,
Or if my destynee be shapen so
That I shal nedes have oon of hem two,
As sende me hym that moost desireth me.
Biboold, goddesse of clene chastitee,
The bittre teeres that on my chekes falle,
Syn thou art mayde, and kepere of us alle,
My maydenhede thou kepe and wel conserve,
And whil I lyve a mayde, I wol thee serve.

THE fires brenne upon the auter cleere
Whil Emelye was thus in hir preyere;
But sodeynly she saugh a sighte queynte,
for right anon, oon of the fyres queynte
And quyked agayn, and after that, anon
That oother fyr was queynt, and al agon,
And as it queynte it made a whistelynge,
As doon thise wete brondes in hir brennynge;
And at the brondes ende out ran anoon
As it were blody dropes many oon;

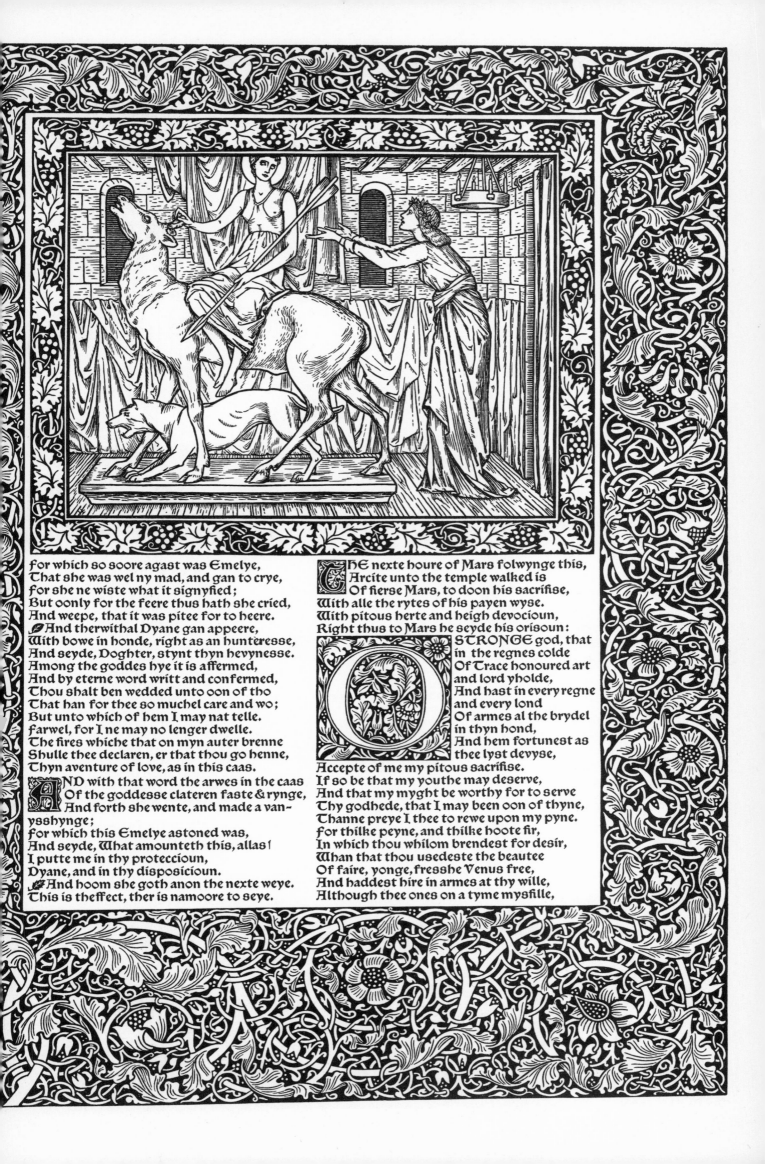

for which so soore agast was Emelye,
That she was wel ny mad, and gan to crye,
for she ne wiste what it signyfied;
But oonly for the feere thus hath she cried,
And weepe, that it was pitee for to heere.
And therwithal Dyane gan appeere,
With bowe in honde, right as an hunteresse,
And seyde, Doghter, stynt thyn hevynesse.
Among the goddes hye it is affermed,
And by eterne word writt and confermed,
Thou shalt ben wedded unto oon of tho
That han for thee so muchel care and wo;
But unto which of hem I may nat telle.
farwel, for I ne may no lenger dwelle.
The fires whiche that on myn auter brenne
Shulle thee declaren, er that thou go henne,
Thyn aventure of love, as in this caas.
AND with that word the arwes in the caas
Of the goddesse clateren faste & rynge,
And forth she wente, and made a van-
ysshynge;
for which this Emelye astoned was,
And seyde, What amounteth this, allas!
I putte me in thy proteccioun,
Dyane, and in thy disposicioun.
And hoom she goth anon the nexte weye.
This is theffect, ther is namoore to seye.

THE nexte houre of Mars folwynge this,
Arcite unto the temple walked is
Of fierse Mars, to doon his sacrifise,
With alle the rytes of his payen wyse.
With pitous herte and heigh devocioun,
Right thus to Mars he seyde his orisoun:
O STRONGE god, that
in the regnes colde
Of Trace honoured art
and lord yholde,
And hast in every regne
and every lond
Of armes al the brydel
in thyn hond,
And hem fortunest as
thee lyst devyse,
Accepte of me my pitous sacrifise.
If so be that my youthe may deserve,
And that my myght be worthy for to serve
Thy godhede, that I may been oon of thyne,
Thanne preye I thee to rewe upon my pyne.
for thilke peyne, and thilke hoote fir,
In which thou whilom brendest for desir,
Whan that thou usedeste the beautee
Of faire, yonge, fresshe Venus free,
And haddest hire in armes at thy wille,
Although thee ones on a tyme mysfille,

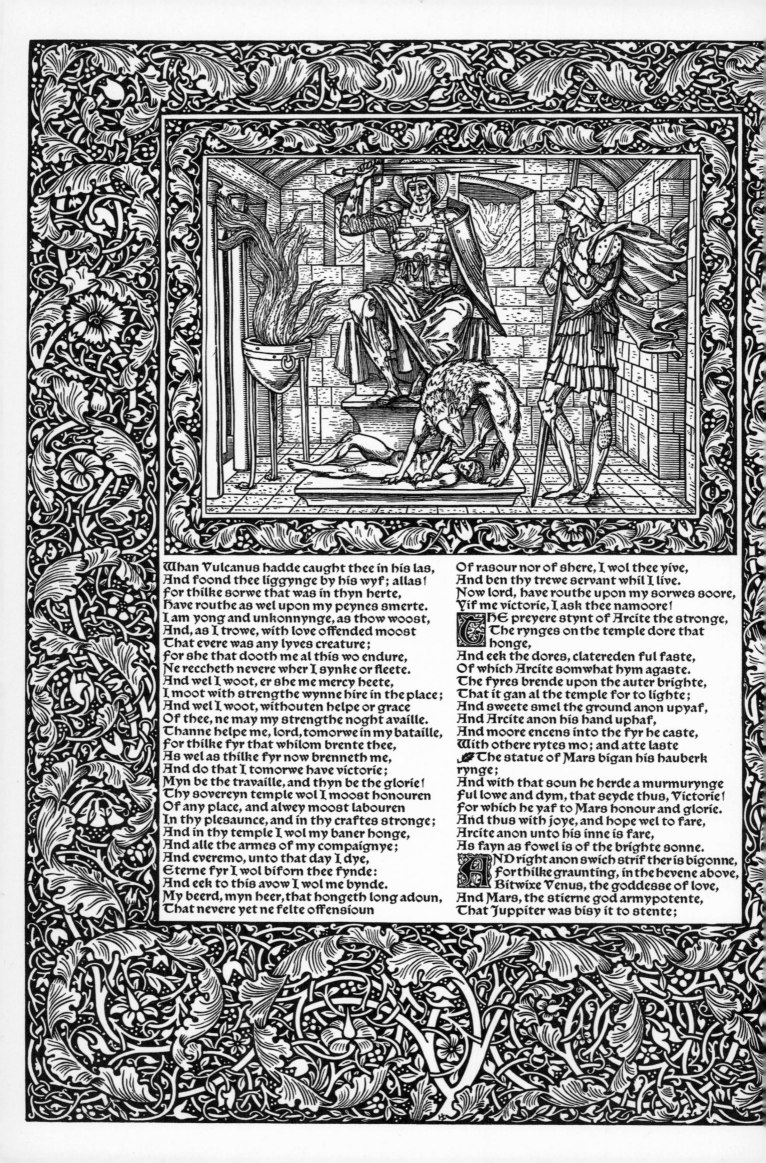

Whan Vulcanus hadde caught thee in his las,
And foond thee liggynge by his wyf; allas!
for thilke sorwe that was in thyn herte,
Have routhe as wel upon my peynes smerte.
I am yong and unkonnynge, as thow woost,
And, as I trowe, with love offended moost
That evere was any lyves creature;
for she that dooth me al this wo endure,
Ne reccheth nevere wher I synke or fleete.
And wel I woot, er she me mercy heete,
I moot with strengthe wynne hire in the place;
And wel I woot, withouten helpe or grace
Of thee, ne may my strengthe noght availle.
Thanne helpe me, lord, tomorwe in my bataille,
for thilke fyr that whilom brente thee,
As wel as thilke fyr now brenneth me,
And do that I tomorwe have victorie;
Myn be the travaille, and thyn be the glorie!
Thy sovereyn temple wol I moost honouren
Of any place, and alwey moost labouren
In thy plesaunce, and in thy craftes stronge,
And in thy temple I wol my baner honge,
And alle the armes of my compaignye;
And everemo, unto that day I dye,
Eterne fyr I wol biforn thee fynde:
And eek to this avow I wol me bynde:
My beerd, myn heer, that hongeth long adoun,
That nevere yet ne felte offensioun

Of rasour nor of shere, I wol thee yive,
And ben thy trewe servant whil I live.
Now lord, have routhe upon my sorwes soore,
Yif me victorie, I ask thee namoore!
THE preyere stynt of Arcite the stronge,
The rynges on the temple dore that honge,
And eek the dores, clatereden ful faste,
Of which Arcite somwhat hym agaste.
The fyres brende upon the auter brighte,
That it gan al the temple for to lighte;
And sweete smel the ground anon upyaf,
And Arcite anon his hand uphaf,
And moore encens into the fyr he caste,
With othere rytes mo; and atte laste
The statue of Mars bigan his hauberk rynge;
And with that soun he herde a murmurynge
ful lowe and dym, that seyde thus, Victorie!
for which he yaf to Mars honour and glorie.
And thus with joye, and hope wel to fare,
Arcite anon unto his inne is fare,
As fayn as fowel is of the brighte sonne.
AND right anon swich strif ther is bigonne,
for thilke graunting, in the hevene above,
Bitwixe Venus, the goddesse of love,
And Mars, the stierne god armypotente,
That Juppiter was bisy it to stente;

Til that the pale Saturnus the colde,
That knew so manye of aventures olde,
Foond in his olde experience an art,
That he ful soone hath plesed every part.
As sooth is seyd, elde hath greet avantage;
In elde is bothe wysdom and usage;
Men may the olde atrenne, and noght atrede.
Saturne anon, to stynten strif and drede,
Al be it that it is agayn his kynde,
Of al this strif he gan remedie fynde.

MY deere doghter Venus, quod Saturne,
My cours, that hath so wyde for to turne,
Hath moore power than woot any man.
Myn is the drenchyng in the see so wan;
Myn is the prison in the derke cote;
Myn is the stranglyng and hangyng by the throte;
The murmure, and the cherles rebellynge,
The groynynge, and the pryvee empoysonynge;
I do vengeance and pleyn correccioun
While I dwelle in the signe of the leoun.
Myn is the ruyne of the hye halles,
The fallynge of the toures and of the walles
Upon the mynour or the carpenter.
I slow Sampsoun in shakynge the piler;
And myne be the maladyes colde,
The derke tresons, and the castes olde;
My lookyng is the fader of pestilence.
Now weepe namoore, I shal doon diligence
That Palamon, that is thyn owene knyght,
Shal have his lady, as thou hast him hight.
Though Mars shal helpe his knyght, yet nathelees
Bitwixe yow ther moot be som tyme pees,
Al be ye noght of o compleccioun,
That causeth al day swich divisioun.
I am thyn aiel, redy at thy wille;
Weep now namoore, I wol thy lust fulfille.

NOW wol I stynten of the goddes above,
Of Mars, and of Venus, goddesse of love,
And telle yow, as pleynly as I kan,
The grete effect, for which that I bygan.
Explicit tercia pars. Sequitur pars quarta.

GREET was the feeste in At-
thenes that day,
And eek the lusty seson of
that May
Made every wight to been in
such plesaunce,
That al that Monday justen
they and daunce,
And spenden it in Venus
heigh servyse;
But, by the cause that they sholde ryse
Eerly, for to seen the grete fight,
Unto hir reste wenten they at nyght.
And on the morwe, whan that day gan sprynge,
Of hors and harneys, noyse and claterynge
Ther was in hostelryes al aboute,
And to the paleys rood ther many a route
Of lordes, upon steedes and palfreys.
Ther maystow seen devisynge of harneys
So unkouth and so riche, and wroght so weel
Of goldsmythrye, of browdynge, and of steel;
The sheeldes bright, testeres, and trappures;

Gold/hewen helmes, hauberkes, cote/armures;
Lordes in paraments on hir courseres,
Knyghtes of retenue, and eek squieres
Nailynge the speres, and helmes bokelynge,
Giggynge of sheeldes, with layneres lacynge;
Ther as nede is, they weren nothyng ydel;
The fomy steedes on the golden brydel
Gnawynge, and faste the armurers also
With fyle and hamer, prikynge to and fro;
Yemen on foote, and communes many oon,
With shorte staves, thikke as they may goon;
Pypes, trompes, nakers, and clariounes,
That in the bataille blowen blody sounes.
The paleys ful of peples up and doun,
Heere thre, ther ten, holdynge hir questioun,
Dyvynynge of thise Thebane knyghtes two.
Somme seyden thus, somme seyde it shal be so;
Somme helden with hym with the blake berd,
Somme with the balled, somme with the thikke
herd;
Somme seyde he looked grymme and he wolde
fighte,
He hath a sparth of twenty pound of wighte.
Thus was the halle ful of divynynge
Longe after that the sonne gan to sprynge.

THE grete Theseus, that of his sleepe awaked
With mynstralcie & noyse that was maked,
Heeld yet the chambre of his paleys riche,
Til that the Thebane knyghtes, bothe yliche
Honoured, were into the paleys fet.
Duc Theseus was at a wyndow set,
Arrayed right as he were a god in trone.
The peple preesseth thiderward ful soone
Hym for to seen, and doon heigh reverence,
And eek to herkne his heste and his sentence.
An heraud on a scaffold made an Hoo!
Til al the noyse of peple was ydo;
And whan he saugh the noyse of peple al stille,
Tho shewed he the myghty dukes wille.

THE lord hath of his heigh discrecioun
Considered, that it were destruccioun
To gentil blood, to fighten in the gyse
Of mortal bataille now in this emprise;
Wherfore, to shapen that they shal nat dye,
He wolde his firste purpos modifye.
No man therfore, up peyne of los of lyf,
No maner shot, ne polax, ne short knyf
Into the lystes sende, ne thider brynge;
Ne short swerd, for to stoke with poynt bitynge,
No man ne drawe, ne bere by his syde.
Ne no man shal unto his felawe ryde
But o cours, with a sharpe ygrounde spere;
Foyne, if hym list, on foote, hymself to were.
And he that is at meschief, shal be take,
And noght slayn, but be broght unto the stake
That shal ben ordeyned on either syde,
But thider he shal by force, and there abyde.
And if so falle, the chieftayn be take
On outher syde, or elles sleen his make,
No lenger shal the turneyinge laste.
God spede you! gooth forth, and ley on faste!
With long swerd & with mace fighteth youre fille.
Gooth now youre wey; this is the lordes wille.

25

HE voys of peple touchede the hevene,
So loude cride they, with murie stevene,
God save swich a lord, that is so good,
He wilneth no destruccion of blood!
UP goon the trompes and the melodye
And to the lystes rit the compaignye
By ordinance, thurghout the citee large,
Hanged with clooth of gold, and nat with sarge.
Ful lik a lord this noble duc gan ryde,
Thise two Thebanes upon either side;
And after rood the queene and Emelye,
And after that another compaignye
Of oon and oother after hir degre.
And thus they passen thurghout the citee,
And to the lystes come they by tyme.
It nas not of the day yet fully pryme
Whan set was Theseus ful riche and hye,
Ypolita the queene and Emelye,
And othere ladys in degrees aboute.
Unto the seetes preesseth al the route;
And westward, thurgh the gates under Marte,
Arcite, and eek the hondred of his parte,
With baner reed, is entred right anon.
And in that selve moment Palamon
Is under Venus, estward in the place,
With baner whyt, and hardy chiere and face.
IN al the world, to seken up and doun,
So evene withouten variacioun,
Ther nere swiche compaignyes tweye;
For ther was noon so wys that koude seye
That any hadde of oother avauntage
Of worthynesse, ne of estaat, ne age,
So evene were they chosen, for to gesse,
And in two renges faire they hem dresse.
Whan that hir names rad were everichoon,
That in hir nombre gyle were ther noon,
Tho were the gates shet, and cried was loude,
Do now youre devoir, yonge knyghtes proude!
THE heraudes lefte hir prikyng up and doun;
Now ryngen trompes loude and clarioun;
Ther is namoore to seyn, but west and est,
In goon the speres ful sadly in arrest;
In gooth the sharpe spore into the syde.
Ther seen men who kan juste, and who kan ryde;
Ther shyveren shaftes upon sheeldes thikke;
He feeleth thurgh the herte-spoon the prikke.
Up spryngen speres twenty foot on highte;
Out gooth the swerdes as the silver brighte;
The helmes they tohewen and toshrede;
Out brest the blood, with stierne stremes rede;
With myghty maces the bones they tobreste.
He, thurgh the thikkeste of the throng gan threste,
Ther, stomblen steedes stronge, and doun
goth al;
He, rolleth under foot as dooth a bal;
He, foyneth on his feet with his tronchoun,
And he, hym hurtleth with his hors adoun;
He, thurgh the body is hurte, and sithen take,
Maugree his heed, and broght unto the stake,
As forward was, right ther he moste abyde;
Another lad is on that oother syde.
And som tyme dooth hem Theseus to reste,
Hem to refresshe and drynken, if hem leste.

26

Ful ofte a day han thise Thebanes two,
Togydre ymet and wroght his felawe wo;
Unhorsed hath ech oother of hem tweye.
Ther nas no tygre in the vale of Galgopheye,
Whan that hir whelpe is stole whan it is lite,
So crueel on the hunte, as is Arcite
For jelous herte upon this Palamoun;
Ne in Belmarye ther nys so fel leoun
That hunted is, or for his hunger wood,
Ne of his praye desireth so the blood,
As Palamoun to sleen his foo Arcite.
The jelous strokes on hir helmes byte;
Out renneth blood on bothe hir sydes rede.
SOM tyme an ende ther is of every dede,
For er the sonne unto the reste wente,
The stronge kyng Emetreus gan hente
This Palamon, as he faught with Arcite,
And made his swerd depe in his flessh to byte;
And by the force of twenty is he take
Unyolden, and ydrawe unto the stake.
And in the rescous of this Palamoun,
The stronge kyng Lygurge is born adoun;
And kyng Emetreus, for al his strengthe,
Is born out of his sadel a swerdes lengthe;
So hitte him Palamoun er he were take;
But al for noght, he was broght to the stake.
His hardy herte myghte hym helpe naught,
He moste abyde, whan that he was caught,
By force, and eek by composicioun.
WHO sorweth now but woful Palamoun,
That moot namoore goon agayn to fighte?
And whan that Theseus hadde seyn this
sighte,
Unto the folk that foghten thus echon
He cryde, Hoo! namoore, for it is don!
I wol be trewe juge, and no partie;
Arcite of Thebes shall have Emelie
That by his fortune hath hire faire ywonne.
ANON ther is a noyse of peple bigonne,
For joye of this, so loude & heighe withalle,
It semed that the lystes sholde falle.
WHAT kan now faire Venus doon above?
What seith she now? what dooth this
queene of love?
But wepeth so, for wantynge of hir wille,
Til that hir teeres in the lystes fille;
She seyde, I am ashamed doutelees.
Saturnus seyde, Doghter, hoold thy pees;
Mars hath his wille, his knyght hath all his boone,
And, by myn heed, thow shalt been esed soone.
THE trompes, with the loude mynstralcie,
The heraudes, that ful loude yolle and crie,
Been in hire wele for joye of daun Arcite.
But herkneth me, and stynteth now a lite,
Which a myracle ther bifel anon.
THIS fierse Arcite hath of his helm ydon,
And on a courser, for to shewe his face,
He priketh endelong the large place,
Lokynge upward upon this Emelye;
And she agayn hym caste a freendlich eye,
For wommen, as to speken in comune,
Thei folwen al the favour of fortune,
And was al his, in chiere, as in his herte.

Out of the ground a furie infernal sterte,
From Pluto sent, at requeste of Saturne,
For which his hors for fere gan to turne,
And leepe aside, and foundred as he leepe,
And er that Arcite may taken keepe,
He pighte hym on the pomel of his heed,
That in the place he lay as he were deed,
His brest tobrosten with his sadelbowe.
As blak he lay as any cole or crowe,
So was the blood yronnen in his face.
Anon he was yborn out of the place
With herte soor, to Theseus paleys.
Tho was he korven out of his harneys,
And in a bed ybrought ful faire and blyve,
For he was yet in memorie and alyve,
And alwey cryinge after Emelye.

DUC Theseus with al his compaignye
Is comen hoom to Atthenes his citee,
With alle blisse and greet solempnitee;
Al be it that this aventure was falle,
He nolde noght disconforten hem alle.
Men seyden eek, that Arcite shal nat dye,
He shal been heeled of his maladye.
And of another thyng they were as fayn,
That of hem alle was ther noon yslayn,
Al were they soore yhurt, and namely oon,
That with a spere was thirled his brest boon.
To othere woundes, and to broken armes,
Somme hadden salves, & somme hadden charmes,
Fermacies of herbes, and eek save
They dronken, for they wolde hir lymes have.
For which this noble duc, as he wel kan,
Conforteth and honoureth every man,
And made revel al the longe nyght,
Unto the straunge lordes, as was right.
Ne ther was holden no disconfitynge,
But as a justes or a tourneyinge;
For soothly ther was no disconfiture,
For fallyng nys nat but an aventure;
Ne to be lad by force unto the stake
Unyolden, and with twenty knyghtes take,
O persone allone, withouten mo,
And haryed forth by arme, foot and too,
And eek his steede dryven forth with staves,
With footmen, bothe yemen and eek knaves,
It nas aretted hym no vileynye,
Ther may no man clepen it cowardye.

FOR which anon duc Theseus leet crye,
To stynten alle rancour and envye,
The gree as wel of o syde as of oother,
And eyther syde ylik as ootheres brother;
And yaf hem yiftes after hir degree,
And fully heeld a feeste dayes three,
And convoyed the kynges worthily
Out of his toun, a journee largely,
And hoom wente every man the righte way.
Ther was namoore, but fare wel! Have good day!
Of this bataille I wol namoore endite,
But speke of Palamon and of Arcyte.

SWELLETH the brest of Arcite, & the soore
Encreesseth at his herte moore and moore.
The clothered blood, for any lechecraft,
Corrupteth, and is in his bouk ylaft,

That neither veyne blood ne ventusynge,
Ne drynke of herbes may ben his helpynge;
The vertu expulsif, or animal,
Fro thilke vertu cleped natural,
Ne may the venym voyden ne expelle.
The pipes of his longes gonne to swelle,
And every lacerte in his brest adoun
Is shent with venym and corrupcioun.
Hym gayneth neither, for to gete his lif,
Vomyt upward, ne dounward laxatif;
Al is tobrosten thilke regioun,
Nature hath now no dominacioun.
And certeinly, ther nature wol nat wirche,
Farewel phisik, go ber the man to chirche.
This al and som, that Arcite moot dye,
For which he sendeth after Emelye,
And Palamon, that was his cosyn deere,
Thanne seyde he thus, as ye shal after heere.

NAUGHT may the woful spirit in myn herte
Declare o point of alle my sorwes smerte
To yow, my lady, that I love moost;
But I biquethe the servyce of my goost
To yow aboven every creature,
Syn that my lyf it may no lenger dure.
Allas, the wo! allas, the peynes stronge,
That I for yow have suffred, and so longe!
Allas, the deeth! allas, myn Emelye!
Allas, departynge of our compaignye!
Allas, myn hertes queene! allas, my wyf!
Myn hertes lady, endere of my lyf!
What is this world? what asketh men to have?
Now with his love, now in his colde grave
Allone, withouten any compaignye.
Farewel, my swete foo! myn Emelye!
And softe taak me in youre armes tweye,
For love of God, and herkneth what I seye.

I HAVE heer with my cosyn Palamon
Had strif and rancour, many a day agon
For love of yow, and for my jalousye.
And Juppiter so wys my soule gye,
To speken of a servaunt proprely,
With alle circumstaunces trewely,
That is to seyn, trouthe, honour, and knyghthede,
Wysdom, humblesse, estaat and heigh kynrede,
Fredom, and al that longeth to that art,
So Juppiter have of my soule part,
As in this world right now ne knowe I non
So worthy to ben loved as Palamon,
That serveth yow, and wol doon al his lyf.
And if that evere ye shul ben a wyf,
Foryet nat Palamon, the gentil man.
And with that word his speche faille gan,
And from his feete up to his brest was come
The coold of deeth, that hadde hym overcome,
And yet mooreover, in his armes two
The vital strengthe is lost, and al ago.
Oonly the intellect, withouten moore,
That dwelled in his herte syk and soore,
Gan faillen when the herte felte deeth,
Dusked his eyen two, and failled breeth.
But on his lady yet caste he his eye;
His laste word was, Mercy, Emelye!
His spirit chaunged hous, and wente ther,

As I cam nevere, I kan nat tellen wher.
Therfore I stynte, I nam no divinistre;
Of soules fynde I nat in this registre,
Ne me ne list thilke opinions to telle
Of hem, though that they writen wher they dwelle.
Arcite is coold, ther Mars his soule gye;
Now wol I speken forth of Emelye.

SHRIGHTE Emelye, and howleth Palamon,
And Theseus his suster took anon
Swownynge, & baar hire fro the corps away.
What helpeth it to tarien forth the day,
To tellen how she weepe, both eve and morwe?
For in swich cas wommen can have swich sorwe,
Whan that hir housbonds ben from hem ago,
That for the moore part they sorwen so,
Or ellis fallen in swich maladye,
That at the laste certeinly they dye.

Infinite been the sorwes and the teeres
Of olde folk, and eek of tendre yeeres,
In all the toun for deeth of this Theban;
For hym ther wepeth bothe child and man;
So greet a wepyng was ther noon certayn,
Whan Ector was ybroght al fressh yslayn
To Troye: Allas! the pitee that was ther,
Cracchynge of chekes, rentynge eek of heer.

Why woldestow be deed? thise wommen crye,
And haddest gold ynough, and Emelye?

NO man ne myghte gladen Theseus,
Savynge his olde fader Egeus,
That knew this worldes transmutacioun,
As he hadde seyn it chaungen, up and doun,
Joye after wo, and wo after gladnesse;
And shewed hem ensamples and liknesse.

Right as ther dyed nevere man, quod he,
That he ne lyvede in erthe in som degree,
Right so ther lyvede nevere man, he seyde,
In al this world, that some tyme he ne deyde.
This world nys but a thurghfare ful of wo,
And we been pilgrymes, passynge to and fro;
Deeth is an ende of every worldly soore.

And over al this yet seyde he muchel moore
To this effect, ful wisely to enhorte
The peple, that they sholde hem reconforte.

DUC Theseus, with all his bisy cure,
Cast busyly wher that the sepulture
Of goode Arcite may best ymaked be,
And eek moost honurable in his degree.
And at the laste he took conclusioun,
That ther as first Arcite and Palamoun
Hadden for love the bataille hem bitwene,
That in that selve grove, swoote and grene,
Ther as he hadde his amorouse desires,
His compleynte, and for love his hoote fires,
He wolde make a fyr in which thoffice
Of funeral he myghte al accomplice;
And leet comande anon to hakke and hewe
The okes olde, and leye hem on a rewe
In colpons, wel arrayed for to brenne.
His officers with swifte feet they renne,
And ryde anon at his comandement.

And after this, Theseus hath ysent
After a beere, and it al overspradde
With clooth of gold, the richeste that he hadde;

28

And of the same suyte he cladde Arcite.
Upon his hondes hadde he gloves white,
Eek on his heed a croune of laurer grene,
And in his hond a swerd ful bright and kene.
He leyde hym, bare the visage, on the beere.
Therwith he weep that pitee was to heere;
And, for the peple sholde seen hym alle,
Whan it was day, he broghte hym to the halle,
That roreth of the crying and the soun.

THO cam this woful Theban Palamoun,
With flotery berd, and rugged asshy heeres,
In clothes blake, ydropped al with teeres;
And passynge othere of wepynge, Emelye,
The rewefulleste of al the compaignye.

In as muche as the servyce sholde be
The moore noble and riche in his degree,
Duc Theseus leet forth thre steedes brynge,
That trapped were in steel al gliterynge,
And covered with the armes of daun Arcite.
Upon thise steedes, that weren grete and white,
Ther sitten folk, of whiche oon baar his sheeld,
Another his spere up in his hondes heeld;
The thridde baar with hym his bowe Turkeys,
Of brend gold was the caas, and eek the harneys,
And riden forth a paas with sorweful cheere
Toward the grove, as ye shul after heere.

THE nobleste of the Grekes that ther were,
Upon hir shuldres caryeden the beere,
With slake paas, and eyen rede and wete,
Thurghout the citee, by the maister-strete,
That sprad was al with blak, and wonder hye
Right of the same is al the strete ywrye.

UPON the right hond wente olde Egeus,
And on that oother syde duc Theseus,
With vessels in hir hond of gold ful fyn
Al ful of hony, milk, and blood, and wyn:
Eek Palamon with ful greet compaignye,
And after that cam woful Emelye,
With fyr in honde, as was that tyme the gyse,
To do thoffice of funeral servyse.

HEIGH labour, and ful greet apparail-
lynge,
Was at the service and the fyr-mak-
ynge,
That with his grene top the heven
raughte,
And twenty fadme of brede the armes straughte,
This is to seyn, the bowes were so brode.
Of stree first ther was leyd ful many a lode;
But how the fyr was maked up on highte,
And eek the names that the trees highte,
As ook, firre, birch, aspe, alder, holm, popeler,
Wylugh, elm, plane, assh, box, chasteyn, lynde,
laurer,
Mapul, thorn, bech, hasel, ew, whippeltre,
How they weren feld, shal nat be toold for me;
Ne how the goddes ronnen up and doun,
Disherited of hire habitacioun,
In whiche they woneden in reste and pees,
Nymphus, and fawnes, and amadrides;
Ne how the beestes and the briddes alle
Fledden for fere, whan the wode was falle;
Ne how the ground agast was of the light,

That was nat wont to seen the sonne bright;
Ne how the fyr was couched first with stree,
And thanne with drye stokkes, cloven a thre,
And thanne with grene wode and spicerye,
And thanne with clooth of gold, and with perrye,
And gerlandes, hangynge with ful many a flour,
The mirre, thencens, with al so greet odour;
Ne how Arcite lay among al this,
Ne what richesse aboute his body is;
Ne how that Emelye, as was the gyse,
Putte in the fyr of funeral servyse;
Ne how she swowned whan men made fyr,
Ne what she spak, ne what was hir desyr,
Ne what jeweles men in the fyre caste,
Whan that the fyr was greet and brente faste;
Ne how somme caste hir sheeld, & somme hir spere,
And of hire vestiments, whiche that they were,
And coppes ful of wyn, and milk, and blood,
Into the fyr, that brente as it were wood;
Ne how the Grekes, with an huge route,
Thryës they riden al the fyr aboute
Upon the left hand, with a loud shoutynge,
And thryës with hir speres claterynge,
And thryës how the ladyes gonne crye;
And how that lad was homward Emelye;
Ne how Arcite is brent to asshen colde;
Ne how that lyche-wake was yholde
Al thilke nyght; ne how the Grekes pleye
The wake-pleyes; ne kepe I nat to seye
Who wrastleth best naked, with oille enoynt,
Ne who that baar hym best, in no disjoynt.
I wol nat tellen eek how that they goon
Hoom til Atthenes whan the pley is doon;
But shortly to the point thanne wol I wende,
And maken of my longe tale an ende.
BY processe and by lengthe of certeyn yeres,
Al styntyd is the moornynge and the teres.
Of Grekes, by oon general assent
Thanne semed me ther was a parlement
At Atthenes, upon certain poynts and caas;
Among the whiche poynts yspoken was,
To have with certein contrees alliaunce,
And have fully of Thebans obeissaunce.
For which this noble Theseus anon
Leet senden after gentil Palamon,
Unwist of hym what was the cause and why;
But in his blake clothes sorwefully
He cam at his comandement in hye.
Tho sente Theseus for Emelye.
Whan they were set, and hust was al the place,
And Theseus abiden hadde a space
Er any word cam fram his wise brest,
His eyen sette he ther as was his lest,
And with a sad visage he siked stille,
And after that right thus he seyde his wille.
THE firste moevere of the cause above,
Whan he first made the faire cheyne of love,
Greet was theffect, & heigh was his entente;
Wel wiste he why, and what therof he mente;
For with that faire cheyne of love he bond
The fyr, the eyr, the water, and the lond,
In certeyn boundes that they may nat flee.
That same prince, and that moevere, quod he,
Hath stablissed, in this wrecched world adoun,

Certeyne dayes and duracioun
To al that is engendred in this place,
Over the whiche day they may nat pace,
Al mowe they yet tho dayes wel abregge;
Ther nedeth noon auctoritee allegge,
For it is preeved by experience,
But that me list declaren my sentence.
Thanne may men by this ordre wel discerne,
That thilke moevere stable is and eterne.
Wel may men knowe, but it be a fool,
That every part dirryveth from his hool.
For nature hath nat take his bigynnyng
Of no partie ne cantel of a thyng,
But of a thyng that parfit is and stable,
Descendynge so, til it be corrumpable.
And therfore of his wise purveiaunce,
He hath so wel biset his ordinaunce,
That speces of thynges and progressiouns
Shullen enduren by successiouns,
And nat eterne, withouten any lye;
This maystow understonde, and seen at eye.
Loo the ook, that hath so long a norisshynge
From tyme that it first bigynneth sprynge,
And hath so long a lif, as we may see,
Yet at the laste wasted is the tree.
Considereth eek how that the harde stoon
Under oure feet, on which we trede and goon,
Yit wasteth it, as it lyth by the weye;
The brode ryver somtyme wexeth dreye;
The grete toures se we wane and wende;
Thanne may ye se that al this thyng hath ende.
Of man and womman seen we wel also,
That nedeth in oon of thise termes two,
This is to seyn, in youthe or elles age,
He moot be deed, the kyng as shal a page;
Som in his bed, som in the depe see,
Som in the large feeld, as men may se;
Ther helpeth noght, al goth that ilke weye:
Thanne may I seyn that al this thyng moot deye.
What maketh this but Juppiter, the kyng?
The which is prince, and cause of alle thyng,
Convertynge al unto his propre welle,
From which it is dirryved, sooth to telle.
And hereagayns no creature on lyve,
Of no degree, availleth for to stryve.
Thanne is it wysdom, as it thynketh me,
To maken vertu of necessitee,
And take it weel that we may not eschue,
And namely that, that to us alle is due.
And whoso gruccheth ought, he dooth folye,
And rebel is to hym that al may gye;
And certeinly a man hath moost honour,
To dyen in his excellence and flour,
Whan he is siker of his goode name.
Thanne hath he doon his freend ne hym no shame,
And gladder oghte his freend been of his deeth,
Whan with honour upyolden is his breeth,
Than whan his name apalled is for age,
For al forgeten is his vassellage.
Thanne is it best, as for a worthy fame,
To dyen whan that he is best of name.
THE contrarie of al this is wilfulnesse.
Why grucchen we, why have we hevynesse
That good Arcite, of chivalrye the flour,

29

Departed is with duetee and honour
Out of this foule prisoun of this lyf?
Why grucchen heere his cosyn and his wyf
Of his welfare that loved hem so weel?
Kan he hem thank? Nay, God woot, never a deel,
That bothe his soule & eek hemself offende,
And yet they mowe hir lustes nat amende.

WHAT may I conclude of this
longe serye,
But after wo, I rede us to be
merye,
And thanken Juppiter of al his
grace?
And er that we departen from this place,
I rede that we make of sorwes two,
O parfit joye, lastynge everemo.
And looketh now, wher moost sorwe is
herinne,
Ther wol we first amenden and bigynne.
🖝 Suster, quod he, this is my fulle assent,
With all thavys heere of my parlement,
That gentil Palamon, thyn owene knyght,
That serveth yow with wille, herte, and myght,
And evere hath doon, syn that ye first hym
knewe,
That ye shul, of your grace, upon hym rewe,
And taken hym for housbonde and for lord;
Lene me youre hond, for this is oure accord.

Lat se now of youre wommanly pitee;
He is a kynges brother sone, pardee,
And though he were a povre bacheler,
Syn he hath served yow so many a yeer
And had for yow so greet adversitee,
It moste been considered, leeveth me,
For gentil mercy oghte to passen right.

THANNE seyde he thus to Palamon ful
right:
I trowe ther nedeth litel sermonyng
To make yow assente to this thyng;
Com neer, and taak youre lady by the hond.
🖝 Bitwixen hem was maad anon the bond
That highte matrimoigne, or mariage,
By al the conseil and the baronage.
And thus with alle blisse and melodye
Hath Palamon ywedded Emelye;
And God, that al this wyde world hath wroght,
Sende hym his love, that it deere aboght.
For now is Palamon in alle wele,
Lyvynge in blisse, in richesse, and in heele;
And Emelye hym loveth so tendrely,
And he hire serveth al so gentilly,
That nevere was ther no word hem bitwene
Of jalousie, or any oother tene.
🖝 Thus endeth Palamon and Emelye,
And God save al this faire compaignye.
Heere is ended the Knyghtes Tale ✤ ✤

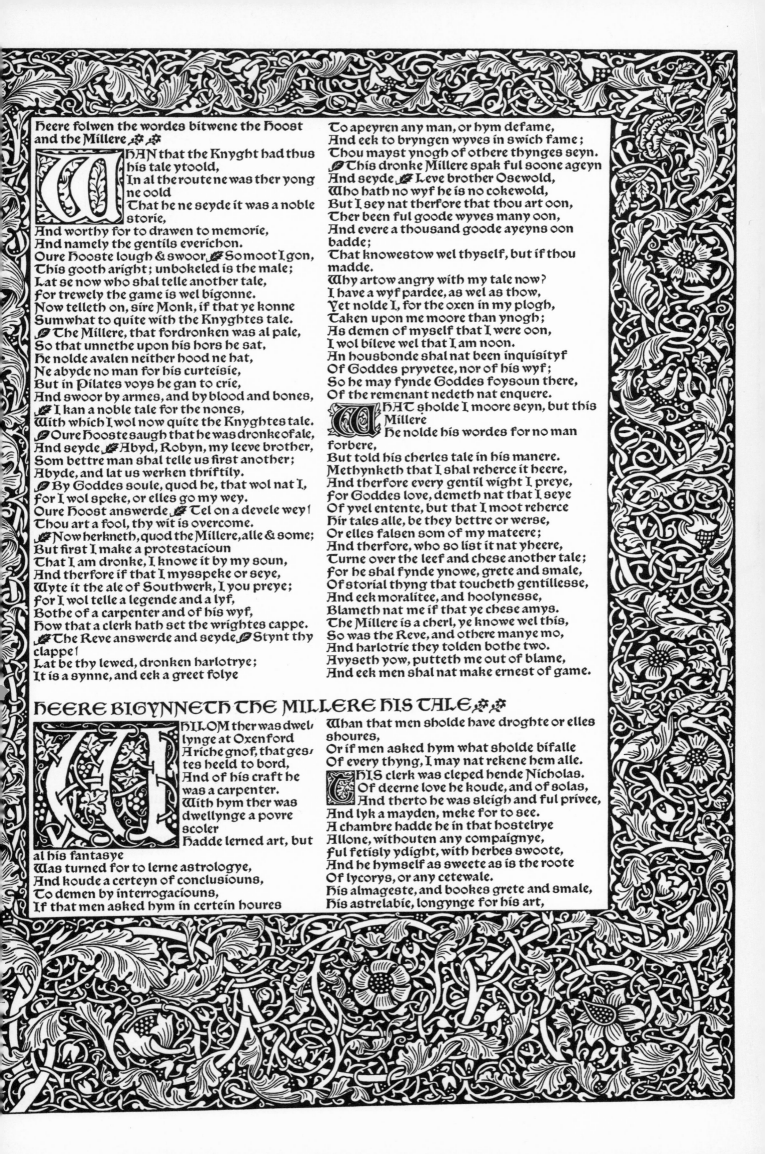

Heere folwen the wordes bitwene the Hoost and the Millere ❧ ❧

WHAN that the Knyght had thus his tale ytoold,
In al the route ne was ther yong ne oold
That he ne seyde it was a noble storie,
And worthy for to drawen to memorie,
And namely the gentils everichon.
Oure Hooste lough & swoor, ❧ So moot I gon,
This gooth aright; unbokeled is the male;
Lat se now who shal telle another tale,
For trewely the game is wel bigonne.
Now telleth on, sire Monk, if that ye konne
Sumwhat to quite with the Knyghtes tale.
❧ The Millere, that fordronken was al pale,
So that unnethe upon his hors he sat,
He nolde avalen neither hood ne hat,
Ne abyde no man for his curteisie,
But in Pilates voys he gan to crie,
And swoor by armes, and by blood and bones,
❧ I kan a noble tale for the nones,
With which I wol now quite the Knyghtes tale.
❧ Oure Hooste saugh that he was dronke of ale,
And seyde, ❧ Abyd, Robyn, my leeve brother,
Som bettre man shal telle us first another;
Abyde, and lat us werken thriftily.
❧ By Goddes soule, quod he, that wol nat I,
For I wol speke, or elles go my wey.
Oure Hoost answerde, ❧ Tel on a devele wey!
Thou art a fool, thy wit is overcome.
❧ Now herkneth, quod the Millere, alle & some;
But first I make a protestacioun
That I am dronke, I knowe it by my soun,
And therfore if that I mysspeke or seye,
Wyte it the ale of Southwerk, I you preye;
For I wol telle a legende and a lyf,
Bothe of a carpenter and of his wyf,
How that a clerk hath set the wrightes cappe.
❧ The Reve answerde and seyde, ❧ Stynt thy clappe!
Lat be thy lewed, dronken harlotrye;
It is a synne, and eek a greet folye

To apeyren any man, or hym defame,
And eek to bryngen wyves in swich fame;
Thou mayst ynogh of othere thynges seyn.
❧ This dronke Millere spak ful soone ageyn
And seyde, ❧ Leve brother Osewold,
Who hath no wyf he is no cokewold,
But I sey nat therfore that thou art oon,
Ther been ful goode wyves many oon,
And evere a thousand goode ayeyns oon badde;
That knowestow wel thyself, but if thou madde.
Why artow angry with my tale now?
I have a wyf pardee, as wel as thow,
Yet nolde I, for the oxen in my plogh,
Taken upon me moore than ynogh;
As demen of myself that I were oon,
I wol bileve wel that I am noon.
An housbonde shal nat been inquisityf
Of Goddes pryvetee, nor of his wyf;
So he may fynde Goddes foysoun there,
Of the remenant nedeth nat enquere.
WHAT sholde I moore seyn, but this Millere
He nolde his wordes for no man forbere,
But told his cherles tale in his manere.
Methynketh that I shal reherce it heere,
And therfore every gentil wight I preye,
For Goddes love, demeth nat that I seye
Of yvel entente, but that I moot reherce
Hir tales alle, be they bettre or werse,
Or elles falsen som of my mateere;
And therfore, who so list it nat yheere,
Turne over the leef and chese another tale;
For he shal fynde ynowe, grete and smale,
Of storial thyng that toucheth gentillesse,
And eek moralitee, and hoolynesse,
Blameth nat me if that ye chese amys.
The Millere is a cherl, ye knowe wel this,
So was the Reve, and othere manye mo,
And harlotrie they tolden bothe two.
Avyseth yow, putteth me out of blame,
And eek men shal nat make ernest of game.

HEERE BIGYNNETH THE MILLERE HIS TALE ❧ ❧

WHILOM ther was dwellynge at Oxenford
A riche gnof, that gestes heeld to bord,
And of his craft he was a carpenter.
With hym ther was dwellynge a povre scoler
Hadde lerned art, but al his fantasye
Was turned for to lerne astrologye,
And koude a certeyn of conclusiouns,
To demen by interrogacioun,
If that men asked hym in certein houres

Whan that men sholde have droghte or elles shoures,
Or if men asked hym what sholde bifalle
Of every thyng, I may nat rekene hem alle.
THIS clerk was cleped hende Nicholas.
Of deerne love he koude, and of solas,
And therto he was sleigh and ful privee,
And lyk a mayden, meke for to see.
A chambre hadde he in that hostelrye
Allone, withouten any compaignye,
Ful fetisly ydight, with herbes swoote,
And he hymself as sweete as is the roote
Of lycorys, or any cetewale.
His almageste, and bookes grete and smale,
His astrelabie, longynge for his art,

His augrym stones, layen faire apart,
On shelves couched at his beddes heed,
His presse ycovered with a faldyng reed,
And all above ther lay a gay sautrie,
On which he made anyghtes melodie
So swetely, that al the chambre rong,
And Angelus ad virginem, he song;
And after that he song the kynges noote;
Ful often blessed was his myrie throte,
And thus this sweete clerk his tyme spente
After his freendes fyndyng and his rente.

THIS carpenter hadde wedded newe a wyf,
Which that he loved moore than his lyf;
Of eighteteene yeer she was of age.
Jalous he was, and heeld hire narwe in cage,
For she was yong and wylde, and he was old,
And demed hymself been lik a cokewold.
He knew nat Catoun, for his wit was rude,
That bad man sholde wedde his symylitude.
Men sholde wedden after hire estaat,
For youthe and elde is often at debaat;
But sith that he was fallen in the snare,
He moste endure, as oother folk, his care.

FAIR was this yonge wyf, and therwithal,
As any wezele, hir body gent and smal,
A ceynt she wered, ybarred al of silk;
A barmclooth eek as whit as morne milk
Upon hir lendes, ful of many a goore;
Whit was hir smok, and broyden al bifoore,
And eek bihynde, on hir coler aboute,
Of colblak silk withinne and eek withoute.
The tapes of hir white voluper
Were of the same suyte of hir coler;
Hir filet brood, of silk and set ful hye;
And sikerly she hadde a likerous eye.
Ful smale ypulled were hire browes two,
And tho were bent, and blake as any sloo.
She was ful moore blisful on to see
Than is the newe perejonette tree,
And softer than the wolle is of a wether;
And by hir girdel heeng a purs of lether,
Tasseled with grene and perled with latoun.
In al this world, to seken up and doun,
Ther nas no man so wys that koude thenche
So gay a popelote, or swich a wenche.
Ful brighter was the shynyng of hir hewe
Than in the Tour the noble yforged newe.

BUT of hir song, it was as loude and yerne
As any swalwe chiterynge on a berne.
Therto she koude skippe and make game,
As any kyde, or calf, folwynge his dame.
Hir mouth was sweete as bragot or the meeth,
Or hoord of apples leyd in hey or heeth.
Wynsynge she was, as is a joly colt;
Long as a mast, and uprighte as a bolt.
A brooch sche baar upon hir love coler,
As brood as is the boos of a bokeler;
Hir shoes were laced on hir legges hye;
She was a prymerole, a piggesnye
For any lord to liggen in his bedde,
Or yet for any good yeman to wedde.

32

NOW, sire, and eft, sire, so bifel the cas,
That on a day this hende Nicholas,
Fil with this yonge wyf to rage and pleye
Whil that hir housbonde was at Oseneye,
As clerkes ben ful subtile and ful queynte,
And prively he caughte hire by the queynte,
And seyde, ywis, But if ich have my wille,
For deerne love of thee, lemman, I spille;
And heeld hire harde by the haunche bones,
And seyde, Lemman, love me al atones,
Or I wol dyen, also God me save!
And she sproong, as a colt doth in the trave,
And with hir heed sche wryed faste awey,
And seyde, I wol nat kisse thee, by my fey!
Why, lat be! quod she, lat be, Nicholas!
Or I wol crie out, Harrow, and Allas!
Do wey youre handes, for your curteisye!

THIS Nicholas gan mercy for to crye,
And spak so faire, and profred him so faste,
That she hir love hym graunted atte laste,
And swoor hir ooth, by Seint Thomas of Kent,
That she wol been at his comandement
Whan that she may hir leyser wel espie.
Myn housbonde is so ful of jalousie,
That but ye wayte wel and been privee,
I woot right wel I nam but deed, quod she;
Ye moste been ful deerne, as in this cas.
Nay, therof care thee noght, quod Nicholas.
A clerk hadde litherly biset his whyle
But if he koude a carpenter bigyle.
And thus they been accorded and ysworn
To wayte a tyme, as I have told biforn.
Whan Nicholas had doon thus everideel,
And thakked hire aboute the lendes weel,
He kist hire sweete, and taketh his sawtrie,
And pleyeth faste, and maketh melodie.
Thanne fil it thus, that to the paryssh chirche,
Christes owene werkes for to wirche,
This goode wyf went on an haliday;
Hir forheed shoon as bright as any day,
So was it wasshen whan she leet hir werk.

NOW was ther of that chirche a parissh clerk,
The which that was ycleped Absolon;
Crul was his heer and as the gold it shoon,
And strouted as a fanne, large and brode,
Ful streight and evene lay his joly shode.
His rode was reed, his eyen greye as goos;
With Powles wyndow corven on his shoos,
In hosen rede he wente fetisly.
Yclad he was ful smal and proprely,
Al in a kirtel of a lyght waget,
Ful faire and thikke been the poyntes set;
And ther upon he hadde a gay surplys,
As whit as is the blosme upon the rys.
A myrie child he was, so God me save,
Wel koude he laten blood, and clippe and shave,
And maken a chartre of lond or acquitaunce.
In twenty manere koude he trippe and daunce,
After the scole of Oxenforde tho,
And with his legges casten to and fro,
And pleyen songes on a small rubible;
Therto he song som tyme a loud quynyble,
And as wel koude he pleye on his giterne.

In al the toun nas brewhous ne taverne
That he ne visited with his solas,
Ther any gaylard tappestere was.
But, sooth to seyn, he was somdel squaymous
Of fartyng, and of speche daungerous.
THIS Absolon, that jolif was and gay,
Gooth with a sencer on the haliday,
Sensynge the wyves of the parisshe faste,
And many a lovely look on hem he caste;
And namely on this carpenteris wyf.
To loke on hire hym thoughte a myrie lyf,
She was so propre, and sweete, and likerous.
I dar wel seyn if she hadde been a mous,
And he a cat, he wold hire hente anon.
This parissh clerk, this joly Absolon,
Hath in his herte swich a love/longynge,
That of no wyf ne took he noon offrynge;
For curteisie, he seyde, he wolde noon.
THE moone, whan it was nyght, ful brighte
shoon,
And Absolon his gyterne hath ytake,
For paramours he thoghte for to wake;
And forth he gooth, jolif and amorous,
Til he cam to the carpenteres hous
A litel after cokkes had ycrowe,
And dressed hym up by a shot/wyndowe
That was upon the carpenteres wal.
He syngeth in his voys gentil and smal,
Now, deere lady, if thy wille be,
I pray yow that ye wole thynke on me,
Ful wel acordaunt to his gyternynge.
This carpenter awook, and herde hym synge,
And spak unto his wyf, and seyde anon,
What, Alison! herestow nat Absolon
That chaunteth thus under oure boures wal?
And she answerde hir housbonde therwithal,
Yis, God woot, John, I heere it every del.
This passeth forth; what wol ye bet than weel?
FRO day to day this joly Absolon
So woweth hire that hym is wo bigon;
He waketh al the nyght and al the day,
He kembeth his lokkes brode, and made hym gay,
He woweth hire by meenes and brocage,
And swoor he wolde been hir owene page;
He syngeth, brokkynge as a nyghtyngale;
He sente hire pyment, meeth, and spiced ale,
And wafres pipyng hoot out of the gleede,
And for she was of toune, he profreth meede;
For som folk wol ben wonnen for richesse,
And somme for strokes, and somme for gen-
tillesse.
Somtyme to shewe his lightnesse & maistrye
He pleyeth Herodes upon a scaffold hye,
But what availeth hym, as in this cas?
She loveth so this hende Nicholas,
That Absolon may blowe the bukkes horn;
He ne had for his labour but a scorn;
And thus she maketh Absolon hire ape,
And al his ernest turneth til a jape.
Ful sooth is this proverbe, it is no lye,
Men seyn right thus, Alwey the nye slye
Maketh the ferre leeve to be looth.
For though that Absolon be wood or wrooth,

d i

Bycause that he fer was from hire sighte,
This nye Nicholas stood in his lighte.
NOW bere thee wel, thou hende Nicholas,
For Absolon may waille and synge, Allas!
And so bifel it on a Saterday,
This carpenter was goon til Osenay,
And hende Nicholas and Alisoun
Acorded been to this conclusioun,
That Nicholas shal shapen hym a wyle,
This sely jalous housbonde to bigyle;
And, if so be the game wente aright,
She sholde slepen in his arm al nyght,
For this was his desir and hire also.
And right anon, withouten wordes mo,
This Nicholas no lenger wolde tarie,
But dooth ful softe unto his chamber carie
Bothe mete and drynke for a day or tweye;
And to hire housbonde bad hire for to seye,
If that he axed after Nicholas,
She sholde seye she nyste where he was;
Of al that day she saugh hym nat with eye;
She trowed that he was in maladye,
For, for no cry, hir mayde koude hym calle,
He nolde answere for nothyng that myghte falle.
This passeth forth al thilke Saterday,
That Nicholas stille in his chambre lay,
And eet and sleepe, or dide what hym leste;
Til Sonday that the sonne gooth to reste
This sely carpenter hath greet merveyle
Of Nicholas, or what thyng myghte hym eyle,
And seyde, I am adrad, by Seint Thomas,
It stondeth nat aright with Nicholas.
God shilde that he deyde sodeynly;
This world is now ful tikel sikerly;
I saugh today a cors yborn to chirche,
That now on Monday last I saugh hym wirche.
Go up, quod he unto his knave anoon,
Clepe at his dore, or knokke with a stoon,
Looke how it is, and tel me boldely.
This knave gooth him up ful sturdily,
And at the chambre dore whil that he stood,
He cride and knokked as that he were wood:
What how! what do ye, maister Nicholay?
How may ye slepen al the longe day?
But al for noght, he herde nat a word.
An hole he foond ful lowe upon a bord,
Ther as the cat was wont in for to crepe;
And at that hole he looked in ful depe,
And at the laste he hadde of hym a sighte.
This Nicholas sat gapyng evere uprighte,
As he had kiked on the newe moone.
Adoun he gooth, and tolde his maister soone
In what array he saugh that ilke man.
THIS carpenter to blessen hym bigan,
And seyde, Help us, Seinte Frydeswyde!
A man woot litel what hym shal bityde;
This man is falle with his astromye
In som woodnesse, or in som agonye.
I thoghte ay wel how that it sholde be,
Men sholde nat knowe of Goddes pryvetee.
Ye, blessed be alwey a lewed man,
That noght but oonly his bileve kan.
So ferde another clerk with astromye;

33

He walked in the feeldes, for to prye
Upon the sterres, what ther sholde bifalle,
Til he was in a marlepit yfalle;
He saugh nat that. But yet, by Seint Thomas,
Me reweth soore of hende Nicholas;
He shal be rated of his studying,
If that I may, by Jhesus, hevene kyng!
Get me a staf, that I may underspore,
Whil that thou, Robyn, hevest of the dore;
He shal out of his studying, as I gesse.
And to the chambre dore he gan hym dresse.
His knave was a strong carl for the nones,
And by the haspe he haaf it of atones,
Into the floore the dore fil anon.
This Nicholas sat ay as stille as stoon,
And evere gaped upward into the eir.
This carpenter wende he were in despeir,
And hente hym by the sholdres myghtily
And shook hym harde, and cride spitously,
What, Nicholay! what how! what! looke adoun!
Awake! and thenk on Cristes passioun!
I crouche thee from elves and fro wightes.
Therwith the nyghtspel seyde he anonrightes,
On foure halves of the hous aboute,
And on the thresshfold of the dore withoute:
Jhesu Crist and Seint Benedight,
Blesse this hous from every wikked wight,
For nyghtes verye the white Pater noster.
Where wentestow, Seint Petres soster?
And atte laste this hende Nicholas
Gan for to sike soore, and seyde Allas!
Shal al this world be lost eftsoones now?
This carpenter answerde What seystow?
What? thynk on God, as we doon, men that
swynke.
This Nicholas answerde Fecche me drynke;
And after wol I speke in pryvetee
Of certeyn thyng that toucheth me and thee;
I wol telle it noon oother man, certeyn.
THIS carpenter goth doun, and comth ageyn,
And broghte of myghty ale a large quart;
And whan that ech of hem had dronke his
part,
This Nicholas his dore faste shette
And doun the carpenter by hym he sette.
He seyde John, myn hooste lief and deere,
Thou shalt upon thy trouthe swere me heere
That to no wight thou shalt this conseil wreye,
For it is Cristes conseil that I seye,
And if thou telle it man thou art forlore,
For this vengeaunce thou shalt han therfore
That if thou wreye me, thou shalt be wood.
Nay, Crist forbede it, for his hooly blood!
Quod tho this sely man, I nam no labbe,
Ne, though I seye, I am nat lief to gabbe;
Sey what thou wolt, I shal it nevere telle
To child ne wyf, by hym that harwed helle!
Now, John, quod Nicholas, I wol nat lye;
I have yfounde in myn astrologye,
As I have looked in the moone bright,
That now, a Monday next, at quarter nyght,
Shal falle a reyn, and that so wilde and wood,
That half so greet was nevere Noees flood.
34

This world, he seyde, in lasse than an hour
Shal al be dreynt, so hidous is the shour;
Thus schal mankynde drenche, and lese hir lyf.
This carpenter answerde Allas, my wyf!
And shal she drenche? Allas! myn Alisoun!
For sorwe of this he fil almoost adoun,
And seyde, Is ther no remedie in this cas?
Why, yis, for Gode, quod hende Nicholas,
If thou wolt werken aftir loore and reed;
Thou mayst nat werken after thyn owene heed,
For thus seith Salomoun, that was ful trewe,
Werk al by conseil, and thou shalt nat rewe;
And if thou werken wolt by good conseil,
I undertake, withouten mast and seyl,
Yet shal I saven hire and thee and me.
Hastow nat herd how saved was Noe,
Whan that oure Lord hadde warned hym biforn
That al the world with water sholde be lorn?
Yis, quod this carpenter, ful yoore ago.
Hastow nat herd, quod Nicholas, also
The sorwe of Noe with his felaweshipe
Er that he myghte brynge his wyf to shipe?
Hym hadde levere, I dar wel undertake,
At thilke tyme, than alle his wetheres blake,
That she hadde had a shipe hirself allone.
And therfore, woostow what is best to doone?
This asketh haste, and of an hastif thyng
Men may nat preche or maken tarying.
Anon go gete us faste into this in
A knedyng-trogh, or ellis a kymelyn,
For ech of us, but loke that they be large,
In whiche we mowe swymme as in a barge,
And han therinne vitaille suffisant
But for a day; fy on the remenant,
The water shal aslake and goon away
Aboute pryme upon the nexte day.
But Robyn may nat wite of this, thy knave,
Ne eek thy mayde Gille I may nat save;
Axe nat why, for though thou aske me,
I wol nat tellen Goddes pryvetee;
Suffiseth thee, but if thy wittes madde,
To han as greet a grace as Noe hadde.
Thy wyf shal I wel saven, out of doute.
Go now thy wey and speed thee heeraboute.
But whan thou hast for hire and thee and me
Ygeten us thise knedyng-tubbes thre,
Thanne shaltow hange hem in the roof ful hye,
That no man of oure purveiaunce spye,
And whan thou thus hast doon as I have seyd,
And hast oure vitaille faire in hem yleyd,
And eek an ax, to smyte the corde atwo
Whan that the water comth, that we may go,
And broke an hole an heigh, upon the gable,
Unto the gardynward, over the stable,
That we may frely passen forth oure way
Whan that the grete shour is goon away.
Thanne shaltow swymme as myrie, I undertake,
As dooth the white doke after hire drake;
Thanne wol I clepe, How Alisoun! how John!
Be myrie, for the flood wol passe anon.
And thou wolt seyn, Hayl, maister Nicholay!
Good morwe, I se thee wel, for it is day!
And thanne shul we be lordes al oure lyf

Of al the world, as Noe and his wyf.
But of o thyng I warne thee ful right,
Be wel avysed on that ilke nyght
That we ben entred into shippes bord,
That noon of us ne speke nat a word,
Ne clepe, ne crie, but been in his preyere;
For it is Goddes owene heeste deere.
Thy wyf and thou moote hange fer atwynne,
For that bitwixe yow shal be no synne,
Na moore in lookyng than ther shal in deede;
This ordinance is seyd; so God thee speede.
Tomorwe at nyght, whan folk ben alle aslepe,
Into our knedyng/tubbes wol we crepe,
And sitten there, abidyng Goddes grace.
Go now thy wey, I have no lenger space
To make of this no lenger sermonyng,
Men seyn thus, Sende the wise and sey no thyng;
Thou art so wys, it needeth thee nat teche,
Go, save oure lyf, and that I the biseche.
THIS sely carpenter goth forth his wey;
Ful ofte he seith Allas, and Weylawey,
And to his wyf he tolde his pryvetee,
And she was war, and knew it bet than he,
What al this queynte cast was for to seye.
But nathelees she ferde as she wolde deye,
And seyde, Allas! go forth thy wey anon,
Help us to scape, or we ben lost echon!
I am thy trewe, verray, wedded wyf,
Go, deere spouse, and help to save oure lyf!
LO! which a greet thyng is affeccioun!
Men may dyen of ymaginacioun,
So depe may impressioun be take.
This sely carpenter bigynneth quake;
Hym thynketh verraily that he may see,
Noeës flood, come walwynge as the see,
To drenchen Alisoun, his hony deere.
He wepeth, weyleth, maketh sory cheere;
He siketh, with ful many a sory swogh,
He gooth and geteth hym a knedyng/trogh,
And after that a tubbe and a kymelyn,
And pryvely he sente hem to his in,
And heng hem in the roof in pryvetee.
His owene hand he made laddres thre,
To clymben by the ronges and the stalkes,
Into the tubbes, hangynge in the balkes;
And hem vitailleth, bothe trogh and tubbe,
With breed and chese and good ale in a jubbe,
Suffisynge right ynogh as for a day.
But er that he hadde maad al this array,
He sente his knave, and eek his wenche also,
Upon his nede to London for to go;
And on the Monday, whan it drow to nyght,
He shette his dore withoute candel/lyght,
And dresseth alle thyng as it shal be;
And shortly, up they clomben alle thre;
They sitten stille, wel a furlong way.
NOW, Pater noster, clom! seyde Nicholay;
And clom, quod John, and clom, seyde
Alisoun.
This carpenter seyde his devocioun,
And stille he sit and biddeth his preyere,
Awaitynge on the reyn, if he it heere.
The dede sleepe for wery bisynesse

fil on this carpenter, right as I gesse
Aboute corfew/tyme, or litel moore;
For travaille of his goost he groneth soore,
And eft he routeth, for his heed myslay.
Doun of the laddre stalketh Nicholay,
And Alisoun, ful softe adoun she spedde;
Withouten wordes mo they goon to bedde
Ther as the carpenter is wont to lye.
Ther was the revel and the melodye;
And thus lith Alisoun and Nicholas,
In bisynesse of myrthe and of solas,
Til that the belle of laudes gan to rynge,
And freres in the chauncel gonne synge.
THIS parissh clerk, this amorous Absolon,
That is for love alwey so wobigon,
Upon the Monday was at Oseneye
With compaignye, hym to disporte and pleye,
And axed upon cas a cloisterer
Ful prively after John the carpenter.
And he drough hym apart out of the chirche,
And seyde, I noot, I saugh hym heere nat wirche
Syn Saterday; I trow that he be went
For tymber, ther our abbot hath hym sent;
For he is wont for tymber for to go,
And dwellen at the grange a day or two;
Or elles he is at his hous, certeyn;
Where that he be, I kan nat soothly seyn.
THIS Absolon ful joly was and light,
And thoghte, Now is tyme to wake al
nyght,
For sikirly I saugh him nat stirynge
Aboute his dore syn day bigan to sprynge.
So moot I thryve, I shal, at cokkes crowe
Ful pryvely knokken at his wyndowe
That stant ful lowe upon his boures wal.
To Alison now wol I tellen al
My love/longynge, for yet I shal nat mysse
That at the leste wey I shal hire kisse.
Som maner confort shal I have, parfay,
My mouth hath icched al this longe day;
That is a signe of kissyng atte leste.
Al nyghte me mette eek, I was at a feeste;
Therfore I wol goon slepe an houre or tweye,
And al the nyght thanne wol I wake and pleye.
WHAN that the firste cok hath crowe, anon
Uprist this joly lovere Absolon,
And hym arraieth gay, at poynt/devys;
But first he cheweth greyn and lycorys,
To smellen sweete, er he hadde kembd his heer.
Under his tonge a trewe/love he beer,
For therby wende he to ben gracious.
He rometh to the carpenteres hous,
And stille he stant under the shot/wyndowe,
Unto his brist it raughte, it was so lowe;
And softe he knokketh with a semy/soun:
What do ye, hony/comb, sweete Alisoun,
My faire bryd, my sweete cynamome?
Awaketh, lemman myn, and speketh to me.
Wel litel thynken ye upon my wo,
That for youre love I swete ther I go.
No wonder is, thogh that I swelte and swete,
I moorne as dooth a lamb after the tete;
Ywis, lemman, I have swich love/longynge,

That lik a turtel trewe is my moornynge;
I may nat ete na moore than a mayde.
Go fro the wyndow, jakke fool, she sayde,
As help me God, it wol nat be, com ba me;
I love another, and elles I were to blame,
Wel bet than thee, by Jhesu, Absolon!
Go forth thy wey, or I wol caste a ston,
And lat me slepe, a twenty devel wey!
Allas, quod Absolon, and weylawey!
That trewe love was evere so ylle biset!
Thanne kysse me, syn it may be no bet,
For Jhesus love, and for the love of me.
Wiltow thanne go thy wey? quod she.
Ye certes, lemman, quod this Absolon.
Thanne make thee redy, quod she, I come anon,
And unto Nicholas she seyde stille,
Now hust, and thou shalt laughen al thy fille.
This Absolon doun sette hym on his knees,
And seyde I am a lord at alle degrees,
For after this I hope ther cometh moore.
Lemman, thy grace, and sweete bryd, thyn oore.
The wyndow she undoth, and that in haste;
Have do, quod she, com of, and speed thee faste,
Lest that oure neighebores thee espie.
THIS Absolon gan wype his mouth ful drie;
Dirk was the nyght as pich, or as the cole,
And at the wyndow out she pitte hir hole,
And Absolon, hym fil no bet ne wers,
But with his mouth he kiste hir naked ers
Ful savourly, er he was war of this.
Abak he stirte, and thoughte it was amys,
For wel he wiste a womman hath no berd;
He felte a thyng al rough and long yherd,
And seyde fy, allas, what have I do?
Tehee! quod she, and clapte the wyndow to;
And Absolon gooth forth a sory pas.
A berd, a berd! quod hende Nicholas,
By Goddes corpus, this goth faire and weel!
This sely Absolon herde every deel,
And on his lippe he gan for anger byte;
And to hymself he seyde I shall thee quyte!
WHO rubbeth now, who froteth now his
lippes
With dust, with sond, with straw, with
clooth, with chippes,
But Absolon? that seith ful ofte Allas!
My soule bitake I unto Sathanas,
But me were levere than al this toun, quod he,
Of this despit awroken for to be.
Allas! quod he, allas! I nadde ybleynt.
His hoote love was coold and al yqueynt;
For fro that tyme that he hadde kiste hir ers,
Of paramours he sette nat a kers;
For he was heeld of his maladie.
Ful ofte paramours he gan deffie,
And weepe as dooth a child that is ybete.
A softe paas he wente over the strete
Until a smyth men cleped daun Gerveys,
That in his forge smythed plough harneys;
He sharpeth shaar and kultour bisily.
This Absolon knokketh al esily,
And seyde Undo, Gerveys, and that anon.
What, who artow? I am heere, Absolon.
36

What, Absolon! for Cristes sweete tree,
Why rise ye so rathe? ey benedicitee!
What eyleth yow? Som gay gerl, God it woot,
Hath brought yow thus upon the viritoot;
By seinte Note, ye woot wel what I mene.
THIS Absolon ne roghte nat a bene
Of al his pley; no word agayn he yaf;
He hadde moore tow on his distaf
Than Gerveys knew, and seyde freend so deere,
That hoote kultour in the chymenee heere,
As lene it me, I have therwith to doone,
And I wol brynge it thee agayn ful soone.
Gerveys answerde Certes, were it gold,
Or in a poke nobles alle untold,
Thou sholdest have, as I am trewe smyth;
Ey, Cristes foo! what wol ye do therwith?
Therof, quod Absolon, be as be may,
I shal wel telle it thee tomorwe day.
And caughte the kultour by the colde stele.
Ful softe out at the dore he gan to stele,
And wente unto the carpenteres wal.
He cogheth first, and knokketh therwithal
Upon the wyndowe, right as he dide er.
This Alisoun answerde Who is ther
That knokketh so? I warante it a theef.
Why nay, quod he, God woot, my sweete leef,
I am thyn Absolon, my deerelyng.
Of gold, quod he, I have thee broght a ryng;
My mooder yaf it me, so God me save;
Ful fyn it is, and therto wel ygrave;
This wol I yeve thee, if thou me kisse.
This Nicholas was risen for to pisse,
And thoughte he wolde amenden al the jape,
He sholde kisse his ers, er that he scape;
And up the wyndowe dide he hastily,
And out his ers he putteth pryvely
Over the buttok, to the haunche bon.
And therwith spak this clerk, this Absolon:
SPEK, sweete bryd, I noot nat where thou art.
This Nicholas anon leet fle a fart,
As greet as it had been a thonder dent,
That with the strook he was almoost yblent;
And he was redy with his iren hoot,
And Nicholas amydde the ers he smoot.
Of gooth the skyn, an hande brede aboute,
The hoote kultour brende so his toute;
And for the smert he wende for to dye.
As he were wood, for wo he gan to crye,
Help! water! water! help, for Goddes herte!
This carpenter out of his slomber sterte,
And herde oon crien Water, as he were wood,
And thoughte Allas, now comth Nowelis flood!
He sit hym up withouten wordes mo,
And with his ax he smoot the corde atwo,
And doun gooth al, he foond neither to selle,
Ne breed ne ale, til he cam to the selle
Upon the floor; and ther aswowne he lay.
UP stirte hire Alison, and Nicholay,
And criden, Out! & Harrow! in the strete.
The neighebores, bothe smale and grete
In ronnen for to gauren on this man
That yet aswowne he lay, bothe pale and wan;
For with the fal he brosten hadde his arm;

But stonde he moste unto his owene harm,
for whan he spak he was anon bore doun
With hende Nicholas and Alisoun.
They tolden every man that he was wood,
He was agast so of Nowelis flood
Thurgh fantasie, that of his vanytee
He hadde yboght hym knedyng tubbes thre,
And hadde hem hanged in the roof above;
And that he preyde hem, for Goddes love,
To sitten in the roof, par compaignye.
THE folk gan laughen at his fantasye;
Into the roof they kiken & they gape,
And turned al his harm unto a jape;
for whatso that this carpenter answerde,
It was for noght, no man his reson herde;
With othes grete he was so sworn adoun,
That he was holden wood in al the toun,
for every clerk anonright heeld with oother;
They seyde, The man was wood, my leeve
broother.
And every wight gan laughen of this stryf.
THUS swyved was this carpenteres wyf,
for al his kepyng and his jalousye;
And Absolon hath kist hir nether eye;
And Nicholas is scalded in the towte:
This tale is doon, and God save al the rowte!
Here endeth the Millere his Tale.

The prologe of the Reves Tale.
WHAN folk hadde laughen at this
nyce cas
Of Absolon & hende Nicholas,
Diverse folk, diversely they
seyde,
But for the moore part, they
loughe and pleyde;
Ne at this tale I saugh no man hym greve,
But it were oonly Osewold the Reve.
Bycause he was of carpenteris craft
A litel ire is in his herte ylaft.
He gan to grucche and blamed it a lite.
So theek, quod he, ful wel koude I yow quite,
With bleryng of a proude millers eye,
If that me liste speke of ribaudye,
But ik am oold, me list no pley for age,
Gras tyme is doon, my fodder is now forage;
This white tope writeth myne olde yeres;
Myn herte is mowled also as myne heres,
But if I fare as dooth an open ers;
That ilke fruyt is ever leng the wers

Til it be roten in mullok, or in stree.
We olde men, I drede, so fare we;
Til we be roten kan we nat be rype.
We hoppen ay, whil that the world wol pype,
for in oure wyl ther stiketh evere a nayl
To have an hoor heed and a grene tayl,
As hath a leek; for thogh oure myght be goon,
Oure wyl desireth folie evere in oon;
for whan we may nat doon, than wol we speke,
Yet in oure asshen olde is fyr yreke.
foure gleedes han we, whiche I shal devyse,
Avaunting, lying, anger, coveitise.
Thise foure sparkles longen unto eelde.
Oure olde lymmes mowe wel been unweelde,
But wyl ne shal nat faillen, that is sooth;
And yet ik have alwey a coltes tooth,
As many a yeer as it is passed henne
Syn that my tappe of lif bigan to renne.
for sikerly, whan I was bore, anon
Deeth drough the tappe of lyf and leet it gon;
And ever sithe hath so the tappe yronne,
Til that almoost al empty is the tonne.
The streem of lyf now droppeth on the chymbe,
The sely tonge may wel rynge and chymbe
Of wrecchednesse that passed is ful yoore;
With olde folk, save dotage, is namoore.
WHAN that oure Hoost hadde herd
this sermonyng,
He gan to speke as lordly as a kyng.
He seide: What amounteth al this wit?
What, shul we speke alday of hooly writ?
The devel made a Reve for to preche,
And of a soutere a shipman or a leche.
Sey forth thy tale, and tarie nat the tyme,
Lo, Depeford, and it is half wey pryme.
Lo, Grenewych, ther many a shrewe is inne;
It were al tyme thy tale to bigynne.
Now, sires, quod this Osewold the Reve,
I pray yow alle that ye nat yow greve,
Thogh I answere and somdeel sette his howve,
for leveful is, with force, force of showve;
This dronke Millere hath ytold us heer,
How that bigyled was a carpenteer,
Peraventure in scorn, for I am oon,
And, by youre leve, I shal him quite anoon.
Right in his cherles termes wol I speke;
I pray to God his nekke mote breke.
He kan wel in myn eye seen a stalke,
But in his owene he kan nat seen a balke.
Thus endeth the prologe of the Reve.

HEERE BIGYNNETH THE REVES TALE.

AT Trumpyngtoun, nat
fer fro Cantebrigge,
Ther gooth a brook, &
over that a brigge,
Upon the whiche brook
ther stant a melle;
And this is verray sooth
that I yow tell.
A millere was ther dwel
lynge many a day,
As eny pecok he was proud and gay.
Pipen he koude, and fisshe, and nettes beete,
And turne coppes, and wel wrastle and sheete;
And by his belt he baar a long panade,
And of a swerd ful trenchant was the blade.
A joly poppere baar he in his pouche,
Ther was no man, for peril, dorste hym touche;
A Sheffeld thwitel baar he in his hose.
Round was his face, and camuse was his nose;
As piled as an ape was his skulle.

He was a market-betere atte fulle;
Ther dorste no wight hand upon hym legge,
That he ne swoor he sholde anon abegge.
A THEEf he was forsooth of corn and mele,
And that a sly and usaunt for to stele.
His name was hoote dëynous Symkyn.
A wyf he hadde, ycomen of noble kyn;
The person of the toun hir fader was;
With hire he yaf ful many a panne of bras
For that Symkyn sholde in his blood allye.
She was yfostred in a nonnerye;
For Symkyn wolde no wyf, as he sayde,
But she were wel ynorissed and a mayde,
To saven his estaat of yomanrye;
And she was proud and peert as is a pye.
A ful fair sighte was it upon hem two
On haly dayes; biforn hire wolde he go
With his typet ybounde about his heed,
And she cam after in a gyte of reed;
And Symkyn hadde hosen of the same.
Ther dorste no wight clepen hire but Dame;
Was noon so hardy that wente by the weye
That with hire dorste rage, or ones pleye,
But if he wolde be slayn of Symkyn
With panade, or with knyf, or boidekyn;
For jalous folk ben perilous everemo;
Algate they wolde hire wyves wenden so.
And eek, for she was somdel smoterlich,
She was as digne as water in a dich,
As ful of hoker, and of bisemare.
Hir thoughte that a lady sholde hire spare,
What for hire kynrede and hir nortelrie
That she hadde lerned in the nonnerie.
A DOGHTER hadde they bitwixe hem two
Of twenty yeer, withouten any mo,
Savynge a child that was of half-yeer age;
In cradel it lay, and was a propre page.
This wenche thikke and wel ygrowen was,
With kamuse nose, and eyen greye as glas;
Buttokes brode, and brestes rounde and hye,
But right fair was hire heer, I wol nat lye.
This person of the toun, for she was feir,
In purpos was to maken hire his heir,
Both of his catel and his mesuage,
And straunge he made it of hir mariage.
His purpos was for to bistowe hire hye
Into som worthy blood of auncetrye;
For hooly chirches good moot been despended
On hooly chirches blood, that is descended;
Therfore he wolde his hooly blood honoure,
Though that he hooly chirche sholde devoure.
Gret sokene hath this millere, out of doute,
With whete and malt of al the land aboute;
And nameliche, ther was a greet college,
Men clepen the Soler Halle at Cantebregge;
Ther was hir whete and eek hir malt ygrounde.
And on a day it happed, in a stounde,
Sik lay the maunciple on a maladye.
Men wenden wisly that he sholde dye;
For which this millere stal bothe mele and corn
An hundred tyme moore than biforn;
For therbiforn he stal but curteisly,
But now he was a theef outrageously;
38

For which the wardeyn chidde and made fare:
But therof sette the millere nat a tare;
He craketh boost, and swoor it was nat so.
THANNE were ther yonge povre clerkes two,
That dwelten in this halle of which I seye;
Testif they were, and lusty for to pleye;
And, oonly for hire myrthe and revelrye,
Upon the wardeyn bisily they crye,
To yeve hem leve, but a litel stounde,
To goon to mille and seen hir corn ygrounde.
And hardily they dorste leye hir nekke,
The millere shold nat stele hem half a pekke
Of corn, by sleighte, ne by force hem reve.
And at the laste the wardeyn yaf hem leve.
John highte that oon, & Aleyn highte that oother;
Of o toun were they born, that highte Strother,
Fer in the North, I kan nat telle where.
This Aleyn maketh redy al his gere,
And on an hors the sak he cast anon.
Forth goth Aleyn the clerk, and also John,
With good swerd and with bokeler by hir side.
John knew the wey, hem nededde no gyde;
And at the mille the sak adoun he layth.
Aleyn spak first, Al hayl, Symond, yfayth!
How fares thy faire doghter, and thy wyf?
Aleyn! welcome, quod Symkyn, by my lyf!
And John also, how now? What do ye heer?
Symond, quod John, by God, nede has na peer,
Hym boes serve hymselue that has na swayn,
Or elles he is a fool, as clerkes sayn.
Oure manciple, I hope he will be deed,
Swa werkes ay the wanges in his heed;
And forthy is I come, and eek Alayn,
To grynde oure corn and carie it ham agayn.
I pray yow spede us heythen that ye may.
It shal be doon, quod Symkyn, by my fay!
What wol ye doon whil that it is in hande?
By God, right by the hopur wil I stande,
Quod John, and se how that the corn gas in;
Yet saugh I nevere, by my fader kyn,
How that the hopur wagges til and fra.
Aleyn answerde, Johan, wiltow swa?
Thanne wil I be bynethe, by my croun!
And se how that the mele falles doun
Into the trough; that sal be my disport;
For John, yfaith, I may been of youre sort,
I is as ille a millere as are ye.
THIS millere smyled of hir nycetee,
And thoghte, Al this nys doon but for a
wyle;
They wene that no man may hem bigile;
But by my thrift, yet shal I blere hir eye,
For al the sleighte in hir philosophye.
The moore queynte crekes that they make,
The moore wol I stele whan I take.
Instede of flour yet wol I yeve hem bren;
The gretteste clerkes been noght wisest men,
As whilom to the wolf thus spak the mare;
Of al hir art I counte noght a tare.
OUT at the dore he gooth ful pryvely,
Whan that he saugh his tyme, softely.
He looketh up and doun til he hath founde
The clerkes hors, ther as it stood ybounde

Bihynde the mille, under a levesel;
And to the hors he goth hym faire and wel;
He strepeth of the brydel right anon,
And whan the hors was laus he gynneth gon
Toward the fen, ther wilde mares renne,
Forth with Wehee! thurgh thikke & thurgh thenne.
¶This millere gooth agayn, no word he seyde,
But dooth his note and with the clerkes pleyde,
Til that hir corn was faire and weel ygrounde;
And whan the mele is sakked and ybounde,
This John goth out, and fynt his hors away,
And gan to crie, Harrow! and, Weylaway!
Our hors is lorn; Alayn, for Goddes banes
Stepe on thy feet; com out man, al at anes!
Allas, our wardeyn has his palfrey lorn!
¶This Aleyn al forgat bothe mele and corn;
Al was out of his mynde his housbondrie.
¶What, whilk way is he geen? he gan to crie.
¶The wyf cam lepynge inward with a ren;
She seyde, Allas, youre hors goth to the fen
With wild mares, as faste as he may go;
Unthank come on his hand that boond hym so,
And he that bettre sholde han knyt the reyne.
¶Allas, quod John, Aleyn, for Cristes peyne,
Lay doun thy swerd, and I wil myn alswa;
I is ful wight, God waat, as is a raa;
By Goddes herte! he sal nat scape us bathe.
Why nadstow pit the capul in the lathe?
Ilhayl, by God, Aleyn, thou is a fonne.
¶THISE sely clerkes han ful faste yronne
Toward the fen, bothe Aleyn and eek John;
And whan the millere saugh that they
were gon,
He half a busshel of hir flour hath take,
And bad his wyf go knede it in a cake.
He seyde, I trowe the clerkes were aferd,
Yet kan a millere make a clerkes berd
For al his art; now lat hem goon hir weye.
Lo wher they goon; ye, lat the children pleye;
They gete hym nat so lightly, by my croun!
¶THISE sely clerkes rennen up and doun
With, Keepe! keepe! stand! stand! Jossa,
warderere!
Ga whistle thou, and I shal kepe hym heere.
¶But shortly, til that it was verray nyght
They koude nat, though they do al hir myght,
Hir capul cacche, he ran alwey so faste,
Til in a dych they caughte hym atte laste.
Wery and weet, as beest is in the reyn,
Comth sely John, and with him comth Aleyn.
Allas! quod John, the day that I was born!
Now are we dryve til hethyng and til scorn;
Oure corn is stoln, men wil us fooles calle,
Bathe the wardeyn and oure felawes alle,
And namely the millere; weylaway!
¶Thus pleyneth John as he gooth by the way
Toward the mille, and Bayard in his hond.
The millere sittynge by the fire he fond,
For it was nyght, and forther myghte they noght;
But for the love of God they hym bisoght
Of herberwe and of ese as for hir peny.
¶The millere seyd agayn, If ther be eny,
Swich as it is, yet shal ye have youre part;

d 4

Myn hous is streit, but ye han lerned art;
Ye konne by argumentes make a place
A myle brood of twenty foot of space.
Lat se now if this place may suffise,
Or make it rowm with speche as is youre gise.
¶Now Symond, seyde John, by Seint Cutberd,
Ay is thou myrie, and this is faire answerd.
I have herd seyd, Man sal taa of twa thynges,
Slyk as he fyndes, or taa slyk as he brynges;
But specially I pray thee, hooste deere,
Get us som mete and drynke, and make us cheere,
And we wil payen trewely atte fulle;
With empty hand men may none haukes tulle;
Loo, heere our silver, redy for to spende.
¶THIS millere into toun his doghter sende
For ale and breed, and rosted hem a goos,
And boond hire hors, it sholde nat goon
loos;
And in his owene chambre hem made a bed,
With sheetes and with chalons faire yspred,
Noght from his owene bed ten foot or twelve.
His doghter hadde a bed al by hirselve,
Right in the same chambre, by and by,
It mighte be no bet, and cause why,
Ther was no roumer herberwe in the place.
They soupen, and they speke, hem to solace,
And drynken evere strong ale atte beste.
Aboute mydnyght wente they to reste.
¶WEL hath this millere vernysshed his heed;
Ful pale he was fordronken, and nat reed.
He yexeth, & he speketh thurgh the nose,
As he were on the quakke, or on the pose.
To bedde he goth, and with hym goth his wyf,
As any jay she light was and jolyf;
So was hir joly whistle wel ywet.
The cradel at hir beddes feet is set,
To rokken, and to yeve the child to sowke;
And whan that dronken al was in the crowke,
To bedde went the doghter right anon;
To bedde wente Aleyn, and also John,
Ther nas na moore; hem nedede no dwale.
¶This millere hath so wisely bibbed ale,
That as an hors he snorteth in his sleepe;
Ne of his tayl bihynde he took no keepe.
His wyf bar him a burdon, a ful strong,
Men myghte hir rowtyng heere two furlong;
The wenche rowteth eek, par compaignye.
¶ALEYN the clerk, that herd this melodye,
He poked John, and seyde, Slepestow?
Herdtow evere slyk a sang er now?
Lo, whilk a complyng is ymel hem alle!
A wilde fyr upon thair bodyes falle!
Wha herkned evere slyk a ferly thyng?
Ye, they sal have the flour of il endyng!
This lange nyght ther tydes me na reste,
But yet, nafors, al sal be for the beste,
For, John, seyde he, als evere moot I thryve,
If that I may, yon wenche wil I swyve.
Som esement has lawe yshapen us;
For John, ther is a lawe that says thus,
That gif a man in a point be ygreved,
That in another he sal be releved.
Oure corn is stoln, shortly it is ne nay,

And we han had an il fit al this day;
And syn I sal have neen amendement
Agayn my los, I wil have esement.
By Goddes sale! it sal neen other bee.
THIS John answerde, Alayn, avyse thee;
The millere is a perilous man, he seyde,
And gif that he out of his sleepe abreyde,
He mighte doon us bathe a vileynye.
Aleyn answerde, I count hym nat a flye.
And up he rist, and by the wenche he crepte.
This wenche lay uprighte, and faste slepte
Til he so ny was, er she myghte espie,
That it had been to late for to crie;
And, shortly for to seyn, they were at on.
Now pley, Aleyn, for I wol speke of John.
This John lith stille a furlong wey or two,
And to hymself he maketh routhe and wo;
Allas! quod he, this is a wikked jape;
Now may I seyn that I is but an ape;
Yet has my felawe somwhat for his harm,
He has the milleris doghter in his arm.
He auntred hym, and has his nedes sped,
And I lye as a draf sek in my bed;
And when this jape is tald another day,
I sal been halde a daf, a cokenay.
I wil arise and auntre it, by my fayth;
Unhardy is unseely, thus men sayth.
And up he roos, and softely he wente
Unto the cradel, and in his hand it hente,
And baar it softe unto his beddes feet.
SOONE after this the wyf hir rowtyng leet,
And gan awake, and wente hire out to pisse,
And cam agayn, and gan hir cradel mysse,
And groped heer and ther, but she foond noon.
Allas! quod she, I hadde almoost mysgoon;
I hadde almoost goon to the clerkes bed.
Ey, benedicite! thanne hadde I foule ysped.
And forth she gooth til she the cradel fond.
She gropeth alwey forther with hir hond,
And foond the bed and thoghte noght but good,
Bycause that the cradel by it stood,
And nyste wher she was, for it was derk,
But faire and wel she creepe in to the clerk;
And lith ful stille, and wolde han caught a sleepe.
Withinne a while this John the clerk up leepe,
And on this goode wyf he leith on soore;
So myrie a fit ne hadde she nat ful yoore;
He priketh harde and depe as he were mad.
This joly lyf han thise two clerkes lad
Til that the thridde cok bigan to synge.
ALEYN wax wery in the dawenynge,
For he had swonken al the longe nyght;
And seyde, fare weel, Malyne, sweete wight!
The day is come, I may no lenger byde;
But everemo, wherso I go or ryde,
I is thyn awen clerk, swa have I seel!
Now, deere lemman, quod she, go, fareweel!
But, er thow go, o thyng I wol thee telle;
Whan that thou wendest homward by the melle,
Right at the entree of the dore bihynde,
Thou shalt a cake of half a busshel fynde,
That was ymaked of thyn owene mele,
Which that I heelpe my fader for to stele;

And, goode lemman, God thee save and kepe!
And with that word almoost she gan to wepe.
Aleyn uprist and thoughte, Er that it dawe,
I wol go crepen in by my felawe;
And fond the cradel with his hand anon.
By God! thoughte he, al wrang I have mysgon;
Myn heed is toty of my swynk tonyght,
That maketh me that I go nat aright.
I woot wel by the cradel I have mysgo;
Heere lith the millere and his wyf also.
And forth he goth, a twenty devel way,
Unto the bed thereas the millere lay.
He wende have cropen by his felawe John,
And by the millere in he creepe anon,
And caughte hym by the nekke, & softe he spak.
He seyde, Thou John, thou swynesheed, awak,
For Cristes saule, and heer a noble game;
For by that lord that called is seint Jame,
As I have thries in this shorte nyght
Swyved the milleres doghter bolt upright,
Whil thow hast as a coward been agast.
YE, false harlot, quod the millere, hast?
A! false traitour! false clerk! quod he,
Thow shalt be deed, by Goddes dignitee!
Who dorste be so boold to disparage
My doghter, that is come of swich lynage?
And by the throte bolle he caughte Alayn;
And he hente hym despitously agayn,
And on the nose he smoot hym with his fest.
Doun ran the blody streem upon his brest,
And in the floor, with nose and mouth tobroke,
They walwe as doon two pigges in a poke;
And up they goon, and doun agayn anon,
Til that the millere sporned at a stoon,
And doun he fil bakward upon his wyf,
That wiste nothyng of this nyce stryf;
For she was falle aslepe a lite wight
With John the clerk, that waked hadde al nyght;
And with the fal, out of hir sleepe she breyde.
Help, hooly croys of Bromeholm, she seyde,
In manus tuas! Lord, to thee I calle!
Awak, Symond! the feend is on us falle!
Myn herte is broken! help! I nam but deed!
Ther lyth oon on my wombe and on myn heed.
Helpe, Symkyn, for the false clerkes fighte!
THIS John stirte up, as soon as ever he myghte,
And graspeth by the walles to and fro
To fynde a staf; and she stirte up also,
And knewe the estres bet than dide this John,
And by the wal a staf she foond anon,
And saugh a litel shymeryng of a light,
For at an hole in shoon the moone bright,
And by that light she saugh hem bothe two,
But sikerly she nyste who was who,
But as she saugh a whit thyng in hir eye:
And whan she gan the white thyng espye,
She wende the clerk hadde wered a volupeer,
And with the staf she drough ay neer and neer,
And wende han hit this Aleyn at the fulle;
And smoot the millere on the pyled skulle,
And doun he gooth, and cride, Harrow! I dye!
Thise clerkes beete hym weel and lete hym lye,

And greythen hem and tooke hir hors anon,
And eek hire mele, and on hir wey they gon,
And at the mille yet they tooke hir cake
Of half a busshel flour ful wel ybake.

THUS is the proude millere wel ybete,
And hath ylost the gryndynge of the whete,
And payed for the soper everideel
Of Aleyn and of John, that bette hym weel;
His wyf is swyved, and his doghter als;
Lo! swich it is a millere to be fals.
And therfore this proverbe is seyd ful sooth,
Hym thar nat wene wel that yvele dooth;
A gylour shal hymself bigyled be,
And God, that sitteth heighe in Trinitee,
Save al this compaignye, grete and smale!
Thus have I quyt the Millere in my tale.
Here is ended the Reves Tale.

The prologe of the Cookes Tale.❀ ❀

THE Cook of London, whil the Reve
spak,
for joye him thoughte he clawed
him on the bak;
Ha, ha! quod he, for Cristes pas-
sioun,
This millere hadde a sharpe conclusioun
Upon his argument of herbergage;
Wel seyde Salomon in his langage,
Ne brynge nat every man into thyn hous;
for herberwynge by nyghte is perilous.
Wel oghte a man avysed for to be

Whom that he broghte into his pryvetee.
I pray to God, so yeve me sorwe and care,
If evere sithe I highte Hogge of Ware,
Herde I a millere bettre yset awerk;
He hadde a jape of malice in the derk.
But God forbede that we stynten heere,
And therfore if ye vouchesauf to heere
A tale of me, that am a povre man,
I wol yow telle as wel as evere I kan
A litel jape that fil in oure citee.
Oure Hoost answerde & seide, I graunte it thee;
Now telle on, Roger, looke that it be good;
for many a pastee hastow laten blood,
And many a jakke of Dovere hastow soold,
That hath been twies hoot and twies coold.
Of many a pilgrym hastow Cristes curs,
for of thy percely yet they fare the wors
That they han eten with thy stubbel goos,
for in thy shoppe is many a flye loos.
Now telle on, gentil Roger, by thy name,
But yet I pray thee be nat wroth for game,
A man may seye ful sooth in game and pley.
Thou seist ful sooth, quod Roger, by my fey!
But sooth pley, quaad pley, as the flemyng seith;
And therfore, Herry Bailly, by thy feith,
Be thou nat wrooth, er we departen heer,
Though that my tale be of an hostileer:
But natheless I wol nat telle it yit;
But er we parte, ywis, thou shalt be quit;
And therwithal he lough and made cheere,
And seyde his tale as ye shul after heere.

HEERE BIGYNNETH THE COOKES TALE ❀ ❀ ❀ ❀ ❀

A PRENTYS whilom dwel-
led in oure citee,
And of a craft of vitailliers
was hee.
Gaillard he was as gold-
fynch in the shawe;
Broun as a berye, a propre
short felawe,
With lokkes blake ykempd
ful fetisly;
Dauncen he koude so wel and jolily,
That he was cleped Perkyn Revelour.
He was as ful of love and paramour
As is the hyve ful of hony sweete.
Wel was the wenche that with hym myghte meete;
At every bridale wolde he synge and hoppe,
He loved bet the taverne than the shoppe.
for whan ther any ridyng was in Chepe,
Out of the shoppe thider wolde he lepe;
Til that he hadde al the sighte yseyn
And daunced wel, he wolde nat come ageyn;
And gadered hym a meynee of his sort
To hoppe and synge and maken swich disport;
And ther they setten stevene for to meete
To pleyen at the dys in swich a streete;
for in the toune nas ther no prentys
That fairer koude cast a paire of dys
Than Perkyn koude, and therto he was free
Of his dispense, in place of pryvetee.

That fond his maister wel in his chaffare;
for often tyme he foond his box ful bare.
for sikerly a prentys revelour,
That haunteth dys, riot, or paramour,
His maister shal it in his shoppe abye,
Al have he no part of the mynstralcye;
for thefte and riot they been convertible,
Al konne he pleye on gyterne or ribible.
Revel and trouthe, as in a lowe degree,
They been ful wrothe al day, as men may see.
THIS joly prentys with his maister bood,
Til he were ny out of his prentishood;
Al were he snybbed bothe erly and late,
And somtyme lad with revel to Newegate;
But atte laste his maister hym bithoghte,
Upon a day whan he his papir soghte,
Of a proverbe that seith this same word,
Wel bet is roten appul out of hoord
Than that it rotie al the remenaunt.
So fareth it by a riotous servaunt;
It is wel lasse harm to lete hym pace
Than he shende alle the servauntz in the place.
Therfore his maister yaf hym acquitance,
And bad hym go with sorwe and with meschance;
And thus this joly prentys hadde his leve.
Now lat him riote al the nyghte or leve.
And for ther is no theef withoute a lowke,
That helpeth hym to wasten and to sowke
Of that he brybe kan or borwe may,

The
Cookes
Tale

Of this
Tale
maked
Chaucer
na more

Anon he sente his bed and his array
Unto a compier of his owene sort
That lovede dys, and revel and disport,
And hadde a wyf that heeld for contenance
A shoppe, and swyved for hir sustenance....

The wordes of the Hoost to the compaignye.

URE Hooste saugh wel
that the brighte sonne
The ark of his artificial day
had ronne
The ferthe part, and half
an houre and moore,
And though he were nat
depe expert in loore,
He wiste it was the eighte-
tethe day
Of Aprill, that is messager to May;
And saugh wel that the shadwe of every tree
Was, as in lengthe, the same quantitee
That was the body erect that caused it;
And therfore by the shadwe he took his wit
That Phebus, which that shoon so clere & brighte,
Degrees was fyve and fourty clombe on highte;
And for that day, as in that latitude,
It was ten at the clokke, he gan conclude;
And sodeynly he plighte his hors aboute.
Lordynges, quod he, I warne yow, al this route
The fourthe party of this day is gon;
Now for the love of God and of Seint John,
Leseth no tyme, as ferforth as ye may.
Lordynges, the tyme wasteth nyght and day,
And steleth from us, what pryvely slepynge,
And what thurgh necligence in oure wakynge,
As dooth the streem, that turneth nevere agayn,
Descendynge fro the montaigne into playn.
WEL kan Senec, and many a philosophre,
Biwaillen tyme moore than gold in cofre;
For losse of catel may recovered be,
But losse of tyme shendeth us, quod he,
It wol nat come agayn, withouten drede,
Namoore than wole Malkyns maydenhede,
Whan she hath lost it in hir wantownesse;
Lat us nat mowlen thus in ydelnesse.
Sire Man of Lawe, quod he, so have ye blis,
Telle us a tale anon, as forward is;
Ye been submytted thurgh youre free assent
To stonde in this cas at my juggement.
Acquiteth yow and holdeth youre biheeste,
Thanne have ye doon youre devoir atte leeste.
Hooste, quod he, depardieux ich assente.
To breke forward is nat myn entente.
Biheste is dette, and I wole holde fayn
Al my biheste; I kan no bettre sayn:
For swich lawe as man yeveth another wight

He sholde hymselven usen it by right;
Thus wole oure text; but nathelees certeyn,
I kan right now no thrifty tale seyn,
But Chaucer, thogh he kan but lewedly
On metres and on ryming craftily,
Hath seyd hem in swich Englissh as he kan
Of olde tyme, as knoweth many a man;
And if he have noght seyd hem, leve brother,
In o book, he hath seyd hem in another.
For he hath toold of loveres up and doun
Mo than Ovide made of mencioun
In his Episteles, that been ful olde.
What sholde I tellen hem, syn they ben tolde?
In youthe he made of Ceys and Alcione,
And sitthe hath he spoken of everichone
Thise noble wyves and thise loveres eke.
Whoso that wole his large volume seke,
Cleped the Seintes Legende of Cupide,
Ther may he seen the large woundes wyde
Of Lucresse, and of Babilan Tesbee;
The swerd of Dido for the false Enee;
The tree of Phillis for hire Demophon;
The pleinte of Dianire and Hermyon;
Of Adriane and of Isiphilee;
The bareyne yle stondynge in the see;
The dreynte Leandre for his Erro;
The teeris of Eleyne, and eek the wo
Of Brixseyde, and of thee, Ladomea;
The crueltee of thee, queene Medea,
Thy litel children hangynge by the hals
For thy Jason that was in love so fals!
O Ypermystra, Penolopee, Alceste,
Youre wifhede he comendeth with the beste!
BUT certeinly no word ne writeth he
Of thilke wikke ensample of Canacee,
That loved hir owene brother synfully;
Of swiche cursed stories I sey fy!
Or ellis of Tyro Appollonius,
How that the cursed kyng Antiochus
Birafte his doghter of hir maydenhede,
That is so horrible a tale for to rede,
Whan he hir threw upon the pavement;
And therfore he, of ful avysement,
Nolde nevere write in none of his sermons
Of swiche unkynde abhomynacions,
Ne I wol noon reherce, if that I may.
But of my tale how shall I doon this day?
Me were looth be likned, douteless,
To Muses that men clepe Pierides,
Methamorphoseos woot what I mene:
But nathelees, I recche noght a bene
Though I come after hym, with hawebake;
I speke in prose, and lat him rymes make.
And with that word, he with a sobre cheere
Bigan his tale, as ye shal after heere.

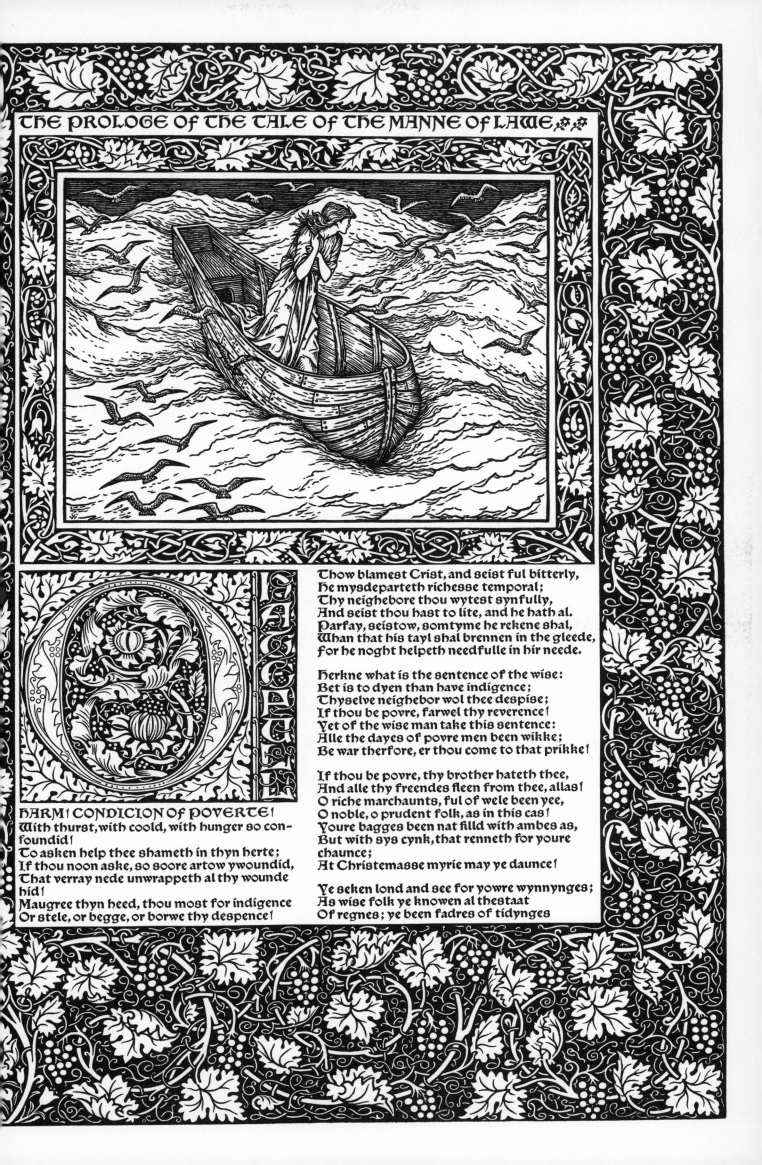

O HARM! CONDICION OF POVERTE!
With thurst, with coold, with hunger so con-
foundid!
To asken help thee shameth in thyn herte;
If thou noon aske, so soore artow ywoundid,
That verray nede unwrappeth al thy wounde
hid!
Maugree thyn heed, thou most for indigence
Or stele, or begge, or borwe thy despence!

Thow blamest Crist, and seist ful bitterly,
He mysdeparteth richesse temporal;
Thy neighebore thou wytest synfully,
And seist thou hast to lite, and he hath al.
Parfay, seistow, somtyme he rekene shal,
Whan that his tayl shal brennen in the gleede,
For he noght helpeth needfulle in hir neede.

Herkne what is the sentence of the wise:
Bet is to dyen than have indigence;
Thyselve neighebor wol thee despise;
If thou be povre, farwel thy reverence!
Yet of the wise man take this sentence:
Alle the dayes of povre men been wikke;
Be war therfore, er thou come to that prikke!

If thou be povre, thy brother hateth thee,
And alle thy freendes fleen from thee, allas!
O riche marchaunts, ful of wele been yee,
O noble, o prudent folk, as in this cas!
Youre bagges been nat filld with ambes as,
But with sys cynk, that renneth for youre
chaunce;
At Christemasse myrie may ye daunce!

Ye seken lond and see for yowre wynnynges;
As wise folk ye knowen al thestaat
Of regnes; ye been fadres of tidynges

And tales, bothe of pees and of debaat.
I were right now of tales desolaat,
Nere that a marchant, goon is many a yeere,
Me taughte a tale, which that ye shal heere.

Heere bigynneth the Man of Lawe his Tale.
Pars prima ✤ ✤

IN Surrye whilom dwelte a compaignye
Of chapmen riche, and therto
sadde and trewe,
That wydewhere senten hir
spicerye,
Clothes of gold, and satyns
riche of hewe.
Hir chaffare was so thrifty and
so newe,
That every wight hath deyntee
to chaffare
With hem, and eek to sellen
hem hire ware.

Now fil it that the maistres of
that sort
Han shapen hem to Rome for
to wende;
Were it for chapmanhode, or
for disport,
Noon oother message wolde they thider sende,
But comen hemself to Rome, this is the ende;
And in swich place, as thoughte hem avantage
for hire entente, they take hir herbergage.

Sojourned han thise marchants in that toun
A certein tyme, as fil to hire plesance;
And so bifel that thexcellent renoun
Of the Emperoures doghter, dame Custance,
Reported was, with every circumstance,
Unto thise Surryen marchants in swich wyse,
fro day to day, as I shal yow devyse.

This was the commune voys of every man:
Oure Emperour of Rome, God hym see!
A doghter hath that syn the world bigan,
To rekene as wel hir goodness as beautee,
Nas nevere swich another as is shee.
I prey to God, in honour hire susteene,
And wolde she were of al Europe the queene!

In hire is heigh beautee, withoute pride,
Yowthe, withoute grenehede or folye;
To alle hire werkes vertu is hir gyde;
Humblesse hath slayn in hire al tirannye;
She is mirour of alle curteisye;
Hir herte is verray chambre of hoolynesse,
Hir hand, ministre of fredam for almesse.

And al this voys was sooth, as God is trewe;
But now to purpos lat us turne agayn;
Thise marchants han doon fraught hir shippes
newe,
And, whan they han this blisful mayden sayn,
Hoom to Surrye been they went ful fayn,

44

And doon hir nedes as they han doon yoore,
And lyven in wele; I kan sey yow na moore.

Now fil it, that thise marchants stode in grace
Of hym that was the sowdan of Surrye;
for whan they cam from any strange place
He wolde, of his benigne curteisye,
Make hem good chiere, and bisily espye
Tidynges of sondry regnes, for to leere
The wondres that they myghte seen or heere.

Amonges othere thynges, specially,
Thise marchants han hym toold of dame Custance,
So greet noblesse in ernest, ceriously,
That this sowdan hath caught so greet plesance
To han hir figure in his remembrance,
That al his lust, and al his busy cure,
Was for to love hire while his lyf may dure.

Paraventure in thilke large book,
Which that men clepe the hevene, ywriten was
With sterres, whan that he his birthe took,
That he for love sholde han his deeth, allas!
for in the sterres, clerer than is glas,
Is written, God woot, whoso koude it rede,
The deeth of every man, withouten drede.

In sterres, many a wynter therbiforn,
Was writen the deeth of Ector, Achilles,
Of Pompei, Julius, er they were born;
The strif of Thebes; and of Ercules,
Of Sampson, Turnus; and of Socrates
The deeth; but mennes wittes ben so dulle,
That no wight kan wel rede it atte fulle.

THIS sowdan for his privee conseil sente,
And, shortly of this matiere for to pace,
He hath to hem declared his entente,
And seyde hem, certein, But he myghte have grace
To han Custance withinne a litel space,
He nas but deed; and charged hem in hye
To shapen for his lyf som remedye.

Diverse men diverse thynges seyden,
They argumenten, casten up and doun;
Many a subtil resoun forth they leyden;
They speken of magyk and abusioun;
But finally, as in conclusioun,
They kan nat seen in that noon avantage,
Ne in noon oother wey, save mariage.

Thanne sawe they therinne swich difficultee,
By wey of reson, for to speke al playn,
Bycause that ther was swich diversitee
Bitwene hir bothe lawes, that they sayn,
They trowe That no cristene prince wolde fayn
Wedden his child under oure lawes sweete,
That us were taught by Mahoun, oure prophete.

And he answerde, Rather than I lese
Custance, I wol be cristned, doutelees;
I moot been hires, I may noon oother chese.
I prey yow hoold youre arguments in pees;
Saveth my lyf, and beth noght reccheless

To geten hire that hath my lyf in cure;
for in this wo I may nat longe endure.

What nedeth gretter dilatacioun?
I seye, by tretys and embassadrie,
And by the popes mediacioun,
And al the chirche, and al the chivalrie,
That in destruccioun of Maumettrie,
And in encrees of Cristes lawe deere,
They been acorded, so as ye shal heere,

How that the sowdan and his baronage
And alle his liges, sholde ycristned be,
And he shal han Custance in mariage,
And certein gold, I noot what quantitee,
And heerto founden sufficient suretee;
This same accord was sworn on eyther syde;
Now, faire Custance, almyghty God thee gyde!

Now wolde som men waiten, as I gesse,
That I sholde tellen al the purveiance
That themperour, of his grete noblesse,
Hath shapen for his doghter, dame Custance.
Wel may men knowen that so greet ordinance
May no man tellen in a litel clause,
As was arrayed for so heigh a cause.

Bisshopes been shapen with hire for to wende,
Lordes, ladies, knyghtes of renoun,
And oother folk ynogh, this is the ende;
And notified is thurghout the toun
That every wight, with greet devocioun,
Sholde preyen Crist, that he this mariage
Receyve in gree, and spede this viage.

THE day is comen of hir departynge,
I seye, the woful day fatal is come,
That ther may be no lenger taryinge,
But forthward they hem dressen, alle and some.
Custance, that was with sorwe al overcome,
ful pale arist, and dresseth hire to wende;
for wel she seeth ther is noon oother ende.

Allas! what wonder is it thogh she wepte,
That shal be sent to strange nacioun,
fro freendes that so tendrely hire kepte,
And to be bounden under subjeccioun
Of oon, she knoweth nat his condicioun.
Housbondes been alle goode, and han ben yoore;
That knowen wyves, I dar say yow na moore.

fader, she seyde, thy wrecched child, Custance,
Thy yonge doghter, fostred up so softe,
And ye, my mooder, my soverayn plesance,
Over alle thyng, outtaken Crist on lofte,
Custance, youre child, hire recomandeth ofte
Unto your grace; for I shal to Surrye,
Ne shal I nevere seen yow moore with eye.

Allas! unto the barbre nacioun
I moste goon, syn that it is youre wille;
But Crist, that starf for our savacioun,
So yeve me grace his heestes to fulfille;
I, wrecche womman, no fors though I spille!

Wommen are born to thraldom and penance,
And to been under mannes governance.

I trowe at Troye, whan Pirrus brak the wal,
Or Ilion brende, at Thebes the citee,
Nat Rome, for the harm thurgh Hanybal,
That Romayns hath venquysshed tymes thre,
Nas herd swich tendre wepyng for pitee,
As in the chambre was for hire departynge;
But forth she moot, wherso she wepe or synge.

O firste moevyng, cruel firmament,
With thy diurnal sweigh that crowdest ay,
And hurlest al from Est til Occident,
That naturelly wolde holde another way;
Thy crowdyng set the hevene in swich array
At the bigynnyng of this fiers viage,
That cruel Mars hath slayn this mariage.

Infortunat ascendent tortuous,
Of which the lord is helplees falle, allas,
Out of his angle into the derkeste hous.
O Mars, O Atazir, as in this cas!
O fieble Moone, unhappy been thy paas!
Thou knyttest thee ther thou art nat receyved,
Ther thou were weel, fro thennes artow weyved.

Imprudent emperour of Rome, allas!
Was ther no philosophre in al thy toun?
Is no tyme bet than oother in swich cas?
Of viage is ther noon eleccioun,
Namely to folk of heigh condicioun,
Noght whan a roote is of a burthe yknowe?
Allas! we been to lewed or to slowe!

TO ship is come this woful faire mayde,
Solempnely, with every circumstance.
Now Jhesu Crist be with yow alle, she sayde.
Ther nys namoore, but, farewel, faire Custance!
She peyneth hire to make good contenance;
And forth I lete hire saille in this manere,
And turne I wole agayn to my matere.

The mooder of the sowdan, welle of vices,
Espied hath hir sones pleyn entente,
How he wol lete his olde sacrifices;
And right anon she for hir conseil sente;
And they been come to knowe what she mente.
And whan assembled was this folk in feere,
She sette hire doun and seyde as ye shal heere.

Lordes, she seyde, ye knowen everichon,
How that my sone in point is for to lete
The hooly lawes of oure Alkaron,
Yeven by Goddes message Makomete;
But oon avow to grete God I hete,
The lyf shal rather out of my body sterte,
Than Makometes lawe out of myn herte!

What sholde us tyden of this newe lawe,
But thraldom to our bodies and penance?
And afterward in helle to be drawe,
for we reneyed Mahoun oure creance?
But, lordes, wol ye maken assurance

45

As I shal seyn, assentynge to my loore,
And I shal make us sauf for everemoore?

They sworen and assenten, every man
To lyve with hire and dye, and by hire stonde;
And everich, in the beste wise he kan,
To strengthen hire shal alle his frendes fonde;
And she hath this emprise ytake on honde,
Which ye shal heren that I shal devyse,
And to hem alle she spak right in this wyse.

We shul first feyne us cristendom to take,
Coold water shal nat greve us but a lite;
And I shal swiche a feeste and revel make,
That, as I trowe, I shal the sowdan quite;
For thogh his wyf be cristned never so white
She shal have nede to wasshe awey the rede,
Thogh she a fontful water with hire lede !

O sowdanesse, roote of iniquitee !
Virago thou, Semyrame the secounde,
O serpent under femynynytee,
Lik to the serpent depe in helle ybounde.
O feyned womman, al that may confounde
Vertu and innocence, thurgh thy malice
Is bred in thee, as nest of every vice !

O Sathan, envious syn thilke day
That thou were chaced from oure heritage,
Wel knowestow to wommen the olde way !
Thou madest Eva brynge us in servage,
Thou wolt fordoon this cristen mariage.
Thyn instrument so, weylawey the while !
Makestow of wommen, whan thou wolt bigile.

This sowdanesse, whom I thus blame & warye,
Leet prively hire conseil goon hire way.
What sholde I in this tale lenger tarye ?
She rydeth to the sowdan on a day,
And seyde hym that she wolde reneye hir lay,
And cristendom of preestes handes fonge,
Repentynge hire she hethen was so longe;

Bisechynge hym to doon hire that honour,
That she moste han the cristen folk to feeste;
To plesen hem, I wol do my labour.
The sowdan seith, I wol doon at youre heeste;
And knelynge, thanketh hire of that requeste;
So glad he was, he nyste what to seye;
She kiste hir sone, and hoome she gooth hir weye.

Explicit pars prima. Sequitur pars secunda

ARRYVED been this cristen
folk to londe,
In Surrye, with a greet
solempne route;
And hastifliche this sowdan
sente his sonde,
First to his mooder, and all
the regne aboute,
And seyde his wyf was
comen, oute of doute,
And preyde hire for to ryde agayne the queene,
The honour of his regne to susteene.

46

Greet was the prees, and riche was tharray
Of Surryens and Romayns met yfeere;
The mooder of the sowdan, riche and gay,
Receyveth hire with al so glad a cheere
As any mooder myghte hir doghter deere,
And to the nexte citee ther bisyde,
A softe paas solempnely they ryde.

Noght trowe I the triumphe of Julius,
Of which that Lucan maketh swich a boost,
Was roialler, ne moore curius,
Than was thassemblee of this blisful hoost;
But this scorpioun, this wikked goost,
The sowdanesse, for all hire flaterynge,
Caste under this ful mortally to stynge.

The sowdan comth hymself soone after this
So roially, that wonder is to telle,
And welcometh hire with alle joye and blis;
And thus in murthe and joye I lete hem dwelle;
The fruyt of this matiere is that I telle.
Whan tyme cam men thoughte it for the beste,
The revel stynte, and men goon to hir reste.

The tyme cam, this olde sowdanesse
Ordeyned hath this feeste of which I tolde,
And to the feeste cristen folk hem dresse
In general, ye, bothe yonge and olde.
Heere may men feeste and roialtee biholde,
And deyntees mo than I kan yow devyse,
But all to deere they boghte it, er they ryse.

O sodeyn wo ! that evere art successour
To worldly blisse, spreynd with bitternesse;
Thende of the joy of oure worldly labour;
Wo occupieth the fyn of oure gladnesse.
Herke this conseil, for thy sikernesse,
Upon thy glade day have in thy mynde
The unwar wo or harm that comth bihynde.

For soothly for to tellen at o word,
The sowdan and the cristen everichone
Been al tohewe and stiked at the bord,
But it were oonly dame Custance allone.
This olde sowdanesse, cursed krone,
Hath with hir freendes doon this cursed dede.
For she hirself wolde all the contree lede.

Ne ther was Surryen noon, that was converted,
That of the conseil of the sowdan woot,
That he nas al tohewe er he asterted,
And Custance han they take anon, foot-hoot,
And in a ship all steereles, God woot,
They han hir set and biddeth hire lerne saille
Out of Surrye, agaynward to Ytaille.

A certein tresor that she with hire ladde,
And, sooth to seyn, vitaille greet plentee,
They han hire yeven, and clothes eek she hadde,
And forth she sailleth in the salte see.
O my Custance, ful of benignytee,
O emperoures yonge doghter deere,
He that is lord of fortune be thy steere !

She blesseth hire, and with ful pitous voys,
Unto the croys of Crist thus seyde she:
O cleere, O weleful auter, hooly croys,
Reed of the lambes blood, ful of pitee,
That wesshe the world fro the olde iniquitee,
Me fro the feend, and fro his clawes kepe,
That day that I shal drenchen in the depe.

Victorious tree, proteccioun of trewe,
That oonly worthy were for to bere
The kyng of hevene with his woundes newe,
The white lamb that hurt was with the spere,
Flemere of feendes out of hym and here,
On which thy lymes feithfully extenden,
Me helpe, and yif me myght my lyf amenden.

ERES and dayes fleteth this creature
    Thurghout the see of Grece unto the
    Strayte
Of Marrok, as it was hire aventure.
On many a sory meel now may she bayte;
After hir deeth ful often may she wayte,
Er that the wilde wawes wol hire dryve
Unto the place ther she shal arryve.

Men myghten asken why she was nat slayn
Eek at the feeste, who myghte hir body save?
And I answere to that demande agayn,
Who saved Danyel in the horrible cave,
Ther every wight save he, maister and knave,
Was with the leoun frete, er he asterte?
No wight but God, that he bar in his herte.

God liste to shewe his wonderful myracle
In hire, for we sholde seen his myghty werkis;
Crist, which that is to every harm triacle,
By certeine meenes ofte, as knowen clerkis,
Dooth thyng for certein ende that ful derk is
To mannes wit, that for oure ignorance
Ne konne noght knowe his prudent purveiance.

Now sith she was nat at the feeste yslawe,
Who kepte hire fro the drenchyng in the see?
Who kepte Jonas in the fisshes mawe,
Til he was spouted up at Nynyvee?
Wel may men knowe it was no wight but he
That kepte peple Ebrayk from hir drenchynge,
With drye feet thurghout the see passynge.

Who bad the foure spirites of tempest,
That power han tanoyen lond and see,
Bothe north and south, and also west and est,
Anoyeth neither see, ne land, ne tree?
Soothly the comandour of that was he
That fro the tempest ay this womman kepte
As wel whan that she wook as whan she slepte.

Where myghte this womman mete & drynke have
Thre yeer and moore? How lasteth hire vitaille?
Who fedde the Egypcien Marie in the cave,
Or in desert? No wight but Crist, sans faille.
Fyve thousand folk it was as greet mervaille
With loves fyve and fisshes two to feede.
God sente his foyson at hir grete neede.

SHE dryveth forth into oure occian,
    Thurghout oure wilde see, til atte laste
    Under an hoold, that nempnen I ne kan,
Fer in Northumberlond the wawe hire caste,
And in the sond hir ship stiked so faste,
That thennes wolde it noght of al a tyde,
The wyl of Crist was that she sholde abyde.

The constable of the castel doun is fare
To seen this wrak, and al the ship he soghte,
And foond this wery womman, ful of care;
He foond also the tresor that she broghte.
In hir langage mercy she bisoghte,
The lyf out of hire body for to twynne,
Hire to delivere of wo that she was inne.

A maner Latyn corrupt was hir speche,
But algates therby was she understonde;
The constable, whan hym list no lenger seche,
This woful womman broghte he to the londe;
She kneleth doun, and thanketh Goddes sonde;
But what she was, she wolde no man seye,
For foul ne fair, thogh that she sholde deye.

She seyde she was so mazed in the see
That she forgat hir mynde, by hir trouthe.
The constable hath of hire so greet pitee,
And eek his wyf, that they wepen for routhe.
She was so diligent, withouten slouthe,
To serve and plesen everich in that place,
That alle hir loven that looken in hir face.

This constable and dame Hermengyld, his wyf,
Were payens, and that contree everywhere;
But Hermengyld loved hire right as hir lyf,
And Custance hath so longe sojourned there,
In orisons, with many a bitter teere,
Til Jhesu hath converted, thurgh his grace,
Dame Hermengyld, constablesse of that place.

In al that lond no cristen dorste route,
Alle cristen folk been fled fro that contree
Thurgh payens, that conquereden al aboute
The plages of the North, by land and see.
To Walys fledde the cristyanytee
Of olde Britons, dwellynge in this ile;
Ther was hir refut for the meene while.

But yet nere cristene Britons so exiled
That ther nere somme, that in hir privetee
Honoured Crist, and hethen folk bigiled;
And ny the castel swiche ther dwelten three,
That oon of hem was blynd and myghte nat see
But it were with thilke eyen of his mynde,
With whiche men seen, after that they ben blynde.

Bright was the sonne as in that someres day,
For which the constable and his wyf also
And Custance, han ytake the righte way
Toward the see, a furlong wey or two,
To pleyen and to romen to and fro;
And in hir walk this blynde man they mette,
Croked and oold, with eyen feste yshette.

47

In name of Crist, criede this olde Britoun,
Dame Hermengyld, yif me my sighte agayn!
This lady weex affrayed of the soun,
Lest that hir housbonde, shortly for to sayn,
Wolde hire for Jhesu Cristes love han slayn;
Til Custance made hire boold, and bad hire wirche
The wyl of Crist, as doghter of his chirche.

The constable weex abasshed of that sight,
And seyde, What amounteth al this fare?
Custance answerde, Sire, it is Cristes myght,
That helpeth folk out of the feendes snare.
And so ferforth she gan oure lay declare,
That she the constable, er that it were eve,
Converteth, and on Crist maketh hym believe.

This constable was nothyng lord of this place
Of which I speke, ther he Custance fond,
But kepte it strongly, many wyntres space,
Under Alla, kyng of al Northhumbrelond,
That was ful wys, and worthy of his hond
Agayn the Scottes, as men may wel heere;
But turne I wole agayn to my mateere.

SATHAN, that evere us waiteth to bigile,
Saugh of Custance al hire perfeccioun,
And caste anon how he myghte quite hir
while,
And made a yong knyght, that dwelte in that toun,
Love hire so hoote, of foul affeccioun,
That verraily hym thoughte he sholde spille
But he of hire myghte ones have his wille.

He woweth hire, but it availleth noght,
She wolde do no synne, by no weye;
And for despit, he compassed in his thoght
To maken hire on shameful deeth to deye.
He wayteth whan the constable was aweye
And pryvely, upon a nyght he crepte
In Hermengyldes chambre whil she slepte.

Wery, forwaked in hire orisouns,
Slepeth Custance, and Hermengyld also.
This knyght, thurgh Sathanas temptaciouns,
All softely is to the bed ygo,
And kitte the throte of Hermengyld atwo,
And leyde the blody knyf by dame Custance,
And wente his wey, ther God yeve hym meschance!

Soone after com'th this constable hoom agayn,
And eek Alla, that kyng was of that lond,
And saugh his wyf despitously yslayn,
For which ful ofte he weepe and wroong his hond,
And in the bed the blody knyf he fond
By dame Custance; allas! what myghte she seye?
For verray wo hir wit was al aweye.

To kyng Alla was toold al this meschance
And eek the tyme, and where, and in what wise
That in a ship was founden dame Custance,
As heerbiforn that ye han herd devyse.
The kynges herte of pitee gan agryse,
Whan he saugh so benigne a creature
Falle in disese, and in mysaventure:

For as the lomb toward his deeth is broght,
So stant this innocent bifore the kyng;
This false knyght that hath this tresoun wroght,
Berth hire on hond that she hath doon thys thyng;
But nathelees, ther was greet moornyng
Among the peple, and seyn, They kan nat gesse
That she had doon so greet a wikkednesse:

For they han seyn hire evere so vertuous,
And lovynge Hermengyld right as hir lyf.
Of this baar witnesse everich in that hous,
Save he that Hermengyld slow with his knyf.
This gentil kyng hath caught a greet motyf
Of this witnesse, and thoghte he wolde enquere
Depper in this, a trouthe for to lere.

Allas! Custance, thou hast no champioun,
Ne fighte kanstow noght, so weylaway!
But he that starf for our redempcioun,
And boond Sathan, and yet lith ther he lay,
So be thy stronge champion this day;
For, but if Crist open myracle kithe,
Withouten gilt thou shalt be slayn as swithe.

She sit hire doun on knees and thus she sayde:
Immortal God that savedest Susanne
Fro false blame, and thou, merciful mayde,
Mary I meene, doghter to Seint Anne,
Bifore whos child angeles synge Osanne,
If I be giltlees of this felonye
My socour be, or elles shal I dye!

Have ye nat seyn som tyme a pale face
Among a prees, of hym that hath be lad
Toward his deeth, wheras hym gat no grace,
And swich a colour in his face hath had,
Men myghte knowe his face, that was bistad,
Amonges alle the faces in that route?
So stant Custance, and looketh hire aboute.

O QUEENES, lyvynge in prosperitee,
Duchesses, and ye ladyes everichone,
Haveth som routhe on hire adversitee;
An emperoures doghter stant allone.
She hath no wight to whom to make hir mone.
O blood roial, that stondest in this drede,
Fer been thy freendes at thy grete nede!

THIS Alla, kyng, hath swich compassioun,
As gentil herte is fulfild of pitee,
That from his eyen ran the water doun.
Now hastily do fecche a book, quod he,
And if this knyght wol sweren how that she
This womman slow, yet wol we us avyse
Whom that we wole that shal been our justise.

A Briton book, written with Evaungiles
Was fet, and on this book he swoor anoon
She gilty was, and in the meene whiles
An hand hym smoot upon the nekke,boon,
That doun he fil atones as a stoon,
And bothe his eyen broste out of his face
In sighte of every body in that place.

A voys was herd in general audience,
And seyde, Thou hast desclaundred, giltelees,
The doghter of hooly chirche in heigh presence;
Thus hastou doon, and yet holde I my pees.
Of this mervaille agast was al the prees;
As mazed folk they stoden everichone,
For drede of wreche, save Custance allone.

Greet was the drede, and eek the repentance,
Of hem that hadden wronge suspecioun
Upon this sely, innocent Custance;
And for this miracle, in conclusioun,
And by Custances mediacioun,
The kyng, and many another in that place,
Converted was, thanked be Cristes grace!

This false knyght was slayn for his untrouthe
By juggement of Alla, hastifly;
And yet Custance hadde of his deeth greet routhe;
And after this Jhesus, of his mercy,
Made Alla wedden, ful solempnely,
This hooly mayden, that is so bright and sheene;
And thus hath Crist ymaad Custance a queene.

BUT who was woful, if I shal nat lye,
Of this weddyng but Donegild, and na mo,
The kynges mooder, ful of tirannye?
Hir thoughte hir cursed herte brast atwo;
She wolde noght hir sone had do so.
Hir thoughte a despit that he sholde take
So strange a creature unto his make.

ME list nat of the chaf, nor of the stree
Maken so long a tale as of the corn.
What sholde I tellen of the roialtee
At mariage, or which cours goth biforn,
Who bloweth in a trumpe, or in an horn?
The fruyt of every tale is for to seye,
They ete, and drynke, and daunce, and synge, and
pleye.

They goon to bedde, as it was skile and right,
For thogh that wyves be ful hooly thynges,
They moste take in pacience at nyght
Swiche manere necessaries as been plesynges
To folk that han ywedded hem with rynges,
And leye a lite hir hoolynesse aside,
As for the tym; it may no bet bitide.

On hire he gat a knave-childe anon,
And to a bisshop, and his constable eke,
He took his wyf to kepe, whan he is gon
To Scotlondward, his foomen for to seke.
Now faire Custance, that is so humble and meke,
So longe is goon with childe, til that stille
She halt hire chambre, abyding Cristes wille.

The tyme is come a knave-child she beer,
Mauricius at the fontstoon they hym calle.
This constable dooth forth come a messageer,
And wroot unto his kyng, that cleped was Alle,
How that this blisful tidyng is bifalle,
And othere tidynges spedeful for to seye.
He taketh the lettre, and forth he gooth his weye.

e I

THIS messager, to doon his avantage,
Unto the kynges mooder rideth swithe,
And salueth hire ful faire in his langage:
Madame, quod he, ye may be glad and blithe,
And thanketh God an hundred thousand sithe,
My lady queene hath child, withouten doute,
To joye and blisse of al this regne aboute.

Lo, heere the lettres seled of this thyng,
That I moot bere with al the haste I may;
If ye wol aught unto youre sone the kyng,
I am youre servant, bothe nyght and day.
Donegild answerde, As now, at this tyme, nay;
But heere al nyght I wol thou take thy reste,
Tomorwe wol I seye thee what me leste.

THIS messager drank sadly ale and wyn,
And stolen were his lettres pryvely,
Out of his box, whil he sleep as a swyn;
And countrefeted was ful subtilly
Another lettre, wroght ful synfully,
Unto the kyng direct of this mateere
Fro his constable, as ye shal after heere.

The lettre spak, The queene delivered was
Of so horrible a feendly creature,
That in the castel noon so hardy was
That any while dorste ther endure.
The mooder was an elf, by aventure
Ycomen, by charmes or by sorcerie,
And everich wight hateth hir compaignye.

Wo was this kyng whan he this lettre had seyn,
But to no wight he tolde his sorwes soore,
But of his owene hand he wroot agayn,
Welcome the sonde of Crist for everemoore
To me, that am now lerned in his loore;
Lord, welcome be thy lust and thy plesaunce
My lust I putte al in thyn ordinaunce.

Kepeth this child, al be it foul or feir,
And eek my wyf unto myn hoomcomynge;
Crist, whan hym list, may sende me an heir
Moore agreable than this to my likynge.
This lettre he seleth, pryvely wepynge,
Which to the messager was take soone,
And forth he gooth; ther is na moore to doone.

O MESSAGER, fulfild of dronkenesse!
Strong is thy breeth, thy lymes faltren ay,
And thou biwreyest alle secreenesse.
Thy mynde is lorn, thou janglest as a jay;
Thy face is turned in a newe array!
Ther dronkenesse regneth in any route,
Ther is no conseil hyd, withouten doute.

O DONEGILD! I ne have noon Englissh
digne
Unto thy malice and thy tirannye,
And therfore to the feend I thee resigne,
Lat hym enditen of thy traitorye!
Fy, mannysh, fy! O nay, by God, I lye,
Fy, feendlych spirit, for I dar wel telle,
Thogh thou heere walke, thy spirit is in helle!

49

HIS messager comth fro the kyng agayn,
And at the kynges moodres court he lighte;
And she was of this messager ful fayn,
And plesed hym, in al that ever she myghte.
He drank, and wel his girdel underpighte;
He slepeth, and he snoreth in his gyse
Al nyghte, until the sonne gan aryse.

Eft were his lettres stolen everychon,
And countrefeted lettres in this wyse:
The king comandeth his constable anon,
Up peyne of hangyng, and on heigh juyse,
That he ne sholde suffren, in no wyse,
Custance inwith his reawme for tabyde
Thre dayes and o quarter of a tyde;

But in the same ship as he hire fond,
Hire and hir yonge sone, and al hir geere
He sholde putte, and croude hire fro the lond,
And chargen hire she never eft coome theere!
O my Custance, wel may thy goost have feere
And slepynge in thy dreem been in penance,
Whan Donegild cast al this ordinance.

This messager on morwe, whan he wook,
Unto the castel halt the nexte way,
And to the constable he the lettre took;
And whan that he this pitous lettre say,
Ful ofte he seyde, Allas! and weylaway!
Lord Crist, quod he, how may this world endure?
So ful of synne is many a creature!

O myghty God, if that it be thy wille,
Sith thou art rightful juge, how may it be
That thou wolt suffren innocents to spille,
And wikked folk regne in prosperitee?
O goode Custance, allas! so wo is me,
That I moot be thy tormentour or deye
On shames deeth; ther is noon oother weye.

WEPEN bothe yonge & olde in al that place,
Whan that the kyng this cursed lettre
sente,
And Custance, with a deedly pale face,
The ferthe day toward the ship she wente;
But nathelees she taketh in good entente
The wyl of Crist, and knelynge on the stronde,
She seyde, Lord! ay welcome be thy sonde!

He that me kepte fro the false blame,
While I was on the lond amonges yow,
He kan me kepe from harm and eek fro shame
In salte see, althogh I se noght how.
As strong as evere he was, he is yet now.
In hym triste I, and in his mooder deere,
That is to me my seyl, and eek my steere.

Hir litel child lay wepyng in hir arm,
And knelynge, pitously to hym she seyde,
Pees, litel sone, I wol do thee noon harm.
With that hir kerchef of hir heed she breyde,
And over his litel eyen she it leyde,
And in hir arm she lulleth it ful faste,
And into hevene hire eyen up she caste.

Mooder, quod she, and mayde bright, Marie,
Sooth is that thurgh wommanes eggement
Mankynde was lorn, and damned ay to dye,
For which thy child was on a croys yrent;
Thy blisful eyen sawe al his torment,
Thanne is ther no comparison bitwene
Thy wo and any wo man may sustene.

Thow sawe thy child yslayn bifore thyne eyen,
And yet now lyveth my litel child, parfay!
Now, lady bright, to whom alle woful cryen,
Thow glorie of wommanhede, thow faire may,
Thow haven of refut, brighte sterre of day,
Rewe on my child, that of thy gentillesse
Ruest on every reweful in distresse.

O litel child, allas! what is thy gilt,
That nevere wroghtest synne as yet, pardee?
Why wil thyn harde fader han thee spilt?
O mercy, deere constable, quod she,
As lat my litel child dwelle heer with thee;
And if thou darst nat saven hym, for blame,
Yet kys hym ones in his fadres name!

THERWITH she looked bakward to the londe,
And seyde, farewel, housbonde routhelees!
And up she rist, & walketh doun the stronde
Toward the ship, hir folweth al the prees,
And evere she preyeth hire child to hold his pees;
And taketh hir leve, and with an hooly entente,
She blissed hire and into ship she wente.

Vitailled was the ship, it is no drede,
Habundantly for hire, ful longe space;
And othere necessaries that sholde nede
She hadde ynogh, heryed be Goddes grace!
For wynd and weder, almyghty God purchace!
And brynge hire hoom, I kan no bettre seye;
But in the see she dryveth forth hir weye.
Explicit secunda pars. Sequitur pars tercia.

LLA the kyng comth hoom,
soon after this,
Unto his castel of the which
I tolde,
And asketh where his wyf
and his child is.
The constable gan aboute
his herte colde,
And pleynly al the manere
he hym tolde,
As ye han herd, I kan telle it no bettre,
And sheweth the kyng his seele and eek his lettre;

And seyde, Lord, as ye comanded me,
Up peyne of deeth, so have I doon, certein.
This messager tormented was til he
Moste biknowe, and tellen plat and pleyn,
Fro nyght to nyght, in what place he had leyn;
And thus, by wit and subtil enquerynge,
Ymagined was by whom this harm gan sprynge.

The hand was knowe that the lettre wroot,
And al the venym of this cursed dede;

But in what wise, certeinly I noot.
Theffect is this, that Alla, out of drede,
His mooder slow, that may men pleynly rede,
For that she traitoure was to hire ligeance.
Thus endeth olde Donegild with meschance.

The sorwe that this Alla nyght and day
Maketh for his wyf, and for his child also,
Ther is no tonge that it telle may;
But now wol I unto Custance go,
That fleteth in the see, in peyne and wo
Fyve yeer and moore, as liked Cristes sonde,
Er that hir ship approched unto londe.

NDER an hethen castel, atte laste,
Of which the name in my text noght I
fynde,
Custance, and eek hir child, the see upcaste.
Almyghty God, that saved al mankynde,
Have on Custance and on hir child som mynde,
That fallen is in hethen hand eftsoone
In point to spille, as I shal telle yow soone.

Doun fro the castel comth ther many a wight,
To gauren on this ship, and on Custance;
But shortly, from the castel, on a nyght,
The lordes styward, God yeve him meschance!
A theef, that hadde reneyed oure creance,
Came into the ship allone, and seyde he sholde
Hir lemman be, wherso she wolde or nolde.

Wo was this wrecched womman tho bigon;
Hir childe cride, and she cride pitously;
But blisful Marie heelp hire right anon,
For with hir struglyng wel and myghtily,
The theef fil overbord al sodeynly,
And in the see he dreynte for vengeance;
And thus hath Crist unwemmed kept Custance!

OFOULE lust of luxurie, lo, thyn ende!
Nat oonly that thou feyntest mannes
mynde,
But verraily thou wolt his body shende.
Thende of thy werk, or of thy lustes blynde,
Is compleynyng: how many oon may men fynde
That noght for werk somtyme, but for thentente
To doon this synne, been outher slayn or shente.

How may this wayke womman han this strengthe
Hire to defende agayn this renegat?
O Golias, unmeasurable of lengthe,
How myghte David make thee so maat?
So yong and of armure so desolaat,
How dorste he looke upon thy dreadful face?
Wel may men seen, it nas but Goddes grace!

WHO yaf Judith corage or hardynesse
To sleen hym, Olofernes, in his tente,
And to deliveren out of wrecchednesse
The peple of God? I seye for this entente,
That right as God spirit of vigour sente
To hem, and saved hem out of meschance,
So sente he myght and vigour to Custance.

e 2

FORTH gooth hir ship thurghout the narwe
mouth
Of Jubaltare and Septe, dryvynge ay,
Somtyme West and sometyme North and South,
And somtyme Est, ful many a wery day,
Til Cristes mooder, blessed be she ay!
Hath shapen, thurgh hir endelees goodnesse,
To make an ende of al hir hevynesse.

NOW lat us stynte of Custance but a throwe,
And speke we of the Romayn emperour,
That out of Surrye hath by lettres knowe
The slaughtre of cristen folk, and dishonour
Doon to his doghter by a fals traytour,
I mene the cursed wikked sowdanesse,
That at the feeste leet sleen both moore and lesse;

For which this emperour hath sent anoon
His senatour with roial ordinance,
And othere lordes, God woot, many oon,
On Surryens to taken heigh vengeance.
They brennen, sleen, & brynge hem to meschance
Ful many a day; but, shortly, this is thende,
Homward to Rome they shapen hem to wende.

This senatour repaireth with victorie
To Romeward, saillynge ful roially,
And mette the ship dryvynge, as seith the storie,
In which Custance sit ful pitously.
Nothyng ne knew he what she was, ne why
She was in swich array; ne she nyl seye
Of hire estaat, althogh she sholde deye.

He bryngeth hire to Rome, and to his wyf
He yaf hire, and hir yonge sone also;
And with the senatour she ladde hir lyf.
Thus kan oure lady bryngen out of wo
Woful Custance, and many another mo.
And longe tyme dwelled she in that place
In hooly werkes evere, as was hir grace.

The senatoures wyf hir aunte was,
But for al that she knew hire never the moore:
I wol no lenger tarien in this cas,
But to kyng Alla, which I spake of yoore,
That wepeth for his wyf and siketh soore,
I wol retourne, and lete I wol Custance
Under the senatoures governance.

KYNG ALLA, which that hadde his mooder
slayn,
Upon a day fil in swich repentance,
That, if I shortly tellen shal and playn,
To Rome he comth, to receyven his penance,
And putte hym in the popes ordinance,
In heigh and logh; and Jhesu Crist bisoghte
Foryeve his wikked werkes that he wroghte.

The fame anon thurghout the toun is born,
How Alla kyng shal come on pilgrymage,
By herbergeours that wenten hym biforn;
For which the senatour, as was usage,
Rood hym agayns, and many of his lynage,

51

As wel to shewen his heighe magnificence,
As to doon any kyng a reverence.

Greet cheere dooth this noble senatour
To kyng Alla, and he to hym also;
Everich of hem dooth oother greet honour;
And so bifel, that in a day or two,
This senatour is to kyng Alla go
To feste, and shortly, if I shal nat lye,
Custances sone wente in his compaignye.

Som men wolde seyn, at requeste of Custance,
This senatour hath lad this child to feeste;
I may nat tellen every circumstance,
Be as be may, ther was he at the leeste;
But sooth is this, that at his moodres heeste,
Biforn Alla, durynge the metes space,
The child stood, lookynge in the kynges face.

This Alla kyng hath of this child greet wonder,
And to the senatour he seyde anon,
Whos is that faire childe that stondeth yonder?
I noot, quod he, by God and by Seint John!
A mooder he hath, but fader hath he noon
That I of woot, but shortly, in a stounde
He tolde Alla how that this child was founde.

But God woot, quod this senatour also,
So vertuous a lyvere in my lyf
Ne saugh I nevere as she, ne herd of mo
Of worldly wommen, mayde ne of wyf;
I dar wel seyn hir hadde levere a knyf
Thurghout hir brest, than ben a womman wikke;
There is no man koude brynge hire to that prikke.

NOW was this child as lyke unto Custance
As possible is a creature to be.
This Alla hath the face in remembrance
Of dame Custance, and theron mused he,
If that the childes mooder were aught she
That is his wyf, and pryvely he sighte,
And spedde hym fro the table that he myghte.

Parfay! thoghte he, fantome is in myn heed!
I oghte deme of skilful juggement,
That in the salte see my wyf is deed;
And afterward he made his argument,
What woot I, if that Crist have hyder ysent
My wyf by see, as wel as he hire sente
To my contree fro thennes that she wente?

And after noon, hoom with the senatour
Goth Alla, for to seen this wonder chaunce.
This senatour dooth Alla greet honour,
And hastifly he sente after Custaunce;
But trusteth weel, hire liste nat to daunce
Whan that she wiste wherfore was that sonde,
Unnethe upon hir feet she myghte stonde.

WHAN Alla saugh his wyf, faire he hire
grette,
And weep, that it was routhe for to see;
For at the firste look he on hire sette,

52

He knew wel verraily that it was she;
And she for sorwe as doumb stant as a tree;
So was hir herte shet in hir distresse
When she remembred his unkyndenesse.

Twyes she swowned in his owene sighte.
He weep, and hym excuseth pitously:
Now God, quod he, and all his halwes brighte,
So wisly on my soul as have mercy,
That of youre harm as giltelees am I,
As is Maurice my sone, so lyk your face;
Elles the feend me fecche out of this place!

Long was the sobbyng and the bitter peyne,
Er that hir woful hertes myghte cesse;
Greet was the pitee for to heere hem pleyne,
Thurgh whiche pleintes gan hir wo encresse.
I pray yow all my labour to relesse,
I may nat telle hir wo until tomorwe,
I am so wery for to speke of sorwe.

But finally, whan that the sothe is wist,
That Alla giltelees was of hir wo,
I trowe an hundred tymes been they kist,
And swich a blisse is ther bitwix hem two,
That, save the joye that lasteth evermo,
Ther is noon lyk, that any creature
Hath seyn, or shal, whil that the world may dure.

Tho preyde she hir housbonde mekely,
In relief of hir longe pitous pyne,
That he wolde preye hir fader specially,
That of his magestee he wolde enclyne
To vouchesauf som day with hym to dyne:
She preyde hym eek he wolde by no weye
Unto hir fader no word of hire seye.

Som men wold seyn how that the child Maurice
Dooth this message unto the emperour;
But, as I gesse, Alla was nat so nyce
To hym, that was of so sovereyn honour
As he that is of cristen folk the flour,
Sente any child, but it is bet to deeme
He wente hymself, and so it may well seeme.

This emperour hath graunted gentilly
To come to dyner, as he hym bisoughte;
And wel rede I, he looked bisily
Upon this child, and on his doghter thoghte.
Alla goth to his in, and, as him oghte,
Arrayed for this feste in every wise,
As ferforth as his konnyng may suffise.

The morwe cam, and Alla gan hym dresse,
And eek his wyf, this emperour to meete;
And forth they ryde in joye and in gladnesse;
And whan she saugh hir fader in the strete,
She lighte doun and falleth hym to feete:
Fader, quod she, youre yonge child, Custance,
Is now ful clene out of youre remembrance.

I am youre doghter Custance, quod she,
That whilom ye han sent unto Surrye.

It am I, fader, that in the salte see
Was put allone, and dampned for to dye.
Now, goode fader, mercy, I yow crye!
Sende me namoore unto noon hethenesse,
But thonketh my lord heere of his kyndenesse.

Who kan the pitous joye tellen al
Bitwixe hem thre, syn they been thus ymette?
But of my tale make an ende I shal;
The day goth faste, I wol no lenger lette.
This glade folk to dyner they hem sette;
In joye and blisse at mete I lete hem dwelle,
A thousand foold wel moore than I kan telle.

This child Maurice was sithen emperour
Maad by the pope and lyved cristenly.
To Cristes chirche he dide greet honour;
But I lete al his storie passen by;
Of Custance is my tale specially.
In the olde Romane geestes may men fynde
Maurices lyf; I bere it noght in mynde.

This kyng Alla, whan he his tyme say,
With his Custance, his hooly wyf so sweete,
To Engelond been they come the righte way,
Wheras they lyve in joye and in quiete;
But litel while it lasteth, I yow heete,
Joye of this world, for tyme wol nat abyde;
Fro day to nyght it changeth as the tyde.

Who lyved evere in swich delit o day
That hym ne moeved outher conscience,
Or ire, or talent, or som kynne affray,
Envye, or pride, or passion, or offence?
I ne seye but for this ende this sentence,
That litel while in joye or in plesance
Lasteth the blisse of Alla with Custance;

For deeth, that taketh of heigh and logh his
rente,
Whan passed was a yeer, evene as I gesse,
Out of this world this kyng Alla he hente,
For whom Custance hath ful greet hevynesse.
Now lat us praye to God his soule blesse!
And dame Custance, finally to seye,
Toward the toun of Rome goth hir weye.

To Rome is come this hooly creature,
And fyndeth ther hire freendes hoole and
sounde:

Now is she scaped al hire aventure;
And whan that she hir fader hath yfounde,
Doun on hir knees falleth she to grounde;
Wepynge for tendrenesse in herte blithe,
She heryeth God an hundred thousand sithe.

In vertu and in hooly almus-dede
They lyven alle, and nevere asonder wende;
Til deeth departed hem this lyf they lede.
And fareth now weel, my tale is at an ende.
Now Jhesu Crist, that of his myght may
sende
Joye after wo, governe us in his grace,
And kepe us alle that been in this place!
Amen.
Heere endeth the Tale of the Man of Lawe.

Next folwith the Shipman his prologe

OURE Hoste upon his stiropes stode anon,
And seyde, Good men, herkeneth, everichon;
This was a thrifty tale for the nones!
Sir Parish Prest, quod he, for Goddes bones,
Telle us a tale, as was thy forward yore;
I se wel that ye lerned men in lore
Can moche good, by Goddes dignitee!
The Persone him answerde, Benedicite!
What eyleth the man, so sinfully to swere?
Oure Hoste answerde, O Jankyn, be ye there?
I smelle a Loller in the wind, quod he.
How! good men, quod our Hoste, herkneth me,
Abydeth, for Goddes digne passioun,
For we shal han a predicacioun;
This Loller here wol prechen us somwhat.
Nay, by my fader soule! that shal he nat!
Seyde the Shipman; here shal he nat preche;
He shal no gospel glosen here ne teche.
We leven alle in the grete God, quod he,
He wolde sowen som difficulte,
Or springen cokkel in our clene corn;
And therfore, Hoste, I warne the biforn,
My joly body shal a tale telle,
And I shal clynken yow so mery a belle,
That I shal waken al this companye;
But it shal nat ben of philosophye,
Ne phislyas, ne termes queynte of lawe;
There is but litel Latin in my mawe.
Here endith the Shipman his prologe.

HEERE BIGYNNETH THE SHIPMANNES TALE.

A MARCHANT whilom dwelled at Seint Denys,
That riche was, for which men helde hym wys;
A wyf he hadde of excellent beautee,
And compaignable and revelous was she,
Which is a thyng that causeth more dispence
Than worth is al the chiere and reverence
That men hem doon at festes & at daunces;
Swiche salutaciouns and contenaunces
Passen as dooth a shadwe upon the wal.
But wo is hym that payen moot for al;
The sely housbonde, algate he moste paye;
He moot us clothe, and he moot us arraye,
Al for his owene worship richely,
In which array we daunce jolily.
And if that he noght may, paraventure,

Or elles list no swich dispence endure,
But thynketh it is wasted and ylost,
Thanne moot another payen for oure cost,
Or lene us gold, and that is perilous.

THIS noble marchaunt heeld a worthy hous,
For which he hadde alday so greet repair
For his largesse, and for his wyf was fair,
That wonder is; but herkneth to my tale.

AMONGES alle his gestes, grete and smale
Ther was a monk, a fair man and a boold,
I trowe of thritty wynter he was oold,
That evere in oon was comynge to that place.
This yonge monk, that was so fair of face,
Aqueynted was so with the goode man
Sith that hir firste knoweliche bigan,
That in his hous as famulier was he
As it possible is any freend to be.
¶And for as muchel as this goode man
And eek this monk, of which that I bigan,
Were bothe two yborn in o village,
The monk hym claymeth as for cosynage;
And he agayn, he seith nat ones nay,
But was as glad therof as fowel of day;
For to his herte it was a greet plesaunce.
Thus been they knyt with eterne alliaunce,
And ech of hem gan oother for tassure
Of bretherhede, whil that hir lyf may dure.
¶Free was Daun John, and namely of dispence,
As in that hous; and ful of diligence
To doon plesaunce, and also greet costage.
He noght forgat to yeve the leeste page
In al that hous, but after hir degree.
He yaf the lord, and sitthe al his meynee,
Whan that he cam, som manere honest thyng,
For which they were as glad of his comyng
As fowel is fayn whan that the sonne upriseth;
Na moore of this as now, for it suffiseth.
¶But so bifel, this marchant on a day
Shoop hym to make redy his array
Toward the toun of Brugges for to fare,
To byen there a porcioun of ware;
For which he hath to Parys sent anon
A messager, and preyed hath Daun John
That he sholde come to Seint Denys to pleye
With hym and with his wyf a day or tweye,
Er he to Brugges wente, in alle wise.

THIS noble monk, of which I yow devyse,
Hath of his abbot, as hym list, licence,
Bycause he was a man of heigh prudence,
And eek an officer, out for to ryde,
To seen hir graunges and hire bernes wyde;
And unto Seint Denys he comth anon.
Who was so welcome as my lord Daun John,
Oure deere cosyn, ful of curteisye?
With hym broghte he a jubbe of malvesye
And eek another, ful of fyn vernage,
And volatyl, as ay was his usage.
And thus I lete hem ete and drynke and pleye,
This marchant and this monk, a day or tweye.

THE thridde day, this marchant up ariseth,
And on his nedes sadly hym avyseth,
And up into his countour/hous gooth he,
To rekene with hymself, as wel may be,

54

Of thilke yeer, how that it with him stood,
And how that he despended hadde his good;
And if that he encressed were or noon.
His bookes and his bagges many oon
He leith biforn hym on his countyng/bord.
Ful riche was his tresor and his hord,
For which ful faste his countour/dore he shette;
And eek he nolde that no man sholde hym lette
Of his accountes, for the meene tyme;
And thus he sit til it was passed pryme.

DAUN JOHN was rysen in the morwe also,
And in the gardyn walketh to and fro,
And hath his thynges seyd ful curteisly.
This goode wyf cam walkinge pryvely
Into the gardyn, there he walketh softe,
And hym saleweth, as she hath doon ofte.
A mayde child cam in hire compaignye,
Which as hir list she may governe and gye,
For yet under the yerde was the mayde.
¶O deere cosyn myn, Daun John, she sayde,
What eyleth yow, so rathe for to ryse?
¶Nece, quod he, it oghte ynough suffise
Fyve houres for to slepe upon a nyght,
But it were for an old appalled wight,
As been thise wedded men, that lye and dare
As in a fourme sit a wery hare,
Were al forstraught with houndes grete & smale.
But deere nece, why be ye so pale?
I trowe certes that oure goode man
Hath yow laboured sith the nyght bigan,
That yow were nede to resten hastily.
And with that word he lough ful murily,
And of his owene thought he wex al reed.
¶This faire wyf gan for to shake hir heed,
And seyde thus: Ye, God woot al, quod she;
Nay, cosyn myn, it stant nat so with me,
For, by that God that yaf me soule and lyf,
In al the reawme of France is ther no wyf
That lasse lust hath to that sory pleye.
For I may synge Allas and weylawey
That I was born; but to no wight, quod she,
Dar I nat telle how that it stant with me.
Wherfore I thynke out of this land to wende,
Or elles of myself to make an ende,
So ful am I of drede and eek of care.

THIS monk bigan upon this wyf to stare,
And seyde, Allas, my nece, God forbede
That ye, for any sorwe or any drede,
Fordo youreself; but tel me of youre grief;
Paraventure I may, in youre meschief,
Conseille or helpe; and therfore telleth me
Al youre anoy, for it shal been secree;
For on my porthors here I make an ooth
That nevere in my lyf, for lief ne looth,
Ne shal I of no conseil yow biwreye.
¶The same agayn to yow, quod she, I seye;
By God and by this porthors, I yow swere,
Though men me wolde al into pieces tere,
Ne shal I nevere, for to goon to helle,
Biwreye a word of thyng that ye me telle,
Nat for no cosynage ne alliance,
But verraily for love and affiance.
¶Thus been they sworn, & heerupon they kiste,

And ech of hem tolde oother what hem liste.
Cosyn, quod she, if that I hadde a space,
As I have noon, and namely in this place,
Thanne wolde I telle a legende of my lyf,
What I have suffred sith I was a wyf
With myn housbonde, al be he youre cosyn.
Nay, quod this monk, by God & Seint Martyn!
He is na moore cosyn unto me
Than is this lief that hangeth on the tree.
I clepe hym so, by Seint Denys of Fraunce!
To have the moore cause of aqueyntaunce
Of yow, which I have loved specially,
Aboven alle wommen sikerly;
This swere I yow on my professioun.
Telleth youre grief lest that he come adoun,
And hasteth yow, and gooth youre wey anon.
MY deere love, quod she, O my Daun John,
Ful lief were me this conseil for to hyde,
But out it moot, I may namoore abyde.
Myn housbonde is to me the worste man
That evere was, sith that the world bigan.
But sith I am a wyf, it sit nat me
To tellen no wight of oure privetee,
Neither a bedde, ne in noon oother place;
God shilde I sholde it tellen, for his grace!
A wyf ne shal nat seyn of hir housbonde
But al honour, as I kan understonde;
Save unto yow, this muche I tellen shal;
As helpe me God, he is noght worth at al
In no degree the value of a flye;
But yet me greveth moost his nygardye.
And wel ye woot that wommen naturelly
Desiren thynges sixe, as wel as I:
They wolde that hir housbondes sholde be
Hardy and wise, and riche, and therto free,
And buxom to his wyf, and fressh abedde.
But, by that ilke Lord that for us bledde,
For his honour, myself for to arraye,
A Sonday next, I moste nedes paye
An hundred frankes, or ellis I am lorn;
Yet were me levere that I were unborn
Than me were doon a sclaundre or vileynye;
And if myn housbonde eek it myghte espye,
I nere but lost, and therfore I yow preye,
Lene me this somme, or ellis moot I deye.
Daun John, I seye, lene me thise hundred frankes;
Pardee, I wol nat faille yow my thankes,
If that yow list to doon that I yow praye;
For at a certeyn day I wol yow paye,
And doon to yow what plesance and servise
That I may doon, right as yow list devise.
And but I do, God take on me vengeance
As foul as evere hadde Genyloun of Fraunce!
THIS gentil monk answerde in this manere:
Now trewely, myn owene lady deere,
I have, quod he, on yow so greet a routhe,
That I yow swere, and plighte yow my trouthe,
That whan youre housbonde is to Flaundres fare,
I wol delyvere yow out of this care;
For I wol brynge yow an hundred frankes.
And with that word he caught hire by the flankes,
And hire embraceth harde, and kiste hire ofte.
Gooth now youre wey, quod he, al stille & softe,

e 4

And lat us dyne as soone as that ye may;
For by my chilyndre it is pryme of day.
Gooth now, and beeth as trewe as I shal be.
Now, elles God forbede, sire, quod she;
And forth she gooth, as jolif as a pye,
And bad the cookes that they sholde hem hye,
So that men myghte dyne, and that anon.
Up to hir housbonde is this wyf ygon,
And knokketh at his countour boldely.
Who is ther? quod he. Peter! it am I,
Quod she; what, sire, how longe wol ye faste?
How longe tyme wol ye rekene and caste
Youre sommes, & youre bookes, & youre thynges?
The devel have part on alle swiche rekenynges!
Ye have ynough, pardee, of Goddes sonde;
Com doun today, and lat youre bagges stonde.
Ne be ye nat ashamed that Daun John
Shal fasting al this day elenge goon?
What! lat us heere a messe, and go we dyne.
WYf, quod this man, litel kanstow devyne
The curious bisynesse that we have;
For of us chapmen, also God me save,
And by that lord that clepid is Seint Yve,
Scarsly amonges twelve, ten shul thryve
Continuelly, lastynge unto oure age.
We may wel make chiere and good visage,
And dryve forth the world as it may be,
And kepen oure estaat in pryvetee
Til we be deed; or elles that we pleye
A pilgrymage, or goon out of the weye.
And therfore have I greet necessitee
Upon this queynte world tavyse me;
For everemoore we moote stonde in drede
Of hap and fortune in oure chapmanhede.
To Flaundres wol I go to morwe at day,
And come agayn, as soone as evere I may,
For which, my deere wyf, I thee biseke
As be to every wight buxom and meke,
And for to kepe oure good be curious,
And honestly governe wel oure hous.
Thou hast ynough in every maner wise,
That to a thrifty houshold may suffise;
Thee lakketh noon array ne no vitaille,
Of silver in thy purs shaltow nat faille.
And with that word his countour-dore he shette,
And doun he gooth, no lenger wolde he lette;
But hastily a messe was ther seyd,
And spedily the tables were yleyd,
And to the dyner faste they hem spedde,
And richely this monk the chapman fedde.
At after dyner Daun John sobrely
This chapman took apart, and prively
He seyde hym thus: Cosyn, it standeth so,
That wel I se to Brugges wol ye go.
God and Seint Austyn spede yow and gyde!
I prey yow, cosyn, wisely that ye ryde;
Governeth yow also of youre diete
Atemprely, and namely in this hete.
Bitwix us two nedeth no strange fare;
Farewel cosyn, God shilde yow fro care.
If anythyng ther be by day or nyght,
If it lye in my power and my myght,
That ye me wol comande in any wyse,

55

It shal be doon, right as ye wol devyse.
O thyng, er that ye goon, if it may be:
I wolde prey yow for to lene me
An hundred frankes, for a wyke or tweye,
for certein beestes that I moste beye,
To stoore with a place that is oures;
God helpe me so, I wolde that it were youres.
I shal nat faille surely at my day,
Nat for a thousand frankes, a mile-way.
But lat this thyng be secree, I yow preye,
for yet tonyght thise beestes moot I beye,
And fare now wel, myn owene cosyn deere,
Graunt mercy of youre cost and of youre cheere!
This noble marchant gentilly anon
Answerde, and seyde, O cosyn myn, Daun John,
Now sikerly this is a smal requeste;
My gold is youres, whan that it yow leste,
And nat oonly my gold, but my chaffare;
Take what yow list, God shilde that ye spare.
But o thyng is, ye knowe it wel ynogh,
Of chapmen, that hir moneie is hir plogh;
We may creaunce whil we have a name,
But goldlees for to be, it is no game;
Paye it agayn whan it lith in youre ese;
After my myght ful fayn wolde I yow plese.
Thise hundred frankes he fette hym forth anon,
And prively he took hem to Daun John;
No wight in al this world wiste of this loone,
Savynge this marchant and Daun John alloone.
They drynke, and speke, & rome awhile, & pleye,
Til that Daun John rideth to his abbeye.
The morwe cam, and forth this marchant rideth
To flaundresward; his prentys wel hym gydeth,
Til he cam into Brugges murily.
Now gooth this marchant faste and bisily
Aboute his nede, and byeth and creaunceth;
He neither pleyeth at the dees, ne daunceth;
But as a marchant, shortly for to telle,
He let his lyf, and there I lete hym dwelle.
THE Sonday next this marchant was agon,
To Seint Denys ycomen is Daun John,
With crowne and berde all fressh and newe
yshave.
In al the hous ther nas so litel a knave,
Ne no wight elles, that he nas ful fayn
for that my lord Daun John was come agayn.
And shortly, to the point right for to gon,
This faire wyf accorded with Daun John
That for thise hundred frankes he sholde al nyght
Have hire in his armes bolt upright,
And this acord parfourned was in dede.
In myrthe al nyght a bisy lyf they lede
Til it was day, that Daun John wente his way,
And bad the meynee, farewel, have good day!
for noon of hem, ne no wight in the toun,
Hath of Daun John right no suspecioun.
And forth he rydeth hoom to his abbeye,
Or where hym list; namoore of hym I seye.
THIS marchant, whan that ended was the
faire,
To Seint Denys he gan for to repaire,
And with his wyf he maketh feeste and cheere,
And telleth hire that chaffare is so deere

That nedes moste he make a chevyssaunce;
for he was bounde in a reconyssaunce,
To paye twenty thousand sheeld anon;
for which this marchant is to Parys gon,
To borwe of certeine freendes that he hadde
A certeyne frankes; and somme with him he ladde.
And whan that he was come into the toun,
for greet chiertee and greet affeccioun,
Unto Daun John he gooth hym first, to pleye;
Nat for to axe or borwe of him moneye,
But for to wite and seen of his welfare,
And for to tellen hym of his chaffare,
As freendes doon whan they been met yfeere.
Daun John hym maketh feeste & murye cheere,
And he hym tolde agayn, ful specially,
How he hadde wel yboght and graciously,
Thanked be God! al hool his marchandise:
Save that he moste, in alle maner wise,
Maken a chevyssaunce, as for his beste,
And thanne he sholde been in joye and reste.
Daun John answerde, Certes I am fayn,
That ye in heele ar comen hom agayn,
And if that I were riche, as have I blisse,
Of twenty thousand sheeld shold ye nat mysse,
for ye so kyndely this oother day
Lente me gold; and as I kan and may
I thanke yow, by God and by Seint Jame!
But nathelees I took unto oure dame,
Youre wyf, at hom, the same gold ageyn
Upon youre bench; she woot it wel, certeyn,
By certeyn tokenes that I kan yow telle.
Now, by youre leve, I may no lenger dwelle;
Oure abbot wole out of this toun anon,
And in his compaignye moot I goon.
Grete wel oure dame, myn owene nece sweete,
And farewel, deere cosyn, til we meete!
THIS marchant, which that was ful war & wys,
Creanced hath, and payd eek in Parys
To certeyn Lumbardes, redy in hir hond
The somme of gold, and hadde of hem his bond;
And hoom he gooth, murie as a papejay.
for wel he knew he stood in swich array
That nedes moste he wynne in that viage
A thousand frankes above al his costage.
His wyf ful redy mette hym atte gate,
As she was wont of oold usage algate,
And al that nyght in myrthe they bisette;
for he was riche and cleerly out of dette.
Whan it was day, this marchant gan embrace
His wyf al newe, and kiste hire on hir face,
And up he gooth and maketh it ful tough.
Namoore, quod she, by God, ye have ynough!
And wantownely agayn with him she pleyde;
Til atte laste, thus this marchant seyde:
By God, quod he, I am a litel wrooth
With yow, my wyf, although it be me looth.
And woot ye why? By God, as that I gesse,
That ye han maad a manere straungenesse
Bitwixen me and my cosyn Daun John;
Ye sholde han warned me, er I had gon,
That he yow hadde an hundred frankes payed
By redy tokene; and heeld hym yvele apayed,
for that I to hym spak of chevyssaunce;

Me semed so as by his contenaunce.
But nathelees, by God, oure hevene kyng,
I thoughte nat to axen hym no thyng.
I prey thee, wyf, ne do namoore so;
Telle me alwey, er that I fro thee go,
If any dettour hath in myn absence
Ypayed thee; lest, thurgh thy necligence,
I myghte hym axe a thing that he hath payed.
THIS wyf was nat afered nor affrayed,
But boldely she seyde, and that anon:
Marie, I deffie the false monk, Daun John!
I kepe nat of his tokenes never a deel,
He took me certeyn gold, that woot I weel.
What! yvel thedom on his monkes snowte!
For, God it woot, I wende, withouten doute,
That he hadde yeve it me bycause of yow,
To doon therwith myn honour and my prow,
For cosynage, and eek for beele cheere
That he hath had ful ofte tymes heere.
But sith I se I stonde in this disjoynt,
I wol answere yow shortly, to the poynt.
Ye han mo slakkere dettours than am I,
For I wol paye yow wel and redily
Fro day to day; and if so be I faille,
I am youre wyf; score it upon my taille,
And I shal paye, as soon as ever I may;
For by my trouthe, I have on myn array,
And nat on wast, bistowed every deel.
And for I have bistowed it so weel
For youre honour, for Goddes sake, I seye,
As be nat wrooth, but lat us laughe and pleye.
Ye shal my joly body have to wedde;
By God! I wol nat paye yow but abedde.
Forgyve it me, myn owene spouse deere;
Turne hiderward, and maketh bettre cheere!
This marchant saugh ther was no remedie,
And for to chide, it nere but greet folie,
Sith that the thyng may nat amended be.
Now, wyf, he seyde, and I foryeve it thee,
But by thy lyf, ne be namoore so large;
Keepe bet oure good, that yeve I thee in charge.
Thus endeth now my tale, and God us sende
Taillynge ynough unto oure lyves ende.
Amen. Heere endeth the Shipmannes Tale.

Bihoold the murie wordes of the Hoost to the
Shipman, and to the lady Prioresse.

WEL seyd! by corpus do-
minus, quod our Hooste;
Now longe moote thou
saille by the coste,
Sire gentil maister,
gentil maryneer!
God yeve this monk a
thousand last quade
yeer!
A ha! felawes, beth ware
of swiche a jape!
The monk putte in the mannes hood an ape,

And in his wyves eek, by Seint Austyn!
Draweth no monkes moore unto youre in.
But now passe over, and lat us seke aboute,
Who shal now telle first, of al this route,
Another tale; and with that word he sayde,
As curteisly as it had ben a mayde,
My lady Prioresse, by youre leve,
So that I wiste I sholde yow nat greve,
I wolde demen that ye tellen sholde
A tale next, if so were that ye wolde.
Now wol ye vouchesauf, my lady deere?
Gladly, quod she, and seyde as ye shal heere.

The prologe of the Prioresses Tale.
Domine, dominus noster.

LORD, oure Lord, thy name
how merveillous
Is in this large world ysprad,
quod she;
For noght oonly thy laude
precious
Parfourned is by men of
dignitee,
But by the mouth of chil-
dren thy bountee
Parfourned is; for on the brest soukynge
Somtyme shewen they thyn heryinge.

Wherfore in laude, as I best kan or may,
Of thee, and of the white lylye flour
Which that thee bar, and is a mayde alway,
To telle a storie I wol do my labour;
Nat that I may encreessen hir honour;
For she hirself is honour, and the roote
Of bountee, next hir sone, and soules boote.

O mooder mayde! O mayde mooder fre!
O bussh unbrent, brennynge in Moyses sighte,
That ravysedest doun fro the Deitee,
Thurgh thyn humblesse, the goost that in tha-
lighte;
Of whos vertu, whan he thyn herte lighte,
Conceyved was the fadres sapience,
Helpe me to telle it in thy reverence!

Lady! thy bountee, thy magnificence,
Thy vertu, and thy grete humylitee
Ther may no tonge expresse in no science;
For somtyme, lady, er men praye to thee,
Thou goost biforn of thy benygnytee,
And getest us the lyght thurgh thy preyere,
To gyden us unto thy sone so deere.

My konnyng is so wayk, O blisful queene,
For to declare thy grete worthynesse,
That I ne may the weighte nat susteene,
But as a child of twelf monthe oold or lesse,
That kan unnethes any word expresse,
Right so fare I, and therfore I yow preye,
Gydeth my song that I shal of yow seye.

WAS IN ASYE, IN A GREET CITEE,
Amonges cristene folk, a Jewerye,
Sustened by a lord of that contree
for foule usure, and lucre of vileynye,
Hateful to Crist and to his compaignye;
And thurgh the strete men myghte ride or
wende,
for it was free, and open at eyther ende.

A litel scole of cristen folk ther stood
Doun at the ferther ende, in which ther were
Children an heepe, ycomen of cristen blood,
That lerned in that scole yeer by yere
Swich manere doctrine as men used there,
This is to seyn, to syngen and to rede,
As smale children doon in hire childhede.

AMONG thise children was a wydwes
sone,
A litel clergeon, seven yeer of age,
That day by day to scole was his wone,
And eek also, whereas he saugh thymage
Of Cristes mooder, hadde he in usage,
As hym was taught, to knele adoun and seye
His Ave Marie, as he goth by the weye.

Thus hath this wydwe hir litel sone ytaught
Oure blisful lady, Cristes mooder deere,
To worshipe ay, and he forgate it naught,
for sely child wol alday soone leere;
But ay, whan I remembre on this mateere,
Seint Nicholas stant evere in my presence,
for he so yong to Crist dide reverence.

This litel child, his litel book lernynge,
As he sat in the scole at his prymer,

He Alma redemptoris herde synge,
As children lerned hire antiphoner;
And, as he dorste, he drough hym ner and ner,
And herkned ay the wordes and the noote,
Til he the firste vers koude al by rote.

Noght wiste he what this Latyn was to seye,
For he so yong and tendre was of age;
But on a day his felawe gan he preye
Texpounden hym this song in his langage,
Or telle him why this song was in usage;
This preyde he hym to construe and declare
Ful often time upon his knowes bare.

His felawe, which that elder was than he,
Answerde hym thus, ☙ This song I have herd seye,
Was maked of oure blisful lady free,
Hire to salue, and eek hire for to preye
To been oure help and socour whan we deye;
I kan na moore expounde in this mateere,
I lerne song, I kan but smal grammeere.

❧ And is this song maked in reverence
Of Cristes mooder? seyde this innocent;
Now certes, I wol do my diligence
To konne it al, er Cristemasse is went;
Though that I for my prymer shal be shent,
And shal be beten thriës in an houre,
I wol it konne, oure lady to honoure!

☙ His felawe taughte hym homward prively
Fro day to day, til he koude it by rote,
And thanne he song it wel and boldely
Fro word to word, acordynge with the note;
Twiës a day it passed thurgh his throte,
To scoleward and homward whan he wente;
On Cristes mooder set was his entente.

As I have seyd, thurghout the Jewerie
This litel child, as he cam to and fro,
Ful murily than wolde he synge and crie
O Alma redemptoris, everemo.
The swetnesse hath his herte perced so
Of Cristes mooder, that, to hire to preye,
He kan nat stynte of syngyng by the weye.

OURE firste foo, the serpent Sathanas,
That hath in Jewes herte his waspes nest,
Up swal, and seide, O Hebrayk peple, allas!
Is this to yow a thyng that is honest,
That swich a boy shal walken as hym lest
In youre despit, and synge of swich sentence,
Which is agayn youre lawes reverence?

Fro thennes forth the Jewes han conspired
This innocent out of this world to chace;
An homycide therto han they hyred,
That in an aleye hadde a privee place;
And as the child gan forby for to pace,
This cursed Jew hym hente and heeld hym faste,
And kitte his throte, and in a pit hym caste.

I seye that in a wardrobe they hym threwe

Whereas thise Jewes purgen hire entraille.
CURSED folk of Herodes al newe!
What may youre yvel entente yow availle?
Mordre wol out, certeyn, it wol nat faille,
And namely, ther thonour of God shal sprede,
The blood out/crieth on youre cursed dede.

O martir, sowded to virginitee,
Now maystow syngen, folwynge evere in oon
The white Lamb celestial, quod she,
Of which the grete Evaungelist, Seint John,
In Pathmos wroot, which seith that they that goon
Biforn this Lamb, and synge a song al newe,
That nevere, fleshly, wommen they ne knewe.

THIS povre wydwe awaiteth al that nyght
After hir litel child, but he cam noght;
For which, as soone as it was dayes lyght,
With face pale of drede and bisy thoght,
She hath at scole and elleswhere hym soght;
Til finally she gan so fer espie
That he last seyn was in the Jewerie.

With moodres pitee in hir brest enclosed,
She gooth, as she were half out of hir mynde,
To every place where she hath supposed
By liklihede hir litel child to fynde;
And evere on Cristes mooder meeke and kynde
She cride, and atte laste thus she wroghte,
Among the cursed Jewes she hym soghte.

She frayneth and she preyeth pitously
To every Jew that dwelte in thilke place,
To telle hire if hir child wente oght forby.
They seyde Nay, but Jhesu of his grace,
Yaf in hir thoght, inwith a litel space,
That in that place after hir sone she cryde,
Where he was casten in a pit bisyde.

O GRETE God, that parfournest thy laude
By mouth of innocents, lo heere thy myght!
This gemme of chastite, this emeraude,
And eek of martirdom the ruby bright,
Ther he, with throte ykorven, lay upright,
He Alma redemptoris gan to synge
So loude, that al the place gan to rynge!

The cristene folk that thurgh the strete wente,
In coomen, for to wondre upon this thyng;
And hastily they for the provost sente;
He cam anon, withouten tarying,
And herieth Crist that is of hevene Kyng,
And eek his mooder, honour of mankynde,
And after that, the Jewes leet he bynde.

This child, with pitous lamentacioun,
Uptaken was, syngynge his song alway;
And with honour of greet processioun
They carien hym unto the next abbay.
His mooder swownynge by the beere lay;
Unnethe myghte the peple that was theere
This newe Rachel brynge fro his beere.

59

WITH torment, and with shameful
deeth echon,
    This provost dooth these Jewes
for to sterve
That of this mordre wiste, and that anon;
He nolde no swich cursednesse observe,
Yvele shal have, that yvele wol deserve,
Therfore with wilde hors he dide hem drawe,
And after that he heng hem, by the lawe.

UPON his beere ay lith this innocent
    Biforn the chief auter, whil masse
    laste,
And after that, the abbot with his covent
Han sped hem for to burien hym ful faste;
And whan they hooly water on hym caste,
Yet spak this child whan spreynd was hooly
water,
And song, O Alma redemptoris mater!

This abbot, which that was an hooly man,
As monkes been, or elles oghten be,
This yonge child to conjure he bigan,
And seyde, O deere child, I halse thee,
In vertu of the hooly Trinitee,
Tel me what is thy cause for to synge,
Sith that thy throte is kut, to my semynge?

My throte is kut unto my nekke, boon,
Seyde this child, and, as by wey of kynde,
I sholde have deyed, ye, longe tyme agon;
But Jhesu Crist, as ye in bookes fynde,
Wil that his glorie laste and be in mynde,
And, for the worship of his mooder deere,
Yet may I synge O Alma, loude and cleere.

This welle of mercy, Cristes mooder sweete,
I loved alwey, as after my konnynge,
And whan that I my lyf sholde forlete,
To me she cam, and bad me for to synge
This anthem verraily in my deyynge,
As ye han herd, and whan that I hadde songe,
Me thoughte she leyde a greyn upon my tonge:

Wherfore I synge, and synge I moot certeyn
In honour of that blisful mayden free,
Til fro my tonge oftaken is the greyn;
And afterward thus seyde she to me,
My litel child, now wol I fecche thee
Whan that the greyn is fro thy tonge ytake;
Be nat agast, I wol thee nat forsake.

THIS hooly monk, this abbot, hym meene I,
    His tonge outcaughte, and took awey
    the greyn,

And he yaf up the goost ful softely.
And whan this abbot hadde this wonder seyn,
His salte teeris trikled doun as reyn,
And gruf he fil, al plat upon the grounde,
And stille he lay as he had ben ybounde.

The covent eek lay on the pavement
Wepynge, and heryen Cristes mooder deere,
And after that they ryse, and forth been went,
And tooke awey this martir from his beere;
And in a tombe of marbul-stones cleere,
Enclosen they his litel body sweete:
Ther he is now, God leve us for to meete!

O yonge Hugh of Lyncoln, slayn also
With cursed Jewes, as it is notable,
For it is but a litel while ago;
Preye eek for us, we synful folk unstable,
That of his mercy, God so merciable,
On us his grete mercy multiplie
For reverence of his mooder, Marie.
Amen. Heere is ended the Prioresses Tale.

Bihoold the murye wordes of the Hoost to
Chaucer.✿✿

HAN seyd was al this miracle, every man
As sobre was, that wonder was to se,
Til that oure hooste japen tho bigan,
And thanne at erst he looked upon me,
And seyde thus: What man artow? quod he;
Thou lookest as thou woldest fynde an hare;
For evere upon the ground I se thee stare.

Approche neer, and looke up murily.
Now war yow, sires, and lat this man have place;
He in the waast is shape as wel as I;
This were a popet in an arm tenbrace
For any womman, smal and fair of face.
He semeth elvyssh by his contenaunce,
For unto no wight dooth he daliaunce.

Sey now somwhat, syn oother folk han sayd;
Telle us a tale of myrthe, and that anon.
🌿 Hooste, quod I, ne beth nat yvele apayd,
For oother tale certes kan I noon,
But of a rym I lerned longe agoon.
🌿 Ye, that is good, quod he, now shul we heere
Som deyntee thyng, methynketh by his cheere.

HEERE BIGYNNETH CHAUCERS TALE OF THOPAS ✿✿✿✿
The first fit.

ISTETH, lordes, in good entent,
And I wol telle verrayment
Of myrthe and of solas;
Al of a knyght was fair and gent
In bataille and in tourney-
ment,
His name was sire Thopas.
Yborn he was in fer contree,
In Flaundres, al biyonde the see,
At Poperyng, in the place;
His fader was a man ful free,
And lord he was of that contree,
As it was Goddes grace.
Sire Thopas wax a doghty swayn;
Whit was his face as payndemayn,
His lippes rede as rose;
His rode is lyk scarlet in grayn,
And I yow telle in good certayn
He hadde a semely nose.
His heer, his berd, was lyk saffroun,
That to his girdel raughte adoun;
His shoon of cordewane.
Of Brugges were his hosen broun,
His robe was of syklatoun
That coste many a jane.
He koude hunte at wilde deer,
And ride an haukyng for riveer
With grey goshauk on honde;
Therto he was a good archeer,
Of wrastlyng was ther noon his peer,
Ther any ram shal stonde.
Ful many a mayde, bright in bour,
They moorne for hym, paramour,

Whan hem were bet to slepe;
But he was chaast, and no lechour,
And sweete as is the brembul-flour
That bereth the red hepe.
AND so bifel upon a day
For sothe, as I yow telle may,
Sire Thopas wolde out ride;
He worth upon his steede gray,
And in his hand a launcegay,
A long swerd by his side.
He priketh thurgh a fair forest,
Therinne is many a wilde best,
Ye, bothe bukke and hare;
And as he priketh north and est
I telle it yow, hym hadde almest
Bitidde a sory care.
Ther spryngen herbes grete and smale,
The lycorys and cetewale,
And many a clowe-gylofre;
And notemuge to putte in ale,
Wheither it be moyste or stale,
Or for to leye in cofre.
The briddes synge, it is no nay,
The sparhauk and the papejay,
That joye it was to heere;
The thrustelcok made eek his lay,
The wodedowve upon the spray
She sang ful loude and cleere.
Sire Thopas fil in love-longynge
Al whan he herde the thrustel synge,
And pryked as he were wood;
His faire steede in his prikynge
So swatte that men myghte hym wrynge,
His sydes were al blood.
Sire Thopas eek so wery was
For prikyng on the softe gras,

61

So fiers was his corage,
That doun he leyde him in that plas
To make his steede som solas,
And yaf hym good forage.
O seinte Marie, benedicite!
What eyleth this love at me
To bynde me so soore?
Me dremed al this nyght, pardee,
An Elf-queene shal my lemman be
And slepe under my goore.
An Elf-queene wol I love, ywis,
For in this world no womman is
Worthy to be my make
In towne;
Alle othere wommen I forsake,
And to an Elf-queene I me take
By dale and eek by downe.

INTO his sadel he clamb anoon,
And priketh over stile and stoon
An Elf-queene for tespye;
Til he so longe hadde riden and goon
That he foond, in a pryve woon,
The contree of fairye
So wilde;
For in that contree was ther noon
That to him dorste ryde or goon,
Neither wyf ne childe;
Til that ther cam a greet geaunt,
His name was sire Olifaunt,
A perilous man of dede;
He seyde, Child, by Termagaunt!
But if thou prike out of myn haunt,
Anon I sle thy steede
With mace!
Heere is the queene of Fayerye,
With harpe, and pipe, and symphonye,
Dwellynge in this place.

THE child seyde, Also moote I thee!
Tomorwe wol I meete thee
Whan I have myn armoure.
And yet I hope, par ma fay,
That thou shalt with this launcegay
Abyen it ful sowre;
Thy mawe
Shal I percen, if I may,
Er it be fully pryme of day,
For heere thow shalt be slawe.
Sire Thopas drow abak ful faste;
This geant at hym stones caste
Out of a fel staf-slynge;
But faire escapeth sire Thopas;
And al it was thurgh Goddes gras,
And thurgh his fair berynge.

YET listeth, lordes, to my tale
Murier than the nightyngale,
For now I wol yow rowne
How sir Thopas with sydes smale,
Prikyng over hill and dale,
Is comen agayn to towne.
His murie men comanded he
To make hym bothe game and glee,
For nedes moste he fighte
With a geaunt with hevedes three,

62

For paramour and jolitee
Of oon that shoon ful brighte.
Do come, he seyde, my mynstrales,
And geestours for to tellen tales,
Anon in myn armynge;
Of romances that ben roiales
Of popes and of cardinales
And eek of love-likynge.
They fette hym first the sweete wyn,
And mede eek in a mazelyn,
And roial spicerye
Of gyngebreed that was ful fyn,
And lycorys, and eek comyn,
With sugre that is so trye.
He dide next his white leere
Of clooth of lake, fyn and cleere,
A breech and eek a sherte;
And next his sherte an aketoun,
And over that an haubergeoun
For percynge of his herte;
And over that a fyn hawberk,
Was al ywroght of Jewes werk,
Ful strong it was of plate;
And over that his cote-armour,
As whit as is a lilye-flour,
In which he wol debate.
His sheeld was al of gold so reed,
And therinne was a bores heed,
A charbocle bisyde;
And there he swoor, on ale and breed,
How that the geaunt shal be deed,
Bityde what bityde!
His jambeux were of quyrboilly,
His swerdes shethe of yvory,
His helm of laton bright;
His sadel was was of rewel-boon;
His brydel as the sonne shoon,
Or as the moone light.
His spere it was of fyn ciprees,
That bodeth werre, and nothyng pees,
The heed ful sharpe ygrounde;
His steede was al dappel-gray,
It gooth an ambil in the way
Ful softely and rounde
In londe.
Loo, lordes myne, heere is a fit!
If ye wol any moore of it,
To telle it wol I fonde.

The Second fit.

NOW holde youre mouth, par charitee,
Bothe knyght and lady free,
And herkneth to my spelle;
Of batailles and of chivalry,
And of ladyes love-drury,
Anon I wol yow telle.
Men speken of romances of prys,
Of Horn child, & of Ypotys,
Of Bevis and of sir Gy,
Of sir Lybeux and Pleyn-damour;
But sir Thopas, he bereth the flour
Of roial chivalry!

His goode steede al he bistrood,
And forth upon his wey he rood,
As sparcle out of the bronde;
Upon his creest he bar a tour,
And therinne stiked a lilie flour,
God shilde his cors fro shonde!
And for he was a knyght auntrous,
He nolde slepen in noon hous,
But liggen in his hoode;
His brighte helm was his wonger,
And by hym baiteth his dextrer
Of herbes fyne and goode.
Hymself drank water of the well,
As dide the knyght sire Percyvell,
So worthy under wede;
Til on a day......

Heere the Hoost stynteth Chaucer of his Tale
of Thopas.❧ ❧

NA moore of this, for Goddes
dignitee!
Quod oure Hooste, for thou
makest me
So wery of thy verray lewednesse
That, also wisly God my soule
blesse,
Min eres aken of thy drasty speche.
Now swich a rym the devel I biteche!
This may wel be rym dogerel, quod he.
❦Why so? quod I; why wiltow lette me
Moore of my tale than another man,
Syn that it is the beste ryme I kan?
❦By God, quod he, for pleynly at a word,
Thy drasty rymyng is nat worth a toord;
Thou doost noght elles but despendest
tyme;
Sire, at o word, thou shalt no lenger ryme.

Lat se wher thou kanst tellen aught in geeste
Or telle in prose somwhat, at the leeste,
In which ther be som murthe, or som
doctryne.
❦Gladly, quod I, by Goddes sweete pyne!
I wol yow telle a litel thyng in prose
That oghte liken yow, as I suppose,
Or elles, certes, ye been to daungerous.
It is a moral tale vertuous,
Al be it told somtyme in sondry wyse
Of sundry folk, as I shal yow devyse.
As thus; ye woot that every Evaungelist,
That telleth us the peyne of Jhesu Crist
Ne seith nat al thyng as his felawe dooth;
But nathelees, hir sentence is al sooth,
And alle acorden as in hire sentence,
Al be ther in hir tellyng difference;
For somme of hem seyn moore, and somme
seyn lesse,
Whan they his pitous passioun expresse,
I meene of Marke, Mathew, Luc and John;
But doutelees hir sentence is al oon.
Therfore, lordynges alle, I yow biseche,
If that ye thynke I varie as in my speche,
As thus, though that I telle somwhat moore
Of proverbes, than ye han herd bifoore,
Comprehended in this litel tretys heere,
To enforce with theffect of my mateere;
And though I nat the same wordes seye,
As ye han herd, yet to yow alle I preye,
Blameth me nat; for as in my sentence
Ye shul not fynden moche difference
Fro the sentence of this tretys lyte
After the which this murye tale I write.
And therfore herkneth what that I shal seye,
And lat me tellen al my tale, I preye.
Explicit.

HEERE BIGYNNETH CHAUCERS TALE OF MELIBEE.❧ ❧ ❧

A YONG man called
Melibeus, myghty &
riche, bigat upon his
wyf, that called was
Prudence, a dogh-
ter which that call-
ed was Sophie ❧
Upon a day bifel,
that he for his des-
port is went into the
feeldes, hym to pleye; his wyf and eek his
doghter hath he left inwith his hous, of
which the dores weren fast yshette. Thre
of his olde foos han it espyed, and setten
laddres to the walles of his hous, and by
wyndowes been entred, & betten his wyf,
and wounded his doghter with fyve mortal
woundes in fyve sondry places; this is to
seyn, in hir feet, in hire handes, in hir erys,
in hir nose, & in hire mouth; and leften hire
for deed, and wenten awey.

WHAN Melibeus retourned was into his hous, & saugh al this meschief, he, lyk a mad man, rentynge
his clothes, gan to wepe & crie. Prudence,
his wyf, as ferforth as she dorste, bisoghte
hym of his wepyng for to stynte; but nat
forthy he gan to crie & wepen evere lenger
the moore.

THIS noble wyf Prudence remembred hire upon the sentence of O-
vide, in his book that cleped is The
Remedie of Love, whereas he seith ❧ He
is a fool that destourbeth the mooder to
wepen in the deeth of hire child, til she have
wept hir fille, as for a certein tyme; & thanne
shal man doon his diligence with amyable
wordes hire to reconforte, and preyen hire
of hir wepyng for to stynte ❧ For which resoun this noble wyf Prudence suffred hir
housbonde for to wepe & crie as for a certein space; and whan she saugh hir tyme,

she seyde hym in this wise: Allas, my lord, quod she, why make ye youreself fro to be lyk a fool? forsothe it aperteneth nat to a wys man to maken swiche a sorwe. Youre doghter, with the grace of God, shal war/ isshe and escape; and, al were it so that she right now were deed, ye ne oughte nat, as for hir deeth, youreself to destroye. Senek seith, ☙ The wise man shal nat take to greet disconfort for the deeth of his children, but certes, he sholde suffren it in pacience as wel as he abideth the deeth of his owene propre persone.

THIS Melibeus answerde anon, and seyde, What man, quod he, sholde of his wepyng stente that hath so greet a cause for to wepe? Jhesu Crist, oure Lord, hymself wepte for the deeth of Lazarus hys freend. ☙ Prudence answerde, Certes, wel I woot, attempree wepyng is nothyng deffended to him that sorweful is amonges folk in sorwe, but it is rather graunted hym to wepe. The Apostle Paul unto the Rom/ ayns writeth, ☙ Man shal rejoyse with hem that maken joye, and wepen with swich folk as wepen. ☙ But though attempree wep/ yng be ygraunted, outrageous wepyng cer/ tes is deffended. Mesure of wepyng sholde be considered, after the loore that techeth us Senek. ☙ Whan that thy frend is deed, quod he, lat nat thyne eyen to moyste been of teeris, ne to muche drye; although the teeris come to thyne eyen, lat hem nat falle; and whan thou hast forgoon thy freend, do diligence to gete another freend; & this is moore wysdom than for to wepe for thy freend which that thou hast lorn; for ther/ inne is no boote. ☙ And therfore, if ye gov/ erne yow by sapience, put awey sorwe out of youre herte. Remembre you that Jhesus Syrak seith. ☙ A man that is joyous and glad in herte, it hym conserveth florissynge in his age; but soothly sorweful herte mak/ eth his bones drye. ☙ He seith eek thus: That sorwe in herte sleeth ful many a man. Salomon seith, ☙ That right as motthes in the shepes flees anoyeth to the clothes, and the smale wormes to the tree, right so an/ oyeth sorwe to the herte. ☙ Wherfore us oghte as wel in the deeth of oure children as in the losse of oure goodes temporels, have pacience.

REMEMBRE yow upon the pacient Job. Whan he hadde lost his children and his temporeel substance, and in his body endured and receyved ful many a grevous tribulacion; yet seyde he thus. ☙ Oure Lord hath sente it me; our Lord hath biraft it me; right as oure Lord hath wold, right so it is doon; blessed be the name of oure Lord. ☙ To thise foreseide thynges answerde Melibeus unto his wyf Prudence: Alle thy wordes, quod he, been sothe, and

64

therwith profitable; but trewely myn herte is troubled with this sorwe so grevously, that I noot what to doon. ☙ Lat calle, quod Prudence, thy trewe freendes alle, & thy ly/ nage whiche that been wise. Telleth youre cas and herkneth what they seye in con/ seillyng, & yow governe after hire sentence. Salomon seith, Werk alle thy thynges by conseil, and thou shalt never repente.

THANNE, by the conseil of his wyf Prudence, this Melibeus leet callen a greet congregacioun of folk; as sur/ giens, phisiciens, olde folk and yonge, and somme of his olde enemys reconsiled, as by hir semblaunt, to his love and into his grace; and therwithal ther coomen somme of his neighebores that diden hym rever/ ence moore for drede than for love, as it happeth ofte. Ther coomen also ful many subtille flatereres, & wise advocats lerned in the lawe.

AND whan this folk togidre assem/ bled weren, this Melibeus in sor/ weful wise shewed hem his cas; & by the manere of his speche it semed wel that in herte he baar a crueel ire, redy to doon vengeance upon his foos, & sodeyn/ ly desired that the werre sholde bigynne, but nathelees, yet axed he here conseil upon this matiere.

A SURGIEN, by licence and assent of swich as weren wise, uproos and to Melibeus seyde as ye may heere: Sire, quod he, as to us surgiens aperteneth that we do to every wight the beste that we kan, wheras we been withholde, and to oure pa/ cients that we do no damage; wherfore it happeth, many tyme & ofte, that whan twey men han everich wounded oother, oon same surgien heeleth hem bothe; wherfore unto oure art it is nat pertinent to norice werre, ne parties to supporte. But certes, as to the warisshynge of youre doghter, albeit so that she perilously be wounded, we shullen do so ententif bisynesse fro day to nyght, that with the grace of God she shal be hool and sound as soone as is possible.

ALMOOST right in the same wise the phisiciens answerden, save that they seyden a fewe woordes moore; That right as maladies been cured by hir contra/ ries, right so shul men warisshe werre by vengeaunce.

HIS neighebores, ful of envye, his feyn/ ed freendes that semeden reconsiled, and his flatereres, maden semblant of wepyng, and empeireden and agreggeden muchel of this matiere, in preisynge greetly Melibee, of myght, of power, of richesse, and of freendes, despisynge the power of his adversaries, and seiden outrely that he anon sholde wreken hym on his foos, and bigynne werre.

A PROOS thanne an advocat that was wys, by leve & by conseil of othere that were wise, & seide: Lordynges, the nede for which we been assembled in this place is a ful hevy thyng, and an heigh matiere, bycause of the wrong and of the wikkednesse that hath be doon, and eek by resoun of the grete damages that in tyme comynge been possible to fallen for this same cause; and eek by resoun of the grete richesse & power of the parties bothe; for the whiche resouns it were a ful greet peril to erren in this matiere. Wherfore, Melibeus, this is oure sentence. We conseille yow aboven alle thyng, that right anon thou do thy diligence in kepynge of thy propre persone, in swich a wise that thou ne wante noon espie ne wacche, thy persone for to save. And after that we conseille, that in thyn hous thou sette suffisant garnisoun, so that they may as wel thy body as thyn hous defende. But certes, for to moeve werre, or sodeynly for to doon vengeaunce, we may nat demen in so litel tyme that it were profitable. Wherfore we axen leyser and espace to have deliberacioun in this cas to deme. For the commune proverbe seith thus, He that soone deemeth, soone shal repente. And eek men seyn that thilke juge is wys, that soone understondeth a matiere and juggeth by leyser; for albeit so that alle tarying be anoyful, algates it is nat to repreve in yevynge of juggement, ne in vengeance-takyng, whan it is suffisant & resonable; and that shewed oure Lord Jhesu Crist by ensample; for whan that the womman that was taken in avowtrie was broght in his presence, to knowen what sholde be doon with hire persone, albeit so that he wiste wel hymself what that he wolde answere, yet ne wolde he nat answere sodeynly, but he wolde have deliberacioun, and in the ground he wroot twies. And by thise causes we axen deliberacioun, and we shal thanne, by the grace of God, conseille thee thyng that shal be profitable.

UP stirten thanne the yong folk atones, & the mooste partie of that compaignye han scorned the olde wise men, & bigonnen to make noyse, and seyden: that Right so as whil that iren is hoot, men sholden smyte, right so, men sholde wreken hir wronges while that they been fresshe and newe. And with loud voys they criden, Werre! werre!

UPROOS tho oon of thise olde wise, & with his hand made contenaunce that men sholde holden hem stille, and yeven hym audience. Lordynges, quod he, there is ful many a man that crieth Werre! werre! that woot ful litel what werre amounteth. Werre at his bigynnyng hath so greet an entryng and so large, that every wight may entre whan hym liketh, & lightly fynde werre; but certes, what ende that shal therof bifalle, it is nat light to knowe. For soothly, whan that werre is ones bigonne, ther is ful many a child unborn of his mooder, that shal sterve yong bycause of that ilke werre, or elles lyve in sorwe & dye in wrecchednesse; and therfore, er that any werre bigynne, men moste have greet conseil & greet deliberacioun. And whan this olde man wende to enforcen his tale by resons, wel ny alle atones bigonne they to rise for to breken his tale, and beden hym ful ofte his wordes for to abregge; for soothly, he that precheth to hem that listen nat heeren his wordes, his sermon hem anoieth. For Jhesus Syrak seith: that Musik in wepynge is a noyous thyng. This is to seyn; as muche availleth to speken bifore folk to whiche his speche anoyeth, as doth to synge biforn hym that wepeth. And whan this wise man saugh that hym wanted audience, al shamefast he sette hym doun agayn. For Salomon seith, Theras thou ne mayst have noon audience, enforce thee nat to speke.

I SEE wel, quod this wise man, that the commune proverbe is sooth, that Good conseil wanteth whan it is moost nede.

YET hadde this Melibeus in his conseil many folk that prively in his eere conseilled hym certeyn thyng, and conseilled hym the contrarie in general audience. Whan Melibeus hadde herde that the gretteste partie of his conseil weren accorded that he sholde maken werre, anoon he consented to hir conseillyng, and fully affermed hire sentence.

THANNE dame Prudence, whan that she saugh how that hir housbonde shoope hym for to wreken hym on his foos, & to bigynne werre, she in ful humble wise, whan she saugh hir tyme, seide to hym thise wordes: My lord, quod she, I yow biseche, as hertely as I dar and kan, ne haste yow nat to faste, & for alle guerdons, as yeveth me audience. For Piers Alfonce seith, Whoso that dooth to that oother good or harm, haste thee nat to quiten it; for in this wise thy freend wole abyde, and thyn enemy shal the lenger lyve in drede. The proverbe seith, He hasteth wel that wisely kan abyde; and in wikked haste is no profit.

THIS Melibee answerde unto his wyf Prudence: I purpose nat, quod he, to werke by thy conseil, for many causes & resouns; for certes, every wight wolde holde me thanne a fool. This is to seyn, if I, for thy conseillyng, wolde chaungen thynges that been ordeyned and affermed by so manye wyse. Secoundly, I seye that alle wommen been wikke, & noon good of hem alle; for ⸿ Of a thousand men, seith Salamon, I foond o good man, but certes, of alle wommen, good womman foond I nevere⸿ And also, certes, if I governed me by thy conseil, it sholde seme that I hadde yeve to thee over me the maistrie; and God forbede that it so were! For Jhesus Syrak seith, That if the wyf have maistrie, she is contrarious to hir housbonde; and Salomon seith⸿ Nevere in thy lyf, to thy wyf, ne to thy child, ne to thy freend, ne yeve no power over thyself; for bettre it were that thy children aske of thy persone thynges that hem nedeth, than thou be thyself in the handes of thy children ⸿ And also, if I wolde werke by thy conseillyng, certes, my conseillyng moste somtyme be secree, til it were tyme that it moste be knowe, and this ne may noght be; for it is written ⸿ The janglerye of wommen can hiden thynges that they witten noght ⸿ Furthermore, the philosophre saith ⸿ In wikked conseyl wommen venquysshe men,⸿ And for thise resouns I ne ow nat usen thy conseil.

WHANNE dame Prudence, ful debonairly & with greet pacience, hadde herd al that hir housbonde liked for to seye, thanne axed she of hym licence for to speke, and seyde in this wise⸿ My lord, quod she, as to youre firste resoun, certes it may lightly been answered; for I seye that it is no folie to chaunge conseil whan the thyng is chaunged; or elles whan the thyng semeth ootherweyes than it was biforn. And mooreover I seye, that though ye han sworn and bihight to perfourne youre emprise, and nathelees ye weyve to perfourne thilke same emprise by juste cause, men sholde nat seyn therfore that ye were a lier ne forsworn. For the book seith that⸿ The wise man maketh no lesyng whan he turneth his corage to the bettre ⸿ And albeit so that youre emprise be establissed & ordeyned by greet multitude of folk, yet thar ye nat accomplice thilke same ordinaunce but yow like; for the trouthe of thynges & the profit been rather founden in fewe folk that been wise and ful of resoun, than by greet multitude of folk, ther every man crieth and clatereth what that hym liketh; soothly, swich multitude is nat honeste.

AS to the seconde resoun, whereas ye seyn that Alle wommen been wikke; save youre grace, certes ye despisen alle wommen in this wyse; & He that alle despiseth alle displeseth, as seith the book; and Senec seith, that whoso wole have sapience, shal no man despreise; but he shal

66

gladly techen the science that he kan, withouten presumpcioun or pride; and swiche thynges as he nought ne kan, he shal nat been ashamed to lerne hem and enquere of lasse folk than hymself. And sire, that ther hath been many a good womman may lightly be preved; for certes, sire, oure Lord Jhesu Crist wolde nevere have descended to be born of a womman, if alle wommen hadden ben wikke. And after that, for the grete bountee that is in wommen, oure Lord Jhesu Crist, whan he was risen fro deeth to lyve, appeered rather to a womman than to his Apostles; & though that Salomon seith that He ne foond nevere womman good, it folweth nat therfore that alle womman ben wikke. For though that he ne foond no good womman, certes, ful many another man hath founden many a womman ful good and trewe. Or elles, peraventure, the entente of Salomon was this; that, as in sovereyn bountee, he foond no womman; this is to seyn, that ther is no wight that hath sovereyn bountee, save God allone; as he hymself recordeth in hys evaungelie. For ther nys no creature so good that hym ne wanteth somwhat of the perfeccioun of God, that is his maker.

YOURE thridde resoun is this; ye seyn, If ye governe yow by my conseil, it sholde seme that ye hadde yeve me the maistrie & the lordshipe over youre persone. Sire, save youre grace, it is nat so. For if it were so, that no man sholde be conseilled but oonly of hem that hadden lordshipe & maistrie of his persone, men wolden nat be conseilled so ofte: for soothly, thilke man that asketh conseil of a purpos, yet hath he free choys, wheither he wole werke by that conseil or noon.

AND as to youre fourthe resoun; ther ye seyn that The janglerie of wommen hath hyd thynges that they wiste noght, as who seith, that A womman kan nat hyde that she woot. Sire thise wordes been understonde of wommen that been jangleresses and wikked; of whiche wommen, men seyn that Thre thynges dryven a man out of his hous; that is to seyn, smoke, droppyng of reyn, and wikked wyves; & of swiche wommen seith Salomon, that It were bettre dwelle in desert, than with a womman that is riotous; and sire, by youre leve, that am nat I; for ye han ful ofte assayed my grete silence and my gret pacience; and eek how wel that I kan hyde and hele thynges that men oghte secreely to hyde.

AND soothly, as to youre fifthe resoun, whereas ye seyn that In wikked conseil wommen venquisshe men; God woot, thilke resoun stant heere in no stede. for, understoond now, ye asken conseil to do wikkednesse; and if ye wole werken wikkednesse, and youre wif restreyneth thilke wikked purpos and overcometh yow by resoun and by good counseil; certes youre wyf oghte rather to be preised than yblamed. Thus sholde ye understonde the philosophre that seith ☙ In wikked conseil wommen venquisshen hir housbondes.

AND theras ye blamen alle wommen and hir resouns, I shal shewe yow by manye ensamples, that many a womman hath ben ful good, and yet been; and hir conseils ful hoolsome and profitable. Eek som men han seyd that The conseillynge of wommen is outher to deere, or elles to litel of pris. But, albeit so that ful many a womman is badde, and hir conseil vile & noght worth, yet han men founde ful many a good womman, and ful discrete and wise in conseillynge.

LOO, Jacob, by good conseil of his mooder Rebekka, wan the benysoun of Ysaak his fader, and the lordshipe over alle his bretheren. Judith, by hire good conseil, delivered the citee of Bethulie, in which she dwelled, out of the handes of Olofernus, that hadde it biseged and wolde have al destroyed it. Abygail delivered Nabal hir housbonde fro David the kyng, that wolde have slayn hym, and apaysed the ire of the kyng by hir wit and by hir good conseillyng. Hester enhaunced greetly by hir good conseil the peple of God in the regne of Assuerus the kyng: and the same bountee in good conseillyng of many a good womman may men telle. And mooreover, whan oure Lord hadde creat Adam oure forme fader, he seyde in this wise: It is nat good to been a man alloone; make we to hym an helpe semblable to hymself.

HEERE may ye see, that if that wommen were nat goode, and hir conseils goode & profitable, oure Lord God of hevene wolde nevere han wroght hem, ne called hem help of man, but rather confusioun of man. And ther seyde oones a clerk in two vers ☙ What is bettre than gold? Jaspre. What is bettre than jaspre? Wisedoom. And what is bettre than wisedoom? Womman. And what is bettre than a good womman? Nothyng ☙ And sire, by manye of othre resouns may ye seen, that manye wommen been goode, & hir conseils goode & profitable. And therfore, sire, if ye wol triste to my conseil, I shal restoore yow youre doghter hool and sound. And eek I wol do to yow so muche, that ye shul have honour in this cause.

WHAN Melibee hadde herd the wordes of his wyf Prudence, he seyde thus: I see wel that the word of Salomon is sooth. He seith that Wordes that been spoken discreetly, by ordinaunce, been honycombes; for they yeven swetnesse to the soule, and hoolsomnesse to the body; and, wyf, bycause of thy sweete wordes, and eek for I have assayed & preved thy grete sapience and thy grete trouthe, I wol governe me by thy conseil in alle thyng.

NOW sire, quod dame Prudence, and syn ye vouchesauf to been governed by my conseil, I wol enforme yow how ye shul governe yourself in chesynge of youre conseillours. Ye shul first, in alle youre werkes mekely biseken to the heighe God that he wol be youre conseillour; & shapeth yow to swich entente, that he yeve yow conseil & confort, as taughte Thobie his sone ☙ At alle tymes thou shalt blesse God, and praye hym to dresse thy weyes; and looke that alle thy conseils been in hym for everemoore. ☙ Seint Jame eek seith ☙ If any of yow have nede of sapience, axe it of God. ☙ And afterward, thanne shul ye taken conseil of youreself and examyne wel youre thoghtes of swich thyng as yow thynketh that is best for youre profit; and thanne shul ye dryve fro youre herte thre thynges that been contrariouse to good conseil, that is to seyn, ire, coveitise, and hastifnesse.

FIRST, he that axeth conseil of hymself, certes he moste been withouten ire, for manye causes. The firste is this: he that hath greet ire and wrathe in hymself, he weneth alwey that he may do thyng that he may nat do. And secoundely, he that is irous and wrooth, he ne may nat wel deme; & he that may nat wel deme, may nat wel conseille. The thridde is this; that He that is irous & wrooth, as seith Senec, ne may nat speke but he blame thynges; & with his viciouse wordes he stireth oother folk to angre and to ire. And eek sire, ye moste dryve coveitise out of youre herte; for the apostle seith that Coveitise is roote of alle harmes; and trust wel that a coveitous man ne kan noght deme ne thynke, but oonly to fulfille the ende of his coveitise; and certes, that ne may nevere been accompliced; for evere the moore habundaunce that he hath of richesse, the moore he desireth. And sire, ye moste also dryve out of youre herte hastifnesse; for certes, ye ne may nat deeme for the beste a sodeyn thought that falleth in youre herte, but ye moste avyse yow on it ful ofte. for as ye herde biforn, the commune proverbe is this, that He that soone deemeth, soone repent-

eth. Sire, ye ne be nat alwey in lyke disposi/
cioun; for certes somthyng that somtyme
semeth to yow that it is good for to do, an/
other tyme it semeth to yow the contrarie.
WHAN ye han taken conseil of youreself, & han demed by good deliberacion swich thyng as you semyth best, thanne rede I yow, that ye kepe it secree. Biwrey nat youre conseil to no persone, but if so be that ye wenen siker/ ly that thurgh youre biwreyyng, youre con/ dicioun shal be to yow the moore profit/ able. for Jhesus Syrak seith. Neither to thy foo ne to thy frend discovere nat thy secree ne thy folie; for they wol yeve yow audience and lookynge and supportacioun in thy presence, and scorne thee in thyn ab/ sence. Another clerk seith, that Scarsly shaltou fynden any persone that may kepe conseil secreely.

THE book seith. Whil that thou kepest thy conseil in thyn herte, thou kepest it in thy prisoun: and whan thou biwreyest thy conseil to any wight, he holdeth thee in his snare. And therfore yow is bettre to hyde youre con/ seil in youre herte, than praye him to whom ye han biwreyed youre conseil, that he wole kepen it cloos & stille; for Seneca seith. If so be that thou ne mayst nat thyn owene conseil hyde, how darstou prayen any oo/ ther wight thy conseil secreely to kepe?

BUT nathelees, if thou wene sikerly that the biwreying of thy conseil to a persone wol make thy condicioun to stonden in the bettre plyt, thanne shaltou tellen hym thy conseil in this wise. first, thou shalt make no semblant wheither thee were levere pees or werre, or this or that, ne shewe hym nat thy wille and thyn entente; for trust wel, that comunly thise conseil/ lours been flatereres, namely the conseil/ lours of grete lordes; for they enforcen hem alwey rather to speken plesante wordes, en/ clynynge to the lordes lust, than wordes that been trewe or profitable. And therfore men seyn, that The riche man hath seeld good conseil but if he have it of hymself.

AND after that, thou shalt considere thy freendes & thyne enemys. And as touchynge thy freendes, thou shalt considere whiche of hem been moost feithful and moost wise, & eldest, & most approved in conseillyng; and of hem shalt thou aske thy conseil as the caas requireth.

I SEYE that first ye shul clepe to youre conseil youre freendes that been trewe, for Salomon seith that Right as the herte of a man deliteth in savour that is soote, right so the conseil of trewe freendes yeveth swetenesse to the soule. He seith also. Ther may nothyng be likned to the trewe freend. for certes,

68

gold ne silver beth nat so muche worth as the goode wyl of a trewe freend. And eek, he seith that. A trewe freend is a strong deffense; whoso that hym fyndeth, certes, he fyndeth a greet tresour.

THANNE shul ye eek considere, if that youre trewe freendes been discrete and wise, for the book seith. Axe alwey thy conseil of hem that been wise. And by this same resoun shul ye clepen to youre conseil of youre freendes that been of age, swiche as han seyn and been expert in manye thynges, & been approved in con/ seillynges; for the book seith that In the olde men is the sapience, & in longe tyme the prudence. And Tullius seith: that Grete thynges ne been nat ay accompliced by strengthe, ne by delivernesse of body, but by good conseil, by auctoritee of persones, and by science; the whiche thre thynges ne been nat fieble by age, but certes, they en/ forcen & encreescen day by day. And thanne shul ye kepe this for a general reule. first shul ye clepen to youre conseil a fewe of youre freendes that been especiale; for Salomon seith. Manye freendes have thou; but among a thousand, chese thee oon to be thy conseillour. for, albeit so that thou first ne telle thy conseil but to a fewe, thou mayst afterward telle it to mo folk, if it be nede. But looke alwey that thy con/ seillours have thilke thre condiciouns that I have seyd bifore; that is to seyn, that they be trewe, wise, and of oold experience. And werke nat alwey in every nede by oon coun/ seillour allone; for somtyme bihooveth it to been conseilled by manye; for Salomon seith. Salvacioun of thynges is wheras ther been manye conseillours.

NOW, sith I have toold yow of which folk ye sholde been counseilled, now wol I teche yow which conseil ye oghte to eschewe. first, ye shul eschue the con/ seillyng of fooles; for Salomon seith. Taak no conseil of a fool, for he ne kan noght conseille but after his owene lust and his affeccioun. The book seith: that The propretee of a fool is this. He trow/ eth lightly harm of every wight, & lightly troweth alle bountee in hymself. Thou shalt eek eschue the conseillyng of alle flatereres, swiche as enforcen hem rather to preise youre persone by flaterye, than for to telle yow the soothfastnesse of thynges.

THERFORE Tullius seith. A/ monges alle the pestilences that been in freendshipe the gretteste is flaterie. And therfore it is moore nede that thou eschue and drede flatereres than any oother peple. The book seith. Thou shalt rather drede and flee fro the sweete wordes of flaterynge preiseres, than fro the egre wordes of thy freend that seith thee thy sothes. Salomon seith: that The wordes of a flaterere is a snare to cacche with innocents He seith also, that He that speketh to his freend wordes of swetnesse & of plesaunce, setteth a net biforn his feet to cacche hym And therfore, seith Tullius Enclyne nat thyne eres to flatereres, ne taaketh no conseil of the wordes of flaterye And Caton seith Avyse thee wel, and eschue the wordes of swetnesse and of plesaunce.

AND eek thou shalt eschue the conseillyng of thyne old enemys that been reconsiled. The book seith: that No wight retourneth saufly into the grace of his olde enemy; and Isope seith Ne trust nat to hem to whiche thou hast had somtyme werre or enemytee, ne telle hem nat thy conseil And Seneca telleth the cause why It may nat be, seith he, that where greet fyr hath longe tyme endured, that ther ne dwelleth som vapour of warmnesse And therfore seith Salomon In thyn olde foo trust nevere for sikerly, though thyn enemy be reconsiled and maketh thee chiere of humylitee, and lowteth to thee with his heed, ne trust hym nevere; for certes, he maketh thilke feyned humilitee moore for his profit than for any love of thy persone; bycause that he deemeth to have victorie over thy persone by swich feyned contenance, the which victorie he myghte nat wynne by strif or werre. And Peter Alfonce seith Make no felawshipe with thyne olde enemys; for if thou do hem bountee, they wol perverten it into wikkednesse.

AND eek thou most eschue the conseillyng of hem that been thy servantz & beren thee greet reverence; for peraventure they doon it moore for drede than for love. And therfore seith a philosophre in this wise Ther is no wight parfitly trewe to hym that he to soore dredeth And Tullius seith Ther nys no myght so greet of any emperour, that longe may endure, but if he have moore love of the peple than drede.

THOU shalt also eschue the conseilling of folk that been dronkelewe; for they kan no conseil hyde. For Salomon seith Ther is no privetee ther as regneth dronkenesse Ye shul also han in suspect the conseillyng of swich folk as conseille yow a thyng prively, and conseille yow the contrarie openly; for Cassidorie seith: that It is a manere sleighte to hyndre, whan he sheweth to doon a thyng openly and werketh prively the contrarie.

THOU shalt also have in suspect the conseillyng of wikked folk; for the book seith The conseillyng of wikked folk is alwey ful of fraude And David seith Blisful is that man that hath nat folwed the conseillyng of shrewes Thou shalt also eschue the conseillyng of yong folk; for hir conseil is nat rype.

NOW sire, sith I have shewed yow of which folk ye shul take youre conseil, and of which folk ye shul folwe the conseil, now wol I teche yow how ye shal examyne youre conseil, after the doctrine of Tullius.

IN the examynynge thanne of youre conseillour, ye shul considere manye thynges. Alderfirst thou shalt considere, that in thilke thyng that thou purposest, & upon what thyng thou wolt have conseil, that verray trouthe be seyd and conserved; this is to seyn, telle trewely thy tale; for he that seith fals may nat wel be conseilled in that cas of which he lieth.

AND after this, thou shalt considere the thynges that acorden to that thou purposest for to do by thy conseillours, if resoun accorde therto; and eek, if thy myght may atteine therto; and if the moore part and the bettre part of thy conseillours acorde therto, or no. Thanne shaltou considere what thyng shal folwe after hir conseillyng; as hate, pees, werre, grace, profit, or damage; and manye othere thynges. And of alle thise thynges, thou shalt chese the beste, and weyve alle othere thynges. Thanne shaltow considere of what roote is engendred the matiere of thy conseil, and what fruyt it may conceyve and engendre. Thou shalt eek considere alle thise causes, fro whennes they been sprongen.

AND whan ye han examyned youre conseil as I have seyd, and which partie is the bettre and moore profitable, and hast approved it by manye wise folk and olde; thanne shaltou considere if thou mayst parfourne it and maken of it a good ende. For certes, resoun wol nat that any man sholde bigynne a thyng, but if he myghte parfourne it as hym oghte. Ne no wight sholde take upon hym so hevy a charge that he myghte nat bere it. For the proverbe seith He that to muche embraceth, distreyneth litel And Catoun seith Assay to do swich thyng as thou hast power to doon, lest that the charge oppresse thee so soore, that thee bihoveth to weyve thyng that thou hast bigonne And if so be that thou be in doute wheither thou mayst parfourne a thing or noon, chese rather to suffre than bigynne. And Piers Alphonce seith If thou hast myght to doon a thyng of which thou most repente thee, it is bettre Nay, than Ye This is to seyn, that thee is bettre holde thy tonge stille, than for to speke.

THANNE may ye understonde by strenger resons that if thou hast power to parfourne a werk of which thou shalt repente, thanne is it bettre that thou suffre than bigynne. Wel seyn they, that defenden every wight to assaye any thyng of which he is in doute, wheither he may parfourne it or no. And after, whan ye han examyned youre conseil, as I have seyd biforn, and knowen wel that ye may parfourne youre emprise, conferme it thanne sadly til it be at an ende.

NOW is it resoun & tyme that I shewe yow, whanne & wherfore that ye may chaunge youre conseillours withouten youre repreve. Soothly, a man may chaungen his purpos and his conseil if the cause cesseth, or whan a newe caas bitydeth; for the lawe seith: that Upon thynges that newely bityden bihoveth newe conseil. And Senec seith If thy conseil is comen to the eeris of thyn enemy, chaunge thy conseil Thou mayst also chaunge thy conseil if so be that thou fynde that, by errour or by oother cause, harm or damage may bityde. Also, if thy conseil be dishonest, or ellis cometh of dishoneste cause, chaunge thy conseil; for the lawes seyn: that Alle bihestes that been dishoneste been of no value; and eek, if it so be that it be inpossible, or may nat goodly be parfourned or kept.

AND take this for a general reule, that every conseil that is affermed so strongly that it may nat be chaunged, for no condicioun that may bityde, I seye that thilke conseil is wikked.

THIS Melibeus, whanne he hadde herd the doctrine of his wyf, dame Prudence, answerde in this wyse Dame, quod he, as yet in to this tyme ye han wel and covenably taught me as in general how I shal governe me in the chesynge and in the withholdynge of my conseillours. But now wolde I fayn that ye wolde condescende in especial, and telle me how liketh yow, or what semeth yow by oure conseillours that we han chosen in oure present nede.

MY lord, quod she, I biseke yow in al humblesse, that ye wol nat wilfully replie agayn my resouns, ne distempre youre herte, thogh I speke thyng that yow displese. For God woot that as in myn entente, I speke it for youre beste, for youre honour, & for youre profite eek; and soothly, I hope that youre benygnytee wol taken it in pacience. Trusteth me wel, quod she, that youre conseil as in this caas ne sholde nat, as to speke properly, be called a conseillyng, but a mocioun or a moevyng of folye; in which conseil ye han erred in many a sondry wise.

FIRST and forward, ye han erred in thassemblynge of youre conseillours; for ye sholde first have cleped a fewe folk to youre conseil, & after ye myghte han shewed it to mo folk, if it hadde been nede. But certes, ye han sodeynly cleped to youre conseil a greet multitude of peple, ful chargeant & ful anoyous for to heere. Also, ye han erred, for thereas ye sholden oonly have cleped to youre conseil youre trewe frendes olde & wise, ye han ycleped straunge folk, and yong folk, false flatereres and enemys reconsiled, & folk that doon yow reverence withouten love. And eek also ye have erred, for ye han broght with yow to youre conseil, ire, coveitise, and hastifnesse; the whiche thre thinges been contrariouse to every conseil honeste and profitable; the whiche thre ye han nat anientissed or destroyed hem, neither in youreself ne in youre conseillours, as yow oghte. Ye han erred also, for ye han shewed to youre conseillours youre talent and youre affeccioun to make werre anon, and for to do vengeance. They han espied by youre wordes to what thyng ye been enclyned; and therfore han they rather conseilled yow to youre talent than to youre profit.

YE han erred also, for it semeth that it suffiseth to han been conseilled by thise conseillours oonly, & with litel avys; whereas in so greet and so heigh a nede, it hadde been necessarie mo conseillours, and moore deliberacioun to parfourne youre emprise.

YE han erred also, for ye han nat examyned youre conseil in the forseyde manere, ne in due manere as the caas requireth. Ye han erred also, for ye han nat maked no divisioun bitwixe youre conseillours; this is to seyn, bitwixen youre trewe freendes & youre feyned conseillours; ne ye han nat knowe the wil of youre trewe freendes, olde and wise; but ye han cast alle hire wordes in an hochepot, and enclyned youre herte to the moore part and to the gretter nombre; and there been ye condescended. And, sith ye woot wel that men shal alwey fynde a gretter nombre of fooles than of wise men, and therfore the conseils that been at congregaciouns and multitudes of folk, thereas men take moore reward to the nombre than to the sapience of persones, ye see wel that in swiche conseillynges fooles han the maistrie.

MELIBEUS answerde agayn, and seyde I graunte wel that I have erred; but thereas thou hast toold me heerbiforn, that he nys nat to blame that chaungeth his conseillours in certein caas, and for certeine juste causes, I am al redy to chaunge my conseillours, right as thow wolt devyse. The proverbe seith: that for to do synne is mannyssh, but certes, for to persevere longe in synne is werk of the devel.

TO this sentence answerde anon dame Prudence, and seyde ◊ Exameneth, quod she, youre conseil and lat us see the whiche of hem han spoken most resonably, and taught yow best conseil. And for asmuche as that the examynacioun is necessarie, lat us bigynne at the surgiens & at the phisiciens that first speeken in this matiere. I sey yow, that the surgiens and phisiciens han seyd yow in youre conseil discreetly, as hem oughte; & in hir speche seyden ful wisely, that to the office of hem aperteneth to doon to every wight honour and profit, and no wight for to anoye; and, in hir craft, to doon greet diligence unto the cure of hem whiche that they han in hir governaunce. And sire, right as they han answered wisely and discreetly, right so rede I that they been heighly & sovereynly guerdoned for hir noble speche; & eek for they sholde do the moore ententif bisynesse in the curacioun of youre doghter deere. For, albeit so that they been youre freendes, therfore shal ye nat suffren that they serve yow for noght; but ye oghte the rather guerdone hem and shewe hem youre largesse.

AND as touchynge the proposicioun which that the phisiciens entreteden in this caas; this is to seyn, that in maladies, that oon contrarie is warisshed by another contrarie; I wolde fayn knowe how ye understonde thilke text, and what is youre sentence.

CERTES, quod Melibeus, I understonde it in this wise: that right as they han doon me a contrarie, right so sholde I doon hem another. For right as they han venged hem on me and doon me wrong, right so shal I venge me upon hem, and doon hem wrong; and thanne have I cured oon contrarie by another.

LO, lo! quod dame Prudence, how lightly is every man enclined to his owene desir and to his owene plesaunce! Certes, quod she, the wordes of the phisiciens ne sholde nat han been understonden in thys wise. For certes, wikkednesse is nat contrarie to wikkednesse, ne vengeaunce to vengeaunce, ne wrong to wrong, but they been semblable; & therfore, o vengeaunce is nat warisshed by another vengeaunce, ne o wroong by another wroong; but everich of hem encreesceth & aggreggeth oother.

BUT certes, the wordes of the phisiciens sholde been understonden in this wise; for good and wikked-

f 4

nesse been two contraries, and pees and werre, vengeaunce and suffraunce, discord and accord, and manye othere thynges. But certes, wikkednesse shal be warisshed by goodnesse, discord by accord, werre by pees, and so forth of othere thynges. And heerto accordeth Seint Paul the Apostle in manye places ◊ He seith; Ne yeldeth nat harm for harm, ne wikked speche for wikked speche; but do wel to hym that dooth thee harm, & blesse hym that seith to thee harm ◊ And in manye othere places he amonesteth pees and accord.

BUT now wol I speke to yow of the conseil which that was yeven to yow by the men of lawe and the wise folk, that seyden alle by oon accord, as ye han herd bifore; that over alle thynges, ye sholde doon your diligence to kepen youre persone & to warnestoore youre hous; and seyden also, that in this caas ye oghten for to werken ful avysely and with greet deliberacioun ◊ And sire, as to the firste point, that toucheth to the kepyng of youre persone; ye shul understonde that he that hath werre shal everemoore mekely and devoutly preyen biforn alle thynges, that Jhesus Crist of his grete mercy wol han hym in his proteccioun & been his sovereyn helpyng at his nede. For certes, in this world ther is no wight that may be conseilled ne kept suffisantly withouten the kepynge of oure Lord Jhesu Crist.

TO this sentence accordeth the prophete David, that seith, ◊ If God ne kepe the citee, in ydel waketh he that it kepeth ◊ Now sire, thanne shul ye committe the kepyng of youre persone to youre trewe freendes that been approved and yknowe; and of hem shul ye axen helpe, youre persone for to kepe; for Catoun seith ◊ If thou hast nede of help, axe it of thy freendes; for ther nys noon so good a phisicien as thy trewe freend.

AND after this, thanne shul ye kepe yow fro alle straunge folk, and fro lyeres, & have alwey in suspect hire compaignye; for Piers Alfonce seith, ◊ Ne taak no compaignye by the weye of a straunge man, but if so be that thou have knowe hym of a lenger tyme. And if so be that he be falle into thy compaignye, paraventure, withouten thyn assent, enquere thanne as subtilly as thou mayst, of his conversacioun, and of his lyf bifore, and feyne thy wey. Seye that thou goost thider as thou wolt nat go; & if he bereth a spere, hoold thee on the right syde, and if he bere a swerd, hoold thee on the lift syde ◊ And after this, thanne shul ye kepe yow wisely from all swich manere peple as I have seyd bifore, and hem and hir conseil eschewe.

71

AND after this, thanne shul ye kepe yow in swich manere, that for any presumpcioun of youre strengthe, that ye ne dispise nat ne acounte nat the myght of youre adversarie so litel, that ye lete the kepyng of youre persone for youre presumpcioun; for every wys man dredeth his enemy; and Salomon seith, Weleful is he that of alle hath drede; for certes, he that thurgh the hardynesse of his herte, & thurgh the hardynesse of hymself, hath to greet presumpcioun, hym shal yvel bityde. Thanne shul ye everemoore countrewayte embusshements & alle espiaille. For Senec seith: that The wise man that dredeth harmes escheweth harmes; ne he ne falleth into perils that perils escheweth. And, albeit so that it seme that thou art in siker place, yet shaltow alwey do thy diligence in kepynge of thy persone; this is to seyn, ne be nat necligent to kepe thy persone; nat oonly fro thy gretteste enemys, but fro thy leeste enemy. Senek seith A man that is wel avysed, he dredeth his leeste enemye. Ovyde seith: that The litel wesele wol slee the grete bole and the wilde hert. And the book seith A litel thorn may prikke a greet kyng ful soore; and an hound wol holde the wilde boor.

BUT nathelees, I sey nat thou shalt be so coward, that thou doute ther wher as is no drede. The book seith: that Somme folk han greet lust to deceyve, but yet they dreden hem to be deceyved. Yet shaltou drede to been empoisoned, & kepe yow from the compaignye of scorneres; for the book seith With scorneres make no compaignye, but flee hire wordes as venym.

NOW as to the seconde point; whereas youre wise conseillours conseilled yow to warnestoore youre hous with gret diligence, I wolde fayn knowe, how that ye understonde thilke wordes, and what is youre sentence.

MELIBEUS answerde and seyde Certes, I understande it in this wise: That I shal warnestoore myn hous with toures, swiche as han castelles and othere manere edifices, and armure & artelries, by whiche thynges I may my persone & myn hous so kepen & defenden, that myne enemys shul been in drede myn hous for to approche.

TO this sentence answerde anon Prudence Warnestooryng, quod she, of heighe toures and of grete edifices appertaineth somtyme to pryde; and eek men make heigh toures and grete edifices with grete costages and with greet travaille; and whan that they been accompliced, yet be they nat worth a stree, but if they be defended by trewe freendes that been olde &

wise. And understoond wel, that the gretteste and strongeste garnyson that a riche man may have, as wel to kepen his persone as his goodes, is that he be biloved amonges hys subgets and with his neighebores; for thus seith Tullius: that Ther is a manere garnysoun that no man may venquysse ne disconfite, and that is, a lord to be biloved of his citezeins and of his peple.

NOW sire, as to the thridde point; whereas youre olde and wise conseillours seyden, that yow ne oghte nat sodeynly ne hastily proceden in this nede, but that yow oghte purveyen and apparaillen yow in this caas with greet diligence and greet deliberacioun; trewely, I trowe that they seyden right wisely & right sooth. For Tullius seith In every nede, er thou bigynne it, apparaille thee with greet diligence Thanne seye I, that in vengeance takyng, in werre, in bataille, and in warnestooryng, er thow bigynne, I rede that thou apparaille thee therto, and do it with greet deliberacioun; for Tullius seith that Longe apparaillyng biforn the bataille maketh short victorie And Cassidorus seith The garnyson is stronger whan it is longe tyme avysed.

BUT now lat us speken of the conseil that was accorded by youre neighebores, swiche as doon yow reverence withouten love, youre olde enemys reconsiled, youre flatereres, that conseilled yow certeyne thynges prively, and openly conseilleden yow the contrarie; the yonge folk also, that conseilleden yow to venge yow, and make werre anon. And certes, sire, as I have seyd biforn, ye han greetly erred to han cleped swich manere folk to youre conseil; which conseillours been ynogh repreved by the resouns aforeseyd.

BUT nathelees, lat us now descende to the special. Ye shuln first procede after the doctrine of Tullius. Certes, the trouthe of this matiere, or of this conseil, nedeth nat diligently enquere; for it is wel wist whiche they been that han doon to yow this trespas and vileynye, and how manye trespassours, and in what manere they han to yow doon al this wrong and al this vileynye. And after this, thanne shul ye examyne the seconde condicioun which that the same Tullius addeth in this matiere. For Tullius put a thyng which that he clepeth Consentynge, this is to seyn; who been they, and how manye, and whiche been they, that consenteden to thy conseil, in thy wilfulnesse to doon hastif vengeance. And lat us considere also who been they, & how manye been they, & whiche been they, that consenteden to youre adversaries And certes, as to the firste poynt, it is wel known which folk been they that consenteden to youre hastif wilfulnesse; for trewely, alle tho that conseilleden yow to maken sodeyn werre, ne been nat youre freendes. LAT us now considere whiche been they that ye holde so greetly youre freendes as to youre persone; for albeit so that ye be myghty and riche, certes, ye ne been nat but allone. For certes, ye ne han no child but a doghter; ne ye ne han bretheren, ne cosyns germayns, ne noon oother neigh kynrede, wherfore that youre enemys, for drede, sholde stinte to plede with yow, or to destroye youre persone. Ye knowen also, that youre richesses mooten been dispended in diverse parties; and whan that every wight hath his part, they ne wollen taken but litel reward to venge thy deeth. But thyne enemys been thre, and they han manie children, bretheren, cosyns, and oother ny kynrede; & though so were that thou haddest slayn of hem two or thre, yet dwellen ther ynowe to wreken hir deeth, and to sle thy persone. And though so be that youre kynrede be moore siker and stedefast than the kyn of youre adversarie, yet nathelees, youre kynrede nys but a fer kynrede; they been but litel syb to yow, and the kyn of youre enemys been ny syb to hem; and certes, as in that, hir condicioun is bet than youres.

THANNE lat us considere also of the conseillyng of hem that conseilleden yow to taken sodeyn vengeaunce, wheither it accorde to resoun. And certes, ye knowe wel Nay. For as by right & resoun, ther may no man taken vengeance on no wight, but the juge that hath the jurisdiccioun of it, whan it is graunted hym to take thilke vengeance, hastily or attemprely, as the lawe requireth. And yet mooreover, of thilke word that Tullius clepeth Consentynge, thou shalt considere if thy myght and thy power may consenten and suffise to thy wilfulnesse and to thy conseillours. And certes, thou mayst wel seyn that Nay. For sikerly, as for to speke proprely, we may do nothyng, but oonly swich thyng as we may doon rightfully; and certes, rightfully ne mowe ye take no vengeance, as of youre propre auctoritee.

THANNE mowe ye seen that youre power ne consenteth nat ne accordeth nat with youre wilfulnesse.

LAT us now examyne the thridde point, that Tullius clepeth Consequent. Thou shalt understonde that the vengeance that thou purposest for to take is the consequent; & therof folweth another vengeaunce, peril, & werre; & othere damages withoute nombre, of whiche we be nat war as at this tyme. And as touchynge the fourthe point, that Tullius clepeth

Engendrynge, thou shalt considere, that this wrong which that is doon to thee is engendred of the hate of thyne enemys; & of the vengeance, takynge upon that, wolde engendre another vengeance, & muchel sorwe and wastynge of richesses, as I seyde.

NOW sire, as to the point that Tullius clepeth Causes, which that is the laste point, thou shalt understonde that the wrong that thou hast receyved hath certeine causes, whiche that clerkes clepen Oriens and Efficiens, & Causa longinqua and Causa propinqua; this is to seyn, the fer cause and the ny cause. The fer cause is Almyghty God, that is cause of alle thynges; the neer cause is thy thre enemys. The cause accidental was hate; the cause material been the fyve woundes of thy doghter. The cause formal is the manere of hir werkynge, that broghten laddres & cloumben in at thy wyndowes. The cause final was for to slee thy doghter; it letted nat inasmuche as in hem was.

BUT for to speken of the fer cause, as to what ende they shul come, or what shal finally bityde of hem in this caas, ne kan I nat deme but by conjectynge and by supposynge. For we shul suppose that they shul come to a wikked ende, bycause that the Book of Decrees seith. Seelden, or with greet peyne, been causes ybroght to good ende whanne they been baddely bigonne.

NOW sire, if men wolde axe me, why that God suffred men to do yow this vileynye, certes, I kan nat wel answere as for no soothfastnesse; for thapostle seith, that the Sciences and the juggements of oure Lord God Almyghty been ful depe, ther may no man comprehende ne serchen hem suffisantly. Nathelees, by certeyne presumpciouns and conjectynges, I holde and bileeve, that God, which that is ful of justice & of rightwisnesse, hath suffred this bityde by juste cause resonable.

THY name is Melibee, this is to seyn, A man that drynketh hony. Thou hast ydronke so muchel hony of sweete temporeel richesses, and delices and honours of this world, that thou art dronken, and hast forgeten Jhesu Crist, thy creatour; thou ne hast nat doon to hym swich honour and reverence as thee oughte; ne thou ne hast nat wel ytaken kepe to the wordes of Ovide, that seith. Under the hony of the goodes of the body is hyd the venym that sleeth the soule. And Salomon seith, If thou hast founden hony, ete of it that suffiseth; for if thou ete of it out of mesure, thou shalt spewe, and be nedy and povre. And peraventure Crist hath thee in despit, and hath turned awey

73

fro thee his face and his eeris of misericorde; and also he hath suffred that thou
hast been punysshed in the manere that
thow hast ytrespassed. Thou hast doon
synne agayn oure Lord Crist; for certes,
the thre enemys of mankynde, that is to
seyn, the flessh, the feend & the world, thou
hast suffred hem entre into thyn herte
wilfully by the wyndowes of thy body, and
hast nat defended thyself suffisantly a-
gayns hire assautes & hire temptaciouns,
so that they han wounded thy soule in five
places; this is to seyn, the deedly synnes
that been entred into thyn herte by thy five
wittes. And in the same manere oure Lord
Crist hath woold and suffred, that thy thre
enemys been entred into thyn hous by the
wyndowes, & han ywounded thy doghter
in the foreseyde manere.

CERTES, quod Melibee, I se wel that
ye enforce yow muchel by wordes
to overcome me in swich manere,
that I shal nat venge me of myne enemys;
shewynge me the perils and the yveles
that myghten falle of this vengeance. But
whoso wolde considere in alle vengeances
the perils and yveles that myghte sewe of
vengeance takynge, a man wolde nevere
take vengeance, & that were harm; for by the
vengeance takynge been the wikked men
dissevered fro the goode men. And they
that han wyl to do wikkednesse restreyne
hir wikked purpos, whan they seen the
punyssynge and chastisynge of the trespassours.

AND to this answerde dame Prudence: Certes, seyde she, I graunte
wel that of vengeance cometh muchel yvel and muchel goode; but vengeance
takynge aperteneth nat unto everichoon,
but only unto juges, & unto hem that han
jurisdiccioun upon the trespassours.

AND yet seye I moore; that right as a
singuler persone synneth in takynge
vengeance of another man, right so
synneth the juge if he do no vengeance of
hem that it han disserved; for Senec seith
thus ✍ That maister, he seith, is good
that proveth shrewes.✍ And, as Cassidore
seith,✍ A man dredeth to do outrages whan
he woot and knoweth that it displeseth to
the juges & sovereyns.✍ And another seith
✍ The juge that dredeth to do right, maketh men shrewes.✍ And Seint Paule the
apostle seith in his epistle, whan he writeth unto the Romayns: that ✍ The juges
beren nat the spere withouten cause; but
they beren it to punysse the shrewes and
mysdoeres, & for to defende the goode men
✍ If ye wol thanne take vengeance of youre
enemys, ye shul retourne or have youre
recours to the juge that hath the jurisdiccioun upon hem; and he shal punysse hem

74

as the lawe axeth and requireth.

A! QUOD Melibee, this vengeance
liketh me no thyng. I bithenke me
now and take heede, how fortune
hath norissed me fro my childhede, and
hath holpen me to passe many a stroong
paas. Now wol I assayen hire, trowynge,
with Goddes helpe, that she shal helpe me
my shame for to venge.

CERTES, quod Prudence, if
ye wol werke by my conseil, ye
shul nat assaye fortune by
no wey; ne ye shul nat lene or
bowe unto hire, after the word
of Senec: for Thynges that
been folily doon, and that been in hope of
fortune, shullen nevere come to good ende.
And, as the same Senec seith, ✍ The moore
cleer and the moore shynyng that fortune
is, the moore brotil and the sonner broken
she is. Trusteth nat in hire, for she nys
nat stidefaste ne stable; for whan thow
trowest to be moost seur or siker of hire
helpe, she wol faille thee and deceyve thee
✍ And whereas ye seyn that fortune hath
norissed yow fro youre childhede, I seye,
that in so muchel shul ye the lasse truste
in hire and in hir wit; for Senec seith,✍
What man that is norissed by fortune she
maketh hym a greet fool.✍ Now thanne,
syn ye desire and axe vengeance, and the
vengeance that is doon after the lawe and
bifore the juge ne liketh yow nat, and the
vengeance that is doon in hope of fortune
is perilous and uncertein, thanne have ye
noon oother remedie, but for to have youre
recours unto the sovereyn juge that vengeth alle vileynyes and wronges; and he shal
venge yow after that hymself witnesseth,
whereas he seith ✍ Leveth the vengeance
to me, and I shal do it.

MELIBEE answerde, If I ne venge
me nat of the vileynye that men han
doon to me, I sompne or warne hem
that han doon to me that vileynye and alle
othere, to do me another vileynye; for it is
writen ✍ If thou take no vengeance of an
oold vileynye, thou sompnest thyne adversaries to do thee a new vileynye.✍ And
also, for my suffrance, men wolden do to me
so muchel vileynye, that I myghte neither
bere it ne susteene; and so sholde I been
put and holden over lowe. For men seyn ✍
In muchel suffrynge shul manye thynges
falle unto thee whiche thou shalt nat mowe
suffre.

CERTES, quod Prudence, I graunte
yow that over muchel suffraunce nys
nat good; but yet ne folweth it nat
therof, that every persone to whom men
doon vileynye take of it vengeance; for that
aperteneth & longeth al oonly to the juges,
for they shul venge the vileynyes and in-

juries. And therfore tho two auctoritees that ye han seyd above, been oonly understonden in the juges; for whan they suffren over muchel the wronges and the vileynyes to be doon withouten punysshynge, they sompne nat a man al oonly for to do newe wronges, but they comanden it ◊ Also, a wys man seith: that The juge that correcteth nat the synnere, comandeth & biddeth hym do synne. And the juges & sovereyns myghten in hir land so muchel suffre of the shrewes and mysdoeres, that they sholden by swich suffrance, by proces of tyme, wexen of swich power & myght, that they sholden putte out the juges & the sovereyns from hir places, and atte laste maken hem lesen hire lordshipes.

BUT lat us now putte, that ye have leve to venge yow. I seye ye been nat of myght & power as now to venge yow. for if ye wole maken comparisoun unto the myght of youre adversaries, ye shul fynde in manye thynges, that I have shewed yow er this, that hire condicioun is bettre than youres; and therfore seye I, that it is good as now that ye suffre and be pacient.

FORTHERMOORE, ye knowen wel that, after the comune sawe, It is a woodnesse a man to stryve with a strenger or a moore myghty man than he is hymself; & for to stryve with a man of evene strengthe that is to seyn, with as stronge a man as he, it is peril; and for to stryve with a weyker man, it is folie; and therfore sholde a man flee stryvynge as muchel as he myghte. for Salomon seith, ◊ It is a greet worshipe to a man to kepen hym fro noyse & stryf ◊ And if it so bifalle or happe that a man of gretter myght and strengthe than thou art do thee grevaunce, studie & bisye thee rather to stille the same grevaunce, than for to venge thee; for Senec seith that ◊ He putteth hym in greet peril that stryveth with a gretter man than he is hymself ◊ And Catoun seith, ◊ If a man of hyer estaat or degree, or moore myghty than thou, do thee anoy or grevaunce, suffre hym; for he that oones hath greved thee, another tyme may releeve thee and helpe.

YET sette I caas, ye have bothe myght and licence for to venge yow; I seye that ther be ful manye thynges that shul restreyne yow of vengeance takynge, and make yow for to enclyne to suffre, and for to han pacience in the thynges that han been doon to yow. first and foreward, if ye wole considere the defautes that been in youre owene persone, for whiche defautes God hath suffred yow have this tribulacioun, as I have seyd yow heerbiforn; for the poete seith, that We oghte paciently taken the tribulacions that comen to us, whan we thynken and consideren that we han disserved to have hem. And Seint Gregorie seith: that Whan a man considereth wel the nombre of his defautes and of his synnes, the peynes and the tribulaciouns that he suffreth semen the lesse unto hym; & inasmuche as hym thynketh his synnes moore hevy and grevous, insomuche semeth his peyne the lighter, & the esier unto him.

ALSO ye owen to enclyne and bowe youre herte to take the pacience of oure Lord Jhesu Crist, as seith Seint Peter in his epistles: Jhesu Crist, he seith, hath suffred for us and yeven ensample to every man to folwe & sewe hym; for he dide nevere synne, ne nevere cam ther a vileynous word out of his mouth; whan men cursed hym, he cursed hem noght; and whan men betten hym, he manaced hem noght ◊ Also the grete pacience which the seintes that been in paradys han had in tribulaciouns that they han ysuffred, withouten hir desert or gilt, oghte muchel stiren yow to pacience. forthermoore, ye sholde enforce yow to have pacience, considerynge that the tribulaciouns of this world but litel while endure, and soone passed been and goone; & the joye that a man seketh to have by pacience in tribulaciouns is perdurable; after that the Apostle seith in his epistle: The joye of God, he seith, is perdurable, that is to seyn, everelastynge.

ALSO troweth & bileveth stedefastly, that he nys nat wel ynorissed, ne wel ytaught, that kan nat have pacience, or wol nat receyve pacience. for Salomon seith: that The doctrine & the wit of a man is knowen by pacience. And in another place he seith: that He that is pacient governeth hym by greet prudence. And the same Salomon seith, ◊ The angry and wrathful man maketh noyses, and the pacient man atempreth hem and stilleth ◊ He seith also: It is moore worth to be pacient, than for to be right strong; & he that may have the lordshipe of his owene herte is moore to preyse than he that by his force or strengthe taketh grete citees; and therfore seith Seint Jame in his epistle: that Pacience is a greet vertu of perfeccioun.

CERTES, quod Melibee, I graunte yow, dame Prudence, that pacience is a greet vertu of perfeccioun; but every man may nat have the perfeccioun that ye seken; ne I nam nat of the nombre of right parfite men, for myn herte may nevere been in pees unto the tyme it be venged. And albeit so that it was greet peril to myn enemys to do me a vileynye in takynge vengeance upon me, yet tooken they noon heede of the peril, but fulfilleden hir wikked wyl, and hir corage. And ther-

75

fore, methynketh men oghten nat repreve me, though I putte me in a litel peril for to venge me, and though I do a greet excesse, that is to seyn, that I venge oon outrage by another.

AI QUOD dame Prudence, ye seyn youre wyl and as yow liketh; but in no caas of the world a man sholde nat doon outrage ne excesse for to vengen hym: for Cassidore seith: that As yvele dooth he that vengeth hym by outrage, as he that dooth the outrage; and therfore, ye shul venge yow after the ordre of right, that is to seyn, by the lawe, and noght by excesse ne by outrage. And also, if ye wol venge yow of the outrage of youre adver-saries in oother manere than right comand-eth, ye synnen; & therfore seith Senec: that A man shal nevere vengen shrewednesse by shrewednesse. And if ye seye, that right axeth a man to defenden violence by vio-lence, and fightyng by fightyng, certes, ye seye sooth, whan the defense is doon anon withouten intervalle or withouten taryinge or delay, for to defenden hym and nat for to vengen hym. And it bihoveth that a man putte swich attemperance in his defense, that men have no cause ne matiere to re-preven hym that defendeth hym of excesse and outrage; for ellis were it agayn resoun Pardee, ye knowen wel, that ye maken no defense as now for to defende yow, but for to venge yow; and so seweth it that ye han no wyl to do youre dede attemprely. And therfore, methynketh that pacience is good, for Salomon seith: that He that is nat pacient shal have greet harm.

CERTES, quod Melibee, I graunte yow, that whan a man is inpacient and wrooth, of that that toucheth hym noght and that aperteneth nat unto hym, though it harme hym, it is no wonder. For the lawe seith that He is coupable that entremetteth or medleth with swych thyng as aperteneth nat unto hym. And Salamon seith, that He that entremetteth hym of the noyse or strif of another man, is lyk to hym that taketh an hound by the eris. For right as he that taketh a straunge hound by the eris is outherwhile biten with the hound, right in the same wise is it resoun that he have harm, that by his inpacience medleth hym of the noyse of another man, wheras it aperteneth nat unto hym. But ye know-en wel that this dede, that is to seyn, my grief and my disese, toucheth me right ny; and therfore, though I be wrooth & inpa-cient, it is no merveille. And, savynge youre grace, I kan nat seen that it myghte greetly harme me though I tooke vengeaunce; for I am richer and moore myghty than myne enemys been. And wel knowen ye, that by moneye & by havynge grete possessions

76

been alle the thynges of this world govern-ed; and Salomon seith: that Alle thynges obeyen to moneye.

WHAN Prudence hadde herd hir housbonde avanten hym of his richesse and of his moneye, dis-preisynge the power of his adversaries, she spak, and seyde in this wise. Certes, deere sire, I graunte yow that ye been riche and myghty, and that the richesses been goode to hem that han wel ygeten hem and wel konne usen hem. For right as the body of a man may nat lyven withoute the soule, namoore may it lyve withouten temporeel goodes; and by richesses may a man gete hym grete freendes. And therfore seith Pamphilles If a netherdes doghter, seith he, be riche, she may chesen of a thousand men which she wol take to hir housbonde; for, of a thousand men, oon wol nat forsaken hire ne refusen hire. And this Pamphilles seith also If thow be right happy, that is to seyn, if thou be right riche, thou shalt fynde a greet nom-bre of felawes & freendes. And if thy for-tune change that thou wexe povre, farewel freendshipe & felaweshipe; for thou shalt be al alloone withouten any compaignye, but if it be the compaignye of povre folk. And yet seith this Pamphilles moreover: that They that been thralle and bonde of lynage shullen been maad worthy & noble by the richesses. And right so as by rich-esses ther comen manye goodes, right so by poverte come ther manye harmes and yveles; for greet poverte constreyneth a man to do manye yveles. And therfore clepeth Cassidore poverte The mooder of ruyne; that is to seyn, the mooder of overthrow-ynge or fallynge doun. And therfore seith Piers Alfonce Oon of the gretteste ad-versitees of this world is whan a free man, by kynde or by burthe, is constreyned by poverte to eten the almesse of his enemy. And the same seith Innocent in oon of his bookes, he seith: that Sorweful and mys-happy is the condicioun of a povre beg-gere, for if he axe nat his mete he dyeth for hunger; and if he axe, he dyeth for shame; and algates necessitee constreyneth hym to axe. And therfore seith Salomon: that Bet it is to dye than for to have swich pov-erte. And as the same Salomon seith Bettre it is to dye of bitter deeth than for to lyven in swich wise By thise resons that I have seid unto yow, and by manye othere resons that I koude seye, I graunte yow that richesses been goode to hem that geten hem wel, and to hem that wel usen tho richesses. And therfore wol I shewe yow how ye shul have yow, & how ye shul bere yow in gaderynge of richesses, and in what manere ye shul usen hem.

FIRST, ye shul geten hem withouten greet desir, by good leyser, sokyngly, & nat over hastily; for a man that is to desirynge to gete richesses abaundoneth hym first to thefte, & to alle other yveles. And therfore seith Salomon He that hasteth hym to bisily to wexe riche shal be noon innocent. He seith also: that The richesse that hastily cometh to a man, soone & lightly gooth & passeth fro a man; but that richesse that cometh litel and litel, wexeth alwey & multiplieth. And sire, ye shul geten richesses by youre wit & by youre travaille unto youre profit; & that withouten wrong or harm-doynge to any oother persone. For the lawe seith: that Ther maketh no man himselven riche, if he do harm to another wight: this is to seyn, that nature defendeth and forbedeth by right, that no man make hymself riche unto the harm of another persone. And Tullius seith: that No sorwe, ne no drede of deeth, ne nothyng that may falle unto a man, is so muchel agayns nature, as a man to encressen his owene profit to the harm of another man. And though the grete men and the myghty men geten richesses moore lightly than thou, yet shaltou nat been ydel ne slow to do thy profit; for thou shalt in alle wise flee ydelnesse; for Salomon seith: that Ydelnesse techeth a man to do manye yveles. And the same Salomon seith: that He that travailleth & bisieth hym to tilien his land, shal eeten breed; but he that is ydel and casteth hym to no bisynesse ne occupacioun, shal falle into poverte, and dye for hunger. And he that is ydel and slow, kan nevere fynde covenable tyme for to doon his profit. For ther is a versifiour seith: that The ydel man excuseth hym in wynter, bycause of the grete coold; and in somer, by enchesoun of the heete. For thise causes seith Caton Waketh and enclyneth nat yow overmuchel for to slepe; for overmuchel reste norisseth and causeth manye vices. And therefore seith Seint Jerome: Dooth somme goode dedes, that the devel, which is oure enemy, ne fynde yow nat unoccupied. For the devel ne taketh nat lightly unto his werkynge swiche as he fyndeth occupied in goode werkes.

THANNE thus in getynge richesses, ye mosten flee ydelnesse; and afterward ye shul use the richesses, whiche ye have geten by youre wit & by youre travaille, in swich a manere, that men holde nat yow to scars, ne to sparynge, ne to fool-large; that is to seyn, overlarge a spendere. For right as men blamen an avaricious man bycause of his scarsetee and chyncherie, in the same wise is he to blame that spend-eth overlargely. And therfore seith Caton Use, he seith, thy richesses that thou hast geten in swich a manere, that men have no matiere ne cause to calle thee neither wrecche ne chynche; for it is a greet shame to a man to have a povere herte and a riche purs. He seith also: The goodes that thou hast ygeten, use hem by mesure, that is to seyn, spende hem mesurably; for they that folily wasten & despenden the goodes that they han, whan they han namoore propre of hir owene, they shapen hem to take the goodes of another man.

I SEYE thanne, that ye shul fleen avarice; usynge youre richesses in swich manere, that men seye nat that youre richesses been yburyed, but that ye have hem in youre myght & in youre weeldynge. For a wys man repreveth the avaricious man, and seith thus, in two vers: Wherto and why burieth a man his goodes by his grete avarice, and knoweth wel that nedes moste he dye; for deeth is the ende of every man, as in this present lyf. And for what cause or enchesoun joyneth he hym, or knytteth he hym, so faste unto his goodes, that alle his wittes mowen nat disseveren hym or departen hym from his goodes; & knoweth wel, or oghte knowe, that whan he is deed he shal nothyng bere with hym out of this world? And therfore seith Seint Augustyn: that The avaricious man is lik-ned unto helle; that the moore it swelweth, the moore desir it hath to swelwe and devoure. And as wel as ye wolde eschewe to be called an avaricious man or chynche, as wel sholde ye kepe yow and governe yow in swich a wise that men calle yow nat fool-large. Therfore seith Tullius The goodes, he seith, of thyn hous ne sholde nat been hyd, ne kept so cloos but that they myght been opened by pitee & debonairetee; that is to seyn, to yeven part to hem that han greet nede; Ne thy goodes shullen nat been so opene, to been every mannes goodes.

AFTERWARD, in getynge of youre richesses & in usynge hem, ye shul alwey have thre thynges in youre herte; that is to seyn, oure Lord God, conscience, and good name. First, ye shul have God in youre herte; and for no richesse ye shullen do nothyng, which may in any manere displese God, that is youre creatour and makere; for after the word of Salomon. It is bettre to have a litel good with the love of God, than to have muchel good & tresour, and lese the love of his Lord God. And the prophete seith: that Bettre it is to been a good man and have litel good and tresour, than to been holden a shrewe, & have grete richesses. And yet seye I ferthermore, that ye sholde alwey doon youre bisynesse to gete yow richesses, so that ye gete hem with good conscience. And thapostle seith:

77

that Ther nys thyng in this world, of which we sholden have so greet joye as whan oure conscience bereth us good witnesse; & the wise man seith: The substance of a man is ful good, whan synne is nat in mannes conscience.

AFTERWARD, in getynge of youre richesses, and in usynge of hem, yow moste have greet bisynesse & greet diligence, that youre goode name be alwey kept & conserved. for Salomon seith: that Bettre it is and moore it availleth a man to have a good name, than for to have grete richesses. And therfore he seith in another place: Do greet diligence, seith Salomon, in kepyng of thy freend and of thy goode name, for it shal lenger abide with thee than any tresour, be it never so precious. And certes, he sholde nat be called a gentil man, that after God and good conscience, alle thynges left, ne dooth his diligence and bisynesse to kepen his good name. And Cassidore seith: that It is signe of gentil herte, whan a man loveth and desireth to han a good name. And therfore seith Seint Augustyn: that Ther been two thynges that arn necessarie and nedefulle, & that is, good conscience and good loos: that is to seyn, good conscience to thyn owene persone inward, and good loos for thy neighebore outward. And he that trusteth hym so muchel in his goode conscience, that he displeseth and setteth at noght his goode name or loos, & rekketh noght though he kepe nat his goode name, nys but a crueel cherl.

SIRE, now have I shewed yow how ye shul do in getynge richesses, & how ye shullen usen hem; & I se wel, that for the trust that ye han in youre richesses, ye wole moeve werre & bataille. I conseille yow, that ye bigynne no werre in trust of youre richesses; for they ne suffisen noght werres to mayntene. And therfore seith a philosophre, That man that desireth & wole algates han werre, shal nevere have suffisaunce; for the richer that he is, the gretter despenses moste he make, if he wole have worshipe & victorie. And Salomon seith: that The gretter richesses that a man hath, the mo despendours he hath. And, deere sire, albeit so that for youre richesses ye mowe have muchel folk, yet bihoveth it nat, ne it is nat good to bigynne werre, whereas ye mowe in oother manere have pees, unto youre worshipe and profit. for the victories of batailles that been in this world, lyen nat in greet nombre or multitude of the peple, ne in the vertu of man; but it lith in the wyl & in the hand of oure Lord God Almyghty.

78

AND therfore Judas Machabeus, which was Goddes knyght, whan he sholde fighte agayn his adversarie that hadde a greet nombre, and a gretter multitude of folk & strenger than was this peple of Machabee, yet he reconforted his litel compaignye, & seyde right in this wise: Als lightly, quod he, may oure Lord God Almyghty yeve victorie to a fewe folk as to many folk, for the victorie of a bataile comth nat by the grete nombre of peple, but it come from oure Lord God of hevene.

AND deere sire, for as muchel as ther is no man certein, if he be worthy that God yeve hym victorie, namore than he is certein whether he be worthy of the love of God or naught, after that Salomon seith, therfore every man sholde greetly drede werres to bigynne. And bycause that in batailles fallen manye perils, & happeth outherwhile that as soone is the grete man slayn as the litel man; and, as it is writen in the seconde book of Kynges, The dedes of batailles been aventurouse & nothyng certeyne; for as lightly is oon hurt with a spere as another. And for ther is gret peril in werre, therfore sholde a man flee and eschue werre, in as muchel as a man may goodly; for Salomon seith: He that loveth peril shal falle in peril.

AFTER that dame Prudence hadde spoken in this manere, Melibee answerde and seyde, I see wel, dame Prudence, that by youre faire wordes, and by youre resouns that ye han shewed me, that the werre liketh yow nothyng; but I have nat yet herd youre conseil, how I shal do in this nede.

CERTES, quod she, I conseille yow that ye accorde with youre adversaries, and that ye have pees with hem; for Seint Jame seith, in his epistles, that By concord & pees the smale richesses wexen grete, and by debaat and discord the grete richesses fallen doun; and ye knowen wel that oon of the gretteste and moost sovereyn thyng that is in this world, is unytee and pees. And therfore seyde oure Lord Jhesu Crist to his apostles in this wise: Wel happy and blessed been they that loven and purchacen pees; for they been called children of God.

A! QUOD Melibee, now se I wel that ye loven nat myn honour ne my worshipe. Ye knowen wel that myne adversaries han bigonnen this debaat and bryge by hire outrage; and ye se wel that they ne requeren ne preyen me nat of pees, ne they asken nat to be reconsiled. Wol ye thanne that I go and meke me and obeye me to hem, and crie hem mercy? forsothe, that were nat my worshipe; for right as men seyn, that Over-greet hoomlynesse engendreth dispreisynge, so fareth it by to greet humylitee or mekenesse.

THANNE bigan dame Prudence to maken semblant of wrathe, and seyde, Certes, sire, sauf youre grace, I love youre honour and your profit as I do myn owene, and evere have doon; ne ye, ne noon oother, syen nevere the contrarie. And yit, if I hadde seyd that ye sholde han purchaced the pees and the reconsiliacioun, I ne hadde nat muchel mystaken me, ne seyd amys; for the wise man seith. The dissensioun bigynneth by another man, and the reconsilyng bygynneth by thyself. And the prophete seith flee shrewednesse & do goodnesse; seke pees and folwe it, as muchel as in thee is. Yet seye I nat that ye shul rather pursue to youre adversaries for pees than they shuln to yow; for I knowe wel that ye been so hardherted, that ye wol do nothyng for me; and Salomon seith. He that hath overhard an herte, atte laste he shal myshappe and mystyde.

WHANNE Melibee hadde herd dame Prudence maken semblant of wrathe, he seyde in this wise: Dame, I prey yow that ye be nat displesed of thynges that I seye; for ye knowe wel that I am angry and wrooth, and that is no wonder; & they that been wrothe witen nat wel what they doon, ne what they seyn. Therfore the prophete seith: that Troubled eyen han no cleer sighte. But seyeth and conseilleth me as yow liketh; for I am redy to do right as ye wol desire; and if ye repreve me of my folye, I am the moore holden to love yow and to preyse yow; for Salomon seith: that He that repreveth hym that dooth folye, he shal fynde gretter grace than he that deceyveth hym by sweete wordes.

THANNE seide dame Prudence, I make no semblant of wrathe ne anger but for youre grete profit; for Salomon seith. He is moore worth, that repreveth or chideth a fool for his folye, shewynge hym semblant of wrathe, than he that supporteth hym and preyseth hym in his mysdoynge, & laugheth at his folye. And this same Salomon seith afterward: that By the sorweful visage of a man, that is to seyn, by the sory & hevy contenaunce of a man, The fool correcteth & amendeth hymself.

THANNE seyde Melibee, I shal nat konne answere to so manye faire resouns as ye putten to me & shewen. Seyeth shortly youre wyl & youre conseil, and I am al redy to fulfille and parfourne it.

THANNE dame Prudence discovered al hir wyl to hym, & seyde, I conseille yow, quod she, aboven alle thynges, that ye make pees bitwene God and yow; and beth reconsiled unto hym and to his grace; for as I have seyd yow heerbiforn, God hath suffred yow to have this tribulacioun and disese for youre synnes. And if ye do as I sey yow, God wol sende youre adversaries unto yow, and maken hem fallen at youre feet, redy to do youre wyl and youre comandements. For Salomon seith. Whan the condicioun of man is plesaunt & likynge to God, he chaungeth the hertes of the mannes adversaries and constreyneth hem to biseken hym of pees and of grace. And I prey yow, lat me speke with youre adversaries in privee place; for they shul nat knowe that it be of youre wyl or youre assent; and thanne, whan I knowe hir wil and hire entente, I may conseille yow the moore seurely.

DAME, quod Melibee, dooth youre wil & youre likynge, for I putte me hoolly in youre disposicioun & ordinaunce. Thanne dame Prudence, whan she saugh the goode wyl of hir housbonde, delibered and took avys in hirself, thinkinge how she myghte brynge this nede unto a good conclusioun and to a good ende. And whan she saugh hir tyme, she sente for thise adversaries to come unto hire into a pryvee place, and shewed wisely unto hem the grete goodes that comen of pees, and the grete harmes and perils that been in werre; and seyde to hem in a goodly manere hou that hem oughten have greet repentaunce of the injurie and wrong that they hadden doon to Melibee hir lord, & to hire, and to hire doghter.

AND whan they herden the goodliche wordes of dame Prudence, they weren so supprised and ravysshed, & hadden so greet joye of hire, that wonder was to telle. A! lady! quod they, ye han shewed unto us The blessynge of swetnesse, after the sawe of David the prophete; for the reconsilynge which we been nat worthy to have in no manere, but we oghte requeren it with greet contricioun & humylitee, ye, of youre grete goodnesse, have presented unto us. Now se we wel that the science & the konnynge of Salomon is ful trewe; for he seith: that Sweete wordes multiplien & encreesen freendes, and maken shrewes to be debonaire and meeke.

CERTES, quod they, we putten oure dede, and al oure matere and cause, al hoolly in youre goode wyl; and been redy to obeye to the speche and comandement of my lord Melibee. And therfore, deere & benygne lady, we preien yow and biseke yow as mekely as we konne

79

and mowen, that it lyke unto youre grete goodnesse to fulfillen in dede youre goodliche wordes; for we consideren & knowelichen that we han offended and greved my lord Melibee out of mesure; so ferforth, that we be nat of power to maken his amendes; & therfore we oblige and bynden us and oure freendes to doon al his wyl & his comandements. But peraventure he hath swich hevynesse and swich wrathe to usward bycause of oure offense, that he wole enjoyne us swich a peyne as we mowe nat bere ne susteene; and therfore, noble lady, we biseke to youre wommanly pitee, to taken swich avysement in this nede, that we, ne oure freendes, be nat desherited ne destroyed thurgh oure folye.

ERTES, quod Prudence, it is an hard thyng and right perilous, that a man putte hym al outrely in the arbitracioun and juggement, & in the myght & power of his enemys; for Salomon seith Leeveth me, and yeveth credence to that I shal seyn; I seye, quod he, ye peple, folk, and governours of hooly chirche, to thy sone, to thy wyf, to thy freend, ne to thy broother, ne yeve thou nevere myght ne maistrie of thy body, whil thou lyvest.

OW sithen he defendeth that man shal nat yeven to his broother, ne to his freend, the myght of his body, by strenger resoun he defendeth and forbedeth a man to yeven hymself to his enemy. And nathelees I conseille you, that ye mystruste nat my lord; for I woot wel and knowe verraily, that he is debonaire and meeke, large, curteys, and nothyng desirous ne coveitous of good ne richesse; for ther nys nothyng in this world that he desireth, save oonly worshipe & honour. forthermoore I knowe wel, and am right seur, that he shal nothyng doon in this nede withouten my conseil. And I shal so werken in this cause that, by grace of oure Lord God, ye shul been reconsiled unto us.

HANNE seyden they with o voys Worshipful lady, we putten us and oure goodes al fully in youre wil and disposicioun; & been redy to comen, what day that it like unto youre noblesse to lymyte us or assigne us, for to maken oure obligacioun & boond as strong as it liketh unto youre goodnesse; that we mowe fulfille the wille of yow & of my lord Melibee.

HAN dame Prudence hadde herd the answeres of thise men, she bad hem goon agayn prively; and she retourned to hir lord Melibee, & tolde hym how she foond his adversaries ful repentant, knowelechynge ful lowely hir synnes and trespas, & how they were redy to suffren al peyne, requirynge and preyinge hym of mercy and pitee.

80

HANNE seyde Melibee He is wel worthy to have pardoun and foryifnesse of his synne, that excuseth nat his synne, but knowelecheth it & repenteth hym, axinge indulgence. for Senec seith Ther is the remissioun and foryifnesse, whereas confessioun is; for confessioun is neighebore to innocence And he seith in another place: He that hath shame for his synne & knowlecheth it, is worthy remyssioun; & therfore I assente and conferme me to have pees; but it is good that we do it nat withouten the assent & wyl of oure freendes.

HANNE was Prudence right glad & joyeful, & seyde, Certes, sire, quod she, ye han wel and goodly answered; for right as by the conseil, assent & helpe of youre freendes, ye han been stired to venge yow and maken werre, right so withouten hire conseil shul ye nat accorden yow, ne have pees with youre adversaries; for the lawe seith Ther nys nothyng so good by wey of kynde as a thyng to been unbounde by hym that it was ybounde.

ND thanne dame Prudence, withouten delay or taryinge, sente anon hire messages for hire kyn, and for hire olde freendes whiche that were trewe and wyse, and tolde hem by ordre, in the presence of Melibee, al this mateere as it is aboven expressed & declared; and preyden hem that they wolde yeven hire avys & conseil what best were to doon in this nede. And whan Melibees freendes hadde taken hire avys and deliberacioun of the forseide mateere, and hadden examyned it by greet bisynesse and greet diligence, they yave ful conseil for to have pees and reste; and that Melibee sholde receyve with good herte his adversaries to foryifnesse and mercy.

ND whan dame Prudence hadde herd the assent of hir lord Melibee, and the conseil of his freendes, accorde with hire wille and hire entencioun, she was wonderly glad in hire herte, and seyde: Ther is an old proverbe, quod she, seith: that the goodnesse that thou mayst do this day, do it, & abide nat ne delaye it nat til tomorwe. And therfore I conseille that ye sende youre messages, swiche as been discrete and wise, unto youre adversaries; tellynge hem on youre bihalve, that if they wole trete of pees and of accord, that they shape hem, withouten delay or tarying, to comen unto us Which thyng parfourned was in dede. And whanne thise trespassours and repentynge folk of hire folies, that is to seyn, the adversaries of Melibee, hadden herd what thise messagers seyden unto hem, they weren right glad & joyeful, and answereden ful mekely and benignely, yeldynge graces & thankynges to hir lord

Melibee & to al his compaignye; & shopen hem, withouten delay to go with the messagers, and obeye to the comandement of hir lord Melibee.

AND right anon they tooken hire wey to the court of Melibee, and tooken with hem somme of hire trewe freendes to maken feith for hem and for to been hire borwes. And whan they were comen to the presence of Melibee, he seyde hem thise wordes ✎ It standeth thus, quod Melibee, and sooth it is, that ye, causelees, and withouten skile and resoun, han doon grete injuries and wronges to me and to my wyf Prudence, & to my doghter also. For ye han entred into myn hous by violence, and have doon swich outrage, that alle men knowen wel that ye have disserved the deeth, and therfore wol I knowe & wite of yow, wheither ye wol putte the punyssement & the chastisynge & the vengeance of this outrage in the wyl of me and of my wyf Prudence; or ye wol nat?

THANNE the wiseste of hem thre answerde for hem alle, and seyde, Sire, quod he, we knowen wel that we been unworthy to comen unto the court of so greet a lord, & so worthy as ye been; for we han so greetly mystaken us, & han offended & agilt in swich a wise agayn youre heigh lordshipe, that trewely we han disserved the deeth. But yet for the grete goodnesse and debonairetee that al the world witnesseth in youre persone, we submytten us to the excellence and benignitee of youre gracious lordshipe, and been redy to obeie to alle youre comandements; bisekynge yow, that of youre merciable pitee ye wol considere oure grete repentaunce and lowe submyssioun, and graunten us foryevenesse of oure outrageous trespas and offense. For wel we knowe that youre liberal grace and mercy strecchen hem ferther into goodnesse, than doon oure outrageouse giltes & trespas into wikkednesse; albeit that cursedly and dampnably we han agilt agayn youre heigh lordshipe.

THANNE Melibee took hem up fro the ground ful benignely, and receyved hire obligaciouns and hire boondes by hire othes upon hire plegges & borwes, and assigned hem a certeyn day to retourne unto his court, for to accepte and receyve the sentence and juggement that Melibee wolde comande to be doon on hem by the causes aforeseyd; whiche thynges ordeyned, every man retourned to his hous.

AND whan that dame Prudence saugh hir tyme, she freyned & axed hir lord Melibee, what vengeance he thoughte to taken of his adversaries.

TO which Melibee answerde and seyde, Certes, quod he, I thynke and purpose me fully to desherite hem of al that evere they han, and for to putte hem in exil for evere.

CERTES, quod dame Prudence, this were a crueel sentence, and muchel agayn resoun; for ye been riche ynough, & han no nede of oother mennes good; & ye myghte lightly in this wise gete yow a coveitous name, which is a vicious thyng, & oghte been eschued of every good man; for after the sawe of the word of the Apostle ✎ Coveitise is roote of alle harmes. ✎ And therfore it were bettre for yow to lese so muchel good of youre owene, than for to taken of hire good in this manere; for bettre it is to lesen with worshipe, than it is to wynne good with vileynye and shame; and everi man oghte to doon his diligence and his bisynesse to geten hym a good name. And yet shal he nat oonly bisie hym in kepynge of his good name, but he shal also enforcen hym alwey to do somthyng by which he may renovelle his good name; for it is writen that ✎ The olde good loos or good name of a man is soone goon and passed, whan it is nat newed ne renovelled.

AND as touchynge that ye seyn, ye wole exile youre adversaries, that thynketh me muchel agayn resoun and out of mesure, considered the power that they han yeve yow upon hemself. And it is writen, that He is worthy to lesen his privilege that mysuseth the myght and the power that is yeven hym. And I sette cas, ye myght enjoyne hem that peyne by right and by lawe, which I trowe ye mowe nat do. I seye, ye mighte nat putten it to execucioun peraventure, and thanne were it likly to retourne to the werre as it was biforn; & therfore if ye wole that men do yow obeisance, ye moste deemen moore curteisly; this is to seyn, ye moste yeven moore esy sentences & juggements. For it is writen, that He that moost curteisly comandeth, to hym men moost obeyen. And therfore I prey yow that in this necessitee & in this nede, ye caste yow to overcome youre herte. For Senec seith: that He that overcometh his herte, overcometh twies; and Tullius seith ✎ Ther is nothyng so comendable in a greet lord as whan he is debonaire & meeke, and appeseth him lightly ✎ And I prey yow that ye wole forbere now to do vengeance, in swich a manere, that youre goode name may be kept and conserved; and that men mowe have cause & mateere to preyse yow of pitee & of mercy, & that ye have no cause to repente yow of thyng that ye doon; for Senec seith ✎ He overcometh in an yvel manere, that repenteth hym of his victorie. ✎ Wherfore, I pray yow, lat mercy been in youre mynde and in youre herte, to theffect & entente that God Almyghty have mercy on yow in his laste juggement; for Seint Jame seith in his epistle, ☙ Juggement withouten mercy shal be doon to hym, that hath no mercy of another wight.

WHANNE Melibee hadde herd the grete skiles & resouns of dame Prudence, & hire wise informaciouns and techynges, his herte gan enclyne to the wil of his wif, consideringe hir trewe entente; & conformed hym anon and assented fully to werken after hir conseil; and thonked God, of whom procedeth al vertu and alle goodnesse, that hym sente a wyf of so greet discrecioun.

AND when the day cam that his adversaries sholde appieren in his presence, he spak unto hem ful goodly, and seyde in this wyse: Albeit so that of youre pride & presumpcioun

The murye wordes of the Hoost to the Monk ☙

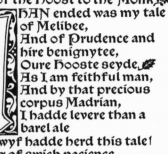

WHAN ended was my tale of Melibee, And of Prudence and hire benignytee, Oure Hooste seyde, ☙ As I am feithful man, And by that precious corpus Madrian, I hadde levere than a barel ale

That goode lief my wyf hadde herd this tale! for she nys nothyng of swich pacience As was this Melibeus wyf Prudence. By Goddes bones! whan I bete my knaves, She bryngeth me forth the grete clobbed staves, And crieth, Slee the dogges everichoon, And brek hem, bothe bak and every boon! And if that any neighebore of myne Wol nat in chirche to my wyf enclyne, Or be so hardy to hire to trespace, Whan she comth home she rampeth in my face, And crieth, false coward! wrek thy wyf! By corpus bones! I wol have thy knyf, And thou shalt have my distaf and go spynne! fro day to nyght right thus she wol bigynne; Allas! she seith, that evere I was shape To wedde a milksop or a coward ape That wol been overlad with every wight! Thou darst nat stonden by thy wyves right!

THIS is my lif, but if that I wol fighte; And out at dore anon I moot me dighte, Or elles I am but lost, but if that I Be lik a wilde leoun, foolhardy. I woot wel she wol do me slee som day Som neighebore, and thanne go my way; for I am perilous with knyf in honde; Albeit that I dar hire nat withstonde, for she is byg in armes, by my feith, That shal he fynde, that hire mysdooth or seith.

82

and folie, and of youre necligence and unkonnynge, ye have mysborn yow and trespassed unto me; yet, forasmuche as I see and biholde youre grete humylitee, & that ye been sory and repentant of youre giltes, it constreyneth me to doon yow grace and mercy. Therfore I receyve yow to my grace, and foryeve yow outrely alle the offenses, injuries, and wronges, that ye have doon agayn me and myne; to this effect and to this ende, that God of his endelees mercy wole at the tyme of oure dyinge foryeven us oure giltes that we han trespassed to hym in this wrecched world; for doutelees, if we be sory and repentant of the synnes and giltes whiche we han trespassed in the sighte of oure Lord God, he is so free and so merciable, that he wole foryeven us oure giltes, and bryngen us to his blisse that nevere hath ende. Amen.

Heere is ended Chaucers Tale of Melibee and of Dame Prudence.

But lat us passe awey fro this mateere. ☙ My lord the Monk, quod he, be myrie of cheere, for ye shul telle a tale trewely. Loo, Rouchestre stant heere faste by! Ryd forth, myn owene lord, brek nat oure game, But by my trouthe, I knowe nat youre name, Wher shal I calle yow my lord daun John, Or daun Thomas, or elles daun Albon? Of what hous be ye, by youre fader kyn? I vowe to God, thou hast a ful fair skyn! It is a gentil pasture ther thow goost; Thou art nat lyk a penant, or a goost. Upon my feith, thou art som officer, Som worthy sexteyn, or some celerer, for by my fader soule, as to my doom, Thou art a maister, whan thou art at hoom; No povre cloysterer, ne no novys, But a governour, both wily and wys, And therwithal of brawnes and of bones, A welfarynge persone for the nones. I pray to God, yeve hym confusioun That first thee broghte unto religioun. Thou woldest han been a tredefowel aright; Haddestow as greet a leeve as thou hast myght To parfourne al thy lust in engendrure, Thou haddest bigeten many a creature. Allas! why werestow so wyd a cope? God yeve me sorwe! but and I were a pope, Nat oonly thou, but every myghty man, Though he were shorn ful hye upon his pan, Sholde have a wyf; for al the world is lorn; Religioun hath take up al the corn Of tredyng, and we borel men been shrympes; Of fieble trees ther comen wrecched ympes. This maketh that oure heires been so sklendre And feble, that they may nat wel engendre. This maketh that oure wyves wole assaye Religious folk, for ye mowe bettre paye Of Venus paiements than mowe we. God woot, no Lussheburghes payen ye!

But be nat wrooth, my lord, for that I pleye,
ful ofte in game a sooth, I have herd seyeſ
THIS worthy Monk took al in pacience,
And seyde, I wol doon al my dili-
gence,
As fer as sowneth into honestee,
To telle yow a tale, or two, or three.
And if yow list to herkne hyderward,
I wol yow seyn the lyf of Seint Edward,
Or ellis, first, tragedies wol I telle,
Of whiche I have an hundred in my celle.
Tragedie is to seyn a certeyn storie,
As olde bookes maken us memorie,
Of hym that stood in greet prosperitee
And is yfallen out of heigh degree

Into myserie, and endeth wrecchedly;
And they ben versified communely
Of six feet, which men clepen exametron.
In prose eek been endited many oon,
And eek in meetre, in many a sondry wyse;
Lo, this declaryng oghte ynogh suffise.
Now herkneth, if yow liketh for to heere;
But first, I yow biseeke in this mateere,
Though I by ordre telle nat thise thynges,
Be it of popes, emperours, or kynges,
After hir ages, as men writen fynde,
But telle hem som bifore and som bihynde,
As it now comth unto my remembraunce;
Have me excused of min ignoraunce.
Explicit.

HEERE BIGYNNETH THE MONKES TALE, DE CASIBUS VIRORUM ILLUSTRIUM

I WOL biwaille, in man-
ere of tragedie,
The harm of hem that
stoode in heigh degree,
And fillen so that ther
nas no remedie
To brynge hem out of
hir adversitee;
for certein, whan that
fortune list to flee,
Ther may no man the cours of hire withholde.
Lat no man truste on blynd prosperitee;
Be war by thise ensamples trewe and olde.

De Lucifero
At Lucifer, though he an angel were,
And nat a man, at hym wol I bigynne;
for, though fortune may noon angel dere,
from heigh degree yet fel he for his synne
Doun into helle, where he yet is inne.
O Luciferſ brightest of angels alle,
Now artow Sathanas, that mayst nat twynne
Out of miserie, in which that thou art falle.

De Adamo
Loo Adam, in the feeld of Damyssene,
With Goddes owene fynger wroght was he,
And nat bigeten of mannes sperme unclene,
And welte al paradys, savynge o tree.
Hadde nevere worldly man so heigh degree
As Adam, til he for mysgovernaunce
Was dryve out of hys hye prosperitee
To labour, and to helle, and to meschaunce.

De Sampsone
LOO Sampson, which that was
annunciat
By thangel, longe er his
nativitee,
And was to God Almyghty
consecrat,
And stood in noblesse, whil he myghte see.
Was nevere swich another as was hee,

To speke of strengthe, and therwith hardynesse;
But to his wyves toolde he his secree,
Thurgh which he slow hymself, for wrecchednesse.

Sampson, this noble almyghty champioun,
Withouten wepene save his handes tweye,
He slow and al torente the leoun,
Toward his weddyng walkynge by the weye.
His false wyf koude hym so plese and preye
Til she his conseil knew; and she untrewe
Unto his foos his conseil gan biwreye,
And hym forsook, and took another newe.

Thre hundred foxes took Sampson for ire,
And alle hir tayles he togydre bond,
And sette the foxes tayles alle on fire,
for he on every tayl had knyt a brond;
And they brende alle the cornes in that lond,
And alle hire olyveres, and vynes eke.
A thousand men he slow eek with his hond,
And hadde no wepene but an asses cheke.

Whan they were slayn, so thursted hym
that he
Was wel ny lorn, for which he gan to preye
That God wolde on his peyne han som pitee,
And sende hym drynke, or elles moste he
deye;
And of this asses cheke, that was dreye,
Out of a wang-tooth sprang anon a welle,
Of which he drank ynogh, shortly to seye,
Thus heelp hym God, as Judicum can telle.

By verray force at Gazan, on a nyght,
Maugree Philistiens of that citee,
The gates of the toun he hath up-plyght,
And on his bak ycaryed hem hath hee
Hye on an hille, that men myghte hem see.
O noble almyghty Sampson, lief and deere,
Had thou nat toold to wommen thy secree,
In al this world ne hadde been thy peereſ

This Sampson nevere ciser drank, ne wyn,
Ne on his heed cam rasour noon, ne sheere,
By precept of the messager divyn;
for alle his strengthes in his heeres weere;
And fully twenty wynter, yeer by yeere,
he hadde of Israel the governaunce;
But soone shal he wepe many a teere,
for wommen shal hym bryngen to meschaunce.

Unto his lemman Dalida he tolde
That in his heeris al his strengthe lay,
And falsly to his foomen she hym solde;
And slepynge in hir barm upon a day
She made to clippe or shere his heer away,
And made his foomen al his craft espyen;
And whan that they hym foond in this array,
They bounde hym faste, and putten out his eyen.

But er his heer were clipped or yshave,
Ther was no boond with which men myghte him
bynde;
But now is he in prison in a cave,
Whereas they made hym at the querne grynde.
O noble Sampson, strongest of mankynde!
O whilom juge in glorie and in richesse!
Now maystow wepen with thyne eyen blynde,
Sith thou fro wele art falle in wrecchednesse.

Thende of this caytyf was as I shal seye;
his foomen made a feeste upon a day,
And made hym as hir fool biforn hem pleye;
And this was in a temple of greet array.
But atte laste he made a foul affray;
for he two pilers shook, and made hem falle,
And doun fil temple and al, and ther it lay,
And slow hymself, and eek his foomen alle.

This is to seyn, the prynces everichoon,
And eek thre thousand bodyes were ther slayn
With fallynge of the grete temple of stoon.
Of Sampson now wol I namoore sayn.
Beth war by this ensample oold and playn
That no men telle hir conseil til hir wyves
Of swich thyng as they wolde han secree fayn,
If that it touche hir lymes or hir lyves.

f Hercules, the sovereyn conquerour,
Syngen his werkes laude and heigh
renoun:
for in his tyme of strengthe he was
the flour.
he slow, and rafte the skyn of the
leoun;
he of Centauros leyde the boost adoun;
he Arpies slow, the crueel bryddes felle;
he golden apples rafte of the dragoun;
he drow out Cerberus, the hound of helle:

he slow the crueel tyrant Busirus,
And made his hors to frete hym, flessh and boon;
he slow the firy serpent venymus;
Of Acheloys two hornes, he brak oon;
And he slow Cacus in a cave of stoon;
he slow the geant Antheus the stronge;
84

he slow the grisly boor, and that anoon;
And bar the hevene on his nekke longe.

Was nevere wight sith that this world bigan.
That slow so manye monstres as dide he;
Thurghout this wyde world his name ran,
What for his strengthe, and for his heigh bountee,
And every reawme wente he for to see.
he was so stroong that no man myghte hym lette;
At bothe the worldes endes, seith Trophee,
In stide of boundes, he a pileer sette.

A lemman hadde this noble champioun,
That highte Dianira, fressh as May;
And as thise clerkes maken mencioun,
She hath hym sent a sherte fressh and gay.
Allas, this sherte, allas, and weylaway!
Envenymed was so subtilly withalle,
That, er that he had wered it half a day,
It made his flessh al from his bones falle.

But nathelees somme clerkes hire excusen
By oon that highte Nessus, that it maked;
Be as be may, I will hire noght accusen;
But on his bak this sherte he wered al naked
Til that his flessh was for the venym blaked;
And whan he saugh noon oother remedye,
In hoote coles he hath hymselven raked;
for with no venym deigned hym to dye.

Thus starf this worthy, myghty Hercules;
Lo! who may truste on fortune any throwe?
for hym that folweth al this world of prees,
Er he be war, is ofte yleyd ful lowe.
ful wys is he that kan hymselven knowe.
Beth war! for whan that fortune list to glose,
Thanne wayteth she hir man to overthrowe
By swich a wey as he wolde leest suppose.

hE myghty trone, the precious
tresor,
The glorious ceptre and roial
magestee
That hadde the kyng Nabugodo-
nosor,
With tonge unnethe may discryved bee.
he twyes wan Jerusalem the citee;
The vessel of the temple he with hym ladde.
At Babiloigne was his sovereyn see,
In which his glorie and his delit he hadde.

The faireste children of the blood roial
Of Israel he leet do gelde anoon,
And maked ech of hem to been his thral.
Amonges othere Daniel was oon,
That was the wiseste child of everychon,
for he the dremes of the kyng expowned,
Whereas in Chaldeye clerk ne was ther noon
That wiste to what fyn his dremes sowned.

This proude kyng leet make a statue of gold,
Sixty cubites long, and sevene in brede,
To which ymage, bothe yonge and oold
Comanded he to loute, and have in drede,

Or in a fourneys ful of flambes rede
He shal be brent that wolde noght obeye.
But nevere wolde assente to that dede
Daniel, ne his yonge felawes tweye.

This kyng of kynges proud was and elaat;
He wende that God that sit in magestee,
Ne myghte hym nat bireve of his estaat:
But sodeynly he loste his dignytee,
And lyk a beest hym semed for to bee,
And eet hey as an oxe, and lay theroute;
In reyn with wilde beestes walked hee,
Til certein tyme was ycome aboute.

And lik an egles fetheres wexe his heres,
His nayles lik a briddes clawes weere;
Til God relessed hym a certeyn yeres,
And yaf hym wit; and thanne with many a teere
He thanked God, and evere his lyf in feere
Was he to doon amys, or moore trespace,
And, til that tyme he leyd was on his beere,
He knew that God was ful of myght and grace.

HIS sone, which that highte Balthasar,
That heeld the regne after his fader day,
He by his fader koude noght be war,
For proud he was of herte and of array;
And eek an ydolastre he was ay.
His hye estaat assured hym in pryde;
But fortune caste hyme doun, and ther he lay,
And sodeynly his regne gan divide.

A feeste he made unto his lordes alle,
Upon a tyme, and bad hem blithe bee;
And thanne his officeres gan he calle,
Gooth, bryngeth forth the vesselles, quod he,
Whiche that my fader, in his prosperitee,
Out of the temple of Jerusalem birafte,
And to oure hye goddes thanke we
Of honour, that oure eldres with us lafte.

Hys wyf, his lordes, and his concubynes
Ay dronken, whil hire appetites laste,
Out of thise noble vessels sondry wynes;
And on a wal this kyng his eyen caste,
And saugh an hand armlees, that wroot ful faste,
For feere of which he quook, and siked soore.
This hand, that Balthasar so soore agaste,
Wroot Mane, techel, phares, and namoore.

In al that land magicien was noon
That koude expounde what this lettre mente;
But Daniel expowned it anoon,
And seyde King, God to thy fader lente
Glorie and honour, regne, tresour, rente:
And he was proud, and nothyng God ne dradde,
And therfore God greet wreche upon hym sente,
And hym birafte the regne that he hadde.

He was out cast of mannes compaignye;
With asses was his habitacioun,
And eet hey as a beest in weet and drye,

g 3

Til that he knew, by grace and by resoun,
That God of hevene hath domynacioun
Over every regne and every creature;
And thanne hadde God of hym compassioun,
And hym restored his regne and his figure.

Eek thou, that art his sone, art proud also,
And knowest alle thise thynges verraily,
And art rebel to God, and art his foo;
Thou drank eek of his vessels boldely;
Thy wyf eek, and thy wenches, synfully
Dronke of the same vessels sondry wynys,
And heryest false goddes cursedly;
Therfore to thee yshapen ful greet pyne ys.

This hand was sent from God, that on the wal
Wroot, Mane, techel, phares, truste me;
Thy regne is doon, thou weyest noght at al;
Dyvyded is thy regne, and it shal be
To Medes and to Perses yeven, quod he.
And thilke same nyght this kyng was slawe,
And Darius occupieth his degree,
Thogh he therto hadde neither right ne lawe.

Lordynges, ensample heerby may ye take,
How that in lordshipe is no sikernesse;
For whan fortune wole a man forsake,
She bereth awey his regne and his richesse,
And eek his freendes, bothe moore and lesse;
For what man that hath freendes thurgh fortune,
Mishap wol make hem enemys, I gesse;
This proverbe is ful sooth and ful commune.

ENOBIA, of Palymerie queene,
As writen Persiens of hir noblesse,
So worthy was in armes and so keene,
That no wight passed hire in hardynesse,
Ne in lynage, nor oother gentilesse.
Of kynges blood of Perce is she descended;
I seye nat that she hadde moost fairnesse,
But of hire shape she myghte nat been amended.

From hire childhede I fynde that she fledde
Office of wommen, and to wode she wente;
And many a wilde hertes blood she shedde
With arwes brode that she to hem sente.
She was so swift that she anon hem hente,
And whan that she was elder, she wolde kille
Leouns, leopardes, and beres al torente,
And in hir armes weelde hem at hir wille.

She dorste wilde beestes dennes seke,
And rennen in the montaignes al the nyght,
And slepen under the bussh; and she koude eke
Wrastlen by verray force and verray myght
With any yong man, were he never so wight;
Ther myghte nothyng in hir armes stonde.
She kepte hir maydenhod from every wight;
To no man deigned hire for to be bonde.

But atte laste hir freendes han hire maried
To Odenake, a prynce of that contree;

Al were it so that she hem longe taried;
And ye shul understonde how that he
Hadde swiche fantasies as hadde she.
But nathelees, whan they were knyt infeere,
They lyved in joye and in felicitee,
For ech of hem hadde oother lief and deere,

Save o thynge, that she wolde nevere assente,
By no wey, that he sholde by hire lye
But ones, for it was hir pleyn entente
To have a child, the world to multiplye;
And al so soone as that she myghte espye
That she was nat with childe with that dede,
Thanne wolde she suffre hym doon his fantasye
Eft soone, and nat but oones, out of drede.

And if she were with childe at thilke cast,
Na moore sholde he pleyen thilke game
Til fully fourty dayes weren past;
Thanne wolde she ones suffre hym do the same.
Al were this Odenake wilde or tame,
He gat na moore of hire, for thus she seyde,
It was to wyves lecherie and shame
In oother caas, if that men with hem pleyde.

Two sones by this Odenake hadde she,
The whiche she kepte in vertu and lettrure;
But now unto our tale turne we.
I seye, so worshipful a creature,
And wys therwith, and large with mesure,
So penyble in the werre, and curteis eke,
Ne moore labour myghte in werre endure
Was noon, though al this world men sholde seke.

Hir riche array ne myghte nat be told,
As wel in vessel as in hire clothyng;
She was al clad in perree and in gold,
And eek she lafte noght, for noon huntyng,
To have of sondry tonges ful knowyng,
Whan that she leyser hadde, and for to entende
To lerne bookes was al hire likyng,
How she in vertu myghte hir lyf dispende.

And, shortly of this storie for to trete,
So doughty was hir housbonde and eek she,
That they conquered manye regnes grete
In the orient, with many a faire citee
Apertenaunt unto the magestee
Of Rome, & with strong hond held hem ful faste;
Ne nevere myghte hir foomen doon hem flee,
Ay whil that Odenakes dayes laste.

Hir batailles, whoso list hem for to rede,
Agayn Sapor the kyng and othere mo,
And how that al this proces fil in dede,
Why she conquered, and what title therto,
And after of hir meschief and hire wo,
How that she was biseged and ytake,
Lat hym unto my maister Petrark go,
That writ ynough of this, I undertake.

Whan Odenake was deed, she myghtily
The regnes heeld, and with hire propre honde
86

Agayn hir foos she faught so cruelly,
That ther nas kyng ne prynce, in al that londe
That he nas glad, if he that grace fonde,
That she ne wolde upon his lond werreye;
With hire they maden alliance by bonde
To been in pees, and lete hire ride and pleye.

The emperour of Rome, Claudius,
Ne hym bifore, the Romayn Galien,
Ne dorste nevere been so corageous
Ne noon Ermyn, ne noon Egipcien,
Ne Surrien, ne noon Arabyen,
Within the feeldes that dorste with hire fighte
Lest that she wolde hem with hir handes slen,
Or with hir meignee putten hem to flighte.

In kynges habit wente hir sones two,
As heires of hir fadres regnes alle,
And Hermanno, and Thymalao
Hir names were, as Persiens hem calle.
But ay fortune hath in hire hony galle:
This myghty queene may no while endure.
Fortune out of hir regne made hire falle
To wrecchednesse and to mysaventure.

Aurelian, whan that the governaunce
Of Rome cam into his handes tweye,
He shoope upon this queene to doon vengeaunce,
And with his legions he took his weye
Toward Cenobie, and, shortly for to seye,
He made hire flee, and atte last hire hente,
And fettred hire, and eek hire children tweye,
And wan the lond, and hoom to Rome he wente.

Amonges othere thynges that he wan,
Hir chaar, that was with gold wroght and perree,
This grete Romayn, this Aurelian,
Hath with hym lad, for that men sholde it see.
Biforen his triumphe walketh shee
With gilte cheynes on hire nekke hangynge;
Corouned was she, after hir degree,
And ful of perree charged hire clothynge.

Allas, fortune! she that whilom was
Dredeful to kynges and to emperoures,
Now gaureth al the peple on hire, allas!
And she that helmed was in starke stoures,
And wan by force townes stronge, and toures,
Shal on hir heed now were a vitremyte;
And she that bar the ceptre ful of floures
Shal bere a distaf, hire cost for to quyte.

NOBLE, o worthy Petro, glorie of
Spayne,
Whom fortune heeld so hye in
magestee,
Wel oghten men thy pitous deeth
complayne!
Out of thy land thy brother made thee flee,
And after, at a seege, by subtiltee,
Thou were bitraysed and lad unto his tente,
Wheras he with his owene hand slow thee,
Succedynge in thy regne and in thy rente.

De P
Reg
Ispa

The feeld of snow, with thegle of blak therinne,
Caught with the lymerod, coloured as the gleede,
He brew this cursednesse and al this synne;
The Wikked nest was werker of this nede;
Noght Charles Olyver, that ay took heede
Of trouthe and honour, but of Armorike
Genylon Olyver, corrupt for meede,
Broghte this worthy kyng in swiche a brike.

 WORTHY Petro, kyng of Cipre,
also,
That Alisandre wan by heigh
maistrye,
Ful many an hethen wroghtestow
ful wo,
Of which thyne owene liges hadde envye,
And, for nothyng but for thy chivalrye,
They in thy bed han slayn thee by the morwe.
Thus kan Fortune hir wheel governe and gye,
And out of joye brynge men to sorwe.

Of Melan, grete Barnabo Viscounte,
God of delit, and scourge of Lumbardye,
Why sholde I nat thyn infortune acounte,
Sith in estaat thow clombe were so hye?
Thy brother sone, that was thy double allye,
For he thy nevew was, and sone/in/lawe,
Withinne his prisoun made thee to dye;
But why, ne how, noot I that thou were slawe.

Of the erl Hugelyn of Pyze the langour
Ther may no tonge telle for pitee;
But litel out of Pize stant a tour,
In whiche tour in prisoun put was he,
And with hym been his litel children thre;
The eldeste scarsly fyf yeer was of age.
Allas, Fortune! it was greet crueltee
Swiche briddes for to putte in swiche a cage!

Dampned was he to dyen in that prisoun,
For Roger, which that bisshope was of Pize,
Hadde on hym maad a fals suggestioun,
Thurgh which the peple gan upon hym rise,
And putten hym to prisoun in swich wise
As ye han herd, and mete and drynke he hadde
So smal, that wel unnethe it may suffise,
And therwithal it was ful povre and badde.

And on a day bifil that, in that hour,
Whan that his mete wont was to be broght,
The gayler shette the dores of the tour.
He herde it wel, but he ne spak right noght,
And in his herte anon ther fil a thoght
That they for hunger wolde doon hym dyen.
Allas! quod he, allas! that I was wroght!
Therwith the teeris fillen from his eyen.

His yonge sone, that thre yeer was of age,
Unto hym seyde, Fader, why do ye wepe?
Whanne wol the gayler bryngen oure potage,
Is ther no morsel breed that ye do kepe?
I am so hungry that I may nat slepe,
Now wolde God that I myghte slepen evere!
g4

Thanne sholde nat hunger in my wombe crepe;
Ther is nothyng, save breed, that me were levere.

Thus day by day this child bigan to crye,
Til in his fadres barm adoun it lay,
And seyde, Farewel, fader, I moot dye,
And kiste his fader, and dyde the same day;
And whan the woful fader deed it say,
For wo his armes two he gan to byte,
And seyde, Allas, Fortune! and weylaway!
Thy false wheel my wo al may I wyte!

His children wende that it for hunger was
That he his armes gnow, and nat for wo,
And seyde, Fader, do nat so, allas!
But rather ete the flessh upon us two;
Oure flessh thou yaf us, take oure flessh us fro,
And ete ynogh. Right thus they to hym seyde,
And after that, withinne a day or two,
They leyde hem in his lappe adoun, and deyde.

Hymself, despeired, eek for hunger starf;
Thus ended is this myghty Erl of Pize;
From heigh estaat Fortune awey hym carf.
Of this tragedie it oghte ynough suffise.
Whoso wol here it in a lenger wise,
Redeth the grete poete of Ytaille,
That highte Dant, for he kan al devyse
Fro point to point, nat o word wol he faille.

 LTHOUGH that Nero were as vicious
As any feend that lith in helle adoun,
Yet he, as telleth us Swetonius,
This wyde world hadde in subjeccioun,
Bothe est and west, south and
septemtrioun;
Of rubies, saphires, and of peerles white,
Were alle his clothes brouded up and doun;
For he in gemmes greetly gan delite.

Moore delicaat, moore pompous of array,
Moore proud, was nevere emperour than he;
That ilke clooth, that he hadde wered o day,
After that tyme he nolde it nevere see.
Nettes of gold/threed hadde he greet plentee
To fisshe in Tybre, whan hym liste pleye.
His lustes were al lawe in his decree,
For Fortune, as his freend, hym wolde obeye.

He Rome brende for his delicasie;
The senatours he slow upon a day,
To heere how men wolde wepe and crie;
And slow his brother, and by his suster lay.
His mooder made he in pitous array;
For he hire wombe slitte, to biholde
Where he conceyved was; so weilaway!
That he so litel of his mooder tolde.

No teere out of his eyen for that sighte
Ne cam, but seyde, A fair womman was she!
Greet wonder is how that he koude or myghte
Be domesman of hire dede beautee;
The wyn to bryngen hym comanded he,
87

And drank anon ; noon oother wo he made.
Whan myght is joyned unto crueltee,
Allas! to depe wol the venym wade!

In yowthe a maister hadde this emperour,
To teche hym letterure and curteisye,
For of moralitee he was the flour,
As in his tyme, but if bookes lye;
And whil this maister hadde of hym maistrye,
He maked hym so konnyng and so sowple,
That longe tyme it was er tirannye,
Or any vice, dorste on hym uncowple.

This Seneca, of which that I devyse,
Bycause Nero hadde of hym swich drede,
For he fro vices wolde hym ay chastise
Discreetly, as by word, and nat by dede;
Sire, wolde he seyn, an emperour moot nede
Be vertuous, and hate tirannye;
For which he in a bath made hym to blede
On bothe his armes, til he moste dye.

This Nero hadde eek of acustumaunce
In youthe agayns his maister for to ryse,
Which afterward hym thoughte a greet grevaunce;
Therfore he made hym dyen in this wise.
But nathelees this Seneca the wise
Chees in a bath to dye in this manere
Rather than han another tormentise;
And thus hath Nero slayn his maister deere.

Now fil it so that fortune liste no lenger
The hye pryde of Nero to cherice;
For though that he were strong, yet was she
strenger;
She thoughte thus By God, I am to nyce,
To sette a man that is fulfild of vice
In heigh degree, and emperour hym calle.
By God! out of his sete I wol hym trice;
Whan he leest weneth, sonnest shal he falle!

The peple roos upon hym on a nyght
For his defaute, and whan he it espied,
Out of his dores anon he hath hym dight
Allone, and, ther he wende han ben allied,
He knokked faste, and ay, the moore he cried,
The faster shette they the dores alle;
Tho wiste he weel he hadde hymself mysgyed,
And wente his wey, no lenger dorste he calle.

The peple cride and rombled up and doun,
That with his erys herde he how they seyde,
Where is this false tiraunt, this Neroun?
For fere almoost out of his wit he breyde,
And to his goddes pitously he preyde
For socour, but it myghte nat bityde.
For drede of this, hym thoughte that he deyde,
And ran into a gardyn, hym to hyde.

And in this gardyn foond he cherles tweye
That seten by a fyr ful greet and reed,
And to thise cherles two he gan to preye
To sleen hym, and to girden of his heed,
That to his body, whan that he were deed,

Were no despit ydoon, for his defame.
Hymself he slow, he koude no bettre reed,
Of which fortune lough, and hadde a game.

WAS nevere capitayn under a kyng
That regnes mo putte in subjeccioun,
Ne strenger was in feeld of alle thyng,
As in his tyme, ne gretter of renoun,
Ne moore pompous in heigh pre-
sumpcioun,
Than Oloferne, which fortune ay kiste
So likerously, and ladde hym up and doun
Til that his heed was of, er that he wiste.

Nat oonly that this world hadde hym in awe
For lesynge of richesse or libertee,
But he made every man reneye his lawe.
Nabugodonosor was god, seyde hee,
Noon oother god ne sholde adoured bee.
Agayns his heeste no wight dorst trespace
Save in Bethulia, a strong citee,
Where Eliachim a preest was of that place.

But taak kepe of the deeth of Oloferne:
Amydde his hoost he dronke lay anyght,
Withinne his tente, large as is a berne,
And yit, for al his pompe and al his myght,
Judith, a womman, as he lay upright
Slepynge, his heed of smoot, and from his tente
Ful pryvely she stal from every wight,
And with his heed unto hir toun she wente.

WHAT nedeth it of kyng Anthiochus
To telle his hye roial magestee,
His hye pride, his werkes venymus?
For swich another was ther noon
as he.
Rede which that he was in Machabee,
And rede the proude wordes that he seyde,
And why he fil fro heigh prosperitee,
And in an hill how wrecchedly he deyde.

Fortune hym hadde enhaunced so in pride
That verraily he wende he myghte attayne
Unto the sterres, upon every syde;
And in balance weyen ech montayne;
And alle the floodes of the see restrayne.
And Goddes peple hadde he moost in hate;
Hem wolde he sleen in torment and in payne,
Wenynge that God ne myghte his pride abate.

And for that Nichanore and Thymothee,
Of Jewes weren vanquysshed myghtily,
Unto the Jewes swich an hate hadde he
That he bad greithe his chaar ful hastily,
And swoor, and seyde, ful despitously,
Unto Jerusalem he wolde eftsoone,
To wreken his ire on it ful cruelly;
But of his purpos he was let ful soone.

God for his manace hym so soore smoot
With invisible wounde, ay incurable,
That in hise guttes carf it so and boot,
That hise peynes weren importable;

And certeinly the wreche was resonable,
for many a mannes guttes dide he peyne;
But from his purpos cursed and dampnable
for al his smert he wolde hym nat restreyne;

But bad anon apparaillen his hoost,
And sodeynly, er he was of it war,
God daunted al his pride and al his boost;
for he so soore fil out of his char,
That it his lemes and his skyn totar,
So that he neyther myghte go ne ryde,
But in a chayer men aboute hym bar
Alle forbrused, bothe bak and syde.

The wreche of God hym smoot so cruelly,
That thurgh his body wikked wormes crepte;
And therwithal he stank so horribly,
That noon of al his meynee that hym kepte,
Wheither so that he wook or ellis slepte,
Ne myghte noght for stynk of hym endure.
In this meschief he wayled and eek wepte,
And knew God lord of every creature.

To al his hoost and to hymself also
ful wlatsom was the stynk of his careyne;
No man ne myghte hym bere to ne fro;
And in this stynk and this horrible peyne,
He starf ful wrecchedly in a monteyne.
Thus hath this robbour and this homycide,
That many a man made to wepe and pleyne,
Swich guerdoun as bilongeth unto pryde.

HE storie of Alisaundre is so
commune
That every wight that hath
discrecioun
Hath herd somwhat or al of his
fortune.
This wyde world, as in conclusioun,
He wan by strengthe, or for his hye renoun
They weren glad for pees unto hym sende.
The pride of man and beest he leyde adoun
Wherso he cam, unto the worldes ende.

Comparisoun myghte nevere yet been maked
Bitwixe hym and another conquerour;
for al this world for drede of hym hath quaked,
He was of knighthod and of fredom flour;
fortune hym made the heir of hire honour;
Save wyn and wommen, nothyng myghte aswage
His hye entente in armes and labour;
So was he ful of leonyn corage.

What preys were it to hym, though I yow tolde
Of Darius, and an hundred thousand mo,
Of kynges, princes, erles, dukes bolde,
Whiche he conquered, and broghte hem into wo?
I seye, as fer as man may ryde or go,
The world was his, what sholde I moore devyse?
for though I write or tolde yow everemo
Of his knyghthode, it myghte nat suffise.

Twelf yeer he regned, as seith Machabee;
Philippes sone of Macidoyne he was,

That first was kyng in Grece the contree.
O worthy gentil Alisandre, allas!
That evere sholde fallen swich a cas!
Empoysoned of thyn owene folk thou weere;
Thy sys, fortune hath turned into aas,
And yet for thee ne weepe she never a teere!

Who shal me yeven teeris to compleyne
The deeth of gentillesse and of franchise,
That al the world weelded in his demeyne,
And yet hym thoughte it myghte nat suffise?
So ful was his corage of heigh emprise.
Allas! who shal me helpe to endite
false fortune, and poyson to despise,
The whiche two of al this wo I wyte?

Y wisedom, manhede, and by greet
labour
from humblehede to roial magestee
Up roos he, Julius the conquerour,
That wan al thoccident by land & see,
By strengthe of hand, or elles by
tretee,
But unto Rome made hem tributarie;
And sitthe of Rome the emperour was he,
Til that fortune weex his adversarie.

O myghty Cesar! that in Thessalie
Agayn Pompeus, fader thyn in lawe,
That of thorient hadde all the chivalrie
As fer as that the day bigynneth dawe,
Thou thurgh thy knyghthod hast hem take & slawe,
Save fewe folk that with Pompeus fledde,
Thurgh which thou puttest al thorient in awe,
Thanke fortune, that so wel thee spedde!

But now a litel while I wol biwaille
This Pompeus, this noble governour
Of Rome, which that fleigh at this bataille.
I seye, oon of his men, a fals traitour,
His heed of smoot, to wynnen hym favour
Of Julius, and hym the heed he broghte.
Allas, Pompeye, of thorient conquerour,
That fortune unto swich a fyn thee broghte!

To Rome agayn repaireth Julius
With his triumphe, lauriat ful hye;
But on a tyme Brutus and Cassius,
That evere hadde of his hye estaat envye,
ful prively had maad conspiracye
Agayns this Julius, in subtil wise,
And caste the place in which he sholde dye
With boydekyns, as I shal yow devyse.

This Julius to the Capitolie wente
Upon a day, as he was wont to goon,
And in the Capitolie anon hym hente
This false Brutus, and his othere foon,
And stiked hym with boydekyns anoon
With many a wounde, and thus they lete hym lye;
But nevere gronte he at no strook but oon,
Or elles at two, but if his storie lye.

So manly was this Julius of herte,
And so wel lovede estaatly honestee,

The
Monkes
Tale

That though his deedly woundes soore smerte,
His mantel over his hypes castyth he
for no man sholde seen his privetee;
And as he lay of dying in a traunce,
And wiste verraily that deed was hee,
Of honestee yet hadde he remembraunce.

Lucan, to thee this storie I recomende,
And to Swetoun, and to Valerius also,
That of this storie writen word and ende,
How that to thise grete conqueroures two
fortune was first freend, and sithen foo.
No man ne truste upon hire favour longe,
But have hire in awayt for everemoo;
Witnesse on alle thise conqueroures stronge.

De Creso
Rege

HIS riche Cresus, whilom kyng of
Lyde,
Of whiche Cresus Cirus soore hym
dradde,
Yet was he caught amyddes al his
pryde,
And to be brent men to the fyr hym ladde;
But swich a reyn doun fro the welkne shadde
That slow the fyr, and made hym to escape;
But to be war no grace yet he hadde,
Til fortune on the galwes made hym gape.

Whanne he escaped was, he kan nat stente
for to bigynne a newe werre agayn.
He wende wel, for that fortune hym sente
Swich hap, that he escaped thurgh the rayn,
That of his foos he myghte nat be slayn;
And eek a swevene upon a nyght he mette,
Of which he was so proud, and eek so fayn,
That in vengeance he al his herte sette.

Upon a tree he was, as that hym thoughte,
Ther Juppiter hym wessh, bothe bak and syde,
And Phebus eek a fair towaille hym broughte
To dryen hym with, and therfore wex his pryde;
And to his doghter, that stood hym bisyde,
Which that he knew in heigh science habounde,
He bad hire telle hym what it signyfyde,
And she his dreem bigan right thus expounde.

☙The tree, quod she, the galwes is to meene;
And Juppiter bitokneth snow and reyn,
And Phebus, with his towaille so clene,
Tho been the sonne‚bemes for to seyn;
Thou shalt anhanged be, fader, certeyn,
Reyn shal thee wasshe, and sonne shal thee drye.
☙Thus warned she hym ful plat and ful pleyn,
His doghter, which that called was Phanye.

☙Anhanged was Cresus, the proude kyng;
His roial trone myghte hym nat availle.
Tragedie is noon oother maner thyng;
Ne kan in syngyng crie ne biwaille,
But for that fortune alwey wole assaille
With unwar strook the regnes that been proude;
For whan men trusteth hire, thanne wol she faille,
And covere hire brighte face with a cloude.
Heere stynteth the Knyght the Monk of his Tale.

90

The prologe of the Nonnes Preestes Tale.❀❀

OO! quod the Knyght, good
sire, namoore of this!
That ye han seyd is right
ynough, ywis,
And muchel moore; for litel
hevynesse
Is right ynough to muche
folk, I gesse.
I seye for me, it is a greet
disese
Whereas men han been in greet welthe and ese,
To heeren of hire sodeyn fal, allas!
And the contrarie is joye and greet solas,
As whan a man hath ben in povre estaat,
And clymbeth up, and wexeth fortunat,
And there abideth in prosperitee,
Swich thyng is gladsom, as it thynketh me,
And of swich thyng were goodly for to telle.
YE, quod oure Hooste, by Seint Poules belle,
Ye seye right sooth; this Monk, he clappeth
lowde;
He spak how fortune covered with a clowde,
I noot nevere what, and als of a Tragedie
Right now ye herde, and, pardee! no remedie
It is for to biwaille, ne compleyne
That that is doon; and als, it is a peyne,
As ye han seyd, to heere of hevynesse.
Sire Monk, namoore of this, so God yow blesse!
Youre tale anoyeth al this compaignye;
Swich talkyng is nat worth a boterflye;
for therinne is ther no desport ne game.
Wherfore, sire Monk, daun Piers by youre name,
I pray yow hertely, telle us somwhat elles,
for sikerly, nere clynkyng of youre belles
That on youre bridel hange on every syde,
By hevene kyng, that for us alle dyde,
I sholde er this han fallen doun for sleepe,
Althogh the slough had never been so deepe;
Thanne hadde your tale al be toold in veyn.
for certeinly, as that thise clerkes seyn,
Whereas a man may have noon audience,
Noght helpeth it to tellen his sentence;
And wel I woot the substance is in me,
If any thyng shal wel reported be.
Sir, sey somwhat of huntyng, I yow preye.
NAY! quod this Monk, I have no lust to
pleye;
Now lat another telle, as I have toold.
☙Thanne spak oure Hoost with rude speche
and boold,
And seyde unto the Nonnes Preest anon,
Com neer, thou preest, come hyder, thou sir John.
Telle us swich thyng as may oure hertes glade;
Be blithe, though thou ryde upon a jade.
What thogh thyn hors be bothe foule and lene,
If he wol serve thee, rekke nat a bene;
Looke that thyn herte be murie everemo.
☙Yis, sir, quod he, yis, Hoost, so moot I go,
But I be myrie, ywis, I wol be blamed.
☙And right anon his tale he hath attamed,
And thus he seyde unto us everichon,
This sweete preest, this goodly man, sir John.

HEERE BIGYNNETH THE NONNES PREESTES TALE OF THE COK AND HEN, CHAUNTECLEER AND PERTELOTE.

A POVRE wydwe, somdel stape in age, Was whilom dwellyng in a narwe cotage, Beside a greve, stondynge in a dale. This wydwe, of which I telle yow my tale, Syn thilke day that she was last a wyf,
In pacience ladde a ful symple lyf,
for litel was hir catel and hir rente.
By housbondrie, of swich as God hire sente,
She foond hirself, and eek hire doghtren two.
Thre large sowes hadde she, and namo;
Three keen, and eek a sheep that highte Malle.
ful sooty was hir bour, and eek hire halle,
In which she eet ful many a sklendre meel;
Of poynaunt sauce hir neded never a deel.
No deyntee morsel passed thurgh hir throte;
Hir diete was accordant to hir cote.
Repleccioun ne made hire nevere sik,
Attempree diete was al hir phisik,
And exercise, and hertes suffisaunce.
The goute lette hire nothyng for to daunce,
Napoplexie ne shente nat hir heed;
No wyn ne drank she, neither whit ne reed;
Hir bord was served moost with whit and blak,
Milk & broun breed, in which she foond no lak,
Seynd bacoun, and somtyme an ey or tweye,
for she was, as it were, a maner deye.

A YEERD she hadde, enclosed al aboute With stikkes, and a drye dych withoute, In which she hadde a cok, heet Chauntecleer.
In al the land of crowyng nas his peer.
His voys was murier than the murie orgon
On messe-dayes that in the chirche gon;
Wel sikerer was his crowyng in his logge,
Than is a clokke, or an abbey orlogge.
By nature he knew eche ascencioun
Of thequynoxial in thilke toun;
for whan degrees fiftene were ascended,
Thanne crewe he, that it myghte nat been amended.
His coomb was redder than the fyn coral,
And batailled, as it were a castel wal;
His byle was blak, and as the jeet it shoon;
Lyk asure were his legges, and his toon;
His nayles whiter than the lylye flour,
And lyk the burned gold was his colour.

T HIS gentil cok hadde in his governaunce Sevene hennes, for to doon al his plesaunce,
Which were his sustres and his paramours,
And wonder lyk to hym, as of colours;
Of whiche the faireste hewed on hir throte
Was cleped faire damoysele Pertelote.

Curteys she was, discreet, and debonaire,
And compaignable, and bar hyrself so faire,
Syn thilke day that she was seven nyght oold,
That trewely she hath the herte in hoold
Of Chauntecleer loken in every lith;
He loved hire so, that wel was hym therwith.
But swiche a joye was it to here hem synge,
Whan that the brighte sonne gan to sprynge,
In sweete accord, My lief is faren in londe,
for thilke tyme, as I have understonde,
Beestes and briddes koude speke and synge.

A ND so bifel, that in the dawenynge, As Chauntecleer among his wyves alle Sat on his perche, that was in the halle,
And next hym sat this faire Pertelote,
This Chauntecleer gan gronen in his throte,
As man that in his dreem is drecched soore.
And whan that Pertelote thus herde hym roore,
She was agast, and seyde, O herte deere!
What eyleth yow, to grone in this manere?
Ye been a verray sleper; fy, for shame!
And he answerde and seyde thus: Madame,
I pray yow that ye take it not agrief;
By God, me thoughte I was in swich meschief
Right now, that yet myn herte is soore afright.
Now God, quod he, my swevene recche aright,
And kepe my body out of foul prisoun.
Me mette, how that I roomed up and doun
Withinne our yeerd, wheeras I saugh a beest
Was lyk an hound, and wolde han maad areest
Upon my body, and wolde han had me deed.
His colour was bitwixe yelow and reed;
And tipped was his tayl, and bothe his eeris,
With blak, unlyk the remenant of his heeris;
His snowte smal, with glowynge eyen tweye.
Yet of his look for feere almoost I deye;
This caused me my gronyng, doutelees.
Avoy! quod she, fy on yow, hertelees!
Allas! quod she, for by that God above!
Now han ye lost myn herte and al my love.
I kan nat love a coward, by my feith!
for certes, whatso any womman seith,
We alle desiren, if it myghte bee,
To han housbondes hardy, wise, and free,
And secree, and no nygard, ne no fool,
Ne hym that is agast of every tool,
Ne noon avauntour, by that God above!
How dorste ye seyn, for shame, unto your love
That any thyng myghte make yow aferd?
Have ye no mannes herte, and han a berd?
Allas! and konne ye been agast of swevenys?
Nothyng, God woot, but vanitee, in swevene is.
Swevenes engendren of replecciouns,
And ofte of fume, and of complecciouns
Whan humours been to habundant in a wight.
C ERTES this dreem, which ye han met tonyght, Cometh of the grete superfluytee

Of youre rede colera, pardee,
Which causeth folk to dreden in hir dremes
Of arwes, and of fyre with rede lemes,
Of grete beestes, that they wol hem byte,
Of contek, and of whelpes, grete and lyte;
Right as the humour of malencolie
Causeth ful many a man, in sleepe, to crie,
For feere of blake beres, or boles blake,
Or elles, blake develes wole hem take.
Of othere humours koude I telle also,
That werken many a man in sleepe ful wo;
But I wol passe as lightly as I kan.
Lo Catoun, which that was so wys a man,
Seyde he nat thus, Ne do no fors of dremes.
℣Now, sire, quod she, whan ye flee fro the bemes,
For Goddes love, as taak som laxatyf.
Up peril of my soule, and of my lyf,
I conseille yow the beste, I wol nat lye,
That bothe of colere and of malencolye
Ye purge yow; and, for ye shal nat tarie,
Though in this toun is noon apothecarie,
I shal myself to herbes techen yow,
That shul been for youre hele, and for youre prow;
And in oure yeerd tho herbes shal I fynde,
The whiche han of hire propretee, by kynde,
To purge yow bynethe, and eek above.
Forget nat this, for Goddes owene love!
Ye been ful coleryk of compleccioun.
Ware the sonne in his ascencioun
Ne fynde yow nat repleet of humours hote;
And if it do, I dar wel leye a grote,
That ye shul have a fevere terciane,
Or an agu, that may be youre bane.
A day or two ye shul have digestyves
Of wormes, er ye take youre laxatyves,
Of lawriol, centaure, and fumetere,
Or elles of ellebor, that groweth there,
Of katapuce, or of gaitrys beryis,
Of herbe yve growyng in oure yeerd, ther mery is;
Pekke hem up right as they growe, and ete hem yn;
Be myrie, housbonde, for youre fader kyn!
Dredeth no dreem; I kan sey yow namoore.

℟ADAME, quod he, graunt mercy of
youre loore,
But nathelees, as touchyng daun
Catoun,
That hath of wysdom swich a greet
renoun,
Though that he bad no dremes for to drede,
By God, men may in olde bookes rede
Of many a man, moore of auctoritee
Than evere Caton was, so moot I thee,
That al the revers seyn of this sentence,
And han wel founden by experience,
That dremes been significaciouns,
As wel of joye as tribulaciouns
That folk enduren in this lif present.
Ther nedeth make of this noon argument;
The verray preeve sheweth it in dede.
℣Oon of the gretteste auctours that men rede
Seith thus, that whilom two felawes wente
On pilgrimage, in a ful good entente;
And happed so, they coomen in a toun,

Wheras ther was swich congregacioun
Of peple, and eek so streit of herbergage,
That they ne founde as muche as o cotage,
In which they bothe myghte ylogged bee;
Wherfore they mosten of necessitee,
As for that nyght, departen compaignye;
And ech of hem gooth to his hostelrye,
And took his loggyng as it wolde falle.
That oon of hem was logged in a stalle
Fer in a yeerd, with oxen of the plough;
That oother man was logged wel ynough,
As was his aventure, or his fortune,
That us governeth alle as in commune.
And so bifel, that longe er it were day,
This man mette in his bed, theras he lay,
How that his felawe gan upon hym calle,
And seyde, Allas! for in an oxes stalle
This nyght I shal be mordred ther I lye.
Now help me, deere brother, or I dye;
In alle haste com to me, he sayde.
℟HIS man out of his sleep for feere abrayde;
But whan that he was wakened of his sleep,
He turned hym and took of it no keep;
Hym thoughte his dreem nas but a vanitee.
Thus twiës in his slepyng dremed hee,
And atte thridde tyme yet his felawe
Cam, as hym thoughte, and seide, I am now slawe;
Bihoold my bloody woundes, depe and wyde!
Arys up erly in the morwe tyde,
And at the west gate of the toun, quod he,
A carte ful of donge ther shaltow se,
In which my body is hid ful prively;
Do thilke carte arresten boldely.
My gold caused my mordre, sooth to sayn,℣
And tolde hym every point how he was slayn,
With a ful pitous face, pale of hewe.
And truste wel, his dreem he foond ful trewe;
For on the morwe, as soone as it was day,
To his felawes in he took the way;
And whan that he cam to this oxes stalle,
After his felawe he bigan to calle.
℣The hostiler answerde hym anon,
And seyde, Sire, your felawe is agon;
As soone as day he wente out of the toun.
℣This man gan fallen in suspecioun,
Remembrynge on his dremes that he mette,
And forth he gooth, no lenger wolde he lette,
Unto the west gate of the toun, and fond
A dong-carte, as it were to donge lond,
That was arrayed in that same wise
As ye han herd the dede man devyse;
And with an hardy herte he gan to crye
Vengeaunce and justice of this felonye:
℣My felawe mordred is this same nyght,
And in this carte he lith gapyng upright.
I crye out on the ministres, quod he,
That sholden kepe and reulen this citee;
Harrow! allas! heere lith my felawe slayn!
℣What sholde I moore unto this tale sayn?
The peple out sterte, and caste the cart to
grounde,
And in the myddel of the dong they founde
The dede man, that mordred was al newe.

O BLISFUL God, that art so just & trewe!
Lo howe that thou biwreyest mordre alway!
Mordre wol out, that se we day by day.
Mordre is so wlatsom, and abhomynable
To God, that is so just and resonable,
That he ne wol nat suffre it heled be,
Though it abyde a yeer, or two, or thre;
Mordre wol out, this my conclusioun.
And right anon, ministres of that toun
Han hent the carter, and so soore hym pyned,
And eek the hostiler so soore engyned,
That they biknewe hire wikkednesse anon,
And were anhanged by the nekke-bon.
Heere may men seen that dremes been to drede;
And certes, in the same book I rede,
Right in the nexte chapitre after this,
I gabbe nat, so have I joye or blis:
TWO men that wolde han passed over see
For certeyn cause, into a fer contree,
If that the wynd ne hadde been contrarie,
That made hem in a citee for to tarie
That stood ful myrie upon an haven-syde;
But on a day, agayn the even-tyde,
The wynd gan chaunge, & blew, right as hem leste.
Jolif and glad they wente unto hir reste,
And casten hem ful erly for to saille.
But to that o man fil a greet mervaille;
That oon of hem in slepyng as he lay,
Hym mette a wonder dreem agayn the day:
Him thoughte a man stood by his beddes syde
And hym comanded, that he sholde abyde,
And seyde hym thus: If thou tomorwe wende,
Thou shalt be dreynt; my tale is at an ende.
He wook, and tolde his felawe what he mette,
And preyde hym his viage for to lette;
As for that day, he preyde him to byde.
His felawe, that lay by his beddes syde,
Gan for to laughe, and scorned him ful faste.
No dreem, quod he, may so myn herte agaste,
That I wol lette for to do my thynges;
I sette nat a straw by thy dremynges,
For swevenes been but vanytees and japes;
Men dreme al day of owles or of apes,
And eek of many a maze therwithal;
Men dreme of thyng that nevere was ne shal.
But sith I see that thou wolt heere abyde,
And thus forslewthen wilfully thy tyde,
God woot it reweth me; and have good day!
And thus he took his leve, and wente his way.
But er that he hadde half his cours yseyled,
Noot I nat why, ne what myschaunce it eyled,
But casuelly the shippes botme rente,
And ship and man under the water wente
In sighte of othere shippes it bisyde,
That with hem seyled at the same tyde.
And therfore, faire Pertelote so deere,
By swiche ensamples olde maistow leere,
That no man sholde been to recchelees
Of dremes, for I seye thee, doutelees,
That many a dreem ful soore is for to drede.
LO, in the lyf of Seint Kenelm I rede,
That was Kenulphus sone, the noble kyng
Of Mercenrike, how Kenelm mette a thyng;

A lite er he was mordred, on a day,
His mordre in his avysioun he say.
His norice hym expowned every deel
His swevene, and bad hym for to kepe hym weel
For traisoun; but he nas but seven yeer oold,
And therfore litel tale hath he toold
Of any dreem, so hooly is his herte.
By God, I hadde levere than my sherte
That ye hadde rad his legende as have I.
Dame Pertelote, I sey yow trewely,
Macrobeus, that writ the avisioun
In Affrike of the worthy Cipioun,
Affermeth dremes, and seith that they been
Warnynge of thynges that men after seen.
And forthermoore, I pray yow looketh wel
In the Olde Testament, of Daniel,
If he heeld dremes any vanitee.
Reed eek of Joseph, and ther shul ye see
Wher dremes be somtyme, I sey nat alle,
Warnynge of thynges that shul after falle.
Looke of Egipt the kyng, daun Pharao,
His baker and his butiller also,
Wher they ne felte noon effect in dremes.
Whoso wol seken actes of sondry remes,
May rede of dremes many a wonder thyng.
LO Cresus, which that was of Lyde kyng,
Mette he nat that he sat upon a tree,
Which signified he sholde anhanged bee?
LO heere Andromacha, Ectores wyf,
That day that Ector sholde lese his lyf,
She dremed on the same nyght biforn,
How that the lyf of Ector sholde be lorn,
If thilke day he wente into bataille;
She warned hym, but it myghte nat availle;
He wente for to fighte natheles,
And he was slayn anon of Achilles.
But thilke tale is al to longe to telle,
And eek it is ny day, I may nat dwelle;
Shortly I seye, as for conclusioun,
That I shal han of this avisioun
Adversitee; and I seye forthermoor,
That I ne telle of laxatyves no stoor,
For they been venymes, I woot it weel;
I hem diffye, I love hem never a deel!
Now let us speke of myrthe, & stynte al this;
Madame Pertelote, so have I blis,
Of o thyng God hath sent me large grace;
For whan I se the beautee of youre face,
Ye been so scarlet-reed aboute youre eyen,
It maketh al my drede for to dyen;
For, also siker as In principio,
Mulier est hominis confusio,
Madame, the sentence of this Latyn is,
Womman is mannes joye, and al his blis.
For whan I feele anyght your softe syde,
Albeit that I may nat on yow ryde,
For that oure perche is maad so narwe, allas!
I am so ful of joye and of solas,
That I diffye bothe swevene and dreem.
AND with that word he fley doun fro the beem,
For it was day, and eek his hennes alle;
And with a chuk he gan hem for to calle,

93

For he hadde founde a corn, lay in the yerd.
Roial he was, he was namoore aferd;
He fethered Pertelote twenty tyme,
And trad as ofte, er that it was pryme.
He looketh as it were a grym leoun;
And on his toos he rometh up and doun,
Hym deigned nat to sette his foot to grounde.
He chukketh, whan he hath a corn yfounde,
And to hym rennen thanne his wyves alle.
Thus roial, as a prince is in an halle,
Leve I this Chauntecleere in his pasture;
And after wol I telle his aventure.
WHAN that the monthe in which the world
bigan,
That highte March, whan God first
maked man,
Was compleet, and ypassed were also,
Syn March bigan, thritty dayes and two,
Bifel that Chauntecleer, in al his pryde,
His sevene wyves walkynge by his syde,
Caste up his eyen to the brighte sonne,
That in the signe of Taurus hadde yronne
Twenty degrees and oon, and somwhat moore;
And knew by kynde, and by noon oother loore,
That it was pryme, and crew with blisful stevene.
The sonne, he seyde, is clomben up on hevene
Fourty degrees and oon, and moore, ywis.
Madame Pertelote, my worldes blis,
Herkneth thise blisful briddes how they synge,
And se the fresshe floures how they sprynge;
Ful is myn herte of revel and solas.
But sodeynly hym fil a sorweful cas;
For evere the latter ende of joy is wo.
God woot that worldly joye is soone ago;
And if a rethor koude faire endite,
He in a cronique saufly myghte it write,
As for a sovereyn notabilitee.
Now every wys man, lat him herkne me;
This storie is al so trewe, I undertake,
As is the book of Launcelot de Lake
That wommen holde in ful greet reverence.
Now wol I come agayn to my sentence.
A COLFOX, ful of sly iniquitee,
That in the grove hadde woned yeres
three,
By heigh ymaginacioun forncast,
The same nyght thurghout the hegges brast
Into the yerd, ther Chauntecleer the faire
Was wont, and eek his wyves, to repaire;
And in a bed of wortes stille he lay,
Til it was passed undren of the day,
Waitynge his tyme on Chauntecleer to falle;
As gladly doon thise homycides alle,
That in await liggen to mordre men.
O false mordrour, lurkynge in thy den!
O newe Scariot, newe Genyloun!
False dissimylour, O Greek Synoun,
That broghtest Troye al outrely to sorwe!
O Chauntecleer, acursed be that morwe,
That thou into that yerd flaugh fro the bemes!
Thou were ful wel ywarned by thy dremes,
That thilke day was perilous to thee.
But what that God forwoot moot nedes bee,

After the opinioun of certein clerkis.
Witnesse on hym, that any parfit clerk is,
That in scole is greet altercacioun
In this mateere, and greet disputisoun,
And hath ben of an hundred thousand men.
But I ne kan nat bulte it to the bren,
As kan the hooly doctour Augustyn,
Or Boece, or the bisshope Bradwardyn,
Wheither that Goddes worthy forwityng
Streyneth me nedefully to doon a thyng,
Nedely clepe I symple necessitee,
Or elles, if free choys be graunted me
To do that same thyng, or do it noght,
Though God forwoot it, er that it was wroght;
Or if his wityng streyneth never a deel
But by necessitee condicioneel.
I wil nat han to do of swich mateere;
My tale is of a cok, as ye may heere,
That took his conseil of his wyf, with sorwe,
To walken in the yerd upon that morwe
That he hadde met that dreem that I of tolde.
WOMMENNES conseils been ful ofte colde;
Wommannes conseil broghte us first to wo,
And made Adam fro Paradys to go,
Theras he was ful myrie and wel at ese;
But, for I noot to whom it myght displese
If I conseil of wommen wolde blame,
Passe over, for I seyde it in my game.
Rede auctours where they trete of swich mateere,
And what they seyn of wommen ye may heere.
Thise been the cokkes wordes, and nat myne;
I kan noon harm of no womman divyne.
FAIRE in the soond, to bathe hire myrily,
Lith Pertelote, and alle hire sustres by,
Agayn the sonne; and Chauntecleer so free
Soong murier than the mermayde in the see;
For Phisiologus seith sikerly,
How that they syngen wel and myrily.
And so bifel that, as he cast his eye,
Among the wortes, on a boterflye,
He was war of this fox that lay ful lowe.
Nothyng ne liste hym thanne for to crowe,
But cride anon, Cok, cok! and up he sterte,
As man that was affrayed in his herte;
For natureelly a beest desireth flee
Fro his contrarie, if he may it see,
Though he never erst hadde seyn it with his eye.
This Chauntecleer, whan he gan hym espye,
He wolde han fled, but that the fox anon
Seyde, Gentil sire, allas! wher wol ye gon?
Be ye affrayed of me that am youre freend?
Now certes, I were worse than a feend,
If I to yow wolde harm or vileynye.
I am nat come your conseil for tespye;
But trewely, the cause of my comynge
Was oonly for to herkne how that ye synge;
For trewely, ye have as myrie a stevene
As any aungel hath that is in hevene.
Therwith ye han in musyk moore feelynge
Than hadde Boece, or any that kan synge.
My lord youre fader, God his soule blesse!
And eek youre mooder, of hire gentillesse,
Han in myn hous ybeen to my greet ese,

And certes, sire, ful fayn wolde I yow plese,
But for men speke of syngyng, I wol seye,
So moote I brouke wel myne eyen tweye,
Save yow, I herde nevere man yet synge
As dide youre fader in the morwenynge.
Certes, it was of herte, al that he song;
And for to make his voys the moore strong,
He wolde so peyne hym that with bothe his eyen
He moste wynke, so loude he wolde cryen,
And stonden on his tiptoon therwithal,
And strecche forth his nekke, long and smal.
And eek he was of swich discrecioun,
That ther nas no man in no regioun
That hym in song or wisedom myghte passe.
I have wel rad in Daun Burnel the Asse,
Among his vers, how that ther was a cok
For that a preestes sone yaf hym a knok
Upon his leg, whil he was yong and nyce,
He made hym for to lese his benefice;
But certeyn, ther nys no comparisoun
Bitwixe the wisedom and discrecioun
Of youre fader, and of his subtiltee.
Now syngeth, sire, for seinte charitee;
Lat se, konne ye youre fader countrefete.
THIS Chauntecleer his wynges gan to bete,
As man that koude his traysoun nat espie,
So was he ravysshed with his flaterie.
Allas, ye lordes, many a fals flatour
Is in youre courtes, and many a losengeour,
That plesen yow yet moore, by my feith,
Than he that soothfastnesse unto yow seith.
Redeth Ecclesiaste of flaterye;
Beth war, ye lordes, of hir trecherye.
This Chauntecleer stood hye upon his toos,
Strecchynge his nekke, and heeld his eyen cloos,
And gan to crowe loude for the nones;
And daun Russell, the fox, stirte up atones
And by the gargat hente Chauntecleer,
And on his bak toward the wode hym beer,
For yet ne was ther no man that hym sewed.
O DESTINEE, that mayst nat been
eschewed!
Allas, that Chauntecleer fleigh fro
the bemes!
Allas, his wyf ne roghte nat of
dremes!
And on a friday fil al this meschaunce.
O Venus, that art goddesse of plesaunce,
Syn that thy servant was this Chauntecleer,
And in thy servyce dide al his poweer,
Moore for delit, than world to multiplye,
Why woldestow suffre hym on thy day to dye?
O Gaufred, deere maister soverayn,
That, whan thy worthy kyng Richard was slayn
With shot, compleynedest his deeth so soore!
Why ne hadde I now thy sentence, and thy loore,
The friday for to chide, as diden ye?
For on a friday, soothly, slayn was he.
Thanne wolde I shewe yow how that I koude
pleyne
For Chauntecleres drede, and for his peyne.
Certes, swich cry ne lamentacioun
Was nevere of ladyes maad, whan Ylioun

Was wonne, and Pirrus, with his streite swerd,
Whan he hadde hent kyng Priam by the berd,
And slayn hym, as seith us Eneydos,
As maden alle the hennes in the clos,
Whan they had seyn of Chauntecleer the sighte.
But sovereynly dame Pertelote shrighte,
Ful louder than dide Hasdrubales wyf,
Whan that hir housbonde hadde lost his lyf,
And that the Romayns hadde brend Cartage;
She was so ful of torment and of rage,
That wilfully into the fyr she sterte,
And brende hirselven with a stedefast herte.
O WOFUL hennes, right so criden ye,
As, whan that Nero brende the citee
Of Rome, cryden the senatours wyves,
For that hir husbondes losten alle hir lyves;
Withouten gilt this Nero hath hem slayn.
Now wole I turne to my tale agayn:
THIS sely wydwe, and eek hir doghtres two,
Herden thise hennes crie and maken wo,
And out at dores stirten they anon,
And syen the fox toward the grove gon,
And bar upon his bak the cok away,
And cryden, Out! harrow! and weylaway!
Ha! ha! the fox! and after hym they ran,
And eek with staves many another man;
Ran Colle, oure dogge, and Talbot, and Gerland,
And Malkyn, with a dystaf in hir hand;
Ran cow and calf, and eek the verray hogges,
Forfered for the berkynge of the dogges,
And shoutyng of the men and wommen eek;
They ronne so, hem thoughte hir herte breek.
They yelleden, as feendes doon in helle;
The dokes cryden, as men wolde hem quelle;
The gees, for feere, flowen over the trees;
Out of the hyve cam the swarm of bees;
So hydous was the noyse, a! benedicitee!
Certes, he Jakke Straw, and his meynee,
Ne made nevere shoutes half so shrille,
Whan that they wolden any flemyng kille,
As thilke day was maad upon the fox.
Of bras they broghten bemes, and of box,
Of horn, of boon, in whiche they blewe & powped,
And therwithal they skriked and they howped;
It semed as that hevene sholde falle.
NOW, goode men, I pray yow herkneth
alle;
Lo, how fortune turneth sodeynly
The hope & pryde eek of hir enemy!
This cok, that lay upon the foxes bak,
In al his drede unto the fox he spak,
And seyde, Sire, if that I were as ye,
Yet wolde I seyn, as wys God helpe me,
Turneth agayn, ye proude cherles alle!
A verray pestilence upon yow falle;
Now am I come unto the wodes syde,
Maugree youre heed, the cok shal heere abyde;
I wol hym ete, in feith, and that anon!
The fox answerde, In feith, it shal be don.
And as he spak that word, al sodeynly
This cok brak from his mouth delyverly
And heighe upon a tree he fleigh anon.
And whan the fox saugh that he was ygon,

95

Allas! quod he, O Chauntecleer, allas!
I have to yow, quod he, ydoon trespas,
Inasmuche as I maked yow aferd,
Whan I yow hente, & broght out of the yerd;
But, sire, I dide it of no wikke entente;
Com doun, and I shal telle yow what I mente;
I shal seye sooth to yow, God help me so!
Nay thanne, quod he, I shrewe us bothe two,
And first I shrewe myself, bothe blood and
bones,
If thou bigyle me ofter than ones.
Thou shalt namoore, thurgh thy flaterye,
Do me to synge, and wynke with myn eye;
for he that wynketh, whan he sholde see,
Al wilfully, God lat him nevere thee!
Nay, quod the fox, but God yeve hym
meschaunce,
That is so undiscreet of governaunce,
That jangleth whan he sholde holde his pees.
LO, swich it is for to be recchelees,
And necligent, and truste on flaterye.
But ye that holden this tale a folye,
As of a fox, or of a cok and hen,
Taketh the moralite, goode men;
for Seint Paul seith, that al that writen is,
To oure doctrine it is ywrite, ywis,
Taketh the fruyt and lat the chaf be stille.

HEERE FOLWETH THE PHISICIENS TALE

THER was, as telleth
Titus Livius,
A knyght that called
was Virginius,
fulfild of honour & of
worthynesse,
And strong of freendes
and of greet richesse.
This knyght a doghter
hadde by his wyf,
No children hadde he mo in al his lyf.
fair was this mayde in excellent beautee
Aboven every wight that man may see;
for Nature hath with sovereyn diligence
Yformed hire in so greet excellence,
As though she wolde seyn, Lo, I, Nature,
Thus kan I forme and peynte a creature
Whan that me list; who kan me countrefete?
Pigmalion noght, though he ay forge and
bete,
Or grave, or peynte; for I dar wel seyn
Apelles, Zanzis, sholde werche in veyn,
Outher to grave, or peynte, or forge, or bete,
If they presumed me to countrefete.
for he that is the former principal
Hath maked me his vicaire general
To forme and peynten erthely creaturis
Right as me list, and ech thyng in my cure is
Under the moone, that may wane and waxe,
And for my werk right nothyng wol I axe;
My lord and I been ful of oon accord;
I made hire to the worship of my lord.
So do I alle myne othere creatures,

Now, goode God, if that it be thy wille,
As seith my lord, so make us alle goode men,
And brynge us to his heighe blisse. Amen.
Heere is ended the Nonnes Preestes Tale.

Words of the Host to the Nonnes Priest

SIRE Nonnes Preest,
oure Hooste seide anoon,
I blessed be thy breche,
and every stoon!
This was a murie tale of
Chaunticleer;
But, by my trouthe, if
thou were seculer,
Thou woldest ben a
tredefoul aright;
for if thou have corage, as thou hast might,
Thee were nede of hennes, as I wene,
Ya, mo than sevene tymes seventene!
Se, whiche braunes hath this gentil preest,
So gret a nekke, and swich a large breest!
He loketh as a sparhawke with his eyen;
Him nedeth nat his colour for to dyen
With brasile, ne with greyn of Portyngale,
Now, sire, faire falle yow for youre tale.
And after that, he with ful merie chere
Seide to another as ye shullen heere.

What colour that they han, or what figures.
Thus semeth me that Nature wolde seye.
THIS mayde of age twelve yeer was and
tweye,
In which that Nature hadde swich
delit;
for, right as she kan peynte a lilie whit,
And reed a rose, right with swich peynture
She peynted hath this noble creature
Er she were born, upon hir lymes fre,
Whereas by right swiche colours sholde be;
And Phebus dyed hath hire treses grete
Lyk to the stremes of his burned heete;
And if that excellent was hire beautee,
A thousand foold moore vertuous was she.
In hire ne lakked no condicioun
That is to preyse, as by discrecioun.
As wel in goost as body chast was she;
for which she floured in virginitee
With alle humylitee and abstinence,
With alle attemperaunce and pacience,
With mesure eek of beryng and array.
Discreet she was in answeryng alway,
Though she were wise as Pallas, dar I seyn;
Hir facound eek, ful wommanly and pleyn;
No countrefeted termes hadde she
To seme wys; but after hir degree
She spak, and alle hire wordes moore & lesse
Sownynge in vertu and in gentillesse;
Shamefast she was, in maydens shame-
fastnesse,
Constant in herte, and evere in bisynesse
To dryve hire out of ydel slogardie.

Bacus hadde of hire mouth right no maistrie;
for wyn and youthe dooth Venus encresse,
As men in fyr wol casten oille or greesse.
And of hir owene vertu unconstreyned,
She hath ful ofte tyme syk hire feyned,
for that she wolde fleen the compaignye
Where likly was to treten of folye,
As is at feestes, revels, and at daunces,
That been occasions of daliaunces.
Swich thynges maken children for to be
To soone rype and boold, as men may se,
Which is ful perilous, and hath been yoore,
for al to soone may she lerne loore
Of booldnesse, whan she woxen is a wyf.
AND ye maistresses, in youre olde lyf,
That lordes doghtres han in governaunce,
Ne taketh of my wordes no displesaunce;
Thenketh that ye been set in governynges
Of lordes doghtres, oonly for two thynges;
Outher for ye han kept youre honestee,
Or elles ye han falle in freletee,
And knowen wel ynough the olde daunce,
And han forsaken fully swich meschaunce
for everemo; therfore, for Cristes sake
To teche hem vertu looke that ye ne slake.
A theef of venysoun, that hath forlaft
His likerousnesse, and al his olde craft,
Kan kepe a forest best of any man;
Now kepeth hem wel, for if ye wol, ye kan;
Looke wel that ye unto no vice assente,
Lest ye be dampned for youre wikke entente;
for who so dooth, a traitour is certeyn;
And taketh kepe of that that I shal seyn;
Of alle tresons, sovereyn pestilence
Is whan a wight bitrayseth innocence.
YE fadres and ye moodres eek, also,
Though ye han children, be it oon or two,
Youre is the charge of al hir surveiaunce
Whil that they been under youre governaunce;
Beth war, that by ensample of youre lyvynge,
Or by youre necligence in chastisynge,
That they ne perisse; for I dar wel seye,
If that they doon, ye shul it deere abeye.
Under a shepherde softe and necligent
The wolf hath many a sheepe and lamb torent.
Suffiseth oon ensample now as heere,
for I moot turne agayne to my matere.
THIS mayde, of which I wol this tale
expresse,
So kepte hirself, hir neded no mais-
tresse;
for in hir lyvyng maydens myghten
rede,
As in a book, every good word or dede
That longeth to a mayden vertuous,
She was so prudent and so bountevous;
for which the fame out sprong on every syde,
Bothe of hir beautee and hir bountee wyde;
That thurgh that land they preised hire echone
That loved vertu, save Envye allone,
That sory is of oother mennes wele,
And glad is of his sorwe and his unheele.
The doctour maketh this descripcioun.

This mayde upon a day wente in the toun
Toward a temple, with hire mooder deere,
As is of yonge maydens the manere.
Now was ther thanne a justice in that toun,
That governour was of that regioun,
And so bifel, this juge his eyen caste
Upon this mayde, avysynge hym ful faste
As she cam forby ther this juge stood.
Anon his herte chaunged and his mood,
So was he caught with beautee of this mayde;
And to hymself ful pryvely he sayde,
This mayde shal be myn, for any man.
Anon the feend into his herte ran,
And taughte hym sodeynly, that he by slyghte
The mayden to his purpos wynne myghte.
for certes, by no force, ne by no meede,
Hym thoughte, he was nat able for to speede;
for she was strong of freendes, and eek she
Confermed was in swich soverayn bountee,
That wel he wiste he myghte hire nevere wynne
As for to make hire with hir body synne;
for which, by greet deliberacioun,
He sente after a cherl, was in the toun,
Which that he knew for subtil and for boold.
This juge unto this cherl his tale hath toold
In secree wise, and made hym to ensure
He sholde telle it to no creature,
And if he dide, he sholde lese his heed.
Whan that assented was this cursed reed,
Glad was this juge, and maked him greet cheere,
And yaf hym yiftes, preciouse and deere.
WHAN shapen was al hire conspiracie,
fro point to point, how that his lecherie
Parfourned sholde been ful subtilly,
As ye shul heere it after openly,
Hoom gooth the cherl, that highte Claudius.
This false juge that highte Apius,
So was his name, for this is no fable,
But knowen for historial thyng notable,
The sentence of it sooth is, out of doute;
This false juge gooth now faste aboute
To hasten his delit al that he may.
And so bifel soone after, on a day,
This false juge, as telleth us the storie,
As he was wont, sat in his consistorie,
And yaf his doomes upon sondry cas.
This false cherl cam forth, a ful greet pas,
And seyde, Lord, if that it be youre wille,
As dooth me right upon this pitous bille,
In which I pleyne upon Virginius;
And if that he wol seyn it is nat thus,
I wol it preeve, and fynde good witnesse
That sooth is that my bille wol expresse.
The juge answerde, Of this, in his absence,
I may nat yeve diffynytyve sentence;
Lat do hym calle, and I wol gladly heere;
Thou shalt have alle right, and no wrong heere.
VIRGINIUS cam to wite the juges wille,
And right anon was rad this cursed bille;
The sentence of it was as ye shul heere:
To yow, my lord, sire Apius so deere,
Sheweth youre povre servant Claudius,
How that a knyght, called Virginius,

Agayns the lawe, agayn al equitee,
Holdeth, expres agayn the wyl of me,
My servant, which that is my thral by right,
Which fro myn hous was stole upon a nyght,
Whil that she was ful yong; this wol I preeve
By witnesse, lord, so that it nat yow greeve.
She nys his doghter nat, what so he seye;
Wherfore to yow, my lord the juge, I preye,
Yeld me my thral, if that it be youre wille.
Lo, this was al the sentence of his bille.
Virginius gan upon the cherl biholde,
But hastily, er he his tale tolde,
And wolde have preeved it, as sholde a knyght,
And eek by witnessyng of many a wight,
That it was fals that seyde his adversarie,
This cursed juge wolde nothyng tarie,
Ne heere a word moore of Virginius,
But yaf his juggement, and seyde thus:
I deeme anon this cherl his servant have;
Thou shalt no lenger in thyn house hir save.
Go, bryng hire forth, and put hire in oure warde,
The cherl shal have his thral; this I awarde.
AND when this worthy knyght, Virginius,
Thurgh sentence of this justice Apius,
Moste by force his deere doghter yiven
Unto the juge, in lecherie to lyven,
He gooth hym hoom, and sette him in his halle,
And leet anon his deere doghter calle,
And, with a face deed as asshen colde,
Upon hir humble face he gan biholde,
With fadres pitee stikynge thurgh his herte,
Al wolde he from his purpos nat converte.
Doghter, quod he, Virginia, by thy name,
Ther been two weyes, outher deeth or shame,
That thou most suffre; allas! that I was bore!
for nevere thou deservedest wherfore
To dyen with a swerd, or with a knyf.
O deere doghter, endere of my lyf,
Which I have fostred up with swich plesaunce,
That thou were nevere out of my remembraunce.
O doghter, which that art my laste wo,
And in my lyf my laste joye also;
O gemme of chastitee! in pacience
Take thou thy deeth, for this is my sentence.
for love, and nat for hate, thou most be deed;
My pitous hand moot smyten of thyn heed!
Allas! that evere Apius the say!
Thus hath he falsly jugged the today.
And tolde hire al the cas, as ye bifore
Han herd; nat nedeth for to telle it moore.
O MERCY, deere fader! quod this mayde,
And with that word she both hir armes
layde
About his nekke, as she was wont to do;
The teeris bruste out of hir eyen two,
And seyde, Goode fader, shal I dye?
Is ther no grace? is ther no remedye?
No, certes, deere doghter myn, quod he.
Thanne yif me leyser, fader myn, quod she,
My deeth for to compleyne a litel space;
for pardee, Jepte yaf his doghter grace
for to compleyne, er he hir slow, allas!
And God it woot, nothyng was hir trespas,

98

But for she ran hir fader first to see,
To welcome hym with greet solempnitee.
And with that word she fil aswowne anon,
And after, whan hir swowning is agon,
She riseth up, and to hir fader sayde,
Blissed be God, that I shal dye a mayde;
Yif me my deeth, er that I have a shame;
Dooth with youre child youre wyl, a Goddes name!
And with that word she preyed hym ful ofte
That with his swerd he wolde smyte softe;
And with that word aswowne doun she fil.
Hir fader, with ful sorweful herte and wil,
Hir heed of smoot, and by the top it hente,
And to the juge he gan it to presente,
As he sat yet in doom in consistorie.
And whan the juge it saugh, as seith the storie,
He bad to take hym and anhange hym faste;
But right anon a thousand peple in thraste,
To save the knyght, for routhe and for pitee,
for knowen was the false iniquitee.
The peple anon hath suspect of this thyng,
By manere of the cherles chalangyng,
That it was by the assent of Apius;
They wisten wel that he was lecherus.
for which unto this Apius they gon,
And caste hym in a prisoun right anon,
Theras he slow hymself; and Claudius,
That servant was unto this Apius,
Was demed for to hange upon a tree;
But that Virginius, of his pitee,
So preyde for hym that he was exiled;
And elles, certes, he had been bigyled.
The remenant were anhanged, moore and lesse,
That were consentant of this cursednesse.
HEERE men may seen how synne hath his
merite.
Beth war, for no man woot whom God wol
smyte
In no degree, ne in which maner wyse
The worm of conscience may agryse
Of wikked lyf, though it so pryvee be
That no man woot therof but God and he;
for be he lewed man, or ellis lered,
He noot how soone that he shal been afered.
Therfore, I rede yow, this conseil take,
forsaketh synne, er synne yow forsake.
Heere endeth the Phisiciens Tale.

The wordes of the Hoost to the Phisicien and the
Pardoner ✲ ✲

URE Hooste gan to swere
as he were wood;
Harrow! quod he, by nayles,
and by blood!
This was a fals cherl and a
fals justise!
As shameful deeth as herte
may devyse
Come to thise juges and
hire advocats!
Algate this sely mayde is slayn, allas!
Allas! to deere boughte she beautee!
Wherfore I seye al day, as men may see,

That yiftes of Fortune and of Nature
Been cause of deeth to many a creature.
Hire beautee was hire deth, I dar wel sayn;
Allas! so pitously as she was slayn!
Of bothe yiftes that I speke of now
Men han ful ofte moore for harm than prow.
BUT trewely, myn owene maister deere,
This is a pitous tale for to heere;
But nathelees, passe over, is no fors;
I pray to God, so save thy gentil cors,
And eek thyne urynals, and thy jurdanes,
Thyn Ypocras, and eek thy Galianes,
And every boyste ful of thy letuarie;
God blesse hem, and oure Lady Seinte Marie!
So moot I theen, thou art a propre man,
And lyk a prelat, by Seint Ronyan!
Seyde I nat wel? I kan nat speke in terme;
But wel I woot, thou doost myn hert to erme,
That I almoost have caught a cardyacle.
By corpus bones! but I have triacle,
Or elles a draughte of moyste and corny ale,
Or but I heere anon a myrie tale,
Myn herte is loste, for pitee of this mayde.
Thou beel amy, thou Pardoner, he sayde,
Telle us som myrthe or japes right anon!
It shal be doon, quod he, by Seint Ronyon!
But first, quod he, heere at this ale stake
I wol bothe drynke, and eten of a cake.
And right anon the gentils gonne to crye,
Nay! lat hym telle us of no ribaudye;
Telle us som moral thyng, that we may leere
Som wit, and thanne wol we gladly heere.
I graunte, ywis, quod he, but I moot thynke
Upon som honeste thyng, while that I drynke.

Heere folweth the prologe of the Pardoners
Tale ❀ ❀

Radix malorum est cupiditas. Ad Timotheum, 6.

LORDYNGES, quod he, in
chirches whan I preche,
I peyne me to han an hauteyn
speche,
And rynge it out as round as
gooth a belle,
for I kan al by rote that I telle.
My theme is alwey oon, and
evere was,
Radix malorum est cupiditas.
first, I pronounce whennes that I come,
And thanne my bulles shewe I, alle and some;
Oure lige lordes seel on my patente,
That shewe I first, my body to warente,
That no man be so boold, ne preest ne clerk,
Me to destourbe of Cristes hooly werk;
And after that thanne telle I forth my tales,
Bulles of popes and of cardynales,
Of patriarkes and bishoppes I shewe;
And in Latyn I speke a wordes fewe,
To saffron with my predicacioun,
And for to stire hem to devocioun.
Thanne shewe I forth my longe cristal stones,
Ycrammed ful of cloutes and of bones;
Relikes been they, as wenen they echoon.

h 2

Thanne have I in latoun a sholder boon
Which that was of an hooly Jewes sheepe.
GOODE men, I seye, taak of my wordes
keepe;
If that this boon be wasshe in any welle,
If cow, or calf, or sheep, or oxe swelle
That any worm hath ete, or worm ystonge,
Taak water of that welle, and wassh his tonge,
And it is hool anon; and forthermoor,
Of pokkes, and of scabbe, and every soor,
Shal every sheep be hool, that of this welle
Drynketh a draughte; taak kepe eek what I telle.
If that the goode man that the beestes oweth
Wol every wyke, er that the cok hym croweth,
fastynge, drinken of this welle a draughte,
As thilke hooly Jew oure eldres taughte,
His beestes and his stoor shal multiplie.
And, sires, also it heeleth jalousie;
for, though a man be falle in jalous rage,
Lat maken with this water his potage,
And nevere shal he moore his wyf mystriste,
Though he the soothe of hir defaute wiste;
Al had she taken preestes two or thre.
Heere is a miteyn eek, that ye may se;
He that his hand wol putte in this miteyn,
He shal have multiplying of his grayn,
Whan he hath sowen, be it whete or otes,
So that he offre pens, or elles grotes.
Goode men & wommen, o thyng warne I yow,
If any wight be in this chirche now
That hath doon synne horrible, that he
Dar nat, for shame, of it yshryven be,
Or any womman, be she yong or old,
That hath ymaked hir housbond cokewold,
Swich folk shal have no power ne no grace
To offren to my relikes in this place;
And whos fyndeth hym out of swich blame,
He wol come up and offre on Goddes name,
And I assoille hym by the auctoritee
Which that by bulle ygraunted was to me.
BY this gaude have I wonne, yeer by yeer,
An hundred mark sith I was Pardoner.
I stonde lyk a clerk in my pulpet,
And whan the lewed peple is doun yset,
I preche, so as ye han herd bifoore,
And telle an hundred false japes moore.
Thanne peyne I me to strecche forth the nekke,
And est and west upon the peple I bekke,
As dooth a dowve sittynge on a berne;
Myne handes and my tonge goon so yerne,
That it is joye to se my bisynesse.
Of avarice and of swich cursednesse
Is al my prechyng, for to make hem free
To geven hir pens, and namely unto me;
for myn entente is nat but for to wynne,
And nothyng for correccioun of synne.
I rekke nevere, whan that they been beryed,
Though that hir soules goon ablakeberyed.
for certes, many a predicacioun
Comth ofte tyme of yvel entencioun;
Som for pleasaunce of folk and flaterye,
To been avaunced by ypocrisye;
And som for veyne glorie, and som for hate.

for, whan I dar noon oother weyes debate,
Thanne wol I stynge hym with my tonge smerte
In prechyng, so that he shal nat asterte
To been defamed falsly, if that he
Hath trespased to my bretheren or to me;
for, though I telle noght his propre name,
Men shal wel knowe that it is the same,
By signes and by othere circumstances.
Thus quyte I folk that doon us displesances;
Thus spitte I out my venym under hewe
Of hoolynesse, to semen hooly and trewe.
BUT, shortly, myn entente I wol devyse;
I preche of nothyng but for coveityse;
Therfore my theme is yet, & evere was,
Radix malorum est cupiditas.
Thus kan I preche agayn that same vice
Which that I use, and that is avarice.
But though myself be gilty in that synne,
Yet kan I maken oother folk to twynne
from avarice, and soore to repente.
But that is nat my principal entente;
I preche nothyng but for coveitise.
Of this mateere it oghte ynogh suffise.
Thanne telle I hem ensamples many oon
Of olde stories, longe tyme agoon:

for lewed peple loven tales olde;
Swiche thynges kan they wel reporte & holde.
What! trowe ye the whiles I may preche,
And wynne gold and silver for I teche,
That I wol lyve in poverte wilfully?
Nat, nay, I thoghte it nevere, trewely!
for I wol preche and begge in sondry landes;
I wol nat do no labour with myne handes,
Ne make baskettes, and lyve therby,
Bycause I wol nat beggen ydelly.
I wol noon of the Apostles countrefete;
I wol have moneie, wolle, chese and whete,
Al were it yeven of the povereste page,
Or of the povereste wydwe in a village,
Al sholde hir children sterve for famyne.
Nay! I wol drynke licour of the vyne,
And have a joly wenche in every toun;
But herkneth, lordynges, in conclusioun.
Youre likyng is that I shal telle a tale.
Now have I dronke a draughte of corny ale,
By God, I hope I shal yow telle a thyng
That shal, by resoun, been at youre likyng;
for though myself be a ful vicious man,
A moral tale yet I yow telle kan,
Which I am wont to preche, for to wynne.
Now hoold your pees, my tale I wol bigynne.

HEERE BIGYNNETH THE PARDONERS TALE

IN flaundres whilom was a compaignye
Of yonge folk, that haunteden folye,
As riot, hasard, stewes and tavernes,
Wheras with harpes, lutes, and gyternes,
They daunce & pleyen at dees, bothe day and nyght,
And eten also and drynken over hir myght,
Thurgh which they doon the devel sacrifise
Withinne that develes temple, in cursed wise,
By superfluytee abhomynable;
Hir othes been so grete and so dampnable,
That it is grisly for to heere hem swere;
Oure blissed Lordes body they totere;
Hem thoughte that Jewes rente hym noght ynough;
And ech of hem at otheres synne lough.
And right anon thanne comen tombesteres
fetys and smale, and yonge frutesteres,
Syngeres with harpes, baudes, wafereres,
Whiche been the verray develes officeres,
To kyndle and blowe the fyr of lecherye,
That is annexed unto glotonye.
The Hooly Writ take I to my witnesse,
That luxurie is in wyn and dronkenesse.
LO, how that dronken Looth, un-kyndely,
Lay by his doghtres two, un-wityngly;

So dronke he was, he nyste what he wroghte.
Herodes, whoso wel the stories soghte,
Whan he of wyn was repleet at his feeste,
Right at his owene table, he yaf his heeste
To sleen the Baptist John, ful giltelees.
Senec seith eek a good word doutelees;
He seith, he kan no difference fynde
Bitwix a man that is out of his mynde
And a man which that is dronkelewe,
But that woodnesse, yfallen in a shrewe,
Persevereth lenger than dooth dronkenesse.
O glotonye, ful of cursednesse;
O cause first of oure confusioun;
O original of oure dampnacioun;
Til Crist hadde boght us with his blood agayn.
LO, how deere, shortly for to sayn,
Aboght was thilke cursed vileynye;
Corrupt was al this world for glotonye.
Adam oure fader, and his wyf also,
fro Paradys to labour and to wo
Were dryven for that vice, it is no drede;
for whil that Adam fasted, as I rede,
He was in Paradys; and whan that he
Eet of the fruyt deffended, on the tree,
Anon he was out cast to wo and peyne.
O glotonye, on thee wel oghte us pleyne!
O, WISTE a man how manye maladyes
folwen of excesse and of glotonyes,
He wolde been the moore mesurable
Of his diete, sittynge at his table.
Allas! the shorte throte, the tendre mouth,
Maketh that, est and west, and north & south,
In erthe, in eir, in water, men to swynke

To gete a glotoun deyntee mete and drynke!
Of this matiere, O Paul, wel kanstow trete;
Mete unto wombe, and wombe eek unto mete,
Shal God destroyen bothe, as Paulus seith.
Allas! a foul thyng is it, by my feith,
To seye this word, and fouler is the dede
Whan man so drynketh of the white and rede,
That of his throte he maketh his pryvee,
Thurgh thilke cursed superfluitee.

The Apostel wepyng seith ful pitously,
Ther walken manye of whiche yow toold have I,
I seye it now, wepyng with pitous voys,
That they been enemys of Cristes croys,
Of whiche the ende is deeth, wombe is hir god.

O wombe! O bely! O stynkyng cod!
Fulfilled of donge and of corrupcioun;
At either ende of thee foul is the soun;
How greet labour and cost is thee to fynde!
Thise cookes, how they stampe, and streyne, and
grynde,
And turnen substaunce into accident,
To fulfille al thy likerous talent.
Out of the harde bones knokke they
The mary, for they caste noght awey
That may go thurgh the golet softe and swoote;
Of spicerie, of leef, and bark, and roote,
Shal been his sauce ymaked by delit,
To make hym yet a newer appetit;
But certes, he that haunteth swiche delices
Is deed, whil that he lyveth in tho vices.

A LECHEROUS thyng is wyn, and dronk-
enesse
Is ful of stryvyng and of wrecchednesse.
O dronke man! disfigured is thy face,
Sour is thy breeth, foul artow to embrace,
And thurgh thy dronke nose semeth the soun
As though thou seydest ay, Sampsoun, Samp-
soun;
And yet, God woot, Sampsoun drank nevere no
wyn.
Thou fallest, as it were a styked swyn,
Thy tonge is lost and al thyn honeste cure;
For dronkenesse is verray sepulture
Of mannes wit and his discrecioun;
In whom that drynke hath dominacioun
He kan no conseil kepe, it is no drede.
Now kepe yow fro the white and fro the rede,
And namely fro the white wyn of Lepe,
That is to selle in Fysshstrete, or in Chepe.
This wyn of Spaigne crepeth subtilly
In othere wynes, growynge faste by,
Of which ther ryseth swich fumositee,
That whan a man hath dronken draughtes thre,
And weneth that he be at hoom in Chepe,
He is in Spaigne, right at the toune of Lepe,
Nat at the Rochele, ne at Burdeux toun;
And thanne wol he seye, Sampsoun, Sampsoun.

But herkneth, lordings, o word, I yow preye,
That alle the sovereyn actes, dar I seye,
Of victories in the Olde Testament,
Thurgh verray God, that is omnipotent,
Were doon in abstinence and in preyere;
Looketh the Bible, and ther ye may it leere.

Looke, Attilla, the grete conquerour,
Deyde in his sleep, with shame and dishonour,
Bledynge ay at his nose in dronkenesse;
A capitayn sholde lyve in sobrenesse.
And over al this, avyseth yow right wel
What was comaunded unto Lamuel, ...
Nat Samuel, but Lamuel seye I;
Redeth the Bible, and fynde it expresly
Of wyn/yevyng to hem that han justise.
Namoore of this, for it may wel suffise.

AND now I have spoken of glotonye,
Now wol I yow deffenden hasardrye.
Hasard is verray mooder of lesynges,
And of deceite, and cursed forswerynges,
Blaspheme of Crist, manslaughtre, and wast also
Of catel and of tyme; and forthermo,
It is repreeve and contrarie of honour
For to ben holde a commune hasardour;
And ever the hyer he is of estaat,
The moore is he holden desolaat.
If that a prynce useth hasardrye
In alle governaunce and policye,
He is, as by commune opinioun,
Yholde the lasse in reputacioun.

Stilbon, that was a wys embassadour,
Was sent to Corynthe, in ful greet honour,
Fro Lacidomye, to maken hire alliaunce;
And whan he cam, hym happede, par chaunce,
That alle the gretteste that were of that lond
Pleyynge atte hasard he hem fond.
For which, as soone as it myghte be,
He stal hym hoom agayn to his contree,
And seyde, Ther wol I nat lese my name,
Ne I wol nat take on me so greet defame,
Yow for to allie unto none hasardours;
Sendeth som othere wise embassadours;
For, by my trouthe, me were levere dye,
Than I yow sholde to hasardours allye;
For ye that been so glorious in honours,
Shul nat allyen yow with hasardours
As by my wyl, ne as by my tretee.

This wise philosophre thus seyde hee.

LOOKE eek that, to the kyng Demetrius,
The kyng of Parthes, as the book seith us,
Sente him a paire of dees of gold, in scorn,
For he hadde used hasard therbiforn;
For which he heeld his glorie or his renoun
At no value or reputacioun.
Lordes may fynden oother maner pley
Honeste ynough to dryve the day awey.

NOW wol I speke of othes false and grete
A word or two, as olde bookes trete.
Gret sweryng is a thyng abhominable,
And fals sweryng is yet moore reprevable.
The heighe God forbad sweryng at al,
Witnesse on Mathew; but in special
Of sweryng seith the hooly Jeremye,
Thou shalt seye sooth thyne othes, and nat lye,
And swere in doom, and eek in rightwisnesse;

But ydel sweryng is a cursednesse.
Bihoold and se, that in the firste table
Of heighe Goddes heestes honurable,
How that the seconde heeste of hym is this:

Take nat my name in ydel, or amys.
Lo, rather he forbedeth swich sweryng
Than homycide, or many a cursed thyng;
I seye that, as by ordre, thus it stondeth;
This knowen, that his heestes understondeth,
How that the seconde heeste of God is that.
And forther over, I wol thee telle al plat
That vengeance shal nat parten from his hous,
That of his othes is to outrageous:
By Goddes precious herte, and by his nayles,
And by the blood of Crist that is in Hayles,
Sevene is my chaunce, and thyn is cynk and treye;
By Goddes armes, if thou falsly pleye,
This daggere shal thurghout thyn herte go!
This fruyt cometh of the bicched bones two,
forsweryng, ire, falsnesse, homycide.
Now for the love of Crist that for us dyde,
Lete youre othes, bothe grete and smale.
But, sires, now wol I telle forth my tale.
THISE riotoures thre, of whiche I
telle,
Longe erst er prime rong of any belle,
Were set hem in a taverne for to
drynke;
And as they sat, they herde a belle
clynke
Biforn a cors, was carried to his grave.
That oon of hem gan callen to his knave:
Go bet, quod he, and axe redily,
What cors is this that passeth heer forby;
And looke that thou reporte his name weel.
Sire, quod this boy, it nedeth neveradeel,
It was me toold, er ye cam heer, two houres;
He was, pardee, an old felawe of youres,
And sodeynly he was yslayn tonyght,
fordronke, as he sat on his bench upright;
Ther cam a privee theef, men clepeth Deeth,
That in this contree al the peple sleeth,
And with his spere he smoot his herte atwo,
And wente his wey withouten wordes mo.
He hath a thousand slayn this pestilence:
And, maister, er ye come in his presence,
Me thynketh that it were necessarie
for to be war of swich an adversarie;
Beth redy for to meete hym everemoore;
Thus taughte me my dame; I sey namoore.
By Seinte Marie! seyde this taverner,
The child seith sooth, for he hath slayn this yeer,
Henne over a mile, withinne a greet village,
Bothe man and womman, child, and hyne, & page;
I trowe his habitacioun be there;
To been avysed greet wysdom it were,
Er that he dide a man a dishonour.
Ye, Goddes armes! quod this riotour,
Is it swich peril with hym for to meete?
I shal hym seke by wey and eek by strete,
I make avow to Goddes digne bones!
Herkneth, felawes, we thre been al ones;
Lat ech of us holde up his hand til oother,
And ech of us bicomen otheres brother,
And we wol sleen this false traytour, Deeth;
He shal be slayn, which that so manye sleeth,
By Goddes dignitee, er it be nyght!
102

TOGIDRES han thise thre hir trouthes
plight,
To lyve and dyen ech of hem for oother,
As though he were his owene yboren brother;
And up they stirte al dronken, in this rage,
And forth they goon towardes that village
Of which the taverner hadde spoke biforn;
And many a grisly ooth thanne han they sworn,
And Cristes blessed body they torente;
Deeth shal be deed, if that they may hym hente.
WHAN they han goon nat fully half a mile,
Right as they wolde han troden over a
stile,
An oold man and a povre with hem mette.
This olde man ful mekely hem grette,
And seyde thus: Now, lordes, God yow see!
The proudeste of thise riotoures three
Answerde agayn: What? carl with sory grace,
Why artow al forwrapped save thy face?
Why lyvestow so longe in so greet age?
This olde man gan looke in his visage,
And seyde thus: for I ne kan nat fynde
A man, though that I walked into Ynde,
Neither in citee nor in no village,
That wolde chaunge his youthe for myn age;
And therfore moot I han myn age stille,
As longe tyme as it is Goddes wille.
Ne Deeth, allas! ne wol nat han my lyf;
Thus walke I, lyk a restelees kaityf,
And on the ground, which is my moodres gate,
I knokke with my staf, bothe erly and late,
And seye: Leeve mooder, leet me in!
Lo, how I vanysshe, flessh, and blood, and skyn;
Allas! whan shul my bones been at reste?
Mooder, with yow wolde I chaunge my cheste,
That in my chambre longe tyme hath be,
Ye! for an heyre clowt to wrappe me!
But yet to me she wol nat do that grace,
for which ful pale and welked is my face.
But, sires, to yow it is no curteisye
To speken to an old man vileynye,
But he trespasse in word, or elles in dede.
In Hooly Writ ye may yourself wel rede,
Agayns an oold man hoor upon his heed,
Ye sholde arise; wherfore I yeve yow reed,
Ne dooth unto an oold man noon harm now,
Namoore than ye wolde men did to yow
In age, if that ye so longe abyde;
And God be with yow wher ye go or ryde;
I moote go thider as I have to go.
NAY, olde cherl, by God, thou shalt nat so!
Seyde this oother hasardour anon;
Thou partest nat so lightly, by Seint John!
Thou spak right now of thilke traytour, Deeth,
That in this contree alle oure freendes sleeth;
Have heer my trouthe, as thou art his espye,
Telle wher he is, or thou shalt it abye,
By God, and by the hooly sacrement!
for soothly thou art oon of his assent,
To sleen us yonge folk, thou false theef!
Now, sires, quod he, if that ye be so leef
To fynde Deeth, turne up this croked wey,
for in that grove I lafte hym, by my fey,

Under a tree, and there he wole abyde;
Nat for youre boost he wole him nothyng hyde.
Se ye that ook? Right there ye shal hym fynde.
God save yow, that boghte agayn mankynde,
And yow amende! Thus seyde this olde man.
And everich of thise riotoures ran
Til he cam to that tree, and ther they founde
Of floryns fyne of gold ycoyned rounde
Wel ny an eighte busshels, as hem thoughte.
No lenger thanne after Deeth they soughte,
But ech of hem so glad was of that sighte,
For that the floryns been so faire and brighte,
That doun they sette hem by this precious hoord.
The worste of hem he spak the firste word.
BRETHEREN, quod he, taak kepe what I seye;
My wit is greet, though that I bourde and pleye.
This tresor hath Fortune unto us yiven,
In myrthe and jolitee oure lyf to lyven,
And lightly as it comth, so wol we spende.
Ey! Goddes precious dignitee! who wende
Today, that we sholde han so fair a grace?
But myghte this gold be caried fro this place
Hoom to myn hous, or elles unto youres,
For wel ye woot that al this gold is oures,
Thanne were we in heigh felicitee.
But trewely, by daye it may nat bee;
Men wolde seyn that we were theves stronge,
And for oure owene tresor doon us honge.
This tresor moste ycaried be by nyghte,
As wisely and as slyly as it myghte.
Wherfore, I rede that cut among us alle
Be drawe, and lat se wher the cut wol falle;
And he that hath the cut, with herte blithe
Shal renne to the towne, and that ful swithe,
And brynge us breed and wyn ful prively;
And two of us shul kepen subtilly
This tresor wel; and if he wol nat tarie,
Whan it is nyght, we wol this tresor carie
By oon assent, wheras us thynketh best.
That oon of hem the cut broghte in his fest,
And bad hem drawe and looke wher it wol falle;
And it fil on the yongeste of hem alle;
And forth toward the toun he wente anon.
AND al so soone as that he was agon,
That oon of hem spak thus unto that oother:
Thow knowest wel thou art my sworne brother;
Thy profit wol I telle thee anon.
Thou woost wel that oure felawe is agon,
And heere is gold, and that ful greet plentee,
That shal departed been among us thre.
But nathelees, if I kan shape it so
That it departed were among us two,
Hadde I nat doon a freendes torn to thee?
That oother answerde, I noot how that may be;
He woot how that the gold is with us tweye;
What shal we doon, what shal we to hym seye?
Shal it be conseil? seyde the firste shrewe,
And I shal tellen in a wordes fewe
What we shal doon, and brynge it wel aboute.
I graunte, quod that oother, out of doute,

h 4

That, by my trouthe, I wol thee nat biwreye.
Now, quod the firste, thou woost wel we be tweye,
And two of us shul strenger be than oon.
Looke whan that he is set, and right anoon
Arys, as though thou woldest with hym pleye,
And I shal ryve hym thurgh the sydes tweye
Whil that thou strogelest with hym as in game,
And with thy dagger looke thou do the same,
And thanne shal al this gold departed be,
My deere freend, bitwixen me and thee.
Thanne may we bothe oure lustes al fulfille,
And pleye at dees right at oure owene wille.
And thus acorded been thise shrewes tweye,
To sleen the thridde, as ye han herd me seye.
THIS yongeste, which that wente unto the toun,
Ful ofte in herte he rolleth up and doun
The beautee of thise floryns newe and brighte.
O Lord! quod he, if so were that I myghte
Have al this tresor to myself allone,
Ther is no man that lyveth under the trone
Of God, that sholde lyve so murye as I!
And atte laste the feend, oure enemy,
Putte in his thought that he sholde poyson beye,
With which he myghte sleen his felawes tweye;
Forwhy the feend foond hym in swich lyvynge,
That he hadde leve hym to sorwe brynge,
For this was outrely his fulle entente
To sleen hem bothe, and nevere to repente.
And forth he gooth, no lenger wolde he tarie,
Into the toun, unto a pothecarie,
And preyde hym that he hym wolde selle
Som poysoun, that he myghte his rattes quelle;
And eek ther was a polcat in his hawe,
That, as he seyde, his capouns hadde yslawe,
And fayn he wolde wreke hym, if he myghte,
On vermyn, that destroyed hym by nyghte.
The pothecarie answerde, And thou shalt have
A thyng that, al so God my soule save!
In al this world ther nis no creature,
That ete or dronke hath of this confiture,
Noght but the montance of a corn of whete,
That he ne shal his lif anon forlete;
Ye, sterve he shal, and that in lasse while
Than thou wolt goon a paas nat but a mile,
This poyson is so strong and violent.
THIS cursed man hath in his hond yhent
This poyson in a box, and sith he ran
Into the nexte strete, unto a man,
And borwed of hym large botels thre,
And in the two his poyson poured he;
The thridde he kept clene for his owene drynke;
For al the nyght he shoop hym for to swynke
In caryinge of the gold out of that place.
And whan this riotour, with sory grace
Hadde filled with wyn his grete botels thre,
To his felawes agayn repaireth he.
WHAT nedeth it to sermone of it moore?
For right as they hadde cast his deeth bifoore,
Right so they han hym slayn, and that anon;
And whan that this was doon thus spak that oon:

Now lat us sitte and drynke, & make us merie,
And afterward we wol his body berie.
And with that word it happed hym, par cas,
To take the botel ther the poysoun was,
And drank and yaf his felawe drynke also,
For which anon they storven bothe two.
But certes, I suppose that Avycen
Wroot nevere in no canon, ne in no fen,
Mo wonder signes of empoisonyng
Than hadde thise wrecches two, er hir endyng.
Thus ended been thise homycides two,
And eek the false empoysoner also.
O CURSED synne, ful of cursednesse!
O traytours homycide! O wikkednesse!
O glotonye, luxurie, and hasardrye!
Thou blasphemour of Crist with vileynye
And othes grete, of usage and of pride!
Allas! mankynde, how may it bitide,
That to thy Creatour which that the wroghte,
And with his precious herte blood thee boghte,
Thou art so fals and so unkynde, allas!
NOW, goode men, God foryeve yow
youre trespas,
And ware yow fro the synne of
avarice.
Myn hooly pardoun may yow alle
warice,
So that ye offre nobles, or sterlynges,
Or elles silver broches, spoones, rynges.
Boweth youre heed under this hooly bulle!
Cometh up, ye wyves, offreth of youre wolle!
Youre names I entre heer in my rolle anon;
Into the blisse of hevene shul ye gon;
I yow assoille by myn heigh power,
Yow that wol offre, as clene and eek as cleer
As ye were born; and lo, sires, thus I preche.
And Jhesu Crist, that is oure soules leche,
So graunte yow his pardoun to receyve;
For that is best; I wol yow nat deceyve.
BUT, sires, o word forgat I in my tale;
I have relikes & pardoun in my male,
As faire as any man in Engelond,
Whiche were me yeven by the popes
hond.
If any of yow wole, of devocioun,
Offren, and han myn absolucioun,
Cometh forth anon, and kneleth heere adoun,
And mekely receyveth my pardoun;
Or elles taketh pardoun as ye wende,
Al newe and fressh, at every miles ende,
So that ye offren alwey newe and newe
Nobles or pens, whiche that be goode and trewe.
It is an honour to everich that is heer
That ye mowe have a suffisant Pardoneer
Tassoille yow, in contree as ye ryde,
For aventures whiche that may bityde.
Paraventure ther may fallen oon or two
Doun of his hors, and breke his nekke atwo.
Looke which a seuretee is it to yow alle
That I am in youre felaweship yfalle,
That may assoille yow, bothe moore and lasse,
Whan that the soule shal fro the body passe.
I rede that oure Hoost heere shal bigynne,

For he is moost envoluped in synne.
Com forth, sire Hoost, and offre first anon,
And thou shalt kisse my relikes everychon,
Ye, for a grote! unbokele anon thy purs.
NAY, nay, quod he, thanne have I Cristes curs!
Lat be, quod he, it shal nat be, so theech!
Thou woldest make me kisse thyn olde
breech,
And swere it were a relyk of a seint,
Though it were with thy fundement depeint!
But, by the croys which that Seint Eleyne fond,
I wolde I hadde thy coillons in myn hond
Instide of relikes or of seintuarie.
Lat kutte hem of, I wol with thee hem carie,
They shul be shryned in an hogges toord.
THIS Pardoner answerde nat a word;
So wrooth he was, no word ne wolde he seye.
Now, quod oure Hoost, I wol no lenger
pleye
With thee, ne with noon oother angry man.
But right anon the worthy Knyght bigan,
Whan that he saugh that al the peple lough:
NAMOORE of this, for it is right ynough!
Sire Pardoner, be glad and myrie of cheere;
And ye, sir Hoost, that been to me so deere,
I prey yow that ye kisse the Pardoner.
And Pardoner, I prey thee drawe thee neer,
And as we diden, lat us laughe and pleye.
Anon they kiste, and ryden forth hir weye.
Heere is ended the Pardoners Tale.

The prologe of the Wyves Tale of Bathe.

EXPERIENCE, though
noon auctoritee
Were in this world, were
right ynogh to me
To speke of wo that is in
mariage;
for, lordynges, sith I twelf
yeer was of age,
Thonked be God, that is
eterne on lyve!
Housbondes at chirche dore I have had fyve;
For I so ofte have ywedded bee;
And alle were worthy men in hir degree.
But me was toold certeyn, nat longe agoon is,
That sith that Crist ne wente nevere but onis
To weddyng in the Cane of Galilee,
That by the same ensample taughte he me
That I ne sholde wedded be but ones.
Herke eek, lo! which a sharp word for the nones!
Beside a welle Jhesus, God and man,
Spak in repreeve of the Samaritan:
Thou hast yhad fyve housbondes, quod he,
And thilke man, the which that hath now thee,
Is noght thyn housbonde. Thus seyde he
certeyn;
What that he mente therby, I kan nat seyn;
But that I axe, why that the fifthe man
Was noon housbonde to the Samaritan?
How manye myghte she have in mariage?
Yet herde I nevere tellen in myn age
Upon this nombre diffinicioun.

Men may devyne, and glosen up and doun,
But wel I woot, expres, withoute lye,
God bad us for to wexe and multiplye.
That gentil text kan I wel understonde;
Eek wel I woot he seyde, myn housbonde
Sholde lete fader and mooder, and take me;
But of no nombre mencioun made he,
Of bigamye, or of octogamye;
Why sholde men speke of it vileynye?

LO, heere the wise kyng, daun Salomon;
I trowe he hadde wyves mo than oon;
As, wolde God, it leveful were to me
To be refresshed half so ofte as he!
Which yifte of God hadde he for alle his wyvys!
No man hath swich, that in this world alyve is.
God woot, this noble kyng, as to my wit,
The firste nyght had many a myrie fit
With ech of hem, so wel was hym on lyve.
Blessed be God, that I have wedded fyve!
Welcome the sixte, whan that evere he shal!
for sothe, I wol nat kepe me chaast in al;
Whan myn housbonde is fro the world ygon,
Som cristen man shal wedde me anon;
for thanne thapostle seith that I am free
To wedde, a Goddes half, wher it liketh me.
He seith that to be wedded is no synne.
Bet is it to be wedded than to brynne.
What rekketh me thogh folk seye vileynye
Of shrewed Lameth and his bigamye?
I woot wel Abraham was an hooly man,
And Jacob eek, as ferforth as I kan;
And ech of hem hadde wyves mo than two;
And many another holy man also.
Whanne saugh ye evere, in any manere age,
That hye God defended mariage
By expres word? I pray you telleth me;
Or where comanded he virginitee?
I woot as wel as ye, it is no drede,
Whan thapostel speketh of maydenhede,
He seyde, that precept therof hadde he noon.
Men may conseille a womman to been oon,
But conseillyng is nat comandement.
He putte it in oure owene juggement;
for hadde God comanded maydenhede,
Thanne hadde he dampned weddyng with the
  dede;
And certes, if ther were no seed ysowe,
Virginitee, wherof thanne sholde it growe?
Poul dorste nat comanden atte leeste,
A thyng of which his maister yaf noon heeste.
The dart is set up for virginitee;
Cacche whoso may, who renneth best lat see!

BUT this word is nat taken of every wight,
But ther as God lust gyve it of his myght.
I woot wel that thapostel was a mayde;
But nathelees, thogh that he wroot and sayde
He wolde that every wight were swich as he,
Al nys but conseil to virginitee;
And for to been a wyf, he yaf me leve
Of indulgence; so it is no repreve
To wedde me, if that my make dye,
Withouten excepcioun of bigamye,
Al were it good no womman for to touche,

He mente as in his bed or in his couche;
for peril is bothe fyr and tow tassemble;
Ye knowe what this ensample may resemble.
This al and som, he heeld virginitee
Moore profiteth than weddyng in freletee:
freeltee clepe I, but if that he and she
Wolde leden al hir lyf in chastitee.
I graunte it wel, I have noon envye
Thogh maydenhede preferre bigamye;
Hem liketh to be clene, body and goost.
Of myn estaat I nyl nat make no boost,
for wel ye knowe, a lord in his houshold,
He nath nat every vessel al of gold;
Somme been of tree, and doon hir lord servyse.
God clepeth folk to hym in sondry wyse,
And everich hath of God a propre yifte,
Som this, som that, as hym liketh to shifte.

VIRGINITEE is greet perfeccioun,
And continence eek with devocioun;
But Crist, that of perfeccioun is welle,
Bad nat every wight he sholde go selle
All that he hadde, and gyve it to the poore,
And in swich wise folwe hym and his foore.
He spak to hem that wolde lyve parfitly;
And, lordynges, by youre leve, that am nat I.
I wol bistowe the flour of al myn age
In the actes and in fruyt of mariage.
Telle me also, to what conclusioun
Were membres maad of generacioun,
And for what profit was a wight ywroght?
Trusteth right wel, they were nat maad for noght.
Glose whoso wole, and seye bothe up and doun,
That they were makyd for purgacioun
Of uryne, and oure bothe thynges smale,
Were eek to knowe a femele from a male,
And for noon oother cause: sey ye no?
The experience woot wel it is noght so;
So that the clerkes be nat with me wrothe,
I seye this, that they maked been for bothe;
This is to seye, for office, and for ese
Of engendrure, ther we nat God displese.
Why sholde men elles in hir bookes sette
That man shal yelde to his wyf hire dette?
Now wherwith sholde he make his paiement,
If he ne used his sely instrument?
Thanne were they maad upon a creature,
To purge uryne, and eek for engendrure.
But I seye noght that every wight is holde,
That hath swich harneys as I to yow tolde,
To goon and usen hem in engendrure;
Than sholde men take of chastitee no cure.
Crist was a mayde, and shapen as a man,
And many a seint, sith that the world bigan,
Yet lyved they evere in parfit chastitee.
I nyl nat envye no virginitee;
Lat hem be breed of pured whete-seed,
And lat us wyves hoten barly-breed;
And yet with barly-breed, Mark telle kan,
Oure Lord Jhesu refresshed many a man.

IN swich estaat as God hath cleped us
I wol persevere, I nam nat precius;
In wyfhode I wol use myn instrument
As frely as my Makere hath it sent.

105

If I be daungerous, God yeve me sorwe;
Myn housbonde shal it have bothe eve and morwe,
Whan that hym list com forth and paye his dette.
An housbonde I wol have, I nyl nat lette,
Which shal be bothe my dettour and my thral,
And have his tribulacioun withal
Upon his flessh, whil that I am his wyf.
I have the power durynge al my lyf
Upon his propre body, and noght he.
Right thus the Apostel tolde it unto me,
And bad oure housbondes for to love us weel;
Al this sentence me liketh every deel.

UP stirte the Pardoner, and that anon;
Now, dame, quod he, by God and by
Seint John,
Ye been a noble prechour in this cas!
I was aboute to wedde a wyf; allas!
What, sholde I bye it on my flessh so
deere?
Yet hadde I levere wedde no wyf toyeere!

ABYDE, quod she, my tale is nat bigonne.
Nay, thou shalt drynken of another tonne,
Er that I go, shal savoure wors than ale.
And whan that I have toold thee forth my tale
Of tribulacioun in mariage,
Of which I am expert in al myn age,
This to seyn, myself have been the whippe;
Than maystow chese wheither thou wolt sippe
Of thilke tonne that I shal abroche.
Be war of it, er thou to ny approche;
For I shal tell ensamples mo than ten.
Whoso that nyl be war by othere men,
By hym shul othere men corrected be.
The same wordes writeth Ptholomee;
Rede it in his Almageste, and take it there.
Dame, I wolde pray yow, if youre wyl it were,
Seyde this Pardoner, as ye bigan
Telle forth youre tale; spareth for no man,
And teche us yonge men of youre praktike.
Gladly, quod she, sith it may yow like;
But yet I praye to al this compaignye,
If that I speke after my fantasye,
As taketh not agrief of that I seye;
For myn entente nis but for to pleye.

NOW sires, now wol I telle forth my
tale.
As evere moote I drynken wyn or ale,
I shal seye sooth, tho housbondes
that I hadde,
As thre of hem were goode, and two
were badde.
The thre were goode men and riche, and olde;
Unnethe myghte they the statut holde
In which that they were bounden unto me;
Ye woot wel what I meene of this, pardee!
As help me God, I laughe whan I thynke
How pitously anyght I made hem swynke!
And, by my fey, I tolde of it no stoor.
They had me yeven hir gold and hir tresoor;
Me neded nat do lenger diligence
To wynne hir love, or doon hem reverence;
They loved me so wel, by God above,
That I ne tolde no deyntee of hir love!

106

A wys womman wol sette hire evere in oon
To gete hire love, theras she hath noon;
But sith I hadde hem hoolly in myn hond,
And sith they hadde me yeven all hir lond,
What sholde I taken heede hem for to plese,
But it were for my profit and myn ese?
I sette hem so a werke, by my fey,
That many a nyght they songen Weilawey!
The bacoun was nat fet for hem, I trowe,
That som men han in Essex at Dunmowe.
I governed hem so wel after my lawe,
That ech of hem ful blisful was and fawe
To brynge me gaye thynges fro the fayre;
They were ful glad whan I spak to hem faire,
For, God it woot, I chidde hem spitously.

NOW herkneth how I baar me proprely,
Ye wise wyves, that kan understonde.
Thus shul ye speke, and bere hem wrong
on honde;
For half so boldely kan ther no man
Swere and lyen as a woman kan.
I sey nat this by wyves that been wyse,
But if it be whan they hem mysavyse.
A wys wyf shal, if that she kan hir good,
Bere hym on honde that the cow is wood,
And take witnesse of hir owene mayde
Of hir assent; but herkneth how I sayde.
Sire, olde kaynard, is this thyn array?
Why is my neighebores wyf so gay?
She is honoured over al ther she gooth;
I sitte at hoom, I have no thrifty clooth.
What dostow at my neighebores hous?
Is she so fair? artow so amorous?
What rowne ye with oure mayde? Benedicite!
Sire olde lechour, lat thy japes be!
And if I have a gossib or a freend,
Withouten gilt, thou chidest as a feend
If that I walke or pleye unto his hous.
Thou comest hoom as dronken as a mous,
And prechest on thy bench, with yvel preef:
Thou seist to me, it is a greet meschief
To wedde a povre womman, for costage;
And if that she be riche, of heigh parage,
Thanne seistow that it is a tormentrie
To soffre hire pride and hire malencolie,
And if that she be fair, thou verray knave,
Thou seyst that every holour wol hire have;
She may no while in chastitee abyde
That is assailled upon ech a syde.
THOU seyst som folk desire us for richesse,
Somme for oure shap, and somme for oure
fairnesse,
And som, for she kan outher synge or daunce,
And som, for gentillesse and daliaunce;
Som, for hir handes and hir armes smale;
Thus goth al to the devel by thy tale,
Thou seyst, men may nat kepe a castel wal;
It may so longe assailled been over al.
And if that she be foul, thou seist that she
Coveiteth every man that she may se;
For as a spaynel she wol on hym lepe,
Til that she fynde som man hire to chepe;
Ne noon so grey goos gooth ther in the lake,

As, seistow, that wol been withoute make.
And seyst, it is an hard thyng for to welde
A thyng that no man wole, his thankes, helde.
Thus seistow, lorel, whan thow goost to bedde,
And that no wys man nedeth for to wedde,
Ne no man that entendeth unto hevene.
With wilde thonder/dynt and firy levene
Moote thy welked nekke be tobroke!
Thow seyst that droppyng houses, and eek smoke,
And chidyng wyves, maken men to flee
Out of hir owene house; a! benedicitee!
What eyleth swich an old man for to chide?
Thow seyst we wyves wol our vices hide
Til we be fast, and thanne we wol hem shewe;
Wel may that be a proverbe of a shrewe.
Thou seist, that oxen, asses, hors, and houndes,
They been assayed at diverse stoundes;
Bacyns, lavoures, er that men hem bye,
Spoones and stooles, and al swich housbondrye,
And so been pottes, clothes, and array;
But folk of wyves maken noon assay
Til they be wedded; olde dotard shrewe!
And thanne, seistow, we wol oure vices shewe.
Thou seist also, that it displeseth me
But if that thou wolt preyse my beautee,
And but thou poure alwey upon my face,
And clepe me, faire dame, in every place;
And but thou make a feeste on thilke day
That I was born, and make me fressh and gay;
And but thou do to my norice honour,
And to my chamberere withinne my bour,
And to my fadres folk and his allyes;
Thus seistow, olde barelful of lyes!
AND yet of oure apprentice Janekyn,
For his crisp heer, shynynge as gold so fyn,
And for he squiereth me bothe up and doun,
Yet hastow caught a fals suspecioun;
I wol hym noght, thogh thou were deed tomorwe!
But tel me this, why hydestow, with sorwe,
The keyes of thy cheste awey fro me?
It is my good, as wel as thyn, pardee!
What! wenestow make an ydiot of oure dame?
Now, by that lord that called is Seint Jame,
Thou shalt nat bothe, thogh that thou were wood,
Be maister of my body and of my good;
That oon thou shalt forgo, maugree thyne eyen!
What nedeth thee of me tenquere or spyen?
I trowe, thou woldest loke me in thy chiste!
Thou sholdest seye: Wyf, go wher thee liste;
Taak youre disport, I wol not leve no talys;
I knowe yow for a trewe wyf, dame Alys.
We love no man that taketh kepe or charge
Wher that we goon; we wol ben at oure large.
Of alle men yblessed moot he be,
The wise astrologien, Daun Ptholome,
That seith this proverbe in his Almageste,
Of alle men his wysdom is hyeste
That rekketh nevere who hath the world in honde.
By this proverbe thou shalt understonde,
Have thou ynogh, what thar thee recche or care
How myrily that othere folkes fare?
For certeyn, olde dotard, by youre leve,

Ye shul have queynte right ynogh at eve.
He is to greet a nygard that wol werne
A man to lighte his candle at his lanterne;
He shal have never the lasse light, pardee!
Have thou ynogh, thee thar nat pleyne thee.
THOU seyst also, that if we make us gay
With clothing, and with precious array,
That it is peril of oure chastitee;
And yet, with sorwe, thou most enforce thee,
And seye thise wordes in thapostles name:
In habit maad with chastitee and shame
Ye wommen shul apparaille yow, quod he,
And noght in tressed heer, and gay perree,
As perles, ne with gold, ne clothes riche.
After thy text, ne after thy rubriche,
I wol nat wirche as muchel as a gnat.
Thou seydest this, that I was lyk a cat;
For whoso wolde senge a cattes skyn,
Thanne wolde the cat wel dwellen in his in;
And if the cattes skyn be slyk and gay,
She wol nat dwelle in house half a day;
But forth she wole, er any day be dawed,
To shewe hir skyn, and goon a caterwawed;
This is to seye, if I be gay, sire shrewe,
I wol renne out, my borel for to shewe.
SIRE olde fool, what eyleth thee to spyen?
Thogh thou preye Argus with his hundred eyen
To be my wardecors, as he kan best,
In feith, he shal nat kepe me but me lest;
Yet koude I make his berd, so moot I thee!
Thou seydest eek, that ther been thynges thre,
The whiche thynges troublen al this erthe,
And that no wight ne may endure the ferthe.
O leeve sire shrewe, Jhesu shorte thy lyf!
Yet prechestow, and seyst, an hateful wyf
Yrekened is for oon of thise meschances.
Been ther none othere maner resemblances
That ye may likne youre parables to,
But if a sely wyf be oon of tho?
Thou liknest eek wommanes love to helle,
To bareyne lond, ther water may nat dwelle;
Thou liknest it also to wilde fyr,
The moore it brenneth, the moore it hath desir
To consume every thyng that brent wole be;
Thou seyst, that right as wormes shende a tree,
Right so a wyf destroyeth hire housbonde;
This knowe they that been to wyves bonde.
LORDYNGES, right thus as ye have understonde,
Baar I stifly myne olde housbondes on honde,
That thus they seyden in hir dronkenesse;
And al was fals, but that I took witnesse
On Janekyn, and on my nece also.
O Lord, the peyne I dide hem and the wo!
Ful giltelees, by Goddes sweete pyne!
For as an hors I koude byte and whyne;
I koude pleyne, thogh I were in the gilt,
Or elles often tyme hadde I been spilt.
Whoso that first to mille comth, first grynt;
I pleyned first, so was oure werre ystynt;
They were ful glad to excusen hem ful blyve

107

Of thyng of which they nevere agilte hir lyve.
Of wenches wolde I beren hym on honde,
Whan that for syk unnethes myghte he stonde;
Yet tikled it his herte, for that he
Wende that I hadde of hym so greet chiertee.
I swoor that al my walkynge out by nyghte
Was for tespye wenches that he dighte.
Under that colour hadde I many a myrthe,
For al swich wit was yeven us in oure byrthe;
Deceite, wepyng, spynnyng, God hath yive
To wommen kyndely, whil they may lyve;
And thus of o thyng I avaunte me,
Atte ende I hadde the bettre in ech degree,
By sleighte, or force, or by som maner thyng,
As by continueel murmur or grucchyng.
Namely abedde hadden they meschaunce;
Ther wolde I chide and do hem no plesaunce;
I wolde no lenger in the bed abyde,
If that I felte his arm over my syde,
Til he had maad his raunsoun unto me;
Thanne wolde I suffre hym do his nycetee.
And therfore every man this tale I telle,
Wynne whoso may, for al is for to selle.
With empty hand men may none haukes lure;
For wynnyng wolde I al his lust endure,
And make me a feyned appetit;
And yet in bacon hadde I nevere delit;
That made me that evere I wolde hem chide;
For thogh the pope hadde seten hem biside,
I wolde nat spare hem at hir owene bord,
For, by my trouthe, I quitte hem word for word.
As help me verray God omnipotent,
Though I right now sholde make my testament,
I ne owe hem nat a word that it nys quit.
I broghte it so aboute by my wit
That they moste yeve it up, as for the beste,
Or elles hadde we nevere been in reste;
For thogh he looked as a wood leoun,
Yet sholde he faille of his conclusioun.
THANNE wolde I seye, Goode lief, taak keep,
How mekely looketh Wilkyn, oure sheep;
Com neer, my spouse, lat me ba thy cheke!
Ye sholde been al pacient and meke,
And han a sweete spiced conscience,
Sith ye so preche of Jobes pacience.
Suffreth alwey, syn ye so wel kan preche,
And, but ye do, certein we shal yow teche
That it is fair to have a wyf in pees.
Oon of us two moste bowen, douteles;
And sith a man is moore resonable
Than womman is, ye moste been suffrable.
What eyleth yow to grucche thus and grone?
Is it for ye wolde have my queynte allone?
Wy, taak it al! lo, have it every deel!
Peter! I shrewe yow but ye love it weel;
For if I wolde selle my bele chose,
I koude walke as fressh as is a rose;
But I wol kepe it for youre owene tooth.
Ye be to blame, by God! I sey yow sooth.
Swiche maner wordes hadde we on honde.

NOW wol I speken of my fourthe
housbonde.
My fourthe housbonde was a
revelour;
This is to seyn, he hadde a para-
mour;
And I was yong and ful of ragerye,
Stibourne and strong, and joly as a pye.
Wel koude I daunce to an harpe smale,
And synge, ywis, as any nyghtyngale,
Whan I had dronke a draughte of sweete wyn.
Metellius, the foule cherl, the swyn,
That with a staf birafte his wyf hire lyf,
For she drank wyn; thogh I hadde been his wyf
He sholde nat han daunted me fro drynke;
And after wyn, on Venus moste I thynke:
For al so siker as cold engendreth hayl,
A likerous mouth moste han a likerous tayl.
In wommen vinolent is no defence,
This knowen lecchours by experience.
But, Lord Crist! whan that it remembreth me
Upon my yowthe, and on my jolitee,
It tikleth me aboute myn herte roote!
Unto this day it dooth myn herte boote
That I have had my world as in my tyme.
But age, allas! that al wole envenyme,
Hath me biraft my beautee and my pith;
Lat go, farewel, the devel go therwith!
The flour is goon, ther is namoore to telle,
The bren, as I best kan, now moste I selle;
But yet to be right myrie wol I fonde.
NOW wol I tellen of my fourthe housbonde.
I seye, I hadde in herte greet despit
That he of any oother had delit;
But he was quit, by God and by Seint Joce!
I made hym of the same wode a croce.
Nat of my body in no foul manere,
But certeinly, I made folk swich cheere,
That in his owene grece I made hym frye
For angre, and for verray jalousye.
By God, in erthe I was his purgatorie,
For which I hope his soule be in glorie!
For God it woot, he sat ful ofte and song
Whan that his shoo ful bitterly hym wrong.
Ther was no wight, save God and he, that wiste,
In many wise, how soore I hym twiste.
He deyde whan I cam fro Jerusalem,
And lith ygrave under the roode/beem;
Al is his tombe noght so curyus
As was the sepulcre of hym, Daryus,
Which that Appelles wroghte subtilly;
It nys but wast to burye hym preciously.
Lat hym fare wel, God yeve his soule reste,
He is now in his grave and in his cheste!
NOW of my fifthe housbonde wol I telle.
God lete his soule nevere come in helle!
And yet was he to me the mooste shrewe;
That feele I on my ribbes al by rewe,
And evere shal, unto myn endyng day.
But in oure bed he was ful fressh and gay;
And therwithal so wel koude he me glose,
Whan that he wolde han my bele chose,
That thogh he hadde me bet on every bon,

He koude wynne agayn my love anon.
I trowe I loved hym beste for that he
Was of his love daungerous to me.
We wommen han, if that I shal nat lye,
In this matere a queynte fantasye;
Wayte what thyng we may nat lightly have,
Therafter wol we crie al day and crave.
Forbede us thyng, and that desiren we;
Preesse on us faste, and thanne wol we fle.
With daunger oute we al oure chaffare;
Greet prees at market maketh deere ware,
And to greet cheepe is holde at litel prys;
This knoweth every womman that is wys.

MY fifthe housbonde, God his soule blesse!
Which that I took for love, and no richesse,
He som tyme was a clerk of Oxen-
ford,
And hadde left scole, and wente at hom to bord
With my gossib, dwellynge in oure toun;
God have hir soule! hir name was Alisoun.
She knew myn herte, and eek my privetee,
Bet than oure parisshe-preest, as moot I thee.
To hire biwreyed I my conseil al;
For hadde myn housbonde pissed on a wal,
Or doon a thyng that sholde han cost his lyf,
To hire, and to another worthy wyf,
And to my nece, which that I loved weel,
I wolde han toold his conseil every deel.
And so I dide ful often, God it woot,
That made his face ful often rede and hoot
For verray shame, and blamed hymself for he
Had toold to me so greet a pryvetee.

AND so bifel that ones, in a Lente,
So often times I to my gossyb wente,
For evere yet I loved to be gay,
And for to walke, in March, Averill and May,
Fro hous to hous, to heere sondry talys,
That Jankyn clerk, and my gossyb, dame Alys,
And I myself, into the feeldes wente.
Myn housbonde was at London al that Lente;
I hadde the bettre leyser for to pleye,
And for to se, and eek for to be seye
Of lusty folk; what wiste I wher my grace
Was shapen for to be, or in what place?
Therfore I made my visitaciouns
To vigilies and to processiouns,
To prechyng eek, and to thise pilgrimages,
To pleyes of myracles, and to mariages,
And wered upon my gaye scarlet gytes.
Thise wormes, ne thise motthes, ne thise mytes,
Upon my peril, frete hem never a deel;
And wostow why? for they were used weel.

NOW wol I tellen forth what happed me.
I seye that in the feeldes walked we
Till trewely we hadde swich daliance,
This clerk and I, that of my purveiance
I spak to hym, and seyde hym, how that he,
If I were wydwe, sholde wedde me;
For certeinly, I sey for no bobance,
Yet was I nevere withouten purveiance
Of mariage, nof othere thynges eek.

I holde a mouses herte nat worth a leek
That hath but oon hole for to sterte to,
And if that faille, thanne is al ydo.
I bar hym on honde he hadde enchanted me,
My dame taughte me that soutiltee,
And eek I seyde, I mette of hym al nyght,
He wolde han slayn me as I lay upright,
And al my bed was ful of verray blood,
But yet I hope that he shal do me good;
For blood bitokeneth gold, as me was taught;
And al was fals, I dremed of it right naught,
But as I folwed ay my dames loore,
As wel of this as othere thynges moore.
But now, sire, lat me se, what I shal seyn?
A! ha! by God, I have my tale ageyn.
Whan that my fourthe housbonde was on beere
I weep algate, and made sory cheere,
As wyves mooten, for it is usage,
And with my coverchief covered my visage;
But, for that I was purveyed of a make,
I wepte but smal, and that I undertake.

TO chirche was myn housbonde born amorwe,
With neighebores, that for hym maden sorwe;
And Jankyn, oure clerk, was oon of tho.
As help me God, whan that I saugh hym go
After the beere, me thoughte he hadde a paire
Of legges and of feet so clene and faire,
That al myn herte I yaf unto his hoold.
He was, I trowe, a twenty wynter oold,
And I was fourty, if I shal seye sooth;
And yet I hadde alwey a coltes tooth.
Gat-tothed I was, and that bicam me weel,
I hadde the prente of seint Venus seel.
As help me God, I was a lusty oon,
And faire, and riche, and yong, and wel bigon;
And trewely, as myne housbondes tolde me,
I hadde the beste quonyam mighte be;
For certes, I am al Venerien
In feelynge, and myn herte is Marcien.
Venus me yaf my lust, my likerousnesse,
And Mars yaf me my sturdy hardynesse.
Myn ascendent was Taur, and Mars therinne.
Allas! allas! that evere love was synne!
I folwed ay myn inclinacioun
By vertu of my constellacioun,
That made me I koude noght withdrawe
My chambre of Venus from a good felawe.
Yet have I Martes mark upon my face,
And also in another, privee, place,
For, God so wys be my savacioun,
I ne loved nevere by no discrecioun,
But evere folwede myn appetit,
Al were he short, or long, or blak, or whit;
I took no kepe, so that he liked me,
How poore he was, ne eek of what degree.

WHAT sholde I seye, but at the monthes
ende
This joly clerk, Jankyn, that was so hende,
Hath wedded me with greet solempnytee,
And to hym yaf I all the lond and fee,
That evere was me yeven therbifoore;
But afterward repented me ful soore.
He nolde suffre nothyng of my list.

By God, he smoot me ones, on the lyst,
for that I rente out of his book a leef,
That of the strook myn ere wax al deef.
Stibourne I was as is a leonesse,
And of my tonge a verray jangleresse;
And walke I wolde, as I had doon biforn,
from hous to hous, although he had it sworn;
for which he often tymes wolde preche,
And me of olde Romayn geestes teche;
How he, Symplicius Gallus, lefte his wyf,
And hire forsok for terme of al his lyf,
Noght but for open-heveded he hir say
Lokynge out at his dore upon a day.
    Another Romayn tolde he me by name,
That, for his wyf was at a someres game
Withouten his wityng, he forsook hire eke.
And thanne wolde he upon his Bible seke
That ilke proverbe of Ecclesiaste,
Where he comandeth and forbedeth faste,
Man shal nat suffre his wyf go roule aboute;
Thanne wolde he seye right thus, withouten doute:
    Whoso that buyldeth his hous al of salwes,
And priketh his blynde hors over the falwes,
And suffreth his wyf to go seken halwes,
Is worthy to been hanged on the galwes.
    But al for noght, I sette noght an hawe
Of his proverbes nof his olde sawe;
Ne I wolde nat of hym corrected be.
I hate hym that my vices telleth me,
And so doo mo, God woot! of us than I.
This made hym with me wood al outrely;
I nolde noght forbere hym in no cas.
    NOW wol I seye yow sooth, by Seint Thomas,
Why that I rente out of his book a leef,
for which he smoot me so that I was deef.
He hadde a book that gladly, nyght and day,
for his desport he wolde rede alway.
He cleped it Valerie and Theofraste,
At whiche book he lough alwey ful faste;
And eek ther was som tyme a clerk at Rome,
A cardinal, that highte Seint Jerome,
That made a book agayn Jovinian,
In whiche book eek ther was Tertulan,
Crisippus, Trotula, and Helowys,
That was abbesse nat fer fro Parys;
And eek the Parables of Salomon,
Ovides Art, and bookes many on;
And alle thise were bounden in o volume.
And every nyght and day was his custume,
Whan he hadde leyser and vacacioun
from oother worldly occupacioun,
To reden on this book of wikked wyves.
He knew of hem mo legendes and lyves
Than been of goode wyves in the Bible.
for, trusteth wel, it is an impossible
That any clerk wol speke good of wyves,
But if it be of hooly Seintes lyves,
Ne of noon oother womman never the mo.
Who peyntede the leoun? Tel me who.
By God! if wommen hadde writen stories,
As clerkes han withinne hire oratories,
They wolde han writen of men moore wikkednesse
Than all the mark of Adam may redresse.
110

The children of Mercurie and of Venus
Been in hir wirkyng ful contrarius;
Mercurie loveth wysdom and science,
And Venus loveth ryot and dispence;
And, for hire diverse disposicioun,
Ech falleth in otheres exaltacioun;
And thus, God woot, Mercurie is desolat
In Pisces, wher Venus is exaltat;
And Venus falleth ther Mercurie is reysed;
Therfore no womman of no clerk is preysed.
The clerk, whan he is oold, and may noght do
Of Venus werkes worth his olde sho,
Thanne sit he doun, and writ in his dotage
That wommen kan nat kepe hir mariage.
    BUT now to purpos, why I tolde thee
    That I was beten for a book, pardee.
    Upon a nyght, Jankyn that was oure sire
Redde on his book, as he sat by the fire,
Of Eva first, that, for hir wikkednesse
Was al mankynde broght to wrecchednesse;
for which that Jhesu Crist hymself was slayn,
That boghte us with his herte-blood agayn.
Lo, heere express of womman may ye fynde,
That womman was the los of al mankynde.
    Tho redde he me how Sampson loste his heres;
Slepynge, his lemman kitte hem with hir sheres;
Thurgh whiche tresoun loste he bothe his eyen.
    Tho redde he me, if that I shal nat lyen,
Of Hercules and of his Dianyre,
That caused hym to sette hymself afyre.
Nothyng forgat he the sorwe and wo
That Socrates hadde with his wyves two;
How Xantippa caste pisse upon his heed.
This sely man sat stille as he were deed;
He wiped his heed, namore dorste he seyn
But, Er that thonder stynte, comth a reyn!
    Of Phasifpha, that was the queene of Crete,
for shrewednesse, hym thoughte the tale swete;
fy! speke namoore; it is a grisly thyng,
Of hire horrible lust and hir likyng!
    Of Clitermystra, for hire lecherye
That falsly made hire housbonde for to dye;
He redde it with ful good devocioun.
    He tolde me eek for what occasioun
Amphiorax at Thebes loste his lyf;
Myn housbonde hadde a legende of his wyf,
    Eriphilem, that for an ouche of gold
Hath prively unto the Grekes told
Wher that hir housbonde hidde hym in a place,
for which he hadde at Thebes sory grace.
    Of Lyma tolde he me, and of Lucye;
They bothe made hir housbondes for to dye;
That oon for love, that oother was for hate;
Lyma, hir housbonde, on an even late,
Empoysoned hath, for that she was his fo;
Lucia, likerous, loved hire housbonde so,
That, for he sholde alwey upon hire thynke,
She yaf hym swich a manere love-drynke
That he was deed, er it were by the morwe;
And thus algates housbondes han sorwe.
    THANNE tolde he me, how oon Latumyus
    Compleyned unto his felawe Arrius
    That in his gardyn growed swich a tree,

On which, he seyde, how that his wyves thre
Hanged hemself for herte despitus.
O leeve brother, quod this Arrius,
Yif me a plante of thilke blissed tree,
And in my gardyn planted it shal be.
Of latter date, of wyves hath he red,
That somme han slayn hir housbondes in hir bed,
And lete hir lecchour dighte hire al the nyght,
Whan that the corps lay in the floor upright;
And somme han dryve nayles in hir brayn
Whil that they slepte, and thus they han hem
slayn.
Somme han hem yeve poysoun in hire drynke;
He spak moore harm than herte may bithynke;
And therwithal, he knew of mo proverbes,
Than in this world ther growen gras or herbes.
Bet is, quod he, thyn habitacioun
Be with a leoun or a foul dragoun,
Than with a womman usynge for to chyde.
Bet is, quod he, hye in the roof abyde,
Than with an angry wyf doun in the hous.
They been so wikked and contrarious,
They haten that hir housbondes loven ay.
He seyde: A womman cast hir shame away
Whan she cast of hir smok; and forther mo,
A fair womman, but she be chaast also,
Is lyk a gold ryng in a sowes nose.
Who wolde wenen, or who wolde suppose,
The wo that in myn herte was, and pyne?
AND whan I saugh he wolde nevere fyne
To reden on this cursed book al nyght,
Al sodeynly thre leves have I plyght
Out of his book, right as he radde, and eke
I with my fest so took hym on the cheke,
That in oure fyr he fil bakward adoun;
And he up stirte as dooth a wood leoun,
And with his fest he smoot me on the heed,
That in the floor I lay as I were deed;
And whan he saugh how stille that I lay,
He was agast, and wolde han fled his way,
Til atte laste out of my swogh I breyde:
O! hastow slayn me, false theef? I seyde;
And for my land thus hastow mordred me?
Er I be deed, yet wol I kisse thee.
And neer he cam, and kneled faire adoun,
And seyde: Deere suster Alisoun!
As help me God, I shal thee nevere smyte;
That I have doon, it is thyself to wyte.
Foryeve it me, and that I thee biseke;
And yet, eftsoones, I hitte hym on the cheke,
And seyde: Theef! thus muchel am I wreke;
Now wol I dye, I may no lenger speke.
But atte laste, with muchel care and wo,

We fille acorded, by us selven two.
He yaf me al the bridel in myn hond,
To han the governance of hous and lond,
And of his tonge, and of his hond also,
And made hym brenne his book anon right tho;
And whan that I hadde geten unto me,
By maistrie, al the soveraynetee,
And that he seyde: Myn owene trewe wyf,
Do as thee lust to terme of al thy lyf,
Keep thyn honour, and keep eek myn estaat.
After that day we hadden never debaat.
God help me so, I was to hym as kynde
As any wyf from Denmark unto Ynde,
And also trewe, and so was he to me.
I prey to God, that sit in magestee,
So blesse his soule, for his mercy deere.
Now wol I seye my tale, if ye wol heere.

Biholde the wordes bitwene the Somonour and
the Frere.

HE Frere lough, whan he hadde herd
al this;
Now, dame, quod he, so have I joye
or blis,
This is a long preamble of a tale!
And whan the Somnour herde
the Frere gale,
Lo! quod the Somnour, Goddes armes two!
A frere wol entremette him everemo.
Lo, goode men, a flye, and eek a frere,
Wol falle in every dyssh and eek mateere.
What spekestow of preambulacioun?
What! amble, or trotte, or pees, or go sit doun;
Thou lettest oure disport in this manere.
Ye, woltow so, sire Somnour? quod the frere;
Now, by my feith! I shal, er that I go,
Telle of a somnour swich a tale or two
That alle the folk shal laughen in this place.
Now elles, frere, I bishrewe thy face!
Quod this Somnour, and I bishrewe me
But if I telle tales, two or thre,
Of freres, er I come to Sidyngborne,
That I shal make thyn herte for to morne,
For wel I woot thy pacience is gon.
OURE Hooste cride, Pees! and that anon!
And seyde: Lat the womman telle hire
tale;
Ye fare as folk that dronken been of ale.
Do, dame, telle forth youre tale, and that is best.
Al redy, sire, quod she, right as yow lest;
If I have licence of this worthy Frere.
Yis, dame, quod he, tel forth, and I wol heere.
Heere endeth the Wyf of Bathe hir prologe.

111

HERE BIGYNNETH THE TALE OF THE WIFE OF BATH ⚜⚜

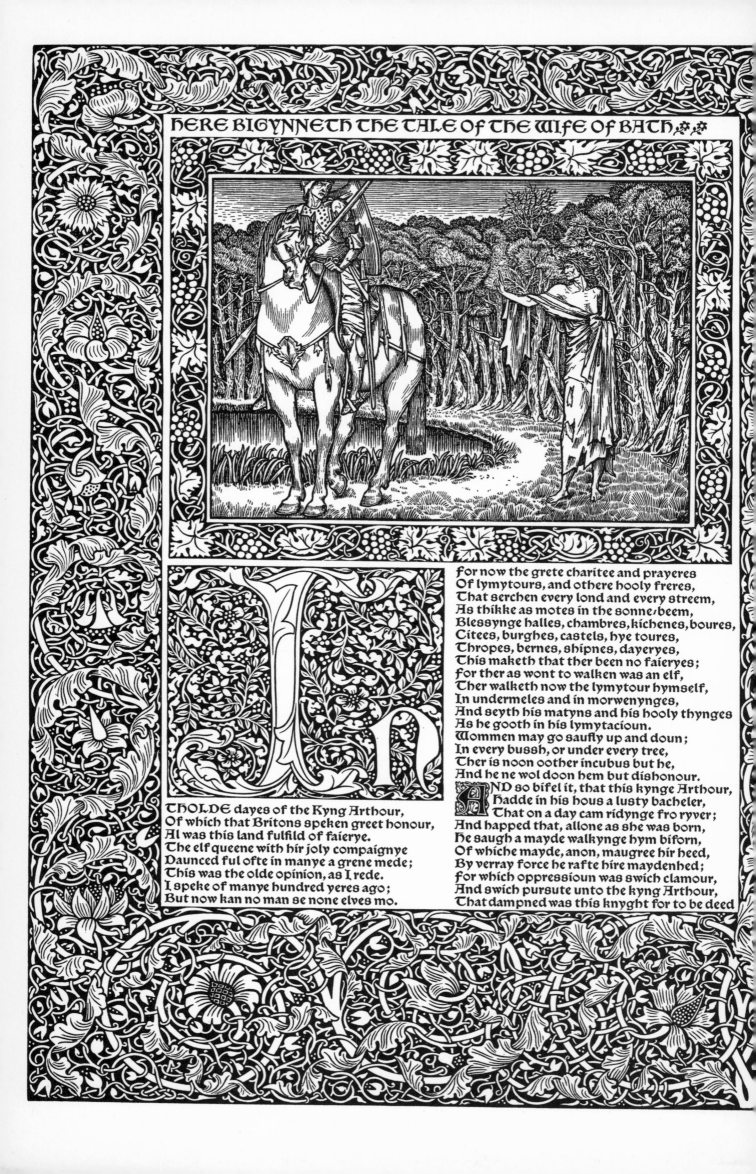

IN THOLDE dayes of the Kyng Arthour,
Of which that Britons speken greet honour,
Al was this land fulfild of faierye.
The elf queene with hir joly compaignye
Daunced ful ofte in manye a grene mede;
This was the olde opinion, as I rede.
I speke of manye hundred yeres ago;
But now kan no man se none elves mo.

For now the grete charitee and prayeres
Of lymytours, and othere hooly freres,
That serchen every lond and every streem,
As thikke as motes in the sonne-beem,
Blessynge halles, chambres, kichenes, boures,
Citees, burghes, castels, hye toures,
Thropes, bernes, shipnes, dayeryes,
This maketh that ther been no faieryes;
For ther as wont to walken was an elf,
Ther walketh now the lymytour hymself,
In undermeles and in morwenynges,
And seyth his matyns and his hooly thynges
As he gooth in his lymytacioun.
Wommen may go saufly up and doun;
In every bussh, or under every tree,
Ther is noon oother incubus but he,
And he ne wol doon hem but dishonour.
AND so bifel it, that this kynge Arthour,
Hadde in his hous a lusty bacheler,
That on a day cam ridynge fro ryver;
And happed that, allone as she was born,
He saugh a mayde walkynge hym biforn,
Of whiche mayde, anon, maugree hir heed,
By verray force he rafte hire maydenhed;
For which oppressioun was swich clamour,
And swich pursute unto the kyng Arthour,
That dampned was this knyght for to be deed

By cours of lawe, and sholde han lost his heed
Paraventure, swich was the statut tho;
But that the queene and othere ladyes mo
So longe preyeden the kyng of grace,
Til he his lyf hym graunted in the place,
And yaf hym to the queene al at hir wille,
To chese, wheither she wolde hym save or spille.
The queene thanketh the kyng with al hir myght,
And after this thus spak she to the knyght,
Whan that she saugh hir tyme, upon a day:
THOU standest yet, quod she, in swich array,
That of thy lyf yet hastow no suretee.
I grante thee lyf, if thou kanst tellen me
What thyng is it that wommen moost desiren;
Be war, and keep thy nekke,boon from iren.
And if thou kanst nat tellen it anon,
Yet shal I yeve thee leve for to gon
A twelfmonth and a day, to seche and leere
An answere suffisant in this mateere;
And suretee wol I han, er that thou pace,
Thy body for to yelden in this place.
WO was this knyght, and sorwefully he
siketh;
But what! he may nat do al as hym liketh;
And at the laste, he chees hym for to wende,
And come agayn, right at the yeres ende,
With swich answere as God wolde hym purveye;
And taketh his leve, and wendeth forth his weye.
HE seketh every hous and every place
Wheras he hopeth for to fynde grace
To lerne, what thyng wommen loven moost;
But he ne koude arryven in no coost
Wheras he myghte fynde in this mateere
Two creatures accordynge in feere.
SOMME seyde, wommen loven best
richesse,
Somme seyde, honour, somme seyde,
jolynesse,
Somme, riche array, somme seyden, lust abedde,
And ofte tyme to be wydwe and wedde.
Somme seyde, that oure hertes been moost esed
Whan that we been yflatered and yplesed.
HE gooth ful ny the sothe, I wol nat lye,
A man shal wynne us best with flaterye;
And with attendance, and with bisynesse,
Been we ylymed, bothe moore and lesse.
AND somme seyn, how that we loven best
for to be free, and do right as us lest,
And that no man repreve us of oure vice,
But seye that we be wise, and nothyng nyce;
for trewely ther is noon of us alle,
If any wight wol clawe us on the galle,
That we nil kike, for he seith us sooth.
Assay, and he shal fynde it, that so dooth,
for, be we never so vicious withinne,
We wol been holden wise, and clene of synne.
AND somme seyn, that greet delit han we
for to been holden stable and eek secree,
And in o purpos stedefastly to dwelle,
And nat biwreye thyng that men us telle;
But that tale is nat worth a rake,stele.
Pardee, we wommen konne nothyng hele;
Witnesse on Myda; wol ye heere the tale?

i 1

VYDE, amonges othere thynges
smale,
Seyde, Myda hadde, under his tonge
heres,
Growynge upon his heed, two asses
eres,
The whiche vice he hydde, as he best myghte,
ful subtilly from every mannes sighte,
That, save his wyf, ther wist of it namo.
He loved hire moost, and trusted hire also;
He preyede hire, that to no creature
She sholde tellen of his disfigure.
She swoor him Nay, for al this world to wynne,
She nolde do that vileynye or synne,
To make hir housbonde han so foul a name;
She nolde nat telle it for hir owene shame.
But nathelees, hir thoughte that she dyde,
That she so longe sholde a conseil hyde;
Hir thoughte it swal so soore aboute hir herte,
That nedely som word hire moste asterte;
And sith she dorste telle it to no man,
Doun to a mareys faste by she ran;
Til she came there, her herte was afyre,
And as a bitore bombleth in the myre,
She leyde hir mouth unto the water doun:
Biwreye me nat, thou water, with thy soun,
Quod she, to thee I telle it, and namo,
Myn housbonde hath longe asses erys two.
Now is myn herte all hool, now is it oute;
I myghte no lenger kepe it, out of doute.
HEERE may ye se, thogh we a tyme abyde,
Yet, out it moot, we can no conseil hyde.
The remenant of the tale if ye wol heere,
Redeth Ovyde, and ther ye may it leere.
THIS knyght, of which my tale is specially,
Whan that he saugh he myghte nat come
therby,
That is to seye, what wommen loven moost,
Withinne his brest ful sorweful was the goost.
But hoom he gooth, he myghte nat sojourne,
The day was come that homward moste he tourne.
And in his wey it happed hym to ryde,
In al this care, under a forest,syde,
Wheras he saugh upon a daunce go
Of ladyes foure and twenty, and yet mo;
Toward the whiche daunce he drow ful yerne,
In hope that som wysdom sholde he lerne;
But certeinly, er he came fully there,
Vanysshed was this daunce, he nyste where.
No creature saugh he that bar lyf,
Save on the grene he saugh sittynge a wyf;
A fouler wight ther may no man devyse.
Agayn the knyght this olde wyf gan ryse,
And seyde: Sire knyght, heerforth ne lith no wey;
Tel me, what that ye seken, by youre fey.
Paraventure it may the bettre be;
Thise olde folk kan muchel thyng, quod she.
My leeve mooder, quod this knyght, certeyn
I nam but deed, but if that I kan seyn
What thyng it is that wommen moost desire:
Koude ye me wisse, I wolde wel quite youre hire.
Plight me thy trouthe heere in myn hand,
quod she,

113

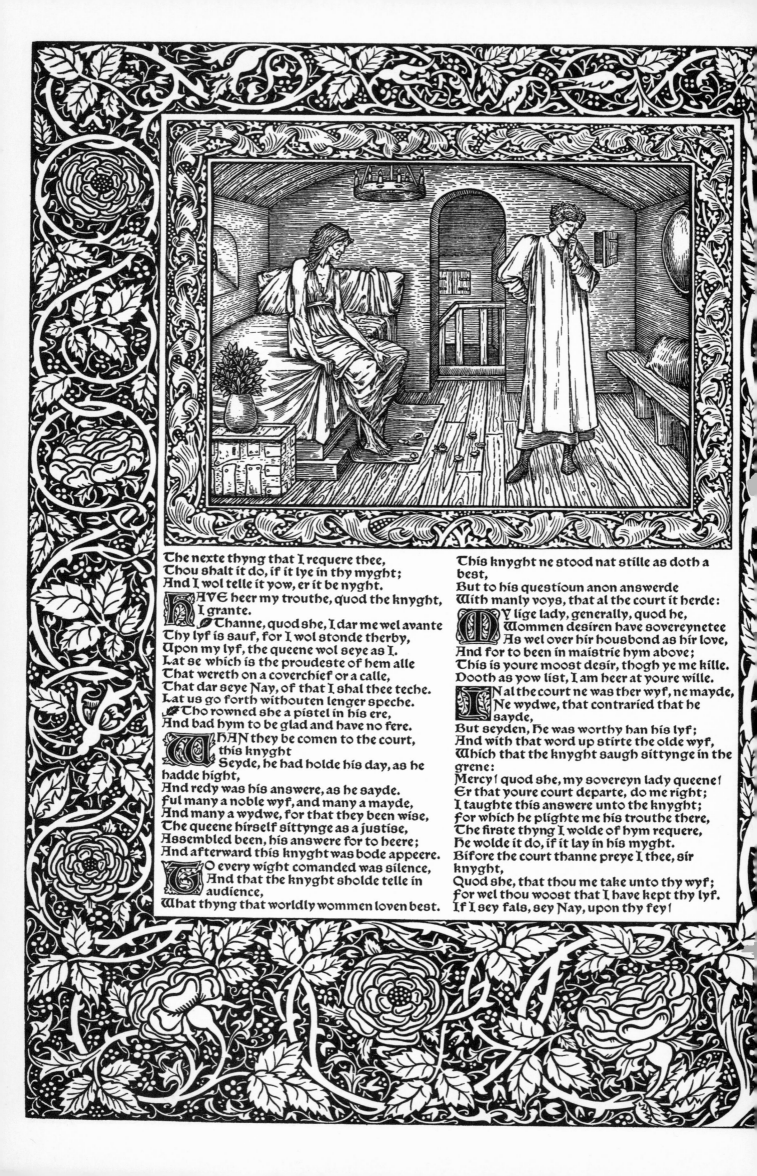

The nexte thyng that I requere thee,
Thou shalt it do, if it lye in thy myght;
And I wol telle it yow, er it be nyght.
HAVE heer my trouthe, quod the knyght,
I grante.
Thanne, quod she, I dar me wel avante
Thy lyf is sauf, for I wol stonde therby,
Upon my lyf, the queene wol seye as I.
Lat se which is the proudeste of hem alle
That wereth on a coverchief or a calle,
That dar seye Nay, of that I shal thee teche.
Lat us go forth withouten lenger speche.
Tho rowned she a pistel in his ere,
And bad hym to be glad and have no fere.

WHAN they be comen to the court, this knyght
Seyde, he had holde his day, as he
hadde hight,
And redy was his answere, as he sayde.
Ful many a noble wyf, and many a mayde,
And many a wydwe, for that they been wise,
The queene hirself sittynge as a justise,
Assembled been, his answere for to heere;
And afterward this knyght was bode appeere.
TO every wight comanded was silence,
And that the knyght sholde telle in
audience,
What thyng that worldly wommen loven best.

This knyght ne stood nat stille as doth a
best,
But to his questioun anon answerde
With manly voys, that al the court it herde:
MY lige lady, generally, quod he,
Wommen desiren have sovereynetee
As wel over hir housbond as hir love,
And for to been in maistrie hym above;
This is youre moost desir, thogh ye me kille.
Dooth as yow list, I am heer at youre wille.
IN al the court ne was ther wyf, ne mayde,
Ne wydwe, that contraried that he
sayde,
But seyden, He was worthy han his lyf;
And with that word up stirte the olde wyf,
Which that the knyght saugh sittynge in the
grene:
Mercy! quod she, my sovereyn lady queene!
Er that youre court departe, do me right;
I taughte this answere unto the knyght;
For which he plighte me his trouthe there,
The firste thyng I wolde of hym requere,
He wolde it do, if it lay in his myght.
Bifore the court thanne preye I thee, sir
knyght,
Quod she, that thou me take unto thy wyf;
For wel thou woost that I have kept thy lyf.
If I sey fals, sey Nay, upon thy fey!

THIS knyght answerde, Allas, and weylawey!
I woot right wel that swich was my biheste.
for Goddes love, as chees a newe requeste!
Taak al my good, and lat my body go.
Nay thanne, quod she, I shrewe us bothe two!
for thogh that I be foul, and oold, and poore,
I nolde for al the metal, ne for oore
That under erthe is grave, or lith above,
But if thy wyf I were, and eek thy love!
MY love? quod he, nay, my dampnacioun!
Allas! that any of my nacioun
Sholde evere so foule disparaged be!
But al for noght, the ende is this, that he
Constreyned was, he nedes moste hire wedde;
And taketh his olde wyf, and gooth to bedde.
NOW wolden som men seye, paraventure,
That, for my necligence, I do no cure
To tellen yow the joye and al tharray,
That at the feeste was that ilke day.
To which thyng shortly answeren I shal;
I seye, ther nas no joye ne feeste at al,
Ther nas but hevynesse, and muche sorwe,
for prively he wedded hire on morwe,
And al day after hidde hym as an owle;

So wo was hym, his wyf looked so foule.
GREET was the wo the knyght hadde in his thoght,
Whan he was with his wyf abedde ybroght.
He walweth, and he turneth to and fro;
His olde wyf lay smylynge everemo,
And seyde, O deere housbonde, benedicitee!
fareth every knyght thus with his wyf as ye?
Is this the lawe of kyng Arthures hous?
Is every knyght of his so dangerous?
I am youre owene love, and eek youre wyf;
I am she which that saved hath youre lyf,
And certes, yet dide I yow nevere unright.
Why fare ye thus with me this firste nyght?
Ye faren lyk a man had lost his wit;
What is my gilt? for Goddes love tel it,
And it shal been amended, if I may.
Amended! quod this knyght, allas! nay, nay!
It wol nat been amended nevere mo,
Thou art so loothly, and so oold also,
And therto comen of so lough a kynde,
That litel wonder is, thogh I walwe and wynde.
So wolde God, myn herte wolde breste!
Is this, quod she, the cause of youre unreste?
Ye, certeinly, quod he, no wonder is.

Now, sire, quod she, I koude amende al this,
If that me liste, er it were dayes thre;
So wel ye myghte bere yow unto me.
But for ye speken of swich gentillesse
As is descended out of old richesse,
That therfore sholden ye be gentil men,
Swich arrogance is nat worth an hen.
Looke who that is moost vertuous alway,
Pryvee and apert, and moost entendeth ay
To do the gentil dedes that he kan,
And taak hym for the grettest gentil man.
Crist wole, we clayme of hym oure gentillesse,
Nat of oure eldres for hire old richesse.
For thogh they yeve us al hir heritage,
For which we clayme to been of heigh parage,
Yet may they nat biquethe, for nothyng,
To noon of us, hir vertuous lyvyng,
That made hem gentil men ycalled be,
And bade us folwen hem in swich degree.
Wel kan the wise poete of Florence,
That highte Dant, speken in this sentence;
Lo in swich maner rym is Dantes tale:
Ful selde up riseth by his branches smale
Prowesse of man, for God, of his goodnesse,
Wole that of hym we clayme our gentillesse;
For of oure eldres may we nothyng clayme,
But temporel thyng, that man may hurte and
mayme.
Eek every wight woot this as wel as I,
If gentilesse were planted naturelly
Unto a certeyn lynage, doun the lyne,
Pryvee ne apert, than wolde they nevere fyne
To doon of gentillesse the faire office;
They myghte do no vileynye or vice.
Taak fyr, and ber it in the derkeste hous
Bitwix this and the mount of Kaukasous,
And lat men shette the dores and go thenne;
Yet wole the fyr as faire lye and brenne,
As twenty thousand men myghte it biholde;
His office natureel ay wol it holde,
Up peril of my lyf, til that it dye.

HEERE may ye se wel, how that genterye
Is nat annexed to possessioun,
Sith folk ne doon hir operacioun
Alwey, as dooth the fyr, lo, in his kynde.
For, God it woot, men may wel often fynde
A lordes sone do shame and vileynye;
And he that wole han pris of his gentrye
For he was boren of a gentil hous,
And hadde his eldres noble and vertuous,
And nyl hymselven do no gentil dedis,
Ne folwe his gentil auncestre that deed is,
He nys nat gentil, be he duc or erl;
For vileyns synful dedes make a cherl.
For gentillesse nys but renomee
Of thyne auncestres, for hire heigh bountee,
Which is a strange thyng to thy persone.
Thy gentillesse cometh fro God allone;
Thanne comth oure verray gentillesse of grace,
It was nothyng biquethe us with oure place.
Thenketh how noble, as seith Valerius,
Was thilke Tullius Hostillius,
That out of poverte roos to heigh noblesse.

116

Redeth Senek, and redeth eek Boece,
Ther shul ye seen expres, that it no drede is,
That he is gentil that dooth gentil dedis;
And therfore, leeve housbonde, I thus conclude,
Al were it that myne auncestres were rude,
Yet may the hye God, and so hope I,
Grante me grace to lyven vertuously;
Thanne am I gentil, whan that I bigynne
To lyven vertuously and weyve synne.
And theras ye of poverte me repreeve,
The hye God, on whom that we bileeve,
In wilful poverte chees to lyve his lyf,
And certes, every man, mayden, or wyf,
May understonde that Jhesus, hevene
kyng,
Ne wolde nat chesen vicious lyvyng.
Glad poverte is an honeste thyng, certeyn;
This wole Senec and othere clerkes seyn.
Whoso that halt hym payd of his poverte,
I holde hym riche, al hadde he nat a sherte.
He that coveiteth is a povere wight,
For he wolde han that is nat in his myght.
But he that noght hath, ne coveiteth have,
Is riche, although ye holde hym but a knave.
Verray poverte, it syngeth proprely;
Juvenal seith of poverte myrily:
The povre man, whan he goth by the weye,
Bifore the theves he may synge and pleye.
Poverte is hateful good, and, as I gesse,
A ful greet bryngere, out of bisynesse;
A greet amender eek of sapience
To hym that taketh it in pacience.
Poverte is this, although it seme alenge:
Possessioun, that no wight wol chalenge,
Poverte ful ofte, whan a man is lowe,
Maketh his God, and eek hymself, to knowe.
Poverte a spectacle is, as thynketh me,
Thurgh which he may his verray freendes see.
And therfore, sire, syn that I noght yow greve,
Of my poverte namoore ye me repreve.

NOW, sire, of elde ye repreve me;
And certes, sire, thogh noon auctoritee
Were in no book, ye gentils of honour
Seyn that men sholde an oold wight doon
favour,
And clepe hym fader, for youre gentillesse;
And auctours shal I fynden, as I gesse.
Now ther ye seye that I am foul and old,
Than drede you noght to been a cokewold;
For filthe and eelde, also moot I thee,
Been grete wardeyns upon chastitee:
But nathelees, syn I knowe youre delit,
I shal fulfille youre worldly appetit.
Chese now, quod she, oon of thise thynges
tweye:
To han me foul and old til that I deye,
And be to yow a trewe humble wyf,
And nevere yow displese in al my lyf;
Or elles ye wol han me yong and fair,
And take youre aventure of the repair
That shal be to youre hous, bycause of me,
Or in som oother place, may wel be;
Now chese yourselven, wheither that yow liketh.

THIS knyght avyseth hym and sore siketh,
But atte laste he seyde in this manere:
My lady and my love, and wyf so deere,
I put me in youre wise governance;
Cheseth youreself which may be moost plesance,
And moost honour to yow and me also;
I do no fors the wheither of the two;
For as yow liketh it suffiseth me.
THANNE have I gete of yow maistrie, quod she,
Syn I may chese, and governe as me lest?
Ye, certes, wyf, quod he, I holde it best.
Kys me, quod she, we be no lenger wrothe;
For, by my trouthe, I wol be to yow bothe,
This is to seyn, ye, bothe fair and good.
I prey to God that I moote sterven wood,
But I to yow be al so good and trewe,
As evere was wyf, syn that the world was newe.
And, but I be tomorn as fair to seene
As any lady, emperice, or queene,
That is bitwixe the est and eek the west,
Dooth with my lyf & deth right as yow lest.
Cast up the curtyn, looke how that it is.
And whan the knyght saugh verraily al this,
That she so fair was, and so yong therto,
For joye he hente hire in his armes two,
His herte bathed in a bath of blisse;
A thousand tyme arewe he gan hire kisse.
And she obeyed hym in every thyng
That myghte doon hym plesance or likyng.
AND thus they lyve unto hir lyves ende,
In parfit joye; and Jhesu Crist us sende
Housbondes meeke, yonge, and fressh abedde,
And grace toverbyde hem that we wedde.
And eek, I praye Jhesu, shorte hir lyves
That wol nat be governed by hir wyves;
And olde and angry nygardes of dispence,
God sende hem soone verray pestilence!
Heere endeth the Wyves Tale of Bath.

The prologe of the freres Tale ❀ ❀

THIS worthy lymytour, this noble Frere,
He made alway a maner louryng chiere
Upon the Somnour, but for honestee
No vileyns word as yet to hym spak he.
But atte laste he seyde unto the Wyf,
Dame, quod he, God yeve yow right good lyf!
Ye han heer touched, also moot I thee,
In scole-matere greet difficultee.
Ye han seyd muchel thyng right wel, I seye;
But dame, heere as we ryden by the weye,
Us nedeth nat to speken but of game,
And lete auctoritees, on Goddes name,
To prechyng, and to scole eek of clergye.
And if it lyke to this compaignye,
I wol yow of a Somnour telle a game.
Pardee, ye may wel knowe by the name,
That of a Somnour may no good be sayd;
I praye that noon of you be yvele apayd.
A Somnour is a renner up and doun
With mandements for fornicacioun,
And is ybet at every townes ende.
OURE Hoost tho spak, A, sire, ye sholde be hende
And curteys, as a man of youre estaat;
In compaignye we wol have no debaat;
Telleth youre tale, and lat the Somnour be.
Nay, quod the Somnour, lat hym seye to me
Whatso hym list; whan it comth to my lot,
By God! I shal hym quiten every grot!
I shal hym tellen which a greet honour
It is to be a flaterynge lymytour;
And his office I shal hym telle, ywis.
Oure Hoost answerde, Pees! namoore of this!
And after this he seyde unto the frere,
Tel forth youre tale, leeve maister deere.
Here endeth the prologe of the frere.

HEERE BIGYNNETH THE FRERES TALE ❀ ❀ ❀ ❀

WHILOM ther was dwellynge in my contree
An erchedekene, a man of heigh degree,
That boldely dide execucioun
In punysshynge of fornicacioun,
Of wicchecraft, and eek of bawderye,
Of diffamacioun, and avowtrye,
Of chirche-reves, and of testaments,
Of contractes, and of lakke of sacraments,
And eek of many another maner cryme,
Which nedeth nat rehercen for this tyme;
Of usure, and of symonye also.
But certes, lecchours dide he grettest wo;
They sholde syngen, if that they were hent;
And smale tytheres weren foule yshent;
If any persone wolde upon hem pleyne
Ther myghte asterte hym no pecunyal peyne.
For smale tithes, and for smal offrynge,
He made the peple pitously to synge;
For er the bisshope caughte hem with his hook,
They weren in the erchedeknes book.
Thanne hadde he, thurgh his jurisdiccioun,
Power to doon on hem correccioun.
HE hadde a Somnour redy to his hond,
A slyer boye was noon in Engelond;
For subtilly he hadde his espiaille,

That taughte hym, wher that hym myghte availle.
He koude spare of lecchours oon or two,
To techen hym to foure and twenty mo.
For thogh this Somnour wood were as an hare,
To telle his harlotrye I wol nat spare;
For we been out of his correccioun,
They han of us no jurisdiccioun,
Ne nevere shullen, terme of alle hir lyves.
Peter! so been the wommen of the styves,
Quod the Somnour, yput out of my cure!
Pees! with myschance and with mysaventure!
Thus seyde our Hoost, and lat hym telle his tale.
Now telleth forth, thogh that the Somnour gale,
Ne spareth nat, myn owene maister deere.
THIS false theef, this Somnour, quod the frere,
Hadde alwey bawdes redy to his hond,
As any hauk to lure in Engelond,
That tolde hym al the secree that they knewe;
For hire acqueyntance was nat come of newe.
They weren his approwours prively;
He took hymself a greet profit therby;
His maister knew nat alwey what he wan.
Withouten mandement, a lewed man
He koude somne, on peyne of Cristes curs,
And they were glade for to fille his purs,
And make hym grete feestes atte nale;
And right as Judas hadde purses smale,
And was a theef, right swich a theef was he;
His maister hadde but half his duëtee.
He was, if I shal yeven hym his laude,
A theef, and eek a Somnour, and a baude.
He hadde eek wenches at his retenue,
That wheither that sir Robert, or sir Huwe,
Or Jakke, or Rauf, or whoso that it were,
That lay by hem, they tolde it in his ere;
Thus was the wenche and he of oon assent.
And he wolde fecche a feyned mandement,
And somne hem to the chapitre bothe two,
And pile the man, and lete the wenche go.
Thanne wolde he seye, Freend, I shal for thy sake
Do striken hire out of oure lettres blake;
Thee thar namoore as in this cas travaille;
I am thy freend, ther I thee may availle.
Certeyn he knew of briberyes mo
Than possible is to telle in yeres two;
For in this world nys dogge for the bowe,
That kan an hurt deer from an hool yknowe,
Bet than this Somnour knew a sly lecchour,
Or an avowtier, or a paramour;
And, for that was the fruyt of al his rente,
Therfore on it he sette al his entente.
AND so bifel, that ones on a day
This Somnour, evere waityng on his pray,
Rode for to somne a widwe, an old ribibe,
Feynynge a cause, for he wolde brybe.
And happed that he saugh bifore hym ryde
A gay yeman, under a forest-syde.
A bowe he bar, and arwes brighte and kene;
He hadde upon a courtepy of grene;
An hat upon his heed with frenges blake.
Sire, quod this Somnour, hayl! and wel atake!
Welcome! quod he, and every good felawe!
118

Wher rydestow under this grene-wode shawe?
Seyde this yeman, wiltow fer to day?
This Somnour hym answerde, and seyde, Nay,
Heere faste by, quod he, is myn entente
To ryden, for to reysen up a rente
That longeth to my lordes duëtee.
Artow thanne a bailly? Ye, quod he.
He dorste nat, for verray filthe and shame,
Seye that he was a Somnour, for the name.
DEPARDIEUX! quod this yeman, deere brother,
Thou art a bailly, and I am another.
I am unknowen as in this contree;
Of thyn aqueyntance I wolde praye thee,
And eek of bretherhede, if that yow leste.
I have gold and silver in my cheste;
If that thee happe to comen in oure shire,
Al shal be thyn, right as thou wolt desire.
Grantmercy! quod this Somnour, by my feith!
Everych in ootheres hand his trouthe leith,
For to be sworne bretheren til they deye.
In daliance they ryden forth hir weye.
THIS Somnour, which that was as ful of jangles,
As ful of venym been thise waryangles,
And evere enqueryng upon every thyng;
Brother, quod he, where is now youre dwellyng,
Another day if that I sholde yow seche?
This yeman hym answerde in softe speche:
Brother, quod he, fer in the north contree,
Where, as I hope, som tyme I shal thee see.
Er we departe, I shal thee so wel wisse,
That of myn hous ne shaltow nevere mysse.
NOW, brother, quod this Somnour, I yow preye,
Teche me, whil that we ryden by the weye,
Syn that ye been a baillif as am I,
Som subtiltee, and tel me feithfully
In myn office how that I may moost wynne,
And spareth nat for conscience ne synne,
But as my brother tel me, how do ye.
Now, by my trouthe, brother deere, seyde he,
As I shal tellen thee a feithful tale,
My wages been ful streite and eek ful smale;
My lord is hard to me and daungerous,
And myn office is ful laborious;
And therfore by extorcions I lyve.
Forsothe, I take al that men wol me yeve,
Algate, by sleyghte or by violence,
Fro yeer to yeer I wynne al my dispence;
I kan no bettre telle feithfully.
Now certes, quod this Somnour, so fare I;
I spare nat to taken, God it woot,
But if it be to hevy or to hoot.
What I may gete in conseil prively;
No maner conscience of that have I;
Nere myn extorcioun, I myghte nat lyven,
Nor of swiche japes wol I nat be shryven.
Stomak, ne conscience, ne knowe I noon;
I shrewe thise shrifte-fadres everychoon.
Wel be we met, by God and by Seint Jame!
But, leeve brother, tel me thanne thy name,
Quod this Somnour; and in this meenewhile
This yeman gan a litel for to smyle.

BROTHER, quod he, wiltow that I thee telle?
I am a feend; my dwellyng is in helle,
And heere I ryde aboute my purchasyng,
To wite wher men wolde yeve me anythyng.
My purchas is theffect of al my rente.
Looke how thou rydest for the same entente,
To wynne good, thou rekkest nevere how;
Right so fare I, for ryde I wolde right now
Unto the worldes ende for a preye.
A! QUOD this Somnour, benedicite! what
sey ye?
I wende ye were a yeman trewely.
Ye han a mannes shap as wel as I;
Han ye a figure thanne determinat
In helle, ther ye been in youre estat?
Nay, certeinly, quod he, ther have we noon;
But whan us liketh, we kan take us oon,
Or elles make yow seme we been shape
Somtym lyk a man, or lyk an ape;
Or lyk an angel kan I ryde or go.
It is no wonder thyng thogh it be so;
A lowsy jogelour kan deceyve thee,
And pardee! yet kan I moore craft than he.
Why, quod the Somnour, ryde ye thanne or
goon
In sondry shap, and nat alwey in oon?
For we, quod he, wol us swiche formes make
As moost able is oure preyes for to take.
What maketh yow to han al this labour?
Ful many a cause, leeve sire Somnour,
Seyde this feend, but alle thyng hath tyme;
The day is short, and it is passed pryme,
And yet ne wan I nothyng in this day;
I wol entende to wynnen, if I may,
And nat entende our wittes to declare.
For, brother myn, thy wit is al to bare
To understonde, althogh I tolde hem thee.
But, for thou axest why labouren we;
For somtyme we been Goddes instruments
And meenes to doon his comandements,
Whan that hym list, upon his creatures,
In divers art and in diverse figures.
Withouten hym we have no myght, certayn,
If that hym list to stonden ther agayn.
And somtyme, at oure prayere, han we leve
Oonly the body and nat the soule greve;
Witnesse on Job, whom that we diden wo;
And somtyme, han we myght of bothe two,
This is to seyn, of soule and body eke.
And somtyme be we suffred for to seke
Upon a man, and doon his soule unreste,
And nat his body, and al is for the beste.
Whan he withstandeth oure temptacioun,
It is the cause of his savacioun;
Albeit that it was nat oure entente
He sholde be sauf, but that we wolde hym hente.
And somtyme be we servant unto man,
As to the erchebisshope Seint Dunstan;
And to the Apostles, servant eek was I.
YET tel me, quod the Somnour, feithfully,
Make ye yow newe bodies thus alway
Of elements? The feend answerde, Nay;
Somtyme we feyne, and somtyme we aryse

14

With dede bodyes in ful sondry wyse,
And speke as renably and faire and wel
As to the Phitonissa dide Samuel;
And yet wol som men seye it was nat he.
I do no fors of youre dyvynytee,
But o thyng warne I thee, I wol nat jape,
Thou wolt algates wite how we been shape;
Thou shalt herafterwardes, my brother deere,
Come there thee nedeth nat of me to leere.
For thou shalt by thyn owene experience
Konne in a chayer rede of this sentence
Bet than Virgile, while he was on lyve,
Or Dant also; now lat us ryde blyve,
For I wole holde compaignye with thee
Til it be so, that thou forsake me.
NAY, quod this Somnour, that shal nat
bityde;
I am a yeman, knowen is ful wyde;
My trouthe wol I holde as in this cas.
For though thou were the devel Sathanas,
My trouthe wol I holde to my brother,
As I am sworn, and ech of us til oother
For to be trewe brother in this cas;
And bothe we goon abouten oure purchas.
Taak thou thy part, what that men wol thee yive,
And I shal myn; thus may we bothe lyve,
And if that any of us have moore than oother,
Lat hym be trewe, and parte it with his brother.
I GRAUNTE, quod the devel, by my fey!
And with that word they ryden forth hir wey.
And right at the entryng of the townes ende,
To which this Somnour shoop hym for to
wende,
They saugh a cart, that charged was with hey,
Which that a carter droof forth in his wey.
Deep was the wey, for which the carte stood;
The carter smoot, and cryde, as he were wood,
Hayt, Brok! hayt, Scot! what spare ye for the
stones?
The feend, quod he, yow fecche body and bones,
As ferforthly as evere were ye foled!
So muche wo as I have with yow tholed!
The devel have al, bothe hors and cart and hey!
THIS Somnour seyde, Heere shal we have
a pley;
And neer the feend he drough, as noght ne
were,
Ful prively, and rowned in his ere:
Herkne, my brother! herkne, by thy feith!
Herestow nat how that the carter seith?
Hent it anon, for he hath yeve it thee,
Bothe hey and cart, and eek his caples thre.
Nay, quod the devel, God woot, never a deel;
It is nat his entente, trust me weel.
Axe hym thyself, if thou nat trowest me,
Or elles stynt awhile, and thou shalt see.
This carter thakketh his hors upon the croupe,
And they bigonne drawen and tostoupe.
Heyt, now! quod he, ther Jhesu Crist yow
blesse!
And al his handwerk, bothe moore and lesse!
That was wel twight, myn owene lyard boy!
I pray God save thee! and Seint Loy!

119

Now is my cart out of the slow, pardee!
Lo! brother, quod the feend, what tolde I thee?
Heere may ye se, myn owene deere brother,
The carl spak o thyng, but he thoghte another.
Lat us go forth abouten oure viage;
Heere wynne I nothyng upon cariage.

WHAN that they coomen somwhat
out of towne,
This Somnour to his brother gan
to rowne:
Brother, quod he, heere woneth an
old rebekke,
That hadde almoost as lief to lese hire nekke
As for to yeve a peny of hir good.
I wole han twelf pens, though that she be wood,
Or I wol sompne hire unto oure office,
And yet, God woot, of hire knowe I no vice.
But, for thou kanst nat, as in this contree,
Wynne thy cost, taak heer ensample of me.
This Somnour clappeth at the wydwes gate:
Come out, quod he, thou olde virytrate!
I trowe thou hast som frere or preest with thee.
Who clappeth? seyde this wyf, benedicitee!
God save you, sire! what is youre sweete wille?
I have, quod he, of somonce here a bille;
Up peyne of cursyng, looke that thou be
Tomorn bifore the erchedeknes knee,
Tanswere to the court of certeyn thynges.
Now, Lord, quod she, Crist Jhesu, kyng of
kynges,
So wisly helpe me, as I ne may!
I have been syk, and that ful many a day.
I may nat go so fer, quod she, ne ryde,
But I be deed, so priketh it in my syde.
May I nat axe a libel, sire Somnour,
And answere there, by my procutour
To swich thyng as men wole opposen me?
Yis, quod this Somnour, pay anon, lat se,
Twelf pens to me, and I wol thee acquite.
I shal no profit han therby but lite,
My maister hath the profit, and nat I.
Com of, and lat me ryden hastily;
Yif me twelf pens, I may no lenger tarye.
Twelf pens! quod she, now lady Seinte Marie
So wisly help me out of care and synne,
This wyde world thogh that I sholde wynne,
Ne have I nat twelf pens withinne myn hoold;
Ye knowen wel that I am povre and oold;
Kithe youre almesse on me povre wrecche.
Nay thanne, quod he, the foule feend me fecche,
If I thexcuse, though thou shul be spilt!
Allas! quod she, God woot, I have no gilt.
Pay me! quod he, or by the sweete Seinte Anne,
As I wol bere awey thy newe panne
for dette, which that thou owest me of old,
Whan that thou madest thyn housbonde coke-
wold,
I payde at hoom for thy correccioun.
Thou lixt, quod she, by my savacioun!
Ne was I nevere er now, wydwe ne wyf,
Somoned unto youre court in al my lyf;
Ne nevere I nas but of my body trewe!
Unto the devel blak and rough of hewe

120

Yeve I thy body and my panne also!
And whan the devel herde hire cursen so
Upon hir knees, he seyde in this manere:
Now, Mabely, myn owene moder deere,
Is this youre wyl in ernest, that ye seye?
The devel, quod she, so fecche hym er he deye,
And panne and al, but he wol hym repente!
Nay, olde stot! that is nat myn entente,
Quod this Somnour, for to repente me
for anythyng that I have had of thee;
I wolde I hadde thy smok and every clooth!
Now, brother, quod the devil, be nat wrooth;
Thy body and this panne been myne by right.
Thou shalt with me to helle yet tonyght,
Where thou shalt knowen of oure privetee
Moore than a maister of dyvynytee.
And with that word this foule feend hym hente;
Body and soule he with the devel wente
Whereas that Somnours han hir heritage.
And God, that maked after his ymage
Mankynde, save and gyde us alle and some,
And leve thise Somnours goode men bicome.

LORDYNGES, I koude han toold
yow, quod this frere,
Hadde I had leyser for this Somnour
heere,
After the text of Crist, and Poul,
and John,
And of oure othere doctours many oon,
Swiche peynes that youre hertes myghte agryse,
Albeit so, no tonge may it devyse,
Thogh that I myghte a thousand wynter telle,
The peyne of thilke cursed hous of helle.
But, for to kepe us fro that cursed place,
Waketh, and preyeth Jhesu for his grace
So kepe us fro the temptour Sathanas.
Herketh this word, beth war, as in this cas.
The leoun sit in his awayt alway
To sle the innocent, if that he may.
Disposeth ay youre hertes to withstonde
The feend that yow wolde make thral and bonde;
He may nat tempte yow over youre myght,
for Crist wol be youre champion and knyght.
And prayeth that thise Somnours hem repente
Of hir mysdedes, er that the feend hem hente.
Heere endeth the freres Tale.

The prologe of the Somonours Tale ❀ ❀

THIS Somnour in his sty-
ropes hye stood;
Upon this frere his herte
was so wood,
That lyk an aspen-leef he
quook for ire.
Lordynges, quod he, but
o thyng I desire;
I yow biseke that, of youre
curteisye,
Syn ye han herd this false frere lye,
As suffereth me I may my tale telle!
This frere bosteth that he knoweth helle,
And God it woot, that it is litel wonder;
freres and feendes been but lyte asonder.

for, pardee! ye han ofte tyme herd telle,
How that a frere ravysshed was to helle
In spirit ones by a visioun;
And as an angel ladde hym up and doun
To shewen hym the peynes that ther were,
In al the place saugh he nat a frere;
Of oother folk he saugh ynowe in wo.
Unto this angel spak the frere tho:
Now, sire, quod he, han freres swich a grace
That noon of hem shal come to this place?
Yis, quod this angel, many a millioun,
And unto Sathanas he ladde hym doun.
And now hath Sathanas, seith he, a tayl,
Brodder than of a carryk is the sayl.
Hold up thy tayl, thou Sathanas! quod he,
Shewe forth thyn ers, and lat the frere se
Where is the nest of freres in this place!
And, er than half a furlong wey of space,

Right so as bees out swarmen from an hyve,
Out of the develes ers ther gonne dryve
Twenty thousand freres in a route,
And thurghout helle swarmeden aboute,
And comen agayn as faste as they may gon,
And in his ers they crepten everychon;
He clapte his tayl agayn, and lay ful stille.
This frere, whan he looked hadde his fille
Upon the torments of this sory place,
His spirit God restored of his grace
Unto his body agayn, and he awook;
But natheles, for fere yet he quook,
So was the develes ers ay in his mynde;
That is his heritage of verray kynde.
God save yow alle, save this cursed frere!
My prologe wol I ende in this manere.
Here endeth the prologe of the Somonours
Tale.

HEERE BIGYNNETH THE SOMONOUR HIS TALE

LORDYNGES, ther is in
Yorkshire, as I gesse,
A mersshy contree
called Holdernesse,
In which ther went a
lymytour aboute,
To preche, and eek to
begge, it is no doute.
And so bifel, that on a
day this frere
Hadde preched at a chirche in his manere,
And specially, aboven every thyng,
Excited he the peple in his prechyng
To trentals, and to yeve for Goddes sake,
Wherwith men myghte hooly houses make,
Ther as divine servyce is honoured,
Nat ther as it is wasted and devoured,
Ne ther it nedeth nat for to be yeve,
As to possessioners, that mowen lyve,
Thanked be God! in wele and habundaunce.
Trentals, seyde he, deliveren fro penaunce
Hir freendes soules, as wel olde as yonge,
Ye, whan that they been hastily ysonge;
Nat for to holde a preest joly and gay,
He syngeth nat but o masse in a day.
Delivereth out, quod he, anon the soules;
Ful hard it is, with flesshhook or with oules
To been yclawed, or to brenne, or bake;
Now spede yow hastily, for Cristes sake.
And whan this frere had seyd al his entente,
With Qui cum patre forth his wey he wente.
Whan folk in chirche had yeve him what
hem leste,
He went his wey, no lenger wolde he reste.
With scrippe and tipped staf, ytukked hye,
In every hous he gan to poure and prye,
And beggeth mele, and chese, or elles corn.
His felawe hadde a staf tipped with horn,
A peyre of tables al of yvory,
And a poyntel polysshed fetisly,
And wroote the names alwey, as he stood,
Of alle folk that yaf hym any good,

Ascaunces that he wolde for hem preye.
Yif us a busshel whete, malt, or reye,
A Goddes kechyl, or a tryp of chese,
Or elles what yow lyst, we may nat cheese;
A Goddes halfpeny, or a masse peny,
Or yif us of youre brawn, if ye have eny;
A dagoun of youre blanket, leeve dame,
Oure suster deere, lo! heere I write youre
name;
Bacoun or beef, or swich thyng as ye fynde.
A sturdy harlot wente ay hem bihynde,
That was hir hostes man, and bar a sak,
And what men yaf hem, leyde it on his bak.
And whan that he was out at dore anon,
He planed awey the names everichon
That he biforn had writen in his tables;
He served hem with nyfles and with fables.
Nay! ther thou lixt, thou Somnour! quod
the frere.
Pees! quod oure Hoost, for Cristes
mooder deere;
Tel forth thy tale and spare it nat at al.
So thryve I, quod this Somnour, so I
shal.
So longe he wente hous by hous, til he
Cam til an hous ther he was wont to be
Refresshed moore than in an hundred placis.
Syk lay the goode man, whos that the place is;
Bedrede upon a couche lowe he lay.
Deus hic! quod he, O Thomas, freend,
good day,
Seyde this frere, curteisly and softe.
Thomas, quod he, God yelde yow! ful ofte
Have I upon this bench faren ful weel,
Heere have I eten many a myrie meel.
And fro the bench he droof awey the cat,
And leyde adoun his potente and his hat,
And eek his scrippe, and sette hym softe
adoun.
His felawe was go walked into toun,
Forth with his knave, into that hostelrye
Wheras he shoop hym thilke nyght to lye.

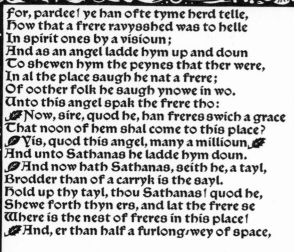

O DEERE maister, quod this sike man,
How han ye fare sith that March bigan?
I saugh yow noght this fourtenyght or
moore.
God woot, quod he, laboured have I ful soore;
And specially for thy savacioun
Have I seyd many a precious orisoun,
And for oure othere freendes, God hem blesse!
I have today been at youre chirche at messe,
And seyd a sermoun after my symple wit,
Nat al after the text of hooly writ;
for it is hard to yow, as I suppose,
And therfore wol I teche yow al the glose.
Glosynge is a glorious thyng, certeyn,
for lettre sleeth, so as we clerkes seyn.
There have I taught hem to be charitable,
And spende hir good ther it is resonable;
And ther I saugh oure dame, a! where is she?
Yond, in the yerd I trowe that she be,
Seyde this man, and she wol come anon.
Ey, maister! welcom be ye, by Seint John!
Seyde this wyf, how fare ye, hertely?
The frere ariseth up ful curteisly,
And hire embraceth in his armes narwe,
And kiste hire sweete, and chirketh as a sparwe
With his lyppes: Dame, quod he, right weel,
As he that is youre servant every deel.
Thanked be God, that yow yaf soule and lyf,
Yet saugh I nat this day so fair a wyf
In al the chirche, God so save me!
Ye, God amende defautes, sire, quod she,
Algates welcome be ye, by my fey!
Graunt mercy, dame, this have I founde alwey,
But of youre grete goodnesse, by youre leve,
I wolde prey yow that ye nat yow greve,
I wole with Thomas speke a litel throwe.
Thise curats been ful necligent and slowe
To grope tendrely a conscience.
In shrift, in prechyng is my diligence,
And studie; in Petres wordes, and in Poules
I walke, and fisshe cristen mennes soules,
To yelden Jhesu Crist his propre rente;
To sprede his word is set al myn entente.
NOW, by youre leve, O deere sire, quod she,
Chideth him weel, for seinte Trinitee!
He is as angry as a pissemyre,
Though that he have al that he kan desire.
Though I him wrye anyght and make hym warm,
And on hym leye my leg, outher myn arm,
He groneth lyk oure boor, lith in oure sty.
Oother desport right noon of hym have I;
I may nat plese hym in no maner cas.
O Thomas! Je vous dy, Thomas! Thomas!
This maketh the feend, this moste ben amended;
Ire is a thyng that hye God defended,
And therof wol I speke a word or two.
Now, maister, quod the wyf, er that I go,
What wol ye dyne? I wol go theraboute.
Now dame, quod he, Je vous dy sanz doute,
Have I nat of a capoun but the lyvere,
And of youre softe breed nat but a shyvere,
And after that a rosted pigges heed,
But that I nolde no beest for me were deed,

Thanne hadde I with yow hoomly suffisaunce.
I am a man of litel sustenaunce.
My spirit hath his fostryng in the Bible.
The body is ay so redy and penyble
To wake, that my stomak is destroyed.
I prey yow, dame, ye be nat anoyed
Though I so freendly yow my conseil shewe;
By God, I wolde nat telle it but a fewe!
NOW, sire, quod she, but o word er I go:
My child is deed withinne thise wykes two,
Soone after that ye wente out of this toun.
His deeth saugh I by revelacioun,
Seith this frere, at hoom in oure dortour.
I dar wel seyn that, er that half an hour
After his deeth, I saugh hym born to blisse
In myn avisioun, so God me wisse!
So dide our sexteyn and oure fermerer,
That han been trewe freres fifty yeer;
They may now, God be thanked of his loone!
Maken hir jubilee, and walke allone.
And up I roos, and al oure covent eke,
With many a teere triklyng on my cheke,
Withouten noyse or claterynge of belles;
Te deum was oure song and nothyng elles,
Save that to Crist I seyde an orisoun,
Thankynge hym of his revelacioun.
for, sire and dame, trusteth me right weel,
Oure orisons been moore effectueel,
And moore we seen of Cristes secree thynges
Than burel folk, although they weren kynges.
We lyve in poverte and in abstinence,
And burell folk in richesse and despence
Of mete and drynke, and in hir foul delit.
We han this worldes lust al in despit.
Lazar and Dives lyveden diversly,
And diverse guerdon hadden they therby.
Whoso wol preye, he moot faste and be clene,
And fatte his soule and make his body lene.
We fare as seith thapostle; clooth and foode
Suffisen us, though they be nat ful goode.
The clennesse and the fastynge of us freres
Maketh that Crist accepteth oure preyeres.
Lo, Moyses fourty dayes and fourty nyght
fasted, er that the heighe God of myght
Spak with hym in the mountayne of Synay.
With empty wombe, fastynge many a day,
Receyved he the lawe that was writen
With Goddes fynger; and Elye, wel ye witen,
In mount Oreb, er he hadde any speche
With hye God, that is oure lyves leche,
He fasted longe, and was in contemplaunce.
Haron, that hadde the temple in governaunce.
And eek the othere preestes everichon,
Into the temple whan they sholde gon
To preye for the peple, and do servyse,
They nolden drynken, in no maner wyse,
No drynke, which that myghte hem dronke make,
But there, in abstinence preye and wake,
Lest that they deyden; taak heede what I seye,
But they be sobre that for the peple preye,
War that! I seye namoore, for it suffiseth.
Oure Lord Jhesu, as hooly writ devyseth,
Yaf us ensample of fastynge and preyeres;

Therfore we mendynants, we sely freres,
Been wedded to poverte and continence,
To charite, humblesse, and abstinence,
To persecucioun for rightwisnesse,
To wepynge, misericorde, and clennesse;
And therfore may ye se that oure preyeres,
I speke of us, we mendynants, we freres,
Been to the hye God moore acceptable
Than youres, with youre feestes at the table.
fro Paradys first, if I shal nat lye,
Was man out chaced for his glotonye;
And chaast was man in Paradys, certeyn.
BUT herkne now, Thomas, what I shal seyn,
I ne have no text of it, as I suppose,
But I shal fynde it in a maner glose,
That specially oure sweete Lord Jhesus
Spak this by freres, when he seyde thus:
Blessed be they that povre in spirit been,
And so forth al the gospel may ye seen,
Wher it be likker oure professioun,
Or hirs that swymmen in possessioun.
fy on hire pompe and on hire glotonye!
And for hir lewednesse, I hem diffye!
Me thynketh they been lyk Jovinyan,
fat as a whale, and walkynge as a swan,
Al vinolent as botel in the spence.
Hir preyere is of ful greet reverence
Whan they for soules seye the Psalm of Davit,
Lo, Buf! they seye, Cor meum eructavit!
Who folweth Cristes gospel and his foore,
But we that humble been and chaast and poore,
Werkers of Goddes word, not auditours?
Therfore, right as an hauk up, at a sours,
Up springeth into their, right so prayeres
Of charitable and chaste bisy freres
Maken hir sours to Goddes eres two.
Thomas! Thomas! so moote I ryde or go,
And by that lord that clepid is Seint Yve,
Nere thou oure brother, sholdestou nat thryve.
In oure chapitre praye we day and nyght
To Crist, that he thee sende heele and myght,
Thy body for to weelden hastily.
GOD woot, quod he, nothyng therof feele I!
As help me Crist, as in a fewe yeres
I han spent upon diverse manere freres
ful many a pound; yet fare I never the bet.
Certeyn my good I have almoost biset,
farwel, my gold, for it is al ago!
The frere answerde, O Thomas, dostow so?
What nedeth yow diverse freres seche?
What nedeth hym that hath a parfit leche
To sechen othere leches in the toun?
Youre inconstance is youre confusioun.
Holde ye thanne me, or elles oure covent,
To praye for yow been insufficient?
Thomas, that jape nys nat worth a myte;
Youre maladye is for we han to lyte.
A! yif that covent half a quarter otes;
A! yif that covent four and twenty grotes;
A! yif that frere a peny, and lat hym go.
Nay, nay, Thomas! it may nothyng be so.
What is a ferthyng worth parted in twelve?
Lo, ech thyng that is oned in itselve

Is moore strong than whan it is toscatered.
Thomas! of me thou shalt nat been yflatered;
Thou woldest han oure labour al for noght.
The hye God, that al this world hath wroght,
Seith that the werkman worthy is his hyre.
Thomas! noght of youre tresor I desire
As for myself, but that al oure covent
To preye for yow is ay so diligent,
And for to buylden Cristes owene chirche.
Thomas! if ye wol lernen for to wirche,
Of buyldynge up of chirches may ye fynde
If it be good, in Thomas lyf of Inde.
Ye lye heere ful of anguish and of ire,
With which the devel set youre herte afyre,
And chiden heere the sely innocent,
Youre wyf, that is so meke and pacient.
And therfore, Thomas, trowe me if thee leste,
Ne stryve nat with thy wyf, as for thy beste;
And ber this word awey now, by thy feith,
Touchynge this thyng, lo, what the wise seith:
Withinne thyn hous ne be thou no leoun;
To thy subgits do noon oppressioun;
Ne make thyne aqueyntance nat to flee,
And, Thomas, yet eftsoones I charge thee,
Be war from hire that in thy bosom slepeth;
War fro the serpent that so slily crepeth
Under the gras, and styngeth subtilly.
Be war, my sone, and herkne paciently,
That twenty thousand men han lost hir lyves
for stryvyng with hir lemmans and hir wyves.
Now sith ye han so hooly and meke a wyf,
What nedeth yow, Thomas, to maken stryf?
Ther nys, ywys, no serpent so cruel,
Whan man tret on his tayl, ne half so fel,
As womman is, whan she hath caught an ire;
Vengeance is thanne al that they desire.
Ire is a synne, oon of the grete of sevene,
Abhomynable unto the God of hevene;
And to hymself it is destruccioun.
This every lewed viker or persoun
Kan seye, how ire engendreth homycide.
Ire is, in sooth, executour of pryde.
I koude of ire seye so muche sorwe,
My tale sholde laste til tomorwe.
And therfore preye I God bothe day and nyght,
An irous man, God sende hym litel myght.
It is greet harme and, certes, greet pitee,
To sette an irous man in heigh degree.
WHILOM ther was an irous potestat,
As seith Senek, that, durynge his
estaat,
Upon a day out ryden knyghtes two,
And as fortune wolde that it were so,
That oon of hem cam hoom, that
oother noght.
Anon the knyght bifore the juge is broght,
That seyde thus: Thou hast thy felawe slayn,
for which I deme thee to the deeth, certayn.
And to another knyght comanded he,
Go lede hym to the deeth, I charge thee!
And happed as they wente by the weye
Toward the place ther he sholde deye,
The knyght cam, which men wenden had be deed.

123

Thanne thoughte they, it was the beste reed,
To lede hem bothe to the juge agayn.
They seiden: Lord, the knyght ne hath nat slayn
His felawe; heere he standeth hool alyve.
Ye shul be deed, quod he, so moot I thryve!
That is to seyn, bothe oon, and two, and thre.
And to the firste knyght right thus spak he:
I dampned thee, thou most algate be deed;
And thou, also, most nedes lese thyn heed,
For thou art cause why thy felawe deyth.
And to the thridde knyght right thus he seith:
Thou hast nat doon that I comanded thee.
And thus he dide doon sleen hem alle thre.
Irous Cambises was eek dronkelewe,
And ay delited hym to been a shrewe.
And so bifel a lord of his meynee,
That loved vertuous moralitee,
Seyde on a day bitwene hem two right thus:
A lord is lost, if he be vicious;
And dronkenesse is eek a foul record
Of any man, and namely in a lord.
Ther is ful many an eye and many an ere,
Awaityng on a lord, and he noot where.
For Goddes love, drynk moore attemprely;
Wyn maketh man to lesen wrecchedly
His mynde, and eek his lymes everichon.
The revers shaltou se, quod he, anon;
And preeve it, by thyn owene experience,
That wyn ne dooth to folk no swich offence.
Ther is no wyn bireveth me my myght
Of hand ne foot, ne of myne eyen sight.
And, for despit, he drank ful muchel moore
An hondred part than he hadde doon bifoore;
And right anon, this irous, cursed wrecche
Lete this knyghtes sone bifore hym fecche,
Comandynge hym he sholde bifore hym stonde.
And sodeynly he took his bowe in honde,
And up the streng he pulled to his ere,
And with an arwe he slow the child right there.
Now, wheither have I a siker hand or noon?
Quod he, is al my myght and mynde agon?
Hath wyn byreved me myne eyen sight?
What sholde I telle thanswere of the knyght?
His sone was slayn, ther is namoore to seye.
Beth war, therfore, with lordes how ye pleye.
Syngeth Placebo, and I shal, if I kan,
But if it be unto a povre man.
To a povre man men sholde his vices telle,
But nat to a lord, thogh he sholde go to helle.
Lo, irous Cirus, thilke Percien,
How he destroyed the ryver of Gysen,
For that an hors of his was dreynt therinne,
Whan that he wente Babiloigne to wynne.
He made that the ryver was so smal
That wommen myghte wade it over al.
Lo, what seyde he that so wel teche kan:
Ne be no felawe to an irous man,
Ne with no wood man walke by the weye,
Lest thee repente; ther is namoore to seye.
NOW Thomas, leeve brother, lef thyn ire;
Thou shalt me fynde as just as is a squyre.
Hoold nat the develes knyf ay at thyn herte;

124

Thyn angre dooth thee al to soore smerte,
But shewe to me al thy confessioun.
Nay, quod the sike man, by Seint Symoun!
I have be shryven this day at my curat;
I have hym toold al hoolly myn estat.
Nedeth namoore to speken of it, seith he,
But if me list, of myn humylitee.
Yif me thanne of thy gold, to make oure cloystre,
Quod he, for many a muscle and many an oystre,
Whan othere men han ben ful wel at eyse,
Hath been oure foode, our cloystre for to reyse.
And yet, God woot, unnethe the fundement
Parfourned is, ne of our pavement
Nys nat a tyle yet withinne oure wones;
By God, we owen fourty pound for stones!
Now help, Thomas, for hym that harwed helle!
For elles moste we oure bookes selle.
And if ye lakke oure predicacioun,
Thanne goth the world al to destruccioun.
For whoso wolde us fro this world bireve,
So God me save, Thomas, by your leve,
He wolde bireve out of this world the sonne;
For who kan teche, and werchen, as we konne?
And that is nat of litel tyme, quod he,
But syn that Elie was, or Elisee,
Han freres been, that fynde I of record,
In charitee, ythanked be our Lord.
Now Thomas, help, for seinte charitee!
And doun anon he sette hym on his knee.
THIS sike man wex wel ny wood for ire;
He wolde that the frere had been on fire
With his false dissymulacioun.
Swich thyng as is in my possessioun,
Quod he, that may I yeven, and noon oother.
Ye sey me thus, how that I am youre brother?
Ye, certes, quod the frere, trusteth weel;
I took oure dame oure lettre with oure seel.
Now wel, quod he, and somwhat shal I yeve
Unto youre hooly covent whil I lyve,
And in thyn hand thou shalt it have anoon;
On this condicioun, and oother noon;
That thou departe it so, my leeve brother,
That every frere have also muche as oother.
This shaltou swere on thy professioun,
Withouten fraude or cavillacioun.
I swere it, quod this frere, by my feith!
And therwithal his hand in his he leith:
Lo, heer my feith! in me shal be no lak.
Now thanne, put thyn hand doun by my bak,
Seyde this man, and grope wel bihynde;
Bynethe my buttok ther shaltow fynde
A thyng that I have hyd in pryvetee.
A! thoghte this frere, this shal go with me!
And doun his hand he launcheth to the clifte,
In hope for to fynde there a yifte.
And whan this sike man felte this frere
Aboute his tuwel grope there and heere,
Amydde his hand he leet the frere a fart.
Ther nys no capul, drawynge in a cart,
That myghte have lete a fart of swich a soun.

The frere up stirte as dooth a wood leoun;
A! false cherl, quod he, for Goddes bones!
This hastow for despit doon, for the nones!
Thou shalt abye this fart, if that I may!
His meynee, whiche that herden this affray,
Cam lepynge in, and chaced out the frere;
And forth he gooth, with a ful angry cheere,
And fette his felawe, theras lay his stoor.
He looked as it were a wilde boor;
He grynte with his teeth, so was he wrooth.
A STURDY paas doun to the court he gooth,
Wheras ther woned a man of greet honour,
To whom that he was alwey confessour;
This worthy man was lord of that village.
This frere cam, as he were in a rage,
Wheras this lord sat etyng at his bord.
Unnethes myghte the frere speke a word,
Til atte laste he seyde: God yow see!
This lord gan looke, and seide: Benedicitee!
What, frere John, what maner world is this?
I trowe som maner thyng ther is amys;
Ye looken as the wode were ful of thevys;
Sit doun anon, and tel me what youre greef is,
And it shal been amended, if I may.
I have, quod he, had a despit this day,
God yelde yow! adoun in youre village,
That in this world is noon so povre a page,
That he nolde have abhomynacioun
Of that I have receyved in youre toun.
And yet ne greveth me nothyng so soore,
As that this olde cherl, with lokkes hoore,
Blasphemed hath oure hooly covent eke.
Now, maister, quod this lord, I yow biseke.
No maister, sire, quod he, but servitour,
Thogh I have had in scole swich honour,
God liketh nat that Raby men us calle,
Neither in market ne in youre large halle.
No fors, quod he, but tel me al youre grief.
Sire, quod this frere, an odious meschief
This day bityd is to myn ordre and me;
And so per consequens to ech degree
Of hooly chirche, God amende it soone!
SIRE, quod the lord, ye woot what is to doone.
Distempre yow noght, ye be my confessour;
Ye been the salt of the erthe and the savour.
For Goddes love youre pacience ye holde;
Tel me youre grief. And he anon hym tolde,
As ye han herd biforn, ye woot wel what.
THE lady of the hous ay stille sat
Til she had herd al what the frere sayde.
Ey! Goddes mooder, quod she, blisful mayde!
Is ther oght elles? telle me feithfully.
Madame, quod he, how thynke ye herby?
How that me thynketh? quod she; so God me speede!
I seye, a cherle hath doon a cherles dede.
What shold I seye? God lat hym nevere thee!
His sike heed is ful of vanytee,
I hold hym in a manere frenesye.
Madame, quod he, by God I shal nat lye;
But I on oother weyes may be wreke,
I shal disclaundre hym, overal ther I speke,

This false blasphemour, that charged me
To parte that wol nat departed be,
To every man yliche, with meschaunce!
THE lord sat stille, as he were in a traunce,
And in his herte he rolled up and doun:
How hadde this cherl ymaginacioun,
To shewe swich a probleme to the frere?
Nevere erst er now herd I of swich mateere;
I trowe the devel putte it in his mynde.
In ars-metrike shal ther no man fynde,
Biforn this day, of swich a questioun,
Certes, it was a shrewed conclusioun,
That every man sholde have yliche his part,
As of the soun or savour of a fart.
O nyce proude cherl! I shrewe his face!
Lo, sires, quod the lord, with harde grace,
Who evere herd of swich a thyng er now?
To every man ylike! tel me how?
It is an inpossible, it may nat be!
Ey, nyce cherl, God lete him nevere thee!
The rumblynge of a fart, and every soun,
Nis but of eir reverberacioun,
And evere it wasteth lite and lite awey.
Ther is no man kan demen, by my fey!
If that it were departed equally.
What, lo, my cherl, lo, yet how shrewedly
Unto my confessour today he spak;
I holde hym certeyn a demonyak!
Now ete youre mete, and let the cherl go pleye,
Lat hym go honge hymself a devel weye!

The wordes of the lordes Squier and his kervere for
departynge of the fart on twelve.

NOW stood the lordes Squier at the bord,
That karf his mete, and herde, word by word,
Of alle thynges whiche that I have sayd;
My lord, quod he, beth nat yvele apayd;
I koude telle, for a gowne-clooth,
To yow, sire frere, so ye be nat wrooth,
How that this fart sholde evene deled be
Among youre covent, if it lyked me.
Tel, quod the lord, and thou shalt have anon
A gowne-clooth, by God and by Seint John!
My lord, quod he, whan that the weder is fair,
Withouten wynd or perturbynge of air,
Lat brynge a cartwheel here into this halle,
But looke that it have his spokes alle;
Twelve spokes hath a cartwheel comunly.
And bryng me thanne twelf freres, woot ye why?
For thrittene is a covent, as I gesse.
The confessour heere, for his worthynesse,
Shal parfourne up the nombre of his covent.
Thanne shal they knele doun, by oon assent,
And to every spokes ende, in this manere,
Ful sadly leye his nose shal a frere.
Youre noble confessour, there God hym save!
Shal hold his nose upright, under the nave.
Thanne shal this cherl, with bely stif and toght
As any tabour, hyder been ybroght;
And sette hym on the wheel right of this cart,

125

Upon the nave, and make hym lete a fart.
And ye shul seen, up peril of my lyf,
By preeve which that is demonstratif,
That equally the soun of it wol wende,
And eek the stynk, unto the spokes ende;
Save that this worthy man, your confessour,
Bycause he is a man of greet honour,
Shal have the firste fruyt, as resoun is.
The noble usage of freres yet is this,
The worthy men of hem shul first be served;
And certeinly, he hath it weel disserved.
He hath today taught us so muchel good
With prechyng in the pulpit ther he stood,
That I may vouchesauf, I sey for me,
He hadde the firste smel of fartes three,
And so wolde al his covent hardily;
He bereth hym so faire and hoolily.
THE lord, the lady, and alle men save the frere,
Seyde that Jankyn spak, in this matere,
As wel as Euclyde, or Protholomee,
Touchynge this cherl; they seyde subtiltee
And heigh wit made hym speken as he spak;
He nys no fool, ne no demonyak;
And Jankyn hath ywonne a newe gowne.
My tale is doon; we been almoost at towne.
Heere endeth the Somonours Tale.

Heere folweth the prologe of the Clerkes Tale of
Oxenford ✤ ✤

IRE Clerk of Oxenford, oure
Hooste sayde,
Ye ryde as coy and stille as
dooth a mayde,
Were newe spoused, sit-
tynge at the bord;
This day ne herde I of youre
tonge a word.
I trowe ye studie aboute som
sophyme;
But Salomon seith, Every thyng hath tyme.
For Goddes sake, as beth of bettre cheere,
It is no tyme for to studien heere.
Telle us some myrie tale, by youre fey;
For what man that is entred in a pley,
He nedes moot unto the pley assente.
But precheth nat, as freres doon in lente,

To make us for oure olde synnes wepe,
Ne that thy tale make us nat to slepe.
Telle us som murie thyng of aventures;
Youre termes, youre colours, and youre figures,
Keepe hem in stoor til so be ye endite
Heigh style, as whan that men to kynges write.
Speketh so pleyn at this tyme, we yow preye,
That we may understonde what ye seye.
THIS worthy clerk benignely answerde,
Hooste, quod he, I am under youre yerde;
Ye han of us, as now, the governance,
And therfore wol I do yow obeisance
As fer as resoun axeth, hardily.
I wol yow telle a tale which that I
Lerned at Padwe of a worthy clerk,
As preved by his wordes and his werk.
He is now deed and nayled in his cheste,
I prey to God so yeve his soule reste!
FRAUNCEYS PETRAK, the lauriat
poete,
Highte this clerk, whos rethorike sweete
Enlumyned al Ytaille of poetrie,
As Lynyan dide of philosophie
Or lawe, or oother art particuler;
But deeth, that wol nat suffre us dwellen heer
But as it were a twynklyng of an eye,
Hem bothe hath slayn, and alle shul we dye.
But forth to tellen of this worthy man
That taughte me this tale, as I bigan,
I seye that first with heigh stile he enditeth,
Er he the body of his tale writeth,
A proheme, in the which discryveth he
Pemond, and of Saluces the contree;
And speketh of Apennyn, the hilles hye
That been the boundes of West Lumbardye,
And of Mount Vesulus in special,
Whereas the Poo, out of a welle smal,
Taketh his firste spryngyng and his sours,
That estward ay encresseth in his cours
To Emeleward, to Ferrare and Venyse:
The which a long thyng were to devyse.
And trewely, as to my juggement,
Me thynketh it a thyng impertinent,
Save that he wole conveyen his mateere:
But this his tale, which that ye may heere.
Here endith the Clerke of Oxenford his prologe.

A markys whilom lord was of that londe,
As were his worthy eldres hym bifore;
And obeisant and redy to his honde
Were alle his liges, bothe lasse and moore,
Thus in delit he lyveth, and hath doon yoore,
Biloved and drad, thurgh favour of fortune,
Bothe of his lordes and of his commune.

Therwith he was, to speke as of lynage,
The gentilleste yborn of Lumbardye;
A fair persone, and strong, and yong of age,
And ful of honour and of curteisye;
Discreet ynogh his contree for to gye,
Save in somme thynges that he was to blame,
And Walter was this yonge lordes name.

I BLAME him thus, that he considereth noght
In tyme comynge what hym myghte bityde;
But in his lust present was al his thoght,
As for to hauke and hunte on every syde;
Wel ny alle othere cures leet he slyde;
And eek he nolde, and that was worst of alle,
Wedde no wyf, for noght that may bifalle.

Oonly that point his peple bar so soore,

IS, AT THE WEST SYDE OF YTAILLE,
Doun at the roote of Vesulus the colde,
A lusty playne, habundant of vitaille,
Where many a tour & toun thou mayst biholde,
That founded were in time of fadres olde,
And many another delitable sighte,
And Saluces this noble contree highte.

That flokmeele on a day they to hym wente,
And oon of hem that wisest was of loore,
Or elles that the lord best wolde assente
That he sholde telle hym what his peple mente,
Or elles koude he shewe wel swich mateere,
He to the markys seyde as ye shul heere.

O noble markys, youre humanitee
Assureth us and yeveth us hardinesse,
As ofte as tyme is of necessitee
That we to yow mowe telle oure hevynesse;
Accepteth, lord, now for youre gentillesse,
That we with pitous herte unto yow pleyne,
And lat youre eres nat my voys desdeyne.

Al have I noght to doone in this mateere
Moore than another man hath in this place,
Yet forasmuche as ye, my lord so deere,
Han alwey shewed me favour and grace,
I dar the bettre aske of yow a space
Of audience, to shewen oure requeste,
And ye, my lord, to doon right as yow leste.

For certes, lord, so wel us liketh yow
And al youre werk, and evere han doon, that we
Ne koude nat us self devysen how
We myghte lyven in moore felicitee,
Save o thyng, lord, if it youre wille be,
That for to been a wedded man yow leste,
Thanne were youre peple in sovereyn hertes reste.

Boweth youre nekke under that blisful yok
Of soveraynetee, noght of servyse,
Which that men clepeth spousaille or wedlok;
And thenketh, lord, among youre thoghtes wyse,
How that oure dayes passe in sondry wyse;
For thogh we slepe, or wake, or rome, or ryde,
Ay fleeth the tyme, it nyl no man abyde.

And thogh youre grene youthe floure as yit,
In crepeth age alwey, as stille as stoon,
And deeth manaceth every age, and smyt
In ech estaat, for ther escapeth noon;
And al so certein as we knowe echoon
That we shul deye, as uncerteyn we alle
Been of that day whan deeth shal on us falle.

Accepteth thanne of us the trewe entente,
That nevere yet refuseden thyn heeste,
And we wol, lord, if that ye wol assente,
Chese yow a wyf in short tyme, atte leeste,
Born of the gentilleste and of the meeste
Of al this land, so that it oghte seme
Honour to God and yow, as we kan deeme.

Delivere us out of al this bisy drede,
And taak a wyf, for hye Goddes sake;
For if it so bifelle, as God forbede,
That thurgh youre deeth youre lyne sholde slake,
And that a straunge successour sholde take
Youre heritage, O, wo were us alyve!
Wherfore we pray yow hastily to wyve.

128

SIR meeke preyere, and hir pitous cheere,
Made the markys herte han pitee.
Ye wol, quod he, myn owene peple deere,
To that I nevere erst thoughte streyne me.
I me rejoysed of my libertee,
That seelde tyme is founde in mariage;
Ther I was free, I moot been in servage.

But nathelees, I se youre trewe entente,
And trust upon youre wit, and have doon ay;
Wherfore, of my free wyl, I wole assente
To wedde me, as soone as evere I may.
But theras ye han profred me this day
To chese me a wyf, I yow relesse
That choys, and prey yow of that profre cesse.

For God it woot, that children ofte been
Unlyk hir worthy eldres hem bifore;
Bountee comth al of God, nat of the streen
Of which they been engendred and ybore;
I truste in Goddes bontee, and therfore
My mariage, and myn estaat and reste,
I hym bitake; he may doon as hym leste.

Lat me allone in chesynge of my wyf,
That charge upon my bak I wol endure;
But I yow preye, and charge upon youre lyf,
That what wyf that I take, ye me assure
To worshipe hire, whil that hir lyf may dure,
In word and werk, bothe heere and everywheere,
As she an emperoures doghter weere.

And forthermoore, this shal ye swere, that ye
Agayn my choys shul neither grucche ne stryve;
For sith I shal forgoon my libertee
At your requeste, as evere moot I thryve,
Theras myn herte is set, ther wol I wyve;
And, but ye wole assente in this manere,
I prey yow, speketh namoore of this matere.

WITH hertely wyl they sworen, and as-
senten
To al this thyng, ther seyde no wight nay;
Bisekynge hym of grace, er that they wenten,
That he wolde graunten hem a certein day
Of his spousaille, as soone as evere he may;
For yet alwey the peple somwhat dredde
Lest that this markys no wyf wolde wedde.

He graunted hem a day, swich as hym leste,
On which he wolde be wedded sikerly,
And seyde, he dide al this at hir requeste;
And they, with humble entente, buxomly
Knelynge upon hir knees ful reverently,
Hym thonken alle; and thus they han an ende
Of hire entente, and hoom agayn they wende.

And heerupon he to his officeres
Comaundeth for the feste to purveye;
And to his privee knyghtes and squieres
Swich charge yaf, as hym liste on hem leye;
And they to his comandement obeye,
And ech of hem dooth al his diligence
To doon unto the feeste reverence.
Explicit prima pars.

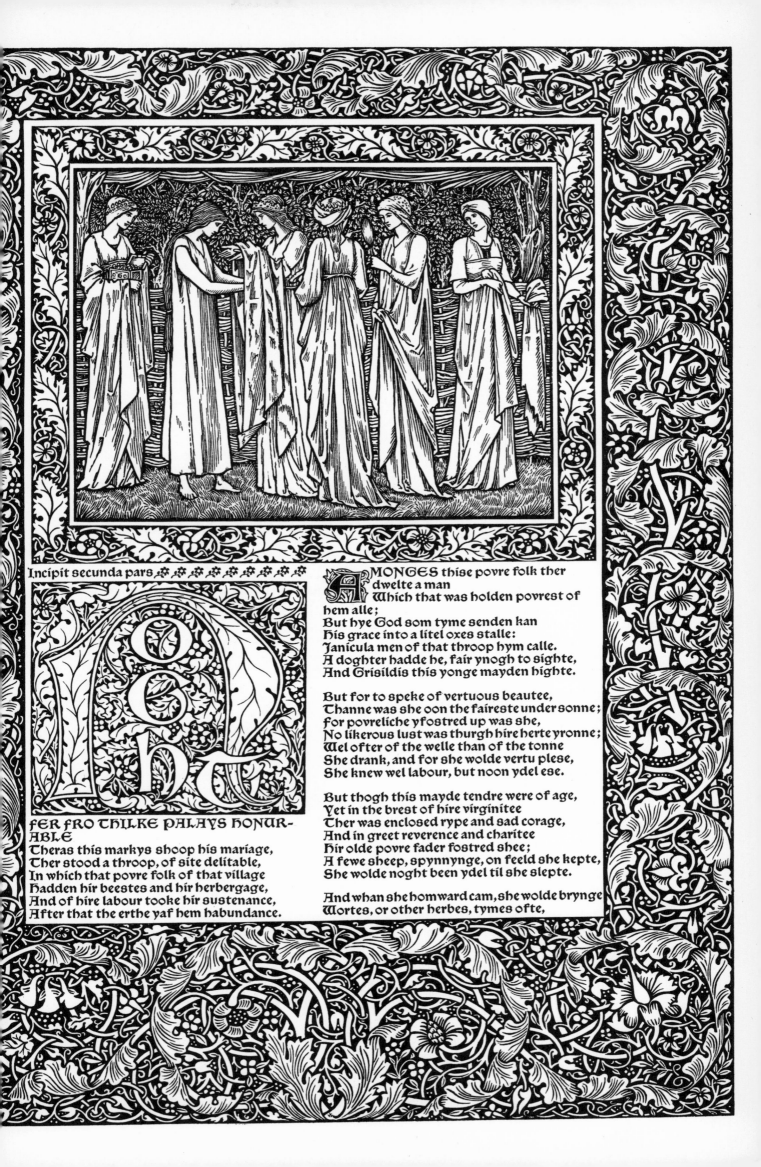

Incipit secunda pars ✾ ✾ ✾ ✾ ✾ ✾

FER FRO THILKE PALAYS HONUR-
ABLE
Theras this markys shoop his mariage,
Ther stood a throop, of site delitable,
In which that povre folk of that village
Hadden hir beestes and hir herbergage,
And of hire labour tooke hir sustenance,
After that the erthe yaf hem habundance.

AMONGES thise povre folk ther
dwelte a man
Which that was holden povrest of
hem alle;
But hye God som tyme senden kan
His grace into a litel oxes stalle:
Janicula men of that throop hym calle.
A doghter hadde he, fair ynogh to sighte,
And Grisildis this yonge mayden highte.

But for to speke of vertuous beautee,
Thanne was she oon the faireste under sonne;
For povreliche yfostred up was she,
No likerous lust was thurgh hire herte yronne;
Wel ofter of the welle than of the tonne
She drank, and for she wolde vertu plese,
She knew wel labour, but noon ydel ese.

But thogh this mayde tendre were of age,
Yet in the brest of hire virginitee
Ther was enclosed rype and sad corage,
And in greet reverence and charitee
Hir olde povre fader fostred shee;
A fewe sheep, spynnynge, on feeld she kepte,
She wolde noght been ydel til she slepte.

And whan she homward cam, she wolde brynge
Wortes, or other herbes, tymes ofte,

The whiche she shredde and seeth for hir lyvynge,
And made hir bed ful harde and nothyng softe;
And ay she kepte hir fadres lyf on lofte
With everich obeisaunce and diligence
That child may doon to fadres reverence.

UPON Grisilde, this povre creature,
Ful ofte sithe this markys sette his eye
As he on huntyng rood paraventure;
And whan it fil that he myghte hire espye,
He noght with wantowne lookyng of folye
His eyen caste on hire, but in sad wyse
Upon hir chiere he gan hym ofte avyse,

Commendynge in his herte hir wommanhede,
And eek hir vertu, passynge any wight
Of so yong age, as wel in chiere as dede.
For thogh the peple hadde no greet insight
In vertu, he considered ful right
Hir bountee, and disposed that he wolde
Wedde hire oonly, if evere he wedde sholde.

THE day of weddyng cam, but no wight kan
Telle what womman that it sholde be;
For which merveille wondred many a man,
And seyden, whan they were in privetee,
Wol nat oure lord yet leve his vanytee?
Wol he nat wedde? allas! allas! the while!
Why wole he thus hymself and us bigile?

But nathelees this markys hath doon make
Of gemmes, set in gold and in asure,
Brooches and rynges, for Grisildis sake;
And of hir clothyng took he the mesure
By a mayden ylyke to hir stature,
And eek of othere ornementes alle
That unto swich a weddyng sholde falle.

THE time of undren of the same day
Approcheth, that this weddyng sholde be;
And al the paleys put was in array,
Bothe halle and chambres, ech in his degree;
Houses of office stuffed with plentee,
Ther maystow seen of deyntevous vitaille
That may be found, as fer as last Ytaille,

This roial markys, richely arrayed,
Lordes and ladyes in his compaignye,
The whiche that to the feeste were yprayed,
And of his retenue the bachelrye,
With many a soun of sondry melodye,
Unto the village, of the which I tolde,
In this array the righte wey han holde.

GRISILDE of this, God woot, ful innocent
That for hire shapen was al this array,
To fecchen water at a welle is went,
And cometh hoom as soone as ever she may.
For wel she hadde herd seyd, that thilke day
The markys sholde wedde, and, if she myghte,
She wolde fayn han seyn som of that sighte.

She thoghte, I wole with othere maydens stonde,
That been my felawes, in oure dore, and se
130

The markysesse, and therfore wol I fonde
To doon at hoom, as soone as it may be,
The labour which that longeth unto me;
And thanne I may at leyser hir biholde,
If she this wey unto the castel holde.

AND as she wolde over hir thresshfold gon
The markys cam, and gan hire for to calle;
And she set doun hir water pot anon
Biside the thresshfold, in an oxes stalle,
And doun upon hir knes she gan to falle,
And with sad contenance kneleth stille
Til she had herd what was the lordes wille.

This thoghtful markys spak unto this mayde
Ful sobrely, and seyde in this manere:
Where is youre fader, Grisildis? he sayde;
And she with reverence, in humble cheere,
Answerde, Lord, he is al redy heere.
And in she gooth withouten lenger lette,
And to the markys she hir fader fette.

HE by the hand thanne took this olde man,
And seyde thus, whan he hym hadde asyde,
Janicula, I neither may ne kan
Lenger the plesance of myn herte hyde.
If that thou vouchesauf, whatso bityde,
Thy doghter wol I take, er that I wende,
As for my wyf, unto hir lyves ende.

Thou lovest me, I woot it wel, certeyn,
And art my feithful lige man ybore;
And al that liketh me, I dar wel seyn,
It liketh thee, and specially therfore,
Tel me that poynt that I have seyd bifore,
If that thou wolt unto that purpos drawe,
To take me as for thy sone-in-lawe?

This sodeyn cas this man astonyed so,
That reed he wex, abayst, and al quakyng
He stood; unnethes seyde he wordes mo,
But oonly thus: Lord, quod he, my willyng
Is as ye wole, ne ayeyns youre likyng
I wol nothyng; ye be my lord so deere;
Right as yow lust governeth this mateere.

Yet wol I, quod this markys softely,
That in thy chambre I and thou and she
Have a collacioun, and wostow why?
For I wol axe if it hire wille be
To be my wyf, and reule hire after me;
And al this shal be doon in thy presence,
I wol noght speke out of thyn audience.

AND in the chambre whil they were aboute
Hir tretys, which as ye shal after heere,
The peple cam unto the hous withoute,
And wondred hem in how honeste manere,
And tentifly, she kepte hir fader deere.
But outrely Grisildis wondre myghte,
For nevere erst ne saugh she swich a sighte.

No wonder is thogh that she were astoned
To seen so greet a gest come in that place;

She nevere was to swiche gestes woned,
for which she looked with ful pale face.
But shortly forth this tale for to chace,
Thise arn the wordes that the markys sayde
To this benigne verray feithful mayde:

Grisilde, he seyde, ye shal wel understonde
It liketh to youre fader and to me
That I yow wedde, and eek it may so stonde,
As I suppose ye wol that it so be;
But thise demandes axe I first, quod he,
That, sith it shal be doon in hastif wyse,
Wol ye assente, or elles yow avyse?

I seye this, be ye redy with good herte
To al my lust, and that I frely may,
As me best thynketh, do yow laughe or smerte,
And nevere ye to grucche it, nyght ne day?
And eek whan I sey Ye, ne sey nat Nay,
Neither by word ne frownyng contenance;
Swere this, and heere I swere oure alliance.

WONDRYNGE upon this word, quak-
ynge for drede,
She seyde, Lord, undigne and unworthy
Am I to thilke honour that ye me beede;
But as ye wole yourself, right so wol I.
And heere I swere that nevere willyngly
In werk ne thoght I nyl yow disobeye,
For to be deed, though me were looth to deye.

This is ynogh, Grisilde myn, quod he,
And forth he gooth with a ful sobre cheere
Out at the dore, and after that cam she,
And to the peple he seyde in this manere,
This is my wyf, quod he, that standeth heere;
Honoureth hire, and loveth hire, I preye,
Whoso me loveth; ther is namoore to seye.

And for that nothing of hir olde geere
She sholde brynge into his hous, he bad
That wommen sholde dispoillen hire right theere;
Of which thise ladyes were nat right glad
To handle hir clothes wherinne she was clad;
But nathelees this mayde, bright of hewe,
Fro foot to heed they clothed han al newe.

Hir heris han they kembd, that lay untressed
Ful rudely, and with hir fyngres smale
A corone on hire heed they han ydressed,
And sette hire ful of nowches grete and smale.
Of hire array what sholde I make a tale?
Unnethe the peple hire knew for hire fairnesse,
Whan she translated was in swich richesse.

THIS markys hath hir spoused with a ryng
Broght for the same cause, and thanne hire
sette
Upon an hors, snow-whit and wel amblyng,
And to his paleys, er he lenger lette,
With joyful peple that hire ladde and mette,
Conveyed hire, and thus the day they spende
In revel, til the sonne gan descende.

k 2

And, shortly forth this tale for to chace,
I seye that to this newe markysesse
God hath swich favour sent hire of his grace,
That it ne semed nat by liklynesse
That she was born and fed in rudenesse,
As in a cote, or in an oxe stalle,
But norissed in an emperoures halle.

To every wight she woxen is so deere
And worshipful, that folk ther she was bore
And from hire birthe knewe hire yeer by yeere,
Unnethe trowed they, but dorste han swore
That to Janicle, of which I spak bifore,
She doghter nas, for, as by conjecture,
Hem thoughte she was another creature.

For though that evere vertuous was she,
She was encressed in swich excellence
Of thewes goode, yset in heigh bountee,
And so discreet and fair of eloquence,
So benigne, and so digne of reverence,
And koude so the peples herte embrace,
That ech hire lovede that looked on hir face.

Noght oonly of Saluces in the toun
Publiced was the bountee of hir name,
But eek biside in many a regioun,
If oon seide wel, another seyde the same.
So spradde of hire heighe bountee the fame,
That men and wommen, as wel yonge as olde,
Goon to Saluce, upon hir to biholde.

Thus Walter lowely, nay, but roially,
Wedded with fortunat honestetee,
In Goddes pees lyveth ful esily
At hoom, and outward grace ynogh had he;
And for he saugh that under lowe degree
Was ofte vertu hid, the peple hym heelde
A prudent man, and that is seyn ful seelde.

Nat oonly this Grisildis thurgh hir wit
Koude al the feet of wyfly homlynesse,
But eek, whan that the cas required it,
The commune profit koude she redresse.
Ther nas discord, rancour, ne hevynesse,
In al that land, that she ne koude apese,
And wisely brynge hem alle in reste and ese.

Though that hire housbonde absent were anon,
If gentil men, or othere of hire contree
Were wrothe, she wolde bryngen hem aton;
So wise and rype wordes hadde she,
And juggements of so greet equitee,
That she from hevene sent was, as men wende,
Peple to save and every wrong tamende.

NAT longe tyme after that this Grisild
Was wedded, she a doghter hath ybore,
Al had hire levere have born a knave child.
Glad was this markys and the folk therfore;
For though a mayde child coome al bifore,
She may unto a knave child atteyne
By liklihede, syn she nys nat bareyne.
Explicit secunda pars.

131

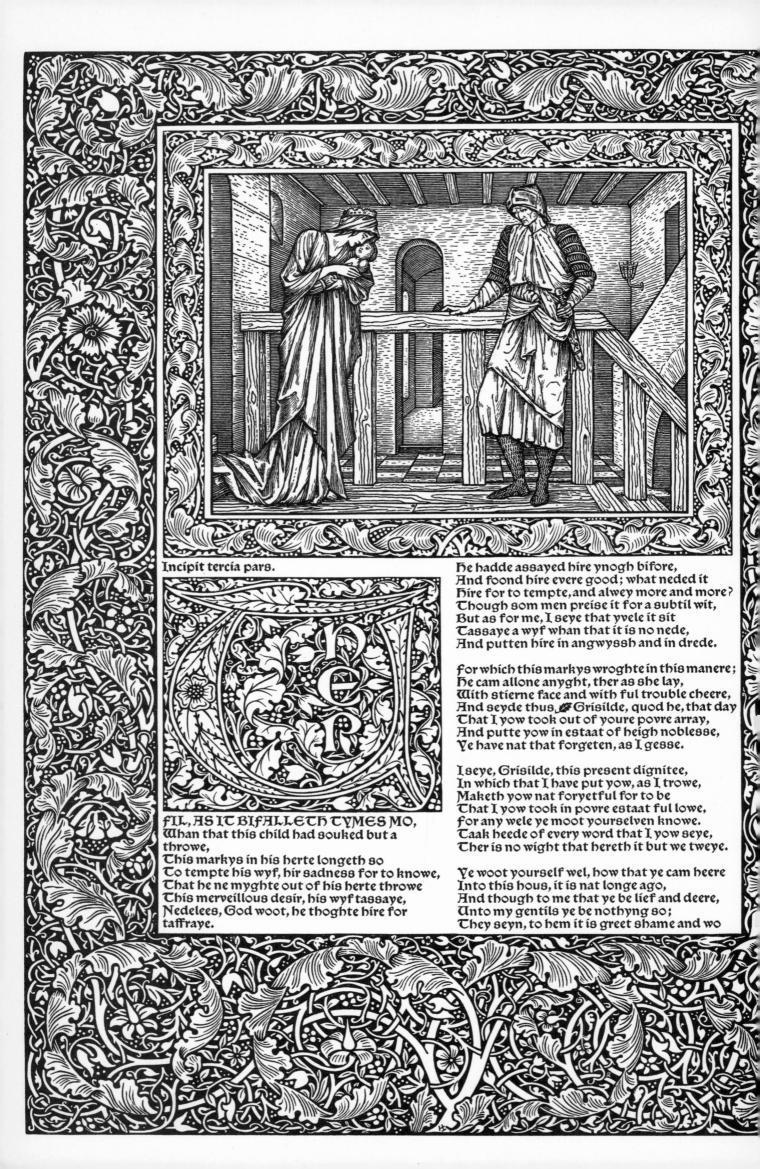

Incipit tercia pars.

He hadde assayed hire ynogh bifore,
And foond hire evere good; what neded it
Hire for to tempte, and alwey more and more?
Though som men preise it for a subtil wit,
But as for me, I seye that yvele it sit
Tassaye a wyf whan that it is no nede,
And putten hire in angwyssh and in drede.

For which this markys wroghte in this manere;
He cam allone anyght, ther as she lay,
With stierne face and with ful trouble cheere,
And seyde thus, Grisilde, quod he, that day
That I yow took out of youre povre array,
And putte yow in estaat of heigh noblesse,
Ye have nat that forgeten, as I gesse.

I seye, Grisilde, this present dignitee,
In which that I have put yow, as I trowe,
Maketh yow nat foryetful for to be
That I yow took in povre estaat ful lowe,
For any wele ye moot yourselven knowe.
Taak heede of every word that I yow seye,
Ther is no wight that hereth it but we tweye.

Ye woot yourself wel, how that ye cam heere
Into this hous, it is nat longe ago,
And though to me that ye be lief and deere,
Unto my gentils ye be nothyng so;
They seyn, to hem it is greet shame and wo

FIL, AS IT BIFALLETH TYMES MO,
Whan that this child had souked but a
throwe,
This markys in his herte longeth so
To tempte his wyf, hir sadness for to knowe,
That he ne myghte out of his herte throwe
This merveillous desir, his wyf tassaye,
Nedelees, God woot, he thoghte hire for
taffraye.

for to be subgets and been in servage
To thee, that born art of a smal village.

And namely sith thy doghter was ybore,
Thise wordes han they spoken doutelees;
But I desire, as I have doon bifore,
To lyve my lyf with hem in reste and pees;
I may nat in this caas be recchelees.
I moot doon with thy doghter for the beste,
Nat as I wolde, but as my peple leste.

And yet, God woot, this is ful looth to me;
But nathelees withoute youre wityng
I wol nat doon, but this wol I, quod he,
That ye to me assente, as in this thyng.
Shewe now youre pacience in youre werkyng
That ye me highte and swore in youre village
That day that maked was oure mariage.

WHAN she had herd al this, she noght ameved,
Neither in word, or chiere, or countenaunce;
for, as it semed, she was nat agreved:
She seyde, Lord, al lyth in youre plesaunce,
My child and I with hertely obeisaunce,
Been youres al, and ye mowe save or spille
Youre owene thyng; werketh after youre wille.

Ther may nothyng, God so my soule save!
Liken to yow that may displese me;
Ne I ne desire nothyng for to have,
Ne drede for to leese, save oonly ye;
This wyl is in myn herte, and ay shal be.
No lengthe of tyme, or deeth, may this deface,
Ne chaunge my corage to another place.

GLAD was this markys of hire answeryng,
But yet he feyned as he were nat so;
Al drery was his cheere and his lookyng,
Whan that he sholde out of the chambre go.
Soone after this, a furlong wey or two,
He prively hath toold al his entente
Unto a man, and to his wyf hym sente.

A maner sergeant was this privee man,
The which that feithful ofte he founden hadde
In thynges grete, and eek swich folk wel kan
Doon execucioun on thynges badde.
The lord knew wel that he hym loved and dradde;
And whan this sergeant wiste his lordes wille,
Into the chambre he stalked hym ful stille.

Madame, he seyde, ye moote foryeve it me,
Though I do thyng to which I am constreyned;
Ye been so wys that ful wel knowe ye
That lordes heestes mowe nat been yfeyned;
They mowe wel been biwailled and compleyned,
But men moote nede unto hire lust obeye,
And so wol I; ther is namoore to seye.

This child I am comanded for to take,
And spak namoore, but out the child he hente
Despitously, and gan a cheere make
As though he wolde han slayn it er he wente.
Grisildis moot al suffren and consente;

And as a lamb she sitteth meke and stille,
And leet this crueel sergeant doon his wille.

Suspecious was the diffame of this man,
Suspect his face, suspect his word also;
Suspect the tyme in which he this bigan.
Allas! hir doghter that she loved so,
She wende he wolde han slawen it right tho.
But nathelees she neither weepe ne syked,
Consentynge hire to that the markys lyked.

But atte laste speken she bigan,
And mekely she to the sergeant preyde,
So as he was a worthy gentil man,
That she moste kisse hir child er that it deyde;
And in hir barm this litel child she leyde
With ful sad face, and gan the child to kisse,
And lulled it, and after gan it blisse.

And thus she seyde in hire benigne voys,
fare weel, my child; I shal thee nevere see!
But, sith I thee have marked with the croys,
Of thilke fader, blessed moote he be,
That for us deyde upon a croys of tree.
Thy soule, litel child, I hym bitake,
for this nyght shaltow dyen for my sake.

I trowe that to a norice in this cas
It had been hard this reuthe for to se;
Wel myghte a mooder thanne han cryd, Allas!
But nathelees, so sad stedefast was she,
That she endured al adversitee,
And to the sergeant mekely she sayde,
Have heer agayn youre litel yonge mayde.

Gooth now, quod she, & dooth my lordes heeste;
But o thyng wol I prey yow of youre grace,
That, but my lord forbad yow, atte leeste
Burieth this litel body in som place
That beestes ne no briddes it torace.
But he no word wol to that purpos seye,
But took the child and wente upon his weye.

THIS sergeant cam unto his lord ageyn,
And of Grisildis wordes and hire cheere
He tolde hym point for point, in short and pleyn,
And hym presenteth with his doghter deere.
Somwhat this lord hath routhe in his manere;
But nathelees his purpos heeld he stille,
As lordes doon whan they wol han hir wille;

And bad his sergeant that he pryvely
Sholde this child ful softe wynde and wrappe
With alle circumstances tendrely,
And carie it in a cofre or in a lappe;
But, upon peyne his heed of for to swappe,
That no man sholde knowe of his entente,
Ne whenne he cam, ne whider that he wente;

But at Boloigne to his suster deere,
That thilke tyme of Panik was countesse,
He sholde it take, and shewe hire this mateere,
Bisekynge hire to doon hire bisynesse
This child to fostre in alle gentillesse;

And whos child that it was he bad hir hyde
From every wight, for oght that may bityde.

¶The sergeant gooth, and hath fulfild this
thyng;
But to this markys now retourne we;
For now gooth he ful faste ymaginyng
If by his wyves cheere he myghte se,
Or by hire word aperceyve that she
Were chaunged; but he nevere hire koude fynde

But evere in oon ylike sad and kynde.

As glad, as humble, as bisy in servyse,
And eek in love, as she was wont to be,
Was she to hym in every maner wyse;
Ne of hir doghter noght a word spak she.
Noon accident for noon adversitee
Was seyn in hire, ne nevere hir doghter name
Ne nempned she, in ernest nor in game.
Explicit tercia pars. Sequitur pars quarta.

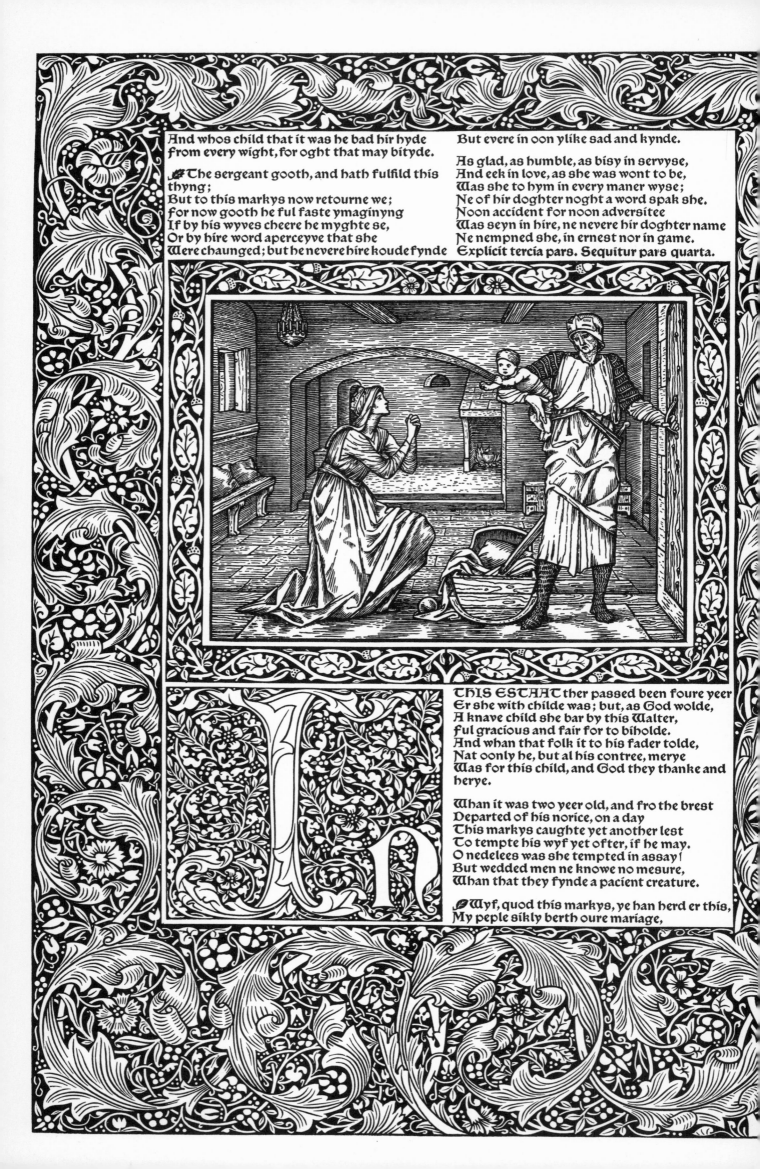

THIS ESTAAT ther passed been foure yeer
Er she with childe was; but, as God wolde,
A knave child she bar by this Walter,
Ful gracious and fair for to biholde.
And whan that folk it to his fader tolde,
Nat oonly he, but al his contree, merye
Was for this child, and God they thanke and
herye.

Whan it was two yeer old, and fro the brest
Departed of his norice, on a day
This markys caughte yet another lest
To tempte his wyf yet ofter, if he may.
O nedelees was she tempted in assay!
But wedded men ne knowe no mesure,
Whan that they fynde a pacient creature.

¶Wyf, quod this markys, ye han herd er this,
My peple sikly berth oure mariage,

And namely, sith my sone yboren is,
Now is it worse than evere in al oure age.
The murmure sleeth myn herte and my corage;
For to myne eres comth the voys so smerte,
That it wel ny destroyed hath myn herte.

Now sey they thus: Whan Walter is agoon,
Thanne shal the blood of Janicle succede
And been oure lord, for oother have we noon;
Swiche wordes seith my peple, out of drede.
Wel oughte I of swich murmur taken heede;
For certeinly I drede swich sentence,
Though they nat pleyn speke in myn audience.

I wolde lyve in pees, if that I myghte;
Wherfore I am disposed outrely,
As I his suster servede by nyghte,
Right so thenke I to serve hym pryvely.
This warne I yow, that ye nat sodeynly
Out of youreself for no wo sholde outreye,
Beth pacient, and therof I yow preye.

I have, quod she, seyd thus, and evere shal,
I wol nothyng, ne nyl nothyng, certayn,
But as yow list; naught greveth me at al,
Though that my doughter and my sone be slayn
At youre comandement; this is to sayn,
I have noght had no part of children tweyne,
But first siknesse, and after wo and peyne.

Ye been oure lord, dooth with youre owene thyng
Right as yow list; axeth no reed at me;
For as I lefte at hoom al my clothyng,
Whan I first cam to yow, right so, quod she,
Lefte I my wyl, and al my libertee,
And took youre clothyng; wherfore I yow preye,
Dooth youre plesaunce, I wol youre lust obeye.

And certes, if I hadde prescience
Youre wyl to knowe er ye youre lust me tolde,
I wolde it doon withouten necligence;
But now I woot youre lust and what ye wolde,
Al youre plesance ferme and stable I holde;
For wiste I that my deeth wolde do yow ese,
Right gladly wolde I dyen, yow to plese.

Deth may noght make no comparisoun
Unto youre love. And whan this markys sey
The constance of his wyf, he caste adoun
His eyen two, and wondreth that she may
In pacience suffre al this array.
And forth he goth with drery contenance,
But to his herte it was ful greet plesance.

THIS ugly sergeant, in the same wyse
That he hire doghter caughte, right so he,
Or worse, if men worse kan devyse,
Hath hent hire sone, that ful was of beautee.
And evere in oon so pacient was she,
That she no chiere maade of hevynesse,
But kiste hir sone, and after gan it blesse;

Save this: she preyde hym, that if he myghte,
Hir litel sone he wolde in erthe grave,

k 4

His tendre lymes, delicaat to sighte,
Fro foweles and fro beestes for to save;
But she noon answere of hym myghte have.
He wente his wey, as hym nothyng ne roghte;
But to Boloigne he tendrely it broghte.

THIS markys wondreth evere lenger the moore
Upon hir pacience, and if that he
Ne hadde soothly knowen therbifoore
That parfitly hir children loved she,
He wolde have wend that of som subtiltee,
And of malice, or for crueel corage,
That she hadde suffred this with sad visage.

But wel he knew, that next hymself, certayn,
She loved hir children best in every wyse.
But now of wommen wolde I axen fayn,
If thise assayes myghte nat suffise?
What koude a sturdy housbonde moore devyse
To preeve hire wyfhod and hir stedefastnesse,
And he continuynge evere in sturdinesse?

But ther been folk of swich condicioun
That, whan they have a certein purpos take,
They kan nat stynte of hire entencioun,
But right as they were bounden to a stake
They wol nat of that firste purpos slake.
Right so this markys fulliche hath purposed
To tempte his wyf, as he was first disposed.

He waiteth, if by word or contenance
That she to hym was changed of corage;
But nevere koude he fynde variance;
She was ay oon in herte and in visage;
And ay the forther that she was in age,
The moore trewe, if that it were possible,
She was to hym in love, and moore penyble.

For which it semed thus, that of hem two
Ther nas but o wyl; for, as Walter leste,
The same lust was hire plesance also;
And, God be thanked, al fil for the beste.
She shewed wel, for no worldly unreste
A wyf, as of hirself, nothing ne sholde
Wille in effect, but as hir housbonde wolde.

The sclaundre of Walter ofte and wyde spradde,
That of a crueel herte he wikkedly,
For he a povre womman wedded hadde,
Hath mordred bothe his children prively.
Swich murmure was among hem comunly.
No wonder is, for to the peples ere
Ther cam no word but that they mordred were.

For which, wheras his peple therbifore
Hadde loved hym wel, the sclaundre of his diffame
Made hem that they hym hatede therfore;
To been a mordrere is an hateful name.
But nathelees, for ernest ne for game,
He of his crueel purpos nolde stente;
To tempte his wyf was set al his entente.

Whan that his doghter twelf yeer was of age,
He to the court of Rome, in subtil wyse

135

Enformed of his wyl, sente his message,
Comaundynge hem swiche bulles to devyse
As to his crueel purpos may suffyse,
How that the pope, as for his peples reste,
Bad hym to wedde another, if hym leste.

I seye, he bad they sholde countrefete
The popes bulles, makynge mencioun
That he hath leve his firste wyf to lete,
As by the popes dispensacioun,
To stynte rancour and dissencioun
Bitwixe his peple and hym; thus seyde the
    bulle,
The which they han publiced atte fulle.

The rude peple, as it no wonder is,
Wenden ful wel that it hadde be right so;
But whan thise tidynges cam to Grisildis,
I deeme that hire herte was ful wo.
But she, ylike sad for everemo,
Disposed was, this humble creature,
Thadversitee of fortune al tendure,

Abidynge evere his lust and his plesance
To whom that she was yeven, herte and al,
As to hire verray worldly suffisance;
But shortly if this storie I tellen shal,
This markys writen hath in special
A lettre in which he sheweth his entente,

And secreely he to Boloigne it sente.

To the erl of Panyk, which that hadde tho
Wedded his suster, preyde he specially
To bryngen hoom agayn his children two
In honurable estaat al openly.
But o thyng he hym preyde outrely,
That he to no wight, though men wolde en-
    quere,
Sholde nat telle, whos children that they
    were,

But seye, the mayden sholde ywedded be
Unto the markys of Saluce anon.
And as this erl was preyed, so dide he;
for at day set he on his wey is goon
Toward Saluce, and lordes many oon
In riche array, this mayden for to gyde,
Hir yonge brother ridynge hire bisyde.

Arrayed was toward hir mariage
This fresshe mayde, ful of gemmes cleere;
Hir brother, which that seven yeer was of age,
Arrayed eek ful fressh in his manere.
And thus in greet noblesse and with glad
    cheere,
Toward Saluces shapynge hir journey,
fro day to day they ryden in hir wey.
Explicit quarta pars.

Sequitur pars quinta.

AL THIS, AFTER HIS WIKKE USAGE,
This markys, yet his wyf to tempte moore
To the outtreste preeve of hir corage,
fully to han experience and loore
If that she were as stedefast as bifoore,
He on a day, in open audience,
ful boistously hath seyd hire this sentence:

Certes, Grisilde, I hadde ynogh plesance
To han yow to my wyf for youre goodnesse
As for youre trouthe & for youre obeisance,
Noght for youre lynage ne for youre richesse;
But now knowe I, in verray soothfastnesse,
That in greet lordshipe, if I wel avyse,
Ther is greet servitute in sondry wyse.

I may nat doon as every plowman may;
My peple me constreyneth for to take
Another wyf, and crien day by day;
And eek the pope, rancour for to slake,
Consenteth it, that dar I undertake;
And treweliche thus muche I wol yow seye,
My newe wyf is comynge by the weye.

Be strong of herte, and voyde anon hir place,
And thilke dowere that ye broghten me,
Taak it agayn, I graunte it of my grace;
Retourneth to youre fadres hous, quod he;
No man may alwey han prosperitee;
With evene herte I rede yow tendure
This strook of fortune or of aventure.

AND she answerde agayn in pacience:
My lord, quod she, I woot, and wiste alway
How that bitwixen youre magnificence
And my poverte no wight kan ne may
Maken comparison; it is no nay.
I ne heeld me nevere digne in no manere
To be your wyf, no, ne your chamberere.

And in this hous, ther ye me lady maade,
The heighe God take I for my witnesse,

And also wysly he my soule glaade,
I nevere heeld me lady ne maistresse,
But humble servant to youre worthynesse,
And evere shal, whil that my lyf may dure,
Aboven every worldly creature.

That ye so longe of youre benignitee
Han holden me in honour and nobleye,
Wheras I was noght worthy for to bee,
That thonke I God and yow, to whom I preye
foryelde it yow; ther is namoore to seye.
Unto my fader gladly wol I wende
And with hym dwelle unto my lyves ende.

Ther I was fostred of a child ful smal,
Til I be deed, my lyf ther wol I lede
A wydwe clene, in body, herte and al.
for sith I yaf to yow my maydenhede,
And am youre trewe wyf, it is no drede,
God shilde swich a lordes wyf to take
Another man to housbonde or to make.

And of youre newe wyf, God of his grace
So graunte yow wele and prosperitee:
for I wol gladly yelden hire my place,
In which that I was blisful wont to bee,
for sith it liketh yow, my lord, quod shee,
That whilom weren al myn hertes reste,
That I shal goon, I wol goon whan yow leste.

But theras ye me profre swich dowaire
As I first broghte, it is wel in my mynde
It were my wrecched clothes, nothyng faire,
The whiche to me were hard now for to fynde.
O goode God! how gentil and how kynde
Ye semed by youre speche and youre visage
The day that maked was oure mariage!

But sooth is seyd, algate I fynde it trewe,
for in effect it preved is on me,
Love is noght oold as whan that it is newe.
But certes, lord, for noon adversitee,
To dyen in the cas, it shal nat bee
That evere in word or werk I shal repente
That I yow yaf myn herte in hool entente.

My lord, ye woot that, in my fadres place,
Ye dide me streepe out of my povre wede,
And richely me cladden, of youre grace.
To yow broghte I noght elles, out of drede,
But feith and nakednesse and maydenhede;
And heere agayn my clothyng I restoore,
And eek my weddyng-ryng, for everemore.

The remenant of youre jueles redy be
Inwith youre chambre, dar I saufly sayn;
Naked out of my fadres hous, quod she,
I cam, and naked moot I turne agayn.
Al youre plesance wol I folwen fayn;
But yet I hope it be nat youre entente
That I smoklees out of youre paleys wente.

Ye koude nat doon so dishoneste a thyng,

That thilke wombe in which youre children leye
Sholde, biforn the peple, in my walkyng,
Be seyn al bare; wherfore I yow preye,
Lat me nat lyk a worm go by the weye:
Remembre yow, myn owene lord so deere,
I was youre wyf, though I unworthy weere.

Wherfore, in guerdon of my maydenhede,
Which that I broghte, and noght agayn I bere,
As voucheth sauf to yeve me, to my meede,
But swich a smok as I was wont to were,
That I therwith may wrye the wombe of here
That was youre wyf; and heer take I my leeve
Of yow, myn owene lord, lest I yow greve.

THE smok, quod he, that thou hast on
thy bak,
Lat it be stille, and bere it forth with
thee.
But wel unnethes thilke word he spak,
But wente his wey for routhe and for pitee.
Biforn the folk hirselven strepeth she,
And in hir smok, with heed and foot al bare,
Toward hir fader hous forth is she fare.

THE folk hire folwe wepynge in hir weye,
And fortune ay they cursen as they
goon;
But she fro wepyng kepte hire eyen dreye,
Ne in this tyme word ne spak she noon.
Hir fader, that this tidynge herde anoon,
Curseth the day and tyme that nature
Shoop hym to been a lyves creature.

For out of doute this olde povre man
Was evere in suspect of hir mariage;
For evere he demed, sith that it bigan,
That whan the lord fulfild hadde his corage,

FRO
BOLOIGNE IS THIS ERL OF PANYK
COME,
Of which the fame up sprang to moore and
lesse,
And in the peples eres alle and some

Hym wolde thynke it were a disparage
To his estaat so lowe for talighte,
And voyden hire as soone as ever he myghte.

AGAYNS his doghter hastiliche goth he,
for he by noyse of folk knew hire
comynge,
And with hire olde coote, as it myghte be,
He covered hire, ful sorwefully wepynge;
But on hire body myghte he it nat brynge,
For rude was the clooth, and moore of age
By dayes fele than at hire mariage.

Thus with hire fader, for a certeyn space,
Dwelleth this flour of wyfly pacience,
That neither by hire wordes ne hire face
Biforn the folk, ne eek in hire absence,
Ne shewed she that hire was doon offence;
Ne of hire heighe estaat no remembraunce
Ne hadde she, as by hire contenaunce.

No wonder is, for in hire grete estaat
Hire goost was evere in pleyn humylitee;
No tendre mouth, noon herte delicaat,
No pompe, no semblant of roialtee,
But ful of pacient benyngnytee,
Discreet and pridelees, ay honurable,
And to hire housbonde evere meke & stable.

Men speke of Job, and moost for his hum-
blesse,
As clerkes, whan hem list, konne wel endite,
Namely of men, but as in soothfastnesse,
Though clerkes preise wommen but a lite,
Ther kan no man in humblesse hym acquite
As womman kan, ne kan been half so trewe
As wommen been, but it be falle of newe.
Explicit quinta pars. Sequitur pars sexta.

Was kouth eek, that a newe markysesse
He with hym broghte, in swich pompe and
richesse,
That nevere was ther seyn with mannes eye
So noble array in al West Lumbardye.

The markys, which that shoop and knew al
this,
Er that this erl was come, sente his message
For thilke sely povre Grisildis;
And she with humble herte and glad visage,
Nat with no swollen thoght in hire corage,
Cam at his heste, and on hire knees hire
sette,
And reverently and wisely she hym grette.

GRISILDE, quod he, my wyl is outrely
This mayden that shal wedded been
to me,
Received be tomorwe as roially
As it possible is in myn hous to be.
And eek that every wight in his degree
Have his estaat in sittyng and servyse
And heigh plesaunce, as I kan best devyse.

I have no wommen suffisaunt certayn
The chambres for tarraye in ordinaunce
After my lust, and therfore wolde I fayn
That thyn were al swich manere governaunce;
Thou knowest eek of old al my plesaunce;
Thogh thyn array be badde and yvel biseye,
Do thou thy devoir at the leeste weye.

NAT oonly, lord, that I am glad, quod she,
To doon youre lust, but I desire also
Yow for to serve and plese in my degree
Withouten feyntyng, and shal everemo;
Ne nevere, for no wele ne no wo,
Ne shal the goost withinne myn herte stente
To love yow best with al my trewe entente.

And with that word she gan the hous to dighte,
And tables for to sette and beddes make;
And peyned hire to doon al that she myghte,
Preyynge the chambereres for Goddes sake
To hasten hem, and faste swepe and shake;
And she, the mooste servysable of alle,
Hath every chambre arrayed and his halle.

ABOUTEN undren gan this erl alighte,
That with him broghte thise noble children tweye,
for which the peple ran to seen the sighte

Of hire array, so richely biseye;
And thanne at erst amonges hem they seye,
That Walter was no fool, thogh that hym leste
To chaunge his wyf, for it was for the beste.

for she is fairer, as they deemen alle,
Than is Grisilde, and moore tendre of age,
And fairer fruyt bitwene hem sholde falle,
And moore plesant, for hire heigh lynage;
Hir brother eek so faire was of visage,
That hem to seen the peple hath caught plesaunce,
Commendynge now the markys governaunce.

Auctor

STORMY peple! unsad and evere untrewe!
Ay undiscreet and chaungynge as a vane,
Delitynge evere in rumbul that is newe,
for lyk the moone ay wexe ye and wane;
Ay ful of clappyng, deere ynogh a jane;
Youre doom is fals, youre constance yvele preeveth,
A ful greet fool is he that on yow leeveth!

Thus seyden sadde folk in that citee
Whan that the peple gazed up and doun,

for they were glad right for the noveltee
To han a newe lady of hir toun.
Namoore of this make I now mencioun;
But to Grisilde agayn wol I me dresse,
And telle hir constance and hir bisynesse.

FUL bisy was Grisilde in everythyng
That to the feeste was apertinent;
Right noght was she abayst of hire
clothyng,
Thogh it were rude and somdeel eek torent.
But with glad cheere to the yate is went,
With oother folk, to greete the markysesse,
And after that dooth forth hire bisynesse.

With so glad chiere his gestes she receyveth,
And konnyngly, everich in his degree,
That no defaute no man aperceyveth;
But ay they wondren what she myghte bee
That in so povre array was for to see,
And koude swich honour and reverence;
And worthily they preisen hire prudence.

In al this meenewhile she ne stente
This mayde and eek hir brother to commende
With al hir herte, in ful benyngne entente,
So wel, that no man koude hir pris amende.
But atte laste, whan that thise lordes wende
To sitten doun to mete, he gan to calle
Grisilde, as she was bisy in his halle.

GRISILDE, quod he, as it were in his pley,
How liketh thee my wyf and hire beautee?
Right wel, quod she, my lord, for, in
good fey,
A fairer saugh I nevere noon than she.
I prey to God yeve hire prosperitee;
And so hope I that he wol to yow sende
Plesance ynogh unto youre lyves ende.

O thyng biseke I yow, and warne also,
That ye ne prikke with no tormentynge
This tendre mayden, as ye han doon mo;
For she is fostred in hire norissynge
Moore tendrely, and, to my supposynge,
She koude nat adversitee endure
As koude a povre fostred creature.

AND whan this Walter saugh hire
pacience,
Hir glade chiere and no malice at al,
And he so ofte had doon to hire offence,
And she ay sad and constant as a wal,
Continuynge evere hire innocence overal,
This sturdy markys gan his herte dresse
To rewen upon hire wyfly stedfastnesse.

THIS is ynogh, Grisilde myn, quod he,
Be now namoore agast ne yvele apayed;
I have thy feith and thy benyngnytee,
As wel as evere womman was, assayed,
In greet estaat, and povreliche arrayed.
Now knowe I, deere wyf, thy stedfastnesse.
And hire in armes took, and gonne hire kesse.

And she for wonder took of it no keep;
She herde nat what thyng he to hire seyde,
She ferde as she had stert out of a sleep,
Til she out of hire mazednesse abreyde.
Grisilde, quod he, by God that for us deyde,
Thou art my wyf, ne noon oother I have,
Ne nevere hadde, as God my soule save!

This is thy doghter, which thou hast supposed
To be my wyf; that oother feithfully
Shal be myn heir, as I have ay purposed;
Thou bare hym in thy body trewely.
At Boloigne have I kept hem prively;
Taak hem agayn, for now maystow nat seye
That thou hast lorn noon of thy children tweye.

And folk that ootherweys han seyd of me,
I warne hem wel that I have doon this deede
For no malice, ne for no crueltee,
But for tassaye in thee thy wommanheede,
And nat to sleen my children, God forbeede!
But for to kepe hem pryvely and stille,
Til I thy purpos knewe and al thy wille.

WHAN she this herde, aswowne doun she
falleth
For pitous joye, & after hire swownynge
She bothe hire yonge children unto hire calleth,
And in hire armes, pitously wepynge,
Embraceth hem, and tendrely kissynge
Ful lyk a mooder, with hire salte teeres
She batheth bothe hire visage and hire heeres.

O, WHICH a pitous thyng it was to se
Hir swownyng, and hire humble voys to
heere!
Grauntmercy, lord! that thanke I yow,
quod she,
That ye han saved me my children deere!
Now rekke I nevere to been deed right heere;
Sith I stonde in youre love and in youre grace,
No fors of deeth, ne whan my spirit pace!

O tendre, O deere, O yonge children myne!
Youre woful mooder wende stedfastly
That crueel houndes or some foul vermyne,
Hadde eten yow; but God, of his mercy,
And youre benyngne fader, tendrely
Hath doon yow kept. And in that same stounde
Al sodeynly she swapte adoun to grounde.

And in hire swough so sadly holdeth she
Hire children two, whan she gan hem tembrace,
That with greet sleighte and greet difficultee
The children from hire arm they goone arace.
O many a teere on many a pitous face
Doun ran of hem that stooden hire bisyde;
Unnethe abouten hire myghte they abyde.

WALTER hire gladeth, and hire sorwe
slaketh;
She riseth up, abaysed, from hire traunce,
And every wight hire joye and feeste maketh,
Til she hath caught agayn hire contenaunce.

Walter hire dooth so feithfully plesaunce,
That it was deyntee for to seen the cheere
Bitwixe hem two, now they been met yfeere.

Thise ladyes, whan that they hir tyme saye,
Han taken hire, and into chambre gon,
And strepen hire out of hire rude array,
And in a clooth of gold that brighte shoon,
With a coroune of many a riche stoon
Upon hire heed, they into halle hire broghte,
And ther she was honured as hire oghte.

Thus hath this pitous day a blisful ende,
For every man and womman dooth his myght
This day in murthe and revel to dispende,
Til on the welkne shoon the sterres lyght.
For more solempne in every mannes syght
This feste was, and gretter of costage,
Than was the revel of hire mariage.

AL many a yeer in heigh prosperitee
Lyven thise two in concord and in
reste,
And richely his doghter maryed he
Unto a lord, oon of the worthieste
Of al Ytaille; and thanne in pees and
reste
His wyves fader in his court he kepeth,
Til that the soule out of his body crepeth.

His sone succedeth in his heritage
In reste and pees, after his fader day;
And fortunat was eek in mariage;
Al putte he nat his wyf in greet assay.
This world is nat so strong, it is no nay,
As it hath been of olde tymes yoore,
And herkneth what this auctour seith therfoore.

This storie is seyd, nat for that wyves sholde
Folwen Grisilde as in humylitee,
For it were inportable, though they wolde;
But for that every wight, in his degree,
Sholde be constant in adversitee
As was Grisilde; therfore Petrak writeth
This storie, which with heigh stile he enditeth.

For sith a womman was so pacient
Unto a mortal man, wel moore us oghte
Receyven al in gree that God us sent;
For greet skile is, he preeve that he wroghte.
But he ne tempteth no man that he boghte,
As seith Seint Jame, if ye his pistel rede;
He preeveth folk al day, it is no drede,

And suffreth us, as for oure exercise,
With sharpe scourges of adversitee
Ful ofte to be bete in sondry wise;
Nat for to know oure wyl, for certes he,
Er we were born, knew al oure freletee;
And for oure beste is al his governaunce;
Lat us thanne lyve in vertuous suffraunce.

But o word, lordynges, herkneth, er I go:
It were ful hard to fynde now a dayes

In al a toun Grisildis thre or two;
For, if that they were put to swiche assayes,
The gold of hem hath now so badde alayes
With bras, that thogh the coyne be fair at eye
It wolde rather breste atwo than plye.

For which heere, for the Wyves love of Bathe,
Whos lyf and al hire secte God mayntene
In heigh maistrie, and elles were it scathe,
I wol with lusty herte fressh and grene
Seyn yow a song to glade yow, I wene;
And lat us stynte of ernestful matere:
Herkneth my song, that seith in this manere.

RISILDE is deed, and eek
hire pacience,
And bothe atones buryed
in Ytaille;
For which I crie in open
audience,
No wedded man so hardy
be tassaille
His wyves pacience in hope
to fynde
Grisildis, for in certein he shal faille!

O noble wyves, ful of heigh prudence,
Lat noon humylitee youre tonge naille,
Ne lat no clerk have cause or diligence
To write of yow a storie of swich mervaille
As of Grisildis pacient and kynde;
Lest Chichevache yow swelwe in hire entraille!

Folweth Ekko, that holdeth no silence,
But evere answereth at the countretaille;
Beth nat bidaffed for youre innocence,
But sharply taak on yow the governaille.
Emprenteth wel this lesson in youre mynde
For commune profit, sith it may availle.

Ye archewyves, stondeth at defense,
Syn ye be strong as is a greet camaille,
Ne suffreth nat that men yow doon offense.
And sklendre wyves, fieble as in bataille,
Beth egre as is a tygre yond in Ynde;
Ay clappeth as a mille, I yow consaille.

Ne dreed hem nat, doth hem no reverence;
For though thyn housbonde armed be in maille,
The arwes of thy crabbed eloquence
Shal perce his brest, and eek his aventaille.
In jalousie I rede eek thou hym bynde,
And thou shalt make hym couche as dooth a
quaille.

If thou be fair, ther folk been in presence
Shewe thou thy visage and thyn apparaille;
If thou be foul, be fre of thy dispence,
To gete thee freendes ay do thy travaille;
Be ay of chiere as light as leef on lynde,
And lat hym care and wepe, and wryng and waille!
Here endith the Clerke of Oxenford his Tale.

The Tale
of the
Clerk of
Oxenford

Lenvoy de
Chaucer

141

The prologe of the Marchantes Tale ❧❧

WEPYNG and waylyng, care and oother sorwe I knowe ynogh, on even and a morwe, Quod the Marchant, and so doon othere mo That wedded been, I trowe that it be so; for wel I woot, it fareth so with me.

I have a wyf, the worste that may be;
for thogh the feend to hire ycoupled were,
She wolde hym overmacche, I dar wel swere.
What sholde I yow reherce in special
Hir hye malice? She is a shrewe at al.
Ther is a long and large difference
Bitwix Grisildis grete pacience
And of my wyf the passyng crueltee.
Were I unbounden, al so moot I thee!
I wolde nevere eft comen in the snare.
We wedded men lyve in sorwe and care.
Assaye whoso wole, and he shal fynde
I seye sooth, by Seint Thomas of Ynde,
As for the moore part, I sey nat alle;
God shilde that it sholde so bifalle!
A! good sir Hoost! I have ywedded bee
Thise monthes two, and moore nat, pardee!
And yet, I trowe, he that al his lyve
Wyflees hath been, though that men wolde
him ryve
Unto the herte, ne koude in no manere
Tellen so muchel sorwe, as I now heere
Koude tellen of my wyves cursednesse!
    Now, quod our Hoost, Marchant, so God
yow blesse!
Syn ye so muchel knowen of that art,
ful hertely I pray yow telle us part.
    Gladly, quod he, but of myn owene soore,
for soory herte, I telle may namoore.

HEERE BIGYNNETH THE MARCHANTES TALE ❧❧

WHILOM
ther was dwellynge in Lumbardye
A worthy knyght, that born was of Pavye,
In which he lyved in greet prosperitee;
And sixty yeer a wyflees man was hee,
And folwed ay his bodily delyt
On wommen, theras was his appetyt,
As doon thise fooles that been seculeer.
And whan that he was passed sixty yeer,
Were it for hoolynesse or for dotage
I kan nat seye, but swich a greet corage
Hadde this knyght to been a wedded man,
That day and nyght he dooth al that he kan
Tespien where he myghte wedded be;
Preyinge oure Lord to granten him, that he
Mighte ones knowe of thilke blisful lyf
That is bitwixe an housbonde and his wyf;
And for to lyve under that hooly bond
With which that first God man and womman
bond.
    Noon oother lyf, seyde he, is worth a bene;
for wedlok is so esy and so clene,
That in this world it is a paradys.
Thus seyde this olde knyght, that was so
wys.
AND certeinly, as sooth as God is kyng,
To take a wyf, it is a glorious thyng;
And namely whan a man is oold and
hoor,
Thanne is a wyf the fruyt of his tresor.
Thanne sholde he take a yong wyf and a feir,
On which he myghte engendren hym an heir,
And lede his lyf in joye and in solas;
Wheras thise bacheleres synge Allas!
Whan that they fynden any adversitee
In love, which nys but childyssh vanytee.
And trewely it sit wel to be so,
That bacheleres have often peyne and wo;
On brotel ground they buylde, & brotelnesse
They fynde, whan they wene sikernesse.
They lyve but as a bryd or as a beest,
In libertee, and under noon arreest,
Theras a wedded man in his estaat
Lyveth a lyf blisful and ordinaat,
Under the yok of mariage ybounde.
Wel may his herte in joye & blisse habounde;
for who kan be so buxom as a wyf?
Who is so trewe, and eek so ententyf
To kepe hym, syk and hool, as is his make?
for wele or wo she wole hym nat forsake.
She nys nat wery hym to love and serve,
Thogh that he lye bedrede til he sterve.
AND yet somme clerkes seyn it nys
nat so,
Of whiche he, Theofraste, is oon of
tho.
What force though Theofraste liste lye?
    Ne take no wyf, quod he, for housbond-
rye,
As for to spare in houshold thy dispence;
A trewe servant dooth moore diligence
Thy good to kepe, than thyn owene wyf,

for she wol clayme half part al hir lyf;
And if that thou be syk, so God me save!
Thy verray freendes or a trewe knave
Wol kepe thee bet than she that waiteth ay
After thy good, and hath doon many a day.
And if thou take a wyf unto thyn hold,
Ful lightly maystow been a cokewold.
¶This sentence, and an hundred thynges worse,
Writeth this man, ther God his bones corse!
But take no kepe of al swich vanytee;
Deffie Theofraste and herke me.
¶A wyf is Goddes yifte verraily;
Alle othere manere yiftes hardily,
As londes, rentes, pasture, or commune,
Or moebles, alle been yiftes of Fortune,
That passen as a shadwe upon a wal.
But dredelees, if pleynly speke I shal,
A wyf wol laste, and in thyn hous endure,
Wel lenger than thee list, paraventure.
MARIAGE is a ful greet sacrement;
He which that hath no wyf, I holde hym
    shent;
He lyveth helplees and al desolat.
I speke of folk in seculer estaat.
And herke why, I sey nat this for noght,
That womman is for mannes help ywroght.
The hye God, whan he hadde Adam maked,
And saugh him al allone, bely-naked,
God of his grete goodnesse seyde than,
Lat us now make an help unto this man
Lyk to hymself; and thanne he made him Eve.
Heere may ye se, and heerby may ye preve,
That wyf is mannes help and his confort,
His Paradys terrestre and his disport;
So buxom and so vertuous is she,
They moste nedes lyve in unitee.
O flessh they been, and o flessh, as I gesse,
Hath but oon herte, in wele and in distresse.
A WYF! a! Seinte Marie, benedicite!
How myghte a man han any adversitee
That hath a wyf? Certes, I kan nat seye.
The blisse which that is bitwixe hem tweye
Ther may no tonge telle, or herte thynke.
If he be povre, she helpeth hym to swynke;
She kepeth his good, and wasteth never a deel;
Al that hire housbonde lust, hire liketh weel;
She seith not ones, Nay, whan he seith, Ye.
¶Do this, seith he. ¶Al redy, sire, seith she.
O BLISFUL ordre of wedlok precious,
Thou art so murye, and eek so vertuous,
And so commended and appreved eek,
That every man that halt hym worth a leek
Upon his bare knees oughte al his lyf
Thanken his God that hym hath sent a wyf;
Or elles preye to God hym for to sende
A wyf, to laste unto his lyves ende;
For thanne his lyf is set in sikernesse;
He may nat be deceyved, as I gesse,
So that he werke after his wyves reed;
Thanne may he boldely kepen up his heed,
They been so trewe, and therwithal so wyse;
For which, if thou wolt werken as the wyse,
Do alwey so as wommen wol thee rede.

LO, how that Jacob, as thise clerkes rede,
By good conseil of his mooder Rebekke,
Boonde the kydes skyn aboute his nekke;
Thurgh which his fadres benysoun he wan.
LO Judith, as the storie telle kan,
By wys conseil she Goddes peple kepte,
And slow hym, Olofernus, whil he slepte.
LO Abigayl, by good conseil how she
Saved hir housbonde, Nabal, whan that he
Sholde han be slayn; & looke, Ester also
By good conseil delyvered out of wo
The peple of God, and made hym, Mardochee,
Of Assuere enhaunced for to be.
THER nys nothyng in gree superlatyf,
As seith Senek, above an humble wyf.
Suffre thy wyves tonge, as Catoun bit;
She shal comande, and thou shalt suffren it;
And yet she wole obeye of curteisye.
A wyf is kepere of thyn housbondrye;
Wel may the sike man biwaille and wepe,
Theras ther nys no wyf the hous to kepe.
I warne thee, if wisely thou wolt wirche,
Love wel thy wyf, as Crist loveth his chirche.
If thou lovest thyself, thou lovest thy wyf,
No man hateth his flessh, but in his lyf
He fostreth it, and therfore bidde I thee,
Cherisse thy wyf, or thou shalt nevere thee.
Housbonde and wyf, whatso men jape or pleye,
Of worldly folk holden the siker weye;
They been so knyt, ther may noon harm bityde;
And namely, upon the wyves syde.
For which this Januarie, of whom I tolde,
Considered hath, inwith his dayes olde,
The lusty lyf, the vertuous quyete,
That is in mariage hony-sweete,
And for his freendes on a day he sente,
To tellen hem theffect of his entente.
WITH face sad, his tale he hath hem
    toold:
He seyde, freendes, I am hoor and
    oold,
And almoost, God woot, on my
    pittes brynke;
Upon my soule somwhat moste I thynke,
I have my body folily despended;
Blessed be God! that it shal been amended!
For I wol be, certeyn, a wedded man,
And that anoon in al the haste I kan,
Unto som mayde fair and tendre of age.
I prey yow, shapeth for my mariage
Al sodeynly, for I wol nat abyde;
And I wol fonde tespien, on my syde,
To whom I may be wedded hastily.
But forasmuche as ye been mo than I,
Ye shullen rather swich a thyng espyen
Than I, and where me best were to allyen.
But o thyng warne I yow, my freendes deere,
I wol noon oold wyf han in no manere.
She shal nat passe twenty yeer, certayn;
Oold fissh and yong flessh wolde I have ful fayn.
Bet is, quod he, a pyk than a pykerel;
And bet than old boef is the tendre veel.
I wol no womman thritty yeer of age,

143

It is but benestraw and greet forage.
And eek this olde wydwes, God it woot,
They konne so muchel craft on Wades boot,
So muchel broken harm, whan that hem leste,
That with hem sholde I nevere lyve in reste;
For sondry scoles maken sotile clerkis;
Womman of manye scoles half a clerk is.
But certeynly, a yong thyng may men gye,
Right as men may warm wex with handes plye.
Wherfore I sey yow pleynly, in a clause,
I wol noon oold wyf han right for this cause.
For if so were, I hadde swich myschaunce
That I in hire ne koude han no plesaunce,
Thanne sholde I lede my lyf in avoutrye,
And go streight to the devel whan I dye.
Ne children sholde I none upon hire geten;
Yet were me levere houndes had me eten,
Than that myn heritage sholde falle
In straunge hand, and this I telle yow alle.
I dote nat; I woot the cause why
Men sholde wedde, and forthermoore woot I
Ther speketh many a man of mariage,
That woot namoore of it than woot my page,
For whiche causes man sholde take a wyf.
If he ne may nat lyven chaast his lyf,
Take hym a wyf with greet devocioun,
Bycause of leveful procreacioun
Of children, to thonour of God above,
And nat oonly for paramour or love;
And for they sholde leccherye eschue,
And yelde hir dettes whan that they ben due;
Or for that ech of hem sholde helpen oother
In meschief, as a suster shal the brother,
And lyve in chastitee ful holily.
But sires, by youre leve, that am nat I.
For, God be thanked, I dar make avaunt,
I feele my lymes stark and suffisaunt
To do al that a man bilongeth to;
I woot myselven best what I may do.
Though I be hoor, I fare as dooth a tree
That blosmeth er that fruyt ywoxen bee;
And blosmy tre nys neither drye ne deed.
I feele me nowher hoor but on myn heed;
Myn herte and alle my lymes been as grene
As laurer thurgh the yeer is for to sene.
And syn that ye han herd al myn entente,
I prey yow to my wyl ye wole assente.

DIVERSE men diversely hym tolde
Of mariage manye ensamples olde.
Somme blamed it, somme preysed it, certeyn;
But atte laste, shortly for to seyn,
As al day falleth altercacioun
Bitwixen freendes in disputisoun,
Ther fil a stryf bitwixe his bretheren two,
Of whiche that oon was cleped Placebo,
Justinus soothly called was that oother.

PLACEBO seyde, O Januarie, brother,
Ful litel nede hadde ye, my lord so deere,
Conseil to axe of any that is heere;
But that ye been so ful of sapience,
That yow ne liketh, for youre heighe prudence,
To weyven fro the word of Salomon.
144

This word seyde he unto us everychon:
Wirk alle thyng by conseil, thus seyde he,
And thanne shaltow nat repente thee
But though that Salomon spak swich a word,
Myn owene deere brother and my lord,
So wysly God my soule brynge at reste,
I holde youre owene conseil is the beste.
For brother myn, of me taak this motyf,
I have now been a court/man al my lyf,
And, God it woot, though I unworthy be,
I have stonden in ful greet degree
Abouten lordes of ful heigh estaat;
Yet hadde I nevere with noon of hem debaat;
I nevere hem contraried, trewely;
I woot wel that my lord kan moore than I.
What that he seith, I holde it ferme and stable;
I seye the same, or elles thyng semblable.
A ful greet fool is any conseillour,
That serveth any lord of heigh honour,
That dar presume, or elles thenken it,
That his conseil sholde passe his lordes wit.
Nay, lordes been no fooles, by my fay!
Ye han youreselven seyed heer today
So heigh sentence, so holily and weel,
That I consente and conferme everydeel
Youre wordes alle, and youre opinioun.
By God, ther nys no man in al this toun,
Nyn al Ytaille, that koude bet han sayd.
Crist halt hym of this conseil wel apayd.
And trewely it is an heigh corage
Of any man that stapen is in age
To take a yong wyf; by my fader kyn,
Youre herte hangeth on a joly pyn!
Dooth now in this matiere right as yow leste,
For, finally, I holde it for the beste.

JUSTINUS, that ay stille sat and herde,
Right in this wise to Placebo answerde:
Now, brother myn, be pacient, I preye,
Syn ye han seyd, and herkneth what I seye.
Senek among his othere wordes wyse
Seith that a man oghte hym right wel avyse
To whom he yeveth his lond or his catel;
And syn I oghte avyse me right wel
To whom I yeve my good awey fro me,
Wel muchel moore I oghte avysed be
To whom I yeve my body for alwey.
I warne yow wel, it is no childes pley
To take a wyf withoute avysement.
Men moste enquere, this is myn assent,
Wher she be wys, or sobre, or dronkelewe,
Or proud, or elles ootherweys a shrewe,
A chidester, or wastour of thy good,
Or riche, or poore, or elles mannyssh wood.
Albeit so that no man fynden shal
Noon in this world that trotteth hool in al,
Ne man ne beest, which as men koude devyse;
But nathelees, it oghte ynough suffise
With any wyf, if so were that she hadde
Mo goode thewes than hire vices badde.
And al this axeth leyser for tenquere;
For, God it woot, I have wept many a teere
Ful pryvely, syn I have had a wyf.
Preyse whoso wole a wedded mannes lyf,

Certein, I fynde in it but cost and care,
And observances, of alle blisses bare.
And yet, God woot, my neighebores aboute,
And namely of wommen many a route,
Seyn that I have the mooste stedefast wyf,
And eek the mekeste oon that bereth lyf;
But I woot best where wryngeth me my sho.
Ye mowe, for me, right as yow liketh do;
Avyseth yow, ye been a man of age,
How that ye entren into mariage,
And namely with a yong wyf and a fair.
By hym that made water, erthe, and air,
The yongest man that is in al this route
Is bisy ynough to bryngen it aboute
To han his wyf allone, trusteth me.
Ye shul nat plesen hire fully yeres thre,
This is to seyn, to doon hire ful plesaunce.
A wyf axeth ful many an observaunce.
I prey yow that ye be nat yvele apayd.

WEL, quod this Januarie, & hastow
sayd?
Straw for thy Senek, and for thy
proverbes!
I counte nat a panyer ful of herbes
Of scole-termes; wyser men than
thow,
As thou hast herd, assenteden right now
To my purpos; Placebo, what sey ye?
I seye, it is a cursed man, quod he,
That letteth matrimoigne, sikerly.
And with that word they rysen sodeynly,
And been assented fully, that he sholde
Be wedded whanne hym list and wher he wolde.

NEIGH fantasye and curious bisynesse
fro day to day gan in the soule impresse
Of Januarie aboute his mariage.
Many fair shap, and many a fair visage
Ther passeth thurgh his herte, nyght by nyght.
As whoso tooke a mirour polisshed bryght,
And sette it in a commune market-place,
Thanne sholde he se ful many a figure pace
By his mirour; and, in the same wyse
Gan Januarie inwith his thoght devyse
Of maydens, whiche that dwelten hym bisyde.
He wiste nat wher that he myghte abyde.
For if that oon have beaute in hir face,
Another stant so in the peples grace
For hire sadnesse, and hire benyngnytee,
That of the peple grettest voys hath she.
And somme were riche, and hadden badde name.
But nathelees, bitwixe ernest and game,
He atte laste apoynted hym on oon,
And leet alle othere from his herte goon,
And chees hire of his owene auctoritee;
For love is blynd al day, and may nat see.
And whan that he was in his bed ybroght,
He purtreyed, in his herte and in his thoght,
Hir fresshe beautee and hir age tendre,
Hir myddel smal, hire armes longe and sklendre,
Hir wise governaunce, hir gentillesse,
Hir wommanly berynge and hire sadnesse.
And whan that he on hire was condescended,
Hym thoughte his choys myghte nat ben amended.

11

For whan that he hymself concluded hadde,
Hym thoughte ech oother mannes wit so badde,
That inpossible it were to replye
Agayn his choys; this was his fantasye.
HIS freendes sente he to, at his instaunce,
And preyed hem to doon hym that plesaunce,
That hastily they wolden to hym come;
He wolde abregge hir labour, alle and some;
Nedeth namoore for hym to go ne ryde,
He was apoynted ther he wolde abyde.
PLACEBO cam, & eek his freendes soone,
And alderfirst he bad hem alle a boone,
That noon of hem none argumentes make
Agayn the purpos which that he hath take;
Which purpos was plesant to God, seyde he,
And verray ground of his prosperitee.
NE seyde, ther was a mayden in the toun,
Which that of beautee hadde greet renoun,
Al were it so she were of smal degree;
Suffiseth hym hir yowthe and hir beautee.
Which mayde, he seyde, he wolde han to his wyf,
To lede in ese and hoolynesse his lyf.
And thanked God that he myghte han hire al,
That no wight of his blisse parten shal;
And preyde hem to labouren in this nede,
And shapen that he faille nat to spede;
For thanne, he seyde, his spirit was at ese.
Thanne is, quod he, nothyng may me displese,
Save o thyng priketh in my conscience,
The which I wol reherce in youre presence.
I HAVE, quod he, herd seyd, ful yoore ago,
Ther may no man han parfite blisses two,
This is to seye, in erthe and eek in hevene.
For though he kepe hym fro the synnes sevene,
And eek from every branche of thilke tree,
Yet is ther so parfit felicitee,
And so greet ese and lust in mariage,
That evere I am agast now in myn age,
That I shal lede now so myrie a lyf,
So delicat, withouten wo and stryf,
That I shal have myn hevene in erthe heere.
For sith that verray hevene is boght so deere
With tribulacioun and greet penaunce,
How sholde I thanne, that lyve in swich plesaunce,
As alle wedded men doon with hire wyvys,
Come to the blisse ther Crist eterne on lyve ys?
This is my drede, and ye, my bretheren tweye,
Assoilleth me this questioun, I preye.
JUSTINUS, which that hated his folye,
Answerde anon, right in his japerye;
And for he wolde his longe tale abregge,
He wolde noon auctoritee allegge,
But seyde, Sire, so ther be noon obstacle
Oother than this, God of his hygh myracle,
And of his mercy, may so for yow wirche,
That, er ye have youre right of hooly chirche,
Ye may repente of wedded mannes lyf,
In which ye seyn ther is no wo ne stryf.
And elles, God forbede but he sente
A wedded man hym grace to repente
Wel ofte rather than a sengle man.
And therfore, sire, the beste reed I kan,
Dispeire yow noght, but have in youre memorie,

145

Paraunter she may be youre purgatorie!
She may be Goddes meene, and Goddes whippe!
Thanne shal youre soule up to hevene skippe
Swifter than dooth an arwe out of the bowe!
I hope to God, herafter shul ye knowe
That ther nys no so greet felicitee
In mariage, ne nevere mo shal bee,
That yow shal lette of youre savacioun,
So that ye use, as skile is and resoun,
The lustes of youre wyf attemprely,
And that ye plese hire nat to amorously,
And that ye kepe yow eek from oother synne.
My tale is doon: for that my witte is thynne.
Beth nat agast herof, my brother deere.
But lat us waden out of this mateere.
The Wyf of Bathe, if ye han understonde,
Of mariage, which ye have on honde,
Declared hath ful wel in litel space.
Fareth now wel, God have yow in his grace.
AND with this word this Justyn & his brother
Han take hir leve, and ech of hem of oother.
For whan they saugh that it moste nedes be,
They wroghten so, by sly and wys tretee,
That she, this mayden, which that Mayus highte,
As hastily as evere that she myghte,
Shal wedded be unto this Januarie.
I trowe it were to longe yow to tarie,
If I yow tolde of every scrit and bond,
By which that she was feffed in his lond;
Or for to herknen of hir riche array.
But finally ycomen is the day
That to the chirche bothe be they went
For to receyve the hooly sacrement.
Forth comth the preest, with stole aboute his
nekke,
And bad hire be lyk Sarra and Rebekke
In wysdom and in trouthe of mariage;
And seyde his orisons as is usage,
And croucheth hem, and bad God sholde hem
blesse,
And made al siker ynogh with hoolynesse.
THUS been they wedded with
solempnitee,
And at the feeste sitteth he and she,
With other worthy folk, upon the
deys.
Al ful of joye & blisse is the paleys,
And ful of instruments, and of vitaille,
The moste deyntevous of al Ytaille.
Biforn hem stoode swich instruments of soun,
That Orpheus, ne of Thebes Amphioun,
Ne maden nevere swich a melodye.
At every cours thanne cam loud mynstralcye
That nevere tromped Joab, for to heere,
Nor he, Theodomas, yet half so cleere,
At Thebes, whan the citee was in doute.
Bacus the wyn hem skynketh al aboute,
And Venus laugheth upon every wight.
For Januarie was bicome hir knyght,
And wolde bothe assayen his corage
In libertee, and eek in mariage.
And with hire fyrbrond in hire hand aboute
Daunceth biforn the bryde and al the route.
146

And certeinly, I dar right wel seyn this,
Ymeneus, that god of weddyng is,
Saugh nevere his lyf so myrie a wedded man.
HOOLD thou thy pees, thou poete Marcian,
That writest us that ilke weddyng murie
Of hire, Philologie, and hym, Mercurie,
And of the songes that the Muses songe.
To smal is bothe thy penne, and eek thy tonge,
For to descryven of this mariage.
Whan tendre youthe hath wedded stoupyng age,
Ther is swich myrthe that it may nat be writen.
Assayeth it yourself, thanne may ye witen
If that I lye or noon in this matiere.
MAYUS, that sit with so benyngne a chiere,
Hire to biholde, it semed faierye.
Queene Ester looked nevere with swich an
eye
On Assuer, so meke a look hath she.
I may yow nat devyse al hir beautee;
But thus muche of hire beautee telle I may,
That she was lyk the brighte morwe of May,
Fulfild of alle beautee and plesaunce.
THIS Januarie is ravysshed in a traunce
At every tyme he looked on hir face;
But in his herte he gan hire to manace,
That he that nyght in armes wolde hire streyne
Harder than evere Parys dide Eleyne.
But nathelees, yet hadde he greet pitee,
That thilke nyght offenden hire moste he;
And thoughte, Allas! O tendre creature!
Now wolde God ye myghte wel endure
Al my corage, it is so sharp and keene;
I am agast ye shul it nat sustene.
But God forbede that I dide al my myght!
Now wolde God that it were woxen nyght,
And that the nyght wolde lasten everemo.
I wolde that al this peple were ago!
And finally, he dooth al his labour,
As he best myghte, savynge his honour,
To haste hem fro the mete in subtil wyse.
THE tyme cam that resoun was to ryse;
And after that, men daunce & drynken faste,
And spices al aboute the hous they caste;
And ful of joye and blisse is every man;
Al but a squyer, highte Damyan,
Which carf biforn the knyght ful many a day.
He was so ravysshed on his lady May,
That for the verray peyne he was ny wood:
Almoost he swelte and swowned ther he stood.
So soore hath Venus hurt hym with hire brond,
As that she bar it daunsynge in hire hond;
And to his bed he wente hym hastily.
Namoore of hym as at this tyme speke I;
But there I lete hym wepe ynogh and pleyne,
Til fresshe May wol rewen on his peyne.
PERILOUS fyr, that in the bed-
straw bredeth!
O famulier foo, that his servyce
bedeth!
O servant traytour, false hoomly
hewe,
Lyk to the naddre in bosom, sly, untrewe,
God shilde us alle from youre aqueyntaunce!

O Januarie, dronken in plesaunce
Of mariage, se how thy Damyan,
Thyn owene squier and thy borne man,
Entendeth for to do thee vileynye.
God graunte thee thyn hoomly fo tespye;
for in this world nys worse pestilence
Than hoomly foo al day in thy presence.

ARFOURNED hath the sonne his
ark diurne,
No lenger may the body of hym
sojurne
On thorisonte, as in that latitude.
Night with his mantel, that is derk
and rude,
Gan oversprede the hemysperie aboute;
for which departed is this lusty route
fro Januarie, with thank on every syde.
Hoom to hir houses lustily they ryde,
Wheras they doon hir thynges as hem leste,
And whan they sye hir tyme, goon to reste.

SOONE after that, this hastif Januarie
Wolde go to bedde, he wolde no lenger tarye.
He drynketh ypocras, clarree, and vernage
Of spices hoote, tencreessen his corage;
And many a letuarie hath he ful fyn,
Swiche as the cursed monk, Daun Constantyn,
Hath writen in his book, De Coitu;
To eten hem alle, he nas nothyng eschu.
And to his privee freendes thus seyde he:

FOR Goddes love, as soone as it may be,
Lat voyden al this hous in curteys wyse.
And they han doon right as he wol devyse.
Men drynken, and the travers drawe anon;
The bryde was broght abedde as stille as stoon;
And whan the bed was with the preest yblessed,
Out of the chambre hath every wight hym dressed.
And Januarie hath faste in armes take
His fresshe May, his paradys, his make.
He lulleth hire, he kisseth hire ful ofte,
With thikke brustles of his berd unsofte,
Lyk to the skyn of houndfyssh, sharpe as brere;
for he was shave al newe in his manere.
He rubbeth hire aboute hir tendre face
And seyde thus, Allas! I moot trespace
To yow, my spouse, and yow greetly offende,
Er tyme come that I wil doun descende.
But nathelees, considereth this, quod he,
Ther nys no werkman, whatsoevere he be,
That may bothe werke wel and hastily;
This wol be doon at leyser parfitly.
It is no fors how longe that we pleye;
In trewe wedlok wedded be we tweye;
And blessed be the yok that we been inne,
for in oure actes we mowe do no synne.
A man may do no synne with his wyf,
Ne hurte hymselven with his owene knyf;
for we han leve to pleye us by the lawe.

THUS laboureth he til that the day gan dawe;
And thanne he taketh a sop in fyne clarree,
And upright in his bed thanne sitteth he;
And after that he sang ful loude and cleere,
And kiste his wyf, and made wantowne cheere.
He was al coltissh, ful of ragerye,

12

And ful of jargon as a flekked pye.
The slakke skyn aboute his nekke shaketh
Whil that he sang; so chaunteth he and craketh.
But God woot what that May thoughte in hire
herte,
Whan she hym saugh up sittynge in his sherte,
In his nyght-cappe, and with his nekke lene;
She preyseth nat his pleyyng worth a bene.

THANNE seide he thus, My reste wol I take;
Now day is come, I may no lenger wake.
And doun he leyde his heed, and sleep til
pryme.
And afterward, whan that he saugh his tyme,
Up ryseth Januarie; but fresshe May
Holdeth hire chambre unto the fourthe day,
As usage is of wyves for the beste;
for every labour som tyme moot han reste,
Or elles longe may he nat endure;
This is to seyn, no lyves creature,
Be it of fyssh, or bryd, or beest, or man.

NOW wol I speke of woful Damyan,
That langwissheth for love, as ye shul heere;
Therfore I speke to hym in this manere:
I seye, O sely Damyan, allas!
Answere to my demaunde, as in this cas,
How shaltow to thy lady, fresshe May,
Telle thy wo? She wole alwey seye Nay.
Eek if thou speke, she wol thy wo biwreye;
God be thyn help, I kan no bettre seye.

This sike Damyan in Venus fyr
So brenneth, that he dyeth for desyr;
for which he putte his lyf in aventure,
No lenger myghte he in this wise endure;
But prively a penner gan he borwe,
And in a lettre wroot he al his sorwe,
In manere of a compleynt or a lay,
Unto his faire fresshe lady May;
And in a purs of silk, heng on his sherte,
He hath it put, and leyde it at his herte.

The moone that, at noon, was, thilke day
That Januarie hath wedded fresshe May,
In two of Tawr, was into Cancre glyden,
So longe hath Mayus in hir chambre byden,
As custume is unto thise nobles alle.
A bryde shal nat eten in the halle,
Til dayes foure or thre dayes atte leeste
Ypassed been; thanne lat hire go to feeste.
The fourthe day compleet fro noon to noon,
Whan that the heighe masse was ydoon,
In halle sit this Januarie, and May
As fressh as is the brighte someres day.
And so bifel, how that this goode man
Remembred hym upon this Damyan,
And seyde, Seynte Marie! how may this be,
That Damyan entendeth nat to me?
Is he ay syk? or how may this bityde?
His squieres, whiche that stooden ther bisyde,
Excused hym bycause of his siknesse,
Which letted hym to doon his bisynesse;
Noon oother cause myghte make hym tarye.

THAT me forthynketh, quod this Januarie,
He is a gentil squier, by my trouthe!
If that he deyde, it were harm and routhe;

147

He is as wys, discreet, and as secree
As any man I woot of his degree;
And therto manly and eek servysable,
And for to been a thrifty man right able.
But after mete, as soone as evere I may,
I wol myself visite hym, and eek May,
To doon hym al the confort that I kan.
⟡And for that word hym blessed every man,
That, of his bountee and his gentillesse,
He wolde so conforten in siknesse
His squier, for it was a gentil dede.
⟡Dame, quod this Januarie, taak good hede,
At after mete, ye with youre wommen alle,
Whan ye han been in chambre out of this halle,
That alle ye go se this Damyan.
Dooth hym disport, he is a gentil man;
And telleth hym that I wol hym visite,
Have I nothyng but rested me a lite;
And spede yow faste, for I wole abyde
Til that ye slepe faste by my syde.
⟡And with that word he gan to hym to calle
A squier, that was marchal of his halle,
And tolde hym certeyn thynges, what he wolde.
THIS fresshe May hath streight hir wey
yholde,
With alle hir wommen, unto Damyan.
Doun by his beddes syde sit she than,
Confortynge hym as goodly as she may.
This Damyan, whan that his tyme he say,
In secree wise his purs, and eek his bille,
In which that he ywriten hadde his wille,
Hath put into hire hand, withouten moore,
Save that he siketh wonder depe and soore,
And softely to hire right thus seyde he:
Mercy! and that ye nat discovere me,
For I am deed, if that this thyng be kyd.
⟡This purs hath she inwith hir bosom hyd,
And wente hire wey; ye gete namoore of me.
But unto Januarie ycomen is she,
That on his beddes syde sit ful softe.
He taketh hire, and kisseth hire ful ofte,
And leyde hym doun to slepe, and that anon.
She feyned hire as that she moste gon
Theras ye woot that every wight moot neede;
And whan she of this bille hath taken heede,
She rente it al to cloutes atte laste,
And in the pryvee softely it caste.
WHO studieth now but faire fresshe May?
Adoun by olde Januarie she lay,
That sleep, til that the coughe hath hym
awaked.
Anon he preyde hire strepen hire al naked;
He wolde of hire, he seyde, han som plesaunce,
And seyde, hir clothes dide hym encombraunce,
And she obeyeth, be hire lief or looth.
But, lest that precious folk be with me wrooth,
How that he wroghte, I dar nat to yow telle;
Or wheither hire thoughte it paradys or helle;
But heere I lete hem werken in hir wyse
Til evensong rong, and that they moste aryse.
⟡Were it by destynee or aventure,
Were it by influence or by nature,
Or constellacion, that in swich estaat

148

The hevene stood, that tyme fortunaat
Was for to putte a bille of Venus werkes,
For alle thyng hath tyme, as seyn thise clerkes,
To any womman, for to gete hire love,
I kan nat seye; but grete God above,
That knoweth that noon act is causelees,
He deme of al, for I wole holde my pees.
But sooth is this, how that this fresshe May
Hath take swich impression that day,
For pitee of this sike Damyan,
That from hire herte she ne dryve kan
The remembrance for to doon hym ese.
⟡Certeyn, thoghte she, whom that this thyng
displese,
I rekke noght, for heere I hym assure,
To love hym best of any creature,
Though he namoore hadde than his sherte.
⟡Lo, pitee renneth soone in gentil herte.
HEERE may ye se how excellent
franchise
In wommen is, whan they hem narwe
avyse.
Som tyrant is, as ther be many oon,
That hath an herte as hard as any
stoon,
Which wolde han lat hym sterven in the place
Wel rather than han graunted hym hire grace;
And hem rejoysen in hire crueel pryde,
And rekke nat to been an homycide.
⟡This gentil May, fulfilled of pitee,
Right of hire hand a lettre made she,
In which she graunteth hym hire verray grace;
Ther lakketh noght oonly but day and place
Wher that she myghte unto his lust suffise;
For it shal be right as he wole devyse.
And whan she saugh hir tyme, upon a day,
To visite this Damyan gooth May,
And sotilly this lettre doun she threste
Under his pilwe, rede it if hym leste.
She taketh hym by the hand, and harde hym
twiste
So secrely, that no wight of it wiste,
And bad hym been al hool; and forth she wente
To Januarie, whan that he for hire sente.
UP riseth Damyan the nexte morwe;
Al passed was his siknesse and his sorwe.
He kembeth hym, he proyneth hym and
pyketh,
He dooth al that his lady lust and lyketh;
And eek to Januarie he gooth as lowe
As evere dide a dogge for the bowe.
He is so plesant unto every man,
For craft is al, whoso that do it kan,
That every wight is fayn to speke hym good;
And fully in his lady grace he stood.
Thus lete I Damyan aboute his nede,
And in my tale forth I wol procede.
SOMME clerkes holden that felicitee
Stant in delit, and therfore certeyn he,
This noble Januarie, with al his myght,
In honeste wyse, as longeth to a knyght,
Shoop hym to lyve ful deliciously.
His housynge, his array, as honestly

To his degree was maked, as a kynges.
Amonges othere of his honeste thynges
He made a gardyn, walled al with stoon;
So fair a gardyn woot I nowher noon.
For out of doute, I verraily suppose
That he that wroot the Romance of the Rose
Ne koude of it the beautee wel devyse;
Ne Priapus ne myghte nat suffise,
Though he be god of gardyns, for to telle
The beautee of the gardyn and the welle,
That stood under a laurer alwey grene.
Ful ofte tyme he, Pluto, and his queene,
Proserpina, and al hire faierye,
Disporten hem and maken melodye
Aboute that welle, and daunced, as men tolde.
THIS noble knyght, this Januarie the olde,
Swich deyntee hath in it to walke and pleye,
That he wol no wight suffren bere the keye
Save he hymself; for of the smale wyket
He baar alwey of silver a smal clyket,
With which, whan that hym leste, he it unshette.
And whan he wolde paye his wyf hir dette
In somer sesoun, thider wolde he go,
And May his wyf, and no wight but they two;
And thynges whiche that were nat doon abedde,
He in the gardyn parfourned hem and spedde.
And in this wyse, many a murye day,
Lyved this Januarie and fresshe May.
But worldly joye may nat alwey dure
To Januarie, ne to no creature.

O SODEYN hap! O thou Fortune
instable!
Lyk to the scorpioun so deceyvable
That flaterest with thyn heed whan
thou wolt stynge;
Thy tayl is deeth, thurgh thyn en-
venymynge.
O brotil joye! O sweete venym queynte!
O monstre, that so subtilly kanst peynte
Thy yiftes, under hewe of stidefastnesse,
That thou deceyvest bothe moore and lesse!
Why hastow Januarie thus deceyved,
That haddest hym for thy ful freend receyved?
And now thou hast biraft hym bothe his eyen,
For sorwe of which desireth he to dyen.
Allas! this noble Januarie free,
Amydde his lust and his prosperitee,
Is woxen blynd, and that al sodeynly!
He wepeth and he wayleth pitously;
And therwithal the fyr of jalousye,
Lest that his wyf sholde falle in som folye,
So brente his herte, that he wolde fayn
That som man bothe hym and hire had slayn;
For neither after his deeth, nor in his lyf,
Ne wolde he that she were love ne wyf,
But evere lyve as wydwe in clothes blake,
Soul as the turtle that lost hath hire make.
BUT atte laste, after a monthe or tweye,
His sorwe gan aswage, sooth to seye;
For whan he wiste it may noon oother be,
He paciently took his adversitee;
Save, out of doute, he may nat forgoon
That he nas jalous everemoore in oon.

l 3

Which jalousye it was so outrageous,
That neither in halle, nyn noon oother hous,
Ne in noon oother place, neverthemo,
He nolde suffre hire for to ryde or go,
But if that he had hond on hire alway;
For which ful ofte wepeth fresshe May,
That loveth Damyan so benyngnely
That she moot outher dyen sodeynly,
Or elles she moot han hym as hir leste;
She wayteth whan hir herte wolde breste.
UPON that oother syde Damyan
Bicomen is the sorwefulleste man
That evere was; for neither nyght ne day
Ne myghte he speke a word to fresshe May,
As to his purpos, of no swich mateere,
But if that Januarie moste it heere,
That hadde an hand upon hire evermo.
But nathelees, by writyng to and fro
And privee signes, wiste he what she mente;
And she knew eek the fyn of his entente.

O JANUARIE! what myghte it thee
availle,
Thou myghtest se as fer as shippes
saille?
For also good is blynd deceyved be,
As be deceyved whan a man may se.
Lo, Argus, which that hadde an hondred eyen,
For al that evere he koude poure or pryen,
Yet was he blent; and, God woot, so been mo,
That wenen wisly that it be nat so.
Passe over is an ese, I sey namoore.
This fresshe May, that I spak of so yoore,
In warm wex hath emprented the clyket
That Januarie bar of the smale wyket,
By which into his gardyn ofte he wente.
And Damyan, that knew al hire entente,
The cliket countrefeted pryvely;
Ther nys namoore to seye; but hastily
Som wonder by this clyket shal bityde,
Which ye shul heeren, if ye wole abyde.

O NOBLE Ovyde! ful sooth seystou,
God woot!
What sleighte is it, thogh it be long
and hoot,
That he nyl fynde it out in som
manere?
By Piramus and Tesbee may men leere;
Thogh they were kept ful longe streite overal,
They been accorded, rownynge thurgh a wal,
Ther no wight koude han founde out swich a
sleighte.
BUT now to purpos: er that dayes eighte
Were passed, er the monthe of Juyl, bifille
That Januarie hath caught so greet a wille,
Thurgh eggyng of his wyf, hym for to pleye
In his gardyn, and no wight but they tweye,
That in a morwe unto this May seith he:
Rys up, my wyf, my love, my lady free;
The turtles voys is herd, my dowve sweete;
The wynter is goon, with alle his reynes weete;
Com forth now, with thyne eyen columbyn!
How fairer been thy brestes than is wyn!
The gardyn is enclosed al aboute;

Com forth, my white spouse! for out of doute,
Thou hast me wounded in myn herte, O wyf!
No spot of thee ne knew I al my lyf;
Come forth, and lat us taken som disport;
I chees thee for my wyf and my confort!
Swiche olde lewed wordes used he.
ON Damyan a signe made she,
That he sholde go biforen with his cliket:
This Damyan thanne hath opened the
wyket,
And in he stirte, and that in swich manere,
That no wight myght it se neither yheere;
And stille he sit under a bussh anoon.
THIS Januarie, as blynd as is a stoon,
With Mayus in his hand, and no wight mo,
Into his fresshe gardyn is ago,
And clapte to the wyket sodeynly.
Now, wyf, quod he, heere nys but thou and I,
That art the creature that I best love;
For, by that Lord that sit in hevene above,
Levere ich hadde to dyen on a knyf,
Than thee offende, trewe deere wyf.
For Goddes sake, thenk how I thee chees,
Noght for no coveitise, doutelees,
But oonly for the love I had to thee.
And though that I be oold, and may nat see,
Beth to me trewe, and I shal telle yow why.
Thre thynges, certes, shul ye wynne therby;
First, love of Crist, and to yourself honour,
And al myn heritage, toun and tour;
I yeve it yow, maketh chartres as yow leste;
This shal be doon tomorwe er sonne reste.
So wisly God my soule brynge in blisse,
I prey yow first, in covenant ye me kisse.
And though that I be jalous, wyte me noght.
Ye been so depe enprented in my thoght,
That, whan that I considere youre beautee,
And therwithal the unlikly elde of me,
I may nat, certes, though I sholde dye,
Forbere to been out of youre compaignye
For verray love; this is withouten doute.
Now kys me, wyf, and lat us rome aboute.
THIS fresshe May, whan she thise wordes
herde,
Benyngnely to Januarie answerde;
But first and forward, she bigan to wepe:
I have, quod she, a soule for to kepe
As wel as ye, and also myn honour,
And of my wyfhod thilke tendre flour,
Which that I have assured in your hond
Whan that the preest to yow my body bond;
Wherfore I wole answere in this manere,
By the leve of yow, my lord so deere,
I prey to God that nevere dawe the day
That I ne sterve, as foule as womman may,
If evere I do unto my kyn that shame,
Or elles I empeyre so my name,
That I be fals; and if I do that lakke,
Do strepe me and put me in a sakke,
And in the nexte ryver do me drenche.
I am a gentil womman and no wenche!
Why speke ye thus? But men been evere untrewe,
And wommen have repreve of yow ay newe.

Ye han noon oother contenance, I leeve,
But speke to us of untrust and repreeve.
And with that word she saugh wher Damyan
Sat in the bussh, and coughen she bigan,
And with hir fynger signes made she
That Damyan sholde clymbe upon a tree,
That charged was with fruyt, and up he wente;
For verraily he knew al hire entente
And every signe that she koude make
Wel bet than Januarie, hir owene make.
For in a lettre she hadde toold hym al
Of this matere, how he werchen shal.
And thus I lete hym sitte upon the pyrie,
And Januarie and May rominge myrie.
BRIGHT was the day, and blew the
firmament,
Phebus of gold his stremes doun
hath sent
To gladen every flour with his warm/
nesse.
He was that tyme in Geminis, as I gesse,
But litel fro his declynacioun
Of Cancer, Jovis exaltacioun.
And so bifel, that brighte morwe/tyde,
That in that gardyn, in the ferther syde,
Pluto, that is the kyng of faierye,
And many a lady in his compaignye,
Folwynge his wyf, the queene Proserpyne,
Ech after oother, right as ony lyne,
Whil that she gadered floures in the mede,
In Claudyan ye may the stories rede,
How in his grisely carte he hire fette.
This kyng of fairye thanne adoun hym sette
Upon a bench of turves, fressh and grene,
And right anon thus seyde he to his queene:
My wyf, quod he, ther may no wight sey nay,
Thexperience so preveth every day
The tresons whiche that wommen doon to man.
Ten hondred thousand stories tellen I kan
Notable of youre untrouthe and brotilnesse.
O Salomon, wys, and richest of richesse,
Fulfild of sapience and of worldly glorie,
Ful worthy been thy wordes to memorie
To every wight that wit and reson kan.
Thus preiseth he yet the bountee of man:
Amonges a thousand men yet foond I oon,
But of wommen alle foond I noon.
THUS seith the kyng that knoweth youre
wikkednesse,
And Jhesus filius Syrak, as I gesse,
Ne speketh of yow but seelde reverence.
A wylde fyr and corrupt pestilence
So falle upon youre bodyes yet tonyght!
Ne se ye nat this honurable knyght?
Bycause, allas! that he is blynd and old,
His owene man shal make hym cokewold.
Lo, heere he sit, the lechour, in the tree!
Now wol I graunten, of my magestee,
Unto this olde, blynde, worthy knyght,
That he shal have ayeyn his eyen syght,
Whan that his wyf wold doon hym vileynye;
Thanne shal he knowen al hire harlotrye
Bothe in repreve of hire and othere mo.

Ye shal? quod Proserpyne; wol ye so?
Now by my moodres sires soule I swere,
That I shal yeven hire suffisant answere,
And alle wommen after, for hir sake;
That, though they be in any gilt ytake,
With face boold they shulle hemself excuse,
And bere hem doun that wolden hem accuse;
for lakke of answere, noon of hem shal dyen.
Al hadde man seyn a thyng with bothe his eyen,
Yit shul we wommen visage it hardily,
And wepe, and swere, and chide subtilly,
So that ye men shul been as lewed as gees.
What rekketh me of youre auctoritees?
I woot wel that this Jew, this Salomon,
foond of us wommen fooles many oon.
But though that he ne foond no good womman,
Yet hath ther founde many another man
Wommen ful trewe, ful goode, and vertuous.
Witnesse on hem that dwelle in Cristes hous;
With martirdom they preved hire constance.
The Romayn Geestes maken remembrance
Of many a verray trewe wyf also.
But, sire, ne be nat wrooth, albeit so,
Though that he seyde he foond no good womman,
I prey yow take the sentence of the man;
He mente thus, that in sovereyn bontee
Nis noon but God, that sit in Trinitee,
Ey! for verray God, that nys but oon,
What make ye so muche of Salomon?
What though he made a temple, Goddes hous?
What though he were riche and glorious?
So made he eek a temple of false goddis,
How myghte he do a thyng that moore forbode is?
Pardee! as faire as ye his name emplastre,
He was a lecchour and an ydolastre,
And in his elde he verray God forsook.
And if that God ne hadde, as seith the book,
Yspared hym for his fadres sake, he sholde
Have lost his regne rather than he wolde.
I sette right noght of al the vileynye
That ye of wommen write, a boterflye!
I am a womman, nedes moot I speke,
Or elles swelle til myn herte breke.
for sithen he seyde that we been jangleresses,
As evere hool I moote brouke my tresses,
I shal nat spare, for no curteisye,
To speke hym harm that wolde us vileynye!

DAME, quod this Pluto, be no lenger wrooth;
I yeve it up! but sith I swoor myn ooth
That I wolde graunten hym his sighte ageyn,
My word shal stonde, I warne yow, certeyn.
I am a kyng, it sit me noght to lye!
And I, quod she, a queene of faierye!
Hir answere shal she have, I undertake;
Lat us namoore wordes heerof make.
forsothe, I wol no lenger yow contrarie.

NOW lat us turne agayn to Januarie,
That in the gardyn with his faire May
Syngeth, ful murier than the papejay:
Yow love I best, and shal, and oother
noon.
So longe aboute the aleyes is he
goon,

14

Til he was come agaynes thilke pyrie
Wheras this Damyan sitteth ful myrie
An heigh, among the fresshe leves grene.
This fresshe May, that is so bright and sheene,
Gan for to syke, and seyde, Allas, my syde!
Now sire, quod she, for aught that may bityde,
I moste han of the peres that I see,
Or I moot dye, so soore longeth me
To eten of the smale peres grene.
Help, for hir love that is of hevene queene!
I telle yow wel, a womman in my plit
May han to fruyt so greet an appetit,
That she may dyen, but she of it have.
Allas! quod he, that I ne had heer a knave
That koude clymbe; Allas! allas! quod he,
That I am blynd. Ye, sire, no fors, quod she:
But wolde ye vouchesauf, for Goddes sake,
The pyrie inwith youre armes for to take,
for wel I woot that ye mystruste me,
Thanne sholde I clymbe wel ynogh, quod she,
So I my foot myghte sette upon youre bak.
Certes, quod he, theron shal be no lak,
Mighte I yow helpen with myn herte blood!
He stoupeth doun, and on his bak she stood,
And caughte hire by a twiste, and up she gooth.
Ladyes, I prey yow that ye be nat wrooth;
I kan nat glose, I am a rude man.
And sodeynly anon this Damyan
Gan pullen up the smok, and in he throng.
And whan that Pluto saugh this grete wrong,
To Januarie he yaf agayn his sighte,
And made hym se as wel as evere he myghte.
And whan that he hadde caught his sighte agayn,
Ne was ther nevere man of thyng so fayn,
But on his wyf his thoght was everemo;
Up to the tree he caste his eyen two,
And saugh that Damyan his wyf had dressed
In swich manere, it may nat been expressed
But if I wolde speke uncurteisly.
And up he yaf a roryng and a cry,
As dooth the mooder whan the child shal dye:
Out! help! allas! harrow! he gan to crye,
O stronge lady stoore, what dostow?
And she answerde, Sire, what eyleth yow?
Have pacience, and resoun in youre mynde,
I have yow holpe on bothe youre eyen
blynde,
Up peril of my soule, I shal nat lyen,
As me was taught, to heele with youre eyen,
Was nothyng bet to make yow to see
Than strugle with a man upon a tree.
God woot, I dide it in ful good entente.
Strugle! quod he, ye, algate in it wente!
God yeve yow bothe on shames deth to dyen!
He swyved thee, I saugh it with myne eyen,
And elles be I hanged by the hals!
Thanne is, quod she, my medicyne fals,
for certeinly, if that ye myghte se,
Ye wolde nat seyn thise wordes unto me;
Ye han som glymsyng, and no parfit sighte.
I se, quod he, as wel as evere I myghte,
Thonked be God! with bothe myne eyen two,
And, by my trouthe, me thoughte he dide thee so.

151

Ye maze, maze, goode sire, quod she;
This thank have I for I have maad yow see;
Allas! quod she, that evere I was so kynde!
Now, dame, quod he, lat al passe out of
mynde.
Com doun, my lief, and if I have myssayd,
God help me so, as I am yvele apayd.
But, by my fader soule! I wende han seyn,
How that this Damyan had by thee leyn,
And that thy smok had leyn upon his brest.
Ye, sire, quod she, ye may wene as yow lest;
But, sire, a man that waketh out of his sleep,
He may nat sodeynly wel taken keep
Upon a thyng, ne seen it parfitly,
Til that he be adawed verraily;
Right so a man, that longe hath blynd ybe,
Ne may nat sodeynly so wel yse,
First whan his sighte is newe come ageyn,
As he that hath a day or two yseyn,
Til that youre sighte ysatled be a while,
Ther may ful many a sighte yow bigile.
Beth war, I prey yow; for, by hevene kyng,
Ful many a man weneth to seen a thyng,
And it is al another than it semeth.
He that mysconceyveth, he mysdemeth.
And with that word she leep doun fro the
tree.
This Januarie, who is glad but he?
He kisseth hire, and clippeth hire ful ofte,
And on hire wombe he stroketh hire ful
softe;
And to his palays hoom he hath hire lad.
Now, goode men, I pray yow to be glad.
Thus endeth heere my tale of Januarie;
God blesse us, and his mooder Seinte Marie!
Heere is ended the Marchantes Tale of
Januarie.

Words of the Host to the Squire
Y! Goddes mercy!
seyde oure Hoost tho,
Now swich a wyf I
pray God kepe me fro!
Lo, whiche sleightes
and subtilitees
In wommen been! for
ay as bisy as bees
Been they, us sely men
for to deceyve;
And from a sothe evere wol they weyve.
By this Marchauntes tale it preveth weel.
But doutelees, as trewe as any steel
I have a wyf, though that she povre be;
But of hir tonge a labbyng shrewe is she,
And yet she hath an heep of vices mo;
Therof no fors, lat alle swiche thynges go.
But wyte ye what? In conseil be it seyd,
Me reweth soore I am unto hire teyd;
For, and I sholde rekenen every vice
Which that she hath, ywis, I were to nyce,
And cause why; it sholde reported be
And toold to hire of somme of this meynee;
Of whom, it nedeth nat for to declare,
Syn wommen konnen outen swich chaffare;
And eek my wit suffiseth nat therto
To tellen al; wherfore my tale is do.
SQUIER, come neer, if it youre wille be,
And sey somwhat of love; for certes, ye
Konnen theron as muche as any man.
Nay, sir, quod he, but I wol seye as I kan
With hertly wyl; for I wol nat rebelle
Agayn youre lust; a tale wol I telle.
Have me excused, if I speke amys,
My wyl is good; and lo, my tale is this.

HEERE BIGYNNETH THE SQUIERES TALE

Incipit prima pars

SARRAY, IN THE LAND OF Tartarye,
Ther dwelte a kyng, that werreyed Russye,

Thurgh which ther deyde many a doughty
man.
This noble kyng was cleped Cambynskan,
Which in his tyme was of so greet renoun
That ther was nowher in no regioun
So excellent a lord in alle thyng;
Hym lakked noght that longeth to a kyng.
As of the secte of which that he was born
He kepte his lay, to which that he was
sworn;
And therto he was hardy, wys, and riche,
And piëtous and just, alwey yliche;
Sooth of his word, benigne and honurable,
Of his corage as any centre stable;
Yong, fressh, and strong, in armes desirous
As any bacheler of al his hous.
A fair persone he was, and fortunat,
And kepte alwey so wel roial estat
That ther was nowher swich another man.
This noble kyng, this Tartre Cambynskan
Hadde two sones on Elpheta his wyf,
Of whiche the eldeste highte Algarsyf,

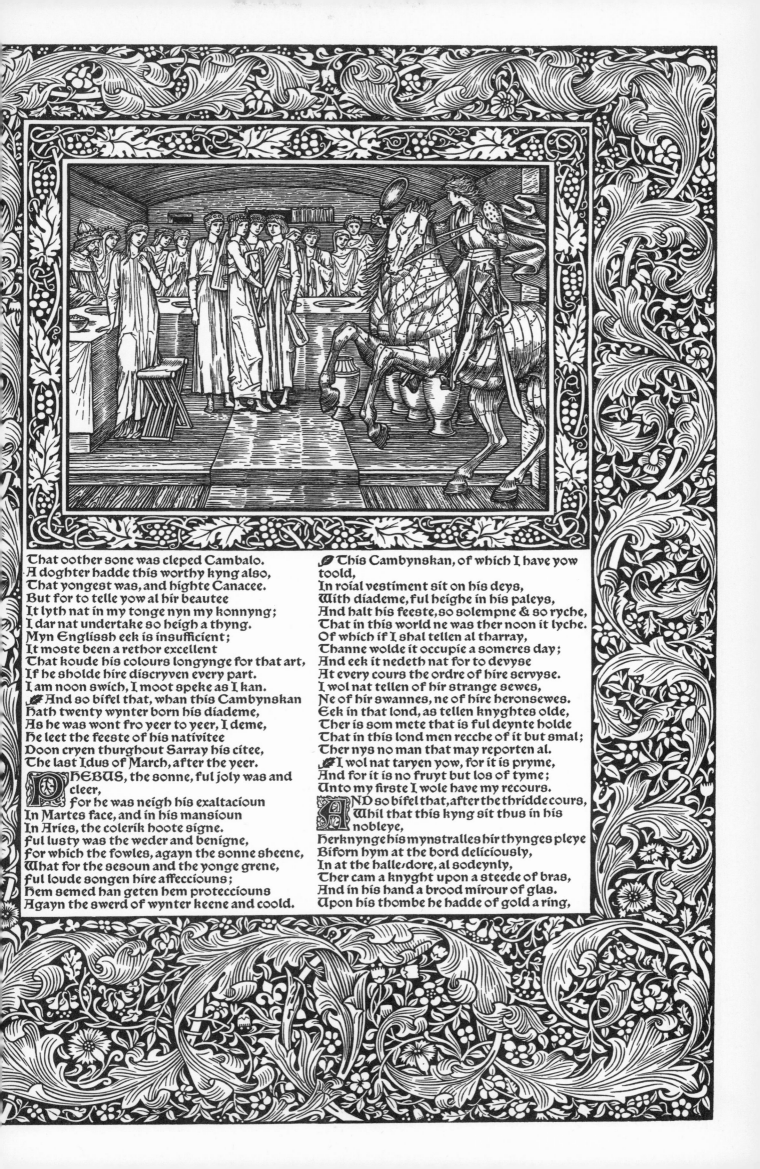

That oother sone was cleped Cambalo.
A doghter hadde this worthy kyng also,
That yongest was, and highte Canacee.
But for to telle yow al hir beautee
It lyth nat in my tonge nyn my konnyng;
I dar nat undertake so heigh a thyng.
Myn Englissh eek is insufficient;
It moste been a rethor excellent
That koude his colours longynge for that art,
If he sholde hire discryven every part.
I am noon swich, I moot speke as I kan.
And so bifel that, whan this Cambynskan
Hath twenty wynter born his diademe,
As he was wont fro yeer to yeer, I deme,
He leet the feeste of his nativitee
Doon cryen thurghout Sarray his citee,
The last Idus of March, after the yeer.
PHEBUS, the sonne, ful joly was and
cleer,
for he was neigh his exaltacioun
In Martes face, and in his mansioun
In Aries, the colerik hoote signe.
ful lusty was the weder and benigne,
for which the fowles, agayn the sonne sheene,
What for the sesoun and the yonge grene,
ful loude songen hire affecciouns;
Hem semed han geten hem protecciouns
Agayn the swerd of wynter keene and coold.

This Cambynskan, of which I have yow
toold,
In roial vestiment sit on his deys,
With diademe, ful heighe in his paleys,
And halt his feeste, so solempne & so ryche,
That in this world ne was ther noon it lyche.
Of which if I shal tellen al tharray,
Thanne wolde it occupie a someres day;
And eek it nedeth nat for to devyse
At every cours the ordre of hire servyse.
I wol nat tellen of hir strange sewes,
Ne of hir swannes, ne of hire heronsewes.
Eek in that lond, as tellen knyghtes olde,
Ther is som mete that is ful deynte holde
That in this lond men recche of it but smal;
Ther nys no man that may reporten al.
I wol nat taryen yow, for it is pryme,
And for it is no fruyt but los of tyme;
Unto my firste I wole have my recours.
AND so bifel that, after the thridde cours,
Whil that this kyng sit thus in his
nobleye,
Herknynge his mynstralles hir thynges pleye
Biforn hym at the bord deliciously,
In at the halle-dore, al sodeynly,
Ther cam a knyght upon a steede of bras,
And in his hand a brood mirour of glas.
Upon his thombe he hadde of gold a ring,

And by his syde a naked swerd hangyng;
And up he rideth to the heighe bord.
In al the halle ne was ther spoken a word
For merveille of this knyght; hym to biholde
Ful bisily ther wayten yonge and olde.
THIS strange knyght, that cam thus sodeynly,
Al armed save his heed ful richely,
Saleweth kyng and queene, and lordes alle,
By ordre, as they seten in the halle,
With so heigh reverence and obeisaunce,
As wel in speche as in his contenaunce,
That Gawayn, with his olde curteisye,
Though he were come ageyn out of Fairye,
Ne koude hym nat amende with a word.
And after this, biforn the heighe bord,
He with a manly voys seith his message
After the forme used in his langage,
Withouten vice of silable or of lettre;
And, for his tale sholde seme the bettre,
Accordant to his wordes was his cheere,
As techeth art of speche hem that it leere.
Albeit that I kan nat sowne his stile,
Ne kan nat clymben over so heigh a style,
Yet seye I this, as to commune entente,
Thus muche amounteth al that evere he mente,
If it so be that I have it in mynde.
HE seyde, The kyng of Arabie and of Inde,
My lige lord, on this solempne day
Saleweth yow, as he best kan & may,
And sendeth yow, in honour of youre feeste,
By me, that am al redy at youre heeste,
This steede of bras, that esily and weel
Kan, in the space of o day natureel,
This is to seyn, in foure and twenty houres,
Wherso yow lyst, in droghte or elles shoures,
Beren youre body into every place
To which youre herte wilneth for to pace,
Withouten wem of yow, thurgh foul or fair;
Or, if yow lyst to fleen as hye in the air
As dooth an egle whan that hym list to soore,
This same steede shal bere yow everemoore,
Withouten harm, til ye be ther yow leste,
Though that ye slepen on his bak or reste;
And turne ayeyn with writhyng of a pyn.
He that it wroghte koude ful many a gyn;
He wayted many a constellacioun
Er he had doon this operacioun;
And knew ful many a seel, and many a bond.
THIS mirrour eek, that I have in myn hond,
Hath swich a myght that men may in it see
Whan ther shal fallen any adversitee
Unto youre regne, or to youreself also;
And openly who is youre freend or foo.
And over al this, if any lady bright
Hath set hire herte on any maner wight,
If he be fals, she shal his tresoun see,
His newe love and al his subtiltee
So openly, that ther shal nothyng hyde.
Wherfore, ageyn this lusty someres tyde,
This mirour and this ryng, that ye may see,
He hath sent to my lady Canacee,
Youre excellente doghter that is heere.

154

THE vertu of the ryng, if ye wol heere,
Is this; that if hire lust it for to were
Upon hir thombe, or in hir purs it bere,
Ther is no fowel that fleeth under the hevene
That she ne shal wel understonde his stevene,
And knowe his menyng openly and pleyn,
And answere hym in his langage ageyn.
And every gras that groweth upon roote
She shal eek knowe, and whom it wol do boote,
Al be his woundes never so depe and wyde.
THIS naked swerd that hangeth by my syde,
Swich vertu hath, that what man so ye smyte,
Thurghout his armure it wole kerve and byte,
Were it as thikke as is a branched ook;
And what man that is wounded with the strook
Shal never be hool til that yow list, of grace,
To stroke hym with the plat in thilke place
Ther he is hurt: this is as muche to seyn,
Ye moote with the platte swerd ageyn
Stroke hym in the wounde, and it wol close.
This is a verray sooth, withouten glose,
It failleth nat whils it is in youre hoold.
AND whan this knyght hath thus his tale toold,
He rideth out of halle, and doun he lighte.
His steede, which that shoon as sonne brighte,
Stant in the court, as stille as any stoon.
This knyght is to his chambre lad anoon
And is unarmed and unto mete yset.
The presentes been ful roially yfet,
This is to seyn, the swerd and the mirour,
And born anon into the heighe tour
With certeine officers ordeyned therfore;
And unto Canacee this ryng was bore
Solempnely, ther she sit at the table.
But sikerly, withouten any fable,
The hors of bras, that may nat be remewed,
It stant as it were to the ground yglewed.
Ther may no man out of the place it dryve
For noon engyn of wyndas ne polyve;
And cause why, for they kan nat the craft.
And therfore in the place they han it laft,
Til that the knyght hath taught hem the manere
To voyden hym, as ye shal after heere.
GREET was the prees that swarmeth to and fro
To gauren on this hors that stondeth so;
For it so heigh was, and so brood and long,
So wel proporcioned for to been strong,
Right as it were a steede of Lumbardye;
Therwith so horsly, and so quyk of eye,
As it a gentil Poilleys courser were.
For certes, fro his tayl unto his ere,
Nature ne art ne koude hym nat amende
In no degree, as al the peple wende.
But everemoore hir mooste wonder was,
How that it koude goon, and was of bras;
It was of Fairye, as the peple semed.
Diverse folk diversely they demed;
As many heddes, as manye wittes ther been.
They murmureden as dooth a swarm of been,
And maden skiles after hir fantasies,

Rehersynge of thise olde poetries;
And seyde that it was lyk the Pegasee,
The hors that hadde wynges for to flee;
Or elles it was the Grekes hors Synoun,
That broghte Troie to destruccioun,
As men in thise olde geestes rede.

MYN herte, quod oon, is everemoore in drede;
I trowe som men of armes been therinne,
That shapen hem this citee for to wynne.
It were right good that al swich thyng were knowe.

Another rowned to his felawe lowe,
And seyde, He lyeth! it is rather lyk
An apparence ymaad by som magyk,
As jogelours pleyen at thise feestes grete.

Of sondry doutes thus they jangle and trete,
As lewed peple demeth comunly
Of thynges that been maad moore subtilly
Than they kan in hir lewednesse comprehende;
They demen gladly to the badder ende.

And somme of hem wondred on the mirour,
That born was up into the maister tour,
How men myghte in it swiche thynges se.

Another answerde, and seyde it myghte wel be
Naturelly, by composiciouns
Of anglis, and of slye reflexiouns;
And seyden, that in Rome was swich oon.
They speken of Alocen and Vitulon,
And Aristotle, that writen in hir lyves
Of queynte mirours and of prospectives,
As knowen they that han hir bookes herd.

AND oother folk han wondred on the swerd
That wolde percen thurghout every thyng;
And fille in speche of Thelophus the kyng,
And of Achilles with his queynte spere,
For he koude with it bothe heele and dere,
Right in swich wise as men may with the swerd
Of which right now ye han yourselven herd.
They speken of sondry hardyng of metal,
And speke of medicynes therwithal,
And how and whanne it sholde yharded be,
Which is unknowe algates unto me.

THO speke they of Canacees ryng,
And seyden alle, that swich a wonder thyng
Of craft of rynges herde they nevere noon;
Save that he, Moyses, and kyng Salomon
Hadde a name of konnyng in swich art.
Thus seyn the peple, and drawen hem apart.

But nathelees, somme seiden that it was
Wonder to maken of fern asshen glas,
And yet nys glas nat lyk asshen of fern;
But for they han yknowen it so fern,
Therfore cesseth hir janglyng and hir wonder.
As soore wondren somme on cause of thonder,
On ebbe, on flood, on gossomer, and on myst,
And alle thyng, til that the cause is wyst.
Thus jangle they, and demen and devyse.
Til that the kyng gan fro the bord aryse.

PHEBUS hath laft the angle meridional,
And yet ascendyng was the beest roial,
The gentil Leon, with his Aldiran,
Whan that this Tartre kyng, this Cambynskan,
Roos fro his bord, ther that he sat ful hye.
Toforn hym gooth the loude mynstralcye

Til he cam to his chambre of parements,
Theras they sownen diverse instruments
That it is lyk an hevene for to heere.
Now dauncen lusty Venus children deere,
For in the fyssh hir lady sat ful hye,
And looketh on hem with a freendly eye.

THIS noble kyng is set up in his trone;
This strange knyght is fet to hym ful sone,
And on the daunce he gooth with Canacee.
Heere is the revel and the jolitee
That is nat able a dul man to devyse.
He moste han knowen love and his servyse,
And been a feestlych man as fressh as May,
That sholde yow devysen swich array.
Who koude telle yow the forme of ddaunces
So unkouthe and so fresshe contenaunces,
Swich subtil lookyng and dissymulynges
For drede of jalouse mennes aperceyvynges?
No man but Launcelot, and he is deed.
Therfore I passe of al this lustiheed;
I sey namoore, but in this jolynesse
I lete hem, til men to the soper dresse.

THE styward bit the spices for to hye,
And eek the wyn, in al this melodye.
The usshers and the squiers been ygoon,
The spices and the wyn is come anoon.
They ete and drynke, and whan this hadde an ende,
Unto the temple, as reson was, they wende.
The service doon, they soupen al by day;
What nedeth me rehercen hire array?
Ech man woot wel, that at a kynges feeste
Hath plentee, to the mooste and to the leeste,
And deyntees mo than been in my knowyng.

AT after soper gooth this noble kyng
To seen this hors of bras, with al the route
Of lordes and of ladyes hym aboute.
Swich wondryng was ther on this hors of bras
That, syn the grete sege of Troie was,
Theras men wondreden on an hors also,
Ne was ther swich a wondryng as was tho.
But fynally the kyng axeth this knyght
The vertu of this courser and the myght,
And preyde hym to telle his governaunce.

THIS hors anoon bigan to trippe and daunce
Whan that this knyght leyde hand upon his reyne,
And seyde, Sire, ther is namoore to seyne,
But, whan yow list to ryden anywhere,
Ye mooten trille a pyn stant in his ere,
Which I shal telle yow bitwix us two.
Ye moote nempne hym to what place also
Or to what contree that yow list to ryde.
And whan ye come ther as yow list abyde,
Bidde hym descende, and trille another pyn,
For therin lith theffect of al the gyn,
And he wol doun descende and doon youre wille;
And in that place he wol abyde stille,
Though al the world the contrarie hadde yswore;
He shal nat thennes been ydrawe ne ybore.
Or, if yow liste bidde hym thennes goon,
Trille this pyn, and he wol vanysshe anoon
Out of the sighte of every maner wight,
And come agayn, be it by day or nyght,
Whan that yow list to clepen hym ageyn

In swich a gyse as I shal to yow seyn
Bitwixe yow and me, and that ful soone.
Ride whan yow list, ther is namoore to doone.
ENFORMED whan the kyng was of
that knyght,
And hath conceyved in his wit aright
The manere and the forme of al this thyng,
ful glad and blithe, this noble doughty kyng
Repeireth to his revel as biforn.

THE brydel is unto the tour yborn
And kept among his jueles leeve and
deere,
The hors vanysshed, I noot in what manere,
Out of hir sighte; ye gete namoore of me;
But thus I lete in lust and jolitee
This Cambynskan his lordes festeyinge,
Til that wel ny the day bigan to sprynge.
Explicit prima pars. Sequitur pars secunda.

HEN
NORICE OF DIGESTIOUN, the sleepe,
Gan on hem wynke, & bad hem taken keepe,
That muchel drynke & labour wolde han reste;
And with a galpyng mouth hem alle he keste,
And seyde, it was tyme to lye adoun,
for blood was in his domynacioun.
Cherisseth blood, natures freend, quod
he,
They thanken hym galpynge, by two, by thre,
And every wight gan drawe hym to his reste
As sleep hem bad; they tooke it for the beste.

HIRE dremes shal nat been ytoold for
me;
ful were hire heddes of fumositee,
That causeth dreem, of which ther nys no
charge.
They slepen til that it was pryme large,
The mooste part, but it were Canacee.

SHE was ful mesurable, as wommen be;
For of hir fader hadde she take leve
To goon to reste, soone after it was eve.
Hir liste nat appalled for to be,
Ne on the morwe unfeestlich for to se;
And slepte hire firste sleep, and thanne awook.
For swich a joye she in hir herte took
Bothe of hir queynte ryng and hire mirour,
That twenty tyme she changed hir colour;
And in hire sleepe, right for impressioun
Of hire mirour, she hadde a visioun.
Wherfore, er that the sonne gan up glyde,
She cleped on hir maistresse hire bisyde,
And seyde, that hire liste for to ryse.

THISE olde wommen that been gladly wyse,
As is hire maistresse, answerde hire anon,
And seyde, Madame, whider wil ye goon
Thus erly? for the folk been alle on reste.
I wol, quod she, arise, for me leste
No lenger for to slepe, and walke aboute.
Hire maistresse clepeth wommen a greet route,
And up they rysen, wel a ten or twelve;
Up riseth fresshe Canacee hirselve,
As rody and bright as dooth the yonge sonne,
That in the Ram is foure degrees up ronne;
Noon hyer was he, whan she redy was;
And forth she walketh esily a pas,
Arrayed after the lusty sesoun soote
Lightly, for to pleye and walke on foote,
Nat but with fyve or sixe of hir meynee,
And in a trench, forth in the park, gooth she.
The vapour, which that fro the erthe glood,
Made the sonne to seme rody and brood;
But nathelees, it was so fair a sighte
That it made alle hire hertes for to lighte,
What for the sesoun, and the morwenynge,
And for the foweles that she herde synge;
For right anon she wiste what they mente
Right by hir song, and knew al hire entente.

THE knotte, why that every tale is toold,
If it be taried til that lust be coold
Of hem that han it after herkned yoore,
The savour passeth ever lenger the moore,
For fulsomnesse of his prolixitee;
And by the same resoun thynketh me,
I sholde to the knotte condescende,
And maken of hir walkyng soone an ende.

AMYDDE a tree fordrye, as whit as chalk,
As Canacee was pleyyng in hir walk,
Ther sat a faucon over hire heed ful hye,
That with a pitous voys so gan to crye
That all the wode resouned of hire cry.
Ybeten hath she hirself so pitously
With bothe hir wynges til the rede blood
Ran endelong the tree theras she stood.
And evere in oon she cryde alwey and shrighte,
And with hir beek hirselven so she prighte,
That ther nys tygre, ne noon so cruel beste,

That dwelleth outher in wode or in foreste
That nolde han wept, if that he wepe koude,
For sorwe of hire, she shrighte alwey so loude.
For ther nas nevere yet no man on lyve,
If that I koude a faucon wel discryve,
That herde of swich another of fairnesse,
As wel of plumage as of gentillesse
Of shap, and al that myghte yrekened be.
A faucon peregryn thanne semed she
Of fremde land; and everemoore, as she stood,
She swowneth now and now for lakke of blood,
Til wel neigh is she fallen fro the tree.

THIS faire kynges doghter, Canacee,
That on hir fynger baar the queynte ryng,
Thurgh which she understood wel every thyng
That any fowel may in his ledene seyn,
And koude answere hym in his ledene ageyn,
Hath understonde what this faucon seyde,
And wel neigh for the routhe almoost she deyde.
And to the tree she gooth ful hastily,
And on this faukon looketh pitously,
And heeld hir lappe abrood, for wel she wiste
That faukon moste fallen fro the twiste,
Whan that it swowned next, for lakke of blood.
A longe while to wayten hire she stood,
Til atte laste she spak in this manere
Unto the hauk, as ye shal after heere:

WHAT is the cause, if it be for to telle,
That ye be in this furial pyne of helle?
Quod Canacee unto the hauk above.
Is this for sorwe of deeth, or los of love?
For, as I trowe, thise been causes two
That causen moost a gentil herte wo.
Of oother harm it nedeth nat to speke,
For ye yourself upon yourself yow wreke,
Which proveth wel that outher love or drede
Moot been enchesoun of youre cruel dede,
Syn that I see noon oother wight yow chace.
For love of God, as dooth yourselven grace
Or what may been youre help; for West nor Eest
Ne saugh I nevere, er now, no bryd ne beest
That ferde with hymself so pitously.
Ye slee me with youre sorwe, verraily;
I have of yow so greet compassioun.
For Goddes love, com fro the tree adoun;
And, as I am a kynges doghter trewe,
If that I verraily the cause knewe
Of youre disese, if it lay in my myght
I wolde amende it, er that it were nyght,
As wisly helpe me grete God of kynde!
And herbes shal I right ynowe yfynde
To heele with youre hurtes hastily.
Tho shrighte this faucon yet moore pitously
Than ever she dide, and fil to grounde anoon,
And lith aswowne, deed, and lyk a stoon,
Til Canacee hath in hire lappe hire take
Unto the tyme she gan of swough awake;
And, after that she of hir swough gan breyde,
Right in hir haukes ledene thus she seyde:
That pitee renneth soone in gentil herte,
Feelynge his similitude in peynes smerte,
Is preved al day, as men may it see

157

As wel by werk as by auctoritee;
For gentil herte kitheth gentillesse.
I se wel, that ye han of my distresse
Compassioun, my faire Canacee,
Of verray wommanly benignytee
That nature in youre principles hath set.
But for noon hope for to fare the bet,
But for to obeye unto youre herte free,
And for to maken othere be war by me,
As by the whelp chasted is the leoun,
Right for that cause and that conclusioun,
Whil that I have a leyser and a space,
Myn harm I wol confessen, er I pace.
And evere, whil that oon hir sorwe tolde,
That oother weep, as she to water wolde,
Til that the faucon bad hire to be stille,
And, with a syk, right thus she seyde hir wille.
HER I was bred, allas! that harde day!
And fostred in a roche of marbul gray
So tendrely, that nothyng eyled me,
I nyste nat what was adversitee,
Til I koude flee ful hye under the sky.
Tho dwelte a tercelet me faste by,
That semed welle of alle gentillesse;
Al were he ful of tresoun and falsnesse,
It was so wrapped under humble cheere,
And under hewe of trouthe in swich manere,
Under plesance, and under bisy peyne,
That I ne koude han wend he koude feyne,
So depe in greyn he dyed his coloures.
Right as a serpent hit hym under floures
Til he may seen his tyme for to byte,
Right so this god of love, this ypocryte.
Dooth so his cerymonyes and obeisaunces,
And kepeth in semblant alle his observaunces
That sowneth into gentillesse of love.
As in a toumbe is al the faire above,
And under is the corps, swich as ye woot,
Swich was this ypocrite, bothe coold and hoot,
And in this wise he served his entente,
That, save the feend, noon wiste what he mente.
Til he so longe hadde wopen and compleyned,
And many a yeer his service to me feyned,
Til that myn herte, to pitous and to nyce,
Al innocent of his crouned malice,
Forfered of his deeth, as thoughte me,
Upon his othes and his seuretee,
Graunted hym love, on this condicioun,
That everemoore myn honour and renoun
Were saved, bothe privee and apert;
This is to seyn, that after his desert,
I yaf hym al myn herte and al my thoght,
God woot and he, that otherwise noght,
And took his herte in chaunge for myn for ay.
But sooth is seyd, goon sithen many a day,
A trewe wight and a theef thenken nat oon.
And whan he saugh the thyng so fer ygoon,
That I hadde graunted hym fully my love,
In swich a gyse as I have seyd above,
And yeven hym my trewe herte, as free
As he swoor he his herte yaf to me;
Anon this tigre, ful of doublenesse
Fil on his knees with so devout humblesse,

158

With so heigh reverence, as by his cheere
So lyk a gentil lovere of manere,
So ravysshed, as it semed, for the joye
That nevere Jason, ne Parys of Troye,
Jason? Certes, ne noon oother man
Syn Lameth was, that alderfirst bigan
To loven two, as writen folk biforn,
Ne nevere, syn the firste man was born,
Ne koude man, by twenty thousand part,
Countrefete the sophymes of his art,
Ne were worthy unbokele his galoche,
Ther doublenesse or feynyng sholde approche
Ne so koude thanke a wight as he dide me!
His manere was an hevene for to see
Til any womman, were she never so wys;
So peynted he and kembde at point/devys,
As wel his wordes as his contenaunce;
And I so loved hym for his obeisaunce,
And for the trouthe I demed in his herte,
That, if so were that any thyng hym smerte,
Al were it never so lite, and I it wiste,
Me thoughte, I felte deeth myn herte twiste.
And shortly, so ferforth this thyng is went,
That my wyl was his willes instrument;
This is to seyn, my wyl obeyed his wyl
In alle thyng, as fer as resoun fil,
Kepynge the boundes of my worship evere.
Ne nevere hadde I thyng so lief, ne levere,
As hym, God woot! ne nevere shal namo.
This lasteth lenger than a yeer or two,
That I supposed of hym noght but good.
But finally, thus atte last it stood,
That Fortune wolde that he moste twynne
Out of that place which that I was inne.
Wher me was wo, that is no questioun;
I kan nat make of it discripcioun,
For o thyng dare I tellen boldely,
I knowe what is the peyne of deeth therby;
Swich harme I felte for he ne myghte bileve.
So on a day of me he took his leve,
So sorwefully eek, that I wende verraily
That he had felt as muche harm as I,
Whan that I herde hym speke, & saugh his hewe;
But nathelees, I thoughte he was so trewe,
And eek that he repaire sholde ageyn
Withinne a litel while, sooth to seyn;
And resoun wolde eek that he moste go
For his honour, as ofte it happeth so,
That I made vertu of necessitee,
And took it wel, syn that it moste be.
As I best myghte, I hidde fro hym my sorwe
And took hym by the hond, Seint John to borwe,
And seyde hym thus: Lo, I am youres al;
Beth swich as I to yow have been, and shal.
What he answerde, it nedeth noght reherce;
Who kan sey bet than he, who kan do werse?
Whan he hath al wel seyd, thanne hath he doon.
Therfore bihoveth him a ful long spoon
That shal ete with a feend, thus herde I seye.
So atte laste he moste forth his weye,
And forth he fleeth, til he cam ther hym leste.
Whan it cam hym to purpos for to reste,
I trowe he hadde thilke text in mynde,

That Alle thyng repeirynge to his kynde
Gladeth hymself, ✤ thus seyn men, as I gesse.
Men loven of propre kynde newefangelnesse,
As briddes doon that men in cages fede;
For though thou nyght and day take of hem hede,
And strawe hir cage faire and softe as silk,
And yeve hem sugre, hony, breed and milk,
Yet right anon, as that his dore is uppe,
He with his feet wol spurne adoun his cuppe,
And to the wode he wole, and wormes ete;
So newefangel been they of hire mete
And loven novelrie of propre kynde;
No gentillesse of blood ne may hem bynde.
SO ferde this tercelet, allas the day!
Though he were gentil born, and fressh
and gay,
And goodlich for to seen, and humble and free,
He saugh upon a tyme a kyte flee,
And sodeynly he loved this kyte so,
That al his love is clene fro me ago,
And hath his trouthe falsed in this wyse;
Thus hath the kyte my love in hire servyse,
And I am lorn withouten remedie.
✦And with that word this faucon gan to crie,
And swowned eft in Canacees barm.
GREET was the sorwe for the haukes
harm
That Canacee and alle hir wommen
made;
They nyste how they myghte the
faucon glade;
But Canacee hom bereth hire in hir lappe,
And softely in plastres gan hire wrappe,
Ther as she with hire beek hadde hurt hirselve.
NOW kan nat Canacee but herbes delve
Out of the ground, and make salves newe
Of herbes preciouse, and fyne of hewe,
To heelen with this hauk; fro day to nyght
She dooth hire bisynesse and hire fulle myght,
And by hire beddes heed she made a mewe,
And covered it with veluettes blewe
In signe of trouthe that is in wommen sene.
And al withoute, the mewe is peynted grene,
In which were peynted alle thise false fowles,
As beth thise tidyves, tercelettes and owles;
Right for despit, were peynted hem bisyde,
And pyes, on hem for to crie and chyde.
THUS lete I Canacee, hir hauk kepyng,
I wol namoore as now speke of hir ryng,
Til it come eft to purpos for to seyn
How that this faucon gat hire love ageyn
Repentant, as the storie telleth us,
By mediacioun of Cambalus,
The kynges sone, of which I to yow tolde;
But hennes forth I wol my proces holde
To speke of aventures and of batailles,
That nevere yet was herd so grete mervailles.
FIRST wol I telle yow of Cambynskan,
That in his tyme many a citee wan;
And after wol I speke of Algarsif,

How that he wan Theodora to his wif,
For whom ful ofte in greet peril he was,
Ne hadde he ben holpen by the steede of bras;
And after wol I speke of Cambalo,
That faught in lystes with the bretheren two
For Canacee, er that he myghte hire wynne;
An ther I lefte I wol ageyn bigynne.
Explicit pars secunda. Incipit pars tercia.
Appollo whirleth up his chaar so hye,
Til that the god Mercurius hous the slye...
There is no more of this Tale done by Chaucer.

Heere folwen the wordes of the Frankelyn to the
Squier, & the wordes of the Hoost to the Frankelyn ❀ ❀

IN feith, Squier, thow hast
thee wel yquit,
And gentilly I preise wel
thy wit,
Quod the Frankeleyn, con-
siderynge thy yowthe,
So feelyngly thou spekest,
sire, I allowe the!
As to my doom, ther is noon
that is heere
Of eloquence that shal be thy peere,
If that thou lyve; God yeve thee good chaunce,
And in vertu sende thee continuaunce;
For of thy speche I have greet deyntee.
I have a sone, and, by the Trinitee!
I hadde levere than twenty pound worth lond,
Though it right now were fallen in myn hond,
He were a man of swich discrecioun
As that ye been! fy on possessioun,
But if a man be vertuous withal.
I have my sone snybbed, and yet shal,
For he to vertu listeth nat entende;
But for to pleye at dees, and to despende,
And lese al that he hath, is his usage.
And he hath levere talken with a page
Than to comune with any gentil wight
There he myghte lerne gentillesse aright.
STRAW for youre gentillesse, quod our
Hoost;
What, Frankeleyn? pardee, sire, wel thou
woost
That ech of yow moot tellen atte leste
A tale or two, or breken his biheste.
✦That knowe I wel, sire, quod the Frankeleyn,
I prey yow, haveth me nat in desdeyn
Though to this man I speke a word or two.
✦Telle on thy tale, withouten wordes mo.
✦Gladly, sire Hoost, quod he, I wole obeye
Unto your wyl; now herkneth what I seye.
I wol yow nat contrarien in no wyse
As fer as that my wittes wol suffyse;
I prey to God that it may plesen yow,
Thanne woot I wel that it is good ynow.
Explicit.

The prologe of the frankeleyns Tale ❧ ❧

THISE olde gentil Britons in hir dayes Of diverse aventures maden layes, Rymeyed in hir firste Briton tonge; Whiche layes with hir instruments they songe, Or elles redden hem for hir plesaunce;
And oon of hem have I in remembraunce,
Which I shal seyn with good wyl as I kan.

But, sires, bycause I am a burel man,
At my bigynnyng first I yow biseche,
Have me excused of my rude speche.
I lerned nevere rethorik certeyn;
Thyng that I speke, it moot be bare and pleyn.
I sleep nevere on the Mount of Pernaso,
Ne lerned Marcus Tullius Cithero.
Colours ne knowe I none, withouten drede,
But swiche colours as growen in the mede,
Or elles swiche as men dye or peynte.
Colours of rethoryk been me to queynte;
My spirit feeleth noght of swich mateere,
But if yow list, my tale shul ye heere.

HEERE BIGYNNETH THE FRANKELEYNS TALE ❧ ❧ ❧ ❧

IN ARMORIK, that called is Britayne,
Ther was a knyght that loved and dide his payne
To serve a lady in his beste wise;
And many a labour, many a greet emprise
He for his lady wroghte, er she were wonne;
For she was oon, the faireste under sonne,
And eek therto come of so heigh kynrede,
That wel unnethes dorste this knyght, for drede,
Telle hire his wo, his peyne, & his distresse.
But atte laste, she, for his worthynesse,
And namely for his meke obeysaunce,
Hath swich a pitee caught of his penaunce,
That pryvely she fil of his accord,
To take hym for hir housbonde and hir lord,
Of swich lordshipe as men han over hir wyves;
And for to lede the moore in blisse hir lyves,
Of his free wyl he swoor hire as a knyght,
That nevere in al his lyf he, day ne nyght,
Ne sholde upon hym take no maistrie
Agayn hir wyl, ne kithe hire jalousie;
But hire obeye, and folwe hir wyl in al,
As any lovere to his lady shal;
Save that the name of soveraynetee,
That wolde he have, for shame of his degree.

She thanked hym, and with ful greet humblesse,
She seyde, Sire, sith of youre gentillesse
Ye profre me to have so large a reyne,
Ne wolde nevere God bitwixe us tweyne,
As in my gilt, were outher werre or stryf.
Sire, I wol be youre humble trewe wyf;
Have heer my trouthe, til that myn herte breste.
Thus been they bothe in quiete & in reste.
For o thyng, sires, saufly dar I seye,
That freendes everych oother moot obeye,
If they wol longe holden compaignye.
Love wol nat been constreyned by maistrye;
Whan maistrie comth, the god of love anon
Beteth his wynges, and farewel! he is gon!
Love is a thyng as any spirit free;
Wommen of kynde desiren libertee,
And nat to been constreyned as a thral;
And so doon men, if I sooth seyen shal.
Looke, who that is moost pacient in love,
He is at his avantage al above.
Pacience is an heigh vertu certeyn;
For it venquysseth, as thise clerkes seyn,
Thynges that rigour sholde nevere atteyne.
For every word men may nat chide or pleyne.
Lerneth to suffre, or elles so moot I goon,
Ye shul it lerne, wherso ye wole or noon;
For in this world, certein, ther no wight is
That he ne dooth or seith somtyme amys.
Ire, siknesse, or constellacioun,
Wyn, wo, or chaungynge of complexioun,
Causeth ful ofte to doon amys or speken.
On every wrong a man may nat be wreken;
After the tyme moste be temperaunce
To every wight that kan on governaunce.
And therfore hath this wise worthy knyght,
To lyve in ese, suffrance hire bihight,
And she to hym ful wisly gan to swere
That nevere sholde ther be defaute in here.
Heere may men seen an humble wys accord;
Thus hath she take hir servant and hir lord,
Servant in love, and lord in mariage,

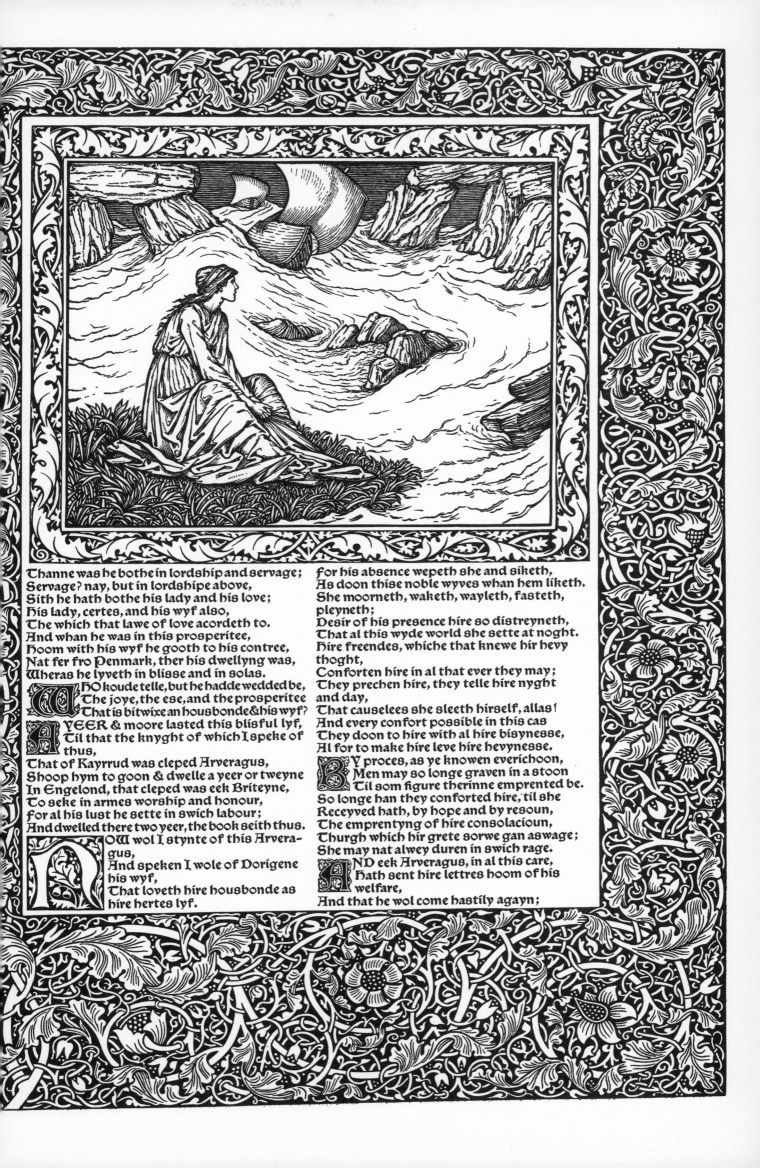

Thanne was he bothe in lordship and servage;
Servage? nay, but in lordshipe above,
Sith he hath bothe his lady and his love;
His lady, certes, and his wyf also,
The which that lawe of love acordeth to.
And whan he was in this prosperitee,
Hoom with his wyf he gooth to his contree,
Nat fer fro Penmark, ther his dwellyng was,
Wheras he lyveth in blisse and in solas.

WHO koude telle, but he hadde wedded be,
The joye, the ese, and the prosperitee
That is bitwixe an housbonde & his wyf?

A YEER & moore lasted this blisful lyf,
Til that the knyght of which I speke of thus,
That of Kayrrud was cleped Arveragus,
Shoop hym to goon & dwelle a yeer or tweyne
In Engelond, that cleped was eek Briteyne,
To seke in armes worship and honour,
for al his lust he sette in swich labour;
And dwelled there two yeer, the book seith thus.

NOW wol I stynte of this Arveragus,
And speken I wole of Dorigene
his wyf,
That loveth hire housbonde as
hire hertes lyf.

for his absence wepeth she and siketh,
As doon thise noble wyves whan hem liketh.
She moorneth, waketh, wayleth, fasteth, pleyneth;
Desir of his presence hire so distreyneth,
That al this wyde world she sette at noght.
Hire freendes, whiche that knewe hir hevy thoght,
Conforten hire in al that ever they may;
They prechen hire, they telle hire nyght and day,
That causelees she sleeth hirself, allas!
And every confort possible in this cas
They doon to hire with al hire bisynesse,
Al for to make hire leve hire hevynesse.

BY proces, as ye knowen everichoon,
Men may so longe graven in a stoon
Til som figure therinne emprented be.
So longe han they conforted hire, til she
Receyved hath, by hope and by resoun,
The emprentyng of hire consolacioun,
Thurgh which hir grete sorwe gan aswage;
She may nat alwey duren in swich rage.

AND eek Arveragus, in al this care,
Hath sent hire lettres hoom of his
welfare,
And that he wol come hastily agayn;

Or elles hadde this sorwe hir herte slayn.
HIRE freendes sawe hir sorwe gan to slake,
And preyde hire on knees, for Goddes sake,
To come and romen hire in compaignye,
Awey to dryve hire derke fantasye.
And finally she graunted that requeste;
for wel she saugh that it was for the beste.
NOW stood hire castel faste by the
see,
And often with hire freendes walketh
shee
Hire to disporte upon the bank an
heigh,
Whereas she many a ship and barge seigh
Seillynge hir cours, wheras hem liste go;
But thanne was that a parcel of hire wo.
for to hirself ful ofte Allas! seith she,
Is ther no ship, of so manye as I se,
Wol bryngen hom my lord? Thanne were myn
herte
Al warisshed of his bittre peynes smerte.
ANOTHER tyme ther wolde she sitte and
thynke,
And caste hir eyen dounward fro the brynke.
But whan she saugh the grisly rokkes blake,
for verray feere so wolde hir herte quake,
That on hire feet she myghte hire noght sustene.
Thanne wolde she sitte adoun upon the grene,
And pitously into the see biholde,
And seyn right thus, with sorweful sikes colde:
Eterne God, that thurgh thy purveiaunce
Ledest the world by certein governaunce,
In ydel, as men seyn, ye nothyng make;
But, Lord, thise grisly feendly rokkes blake,
That semen rather a foul confusioun
Of werk than any fair creacioun
Of swich a parfit wys God and a stable,
Why han ye wroght this werk unresonable?
for by this werk, south, north, ne west, ne eest,
Ther nys yfostred man, ne bryd, ne beest;
It dooth no good, to my wit, but anoyeth.
Se ye nat, Lord, how mankynde it destroyeth?
An hundred thousand bodyes of mankynde
Han rokkes slayn, al be they nat in mynde,
Which mankynde is so fair part of thy werk
That thou it madest lyk to thyn owene merk.
Thanne semed it ye hadde a greet chiertee
Toward mankynde; but how thanne may it bee
That ye swiche meenes make it to destroyen,
Whiche meenes do no good, but evere anoyen?
I woot wel clerkes wol seyn, as hem leste,
By arguments, that al is for the beste,
Though I ne kan the causes nat yknowe.
But thilke God, that made wynd to blowe,
As kepe my lord! this my conclusioun;
To clerkes lete I al disputisoun.
But wolde God that alle thise rokkes blake
Were sonken into helle for his sake.
Thise rokkes sleen myn herte for the feere.
Thus wolde she seyn with many a pitous teere.
HIRE freendes sawe that it was no disport
To romen by the see, but disconfort;
And shopen for to pleyen somwher elles.

162

They leden hire by ryveres and by welles,
And eek in othere places delitables;
They dauncen, and they pleyen at ches and tables.
So on a day, right in the morwe tyde,
Unto a gardyn that was ther bisyde,
In which that they hadde maad hir ordinaunce
Of vitaille and of oother purveiaunce,
They goon and pleye hem al the longe day;
And this was in the sixte morwe of May,
Which May hadde peynted with his softe shoures
This gardyn ful of leves and of floures;
And craft of mannes hand so curiously
Arrayed hadde this gardyn, trewely,
That nevere was ther gardyn of swich prys,
But if it were the verray Paradys.
The odour of floures and the fresshe sighte
Wolde han maked any herte lighte
That evere was born, but if to greet siknesse,
Or to greet sorwe, helde it in distresse;
So ful it was of beautee with plesaunce.
AT after dyner gonne they to daunce,
And synge also, save Dorigen allone,
Which made alwey hir compleint and hir
moone;
for she ne saugh hym on the daunce go,
That was hir housbonde and hir love also.
But nathelees she moste a tyme abyde,
And with good hope lete hir sorwe slyde.
UPON this daunce, amonges
othere men,
Daunced a squier biforen Dorigen,
That fressher was, and jolyer of
array,
As to my doom, than is the
monthe of May;
He syngeth, daunceth, passynge any man
That is, or was, sith that the world bigan.
Therwith he was, if men sholde hym discryve,
Oon of the beste farynge man on lyve;
Yong, strong, right vertuous, and riche and wys,
And wel biloved, and holden in greet prys.
And shortly, if the sothe I tellen shal,
Unwityng of this Dorigen at al,
This lusty squier, servant to Venus,
Which that ycleped was Aurelius,
Hadde loved hire best of any creature
Two yeer and moore, as was his aventure,
But nevere dorste he telle hire his grevaunce;
Withouten coppe he drank al his penaunce.
He was despeyred, nothyng dorste he seye,
Save in his songes somwhat wolde he wreye
His wo, as in a general compleynyng;
He seyde he lovede, and was biloved nothyng.
Of swich matere made he manye layes,
Songes, compleintes, roundels, virelayes;
How that he dorste nat his sorwe telle,
But langwissheth, as a furye dooth in helle;
And dye he moste, he seyde, as dide Ekko
for Narcisus, that dorste nat telle hir wo.
In oother manere than ye heer me seye,
Ne dorste he nat to hire his wo biwreye;
Save that, paraventure, som tyme at daunces,
Ther yonge folk kepen hir observaunces,

It may wel be he looked on hir face
In swich a wise, as man that asketh grace;
But nothyng wiste she of his entente.
Nathelees, it happed, er they thennes wente,
Bycause that he was hire neighebour,
And was a man of worship and honour,
And hadde yknowen hym of tyme yoore,
They fille in speche; and forth moore and
moore
Unto his purpos drough Aurelius,
And whan he saugh his tyme, he sayde thus:

MADAME, quod he, by God that this
world made,
So that I wiste it myghte youre herte
glade,
I wolde, that day that youre Arveragus
Wente over the see, that I, Aurelius,
Hadde went ther nevere I sholde have come
agayn;
for wel I woot my servyce is in vayn.
My guerdoun is but brestyng of myn herte;
Madame, reweth upon my peynes smerte;
for with a word ye may me sleen or save,
Heere at youre feet God wolde that I were
grave!
I ne have as now no leyser moore to seye;
Have mercy, sweete, or ye wol do me deye!

SHE gan to looke upon Aurelius:
Is this your wyl, quod she, and sey ye
thus?
Nevere erst, quod she, ne wiste I what ye
mente;
But now, Aurelie, I knowe youre entente,
By thilke God that yaf me soule and lyf,
Ne shal I nevere been untrewe wyf
In word ne werk; as fer as I have wit,
I wol been his to whom that I am knyt!
Taak this for fynal answere as of me.
But after that in pley thus seyde she:
Aurelie, quod she, by heighe God above!
Yet wolde I graunte yow to been youre love,
Syn I yow se so pitously complayne;
Looke what day that, endelong Britayne,
Ye remoeve alle the rokkes, stoon by stoon,
That they ne lette ship ne boot to goon,
I seye, whan ye han maad the coost so clene
Of rokkes, that ther nys no stoon ysene,
Thanne wol I love yow best of any man;
Have heer my trouthe in al that evere I kan!

IS ther noon oother grace in yow? quod
he.
No, by that Lord, quod she, that
maked me!
for wel I woot that it shal never bityde.

Lat swiche folies out of youre herte slyde.
What deyntee sholde a man han in his lyf
for to go love another mannes wyf,
That hath hir body whan so that hym lyketh?
Aurelius ful ofte soore siketh.

O was Aurelie, whan that he this herde,
And with a sorweful herte he thus
answerde:
Madame, quod he, this were an inpossible,
Thanne moot I dye of sodeyn deth horrible!
And with that word he turned hym anon.
Tho come hir othere freendes many oon,
And in the aleyes romeden up and doun,
And nothyng wiste of this conclusioun,
But sodeynly bigonne revel newe,
Til that the brighte sonne loste his hewe;
For thorisonte hath reft the sonne his lyght;
This is as muche to seye as it was nyght;
And hoom they goon in joye and in solas,
Save oonly wrecche Aurelius, allas!

HE to his hous is goon with sorweful herte;
He seeth he may nat fro his deeth asterte.
Hym semed that he felte his herte colde;
Up to the hevene his handes he gan holde,
And on his knowes bare he sette hym doun,
And in his ravyng seyde his orisoun.
For verray wo out of his wit he breyde.
He nyste what he spak, but thus he seyde;
With pitous herte his pleynt hath he bigonne
Unto the goddes, and first unto the sonne:

HE seyde, Appollo, god and governour,
Of every plaunte, herbe, tree and flour,
That yevest, after thy declinacioun,
To ech of hem his tyme and his sesoun,
As thyn herberwe chaungeth lowe or heighe;
Lord Phebus, cast thy merciable eighe
On wrecche Aurelie, which that am but lorn.
Lo, lord! my lady hath my deeth ysworn
Withoute gilt, but thy benignytee
Upon my dedly herte have som pitee!
For wel I woot, lord Phebus, if yow lest,
Ye may me helpen, save my lady, best.
Now vouchethsauf that I may yow devyse
How that I may been holpe and in what wyse.
Youre blisful suster, Lucina the sheene,
That of the see is chief goddesse and queene,
Though Neptunus have deitee in the see,
Yet Emperesse aboven hym is she:
Ye knowen wel, lord, that right as hir desir
Is to be quyked and lightned of youre fir,
For which she folweth yow ful bisily,
Right so the see desireth naturelly
To folwen hire, as she that is goddesse
Bothe in the see and ryveres moore and lesse.
Wherfore, lord Phebus, this is my requeste,
Do this miracle, or do myn herte breste;
That now, next at this opposicioun,
Which in the signe shal be of the Leoun,
As preieth hire so greet a flood to brynge,
That fyve fadme at the leeste it oversprynge
The hyeste rokke in Armorik Briteyne;
And lat this flood endure yeres tweyne;
Thanne certes to my lady may I seye:

164

Holdeth youre heste, the rokkes been aweye.

LORD PHEBUS, dooth this miracle
for me;
Preye hire she go no faster cours than ye;
I seye, preyeth your suster that she go
No faster cours than ye thise yeres two.
Thanne shal she been evene atte fulle alway,
And spryng-flood laste bothe nyght and day.
And, but she vouchesauf in swich manere
To graunte me my sovereyn lady deere,
Prey hire to synken every rok adoun
Into hir owene derke regioun
Under the ground, ther Pluto dwelleth inne,
Or nevere mo shal I my lady wynne.
Thy temple in Delphos wol I barefoot seke;
Lord Phebus, se the teeris on my cheke,
And of my peyne have som compassioun!
And with that word in swowne he fil adoun,
And longe tyme he lay forth in a traunce.

HIS brother, which that knew of his penaunce,
Up caughte hym, and to bedde he hath hym
broght.
Dispeyred in this torment and this thoght
Lete I this woful creature lye;
Chese he, for me, whether he wol lyve or dye.

ARVERAGUS, with heele and greet
honour,
As he that was of chivalrie the flour,
Is comen hoom, and othere worthy
men.
O blisful artow now, thou Dorigen!
That hast thy lusty housbonde in thyne armes,
The fresshe knyght, the worthy man of armes,
That loveth thee, as his owene hertes lyf.
Nothyng list hym to been ymaginatyf
If any wight had spoke, whil he was oute,
To hire of love; he hadde of it no doute.
He noght entendeth to no swich mateere,
But daunceth, justeth, maketh hire good cheere;
And thus in joye and blisse I lete hem dwelle,
And of the sike Aurelius wol I telle.

IN langour and in torment furyus,
Two yeer and moore lay wrecche
Aurelyus,
Er any foot he myghte on erthe gon;
Ne confort in this tyme hadde he
noon,
Save of his brother, which that was a clerk;
He knew of al this wo and al this werk.
For to noon oother creature certeyn
Of this matere he dorste no word seyn.
Under his brest he baar it moore secree
Than evere dide Pamphilus for Galathee.
His brest was hool, withoute for to sene,
But in his herte ay was the arwe kene;
And wel ye knowe that of a sursanure
In surgerye is perilous the cure,
But men myghte touche the arwe, or come therby.

HIS brother weep and wayled pryvely,
Til atte laste hym fil in remembraunce
That whiles he was at Orliens in Fraunce,
As yonge clerkes, that been lykerous
To reden artes that been curious,

Seken in every halke and every herne
Particuler sciences for to lerne,
He hym remembred, that upon a day,
At Orliens in studie a book he say
Of magyk natureel, which his felawe,
That was that time a bacheler of lawe,
Al were he ther to lerne another craft,
Hadde prively upon his desk yplaft;
Which book spak muchel of the operaciouns
Touchynge the eighte and twenty mansiouns
That longen to the moone, and swich folye,
As in oure dayes is nat worth a flye;
For hooly chirches feith in oure bileve,
Ne suffreth noon illusion us to greve.
And whan this book was in his remembraunce,
Anon for joye his herte gan to daunce,
And to hymself he seyde pryvely:
My brother shal be warisshed hastily;
For I am siker that ther be sciences
By whiche men make diverse apparences,
Swiche as thise subtile tregetoures pleye.
For ofte at feestes have I wel herd seye,
That tregetours, withinne an halle large,
Have maad come in a water and a barge,
And in the halle rowen up and doun.
Somtyme hath semed come a grym leoun;
And somtyme floures sprynge as in a mede;
Somtyme a vyne, and grapes white and rede;

Somtyme a castel, al of lym and stoon;
And whan hym lyked, voyded it anoon.
Thus semed it to every mannes sighte.
Now thanne conclude I thus, that if I myghte
At Orliens som oold felawe yfynde,
That hadde this moones mansions in mynde,
Or oother magyk natureel above,
He sholde wel make my brother han his love.
For with an apparence a clerk may make
To mannes sighte, that alle the rokkes blake
Of Britaigne weren yvoyded everichon,
And shippes by the brynke comen and gon,
And in swich forme endure a wowke or two.
Thanne were my brother warisshed of his wo.
Thanne moste she nedes holden hire biheste,
Or elles he shal shame hire atte leeste.

WHAT sholde I make a lenger tale of
this?
Unto his brotheres bed he comen is,
And swich confort he yaf hym for to gon
To Orliens, that he up stirte anon,
And on his wey forthward thanne is he fare,
In hope for to been lissed of his care.
Whan they were come almoost to that
citee,
But if it were a two furlong or thre,
A yong clerk romynge by hymself they mette
Which that in Latyn thriftily hem grette,

And after that he seyde a wonder thyng:
I knowe, quod he, the cause of youre comyng;
And er they ferther any foote wente,
He tolde hem al that was in hire entente.
This Briton clerk hym asked of felawes
The whiche that he had knowe in olde dawes;
And he answerde hym that they dede were,
For which he weep ful ofte many a teere.
Doun of his hors Aurelius lighte anon,
And forth with this magicien is he gon
Hoom to his hous, and made hem wel at ese.
Hem lakked no vitaille that myghte hem plese;
So wel arrayed hous as ther was oon
Aurelius in his lyf saugh nevere noon.
He shewed hym, er he wente to soper,
Forestes, parkes ful of wilde deer;
Ther saugh he hertes with hir hornes hye,
The gretteste that evere were seyn with eye.
He saugh of hem an hondred slayn with houndes,
And somme with arwes blede of bittre woundes.
He saugh, whan voyded were thise wilde deer,
Thise fauconers upon a fair ryver,
That with hir haukes han the heroun slayn.
Tho saugh he knyghtes justyng in a playn;
And after this, he dide hym swich plesaunce,
That he hym shewed his lady on a daunce,
On which hymself he daunced, as hym thoughte.
And whan this maister, that this magyk wroughte,
Saugh it was tyme, he clapte his handes two,
And, farewel! al oure revel was ago.
And yet remoeved they nevere out of the hous,
Whil they saugh al this sighte merveillous,
But in his studie, theras his bookes be,
They seten stille, and no wight but they thre.
To hym this maister called his squier,
And seyde hym thus: Is redy oure soper?
Almoost an houre it is, I undertake,
Sith I yow bad oure soper for to make,
Whan that thise worthy men wenten with me
Into my studie, theras my bookes be.
Sire, quod this squier, whan it liketh yow,
It is al redy, though ye wol right now.
Go we thanne soupe, quod he, as for the beste;
This amorous folk som tyme moote han hir reste.
At after soper fille they in tretee
What somme sholde this maistres
guerdon be,
To remoeven alle the rokkes of Britayne,
And eek from Gerounde to the mouth of Sayne.
He made it straunge, and swoor, so God hym
save!
Lasse than a thousand pound he wolde nat have,
Ne gladly for that somme he wolde nat goon.
AURELIUS, with blisful herte anoon,
Answerde thus: Fy on a thousand pound!
This wyde world, which that men seye is
round,
I wolde it yeve, if I were lord of it!
This bargayn is ful dryve, for we been knyt.
Ye shal be payed trewely, by my trouthe!
But looketh now, for no necligence or slouthe,
Ye tarie us heere no lenger than tomorwe.
Nay, quod this clerk, have heer my feith to borwe.

To bedde is goon Aurelius whan hym leste,
And wel ny al that nyght he hadde his reste;
What for his labour and his hope of blisse,
His woful herte of penaunce hadde a lisse.
Upon the morwe, whan that it was day,
To Britaigne tooke they the righte way,
Aurelius, and this magicien bisyde;
And been descended ther they wolde abyde;
And this was, as thise bookes me remembre,
The colde frosty sesoun of Decembre.
PHEBUS wex old, and hewed lyk
latoun,
That in his hoote declynacioun
Shoon as the burned gold with
stremes brighte;
But now in Capricorn adoun he
lighte,
Wheras he shoon ful pale, I dar wel seyn.
The bittre frostes, with the sleet and reyn,
Destroyed hath the grene in every yerd.
Janus sit by the fyr, with double berd,
And drynketh of his bugle-horn the wyn.
Biforn hym stant brawn of the tusked swyn,
And Nowel crieth every lusty man.
Aurelius, in al that evere he kan,
Dooth to his maister chiere and reverence,
And preyeth hym to doon his diligence
To bryngen hym out of his peynes smerte,
Or with a swerd that he wolde slitte his herte.
This subtil clerk swich routhe had of this man,
That nyght and day he spedde hym that he kan,
To wayten a tyme of his conclusioun;
This is to seye, to maken illusioun,
By swich an apparence or jogelrye,
I ne kan no termes of astrologye,
That she and every wight sholde wene and seye,
That of Britaigne the rokkes were aweye,
Or ellis they were sonken under grounde.
So atte laste he hath his tyme yfounde
To maken his japes and his wrecchednesse
Of swich a supersticious cursednesse.
His tables Tolletanes forth he brought,
Ful wel corrected, ne ther lakked nought,
Neither his collect, ne his expans yeeris,
Ne his rootes, ne his othere geeris,
As been his centris and his arguments,
And his proporcionels convenients
For his equacions in every thyng.
And, by his eighte speere in his wirkyng,
He knew ful wel how fer Alnath was shove
Fro the heed of thilke fixe Aries above,
That in the ninthe speere considered is;
Ful subtilly he kalkuled al this.
Whan he hadde founde his firste mansioun,
He knew the remenaunt by proporcioun;
And knew the arisyng of his moone weel,
And in whos face, and terme, and everydeel;
And knew ful weel the moones mansioun
Acordaunt to his operacioun;
And knew also his othere observaunces
For swiche illusiouns & swiche meschaunces
As hethen folk useden in thilke dayes;
For which no lenger maked he delayes;

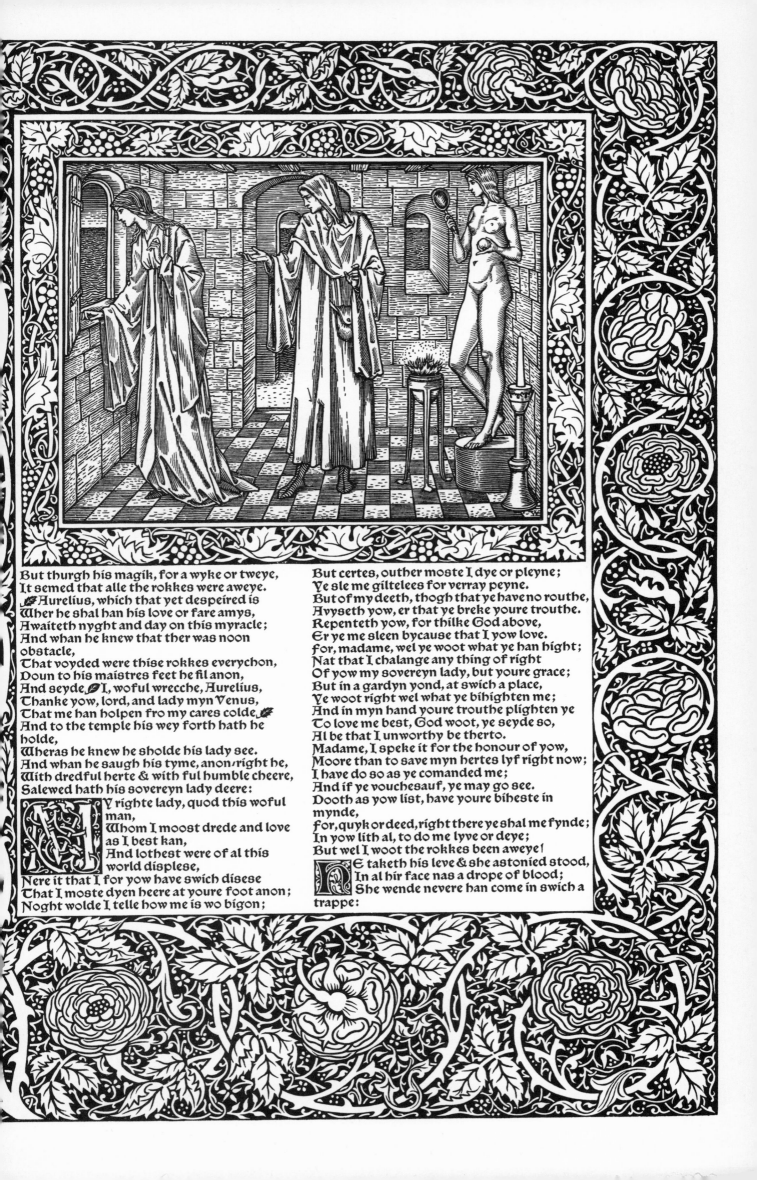

But thurgh his magik, for a wyke or tweye,
It semed that alle the rokkes were aweye.
Aurelius, which that yet despeired is
Wher he shal han his love or fare amys,
Awaiteth nyght and day on this myracle;
And whan he knew that ther was noon obstacle,
That voyded were thise rokkes everychon,
Doun to his maistres feet he fil anon,
And seyde, I, woful wrecche, Aurelius,
Thanke yow, lord, and lady myn Venus,
That me han holpen fro my cares colde,
And to the temple his wey forth hath he holde,
Wheras he knew he sholde his lady see.
And whan he saugh his tyme, anon right he,
With dredful herte & with ful humble cheere,
Salewed hath his sovereyn lady deere:

M
Y righte lady, quod this woful man,
Whom I moost drede and love
as I best kan,
And lothest were of al this
world displese,
Nere it that I for yow have swich disese
That I moste dyen heere at youre foot anon;
Noght wolde I telle how me is wo bigon;

But certes, outher moste I dye or pleyne;
Ye sle me giltelees for verray peyne.
But of my deeth, thogh that ye have no routhe,
Avyseth yow, er that ye breke youre trouthe.
Repenteth yow, for thilke God above,
Er ye me sleen bycause that I yow love.
For, madame, wel ye woot what ye han hight;
Nat that I chalange any thing of right
Of yow my sovereyn lady, but youre grace;
But in a gardyn yond, at swich a place,
Ye woot right wel what ye bihighten me;
And in myn hand youre trouthe plighten ye
To love me best, God woot, ye seyde so,
Al be that I unworthy be therto.
Madame, I speke it for the honour of yow,
Moore than to save myn hertes lyf right now;
I have do so as ye comanded me;
And if ye vouchesauf, ye may go see.
Dooth as yow list, have youre biheste in mynde,
For, quyk or deed, right there ye shal me fynde;
In yow lith al, to do me lyve or deye;
But wel I woot the rokkes been aweye!

S
E taketh his leve & she astonied stood,
In al hir face nas a drope of blood;
She wende nevere han come in swich a trappe:

*Allas! quod she, that evere this sholde happe!
For wende I nevere, by possibilitee,
That swich a monstre or merveille myghte be!
It is agayns the proces of nature:
*And hoom she goth a sorweful creature.
For verray feere unnethe may she go,
She wepeth, wailleth, al a day or two,
And swowneth, that it routhe was to see;
But why it was, to no wight tolde shee,
For out of towne was goon Arveragus.
But to hirself she spak, and seyde thus,
With face pale and with ful sorweful cheere,
In hire compleynt, as ye shal after heere.
*Allas! quod she, on thee, Fortune, I pleyne,
That unwar wrapped hast me in thy cheyne;
For which, tescape, woot I no socour,
Save oonly deeth or elles dishonour;
Oon of thise two bihoveth me to chese.
But nathelees, yet have I levere to lese
My lif than of my body have a shame,
Or knowe myselven fals, or lese my name;
And with my deth I may be quyt, ywis.
Hath ther nat many a noble wyf, er this,
And many a mayde, yslayn hirself, allas!
Rather than with hir body doon trespas?
YIS, certes, lo, thise stories beren witnesse;
Whan thretty tirauntz, ful of cursednesse,
Hadde slayn Phidoun in Athenes, atte feste,
They comanded his doghtres for tareste,
And bryngen hem biforn hem in despit
Al naked, to fulfille hir foul delit,
And in hir fadres blood they made hem daunce
Upon the pavement, God yeve hem myschaunce!
For which thise woful maydens, ful of drede,
Rather than they wolde lese hir maydenhede
They prively been stirt into a welle,
And dreynte hemselven, as the bookes telle.
*They of Messene leete enquere and seke
Of Lacedomye fifty maydens eke,
On whiche they wolden doon hir lecherye;
But was ther noon of al that compaignye
That she nas slayn, and with a good entente
Chees rather for to dye than assente
To been oppressed of hir maydenhede.
Why sholde I thanne to dye been in drede?
*Lo, eek, the tiraunt Aristoclides,
That loved a mayden heet Stymphalides,
Whan that hir fader slayn was on a nyght,
Unto Dianes temple goth she right,
And hente the ymage in hir handes two,
Fro which ymage wolde she nevere go:
No wight ne myghte hir handes of it arace
Til she was slayn right in the selve place.
NOW sith that maydens hadden swich despit
To been defouled with mannes foul delit,
Wel oghte a wyf rather hirselven slee
Than be defouled, as it thynketh me.
*What shal I seyn of Hasdrubales wyf,
That at Cartage birafte hirself hir lyf?
For whan she saugh that Romayns wan the toun,
She took hir children alle, and skipte adoun

168

Into the fyr, and chees rather to dye
Than any Romayn dide hire vileynye.
*Hath nat Lucresse yslayn hirself, allas!
At Rome, whan that she oppressed was
Of Tarquyn, for hire thoughte it was a shame
To lyven whan she hadde lost hir name?
*The sevene maydens of Melesie, also,
Han slayn hemself, for verray drede and wo,
Rather than folk of Gawle hem sholde oppresse.
Mo than a thousand stories, as I gesse,
Koude I now telle as touchynge this mateere.
*Whan Habradate was slayn, his wyf so deere
Hirselven slow, and leet hir blood to glyde
In Habradates woundes depe and wyde,
And seyde, My body, at the leeste way,
Ther shal no wight defoulen, if I may.
WHAT sholde I mo ensamples heerof sayn,
Sith that so manye han hemselven slayn
Wel rather than they wolde defouled be?
I wol conclude, that it is bet for me
To sleen myself, than been defouled thus.
I wol be trewe unto Arveragus,
Or rather sleen myself in som manere,
*As dide Demociones doghter deere,
Bycause that she wolde nat defouled be.
*O Cedasus! it is ful greet pitee
To reden how thy doghtren deyde, allas!
That slowe hemselven for swich maner cas.
*As greet a pitee was it, or wel moore,
The Theban mayden, that for Nichanore
Hirselven slow, right for swich manere wo.
*Another Theban mayden dide right so;
For oon of Macidoyne hadde hire oppressed,
She with hir deeth hir maydenhede redressed.
*What shal I seye of Nicerates wyf,
That for swich cas birafte hirself hir lyf?
*How trewe eek was to Alcebiades
His love, that rather for to dyen chees
Than for to suffre his body unburyed be?
*Lo which a wyf was Alceste, quod she.
*What seith Omer of goode Penalopee?
Al Grece knoweth of hire chastitee.
*Pardee, of Laodomya is writen thus,
That whan at Troie was slayn Protheselaus,
No lenger wolde she lyve after his day.
*The same of noble Porcia telle I may;
Withoute Brutus koude she nat lyve,
To whom she hadde al hool hir herte yive.
*The parfit wyfhod of Arthemesie
Honoured is thurgh al the Barbarie.
*O Teuta, queene! thy wyfly chastitee
To alle wyves may a mirour bee.
*The same thyng I seye of Bilyea,
Of Rodogone, and eek Valeria.
THUS pleyned Dorigene a day or tweye,
Purposynge evere that she wolde deye.
But nathelees, upon the thridde nyght
Hoom cam Arveragus, this worthy knyght,
And asked hire, why that she weep so soore;
And she gan wepen ever lenger the moore.

Allas! quod she, that evere I was born!
Thus have I seyd, quod she, thus have I
sworn,
And toold hym al as ye han herd bifore;
It nedeth nat reherce it yow namoore.
This housbonde, with glad chiere, in freendly
wyse,
Answerde and seyde as I shal yow devyse:
Is ther oght elles, Dorigen, but this?
Nay, nay, quod she, God help me so, as
wys!
This is to muche, and it were Goddes wille.
Ye, wyf, quod he, lat sleepen that is stille;
It may be wel, paraventure, yet today.
Ye shul youre trouthe holden, by my fay!
For God so wisly have mercy upon me,
I hadde wel levere ystiked for to be,
For verray love which that I to yow have,
But if ye sholde youre trouthe kepe and save!
Trouthe is the hyeste thyng that man may
kepe:
BUT with that word he brast anon to
wepe,
And seyde, I yow forbede, up peyne of
deeth,
That nevere, whil thee lasteth lyf ne breeth,
To no wight tel thou of this aventure.

As I may best, I wol my wo endure,
Ne make no contenance of hevynesse,
That folk of yow may demen harm or gesse.
AND forth he cleped a squier & a mayde:
Gooth forth anon with Dorigen, he
sayde,
And bryngeth hire to swich a place anon.
They take hir leve, and on hir wey they gon;
But they ne wiste why she thider wente.
He nolde no wight tellen his entente.
PARAVENTURE an heep of yow,
ywis,
Wol holden hym a lewed man in this,
That he wol putte his wyf in jupartie;
Herkneth the tale, er ye upon hir crie.
She may have bettre fortune than yow semeth;
And whan that ye han herd the tale, demeth.
THIS squier, which that highte Aurelius,
On Dorigen that was so amorous,
Of aventure happed hire to meete
Amydde the toun, right in the quykkest
strete,
As she was bown to goon the wey forthright
Toward the gardyn theras she had hight;
And he was to the gardynward also;
For wel he spyed, whan she wolde go
Out of hir hous to any maner place.

But thus they mette, of aventure or grace;
And he saleweth hire with glad entente,
And asked of hire whiderward she wente.
And she answerde, half as she were mad,
Unto the gardyn, as myn housbonde bad,
My trouthe for to holde, allas! allas!

AURELIUS gan wondren on this cas,
And in his herte hadde greet com-
passioun
Of hire and of hire lamentacioun,
And of Arveragus, the worthy knyght,
That bad hire holden al that she had hight,
So looth hym was his wyf sholde breke hir
trouthe;
And in his herte he caughte of this greet
routhe,
Consideryinge the beste on every syde,
That fro his lust yet were hym levere abyde,
Than doon so heigh a cherlyssh wrecched-
nesse
Agayns franchise and alle gentillesse;
for which in fewe wordes seyde he thus:

MADAME, seyeth to youre lord,
Arveragus,
That sith I se his grete gentillesse
To yow, and eek I se wel youre distresse,

That him were levere han shame, and that
were routhe,
Than ye to me sholde breke thus youre
trouthe,
I have wel levere evere to suffre wo,
Than I departe the love bitwix yow two.
I yow relesse, madame, into youre hond
Quyt every surement and every bond,
That ye han maad to me as heer biforn,
Sith thilke tyme which that ye were born.
My trouthe I plighte, I shal yow never repreve
Of no biheste, and heere I take my leve,
As of the treweste and the beste wyf
That evere yet I knew in al my lyf.
But every wyf be war of hire biheeste,
On Dorigene remembreth atte leeste.
Thus kan a squier doon a gentil dede,
As wel as kan a knyght, withouten drede.

SHE thonketh hym upon hir knees al
bare,
And hoom unto hir housbonde is she
fare,
And tolde hym al as ye han herd me sayd;
And be ye siker, he was so weel apayd
That it were inpossible me to wryte.
What sholde I lenger of this cas endyte?

Arveragus and Dorigene his wyf
In sovereyn blisse leden forth hir lyf.
Nevere eft ne was ther angre hem bitwene;
He cherisseth hire as though she were a
queene;
And she was to hym trewe for everemoore.
Of thise two folk ye gete of me namoore.

AURELIUS, that his cost hath al
forlorn,
Curseth the tyme that evere he
was born:
Allas! quod he, allas! that I
bihighte
Of pured gold a thousand pound of wighte
Unto this philosophre! How shal I do?
I se namoore but that I am fordo.
Myn heritage moot I nedes selle,
And been a begger; heere may I nat dwelle,
And shamen al my kynrede in this place,
But I of hym may gete bettre grace.
But nathelees, I wol of hym assaye,
At certeyn dayes, yeer by yeer, to paye,
And thanke hym of his grete curteisye;
My trouthe wol I kepe, I wol nat lye.
With herte soor he gooth unto his cofre,
And broghte gold unto this philosophre,
The value of fyve hundred pound, I gesse,
And hym bisecheth, of his gentillesse,
To graunte hym dayes of the remenaunt,
And seyde, Maister, I dar wel make avaunt,
I failled nevere of my trouthe as yit;
For sikerly my dette shal be quyt
Towardes yow, howevere that I fare
To goon a begged in my kirtle bare.
But wolde ye vouchesauf, upon seuretee,
Two yeer or thre for to respiten me,
Thanne were I wel; for elles moot I selle
Myn heritage; ther is namoore to telle.

THIS philosophre sobrely answerde
And seyde thus, whan he thise wordes
herde:
Have I nat holden covenant unto thee?
Yes, certes, wel and trewely, quod he.
Hastow nat had thy lady as thee liketh?
No, no, quod he, and sorwefully he siketh.
What was the cause? tel me if thou kan.
Aurelius his tale anon bigan,
And tolde hym al, as ye han herd bifoore;
It nedeth nat to yow reherce it moore.

HE seide, Arveragus, of gentillesse,
Hadde levere dye in sorwe and in distresse
Than that his wyf were of hir trouthe
fals.
The sorwe of Dorigen he tolde hym als,
How looth hire was to been a wikked wyf,
And that she levere had lost that day hir lyf,
And that hir trouthe she swoor, thurgh in-
nocence:
She nevere erst herde speke of apparence;
That made me han of hire so greet pitee.
And right as frely as he sente hire me,
As frely sente I hire to hym ageyn.
This al and som, ther is namoore to seyn.

HIS philosophre answerde, Leeve
brother,
Everich of yow dide gentilly til
oother.
Thou art a squier, and he is a
knyght;
But God forbede, for his blisful myght,
But if a clerk koude doon a gentil dede
As wel as any of yow, it is no drede.
Sire, I releesse thee thy thousand pound,
As thou right now were cropen out of the ground,
Ne nevere er now ne haddest knowen me.
For sire, I wol nat taken a peny of thee
For al my craft, ne noght for my travaille.
Thou hast ypayed wel for my vitaille;
It is ynogh, and farewel, have good day!
And took his hors, and forth he goth his way.
Lordynges, this question wolde I aske now,
Which was the mooste fre, as thynketh yow?
Now telleth me, er that ye ferther wende.
I kan namoore, my tale is at an ende.
Heere is ended the Frankeleyns Tale.

The prologe of the Seconde Nonnes Tale ✿ ✿

HE ministre & the norice unto vices,
Which that men clepe in Englissh
ydelnesse,
That porter of the gate is of delices,
To eschue, and by hire contrarie hire
oppresse,
That is to seyn, by leveful bisynesse,
Wel oghten we to doon al oure entente,
Lest that the feend thurgh ydelnesse us hente.

For he, that with his thousand cordes slye
Continuelly us waiteth to biclappe,
Whan he may man in ydelnesse espye,
He kan so lightly cacche hym in his trappe,
Til that a man be hent right by the lappe,
He nys nat war the feend hath hym in honde;
Wel oghte us werche, and ydelnesse withstonde.

And though men dradden nevere for to dye,
Yet seen men wel by resoun doutelees,
That ydelnesse is roten slogardye,
Of which ther nevere comth no good encrees;
And seen, that slouthe it holdeth in a lees
Oonly to slepe, and for to ete and drynke,
And to devouren al that othere swynke.

And for to putte us fro swich ydelnesse,
That cause is of so greet confusioun,
I have heer doon my feithful bisynesse,
After the legende, in translacioun,
Right of thy glorious lif and passioun,
Thou with thy gerland wroght of rose and lilie,
Thee, meene I, mayde and martir, Seynt Cecilie!

Invocacio ad Mariam.

AND thow that flour of virgines art
alle,
Of whom that Bernard list so wel
to write,
To thee, at my bigynnyng, first I
calle;

171

Thou confort of us wrecches, do me endite
Thy maydens deeth, that wan thurgh hire merite
The eterneel lyf, and of the feend victorie,
As man may after reden in hire storie.

Thow mayde and mooder, doghter of thy sone,
Thow welle of mercy, synful soules cure,
In whom that God, for bountee, chees to wone,
Thow humble, and heigh over every creature,
Thow nobledest so ferforth oure nature,
That no desdeyn the Makere hadde of kynde,
His sone in blood and flessh to clothe and wynde.

Withinne the cloistre blisful of thy sydis
Took mannes shap the eterneel love and pees,
That of the tryne compas lord and gyde is,
Whom erthe, and see, and hevene, out of relees,
Ay heryen; and thou, virgine wemmelees,
Baar of thy body, and dweltest mayden pure,
The creatour of every creature.

Assembled is in thee magnificence,
With mercy, goodnesse, and with swich pitee,
That thou, that art the sonne of excellence,
Nat oonly helpest hem that preyen thee,
But often tyme, of thy benygnytee,
Ful frely, er that men thyn help biseche,
Thou goost biforn, and art hir lyves leche.

NOW help, thow meeke and blisful faire
mayde,
Me, flemed wrecche, in this desert of galle;
Thynk on the womman Cananee, that sayde
That whelpes eten somme of the crommes alle
That from hir lordes table been yfalle;
And though that I, unworthy sone of Eve,
Be synful, yet accepte my bileve.

And, for that feith is deed withouten werkis,
So for to werken yif me wit and space,
That I be quit fro thennes that moost derk is.
O thou, that art so fair and ful of grace,
Be myn advocat in that heighe place
Theras withouten ende is songe Osanne,
Thow Cristes mooder, doghter deere of Anne!

And of thy light my soule in prison lighte,
That troubled is by the contagioun
Of my body, and also by the wighte
Of erthely lust and fals affeccioun;
O havene of refut, O salvacioun
Of hem that been in sorwe and in distresse,
Now help, for to my werk I wol me dresse!

Yet preye I yow that reden that I write,
Foryeve me, that I do no diligence
This ilke storie subtilly to endite;
For bothe have I the wordes and sentence
Of hym that at the seintes reverence
The storie wroot, and folwen hire legende,
I pray yow that ye wole my werk amende.

Interpretacio nominis Cecilie, quam ponit frater
Jacobus Januensis in Legenda Aurea.

FIRST wolde I yow the name of
Seinte Cecilie
Expowne, as men may in hir
storie see,
It is to seye in Englissh Hevenes
lilie,
For pure chaastnesse of virginitee;
Or, for she whitnesse hadde of honestee,
And grene of conscience, and of good fame
The soote savour, Lilie was hir name;

Or Cecile is to seye The wey to blynde,
For she ensample was by good techynge;
Or elles Cecile, as I writen fynde,
Is joyned, by a manere conjoynynge
Of Hevene and Lia, and heere, in figurynge,
The Hevene is set for thoght of hoolynesse,
And Lia for hire lastynge bisynesse.

Cecile may eek be seyd in this manere;
Wantynge of blyndnesse, for hir grete light
Of sapience, and for hire thewes cleere;
Or elles, loo! this maydens name bright
Of Hevene and Leos comth, for which by right
Men myghte hire wel, The hevene of peple, calle,
Ensample of goode and wise werkes alle.

For, Leos, Peple in Englissh is to seye,
And right as men may in the hevene see
The sonne and moone and sterres every weye,
Right so men goostly, in this mayden free,
Seyen of feith the magnanymytee,
And eek the cleernesse hool of sapience,
And sondry werkes, brighte of excellence.

And right so as thise philosophres write
That hevene is swift and round & eek brennynge,
Right so was faire Cecilie the white
Ful swift and bisy evere in good werkynge,
And round and hool in good perseverynge,
And brennynge evere in charite ful brighte;
Now have I yow declared what she highte.
Explicit.

HEERE BIGYNNETH THE SECONDE NONNES TALE OF THE LYF OF SEINTE CECILE

THIS mayden bright
Cecile, as hir lif seith,
Was comen of Ro-
mayns, & of noble kynde,
And from hir cradel up/
fostred in the feith
Of Crist, and bar his
gospel in hir mynde;
She nevere cessed, as I
writen fynde,
Of hir preyere, and God to love and drede,
Bisekynge hym to kepe hir maydenhede.

And whan this mayden sholde unto a man
Ywedded be, that was ful yong of age,
Which that ycleped was Valerian,
And day was comen of hir mariage,
She, ful devout and humble in hire corage,
Under hir robe of gold, that sat ful faire,
Hadde next hire flessh yclad hire in an haire.

And whil the orgues maden melodie,
To God allone in herte thus sang she:
O Lord, my soule and eek my body gye
Unwemmed, lest that I confounded be:
And, for his love that deyde upon a tree,
Every seconde or thridde day she faste,
Ay biddynge in hire orisons ful faste.

The nyght cam, and to bedde moste she gon
With hire housbonde, as ofte is the manere,
And pryvely to hym she seyde anon,
O sweete and wel/biloved spouse deere,
Ther is a conseil, and ye wolde it heere,
Which that right fayn I wolde unto yow seye,
So that ye swere ye shul me nat biwreye.

Valerian gan faste unto hire swere
That for no cas, ne thyng that myghte be,
He sholde neveremo biwreyen here;
And thanne at erst to hym thus seyde she:
I have an aungel which that loveth me,
That with greet love, wherso I wake or
sleepe,
Is redy ay my body for to kepe.

And if that he may feelen, out of drede,
That ye me touche or love in vileynye,
He right anon wol sle yow with the dede,
And in youre yowthe thus ye sholden dye;
And if that ye in clene love me gye,
He wol yow loven as me, for youre clennesse,
And shewen yow his joye and his brightnesse.

Valerian, corrected as God wolde,
Answerde agayn, If I shal trusten thee
Lat me that aungel se, and hym biholde;
And if that it a verray angel bee,
Thanne wol I doon as thou hast prayed me;

And if thou love another man, forsothe,
Right with this swerd thanne wol I sle yow
bothe.

CECILE answerde anon right in this
wise:
If that yow list, the angel shul ye see,
So that ye trowe on Crist, and yow baptize.
Gooth forth to Via Apia, quod shee,
That fro this toun ne stant but miles three,
And, to the povre folkes that ther dwelle
Sey hem right thus, as that I shal yow telle.

Tell hem that I, Cecile, yow to hem sente,
To shewen yow the goode Urban the olde,
For secree thynges, and for good entente.
And whan that ye Seint Urban han biholde,
Telle hym the wordes whiche I to yow tolde;
And whan that he hath purged yow fro synne,
Thanne shul ye se that angel, er ye twynne.

VALERIAN is to the place ygon,
And right as hym was taught by
his lernynge,
He foond this hooly olde Urban
anon,
Among the seintes buryeles
lotynge.
And he anon, withouten taryinge,
Dide his message; and whan that he it tolde,
Urban for joye his handes gan upholde;

The teeris from his eyen leet he falle:
Almyghty Lord! O Jhesu Crist, quod he,
Sower of chast conseil, hierde of us alle,
The fruyt of thilke seed of chastitee
That thou hast sowe in Cecile, taak to thee!
Lo, lyk a bisy bee, withouten gile,
Thee serveth ay thyn owene thral Cecile!

For thilke spouse, that she took right now
Ful lyk a fiers leoun, she sendeth heere,
As meke as evere was any lamb, to yow.
And with that word, anon ther gan appere
An oold man, clad in white clothes cleere,
That hadde a book with lettre of gold in
honde,
And gan biforn Valerian to stonde.

Valerian as deed fil doun for drede
Whan he hym saugh, & he up hente hym tho,
And on his book right thus he gan to rede:
Oo Lord, oo feith, oo God, withouten mo;
Oo Cristendom, and fader of alle also,
Aboven alle, and over al everywhere.
Thise wordes al with gold ywriten were.

Whan this was rad, thanne seyde this olde
man,
Leevestow this thyng or no? Sey ye or nay.

I leeve al this thyng, quod Valerian,
for sother thyng than this, I dar wel say,
Under the hevene no wight thynke may.
Tho vanysshed this olde man, he nyste where,
And Pope Urban hym cristened right there.

VALERIAN gooth hoom and fynt Cecilie
Withinne his chambre with an angel
stonde;
This angel hadde of roses and of lilie
Corones two, the which he bar in honde;
And first to Cecile, as I understonde,
He yaf that oon, and after gan he take
That oother to Valerian, hir make.

With body clene, and with unwemmed thoght,
Kepeth ay wel thise corones, quod he;
fro Paradys to yow have I hem broght,
Ne nevere mo ne shal they roten bee,
Ne lese hir soote savour, trusteth me;
Ne nevere wight shal seen hem with his eye,
But he be chaast and hate vileynye.

And thow, Valerian, for thow so soone
Assentedest to good conseil also,
Sey what thee list, and thou shalt han thy boone.
I have a brother, quod Valerian tho,
That in this world I love no man so.
I pray yow that my brother may han grace
To knowe the trouthe, as I do in this place.

THE angel seyde, God liketh thy requeste,
And bothe, with the palm of martirdom,
Ye shullen come unto his blisful feste.
And with that word Tiburce his brother coom.
And whan that he the savour undernoom
Which that the roses and the lilies caste,
Withinne his herte he gan to wondre faste,

And seyde: I wondre, this tyme of the yeer,
Whennes that soote savour cometh so
Of rose and lilies that I smelle heer;
for though I hadde hem in myne handes two
The savour myghte in me no depper go.
The sweete smel that in myn herte I fynde
Hath chaunged me al in another kynde.

VALERIAN seyde, Two corones han we,
Snow-white and rose-reed, that shynen
cleere,
Whiche that thyne eyen han no myght to see;
And as thou smellest hem thurgh my preyere,
So shaltow seen hem, leeve brother deere,
If it so be thou wolt, withouten slouthe,
Bileve aright and knowen verray trouthe.

TIBURCE answerde: Seistow this to me
In soothnesse, or in dreem I herkne this?
In dremes, quod Valerian, han we be
Unto this tyme, brother myn, ywis;
But now at erst in trouthe our dwellyng is.
How woostow this, quod Tiburce, in what
wyse?
Quod Valerian: That shal I thee devyse.

174

The aungel of God hath me the trouthe ytaught
Which thou shalt seen, if that thou wolt reneye
The ydoles and be clene, and elles naught.
And of the myracle of thise corones tweye,
Seint Ambrose in his preface list to seye;
Solempnely this noble doctour deere
Commendeth it, and seith in this manere:

The palm of martirdom for to receyve
Seinte Cecile, fulfild of Goddes yifte,
The world and eek hire chambre gan she weyve;
Witnesse Tyburces and Valerians shrifte,
To which God of his bountee wolde shifte
Corones two of floures wel smellynge,
And made his angel hem the corones brynge:

The mayde hath broght thise men to blisse above;
The world hath wist what it is worth, certeyn,
Devocioun of chastitee to love.
Tho shewed hym Cecile, al open and pleyn,
That alle ydoles nys but a thyng in veyn;
for they been dombe, and therto they been deve,
And charged hym his ydoles for to leve.

WHOSO that troweth nat this, a beest he is,
Quod tho Tiburce, if that I shal nat lye.
And she gan kisse his brest, that herde
this,
And was ful glad he koude trouthe espye.
This day I take thee for myn allye,
Seyde this blissful faire mayde, deere;
And after that she seyde as ye may heere:

Lo, right so as the love of Crist, quod she,
Made me thy brotheres wyf, right in that wise
Anon for myn allye heer take I thee,
Syn that thou wolt thyne ydoles despise.
Go with thy brother now, and thee baptise,
And make thee clene; so that thou mowe biholde
The angeles face of which thy brother tolde.

TIBURCE answerde and seyde, Brother dere,
first tel me whider I shal, and to what man?
To whom? quod he, com forth with right
good cheere;
I wol thee lede unto the Pope Urban.
Til Urban? brother myn Valerian,
Quod tho Tiburce; woltow me thider lede?
Me thynketh that it were a wonder dede.

Ne menestow nat Urban, quod he tho,
That is so ofte dampned to be deed,
And woneth in halkes alwey to and fro,
And dar nat ones putte forth his heed?
Men sholde hym brennen in a fyr so reed
If he were founde, or that men myghte hym spye,
And we also, to bere hym compaignye;

And whil we seken thilke divinitee
That is yhid in hevene pryvely,
Algate ybrend in this world shul we be!
To whom Cecile answerde boldely,
Men myghten dreden wel and skilfully

This lyf to lese, myne owene deere brother,
If this were lyvynge oonly and noon oother.

But ther is bettre lif in oother place,
That nevere shal be lost, ne drede thee noght,
Which Goddes sone us tolde thurgh his grace;
That fadres son hath alle thyng ywroght,
And al that wroght is with a skilful thoght,
The Goost, that fro the fader gan procede,
Hath sowled hem, withouten any drede.

By word and by myracle Goddes sone,
Whan he was in this world, declared heere
That ther was oother lyf ther men may wone.
To whom answerde Tiburce, O suster deere,
Ne seydestow right now in this manere,
Ther nys but oo God, lord in soothfastnesse;
And now of three how maystow bere witnesse?

That shal I telle, quod she, er I go.
Right as a man hath sapiences three,
Memorie, engyn, and intellect also,
So in oo beynge of divinitee
Thre persones may ther right wel bee.
Tho gan she hym ful bisily to preche
Of Cristes come, and of his peynes teche,

And many pointes of his passioun;
How Goddes sone in this world was withholde,
To doon mankynde pleyn remissioun,
That was ybounde in synne and cares colde:
Al this thynge she unto Tiburce tolde.
And after this Tiburce, in good entente,
With Valerian to Pope Urban he wente,

That thanked God; and with glad herte and light
He cristned hym, and made hym in that place
Parfit in his lernynge, Goddes knyght.
And after this Tiburce gat swich grace,
That every day he saugh, in tyme and space,
The aungel of God; and every maner boone
That he God axed, it was sped ful soone.

IT were ful hard by ordre for to seyn
How manye wondres Jhesus for hem
wroghte;
But atte laste, to tellen short and pleyn,
The sergeants of the toun of Rome hem soghte,
And hem biforn Almache the Prefect broghte,
Which hem opposed, and knew al hire entente,
And to the ymage of Juppiter hem sente,

And seyde: Whoso wol nat sacrifise,
Swap of his heed; this my sentence heer!
Anon thise martirs that I yow devyse,
Oon Maximus, that was an officer
Of the Prefectes, and his corniculer,
Hem hente; and whan he forth the seintes ladde,
Hymself he weep, for pitee that he hadde.

Whan Maximus had herd the seintes loore,
He gat hym of the tormentoures leve,
And ladde hem to his hous withoute moore,
And with hir prechyng, er that it were eve,

They gonnen fro the tormentours to reve,
And fro Maxime, and fro his folk echone,
The false feith, to trowe in God allone.

Cecilie cam, whan it was woxen nyght,
With preestes that hem cristned all yfeere;
And afterward, whan day was woxen light,
Cecile hem seyde with a ful stedefast cheere,
Now, Cristes owene knyghtes leeve and deere,
Cast alle awey the werkes of derknesse,
And armeth yow in armure of brightnesse.

Ye han, for sothe ydoon a greet bataille,
Youre cours is doon, youre feith han ye conserved,
Gooth to the corone of lyf that may nat faille;
The rightful Juge, which that ye han served,
Shal yeve it yow, as ye han it deserved.
And whan this thing was seyd as I devyse,
Men ledde hem forth to doon the sacrefise.

But whan they weren to the place broght,
To tellen shortly the conclusioun,
They nolde encense ne sacrifise right noght,
But on hir knees they setten hem adoun
With humble herte and sad devocioun,
And losten bothe hir hevedes in the place;
Hir soules wenten to the kyng of grace.

THIS Maximus, that saugh this thyng bityde,
With pitous teeris tolde it anon right,
That he hir soules saugh to hevene glyde
With aungels ful of cleernesse and of light,
And with his word converted many a wight;
For which Almachius dide hym so tobete,
With whippe of leed, til he the lif gan lete.

CECILE hym took, and buryed hym anoon
By Tiburce and Valerian softely,
Withinne hire burying-place, under the stoon.
And after this Almachius hastily
Bad his ministres fecchen openly
Cecile, so that she myghte in his presence
Doon sacrifice, and Juppiter encense.

But they, converted at hir wise loore,
Wepten ful soore, and yaven ful credence
Unto hire word, and cryden moore and moore,
Crist, Goddes sone, withouten difference
Is verray God, this is al oure sentence,
That hath so good a servant hym to serve;
This with oo voys we trowen, thogh we sterve!

ALMACHIUS, that herde of this doynge,
Bad fecchen Cecile, that he myghte hire see;
And alderfirst, lo! this was his axynge:
What maner womman artow? tho quod he.
I am a gentil womman born, quod she.
I axe thee, quod he, though it thee greeve;
Of thy religioun and of thy bileeve.

YE han bigonne youre question folily,
Quod she, that wolden two answeres
conclude
In oo demande; ye axed lewedly.

175

Almache answerde unto that similitude,
Of whennes comth thyn answering so rude?
Of whennes? quod she, whan that she was freyned,
Of conscience and of good feith unfeyned.

Almachius seyde: Ne takestow noon heede
Of my power? And she answerde hym this:
Youre myght, quod she, ful litel is to dreede;
for every mortal mannes power nys
But lyke a bladdre, ful of wynd, ywys.
for with a nedles poynt, whan it is blowe,
May al the boost of it be leyd ful lowe.

FUL wrongfully bigonne thow, quod he,
And yet in wrong is thy perseveraunce;
Wostow nat how oure myghty princes free
Han thus comanded and maad ordinaunce,
That every cristen wight shal han penaunce
But if that he his cristendom withseye,
And goon al quit, if he wole it reneye?

YOWRE princes erren, as youre nobleye dooth,
Quod tho Cecile, and with a wood sentence
Ye make us gilty, and it is nat sooth;
for ye, that knowen wel oure innocence,
for as muche as we doon a reverence
To Crist, and for we bere a cristen name,
Ye putte on us a cryme, and eek a blame.

But we that knowen thilke name so
for vertuous, we may it not withseye.
Almache answerde, Chees oon of thise two,
Do sacrifice, or cristendom reneye,
That thou mowe now escapen by that weye.
At which the hooly blisful faire mayde
Gan for to laughe, and to the juge sayde,

O juge, confus in thy nycetee,
Woltow that I reneye innocence,
To make me a wikked wight? quod she;
Lo! he dissymuleth heere in audience,
He stareth and woodeth in his advertence!
To whom Almachius, Unsely wrecche!
Ne woostow nat how far my myght may
strecche?

Han noght oure myghty princes to me yeven,
Ye, bothe power and auctoritee
To maken folk to dyen or to lyven?
Why spekestow so proudly thanne to me?
I speke noght but stedfastly, quod she,
Nat proudly, for I seye, as for my syde,
We haten deedly thilke vice of pryde.

And if thou drede nat a sooth to heere,
Thanne wol I shewe al openly, by right,
That thou hast maad a ful gret lesyng heere.
Thou seyst, thy princes han thee yeven myght
Bothe for to sleen and for to quyken a wight;
Thou, that ne mayst but oonly lyf bireve,
Thou hast noon oother power, ne no leve!

But thou mayst seyn, thy princes han thee maked
Ministre of deeth; for if thou speke of mo,
176

Thou lyest, for thy power is ful naked.
Do wey thy booldnesse! seyde Almachius tho,
And sacrifice to oure goddes, er thou go;
I recche nat what wrong that thou me profre,
for I can suffre it as a philosophre;

But thilke wronges may I nat endure
That thou spekest of oure goddes heere, quod he.
Cecile answerde, O nyce creature!
Thou seydest no word syn thou spak to me
That I ne knew therwith thy nycetee;
And that thou were, in every maner wise,
A lewed officer and a veyn justise!

Ther lakketh nothyng to thyne outter eyen
That thou nart blynd, for thyng that we seen alle
That it is stoon, that men may wel espyen,
That ilke stoon a god thow wolt it calle.
I rede thee, lat thyn hand upon it falle,
And taste it wel, and stoon thou shalt it fynde,
Syn that thou seest nat with thyne eyen blynde.

It is a shame that the peple shal
So scorne thee, and laughe at thy folye;
for comunly men woot it wel overal,
That myghty God is in his hevenes hye,
And thise ymages, wel thou mayst espye,
To thee, ne to hemself, mowe noght profite,
for in effect they been nat worth a myte.

THISE wordes and swiche other seyde she;
And he weex wrooth, and bad men sholde hir
lede
Hom til hir hous, And in hire hous, quod he,
Brenne hire right in a bath of flambes rede.
And as he bad, right so was doon in dede;
for in a bath they gonne hire faste shetten,
And nyght and day greet fyre they under betten.

The longe nyght, and eek a day also,
for al the fyr and eek the bathes heete,
She sat al coold, and feelede no wo,
It made hire nat a drope for to sweete.
But in that bath hir lyf she moste lete;
for he, Almachius, with ful wikke entente
To sleen hire in the bath his sonde sente.

THRE strokes in the nekke he smoot hire tho,
The tormentour, but for no maner chaunce
He myghte noght smyte al hir nekke atwo;
And for ther was that tyme an ordinaunce,
That no man sholde doon men swich penaunce
The ferthe strook to smyten, softe or soore,
This tormentour ne dorste do namoore;

But half deed, with hir nekke ycorven there,
He lefte hir lye, and on his wey is went.
The cristen folk, which that aboute hire were,
With sheetes han the blood ful faire yhent.
Thre dayes lyved she in this torment,
And nevere cessed hem the feith to teche;
That she hadde fostred, hem she gan to preche;

And hem she yaf hir moebles and hir thyng,
And to the Pope Urban bitook hem tho,

And seyde, I axed this at hevene kyng,
To han respit thre dayes and namo,
To recomende to yow, er that I go,
Thise soules, lo! and that I myghte do werche
Heere of myn hous perpetuelly a cherche.

SEINT URBAN, with his deknes, prively
The body fette, and buryed it by nyghte
Among his other seintes honestly.
Hir hous the chirche of Seinte Cecilie highte;
Seint Urban halwed it, as he wel myghte;
In which, into this day, in noble wyse,
Men doon to Crist and to his seinte servyse.
Heere is ended the Seconde Nonnes Tale.

The prologe of the Chanons Yemannes Tale.❀ ❀

HAN toold was al the lyf
of Seinte Cecile,
Er we hadde riden fully
fyve mile,
At Boghton under Blee
us gan atake
A man, that clothed was
in clothes blake,
And undernethe he wered
a surplys;
His hakeney, that was al pomely grys,
So swatte, that it wonder was to see;
It semed as he had priked miles three.
The hors eek that his Yeman rood upon
So swatte, that unnethe myghte it gon.
Aboute the peytrel stood the foom ful hye,
He was of foom al flekked as a pye.
A male tweyfoold on his croper lay,
It semed that he caried lite array.
Al light for somer rood this worthy man,
And in myn herte wondren I bigan
What that he was, til that I understood
How that his cloke was sowed to his hood;
for which, whan I hadde longe avysed me,
I demed hym som chanoun for to be.
His hat heeng at his bak doun by a laas,
for he hadde riden moore than trot or paas;
He hadde ay priked lik as he were wood.
A cloteleef he hadde under his hood
for swoot, and for to kepe his heed from heete;
But it was joye for to seen hym swete!
His forheed dropped as a stillatorie
Were ful of plantayne and of paritorie.
And whan that he was come, he gan to crye,
God save, quod he, this joly compaignye!
faste have I priked, quod he, for your sake,
Bycause that I wolde yow atake,
To riden in this myrie compaignye.
His yeman eek was ful of curteisye,
And seyde, Sires, now in the morwetyde,
Out of youre hostelrie I saugh you ryde,
And warned heer my lord and my soverayn,
Which that to ryden with yow is ful fayn
for his desport; he loveth daliaunce.
freend, for thy warnyng God yeve thee good
chaunce!
Thanne seyde oure Hoost, for certes it wolde seme

n 1

Thy lord were wys, and so I may wel deme;
He is ful jocunde also, dar I leye.
Can he oght telle a myrie tale or tweye,
With which he glade may this compaignye?

WHO, sire? my lord? ye, ye, withouten lye!
He kan of murthe, and eek of jolitee
Nat but ynough; also sire, trusteth me,
And ye hym knewe as wel as that do I,
Ye wolde wondre how wel and craftily
He koude werke, and that in sondry wise.
He hath take on hym many a greet emprise,
Which were ful hard for any that is heere
To brynge aboute, but they of hym it leere.
As hoomely as he rit amonges yow,
If ye hym knewe, it wolde be for youre prow;
Ye wolde nat forgoon his aqueyntaunce
for muchel good, I dar leye in balaunce
Al that I have in my possessioun.
He is a man of heigh discrecioun;
I warne yow wel, he is a passyng man.

WEL, quod oure Hoost, I pray thee tel me
than,
Is he a clerk or noon? Telle what he is.
Nay, he is gretter than a clerk, ywis,
Seyde this yeman, and in wordes fewe,
Hoost, of his craft somwhat I wol yow shewe.
I seye, my lord kan swich subtilitee,
But al his craft ye may nat wite for me,
And som what helpe I yet to his wirkyng,
That al this ground on which we been ridyng,
Til that we come to Caunterbury toun,
He koude al clene turne it up-so-doun,
And pave it al of silver and of gold.

AND whan this yeman hadde this tale ytold
Unto oure Hoost, he seyde, Benedicitee!
This thyng is wonder merveillous to me,
Syn that thy lord is of so heigh prudence,
Bycause of which men sholde hym reverence,
That of his worship rekketh he so lite;
His overslope nys nat worth a myte,
As in effect, to hym, so moot I go!
It is al baudy and totore also.
Why is thy lord so sluttish, I the preye,
And is of power bettre clooth to beye,
If that his dede accorde with thy speche?
Telle me that, and that I thee biseche.

WHY? quod this yeman, wherto axe ye me?
God help me so, for he shal nevere thee!
But I wol nat avowe that I seye,
And therfore keep it secree, I yow preye,
He is to wys, in feith, as I bileeve;
That that is overdoon, it wol nat preeve
Aright, as clerkes seyn, it is a vice.
Wherfore in that I holde hym lewed and nyce.
for whan a man hath overgreet a wit,
ful oft hym happeth to mysusen it;
So dooth my lord, and that me greveth soore.
God it amende! I kan sey yow namoore.

THEROf no fors, good yeman, quod oure
Hoost,
Syn of the konnyng of thy lord thow woost,
Telle how he dooth, I pray thee hertely,
Syn that he is so crafty and so sly.

Where dwellen ye, if it to telle be?
IN the suburbes of a toun, quod he,
Lurkynge in hernes and in lanes blynde,
Wheras thise robbours and thise
theves by kynde,
Holden hir pryvee fereful residence,
As they that dar not shewen hir presence,
So faren we, if I shall seye the sothe.
Now, quod oure Hoost, yit lat me talke to the;
Why artow so discoloured of thy face?
Peter! quod he, God yeve it harde grace,
I am so used in the fyr to blowe,
That it hath chaunged my colour, I trowe.
I am nat wont in no mirour to prie,
But swynke soore, and lerne multiplie.
We blondren evere, and pouren in the fir,
And for al that we faille of our desir,
For evere we lakken oure conclusioun.
To muchel folk we doon illusioun,
And borwe gold, be it a pound or two,
Or ten, or twelve, or manye sommes mo,
And make hem wenen, at the leeste weye,
That of a pound we koude make tweye!
Yet is it fals; but ay we han good hope
It for to doon, and after it we grope.
But that science is so fer us biforn,
We mowen nat, although we hadde it sworn,
It overtake, it slit awey so faste;
It wol us maken beggers atte laste.
WHIL this yeman was thus in his talkyng,
This chanoun drough hym neer, and herde al thyng
Which this yeman spak, for suspecioun
Of mennes speche evere hadde this chanoun.
For Catoun seith, that he that gilty is

Demeth alle thyng be spoke of hym, ywis.
That was the cause he gan so ny hym drawe
To his yeman, to herknen al his sawe.
And thus he seyde unto his yeman tho:
HOOLD thou thy pees, and spek no wordes mo!
For if thou do, thou shalt it deere abye!
Thou sclaundrest me heere in this compaignye,
And eek discoverest that thou sholdest hyde.
Ye? quod our Hoost, telle on, what so bityde;
Of al his thretyng rekke nat a myte!
In feith, quod he, namoore I do but lyte.
AND whan this chanoun saugh it wolde nat be,
But his yeman wolde telle his pryvetee,
He fledde awey for verray sorwe and shame.
A! quod the yeman, heere shal arise game,
Al that I kan anon now wol I telle,
Syn he is goon, the foule feend hym quelle!
For nevere heerafter wol I with hym meete
For peny ne for pound, I yow biheete!
He that me broghte first unto that game,
Er that he dye, sorwe have he and shame!
For it is ernest to me, by my feith;
That feele I wel, whatso any man seith.
And yet, for al my smert, and al my grief,
For al my sorwe, labour, and meschief,
I koude nevere leve it in no wise.
Now wolde God, my wit myghte suffise
To tellen al that longeth to that art!
And nathelees yow wol I tellen part;
Syn that my lord is goon, I wol nat spare;
Swich thyng as that I knowe, I wol declare.
Heere endeth the prologe of the Chanouns
Yemannes Tale.

HEERE BIGYNNETH THE CHANOUNS YEMAN HIS TALE.

Prima pars.

WITH this chanoun I dwelt have seven yeer,
And of his science am I never the neer.
Al that I hadde I have ylost therby;
And, God woot, so hath many mo than I.
Ther I was wont to be right fressh and gay
Of clothyng and of oother good array,
Now may I were an hose upon myn heed;
And wher my colour was bothe fressh & reed,
Now is it wan and of a leden hewe;
Whoso it useth, soore shal he rewe.
And of my swynk yet blered is myn eye;
Lo! which avantage is to multiplie!
That slidynge science hath me maad so bare,
That I have no good, wher that evere I fare,
And yet I am endetted so therby,

Of gold that I have borwed, trewely,
That whil I lyve, I shal it quite nevere.
Lat every man be war by me for evere!
What maner man that casteth hym therto,
If he continue, I holde his thrift ydo.
So help me God, therby shal he nat wynne,
But empte his purs, and make his wittes thynne.
And whan he, thurgh his madnesse and folye
Hath lost his owene good thurgh jupartye,
Thanne he exciteth oother folk therto,
To lese hir good as he hymself hath do.
For unto shrewes joye it is and ese
To have hir felawes in peyne and disese,
Thus was I ones lerned of a clerk.
Of that no charge, I wol speke of oure werk.
Whan we been there as we shul excercise
Oure elvysshe craft, we semen wonder wise,
Oure termes been so clergial and so queynte.
I blowe the fir til that myn herte feynte.

WHAT sholde I tellen eche proporcioun
Of thynges whiche that we werche upon,
As on fyve or sixe ounces, may wel be,
Of silver or som oother quantite,
And bisye me to telle yow the names
Of orpyment, brent bones, iren squames,
That into poudre grounden been ful smal?
And in an erthen pot how put is al,
And salt yput in, and also papeer,
Biforn thise poudres that I speke of heer,
And wel ycovered with a lampe of glas;
And muchel oother thyng which that ther was?
And of the pot and glasses enlutyng,
That of the eyre myghte passe out nothyng,
And of the esy fir and smart also,
Which that was maad, and of the care and wo
That we hadde in oure matires sublymyng,
And in amalgamyng and calcenyng
Of quyksilver, yclept mercurie crude?
For alle our sleightes we kan nat conclude.
Oure orpyment and sublymed mercurie,
Oure grounden litarge eek on the porfurie,
And ech of thise of ounces a certeyn,
Noght helpeth us, oure labour is in veyn.
Ne eek oure spirites ascencioun,
Ne oure matires that lyen al fix adoun,
Mowe in oure werkyng nothyng us availle.
For lost is al oure labour and travaille,
And al the cost, a twenty devel way,
Is lost also, which we upon it lay.

THER is also ful many another thyng
That is unto oure craft apertenyng;
Though I by ordre hem nat reherce kan,
Bycause that I am a lewed man,
Yet wol I telle hem as they come to mynde,
Thogh I ne kan nat sette hem in hir kynde;
As boole armonyak, vertgrees, boras,
And sondry vessels maad of erthe and glas,
Oure urynales, and our descensories,
Violes, croslets, and sublymatories,
Cucurbites, and alambikes eek,
And othere swiche, deere ynough a leek.
Nat nedeth it for to reherce hem alle,
Watres rubifiyng, and boles galle,
Arsenyk, sal armonyak, and brymstoon;
And herbes koude I telle eek many oon,
As egremoyne, valerian, and lunarie,
And othere swiche, if that me liste tarie.
Oure lampes brennyng bothe nyght and day,
To brynge aboute oure purpos if we may;
Oure fourneys eek of calcinacioun,
And of watres albificacioun,
Unslekked lym, chalk, and gleyre of an ey,
Poudres diverse, asshes, donge, pisse, and cley,
Cered pokets, sal peter, vitriole,
And diverse fires maad of wode and cole;
Sal tartre, alkaly, and sal preparat,
And combust matires, and coagulat,
Cley maad with hors or mannes heer, and oille
Of tartre, alum, glas, berme, wort, and argoille,
Resalgar, and oure matires enbibyng;
And eek of oure matires encorporyng,
And of oure silver citrinacioun,

Oure cementyng and fermentacioun,
Oure yngottes, testes, and many mo.

I WOL yow telle, as was me taught also,
The foure spirites and the bodies sevene,
By ordre, as ofte I herde my lord hem
nevene.
The firste spirit quyksilver called is,
The seconde orpyment, the thridde, ywis,
Sal armonyak, and the ferthe brymstoon.
The bodyes sevene eek, lo! hem heere anoon:
Sol gold is, and Luna silver we threpe,
Mars iren, Mercurie quyksilver we clepe,
Saturnus leed, and Juppiter is tyn,
And Venus coper, by my fader kyn!
This cursed craft whoso wole excercise,
He shal no good han that hym may suffise;
For al the good he spendeth theraboute,
He lese shal, therof have I no doute.
Whoso that listeth outen his folie,
Lat hym come forth, and lerne multiplie;
And every man that oght hath in his cofre,
Lat hym appiere, and wexe a philosophre.
Ascaunce that craft is so light to leere?
Nay, nay, God woot, al be he monk or frere,
Preest or chanoun, or any oother wyght,
Though he sitte at his book bothe day and night
In lernyng of this elvysshe nyce loore,
Al is in veyn, and parde, muchel moore!
To lerne a lewed man this subtiltee,
Fy! spek nat therof, for it wol nat bee;
And konne he letterure, or konne he noon,
As in effect, he shal fynde it al oon.
For bothe two, by my savacioun,
Concluden, in multiplicacioun,
Ylike wel, whan they han al ydo;
This is to seyn, they faillen bothe two.

YET forgat I to maken rehersaille
Of watres corosif, and of lymaille,
And of bodies mollificacioun,
And also of hire induracioun,
Oilles, ablucions, and metal fusible,
To tellen al wolde passen any bible
That owher is; wherfore, as for the beste,
Of alle thise names now wol I me reste.
For as I trowe, I have yow toold ynowe
To reyse a feend, al looke he never so rowe.
A! nay! lat be; the philosophres stoon,
Elixir clept, we sechen faste echoon,
For hadde we hym, thanne were it siker ynow.
But, unto God of hevene I make avow,
For al oure craft, whan we han al ydo,
With al oure sleighte, he wol nat come us to.
He hath ymaad us spenden muchel good,
For sorwe of which almoost we wexen wood,
But that good hope crepeth in oure herte,
Supposynge ever, though we sore smerte,
To be releeved by hym afterward.
Swich supposyng and hope is sharpe and hard;
I warne yow wel it is to seken evere;
That futur temps hath maad men to dissevere,
In trust therof, from al that evere they hadde.
Yet of that art they kan nat wexen sadde,
For unto hem it is a bitter sweete;

So semeth it; for nadde they but a sheete
Which that they myghte wrappe hem inne at nyght,
And a bak to walken inne by daylyght,
They wolde hem selle and spenden on the craft;
They kan nat stynte til nothyng be laft.
And everemoore, where that evere they goon
Men may hem knowe by smel of brymstoon;
for al the world, they stynken as a goot;
Hir savour is so rammyssh and so hoot,
That, though a man from hem a mile be,
The savour wole infecte hym, trusteth me;
Lo, thus by smelling, and threedbare array,
If that men liste, this folk they knowe may.
And if a man wole aske hem pryvely,
Why they been clothed so unthriftily,
They right anon wol rownen in his ere
And seyn, that if that they espied were,
Men wolde hem slee, bycause of hir science;
Lo, thus this folk bitrayen innocence!

Passe over this; I go my tale unto.
Er that the pot be on the fire ydo,
Of metals with a certeyn quantite,
My lord hem trempeth, and no man but he,
Now he is goon, I dare seyn boldely,
for, as men seyn, he kan doon craftily;
Algate I woot wel he hath swich a name,
And yet ful ofte he renneth in a blame;
And wite ye how? ful ofte it happeth so,
The pot tobreketh, and farewel! al is go!
Thise metals been of so greet violence,
Oure walles mowe nat make hem resistence,
But if they weren wroght of lym and stoon;
They percen so, and thurgh the wal they goon,
And somme of hem synken into the ground,
Thus han we lost by tymes many a pound,
And somme are scatered al the floor aboute,
Somme lepe into the roof; withouten doute,
Though that the feend noght in oure sighte hym shewe,
I trowe he with us be, that ilke shrewe!
In helle where that he lord is and sire,
Nis ther moore wo, ne moore rancour ne ire.
Whan that oure pot is broke, as I have sayd,
Every man chit, and halt hym yvele apayd.
Somme seyde, it was long on the fir makyng,
Somme seyde, nay! it was on the blowyng;
Thanne was I fered, for that was myn office;
Straw! quod the thridde, ye been lewed & nyce,
It was nat tempred as it oghte be.
Nay! quod the fourthe, stynt, and herkne me;
Bycause our fir ne was nat maad of beech,
That is the cause, and oother noon, so theech!
I kan nat telle wheron it was along,
But wel I woot greet strif is us among.
What! quod my lord, ther is namoore to doone,
Of thise perils I wol be war eftsoone;
I am right siker that the pot was crased.
Be as be may, be ye nothyng amased;
As usage is, lat swepe the floor as swithe,
Plukke up your hertes, and beeth glad and blithe!
The mullok on an heep ysweped was,
And on the floor ycast a canevas,
And al this mullok in a syve ythrowe,

180

And sifted, and ypiked many a throwe.
Pardee! quod oon, somwhat of oure metal
Yet is ther heere, though that we han nat al.
Although this thyng myshapped have as now,
Another tyme it may be wel ynow.
Us moste putte oure good in aventure;
A marchant, pardee! may nat ay endure,
Trusteth me wel, in his prosperitee;
Somtyme his good is drenched in the see,
And somtyme comth it sauf unto the londe.
Pees! quod my lord, the nexte tyme I shal fonde
To bryngen oure craft al in another plite;
And but I do, sires, lat me han the wite;
Ther was defaute in somwhat, wel I woot.
ANOTHER seyde the fir was over hoot:
But, be it hoot or coold, I dar seye this,
That we concluden everemoore amys.
We faille of that which that we wolden have,
And in oure madnesse everemoore we rave.
And whan we been togidres everichoon,
Every man semeth a Salomon.
But every thyng which shyneth as the gold,
Nis nat gold, as that I have herd it told;
Ne every appul that is fair to eye
Ne is nat good, what so men clappe or crye.
Right so, lo! fareth it amonges us;
He that semeth the wiseste, by Jhesus!
Is moost fool, whan it cometh to the preef;
And he that semeth trewest is a theef;
That shul ye knowe, er that I fro yow wende,
By that I of my tale have maad an ende.
Explicit prima pars. Et sequitur pars secunda.

HER is a chanoun of religioun
Amonges us, wolde infecte al a toun,
Thogh it as greet were as was Nynyvee,
Rome, Alisaundre, Troye, and othere three.
His sleightes and his infinit falsnesse
Ther koude no man writen, as I gesse,
Though that he myghte lyven a thousand yeer.
In al this world of falshede nis his peer;
for in his termes so he wolde hym wynde,
And speke his wordes in so sly a kynde,
Whanne he commune shal with any wight,
That he wol make hym doten anon right,
But it a feend be, as hymselven is.
ful many a man hath he begiled er this,
And wole, if that he lyve may a while;
And yet men ride and goon ful many a mile
Hym for to seke and have his aqueyntaunce,
Noght knowynge of his false governaunce;
And if yow list to yeve me audience,
I wol it tellen heere in youre presence.
BUT, worshipful chanouns religious,
Ne demeth nat that I sclaundre youre hous,
Although that my tale of a chanoun bee;
Of every ordre som shrewe is, pardee,
And God forbede that al a compaignye

Sholde rewe oo singuleer mannes folye.
To sclaundre yow is nothyng myn entente,
But to correcten that is mys I mente.
This tale was nat oonly toold for yow,
But eek for othere mo; ye woot wel how
That, among Cristes apostelles twelve,
Ther nas no traytour but Judas hymselve.
Thanne why sholde al the remenant have blame
That giltlees were? By yow I seye the same.
Save oonly this, if ye wol herkne me,
If any Judas in youre covent be,
Remoeveth hym bitymes, I yow rede,
If shame or los may causen any drede.
And beeth nothyng displesed, I yow preye,
But in this cas herkneth what I shal seye.

IN Londoun was a preest, an annueleer,
That therinne dwelled hadde many a yeer,
Which was so plesaunt and so servysable
Unto the wyf, wheras he was at table,
That she wolde suffre hym nothyng for to paye
For bord ne clothyng, wente he never so gaye;
And spendyng silver hadde he right ynow.
Therof no fors; I wol procede as now,
And telle forth my tale of the chanoun,
That broghte this preest to confusioun.

THIS false chanoun cam upon a day
Unto this preestes chambre, wher he lay,
Bisechynge hym to lene hym a certeyn
Of gold, and he wolde quite it hym ageyn.
Leene me a marc, quod he, but dayes three,
And at my day I wol it quiten thee.
And if so be that thow me fynde fals,
Another day do hange me by the hals!
This preest hym took a marc, and that as swithe,
And this chanoun hym thanked ofte sithe,
And took his leve, and wente forthe his weye,
And at the thridde day broghte his moneye,
And to the preest he took his gold agayn,
Wherof this preest was wonder glad and fayn.
Certes, quod he, nothyng anoyeth me
To lene a man a noble, or two or thre,
Or what thyng were in my possessioun,
Whan he so trewe is of condicioun,
That in no wise he breke wole his day;
To swich a man I kan never seye nay.

WHAT! quod this chanoun, sholde I be untrewe?
Nay, that were thyng yfallen al of newe.
Trouthe is a thyng that I wol evere kepe,
Unto that day in which that I shal crepe
Into my grave, or ellis God forbede!
Bileveth this as siker as the Crede.
God thanke I, and in good tyme be it sayd,
That ther was nevere man yet yvele apayd
For gold ne silver that he to me lente,
Ne nevere falshede in myn herte I mente.
And, sire, quod he, now of my pryvetee,
Syn ye so goodlich han been unto me,
And kithed to me so greet gentillesse,
Somwhat to quyte with youre kyndenesse,
I wol yow shewe, if that yow list to leere,

I wol yow teche pleynly the manere,
How I kan werken in philosophie.
Taketh good heede ye shul wel seen at eye,
That I wol doon a maistrie er I go.
Ye, quod the preest, ye, sire, and wol ye so?
Marie! therof I pray yow hertely!
At youre comandement, sire, trewely,
Quod the chanoun, and ellis God forbeede!
Loo, how this theef koude his servyse beede!
Ful sooth it is, that swiche profred servyse
Stynketh, as witnessen thise olde wyse;
And that ful soone I wol it verifie
In this chanoun, roote of alle trecherie,
That everemoore delit hath and gladnesse,
Swiche feendly thoughtes in his herte impresse,
How Cristes peple he may to meschief brynge;
God kepe us from his false dissymulynge!

NOGHT wiste this preest with whom that he delte,
Ne of his harm comynge he nothyng felte.
O sely preest! O sely innocent!
With coveitise anon thou shalt be blent!
O gracelees, ful blynd is thy conceite,
Nothyng ne artow war of the deceite
Which that this fox yshapen hath for thee;
His wily wrenches thou ne mayst nat flee.
Wherfore, to go to the conclusioun
That refereth to thy confusioun,
Unhappy man! anon I wol me hye
To tellen thyn unwit and thy folye,
And eek the falsnesse of that oother wrecche,
As ferforth as that my konnyng may strecche.
This chanoun was my lord, ye wolden weene;
Sire Hoost, in feith, and by the hevenes queene,
It was another chanoun, and nat hee,
That kan an hundred foold moore subtiltee!
He hath bitrayed folkes many tyme;
Of his falshede it dulleth me to ryme.
Evere whan that I speke of his falshede,
For shame of hym my chekes wexen rede,
Algates, they bigynnen for to glowe,
For reednesse have I noon, right wel I knowe,
In my visage; for fumes diverse
Of metals, whiche ye han herd me reherce,
Consumed and wasted han my reednesse.
Now taak heede of this chanouns cursednesse!
Sire, quod he to the preest, lat youre man gon
For quyksilver, that we hadde it anon,
And lat hym bryngen ounces two or three;
And whan he comth, as faste shul ye see
A wonder thyng, which ye saugh nevere er this.
Sire, quod the preest, it shal be doon ywis.
He bad his servant fecchen hym this thyng,
And he al redy was at his biddyng,
And wente hym forth, and cam anon agayn
With this quyksilver, soothly for to sayn,
And toke thise ounces thre to the chanoun;
And he hem leyde faire and wel adoun,
And bad the servant coles for to brynge,
That he anon myghte go to his werkynge.
THE coles right anon weren yfet,
And this chanoun took out a crosselet
Of his bosom, and shewed it to the preest.

n 3

*This instrument, quod he, which that thou
seest,
Taak in thyn hand, and put thyself therinne
Of this quyksilver an ounce, and heer bigynne,
In the name of Crist, to wexe a philosofre.
Ther been ful fewe, whiche that I wolde profre
To shewen hem thus muche of my science.
For ye shul seen heer, by experience,
That this quyksilver wol I mortifye
Right in youre sighte anon, I wol nat lye,
And make it as good silver and as fyn
As ther is any in youre purse or myn,
Or elleswhere, and make it malliable;
And elles, holdeth me fals and unable
Amonges folk for evere to appeere!
I have a poudre heer, that coste me deere,
Shal make al good, for it is cause of al
My konnyng, which that I yow shewen shal.
Voydeth youre man, and lat hym be theroute,
And shette the dore, whils we been aboute
Oure pryvetee, that no man us espie
Whils that we werke in this philosophie.

*AL as he bad fulfilled was in dede;
This ilke servant anonright out yede,
And his maister shette the dore anon,
And to hire labour spedily they gon.

*This preest, at this cursed chanouns biddyng
Upon the fir anon sette this thyng,
And blew the fir, and bisyed hym ful faste;
And this chanoun into the crosselet caste
A poudre, noot I wherof that it was
Ymaad, outher of chalk, outher of glas,
Or somwhat elles, was nat worth a flye,
To blynde with the preest; and bad hym hye
The coles for to couchen al above
The crosselet.*For, in tokenyng I thee love,
Quod this chanoun, thyne owene handes two
Shul werche al thyng which that shal heer be do.

*GRAUNT mercy! quod the preest, and was
ful glad,
And couched coles as that chanoun bad;
And while he bisy was, this feendly wrecche,
This false chanoun, the foule feend hym fecche!
Out of his bosom took a bechen cole,
In which ful subtilly was maad an hole,
And therinne put was of silver lemaille
An ounce, and stopped was, withouten faille,
The hole with wex, to kepe the lemaille in;
And understondeth, that this false gyn
Was nat maad ther, but it was maad bifore;
And othere thynges I shal telle moore
Herafterward, whiche that he with hym broghte;
Er he cam ther, hym to bigile he thoghte;
And so he dide, er that they wente atwynne;
Til he had terved hym, he koude nat blynne.
It dulleth me whan that I of hym speke,
On his falshede fayn wolde I me wreke,
If I wiste how; but he is heere and there;
He is so variaunt, he abit nowhere.

*BUT taketh heede now, sires, for Goddes love!
He took this cole of which I spak above,
And in his hand he baar it pryvely.
And whyles the preest couchede bisily
182

The coles, as I tolde yow er this,
This chanoun seyde, freend, ye doon amys;
This is nat couched as it oghte be;
But soone I shal amenden it, quod he.
Now lat me medle therwith but a while,
For of yow have I pitee, by Seint Gile!
Ye been right hoot, I se wel how ye swete;
Have heer a clooth, and wipe awey the wete.

*And whyles that the preest wiped his face,
This chanoun took his cole with harde grace,
And leyde it above, upon the myddeward
Of the crosselet, and blew wel afterward,
Til that the coles gonne faste brenne.

*NOW yeve us drynke, quod the chanoun
thenne,
As swithe al shal be wel, I undertake;
Sitte we doun, and let us myrie make.

*And whan that this chanounes bechen cole
Was brent, al the lemaille, out of the hole,
Into the crosselet fil anon adoun;
And so it moste nedes, by resoun,
Syn it so evene aboven couched was;
But therof wiste the preest nothyng, alas!
He demed alle the coles yliche good,
For of that sleighte he nothyng understood.
And whan this alkamystre saugh his tyme,
*Ris up, quod he, sire preest, & stondeth by me,
And for I woot wel ingot have ye noon,
Gooth, walketh forth, and bringe us a chalk stoon;
For I wol make oon of the same shap
That is an ingot, if I may han hap;
And bryngeth eek with yow a bolle or a panne
Ful of water, and ye shul se wel thanne
How that oure bisynesse shal thryve and preeve.
And yet, for ye shal han no mysbileeve,
Ne wrong conceite of me in youre absence,
I ne wol nat been out of youre presence,
But go with yow, and come with yow ageyn.

*The chambre dore, shortly for to seyn,
They opened and shette, and went hir weye.
And forth with hem they carieden the keye,
And coome agayn withouten any delay.
What sholde I tarien al the longe day?
He took the chalk, and shoop it in the wise
Of an ingot, as I shal yow devyse.

*I seye, he took out of his owene sleeve,
A teyne of silver, yvele moot he cheeve!
Which that ne was nat but an ounce of weighte;
And taketh heed now of his cursed sleighte!
He shoop his ingot, in lengthe and eek in breede
Of this teyne, withouten any drede,
So slyly, that the preest it nat espide;
And in his sleeve agayn he gan it hide;
And fro the fir he took up his mateere,
And in thyngot putte it with myrie cheere,
And in the water-vessel he it caste
Whan that hym luste, and bad the preest as faste,
*Loke what ther is, put in thin hand and grope,
Thow fynde shalt ther silver, as I hope.

*What, devel of helle! sholde it ellis be?
Shavyng of silver silver is, pardee!
He putte his hand in, and took up a teyne
Of silver fyn, and glad in every veyne

Was this preest, whan he saugh that it was so.
Goddes blessyng, and his moodres also,
And alle halwes have ye, sire chanoun!
Seyde this preest, and I hir malisoun,
But, and ye vouchesauf to techen me
This noble craft and this subtilitee,
I wol be youre, in al that evere I may.
QUOD the chanoun, Yet wol I make assay
The seconde tyme, that ye may taken heede
And been expert of this, & in youre neede
Another daye assaye in myn absence
This disciplyne, and this crafty science.
Lat take another ounce, quod he tho,
Of quyksilver, withouten wordes mo,
And do therwith as ye han doon er this
With that oother, which that now silver is.
This preest hym bisieth in al that he kan
To doon as this chanoun, this cursed man,
Comanded hym, and faste he blew the fir,
For to come to theffect of his desir.
And this chanoun, right in the meene while,
Al redy was, the preest eft to bigile,
And, for a countenaunce, in his hand he bar
An holwe stikke, taak kepe and be war!
In the ende of which an ounce, and namoore,
Of silver lemaille put was, as bifore
Was in his cole, and stopped with wex weel,
Fo to kepe in his lemaille every deel.
And whil this preest was in his bisynesse,
This chanoun with his stikke gan hym dresse
To hym anon, and his pouder caste in
As he did er; The devel out of his skyn
Hym terve, I pray to God, for his falshede!
For he was evere fals in thoght and dede;
And with this stikke, above the crosselet,
That was ordeyned with that false get,
He stired the coles, til relente gan
The wex agayn the fir, as every man,
But it a fool be, woot wel it moot nede,
And al that in the stikke was out yede,
And in the crosselet hastily it fel.
NOW, goode sires, what wol ye bet than wel?
Whan that this preest thus was bigiled
ageyn,
Supposynge noght but trouthe, sooth to seyn,
He was so glad, that I kan nat expresse
In no manere his myrthe and his gladnesse;
And to the chanoun he profred eftsoone
Body and good. Ye, quod the chanoun soone,
Though povre I be, crafty thou shalt me fynde;
I warne thee, yet is ther moore bihynde.
Is ther any coper herinne? seyde he.
Ye, quod the preest, sire, I trowe wel ther be.
Elles go bye us som, and that as swithe,
Now, goode sire, go forth thy wey and hy the.
He wente his wey, and with the coper cam,
And this chanoun it in his handes nam,
And of that coper weyed out but an ounce.
Al to symple is my tonge to pronounce,
As ministre of my wit, the doublenesse
Of this chanoun, roote of alle cursednesse.
He semed freendly to hem that knewe hym noght,
But he was feendly bothe in herte and thoght.

n 4

It werieth me to telle of his falsnesse,
And nathelees yet wol I it expresse,
To thentente that men may be war therby,
And for noon oother cause, trewely.
He putte the ounce of coper in the crosselet,
And on the fir as swithe he hath it set,
And caste in poudre, and made the preest to blowe,
And in his werkyng for to stoupe lowe,
As he dide er, and al nas but a jape;
Right as hym liste, the preest he made his ape;
And afterward in the ingot he it caste,
And in the panne putte it at the laste
Of water, and in he putte his owene hand;
And in his sleve, as ye biforne hand
Herde me telle, he hadde a silver teyne.
He slyly tooke it out, this cursed heyne,
Unwityng this preest of his false craft,
And in the pannes botme he hath it laft;
And in the water rombled to and fro,
And wonder pryvely took up also
The coper teyne, noght knowynge this preest,
And hidde it, and hym hente by the breest,
And to hym spak and thus seyde in his game,
Stoupeth adoun, by God, ye be to blame,
Helpeth me now, as I dide yow whileer,
Putte in youre hand, and looketh what is theer.
This preest took up this silver teyne anon,
And thanne seyde the chanoun: Lat us gon
With thise thre teynes, whiche that we han wroght
To som goldsmyth, and wite if they been oght.
For, by my feith, I nolde, for myn hood,
But if that they were silver, fyn and good,
And that as swithe preeved shal it bee.
UNTO the goldsmyth with this eteynes three
They wente, and putte thise teynes in assay
To fir and hamer; myghte no man seye nay,
But that they weren as hem oghte be.
THIS sotted preest, who was gladder than he?
Was nevere brid gladder agayn the day,
Ne nyghtyngale, in the sesoun of May.
Nas nevere man that luste bet to synge;
Ne ladye lustier in carolynge
Or for to speke of love and wommanhede,
Ne knyght in armes to doon an hardy dede
To stonde in grace of his lady deere,
Than hadde this preest this sory craft to leere;
And to the chanoun thus he spak and seyde:
FOR love of God, that for us alle deyde,
And as I may deserve it unto yow,
What shal this receite coste? telleth now!
By oure lady, quod this chanoun, it is deere,
I warne yow wel; for save I and a frere
In Engelond ther kan no man it make.
No fors, quod he, now, sire, for Goddes sake,
What shal I paye? Telleth me, I preye.
Ywis, quod he, it is ful deere, I seye;
Sire, at oo word, if that thee list it have,
Ye shul paye fourty pound, so God me save!
And, nere the freendshipe that ye dide er this
To me, ye sholde paye moore, ywis.
THIS preest the somme of fourty pound
anon
Of nobles fette, and took hem everichon

183

To this chanoun, for this ilke receit;
Al his werkyng nas but fraude and deceit.
Sire preest, he seyde, I kepe han no loos
Of my craft, for I wolde it kept were cloos;
And, as ye love me, kepeth it secree;
for, and men knewen al my soutiltee,
By God, they wolden han so greet envye
To me, bycause of my philosophye,
I sholde be deed, ther were noon oother weye.
God it forbeede! quod the preest; what sey ye?
Yet hadde I levere spenden al the good
Which that I have, or elles wexe I wood!
Than that ye sholden falle in swiche mescheef.
for youre good wyl, sire, have ye right good
preef,
Quod the chanoun, and farwel, grant mercy!
HE wente his wey, and never the preest hym sy
After that day; and whan that this preest
sholde
Maken assay, at swich tyme as he wolde
Of this receit, farwel! it wolde nat be!
Lo, thus byjaped and bigiled was he!
Thus maketh he his introduccioun,
To brynge folk to hir destruccioun.
Considereth sires, how that in ech estaat,
Bitwixe men and gold ther is debaat
So ferforth, that unnethes is ther noon.
This multiplying blent so many oon,
That, in good feith, I trowe that it bee
The cause grettest of swich scarsetee.
Philosophres speken so mystily
In this craft, that men kan nat come therby,
for any wit that men han now adayes.
They mowe wel chiteren as that doon jayes,
And in hir termes sette hir lust and peyne,
But to hir purpos shul they nevere atteyne.
A man may lightly lerne, if he have aught,
To multiplie, and brynge his good to naught!
Lo! swich a lucre is in this lusty game,
A mannes myrthe it wol turne unto grame,
And empten also grete and hevy purses,
And maken folk for to purchasen curses
Of hem that han hir good therto ylent.
O fy! for shame! they that han been brent,
Allas! kan they nat flee the fires heete?
Ye that it use, I rede ye it leete,
Lest ye lese al; for Bet than nevere is late.
Nevere to thryve were to long a date.
Though ye prolle ay, ye shul it nevere fynde;
Ye been as boold as is Bayard the blynde,
That blondreth forth, and peril casteth noon;
He is as boold to renne agayn a stoon,
As for to goon besides in the weye.
So faren ye that multiplie, I seye.
If that youre eyen kan nat seen aright,
Looke that youre mynde lakke noght his sight.
for though ye looke never so brode, and stare,
Ye shul nat wynne a myte on that chaffare,
But wasten al that ye may rape and renne.
Withdrawe the fir, lest it to faste brenne;
Medleth namoore with that art, I mene,

for, if ye doon, youre thrift is goon ful clene.
And right as swithe I wol yow tellen heere,
What philosophres seyn in this mateere.
LO, thus seith Arnold of the Newe Toun,
As his Rosarie maketh mencioun;
He seith right thus, withouten any lye,
Ther may no man mercurie mortifie,
But it be with his brother knowlechyng.
HOW that he, which that first seyde this thyng,
Of philosophres fader was, Hermes;
He seith, how that the dragon, doutelees,
Ne dyeth nat, but if that he be slayn
With his brother; and that is for to sayn,
By the dragon, Mercurie and noon oother,
He understood; and Brymstoon by his brother,
That out of Sol and Luna were ydrawe.
And therfore, seyde he, taak heede to my sawe;
Lat no man bisye hym this art for to seche,
But if that he thentencioun and speche
Of philosophres understonde kan;
And if he do, he is a lewed man.
for this science and this konnyng, quod he,
Is of the secree of secrees, pardee.
ALSO ther was a disciple of Plato
That on a tyme seyde his maister to,
As his book Senior wol bere witnesse,
And this was his demande, in soothfastnesse:
Telle me the name of the privee stoon.
And Plato answerde unto hym anoon,
Take the stoon that Titanos men name.
Which is that? quod he. Magnesia is the
same,
Seyde Plato. Ye, sire, and is it thus?
This is ignotum per ignotius.
What is Magnesia, good sire, I yow preye?
It is a water that is maad, I seye,
Of elementes foure, quod Plato.
Telle me the roote, good sire, quod he tho,
Of that water, if that it be youre wille.
Nay, nay, quod Plato, certein that I nylle.
The philosophres sworn were everychoon
That they sholden discovere it unto noon,
Ne in no book it write in no manere;
for unto Crist it is so lief and deere,
That he wol nat that it discovered bee,
But where it liketh to his deitee
Man for tenspire, and eek for to deffende
Whom that hym liketh; lo, this is the ende.
THANNE conclude I thus, sith God of
hevene
Ne wil nat that the philosophres nevene
How that a man shal come unto this stoon,
I rede, as for the beste, lete it goon.
for whoso maketh God his adversarie,
As for to werken anythyng in contrarie
Of his wil, certes never shal he thryve,
Thogh that he multiplie terme of his lyve.
And there a poynt; for ended is my tale;
God sende every trewe man boote of his bale!
Amen.
Heere is ended the Chanouns Yemannes Tale.

Heere folweth the prologe of the Maunciples Tale.

WITE ye nat where ther
stant a litel toun
Which that ycleped is
Bobbe-up-and-doun,
Under the Blee, in Caun-
terbury weye?
Ther gan oure Hooste for
to jape and pleye,
And seyde, Sires, what!
Dun is in the Myre!
Is ther no man, for preyere ne for hyre,
That wole awake oure felawe al bihynde?
A theef myghte hym ful lightly robbe and bynde.
See how he nappeth! see, for cokkes bones!
As he wol falle fro his hors atones.
Is that a cook of Londoun, with meschaunce?
Do hym come forth, he knoweth his penaunce,
For he shal telle a tale, by my fey!
Although it be nat worth a botel hey.
Awake, thou cook, quod he, God yeve thee sorwe!
What eyleth thee to slepe by the morwe?
Hastow had fleen al nyght, or artow dronke?
Or hastow with some quene al nyght yswonke,
So that thou mayst nat holden up thyn heed?
This cook, that was ful pale and nothyng reed,
Seyde to oure Hoost, So God my soule blesse,
As ther is falle on me swich hevynesse,
Noot I nat why, that me were levere slepe
Than the beste galon wyn in Chepe.
Wel, quod the maunciple, if it may doon ese
To thee, sire cook, and to no wight displese
Which that heere rideth in this compaignye,
And that oure Hoost wol, of his curteisye,
I wol as now excuse thee of thy tale,
For, in good feith, thy visage is ful pale,
Thyne eyen daswen eek, as that me thynketh,
And wel I woot, thy breeth ful soure stynketh,
That sheweth wel thou art nat wel disposed;
Of me, certeyn, thou shal nat been yglosed.
See how he ganeth, lo, this dronken wight!
As though he wolde swolwe us anonright.
Hoold cloos thy mouth, man, by thy fader kyn!
The devel of helle sette his foot therin!
Thy cursed breeth infecte wole us alle;
Fy, stynkyng swyn! fy, foule moote thee falle!
A! taketh heede, sires, of this lusty man.
Now, sweete sire, wol ye justen atte fan?
Therto me thynketh ye been wel yshape!
I trowe that ye dronken han wyn ape,
And that is whan men pleyen with a straw.
AND with this speche the cook wex wrooth
and wraw,
And on the maunciple he gan nodde faste
For lakke of speche, and doun the hors hym caste,
Wheras he lay, til that men up hym took;
This was a fair chyvachee of a cook!

Allas! he nadde holde hym by his ladel!
And, er that he agayn were in his sadel,
Ther was greet showvyng bothe to and fro,
To lifte hym up, and muchel care and wo,
So unweeldy was this sory palled goost;
And to the maunciple thanne spak oure Hoost:
Bycause drynke hath dominacioun
Upon this man, by my savacioun,
I trowe he lewedly wolde telle his tale,
For were it wyn, or oold or moysty ale,
That he hath dronke, he speketh in his nose,
And fneseth faste, and eek he hath the pose.
He hath also to do moore than ynough
To kepe hym and his capul out of slough;
And, if he falle from his capul eftsoone,
Thanne shul we alle have ynough to doone,
In liftyng up his hevy dronken cors;
Telle on thy tale, of hym make I no fors.
BUT yet, maunciple, in feith thou art to nyce,
Thus openly repreve hym of his vice.
Another day he wole, peraventure,
Reclayme thee, and brynge thee to lure;
I meene, he speke wole of smale thynges,
As for to pynchen at thy rekenynges,
That were nat honeste, if it cam to preef.
No, quod the maunciple, that were a greet
mescheef!
So myghte he lightly brynge me in the snare.
Yet hadde I levere payen for the mare
Which he rit on, than he sholde with me stryve;
I wol nat wratthe hym, al so moot I thryve!
That that I spak, I seyde it in my bourde;
And wite ye what? I have heer, in a gourde,
A draughte of wyn, ye, of a ripe grape,
And right anon ye shul seen a good jape.
This cook shal drynke therof, if I may;
Up peyne of deeth, he wol nat seye me nay!
And certeynly, to tellen as it was,
Of this vessel the cook drank faste, allas!
What neded hym? he drank ynough biforn.
And whan he hadde pouped in this horn,
To the maunciple he took the gourde agayn,
And of that drynke the cook was wonder fayn,
And thanked hym in swich wise as he koude.
Thanne gan oure Hoost to laughen wonder
loude,
And seyde, I se wel it is necessarie,
Where that we goon, good drynke we with us carie;
For that wol turne rancour and disese
Tacord and love, and many a wrong apese.
O thou Bachus! yblessed be thy name
That so kanst turnen ernest into game!
Worship and thank be to thy deitee!
Of that mateere ye gete namoore of me.
Telle on thy tale, maunciple, I thee preye.
Wel, sire, quod he, now herkneth what I seye.
Thus endeth the prologe of the Maunciple.

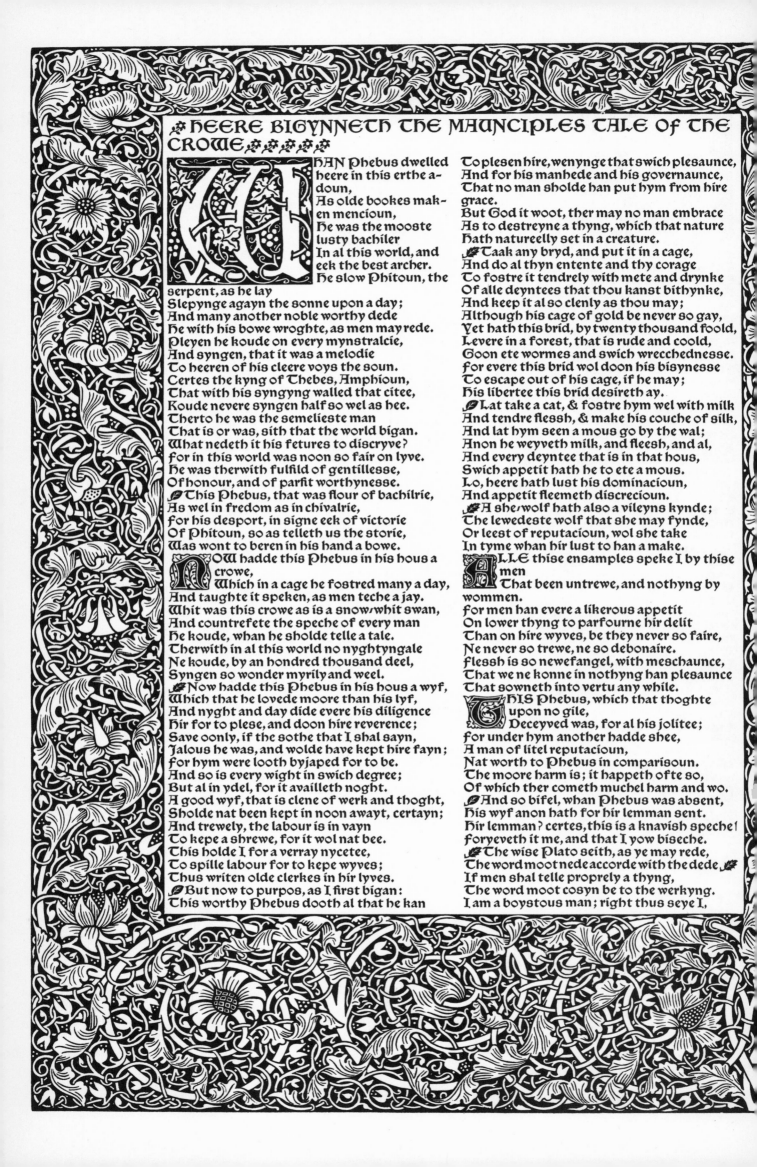

¶ HEERE BIGYNNETH THE MAUNCIPLES TALE OF THE CROWE ❦❦❦❦

WHAN Phebus dwelled
heere in this erthe a-
doun,
As olde bookes mak-
en mencioun,
He was the mooste
lusty bachiler
In al this world, and
eek the best archer.
He slow Phitoun, the
serpent, as he lay
Slepynge agayn the sonne upon a day;
And many another noble worthy dede
He with his bowe wroghte, as men may rede.
Pleyen he koude on every mynstralcie,
And syngen, that it was a melodie
To heeren of his cleere voys the soun.
Certes the kyng of Thebes, Amphioun,
That with his syngyng walled that citee,
Koude nevere syngen half so wel as hee.
Therto he was the semelieste man
That is or was, sith that the world bigan.
What nedeth it his fetures to discryve?
For in this world was noon so fair on lyve.
He was therwith fulfild of gentillesse,
Of honour, and of parfit worthynesse.
¶ This Phebus, that was flour of bachilrie,
As wel in fredom as in chivalrie,
For his desport, in signe eek of victorie
Of Phitoun, so as telleth us the storie,
Was wont to beren in his hand a bowe.
NOW hadde this Phebus in his hous a
crowe,
Which in a cage he fostred many a day,
And taughte it speken, as men teche a jay.
Whit was this crowe as is a snow-whit swan,
And countrefete the speche of every man
He koude, whan he sholde telle a tale.
Therwith in al this world no nyghtyngale
Ne koude, by an hondred thousand deel,
Syngen so wonder myrily and weel.
¶ Now hadde this Phebus in his hous a wyf,
Which that he lovede moore than his lyf,
And nyght and day dide evere his diligence
Hir for to plese, and doon hire reverence;
Save oonly, if the sothe that I shal sayn,
Jalous he was, and wolde have kept hire fayn;
For hym were looth byjaped for to be.
And so is every wight in swich degree;
But al in ydel, for it availleth noght.
A good wyf, that is clene of werk and thoght,
Sholde nat been kept in noon awayt, certayn;
And trewely, the labour is in vayn
To kepe a shrewe, for it wol nat bee.
This holde I for a verray nycetee,
To spille labour for to kepe wyves;
Thus writen olde clerkes in hir lyves.
¶ But now to purpos, as I first bigan:
This worthy Phebus dooth al that he kan

To plesen hire, wenynge that swich plesaunce,
And for his manhede and his governaunce,
That no man sholde han put hym from hire
grace.
But God it woot, ther may no man embrace
As to destreyne a thyng, which that nature
Hath natureelly set in a creature.
¶ Taak any bryd, and put it in a cage,
And do al thyn entente and thy corage
To fostre it tendrely with mete and drynke
Of alle deyntees that thou kanst bithynke,
And keep it al so clenly as thou may;
Although his cage of gold be never so gay,
Yet hath this brid, by twenty thousand foold,
Levere in a forest, that is rude and coold,
Goon ete wormes and swich wrecchednesse.
For evere this brid wol doon his bisynesse
To escape out of his cage, if he may;
His libertee this brid desireth ay.
¶ Lat take a cat, & fostre hym wel with milk
And tendre flessh, & make his couche of silk,
And lat hym seen a mous go by the wal;
Anon he weyveth milk, and fleesh, and al,
And every deyntee that is in that hous,
Swich appetit hath he to ete a mous.
Lo, heere hath lust his dominacioun,
And appetit fleemeth discrecioun.
¶ A she-wolf hath also a vileyns kynde;
The lewedeste wolf that she may fynde,
Or leest of reputacioun, wol she take
In tyme whan hir lust to han a make.
ALLE thise ensamples speke I by thise
men
That been untrewe, and nothyng by
wommen.
For men han evere a likerous appetit
On lower thyng to parfourne hir delit
Than on hire wyves, be they never so faire,
Ne never so trewe, ne so debonaire.
Flessh is so newefangel, with meschaunce,
That we ne konne in nothyng han plesaunce
That sowneth into vertu any while.
THIS Phebus, which that thoghte
upon no gile,
Deceyved was, for al his jolitee;
For under hym another hadde shee,
A man of litel reputacioun,
Nat worth to Phebus in comparisoun.
The moore harm is; it happeth ofte so,
Of which ther cometh muchel harm and wo.
¶ And so bifel, whan Phebus was absent,
His wyf anon hath for hir lemman sent.
Hir lemman? certes, this is a knavish speche!
Foryeveth it me, and that I yow biseche.
¶ The wise Plato seith, as ye may rede,
The word moot nede accorde with the dede.
If men shal telle proprely a thyng,
The word moot cosyn be to the werkyng.
I am a boystous man; right thus seye I,

Ther nys no difference, trewely
Bitwixe a wyf that is of heigh degree,
If of hire body dishoneste she be,
And a povre wenche, oother than this,
If it so be, they werke bothe amys,
But that the gentile, in hire staat above,
She shal be cleped his lady, as in love;
And for that oother is a povre womman,
She shal be cleped his wenche, or his lemman.
And, God it woot, myn owene deere brother,
Men leyn that oon as lowe as lith that oother.
Right so, bitwixe a titlelees tiraunt
And an outlawe, or a theef erraunt,
The same I seye, ther is no difference.
To Alisaundre toold was this sentence;
That, for the tiraunt is of gretter myght,
By force of meynee for to sleen dounright,
And brennen hous and hoom, and make al playn,
Lo, therfore is he cleped a capitayn;
And, for the outlawe hath but smal meynee,
And may nat doon so greet an harm as he,
Ne brynge a contree to so greet mescheef,
Men clepen hym an outlawe or a theef.
But, for I am a man noght textueel,
I wol noght telle of textes never a deel;
I wol go to my tale, as I bigan.
WHAN Phebus wyf had sent for hir
lemman,
Anon they wroghten al hire lust volage.
The white crowe, that heeng ay in the cage,
Biheeld hire werk, and seyde never a word.
And whan that hoom was come Phebus, the lord,
This crowe sang Cokkow! cokkow! cokkow!
What, bryd? quod Phebus, what song
syngestow?
Ne were thow wont so myrily to synge
That to myn herte it was a rejoysynge
To heere thy voys? Allas! what song is this?
By God! quod he, I synge nat amys.
Phebus, quod he, for al thy worthynesse,
For al thy beautee and thy gentilesse,
For al thy song and al thy mynstralcye,
For al thy waityng, blered is thyn eye
With oon of litel reputacioun,
Noght worth to thee, as in comparisoun,
The montance of a gnat; so moote I thryve!
For on thy bed thy wyf I saugh hym swyve.
What wol ye moore? The crowe anon hym
tolde
By sadde tokenes and by wordes bolde,
How that his wyf had doon hire lecherye,
Hym to greet shame and to greet vileynye;
And tolde hym ofte, he saugh it with his eyen.
THIS Phebus gan aweyward for to wryen,
And thoughte his sorweful herte brast
atwo;
His bowe he bente, and sette therinne a flo,
And in his ire his wyf thanne hath he slayn.
This is theffect, ther is namoore to sayn;
For sorwe of which he brak his mynstralcie,
Bothe harpe, and lute, and gyterne, and sautrie;
And eek he brak his arwes and his bowe,
And after that, thus spak he to the crowe:

TRAITOUR, quod he, with tonge of scor-
pioun,
Thou hast me broght to my confusioun!
Allas! that I was wroght! why nere I deed?
O deere wyf! O gemme of lustiheed!
That were to me so sad and eek so trewe,
Now listow deed, with face pale of hewe,
Ful giltelees, that dorste I swere, ywys!
O rakel hand! to doon so foule amys!
O trouble wit! O ire reccheless!
That unavysed smytest giltelees!
O wantrust! ful of fals suspecioun,
Where was thy wit and thy discrecioun?
O every man, bewar of rakelnesse,
Ne trowe nothyng withouten strong witnesse.
Smyt nat to soone, er that ye witen why,
And beeth avysed wel and sobrely,
Er ye doon any execucioun
Upon youre ire, for suspecioun.
Allas! a thousand folk hath rakel ire
Fully fordoon, and broght hem in the mire.
Allas! for sorwe I wol myselven slee!
And to the crowe, O false theef! seyde he,
I wol thee quite anon thy false tale!
Thou songe whilom lyk a nyghtyngale;
Now shaltow, false theef, thy song forgon,
And eek thy white fetheres everichon,
Ne nevere in al thy lif ne shaltou speke.
Thus shal men on a traytour been awreke;
Thou and thyn ofspryng evere shul be blake,
Ne nevere sweete noyse shul ye make,
But evere crie agayn tempest and rayn,
In tokenynge that thurgh thee my wyf is slayn.
And to the crowe he stirte, and that anon,
And pulled his white fetheres everychon,
And made hym blak, and refte hym al his song,
And eek his speche, and out at dore hym slong
Unto the devel, which I hym bitake;
And for this caas been alle crowes blake.
LORDYNGES, by this ensample I yow
preye,
Beth war, and taketh kepe what I seye;
Ne telleth nevere no man in youre lyf
How that another man hath dight his wyf;
He wol yow haten mortally, certeyn.
Daun Salomon, as wise clerkes seyn,
Techeth a man to kepen his tonge weel;
But as I seyde, I am noght textueel.
But nathelees, thus taughte me my dame:
My sone, thenk on the crowe, a Goddes name;
My sone, keep wel thy tonge and keep thy freend.
A wikked tonge is worse than a feend.
My sone, from a feend men may hem blesse;
My sone, God of his endelees goodnesse
Walled a tonge with teeth and lippes eke,
For man sholde hym avyse what he speeke;
My sone, ful ofte, for to muche speche,
Hath many a man been spilt, as clerkes teche;
But for a litel speche avysely
Is no man shent, to speke generally.
My sone, thy tonge sholdestow restreyne
At alle tymes, but whan thou doost thy peyne
To speke of God, in honour and preyere.

The firste vertu, sone, if thou wolt leere,
Is to restreyne and kepe wel thy tonge;
Thus lerne children whan that they been yonge.
My sone, of muchel spekyng yvele avysed,
Ther lasse spekyng hadde ynough suffised,
Comth muchel harm, thus was me toold and taught.
In muchel speche synne wanteth naught.
Wostow wherof a rakel tonge serveth?
Right as a swerd forkutteth and forkerveth
An arm atwo, my deere sone, right so
A tonge kutteth freendshipe al atwo.
A jangler is to God abhomynable;
Reed Salomon, so wys and honurable;
Reed David in his Psalmes, reed Senekke.
My sone, spek nat, but with thyn heed thou bekke.
Dissimule as thou were deef, if that thou heere
A jangler speke of perilous mateere.
The Flemyng seith, and lerne it if thee leste,
That Litel janglyng causeth muchel reste.
My sone, if thou no wikked word hast seyd,
Thee thar nat drede for to be biwreyd;
But he that hath mysseyd, I dar wel sayn,
He may by no wey clepe his word agayn.
Thyng that is seyd, is seyd; and forth it gooth,
Though hym repente, or be hym leef or looth.
He is his thral to whom that he hath sayd
A tale, of which he is now yvele apayd.
My sone, be war, and be noon auctour newe
Of tidynges, wheither they been false or trewe.
Wherso thou come, amonges hye or lowe,
Kepe wel thy tonge, and thenk upon the crowe.
Heere is ended the Maunciples Tale of the Crowe.

Here folweth the prologe of the Persones Tale.

Y that the maunciple hadde
his tale al ended,
The sonne fro the south
lyne was descended
So lowe, that he nas nat, to
my sighte
Degreës nyne-and-twenty
as in highte.
Foure of the clokke it was
tho, as I gesse;
For elevene foot, or litel moore or lesse,
My shadwe was at thilke tyme, as there
Of swiche feet as my lengthe parted were
In sixe feet equal of proporcioun.
Therwith the moones exaltacioun,
I meene Libra, alwey gan ascende,
As we were entryng at a thropes ende;
For which our Hoost, as he was wont to gye,
As in this caas, oure joly compaignye,
Seyde in this wise, Lordynges everichoon,
Now lakketh us no tales mo than oon.
Fulfilled is my sentence and my decree;
I trowe that we han herd of ech degree.

Almoost fulfild is al myn ordinaunce;
I pray to God so yeve hym right good chaunce
That telleth this tale to us lustily.
Sire preest, quod he, artow a vicary?
Or arte a person? sey sooth, by thy fey!
Be what thou be, ne breke thou nat oure pley;
For every man, save thou, hath toold his tale,
Unbokele, and shewe us what is in thy male;
For trewely, me thynketh, by thy cheere,
Thou sholdest knytte up wel a greet mateere.
Telle us a fable anon, for cokkes bones!
THIS persoune, him answerde al atones,
Thou getest fable noon ytoold for me,
For Paul, that writeth unto Thymothee,
Repreveth hem that weyveth soothfastnesse,
And tellen fables and swich wrecchednesse.
Why sholde I sowen draf out of my fest,
Whan I may sowen whete, if that me lest?
For which I seye, if that yow list to heere
Moralitee and vertuous mateere,
And thanne that ye wol yeve me audience,
I wol ful fayn, at Cristes reverence,
Do yow plesaunce leefful, as I kan.
But trusteth wel, I am a southren man,
I kan nat geeste rum, ram, ruf, by lettre,
Ne, God woot, rym holde I but litel bettre;
And therfore, if yow list, I wol nat glose.
I wol yow telle a myrie tale in prose
To knytte up al this feeste, and make an ende.
And Jhesu, for his grace, wit me sende
To shewe yow the wey, in this viage,
Of thilke parfit glorious pilgrymage
That highte Jerusalem celestial.
And, if ye vouchesauf, anon I shal
Bigynne upon my tale, for whiche I preye
Telle youre avys, I kan no bettre seye.
But nathelees, this meditacioun
I putte it ay under correccioun
Of clerkes, for I am nat textueel;
I take but the sentence, trusteth weel.
Therfore I make protestacioun
That I wol stonde to correccioun.
UPON this word we han assented soone,
For, as us semed, it was for to doone,
To enden in som vertuous sentence,
And for to yeve hym space and audience;
And bede oure Hoost he sholde to hym seye,
That alle we to telle his tale hym preye.
Oure Hoost hadde the wordes for us alle:
Sire preest, quod he, now faire yow bifalle!
Sey what yow list, and we wol gladly heere;
And with that word, he seyde in this manere:
Telleth, quod he, youre meditacioun.
But hasteth yow, the sonne wol adoun;
Beth fructuous, and that in litel space,
And to do wel God sende yow his grace.
Explicit prohemium.

188

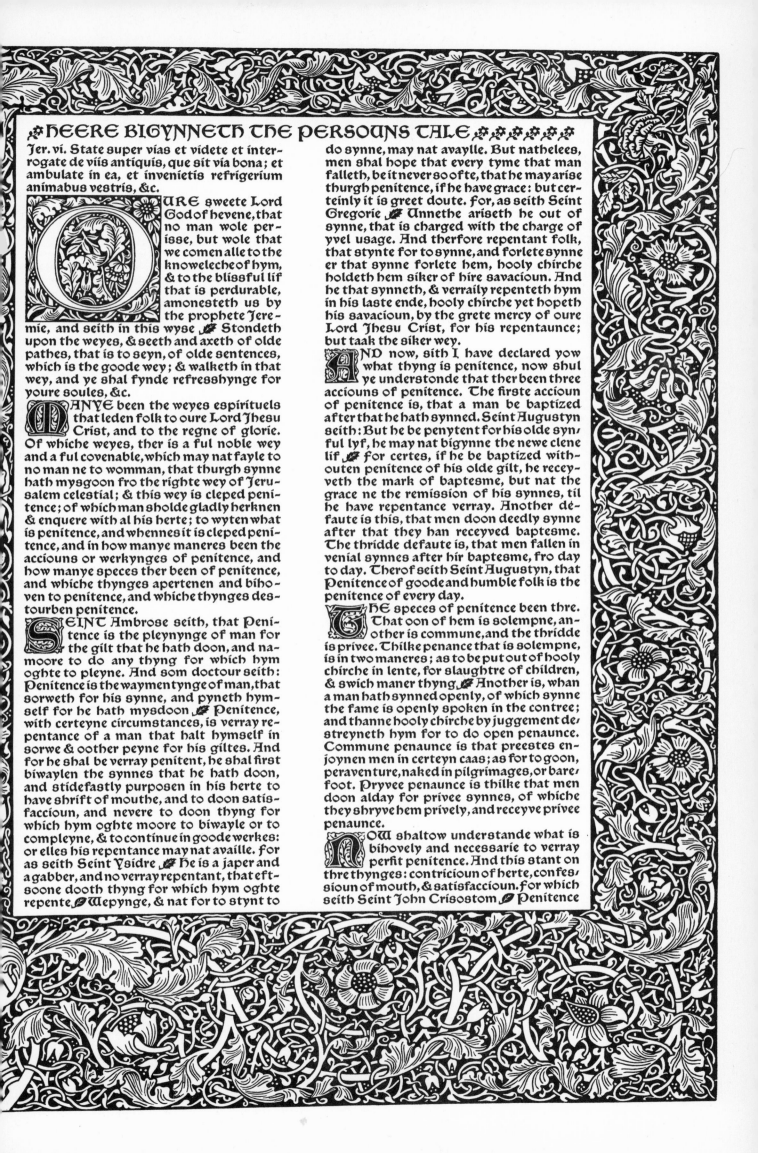

❧HEERE BIGYNNETH THE PERSOUNS TALE ❧❧❧❧❧

Jer. vi. State super vias et videte et inter-
rogate de viis antiquis, que sit via bona; et
ambulate in ea, et invenietis refrigerium
animabus vestris, &c.

OURE sweete Lord
God of hevene, that
no man wole per-
isse, but wole that
we comen alle to the
knoweleche of hym,
& to the blissful lif
that is perdurable,
amonesteth us by
the prophete Jere-
mie, and seith in this wyse ❧ Stondeth
upon the weyes, & seeth and axeth of olde
pathes, that is to seyn, of olde sentences,
which is the goode wey; & walketh in that
wey, and ye shal fynde refresshynge for
youre soules, &c.

MANYE been the weyes espirituels
that leden folk to oure Lord Jhesu
Crist, and to the regne of glorie.
Of whiche weyes, ther is a ful noble wey
and a ful covenable, which may nat fayle to
no man ne to womman, that thurgh synne
hath mysgoon fro the righte wey of Jerusalem celestial; & this wey is cleped penitence; of which man sholde gladly herknen
& enquere with al his herte; to wyten what
is penitence, and whennes it is cleped penitence, and in how manye maneres been the
acciouns or werkynges of penitence, and
how manye speces ther been of penitence,
and whiche thynges apertenen and biho-
ven to penitence, and whiche thynges destourben penitence.

SEINT Ambrose seith, that Penitence is the pleynynge of man for
the gilt that he hath doon, and namoore to do any thyng for which hym
oghte to pleyne. And som doctour seith:
Penitence is the waymentynge of man, that
sorweth for his synne, and pyneth hymself for he hath mysdoon ❧ Penitence,
with certeyne circumstances, is verray repentance of a man that halt hymself in
sorwe & oother peyne for his giltes. And
for he shal be verray penitent, he shal first
biwaylen the synnes that he hath doon,
and stidefastly purposen in his herte to
have shrift of mouthe, and to doon satisfaccioun, and nevere to doon thyng for
which hym oghte moore to biwayle or to
compleyne, & to continue in goode werkes:
or elles his repentance may nat availle. for
as seith Seint Ysidre ❧ He is a japer and
a gabber, and no verray repentant, that eftsoone dooth thyng for which hym oghte
repente ❧ Wepynge, & nat for to stynt to

do synne, may nat avaylle. But nathelees,
men shal hope that every tyme that man
falleth, be it never so ofte, that he may arise
thurgh penitence, if he have grace: but certeinly it is greet doute. for, as seith Seint
Gregorie ❧ Vnnethe ariseth he out of
synne, that is charged with the charge of
yvel usage. And therfore repentant folk,
that stynte for to synne, and forlete synne
er that synne forlete hem, hooly chirche
holdeth hem siker of hire savacioun. And
he that synneth, & verraily repenteth hym
in his laste ende, hooly chirche yet hopeth
his savacioun, by the grete mercy of oure
Lord Jhesu Crist, for his repentaunce;
but taak the siker wey.

AND now, sith I have declared yow
what thyng is penitence, now shul
ye understonde that ther been three
acciouns of penitence. The firste accioun
of penitence is, that a man be baptized
after that he hath synned. Seint Augustyn
seith: But he be penytent for his olde synful lyf, he may nat bigynne the newe clene
lif ❧ for certes, if he be baptized withouten penitence of his olde gilt, he receyveth the mark of baptesme, but nat the
grace ne the remission of his synnes, til
he have repentance verray. Another defaute is this, that men doon deedly synne
after that they han receyved baptesme.
The thridde defaute is, that men fallen in
venial synnes after hir baptesme, fro day
to day. Therof seith Seint Augustyn, that
Penitence of goode and humble folk is the
penitence of every day.

THE speces of penitence been thre.
That oon of hem is solempne, another is commune, and the thridde
is privee. Thilke penance that is solempne,
is in two maneres; as to be put out of hooly
chirche in lente, for slaughtre of children,
& swich maner thyng. ❧ Another is, whan
a man hath synned openly, of which synne
the fame is openly spoken in the contree;
and thanne hooly chirche by juggement destreyneth hym for to do open penaunce.
Commune penaunce is that preestes en-
joynen men in certeyn caas; as for to goon,
peraventure, naked in pilgrimages, or barefoot. Pryvee penaunce is thilke that men
doon alday for privee synnes, of whiche
they shryve hem prively, and receyve privee
penaunce.

NOW shaltow understande what is
bihovely and necessarie to verray
perfit penitence. And this stant on
thre thynges: contricioun of herte, confessioun of mouth, & satisfaccioun. for which
seith Seint John Crisostom ❧ Penitence

destreyneth a man to accepte benygnely every peyne that hym is enjoyned, with contricioun of herte, and shrift of mouth, with satisfaccioun; & in werkynge of alle manere humylitee. And this is fruytful penitence agayn thre thynges in whiche we wratthe oure Lord Jhesu Crist: this is to seyn, by delit in thynkynge, by reccheleesnesse in spekynge, & by wikked synful werkynge. And agayns thise wikkede giltes is penitence, that may be likned unto a tree.

THE roote of this tree is contricioun, that hideth hym in the herte of hym that is verray repentaunt, right as the roote of a tree hydeth hym in the erthe. Of the roote of contricioun spryngeth a stalke, that bereth braunches and leves of confessioun, & fruyt of satisfaccioun. For which Crist seith in his gospel. Dooth digne fruyt of penitence. For by this fruyt may men knowe this tree, and nat by the roote that is hyd in the herte of man, ne by the braunches, ne by the leves of confessioun. And therfore oure Lord Jhesu Crist seith thus. By the fruyt of hem ye shul knowen hem. Of this roote eek spryngeth a seed of grace, the which seed is mooder of sikerness, and this seed is egre and hoot. The grace of this seed spryngeth of God, thurgh remembrance of the day of doome and on the peynes of helle. Of this matere seith Salomon, that. In the drede of God man forleteth his synne. The heete of this seed is the love of God, & the desiryng of the joye perdurable. This hete draweth the herte of a man to God, and dooth hym haten his synne. For soothly, ther is nothyng that savoureth so wel to a child as the milk of his norice, ne nothyng is to hym moore abhomynable than thilke milk whan it is medled with oother mete. Right so the synful man that loveth his synne, hym semeth that it is to him moost sweete of anythyng; but fro that tyme that he loveth sadly oure Lord Jhesu Crist, and desireth the lif perdurable, ther nys to hym nothyng moore abhomynable. For soothly, the lawe of God is the love of God; for which David the prophete seith: I have loved thy lawe and hated wikkednesse and hate; he that loveth God kepeth his lawe and his word. This tree saugh the prophete Daniel in spirit, upon the avysioun of the kyng Nabugodonosor, whan he conseiled hym to do penitence. Penaunce is the tree of lyf to hem that it receyven, & he that holdeth hym in verray penitence is blessed; after the sentence of Salomon.

IN this penitence or contricioun man shal understonde foure thynges; that is to seyn, what is contricioun: and whiche been the causes that moeven a

190

man to contricioun: and how he sholde be contrit: and what contricioun availleth to the soule. Thanne is it thus: that contricioun is the verray sorwe that a man receyveth in his herte for his synnes, with sad purpos to shryve hym, and to do penaunce, and neveremoore to do synne. And this sorwe shal been in this manere, as seith Seint Bernard. It shal been hevy and grevous, and ful sharpe and poynant in herte. First, for man hath agilt his Lord and his Creatour; and moore sharpe and poynaunt, for he hath agilt hys fader celestial; and yet moore sharpe & poynaunt, for he hath wrathed and agilt hym that boghte hym; which with his precious blood hath delivered us fro the bondes of synne, and fro the crueltee of the devel, and fro the peynes of helle.

THE causes that oghte moeve a man to contricioun been sexe. First, a man shal remembre hym of his synnes; but looke he that thilke remembrance ne be to hym no delit by no wey, but greet shame and sorwe for his gilt. For Job seith: Synful men doon werkes worthy of confessioun. And therfore seith Ezechie: I wol remembre me alle the yeres of my lyf, in bitternesse of myn herte. And God seith in the Apocalips: Remembreth yow fro whennes that ye been falle. For biforn that tyme that ye synned ye were the children of God, and lymes of the regne of God; but for youre synne ye been woxen thral and foul, and membres of the feend, hate of aungels, sclaundre of hooly chirche, and foode of the false serpent; perpetueel matere of the fir of helle. And yet moore foul and abhomynable, for ye trespassen so ofte tyme, as dooth the hound that retourneth to eten his spewyng. And yet be ye fouler for youre longe continuyng in synne & youre synful usage, for which ye be roten in your synne, as a beest in his dong. Swiche manere of thoghtes maken a man to have shame of his synne, and no delit, as God seith by the prophete Ezechiel: Ye shal remembre yow of youre weyes, & they shuln displese yow. Soothly, synnes been the weyes that leden folk to helle.

THE seconde cause that oghte make a man to have desdeyn of synne is this: that, as seith Seint Peter: Whoso that dooth synne is thral of synne. And synne put a man in greet thraldom. And therfore seith the prophete Ezechiel: I wente sorweful in desdayn of myself. And certes, wel oghte a man have desdayn of synne, and withdrawe hym from that thraldom and vileynye. And lo, what seith Seneca in this matere. He seith thus: Though I wiste that neither God ne man ne sholde nevere knowe it, yet wolde I have desdayn for to do synne. And the same Seneca also seith: I am born to gretter thynges than to be thral to my body, or than for to maken of my body a thral. Ne a fouler thral may no man ne womman maken of his body, than for to yeven his body to synne. Al were it the fouleste cherl, or the fouleste womman that lyveth, & leest of value, yet is he thanne moore foule and moore in servitute. Evere fro the hyer degree that man falleth, the moore is he thral, and moore to God & to the world vile and abhomynable. O goode God! wel oghte man have desdayn of synne; sith that, thurgh synne, ther he was free, now is he maked bonde. And therfore seyth Seint Augustyn: If thou hast desdayn of thy servant, if he agilte or synne, have thou thanne desdayn that thou thyself sholdest do synne. Take reward of thy value, that thou ne be to foul to thyself. Allas! wel oghten they thanne have desdayn to been servaunts and thralles to synne, and soore been ashamed of hemself, that God of his endelees goodnesse hath set hem in heigh estaat, or yeven hem wit, strengthe of body, heele, beautee, prosperitee, and boghte hem fro the deeth with his herte blood, that they so unkyndely, agayns his gentilesse, quiten hym so vileynsly, to slaughtre of hir owene soules. O goode God! ye wommen that been of so greet beautee, remembreth yow of the proverbe of Salomon, that seith: He likneth a fair womman that is a fool of hire body, lyk to a ryng of gold that were in the groyn of a soughe. For right as a soughe wroteth in everich ordure, so wroteth she hire beautee in the stynkynge ordure of synne.

THE thridde cause that oghte moeve a man to contricioun, is drede of the day of doome, and of the horrible peynes of helle. For as Seint Jerome seith: At every tyme that me remembreth of the day of doome, I quake; for whan I ete or drynke, or whatso that I do, evere semeth me that the trompe sowneth in myn ere: Riseth up, ye that been dede, & cometh to the juggement. O goode God! muchel oghte a man to drede swich a juggement, Theras we shullen been alle, as Seint Poul seith, biforn the seete of oure Lord Jhesu Crist; wheras he shal make a general congregacioun, wheras no man may been absent. For certes, there availleth noon essoyne ne excusacioun. And nat oonly that oure defautes shullen be jugged, but eek that alle oure werkes shullen openly be knowe. And as seith Seint Bernard: Ther ne shal no pledynge availle, ne no sleighte; we shullen yeven rekenynge of everich ydel word. Ther shul we han a juge that may

nat been deceyved ne corrupt. And why? for certes, alle oure thoghtes been discovered as to hym; ne for preyere ne for meede he shal nat been corrupt. And therfore seith Salomon: The wratthe of God ne wol nat spare no wight, for preyere ne for yifte. And therfore, at the day of doom, ther nys noon hope to escape.

WHERFORE, as seith Seint Anselm: Ful greet angwyssh shul the synful folk have at that tyme. Ther shal the stierne & wrothe juge sitte above, and under hym the horrible put of helle open to destroyen hym that moot biknowen his synnes, whiche synnes openly been shewed biforn God and biforn every creature. And on the left syde, mo develes than herte may bithynke, for to harye and drawe the synful soules to the peyne of helle. And withinne the hertes of folk shal be the bitynge conscience, and withouteforth shal be the world al brennynge. Whider shal thanne the wrecched synful man flee to hiden hym? Certes, he may nat hyden hym; he moste come forth & shewen hym. For certes, as seith Seint Jerome: The erthe shal casten hym out of hym, and the see also; and the eyr also, that shal be ful of thonder-clappes and lightnynges.

NOW soothly, whoso wel remembreth hym of thise thynges, I gesse that his synne shal nat turne hym into delit, but to greet sorwe, for drede of the peyne of helle. And therfore seith Job to God: Suffre, Lord, that I may awhile biwaille, and wepe, er I go withoute returnyng to the derke lond, covered with the derknesse of deeth; to the lond of mysese and of derknesse, whereas is the shadwe of deeth; whereas ther is noon ordre or ordinaunce, but grisly drede that evere shal laste. Loo, heere may ye seen that Job preyde respit awhile, to biwepe and waille his trespas; for soothly, oo day of respit is bettre than al the tresor of the world. And forasmuche as a man may acquiten hymself biforn God by penitence in this world, & nat by tresor, therfore sholde he preye to God to yeve hym respit awhile, to biwepe and biwaillen his trespas. For certes, al the sorwe that a man myghte make fro the bigynnyng of the world, nys but a litel thyng at regard of the sorwe of helle.

THE cause why that Job clepeth helle the lond of derknesse: understondeth that he clepeth it londe or erthe, for it is stable, and nevere shal faille; derk, for he that is in helle hath defaute of light material. For certes, the derke light, that shal come out of the fyr that evere shal brenne, shal turne hym al to peyne that is in helle; for it sheweth hym to the horrible

191

develes that hym tormenten. Covered with the derknesse of deeth: that is to seyn, that he that is in helle shal have defaute of the sighte of God; for certes, the sighte of God is the lyf perdurable. The derknesse of deeth, been the synnes that the wrecched man hath doon, whiche that destourben hym to see the face of God; right as dooth a derk clowde bitwixe us and the sonne. Lond of misese: bycause that ther been three maneres of defautes, agayn thre thynges that folk of this world han in this present lyf; that is to seyn, honours, delices, and richesses. Agayns honour, have they in helle shame and confusioun. For wel ye woot that men clepen honour the reverence that man doth to man; but in helle is noon honour ne reverence. For certes, namoore reverence shal be doon there to a kyng than to a knave. For which God seith by the prophete Jeremye: Thilke folk that me despisen shul been in despit. Honour is eek cleped greet lordshipe; ther shal no wight serven oother but of harm & torment. Honour is eek cleped greet dignytee and heighnesse; but in helle shul they been al fortroden of develes. And God seith: The horrible develes shulle goon & comen upon the hevedes of the dampned folk. And this is forasmuche as, the hyer that they were in this present lyf, the moore shulle they been abated & defouled in helle. Agayns the richesses of this world, shul they han mysese of poverte; and this poverte shal been in foure thynges: in defaute of tresor, of which that David seith: The riche folk that embraceden and oneden al hire herte to tresor of this world, shul slepe in the slepynge of deeth; & nothyng ne shal they fynden in hir handes of al hire tresor. And mooreover, the myseyse of helle shul been in defaute of mete and drinke. For God seith thus by Moyses: They shul been wasted with hunger, and the briddes of helle shul devouren hem with the bitter deeth, and the galle of the dragon shal been hire drynke, and the venym of the dragon hire morsels. And fortherover, hire myseyse shal been in defaute of clothyng; for they shulle be naked in body as of clothyng, save the fyr in which they brenne and oothere filthes; and naked shul they been of soule, of alle manere vertues, which that is the clothyng of the soule. Where been thanne the gaye robes, & the softe shetes, and the smale shertes? Loo, what seith God of hem by the prophete Ysaye: that Under hem shul been strawed motthes, & hire covertures shulle been of wormes of helle. And fortherover, hir myseyse shal been in defaute of freendes; for he nys nat povre that hath goode freendes, but there

192

is no frend; for neither God ne no creature shal been freend to hem, and everich of hem shal haten oother with deedly hate. The sones and the doghtren shullen rebellen agayns fader and mooder, and kynrede agayns kynrede, and chiden and despisen everich of hem oother, bothe day and nyght, as God seith by the prophete Michias. And the lovynge children, that whilom loveden so flesshly everich oother, wolden everich of hem eten oother if they mighte. For how sholden they love hem togidre in the peyne of helle, whan they hated ech of hem oother in the prosperitee of this lyf? For truste wel, hir flesshly love was deedly hate; as seith the prophete David: Whoso that loveth wikkednesse he hateth his soule. And whoso hateth his owene soule, certes, he may love noon oother wight in no manere. And therfore in helle is no solas ne no freendshipe, but evere the moore flesshly kynredes that been in helle, the moore cursynges, the moore chidynges, and the moore deedly hate ther is among hem.

AND fortherover they shul have defaute of alle manere delices; for certes, delices been after the appetites of the five wittes, as sighte, herynge, smellynge, savorynge, & touchynge. But in helle hir sighte shal be ful of derknesse and of smoke, and therfore ful of teeres; and hir herynge, ful of waymentynge and of gryntynge of teeth, as seith Jhesu Crist; hir nosethirles shullen be ful of stynkynge stynk. And as seith Ysaye the prophete: Hir savoryng shal be ful of bitter galle. And touchynge of al hir body, ycovered with fir that nevere shal quenche, and with wormes that nevere shul dyen, as God seith by the mouth of Ysaye. And forasmuche as they shul nat wene that they may dyen for peyne, and by hir deeth flee fro peyne, that may they understonden by the word of Job, that seith: Theras is the shadwe of deeth. Certes, a shadwe hath the liknesse of the thyng of which it is shadwe, but shadwe is nat the same thyng of which it is shadwe. Right so fareth the peyne of helle; it is lyk deeth for the horrible angwissh; and why? For it peyneth hem evere, as though they sholde dye anon; but certes, they shal nat dye. For as seith Seint Gregorie: To wrecche caytyves shal be deeth withoute deeth, & ende withouten ende, and defaute withoute failynge. For hir deeth shal alwey lyven, and hir ende shal everemo bigynne, and hir defaute shal nat faille. And therfore seith Seint John the Evaungelist: They shullen folwe deeth, and they shul nat fynde hym; and they shul desiren to dye, and deeth shal flee fro hem.

AND eek Job seith: that In helle is noon ordre of rule; & albeit so that God hath creat alle thynges in right ordre, and nothyng withouten ordre, but alle thynges been ordeyned and nombred; yet nathelees, they that been dampned been nothyng in ordre, ne holden noon ordre; for the erthe ne shal bere hem no fruyt. For, as the prophete David seith: God shal destroie the fruyt of the erthe as fro hem; ne water ne shal yeve hem no moisture; ne the eyr no refresshng, ne fyr no light. For as seith Seint Basilie: The brennynge of the fyr of this world shal God yeven in helle to hem that been dampned; but the light and the cleernesse shal be yeven in hevene to his children; right as the goode man yeveth flessh to his children, and bones to his houndes. And for they shullen have noon hope to escape, seith Seint Job atte laste: that Ther shal horrour & grisly drede dwellen withouten ende.

HORROUR is alwey drede of harm that is to come, and this drede shal evere dwelle in the hertes of hem that been dampned; and therfore han they lorn al hire hope for sevene causes. First, for God that is hir juge shal be withouten mercy to hem; and they may nat plese hym ne noon of his halwes; ne they ne may yeve nothyng for hir raunsoun; ne they have no voys to speke to hym; ne they may nat fle fro peyne; ne they have no goodnesse in hem, that they mowe shewe to delivere hem fro peyne. And therfore seith Salomon: The wikked man dyeth; and whan he is deed, he shal have noon hope to escape fro peyne. Whoso thanne wolde wel understande these peynes, and bithynke hym weel that he hath deserved thilke peynes for his synnes, certes, he sholde have moore talent to siken and to wepe, than for to syngen & to pleye. For as that seith Salomon: Whoso that hadde the science to knowe the peynes that been establissd and ordeyned for synne, he wolde make sorwe. Thilke science, as seith Seint Augustyn, maketh a man to waymenten in his herte.

THE fourthe point, that oghte maken a man to have contricioun, is the sorweful remembraunce of the good that he hath left to doon heere in erthe; & eek the good that he hath lorn. Soothly, the goode werkes that he hath left, outher they been the goode werkes that he hath wroght er he fel into deedly synne, or elles the goode werkes that he wroghte while he lay in synne. Soothly, the goode werkes that he dide biforn that he fil in synne, been al mortefied and astoned and dulled by the ofte synnyng. The othere goode werkes that he wroghte while he lay in deedly synne, thei been outrely dede as to the lyf perdurable in hevene. Thanne thilke goode werkes that been mortefied by ofte synnyng, whiche goode werkes he dide whil he was in charitee, ne mowe nevere quyken agayn withouten verray penitence. And therof seith God, by the mouth of Ezechiel: that, If the rightful man returne agayn from his rightwisnesse and werke wikkednesse, shal he lyve? Nay; for alle the goode werkes that he hath wroght ne shul nevere been in remembrance; for he shal dyen in his synne. And upon thilke chapitre seith Seint Gregorie thus: That we shulle understonde this principally; that whan we doon deedly synne, it is for noght thanne to rehercen or drawen into memorie the goode werkes that we han wroght biforn. For certes, in the werkynge of the deedly synne, ther is no trust to no good werk that we han doon biforn; that is to seyn, as for to have therby the lyf perdurable in hevene. But nathelees, the goode werkes quyken agayn, and comen agayn, and helpen, & availlen to have the lyf perdurable in hevene, whan we han contricioun. But soothly, the goode werkes that men doon whil they been in deedly synne, forasmuche as they were doon in deedly synne, they may nevere quyken agayn. For certes, thyng that nevere hadde lyf may nevere quykene; and nathelees, albeit that they ne availle noght to han the lyf perdurable, yet availlen they to abregge of the peyne of helle, or elles to geten temporal richesse, or elles that God wole the rather enlumyne and lightne the herte of the synful man to have repentaunce. And eek they availlen for to usen a man to doon goode werkes, that the feend have the lasse power of his soule. And thus the curteis Lord Jhesu Crist wole that no good werk be lost; for in somwhat it shal availle. But, forasmuche as the goode werkes that men doon whil they been in good lyf, been al mortefied by synne folwynge; and eek, sith that alle the goode werkes that men doon whil they been in deedly synne, been outrely dede as for to have the lyf perdurable; wel may that man, that no good werk ne dooth, synge thilke newe frenshe song: Jay tout perdu mon temps et mon labour.

FOR certes, synne bireveth a man bothe goodnesse of nature and eek the goodnesse of grace. For soothly, the grace of the Hooly Goost fareth lyk fyr, that may nat been ydel; for fyr fayleth anoon as it forleteth his wirkynge, & right so grace fayleth anoon as it forleteth his werkynge. Then leseth the synful man the goodnesse of glorie, that oonly is bihight to goode men that labouren and werken.

Wel may he be sory thanne, that oweth al his lif to God, as longe as he hath lyved, and eek as longe as he shal lyve, that no goodnesse ne hath to paye with his dette to God, to whom he oweth al his lyf. For, trust wel: He shal yeven acountes, as seith Seint Bernard, of alle the goodes that han be yeven hym in this present lyf, and how he hath hem despended; insomuche that ther shal nat perisse an heer of his heed, ne a moment of an houre ne shal nat perisse of his tyme, that he ne shal yeve of it a rekenyng.

THE fifthe thyng that oghte moeve a man to contricioun, is remembrance of the passioun that oure Lord Jhesu Crist suffred for oure synnes. For, as seith Seint Bernard: Whil that I lyve, I shal have remembrance of the travailles that oure Lord Crist suffred in prechyng; his werynesse in travaillyng, his temptaciouns whan he fasted, his longe wakynges whan he preyde, his teeres whan that he weepe for pitee of good peple; the wo and the shame and the filthe that men seyden to hym; of the foule spittyng that men spitte in his face, of the buffettes that men yaven hym, of the foule mowes, and of the repreves that men to hym seyden; of the nayles with whiche he was nayled to the croys, and of al the remenaunt of his passioun that he suffred for my synnes, and nothyng for his gilt. And ye shul understonde, that in mannes synne is every manere of ordre or ordinaunce turned up-so-doun. For it is sooth, that God, & resoun, and sensualitee, and the body of man, been so ordeyned, that everich of thise foure thynges sholde have lordshipe over that oother; as thus: God sholde have lordshipe over resoun, & resoun over sensualitee, and sensualitee over the body of man. But soothly, whan man synneth, al this ordre or ordinaunce is turned up-so-doun. And therfore thanne, forasmuche as the resoun of man ne wol nat be subget ne obeisant to God, that is his lord by right, therfore leseth it the lordshipe that it sholde have over sensualitee, and eek over the body of man. And why? For sensualitee rebelleth thanne agayns resoun; & by that wey leseth resoun the lordshipe over sensualitee and over the body. For right as resoun is rebel to God, right so is bothe sensualitee rebel to resoun and the body also.

AND certes, this disordinaunce & this rebellioun oure Lord Jhesu Crist aboghte upon his precious body ful deere, and herkneth in which wise. Forasmuche thanne as resoun is rebel to God, therfore is man worthy to have sorwe and to be deed. This suffred oure Lord Jhesu Crist for man, after that he hadde be bi-

traysed of his disciple, & distreyned and bounde, So that his blood brast out at every nayl of his handes, as seith Seint Augustyn. And fortherover, forasmuchel as resoun of man ne wol nat daunte sensualitee whan it may, therfore is man worthy to have shame; and this suffred oure Lord Jhesu Crist for man, whan they spetten in his visage. And fortherover, forasmuchel thanne as the caytyf body of man is rebel bothe to resoun and to sensualitee, therfore is it worthy the deeth. And this suffred oure Lord Jhesu Crist for man upon the croys, whereas ther was no part of his body free, withouten greet peyne and bitter passioun.

AND al this suffred Jhesu Crist, that nevere forfeted. And therfore resonably may be said of Jhesu in this manere: To muchel am I peyned for the thynges that I nevere deserved, & to muche defouled for shendshipe that man is worthy to have. And therfore may the synful man wel seye, as seith Seint Bernard: A-cursed be the bitternesse of my synne, for which ther moste be suffred so muchel bitternesse. For certes, after the diverse disconcordaunces of oure wikkednesses, was the passioun of Jhesu Crist ordeyned in diverse thynges, as thus. Certes, synful mannes soule is bitraysed of the devel by coveitise of temporeel prosperitee, and scorned by deceite whan he cheseth flesshly delices; and yet is it tormented by inpacience of adversitee, and byspet by servage and subjeccioun of synne; and atte laste it is slayn fynally. For this disordinaunce of synful man was Jhesu Crist fyrst bitraysed, and after that was he bounde, that cam for to unbynden us of synne and peyne. Thanne was he byscorned, that oonly sholde han been honoured in alle thynges & of alle thynges. Thanne was his visage, that oghte be desired to be seyn of al mankynde, in which visage aungels desiren to looke, vileynsly bispet. Thanne was he scourged that nothyng hadde agilt; and finally, thanne was he crucified and slayn. Thanne was acompliced the word of Ysaye: He was wounded for oure mysdedes, & defouled for oure felonies. Now sith that Jhesu Crist took upon hymself the peyne of alle oure wikkednesses, muchel oghte synful man wepen & biwayle, that for his synnes Goddes sone of hevene sholde al this peyne endure.

THE sixte thyng that oghte moeve a man to contricioun, is the hope of thre thynges; that is to seyn, foryifnesse of synne, and the yifte of grace wel for to do, and the glorie of hevene, with which God shal guerdone a man for his goode dedes.

AND, forasmuche as Jhesu Crist yeveth us thise yiftes of his largesse, and of his sovereyn bountee, therfore is he cleped Jhesus Nazarenus, rex Judæorum. Jhesus is to seyn Saveour or Salvacioun, on whom men shul hope to have foryifnesse of synnes, which that is proprely salvacioun of synnes. And therfore seyde the aungel to Joseph: Thou shalt clepen his name Jhesus, that shal saven his peple of hir synnes And heerof seith Seint Peter: Ther is noon oother name under hevene that is yeve to any man, by which a man may be saved, but oonly Jhesus Nazarenus is as muche for to seye as florisshynge, in which a man shal hope, that he that yeveth hym remissioun of synnes shal yeve hym eek grace wel for to do. For in the flour is hope of fruyt in tyme comynge; and in foryifnesse of synnes, hope of grace wel for to do. I was atte dore of thyn herte, seith Jhesus, and cleped for to entre; he that openeth to me shal have foryifnesse of synne. I wol entre into hym by my grace, and soupe with hym, by the goode werkes that he shal doon; whiche werkes been the foode of God; and he shal soupe with me, by the grete joye that I shal yeven hym Thus shal man hope, for his werkes of penaunce, that God shal yeven hym his regne; as he bihooteth hym in the gospel.

NOW shal a man understonde, in which manere shal been his contricioun. I seye, that it shal been universal and total; this is to seyn, a man shal be verray repentaunt for alle his synnes that he hath doon in delit of his thoght; for delit is ful perilous. For ther been two manere of consentynges; that oon of hem is cleped consentynge of affeccioun, whan a man is moeved to do synne, and deliteth hym longe for to thynke on that synne; and his resoun aperceyveth it wel, that it is synne agayns the lawe of God, and yet his resoun refreyneth nat his foul delit or talent, though he se wel apertly that it is agayns the reverence of God; although his resoune consente noght to doon that synne in dede, yet seyn somme doctours that swich delit that dwelleth longe, it is ful perilous, al be it nevere so lite. And also a man sholde sorwe, namely, for al that evere he hath desired agayn the lawe of God with perfit consentynge of his resoun; for therof is no doute, that it is deedly synne in consentynge. For certes, ther is no deedly synne that it nas first in mannes thought, & after that in his delit; & so forth into consentynge, and into dede Wherfore I seye, that many men ne repenten hem nevere of swiche thoghtes & delites, ne nevere shryven hem of it, but oonly of the dede of grete synnes outward. Wherfore I seye, that

02

swiche wikked delites & wikked thoghtes been subtile bigileres of hem that shullen be dampned.

MOOREOVER, man oghte to sorwe for his wikkede wordes, as wel as for his wikkede dedes; for certes, the repentaunce of a synguler synne, and nat repente of alle his othere synnes, or elles repenten hym of alle his othere synnes & nat of a synguler synne, may nat availle. For certes, God Almyghty is al good; and therfore he foryeveth al, or elles right noght. And heerof seith Seint Augustyn: I woot certeinly that God is enemy to everich synnere; and how thanne? He that observeth o synne, shal he have foryifnesse of the remenaunt of his othere synnes? Nay.

AND fortherover, contricioun sholde be wonder sorweful & angwissous, & therfore yeveth hym God pleynly his mercy; & therfore, whan my soule was angwissous withinne me, I hadde remembrance of God, that my preyere myghte come to hym fortherover, contricioun moste be continueel, & that man have stedefast purpos to shriven hym, and for to amenden hym of his lyf. For soothly, whil contricioun lasteth, man may evere have hope of foryifnesse; & of this comth hate of synne, that destroyeth synne bothe in himself, & eek in oother folk, at his power. For which seith David: Ye that loven God hateth wikkednesse, for trusteth wel, to love God is for to love that he loveth, and hate that he hateth.

THE laste thyng that man shal understonde in contricioun is this; wherof availeth contricioun. I seye, that somtyme contricioun delivereth a man fro synne; of which that David seith: I seye, quod David, that is to seyn, I purposed fermely to shryve me; & thow, Lord, relesedest my synne. And right so as contricioun availleth noght, withouten sad purpos of shrifte, if man have oportunitee, right so litel worth is shrifte or satisfaccioun withouten contricioun. And mooreover contricioun destroyeth the prisoun of helle, and maketh wayk and fieble alle the strengthes of the develes, and restoreth the yiftes of the Hooly Goost and of alle goode vertues; and it clenseth the soule of synne, & delivereth the soule fro the peyne of helle, & fro the compaignye of the devel, and fro the servage of synne, & restoreth it to alle goodes espirituels, & to the compaignye & communyoun of hooly chirche.

AND fortherover, it maketh hym that whilom was sone of ire, to be sone of grace; and alle thise thynges been preved by hooly writ. And therfore, he that wolde sette his entente to thise thynges,

195

he were ful wys; for soothly, he ne sholde nat thanne in al his lyf have corage to synne, but yeven his body and al his herte to the service of Jhesu Crist, & therof doon hym hommage. for soothly, oure sweete Lord Jhesu Crist hath spared us so debonairly in our folies, that if he ne hadde pitee of mannes soule, a sory song we myghten alle synge.

Explicit prima pars Penitentie; et sequitur secunda pars eiusdem.

HE seconde partie of penitence is confessioun, that is signe of contricioun. Now shul ye understonde what is confessioun, and wheither it oghte nedes be doon or noon, and whiche thynges been covenable to verray confessioun ✒ first shaltow understonde that confessioun is verray shewynge of synnes to the preest; this is to seyn, Verray, for he moste confessen hym of alle the condiciouns that bilongen to his synne, as ferforth as he kan. Al moot be seyd, and nothyng excused, ne hyd, ne forwrapped, and noght avaunte him of his goode werkes. And fortherover, it is necessarie to understonde whennes that synnes spryngen, and how they encreessen, and whiche they been ✒ Of the spryngynge of synnes seith Seint Paul in this wise: that Right as by a man synne entred first into this world, and thurgh that synne deeth, right so thilke deeth entred into alle men that synneden. And this man was Adam, by whom synne entred into this world whan he brak the comaundement of God. And therfore, he that first was so myghty that he sholde nat have dyed, bicam swich oon that he moste nedes dye, wheither he wolde or noon; and al his progenye in this world that in thilke man synneden.

OOKE, that in thestaat of innocence, whan Adam and Eve naked weren in Paradys, and nothyng ne hadden shame of hir nakednesse, how that the serpent, that was moost wily of alle othere beestes that God hadde maked, seyde to the woman: Why comaunded God to yow, ye sholde nat eten of every tree in Paradys? ✒ The womman answerde: Of the fruyt, quod she, of the trees in Paradys we feden us, but soothly, of the fruyt of the tree that is in the myddel of Paradys, God forbad us for to ete, ne nat touchen it, lest peraventure we sholde dyen ✒ The serpent seyde to the womman: Nay, nay, ye shul nat dyen of deeth; for sothe, God woot, that what day that ye eten therof, youre eyen shul opene, and ye shul been as goddes, knowynge good and harm.

HE womman thanne saugh that the tree was good to feedyng, and fair to the eyen, and delitable to the sighte; she took of the fruyt of the tree, and eet it, and yaf to hire housbonde, and he eet; and anoon the eyen of hem bothe openeden. And whan that they knewe that they were naked, they sowed of fige-leves a manere of breches, to hiden hire membres. There may ye seen that deedly synne hath first suggestioun of the feend, as sheweth heere by the naddre; and afterward, the delit of the flessh, as sheweth heere by Eve; and after that, the consentynge of resoun, as sheweth heere by Adam. For trust wel, though so were that the feend tempted Eve, that is to seyn the flessh, & the flessh hadde delit in the beautee of the fruyt defended, yet certes, til that resoun, that is to seyn, Adam, consented to the etynge of the fruyt, yet stood he in thestaat of innocence. Of thilke Adam tooke we thilke synne original; for of hym flesshly descended be we alle, and engendred of vile and corrupt mateere. And whan the soule is put in oure body, right anon is contract original synne; & that, that was erst but oonly peyne of concupiscence, is afterward both peyne and synne. And therfore be we alle born sones of wratthe and of dampnacioun perdurable, if it nere baptesme that we receyven, which bynymeth us the culpe; but forsothe, the peyne dwelleth with us, as to temptacioun, which peyne highte concupiscence. Whan it is wrongfully disposed or ordeyned in man, it maketh hym coveite, by coveitise of flessh, flesshly synne, by sighte of his eyen as to erthely thynges, and coveitise of hynesse by pride of herte.

OW, as for to speken of the firste coveitise, that is concupiscence after the lawe of oure membres, that weren lawefulliche ymaked and by rightful juggement of God; I seye, forasmuche as man is nat obeisaunt to God, that is his Lord, therfore is the flessh to hym disobeisaunt thurgh concupiscence, which yet is cleped norrissynge of synne, & occasion of synne. Therfore, al the while that a man hath in hym the peyne of concupiscence, it is impossible but he be tempted somtime, and moeved in his flessh to synne. And this thyng may nat faille as longe as he lyveth; it may wel wexe fieble & faille, by vertu of baptesme & by the grace of God thurgh penitence; but fully ne shal it nevere quenche, that he ne shal somtyme be moeved in hymself, but if he were al refreyded by siknesse, or by malefice of sorcerie, or colde drynkes. For lo, what seith Seint Paul: The flessh coveiteth agayn the spirit, and the spirit agayn the flessh ✒ they been so contrarie &

so stryven, that a man may nat alwey doon as he wolde. The same Seint Paul, after his grete penaunce in water and in lond; in water by nyght & by day, in greet peril and in greet peyne, in lond, in famyne, in thurst, in coold, and cloothlees, and ones stoned almoost to the deeth, yet seyde he: Allas! I, caytyf man, who shal delivere me fro the prisoun of my caytyf body? And Seint Jerome, whan he longe tyme hadde woned in desert, whereas he hadde no compaignye but of wilde beestes, whereas he ne hadde no mete but herbes, & water to his drynke, ne no bed but the naked erthe, for which his flessh was blak as an Ethiopeen for heete, & ny destroyed for coold, yet seyde he: that The brennynge of lecherie boyled in al his body. Wherfore, I woot wel syker-ly, that they been deceyved that seyn, that they ne be nat tempted in hir body. Wit-nesse on Seint Jame the Apostel, that seith: that Every wight is tempted in his owene concupiscence; that is to seyn, that everich of us hath matere and occasioun to be tempted of the norissynge of synne that is in his body. And therfore seith Seint John the evaungelist: If that we seyn that we beth withoute synne, we deceyve us selve, and trouthe is nat in us.

NOW shal ye understonde in what ma-nere that synne wexeth or encreeseth in man. The firste thyng is thilke norissynge of synne, of which I spak bi-forn, thilke flesshly concupiscence. And after that comth the subjeccioun of the devel, this is to seyn, the develes bely, with which he bloweth in man the fir of flesshly concupiscence. And after that, a man bi-thynketh hym wheither he wol doon, or no, thilke thing to which he is tempted. And thanne, if that a man withstonde & weyve the firste entisynge of his flessh and of the feend, thanne is it no synne; and if it so be that he do nat so, thanne feeleth he anoon a flambe of delit. And thanne is it good to be war, and kepen hym wel, or elles he wol falle anon into consentynge of synne; and thanne wol he do it, if he may have tyme & place. And of this matere seith Moyses by the devel in this manere: The feend seith, I wole chace and pursue the man by wikked suggestioun, and I wole hente hym by moevynge or stirynge of synne. I wol departe my prise or my praye by delibera-cioun, and my lust shal been accompliced in delit; I wol drawe my swerd in consent-ynge: for certes, right as a swerd depart-eth a thyng in two peces, right so consent-ynge departeth God fro man: And thanne wol I sleen hym with myn hand in dede of synne; thus seith the feend, for certes, thanne is a man al deed in soule. And thus is synne accompliced by temptacioun, by delit, and by consentynge; and thanne is the synne cleped actueel.

FORSOTHE, synne is in two man-eres; outher it is venial, or deedly synne. Soothly, whan man loveth any creature moore than Jhesu Crist oure Creatour, thanne is it deedly synne. And venial synne is it, if man love Jhesu Crist lasse than hym oghte. Forsothe, the dede of this venial synne is ful perilous; for it amenuseth the love that men sholde han to God moore and moore. And therfore if a man charge hymself with manye swiche ve-nial synnes, certes, but if so be that he som-tyme descharge hym of hem by shrifte, they mowe ful lightly amenuse in hym al the love that he hath to Jhesu Crist; and in this wise skippeth venial into deedly synne. For certes, the moore that a man chargeth his soule with venial synnes, the moore is he enclyned to fallen into deedly synne. And therfore, lat us nat be necli-gent to deschargen us of venial synnes; for the proverbe seith: that Manye smale maken a greet. And herkne this ensample. A greet wawe of the see comth somtyme with so greet a violence that it drencheth the ship. And the same harm dooth som-tyme the smale dropes of water, that en-tren thurgh a litel crevace into the thurrok, and into the botme of the ship, if men be so necligent that they ne descharge hem nat by tyme. And therfore, although ther be a difference bitwixe thise two causes of drenchynge, algates the ship is dreynt. Right so fareth it somtyme of deedly synne, and of anoyouse veniale synnes, whan they multiplie in a man so greetly, that thilke worldly thynges that he loveth, thurgh whiche he synneth venyally, is as greet in his herte as the love of God, or moore. And therfore, the love of every thyng that is nat biset in God, ne doon principally for Goddes sake, although that a man love it lasse than God, yet is it venial synne; and deedly synne, whan the love of any thyng weyeth in the herte of man as muchel as the love of God, or moore. Deed-ly synne, as seith Seint Augustyn: Is, whan a man turneth his herte fro God, which that is verray sovereyn bountee, that may nat chaunge, and yeveth his herte to thyng that may chaunge and flitte. And certes, that is every thyng, save God of hevene. For sooth is, that if a man yeve his love, the which that he oweth al to God with al his herte, unto a creature, certes, as muche as he yeveth of his love to thilke creature, so muche he bireveth fro God; and therfore dooth he synne. For he that is dettour to God, ne yeldeth nat to God al his dette, that is to seyn, al the love of his herte.

NOW sith man understondeth gene∕
rally, which is venial synne, thanne
is it covenable to tellen specially of
synnes whiche that many a man peraven∕
ture ne demeth hem nat synnes, & ne shry∕
veth him nat of the same thynges; and yet
nathelees they been synnes. Soothly, as
thise clerkes writen, this is to seyn, that at
every tyme that a man eteth or drynketh
moore than suffiseth to the sustenaunce
of his body, in certein he dooth synne. And
eek when he speketh moore than nedeth, it
is synne. Eke when he herkneth nat benignely the compleint of the povre. Eke
when he is in heele of body & wol nat faste,
when othere folk faste, withouten cause
resonable. Eke when he slepeth moore
than nedeth, or when he comth by thilke
enchesoun to late to chirche, or to othere
werkes of charite. Eke when he useth his
wyf, withouten sovereyn desir of engendrure, to the honour of God, or for the entente to yelde to hys wyf the dette of his
body. Eke when he wol nat visite the sike
& the prisoner, if he may. Eke if he love wyf
or child, or oother worldly thyng, moore
than resoun requireth. Eke if he flatere or
blandise moore than hym oghte for any
necessitee. Eke if he amenuse or withdrawe the almesse of the povre. Eke if he
apparailleth his mete moore deliciously
than nede is, or ete it to hastily by likerousnesse. Eke if he tale vanytees at chirche
or at Goddes service, or that he be a talker
of ydel wordes of folye or of vileynye;
for he shal yelden acountes of it at the day
of doome. Eke when he bibeteth or assureth to do thynges that he may nat perfourne. Eke when that he, by lightnesse or
folie, mysseyeth or scorneth his neighebore. Eke when he hath any wikked suspecioun of thyng, ther he ne woot of it no
soothfastnesse. Thise thynges and mo
withoute nombre been synnes, as seith
Seint Augustyn.

NOW shal men understonde that albeit so that noon erthely man may
eschue alle venial synnes, yet may he
refreyne hym by the brennynge love that
he hath to oure Lord Jhesu Crist, and by
preyeres and confessioun & othere goode
werkes, so that it shal but litel greve. For,
as seith Seint Augustyn: If a man love
God in swich manere, that al that evere he
dooth is in the love of God, & for the love
of God verraily, for he brenneth in the love
of God: looke, how muche that a drope of
water that falleth in a fourneys ful of fyr
anoyeth or greveth, so muche anoyeth a
venial synne unto a man that is perfit in the
love of Jhesu Crist ◦ Men may also refreyne venial synne by receyvynge worthily of the precious body of Jhesu Crist;
198

by receyvynge eek of hooly water; by almes-
dede; by general confessioun of Confiteor
at masse and at complyn; & by blessynge
of bisshopes & of preestes, & by oothere
goode werkes.

Explicit secunda pars Penitentie. Sequitur
de septem peccatis mortalibus, et eorum
dependenciis circumstanciis et speciebus.

NOW is it bihovely thyng to
telle whiche been the deedly
synnes, this is to seyn, chief∕
taynes of synnes; alle they
renne in o lees, but in diverse
maneres. Now been they clep∕
ed chieftaynes, forasmuche as they been
chief, and spryngers of alle othere synnes.
Of the roote of thise sevene synnes thanne
is pride, the general roote of alle harmes;
for of this roote spryngen certein braunch∕
es, as ire; envye; accidie or slewthe; avarice
or coveitise, to commune understondynge;
glotonye, & lecherye. And everich of thise
chief synnes hath his braunches and his
twigges, as shal be declared in hire chapitres folwynge.

De Superbia.

AND thogh so be that no man
kan outrely telle the nombre of
the twigges & of the harmes
that cometh of pride, yet wol
I shewe a partie of hem, as ye
shul understonde. Ther is in∕
obedience, avauntynge, ypocrisie, despit,
arrogance, inpudence, swellynge of herte,
insolence, elacioun, inpacience, strif, con-
tumacie, presumpcioun, irreverence, pertinacie, veyne glorie; and many another twig
that I kan nat declare.

INOBEDIENT, is he that disobey∕
eth for despit to the comandements
of God and to his sovereyns, and to
his goostly fader. Avauntour, is he that
bosteth of the harm or of the bountee that
he hath doon. Ypocrite, is he that hideth to
shewe hym swich as he is, and sheweth
hym swich as he noght is. Despitous, is he
that hath desdeyn of his neighebore, that
is to seyn, of his evene∕Cristene, or hath
despit to doon that hym oghte to do. Ar-
rogant, is he that thynketh that he hath
thilke bountees in hym that he hath noght,
or weneth that he sholde have hem by his
desertes; or elles he demeth that he be that
he nys nat. Inpudent, is he that for his
pride hath no shame of his synnes. Swellynge of herte, is whan a man rejoyseth hym
of harm that he hath doon. Insolent, is
that despiseth in his juggement alle othere folk as to regard of his value, and of
his konnyng, and of his spekyng, and
of his beryng. Elacioun, is whan he
ne may neither suffre to have maister ne

felawe. Inpacient, is he that wol nat been ytaught ne undernome of his vice, and by strif werreieth trouthe wityngly, and deffendeth his folye. Contumax, is he that thurgh his indignacioun is agayns everich auctoritee or power of hem that been his sovereyns. Presumpcioun, is whan a man undertaketh an emprise that hym oghte nat do, or elles that he may nat do; and this is called surquidrie. Irreverence, is whan men do nat honour theras hem oghte to doon, and waiten to be reverenced. Pertinacie, is whan man deffendeth his folye, & trusteth to muchel in his owene wit. Veyneglorie, is for to have pompe and delit in his temporeel hynesse, and glorifie hym in this worldly estaat. Janglynge, is whan men speken to muche biforn folk, & clappen as a mille, and taken no kepe what they seye. And yet is ther a privee spece of pride, that waiteth first to be salewed er he wole salewe, al be he lasse worth than that oother is, peraventure; & eek he waiteth or desireth to sitte, or elles to goon above hym in the wey, or kisse pax, or been encensed, or goon to offryng biforn his neighebore, & swiche semblable thynges; agayns his duetee, peraventure, but that he hath his herte and his entente in swich a proud desir to be magnified and honoured biforn the peple. Now been ther two maneres of pride. That oon of hem is withinne the herte of man, and that oother is withoute; of whiche soothly thise forseyde thynges, & mo than I have seyd, apertenen to pride that is in the herte of man; & that othere speces of pride been withoute. But natheles that oon of thise speces of pride is signe of that oother, right as the gaye leefsel atte taverne is signe of the wyn that is in the celer. And this is in manye thynges: as in speche & contenaunce, and in outrageous array of clothyng; for certes, if ther ne hadde be no synne in clothyng, Crist wolde nat have noted and spoken of the clothyng of thilke riche man in the gospel. And, as seith Seint Gregorie: that Precious clothyng is cowpable for the derthe of it, and for his softenesse, and for his strangenesse and degisynesse, & for the superfluitee, and for the inordinat scantnesse of it. Allas! may men nat seen, as in oure dayes, the synful costlewe array of clothynge, and namely in to muche superfluitee, or elles in to desordinat scantnesse?

S to the firste synne, that is in superfluitee of clothynge, which that maketh it so deere, to harm of the peple; nat oonly the cost of embrowdynge, the degise endentynge or barrynge, owndynge, palynge, wyndynge or bendynge, and semblable wast of clooth in vanitee;

but ther is also costlewe furrynge in hir gownes, so muche pownsonynge of chisels to maken holes, so muche daggynge of sheres; forthwith the superfluitee in lengthe of the forseide gownes, trailynge in the dong and in the mire, on horse & eek on foote, as wel of men as of wommen, that al thilke trailyng is verraily as in effect wasted, consumed, thredbare, and roten with donge, rather than it is yeven to the povre; to greet damage of the forseyde povre folk. And that in sondry wise; this is to seyn, that the moore that clooth is wasted, the moore it costeth to the peple for the scantnesse. And fortherover, if so be that they wolde yeven swich pownsoned and dagged clothyng to the povre folk, it is nat convenient to were for hire estaat, ne suffisant to beete hire necessitee, to kepe hem fro the distemperance of the firmament.

PON that oother side to speken of the horrible disordinat scantnesse of clothyng, as been thise kutted sloppes or haynselyns, that thurgh hire shortnesse ne covere nat the shameful membres of man, to wikked entente. Allas! somme of hem shewen the boce of hir shap, & the horrible swollen membres, that semeth lik the maladie of hirnia, in the wrappynge of hir hoses; and eek the buttokes of hem faren as it were the hyndre part of a she-ape in the fulle of the moone. And mooreover the wrecched swollen membres that they shewe thurgh the degisynge, in departynge of hire hoses in whit and reed, semeth that half hir shameful privee membres weren flayne. And if so be that they departen hire hoses in othere colours, as is whit and blak, or whit and blew, or blak and reed, and so forth; thanne semeth it, as by variaunce of colour, that half the partie of hire privee membres were corrupt by the fir of Seint Antony, or by cancre, or by oother swich meschaunce. Of the hyndre part of hir buttokes, it is ful horrible for to see. For certes, in that partie of hir body theras they purgen hir stynkynge ordure, that foule partie shewe they to the peple prowdly in despit of honestitee, the which honestitee that Jhesu Crist and his freendes observede to shewen in hir lyve.

OW of the outrageous array of wommen, God woot, that though the visages of somme of hem seme ful chaast and debonaire, yet notifie they in hire array of atyr, likerousnesse and pride. I sey nat that honestitee in clothynge of man or womman is uncovenable, but certes the superfluitee or disordinat scantitee of clothynge is reprevable. Also the synne of aornement or of apparaille is in thynges that apertenen to ridynge, as in to manye delicat horses that been hoolden for delit, that been so faire, fatte, and costlewe; and also to many a vicious knave that is sustened by cause of hem; in to curious harneys, as in sadeles, in crouperes, peytrels, and bridles covered with precious clothyng and riche, barres and plates of gold and of silver. for which God seith by Zakarie the prophete: I wol confounde the rideres of swiche horses. This folk taken litel reward of the ridynge of Goddes sone of hevene, and of his harneys whan he rood upon the asse, and ne hadde noon oother harneys but the povre clothes of his disciples; ne we ne rede nat that evere he rood on oother beest. I speke this for the synne of superfluitee, and nat for resonable honestitee, whan reson it requireth.

AND forther, certes pride is greetly notified in holdynge of greet meynee, whan they be of litel profit or of right no profit. And namely, whan that meynee is felonous and damageous to the peple, by hardynesse of heigh lordshipe, or by wey of offices. for certes, swiche lordes sellen thanne hir lordshipe to the devel of helle, whanne they sustenen the wikkednesse of hir meynee. Or elles whan this folk of lowe degree, as thilke that holden hostelries, sustenen the thefte of hire hostilers, and that is in many manere of deceites. Thilke manere of folk been the flyes that folwen the hony, or elles the houndes that folwen the careyne. Swich forseyde folk stranglen spiritually hir lordshipes; for which thus seith David the prophete: Wikked deeth moote come upon thilke lordshipes, and God yeve that they moote descenden into helle al doun; for in hire houses been iniquitees and shrewednesses, and nat God of hevene. And certes, but if they doon amendement, right as God yaf his benysoun to Laban by the service of Jacob, and to Pharao by the service of Joseph, right so God wol yeve his malisoun to swiche lordshipes as sustenen the wikkednesse of hir servaunts, but if they come to amendement.

PRIDE of the table appeereth eek ful ofte; for certes, riche men been cleped to festes, & povre folk been put awey and rebuked. Also in excess of diverse metes and drynkes; and namely, swiche manere bake-metes & dissh-metes brennynge of wilde fir, and peynted and castelled with papir, and semblable wast; so that it is abusioun for to thynke. And eek in to greet preciousnesse of vessel and curiositee of mynstralcie, by whiche a man is stired the moore to delices of luxurie, if so be that he sette his herte the lasse upon oure Lord Jhesu Crist, certeyn it is a synne; and certeinly the delices myghte been so
200

grete in this caas, that man myghte lightly falle by hem into deedly synne. The especes that sourden of pride, soothly whan they sourden of malice ymagined, avised, & forncast, or elles of usage, been deedly synnes, it is no doute. And whan they sourden by freletee unavysed sodeynly, and sodeynly withdrawen ayeyn, al been they grevouse synnes, I gesse that they ne been nat deedly.

NOW myghte men axe wherof that pride sourdeth and spryngeth, and I seye: somtyme it spryngeth of the goodes of nature, and somtyme of the goodes of fortune, and somtyme of the goodes of grace. Certes, the goodes of nature stonden outher in goodes of body or in goodes of soule. Certes, goodes of body been heele of body, as strengthe, delivernesse, beautee, gentrie, franchise. Goodes of nature of the soule been good wit, sharpe understondynge, subtilengyn, vertu natureel, good memorie. Goodes of fortune been richesses, hyghe degrees of lordshipes, preisynges of the peple. Goodes of grace been science, power to suffre spiritueel travaille, benignitee, vertuous contemplacioun, withstondynge of temptacioun, and semblable thynges. Of which forseyde goodes, certes, it is a ful greet folye a man to priden hym in any of hem alle. Now as for to speken of goodes of nature; God woot that somtyme we han hem in nature as muche to oure damage as to oure profit. As for to speken of heele of body; certes, it passeth ful lightly, and eek it is ful ofte enchesoun of the siknesse of oure soule; for God woot, the flessh is a ful greet enemy to the soule: and therfore, the moore that the body is hool, the moore be we in peril to falle. Eke for to pride hym in his strengthe of body, it is an heigh folye; for certes, the flessh coveiteth agayn the spirit, & ay the moore strong that the flessh is, the sorier may the soule be: and, over al this, strengthe of body and worldly hardynesse causeth ful ofte many a man to peril and meschaunce. Eek for to pride hym of his gentrie is ful greet folie; for ofte tyme the gentrie of the body binymeth the gentrie of the soule; & eek we ben alle of o fader & of o mooder; and alle we been of o nature, roten and corrupt, bothe riche and povre. forsothe, o manere gentrie is for to preise, that apparailleth mannes corage with vertues and moralitees, and maketh hym Cristes child. for truste wel, that over what man that synne hath maistrie, he is a verray cherl to synne.

NOW been ther generale signes of gentillesse; as eschewynge of vice and ribaudye and servage of synne, in word, in werk, and contenaunce; and usynge vertu, curteisye, and clennesse, and to be liberal, that is to seyn, large by mesure; for thilke that passeth mesure is folie and synne. ✒Another is, to remembre hym of bountee that he of oother folk hath receyved. Another is, to be benigne to his goode subgetis; wherfore, as seith Senek: Ther is nothyng moore covenable to a man of heigh estaat, than debonairetee & pitee ✒And therfor thise flyes that men clepeth bees, whan they maken hir kyng, they chesen oon that hath no prikke wherwith he may stynge. ✒Another is, a man to have a noble herte and a diligent, to attayne to heighe vertuouse thynges. Now certes, a man to pride hym in the goodes of grace is eek an outrageous folie; for thilke yifte of grace that sholde have turned hym to goodnesse and to medicine, turneth hym to venym and to confusioun, as seith Seint Gregorie. Certes also, whoso prideth hym in the goodes of fortune, he is a ful greet fool; for somtyme is a man a greet lord by the morwe, that is a caytyf and a wrecche er it be nyght: and somtyme the richesse of a man is cause of his deth; somtyme the delices of a man is cause of the grevous maladye thurgh which he dyeth. Certes, the commendacioun of the peple is somtyme ful fals and ful brotel for to triste; this day they preyse, tomorwe they blame. God woot, desir to have commendacioun of the peple hath caused deeth to many a bisy man.

Remedium contra peccatum Superbie.

NOW sith that so is, that ye han understonde what is pride, & whiche been the speces of it, and whennes pride sourdeth & spryngeth; now shul ye understonde which is the remedie agayns the synne of pride, & that is, humylitee or mekenesse. That is a vertu thurgh which a man hath verray knoweleche of hymself, & holdeth of hymself no pris ne deyntee as in regard of his desertes, considerynge evere his freletee ✒Now been ther thre maneres of humylitee; as humylitee in herte, and another humylitee in his mouth, the thridde in his werkes. ✒The humilitee in herte is in foure maneres: that oon is, whan a man holdeth hymself as noght worth biforn God of hevene. Another is, whan he ne despiseth noon oother man. The thridde is, whan he rekketh nat though men holde hym noght worth. The ferthe is, whan he nys nat sory of his humiliacioun. ✒Also, the humilitee of mouth is in foure thynges: in attempree speche, & in humblesse of speche; and whan he biknoweth with his owene mouth that he is

swich as hym thynketh that he is in his herte. Another is, whan he preiseth the bountee of another man, & nothyng therof amenuseth ✒Humilitee eek in werkes is in foure maneres: the firste is, whan he putteth othere men biforn hym. The seconde is, to chese the loweste place over al. The thridde is, gladly to assente to good conseil. The ferthe is, to stonde gladly to the award of his sovereyns, or of hym that is in hyer degree; certein, this is a greet werk of humylitee.

Sequitur de Invidia.

AfTER pride wol I speken of the foule synne of envye, which is, as by the word of the philosophre, sorwe of oother mannes prosperitee; & after the word of Seint Augustyn, it is sorwe of oother mannes wele, and joye of othere mennes harm. This foule synne is platly agayns the Hooly Goost. Albeit so that every synne is agayns the Hooly Goost, yet nathelees, forasmuche as bountee aperteneth proprely to the Hooly Goost, & envye comth proprely of malice, therfor it is proprely agayn the bountee of the Hooly Goost.

NOW hath malice two speces, that is to seyn, hardnesse of herte in wikkednesse, or elles the flessh of man is so blynd, that he considereth nat that he is in synne, or rekketh nat that he is in synne; which is the hardnesse of the devel. ✒That oother spece of malice is, whan a man werreyeth trouthe, whan he woot that it is trouthe. And eek, whan he werreyeth the grace that God hath yeve to his neighebore; & al this is by envye. Certes, thanne is envye the worste synne that is. For soothly, alle othere synnes been somtyme oonly agayns o special vertu; but certes, envye is agayns alle vertues, and agayns alle goodnesses; for it is sory of alle the bountees of his neighebore; and in this manere it is divers from alle othere synnes. For wel unnethe is ther any synne that it ne hath som delit in itself, save oonly envye, that evere hath in itself angwissh and sorwe.

THE speces of envye been thise: ther is first, sorwe of oother mannes goodnesse and of his prosperitee; and prosperitee is kyndely matere of joye; thanne is envye a synne agayns kynde. The seconde spece of envye is joye of oother mannes harm; & that is proprely lyk to the devel, that evere rejoyseth hym of mannes harm.

Of thise two speces comth bakbityng; and this synne of bakbityng or detraccion hath certeine speces, as thus. Som man preiseth his neighebore

201

by a wikke entente; for he maketh alwey a wikked knotte atte laste ende. Alwey he maketh a But, atte laste ende, that is digne of moore blame, than worth is al the preisynge. The seconde spece is, that if a man be good, & dooth or seith a thing to good entente, the bakbiter wol turne all thilke goodnesse up-so-doun, to his shrewed entente. The thridde is, to amenuse the bountee of his neighebore. The fourthe spece of bakbityng is this; that if men speke goodnesse of a man, thanne wol the bakbiter seyn: Pardee! swich a man is yet bet than he; in dispreisynge of hym that men preise. The fifte spece is this; for to consente gladly & herkne gladly to the harm that men speke of oother folk. This synne is ful greet, and ay encreeseth after the wikked entente of the bakbiter. After bakbityng cometh grucchyng or murmuracioun; and somtyme it spryngeth of inpacience agayns God, & somtyme agayns man. Agayns God it is, whan a man gruccheth agayn the peynes of helle, or agayns poverte, or los of catel, or agayn reyn or tempest; or elles gruccheth that shrewes han prosperitee, or elles for that goode men han adversitee. And alle thise thinges sholde men suffre paciently, for they comen by the rightful juggement and ordinance of God. Somtyme comth grucching of avarice; as Judas grucched agayns the Magdaleyne, whan she enoynte the heved of oure Lord Jhesu Crist with hir precious oynement. This maner murmure is swich as whan man gruccheth of goodnesse that hymself dooth, or that oother folk doon of hir owene catel.

SOMTYME comth murmure of pride; as whan Simon the Pharisee gruccched agayn the Magdaleyne, whan she approched to Jhesu Crist, and weep at his feet for hire synnes. And somtyme grucchyng sourdeth of envye; whan men discovereth a mannes harm that was pryvee, or bereth hym on hond thyng that is fals.

MURMURE eek is ofte amonges servaunts that grucchen whan hir sovereyns bidden hem doon leveful thynges; and, forasmuche as they dar nat openly withseye the comaundements of hir sovereyns, yet wol they seyn harm, and grucche, and murmure prively, for verray despit; which wordes men clepen: The develes Pater noster, though so be that the devel ne hadde nevere Pater noster, but that lewed folk yeven it swich a name. Somtyme grucchyng comth of ire, or prive hate, that norisseth rancour in herte, as afterward I shal declare. Thanne cometh eek bitternesse of herte; thurgh which bitternesse every good dede of his neighebor semeth to hym bitter and

202

unsavory. Thanne cometh discord, that unbyndeth alle manere of freendshipe. Thanne comth scornynge, as whan a man seketh occasioun to anoyen his neighebor, al do he never so weel. Thanne comth accusynge, as whan a man seketh occasioun to anoyen his neighebor, which that is lyk to the craft of the devel, that waiteth bothe nyght and day to accusen us alle. Thanne comth malignitee, thurgh which a man anoyeth his neighebor prively if he may; & if he noght may, algate his wikked wil ne shal nat wante, as for to brennen his hous pryvely, or empoysone or sleen his beestes, and semblable thynges.

Remedium contra peccatum Invidie.

NOW wol I speke of the remedie agayns the foule synne of envye. First, is the lovynge of God principal, & lovyng of his neigheboras hymself; for soothly, that oon ne may nat been withoute that oother. And truste wel, that in the name of thy neighebore thou shalt understonde the name of thy brother; for certes, alle we have o fader flesshly, and o mooder, that is to seyn, Adam and Eve; and eek o fader espiritueel, and that is God of hevene. Thy neighebore artow holden for to love, & wilne hym alle goodnesse; and therfore seith God: Love thy neighebore as thyselve; that is to seyn, to salvacioun of lyf & of soule. And mooreover, thou shalt love hym in word, & in benigne amonestynge, and chastisynge; and conforten hym in his anoyes, and preye for hym with al thyn herte. And in dede thou shalt love hym in swich wise that thou shalt doon to hym in charitee as thou woldest that it were doon to thyn owene persone. And therfore, thou ne shalt doon hym no damage in wikked word, ne harm in his body, ne in his catel, ne in his soule by entisyng of wikked ensample. Thou shalt nat desiren his wyf, ne none of his thynges. Understoond eek, that in the name of neighebor is comprehended his enemy. Certes man shal loven his enemy by the comandement of God; & soothly, thy freend shaltow love in God. I seye, thyn enemy shaltow love for Goddes sake, by his comandement. For if it were reson that a man sholde haten his enemy, forsothe God nolde nat receyven us to his love that been his enemys Agayns thre manere of wronges that his enemy dooth to hym, he shal doon thre thynges, as thus. Agayns hate & rancour of herte, he shal love hym in herte. Agayns chidyng and wikked wordes, he shal preye for his enemy. And agayn wikked dede of his enemy, he shal doon hym bountee. For Crist seith: Loveth youre enemys, & preyeth for hem that speke yow harm; and eek for hem that yow chacen & pursewen, and dooth bountee to hem that yow haten. Loo, thus comaundeth us oure Lord Jhesu Crist to do to oure enemys. For soothly, nature dryveth us to loven oure freendes, and parfey, oure enemys han moore nede to love than oure freendes; and they that moore nede have, certes, to hem shal men doon goodnesse; and certes, in thilke dede have we remembrance of the love of Jhesu Crist, that deyde for his enemys. And inasmuche as thilke love is the moore grevous to perfourne, insomuche is the moore gretter the merite; & therfor the lovynge of our enemy hath confounded the venym of the devel. For right as the devel is disconfited by humylitee, right so is he wounded to the deeth by love of oure enemy. Certes, thanne is love the medicine that casteth out the venym of envye fro mannes herte. The speces of this paas shullen be moore largely in hir chapitres folwynge declared.

Sequitur de Ira.

AFTER envye wol I discryven the synne of ire. For soothly, whoso hath envye upon his neighebor, anon he wole comunly fynde hym a matere of wratthe, in word, or in dede, agayns hym to whom he hath envye. And as wel comth ire of pride as of envye; for soothly, he that is proude or envyous is lightly wrooth. This synne of ire, after the discryvyng of Seint Augustyn, is wikked wil to been avenged by word or by dede. Ire, after the philosophre, is the fervent blood of man yquyked in his herte, thurgh which he wole harm to hym that he hateth. For certes, the herte of man, by eschawfynge & moevynge of his blood, wexeth so trouble, that he is out of alle juggement of resoun. But ye shal understonde that ire is in two maneres; that oon of hem is good, & that oother is wikked. The goode ire is by jalousie of goodnesse, thurgh which a man is wrooth with wikkednesse and agayns wikkednesse; & therfore seith a wys man: that Ire is bet than pley. This ire is with debonairetee, and it is wrooth withouten bitternesse; nat wrooth agayns the man, but wrooth with the mysdede of the man; as seith the prophete David: Irascimini et nolite peccare.

NOW understondeth, that wikked ire is in two maneres, that is to seyn, sodeyn ire, or hastif ire, withouten avisement & consentynge of resoun. The menyng and the sens of this is, that the resoun of man ne consente nat to thilke sodeyn ire; & thanne it is venial. Another

ire is ful wikked, that comth of felonie of herte avysed and cast biforn; with wikked wil to do vengeance, and therto his resoun consenteth; and soothly, this is deedly synne. This ire is so displesant to God, that it troubleth his hous and chaceth the Hooly Goost out of mannes soule, and wasteth and destroyeth the liknesse of God, that is to seyn, the vertu that is in mannes soule; and put in hym the liknesse of the devel, and bynymeth the man fro God that is his rightful lord. This ire is a ful greet plesaunce to the devel; for it is the develes fourneys, that is eschawfed with the fir of helle. For certes, right so as fir is moore mighty to destroyen erthely thynges than any oother element, right so ire is myghty to destroyen alle spiritueel thynges.

LOOKE how that fir of smale gleedes, that been almoost dede under asshen, wollen quike agayn whan they been touched with brymstoon. Right so ire wol everemo quyken agayn, whan it is touched by the pride that is covered in mannes herte. For certes, fir ne may nat comen out of nothyng, but if it were first in the same thyng natureely; as fir is drawen out of flyntes with steel. And, right so as pride is ofteryme matere of ire, right so is rancour norice and keper of ire. Ther is a maner tree, as seith Seint Ysidre, that whan men maken fir of thilke tree, and covere the coles of it with asshen, soothly the fir of it wol lasten al a yeer or moore. And right so fareth it of rancour; whan it is ones conceyved in the hertes of som men, certein it wol lasten peraventure from oon Estre-day unto another Estre-day, and moore. But certes, thilke man is ful fer fro the mercy of God al thilke while.

IN this forseyde develes fourneys ther forgen thre shrewes: pride, that ay bloweth & encreesseth the fir by chidynge & wikked wordes. Thanne stant envye, and holdeth the hoote iren upon the herte of man with a peire of longe toonges of long rancour. And thanne stant the synne of contumelie or strif & cheeste, and batereth and forgeth by vileyns reprevynges. Certes, this cursed synne anoyeth bothe to the man hymself and eek to his neighebore. For soothly, almoost al the harm that any man dooth to his neighebore comth of wratthe. For certes, outrageous wratthe dooth al that evere the devel hym comaundeth; for he ne spareth neither Crist, ne his sweete mooder. And in his outrageous anger and ire, allas! allas! ful many oon at that tyme feeleth in his herte ful wikkedly, both of Crist and of alle his halwes. Is nat this a cursed vice? Yis, certes. Allas! it bynymeth from man

203

his wit and his resoun, and al his debonaire lif espiritueel, that sholde kepen his soule. Certes, it bynymeth eek Goddes due lord/ shipe, and that is mannes soule, & the love of his neighebores. It stryveth eek alday agayn trouthe. It reveth hym the quiete of his herte, and subverteth his soule.

Of ire comen thise stynkynge en/ gendrures: first hate, that is oold wratthe; discord, thurgh which a man forsaketh his olde freend that he hath lovede ful longe. And thanne cometh werre, and every manere of wrong that man dooth to his neighebore, in body or in catel. Of this cursed synne of ire cometh eek man/ slaughtre. And understonde wel, that ho/ mycide, that is manslaughtre, is in diverse wise. Som manere of homycide is spiritu/ eel, and som is bodily.

SPIRITUEEL manslaughtre is in sixe thynges. First, by hate; as Seint John seith: He that hateth his bro/ ther is homycide. Homycide is eek by bakbitynge; of whiche bakbiteres seith Sa/ lomon: that They han two swerdes with whiche they sleen hire neighebores. For soothly, as wikke is to bynyme his good name, as his lyf. Homycide is eek in yev/ ynge of wikked conseil by fraude; as for to yeven conseil to areysen wrongful cus/ tumes and taillages. Of whiche seith Salo/ mon: Leoun rorynge and bere hongry been like to the crueel lordshipes, in withhold/ ynge or abreggynge of the shepe, or the hyre, or of the wages of servaunts, or elles in usure or in withdrawynge of the alm/ esse of povre folk. For which the wise man seith: Fedeth hym that almoost dy/ eth for honger. For soothly, but if thow feede hym, thou sleest hym; and alle thise been deedly synnes. Bodily manslaughtre is, whan thow sleest him with thy tonge in oother manere; as whan thou comandest to sleen a man, or elles yevest hym conseil to sleen a man.

MANSLAUGHTRE in dede is in foure maneres. That oon is by lawe; right as a justice dampneth hym that is coupable to the deeth. But lat the justice be war that he do it rightfully, and that he do it nat for delit to spille blood, but for kepynge of rightwisenesse. Ano/ ther homycide is, that is doon for neces/ sitee, as whan o man sleeth another in his defendaunt, & that he ne may noon ooth/ erwise escape from his owene deeth. But certeinly, if he may escape withouten man/ slaughtre of his adversarie, & sleeth hym, he dooth synne, and he shal bere penance as for deedly synne. Eek if a man, by caas or aventure, shete an arwe or caste a stoon with which he sleeth a man, he is homycide. Eek if a womman by necligence overlyeth

204

hir child in hir slepyng, it is homycide and deedly synne. Eek whan man destourb/ eth concepcioun of a child, and maketh a womman outher bareyne by drynkynge venenouse herbes, thurgh which she may nat conceyve, or sleeth a child by drynkes wilfully, or elles putteth certeine material thynges in hire secree places to slee the child; or elles dooth unkyndely synne, by which man or womman shedeth hire na/ ture in manere or in place theras a child may nat be conceived; or elles, if a woman have conceyved and hurt hirself, and sleeth the child, yet it is homycide. What seye we eek of wommen that mordren hir children for drede of worldly shame? Certes, an horri/ ble homicide. Homycide is eek if a man ap/ procheth to a womman by desir of lecherie, thurgh which the child is perissed, or elles smyteth a womman wityngly, thurgh which she leseth hir child. Alle thise been homy/ cides and horrible deedly synnes.

YET comen ther of ire manye mo synnes, as wel in word, as in thoght & in dede; as he that arretteth upon God, or blameth God, of thyng of which he is hymself gilty; or despiseth God and alle his halwes, as doon thise cursede ha/ sardours in diverse contrees. This cursed synne doon they, whan they feelen in hir hertes ful wikkedly of God and of his hal/ wes. Also, whan they treten unreverently the sacrament of the auter. Thilke synne is so greet, that unnethe may it been re/ leessed, but that the mercy of God pas/ seth alle his werkes; it is so greet, and he so benigne.

THANNE comth of ire, attry angre; whan a man is sharply amonested in his shrifte to forleten his synne, thanne wole he be angry and answeren ho/ kerly and angrily, and deffenden or excus/ en his synne by unstedefastnesse of his flessh; or elles he dide it for to holde com/ paignye with his felawes; or elles, he seith, the feend enticed hym; or elles he dide it for his youthe; or elles his conpleccioun is so corageous, that he may nat forbere; or elles it is his destinee, as he seith, unto a cer/ tein age; or elles, he seith, it cometh hym of gentillesse of his auncestres; and sem/ blable thynges. Alle this manere of folk so wrappen hem in hir synnes, that they ne wol nat delivere hemself. For soothly, no wight that excuseth hym wilfully of his synne may nat been delivered of his synne, til that he mekely biknoweth his synne.

AFTER this, thanne cometh sweryng, that is expres agayn the comande/ ment of God; and this bifalleth ofte of anger and of ire. God seith: Thow shalt nat take the name of thy Lord God in veyn,

or in ydel. Also oure Lord Jhesu Crist
seith, by the word of Seint Mathew: Nolite
jurare omnino: Ne wol ye nat swere in alle
manere; neither by hevene, for it is Goddes
trone; ne by erthe, for it is the bench of his
feet; ne by Jerusalem, for it is the citee of
a greet kyng; ne be thyn heed, for thou
mayst nat make an heer whit ne blak. But
seyeth by youre word, Ye, ye, and Nay,
nay; and what that is moore, it is of yvel,
seith Crist. For Cristes sake, ne swereth
nat so synfully, in dismembrynge of Crist
by soule, herte, bones, & body. For certes,
it semeth that ye thynke that the cursede
Jewes ne dismembred nat ynough the preciouse persone of Crist, but ye dismembre
hym moore. And if so be that the lawe com-
pelle yow to swere, thanne rule yow after
the lawe of God in youre sweryng, as seith
Jeremye, quarto capitulo: Jurabis in veri-
tate, in judicio et in justicia: thou shalt
kepe thre condicions; thou shalt swere in
trouthe, in doom, and in rightwisnesse.
This is to seyn, thou shalt swere sooth;
for every lesynge is agayns Crist; for Crist
is verray trouthe. And thynk wel this, that
every greet swerere, nat compelled lawefully to swere, the wounde shal nat departe
from his hous whil he useth swich unleveful sweryng. Thou shalt sweren eek in
doom, whan thou art constreyned by thy
domesman to witnessen the trouthe. Eek
thow shalt nat swere for envye, ne for favour, ne for meede, but for rightwisnesse;
& for declaracioun of it, to the worship of
God and helpyng of thyne evene Cristene. And therfore, every man that taketh
Goddes name in ydel, or falsly swereth
with his mouth, or elles taketh on hym the
name of Crist, to be called a Cristene man,
and lyveth agayns Cristes lyvynge and his
techynge, alle they taken Goddes name in
ydel.

LOOKE eek what seint Peter seith,
Actuum quarto capitulo: Non est
aliud nomen sub celo, etc. Ther
nys noon oother name, seith Seint Peter,
under hevene, yeven to men, in which they
mowe be saved. that is to seyn, but the
name of Jhesu Crist. Take kepe eek how
that the precious name of Crist, as seith
Seint Paul ad Philipenses secundo: In no-
mine Jhesu, etc.: that In the name of Jhesu
every knee of hevenely creatures, or erthely,
or of helle, sholden bowe. for it is so
heigh and so worshipful that the cursede
feend in helle sholde tremblen to heeren it
ynempned. Thanne semeth it, that men
that sweren so horribly by his blessed
name, that they despise hym moore
booldely than dide the cursede Jewes, or
elles the devel, that trembleth whan he
heereth his name.

NOW certes, sith that sweryng, but
if it be lawefully doon, is so heighly
deffended, muche worse is forsweryng falsly, and yet nedelees.

WHAT seye we eek of hem that de-
liten hem in sweryng, and holden
it a gentrie or a manly dede to
swere grete othes? And what of hem that,
of verray usage, ne cesse nat to swere grete
othes, al be the cause nat worth a straw?
Certes, it is horrible synne. Swerynge sodeynly, withoute avysement, is eek a synne.
But lat us go now to thilke horrible sweryng of adjuracioun and conjuracioun, as
doon thise false enchauntours or nigro-
manciens, in bacyns ful of water, or in a
bright swerd, in a cercle, or in a fir, or in a
shulder-boon of a sheepe. I kan nat seye
but that they doon cursedly and damna-
bly, agayns Crist and al the feith of hooly
chirche.

WHAT seye we of hem that bileeven
in divynailes, as by flight or by
noyse of briddes, or of beestes,
or by sort, by geomancie, by dremes, by
chirkynge of dores, or crakynge of houses,
by gnawynge of rattes, and swich manere
wrecchednesse? Certes, al this thyng is
deffended by God, and by al hooly chirche.
For which they been acursed til they come
to amendement, that on swich filthe setten
hire bileeve. Charmes for woundes or maladie of men, or of beestes, if they taken
any effect, it be peraventure that God suffreth it, for folk sholden yeve the moore
feith and reverence to his name. Now wol
I speken of lesynges, which generally is
fals signyficacioun of word, in entente to
deceyven his evene cristene. Some lesynge
is, of which ther comth noon avantage to
no wight; and some lesynge turneth to the
ese and profit of o man, and to disese and
damage of another man. Another lesynge
is for to saven his lyf or his catel. Another
lesynge comth of delit for to lye, in which
delit they wol forge a long tale, & peynten
it with alle circumstaunces, where al the
ground of the tale is fals. Som lesynge
comth for he wole sustene his word; & som
lesynge comth of reccheleesnesse, withouten avysement; and semblable thynges.

LAT us now touche the vice of flaterynge, which ne comth nat gladly, but for drede, or for coveitise.
Flaterye is generally wrongful preisynge.
Flatereres been the develes norices, that
norissen his children with milk of losengerie. Forsothe, Salomon seith: that flaterie is wors than detraccioun. For somtyme detraccion maketh an hauteyn man
be the moore humble, for he dredeth detraccion; but certes, flaterye, that maketh
a man to enchauncen his herte and his con-

205

The
Persouns
Tale

tenaunce. flatereres been the develes enchauntours; for they make a man to wene
of hymself be lyk that he nys nat lyk. They
been lyk to Judas, that bitraysed God; and
thise flaterers bitraysen a man to sellen
hym to his enemy, that is, to the devel.
flatereres been the develes chapelleyns,
that syngen evere Placebo. I rekene flaterie
in the vices of ire; for ofte tyme, if o man
be wrooth with another, thanne wole he
flatere som wight to sustene hym in his
querele.

SPEKE we now of swich cursynge
as comth of irous herte. Malisoun
generally may be seyd every maner
power or harm. Swich cursynge bireveth
man fro the regne of God, as seith Seint
Paul. And ofte tyme swich cursynge
wrongfully retorneth agayn to hym that
curseth, as a bryd that retorneth agayn to
his owene nest. And over alle thyng men
oghten eschewe to cursen hire children, &
yeven to the devel hire engendrure, as ferforth as in hem is; certes, it is greet peril
and greet synne.

LAT us thanne speken of chidynge
and reproche, whiche been ful grete
woundes in mannes herte; for they
unsowen the semes of freendshipe in
mannes herte. for certes, unnethes may a
man pleynly been accorded with hym that
hath hym openly revyled and repreved in
disclaundre. This is a ful grisly synne, as
Crist seith in the gospel. And taak kepe
now, that he that repreveth his neighebor,
outher he repreveth hym by som harm of
peyne that he hath on his body, as Mesel,
Croked harlot, or by som synne that he
dooth. Now if he repreve hym by harm of
peyne, thanne turneth the repreve to Jhesu
Crist; for peyne is sent by the rightwys
sonde of God, and by his suffrance, be it
meselrie, or maheym, or maladie. And if he
repreve hym uncharitably of synne, as,
Thou holour, Thou dronkelewe harlot, &
so forth; thanne aperteneth that to the
rejoysynge of the devel, that evere hath
joye that men doon synne. And certes,
chidynge may nat come but out of a vileyns
herte. for after the habundance of the herte
speketh the mouth ful ofte. And ye shul
understonde that looke, by any wey, whan
any man shal chastise another, that he be
war from chidynge and reprevynge. for
trewely, but he be war, he may ful lightly
quyken the fir of angre and of wratthe,
which that he sholde quenche, and peraventure sleeth hym which that he myghte
chastise with benignitee. for as seith Salomon: The amyable tonge is the tree of lyf;
that is to seyn, of lyf espiritueel, & soothly, a deslavee tonge sleeth the spirites of
hym that repreveth, and eek of hym that is
repreved. Loo, what seith Seint Augus-
206

tyn: Ther is nothyng so lyk the develes
child as he that ofte chideth. Seint Paul
seith eek: I, servant of God, bihove nat to
chide. And how that chidynge be a vileyns
thyng bitwixe alle manere folk, yet is it,
certes, moost uncovenable bitwixe a man
and his wyf; for there is nevere reste. And
therfore seith Salomon: An hous that is
uncovered and droppynge, and a chidynge
wyf, been lyke. A man that is in a droppynge hous in manye places, though he eschewe the droppynge in o place, it droppeth
on hym in another place; so fareth it by a
chydynge wyf; but she chide hym in o place,
she wol chide hym in another. And therefore: Bettre is a morsel of breed with joye
than an hous ful of delices, with chidynge,
seith Salomon. Seint Paul seith: O ye
wommen, be ye subgetes to youre housbondes as bihoveth in God; & ye men, loveth youre wyves: Ad Colossenses, tertio.

AFTERWARD speke we of scornynge, which is a wikked synne, and
namely, whan he scorneth a man for
his goode werkes. for certes, swiche scorneres faren lyk the foule tode, that may nat
endure to smelle the soote savour of the
vyne whanne it florissheth. Thise scorneres been partyng-felawes with the devel;
for they han joye whan the devel wynneth,
and sorwe whan he leseth. They been adversaries of Jhesu Crist; for they haten
that he loveth, that is to seyn, salvacioun
of soule.

SPEKE we now of wikked conseil;
for he that wikked conseil yeveth is
a traytour; for he deceyveth hym
that trusteth in hym: At Achitofel ad Ab-
solonem. But nathelees, yet is his wikked
conseil first agayn hymself. for, as seith
the wise man: Every fals livynge man hath
this propertee in hymself, that he that
wol anoye another man, he anoyeth first
hymself. And men shul understonde,
that man shal nat taken his conseil of fals
folk, ne of angry folk, or grevous folk,
ne of folk that loven specially to muchel
hir owene profit, ne to muche worldly folk;
namely, in conseilynge of soules.

NOW comth the synne of hem that
sowen & maken discord amonges
folk, which is a synne that Crist
hateth outrely; and no wonder is. for he
deyde for to make concord. And moore
shame do they to Crist, than dide they
that hym crucifiede; for God loveth bettre,
that freendshipe be amonges folk, than
he dide his owene body, the which that he
yaf for unitee. Therfore been they likned
to the devel, that evere been aboute to
maken discord.

NOW comth the synne of double
tonge; swiche as speken faire byforn folk, and wikkedly bihynde;

or elles they maken semblant as though they speke of good intencioun, or elles in game and pley, & yet they speke of wikked entente.

NOW comth biwreying of conseil, thurgh which a man is defamed; certes, unnethe may he restoore the damage.

NOW comth manace, that is an open folye; for he that ofte manaceth, he threteth moore than he may perfourne ful ofte tyme.

NOW cometh ydel wordes, that is withouten profit of hym that speketh tho wordes, and eek of hym that herkneth tho wordes. Or elles ydel wordes been tho that been nedelees, or withouten entente of natureel profit. And albeit that ydel wordes been som tyme venial synne, yet sholde men douten hem; for we shul yeve rekenynge of hem bifore God.

NOW comth janglynge, that may nat been withoute synne. And as seith Salomon: It is a synne of apert folye. And therfore a philosophre seyde, whan men axed hym how that men sholde plese the peple; & he answerde: Do manye goode werkes, and spek fewe jangles.

AFTER this comth the synne of japeres, that been the develes apes; for they maken folk to laughe at hire japerie, as folk doon at the gawdes of an ape. Swich japeres deffendeth Seint Paul. Looke how that vertuouse wordes and hooly conforten hem that travaillen in the service of Crist; right so conforten the vileyns wordes & knakkes of japeris, hem that travaillen in the service of the devel. Thise been the synnes that comen of the tonge, that comen of ire, and of othere synnes mo.

Sequitur remedium contra peccatum Ire.

THE remedie agayns ire is a vertu that men clepen mansuetude, that is debonairetee; and eek another vertu, that men callen pacience, or suffrance. Debonairetee withdraweth and refreyneth the stirynges and the moevynges of mannes corage in his herte, in swich manere that they ne skippe nat out by angre ne by ire.

SUFFRANCE suffreth swetely alle the anoyaunces & the wronges that men doon to man outward. Seint Jerome seith thus of debonairetee: that It dooth noon harm to no wight, ne seith; ne for noon harm that men doon or seyn, he ne eschawfeth nat agayns his resoun. This vertu somtyme comth of nature; for, as seith the philosophre: A man is a quyk thyng, by nature debonaire and tretable to goodnesse. But whan debonairetee is enformed of grace, thanne is it the moore worth.

PACIENCE, that is another remedie agayns ire, is a vertu that suffreth swetely every mannes goodnesse, and is nat wrooth for noon harm that is doon to hym. The philosophre seith: that Pacience is thilke vertu that suffreth debonairely alle the outrages of adversitee & every wikked word. This vertu maketh a man lyk to God, and maketh hym Goddes owene deere childe, as seith Crist. This vertu disconfiteth thyn enemy. And therfore seith the wise man: If thow wolt venquysse thyn enemy, lerne to suffre. And thou shalt understonde, that man suffreth foure manere of grevances in outward thynges; agayns the whiche foure he moot have foure manere of paciences.

THE firste grevance is of wikkede wordes; thilke suffred Jhesu Crist withouten grucchyng, ful paciently, whan the Jewes despised and repreved hym ful ofte. Suffre thou therfore paciently; for the wise man seith: If thou stryve with a fool, though the fool be wrooth or though he laughe, algate thou shalt have no reste.

THAT oother grevance outward is to have damage of thy catel. Theragayns suffred Crist ful paciently, whan he was despoyled of al that he hadde in this lyf, and that nas but his clothes.

THE thridde grevance is a man to have harm in his body. That suffred Crist ful paciently in al his passioun.

THE fourthe grevance is in outrageous labour in werkes. Wherfore I seye, that folk that maken hir servants to travaillen so grevously, or out of tyme, as on halydayes, soothly they do greet synne. Heeragayns suffred Crist ful paciently, & taughte us pacience, whan he baar upon his blissed shulder the croys, upon which he sholde suffren despitous deeth. Heere may men lerne to be pacient; for certes, noght oonly Cristen men been pacient for love of Jhesu Crist, & for guerdoun of the blisful lyf that is perdurable; but certes, the olde payens, that nevere were Cristene, commendeden & useden the vertu of pacience.

A PHILOSOPHRE upon a tyme, that wolde have beten his disciple for his grete trespas, for which he was greetly amoeved, and broghte a yerde to scourge the child; and whan this child saugh the yerde, he seyde to his maister: What thenke ye to do? I wol bete thee, quod the maister, for thy correccioun. forsothe, quod the child; ye oghten first correcte youreself, that han lost al youre pacience for the gilt of a child. forsothe, quod the maister, al wepynge, thow seyst

207

sooth; have thow the yerde, my deere sone, and correcte me for myn inpacience ✒ Of pacience comth obedience, thurgh which a man is obedient to Crist, and to alle hem to whiche he oghte to been obedient in Crist. And understond wel that obedience is perfit, whan that a man dooth gladly and hastily, with good herte entierly, al that he sholde do. Obedience generally, is to perfourne the doctrine of God and of his sovereyns, to whiche hym oghte to ben obeisaunt in alle rightwisnesse.

Sequitur de Accidia.

fTER the synnes of envye and of ire, now wol I speken of the synne of accidie. For envye blyndeth the herte of a man, & ire troubleth a man; & accidie maketh hym hevy, thoghtful & wrawful. Envye & ire maken bitternesse in herte; which bitternesse is mooder of accidie, and bynymeth hym the love of alle goodnesse. Thanne is accidie the angwissh of a trouble herte; and Seint Augustyn seith: It is anoy of goodnesse and joye of harm. ✒ Certes, this is a dampnable synne; for it dooth wrong to Jhesu Crist, inasmuche as it bynymeth the service that men oghte doon to Crist with alle diligence, as seith Salomon. But accidie dooth no swich diligence; he dooth alle thyng with anoy, and with wrawnesse, slaknesse, and excusacioun, and with ydelnesse, & unlust; for which the book seith: Acursed be he that dooth the service of God necligently.

THANNE is accidie enemy to everich estaat of man; for certes, the estaat of man is in thre maneres. Outher it is thestaat of innocence, as was thestaat of Adam biforn that he fil into synne; in which estaat he was holden to wirche as in heryinge & adowrynge of God. Another estaat is the estaat of synful men, in which estaat men been holden to laboure in preyinge to God for amendement of hire synnes, and that he wole graunte hem to arysen out of hir synnes. Another estaat is thestaat of grace, in which estaat he is holden to werkes of penitence; & certes, to alle thise thynges is accidie enemy & contrarie. For he loveth no bisynesse at al. Now certes, this foule synne, accidie, is eek a ful greet enemy to the liflode of the body; for it ne hath no purveaunce agayn temporeel necessitee; for it forsleweth and forsluggeth, and destroyeth alle goodes temporeles by recchelesnesse.

THE fourthe thyng is, that accidie is lyk to hem that been in the peyne of helle, bycause of hir slouthe and of hire hevynesse; for they that been dampned been so bounde, that they ne may

208

neither wel do ne wel thynke. Of accidie comth first, that a man is anoyed and encombred for to doon any goodnesse, and maketh that God hath abhomynacion of swich accidie, as seith Seint John ✒ Now cometh slouthe, that wol nat suffre noon hardnesse ne no penaunce. For soothly, slouthe is so tendre, & so delicat, as seith Salomon, that he wol nat suffre noon hardnesse ne penaunce, & therfore he shendeth al that he dooth. Agayns this roten-herted synne of accidie and slouthe sholde men exercise hemself to doon goode werkes, & manly and vertuously cacchen corage wel to doon; thynkynge that oure Lord Jhesu Crist quiteth every good dede, be it never so lite. Usage of labour is a greet thyng; for it maketh, as seith Seint Bernard, the laborer to have stronge armes and harde synwes; and slouthe maketh hem feble and tendre. Thanne comth drede to bigynne to werke anye goode werkes; for certes, he that is enclyned to synne, hym thynketh it is so greet an emprise for to undertake to doon werkes of goodnesse, and casteth in his herte that the circumstaunces of goodnesse been so grevouse and so chargeaunt for to suffre, that he dar nat undertake to do werkes of goodnesse, as seith Seint Gregorie.

NOW comth wanhope, that is despeir of the mercy of God, that comth somtyme of to muche outrageous sorwe, and somtyme of to muche drede; ymaginynge that he hath doon so muche synne, that it wol nat availlen hym, though he wolde repenten hym and forsake synne; thurgh which despeir or drede he abaundoneth al his herte to every maner synne, as seith Seint Augustin. Which dampnable synne, if that it continue unto his ende, it is cleped synnyng in the Hooly Goost. This horrible synne is so perilous, that he that is despeired, ther nys no felonye ne no synne that he douteth for to do; as shewed wel by Judas ✒ Certes, aboven alle synnes thanne is this synne moost displesant to Crist and moost adversarie. ✒ Soothly, he that despeireth hym is lyke the coward champioun recreant, that seith Creaunt, withoute nede. Alas! alas! nedeles is he recreaunt, and nedelees despeired. Certes, the mercy of God is evere redy to every penitent, and is aboven alle his werkes. Allas! kan a man nat bithynke hym on the gospel of Seint Luc, xv., whereas Crist seith: that As wel shal ther be joye in hevene upon a synful man that dooth penitence, as upon nynety and nyne rightful men that nevere ne dede synne, ne neden no penitence? ✒ Looke forther, in the same gospel, the joye and the feeste of the goode man that hadde lost his sone, whan his sone with repentaunce was retourned to his fader. Kan they nat remembren hem eek, that, as seith Seint Luc xxiii. capitulo, how that the theef that was hanged bisyde Jhesu Crist seyde: Lord, remembre of me, whan thow comest into thy regne. Forsothe, seyde Crist: I seye to thee, today shaltow been with me in paradys Certes, ther is noon so horrible synne of man, that it ne may, in his lyf, be destroyed by penitence, thurgh vertu of the passion & of the deeth of Crist. Allas! what nedeth man thanne to been despeired, sith that his mercy so redy is and large? Axe and have. Thanne cometh sompnolence, that is, sloggy slombrynge, which maketh a man be hevy and dul, in body and in soule. And this synne comth of slouthe. And certes, the tyme that, by wey of resoun, men sholde nat slepe, that is by the morwe; but if ther were cause resonable. For soothly, the morwe-tyde is moost covenable a man to seye his preyeres, and for to thynken on God, and for to honoure God, and to yeven almesse to the povre, that first cometh in the name of Crist. Lo! what seith Salomon: Whoso wolde by the morwe awaken & seke me, he shal fynde. Thanne cometh necligence, or reccheleesnesse, that rekketh of nothyng. And how that ignoraunce be mooder of alle harm, certes, necligence is the norice. Necligence ne dooth no fors, whan he shal doon a thyng, wheither he do it weel or baddely. Of the remedie of thise two synnes, as seith the wise man: that He that dredeth God, he spareth nat to doon that him oghte doon. And he that loveth God he wol doon diligence to plese God by his werkes, and abaundone hymself, with al his myght, wel for to doon. Thanne comth ydelnesse, that is the yate of alle harmes. An ydel man is lyk to a place that hath no walles; the develes may entre on every syde and sheten at hym at discovert, by temptacion on every syde. This ydelnesse is the thurrok of alle wikked and vileyns thoghtes, & of alle jangles, trufles, and of alle ordure. Certes, the hevene is yeven to hem that wol labouren, and nat to ydel folk. Eek David seith: that They ne been nat in the labour of men, ne they shul nat been whipped with men, that is to seyn, in purgatorie. Certes, thanne semeth it, they shul be tormented with the devel in helle, but if they doon penitence.

THANNE comth the synne that men clepen Tarditas, as whan a man is to laterede or taryinge, er he wole turne to God; and certes, that is a greet folie. He is lyk to hym that falleth in the dych, and wol nat arise. And this vice comth of a fals hope, that he thynketh that he shal lyve longe; but that hope faileth ful ofte.

THANNE comth lachesse; that is he that whan he biginneth any good werk, anon he shal forleten it, and stynten; as doon they that han any wight to governe, and ne taken of hym namoore kepe, anon as they fynden any contrarie or any anoy. Thise been the newe sheepherdes, that leten hir sheep wityngly go renne to the wolf that is in the breres, or do no fors of hir owene governaunce. Of this comth poverte & destruccioun, bothe of spiritueel and temporeel thynges. Thanne comth a manere cooldnesse, that freseth al the herte of a man. Thanne comth undevocioun, thurgh which a man is so blent, as seith Seint Bernard, and hath swich langour in soule, that he may neither rede ne singe in hooly chirche, ne heere ne thynke of no devocioun, ne travaille with his handes in no good werk, that it nys hym unsavory and al apalled. Thanne wexeth he slough and slombry, and soone wol be wrooth, and soone is enclyned to hate and to envye. Thanne comth the synne of worldly sorwe, which as is cleped Tristicia, that sleeth man, as Seint Paul seith. For certes, swich sorwe werketh to the deeth of the soule and of the body also; for therof comth, that a man is anoyed of his owene lif. Wherfore swich sorwe shorteth ful ofte the lif of a man, er that his tyme be come by wey of kynde.

Remedium contra peccatum Accidie.

AGAYNS this horrible synne of accidie, and the branches of the same, ther is a vertu that is called fortitudo, or strengthe; that is, an affeccioun thurgh which a man despiseth anoyouse thinges. This vertu is so myghty and so vigorous, that it dar withstonde myghtily, & wisely kepen hymself fro perils that been wikked, & wrastle agayn the assautes of the devel. For it enhaunceth & enforceth the soule, right as accidie abateth it, and maketh it fieble. For this fortitudo may endure by long suffraunce the travailles that been covenable. This vertu hath manye speces; and the firste is cleped magnanimitee, that is to seyn, greet corage. For certes, ther bihoveth greet corage agains accidie, lest that it ne swolwe the soule by the synne of sorwe, or destroye it by wanhope. This vertu maketh folk to undertake harde thynges and grevouse thynges, by hir owene wil, wisely & resonably. And for as muchel as the devel fighteth agayns a man moore by queyntise and by sleighte than by strengthe, therfore men shal withstonden hym by wit & by resoun and by discrecioun. Thanne arn ther the vertues of feith and hope in God, and in his seintes, to acheve and ac-

p 1

209

complice the goode werkes in the whiche he purposeth fermely to continue. Thanne comth seuretee, or sikernesse; and that is, whan a man ne douteth no travaille in tyme comynge of the goode werkes that a man hath bigonne. Thanne comth magnificence, that is to seyn, whan a man dooth and perfourneth grete werkes of goodnesse that he hath bigonne; and that is the ende why that men sholde do goode werkes; for in the acomplissynge of grete goode werkes lith the grete guerdoun. ‎Thanne is ther constaunce, that is stablenesse of corage; and this sholde been in herte by stedefast feith, and in mouth, and in berynge, and in chiere, and in dede. Eke ther been mo speciale remedies agains accidie, in diverse werkes, & in consideracioun of the peynes of helle, and of the joyes of hevene, and in trust of the grace of the Holy Goost, that wole yeve hym myght to perfourne his goode entente.

Sequitur de Avaricia.

fTER accidie wol I speke of avarice and of coveitise, of which synne seith Seint Paule: that The roote of alle harmes is coveitise: Ad Thimotheum, sexto capitulo. For soothly, whan the herte of a man is confounded in itself, and troubled, and that the soule hath lost the confort of God, thanne seketh he an ydel solas of worldly thynges.

VARICE, after the descripcion of Seint Augustyn, is likerousnesse in herte to have erthely thynges. Som oother folk seyn, that avarice is, for to purchacen manye erthely thynges, and no thyng yeve to hem that han nede. And understoond, that avarice ne stant nat oonly in lond ne catel, but somtyme in science & in glorie, & in every manere of outrageous thyng is avarice and coveitise. ‎And the difference bitwixe avarice and coveitise is this. Coveitise is for to coveite swiche thynges as thou hast nat; and avarice is for to witholde & kepe swiche thynges as thou hast, withoute rightful nede. Soothly, this avarice is a synne that is ful dampnable; for al hooly writ curseth it, & speketh agayns that vice; for it dooth wrong to Jhesu Crist. For it bireveth hym the love that men to hym owen, and turneth it bakward agayns alle resoun; and maketh that the avaricious man hath moore hope in his catel than in Jhesu Crist, and dooth moore observance in kepynge of his tresor than he dooth to service of Jhesu Crist. And therfore seith Seint Paul, ad Ephesios quinto, that An avaricious man is in the thraldom of ydolatrie ‎What difference is betwixe an ydolastre and an avaricious

man, but that an ydolastre, peraventure, ne hath but o mawmet or two, and the avaricious man hath manye? For certes, every floryn in his cofre is his mawmet. And certes, the synne of mawmettrie is the firste thyng that God deffended in the ten comaundments, as bereth witnesse Exodi, capitulo xx: Thou shalt have no false goddes bifore me, ne thou shalt make to thee no grave thyng. ‎Thus is an avaricious man, that loveth his tresor biforn God, an ydolastre, thurgh this cursed synne of avarice.

f coveitise comen thise harde lordshipes, thurgh whiche men been distreyned by taylages, custumes, and cariages, moore than hire duetee or resoun is. And eek they taken of hire bondemen amerciments, whiche myghten moore resonably ben cleped extorciouns than amerciments. Of whiche amerciments and raunsonynge of bondemen, somme lordes stywardes seyn, that it is rightful; forasmuche as a cherl hath no temporeel thyng that it ne is his lordes, as they seyn. But certes, thise lordshipes doon wrong, that bireven hire bondefolk thynges that they nevere yave hem. Augustinus de Civitate Dei, libro nono. Sooth is, that the condicioun of thraldom, and the firste cause of thraldom is for synne. Genesis nono. ‎Thus may ye seen that the gilt disserveth thraldom, but nat nature. Wherfore thise lordes ne sholde nat muche glorifien hem in hir lordshipes, sith that by natureel condicioun they been nat lordes of thralles; but that thraldom comth first by the desert of synne. And fortherover, theras the lawe seith, that temporeel goodes of boondefolk been the goodes of hir lordshipes, ye, that is for to understonde, the goodes of the emperour, to deffenden hem in hir right, but nat for to robben hem ne reven hem. And therfore seith Seneca: Thy prudence sholde lyve benignely with thy thralles. Thilke that thou clepest thy thralles been Goddes peple; for humble folk been Cristes freendes; they been contubernyal with the Lord. ‎Thynk eek, that of swich seed as cherles spryngeth, of swich seed spryngen lordes. As wel may the cherl be saved as the lord. The same deeth that taketh the cherl, swich deeth taketh the lord. Wherfore I rede, do right so with thy cherl, as thou woldest that thy lord dide with thee, if thou were in his plit. Every synful man is a cherl to synne. I rede thee, certes, that thou, lord, werke in swiche wise with thy cherles, that they rather love thee than drede. I woot wel ther is degree above degree, as reson is; and skile it is, that men do hir devoir theras it is due; but certes, extorcions & despit of youre underlynges is dampnable.

AND fortherover understoond well that thise conquerours, or tiraunts maken ful ofte thralles of hem that been born of as roial blood as been they that hem conqueren. This name of thraldom was nevere erst kowth, til that Noe seyde, that his sone Canaan sholde be thral to his bretheren for his synne. What seye we thanne of hem that pilen & doon extorcions to hooly chirche? Certes, the swerd, that men yeven first to a knyght whan he is newe dubbed, signifieth that he sholde deffenden hooly chirche, and nat robben it ne pilen it; and whoso dooth, is traitour to Crist. And, as seith Seint Augustyn: They been the develes wolves, that stranglen the sheep of Jhesu Crist; and doon worse than wolves ❧ for soothly, whan the wolf hath ful his wombe, he stynteth to strangle sheep. But soothly, the pilours and destroyours of Goddes hooly chirche ne do nat so; for they ne stynte nevere to pile.

NOW, as I have seyd, sith so is that synne was first cause of thraldom, thanne is it thus; that thilke tyme that al this world was in synne, thanne was al this world in thraldom and subjeccioun. But certes, sith the time of grace cam, God ordeyned that som folk sholde be moore heigh in estaat and in degree, and som folk moore lough, and that everich sholde be served in his estaat and in his degree. And therfore, in somme contrees ther they byen thralles, whan they han turned hem to the feith, they maken hire thralles free out of thraldom. And therfore, certes, the lord oweth to his man that the man oweth to his lord. The pope calleth hymself servaunt of the servaunts of God; but forasmuche as the estaat of hooly chirche ne myghte nat han be, ne the commune profit myghte nat han be kept, ne pees and reste in erthe, but if God hadde ordeyned that som men hadde hyer degree & som men lower: therfore was sovereyntee ordeyned to kepe and mayntene and deffenden hire underlynges or hire subgets in resoun, as ferforth as it lith in hire power; & nat to destroyen hem ne confounde.

THERFORE I seye, that thilke lordes that been lyk wolves, that devouren the possessiouns or the catel of povre folk wrongfully, without-en mercy or mesure, they shul receyven, by the same mesure that they han mesured to povre folk, the mercy of Jhesu Crist, but if it be amended ❧ Now comth deceite bitwixe marchaunt and marchaunt. And thow shalt understonde, that marchandise is in two maneres; that oon is bodily, & that oother is goostly. That oon is honeste and leveful, and that oother is deshoneste & unleveful. Of thilke bodily marchandise, that is leveful and honeste,

is this; that, thereas God hath ordeyned that a regne or a contree is suffisaunt to hymself, thanne is it honeste and leveful, that of habundaunce of this contree, that men helpe another contree that is moore nedy. And therfore, ther moote been marchants to bryngen fro that o contree to that oother hire marchandises.

THAT oother marchandise, that men haunten with fraude and trecherie & deceite, with lesynges & false othes, is cursed and dampnable ❧ Espiritueel marchandise is proprely symonye, that is, ententif desir to byen thyng espiritueel, that is, thyng that aperteneth to the seintuarie of God & to cure of the soule. This desir, if so be that a man do his diligence to parfournen it, albeit that his desir ne take noon effect, yet is it to hym a deedly synne; and if he be ordred, he is irreguleer. Certes, symonye is cleped of Simon Magus, that wolde han boght, for temporeel catel, the yifte that God hadde yeven, by the Hooly Goost, to Seint Peter and to the Apostles. And therfore understoond, that bothe he that selleth and he that beyeth thynges espirituels, been cleped Symonyals; be it by catel, be it by procurynge, or by flesshly preyere of his freendes, flesshly freendes, or espiritueel freendes. flesshly in two maneres; as by kynrede, or othere freendes. Soothly, if they praye for hym that is nat worthy and able, it is symonye, if he take the benefice; and if he be worthy and able, ther nys noon.

THAT oother manere is, whan a man or womman preyen for folk to avauncen hem, oonly for wikked flesshly affeccioun that they have unto the persone; and that is foul symonye. But certes, in service, for which men yeven thynges espirituels unto hir servants, it moot been understonde that the service moot been honeste, and elles nat; and eek that it be withouten bargaynynge, and that the persone be able. for, as seith Seint Damasie: Alle the synnes of the world, at regard of this synne, arn as thyng of noght; for it is the gretteste synne that may be, after the synne of Lucifer and Antecrist ❧ for by this synne, God forleseth the chirche, and the soule that he boghte with his precious blood, by hem that yeven chirches to hem that been nat digne. for they putten in theves, that stelen the soules of Jhesu Crist and destroyen his patrimoyne. By swiche undigne preestes and curates han lewed men the lasse reverence of the sacraments of hooly chirche; & swiche yeveres of chirches putten out the children of Crist, & putten into the chirche the develes owene sone. They sellen the soules that lambes sholde kepen, to the wolf that strangleth hem. And therfore shul they nevere han part of the pasture of lambes, that is, the blisse of hevene.

NOW comth hasardrie, with his apurtenaunces, as tables and rafles; of which comth deceite, false othes, chidynges, & alle ravynes, blasphemynge and reneyinge of God, and hate of his neighebores, wast of goodes, mysspendynge of tyme, and somtyme manslaughtre. Certes, hasardours ne mowe nat been withouten greet synne whiles thei haunte that crafte. Of avarice comen eek lesynges, thefte, fals witnesse, and false othes. And ye shul understonde that thise been grete synnes, and expres agayn the comaundements of God, as I have seyd. Fals witnesse is in word and eek in dede. In word, as for to bireve thy neighebores goode name by thy fals witnessyng, or bireven hym his catel or his heritage by thy fals witnessyng; whan thou, for ire or for meede, or for envye, berest fals witnesse, or accusest hym, or excusest hym, by thy fals witnesse, or elles excusest thyself falsly. Ware yow, questemongeres and notaries! Certes, for fals witnessyng was Susanna in ful gret sorwe and peyne, and many another mo. The synne of thefte is eek expres agayns Goddes heeste, and in two maneres, corporeel and espiritueel. Corporeel, as for to take thy neighebores catel agayn his wyl, be it by force or by sleighte, be it by met or by mesure. By stelyng eek of fals enditements upon hym, and in borwynge of thy neighebores catel, in entente nevere to payen it agayn, and semblable thynges.

SPIRITUEEL thefte is sacrilege, that is to seyn, hurtynge of hooly thynges, or of thynges sacred to Crist, in two maneres; by reson of the hooly place, as chirches or chirche hawes, for which every vileyns synne that men doon in swiche places may be cleped sacrilege, or every violence in the semblable places. Also, they that withdrawen falsly the rightes that longen to hooly chirche. And pleynly and generally, sacrilege is to reven hooly thyng fro hooly place, or unhooly thyng out of hooly place, or hooly thyng out of unhooly place.

Relevacio contra peccatum Avaricie.

NOW shul ye understonde, that the releevynge of avarice is misericorde, & pitee largely taken. And men myghten axe, why that misericorde & pitee is releevynge of avarice. Certes, the avaricious man sheweth no pitee ne misericorde to the nedeful man; for he deliteth hym in the kepynge of his tresor, and nat in the rescowynge ne releevynge of his evene cristene. And therfore speke I first of misericorde.

THANNE is misericorde, as seith the philosophre, a vertu, by which the corage of man is stired by the mysese of hym that is mysesed. Upon which misericorde folweth pitee, in parfournynge of charitable werkes of misericorde. And certes, thise thynges moeven a man to misericorde of Jhesu Crist, that he yaf hymself for oure gilt, and suffred deeth for misericorde, and forgaf us oure originale synnes; and therby relessed us fro the peynes of helle, and amenused the peynes of purgatorie by penitence, and yeveth grace wel to do, and atte laste the blisse of hevene. The speces of misericorde been, as for to lene and for to yeve, and to foryeven & relesse, and for to han pitee in herte, and compassioun of the meschief of his evene Cristene, and eek to chastise there as nede is.

ANOTHER manere of remedie agayns avarice is resonable largesse; but soothly, heere bihoveth the consideracioun of the grace of Jhesu Crist, & of his temporeel goodes, and eek of the goodes perdurables that Crist yaf to us; and to han remembrance of the deeth that he shal receyve, he noot whanne, where, ne how; and eek that he shal forgon al that he hath, save oonly that he hath despended in good werkes. But, forasmuche as som folk been unmesurable, men oughten eschue fool largesse, that men clepen wast. Certes, he that is fool large ne yeveth nat his catel, but he leseth his catel. Soothly, what thyng that he yeveth for veyne glorie, as to mynstrals & to folk, for to beren his renoun in the world, he hath synne therof, and noon almesse. Certes, he leseth foule his good, that ne seketh with the yifte of his good nothyng but synne. He is lyk to an hors that seketh rather to drynken drovy or trouble water, than for to drynken water of the clere welle. And forasmuche las they yeven theras they sholde nat yeven, to hem aperteneth thilke malisoun that Crist shal yeven at the day of doome to hem that shullen been dampned.

Sequitur de Gula.

AFTER avarice comth glotonye, which is expres eek agayn the comandement of God. Glotonye is unmesurable appetit to ete or to drynke, or elles to doon ynogh to the unmesurable appetit & disordeynee coveitise to eten or to drynke. This synne corrumped al this world, as is wel shewed in the synne of Adam and of Eve. Looke eek, what seith Seint Paul of glotonye: Manye, seith Seint Paul, goon, of whiche I have ofte seyd to yow, & now I seye it wepynge, that they been the enemys of the croys of Crist; of whiche the ende is deeth, and of whiche hire wombe is hire God, and hire glorie in confusioun of hem that so devouren erthely thynges ✣ He that is usaunt to this synne of glotonye, he ne may no synne withstonde. He moot been in servage of alle vices, for it is the develes hoord ther he hideth hym and resteth.

THIS synne hath manye speces. The firste is dronkenesse, that is the horrible sepulture of mannes resoun; & therfore, whan a man is dronken, he hath lost his resoun; and this is deedly synne. But soothly, whan that a man is nat wont to strong drynke, & peraventure ne knoweth nat the strengthe of the drynke, or hath feblesse in his heed, or hath travailed, thurgh which he drynketh the moore, al be he sodeynly caught with drynke, it is no deedly synne, but venyal ✣ The seconde spece of glotonye is, that the spirit of a man wexeth al trouble; for dronkenesse bireveth hym the discrecioun of his wit ✣ The thridde spece of glotonye is, whan a man devoureth his mete, and hath no rightful manere of etynge ✣ The fourthe is whan, thurgh the grete habundaunce of his mete, the humours in his body been destempred ✣ The fifthe is, foryetelnesse by to muchel drynkynge; for which somtyme a man foryeteth er the morwe what he dide at even, or on the nyght biforn.

IN oother manere been distinct the speces of glotonye, after Seint Gregorie. The firste is, for to ete biforn tyme to ete. The seconde is, whan a man get hym to delicaat mete or drynke. The thridde is, whan men taken to muche over mesure. The fourthe is, curiositee, with greet entente to maken and apparaillen his mete. The fifthe is, for to eten to gredily. Thise been the fyve fyngres of the develes hand, by whiche he draweth folk to synne.

Remedium contra peccatum Gule.

AGAYNS glotonye is the remedie abstinence, as seith Galien; but that holde I nat meritorie, if he do it oonly for the heele of his body ✣ Seint Augustyn wole, that abstinence be doon for vertu and with pacience. Abstinence, he seith, is litel worth, but if a man have good wil therto, and but it be enforced by pacience and by charitee, and that men doon it for Godes sake, and in hope to have the blisse of hevene ✣ The felawes of abstinence been attemperaunce, that holdeth the meene in alle thynges: eek shame, that eschueth alle dishonestee: suffisance, that seketh no riche metes ne drynkes, ne dooth no fors of too outrageous apparailynge of mete. Mesure also, that restreyneth by resoun the deslavee appetit of etynge: sobrenesse also, that

p 3

restreyneth the outrage of drynke: sparynge also, that restreyneth the delicaat ese to sitte longe at his mete and softely; wherfore som folk stonden, of hir owene wyl, to eten at the lasse leyser.

Sequitur de Luxuria.

AFTER glotonye, thanne comth lecherie; for thise two synnes been so ny cosyns, that ofte tyme they wol nat departe. God woot, this synne is ful displesaunt thyng to God; for he seyde himself: Do no lecherie ✣ And therfore he putte grete peynes agayns this synne in the olde lawe. If womman thral were taken in this synne, she sholde be beten with staves to the deeth. And if she were a gentil womman, she sholde be slayn with stones. And if she were a bisshopes doghter, she sholde been brent, by Goddes comandement. for therover, by the synne of lecherie, God dreynte al the world at the diluge. And after that, he brente five citees with thonderleyt, and sank hem into helle.

NOW lat us speke thanne of thilke stynkynge synne of lecherie that men clepe avowtrie of wedded folk; that is to seyn, if that oon of hem be wedded, or elles bothe. Seint John seith, that avowtiers shullen been in helle in a stank brennynge of fyr and of brymston; in fyr, for the lecherie; in brymston, for the stynk of hire ordure. Certes, the brekynge of this sacrement is an horrible thyng; it was maked of God hymself in paradys, and confermed by Jhesu Crist, as witnesseth Seint Mathew in the gospel: A man shal lete fader and mooder, and taken hym to his wif, and they shullen be two in o flessh ✣ This sacrement bitokneth the knyttynge togidre of Crist and of hooly chirche. And nat oonly that God forbad avowtrie in dede, but eek he comanded that thou sholdest nat coveite thy neighebores wyf. In this heeste, seith Seint Augustyn, is forboden alle manere coveitise to doon lecherie. Lo, what seith Seint Mathew in the gospel: that Whoso seeth a womman to coveitise of his lust, he hath doon lecherie with hire in his herte ✣ Heere may ye seen that nat oonly the dede of this synne is forboden, but eek the desir to doon that synne.

THIS cursed synne anoyeth grevousliche hem that it haunten. And first, to hire soule; for he obligeth it to synne and to peyne of deeth that is perdurable. Unto the body anoyeth it grevously also, for it dreyeth hym, and wasteth, and shenteth hym, and of his blood he maketh sacrifice to the feend of helle; it wasteth his catel and his substaunce. And certes, if it be a foul thyng, a man to waste his catel on wommen, yet is it a fouler thyng, whan that, for swich ordure, wommen dispenden upon men hir catel and substaunce. This synne, as seith the prophete, bireveth man and womman hir goode fame, and al hire honour; and it is ful plesaunt to the devel; for therby wynneth he the mooste partie of this world. And, right as a marchant deliteth hym moost in chaffare that he hath moost avantage of, right so deliteth the fend in this ordure.

THIS is that oother hand of the devel, with five fyngres, to cacche the peple to his vileynye. The firste fynger is the fool lookynge of the fool womman, and of the fool man, that sleeth right as the basilicok sleeth folk by the venym of his sighte; for the coveitise of eyen folweth the coveitise of the herte. The seconde fynger is the vileyns touchynge in wikkede manere; and therfore, seith Salomon: that Whoso toucheth and handleth a womman, he fareth lyk hym that handleth the scorpioun that styngeth and sodeynly sleeth thurgh his envenymynge; as whoso toucheth warm pych, it shent his fyngres. The thridde, is foule wordes, that fareth lyk fyr, that right anon brenneth the herte. The fourthe fynger is the kissynge; and trewely he were a greet fool that wolde kisse the mouth of a brennynge ovene, or of a fourneys. And moore fooles been they that kissen in vileynye; for that mouth is the mouth of helle: & namely thise olde dotardes holours, yet wol they kisse though they may nat do, and smatre hem. Certes, they been lyk to houndes; for an hound whan he comth by the roser, or by othere beautees, though he may nat pisse, yet wole he heve up his leg and make a contenaunce to pisse. And for that many man weneth that he may nat synne, for no likerousnesse that he dooth with his wyf; certes, that opinioun is fals. God woot, a man may sleen hymself with his owene knyf, and make hymselven dronken of his owene tonne. Certes, be it wyf, be it child, or any worldly thyng that he loveth biforn God, it is his mawmet, and he is an ydolastre. Man sholde loven his wyf by discrecioun, paciently & atemprely; and thanne is she as though it were his suster. The fifthe fynger of the develes hand is the stynkynge dede of leccherie. Certes, the five fyngres of glotonie the feend put in the wombe of a man, & with his five fyngres of lecherie he gripeth hym by the reynes, for to throwen hym into the fourneys of helle; theras they shul han the fyr and the wormes that evere shul lasten, & wepynge and wailynge, sharp hunger & thurst, and grymnesse of develes that shullen al totrede hem, withouten respit and withouten ende.

214

Of leccherie, as I seyde, sourden diverse speces; as fornicacioun that is bitwixe man and womman that been nat maried; and this is deedly synne and agayns nature. Al that is enemy and destruccioun to nature is agayns nature. Parfay, the resoun of a man telleth eek hym wel that it is deedly synne, forasmuche as God forbad leccherie. And Seint Paul yeveth hem the regne, that nys dewe to no wight but to hem that doon deedly synne. Another synne of leccherie is to bireve a mayden of hir maydenhede; for he that so dooth, certes, he casteth a mayden out of the hyeste degree that is in this present lif, and bireveth hire thilke precious fruyt that the book clepeth: The hundred fruyt. I ne kan seye it noon oother weyes in Englissh, but in Latyn it highte: Centesimus fructus. Certes, he that so dooth is cause of manye damages and vileynyes, mo than any man kan rekene; right as he somtyme is cause of alle damages that beestes don in the feeld, that breketh the hegge or the closure; thurgh which he destroyeth that may nat been restoored. For certes, namoore may maydenhede be restoored than an arm that is smyten fro the body may retourne agayn to wexe. She may have mercy; this woot I wel, if she do penitence; but nevere shal it be that she nas corrupt.

AND, albeit so that I have spoken somwhat of avowtrie, it is good to shewen mo perils that longen to avowtrie, for to eschue that foule synne. Avowtrie in Latyn is for to seyn, approchynge of oother mannes bed, thurgh which tho that whilom weren o flessh abawndone hir bodyes to othere persones. Of this synne, as seith the wise man, folwen manye harmes. First, brekynge of feith; & certes, in feith is the keye of Cristendom. And whan that feith is broken and lorn, soothly, Cristendom stant veyn & withouten fruyt. This synne is eek a thefte; for thefte generally is for to reve a wight his thyng agayns his wille. Certes, this is the fouleste thefte that may be, whan a womman steleth hir body from hir housbonde, and yeveth it to hire holour to defoulen hire; & steleth hir soule fro Crist, & yeveth it to the devel. This is a fouler thefte, than for to breke a chirche and stele the chalice; for thise avowtiers breken the temple of God spiritually, and stelen the vessel of grace, that is, the body and the soule, for which Crist shal destroyen hem, as seith Seint Paul.

SOOTHLY of this thefte douted gretly Joseph, whan that his lordes wyf preyed hym of vileynye, whan he seyde: Lo, my lady, how my lord hath take to me under my warde al that he hath in this world; ne no thyng of his thynges is out of my power, but oonly ye, that been his wyf. And how sholde I thanne do this wikkednesse, & synne so horribly agayns God, & agayns my lord? God it forbeede! Allas! al to litel is swich trouthe now yfounde.

THE thridde harm is the filthe thurgh which they breken the comandement of God, and defoulen the auctour of matrimoyne, that is, Crist. For certes, insomuche as the sacrement of mariage is so noble and so digne, so muche is it gretter synne for to breken it; for God made mariage in paradys, in the estaat of innocence, to multiplye mankynde to the service of God. And therfore is the brekynge therof the moore grevous. Of which brekynge comen false heires ofte tyme, that wrongfully occupien folkes heritages. And therfore wol Crist putte hem out of the regne of hevene, that is heritage to goode folk. Of this brekynge comth eek ofte tyme, that folk unwar wedden or synnen with hire owene kynrede; and namely thilke harlottes that haunten bordels of thise fool wommen, that mowe be likned to a commune gonge, whereas men purgen hire ordure.

WHAT seye we eek of putours, that lyven by the horrible synne of putrie, and constreyne wommen to yelden to hem a certeyn rente of hire bodily puterie; ye, somtyme of his owene wyf or his child; as doon thise bawdes? Certes, thise been cursede synnes. Understoond eek, that avowtrie is set gladly in the ten comandements bitwixe thefte and manslaughtre; for it is the gretteste thefte that may be; for it is thefte of body and of soule. And it is lyk to homycide; for it kerveth atwo and breketh atwo hem that first were maked o flessh, and therfore, by the olde lawe of God, they sholde be slayn. But nathelees, by the lawe of Jhesu Crist, that is lawe of pitee, whan he seyde to the womman that was founden in avowtrie, & sholde han been slayn with stones, after the wyl of the Jewes, as was hir lawe: Go, quod Jhesu Crist, and have namoore wyl to synne, or, wille namoore to do synne. Soothly, the vengeaunce of avowtrie is awarded to the peynes of helle, but if so be that it be destourbed by penitence.

YET been ther mo speces of this cursed synne; as whan that oon of hem is religious, or elles bothe; or of folk that been entred into ordre, as subdekne or dekne, or preest, or hospitaliers. And evere the hyer that he is in ordre, the gretter is the synne. The thynges that gretly agreggen hire synne, is the brekynge of hire avow of chastitee, whan they recevyed the ordre. And fortherover, sooth is, that hooly ordre is chief of al the tre-

sorie of God, and his especial signe and mark of chastitee; to shewe that they been joyned to chastitee, which that is moost precious lyf that is. And thise ordred folk been specially titled to God, and of the special meignee of God; for which, whan they doon deedly synne, they been the special traytours of God and of his peple; for they lyven of the peple, to preye for the peple, and while they been suche traytours here preyers availen nat to the peple.

PREESTES been aungeles, as by the dignitee of hir mysterye; but forsothe Seint Paul seith: that Sathanas transformeth hym in an aungel of light. Soothly, the preest that haunteth deedly synne, he may be likned to the aungel of derknesse transformed in the aungel of light; he semeth aungel of light, but forsothe he is aungel of derknesse. Swiche preestes been the sones of Helie, as sheweth in the book of Kynges, that they weren the sones of Belial, that is, the devel. Belial is to seyn Withouten juge; and so faren they; hem thynketh they been free, and han no juge, namoore than hath a free bole that taketh which cow that hym liketh in the toun. So faren they by wommen. For right as a free bole is ynough for al a toun, right so is a wikked preest corrupcion ynough for al a parisshe, or for al a contree.

THISE preestes, as seith the book, ne konne nat the mysterie of preesthode to the peple, ne God ne knowe they nat; they ne helde hem nat apayd, as seith the book, of soden flessh that was to hem offred, but they tooke by force the flessh that is rawe. Certes, so thise shrewes ne holden hem nat apayed of roosted flessh and sode flessh, with which the peple fedden hem in greet reverence, but they wole have raw flessh of folkes wyves and hir doghtres. And certes, thise wommen that consenten to hire harlotrie, doon greet wrong to Crist and to hooly chirche & alle halwes, and to alle soules; for they bireven alle thise, hym that sholde worshipe Crist and hooly chirche, and preye for cristene soules. And therfore han swiche preestes, and hire lemmanes eek that consenten to hir leccherie, the malisoun of al the court cristen, til they come to amendement.

THE thridde spece of avowtrie is somtyme bitwixe a man & his wyf; and that is whan they take no reward in hire assemblynge, but oonly to hire flesshly delit, as seith Seint Jerome; and ne rekken of nothyng but that they been assembled; bycause that they been maried, al is good ynough, as thynketh to hem. But in swich folk hath the devel power, as seyde the aungel Raphael to Thobie; for in hire assemblynge they putten Jhesu Crist out of hire herte, and yeven hemself to alle ordure. The fourthe spece is, the assemblee of hem that been of hire kynrede, or of hem that been of oon affynytee, or elles with hem with whiche hir fadres or hir kynrede han deled in the synne of lecherie. This synne maketh hem lyk to houndes, that taken no kepe to kynrede. And certes, parentele is in two maneres, outher goostly or flesshly: goostly, as for to deelen with his godsibbes. for right so as he that engendreth a child is his flesshly fader, right so is his godfader his fader espiritueel. for which a womman may in no lasse synne assemblen with hire godsib than with hire owene flesshly brother.

THE fifthe spece is thilke abhomynable synne, of which that no man unnethe oghte speke ne write, nathelees it is openly reherced in holy writ. This cursednesse doon men & wommen in diverse entente, and in diverse manere; but though that hooly writ speke of horrible synne, certes, hooly writ may nat been defouled, namoore than the sonne that shyneth on the mixen.

ANOTHER synne aperteneth to lecherie, that comth in slepynge; & this synne cometh ofte to hem that been maydenes, and eek to hem that been corrupt; & this synne men clepen pollucioun, that comth in four maneres. Somtyme, of langwissynge of body; for the humours been to ranke and habundaunt in the body of man. Somtyme, of infermetee; for the fieblesse of the vertu retentif, as phisik maketh mencioun. Somtyme, for surfeet of mete & drynke. And somtyme, of vileyns thoghtes, that been enclosed in mannes mynde whan he gooth to slepe; which may nat been withoute synne. for which men moste kepen hem wisely, or elles may men synnen ful grevously.

Remedium contra peccatum Luxurie.

NOW comth the remedie agayns leccherie, and that is generally, chastitee and continence, that restreyneth alle the desordeynee moevynges that comen of flesshly talentes. And evere the gretter merite shal he han, that most restreyneth the wikkede eschawfynges of the ordure of this synne. And this is in two maneres; that is to seyn, chastitee in mariage, & chastitee of widwehode. Now shaltow understonde, that matrimoyne is leefful assemblynge of man & of womman, that receyven, by vertu of the sacrement the boond, thurgh which they may nat be departed in al hir lyf, that is to seyn, whil that they lyven bothe. This, as seith the book, is a ful greet sacrement. God maked it, as I have seyd, in paradys,
216

and wolde hymself be born in mariage. And, for to halwen mariage, he was at a weddynge, whereas he turned water into wyn; which was the firste miracle that he wroghte in erthe biforn his disciples.

TREWE effect of mariage clenseth fornicacioun & replenysseth hooly chirche of good lynage; for that is the ende of mariage; & it chaungeth deedly synne into venial synne bitwixe hem that been ywedded, and maketh the hertes al oon of hem that been ywedded, as wel as the bodies. This is verray mariage that was establissed by God er that synne bigan, whan natureel lawe was in his right poynt in paradys; & it was ordeyned that o man sholde have but o womman, & o womman but o man, as seith Seint Augustyn, by manye resouns.

FIRST, for mariage is figured bitwixe Crist & holy chirche. And that oother is, for a man is heved of a womman; algate, by ordinaunce it sholde be so. for if a womman hadde mo men than oon, thanne sholde she have moo hevedes than oon, & that were an horrible thyng biforn God; and eek a womman ne myghte nat plese to many folk at oones. And also ther ne sholde nevere be pees ne reste amonges hem; for everich wolde axen his owene thyng. And fortherover, no man ne sholde knowe his owene engendrure, ne who sholde have his heritage; and the womman sholde been the lasse biloved, fro the tyme that she were conjoynt to many men.

NOW comth, how that a man sholde bere hym with his wif; and namely in two thynges, that is to seyn, in suffraunce and reverence, as shewed Crist whan he made first womman. for he ne made hire nat of the heved of Adam, for she sholde nat clayme to greet lordshipe; for theras the womman hath the maistrie, she maketh to muche desray; ther neden none ensamples of this; the experience of day by day oghte suffise. Also certes, God ne made nat womman of the foot of Adam, for she ne sholde nat been holden to lowe; for she kan nat paciently suffre: but God made womman of the ryb of Adam, for womman sholde be felawe unto man. Man sholde bere hym to his wyf in feith, in trouthe, and in love, as seith Seint Paul: that A man sholde loven his wyf as Crist loved hooly chirche, that loved it so wel that he deyde for it. So sholde a man for his wyf, if it were nede.

NOW how that a womman sholde be subget to hire housbonde, that telleth Seint Peter. first, in obedience. And eek, as seith the decree, a womman that is wyf, as longe as she is a wyf, she hath noon auctoritee to swere ne bere witnesse withoute leve of hir housbonde, that

is hire lord; algate he sholde be so by resoun. She sholde eek serven hym in alle
honestee, and been attempree of hire array.
I woot wel that they sholde setten hire entente to plesen hir housbondes, but nat by
hire queyntise of array. Seint Jerome seith,
that wyves that been apparailled in silk &
in precious purpre ne mowe nat clothen
hem in Jhesu Crist. What seith Seint John
eek in thys matere? Seint Gregorie eek seith
that no wight seketh precious array but
oonly for veyne glorie, to been honoured
the moore biforn the peple. It is a greet
folye, a womman to have a fair array outward and in hirself be foul inward. A wyf
sholde eek be mesurable in lookynge, and
in berynge, and in lawghynge, and discreet
in alle hire wordes and hire dedes. And a-
boven alle worldly thyng she sholde loven
hire housbonde with al hire herte, and to
hym be trewe of hir body; so sholde an
housbonde eek be to his wyf. For sith that
al the body is the housbondes, so sholde
hire herte been, or elles ther is bitwixe hem
two, as in that, no parfit mariage.

THANNE shal men understonde that
for thre thynges a man and his wyf
flesshly mowen assemble. The firste
is in entente of engendrure of children to
the service of God, for certes, that is the
cause final of matrimoyne. Another cause
is, to yelden everich of hem to oother the
dette of hire bodies, for neither of hem hath
power over his owene body. The thridde is,
for to eschewe leccherye and vileynye. The
ferthe is forsothe deedly synne. As to the
firste, it is meritorie; the seconde also; for,
as seith the decree, that she hath merite of
chastitee that yeldeth to hire housbonde
the dette of hir body, ye, though it be agayn
hir likynge and the lust of hire herte. The
thridde manere is venyal synne, & trewely,
scarsly may ther any of thise be withoute
venial synne, for the corrupcioun & for the
delit. The fourthe manere is for to understonde, if they assemble oonly for amorous
love, and for noon of the foreseyde causes,
but for to accomplice thilke brennynge delit, they rekke nevere how ofte, soothly it
is deedly synne; & yet, with sorwe, somme
folk wol peynen hem moore to doon than
to hire appetit suffiseth.

THE seconde manere of chastitee is
for to been a clene wydewe, and eschue the embracynges of man, and
desiren the embracynge of Jhesu Crist.
Thise been tho that han been wyves & han
forgoon hire housbondes, & eek wommen
that han doon leccherie & been releeved by
penitence. And certes, if that a wyf koude
kepen hire al chaast by licence of hire housbonde, so that she yeve nevere noon occasion that he agilte, it were to hire a greet
merite. Thise manere wommen that observ-

en chastitee moste be clene in herte, as wele
as in body and in thought, and mesurable
in clothynge and in contenaunce; and been
abstinent in etynge & drynkynge, in spekynge, and in dede. They been the vessel, or
the boyste of the blissed Magdelene, that
fulfilleth hooly chirche of good odour.

THE thridde manere of chastitee is virginitee, and it bihoveth that she be
hooly in herte & clene of body; thanne
is she spouse to Jhesu Crist, and she is the
lyf of angeles. She is the preisynge of this
world, & she is as thise martirs in egalitee.
She hath in hire that tonge may nat telle,
ne herte thynke. Virginitee baar oure Lord
Jhesu Crist, and virgine was hymselve.

ANOTHER remedie agayns leccherie is, specially to withdrawen swiche
thynges as yeve occasion to thilke
vileynye; as ese, etynge & drynkynge; for
certes, whan the pot boyleth strongly, the
beste remedie is to withdrawe the fyr. Slepynge longe in greet quiete is eek a greet norice to leccherie.

ANOTHER remedie agayns leccherie is, that a man or a womman eschue the compaignye of hem by
whiche he douteth to be tempted; for albeit
so that the dede is withstonden, yet is ther
greet temptacioun. Soothly, a whit wal, although it ne brenne noght fully by stikynge of a candele, yet is the wal blak of the
leyt. Ful ofte tyme I rede, that no man truste
in his owene perfeccioun, but he be stronger than Sampsoun, and hoolier than David,
& wiser than Salomon. Now after that I
have declared yow, as I kan, the sevene deedly synnes, & somme of hire braunches and
hire remedies, soothly, if I koude, I wolde
telle yow the ten comandements. But so
heigh a doctrine I lete to divines. Nathelees, I hope to God they been touched in
this tretice, everich of hem alle.

Sequitur secunda pars Penitencie.

NOW, forasmuche as the seconde partie of penitence stant
in confessioun of mouth, as
I bigan in the firste chapitre,
I seye, Seint Augustyn seith:
Synne is every word & every
dede, and al that men coveiten agayn the
lawe of Jhesu Crist; & this is for to synne
in herte, in mouth, and in dede, by thy five
wittes, that been sighte, herynge, smellynge, tastynge or savourynge, & feelynge.

NOW is it good to understonde that
that aggreggeth muchel every synne.
Thow shalt considere what thow art
that doost the synne; wheither thou be
male or femele, yong or oold, gentil or thral,
free or servant, hool or syk, wedded or sengle, ordred or unordred, wys or fool, clerk
or seculeer; if she be of thy kynrede, bodily

217

or goostly, or noon; if any of thy kynrede have synned with hire or noon, and manye mo thinges ✿ Another circumstaunce is this; wheither it be doon in fornicacioun, or in avowtrie, or noon; incest, or noon; mayden, or noon; in manere of homicide, or noon; horrible grete synnes or smale; & how longe thou hast continued in synne. ✿ The thridde circumstaunce is the place ther thou hast do synne; wheither in oother mennes hous or in thyn owene; in feeld or in chirche, or in chirchehawe; in chirche dedicaat, or noon. For if the chirche be hal wed, and man or womman spille his kynde inwith that place by wey of synne, or by wikked temptacioun, the chirche is entredited til it be reconsiled by the bysshop; and the preest that dide swich a vileynye, to terme of al his lif, he sholde namoore synge masse; & if he dide, he sholde doon deedly synne at every time that he so songe masse ✿ The fourthe circumstaunce is, by whiche mediatours or by whiche messagers, as for enticement, or for consentement to bere compaignye with felaweshipe; for many a wrecche, for to bere compaignye, wil go to the devel of helle. Wherfore they that eggen or consenten to the synne been parteners of the synne, & of the dampnacioun of the synner ✿ The fifthe circumstance is, how manye tymes that he hath synned, if it be in his mynde, and how ofte that he hath falle. For he that ofte falleth in synne, he despiseth the mercy of God, and encreesseth hys synne, & is unkynde to Crist; and he wexeth the moore fieble to withstonde synne, and synneth the moore lightly, and the latter ariseth, and is the moore eschew for to shryven hym, namely, to hym that is his confessour. For which that folk, whan they falle agayn in hir olde folies, outher they forleten hir olde confessours al outrely, or elles they departen hir shrift in diverse places; but soothly, swich departed shrift deserveth no mercy of God of his synnes ✿ The sixte circumstaunce is, why that a man synneth, as by temptacioun; & if hymself procure thilke temptacioun, or by the excitynge of oother folke; or if he synne with a womman by force, or by hire owene assent; or if the womman, maugree hir hed, hath been afforced, or noon; this shal she telle; for coveitise, or for poverte, and if it was hire procurynge or noon; & swiche manere harneys ✿ The seventhe circumstaunce is, in what manere he hath doon his synne, or how that she hath suffred that folk han doon to hire. And the same shal the man telle pleynly, with alle circumstaunces; and wheither he hath synned with comune bordel wommen, or noon; or doon his synne in hooly tymes, or noon; in fastynge tymes, or noon; or biforn his shrifte, or after his latter shrifte;

218

and hath, peraventure, broken therfore his penance enjoyned; by whos help and whos conseil; by sorcerie or craft; al moste be toold. Alle thise thynges, after that they been grete or smale, engreggen the conscience of man. And eek the preest that is thy juge, may the bettre been avysed of his jugement in yevynge of thy penaunce, & that is after thy contricioun. For understond wel, that after tyme that a man hath defouled his baptesme by synne, if he wole come to salvacioun, ther is noon other wey but by penitence & shrifte and satisfaccioun; and namely by the two, if ther be a confessour to which he may shriven hym; and the thridde, if he have lyf to parfournen it.

THANNE shal man looke and considere, that if he wole maken a trewe and a profitable confessioun, ther moste be foure condiciouns. First, it moot been in sorweful bitternesse of herte, as seyde the kyng Ezechias to God: I wol remembre me alle the yeres of my lif in bitternesse of myn herte ✿ This condicioun of bitternesse hath fyve signes. The firste is, that confessioun moste be shamefast, nat for to covere ne hyden his synne, for he hath agilt his God & defouled his soule. And therof seith Seint Augustyn: The herte travailleth for shame of his synne; and for he hath greet shamefastnesse, he is digne to have greet mercy of God ✿ Swich was the confessioun of the publican, that wolde nat heven up his eyen to hevene, for he hadde offended God of hevene; for which shamefastnesse he hadde anon the mercy of God. And therof seith Seint Augustyn, that swich shamefast folk been next foryevenesse and remissioun ✿ Another signe is humylitee in confessioun; of which seith Seint Peter: Humbleth yow under the myghty of God ✿ The hond of God is myghty in confessioun, for therby God foryeveth thee thy synnes; for he allone hath the power. And this humylitee shal been in herte, and in signe outward; for right as he hath humylitee to God in his herte, right so sholde he humble his body outward to the preest that sit in Goddes place. For which in no manere, sith that Crist is sovereyn and the preest meene and mediatour bitwixe Crist and the synnere, and the synnere is the laste by wey of resoun, thanne sholde nat the synnere sitte as heighe as his confessour, but knele biforn hym or at his feet, but if maladie destourbe it. For he shal nat taken kepe who sit there, but in whos place that he sitteth. A man that hath trespased to a lord, and comth for to axe mercy and maken his accord, and set him doun anon by the lord, men wolde holden hym outrageous, and nat worthy so soone for to have remissioun ne mercy ✿ The thridde signe is,

how that thy shrift sholde be ful of teeris,
if man may; and if man may nat wepe with
his bodily eyen, lat hym wepe in herte.
Swich was the confessioun of Seint Peter;
for after that he hadde forsake Jhesu Crist,
he wente out and weep ful bitterly. The
fourthe signe is, that he ne lette nat for
shame to shewen his confessioun. Swich
was the confessioun of the Magdelene,
that ne spared for no shame of hem that
weren atte feeste, for to go to oure Lord
Jhesu Crist & biknowe to hym hire synnes.
The fifthe signe is, that a man or a womman be obeisant to receyven the penaunce
that hym is enjoyned for his synnes; for
certes, Jhesu Crist, for the giltes of a man,
was obedient to the deeth.

THE seconde condicion of verray confession is, that it be hastily doon;
for certes, if a man hadde a deedly
wounde, evere the lenger that he taried to
warisshe hymself, the moore wolde it cor-
rupte and haste hym to his deeth; and eek
the wounde wolde be the wors for to heele.
And right so fareth synne, that longe tyme
is in a man unshewed. Certes, a man
oghte hastily shewen his synnes for manye
causes; as for drede of deeth, that cometh
ofte sodenly, & is in no certeyn what tyme
it shal be, ne in what place; & eek the drec-
chynge of o synne draweth in another; and
eek the lenger that he tarieth, the ferther
he is fro Crist. And if he abide to his laste
day, scarsly may he shryven hym, or remembre hym of his synnes, or repenten
hym, for the grevous maladie of his deeth.
And forasmuche as he ne hath nat in his
lyf herkned Jhesu Crist, whanne he hath
spoken, he shal crie to Jhesu Crist at his
laste day, and scarsly wol he herkne hym.
And understond that this condicioun
moste han foure thynges. Thi shrift
moste be purveyed bifore and avysed; for
wikked haste dooth no profit; and that a
man konne shryve hym of his synnes, be it
of pride, or of envye, and so forth of the
speces and circumstances; & that he have
comprehended in hys mynde the nombre
and the greetnesse of his synnes, and how
longe that he hath leyn in synne; & eek that
he be contrit of his synnes, and in stidefast purpos, by the grace of God, nevere
eft to falle in synne; and eek that he drede
& countrewaite hymself, that he fle the oc-
casiouns of synne to whiche he is enclyned.

ALSO thou shalt shryve thee of alle
thy synnes too man, and nat a parcel
to o man and a parcel to another; that
is to understonde, in entente to departe
thy confessioun as for shame or drede; for
it nys but stranglynge of thy soule. For
certes, Jhesu Crist is entierly al good; in
hym nys noon inperfeccioun; and therfore

outher he foryeveth al parfitly, or never a
deel. I seye nat that if thow be assigned to
the penitauncer for certein synne, that thow
art bounde to shewen hym al the remenaunt
of the synnes, of which thow hast be shryven to thy curaat, but if it like to thee of
thyn humylitee; this is no departynge of
shrifte. Ne I seye nat, theras I speke of
divisioun of confessioun, that if thou have
licence for to shryve thee to a discreet and
an honeste preest, where thee liketh, and
by licence of thy curaat, that thow ne mayst
wel shryve thee to him of alle thy synnes.
But lat no blotte be bihynde; lat no synne
been untoold, as fer as thow hast remembraunce. And whan thou shalt be shryven
to thy curaat, telle hym eek alle the synnes
that thow hast doon syn thou were last
yshryven; this is no wikked entente of divisioun of shrifte.

ALSO, the verray shrifte axeth certeine
condiciouns. First, that thow shryve
thee by thy free wil, noght constreyned, ne for shame of folk, ne for maladie, ne
swiche thynges; for it is resoun that he
that trespasseth by his free wyl, that by
his free wyl he confesse his trespas; and
that noon oother man telle his synne but
he hymself; ne he shal nat nayte ne denye
his synne, ne wratthe hym agayn the preest
for his amonestynge to leve synne.

THE seconde condicioun is, that thy
shrift be laweful; that is to seyn,
that thow that shryvest thee, and
eek the preest that hereth thy confessioun,
been verraily in the feith of hooly chirche;
and that a man ne be nat despeired of the
mercy of Jhesu Crist, as Caym or Judas.
And eek a man moot accusen hymself of
his owene trespas, and nat another; but he
shal blame and wyten hymself & his owene
malice of his synne, and noon oother; but
nathelees, if that another man be occasioun or enticere of his synne, or the estaat
of a persone be swich thurgh which his
synne is agregged, or elles that he may nat
pleynly shryven hym but he telle the persone with which he hath synned; thanne
may he telle; so that his entente ne be nat
to bakbite the persone, but oonly to declaren his confessioun. Thou ne shalt
nat eek make no lesynges in thy confessioun; for humylitee, peraventure, to seyn
that thow hast doon synnes of whiche that
thow were nevere gilty. For Seint Augustyn seith: If thou, bycause of thyn humylitee makest lesynges on thyself, though
thow ne were nat in synne biforn, yet artow
thanne in synne thurgh thy lesynges.
Thou most eek shewe thy synne by thyn
owene propre mouth, but thow be woxe
dowmb, and nat by no lettre; for thow that
hast doon the synne, thou shalt have the
219

shame therfore. Thow shalt nat eek peynte thy confessioun by faire subtile wordes, to covere the moore thy synne; for thanne bigilestow thyself & nat the preest; thow most tellen it pleynly, be it nevere so foul ne so horrible.

THOW shalt eek shryve thee to a preest that is discreet to conseille thee, and eek thou shalt nat shryve thee for veyne glorie, ne for ypocrisye, ne for no cause, but oonly for the doute of Jhesu Crist and the heele of thy soule. Thow shalt nat eek renne to the preest sodeynly, to tellen hym lightly thy synne, as whoso telleth a jape or a tale, but avysely, & with greet devocioun. And generally, shryve thee ofte. If thou ofte falle, ofte thou arise by confessioun. And though thou shryve thee ofter than ones of synne, of which thou hast be shryven, it is the moore merite. And, as seith Seint Augustyn, thow shalt have the moore lightly relesyng & grace of God, bothe of synne & of peyne. And certes, oones a yeere atte leeste wey it is laweful for to been housled; for certes, oones a yeere alle thynges renovellen. Now have I toolde you of verray confessioun, that is the seconde partie of penitence.

Explicit secunda pars Penitencie; et sequitur tercia pars ejusdem.

THE thridde partie of penitence is satisfaccioun; and that stant moost generally in almesse, & in bodily peyne. Now been ther thre manere of almesses: contricioun of herte, where a man offreth hymself to God; another is, to han pitee of defaute of his neighebores; and the thridde is in yevynge of good conseil goostly and bodily, where men han nede, and namely in sustenaunce of mannes foode. And tak keep, that a man hath nede of thise thinges generally; he hath nede of foode, he hath nede of clothyng & herberwe, he hath nede of charitable conseil, and visitynge in prisone and in maladie, and sepulture of his dede body. And if thow mayst nat visite the nedeful with thy persone, visite hym by thy message and by thy yiftes. Thise been generally almesses or werkes of charitee of hem that han temporeel richesses or discrecioun in conseilynge. Of thise werkes shaltow heren at the day of doome.

THISE almesses shaltow doon of thyne owene propre thynges, and hastily, and prively if thow mayst; but nathelees, if thow mayst nat doon it prively, thow shalt nat forbere to doon almesse though men seen it; so that it be nat doon for thank of the world, but oonly for thank of Jhesu Crist. For, as witnesseth Seint Mathew, capitulo quinto: A citee may nat been hyd that is set on a mon-

tayne; ne men lighte nat a lanterne and put it under a busshel; but men sette it on a candlestikke, to yeve light to the men in the hous. Right so shal youre light lighten bifore men, that they may seen youre goode werkes, and glorifie youre fader that is in hevene.

NOW as to speken of bodily peyne; it stant in preyeres, in wakynges, in fastynges, in vertuouse techinges of orisouns. And ye shul understonde that orisouns or preyeres is for to seyn a pitous wyl of herte, that redresseth it in God and expresseth it by word outward, to remoeven harmes and to han thynges espiritueel & durable, and somtyme temporele thynges; of whiche orisouns, certes, in the orison of the Pater noster, hath Jhesu Crist enclosed moost thynges. Certes, it is privyleged of thre thynges in his dignytee, for which it is moore digne than any oother preyere; for that Jhesu Crist hymself maked it; and it is short, for it sholde be koud the moore lightly, and for to withholden it the moore esily in herte, & helpen hymself the ofter with the orisoun; and for a man sholde be the lasse wery to seyen it, and for a man may nat excusen hym to lerne it, it is so short and so esy; and for it comprehendeth in itself alle goode preyeres. The exposicioun of this hooly preyere, that is so excellent and digne, I bitake to thise maistres of theologie; save thus muchel wol I seyn: that whan thow prayest that God sholde foryeve thee thy giltes as thou foryevest hem that agilten to thee, be ful wel war that thow be nat out of charitee. This hooly orisoun amenuseth eek venyal synne; & therfore it aperteneth specially to penitence. This preyere moste be trewely seyd, and in verray feith, & that men preye to God ordinatly and discreetly and devoutly; and alwey a man shal putten his wyl to be subget to the wille of God. This orisoun moste eek been seyd with greet humblesse and ful pure; honestly, and nat to the anoyaunce of any man or womman. It moste eek been continued with the werkes of charitee. It avayleth eek agayn the vices of the soule; for, as seith Seint Jerome: By fastynge been saved the vices of the flessh, and by preyere the vices of the soule. After this, thou shalt understonde, that bodily peyne stant in wakynge; for Jhesu Crist seith: Waketh, and preyeth that ye ne entre in wikked temptacioun. Ye shul understanden also, that fastynge stant in thre thynges; in forberynge of bodily mete and drynke, and in forberynge of worldly jolitee, and in forberynge of deedly synne; this is to seyn, that a man shal kepen hym fro deedly synne with al his myght.

AND thou shalt understanden eek, that God ordeyned fastynge; and to fastynge appertenen foure thinges: largenesse to povre folk, gladnesse of herte espiritueel, nat to been angry ne anoyed, ne grucche for he fasteth; and also resonable houre for to ete by mesure; that is for to seyn, a man shal nat ete in untyme, ne sitte the lenger at his table to ete for he fasteth. Thanne shaltow understonde, that bodily peyne stant in disciplyne or techynge, by word and by writynge, or in ensample. Also in werynge of heyres or of stamyn, or of haubergeons on hire naked flessh, for Cristes sake, & swiche manere penaunces. But war thee wel that swiche manere penaunces on thy flessh ne make nat thyn herte bitter or angry or anoyed of thyself; for bettre is to caste awey thyn heyre, than for to caste awey the sikernesse of Jhesu Crist. And therfore seith Seint Paul: Clothe yow, as they that been chosen of God, in herte of misericorde, debonairetee, suffraunce, & swiche manere of clothynge; of whiche Jhesu Crist is moore apayed than of heyres, or haubergeons, or hauberkes. Thanne is discipline eek in knokkynge of thy brest, in scourgynge with yerdes, in knelynges, in tribulaciouns; in suffrynge paciently wronges that been doon to thee, and eek in pacient suffraunce of maladies, or lesynge of worldly catel, or of wyf, or of child, or othere freendes.

THANNE shaltow understonde, whiche thynges destourben penaunce; and this is in foure maneres; that is, drede, shame, hope, and wanhope, that is, desperacioun. And for to speke first of drede; for which he demeth that he may suffre no penaunce. Theragayns is remedie for to thynke that bodily penaunce is but short & litel, at regard of the peynes of helle, that is so cruel and so long that it lasteth withouten ende. Now agayn, the shame that a man hath to shryven hym, & namely, thise ypocrites that wolden been holden so parfite that they han no nede to shryven hem. Agayns that shame, sholde a man thynke that, by wey of resoun, that he that hath nat been ashamed to doon foule thinges, certes hym oghte nat been ashamed to do faire thynges, & that is confessiouns. A man sholde eek thynke that God seeth & woot alle his thoghtes and alle his werkes; to hym may no thyng been hyd ne covered. Men sholden eek remembren hem of the shame that is to come at the day of doome to hem that been nat penitent and shryven in this present lyf. For alle the creatures in erthe & in helle shullen seen apertly al that they hyden in this world.

NOW for to speken of hope of hem that been necligent and slowe to shryven hem; that stant in two maneres. That oon is, that he hopeth for to lyve longe and for to purchacen muche richesse for his delit, and thanne he wol shryven hym; &, as he seith, hym semeth thanne tymely ynough to come to shrifte. Another is, surquidrie that he hath in Cristes mercy. Agayns the firste vice, he shal thynke, that oure life is in no sikernesse; & eek that alle the richesses in this world ben in aventure, and passen as a shadwe on the wal. And, as seith Seint Gregorie, that it aperteneth to the grete rightwisnesse of God, that nevere shal the peyne stynte, of hem that nevere wolde withdrawen hem fro synne, hir thankes, but ay continue in synne; for thilke perpetueel wil to do synne shul they han perpetueel peyne.

WANHOPE is in two maneres: the firste wanhope is in the mercy of Crist; that oother is that they thynken that they ne myghte nat longe persevere in goodnesse. The firste wanhope comth of that he demeth that he hath synned so greetly and so ofte, & so longe leyn in synne, that he shal nat be saved. Certes, agayns that cursed wanhope sholde he thynke, that the passion of Jhesu Crist is moore strong for to unbynde thanne synne is strong for to bynde. Agayns the seconde wanhope, he shal thynke, that as ofte as he falleth he may arise agayn by penitence; & though he never so longe have leyn in synne, the mercy of Crist is alwey redy to receiven hym to mercy. Agayns the wanhope, that he demeth that he sholde nat longe persevere in goodnesse, he shal thynke that the feblesse of the devel may nothyng doon but if men wol suffren hym; & eek he shal han strengthe of the help of God, and of al hooly chirche, and of the proteccioun of aungels, if hym list.

THANNE shal men understonde what is the fruyt of penaunce; and, after the word of Jhesu Crist, it is the endelees blisse of hevene. Ther joye hath no contrariousteeof wo ne grevaunce; theralle harmes been passed of this present lyf; theras is the sikernesse fro the peyne of helle; theras is the blisful compaignye that rejoysen hem everemo, everich of otheres joye; theras the body of man, that whilom was foul and derk, is moore cleer than the sonne; theras the body, that whilom was syk, freele, and fieble, and mortal, is inmortal, and so strong and so hool that ther may nothyng apeyren it; theras ne is neither hunger, thurst, ne coold, but every soule replenyssed with the sighte of the parfit knowynge of God. This blisful regne may men purchace by povertee espiritueel, and the glorie by lowenesse; the plentee of joye by hunger and thurst, & the reste by travaille; and the lyf by deeth and mortificacioun of synne.

221

Here taketh the makere of this book his leve.

NOW preye I to hem alle that herkne this litel tretys or rede, that if ther be any thyng in it that liketh hem, that therof they thanken oure Lord Jhesu Crist, of whom procedeth al wit and al goodnesse. And if ther be any thyng that displese hem, I preye hem also that they arrette it to the defaute of myn unkonnynge, and nat to my wyl, that wolde ful fayn have seyd bettre if I hadde had konnynge. For oure boke seith: Al that is writen is writen for oure doctrine, and that is myn entente. Wherfore I biseke yow mekely, for the mercy of God, that ye preye for me, that Crist have mercy on me & foryeve me my giltes: and namely, of my translaciouns and enditynges of worldly vanitees, the whiche I revoke in my retracciouns: as is The book of Troylus; The book also of Fame; The book of the Nynetene Ladies; The book of the Duchesse; The book of Seint Valentynes day of the Parlement of Briddes; The Tales of Caunterbury, thilke that sownen into synne; The book of the Leoun; and many another book, if they were in my remembrance; and many a song, and many a leccherous lay; that Crist, for his grete mercy, foryeve me the synne. But of the translacioun of Boece de Consolacione, & othere bookes of Legendes of Seintes, and omelies, and moralitee, & devocioun, that thanke I oure Lord Jhesu Crist and his blisful mooder, & alle the seintes of hevene; bisekynge hem that they from hennesforth, unto my lyves ende, sende me grace to biwayle my giltes, & to studie to the salvacioun of my soule: and graunte me grace of verray penitence, confessioun and satisfaccioun to doon in this present lyf; thurgh the benigne grace of hym that is kyng of kynges, and preest over alle preestes, that boghte us with the precious blood of his herte; so that I may been oon of hem at the day of doome that shulle be saved. Qui cum Patre et Spiritu Sancto vivis et regnas Deus per omnia secula. Amen.

Heere is ended the book of the Tales of Caunterbury, compiled by Geffrey Chaucer, of whos soule Jhesu Crist have mercy. Amen.

❧ ❧ AN A.B.C. OF GEOFFREY CHAUCER ❧ ❧ ❧ ❧ ❧ ❧ ❧ ❧ ❧ ❧

Incipit carmen secundum ordinem literarum
Alphabeti.

To thee I flee, confounded in errour!
Help and releve, thou mighty debonaire,
Have mercy on my perilous langour!
Venquisshed me hath my cruel adversaire.

BOUNTEE so fix hath in thyn herte
his tente,
That wel I wot thou wolt my
socour be,
Thou canst not warne him that, with good
entente,
Axeth thyn help. Thyn herte is ay so free,
Thou art largesse of pleyn felicitee,
Haven of refut, of quiete and of reste.
Lo, how that theves seven chasen me!
Help, lady bright, er that my ship to-breste!

COMFORT is noon, but in yow, lady
dere,
For lo, my sinne and my confusioun,
Which oughten not in thy presence appere,
Han take on me a grevous accioun
Of verrey right and desperacioun;
And, as by right, they mighten wel sustene
That I were worthy my dampnacioun,
Nere mercy of you, blisful hevene quene.

AND AL MERCIABLE QUENE,
To whom that al this world fleeth for
socour,
To have relees of sinne, sorwe and tene,
Glorious virgine, of alle floures flour,

DOUTE is ther noon, thou queen of misericorde,
That thou nart cause of grace and mercy here;
God vouched sauf thurgh thee with us tacorde.
For certes, Cristes blisful moder dere,
Were now the bowe bent in swich manere,
As it was first, of justice and of yre,
The rightful God nolde of no mercy here;
But thurgh thee han we grace, as we desyre.

EVER hath myn hope of refut been in thee,
For heerbiforn ful ofte, in many a wyse,
Hast thou to misericorde receyved me.
But mercy, lady, at the grete assyse,
Whan we shul come bifore the hye justyse!
So litel fruit shal thanne in me be founde,
That, but thou er that day me wel chastyse,
Of verrey right my werk me wol confounde.

FLEEING, I flee for socour to thy tente
Me for to hyde from tempest ful of drede,
Biseching you that ye you not absente,
Though I be wikke. O help yit at this nede!
Al have I been a beste in wille and dede,
Yit, lady, thou me clothe with thy grace.
Thyn enemy and myn, lady, tak hede,
Unto my deth in poynt is me to chace.

GLORIOUS mayde and moder, which that never
Were bitter, neither in erthe nor in see,
But ful of swetnesse and of mercy ever,
Help that my fader be not wroth with me!
Spek thou, for I ne dar not him ysee.
So have I doon in erthe, allas therwhyle!
That certes, but if thou my socour be,
To stink eterne he wol my gost exyle.

HE vouched sauf, tel him, as was his wille,
Bicome a man, to have our alliaunce,
And with his precious blood he wroot the bille
Upon the crois, as general acquitaunce,
To every penitent in ful creaunce;
And therfor, lady bright, thou for us praye.
Than shalt thou bothe stinte al his grevaunce,
And make our foo to failen of his praye.

I WOT it wel, thou wolt ben our socour,
Thou art so ful of bountee, in certeyn.
For whan a soule falleth in errour,
Thy pitee goth and haleth him ayeyn.
Than makest thou his pees with his sovereyn,
And bringest him out of the crooked strete.
Whoso thee loveth he shal not love in veyn,
That shal he finde, as he the lyf shal lete.

KALENDERES enlumined ben they
That in this world ben lighted with thy name,
And whoso goth to you the righte wey,
224

Him thar not drede in soule to be lame.
Now, queen of comfort, sith thou art that same
To whom I seche for my medicyne,
Lat not my foo no more my wounde entame,
Myn hele into thyn hand al I resigne.

LADY, thy sorwe can I not portreye
Under the cros, ne his grevous penaunce.
But, for your bothes peynes, I you preye,
Lat nat our alder foo make his bobaunce,
That he hath in his listes of mischaunce
Convict that ye bothe have bought so dere.
As I seide erst, thou ground of our substaunce,
Continue on us thy pitous eyen clere!

MOISES, that saugh the bush with flaumes rede
Brenninge, of which ther never a stikke brende,
Was signe of thyn unwemmed maidenhede.
Thou art the bush on which ther gan descende
The Holy Gost, the which that Moises wende
Had ben a-fyr; and this was in figure.
Now lady, from the fyr thou us defende
Which that in helle eternally shal dure.

NOBLE princesse, that never haddest pere,
Certes, if any comfort in us be,
That cometh of thee, thou Cristes moder dere,
We han non other melodye or glee
Us to rejoyse in our adversitee,
Ne advocat noon that wol and dar so preye
For us, and that for litel hyre as ye,
That helpen for an Ave-Marie or tweye.

O VERREY light of eyen that ben blinde,
O verrey lust of labour and distresse,
O tresorere of bountee to mankinde,
Thee whom God chees to moder for humblesse!
From his ancille he made thee maistresse
Of hevene and erthe, our bille up for to bede.
This world awaiteth ever on thy goodnesse,
For thou ne failest never wight at nede.

PURPOS I have sum tyme for tenquere,
Wherfore and why the Holy Gost thee soughte,
Whan Gabrielles vois cam to thyn ere.
He not to werre us swich a wonder wroughte,
But for to save us that he sithen boughte.
Than nedeth us no wepen us for to save,
But only ther we did not, as us oughte,
Do penitence, and mercy axe and have.

QUEEN of comfort, yit whan I me bithinke
That I agilt have bothe, him and thee,
And that my soule is worthy for to sinke,
Allas, I, caitif, whider may I flee?
Who shal unto thy sone my mene be?
Who, but thyself, that art of pitee welle?
Thou hast more reuthe on our adversitee
Than in this world mighte any tunge telle.

REDRESSE me, moder, and me chastyse,
for, certeynly, my fadres chastisinge
That dar I nought abyden in no wyse:
So hidous is his rightful rekeninge.
Moder, of whom our mercy gan to springe,
Beth ye my juge and eek my soules leche;
for ever in you is pitee haboundinge
To ech that wol of pitee you biseche.

SOTH is, that God ne graunteth no pitee
Withoute thee; for God, of his goodnesse,
foryiveth noon, but it like unto thee.
He hath thee maked vicaire and maistresse
Of al the world, and eek governeresse
Of hevene, and he represseth his justyse
After thy wille, and therefore in witnesse
He hath thee crouned in so ryal wyse.

TEMPLE devout, ther God hath his woninge,
fro which these misbileved pryved been,
To you my soule penitent I bringe.
Receyve me! I can no ferther fleen!
With thornes venimous, O hevene queen,
for which the erthe acursed was ful yore,
I am so wounded, as ye may wel seen,
That I am lost almost; it smert so sore.

VIRGINE, that art so noble of apparaile,
And ledest us into the hye tour
Of Paradys, thou me wisse and counsaile,
How I may have thy grace and thy socour;
Al have I been in filthe and in errour.
Lady, unto that court thou me ajourne
That cleped is thy bench, O fresshe flour!
Theras that mercy ever shal sojourne.

XRISTUS, thy sone, that in this world
alighte,
Upon the cros to suffre his passioun,
And suffred eek, that Longius him pighte,
And made his herte blood to renne adoun;
And al was this for my salvacioun;
And I to him am fals and eek unkinde,
And yit he wol not my dampnacioun,
This thanke I you, socour of al mankinde.

YSAAC was figure of his deeth, certeyn,
That so ferforth his fader wolde obeye
That him ne roughte nothing to be slayn;
Right so thy sone list, as a lamb, to deye.
Now lady, ful of mercy, I you preye,
Sith he his mercy mesured so large,
Be ye not skant; for alle we singe and seye
That ye ben from vengeaunce ay our targe.

ZACHARIE you clepeth the open welle
To wasshe sinful soule out of his gilt.
Therfore this lessoun oughte I wel to telle
That, nere thy tender herte, we weren spilt.
Now lady brighte, sith thou canst and wilt
Ben to the seed of Adam merciable,
So bring us to that palais that is bilt
To penitents that ben to mercy able. Amen.
Explicit carmen.

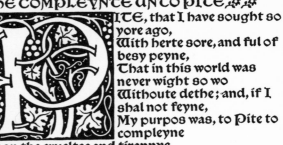

PITE, that I have sought so
yore ago,
With herte sore, and ful of
besy peyne,
That in this world was
never wight so wo
Withoute dethe; and, if I
shal not feyne,
My purpos was, to Pite to
compleyne
Upon the crueltee and tirannye
Of Love, that for my trouthe doth me dye.

And when that I, by lengthe of certeyn yeres,
Had ever in oon a tyme sought to speke,
To Pite ran I, al bespreynt with teres,
To preyen hir on Crueltee me awreke.
But, er I might with any worde outbreke,
Or tellen any of my peynes smerte,
I fond hir deed, and buried in an herte.

Adoun I fel, whan that I saugh the herse,
Deed as a stoon, whyl that the swogh me laste;
But up I roos, with colour ful diverse,
And pitously on hir myn yën caste,
And ner the corps I gan to presen faste,
And for the soule I shoop me for to preye;
I nas but lorn; ther nas no more to seye.

Thus am I slayn, sith that Pite is deed;
Allas! that day! that ever hit shulde falle!
What maner man dar now holde up his heed?
To whom shal any sorwful herte calle?
Now Crueltee hath cast to sleen us alle,
In ydel hope, folk redelees of peyne,
Sith she is deed, to whom shul we compleyne?

But yet encreseth me this wonder newe,
That no wight woot that she is deed, but I;
So many men as in hir tyme hir knewe,
And yet she dyed not so sodeynly;
for I have sought hir ever ful besily
Sith first I hadde wit or mannes mynde;
But she was deed, er that I coude hir fynde.

Aboute hir herse ther stoden lustily,
Withouten any wo, as thoughte me,
Bountee parfit, wel armed and richely,
And fresshe Beautee, Lust, and Jolitee,
Assured Maner, Youthe, and Honestee,
Wisdom, Estaat, and Dreed, and Governaunce,
Confedred bothe by bonde and alliaunce.

A compleynt hadde I, writen, in myn hond,
for to have put to Pite as a bille,
But whan I al this companye ther fond,
That rather wolden al my cause spille
Than do me help, I held my pleynte stille;
for to that folk, withouten any faile,
Withoute Pite may no bille availe.

Then leve I al thise virtues, sauf Pite,
Keping the corps, as ye have herd me seyn,

Confedred alle by bonde of Crueltee,
And been assented that I shal be sleyn.
And I have put my compleynt up ageyn;
for to my foos my bille I dar not shewe,
Theffect of which seith thus, in wordes fewe:

The Bille.

UMBLEST of herte, hyest
of reverence,
Benigne flour, coroune of
vertues alle,
Sheweth unto your rial
excellence
Your servaunt, if I durste
me so calle,
His mortal harm, in which he
is yfalle,
And noght al only for his evel fare,
But for your renoun, as he shal declare.

Hit stondeth thus: your contraire, Crueltee,
Allyed is ageynst your regalye
Under colour of womanly Beautee,
for men ne shuld not knowe hir tirannye,
With Bountee, Gentilesse, and Curtesye,
And hath depryved you now of your place
That hight Beautee, apertenant to Grace.

for kyndly, by your heritage right,
Ye been annexed ever unto Bountee;
And verrayly ye oughte do your might
To helpe Trouthe in his adversitee.
Ye been also the coroune of Beautee;
And certes, if ye wanten in thise tweyne,
The world is lore; ther nis no more to seyne.

Eek what availeth Maner and Gentilesse
Withoute you, benigne creature?
Shal Crueltee be your governeresse?
Allas! what herte may hit longe endure?
Wherfor, but ye the rather take cure
To breke that perilous alliaunce,
Ye sleen hem that ben in your obeisaunce.

And further over, if ye suffre this,
Your renoun is fordo than in a throwe;
Ther shal no man wite wel what Pite is.
Allas! that your renoun shul be so lowe!
Ye be than fro your heritage ythrowe
By Crueltee, that occupieth your place;
And we despeired, that seken to your grace.

Have mercy on me, thou Herenus quene,
That you have sought so tenderly and yore;
Let som streem of your light on me be sene
That love and drede you, ay lenger the more.
for, sothly for to seyne, I bere the sore,
And, though I be not cunning for to pleyne,
for Goddes love, have mercy on my peyne!

My peyne is this, that whatso I desire
That have I not, ne nothing lyk therto;
And ever set Desire myn herte on fire;

226

Eek on that other syde, wherso I go,
What maner thing that may encrese wo
That have I redy, unsoght, everywhere;
Me ne lakketh but my deth, and than my bere.

What nedeth to shewe parcel of my peyne?
Sith every wo that herte may bethinke
I suffre, and yet I dar not to you pleyne;
for wel I woot, although I wake or winke,
Ye rekke not whether I flete or sinke.
But natheles, my trouthe I shal sustene
Unto my deth, and that shal wel be sene.

This is to seyne, I wol be youres ever;
Though ye me slee by Crueltee, your fo,
Algate my spirit shal never dissever
fro your servyse, for any peyne or wo.
Sith ye be deed, allas! that hit is so!
Thus for your deth I may wel wepe and pleyne
With herte sore and ful of besy peyne.
Here endeth the exclamacion of the Deth of
Pyte.

THE COMPLEYNT OF MARS ❀ ❀
The Proem.

LADETH, ye foules, of the
morow gray,
Lo! Venus risen among yon
rowes rede!
And floures fresshe, hon-
oureth ye this day;
for when the sonne uprist,
then wol ye sprede.
But ye lovers, that lye in any
drede,
fleeth, lest wikked tonges yow espye;
Lo! yond the sonne, the candel of jelosye!

With teres blewe, and with a wounded herte
Taketh your leve; and, with seynt John to
borow,
Apeseth somwhat of your sorowes smerte,
Tyme cometh eft, that cese shal your sorow;
The glade night is worth an hevy morow!
(Seynt Valentyne! a foul thus herde I singe
Upon thy day, er sonne gan upspringe).

Yet sang this foul: I rede yow al awake,
And ye, that han not chosen in humble wyse,
Without repenting cheseth yow your make.
And ye, that han ful chosen as I devyse,
Yet at the leste renoveleth your servyse;
Confermeth it perpetuely to dure,
And paciently taketh your aventure.

And for the worship of this hye feste,
Yet wol I, in my briddes wyse, singe
The sentence of the compleynt, at the leste,
That woful Mars made atte departinge
fro fresshe Venus in a morweninge,
Whan Phebus, with his fyry torches rede,
Ransaked every lover in his drede.

 HYLOM the thridde
hevenes lord above,
As wel by hevenish
revolucioun
As by desert, hath wonne
Venus his love,
And she hath take him in
subjeccioun,
And as a maistresse
taught him his lessoun,
Comaunding him that never, in hir servyse,
He nere so bold no lover to despyse.

For she forbad him jelosye at alle,
And cruelte, and bost, and tirannye;
She made him at hir lust so humble and talle,
That when hir deyned caste on hym her yë
He took in pacience to live or dye;
And thus she brydeleth him in hir manere,
With nothing but with scourging of hir chere.

Who regneth now in blisse, but Venus,
That hath this worthy knight in governaunce?
Who singeth now but Mars, that serveth thus
The faire Venus, causer of plesaunce?
He bynt him to perpetual obeisaunce,
And she bynt hir to loven him for ever,
But so be that his trespas hit dissever.

Thus be they knit, and regnen as in heven
By loking most; til hit fil, on a tyde,
That by hir bothe assent was set a steven,
That Mars shal entre, as faste as he may glyde,
Into hir nexte paleys, to abyde,
Walking his cours til she had him atake,
And he preyde hir to haste hir for his sake.

Then seyde he thus: Myn hertes lady swete,
Ye knowe wel my mischef in that place;
For sikerly, til that I with yow mete,
My lyf stant ther in aventure and grace;
But when I see the beaute of your face,
Ther is no dreed of deth may do me smerte,
For al your lust is ese to myn herte.

 She hath so gret compassion of hir knight,
That dwelleth in solitude til she come;
For hit stood so, that ilke tyme, no wight
Counseyled him, ne seyde to him welcome,
That nigh hir wit for wo was overcome;
Wherfore she spedde hir as faste in hir weye,
Almost in oon day, as he dide in tweye.

The grete joye that was bitwix hem two,
Whan they be met, ther may no tunge telle,
Ther is no more, but unto bed they go,
And thus in joye and blisse I lete hem dwelle;
This worthy Mars, that is of knighthod welle,
The flour of fairnes lappeth in his armes,
And Venus kisseth Mars, the god of armes.

Sojourned hath this Mars, of which I rede,
In chambre amid the paleys prively

q 2

A certeyn tyme, til him fel a drede,
Through Phebus, that was comen hastely
Within the paleys-yates sturdely,
With torche in honde, of which the stremes brighte
On Venus chambre knokkeden ful lighte.

The chambre, ther as lay this fresshe quene,
Depeynted was with whyte boles grete,
And by the light she knew, that shoon so shene,
That Phebus cam to brenne hem with his hete;
This sely Venus, dreynt in teres wete,
Enbraceth Mars, and seyde, Alas! I dye!
The torch is come, that al this world wol wrye.

Up sterte Mars, him liste not to slepe,
Whan he his lady herde so compleyne;
But, for his nature was not for to wepe,
Instede of teres, fro his eyen tweyne
The fyry sparkes brosten out for peyne;
And hente his hauberk, that lay him besyde;
Flee wolde he not, ne mighte himselven hyde.

He throweth on his helm of huge wighte,
And girt him with his swerde; and in his honde
His mighty spere, as he was wont to fighte,
He shaketh so that almost it towonde;
Ful hevy he was to walken over londe;
He may not holde with Venus companye,
But bad hir fleen, lest Phebus hir espye.

O woful Mars! alas! what mayst thou seyn,
That in the paleys of thy disturbaunce
Art left behinde, in peril to be sleyn?
And yet therto is double thy penaunce,
For she, that hath thyn herte in governaunce,
Is passed halfe the stremes of thyn yën;
That thou nere swift, wel mayst thou wepe
and cryen.

Now fleeth Venus unto Cylenius tour,
With voide cours, for fere of Phebus light.
Alas! and ther ne hath she no socour,
For she ne fond ne saw no maner wight;
And eek as ther she had but litil might;
Wherfor, hirselven for to hyde and save,
Within the gate she fledde into a cave.

Derk was this cave, and smoking as the helle,
Not but two pas within the gate hit stood;
A naturel day in derk I lete hir dwelle.
Now wol I speke of Mars, furious and wood;
For sorow he wolde have seen his herte blood;
Sith that he mighte hir don no companye,
He ne roghte not a myte for to dye.

So feble he wex, for hete and for his wo,
That nigh he swelt, he mighte unnethe endure;
He passeth but oo steyre in dayes two,
But ner the les, for al his hevy armure,
He foloweth hir that is his lyves cure;
For whos departing he took gretter yre
Thanne for al his brenning in the fyre.

227

After he walketh softely a pas,
Compleyning, that hit pite was to here.
He seyde, O lady bright, Venus! alas!
That ever so wyde a compas is my spere!
Alas! whan shal I mete yow, herte dere,
This twelfte day of April I endure,
Through jelous Phebus, this misaventure.

Now God helpe sely Venus allone!
But, as God wolde, hit happed for to be,
That, whyl that Venus weping made hir mone,
Cylenius, ryding in his chevauchè,
fro Venus valance mighte his paleys see,
And Venus he salueth, and maketh chere,
And hir receyveth as his frend ful dere.

Mars dwelleth forth in his adversite,
Compleyning ever on hir departinge;
And what his compleynt was, remembreth me;
And therfore, in this lusty morweninge,
As I best can, I wol hit seyn and singe,
And after that I wol my leve take;
And God yeve every wight joye of his make!

THE COMPLEYNT OF MARS.
The Proem of the Compleynt.

HE ordre of compleynt re-
quireth skilfully,
That if a wight shal pleyne
pitously,
Ther mot be cause wherfor
that men pleyne;
Or men may deme he pleyn-
eth folily
And causeles; alas! that I
am not I!
Wherfor the ground and cause of al my peyne,
So as my troubled wit may hit ateyne,
I wol reherse; not for to have redresse,
But to declare my ground of hevinesse.

HE firste tyme, alas! that I
was wroght,
And for certeyn effectes
hider broght
By him that lordeth ech
intelligence,
I yaf my trewe servise and
my thoght,
for evermore...how dere I
have hit boght!...
To hir, that is of so gret excellence,
That what wight that first sheweth his presence,
When she is wroth and taketh of him no cure,
He may not longe in joye of love endure.

This is no feyned mater that I telle;
My lady is the verrey sours and welle
Of beaute, lust, fredom, and gentilnesse,
Of riche aray...how dere men hit selle!...
Of al disport in which men frendly dwelle,
Of love and pley, and of benigne humblesse,
Of soune of instruments of al swetnesse;
And therto so wel fortuned and thewed,

228

That through the world hir goodnesse is yshewed.

What wonder is then, thogh that I besette
My servise on suche oon, that may me knette
To wele or wo, sith hit lyth in hir might?
Therfor my herte for ever I to hir hette;
Ne trewly, for my dethe, I shal not lette
To ben hir trewest servaunt and hir knight.
I flater noght, that may wite every wight;
for this day in hir servise shal I dye;
But grace be, I see hir never with yè.

O whom shal I than pleyne
of my distresse?
Who may me helpe, who
may my harm redresse?
Shal I compleyne unto my
lady free?
Nay, certes! for she hath
such hevinesse,
for fere and eek for wo,
that, as I gesse,
In litil tyme hit wol hir bane be.
But were she sauf, hit were no fors of me.
Alas! that ever lovers mote endure,
for love, so many a perilous aventure!

for thogh so be that lovers be as trewe
As any metel that is forged newe,
In many a cas hem tydeth ofte sorowe.
Somtyme hir ladies will not on hem rewe,
Somtyme, yif that jelosye hit knewe,
They mighten lightly leye hir heed to borowe;
Somtyme envyous folk with tunges horowe
Depraven hem; alas! whom may they plese?
But he be fals, no lover hath his ese.

But what availeth suche a longe sermoun
Of aventures of love, up and doun?
I wol returne and speken of my peyne;
The point is this of my destruccioun,
My righte lady, my salvacioun,
Is in affray, and not to whom to pleyne.
O herte swete, O lady sovereyne!
for your disese, wel oghte I swoune and swelte,
Thogh I non other harm ne drede felte.

O what fyn made the god
that sit so hye,
Benethen him, love other
companye,
And streyneth folk to love,
malgre hir hede?
And then hir joye, for oght
I can espye,
Ne lasteth not the twinkel-
ing of an yè,
And somme han never joye til they be dede.
What meneth this? what is this mistihede?
Wherto constreyneth he his folk so faste
Thyng to desyre, but hit shulde laste?

And thogh he made a lover love a thing,

And maketh hit seme stedfast and during,
Yet putteth he in hit such misaventure,
That reste nis ther noon in his yeving.
And that is wonder, that so just a king
Doth such hardnesse to his creature.
Thus, whether love breke or elles dure,
Algates he that hath with love to done
Hath ofter wo then changed is the mone.

Hit semeth he hath to lovers enmite,
And lyk a fissher, as men alday may see,
Baiteth his angle-hook with som plesaunce,
Til mony a fish is wood til that he be
Sesed therwith; and then at erst hath he
Al his desyr, and therwith al mischaunce;
And thogh the lyne breke, he hath penaunce;
For with the hoke he wounded is so sore,
That he his wages hath for evermore.

HE broche of Thebes was
of suche a kinde,
So ful of rubies and of
stones Inde,
That every wight, that
sette on hit an yë,
He wende anon to worthe
out of his minde;
So sore the beaute wold
his herte binde,
Til he hit hadde, him thoghte he moste dye;
And whan that hit was his, than shulde he drye
Such wo for drede, ay whyl that he hit hadde,
That welnigh for the fere he shulde madde.

And whan hit was fro his possessioun,
Than had he double wo and passioun
For he so fair a tresor had forgo;
But yet this broche, as in conclusioun,
Was not the cause of this confusioun;
But he that wroghte hit enfortuned hit so,
That every wight that had it shuld have wo;
And therfor in the worcher was the vyce,
And in the covetour that was so nyce.

So fareth hit by lovers and by me;
For thogh my lady have so gret beaute,
That I was mad til I had gete hir grace,
She was not cause of myn adversite,
But he that wroghte hir, also mot I thee,
That putte suche a beaute in hir face,
That made me to covete and purchace
Myn owne deth; him wyte I that I dye,
And myn unwit, that ever I clomb so hye.

UT to yow, hardy knightes
of renoun,
Sin that ye be of my divisioun,
Al be I not worthy so grete
a name,
Yet, seyn these clerkes, I
am your patroun;
Therfor ye oghte have som
compassioun

q 3

Of my disese, and take it noght agame.
The proudest of yow may be mad ful
tame;
Wherfor I prey yow, of your gentilesse,
That ye compleyne for myn hevinesse.

And ye, my ladies, that ben trewe and
stable,
By way of kinde, ye oghten to be able
To have pite of folk that be in peyne:
Now have ye cause to clothe yow in sable;
Sith that your emperice, the honorable,
Is desolat, wel oghte ye to pleyne;
Now shuld your holy teres falle and reyne.
Alas! your honour and your emperice,
Nigh deed for drede, ne can hir not chevise.

Compleyneth eek, ye lovers, al in fere,
For hir that, with unfeyned humble chere,
Was ever redy to do yow socour;
Compleyneth hir that ever hath had yow
dere;
Compleyneth beaute, fredom, and manere;
Compleyneth hir that endeth your labour;
Compleyneth thilke ensample of al
honour,
That never dide but al gentilesse;
Kytheth therfor on hir some kindenesse.

THE COMPLEYNT OF VENUS. ❀ ❀

HER nis so hy comfort
to my plesaunce,
Whan that I am in any
hevinesse,
As for to have leyser of
remembraunce
Upon the manhod and
the worthinesse,
Upon the trouthe, and
on the stedfastnesse
Of him whos I am al, whyl I may dure;
Ther oghte blame me no creature,
For every wight preiseth his gentilesse.

In him is bountee, wisdom, governaunce
Wel more then any mannes wit can gesse;
For grace hath wold so ferforth him
avaunce
That of knighthode he is parfit richesse.
Honour honoureth him for his noblesse;
Therto so wel hath formed him Nature,
That I am his for ever, I him assure,
For every wight preiseth his gentilesse.

And notwithstanding al his suffisaunce,
His gentil herte is of so greet humblesse
To me in worde, in werke, in contenaunce,
And me to serve is al his besinesse,
That I am set in verrey sikernesse.
Thus oghte I blesse wel myn aventure,
Sith that him list me serven and honoure;
For every wight preiseth his gentilesse.

OW certes, Love, hit is right
covenable
That men ful dere bye thy
noble thing,
As wake abedde, and fasten
at the table,
Weping to laughe, & singe
in compleyning,
And doun to caste visage
and loking,
Often to chaungen hewe and contenaunce,
Pleyne in sleping, and dremen at the daunce,
Al the revers of any glad feling.

Jalousye be hanged by a cablef
She wolde al knowe through hir espying;
Ther doth no wight nothing so resonable,
That al nis harm in hir imagening.
Thus dere abought is love in yeving,
Which ofte he yiveth withouten ordinaunce,
As sorow ynogh, and litel of plesaunce,
Al the revers of any glad feling.

A litel tyme his yift is agreable,
But ful encomberous is the using;
for sotel jalousye, the deceyvable,
ful oftentyme causeth destourbing.
Thus be we ever in drede and suffering,
In nouncerteyn we languisshe in penaunce,
And han ful often many an hard meschaunce,
Al the revers of any glad feling.

UT certes, Love, I sey nat in
such wyse
That for tescape out of your
lace I mente;
for I so longe have been in
your servyse
That for to lete of wol I
never assente;
No force thogh jalousye me
tormente;
Suffyceth me to see him when I may,
And therfore certes, to myn ending-day
To love him best ne shal I never repente.

And certes, Love, whan I me wel avyse
On any estat that man may represente,
Than have ye maked me, through your franchyse,
Chese the best that ever on erthe wente.
Now love wel, herte, and look thou never stente;
And let the jelous putte hit in assay
That, for no peyne wol I nat sey nay;
To love him best ne shal I never repente.

Herte, to thee hit oghte ynogh suffyse
That Love so hy a grace to thee sente,
To chese the worthiest in alle wyse
And most agreable unto myn entente.
Seche no ferther, neyther wey ne wente,
Sith I have suffisaunce unto my pay.
Thus wol I ende this compleynt or lay;
To love him best ne shal I never repente.
230

Lenvoy.

RINCESS, receyveth this
compleynt in gree,
Unto your excellent be-
nignitee
Direct after my litel suf-
fisaunce.
for eld, that in my spirit
dulleth me,
Hath of endyting al the
soteltee
Wel ny bereft out of my remembraunce;
And eek to me hit is a greet penaunce,
Sith rym in English hath swich scarsitee,
To folowe word by word the curiositee
Of Graunson, flour of hem that make in Fraunce.

ANELIDA AND ARCITE ❦ ❦
The Compleynt of feire Anelida and fals Arcite.
Proem.

HOU ferse god of armes,
Mars the rede,
That in the frosty country
called Trace,
Within thy grisly temple
ful of drede
Honoured art, as patroun
of that placef
With thy Bellona, Pallas,
ful of grace,
Be present, and my song continue and gye;
At my beginning thus to thee I crye.

for hit ful depe is sonken in my minde,
With pitous herte in English for tendyte
This olde storie, in Latin which I finde,
Of quene Anelida and fals Arcite,
That elde, which that al can frete and byte,
As hit hath freten mony a noble storie,
Hath nigh devoured out of our memorie.

Be favorable eek, thou Polymnia,
On Parnaso that, with thy sustres glade,
By Elicon, not fer from Cirrea,
Singest with vois memorial in the shade,
Under the laurer which that may not fade,
And do that I my ship to haven winne;
first folow I Stace, and after him Corinne.

Iamque domos patrias, &c.: Statii Thebais, xii.519.

HAN Theseus, with werres
longe and grete,
The aspre folk of Cithe
had overcome,
With laurer crouned, in his
char gold-bete,
Hoom to his contre-houses
is ycome;...
for which the peple blis-
ful, al and somme,
So cryden, that unto the sterres hit wente,
And him to honouren dide al hir entente;...

Beforn this duk, in signe of hy victorie,
The trompes come, and in his baner large
The image of Mars; and, in token of glorie,
Men mighten seen of tresor many a charge,
Many a bright helm, and many a spere and targe,
Many a fresh knight, and many a blisful route,
On hors, on fote, in al the felde aboute.

Ipolita his wyf, the hardy quene
Of Cithia, that he conquered hadde,
With Emelye, hir yonge suster shene,
Faire in a char of golde he with him ladde,
That al the ground aboute hir char she spradde
With brightnesse of the beautee in hir face,
Fulfild of largesse and of alle grace.

With his triumphe and laurer-crouned thus,
In al the floure of fortunes yevinge,
Lete I this noble prince Theseus
Toward Athenes in his wey rydinge,
And founde I wol in shortly for to bringe
The slye wey of that I gan to wryte,
Of quene Anelida and fals Arcite.

Mars, which that through his furious course of
yre,
The olde wrath of Juno to fulfille,
Hath set the peples hertes bothe on fyre
Of Thebes and Grece, everich other to kille
With blody speres, ne rested never stille,
But throng now her, now ther, among hem bothe,
That everich other slough, so wer they wrothe.

For whan Amphiorax and Tydeus,
Ipomedon, Parthonopee also
Were dede, and slayn was proud Campaneus,
And whan the wrecches Thebans, bretheren two,
Were slayn, and king Adrastus hoom ago,
So desolat stood Thebes and so bare,
That no wight coude remedie of his care.

And whan the olde Creon gan espye
How that the blood roial was broght adoun,
He held the cite by his tirannye,
And did the gentils of that regioun
To been his frendes, and dwellen in the toun.
So what for love of him, and what for awe,
The noble folk wer to the toun ydrawe.

Among al these, Anelida the quene
Of Ermony was in that toun dwellinge,
That fairer was then is the sonne shene;
Throughout the world so gan hir name springe,
That hir to seen had every wight lykinge;
For, as of trouthe, is ther noon hir liche,
Of al the women in this worlde riche.

Yong was this quene, of twenty yeer of elde,
Of midel stature, and of swich fairnesse,
That nature had a joye hir to beholde;
And for to speken of hir stedfastnesse,
She passed hath Penelope and Lucresse,
And shortly, if she shal be comprehended,
In hir ne mighte nothing been amended.

q 4

This Theban knight Arcite eek, sooth to seyn,
Was yong, and therwithal a lusty knight,
But he was double in love and nothing pleyn,
And subtil in that crafte over any wight,
And with his cunning wan this lady bright;
For so ferforth he gan hir trouthe assure,
That she him trust over any creature.

What shuld I seyn? she loved Arcite so,
That, whan that he was absent any throwe,
Anon hir thoghte hir herte brast atwo;
For in hir sight to hir he bar him lowe,
So that she wende have al his herte yknowe;
But he was fals; it nas but feyned chere,
As nedeth not to men such craft to lere.

But nevertheles ful mikel besinesse
Had he, er that he mighte his lady winne,
And swoor he wolde dyen for distresse,
Or from his wit he seyde he wolde twinne.
Alas, the whyle! for hit was routhe and sinne,
That she upon his sorowes wolde rewe,
But nothing thenketh the fals as doth the trewe.

Hir fredom fond Arcite in swich manere,
That al was his that she hath, moche or lyte,
Ne to no creature made she chere
Ferther than that hit lyked to Arcite;
Ther was no lak with which he mighte hir wyte,
She was so ferforth yeven him to plese,
That al that lyked him, hit did hir ese.

Ther nas to hir no maner lettre ysent
That touched love, from any maner wight,
That she ne shewed hit him, er hit was brent;
So pleyn she was, and did hir fulle might,
That she nil hyden nothing from hir knight,
Lest he of any untrouthe hir upbreyde;
Withouten bode his heste she obeyde.

And eek he made him jelous over here,
That, what that any man had to hir seyd,
Anoon he wolde preyen hir to swere
What was that word, or make him evel apayd;
Than wende she out of hir wit have brayd;
But al this nas but sleight and flaterye,
Withouten love he feyned jelosye.

And al this took she so debonerly,
That al his wille, hir thoghte hit skilful thing,
And ever the lenger loved him tenderly,
And did him honour as he were a king.
Hir herte was wedded to him with a ring;
So ferforth upon trouthe is hir entente,
That wher he goth, hir herte with him wente.

Whan she shal ete, on him is so hir thoght,
That wel unnethe of mete took she keep;
And whan that she was to hir reste broght,
On him she thoghte alwey til that she sleep;
Whan he was absent, prevely she weep;
Thus liveth fair Anelida the quene
For fals Arcite, that did hir al this tene.

This fals Arcite, of his new-fangelnesse,
For she to him so lowly was and trewe,
Took lesse deyntee for hir stedfastnesse,
And saw another lady, proud and newe,
And right anon he cladde him in hir hewe,
Wot I not whether in whyte, rede, or grene,
And falsed fair Anelida the quene.

But nevertheles, gret wonder was hit noon
Thogh he wer fals, for hit is kinde of man,
Sith Lamek was, that is so longe agoon,
To been in love as fals as ever he can;
He was the firste fader that began
To loven two, and was in bigamye;
And he found tentes first, but if men lye.

This fals Arcite sumwhat moste he feyne,
Whan he wex fals, to covere his traitorye,
Right as an hors, that can both byte and pleyne;
For he bar hir on honde of trecherye,
And swoor he coude hir doublenesse espye,
And al was falsnes that she to him mente;
Thus swoor this theef, & forth his way he wente.

Alas! what herte might enduren hit,
For routhe or wo, hir sorow for to telle?
Or what man hath the cunning or the wit?
Or what man might within the chambre dwelle,
If I to him rehersen shal the helle,
That suffreth fair Anelida the quene
For fals Arcite, that did hir al this tene?

She wepeth, waileth, swowneth pitously,
To grounde deed she falleth as a stoon;
Al crampissheth hir limes crokedly,
She speketh as hir wit were al agoon;
Other colour then asshen hath she noon,
Noon other word she speketh moche or lyte,
But Mercy, cruel herte myn, Arcite!

And thus endureth, til that she was so mate
That she ne hath foot on which she may sustene;
But forth languisshing ever in this estate,
Of which Arcite hath nother routhe ne tene;
His herte was elleswhere, newe and grene,
That on hir wo ne deyneth him not to thinke,
Him rekketh never wher she flete or sinke.

His newe lady holdeth him so narowe
Up by the brydel, at the staves ende,
That every word, he dradde hit as an arowe;
Hir daunger made him bothe bowe and bende,
And as hir liste, made him turne or wende;
For she ne graunted him in hir livinge
No grace, why that he hath lust to singe;

But drof him forth, unnethe liste hir knowe
That he was servaunt to hir ladyshippe,
But lest that he wer proude, she held him lowe;
Thus serveth he, withouten fee or shipe,
She sent him now to londe, now to shippe;
And for she yaf him daunger al his fille,
Therfor she had him at hir owne wille.

232

Ensample of this, ye thrifty wimmen alle,
Take here Anelida and fals Arcite,
That for hir liste him Dere herte calle,
And was so meek, therfor he loved hir lyte;
The kinde of mannes herte is to delyte
In thing that straunge is, also God me save!
For what he may not gete, that wolde he have.

Now turne we to Anelida ageyn,
That pyneth day by day in languisshing;
But whan she saw that hir ne gat no geyn,
Upon a day, ful sorowfully weping,
She caste hir for to make a compleyning,
And with hir owne honde she gan hit wryte;
And sente hit to hir Theban knight Arcite.

The Compleynt of Anelida the Quene upon fals
Arcite.
Proem.

SO thirleth with the poynt
of remembraunce,
The swerd of sorowe,
ywhet with fals plesaunce,
Myn herte, bare of blis and
blak of hewe,
That turned is in quaking
al my daunce,
My suretee in awhaped
countenaunce;
Sith hit availeth not for to ben trewe;
For whoso trewest is, hit shal hir rewe,
That serveth love and doth hir observaunce
Alwey to oon, and chaungeth for no newe.

I WOT myself as wel as any wight;
For I loved oon with al my herte and
might
More then myself, an hundred
thousand sythe,
And called him my hertes lyf, my
knight,
And was al his, as fer as hit was right;
And whan that he was glad, than was I blythe,
And his disese was my deeth as swythe;
And he ayein his trouthe me had plight
For evermore, his lady me to kythe.

NOW is he fals, alas! and causeles,
And of my wo he is so routheles,
That with a worde him list not ones deyne
To bring ayein my sorowful herte in pees,
For he is caught up in another lees.
Right as him list, he laugheth at my peyne,
And I ne can myn herte not restreyne,
That I ne love him alwey, nevertheles;
And of al this I not to whom me pleyne.

AND shal I pleyne ... alas! the harde
stounde...
Unto my foo that yaf my herte a wounde,
And yet desyreth that myn harm be more?
Nay, certes! ferther wol I never founde
Non other help, my sores for to sounde.

My desteny hath shapen it ful yore;
I wil non other medecyne ne lore;
I wil ben ay ther I was ones bounde,
That I have seid, be seid for evermore!

ALAS! wher is become your gentilesse!
Your wordes ful of plesaunce and
humblesse?
Your observaunces in so low manere,
And your awayting and your besinesse
Upon me, that ye calden your maistresse,
Your sovereyn lady in this worlde here?
Alas! and is ther nother word ne chere
Ye vouchesauf upon myn hevinesse?
Alas! your love, I bye hit al to dere.

NOW certes, swete, thogh that ye
Thus causeles the cause be
Of my dedly adversitee,
Your manly reson oghte it to respyte
To slee your frend, and namely me,
That never yet in no degree
Offended yow, as wisly he,
That al wot, out of wo my soule quyte!

UT for I shewed yow,
Arcite,
Al that men wolde to me
wryte,
And was so besy, yow to
delyte...
My honour save...meke,
kinde, and free,
Therfor ye putte on me the
wyte,
And of me recche not a myte,
Thogh that the swerd of sorow byte
My woful herte through your crueltee.

MY swete foo, why do ye so, for shame?
And thenke ye that furthered be your
name,
To love a newe, and been untrewe? nay!
And putte yow in sclaunder now and blame,
And do to me adversitee and grame,
That love yow most, God, wel thou wost! alway?
Yet turn ayeyn, and be al pleyn som day,
And than shal this that now is mis be game,
And al foryive, whyl that I live may.

O!herte myn, al this is for
to seyne,
As whether shal I preye or
elles pleyne?
Whiche is the wey to doon
yow to be trewe?
For either mot I have yow
in my cheyne,
Or with the dethe ye mot
departe us tweyne;
Ther ben non other mene weyes newe;
For God so wisly on my soule rewe,

As verily ye sleen me with the peyne;
That may ye see unfeyned of myn hewe.

FOR thus ferforth have I my deth ysoght,
Myself I mordre with my prevy thoght;
for sorow and routhe of your unkinde-
nesse
I wepe, I wake, I faste; al helpeth noght;
I weyve joy that is to speke of oght,
I voyde companye, I flee gladnesse;
Who may avaunte hir bet of hevinesse
Then I? and to this plyte have ye me broght,
Withoute gilt; me nedeth no witnesse.

AND sholde I preye, and weyve woman-
hede?
Nay! rather deth then do so foul a dede,
And axe mercy gilteles! what nede?
And if I pleyne what lyf that I lede,
Yow rekketh not; that know I, out of drede;
And if I unto yow myn othes bede
For myn excuse, a scorn shal be my mede;
Your chere floureth, but hit wol not sede;
Ful longe agoon I oghte have take hede.

FOR thogh I hadde yow tomorow ageyn,
I might as wel holde Averill fro reyn,
As holde yow, to make yow stedfast.
Almighty god, of trouthe sovereyn,
Wher is the trouthe of man? who hath hit
sleyn?
Who that hem loveth shal hem fynde as fast
As in a tempest is a roten mast.
Is that a tame best that is ay feyn
To renne away, when he is leest agast?

NOW mercy, swete, if I misseye,
Have I seyd oght amis, I preye?
I not; my wit is al aweye.
I fare as doth the song of Chaunte/pleure.
For now I pleyne, and now I pleye,
I am so mased that I deye,
Arcite hath born awey the keye
Of al my worlde, and my good aventure!

FOR in this worlde nis creature
Wakinge, in more discomfiture
Then I, ne more sorow endure;
And if I slepe a furlong/wey or tweye,
Than thinketh me, that your figure
Before me stant, clad in asure,
To profren eft a newe assure
For to be trewe, and mercy me to preye.

THE longe night this wonder sight I drye,
And on the day for this afray I dye,
And of al this right noght, ywis, ye recche.
Ne never mo myn yen two be drye,
And to your routhe and to your trouthe I crye.
But welawey! to fer be they to fecche;
Thus holdeth me my destinee a wrecche.
But me to rede out of this drede or gye
Ne may my wit, so weyk is hit, not strecche.

233

THAN ende I thus, sith I
may do no more,
I yeve hit up for now and
evermore;
for I shal never eft putten
in balaunce
My sekernes, ne lerne of
love the lore.
But as the swan, I have
herd seyd ful yore,
Ayeins his deth shal singe in his penaunce,
So singe I here my destiny or chaunce,
How that Arcite Anelida so sore
Hath thirled with the poynt of remembraunce!

WHAN that Anelida this woful
quene
Hath of hir hande writen in this
wyse,
With face deed, betwixe pale and
grene,
She fel a,swowe; and sith ye gan to ryse,
And unto Mars avoweth sacrifyse
Within the temple, with a sorowful chere,
That shapen was as ye shal after here.
Unfinished.

CHAUCERS WORDES UNTO ADAM, HIS OWNE SCRIVEYN ❀ ❀

ADAM scriveyn, if ever it thee
bifalle
Boece or Troilus to wryten
newe,
Under thy lokkes thou
most have the scalle,
But after my making thou
wryte trewe.
So ofte a daye I mot thy
werk renewe,
Hit to correcte and eek to rubbe and scrape;
And al is through thy negligence and rape.

THE FORMER AGE ❀ ❀

A BLISFUL lyf, a paisible
and a swete
Ledden the peples in the
former age;
They helde hem payed of
fruites, that they ete,
Which that the feldes yave
hem by usage;
They ne were nat forpam-
pred with outrage;
Unknowen was the quern and eek the melle;
They eten mast, hawes, and swich pounage,
And dronken water of the colde welle.

Yit nas the ground nat wounded with the
plough,
But corn up,sprong, unsowe of mannes
hond,

The which they gniden, and eete nat half
ynough.
No man yit knew the forwes of his lond;
No man the fyr out of the flint yit fond;
Unkorven and ungrobbed lay the vyne;
No man yit in the morter spyces grond
To clarre, ne to sause of galantyne.

No mader, welde, or wood no litestere
Ne knew; the flees was of his former hewe;
No flesh ne wiste offence of egge or spere;
No coyn ne knew man which was fals or trewe;
No ship yit karf the wawes grene and blewe;
No marchaunt yit ne fette outlandish ware;
No trompes for the werres folk ne knewe,
No toures heye, and walles rounde or square.

What sholde it han avayled to werreye?
Ther lay no profit, ther was no richesse,
But cursed was the tyme, I dar wel seye,
That men first dide hir swety bysinesse
To grobbe up metal, lurkinge in darknesse,
And in the riveres first gemmes soghte.
Allas! than sprong up al the cursednesse
Of covetyse, that first our sorwe broghte!

Thise tyraunts putte hem gladly nat in pres,
No wildnesse, ne no busshes for to winne
Ther poverte is, as seith Diogenes,
Ther as vitaile is eek so skars and thinne
That noght but mast or apples is therinne.
But, ther as bagges been and fat vitaile,
Ther wol they gon, and spare for no sinne
With al hir ost the cite for tassaile.

Yit were no paleis,chaumbres, ne non halles;
In caves and in wodes softe and swete
Slepten this blissed folk withoute walles,
On gras or leves in parfit quiete.
No doun of fetheres, ne no bleched shete
Was kid to hem, but in seurtee they slepte;
Hir hertes were al oon, withoute galles,
Everich of hem his feith to other kepte.

Unforged was the hauberk and the plate;
The lambish peple, voyd of alle vyce,
Hadden no fantasye to debate,
But ech of hem wolde other wel cheryce;
No pryde, non envye, non avaryce,
No lord, no taylage by no tyrannye;
Humblesse and pees, good feith, the emperice,
fulfilled erthe of olde curtesye.

Yit was not Jupiter the likerous,
That first was fader of delicacye,
Come in this world; ne Nembrot, desirous
To reynen, had nat maad his toures hye.
Allas, allas! now may men wepe and crye!
For in our dayes nis but covetyse
And doublenesse, and tresoun and envye,
Poysoun, manslauhtre, and mordre in sondry
wyse.
finit Etas prima. Chaucers.

BALADE DE BON CONSEYL ❧ ❧

FLEE fro the prees, and
dwelle with sothfastnesse,
Suffyce unto thy good,
though hit be smal;
For hord hath hate, and
climbing tikelnesse,
Prees hath envye, and wele
blent overal;
Savour no more than thee
bihove shal;
Werk wel thyself, that other folk canst rede;
And trouthe shal delivere, hit is no drede.

Tempest thee noght al croked to redresse,
In trust of hir that turneth as a bal:
Gret reste stant in litel besinesse;
And eek be war to sporne ageyn an al;
Stryve noght, as doth the crokke with the wal.
Daunte thyself, that dauntest otheres dede;
And trouthe shal delivere, hit is no drede.

That thee is sent, receyve in buxumnesse,
The wrastling for this worlde axeth a fal.
Her nis non hoom, her nis but wildernesse:
Forth, pilgrim, forth! forth, beste, out of thy
stal!
Know thy contree, look up, thank God of al;
Holde the hye wey, and lat thy gost thee lede:
And trouthe shal delivere, hit is no drede.

Envoy.

THERFORE, thou vache, leve thyn
old wrecchednesse
Unto the worlde; leve now to be thral;
Crye him mercy, that of his hy
goodnesse
Made thee of noght, and in especial
Draw unto him, and pray in general
For thee, and eek for other, hevenlich mede;
And trouthe shal delivere, hit is no drede.
Explicit Le bon counseill de G. Chaucer.

TO ROSEMOUNDE. A BALADE ❧ ❧

MADAME, ye ben of al beautè
shryne
As fer as cercled is the
mappemounde;
For as the cristal glorious
ye shyne,
And lyke ruby ben your
chekes rounde.
Therwith ye ben so mery
and so jocounde,
That at a revel whan that I see you daunce,
It is an oynement unto my wounde,
Thogh ye to me ne do no daliaunce.

For thogh I wepe of teres ful a tyne,
Yet may that wo myn herte nat confounde;
Your seemly voys that ye so smal out-twyne
Maketh my thoght in joye and blis habounde.
So curteisly I go, with love bounde,

That to myself I sey, in my penaunce,
Suffyseth me to love you, Rosemounde,
Thogh ye to me ne do no daliaunce.

Nas never pyk walwed in galauntyne
As I in love am walwed and ywounde;
For which ful ofte I of myself divyne
That I am trewe Tristam the secounde.
My love may not refreyd be nor afounde;
I brenne ay in an amorous plesaunce.
Do what you list, I wil your thral be founde,
Thogh ye to me ne do no daliaunce.
Tregentil. Chaucer.

PROVERBE OF CHAUCER ❧ ❧

WHAT shul thise clothes
manyfold,
Lo! this hote somers
day?...
After greet heet cometh
cold;
No man caste his pilche
away.
Of al this world the wyde
compas
Hit wol not in myn armes tweyne. ...
Whoso mochel wol embrace
Litel therof he shal distreyne.

LENVOY DE CHAUCER A SCOGAN ❧ ❧

TO-BROKEN been the
statuts hye in hevene
That creat were eternally to
dure,
Sith that I see the brighte
goddes sevene
Mow wepe and wayle, and
passioun endure,
As may in erthe a mortal
creature.
Allas, fro whennes may this thing procede?
Of whiche errour I deye almost for drede.

By worde eterne whylom was hit shape
That fro the fifte cercle, in no manere,
Ne mighte a drope of teres doun escape.
But now so wepeth Venus in hir spere,
That with hir teres she wol drenche us here.
Allas, Scogan! this is for thyn offence!
Thou causest this deluge of pestilence.

Hast thou not seyd, in blaspheme of this goddes,
Through pryde, or through thy grete rakelnesse,
Swich thing as in the lawe of love forbode is?
That, for thy lady saw nat thy distresse,
Therfor thou yave hir up at Michelmesse!
Allas, Scogan! of olde folk ne yonge
Was never erst Scogan blamed for his tonge!

Thou drowe in scorn Cupyde eek to record
Of thilke rebel word that thou hast spoken,
For which he wol no lenger be thy lord.
And, Scogan, thogh his bowe be nat broken,

235

He wol nat with his arwes been ywroken
On thee, ne me, ne noon of our figure;
We shul of him have neyther hurt ne cure.

Now certes, frend, I drede of thyn unhappe,
Lest for thy gilt the wreche of Love procede
On alle hem that ben hore and rounde of shape,
That ben so lykly folk in love to spede.
Than shul we for our labour han no mede;
But wel I wot, thou wilt answere and seye:
Lo! olde Grisel list to ryme and pleye!

Nay, Scogan, sey not so, for I mexcuse,
God help me so! in no rym, doutelees,
Ne thinke I never of slepe wak my muse,
That rusteth in my shethe stille in pees.
Whyl I was yong, I putte hir forth in prees,
But al shal passe that men prose or ryme;
Take every man his turn, as for his tyme.

Envoy.

COGAN, that knelest at the stremes
heed
Of grace, of alle honour & worthinesse,
In thende of which streme I am dul
as deed,
Forgete in solitarie wildernesse;
Yet, Scogan, thenke on Tullius kindenesse,
Minne thy frend, ther it may fructifye!
Farwel, and lok thou never eft Love defye!

LENVOY DE CHAUCER A BUKTON.
The counseil of Chaucer touching Mariage, which
was sent to Bukton.

Y maister Bukton, whan of
Criste our kinge
Was axed, what is trouthe
or sothfastnesse,
He nat a word answerde to
that axinge,
As who saith: No man is al
trewe, I gesse.
And therfor, thogh I
highte to expresse
The sorwe and wo that is in mariage,
I dar not wryte of hit no wikkednesse,
Lest I myself falle eft in swich dotage.

I wol nat seyn, how that hit is the cheyne
Of Sathanas, on which he gnaweth ever,
But I dar seyn, were he out of his peyne,
As by his wille, he wolde be bounde never.
But thilke doted fool that eft hath lever
Ycheyned be than out of prisoun crepe,
God lete him never fro his wo dissever,
Ne no man him bewayle, though he wepe.

But yit, lest thou do worse, tak a wyf;
Bet is to wedde, than brenne in worse wyse.
But thou shalt have sorwe on thy flesh, thy lyf,
And been thy wyves thral, as seyn these wyse,
And if that holy writ may nat suffise,
Experience shal thee teche, so may happe,
That thee were lever to be take in Fryse
Than eft to falle of wedding in the trappe.

236

Envoy.

HIS litel writ, proverbes, or figure
I sende you, tak kepe of hit, I rede:
Unwys is he that can no wele endure.
If thou be siker, put thee nat in drede.
The Wyf of Bathe I pray you that
ye rede
Of this matere that we have on honde.
God graunte you your lyf frely to lede
In fredom; for ful harde is to be bonde.
Explicit.

GENTILESSE. MORAL BALADE OF CHAUCER.

HE firste stok, fader of
gentilesse...
What man that claymeth
gentil for to be,
Must folowe his trace, and
alle his wittes dresse
Vertu to sewe, and vyces
for to flee.
For unto vertu longeth
dignitee,
And noght the revers, saufly dar I deme,
Al were he mytre, croune, or diademe.

This firste stok was ful of rightwisnesse,
Trewe of his word, sobre, pitous, and free,
Clene of his goste, and loved besinesse,
Ageinst the vyce of slouthe, in honestee;
And, but his heir love vertu, as dide he,
He is noght gentil, thogh he riche seme,
Al were he mytre, croune, or diademe.

Vyce may wel be heir to old richesse;
But ther may no man, as men may wel see,
Bequethe his heir his vertuous noblesse;
That is appropred unto no degree,
But to the firste fader in magestee,
That maketh him his heir, that can him queme,
Al were he mytre, croune, or diademe.

LAK OF STEDFASTNESSE. BALADE

OM tyme this world was so
stedfast and stable
That mannes word was
obligacioun,
And now hit is so fals and
deceivable,
That word and deed, as in
conclusioun,
Ben nothing lyk, for turned
up so doun
Is al this world for mede and wilfulnesse,
That al is lost, for lak of stedfastnesse.

What maketh this world to be so variable
But lust that folk have in dissensioun?
Among us now a man is holde unable,
But if he can, by som collusioun,
Don his neighbour wrong or oppressioun.
What causeth this, but wilful wrecchednesse,
That al is lost, for lak of stedfastnesse?

Trouthe is put doun, resoun is holden fable;
Vertu hath now no dominacioun,
Pitee exyled, no man is merciable.
Through covetyse is blent discrecioun;
The world hath mad a permutacioun
Fro right to wrong, fro trouthe to fikelnesse,
That al is lost, for lak of stedfastnesse.

Lenvoy to King Richard.

PRINCE, desyre to be honourable,
Cherish thy folk and hate ex-
torcioun!
Suffre no thing, that may be
reprevable
To thyn estat, don in thy regioun.
Shew forth thy swerd of castigacioun,
Dred God, do law, love trouthe and worthinesse,
And wed thy folk ageîn to stedfastnesse.
Explicit.

BALADES DE VISAGE SANZ PEINTURE.
Le Pleintif countre fortune.

HIS wrecched worldes
transmutacioun,
As wele or wo, now povre
and now honour,
Withouten ordre or wys
discrecioun
Governed is by fortunes
errour;
But natheles, the lak of hir
favour
Ne may nat don me singen, though I dye,
Jay tout perdu mon temps et mon labour:
For fynally, Fortune, I thee defye!

Yit is me left the light of my resoun,
To knowen frend fro fo in thy mirour.
So muche hath yit thy whirling up and doun
Ytaught me for to knowen in an hour.
But trewely, no force of thy reddour
To him that over himself hath the maystrye!
My suffisaunce shal be my socour:
For fynally, Fortune, I thee defye!

O Socrates, thou stedfast champioun,
She never mighte be thy tormentour;
Thou never dreddest hir oppressioun,
Ne in hir chere founde thou no savour.
Thou knewe wel deceit of hir colour,
And that hir moste worshipe is to lye.
I knowe hir eek a fals dissimulour:
For fynally, Fortune, I thee defye!

La respounse de fortune au Pleintif.

O man is wrecched, but himself hit
wene,
And he that hath himself hath
suffisaunce.
Why seystow thanne I am to thee
so kene,
That hast thyself out of my governaunce?
Sey thus: Graunt mercy of thyn haboundaunce

That thou hast lent or this. Why wolt thou stryve?
What wostow yit, how I thee wol avaunce?
And eek thou hast thy beste frend alyve!

I have thee taught divisioun bitwene
Frend of effect, and frend of countenaunce;
Thee nedeth nat the galle of noon hyene,
That cureth eyen derke fro hir penaunce;
Now seestow cleer, that were in ignoraunce.
Yit halt thyn ancre, and yit thou mayst arryve
Ther bountee berth the keye of my substaunce:
And eek thou hast thy beste frend alyve.

How many have I refused to sustene,
Sin I thee fostred have in thy plesaunce!
Woltow than make a statut on thy quene
That I shal been ay at thyn ordinaunce?
Thou born art in my regne of variaunce,
Aboute the wheel with other most thou dryve.
My lore is bet than wikke is thy grevaunce,
And eek thou hast thy beste frend alyve.

La respounse du Pleintif countre fortune.

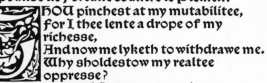HY lore I dampne, hit is adversitee.
My frend maystow nat reven, blind
goddesse!
That I thy frendes knowe, I thanke
hit thee.
Tak hem agayn, lat hem go lye on
presse!
The negardye in keping hir richesse
Prenostik is thou wolt hir tour assayle;
Wikke appetyt comth ay before seknesse:
In general, this reule may nat fayle.

La respounse de fortune countre le Pleintif.

HOU pinchest at my mutabilitee,
For I thee lente a drope of my
richesse,
And now me lyketh to withdrawe me.
Why sholdestow my realtee
oppresse?
The see may ebbe and flowen more or lesse;
The welkne hath might to shyne, reyne, or hayle;
Right so mot I kythen my brotelnesse.
In general, this reule may nat fayle.

Lo, thexecucion of the magestee
That al purveyeth of his rightwisnesse,
That same thing fortune clepen ye,
Ye blinde bestes, ful of lewednesse!
The hevene hath propretee of sikernesse,
This world hath ever resteles travayle;
Thy laste day is ende of myn intresse:
In general, this reule may nat fayle.

Lenvoy de fortune.

RINCES, I prey you of your
gentilesse,
Lat nat this man on me thus crye
and pleyne,
And I shal quyte you your bisinesse
At my requeste, as three of you or
tweyne;

237

And, but you list releve him of his peyne,
Preyeth his beste frend, of his noblesse,
That to som beter estat he may atteyne.
Explicit.

THE COMPLEINT OF CHAUCER TO HIS EMPLY PURSE ✿ ✿

O you, my purse, & to non other wight
Compleyne I, for ye be my lady dere!
I am so sory, now that ye be light;
for certes, but ye make me hevy chere,
Me were as leef be leyd upon my bere;
for whiche unto your mercy thus I crye:
Beth hevy ageyn, or elles mot I dye!

Now voucheth sauf this day, or hit be night,
That I of you the blisful soun may here,
Or see your colour lyk the sonne bright,
That of yelownesse hadde never pere.
Ye be my lyf, ye be myn hertes stere,
Quene of comfort and of good companye:
Beth hevy ageyn, or elles mot I dye!

Now purs, that be to me my lyves light,
And saveour, as doun in this worlde here,
Out of this toune help me through your might,
Sin that ye wole nat been my tresorere;
for I am shave as nye as any frere.
But yit I pray unto your curtesye:
Beth hevy ageyn, or elles mot I dye!

Lenvoy de Chaucer.

O CONQUEROUR of Brutes Albioun!
Which that by lyne and free eleccioun
Ben verray king, this song to you I sende;
And ye, that mowen al our harm amende,
Have minde upon my supplicacioun!

MERCILES BEAUTE: A TRIPLE ROUNDEL ✿ ✿

OUR yën two wol slee me sodenly,
I may the beautè of hem not sustene,
So woundeth hit throughout my herte kene.
And but your word wol helen hastily
My hertes wounde, whyl that hit is grene,
Your yën two wol slee me sodenly,
I may the beautè of hem not sustene.

Upon my trouthe I sey yow feithfully,
That ye ben of my lyf and deeth the quene;
for with my deeth the trouthe shal be sene.

238

Your yën two wol slee me sodenly,
I may the beautè of hem not sustene,
So woundeth hit throughout my herte kene.

SO hath youre beautè fro your herte chaced
Pitee, that me ne availeth not to pleyne;
for Daunger halt your mercy in his cheyne.
Giltles my deeth thus han ye me purchaced;
I sey yow sooth, me nedeth not to feyne;
So hath your beautè fro your herte chaced
Pitee, that me ne availeth not to pleyne.

Allas! that nature hath in yow compassed
So greet beautè, that no man may atteyne
To mercy, though he sterve for the peyne.
So hath your beautè fro your herte chaced
Pitee, that me ne availeth not to pleyne;
for Daunger halt your mercy in his cheyne.

SIN I fro Love escaped am so fat,
I never thenk to ben in his prison lene;
Sin I am free, I counte him not a bene.

He may answere, and seye this or that;
I do no fors, I speke right as I mene.
Sin I fro Love escaped am so fat,
I never thenk to ben in his prison lene.

Love hath my name ystrike out of his sclat,
And he is strike out of my bokes clene
for evermo; ther is non other mene.
Sin I fro Love escaped am so fat,
I never thenk to ben in his prison lene;
Sin I am free, I counte him not a bene.
Explicit.

A COMPLEINT TO HIS LADY ✿ ✿
I.

THE longe night, whan every creature
Shulde have hir rest in som/what, as by kinde,
Or elles ne may hir lyf nat long endure,
Hit falleth most into my woful minde
How I so fer have broght myself behinde,
That, sauf the deeth, ther may nothing me lisse,
So desespaired I am from alle blisse.

This same thoght me lasteth til the morwe,
And from the morwe forth til hit be eve;
Ther nedeth me no care for to borwe,
for bothe I have good leyser and good leve;
Ther is no wight that wol me wo bereve
To wepe ynogh, and wailen al my fille;
The sore spark of peyne doth me spille.

II.
The sore spark of peyne doth me spille;
This Love hath eek me set in swich a place
That my desyr he never wol fulfille;
for neither pitee, mercy, neither grace

Can I nat finde; and fro my sorwful herte,
For to be deed, I can hit nat arace.
The more I love, the more she doth me smerte;
Through which I see, withoute remedye,
That from the deeth I may no wyse asterte;
For this day in hir servise shal I dye.

III.

Thus am I slain, with sorwes ful dyverse;
Ful longe agoon I oghte have taken hede.
Now sothly, what she hight I wol reherse;
Hir name is Bountee, set in womanhede,
Sadnesse in youthe, and Beautee prydelees,
And Plesaunce, under governaunce and drede;
Hir surname eek is faire Rewthelees,
The Wyse, yknit unto Good Aventure,
That, for I love hir, sleeth me giltelees.
Hir love I best, and shal, whyl I may dure,
Bet than myself an hundred thousand deel,
Than al this worldes richesse or creature.
Now hath nat Love me bestowed weel
To love, ther I never shal have part?
Allas! right thus is turned me the wheel,
Thus am I slayn with loves fyry dart.
I can but love hir best, my swete fo;
Love hath me taught no more of his art
But serve alwey, and stinte for no wo.

IV.

Within my trewe careful herte ther is
So moche wo, and eek so litel blis,
That wo is me that ever I was bore;
For al that thing which I desyre I mis,
And al that ever I wolde nat, I wis,
That finde I redy to me evermore;
And of al this I not to whom me pleyne.
For she that mighte me out of this bringe
Ne reccheth nat whether I wepe or singe;
So litel rewthe hath she upon my peyne.

Allas! whan sleping-time is, than I wake,
Whan I shulde daunce, for fere than I quake;
Yow rekketh never wher I flete or sinke;
This hevy lyf I lede for your sake,
Thogh ye therof in no wyse hede take,
For on my wo yow deyneth not to thinke.
My hertes lady, and hool my lyves quene!
For trewly dorste I seye, as that I fele,
Me semeth that your swete herte of stele
Is whetted now ageynes me to kene.

My dere herte, and best beloved fo,
Why lyketh yow to do me al this wo,
What have I doon that greveth yow, or sayd,
But for I serve and love yow and no mo?
And whylst I live, I wol do ever so;
And therfor, swete, ne beth nat evil apayd.
For so good and so fair as that ye be,
Hit were a right gret wonder but ye hadde
Of alle servants, bothe goode and badde;
And leest worthy of alle hem, I am he.

But nevertheles, my righte lady swete,

Thogh that I be unconning and unmete
To serve as I best coude ay your hynesse,
Yit is ther fayner noon, that wolde I hete,
Than I, to do yow ese, or elles bete
Whatso I wiste were to yow distresse.
And hadde I might as good as I have wille,
Than shulde ye fele wher it wer so or noon;
For in this worlde living is ther noon
That fayner wolde your hertes wil fulfille.

For bothe I love, and eek dreed yow so sore,
And algates moot, and have doon yow, ful
    yore,
That bet loved is noon, ne never shal;
And yit I wolde beseche yow of no more
But leveth wel, and be nat wrooth therfore,
And lat me serve yow forth; lo! this is al.
For I am nat so hardy ne so wood
For to desire that ye shulde love me;
For wel I wot, allas! that may nat be;
I am so litel worthy, and ye so good.

For ye be oon the worthiest on-lyve,
And I the most unlykly for to thryve;
Yit, for al this, now witeth ye right wele,
That ye ne shul me from your service dryve
That I nil ay, with alle my wittes fyve,
Serve yow trewly, what wo so that I fele.
For I am set on yow in swich manere
That, thogh ye never wil upon me rewe,
I moste yow love, and ever been as trewe
As any can or may on-lyve here.

The more that I love yow, goodly free,
The lasse fynde I that ye loven me;
Allas! whan shal that harde wit amende?
Wher is now al your wommanly pitee,
Your gentilesse and your debonairtee,
Wil ye nothing therof upon me spende?
And so hool, swete, as I am youres al,
And so gret wil as I have yow to serve,
Now, certes, and ye lete me thus sterve,
Yit have ye wonne theron but a smal.

For, at my knowing, I do nothing why,
And this I wol beseche yow hertely,
That, ther ever ye finde, whyl ye live,
A trewer servant to yow than am I,
Leveth me thanne, and sleeth me hardely,
And I my deeth to you wol al forgive.
And if ye finde no trewer man than me,
Why will ye suffre than that I thus spille,
And for no maner gilt but my good wille?
As good wer thanne untrewe as trewe to be.

But I, my lyf and deeth, to yow obeye,
And with right buxom herte hoolly I preye,
As is your moste plesure, so doth by me;
Wel lever is me lyken yow and deye
Than for to any thing or thinke or seye
That mighte yow offende in any tyme.
And therfor, swete, rewe on my peynes
    smerte,

And of your grace granteth me som drope;
For elles may me laste ne blis ne hope,
Ne dwellen in my trouble careful herte.

WOMANLY NOBLESSE.
Balade that Chaucier made.

O hath my herte caught
in rémembraunce
Your beautè hool, and
stedfast governaunce,
Your vertues allè, and
your hy noblesse,
That you to serve is set
al my plesaunce;
So wel me lykth your
womanly contenaunce,
Your fresshe fetures and your comlinesse,
That, whyl I live, my herte to his maistresse,
You hath ful chose, in trew persèveraunce,
Never to chaunge, for no maner distresse.

And sith I you shal do this observaunce
Al my lyf, withouten displesaunce,
You for to serve with al my besinesse,
Taketh me, lady, in your obeisaunce,
And have me somwhat in your souvenaunce.
My woful herte suffreth greet duresse;
And loke how humblely, with al simplesse,
My wil I cónforme to your ordenaunce,
As you best list, my peynes to redresse.

Considring eek how I hange in balaunce
In your servysè; swich, lof is my chaunce,
Abyding grace, whan that your gentilnesse
Of my gret wo list doon allegeaunce,
And with your pitè me som wyse avaunce,
In ful rebating of my hevinesse;
And thinkth, by reson, wommanly noblesse
Shuld nat desyre for to doon outrance
Theras she findeth noon unbuxumnesse.

Lenvoye.

UCTOUR of norture, lady of
plesaunce,
Soveraine of beautè, flour of
wommanhede,
Take ye non hede unto myn
ignoraunce,
But this receyveth of your goodlihede,
Thinking that I have caught in rémembraunce
Your beautè hool, your stedfast governaunce.

HEERE BIGYNNETH THE ROMAUNT OF THE ROSE

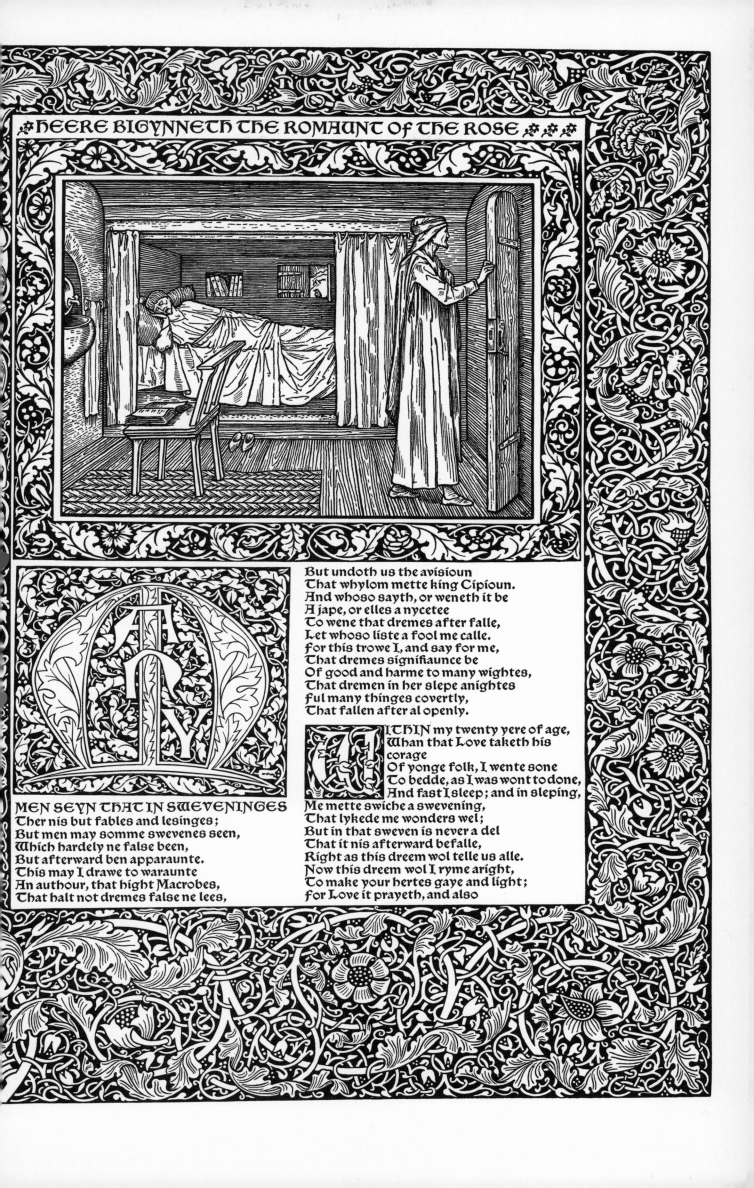

But undoth us the avisioun
That whylom mette king Cipioun.
And whoso sayth, or weneth it be
A jape, or elles a nycetee
To wene that dremes after falle,
Let whoso liste a fool me calle.
for this trowe I, and say for me,
That dremes signifiaunce be
Of good and harme to many wightes,
That dremen in her slepe anightes
ful many thinges covertly,
That fallen after al openly.

ITHIN my twenty yere of age,
Whan that Love taketh his
corage
Of yonge folk, I wente sone
To bedde, as I was wont to done,
And fast I sleep; and in sleping,
Me mette swiche a swevening,
That lykede me wonders wel;
But in that sweven is never a del
That it nis afterward befalle,
Right as this dreem wol telle us alle.
Now this dreem wol I ryme aright,
To make your hertes gaye and light;
for Love it prayeth, and also

MEN SEYN THAT IN SWEVENINGES
Ther nis but fables and lesinges;
But men may somme swevenes seen,
Which hardely ne false been,
But afterward ben apparaunte.
This may I drawe to waraunte
An authour, that hight Macrobes,
That halt not dremes false ne lees,

Commaundeth me that it be so
And if ther any aske me,
Whether that it be he or she,
How that this book the which is here
Shal hote, that I rede you here;
It is the Romance of the Rose,
In which al the art of love I close.

THE mater fair is of to make;
God graunte in gree that she it take
For whom that it begonnen is!
And that is she that hath, ywis,
So mochel prys; and therto she
So worthy is biloved be,
That she wel oughte, of prys and right,
Be cleped Rose of every wight.

THAT it was May me thoughte tho,
It is fyve yere or more ago;
That it was May, thus dremed me,
In tyme of love and jolitee,
That al thing ginneth waxen gay,
For ther is neither busk nor hay
In May, that it nil shrouded been,
And it with newe leves wreen.
These wodes eek recoveren grene,
That drye in winter been to sene;
And the erthe wexeth proud withalle,
For swote dewes that on it falle,
And al the pore estat forget
In which that winter hadde it set,
And than bicometh the ground so proud
That it wol have a newe shroud,
And maketh so queynt his robe and fayr
That it hath hewes an hundred payr
Of gras and floures, inde and pers,
And many hewes ful dyvers:
That is the robe I mene, ywis,
Through which the ground to preisen is.

THE briddes, that han left hir song,
Whyl they han suffred cold so strong
In wedres grille, and derk to sighte,
Ben in May, for the sonne brighte,
So glade, that they shewe in singing,
That in hir herte is swich lyking,
That they mote singen and be light.
Than doth the nightingale hir might
To make noyse, and syngen blythe.
Than is blisful, many a sythe,
The chelaundre and the papingay.
Than yonge folk entenden ay
For to ben gay and amorous,
The tyme is than so savorous.
Hard is his herte that loveth nought
In May, whan al this mirth is wrought;
Whan he may on these braunches here
The smale briddes singen clere
Hir blisful swete song pitous;
And in this sesoun delytous,
Whan love affrayeth alle thing,
Me thoughte anight, in my sleping,
Right in my bed, ful redily,
That it was by the morowe erly,
And up I roos, and gan me clothe;
Anoon I wissh myn hondes bothe;
A sylvre nedle forth I drogh

Out of an aguiler queynt ynogh,
And gan this nedle threde anon;
For out of toun me list to gon
The sowne of briddes for to here,
That on thise busshes singen clere.
And in the swete sesoun that leef is,
With a threde basting my slevis,
Aloon I wente in my playing,
The smale foules song harkning;
That peyned hem ful many a payre
To singe on bowes blosmed fayre.
Jolif and gay, ful of gladnesse,
Toward a river I gan me dresse,
That I herde renne faste by;
For fairer playing non saugh I
Than playen me by that riveer,
For from an hille that stood ther neer
Cam doun the streem ful stif and bold.
Cleer was the water, and as cold
As any welle is, sooth to seyne;
And somdel lasse it was than Seine,
But it was straighter wel away.
And never saugh I, er that day,
The water that so wel lyked me;
And wonder glad was I to see
That lusty place, and that riveer;
And with that water that ran so cleer
My face I wissh. Tho saugh I wel
The botme paved everydel
With gravel, ful of stones shene.
The medewe softe, swote, and grene,
Beet right on the watersyde.
Ful cleer was than the morowtyde,
And ful attempre, out of drede.
Tho gan I walke through the mede,
Dounward ay in my pleying,
The riversyde costeying.

AND whan I had a whyle goon,
I saugh a Gardin right anoon,
Ful long and brood, and everydel
Enclos it was, and walled wel,
With hye walles enbat-
ailled,
Portrayed without, and wel entailled
With many riche portraitures;
And bothe images and peyntures
Gan I biholde bisily.
And I wol telle you, redily,
Of thilke images the semblaunce,
As fer as I have remembraunce.

AMIDDE saugh I Hate stonde,
That for hir wrathe, ire, and onde,
Semed to been a moveresse,
An angry wight, a chideresse;
And ful of gyle, and fel corage,
By semblaunt was that ilke image.
And she was nothing wel arrayed,
But lyk a wood womman afrayed;
Yfrounced foule was hir visage,
And grenning for dispitous rage;

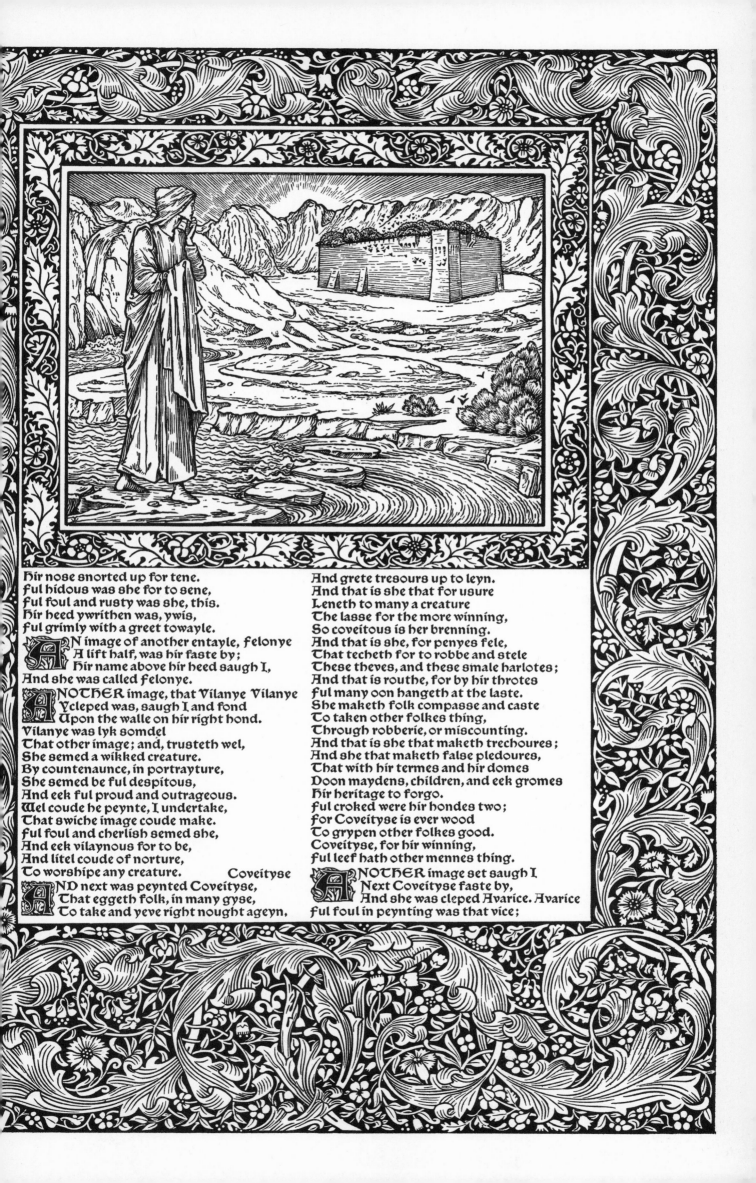

Hir nose snorted up for tene.
ful hidous was she for to sene,
ful foul and rusty was she, this.
Hir heed ywrithen was, ywis,
ful grimly with a greet towayle.

AN image of another entayle, Felonye
A lift half, was hir faste by;
Hir name above hir heed saugh I,
And she was called Felonye.

ANOTHER image, that Vilanye Vilanye
Ycleped was, saugh I and fond
Upon the walle on hir right hond.
Vilanye was lyk somdel
That other image; and, trusteth wel,
She semed a wikked creature.
By countenaunce, in portrayture,
She semed be ful despitous,
And eek ful proud and outrageous.
Wel coude he peynte, I undertake,
That swiche image coude make.
ful foul and cherlish semed she,
And eek vilaynous for to be,
And litel coude of norture,
To worshipe any creature.   Coveityse

AND next was peynted Coveityse,
That eggeth folk, in many gyse,
To take and yeve right nought ageyn,

And grete tresours up to leyn.
And that is she that for usure
Leneth to many a creature
The lasse for the more winning,
So coveitous is her brenning.
And that is she, for penyes fele,
That techeth for to robbe and stele
These theves, and these smale harlotes;
And that is routhe, for by hir throtes
ful many oon hangeth at the laste.
She maketh folk compasse and caste
To taken other folkes thing,
Through robberie, or miscounting.
And that is she that maketh trechoures;
And she that maketh false pledoures,
That with hir termes and hir domes
Doon maydens, children, and eek gromes
Hir heritage to forgo.
ful croked were hir hondes two;
for Coveityse is ever wood
To grypen other folkes good.
Coveityse, for hir winning,
ful leef hath other mennes thing.

ANOTHER image set saugh I
Next Coveityse faste by,
And she was cleped Avarice. Avarice
ful foul in peynting was that vice;

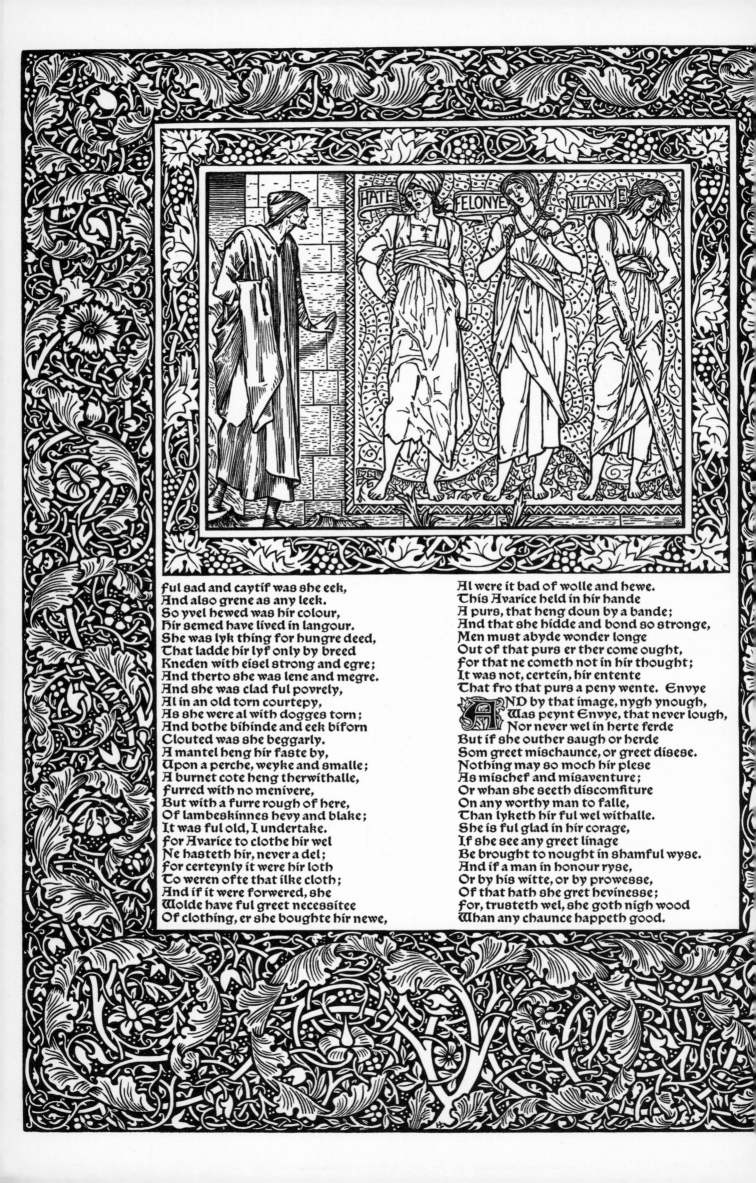

ful sad and caytif was she eek,
And also grene as any leek.
So yvel hewed was hir colour,
Hir semed have lived in langour.
She was lyk thing for hungre deed,
That ladde hir lyf only by breed
Kneden with eisel strong and egre;
And therto she was lene and megre.
And she was clad ful povrely,
Al in an old torn courtepy,
As she were al with dogges torn;
And bothe bihinde and eek biforn
Clouted was she beggarly.
A mantel heng hir faste by,
Upon a perche, weyke and smalle;
A burnet cote heng therwithalle,
furred with no menivere,
But with a furre rough of here,
Of lambeskinnes hevy and blake;
It was ful old, I undertake.
for Avarice to clothe hir wel
Ne hasteth hir, never a del;
for certeynly it were hir loth
To weren ofte that ilke cloth;
And if it were forwered, she
Wolde have ful greet necessitee
Of clothing, er she boughte hir newe,

Al were it bad of wolle and hewe.
This Avarice held in hir hande
A purs, that heng doun by a bande;
And that she hidde and bond so stronge,
Men must abyde wonder longe
Out of that purs er ther come ought,
for that ne cometh not in hir thought;
It was not, certein, hir entente
That fro that purs a peny wente. Envye
AND by that image, nygh ynough,
Was peynt Envye, that never lough,
Nor never wel in herte ferde
But if she outher saugh or herde
Som greet mischaunce, or greet disese.
Nothing may so moch hir plese
As mischef and misaventure;
Or whan she seeth discomfiture
On any worthy man to falle,
Than lyketh hir ful wel withalle.
She is ful glad in hir corage,
If she see any greet linage
Be brought to nought in shamful wyse.
And if a man in honour ryse,
Or by his witte, or by prowesse,
Of that hath she gret hevinesse;
for, trusteth wel, she goth nigh wood
Whan any chaunce happeth good.

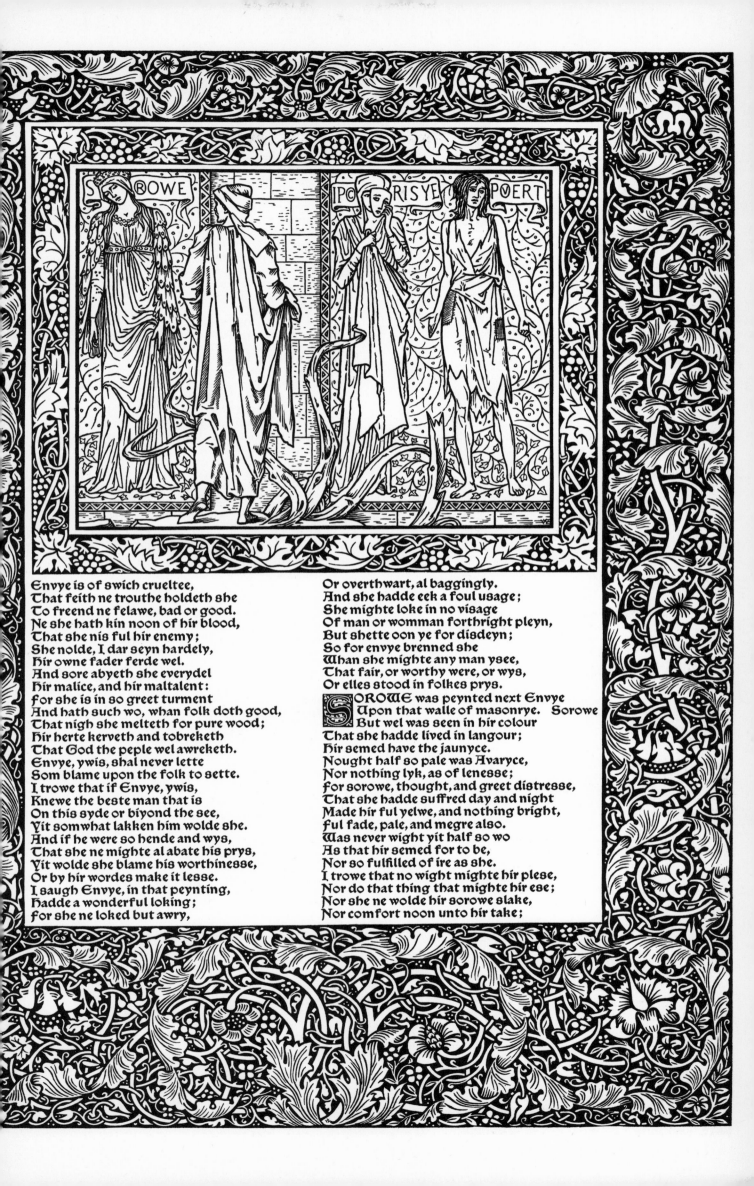

Envye is of swich crueltee,
That feith ne trouthe holdeth she
To freend ne felawe, bad or good.
Ne she hath kin noon of hir blood,
That she nis ful hir enemy;
She nolde, I dar seyn hardely,
Hir owne fader ferde wel.
And sore abyeth she everydel
Hir malice, and hir maltalent:
for she is in so greet turment
And hath such wo, whan folk doth good,
That nigh she melteth for pure wood;
Hir herte kerveth and tobreketh
That God the peple wel awreketh.
Envye, ywis, shal never lette
Som blame upon the folk to sette.
I trowe that if Envye, ywis,
Knewe the beste man that is
On this syde or biyond the see,
Yit somwhat lakken him wolde she.
And if he were so hende and wys,
That she ne mighte al abate his prys,
Yit wolde she blame his worthinesse,
Or by hir wordes make it lesse.
I saugh Envye, in that peynting,
Hadde a wonderful loking;
for she ne loked but awry,

Or overthwart, al baggingly.
And she hadde eek a foul usage;
She mighte loke in no visage
Of man or womman forthright pleyn,
But shette oon ye for disdeyn;
So for envye brenned she
Whan she mighte any man ysee,
That fair, or worthy were, or wys,
Or elles stood in folkes prys.
SOROWE was peynted next Envye
Upon that walle of masonrye. Sorowe
But wel was seen in hir colour
That she hadde lived in langour;
Hir semed have the jaunyce.
Nought half so pale was Avaryce,
Nor nothing lyk, as of lenesse;
for sorowe, thought, and greet distresse,
That she hadde suffred day and night
Made hir ful yelwe, and nothing bright,
ful fade, pale, and megre also.
Was never wight yit half so wo
As that hir semed for to be,
Nor so fulfilled of ire as she.
I trowe that no wight mighte hir plese,
Nor do that thing that mighte hir ese;
Nor she ne wolde hir sorowe slake,
Nor comfort noon unto hir take;

So depe was hir wo bigonnen,
And eek hir herte in angre ronnen;
A sorowful thing wel semed she.
Nor she hadde nothing slowe be
for to forcracchen al hir face,
And for to rende in many place
Hir clothes, and for to tere hir swire,
As she that was fulfilled of ire;
And al totorn lay eek hir here
Aboute hir shuldres, here and there,
As she that hadde it al torent
for angre and for maltalent.
And eek I telle you certeynly
How that she weep ful tenderly.
In world nis wight so hard of herte
That hadde seen hir sorowes smerte,
That nolde have had of hir pitee,
So wobigoon a thing was she.
She al todasshte hirself for wo,
And smoot togider her handes two.
To sorwe was she ful ententyf,
That woful recchelees caityf;
Hir roughte litel of pleying,
Or of clipping or of kissing;
for whoso sorweful is in herte
Him liste not to pleye ne sterte,
Nor for to daunsen, ne to singe,
Ne may his herte in temper bringe
To make joye on even or morowe;
for joye is contraire unto sorowe.

ELDE was peynted after this,
That shorter was a foot, ywis,
Than she was wont in her yonghede.
Unnethe hirself she mighte fede;
So feble and eek so old was she
That faded was al hir beautee.
ful salowe was waxen hir colour,
Hir heed forhoor was, whyt as flour.
Ywis, gret qualm ne were it noon,
Ne sinne, although hir lyf were gon.
Al woxen was hir body unwelde,
And drye, and dwyned al for elde.
A foul forwelked thing was she
That whylom round and softe had be.
Hir eres shoken fast withalle,
As from her heed they wolde falle.
Hir face frounced and forpyned,
And bothe hir hondes lorn, fordwyned.
So old she was that she ne wente
A foot, but it were by potente.

THE Tyme, that passeth night and day,
And restelees travayleth ay,
And steleth from us so prively,
That to us seemeth sikerly
That it in oon point dwelleth ever,
And certes, it ne resteth never,
But goth so faste, and passeth ay,
That ther nis man that thinke may
What tyme that now present is:
Asketh at these clerkes this;
for er men thinke it redily,
Three tymes been ypassed by.
The tyme, that may not sojourne,
But goth, and never may retourne,

As water that doun renneth ay,
But never drope retourne may;
Ther may nothing as tyme endure,
Metal, nor erthely creature;
for alle thing it fret and shal:
The tyme eek, that chaungeth al,
And al doth waxe and fostred be,
And alle thing distroyeth he:
The tyme, that eldeth our auncessours
And eldeth kinges and emperours,
And that us alle shal overcomen
Er that deeth us shal have nomen:
The tyme, that hath al in welde
To elden folk, had maad hir elde
So inly, that, to my witing,
She mighte helpe hirself nothing,
But turned ageyn unto childhede;
She had nothing hirself to lede,
Ne wit ne pith inwith hir holde
More than a child of two yeer olde.
But natheles, I trowe that she
Was fair sumtyme, and fresh to see,
Whan she was in hir rightful age:
But she was past al that passage
And was a doted thing bicomen.
A furred cope on had she nomen;
Wel had she clad hirself and warm,
for cold mighte elles doon hir harm.
These olde folk have alwey colde,
Hir kinde is swiche, whan they ben olde.

ANOTHER thing was doon ther write,
That semede lyk an ipocrite,
And it was cleped Pope holy.
That ilke is she that prively
Ne spareth never a wikked dede,
Whan men of hir taken non hede;
And maketh hir outward precious,
With pale visage and pitous,
And semeth a simple creature;
But ther nis no misaventure
That she ne thenketh in hir corage.
ful lyk to hir was that image,
That maked was lyk hir semblaunce.
She was ful simple of countenaunce,
And she was clothed and eek shod,
As she were, for the love of God,
Yolden to religioun,
Swich semed hir devocioun.
A sauter held she faste in honde,
And bisily she gan to fonde
To make many a feynt prayere
To God, and to his seyntes dere.
Ne she was gay, fresh, ne jolyf,
But semed be ful ententyf
To gode werkes, and to faire,
And therto she had on an haire.
Ne certes, she was fat nothing,
But semed wery for fasting;
Of colour pale and deed was she.
from hir the gate shal werned be
Of paradys, that blisful place;
for swich folk maketh lene hir face,
As Crist seith in his evangyle,
To gete hem prys in toun a whyle;

And for a litel glorie veine
They lesen God and eek his reine.
AND alderlast of everichoon,
Was peynted Povert al aloon,
That not a peny hadde in wolde,
Although that she hir clothes solde,
And though she shulde anhonged be;
For naked as a worm was she.
And if the weder stormy were,
For colde she shulde have deyed there.
She nadde on but a streit old sak,
And many a clout on it ther stak;
This was hir cote and hir mantel,
No more was there, never a del,
To clothe her with; I undertake,
Gret leyser hadde she to quake.
And she was put, that I of talke,
Fer fro these other, up in an halke;
There lurked and there coured she,
For povre thing, wherso it be,
Is shamfast, and despysed ay.
Acursed may wel be that day,
That povre man conceyved is;
For God wot, al to selde, ywis,
Is any povre man wel fed,
Or wel arayed or ycled,
Or wel biloved, in swich wyse
In honour that he may aryse.
ALLE these thinges, wel avysed,
As I have you er this devysed,
With gold and asure over alle
Depeynted were upon the walle.
Squar was the wal, & high somdel;
Enclosed, and ybarred wel,
In stede of hegge, was that gardin;
Com never shepherde therin.
Into that gardyn, wel ywrought,
Whoso that me coude have brought,
By laddre, or elles by degree,
It wolde wel have lyked me.
For swich solace, swich joye, and play,
I trowe that never man ne say,
As in that place delitous.
The gardin was not daungerous
To herberwe briddes many oon.
So riche a yerd was never noon
Of briddes songe, and braunches grene.
Therin were briddes mo, I wene,
Than been in alle the rewme of Fraunce.
Ful blisful was the accordaunce
Of swete and pitous songe they made,
For al this world it oughte glade.
And I myself so mery ferde,
Whan I hir blisful songes herde,
That for an hundred pound nolde I,
If that the passage openly
Hadde been unto me free
That I nolde entren for to see
Thassemblee, God kepe it fro care!
Of briddes, whiche therinne were,
That songen, through hir mery throtes,
Daunces of love, and mery notes.
Whan I thus herde foules singe,
I fel faste in a weymentinge,

r 4

By which art, or by what engyn
I mighte come in that gardyn;
But way I couthe finde noon
Into that gardin for to goon.
Ne nought wiste I if that ther were
Eyther hole or place o,where,
By which I mighte have entree;
Ne ther was noon to teche me;
For I was al aloon, ywis,
Ful wo and anguissous of this.
Til atte laste bithoughte I me,
That by no weye ne mighte it be;
That ther nas laddre or wey to passe,
Or hole, into so fair a place.
THO gan I go a ful gret pas
Envyroning even in compas
The closing of the square wal,
Til that I fond a wiket smal
So shet, that I ne mighte in goon,
And other entree was ther noon.
UPON this dore I gan to smyte,
That was so fetys and so lyte;
For other wey coude I not seke.
Ful long I shoof, and knokked eke,
And stood ful long & oft herkning
If that I herde a wight coming;
Til that the dore of thilke entree
A mayden curteys opened me.
Hir heer was as yelowe of hewe
As any basin scoured newe.
Hir flesh as tendre as is a chike,
With bente browes, smothe and slike;
And by mesure large were
The opening of hir yën clere.
Hir nose of good proporcioun,
Hir yën greye as a faucoun,
With swete breeth and wel savoured.
Hir face whyt and wel coloured,
With litel mouth, and round to see;
A clove chin eek hadde she.
Hir nekke was of good fasoun
In lengthe and gretnesse, by resoun,
Withoute bleyne, scabbe, or royne.
Fro Jerusalem unto Burgoyne
Ther nis a fairer nekke, ywis,
To fele how smothe and softe it is.
Hir throte, also whyt of hewe
As snow on braunche snowed newe.
Of body ful wel wrought was she
Men neded not, in no cuntree,
A fairer body for to seke.
And of fyn orfrays had she eke
A chapelet: so semly oon
Ne wered never mayde upon;
And faire above that chapelet
A rose gerland had she set.
She hadde in honde a gay mirour,
And with a riche gold tressour
Hir heed was tressed queyntely;
Hir sleves sewed fetisly.
And for to kepe hir hondes faire
Of gloves whyte she hadde a paire.
And she hadde on a cote of grene
Of cloth of Gaunt; withouten wene,

The
Romaunt
of the
Rose

The
Door

Ydel-
nesse

247

Wel semed by hir apparayle
She was not wont to greet travayle.
for whan she kempt was fetisly,
And wel arayed and richely,
Thanne had she doon al hir journee;
for mery and wel bigoon was she.
She ladde a lusty lyf in May,
She hadde no thought, by night ne day,
Of nothing, but it were oonly
To graythe hir wel and uncouthly.

WHAN that this dore hadde opened me
This mayden, semely for to see,
I thanked hir as I best mighte,
And axede hir how that she highte,
And what she was, I axede eke.
And she to me was nought unmeke,
Ne of hir answer daungerous,
But faire answerde, and seide thus:

LO, sir, my name is Ydelnesse;
So clepe men me, more & lesse.
ful mighty and ful riche am I,
And that of oon thing, namely;
for I entende to nothing
But to my joye, and my pleying,
And for to kembe and tresse me.
Aqueynted am I, and privee
With Mirthe, lord of this gardyn,

That fro the lande of Alexandryn
Made the trees be hider fet,
That in this gardin been yset.
And whan the trees were woxen on highte,
This wal, that stant here in thy sighte,
Dide Mirthe enclosen al aboute;
And these images, al withoute,
He dide hem bothe entaile and peynte,
That neither ben jolyf ne queynte,
But they ben ful of sorowe and wo,
As thou hast seen a whyle ago.

AND ofte tyme, him to solace
Sir Mirthe cometh into this place,
And eek with him cometh his meynee,
That liven in lust and jolitee.
And now is Mirthe therin, to here
The briddes, how they singen clere,
The mavis and the nightingale,
And other joly briddes smale.
And thus he walketh to solace
Him and his folk; for swetter place
To pleyen in he may not finde,
Although he soughte oon intil Inde.
The altherfairest folk to see
That in this world may founde be
Hath Mirthe with him in his route,
That folowen him alwayes aboute.

WHEN Ydelnesse had told al this,
And I hadde herkned wel, ywis,
Than seide I to dame Ydelnesse:
Now also wisly God me blesse,
Sith Mirthe, that is so fair and free,
Is in this yerde with his meynee,
fro thilke assemblee, if I may,
Shal no man werne me today,
That I this night ne mote it see.
for, wel wene I, ther with him be
A fair and joly companye
fulfilled of alle curtesye.
And forth, withoute wordes mo,
In at the wiket wente I tho,
That Ydelnesse hadde opened me,
Into that gardin fair to see.

AND whan I was therin, ywis,
Myn herte was ful glad of
this.
for wel wende I ful sikerly
Have been in paradys
erthely;
So fair it was, that, trusteth
wel,
It semed a place espirituel.
for certes, as at my devys,
Ther is no place in paradys
So good in for to dwelle or be
As in that Gardin, thoughte me;
for there was many a brid singing,
Throughout the yerde al thringing.
In many places were nightingales,
Alpes, finches, and wodewales,
That in her swete song delyten
In thilke place as they habyten.
Ther mighte men see many flokkes
Of turtles and of laverokkes.
Chalaundres fele saw I there,
That wery, nigh forsongen were.
And thrustles, terins, and mavys,
That songen for to winne hem prys,
And eek to sormounte in hir song
These other briddes hem among.
By note made fair servyse
These briddes, that I you devyse;
They songe hir song as faire and wel
As angels doon espirituel.
And, trusteth wel, whan I hem herde,
full lustily and wel I ferde;
for never yit swich melodye
Was herd of man that mighte dye.
Swich swete song was hem among,
That me thoughte it no briddes song,
But it was wonder lyk to be
Song of mermaydens of the see;
That, for her singing is so clere,
Though we mermaydens clepe hem here
In English, as in our usaunce,
Men clepen hem sereyns in fraunce.
Ententif weren for to singe
These briddes, that nought unkunninge
Were of hir craft, and apprentys,
But of hir song sotyl and wys.

And certes, whan I herde hir song,
And saw the grene place among,
In herte I wex so wonder gay,
That I was never erst, er that day,
So jolyf, nor so wel bigo,
Ne mery in herte, as I was tho.
And than wiste I, and saw ful wel,
That Ydelnesse me served wel,
That me putte in swich jolitee.
Hir freend wel oughte I for to be,
Sith she the dore of that gardyn
Hadde opened, and me leten in.
from hennesforth how that I wroughte,
I shal you tellen, as me thoughte.
first, wherof Mirthe served there,
And eek what folk ther with him were,
Withoute fable I wol descryve.
And of that gardin eek as blyve
I wol you tellen after this.
The faire fasoun al, ywis,
That wel ywrought was for the nones,
I may not telle you al at ones:
But as I may and can, I shal
By ordre tellen you it al.
ful fair servyse and eek ful swete
These briddes maden as they sete.
Layes of love, ful wel sowning
They songen in hir jargoning;
Summe highe and summe eek lowe songe
Upon the braunches grene yspronge.
The sweetnesse of hir melodye
Made al myn herte in reverdye.
And whan that I hadde herd, I trowe,
These briddes singing on a rowe,
Than mighte I not withholde me
That I ne wente in for to see
Sir Mirthe; for my desiring
Was him to seen, over alle thing,
His countenaunce and his manere:
That sighte was to me ful dere.

THO wente I forth on my right hond
Doun by a litel path I fond
Of mentes ful, and fenel grene;
And faste by, withoute wene,
Sir Mirthe I fond; and right anoon
Unto sir Mirthe gan I goon,
Theras he was, him to solace.
And with him, in that lusty place,
So fair folk and so fresh hadde he,
That whan I saw, I wondred me
fro whennes swich folk mighte come,
So faire they weren, alle and some;
for they were lyk, as to my sighte,
To angels, that ben fethered brighte.

THIS folk, of which I telle you so,
Upon a carole wenten tho.
A lady caroled hem, that highte
Gladnes, the blisful and the lighte;
Wel coude she singe and lustily,
Non half so wel and semely,
And make in song swich refreininge,
It sat hir wonder wel to singe.
Hir vois ful cleer was and ful swete.

249

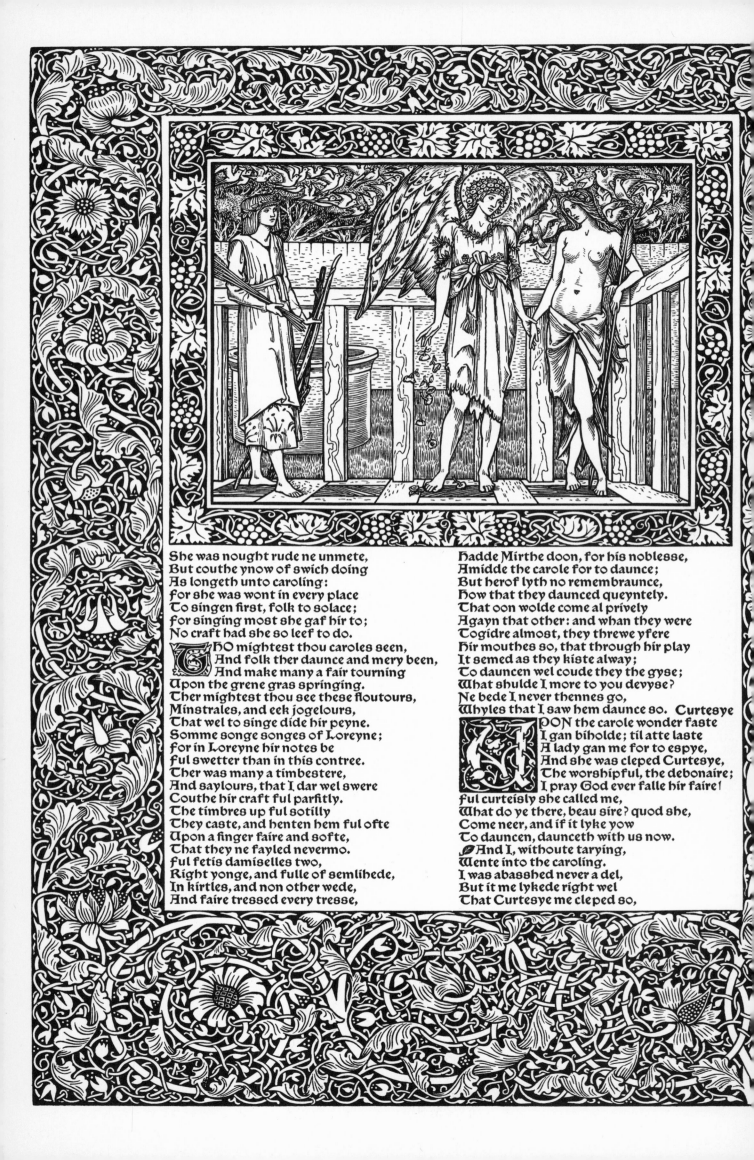

She was nought rude ne unmete,
But couthe ynow of swich doing
As longeth unto caroling:
for she was wont in every place
To singen first, folk to solace;
for singing most she gaf hir to;
No craft had she so leef to do.
THO mightest thou caroles seen,
And folk ther daunce and mery been,
And make many a fair tourning
Upon the grene gras springing.
Ther mightest thou see these floutours,
Minstrales, and eek jogelours,
That wel to singe dide hir peyne.
Somme songe songes of Loreyne;
for in Loreyne hir notes be
ful swetter than in this contree.
Ther was many a timbestere,
And saylours, that I dar wel swere
Couthe hir craft ful parfitly.
The timbres up ful sotilly
They caste, and henten hem ful ofte
Upon a finger faire and softe,
That they ne fayled nevermo.
ful fetis damiselles two,
Right yonge, and fulle of semlihede,
In kirtles, and non other wede,
And faire tressed every tresse,

Hadde Mirthe doon, for his noblesse,
Amidde the carole for to daunce;
But herof lyth no remembraunce,
How that they daunced queyntely.
That oon wolde come al prively
Agayn that other: and whan they were
Togidre almost, they threwe yfere
Hir mouthes so, that through hir play
It semed as they kiste alway;
To dauncen wel coude they the gyse;
What shulde I more to you devyse?
Ne bede I never thennes go,
Whyles that I saw hem daunce so. Curtesye
UPON the carole wonder faste
I gan biholde; til atte laste
A lady gan me for to espye,
And she was cleped Curtesye,
The worshipful, the debonaire;
I pray God ever falle hir faire!
ful curteisly she called me,
What do ye there, beau sire? quod she,
Come neer, and if it lyke yow
To dauncen, daunceth with us now.
And I, withoute tarying,
Wente into the caroling.
I was abasshed never a del,
But it me lykede right wel
That Curtesye me cleped so,

And bad me on the daunce go.
For if I hadde durst, certeyn
I wolde have caroled right fayn,
As man that was to daunce blythe.
Than gan I loken ofte sythe
The shap, the bodies, and the cheres,
The countenaunce and the maneres
Of alle the folk that daunced there,
And I shal telle what they were.

AL fair was Mirthe, ful long & high;
A fairer man I never sigh.
As round as appel was his face,
Ful rody and whyt in every place.
Fetys he was and wel beseye,
With metely mouth and yën greye;
His nose by mesure wrought ful right;
Crisp was his heer, and eek ful bright.
His shuldres of a large brede,
And smalish in the girdilstede.
He semed lyk a portreiture,
So noble he was of his stature,
So fair, so joly, and so fetys,
With limes wrought at poynt devys,
Deliver, smert, and of gret might;
Ne sawe thou never man so light.
Of berde unnethe hadde he nothing,
For it was in the firste spring.
Ful yong he was, and mery of thought,
And in samyt, with briddes wrought,
And with gold beten fetisly,
His body was clad ful richely.
Wrought was his robe in straunge gyse,
And al toslitered for queyntyse
In many a place, lowe and hye.
And shod he was with greet maistrye,
With shoon decoped, and with laas.
By druerye, and by solas,
His leef a rosen chapelet
Had maad, and on his heed it set.

AND wite ye who was his leef?
Dame Gladnes ther was him so leef,
That singeth so wel with glad
corage,
That from she was twelve yeer of
age,
She of hir love graunt him made.
Sir Mirthe hir by the finger hadde
In daunsing, and she him also;
Gret love was atwixe hem two.
Bothe were they faire and brighte of hewe;
She semede lyk a rose newe
Of colour, and hir flesh so tendre,
That with a brere smale and slendre
Men mighte it cleve, I dar wel sayn.
Hir forheed, frounceles al playn.
Bente were hir browes two,
Hir yën greye, and gladde also,
That laughede ay in hir semblaunt,
First or the mouth, by covenaunt.
I not what of hir nose descryve;
So fair hath no womman alyve.
Hir heer was yelowe, and cleer shyning,
I wot no lady so lyking.
Of orfrays fresh was hir gerland;

I, whiche seen have a thousand,
Saugh never, ywis, no gerlond yit,
So wel ywrought of silk as it.
And in an over-gilt samyt
Clad she was, by gret delyt,
Of which hir leef a robe werde,
The myrier she in herte ferde.

AND next hir wente, on hir other syde,
The God of Love, that can devyde
Love, as him lyketh it to be.
But he can cherles daunten, he,
And maken folkes pryde fallen.
And he can wel these lordes thrallen,
And ladies putte at lowe degree,
Whan he may hem to proude see.

THIS God of Love of his fasoun
Was lyk no knave, ne quistroun;
His beautee gretly was to pryse.
But of his robe to devyse
I drede encombred for to be.
For nought yclad in silk was he,
But al in floures and flourettes,
Ypainted al with amorettes;
And with losenges and scochouns,
With briddes, libardes, and lyouns,
And other beestes wrought ful wel.
His garnement was everydel
Yportreyd and ywrought with floures,
By dyvers medling of coloures.
Floures ther were of many gyse
Yset by compas in assyse;
Ther lakked no flour, to my dome,
Ne nought so muche as flour of brome,
Ne violete, ne eek pervenke,
Ne flour non, that man can on thenke,
And many a roseleef ful long
Was entermedled theramong:
And also on his heed was set
Of roses rede a chapelet.
But nightingales, a ful gret route,
That flyen over his heed aboute,
The leves felden as they flyen;
And he was al with briddes wryen,
With popinjay, with nightingale,
With chalaundre, and with wodewale,
With finch, with lark, and with archaungel.
He semede as he were an aungel
That doun were comen fro hevene clere.

LOVE hadde with him a bachelere,
That he made alweyes with him be;
Swete-Loking cleped was he.
This bachelere stood biholding
The daunce, and in his honde holding
Turke bowes two hadde he.
That oon of hem was of a tree
That bereth a fruyt of savour wikke;
Ful croked was that foule stikke,
And knotty here and there also,
And blak as bery, or any slo.
That other bowe was of a plante
Withoute wem, I dar warante,
Ful even, and by proporcioun
Tretys and long, of good fasoun.
And it was peynted wel and thwiten,

251

And over-al diapred and writen
With ladies and with bacheleres,
Ful lightsom and ful glad of cheres.
These bowes two held Swete-Loking,
That semed lyk no gadeling.
And ten brode arowes held he there,
Of which five in his right hond were.
But they were shaven wel and dight,
Nokked and fethered aright;
And al they were with gold bigoon,
And stronge poynted everichoon,
And sharpe for to kerven weel.
But iren was ther noon ne steel;
For al was gold, men mighte it see,
Out-take the fetheres and the tree.

THE swiftest of these arowes fyve
Out of a bowe for to dryve,
And best yfethered for to flee,
And fairest eek, was cleped Beautee. Beautee
That other arowe, that hurteth lesse,
Was cleped, as I trowe, Simplesse. Simplesse
The thridde cleped was Fraunchyse, fraun-
That fethered was, in noble wyse, chyse
With valour and with curtesye.
The fourthe was cleped Companye, Com-
That hevy for to sheten is; panye
But whoso sheteth right, ywis,

May therwith doon gret harm and wo.
The fifte of these, and laste also,
Fair-Semblaunt men that arowe calle, Fair-
The leeste grevous of hem alle; Semblaunt
Yit can it make a ful gret wounde,
But he may hope his sores sounde,
That hurt is with that arowe, ywis;
His wo the bet bistowed is.
For he may soner have gladnesse,
His langour oughte be the lesse.

FYVE arowes were of other gyse,
That been ful foule to devyse;
For shaft and ende, sooth to telle,
Were al so black as feend in helle.

THE first of hem is called Pryde; Pryde
That other arowe next him bisyde,
It was ycleped Vilanye; Vilanye
That arowe was as with felonye
Envenimed, and with spitous blame.
The thridde of hem was cleped Shame. Shame
The fourthe, Wanhope cleped is, Wanhope
The fifte, the Newe-Thought, ywis. Newe-
Thought
THESE arowes that I speke Thought
of here,
Were alle fyve of oon manere,
And alle were they resemblable.
To hem was wel sitting and able

The foule croked bowe hidous,
That knotty was, and al roynous.
That bowe semede wel to shete
These arowes fyve, that been unmete,
Contrarie to that other fyve.
But though I telle not as blyve
Of hir power, ne of hir might,
Herafter shal I tellen right
The sothe, and eek signifiaunce,
As fer as I have remembraunce:
Al shal be seid, I undertake,
Er of this boke an ende I make.

OW come I to my tale ageyn.
But alderfirst, I wol you seyn
The fasoun and the counten-
aunces
Of al the folk that on the
daunce is.
The God of Love, jolyf and light,
Ladde on his honde a lady bright,
Of high prys, and of greet degree.
This lady called was Beautee,
As was an arowe, of which I tolde.
Ful wel ythewed was she holde;
Ne she was derk ne broun, but bright,
And cleer as is the monelight,
Ageyn whom alle the sterres semen
But smale candels, as we demen.

Hir flesh was tendre as dewe of flour,
Hir chere was simple as byrde in bour;
As whyt as lilie or rose in rys,
Hir face gentil and tretys.
Fetys she was, and smal to see;
No windred browes hadde she,
Ne popped hir, for it neded nought
To windre hir, or to peynte hir ought.
Hir tresses yelowe and longe straughten,
Unto hir heles doun they raughten:
Hir nose, hir mouth, and eye and cheke
Wel wrought, and al the remenaunt eke.
A ful grete savour and a swote
Me thinketh in myn herte rote,
As helpe me God, whan I remembre
Of the fasoun of every membre!
In world is noon so fair a wight;
For yong she was, and hewed bright,
Sadde, plesaunt, and fetys withalle,
Gente, and in hir middel smalle.   Richesse

ISYDE Beaute yede Richesse,
An high lady of greet noblesse,
And greet of prys in every place.
But whoso durste to hir
trespace,
Or til hir folk, in worde or dede,
He were ful hardy, out of drede;
For bothe she helpe and hindre may:

And that is nought of yisterday
That riche folk have ful gret might
To helpe, and eek to greve a wight.
The beste and grettest of valour
Diden Richesse ful gret honour,
And besy weren hir to serve;
For that they wolde hir love deserve,
They cleped hir Lady, grete and smalle;
This wyde world hir dredeth alle;
This world is al in hir daungere.
Hir court hath many a losengere,
And many a traytour envious,
That ben ful besy and curious
For to dispreisen, and to blame
That best deserven love and name.
Bifore the folk, hem to bigylen,
These losengeres hem preyse, and smylen,
And thus the world with word anoynten;
But afterward they prikke and poynten
The folk right to the bare boon
Bihinde her bak whan they ben goon,
And foule abate the folkes prys.
Ful many a worthy man and wys,
An hundred, have they don to dye,
These losengeres, through flaterye;
And maketh folk ful straunge be,
Theras hem oughte be prive.
Wel yvel mote they thryve and thee,
And yvel aryved mote they be,
These losengeres, ful of envye!
No good man loveth hir companye.
RICHESSE a robe of purpre on hadde,
Ne trowe not that I lye or madde;
For in this world is noon it liche,
Ne by a thousand deel so riche,
Ne noon so fair; for it ful wel
With orfrays leyd was everydel,
And portrayed in the ribaninges
Of dukes stories, and of kinges.
And with a bend of gold tasseled,
And knoppes fyne of gold ameled.
Aboute hir nekke of gentil entaile
Was shet the riche chevesaile,
In which ther was ful gret plentee
Of stones clere and bright to see.
RYCHESSE a girdel hadde upon,
The bokel of it was of a stoon
Of vertu greet, and mochel of might;
For whoso bar the stoon so bright,
Of venim thurte him nothing doute,
While he the stoon hadde him aboute.
That stoon was greetly for to love,
And til a riche mannes bihove
Worth al the gold in Rome and Fryse.
The mourdaunt, wrought in noble wyse,
Was of a stoon ful precious,
That was so fyn and vertuous,
That hool a man it coude make
Of palasye, and of toothake.
And yit the stoon hadde suche a grace,
That he was siker in every place,
Al thilke day, not blind to been,
That fasting mighte that stoon seen.

The barres were of gold ful fyne,
Upon a tissu of satyne,
Ful hevy, greet, and nothing light,
In everich was a besaunt-wight.
UPON the tresses of Richesse
Was set a cercle, for noblesse,
Of brend gold, that ful lighte shoon;
So fair, trowe I, was never noon.
But he were cunning, for the nones,
That coude devysen alle the stones
That in that cercle shewen clere;
It is a wonder thing to here.
For no man coude preyse or gesse
Of hem the valewe or richesse.
Rubyes there were, saphyres, jagounces,
And emeraudes, more than two ounces.
But al bifore, ful sotilly,
A fyn carboucle set saugh I.
The stoon so cleer was and so bright,
That, also sone as it was night,
Men mighte seen to go, for nede,
A myle or two, in lengthe and brede.
Swich light tho sprang out of the stoon,
That Richesse wonder brighte shoon,
Bothe hir heed, and al hir face,
And eke aboute hir al the place.
DAME Richesse on hir hond gan lede
A yong man ful of semelihede,
That she best loved of any thing;
His lust was muche in housholding.
In clothing was he ful fetys,
And lovede wel have hors of prys.
He wende to have reproved be
Of thefte or mordre, if that he
Hadde in his stable an hakeney.
And therfore he desyred ay
To been aqueynted with Richesse;
For al his purpos, as I gesse,
Was for to make greet dispense,
Withoute werning or defence.
And Richesse mighte it wel sustene,
And hir dispenses wel mayntene,
And him alwey swich plentee sende
Of gold and silver for to spende
Withoute lakking or daungere,
As it were poured in a garnere.
AND after on the daunce wente
Largesse, that sette al hir entente
For to be honourable and free;
Of Alexandres kin was she;
Hir moste joye was, ywis,
Whan that she yaf, & seide Have this.
Not Avarice, the foule caytyf,
Was half to grype so ententyf,
As Largesse is to yeve and spende.
And God ynough alwey hir sende,
So that the more she yaf away,
The more, ywis, she hadde alwey.
Gret loos hath Largesse, and gret prys;
For bothe wys folk and unwys
Were hoolly to hir baundon brought,
So wel with yiftes hath she wrought.
And if she hadde an enemy,

I trowe, that she coude craftily
Make him ful sone hir freend to be,
So large of yift and free was she;
Therfore she stood in love and grace
Of riche and povre in every place.
A ful gret fool is he, ywis,
That bothe riche and nigard is.
A lord may have no maner vice
That greveth more than avarice.
For nigard never with strengthe of hond
May winne him greet lordship or lond.
For freendes al to fewe hath he
To doon his wil perfourmed be.
And whoso wol have freendes here,
He may not holde his tresour dere.
For by ensample I telle this,
Right as an adamaunt, ywis,
Can drawen to him sotilly
The yren, that is leyd therby,
So draweth folkes hertes, ywis,
Silver and gold that yeven is.

LARGESSE hadde on a robe fresshe
Of riche purpur Sarsinesshe.
Wel fourmed was hir face and clere,
And opened had she hir colere;
For she right there hadde in present
Unto a lady maad present
Of a gold broche, ful wel wrought.
And certes, it missat hir nought;
For through hir smokke, wrought with silk,
The flesh was seen, as whyt as milk.
Largesse, that worthy was and wys,
Held by the honde a knight of prys,
Was sib to Arthour of Bretaigne.
And that was he that bar the enseigne
Of worship, and the gonfanoun.
And yit he is of swich renoun,
That men of him seye faire thinges
Bifore barouns, erles, and kinges.
This knight was comen al newely
Fro tourneyinge faste by;
Ther hadde he doon gret chivalrye
Through his vertu and his maistrye;
And for the love of his lemman
Had cast doun many a doughty man.

AND next him daunced dame
Fraunchyse,
Arrayed in ful noble gyse.
She was not broun ne dun of
hewe,
But whyt as snowe yfallen newe.
Hir nose was wrought at poynt devys,
For it was gentil and tretys;
With eyen gladde, and browes bente;
Hir heer doun to hir heles wente.
And she was simple as dowve on tree,
Ful debonaire of herte was she.
She durste never seyn ne do
But that thing that hir longed to.
And if a man were in distresse,
And for hir love in hevinesse,
Hir herte wolde have ful greet pitee,
She was so amiable and free.

For were a man for hir bistad,
She wolde ben right sore adrad
That she dide over greet outrage,
But she him holpe his harm to aswage;
Hir thoughte it elles a vilanye.
And she hadde on a sukkenye,
That not of hempen herdes was;
So fair was noon in alle Arras.
Lord, it was rideled fetysly!
Ther nas nat oo poynt, trewely,
That it nas in his right assyse.
Ful wel yclothed was Fraunchyse;
For ther is no cloth sitteth bet
On damiselle, than doth roket.
A womman wel more fetys is
In roket than in cote, ywis.
The whyte roket, rideled faire,
Bitokened, that ful debonaire
And swete was she that it bere.

BY hir daunced a bachelere;
I can not telle you what he highte,
But fair he was, and of good highte,
Al hadde he be, I sey no more,
The lordes sone of Windesore.

AND next that daunced Curtesye,
That preised was of lowe and hye,
For neither proud ne fool was she.
She for to daunce called me,
I pray God yeve hir right good
grace!
Whan I com first into the place.
She was not nyce, ne outrageous,
But wys and war, and vertuous,
Of faire speche, and faire answere;
Was never wight misseid of here;
She bar no rancour to no wight.
Cleer broun she was, and therto bright
Of face, of body avenaunt;
I wot no lady so plesaunt.
She were worthy for to bene
An emperesse or crouned quene.

AND by hir wente a knight dauncing
That worthy was and wel speking,
And ful wel coude he doon honour.
The knight was fair and stif in stour,
And in armure a semely man,
And wel biloved of his lemman.

HIR Ydelnesse than saugh I,
That alwey was me faste by.
Of hir have I, withouten fayle,
Told yow the shap and apparayle,
For, as I seide, lo, that was she
That dide me so greet bountee,
That she the gate of the gardin
Undide, and leet me passen in.

AND after daunced, as I gesse,
Youthe fulfild of lustinesse,
That nas not yit twelve yeer of age,
With herte wilde, & thought volage;
Nyce she was, but she ne mente
Noon harm ne slight in hir entente,
But only lust and jolitee.
For yonge folk, wel witen ye,

Youthe

255

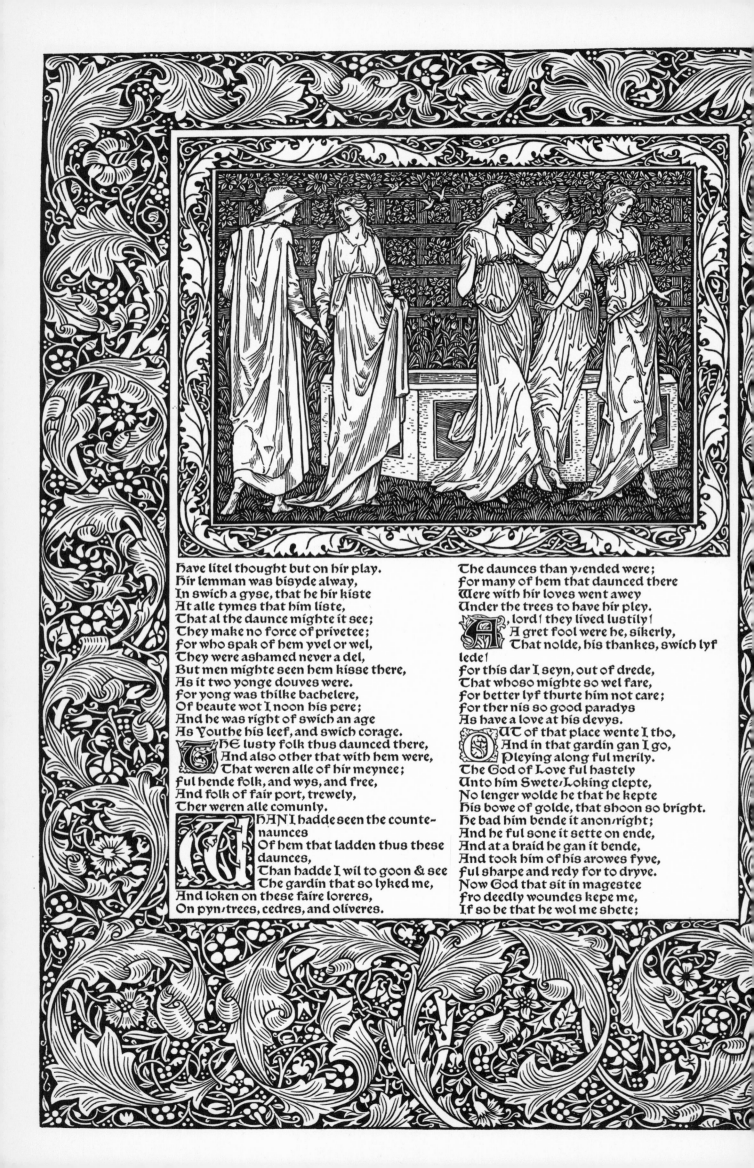

Have litel thought but on hir play.
Hir lemman was bisyde alway,
In swich a gyse, that he hir kiste
At alle tymes that him liste,
That al the daunce mighte it see;
They make no force of privetee;
for who spak of hem yvel or wel,
They were ashamed never a del,
But men mighte seen hem kisse there,
As it two yonge douves were.
for yong was thilke bachelere,
Of beaute wot I noon his pere;
And he was right of swich an age
As Youthe his leef, and swich corage.
¶HE lusty folk thus daunced there,
    And also other that with hem were,
    That weren alle of hir meynee;
ful hende folk, and wys, and free,
And folk of fair port, trewely,
Ther weren alle comunly.
¶HAN I hadde seen the counte-
        naunces
        Of hem that ladden thus these
        daunces,
        Than hadde I wil to goon & see
        The gardin that so lyked me,
And loken on these faire loreres,
On pyn-trees, cedres, and oliveres.

The daunces than y-ended were;
for many of hem that daunced there
Were with hir loves went awey
Under the trees to have hir pley.
¶A, lord! they lived lustily!
    A gret fool were he, sikerly,
    That nolde, his thankes, swich lyf
lede!
for this dar I seyn, out of drede,
That whoso mighte so wel fare,
for better lyf thurte him not care;
for ther nis so good paradys
As have a love at his devys.
¶UT of that place wente I tho,
    And in that gardin gan I go,
    Pleying along ful merily.
The God of Love ful hastely
Unto him Swete-Loking clepte,
No lenger wolde he that he kepte
His bowe of golde, that shoon so bright.
He bad him bende it anon-right;
And he ful sone it sette on ende,
And at a braid he gan it bende,
And took him of his arowes fyve,
ful sharpe and redy for to dryve.
Now God that sit in magestee
fro deedly woundes kepe me,
If so be that he wol me shete;

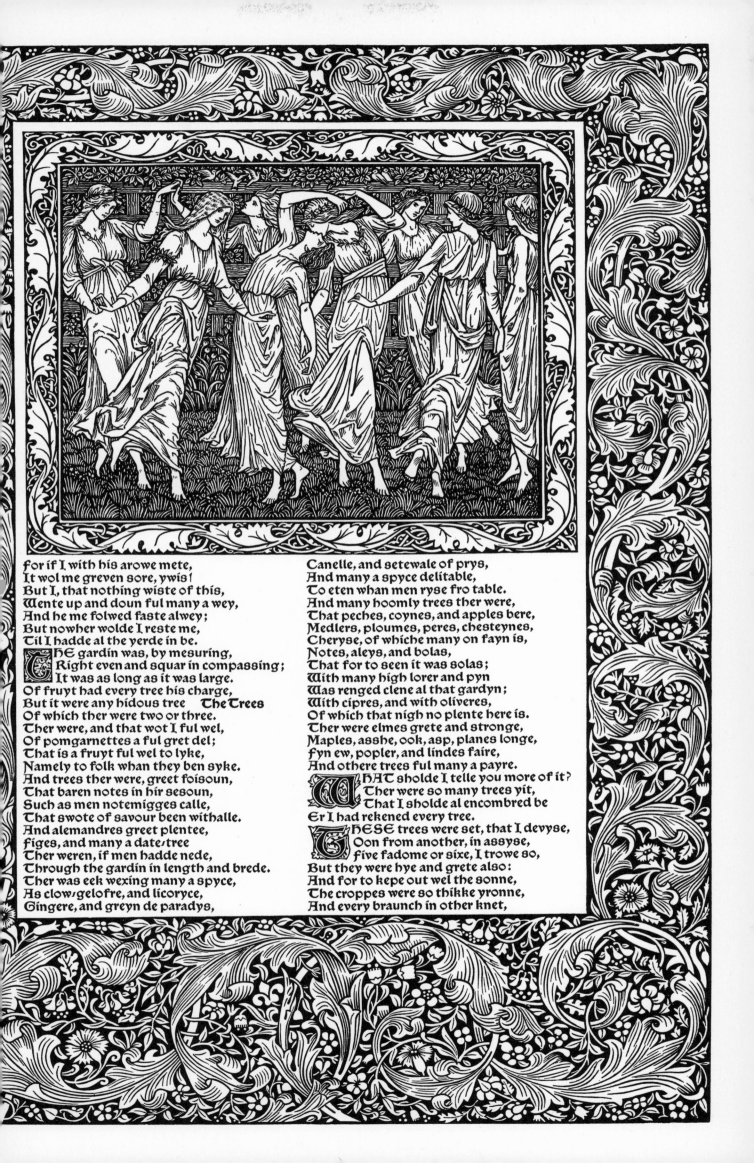

for if I with his arowe mete,
It wol me greven sore, ywis!
But I, that nothing wiste of this,
Wente up and doun ful many a wey,
And he me folwed faste alwey;
But nowher wolde I reste me,
Til I hadde al the yerde in be.
THE gardin was, by mesuring,
Right even and squar in compassing;
It was as long as it was large.
Of fruyt had every tree his charge,
But it were any hidous tree   The Trees
Of which ther were two or three.
Ther were, and that wot I ful wel,
Of pomgarnettes a ful gret del;
That is a fruyt ful wel to lyke,
Namely to folk whan they ben syke.
And trees ther were, greet foisoun,
That baren notes in hir sesoun,
Such as men notemigges calle,
That swote of savour been withalle.
And alemandres greet plentee,
figes, and many a date/tree
Ther weren, if men hadde nede,
Through the gardin in length and brede.
Ther was eek wexing many a spyce,
As clow/gelofre, and licoryce,
Gingere, and greyn de paradys,

Canelle, and setewale of prys,
And many a spyce delitable,
To eten whan men ryse fro table.
And many hoomly trees ther were,
That peches, coynes, and apples bere,
Medlers, ploumes, peres, chesteynes,
Cheryse, of whiche many on fayn is,
Notes, aleys, and bolas,
That for to seen it was solas;
With many high lorer and pyn
Was renged clene al that gardyn;
With cipres, and with oliveres,
Of which that nigh no plente here is.
Ther were elmes grete and stronge,
Maples, asshe, ook, asp, planes longe,
fyn ew, popler, and lindes faire,
And othere trees ful many a payre.
WHAT sholde I telle you more of it?
Ther were so many trees yit,
That I sholde al encombred be
Er I had rekened every tree.
THESE trees were set, that I devyse,
Oon from another, in assyse,
five fadome or sixe, I trowe so,
But they were hye and grete also:
And for to kepe out wel the sonne,
The croppes were so thikke yronne,
And every braunch in other knet,

And ful of grene leves set,
That sonne mighte noon descende,
Lest it the tendre grasses shende.
Ther mighte men does and roes ysee,
And of squirels ful greet plentee,
From bough to bough alwey leping.
Conies ther were also playing,
That comen out of hir claperes
Of sondry colours and maneres,
And maden many a turneying
Upon the fresshe gras springing.

IN places saw I Welles there,
In whiche ther no frogges were,
And fair in shadwe was every welle;
But I ne can the nombre telle
Of stremes smale, that by devys
Mirthe had don come through condys,
Of which the water, in renning,
Gan make a noyse ful lyking.

ABOUT the brinkes of thise welles,
And by the stremes overal elles
Sprang up the gras, as thikke yset
And softe as any veluet,
On which men mighte his lemman leye,
As on a fetherbed, to pleye,
For therthe was ful softe and swete.
Through moisture of the welle wete
Sprang up the sote grene gras,
As fair, as thikke, as mister was.
But muche amended it the place,
That therthe was of swich a grace
That it of floures had plente,
That both in somer and winter be.

THER sprang the violete al newe,
And fresshe pervinke, riche of hewe,
And floures yelowe, whyte, and rede;
Swich plentee grew ther never in mede.
Ful gay was al the ground, and queynt,
And poudred, as men had it peynt,
With many a fresh and sondry flour,
That casten up ful good savour.

I WOL not longe holde you in fable
Of al this gardin delitable.
I moot my tonge stinten nede,
For I ne may, withouten drede,
Naught tellen you the beautee al,
Ne half the bountee therewithal.

I WENTE on right honde and on left
Aboute the place; it was not left,
Til I hadde al the yerde in been,
In the estres that men mighte seen.
And thus whyle I wente in my pley,
The God of Love me folowed ay,
Right as an hunter can abyde
The beste, til he seeth his tyde
To shete, at good mes, to the dere,
Whan that him nedeth go no nere.

AND so befil, I rested me
Besyde a welle, under a tree,
Which tree in fraunce men calle a pyn.
But, sith the tyme of kyng Pepyn,
Ne grew ther tree in mannes sighte
So fair, ne so wel woxe in highte;
In al that yerde so high was noon.

258

And springing in a marble-stoon
Had nature set, the sothe to telle,
Under that pyn-tree a welle.
And on the border, al withoute,
Was writen, in the stone aboute,
Lettres smale, that seyden thus:
Here starf the faire Narcisus.

NARCISUS was a bachelere,
That Love had caught in his
daungere,
And in his net gan him so streyne,
And dide him so to wepe and pleyne,
That nede him muste his lyf forgo.
For a fair lady, hight Echo,
Him loved over any creature,
And gan for him swich peyne endure,
That on a tyme she him tolde,
That, if he hir loven nolde,
That hir behoved nedes dye,
Ther lay non other remedye.
But natheles, for his beautee,
So fiers and daungerous was he,
That he nolde graunten hir asking,
For weping, ne for fair praying.
And whan she herde him werne hir so,
She hadde in herte so gret wo,
And took it in so gret dispyt,
That she, withoute more respyt,
Was deed anoon. But, er she deyde,
Ful pitously to God she preyde,
That proude-herted Narcisus,
That was in love so daungerous,
Mighte on a day ben hampred so
For love, and been so hoot for wo,
That never he mighte joye atteyne;
Than shulde he fele in every veyne
What sorowe trewe lovers maken,
That been so vilaynsly forsaken.
This prayer was but resonable,
Therfor God held it ferme and stable:
For Narcisus, shortly to telle,
By aventure com to that welle
To reste him in that shadowing
A day, whan he com fro hunting.
This Narcisus had suffred paynes
For renning alday in the playnes,
And was for thurst in greet distresse
Of hete, and of his werinesse
That hadde his breeth almost binomen.
Whan he was to that welle ycomen,
That shadwed was with braunches grene,
He thoughte of thilke water shene
To drinke and fresshe him wel withalle;
And doun on knees he gan to falle,
And forth his heed and nekke out-straughte
To drinken of that welle a draughte.
And in the water anoon was sene
His nose, his mouth, his yen shene,
And he therof was al abasshed;
His owne shadowe had him bitrasshed.
For wel wende he the forme see
Of a child of greet beautee.
Wel couthe Love him wreke tho
Of daunger and of pryde also,

HERE·STARF·THE·FAIRE·NARCISSVS

That Narcisus somtyme him bere.
He quitte him wel his guerdon there;
for he so musede in the welle,
That, shortly al the sothe to telle,
He lovede his owne shadowe so,
That atte laste he starf for wo.
for whan he saugh that he his wille
Mighte in no maner wey fulfille,
And that he was so faste caught
That he him couthe comfort naught,
He loste his wit right in that place,
And deyde within a litel space.
And thus his warisoun he took
for the lady that he forsook.
LADYES, I preye ensample taketh,
Ye that ayeins your love mistaketh:
for if hir deeth be yow to wyte,
God can ful wel your whyle quyte.
WHAN that this lettre, of whiche
I telle,
Had taught me that it was the welle
Of Narcisus in his beautee,
I gan anoon withdrawe me,
Whan it fel in my remembraunce,
That him bitidde swich mischaunce.
But at the laste than thoughte I,
That scatheles, ful sikerly,

I mighte unto The Welle go.   The Welle
Wherof shulde I abasshen so?
Unto the welle than wente I me,
And doun I louted for to see
The clere water in the stoon,
And eek the gravel, which that shoon
Down in the botme, as silver fyn;
for of the welle, this is the fyn,
In world is noon so cleer of hewe.
The water is ever fresh and newe
That welmeth up with wawes brighte
The mountance of two finger highte.
Abouten it is gras springing,
for moiste so thikke and wel lyking,
That it ne may in winter dye,
No more than may the see be drye.
DOWN at the botme set saw I
Two cristal stones craftely
In thilke fresshe and faire welle.
But o thing soothly dar I telle,
That ye wol holde a greet mervayle
Whan it is told, withouten fayle.
for whan the sonne, cleer in sighte,
Cast in that welle his bemes brighte,
And that the heet descended is,
Than taketh the cristal stoon, ywis,
Agayn the sonne an hundred hewes,
Blewe, yelowe, & rede, that fresh and newe is.

Yit hath the merveilous cristal
Swich strengthe, that the place overal,
Bothe fowl and tree, and leves grene,
And al the yerd in it is sene.
And for to doon you understonde,
To make ensample wol I fonde;
Right as a mirour openly
Sheweth al thing that stant therby,
As wel the colour as the figure,
Withouten any coverture;
Right so the cristal stoon, shyning,
Withouten any disceyving,
The estres of the yerde accuseth
To him that in the water museth;
For ever, in which half that he be,
He may wel half the gardin see;
And if he turne, he may right wel
Seen the remenaunt everydel.
For ther is noon so litel thing
So hid, ne closed with shitting,
That it ne is sene, as though it were
Peynted in the cristal there.
THIS is the mirour perilous,
In which the proude Narcisus
Saw al his face fair and bright,
That made him sith to lye upright.
For whoso loke in that mirour,
Ther may nothing ben his socour
That he ne shal ther seen som thing
That shal him lede into loving.
Ful many a worthy man hath it
Yblent; for folk of grettest wit
Ben sone caught here and awayted;
Withouten respyt been they bayted.
Heer comth to folk of newe rage,
Heer chaungeth many wight corage;
Heer lyth no reed ne wit therto;
For Venus sone, daun Cupido,
Hath sowen there of love the seed,
That help ne lyth ther noon, ne reed,
So cercleth it the welle aboute.
His ginnes hath he set withoute
Right for to cacche in his panteres
These damoysels and bacheleres.
Love will noon other bridde cacche,
Though he sette either net or lacche.
And for the seed that heer was sowen,
This welle is cleped, as wel is knowen,
The Welle of Love, of verray right,
Of which ther hath ful many a wight
Spoke in bokes dyversely.
But they shulle never so verily
Descripcioun of the welle here,
Ne eek the sothe of this matere,
As ye shulle, whan I have undo
The craft that hir bilongeth to.
ALWAY me lyked for to dwelle,
To seen the cristal in the welle,
That shewed me ful openly
A thousand thinges faste by.
But I may saye, in sory houre
Stood I to loken or to poure;
For sithen have I sore syked,
That mirour hath me now entryked.
But hadde I first knowen in my wit

260

The vertue and the strengthe of it,
I nolde not have mused there;
Me hadde bet ben elleswhere;
For in the snare I fel anoon,
That hath bitraisshed many oon.
N thilke mirour saw I tho,
Among a thousand thinges mo,
A Roser charged ful of roses,
That with an hegge aboute enclos
is.
Tho had I swich lust and envye,
That, for Parys ne for Pavye,
Nolde I have left to goon and see
Ther grettest hepe of roses be.
Whan I was with this rage hent,
That caught hath many a man and shent,
Toward the roser gan I go.
And whan I was not fer therfro,
The savour of the roses swote
Me smoot right to the herte rote,
As I hadde al embawmed be.
And if I ne hadde endouted me
To have ben hated or assailed,
My thankes, wolde I not have failed
To pulle a rose of al that route
To beren in myn honde aboute,
And smellen to it wher I wente;
But ever I dredde me to repente,
And lest it greved or forthoughte
The lord that thilke gardyn wroughte.
Of roses were ther gret woon,
So faire wexe never in roon.
Of knoppes clos, som saw I there,
And some wel beter woxen were;
And some ther been of other moysoun,
That drowe nigh to hir sesoun,
And spedde hem faste for to sprede;
I love wel swiche roses rede;
For brode roses, and open also,
Ben passed in a day or two;
But knoppes wilen fresshe be
Two dayes atte leest, or three.
The knoppes gretly lyked me,
For fairer may ther no man see.
Whoso mighte haven oon of alle,
It oughte him been ful leef withalle.
Mighte I a gerlond of hem geten,
For no richesse I wolde it leten.
Among the Knoppes I chees oon
So fair, that of the remenaunt noon
Ne preyse I half so wel as it,
Whan I avyse it in my wit.
For it so wel was enlumyned
With colour reed, as wel yfyned
As nature couthe it make faire.
And it had leves wel foure paire,
That Kinde had set through his knowing
Aboute the rede rose springing.
The stalke was as risshe right,
And theron stood the knoppe upright,
That it ne bowed upon no syde.
The swote smelle sprong so wyde
That it dide al the place aboute…

Thus far Geffrey Chaucer; what follows is
thought to be by another hand.

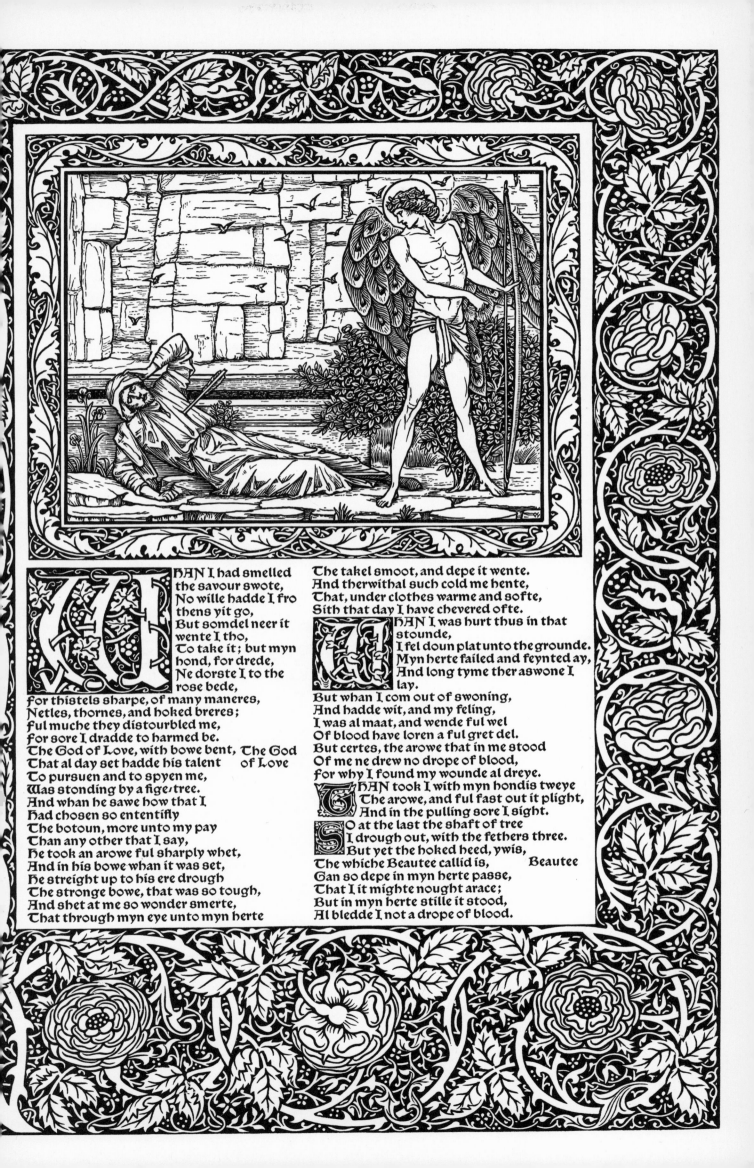

WHAN I had smelled the savour swote,
No wille hadde I fro thens yit go,
But somdel neer it wente I tho,
To take it; but myn hond, for drede,
Ne dorste I to the rose bede,
For thistels sharpe, of many maneres,
Netles, thornes, and hoked breres;
Ful muche they distourbled me,
For sore I dradde to harmed be.
The God of Love, with bowe bent,   The God
That al day set hadde his talent   of Love
To pursuen and to spyen me,
Was stonding by a fige-tree.
And whan he sawe how that I
Had chosen so ententifly
The botoun, more unto my pay
Than any other that I say,
He took an arowe ful sharply whet,
And in his bowe whan it was set,
He streight up to his ere drough
The stronge bowe, that was so tough,
And shet at me so wonder smerte,
That through myn eye unto myn herte

The takel smoot, and depe it wente.
And therwithal such cold me hente,
That, under clothes warme and softe,
Sith that day I have chevered ofte.

WHAN I was hurt thus in that stounde,
I fel doun plat unto the grounde.
Myn herte failed and feynted ay,
And long tyme ther aswone I lay.
But whan I com out of swoning,
And hadde wit, and my feling,
I was al maat, and wende ful wel
Of blood have loren a ful gret del.
But certes, the arowe that in me stood
Of me ne drew no drope of blood,
For why I found my wounde al dreye.

THAN took I with myn hondis tweye
The arowe, and ful fast out it plight,
And in the pulling sore I sight.

SO at the last the shaft of tree
I drough out, with the fethers three.
But yet the hoked heed, ywis,
The whiche Beautee callid is,   Beautee
Gan so depe in myn herte passe,
That I it mighte nought arace;
But in myn herte stille it stood,
Al bledde I not a drope of blood.

I was bothe anguissous and trouble
For the peril that I saw double;
I niste what to seye or do,
Ne gete a leche my woundis to;
For neithir thurgh gras ne rote,
Ne hadde I help of hope ne bote.
But to the botoun evermo
Myn herte drew; for al my wo,
My thought was in non other thing.
For hadde it been in my keping,
It wolde have brought my lyf agayn.
For certeinly, I dar wel seyn,
The sight only, and the savour,
Alegged muche of my langour.

Simplesse

WHAN gan I for to drawe me
Toward the botoun fair to see;
And Love hadde gete him, in a
throwe,
Another arowe into his bowe,
And for to shete gan him dresse;
The arowis name was Simplesse.
And whan that Love gan nyghe me nere,
He drow it up, withouten were,
And shet at me with al his might,
So that this arowe anon right
Thourghout myn eigh, as it was founde,
Into myn herte hath maad a wounde.
Thanne I anoon dide al my crafte
For to drawen out the shafte,
And therwithal I sighed eft.
But in myn herte the heed was left,
Which ay encresid my desyre,
Unto the botoun drawe nere;
And ever, mo that me was wo,
The more desyr hadde I to go
Unto the roser, where that grew
The fresshe botoun so bright of hewe.
Betir me were have leten be;
But it bihoved nedes me
To don right as myn herte bad.
For ever the body must be lad
Aftir the herte; in wele and wo,
Of force togidre they must go.
But never this archer wolde fyne
To shete at me with alle his pyne,
And for to make me to him mete.

Curtesye

HE thridde arowe he gan to shete,
Whan best his tyme he mighte
espye,
The which was named Curtesye;
Into myn herte it dide avale.
Aswone I fel, bothe deed and pale;
Long tyme I lay, and stired nought,
Til I abraid out of my thought.
And faste than I avysed me
To drawen out the shafte of tree;
But ever the heed was left bihinde
For ought I couthe pulle or winde.
So sore it stikid whan I was hit,
That by no craft I might it flit;
But anguissous and ful of thought,
I felte such wo, my wounde ay wrought,
That somoned me alway to go

262

Toward the rose, that plesed me so;
But I ne durste in no manere,
Bicause the archer was so nere.
For evermore gladly, as I rede,
Brent child of fyr hath muche drede.
And, certis yit, for al my peyne,
Though that I sigh yit arwis reyne,
And grounde quarels sharpe of stele,
Ne for no payne that I might fele,
Yit might I not mysilf withholde
The faire roser to biholde;
For Love me yaf sich hardement
For to fulfille his comaundement.

UPON my feet I roos up than
Feble, as a forwoundid man;
And forth to gon my might I sette,
And for the archer nolde I lette.
Toward the roser fast I drow;
But thornes sharpe mo than ynow
Ther were, and also thistels thikke,
And breres, brimme for to prikke,
That I ne mighte gete grace
The rowe thornes for to passe,
To sene the roses fresshe of hewe.
I must abide, though it me rewe,
The hegge aboute so thikke was,
That closid the roses in compas.
But o thing lyked me right wele;
I was so nygh, I mighte fele
Of the botoun the swote odour,
And also see the fresshe colour;
And that right gretly lyked me,
That I so neer it mighte see.
Sich joye anoon therof hadde I,
That I forgat my malady.
To sene it hadde I sich delyt,
Of sorwe and angre I was al quit,
And of my woundes that I had thar;
For nothing lyken me might mar
Than dwellen by the roser ay,
And thennes never to passe away.

Compa[ny]

BUT whan a whyle I had be thar,
The God of Love, which al toshar
Myn herte with his arwis kene,
Caste him to yeve me woundis
grene.
He shet at me ful hastily
An arwe named Company,
The whiche takel is ful able
To make these ladies merciable.
Than I anoon gan chaungen hewe
For grevaunce of my wounde newe,
That I agayn fel in swoning,
And sighed sore in compleyning.
Sore I compleyned that my sore
On me gan greven more and more.
I had non hope of allegeaunce;
So nigh I drow to desperaunce,
I rought of dethe ne of lyf,
Whither that love wolde me dryf.
If me a martir wolde he make,
I might his power nought forsake.
And whyl for anger thus I wook,

HE God of Love an arowe took;
Ful sharp it was and ful pugnaunt,
And it was callid Fair-Semblaunt,
The which in no wys wol consente,
That any lover him repente
To serve his love with herte and alle,
For any peril that may bifalle.
But though this arwe was kene grounde
As any rasour that is founde,
To cutte and kerve, at the poynt,
The God of Love it hadde anoynt
With a precious oynement,
Somdel to yeve aleggement
Upon the woundes that he had
Through the body in my herte maad,
To helpe hir sores, and to cure,
And that they may the bet endure.
But yit this arwe, withoute more,
Made in myn herte a large sore,
That in ful gret peyne I abood.
But ay the oynement wente abroad;
Throughout my woundes large and wyde
It spredde aboute in every syde;
Through whos vertu and whos might
Myn herte joyful was and light.
I had ben deed and al toshent
But for the precious oynement.
The shaft I drow out of the arwe,
Roking for wo right wondir narwe;
But the heed, which made me smerte,
Lefte bihinde in myn herte
With other foure, I dar wel say,
That never wol be take away;
But the oynement halp me wele.
And yit sich sorwe dide I fele,
Of my woundes fresshe and newe,
That alday I chaunged hewe,
As men might see in my visage.
The arwis were so fulle of rage,
So variaunt of diversitee,
That men in everich mighte see
Bothe gret anoy and eek swetnesse,
And joye meynt with bittirnesse.
Now were they esy, now were they wood,
In hem I felte bothe harm and good;
Now sore without aleggement,
Now softening with oynement;
It softned here, and prikked there,
Thus ese and anger togider were.

HE God of Love deliverly
Com lepand to me hastily,
And seide to me, in gret rape:
Yeld thee, for thou may not escape!
May no defence availe thee heere;
Therfore I rede mak no daungere.
If thou wolt yelde thee hastily,
Thou shalt the rather have mercy.
He is a fool in sikernesse,
That with daunger or stoutnesse
Rebellith ther that he shulde plese;
In such folye is litel ese.
Be meek, wher thou must nedis bowe;
To stryve ageyn is nought thy prowe.

Come at ones, and have ydo,
For I wol that it be so.
Than yeld thee here debonairly.

AND I answerid ful humbly:
Gladly, sir; at your bidding,
I wol me yelde in alle thing.
To your servyse I wol me take;
For God defende that I shulde make
Ageyn your bidding resistence;
I wol not doon so gret offence;
For if I dide, it were no skile.
Ye may do with me what ye wile,
Save or spille, and also sloo;
Fro you in no wyse may I go.
My lyf, my deth, is in your honde,
I may not laste out of your bonde.
Pleyn at your list I yelde me,
Hoping in herte, that sumtyme ye
Comfort and ese shulle me sende;
Or ellis shortly, this is the ende,
Withouten helthe I moot ay dure,
But if ye take me to your cure.
Comfort or helthe how shuld I have,
Sith ye me hurte, but ye me save?
The helthe of lovers moot be founde
Wheras they token firste hir wounde.
And if ye list of me to make
Your prisoner, I wol it take
Of herte and wil, fully at gree.
Hoolly and pleyn I yelde me,
Withoute feyning or feyntyse,
To be governed by your empryse.
Of you I here so much prys,
I wol ben hool at your devys
For to fulfille your lyking
And repente for nothing,
Hoping to have yit in som tyde
Mercy, of that that I abyde.
And with that covenaunt yeld I me,

ANOON doun kneling upon my knee,
Profering for to kisse his feet;
But for nothing he wolde me lete,
And seide: I love thee bothe and preyse,
Sen that thyn answer doth me ese,
For thou answerid so curteisly.
For now I wot wel uttirly,
That thou art gentil, by thy speche.
For though a man fer wolde seche,
He shulde not finden, in certeyn,
No sich answer of no vileyn;
For sich a word ne mighte nought
Isse out of a vilayns thought.
Thou shalt not lesen of thy speche,
For to thy helping wol I eche,
And eek encresen that I may.
But first I wol that thou obay
Fully, for thyn avauntage,
Anon to do me here homage.
And sithen kisse thou shalt my mouth,
Which to no vilayn was never couth
For to aproche it, ne for to touche;
For sauf of cherlis I ne vouche
That they shulle never neigh it nere.

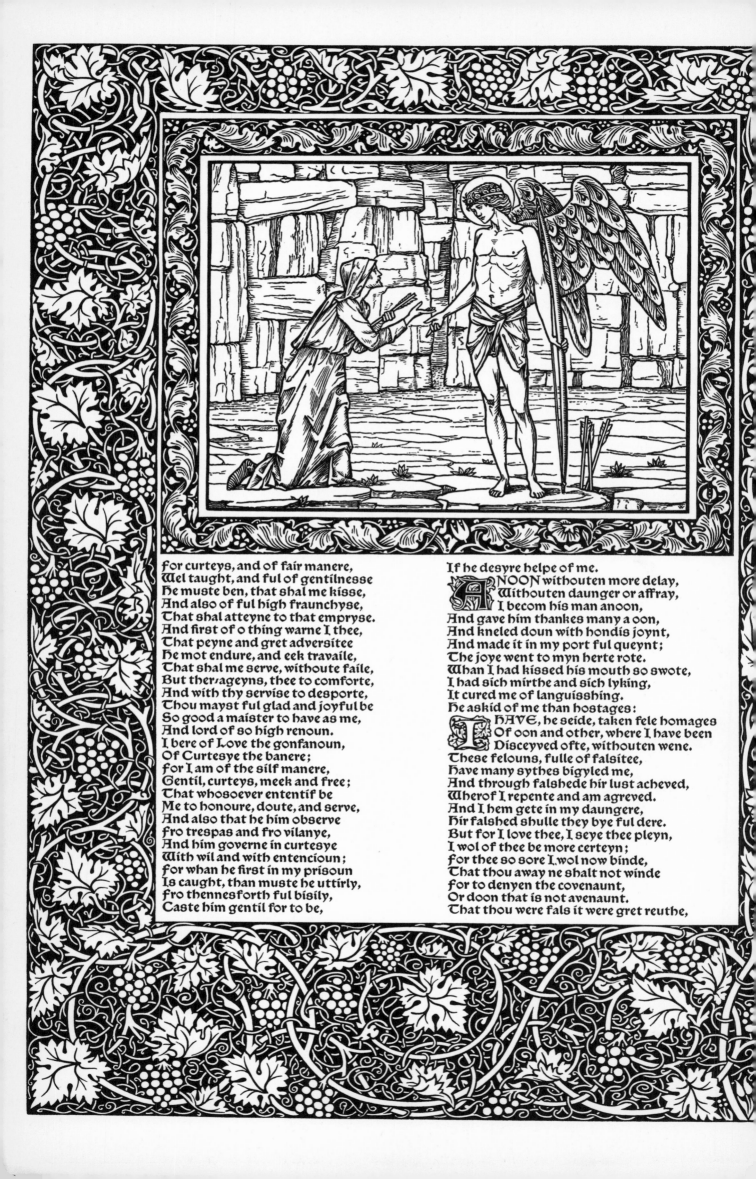

for curteys, and of fair manere,
Wel taught, and ful of gentilnesse
He muste ben, that shal me kisse,
And also of ful high fraunchyse,
That shal atteyne to that empryse.
And first of o thing warne I thee,
That peyne and gret adversitee
He mot endure, and eek travaile,
That shal me serve, withoute faile,
But ther/ageyns, thee to comforte,
And with thy servise to desporte,
Thou mayst ful glad and joyful be
So good a maister to have as me,
And lord of so high renoun,
I bere of Love the gonfanoun,
Of Curtesye the banere;
for I am of the silf manere,
Gentil, curteys, meek and free;
That whosoever ententif be
Me to honoure, doute, and serve,
And also that he him observe
fro trespas and fro vilanye,
And him governe in curtesye
With wil and with entencioun;
for whan he first in my prisoun
Is caught, than muste he uttirly,
fro thennesforth ful bisily,
Caste him gentil for to be,

If he desyre helpe of me.
ANOON withouten more delay,
Withouten daunger or affray,
I becom his man anoon,
And gave him thankes many a oon,
And kneled doun with hondis joynt,
And made it in my port ful queynt;
The joye went to myn herte rote.
Whan I had kissed his mouth so swote,
I had sich mirthe and sich lyking,
It cured me of languisshing.
He askid of me than hostages:
I HAVE, he seide, taken fele homages
Of oon and other, where I have been
Disceyved ofte, withouten wene.
These felouns, fulle of falsitee,
Have many sythes bigyled me,
And through falshede hir lust acheved,
Wherof I repente and am agreved.
And I hem gete in my daungere,
Hir falshed shulle they bye ful dere.
But for I love thee, I seye thee pleyn,
I wol of thee be more certeyn;
for thee so sore I wol now binde,
That thou away ne shalt not winde
for to denyen the covenaunt,
Or doon that is not avenaunt.
That thou were fals it were gret reuthe,

Sith thou semest so ful of treuthe.
SIRE, if thee list to undirstande,
I merveile thee asking this demande.
For why or wherfore shulde ye
Ostages or borwis aske of me,
Or any other sikirnesse,
Sith ye wote, in sothfastnesse,
That ye have me surprysed so,
And hool myn herte taken me fro,
That it wol do for me nothing
But if it be at your bidding?
Myn herte is yours, and myn right nought,
As it bihoveth, in dede and thought,
Redy in alle to worche your wille,
Whether so it turne to good or ille.
So sore it lustith you to plese,
No man therof may you disseise,
Ye have theron set sich justise,
That it is werreyd in many wise.
And if ye doute it nolde obeye,
Ye may therof do make a keye,
And holde it with you for ostage.
NOW certis, this is noon outrage,
Quoth Love, and fully I accord;
For of the body he is ful lord
That hath the herte in his tresor;
Outrage it were to asken more.
THAN of his aumener he drough
A litel keye, fetys ynough,
Which was of gold polisshed clere,
And seide to me: With this keye here
Thyn herte to me now wol I shette;
For al my jowellis loke and knette
I binde under this litel keye,
That no wight may carye aweye;
This keye is ful of gret poeste.
WITH which anoon he touchid me
Undir the syde ful softely,
That he myn herte sodeynly
Without al anoy had spered,
That yit right nought it hath me dered.
Whan he had doon his wil al out,
And I had put him out of dout,
SIRE, I seide, I have right gret wille
Your lust and plesaunce to fulfille.
Til ye my servise take at gree,
By thilke feith ye owe to me.
I seye nought for recreaundyse,
For I nought doute of your servyse.
But the servaunt traveileth in vayne,
That for to serven doth his payne
Unto that lord, which in no wyse
Can him no thank for his servyse.
LOVE seide: Dismaye thee nought,
Sin thou for sucour hast me sought,
In thank thy servise wol I take,
And high of degree I wol thee make,
If wikkidnesse ne hindre thee;
But, as I hope, it shal nought be.
To worship no wight by aventure
May come, but if he peyne endure.
Abyde and suffre thy distresse;
That hurtith now, it shal be lesse;

I wot mysilf what may thee save,
What medicyne thou woldist have.
And if thy trouthe to me thou kepe,
I shal unto thyn helping eke,
To cure thy woundes and make hem clene,
Wherso they be olde or grene;
Thou shalt be holpen, at wordis fewe.
For certeynly thou shalt wel shewe
Wher that thou servest with good wille,
For to complisshen and fulfille
My comaundementis, day and night,
Whiche I to lovers yeve of right.
AH, sire, for Goddis love, seide I,
Er ye passe hens, ententifly
Your comaundementis to me ye say,
And I shal kepe hem, if I may;
For hem to kepen is al my thought.
And if so be I wot hem nought,
Than may I sinne unwitingly.
Wherfore I pray you enterely,
With al myn herte, me to lere,
That I trepasse in no manere.
THE god of love than chargid me
Anoon, as ye shal here and see,
Word by word, by right empryse,
So as the Romance shal devyse.
The maister lesith his tyme to lere,
Whan the disciple wol not here.
It is but veyn on him to swinke,
That on his lerning wol not thinke.
Whoso lust love, let him entende,
For now the Romance ginneth amende.
Now is good to here, in fay,
If any be that can it say,
And poynte it as the resoun is
Set; for othergate, ywis,
It shal nought wel in alle thing
Be brought to good undirstonding:
For a reder that poyntith ille
A good sentence may ofte spille.
The book is good at the ending,
Maad of newe and lusty thing;
For whoso wol the ending here,
The crafte of love he shal now lere,
If that he wol so long abyde,
Til I this Romance may unhyde,
And undo the signifiaunce
Of this dreme into Romaunce.
The sothfastnesse that now is hid,
Without coverture shal be kid,
Whan I undon have this dreming,
Wherin no word is of lesing.
VILANY, at the biginning,
I wol, sayd Love, over alle thing,
Thou leve, if thou wolt not be
fals, and trespasse ageynes me.
I curse and blame generally
Alle hem that loven vilany;
For vilany makith vilayn,
And by his dedis a cherle is seyn.
Thise vilayns arn without pitee,
Frendshipe, love, and al bounte.
I nil receyve to my servyse

265

Hem that ben vilayns of empryse.
But undirstonde in thyn entent,
That this is not myn entendement,
To clepe no wight in no ages
Only gentil for his linages.
But whoso that is vertuous,
And in his port nought outrageous,
Whan sich oon thou seest thee biforn,
Though he be not gentil born,
Thou mayst wel seyn, this is a soth,
That he is gentil, bicause he doth
As longeth to a gentilman;
Of hem non other deme I can.
For certeynly, withouten drede,
A cherl is demed by his dede,
Of hye or lowe, as ye may see,
Or of what kinrede that he be.
Ne say nought, for noon yvel wille,
Thing that is to holden stille;
It is no worship to misseye.
Thou mayst ensample take of Keye,
That was somtyme, for misseying,
Hated both of olde and ying;
As fer as Gaweyn, the worthy,
Was preysed for his curtesy,
Keye was hated, for he was fel,
Of word dispitous and cruel.
Wherfore be wyse and aqueyntable,
Goodly of word, and resonable
Bothe to lesse and eek to mar.
And whan thou comest ther men ar,
Loke that thou have in custom ay
First to salue hem, if thou may:
And if it falle, that of hem som
Salue thee first, be not dom,
But quyte him curteisly anoon
Without abiding, er they goon.
FOR nothing eek thy tunge applye
To speke wordis of ribaudye.
To vilayn speche in no degree
Lat never thy lippe unbounden be.
For I nought holde him, in good feith,
Curteys, that foule wordis seith.
And alle wimmen serve and preyse,
And to thy power hir honour reyse.
And if that any missayere
Dispyse wimmen, that thou mayst here,
Blame him, and bidde him holde him stille.
And set thy might and al thy wille
Wimmen and ladies for to plese,
And to do thing that may hem ese,
That they ever speke good of thee,
For so thou mayst best preysed be.
LOKE fro pryde thou kepe thee wele;
For thou mayst bothe perceyve and fele,
That pryde is bothe foly and sinne;
And he that pryde hath, him withinne,
Ne may his herte, in no wyse,
Meken ne souplen to servyse.
For pryde is founde, in every part,
Contrarie unto Loves art.
And he that loveth trewely
Shulde him contene jolily,

Withouten pryde in sondry wyse,
And him disgysen in queyntyse.
For queynt array, withouten drede,
Is nothing proud, who takith hede;
For fresh array, as men may see,
Withouten pryde may ofte be.
MAYNTENE thysilf aftir thy rent,
Of robe and eek of garnement;
For many sythe fair clothing
A man amendith in mich thing.
And loke alwey that they be shape,
What garnement that thou shalt make,
Of him that can hem beste do,
With al that perteyneth therto.
Poyntis and sleves be wel sittand,
Right and streight upon the hand.
Of shoon and botes, newe and faire,
Loke at the leest thou have a paire;
And that they sitte so fetisly,
That these rude may uttirly
Merveyle, sith that they sitte so pleyn,
How they come on or of ageyn.
Were streite gloves, with aumenere
Of silk; and alwey with good chere
Thou yeve, if thou have richesse;
And if thou have nought, spend the lesse.
Alwey be mery, if thou may,
But waste not thy good alway.
Have hat of floures fresh as May,
Chapelet of roses of Whitsonday;
For sich aray ne cost but lyte.
Thyn hondis wasshe, thy teeth make whyte,
And let no filthe upon thee be.
Thy nailes blak if thou mayst see,
Voide it awey deliverly,
And kembe thyn heed right jolily.
Fard not thy visage in no wyse,
For that of love is not thempryse;
For love doth haten, as I finde,
A beaute that cometh not of kinde.
ALWEY in herte I rede thee
Glad and mery for to be,
And be as joyful as thou can;
Love hath no joye of sorowful man.
That yvel is ful of curtesye
That lauhwith in his maladye;
For ever of love the siknesse
Is meynd with swete and bitternesse.
The sore of love is merveilous;
For now the lover is joyous,
Now can he pleyne, now can he grone,
Now can he singen, now maken mone.
To-day he pleyneth for hevinesse,
To-morowe he pleyeth for jolynesse.
The lyf of love is ful contrarie,
Which stoundemele can ofte varie.
But if thou canst som mirthis make,
That men in gree wole gladly take,
Do it goodly, I comaunde thee;
For men sholde, whersoever they be,
Do thing that hem best sitting is,
For therof cometh good loos and pris.
Wherof that thou be vertuous,

Ne be not straunge ne daungerous.
OR if that thou good rider be,
Prike gladly, that men may se.
In armes also if thou conne,
Pursue, til thou a name hast wonne.
ND if thy voice be fair and clere,
Thou shalt maken no gret daungere
Whan to singe they goodly preye;
It is thy worship for to obeye.
Also to you it longith ay
To harpe and giterne, daunce and play;
For if he can wel foote and daunce,
It may him greetly do avaunce.
Among eek, for thy lady sake,
Songes and complayntes that thou make;
For that wol meve hem in hir herte,
Whan they reden of thy smerte.
OKE that no man for scarce thee holde,
For that may greve thee manyfolde.
Resoun wol that a lover be
In his yiftes more large and free
Than cherles that been not of loving.
For who therof can any thing,
He shal be leef ay for to yeve,
In Loves lore who so wolde leve;
For he that, through a sodeyn sight,
Or for a kissing, anonright
Yaf hool his herte in wille and thought,
And to himsilf kepith right nought,
Aftir swich yift, is good resoun,
He yeve his good in abandoun.
OW wol I shortly here reherce,
Of that that I have seid in verse,
Al the sentence by and by,
In wordis fewe compendiously,
That thou the bet mayst on hem
thinke,
Whether so it be thou wake or winke;
For that the wordis litel greve
A man to kepe, whanne it is breve.
HOSO with Love wol goon or ryde
He mot be curteys, and void of pryde,
Mery and fulle of jolite,
And of largesse alosed be.
IRST I joyne thee, here in penaunce,
That ever, withoute repentaunce,
Thou set thy thought in thy loving,
To laste withoute repenting;
And thenke upon thy mirthis swete,
That shal folowe aftir whan ye mete.
ND for thou trewe to love shalt be,
I wol, and eek comaunde thee,
That in oo place thou sette, al hool,
Thyn herte, withouten halfen dool,
For trecherie, in sikernesse;
For I lovede never doublenesse.
To many his herte that wol depart,
Everiche shal have but litel part.
But of him drede I me right nought,
That in oo place settith his thought.
Therfore in oo place it sette,
And lat it never thennes flette.
For if thou yevest it in lening,

I holde it but a wrecchid thing:
Therfore yeve it hool and quyte,
And thou shalt have the more merite.
If it be lent, than aftir soon,
The bountee and the thank is doon;
But, in love, free yeven thing
Requyrith a gret guerdoning.
Yeve it in yift al quit fully,
And make thy yift debonairly;
For men that yift wol holde more dere
That yeven is with gladsome chere.
That yift nought to preisen is
That man yeveth, maugre his.
Whan thou hast yeven thyn herte, as I
Have seid thee here al openly,
Than aventures shulle thee falle,
Which harde and hevy been withalle.
For ofte whan thou bithenkist thee
Of thy loving, wherso thou be,
Fro folk thou must depart in hy,
That noon perceyve thy malady,
But hyde thyn harm thou must alone,
And go forth sole, and make thy mone.
Thou shalt no whyl be in oo stat,
But whylom cold and whylom hat;
Now reed as rose, now yelowe and fade.
Such sorowe, I trowe, thou never hade;
Cotidien, ne yit quarteyne,
It is nat so ful of peyne.
For ofte tymes it shal falle
In love, among thy peynes alle,
That thou thyself, al hoolly,
Foryeten shalt so utterly,
That many tymes thou shalt be
Stille as an image of tree,
Dom as a stoon, without stering
Of foot or hond, without speking.
Than, sone after al thy peyne,
To memorie shalt thou come ageyn,
As man abasshed wondre sore,
And after sighen more and more.
For wit thou wel, withouten wene,
In swich astat ful oft have been
That have the yvel of love assayd,
Wherthrough thou art so dismayd.
FTER, a thought shal take thee so,
That thy love is to fer thee fro:
Thou shalt say: God, what may this be,
That I ne may my lady see?
Myne herte aloon is to her go,
And I abyde al sole in wo,
Departed fro myn owne thought,
And with myne eyen see right nought.
Alas, myn eyen sende I ne may,
My careful herte to convay!
Myn hertes gyde but they be,
I praise nothing whatever they see.
Shul they abyde thanne? nay;
But goon visyte without delay
That myn herte desyreth so.
For certeynly, but if they go,
A fool myself I may wel holde,
Whan I ne see what myn herte wolde.

Wherfore I wol gon her to seen,
Or esed shal I never been,
But I have som tokening.
THEN gost thou forth without dwelling;
But ofte thou faylest of thy desyre,
Er thou mayst come hir any nere,
And wastest in vayn thy passage.
Than fallest thou in a newe rage;
For want of sight thou ginnest morne,
And homward pensif dost retorne.
In greet mischeef than shalt thou be,
For than agayn shal come to thee
Sighes and pleyntes, with newe wo,
That no icching prikketh so.
Who wot it nought, he may go lere
Of hem that byen love so dere.
Nothing thyn herte appesen may,
That oft thou wolt goon and assay,
If thou mayst seen, by aventure,
Thy lyves joy, thyn hertis cure;
So that, by grace if thou might
Atteyne of hir to have a sight,
Than shalt thou doon non other dede
But with that sight thyn eyen fede.
That faire fresh whan thou mayst see,
Thyn herte shal so ravisshed be,
That never thou woldest, thy thankis, lete,
Ne remove, for to see that swete.
The more thou seest in sothfastnesse,
The more thou coveytest of that swetnesse;
The more thyn herte brenneth in fyr,
The more thyn herte is in desyr.
For who considreth every del,
It may be lykned wondir wel,
The peyne of love, unto a fere;
For ever the more thou neighest nere
Thought, or whoso that it be,
For verray sothe I telle it thee,
The hatter ever shal thou brenne,
As experience shal thee kenne.
Wherso thou comest in any cost,
Who is next fyr, he brenneth most.
And yit forsothe, for al thyn hete,
Though thou for love swelte and swete,
Ne for nothing thou felen may,
Thou shalt not willen to passe away.
And though thou go, yet must thee nede
Thenke alday on hir fairhede,
Whom thou bihelde with so good wille;
And holde thysilf bigyled ille,
That thou ne haddest non hardement
To shewe hir ought of thyn entent.
Thyn herte ful sore thou wolt dispyse,
And eek repreve of cowardyse,
That thou, so dulle in every thing,
Were dom for drede, without speking.
Thou shalt eek thenke thou didest foly,
That thou were hir so faste by,
And durst not auntre thee to say
Somthing, er thou cam away;
For thou haddist no more wonne,
To speke of hir whan thou bigonne:
But yif she wolde, for thy sake,
268

In armes goodly thee have take,
It shulde have be more worth to thee
Than of tresour greet plentee.
THUS shalt thou morne and eek compleyn,
And gete enchesoun to goon ageyn
Unto thy walk, or to thy place,
Where thou biheld hir fleshly face.
And never, for fals suspeccioun,
Thou woldest finde occasioun
For to gon unto hir hous.
So art thou thanne desirous
A sight of hir for to have,
If thou thine honour mightest save,
Or any erand mightist make
Thider, for thy loves sake;
Ful fayn thou woldist, but for drede
Thou gost not, lest that men take hede.
Wherfore I rede, in thy going,
And also in thyn ageyn-coming,
Thou be wel war that men ne wit;
Feyne thee other cause than it
To go that weye, or faste by;
To hele wel is no folye.
And if so be it happe thee
That thou thy love ther mayst see,
In siker wyse thou hir salewe,
Wherwith thy colour wol transmewe,
And eke thy blood shal al toquake,
Thyn hewe eek chaungen for hir sake.
But word and wit, with chere ful pale,
Shul wante for to telle thy tale.
And if thou mayst so ferforth winne,
That thou thy resoun durst biginne,
And woldist seyn three thingis or mo,
Thou shalt ful scarsly seyn the two.
Though thou bithenke thee never so wel,
Thou shalt foryete yit somdel,
But if thou dele with trecherye.
For fals lovers mowe al folye
Seyn, what hem lust, withouten drede,
They be so double in hir falshede;
For they in herte cunne thenke a thing
And seyn another, in hir speking.
And whan thy speche is endid al,
Right thus to thee it shal bifal;
If any word than come to minde,
That thou to seye hast left bihinde,
Than thou shalt brenne in greet martyr;
For thou shalt brenne as any fyr.
This is the stryf and eke the affray,
And the batail that lastith ay.
This bargeyn ende may never take,
But if that she thy pees wil make.
AND whan the night is comen, anon
A thousand angres shal come upon.
To bedde as fast thou wolt thee dight,
Where thou shalt have but smal delyt;
For whan thou wenest for to slepe,
So ful of peyne shalt thou crepe,
Sterte in thy bedde aboute ful wyde,
And turne ful ofte on every syde;
Now dounward groffe, and now upright,
And walowe in wo the longe night,

Thyne armis shalt thou sprede abrede,
As man in werre were forwerreyd.
Than shal thee come a remembraunce
Of hir shape and hir semblaunce,
Wherto non other may be pere.
And wite thou wel, withoute were,
That thee shal seme, somtyme that night,
That thou hast hir, that is so bright,
Naked bitwene thyn armes there,
Al sothfastnesse as though it were.
Thou shalt make castels than in Spayne,
And dreme of joye, al but in vayne,
And thee delyten of right nought,
Whyl thou so slomrest in that thought,
That is so swete and delitable,
The which, in soth, nis but a fable,
For it ne shal no whyle laste.
Than shalt thou sighe and wepe faste,
And say: Dere God, what thing is this?
My dreme is turned al amis,
Which was ful swete and apparent,
But now I wake, it is al shent!
Now yede this mery thought away!
Twenty tymes upon a day
I wolde this thought wolde come ageyn,
For it alleggith wel my peyn.
It makith me ful of joyful thought,
It sleeth me, that it lastith noght.
A, Lord! why nil ye me socoure,
The joye, I trowe, that I langoure?
The deth I wolde me shulde slo
Whyl I lye in hir armes two.
Myn harm is hard, withouten wene,
My greet unese ful ofte I mene.
But wolde Love do so I might
Have fully joye of hir so bright,
My peyne were quit me richely.
Allas, to greet a thing aske I!
It is but foly, and wrong wening,
To aske so outrageous a thing.
And whoso askith folily,
He moot be warned hastily;
And I ne wot what I may say,
I am so fer out of the way;
For I wolde have ful gret lyking
And ful gret joye of lasse thing.
For wolde she, of hir gentilnesse,
Withouten more, me onis kesse,
It were to me a greet guerdoun,
Relees of al my passioun.
But it is hard to come therto;
Al is but foly that I do,
So high I have myn herte set,
Where I may no comfort get.
I noot wher I sey wel or nought;
But this I wot wel in my thought,
That it were bet of hir aloon,
For to stinte my wo and moon,
A loke on me ycast goodly,
Than for to have, al utterly,
Of another al hool the pley.
A! Lord! wher I shal byde the day
That ever she shal my lady be?

He is ful cured that may hir see.
A! God! whan shal the dawning spring?
To ly thus is an angry thing;
I have no joye thus here to ly
Whan that my love is not me by.
A man to lyen hath gret disese,
Which may not slepe ne reste in ese.
I wolde it dawed, and were now day,
And that the night were went away;
For were it day, I wolde upryse.
A! slowe sonne, shew thyn enpryse!
Speed thee to sprede thy bemis bright,
And chace the derknesse of the night,
To putte away the stoundes stronge,
Which in me lasten al to longe.
THE night shalt thou contene so,
Withoute rest, in peyne and wo;
If ever thou knewe of love distresse,
Thou shalt mowe lerne in that siknesse.
And thus enduring shalt thou ly,
And ryse on morwe up erly
Out of thy bedde, and harneys thee
Er ever dawning thou mayst see.
Al privily than shalt thou goon,
What weder it be, thysilf aloon,
For reyn, or hayl, for snow, for slete,
Thider she dwellith that is so swete,
The which may falle aslepe be,
And thenkith but litel upon thee.
Than shalt thou goon, ful foule aferd;
Loke if the gate be unsperd,
And waite without in wo and peyn,
Ful yvel acold in winde and reyn.
Than shalt thou go the dore bifore,
If thou maist fynde any score,
Or hole, or reft, whatever it were;
Than shalt thou stoupe, and lay to ere,
If they within aslepe be;
I mene, alle save thy lady free.
Whom waking if thou mayst aspye,
Go put thysilf in jupartye,
To aske grace, and thee bimene,
That she may wite, withouten wene,
That thou anight no rest hast had,
So sore for hir thou were bistad.
Wommen wel ought pite to take
Of hem that sorwen for hir sake.
And loke, for love of that relyke,
That thou thenke non other lyke,
For whom thou hast so greet annoy,
Shal kisse thee er thou go away,
And hold that in ful gret deyntee.
And, for that no man shal thee see
Bifore the hous, ne in the way,
Loke thou be goon ageyn er day.
Suche coming, and such going,
Such hevinesse, and such walking,
Makith lovers, withouten wene,
Under hir clothes pale and lene,
For Love leveth colour ne cleernesse;
Who loveth trewe hath no fatnesse.
Thou shalt wel by thyselfe see
That thou must nedis assayed be.

269

For men that shape hem other wey
Falsly her ladies to bitray,
It is no wonder though they be fat;
With false othes hir loves they gat;
For oft I see suche losengeours
Fatter than abbatis or priours.

YET with o thing I thee charge,
That is to seye, that thou be large
Unto the mayd that hir doth serve,
So best hir thank thou shalt deserve.
Yeve hir yiftes, and get hir grace,
For so thou may hir thank purchace,
That she thee worthy holde and free,
Thy lady, and alle that may thee see.
Also hir servauntes worshipe ay,
And plese as muche as thou may;
Gret good through hem may come to thee,
Bicause with hir they been prive.
They shal hir telle how they thee fand
Curteis and wys, and wel doand,
And she shal preyse thee wel the mare.
Loke out of londe thou be not fare;
And if such cause thou have, that thee
Bihoveth to gon out of contree,
Leve hool thyn herte in hostage,
Til thou ageyn make thy passage.
Thenk long to see the swete thing
That hath thyn herte in hir keping.

NOW have I told thee, in what wyse
A lover shal do me servyse.
Do it than, if thou wolt have
The mede that thou aftir crave.

WHAN Love al this had boden me,
I seide him: Sire, how may it be
That lovers may in such manere
Endure the peyne ye have seid here?
I merveyle me wonder faste,
How any man may live or laste
In such peyne, and such brenning,
In sorwe and thought, and such sighing,
Ay unrelesed wo to make,
Whether so it be they slepe or wake.
In such annoy continuely,
As helpe me God, this merveile I,
How man, but he were maad of stele,
Might live a month, such peynes to fele.

THE God of Love than seide me:
Freend, by the feith I owe to thee,
May no man have good, but he it by.
A man loveth more tendirly
The thing that he hath bought most dere.
For wite thou wel, withouten were,
In thank that thing is taken more,
For which a man hath suffred sore.
Certis, no wo ne may atteyne
Unto the sore of loves peyne.
Non yvel therto ne may amounte,
No more than a man may counte
The dropes that of the water be.
For drye as wel the grete see
Thou mightist, as the harmes telle
Of hem that with Love dwelle
In servyse; for peyne hem sleeth,

270

And that ech man wolde flee the deeth,
And trowe they shulde never escape,
Nere that hope couthe hem make
Glad as man in prisoun set,
And may not geten for to et
But barly-breed, and watir pure,
And lyeth in vermin and in ordure;
With alle this, yit can he live,
Good hope such comfort hath him yive,
Which maketh wene that he shal be
Delivered and come to liberte;
In fortune is his fulle trust.
Though he lye in strawe or dust,
In hope is al his susteyning.

AND so for lovers, in hir wening,   Good Ho
Whiche Love hath shit in his prisoun;
Good-Hope is hir salvacioun.
Good-Hope, how sore that they smerte,
Yeveth hem bothe wille and herte
To profre hir body to martyre;
For Hope so sore doth hem desyre
To suffre ech harm that men devyse,
For joye that aftir shal aryse.
Hope, in desire to cacche victorie;
In Hope, of love is al the glorie,
For Hope is al that love may yive;
Nere Hope, ther shulde no lover live,
Blessid be Hope, which with desyre
Avaunceth lovers in such manere.
Good-Hope is curteis for to plese,
To kepe lovers from al disese.
Hope kepith his lond, and wol abyde,
For any peril that may betyde;
For Hope to lovers, as most cheef,
Doth hem enduren al mischeef;
Hope is her help, whan mister is.
And I shal yeve thee eek, ywis,
Three other thingis, that greet solas
Doth to hem that be in my las.   Swete Thou

THE firste good that may be founde,
To hem that in my lace be bounde,
Is Swete-Thought, for to recorde
Thing wherwith thou canst accorde
Best in thyn herte, wher she be;
Thought in absence is good to thee.
Whan any lover doth compleyne,
And liveth in distresse and peyne,
Than Swete-Thought shal come, as blyve,
Awey his angre for to dryve.
It makith lovers have remembrance
Of comfort, and of high plesaunce,
That Hope hath hight him for to winne.
For Thought anoon than shal biginne,
As fer, God wot, as he can finde,
To make a mirrour of his minde;
For to biholde he wol not lette.
Hir person he shal afore him sette,
Hir laughing eyen, persaunt and clere,
Hir shape, hir fourme, hir goodly chere,
Hir mouth that is so gracious,
So swete, and eek so saverous;
Of alle hir fetures he shal take heede,
His eyen with alle hir limes fede.

THUS Swete-Thenking shal aswage
The peyne of lovers, and hir rage.
Thy joye shal double, withoute gesse,
Whan thou thenkist on hir semlinesse,
Or of hir laughing, or of hir chere,
That to thee made thy lady dere.
This comfort wol I that thou take;
And if the next thou wolt forsake
Which is not lesse saverous,
Thou shuldist been to daungerous.

THE secounde shal be Swete-Speche,
That hath to many oon be leche,
To bringe hem out of wo and were,
And helpe many a bachilere;
And many a lady sent socoure,
That have loved par amour,
Through speking, whan they mighten here
Of hir lovers, to hem so dere.
To hem it voidith al hir smerte,
The which is closed in hir herte.
In herte it makith hem glad and light,
Speche, whan they mowe have sight.
And therfore now it cometh to minde,
In olde dawes, as I finde,
That clerkis writen that hir knewe,
Ther was a lady fresh of hewe,
Which of hir love made a song
On him for to remembre among,
In which she seide: Whan that I here
Speken of him that is so dere,
To me it voidith al my smerte,
Ywis, he sit so nere myn herte.
To speke of him, at eve or morwe,
It cureth me of al my sorwe.
To me is noon so high plesaunce
As of his persone daliaunce.
She wist ful wel that Swete-Speking
Comfortith in ful muche thing,
Hir love she had ful wel assayed,
Of him she was ful wel apayed;
To speke of him hir joye was set.
Therfore I rede thee that thou get
A felowe that can wel concele
And kepe thy counsel, and wel hele,
To whom go shewe hoolly thyn herte,
Bothe wele and wo, joye and smerte:
To gete comfort to him thou go,
And privily, bitwene yow two,
Ye shal speke of that goodly thing,
That hath thyn herte in hir keping;
Of hir beaute and hir semblaunce,
And of hir goodly countenaunce.
Of al thy state thou shalt him sey,
And aske him counseil how thou may
Do any thing that may hir plese;
For it to thee shal do gret ese,
That he may wite thou trust him so,
Bothe of thy wele and of thy wo.
And if his herte to love be set,
His companye is muche the bet,
For resoun wol, he shewe to thee
Al uttirly his privite;
And what she is he loveth so,

To thee pleynly he shal undo,
Withoute drede of any shame,
Bothe telle hir renoun and hir name.
Than shal he forther, ferre and nere,
And namely to thy lady dere,
In siker wyse; ye, every other
Shal helpen as his owne brother,
In trouthe withoute doublenesse,
And kepen cloos in sikernesse.
For it is noble thing, in fay,
To have a man thou darst say
Thy prive counsel every del;
For that wol comfort thee right wel,
And thou shalt holde thee wel apayed,
Whan such a freend thou hast assayed.

THE thridde good of greet comfort
That yeveth to lovers most dis-
port,
Comith of sight and biholding,
That clepid is Swete-Loking,
The whiche may noon ese do,
Whan thou art fer thy lady fro;
Wherfore thou prese alwey to be
In place, where thou mayst hir se.
For it is thing most amerous,
Most delitable and saverous,
For to aswage a mannes sorowe,
To sene his lady by the morowe.
For it is a ful noble thing
Whan thyn eyen have meting
With that relyke precious,
Wherof they be so desirous.
But al day after, soth it is,
They have no drede to faren amis,
They dreden neither wind ne reyn,
Ne yit non other maner peyn.
For whan thyn eyen were thus in blis,
Yit of hir curtesye, ywis,
Aloon they can not have hir joye,
But to the herte they it convoye;
Part of hir blis to him they sende,
Of al this harm to make an ende.
The eye is a good messangere,
Which can to the herte in such manere
Tidyngis sende, that he hath seen,
To voide him of his peynes cleen.
Wherof the herte rejoyseth so
That a gret party of his wo
Is voided, and put awey to flight.
Right as the derknesse of the night
Is chased with clerenesse of the mone,
Right so is al his wo ful sone
Devoided clene, whan that the sight
Biholden may that fresshe wight
That the herte desyreth so,
That al his derknesse is ago;
For than the herte is al at ese,
Whan they seen that that may hem plese.

NOW have I thee declared al out,
Of that thou were in drede and dout;
For I have told thee feithfully
What thee may curen utterly,
And alle lovers that wole be

The
Romaunt
of the
Rose

Swete-
Speche

Swete-
Loking

271

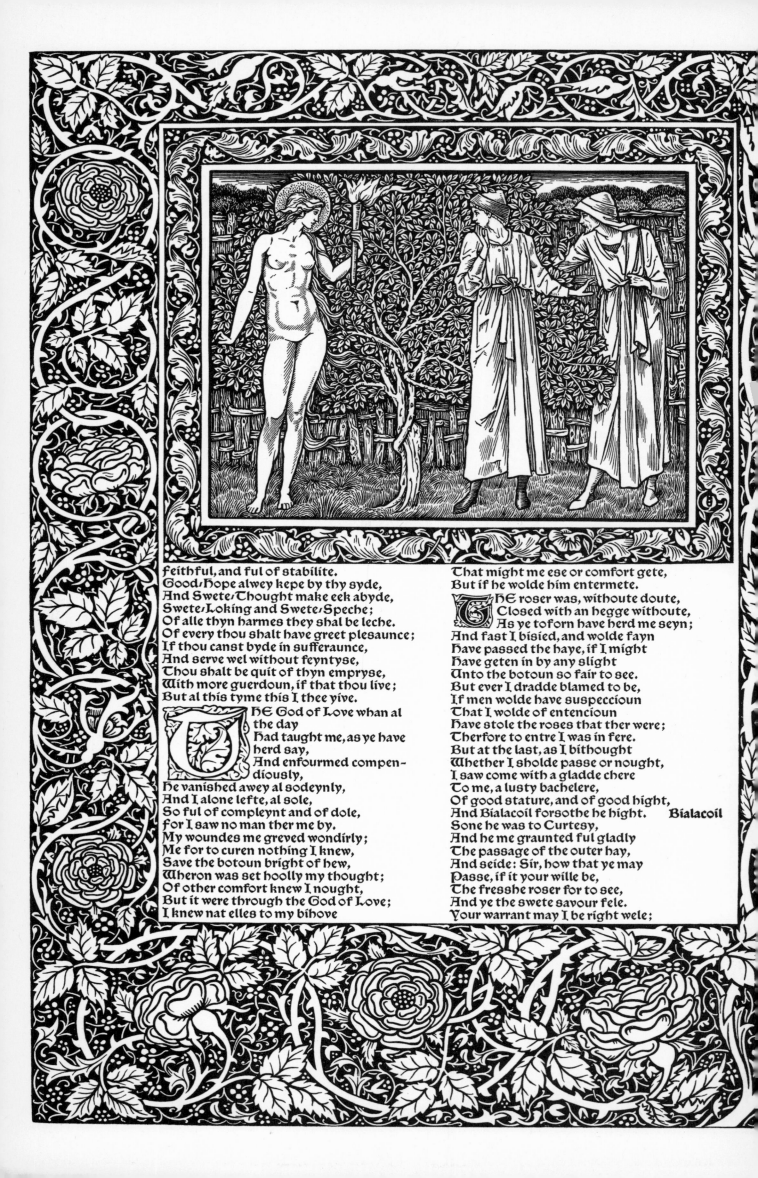

feithful, and ful of stabilite.
Good Hope alwey kepe by thy syde,
And Swete Thought make eek abyde,
Swete Loking and Swete Speche;
Of alle thyn harmes they shal be leche.
Of every thou shalt have greet plesaunce;
If thou canst byde in sufferaunce,
And serve wel without feyntyse,
Thou shalt be quit of thyn empryse,
With more guerdoun, if that thou live;
But al this tyme this I thee yive.

THE God of Love whan al the day
Had taught me, as ye have herd say,
And enfourmed compen-
diously,
He vanished awey al sodeynly,
And I alone lefte, al sole,
So ful of compleynt and of dole,
for I saw no man ther me by.
My woundes me greved wondirly;
Me for to curen nothing I knew,
Save the botoun bright of hew,
Wheron was set hoolly my thought;
Of other comfort knew I nought,
But it were through the God of Love;
I knew nat elles to my bihove

That might me ese or comfort gete,
But if he wolde him entermete.

THE roser was, withoute doute,
Closed with an hegge withoute,
As ye toforn have herd me seyn;
And fast I bisied, and wolde fayn
Have passed the haye, if I might
Have geten in by any slight
Unto the botoun so fair to see.
But ever I dradde blamed to be,
If men wolde have suspeccioun
That I wolde of entencioun
Have stole the roses that ther were;
Therfore to entre I was in fere.
But at the last, as I bithought
Whether I sholde passe or nought,
I saw come with a gladde chere
To me, a lusty bachelere,
Of good stature, and of good hight,
And Bialacoil forsothe he hight. **Bialacoil**
Sone he was to Curtesy,
And he me graunted ful gladly
The passage of the outer hay,
And seide: Sir, how that ye may
Passe, if it your wille be,
The fresshe roser for to see,
And ye the swete savour fele.
Your warrant may I be right wele;

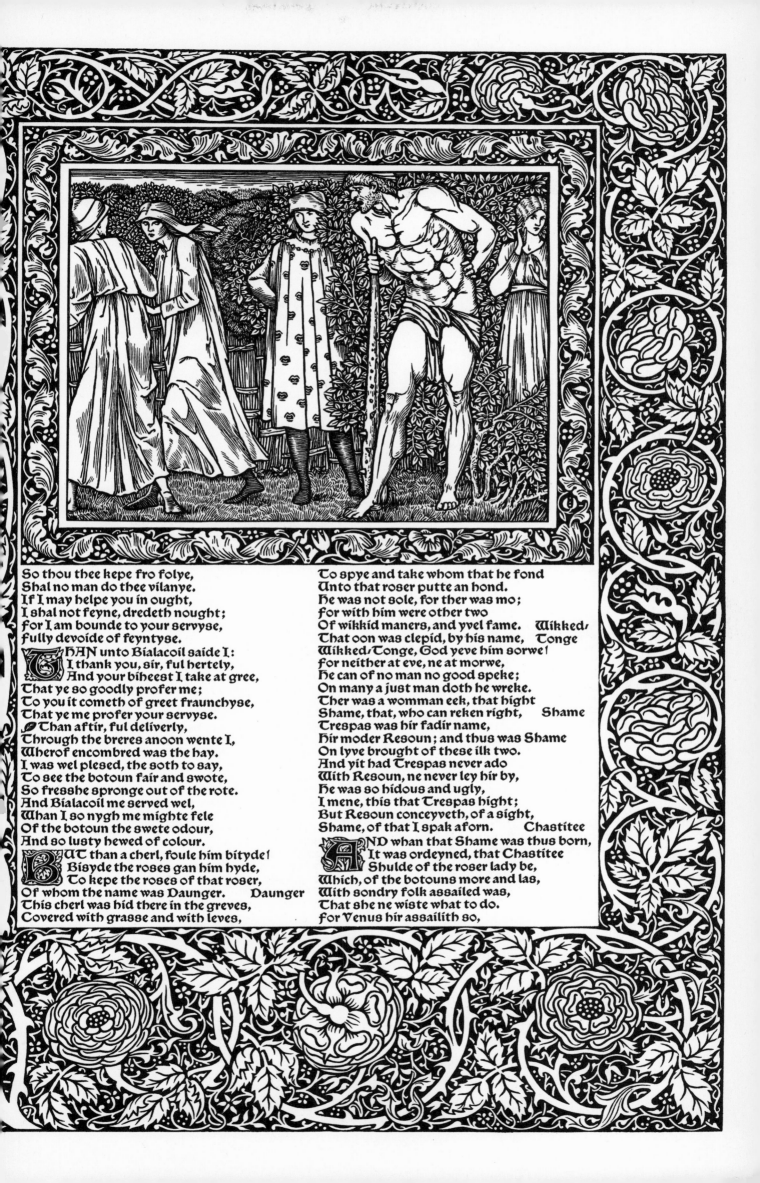

So thou thee kepe fro folye,
Shal no man do thee vilanye.
If I may helpe you in ought,
I shal not feyne, dredeth nought;
for I am bounde to your servyse,
fully devoide of feyntyse.
THAN unto Bialacoil saide I:
I thank you, sir, ful hertely,
And your biheest I take at gree,
That ye so goodly profer me;
To you it cometh of greet fraunchyse,
That ye me profer your servyse.
Than aftir, ful deliverly,
Through the breres anoon wente I,
Wherof encombred was the hay.
I was wel plesed, the soth to say,
To see the botoun fair and swote,
So fresshe sponge out of the rote.
And Bialacoil me served wel,
Whan I so nygh me mighte fele
Of the botoun the swete odour,
And so lusty hewed of colour.
BUT than a cherl, foule him bityde!
Bisyde the roses gan him hyde,
To kepe the roses of that roser,
Of whom the name was Daunger.   Daunger
This cherl was hid there in the greves,
Covered with grasse and with leves,

To spye and take whom that he fond
Unto that roser putte an hond.
He was not sole, for ther was mo;
for with him were other two
Of wikkid maners, and yvel fame.   Wikked-
That oon was clepid, by his name,   Tonge
Wikked-Tonge, God yeve him sorwe!
for neither at eve, ne at morwe,
He can of no man no good speke;
On many a just man doth he wreke.
Ther was a womman eek, that hight
Shame, that, who can reken right,   Shame
Trespas was hir fadir name,
Hir moder Resoun; and thus was Shame
On lyve brought of these ilk two.
And yit had Trespas never ado
With Resoun, ne never ley hir by,
He was so hidous and ugly,
I mene, this that Trespas hight;
But Resoun conceyveth, of a sight,
Shame, of that I spak aforn.   Chastitee
AND when that Shame was thus born,
It was ordeyned, that Chastitee
Shulde of the roser lady be,
Which, of the botouns more and las,
With sondry folk assailed was,
That she ne wiste what to do.
for Venus hir assailith so,

That night and day from hir she stal
Botouns and roses over al.
To Resoun than prayeth Chastitee,
Whom Venus flemed over the see,
That she hir doughter wolde hir lene,
To kepe the roser fresh and grene.
Anoon Resoun to Chastitee
Is fully assented that it be,
And grauntid hir, at hir request,
That Shame, bicause she is honest,
Shal keper of the roser be.
And thus to kepe it ther were three,
That noon shulde hardy be ne bold,
Were he yong, or were he old,
Ageyn hir wille awey to bere
Botouns ne roses, that ther were.
I had wel sped, had I not been
Awayted with these three, and seen.
For Bialacoil, that was so fair,
So gracious and debonair,
Quitte him to me ful curteisly,
And, me to plese, bad that I
Shuld drawe me to the botoun nere;
Prese in, to touche the rosere
Which bar the roses, he yaf me leve;
This graunt ne might but litel greve.
And for he saw it lyked me,
Right nygh the botoun pullede he
A leef al grene, and yaf me that,
The which ful nygh the botoun sat;
I made me of that leef ful queynt.
And whan I felte I was aqueynt
With Bialacoil, and so prive,
I wende al at my wille had be.
THAN wex I hardy for to tel
To Bialacoil how me bifel
Of Love, that took and wounded me,
And seide: Sir, so mote I thee,
I may no joye have in no wyse,
Upon no syde, but it ryse;
For sithe, if I shal not feyne,
In herte I have had so gret peyne,
So gret annoy, and such affray,
That I ne wot what I shal say;
I drede your wrath to disserve.
Lever me were, that knyves kerve
My body shulde in pecis smalle,
Than in any wyse it shulde falle
That ye wratthed shulde been with me.
Sey boldely thy wille, quod he,
I nil be wroth, if that I may,
For nought that thou shalt to me say.
Thanne seide I: Sir, not you displese
To knowen of my greet unese,
In which only Love hath me brought;
For peynes greet, disese and thought,
Fro day to day he doth me drye;
Supposeth not, sir, that I lye.
In me fyve woundes dide he make,
The sore of whiche shal never slake
But ye the botoun graunte me,
Which is most passaunt of beautee,
My lyf, my deth, and my martyre,
And tresour that I most desyre.

274

THAN Bialacoil, affrayed all,
Seyde: Sir, it may not fall;
That ye desire, it may not ryse.
What? wolde ye shende me in this wyse?
A mochel foole than I were,
If I suffrid you awey to bere
The fresh botoun, so fair of sight.
For it were neither skile ne right
Of the roser ye broke the rind,
Or take the rose aforn his kind;
Ye ar not courteys to aske it.
Lat it stil on the roser sit,
And growe til it amended be,
And parfitly come to beaute.
I nolde not that it pulled wer
Fro the roser that it ber,
To me it is so leef and dere.
WITH that sterte out anoon Daungere,
Out of the place where he was hid.
His malice in his chere was kid;
Ful greet he was, and blak of hewe,
Sturdy and hidous, whoso him knewe;
Like sharp urchouns his here was growe,
His eyes rede as the fire-glow;
His nose frounced ful kirked stood,
He com criand as he were wood,
And seide: Bialacoil, tel me why
Thou bringest hider so boldly
Him that so nygh is the roser?
Thou worchist in a wrong maner;
He thenkith to dishonour thee,
Thou art wel worthy to have maugree
To late him of the roser wit;
Who serveth a feloun is yvel quit.
Thou woldist have doon greet bountee,
And he with shame wolde quyte thee.
Flee hennes, felowe! I rede thee go!
It wanteth litel I wol thee slo;
For Bialacoil ne knew thee nought,
Whan thee to serve he sette his thought;
For thou wolt shame him, if thou might,
Bothe ageyn resoun and right.
I wol no more in thee affye,
That comest so slyghly for tespye;
For it preveth wonder wel,
Thy slight and tresoun every del.
I DURST no more ther make abode,
For the cherl, he was so wode;
So gan he threten and manace,
And thurgh the haye he did me chace.
For feer of him I tremblid and quook,
So cherlishly his heed he shook;
And seide, if eft he might me take,
I shulde not from his hondis scape.
THAN Bialacoil is fled and mate,
And I al sole, disconsolate,
Was left aloon in peyne and thought;
For shame, to deth I was nygh brought.
Than thought I on myn high foly,
How that my body, utterly,
Was yeve to peyne and to martyre;
And therto hadde I so gret yre,
That I ne durst the hayes passe;
Ther was non hope, ther was no grace.

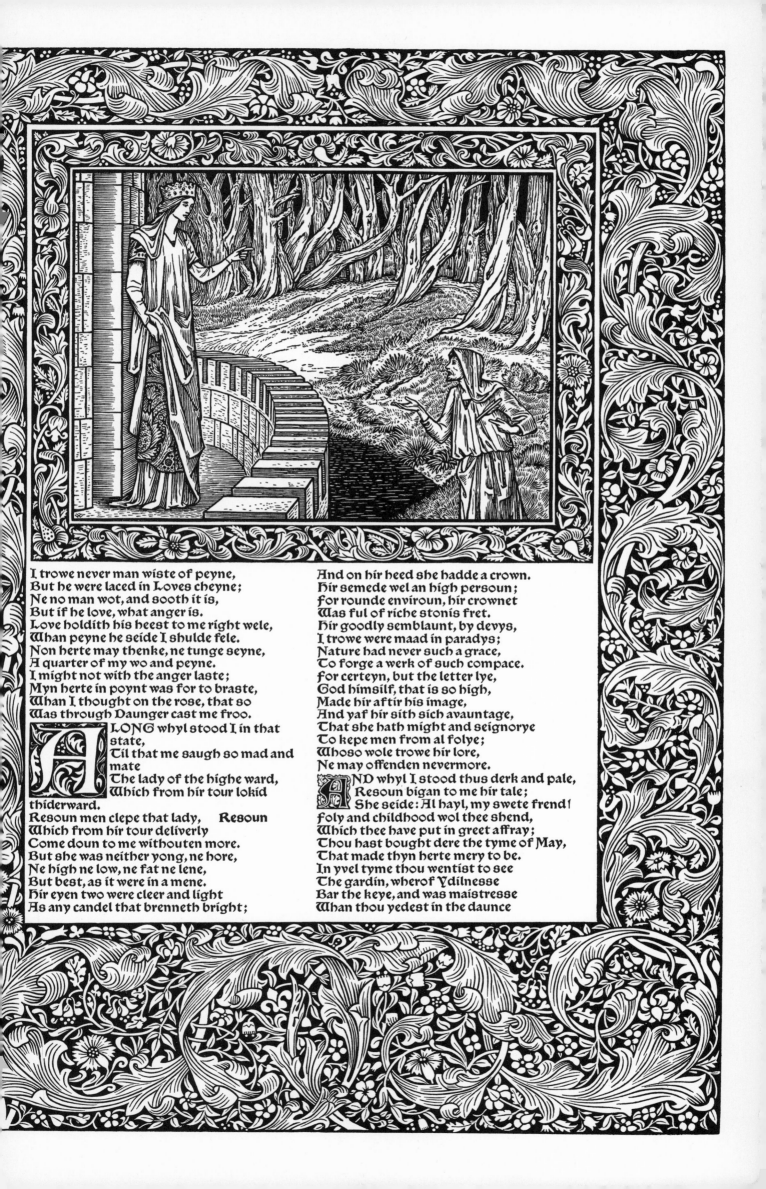

I trowe never man wiste of peyne,
But he were laced in Loves cheyne;
Ne no man wot, and sooth it is,
But if he love, what anger is.
Love holdith his heest to me right wele,
Whan peyne he seide I shulde fele.
Non herte may thenke, ne tunge seyne,
A quarter of my wo and peyne.
I might not with the anger laste;
Myn herte in poynt was for to braste,
Whan I thought on the rose, that so
Was through Daunger cast me froo.

ALONG whyl stood I in that state,
Til that me saugh so mad and mate
The lady of the highe ward,
Which from hir tour lokid thiderward.
Resoun men clepe that lady,   Resoun
Which from hir tour deliverly
Come doun to me withouten more.
But she was neither yong, ne hore,
Ne high ne low, ne fat ne lene,
But best, as it were in a mene.
Hir eyen two were cleer and light
As any candel that brenneth bright;

And on hir heed she hadde a crown.
Hir semede wel an high persoun;
for rounde enviroun, hir crownet
Was ful of riche stonis fret.
Hir goodly semblaunt, by devys,
I trowe were maad in paradys;
Nature had never such a grace,
To forge a werk of such compace.
for certeyn, but the letter lye,
God himsilf, that is so high,
Made hir aftir his image,
And yaf hir sith sich avauntage,
That she hath might and seignorye
To kepe men from al folye;
Whoso wole trowe hir lore,
Ne may offenden nevermore.

AND whyl I stood thus derk and pale,
Resoun bigan to me hir tale;
She seide: Al hayl, my swete frend!
foly and childhood wol thee shend,
Which thee have put in greet affray;
Thou hast bought dere the tyme of May,
That made thyn herte mery to be.
In yvel tyme thou wentist to see
The gardin, wherof Ydilnesse
Bar the keye, and was maistresse
Whan thou yedest in the daunce

With hir, and haddest aqueyntaunce:
Hir aqueyntaunce is perilous,
First softe, and aftirward noyous;
She hath thee trasshed, withoute ween;
The God of Love had thee not seen,
Ne hadde Ydilnesse thee conveyed
In the verger where Mirthe him pleyed.
If foly have supprised thee,
Do so that it recovered be;
And be wel war to take no more
Counsel, that greveth aftir sore;
He is wys that wol himsilf chastyse.
And though a young man in any wyse
Trespace among, and do foly,
Lat him not tarye, but hastily
Lat him amende what so be mis.
And eek I counseile thee, ywis,
The God of Love hoolly foryet,
That hath thee in sich peyne set,
And thee in herte tormented so.
I can nat seen how thou mayst go
Other weyes to garisoun;
For Daunger, that is so feloun,
Felly purposith thee to werrey,
Which is ful cruel, the soth to sey.
And yit of Daunger cometh no blame,
In reward of my doughter Shame,
Which hath the roses in hir warde,
As she that may be no musarde.
And Wikked-Tunge is with these two,
That suffrith no man thider go;
For er a thing be do, he shal,
Where that he cometh, over al,
In fourty places, if it be sought,
Seye thing that never was doon ne wrought;
So moche tresoun is in his male,
Of falsnesse for to feyne a tale.
Thou delest with angry folk, ywis;
Wherfor to thee it bettir is
From these folk awey to fare,
For they wol make thee live in care.
This is the yvel that Love they calle,
Wherin ther is but foly alle,
For love is foly everydel;
Who loveth, in no wyse may do wel,
Ne sette his thought on no good werk.
His scole he lesith, if he be clerk;
Of other craft eek if he be,
He shal not thryve therin; for he
In love shal have more passioun
Than monke, hermyte, or chanoun.
The peyne is hard, out of mesure,
The joye may eek no whyl endure;
And in the possessioun
Is muche tribulacioun;
The joye it is so short-lasting,
And but in happe is the geting;
For I see ther many in travaille,
That atte laste foule fayle.
I was nothing thy counseler,
Whan thou were maad the homager
Of God of Love to hastily;
Ther was no wisdom, but foly.

Thyn herte was joly, but not sage,
Whan thou were brought in sich a rage,
To yelde thee so redily,
And to Love, of his gret maistry.
I rede thee Love awey to dryve,
That makith thee recche not of thy lyve.
The foly more fro day to day
Shal growe, but thou it putte away.
Take with thy teeth the bridel faste,
To daunte thyn herte; and eek thee caste,
If that thou mayst, to gete defence
For to redresse thy first offence.
Whoso his herte alwey wol leve,
Shal finde among that shal him greve.
WHAN I hir herd thus me chastyse,
I answerd in ful angry wyse.
I prayed hir cessen of hir speche,
Outher to chastyse me or teche,
To bidde me my thought refreyne,
Which Love hath caught in his demeyne:
What? wene ye Love wol consent,
That me assailith with bowe bent,
To draw myn herte out of his honde,
Which is so quikly in his bonde?
That ye counsayle, may never be;
For whan he first arested me,
He took myn herte so hool him til,
That it is nothing at my wil;
He taughte it so him for to obey,
That he it sparred with a key.
I pray yow lat me be al stille.
For ye may wel, if that ye wille,
Your wordis waste in idilnesse;
For utterly, withouten gesse,
Al that ye seyn is but in veyne.
Me were lever dye in the peyne,
Than Love to meward shulde arette
Falsheed, or tresoun on me sette.
I wol me gete prys or blame,
And love trewe, to save my name;
Who me chastysith, I him hate.
WITH that word Resoun wente hir gate,
Whan she saugh for no sermoning
She might me fro my foly bring.
Than dismayed, I lefte al sool,
Forwery, forwandred as a fool,
For I ne knew no chevisaunce.
Than fel into my remembraunce,
How Love bade me to purveye
A felowe, to whom I mighte seye
My counsel and my privete,
For that shulde muche availe me.
With that bithought I me, that I
Hadde a felowe faste by,
Trewe and siker, curteys, and hend,
And he was called by name a freend;
A trewer felowe was nowher noon.
In haste to him I wente anoon,
And to him al my wo I tolde,
Fro him right nought I wold withholde.
I tolde him al withoute were,
And made my compleynt on Daungere,
How for to see he was hidous,

And to meward contrarious;
The whiche through his cruelte
Was in poynt to have meygned me;
With Bialacoil whan he me sey
Within the gardyn walke and pley,
fro me he made him for to go,
And I bilefte aloon in wo;
I durst no lenger with him speke,
for Daunger seide he wolde be wreke,
Whan that he sawe how I wente
The fresshe botoun for to hente,
If I were hardy to come neer
Bitwene the hay and the roser.
THIS freend, whan he wiste of my thought,
He discomforted me right nought,
But seide: felowe, be not so mad,
Ne so abaysshed nor bistad.
Mysilf I knowe ful wel Daungere,
And how he is feers of his chere,
At prime temps, Love to manace;
ful ofte I have ben in his caas.
A feloun first though that he be,
Aftir thou shalt him souple see.
Of long passed I knew him wele;
Ungoodly first though men him fele,
He wol meek aftir, in his bering,
Been, for service and obeysshing.
I shal thee telle what thou shalt do:
Mekely I rede thou go him to,
Of herte pray him specialy
Of thy trespace to have mercy,
And hote him wel, him here to plese,
That thou shalt nevermore him displese.
Who can best serve of flatery,
Shal plese Daunger most uttirly.
MY freend hath seid to me so wel,
That he me esid hath somdel,
And eek allegged of my torment;
for through him had I hardement
Again to Daunger for to go,
To preve if I might meke him so.
TO Daunger cam I, al ashamed,
The which aforn me hadde blamed,
Desyring for to pese my wo;
But over hegge durst I not go,
for he forbad me the passage.
I fond him cruel in his rage,
And in his hond a gret burdoun.
To him I knelid lowe adoun,
ful meke of port, and simple of chere,
And seide: Sir, I am comen here
Only to aske of you mercy.
That greveth me, sir, ful gretly
That ever my lyf I wratthed you,
But for to amende I am come now,
With al my might, bothe loude and stille,
To doon right at your owne wille;
for Love made me for to do
That I have trespassed hidirto;
fro whom I ne may withdrawe myn herte;
Yit shal I never, for joy ne smerte,
What so bifalle, good or ille,
Offende more ageyn your wille.

t 3

Lever I have endure disese
Than do that shulde you displese.
I you require and pray, that ye
Of me have mercy and pitee,
To stinte your yre that greveth so,
And I wol swere for evermo
To be redressid at your lyking,
If I trespasse in any thing;
Save that I pray thee graunte me
A thing that may nat warned be,
That I may love, al only;
Non other thing of you aske I.
I shal doon elles wel, ywis,
If of your grace ye graunte me this.
And ye ne may not letten me,
for wel wot ye that love is free,
And I shal loven, sith that I wil,
Whoever lyke it wel or il;
And yit ne wold I, for al fraunce,
Do thing to do you displesaunce.
WHAN Daunger fil in his entent
for to foryeve his maltalent;
But al his wratthe yit at laste
He hath relesed, I preyde so faste:
Shortly he seide: Thy request
Is not to mochel dishonest;
Ne I wol not werne it thee,
for yit nothing engreveth me.
for though thou love thus evermore,
To me is neither softe ne sore.
Love wher thee list; what recchith me,
So thou fer fro my roses be?
Trust not on me, for noon assay,
In any time to passe the hay.
Thus hath he graunted my prayere.
WHAN wente I forth, withouten were,
Unto my freend, and tolde him al,
Which was right joyful of my tale.
He seide: Now goth wel thyn affaire,
He shal to thee be debonaire.
Though he aforn was dispitous,
He shal heeraftir be gracious.
If he were touchid on som good veyne,
He shuld yit rewen on thy peyne.
Suffre, I rede, and no boost make,
Til thou at good mes mayst him take.
By suffraunce, and by wordis softe,
A man may overcomen ofte
Him that aforn he hadde in drede,
In bookis sothly as I rede.
THUS hath my freend with gret comfort
Avaunced me with high disport,
Which wolde me good as mich as I.
And thanne anoon ful sodeynly
I took my leve, and streight I went
Unto the hay; for gret talent
I had to seen the fresh botoun,
Wherin lay my salvacioun;
And Daunger took kepe, if that I
Kepe him covenaunt trewly.
So sore I dradde his manasing,
I durst not breken his bidding;
for, lest that I were of him shent,

I brak not his comaundement,
for to purchase his good wil.
It was hard for to come thertil,
His mercy was to fer bihinde;
I wepte, for I ne might it finde.
I compleyned and sighed sore,
And languisshed evermore,
for I durst not over go
Unto the rose I loved so.
Thurghout my deming outerly,
Than had he knowlege certeinly,
That Love me ladde in sich a wyse,
That in me ther was no feyntyse,
falsheed, ne no trecherye.
And yit he, ful of vilanye,
Of disdeyne, and cruelte,
On me ne wolde have pite,
His cruel wil for to refreyne,
Though I wepe alwey, and compleyne.

AND while I was in this torment,
Were come of grace, by God
sent,
fraunchyse, and with hir Pite
fulfild the botoun of bountee.
They go to Daunger anon-right
To forther me with al hir might,
And helpe in worde and in dede,
for wel they saugh that it was nede.
first, of hir grace, dame fraunchyse
Hath taken word of this empryse:

SHE seide: Daunger, gret wrong ye do
To worche this man so muche wo,
Or pynen him so angerly;
It is to you gret vilany.
I can not see why, ne how,
That he hath trespassed ageyn you,
Save that he loveth; wherfore ye shulde
The more in cherete of him holde.
The force of love makith him do this;
Who wolde him blame he dide amis?
He leseth more than ye may do;
His peyne is hard, ye may see, lo!
And Love in no wyse wolde consente
That he have power to repente;
for though that quik ye wolde him sloo,
fro Love his herte may not go.
Now, swete sir, is it your ese
Him for to angre or disese?
Allas, what may it you avaunce
To doon to him so greet grevaunce?
What worship is it agayn him take,
Or on your man a werre make,
Sith he so lowly every wyse
Is redy, as ye lust devyse?
If Love hath caught him in his lace,
You for tobeye in every caas,
And been your suget at your wille,
Shulde ye therfore willen him ille?
Ye shulde him spare more, about,
Than him that is bothe proud and stout.
Curtesye wol that ye socour
Hem that ben meke undir your cure.
His herte is hard, that wole not meke,

278

Whan men of mekenesse him biseke.
THAT is certeyn, seide Pite;
We see ofte that humilitee
Bothe ire, and also felonye
Venquissheth, and also melancolye;
To stonde forth in such duresse,
This crueltee and wikkednesse.
Wherfore I pray you, sir Daungere,
for to mayntene no lenger here
Such cruel werre agayn your man,
As hoolly youres as ever he can;
Nor that ye worchen no more wo
On this caytif that languisshith so,
Which wol no more to you trespasse,
But put him hoolly in your grace.
His offense ne was but lyte;
The God of Love it was to wyte,
That he your thral so gretly is,
And if ye harm him, ye doon amis;
for he hath had ful hard penaunce,
Sith that ye refte him thaqueyntaunce
Of Bialacoil, his moste joye,
Which alle his peynes might acoye.
He was biforn anoyed sore,
But than ye doubled him wel more;
for he of blis hath ben ful bare,
Sith Bialacoil was fro him fare.
Love hath to him do greet distresse,
He hath no nede of more duresse.
Voideth from him your ire, I rede;
Ye may not winnen in this dede.
Makith Bialacoil repeire ageyn,
And haveth pite upon his peyn;
for fraunchise wol, and I, Pite,
That merciful to him ye be;
And sith that she and I accorde,
Have upon him misericorde;
for I you pray, and eek moneste,
Nought to refusen our requeste;
for he is hard and fel of thought,
That for us two wol do right nought.
DAUNGER ne might no more endure,
He meked him unto mesure.
I wol in no wyse, seith Daungere,
Denye that ye have asked here;
It were to greet uncurtesye.
I wol ye have the companye
Of Bialacoil, as ye devyse;
I wol him letten in no wyse.
To Bialacoil than wente in by
fraunchyse, and seide ful curteisly:
Ye have to longe be deignous
Unto this lover, and daungerous,
fro him to withdrawe your presence,
Which hath do to him grete offence,
That ye not wolde upon him see;
Wherfore a sorowful man is he.
Shape ye to paye him, and to plese,
Of my love if ye wol have ese.
fulfil his wil, sith that ye knowe
Daunger is daunted and brought lowe
Thurgh help of me and of Pite;
You thar no more afered be.

I SHAL do right as ye wil,
Saith Bialacoil, for it is skil,
Sith Daunger wol that it so be.
THAN fraunchise hath him sent to me.
Bialacoil at the biginning
Salued me in his coming.
No straungenes was in him seen,
No more than he ne had wrathed been.
As faire semblaunt than shewed he me,
And goodly, as aforn did he;
And by the honde, withouten doute,
Within the haye, right al aboute
He ladde me, with right good chere,
Al environ the vergere,
That Daunger had me chased fro.
Now have I leve overal to go;
Now am I raised, at my devys,
Fro helle unto paradys.
Thus Bialacoil, of gentilnesse,
With alle his peyne and besinesse,
Hath shewed me, only of grace,
The estres of the swote place.
I SAW the rose, whan I was nigh,
Was gretter woxen, and more high,
Fresh, rody, and faire of hewe,
Of colour ever yliche newe.
And whan I had it longe seen,
I saugh that through the leves grene
The rose spredde to spanishing;
To sene it was a goodly thing.
But it ne was so spred on brede,
That men within might knowe the sede;
For it covert was and enclose
Bothe with the leves and with the rose.
The stalk was even and grene upright,
It was theron a goodly sight;
And wel the better, withouten wene,
For the seed was not ysene.
Ful faire it spradde, God it blesse!
For suche another, as I gesse,
Aforn ne was, ne more vermayle.
I was abawed for merveyle,
For ever, the fairer that it was,
The more I am bounden in Loves laas.
LONGE I abood there, soth to
saye,
Til Bialacoil I gan to praye,
Whan that I sawe him in no wyse
To me warnen his servyse,
That he me wolde graunte a thing,
Which to remembre is wel sitting;
This is to sayne, that of his grace
He wolde me yeve leyser and space
To me that was so desirous
To have a kissing precious
Of the goodly freshe rose,
That swetely smelleth in my nose;
For if it you displesed nought,
I wolde gladly, as I have sought,
Have a cos therof freely
Of your yeft; for certainly
I wol non have but by your leve,
So loth me were you for to greve.

HE sayde: frend, so God me spede,
Of Chastite I have suche drede,
Thou shuldest not warned be for me,
But I dar not, for Chastite.
Agayn hir dar I not misdo,
For alwey biddeth she me so
To yeve no lover leve to kisse;
For who therto may winnen, ywis,
He of the surplus of the pray
May live in hope to get som day.
For who so kissing may attayne,
Of loves peyne hath, soth to sayne,
The beste and most avenaunt,
And ernest of the remenaunt.
OF his answere I syghed sore;
I durst assaye him tho no more,
I had such drede to greve him ay.
A man shulde not to muche assaye
To chafe his frend out of mesure,
Nor put his lyf in aventure;
For no man at the firste stroke
Ne may nat felle doun an oke;
Nor of the reisins have the wyne,
Til grapes rype and wel afyne
Be sore empressid, I you ensure,
And drawen out of the pressure.
But I, forpeyned wonder stronge,
Thought that I abood right longe
Aftir the kis, in peyne and wo,
Sith I to kis desyred so:
Til that, rewing on my distresse,
Ther to me Venus the goddesse,   Venus
Which ay werreyeth Chastite,
Came of hir grace, to socoure me,
Whos might is knowe fer and wyde,
For she is modir of Cupyde,
The God of Love, blinde as stoon,
That helpith lovers many oon.
This lady brought in hir right hond
Of brenning fyr a blasing brond;
Wherof the flawme and hote fyr
Hath many a lady in desyr
Of love brought, and sore het,
And in hir servise hir hertes set.
THIS lady was of good entayle,
Right wondirful of apparayle;
By hir atyre so bright and shene,
Men might perceyve wel, and sene,
She was not of religioun.
Nor I nil make mencioun
Nor of hir robe, nor of tresour,
Of broche, nor of hir riche attour;
Ne of hir girdil aboute hir syde,
For that I nil not long abyde.
But knowith wel, that certeynly
She was arayed richely.
Devoyd of pryde certeyn she was.
TO Bialacoil she wente a pas,
And to him shortly, in a clause,
She seide: Sir, what is the cause
Ye been of port so daungerous
Unto this lover, and deynous,
To graunte him nothing but a kis?

To werne it him ye doon amis;
Sith wel ye wote, how that he
Is Loves servaunt, as ye may see,
And hath beaute, wherthrough he is
Worthy of love to have the blis.
How he is semely, biholde and see,
How he is fair, how he is free,
How he is swote and debonair,
Of age yong, lusty, and fair.
Ther is no lady so hauteyne,
Duchesse, countesse, ne chasteleyne,
That I nolde holde hir ungoodly
For to refuse him outerly.
His breeth is also good and swete,
And eke his lippis rody, and mete
Only to pleyen, and to kisse.
Graunte him a kis, of gentilnesse!
His teeth arn also whyte and clene;
Me thinkith wrong, withouten wene,
If ye now werne him, trustith me,
To graunte that a kis have he;
The lasse to helpe him that ye haste,
The more tyme shul ye waste.

WHAN the flawme of the verry brond,
That Venus brought in hir right hond,
Had Bialacoil with hete smete,
Anoon he bad, withouten lette,
Graunte to me the rose kisse.
Than of my peyne I gan to lisse,
And to the rose anoon wente I,
And kissid it ful feithfully.
Thar no man aske if I was blythe,
Whan the savour softe and lythe
Strook to myn herte withoute more,
And me alegged of my sore,
So was I ful of joye and blisse.
It is fair sich a flour to kisse,
It was so swote and saverous.
I might not be so anguisshous,
That I mote glad and joly be,
Whan that I remembre me.
Yit ever among, sothly to seyn,
I suffre noye and moche peyn.

THE see may never be so stil,
That with a litel winde it nil
Overwhelme and turne also,
As it were wood, in wawis go.
Aftir the calm the trouble sone
Mot folowe, and chaunge as the mone.
Right so farith Love, that selde in oon
Holdith his anker; for right anoon
Whan they in ese wene best to live,
They been with tempest al fordrive.
Who serveth Love, can telle of wo;
The stoundemele joye mot overgo.
Now he hurteth, and now he cureth,
For selde in oo poynt Love endureth.
Now is it right me to procede,
How Shame gan medle and take hede,
Thurgh whom felle angres I have had;
And how the stronge wal was maad,
And the castell of brede and lengthe,
That God of Love wan with his strengthe.

280

Al this in romance wil I sette,
And for nothing ne wil I lette,
So that it lyking to hir be,
That is the flour of beaute;
For she may best my labour quyte,
That I for hir love shal endyte.

WIKKID-TUNGE, that the covyne
Of every lover can devyne
Worst, and addith more somdel,
For Wikkid-Tunge seith never wel,
To meward bar he right gret hate,
Espying me erly and late,
Til he hath seen the grete chere
Of Bialacoil and me yfere.
He mighte not his tunge withstonde
Worse to reporte than he fonde,
He was so ful of cursed rage;
It sat him wel of his linage,
For him an Irish womman bar.
His tunge was fyled sharp, and squar,
Poignaunt and right kerving,
And wonder bitter in speking.
For whan that he me gan espye,
He swoor, afferming sikirly,
Bitwene Bialacoil and me
Was yvel aquayntaunce and privee.
He spak therof so folily,
That he awakid jelousy;
Which, al afrayed in his rysing,
Whan that he herde him jangling,
He ran anoon, as he were wood,
To Bialacoil ther that he stood;
Which hadde lever in this caas
Have been at Reynes or Amyas;
For foot-hoot, in his felonye
To him thus seide Jelousye:

WHY hast thou been so necligent,
To kepen, whan I was absent,
This verger here left in thy ward?
To me thou haddist no reward,
To truste, to thy confusioun,
Him thus, to whom suspeccioun
I have right greet, for it is nede;
It is wel shewed by the dede.
Greet faute in thee now have I founde;
By God, anoon thou shalt be bounde,
And faste loken in a tour,
Withoute refuyt or socour.
For Shame to long hath be thee fro;
Over sone she was agoo.
Whan thou hast lost bothe drede and fere,
It semed wel she was not here.
She was not bisy, in no wyse,
To kepe thee and to chastyse,
And for to helpen Chastitee
To kepe the roser, as thinkith me.
For than this boy-knave so boldely
Ne sholde not have be hardy,
Ne in this verger had such game,
Which now me turneth to gret shame.

BIALACOIL nist what to sey;
Ful fayn he wolde have fled awey,
For fere han hid, nere that he

Al sodeynly took him with me.
And whan I saugh he hadde so,
This Jelousye, take us two,
I was astoned, and knew no rede,
But fledde awey for verrey drede.
THAN Shame cam forth ful simply;
She wende have trespaced ful gretly;
Humble of hir port, and made it simple,
Wering a vayle in stede of wimple,
As nonnis doon in hir abbey.
Bicause hir herte was in affray,
She gan to speke, within a throwe,
To Jelousye, right wonder lowe.
First of his grace she bisought,
And seide: Sire, ne leveth nought
Wikkid-Tunge, that fals espye,
Which is so glad to feyne and lye.
He hath you maad, thurgh flatering,
On Bialacoil a fals lesing.
His falsnesse is not now anew,
It is to long that he him knew.
This is not the firste day;
For Wikkid-Tunge hath custom ay
Yonge folkis to bewreye,
And false lesinges on hem leye.
Yit nevertheles I see among,
That the loigne it is so longe
Of Bialacoil, hertis to lure,
In Loves servise for to endure,
Drawing suche folk him to,
That he had nothing with to do;
But in sothnesse I trowe nought,
That Bialacoil hadde ever in thought
To do trespace or vilanye;
But, for his modir Curtesye
Hath taught him ever for to be
Good of aqueyntaunce and privee;
For he loveth non hevinesse,
But mirthe and pley, and al gladnesse;
He hateth alle trecherous,
Soleyn folk and envious;
For wel ye witen how that he
Wol ever glad and joyful be
Honestly with folk to pley.
I have be negligent, in good fey,
To chastise him; therfore now I
Of herte crye you here mercy,
That I have been so recheles
To tamen him, withouten lees.
Of my foly I me repente;
Now wol I hool sette myn entente
To kepe, bothe loude and stille,
Bialacoil to do your wille.
SHAME, Shame, seyde Jelousy,
To be bitrasshed gret drede have I.
Lecherye hath clombe so hye,
That almost blered is myn ye;
No wonder is, if that drede have I.
Overal regnith Lechery,
Whos might yit growith night and day.
Bothe in cloistre and in abbey
Chastite is werreyed overal.
Therfore I wol with siker wal

Close bothe roses and roser.
I have to longe in this maner
Left hem unclosid wilfully;
Wherfore I am right inwardly
Sorowful and repente me.
But now they shal no lenger be
Unclosid; and yit I drede sore,
I shal repente ferthermore,
For the game goth al amis.
Counsel I mot take newe, ywis.
I have to longe tristed thee,
But now it shal no lenger be;
For he may best, in every cost,
Disceyve, that men tristen most.
I see wel that I am nygh shent,
But if I sette my ful entent
Remedye to purveye.
Therfore close I shal the weye
Fro hem that wol the rose espye,
And come to wayte me vilanye,
For, in good feith and in trouthe,
I wol not lette, for no slouthe,
To live the more in sikirnesse,
To make anoon a forteresse,
To enclose the roses of good savour.
In middis shal I make a tour
To putte Bialacoil in prisoun,
For ever I drede me of tresoun.
I trowe I shal him kepe so,
That he shal have no might to go
Aboute to make companye
To hem that thenke of vilanye;
Ne to no such as hath ben here
Aforn, and founde in him good chere,
Which han assailed him to shende,
And with hir trowandyse to blende.
A fool is eyth for to bigyle;
But may I lyve a litel while,
He shal forthenke his fair semblaunt.
AND with that word cam Drede avaunt,   Drede
Which was abasshed, and in gret fere,
Whan he wiste Jelousye was there.
He was for Drede in such affray,
That not a word durste he say,
But quaking stood ful stille aloon,
Til Jelousye his wey was goon,
Save Shame, that him not forsook;
Bothe Drede and she ful sore quook;
Til that at laste Drede abreyde,
And to his cosin Shame seyde:
O Shame, he seide, in sothfastnesse,
To me it is gret hevinesse,
That the noyse so fer is go,
And the sclaundre of us two.
But sith that it is so bifalle,
We may it not ageyn do calle,
Whan onis sprongen is a fame.
For many a yeer withouten blame
We han been, and many a day;
For many an April and many a May
We han ypassed, not ashamed,
Til Jelousye hath us blamed
Of mistrust and suspecioun

Causeles, withouten enchesoun.
Go we to Daunger hastily,
And late us shewe him openly,
That he hath not aright ywrought,
Whan that he sette nought his thought
To kepe better the purpryse;
In his doing he is not wyse.
He hath to us ydo gret wrong,
That hath suffred now so long
Bialacoil to have his wille,
Alle his lustes to fulfille.
He must amende it utterly,
Or ellis shal he vilaynsly
Exyled be out of this londe;
for he the werre may not withstonde
Of Jelousye, nor the greef,
Sith Bialacoil is at mischeef.
To Daunger, Shame and Drede anoon
The righte wey ben bothe agoon.
The cherl they founden hem aforn
Ligging undir an hawethorn.
Undir his heed no pilowe was,
But in the stede a trusse of gras.
He slombred, and a nappe he took,
Til Shame pitously him shook,
And greet manace on him gan make.
Why slepist thou whan thou shulde wake?
Quod Shame; thou dost us vilanye!
Who tristith thee, he doth folye,
To kepe roses or botouns,
Whan they ben faire in hir sesouns.
Thou art woxe to familiere
Where thou shulde be straunge of chere,
Stout of thy port, redy to greve.
Thou dost gret foly for to leve
Bialacoil herein, to calle
The yonder man to shenden us alle.
Though that thou slepe, we may here
Of Jelousie gret noyse here.
Art thou now late? ryse up in hy,
And stoppe sone and deliverly
Alle the gappis of the hay;
Do no favour, I thee pray.
It fallith nothing to thy name
Make fair semblaunt, where thou maist blame.
If Bialacoil be swete and free,
Dogged and fel thou shuldist be;
froward and outrageous, ywis;
A cherl chaungeth that curteis is.
This have I herd ofte in seying,
That man ne may, for no daunting,
Make a sperhauke of a bosarde.
Alle men wole holde thee for musarde,
That debonair have founden thee;
It sit thee nought curteis to be;
To do men plesaunce or servyse,
In thee it is recreaundyse.
Let thy werkis, fer and nere,
Be lyke thy name, which is Daungere.
Than, al abawid in shewing,
Anoon spak Dreed, right thus seying,
And seide: Daunger, I drede me
That thou ne wolt not bisy be

To kepe that thou hast to kepe;
Whan thou shuldist wake, thou art aslepe.
Thou shalt be greved certeynly
If thee aspye Jelousy,
Or if he finde thee in blame.
He hath today assailed Shame,
And chased awey, with gret manace,
Bialacoil out of this place,
And swereth shortly that he shal
Enclose him in a sturdy wal;
And al is for thy wikkednesse,
for that thee faileth straungenesse.
Thyn herte, I trowe, be failed al;
Thou shalt repente in special,
If Jelousye the sothe knewe;
Thou shalt forthenke, and sore rewe.
With that the cherl his clubbe gan shake,
frouning his eyen gan to make,
And hidous chere; as man in rage,
for ire he brente in his visage.
Whan that he herde him blamed so,
He seide: Out of my wit I go;
To be discomfit I have gret wrong.
Certis, I have now lived to long,
Sith I may not this closer kepe;
Al quik I wolde be dolven depe,
If any man shal more repeire
Into this garden, for foule or faire.
Myn herte for ire goth afere,
That I lete any entre here.
I have do foly, now I see,
But now it shal amended bee.
Who settith foot here any more,
Truly, he shal repente it sore;
for no man mo into this place
Of me to entre shal have grace.
Lever I hadde, with swerdis tweyne
Thurghout myn herte, in every veyne
Perced to be, with many a wounde,
Than slouthe shulde in me be founde.
from hennesforth, by night or day,
I shal defende it, if I may,
Withouten any excepcioun
Of ech maner condicioun;
And if I any man it graunte,
Holdeth me for recreaunte.
Than Daunger on his feet gan stonde,
And hente a burdoun in his honde.
Wroth in his ire, ne lefte he nought,
But thurgh the verger he hath sought.
If he might finde hole or trace,
Wherthurgh that men mot forthby pace,
Or any gappe, he dide it close,
That no man mighte touche a rose
Of the roser al aboute;
He shitteth every man withoute.
Thus day by day Daunger is wers,
More wondirful and more divers,
And feller eek than ever he was;
for him ful oft I singe Allas!
for I ne may nought, thurgh his ire,
Recover that I most desire.
Myn herte, allas, wol brest atwo,

For Bialacoil I wratthed so.
For certeynly, in every membre
I quake, whan I me remembre
Of the botoun, which that I wolde
Fulle ofte a day seen and biholde.
And whan I thenke upon the kisse,
And how muche joye and blisse
I hadde thurgh the savour swete,
For wante of it I grone and grete.
Me thenkith I fele yit in my nose
The swete savour of the rose.
And now I woot that I mot go
So fer the fresshe floures fro,
To me ful welcome were the deeth;
Absens therof, allas, me sleeth!
For whylom with this rose, allas,
I touched nose, mouth, and face;
But now the deeth I must abyde.
But Love consente, another tyde,
That onis I touche may and kisse,
I trowe my peyne shal never lisse.
Theron is al my coveityse,
Which brent myn herte in many wyse.

NOW shal repaire agayn sighinge,
Long wacche on nightis, and no slepinge;
Thought in wisshing, torment, and wo,
With many a turning to and fro,
That half my peyne I can not telle.
For I am fallen into helle
From paradys and welthe, the more
My turment greveth; more and more
Anoyeth now the bittirnesse,
That I toforn have felt swetnesse.
And Wikkid-Tunge, thurgh his falshede,
Causeth al my wo and drede.
On me he leyeth a pitous charge,
Bicause his tunge was to large.

NOW it is tyme, shortly that I
Telle you somthing of
Jelousy,
That was in gret suspe-
cioun.
Aboute him lefte he no
masoun,
That stoon coude leye, ne
querrour;
He hired hem to make a tour.
And first, the roses for to kepe,
Aboute hem made he a diche depe,
Right wondir large, and also brood;
Upon the whiche also stood
Of squared stoon a sturdy wal,
Which on a cragge was founded al,
And right gret thikkenesse eek it bar.
Abouten, it was founded squar,
An hundred fadome on every syde,
It was al liche longe and wyde.
Lest any tyme it were assayled,
Ful wel aboute it was batayled;
And rounde enviroun eek were set
Ful many a riche and fair touret.
At every corner of this wal
Was set a tour ful principal;

And everich hadde, withoute fable,
A porte-colys defensable
To kepe of enemies, and to greve,
That there hir force wolde preve.

AND eek amidde this purpryse
Was maad a tour of gret maistryse;
A fairer saugh no man with sight,
Large and wyde, and of gret might.
They ne dredde noon assaut
Of ginne, gunne, nor skaffaut.
For the temprure of the mortere
Was maad of licour wonder dere;
Of quikke lyme persant and egre,
The which was tempred with vinegre.
The stoon was hard as ademant,
Wherof they made the foundement.
The tour was rounde, maad in compas;
In al this world no richer was,
Ne better ordeigned therwithal.

ABOUTE the tour was maad a wal,
So that, bitwixt that and the tour,
Rosers were set of swete savour,
With many roses that they bere.

AND eek within the castel were
Springoldes, gunnes, bows, archers;
And eek above, atte corners,
Men seyn over the walle stonde
Grete engynes, whiche were nigh honde;
And in the kernels, here and there,
Of arblasters gret plentee were.
Noon armure might hir stroke withstonde,
It were foly to prece to honde.
Without the diche were listes made,
With walles batayled large and brade,
For men and hors shulde not atteyne
To neigh the diche over the pleyne.

THUS Jelousye hath enviroun
Set aboute his garnisoun
With walles rounde, and diche depe,
Only the roser for to kepe.
And Daunger eek, erly and late
The keyes kepte of the utter gate,
The which openeth toward the eest.
And he hadde with him atte leest
Thritty servauntes, echon by name.

THAT other gate kepte Shame,
Which openede, as it was couth,
Toward the parte of the south.
Sergeauntes assigned were
hir to
Ful many, hir wille for to do.

THAN Drede hadde in hir baillye
The keping of the conestablerye,
Toward the north, I undirstonde,
That opened upon the left honde,
The which for nothing may be sure,
But if she do hir bisy cure
Erly on morowe and also late,
Strongly to shette and barre the gate.
Of every thing that she may see
Drede is aferd, wherso she be;
For with a puff of litel winde
Drede is astonied in hir minde.

Therfore, for stelinge of the rose,
I rede hir nought the yate unclose.
A foulis flight wol make hir flee,
And eek a shadowe, if she it see.

THANNE Wikked-Tunge, ful of
envye,
With soudiours of Normandye,
As he that causeth al the bate,
Was keper of the fourthe gate,
And also to the tother three
He went ful ofte, for to see.
Whan his lot was to wake anight,
His instrumentis wolde he dight,
For to blowe and make soun,
Ofter than he hath enchesoun;
And walken oft upon the wal,
Corners and wikettis overal
Ful narwe serchen and espye;
Though he nought fond, yit wolde he lye.
Discordaunt ever fro armonye,
And distoned from melodye,
Controve he wolde, and foule fayle,
With hornpypes of Cornewayle.
In floytes made he discordaunce,
And in his musik, with mischaunce,
He wolde seyn, with notes newe,
That he ne fond no womman trewe,
Ne that he saugh never, in his lyf,
Unto hir husbonde a trewe wyf;
Ne noon so ful of honestee,
That she nil laughe and mery be
Whan that she hereth, or may espye,
A man speken of lecherye.
Everich of hem hath somme vyce;
Oon is dishonest, another is nyce;
If oon be ful of vilanye,
Another hath a likerous ye;
If oon be ful of wantonesse,
Another is a chideresse.

THUS Wikked-Tunge, God yeve him shame!
Can putte hem everichone in blame
Withoute desert and causeles;
He lyeth, though they been giltles.
I have pite to seen the sorwe,
That waketh bothe eve and morwe,
To innocents doth such grevaunce;
I pray God yeve him evel chaunce,
That he ever so bisy is
Of any womman to seyn amis!

EK Jelousye God con-
founde,
That hath ymaad a tour so
rounde,
And made aboute a gari-
soun
To sette Bialacoil in pri-
soun;
The which is shet there in
the tour,
Ful longe to holde there soiour,
There for to liven in penaunce.
And for to do him more grevaunce,
Ther hath ordeyned Jelousye

An olde vekke, for to espye
The maner of his governaunce;
The whiche devel, in hir enfaunce,
Had lerned muche of Loves art,
And of his pleyes took hir part;
She was expert in his servyse.
She knewe ech wrenche and every gyse
Of love, and every loveres wyle,
It was the harder hir to gyle.
Of Bialacoil she took ay hede,
That ever he liveth in wo and drede.
He kepte him coy and eek privee,
Lest in him she hadde see
Any foly countenaunce,
For she knew al the olde daunce.
And aftir this, whan Jelousye
Had Bialacoil in his baillye
And shette him up that was so free,
For seure of him he wolde be,
He trusteth sore in his castel;
The stronge werk him lyketh wel.
He dradde nat that no glotouns
Shulde stele his roses or botouns.
The roses weren assured alle,
Defenced with the stronge walle.

NOW Jelousye ful wel may be
Of drede devoid, in libertee,
Whether that he slepe or wake;
For of his roses may noon be take.

BUT I, allas, now morne shal;
Bicause I was without the wal,
Ful moche dole and mone I made.
Who hadde wist what wo I hadde,
I trowe he wolde have had pitee.
Love to deere had sold to me
The good that of his love hadde I.
I wende a bought it al queyntly;
But now, thurgh doubling of my peyn,
I see he wolde it selle ageyn,
And me a newe bargeyn lere,
The which al-out the more is dere,
For the solace that I have lorn,
Than if I hadde it never aforn.
Certayn I am ful lyk, indeed,
To him that cast in erthe his seed;
And hath joie of the newe spring,
Whan it greneth in the ginning,
And is also fair and fresh of flour,
Lusty to seen, swote of odour;
But er he it in sheves shere,
May falle a weder that shal it dere,
And maken it to fade and falle,
The stalk, the greyn, and floures alle;
That to the tilier is fordone
The hope that he hadde to sone.
I drede, certeyn, that so fare I;
For hope and travaile sikerly
Ben me biraft al with a storm;
The floure nil seden of my corn.
For Love hath so avaunced me,
Whan I bigan my privitee
To Bialacoil al for to telle,
Whom I ne fond froward ne felle,

But took agree al hool my play.
But Love is of so hard assay,
That al at onis he reved me,
Whan I wend best aboven have be.
It is of Love, as of Fortune,
That chaungeth ofte, and nil contune;
Which whylom wol on folke smyle,
And gloumbe on hem another whyle;
Now freend, now foo, thou shalt hir fele,
For in a twinkling tourneth hir wheele.
She can wrythe hir heed awey,
This is the concours of hir pley;
She can areyse that doth morne,
And whirle adown, and overturne
Who sittith hieghst, al as hir list;
A fool is he that wol hir trist.
For it am I that am com doun
Thurgh change and revolucioun!
Sith Bialacoil mot fro me twinne,
Shet in the prisoun yond withinne,
His absence at myn herte I fele;
For al my joye and al myn hele
Was in him and in the rose,
That but yon wal, which him doth close,
Open, that I may him see,
Love nil not that I cured be
Of the peynes that I endure,
Nor of my cruel aventure.
BIALACOIL, myn owne dere!
Though thou be now a prisonere,
Kepe atte leste thyn herte to me,
And suffre not that it daunted be;
Ne lat not Jelousye, in his rage,
Putten thyn herte in no servage.
Although he chastice thee withoute,
And make thy body unto him loute,
Have herte as hard as dyamaunt,
Stedefast, and nought pliaunt;
In prisoun though thy body be,
At large kepe thyn herte free.
A trewe herte wol not plye
For no manace that it may drye.
If Jelousye doth thee payne,
Quyte him his whyle thus agayne,
To venge thee, atte leest in thought,
If other way thou mayest nought;
And in this wyse sotilly
Worche, and winne the maistry.
But yit I am in gret affray
Lest thou do not as I say;
I drede thou canst me greet maugree,
That thou emprisoned art for me;
But that is not for my trespas,
For thurgh me never discovered was
Yit thing that oughte be secree.
Wel more anoy ther is in me,
Than is in thee, of this mischaunce;
For I endure more hard penaunce
Than any man can seyn or thinke,
That for the sorwe almost I sinke.
Whan I remembre me of my wo,
Ful nygh out of my wit I go.
Inward myn herte I fele blede,

For comfortles the deeth I drede.
Ow I not wel to have distresse,
Whan false, thurgh hir wikkednesse,
And traitours, that arn envyous,
To noyen me be so coragious?
A, BIALACOIL! ful wel I see,
That they hem shape to disceyve thee,
To make thee buxom to hir lawe,
And with hir corde thee to drawe
Wherso hem lust, right at hir wil;
I drede they have thee brought thertil.
Withoute comfort, thought me sleeth;
This game wol bringe me to my deeth.
For if your gode wille I lese,
I mote be deed; I may not chese.
And if that thou foryete me,
Myn herte shal never in lyking be;
Nor elleswhere finde solace,
If I be put out of your grace,
As it shal never been, I hope;
Than shulde I fallen in wanhope.
Here ends the work of Guillaume de Lorris; and
begins the work of Jean de Meun.
ALLAS, in wanhope?... nay, pardee!
For I wol never dispeired be.
If Hope me faile, than am I
Ungracious and unworthy;
In Hope I wol comforted be,
For Love, whan he bitaught hir me,
Seide, that Hope, wherso I go,
Shulde ay be relees to my wo.
But what and she my balis bete,
And be to me curteis and swete?
She is in nothing ful certeyn.
Lovers she put in ful gret peyn,
And makith hem with wo to dele.
Hir fair biheest disceyveth fele,
For she wol bihote, sikirly,
And failen aftir outrely.
A! that is a ful noyous thing!
For many a lover, in loving,
Hangeth upon hir, and trusteth fast,
Whiche lese hir travel at the last.
Of thing to comen she woot right nought;
Therfore, if it be wysly sought,
Hir counseille, foly is to take.
For many tymes, whan she wol make
A ful good silogisme, I drede
That aftirward ther shal in dede
Folwe an evel conclusioun;
This put me in confusioun.
For many tymes I have it seen,
That many have bigyled been,
For trust that they have set in Hope,
Which fel hem aftirward aslope.
BUT natheles yit, gladly she wolde,
That he, that wol him with hir holde,
Hadde alle tymes his purpos clere,
Withoute deceyte, or any were.
That she desireth sikirly;
Whan I hir blamed, I did foly.
But what avayleth hir good wille,
Whan she ne may staunche my wounde ille?

That helpith litel, that she may do,
Outake biheest unto my wo.
And heeste certeyn, in no wyse,
Withoute yift, is not to pryse.
Whan heest and deed asundir varie,
They doon me have a gret contrarie.
THUS am I possed up and doun
With dool, thought, and confusioun;
Of my disese ther is no noumbre.
Daunger and Shame me encumbre,
Drede also, and Jelousye,
And Wikked-Tunge, ful of envye,
Of whiche the sharpe and cruel ire
Ful oft me put in gret martire.
They han my joye fully let,
Sith Bialacoil they have bishet
Fro me in prisoun wikkidly,
Whom I love so entierly,
That it wol my bane be,
But I the soner may him see.
And yit moreover, wurst of alle,
Ther is set to kepe, foule hir bifalle!
A rimpled vekke, fer ronne in age,
Frowning and yelowe in hir visage,
Which in awayte lyth day and night,
That noon of hem may have a sight.
Now moot my sorwe enforced be.
FUL soth it is, that Love yaf me
Three wonder yiftes of his grace,
Which I have lorn now in this place,
Sith they ne may, withoute drede,
Helpen but litel, who taketh hede.
For here availeth no Swete-Thought,
And Swete-Speche helpith right nought.
The thridde was called Swete-Loking,
That now is lorn, without lesing.
The yiftes were fair, but not forthy
They helpe me but simply,
But Bialacoil may loosed be,
To gon at large and to be free.
For him my lyf lyth al in dout,
But if he come the rather out.
Allas! I trowe it wol not been!
For how shuld I evermore him seen?
He may not out, and that is wrong,
Bicause the tour is so strong.
How shulde he out? by whos prowesse,
Out of so strong a forteresse?
By me, certeyn, it nil be do;
God woot, I have no wit therto!
But wel I woot I was in rage,
Whan I to Love dide homage.
WHO was in cause, in sothfastnesse,
But hirsilf, dame Idelnesse,
Which me conveyed, thurgh fair prayere,
To entre into that fair vergere?
She was to blame me to leve,
The which now doth me sore greve.
A foolis word is nought to trowe,
Ne worth an appel for to lowe;
Men shulde him snibbe bittirly,
At pryme temps of his foly.
I was a fool, and she me leved,
286

Thurgh whom I am right nought releved.
She accomplisshed al my wil,
That now me greveth wondir il.
Resoun me seide what shulde falle.
A fool mysilf I may wel calle,
That love asyde I had not leyde,
And trowed that dame Resoun seyde.
Resoun had bothe skile and right,
Whan she me blamed, with al hir might,
To medle of love, that hath me shent;
But certeyn now I wol repent.
AND shulde I repent? Nay parde!
A fals traitour than shulde I be.
The develles engins wolde me take,
If I my lorde wolde forsake,
Or Bialacoil falsly bitraye.
Shulde I at mischeef hate him? nay,
Sith he now, for his curtesye,
Is in prisoun of Jelousye.
Curtesye certeyn dide he me,
So muche, it may not yolden be,
Whan he the hay passen me lete,
To kisse the rose, faire and swete;
Shulde I therfore cunne him maugree?
Nay, certeynly, it shal not be;
For Love shal never, if God wil,
Here of me, thurgh word or wil,
Offence or complaynt, more or lesse,
Neither of Hope nor Idilnesse;
For certis, it were wrong that I
Hated hem for hir curtesye.
Ther is not ellis, but suffre and thinke,
And waken whan I shulde winke;
Abyde in hope, til Love, thurgh chaunce,
Sende me socour or allegeaunce,
Expectant ay til I may mete
To geten mercy of that swete.
Whylom I thinke how Love to me
Seyde he wolde taken atte gree
My servise, if unpacience
Caused me to doon offence.
He seyde: In thank I shal it take,
And high maister eek thee make,
If wikkednesse ne reve it thee;
But sone, I trowe, that shal not be.
THESE were his wordis by and by;
It semed he loved me trewly.
Now is ther not but serve him wele,
If that I thinke his thank to fele.
My good, myn harm, lyth hool in me;
In Love may no defaute be;
For trewe Love ne failid never man.
Sothly, the faute mot nedis than
As God forbede! be founde in me,
And how it cometh, I can not see.
Now lat it goon as it may go;
Whether Love wol socoure me or slo,
He may do hool on me his wil.
I am so sore bounde him til,
From his servyse I may not fleen;
For lyf and deth, withouten wene,
Is in his hand; I may not chese;
He may me do bothe winne and lese.

And sith so sore he doth me greve,
Yit, if my lust he wolde acheve
To Bialacoil goodly to be,
I yeve no force what felle on me.
For though I dye, as I mot nede,
I praye Love, of his goodlihede,
To Bialacoil do gentilnesse,
For whom I live in such distresse,
That I mote deyen for penaunce.
But first, withoute repentaunce,
I wol me confesse in good entent,
And make in haste my testament,
As lovers doon that felen smerte:
To Bialacoil leve I myn herte
Al hool, withoute departing,
Or doublenesse of repenting.

Coment Raisoun vient a L'amant.

THUS as I made my passage
In compleynt, and in cruel
rage,
And I not wher to finde a
leche
That couthe unto myn
helping eche,
Sodeynly agayn comen
doun
Out of hir tour I saugh
Resoun,
Discrete and wys, and ful plesaunt,
And of hir porte ful avenaunt.
The righte wey she took to me,
Which stood in greet perplexite,
That was posshed in every side,
That I nist where I might abyde,
Til she, demurely sad of chere,
Seide to me as she com nere:
MYN owne freend, art thou yit greved?
How is this quarel yit acheved
Of Loves syde? Anoon me telle;
Hast thou not yit of love thy fille?
Art thou not wery of thy servyse
That thee hath pyned in sich wyse?
What joye hast thou in thy loving?
Is it swete or bitter thing?
Canst thou yit chese, lat me see,
What best thy socour mighte be?
Thou servest a ful noble lord,
That maketh thee thral for thy reward,
Which ay renewith thy turment,
With foly so he hath thee blent.
Thou felle in mischeef thilke day,
Whan thou didest, the sothe to say,
Obeysaunce and eek homage;
Thou wroughtest nothing as the sage.
Whan thou bicam his liege man,
Thou didist a gret foly than;
Thou wistest not what fel therto,
With what lord thou haddist to do.
If thou haddist him wel knowe,
Thou haddist nought be brought so lowe;
For if thou wistest what it were,
Thou noldist serve him half a yeer,

Not a weke, nor half a day,
Ne yit an hour withoute delay,
Ne never han loved paramours,
His lordship is so ful of shoures.
Knowest him ought?
L'Amaunt. Ye, dame, parde!
Raisoun. Nay, nay.
L'Amaunt. Yes, I.
Raisoun. Wherof, lat see?
L'Amaunt. Of that he seyde I shulde be
Glad to have sich lord as he,
And maister of sich seignory.
Raisoun. Knowist him no more?
L'Amaunt. Nay, certis, I,
Save that he yaf me rewles there,
And wente his wey, I niste where,
And I abood bounde in balaunce.
Raisoun.
LO, there a noble conisaunce!
But I wil that thou knowe him now
Ginning and ende, sith that thou
Art so anguisshous and mate,
Disfigured out of astate;
Ther may no wrecche have more of wo,
Ne caitif noon enduren so.
It were to every man sitting
Of his lord have knowleching.
For if thou knewe him, out of dout,
Lightly thou shulde escapen out
Of the prisoun that marreth thee.
L'Amaunt.
YE, dame! sith my lord is he,
And I his man, maad with myn honde,
I wolde right fayn undirstonde
To knowen of what kinde he be,
If any wolde enforme me.
I WOLDE, seid Resoun, thee lere,
Sith thou to lerne hast sich desire,
And shewe thee, withouten fable,
A thing that is not demonstrable.
Thou shalt here lerne without science,
And knowe, withoute experience,
The thing that may not knowen be,
Ne wist ne shewid in no degree.
Thou mayst the sothe of it not witen,
Though in thee it were writen.
Thou shalt not knowe therof more
Whyle thou art reuled by his lore;
But unto him that love wol flee,
The knotte may unclosed be,
Which hath to thee, as it is founde,
So long be knet and not unbounde.
Now sette wel thyn entencioun,
To here of love discripcioun.
LOVE, it is an hateful pees,
A free acquitaunce, without relees,
A trouthe, fret full of falshede,
A sikernesse, al set in drede;
In herte is a dispeiring hope,
And fulle of hope, it is wanhope;
Wyse woodnesse, and wood resoun,
A swete peril, in to droune,
An hevy birthen, light to bere,

287

A wikked wawe awey to were.
It is Caribdis perilous,
Disagreable and gracious.
It is discordaunce that can accorde,
And accordaunce to discorde.
It is cunning withoute science,
Wisdom withoute sapience,
Wit withoute discrecioun,
Havoir, withoute possessioun.
It is sike hele and hool siknesse,
A thrust drowned in dronkenesse,
An helthe ful of maladye,
A charitee ful of envye,
An hunger ful of habundaunce,
And a gredy suffisaunce;
Delyt right ful of hevinesse,
And drerihed ful of gladnesse;
Bitter swetnesse and swete errour,
Right evel savoured good savour;
Sinne that pardoun hath withinne,
And pardoun spotted without with sinne;
A peyne also it is, joyous,
And felonye right pitous;
Also pley that selde is stable,
And stedefast stat, right mevable;
A strengthe, weyked to stonde upright,
And feblenesse, ful of might;
Wit unavysed, sage folye,
And joye ful of turmentrye;
A laughter it is, weping ay,
Rest, that traveyleth night and day;
Also a swete helle it is,
And a sorowful Paradys;
A plesaunt gayl and esy prisoun,
And, ful of froste, somer sesoun;
Pryme temps, ful of frostes whyte,
And May, devoide of al delyte,
With seer braunches, blossoms ungrene;
And newe fruyt, fillid with winter tene.
It is a slowe, may not forbere
Ragges, ribaned with gold, to were;
For al so wel wol love be set
Under ragges as riche rochet;
And eek as wel be amourettes
In mourning blak, as bright burnettes.
For noon is of so mochel prys,
Ne no man founden is so wys,
Ne noon so high is of parage,
Ne no man founde of wit so sage,
No man so hardy ne so wight,
Ne no man of so mochel might,
Noon so fulfilled of bounte,
But he with love may daunted be.
Al the world holdith this way;
Love makith alle to goon miswey,
But it be they of yvel lyf,
Whom Genius cursith, man and wyf,
That wrongly werke ageyn nature.
Noon suche I love, ne have no cure
Of suche as Loves servaunts been,
And wol not by my counsel fleen.
For I ne preyse that loving,
Wherthurgh man, at the laste ending,

Shal calle hem wrecchis fulle of wo,
Love greveth hem and shendith so.
But if thou wolt wel Love eschewe,
For to escape out of his mewe,
And make al hool thy sorwe to slake,
No bettir counsel mayst thou take,
Than thinke to fleen wel, ywis;
May nought helpe elles; for wite thou this:
If thou flee it, it shal flee thee;
Folowe it, and folowen shal it thee.

L'Amaunt.

WHAN I hadde herd al Resoun seyn,
Which hadde spilt hir speche in
veyn:
Dame, seyde I, I dar wel sey
Of this avaunt me wel I may
That from your scole so deviaunt
I am, that never the more avaunt
Right nought am I, thurgh your doctryne;
I dulle under your disciplyne;
I wot no more than I wist er,
To me so contrarie and so fer
Is every thing that ye me lere;
And yit I can it al par cuere.
Myn herte foryetith therof right nought,
It is so writen in my thought;
And depe graven it is so tendir
That al by herte I can it rendre,
And rede it over comunely;
But to mysilf lewedist am I.
But sith ye love discreven so,
And lakke and preise it, bothe two,
Defyneth it into this letter,
That I may thenke on it the better;
For I herde never diffyne it ere,
And wilfully I wolde it lere.

Raisoun.

IF love be serched wel and sought,
It is a sykenesse of the thought
Annexed and knet bitwixe tweyne,
Which male and female, with oo cheyne,
So frely byndith, that they nil twinne,
Whether so therof they lese or winne.
The roote springith, thurgh hoot brenning,
Into disordinat desiring
For to kissen and enbrace,
And at her lust them to solace.
Of other thing love recchith nought,
But setteth hir herte and al hir thought
More for delectacioun
Than any procreacioun
Of other fruyt by engendring;
Which love to God is not plesing;
For of hir body fruyt to get
They yeve no force, they are so set
Upon delyt, to pley in fere.
And somme have also this manere,
To feynen hem for love seke;
Sich love I preise not at a leke.
For paramours they do but feyne;
To love truly they disdeyne.
They falsen ladies traitoursly,
And sweren hem othes utterly,

With many a lesing, and many a fable,
And al they finden deceyvable.
And, whan they her lust han geten,
The hoote ernes they al foryeten.
Wimmen, the harm they byen ful sore;
But men this thenken evermore,
That lasse harm is, so mote I thee,
Disceyve them, than disceyved be;
And namely, wher they ne may
Finde non other mene wey.
For I wot wel, in sothfastnesse,
That who doth now his bisynesse
With any womman for to dele,
For any lust that he may fele,
But if it be for engendrure,
He doth trespasse, I you ensure.
For he shulde setten al his wil
To geten a likly thing him til,
And to sustenen, if he might,
And kepe forth, by kindes right,
His owne lyknesse and semblable,
For bicause al is corumpable,
And faile shulde successioun,
Ne were ther generacioun
Our sectis strene for to save.
Whan fader or moder arn in grave,
Hir children shulde, whan they ben deede,
Ful diligent ben, in hir steede,
To use that werke on such a wyse,
That oon may thurgh another ryse.
Therfore set Kinde therin delyt,
For men therin shulde hem delyte,
And of that dede be not erke,
But ofte sythes haunt that werke.
For noon wolde drawe therof a draught
Ne were delyt, which hath him caught.
This hadde sotil dame Nature;
For noon goth right, I thee ensure,
Ne hath entent hool ne parfyt;
For hir desir is for delyt,
The which fortened crece and eke
The pley of love for-ofte seke,
And thralle hemsilf, they be so nyce,
Unto the prince of every vyce.
For of ech sinne it is the rote,
Unlefulle lust, though it be sote,
And of al yvel the racyne,
As Tullius can determyne,
Which in his tyme was ful sage,
In a boke he made of Age,
Wher that more he preyseth Elde,
Though he be croked and unwelde,
And more of commendacioun,
Than Youthe in his discripcioun.
For Youthe set bothe man and wyf
In al perel of soule and lyf;
And perel is, but men have grace,
The tyme of youthe for to pace,
Withoute any deth or distresse,
It is so ful of wildenesse,
So ofte it doth shame or damage
To him or to his linage.
It ledith man now up, now doun,

u 1

In mochel dissolucioun,
And makith him love ill company,
And lede his lyf disrewlily,
And halt him payed with noon estate.
Within himsilf is such debate,
He chaungith purpos and entent,
And yalt him into som covent,
To liven aftir her empryse,
And lesith fredom and fraunchyse,
That Nature in him hadde set,
The which ageyn he may not get,
If he there make his mansioun
For to abyde professioun.
Though for a tyme his herte absente,
It may not fayle, he shal repente,
And eke abyde thilke day
To leve his abit, and goon his way,
And lesith his worship and his name,
And dar not come ageyn for shame;
But al his lyf he doth so mourne,
Bicause he dar not hoom retourne.
Fredom of kinde so lost hath he
That never may recured be,
But if that God him graunte grace
That he may, er he hennes pace,
Conteyne undir obedience
Thurgh the vertu of pacience.
For Youthe set man in al folye,
In unthrift and in ribaudye,
In leccherye, and in outrage,
So ofte it chaungith of corage.
Youthe ginneth ofte sich bargeyn,
That may not ende withouten peyn.
In gret perel is set youth-hede,
Delyt so doth his bridil lede.
Delyt thus hangith, drede thee nought,
Bothe mannis body and his thought,
Only thurgh Youthe, his chamberere,
That to don yvel is customere,
And of nought elles taketh hede
But only folkes for to lede
Into disporte and wildenesse,
So is she froward from sadnesse.
BUT Elde drawith hem therfro;
Who wot it nought, he may wel go
Demand of hem that now arn olde,
That whylom Youthe hadde in holde,
Which yit remembre of tendir age,
How it hem brought in many a rage,
And many a foly therin wrought.
But now that Elde hath hem thurgh-sought,
They repente hem of her folye,
That Youthe hem putte in jupardye,
In perel and in muche wo,
And made hem ofte amis to do,
And suen yvel companye,
Riot and avouterye.
BUT Elde can ageyn restreyne
From suche foly, and refreyne,
And set men, by hir ordinaunce,
In good reule and in governaunce.
But yvel she spendith hir servyse,
For no man wol hir love, ne pryse;

She is hated, this wot I wele.
Hir acqueyntaunce wolde no man fele,
Ne han of Elde companye,
Men hate to be of hir alye.
For no man wolde bicomen olde,
Ne dye, whan he is yong and bolde.
And Elde merveilith right gretly,
Whan they remembre hem inwardly
Of many a perelous empryse,
Whiche that they wrought in sondry wyse,
How ever they might, withoute blame,
Escape awey withoute shame,
In youthe, withouten damage
Or repreef of her linage,
Losse of membre, sheding of blode,
Perel of deth, or losse of good.
WOST thou nought where Youthe abit,
That men so preisen in her wit?
With Delyt she halt sojour,
For bothe they dwellen in oo tour.
As longe as Youthe is in sesoun,
They dwellen in oon mansioun.
Delyt of Youthe wol have servyse
To do what so he wol devyse;
And Youthe is redy evermore
For to obey, for smerte of sore,
Unto Delyt, and hym to yive
Hir servise, whyl that she may live.
WHERE Elde abit, I wol thee telle
Shortly, and no whyle dwelle,
For thider bihoveth thee to go.
If Deth in youthe thee not slo,
Of this journey thou maist not faile.
With hir Labour and Travaile
Logged been, with Sorwe and Wo,
That never out of hir courte go.
Peyne and Distresse, Syknesse and Ire,
And Malencoly, that angry sire,
Ben of hir paleys senatours;
Groning and Grucching, hir herbergeours,
The day and night, hir to turment,
With cruel Deth they hir present,
And tellen hir, erliche and late,
That Deth stant armed at hir gate.
Than bringe they to hir remembraunce
The foly dedis of hir infaunce,
Which causen hir to mourne in wo
That Youthe hath hir bigiled so,
Which sodeynly awey is hasted.
She wepeth the tyme that she hath wasted,
Compleyning of the preterit,
And the present, that not abit,
And of hir olde vanitee,
That, but aforn hir she may see
In the future som socour,
To leggen hir of hir dolour,
To graunt hir tyme of repentaunce,
For hir sinnes to do penaunce,
And at the laste so hir governe
To winne the joy that is eterne,
Fro which go bakward Youthe hir made,
In vanitee to droune and wade.
For present tyme abidith nought,
290

It is more swift than any thought;
So litel whyle it doth endure
That ther nys compte ne mesure.
BUT how that ever the game go,
Who list have joye and mirth also
Of love, be it he or she,
High or lowe, whoso it be,
In fruyt they shulde hem delyte;
Her part they may not elles quyte,
To save hemsilf in honestee.
And yit ful many oon I see
Of wimmen, sothly for to seyne,
That ay desire and wolde fayne
The pley of love, they be so wilde,
And not coveite to go with childe.
And if with child they be perchaunce,
They wole it holde a gret mischaunce;
But whatsomever wo they fele,
They wol not pleyne, but concele;
But if it be any fool or nyce,
In whom that shame hath no justyce.
For to delyt echon they drawe,
That haunte this werk, bothe high and lawe,
Save sich that aren worth right nought,
That for money wol be bought.
Such love I preise in no wyse,
Whan it is given for coveitise.
I preise no womman, though she be wood,
That yeveth hirsilf for any good.
For litel shulde a man telle
Of hir, that wol hir body selle,
Be she mayde, be she wyf,
That quik wol selle hir, by hir lyf.
How faire chere that ever she make,
He is a wrecche, I undirtake,
That loveth such one, for swete or sour,
Though she him calle hir paramour,
And laugheth on him, and makith him feeste.
For certeynly no suche a beeste
To be loved is not worthy,
Or bere the name of druery.
Noon shulde hir please, but he were wood,
That wol dispoile him of his good.
Yit nevertheles, I wol not sey
But she, for solace and for pley,
May a jewel or other thing
Take of her loves free yeving;
But that she aske it in no wyse,
For drede of shame of coveityse.
And she of hirs may him, certeyn,
Withoute sclaundre, yeven ageyn,
And joyne her hertes togidre so
In love, and take and yeve also.
Trowe not that I wolde hem twinne,
Whan in her love ther is no sinne;
I wol that they togedre go,
And doon al that they han ado,
As curteis shulde and debonaire,
And in her love beren hem faire,
Withoute vyce, bothe he and she;
So that alwey, in honestee,
Fro foly love they kepe hem clere
That brenneth hertis with his fere;

And that her love, in any wyse,
Be devoid of coveityse.
Good love shulde engendrid be
Of trewe herte, just, and secree,
And not of such as sette her thought
To have her lust, and ellis nought,
So are they caught in Loves lace,
Truly, for bodily solace.
FLESHLY delyt is so present
With thee, that sette al thyn entent,
Withoute more, what shulde I glose?
For to gete and have the Rose;
Which makith thee so mate and wood
That thou desirest noon other good.
But thou art not an inche the nerre,
But ever abydest in sorwe and werre,
As in thy face it is sene;
It makith thee bothe pale and lene;
Thy might, thy vertu goth away.
A sory gest, in goode fay,
Thou herberedest than in thyn inne,
The God of Love whan thou let inne!
Wherfore I rede, thou shette him out,
Or he shal greve thee, out of doute;
For to thy profit it wol turne,
If he nomore with thee sojourne.
In gret mischeef and sorwe sonken
Ben hertis, that of love arn dronken,
As thou peraventure knowen shal,
Whan thou hast lost thy tyme al,
And spent thy youthe in ydilnesse,
In waste, and woful lustinesse;
If thou maist live the tyme to see
Of love for to delivered be,
Thy tyme thou shalt biwepe sore
The whiche never thou maist restore.
For tyme lost, as men may see,
For nothing may recured be.
And if thou scape yit, atte laste,
Fro Love, that hath thee so faste
Knit and bounden in his lace,
Certeyn, I holde it but a grace.
For many oon, as it is seyn,
Have lost, and spent also in veyn,
In his servyse, withoute socour,
Body and soule, good, and tresour,
Wit, and strengthe, and eek richesse,
Of which they hadde never redresse.
THUS taught and preched hath
Resoun,
But Love spilte hir sermoun,
That was so imped in my thought,
That hir doctrine I sette at nought.
And yit ne seide she never a dele,
That I ne understode it wele,
Word by word, the mater al.
But unto Love I was so thral,
Which callith overal his pray,
He chasith so my thought alway,
And holdith myn herte undir his sele,
As trust and trew as any stele;
So that no devocioun
Ne hadde I in the sermoun
Of dame Resoun, ne of hir rede;
It toke no sojour in myn hede.
For alle yede out at oon ere
That in that other she dide lere;
Fully on me she lost hir lore,
Hir speche me greved wondir sore.
WHAN unto hir for ire I seide,
For anger, as I dide abraide:
Dame, and is it your wille algate,
That I not love, but that I hate
Alle men, as ye me teche?
For if I do aftir your speche,
Sith that ye seyn love is not good,
Than must I nedis say with mood,
If I it leve, in hatrede ay
Liven, and voide love away
From me, and been a sinful wrecche,
Hated of all that love that tecche.
I may not go noon other gate,
For either must I love or hate.
And if I hate men of newe
More than love, it wol me rewe,
As by your preching semeth me,
For Love nothing ne preisith thee.
Ye yeve good counseil, sikirly,
That prechith me al day, that I
Shulde not Loves lore alowe;
He were a fool, wolde you not trowe!
In speche also ye han me taught
Another love, that knowen is naught,
Which I have herd you not repreve,
To love ech other; by your leve,
If ye wolde diffyne it me,
I wolde gladly here, to see,
At the leest, if I may lere
Of sondry loves the manere.
Raison.

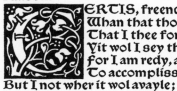

CERTIS, freend, a fool art thou
Whan that thou nothing wolt allowe
That I thee for thy profit say.
Yit wol I sey thee more, in fay;
For I am redy, at the leste,
To accomplisshe thy requeste,
But I not wher it wol avayle;
In veyne, perauntre, I shal travayle.
LOVE ther is in sondry wyse,
As I shal thee here devyse.
For som love leful is and good;
I mene not that which makith thee wood,
And bringith thee in many a fit,
And ravisshith fro thee al thy wit,
It is so merveilous and queynt;
With such love be no more aqueynt.
Comment Raisoun diffinist Amistie.

LOVE of frendshipe also
ther is,
Which makith no man doon
amis,
Of wille knit bitwixe two,
That wol not breke for wele
ne wo;
Which long is lykly to contune,
Whan wille and goodis ben
in comune;

Grounded by Goddis ordinaunce,
Hool, withoute discordaunce;
With hem holding comuntee
Of al her goode in charitee,
That ther be noon excepcioun
Thurgh chaunging of entencioun;
That ech helpe other at hir neede,
And wysly hele bothe word and dede;
Trewe of mening, devoid of slouthe,
For wit is nought withoute trouthe;
So that the ton dar al his thought
Seyn to his freend, and spare nought,
As to himsilf, without dreding
To be discovered by wreying.
For glad is that conjunccioun,
Whan ther is noon suspecioun
Ne lak in hem, whom they wolde prove
That trew and parfit weren in love.
For no man may be amiable,
But if he be so ferme and stable,
That fortune chaunge him not, ne blinde,
But that his freend alwey him finde,
Bothe pore and riche, in oon estate.
For if his freend, thurgh any gate,
Wol compleyne of his povertee,
He shulde not byde so long, til he
Of his helping him requere;
For good deed, done but thurgh prayere,
Is sold, and bought to dere ywis,
To hert that of gret valour is.
For hert fulfilled of gentilnesse
Can yvel demene his distresse.
And man that worthy is of name
To asken often hath gret shame.
A GOOD man brenneth in his thought
For shame, whan he axeth ought.
He hath gret thought, and dredith ay
For his disese, whan he shal pray
His freend, lest that he warned be,
Til that he preve his stabiltee.
But whan that he hath founden oon
That trusty is and trew as stone,
And hath assayed him at al,
And found him stedefast as a wal,
And of his freendship be certeyne,
He shal him shewe bothe joye and peyne,
And al that he dar thinke or sey,
Withoute shame, as he wel may.
For how shulde he ashamed be
Of sich oon as I tolde thee?
For whan he woot his secree thought,
The thridde shal knowe therof right nought;
For tweyn in nombre is bet than three
In every counsel and secree.
Repreve he dredeth never a del,
Who that biset his wordis wel;
For every wys man, out of drede,
Can kepe his tunge til he see nede;
And fooles can not holde hir tunge;
A fooles belle is sone runge.
WIT shal a trewe freend do more
To helpe his felowe of his sore,
And socoure him, whan he hath nede,

In al that he may doon in dede;
And gladder be that he him plesith
Than is his felowe that he esith.
And if he do not his requeste,
He shal as mochel him moleste
As his felow, for that he
May not fulfille his voluntee
As fully as he hath requered.
If bothe the hertis Love hath fered,
Joy and wo they shul depart,
And take evenly ech his part.
Half his anoy he shal have ay,
And comfort him what that he may;
And of his blisse parte shal he,
If love wol departed be.
And whilom of this amitee
Spak Tullius in a ditee:
A MAN shulde maken his request
Unto his freend, that is honest;
And he goodly shulde it fulfille,
But it the more were out of skile,
And otherwise not graunt therto,
Except only in cases two:
If men his freend to deth wolde dryve,
Lat him be bisy to save his lyve.
Also if men wolen him assayle,
Of his wurship to make him faile,
And hindren him of his renoun,
Lat him, with ful entencioun,
His dever doon in ech degree
That his freend ne shamed be
In this two cases with his might,
Taking no kepe to skile nor right,
As ferre as love may him excuse;
This oughte no man to refuse.
This love that I have told to thee
Is nothing contrarie to me;
This wol I that thou folowe wel,
And leve the tother everydel.
This love to vertu al attendith,
The tothir fooles blent and shendith.
ANOTHER love also there is,
That is contrarie unto this,
Which desyre is so constreyned
That it is but wille feyned;
Awey fro trouthe it doth so varie,
That to good love it is contrarie;
For it maymeth, in many wyse,
Syke hertis with coveityse;
Al in winning and in profyt
Sich love settith his delyt.
This love so hangeth in balaunce
That, if it lese his hope, perchaunce,
Of lucre, that he is set upon,
It wol faile, and quenche anon;
For no man may be amorous,
Ne in his living vertuous,
But if he love more, in mood,
Men for hemsilf than for hir good.
For love that profit doth abyde
Is fals, and bit not in no tyde.
This love cometh of dame Fortune,
That litel whyle wol contune;

for it shal chaungen wonder sone,
And take eclips right as the mone,
Whan she is from us ylet
Thurgh erthe, that bitwixe is set
The sonne and hir, as it may falle,
Be it in party, or in alle;
The shadowe maketh her bemis merke,
And hir hornes to shewe derke,
That part where she hath lost hir lyght
Of Phebus fully, and the sight;
Til, whan the shadowe is overpast,
She is enlumined ageyn as faste,
Thurgh brightnesse of the sonne bemes
That yeveth to hir ageyn hir lemes.
That love is right of sich nature;
Now is it fair, and now obscure,
Now bright, now clipsy of manere,
And whylom dim, and whylom clere.
As sone as Poverte ginneth take,
With mantel and with wedis blake
It hidith of Love the light awey,
That into night it turneth day;
It may not see Richesse shyne
Til the blakke shadowes fyne.
for, whan Richesse shyneth bright,
Love recovereth ageyn his light;
And whan it failith, he wol flit,
And as she groweth, so groweth it.
Of this love, here what I sey:
     The riche men are loved ay,
     And namely tho that sparand bene,
That wol not wasshe hir hertes clene
Of the filthe, nor of the vyce
Of gredy brenning avaryce.
The riche man ful fond is, ywis,
That weneth that he loved is.
If that his herte it undirstood,
It is not he, it is his good;
He may wel witen in his thought,
His good is loved, and he right nought.
for if he be a nigard eke,
Men wole not sette by him a leke,
But haten him; this is the soth.
Lo, what profit his catel doth!
Of every man that may him see,
It geteth him nought but enmitee.
But he amende him of that vyce,
And knowe himsilf, he is not wys.
CERTIS, he shulde ay freendly be,
     To gete him love also ben free,
     Or ellis he is not wyse ne sage
No more than is a gote ramage.
That he not loveth, his dede proveth,
Whan he his richesse so wel loveth,
That he wol hyde it ay and spare,
His pore freendis seen forfare;
To kepe it ay is his purpose,
Til for drede his eyen close,
And til a wikked deth him take,
Him hadde lever asondre shake,
And late his limes asondre ryve,
Than leve his richesse in his lyve.
He thenkith parte it with no man;

Certayn, no love is in him than.
How shulde love within him be,
Whan in his herte is no pite?
That he trespasseth, wel I wat,
for ech man knowith his estat;
for wel him oughte be reproved
That loveth nought, ne is not loved.
BUT sith we arn to fortune comen,
     And han our sermoun of hir nomen,
     A wondir wil I telle thee now,
Thou herdist never sich oon, I trow.
I not wher thou me leven shal,
Though sothfastnesse it be in al,
As it is writen, and is sooth,
That unto men more profit doth
The froward fortune and contraire,
Than the swote and debonaire:
And if thee thinke it is doutable,
It is thurgh argument provable.
for the debonaire and softe
falsith and bigylith ofte;
for liche a moder she can cherishe
And milken as doth a norys;
And of hir goode to hem deles,
And yeveth hem part of her joweles,
With grete richesse and dignitee;
And hem she hoteth stabilitee
In a state that is not stable,
But chaunging ay and variable;
And fedith hem with glorie veyne,
And worldly blisse noncerteyne.
Whan she hem settith on hir whele,
Than wene they to be right wele,
And in so stable state withalle,
That never they wene for to falle.
And whan they set so highe be,
They wene to have in certeintee
Of hertly frendis so gret noumbre,
That nothing mighte her stat encombre:
They truste hem so on every syde,
Wening with hem they wolde abyde
In every perel and mischaunce,
Withoute chaunge or variaunce,
Bothe of catel and of good;
And also for to spende hir blood
And alle hir membris for to spille,
Only to fulfille hir wille.
They maken it hole in many wyse,
And hoten hem hir ful servyse,
How sore that it do hem smerte,
Into hir very naked sherte!
Herte and al, so hole they yeve,
for the tyme that they may live,
So that, with her flaterye,
They maken foolis glorifye
Of hir wordis greet speking,
And han thereof a rejoysing,
And trowe hem as the Evangyle;
And it is al falsheed and gyle,
As they shal afterwardes see,
Whan they arn falle in povertee,
And been of good and catel bare;
Than shulde they seen who freendis ware.

for of an hundred, certeynly,
Nor of a thousand ful scarsly,
Ne shal they fynde unnethis oon,
Whan povertee is comen upon.
for this fortune that I of telle,
With men whan hir lust to dwelle,
Makith hem to lese hir conisaunce,
And nourishith hem in ignoraunce.
BUT froward fortune and perverse,
Whan high estatis she doth reverse,
And maketh hem to tumble doun
Of hir whele, with sodeyn tourn,
And from hir richesse doth hem flee,
And plongeth hem in povertee,
As a stepmoder envyous,
And leyeth a plastre dolorous
Unto her hertis, wounded egre,
Which is not tempred with vinegre,
But with poverte and indigence,
for to shewe, by experience,
That she is fortune verely
In whom no man shulde affy,
Nor in hir yeftis have fiaunce,
She is so ful of variaunce.
Thus can she maken high and lowe,
Whan they from richesse aren throwe,
fully to knowen, withouten were,
freend of effect, and freend of chere;
And which in love weren trew and stable,
And whiche also weren variable,
After fortune, hir goddesse,
In poverte, outher in richesse;
for al she yeveth, out of drede,
Unhappe bereveth it in dede;
for Infortune lat not oon
Of freendis, whan fortune is goon;
I mene tho freendis that wol flee
Anoon as entreth povertee.
And yit they wol not leve hem so,
But in ech place where they go
They calle hem Wrecche, scorne and blame,
And of hir mishappe hem diffame,
And, namely, siche as in richesse
Pretendith most of stablenesse,
Whan that they sawe him set onlofte,
And weren of him socoured ofte,
And most ybolpe in al hir nede:
But now they take no maner hede,
But seyn, in voice of flaterye,
That now apperith hir folye,
Overal whereso they fare,
And singe: Go, farewel feldefare.
Alle suche freendis I beshrewe,
for of the trewe ther be to fewe;
But sothfast freendis, what so bityde,
In every fortune wolen abyde;
They han hir hertis in suche noblesse
That they nil love for no richesse;
Nor, for that fortune may hem sende,
They wolen hem socoure and defende;
And chaunge for softe ne for sore,
for who is freend, loveth evermore.
Though men drawe swerd his freend to slo,
294

He may not hewe hir love atwo.
BUT, in the case that I shal sey,
for pride and ire lese it he may,
And for reprove by nycetee,
And discovering of privitee,
With tonge wounding, as feloun,
Thurgh venemous detraccioun.
frend in this case wol gon his way,
for nothing greve him more ne may;
And for nought ellis wol he flee,
If that he love in stabilitee.
And certeyn, he is wel bigoon
Among a thousand that fyndith oon.
for ther may be no richesse,
Ageyns frendship, of worthinesse;
for it ne may so high atteigne
As may the valoure, sooth to seyne,
Of him that loveth trew and wel;
frendship is more than is catel.
for freend in court ay better is
Than peny in his purs, certis;
And fortune, mishapping,
Whan upon men she is falling,
Thurgh misturning of hir chaunce,
And casteth hem oute of balaunce,
She makith, thurgh hir adversitee,
Men ful cleerly for to see
Him that is freend in existence
from him that is by apparence.
for Infortune makith anoon
To knowe thy freendis fro thy foon,
By experience, right as it is;
The which is more to preyse, ywis,
Than is miche richesse and tresour;
for more doth profit and valour
Poverte, and such adversitee,
Bifore than doth prosperitee;
for the toon yeveth conisaunce,
And the tother ignoraunce.
AND thus in poverte is in dede
Trouthe declared fro falsehede;
for feynte frendis it wol declare,
And trewe also, what wey they fare.
for whan he was in his richesse,
These freendis, ful of doublenesse,
Offrid him in many wyse
Hert and body, and servyse.
What wolde he than ha yeve to ha bought
To knowen openly her thought,
That he now hath so clerly seen?
The lasse bigyled he sholde have been
And he hadde than perceyved it,
But richesse nold not late him wit.
Wel more avauntage doth him than,
Sith that it makith him a wys man,
The greet mischeef that he receyveth,
Than doth richesse that him deceyveth.
Richesse riche ne makith nought
Him that on tresour set his thought;
for richesse stont in suffisaunce
And nothing in habundaunce;
for suffisaunce alonly
Makith men to live richely.

for he that hath but miches tweyne,
Ne more value in his demeigne,
Liveth more at ese, and more is riche,
Than doth he that is so chiche,
And in his bern hath, soth to seyn,
An hundred muwis of whete greyn,
Though he be chapman or marchaunt,
And have of golde many besaunt.
for in the geting he hath such wo,
And in the keping drede also,
And set evermore his bisynesse
for to encrese, and not to lesse,
for to augment and multiply.
And though on hepis it lye him by,
Yit never shal make his richesse
Asseth unto his gredinesse.
But the povre that recchith nought,
Save of his lyflode, in his thought,
Which that he getith with his travaile,
He dredith nought that it shal faile,
Though he have lytel worldis good,
Mete and drinke, and esy food,
Upon his travel and living,
And also suffisaunt clothing.
Or if in syknesse that he falle,
And lothe mete and drink withalle,
Though he have nought, his mete to by,
He shal bithinke him hastely,
To putte him out of al daunger,
That he of mete hath no mister;
Or that he may with litel eke
Be founden, whyl that he is seke;
Or that men shul him bere in hast,
To live, til his syknesse be past,
To somme maysondewe bisyde;
He cast nought what shal him bityde.
He thenkith nought that ever he shal
Into any syknesse falle.
AND though it falle, as it may be,
That al betyme spare shal he
As mochel as shal to him suffyce,
Whyl he is syke in any wyse,
He doth it, for that he wol be
Content with his povertee
Withoute nede of any man.
So miche in litel have he can,
He is apayed with his fortune;
And for he nil be importune
Unto no wight, ne onerous,
Nor of hir goodes coveitous;
Therfore he spareth, it may wel been,
His pore estat for to sustene.
OR if him lust not for to spare,
But suffrith forth, as nought ne ware,
Atte last it hapneth, as it may,
Right unto his laste day,
And taketh the world as it wolde be;
for ever in herte thenkith he,
The soner that the deeth him slo,
To paradys the soner go
He shal, there for to live in blisse,
Where that he shal no good misse.
Thider he hopith God shal him sende
u 4

Aftir his wrecchid lyves ende.
Pictagoras himsilf reherses,
In a book that the Golden Verses
Is clepid, for the nobilitee
Of the honourable ditee:
THAN, whan thou gost thy body fro,
free in the eir thou shalt up go,
And leven al humanitee,
And purely live in deitee.
He is a fool, withouten were,
That trowith have his countre here.
In erthe is not our countree,
That may these clerkis seyn and see
In Boece of Consolacioun,
Where it is maked mencioun
Of our countree pleyn at the eye,
By teching of philosophye,
Where lewid men might lere wit,
Whoso that wolde translaten it.
If he be siche that can wel live
Aftir his rente may him yive,
And not desyreth more to have,
That may fro povertee him save:
A wys man seide, as we may seen,
Is no man wrecched, but he it wene,
Be he king, knight, or ribaud.
And many a ribaud is mery and baud,
That swinkith, and berith, bothe day and night,
Many a burthen of gret might,
The whiche dothe him lasse offense,
for he suffrith in pacience.
They laugh and daunce, trippe and singe,
And ley not up for her living,
But in the tavern al dispendith
The winning that God hem sendith.
Than goth he, fardels for to bere,
With as good chere as he dide ere;
To swinke and traveile he not feynith,
for for to robben he disdeynith;
But right anoon, aftir his swinke,
He goth to tavern for to drinke.
Alle these ar riche in abundaunce,
That can thus have suffisaunce
Wel more than can an usurere,
As God wel knowith, withoute were.
for an usurer, so God me see,
Shal never for richesse riche bee,
But evermore pore and indigent,
Scarce, and gredy in his entent.
FOR soth it is, whom it displese,
Ther may no marchaunt live at ese,
His herte in sich a were is set,
That it quik brenneth more to get,
Ne never shal enough have geten;
Though he have gold in gerners yeten,
for to be nedy he dredith sore.
Wherfore to geten more and more
He set his herte and his desire;
So hote he brennith in the fire
Of coveitise, that makith him wood
To purchase other mennes good.
He undirfongith a gret peyne,
That undirtakith to drinke up Seyne;

For the more he drinkith, ay
The more he leveth, the soth to say.
This is the thurst of fals geting,
That last ever in coveiting,
And the anguisshe and distresse
With the fire of gredinesse.
She fighteth with him ay, and stryveth,
That his herte asondre ryveth;
Such gredinesse him assaylith,
That whan he most hath, most he faylith.
PHISICIENS and advocates
Gon right by the same yates;
They selle hir science for winning,
And haunte hir crafte for greet geting.
Hir winning is of such swetnesse,
That if a man falle in sikenesse,
They are ful glad, for hir encrese;
For by hir wille, withoute lees,
Everiche man shulde be seke,
And though they dye, they set not a leke.
After, whan they the gold have take,
Ful litel care for hem they make.
They wolde that fourty were seke at onis,
Ye, two hundred, in flesh and bonis,
And yit two thousand, as I gesse,
For to encresen her richesse.
They wol not worchen, in no wyse,
But for lucre and coveityse;
For fysyk ginneth first by fy,
The fysycien also sothely;
And sithen it goth fro fy to sy;
To truste on hem, it is foly;
For they nil, in no maner gree,
Do right nought for charitee.
EKE in the same secte are set
Alle tho that prechen for to get
Worshipes, honour, and richesse.
Her hertis arn in greet distresse,
That folk ne live not holily.
But aboven al, specialy,
Sich as prechen for veynglorie,
And toward God have no memorie,
But forth as ypocrites trace,
And to her soules deth purchace,
And outward shewen holynesse,
Though they be fulle of cursidnesse.
Not liche to the apostles twelve,
They deceyve other and hemselve;
Bigyled is the gyler than.
For preching of a cursed man,
Though it to other may profyte,
Himsilf availeth not a myte;
For oft good predicacioun
Cometh of evel entencioun.
To him not vailith his preching,
Al helpe he other with his teching;
For where they good ensaumple take,
There is he with veynglorie shake.
But lat us leven these prechoures,
And speke of hem that in her toures
Hepe up her gold, and faste shette,
And sore theron her herte sette.
They neither love God, ne drede;
296

They kepe more than it is nede,
And in her bagges sore it binde,
Out of the sonne, and of the winde;
They putte up more than nede ware,
Whan they seen pore folk forfare,
For hunger dye, and for cold quake;
God can wel vengeaunce therof take.
Thre gret mischeves hem assailith,
And thus in gadring ay travaylith;
With moche peyne they winne richesse;
And drede hem holdith in distresse,
To kepe that they gadre faste;
With sorwe they leve it at the laste;
With sorwe they bothe dye and live,
That to richesse her hertis yive,
And in defaute of love it is,
As it shewith ful wel, ywis.
For if these gredy, the sothe to seyn,
Loveden, and were loved ageyn,
And good love regned over alle,
Such wikkidnesse ne shulde falle;
But he shulde yeve that most good had
To hem that weren in nede bistad,
And live withoute fals usure,
For charitee ful clene and pure.
If they hem yeve to goodnesse,
Defending hem from ydelnesse,
In al this world than pore noon
We shulde finde, I trowe, not oon.
But chaunged is this world unstable;
For love is overal vendable.
We see that no man loveth now
But for winning and for prow;
And love is thralled in servage
Whan it is sold for avauntage;
Yit wommen wol hir bodies selle;
Suche soules goth to the devel of helle.
Here is lacking from 5170 of the french to 10717 of
the same.

❀❀❀❀❀❀❀❀❀❀❀❀❀❀❀❀❀❀

WHAN Love had told hem his entente,
The baronage to councel wente;
In many sentences they fille,
And dyversly they seide hir wille:
But aftir discord they accorded,
And hir accord to Love recorded.
Sir, seiden they, we been at oon,
By even accord of everichoon,
Outtake Richesse alonly,
That sworen hath ful hauteynly,
That she the castel nil assaile,
Ne smyte a stroke in this bataile,
With dart, ne mace, spere, ne knyf,
For man that speketh or bereth the lyf,
And blameth your empryse, ywis,
And from our hoost departed is,
At leeste wey, as in this plyte,
So hath she this man in dispyte;
For she seith he ne loved hir never,
And therfor she wol hate him ever.
For he wol gadre no tresore,
He hath hir wrath for evermore.

He agilte hir never in other caas,
Lo, here al hoolly his trespas!
She seith wel, that this other day
He asked hir leve to goon the way
That is clepid To-moche-Yeving,
And spak ful faire in his praying;
But whan he prayde hir, pore was he,
Therfore she warned him the entree.
Ne yit is he not thriven so
That he hath geten a peny or two,
That quitly is his owne in hold.

THUS hath Richesse us alle told;
And whan Richesse us this recorded,
Withouten hir we been accorded.

AND we finde in our accordaunce,
That False-Semblant and Abstinaunce,
With alle the folk of hir bataile,
Shulle at the hinder gate assayle,
That Wikkid-Tunge hath in keping,
With his Normans, fulle of jangling.
And with hem Curtesie and Largesse,
That shulle shewe hir hardinesse
To the olde wyf that kepeth so harde
Fair-Welcoming within hir warde.

THAN shal Delyte and Wel-Helinge
Fonde Shame adoun to bringe;
With al hir hoost, erly and late,
They shulle assailen thilke gate.

AGAYNES Drede shal Hardinesse
Assayle, and also Sikernesse,
With al the folk of hir leding,
That never wist what was fleing.

FRAUNCHYSE shal fighte, and eek
Pitee,
With Daunger ful of crueltee.
Thus is your hoost ordeyned wel;
Doun shal the castel every del,
If everiche do his entente,
So that Venus be presente,
Your modir, ful of vassalage,
That can ynough of such usage;
Withouten hir may no wight spede
This werk, neither for word ne dede.
Therfore is good ye for hir sende,
For thurgh hir may this werk amende.
Amour.

LORDINGES, my modir, the god-
desse,
That is my lady, and my mais-
tresse,
Nis not at al at my willing,
Ne doth not al my desyring.
Yit can she somtyme doon labour,
Whan that hir lust, in my socour,
Al my nedis for to acheve,
But now I thenke hir not to greve.
My modir is she, and of childhede.
I bothe worshipe hir, and eek drede;
For who that dredith sire ne dame
Shal it abye in body or name.
And, natheles, yit cunne we
Sende aftir hir, if nede be;
And were she nigh, she comen wolde,

I trowe that nothing might hir holde.

MY modir is of greet prowesse;
She hath tan many a forteresse,
That cost hath many a pound er this;
Ther I nas not present, ywis;
And yit men seide it was my dede;
But I come never in that stede;
Ne me ne lykith, so mote I thee,
Such toures take withoute me.
Forwhy me thenketh that, in no wyse,
It may ben cleped but marchandise.

GO bye a courser, blak or whyte,
And pay therfor; than art thou quyte.
The marchaunt oweth thee right
nought,
Ne thou him, whan thou hast it bought.
I wol not selling clepe yeving,
For selling axeth no guerdoning;
Here lyth no thank, ne no meryte,
That oon goth from that other al quyte.
But this selling is not semblable;
For, whan his hors is in the stable,
He may it selle ageyn, pardee,
And winne on it, such hap may be;
Al may the man not lese, ywis,
For at the leest the skin is his.
Or elles, if it so bityde
That he wol kepe his hors to ryde,
Yit is he lord ay of his hors.

BUT thilke chaffare is wel wors,
There Venus entremeteth nought;
For whoso such chaffare hath
bought,
He shal not worchen so wysly,
That he ne shal lese al outerly
Bothe his money and his chaffare;
But the seller of the ware
The prys and profit have shal.
Certeyn, the byer shal lese al;
For he ne can so dere it bye
To have lordship and ful maistrye,
Ne have power to make letting
Neither for yift ne for preching,
That of his chaffare, maugre his,
Another shal have as moche, ywis,
If he wol yeve as moche as he,
Of what contrey so that he be;
Or for right nought, so happe may,
If he can flater hir to hir pay.
Ben than suche marchaunts wyse?
No, but fooles in every wyse,
Whan they bye such thing wilfully,
Theras they lese her good fully.
But natheles, this dar I saye,
My modir is not wont to paye,
For she is neither so fool ne nyce,
To entremete hir of sich vyce.
But truste wel, he shal paye al,
That repente of his bargeyn shal,
Whan Poverte put him in distresse,
Al were he scoler to Richesse,
That is for me in gret yerning,
Whan she assenteth to my willing.

BUT, by my modir seint Venus,
And by hir fader Saturnus,
That hir engendrid by his lyf,
But not upon his weddid wyf!
Yet wol I more unto you swere,
To make this thing the seurere;
Now by that feith, and that leautee
I owe to alle my brethren free,
Of which ther nis wight under heven
That can her fadris names neven,
So dyvers and so many ther be
That with my modir have be privee!
Yit wolde I swere, for sikirnesse,
The pole of helle to my witnesse,
Now drinke I not this yeer clarree,
If that I lye, or forsworn be!
(for of the goddes the usage is,
That whoso him forswereth amis,
Shal that yeer drinke no clarree).

NOW have I sworn ynough, pardee;
If I forswere me, than am I lorn,
But I wol never be forsworn.
Sith Richesse hath me failed here,
She shal abye that trespas dere,
At leeste wey, but she hir arme
With swerd, or sparth, or gisarme.
For certes, sith she loveth not me,
Fro thilke tyme that she may see
The castel and the tour toshake,
In sory tyme she shal awake.
If I may grype a riche man,
I shal so pulle him, if I can,
That he shal, in a fewe stoundes,
Lese alle his markes and his poundes.
I shal him make his pens outslinge,
But if they in his gerner springe,
Our maydens shal eek plukke him so,
That him shal neden fetheres mo,
And make him selle his lond to spende,
But he the bet cunne him defende.

PORE men han maad hir lord of me;
Although they not so mighty be,
That they may fede me in delyt,
I wol not have hem in despyt.
No good man hateth hem, as I gesse,
For chinche and feloun is Richesse,
That so can chase hem and dispyse,
And hem defoule in sondry wyse.
They loven ful bet, so God me spede,
Than doth the riche, chinchy grede,
And been, in good feith, more stable
And trewer, and more serviable;
And therfore it suffysith me
Hir goode herte, and hir leautee.
They han on me set al hir thought,
And therfore I forgete hem nought.
I wolde hem bringe in greet noblesse,
If that I were God of Richesse,
As I am God of Love, sothly,
Such routhe upon hir pleynt have I.

THERFORE I must his socour be,
That peyneth him to serven me,
For if he deyde for love of this,
298

Than semeth in me no love ther is.

SIR, seide they, sooth is, every del,
That ye reherce, and we wot wel
Thilk oth to holde is resonable;
For it is good and covenable,
That ye on riche men han sworn.
For, sir, this wot we wel biforn;
If riche men doon you homage,
That is as fooles doon outrage;
But ye shul not forsworen be,
Ne let therfore to drinke clarree,
Or piment maked fresh and newe.
Ladyes shulle hem such pepir brewe,
If that they falle into hir laas,
That they for wo mowe seyn Allas!
Ladyes shuln ever so curteis be,
That they shal quyte your oth al free.
Ne seketh never other vicaire,
For they shal speke with hem so faire
That ye shal holde you payed ful wel,
Though ye you medle never a del.
Lat ladies worche with hir thinges,
They shal hem telle so fele tydinges,
And moeve hem eke so many requestis
By flatery, that not honest is,
And therto yeve hem such thankinges,
What with kissing, and with talkinges,
That certes, if they trowed be,
Shal never leve hem lond ne fee
That it nil as the moeble fare,
Of which they first delivered are.
Now may ye telle us al your wille,
And we your hestes shal fulfille.

BUT fals-Semblant dar not, for drede
Of you, sir, medle him of this dede,
For he seith that ye been his fo;
He not, if ye wol worche him wo.
Wherfore we pray you alle, beausire,
That ye forgive him now your ire,
And that he may dwelle, as your man,
With Abstinence, his dere lemman;
This our accord and our wil now.

PARFAY, seide Love, I graunte
it yow;
I wol wel holde him for my
man;
Now lat him come: and he forth
ran.

FALS-SEMBLANT, quod Love, in this
wyse
I take thee here to my servyse,
That thou our freendis helpe alway,
And hindre hem neithir night ne day,
But do thy might hem to releve,
And eek our enemies that thou greve.
Thyn be this might, I graunt it thee,
My king of harlotes shalt thou be;
We wol that thou have such honour.
Certeyn, thou art a fals traitour,
And eek a theef; sith thou were born,
A thousand tyme thou art forsworn.
But, natheles, in our hering,
To putte our folk out of douting,

I bid thee teche hem, wostow how?
By somme general signe now,
In what place thou shalt founden be,
If that men had mister of thee;
And how men shal thee best espye,
For thee to knowe is greet maistrye;
Tel in what place is thyn haunting.
Fals-Semblant.
SIR, I have fele dyvers woning,
That I kepe not rehersed be,
So that ye wolde respyten me.
For if that I telle you the sothe,
I may have harm and shame bothe.
If that my felowes wisten it,
My tales shulden me be quit;
For certeyn, they wolde hate me,
If ever I knewe hir cruelte;
For they wolde overal holde hem stille
Of trouthe that is ageyn hir wille;
Suche tales kepen they not here.
I might eftsone bye it ful dere,
If I seide of hem any thing,
That ought displeseth to hir hering.
For what word that hem prikke or byteth,
In that word noon of hem delyteth,
Al were it gospel, the evangyle,
That wolde reprove hem of hir gyle,
For they are cruel and hauteyn.
And this thing wot I wel, certeyn,
If I speke ought to peire hir loos,
Your court shal not so wel be cloos,
That they ne shal wite it atte last.
Of good men am I nought agast,
For they wol taken on hem nothing,
Whan that they knowe al my mening;
But he that wol it on him take,
He wol himself suspecious make,
That he his lyf let covertly,
In Gyle and in Ipocrisy,
That me engendred and yaf fostring.
THEY made a ful good engendring,
Quod Love, for whoso soothly
telle,
They engendred the devel of helle!
But nedely, howsoever it be,
Quod Love, I wol and charge thee,
To telle anoon thy woning-places,
Hering ech wight that in this place is;
And what lyf that thou livest also,
Hyde it no lenger now; wherto?
Thou most discover al thy wurching,
How thou servest, and of what thing,
Though that thou shuldest for thy soth-sawe
Ben al tobeten and todrawe;
And yit art thou not wont, pardee,
But natheles, though thou beten be,
Thou shalt not be the first, that so
Hath for soth-sawe suffred wo.
Fals-Semblant.
SIR, sith that it may lyken you,
Though that I shulde be slayn right now,
I shal don your comaundement,
For therto have I gret talent.

WITHOUTEN wordes mo, right
than
Fals-Semblant his sermon
bigan,
And seide hem thus in
audience:
BAROUNS, tak hede of my sentence!
That wight that list to have knowing
Of Fals-Semblant, ful of flatering,
He must in worldly folk him seke,
And, certes, in the cloistres eke;
I wone nowhere but in hem tweye;
But not lyk even, sooth to seye;
Shortly, I wol herberwe me
There I hope best to hulstred be;
And certeynly, sikerest hyding
Is undirneth humblest clothing.
RELIGIOUS folk been ful covert;
Seculer folk ben more appert.
But natheles, I wol not blame
Religious folk, ne hem diffame
In what habit that ever they go:
Religioun humble, and trewe also,
Wol I not blame, ne dispyse,
But I nil love it, in no wyse.
I mene of fals religious,
That stoute ben, and malicious;
That wolen in an abit go,
And setten not hir herte therto.
RELIGIOUS folk ben al pitous;
Thou shalt not seen oon dispitous.
They loven no pryde, ne no stryf,
But humbly they wol lede hir lyf;
With swich folk wol I never be.
And if I dwelle, I feyne me
I may wel in her abit go;
But me were lever my nekke atwo,
Than lete a purpose that I take,
What covenaunt that ever I make.
I dwelle with hem that proude be,
And fulle of wyles and subtelte;
That worship of this world coveyten,
And grete nedes cunne espleyten;
And goon and gadren greet pitaunces,
And purchace hem the acqueyntaunces
Of men that mighty lyf may leden;
And feyne hem pore, and hemself feden
With gode morcels delicious,
And drinken good wyn precious,
And preche us povert and distresse,
And fisshen hemself greet richesse
With wyly nettis that they caste:
It wol come foul out at the laste.
They ben fro clene religioun went;
They make the world an argument
That hath a foul conclusioun.
I have a robe of religioun,
Than am I al religious:
This argument is al roignous;
It is not worth a croked brere;
Habit ne maketh monk ne frere,
But clene lyf and devocioun
Maketh gode men of religioun.

Nathelesse, ther can noon answere,
How high that ever his heed he shere
With rasour whetted never so kene,
That Gyle in braunches cut thrittene;
Ther can no wight distincte it so,
That he dar sey a word therto.

BUT what herberwe that ever I take,
Or what semblant that ever I make,
I mene but gyle, and folowe that;
For right no mo than Gibbe our cat
Fro myce and rattes went his wyle,
Ne entende I not but to begyle;
Ne no wight may, by my clothing,
Wite with what folk is my dwelling;
Ne by my wordis yet, pardee,
So softe and so plesaunt they be.
Bihold the dedis that I do;
But thou be blind, thou oughtest so;
For, varie hir wordis fro hir dede,
They thenke on gyle, withouten drede,
What maner clothing that they were,
Or what estat that ever they bere,
Lered or lewd, lord or lady,
Knight, squier, burgeis, or bayly.

RIGHT thus whyl Fals-Semblant
sermoneth,
Eftsones Love him aresoneth,
And brak his tale in the speking
As though he had him told lesing;
And seide: What, devel, is that I here?
What folk hast thou us nempned here?
May men finde religioun
In worldly habitacioun?
Fals-Semblant.

YE, sir; it foloweth not that they
Shulde lede a wikked lyf, parfey,
Ne not therfore her soules lese,
That hem to worldly clothes chese;
For, certis, it were gret pitee.
Men may in seculer clothes see
Florisshen holy religioun.
Ful many a seynt in feeld and toun,
With many a virgin glorious,
Devout, and ful religious,
Had deyed, that comun clothe ay beren,
Yit seyntes nevertheles they weren.
I coude reken you many a ten;
Ye, wel nigh alle these holy wimmen,
That men in chirchis herie and seke,
Bothe maydens, and these wyves eke,
That baren many a fair child here,
Wered alwey clothis seculere,
And in the same dyden they,
That seyntes weren, and been alwey.
The eleven thousand maydens dere,
That beren in heven hir ciergis clere,
Of which men rede in chirche, and singe,
Were take in seculer clothing,
Whan they resseyved martirdom,
And wonnen heven unto her hoom.
Good herte makith the gode thought;
The clothing yeveth ne reveth nought.
The gode thought and the worching,

300

That maketh religioun flowring,
Ther lyth the good religioun
Aftir the right entencioun.

WHOSO toke a wethers skin,
And wrapped a gredy wolf therin,
For he shulde go with lambis whyte,
Wenest thou not he wolde hem byte?
Yis! neverthelas, as he were wood,
He wolde hem wery, and drinke the blood;
And wel the rather hem disceyve,
For, sith they coude not perceyve
His treget and his crueltee,
They wolde him folowe, al wolde he flee.

IF ther be wolves of sich hewe
Amonges these apostlis newe,
Thou, holy chirche, thou mayst be wayled!
Sith that thy citee is assayled
Thourgh knightis of thyn owne table,
God wot thy lordship is doutable!
If they enforce hem it to winne,
That shulde defende it fro withinne,
Who might defence ayens hem make?
Withouten stroke it mot be take
Of trepeget or mangonel;
Without displaying of pensel.
And if God nil don it socour,
But lat hem renne in this colour,
Thou moost thyn heestis laten be.
Than is ther nought, but yelde thee,
Or yeve hem tribute, doutelees,
And holde it of hem to have pees:
But gretter harm bityde thee,
That they al maister of it be.
Wel conne they scorne thee withal;
By day stuffen they the wal,
And al the night they mynen there.
Nay, thou most planten elleswhere
Thyn impes, if thou wolt fruyt have;
Abyd not there thyself to save.

BUT now pees! here I turne ageyn;
I wol no more of this thing seyn,
If I may passen me herby;
I mighte maken you wery.
But I wol heten you alway
To helpe your freendis what I may,
So they wollen my company;
For they be shent al outerly
But if so falle, that I be
Oft with hem, and they with me.
And eek my lemman mot they serve,
Or they shul not my love deserve.
Forsothe, I am a fals traitour;
God jugged me for a theef trichour;
Forsworn I am, but wel nygh non
Wot of my gyle, til it be don.

THOURGH me hath many oon deth res-
seyved,
That my treget never aperceyved;
And yit resseyveth, and shal resseyve,
That my falsnesse never aperceyve:
But whoso doth, if he wys be,
Him is right good be war of me.
But so sligh is the deceyving

That to hard is the aperceyving.
For Protheus, that coude him chaunge
In every shap, hoomly and straunge,
Coude never sich gyle ne tresoun
As I; for I com never in toun
Theras I mighte knowen be,
Though men me bothe might here and see.
WEl wel I can my clothis chaunge,
Take oon, and make another straunge.
Now am I knight, now chasteleyn;
Now prelat, and now chapeleyn;
Now preest, now clerk, and now forstere;
Now am I maister, now scolere;
Now monk, now chanoun, now baily;
Whatever mister man am I.
Now am I prince, now am I page,
And can by herte every langage.
Somtyme am I hoor and old;
Now am I yong, and stout, and bold;
Now am I Robert, now Robyn;
Now frere Menour, now Jacobyn;
And with me folweth my loteby,
To don me solas and company,
That hight dame Abstinence/Streyned,
In many a queynt array yfeyned.
Right as it cometh to hir lyking,
I fulfille al hir desiring.
Somtyme a wommans cloth take I;
Now am I mayde, now lady.
Somtyme I am religious;
Now lyk an anker in an hous.
Somtyme am I prioresse,
And now a nonne, and now abbesse;
And go thurgh alle regiouns,
Seking alle religiouns.
But to what ordre that I am sworn,
I lete the strawe, and take the corn;
To blynde folk ther I enhabite,
I axe no more but hir abite.
WHAT wol ye more? in every wyse,
Right as me list, I me disgyse.
Wel can I bere me under weed;
Unlyk is my word to my deed.
Thus make I in my trappis falle,
Thurgh my pryvileges, alle
That ben in Cristendom alyve.
I may assoile, and I may shryve,
That no prelat may lette me,
Al folk, wherever they founde be:
I noot no prelat may don so,
But if the pope be, and no mo,
That made thilk establisshing.
NOW is not this a propre thing?
But, were my sleightis aperceyved,
Ne shulde I more been receyved
As I was wont; and wostow why?
For I dide hem a tregetry;
But therof yeve I litel tale,
I have the silver and the male;
So have I preched and eek shriven,
So have I take, so have me yiven,
Thurgh hir foly, husbond and wyf,
That I lede right a joly lyf,

Thurgh simplesse of the prelacye;
They know not al my tregetrye.
BUT for as moche as man and wyf
Shuld shewe hir paroche/prest hir lyf
Ones a yeer, as seith the book,
Er any wight his housel took,
Than have I pryvilegis large,
That may of moche thing discharge;
For he may seye right thus, pardee:
Sir Preest, in shrift I telle it thee,
That he, to whom that I am shriven,
Hath me assoiled, and me yiven
Penaunce soothly, for my sinne,
Which that I fond me gilty inne;
Ne I ne have never entencioun
To make double confessioun,
Ne reherce eft my shrift to thee;
O shrift is right ynough to me.
This oughte thee suffyce wel,
Ne be not rebel never/a/del;
For certis, though thou haddest it sworn,
I wot no prest ne prelat born
That may to shrift eft me constreyne.
And if they don, I wol me pleyne;
For I wot where to pleyne wel.
Thou shalt not streyne me a del,
Ne enforce me, ne yit me trouble,
To make my confessioun double.
Ne I have none affeccioun
To have double absolucioun.
The firste is right ynough to me;
This latter assoiling quyte I thee.
I am unbounde; what mayst thou finde
More of my sinnes me to unbinde?
For he, that might hath in his hond,
Of alle my sinnes me unbond,
And if thou wolt me thus constreyne,
That me mot nedis on thee pleyne,
There shal no jugge imperial,
Ne bisshop, ne official,
Don jugement on me; for I
Shal gon and pleyne me openly
Unto my shrift/fadir newe,
That hight not frere Wolf untrewe!
And he shal chevise him for me,
For I trowe he can hampre thee.
But, lord! he wolde be wrooth withalle,
If men him wolde frere Wolf calle!
For he wolde have no pacience,
But don al cruel vengeaunce!
He wolde his might don at the leest,
Ne nothing spare for goddis heest.
And, God so wis be my socour,
But thou yeve me my Saviour
At Ester, whan it lyketh me,
Withoute presing more on thee,
I wol forth, and to him goon,
And he shal housel me anoon,
For I am out of thy grucching;
I kepe not dele with thee nothing.
Thus may he shryve him, that forsaketh
His paroche/prest, and to me taketh.
And if the prest wol him refuse,

I am ful redy him to accuse,
And him punisshe and hampre so,
That he his chirche shal forgo.
But whoso hath in his feling
The consequence of such shryving,
Shal seen that prest may never have might
To knowe the conscience aright
Of him that is under his cure.
And this ageyns holy scripture,
That biddeth every herde honeste
Have verry knowing of his beste.
But pore folk that goon by strete,
That have no gold, ne sommes grete,
Hem wolde I lete to her prelates,
Or lete hir prestis knowe hir states,
For to me right nought yeve they.
Amour.

AND why is it?
Fals-Semblant. For they ne may.
They ben so bare, I take no keep;
But I wol have the fatte sheep;
Lat parish prestis have the lene,
I yeve not of hir harm a bene{
And if that prelats grucchen it,
That oughten wroth be in hir wit,
To lese her fatte bestes so,
I shal yeve hem a stroke or two,
That they shal lesen with the force,
Ye, bothe hir mytre and hir croce.
Thus jape I hem, and have do longe,
My previleges been so stronge.

FALS-SEMBLANT wolde have
stinted here,
But Love ne made him no such chere
That he was wery of his sawe;
But for to make him glad and fawe,
He seide: Tel on more specialy,
How that thou servest untrewly.
Tel forth, and shame thee never a del;
For as thyn abit shewith wel,
Thou semest an holy heremyte.
Fals-Semblant. Soth is, but I am an ypocryte.
Amour. Thou gost and prechest povertee?
Fals-Semblant. Ye, sir; but richesse hath poustee.
Amour. Thou prechest abstinence also?
Fals-Semblant.

SIR, I wol fillen, so mote I go,
My paunche of gode mete and wyne,
As shulde a maister of divyne;
For how that I me pover feyne,
Yit alle pore folk I disdeyne.
I love bet the acqueyntaunce
Ten tymes, of the king of Fraunce,
Than of pore man of mylde mode,
Though that his soule be also gode.
For whan I see beggers quaking,
Naked on mixens al stinking,
For hungre crye, and eek for care,
I entremete not of hir fare.
They been so pore, and ful of pyne,
They might not ones yeve me dyne,
For they have nothing but hir lyf;
What shulde he yeve that likketh his knyf?

It is but foly to entremete,
To seke in houndes nest fat mete.
Let bere hem to the spitel anoon,
But, for me, comfort gete they noon.
But a riche sike usurere
Wolde I visyte and drawe nere;
Him wol I comforte and rehete,
For I hope of his gold to gete.
And if that wikked deth him have,
I wol go with him to his grave.
And if ther any reprove me,
Why that I lete the pore be,
Wostow how I mot ascape?
I sey, and swere him ful rape,
That riche men han more tecches
Of sinne, than han pore wrecches,
And han of counseil more mister;
And therfore I wol drawe hem ner.
But as gret hurt, it may so be,
Hath soule in right gret poverte,
As soul in gret richesse, forsothe,
Albeit that they hurten bothe.
For richesse and mendicitees
Ben cleped two extremitees;
The mene is cleped suffisaunce,
Ther lyth of vertu the aboundaunce.

FOR Salamon, ful wel I woot,
In his Parables us wroot,
As it is knowe of many a wight,
In his thrittethe chapitre right:
God, thou me kepe, for thy poustee,
Fro richesse and mendicitee;
For if a riche man him dresse
To thenke to moche on his richesse,
His herte on that so fer is set,
That he his creatour foryet;
And him, that begging wol ay greve,
How shulde I by his word him leve?
Unnethe that he nis a micher,
Forsworn, or elles God is lyer.

Thus seith Salamones sawes;
Ne we finde writen in no lawes,
And namely in our Cristen lay,
Who seith Ye, I dar sey Nay,
That Crist, ne his apostlis dere,
Whyl that they walkede in erthe here,
Were never seen her bred begging,
For they nolde beggen for nothing.
And right thus were men wont to teche;
And in this wyse wolde it preche
The maistres of divinitee
Somtyme in Paris the citee.

AND if men wolde thergeyn appose
The naked text, and lete the glose,
It mighte sone assoiled be;
For men may wel the sothe see,
That, parde, they might axe a thing
Pleynly forth, without begging.
For they weren Goddis herdis dere,
And cure of soules hadden here,
They nolde nothing begge hir fode;
For aftir Crist was don on rode,
With hir propre hondis they wrought,

And with travel, and elles nought,
They wonnen al hir sustenaunce,
And liveden forth in hir penaunce,
And the remenaunt yeve awey
To other pore folk alwey.
They neither bilden tour ne halle,
But leye in houses smale withalle.
A mighty man, that can and may,
Shulde with his honde and body alway
Winne him his food in laboring,
If he ne have rent or sich a thing,
Although he be religious,
And God to serven curious.
Thus mote he don, or do trespas,
But if it be in certeyn cas,
That I can reherce, if mister be,
Right wel, whan the tyme I see.

EKE the book of Seynt Austin,
Be it in paper or perchemin,
Thereas he writ of these worchinges,
Thou shalt seen that non excusinges
A parfit man ne shulde seke
By wordis, ne by dedis eke,
Although he be religious,
And God to serven curious,
That he ne shal, so mote I go,
With propre hondis and body also,
Gete his food in laboring,
If he ne have propretee of thing.
Yit shulde he selle al his substaunce,
And with his swink have sustenaunce,
If he be parfit in bountee.
Thus han tho bookes tolde me:
For he that wol gon ydilly,
And useth it ay besily
To haunten other mennes table,
He is a trechour, ful of fable;
Ne he ne may, by gode resoun,
Excuse him by his orisoun,
For men bihoveth, in som gyse,
Somtyme leven Goddes servyse
To gon and purchasen her nede.
Men mote eten, that is no drede,
And slepe, and eek do other thing;
So longe may they leve praying.
So may they eek hir prayer blinne,
While that they werke, hir mete to winne.

EYNT AUSTIN wol therto accorde,
In thilke book that I recorde.
Justinian eek, that made lawes,
Hath thus forboden, by olde dawes:
No man, up peyne to be deed,
Mighty of body, to begge his breed,
If he may swinke, it for to gete;
Men shulde him rather mayme or bete,
Or doon of him apert justice,
Than suffren him in such malice.

HEY don not wel, so mote I go,
That taken such almesse so,
But if they have som privelege,
That of the peyne hem wol allege.
But how that is, can I not see,
But if the prince disseyved be;

Ne I ne wene not, sikerly,
That they may have it rightfully.
But I wol not determyne
Of princes power, ne defyne,
Ne by my word comprende, ywis,
If it so fer may strecche in this.
I wol not entremete a del;
But I trowe that the book seith wel,
Who that taketh almesses, that be
Dewe to folk that men may see
Lame, feble, wery, and bare,
Pore, or in such maner care,
That conne winne hem nevermo,
For they have no power therto,
He eteth his owne dampning,
But if he lye, that made al thing.
And if ye such a truaunt finde,
Chastise him wel, if ye be kinde.
But they wolde hate you, percas,
And, if ye fillen in hir laas,
They wolde eftsones do you scathe,
If that they mighte, late or rathe;
For they be not ful pacient,
That han the world thus foule blent.
And witeth wel, wher that God bad
The good man selle al that he had,
And folowe him, and to pore it yive,
He wolde not therfore that he live
To serven him in mendience,
For it was never his sentence;
But he bad wirken whan that nede is,
And folwe him in goode dedis.

EYNT POULE, that loved al holy chirche,
He bade thapostles for to wirche,
And winnen hir lyflode in that wyse,
And hem defended truaundyse,
And seide: Wirketh with your honden;
Thus shul the thing be undirstonden.
He nolde, ywis, bidde hem begging,
Ne sellen gospel, ne preching,
Lest they berafte, with hir asking,
Folk of hir catel or of hir thing.

OR in this world is many a man
That yeveth his good, for he ne can
Werne it for shame, or elles he
Wolde of the asker delivered be;
And, for he him encombreth so,
He yeveth him his good to late him go;
But it can him nothing profyte,
They lese the yift and the meryte.
The goode folk, that Poule to preched,
Profred him ofte, whan he hem teched
Som of hir good in charite;
But therof right nothing took he;
But of his hondwerk wolde he gete
Clothes to wryen him, and his mete.
Amour.

EL me than how a man may liven,
That al his good to pore hath yiven,
And wol but only bidde his bedis,
And never with honde laboure his nedis:
May he do so?

303

Fals-Semblant. Ye, sir.
Amour. And how?
Fals-Semblant. Sir, I wol gladly telle yow:
Seynt Austin seith, a man may be
In houses that han propretee,
As templers and hospitelers,
And as these chanouns regulers,
Or whyte monkes, or these blake,
I wole no mo ensamplis make,
And take therof his sustening,
For therin ne lyth no begging;
But otherweyes not, ywis,
If Austin gabbeth not of this.
And yit ful many a monk laboureth,
That God in holy chirche honoureth;
For whan hir swinking is agoon,
They rede and singe in chirche anoon.

AND for ther hath ben greet discord,
As many a wight may bere record,
Upon the estate of mendience,
I wol shortly, in your presence,
Telle how a man may begge at nede,
That hath not wherwith him to fede,
Maugre his felones jangelinges,
For sothfastnesse wol non hidinges;
And yit, percas, I may abey,
That I to yow sothly thus sey.

LO, here the caas especial:
If a man be so bestial
That he of no craft hath science,
And nought desyreth ignorence,
Than may he go a-begging yerne,
Til he som maner craft can lerne,
Thurgh which, withoute truaunding,
He may in trouthe have his living.
Or if he may don no labour,
For elde, or syknesse, or langour,
Or for his tendre age also,
Than may he yit a-begging go.

OR if he have, peraventure,
Thurgh usage of his noriture,
Lived over deliciously,
Than oughten good folk comunly
Han of his mischeef som pitee,
And suffren him also, that he
May gon aboute and begge his breed,
That he be not for hungur deed.
Or if he have of craft cunning,
And strengthe also, and desiring
To wirken, as he hadde what,
But he finde neither this ne that,
Than may he begge, til that he
Have geten his necessitee.

OR if his winning be so lyte,
That his labour wol not acquyte
Sufficiantly al his living,
Yit may he go his breed begging;
Fro dore to dore he may go trace,
Til he the remenaunt may purchace.
Or if a man wolde undirtake
Any empryse for to make,
In the rescous of our lay,
And it defenden as he may,

304

Be it with armes or lettrure,
Or other covenable cure,
If it be so he pore be,
Than may he begge, til that he
May finde in trouthe for to swinke,
And gete him clothes, mete, and drinke.
Swinke he with hondis corporel,
And not with hondis espirituel.

IN al thise caas, and in semblables,
If that ther ben mo resonables,
He may begge, as I telle you here,
And elles nought, in no manere;
As William Seynt Amour wolde preche,
And ofte wolde dispute and teche
Of this matere alle openly
At Paris ful solempnely.
And also God my soule blesse,
As he had, in this stedfastnesse,
The accord of the universitee,
And of the puple, as semeth me.

NO good man oughte it to refuse,
Ne oughte him therof to excuse,
Be wrooth or blythe whoso be;
For I wol speke, and telle it thee,
Al shulde I dye, and be put doun,
As was Seynt Poul, in derk prisoun;
Or be exiled in this caas
With wrong, as maister William was,
That my moder Ypocrisye
Banisshed for hir greet envye.

MY moder flemed him, Seynt Amour:
This noble dide such labour
To susteyne ever the loyaltee,
That he to moche agilte me.
He made a book, and leet it wryte,
Wherin his lyf he dide al wryte,
And wolde ich reneyed begging,
And lived by my traveyling,
If I ne had rent ne other good.
What? wened he that I were wood?
For labour might me never plese,
I have more wil to been at ese;
And have wel lever, sooth to sey,
Bifore the puple patre and prey,
And wrye me in my foxerye
Under a cope of papelardye.

QUOD Love: What devel is this I here?
What wordis tellest thou me here?
Fals-Semblant. What, sir?
Amour. Falsnesse, that apert is;
Than dredist thou not God?
Fals-Semblant.
NO, certis:
For selde in greet thing shal he spede
In this world, that God wol drede.
For folk that hem to vertu yiven,
And truly on her owne liven,
And hem in goodnesse ay contene,
On hem is litel thrift ysene;
Such folk drinken gret misese;
That lyf ne may me never plese.
But see what gold han usurers,
And silver eek in hir garners,

Taylagiers, and these monyours,
Bailifs, bedels, provost, countours;
These liven wel nygh by ravyne;
The smale puple hem mote enclyne,
And they as wolves wol hem eten.
Upon the pore folk they geten
ful moche of that they spende or
kepe;
Nis none of hem that he nil strepe,
And wryen himself wel atte fulle;
Withoute scalding they hem pulle.
The stronge the feble overgoth;
But I, that were my simple cloth,
Robbe bothe robbed and robbours,
And gyle gyled and gylours.
By my treget, I gadre and threste
The greet tresour into my cheste,
That lyth with me so faste bounde.
Myn highe paleys do I founde,
And my delytes I fulfille
With wyne at feestes at my wille,
And tables fulle of entremees;
I wol no lyf, but ese and pees,
And winne gold to spende also.
for whan the grete bagge is go,
It cometh right with my japes.
Make I not wel tumble myn apes?
To winne is alwey myn entent;
My purchas is better than my rent;
for though I shulde beten be,
Overal I entremete me;
Withoute me may no wight dure.
I walke soules for to cure.
Of al the worlde cure have I
In brede and lengthe; boldely
I wol bothe preche and eek counceilen;
With hondis wille I not traveilen,
for of the pope I have the bulle;
I ne holde not my wittes dulle.
I wol not stinten, in my lyve,
These emperouris for to shryve,
Or kyngis, dukis, and lordis grete;
But pore folk al quyte I lete.
I love no such shryving, pardee,
But it for other cause be.
I rekke not of pore men,
Hir astate is not worth an hen.
Where fyndest thou a swinker of labour
Have me unto his confessour?
But emperesses, and duchesses,
Thise quenes, and eek thise countesses,
Thise abbesses, and eek Bigyns,
These grete ladyes palasyns,
These joly knightes, and baillyves,
Thise nonnes, and thise burgeis wyves,
That riche been, and eek plesing,
And thise maidens welfaring,
Wherso they clad or naked be,
Uncounceiled goth ther noon fro me.
And, for her soules savetee,
At lord and lady, and hir meynee,
I axe, whan they hem to me shryve,

X 1

The propretee of al hir lyve,
And make hem trowe, bothe meest and
leest,
Hir paroch-prest nis but a beest
Ayens me and my company,
That shrewis been as greet as I;
for whiche I wol not hyde in hold
No privetee that me is told,
That I by word or signe, ywis,
Nil make hem knowe what it is,
And they wolen also tellen me;
They hele fro me no privetee.
And for to make yow hem perceyven,
That usen folk thus to disceyven,
I wol you seyn, withouten drede,
What men may in the gospel rede
Of Seynt Mathew, the gospelere,
That seith, as I shal you sey here.
UPON the chaire of Moyses
Thus is it glosed, douteles:
That is the olde testament,
for therby is the chaire ment
Sitte Scribes and Pharisen;
That is to seyn, the cursid men
Whiche that we ypocritis calle
Doth that they preche, I rede you alle,
But doth not as they don a del,
That been not wery to seye wel,
But to do wel, no wille have they;
And they wolde binde on folk alwey,
That ben to be begyled able,
Burdens that ben importable;
On folkes shuldres thinges they
couchen
That they nil with her fingres touchen.
Amour.
AND why wol they not touche it?
fals-Semblant. Why?
for hem ne list not, sikirly;
for sadde burdens that men taken
Make folkes shuldres aken.
And if they do ought that good be,
That is for folk it shulde see:
Her burdens larger maken they,
And make hir hemmes wyde alwey,
And loven setes at the table,
The firste and most honourable;
And for to han the first chaieris
In synagoges, to hem ful dere is;
And willen that folk hem loute and
grete,
Whan that they passen thurgh the strete,
And wolen be cleped Maister also.
But they ne shulde not willen so;
The gospel is therageyns, I gesse:
That sheweth wel hir wikkidnesse.
ANOTHER custom use we:
Of hem that wol ayens us be,
We hate hem deedly everichoon,
And we wol werrey hem, as oon.
Him that oon hatith, hate we alle,
And conjecte how to doon him falle.

305

And if we seen him winne honour,
Richesse or preys, thurgh his valour,
Provende, rent, or dignitee,
Ful fast, ywis, compassen we
By what ladder he is clomben so;
And for to maken him doun to go,
With traisoun we wole him defame,
And doon him lese his gode name.
Thus from his ladder we him take,
And thus his freendis foes we make;
But word ne wite shal he noon,
Til alle his freendis been his foon.
For if we dide it openly,
We might have blame redily;
For hadde he wist of our malyce,
He hadde him kept, but he were nyce.
ANOTHER is this, that, if so falle
That ther be oon among us alle
That doth a good turn, out of
drede,
We seyn it is our alder dede.
Ye, sikerly, though he it feyned,
Or that him list, or that him deyned
A man thurgh him avaunced be;
Therof alle parceners be we,
And tellen folk, wherso we go,
That man thurgh us is sprongen so.
And for to have of men preysing,
We purchace, thurgh our flatering,
Of riche men, of gret poustee,
Lettres, to witnesse our bountee;
So that man weneth, that may us see,
That alle vertu in us be.
And alwey pore we us feyne;
But how so that we begge or pleyne,
We ben the folk, without lesing,
That al thing have without having.
Thus be we dred of the puple, ywis.
And gladly my purpos is this:
I dele with no wight, but he
Have gold and tresour gret plentee;
Hir acqueyntaunce wel love I;
This is moche my desyr, shortly.
I entremete me of brocages,
I make pees and mariages,
I am gladly executour,
And many tymes procuratour;
I am somtyme messager;
That falleth not to my mister.
And many tymes I make enquestes;
For me that office not honest is;
To dele with other mennes thing,
That is to me a gret lyking.
And if that ye have ought to do
In place that I repeire to,
I shal it speden thurgh my wit,
As sone as ye have told me it.
So that ye serve me to pay,
My servyse shal be your alway.
But whoso wol chastyse me,
Anoon my love lost hath he;
For I love no man in no gyse,
306

That wol me repreve or chastyse;
But I wolde al folk undirtake,
And of no wight no teching take;
For I, that other folk chastye,
Wol not be taught fro my folye.
I LOVE noon hermitage more;
Alle desertes, and holtes hore,
And grete wodes everichoon,
I lete hem to the Baptist Johan.
I quethe him quyte, and him relesse
Of Egipt al the wildirnesse;
To fer were alle my mansiouns
Fro alle citees and goode tounes.
My paleis and myn hous make I
There men may renne in openly,
And sey that I the world forsake.
But al amidde I bilde and make
My hous, and swimme and pley therinne
Bet than a fish doth with his finne.
Of Antecristes men am I,
Of whiche that Crist seith openly,
They have abit of holinesse,
And liven in such wikkednesse.
Outward, lambren semen we,
Fulle of goodnesse and of pitee,
And inward we, withouten fable,
Ben gredy wolves ravisable.
We enviroune bothe londe and see;
With al the world werreyen we;
We wol ordeyne of alle thing,
Of folkes good, and her living.
If ther be castel or citee
Wherin that any bougerons be,
Although that they of Milayne
were,
For therof ben they blamed there:
Or if a wight, out of mesure,
Wolde lene his gold, and take usure,
For that he is so coveitous:
Or if he be to leccherous,
Or thefe, or haunte simonye;
Or provost, ful of trecherye,
Or prelat, living jolily,
Or prest that halt his quene him by;
Or olde hores hostilers,
Or other bawdes or bordillers,
Or elles blamed of any vyce,
Of whiche men shulden doon justice:
By alle the seyntes that we pray,
But they defende hem with lamprey,
With luce, with elis, with samons,
With tendre gees, and with capons,
With tartes, or with cheses fat,
With deynte flawnes, brode and flat,
With caleweys, or with pullaille,
With coninges, or with fyn vitaille,
That we, undir our clothes wide,
Maken thurgh our golet glyde:
Or but he wol do come in haste
Roo-venisoun, ybake in paste;
Whether so that he loure or groine,
He shal have of a corde a loigne,

With whiche men shal him binde and lede,
To brenne him for his sinful dede,
That men shulle here him crye and rore
A myle-wey aboute, and more.
Or elles he shal in prisoun dye,
But if he wol our frendship bye,
Or smerten that that he hath do,
More than his gilt amounteth to.
But, and he couthe thurgh his sleight
Do maken up a tour of height,
Nought roughte I whether of stone or tree,
Or erthe, or turves though it be,
Though it were of no younde stone,
Wrought with squyre and scantilone,
So that the tour were stuffed wel
With alle richesse temporel;
And thanne, that he wolde updresse
Engyns, bothe more and lesse,
To caste at us, by every syde,
To bere his goode name wyde,
Such sleightes as I shal yow nevene,
Barelles of wyne, by sixe or sevene,
Or gold in sakkes gret plente,
He shulde sone delivered be.
And if he have noon sich pitaunces,
Late him study in equipolences,
And lete lyes and fallaces,
If that he wolde deserve our graces;
Or we shal bere him such witnesse
Of sinne, and of his wrecchidnesse,
And doon his loos so wyde renne,
That al quik we shulde him brenne,
Or elles yeve him suche penaunce,
That is wel wors than the pitaunce.
FOR thou shalt never, for nothing,
Con knowen aright by her clothing
The traitours fulle of trecherye,
But thou her werkis can aspye.
And ne hadde the good keping be
Whylom of the universitee,
That kepeth the key of Cristendome,
They had been turmented, alle and some.
Suche been the stinking fals prophetis;
Nis non of hem, that good prophete is;
For they, thurgh wikked entencioun,
The yeer of the incarnacioun
A thousand and two hundred yeer,
Fyve and fifty, ferther ne ner,
Broughten a book, with sory grace,
To yeven ensample in comune place,
That seide thus, though it were fable:
This is the Gospel Perdurable,
That fro the Holy Goost is sent.
Wel were it worth to ben ybrent.
Entitled was in such manere
This book, of which I telle here.
Ther nas no wight in al Parys,
Biforn Our Lady, at parvys,
That he ne mighte bye the book,
To copy, if him talent took.
Ther might he see, by greet tresoun,
Ful many fals comparisoun:

As moche as, thurgh his grete might,
Be it of hete, or of light,
The sunne sourmounteth the mone,
That troubler is, and chaungeth sone,
And the note-kernel the shelle
(I scorne nat that I yow telle)
Right so, withouten any gyle,
Sourmounteth this noble Evangyle
The word of any evangelist.
And to her title they token Christ;
And many such comparisoun,
Of which I make no mencioun,
Might men in that boke finde,
Whoso coude of hem have minde.
THE universitee, that tho was aslepe,
Gan for to braide, and taken kepe;
And at the noys the heed upcaste,
Ne never sithen slepte it faste,
But up it sterte, and armes took
Ayens this fals horrible book,
Al redy bateil for to make,
And to the juge the book to take.
But they that broughten the book there
Hente it anoon awey, for fere;
They nolde shewe it more a del,
But thenne it kepte, and kepen wil,
Til such a tyme that they may see
That they so stronge woxen be,
That no wight may hem wel withstonde;
For by that book they durst not stonde.
Away they gonne it for to bere,
For they ne durste not answere
By exposicioun ne glose
To that that clerkis wole appose
Ayens the cursednesse, ywis,
That in that boke writen is.
Now wot I not, ne I can not see
What maner ende that there shal be
Of al this boke that they hyde;
But yit algate they shal abyde
Til that they may it bet defende;
This trowe I best, wol be hir ende.
THUS Antecrist abyden we,
For we ben alle of his meynee;
And what man that wol not be so,
Right sone he shal his lyf forgo.
We wol a puple on him areyse,
And thurgh our gyle doon him seise,
And him on sharpe speris ryve,
Or other weyes bringe him fro lyve,
But if that he wol folowe, ywis,
That in our boke writen is.
Thus moche wol our book signifye,
That whyl that Peter hath maistrye,
May never Johan shewe wel his might.
NOW have I you declared right
The mening of the bark and rinde
That makith the entenciouns blinde.
But now at erst I wol biginne
To expowne you the pith withinne:

And first, by Peter, as I wene,
The Pope himself we wolden mene,
And eek the seculers comprehende,
That Cristes lawe wol defende,
And shulde it kepen and mayntenen
Ayeines hem that al sustenen,
And falsly to the puple techen.
And Johan bitokeneth hem that prechen,
That ther nis lawe covenable
But thilke Gospel Perdurable,
That fro the Holy Gost was sent
To turne folk that been miswent.
The strengthe of Johan they undirstonde
The grace in which, they seye, they stonde,
That doth the sinful folk converte,
And hem to Jesus Crist reverte.
AL many another horriblete
May men in that boke see,
That ben comaunded, douteles,
Ayens the lawe of Rome expres;
And alle with Antecrist they holden,
As men may in the book biholden.
And than comaunden they to sleen
Alle tho that with Peter been;
But they shal nevere have that might,
And, God toforn, for stryf to fight,
That they ne shal ynough men finde
That Peters lawe shal have in minde,
And ever holde, and so mayntene,
That at the last it shal be sene
That they shal alle come therto,
For ought that they can speke or do.
And thilke lawe shal not stonde,
That they by Johan have undirstonde;
But, maugre hem, it shal adoun,
And been brought to confusioun.
But I wol stinte of this matere,
For it is wonder long to here;
But hadde that ilke book endured,
Of better estate I were ensured;
And freendis have I yit, pardee,
That han me set in greet degree.
Of all this world is emperour
Gyle my fader, the trechour,
And emperesse my moder is,
Maugre the Holy Gost, ywis.
Our mighty linage and our route
Regneth in every regne aboute;
And wel is worth we maistres be,
For al this world governe we,
And can the folk so wel disceyve,
That noon our gyle can perceyve;
And though they doon, they dar not
saye;
The sothe dar no wight biwreye.
But he in Cristis wrath him ledeth,
That more than Crist my bretheren
dredeth.
He nis no ful good champioun,
That dredith such similacioun;
Nor that for peyne wole refusen
Us to correcten and accusen.

308

He wol not entremete by right,
Ne have God in his eyesight,
And therfore God shal him punyce:
But me ne rekketh of no vyce,
Sithen men us loven comunably,
And holden us for so worthy,
That we may folk repreve echoon,
And we nil have repref of noon.
Whom shulden folk worshipen so
But us, that stinten never mo
To patren whyl that folk us see,
Though it not so bihinde hem be?
AND where is more wood folye,
Than to enhaunce chivalrye,
And love noble men and gay,
That joly clothis weren alway?
If they be sich folk as they semen,
So clene, as men her clothis demen,
And that her wordis folowe her dede,
It is gret pite, out of drede,
For they wol be noon ypocritis!
Of hem, me thinketh it gret spite is;
I can not love hem on no syde.
But Beggers with these hodes wyde,
With sleighe and pale faces lene,
And greye clothis not ful clene,
But fretted ful of tatarwagges,
And highe shoes, knopped with dagges,
That frouncen lyke a quaile-pype,
Or botes riveling as a gype;
To such folk as I you devyse
Shuld princes and these lordes wyse
Take alle her londes and her thinges,
Bothe werre and pees, in governinges;
To such folk shulde a prince him yive,
That wolde his lyf in honour live.
And if they be not as they seme,
That serven thus the world to queme,
There wolde I dwelle, to disceyve
The folk, for they shal not perceyve.
BUT I ne speke in no such wyse,
That men shulde humble abit
dispyse,
So that no pryde therunder be.
No man shulde hate, as thinketh me,
The pore man in sich clothing.
But God ne preiseth him nothing,
That seith he hath the world forsake,
And hath to worldly glorie him take,
And wol of siche delyces use;
Who may that Begger wel excuse?
That papelard, that him yeldeth so,
And wol to worldly ese go,
And seith that he the world hath left,
And gredily it grypeth eft,
He is the hound, shame is to seyn,
That to his casting goth ageyn.
BUT unto you dar I not lye:
But mighte I felen or aspye,
That ye perceyved it nothing,
Ye shulden have a stark lesing
Right in your hond thus, to biginne,

I nolde it lette for no sinne.
THE god lough at the wonder tho,
And every wight gan laughe also,
And seide: Lo here a man aright
for to be trusty to every wight!

FALS-SEMBLANT, quod Love, sey to me,
Sith I thus have avaunced thee,
That in my court is thy dwelling,
And of ribaudes shalt be my king,
Wolt thou wel holden my for-
wardis?

fals-Semblant.
YE, sir, from hennes forewardis;
Hadde never your fader herebiforn
Servaunt so trewe, sith he was born.

Amour. That is ayeines al nature.

fals-Semblant.
SIR, put you in that aventure;
for though ye borowes take of me,
The sikerer shal ye never be
for ostages, ne sikirnesse,
Or chartres, for to bere witnesse.
I take yourself to record here,
That men ne may, in no manere,
Teren the wolf out of his hyde,
Til he be flayn, bak and syde,
Though men him bete and al defyle;
What? wene ye that I wole bigyle?
for I am clothed mekely,
Therunder is al my trechery;
Myn herte chaungeth never the mo
for noon abit, in which I go.
Though I have chere of simplenesse,
I am not wery of shrewednesse.
My lemman, Streyned-Abstinence,   **Streyned-**
Hath mister of my purveaunce;   **Abstinence**
She hadde ful longe ago be deed,
Nere my councel and my reed;
Lete hir allone, and you and me.

AND Love answerde: I truste thee
Withoute borowe, for I wol noon.
And fals-Semblant, the theef,
anoon,
Right in that ilke same place,
That hadde of tresoun al his face
Right blak withinne, and whyt withoute,
Thanketh him, gan on his knees loute.

THAN was ther nought, but
Every man
Now to assaut, that sailen
can,
Quod Love, and that ful
hardily.
Than armed they hem communly
Of sich armour as to hem fel.
Whan they were armed, fers and fel,
They wente hem forth, alle in a route,
And set the castel al aboute;
They wil nought away, for no drede,
Til it so be that they ben dede,
Or til they have the castel take.

X 3

And foure batels they gan make,
And parted hem in foure anoon,
And toke her way, and forth they goon,
The foure gates for to assaile,
Of whiche the kepers wol not faile;
for they ben neither syke ne dede,
But hardy folk, and strong in dede.

NOW wole I seyn the counte-
naunce
Of fals-Semblant, and
Abstinaunce,
That ben to Wikkid-Tonge
went.
But first they helde her parlement,
Whether it to done were
To maken hem be knowen there,
Or elles walken forth disgysed.
But at the laste they devysed,
That they wold goon in tapinage,
As it were in a pilgrimage,
Lyk good and holy folk unfeyned.
And Dame Abstinence-Streyned
Took on a robe of camelyne,
And gan hir graithe as a Begyne.
A large coverchief of threde
She wrapped al aboute hir hede,
But she forgat not hir sautere;
A peire of bedis eek she bere
Upon a lace, al of whyt threde,
On which that she hir bedes bede;
But she ne boughte hem never a del,
for they were geven her, I wot wel,
God wot, of a ful holy frere,
That seide he was hir fader dere,
To whom she hadde ofter went
Than any frere of his covent.
And he visyted hir also,
And many a sermoun seide hir to;
He nolde lette, for man on lyve,
That he ne wolde hir ofte shryve.
And with so gret devocion
They maden her confession,
That they had ofte, for the nones,
Two hedes in one hood at ones.

Of fair shape I devyse her thee,
But pale of face somtyme was
she;
That false traitouresse untrewe
Was lyk that salowe hors of hewe,
That in the Apocalips is shewed,
That signifyeth tho folk beshrewed,
That been al ful of trecherye,
And pale, thurgh hypocrisye;
for on that hors no colour is,
But only deed and pale, ywis.
Of suche a colour enlangoured
Was Abstinence, ywis, coloured;
Of her estat she her repented,
As her visage represented.

SHE had a burdoun al of Thefte,
That Gyle had yeve her of his
yefte;

309

And a scrippe of fainte Distresse,
That ful was of elengenesse,
And forth she walked sobrely:
And false-Semblant saynt, je vous die,
Had, as it were for such mistere,
Don on the cope of a frere,
With chere simple, and ful pitous;
His looking was not disdeinous,
Ne proud, but meke and ful pesible.
About his nekke he bar a bible,
And squierly forth gan he gon;
And, for to reste his limmes upon,
He had of Treson a potente;
As he were feble, his way he wente.
But in his sleve he gan to thringe
A rasour sharp, and wel bytinge,
That was forged in a forge,
Which that men clepen Coupegorge.

So longe forth hir way they nomen,
Til they to Wicked-Tonge comen,
That at his gate was sitting,
And saw folk in the way passing.
The pilgrimes saw he faste by,
That beren hem ful mekely,
And humblely they with him mette.
Dame Abstinence first him grette,
And sith him false-Semblant salued,
And he hem; but he not remued,
for he ne dredde hem not a del.
for when he saw hir faces wel,
Alway in herte him thoughte so,
He shulde knowe hem bothe two;
for wel he knew Dame Abstinaunce,
But he ne knew not Constreynaunce.
He knew nat that she was constrayned,
Ne of her theves lyfe feyned,
But wende she com of wil al free;
But she com in another degree;
And if of good wil she began,
That wil was failed her as than.

And fals-Semblant had he seyn als,
But he knew nat that he was fals.
Yet fals was he, but his falsnesse
Ne coude he not espye, nor gesse;
for semblant was so slye wrought,
That falsnesse he ne espyed nought.
But haddest thou knowen him biforn,
Thou woldest on a boke have sworn,
Whan thou him saugh in thilke aray
That he, that whylom was so gay,
And of the daunce Joly Robin,
Was tho become a Jacobin.
But sothely, what so men him calle,
freres Prechours been good men alle;
Hir order wickedly they beren,
Suche minstrelles if that they weren.
So been Augustins and Cordileres,
And Carmes, and eek Sakked freres,
And alle freres, shodde and bare,
(Though some of hem ben grete and
square),
ful holy men, as I hem deme;
310

Everich of hem wolde good man seme.
But shalt thou never of apparence
Seen conclude good consequence
In none argument, ywis,
If existence al failed is.
for men may finde alway sophyme
The consequence to envenyme,
Whoso that hath the subteltee
The double sentence for to see.

WHAN the pilgrymes commen were
To Wicked-Tonge, that dwelled
there,
Hir harneis nigh hem was algate;
By Wicked-Tonge adoun they sate,
That bad hem ner him for to come,
And of tydinges telle him some,
And sayde hem: What cas maketh yow
To come into this place now?

SIR, seyde Strained-Abstinaunce,
We, for to drye our penaunce,
With hertes pitous and devoute,
Are commen, as pilgrimes gon aboute;
Wel nigh on fote alway we go;
ful dusty been our heles two;
And thus bothe we ben sent
Thurghout this world that is miswent,
To yeve ensample, and preche also.
To fisshen sinful men we go,
for other fisshing ne fisshe we.
And, sir, for that charitee,
As we be wont, herberwe we crave,
Your lyf to amende; Crist it save!
And, so it shulde you nat displese,
We wolden, if it were your ese,
A short sermoun unto you seyn.
And Wikked-Tonge answerde ageyn:
The hous, quod he, such as ye see,
Shal nat be warned you for me,
Sey what you list, and I wol here.
Graunt mercy, swete sire dere!
Quod alderfirst Dame Abstinence,
And thus began she hir sentence:
Constreyned-Abstinence.

SIR, the first vertue, certeyn,
The gretest, and most sovereyn
That may be founde in any man,
for having, or for wit he can,
That is, his tonge to refreyne;
Therto ought every wight him peyne.
for it is better stille be
Than for to speken harm, pardee!
And he that herkeneth it gladly,
He is no good man, sikerly.
And, sir, aboven al other sinne,
In that art thou most gilty inne.
Thou spake a jape not long ago,
And, sir, that was right yvel do,
Of a yong man that here repaired,
And never yet this place apaired.
Thou seydest he awaited nothing
But to disceyve fair-Welcoming.
Ye seyde nothing sooth of that;

But, sir, ye lye; I tell you plat;
He ne cometh no more, ne goth, pardee!
I trow ye shal him never see.
Fair-Welcoming in prison is,
That ofte hath pleyed with you, er this,
The fairest games that he coude,
Withoute filthe, stille or loude;
Now dar he nat himself solace.
Ye han also the man do chace,
That he dar neither come ne go.
What meveth you to hate him so
But properly your wikked thought,
That many a fals lesing hath thought,
That meveth your foole eloquence,
That jangleth ever in audience,
And on the folk areyseth blame,
And doth hem dishonour and shame,
For thing that may have no preving,
But lyklinesse, and contriving.
For I dar seyn, that Reson demeth,
It is not al sooth thing that semeth,
And it is sinne to controve
Thing that is for to reprove;
This wot ye wel; and, sir, therefore
Ye arn to blame wel the more.
And, nathelesse, he rekketh lyte;
He yeveth nat now thereof a myte;
For if he thoughte harm, parfay,
He wolde come and gon al day;
He coude himselfe nat abstene.
Now cometh he nat, and that is sene,
For he ne taketh of it no cure,
But if it be through aventure,
And lasse than other folk, algate.
And thou here watchest at the gate,
With spere in thyne arest alway;
There muse, musard, al the day.
Thou wakest night and day for thought;
Ywis, thy traveyl is for nought.
And jelousye, withouten faile,
Shal never quyte thee thy travaile.
And scathe is, that Fair-Welcoming,
Withouten any trespassing,
Shal wrongfully in prison be,
Ther wepeth and languissheth he.
And though thou never yet, ywis,
Agiltest man no more but this,
Take not agreef, it were worthy
To putte thee out of this baily,
And afterward in prison lye,
And fettre thee til that thou dye;
For thou shalt for this sinne dwelle
Right in the devils ers of helle,
But if that thou repente thee.
A fay, thou lyest falsly! quod he.
What? welcome with mischaunce now!
Have I therfore herbered you
To seye me shame, and eek reprove?
With sory happe, to your bihove,
Am I today your herbergere!
Go, herber you elleswhere than here,

That han a lyer called me!
Two tregetours art thou and he,
That in myn hous do me this shame,
And for my sothsawe ye me blame.
Is this the sermoun that ye make?
To alle the develles I me take,
Or elles, God, thou me confounde!
But er men diden this castel founde,
It passeth not ten dayes or twelve,
But it was told right to myselve,
And as they seide, right so tolde I,
He kiste the Rose privily!
Thus seide I now, and have seid yore;
I not wher he dide any more.
Why shulde men sey me such a thing,
If it hadde been gabbing?
Right so seide I, and wol seye yit;
I trowe, I lyed not of it;
And with my bemes I wol blowe
To alle neighboris a-rowe,
How he hath bothe comen and gon.
THO spak fals-Semblant right
anon,
Al is not gospel, out of doute,
That men seyn in the toune aboute;
Ley no deef ere to my speking;
I swere yow, sir, it is gabbing!
I trowe ye wot wel certeynly,
That no man loveth him tenderly
That seith him harm, if he wot it,
Al be he never so pore of wit.
And sooth is also sikerly,
This knowe ye, sir, as wel as I,
That lovers gladly wol visyten
The places ther hir loves habyten.
This man you loveth and eek honoureth;
This man to serve you laboureth;
And clepeth you his freend so dere,
And this man maketh you good chere,
And everywher that he you meteth,
He you saleweth, and he you greteth.
He preseth not so ofte, that ye
Ought of his come encombred be;
Ther presen other folk on yow
Ful ofter than that he doth now.
And if his herte him streyned so
Unto the Rose for to go,
Ye shulde him seen so ofte nede,
That ye shulde take him with the dede.
He coude his coming not forbere,
Though ye him thrilled with a spere;
It nere not thanne as it is now.
But trusteth wel, I swere it yow,
That it is clene out of his thought.
Sir, certes, he ne thenketh it nought;
No more ne doth Fair-Welcoming,
That sore abyeth al this thing.
And if they were of oon assent,
Ful sone were the Rose hent;
The maugre youres wolde be.
And sir, of o thing herkeneth me:
Sith ye this man, that loveth yow,

Han seid such harm and shame now,
Witeth wel, if he gessed it,
Ye may wel demen in your wit,
He nolde nothing love you so,
Ne callen you his freend also,
But night and day he wolde wake,
The castel to destroye and take,
If it were sooth as ye devyse;
Or som man in som maner wyse
Might it warne him everydel,
Or by himself perceyven wel;
For sith he might not come and gon
As he was whylom wont to don,
He might it sone wite and see;
But now al otherwyse doth he.
Than have ye, sir, al outerly
Deserved helle, and jolyly
The deth of helle, douteles,
That thrallen folk so gilteles.

FALS-SEMBLANT proveth so
        this thing
        That he can noon answering,
And seeth alwey such apparaunce,
That nygh he fel in repentaunce,
And seide him : Sir, it may wel be.
Semblant, a good man semen ye;
And, Abstinence, ful wyse ye seme;
Of o talent you bothe I deme.

What counceil wole ye to me yeven?
Fals-Semblant.
RIGHT here anoon thou shalt be
        shriven,
        And sey thy sinne withoute more;
Of this shalt thou repente sore;
For I am preest, and have poustee
To shryve folk of most dignitee
That been, as wyde as world may dure.
Of al this world I have the cure,
And that had never yit persoun,
No vicarie of no maner toun.
And, God wot, I have of thee
A thousand tymes more pitee
Than hath thy preest parochial,
Though he thy freend be special.
I have avauntage, in o wyse,
That your prelates ben not so wyse
Ne half so lettred as am I.
I am licenced boldely
In divinitee to rede,
And to confessen, out of drede.
If ye wol you now confesse,
And leve your sinnes more and lesse,
Without abood, knele doun anon,
And you shal have absolucion.
Here ends all that is done of The Romance
of the Rose.

✤ ✤ THE PARLEMENT OF FOULES ✤ ✤ THE PROEM. ✤ ✤ ✤

For al be that I knowe not love in dede,
Ne wot how that he quyteth folk hir hyre,
Yet happeth me ful ofte in bokes rede
Of his miracles, and his cruel yre;
Ther rede I wel he wol be lord and syre,
I dar not seyn, his strokes been so sore,
But God save swich a lord! I can no more.

Of usage, what for luste what for lore,
On bokes rede I ofte, as I yow tolde.
But wherfor that I speke al this? not yore
Agon, hit happed me for to beholde
Upon a boke, was write with lettres olde;
And therupon, a certeyn thing to lerne,
The longe day ful faste I radde and yerne.

For out of olde feldes, as men seith,
Cometh al this newe corn fro yeer to yere;
And out of olde bokes, in good feith,
Cometh al this newe science that men lere.
But now to purpos as of this matere...
To rede forth hit gan me so delyte,
That al the day me thoughte but a lyte.

This book of which I make mencioun,
Entitled was al thus, as I shal telle,
Tullius of the dreme of Scipioun;

THE LYF SO SHORT, THE CRAFT SO LONG
to lerne,
Thassay so hard, so sharp the conquering,
The dredful joy, that alwey slit so yerne,
Al this mene I by love, that my feling
Astonyeth with his wonderful worching
So sore ywis, that whan I on him thinke,
Nat wot I wel wher that I wake or winke.

Chapitres seven hit hadde, of hevene and
helle,
And erthe, and soules that therinne dwelle,
Of whiche, as shortly as I can hit trete,
Of his sentence I wol you seyn the grete.

First telleth hit, whan Scipioun was come
In Afrik, how he mette Massinisse,
That him for joye in armes hath ynome.
Than telleth hit hir speche and al the blisse
That was betwix hem, til the day gan misse;
And how his auncestre, African so dere,
Gan in his slepe that night to him appere.

Than telleth hit that, fro a sterry place,
How African hath him Cartage shewed,
And warned him before of al his grace,
And seyde him, what man, lered other lewed,
That loveth comun profit, wel ythewed,
He shal unto a blisful place wende,
Ther as joye is that last withouten ende.

Than asked he, if folk that heer be dede
Have lyf and dwelling in another place;
And African seyde: Ye, withoute drede,
And that our present worldes lyves space
Nis but a maner deth, what wey we trace,
And rightful folk shal go, after they dye,
To heven; and shewed him the galaxye.

Than shewed he him the litel erthe, that
heer is,
At regard of the hevenes quantite;
And after shewed he him the nyne speres,
And after that the melodye herde he
That cometh of thilke speres thryes three,
That welle is of musyke and melodye
In this world heer, and cause of armonye.

Than bad he him, sin erthe was so lyte,
And ful of torment and of harde grace,
That he ne shulde him in the world delyte.
Than tolde he him, in certeyn yeres space,
That every sterre shulde come into his place
Ther hit was first; and al shulde out of minde
That in this worlde is don of al mankinde.

Than prayde him Scipioun to telle him al
The wey to come unto that hevene blisse;
And he seyde: Know thyself first immortal,
And loke ay besily thou werke and wisse
To comun profit, and thou shalt nat misse
To comen swiftly to that place dere,
That ful of blisse is and of soules clere.

But brekers of the lawe, soth to seyne,
And lecherous folk, after that they be dede,
Shul alwey whirle aboute therthe in peyne,
Til many a world be passed, out of drede,
And than, foryeven alle hir wikked dede,
Than shul they come unto that blisful place,
To which to comen God thee sende his grace!

The day gan failen, and the derke night,
314

That reveth bestes from hir besinesse,
Berafte me my book for lakke of light,
And to my bedde I gan me for to dresse,
Fulfild of thought and besy hevinesse;
For bothe I hadde thing which that I nolde,
And eek I ne hadde that thing that I wolde.

But fynally my spirit, at the laste,
Forwery of my labour al the day,
Took rest, that made me to slepe faste,
And in my slepe I mette, as I lay,
How African, right in that selfe aray
That Scipioun him saw before that tyde,
Was comen, and stood right at my beddes
syde.

The wery hunter, slepinge in his bed,
To wode ayein his minde goth anoon;
The juge dremeth how his plees ben sped;
The carter dremeth how his cartes goon;
The riche, of gold; the knight fight with his
foon,
The seke met he drinketh of the tonne;
The lover met he hath his lady wonne.

Can I nat seyn if that the cause were
For I had red of African beforn,
That made me to mete that he stood there;
But thus seyde he: Thou hast thee so wel
born
In loking of myn olde book totorn,
Of which Macrobie roghte nat a lyte,
That somdel of thy labour wolde I quyte!

Cithereal thou blisful lady swete,
That with thy fyr/brand dauntest whom thee
lest,
And madest me this sweven for to mete,
Be thou my help in this, for thou mayst best;
As wisly as I saw thee north/north/west,
When I began my sweven for to wryte,
So yif me might to ryme hit and endyte!

The Story.

THIS forseid African me hente
anoon,
And forth with him unto a gate
broghte
Right of a parke, walled with
grene stoon;
And over the gate, with lettres large ywroghte,
Ther weren vers ywriten, as me thoghte,
On eyther halfe, of ful gret difference,
Of which I shal yow sey the pleyn sentence.

Thorgh me men goon into that blisful
place
Of hertes hele and dedly woundes cure;
Thorgh me men goon unto the welle of Grace,
Ther grene and lusty May shal ever endure;
This is the wey to al good aventure;
Be glad, thou reder, and thy sorwe of/caste,
Al open am I; passe in, and by thee faste!

Thorgh me men goon, than spak that
other syde,
Unto the mortal strokes of the spere,
Of which Disdayn and Daunger is the gyde,
Ther tree shal never fruyt ne leves bere.
This streem you ledeth to the sorwful were,
Ther as the fish in prison is al drye;
Theschewing is only the remedye.

Thise vers of gold and blak ywriten were,
The whiche I gan a stounde to beholde,
For with that oon encresed ay my fere,
And with that other gan myn herte bolde;
That oon me hette, that other did me colde,
No wit had I, for errour, for to chese,
To entre or flee, or me to save or lese.

Right as, betwixen adamauntes two
Of even might, a pece of iren yset,
That hath no might to meve to ne fro,
For what that on may hale, that other let,
Ferde I, that niste whether me was bet,
To entre or leve, til African my gyde
Me hente, and shoof in at the gates wyde,

And seyde: Hit stondeth writen in thy face,
Thyn errour, though thou telle it not to me;
But dred thee nat to come into this place,

For this wryting is nothing ment by thee,
Ne by noon, but he Loves servant be;
For thou of love hast lost thy tast, I gesse,
As seek man hath of swete and bitternesse.

But natheles, although that thou be dulle,
Yit that thou canst not do, yit mayst thou
see;
For many a man that may not stonde a pulle,
Yit lyketh him at the wrastling for to be,
And demeth yit wher he do bet or he;
And if thou haddest cunning for tendyte,
I shal thee shewen mater of to wryte.

With that my hond in his he took anoon,
Of which I comfort caughte, and wente in
faste;
But lord! so I was glad and wel begoon!
For overal, wher that I myn eyen caste,
Were treës clad with leves that ay shal laste,
Eche in his kinde, of colour fresh and grene
As emeraude, that joye was to sene.

The bilder ook, and eek the hardy asshe;
The piler elm, the cofre unto careyne;
The boxtree piper; holm to whippes lasshe;
The sayling firr; the cipres, deth to pleyne;
The sheter ew, the asp for shaftes pleyne;

The olyve of pees, and eek the drunken vyne,
The victor palm, the laurer to devyne.

A garden saw I, ful of blosmy bowes,
Upon a river, in a grene mede,
Ther as that swetnesse evermore ynow is,
With floures whyte, blewe, yelowe, and rede;
And colde welle streames, nothing dede,
That swommen ful of smale fisshes lighte,
With finnes rede and scales silver brighte.

On every bough the briddes herde I singe,
With voys of aungel in hir armonye,
Som besyed hem hir briddes forth to bringe;
The litel conyes to hir pley gunne hye,
And further al aboute I gan espye
The dredful roo, the buk, the hert and hinde,
Squerels, and bestes smale of gentil kinde.

Of instruments of strenges in acord
Herde I so pleye a ravisshing swetnesse,
That God, that maker is of al and lord,
Ne herde never better, as I gesse;
Therwith a wind, unnethe hit might be lesse,
Made in the leves grene a noise softe
Acordant to the foules songe on lofte.

The air of that place so attempre was

That never was grevaunce of hoot ne cold;
Ther wex eek every holsom spyce and gras,
Ne no man may ther wexe seek ne old;
Yet was ther joye more a thousand fold
Then man can telle; ne never wolde it nighte,
But ay cleer day to any mannes sighte.

Under a tree, besyde a welle, I say
Cupyde our lord his arwes forge and fyle;
And at his fete his bowe al redy lay,
And wel his doghter tempred al the whyle
The hedes in the welle, and with hir wyle
She couched hem after as they shulde serve,
Som for to slee, and som to wounde and kerve.

Tho was I war of Plesaunce anon right,
And of Aray, and Lust, and Curtesye;
And of the Craft that can and hath the might
To doon by force a wight to do folye,
Disfigurat was she, I nil not lye;
And by himself, under an oke, I gesse,
Sawe I Delyt, that stood with Gentilnesse.

I saw Beautee, withouten any atyr,
And Youthe, ful of game and jolyte,
fool hardinesse, flatery, and Desyr,
Messagerye, and Mede, and other three,
Hir names shul noght here be told for me,

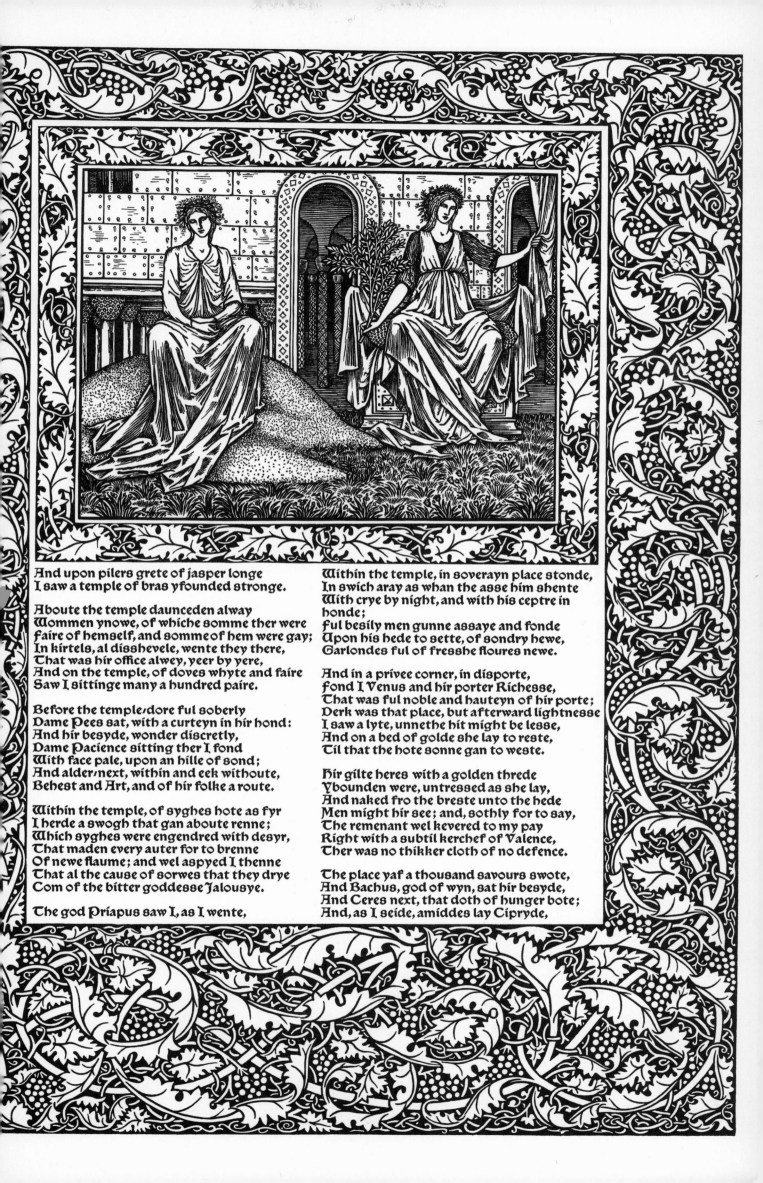

And upon pilers grete of jasper longe
I saw a temple of bras yfounded stronge.

Aboute the temple daunceden alway
Wommen ynowe, of whiche somme ther were
Faire of hemself, and somme of hem were gay;
In kirtels, al disshevele, wente they there,
That was hir office alwey, yeer by yere,
And on the temple, of doves whyte and faire
Saw I sittinge many a hundred paire.

Before the temple-dore ful soberly
Dame Pees sat, with a curteyn in hir hond:
And hir besyde, wonder discretly,
Dame Pacience sitting ther I fond
With face pale, upon an hille of sond;
And alder-next, within and eek withoute,
Behest and Art, and of hir folke a route.

Within the temple, of syghes hote as fyr
I herde a swogh that gan aboute renne;
Which syghes were engendred with desyr,
That maden every auter for to brenne
Of newe flaume; and wel aspyed I thenne
That al the cause of sorwes that they drye
Com of the bitter goddesse Jalousye.

The god Priapus saw I, as I wente,

Within the temple, in soverayn place stonde,
In swich aray as whan the asse him shente
With crye by night, and with his ceptre in
honde;
Ful besily men gunne assaye and fonde
Upon his hede to sette, of sondry hewe,
Garlondes ful of fresshe floures newe.

And in a privee corner, in disporte,
Fond I Venus and hir porter Richesse,
That was ful noble and hauteyn of hir porte;
Derk was that place, but afterward lightnesse
I saw a lyte, unnethe hit might be lesse,
And on a bed of golde she lay to reste,
Til that the hote sonne gan to weste.

Hir gilte heres with a golden threde
Ybounden were, untressed as she lay,
And naked fro the breste unto the hede
Men might hir see; and, sothly for to say,
The remenant wel kevered to my pay
Right with a subtil kerchef of Valence,
Ther was no thikker cloth of no defence.

The place yaf a thousand savours swote,
And Bachus, god of wyn, sat hir besyde,
And Ceres next, that doth of hunger bote;
And, as I seide, amiddes lay Cipryde,

To whom on knees two yonge folkes cryde
To ben hir help; but thus I leet hir lye,
And ferther in the temple I gan espye

That, in dispyte of Diane the chaste,
ful many a bowe ybroke heng on the wal
Of maydens, suche as gunne hir tymes waste
In hir servyse; and peynted over al
Of many a story, of which I touche shal
A fewe, as of Calixte and Athalaunte,
And many a mayde, of which the name I
wante;

Semyramus, Candace, and Ercules,
Biblis, Dido, Tisbe and Piramus,
Tristram, Isoude, Paris, and Achilles,
Eleyne, Cleopatre, and Troilus,
Silla, and eek the moder of Romulus...
Alle these were peynted on that other syde,
And al hir love, and in what plyte they dyde.

Whan I was come ayen into the place
That I of spak, that was so swote & greene,
forth welk I tho, myselven to solace.
Tho was I war wher that ther sat a quene
That, as of light the somer-sonne shene
Passeth the sterre, right so over mesure
She fairer was than any creature.

And in a launde, upon an hille of floures,
Was set this noble goddesse Nature;
Of braunches were hir halles and hir boures,
Ywrought after hir craft and hir mesure;
Ne ther nas foul that cometh of engendrure,
That they ne were prest in hir presence,
To take hir doom and yeve hir audience.

For this was on seynt Valentynes day,
Whan every foul cometh ther to chese his
make,
Of every kinde, that men thenke may;
And that so huge a noyse gan they make,
That erthe and see, and tree, and every lake
So ful was, that unnethe was ther space
For me to stonde, so ful was al the place.

And right as Aleyn, in the Pleynt of Kinde,
Devyseth Nature of aray and face,
In swich aray men mighten hir ther finde.
This noble emperesse, ful of grace,
Bad every foul to take his owne place,
As they were wont alwey fro yeer to yere,
Seynt Valentynes day, to stonden there.

That is to sey, the foules of ravyne
Were hyest set; and than the foules smale,
That eten as hem nature wolde enclyne,

As worm, or thing of whiche I telle no tale;
But water-foul sat lowest in the dale;
And foul that liveth by seed sat on the grene,
And that so fele, that wonder was to sene.

Ther mighte men the royal egle finde,
That with his sharpe look perceth the sonne;
And other egles of a lower kinde,
Of which that clerkes wel devysen conne.
Ther was the tyraunt with his fethres donne
And greye, I mene the goshauk, that doth pyne
To briddes for his outrageous ravyne.

The gentil faucon, that with his feet distreyneth
The kinges hond; the hardy sperhauk eke,
The quayles foo; the merlion that peyneth
Himself ful ofte, the larke for to seke;
Ther was the douve, with hir eyen meke;
The jalous swan, ayens his deth that singeth;
The oule eek, that of dethe the bode bringeth;

The crane the geaunt, with his trompes soune;
The theef, the chogh; and eek the jangling pye;
The scorning jay; the eles foo, the heroune;
The false lapwing, ful of trecherye;
The stare, that the counseyl can bewrye;
The tame ruddok; and the coward kyte;
The cok, that orloge is of thorpes lyte;

The sparow, Venus sone; the nightingale,
That clepeth forth the fresshe leves newe;
The swalow, mordrer of the flyës smale
That maken hony of floures fresshe of hewe;
The wedded turtel, with hir herte trewe;
The pecok, with his aungels fethres brighte;
The fesaunt, scorner of the cok by nighte;

The waker goos; the cukkow ever unkinde;
The popinjay, ful of delicasye;
The drake, stroyer of his owne kinde;
The stork, the wreker of avouterye;
The hote cormeraunt of glotonye;
The raven wys, the crow with vois of care;
The throstel olde; the frosty feldefare.

What shulde I seyn? of foules every kinde
That in this worlde han fethres and stature,
Men mighten in that place assembled finde
Before the noble goddesse Nature.
And everich of hem did his besy cure
Benignely to chese or for to take,
By hir acord, his formel or his make.

But to the poynt...Nature held on hir honde
A formel egle, of shap the gentileste
That ever she among hir werkes fonde,
The most benigne and the goodlieste;
In hir was every vertu at his reste,
So ferforth, that Nature hirself had blisse
To loke on hir, and ofte hir bek to kisse.

Nature, the vicaire of thalmyghty lorde,
That hoot, cold, hevy, light, and moist and dreye

Hath knit by even noumbre of acorde,
In esy vois began to speke and seye:
Foules, tak hede of my sentence, I preye,
And, for your ese, in furthering of your nede,
As faste as I may speke, I wol me spede.

Ye know wel how, seynt Valentynes day,
By my statut and through my governaunce,
Ye come for to chese, and flee your way,
Your makes, as I prik yow with plesaunce.
But natheles, my rightful ordenaunce
May I not lete, for al this world to winne,
That he that most is worthy shal beginne.

The tercel egle, as that ye knowen wel,
The foul royal above yow in degree,
The wyse and worthy, secree, trewe as stel,
The which I formed have, as ye may see,
In every part as hit best lyketh me,
Hit nedeth noght his shap yow to devyse,
He shal first chese and speken in his gyse.

And after him, by order shul ye chese,
After your kinde, everich as yow lyketh,
And, as your hap is, shul ye winne or lese;
But which of yow that love most entryketh,
God sende him hir that sorest for him syketh.
🖋 And therwithal the tercel gan she calle,
And seyde: My sone, the choys is to thee falle.

But natheles, in this condicioun
Mot be the choys of everich that is here,
That she agree to his eleccioun,
Whoso he be that shulde been hir fere;
This is our usage alwey, fro yeer to yere;
And who so may at this time have his grace,
In blisful tyme he com into this place.

🖋 With hed enclyned and with ful humble chere
This royal tercel spak and taried nought:
Unto my sovereyn lady, and noght my fere,
I chese, and chese with wille and herte & thought,
The formel on your hond so wel ywrought,
Whos I am al and ever wol hir serve,
Do what hir list, to do me live or sterve.

Beseching hir of mercy and of grace,
As she that is my lady sovereyne;
Or let me dye present in this place.
For certes, long may I not live in peyne;
For in myn herte is corven every veyne;
Having reward al only to my trouthe,
My dere herte, have on my wo som routhe.

And if that I to hir be founde untrewe,
Disobeysaunt, or wilful negligent,
Avauntour, or in proces love a newe,
I pray to you this be my jugement,
That with these foules I be al torent,
That ilke day that ever she me finde
To hir untrewe, or in my gilte unkinde.

And sin that noon loveth hir so wel as I,

319

Al be she never of love me behette,
Than oghte she be myn thourgh hir mercy,
For other bond can I noon on hir knette.
For never, for no wo, ne shal I lette
To serven hir, how fer so that she wende;
Sey what yow list, my tale is at an ende.

Right as the fresshe, rede rose newe
Ayen the somer/sonne coloured is,
Right so for shame al wexen gan the hewe
Of this formel, whan that she herde al this;
She neyther answerde Wel, ne seyde amis,
So sore abasshed was she, til that Nature
Seyde, Doghter, drede yow noght, I yow
assure.

Another tercel egle spak anoon
Of lower kinde, and seyde: That shal not be;
I love hir bet than ye do, by seynt John,
Or atte leste I love hir as wel as ye;
And lenger have served hir, in my degree,
And if she shulde have loved for long loving,
To me allone had been the guerdoning.

I dar eek seye, if she me finde fals,
Unkinde, jangler, or rebel any wyse,
Or jalous, do me hongen by the hals!
And but I bere me in hir servyse
As wel as that my wit can me suffyse,
Fro poynt to poynt, hir honour for to save,
Tak she my lyf, and al the good I have.

The thridde tercel egle answerde tho:
Now, sirs, ye seen the litel leyser here;
For every foul cryeth out to been ago
Forth with his make, or with his lady dere;
And eek Nature hirself ne wol nought here,
For tarying here, noght half that I wolde seye;
And but I speke, I mot for sorwe deye.

Of long servyse avaunte I me nothing,
But as possible is me to dye today
For wo, as he that hath ben languisshing
Thise twenty winter, and wel happen may
A man may serven bet and more to pay
In half a yere, although hit were no more,
Than som man doth that hath served ful yore.

I ne say not this by me, for I ne can
Do no servyse that may my lady plese;
But I dar seyn, I am hir trewest man
As to my dome, and feynest wolde hir ese;
At shorte wordes, til that deth me sese,
I wol ben hires, whether I wake or winke,
And trewe in al that herte may bethinke.

Of al my lyf, sin that day I was born,
So gentil plee in love or other thing
Ne herde never no man me biforn,
Whoso that hadde leyser and cunning
For to reherse hir chere and hir speking;
And from the morwe gan this speche laste
Til dounward drow the sonne wonder faste.

320

The noyse of foules for to ben delivered
So loude rong, Have doon and let us wende!
That wel wende I the wode had al toshivered.
Come of! they cryde, allas! ye wil us shende!
Whan shal your cursed pleding have an ende?
How shulde a juge eyther party leve,
For yee or nay, withouten any preve?

The goos, the cokkow, and the doke also
So cryden Kek, kek! kukkow! quek, quek! hye,
That thorgh myn eres the noyse wente tho.
The goos seyde: Al this nis not worth a flye!
But I can shape hereof a remedye,
And I wol sey my verdit faire and swythe
For water/foul, whoso be wrooth or blythe.

And I for worm/foul, seyde the fool cukkow,
For I wol, of myn owne auctoritè,
For comune spede, take the charge now,
For to delivere us is gret charitè.
Ye may abyde a whyle yet, pardè!
Seide the turtel, if hit be your wille
A wight may speke, him were as good be stille.

I am a seed/foul, oon the unworthieste,
That wot I wel, and litel of kunninge;
But bet is that a wightes tonge reste
Than entremeten him of such doinge
Of which he neyther rede can nor singe.
And whoso doth, ful foule himself acloyeth,
For office uncommitted ofte anoyeth.

Nature, which that alway had an ere
To murmour of the lewednes behinde,
With facound voys seide: Hold your tonges there!
And I shal sone, I hope, a counseyl finde
You to delivere, and fro this noyse unbinde;
I juge, of every folk men shal oon calle
To seyn the verdit for you foules alle.

Assented were to this conclusioun
The briddes alle; and foules of ravyne
Han chosen first, by pleyn eleccioun,
The tercelet of the faucon, to diffyne
Al hir sentence, and as him list, termyne;
And to Nature him gonnen to presente,
And she accepteth him with glad entente.

The tercelet seide than in this manere:
Ful hard were hit to preve hit by resoun
Who loveth best this gentil formel here;
For everich hath swich replicacioun,
That noon by skilles may be broght adoun;
I can not seen that arguments avayle;
Than semeth hit ther moste be batayle.

Al redy! quod these egles tercels tho.
Nay, sirs! quod he, if that I dorste it seye,
Ye doon me wrong, my tale is not ydo!
For sirs, ne taketh noght agref, I preye,
It may noght gon, as ye wolde, in this weye;
Oure is the voys that han the charge in honde,
And to the juges dome ye moten stonde;

And therfor pees! I seye, as to my wit,
Me wolde thinke how that the worthieste
Of knighthode, and lengest hath used hit,
Moste of estat, of blode the gentileste,
Were sittingest for hir, if that hir leste;
And of these three she wot hirself, I trowe,
Which that he be, for hit is light to knowe.

The water-foules han her hedes leyd
Togeder, and of short avysement,
Whan everich had his large golee seyd,
They seyden sothly, al by oon assent,
How that The goos, with hir facounde gent,
That so desyreth to pronounce our nede,
Shal telle our tale, and preyde God hir spede.

And for these water-foules tho began
The goos to speke, and in hir cakelinge
She seyde: Pees! now tak kepe every man,
And herkeneth which a reson I shal bringe;
My wit is sharp, I love no taryinge;
I seye, I rede him, though he were my brother,
But she wol love him, lat him love another!

Lo here! a parfit reson of a goos!
Quod the sperhauk; never mot she thee!
Lo, swich hit is to have a tonge loos!
Now parde, fool, yet were hit bet for thee
Have holde thy pees, than shewed thy nycete!
Hit lyth not in his wit nor in his wille,
But sooth is seyd, A fool can noght be stille.

The laughter aroos of gentil foules alle,
And right anoon the seed-foul chosen hadde
The turtel trewe, and gunne hir to hem calle,
And preyden hir to seye the sothe sadde
Of this matere, and asked what she radde;
And she answerde, that pleynly hir entente
She wolde shewe, and sothly what she mente.

Nay, God forbede a lover shulde chaunge!
The turtel seyde, and wex for shame al reed;
Thogh that his lady evermore be straunge,
Yet let him serve hir ever, til he be deed;
For sothe, I preyse noght the gooses reed;
For thogh she deyed, I wolde non other make,
I wol ben hires, til that the deth me take.

Wel bourded! quod the doke, by my hat!
That men shulde alwey loven, causeles,
Who can a reson finde or wit in that?
Daunceth he mury that is mirtheles?
Who shulde recche of that is reccheles?
Ye, quek! yit quod the doke, ful wel and faire,
Ther been mo sterres, God wot, than a paire!

Now fy, cherl! quod the gentil tercelet,
Out of the dunghil com that word ful right,
Thou canst noght see which thing is wel beset:
Thou farest by love as oules doon by light,
The day hem blent, ful wel they see by night;
Thy kind is of so lowe a wrechednesse,
That what love is, thou canst nat see ne gesse.

y 1

Tho gan the cukkow putte him forth in prees
For foul that eteth worm, and seide blyve:
So I, quod he, may have my make in pees,
I recche not how longe that ye stryve;
Lat ech of hem be soleyn al hir lyve,
This is my reed, sin they may not acorde;
This shorte lesson nedeth noght recorde.

Ye! have the glotoun fild ynogh his paunche,
Than are we wel! seyde the merlioun;
Thou mordrer of the heysugge on the braunche
That broghte thee forth, thou rewthelees glotoun!
Live thou soleyn, wormes corrupcioun!
For no fors is of lakke of thy nature!
Go, lewed be thou, whyl the world may dure!

Now pees, quod Nature, I comaunde here;
For I have herd al your opinioun,
And in effect yet be we never the nere;
But fynally, this is my conclusioun,
That she hirself shal han the eleccioun
Of whom hir list, whoso be wrooth or blythe,
Him that she cheest, he shal hir have as swythe.

For sith hit may not here discussed be
Who loveth hir best, as seide the tercelet,
Than wol I doon hir this favour, that she
Shal have right him on whom hir herte is set,
And he hir that his herte hath on hir knet.
This juge I, Nature, for I may not lyë;
To noon estat I have non other yë.

But as for counseyl for to chese a make,
If hit were reson, certes, than wolde I
Counseyle yow the royal tercel take,
As seide the tercelet ful skilfully,
As for the gentilest and most worthy,
Which I have wroght so wel to my plesaunce;
That to yow oghte been a suffisaunce.

With dredful vois the formel hir answerde:
My rightful lady, goddesse of Nature,
Soth is that I am ever under your yerde,
Lyk as is everiche other creature,
And moot be youres whyl my lyf may dure;
And therfor graunteth me my firste bone,
And myn entente I wol yow sey right sone.

I graunte it you, quod she; and right anoon
This formel egle spak in this degree:
Almighty quene, unto this yeer be doon
I aske respit for to avysen me.
And after that to have my choys al free;
This al and som, that I wolde speke and seye;
Ye gete no more, although ye do me deye.

I wol noght serven Venus ne Cupyde
For sothe as yet, by no manere weye.
Now sin it may non other wyse betyde,
Quod tho Nature, here is no more to seye;
Than wolde I that these foules were aweye
Ech with his make, for tarying lenger here,
And seyde hem thus, as ye shul after here.

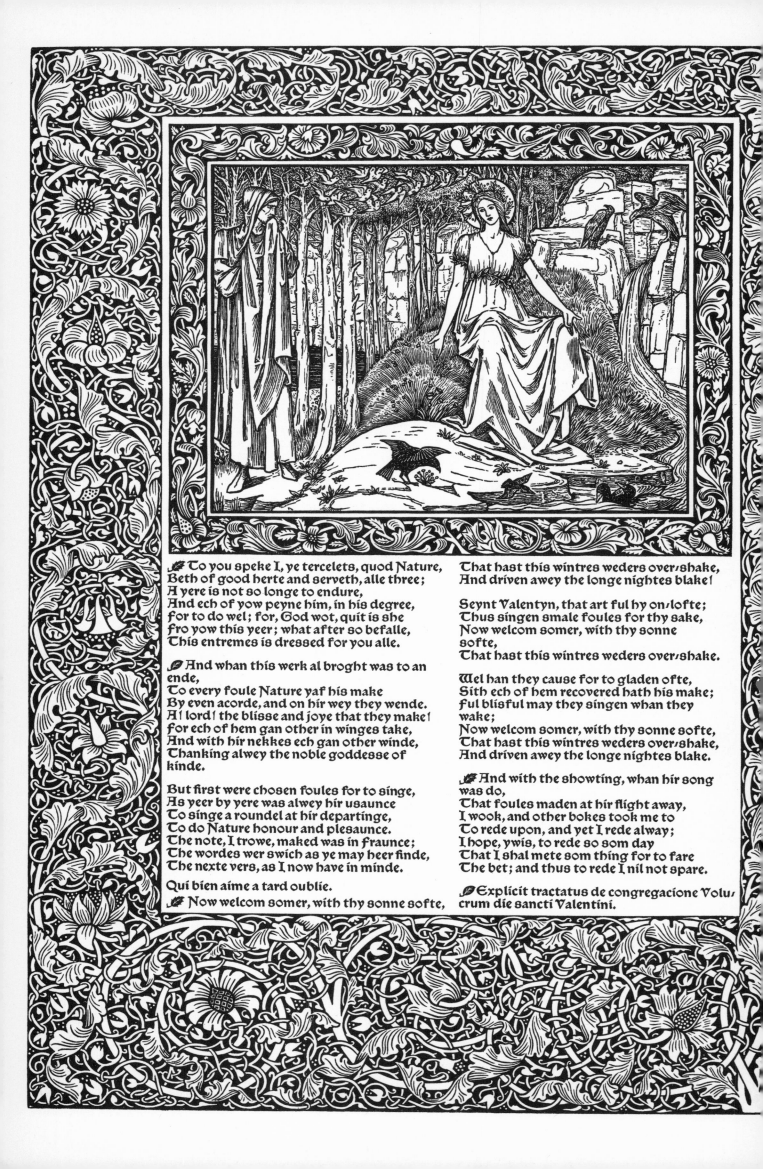

To you speke I, ye tercelets, quod Nature,
Beth of good herte and serveth, alle three;
A yere is not so longe to endure,
And ech of yow peyne him, in his degree,
For to do wel; for, God wot, quit is she
Fro yow this yeer; what after so befalle,
This entremes is dressed for you alle.

And whan this werk al broght was to an
ende,
To every foule Nature yaf his make
By even acorde, and on hir wey they wende.
A! lord! the blisse and joye that they make!
For ech of hem gan other in winges take,
And with hir nekkes ech gan other winde,
Thanking alwey the noble goddesse of
kinde.

But first were chosen foules for to singe,
As yeer by yere was alwey hir usaunce
To singe a roundel at hir departinge,
To do Nature honour and plesaunce.
The note, I trowe, maked was in fraunce;
The wordes wer swich as ye may heer finde,
The nexte vers, as I now have in minde.

Qui bien aime a tard oublie.

Now welcom somer, with thy sonne softe,

That hast this wintres weders over-shake,
And driven awey the longe nightes blake!

Seynt Valentyn, that art ful hy on-lofte;
Thus singen smale foules for thy sake,
Now welcom somer, with thy sonne
softe,
That hast this wintres weders over-shake.

Wel han they cause for to gladen ofte,
Sith ech of hem recovered hath his make;
Ful blisful may they singen whan they
wake;
Now welcom somer, with thy sonne softe,
That hast this wintres weders over-shake,
And driven awey the longe nightes blake.

And with the showting, whan hir song
was do,
That foules maden at hir flight away,
I wook, and other bokes took me to
To rede upon, and yet I rede alway;
I hope, ywis, to rede so som day
That I shal mete som thing for to fare
The bet; and thus to rede I nil not spare.

Explicit tractatus de congregacione Volu-
crum die sancti Valentini.

BOETHIUS DE CONSOLATIONE PHILOSOPHIE ❧ BOOK I. ❧

Metre I. ❀❀❀❀❀❀❀❀❀❀❀❀❀❀
Carmina qui quondam studio florente peregi.

I, WEPING, AM CONSTREINED TO biginnen vers of sorowful matere, that whylom in florisching studie made delitable ditees. for lo! rendinge Muses of poetes endyten to me thinges to be writen; and drery vers of wrecchednesse weten my face with verray teres. At the leeste, no drede ne mighte overcomen tho Muses, that they ne weren felawes, and folweden my wey, that is to seyn, whan I was exyled; they that weren glorie of my youthe, whylom weleful and grene, comforten now the sorowful werdes of me, olde man ✍ for elde is comen unwarly upon me, hasted by the harmes that I have, and sorow hath comaunded his age to be in me. Heres hore ben shad overtymeliche upon myn heved, & the slake skin trembleth upon myn empted body. Thilke deeth of men is weleful that ne cometh not in yeres that ben swete, but cometh to wrecches, often ycleped.

ALLAS! allas! with how deef an ere deeth, cruel, torneth awey fro wrecches, and naiteth to closen wepinge eyen! Whyl fortune, unfeithful, favorede me with lighte goodes, the sorowful houre, that is to seyn, the deeth, hadde almost dreynt myn heved. But now, for fortune cloudy hath chaunged hir deceyvable chere to meward, myn unpitous lyf draweth along unagreable dwellinges in me. O ye, my frendes, what or wherto avauntede ye me to ben weleful? for he that hath fallen stood nat in stedefast degree.

Prose I.
Hec dum mecum tacitus ipse reputarem.

HYLE that I stille recordede thise thinges with myself, and markede my weeply compleynte with office of pointel, I saw, stondinge aboven the heighte of myn heved, a woman of ful greet reverence by semblaunt, hir eyen brenninge and cleerseinge over the comune might of men; with a lyfly colour, and with swich vigour & strengthe that it ne mighte nat ben empted; al were it so that she was ful of so greet age, that men ne wolde nat trowen, in no manere, that she were of oure elde. The stature of hir was of a doutous jugement; for somtyme she constreinede and shronk hirselven lyk to the comune mesure of men, and sumtyme it semede that she touchede the hevene with the heighte of hir heved; and whan she heef hir heved hyer, she percede the selve hevene, so that the sighte of men looking was in ydel. Hir clothes weren maked of right delye thredes and subtil crafte, of perdurable matere; the whiche clothes she hadde woven with hir owene hondes, as I knew wel after by hirself, declaringe & shewinge to me the beautee; the whiche clothes a derknesse of a forleten & dispysed elde hadde dusked and derked, as it is wont to derken bismokede images.

IN the nethereste hem or bordure of thise clothes men redden, ywoven in, a Grekissh P, that signifyeth the lyf Actif; and aboven that lettre, in the heyeste bordure, a Grekissh T, that signifyeth the lyf Contemplatif. And bitwixen these two lettres ther weren seyn degrees, nobly ywroght in manere of laddres; by whiche degrees men mighten climben fro the nethereste lettre to the uppereste. Natheles, handes of some men hadde corven that cloth by violence & by strengthe; and everiche man of hem hadde born awey swiche peces as he mighte geten. And forsothe, this forseide woman bar smale bokes in hir right hand, & in hir left hand she bar a ceptre.

AND whan she say thise poetical Muses aprochen aboute my bed, and endytinge wordes to my wepinges, she was a litel amoved, and glowede with cruel eyen. Who, quod she, hath suffred aprochen to this syke man thise comune strompetes of swich a place that men clepen the theatre? The whiche nat only ne asswagen nat hise sorwes with none remedies, but they wolden feden & norrisshen hem with swete venim. Forsothe, thise ben tho that with thornes and prikkinges of talents or affecciouns, whiche that ne ben nothing fructefyinge nor profitable, destroyen the corn plentevous of fruites of resoun; for they holden the hertes of men in usage, but they ne delivere nat folk fro maladye. But if ye Muses hadden withdrawen fro me, with your flateryes, any uncunninge and unprofitable man, as men ben wont to finde comunly amonges the poeple, I wolde wene suffre the lasse grevously; for why, in swiche an unprofitable man, myn ententes ne weren nothing endamaged. But ye withdrawen me this man, that hath be norisshed in the studies or scoles of Eleaticis and of Achademicis in Grece. But goth now rather awey, ye mermaidenes, whiche that ben swete til it be at the laste, and suffreth this man to be cured and heled by myne Muses, that is to seyn, by noteful sciences.

AND thus this companye of Muses yblamed casten wrothly the chere dounward to the erthe; and, shewinge by reednesse hir shame, they passeden sorowfully the threshfold.

AND I, of whom the sighte, plounged in teres, was derked so that I ne mighte not knowen what that womman was, of so imperial auctoritee, I wex al abaisshed and astoned, and caste my sighte doun to the erthe, and bigan stille for to abyde what she wolde don afterward. Tho com she ner, and sette hir doun upon the uttereste corner of my bed; and she, biholdinge my chere, that was cast to the erthe, hevy and grevous of wepinge, compleinede, with thise wordes that I shal seyen, the perturbacioun of my thought.

Metre II.
Heu quam precipiti mersa profundo.

LLAS! how the thought of man, dreint in overthrowinge deepnesse, dulleth, and forleteth his propre cleernesse, mintinge to goon into foreine derknesses, as ofte as his anoyous bisinesse wexeth withoute mesure, that is driven to and fro with worldly windes! This man, that whylom was free, to whom the hevene was open and knowen, and was wont to goon in heveneliche pathes, and saugh the lightnesse of the rede sonne, & saugh the sterres of the colde mone, & whiche sterre in hevene useth wandering recourses, yflit by dyverse speres; this man, overcomer, hadde comprehended al this by noumbre of acountinge in astronomye. And over this, he was wont to seken the causes whennes

the souning windes moeven and bisien the
smothe water of the see; & what spirit torn,
eth the stable hevene; and why the sterre
aryseth out of the rede eest, to fallen in the
westrene wawes; and what atempreth the
lusty houres of the firste somer sesoun,
that highteth and apparaileth the erthe with
rosene flowres; and who maketh that plen,
tevouse autompne, in fulle yeres, fleteth with
hevy grapes. And eek this man was wont to
telle the dyverse causes of nature that weren
yhidde. Allas! now lyeth he empted of light
of his thought; & his nekke is pressed with
hevy cheynes; and bereth his chere enclyned
adoun for the grete weighte, & is constrein,
ed to looken on the fool erthe!

Prose II.
Set medicine, inquit, tempus est.

AT tyme is now, quod
she, of medicine more
than of compleinte; 🍃
forsothe than she en,
tendinge to meward
with alle the lookinge
of hir eyen, seide: Art
nat thou he, quod she,
that whylom ynoris,
shed with my milk, &

fostered with myne metes, were escaped and
comen to corage of a parfit man? Certes, I yaf
thee swiche armures that, yif thou thyself ne
haddest first cast hem awey, they shulden han
defended thee in sikernesse that may nat ben
overcomen. Knowest thou me nat? Why art
thou stille? Is it for shame or for astoninge?
It were me lever that it were for shame; but
it semeth me that astoninge hath oppres,
sed thee 🍃 And whan she say me nat only
stille, but withouten office of tunge & al doumb,
she leide hir hand softely upon my brest, and
seide: Here nis no peril, quod she; he is fallen
into a litargie, whiche that is a comune syke,
nes to hertes that ben deceived. He hath a litel
foryeten himself, but certes he shal lightly
remembren himself, yif so be that he hath
knowen me or now; & that he may so don, I
wil wypen a litel his eyen, that ben derked by
the cloude of mortal thinges 🍃 Thise wordes
seide she, and with the lappe of hir garment,
yplyted in a frounce, she dryede myn eyen,
that weren fulle of the wawes of my wepinges.

Metre III.
Tunc me discussa liquerunt nocte tenebre.

HUS, when that night was discussed
& chased awey, derknesses forleften
me, and to myn eyen repeirede ayein

hir firste strengthe. And, right by ensaum/
ple as the sonne is hid whan the sterres ben
clustred (that is to seyn, whan sterres ben
covered with cloudes) by a swifte winde
that highte Chorus, & that the firmament
stant derked by wete ploungy cloudes, &
that the sterres nat apperen upon hevene,
so that the night semeth sprad upon
erthe: yif thanne the wind that highte Bo/
rias, ysent out of the caves of the contree
of Trace, beteth this night (that is to seyn,
chaseth it awey), & descovereth the closed
day: than shyneth Phebus yshaken with
sodein light, and smyteth with his bemes
in mervelinge eyen.

Prose III.
Haud aliter tristicie nebulis dissolutis.

RIGHT so, & non oth/
er wyse, the cloudes
of sorwe dissolved
and don awey, I took
hevene, and receiv/
ede minde to know/
en the face of my
fysicien; so that I
sette myn eyen on
hir, & fastnede my
lookinge. I beholde my norice Philosophie, in whos houses I hadde conversed
& haunted fro my youthe; & I seide thus:
O thou maistresse of alle vertues, descend/
ed from the soverein sete, why artow comen
into this solitarie place of myn exil? Artow
comen for thou art maked coupable with
me of false blames?

O, QUOD she, my norry, sholde I
forsaken thee now, and sholde I
nat parten with thee, by comune
travaile, the charge that thou hast suffred
for envie of my name? Certes, it nere not
leveful ne sittinge thing to Philosophie,
to leten withouten companye the wey of
him that is innocent. Sholde I thanne re-
doute my blame, & agrysen as though ther
were bifallen a new thing? quasi diceret,
non. For trowestow that Philosophie be
now alderfirst assailed in perils by folk of
wikkede maneres? Have I nat striven with
ful greet stryf, in olde tyme, bifore the age
of my Plato, ayeines the foolhardinesse
of folye? And eek, the same Plato livinge,
his maister Socrates deservede victorie of
unrightful deeth in my presence. The heri/
tage of which Socrates ... the heritage is to
seyn the doctrine of the whiche Socrates in
his opinioun of felicitee, that I clepe welefulnesse ... whan that the poeple of Epicuriens and Stoiciens and many othre en-
forceden hem to go ravisshe everich man
for his part ... that is to seyn, that everich
of hem wolde drawen to the defence of his
opinioun the wordes of Socrates ... they,

326

as in partie of hir preye, todrowen me, cryinge and debatinge therayeins, and corven
& torenten my clothes that I hadde woven
with myn handes; & with tho cloutes that
they hadden araced out of my clothes they
wenten awey, weninge that I hadde gon
with hem everydel.

IN whiche Epicuriens and Stoiciens,
for as moche as ther semede some
traces or steppes of myn habite, the
folye of men, weninge tho Epicuriens and
Stoiciens my famuleres, perverted (sc.
persequendo) some through the errour of
the wikkede or uncunninge multitude of
hem. This is to seyn that, for they semede
philosophres, they weren pursued to the
deeth & slayn. So yif thou hast nat know-
en the exilinge of Anaxogore, ne the enpoy/
soninge of Socrates, ne the tourments
of Zeno, for they weren straungeres: yit
mightestow han knowen the Senecciens
and the Canios and the Sorans, of whiche
folk the renoun is neither over olde ne un-
solempne. The whiche men, nothing elles
ne broughte hem to the deeth but only for
they weren enfourmed of myne maneres,
and semeden most unlyke to the studies
of wikkede folk. And forthy thou oughtest
nat to wondren though that I, in the bittre
see of this lyf, be fordriven with tempestes
blowinge aboute, in the whiche tempestes
this is my most purpos, that is to seyn,
to displesen to wikkede men. Of whiche
shrewes, al be the ost never so greet, it is
to dispyse; for it nis governed with no
leder of resoun, but it is ravisshed only by
fletinge errour folyly and lightly. And if
they somtyme, makinge an ost ayeins us,
assaile us as as strenger, our leder draweth
togidere hise richesses into his tour, & they
ben ententif aboute sarpulers or sachels
unprofitable for to taken. But we that ben
heye aboven, siker fro alle tumulte & wode
noise, warnestored and enclosed in swich
a palis, whider as that chateringe or anoyinge folye ne may nat atayne, we scorne
swiche ravineres and henteres of fouleste
thinges.

Metre IV.
Quisquis composito serenus evo.

WHOSO it be that is cleer of
vertu, sad, & wel ordinat of
livinge, that hath put under
foot the proude werdes, and
looketh upright upon either
fortune, he may hold his chere
undiscomfited. The rage ne the manaces
of the see, commoevinge or chasing upward hete fro the botme, ne shal not moeve
that man; ne the unstable mountaigne
that highte Vesevus, that wrytheth out
through his brokene chiminees smokinge

fyres. Ne the wey of thonder/leit, that is wont to smyten heye toures, ne shal nat moeve that man. Wherto thanne, o wrecch/es, drede ye tirauntes that ben wode and felonous withoute any strengthe? Hope after nothing, ne drede nat; & so shaltow desarmen the ire of thilke unmighty tiraunt. But whoso that, quakinge, dredeth or desireth thing that nis nat stable of his right, that man that so doth hath cast awey his sheld & is removed fro his place, and enlaceth him in the cheyne with the which he may ben drawen.

Prose IV.
Sentisne, inquit, hec.

ELESTOW, quod she, thise thinges, & entren they aught in thy corage? Artow lyke an asse to the harpe? Why wepestow, why spillestow teres? Yif thou abydest after help of thy leche, thee bihoveth discovere thy wounde.

THO I, that hadde gadered strengthe in my corage, answerede and seide: And nedeth it yit, quod I, of rehersinge or of amonicioun; and sheweth it nat ynough by himself the sharpnesse of fortune, that wexeth wood ayeins me? Ne moeveth it nat thee to seen the face or the manere of this place (i. prisoun)? Is this the librarie whiche that thou haddest chosen for a right certein sete to thee in myn hous, theras thou desputedest ofte with me of the sciences of thinges touchinge divinitee and touchinge mankinde? Was thanne myn habite swich as it is now? Was than my face or my chere swiche as now (quasi diceret, non), whan I soughte with thee secrets of nature, whan thou enformedest my maneres and the resoun of alle my lyf to the ensaumple of the ordre of hevene? Is nat this the guerdoun that I referre to thee, to whom I have be obeisaunt? Certes, thou confermedest, by the mouth of Plato, this sentence, that is to seyn, that comune thinges or comualitees weren blisful, yif they that hadden studied al fully to wisdom governeden thilke thinges, or elles yif it so bifille that the governoures of comunalitees studieden to geten wisdom.

THOU seidest eek, by the mouth of the same Plato, that it was a necessarie cause, wyse men to taken and desire the governaunce of comune thinges, for that the governements of citees, yleft in the handes of felonous tormentours citizenes, ne sholde nat bringe in pestilence & destruccioun to gode folk. And therfor I, folwinge thilke auctoritee (sc. Platonis), desired to putten forth in execucioun and in acte of comune administracioun thilke thinges that I hadde lerned of thee among my secree resting/whyles. Thou, and God that putte thee in the thoughtes of wyse folk, ben knowinge with me, that nothing ne broughte me to maistrie or dignitee, but the comune studie of alle goodnesse. And therof comth it that bitwixen wikked folk and me han ben grevous discordes, that ne mighten ben relesed by preyeres; for this libertee hath the freedom of conscience, that the wratthe of more mighty folk hath alwey ben despysed of me for savacioun of right.

HOW ofte have I resisted and withstonde thilke man that highte Conigaste, that made alwey assautes ayeins the prospre fortunes of pore feble folk? How ofte eek have I put of or cast out him, Trigwille, provost of the kinges hous, bothe of the wronges that he hadde bigunne to don, and eek fully performed? How ofte have I covered & defended by the auctoritee of me, put ayeins perils... that is to seyn, put myn auctoritee in peril for... the wrecched pore folk, that the covetyse of straungeres unpunished tourmenteden alwey with miseyses & grevaunces out of noumbre? Never man ne drow me yit fro right to wronge. Whan I say the fortunes and the richesses of the poeple of the provinces ben harmed or amenused, outher by privee ravynes or by comune tributes or cariages, as sory was I as they that suffreden the harm.

Glossa. Whan that Theodoric, the king of Gothes, in a dere yere, hadde hise gerneres ful of corn, and comaundede that no man ne sholde byen no corn til his corn were sold, & that at a grevous dere prys, Boece withstood that ordinaunce, and overcom it, knowinge al this the king himself.

Textus.

WHAN it was in the soure hungry tyme, ther was establisshed or cryed grevous and inplitable coempcioun, that men sayen wel it sholde greetly turmenten & endamagen al the province of Campaigne, I took stryf ayeins the provost of the pretorie for comune profit. And, the king knowinge of it, I overcom it, so that the coempcioun ne was not axed ne took effect.

Glossa. Coempcioun, that is to seyn, comune achat or bying togidere, that were establisshed upon the poeple by swiche a manere imposicioun, as whoso boughte a busshel corn, he moste yeve the king the fifte part.

Textus.

PAULIN, a counseiller of Rome, the richesses of the whiche Paulin the houndes of the palays, that is to seyn, the officeres, wolden han devoured by hope and covetise, yit drow I him out of the jowes (sc. faucibus) of hem that gapeden. And for as moche as the peyne of the accusacioun ajuged biforn ne sholde nat sodeinly henten ne punisshen wrongfully Albin, a counseiller of Rome, I putte me ayeins the hates and indignaciouns of the accusor Ciprian. Is it nat thanne ynough yseyn, that I have purchased grete discordes ayeins myself? But I oughte be the more assured ayeins alle othre folk (s. Romayns), that for the love of rightwisnesse I ne reserved never nothing to myself to hemward of the kinges halle, sc. officers, by the whiche I were the more siker. But thorugh tho same accusors accusinge, I am condempned. Of the noumbir of the whiche accusors oon Basilius, that whylom was chased out of the kinges service, is now compelled in accusinge of my name, for nede of foreine moneye. Also Opilion and Gaudencius han accused me, al be it so that the justice regal hadde whylom demed hem bothe to go into exil for hir trecheryes and fraudes withoute noumbir. To whiche jugement they nolden nat obeye, but defendeden hem by the sikernesse of holy houses, that is to seyn, fledden into seintuaries; and whan this was aperceived to the king, he comaundede, that but they voidede the citee of Ravenne by certein day assigned, that men sholde merken hem on the forheved with an hoot yren & chasen hem out of the toune. Now what thing, semeth thee, mighte ben lykned to this crueltee? For certes, thilke same day was received the accusinge of my name by thilke same accusors. What may ben seid herto? (quasi diceret, nichil). Hath my studie and my cunninge deserved thus; or elles the forseide dampnacioun of me, made that hem rightful accusors or no? (quasi diceret, non). Was not fortune ashamed of this? Certes, al hadde nat fortune ben ashamed that innocence was accused, yit oughte she han had shame of the filthe of myne accusours.

BUT, axestow in somme, of what gilt I am accused? men seyn that I wolde save the companye of the senatours. And desirest thou to heren in what manere? I am accused that I sholde han destourbed the accusor to beren lettres, by whiche he sholde han maked the senatoures gilty ayeins the kinges real majestee. O maistresse, what demestow of this? Shal I forsake this blame, that I ne be no shame to thee? (quasi diceret, non). Certes,
328

I have wold it, that is to seyn, the savacioun of the senat, ne I shal never leten to wilne it, and that I confesse & am aknowe; but the entente of the accusor to be destourbed shal cese. For shal I clepe it thanne a felonie or a sinne that I have desired the savacioun of the ordre of the senat? (quasi diceret, dubito quid). And certes yit hadde thilke same senat don by me, thorugh hir decrets & hir jugements, as though it were a sinne or a felonie; that is to seyn, to wilne the savacioun of hem (sc. senatus). But folye, that lyeth alwey to himself, may not chaunge the merite of thinges. Ne I trowe nat, by the jugement of Socrates, that it were leveful to me to hyde the sothe, ne assente to lesinges. But certes, how so ever it be of this, I putte it to gessen or preisen to the jugement of thee & of wyse folk. Of whiche thing al the ordinaunce & the sothe, for as moche as folke that ben to comen after our dayes shullen knowen it, I have put it in scripture and in remembraunce. For touching the lettres falsly maked, by whiche lettres I am accused to han hoped the fredom of Rome, what aperteneth me to speke therof? Of whiche lettres the fraude hadde ben shewed apertly, yif I hadde had libertee for to han used & ben at the confessioun of myne accusours, the whiche thing in alle nedes hath greet strengthe. For what other fredom may men hopen? Certes, I wolde that som other fredom mighte ben hoped. I wolde thanne han answered by the wordes of a man that highte Canius; for whan he was accused by Gaius Cesar, Germeynes sone, that he (Canius) was knowinge and consentinge of a conjuracioun ymaked ayeins him (sc. Gaius), this Canius answerede thus: Yif I hadde wist it, thou haddest nat wist it. In which thing sorwe hath nat so dulled my wit, that I pleyne only that shrewede folk aparailen felonies ayeins vertu; but I wondre greetly how that they may performe thinges that they hadde hoped for to don. Forwhy, to wilne shrewednesse, that comth peraventure of oure defaute; but it is lyk a monstre and a mervaille, how that, in the present sighte of God, may ben acheved and performed swiche thinges as every felonous man hath conceived in his thought ayeins innocents. For which thing oon of thy famileres nat unskilfully axed thus: Yif God is, whennes comen wikkede thinges? And yif God ne is, whennes comen gode thinges? But al hadde it ben leveful that felonous folk, that now desiren the blood & the deeth of alle gode men and eek of alle the senat, han wilned to gon destroyen me, whom they han seyen alwey batailen & defenden gode men and eek al the senat, yit had I nat des-served of the faderes, that is to seyn, of the senatoures, that they sholden wilne my destruccioun.

THOU remembrest wel, as I gesse, that whan I wolde doon or seyen any thing, thou thyself, alwey present, rewledest me. At the city of Verone, whan that the king, gredy of comune slaughter, caste him to transporten up al the ordre of the senat the gilt of his real majestee, of the whiche gilt that Albin was accused, with how gret sikernesse of peril to me defendede I al the senat! Thou wost wel that I seye sooth, ne I ne avauntede me never in preysinge of myself. For alwey, whan any wight receiveth precious renoun in avauntinge himself of his werkes, he amenuseth the secree of his conscience. But now thou mayst wel seen to what ende I am comen for myne innocence; I receive peyne of fals felonye for guerdon of verray vertu. And what open confessioun of felonye hadde ever juges so acordaunt in crueltee, that is to seyn, as myn accusinge hath, that either errour of mannes wit or elles condicioun of Fortune, that is uncertein to alle mortal folk, ne submittede some of hem, that is to seyn, that it ne enclynede som juge to han pitee or compassioun? For althogh I hadde ben accused that I wolde brenne holy houses, and strangle preestes with wikkede swerde, or that I hadde greythed deeth to al gode men, algates the sentence sholde han punisshed me, present, confessed, or convict. But now I am remewed fro the citee of Rome almost fyve hundred thousand pas, I am withoute defence dampned to proscripcioun and to the deeth, for the studie and bountees that I have doon to the senat. But O, wel ben they worthy of merite (as who seith, nay), ther mighte never yit non of hem be convict of swiche a blame as myne is! Of whiche trespas, myne accusours sayen ful wel the dignitee; the whiche dignitee, for they wolden derken it with medeling of som felonye, they baren me on hand, and lyeden, that I hadde polut and defouled my conscience with sacrilege, for coveitise of dignitee. And certes, thou thyself, that are plaunted in me, chacedest out of the sege of my corage al coveitise of mortal thinges; ne sacrilege hadde no leve to han a place in me biforn thyne eyen. For thou droppedest every day in myne eres and in my thought thilke comaundement of Pictagoras, that is to seyn, men shal serve to Godde, & not to goddes. Ne it was nat convenient, ne no nede, to taken help of the foulest spirites; I, that thou hast ordeined & set in swiche excellence that thou makedest me lyk to God. And over this, the right clene secree chaumbre of myne

hous, that is to seyn, my wyf, & the companye of myn honest freendes, and my wyves fader, as wel holy as worthy to ben reverenced thorugh his owne dedes, defenden me from alle suspecioun of swich blame. But O malice! for they that accusen me taken of thee, Philosophie, feith of so gret blame! for they trowen that I have had affinitee to malefice or enchauntement, bycause that I am replenisshed and fulfilled with thy techinges, and enformed of thy maneres. And thus it suffiseth not only, that thy reverence ne availe me not, but yif that thou, of thy free wille, rather be blemished with myn offencioun. But certes, to the harmes that I have, ther bitydeth yit this encrees of harm, that the gessinge & the jugement of moche folk ne looken nothing to the desertes of thinges, but only to the aventure of fortune; and jugen that only swiche thinges ben purveyed of God, whiche that temporel welefulnesse commendeth.
Glose. As thus: that, yif a wight have prosperitee, he is a good man and worthy to han that prosperitee; and whoso hath adversitee, he is a wikked man, and God hath forsake him, and he is worthy to han that adversitee. This is the opinioun of some folk.

AND therof comth that good gessinge, first of alle thing, forsaketh wrecches: certes, it greveth me to thinke right now the dyverse sentences that the poeple seith of me. And thus moche I seye, that the last charge of contrarious fortune is this: that, whan that any blame is leyd upon a caitif, men wenen that he hath deserved that he suffreth. And I, that am put awey fro gode men, and despoiled of dignitees, & defouled of my name by gessinge, have suffred torment for my gode dedes. Certes, me semeth that I see the felonous covines of wikked men habounden in joye and in gladnesse. And I see that every lorel shapeth him to finde out newe fraudes for to accuse gode folk. And I see that gode men beth overthrowen for drede of my peril; & every luxurious tourmentour dar doon alle felonye unpunisshed & ben excited therto by yiftes; and innocents ne ben not only despoiled of sikernesse but of defence; and therfore me list to cryen to God in this wyse:

Metre V.
O stelliferi conditor orbis.

THOU maker of the whele that bereth the sterres, which that art yfastned to thy perdurable chayer, and tornest the hevene with a ravisshing sweigh, and constreinest the
329

sterres to suffren thy lawe; so that the mone somtyme shyning with hir ful hornes, meting with alle the bemes of the sonne hir brother, hydeth the sterres that ben lesse; and somtyme, whan the mone, pale with hir derke hornes, approcheth the sonne, leseth hir lightes; and that the eve-sterre Hesperus, whiche that in the firste tyme of the night bringeth forth hir colde arysinges, cometh eft ayein hir used cours, & is pale by the morwe at the rysing of the sonne, and is thanne cleped Lucifer. Thou restreinest the day by shorter dwelling, in the tyme of colde winter that maketh the leves to falle. Thou dividest the swifte tydes of the night, whan the hote somer is comen. Thy might atempreth the variaunts sesons of the yere; so that Zephirus the deboneir wind bringeth ayein, in the first somer sesoun, the leves that the wind that highte Boreas hath reft awey in autumpne, that is to seyn, in the laste ende of somer; and the sedes that the sterre that highte Arcturus saw, ben waxen heye cornes whan the sterre Sirius eschaufeth hem. Ther nis nothing unbounde from his olde lawe, ne forleteth the werke of his propre estat.

THOU governour, governinge alle thinges by certein ende, why refusestow only to governe the werkes of men by dewe manere? Why suffrest thou that slydinge fortune torneth so grete entrechaunginges of thinges, so that anoyous peyne, that sholde dewely punisshe felouns, punissheth innocents? And folk of wikkede maneres sitten in heye chayres, and anoyinge folk treden, & that unrightfully, on the nekkes of holy men? And vertu clershyninge naturelly is hid in derke derkenesses, and the rightful man bereth the blame and the peyne of the feloun. Ne forsweringe ne the fraude, covered and kembd with a fals colour, ne anoyeth nat to shrewes; the whiche shrewes, whan hem list to usen hir strengthe, they rejoysen hem to putten under hem the sovereyne kinges, whiche that poeple withouten noumbre dreden.

THOU, what so ever thou be that knittest alle bondes of thinges, loke on thise wrecchede erthes; we men that ben nat a foule party, but a fayr party of so grete a werk, we ben tormented in this see of fortune. Thou governour, withdraw and restreyne the ravisshinge flodes, and fastne and ferme thise erthes stable with thilke bonde, with whiche thou governest the hevene that is so large.

Prose V.
Hic ubi continuato dolore delatravi.

WHAN I hadde, with a continuel sorwe, sobbed or borken out thise thinges, she with hir chere pesible, and nothing amoeved with my compleintes, seide thus: Whan I say thee, quod she, sorweful and wepinge, I wiste anon that thou were a wrecche and exiled; but I wiste never how fer thyne exile was, yif thy tale ne hadde shewed it to me. But certes, al be thou fer fro thy contree, thou nart nat put out of it; but thou hast failed of thy weye and gon amis. And yif thou hast lever for to wene that thou be put out of thy contree, than hast thou put out thyself rather than any other wight hath. For no wight but thyself ne mighte never han don that to thee. For yif thou remembre of what contree thou art born, it nis nat governed by emperours, ne by governement of multitude, as weren the contrees of hem of Athenes; but oo lord and oo king, and that is God, that is lord of thy contree, whiche that rejoyseth him of the dwelling of his citezenes, and nat for to putte hem in exil; of the whiche lorde it is a soverayne fredom to be governed by the brydel of him and obeye to his justice. Hastow foryeten thilke right olde lawe of thy citee, in the whiche citee it is ordeined and establisshed, that for what wight that hath lever founden therin his sete or his hous than elleswher, he may nat be exiled by no right from that place? For whoso that is contened inwith the palis and the clos of thilke citee, ther nis no drede that he may deserve to ben exiled. But whoso that leteth the wil for to enhabite there, he forleteth also to deserve to ben citezein of thilke citee. So that I sey, that the face of this place ne moveth me nat so mochel as thyne owne face. Ne I axe nat rather the walles of thy librarie, aparayled and wrought with yvory & with glas, than after the sete of thy thought. In whiche I putte nat whylom bokes, but I putte that that maketh bokes worthy of prys or precious, that is to seyn, the sentence of my bokes. And certeinly of thy desertes, bistowed in comune good, thou hast seid sooth, but after the multitude of thy gode dedes, thou hast seid fewe; & of the honestee or of the falsnesse of thinges that ben aposed ayeins thee, thou hast remembred thinges that ben knowen to alle folk. And of the felonyes and fraudes of thyne accusours, it semeth thee have ytouched it forsothe rightfully & shortly, al mighten tho same thinges betere and more plenti-vousely ben couth in the mouthe of the poeple that knoweth al this.

THOU hast eek blamed gretly and com-pleined of the wrongful dede of the senat. And thou hast sorwed for my blame, & thou hast wopen for the damage of thy renoun that is apayred; and thy laste sorwe eschaufede ayeins fortune, & com-pleinest that guerdouns ne ben nat even-liche yolden to the desertes of folk. And in the latere ende of thy wode Muse, thou preyedest that thilke pees that governeth the hevene sholde governe the erthe. But for that manye tribulaciouns of affecciouns han assailed thee, and sorwe and ire & wep-inge todrawen thee dyversely; as thou art now feble of thought, mightier remedies ne shullen nat yit touchen thee, for whiche we wol usen somdel lighter medicines: so that thilke passiouns that ben woxen harde in swellinge, by perturbaciouns flowing into thy thought, mowen wexen esy and softe, to receiven the strengthe of a more mighty and more egre medicine, by an esier touchinge.

Metre VI.

Cum Phebi radiis grave
Cancri sidus inestuat.

WHAN that the hevy sterre of the Cancre eschaufeth by the bemes of Phebus, that is to seyn, whan that Phebus the sonne is in the signe of the Cancre, who so yeveth thanne largely hise sedes to the feldes that refu-sen to receiven hem, lat him gon, bigyled of trust that he hadde to his corn, to acorns of okes. Yif thou wolt gadre violettes, ne go thou not to the purpur wode whan the feld, chirkinge, agryseth of colde by the felnesse of the winde that highte Aquilon. Yif thou desirest or wolt usen grapes, ne seke thou nat, with a glotonous hond, to streyne and presse the stalkes of the vine in the ferst somer sesoun; for Bachus, the god of wyne, hath rather yeven his yiftes to autumpne, the later ende of somer.

GOD tokneth & assigneth the tymes, ablinge hem to hir propres offices; ne he ne suffreth nat the stoundes whiche that himself hath devyded and con-streyned to ben ymedled togidere. And forthy he that forleteth certein ordinaunce of doinge by overthrowinge wey, he ne hath no glade issue or ende of his werkes.

Prose VI.

Primum igitur paterisne me pauculis ro-gacionibus.

FIRST woltow suf-fre me to touche & assaye the estat of thy thought by a fewe demaundes, so that I may under-stonde what be the manere of thy cura-cioun ? Axe me, quod I, at thy wille, what thou wolt, and I shal answere.

WHO seide she thus: Whether wene-stow, quod she, that this world be governed by foolish happes and fortunous, or elles that ther be in it any governement of resoun?

CERTES, quod I, I ne trowe nat in no manere, that so certein thinges sholde be moeved by fortunous for-tune; but I wot wel that God, maker and mayster, is governour of his werk. Ne never nas yit day that mighte putte me out of the sothnesse of that sentence.

SO is it, quod she; for the same thing songe thou a litel herbiform, and bi-weyledest and biweptest, that only men weren put out of the cure of God. For of alle other thinges thou ne doutedest nat that they nere governed by resoun. But owh! (i. pape!) I wondre gretly, certes, why that thou art syk, sin that thou art put in so holsom a sentence. But lat us seken dep-per; I conjecte that ther lakketh I not nere what. But sey me this: sin that thou ne doutest nat that this world be governed by God, with whiche governailes takestow hede that it is governed?

UNNETHE, quod I, knowe I the sen-tence of thy questioun; so that I ne may nat yit answeren to thy de-maundes.

I NAS nat deceived, quod she, that ther ne faileth somwhat, by whiche the maladye of thy perturbacioun is crept into thy thought, so as the strengthe of the palis chyning is open. But sey me this: remembrest thou what is the ende of thinges, and whider that the entencioun of alle kinde tendeth?

I HAVE herd it told somtyme, quod I; but drerinesse hath dulled my memorie.

CERTES, quod she, thou wost wel whennes that alle thinges ben com-en and procedeth?

I wot well, quod I, and answerede, that God is beginning of al.

AND how may this be, quod she, that, sin thou knowest the beginning of thinges, that thou ne knowest nat what is the ende of thinges? But swiche

331

ben the customes of perturbaciouns, and this power they han, that they may moeve a man out of his place, that is to seyn, fro the stablenes & perfeccioun of his knowinge; but, certes, they may nat a1 arace him, ne aliene him in al. But I wolde that thou woldest answere to this: remembrestow that thou art a man?

 Why sholde I nat remembre that? quod I.

 Maystow nat telle me thanne, quod she, what thing is a man?

AXESTOW me nat, quod I, whether that I be a resonable mortal beest? I woot wel, & I confesse wel that I am it.

 Wistestow never yit that thou were any other thing? quod she.

 No, quod I.

NOW woot I, quod she, other cause of thy maladye, and that right grete. Thou hast left for to knowen thyself, what thou art; thorugh whiche I have pleynly founden the cause of thy maladye, or elles the entree of recoveringe of thyn hele. For why, for thou art confounded with foryeting of thyself, forthy sorwestow that thou art exiled of thy propre goodes. And for thou ne wost what is the ende of thinges, forthy demestow that felonous and wikked men ben mighty and weleful. And for thou hast foryeten by whiche governements the world is governed, forthy wenestow that thise mutaciouns of fortune fleten withoute governour ✿ Thise ben grete causes not only to maladye, but, certes, grete causes to deeth. But I thanke the auctor and the maker of hele, that nature hath not al forleten thee. I have grete norisshinges of thyn hele, and that is, the sothe sentence of governaunce of the worlde; that thou bilevest that the governinge of it nis nat subject ne underput to the folie of thise happes aventurous, but to the resoun of God. And therfor doute

thee nothing; for of this litel spark thyn hete of lyf shal shyne.

BUT for as moche as it is nat time yit of faster remedies, and the nature of thoughtes deceived is this, that as ofte as they casten awey sothe opiniouns, they clothen hem in false opiniouns, of which false opiniouns the derkenesse of perturbacioun wexeth up, that confoundeth the verray insighte: & that derkenesse shal I assaye somwhat to maken thinne & wayk by lighte and meneliche remedies; so that, after that the derkenesse of deceivinge desiringes is don awey, thou mowe knowe the shyninge of verray light.

Metre VII.
Nubibus atris.

THE sterres, covered with blake cloudes, ne mowen yeten adoun no light. Yif the trouble wind that hight Auster, turning & walwinge the see, medleth the hete, that is to seyn, the boylinge up from the botme; the wawes, that whylom weren clere as glas & lyke to the faire clere dayes, withstande anon the sightes of men by the filthe and ordure that is resolved. And the fletinge streem, that royleth doun dyversly fro heye mountaignes, is arested and resisted ofte tyme by the encountringe of a stoon that is departed and fallen from som roche.

AND forthy, yif thou wolt loken and demen sooth with cleer light, and holden the wey with a right path, weyve thou joye, dryf fro thee drede, fleme thou hope, ne lat no sorwe aproche; that is to seyn, lat non of thise four passiouns overcomen thee or blende thee. For cloudy and derke is thilke thought, and bounde with brydles, wheras thise thinges regnen. Explicit Liber Primus.

DE CONSOLATIONE PHILOSOPHIE. ✿ BOOK II. PROSE I. ✿
Postea paulisper conticuit.

AFTER THIS SHE STINTE A LITEL; AND, after that she hadde gadered by atempre stillenesse myn attencioun, she seide thus: ✿ (As who mighte seyn thus: After thise thinges she stinte a litel; and whan she aperceived by atempre stillenesse that I was ententif to herkene hir, she bigan to speke in this wyse): Yif I, quod she, have understonden and knowen outrely the causes and the habit of thy maladye, thou languissest

and art defeted for desyr and talent of thy rather fortune. She, that ilke fortune only, that is chaunged, as thou feynest, to theeward, hath perverted the cleernesse and the estat of thy corage. I understonde the felefolde colours and deceites of thilke merveilous monstre fortune, & how she useth ful flateringe familaritee with hem that she enforceth to bigyle; so longe, til that she confounde with unsufferable sorwe hem that she hath left in despeyr unpurveyed. And yif thou remembrest wel the kinde, the maneres, and the desert of thilke fortune, thou shalt wel knowe that, as in hir, thou never ne haddest ne hast ylost any fair thing. But, as I trowe, I shal nat gretly travailen to do thee remembren on thise thinges. For thou were wont to hurtelen and despysen hir, with manly wordes, whan she was blaundissinge and present, & pursewedest hir with sentences that were drawen out of myn entree, that is to seyn, out of myn informacioun. But no sodein mutacioun ne bitydeth nat withoute a manere chaunginge of corages; and so is it befallen that thou art a litel departed fro the pees of thy thought.

BUT now is tyme that thou drinke and ataste some softe and delitable thinges; so that, whan they ben entred within thee, it mowe maken wey to strengere drinkes of medicynes. Com now forth therfore the suasioun of swetenesse rethorien, whiche that goth only the right wey, whyl she forsaketh nat myne estatuts. And with Rhetorice com forth Musice, a damisel of our hous, that singeth now lighter moedes or prolaciouns, now hevyer. What eyleth thee, man? What is it that hath cast thee into morninge and into wepinge? I trowe that thou hast seyn som new thing and uncouth. Thou wenest that Fortune be chaunged ayein thee; but thou wenest wrong, yif thou that wene. Alwey tho ben hir maneres; she hath rather kept, as to theeward, hir propre stablenesse in the chaunginge of hirself. Rights swich was she whan she flatered thee, & deceived thee with unleveful lykinges of fals welefulnesse. Thou hast now knowen and atthis doutous or double visage of thilke blinde goddesse Fortune. She, that yit covereth hir and wimpleth hir to other folk, hath shewed hir everydel to thee. Yif thou aprovest hir and thenkest that she is good, use hir maneres and pleyne thee nat. And yif thou agrysest hir false trecherye, despyse and cast awey hir that pleyeth so harmfully; for she, that is now cause of so muche sorwe to thee, sholde ben cause to thee of pees & of joye. She hath forsaken thee, forsothe; the whiche that never man may ben siker that she ne shal forsake him. Glose. But natheles, some bokes han the text thus: for sothe, she hath forsaken thee, ne ther nis no man siker that she ne hath nat forsaken.

HOLDESTOW than thilke welefulnesse precious to thee that shal passen? And is present fortune dereworthe to thee, which that nis nat feithful for to dwelle; and, whan she goth awey, that she bringeth a wight in sorwe? For sin she may nat ben withholden at a mannes wille, she maketh him a wrecche whan she departeth fro him. What other thing is flittinge fortune but a maner shewinge of wrecchednesse that is to comen? Ne it ne suffyseth not only to loken on thinge that is present biforn the eyen of a man. But

wisdom loketh and amesureth the ende of thinges; & the same chaunginge from oon into another, that is to seyn, from adversitee into prosperitee, maketh that the manaces of fortune ne ben not for to dreden, ne the flateringes of hir to ben desired. Thus, at the laste, it bihoveth thee to suffren with evene wille in pacience al that is don inwith the floor of fortune, that is to seyn, in this world, sin thou hast ones put thy nekke under the yok of hir. For yif thou wolt wryten a lawe of wendinge & of dwellinge to fortune, whiche that thou hast chosen frely to ben thy lady, artow nat wrongful in that, & makest fortune wroth and aspere by thyn inpatience, & yit thou mayst nat chaunge hir?

YIf thou committest and bitakest thy sailes to the winde, thou shalt be shoven, not thider that thou woldest, but whider that the wind shoveth thee. Yif thou castest thy sedes into the feldes, thou sholdest han in minde that the yeres ben, amonges, otherwhyle plentevous and otherwhyle bareyne. Thou hast bitaken thyself to the governaunce of fortune, and forthy it bihoveth thee to ben obeisaunt to the maneres of thy lady. Enforcest thou thee to aresten or withholden the swiftnesse & the sweigh of hir turninge whele? O thou fool of alle mortal fooles, if fortune bigan to dwelle stable, she cesede thanne to ben fortune!

Metre I.
Hec cum superba verterit vices dextra.

WHAN fortune with a proud right hand hath torned hir chaunginge stoundes, she fareth lyk the maneres of the boilinge Eurype. Glosa. Eurype is an arm of the see that ebbeth and floweth; and somtyme the streem is on o syde, and somtyme on the other. Text. She, cruel fortune, casteth a doun kinges that whylom weren ydrad; & she, deceivable, enhaunseth up the humble chere of him that is discomfited. Ne she neither hereth ne rekketh of wrecchede wepinges; & she is so hard that she laugheth and scorneth the wepinges of hem, the whiche she hath maked wepe with hir free wille. Thus she pleyeth, & thus she proeveth hir strengthes; and sheweth a greet wonder to alle hir servauntes, yif that a wight is seyn weleful, and overthrowe in an houre.

Prose II.
Vellem autem pauca tecum.

CERTES, I wolde pleten with thee a fewe thinges, usinge the wordes of fortune; tak hede now thyself, yif that she axeth right: O thou man, wherfore makest thou me gilty by thyne everydayes pleyninges? What wrong have I don thee? What goodes have I bireft thee that weren thyne? Stryf or plete with me, bifore what juge that thou wolt, of the possessioun of richesses or of dignitees. And yif thou mayst shewen me that ever any mortal man hath received any of tho thinges to ben hise in propre, than wol I graunte frely that alle thilke thinges weren thyne whiche that thou axest. Whan that nature broughte thee forth out of thy moder wombe, I receyved thee naked and nedy of alle thinges, and I norisshede thee with my richesses, and was redy and ententif through my favour to susteyne thee; and that maketh thee now inpacient ayeins me; and I envirounde thee with alle the aboundance and shyninge of alle goodes that ben in my right. Now it lyketh me to withdrawen my hand; thou hast had grace as he that hath used of foreine goodes: thou hast no right to pleyne thee, as though thou haddest outrely forlorn alle thy thinges. Why pleynest thou thanne? I have done thee no wrong. Richesses, honours, and swiche other thinges ben of my right. My servauntes knowen me for hir lady; they comen with me, & departen whan I wende. I dar wel affermen hardily, that yif tho thinges of which thou pleynest that thou hast forlorn, hadde ben thyne, thou ne haddest not lorn hem. Shal I thanne only ben defended to usen my right?

CERTES, it is leveful to the hevene to make clere dayes, &, after that, to coveren tho same dayes with derke nightes. The yeer hath eek leve to apparailen the visage of the erthe, now with floures and now with fruit, & to confounden hem somtyme with reynes and with coldes. The see hath eek his right to ben somtyme calme & blaundishing with smothe water, and somtyme to ben horrible with wawes and with tempestes. But the covetise of men, that may nat ben stanched, shal it binde me to ben stedefast, sin that stedefastnesse is uncouth to my maneres? Swich is my strengthe, & this pley I pleye continuely. I torne the whirlinge wheel with the torninge cercle; I am glad to chaungen the lowest to the heyest, and the

heyest to the lowest. Worth up, if thou wolt, so it be by this lawe, that thou ne holde nat that I do thee wronge thogh thou descende adoun, whan the resoun of my pley axeth it.

WISTEST thou nat how Cresus, the king of Lydiens, of whiche king Cyrus was ful sore agast a litel biforn, that this rewliche Cresus was caught of Cyrus and lad to the fyr to ben brent, but that a rayn descendede doun fro hevene that rescowede him? And is it out of thy minde how that Paulus, consul of Rome, whan he hadde taken the king of Perciens, weep pitously for the captivitee of the self kinge? What other thing biwailen the cryinges of tragedies but only the dedes of fortune, that with an unwar stroke overtorneth realmes of grete nobley? Glose. Tragedie is to seyn, a ditee of a prosperitee for a tyme, that endeth in wrecchednesse.

LERNEDEST nat thou in Greke, whan thou were yonge, that in the entree, or in the celere, of Jupiter, ther ben couched two tonnes; that on is ful of good, that other is ful of harm? What right hast thou to pleyne, yif thou hast taken more plentevously of the goode syde, that is to seyn, of my richesses and prosperites; and what eek if I ne be nat al departed fro thee? What eek yif my mutabilitee yiveth thee rightful cause of hope to han yit beter thinges? Natheles dismaye thee nat in thy thought; and thou that art put in the comune realme of alle, ne desyre nat to liven by thyn only propre right.

Metre II.
Si quantas rapidis flatibus incitus.

THOUGH Plentee, that is goddesse of richesses, hielde adoun with ful horn, and withdraweth nat hir hand, as many richesses as the see torneth upward sandes whan it is moeved with ravisshinge blastes, or elles as many richesses as ther shynen brighte sterres on hevene on the sterry nightes; yit, for al that, mankinde nolde not cese to wepe wrecchede pleyntes. And al be it so that God receyveth gladly hir preyers, and yiveth them (as fool-large) moche gold, & aparaileth coveitous men with noble or clere honours: yit semeth hem haven ygeten nothing, but alwey hir cruel ravyne, devouringe al that they han geten, sheweth other gapinges; that is to seyn, gapen and desyren yit after mo richesses. What brydles mighten withholden, to any certein ende, the desordenee covetise of men, whan, ever the rather that it fleteth in large yiftes, the more ay brenneth in hem the thurst of havinge? Certes he that, quakinge & dred／ful, weneth himselven nedy, he ne liveth nevermore riche.

Prose III.

Hiis igitur si pro se tecum fortuna loqueretur.

HERFOR, yif that fortune spake with thee for hirself in this manere, forsothe thou ne haddest nat what thou mightest answere. And, if thou hast anything wherwith thou mayest rightfully defenden thy compleint, it behoveth thee to shewen it; & I wol yeven thee space to tellen it.

CERTEYNLY, quod I thanne, thise beth faire thinges, & enointed with hony swetenesse of rethorike and musike; and only whyl they ben herd they ben delicious. But to wrecches is a depper felinge of harm; this is to seyn, that wrecches felen the harmes that they suffren more grevously than the remedies or the delites of thise wordes mowen gladen or comforten hem; so that, whan thise thinges stinten for to soune in eres, the sorwe that is inset greveth the thought.

RIGHT so is it, quod she. For thise ne ben yit none remedies of thy maladye; but they ben a maner norisshinges of thy sorwe, yit rebel ayein thy cura／cioun. For whan that tyme is, I shal moeve swiche thinges that percen hemself depe. But natheles, that thou shalt not wilne to leten thyself a wrecche, hast thou foryeten the noumber and the manere of thy welefulnesse? I holde me stille, how that the soverayne men of the citee token thee in cure and kepinge, whan thou were orphelin of fader and moder, and were chosen in af／finitee of princes of the citee; and thou bigunne rather to be leef and dere than for to ben a neighbour; the whiche thing is the most precious kinde of any propinquitee or alyaunce that may ben. Who is it that ne seide tho that thou were right weleful, with so grete a nobleye of thy fadres／in／lawe, and with the chastitee of thy wyf, and with the oportunitee and noblesse of thy masculin children, that is to seyn, thy sones? And over al this, me list to passen the comune thinges, how thou haddest in thy youthe dignitees that weren werned to olde men. But it delyteth me to comen now to the singuler uphepinge of thy welefulnesse. Yif any fruit of mortal thinges may han any weighte or prys of welefulnesse, mightest thou ever foryeten, for any charge

of harm that mighte bifalle, the remembraunce of thilke day that thou saye thy two sones maked conseileres, and ylad to／gedere fro thyn house under so greet assemblee of senatoures & under the blythe／nesse of poeple; and whan thou saye hem set in the court in here chayeres of dignitees? Thou, rethorien or pronouncere of kinges preysinges, deservedest glorie of wit and of eloquence, whan thou, sittinge bitwene thy two sones, conseileres, in the place that highte Circo, fulfuldest the abydinge of the multitude of poeple that was sprad abouten thee, with so large prey／singe & laude, as men singen in victories. Tho yave thou wordes to fortune, as I trowe, that is to seyn, tho feffedest thou fortune with glosinge wordes & deceived／est hir, whan she acoyede thee and norisshede thee as hir owne delyces. Thou bere away of fortune a yifte, that is to seyn, swiche guerdoun, that she never yaf to privee man. Wilt thou therfor leye a reken／inge with fortune? She hath now twinkled first upon thee with a wikkede eye. Yif thou considere the noumbre and the manere of thy blisses and of thy sorwes, thou mayst nat forsaken that thou art yit blisful. For if thou therfor wenest thyself nat weleful, for thinges that tho semeden joyful ben passed, ther nis nat why thou sholdest wene thyself a wrecche; for thinges that semen now sorye passen also.

ART thou now comen first, a sodein gest, into the shadwe or tabernacle of this lyf; or trowest thou that any stedefastnesse be in mannes thinges, whan ofte a swift houre dissolveth the same man; that is to seyn, whan the soule departeth fro the body?For, although that selde is ther any feith that fortunous thinges wolen dwellen, yit natheles the laste day of a mannes lyf is a manere deeth to fortune, and also to thilke that hath dwelt. And therfor, what, wenestow, thar thee recche, yif thou forlete hir in deyinge, or elles that she, fortune, forlete thee in fleeinge awey?

Metre III.

Cum polo Phebus roseis quadrigis.

WHAN Phebus, the sonne, bi／ginneth to spreden his cleer／nesse with rosene chariettes, thanne the sterre, ydimmed, paleth hir whyte cheres, by the flambes of the sonne that overcometh the sterrelight ✦ This is to seyn, whan the sonne is risen, the deysterre wexeth pale, and leseth hir light for the grete brightnesse of the sonne.

HAN the wode wexeth rody of rosene floures, in the first somer sesoun, thorugh the brethe of the winde Zephirus that wexeth warm, yif the cloudy wind Auster blowe felliche, than goth awey the fairenesse of thornes.

OfTE the see is cleer and calm withoute moevinge flodes; and ofte the horrible wind Aquilon moeveth boilinge tempestes and overwhelveth the see.

YIf the forme of this worlde is so selde stable, and yif it turneth by so many entrechaunginges, wolt thou thanne trusten in the tomblinge fortunes of men? Wolt thou trowen on flittinge goodes? It is certein and establisshed by lawe perdurable, that nothing that is engendered nis stedefast ne stable.

Prose IV.
Tunc ego, vera, inquam, commemoras.

HANNE SEIDE I thus: O norice of alle vertues, thou seist ful sooth; ne I ne may nat forsake the right swifte cours of my prosperitee; that is to seyn, that prosperitee ne be comen to me wonder swiftly and sone. But this is a thing that greetly smerteth me whan it remembreth me. for in all adversitee of fortune, the most unsely kinde of contrarious fortune is to han ben weleful.

BUT that thou, quod she, abyest thus the torment of thy false opinioun, that mayst thou nat rightfully blamen ne aretten to thinges: as who seith, for thou hast yit many habundaunces of thinges.

Text.
FOR al be it so that the ydel name of aventurous welefulnesse moeveth thee now, it is leveful that thou rekne with me of how manye grete thinges thou hast yit plentee ✪ And therfor, yif that thilke thing that thou haddest for most precious in al thy richesse of fortune be kept to thee yit, by the grace of God, unwemmed and undefouled, mayst thou thanne pleyne rightfully upon the meschef of fortune, sin thou hast yit thy beste thinges? Certes, yit liveth in good point thilke precious honour of mankinde, Symacus, thy wyves fader, which that is a man maked alle of sapience and of vertu; the whiche man thou woldest byen redely with the prys of thyn owne lyf. He biwayleth the wronges that men don to thee, and nat for himself; for he liveth in sikernesse of

any sentences put ayeins him. And yit liveth thy wyf, that is atempre of wit, & passinge other wimmen in clennesse of chastetee; and for I wol closen shortely hir bountees, she is lyk to hir fader. I telle thee wel, that she liveth looth of this lyf, and kepeth to thee only hir goost; and is al maat and overcomen by wepinge and sorwe for desyr of thee, in the whiche thing only I moot graunten that thy welefulnesse is amenused. What shal I seyn eek of thy two sones, conseilours, of whiche, as of children of hir age, ther shyneth the lyknesse of the wit of hir fader or of hir elder fader? And sin the sovereyn cure of alle mortel folk is to saven hir owen lyves, O how weleful art thou, yif thou knowe thy goodes! for yit ben ther thinges dwelled to theeward, that no man douteth that they ne ben more dereworthe to thee than thyn owen lyf. And forthy drye thy teres, for yit nis nat everich fortune al hateful to theeward, ne over greet tempest hath nat yit fallen upon thee, whan that thyn ancres cleven faste, that neither wolen suffren the counfort of this tyme present ne the hope of tyme cominge to passen ne to faylen.

AND I preye, quod I, that faste moten they halden; for whyles that they halden, howsoever that thinges ben, I shal wel fleten forth & escapen; but thou mayst wel seen how grete aparayles and aray that me lakketh, that ben passed away fro me.

I HAVE somwhat avaunced and forthered thee, quod she, yif that thou anoye nat or forthinke nat of al thy fortune: as who seith, I have somwhat comforted thee, so that thou tempest thee nat thus with al thy fortune, sin thou hast yit thy beste thinges. But I may nat suffren thy delices, that pleynest so wepinge & anguissous, for that ther lakketh somwhat to thy welefulnesse. for what man is so sad or of so parfit welefulnesse, that he ne stryveth & pleyneth on som halve ayen the qualitee of his estat? forwhy ful anguissous thing is the condicioun of mannes goodes; for either it cometh nat altogider to a wight, or elles it last nat perpetuel. for sum man hath grete richesses, but he is ashamed of his ungentel linage; and som is renowned of noblesse of kinrede, but he is enclosed in so grete anguissshe of nede of thinges, that him were lever that he were unknowe. And som man haboundeth both in richesse and noblesse, but yit he bewaileth his chaste lyf, for he ne hath no wyf. And som man is wel & selily ymaried, but he hath no children, and norissheth his richesses to the eyres of strange folkes. And som man is gladed with children, but he wepeth ful sory for the trespas of his

sone or of his doughter. And for this ther
ne acordeth no wight lightly to the condicioun of his fortune; for alwey to every man
ther is in somwhat that, unassayed, he ne
wot nat; or elles he dredeth that he hath
assayed. And adde this also, that every
weleful man hath a ful delicat felinge; so
that, but yif alle thinges bifalle at his owne
wil, for he is impacient, or is nat used to han
non adversitee, anon he is thrown adoun
for every litel thing. And ful litel thinges
ben tho that withdrawen the somme or the
perfeccioun of blisfulnesse fro hem that
ben most fortunat. How many men, trowest thou, wolden demen hemself to ben almost in hevene, yif they mighten atayne to
the leest party of the remnaunt of thy fortune? This same place that thou clepest
exil, is contree to hem that enhabiten heer,
and forthy nothing is wrecched but whan
thou wenest it: as who seith, thou thyself,
ne no wight elles, nis a wrecche, but whan
he weneth himself a wrecche by reputacioun
of his corage. And ayeinward, alle fortune
is blisful to a man by the agreabletee or by
the egalitee of him that suffreth it.

W̶HAT man is that, that is so weleful, that nolde changen his estat
whan he hath lost pacience? ✤
The swetnesse of mannes welefulnesse
is sprayned with many biternesses; the
whiche welefulnesse, although it seme
swete and joyful to hem that useth it, yit
may it nat ben withholden that it ne goth
away whan it wole. Thanne is it wel sene,
how wrecched is the blisfulnesse of mortal
thinges, that neither it dureth perpetuel
with hem that every fortune receiven agre-
ably or egaly, ne it delyteth nat in al to hem
that ben anguissous. O ye mortal folk, what
seke ye thanne blisfulnesse out of yourself, whiche that is put in yourself? Errour
and folye confoundeth yow.

I̶ SHAL shewe thee shortely the poynt
of sovereyne blisfulnesse. Is ther
anything more precious to thee than
thyself? Thou wolt answere, Nay. Thanne,
yif it so be that thou art mighty over thyself, that is to seyn, by tranquillitee of thy
sowle, than hast thou thing in thy power
that thou noldest never lesen, ne fortune
ne may nat beneme it thee. And that thou
mayst knowe that blisfulnesse ne may nat
standen in thinges that ben fortunous and
temporel, now understonde and gader it
togidere thus: Yif blisfulnesse be the sovereyn good of nature that liveth by resoun,
ne thilke thing nis nat sovereyn good that
may be taken awey in any wyse, (for more
worthy thing & more digne is thilke thing
that may nat ben taken awey); than sheweth it wel, that the unstablenesse of fortune may nat atayne to receiven verray blis-

fulnesse. And yit moreover: what man that
this toumbling welefulnesse ledeth, either
he woot that it is chaungeable, or elles he
woot it nat. And yif he woot it nat, what
blisful fortune may ther be in the blindnesse of ignorance? And yif he woot that
it is chaungeable, he moot alwey ben adrad
that he ne lese that thing that he ne doubt-
eth nat but that he may lesen it; as who
seith, he mot ben alwey agast, lest he lese
that he wot wel he may lese it. For which, the
continuel dreed that he hath, ne suffreth
him nat to ben weleful. Or yif he lese it, he
weneth to be dispysed and forleten. Certes
eek, that is a ful litel good that is born with
evene herte whan it is lost; that is to seyn,
that men do no more fors of the lost than of
the havinge. And for as moche as thou thyself art he, to whom it hath ben shewed and
proved by ful manye demonstraciouns, as
I wot wel, that the sowles of men ne mowe
nat deyen in no wyse; and eek sin it is cleer
and certein, that fortunous welefulnesse
endeth by the deeth of the body; it may
nat ben douted that, yif that deeth may
take awey blisfulnesse, that alle the kinde
of mortal thinges ne descendeth into wrecchednesse by the ende of the deeth. ✤
And sin we knowen wel, that many a man
hath sought the fruit of blisfulnesse nat
only with suffringe of deeth, but eek with
suffringe of peynes and tormentes; how
mighte than this present lyf maken men
blisful, sin that, whan thilke selve lyf is
ended, it ne maketh folk no wrecches?

Metre IV.
Quisquis volet perennem Cautus ponere
sedem.

W̶HAT maner man, stable &
war, that wole founden him
a perdurable sete, & ne wole
nat ben cast down with the
loude blastes of the wind
Eurus; & wole despyse the
see, manasinge with flodes; lat him eschewen to bilde on the cop of the mountaigne or in the moiste sandes. For the felle
wind Auster tormenteth the cop of the
mountaigne with all his strengthes; and
the lause sandes refusen to beren the hevy
wighte.

A̶ND forthy, if thou wolt fleen the
perilous aventure, that is to seyn,
of the worlde; have minde certeinly
to ficchen thyn hous of a merye site in a
lowe stoon. For although the wind, troub-
ling the see, thondre with over-throwing-
es, thou that art put in quiete, and weleful
by strengthe of thy palis, shalt leden a
cleer age, scorninge the woodnesses and
the ires of the eyr.

Prose V.
Set cum rationum jam in te.

BUT for as moche as the norisshinges of my resouns descenden now into thee, I trowe it were tyme to usen a litel strenger medicynes. Now understond heer, al were it so that the yiftes of fortune ne were nat brutel ne transitorie, what is ther in hem that may be thyn in any tyme, or elles that it nis foul, yif that it be considered and loked perfitly? Richesses, ben they precious by the nature of hemself, or elles by the nature of thee? What is most worth of richesses? Is it nat gold or might of moneye assembled? Certes, thilke gold and thilke moneye shyneth & yeveth betere renoun to hem that despenden it thanne to thilke folk that mokeren it; for avarice maketh alwey mokereres to ben hated, and largesse maketh folk cleer of renoun. For sin that swich thing as is transferred fram o man to another ne may nat dwellen with no man; certes, thanne is thilke moneye precious whan it is translated into other folk and stenteth to ben had, by usage of large yevinge of him that hath yeven it. And also: yif that al the moneye that is overal in the worlde were gadered toward o man, it sholde maken alle other men to ben nedy as of that. And certes a voys al hool, that is to seyn, withoute amenusinge, fulfilleth togidere the hering of moche folk; but certes, youre richesses ne mowen nat passen into moche folke withoute amenusinge. And whan they ben apassed, nedes they maken hem pore that forgon the richesses.

O STREITE and nedy clepe I this richesse, sin that many folk ne may nat han it al, ne al may it nat comen to o man withouten povertee of alle other folk! And the shyninge of gemmes, that I clepe precious stones, draweth it nat the eyen of folk to hemward, that is to seyn, for the beautee? But certes, yif ther were beautee or bountee in the shyninge of stones, thilke cleernesse is of the stones hemself, and nat of men; for whiche I wondre gretly that men mervailen on swiche thinges. For why, what thing is it, that yif it wanteth moeving and joynture of sowle and body, that by right mighte semen a fair creature to him that hath a sowle of resoun? For al be it so that gemmes drawen to hemself a litel of the laste beautee of the world, through the entente of hir creatour and through the distinccioun of hemself; yit, for as mochel as they ben put under youre excellence, they ne han nat deserved by no wey that ye sholden mervailen on hem. And the beautee of feldes, delyteth it nat mochel unto yow?

338

Boece. Why sholde it nat delyten us, sin that it is a right fair porcioun of the right faire werke, that is to seyn, of this world? And right so ben we gladed somtyme of the face of the see whan it is cleer; and also mervailen we on the hevene and on the sterres, and on the sonne & on the mone.

Philosophye.

APERTENETH, quod she, any of thilke thinges to thee? Why darst thou glorifyen thee in the shyninge of any swiche thinges? Art thou distingwed and embelised by the springinge floures of the first somer sesoun, or swelleth thy plentee in the fruites of somer? Why art thou ravisshed with ydel joyes? Why embracest thou straunge goodes as they weren thyne? Fortune ne shal never maken that swiche thinges ben thyne, that nature of thinges hath maked foreine fro thee. Sooth is that, withouten doute, the frutes of the erthe owen to ben to the norissinge of bestes. And yif thou wolt fulfille thy nede after that it suffyseth to nature, than is it no nede that thou seke after the superfluitee of fortune. For with ful fewe things and with ful litel thinges nature halt hir apayed; and yif thou wolt achoken the fulfillinge of nature with superfluitees, certes, thilke thinges that thou wolt thresten or pouren into nature shullen ben unjoyful to thee, or elles anoyous. Wenest thou eek that it be a fair thing to shyne with dyverse clothinge? Of whiche clothinge yif the beautee be agreeable to loken upon, I wol mervailen on the nature of the matere of thilke clothes, or elles on the werkman that wroughte hem. But also a long route of meynee, maketh that a blisful man? The whiche servants, yif they ben vicious of condiciouns, it is a greet charge and a distruccioun to the hous, & a greet enemy to the lord himself. And yif they ben goode men, how shal straunge or foreine goodnesse ben put in the noumbre of thy richesse? So that, by alle these forseide thinges, it is clearly yshewed, that never oon of thilke thinges that thou acountedest for thyne goodes nas nat thy good. In the whiche thinges, yif ther be no beautee to ben desyred, why sholdest thou ben sory yif thou lese hem, or why sholdest thou rejoysen thee to holden hem? For yif they ben faire of hir owne kinde, what aperteneth that to thee? For also wel sholden they han ben faire by hemselve, though they weren departed fram alle thyn richesses. Forwhy faire ne precious ne weren they nat, for that they comen among thy richesses; but, for they semeden faire and precious, therfor thou haddest lever rekne hem amonges thy richesses.

BUT what desirest thou of fortune with so grete a noise, and with so grete a fare? ꝯ I trowe thou seke to drive awey nede with habundaunce of thinges; but certes, it torneth to you al in the contrarie. Forwhy certes, it nedeth of ful manye helpinges to kepen the diversitee of precious ostelments. And sooth it is, that of manye thinges han they nede that many thinges han; and ayeinward, of litel nedeth hem that mesuren hir fille after the nede of kinde, and nat after the outrage of coveityse. Is it thanne so, that ye men ne han no proper good yset in you, for which ye moten seken outward youre goodes in foreine and subgit thinges? So is thanne the condicioun of thinges torned upsodown, that a man, that is a devyne beest by merite of his resoun, thinketh that himself nis neither faire ne noble, but yif it be thorugh possessioun of ostelments that ne han no sowles. And certes, al other thinges ben apayed of hir owne beautee; but ye men, that ben semblable to God by your resonable thought, desiren to aparailen your excellent kinde of the lowest thinges; ne ye understonden nat how greet a wrong ye don to your creatour ꝯ for he wolde that mankinde were most worthy & noble of any othre erthely thinges; and ye threste adoun your dignitees benethe the lowest thinges. For yif that al the good of every thinge be more precious than is thilke thing whos that the good is: sin ye demen that the fouleste thinges ben youre goodes, thanne submitten ye and putten yourselven under tho fouleste thinges by your estimacioun; & certes, this tydeth nat withoute youre desertes. For certes, swiche is the condicioun of alle mankinde, that only whan it hath knowinge of itselve, than passeth it in noblesse alle other thinges; and whan it forleteth the knowinge of itself, than is it brought binethen alle beestes. ꝯ forwhy al other livinge beestes han of kinde to knowe nat hemself; but whan that men leten the knowinge of hemself, it cometh hem of vice. But how brode sheweth the errour and the folye of yow men, that wenen that any thing may ben aparailed with straunge aparailements! ꝯ But for sothe that may nat ben doon. For yif a wight shyneth with thinges that ben put to him, as thus, if thilke thinges shynen with which a man is aparailed, certes, thilke thinges ben comended and preysed with which he is aparailed; but natheles, the thing that is covered and wrapped under that dwelleth in his filthe.

AND I denye that thilke thing be good that anoyeth him that hath it. Gabbe I of this? Thou wolt seye Nay. Certes, richesses han anoyed ful ofte hem that han tho richesses; sin that every wikked shrewe, (and for his wikkednesse the more gredy after other folkes richesses, wher-so ever it be in any place, be it gold or precious stones), weneth him only most worthy that hath hem. Thou thanne, that so bisy dredest now the swerd and now the spere, yif thou haddest entred in the path of this life a voide wayferinge man, than woldest thou singe biforn the theef; as who seith, a pore man, that berth no richesse on him by the weye, may boldely singe biforn theves, for he hath nat wherof to ben robbed. O precious and right cleer is the blisfulnesse of mortal richesses, that, whan thou hast geten it, than hast thou lorn thy sikernesse!

Metre V.
felix nimium prior etas.

BLISFUL was the first age of men! They helden hem apayed with the metes that the trewe feldes broughten forth. They ne distroyede nor deceivede nat hemself without-rage. They weren wont lightly to slaken hir hunger at even with acornes of okes. They ne coude nat medly the yifte of Bachus to the cleer hony; that is to seyn, they coude make no piment nor clarree; ne they coude nat medle the brighte fleeses of the contree of Seriens with the venim of Tyrie; this is to seyn, they coude nat deyen whyte fleeses of Serien contree with the blode of a maner shelfisshe that men finden in Tyrie, with whiche blood men deyen purpur. They slepen hoolsom slepes upon the gras, & dronken of the renninge wateres; and layen under the shadwes of the heye pyn-trees. Ne no gest ne straungere ne carf yit the heye see with ores or with shippes; ne they ne hadde seyn yit none newe strondes, to leden marchaundyse into dyverse contrees. Tho weren the cruel clariouns ful hust and ful stille, ne blood yshad by egre hate ne hadde nat deyed yit armures. For wherto or which woodnesse of enemys wolde first moeven armes, whan they seyen cruel woundes, ne none medes be of blood yshad?

I WOLDE that oure tymes sholde torne ayein to the olde maneres! But the anguissous love of havinge brenneth in folk more cruely than the fyr of the mountaigne Ethna, that ay brenneth ꝯ Allas! what was he that first dalf up the gobetes or the weightes of gold covered under erthe, and the precious stones that wolden han ben hid? He dalf up precious perils. That is to seyn, that he that hem first up dalf, he dalf up a precious peril; forwhy for the preciousnesse of swiche thinge, hath many man ben in peril.

Prose VI.
Quid autem de dignitatibus.

UT what shal I seye of dignitees and of powers, the whiche ye men, that neither knowen verray dignitee ne verray power, areysen hem as heye as the hevene? The whiche dignitees and powers, yif they comen to any wikked man, they don as grete damages & destruccions as doth the flaumbe of the mountaigne Ethna, whan the flaumbe walweth up; ne no deluge ne doth so cruel harmes. Certes, thee remembreth wel, as I trowe, that thilke dignitee that men clepen the imperie of consulers, the whiche that whylom was biginninge of fredom, youre eldres coveiteden to han don away that dignitee, for the pryde of the consulers. And right for the same pryde your eldres, biforn that tyme, hadden don awey, out of the citee of Rome, the kinges name; that is to seyn, they nolde han no lenger no king. But now, yif so be that dignitees & powers be yeven to goode men, the whiche thing is ful selde, what a greable thing is ther in tho dignitees or powers but only the goodnesse of folkes that usen hem? And therfor it is thus, that honour ne comth nat to vertu for cause of dignitee, but ayeinward honour comth to dignitee for cause of vertu. But whiche is thilke youre dereworthe power, that is so cleer and so requerable? O ye ertheliche bestes, considere ye nat over which thinge that it semeth that ye han power? Now yif thou saye a mous amonges other mys, that chalaunged to himselfward right & power over alle other mys, how greet scorn woldest thou han of it! Glosa. So fareth it by men; the body hath power over the body.🐦 For yif thou loke wel upon the body of a wight, what thing shalt thou finde more freele than is mankinde; the whiche men wel ofte ben slayn with bytinge of smale flyes, or elles with the entringe of crepinge wormes into the privetees of mannes body? But wher shal man finden any man that may exercen or haunten any right upon another man, but only upon his body, or elles upon thinges that ben lowere than the body, the whiche I clepe fortunous possessiouns? Mayst thou ever have any comaundement over a free corage? Mayst thou

remuen fro the estat of his propre reste a thought that is clyvinge togidere in himself by stedefast resoun? As whylom a tyraunt wende to confounde a free man of corage, and wende to constreyne him by torment, to maken him discoveren & acusen folk that wisten of a conjuracioun, which I clepe a confederacie, that was cast ayeins this tyraunt; but this free man boot of his owne tonge and caste it in the visage of thilke wode tyraunt; so that the torments that this tyraunt wende to han maked matere of crueltee, this wyse man maked it matere of vertu.

UT what thing is it that a man may don to another man, that he ne may receyven the same thing of othre folk in himself: or thus, what may a man don to folk, that folk ne may don him the same? I have herd told of Busirides, that was wont to sleen his gestes that herberweden in his hous; and he was sleyn himself of Ercules that was his gest. Regulus hadde taken in bataile many men of Affrike and cast hem into feteres; but sone after he moste yeve his handes to ben bounde with the cheynes of hem that he hadde whylom overcomen. Wenest thou thanne that he be mighty, that hath no power to don a thing, that othre ne may don in him that he doth in othre? And yit moreover, yif it so were that thise dignitees or poweres hadden any propre or natural goodnesse in hemself, never nolden they comen to shrewes. For contrarious thinges ne ben nat wont to ben yfelawshiped togidere. Nature refuseth that contrarious thinges ben yjoigned. And so, as I am in certein that right wikked folk han dignitees ofte tyme, than sheweth it wel that dignitees and powers ne ben nat goode of hir owne kinde; sin that they suffren hemself to cleven or joinen hem to shrewes. And certes, the same thing may I most digneliche jugen and seyn of alle the yiftes of fortune that most plentevously comen to shrewes; of the whiche yiftes, I trowe that it oughte ben considered, that no man douteth that he nis strong in whom he seeth strengthe; and in whom that swiftnesse is, sooth it is that he is swift. Also musike maketh musiciens, and phisike maketh phisiciens, and rethorike rethoriens. Forwhy the nature of every thing maketh his propretee, ne it is nat entremedled with the effects of the contrarious thinges; and, as of wil, it chaseth out thinges that ben to it contrarie. But certes, richesse may not restreyne avarice unstaunched; ne power ne maketh nat a man mighty over himself, whiche that vicious lustes holden destreyned with cheynes that ne mowen nat be unbounden. And dignitees that ben yeven to shrewede

folk nat only ne maketh hem nat digne, but
it sheweth rather al openly that they ben
unworthy & undigne. And why is it thus?
Certes, for ye han joye to clepen thinges
with false names that beren hem alle in the
contrarie; the whiche names ben ful ofte re-
proeved by the effecte of the same thinges;
so that thise ilke richesses ne oughten nat
by right to ben cleped richesses; ne swich
power ne oughte nat ben cleped power; ne
swich dignitee ne oughte nat ben cleped
dignitee.

ND at the laste, I may conclude the
same thing of alle the yiftes of fortune, in which ther nis nothing to
ben desired, ne that hath in himself naturel
bountee, as it is ful wel ysene. For neither
they ne joignen hem nat alwey to goode
men, ne maken hem alwey goode to whom
that they ben yjoigned.

Metre VI.
Novimus quantas dederit ruinas.

E han wel knowen how many
grete harmes and destruc-
ciouns weren don by the em-
peror Nero. He leet brenne the
citee of Rome, & made sleen
the senatoures. And he, cruel,
whylom slew his brother; & he was maked
moist with the blood of his moder; that is
to seyn, he leet sleen and slitten the body
of his moder, to seen wher he was conceived; and he loked on every halve upon her
cold dede body, ne no tere ne wette his face,
but he was so hard-herted that he mighte
ben domes-man or juge of hir dede beautee. And natheles, yit governede this Nero
by ceptre alle the poeples that Phebus the
sonne may seen, cominge from his outer-
este arysinge til he hyde his bemes under
the wawes; that is to seyn, he governed alle
the poeples by ceptre imperial that the
sonne goth aboute, from est to west. And
eek this Nero governed by ceptre alle the
poeples that ben under the colde sterres
that highten Septem triones; this is to
seyn, he governede alle the poeples that
ben under the party of the north. And eek
Nero governed alle the poeples that the
violent wind Nothus scorkleth, & baketh
the brenninge sandes by his drye hete; that
is to seyn, alle the poeples in the south.
But yit ne mighte nat al his hye power
torne the woodnesse of this wikked Nero.
Allas! it is a grevous fortune, as ofte as
wikked swerd is joigned to cruel venim;
that is to seyn, venimous crueltee to lord-
shippe.

Prose VII.
Tum ego, scis, inquam.

HANNE seyde I
thus: Thou wost
wel thyself that the
coveitise of mortal
thinges ne hadde
never lordshipe of
me; but I have wel
desired matere of
thinges to done, as
who seith, I desire
to han matere of governaunce over comunalitees, for vertu, stille, ne sholde nat
elden; that is to seyn, that him leste that,
or he wex olde, his vertu, that lay now ful
stille, ne should nat perisshe unexercised
in governaunce of comune; for which men
mighten speken or wryten of his goode
governement.

Philosophye.
OR sothe, quod she, and that is a
thing that may drawen to governaunce swiche hertes as ben worthy
& noble of hir nature; but natheles, it may
nat drawen or tollen swiche hertes as ben
ybrought to the fulle perfeccioun of vertu,
that is to seyn, coveitise of glorie and renoun to han wel administred the comune
thinges or don gode desertes to profit of
the comune. For see now & considere, how
litel and how voide of alle prys is thilke
glorie. Certein thing is, as thou hast lerned
by the demonstracioun of astronomye,
that al the environinge of the erthe aboute
ne halt nat but the resoun of a prikke at regard of the greetnesse of hevene; that is
to seyn, that yif ther were maked comparisoun of the erthe to the greetnesse of
hevene, men wolden jugen in al, that the
erthe ne helde no space. Of the whiche litel
regioun of this worlde, the ferthe partye
is enhabited with livinge bestes that we
knowen, as thou thyself hast ylerned by
Tholomee that proveth it. And yif thou
haddest withdrawen and abated in thy
thought fro thilke ferthe partye as moche
space as the see & the mareys contenen &
overgoon, & as moche space as the regioun
of droughte overstreccheth, that is to seyn,
sandes and desertes, wel unnethe sholde
ther dwellen a right streit place to the habitacioun of men. And ye thanne, that ben
environed & closed within the leste prikke
of thilke prikke, thinken ye to manifesten
your renoun & don youre name to ben born
forth? But your glorie, that is so narwe and
so streite ythrongen into so litel boundes,
how mochel coveiteth it in largesse and in
greet doinge? And also sette this thereto:
that many a nacioun, dyverse of tonge and
of maneres and eek of resoun of hir livinge,
ben enhabited in the clos of thilke litel ha-

bitacle; to the whiche naciouns, what for difficultee of weyes and what for dyversitee of langages, and what for defaute of un-usage and entrecomuninge of marchaun-dise, nat only the names of singuler men ne may nat strecchen, but eek the fame of citees ne may nat strecchen. At the laste, certes, in the tyme of Marcus Tullius, as himself writ in his book, that the renoun of the comune of Rome ne hadde nat yit passed ne cloumben over the mountaigne that highte Caucasus; and yit was, thilke tyme, Rome wel waxen & greetly redouted of the Parthes and eek of other folk enha-bitinge aboute. Seestow nat thanne how streit and how compressed is thilke glorie that ye travailen aboute to shewe and to multiplye? May thanne the glorie of a sin-guler Romaine strecchen thider as the fame of the name of Rome may nat climben ne passen? And eek, seestow nat that the maneres of dyverse folk and eek hir lawes ben discordaunt among hemself; so that thilke thing that som men jugen worthy of preysinge, other folk jugen that it is wor-thy of torment? And therof comth it that, though a man delyte him in preysinge of his renoun, he may nat in no wyse bringen forth ne spreden his name to many maner poeples. Therefor every man oughte to ben apayed of his glorie that is publisshed a-mong his owne neighbours; and thilke noble renoun shal ben restreyned within the boundes of o manere folke. But how many a man, that was ful noble in his tyme, hath the wrecched and nedy foryetinge of wryteres put out of minde and don awey! Al be it so that, certes, thilke wrytinges profiten litel; the whiche wrytinges long and derk elde doth awey, bothe hem & eek hir autours. But ye men semen to geten yow a perdurabletee, whan ye thenken that, in tyme tocominge, your fame shal lasten. But natheles, yif thou wolt maken com-parisoun to the endeles spaces of eterni-tee, what thing hast thou by whiche thou mayst rejoysen thee of long lastinge of thy name? For yif ther were maked com-parisoun of the abydinge of a moment to ten thousand winter, for as mochel as bothe the spaces ben ended, yit hath the moment som porcioun of it, although it litel be. But natheles, thilke selve noum-bre of yeres, & eek as many yeres as therto may be multiplyed, ne may nat, certes, ben comparisoned to the perdurabletee that is endeles; for of thinges that han ende may be maked comparisoun, but of thinges that ben withouten ende, to thinges that han ende, may be maked no comparisoun. And forthy is it that, although renoun, of as long tyme as ever thee list to thinken, were thought to the regard of eternitee,

that is unstaunchable & infinit, it ne sholde nat only semen litel, but pleynliche right naught. But ye men, certes, ne conne don nothing aright, but yif it be for the audi-ence of poeple and for ydel rumours; and ye forsaken the grete worthinesse of con-science and of vertu, & ye seken your guer-douns of the smale wordes of straunge folk.

HAVE now heer and understonde, in the lightnesse of swich pryde and veine glorie, how a man scornede festivaly & merily swich vanitee. Whylom ther was a man that hadde assayed with stryvinge wordes another man, the whiche, nat for usage of verray vertu but for proud veine glorie, had taken upon him falsly the name of a philosophre. This rather man that I spak of thoughte he wolde assaye, wher he, thilke, were a philosophre or no; that is to seyn, yif that he wolde han suf-fred lightly in pacience the wronges that weren don unto him. This feynede philo-sophre took pacience a litel whyle, &, whan he hadde received wordes of outrage, he, as in stryvinge ayein and rejoysinge of him-self, seyde at the laste right thus: Under-stondest thou nat that I am a philosophre? That other man answerde ayein ful byt-ingly, & seyde: I hadde wel understonden it, yif thou haddest holden thy tonge stille. But what is it to thise noble worthy men (for, certes, of swiche folke speke I) that seken glorie with vertu? What is it? quod she; what atteyneth fame to swiche folk, whan the body is resolved by the deeth at the laste? For yif it so be that men dyen in al, that is to seyn, body and sowle, the whiche thing our resoun defendeth us to bileven, thanne is ther no glorie in no wyse. For what sholde thilke glorie ben, whan he, of whom thilke glorie is seyde to be, nis right naught in no wyse? And yif the sowle, which that hath in itself science of goode werkes, unbounden fro the prison of the erthe, wendeth frely to the hevene, despy-seth it nat thanne alle erthely occupacioun; and, being in hevene, rejoyseth that it is exempt fro alle erthely thinges? As who seith, thanne rekketh the sowle of no glorie of renoun of this world.

Metre VII.
Quicunque solam mente praecipiti petit.

WHOSO that, with overthrow-inge thought, only seketh glorie of fame, and weneth that it be sovereyn good: lat him loken upon the brode shewinge contrees of hevene, and upon the streite site of this erthe; and he shal ben ashamed of the encrees of his name, that may nat fulfille the litel compas of the erthe. O! what coveiten proude folk to liften up hir nekkes in ydel in the dedly yok of this worlde? For although that renoun ysprad, passinge to ferne poeples, goth by dyverse tonges; & although that grete houses or kinredes shynen with clere titles of honours; yit, natheles, deeth despyseth alle heye glorie of fame: and deeth wrappeth togidere the heye hevedes & the lowe, and maketh egal & evene the heyeste to the loweste. Wher wonen now the bones of trewe Fabricius? What is now Brutus, or stierne Catoun? The thinne fame, yit lastinge, of hir ydel names, is marked with a fewe lettres; but although that we han knowen the faire wordes of the fames of hem, it is nat yeven to knowe hem that ben dede & consumpte. Liggeth thanne stille, al outrely unknowable; ne fame ne maketh yow nat knowe. And yif ye wene to liven the longer for winde of your mortal name, whan o cruel day shal ravisshe yow, thanne is the seconde deeth dwellinge unto yow. Glose. The first deeth he clepeth heer the departinge of the body and the sowle; and the seconde deeth he clepeth, as heer, the stintinge of the renoun of fame.

Prose VIII.
Set ne me inexorabile contra fortunam.

UT for as mochel as thou shalt nat wenen, quod she, that I bere untretable bataile ayeins fortune, yit somtyme it bifalleth that she, deceyvable, deserveth to han right good thank of men; and that is, whan she hirself opneth, and whan she descovereth hir frount, and sheweth hir maneres. Peraventure yit understondest thou nat that I shal seye. It is a wonder that I desire to telle, and forthy unnethe may I unpleyten my sentence with wordes; for I deme that contrarious fortune profiteth more to men than fortune debonaire. For alwey, whan fortune semeth debonaire, than she lyeth falsly in bihetinge the hope of welefulnesse; but forsothe contrarious fortune is alwey soothfast, whan she sheweth hirself unstable thorugh hir chaunginge. The amiable fortune deceyveth folk; the contrarie fortune techeth. The amiable fortune bindeth with the beautee of false goodes the hertes of folk that usen hem; the contrarie fortune unbindeth hem by the knowinge of freele welefulnesse. The amiable fortune mayst thou seen alwey windy and flowinge, and ever misknowinge of hirself; the contrarie fortune is atempre and restreyned, & wys

Z 4

thorugh exercise of hir adversitee. At the laste, amiable fortune with hir flateringes draweth miswandringe men fro the sovereyne good; the contrarious fortune ledeth ofte folk ayein to soothfast goodes, and haleth hem ayein as with an hooke. Wenest thou thanne that thou oughtest to leten this a litel thing, that this aspre and horrible fortune hath discovered to thee the thoughtes of thy trewe freendes? Forwhy this ilke fortune hath departed and uncovered to thee bothe the certein visages & eek the doutous visages of thy felawes. Whan she departed awey fro thee, she took awey hir freendes, and lafte thee thyne freendes. Now whan thou were riche and weleful, as thee semede, with how mochel woldest thou han bought the fulle knowinge of this, that is to seyn, the knowinge of thy verray freendes? Now pleyne thee nat thanne of richesse ylorn, sin thou hast founden the moste precious kinde of richesses, that is to seyn, thy verray freendes.

Metre VIII.
Quod mundus stabili fide.

HAT the world with stable feith varieth acordable chaunginges; that the contrarious qualitee of elements holden among hemself aliaunce perdurable; that Phebus the sonne with his goldene chariet bringeth forth the rosene day; that the mone hath commaundement over the nightes, which nightes Hesperus the evesterre hath brought; that the see, greedy to flowen, constreyneth with a certein ende hise flodes, so that it is nat leveful to strecche hise brode termes or boundes upon the erthes, that is to seyn, to covere al the erthe: al this acordaunce of thinges is bounden with Love, that governeth erthe and see, and hath also commaundements to the hevenes. And yif this Love slakede the brydeles, alle thinges that now loven hem togederes wolden maken a bataile continuely, and stryven to fordoon the fasoun of this worlde, the whiche they now leden in acordable feith by faire moevinges. This Love halt togideres poeples joigned with an holy bond, and knitteth sacrement of mariages of chaste loves; & Love endyteth lawes to trewe felawes. O! weleful were mankinde, yif thilke Love that governeth hevene governed youre corages!
Explicit Liber secundus.

343

Iam cantum illa finierat.

BY this she hadde ended hir song, whan the sweetnesse of hir ditee hadde thorugh-perced me that was desirous of herkninge, and I astoned hadde yit streighte myn eres, that is to seyn, to herkne the bet what she wolde seye; so that a litel here-after I seyde thus: O thou that art sovereyn comfort of anguissous corages, so thou hast remounted & norisshed me with the weighte of thy sentences and with delyt of thy singinge; so that I trowe nat now that I be unparigal to the strokes of fortune: as who seyth, I dar wel now suffren al the assautes of fortune, and wel defende me fro hir. And tho remedies which that thou seydest herbiforn weren right sharpe, nat only that I am nat agrisen of hem now, but I, desirous of heringe, axe gretely to heren the remedies.

THAN seyde she thus: That felede I ful wel, quod she, whan that thou, ententif & stille, ravisshedest my wordes; and I abood til that thou haddest swich habite of thy thought as thou hast now; or elles til that I myself hadde maked to thee the same habit, which that is a more verray thing. And certes, the remenaunt of thinges that ben yit to seye ben swiche, that first whan men tasten hem they ben bytinge, but whan they ben receyved with-inne a wight, than ben they swete. But for thou seyst that thou art so desirous to herkne hem, with how gret brenninge woldest thou glowen, yif thou wistest whider I wol leden thee!

WHIDER is that? quod I. ✍ To thilke verray welefulnesse, quod she, of whiche thyn herte dremeth; but for as moche as thy sighte is ocupied and distorbed by imaginacioun of erthely thinges, thou mayst nat yit seen thilke selve welefulnesse.

DO, quod I, and shewe me what is thilke verray welefulnesse, I preye thee, withoute taryinge. ✍ That wole I gladly don, quod she, for the cause of thee; but I wol first marken thee by wordes and I wol enforcen me to enformen thee thilke false cause of blisfulnesse that thou more knowest; so that, whan thou hast fully biholden thilke false goodes, & torned thyn eyen to that other syde, thou mowe knowe the cleernesse of verray blisfulnesse.

Metre I.

Qui serere ingenuum volet agrum.

WHOSO wole sowe a feeld plentivous, lat him first delivere it fro thornes, and kerve a-sunder with his hook the busshes & the fern, so that the corn may comen hevy of eres & of greynes. Hony is the more swete, yif mouthes han first tasted savoures that ben wikkid. The sterres shynen more a-greably whan the wind Nothus leteth his ploungy blastes; & after that Lucifer the day-sterre hath chased awey the derke night, the day the fairere ledeth the rosene hors of the sonne. And right so thou, bi-holdinge first the false goodes, bigin to withdrawen thy nekke fro the yok of erthe-ly affecciouns; and afterward the verray goodes shollen entren into thy corage.

Prose II.

Tunc defixo paullulum visu.

THO fastnede she a litel the sighte of hir eyen, and with-drow hir right as it were into the streite sete of hir thought; and bigan to speke right thus: Alle the cures, quod she, of mortal folk, whiche that travaylen hem in many maner studies, goon certes by diverse weyes, but natheles they enforcen hem alle to comen only to oon ende of blisfulnesse. And blisfulnesse is swiche a good, that whoso that hath geten it, he ne may, over that, nothing more desyre. And this thing is forsothe the sovereyn good that conteyneth in him-self alle maner goodes; to the whiche good yif ther failede any thing, it mighte nat ben cleped sovereyn good: for thanne were ther som good, out of this ilke sovereyn good, that mighte ben desired. Now is it cleer and certein thanne, that blisfulnesse is a parfit estat by the congregacioun of alle goodes; the whiche blisfulnesse, as I have seyd, alle mortal folk enforcen hem to geten by diverse weyes. for why the coveitise of verray good is naturelly yplaunted in the hertes of men; but the miswandringe errour mis-ledeth hem into false goodes. Of the whiche men, som of hem wenen that sovereyn good be to liven withoute nede of any thing, and travaylen hem to be haboundaunt of rich-esses. And som other men demen that sov-ereyn good be, for to ben right digne of re-verence; & enforcen hem to ben reverenced

among hir neighbours by the honours that they han ygeten. And some folk ther ben that holden, that right heigh power be sovereyn good, & enforcen hem for to regnen, or elles to joignen hem to hem that regnen. And it semeth to some other folk, that noblesse of renoun be the sovereyn good; and hasten hem to geten glorious name by the arts of werre and of pees. And many folk mesuren and gessen that sovereyn good be joye and gladnesse, & wenen that it be right blisful thing to ploungen hem in voluptuous delyt. And ther ben folk that entrechaungen the causes and the endes of thise forseyde goodes, as they that desiren richesses to han power & delytes; or elles they desiren power for to han moneye, or for cause of renoun. In thise thinges, and in swiche othre thinges, is torned alle the entencioun of desiringes and of werkes of men; as thus: noblesse and favour of people, whiche that yeveth to men, as it semeth hem, a maner cleernesse of renoun; & wyf and children, that men desiren for cause of delyt and of merinesse. But forsothe, frendes ne sholden nat be rekned among the goodes of fortune, but of vertu; for it is a ful holy maner thing. Alle thise othre thinges, forsothe, ben taken for cause of power or elles for cause of delyt.

CERTES, now am I redy to referren the goodes of the body to thise forseide thinges aboven; for it semeth that strengthe & gretnesse of body yeven power and worthinesse, and that beautee and swiftnesse yeven noblesses & glorie of renoun; and hele of body semeth yeven delyt. In alle thise thinges it semeth only that blisfulnesse is desired. Forwhy thilke thing that every man desireth most over alle thinges, he demeth that it be the sovereyn good; but I have defyned that blisfulnesse is the sovereyn good; for which every wight demeth, that thilke estat that he desireth over alle thinges, that it be blisfulnesse.

NOW hast thou thanne biforn thyn eyen almest al the purposed forme of the welefulnesse of mankinde, that is to seyn, richesses, honours, power, and glorie, and delyts. The whiche delyt only considerede Epicurus, and juged and establisshed that delyt is the sovereyn good; for as moche as alle othre thinges, as him thoughte, birefte awey joye & mirthe fram the herte. But I retorne ayein to the studies of men, of whiche men the corage alwey reherseth and seketh the sovereyn good, al be it so that it be with a derked memorie; but he not by whiche path, right as a dronken man not nat by whiche path he may retorne him to his hous. Semeth it thanne that folk folyen and erren that enforcen hem to have nede of nothing?

Certes, ther nis non other thing that may so wel performe blisfulnesse, as an estat plentivous of alle goodes, that ne hath nede of non other thing, but that is suffisaunt of himself unto himself. And folyen swiche folk thanne, that wenen that thilke thing that is right good, that it be eek right worthy of honour & of reverence? Certes, nay. For that thing nis neither foul ne worthy to ben despised, that wel neigh al the entencioun of mortal folk travaylen for to geten it. And power, oughte nat that eek to ben rekened amonges goodes? What elles? For it is nat to wene that thilke thing, that is most worthy of alle thinges, be feble and withoute strengthe. And cleernesse of renoun, oughte that to ben despised? Certes, ther may no man forsake, that al thing that is right excellent and noble, that it ne semeth to ben right cleer and renomed. For certes, it nedeth nat to seye, that blisfulnesse be nat anguissous ne drery, ne subgit to grevaunces ne to sorwes, sin that in right litel thinges folk seken to have and to usen that may delyten hem. Certes, thise ben the thinges that men wolen & desiren to geten. And for this cause desiren they richesses, dignitees, regnes, glorie, and delices. For therby wenen they to han suffisaunce, honour, power, renoun, and gladnesse. Than is it good, that men seken thus by so many diverse studies. In whiche desyr it may lightly ben shewed how gret is the strengthe of nature; for how so that men han diverse sentences and discordinge, algates men acorden alle in lovinge the ende of good.

Metre II.
Quantas rerum flectat habenas.

IT lyketh me to shewe, by subtil song, with slakke and delitable soun of strenges, how that Nature, mighty, enclineth and flitteth the governements of thinges, and by whiche lawes she, purveyable, kepeth the grete world; & how she, bindinge, restreyneth alle thinges by a bonde that may nat ben unbounde. Al be it so that the lyouns of the contre of Pene beren the faire chaynes, and taken metes of the handes of folk that yeven it hem, and dreden hir sturdy maystres of whiche they ben wont to suffren betinges: yif that hir horrible mouthes ben bebled, that is to seyn, of bestes devoured, hir corage of time passed, that hath ben ydel & rested, repeyreth ayein; and they roren grevously and remembren on hir nature, & slaken hir nekkes fram hir chaynes unbounde; and hir mayster, first totorn with blody tooth, assayeth the wode wrathes of hem; this is to seyn, they freten hir mayster. And the jangel-

345

inge brid that singeth on the heye braunch,
es, that is to seyn, in the wode, and after
is enclosed in a streyt cage: although that
the pleyinge bisinesse of men yeveth hem
honiede drinkes & large metes with swete
studie, yit natheles, yif thilke brid, skip,
pinge out of hir streyte cage, seeth the a,
greables shadewes of the wodes, she de,
fouleth with hir feet hir metes yshad, and
seketh mourninge only the wode; & twit,
ereth, desiringe the wode, with hir swete
vois. The yerde of a tree, that is haled a,
doun by mighty strengthe, boweth redily
the crop adoun: but yif that the hand of
him that it bente lat it gon ayein, anon the
crop loketh upright to hevene. The sonne
Phebus, that falleth at even in the west,
rene wawes, retorneth ayein eftsones his
carte, by privee path, theras it is wont a,
ryse. Alle thinges seken ayein to hir propre
cours, and alle thinges rejoysen hem of hir
retorninge ayein to hir nature. Ne non or,
dinaunce nis bitaken to thinges, but that
that hath joyned the endinge to the begin,
ninge, and hath maked the cours of itself
stable, that it chaungeth nat from his
propre kinde.

Prose III.
Vos quoque, o terrena animalia.

ERTES also ye
men, that ben erthe,
liche beestes, dre,
men alwey youre be,
ginninge, although
it be with a thinne
imaginacioun; & by
a maner thoughte,
albe it nat cleerly ne
parfitly, ye loken
fram afer to thilke verray fyn of blisful,
nesse; & therfore naturel entencioun ledeth
you to thilke verray good, but many maner
errours mistorneth you therfro. Consider
now yif that by thilke thinges, by whiche
a man weneth to geten him blisfulnesse,
yif that he may comen to thilke ende that
he weneth to come by nature. For yif that
moneye or honours, or thise other for,
seyde thinges bringen to men swich a thing
that no good ne fayle hem ne semeth fayle,
certes than wole I graunte that they ben
maked blisful by thilke thinges that they
han geten. But yif so be that thilke thinges
ne mowen nat performen that they biheten,
and that ther be defaute of manye goodes,
sheweth it nat thanne cleerly that fals
beautee of blisfulnesse is knowen and a,
teint in thilke thinges? First and forward
thou thyself, that haddest habundaunces
of richesses nat long agon, I axe yif that,
in the habundaunce of alle thilke richesses,
thou were never anguissous or sory in thy

corage of any wrong or grevaunce that bi,
tidde thee on any syde?

ERTES, quod I, it ne remembreth
me nat that evere I was so free of
my thought that I ne was alwey in
anguissh of somwhat.

AND was nat that, quod she, for that
thee lakked somwhat that thou nold,
est nat han lakked, or elles thou had,
dest that thou noldest nat han had?
Right so is it, quod I.

THANNE desiredest thou the pre,
sence of that oon and the absence
of that other? I graunte wel,
quod I. Forsothe, quod she, than nedeth
ther somwhat that every man desireth?
Ye, ther nedeth, quod I.

ERTES, quod she, & he that hath
lakke or nede of aught nis nat in
every wey suffisaunt to himself?
No, quod I.

AND thou, quod she, in al the plentee of
thy richesses haddest thilke lakke of
suffisaunse? What elles? quod I.

THANNE may nat richesses maken
that a man nis nedy, ne that he be
suffisaunt to himself; & that was
it that they bihighten, as it semeth. And
eek certes I trowe, that this be gretly to
considere, that moneye ne hath nat in his
owne kinde that it ne may ben binomen of
hem that han it, maugre hem? I biknowe
it wel, quod I.

WHY sholdest thou nat biknowen
it, quod she, whan every day the
strenger folk binemen it fro the
febler, maugre hem? For whennes comen
elles alle thise foreyne compleyntes or
quereles of pletinges, but for that men
axen ayein here moneye that hath ben bi,
nomen hem by force or by gyle, and alwey
maugre hem? Right so is it, quod I.

THAN, quod she, hath a man nede to
seken him foreyne helpe by whiche
he may defende his moneye? Who
may sey nay? quod I.

ERTES, quod she; & him nedede
non help, yif he ne hadde no moneye
that he mighte lese? That is
douteles, quod I.

THAN is this thinge torned into the
contrarye, quod she. For richesses,
that men wenen sholde make suffi,
saunce, they maken a man rather han nede
of foreyne help. Which is the manere or the
gyse, quod she, that richesse may dryve
awey nede? Riche folk, may they neither
han hunger ne thurst? Thise riche men,
may they fele no cold on hir limes on win,
ter? But thou wolt answeren, that riche
men han ynow wherwith they may staunch,
en hir hunger, slaken hir thurst, and don
awey cold. In this wyse may nede be coun,

forted by richesses; but certes, nede ne may nat al outrely ben don awey. for though this nede, that is alwey gapinge and gredy, be fulfild with richesses, & axe any thing, yit dwelleth thanne a nede that mighte be fulfild. I holde me stille, & telle nat how that litel thing suffiseth to nature; but certes to avarice ynough ne suffiseth nothing. for sin that richesses ne may nat al don awey nede, but richesses maken nede, what may it thanne be, that ye wenen that richesses mowen yeven you suffisaunce?

Metre III.
Quamvis fluente dives auri gurgite.

 L were it so that a riche covey-tous man hadde a river flet-inge al of gold, yit sholde it never staunchen his coveit-ise; and though he hadde his nekke ycharged with preci-ous stones of the rede see, and though he do ere his feldes plentivous with an hun-dred oxen, never ne shal his bytinge bisi-nesse forleten him whyl he liveth, ne the lighte richesses ne sholle nat beren him companye whan he is ded.

Prose IV.
Set dignitates.

 AT dignitees, to whom they ben comen, mak-en they him honorable & reverent? Han they nat so gret strengthe, that they may putte vertues in the hertes of folk that usen the lordshipes of hem? Or elles may they don awey the vyces? Certes, they ne ben at wont to don awey wikkednesse, but they ben wont rather to shewen wikkednesse. And therof comth it that I have right grete des-deyn, that dignitees ben yeven ofte to wik-ked men; for which thing Catullus cleped a consul of Rome, that highte Nonius, Postum or Boch; as who seyth, he cleped him a congregacioun of vyces in his brest, as a postum is ful of corupcioun, al were this Nonius set in a chayre of dignitee. Seest thou nat thanne how gret vilenye dignitees don to wikked men? Certes, un-worthinesse of wikked men sholde be the lasse ysene, yif they nere renomed of none honours. Certes, thou thyself ne mightest nat ben brought with as manye perils as thou mightest suffren that thou woldest beren the magistrat with Decorat; that is to seyn, that for no peril that mighte be-fallen thee by offence of the king Theo-dorike, thou noldest nat be felawe in gov-ernaunce with Decorat; whan thou saye

that he hadde wikked corage of a likerous shrewe and of an accusor. Ne I ne may nat, for swiche honours, jugen hem worthy of reverence, that I deme and holde unworthy to han thilke same honours. Now yif thou saye a man that were fulfild of wisdom, certes, thou ne mightest nat deme that he were unworthy to the honour, or elles to the wisdom of which he is fulfild? No, quod I. Certes, dignitees, quod she, a-pertienen proprely to vertu; & vertu trans-porteth dignitee anon to thilke man to which she hirself is conjoigned. And for as moche as honours of poeple ne may nat maken folk digne of honour, it is wel seyn cleerly that they ne han no propre beautee of dignitee. And yit men oughten taken more heed in this. for yif it so be that a wikked wight be so mochel the foulere and the more outcast, that he is despysed of most folk, so as dignitee ne may nat mak-en shrewes digne of reverence, the which shrewes dignitee sheweth to moche folk, thanne maketh dignitee shrewes rather so moche more despysed than preysed; and forsothe nat unpunisshed: that is for to seyn, that shrewes revengen hem ayein-ward upon dignitees; for they yilden ayein to dignitees as gret guerdoun, whan they bispotten and defoulen dignitees with hir vilenye. And for as mochel as thou mowe knowe that thilke verray reverence ne may nat comen by thise shadewy transitorie dignitees, undirstond now thus: yif that a man hadde used & had many maner dig-nitees of consules, and were comen pera-venture amonge straunge naciouns, sholde thilke honour maken him worshipful and redouted of straunge folk? Certes, yif that honour of poeple were a naturel yift to dignitees, it ne mighte never cesen no-wher amonges no maner folk to don his office, right as fyr in every contree ne stint-eth nat to eschaufen and to ben hoot. But for as moche as for to ben holden honour-able or reverent ne cometh nat to folk of hir propre strengthe of nature, but only of the false opinioun of folk, that is to seyn, that wenen that dignitees maken folk dig-ne of honour; anon therfore whan that they comen theras folk ne knowen nat thilke dignitees, hir honours vanisshen awey, & that anon. But that is amonges straunge folk, mayst thou seyn; but amonges hem ther they weren born, ne duren nat thilke dignitees alwey? Certes, the dignitee of the provostrie of Rome was whylom a gret power; now is it nothing but an ydel name, & the rente of the senatorie a gret charge. And yif a wight whylom hadde the office to taken hede to the vitailes of the poeple, as of corn & other thinges, he was holden a-monges grete; but what thing is now more

347

outcast thanne thilke provostrie? And, as I have seyd a litel herbiforn, that thilke thing that hath no propre beautee of him-self receiveth somtyme prys & shyninge, and somtyme leseth it by the opinioun of usaunces. Now yif that dignitees thanne ne mowen nat maken folk digne of rever-ence, and yif that dignitees wexen foule of hir wille by the filthe of shrewes, & yif that dignitees lesen hir shyninge by chaung-inge of tymes, and yif they wexen foule by estimacioun of poeple: what is it that they han in hemself of beautee that oughte ben desired? as who seyth, non; thanne ne mowen they yeven no beautee of dignitee to non other.

Metre IV.

Quamvis se, Tyrio superbus ostro.

AL be it so that the proude Nero, with alle his wode luxu-rie, kembde him & aparailede him with faire purpres of Tirie, and with whyte perles, algates yit throf he hateful to alle folk: this is to seyn, that al was he behated of alle folk. Yit this wikked Nero hadde gret lordship, and yaf whylom to the reverents senatours the unworshipful setes of dignitees. Unworshipful setes he clepeth here, for that Nero, that was so wikked, yaf tho dignitees. Whoso wolde thanne resonably wenen, that blisfulnesse were in swiche honours as ben yeven by vicious shrewes?

Prose V.

An vero regna regumque familiaritas.

AT regnes and fami-liaritees of kinges, may they maken a man to ben mighty? How elles, whan hir blisful-nesse dureth perpetu-ely? But certes, the olde age of tyme pass-ed, and eek of present tyme now, is ful of en-saumples how that kinges ben chaunged into wrecchednesse out of hir welefulnesse. O! a noble thing and a cleer thing is power, that is nat founden mighty to kepen itself! And yif that power of reaumes be auctour and maker of blisfulnesse, yif thilke power lakketh on any syde, amen-useth it nat thilke blisfulnesse and bring-eth in wrecchednesse? But yit, al be it so that the reaumes of mankinde strecchen brode, yit mot ther nede ben moche folk, over whiche that every king ne hath no lord-shipe ne comaundement. And certes, upon thilke syde that power faileth, which that maketh folk blisful, right on that same

348

syde noun-power entreth undernethe, that maketh hem wrecches; in this manere thanne moten kinges han more porcioun of wrecchednesse than of welefulnesse. A tyraunt, that was king of Sisile, that hadde assayed the peril of his estat, shew-ede by similitude the dredes of reaumes by gastnesse of a swerd that heng over the heved of his familier. What thing is thanne this power, that may nat don awey the by-tinges of bisinesse, ne eschewe the prikkes of drede? And certes, yit wolden they liven in sikernesse, but they may nat; and yit they glorifye hem in hir power. Holdest thou thanne that thilke man be mighty, that thou seest that he wolde don that he may nat don? And holdest thou thanne him a mighty man, that hath envirownede his sydes with men of armes or serjaunts, & dredeth more hem that he maketh agast than they dreden him, and that is put in the handes of his servaunts for he sholde seme mighty? But of familieres or ser-vaunts of kinges what sholde I telle thee anything, sin that I myself have shewed thee that reaumes hemself ben ful of gret feblesse? The whiche familieres, certes, the ryal power of kinges, in hool estat and in estat abated, ful ofte throweth adown. Nero constreynede Senek, his familier and his mayster, to chesen on what deeth he wolde deyen. Antonius comaundede that knightes slowen with hir swerdes Papin-ian his familier, which Papinian hadde ben longe tyme ful mighty amonges hem of the court. And yit, certes, they wolden bothe han renounced hir power; of whiche two Senek enforcede him to yeven to Nero his richesses, & also to han gon into solitarie exil. But whan the grete weighte, that is to seyn, of lordes power or of fortune, draw-eth hem that shullen falle, neither of hem ne mighte do that he wolde. What thing is thanne thilke power, that though men han it, yit they ben agast; and whanne thou woldest han it, thou nart nat siker; & yif thou woldest forleten it, thou mayst nat eschuen it? But whether swiche men ben frendes at nede, as ben conseyled by for-tune and nat by vertu? Certes, swiche folk as weleful fortune maketh freendes, con-trarious fortune maketh hem enemys. And what pestilence is more mighty for to a-noye a wight than a familier enemy?

Metre V.

Qui se volet esse potentem.

HOSO wol be mighty, he mot daunten his cruel corage, ne putte nat his nekke, overco-men, under the foule reynes of lecherye. For albeit so that thy lordshipe strecche so fer, that the contree of Inde quaketh at thy comaundements or at thy lawes, and that the last ile in the see, that hight Tyle, be thral to thee, yit, yif thou mayst nat putten awey thy foule derke desyrs, & dryven out fro thee wrecched complaintes, certes, it nis no power that thou hast.

Prose VI.
Gloria vero quam fallax saepe.

BUT glorie, how deceivable and how foul is it ofte! For which thing nat unskilfully a tragedien, that is to seyn, a maker of ditees that highten tragedies, cryde & seide: O glorie, glorie, quod he, thou art nothing elles to thousandes of folkes but a greet sweller of eres! For manye han had ful greet renoun by the false opinioun of the poeple, and what thing may ben thought fouler than swiche preysinge? For thilke folk that ben preysed falsly, they moten nedes han shame of hir preysinges. And yif that folk han geten hem thonk or preysinge by hir desertes, what thing hath thilke prys eched or encresed to the conscience of wyse folk, that mesuren hir good, nat by the rumour of the poeple, but by the soothfastnesse of conscience? And yif it seme a fair thing, a man to han encresed and spred his name, than folweth it that it is demed to ben a foul thing, yif it ne be ysprad and encresed. But, as I seyde a litel herbiforn that, sin ther mot nedes ben many folk, to whiche folk the renoun of a man ne may nat comen, it befalleth that he, that thou wenest be glorious and renomed, semeth in the nexte partie of the erthes to ben withoute glorie and withoute renoun.

AND certes, amonges thise thinges I ne trowe nat that the prys & grace of the poeple nis neither worthy to ben remembred, ne cometh of wyse jugement, ne is ferme perdurably. But now, of this name of gentilesse, what man is it that ne may wel seen how veyn & how flittinge a thing it is? For yif the name of gentilesse be referred to renoun & cleernesse of linage, thanne is gentil name but a foreine thing, that is to seyn, to hem that glorifyen hem of hir linage. For it semeth that gentilesse be a maner preysinge that comth of the deserte of ancestres. And yif preysinge maketh gentilesse, thanne moten they nedes be gentil that ben preysed. For which thing it folweth, that yif thou ne have no gentilesse of thyself, that is to seyn, preyse that comth of thy deserte,

foreine gentilesse ne maketh thee nat gentil. But certes, yif ther be any good in gentilesse, I trowe it be alonly this, that it semeth as that a maner necessitee be imposed to gentil men, for that they ne sholden nat outrayen or forliven fro the virtues of hir noble kinrede.

Metre VI.
Omne hominum genus in terris.

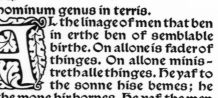

AL the linage of men that ben in erthe ben of semblable birthe. On allone is fader of thinges. On allone ministreth alle thinges. He yaf to the sonne hise bemes; he yaf to the mone hir hornes. He yaf the men to the erthe; he yaf the sterres to the hevene. He encloseth with membres the soules that comen fro his hye sete. Thanne comen alle mortal folk of noble sede; why noisen ye or bosten of youre eldres? For yif thou loke your biginninge, and God your auctor & your maker, thanne nis ther no forlived wight, but yif he norisshe his corage unto vyces, and forlete his propre burthe.

Prose VII.
Quid autem de corporis voluptatibus.

BUT what shal I seye of delices of body, of whiche delices the desiringes ben ful of anguissh, & the fulfillinges of hem ben ful of penaunce? How greet syknesse and how grete sorwes unsufferable, right as a maner fruit of wikkednesse, ben thilke delices wont to bringen to the bodies of folk that usen hem! Of whiche delices I not what joye may ben had of hir moevinge. But this wot I wel, that whosoever wole remembren him of hise luxures, he shal wel understonde that the issues of delices ben sorwful & sorye. And yif thilke delices mowen maken folk blisful, than by the same cause moten thise bestes ben cleped blisful; of whiche bestes al the entencioun hasteth to fulfille hir bodily jolitee. And the gladnesse of wyf and children were an honest thing, but it hath ben seyd that it is over muchel ayeins kinde, that children han ben founden tormentours to hir fadres, I not how manye: of whiche children how bytinge is every condicioun, it nedeth nat to tellen it thee, that hast or this tyme assayed it, and art yit now anguissous. In this approve I the sentence of my disciple Euripidis, that seyde, that He that hath no children is weleful by infortune.

Metre VII.
Habet omnis hoc voluptas.

EVERY delyt hath this, that it anguissheth hem with prikkes that usen it. It resembleth to thise flyinge flyes that we clepen been, that, after that he hath shad hise agreable honies, he fleeth awey, and stingeth the hertes, of hem that ben ysmite, with bytinge overlonge holdinge.

Prose VIII.
Nihil igitur dubium est.

OW is it no doute thanne that thise weyes ne ben a maner misledinges to blisfulnesse, ne that they ne mowe nat leden folk thider as they biheten to leden hem. But with how grete harmes thise forseyde weyes ben enlaced, I shal shewe thee shortly. Forwhy yif thou enforcest thee to asemble moneye, thou most bireven him his moneye that hath it. And yif thou wolt shynen with dignitees, thou most bisechen & supplien hem that yeven tho dignitees. And yif thou coveitest by honour to gon biforn other folk, thou shalt defoule thyself thorugh humblesse of axinge. Yif thou desirest power, thou shalt by awaytes of thy subgits anoyously ben cast under manye periles. Axest thou glorie? Thou shalt ben so destrat by aspre thinges that thou shalt forgoon sikernesse. And yif thou wolt leden thy lyf in delices, every wight shal despisen thee and forleten thee, as thou that art thral to thing that is right foul & brotel; that is to seyn, servaunt to thy body. Now is it thanne wel seen, how litel & how brotel possessioun they coveiten, that putten the goodes of the body aboven hir owne resoun. For mayst thou sormounten thise olifaunts in gretnesse or weight of body? Or mayst thou ben stronger than the bole? Mayst thou ben swifter than the tygre? Bihold the spaces and the stablenesse & the swifte cours of the hevene, and stint somtyme to wondren on foule thinges; the which hevene, certes, nis nat rather for thise thinges to ben wondred upon, than for the resoun by which it is governed. But the shyning of thy forme, that is to seyn, the beautee of thy body, how swiftly passinge is it, and how transitorie; certes, it is more flittinge than the mutabilitee of flowers of the somer sesoun. For so Aristotle telleth, that yif that men hadden eyen of a beest that highte lynx, so that the lokinge of folk mighte percen

thorugh the thinges that withstonden it, whoso loked thanne in the entrailes of the body of Alcibiades, that was ful fayr in the superfice withoute, it shold seme right foul. And forthy, yif thou semest fayr, thy nature maketh nat that, but the desceivaunce of the feblesse of the eyen that loken. But preyse the goodes of the body as mochel as ever thee list; so that thou knowe algates that, whatso it be, that is to seyn, of the goodes of thy body, which that thou wondrest upon, may ben desstroyed or dissolved by the hete of a fevere of three dayes. Of alle whiche forseyde thinges I may reducen this shortly in a somme, that thise worldly goodes, whiche that ne mowen nat yeven that they biheten, ne ben nat parfit by the congregacioun of alle goodes; that they ne ben nat weyes ne pathes that bringen men to blisfulnesse, ne maken men to ben blisful.

Metre VIII.
Eheu! quae miseros tramite devios.

LLAS! which folye and which ignoraunce misledeth wandringe wrecches fro the path of verray goode! Certes, ye ne seken no gold in grene trees, ne ye ne gaderen nat precious stones in the vynes, ne ye ne hyden nat your ginnes in the hye mountaignes to cacchen fish of whiche ye may maken riche festes. And yif yow lyketh to hunte to roes, ye ne gon nat to the fordes of the water that highte Tyrene. And over this, men knowen wel the crykes and the cavernes of the see yhid in the flodes, and knowen eek which water is most plentivous of whyte perles, and knowen which water haboundeth most of rede purpre, that is to seyn, of a maner shelle-fish with which men dyen purpre; & knowen which strondes habounden most with tendre fisshes, or of sharpe fisshes that highten echines. But folk suffren hemself to ben so blinde, that hem ne reccheth nat to knowe where thilke goodes ben yhid whiche that they coveiten, but ploungen hem in erthe & seken there thilke good that sormounteth the hevene that bereth the sterres. What preyere may I maken that be digne to the nyce thoughtes of men? But I preye that they coveiten richesse and honours, so that, whan they han geten tho false goodes with greet travaile, that therby they mowe knowen the verray goodes.

Prose IX.
Hactenus mendacis formam.

IT SUFFYSETH that I have shewed hiderto the forme of false welefulnesse, so that, yif thou loke now cleerly, the order of myn entencioun requireth from hennesforth to shewen thee the verray welefulnesse.

FOR sothe, quod I, I see wel now that suffisaunce may nat comen by richesses, ne power by reames, ne reverence by dignitees, ne gentilesse by glorie, ne joye by delices. And hast thou wel knowen the causes, quod she, why it is?

CERTES, me semeth, quod I, that I see hem right as though it were thorugh a litel clifte; but me were levere knowen hem more openly of thee.

CERTES, quod she, the resoun is al redy. For thilke thing that simply is o thing, withouten any devisioun, the errour and folye of mankinde departeth and devydeth it, and misledeth it and transporteth from verray and parfit good to goodes that ben false and unparfit. But sey me this. Wenest thou that he, that hath nede of power, that him ne lakketh nothing? Nay, quod I.

CERTES, quod she, thou seyst aright. For yif so be that ther is a thing, that in any partye be febler of power, certes, as in that, it mot nedes ben nedy of foreine help. Right so is it, quod I.

SUFFISAUNCE & power ben thanne of o kinde? So semeth it, quod I. And demest thou, quod she, that a thing that is of this manere, that is to seyn, suffisaunt and mighty, oughte ben despysed, or elles that it be right digne of reverence aboven alle thinges? Certes, quod I, it nis no doute, that it is right worthy to ben reverenced.

LAT us, quod she, adden thanne reverence to suffisaunce & to power, so that we demen that thise three thinges ben al o thing. Certes, quod I, lat us adden it, yif we wolen graunten the sothe.

WHAT demest thou thanne? quod she; is that a derk thing and nat noble, that is suffisaunt, reverent, and mighty, or elles that it is right noble & right cleer by celebritee of renoun? Consider thanne, quod she, as we han graunted herbiforn, that he that ne hath nede of nothing, and is most mighty & most digne of honour, yif him nedeth any cleernesse

of renoun, which cleernesse he mighte nat graunten of himself, so that, for lakke of thilke cleernesse, he mighte seme the febeler on any syde or the more outcast? Glose. This is to seyn, nay; for whoso that is suffisaunt, mighty, & reverent, cleernesse of renoun folweth of the forseyde thinges; he hath it al redy of his suffisaunce. Boece. I may nat, quod I, denye it; but I mot graunte as it is, that this thing be right celebrable by cleernesse of renoun and noblesse.

THANNE folweth it, quod she, that we adden cleernesse of renoun to the three forseyde thinges, so that ther ne be amonges hem no difference? This is a consequence, quod I.

THIS thing thanne, quod she, that ne hath nede of no foreine thing, & that may don alle thinges by hise strengthes, and that is noble and honourable, nis nat that a mery thing & a joyful? But whennes, quod I, that any sorwe mighte comen to this thing that is swiche, certes, I may nat thinke.

THANNE moten we graunte, quod she, that this thing be ful of gladnesse, yif the forseyde thinges ben sothe; and certes, also mote we graunten that suffisaunce, power, noblesse, reverence, and gladnesse ben only dyverse by names, but hir substaunce hath no diversitee. It mot needly been so, quod I.

THILKE thing thanne, quod she, that is oon & simple in his nature, the wikkednesse of men departeth it and devydeth it; and whan they enforcen hem to geten partye of a thing that ne hath no part, they ne geten hem neither thilke partye that nis non, ne the thing al hool that they ne desire nat. In which manere? quod I.

THILKE man, quod she, that secheth richesses to fleen povertee, he ne travaileth him nat for to gete power; for he hath levere ben derk and vyl; and eek withdraweth from himself many naturel delyts, for he nolde lese the moneye that he hath assembled. But certes, in this manere he ne geteth him nat suffisaunce that power forleteth, and that molestie prikketh, and that filthe maketh outcast, and that derkenesse hydeth. And certes, he that desireth only power, he wasteth and scatereth richesse, and despyseth delyts, & eek honour that is withoute power, ne he ne preyseth glorie nothing. Certes, thus seest thou wel, that manye thinges faylen to him; for he hath somtyme defaute of many necessitees, and many anguisshes byten him; and whan he ne may nat don tho defautes awey, he forleteth to ben mighty, and that is the thing that he

351

most desireth. And right thus may I maken semblable resouns of honours, and of glorie, and of delyts. For so as every of thise forseyde thinges is the same that thise other thinges ben, that is to seyn, al oon thing, whoso that ever seketh to geten that oon of thise, and nat that other, he ne geteth nat that he desireth. Boece. What seyst thou thanne, yif that a man coveiteth to geten alle thise thinges togider? Philosophie.

CERTES, quod she, I wolde seye, that he wolde geten him sovereyn blisfulnesse; but that shal he nat finde in tho thinges that I have shewed, that ne mowen nat yeven that they beheten. Certes, no, quod I.

THANNE, quod she, ne sholden men nat by no wey seken blisfulnesse in swiche thinges as men wene that they ne mowen yeven but o thing senglely of alle that men seken. I graunte wel, quod I; ne no sother thing ne may ben sayd.

NOW hast thou thanne, quod she, the forme and the causes of false welefulnesse. Now torne and flitte the eyen of thy thought; for ther shalt thou sen anon thilke verray blisfulnesse that I have bihight thee. Certes, quod I, it is cleer and open, thogh it were to a blinde man; and that shewedest thou me ful wel a litel herbiforn, whan thou enforcedest thee to shewe me the causes of the false blisfulnesse. For but yif I be bigyled, thanne is thilke the verray blisfulnesse parfit, that parfitly maketh a man suffisaunt, mighty, honourable, noble, and ful of gladnesse. And, for thou shalt wel knowe that I have wel understonden thise thinges within my herte, I knowe wel that thilke blisfulnesse, that may verrayly yeven oon of the forseyde thinges, sin they ben al oon, I knowe, douteles, that thilke thing is the fulle blisfulnesse. Philosophie.

O MY norie, quod she, by this opinioun I seye that thou art blisful, yif thou putte this therto that I shal seyn. What is that? quod I.

TROWEST thou that ther be any thing in thise erthely mortal toumbling thinges that may bringen this estat? Certes, quod I, I trowe it naught; and thou hast shewed me wel that over thilke good ther nis nothing more to ben desired.

THISE thinges thanne, quod she, that is to sey, erthely suffisaunce & power & swiche thinges, either they semen lykenesses of verray good, or elles it semeth that they yeve to mortal folk a maner of goodes that ne ben nat parfit; but thilke good that is verray and parfit, that may

they nat yeven. I acorde me wel, quod I.

THANNE, quod she, for as mochel as thou hast knowen which is thilke verray blisfulnesse, and eek whiche thilke thinges ben that lyen falsly blisfulnesse, that is to seyn, that by deceite semen verray goodes, now behoveth thee to knowe whennes and where thou mowe seke thilke verray blisfulnesse. Certes, quod I, that desire I greetly, and have abiden longe tyme to herknen it.

BUT for as moche, quod she, as it lyketh to my disciple Plato, in his book of In Timeo, that in right litel thinges men sholden bisechen the help of God, what jugest thou that be now to done, so that we may deserve to finde the sete of thilke verray good? Certes, quod I, I deme that we shollen clepen the fader of alle goodes; for withouten him nis ther nothing founden aright. Thou seyst aright, quod she; and bigan anon to singen right thus:

Metre IX.
O qui perpetua mundum ratione gubernas.

THOU fader, creator of hevene and of erthes, that governest this world by perdurable resoun, that comaundest the tymes to gon from sin that age hadde beginninge; thou that dwellest thyself ay stedefast and stable, & yevest alle othre thinges to ben moeved; ne foreine causes necesseden thee never to compoune werk of floteringe matere, but only the forme of soverein good yset within thee withoute envye, that moevede thee freely. Thou that art alder-fayrest, beringe the faire world in thy thought, formedest this world to the lyknesse semblable of that faire world in thy thought. Thou drawest al thing of thy soverein ensaumpler, & comaundest that this world, parfitliche ymaked, have freely & absolut his parfit parties. Thou bindest the elementes by noumbres proporcionables, that the colde thinges mowen acorden with the hote thinges, and the drye thinges with the moiste thinges; that the fyr, that is purest, ne flee nat over hye, ne that the hevinesse ne drawe nat adoun over-lowe the erthes that ben plounged in the wateres. Thou knittest togider the mene sowle of treble kinde, moevinge alle thinges, and devydest it by membres acordinge; & whan it is thus devyded, it hath asembled a moevinge into two roundes; it goth to torne ayein to himself, and envirouneth a ful deep thought, and torneth the hevene by semblable image. Thou by evene-lyke causes enhansest the sowles & the lasse lyves, and, ablinge hem heye by lighte cartes, thou sowest hem into hevene and into erthe; & whan they ben converted to thee by thy benigne lawe, thou makest hem retorne ayein to thee by ayein-ledinge fyr.

O FADER, yive thou to the thought to styen up into thy streite sete, and graunte him to enviroune the welle of good; and, the lighte yfounde, graunte him to fichen the clere sightes of his corage in thee. And scater thou and to-breke thou the weightes & the cloudes of erthely hevinesse, and shyne thou by thy brightnesse. for thou art cleernesse; thou art peysible reste to debonaire folk; thou thyself art biginninge, berer, leder, path, & terme; to loke on thee, that is our ende.

Prose X.
Quoniam igitur quae sit imperfecti.

FOR as moche thanne as thou hast seyn, which is the forme of good that nis nat parfit, & which is the forme of good that is parfit, now trowe I that it were good to shewe in what this perfeccioun of blisfulnesse is set. And in this thing, I trowe that we sholden first enquere for to witen, yif that any swiche maner good as thilke good that thou hast diffinisshed a litel heer-biforn, that is to seyn, soverein good, may ben founde in the nature of thinges; forthat veyn imaginacioun of thought ne deceyve us nat, and putte us out of the sothfast-nesse of thilke thing that is summitted unto us. But it may nat ben deneyed that thilke good ne is, and that it nis right as welle of alle goodes. for al thing that is cleped inparfit is proeved inparfit by the a-menusinge of perfeccioun or of thing that is parfit. And therof comth it, that in every thing general, yif that men sen anything that is inparfit, certes, in thilke general ther mot ben somthing that is parfit; for yif so be that perfeccioun is don awey, men may nat thinke ne seye fro whennes thilke thing is that is cleped inparfit. for the nature of thinges ne took nat hir beginninge of thinges amenused and inparfit, but it pro-cedeth of thinges that ben al hoole & ab-solut, and descendeth so doun into outter-est thinges, and into thinges empty and withouten frut. But, as I have yshewed a litel herbiforn, that yif ther be a blisful-nesse that be freele and veyn and inparfit, ther may no man doute that ther nis som blisfulnesse that is sad, stedefast, and parfit. Boece. This is concluded, quod I, fermely and sothfastly.

a a 1

BUT considere also, quod she, in wham this blisfulnesse enhabiteth. The comune acordaunce and conceite of the corages of men proeveth & graunteth, that God, prince of alle thinges, is good. for, so as nothing ne may ben thought bettre than God, it may nat ben douted thanne that he, that nothing nis bettre, that he nis good. Certes, resoun sheweth that God is so good, that it proveth by verray force that parfit good is in him. for yif God ne is swich, he ne may nat ben prince of alle thinges; for certes somthing possessing in itself parfit good, sholde ben more worthy than God, and it sholde semen that thilke thing were first, & eld-er than God. for we han shewed apertly that alle thinges that ben parfit ben first or thinges that ben unparfit; and forthy, for as moche as that my resoun or my proces ne go nat awey withoute an ende, we owen to graunten that the soverein God is right ful of soverein parfit good. And we han establisshed that the soverein good is ver-ray blisfulnesse: thanne mot it nedes be, that verray blisfulnesse is set in soverein God. This take I wel, quod I, ne this ne may nat ben withseid in no manere.

BUT I preye, quod she, see now how thou mayst proeven, holily & with-oute corupcioun, this that I have seyd, that the soverein God is right ful of soverein good. In which manere? quod I.

WENEST thou aught, quod she, that this prince of alle thinges have ytake thilke soverein good anywher out of himself, of which soverein good men proveth that he is ful, right as thou mightest thinken that God, that hath blisfulnesse in himself, and thilke blisful-nesse that is in him, weren dyvers in sub-staunce? for yif thou wene that God have received thilke good out of himself, thou mayst wene that he that yaf thilke good to God be more worthy than is God. But I am biknowen and confesse, and that right dignely, that God is right worthy aboven alle thinges; and, yif so be that this good be in him by nature, but that it is dyvers fro him by weninge resoun, sin we speke of God prince of alle thinges: feigne who-so feigne may, who was he that hath con-joigned thise dyverse thinges togider? And eek, at the laste, see wel that a thing that is dyvers from any thing, that thilke thing nis nat that same thing fro which it is un-derstonden to ben dyvers. Thanne folweth it, that thilke thing that by his nature is dyvers fro soverein good, that that thing nis nat soverein good; but certes, that were a felonous corsednesse to thinken that of him that nothing nis more worth.

353

for alwey, of alle thinges, the nature of hem ne may nat ben bettre than his biginning; for which I may concluden, by right verray resoun, that thilke that is biginning of alle thinges, thilke same thing is soverein good in his substaunce ✒ Boece. Thou hast seyd rightfully, quod I. Philosophie.

BUT we han graunted, quod she, that the soverein good is blisfulnesse.✒ And that is sooth, quod I.

THANNE, quod she, moten we nedes graunten and confessen that thilke same soverein good be God.✒ Certes, quod I, I ne may nat denye ne withstonde the resouns purposed; and I see wel that it folweth by strengthe of the premisses.

LOKE now, quod she, yif this be proved yit more fermely thus: that ther ne mowen nat ben two soverein goodes that ben dyverse amonge hemself. For certes, the goodes that ben dyverse amonges hemself, that oon nis nat that that other is; thanne ne may neither of hem ben parfit, so as either of hem lakketh to other. But that that nis nat parfit, men may seen apertly that it nis nat soverein. The thinges, thanne, that ben sovereinly goode, ne mowen by no wey ben dyverse. But I have wel concluded that blisfulnesse and God ben the soverein good; for whiche it mot nedes ben, that soverein blisfulnesse is soverein divinitee ✒ Nothing, quod I, nis more soothfast than this, ne more ferme by resoun; ne a more worthy thing than God may nat ben concluded.

UPON thise thinges thanne, quod she, right as thise geometriens, whan they han shewed hir proposiciouns, ben wont to bringen in thinges that they clepen porismes, or declaraciouns of forseide thinges, right so wole I yeve thee heer as a corollarie, or a mede of coroune. Forwhy, for as moche as by the getinge of blisfulnesse men ben maked blisful, and blisfulnesse is divinitee: thanne is it manifest and open, that by the getinge of divinitee men ben maked blisful. Right as by the getinge of justice they ben maked just, & by the getinge of sapience they ben maked wyse: right so, nedes, by the semblable resoun, whan they han geten divinitee, they ben maked goddes. Thanne is every blisful man God; but certes, by nature, ther nis but o God; but, by the participacioun of divinitee, ther ne let ne desturbeth nothing that ther ne ben manye goddes.✒ This is, quod I, a fair thing and a precious, clepe it as thou wolt; be it porisme or corollarie, or mede of coroune or declaringes.

354

CERTES, quod she, nothing nis fayrer than is the thing that by resoun sholde ben added to thise forseide thinges.✒ What thing? quod I.

SO, quod she, as it semeth that blisfulnesse conteneth many thinges, it were for to witen whether that alle thise thinges maken or conjoignen as a maner body of blisfulnesse, by dyversitee of parties or of membres; or elles, yif that any of alle thilke thinges be swich that it acomplisshe by himself the substaunce of blisfulnesse, so that alle thise othre thinges ben referred and brought to blisfulnesse, that is to seyn, as to the cheef of hem ✒ I wolde, quod I, that thou makedest me cleerly to understonde what thou seyst, & that thou recordedest me the forseyde thinges.

HAVE I nat juged, quod she, that blisfulnesse is good?✒ Yis, forsothe, quod I; and that soverein good.

ADDE thanne, quod she, thilke good, that is maked blisfulnesse, to alle the forseide thinges; for thilke same blisfulnesse that is demed to ben soverein suffisaunce, thilke selve is soverein power, soverein reverence, soverein cleernesse or noblesse, and soverein delyt. Conclusio. What seyst thou thanne of alle thise thinges, that is to seyn, suffisaunce, power, and thise othre thinges; ben they thanne as membres of blisfulnesse, or ben they referred and brought to soverein good, right as alle thinges that ben brought to the chief of hem?✒ I understonde wel; quod I, what thou purposest to seke; but I desire for to herkne that thou shewe it me.

TAK now thus the discrecioun of this questioun, quod she. Yif alle thise thinges, quod she, weren membres to felicitee, than weren they dyverse that oon from that other; and swich is the nature of parties or of membres, that dyverse membres compounen a body ✒ Certes, quod I, it hath wel ben shewed heerbiforn, that alle thise thinges ben alle o thing.

THANNE ben they none membres, quod she; for elles it sholde seme that blisfulnesse were conjoigned al of on membre allone; but that is a thing that may nat be don ✒ This thing, quod I, nis nat doutous; but I abyde to herknen the remnaunt of thy questioun.

THIS is open and cleer, quod she, that alle othre thinges ben referred & brought to good. For therefore is suffisaunce requered, for it is demed to ben good; and forthy is power requered, for men trowen also that it be good; & this same thing mowen we thinken & conjecten of reverence, and of noblesse, and of delyt.

Thanne is soverein good the somme and the cause of al that aughte ben desired; forwhy thilke thing that withholdeth no good in itself, ne semblaunce of good, it ne may nat wel in no manere be desired ne requered. And the contrarie: for thogh that thinges by hir nature ne ben nat goode, al-gates, yif men wene that ben goode, yit ben they desired as though that they weren verrayliche goode. And therfor is it that men oughten to wene by right, that boun-tee be the soverein fyn, and the cause of alle the thinges that ben to requeren. But certes, thilke that is cause for which men requeren any thing, it semeth that thilke same thing be most desired. As thus: yif that a wight wolde ryden for cause of hele, he ne desireth nat so mochel the moevinge to ryden, as the effect of his hele. Now thanne, sin that alle thinges ben requered for the grace of good, they ne ben nat de-sired of alle folk more thanne the same good. But we han graunted that blisful-nesse is that thing, for whiche that alle thise othre thinges ben desired; thanne is it thus: that, certes, only blisfulnesse is requered and desired. By whiche thing it sheweth cleerly, that of good and of blis-fulnesse is al oon & the same substaunce. ◆ I see nat, quod I, wherfore that men mighten discorden in this.

AND we han shewed that God & verray blisfulnesse is al oo thing ◆ That is sooth, quod I.

THANNE mowen we conclude siker-ly, that the substaunce of God is set in thilke same good, and in non other place.

Metre X.
Huc omnes pariter venite capti.

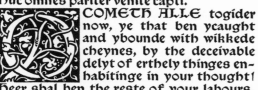COMETH ALLE togider now, ye that ben ycaught and ybounde with wikkede cheynes, by the deceivable delyt of erthely thinges en-habitinge in your thought! Heer shal ben the reste of your labours, heer is the havene stable in peysible quiete; this allone is the open refut to wrecches. Glosa. This is to seyn, that ye that ben combred and deceived with worldely affec-ciouns, cometh now to this soverein good, that is God, that is refut to hem that wolen comen to him. Textus. Alle the thinges that the river Tagus yeveth yow with his goldene gravailes, or elles alle the thinges that the river Hermus yeveth with his rede brinke, or that Indus yeveth, that is next the hote party of the world, that medleth the grene stones with the whyte, ne sholde nat cleeren the lookinge of your thought, but hyden rather your blinde corages with-

a a 2

in hir derknesse. Al that lyketh yow heer, and excyteth & moeveth your thoughtes, the erthe hath norisshed it in hise lowe caves. But the shyninge, by whiche the he-vene is governed and whennes he hath his strengthe, that eschueth the derke over-throwinge of the sowle; and whoso may knowen thilke light of blisfulnesse, he shal wel seyn, that the whyte bemes of the sonne ne ben nat cleer.

Prose XI.
Assentior, inquam.
Boece.

ASSENTE ME, quod I; for alle thise thinges ben strongly bounden with right ferme resouns ◆ Philosophie. How mochel wilt thou preysen it, quod she, yif that thou knowe what thilke good is? ◆ I wol preyse it, quod I, by prys with-outen ende, yif it shal bityde me to knowe also togider God that is good.

CERTES, quod she, that shal I do thee by verray resoun, yif that tho thinges that I have concluded a litel herbiforn dwellen only in hir first graunt-ing ◆ They dwellen graunted to thee, quod I; this is to seyn, as who seith: I graunte thy forseide conclusiouns.

HAVE I nat shewed thee, quod she, that the thinges that ben requered of many folkes ne ben nat verray goodes ne parfite, for they ben dyverse that oon fro that othre; and so as ech of hem is lakkinge to other, they ne han no power to bringen a good that is ful and absolut? But thanne at erst ben they verray good, whanne they ben gadered togider alle into o forme & into oon wirkinge, so that thilke thing that is suffisaunce, thilke same be power, and reverence, and noblesse, and mirthe; and forsothe, but yif alle thise thinges ben alle oon same thing, they ne han nat wherby that they mowen ben put in the noumber of thinges that oughten ben requered or desired ◆ It is shewed, quod I; ne herof may ther no man douten.

THE thinges thanne, quod she, that ne ben no goodes whanne they ben dyverse, & whan they biginnen to ben alle oon thing thanne ben they goodes, ne comth it hem nat thanne by the getinge of unitee, that they ben maked goodes? ◆ So it semeth, quod I.

BUT al thing that is good, quod she, grauntest thou that it be good by the participacioun of good or no? ◆ I graunte it, quod I.

355

THANNE most thou graunten, quod she, by semblable resoun, that oon and good be oo same thing. For of thinges, of whiche that the effect nis nat naturelly diverse, nedes the substance mot be oo same thing. I ne may nat denye that, quod I.

HAST thou nat knowen wel, quod she, that al thing that is hath so longe his dwellinge & his substaunce as longe as it is oon; but whan it forleteth to ben oon, it mot nedes dyen and corumpe togider? In which manere? quod I.

RIGHT as in bestes, quod she, whan the sowle and the body ben conjoigned in oon and dwellen togider, it is cleped a beest. And whan hir unitee is destroyed by the disseveraunce of that oon from that other, than sheweth it wel that it is a ded thing, & that it nis no lenger no beest. And the body of a wight, whyl it dwelleth in oo forme by conjunccioun of membres, it is wel seyn that it is a figure of mankinde. And yif the parties of the body ben so devyded and dissevered, that oon fro that other, that they destroyen unitee, the body forleteth to ben that it was biforn. And, whoso wolde renne in the same manere by alle thinges, he sholde seen that, withoute doute, every thing is in his substaunce as longe as it is oon; and whan it forleteth to ben oon, it dyeth and perissheth. Whan I considere, quod I, manye thinges, I see non other.

IS ther anything thanne, quod she, that, in as moche as it liveth naturelly, that forleteth the talent or appetyt of his beinge, and desireth to come to deeth and to corupcioun? Yif I considere, quod I, the beestes that han any maner nature of wilninge and of nillinge, I ne finde no beest, but yif it be constreined fro withoute forth, that forleteth or despyseth the entencioun to liven and to duren, or that wole, his thankes, hasten him to dyen. For every beest travaileth him to deffende and kepe the savacioun of his lyf, and eschueth deeth and destruccioun. But certes, I doute me of herbes and of trees, that is to seyn, that I am in a doute of swiche thinges as herbes or trees, that ne han no felinge sowles, ne no naturel wirkinges servinge to appetytes as bestes han, whether they han appetyt to dwellen and to duren.

CERTES, quod she, ne therof thar thee nat doute. Now loke upon thise herbes and thise trees; they wexen first in swiche places as ben covenable to hem, in whiche places they ne mowen nat sone dyen ne dryen, as longe as hir nature may deffenden hem. For som of hem waxen in feeldes, and som in mountaignes, and

othre waxen in mareys, and othre cleven on roches, and somme waxen plentivous in sondes; & yif that any wight enforce him to beren hem into othre places, they wexen drye. For nature yeveth to every thing that that is convenient to him, and travaileth that they ne dye nat, as longe as they han power to dwellen & to liven. What woltow seyn of this, that they drawen alle hir norisshinges by hir rotes, right as they hadden hir mouthes yplounged within the erthes, and sheden by hir maryes hir wode and hir bark? And what woltow seyn of this, that thilke thing that is right softe, as the marye is, that is alwey hid in the sete, al withinne, and that is defended fro withoute by the stedefastnesse of wode? and that the uttereste bark is put ayeins the destemperaunce of the hevene, as a defendour mighty to suffren harm? And thus, certes, maystow wel seen how greet is the diligence of nature; for alle thinges renovelen and puplisshen hem with seed ymultiplyed; ne ther nis no man that ne wot wel that they ne ben right as a foundement and edifice, for to duren nat only for a tyme, but right as for to duren perdurably by generacioun. And the thinges eek that men wenen ne haven none sowles, ne desire they nat ech of hem by semblable resoun to kepen that is hirs, that is to seyn, that is acordinge to hir nature in conservacioun of hir beinge & enduringe? For wher for elles bereth lightnesse the flaumbes up, and the weighte presseth the erthe adoun, but for as moche as thilke places and thilke moevinges ben covenable to everich of hem? And forsothe every thing kepeth thilke that is acordinge & propre to him, right as thinges that ben contraries and enemys corompen hem. And yit the harde thinges, as stones, clyven & holden hir parties togider right faste and harde, and deffenden hem in withstondinge that they ne departe nat lightly atwinne. And the thinges that ben softe and fletinge, as is water and eyr, they departen lightly, and yeven place to hem that breken or devyden hem; but natheles, they retornen sone ayein into the same thinges fro whennes they ben arraced. But fyr fleeth & refuseth al devisioun. Ne I ne trete nat heer now of wilful moevinges of the sowle that is knowinge, but of the naturel entencioun of thinges, as thus: right as we swolwe the mete that we receiven and ne thinke nat on it, and as we drawen our breeth in slepinge that we wite it nat whyle we slepen. For certes, in the beestes, the love of hir livinges ne of hir beinges ne comth nat of the wilninges of the sowle, but of the biginninges of nature. For certes, thurgh constreininge causes, wil desireth & embraceth ful ofte tyme the deeth that nature dredeth; that is to seyn as thus: that a man may ben constreyned so, by som cause, that his wil desireth and taketh the deeth which that nature hateth & dredeth ful sore. And somtyme we seeth the contrarye, as thus: that the wil of a wight destorbeth & constreyneth that that nature desireth & requereth alwey, that is to seyn, the werk of generacioun, by the whiche generacioun only dwelleth and is sustened the long durabletee of mortal thinges.

AND thus this charitee and this love, that every thing hath to himself, ne comth nat of the moevinge of the sowle, but of the entencioun of nature. for the purviaunce of God hath yeven to thinges that ben creat of him this, that is a ful gret cause to liven and to duren; for which they desiren naturelly hir lyf as longe as ever they mowen. for which thou mayst nat drede, by no manere, that alle the thinges that ben anywhere, that they ne requeren naturelly the ferme stablenesse of perdurable dwellinge, and eek the eschuinge of destruccioun ✒ Boece. Now confesse I wel, quod I, that I see now wel certeinly, withoute doutes, the thinges that whylom semeden uncertain to me.

BUT, quod she, thilke thing that desireth to be and to dwellen perdurably, he desireth to ben oon; for yif that that oon were destroyed, certes, beinge ne shulde ther non dwellen to no wight.✒That is sooth, quod I.✒Thanne, quod she, desiren alle thinges oon?✒I assente, quod I.✒And I have shewed, quod she, that thilke same oon is thilke that is good.✒Ye, for sothe, quod I.

ALLE thinges thanne, quod she, requiren good; & thilke good thanne mayst thou descryven right thus: good is thilke thing that every wight desireth.

THER ne may be thought, quod I, no more verray thing. for either alle thinges ben referred & brought to nought, & floteren withoute governour, despoiled of oon as of hir propre heved; or elles, yif ther be any thing to which that alle thinges tenden and hyen, that thing moste ben the sovereingood of alle goodes.

THANNE seyde she thus: O my nory, quod she, I have gret gladnesse of thee; for thou hast ficched in thyn herte the middel soothfastnesse, that is to seyn, the prikke; but this thing hath ben descovered to thee, in that thou seydest that thou wistest nat a litel herbiforn. ✒What was that? quod I.

THAT thou ne wistest nat, quod she, which was the ende of thinges; and certes, that is the thing that every

a a 3

wight desireth; and for as mochel as we han gadered and comprehended that good is thilke thing that is desired of alle, thanne moten we nedes confessen, that good is the fyn of alle thinges.

Metre XI.
Quisquis profunda mente vestigat verum.

WHOSO that seketh sooth by a deep thoght, and coveiteth nat to ben deceived by no misweyes, lat him rollen and trenden withinne himself the light of his inward sighte; & lat him gadere ayein, enclyninge into a compas, the longe moevinges of his thoughtes; and lat him techen his corage that he hath enclosed and hid in his tresors, al that he compasseth or seketh fro withoute. And thanne thilke thinge, that the blake cloude of errour whylom hadde ycovered, shal lighten more cleerly thanne Phebus himself ne shyneth.

Glosa.

WHOSO WOLE seken the deep grounde of sooth in his thought, and wol nat be deceived by false proposiciouns that goon amis fro the trouthe, lat him wel examine and rolle withinne himself the nature and the propretees of the thing; and lat him yit eftsones examine and rollen his thoughtes by good deliberacioun, or that he deme; and lat him techen his sowle that it hath, by natural principles kindeliche yhid within itself, alle the trouthe the whiche he imagineth to ben in thinges withoute. And thanne alle the derknesse of his misknowinge shal seme more evidently to sighte of his understondinge thanne the sonne ne semeth to sighte withouteforth.

FOR certes the body, bringinge the weighte of foryetinge, ne hath nat chased out of your thoughte al the cleernesse of your knowinge; for certeinly the seed of sooth haldeth & clyveth within your corage, and it is awaked and excyted by the winde & by the blastes of doctrine. for wherfor elles demen ye of your owne wil the rightes, whan ye ben axed, but yif so were that the norisshinge of resoun ne livede yplounged in the depthe of your herte? this is to seyn, how sholden men demen the sooth of any thing that were axed, yif ther nere a rote of soothfastnesse that were yplounged & hid in naturel principles, the whiche soothfastnesse lived within the deepnesse of the thought. And yif so be that the Muse and the doctrine of Plato singeth sooth, al that every wight lerneth, he ne doth nothing elles thanne but recordeth, as men recorden thinges that ben foryeten.

357

Prose XII.
Tum ego, Platoni, inquam.

THANNE seide I thus: I acorde me gretly to Plato, for thou remembrest & recordest me thise thinges yit the secounde tyme; that is to seyn, first whan I loste my memorie by the contagious conjunccioun of the body with the sowle; & eftsones afterward, whan I loste it, confounded by the charge and by the burdene of my sorwe.

AND thanne seide she thus: yif thou loke, quod she, first the thinges that thou hast graunted, it ne shal nat ben right fer that thou ne shalt remembren thilke thing that thou seydest that thou nistest nat. What thing? quod I. By whiche governement, quod she, that this world is governed. Me remembreth it wel, quod I; and I confesse wel that I ne wiste it naught. But albeit so that I see now from afer what thou purposest, algates, I desire yit to herkene it of thee more pleynly. Thou wendest nat, quod she, a litel herbiforn, that men sholden doute that this world nis governed by God.

CERTES, quod I, ne yit ne doute I it naught, ne I nel never wene that it were to doute; as who seith, but I wot wel that God governeth this world; & I shal shortly answeren thee by what resouns I am brought to this. This world, quod I, of so manye dyverse & contrarious parties, ne mighte never han ben assembled in o forme, but yif ther nere oon that conjoignede so manye dyverse thinges; and the same dyversitee of hir natures, that so discorden that oon fro that other, moste departen and unjoignen the thinges that ben conjoigned, yif ther ne were oon that contenede that he hath conjoined and ybounde. Ne the certein ordre of nature ne sholde nat bringe forth so ordenee moevinges, by places, by tymes, by doinges, by spaces, by qualitees, yif ther ne were oon that were ay stedefast dwellinge, that ordeynede and disponede thise dyversitees of moevinges. And thilke thing, whatsoever it be, by which that alle thinges ben ymaked and ylad, I clepe him God; that is a word that is used to alle folk.

THANNE seyde she: sin thou felest thus thise thinges, quod she, I trowe that I have litel more to done that thou, mighty of welefulnesse, hool and sounde, ne see eftsones thy contree. But lat us loken the thinges that we han purposed herbiforn. Have I nat noumbred and

358

seyd, quod she, that suffisaunce is in blisfulnesse, and we han acorded that God is thilke same blisfulnesse? Yis, forsothe, quod I. And that, to governe this world, quod she, ne shal he never han nede of non help fro withoute? for elles, yif he hadde nede of any help, he ne sholde nat have no ful suffisaunce? Yis, thus it mot nedes be, quod I. Thanne ordeineth he by himself alone alle thinges? quod she. That may nat be deneyed, quod I. And I have shewed that God is the same good? It remembreth me wel, quod I.

THANNE ordeineth he alle thinges by thilke good, quod she; sin he, which that we han acorded to be good, governeth alle thinges by himself; and he is as a keye & a stere by which that the edifice of this world is ykept stable & withoute coroumpinge.

I ACORDE me greetly, quod I; and I aperceivede a litel herbiforn that thou woldest seye thus; albeit so that it were by a thinne suspecioun.

I TROWE it wel, quod she; for, as I trowe, thou ledest now more ententifly thyne eyen to loken the verray goodes. But natheles the thing that I shal telle thee yit ne sheweth nat lasse to loken. What is that? quod I.

SO as men trowen, quod she, and that rightfully, that God governeth alle thinges by the keye of his goodnesse, & alle thise same thinges, as I have taught thee, hasten hem by naturel entencioun to comen to good: ther may no man douten that they ne be governed voluntariely, and that they ne converten hem of hir owne wil to the wil of hir ordenour, as they that ben acordinge and enclyninge to hir governour and hir king. It mot nedes be so, quod I; for the reaume ne sholde nat semen blisful yif ther were a yok of misdrawinges in dyverse parties; ne the savinge of obedient thinges ne sholde nat be. Thanne is ther nothing, quod she, that kepeth his nature, that enforceth him to goon ayein God? No, quod I.

AND yif that anything enforcede him to withstonde God, mighte it availen at the laste ayeins him, that we han graunted to ben almighty by the right of blisfulnesse? Certes, quod I, al outrely it ne mighte nat availen him. Thanne is ther nothing, quod she, that either wole or may withstonden to this soverein good? I trowe nat, quod I. Thanne is thilke the soverein good, quod she, that alle thinges governeth strongly, and ordeyneth hem softely.

THANNE seyde I thus: I delyte me, quod I, nat only in the endes or in the somme of the resouns that thou hast concluded and proeved, but thilke wordes that thou usest delyten me moche more; so, at the laste, fooles that sumtyme renden grete thinges oughten ben ashamed of hemself; that is to seyn, that we fooles that reprehenden wikkedly the thinges that touchen Goddes governaunce, we oughten ben ashamed of ourself: as I, that seyde that God refuseth only the werkes of men, and ne entremeteth nat of hem.

ÞOU hast wel herd, quod she, the fables of the poetes, how the giaunts assaileden the hevene with the goddes; but forsothe, the debonair force of God deposede hem, as it was worthy; that is to seyn, destroyede the giaunts, as it was worthy. But wilt thou that we joignen togider thilke same resouns? for peraventure, of swich conjuncioun may sterten up som fair sparkle of sooth. Do, quod I, as thee liste. Wenest thou, quod she, that God ne be almighty? No man is in doute of it. Certes, quod I, no wight ne douteth it, yif he be in his minde. But he, quod she, that is almighty, ther nis nothing that he ne may. That is sooth, quod I. May God don yvel? quod she. Nay, forsothe, quod I. Thanne is yvel nothing, quod she, sin that he ne may nat don yvel that may don alle thinges.

SCORNEST thou me? quod I; or elles pleyest thou or deceivest thou me, that hast so woven me with thy resouns the hous of Dedalus, so entrelaced that it is unable to be unlaced; thou that otherwhyle entrest ther thou issest, and otherwhyle issest ther thou entrest, ne foldest thou nat togider, by replicacioun of wordes, a maner wonderful cercle or environinge of the simplicitee devyne? for certes, a litel herbiform, whan thou bigunne at blisfulnesse, thou seydest that it is sovereyn good; and seydest that it is set in sovereyn God; and seydest that God himself is sovereyn good; and that God is the fulle blisfulnesse; for which thou yave me as a covenable yift, that is to seyn, that no wight nis blisful but yif he be God also therwith. And seidest eek, that the forme of good is the substaunce of God and of blisfulnesse; & seidest, that thilke same oon is thilke same good, that is requered & desired of alle the kinde of thinges. And thou proevedest, in disputinge, that God governeth alle the thinges of the world by the governements of bountee, and seydest, that alle thinges wolen obeyen to him; and seydest, that the nature of yvel nis nothing. And thise thinges ne shewedest thou nat with none resouns ytaken fro withoute, but by proeves in cercles & boomlich knowen; the whiche proeves drawen to hemself hir feith and hir acord, everich of

aa4

hem of other.

ÞANNE seyde she thus: I ne scorne thee nat, ne pleye, ne deceive thee; but I have shewed thee the thing that is grettest over alle thinges by the yift of God, that we whylom preyeden. for this is the forme of the devyne substaunce, that is swich that it ne slydeth nat into outterest foreine thinges, ne ne receiveth no straunge thinges in him; but right as Parmenides seyde in Greek of thilke devyne substaunce; he seyde thus: that Thilke devyne substaunce torneth the world and the moevable cercle of thinges, whyl thilke devyne substaunce kepeth itself withoute moevinge; that is to seyn, that it ne moeveth nevermo, and yit it moeveth alle othre thinges. But natheles, yif I have stired resouns that ne ben nat taken fro withoute the compas of thing of which we treten, but resouns that ben bistowed within that compas, ther nis nat why that thou sholdest merveilen; sin thou hast lerned by the sentence of Plato, that Nedes the wordes moten be cosines to the thinges of which they speken.

Metre XII.
Felix, qui potuit boni.

BLISFUL is that man that may seen the clere welle of good; blisful is he that may unbinden him fro the bondes of the hevy erthe. The poete of Trace, Orpheus, that whylom hadde right greet sorwe for the deeth of his wyf, after that he hadde maked, by his weeply songes, the wodes, moevable, to rennen; and hadde maked the riveres to stonden stille; & hadde maked the hertes and the hindes to joignen, dredeles, hir sydes to cruel lyouns, for to herknen his songe; & hadde maked that the hare was nat agast of the hounde, which that was plesed by his songe: so, whan the moste ardaunt love of his wif brende the entrailes of his brest, ne the songes that hadden overcomen alle thinges ne mighten nat asswagen hir lord Orpheus, he pleynede him of the hevene goddes that weren cruel to him; he went him to the houses of helle. And there he temprede hise blaundisshinge songes by resowninge strenges, and spak and song in wepinge al that ever he hadde received and laved out of the noble welles of his moder Calliope the goddesse; and he song with as mochel as he mighte of wepinge, and with as moche as love, that doublede his sorwe, mighte yeve him and techen him; and he commoevede the helle, & requerede & bisoughte by swete preyere the lordes of sowles in helle, of relesinge; that is to seyn, to yilden him his wyf.

359

CERBERUS, the porter of helle, with his three hevedes, was caught and al abayst for the newe song; and the three goddesses, Furies, and vengeresses of felonyes, that tormenten and agasten the sowles by anoy, woxen sorwful and sory, & wepen teres for pitee. Tho ne was nat the heved of Ixion ytormented by the overthrowinge wheel; and Tantalus, that was destroyed by the woodnesse of longe thurst, despyseth the flodes to drinke; the fowl that highte voltor, that eteth the stomak or the giser of Tityus, is so fulfild of his song that it nil eten ne tyren no more. At the laste the lord and juge of sowles was moeved to misericordes and cryde, We ben overcomen, quod he; yive we to Orpheus his wyf to bere him companye; he hath wel ybought hir by his song and his ditee; but we wol putte a lawe in this, and covenaunt in the yifte: that is to seyn, that, til he be out of helle, yif he loke behinde him, that his wyf shal comen ayein unto us.

BUT what is he that may yive a lawe to loveres? Love is a gretter lawe and a strenger to himself than any lawe that men may yeven. Allas! whan Orpheus and his wyf weren almost at the termes of the night, that is to seyn, at the laste boundes of helle, Orpheus lokede abakward on Eurydice his wyf, and loste hir, and was deed.

THIS fable aperteineth to yow alle, whosoever desireth or seketh to lede his thought into the soverein day, that is to seyn, the cleernesse of soverein good. For whoso that ever be so overcomen that he ficche his eyen into the putte of helle, that is to seyn, whoso sette his thoughtes in erthely thinges, al that ever he hath drawen of the noble good celestial, he leseth it whan he loketh the helles, that is to seyn, into lowe thinges of the erthe. Explicit Liber tercius.

DE CONSOLATIONE PHILOSOPHIE. ❧ BOOK IV. PROSE I. ❧

Hec cum Philosophia, dignitate vultus.

WHAN PHILOSOPHYE hadde songen softely and delitably the forseide thinges, kepinge the dignitee of hir chere and the weighte of hir wordes, I thanne, that ne hadde nat al outerly foryeten the wepinge and the mourninge that was set in myn herte, forbrak the entencioun of hir that entendede yit to seyn some othre thinges. O, quod I, thou that art gyderesse of verrey light; the thinges that thou hast seid me hiderto ben so clere to me and so shewinge by the devyne lookinge of hem, & by thy resouns, that they ne mowen ben overcomen. And thilke thinges that thou toldest me, albeit so that I hadde whylom foryeten hem, for the sorwe of the wrong that hath ben don to me, yit natheles they ne weren nat al outrely unknowen to me. But this same is, namely, a right greet cause of my sorwe, so as the governour of thinges is good, yif that yveles mowen ben by any weyes; or elles yif that yveles passen withoute punisshinge. The whiche thing only, how worthy it is to ben wondred upon, thou considerest it wel thyself certeinly. But yit to this thing ther is yit another thing yjoigned, more to ben wondred upon. For felonye is emperesse, and floureth ful of richesses; and vertu nis nat alonly withoute medes, but it is cast under & fortroden under the feet of felonous folk; and it abyeth the torments in stede of wikkede felounes. Of alle whiche thinges ther nis no wight that may merveylen ynough, ne compleine, that swiche thinges ben doon in the regne of God, that alle thinges woot & alle thinges may, and ne wole nat but only gode thinges.

THANNE seyde she thus: Certes, quod she, that were a greet merveyle, & an enbasshinge withouten ende, and wel more horrible than alle monstres, yif it were as thou wenest; that is to seyn, that in the right ordenee hous of so mochel a fader & an ordenour of meynee, that the vesseles that ben foule and vyle sholden ben honoured and heried, and the precious vesseles sholden ben defouled & vyle; but it nis nat so. For yif tho thinges that I have concluded a litel herbiforn ben kept hole & unraced, thou shalt wel knowe by the autoritee of God, of the whos regne I speke, that certes the gode folk ben alwey mighty, and shrewes ben alwey outcast and feble; ne the vyces ne ben nevermo withoute peyne, ne the vertues ne ben nat withoute mede; & that blisfulnesses comen alwey to goode folk, and infortune comth alwey to wikked folk. And thou shalt wel knowe many thinges of this kinde, that shollen cesen thy pleintes, and strengthen thee with stedefast sadnesse. And for thou hast seyn the forme of the verray blisfulnesse by me, that have whylom shewed it thee, and thou hast knowen in whom blisfulnesse is yset, alle thinges ytreted that I trowe ben necessarie to putten forth, I shal shewe thee the wey that shal bringen thee ayein unto thyn hous. And I shal ficchen fetheres in thy thought, by whiche it may arysen in heighte, so that, alle tribulacioun ydon awey, thou, by my gydinge and by my path & by my sledes, shalt mowe retorne hool and sound into thy contree.

Metre I.
Sunt etenim pennae volucres mihi.

I HAVE, forsothe, swifte fetheres that surmounten the heighte of hevene. Whan the swifte thought hath clothed itself in tho fetheres, it despyseth the hateful erthes, and surmounteth the roundnesse of the grete ayr; and it seeth the cloudes behinde his bak; and passeth the heighte of the region of the fyr, that eschaufeth by the swifte moevinge of the firmament, til that he areyseth him into the houses that beren the sterres, & joyneth his weyes with the sonne Phebus, and felawshipeth the wey of the olde colde Saturnus; & he ymaked a knight of the clere sterre; that is to seyn, that the thought is maked Goddes knight by the sekinge of trouthe to comen to the verray knowleche of God. And thilke thoght renneth by the cercle of the sterres, in alle places theras the shyninge night is peinted; that is to seyn, the night that is cloudeles; for on nightes that ben cloudeles it semeth as the hevene were peinted with dyverse images of sterres. And whanne he hath ydoon ther ynough, he shal forleten the laste hevene, and he shal pressen & wenden on the bak of the swifte firmament, and he shal ben maked parfit of the worshipful light of God. Ther halt the lord of kinges the ceptre of his might, and atempreth the governements of the world, and the shyninge juge of thinges, stable in himself, governeth the swifte cart or wayn, that is to seyn, the circuler moevinge of the sonne. And yif thy wey ledeth thee ayein so that thou be brought thider, thanne wolt thou seye now that that is the contree that thou requerest, of which thou ne haddest no minde: But now it remembreth me wel, heer was I born, heer wol I fastne my degree, heer wole I dwelle. But yif thee lyketh thanne to loken on the derknesse of the erthe that thou hast forleten, thanne shalt thou seen that thise felonous tyraunts, that the wrecchede peple dredeth, now shollen ben exyled fro thilke fayre contree.

Prose II.
Tum ego, Papae, inquam.

THAN seyde I thus: Owh! I wondre me that thou bihetest me so grete thinges; ne I ne doute nat that thou ne mayst wel performe that thou bihetest. But I preye thee only this, that thou ne tarye nat to telle me thilke thinges that thou hast moeved.

FIRST, quod she, thou most nedes knowen, that goode folk ben alwey stronge & mighty, & the shrewes ben feble and desert and naked of alle strengthes. And of thise thinges, certes, everich of hem is declared and shewed by other. For so as good and yvel ben two contraries, yif so be that good be stedefast, than sheweth the feblesse of yvel al openly; & yif thou knowe cleerly the frelesnesse of yvel, the stedefastnesse of good is knowen. But for as moche as the fey of my sentence shal be the more ferme and habboundaunt, I will gon by that oo wey and by that other; and I wole conferme the thinges that ben purposed, now on this syde and now on that syde. Two thinges ther ben in whiche the effect of alle the dedes of mankinde standeth, that is to seyn, wil and power; and yif that oon of thise two fayleth, ther nis nothing that may be don. For yif that wil lakketh, ther nis no wight that undertaketh to don that he wol nat don; and yif power fayleth, the wil nis but in ydel and stant for naught. And therof cometh it, that yif thou see a wight that wolde geten that he may nat geten, thou mayst nat douten that power ne fayleth him to haven that he wolde. This is open and cleer, quod I; ne it may nat ben deneyed in no manere. And yif thou see a wight, quod she, that hath doon that he wolde doon, thou nilt nat douten that he ne hath had power to don it? No, quod I. And in that that every wight may, in that men may holden him mighty; as who seyth, in so moche as man is mighty to don a thing, in so mochel men halt him mighty; and in that that he ne may, in that men demen him to be feble. I confesse it wel, quod I. Remembreth thee, quod she, that I have gadered & shewed by forseyde resouns that al the entencioun of the wil of mankinde, which that is lad by dyverse studies, hasteth to comen to blisfulnesse? It remembreth me wel, quod I, that it hath ben shewed. And recordeth thee nat thanne, quod she, that blisfulnesse is thilke same good that men requeren; so

361

that, whan that blisfulnesse is requered of alle, that good also is requered and desired of alle? ℗ It ne recordeth me nat, quod I; for I have it gretly alwey ficched in my memorie. ℘ Alle folk thanne, quod she, goode and eek badde, enforcen hem withoute difference of entencioun to comen to good? ℘ This is a verray consequence, quod I. ℘ And certein is, quod she, that by the getinge of good ben men ymaked goode? ℗ This is certein, quod I. ℘ Thanne geten goode men that they desiren? ℘ So semeth it, quod I. ℘ But wikkede folk, quod she, yif they geten the good that they desiren, they ne mowe nat be wikkede? ℘ So is it, quod I.

THANNE, so as that oon and that other, quod she, desiren good; and the goode folk geten good, & nat the wikke folk; thanne nis it no doute that the goode folk ne ben mighty & the wikkede folk ben feble? ℘ Whoso that ever, quod I, douteth of this, he ne may nat considere the nature of thinges ne the consequence of resouns.

AND over this, quod she, yif that ther be two thinges that han oo same purpose by kinde, and that oon of hem pursueth & parformeth thilke same thing by naturel office, and that other ne may nat doon thilke naturel office, but folweth, by other manere thanne is convenable to nature, him that acomplissheth his purpos kindely, and yit he ne acomplissheth nat his owne purpos: whether of thise two demestow for more mighty? ℘ Yif that I conjecte, quod I, that thou wolt seye, algates yit I desire to herkne it more pleynly of thee. ℗ Thou wilt nat thanne deneye, quod she, that the moevement of goinge nis in men by kinde? ℘ No, forsothe, quod I. ℗ Ne thou ne doutest nat, quod she, that thilke naturel office of goinge ne be the office of feet? ℗ I ne doute it nat, quod I.

THANNE, quod she, yif that a wight be mighty to moeve and goth upon his feet, and another, to whom thilke naturel office of feet lakketh, enforceth him to gon crepinge upon his handes: whiche of thise two oughte to ben holden the more mighty by right?

KNIT forth the remenaunt, quod I; for no wight ne douteth that he that may gon by naturel office of feet ne be more mighty than he that ne may nat.

BUT the soverein good, quod she, that is eveneliche purposed to the gode folk & to badde, the gode folk seken it by naturel office of vertues, & the shrewes enforcen hem to geten it by dyverse coveityse of erthely thinges, which that nis no naturel office to geten thilke same soverein good. Trowestow that it be any other

362

wyse?

NAY, quod I; for the consequence is open and shewinge of thinges that I have graunted; that nedes gode folk moten ben mighty, and shrewes feeble and unmighty.

THOU rennest aright biforn me, quod she, and this is the jugement; that is to seyn, I juge of thee right as thise leches ben wont to hopen of syke folk, whan they aperceyven that nature is redressed and withstondeth to the maladye. But, for I see thee now al redy to the understondinge, I shal shewe thee more thikke & continuel resouns. For loke now how greetly sheweth the feblesse and infirmitee of wikkede folk, that ne mowen nat comen to that hir naturel entencioun ledeth hem, and yit almost thilke naturel entencioun constreineth hem. And what were to demen thanne of shrewes, yif thilke naturel help hadde forleten hem, the which naturel help of intencioun goth awey biforn hem, and is so greet that unnethe it may ben overcome? Consider thanne how greet defaute of power and how greet feblesse ther is in wikkede felonous folk; as who seyth, the gretter thing that is coveited and the desire nat acomplisshed, of the lasse might is he that coveiteth it and may nat acomplisshe. And forthy Philosophie seyth thus by soverein good: Ne shrewes ne requeren nat lighte medes ne veyne games, whiche they ne may folwen ne holden; but they failen of thilke somme and of the heighte of thinges, that is to seyn, soverein good; ne thise wrecches ne comen nat to the effect of soverein good, the which they enforcen hem only to geten, by nightes and by dayes; in the getinge of which good the strengthe of good folk is ful wel ysene. For right so as thou mightest demen him mighty of goinge, that gooth on his feet til he mighte come to thilke place, fro the whiche place ther ne laye no wey forther to ben gon; right so most thou nedes demen him for right mighty, that geteth & ateyneth to the ende of alle thinges that ben to desire, biyonde the whiche ende ther nis nothing to desire. Of the which power of good folk men may conclude, that the wikked men semen to be bareine & naked of alle strengthe. Forwhy forleten they vertues & folwen vyces? Nis it nat for that they ne knowen nat the goodes? But what thing is more feble and more caitif thanne is the blindnesse of ignoraunce? Or elles they knowen ful wel whiche thinges that they oughten folwe, but lecherye and coveityse overthroweth hem mistorned; and certes, so doth distemperaunce to feble men, that ne mowen nat wrastlen ayeins the vyces. Ne knowen

they nat thanne wel that they forleten the
good wilfully, and tornen hem wilfully to
vyces? And in this wyse they ne forleten
nat only to ben mighty, but they forleten
al outrely in any wyse for to ben. For they
that forleten the comune fyn of alle thinges
that ben, they forleten also therwithal for
to ben.

AND peraventure it sholde semen to
som folk that this were a merveile to
seyen: that shrewes, whiche that contienen the more partye of men, ne ben nat ne
han no beinge; but natheles, it is so, & thus
stant this thing. For they that ben shrewes, I deneye nat that they ben shrewes;
but I deneye, and seye simpely & pleinly,
that they ne ben nat, ne han no beinge. For
right as thou mightest seyen of the ca-
rayne of a man, that it were a deed man, but
thou ne mightest nat simpely callen it a
man; so graunte I wel forsothe, that vicious folk ben wikked, but I ne may nat
graunten absolutly and simpely that they
ben. For thilke thing that withholdeth ordre and kepeth nature, thilke thing is and
hath beinge; but what thing that faileth
of that, that is to seyn, that he forleteth
naturel ordre, he forleteth thilke thing that
is set in his nature. But thou wolt seyn,
that shrewes mowen. Certes, that ne deneye I nat; but certes, hir power ne descendeth nat of strengthe, but of feblesse.
For they mowen don wikkednesses; the
whiche they ne mighte nat don, yif they
mighten dwellen in the forme & in the doinge of good folk. And thilke power sheweth ful evidently that they ne mowen right
naught. For so as I have gadered & proeved
a litel herbiforn, that yvel is naught; and
so as shrewes mowen only but shrewednesses, this conclusioun is al cleer, that
shrewes ne mowen right naught, ne han
no power. And for as moche as thou understonde which is the strengthe of this
power of shrewes, I have definisshed a litel
herbiforn, that nothing is so mighty as
soverein good. That is sooth, quod I.
And thilke same soverein good may don
non yvel? Certes, no, quod I. Is ther
any wight thanne, quod she, that weneth
that men mowen doon alle thinges? No
man, quod I, but yif he be out of his witte.
But, certes, shrewes mowen don yvel,
quod she. Ye, wolde God, quod I, that
they mighten don non!

THANNE, quod she, so as he that
is mighty to doon only but goode
thinges may don alle thinges; and
they that ben mighty to don yvele thinges
ne mowen nat alle thinges: thanne is it
open thing and manifest, that they that
mowen don yvel ben of lasse power. And
yit, to proeve this conclusioun, ther helpeth me this, that I have yshewed herbiforn,
that alle power is to be noumbred among
thinges that men oughten requere. And I
have shewed that alle thinges, that ought-
en ben desired, ben referred to good, right
as to a maner heighte of hir nature. But
for to mowen don yvel and felonye ne may
nat ben referred to good. Thanne nis nat
yvel of the noumbir of thinges that oughte
ben desired. But alle power oughte ben desired & requered. Than is it open and cleer
that the power ne the mowinge of shrewes
nis no power; and of alle thise thinges it
sheweth wel, that the goode folke ben certeinly mighty, and the shrewes douteles
ben unmighty. And it is cleer and open
that thilke opinioun of Plato is verray and
sooth, that seith, that only wyse men may
doon that they desiren; & shrewes mowen
haunten that hem lyketh, but that they
desiren, that is to seyn, to comen to sovereign good, they ne han no power to acom-
plisshen that. For shrewes don that hem
list, whan, by tho thinges in which they delyten, they wenen to ateine to thilke good
that they desiren; but they ne geten ne
ateinen nat therto, for vyces ne comen nat
to blisfulnesse.

Metre II.
Quos vides sedere celsos.

WHOSO THAT the cover-
toures of hir veyne apa-
railes mighte strepen of
thise proude kinges, that
thou seest sitten on heigh
in hir chaires gliteringe in
shyninge purpre, envirouned with sorwful armures, manasinge with cruel mouth,
blowinge by woodnesse of herte, he shulde
seen thanne that thilke lordes beren withinne hir corages ful streite cheines. For
lecherye tormenteth hem in that oon syde
with gredy venims; and troublable ire,
that araiseth in him the flodes of troub-
linges, tormenteth upon that other syde
hir thought; or sorwe halt hem wery and
ycaught; or slydinge and deceivinge hope
tormenteth hem. And therfore, sen thou
seest oon heed, that is to seyn, oon tyraunt, beren so manye tyrannyes, thanne
ne doth thilke tyraunt nat that he desireth, sin he is cast doun with so manye wikkede lordes; that is to seyn, with so manye
vyces, that han so wikkedly lordshipes
over him.

Prose III.
Videsne igitur quanto in coeno.

EESTOW NAT thanne in how grete filthe thise shrewes ben ywrapped, and with which cleernesse thise good folk shynen? In this sheweth it wel, that to goode folk ne lakketh nevermo hir medes, ne shrewes lakken nevermo torments. For of alle thinges that ben ydoon, thilke thing, for which anything is don, it semeth as by right that thilke thing be the mede of that; as thus: yif a man renneth in the stadie, or in the forlong, for the corone, thanne lyth the mede in the corone for which he renneth. And I have shewed that blisfulnesse is thilke same good for which that alle thinges ben doon. Thanne is thilke same good purposed to the workes of mankinde right as a comune mede; which mede ne may ben dissevered fro good folk. For no wight as by right, fro thennesforth that him lakketh goodnesse, ne shal ben cleped good. For which thing, folk of goode maneres, hir medes ne forsaken hem nevermo. For albeit so that shrewes wexen as wode as hem list ayeins goode folk, yit neverthelesse the corone of wyse men shal nat fallen ne faden. For foreine shrewednesse ne binimeth nat fro the corages of goode folk hir propre honour. But yif that any wight rejoyse him of goodnesse that he hadde take fro withoute (as who seith, yif that any wight hadde his goodnesse of any other man than of himself), certes, he that yaf him thilke goodnesse, or elles som other wight, mighte binime it him. But for as moche as to every wight his owne propre bountee yeveth him his mede, thanne at erst shal he failen of mede whan he forleteth to ben good. And at the laste, so as alle medes ben requered for men wenen that they ben goode, who is he that wolde deme, that he that is right mighty of good were partles of mede? And of what mede shal he be guerdoned? Certes, of right faire mede and right grete aboven alle medes. Remembre thee of thilke noble corolarie that I yaf thee a litel herbiforn; and gader it togider in this manere: so as good himself is blisfulnesse, thanne is it cleer and certein, that alle good folk ben maked blisful for they ben goode; & thilke folk that ben blisful, it acordeth and is covenable to ben goddes. Thanne is the mede of goode folk swich that no day shal enpeiren it, ne no wikkednesse ne shal derken it, ne power of no wight ne shal nat amenusen it, that is to seyn, to ben maked goddes.

364

AND sin it is thus, that goode men ne failen nevermo of hir mede, certes, no wys man ne may doute of undepartable peyne of the shrewes; that is to seyn, that the peyne of shrewes ne departeth nat from hemself nevermo. For so as goode and yvel, and peyne and medes ben contrarye, it mot nedes ben, that right as we seen bityden in guerdoun of goode, that also mot the peyne of yvel answery, by the contrarye party, to shrewes. Now thanne, so as bountee and prowesse ben the mede to goode folk, also is shrewednesse itself torment to shrewes. Thanne, whoso that ever is entecched and defouled with peyne, he ne douteth nat, that he is entecched & defouled with yvel. Yif shrewes thanne wolen preysen hemself, may it semen to hem that they ben withouten party of torment, sin they ben swiche that the uttereste wikkednesse (that is to seyn, wikkede thewes, which that is the uttereste & the worste kinde of shrewednesse) ne defouleth ne enteccheth nat hem only, but infecteth & envenimeth hem gretly? And also look on shrewes, that ben the contrarie party of goode men, how greet peyne felawshipeth & folweth hem! for thou hast lerned a litel herbiforn, that al thing that is & hath beinge is oon, and thilke same oon is good; thanne is this the consequence, that it semeth wel, that al that is & hath beinge is good; this is to seyn, as who seyth, that beinge and unitee and goodnesse is al oon. And in this manere it folweth thanne, that al thing that faileth to ben good, it stinteth for to be and for to han any beinge; wherfore it is, that shrewes stinten for to ben that they weren. But thilke other forme of mankinde, that is to seyn, the forme of the body withoute, sheweth yit that thise shrewes weren whylom men; wherfor, whan they ben perverted and torned into malice, certes, than han they forlorn the nature of mankinde. But so as only bountee and prowesse may enhaunsen every man over other men; thanne mot it nedes be that shrewes, which that shrewednesse hath cast out of the condicioun of mankinde, ben put under the merite and the desert of men. Thanne bitydeth it, that yif thou seest a wight that be transformed into vyces, thou ne mayst nat wene that he be a man.

FOR yif he be ardaunt in avaryce, and that he be a ravinour by violence of foreine richesse, thou shalt seyn that he is lyke to the wolf. And yif he be felonous and withoute reste, and exercyse his tonge to chydinges, thou shalt lykne him to the hound. And yif he be a prevey awaitour yhid, and rejoyseth him to ravisshe by wyles, thou shalt seyn him lyke to the fox-whelpes. And yif he be distempre and quaketh for ire, men shal wene that he bereth the corage of a lyoun. And yif he be dredful and fleinge, and dredeth thinges that ne oughten nat to ben dred, men shal holden him lyk to the hert. And yif he be slow and astoned and lache, he liveth as an asse. And yif he be light and unstedefast of corage, & chaungeth ay his studies, he is lykned to briddes. And if he be plounged in foule and unclene luxuries, he is withholden in the foule delyces of the foule sowe. Thanne folweth it, that he that forleteth bountee and prowesse, he forleteth to ben a man; sin he may nat passen into the condicioun of God, he is torned into a beest.

Metre III.
Vela Neritii dulcis.

EURUS the wind aryvede the sailes of Ulixes, duk of the contree of Narice, & his wandringe shippes by the see, into the ile theras Circes, the faire goddesse, doughter of the sonne, dwelleth; that medleth to hir newe gestes drinkes that ben touched and maked with enchauntements. And after that hir hand, mighty over the herbes, hadde chaunged hir gestes into dyverse maneres; that oon of hem, is covered his face with forme of a boor; that other is chaunged into a lyoun of the contree of Marmorike, and his nayles and his teeth wexen; that other of hem is neweliche chaunged into a wolf, & howleth whan he wolde wepe; that other goth debonairely in the hous as a tygre of Inde.

BUT albeit so that the godhed of Mercurie, that is cleped the brid of Arcadie, hath had mercy of the duke Ulixes, biseged with dyverse yveles, and hath unbounden him fro the pestilence of his ostesse, algates the roweres and the marineres hadden by this ydrawen into hir mouthes & dronken the wikkede drinkes. They that weren woxen swyn hadden by this ychaunged hir mete of breed, for to eten akornes of okes. Non of hir limes ne dwelleth with hem hole, but they han lost the voice and the body; only hir thought dwelleth with hem stable, that wepeth and biweileth the monstruous chaunginge that they suffren. O overlight hand (as who seyth, O! feble and light is the hand of Circes the enchaunteresse, that chaungeth the bodyes of folkes into bestes, to regard and to comparisoun of mutacioun that is maked by vyces); ne the herbes of Circes ne ben nat mighty. For albeit so that they may chaungen the limes of the body, algates yit they may nat chaunge the hertes;

for withinne is yhid the strengthe & vigor of men, in the secree tour of hir hertes; that is to seyn, the strengthe of resoun. But thilke venims of vyces to drawen a man to hem more mightily than the venim of Circes; for vyces ben so cruel that they percen and thurgh-passen the corage withinne; and, thogh they ne anoye nat the body, yit vyces wooden to destroye men by wounde of thought.

Prose IV.
Tum ego, fateor, inquam.

THAN seyde I thus: I confesse and am aknowe it, quod I; ne I ne see nat that men may sayn, as by right, that shrewes ne ben chaunged into bestes by the qualitee of hir soules, albeit so that they kepen yit the forme of the body of mankinde. But I nolde nat of shrewes, of which the thought cruel woodeth alwey into destruccioun of goode men, that it were leveful to hem to don that.

CERTES, quod she, ne is nis nat leveful to hem, as I shal wel shewe thee in covenable place; but natheles, yif so were that thilke that men wenen be leveful to shrewes were binomen hem, so that they ne mighte nat anoyen or doon harm to goode men, certes, a greet partye of the peyne to shrewes sholde ben allegged and releved. For albeit so that this ne seme nat credible thing, peraventure, to some folk, yit moot it nedes be, that shrewes ben more wrecches and unsely whan they may doon & performe that they coveiten, than yif they mighte nat complisshen that they coveiten. For yif so be that it be wrecchednesse to wilne to don yvel, than is more wrecchednesse to mowen don yvel; withoute whiche mowinge the wrecched wil sholde languisshe withoute effect. Than, sin that everiche of thise thinges hath his wrecchednesse, that is to seyn, wil to don yvel & mowinge to don yvel, it moot nedes be that they ben constreyned by three unselinesses, that wolen and mowen & performen felonyes and shrewednesses. I acorde me, quod I; but I desire gretly that shrewes losten sone thilke unselinesse, that is to seyn, that shrewes weren despoyled of mowinge to don yvel.

SO shullen they, quod she, soner, peraventure, than thou woldest; or soner than they hemself wene to lakken mowinge to don yvel. For ther nis nothing so late in so shorte boundes of this lyf, that is long to abyde, nameliche, to a corage inmortel; of whiche shrewes the grete hope, & the hye compassinges of shrewednesses, is ofte destroyed by a sodeyn ende, or they ben war; & that thing estableth to shrewes the ende of hir shrewednesse. For yif that shrewednesse maketh wrecches, than mot he nedes ben most wrecched that lengest is a shrewe; the whiche wikked shrewes wolde I demen aldermost unsely and caitifs, yif that hir shrewednesse ne were finisshed, at the leste way, by the outtereste deeth. For yif I have concluded sooth of the unselinesse of shrewednesse, than sheweth it cleerly that thilke wrecchednesse is withouten ende, the whiche is certein to ben perdurable. Certes, quod I, this conclusioun is hard & wonderful to graunte; but I knowe wel that it acordeth moche to the thinges that I have graunted herbiforn.

THOU hast, quod she, the right estimacioun of this; but whosoever wene that it be a hard thing to acorde him to a conclusioun, it is right that he shewe that some of the premisses ben false; or elles he moot shewe that the collacioun of proposiciouns nis nat speedful to a necessarie conclusioun. And yif it be nat so, but that the premisses ben ygraunted, ther is not why he sholde blame the argument. For this thing that I shal telle thee now ne shal nat seme lasse wonderful; but of the thinges that ben taken also it is necessarie; as who seyth, it folweth of that which that is purposed biforn. What is that? quod I.

CERTES, quod she, that is, that thise wikked shrewes ben more blisful, or elles lasse wrecches, that abyen the torments that they han deserved, than yif no peyne of justice ne chastysede hem. Ne this ne seye I nat now, for that any man mighte thenke, that the maners of shrewes ben coriged and chastysed by venjaunce, and that they ben brought to the right wey by the drede of the torment, ne for that they yeven to other folk ensaumple to fleen fro vyces; but I understande yit in another manere, that shrewes ben more unsely whan they ne ben nat punisshed, albeit so that ther ne be had no resoun or lawe of correccioun, ne non ensaumple of lokinge. And what manere shal that ben, quod I, other than hath be told herbiforn? Have we nat thanne graunted, quod she, that goode folk ben blisful, and shrewes ben wrecches? Yis, quod I. Thanne, quod she, yif that any good were added to the wrecchednesse of any wight, nis he nat more weleful than he that ne hath no medlinge of good in his solitarie wrecchednesse? So semeth it, quod I.

366

AND what seystow thanne, quod she, of thilke wrecche that lakketh alle goodes, so that no good nis medled in his wrecchednesse, & yit, over al his wikkednesse for which he is a wrecche, that ther be yit another yvel anexed and knit to him, shal nat men demen him more unsely than thilke wrecche of whiche the unselinesse is releved by the participacioun of som good? Why sholde he nat? quod I.

THANNE, certes, quod she, han shrewes, whan they ben punisshed, somwhat of good anexed to hir wrecchednesse, that is to seyn, the same peyne that they suffren, which that is good by the resoun of justice; and whan thilke same shrewes ascapen withoute torment, than han they somwhat more of yvel yit over the wikkednesse that they han don, that is to seyn, defaute of peyne; which defaute of peyne, thou hast graunted, is yvel for the deserte of felonye. I ne may nat denye it, quod I. Moche more thanne, quod she, ben shrewes unsely, whan they ben wrongfully delivered fro peyne, than whan they ben punisshed by rightful venjaunce. But this is open thing & cleer, that it is right that shrewes ben punisshed, and it is wikkednesse & wrong that they escapen unpunisshed. Who mighte deneye that? quod I. But, quod she, may any man denye that al that is right nis good; & also the contrarie, that al that is wrong is wikke? Certes, quod I, these thinges ben clere ynough; and that we han concluded a litel herbiforn. But I praye thee that thou telle me, yif thou acordest to leten no torment to sowles, after that the body is ended by the deeth; this is to seyn, understandestow aught that sowles han any torment after the deeth of the body?

CERTES, quod she, ye; & that right greet; of which sowles, quod she, I trowe that some ben tormented by asprenesse of peyne; and some sowles, I trowe, ben exercised by a purginge mekenesse. But my conseil nis nat to determinye of thise peynes. But I have travailed and told yit hiderto, for thou sholdest knowe that the mowinge of shrewes, which mowinge thee semeth to ben unworthy, nis no mowinge: & eek of shrewes, of which thou pleinedest that they ne were nat punisshed, that thou woldest seen that they ne weren nevermo withouten the torments of hir wikkednesse: and of the licence of the mowinge to don yvel, that thou preydest that it mighte sone ben ended, & that thou woldest fayn lernen that it ne sholde nat longe dure: and that shrewes ben more unsely yif they were of lenger duringe, and most unsely yif they weren perdurable.

And after this, I have shewed thee that more unsely ben shrewes, whan they escapen withoute hir rightful peyne, than whan they ben punisshed by rightful venjaunce. And of this sentence folweth it, that thanne ben shrewes constreined at the laste with most grevous torment, whan men wene that they ne be nat punisshed.

WHAN I consider thy resouns, quod I, I ne trowe nat that men seyn anything more verayly. And yif I torne ayein to the studies of men, who is he to whom it sholde seme that he ne sholde nat only leven thise thinges, but eek gladly herkne hem?

CERTES, quod she, so it is; but men may nat. For they han hir eyen so wont to the derknesse of erthely thinges, that they ne may nat liften hem up to the light of cleer sothfastnesse; but they ben lyke to briddes, of which the night lightneth hir lokinge, and the day blindeth hem. For whan men loken nat the ordre of thinges, but hir lustes and talents, they wene that either the leve or the mowinge to don wikkednesse, or elles the scapinge withoute peyne, be weleful. But consider the jugement of the perdurable lawe. For yif thou conferme thy corage to the beste thinges, thou ne hast no nede of no juge to yeven thee prys or mede; for thou hast joyned thyself to the most excellent thing. And yif thou have enclyned thy studies to the wikked thinges, ne seek no foreyne wreker out of thyself; for thou thyself hast thrist thyself into wikke thinges: right as thou mightest loken by dyverse tymes the foul erthe and the hevene, and that alle other thinges stinten fro withoute, so that thou nere neither in hevene ne in erthe, ne saye nothing more; than it sholde semen to thee, as by only resoun of lokinge, that thou were now in the sterres and now in the erthe. But the poeple ne loketh nat on thise thinges. What thanne? Shal we thanne aprochen us to hem that I have shewed that they ben lyk to bestes? And what woltow seyn of this: yif that a man hadde al forlorn his sighte and hadde foryeten that he ever saugh, and wende that nothing ne faylede him of perfeccioun of mankinde, now we that mighten seen the same thinges, wolde we nat wene that he were blinde? Ne also ne acordeth nat the poeple to that I shal seyn, the which thing is sustened by a stronge foundement of resouns, that is to seyn, that more unsely ben they that don wrong to othre folk than they that the wrong suffren ✿ I wolde heren thilke same resouns, quod I. ✿ Denyestow, quod she, that alle shrewes ne ben worthy to han torment? ✿ Nay, quod I ✿ But,

quod she, I am certein, by many resouns, that shrewes ben unsely ✿ It acordeth, quod I. ✿ Thanne ne doutestow nat, quod she, that thilke folk that ben worthy of torment, that they ne ben wrecches? ✿ It acordeth wel, quod I ✿ Yif thou were thanne, quod she, yset a juge or a knower of thinges, whether, trowestow, that men sholden tormenten him that hath don the wrong, or elles him that hath suffred the wrong? ✿ I ne doute nat, quod I, that I nolde don suffisaunt satisfaccioun to him that hadde suffred the wrong by the sorwe of him that hadde don the wrong ✿ Thanne semeth it, quod she, that the doere of wrong is more wrecche than he that suffred wrong? ✿ That folweth wel, quod I.

THAN, quod she, by these causes & by othre causes that ben enforced by the same rote, filthe or sinne, by the propre nature of it, maketh men wrecches; & it sheweth wel, that the wrong that men don nis nat the wrecchednesse of him that receyveth the wrong, but the wrecchednesse of him that doth the wrong. But certes, quod she, thise oratours or advocats don al the contrarye; for they enforcen hem to commoeve the juges to han pitee of hem that han suffred & receyved the thinges that ben grevous and aspre, and yit men sholden more rightfully han pitee of hem that don the grevaunces and the wronges; the whiche shrewes, it were a more covenable thing, that the accusours or advocats, nat wroth but pitous & debonair, ledden tho shrewes that han don wrong to the jugement, right as men leden syke folk to the leche, for that they sholde seken out the maladyes of sinne by torment. And by this covenaunt, either the entente of deffendours or advocats sholde faylen and cesen in al, or elles, yif the office of advocats wolde bettre profiten to men, it sholde ben torned into the habite of accusacioun; that is to seyn, they sholden accuse shrewes, and nat excuse hem. And eek the shrewes hemself, yif hit were leveful to hem to seen at any clifte the vertu that they han forleten, & sawen that they sholden putten adoun the filthes of hir vyces, by the torments of peynes, they ne oughte nat, right for the recompensacioun for to geten hem bountee and prowesse which that they han lost, demen ne holden that thilke peynes weren torments to hem; & eek they wolden refuse the attendaunce of hir advocats, and taken hemself to hir juges and to hir accusors. For which it bitydeth that, as to the wyse folk, ther nis no place yleten to hate; that is to seyn, that ne hate hath no place amonges wyse men. For no wight nil haten goode men, but yif he were overmochel a fool; and for to haten shrewes, it nis no resoun. for right so as languissinge is maladye of body, right so ben vyces & sinne maladye of corage. And so as we ne deme nat, that they that ben syke of hir body ben worthy to ben hated, but rather worthy of pitee: wel more worthy, nat to ben hated, but for to ben had in pitee, ben they of whiche the thoughtes ben constreined by felonous wikkednesse, that is more cruel than any languissinge of body.

Metre IV.
Quid tantos juvat excitare motus.

HAT delyteth you to excyten so grete moevinges of hateredes, & to hasten and bisien the fatal disposicioun of your deeth with your propre handes? that is to seyn, by batailes or by contek. for yif ye axen the deeth, it hasteth him of his owne wil; ne deeth ne tarieth nat his swifte hors. And the men that the serpent and the lyoun and the tygre and the bere and the boor seken to sleen with hir teeth, yit thilke same men seken to sleen everich of hem other with swerd. Lo! for hir maneres ben dyverse and descordaunt, they moeven unrightful ostes and cruel batailes, & wilnen to perisshe by entrechauninge of dartes. But the resoun of crueltee nis nat ynough rightful.

ILTOW thanne yelden a covenable guerdoun to the desertes of men? Love rightfully goode folk, and have pitee on shrewes.

Prose V.
Hic ego video inquam.

HUS see I wel, quod I, either what blisfulnesse or elles what unselinesse is establisshed in the desertes of goode men and of shrewes. But in this ilke fortune of poeple I see somwhat of good & somwhat of yvel. for no wyse man hath lever ben exyled, poore and nedy, and nameles, than for to dwellen in his citee and flouren of richesses, and be redoutable by honour, and strong of power. for in this wyse more cleerly and more witnesfully is the office of wyse men ytreted, whan the blisfulnesse and the poustee of governours is, as it were, yshad amonges poeples that be neighebours & subgits; sin that, namely, prisoun, lawe, & thise othre torments of laweful peynes ben rather owed to fe-

368

lonous citezeins, for the whiche felonous citezeins tho peynes ben establissched, than for good folk. Thanne I mervaile me greetly, quod I, why that the thinges ben so mis entrechaunged, that torments of felonyes pressen and confounden goode folk, & shrewes ravisshen medes of vertu, and ben in honours & in gret estats. And I desyre eek for to witen of thee, what semeth thee to ben the resoun of this so wrongful a conclusioun? for I wolde wondre wel the lasse, yif I trowede that al thise thinges weren medled by fortunous happe; but now hepeth & encreseth myn astonyinge God, governour of thinges, that, so as God yeveth ofte tymes to gode men godes and mirthes, and to shrewes yveles and aspre thinges: and yeveth a-yeinward to gode folk hardnesses, and to shrewes he graunteth hem hir wil and that they desyren: what difference thanne may ther be bitwixen that that God doth, and the happe of fortune, yif men ne knowe nat the cause why that it is?

E it nis no mervaile, quod she, though that men wenen that ther be somewhat folissh and confuse, whan the resoun of the ordre is unknowe. But although that thou ne knowe nat the cause of so greet a disposicioun, natheles, for as moche as God, the gode governour, a-tempreth & governeth the world, ne doute thee nat that alle thinges ben doon aright.

Metre V.
Si quis Arcturi sidera nescit.

HOSO that ne knowe nat the sterres of Arcture, ytorned neigh to the soverein contree or point, that is to seyn, ytorned neigh to the soverein pool of the firmament, & wot nat why the sterre Bootes passeth or gadereth his weynes, and drencheth his late flambes in the see, & why that Bootes the sterre unfoldeth his over-swifte arys-inges, thanne shal he wondren of the lawe of the heye eyr.

ND eek, yif that he ne knowe nat why that the hornes of the fulle mone wexen pale & infect by the boundes of the derke night; and how the mone, derk and confuse, discovereth the sterres that she hadde ycovered by hir clere visage. The comune errour moeveth folk, and maketh wery hir basins of bras by thikke strokes; that is to seyn, that ther is a maner of poeple that highte Coribantes, that wenen that, whan the mone is in the eclipse, that it be enchaunted; and therfore, for to rescowe the mone, they beten hir basins with thikke strokes.

NE no man ne wondreth whan the blastes of the wind Chorus beten the strondes of the see by quakinge flodes; ne no man ne wondreth whan the weighte of the snowe, yharded by the colde, is resolved by the brenninge hete of Phebus the sonne; for heer seen men redely the causes.

BUT the causes yhid, that is to seyn, in hevene, troublen the brestes of men; the moevable poeple is astoned of alle thinges that comen selde & sodeinly in our age. But yif the troubly errour of our ignoraunce departede fro us, so that we wisten the causes why that swiche thinges bityden, certes, they sholden cese to seme wondres.

Prose VI.
Ita est, inquam.

THUS is it, quod I. But so as thou hast yeven or bihight me to unwrappen the hid causes of thinges, & to discovere me the resouns covered with derknesses, I prey thee that thou devyse and juge me of this matere, and that thou do me to understonden it; for this miracle or this wonder troubleth me right gretly.

AND thanne she, a litel what smylinge, seyde: Thou clepest me, quod she, to telle thing that is grettest of alle thinges that mowen ben axed, and to the whiche questioun unnethes is ther aught ynough to laven it; as who seyth, unnethes is ther suffisauntly anything to answere parfitly to thy questioun. For the matere of it is swich, that whan o doute is determined & cut awey, ther wexen other doutes withoute number; right as the hevedes wexen of Ydre, the serpent that Ercules slowh. Ne ther ne were no manere ne non ende, but yif that a wight constreinede tho doutes by a right lyfly and quik fyr of thought; that is to seyn, by vigour and strengthe of wit. For in this manere men weren wont to maken questions of the simplicitee of the purviaunce of God, and of the order of destinee, & of sodein happe, and of the knowinge and predestinacioun divyne, and of the libertee of free wille; the whiche thinges thou thyself aperceyvest wel, of what weight they ben. But for as mochel as the knowinge of thise thinges is a maner porcioun of the medicine of thee, albeit so that I have litel tyme to don it, yit natheles I wol enforcen me to shewe somwhat of it. But althogh the norisshinges of ditee of musike delyteth thee, thou

b b i

most suffren and forberen a litel of thilke delyte, whyle that I weve to thee resouns yknit by ordre.

AS it lyketh to thee, quod I, so do. Tho spak she right as by another biginninge, and seyde thus. The engendringe of alle thinges, quod she, and alle the progressiouns of muable nature, and al that moeveth in any manere, taketh his causes, his ordre, and his formes, of the stablenesse of the divyne thoght; & thilke divyne thought, that is yset and put in the tour, that is to seyn, in the heighte, of the simplicitee of God, stablissheth many maner gyses to thinges that ben to done; the whiche maner, whan that men loken it in thilke pure clennesse of the divyne intelligence, it is ycleped purviaunce; but whan thilke maner is referred by men to thinges that it moeveth & disponeth, thanne of olde men it was cleped destinee. The whiche thinges, yif that any wight loketh wel in his thought the strengthe of that oon & of that other, he shal lightly mowen seen, that thise two thinges ben dyverse. For purviaunce is thilke divyne reson that is establisshed in the soverein prince of thinges; the whiche purviaunce disponeth alle thinges. But destinee is the disposicioun and ordinaunce clyvinge to moevable thinges, by the whiche disposicioun the purviaunce knitteth alle thinges in hir ordres; for purviaunce embraceth alle thinges tohepe, althogh that they ben dyverse, & althogh they ben infinite; but destinee departeth & ordeineth alle thinges singulerly, and divyded in moevinges, in places, in formes, in tymes, as thus: lat the unfoldinge of temporel ordinaunce, assembled and ooned in the lokinge of the divyne thought, be cleped purviaunce; and thilke same assemblinge and ooninge, divyded and unfolden by tymes, lat that ben called destinee. And albeit so that thise thinges ben dyverse, yit natheles hangeth that oon on that other; forwhy the order destinal procedeth of the simplicitee of purviaunce. For right as a werkman, that aperceyveth in his thoght the forme of the thing that he wol make, and moeveth the effect of the werk, and ledeth that he hadde loked biforn in his thoght simply & presently, by temporel ordinaunce: certes, right so God disponeth in his purviaunce, singulerly and stably, the thinges that ben to done, but he aministreth in many maneres and in dyverse tymes, by destinee, thilke same thinges that he hath disponed.

THANNE, whether that destinee be exercysed outher by some divyne spirits, servaunts to the divyne purviaunce, or elles by som sowle, or elles by alle nature servinge to God, or elles by the celestial moevinges of sterres, or elles by the vertu of angeles, or elles by the dyverse subtilitee of develes, or elles by any of hem, or elles by hem alle, the destinal ordinaunce is ywoven and acomplissed. Certes, it is open thing, that the purviaunce is an unmoevable and simple forme of thinges to done; & the moevable bond and the temporel ordinaunce of thinges, whiche that the divyne simplicitee of purviaunce hath ordeyned to done, that is destinee. For which it is, that alle thinges that ben put under destinee ben, certes, subgits to purviaunce, to whiche purviaunce destinee itself is subgit and under. But some thinges ben put under purviaunce, that surmounten the ordinaunce of destinee; and tho ben thilke that stably ben yficched negh to the firste godhed: they surmounten the ordre of destinal moevabletee. For right as of cercles that tornen aboute a same centre or aboute a poynt, thilke cercle that is innerest or most withinne joyneth to the simplesse of the middel, and is, as it were, a centre or a poynt to that other cercles that tornen abouten him; and thilke that is outterest, compassed by larger envyronninge, is unfolden by larger spaces, in so moche as it is forthest fro the middel simplicitee of the poynt; and yif ther be anything that knitteth and felawshippeth himself to thilke middel poynt, it is constreined into simplicitee, that is to seyn, into unmoevabletee, & it ceseth to be shad & to fleten dyversely: right so, by semblable resoun, thilke thing that departeth forthest fro the first thoght of God, it is unfolden & summitted to gretter bondes of destinee: and in so moche is the thing more free and laus fro destinee, as it axeth and holdeth him ner to thilke centre of thinges, that is to seyn, God. And yif the thing clyveth to the stedefastnesse of the thoght of God, and be withoute moevinge, certes, it sormounteth the necessitee of destinee. Thanne right swich comparisoun as it is of skilinge to understondinge, & of thing that is engendred to thing that is, and of tyme to eternitee, and of the cercle to the centre, right so is the ordre of moevable destinee to the stable simplicitee of purviaunce.

THILKE ordinaunce moeveth the hevene and the sterres, and atempreth the elements togider amonges hemself, and transformeth hem by entrechaungeable mutacioun; and thilke same ordre neweth ayein alle thinges growinge and fallinge adoun, by semblable progressiouns of sedes & of sexes, that is to seyn, male and femele. And this ilke ordre constreineth the fortunes & the dedes of men by a bond of causes, nat able to ben un-

bounde; the whiche destinal causes, whan they passen out fro the biginninges of the unmoevable purviaunce, it mot nedes be that they ne be nat mutable. And thus ben the thinges ful wel ygoverned, yif that the simplicitee dwellinge in the divyne thoght sheweth forth the ordre of causes, unable to ben ybowed; and this ordre constreineth by his propre stabletee the moevable thinges, or elles they sholden fleten folily. For which it is, that alle thinges semen to ben confus and trouble to us men, for we ne mowen nat considere thilke ordinaunce; natheles, the propre maner of every thinge, dressinge hem to goode, disponeth hem alle.

FOR ther nis nothing don for cause of yvel; ne thilke thing that is don by wikkede folk nis nat don for yvel. The whiche shrewes, as I have shewed ful plentivously, seken good, but wikked errour mistorneth hem, ne the ordre cominge fro the poynt of soverein good ne declyneth nat fro his biginninge. But thou mayst seyn, what unreste may ben a worse confusioun than that gode men han somtyme adversitee and somtyme prosperitee, and shrewes also now han thinges that they desiren, and now thinges that they haten? Whether men liven now in swich hoolnesse of thoght, (as who seyth, ben men now so wyse), that swiche folk as they demen to ben gode folk or shrewes, that it moste nedes ben that folk ben swiche as they wenen? But in this manere the domes of men discorden, that thilke men that some folk demen worthy of mede, other folk demen hem worthy of torment. But lat us graunte, I pose that som man may wel demen or knowen the gode folk and the badde; may he thanne knowen & seen thilke innereste atempraunce of corages, as it hath ben wont to be seyd of bodies; as who seyth, may a man speken & determinen of atempraunces in corages, as men were wont to demen or speken of complexiouns and atempraunces of bodies? Ne it ne is nat an unlyk miracle, to hem that ne knowen it nat, (as who seith, but it is lyke a merveil or a miracle to hem that ne knowen it nat), why that swete thinges ben covenable to some bodies that ben hole, and to some bodies bittere thinges ben covenable; and also, why that some syke folk ben holpen with lighte medicynes, & some folk ben holpen with sharpe medicynes. But natheles, the leche that knoweth the manere and the atempraunce of hele & of maladye, ne merveileth of it nothing. But what other thing semeth hele of corages but bountee and prowesse? And what other thing semeth maladye of corages but vyces? Who is elles kepere of good or dryver awey of yvel, but

God, governour and lecher of thoughtes? The whiche God, whan he hath biholden from the heye tour of his purveaunce, he knoweth what is covenable to every wight, and leneth hem that he wot that is covenable to hem. Lo, herof comth and herof is don this noble miracle of the ordre destinal, whan God, that al knoweth, doth swiche thing, of which thing that unknowinge folk ben astoned. But for to constreine, as who seyth, but for to comprehende & telle a fewe thinges of the divyne deepnesse, the whiche that mannes resoun may understonde, thilke man that thou wenest to ben right juste and right kepinge of equitee, the contrarie of that semeth to the divyne purveaunce, that al wot. And Lucan, my familer, telleth that The victorious cause lykede to the goddes, and the cause overcomen lykede to Catoun. Thanne, whatsoever thou mayst seen that is don in this werld unhoped or unwened, certes, it is the right ordre of thinges; but, as to thy wikkede opinioun, it is a confusioun. But I suppose that som man be so wel ythewed, that the divyne jugement & the jugement of mankinde acorden hem togider of him; but he is so unstedefast of corage, that, yif any adversitee come to him, he wol forleten, paraventure, to continue innocence, by the whiche he ne may nat withholden fortune. Thanne the wyse dispensacioun of God spareth him, the whiche man adversitee mighte enpeyren; for that God wol nat suffren him to travaile, to whom that travaile nis nat covenable. Another man is parfit in alle vertues, and is an holy man, & negh to God, so that the purviaunce of God wolde demen, that it were a felonye that he were touched with any adversitees; so that he wol nat suffre that swich a man be moeved with any bodily maladye. But so as seyde a philosophre, the more excellent by me: he seyde in Grek, that Vertues han edified the body of the holy man. And ofte tyme it bitydeth, that the somme of thinges that ben to done is taken to governe to gode folk, for that the malice haboundaunt of shrewes sholde ben abated. And God yeveth & departeth to othre folk prosperitees and adversitees ymedled tohepe, after the qualitee of hir corages, and remordeth som folk by adversitee, for they ne sholde nat wexen proude by longe welefulnesse. And other folk he suffreth to ben travailed with harde thinges, for that they sholden confermen the vertues of corage by the usage and exercitacioun of pacience. And other folk dreden more than they oughten that whiche they mighten wel beren; and somme dispyse that they mowe nat beren; & thilke folk God ledeth into experience of himself by aspre and

b b 2

sorwful thinges. And many othre folk han bought honourable renoun of this world by the prys of glorious deeth. And som men, that ne mowen nat ben overcomen by torments, have yeven ensaumple to othre folk, that vertu may nat ben overcomen by adversitees; and of alle thinges ther nis no doute, that they ne ben don rightfully and ordenely, to the profit of hem to whom we seen thise thinges bityde. For certes, that adversitee comth somtyme to shrewes, & somtyme that that they desiren, it comth of thise forseide causes. And of sorwful thinges that bityden to shrewes, certes, no man ne wondreth; for alle men wenen that they han wel deserved it, and that they ben of wikkede merite; of whiche shrewes the torment somtyme agasteth othre to don felonyes, and somtyme it amendeth hem that suffren the torments. And the prosperitee that is yeven to shrewes sheweth a greet argument to gode folk, what thing they sholde demen of thilke welefulnesse, the whiche prosperitee men seen ofte serven to shrewes. In the which thing I trowe that God dispenseth; for peraventure, the nature of som man is so overthrowinge to yvel, and so uncovenable, that the nedy povertee of his houshold mighte rather egren him to don felonyes. And to the maladye of him God putteth remedie, to yeven him richesses. And som other man biholdeth his conscience defouled with sinnes, and maketh comparisoun of his fortune and of himself; and dredeth, peraventure, that his blisfulnesse, of which the usage is joyeful to him, that the lesinge of thilke blisfulnesse ne be nat sorwful to him; and therfor he wol chaunge his maneres, and, for he dredeth to lese his fortune, he forleteth his wikkednesse. To othre folk is welefulnesse y-yeven unworthily, the whiche overthroweth hem into distruccioun that they han deserved. And to som othre folk is yeven power to punisshen, for that it shal be cause of continuacioun and exercysinge to gode folk and cause of torment to shrewes. For so as ther nis non alyaunce bytwixe gode folk and shrewes, ne shrewes ne mowen nat acorden amonges hemself. And why nat? For shrewes discorden of hemself by hir vyces, the whiche vyces al torenden hir consciences; & don ofte tyme thinges, the whiche thinges, whan they han don hem, they demen that tho thinges ne sholden nat han ben don. For which thing thilke soverein purveaunce hath maked ofte tyme fair miracle; so that shrewes han maked shrewes to ben gode men. For whan that som shrewes seen that they suffren wrongfully felonyes of othre shrewes, they wexen eschaufed into hate of hem that anoye-

371

den hem, and retornen to the frut of vertu, whan they studien to ben unlyk to hem that they han hated. Certes, only this is the divyne might, to the whiche might yveles ben thanne gode, whan it useth tho yveles covenably, & draweth out the effect of any gode; as who seyth, that yvel is good only to the might of God, for the might of God ordeyneth thilke yvel to good.

FOR oon ordre embraseth alle thinges, so that what wight that departeth fro the resoun of thilke ordre which that is assigned to him, algates yit he slydeth into another ordre, so that nothing nis leveful to folye in the reame of the divyne purviaunce; as who seyth, nothing nis withouten ordinaunce in the reame of the divyne purviaunce; sin that the right stronge God governeth alle thinges in this world. For it nis nat leveful to man to comprehenden by wit, ne unfolden by word, alle the subtil ordinaunces and disposiciouns of the divyne entente. For only it oughte suffise to han loked, that God himself, maker of alle natures, ordeineth and dresseth alle thinges to gode; whyl that he hasteth to withholden the thinges that he hath maked into his semblaunce, that is to seyn, for to withholden thinges into good, for he himself is good, he chaseth out al yvel fro the boundes of his comunalitee by the ordre of necessitee destinable. For which it folweth, that yif thou loke the purviaunce ordeininge the thinges that men wenen ben outrageous or haboundant in erthes, thou ne shalt nat seen in no place nothing of yvel. But I see now that thou art charged with the weighte of the questioun, & wery with the lengthe of my resoun; and that thou abydest som sweetnesse of songe. Tak thanne this draught; and whan thou art wel refresshed & refect, thou shal be more stedefast to stye into heyere questiouns.

Metre VI.
Si vis celsi jura tonantis.

If thou, wys, wilt demen in thy pure thought the rightes or the lawes of the heye thonderer, that is to seyn, of God, loke thou and bihold the heightes of the soverein hevene. There kepen the sterres, by rightful alliaunce of thinges, hir olde pees. The sonne, ymoeved by his rody fyr, ne distorbeth nat the colde cercle of the mone. Ne the sterre ycleped The Bere, that enclyneth his ravisshinge courses abouten the soverein heighte of the worlde, ne the same sterre Ursa nis nevermo wasshen in the depe westrene see, ne coveiteth nat to deyen his flaumbes in the see of the occian, al

372

thogh he see othre sterres yplounged in the see. And Hesperus the sterre bodeth & telleth alwey the late nightes; & Lucifer the sterre bringeth ayein the clere day.

AND thus maketh Love entrechaungeable the perdurable courses; & thus is discordable bataile yput out of the contree of the sterres. This acordaunce atempreth by evenelyk maneres the elements, that the moiste thinges, stryvinge with the drye thinges, yeven place by stoundes; & the colde thinges joynen hem by feyth to the hote thinges; and that the lighte fyr aryseth into heighte; and the hevy erthes avalen by hir weightes. By thise same causes the floury yeer yildeth swote smelles in the firste somer-sesoun warminge; and the hote somer dryeth the cornes; & autumpne comth ayein, hevy of apples; and the fletinge reyn bideweth the winter. This atempraunce norissheth and bringeth forth al thing that bretheth lyf in this world; & thilke same atempraunce, ravisshinge, hydeth and binimeth, and drencheth under the laste deeth, alle thinges yborn.

AMONGES thise thinges sitteth the heye maker, king and lord, welle and biginninge, lawe & wys juge, to don equitee; and governeth and enclyneth the brydles of thinges. And tho thinges that he stereth to gon by moevinge, he withdraweth and aresteth; and affermeth the moevable or wandringe thinges. For yif that he ne clepede ayein the right goinge of thinges, and yif that he ne constreinede hem nat eftsones into roundnesses enclynede, the thinges that ben now continued by stable ordinaunce, they sholden departen from hir welle, that is to seyn, from hir biginninge, and faylen, that is to seyn, torne into nought.

THIS is the comune Love to alle thinges; and alle thinges axen to ben holden by the fyn of good. For elles ne mighten they nat lasten, yif they ne come nat eftsones ayein, by Love retorned, to the cause that hath yeven hem beinge, that is to seyn, to God.

Prose VII.
Jamne igitur vides.

SEESTOW NAT thanne what thing folweth alle the thinges that I have seyd? Boece. What thing? quod I ✍ Certes, quod she, al outrely, that alle fortune is good. ✍ And how may that be? quod I.

NOW understand, quod she, so as alle fortune, whether so it be joyeful fortune or aspre fortune, is yeven either by cause of guerdoning or elles of exercysinge of good folk, or elles by cause to punisshen or elles chastysen shrewes; thanne is alle fortune good, the whiche fortune is certein that it be either rightful or elles profitable.

FORSOTHE, this is a ful verray resoun, quod I; & yif I consider the purviaunce and the destinee that thou taughtest me a litel herbiforn, this sentence is sustened by stedefast resouns. But yif it lyke unto thee, lat us noumbren hem amonges thilke thinges, of whiche thou seydest a litel herbiforn, that they ne were nat able to ben wened to the poeple. Why so? quod she. For that the comune word of men, quod I, misuseth this maner speche of fortune, & seyn ofte tymes that the fortune of som wight is wikkede. Wiltow thanne, quod she, that I aproche a litel to the wordes of the poeple, so that it seme nat to hem that I be overmoche departed as fro the usage of mankinde? As thou wolt, quod I. Demestow nat, quod she, that al thing that profiteth is good? Yis, quod I. And certes, thilke thing that exercyseth or corigeth, profiteth? I confesse it wel, quod I. Thanne is it good? quod she. Why nat? quod I.

BUT this is the fortune, quod she, of hem that either ben put in vertu and batailen ayeins aspre thinges, or elles of hem that eschuen & declynen fro vyces and taken the wey of vertu. This ne may I nat denye, quod I. But what seystow of the mery fortune that is yeven to good folk in guerdoun? Demeth aught the poeple that it is wikked? Nay, forsothe quod I; but they demen, as it sooth is, that it is right good.

AND what seystow of that other fortune, quod she, that, althogh that it be aspre, & restreineth the shrewes by rightful torment, weneth aught the poeple that it be good? Nay, quod I, but the poeple demeth that it is most wrecched of alle thinges that may ben thought. War now, & loke wel, quod she, lest that we, in folwinge the opinioun of the poeple, have confessed and concluded thing that is unable to be wened to the poeple. What is that? quod I.

CERTES, quod she, it folweth or comth of thinges that ben graunted, that alle fortune, whatsoever it be, of hem that ben either in possessioun of vertu, or in the encres of vertu, or elles in the purchasinge of vertu, that thilke fortune is good; and that alle fortune is right wikkede to hem that dwellen in shrewednesse; as who seyth, and thus weneth nat

the poeple. That is sooth, quod I, albeit so that no man dar confesse it ne biknowen it.

WHY so? quod she; for right as the stronge man ne semeth nat to abaissen or disdaignen as ofte tyme as he hereth the noise of the bataile, ne also it ne semeth nat, to the wyse man, to beren it grevously, as ofte as he is lad into the stryf of fortune. For bothe to that oon man and eek to that other thilke difficultee is the matere; to that oon man, of encres of his glorious renoun, and to that other man, to conforme his sapience, that is to seyn, to the asprenesse of his estat. For therfore is it called Vertu, for that it susteneth & enforseth, by hise strengthes, that it nis nat overcomen by adversitees. Ne certes, thou that art put in the encres or in the heighte of vertu, ne hast nat comen to fleten with delices, and for to welken in bodily luste; thou sowest or plauntest a ful egre bataile in thy corage ayeins every fortune: for that the sorwful fortune ne confounde thee nat, ne that the merye fortune ne corumpe thee nat, occupye the mene by stedefast strengthes. For al that ever is under the mene, or elles al that overpasseth the mene, despyseth welefulnesse (as who seyth, it is vicious), & ne hath no mede of his travaile. For it is set in your hand (as who seyth, it lyth in your power) what fortune yow is levest, that is to seyn, good or yvel. For alle fortune that semeth sharp or aspre, yif it ne exercyse nat the gode folk ne chastyseth the wikked folk, it punissheth.

Metre VII.
Bella bis quinis operatus annis.

THE wreker Attrides, that is to seyn, Agamenon, that wroughte and continuede the batailes by ten yeer, recovered & purgede in wrekinge, by the destruccioun of Troye, the loste chaumbres of mariage of his brother; this is to seyn, that he, Agamenon, wan ayein Eleyne, that was Menelaus wyf his brother. In the mene whyle that thilke Agamenon desirede to yeven sayles to the Grekissh navye, and boughte ayein the windes by blood, he unclothede him of pitee of fader; & the sory preest yiveth in sacrifyinge the wrecched cuttinge of throte of the doughter; that is to seyn, that Agamenon let cutten the throte of his doughter by the preest, to maken allyaunce with his goddes, & for to han winde with whiche he mighte wenden to Troye.

ITACUS, that is to seyn, Ulixes, biwepte his felawes ylorn, the whiche felawes the ferse Poliphemus, ligginge in his grete cave, hadde freten and dreynt in his empty wombe. But natheles Poliphemus, wood for his blinde visage, yald to Ulixes joye by his sorwful teres; this is to seyn, that Ulixes smoot out the eye of Poliphemus that stood in his forehed, for which Ulixes hadde joye, whan he say Poliphemus wepinge and blinde.

HERCULES is celebrable for his harde travailes; he dauntede the proude Centaures, half hors, half man; and he birafte the dispoylinge fro the cruel lyoun, that is to seyn, he slowh the lyoun & rafte him his skin. He smoot the briddes that highten Arpyes with certein arwes. He ravisshede apples fro the wakinge dragoun, and his hand was the more hevy for the goldene metal. He drow Cerberus, the hound of helle, by his treble cheyne. He, overcomer, as it is seyd, hath put an unmeke lord foddre to his cruel hors; this is to seyn, that Hercules slowh Diomedes, & made his hors to freten him. And he, Hercules, slowh Ydra the serpent, and brende the venim. And Achelous the flood, defouled in his forhed, dreynte his shamefast visage in his strondes; this is to seyn, that Achelous coude transfigure himself into dyverse lyknesses; and, as he faught with Hercules, at the laste he tornede him into a bole; and Hercules brak of oon of his hornes, and he, for shame, hidde him in his river. And he, Hercules, caste adoun Antheus the gyaunt in the strondes of Libie; & Cacus apaysede the wratthes of Evander; this is to seyn, that Hercules slowh the monstre Cacus, and apaysede with that deeth the wratthe of Evander. And the bristlede boor markede with scomes the shuldres of Hercules, the whiche shuldres the heye cercle of hevene sholde thriste. And the laste of his labours was, that he sustened the hevene upon his nekke unbowed; & he deservede eftsones the hevene, to ben the prys of his laste travaile.

GOTH now thanne, ye stronge men, theras the heye wey of the grete ensaumple ledeth yow. O nyce men, why nake ye youre bakkes? As who seyth: O ye slowe and delicat men, why flee ye adversitees, and ne fighten nat ayeins hem by vertu, to winnen the mede of the hevene? for the erthe, overcomen, yeveth the sterres; this is to seyn, that, whan that erthely lust is overcomen, a man is maked worthy to the hevene.

DE CONSOLATIONE PHILOSOPHIE. BOOK V. PROSE I.

Dixerat, orationisque cursum.

HE hadde seyd, and torned the cours of hir resoun to some othre thinges to ben treted and to ben y-sped. Thanne seyde I: Certes, rightful is thyn amonestinge and ful digne by auctoritee. But that thou seidest whylom, that the questioun of the divyne purviaunce is enlaced with many other questiouns, I understonde wel and proeve it by the same thing. But I axe yif that thou wenest that hap be any thing in any weys; and, yif thou wenest that hap be any thing, what is it? Thanne quod she, I haste me to yilden and assoilen to thee the dette of my bihest, and to shewen and opnen the wey, by which wey thou mayst come ayein to thy contree. But albeit so that the thinges which that thou axest ben right profitable to knowe, yit ben they diverse somwhat fro the path of my purpos; and it is to douten that thou ne be maked wery by misweyes, so that thou ne mayst nat suffyce to mesuren the right wey.

NE doute thee therof nothing, quod I. for, for to knowen thilke thinges togedere, in the whiche thinges I delyte me greetly, that shal ben to me in stede of reste; sin it is nat to douten of the thinges folwinge, whan every syde of thy disputacioun shal han be stedefast to me by undoutous feith.

THANNE seyde she: That manere wol I don thee; & bigan to speken right thus. Certes, quod she, yif any wight diffinisshe hap in this manere, that is to seyn, that Hap is bitydinge ybrought forth by foolish moevinge and by no knettinge of causes, I conferme that hap nis right naught in no wyse; and I deme aloutrely that hap nis, ne dwelleth but a voice, as who seith, but an ydel word, withouten any significacioun of thing submitted to that vois. for what place mighte ben left, or dwellinge, to folye and to disordenaunce, sin that God ledeth and constreineth alle thinges by ordre? for this sentence is verray & sooth, that Nothing ne hath his beinge of naught; to the whiche sentence none of thise olde folk ne withseyde never; albeit so that they ne understoden ne meneden it naught by God, prince and beginnere of werkinge, but they casten it as a manere foundement of subject material, that is to seyn, of the nature of alle resoun. And yif that any thing is woxen or comen of no causes, than shal it seme that thilke thing is comen or woxen of naught; but yif this ne may nat ben don, thanne is it nat possible, that hap be any swich thing as I have diffinisshed a litel heerbiforn. How shal it thanne be? quod I. Nis ther thanne nothing that by right may be cleped either Hap or elles Aventure of fortune; or is ther aught, albeit so that it is hid fro the peple, to which these wordes ben covenable? Myn Aristotulis, quod she, in the book of his Phisik, diffinissheth this thing by short resoun, & neigh to the sothe. In which manere? quod I.

AS ofte, quod she, as men doon any thing for grace of any other thing, and another thing than thilke thing that men entenden to don bitydeth by some causes, it is cleped Hap. Right as a man dalf the erthe by cause of tilyinge of the feeld, and founde ther a gobet of gold bidolven, thanne wenen folk that it is bifalle by fortunous bitydinge. But, for sothe, it nis nat of naught, for it hath his propre causes; of whiche causes the cours unforeseyn & unwar semeth to han maked hap. For yif the tilyere of the feld ne dolve nat in the erthe, and yif the hyder of the gold ne hadde hid the gold in thilke place, the gold ne hadde nat been founde. Thise ben thanne the causes of the abregginge of fortuit hap, the which abregginge of fortuit hap comth of causes encountringe and flowinge togidere to hemself, and nat by the entencioun of the doer. For neither the hyder of the gold ne the delver of the feeld ne understoden nat that the gold sholde han ben founde; but, as I sayde, it bitidde and ran togidre that he dalf theras that other hadde hid the gold. Now may I thus diffinisshe Hap. Hap is an unwar bitydinge of causes assembled in thinges that ben don for som other thing. But thilke ordre, procedinge by an uneschuable bindinge togidre, which that descendeth fro the welle of purviaunce that ordeineth alle thinges in hir places and in hir tymes, maketh that the causes rennen and assemblen togidere.

Metre I.
Rupis Achemenie scopulis, ubi versa sequentum.

TIGRIS & Eufrates resolven and springen of oo welle, in the cragges of the roche of the contree of Achemenie, theras the fleinge bataile ficcheth hir dartes, retorned in the brestes of hem that folwen hem. And sone after tho same riveres, Tigris & Eufrates, unjoinen and departen hir wateres. And yif they comen togideres, and ben assembled and cleped togidere into o cours, thanne moten thilke thinges fleten togi-

dere which that the water of the entrechauninge flood bringeth. The shippes & the stokkes arraced with the flood moten assemblen; & the wateres ymedled wrappeth or implyeth many fortunel happes or maneres; the whiche wandringe happes, natheles, thilke declyninge lownesse of the erthe and the flowinge ordre of the slydinge water governeth. Right so fortune, that semeth as that it fleteth with slaked or ungovernede brydles, it suffereth brydles, that is to seyn, to be governed, and passeth by thilke lawe, that is to seyn, by thilke divyne ordenaunce.

Prose II.
Animadverto, inquam.

HIS understonde I wel, quod I, and I acorde wel that it is right as thou seyst. But I axe yif ther be any libertee of free wil in this ordre of causes that clyven thus togidere in hemself; or elles I wolde witen yif that the destinal cheyne constreineth the movinges of the corages of men?

YIS, quod she; ther is libertee of free wil. Ne ther ne was nevere no nature of resoun that it ne hadde libertee of free wil. For every thing that may naturely usen resoun, it hath doom by which it decerneth & demeth every thing; thanne knoweth it, by itself, thinges that ben to fleen and thinges that ben to desiren. And thilke thing that any wight demeth to ben desired, that axeth or desireth he; & fleeth thilke thing that he troweth ben to fleen. Wherfore in alle thinges that resoun is, in hem also is libertee of willinge and of nillinge. But I ne ordeyne nat, as who seyth, I ne graunte nat, that this libertee be evenelyk in alle thinges. Forwhy in the sovereines devynes substaunces, that is to seyn, in spirits, jugement is more cleer, and wil nat ycorumped, and might redy to speden thinges that ben desired. But the soules of men moten nedes be more free whan they loken hem in the speculacioun or lokinge of the devyne thought, and lasse free whan they slyden into the bodies; and yit lasse free whan they ben gadered togidere & comprehended in erthely membres. But the laste servage is whan that they ben yeven to vyces, & han yfalle from the possessioun of hir propre resoun. For after that they han cast awey hir eyen fro the light of the sovereyn soothfastnesse to lowe thinges and derke, anon they derken by the cloude of ignoraunce & ben troubled by felonous talents; to the whiche talents whan they aprochen and asenten, they hepen & encresen the servage which they han joyned to hemself; and in this manere they ben caitifs fro hir propre libertee. The whiche thinges, nathelesse, the lokinge of the devyne purviaunce seeth, that alle thinges biholdeth and seeth fro eterne, & ordeineth hem everich in hir merites as they ben predestinat: & it is seyd in Greek, that Alle thinges he seeth and alle thinges he hereth.

Metre II.

Puro clarum lumine Phebum.

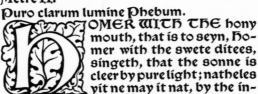 OMER WITH THE hony mouth, that is to seyn, Homer with the swete ditees, singeth, that the sonne is cleer by pure light; natheles yit ne may it nat, by the infirme light of his bemes, breken or percen the inwarde entrailes of the erthe, or elles of the see. So ne seeth nat God, maker of the grete world: to him, that loketh alle thinges from an heigh, ne withstondeth nat no thinges by hevinesse of erthe; ne the night ne withstondeth nat to him by the blake cloudes. Thilke God seeth, in oo strok of thought, alle thinges that ben, or weren, or sholle comen; & thilke God, for he loketh & seeth alle thinges alone, thou mayst seyn that he is the verray sonne.

Prose III.

Tum ego, en, inquam.

 HANNE SEYDE I, NOW AM I confounded by a more hard doute than I was ✠ What doute is that? quod she. For certes, I conjecte now by whiche thinges thou art troubled.

IT semeth, quod I, to repugnen & to contrarien greetly, that God knoweth biforn alle thinges, and that ther is any freedom of libertee. For yif so be that God loketh alle thinges biforn, ne God ne may nat ben desseived in no manere, than mot it nedes been, that alle thinges bityden the whiche that the purviaunce of God hath seyn biforn to comen. For which, yif that God knoweth biforn nat only the werkes of men, but also hir conseiles and hir willes, thanne ne shal ther be no libertee of arbitre; ne, certes, ther ne may be noon other dede, ne no wil, but thilke which that the divyne purviaunce, that may nat ben desseived, hath feled biforn. For yif that they mighten wrythen awey in othre manere than they ben purveyed, than sholde ther be no stedefast prescience of thing

376

to comen, but rather an uncertein opinioun; the whiche thing to trowen of God, I deme it felonye and unleveful. Ne I ne proeve nat thilke same resoun, as who seyth, I ne alowe nat, or I ne preyse nat, thilke same resoun, by which that som men wenen that they mowen assoilen and unknitten the knotte of this questioun. For, certes, they seyn that thing nis nat to comen for that the purviaunce of God hath seyn it biforn that is to comen, but rather the contrarye, and that is this: that, for that the thing is to comen, therfore ne may it nat ben hid fro the purviaunce of God; & in this manere this necessitee slydeth ayein into the contrarye partye: ne it ne bihoveth nat, nedes, that thinges bityden that ben purvyed, but it bihoveth, nedes, that thinges that ben to comen ben yporveyed: but as it were ytravailed, as who seyth, that thilke answere procedeth right as thogh men travaileden, or weren bisy to enqueren, the whiche thing is cause of the whiche thing: as, whether the prescience is cause of the necessitee of thinges to comen, or elles that the necessitee of thinges to comen is cause of the purviaunce. But I ne enforce me nat now to shewen it, that the bitydinge of thinges ywist biforn is necessarie, how so or in what manere that the ordre of causes hath itself; althogh that it ne seme nat that the prescience bringe in necessitee of bitidinge to thinges to comen. For certes, yif that any wight sitteth, it bihoveth by necessitee that the opinioun be sooth of him that conjecteth that he sitteth; and ayeinward also is it of the contrarye: yif the opinioun be sooth of any wight for that he sitteth, it bihoveth by necessitee that he sitte. Thanne is heer necessitee in that oon and in that other: for in that oon is necessitee of sittinge, and, certes, in that other is necessitee of sooth. But therfore ne sitteth nat a wight, for that the opinioun of the sittinge is sooth; but the opinioun is rather sooth, for that a wight sitteth biforn. And thus, althogh that the cause of the sooth cometh of that other syde (as who seyth, that althogh the cause of sooth comth of the sitting, and nat of the trewe opinioun), algates yit is ther comune necessitee in that oon and in that other. Thus sheweth it, that I may make semblable skiles of the purviaunce of God & of thinges to comen. For althogh that, for that thinges ben to comen, therfore ben they purveyed, nat, certes, for that they ben purveyed, therfore ne bityde they nat. Yit natheles, bihoveth it by necessitee, that either the thinges to comen ben ypurveyed of God, or elles that the thinges that ben purveyed of God bityden. And this thing only suffiseth ynough to destroyen the freedom of oure arbitre, that is to seyn, of oure free wil. But now, certes, sheweth it wel, how fer fro the sothe and how upsodoun is this thing that we seyn, that the bitydinge of temporel thinges is cause of the eterne prescience. But for to wenen that God purvyeth the thinges to comen for they ben to comen, what other thing is it but for to wene that thilke thinges that bitidden whylom ben causes of thilke soverein purvyaunce that is in God? And herto I adde yit this thing: that, right as whan that I wot that a thing is, it bihoveth by necessitee that thilke selve thing be; and eek, whan I have knowe that any thing shal bityden, so byhoveth it by necessitee that thilke thing bityde: so folweth it thanne, that the bitydinge of the thing ywist biforn ne may nat ben eschued. And at the laste, yif that any wight wene a thing to ben other weyes thanne it is, it is nat only unscience, but it is deceivable opinioun ful diverse and fer fro the sothe of science. Wherfore, yif any thing be so to comen, that the bitydinge of hit ne be nat certein ne necessarie, who may weten biforn that thilke thing is to comen? For right as science ne may nat ben medled with falsnesse (as who seyth, that yif I wot a thing, it ne may nat be false that I ne wot it), right so thilke thing that is conceived by science ne may nat ben non other weys than as it is conceived. For that is the cause why that science wanteth lesing (as who seyth, why that witinge ne receiveth nat lesinge of that it wot); for it bihoveth, by necessitee, that every thing be right as science comprehendeth it to be. What shal I thanne seyn? In whiche manere knoweth God biforn the thinges to comen, yif they ne be nat certein? For yif that he deme that they ben to comen uneschewably, & so may be that it is possible that they ne shollen nat comen, God is deceived. But nat only to trowen that God is deceived, but for to speke it with mouth, it is a felonous sinne. But yif that God wot that, right so as thinges ben to comen, so shullen they comen...so that he wite egaly, as who seyth, indifferently, that thinges mowen ben doon or elles nat ydoon...what is thilke prescience that ne comprehendeth no certein thing ne stable? Or elles what difference is ther bitwixe the prescience & thilke jape-worthy divyninge of Tiresie the divynour, that seyde: Al that I seye, quod he, either it shal be, or elles it shal nat be? Or elles how mochel is worth the devyne prescience more than the opinioun of mankinde, yif so be that it demeth the thinges uncertein, as men doon; of the whiche domes of men the bitydinge nis nat certein? But yif so be that non uncertein thing ne may ben in him that is right certein welle of alle thinges,

thanne is the bitydinge certein of thilke thinges whiche he hath wist biforn fermely to comen. For which it folweth, that the freedom of the conseiles & of the werkes of mankind nis non, sin that the thoght of God, that seeth alle thinges without errour of falsnesse, bindeth & constreineth hem to a bitydinge by necessitee. And yif this thing be ones ygraunted and received, that is to seyn, that ther nis no free wille, than sheweth it wel, how greet destruccioun and how grete damages ther folwen of thinges of mankinde. For in ydel ben ther thanne purposed and bihight medes to gode folk, and peynes to badde folk, sin that no moevinge of free corage voluntarie ne hath nat deserved hem, that is to seyn, neither mede ne peyne; and it sholde seme thanne, that thilke thing is alderworst, which that is now demed for aldermost just and most rightful, that is to seyn, that shrewes ben punisshed, or elles that gode folk ben ygerdoned: the whiche folk, sin that hir propre wil ne sent hem nat to that oon ne to that other, that is to seyn, neither to gode ne to harm, but constreineth hem certein necessitee of thinges to comen: thanne ne shollen ther nevere ben, ne nevere weren, vyce ne vertu, but it sholde rather ben confusioun of alle desertes medled withouten discrecioun. And yit ther folweth another inconvenient, of the whiche ther ne may ben thoght no more felonous ne more wikke; and that is this: that, so as the ordre of thinges is yled and comth of the purviaunce of God, ne that nothing nis leveful to the conseiles of mankinde (as who seyth, that men han no power to doon nothing, ne wilne nothing), than folweth it, that oure vyces ben referred to the maker of alle good (as who seyth, than folweth it, that God oughte han the blame of oure vyces, sin he constreineth us by necessitee to doon vyces). Thanne is ther no resoun to hopen in God, ne for to preyen to God; for what sholde any wight hopen to God, or why sholde he preyen to God, sin that the ordenaunce of destinee, which that ne may nat ben inclyned, knitteth and streineth alle thinges that men may desiren? Thanne sholde ther be doon awey thilke only allyaunce bitwixen God and men, that is to seyn, to hopen & to preyen. But by the prys of rightwisnesse & of verray mekenesse we deserven the gerdoun of the divyne grace, which that is inestimable, that is to seyn, that it is so greet, that it ne may nat ben ful ypreysed. And this is only the manere, that is to seyn, hope & preyeres, for which it semeth that men mowen speke with God, & by resoun of supplicacioun be conjoined to thilke cleernesse, that nis nat aproched no rather or that men beseken it & impetren it. And

yif men wene nat that hope ne preyeres ne
han no strengthes, by the necessitee of
thinges to comen yreceived, what thing is
ther thanne by whiche we mowen ben conjoined and clyven to thilke soverein prince
of thinges? For which it bihoveth, by necessitee, that the linage of mankinde, as
thou songe a litel herbiforn, be departed
and unjoined from his welle, and failen of
his biginninge, that is to seyn, God.

Metre III.
Quenam discors federa rerum.

HAT discordable cause
hath torent & unjoined the
bindinge, or the alliaunce,
of thinges, that is to seyn,
the conjunccioun of God &
man? Whiche God hath es-
tablisshed so greet bataile bitwixen thise
two soothfast or verray thinges, that is to
seyn, bitwixen the purviaunce of God and
free wil, that they ben singuler & devyded,
ne that they ne wolen nat be medeled ne
coupled togidere? But ther nis no discord
to the verray thinges, but they clyven, certein, alwey to hemself. But the thought of
man, confounded and overthrowen by the
dirke membres of the body, ne may nat, by
fyr of his derked looking, that is to seyn,
by the vigour of his insighte, whyl the
soule is in the body, knowe the thinne subtil knittinges of thinges. But wherfore enchaufeth it so, by so greet love, to finden
thilke notes of sooth ycovered; that is to
seyn, wherfore enchaufeth the thoght of
man by so greet desyr to knowen thilke
notificacions that ben yhid under the cover-
toures of sooth? Wot it aught thilke thing
that it, anguissous, desireth to knowe?
As who seith, nay; for no man travaileth
for to witen thinges that he wot. And therfore the texte seith thus: but who travaileth to witen thinges yknowe? And yif that
he ne knoweth hem nat, what seketh thilke
blinde thoght? What is he that desireth
any thing of which he wot right naught?
As who seith, who so desireth any thing,
nedes, somwhat he knoweth of it; or elles,
he ne coude nat desire it. Or who may folwen thinges that ne ben nat ywist? And
thogh that he seke tho thinges, wher shal
he finde hem? What wight, that is al un-
conninge and ignoraunt, may knowen the
forme that is yfounde? But whan the
soule biholdeth & seeth the heye thoght,
that is to seyn, God, than knoweth it togidere the somme and the singularitees,
that is to seyn, the principles and everich
by himself.

UT now, whyl the soule is hid in the
cloude and in the derkenesse of the
membres of the body, it ne hath nat
al foryeten itself, but it withholdeth the

378

somme of thinges, & leseth the singularitees. Thanne, whoso that seeketh soothnesse, he nis in neither nother habite; for
he noot nat al, ne he ne hath nat al foryet-
en: but yit him remembreth the somme of
thinges that he withholdeth, & axeth conseil, and retreteth deepliche thinges yseyn
biforn, that is to seyn, the grete somme
in his minde: so that he mowe adden the
parties that he hath foryeten to thilke that
he hath withholden.

Prose IV.
Tum illa: Vetus, inquit, hec est.

HANNE seide she:
this is, quod she, the
olde question of the
purviaunce of God;
and Marcus Tullius,
whan he devyded the
divynaciouns, that is
to seyn, in his book
that he wroot of di-
vynaciouns, he moev-
ede gretly this questioun; and thou thyself has ysought it mochel, & outrely, and
longe; but yit ne hath it nat ben determined ne ysped fermely and diligently of any
of yow. And the cause of this derkenesse
and of this difficultee is, for that the moevinge of the resoun of mankinde ne may
nat moeven to (that is to seyn, applyen or
joinen to) the simplicitee of the devyne
prescience; the whiche simplicitee of the
devyne prescience, yif that men mighten
thinken it in any maner, that is to seyn,
that yif men mighten thinken & comprehenden the thinges as God seeth hem,
thanne ne sholde ther dwellen outrely no
doute: the whiche resoun & cause of difficultee I shal assaye at the laste to shewe
and to speden, whan I have first ys(p)ended
& answered to tho resouns by which thou
art ymoeved. For I axe why thou wenest
that thilke resouns of hem that assoilen
this questioun ne ben nat speedful ynough
ne sufficient: the whiche solucioun, or the
whiche resoun, for that it demeth that the
prescience nis nat cause of necessitee to
thinges to comen, than ne weneth it nat
that freedom of wil be destorbed or ylet
by prescience. For ne drawestow nat arguments from elleswhere of the necessitee
of thinges to comen (as who seith, any other wey than thus) but that thilke thinges
that the prescience wot biforn ne mowen
nat unbityde? That is to seyn, that they
moten bityde. But thanne, yif that prescience ne putteth no necessitee to thinges
to comen, as thou thyself hast confessed
it & biknowen a litel herbiforn, what cause
or what is it (as who seith, ther may no
cause be) by which that the endes voluntarie of thinges mighten be constreined

to certein bitydinge? for by grace of po-
sitioun, so that thou mowe the betere understonde this that folweth, I pose, per
impossibile, that ther be no prescience.
Thanne axe I, quod she, in as mochel as
apertieneth to that, sholden thanne thinges that comen of free wil ben constreined
to bityden by necessitee? Boece. Nay,
quod I.

THanne ayeinward, quod she, I
suppose that ther be prescience,
but that it ne putteth no necessitee
to thinges; thanne trowe I, that thilke
selve freedom of wil shal dwellen al hool
and absolut & unbounden. But thou wolt
seyn that, albeit so that prescience nis nat
cause of the necessitee of bitydinge to
thinges to comen, algates yit it is a signe
that the thinges ben to bityden by necessitee. By this manere thanne, althogh the
prescience ne hadde never yben, yit algate
or at the leeste weye it is certein thing, that
the endes and bitydinges of thinges to
comen sholden ben necessarie. for every
signe sheweth and signifyeth only what
the thing is, but it ne maketh nat the thing
that it signefyeth. for which it bihoveth
first to shewen, that nothing ne bitydeth
that it ne bitydeth by necessitee, so that
it may appere that the prescience is signe
of this necessitee; or elles, yif ther nere
no necessitee, certes, thilke prescience ne
mighte nat be signe of thing that nis nat.
But certes, it is now certein that the proeve
of this, ysustened by stidefast resoun, ne
shal nat ben lad ne proeved by signes ne
by arguments ytaken fro withoute, but by
causes covenable and necessarie. But thou
mayst seyn, how may it be that the thinges
ne bityden nat that ben ypurveyed to com-
en? But, certes, right as we trowen that
tho thinges which that the purviaunce wot
biforn to comen ne ben nat to bityden; but
that ne sholden we nat demen; but rather,
althogh that they shal bityden, yit ne have
they no necessitee of hir kinde to bityden.
And this maystow lightly aperceiven by
this that I shal seyn. for we seen many
thinges whan they ben don biforn oure
eyen, right as men seen the cartere work-
en in the torninge or atempringe or adres-
singe of hise cartes or charietes. And by
this manere (as who seith, maystow understonde) of alle othere workmen. Is ther
thanne any necessitee, as who seith, in oure
lokinge, that constreineth or compelleth
any of thilke thinges to ben don so?
Boece.

NAY, quod I; for in ydel and in veyn
were al the effect of craft, yif that
alle thinges weren moeved by constreininge; that is to seyn, by constreininge of oure eyen or of oure sight.

THE thinges thanne, quod she, that
whan men doon hem, ne han no necessitee that men doon hem, eek tho
same thinges, first or they ben doon, they
ben to comen withoute necessitee. forwhy
ther ben somme thinges to bityden, of
which the endes & the bitydinges of hem
ben absolut and quit of alle necessitee. for
certes, I ne trowe nat that any man wolde
seyn this: that tho thinges that men doon
now, that they ne weren to bityden first or
they weren ydoon; & thilke same thinges,
althogh that men had ywist hem biforn,
yit they han free bitydinges. for right as
science of thinges present ne bringeth in
no necessitee to thinges that men doon,
right so the prescience of thinges to com-
en ne bringeth in no necessitee to thinges
to bityden. But thou mayst seyn, that of
thilke same it is ydouted, as whether that
of thilke thinges that ne han non issues &
bitydinges necessaries, yif therof may ben
any prescience; for certes, they semen to
discorden. for thou wenest that, yif that
thinges ben yseyn biforn, that necessitee
folweth hem; and yif necessitee faileth
hem, they ne mighten nat ben wist biforn,
& that nothing ne may ben comprehended
by science but certein; and yif tho thinges
that ne han no certein bitydinges ben purveyed as certein, it sholde ben dirknesse of
opinioun, nat soothfastnesse of science.
And thou wenest that it be diverse fro the
hoolnesse of science that any man sholde
deme a thing to ben otherweys thanne it
is itself. And the cause of this erroure is,
that of alle the thinges that every wight
hath yknowe, they wenen that tho thinges
been yknowe aloonly by the strengthe & by
the nature of the thinges that ben ywist or
yknowe; & it is al the contrarie. for al that
ever is yknowe, it is rather comprehended
and knowen, nat after his strengthe and
his nature, but after the facultee, that is to
seyn, the power and the nature, of hem
that knowen. And, for that this thing shal
mowen shewen by a short ensaumple: the
same roundnesse of a body, otherweys
the sighte of the eye knoweth it, & otherweyes the touchinge. The lokinge by cast-
inge of his bemes, waiteth and seeth from
afer al the body togidere, withoute moevinge of itself; but the touchinge clyveth &
conjoineth to the rounde body, & moeveth
aboute the environinge, and comprehendeth by parties the roundnesse. And the man
himself, otherweys wit biholdeth him, and
otherweys imaginacioun, & otherweys resoun, & otherweys intelligence. for the wit
comprehendeth withouteforth the figure
of the body of the man that is establissed
in the matere subject; but the imaginacioun
comprehendeth only the figure withoute

379

the matere. Resoun surmounteth imaginacioun, and comprehendeth by universal
lokinge the comune spece that is in the
singuler peces. But the eye of intelligence
is heyere; for it surmounteth the environinge of the universitee, and looketh, over
that, by pure subtilitee of thoght, thilke
same simple forme of man that is perdurably in the divyne thoght. In whiche
this oughte greetly to ben considered, that
the heyeste strengthe to comprehenden
thinges enbraseth and contieneth the lowere strengthe; but the lowere strengthe
ne aryseth nat in no manere to heyere
strengthe. For wit ne may nothing comprehende out of matere, ne the imaginacioun ne loketh nat the universels speces,
ne resoun taketh nat the simple forme so
as intelligence taketh it; but intelligence,
that looketh al aboven, whan it hath comprehended the forme, it knoweth & demeth
alle the thinges that ben under that forme.
But she knoweth hem in thilke manere in
the whiche it comprehendeth thilke same
simple forme that ne may never ben know-
en to none of that other; that is to seyn, to
none of tho three forseide thinges of the
sowle. For it knoweth the universitee of
resoun, & the figure of the imaginacioun,
and the sensible material conceived by wit;
ne it ne useth nat nor of resoun ne of
imaginacioun ne of wit withouteforth;
but it biholdeth alle thinges, so as I shal
seye, by a strok of thought formely, withoute discours or collacioun. Certes resoun,
whan it looketh anything universel, it ne
useth nat of imaginacioun, nor of witte, &
algates yit it comprehendeth the thinges
imaginable and sensible; for resoun is she
that diffinisseth the universel of hir con-
seyte right thus: man is a resonable two-
foted beest. And how so that this knowinge is universel, yet nis ther no wight that
ne woot wel that a man is a thing imaginable and sensible; & this same considereth
wel resoun; but that nis nat by imaginacioun nor by wit, but it looketh it by a resonable concepcioun. Also imaginacioun,
albeit so that it taketh of wit the biginninges to seen and to formen the figures,
algates, althogh that wit ne were nat present, yit it environeth and comprehendeth
alle thinges sensible; nat by resoun sensible of deminge, but by resoun imaginatif.
Seestow nat thanne that alle the thinges, in
knowinge, usen more of hir facultee or of
hir power than they doon of the facultee or
power of thinges that ben yknowe? Ne that
nis nat wrong; for so as every jugement is
the dede or doinge of him that demeth, it bihoveth that every wight performe the werk
and his entencioun, nat of foreine power,
but of his propre power.

Metre IV.
Quondam porticus attulit.

HE Porche, that is to seyn, a
gate of the town of Athenes
theras philosophres hadden
hir congregacioun to desput-
en, thilke Porche broughte
somtyme olde men, fulderke
in hir sentences, that is to seyn, philosophres that highten Stoiciens, that wenden
that images and sensibilitees, that is to
seyn, sensible imaginaciouns, or elles imaginaciouns of sensible thinges, weren empreinted into sowles fro bodies withouteforth; as who seith, that thilke Stoiciens
wenden that the sowle hadde ben naked of
itself, as a mirour or a clene parchemin, so
that alle figures mosten first comen fro
thinges fro withouteforth into sowles, &
ben empreinted into sowles: Text: right as
we ben wont somtyme, by a swifte pointel,
to ficchen lettres empreinted in the smoth-
enesse or in the pleinnesse of the table of
wex or in parchemin that ne hath no figure
ne note in it. Glose. But now argueth Boece
ayeins that opinioun, and seith thus: But
yif the thryvinge sowle ne unpleyteth nothing, that is to seyn, ne doth nothing, by
his propre moevinges, but suffreth and
lyth subgit to tho figures and to tho notes
of bodies withouteforth, and yildeth images ydel and veyn in the manere of a mirour, whennes thryveth thanne or whennes
comth thilke knowinge in our sowle, that
discerneth & biholdeth alle thinges? And
whennes is thilke strengthe that biholdeth the singuler thinges; or whennes is the
strengthe that devydeth thinges yknowe;
& thilke strengthe that gadereth togidere
the thinges devyded; and the strengthe
that cheseth his entrechaunged wey? For
somtyme it heveth up the heved, that is to
seyn, that it heveth up the entencioun to
right heye thinges; & somtyme it descendeth into right lowe thinges. And whan it retorneth into himself, it reproeveth & destroyeth the false thinges by the trewe
thinges. Certes, this strengthe is cause
more efficient, and mochel more mighty to
seen & to knowe thinges, than thilke cause
that suffreth and receiveth the notes and
the figures impressed in maner of matere.
Algates the passioun, that is to seyn, the
suffraunce or the wit, in the quike body,
goth biforn, excitinge and moevinge the
strengthes of the thought. Right so as
whan that cleernesse smyteth the eyen &
moeveth hem to seen, or right so as vois or
soun hurteleth to the eres and commoev-
eth hem to herkne, than is the strengthe
of the thought ymoeved and excited, and
clepeth forth, to semblable moevinges, the
speces that it halt withinne itself; and addeth tho speces to the notes and to the

thinges withouteforth, and medleth the images of thinges withouteforth to tho formes yhidde withinne himself.

Prose V.
Quod si in corporibus sentiendis.

BVT what yif that in bodies to ben feled, that is to seyn, in the takinge of knowe-lechinge of bodily thinges, and albeit so that the quali-tees of bodies, that ben objecte fro with-outeforth, moeven & entalenten the instruments of the wittes; and albeit so that the passioun of the body, that is to seyn, the wit or the suffraunce, goth toforn the strengthe of the workinge corage, the which passioun or suffraunce clepeth forth the dede of the thoght in himself, and moeveth and exciteth in this mene whyle the formes that resten with-inneforth; and yif that, in sensible bodies, as I have seyd, our corage nis nat ytaught or empreinted by passioun to knowe thise thinges, but demeth and knoweth, of his owne strengthe, the passioun or suffraunce subject to the body: moche more thanne tho thinges that ben absolut and quite fro alle talents or affecciouns of bodies, as God or his aungeles, ne folwen nat in discern-inge thinges object fro withouteforth, but they accomplisshen and speden the dede of hir thoght. By this resoun thanne ther comen many maner knowinges to dyverse and differinge substaunces. For the wit of the body, the whiche wit is naked and de-spoiled of alle other knowinges, thilke wit comth to beestes that ne mowen nat moev-en hemself her and ther, as oystres and muscules, and other swiche shelle-fish of the see, that clyven and ben norisshed to roches. But the imaginacioun comth to remuable beestes, that semen to han talent to fleen or to desiren any thing. But resoun is alonly to the linage of mankinde, right as intelligence is only to the devyne nature: of which it folweth, that thilke knowinge is more worth than thise othre, sin it know-eth by his propre nature nat only his sub-ject, as who seith, it ne knoweth nat alonly that apertieneth properly to his knowinge, but it knoweth the subjects of alle other knowinges. But how shal it thanne be, yif that wit and imaginacioun stryven ayein resoninge, & seyn, that of thilke universel thing that resoun weneth to seen, that it nis right naught? For wit & imaginacioun seyn that that, that is sensible or imagin-able, it ne may nat be universel. Thanne is either the jugement of resoun sooth, ne that ther nis nothing sensible; or elles, for

that resoun wot wel that many thinges ben subject to wit and to imaginacioun, thanne is the concepcioun of resoun veyn & false, which that loketh & comprehendeth that that is sensible and singuler as universel. And yif that resoun wolde answeren ayein to thise two, that is to seyn, to witte & to imaginacioun, and seyn, that soothly she hirself, that is to seyn, resoun, loketh and comprehendeth, by resoun of universali-tee, bothe that that is sensible & that that is imaginable; and that thilke two, that is to seyn, wit and imaginacioun, ne mowen nat strecchen ne enhansen hemself to the knowinge of universalitee, for that the knowinge of hem ne may exceden ne sur-mounte the bodily figures: certes, of the knowinge of thinges, men oughten rather yeven credence to the more stedefast and to the more parfit jugement. In this maner stryvinge thanne, we that han strengthe of resoninge & of imagininge and of wit, that is to seyn, by resoun and by imagina-cioun and by wit, we sholde rather preyse the cause of resoun; as who seith, than the cause of wit and of imaginacioun. SEMBLABLE thing is it, that the re-soun of mankinde ne weneth nat that the devyne intelligence biholdeth or knoweth thinges to comen, but right as the resoun of mankinde knoweth hem. For thou arguest and seyst thus: that yif it ne seme nat to men that some thinges han certein & necessarie bitydinges, they ne mowen nat ben wist biforn certeinly to bityden. And thanne nis ther no prescience of thilke thinges; and yif we trowe that prescience be in thise thinges, thanne is ther nothing that it ne bitydeth by neces-sitee. But certes, yif we mighten han the jugement of the devyne thoght, as we ben parsoneres of resoun, right so as we han demed that it behoveth that imaginacioun and wit be binethe resoun, right so wolde we demen that it were rightful thing, that mannes resoun oughte to submitten itself and to ben binethe the divyne thoght. For which, yif that we mowen, as who seith, that, yif that we mowen, I counseyle, that we enhanse us into the heighte of thilke sovereyn intelligence; for ther shal resoun wel seen that, that it ne may nat biholden in itself. And certes that is this, in what maner the prescience of God seeth alle thinges certeins and diffinisshed, althogh they ne han no certein issues or bityding-es; ne this is non opinioun, but it is rather the simplicitee of the sovereyn science, that nis nat enclosed nor yshet within none boundes.

Metre V.
Quam variis terris animalia permeant
figuris.

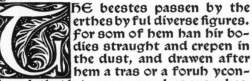HE beestes passen by the
erthes by ful diverse figures.
For som of hem han hir bodies straught and crepen in
the dust, and drawen after
hem a tras or a forub ycon-
tinued; that is to seyn, as nadres or snakes.
And other beestes, by the wandringe lightnesse of hir winges, beten the windes, and
over-swimmen the spaces of the longe eyr
by moist fleeinge. And other beestes glad-
en hemself to diggen hir tras or hir steppes in the erthe with hir goings or with hir
feet, & to goon either by the grene feldes,
or elles to walken under the wodes. And
albeit so that thou seest that they alle discorden by diverse formes, algates hir faces,
enclined, hevieth hir dulle wittes. Only the
linage of man heveth heyeste his heye heved, and stondeth light with his upright
body, and biholdeth the erthes under him.
And, but yif thou, erthely man, wexest
yvel out of thy wit, this figure amonesteth
thee, that axest the hevene with thy righte
visage, and hast areysed thy foreheved, to
beren up aheigh thy corage; so that thy
thoght ne be nat yhevied ne put lowe under
fote, sin that thy body is so heye areysed.

Prose VI.
Quoniam igitur, uti paullo ante.

HERFOR thanne,
as I have shewed a
litel herbiform, that
althing that is ywist
nis nat knowen by
his nature propre,
but by the nature of
hem that compre-
henden it, lat us loke
now, in as mochel as
it is leveful to us, as who seith, lat us loke
now as we mowen, which that the estat is
of the devyne substaunce; so that we mow-
en eek knowen what his science is. The
commune jugement of alle creatures resonables thanne is this: that God is eterne.
Lat us considere thanne what is eternitee;
for certes that shal shewen us togidere the
devyne nature and the devyne science.
TERNITEE, thanne, is parfit possessioun & altogidere of lyf interminable; and that sheweth more
cleerly by the comparisoun or the collacioun of temporel thinges. For al thing
that liveth in tyme it is present, and procedeth fro preterits into futures, that is
to seyn, fro tyme passed into tyme cominge; ne ther nis nothing establisshed in
tyme that may embracen togider al the
space of his lyf. For certes, yit ne hath it

taken the tyme of tomorwe, and it hath
lost the tyme of yisterday. And certes, in
the lyf of this day, ye ne liven no more but
right as in the moevable & transitorie moment. Thanne thilke thing that suffreth
temporel condicioun, althogh that it never
bigan to be, ne thogh it never cese for to
be, as Aristotle demed of the world, and
althogh that the lyf of it be strecched with
infinitee of tyme, yit algates nis it no swich
thing that men mighten trowen by right
that it is eterne. For althogh that it comprehende and embrace the space of lyf infinit, yit algates ne embraceth it nat the
space of the lyf altogider; for it ne hath
nat the futures that ne ben nat yit, ne it ne
hath no lenger the preterits that ben ydoon
or ypassed. But thilke thing thanne, that
hath & comprehendeth togider al the plentee of the lyf interminable, to whom ther ne
faileth naught of the future, and to whom
ther nis naught of the preterit escaped nor
ypassed, thilke same is ywitnessed and
yproeved by right to be eterne. And it bihoveth by necessitee that thilke thing be
alwey present to himself, and compotent;
as who seith, alwey present to himself, &
so mighty that al be right at his plesaunce;
& that he have al present the infinitee of the
moevable tyme. Wherfor som men trowen
wrongfully that, whan they heren that it
semede to Plato that this world ne hadde
never biginninge of tyme, ne that it never
shal han failinge, they wenen in this maner
that this world be maked coeterne with his
maker; as who seith, they wene that this
world and God ben maked togider eterne,
and that is a wrongful weninge. For other
thing is it to ben ylad by lyf interminable,
as Plato graunted to the world, and other
thing is it to embrace togider al the present
of the lyf interminable, the whiche thing
it is cleer and manifest that it is propre to
the devyne thoght.
NE it ne sholde nat semen to us, that
God is elder thanne thinges that ben
ymaked by quantitee of tyme, but
rather by the propretee of his simple nature. For this ilke infinit moevinge of temporel thinges folweth this presentarie estat of lyf unmoevable; and so as it ne may
nat countrefeten it ne feynen it ne be even-
lyke to it for the inmoevabletee, that is
to seyn, that is in the eternitee of God, it
faileth and falleth into moevinge fro the
simplicitee of the presence of God, and
disencreseth into the infinit quantitee of
future and of preterit: and so as it ne may
nat han togider al the plentee of the lyf, algates yit, for as moche as it ne ceseth never
for to ben in som maner, it semeth somdel
to us, that it folweth & resembleth thilke
thing that it ne may nat atayne to ne fulfillen, and bindeth itself to som maner pre-

sence of this litel and swifte moment: the which presence of this litel & swifte moment, for that it bereth a maner image or lyknesse of the ay⁄dwellinge presence of God, it graunteth, to swiche maner thinges as it bitydeth to, that it semeth hem as thise thinges han yben, and ben.

AND, for that the presence of swich litel moment ne may nat dwelle, therfor it ravisshed and took the infinit wey of tyme, that is to seyn, by successioun; and by this maner is it y⁄doon, for that it sholde continue the lyf in goinge, of the whiche lyf it ne mighte nat enbrace the plentee in dwellinge. And forthy, yif we wollen putten worthy names to thinges, and folwen Plato, lat us seye thanne soothly, that God is eterne, & the world is perpetuel. Thanne, sin that every jugement knoweth and comprehendeth by his owne nature thinges that ben subject unto him, ther is soothly to God, alweys, an eterne and presentarie estat; and the science of him, that over⁄passeth al temporel moevement, dwelleth in the simplicitee of his presence, and embraceth and considereth alle the infinit spaces of tymes, preterits and futures, and loketh, in his simple knowinge, alle thinges of preterit right as they weren ydoon presently right now. Yif thou wolt thanne thenken & avyse the prescience, by which it knoweth alle thinges, thou ne shal nat demen it as prescience of thinges to com⁄en, but thou shalt demen it more rightfully that it is science of presence or of instaunce, that never ne faileth. For which it nis nat ycleped Previdence, but it sholde rather ben cleped Purviaunce, that is establisshed ful fer fro right lowe thinges, & biholdeth from afer alle thinges, right as it were fro the heye heighte of thinges. Why axestow thanne, or why desputestow thanne, that thilke thinges ben doon by necessitee whiche that ben yseyn and knowen by the devyne sighte, sin that, forsothe, men ne maken nat thilke thinges necessarie which that seen ben ydoon in hir sighte? For addeth thy biholdinge any necessitee to thilke thinges that thou biholdest presente? ⌐ Nay, quod I. Philosophie.

CERTES, thanne, if men mighte maken any digne comparisoun or collacioun of the presence devyne and of the presence of mankinde, right so as ye seen some thinges in this temporel present, right so seeth God alle thinges by his eterne present. Wherfore this devyne prescience ne chaungeth nat the nature ne the propretee of thinges, but biholdeth swiche thinges present to himward as they shullen bityde to yowward in tyme to comen. Ne it confoundeth nat

the jugement of thinges; but by o sighte of his thought, he knoweth the thinges to comen, as wel necessarie as nat necessarie. Right so as whan ye seen togider a man walken on the erthe and the sonne arysen in the hevene, albeit so that ye seen and biholden that oon and that other togider, yit natheles ye demen and discernen that that oon is voluntarie and that other necessarie. Right so thanne the devyne lookinge, biholdinge alle thinges under him, ne troubleth nat the qualitee of thing⁄es that ben certeinly present to himward; but, as to the condicioun of tyme, forsothe, they ben future. For which it folweth, that this nis noon opinioun, but rather a stedefast knowinge, ystrengthed by soothnesse, that, whanne that God knoweth any thing to be, he ne unwot nat that thilke thing wanteth necessitee to be; this is to seyn, that, whan that God knoweth any thing to bityde, he wot wel that it ne hath no necessitee to bityde.

AND yif thou seyst heer, that thilke thing that God seeth to bityde, it ne may nat unbityde (as who seith, it mot bityde), and thilke thing that ne may nat unbityde it mot bityde by necessitee, and that thou streyne me by this name of necessitee: certes, I wol wel confessen and biknowe a thing of ful sad trouthe, but unnethe shal ther any wight mowe seen it or come therto, but yif that he be biholder of the devyne thoght. For I wol answeren thee thus: that thilke thing that is future, whan it is referred to the devyne knowinge, thanne is it necessarie; but certes, whan it is understonden in his owne kinde, men seen it is outrely free, & absolut fro alle necessitee.

FOR certes, ther ben two maneres of necessitee. That oon necessitee is simple, as thus: that it bihoveth by necessitee, that alle men be mortal or deedly. Another necessitee is condicionel, as thus: yif thou wost that a man walketh, it bihoveth by necessitee that he walke. Thilke thing thanne that any wight hath yknowe to be, it ne may ben non other weyes thanne he knoweth it to be. But this condicioun ne draweth nat with hir thilke necessitee simple. For certes, this necessitee condicionel, the propre nature of it ne maketh it nat, but the adjeccioun of the condicioun maketh it. For no necessitee ne constreyneth a man to gon, that goth by his propre wil; albeit so that, whan he goth, that it is necessarie that he goth. Right on this same maner thanne, yif that the purviaunce of God seeth any thing present, than mot thilke thing ben by necessitee, althogh that it ne have no necessitee of his owne nature. But certes, the futures that bityden by freedom of

383

arbitre, God seeth hem alle togider present. Thise thinges thanne, yif they ben referred to the devyne sighte, thanne ben they maked necessarie by the condicioun of the devyne knowinge. But certes, yif thilke thinges be considered by hemself, they ben absolut of necessitee, and ne forleten nat ne cesen nat of the libertee of hir owne nature. Thanne, certes, withoute doute, alle the thinges shollen ben doon which that God wot biforn that they ben to comen. But som of hem comen and bityden of free arbitre or of free wille, that, albeit so that they bityden, yit algates ne lese they nat hir propre nature in beinge; by the which first, or that they weren ydoon, they hadden power nat to han bitid.

Boece.

WHAT is this to seyn thanne, quod I, that thinges ne ben nat necessarie by hir propre nature, so as they comen in alle maneres in the lyknesse of necessitee by the condicioun of the devyne science?

Philosophie.

THIS is the difference, quod she; that tho thinges that I purposede thee a litel heerbiforn, that is to seyn, the sonne arysinge and the man walkinge, that, therwhyles that thilke thinges been ydoon, they ne mighte nat ben undoon; natheles, that oon of hem, or it was ydoon, it bihoved by necessitee that it was ydoon, but nat that other. Right so is it here, that the thinges that God hath present, withoute doute they shollen been. But som of hem descendeth of the nature of thinges, as the sonne arysinge; and som descendeth of the power of the doeres, as the man walkinge. Thanne seide I no wrong, that yif these thinges ben referred to the devyne knowinge, thanne ben they necessarie; and yif they ben considered by hemself, thanne ben they absolut fro the bond of necessitee. Right so as alle thinges that apereth or sheweth to the wittes, yif thou referre it to resoun, it is universel; and yif thou referre it or loke it to itself, than is it singuler. But now, yif thou seyst thus, that yif it be in my power to chaunge my purpos, than shal I voide the purviaunce of God, whan that, peraventure, I shal han chaunged the thinges that he knoweth biforn, thanne shal I answere thee thus. Certes, thou mayst wel chaunge thy purpos; but, for as mochel as the present soothnesse of the devyne purviaunce biholdeth that thou mayst chaunge thy purpos, and whether thou wolt chaunge it or no, & whiderward that thou torne it, thou ne mayst nat eschuen the devyne prescience; right as thou ne mayst nat fleen the sighte of the presente eye, although that thou torne thyself by thy free wil into

384

dyverse acciouns. But thou mayst seyn ayein: How shal it thanne be? Shal nat the devyne science be chaunged by my disposicioun, whan that I wol o thing now, and now another? And thilke prescience, ne semeth it nat to entrechaunge stoundes of knowinge; as who seith, ne shal it nat seme to us, that the devyne prescience entrechaungeth hise dyverse stoundes of knowinge, so that it knowe sumtyme o thing and sumtyme the contrarie of that thing? No, forsothe, quod I.

Philosophie.

FOR the devyne sighte renneth toforn and seeth alle futures, and clepeth hem ayein, and retorneth hem to the presence of his propre knowinge; ne he ne entrechaungeth nat, so as thou wenest, the stoundes of forknowinge, as now this, now that; but he ay dwellinge comth biforn, and embraceth at o strook alle thy mutaciouns. And this presence to comprehenden and to seen alle thinges, God ne hath nat taken it of the bitydinge of thinges to come, but of his propre simplicitee. And herby is assoiled thilke thing that thou puttest a litel herbiforn, that is to seyn, that it is unworthy thing to seyn, that our futures yeven cause of the science of God. For certes, this strengthe of the devyne science, which that embraceth alle thinges by his presentarie knowinge, establissheth maner to alle thinges, and it ne oweth naught to latter thinges; and sin that these thinges ben thus, that is to seyn, sin that necessitee nis nat in thinges by the devyne prescience, than is ther freedom of arbitre, that dwelleth hool and unwemmed to mortal men. Ne the lawes ne purposen nat wikkedly medes and peynes to the willinges of men that ben unbounden and quite of alle necessitee. And God, biholder & forwiter of alle thinges, dwelleth above; and the present eternitee of his sighte renneth alwey with the dyverse qualitee of oure dedes, despensinge & ordeyninge medes to goode men, and torments to wikked men. Ne in ydel ne in veyn ne ben ther nat put in God hope and preyeres, that ne mowen nat ben unspeedful ne withoute effect, whan they ben rightful.

WITHSTOND thanne and eschue thou vyces; worshipe & love thou virtues; areys thy corage to rightful hopes; yilde thou humble preyeres aheigh. Gret necessitee of prowesse & vertu is encharged & commaunded to yow, yif ye nil nat dissimulen; sin that ye worken and doon, that is to seyn, your dedes or your workes, biforn the eyen of the Juge that seeth and demeth alle thinges. To whom be glorye and worshipe by infinit tymes. Amen.

I HAVE GRET WONDER, BY THIS LIGHTE,
How that I live, for day ne nighte
I may nat slepe wel nigh noght;
I have so many an ydel thoght
Purely for defaute of slepe,
That, by my trouthe, I take kepe
Of nothing, how hit cometh or goth,
Ne me nis nothing leef nor loth.

Al is yliche good to me,
Joye or sorowe, wherso hit be,
For I have feling in nothing,
But, as it were, a mased thing,
Alway in point to falle adoun;
For sory imaginacioun
Is alway hoolly in my minde.
AND wel ye wite, agaynes kinde
Hit were to liven in this wyse;
For nature wolde nat suffyse
To noon erthely creature
Not longe tyme to endure
Withoute slepe, and been in sorwe;
And I ne may, ne night ne morwe,
Slepe; and thus melancolye,
And dreed I have for to dye,
Defaute of slepe, and hevinesse
Hath sleyn my spirit of quiknesse,
That I have lost al lustihede.
Suche fantasyes ben in myn hede
So I not what is best to do.
BUT men mighte axe me, why so
I may not slepe, and what me is?
But natheles, who aske this
Leseth his asking trewely.
Myselven can not telle why
The sooth; but trewely, as I gesse,

I holde hit be a siknesse
That I have suffred this eight yere,
And yet my bote is never the nere;
For ther is phisicien but oon,
That may me hele; but that is doon.
Passe we over until eft;
That wil not be, moot nede be left;
Our first matere is good to kepe.
So whan I saw I might not slepe,
Til now late, this other night,
Upon my bedde I sat upright,
And bad oon reche me a book,
A romaunce, and he hit me took
To rede and dryve the night away;
For me thoghte it better play
Then playen either at chesse or tables.
AND in this boke were writen fables
That clerkes hadde, in old tyme,
And other poets, put in ryme
To rede, and for to be in minde
Whyl men loved the lawe of kinde.
This book ne spak but of such thinges,
Of quenes lyves, and of kinges,
And many othere thinges smale.
Amonge al this I fond a tale
That me thoughte a wonder thing.
THIS was the tale: Ther was a king
That highte Seys, and hadde a wyf,
The beste that mighte bere lyf;
And this quene highte Alcyone.
So hit befel, therafter sone,
This king wolde wenden over see.
To tellen shortly, whan that he
Was in the see, thus in this wyse,
Soche a tempest gan to ryse
That brak hir mast, and made it falle,
And clefte hir ship, and dreinte hem alle,
That never was founden, as it telles,
Bord ne man, ne nothing elles.
Right thus this king Seys loste his lyf.
NOW for to speken of his wyf:
This lady, that was left at home,
Hath wonder, that the king ne come
Hoom, for hit was a longe terme.
Anon her herte gan to erme;
And for that hir thoughte evermo
Hit was not wel he dwelte so,
She longed so after the king
That certes, hit were a pitous thing
To telle hir hertely sorwful lyf
That hadde, alas! this noble wyf;
For him she loved alderbest.
Anon she sente bothe eest and west
To seke him, but they founde nought.
ALAS! quoth she, that I was wroughtt!
And wher my lord, my love, be deed?
Certes, I nil never ete breed,
I make avowe to my god here,
But I mowe of my lorde here!
Such sorwe this lady to her took
That trewely I, which made this book,
Had swich pite and swich rowthe
To rede hir sorwe, that, by my trowthe,
386

I ferde the worse al the morwe
After, to thenken on her sorwe.
SO whan she coude here no word
That no man mighte fynde hir lord,
Ful oft she swouned, and seide Alas!
For sorwe ful nigh wood she was,
Ne coude she no reed but oon;
But doun on knees she sat anoon,
And weep, that pite was to here.
A! MERCY! swete lady dere!
Quod she to Juno, hir goddesse;
Help me out of this distresse,
And yeve me grace my lord to see
Sone, or wite wherso he be,
Or how he fareth, or in what wyse,
And I shal make you sacrifyse,
And hoolly youres become I shal
With good wil, body, herte, and al;
And but thou wilt this, lady swete,
Send me grace to slepe, and mete
In my slepe som certeyn sweven,
Wherthrough that I may knowen even
Whether my lord be quik or deed.
With that word she heng doun the heed,
And fil aswown as cold as ston;
Hir women caughte her up anon,
And broghten hir in bed al naked,
And she, forweped and forwaked,
Was wery, and thus the dede sleep
Fil on her, or she toke keep,
Through Juno, that had herd hir bone,
That made hir for to slepe sone;
For as she prayde, so was don,
In dede; for Juno, right anon,
Called thus her messagere
To do her erande, and he com nere.
Whan he was come, she bad him thus:
GO bet, quod Juno, to Morpheus,
Thou knowest him wel, the god of sleep;
Now understond wel, and tak keep.
Sey thus on my halfe, that he
Go faste into the grete see,
And bid him that, on alle thing,
He take up Seys body the king,
That lyth ful pale and nothing rody.
Bid him crepe into the body,
And do it goon to Alcyone
The quene, ther she lyth alone,
And shewe hir shortly, hit is no nay,
How hit was dreynt this other day;
And do the body speke so
Right as hit was wont to do,
The whyles that hit was on lyve.
Go now faste, and hy thee blyve!
THIS messager took leve and wente
Upon his weye, and never ne stente
Til he com to the derke valeye
That stant bytwene roches tweye,
Ther never yet grew corn ne gras,
Ne tree, ne nothing that ought was,
Beste, ne man, ne nothing elles,
Save there were a fewe welles
Came renning fro the cliffes adoun,

That made a deedly sleping soun,
And ronnen doun right by a cave
That was under a rokke ygrave
Amid the valey, wonder depe.
Ther thise goddes laye and slepe,
Morpheus, and Eclympasteyre,
That was the god of slepes heyre,
That slepe and did non other werk.

THIS cave was also as derk
As helle pit overal aboute;
They had good leyser for to route
To envye, who might slepe beste;
Some henge hir chin upon hir breste
And slepe upright, hir heed yhed,
And some laye naked in hir bed,
And slepe whyles the dayes laste.

THIS messager com flying faste,
And cryed: O ho! awak anon!
Hit was for noght; ther herde him non.
Awak! quod he, who is, lyth there?
And blew his horn right in hir ere,
And cryed Awaketh! wonder hyë.
This god of slepe, with his oon yë
Cast up, axed: Who clepeth there?
Hit am I, quod this mesagere;
Juno bad thou shuldest goon.
And tolde him what he shulde doon
As I have told yow heretofore;
Hit is no need reherse hit more;
And wente his wey, whan he had sayd.

ANON this god of slepe abrayd
Out of his slepe, and gan to goon,
And did as he had bede him doon;
Took up the dreynte body sone,
And bar hit forth to Alcyone,
His wyf the quene, theras she lay,
Right even a quarter before day,
And stood right at hir beddes fete,
And called hir, right as she hete,
By name, and seyde: My swete wyf,
Awak! let be your sorwful lyf!
For in your sorwe ther lyth no reed;
For certes, swete, I nam but deed;
Ye shul me never on lyve ysee.
But good swete herte, look that ye
Bury my body, at whiche a tyde
Ye mowe hit finde the see besyde;
And farwel, swete, my worldes blisse!
I praye god your sorwe lisse;
To litel whyl our blisse lasteth!

WITH that hir eyen up she casteth,
And saw noght: A! quod she, for sorwe!
And deyed within the thridde morwe.
But what she sayde more in that swow
I may not telle yow as now,
Hit were to longe for to dwelle;
My first matere I wil yow telle,
Wherfor I have told this thing
Of Alcione and Seys the king.

OR thus moche dar I saye wel,
I had be dolven everydel,
And deed, right through defaute of
sleep,
If I nad red and taken keep
Of this tale next before:
And I wol telle yow wherfore;
For I ne might, for bote ne bale,
Slepe, or I had red this tale
Of this dreynte Seys the king,
And of the goddes of sleping.
Whan I had red this tale wel,
And overloked hit everydel,
Me thoughte wonder if hit were so;
For I had never herd speke, or tho,
Of no goddes that coude make
Men for to slepe, ne for to wake;
For I ne knew never god but oon.
And in my game I sayde anoon,
And yet me list right evel to pleye:
Rather then that I shulde deye
Through defaute of sleping thus,
I wolde yive thilke Morpheus,
Or his goddesse, dame Juno,
Or som wight elles, I ne roghte who,
To make me slepe and have som reste;
I wil yive him the alderbeste
Yift that ever he abood his lyve,
And here on warde, right now, as blyve;
If he wol make me slepe a lyte,
Of downe of pure dowves whyte
I wil yive him a fether-bed,
Rayed with golde, and right wel cled
In fyn blak satin doutremere,
And many a pilow, and every bere
Of clothe of Reynes, to slepe softe;
Him thar not nede to turnen ofte.
And I wol yive him al that falles
To a chambre; and al his halles
I wol do peynte with pure golde,
And tapite hem ful many folde
Of oo sute; this shal he have,
If I wiste wher were his cave,
If he can make me slepe sone,
As did the goddesse Alcione.
And thus this ilke god, Morpheus,
May winne of me mo feës thus
Than ever he wan; and to Juno,
That is his goddesse, I shal so do,
I trow that she shal holde her payd.

I HADDE unneth that word ysayd
Right thus as I have told hit yow,
That sodeynly, I niste how,
Swich a lust anoon me took
To slepe, that right upon my book
I fil aslepe, and therwith even
Me mette so inly swete a sweven,
So wonderful, that never yit
I trowe no man hadde the wit
To conne wel my sweven rede;
No, not Joseph, withoute drede,
Of Egipte, he that redde so
The kinges meting Pharao,

No more than coude the leste of us;
Ne nat scarsly Macrobeus,
(He that wroot al thavisioun
That he mette, king Scipioun,
The noble man, the Affrican,
Swiche mervayles fortuned than)
I trowe, arede my dremes even.
Lo, thus hit was, this was my sweven.

The Dream.

E thoughte thus: that hit
was May,
And in the dawning ther I
lay,
Me mette thus, in my bed
al naked:
I loked forth, for I was
waked
With smale foules a gret
hepe,
That had affrayed me out of slepe
Through noyse and swetnesse of hir song;
And, as me mette, they sate among,
Upon my chambre roof withoute,
Upon the tyles, al aboute,
And songen, everich in his wyse,
The moste solempne servyse
By note, that ever man, I trowe,
Had herd; for som of hem song lowe,
Som hye, and al of oon acorde.
To telle shortly, at oo worde,
Was never yherd so swete a steven,
But hit had be a thing of heven;
So mery a soun, so swete entunes,
That certes, for the toune of Tewnes,
I nolde but I had herd hem singe,
For al my chambre gan to ringe
Through singing of hir armonye.
For instrument nor melodye
Was nowher herd yet half so swete,
Nor of acorde half so mete;
For ther was noon of hem that feyned
To singe, for ech of hem him peyned
To finde out mery crafty notes;
They ne spared not hir throtes.
And, sooth to seyn, my chambre was
Ful wel depeynted, and with glas
Were al the windowes wel yglased,
Ful clere, and nat an hole ycrased,
That to beholde hit was gret joye.
For hoolly al the storie of Troye
Was in the glasing ywroght thus,
Of Ector and king Priamus,
Of Achilles and Lamedon,
Of Medea and of Jason,
Of Paris, Eleyne, and Lavyne.
And alle the walles with colours fyne
Were peynted, bothe text and glose,
Of al the Romaunce of the Rose.
My windowes weren shet echon,
And through the glas the sunne shon
Upon my bed with brighte bemes,
With many glade gilden stremes;

388

And eek the welken was so fair,
Blew, bright, clere was the air,
And ful atempre, for sothe, hit was;
For nother cold nor hoot hit nas,
Ne in al the welken was a cloude.
AND as I lay thus, wonder loude
Me thoughte I herde an hunte blowe
T'assaye his horn, and for to knowe
Whether hit were clere or hors of soune.
I HERDE goinge, up and doune,
Men, hors, houndes, and other thing;
And al men speken of hunting,
How they wolde slee the hert with strengthe,
And how the hert had, upon lengthe,
So moche embosed, I not now what.
Anon-right, whan I herde that,
How they wolde on huntinge goon,
I was right glad, and up anoon;
I took my hors, and forth I wente
Out of my chambre; I never stente
Til I com to the feld withoute.
Ther overtook I a gret route
Of huntes and eek of foresteres,
With many relayes and lymeres,
And hyed hem to the forest faste,
And I with hem; so at the laste
I asked oon, ladde a lymere:
Say, felow, who shal hunten here
Quod I; and he answerde ageyn:
Sir, themperour Octovien,
Quod he, and is heer faste by.
A goddes halfe, in good tyme, quod I,
Go we faste! and gan to ryde.
Whan we came to the forest-side,
Every man dide, right anoon,
As to hunting fil to doon.
The mayster-hunte anoon, fot-hoot,
With a gret horne blew three moot
At the uncoupling of his houndes.
Within a whyl the hert yfounde is,
Yhalowed, and rechased faste
Longe tyme; and at the laste,
This hert rused and stal away
Fro alle the houndes a prevy way.
The houndes had overshote hem alle,
And were on a defaute yfalle;
Therwith the hunte wonder faste
Blew a forloyn at the laste.
I WAS go walked fro my tree,
And as I wente, ther cam by me
A whelp, that fauned me as I stood,
That hadde yfolowed, and coude no good.
Hit com and creep to me as lowe,
Right as hit hadde me yknowe,
Hild down his heed and joyned his eres,
And leyde al smothe doun his heres.
I wolde han caught hit, and anoon
Hit fledde, and was fro me goon;
And I him folwed, and hit forth wente
Doun by a floury grene wente
Ful thikke of gras, ful softe and swete,
With floures fele, faire under fete,
And litel used, hit seemed thus;

for bothe flora and Zephirus,
They two that make floures growe,
Had mad hir dwelling ther, I trowe;
for hit was, on to beholde,
As thogh the erthe envye wolde
To be gayer than the heven,
To have mo floures, swiche seven
As in the welken sterres be.
Hit had forgete the povertee
That winter, through his colde morwes,
Had mad hit suffren, and his sorwes;
Al was forgeten, and that was sene.
for al the wode was waxen grene,
Swetnesse of dewe had mad it waxe.

HIT is no need eek for to axe
Wher ther were many grene greves,
Or thikke of trees, so ful of leves;
And every tree stood by himselve
fro other wel ten foot or twelve.
So grete trees, so huge of strengthe,
Of fourty or fifty fadme lengthe,
Clene withoute bough or stikke,
With croppes brode, and eek as thikke,
They were nat an inche asonder,
That hit was shadwe overal under;
And many an hert and many an hinde
Was both before me and bihinde.
Of founes, soures, bukkes, does
Was ful the wode, and many roes,
And many squirelles, that sete
ful hye upon the trees, and ete,
And in hir maner made festes.
Shortly, hit was so ful of bestes,
That thogh Argus, the noble countour,
Sete to rekene in his countour,
And rekened with his figures ten,
for by tho figures mowe al ken,
If they be crafty, rekene and noumbre,
And telle of every thing the noumbre,
Yet shulde he fayle to rekene even
The wondres, me mette in my sweven.

BUT forth they romed wonder faste
Doun the wode; so at the laste
I was war of a man in blak,
That sat and had yturned his bak
To an oke, an huge tree.
Lord, thoghte I, who may that be?
What ayleth him to sitten here?
Anoon-right I wente nere;
Than fond I sitte even upright
A wonder wel-faringe knight,
By the maner me thoughte so,
Of good mochel, and yong therto,
Of the age of four and twenty yeer.
Upon his berde but litel heer,
And he was clothed al in blakke.
I stalked even unto his bakke,
And ther I stood as stille as ought,
That, sooth to saye, he saw me nought,
forwhy he heng his heed adoune.
And with a deedly sorwful soune
He made of ryme ten vers or twelve,
Of a compleynt to himselve,

The moste pite, the moste rowthe,
That ever I herde; for, by my trowthe,
Hit was gret wonder that nature
Might suffren any creature
To have swich sorwe, and be not deed.
ful pitous, pale, and nothing reed,
He sayde a lay, a maner song,
Withoute note, withoute song,
And hit was this; for wel I can
Reherse hit; right thus hit began:

I HAVE of sorwe so gret woon,
That joye gete I never noon,
Now that I see my lady bright,
Which I have loved with al my might,
Is fro me deed, and is agoon.
Allas, o deeth! what ayleth thee,
That thou noldest have taken me,
Whan that thou toke my lady swete?
That was so fayr, so fresh, so free,
So good, that men may wel ysee
Of al goodnesse she had no mete!

WHAN he had mad thus his complaynte,
His sorowful herte gan faste faynte,
And his spirites wexen dede;
The blood was fled, for pure drede,
Doun to his herte, to make him warm,
for wel hit feled the herte had harm,
To wite eek why hit was adrad
By kinde, and for to make hit glad;
for hit is membre principal
Of the body; and that made al
His hewe chaunge and wexe grene
And pale, for no blood was sene
In no maner lime of his.

ANOON therwith whan I saw this,
He ferde thus evel ther he sete,
I wente and stood right at his fete,
And grette him, but he spak noght,
But argued with his owne thoght,
And in his witte disputed faste
Why and how his lyf might laste;
Him thoghte his sorwes were so smerte
And lay so colde upon his herte;
So, through his sorwe and hevy thoght,
Made him that he ne herde me noght;
for he had wel nigh lost his minde,
Thogh Pan, that men clepe god of kinde,
Were for his sorwes never so wrooth.

BUT at the laste, to sayn right sooth,
He was war of me, how I stood
Before him, and dide of myn hood,
And grette him, as I best coude.
Debonairly, and nothing loude,
He sayde: I prey thee, be not wrooth,
I herde thee not, to sayn the sooth,
Ne I saw thee not, sir, trewely.

A! GOODE sir, no fors, quod I,
I am right sory if I have ought
Destroubled yow out of your thought;
foryive me if I have mistake.
YIS, thamendes is light to make,
Quod he, for ther lyth noon therto;
Ther is nothing missayd nor do.

LO! how goodly spak this knight,
As it had been another wight;
He made it nouther tough ne queynte.
And I saw that, and gan me aqueynte
With him, and fond him so tretable,
Right wonder skilful and resonable,
As me thoghte, for al his bale.
Anoon-right I gan finde a tale
To him, to loke wher I might ought
Have more knowing of his thought.
SIR, quod I, this game is doon;
I holde that this hert be goon;
Thise huntes conne him nowher see.
I do no fors therof, quod he,
My thought is theron never a del.
BY our lord, quod I, I trow yow wel,
Right so me thinketh by your chere.
But, sir, oo thing wol ye here?
Me thinketh, in gret sorwe I yow see;
But certes, good sir, yif that ye
Wolde ought discure me your wo,
I wolde, as wis God helpe me so,
Amende hit, yif I can or may;
Ye mowe preve hit by assay.
For, by my trouthe, to make yow hool,
I wol do al my power hool;
And telleth me of your sorwes smerte,
Paraventure hit may ese your herte,
That semeth ful seke under your syde.
With that he loked on me asyde,
As who sayth, Nay, that wol not be.
Graunt mercy, goode frend, quod he,
I thanke thee that thou woldest so,
But hit may never the rather be do.
No man may my sorwe glade,
That maketh my hewe to falle and fade,
And hath myn understonding lorn,
That me is wo that I was born!
May noght make my sorwes slyde,
Nought the remedies of Ovyde;
Ne Orpheus, god of melodye,
Ne Dedalus, with playes slye;
Ne hele me may phisicien,
Noght Ypocras, ne Galien;
Me is wo that I live houres twelve;
But who so wol assaye himselve
Whether his herte can have pite
Of any sorwe, lat him see me.
I wrecche, that deeth hath mad al naked
Of alle blisse that was ever maked,
Yworthe worste of alle wightes,
That hate my dayes and my nightes;
My lyf, my lustes be me lothe,
For al welfare and I be wrothe.
The pure deeth is so my fo,
Thogh I wolde deye, hit wolde not so;
For whan I folwe hit, hit wol flee;
I wolde have hit, hit nil not me.
This is my peyne withoute reed,
Alway deying, and be not deed,
That Sesiphus, that lyth in helle,
May not of more sorwe telle.
And who so wiste al, by my trouthe,

390

My sorwe, but he hadde routhe
And pite of my sorwes smerte,
That man hath a feendly herte.
For who so seeth me first on morwe
May seyn, he hath ymet with sorwe;
For I am sorwe and sorwe is I.
ALLAS! and I wol telle the why;
My song is turned to pleyning,
And al my laughter to weping,
My glade thoghtes to hevinesse,
In travaile is myn ydelnesse
And eek my reste; my wele is wo.
My good is harm, and evermo
In wrathe is turned my pleying,
And my delyt into sorwing.
Myn hele is turned into seeknesse,
In drede is al my sikernesse.
To derke is turned al my light,
My wit is foly, my day is night,
My love is hate, my sleep waking,
My mirthe and meles is fasting,
My countenaunce is nycete,
And al abaved wherso I be,
My pees, in pleding and in werre;
Allas! how mighte I fare werre?
MY boldnesse is turned to shame,
For fals Fortune hath pleyd a game
Atte ches with me, allas! the whyle!
The trayteresse fals and ful of gyle,
That al behoteth and nothing halt,
She goth upryght and yet she halt,
That baggeth foule and loketh faire,
The dispitouse debonaire,
That scorneth many a creature!
An ydole of fals portraiture
Is she, for she wil sone wryen;
She is the monstres heed ywryen,
As filth over ystrawed with floures;
Hir moste worship and hir flour is
To lyen, for that is hir nature;
Withoute feyth, lawe, or mesure
She is fals; and ever laughinge
With oon eye, and that other wepinge.
That is broght up, she set al doun.
I lykne hir to the scorpioun,
That is a fals flatering beste;
For with his hede he maketh feste,
But al amid his flateringe
With his tayle he wol stinge,
And envenyme; and so wol she.
She is thenvyous charite
That is ay fals, and semeth wele,
So turneth she hir false whele
Aboute, for it is nothing stable,
Now by the fyre, now at table;
Ful many oon hath she thus yblent.
She is pley of enchauntement,
That semeth oon and is nat so,
The false theef! what hath she do,
Trowest thou? by our Lord, I wol thee seye.
Atte ches with me she gan to pleye;
With hir false draughtes divers
She stal on me, and took my fers.

And whan I saw my fers aweye,
Alas! I couthe no lenger pleye,
But seyde, farwel, swete, ywis,
And farwel al that ever ther is!
Therwith fortune seyde Chek here!
And Mate! in mid pointe of the chekkere
With a poune erraunt, allas!
Ful craftier to pley she was
Than Athalus, that made the game
First of the ches: so was his name.
But God wolde I had ones or twyes
Ykoud and knowe the jeupardyes
That coude the Grek Pithagores!
I shulde have pleyd the bet at ches,
And kept my fers the bet therby;
And thogh wherto? for trewely
I hold that wish nat worth a stree!
Hit had be never the bet for me.
For fortune can so many a wyle,
Ther be but fewe can hir begyle,
And eek she is the las to blame;
Myself I wolde have do the same,
Before God, hadde I been as she;
She oghte the more excused be.
For this I say yet more therto,
Hadde I be God and mighte have do
My wille, whan my fers she caughte,
I wolde have drawe the same draughte.
For, also wis God yive me reste,
I dar wel swere she took the beste!
BUT through that draughte I have lorn
My blisse; allas! that I was born!
For evermore, I trowe trewly,
For al my wil, my lust hoolly
Is turned; but yet, what to done?
By our Lord, hit is to deye sone;
For nothing I ne leve it noght,
But live and deye right in this thoght.
Ther nis planete in firmament,
Ne in air, ne in erthe, noon element,
That they ne yive me a yift echoon
Of weping, whan I am aloon.
For whan that I avyse me wel,
And bethenke me everydel,
How that ther lyth in rekening,
In my sorwe, for nothing;
And how ther leveth no gladnesse
May gladde me of my distresse,
And how I have lost suffisance,
And therto I have no plesance,
Than may I say, I have right noght.
And whan al this falleth in my thoght,
Allas! than am I overcome!
For that is doon is not to come!
I have more sorwe than Tantale.
AND whan I herde him telle this tale
Thus pitously, as I yow telle,
Unnethe mighte I lenger dwelle,
Hit dide myn herte so moche wo.
A! GOOD sir! quod I, say not so!
Have som pite on your nature
That formed yow to creature;
Remembre yow of Socrates;

For he ne counted nat three strees
Of noght that fortune coude do.
No, quod he, I can not so.
WHY so? good sir! parde! quod I;
Ne say noght so, for trewely,
Thogh ye had lost the ferses twelve,
And ye for sorwe mordred yourselve,
Ye sholde be dampned in this cas
By as good right as Medea was,
That slow hir children for Jason;
And Phyllis als for Demophon
Heng hirself, so weylaway!
For he had broke his terme-day
To come to hir. Another rage
Had Dydo, quene eek of Cartage,
That slow hirself, for Eneas
Was fals; a! whiche a fool she was!
And Ecquo dyed for Narcisus
Nolde nat love hir; and right thus
Hath many another foly don.
And for Dalida dyed Sampson,
That slow himself with a pilere.
But ther is noon alyve here
Wolde for a fers make this wo!
WHY so? quod he; hit is nat so;
Thou wost ful litel what thou menest;
I have lost more than thou wenest.
Lo, sir, how may that be? quod I;
Good sir, tel me al hoolly
In what wyse, how, why, and wherfore
That ye have thus your blisse lore.
BLYTHLY, quod he, com sit adoun;
I telle thee up condicioun
That thou hoolly, with al thy wit,
Do thyn entent to herkene hit.
Yis, sir. Swere thy trouthe therto.
Gladly. Do than holde herto!
I shal right blythly, so God me save,
Hoolly, with al the witte I have,
Here yow, as wel as I can.
A GODDES half! quod he, and began:
Sir, quod he, sith first I couthe
Have any maner wit fro youthe,
Or kyndely understonding
To comprehende, in any thing,
What love was, in myn owne wit,
Dredeles, I have ever yit
Be tributary, and yiven rente
To love hoolly with goode entente,
And through plesaunce become his thral,
With good wil, body, herte, and al.
Al this I putte in his servage,
As to my lorde, and dide homage;
And ful devoutly prayde him to,
He shulde besette myn herte so,
That it plesaunce to him were,
And worship to my lady dere.
AND this was longe, and many a yeer
Or that myn herte was set owher,
That I did thus, and niste why;
I trowe hit cam me kindely.
Paraunter I was therto most able
As a whyt wal or a table;

For hit is redy to cacche and take
Al that men wil therin make,
Wherso men wol portreye or peynte,
Be the werkes never so queynte.

AND thilke tyme I ferde so
I was able to have lerned tho,
And to have coud as wel or better,
Paraunter, other art or letter.
But for love cam first in my thought,
Therfore I forgat it nought.
I chees love to my firste craft,
Therfor hit is with me ylaft.
Forwhy I took hit of so yong age,
That malice hadde my corage,
Nat that tyme turned to nothing
Through to mochel knowleching.
For that tyme youthe, my maistresse,
Governed me in ydelnesse;
For hit was in my firste youthe,
And tho ful litel good I couthe;
For al my werkes were flittinge,
And al my thoghtes varyinge;
Al were to me yliche good,
That I knew tho; but thus hit stood.

HIT happed that I cam on a day
Into a place, ther I say,
Trewly, the fayrest companyë
Of ladies, that ever man with yë
Had seen togedres in oo place.
Shal I clepe hit hap other grace
That broghte me ther? nay, but Fortune,
That is to lyen ful comune,
The false trayteresse, pervers,
God wolde I coude clepe hir wers!
For now she worcheth me ful wo,
And I wol telle sone why so.

AMONG thise ladies thus echoon,
Soth to seyn, I saw ther oon
That was lyk noon of al the route;
For I dar swere, withoute doute,
That as the someres sonne bright
Is fairer, clerer, and hath more light
That any planete, is in heven,
The mone, or the sterres seven,
For al the worlde, so had she
Surmounted hem alle of beaute,
Of maner and of comlinesse,
Of stature and wel set gladnesse,
Of goodlihede so wel beseye...
Shortly, what shal I more seye?
By God, and by his halwes twelve,
It was my swete, right as hirselve!
She had so stedfast countenaunce,
So noble port and meyntenaunce.
And Love, that had herd my bone,
Had espyed me thus sone,
That she ful sone, in my thoght,
As helpe me God, so was ycaught
So sodenly, that I ne took
No maner reed but at hir look
And at myn herte; forwhy hir eyen
So gladly, I trow, myn herte seyen,
That purely tho myn owne thoght

392

Seyde hit were bet serve hir for noght
Than with another to be wel.
And hit was sooth, for, everydel,
I wil anoon/right telle thee why.

I SAW hir daunce so comlily,
Carole and singe so swetely,
Laughe and pleye so womanly,
And loke so debonairly,
So goodly speke and so frendly,
That certes, I trow, that evermore
Nas seyn so blisful a tresore.
For every heer upon hir hede,
Soth to seyn, hit was not rede,
Ne nouther yelw, ne broun hit nas;
Me thoghte, most lyk gold hit was.
And whiche eyen my lady hadde!
Debonair, goode, glade, and sadde,
Simple, of good mochel, noght to wyde;
Therto hir look nas not asyde,
Ne overthwert, but beset so wel,
Hit drew and took up, everydel,
Alle that on hir gan beholde.
Hir eyen semed anoon she wolde
Have mercy; fooles wenden so;
But hit was never the rather do.
Hit nas no countrefeted thing,
It was hir owne pure loking,
That the goddesse, dame Nature,
Had made hem opene by mesure,
And close; for, were she never so glad,
Hir loking was not foly sprad,
Ne wildely, thogh that she pleyde;
But ever, me thoghte, hir eyen seyde,
By God, my wrathe is al foryive!

THERWITH hir liste so wel to live,
That dulnesse was of hir adrad.
She nas to sobre ne to glad;
In alle thinges more mesure
Had never, I trowe, creature.
But many oon with hir loke she herte,
And that sat hir ful lyte at herte,
For she knew nothing of hir thoght;
But whether she knew, or knew hit noght,
Algate she ne roghte of hem a stree!
To gete hir love no ner nas he
That woned at home, than he in Inde;
The formest was alway behinde.
But goode folk, over al other,
She loved as man may do his brother;
Of whiche love she was wonder large,
In skilful places that bere charge.

WHICH a visage had she therto!
Allas! myn herte is wonder wo
That I ne can discryven hit!
Me lakketh bothe English and wit
For to undo hit at the fulle;
And eek my spirits be so dulle
So greet a thing for to devyse.
I have no wit that can suffyse
To comprehenden hir beaute;
But thus moche dar I seyn, that she
Was rody, fresh, and lyvely hewed;
And every day hir beautee newed.

And negh hir face was alderbest;
For certes, Nature had swich lest
To make that fair, that trewly she
Was hir cheef patron of beautee,
And cheef ensample of al hir werke,
And moustre; for, be hit never so derke,
Me thinketh I see hir evermo.
And yet moreover, thogh alle tho
That ever lived were now alyve,
They ne sholde have founde to discryve
In al hir face a wikked signe;
For hit was sad, simple, and benigne.
AND which a goodly softe speche
Had that swete, my lyves leche!
So frendly, and so wel ygrounded,
Up al resoun so wel yfounded,
And so tretable to alle gode,
That I dar swere by the rode,
Of eloquence was never founde
So swete a sowninge facounde,
Ne trewer tonged, ne scorned lasse,
Ne bet coude hele; that, by the masse
I durste swere, thogh the pope hit songe,
That ther was never through hir tonge
Man ne woman gretly harmed;
As for hir, ther was al harm hid;
Ne lasse flatering in hir worde,
That purely, hir simple recorde
Was founde as trewe as any bonde,
Or trouthe of any mannes honde.
Ne chyde she coude never a del,
That knoweth al the world ful wel.
BUT swich a fairnesse of a nekke
Had that swete, that boon nor brekke
Nas ther non sene, that mis-sat.
Hit was whyt, smothe, streght, and flat,
Withouten hole; and canel-boon,
As by seming, had she noon.
Hir throte, as I have now memoire,
Semed a round tour of yvoire,
Of good gretnesse, and noght to grete.
AND gode faire Whyte she hete,
That was my lady name right.
She was bothe fair and bright,
She hadde not hir name wrong.
Right faire shuldres, and body long
She hadde, and armes, every lith
Fattish, fleshly, not greet therwith;
Right whyte handes, and nayles rede,
Rounde brestes; and of good brede
Hir hippes were, a streight flat bak.
I knew on hir non other lak
That al hir limmes nere sewing,
In as fer as I had knowing.
THERTO she coude so wel pleye,
Whan that hir liste, that I dar seye,
That she was lyk to torche bright,
That every man may take of light
Ynogh, and hit hath never the lesse.
Of maner and of comlinesse
Right so ferde my lady dere;
For every wight of hir manere
Might cacche ynogh, if that he wolde,

If he had eyen hir to beholde.
For I dar sweren, if that she
Had among ten thousand be,
She wolde have be, at the leste,
A cheef mirour of al the feste,
Thogh they had stonden in a rowe,
To mennes eyen that coude have knowe.
For wherso men had pleyd or waked,
Me thoghte the felawship as naked
Withouten hir, that saw I ones,
As a coroune withoute stones.
Trewely she was, to myn yë,
The soleyn fenix of Arabyë,
For ther liveth never but oon;
Ne swich as she ne knew I noon.
TO speke of goodnesse; trewly she
Had as moche debonairte
As ever had Hester in the bible,
And more, if more were possible.
And, soth to seyne, therwithal
She had a wit so general,
So hool enclyned to alle gode,
That al hir wit was set, by the rode,
Withoute malice, upon gladnesse;
Therto I saw never yet a lesse
Harmful, than she was in doing.
I sey nat that she ne had knowing
What was harm; or elles she
Had coud no good, so thinketh me.
AND trewly, for to speke of trouthe,
But she had had, hit had be routhe.
Therof she had so moche hir del,
And I dar seyn and swere hit wel,
That Trouthe himself, over al and al,
Had chose his maner principal
In hir, that was his resting-place.
Therto she hadde the moste grace,
To have stedfast perseveraunce,
And esy, atempre governaunce,
That ever I knew or wiste yit;
So pure suffraunt was hir wit.
And reson gladly she understood,
Hit folowed wel she coude good.
She used gladly to do wel;
These were hir maners every-del.
THERWITH she loved so wel right,
She wrong do wolde to no wight;
No wight might do hir no shame,
She loved so wel hir owne name.
Hir luste to holde no wight in honde;
Ne, be thou siker, she nolde fonde
To holde no wight in balaunce,
By half word ne by countenaunce,
But if men wolde upon hir lye;
Ne sende men into Walakye,
To Pruyse and into Tartarye,
To Alisaundre, ne into Turkye,
And bidde him faste, anoon that he
Go hoodles to the drye see,
And come hoom by the Carrenare;
And seye: Sir, be now right ware
That I may of yow here seyn
Worship, or that ye come ageyn!

She ne used no suche knakkes smale.
BUT wherfor that I telle my tale?
Right on this same, as I have seyd,
Was hoolly al my love leyd;
for certes, she was, that swete wyf,
My suffisaunce, my lust, my lyf,
Myn hap, myn hele, and al my blisse,
My worldes welfare and my lisse,
And I hirs hooly, everydel.
YOur Lord, quod I, I trowe yow wel!
Hardely, your love was wel beset,
I not how ye mighte have do bet.
Bet? ne no wight so wel! quod he.
I trowe hit, sir, quod I, parde!
Nay, leve hit wel! Sir, so do I;
I leve you wel, that trewely
Yow thoghte, that she was the beste,
And to beholde the alderfaireste,
Who so had loked with your eyen.
WITH myn? nay, alle that hir seyen
Seyde, and sworen hit was so.
And thogh they ne hadde, I wolde tho
Have loved best my lady fre,
Thogh I had had al the beautee
That ever had Alcipyades,
And al the strengthe of Ercules,
And therto had the worthinesse
Of Alisaundre, and al the richesse
That ever was in Babiloyne,
In Cartage, or in Macedoyne,
Or in Rome, or in Ninive;
And therto also hardy be
As was Ector, so have I joye,
That Achilles slow at Troye,
And therfor was he slayn also
In a temple, for bothe two
Were slayn, he and Antilogus,
And so seyth Dares Frigius,
for love of hir Polixena,
Or ben as wys as Minerva,
I wolde ever, withoute drede,
Have loved hir, for I moste nede!
Nede! nay, I gabbe now,
Noght Nede, and I wol telle how,
for of good wille myn herte hit wolde,
And eek to love hir I was holde
As for the fairest and the beste.
SHE was as good, so have I reste,
As ever was Penelope of Grece,
Or as the noble wyf Lucrece,
That was the beste, he telleth thus,
The Romain Tytus Livius,
She was as good, and nothing lyke,
Thogh hir stories be autentyke;
Algate she was as trewe as she.
BUT wherfor that I telle thee
Whan I first my lady sey?
I was right yong, the sooth to sey,
And ful gret need I hadde to lerne;
Whan my herte wolde yerne
To love, it was a greet empryse.
But as my wit coude best suffyse,
After my yonge childly wit,

Withoute drede, I besette hit
To love hir in my beste wyse,
To do hir worship and servyse
That I tho coude, by my trouthe,
Withoute feyning outher slouthe;
for wonder fayn I wolde hir see.
So mochel hit amended me,
That, whan I saw hir first amorwe,
I was warished of al my sorwe
Of al day after, til hit were eve;
Me thoghte nothing mighte me greve,
Were my sorwes never so smerte.
And yit she sit so in myn herte,
That, by my trouthe, I nolde noght,
for al this worlde, out of my thoght
Leve my lady; no, trewly!
NOW, by my trouthe, sir, quod I,
Me thinketh ye have such a chaunce
As shrift withoute repentaunce.
REPENTAUNCE! nay fy, quod he;
Shulde I now repente me
To love? nay, certes, than were I wel
Wers than was Achitofel,
Or Anthenor, so have I joye,
The traytour that betraysed Troye,
Or the false Genelon,
He that purchased the treson
Of Rowland and of Olivere.
Nay, whyl I am alyve here
I nil foryete hir nevermo.
NOW, goode sir, quod I right tho,
Ye han wel told me herbefore.
It is no need reherse hit more
How ye sawe hir first, and where;
But wolde ye telle me the manere,
To hir which was your firste speche,
Therof I wolde yow beseche,
And how she knewe first your thoght,
Whether ye loved hir or noght,
And telleth me eek what ye have lore;
I herde yow telle herbefore.
YE, seyde he, thou nost what thou menest;
I have lost more than thou wenest.
What los is that, sir? quod I tho;
Nil she not love yow? is hit so?
Or have ye oght ydoon amis,
That she hath left yow? is hit this?
for Goddes love, tel me al.
BEfORE God, quod he, and I shal.
I saye right as I have seyd,
On hir was al my love leyd;
And yet she niste hit never a del
Noght longe tyme, leve hit wel.
for be right siker, I durste noght
for al this worlde telle hir my thoght,
Ne I wolde have wratthed hir, trewly.
for wostow why? she was lady
Of the body; she had the herte,
And who hath that, may not asterte.
BUT, for to kepe me fro ydelnesse,
Trewly I did my besinesse
To make songes, as I best coude,
And ofte tyme I song hem loude;

And made songes a gret del,
Althogh I coude not make so wel
Songes, ne knowe the art al,
As coude Lamekes sone Tubal,
That fond out first the art of songe;
For, as his brothers hamers ronge
Upon his anvelt up and doun,
Therof he took the firste soun;
But Grekes seyn, Pictagoras,
That he the firste finder was
Of the art; Aurora telleth so,
But therof no fors, of hem two.
Algates songes thus I made
Of my feling, myn herte to glade;
And lo! this was the altherfirste,
I not wher that hit were the werste.

LORD, hit maketh myn herte light,
When I thenke on that swete wight
That is so semely on to see;
And wisshe to God hit might so be,
That she wolde holde me for hir knight,
My lady, that is so fair and bright!

NOW have I told thee, sooth to saye,
My firste song. Upon a daye
I bethoghte me what wo
And sorwe that I suffred tho
For hir, and yet she wiste hit noght,
Ne telle hir durste I nat my thoght.
Allas! thoghte I, I can no reed;
And, but I telle hir, I nam but deed;
And if I telle hir, to seye sooth,
I am adred she wol be wrooth;
Allas! what shal I thanne do?

IN this debat I was so wo,
Me thoghte myn herte braste atweyn!
So atte laste, soth to seyn,
I me bethoghte that nature
Ne formed never in creature
So moche beaute, trewely,
And bounte, withouten mercy.

IN hope of that, my tale I tolde
With sorwe, as that I never sholde,
For nedes; and, maugree my heed,
I moste have told hir or be deed.
I not wel how that I began,
Ful evel rehersen hit I can;
And eek, as helpe me God withal,
I trowe hit was in the dismal,
That was the ten woundes of Egipte;
For many a word I over-skipte
In my tale, for pure fere
Lest my wordes mis-set were.
With sorweful herte, and woundes dede,
Softe and quaking for pure drede
And shame, and stinting in my tale
For ferde, and myn hewe al pale,
Ful ofte I wex bothe pale and reed;
Bowing to hir, I heng the heed;
I durste nat ones loke hir on,
For wit, manere, and al was gon.
I seyde Mercy! and no more;
Hit nas no game, hit sat me sore.

SO atte laste, sooth to seyn,
When that myn herte was come ageyn,
To telle shortly al my speche,
With hool herte I gan hir beseche
That she wolde be my lady swete;
And swor, and gan hir hertely hete
Ever to be stedfast and trewe,
And love hir alwey freshly newe,
And never other lady have,
And al hir worship for to save
As I best coude; I swor hir this:
For youres is al that ever ther is
For evermore, myn herte swete!
And never false yow, but I mete,
I nil, as wis God helpe me so!

AND when I had my tale ydo,
God wot, she acounted nat a stree
Of al my tale, so thoghte me.
To telle shortly as hit is,
Trewly hir answere, hit was this;
I can not now wel counterfete
Hir wordes, but this was the grete
Of hir answere; she sayde, Nay
Al-outerly. Allas! that day
The sorwe I suffred, and the wo!
That trewly Cassandra, that so
Bewayled the destruccioun
Of Troye and of Ilioun,
Had never swich sorwe as I tho.
I durste no more say therto
For pure fere, but stal away;
And thus I lived ful many a day:
That trewely, I hadde no need
Ferther than my beddes heed
Never a day to seche sorwe;
I fond hit redy every morwe,
Forwhy I loved hir in no gere.

SO hit befel, another yere,
I thoughte ones I wolde fonde
To do hir knowe and understonde
My wo; and she wel understood
That I ne wilned thing but good,
And worship, and to kepe hir name
Over al thing, and drede hir shame,
And was so besy hir to serve;
And pite were I shulde sterve,
Sith that I wilned noon harm, ywis.
So when my lady knew al this,
My lady yaf me al hoolly
The noble yift of hir mercy,
Saving hir worship, by al weyes;
Dredles, I mene noon other weyes.
And therwith she yaf me a ring;
I trowe hit was the firste thing;
But if myn herte was ywaxe
Glad, that is no need to axe!
As helpe me God, I was as blyve,
Reysed, as fro dethe to lyve,
Of alle happes the alderbeste,
The gladdest and the moste at reste.
For trewely, that swete wight,
When I had wrong and she the right,
She wolde alwey so goodely

foryeve me so debonairly.
In alle my youthe, in alle chaunce,
She took me in hir governaunce.
THERWITH she was alway so trewe,
Our joye was ever yliche newe;
Our hertes wern so even a payre,
That never nas that oon contrayre
To that other, for no wo.
for sothe, yliche they suffred tho
Oo blisse and eek oo sorwe bothe;
Yliche they were bothe gladde and wrothe;
Al was us oon, withoute were.
And thus we lived ful many a yere
So wel, I can nat telle how.
Sir, quod I, wher is she now?
Now! quod he, and stinte anoon.
THERWITH he wex as deed as stoon,
And seyde: Allas! that I was bore!
That was the los, that herbefore
I tolde thee, that I had lorn.
Bethenk how I seyde herbeforn,
Thou wost ful litel what thou menest;
I have lost more than thou wenest...
God wot, allas! right that was she!
ALLAS! sir, how? what may that be?
She is deed! Nay! Yis, by my
trouthe!

Is that your los? by God, hit is routhe!
AND with that worde, right anoon,
They gan to strake forth; al was doon,
for that tyme, the hert-hunting.
WITH that, me thoghte, that this king
Gan quikly hoomward for to ryde
Unto a place ther besyde,
Which was from us but a lyte,
A long castel with walles whyte,
By seynt Johan! on a riche hil,
As me mette; but thus it fil.
RIGHT thus me mette, as I yow telle,
That in the castel was a belle,
As hit had smiten houres twelve.
THERWITH I awook myselve,
And fond me lying in my bed;
And the book that I had red,
Of Alcyone and Seys the king,
And of the goddes of sleping,
I fond it in myn honde ful even.
THOGHTE I, this is so queynt a sweven,
That I wol, by processe of tyme,
fonde to putte this sweven in ryme
As I can best; and that anoon.
This was my sweven; now hit is doon.
Explicit the Boke of the Duchesse.

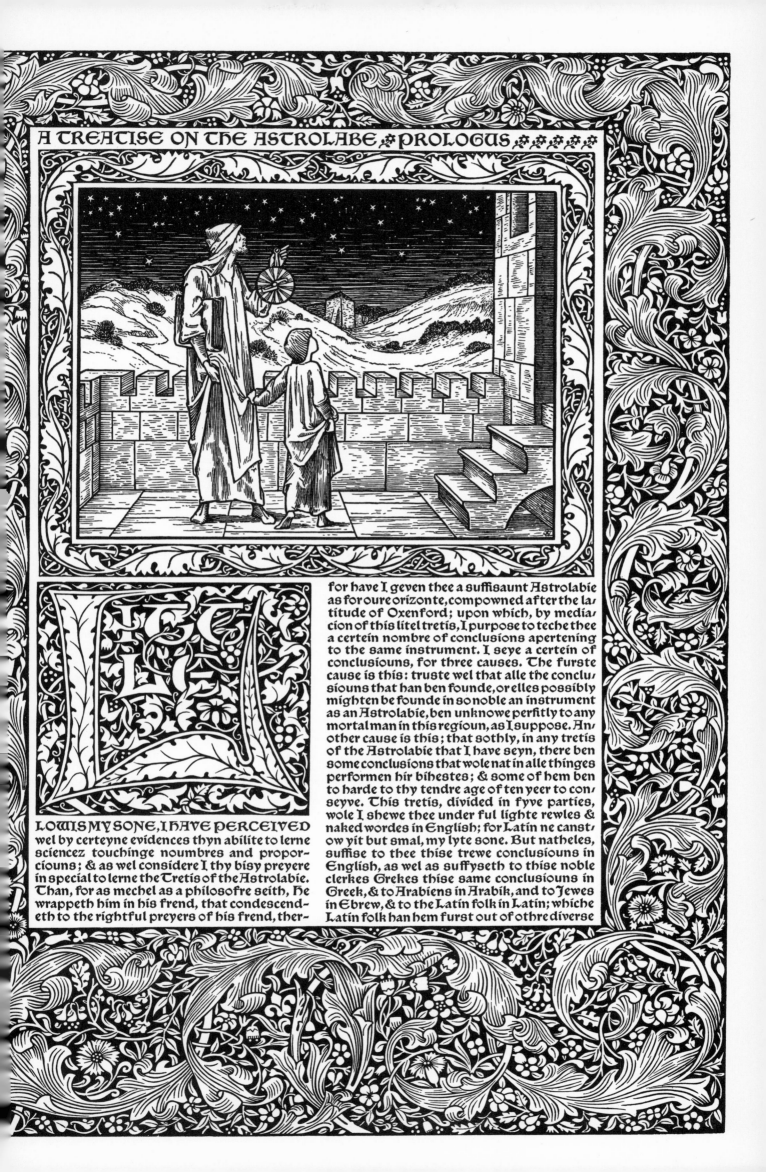

LOWIS MY SONE, I HAVE PERCEIVED wel by certeyne evidences thyn abilite to lerne sciencez touchinge noumbres and proporcïouns; & as wel considere I thy bisy preyere in special to lerne the Tretis of the Astrolabie. Than, for as mechel as a philosofre seith, He wrappeth him in his frend, that condescendeth to the rightful preyers of his frend, therfor have I geven thee a suffisaunt Astrolabie as for oure orizonte, compowned after the latitude of Oxenford; upon which, by mediacïon of this litel tretis, I purpose to teche thee a certein nombre of conclusions apertening to the same instrument. I seye a certein of conclusiouns, for three causes. The furste cause is this: truste wel that alle the conclusiouns that han ben founde, or elles possibly mighten be founde in so noble an instrument as an Astrolabie, ben unknowe perfitly to any mortal man in this regïoun, as I suppose. Another cause is this; that sothly, in any tretis of the Astrolabie that I have seyn, there ben some conclusions that wole nat in alle thinges performen hir bihestes; & some of hem ben to harde to thy tendre age of ten yeer to conseyve. This tretis, divided in fyve parties, wole I shewe thee under ful lighte rewles & naked wordes in English; for Latin ne canstow yit but smal, my lyte sone. But natheles, suffise to thee thise trewe conclusiouns in English, as wel as suffyseth to thise noble clerkes Grekes thise same conclusiouns in Greek, & to Arabiens in Arabik, and to Jewes in Ebrew, & to the Latin folk in Latin; whiche Latin folk han hem furst out of othre diverse

langages, & writen in hir owne tonge, that
is to sein, in Latin. And God wot, that in
alle thise langages, and in many mo, han
thise conclusiouns ben suffisauntly lerned
& taught, & yit by diverse rewles, right as
diverse pathes leden diverse folk the righte
wey to Rome. Now wol I prey meekly every
discret persone that redeth or hereth this
litel tretis, to have my rewde endyting for
excused, and my superfluite of wordes, for
two causes. The firste cause is, for that
curious endyting and hard sentence is ful
hevy atones for swich a child to lerne. And
the seconde cause is this, that sothly me
semeth betre to wryten unto a child twyes
a good sentence, than he forgete it ones.
And Lowis, yif so be that I shewe thee in
my lighte English as trewe conclusiouns
touching this matere, and naught only as
trewe but as many and as subtil conclusiouns as ben shewed in Latin in any commune tretis of the Astrolabie, con me the
more thank; and preye God save the king,
that is lord of this langage, and alle that
him feyth bereth and obeyeth, everech in
his degree, the more & the lasse. But considere wel, that I ne usurpe nat to have
founde this werk of my labour or of myn
engin. I nam but a lewd compilatour of the
labour of olde Astrologiens, and have hit
translated in myn English only for thy doctrine; & with this swerd shal I sleen envye.

I.

HE firste partie of this tretis
shal reherse the figures and
the membres of thyn Astrolabie, bicause that thou shalt
han the grettre knowing of
thyn owne instrument.

II.

HE second partie shal teche thee werk-
en the verrey practik of the forseide
conclusiouns, as ferforth and as narwe as may be shewed in so smal an instrument portatif aboute. For wel wot every
astrologien that smalest fraccions ne wol
nat ben shewed in so smal an instrument,
as in subtil tables calculed for a cause.

III.

HE thridde partie shal contienen diverse tables of longitudes and latitudes of sterres fixe for the Astrolabie, & tables of declinacions of the sonne,
and tables of longitudes of citeez and of
townes; and as wel for the governance of a
clokke as for to finde the altitude meridian;
& many another notable conclusioun, after the kalendres of the reverent clerkes,
frere I. Somer and frere N. Lenne.

IV.

HE ferthe partie shal ben a theorik
to declare the moevinge of the celestial bodies with the causes. The

398

whiche ferthe partie in special shal shewen
a table of the verray moeving of the mone
from houre to houre, every day and in every
signe, after thyn almenak; upon which table
ther folwith a canon, suffisant to teche as
wel the maner of the wyrking of that same
conclusioun, as to knowe in oure orizonte
with which degree of the zodiac that the
mone ariseth in any latitude; and the arising of any planete after his latitude fro the
ecliptik lyne.

v.

HE fifte partie shal ben an intro-
ductorie after the statutz of oure
doctours, in which thou maist lerne
a gret part of the general rewles of theorik
in astrologie. In which fifte partie shaltow
finde tables of equacions of houses aftur
the latitude of Oxenford; and tables of
dignetes of planetes, and other noteful
thinges, yif God wol vouchesauf and his
modur the mayde, mo than I behete, &c.

Part I.
Here biginneth the descripcion of the Astrolabie.

1.

HYN Astrolabie hath
a ring to putten on
the thoumbe of thy
right hand in taking
the heighte of thing-
es. And tak keep, for
from hennesforth-
ward, I wol clepe the
heighte of any thing
that is taken by thy
rewle, the altitude, withoute mo wordes.

2.

HIS ring renneth in a maner turet,
fast to the moder of thyn Astrolabie, in so rowm a space that hit
desturbeth nat the instrument to hangen
after his righte centre.

3.

HE Moder of thyn Astrolabie is the
thikkeste plate, perced with a large
hole, that resseyveth in hir wombe
the thinne plates compowned for diverse
clymatz, and thy riet shapen in manere of
a net or of a webbe of a loppe; and for the
more declaracioun, lo here the figure.

4.

HIS moder is devyded on the bak-
half with a lyne, that cometh des-
sendinge fro the ring down to the
nethereste bordure. The whiche lyne, fro
the forseide ring unto the centre of the
large hole amidde, is cleped the south
lyne, or elles the lyne meridional. And the
remenant of this lyne downe to the bordure is cleped the north lyne, or elles the
lyne of midnight. And for the more de-

claracioun, lo here the figure.

5. OVERTHWART THIS forseide longe lyne, ther crosseth him another lyne of the same lengthe fro est to west. Of the whiche lyne, from a little croys ✠ in the bordure unto the centre of the large hole, is cleped the Est lyne, or elles the lyne Orientale; & the remenant of this lyne fro the forseide ✠ unto the bordure, is cleped the West lyne, or the lyne Occidentale. Now hastow here the foure quarters of thin Astrolabie, devyded after the foure principals plages or quarters of the firmament. And for the more declaracioun, lo here thy figure.

6. THE est side of thyn Astrolabie is cleped the right side, and the west side is cleped the left side. Forget nat this, litel Lowis. Put the ring of thyn Astrolabie upon the thoumbe of thy right hand, and thanne wole his right syde be toward thy left syde, & his left syde wol be toward thy right syde; tak this rewle general, as wel on the bak as on the wombe-side. Upon the ende of this est lyne, as I first seide, is marked a litel ✠, wheras everemo generaly is considered the entring of the first degree in which the sonne aryseth. And for the more declaracioun, lo here the figure.

7. FRO this litel ✠ up to the ende of the lyne meridional, under the ring, shaltow finden the bordure devyded with 90 degrees; and by that same proporcioun is every quarter of thin Astrolabie devyded. Over the whiche degrees ther ben noumbres of augrim, that devyden thilke same degrees fro fyve to fyve, as sheweth by longe strykes bytwene. Of whiche longe strykes the space bytwene contienith a mile-wey. And every degree of the bordure contieneth foure minutes, that is to seyn, minutes of an houre. And for more declaracioun, lo here the figure.

8. UNDER the compas of thilke degrees ben writen the names of the Twelve Signes, as Aries, Taurus, Gemini, Cancer, Leo, Virgo, Libra, Scorpio, Sagittarius, Capricornus, Aquarius, Pisces; and the nombres of the degrees of tho signes ben writen in augrim above, and with longe devisiouns, fro fyve to fyve; devyded fro tyme that the signe entreth unto the laste ende. But understond wel, that thise degrees of signes ben everich of hem considered of 60 minutes, and every minute of 60 secondes, and so forth into smale fracciouns infinit, as seith Alkabucius. And therfor, know wel, that a degree of the bordure contieneth foure minutes,

and a degree of a signe contieneth 60 minutes, and have this in minde. And for the more declaracioun, lo here thy figure.

9. NEXT this folweth the Cercle of the Dayes, that ben figured in maner of degrees, that contienen in noumbre 365; divyded also with longe strykes fro fyve to fyve, and the nombres in augrim writen under that cercle. And for more declaracioun, lo here thy figure.

10. NEXT the Cercle of the Dayes, folweth the Cercle of the names of the Monthes; that is to seyn, Januare, Februare, Marcius, Aprile, Mayus, Juin, Julius, Augustus, Septembre, October, Novembre, Decembre. The names of thise monthes were cleped in Arabiens, somme for hir propretees, and some by statutz of lordes, some by other lordes of Rome. Eek of thise monthes, as lyked to Julius Cesar and to Cesar Augustus, some were compowned of diverse nombres of dayes, as Juil and August.✒ Thanne hath Januare 31 dayes, Februare 28, March 31, Aprille 30, May 31, Junius 30, Julius 31, Augustus 31, September 30, Octobre 31, Novembre 30, December 31. Natheles, although that Julius Cesar took 2 dayes out of Feverer and put hem in his moneth of Juille, and Augustus Cesar cleped the moneth of August after his name, and ordeyned it of 31 dayes, yit truste wel, that the sonne dwelleth therfor nevere the more ne lesse in oon signe than in another.

11. THAN folwen the names of the Halidayes in the Kalender, and next hem the lettres of the Abc. on which they fallen. And for the more declaracioun, lo here thy figure.

12. NEXT the forseide Cercle of the Abc., under the cros-lyne, is marked the scale, in maner of two squyres, or elles in manere of laddres, that serveth by hise 12 poyntes and his devisiouns of ful many a subtil conclusioun. Of this forseide scale, fro the croos-lyne unto the verre angle, is cleped umbra versa, and the nether partie is cleped the umbra recta, or elles umbra extensa. And for the more declaracioun, lo here the figure.

13. THANNE hastow a brood Rewle, that hath on either ende a square plate perced with a certein holes, some more and some lesse, to resseyven the stremes of the sonne by day, and eek by mediacioun of thyn eye, to knowe the altitude of sterres by nighte. And for the more declaracioun, lo here thy figure.

399

14.

THANNE is ther a large Pyn, in maner of an extree, that goth thorow the hole, that halt the tables of the clymates and the riet in the wombe of the Moder, thorw which Pyn ther goth a litel wegge which that is cleped The Hors, that streyneth alle thise parties tohepe; this forseide grete Pyn, in maner of an extree, is imagined to be the Pol Artik in thyn Astrolabie. And for the more declaracioun, lo here the figure.

15.

THE wombe-side of thyn Astrolabie is also devyded with a longe croys in foure quarters from est to west, fro south to north, fro right syde to left syde, as is the bak-syde. And for the more declaracioun, lo here thy figure.

16.

THE bordure of which wombe-side is devyded fro the poynt of the est lyne unto the poynt of the south lyne under the ring, in 90 degres; & by that same proporcioun is every quarter devyded as is the bak-syde, that amonteth 360 degrees. And understond wel, that degrees of this bordure ben answering and consentrik to the degrees of the Equinoxial, that is devyded in the same nombre as every othere cercle is in the heye hevene. This same bordure is devyded also with 23 lettres capitals and a smal croys ✠ above the south lyne, that sheweth the 24 houres equals of the clokke; and, as I have said, 5 of thise degrees maken a mile-wey, and 3 mile-wey maken an houre. And every degree of this bordure conteneth 4 minutes, and every minut 60 secoundes; now have I told thee twye. And for the more declaracioun, lo here the figure.

17.

THE plate under thy riet is descryved with 3 principal cercles; of whiche the leste is cleped the cercle of Cancer, bycause that the heved of Cancer turneth evermor consentrik upon the same cercle. In this heved of Cancer is the grettest declinacioun northward of the sonne. And therfor is he cleped the Solsticioun of Somer; whiche declinacioun, aftur Ptholome, is 23 degrees and 50 minutes, as wel in Cancer as in Capricorne. This signe of Cancre is cleped the Tropik of Somer, of tropos, that is to seyn, agaynward; for thanne byginneth the sonne to passe fro usward. And for the more declaracioun, lo here the figure.

THE middel cercle in wydnesse, of thise 3, is cleped the Cercle Equinoxial; upon whiche turneth evermo the hedes of Aries and Libra. And understond wel, that evermo this Cercle

Equinoxial turneth justly fro verrey est to verrey west; as I have shewed thee in the spere solide. This same cercle is cleped also the Weyere, equator, of the day; for whan the sonne is in the hevedes of Aries and Libra, than ben the dayes & the nightes ilyke of lengthe in al the world. And therfore ben thise two signes called the Equinoxies. And alle that moeveth within the hevedes of thise Aries & Libra, his moeving is cleped northward; & alle that moeveth withoute thise hevedes, his moeving is cleped southward as fro the equinoxial. ☞ Tak keep of thise latitudes north and sowth, and forget it nat. By this Cercle Equinoxial ben considered the 24 houres of the clokke; for everemo the arysing of 15 degrees of the equinoxial maketh an houre equal of the clokke. This equinoxial is cleped the girdel of the firste moeving, or elles of the angulus primi motus vel primi mobilis. And nota, that firste moeving is cleped Moeving of the firste moevable of the 8 spere, whiche moeving is fro est to west, & eft agayn into est; also it is clepid Girdel of the first moeving, for it departeth the firste moevable, that is to seyn, the spere, in two ilyke parties, evene-distantz fro the poles of this world. ☞ The wydeste of thise three principal cercles is cleped the Cercle of Capricorne, bycause that the heved of Capricorne turneth evermo consentrik upon the same cercle. In the heved of this forseide Capricorne is the grettest declinacioun southward of the sonne, and therfor is it cleped the Solsticioun of Winter. This signe of Capricorne is also cleped the Tropik of Winter, for thanne byginneth the sonne to come agayn to usward. And for the more declaracioun, lo here thy figure.

18.

UPON this forseide plate ben compassed certein cercles that highten Almicanteras, of which som of hem semen perfit cercles, and somme semen inperfit. The centre that standith amiddes the narwest cercle is cleped the Senith; & the netherest cercle, or the firste cercle, is clepid the Orisonte, that is to seyn, the cercle that devydeth the two emisperies, that is, the partie of the hevene above the erthe and the partie benethe. Thise Almicanteras ben compowned by two and two, albeit so that on divers Astrolabies some Almicanteras ben devyded by oon, & some by two, and somme by three, after the quantite of the Astrolabie. This forseide senith is imagened to ben the verrey point over the crowne of thyn heved; and also this senith is the verrey pool of the orisonte in every regioun. And for the more declaracioun, lo here thy figure.

19.

FROM this senith, as it semeth, ther come a maner crokede strykes lyke to the clawes of a loppe, or elles like to the werk of a womanes calle, in kerving overthwart the Almikanteras. And thise same strykes or divisiouns ben cleped Azimuthz. And they devyden the orisonte of thyn Astrolabie in four and twenty devisiouns. And thise Azimutz serven to knowe the costes of the firmament, and to othre conclusiouns, as for to knowe the cenith of the sonne and of every sterre. And for more declaracioun, lo here thy figure.

20.

NEXT this azimutz, under the Cercle of Cancer, ben ther twelve devisiouns embelif, moche like to the shap of the azimutes, that shewen the spaces of the houres of planetes; and for more declaracioun, lo here thy figure.

21.

THE Riet of thyn Astrolabie with thy zodiak, shapen in maner of a net or of a loppe-webbe after the olde descripcioun, which thow mayst tornen up and doun as thyself lyketh, conteneth certein nombre of sterres fixes, with hir longitudes and latitudes determinat; yif so be that the makere have nat erred. The names of the sterres ben writen in the margin of the riet ther as they sitte; of whiche sterres the smale poynt is cleped the Centre. And understond also that alle sterres sittinge within the zodiak of thyn Astrolabie ben cleped Sterres of the north, for they arysen by northe the est lyne. And alle the remenant fixed, out of the zodiak, ben cleped Sterres of the south; but I sey nat that they arysen alle by southe the est lyne; witnesse on Aldeberan and Algomeysa. Generally understond this rewle, that thilke sterres that ben cleped sterres of the north arysen rather than the degree of hir longitude, & alle the sterres of the south arysen after the degree of hir longitude; this is to seyn, sterres fixed in thyn Astrolabie. The mesure of this longitude of sterres is taken in the lyne ecliptik of hevene, under which lyne, whan that the sonne & the mone ben lyne-right or elles in the superfice of this lyne, than is the eclips of the sonne or of the mone; as I shal declare, and eek the cause why. But sothly the Ecliptik Lyne of thy zodiak is the outtereste bordure of thy zodiak, ther the degrees ben marked. Thy Zodiak of thyn Astrolabie is shapen as a compas which that conteneth a large brede, as after the quantite of thyn Astrolabie; in ensample that the zodiak in hevene is imagened to ben a superfice contening a latitude of twelve degrees, wheras al the remenant of cercles in the hevene ben imagined verrey lynes withoute eny latitude. Amiddes this celestial zodiak ys imagined a lyne, which that is cleped the Ecliptik Lyne, under which lyne is evermo the wey of the sonne. Thus ben ther six degrees of the zodiak on that on side of the lyne, and six degrees on that other. This zodiak is devided in twelve principal devisiouns, that departen the twelve signes. And, for the streitnes of thin Astrolabie, than is every smal devisioun in a signe departid by two degrees and two; I mene degrees conteining sixty minutes. And this forseide hevenissh zodiak is cleped the Cercle of the Signes, or the Cercle of the Bestes; for zodia in langage of Greek sowneth Bestes in Latin tonge; and in the zodiak ben the twelve signes that han name of bestes; or elles, for whan the sonne entreth in any of the signes, he taketh the propretee of swich bestes; or elles, for that the sterres that ben there fixed ben disposed in signes of bestes, or shape like bestes; or elles, whan the planetes ben under thilke signes, they causen us by hir influence operaciouns & effectes lyk to the operaciouns of bestes. And understonde also, that whan an hot planete cometh into an hot signe, than encresseth his hete; & yif a planete be cold, thanne amenuseth his coldnesse, bycause of the hote signe. And by this conclusioun maystow take ensample in alle the signes, be they moist or drye, or moeble or fix; rekening the qualitee of the planete as I first seide. And everich of thise twelve signes hath respecte to a certein parcelle of the body of a man and hath it in governance; as Aries hath thyn heved, and Taurus thy nekke & thy throte, Gemini thyn armholes & thyn armes, and so forth; as shal be shewed more pleyn in the fifte partie of this tretis. This zodiak, which that is part of the eighte spere, over-kerveth the equinoxial; & he over-kerveth him again in evene parties; & that on half declineth southward, & that other northward, as pleynly declareth the tretis of the spere. And for more declaracioun, lo here thy figure.

22.

THANNE hastow a label, that is schapen lyk a rewle, save that it is streit & hath no plates on either ende with holes; but, with the smale point of the forseide label, shaltow calcule thyne equaciouns in the bordure of thin Astrolabie, as by thyn almury. And for the more declaracioun, lo here thy figure.

23.

THYN Almury is cleped the Denticle of Capricorne, or elles the Calculer. This same Almury sit fix in the hed of Capricorne, and it serveth of many a necessarie conclusioun in equaciouns of thinges, as shal be shewed; and for the more declaracioun, lo here thy figure.

Here endeth the descripcion of the Astrolabie.

Part II.

Here biginnen the Conclusions of the Astrolabie.

1. To fynde the degree in which the sonne is day by day, after hir cours aboute.

(Hic incipiunt Conclusiones Astrolabii; et prima est ad inveniendum gradus solis in quibus singulis diebus secundum cursum sol est existens.)

REKENE and knowe which is the day of thy monthe; and ley thy rewle up that same day; & thanne wol the verray point of thy rewle sitten in the bordure, upon the degree of thy sonne. Ensample as thus; the yeer of oure Lord 1391, the 12 day of March at midday, I wolde knowe the degree of the sonne. I soughte in the bak-half of myn Astrolabie, and fond the cercle of the dayes, the which I knowe by the names of the monthes writen under the same cercle. Tho leide I my rewle over this forseide day, & fond the point of my rewle in the bordure upon the firste degree of Aries, a litel within the degree; and thus knowe I this conclusioun. Another day, I wolde knowe the degree of my sonne, and this was at midday in the 13 day of Decembre; I fond the day of the monthe in maner as I seide; tho leide I my rewle upon this forseide 13 day, and fond the point of my rewle in the bordure upon the first degree of Capricorne, a lite within the degree; and than hadde I of this conclusioun the ful experience. And for the more declaracioun, lo here thy figure.

2. To knowe the altitude of the sonne, or of othre celestial bodies.

(De altitudine solis et aliorum corporum supra celestium.)

PUT the ring of thyn Astrolabie upon thy right thoumbe, and turne thy lift syde agayn the light of the sonne. And remeve thy rewle up & doun, til that the stremes of the sonne shyne thorgh bothe holes of thy rewle. Loke thanne how many degrees thy rewle is areised fro the litel crois upon thyn est line, and tak ther the altitude of thy sonne. And in this same wyse maistow knowe by nighte the altitude of the mone, or of brighte sterres. This chapitre is so

402

general ever in oon, that ther nedith no more declaracion; but forget it nat. And for the more declaracioun, lo here the figure.

3. To knowe every tyme of the day by light of the sonne, and every tyme of the night by the sterres fixe, & eke to knowe by night or by day the degree of any signe that assendeth on the Est Orisonte, which that is cleped communly the Assendent, or elles Oruscupum.

(Ad cognoscendum quodlibet tempus diei per solis indicacionem, et quodlibet tempus noctis per quasdam stellas in celo fixas; ac eciam ad inveniendum et cognoscendum signum super orizontem qui communiter vocatur ascendens.)

TAK the altitude of the sonne whan thee list, as I have said; & set the degree of the sonne, in cas that it be byforn the middel of the day, among thyn almikanteras on the est side of thyn Astrolabie; and yif it be after the middel of the day, set the degree of thy sonne upon the west side; tak this manere of setting for a general rewle, ones for evere. And whan thou hast set the degree of thy sonne up as many almikanteras of heyghte as was the altitude of the sonne taken by thy rewle, ley over thy label, upon the degree of the sonne; and thanne wol the point of thy label sitten in the bordure, upon the verrey tyd of the day. Ensample as thus: the yeer of oure Lord 1391, the 12 day of March, I wold knowe the tyd of the day. I took the altitude of my sonne, and fond that it was 25 degrees and 30 of minutes of heyghte in the bordure on the bak-syde. Tho turnede I myn Astrolabie, and bycause that it was byforn midday, I turnede my riet, & sette the degree of the sonne, that is to seyn, the 1 degree of Aries, on the right syde of myn Astrolabie, upon that 25 degrees & 30 of minutes of heyghte among myn almikanteras; tho leide I my label upon the degree of my sonne, & fond the poynte of my label in the bordure, upon a capital lettre that is cleped an X; tho rekened I alle the capitalles lettres fro the lyne of midnight unto this forseide lettre X, and fond that it was 9 of the clokke of the day. Tho loked I down upon the est orisonte, and fond ther the 20 degree of Geminis assending; which that I tok for myn assendent. And in this wyse hadde I the experience for evermo in which maner I sholde knowe the tyd of the day, and eek myn assendent. Tho wolde I wite the same night folwing the hour of the night, and wroughte in this wyse. Among an heep of sterris fixe, it lyked me for to take the altitude of the feire white sterre that is cleped Alhabor; and fond hir sitting on the west side of the lyne of midday, 18 degres of heighte taken by my rewle on the bak-syde. Tho sette I the centre of this Alhabor upon 18 degrees among myn almikanteras, upon the west side; bycause that she was founden on the west syde. Tho leide I my label over the degree of the sonne that was descended under the weste orisonte, and rikened alle the lettres capitals fro the lyne of midday unto the point of my label in the bordure; and fond that it was passed 8 of the clokke the space of 2 degrees. Tho loked I doun upon myn est orisonte, and fond ther 23 degrees of Libra assending, whom I tok for myn assendent; and thus lerned I to knowe ones for ever in which manere I shuld come to the houre of the night and to myn assendent; as verreyly as may be taken by so smal an instrument. But natheles, in general, wolde I warne thee for evere, ne mak thee nevere bold to have take a just ascendent by thyn Astrolabie, or elles to have set justly a clokke, whan any celestial body by which that thow wenest governe thilke thinges ben ney the south lyne; for trust wel, whan that the sonne is ney the meridional lyne, the degree of the sonne renneth so longe consentrik upon the almikanteras, that sothly thou shalt erre fro the just assendent. The same conclusioun sey I by the centre of any sterre fix by night; and moreover, by experience, I wot wel that in oure orisonte, from 11 of the clokke unto oon of the clokke, in taking of a just assendent in a portatif Astrolabie, hit is to hard to knowe. I mene, from 11 of the clokke biforn the houre of noon til oon of the clok next folwing. And for the more declaracion, lo here thy figure.

4. Special declaracion of the assendent. (Specialis declaracio de ascendente.)

THE assendent sothly, as wel in alle nativitez as in questiouns & elecciouns of tymes, is a thing which that thise astrologiens gretly observen; wherfore me semeth convenient, sin that I speke of the assendent, to make of it special declaracioun. The assendent sothly, to take it at the largeste, is thilke degree that assendeth at any of thise forseide tymes upon the est orisonte; and therefor, yif that any planet assende at that same tyme in thilke forseide degree of his longitude, men seyn that thilke planete is in horoscopo. But sothly, the hous of the assendent, that is to seyn, the firste hous or the est angle, is a thing more brood and large. For after the statutz of astrologiens, what celestial body that is 5 degrees above thilk degree that assendeth, or within that noumbre, d d 2

that is to seyn, nere the degree that assendeth, yit rikne they thilke planet in the assendent. And what planete that is under thilke degree that assendith the space of 25 degrees, yit seyn they that thilke planete is lyk to him that is in the hous of the assendent; but sothly, yif he passe the bondes of thise forseide spaces, above or bynethe, they seyn that the planete is failling fro the assendent. Yit sein thise astrologiens, that the assendent, & eke the lord of the assendent, may be shapen for to be fortunat or infortunat, as thus: a fortunat assendent clepen they whan that no wykkid planete, as Saturne or Mars, or elles the Tail of the Dragoun, is in the hous of the assendent, ne that no wikked planete have non aspecte of enemite upon the assendent; but they wol caste that they have a fortunat planete in hir assendent and yit in his felicitee, and than sey they that it is wel. Fortherover, they seyn that the infortuning of an assendent is the contrarie of thise forseide thinges. The lord of the assendent, sey they, that he is fortunat, whan he is in good place fro the assendent as in angle; or in a succedent, whereas he is in his dignitee and conforted with frendly aspectes of planetes and wel resceived, and eek that he may seen the assendent, and that he be nat retrograd ne combust, ne joigned with no shrewe in the same signe; ne that he be nat in his descencioun, ne joigned with no planete in his discencioun, ne have upon him non aspecte infortunat; and than sey they that he is wel. Natheles, thise ben observauncez of judicial matiere and rytes of payens, in which my spirit ne hath no feith, ne no knowing of hir horoscopum; for they seyn that every signe is departed in 3 evene parties by 10 degrees, and thilke porcioun they clepe a face. And althogh that a planete have a latitude fro the ecliptik, yit sey some folk, so that the planete aryse in that same signe with any degree of the forseide face in which his longtitude is rekned, that yit is the planete in horoscopo, be it in nativite or in eleccioun, &c. And for the more declaracioun, lo here the figure.

5. To knowe the verrey equacioun of the degree of the sonne, yif so be that it falle bytwixe thyn Almikanteras.

(Ad cognoscendum veram equacionem de gradu solis, si contigerit fore in duas Almicanteras.)

FOR as moche as the almikanteras in thyn Astrolabie been compouned by two and two, whereas some almikanteras in sondry Astrolabies ben compouned by on and on, or elles by two and two, it is necessarie to thy lerning to teche thee first to knowe and worke with thyn owne instrument. Wherfor, whan that the degree of thy sonne falleth bytwixe two almikanteras, or elles yif thyn almikanteras ben graven with over gret a point of a compas (for bothe thise thinges may causen errour as wel in knowing of the tyd of the day as of the verrey assendent),thou most werken in this wyse. Set the degree of thy sonne upon the heyer almikanteras of bothe, and waite wel wher as thin almury toucheth the bordure, and set ther a prikke of inke. Set doun agayn the degree of thy sonne upon the nethere almikanteras of bothe, and set ther another prikke. Remewe thanne thyn almury in the bordure evene amiddes bothe prikkes, and this wol lede justly the degree of thy sonne to sitte bytwixe bothe almikanteras in his right place. Ley thanne thy label over the degree of thy sonne; and find in the bordure the verrey tyde of the day or of the night. And as verreyly shaltow finde upon thyn est orisonte thyn assendent. And for more declaracioun, lo here thy figure.

6. To knowe the spring of the dawing and the ende of the evening,the which ben called the two crepusculis.

(Ad cognoscendum ortum solis et ejus occasum, que vocatur vulgariter crepusculum.)

SET the nadir of thy sonne upon 18 degrees of heighte among thyn almikanteras on the west syde, & ley thy label on the degree of thy sonne, and thanne shal the poynt of thy label schewe the spring of day. Also set the nadir of thy sonne upon 18 degrees of heighte among thyn almikanteras on the est side, and ley over thy label upon the degree of the sonne, and with the point of thy label find in the bordure the ende of the evening, that is, verrey night. The nadir of the sonne is thilke degree that is opposit to the degree of the sonne, in the seventhe signe, as thus: every degree of Aries by ordre is nadir to every degree of Libra by ordre; and Taurus to Scorpion; Gemini to Sagittare; Cancer to Capricorne; Leo to Aquarie; Virgo to Pisces; and yif any degree in thy zodiak be dirk, his nadir shal declare him. And for the more declaracioun, lo here thy figure.

7. To knowe the arch of the day, that some folk callen the day artificial, from the sonne arysing til hit go to reste.

(Ad cognoscendum archum diei, quem vulgus vocat diem artificialem, in hoc, ab ortu solis usque ad occasum.)

SET the degree of thy sonne upon thyn est orisonte, & ley thy label on the degree of the sonne, and at the poynt of thy label in the bordure set a prikke. Turn thanne thy riet aboute til the degree of the sonne sit upon the west orisonte, and ley thy label upon the same degree of the sonne, and at the point of thy label set another prikke. Rekne thanne the quantitee of tyme in the bordure bytwixe bothe prikkes, and tak ther thyn ark of the day. The remenant of the bordure under the orisonte is the ark of the night. Thus maistow rekne bothe arches, or every porcion, of whether that thee lyketh. And by this manere of wyrking maistow see how longe that any sterre fix dwelleth above the erthe, fro tyme that he ryseth til he go to reste. But the day natural, that is to seyn 24 houres, is the revolucioun of the equinoxial with as moche partie of the zodiak as the sonne of his propre moevinge passeth in the mene whyle. And for the more declaracioun, lo here thy figure.

8. To turn the houres inequales in houres equales.

(Ad convertendum horas inequales in horas equales.)

KNOWE the nombre of the degrees in the houres inequales, and departe hem by 15, and tak ther thyn houres equales. And for the more declaracioun, lo here thy figure.

9. To knowe the quantitee of the day vulgare, that is to seyen, from spring of the day unto verrey night.

(Ad cognoscendum quantitatem diei vulgaris, viz. ab ortu diei usque ad noctem.)

NOW the quantitee of thy crepusculis, as I have taught in the chapitre biforn, and adde hem to the arch of thy day artificial; and tak ther the space of alle the hole day vulgar, unto verrey night. The same manere maystow worke, to knowe the quantitee of the vulgar night. And for the more declaracioun, lo here the figure.

10. To knowe the quantite of houres inequales by day.

(Ad cognoscendum horas inequales in die.)

UNDERSTOND WEL, that thise houres inequales ben cleped houres of planetes, & understond wel that somtyme ben they lengere by day than by night, and somtyme the contrarie. But understond wel, that evermo, generaly, the hour inequal of the day with the houre inequal of the night contenen 30 degrees of the bordure, whiche bordure is evermo answering to the degrees of the equinoxial; wherfor departe the arch of the day artificial in 12, and tak ther the quantitee of the houre inequal by day. And yif thow abate the quantitee of the houre inequal by daye out of 30, than shal the remenant that leveth performe the houre inequal by night. And for the more declaracioun, lo here the figure.

11. To knowe the quantite of houres equales.

(Ad cognoscendum quantitatem horarum equalium.)

THE quantitee of houres equales, that is to seyn, the houres of the clokke, ben departed by 15 degrees alredy in the bordure of thyn Astrolalabie, as wel by night as by day, generaly for evere. What nedeth more declaracioun? Wherfor, whan thee list to know how manye houres of the clokke ben passed, or any part of any of thise houres that ben passed, or elles how many houres or partie of houres ben to come, fro swich a tyme to swich a tyme, by day or by nighte, knowe the degree of thy sonne, and ley thy label on it; turne thy riet aboute joyntly with thy label, & with the point of it rekne in the bordure fro the sonne aryse unto the same place ther thou desirest, by day as by nighte. This conclusioun wol I declare in the laste chapitre of the 4 partie of this tretis so openly, that ther shal lakke no worde that nedeth to the declaracioun. And for the more declaracioun, lo here the figure.

12. Special declaracioun of the houres of planetes.

(Specialis declaracio de horis planetarum.)

UNDERSTOND WEL, that everemo, fro the arysing of the sonne til it go to reste, the nadir of the sonne shal shewe the houre of the planete, & fro that tyme forward al the night til the sonne aryse; than shal the verrey degree of the sonne shewe the houre of the planete. Ensample as thus. The 13 day of March fil upon a Saterday per aventure, and, at the arising of the sonne, I fond the secounde degree of Aries sitting upon myn est orisonte, albeit that it was but lite; than fond I the 2 degree of Libra, nadir of my sonne, dessending on my west orisonte, upon which west orisonte every day generally, at the sonne ariste, entreth the houre of any planete, after which planete the day bereth his name; and endeth in the nexte stryk of the plate under the forseide west orisonte; & evere,

d d.3

as the sonne climbeth uppere and uppere, so goth his nadir dounere and dounere, teching by swich strykes the houres of planetes by ordre as they sitten in the hevene. The first houre inequal of every Satterday is to Saturne; and the secounde, to Jupiter; the 3, to Mars; the 4, to the Sonne; the 5, to Venus; the 6, to Mercurius; the 7, to the Mone; and thanne agayn, the 8 is to Saturne; the 9, to Jupiter; the 10, to Mars; the 11, to the Sonne; the 12, to Venus; and now is my sonne gon to reste as for that Setterday. Thanne sheweth the verrey degree of the sonne the houre of Mercurie entring under my west orisonte at eve; and next him succedeth the Mone; and so forth by ordre, planete after planete, in houre after houre, al the night longe til the sonne aryse. Now ryseth the sonne that Sonday by the morwe; and the nadir of the sonne, upon the west orizonte, sheweth me the entring of the houre of the forseide sonne. And in this maner succedeth planete under planete, fro Saturne unto the Mone, and fro the Mone up agayn to Saturne, houre after houre generaly. And thus knowe I this conclusioun. And for the more declaracioun, lo here the figure.

13. To knowe the altitude of the sonne in middes of the day, that is cleped the altitude meridian.

(Ad cognoscendum altitudinem solis in medio diei, que vocatur altitudo meridiana.)

SET the degree of the sonne upon the lyne meridional, & rikene how many degrees of almikanteras ben bytwixe thyn est orisonte & the degree of the sonne. And tak ther thyn altitude meridian; this is to seyne, the heyest of the sonne as for that day. So maystow knowe in the same lyne, the heyest cours that any sterre fix climbeth by night; this is to seyn, that whan any sterre fix is passed the lyne meridional, than byginneth it to descende, and so doth the sonne. And for the more declaracioun, lo here thy figure.

14. To knowe the degree of the sonne by thy riet, for a maner curiositee, &c.

(Ad cognoscendum gradum solis curiose.)

SEK bysily with thy rewle the heyest of the sonne in midde of the day; turne thanne thyn Astrolabie, & with a prikke of ink marke the nombre of that same altitude in the lyne meridional. Turne thanne thy riet aboute til thou fynde a degree of thy zodiak according with the prikke, this is to seyn, sittinge on the prikke; and in sooth, thou shalt finde but two degrees in al the zodiak of that condicioun; and yit thilke two degrees ben in diverse signes; than maistow lightly by the sesoun of the yere knowe the signe in whiche that is the sonne. And for the more declaracioun, lo here thy figure.

15. To know which day is lyk to which day as of lengthe, &c.

(Ad cognoscendum quales dies in longitudine sunt similes.)

OKE whiche degrees ben ylyke fer fro the hevedes of Cancer and Capricorn; and lok, whan the sonne is in any of thilke degrees, than ben the dayes ylyke of lengthe. This is to seyn, that as long is that day in that monthe, as was swich a day in swich a month; ther varieth but lite. Also, yif thou take two dayes naturaly in the yer ylyke fer fro eyther pointe of the equinoxial in the opposit parties, than as long is the day artificial of that on day as is the night of that othere, and the contrarie. And for the more delaracioun, lo here thy figure.

16. This chapitre is a maner declaracioun to conclusiouns that folwen.

(Illud capitulum est quedam declaracio ad certas conclusiones sequentes.)

NDERSTOND wel that thy zodiak is departid in two halfe cercles, as fro the heved of Capricorne unto the heved of Cancer; & agaynward fro the heved of Cancer unto the heved of Capricorne. The heved of Capricorne is the lowest point, wheras the sonne goth in winter; and the heved of Cancer is the heyest point, in whiche the sonne goth in somer. And therfor understond wel, that any two degrees that ben ylyke fer fro any or thise two hevedes, truste wel that thilke two degrees ben of ylyke declinacioun, be it southward or northward; and the dayes of hem ben ylyke of lengthe, and the nightes also; & the shadwes ylyke, and the altitudes ylyke at midday for evere. And for more declaracioun, lo here thy figure.

17. To knowe the verrey degree of any maner sterre straunge or unstraunge after his longitude, though he be indeterminat in thyn Astrolabie; sothly to the trowthe, thus he shal be knowe.

(Ad cognoscendum verum gradum alicujus stelle aliene secundum ejus longitudinem, quamvis sit indeterminata in astrolabio; veraciter isto modo.)

AK the altitude of this sterre whan he is on the est side of the lyne meridional, as ney as thou mayst gesse; & tak an assendent anon right by som maner sterre fix which

that thou knowest; and forget nat the altitude of the firste sterre, ne thyn assendent. And whan that this is don, espye diligently whan this same firste sterre passeth anything the south westward, & hath him anon right in the same noumbre of altitude on the west side of this lyne meridional as he was caught on the est side; and tak a newe assendent anon right by some maner sterre fixe which that thou knowest; and forget nat this secounde assendent. And whan that this is don, rikne thanne how manye degrees ben bytwixe the firste assendent and the seconde assendent, & rikne wel the middel degree bytwene bothe assendentes, & set thilke middel degree upon thin estorisonte; and waite thanne what degree that sit upon the lyne meridional, & tak ther the verrey degree of the ecliptik in which the sterre stondeth for the tyme. For in the ecliptik is the longitude of a celestial body rekened, evene fro the heved of Aries unto the ende of Pisces. And his latitude is rikned after the quantite of his declinacion, north or south towarde the poles of this world; as thus. Yif it be of the sonne or of any fix sterre, rekene his latitude or his declinacioun fro the equinoxial cercle; and yif it be of a planete, rekne than the quantitee of his latitude fro the ecliptik lyne. Albeit so that fro the equinoxial may the declinacion or the latitude of any body celestial be rikned, after the site north or south, and after the quantitee of his declinacion. And right so may the latitude or the declinacion of any body celestial, save only of the sonne, after his site north or south, and after the quantitee of his declinacioun, be rekned fro the ecliptik lyne; fro which lyne alle planetes som tyme declynen north or south, save only the forseide sonne. And for the more declaracioun, lo here thy figure.

18. To knowe the degrees of the longitudes of fixe sterres after that they ben determinat in thin Astrolabie, yif so be that they ben trewly set.

(Ad cognoscendum gradus longitudinis de stellis fixis que determinantur in astrolabio, sicut in suis locis recte locentur.)

ET the centre of the sterre upon the lyne meridional, & tak keep of thy zodiak, and loke what degree of any signe that sit on the same lyne meridional at that same tyme, & tak the degree in which the sterre standeth; and with that same degree comth that same sterre unto that same lyne fro the orisonte. And for more declaracioun, lo here thy figure.

19. To knowe with which degree of the
zodiak any sterre fixe in thyn Astrolabie
aryseth upon the est orisonte, althogh his
dwelling be in another signe.

(Ad cognoscendum cum quibus gradibus
zodiaci que stella fixa in astrolabio ascen-
dit super orizontem orientalem, quamvis
ejus statio sit in alio signo.)

SET the centre of the sterre
upon the est orisonte, and
loke what degree of any signe
that sit upon the same orisonte at that same tyme.
And understond wel, that
with that same degree aryseth that same
sterre; and this merveyllous arysing with
a strange degree in another signe is bycause that the latitude of the sterre fix is
either north or south fro the equinoxial.
But sothly, the latitudes of planetes ben
comunly rekned fro the ecliptik, bicause
that non of hem declineth but fewe degrees out fro the brede of the zodiak. And
tak good keep of this chapitre of arysing
of the celestial bodies; for truste wel, that
neyther mone ne sterre as in oure embelif
orisonte aryseth with that same degree of
his longitude, save in o cas; and that is,
whan they have no latitude fro the ecliptik lyne. But natheles, som tyme is everiche
of thise planetes under the same lyne. And
for more declaracioun, lo here thy figure.

20. To knowe the declinacioun of any degree in the zodiak fro the equinoxial cercle,
&c.

(Ad cognoscendum declinacionem alicujus
gradus in zodiaco a circulo equinoctiali.)

SET the degree of any signe
upon the lyne meridional, &
rikne his altitude in almikanteras fro the est orizonte up
to the same degree set in the
forseide lyne, and set ther a
prikke. Turne up thanne thy riet, and set
the heved of Aries or Libra in the same meridional lyne, and set ther another prikke.
And whan that this is don, considere the
altitudes of hem bothe; for sothly the difference of thilke altitudes is the declinacion of thilke degree fro the equinoxial.
And yif so be that thilke degree be northward fro the equinoxial, than is his declinacion north; yif it be southward, than is it
south. And for the more declaracioun, lo
here thy figure.

21. To knowe for what latitude in any regioun the almikanteras of any table ben
compouned.

(Ad cognoscendum pro qua latitudine in
aliqua regione almicantre tabule mee sunt
composite.)

RIKNE how manye degrees of
almikanteras, in the meridional lyne, be fro the cercle
equinoxial unto the senith;
or elles fro the pool artik unto the north orisonte; & for
so gret a latitude or for so smal a latitude
is the table compouned. And for more declaracion, lo here thy figure.

22. To knowe in special the latitude of oure
countray, I mene after the latitude of Oxenford, and the heighte of oure pol.

(Ad cognoscendum specialiter latitudinem
nostri regionis, scilicet latitudinem Oxonie, et altitudinem poli nostri.)

UNDERSTOND wel, that as
fer is the heved of Aries or
Libra in the equinoxial from
oure orisonte as is the senith
from the pole artik; & as hey is
the pol artik fro the orisonte,
as the equinoxial is fer fro the senith. I
prove it thus by the latitude of Oxenford.
Understond wel, that the heyghte of oure
pool artik fro oure north orisonte is 51 degrees and 50 minutes; than is the senith
from oure pool artik 38 degrees and 10
minutes; than is the equinoxial from oure
senith 51 degrees and 50 minutes; than is
oure south orisonte from oure equinoxial
38 degrees and 10 minutes. Understond
wel this rekning. Also forget nat that the
senith is 90 degrees of heyghte fro the
orisonte, and oure equinoxial is 90 degrees
from oure pool artik. Also this shorte rewle
is soth, that the latitude of any place in a regioun is the distance fro the senith unto
the equinoxial. And for more declaracioun,
lo here thy figure.

23. To prove evidently the latitude of any
place in a regioun, by the preve of the
heyghte of the pol artik in that same place.

(Ad probandum evidenter latitudinem alicujus loci in aliqua regione, per probaci-
onem altitudinis de polo artico in eodem
loco.)

IN some winters night, whan
the firmament is clere and
thikke-sterred, waite a tyme
til that any sterre fix sit lyne-
right perpendiculer over the
pol artik, & clepe that sterre
A. And wayte another sterre that sit lyne-
right under A, and under the pol, & clepe
that sterre f. And understond wel, that f
is nat considered but only to declare that A
sit evene overe the pool. Tak thanne anon
right the altitude of A from the orisonte,
and forget it nat. Lat A and f go farwel til
agayns the dawening a gret whyle; & come
thanne agayn, and abyd til that A is evene
under the pol and under f; for sothly, than
wol f sitte over the pool, and A wol sitte

under the pool. Tak than eftsones the altitude of A from the orisonte, and note as wel his secounde altitude as his firste altitude; and whan that this is don, rikne how manye degrees that the firste altitude of A excedeth his seconde altitude, and tak half thilke porcioun that is exceded, and adde it to his seconde altitude; & tak ther the elevacioun of thy pool, and eke the latitude of thy regioun. For thise two ben of a nombre; this is to seyn, as manye degrees as thy pool is elevat, so michel is the latitude of the regioun. Ensample as thus: par aventure, the altitude of A in the evening is 56 degrees of heyghte. Than wol his seconde altitude or the dawing be 48; that is 8 lasse than 56, that was his firste altitude at even. Take thanne the half of 8, & adde it to 48, that was his seconde altitude, & than hastow 52. Now hastow the heyghte of thy pol, and the latitude of the regioun. But understond wel, that to prove this conclusioun & many another fair conclusioun, thou most have a plomet hanging on a lyne heyer than thin heved on a perche; & thilke lyne mot hange evene perpendiculer bytwixe the pool & thyn eye; & thanne shaltow seen yif A sitte evene over the pool and over f at evene; and also yif f sitte evene over the pool and over A or day. And for more declaracion, lo here thy figure.

24. Another conclusioun to prove the heyghte of the pool artik fro the orisonte. (Alia conclusio ad probandum altitudinem de polo artico ab orizonte.)

TAK any sterre fixe that nevere dissendeth under the orisonte in thilke regioun, and considere his heyest altitude & his lowest altitude fro the orisonte; and make a nombre of bothe thise altitudes. Tak thanne and abate half that nombre, and tak ther the elevacioun of the pol artik in that same regioun. And for more declaracioun, lo here thy figure.

25. Another conclusioun to prove the latitude of the regioun, &c. (Alia conclusio ad probandum latitudinem regionis.)

UNDERSTOND wel that the latitude of any place in a regioun is verreyly the space bytwixe the senith of hem that dwellen there & the equinoxial cerkle, north or southe, taking the mesure in the meridional lyne, as sheweth in the almikanteras of thyn Astrolabie. And thilke space is as moche as the pool artik is hey in the same place fro the orisonte. And than is the depressioun of the pol antartik, that is to seyn, than is the pol antartik bynethe the orisonte, the same

quantite of space, neither more ne lasse. Thanne, yif thow desire to knowe this latitude of the regioun, tak the altitude of the sonne in the middel of the day, whan the sonne is in the hevedes of Aries or of Libra; (for thanne moeveth the sonne in the lyne equinoxial); and abate the nombre of that same sonnes altitude out of 90, and thanne is the remenaunt of the noumbre that leveth the latitude of the regioun. As thus: I suppose that the sonne is thilke day at noon 38 degrees and 10 minutes of heyghte. Abate thanne thise degrees and minutes out of 90; so leveth there 51 degrees & 50 minutes, the latitude. I sey nat this but for ensample; for wel I wot the latitude of Oxenforde is certein minutes lasse, as I mighte prove. Now yif so be that thee semeth to long a tarying, to abyde til that the sonne be in the hevedes of Aries or of Libra, thanne waite whan the sonne is in any other degree of the zodiak, & considere the degree of his declinacion fro the equinoxial lyne; & yif it so be that the sonnes declinacion be northward fro the equinoxial, abate thanne fro the sonnes altitude at noon the nombre of his declinacion, and thanne hastow the heyghte of the hevedes of Aries & Libra. As thus: my sonne is, par aventure, in the firste degre of Leoun, 58 degrees and 10 minutes of heyghte at noon and his declinacion is almost 20 degrees northward fro the equinoxial; abate thanne thilke 20 degrees of declinacion out of the altitude at noon, than leveth thee 38 degrees and odde minutes; lo ther the heved of Aries or Libra, & thyn equinoxial in that regioun. Also yif so be that the sonnes declinacioun be southward fro the equinoxial, adde thanne thilke declinacion to the altitude of the sonne at noon; and tak ther the hevedes of Aries and Libra, and thyn equinoxial. Abate thanne the heyghte of the equinoxial out of 90 degrees, and thanne leveth there the distans of the pole, 51 degrees & 50 minutes, of that regioun fro the equinoxial. Or elles, yif thee lest, take the heyest altitude fro the equinoxial of any sterre fix that thou knowest, and tak his nethere elongacioun lengthing fro the same equinoxial lyne, and wirke in the maner forseid. And for more declaracion, lo here thy figure.

26. Declaracioun of the assensioun of signes, &c. (Declaracio de ascensione signorum.)

THE excellence of the spere solide, amonges other noble conclusiouns, sheweth manifeste the diverse assenciouns of signes in diverse places, as wel in the righte cercle as

in the embelif cercle. Thise auctours wryt-
en that thilke signe is cleped of right ascensioun, with which more part of the cercle equinoxial and lasse part of the zodiak
ascendeth; & thilke signe assendeth embelif, with which lasse part of the equinoxial and more part of the zodiak assendeth.
Fertherover they seyn, that in thilke cun-
trey where as the senith of hem that dwellen there is in the equinoxial lyne, & her orisonte passing by the poles of this worlde,
thilke folke han this right cercle and the
right orisonte; and everemo the arch of the
day and the arch of the night is ther ylike
long, and the sonne twyes every yeer passinge thorow the senith of her heved; and
two someres & two winteres in a yeer han
this forseide poeple. And the almikanteras
in her Astrolabies ben streighte as a lyne,
so as sheweth in this figure. The utilite to
knowe the assenciouns in the righte cercle
is this: truste wel that by mediacioun of
thilke assenciouns thise astrologiens, by
hir tables & hir instrumentz, knowen verreyly the assencioun of every degree and
minut in al the zodiak, as shal be shewed. And nota, that this forseid righte orisonte, that is cleped orison rectum, divyd-
eth the equinoxial into right angles; and
the embelif orisonte, wheras the pol is en-
haused upon the orisonte, overkerveth the
equinoxial in embelif angles, as sheweth
in the figure. And for the more declaracioun, lo here the figure.

27. This is the conclusioun to knowe the
assenciouns of signes in the right cercle,
that is, circulus directus, &c.
(Ad cognoscendum ascenciones signorum in recto circulo, qui vocatur circulus
directus.)

SET THE HEVED of what
signe thee liste to knowe his
assending in the right cercle
upon the lyne meridional; and
waite wher thyn almury toucheth the bordure, and set ther a
prikke. Turne thanne thy riet westward til
that the ende of the forseide signe sitte
upon the meridional lyne; and eftsones
waite wher thyn almury toucheth the bordure, and set ther another prikke. Rikne
thanne the nombre of degrees in the bordure bytwixe bothe prikkes, & tak the assencioun of the signe in the right cercle.
And thus maystow wyrke with every porcioun of thy zodiak, &c. And for the more
declaracioun, lo here thy figure.

28. To knowe the assencions of signes in
the embelif cercle in every regioun, I mene,
in circulo obliquo.
(Ad cognoscendum ascenciones signorum in circulo obliquo, in omni regione.)

SET the heved of the signe
which as thee list to knowe
his ascensioun upon the est
orisonte, & waite wher thyn
almury toucheth the bor-
dure, and set ther a prikke.
Turne thanne thy riet upward til that the
ende of the same signe sitte upon the est
orisonte, and waite eftsones wher as thyn
almury toucheth the bordure, and set ther
another prikke. Rikne thanne the noumbre
of degrees in the bordure bytwixe bothe
prikkes, & tak ther the assencioun of the
signe in the embelif cercle. And understond wel, that alle signes in thy zodiak,
fro the heved of Aries unto the ende of
Virgo, ben cleped signes of the north fro
the equinoxial; & these signes arysen bytwixe the verrey est and the verrey north
in oure orisonte generaly for evere. And
alle signes fro the heved of Libra unto the
ende of Pisces ben cleped signes of the
south fro the equinoxial; and thise signes
arysen evermo bytwixe the verrey est and
the verrey south in oure orisonte. Also
every signe bytwixe the heved of Capricorne unto the ende of Geminis aryseth on
oure orisonte in lasse than two houres e-
quales; and thise same signes, fro the heved of Capricorne unto the ende of Geminis, ben cleped Tortuos signes or Croked
signes, for they arisen embelif on oure orisonte; and thise crokede signes ben obedient to the signes that ben of right assencioun. The signes of right assencioun ben
fro the heved of Cancer to the ende of Sagittare; and thise signes arysen more upright, and they ben called eke sovereyn
signes; & everich of hem aryseth in more
space than in two houres. Of which signes,
Gemini obeyeth to Cancer; and Taurus to
Leo; Aries to Virgo; Pisces to Libra; A-
quarius to Scorpioun; and Capricorne to
Sagittare. And thus evermo two signes,
that ben ylyke fer fro the heved of Capricorne, obeyen everich of hem til other. And
for more declaracioun, lo here the figure.

29. To knowe justly the foure quarters of
the world, as est, west, north, and sowth.
(Ad cognoscendum evidenter quatuor par-
tes mundi, scilicet, orientem, austrum, a-
quilonem, et occidentem.)

TAKE the altitude of thy sonne
whan thee list, and note wel
the quarter of the world in
which the sonne is for the
tyme by the azimutz. Turne
thanne thyn Astrolabie, and
set the degree of the sonne in the almikanteras of his altitude, on thilke side that the
sonne stant, as is the manere in taking of
houres; and ley thy label on the degree of
the sonne, and rikene how many degrees of

the bordure ben bytwixe the lyne meridional and the point of thy label; & note wel that noumbre. Turne thanne agayn thyn Astrolabie, and set the point of thy gret rewle, ther thou takest thyne altitudes, upon as many degrees in his bordure fro his meridional as was the point of thy label fro the lyne meridional on the wombe-syde. Tak thanne thyn Astrolabie with bothe handes sadly and slely, and lat the sonne shyne thorow bothe holes of thy rewle; & slely, in thilke shyninge, lat thyn Astrolabie couch adoun evene upon a smothe grond, & thanne wol the verrey lyne meridional of thyn Astrolabie lye evene south, and the est lyne wole lye est, and the west lyne west, and north lyne north, so that thou werke softly and avisely in the couching; and thus hastow the 4 quarters of the firmament. And for the more declaracioun, lo here the figure.

30. To knowe the altitude of planetes fro the wey of the sonne, whether so they be north or south fro the forseide wey.

(Ad cognoscendum altitudinem planetarum a cursu solis, utrum sint in parte australi vel boreali a cursu supra dicto.)

LOK whan that a planete is in the lyne meridional, yif that hir altitude be of the same heyghte that is the degree of the sonne for that day, and than is the planete in the verrey wey of the sonne, & hath no latitude. And yif the altitude of the planete be heyere than the degree of the sonne, than is the planete north fro the wey of the sonne swich a quantite of latitude as sheweth by thyn almikanteras. And yif the altitude of the planete be lasse than the degree of the sonne, thanne is the planete south fro the wey of the sonne swich a quantite of latitude as sheweth by thyn almikanteras. This is to seyn, fro the wey wheras the sonne wente thilke day, but nat from the wey of the sonne in every place of the zodiak. And for the more declaracioun, lo here the figure.

31. To knowe the senith of the arysing of the sonne, this is to seyn, the partie of the orisonte in which that the sonne aryseth.

(Ad cognoscendum signum de ortu solis, scilicet, illam partem orientis in qua oritur sol.)

THOU most first considere that the sonne aryseth nat alwey verrey est, but some tyme by north the est, & som tyme by southe the est. Sothly, the sonne aryseth nevermo verrey est in oure orisonte, but he be in the heved of Aries or Libra. Now is thyn orisonte departed in 24 parties by thy azimutz, in significacion of 24 partiez of the

410

world; albeit so that shipmen rikne thilke partiez in 32. Thanne is ther no more but waite in which azimut that thy sonne entreth at his arysing; & take ther the senith of the arysing of the sonne. The manere of the devisioun of thyn Astrolabie is this; I mene, as in this cas. First is it devided in 4 plages principalx with the lyne that goth from est to west, and than with another lyne that goth fro south to north. Than is it devided in smale partiez of azimutz, as est, and est by southe, whereas is the firste azimut above the est lyne; & so forth, fro partie to partie, til that thou come agayn unto the est lyne. Thus maistow understond also the senith of any sterre, in which partie he ryseth, &c. And for the more declaracion, lo here the figure.

32. To knowe in which partie of the firmament is the conjunccioun.

(Ad cognoscendum in qua parte firmamenti sunt conjuncciones solis et lune.)

CONSIDERE the tyme of the conjunccion by thy kalender, as thus; lok how many houres thilke conjunccion is fro the midday of the day precedent, as sheweth by the canoun of thy kalender. Rikne thanne thilke nombre of houres in the bordure of thyn Astrolabie, as thou art wont to do in knowing of the houres of the day or of the night; and ley thy label over the degree of the sonne; and thanne wol the point of thy label sitte upon the hour of the conjunccion. Loke thanne in which azimut the degree of thy sonne sitteth, and in that partie of the firmament is the conjunccioun. And for the more declaracioun, lo here thy figure.

33. To knowe the senith of the altitude of the sonne, &c.

(Ad cognoscendum signa de altitudine solis.)

THIS is no more to seyn but any tyme of the day tak the altitude of the sonne; and by the azimut in which he stondeth, maystou seen in which partie of the firmament he is. And in the same wyse maystou seen, by the night, of any sterre, whether the sterre sitte est or west or north, or any partie bytwene, after the name of the azimut in which is the sterre. And for the more declaracioun, lo here the figure.

34. To knowe sothly the degree of the longitude of the mone, or of any planete that hath no latitude for the tyme fro the ecliptik lyne.

(Ad cognoscendum veraciter gradum de longitudine lune, vel alicujus planete qui non habet longitudinem pro tempore causante linea ecliptica.)

TAK the altitude of the mone, and rikne thyn altitude up among thyne almikanteras on which syde that the mone stande; & set there a prikke. Tak thenne anon-right, upon the mones syde, the altitude of any sterre fix which that thou knowest, and set his centre upon his altitude among thyn almikanteras ther the sterre is founde. Waite thanne which degree of the zodiak toucheth the prikke of the altitude of the mone, and tak ther the degree in which the mone standeth. This conclusioun is verrey soth, yif the sterres in thyn Astrolabie stonden after the trowthe; of comune, tretis of Astrolabie ne make non excepcioun whether the mone have latitude, or non; ne on whether syde of the mone the altitude of the sterre fix be taken. And nota, that yif the mone shewe himself by light of day, than maystow wyrke this same conclusioun by the sonne, as wel as by the fix sterre. And for the more declaracioun, lo here thy figure.

35. This is the workinge of the conclusioun, to knowe yif that any planete be directe or retrograde.

(Hec conclusio operatur ad cognoscendum si aliqua planeta sit directa vel retrograda.)

TAK the altitude of any sterre that is cleped a planete, and note it wel. And tak eek anon the altitude of any sterre fix that thou knowest, & note it wel also. Come thanne agayn the thridde or the ferthe night next folwing; for thanne shaltow aperceyve wel the moeving of a planete, whether so he moeve forthward or bakward. Awaite wel thanne whan that thy sterre fix is in the same altitude that she was whan thou toke hir firste altitude; and tak than eftsones the altitude of the forseide planete, and note it wel. For trust wel, yif so be that the planete be on the right syde of the meridional lyne, so that his seconde altitude be lasse than his firste altitude was, thanne is the planete directe. And yif he be on the west syde in that condicion, thanne is he retrograd. And yif so be that this planete be upon the est syde whan his altitude is taken, so that his secounde altitude be more than his firste altitude, thanne is he retrograde, and yif he be on the west syde, than is he directe. But the contrarie of thise parties is of the cours of the mone; for sothly, the mone moeveth the contrarie from othere planetes as in hir episicle, but in non other manere. And for the more declaracioun, lo here thy figure.

36. The conclusiouns of equaciouns of houses, after the Astrolabie, &c.

(Conclusio de equacione domorum.)

SET the byginning of the degree that assendeth upon the ende of the 8 houre inequal; thanne wol the byginning of the 2 hous sitte upon the lyne of midnight. Remeve thanne the degree that assendeth, and set him on the ende of the 10 hour inequal; & thanne wol the byginning of the 3 hous sitte upon the midnight lyne. Bring up agayn the same degree that assendeth first, and set him upon the orisonte; and thanne wol the beginning of the 4 hous sitte upon the lyne of midnight. Tak thanne the nadir of the degree that first assendeth, and set him on the ende of the 2 houre inequal; and thanne wol the byginning of the 5 hous sitte upon the lyne of midnight; set thanne the nadir of the assendent on the ende of the 4 houre, than wol the byginning of the 6 house sitte on the midnight lyne. The byginning of the 7 hous is nadir of the assendent, and the byginning of the 8 hous is nadir of the 2; and the byginning of the 9 hous is nadir of the 3; and the byginning of the 10 hous is the nadir of the 4; & the byginning of the 11 hous is nadir of the 5; and the byginning of the 12 hous is nadir of the 6. And for the more declaracion, lo here the figure.

37. Another manere of equaciouns of houses by the Astrolabie.

(De aliqua forma equacionis domorum secundum astrolabium.)

TAK thyn assendent, & thanne hastow thy 4 angles; for wel thou wost that the opposit of thyn assendent, that is to seyn, thy byginning of the 7 hous, sit upon the west orizonte; and the byginning of the 10 hous sit upon the lyne meridional; and his opposit upon the lyne of midnight. Thanne ley thy label over the degree that assendeth, and rekne fro the point of thy label alle the degrees in the bordure, til thou come to the meridional lyne; and departe alle thilke degrees in 3 evene parties, and take the evene equacion of 3; for ley thy label over everich of 3 parties, and than maistow see by thy label in which degree of the zodiak is the byginning of everich of thise same houses fro the assendent: that is to seyn, the beginning of the 12 house next above thyn assendent; and thanne the beginning of the 11 house; and thanne the 10, upon the meridional lyne; as I first seide. The same wyse wirke thou fro the assendent doun to the lyne of midnight; and thanne thus hastow other 3 houses, that is to seyn, the byginning of the 2, and the 3, and the 4 houses; thanne

411

is the nadir of thise 3 houses the byginning of the 3 houses that folwen. And for the more declaracioun, lo here thy figure.

38. To finde the lyne merydional to dwelle fix in any certein place.

(Ad inveniendum lineam meridionalem per subtiles operaciones.)

 TAK a rond plate of metal; for warping, the brodere the bettre; & make therupon a just compas, a lite within the bordure; and ley this ronde plate upon an evene grond, or on an evene ston, or on an evene stok fix in the gronde; and ley it even by a level. And in centre of the compas stike an evene pin or a wyr upright; the smallere the betere. Set thy pin by a plomrewle evene upright; & let this pin be no lengere than a quarter of the diametre of thy compas, fro the centre. And waite bisily, aboute 10 or 11 of the clokke and whan the sonne shyneth, whan the shadwe of the pin entreth anything within the cercle of thy plate an heermele, and mark ther a prikke with inke. Abyde thanne stille waiting on the sonne after 1 of the clokke, til that the schadwe of the wyr or of the pin passe onything out of the cercle of the compas, be it never so lyte; and set ther another prikke of inke. Take than a compas, and mesure evene the middel bytwixe bothe prikkes; and set ther a prikke. Take thanne a rewle, and draw a stryke, evene a lyne fro the pin unto the middel prikke; & tak ther thy lyne meridional for everemo, as in that same place. And yif thow drawe a croslyne overthwart the compas, justly over the lyne meridional, than hastow est and west and south; and, par consequence, than the nadir of the south lyne is the north lyne. And for more declaracioun, lo here thy figure.

39. Descripcion of the meridional lyne, of longitudes, and latitudes of citees and townes from on to another of clymatz.

THIS lyne meridional is but a maner descripcion of lyne imagined, that passeth upon the poles of this world & by the senith of oure heved. And hit is ycleped the lyne meridional; for in what place that any maner man is at any tyme of the yeer, whan that the sonne by moeving of the firmament cometh to his verrey meridian place, than is hit verrey midday, that we clepen oure noon, as to thilke man; and therfore is it cleped the lyne of midday. And nota, for evermo, of 2 citees or of 2 tounes, of whiche that o toun aprocheth more toward the est than doth that other toun, truste wel that thilke tounes han diverse meridians. Nota also, that the arch of the equinoxial, that

412

is conteyned or bounded bytwixe the 2 meridians, is cleped the longitude of the toun. And yif so be that two tounes have ylyke meridian, or oon meridian, than is the distance of hem bothe ylyke fer fro the est; and the contrarie. And in this manere they chaunge nat her meridian, but sothly they chaungen her almikanteras; for the enhausing of the pool and the distance of the sonne. The longitude of a clymat is a lyne imagined fro est to west, ylyke distant bytwene them alle. The latitude of a clymat is a lyne imagined from north to south the space of the erthe, fro the byginning of the firste clymat unto the verrey ende of the same climat, evene directe agayns the pole artik. Thus seyn some auctours; and somme of hem seyn that yif men clepen the latitude, thay mene the arch meridian that is contiened or intercept bytwixe the senith & the equinoxial. Thanne sey they that the distaunce fro the equinoxial unto the ende of a clymat, evene agayns the pole artyk, is the latitude of a clymat for sothe. And for more declaracioun, lo here thy figure.

40. To knowe with which degree of the zodiak that any planete assendith on the orisonte, whether so that his latitude be north or south.

 KNOWE by thyn almenak the degree of the ecliptik of any signe in which that the planete is rekned for to be, and that is cleped the degree of his longitude; and knowe also the degree of his latitude fro the ecliptik, north or south. And by thise samples folwinge in special, maystow wirke for sothe in every signe of the zodiak. The degree of the longitude, par aventure, of Venus or of another planete, was 6 of Capricorne, & the latitude of him was northward 2 degrees fro the ecliptik lyne. I tok a subtil compas, and cleped that oon poynt of my compas A, and that other poynt f. Than tok I the point of A, and set it in the ecliptik lyne evene in my zodiak, in the degree of the longitude of Venus, that is to seyn, in the 6 degree of Capricorne; and thanne sette I the point of f upward in the same signe, bycause that the latitude was north, upon the latitude of Venus, that is to seyn, in the 6 degree fro the heved of Capricorne; and thus have I 2 degrees bytwixe my two prikkes. Than leide I doun softely my compas, and sette the degree of the longitude upon the orisonte; tho tok I & wexede my label in maner of a peyre tables to resceyve distinctly the prikkes of my compas. Tho tok I this forseide label, and leide it fix over the degree of my longitude; tho tok I up my compas, and sette the point of

A in the wex on my label, as evene as I coude
gesse over the ecliptik lyne, in the ende of
the longitude; & sette the point of f endlang in my label upon the space of the latitude, inwarde and over the zodiak, that is
to seyn, northward fro the ecliptik. Than
leide I doun my compas, and lokede wel in
the wey upon the prikke of A and of f; tho
turned I my riet til that the prikke of f sat
upon the orisonte; than saw I wel that the
body of Venus, in hir latitude of 2 degrees
septentrionalis, assended, in the ende of
the 6 degree, in the heved of Capricorne.
And nota, that in the same maner maistow
wirke with any latitude septentrional in alle
signes; but sothly the latitude meridional
of a planete in Capricorne may not be take,
bycause of the litel space bytwixe the ecliptik and the bordure of the Astrolabie; but
sothly, in alle other signes it may. Also the
degree, par aventure, of Juppiter or of a-
nother planete, was in the first degree of
Pisces in longitude, and his latitude was
3 degrees meridional; tho tok I the point
of A, and sette it in the firste degree of
Pisces on the ecliptik, and thanne sette I
the point of f dounward in the same signe,
bycause that the latitude was south 3 degrees, that is to seyn, fro the heved of
Pisces; and thus have I 3 degrees bytwixe
bothe prikkes; thanne sette I the degree
of the longitude upon the orisonte. Tho
tok I my label, and leide it fix upon the degree of the longitude; tho sette I the point
of A on my label, evene over the ecliptik
lyne, in the ende evene of the degree of the
longitude, & sette the point of f endlang
in my label the space of 3 degrees of the latitude fro the zodiak, this is to seyn, southward fro the ecliptik, toward the bordure;
and turned my riet til the prikke of f sat
upon the orisonte; thanne saw I wel that
the body of Juppiter, in his latitude of 3
degrees meridional, ascended with 14 degrees of Pisces in horoscopo. And in this
maner maistow wirke with any latitude
meridional, as I first seide, save in Capricorne. And yif thou wolt pleye this craft
with the arysing of the mone, loke thou
rekne wel hir cours houre by houre; for she
ne dwelleth nat in a degree of hir longitude
but a litel whyle, as thou wel knowest; but
natheles, yif thou rekne hir verreye moeving by thy tables houre after houre, thou
shalt do wel ynow.
Explicit tractatus de Conclusionibus Astrolabii, compilatus per Galfridum Chau-
ciers ad filium suum Lodewicum, scola-
rem tunc temporis Oxonie, ac sub tutela
illius nobilissimi philosophi Magistri N.
Strode, etc.

41. Umbra Recta.

YIF IT SO BE that thou wilt
werke by umbra recta, and
thou may come to the bas of
the toure, in this maner thou
schalt werke. Tak the altitude of the tour by bothe
holes, so that thy rewle ligge even in a
poynt. Ensample as thus: I see him thorw
at the poynt of 4; then mete I the space
between me and the tour, and I finde it 20
feet; than beholde I how 4 is to 12, right so
is the space betwixe thee & the tour to the
altitude of the tour. For 4 is the thridde
part of 12, so is the space between thee &
the tour the thridde part of the altitude of
the tour; than thryes 20 feet is the heyghte
of the tour, with adding of thyn owne persone to thyn eye. And this rewle is so general in umbra recta, fro the poynt of oon
to 12. And yif thy rewle falle upon 5, than
is 5 12/partyes of the heyght the space between thee and the toure; with adding of
thyn owne heyght.
42. Umbra Versa.

ANOTHER maner of werk-
inge, by umbra versa. Yif so
be that thou may nat come
to the bas of the tour, I see
him thorw the nombre of 1;
I sette ther a prikke at my
fote; than go I neer to the tour, and I see
him thorw at the poynt of 2, and there I
sette another prikke; and I beholde how 1
hath him to 12, and ther finde I that it hath
him twelfe sythes; than beholde I how 2
hath him to 12, and thou shalt finde it sexe
sythes; than thou shalt finde that as 12 a-
bove 6 is the numbre of 6, right so is the
space between thy two prikkes the space of
6 tymes thyn altitude. And note, that at the
ferste altitude of 1, thou settest a prikke;
and afterward, whan thou seest him at 2,
ther thou settest another prikke; than thou
findest between two prikkys 60 feet; than
thou shalt finde that 10 is the 6/party of
60. And then is 10 feet the altitude of the
tour. For other poyntis, yif it fille in umbra
versa, as thus: I sette caas it fill upon 2,
& at the secunde upon 3; than schalt thou
finde that 2 is 6 partyes of 12; & 3 is 4 partyes of 12; than passeth 6 4, by nombre
of 2; so is the space between two prikkes
twyes the heyghte of the tour. And yif the
differens were thryes, than shulde it be
three tymes; and thus mayst thou werke
fro 2 to 12; and yif it be 4, 4 tymes; or 5, 5
tymes; et sic de ceteris.

413

43. Umbra Recta.

NOTHER maner of wyrking be umbra recta. Yif it so be that thou mayst nat come to the baas of the tour, in this maner thou schalt werke. Sette thy rewle upon 1 till thou see the altitude, and sette at thy foot a prikke. Than sette thy rewle upon 2, and beholde what is the differense between 1 & 2 & thou shalt finde that it is 1. Than mete the space between two prikkes, and that is the 12 partie of the altitude of the tour. And yif ther were 2, it were the 6 partye; and yif ther were 3, the 4 partye; et sic deinceps. And note, yif it were 5, it were the 5 party of 12; and 7, 7 party of 12; and note, at the altitude of thy conclusioun, adde the stature of thyn heyghte to thyn eye.

44. Another maner conclusion, to knowe the mene mote and the argumentis of any planete. To know the mene mote & the argumentis of every planete fro yere to yere, from day to day, from houre to houre, and from smale fraccionis infinite.

(Ad cognoscendum medios motus et argumenta de hora in horam cujuslibet planete, de anno in annum, de die in diem.)

N THIS maner shalt thou worche: consider thy rote first, the whiche is made the beginning of the tables fro the yere of oure lord 1397, and entere hit into thy slate for the laste meridie of December; & than consider the yere of oure lord, what is the date, & behold whether thy date be more or lasse than the yere 1397. And yf hit so be that hit be more, loke how many yeres hit passeth, and with so many entere into thy tables in the first lyne theras is writen anni collecti et expansi. And loke where the same planet is writen in the hede of thy table, and than loke what thou findest in directe of the same yere of oure lord whiche is passid, be hit 8, or 9, or 10, or what nombre that evere it be, til the tyme that thou come to 20, or 40, or 60. And that thou findest in directe wryte in thy slate under thy rote, and adde hit togeder, and that is thy mene mote, for the laste meridian of the December, for the same yere whiche that thou hast purposed. And if hit so be that hit passe 20, consider wel that fro 1 to 20 ben anni expansi, and fro 20 to 3000 ben anni collecti; and if thy nombere passe 20, than take that thou findest in directe of 20, and if hit be more, as 6 or 18, than take that thou findest in directe thereof, that is to sayen, signes, degrees, minutes, and secoundes, and adde togedere unto thy rote; and thus to make rotes; and note, that if hit so be

414

that the yere of oure lord be lasse than the rote, whiche is the yere of oure lord 1397, than shalt thou wryte in the same wyse furst thy rote in thy slate, and after entere into thy table in the same yere that be lasse, as I taught before; & than consider how many signes, degrees, minutes, and secoundes thyn entringe conteyneth. And so be that ther be 2 entrees, than adde hem togeder, & after withdrawe hem from the rote, the yere of oure lord 1397; and the residue that leveth is thy mene mote fro the laste meridie of December, the whiche thou hast purposed; and if hit so be that thou wolt weten thy mene mote for any day, or for any fraccioun of day, in this maner thou shalt worche. Make thy rote fro the laste day of Decembere in the maner as I have taught, and afterward behold how many monethis, dayes, & houres ben passid from the meridie of Decembere, & with that entere with the laste moneth that is ful passed, and take that thou findest in directe of him, and wryte hit in thy slate; and entere with as mony dayes as be more, and wryte that thou findest in directe of the same planete that thou worchest for; & in the same wyse in the table of houres, for houres that ben passed, and adde alle these to thy rote; and the residue is the mene mote for the same day and the same houre.

45. Another manere to knowe the mene mote.

HAN THOU wolt make the mene mote of eny planete to be by Arsechieles tables, take thy rote, the whiche is for the yere of oure lord 1397; and if so be that thy yere be passid the date, wryte that date, and than wryte the nombere of the yeres. Than withdrawe the yeres out of the yeres that ben passed that rote. Ensampul as thus: the yere of oure lord 1400, I wolde witen, precise, my rote; than wroot I furst 1400. And under that nombere I wrote a 1397; than withdrow I the laste nombere out of that, and than fond I the residue was 3 yere; I wiste that 3 yere was passed fro the rote, the whiche was writen in my tables. Than afterward soghte I in my tables the annis collectis et expansis, & amonge myn expanse yeres fond I 3 yeer. Than tok I alle the signes, degrees, & minutes, that I fond directe under the same planete that I wroghte for, and wroot so many signes, degrees, and minutes in my slate, and afterward added I to signes, degrees, minutes, and secoundes, the whiche I fond in my rote the yere of oure lord 1397; and kepte the residue; and than had I the mene mote for the laste day of Decembere. And if thou woldest wete the mene mote of any planete in March, Aprile, or May, other in any other tyme or moneth of the yere, loke how many monethes and dayes ben passed from the laste day of Decembere, the yere of oure lord 1400; and so with monethes & dayes entere into thy table ther thou findest thy mene mote ywriten in monethes & dayes, and take alle the signes, degrees, minutes, and secoundes that thou findest ywrite in directe of thy monethes, & adde to signes, degrees, minutes, & secoundes that thou findest with thy rote the yere of oure lord 1400, & the residue that leveth is the mene mote for that same day. And note, if hit so be that thou woldest wete the mene mote in ony yere that is lasse than thy rote, with/drawe the nombere of so many yeres as hit is lasse than the yere of oure lord a 1397, and kepe the residue; and so many yeres, monethes, & dayes entere into thy tabelis of thy mene mote. And take alle the signes, degrees, and minutes, and secoundes, that thou findest in directe of alle the yeris, monethes, & dayes, and wryte hem in thy slate; and above thilke nombere wryte the signes, degrees, minutes, and secoundes, the whiche thou findest with thy rote the yere of oure lord a 1397; and withdrawe alle the nethere signes and degrees fro the signes and degrees, minutes, & secoundes of other signes with thy rote; and thy re/sidue that leveth is thy mene mote for that day.

46. For to knowe at what houre of the day, or of the night, shal be flode or ebbe.

IRST wite thou certeinly, how that haven stondeth, that thou list to werke for; that is to say in whiche place of the firmament the mone being, maketh fulle see. Than awayte thou redily in what degree of the zodiak that the mone at that tyme is inne.

Bringe furth than the labelle, and set the point therof in that same cost that the mone maketh flode, and set thou there the degree of the mone according with the egge of the label. Than afterward awayte where is than the degree of the sonne, at that tyme. Remeve thou than the label fro the mone, and bringe and sette it justly upon the degree of the sonne. And the point of the label shal than declare to thee, at what houre of the day or of the night shal be flode. And there also maist thou wite by the same point of the label, whether it be, at that same tyme, flode or ebbe, or half flode, or quarter flode, or ebbe, or half or quarter ebbe; or ellis at what houre it was last, or shal be next by night or by day, thou than shalt esely knowe, &c. Further-more, if it so be that thou happe to worke for this matere aboute the tyme of the con/junccioun, bringe furthe the degree of the mone with the labelle to that coste as it is before seyd. But than thou shalt under-stonde that thou may not bringe furthe the label fro the degree of the mone as thou dide before; forwhy the sonne is than in the same degree with the mone. And so thou may at that tyme by the point of the labelle unremeved knowe the houre of the flode or of the ebbe, as it is before seyd, &c. And evermore as thou findest the mone passe fro the sonne, so remeve thou the labelle than fro the degree of the mone, & bringe it to the degree of the sonne. And worke thou than as thou dide before, &c. Or elles knowe thou what houre it is that thou art inne, by thyn instrument. Than bringe thou furth fro thennes the labelle and ley it upon the degree of the mone, and therby may thou wite also whan it was flode, or whan it wol be next, be it night or day; &c.

Here end Chaucer's Propositions supple/mentary to his Treatise on the Astrolabe.

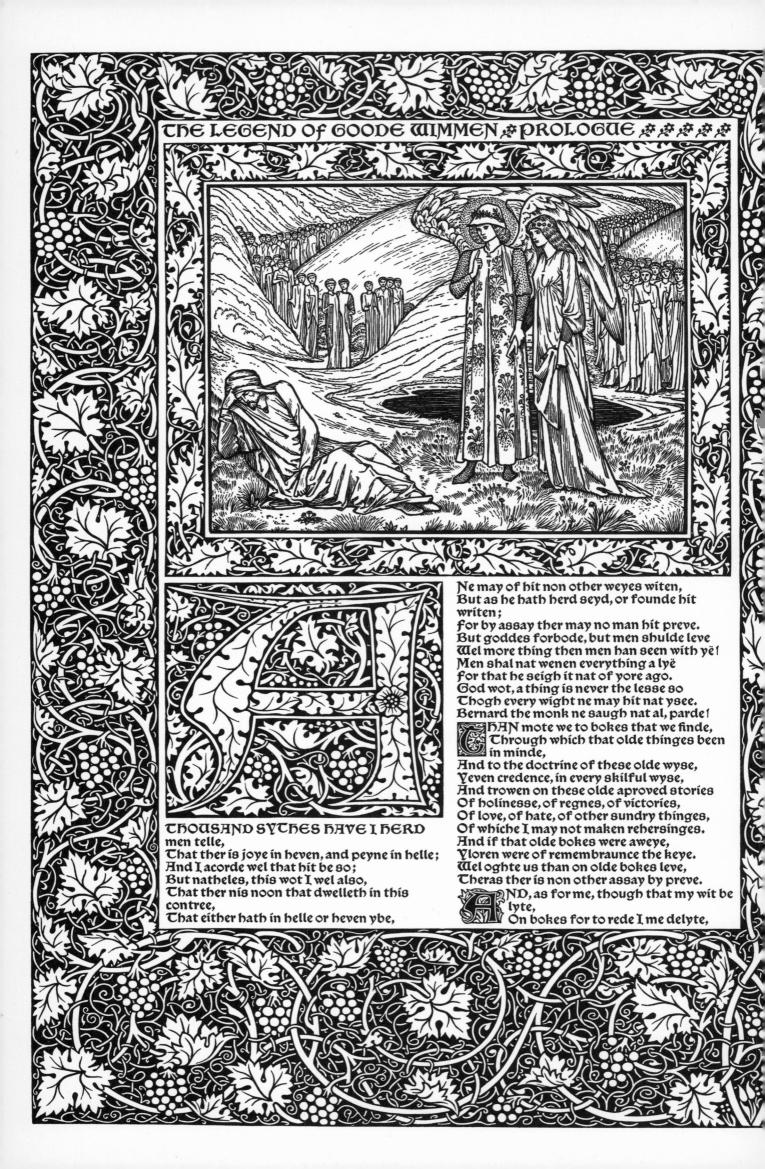

A THOUSAND SYTHES HAVE I HERD
men telle,
That ther is joye in heven, and peyne in helle;
And I acorde wel that hit be so;
But natheles, this wot I wel also,
That ther nis noon that dwelleth in this
contree,
That either hath in helle or heven ybe,

Ne may of hit non other weyes witen,
But as he hath herd seyd, or founde hit
writen;
For by assay ther may no man hit preve.
But goddes forbode, but men shulde leve
Wel more thing then men han seen with yë!
Men shal nat wenen everything a lyë
For that he seigh it nat of yore ago.
God wot, a thing is never the lesse so
Thogh every wight ne may hit nat ysee.
Bernard the monk ne saugh nat al, parde!
THAN mote we to bokes that we finde,
Through which that olde thinges been
in minde,
And to the doctrine of these olde wyse,
Yeven credence, in every skilful wyse,
And trowen on these olde aproved stories
Of holinesse, of regnes, of victories,
Of love, of hate, of other sundry thinges,
Of whiche I may not maken rehersinges.
And if that olde bokes were aweye,
Yloren were of remembraunce the keye.
Wel oghte us than on olde bokes leve,
Theras ther is non other assay by preve.
AND, as for me, though that my wit be
lyte,
On bokes for to rede I me delyte,

And in myn herte have hem in reverence;
And to hem yeve swich lust and swich credence,
That ther is wel unethe game noon
That from my bokes make me to goon,
But hit be other upon the halyday,
Or elles in the joly tyme of May;
Whan that I here the smale foules singe,
And that the floures ginne for to springe,
Farwel my studie, as lasting that sesoun!
NOW have I therto this condicioun
That, of alle the floures in the mede,
Than love I most these floures whyte
and rede,
Swiche as men callen daysies in our toun.
To hem have I so greet affeccioun,
As I seyde erst, whan comen is the May,
That in my bed ther daweth me no day
That I nam up, and walking in the mede
To seen these floures agein the sonne sprede,
Whan hit upriseth by the morwe shene,
The longe day, thus walking in the grene.
And whan the sonne ginneth for to weste,
Than closeth hit, and draweth hit to reste.
So sore hit is afered of the night,
Til on the morwe, that hit is dayes light.
This dayesye, of alle floures flour,
Fulfild of vertu and of alle honour,
And ever ylyke fair and fresh of hewe,
As wel in winter as in somer newe,
Fain wolde I preisen, if I coude aright;
But wo is me, hit lyth nat in my might!
FOR wel I wot, that folk han herbeforn
Of making ropen, and lad awey the
corn;
And I come after, glening here and
there,
And am ful glad if I may finde an ere
Of any goodly word that they han left.
And, if hit happe me rehersen eft
That they han in her fresshe songes sayd,
I hope that they wil nat ben evel apayd,
Sith hit is seid in forthering and honour
Of hem that either serven leef or flour.
For trusteth wel, I ne have nat undertake
As of the leef, ageyn the flour, to make;
Ne of the flour to make, ageyn the leef,
No more than of the corn ageyn the sheef.
For, as to me, is leefer noon ne lother;
I am withholde yit with never nother.
I not who serveth leef, ne who the flour;
That nis nothing the entent of my labour.
For this werk is al of another tunne,
Of olde story, er swich stryf was begunne.
But wherfor that I spak, to yeve credence
To bokes olde and doon hem reverence,
Is for men shulde autoritees beleve,
Ther as ther lyth non other assay by preve.
For myn entent is, or I fro yow fare,
The naked text in English to declare
Of many a story, or elles of many a geste,
As autours seyn; leveth hem if yow leste!

WHAN passed was almost the month
of May,
And I had romed, al the someres
day,
The grene medew, of which that I
yow tolde,
Upon the fresshe daysy to beholde,
And that the sonne out of the south gan weste,
And closed was the flour and goon to reste
For derknesse of the night, of which she dredde,
Hoom to myn hous ful swiftly I me spedde;
And, in a litel erber that I have,
Ybenched newe with turves fresshe ygrave,
I bad men shulde me my couche make;
For deyntee of the newe someres sake,
I bad hem strowe floures on my bed.
Whan I was layd, and had myn eyen hed,
I fel aslepe within an houre or two.
Me mette how I was in the medew tho,
And that I romed in that same gyse,
To seen that flour, as ye han herd devyse.
Fair was this medew, as thoughte me overal;
With floures swote enbrowded was it al;
As for to speke of gomme, or erbe, or tree,
Comparisoun may noon ymaked be.
For hit surmounted pleynly alle odoures,
And eek of riche beaute alle floures.
Forgeten had the erthe his pore estat
Of winter, that him naked made and mat,
And with his swerd of cold so sore had greved.
Now had the atempre sonne al that releved,
And clothed him in grene al newe agayn.
The smale foules, of the seson fayn,
That from the panter and the net ben scaped,
Upon the fouler, that hem made awhaped
In winter, and distroyed had hir brood,
In his despyt, hem thoughte hit did hem good
To singe of him, and in hir song despyse
The foule cherl that, for his covetyse,
Had hem betrayed with his sophistrye.
This was hir song: The fouler we defye!
Somme songen layes on the braunches clere
Of love and May, that joye hit was to here,
In worship and in preysing of hir make,
And of the newe blisful someres sake,
That songen, Blissed be seynt Valentyn!
For at his day I chees yow to be myn,
Withoute repenting, myn herte swete!
And therwithal hir bekes gonnen mete.
They dide honour and humble obeisaunces,
And after diden other observaunces
Right plesing unto love and to nature;
So ech of hem doth wel to creature.
This song to herkne I dide al myn entente,
Forwhy I mette I wiste what they mente.
Til at the laste a larke song above:
I see, quod she, the mighty god of love!
Lo! yond he cometh, I see his winges sprede!
Tho gan I loken endelong the mede,
And saw him come, and in his hond a quene,
Clothed in ryal abite al of grene.
A fret of gold she hadde next hir heer,
And upon that a whyt coroun she beer

With many floures, and I shal nat lye;
for al the world, right as the dayesye
Icoroned is with whyte leves lyte,
Swich were the floures of hir coroun whyte.
for of o perle fyn and oriental
Hir whyte coroun was ymaked al;
for which the whyte coroun, above the grene,
Made hir lyk a daysie for to sene,
Considered eek the fret of gold above.

CLOTHED was this mighty god of love
Of silk, ybrouded ful of grene greves;
A garlond on his heed of rose-leves
Steked al with lilie floures newe;
But of his face I can nat seyn the hewe,
for sekirly his face shoon so brighte,
That with the gleem astoned was the sighte;
A furlong-wey I mighte him nat beholde.
But at the laste in hande I saw him holde
Two fyry dartes, as the gledes rede;
And aungellich his wenges gan he sprede.
And al be that men seyn that blind is he,
Algate me thoughte he mighte wel ysee;
for sternely on me he gan biholde,
So that his loking doth myn herte colde.

AND by the hande he held the noble quene,
Corouned with whyte, & clothed al in grene,
So womanly, so benigne, and so meke,
That in this world, thogh that men wolde seke,
Half hir beautee shulde men nat finde
In creature that formed is by kinde,
Hir name was Alceste the debonayre;
I prey to God that ever falle she fayre!
for ne hadde confort been of hir presence,
I had be deed, withouten any defence,
for drede of Loves wordes and his chere,
As, whan tyme is, herafter ye shal here.
Byhind this god of love, upon this grene,
I saw cominge of ladyës nyntene
In ryal abite, a ful esy pas,
And after hem com of wemen swich a tras
That, sin that God Adam had made of erthe,
The thredde part of wemen, ne the ferthe,
Ne wende I nat by possibilitee
Hadden ever in this world ybe;
And trewe of love thise wemen were echoon.

NOW whether was that a wonder thing or noon,
That, right anoon as that they gonne espye
This flour, which that I clepe the dayesye,
ful sodeinly they stinten alle atones,
And kneled adoun, as it were for the nones.
And after that they wenten in compas,
Daunsinge aboute this flour an esy pas,
And songen, as it were in carole-wyse,
This balade, which that I shal yow devyse.

Balade.

HYD, Absolon, thy gilte tresses clere;
Ester, ley thou thy meknesse al adoun;
Hyd, Jonathas, al thy frendly manere;
Penalopee, and Marcia Catoun,

Mak of your wyfhod no comparisoun;
Hyde ye your beautes, Isoude and Eleyne,
Alceste is here, that al that may desteyne.

THY faire body, lat hit nat appere,
Lavyne; and thou, Lucresse of Rome toun,
And Polixene, that boghte love so dere,
Eek Cleopatre, with al thy passioun,
Hyde ye your trouthe in love and your renoun;
And thou, Tisbe, that hast for love swich peyne:
Alceste is here, that al that may desteyne.

HERRO, Dido, Laudomia, alle infere,
Eek Phyllis, hanging for thy Demophoun,
And Canace, espyed by thy chere,
Ysiphile, betrayed with Jasoun,
Mak of your trouthe in love no bost ne soun;
Nor Ypermistre or Adriane, ne pleyne;
Alceste is here, that al that may desteyne.

WHAN that this balade al ysongen was,
Upon the softe and swote grene gras
They setten hem ful softely adoun,
By ordre alle in compas, alle enveroun.
first sat the god of love, and than this quene
With the whyte coroun, clad in grene;
And sithen al the remenant by and by,
As they were of degree, ful curteisly;
Ne nat a word was spoken in the place
The mountance of a furlong-wey of space.

I, LENING faste by under a bente,
Abood, to knowen what this peple mente,
As stille as any stoon; til at the laste,
The god of love on me his eye caste,
And seyde, Who resteth ther? and I answerde
Unto his axing, whan that I him herde,
And seyde, Sir, hit am I; and cam him neer,
And salued him. Quod he: What dostow heer
In my presence, and that so boldely?
for it were better worthy, trewely,
A werm to comen in my sight than thou.
And why, sir, quod I, and hit lyke yow?
for thou, quod he, art therto nothing able.
My servaunts been alle wyse and honourable.
Thou art my mortal fo, and me warreyest,
And of myne olde servaunts thou misseyest,
And hinderest hem with thy translacioun,
And lettest folk to han devocioun
To serven me, and haldest hit folye
To troste on me. Thou mayst hit nat denye;
for in pleyn text, hit nedeth nat to glose,
Thou hast translat the Romauns of the Rose,
That is an heresye ageyns my lawe,
And makest wyse folk fro me withdrawe.
And thinkest in thy wit, that is ful cool,
That he nis but a verray propre fool
That loveth paramours, to harde and hote.
Wel wot I therby thou beginnest dote
As olde foles, whan hir spirit fayleth;
Than blame they folk, & wite nat what hem ayleth.
Hast thou nat mad in English eek the book
How that Crisseyde Troilus forsook,
In shewinge how that wemen han don mis?

But natheles, answere me now to this,
Why noldest thou as wel han seyd goodnesse
Of wemen, as thou hast seyd wikkednesse?
Was ther no good matere in thy minde,
Ne in alle thy bokes coudest thou nat finde
Sum story of wemen that were goode and trewe?
Yis! God wot, sixty bokes olde and newe
Hast thou thyself, alle fulle of stories grete,
That bothe Romains and eek Grekes trete
Of sundry wemen, which lyf that they ladde,
And ever an hundred gode ageyn oon badde.
This knoweth God, and alle clerkes eke,
That usen swiche materes for to seke.
What seith Valerie, Titus, or Claudian?
What seith Jerome ageyns Jovinian?
How clene maydens, and how trewe wyves,
How stedfast widwes during al hir lyves,
Telleth Jerome; and that nat of a fewe,
But, I dar seyn, an hundred on a rewe;
That hit is pitee for to rede, and routhe,
The wo that they enduren for hir trouthe.
For to hir love were they so trewe,
That, rather than they wolde take a newe,
They chosen to be dede in sundry wyse,
And deyden, as the story wol devyse;
And some were brend, and some were cut the hals,
And some dreynt, for they wolden nat be fals.
For alle keped they hir maydenhed,
Or elles wedlok, or hir widwehed.
And this thing was nat kept for holinesse,
But al for verray vertu and clennesse,
And for men shulde sette on hem no lak;
And yit they weren hethen, al the pak,
That were so sore adrad of alle shame.
These olde wemen kepte so hir name,
That in this world I trow men shal nat finde
A man that coude be so trewe and kinde,
As was the leste woman in that tyde.
What seith also the epistels of Ovyde
Of trewe wyves, and of hir labour?
What Vincent, in his Storial Mirour?
Eek al the world of autours maystow here,
Cristen and hethen, trete of swich matere;
It nedeth nat alday thus for tendyte.
But yit I sey, what eyleth thee to wryte
The draf of stories, and forgo the corn?
By seint Venus, of whom that I was born,
Although that thou reneyed hast my lay,
As othere olde foles many a day,
Thou shalt repente hit, that hit shal be sene!
THAN spak Alceste, the worthieste quene,
And seyde: God, right of your curtesye,
Ye moten herknen if he can replye
Ageyns these points that ye han to him meved;
A god ne sholde nat be thus agreved,
But of his deitee he shal be stable,
And therto rightful and eek merciable.
He shal nat rightfully his yre wreke
Or he have herd the tother party speke.
Al ne is nat gospel that is to yow pleyned;
The god of love herth many a tale yfeyned.
For in your court is many a losengeour,
And many a queynte totelere accusour,

That tabouren in your eres many a thing
For hate, or for jelous imagining,
And for to han with yow som daliaunce.
Envye (I preye to God yeve hir mischaunce!)
Is lavender in the grete court alway.
For she ne parteth, neither night ne day,
Out of the hous of Cesar; thus seith Dante;
Whoso that goth, alwey she moot nat wante.
This man to yow may wrongly been accused,
Ther as by right him oghte ben excused.
Or elles, sir, for that this man is nyce,
He may translate a thing in no malyce,
But for he useth bokes for to make,
And takth non heed of what matere he take;
Therfor he wroot the Rose and eek Crisseyde
Of innocence, and niste what he seyde;
Or him was boden make thilke tweye
Of som persone, and durste hit nat withseye;
For he hath writen many a book er this.
He ne hath nat doon so grevously amis
To translaten that olde clerkes wryten,
As thogh that he of malice wolde endyten
Despyt of love, and hadde himself ywroght.
This shulde a rightwys lord han in his thoght,
And nat be lyk tiraunts of Lumbardye,
That usen wilfulhed and tirannye,
For he that king or lord is naturel,
Him oghte nat be tiraunt ne cruel,
As is a fermour, to doon the harm he can.
He moste thinke hit is his lige man,
And that him oweth, of verray duetee,
Shewen his peple pleyn benignitee,
And wel to here hir excusaciouns,
And hir compleyntes and peticiouns,
In duewe tyme, whan they shal hit profre.
This is the sentence of the philosophre:
A king to kepe his liges in justyce;
Withouten doute, that is his offyce.
And therto is a king ful depe ysworn,
Ful many an hundred winter heerbiforn;
And for to kepe his lordes hir degree,
As hit is right and skilful that they be
Enhaunced and honoured, and most dere,
For they ben half-goddes in this world here,
This shal he doon, bothe to pore and riche,
Al be that here stat be nat aliche,
And han of pore folk compassioun.
For lo, the gentil kind of the lioun!
For whan a flye offendeth him or byteth,
He with his tayl awey the flye smyteth
Al esily; for, of his genterye,
Him deyneth nat to wreke him on a flye,
As doth a curre or elles another beste.
In noble corage oghte been areste,
And weyen every thing by equitee,
And ever han reward to his owen degree.
For, sir, hit is no maystrie for a lord
To dampne a man withoute answere or word;
And, for a lord, that is ful foul to use.
And if so be he may him nat excuse,
But axeth mercy with a sorweful herte,
And profreth him, right in his bare sherte,
To been right at your owne jugement,

ee2

Than oghte a god, by short avysement,
Considre his owne honour and his trespas.
for sith no cause of deeth lyth in this cas,
Yow oghte been the lighter merciable;
Leteth your yre, and beth somwhat tretable!
The man hath served yow of his conning,
And forthered your lawe with his making.
Whyl he was yong, he kepte your estat;
I not wher he be now a renegat.
But wel I wot, with that he can endyte,
He hath maked lewed folk delyte
To serve you, in preysing of your name.
He made the book that hight the Hous of fame,
And eek the Deeth of Blaunche the Duchesse,
And the Parlement of foules, as I gesse,
And al the love of Palamon and Arcyte
Of Thebes, thogh the story is knowen lyte;
And many an ympne for your halydayes,
That highten Balades, Roundels, Virelayes;
And for to speke of other besinesse,
He hath in prose translated Boëce;
And of the Wreched Engendring of Mankinde,
As man may in pope Innocent yfinde;
And mad the Lyf also of seynt Cecyle;
He made also, goon sithen a greet whyl,
Origenes upon the Maudeleyne;
Him oghte now to have the lesse peyne;
He hath mad many a lay and many a thing.

NOW as ye been a god, and eek a king,
I, your Alceste, whylom quene of Trace,
I axe yow this man, right of your grace,
That ye him never hurte in al his lyve;
And he shal sweren yow, and that as blyve,
He shal no more agilten in this wyse;
But he shal maken, as ye wil devyse,
Of wemen trewe in lovinge al hir lyve,
Wherso ye wil, of maiden or of wyve,
And forthren yow, as muche as he misseyde
Or in the Rose or elles in Crisseyde.

THE god of love answerde hir thus
anoon:
Madame, quod he, hit is so long
agoon
That I yow knew so charitable and
trewe,
That never yit, sith that the world was newe,
To me ne fond I better noon than ye.
That, if that I wol save my degree,
I may ne wol nat warne your requeste;
Al lyth in yow, doth with him what yow leste
And al foryeve, withouten lenger space;
for whoso yeveth a yift, or doth a grace,
Do hit by tyme, his thank is wel the more;
And demeth ye what he shal do therfore.
Go thanke now my lady heer, quod he.

I ROOS, and doun I sette me on my knee,
And seyde thus: Madame, the God above
foryelde yow, that ye the god of love
Han maked me his wrathe to foryive;
And yeve me grace so long for to live,
That I may knowe soothly what ye be
That han me holpen, and put in swich degree.
But trewely I wende, as in this cas,

420

Naught have agilt, ne doon to love trespas.
forwhy a trewe man, withouten drede,
Hath nat to parten with a theves dede;
Ne a trewe lover oghte me nat blame,
Thogh that I speke a fals lover som shame.
They oghte rather with me for to holde,
for that I of Creseyde wroot or tolde,
Or of the Rose; whatso myn auctour mente,
Algate, God wot, hit was myn entente
To forthren trouthe in love and hit cheryce;
And to be war fro falsnesse and fro vyce
By swich ensample; this was my meninge.

AND she answerde: Lat be thyn arguinge;
for Love ne wol nat countrepleted be
In right ne wrong; and lerne this at me!
Thou hast thy grace, and hold thee right therto.
Now wol I seyn what penance thou shalt do
for thy trespas, and understond hit here:
Thou shalt, whyl that thou livest, yeer by yere,
The moste party of thy lyve spende
In making of a glorious Legende
Of Gode Wemen, maidenes and wyves,
That were trewe in lovinge al hir lyves;
And telle of false men that hem bitrayen,
That al hir lyf ne doon nat but assayen
How many wemen they may doon a shame;
for in your world that is now holden game.
And thogh thee lesteth nat a lover be,
Spek wel of love; this penance yeve I thee.
And to the god of love I shal so preye,
That he shal charge his servants, by any weye,
To forthren thee, and wel thy labour quyte;
Go now thy wey, thy penance is but lyte.

THE god of love gan smyle, and than he seyde:
Wostow, quod he, wher this be wyf or mayde,
Or quene, or countesse, or of what degree,
That hath so litel penance yeven thee,
That hast deserved sorer for to smerte?
But pitee renneth sone in gentil herte;
That mayst thou seen, she kytheth what she is.
And I answerde: Nay, sir, so have I blis,
No more but that I see wel she is good.

THAT is a trewe tale, by myn hood,
Quod Love, and that thou knowest wel, pardee,
If hit be so that thou avyse thee.
Hastow nat in a book, lyth in thy cheste,
The grete goodnesse of the quene Alceste,
That turned was into a dayesye:
She that for hir husbonde chees to dye,
And eek to goon to helle, rather than he,
And Ercules rescued hir, pardee,
And broghte hir out of helle agayn to blis?

AND I answerde ageyn, and seyde: Yis,
Now knowe I hir! And is this good Alceste,
The dayesye, and myn owne hertes reste?
Now fele I wel the goodnesse of this wyf,
That bothe after hir deeth, and in hir lyf,
Hir grete bountee doubleth hir renoun!
Wel hath she quit me myn affeccioun
That I have to hir flour, the dayesye!
No wonder is thogh Jove hir stellifye,
As telleth Agaton, for hir goodnesse!

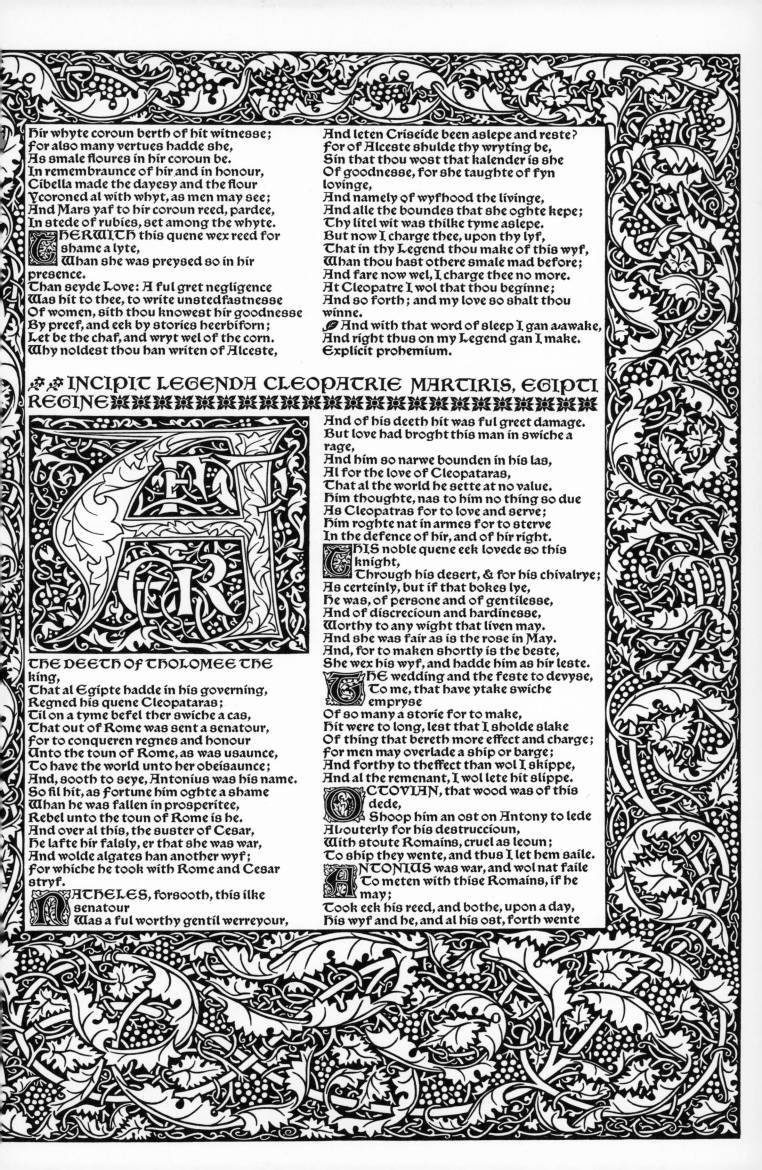

Hir whyte coroun berth of hit witnesse;
For also many vertues hadde she,
As smale floures in hir coroun be.
In remembraunce of hir and in honour,
Cibella made the dayesy and the flour
Ycoroned al with whyt, as men may see;
And Mars yaf to hir coroun reed, pardee,
In stede of rubies, set among the whyte.

THERWITH this quene wex reed for shame a lyte,
Whan she was preysed so in hir presence.
Than seyde Love: A ful gret negligence
Was hit to thee, to write unstedfastnesse
Of women, sith thou knowest hir goodnesse
By preef, and eek by stories heerbiforn;
Let be the chaf, and wryt wel of the corn.
Why noldest thou han writen of Alceste,

And leten Criseide been aslepe and reste?
For of Alceste shulde thy wryting be,
Sin that thou wost that kalender is she
Of goodnesse, for she taughte of fyn lovinge,
And namely of wyfhood the livinge,
And alle the boundes that she oghte kepe;
Thy litel wit was thilke tyme aslepe.
But now I charge thee, upon thy lyf,
That in thy Legend thou make of this wyf,
Whan thou hast othere smale mad before;
And fare now wel, I charge thee no more.
At Cleopatre I wol that thou beginne;
And so forth; and my love so shalt thou winne.
And with that word of sleep I gan awake,
And right thus on my Legend gan I make.
Explicit prohemium.

INCIPIT LEGENDA CLEOPATRIE MARTIRIS, EGIPTI REGINE

And of his deeth hit was ful greet damage.
But love had broght this man in swiche a rage,
And him so narwe bounden in his las,
Al for the love of Cleopataras,
That al the world he sette at no value.
Him thoughte, nas to him no thing so due
As Cleopatras for to love and serve;
Him roghte nat in armes for to sterve
In the defence of hir, and of hir right.

THIS noble quene eek lovede so this knight,
Through his desert, & for his chivalrye;
As certeinly, but if that bokes lye,
He was, of persone and of gentilesse,
And of discrecioun and hardinesse,
Worthy to any wight that liven may.
And she was fair as is the rose in May.
And, for to maken shortly is the beste,
She wex his wyf, and hadde him as hir leste.

THE wedding and the feste to devyse,
To me, that have ytake swiche empryse
Of so many a storie for to make,
Hit were to long, lest that I sholde slake
Of thing that bereth more effect and charge;
For men may overlade a ship or barge;
And forthy to theffect than wol I skippe,
And al the remenant, I wol lete hit slippe.

OCTOVIAN, that wood was of this dede,
Shoop him an ost on Antony to lede
Al outerly for his destruccioun,
With stoute Romains, cruel as leoun;
To ship they wente, and thus I let hem saile.

ANTONIUS was war, and wol nat faile
To meten with thise Romains, if he may;
Took eek his reed, and bothe, upon a day,
His wyf and he, and al his ost, forth wente

THE DEETH OF THOLOMEE THE king,
That al Egipte hadde in his governing,
Regned his quene Cleopataras;
Til on a tyme befel ther swiche a cas,
That out of Rome was sent a senatour,
For to conqueren regnes and honour
Unto the toun of Rome, as was usaunce,
To have the world unto her obeisaunce;
And, sooth to seye, Antonius was his name.
So fil hit, as fortune him oghte a shame
Whan he was fallen in prosperitee,
Rebel unto the toun of Rome is he.
And over al this, the suster of Cesar,
He lafte hir falsly, er that she was war,
And wolde algates han another wyf;
For whiche he took with Rome and Cesar stryf.

NATHELES, forsooth, this ilke senatour
Was a ful worthy gentil werreyour,

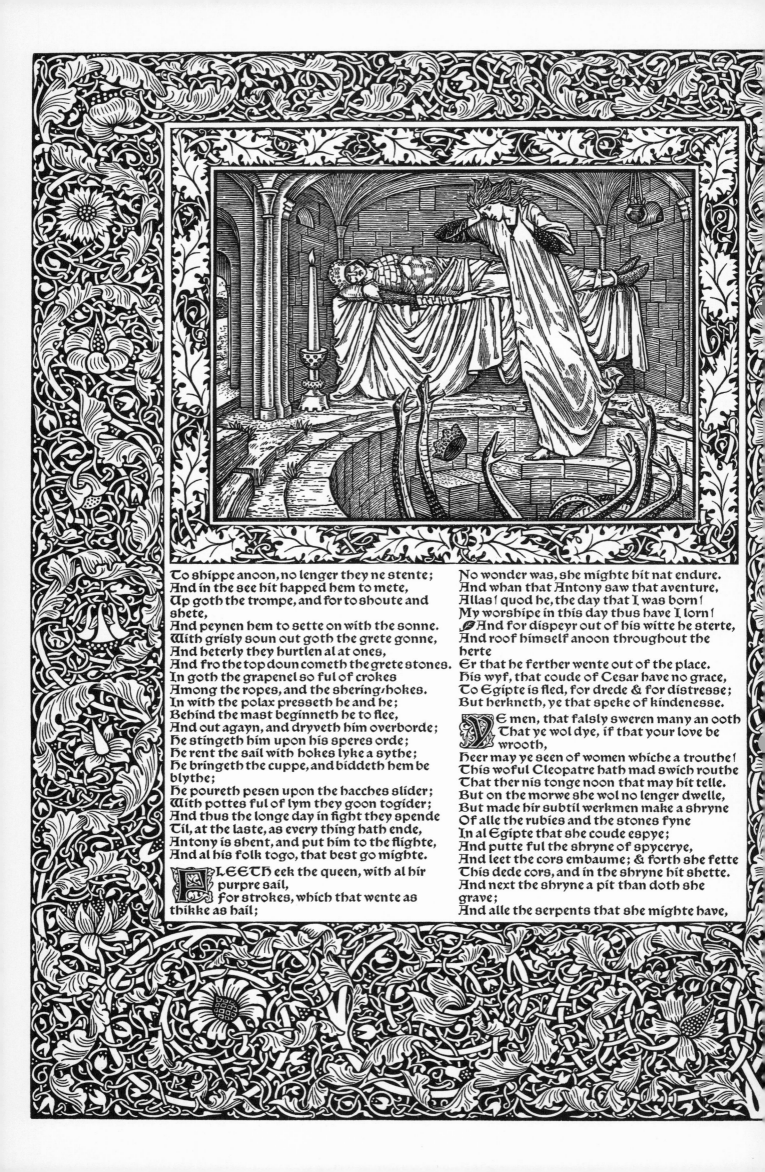

To shippe anoon, no lenger they ne stente;
And in the see hit happed hem to mete,
Up goth the trompe, and for to shoute and shete,
And peynen hem to sette on with the sonne.
With grisly soun out goth the grete gonne,
And heterly they hurtlen al at ones,
And fro the top doun cometh the grete stones.
In goth the grapenel so ful of crokes
Among the ropes, and the shering-hokes.
In with the polax presseth he and he;
Behind the mast beginneth he to flee,
And out agayn, and dryveth him overborde;
He stingeth him upon his speres orde;
He rent the sail with hokes lyke a sythe;
He bringeth the cuppe, and biddeth hem be blythe;
He poureth pesen upon the hacches slider;
With pottes ful of lym they goon togider;
And thus the longe day in fight they spende
Til, at the laste, as every thing hath ende,
Antony is shent, and put him to the flighte,
And al his folk togo, that best go mighte.

FLEETH eek the queen, with al hir purpre sail,
For strokes, which that wente as thikke as hail;

No wonder was, she mighte hit nat endure.
And whan that Antony saw that aventure,
Allas! quod he, the day that I was born!
My worshipe in this day thus have I lorn!
And for dispeyr out of his witte he sterte,
And roof himself anoon throughout the herte
Er that he ferther wente out of the place.
His wyf, that coude of Cesar have no grace,
To Egipte is fled, for drede & for distresse;
But herkneth, ye that speke of kindenesse.

YE men, that falsly sweren many an ooth
That ye wol dye, if that your love be wrooth,
Heer may ye seen of women whiche a trouthe!
This woful Cleopatre hath mad swich routhe
That ther nis tonge noon that may hit telle.
But on the morwe she wol no lenger dwelle,
But made hir subtil werkmen make a shryne
Of alle the rubies and the stones fyne
In al Egipte that she coude espye;
And putte ful the shryne of spycerye,
And leet the cors embaume; & forth she fette
This dede cors, and in the shryne hit shette.
And next the shryne a pit than doth she grave;
And alle the serpents that she mighte have,

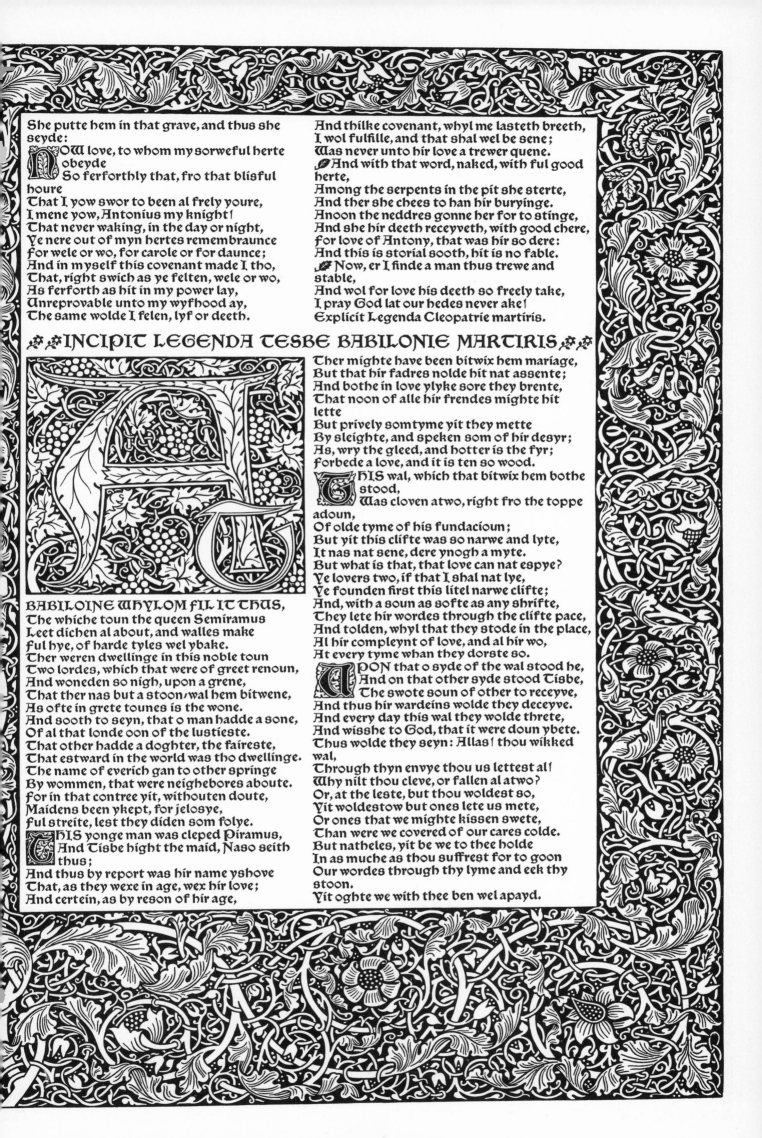

She putte hem in that grave, and thus she
seyde:
NOW love, to whom my sorweful herte
obeyde
So ferforthly that, fro that blisful
houre
That I yow swor to been al frely youre,
I mene yow, Antonius my knight!
That never waking, in the day or night,
Ye nere out of myn hertes remembraunce
For wele or wo, for carole or for daunce;
And in myself this covenant made I tho,
That, right swich as ye felten, wele or wo,
As ferforth as hit in my power lay,
Unreprovable unto my wyfhood ay,
The same wolde I felen, lyf or deeth.

And thilke covenant, whyl me lasteth breeth,
I wol fulfille, and that shal wel be sene;
Was never unto hir love a trewer quene.
And with that word, naked, with ful good
herte,
Among the serpents in the pit she sterte,
And ther she chees to han hir buryinge.
Anoon the neddres gonne her for to stinge,
And she hir deeth receyveth, with good chere,
For love of Antony, that was hir so dere:
And this is storial sooth, hit is no fable.
Now, er I finde a man thus trewe and
stable,
And wol for love his deeth so freely take,
I pray God lat our hedes never ake!
Explicit Legenda Cleopatrie martiris.

INCIPIT LEGENDA TESBE BABILONIE MARTIRIS

BABILOINE WHYLOM FIL IT THUS,
The whiche toun the queen Semiramus
Leet dichen al about, and walles make
Ful hye, of harde tyles wel ybake.
Ther weren dwellinge in this noble toun
Two lordes, which that were of greet renoun,
And woneden so nigh, upon a grene,
That ther nas but a stoon-wal hem bitwene,
As ofte in grete tounes is the wone.
And sooth to seyn, that o man hadde a sone,
Of al that londe oon of the lustieste.
That other hadde a doghter, the faireste,
That estward in the world was tho dwellinge.
The name of everich gan to other springe
By wommen, that were neighebores aboute.
For in that contree yit, withouten doute,
Maidens been ykept, for jelosye,
Ful streite, lest they diden som folye.
THIS yonge man was cleped Piramus,
And Tisbe highte the maid, Naso seith
thus;
And thus by report was hir name yshove
That, as they wexe in age, wex hir love;
And certein, as by reson of hir age,

Ther mighte have been bitwix hem mariage,
But that hir fadres nolde hit nat assente;
And bothe in love ylyke sore they brente,
That noon of alle hir frendes mighte hit
lette
But prively somtyme yit they mette
By sleighte, and speken som of hir desyr;
As, wry the gleed, and hotter is the fyr;
Forbede a love, and it is ten so wood.
THIS wal, which that bitwix hem bothe
stood,
Was cloven atwo, right fro the toppe
adoun,
Of olde tyme of his fundacioun;
But yit this clifte was so narwe and lyte,
It nas nat sene, dere ynogh a myte.
But what is that, that love can nat espye?
Ye lovers two, if that I shal nat lye,
Ye founden first this litel narwe clifte;
And, with a soun as softe as any shrifte,
They lete hir wordes through the clifte pace,
And tolden, whyl that they stode in the place,
Al hir compleynt of love, and al hir wo,
At every tyme whan they dorste so.
UPON that o syde of the wal stood he,
And on that other syde stood Tisbe,
The swote soun of other to receyve,
And thus hir wardeins wolde they deceyve.
And every day this wal they wolde threte,
And wisshe to God, that it were doun ybete.
Thus wolde they seyn: Allas! thou wikked
wal,
Through thyn envye thou us lettest al!
Why nilt thou cleve, or fallen al atwo?
Or, at the leste, but thou woldest so,
Yit woldestow but ones lete us mete,
Or ones that we mighte kissen swete,
Than were we covered of our cares colde.
But natheles, yit be we to thee holde
In as muche as thou suffrest for to goon
Our wordes through thy lyme and eek thy
stoon.
Yit oghte we with thee ben wel apayd.

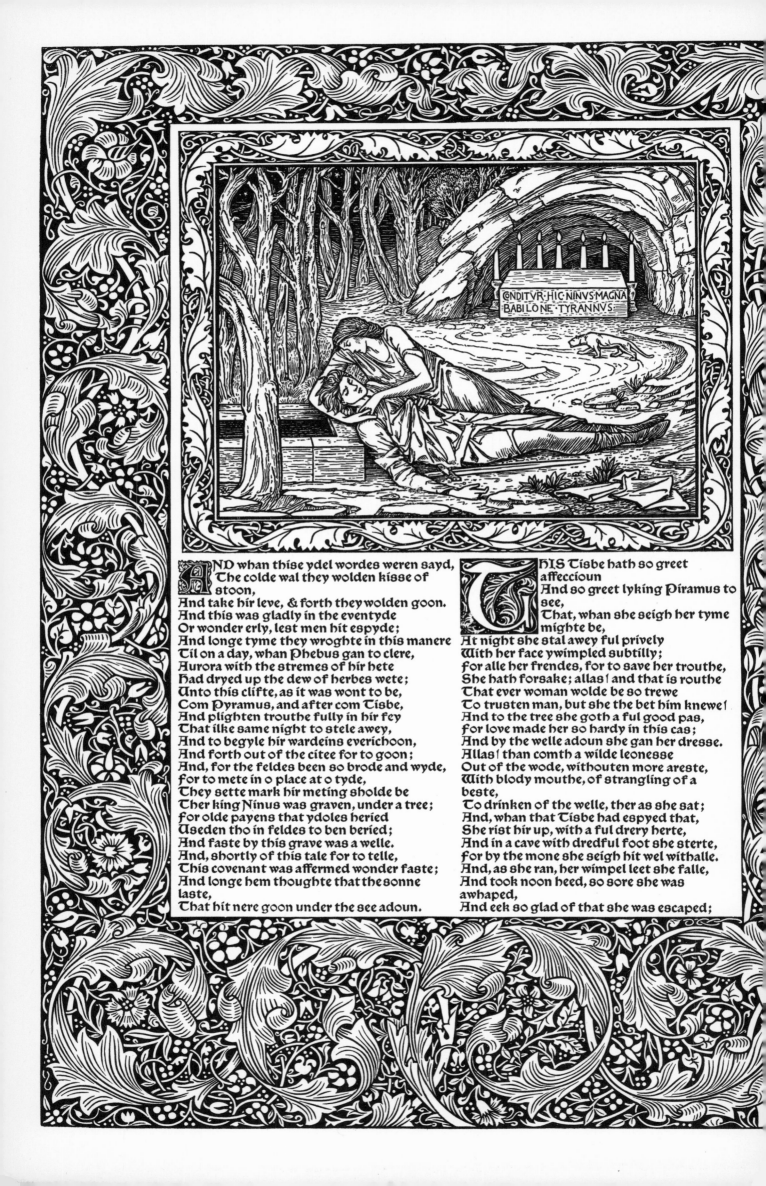

AND when thise ydel wordes weren sayd,
The colde wal they wolden kisse of stoon,
And take hir leve, & forth they wolden goon.
And this was gladly in the eventyde
Or wonder erly, lest men hit espyde;
And longe tyme they wroghte in this manere
Til on a day, whan Phebus gan to clere,
Aurora with the stremes of hir hete
Had dryed up the dew of herbes wete;
Unto this clifte, as it was wont to be,
Com Pyramus, and after com Tisbe,
And plighten trouthe fully in hir fey
That ilke same night to stele awey,
And to begyle hir wardeins everichoon,
And forth out of the citee for to goon;
And, for the feldes been so brode and wyde,
For to mete in o place at o tyde,
They sette mark hir meting sholde be
Ther king Ninus was graven, under a tree;
For olde payens that ydoles heried
Useden tho in feldes to ben beried;
And faste by this grave was a welle.
And, shortly of this tale for to telle,
This covenant was affermed wonder faste;
And longe hem thoughte that the sonne laste,
That hit nere goon under the see adoun.

THIS Tisbe hath so greet affeccioun
And so greet lyking Piramus to see,
That, whan she seigh her tyme mighte be,
At night she stal awey ful prively
With her face ywimpled subtilly;
For alle her frendes, for to save her trouthe,
She hath forsake; allas! and that is routhe
That ever woman wolde be so trewe
To trusten man, but she the bet him knewe!
And to the tree she goth a ful good pas,
For love made her so hardy in this cas;
And by the welle adoun she gan her dresse.
Allas! than comth a wilde leonesse
Out of the wode, withouten more areste,
With blody mouthe, of strangling of a beste,
To drinken of the welle, ther as she sat;
And, whan that Tisbe had espyed that,
She rist hir up, with a ful drery herte,
And in a cave with dredful foot she sterte,
For by the mone she seigh hit wel withalle.
And, as she ran, her wimpel leet she falle,
And took noon heed, so sore she was awhaped,
And eek so glad of that she was escaped;

And thus she sit, and darketh wonder stille.
Whan that this leonesse hath dronke her fille,
Aboute the welle gan she for to winde,
And right anoon the wimpel gan she finde,
And with her blody mouth hit al torente.
Whan this was doon, no lenger she ne stente,
But to the wode her wey than hath she nome.
AND, at the laste, this Piramus is come,
But al to longe, allas! at hoom was he.
The mone shoon, men mighte wel ysee,
And in his weye, as that he com ful faste,
His eyen to the grounde adoun he caste,
And in the sonde, as he beheld adoun,
He seigh the steppes brode of a leoun,
And in his herte he sodeinly agroos,
And pale he wex, therwith his heer aroos,
And neer he com, and fond the wimpel torn.
Allas! quod he, the day that I was born!
This o night wol us lovers bothe slee!
How sholde I axen mercy of Tisbe
Whan I am he that have yow slain, allas!
My bidding hath yow slain, as in this cas.
Allas! to bidde a woman goon by nighte
In place ther as peril fallen mighte,
And I so slow! allas, I ne hadde be
Here in this place a furlong-wey or ye!
Now what leoun that be in this foreste,
My body mote he renden, or what beste
That wilde is, gnawen mote he now myn herte!
And with that worde he to the wimpel sterte,
And kiste hit ofte, and weep on hit ful sore,
And seide: Wimpel, allas, ther nis no more
But thou shalt fele as wel the blood of me
As thou hast felt the bleding of Tisbe!
And with that worde he smoot him to the herte.
The blood out of the wounde as brode sterte
As water, whan the conduit broken is.
NOW Tisbe, which that wiste nat of this,
But sitting in her drede, she thoghte thus:
If hit so falle that my Piramus
Be comen hider, and may me nat yfinde,
He may me holden fals and eek unkinde.
And out she comth, and after him gan espyen
Bothe with her herte and with her yën,
And thoghte, I wol him tellen of my drede
Bothe of the leonesse and al my dede.
And at the laste her love than hath she founde
Beting with his heles on the grounde,
Al blody, and therwithal abak she sterte,
And lyke the wawes quappe gan her herte,
And pale as box she wex, and in a throwe
Avysed her, and gan him wel to knowe,
That hit was Piramus, her herte dere.
Who coude wryte whiche a deedly chere
Hath Tisbe now, and how her heer she rente,

And how she gan herselve to turmente,
And how she lyth and swowneth on the grounde,
And how she weep of teres ful his wounde,
How medeleth she his blood with her compleynte,
And with his blood herselven gan she peynte;
How clippeth she the dede cors, allas!
How doth this woful Tisbe in this cas!
How kisseth she his frosty mouth so cold!
Who hath doon this, & who hath been so bold
To sleen my leef? O spek, my Piramus!
I am thy Tisbe, that thee calleth thus!
And therwithal she lifteth up his heed.
THIS woful man, that was nat fully deed,
Whan that he herde the name of Tisbe cryen,
On her he caste his hevy deedly yën
And doun again, and yeldeth up the gost.
TISBE rist up, withouten noise or bost,
And seigh her wimpel and his empty shethe,
And eek his swerd, that him hath doon to dethe;
Than spak she thus: My woful hand, quod she,
Is strong ynogh in swiche a werk to me;
For love shal yive me strengthe and hardinesse
To make my wounde large ynogh, I gesse.
I wol thee folwen deed, and I wol be
Felawe and cause eek of thy deeth, quod she.
And thogh that nothing save the deeth only
Mighte thee fro me departe trewely,
Thou shalt no more departe now fro me
Than fro the deeth, for I wol go with thee!
AND now, ye wrecched jelous fadres oure,
We, that weren whylom children youre,
We prayen yow, withouten more envye,
That in o grave yfere we moten lye,
Sin love hath brought us to this pitous ende!
And rightwis God to every lover sende,
That loveth trewely, more prosperitee
Than ever hadde Piramus and Tisbe!
And lat no gentil woman her assure
To putten her in swiche an aventure.
But God forbede but a woman can
Been as trewe and loving as a man!
And, for my part, I shal anoon it kythe!
And, with that worde, his swerd she took as swythe,
That warm was of her loves blood and hoot,
And to the herte she herselven smoot.
AND thus ar Tisbe and Piramus ago.
Of trewe men I finde but fewe mo
In alle my bokes, save this Piramus,
And therfor have I spoken of him thus.
For hit is deyntee to us men to finde
A man that can in love be trewe and kinde.
Heer may ye seen, what lover so he be,
A woman dar and can as wel as he.
Explicit legenda Tesbe.

425

AND HONOUR, VIRGIL MANTUAN,
Be to thy names! and I shal, as I can,
folow thy lantern, as thou gost biforn,
How Eneas to Dido was forsworn.
In thyn Eneid and Naso wol I take
The tenour, and the grete effectes make.

WHAN Troye broght was to de-
struccioun
By Grekes sleighte, and namely
by Sinoun,
feyning the hors y-offred to Minerve,
Through which that many a Troyan moste
sterve;
And Ector had, after his deeth, appered,
And fyr so wood, it mighte nat be stered,
In al the noble tour of Ilioun,
That of the citee was the cheef dungeoun;
And al the contree was so lowe ybroght,
And Priamus the king fordoon and noght;
And Eneas was charged by Venus
To fleen awey, he took Ascanius,
That was his sone, in his right hand, and
fledde;
And on his bakke he bar and with him ledde
His olde fader, cleped Anchises,
And by the weye his wyf Creusa he lees.
And mochel sorwe hadde he in his minde
Er that he coude his felawshippe finde.
But, at the laste, whan he had hem founde,
He made him redy in a certein stounde,
And to the see ful faste he gan him hye,

And saileth forth with al his companye
Toward Itaile, as wolde destinee.
But of his aventures in the see
Nis nat to purpos for to speke of here,
For hit acordeth nat to my matere.
But, as I seide, of him and of Dido
Shal be my tale, til that I have do.
So longe he sailed in the salte see
Til in Libye unnethe aryved he,
With shippes seven and with no more navye;
And glad was he to londe for to hye,
So was he with the tempest al toshake.
And whan that he the haven had ytake,
He had a knight, was called Achates;
And him of al his felawshippe he chees
To goon with him, the contre for tespye;
He took with him no more companye.
But forth they goon, and lafte his shippes ryde,
His fere and he, withouten any gyde.
So longe he walketh in this wildernesse
Til, at the laste, he mette an hunteresse.
A bowe in honde and arwes hadde she,
Her clothes cutted were unto the knee;
But she was yit the fairest creature
That ever was yformed by nature;
And Eneas and Achates she grette,
And thus she to hem spak, whan she hem mette.
*Sawe ye, quod she, as ye han walked wyde,
Any of my sustren walke yow besyde,
With any wilde boor or other beste
That they han hunted to, in this foreste,
Ytukked up, with arwes in her cas?
*Nay, soothly, lady, quod this Eneas;
But, by thy beaute, as hit thinketh me,
Thou mightest never erthely womman be,
But Phebus suster artow, as I gesse.
And, if so be that thou be a goddesse,
Have mercy on our labour and our wo.
I NAM no goddes, soothly, quod she tho;
for maidens walken in this contree here,
With arwes and with bowe, in this manere.
This is the regne of Libie, ther ye been,
Of which that Dido lady is and queen.
*And shortly tolde him al the occasioun
Why Dido com into that regioun,
Of which as now me lusteth nat to ryme;
Hit nedeth nat; hit nere but los of tyme.
For this is al and som, it was Venus,
His owne moder, that spak with him thus;
And to Cartage she bad he sholde him dighte,
And vanished anoon out of his sighte.
I coude folwe, word for word, Virgyle,
But it wolde lasten al to longe a whyle.
THIS noble queen, that cleped was Dido,
That whylom was the wyf of Sitheo,
That fairer was then is the brighte sonne,
This noble toun of Cartage hath begonne;
In which she regneth in so greet honour,
That she was holde of alle quenes flour,
Of gentilnesse, of freedom, of beautee;
That wel was him that mighte her ones see;
Of kinges and of lordes so desyred,
That al the world her beaute hadde yfyred;

She stood so wel in every wightes grace.
WHAN Eneas was come unto that place,
Unto the maister-temple of al the toun
Ther Dido was in her devocioun,
Ful prively his wey than hath he nome.
Whan he was in the large temple come,
I can nat seyn if that hit be possible,
But Venus hadde him maked invisible;
Thus seith the book, withouten any lees.
And whan this Eneas and Achates
Hadden in this temple been overal,
Than founde they, depeynted on a wal,
How Troye and al the lond destroyed was.
*Allas! that I was born, quod Eneas,
Throughout the world our shame is kid so wyde,
Now it is peynted upon every syde!
We, that weren in prosperitee,
Be now disslaundred, and in swich degre,
No lenger for to liven I ne kepe!
*And, with that worde, he brast out for to wepe
So tendrely, that routhe hit was to sene.
This fresshe lady, of the citee quene,
Stood in the temple, in her estat royal,
So richely, and eek so fair withal,
So yong, so lusty, with her eyen glade,
That, if that God, that heven and erthe made,
Wolde han a love, for beaute and goodnesse,
And womanhod, and trouthe, and seemlinesse,
Whom sholde he loven but this lady swete?
There nis no womman to him half so mete.
FORTUNE, that hath the world in govern-
aunce,
Hath sodeinly broght in so newe a chaunce,
That never was ther yit so fremd a cas.
For al the companye of Eneas,
Which that he wende han loren in the see,
Aryved is, nat fer fro that citee;
For which, the grettest of his lordes some
By aventure ben to the citee come,
Unto that same temple, for to seke
The quene, and of her socour her beseke;
Swich renoun was ther spronge of her goodnesse.
And, whan they hadden told al hir distresse,
And al hir tempest and hir harde cas,
Unto the quene appered Eneas,
And openly beknew that hit was he.
Who hadde joye than but his meynee,
That hadden founde hir lord, hir governour?
THE quene saw they dide him swich honour,
And had herd ofte of Eneas, er tho,
And in her herte she hadde routhe and wo
That ever swich a noble man as he
Shal been disherited in swich degree;
And saw the man, that he was lyk a knight,
And suffisaunt of persone and of might,
And lyk to been a veray gentil man;
And wel his wordes he besette can,
And had a noble visage for the nones,
And formed wel of braunes and of bones.
For, after Venus, hadde he swich fairnesse,
That no man might be half so fair, I gesse.
And wel a lord he semed for to be.
And, for he was a straunger, somwhat she

427

Lyked him the bet, as, God do bote,
To som folk ofte newe thing is swote.
Anoon her herte hath pitee of his wo,
And, with that pitee, love com in also;
And thus, for pitee and for gentilesse,
Refresshed moste he been of his distresse.
She seide, certes, that she sory was
That he hath had swich peril and swich cas;
And, in her frendly speche, in this manere
She to him spak, and seide as ye may here.

BE ye nat Venus sone and Anchises?
In good feith, al the worship and encrees
That I may goodly doon yow, ye shul have.
Your shippes and your meynee shal I save;
And many a gentil word she spak him to;
And comaunded her messageres go
The same day, withouten any faile,
His shippes for to seke, and hem vitaile.
She many a beste to the shippes sente,
And with the wyn she gan hem to presente;
And to her royal paleys she her spedde,
And Eneas alwey with her she ledde.
What nedeth yow the feste to descryve?
He never beter at ese was his lyve.
Ful was the feste of deyntees and richesse,
Of instruments, of song, and of gladnesse,
And many an amorous loking and devys.

THIS Eneas is come to Paradys
Out of the swolow of helle, & thus in joye
Remembreth him of his estat in Troye.
To dauncing-chambres ful of parements,
Of riche beddes, and of ornaments,
This Eneas is lad, after the mete.
And with the quene whan that he had sete,
And spyces parted, and the wyn agoon,
Unto his chambres was he lad anoon
To take his ese and for to have his reste,
With al his folk, to doon what so hem leste.

THER nas coursere wel ybrydled noon,
Ne stede, for the justing wel to goon,
Ne large palfrey, esy for the nones,
Ne juwel, fretted ful of riche stones,
Ne sakkes ful of gold, of large wighte,
Ne ruby noon, that shynede by nighte,
Ne gentil hautein faucon heronere,
Ne hound, for hert or wilde boor or dere,
Ne coupe of gold, with florins newe ybete,
That in the lond of Libie may be gete,
That Dido ne hath hit Eneas ysent;
And al is payed, what that he hath spent.
Thus can this noble quene her gestes calle,
As she that can in freedom passen alle.

ENEAS sothly eek, withouten lees,
Hath sent unto his shippe, by Achates,
After his sone, and after riche thinges,
Both ceptre, clothes, broches, and eek ringes,
Som for to were, and som for to presente
To her, that al thise noble thinges him sente;
And bad his sone, how that he sholde make
The presenting, and to the quene hit take.

REPAIRED is this Achates again,
And Eneas ful blisful is and fain
To seen his yonge sone Ascanius.

428

But natheles, our autour telleth us,
That Cupido, that is the god of love,
At preyere of his moder, hye above,
Hadde the lyknes of the child ytake,
This noble quene enamoured to make
On Eneas; but, as of that scripture,
Be as be may, I make of hit no cure.
But sooth is this, the quene hath mad swich chere
Unto this child, that wonder is to here;
And of the present that his fader sente
She thanked him ful ofte, in good entente.

THUS is this quene in plesaunce & in joye,
With al this newe lusty folk of Troye.
And of the dedes hath she more enquered
Of Eneas, and al the story lered
Of Troye; and al the longe day they tweye
Entendeden to speken and to pleye;
Of which ther gan to breden swich a fyr,
That sely Dido hath now swich desyr
With Eneas, her newe gest, to dele,
That she hath lost her hewe, and eek her hele.
Now to theffect, now to the fruit of al,
Why I have told this story, and tellen shal.

THUS I beginne; hit fil, upon a night,
When that the mone upreysed had her light,
This noble quene unto her reste wente;
She syketh sore, and gan herself turmente.
She waketh, walweth, maketh many a brayd,
As doon thise loveres, as I have herd sayd.
And at the laste, unto her suster Anne
She made her moon, & right thus spak she thanne.

NOW, dere suster myn, what may hit be
That me agasteth in my dreme? quod she.
This ilke Troyan is so in my thoght,
For that me thinketh he is so wel ywroght,
And eek so lykly for to be a man,
And therwithal so mikel good he can,
That al my love and lyf lyth in his cure.
Have ye not herd him telle his aventure?
Now certes, Anne, if that ye rede hit me,
I wolde fain to him ywedded be;
This is theffect; what sholde I more seye?
In him lyth al, to do me live or deye.

HER suster Anne, as she that coude her good,
Seide as her thoughte, and somdel hit with-
stood.
But herof was so long a sermoning,
Hit were to long to make rehersing;
But fynally, hit may not been withstonde;
Love wol love, for no wight wol hit wonde.

THE dawening uprist out of the see;
This amorous quene chargeth her meynee
The nettes dresse, and speres brode & kene;
An hunting wol this lusty fresshe quene;
So priketh her this newe joly wo.
To hors is al her lusty folk ygo;
Unto the court the houndes been ybroght,
And upon coursers, swift as any thoght,
Her yonge knightes hoven al aboute,
And of her wommen eek an huge route.
Upon a thikke palfrey, paper-whyt,
With sadel rede, enbrouded with delyt,
Of gold the barres up-enbossed hye,

Sit Dido, al in gold and perre wrye;
And she is fair, as is the brighte morwe,
That heleth seke folk of nightes sorwe.
UPON a courser, startling as the fyr,
Men mighte turne him with a litel wyr,
Sit Eneas, lyk Phebus to devyse;
So was he fresshe arayed in his wyse.
The fomy brydel with the bit of gold
Governeth he, right as himself hath wold.
And forth this noble quene thus lat I ryde
An hunting, with this Troyan by her syde.
THE herd of hertes founden is anoon,
With: Hey! go bet! prik thou! lat goon, lat
goon!
Why nil the leoun comen or the bere,
That I mighte ones mete him with this spere?
Thus seyn thise yonge folk, and up they kille
These hertes wilde, and han hem at hir wille.
AMONG al this to romblen gan the heven,
The thunder rored with a grisly steven;
Doun com the rain, with hail & sleet so faste,
With hevenes fyr, that hit so sore agaste
This noble quene, and also her meynee,
That ech of hem was glad awey to flee.
And shortly, fro the tempest her to save,
She fledde herself into a litel cave,
And with her wente this Eneas also;
I noot, with hem if ther wente any mo;
The autour maketh of hit no mencioun.
And heer began the depe affeccioun
Betwix hem two; this was the firste morwe
Of her gladnesse, and ginning of her sorwe.
For ther hath Eneas ykneled so,
And told her al his herte, and al his wo,
And sworn so depe, to her to be trewe,
For wele or wo, and chaunge for no newe,
And as a fals lover so wel can pleyne,
That sely Dido rewed on his peyne,
And took him for husband, to been his wyf
For evermo, whyl that hem laste lyf.
And after this, whan that the tempest stente,
With mirth out as they comen, hoom they wente.
THE wikked fame up roos, and that anon,
How Eneas hath with the quene ygon
Into the cave; and demed as hem liste;
And whan the king, that Yarbas hight, hit wiste,
As he that had her loved ever his lyf,
And wowed her, to have her to his wyf,
Swich sorwe as he hath maked, and swich chere,
Hit is a routhe and pitee for to here.
But, as in love, alday hit happeth so,
That oon shal laughen at anothers wo;
Now laugheth Eneas, and is in joye
And more richesse than ever he was in Troye.
O SELY womman, ful of innocence,
Ful of pitee, of trouthe, and conscience,
What maked yow to men to trusten so?
Have ye swich routhe upon hir feined wo,
And han swich olde ensamples yow beforn?
See ye nat alle, how they been forsworn?
Wher see ye oon, that he ne hath laft his leef,
Or been unkinde, or doon her som mischeef,
Or pilled her, or bosted of his dede?

Ye may as wel hit seen, as ye may rede;
Tak heed now of this grete gentilman,
This Troyan, that so wel her plesen can,
That feineth him so trewe and obeising,
So gentil and so privy of his doing,
And can so wel doon alle his obeisaunces,
And waiten her at festes and at daunces,
And whan she goth to temple and hoom ageyn,
And fasten til he hath his lady seyn,
And bere in his devyses, for her sake,
Noot I nat what; and songes wolde he make,
Justen, and doon of armes many thinges,
Sende her lettres, tokens, broches, ringes,
Now herkneth, how he shal his lady serve!
Theras he was in peril for to sterve
For hunger, and for mischeef in the see,
And desolat, and fled from his contree,
And al his folk with tempest al todriven,
She hath her body and eek her reame yiven
Into his hond, theras she mighte have been
Of other lond than of Cartage a queen,
And lived in joye ynogh; what wolde ye more?
THIS Eneas, that hath so depe yswore,
Is wery of his craft within a throwe;
The hote ernest is al overblowe.
And prively he doth his shippes dighte,
And shapeth him to stele awey by nighte.
THIS Dido hath suspecioun of this,
And thoughte wel, that hit was al amis;
For in his bedde he lyth anight & syketh;
She asketh him anoon, what him mislyketh:
My dere herte, which that I love most?
Certes, quod he, this night my fadres gost
Hath in my sleep so sore me tormented,
And eek Mercurie his message hath presented,
That nedes to the conquest of Itaile
My destinee is sone for to saile;
For which, me thinketh, brosten is myn herte!
Therwith his false teres out they sterte;
And taketh her within his armes two.
IS that in ernest, quod she; wil ye so?
Have ye nat sworn to wyve me to take,
Alas! what womman wil ye of me make?
I am a gentilwoman and a queen,
Ye wil nat fro your wyf thus foule fleen?
That I was born! allas! what shal I do?
TO telle in short, this noble queen Dido,
She seketh halwes, and doth sacrifyse;
She kneleth, cryeth, that routhe is to devyse;
Conjureth him, and profreth him to be
His thral, his servant in the leste gree;
She falleth him to fote, and swowneth there
Dischevele, with her brighte gilte here,
And seith: Have mercy! let me with yow ryde!
Thise lordes, which that wonen me besyde
Wil me destroyen only for your sake.
And, so ye wil me now to wyve take,
As ye han sworn, than wol I yive yow leve
To sleen me with your swerd now sone at eve!
For than yit shal I dyen as your wyf.
I am with childe, and yive my child his lyf.
O mercy, lord! have pite in your thoght!
But al this thing availeth her right noght;

429

for on a night, slepinge, he let her lye,
And stal awey unto his companye,
And, as a traitour, forth he gan to saile
Toward the large contree of Itaile.
Thus hath he laft Dido in wo and pyne;
And wedded ther a lady hight Lavyne.

A CLOTH he lafte, and eek his swerd stonding,
Whan he fro Dido stal in her sleping,
Right at her beddes heed, so gan he hye
Whan that he stal awey to his navye;
Which cloth, whan sely Dido gan awake,
She hath hit kist ful ofte for his sake;
And seide: O cloth, whyl Jupiter hit leste,
Tak now my soule, unbind me of this unreste!
I have fulfild of fortune al the cours.
And thus, allas! withouten his socours,
Twenty tyme yswowned hath she thanne.
And, whan that she unto her suster Anne
Compleyned had, of which I may nat wryte,
So greet a routhe I have hit for tendyte,
And bad her norice and her suster goon
To fecchen fyr and other thing anoon,
And seide, that she wolde sacrifye.

And, whan she mighte her tyme wel espye,
Upon the fyr of sacrifys she sterte,
And with his swerd she roof her to the herte.

BUT, as myn autour seith, right thus she seyde;
Or she was hurt, before that she deyde,
She wroot a lettre anoon, that thus began:
Right so, quod she, as that the whyte swan
Ayeins his deeth beginneth for to singe,
Right so to yow make I my compleyninge.
Nat that I trowe to geten yow again,
For wel I woot that it is al in vain,
Sin that the goddes been contraire to me.
But sin my name is lost through yow, quod she,
I may wel lese a word on yow, or letter,
Albeit that I shal be never the better;
For thilke wind that blew your ship awey,
The same wind hath blowe awey your fey.
But who wol al this letter have in minde,
Rede Ovide, and in him he shal hit finde.
Explicit Legenda Didonis martiris, Cartaginis regine.

INCIPIT LEGENDA YSIPHILE ET MEDEE MARTIRUM.

ROTE OF FALSE LOVERS, DUK JASOUN!
Thou sly devourer and confusioun
Of gentilwommen, tender creatures,
Thou madest thy reclaiming and thy lures
To ladies of thy statly apparaunce,
And of thy wordes, farced with plesaunce,
And of thy feyned trouthe and thy manere,
With thyn obeisaunce and thy humble chere,
And with thy counterfeted peyne and wo.
Ther other falsen oon, thou falsest two!
O! ofte swore thou that thou woldest dye
For love, whan thou ne feltest maladye
Save foul delyt, which that thou callest love!
If that I live, thy name shal be shove
In English, that thy sleighte shal be knowe!

Have at thee, Jasoun! now thyn horn is blowe!
But certes, hit is bothe routhe and wo
That love with false loveres werketh so;
For they shul have wel better love and chere
Than he that hath aboght his love ful dere,
Or had in armes many a blody box.
For ever as tendre a capoun et the fox,
Thogh he be fals and hath the foul betrayed,
As shal the goodman that therfor hath payed;
Al have he to the capoun skille and right,
The false fox wol have his part at night.
On Jasoun this ensample is wel ysene
By Isiphile and Medea the quene.

IN Tessalye, as Guido telleth us,
Ther was a king that highte Pelleus,
That had a brother, which that highte Eson;
And, whan for age he mighte unnethes gon,
He yaf to Pelleus the governing
Of al his regne, and made him lord and king.
Of which Eson this Jasoun geten was,
That, in his tyme, in al that lond, ther nas
Nat swich a famous knight of gentilesse,
Of freedom, & of strengthe and lustinesse.
After his fader deeth, he bar him so
That ther nas noon that liste been his fo,
But dide him al honour and companye;
Of which this Pelleus hath greet envye,
Imagining that Jasoun mighte be
Enhaunsed so, and put in swich degree
With love of lordes of his regioun,
That from his regne he may be put adoun.
And in his wit, anight, compassed he
How Jasoun mighte best destroyed be
Withoute slaunder of his compasment.

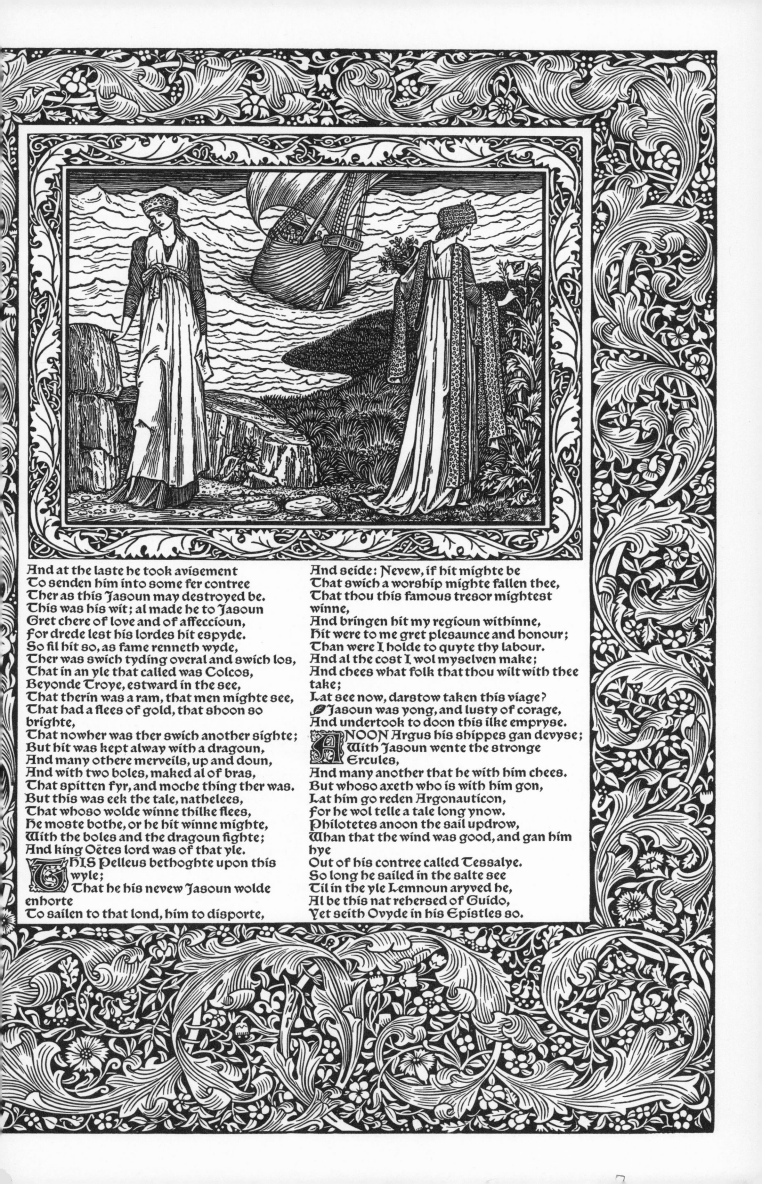

And at the laste he took avisement
To senden him into some fer contree
Ther as this Jasoun may destroyed be.
This was his wit; al made he to Jasoun
Gret chere of love and of affeccioun,
For drede lest his lordes hit espyde.
So fil hit so, as fame renneth wyde,
Ther was swich tyding overal and swich los,
That in an yle that called was Colcos,
Beyonde Troye, estward in the see,
That therin was a ram, that men mighte see,
That had a flees of gold, that shoon so
brighte,
That nowher was ther swich another sighte;
But hit was kept alway with a dragoun,
And many othere merveils, up and doun,
And with two boles, maked al of bras,
That spitten fyr, and moche thing ther was.
But this was eek the tale, nathelees,
That whoso wolde winne thilke flees,
He moste bothe, or he hit winne mighte,
With the boles and the dragoun fighte;
And king Oëtes lord was of that yle.
THIS Pelleus bethoghte upon this
wyle;
That he his nevew Jasoun wolde
enhorte
To sailen to that lond, him to disporte,

And seide: Nevew, if hit mighte be
That swich a worship mighte fallen thee,
That thou this famous tresor mightest
winne,
And bringen hit my regioun withinne,
Hit were to me gret plesaunce and honour;
Than were I holde to quyte thy labour.
And al the cost I wol myselven make;
And chees what folk that thou wilt with thee
take;
Lat see now, darstow taken this viage?
Jasoun was yong, and lusty of corage,
And undertook to doon this ilke empryse.
ANOON Argus his shippes gan devyse;
With Jasoun wente the stronge
Ercules,
And many another that he with him chees.
But whoso axeth who is with him gon,
Lat him go reden Argonauticon,
For he wol telle a tale long ynow.
Philotetes anoon the sail updrow,
Whan that the wind was good, and gan him
hye
Out of his contree called Tessalye.
So long he sailed in the salte see
Til in the yle Lemnoun aryved he,
Al be this nat rehersed of Guido,
Yet seith Ovyde in his Epistles so.

And of this yle lady was and quene
The faire yonge Isiphilee, the shene,
That whylom Thoas doghter was, the king.
ISIPHILEE was goon in her playing;
And, roming on the clyves by the see,
Under a banke anoon espyed she
Wher that the ship of Jasoun gan aryve.
Of her goodnesse adoun she sendeth blyve
To witen yif that any straunge wight
With tempest thider were yblowe anight,
To doon him socour; as was her usaunce
To forthren every wight, and doon plesaunce
Of veray bountee and of curtesye.
THIS messagere adoun him gan to hye,
And fond Jasoun, and Ercules also,
That in a cogge to londe were ygo
Hem to refresshen and to take the eyr.
The morwening atempre was and fair;
And in his wey the messagere hem mette.
Ful cunningly thise lordes two he grette,
And dide his message, axing hem anoon
Yif they were broken, or oght wo begoon,
Or hadde nede of lodesmen or vitaile;
For of socour they shulde nothing faile,
For hit was utterly the quenes wille.
JASOUN answerde, mekely and stille:
My lady, quod he, thanke I hertely
Of hir goodnesse; us nedeth, trewely,
Nothing as now, but that we wery be,
And come for to pleye, out of the see,
Til that the wind be better in our weye.
THIS lady rometh by the clif to pleye,
With her meynee, endelong the stronde,
And fynt this Jasoun and this other stonde,
In spekinge of this thing, as I yow tolde.
THIS Ercules and Jasoun gan beholde
How that the quene hit was, and faire her
grette
Anon-right as they with this lady mette;
And she took heed, and knew, by hir manere,
By hir aray, by wordes and by chere,
That hit were gentilmen, of greet degree.
And to the castel with her ledeth she
Thise straunge folk, and doth hem greet honour,
And axeth hem of travail and labour
That they han suffred in the salte see;
So that, within a day, or two, or three,
She knew, by folk that in his shippes be,
That hit was Jasoun, ful of renomee,
And Ercules, that had the grete los,
That soghten the aventures of Colcos;
And dide hem honour more then before,
And with hem deled ever lenger the more,
For they ben worthy folk, withouten lees.
And namely, most she spak with Ercules;
To him her herte bar, he sholde be
Sad, wys, and trewe, of wordes avisee,
Withouten any other affeccioun
Of love, or evil imaginacioun.
THIS Ercules hath so this Jasoun preysed,
That to the sonne he hath him up areysed,
That half so trewe a man ther nas of love
Under the cope of heven that is above;

432

And he was wys, hardy, secree, and riche.
Of thise three pointes ther nas noon him liche;
Of freedom passed he, and lustihede,
Alle tho that liven or ben dede;
Therto so greet a gentilman was he,
And of Tessalie lykly king to be.
Ther nas no lak, but that he was agast
To love, and for to speke shamefast.
He hadde lever himself to mordre, and dye
Than that men shulde a lover him espye:
As wolde almighty God that I had yive
My blood and flesh, so that I mighte live,
With the nones that he hadde owher a wyf
For his estat; for swich a lusty lyf
She sholde lede with this lusty knight!
AND al this was compassed on the night
Betwixe him Jasoun and this Ercules.
Of thise two heer was mad a shrewed lees
To come to hous upon an innocent;
For to bedote this queen was hir assent.
And Jasoun is as coy as is a maide,
He loketh pitously, but noght he saide,
But frely yaf he to her conseileres
Yiftes grete, and to her officeres.
As wolde God I leiser hadde, and tyme,
By proces al his wowing for to ryme.
But in this hous if any fals lover be,
Right as himself now doth, right so dide he,
With feyning and with every sotil dede.
Ye gete no more of me, but ye wil rede
Thoriginal, that telleth al the cas.
THE somme is this, that Jasoun wedded was
Unto this quene, and took of her substaunce
Whatso him liste, unto his purveyaunce;
And upon her begat he children two,
And drow his sail, and saw her nevermo.
A LETTRE sente she to him certein,
Which were to long to wryten and to sein,
And him repreveth of his grete untrouthe,
And preyeth him on her to have som routhe.
And of his children two, she seide him this,
That they be lyke, of alle thing, ywis,
To Jasoun, save they coude nat begyle;
And preyed God, or hit were longe whyle,
That she, that had his herte yraft her fro,
Moste finden him to her untrewe also,
And that she moste bothe her children spille,
And alle tho that suffreth him his wille.
And trew to Jasoun was she al her lyf,
And ever kepte her chast, as for his wyf;
Ne never had she joye at her herte,
But dyed, for his love, of sorwes smerte.

TO Colcos comen is this duk Jasoun,
That is of love devourer and dragoun.
As matere appetyteth forme alwey,
And from forme into forme hit passen may,
Or as a welle that were botomlees,

Right so can this fals Jasoun have no pees.
For, to desyren, through his appetyt,
To doon with gentil wommen his delyt,
This is his lust and his felicitee.
JASOUN is romed forth to the citee,
That whylom cleped was Jaconitos,
That was the maister-toun of al Colcos,
And hath ytold the cause of his coming
Unto Oëtes, of that contre king,
Preying him that he moste doon his assay
To gete the flees of gold, if that he may;
Of which the king assenteth to his bone,
And doth him honour, as hit is to done,
So ferforth, that his doghter and his eyr,
Medea, which that was so wys and fair
That fairer saw ther never man with yë,
He made her doon to Jasoun companye
At mete, and sitte by him in the halle.
NOW was Jasoun a semely man withalle,
And lyk a lord, and had a greet renoun,
And of his loke as real as leoun,
And goodly of his speche, and famulere,
And coude of love al craft and art plenere
Withoute boke, with everich observaunce.
And, as fortune her oghte a foul meschaunce,
She wex enamoured upon this man.
JASOUN, quod she, for ought I see or can,
As of this thing the which ye been aboute,
Ye han yourself yput in moche doute.
For, whoso wol this aventure acheve,
He may nat wel asterten, as I leve,
Withouten deeth, but I his helpe be.
But natheles, Hit is my wille, quod she,
To forthren yow, so that ye shal nat dye,
But turnen, sound, hoom to your Tessalye.
MY righte lady, quod this Jasoun tho,
That ye han of my dethe or of my wo
Any reward, and doon me this honour,
I wot wel that my might ne my labour
May nat deserve hit in my lyves day;
God thanke yow, ther I ne can ne may.
Your man am I, and lowly you beseche,
To been my help, withoute more speche;
But certes, for my deeth shal I nat spare.
THO gan this Medea to him declare
The peril of this cas, fro point to point,
And of his batail, and in what disjoint
He mote stande, of which no creature,

Save only she, ne mighte his lyf assure.
And shortly, to the point right for to go,
They been accorded ful, betwix hem two,
That Jasoun shal her wedde, as trewe knight;
And term yset, to come sone at night
Unto her chambre, and make ther his ooth,
Upon the goddes, that he, for leef ne looth,
Ne sholde her never falsen, night ne day,
To been her husbond, whyl he liven may,
As she that from his deeth him saved here.
And herupon, at night they mette yfere,
And doth his ooth, and goth with her to bedde.
And on the morwe, upward he him spedde;
For she hath taught him how he shal nat faile
The flees to winne, and stinten his bataile;
And saved him his lyf and his honour;
And gat him greet name as a conquerour
Right through the sleight of her enchantement.
NOW hath Jasoun the flees, and hoom is went
With Medea, and tresor ful gret woon.
But unwist of her fader is she goon
To Tessaly, with duk Jasoun her leef,
That afterward hath broght her to mescheef.
For as a traitour he is from her go,
And with her lafte his yonge children two,
And falsly hath betrayed her, allas!
And ever in love a cheef traitour he was;
And wedded yit the thridde wyf anon,
That was the doghter of the king Creon.
THIS is the meed of loving and guerdoun
That Medea received of Jasoun
Right for her trouthe and for her kindenesse,
That loved him better than herself, I gesse,
And lafte her fader and her heritage.
And of Jasoun this is the vassalage,
That, in his dayes, nas ther noon yfounde
So fals a lover going on the grounde.
And therfor in her lettre thus she seyde
First, whan she of his falsnesse him umbreyde,
Why lyked me thy yelow heer to see
More then the boundes of myn honestee,
Why lyked me thy youthe and thy fairnesse,
And of thy tonge the infinit graciousnesse?
O, haddest thou in thy conquest deed y-be,
Ful mikel untrouthe hath ther dyed with thee!
Wel can Ovyde her lettre in vers endyte,
Which were as now to long for me to wryte.
Explicit Legenda Ysiphile et Medee martirum.

INCIPIT LEGENDA LUCRECIE ROME MARTIRIS. ❦❦❦

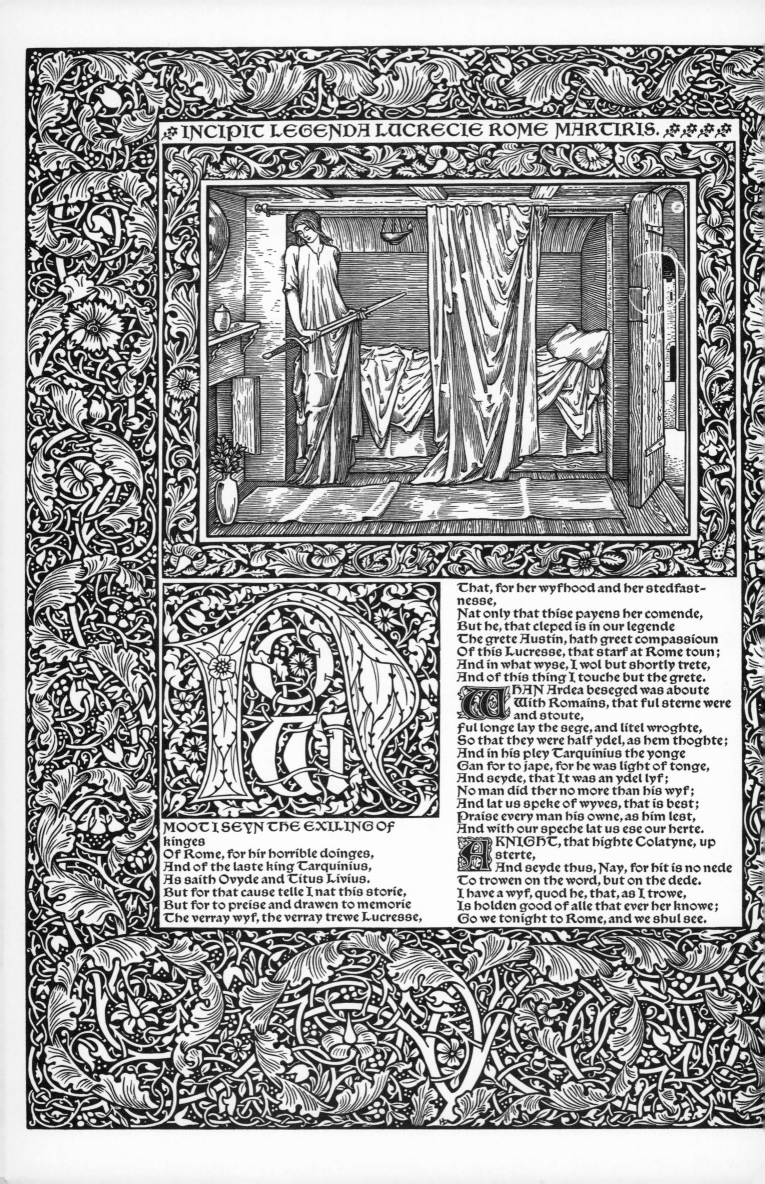

That, for her wyfhood and her stedfast-
nesse,
Nat only that thise payens her comende,
But he, that cleped is in our legende
The grete Austin, hath greet compassioun
Of this Lucresse, that starf at Rome toun;
And in what wyse, I wol but shortly trete,
And of this thing I touche but the grete.

WHAN Ardea beseged was aboute
With Romains, that ful sterne were
and stoute,
Ful longe lay the sege, and litel wroghte,
So that they were half ydel, as hem thoghte;
And in his pley Tarquinius the yonge
Gan for to jape, for he was light of tonge,
And seyde, that It was an ydel lyf;
No man did ther no more than his wyf;
And lat us speke of wyves, that is best;
Praise every man his owne, as him lest,
And with our speche lat us ese our herte.

A KNIGHT, that highte Colatyne, up
sterte,
And seyde thus, Nay, for hit is no nede
To trowen on the word, but on the dede.
I have a wyf, quod he, that, as I trowe,
Is holden good of alle that ever her knowe;
Go we tonight to Rome, and we shul see.

MOOT I SEYN THE EXILING OF
kinges
Of Rome, for hir horrible doinges,
And of the laste king Tarquinius,
As saith Ovyde and Titus Livius.
But for that cause telle I nat this storie,
But for to preise and drawen to memorie
The verray wyf, the verray trewe Lucresse,

TARQUINIUS answerde, That lyketh me.
To Rome be they come, & faste hem dighte
To Colatynes hous, and doun they lighte,
Tarquinius, and eek this Colatyne.
The husbond knew the estres wel and fyne,
And prively into the hous they goon;
Nor at the gate porter was ther noon;
And at the chambre-dore they abyde.
This noble wyf sat by her beddes syde
Dischevele, for no malice she ne thoghte;
And softe wolle our book seith that she wroghte
To kepen her fro slouthe and ydelnesse;
And bad her servants doon hir businesse,
And axeth hem: What tydings heren ye?
How seith men of the sege, how shal hit be?
God wolde the walles weren falle adoun;
Myn husbond is so longe out of this toun,
For which the dreed doth me so sore smerte,
Right as a swerd hit stingeth to myn herte
Whan I think on the sege or of that place;
God save my lord, I preye him for his grace:
And therwithal ful tenderly she weep,
And of her werk she took no more keep,
But mekely she leet her eyen falle;
And thilke semblant sat her wel withalle.
And eek her teres, ful of honestee,
Embelisshed her wyfly chastitee;
Her countenaunce is to her herte digne,
For they acordeden in dede and signe.
And with that word her husbond Colatyn,
Or she of him was war, com sterting in,
And seide, Dreed the noght, for I am here!
And she anoon up roos, with blisful chere,
And kiste him, as of wyves is the wone.

TARQUINIUS, this proude kinges sone,
Conceived hath her beautee and her chere,
Her yelow heer, her shap, and her manere,
Her hew, her wordes that she hath compleyned,
And by no crafte her beautee nas nat feyned;
And caughte to this lady swich desyr,
That in his herte brende as any fyr
So woodly, that his wit was al forgeten.
For wel, thoghte he, she sholde nat be geten;
And ay the more that he was in dispair,
The more he coveteth and thoghte her fair.
His blinde lust was al his covetinge.

A-MORWE, whan the brid began to singe,
Unto the sege he comth ful privily,
And by himself he walketh sobrely,
Thimage of her recording alwey newe;
Thus lay her heer, and thus fresh was her hewe;
Thus sat, thus spak, thus span; this was her chere,
Thus fair she was, and this was her manere.
Al this conceit his herte hath now ytake.
And, as the see, with tempest al toshake,
That, after whan the storm is al ago,
Yet wol the water quappe a day or two,
Right so, thogh that her forme wer absent,
The plesaunce of her forme was present;
But natheles, nat plesaunce, but delyt,
Or an unrightful talent with despyt;
For, maugre her, she shal my lemman be;
Hap helpeth hardy man alday, quod he;
What ende that I make, hit shal be so;

And girt him with his swerde, and gan to go;
And forth he rit til he to Rome is come,
And al aloon his wey than hath he nome
Unto the house of Colatyn ful right.
Doun was the sonne, and day hath lost his light;
And in he com unto a privy halke,
And in the night ful theefly gan he stalke,
Whan every night was to his reste broght,
Ne no wight had of tresoun swich a thoght.
Were hit by window or by other gin,
With swerde ydrawe, shortly he comth in
Ther as she lay, this noble wyf Lucresse.
And, as she wook, her bed she felte presse.
What beste is that, quod she, that weyeth thus?
I am the kinges sone, Tarquinius,
Quod he, but and thou crye, or noise make,
Or if thou any creature awake,
By thilke God that formed man on lyve,
This swerd throughout thyn herte shal I ryve.
And therwithal unto her throte he sterte,
And sette the point al sharp upon her herte.
No word she spak, she hath no might therto.
What shal she sayn? her wit is al ago.
Right as a wolf that fynt a lomb aloon,
To whom shal she compleyne, or make moon?
What! shal she fighte with an hardy knight?
Wel wot men that a woman hath no might.
What! shal she crye, or how shal she asterte
That hath her by the throte, with swerde at herte?
She axeth grace, and seith al that she can.
Ne wolt thou nat, quod he, this cruel man,
As wisly Jupiter my soule save,
As I shal in the stable slee thy knave,
And leye him in thy bed, and loude crye,
That I thee finde in suche avouterye;
And thus thou shalt be deed, and also lese
Thy name, for thou shalt non other chese.

THISE Romain wyves loveden so hir name
At thilke tyme, and dredden so the shame,
That, what for fere of slaundre and drede
of deeth,
She loste bothe atones wit and breeth,
And in a swough she lay and wex so deed,
Men mighte smyten of her arm or heed;
She feleth nothing, neither foul ne fair.

TARQUINIUS, that art a kinges eyr,
And sholdest, as by linage and by right,
Doon as a lord and as a verray knight,
Why hastow doon dispyt to chivalrye?
Why hastow doon this lady vilanye?
Allas! of thee this was a vileins dede!

BUT now to purpos; in the story I rede,
Whan he was goon, al this mischaunce is
falle.
This lady sente after her frendes alle,
Fader, moder, husbond, al yfere;
And al dischevele, with her heres clere,
In habit swich as women used tho
Unto the burying of her frendes go,
She sit in halle with a sorweful sighte.
Her frendes axen what her aylen mighte,
And who was deed? And she sit ay wepinge,
A word for shame ne may she forth outbringe,
Ne upon hem she dorste nat beholde.

But atte laste of Tarquiny she hem tolde,
This rewful cas, and al this thing horrible.
The wo to tellen hit were impossible,
That she and alle her frendes made atones.
Al hadde folkes hertes been of stones,
Hit mighte have maked hem upon her rewe,
Her herte was so wyfly and so trewe.
She seide, that, for her gilt ne for her blame,
Her husbond sholde nat have the foule name,
That wolde she nat suffre, by no wey.
And they answerden alle, upon hir fey,
That they foryeve hit her, for hit was right;
Hit was no gilt, hit lay nat in her might;
And seiden her ensamples many oon.
But al for noght; for thus she seide anoon:
Be as be may, quod she, of forgiving,
I wol nat have no forgift for nothing.
  But prively she caughte forth a knyf,
And therwithal she rafte herself her lyf;
And as she fel adoun, she caste her look,
And of her clothes yit she hede took;
for in her falling yit she hadde care
Lest that her feet or swiche thing lay bare;
So wel she loved clennesse and eek trouthe.
  Of her had al the toun of Rome routhe,

And Brutus by her chaste blode hath swore
That Tarquin sholde ybanisht be therfore,
And al his kin; and let the peple calle,
And openly the tale he tolde hem alle,
And openly let carie her on a bere
Through al the toun, that men may see & here
The horrible deed of her oppressioun.
Ne never was ther king in Rome toun
Sin thilke day; and she was holden there
A seint, and ever her day yhalwed dere
As in hir lawe: and thus endeth Lucresse,
The noble wyf, as Titus bereth witnesse.
I TELL hit, for she was of love so trewe,
Ne in her wille she chaunged for no newe.
And for the stable herte, sad and kinde,
That in these women men may alday finde;
Ther as they caste hir herte, ther hit dwelleth.
for wel I wot, that Crist himselve telleth,
That in Israel, as wyd as is the lond,
That so gret feith in al the lond he ne fond
As in a woman; and this is no lye.
And as of men, loketh which tirannye
They doon alday; assay hem who so liste,
The trewest is ful brotel for to triste.
  Explicit Legenda Lucrecie Rome martiris.

INCIPIT LEGENDA ADRIANE DE ATHENES

IUGE INFERNAL, MINOS, OF CRETE KING, NOW COMETH THY LOT, NOW COMESTOW ON THE RING; NAT FOR THY SAKE ONLY WRYTE I THIS STORIE, BUT FOR TO CLEPE A-GEIN UNTO MEMORIE OF THESEUS THE GRETE UNTROUTHE OF LOVE; FOR WHICH THE GODDES OF THE HEVEN ABOVE BEN WROTHE, AND WRECHE HAN TAKE FOR THY SINNE. BE REED FOR SHAME! NOW I THY LYF BE-GINNE.

MINOS, that was the mighty king of Crete,
  That hadde an hundred citees stronge and grete,
To scole hath sent his sone Androgeus,
To Athenes; of the whiche hit happed thus,
That he was slayn, lerning philosophye,
Right in that citee, nat but for envye.
THE grete Minos, of the whiche I speke,
His sones deeth is comen for to wreke;
Alcathoe he bisegeth harde and longe.
But natheles the walles be so stronge,
And Nisus, that was king of that citee,
So chivalrous, that litel dredeth he;
Of Minos or his ost took he no cure,

Til on a day befel an aventure,
That Nisus doghter stood upon the wal,
And of the sege saw the maner al.
So happed hit, that, at a scarmishing,
She caste her herte upon Minos the king,
for his beautee and for his chivalrye,
So sore, that she wende for to dye.
And, shortly of this proces for to pace,
She made Minos winnen thilke place,
So that the citee was al at his wille,
To saven whom him list, or elles spille;
But wikkedly he quitte her kindenesse,
And let her drenche in sorowe and distresse
Nere that the goddes hadde of her pite;
But that tale were to long as now for me.
ATHENES wan this king Minos also,
And Alcathoe and other tounes mo;
And this theffect, that Minos hath so driven
Hem of Athenes, that they mote him yiven
fro yere to yere her owne children dere
for to be slayn, as ye shul after here.
THIS Minos hath a monstre, a wikked beste,
That was so cruel that, without areste,
Whan that a man was broght in his presence,
He wolde him ete, ther helpeth no defence.
And every thridde yeer, withouten doute,
They casten lot, and, as hit com aboute
On riche, on pore, he moste his sone take,
And of his child he moste present make
Unto Minos, to save him or to spille,
Or lete his beste devoure him at his wille.
And this hath Minos don, right in despyt;
To wreke his sone was set al his delyt,

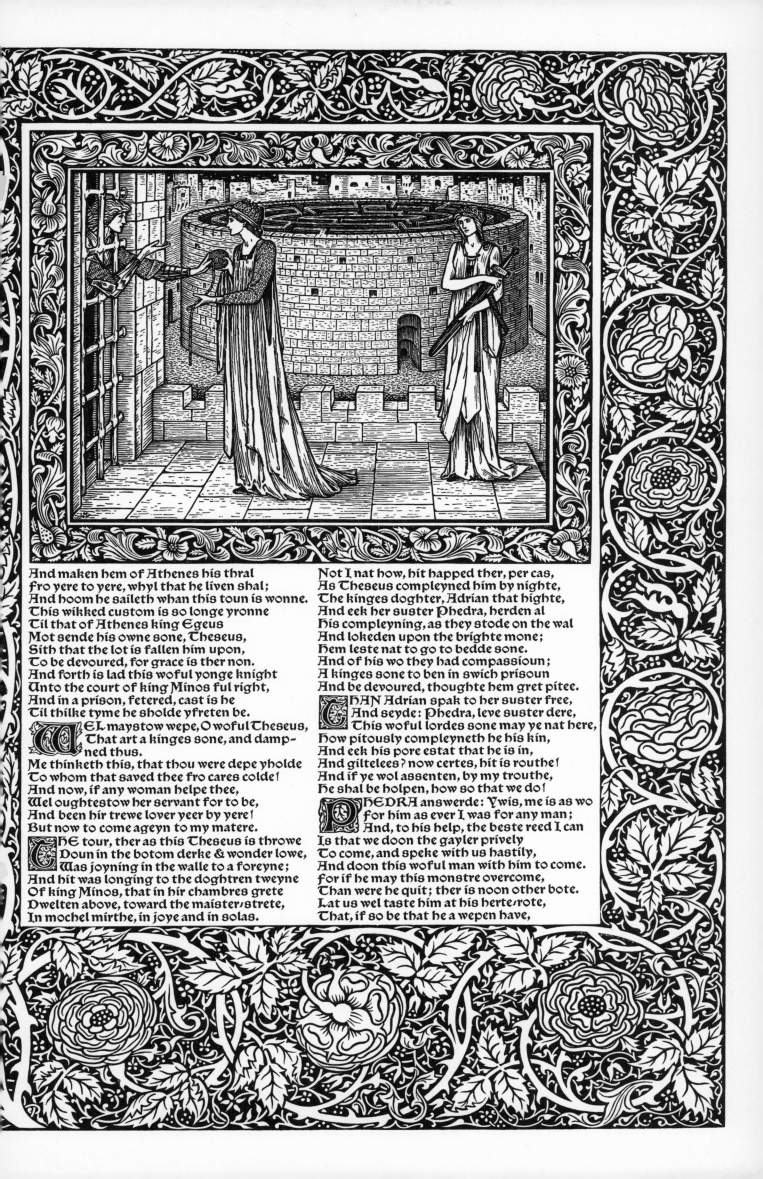

And maken hem of Athenes his thral
Fro yere to yere, whyl that he liven shal;
And hoom he saileth whan this toun is wonne.
This wikked custom is so longe yronne
Til that of Athenes king Egeus
Mot sende his owne sone, Theseus,
Sith that the lot is fallen him upon,
To be devoured, for grace is ther non.
And forth is lad this woful yonge knight
Unto the court of king Minos ful right,
And in a prison, fetered, cast is he
Til thilke tyme he sholde yfreten be.

WEL maystow wepe, O woful Theseus,
That art a kinges sone, and damp-
ned thus.
Me thinketh this, that thou were depe yholde
To whom that saved thee fro cares colde!
And now, if any woman helpe thee,
Wel oughtestow her servant for to be,
And been hir trewe lover yeer by yere!
But now to come ageyn to my matere.

THE tour, ther as this Theseus is throwe
Doun in the botom derke & wonder lowe,
Was joyning in the walle to a foreyne;
And hit was longing to the doghtren tweyne
Of king Minos, that in hir chambres grete
Dwelten above, toward the maister-strete,
In mochel mirthe, in joye and in solas.

Not I nat how, hit happed ther, per cas,
As Theseus compleyned him by nighte,
The kinges doghter, Adrian that highte,
And eek her suster Phedra, herden al
His compleyning, as they stode on the wal
And lokeden upon the brighte mone;
Hem leste nat to go to bedde sone.
And of his wo they had compassioun;
A kinges sone to ben in swich prisoun
And be devoured, thoughte hem gret pitee.

THAN Adrian spak to her suster free,
And seyde: Phedra, leve suster dere,
This woful lordes sone may ye nat here,
How pitously compleyneth he his kin,
And eek his pore estat that he is in,
And giltelees? now certes, hit is routhe!
And if ye wol assenten, by my trouthe,
He shal be holpen, how so that we do!

PHEDRA answerde: Ywis, me is as wo
For him as ever I was for any man;
And, to his help, the beste reed I can
Is that we doon the gayler prively
To come, and speke with us hastily,
And doon this woful man with him to come.
For if he may this monstre overcome,
Than were he quit; ther is noon other bote.
Lat us wel taste him at his herte-rote,
That, if so be that he a wepen have,

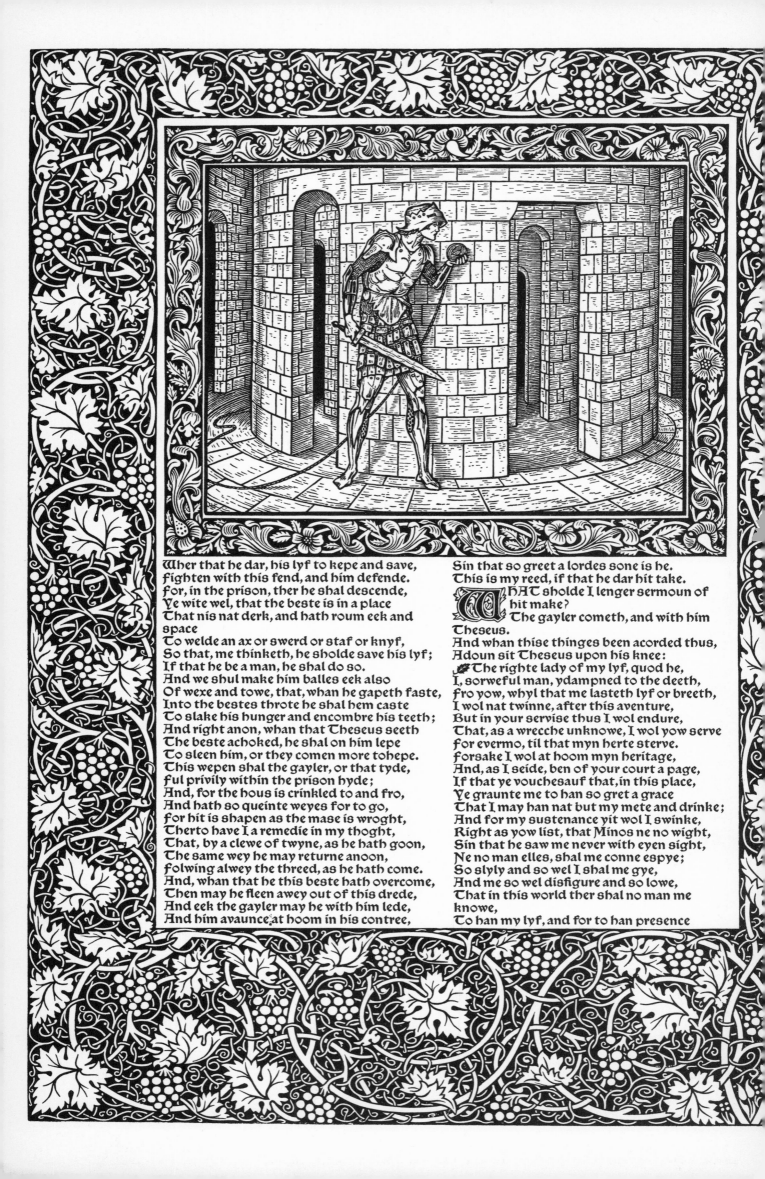

Wher that he dar, his lyf to kepe and save,
fighten with this fend, and him defende.
for, in the prison, ther he shal descende,
Ye wite wel, that the beste is in a place
That nis nat derk, and hath roum eek and
space
To welde an ax or swerd or staf or knyf,
So that, me thinketh, he sholde save his lyf;
If that he be a man, he shal do so.
And we shul make him balles eek also
Of wexe and towe, that, whan he gapeth faste,
Into the bestes throte he shal hem caste
To slake his hunger and encombre his teeth;
And right anon, whan that Theseus seeth
The beste achoked, he shal on him lepe
To sleen him, or they comen more tohepe.
This wepen shal the gayler, or that tyde,
ful privily within the prison hyde;
And, for the hous is crinkled to and fro,
And hath so queinte weyes for to go,
for hit is shapen as the mase is wroght,
Therto have I a remedie in my thoght,
That, by a clewe of twyne, as he hath goon,
The same wey he may returne anoon,
folwing alwey the threed, as he hath come.
And, whan that he this beste hath overcome,
Then may he fleen awey out of this drede,
And eek the gayler may he with him lede,
And him avaunce at hoom in his contree,

Sin that so greet a lordes sone is he.
This is my reed, if that he dar hit take.
WHAT sholde I lenger sermoun of
hit make?
The gayler cometh, and with him
Theseus.
And whan thise thinges been acorded thus,
Adoun sit Theseus upon his knee:
The righte lady of my lyf, quod he,
I, sorweful man, ydampned to the deeth,
fro yow, whyl that me lasteth lyf or breeth,
I wol nat twinne, after this aventure,
But in your servise thus I wol endure,
That, as a wrecche unknowe, I wol yow serve
for evermo, til that myn herte sterve.
forsake I wol at hoom myn heritage,
And, as I seide, ben of your court a page,
If that ye vouchesauf that, in this place,
Ye graunte me to han so gret a grace
That I may han nat but my mete and drinke;
And for my sustenance yit wol I swinke,
Right as yow list, that Minos ne no wight,
Sin that he saw me never with eyen sight,
Ne no man elles, shal me conne espye;
So slyly and so wel I shal me gye,
And me so wel disfigure and so lowe,
That in this world ther shal no man me
knowe,
To han my lyf, and for to han presence

Of yow, that doon to me this excellence.
And to my fader shal I senden here
This worthy man, that is now your gaylere,
And, him to guerdon, that he shal wel be
Oon of the grettest men of my contree.
And yif I dorste seyn, my lady bright,
I am a kinges sone, and eek a knight;
As wolde God, yif that hit mighte be
Ye weren in my contree, alle three,
And I with yow, to bere yow companye,
Than shulde ye seen yif that I therof lye!
And, if I profre yow in low manere
To ben your page and serven yow right here,
But I yow serve as lowly in that place,
I prey to Mars to yive me swiche a grace
That shames deeth on me ther mote falle,
And deeth and povert to my frendes alle;
And that my spirit by nighte mote go
After my deeth, and walke to and fro;
That I mote of a traitour have a name,
For which my spirit go, to do me shame!
And yif I ever claime other degree,
But if ye vouchesauf to yive hit me,
As I have seid, of shames deeth I deye!
And mercy, lady! I can nat elles seye!
A SEEMLY knight was Theseus to see,
And yong, but of a twenty yeer and three;
But whoso hadde yseyn his countenaunce,
He wolde have wept, for routhe of his penaunce;
For which this Adriane in this manere
Answerde to his profre and to his chere.
A kinges sone, and eek a knight, quod she,
To been my servant in so low degree,
God shilde hit, for the shame of women alle!
And leve me never swich a cas befalle!
But sende yow grace and sleighte of herte also,
Yow to defende and knightly sleen your fo,
And leve herafter that I may yow finde
To me and to my suster here so kinde,
That I repente nat to give yow lyf!
Yit were hit better that I were your wyf,
Sin that ye been as gentil born as I,
And have a reäume, nat but faste by,
Then that I suffred giltles yow to sterve,
Or that I let yow as a page serve;
Hit is not profit, as unto your kinrede;
But what is that that man nil do for drede?
And to my suster, sin that hit is so
That she mot goon with me, if that I go,
Or elles suffre deeth as wel as I,
That ye unto your sone as trewely
Doon her be wedded at your hoom-coming.
This is the fynal ende of al this thing;
Ye swere hit heer, on al that may be sworn.
YE, lady myn, quod he, or elles torn
Mote I be with the Minotaur tomorwe!
And haveth herof my herte-blood to borwe,
Yif that ye wile; if I had knyf or spere,
I wolde hit leten out, and theron swere,
For than at erst I wot ye wil me leve.
By Mars, that is the cheef of my bileve,
So that I mighte liven and nat faile
Tomorwe for tacheve my bataile,
I nolde never fro this place flee,
Til that ye shuld the verray preve see.

For now, if that the sooth I shal yow say,
I have yloved yow ful many a day,
Thogh ye ne wiste hit nat, in my contree.
And aldermost desyred yow to see
Of any erthly living creature;
Upon my trouthe I swere, and yow assure,
Thise seven yeer I have your servant be;
Now have I yow, and also have ye me,
My dere herte, of Athenes duchesse!
THIS lady smyleth at his stedfastnesse,
And at his hertly wordes, and his chere,
And to her suster seide in this manere,
Al softely: Now, suster myn, quod she,
Now be we duchesses, bothe I and ye,
And sikered to the regals of Athenes,
And bothe herafter lykly to be quenes,
And saved fro his deeth a kinges sone,
As ever of gentil women is the wone
To save a gentil man, emforth hir might,
In honest cause, and namely in his right.
Me thinketh no wight oghte herof us blame,
Ne beren us therfor an evel name.
AND shortly of this matere for to make,
This Theseus of her hath leve ytake,
And every point performed was in dede
As ye have in this covenant herd me rede.
His wepen, his clew, his thing that I have said,
Was by the gayler in the hous ylaid
Ther as this Minotaur hath his dwelling,
Right faste by the dore, at his entring.
And Theseus is lad unto his deeth,
And forth unto this Minotaur he geeth,
And by the teching of this Adriane
He overcom this beste, and was his bane;
And out he cometh by the clewe again
Ful prevely, whan he this beste hath slain;
And by the gayler geten hath a barge,
And of his wyves tresor gan hit charge,
And took his wyf, and eek her suster free,
And eek the gayler, and with hem alle three
Is stole awey out of the lond by nighte,
And to the contre of Ennopye him dighte
Ther as he had a frend of his knowinge.
Ther festen they, ther dauncen they and singe;
And in his armes hath this Adriane,
That of the beste hath kept him from his bane;
And gat him ther a newe barge anoon,
And of his contree-folk a ful gret woon,
And taketh his leve, and hoomward saileth he.
And in an yle, amid the wilde see,
Ther as ther dwelte creature noon
Save wilde bestes, and that ful many oon,
He made his ship alonde for to sette;
And in that yle half a day he lette,
And seide, that on the lond he moste him reste.
His mariners han doon right as him leste;
And, for to tellen shortly in this cas,
When Adriane his wyf aslepe was,
For that her suster fairer was than she,
He taketh her in his hond, and forth goth he
To shippe, and as a traitour stal his way
Whyl that this Adriane aslepe lay,
And to his contree-ward he saileth blyve,
A twenty devil way the wind him dryve!
And fond his fader drenched in the see.

ME list no more to speke of him, parde;
Thise false lovers, poison be hir bane!
But I wol turne again to Adriane
That is with slepe for werinesse atake.
Ful sorwefully her herte may awake.
Allas! for thee my herte hath now pite!
Right in the dawening awaketh she,
And gropeth in the bedde, and fond right noght.
Allas! quod she, that ever I was wroght!
I am betrayed! and her heer torente,
And to the stronde barfot faste she wente,
And cryed: Theseus! myn herte swete!
Wher be ye, that I may nat with yow mete,
And mighte thus with bestes been yslain?
THE holwe rokkes answerde her again;
No man she saw, and yit shyned the mone,
And hye upon a rokke she wente sone,
And saw his barge sailing in the see.
Cold wex her herte, and right thus seide she:
Meker than ye finde I the bestes wilde!
Hadde he nat sinne, that her thus begylde?
She cryed: O turne again, for routhe and sinne!
Thy barge hath nat al his meiny inne!
Her kerchef on a pole up stikked she,
Ascaunce that he sholde hit wel ysee,

And him remembre that she was behinde,
And turne again, and on the stronde her finde;
But al for noght; his wey he is ygoon.
And doun she fil aswown upon a stoon;
And up she rist, and kiste, in al her care,
The steppes of his feet, ther he hath fare,
And to her bedde right thus she speketh tho:
Thou bed, quod she, that hast receyved two,
Thou shalt answere of two, and nat of oon!
Wher is thy gretter part away ygoon?
Allas! wher shal I, wrecched wight, become!
For, thogh so be that ship or boot heer come,
Hoom to my contree dar I nat for drede;
I can myselven in this cas nat rede!
WHAT shal I telle more her com-
pleining?
Hit is so long, hit were an hevy thing.
In her epistle Naso telleth al;
But shortly to the ende I telle shal.
The goddes have her holpen, for pitee;
And, in the signe of Taurus, men may see
The stones of her coroun shyne clere.
I WOL no more speke of this matere;
But thus this false lover can begyle
His trewe love. The devil quyte him his whyle!
Explicit Legenda Adriane de Athenes.

INCIPIT LEGENDA PHILOMENE.

Deus dator formarum.

T HOU

YIVER OF THE FORMES, THAT HAST
wroght
The faire world, and bare hit in thy thoght
Eternally, or thou thy werk began,
Why madest thou, unto the slaundre of man,
Or, al be that hit was not thy doing,

As for that fyn to make swiche a thing,
Why suffrest thou that Tereus was bore,
That is in love so fals and so forswore,
That, fro this world up to the firste hevene,
Corrumpeth, whan that folk his name nevene?
And, as to me, so grisly was his dede,
That, whan that I his foule story rede,
Myn eyen wexen foule and sore also;
Yit last the venim of so longe ago,
That hit enfecteth him that wol beholde
The story of Tereus, of which I tolde.
O f Trace was he lord, and kin to Marte,
The cruel god that stant with blody
darte;
And wedded had he, with a blisful chere,
King Pandiones faire doghter dere,
That highte Progne, flour of her contree,
Thogh Juno list nat at the feste be,
Ne Ymeneus, that god of wedding is;
But at the feste redy been, ywis,
The furies three, with alle hir mortel brond.
The owle al night aboute the balkes wond,
That prophet is of wo and of mischaunce.
This revel, ful of songe and ful of daunce,
Lasteth a fourtenight, or litel lasse.
But, shortly of this story for to passe,

for I am wery of him for to telle,
five yeer his wyf and he togeder dwelle,
Til on a day she gan so sore longe
To seen her suster, that she saw nat longe,
That for desyr she niste what to seye.
But to her husband gan she for to preye,
for Goddes love, that she moste ones goon
Her suster for to seen, and come anoon,
Or elles, but she moste to her wende,
She preyde him, that he wolde after her sende;
And this was, day by day, al her prayere
With al humblesse of wyfhood, word, and chere.
THIS Tereus let make his shippes yare,
And into Grece himself is forth yfare
Unto his fader in lawe, and gan him preye
To vouchesauf that, for a month or tweye,
That Philomene, his wyves suster, mighte
On Progne his wyf but ones have a sighte,
And she shal come to yow again anoon.
Myself with her wol bothe come and goon,
And as myn hertes lyf I wol her kepe.
THIS olde Pandion, this king, gan wepe
for tendernesse of herte, for to leve
His doghter goon, and for to yive her leve;
Of al this world he lovede nothing so;
But at the laste leve hath she to go.
for Philomene, with salte teres eke,
Gan of her fader grace to beseke
To seen her suster, that her longeth so;
And him embraceth with her armes two.
And therwithal so yong and fair was she
That, whan that Tereus saw her beautee,
And of array that ther was noon her liche,
And yit of bountee was she two so riche,
He caste his fyry herte upon her so
That he wol have her, how so that hit go,
And with his wyles kneled and so preyde,
Til at the laste Pandion thus seyde:
NOW, sone, quod he, that art to me so dere,
I thee betake my yonge doghter here,
That bereth the key of al my hertes lyf.
And grete wel my doghter and thy wyf,
And yive her leve somtyme for to pleye,
That she may seen me ones er I deye.
And soothly, he hath mad him riche feste,
And to his folk, the moste and eek the leste,
That with him com; and yaf him yiftes grete,
And him conveyeth through the maister-strete
Of Athenes, and to the see him broghte,
And turneth hoom; no malice he ne thoghte.
HE ores pulleth forth the vessel faste,
And into Trace arriveth at the laste,
And up into a forest he her ledde,
And to a cave privily him spedde;
And, in this derke cave, yif her leste,
Or leste noght, he bad her for to reste;
Of whiche her herte agroos, and seyde thus:
Wher is my suster, brother Tereus?
And therwithal she wepte tenderly,
And quook for fere, pale and pitously,
Right as the lamb that of the wolf is biten;
Or as the colver, that of the egle is smiten,
And is out of his clawes forth escaped,

442

Yet hit is sore afered and awhaped
Lest hit be hent eftsones, so sat she.
But utterly hit may non other be.
By force hath he, this traitour, doon that dede,
That he hath reft her of her maydenhede,
Maugree her heed, by strengthe and by his might.
Lo! here a dede of men, and that a right!
She cryeth Suster! with ful loude stevene,
And fader dere! and Help me, God in hevene!
Al helpeth nat; and yet this false theef
Hath doon this lady yet a more mischeef,
for fere lest she sholde his shame crye,
And doon him openly a vilanye,
And with his swerd her tong of kerveth he,
And in a castel made her for to be
ful privily in prison evermore,
And kepte her to his usage and his store,
So that she mighte him nevermore asterte.
O sely Philomene! wo is thyn herte;
God wreke thee, and sende thee thy bone!
Now is hit tyme I make an ende sone.
THIS Tereus is to his wyf ycome,
And in his armes hath his wyf ynome,
And pitously he weep, and shook his heed,
And swor her that he fond her suster deed;
for which this sely Progne hath swich wo,
That ny her sorweful herte brak atwo;
And thus in teres lete I Progne dwelle,
And of her suster forth I wol yow telle.
THIS woful lady lerned had in youthe
So that she werken & embrouden couthe,
And weven in her stole the radevore
As hit of women hath be woned yore.
And, shortly for to seyn, she hath her fille
Of mete and drink, and clothing at her wille,
And coude eek rede, and wel ynogh endyte,
But with a penne coude she nat wryte;
But lettres can she weven to and fro,
So that, by that the yeer was al ago,
She had ywoven in a stamin large
How she was broght from Athenes in a barge,
And in a cave how that she was broght;
And al the thing that Tereus hath wroght,
She waf hit wel, and wroot the story above,
How she was served for her suster love;
And to a knave a ring she yaf anoon,
And prayed him, by signes, for to goon
Unto the quene, and beren her that clooth,
And than by signes swor him many an ooth,
She sholde him yeve what she geten mighte.
THIS knave anoon unto the quene him
dighte,
And took hit her, and al the maner tolde.
And, whan that Progne hath this thing beholde,
No word she spak, for sorwe and eek for rage;
But feyned her to goon on pilgrimage
To Bachus temple; and, in a litel stounde,
Her dombe suster sitting hath she founde,
Weping in the castel her aloon.
Allas! the wo, the compleint, and the moon
That Progne upon her dombe suster maketh!
In armes everich of hem other taketh,
And thus I lete hem in hir sorwe dwelle.

THE remenant is no charge for to telle,
for this is al & som, thus was she served,
That never harm agilte ne deserved
Unto this cruel man, that she of wiste.
Ye may be war of men, yif that yow liste.
for, al be that he wol nat, for his shame,

Doon so as Tereus, to lese his name,
Ne serve yow as a mordrour or a knave,
ful litel whyle shul ye trewe him have,
That wol I seyn, al were he now my brother,
But hit so be that he may have non other.
Explicit Legenda Philomene.

INCIPIT LEGENDA PHILLIS.

That wikked fruit cometh of a wikked tree,
That may ye finde, if that it lyketh yow.
But for this ende I speke this as now,
To telle you of false Demophon.
In love a falser herde I never non,
But if hit were his fader Theseus.
God, for his grace, fro swich oon kepe us!
Thus may thise women prayen that hit here.
Now to theffect turne I of my matere.

DESTROYED is of Troye the citee;
This Demophon com sailing in the see
Toward Athenes, to his paleys large;
With him com many a ship and many a barge
ful of his folk, of which ful many oon
Is wounded sore, and seek, and wo begoon.
And they han at the sege longe ylain.
Behinde him com a wind and eek a rain
That shoof so sore, his sail ne mighte stonde,
Him were lever than al the world alonde,

PREVE AS WEL AS BY AUCTORITEE,

So hunteth him the tempest to and fro.
So derk hit was, he coude nowher go;
And with a wawe brosten was his stere.
His ship was rent so lowe, in swich manere,
That carpenter ne coude hit nat amende.
The see, by nighte, as any torche brende
For wood, and posseth him now up now doun,
Til Neptune hath of him compassioun,
And Thetis, Chorus, Triton, and they alle,
And maden him upon a lond to falle,
Wherof that Phillis lady was and quene,
Ligurgus doghter, fairer on to sene
Than is the flour again the brighte sonne.
Unnethe is Demophon to londe ywonne,
Wayk and eek wery, and his folk forpyned
Of werinesse, and also enfamyned;
And to the deeth he almost was ydriven.
His wyse folk to conseil han him yiven
To seken help and socour of the queen,
And loken what his grace mighte been,
And maken in that lond som chevisaunce,
To kepen him fro wo and fro mischaunce.
For seek was he, and almost at the deeth;
Unnethe mighte he speke or drawe his breeth,
And lyth in Rodopeya him for to reste.
When he may walke, him thoughte hit was the beste
Unto the court to seken for socour.
Men knewe him wel, and diden him honour;
For at Athenes duk and lord was he,
As Theseus his fader hadde ybe,
That in his tyme was of greet renoun,
No man so greet in al his regioun;
And lyk his fader of face and of stature,
And fals of love; hit com him of nature;
As doth the fox Renard, the foxes sone,
Of kinde he coude his olde faders wone
Withoute lore, as can a drake swimme,
When hit is caught and caried to the brimme.
This honourable Phillis doth him chere,
Her lyketh wel his port and his manere.
But for I am agroted heerbiforn
To wryte of hem that been in love forsworn,
And eek to haste me in my legende,
Which to performe God me grace sende,
Therfor I passe shortly in this wyse;
Ye han wel herd of Theseus devyse
In the betraising of fair Adriane,
That of her pite kepte him from his bane.
At shorte wordes, right so Demophon
The same wey, the same path hath gon
That dide his false fader Theseus.
For unto Phillis hath he sworen thus,
To wedden her, and her his trouthe plighte,
And piked of her al the good he mighte,
When he was hool and sound and hadde his reste;
And doth with Phillis what so that him leste.
And wel coude I, yif that me leste so,
Tellen al his doing to and fro.
HE seide, unto his contree moste he saile,
For ther he wolde her wedding apparaile
As fil to her honour and his also.

444

And openly he took his leve tho,
And hath her sworn, he wolde nat sojorne,
But in a month he wolde again retorne.
And in that lond let make his ordinaunce
As verray lord, and took the obeisaunce
Wel and hoomly, and let his shippes dighte,
And hoom he goth the nexte wey he mighte;
For unto Phillis yit ne com he noght.
And that hath she so harde and sore aboght,
Allas! that, as the stories us recorde,
She was her owne deeth right with a corde,
When that she saw that Demophon her trayed.
BUT to him first she wroot and faste him prayed
He wolde come, and her deliver of peyne
As I reherse shal a word or tweyne.
Me list nat vouchesauf on him to swinke,
Ne spende on him a penne ful of inke,
For fals in love was he, right as his syre;
The devil sette hir soules bothe afyre!
But of the lettre of Phillis wol I wryte
A word or tweyne, althogh hit be but lyte.
THYN hostesse, quod she, O Demophon,
Thy Phillis, which that is so wo begon,
Of Rodopeye, upon yow moot compleyne,
Over the terme set betwix us tweyne,
That ye ne holden forward, as ye seyde;
Your anker, which ye in our haven leyde,
Highte us, that ye wolde comen, out of doute,
Or that the mone ones wente aboute.
But tymes foure the mone hath hid her face
Sin thilke day ye wente fro this place,
And foure tymes light the world again.
But for al that, yif I shal soothly sain,
Yit hath the streem of Sitho nat ybroght
From Athenes the ship; yit comth hit noght.
And, yif that ye the terme rekne wolde,
As I or other trewe lovers sholde,
I pleyne not, God wot, beforn my day.
BUT al her lettre wryten I ne may
By ordre, for hit were to me a charge;
Her lettre was right long and therto large;
But here and there in ryme I have hit laid,
Ther as me thoughte that she wel hath said.
SHE seide: Thy sailes comen nat again,
Ne to thy word ther nis no fey certein;
But I wot why ye come nat, quod she;
For I was of my love to you so free.
And of the goddes that ye han forswore,
Yif that hir vengeance falle on yow therfore,
Ye be nat suffisaunt to bere the peyne.
To moche trusted I, wel may I pleyne,
Upon your linage and your faire tonge,
And on your teres falsly out ywronge,
How coude ye wepe so by craft? quod she;
May ther swiche teres feyned be?
Now certes, yif ye wolde have in memorie,
Hit oghte be to yow but litel glorie
To have a sely mayde thus betrayed!
To God, quod she, preye I, and ofte have prayed,
That hit be now the grettest prys of alle,
And moste honour that ever yow shal befalle!
And when thyn olde auncestres peynted be,

In which men may hir worthinesse see,
Than, preye I God, thou peynted be also,
That folk may reden, forby as they go,
Lo! this is he, that with his flaterye
Betrayed hath and doon her vilanye
That was his trewe love in thoghte and dede!
But sothly, of oo point yit may they rede,
That ye ben lyk your fader as in this;
for he begyled Adriane, ywis,
With swiche an art and swiche sotelte
As thou thyselven hast begyled me.
As in that point, althogh hit be nat fayr,
Thou folwest him, certein, and art his eyr.

But sin thus sinfully ye me begyle,
By body mote ye seen, within a whyle,
Right in the haven of Athenes fletinge,
Withouten sepulture and buryinge;
Thogh ye ben harder than is any stoon.
And, whan this lettre was forth sent anoon
And knew how brotel and how fals he was,
She for dispeyr fordide herself, allas!
Swich sorwe hath she, for she besette her so.
Be war, ye women, of your sotil fo,
Sin yit this day men may ensample see;
And trusteth, as in love, no man but me.
Explicit Legenda Phillis.

INCIPIT LEGENDA YPERMISTRE.

IN GRECE WHYLOM WEREN brethren two,
Of whiche that oon was called Danao,
That many a sone hath of his body wonne,
As swiche false lovers ofte conne.
Among his sones alle ther was oon
That aldermost he lovede of everichoon.
And whan this child was born, this Danao
Shoop him a name, and called him Lino.
That other brother called was Egiste,
That was of love as fals as ever him liste,
And many a doghter gat he in his lyve;
Of which he gat upon his righte wyve
A doghter dere, and dide her for to calle
Ypermistra, yongest of hem alle;
The whiche child, of her nativitee,
To alle gode thewes born was she,
As lyked to the goddes, or she was born,
That of the shefe she sholde be the corn;
The Wirdes, that we clepen Destinee,
Hath shapen her that she mot nedes be
Pitouse, sadde, wyse, and trewe as steel;
And to this woman hit accordeth weel.
for, though that Venus yaf her greet beautee,
With Jupiter compouned so was she
That conscience, trouthe, and dreed of shame,
And of her wyfhood for to kepe her name,
This, thoughte her, was felicitee as here.

And rede Mars was, that tyme of the yere,
So feble, that his malice is him raft,
Repressed hath Venus his cruel craft;
What with Venus and other oppressioun
Of houses, Mars his venim is adoun,
That Ypermistra dar nat handle a knyf
In malice, thogh she sholde lese her lyf.
But natheles, as heven gan tho turne,
To badde aspectes hath she of Saturne,
That made her for to deyen in prisoun,
As I shal after make mencioun.
O Danao and Egistes also,
Althogh so be that they were brethren two,
for thilke tyme nas spared no linage,
Hit lyked hem to maken mariage
Betwix Ypermistra and him Lino,
And casten swiche a day hit shal be so;
And ful acorded was hit witterly;
The array is wroght, the tyme is faste by.
And thus Lino hath of his fadres brother
The doghter wedded, and eche of hem hath
other.
THE torches brennen & the lampes
brighte,
The sacrifices been ful redy dighte;
Thencens out of the fyre reketh sote,
The flour, the leef is rent up by the rote
To maken garlands and corounes hye;
ful is the place of soun of minstralcye,
Of songes amorous of mariage,
As thilke tyme was the pleyn usage.
And this was in the paleys of Egiste,
That in his hous was lord, right as him liste;
And thus the day they dryven to an ende;
The frendes taken leve, and hoom they
wende.
The night is come, the bryd shal go to bedde;
Egiste to his chambre faste him spedde,
And privily he let his doghter calle.
Whan that the hous was voided of hem alle,
He loked on his doghter with glad chere,
And to her spak, as ye shul after here.
MY righte doghter, tresor of myn herte!
Sin first that day that shapen was my
sherte,

Or by the fatal sustren had my dom,
So ny myn herte never thing me com
As thou, myn Ypermistra, doghter dere!
Tak heed what I thy fader sey thee here,
And werk after thy wyser evermo.
for alderfirste, doghter, I love thee so
That al the world to me nis half so leef;
Ne I nolde rede thee to thy mischeef
for al the gode under the colde mone;
And what I mene, hit shal be seid right sone,
With protestacioun, as in this wyse,
That, but thou do as I shal thee devyse,
Thou shalt be deed, by him that al hath wroght!
At shorte wordes, thou nescapest noght
Out of my paleys, or that thou be deed,
But thou consente and werke after my reed;
Tak this to thee for ful conclusioun.
THIS Ypermistra caste her eyen doun,
And quook as dooth the leef of aspe
    grene;
Deed wex her hewe, and lyk as ash to sene,
And seyde: Lord and fader, al your wille,
After my might, God wot, I shal fulfille,
So hit to me be no confusioun.
NIL, quod he, have noon excepcioun;
And out he caughte a knyf, as rasour
    kene;

Hyd this, quod he, that hit be nat ysene;
And, whan thyn husbond is to bedde ygo,
Whyl that he slepeth, cut his throte atwo.
for in my dremes hit is warned me
How that my nevew shal my bane be,
But whiche I noot, wherfor I wol be siker.
Yif thou sey nay, we two shul have a biker
As I have seyd, by him that I have sworn.
THIS Ypermistra hath ny her wit for-
    lorn;
    And, for to passen harmles of that
place,
She graunted him; ther was non other grace.
And therwithal a costrel taketh he,
And seyde: Herof a draught, or two or three,
Yif him to drinke, whan he goth to reste,
And he shal slepe as longe as ever thee leste,
The narcotiks and opies been so stronge:
And go thy wey, lest that him thinke longe.
OUT comth the bryd, & with ful sober
    chere,
    As is of maidens ofte the manere,
To chambre is broght with revel and with
songe,
And shortly, lest this tale be to longe,
This Lino and she ben sone broght to bedde;
And every wight out at the dore him spedde.

THE night is wasted, and he fel aslepe;
Ful tenderly beginneth she to wepe.
  She rist her up, and dredfully she quaketh,
As doth the braunche that Zephirus shaketh,
And husht were alle in Argon that citee.
As cold as any frost now wexeth she;
For pite by the herte her streyneth so,
And dreed of deeth doth her so moche wo,
That thryes doun she fil in swiche a were.
She rist her up, and stakereth heer and there,
And on her handes faste loketh she.
  Allas! and shul my handes blody be?
I am a maid, and, as by my nature,
And by my semblant and by my vesture,
Myn handes been nat shapen for a knyf,
As for to reve no man fro his lyf,
What devil have I with the knyf to do?
And shal I have my throte corve atwo?
Than shal I blede, allas! and me beshende;
And nedes cost this thing mot have an ende;
Or he or I mot nedes lese our lyf.
Now certes, quod she, sin I am his wyf,
And hath my feith, yit is it bet for me
For to be deed in wyfly honestee

Than be a traitour living in my shame.
Be as be may, for ernest or for game,
He shal awake, and ryse and go his way
Out at this goter, or that hit be day!
  And weep ful tenderly upon his face,
And in her armes gan him to embrace,
And him she roggeth and awaketh softe;
And at the window leep he fro the lofte
Whan she hath warned him, and doon him
bote.

THIS Lino swifte was, and light of fote,
And from his wyf he ran a ful good pas.
  This sely woman is so wayk, allas!
And helples so, that, or that she fer wente,
Her cruel fader dide her for to hente.
Allas! Lino! why art thou so unkinde?
Why ne haddest thou remembred in thy minde
To taken her, and lad her forth with thee?
For, whan she saw that goon awey was he,
And that she mighte nat so faste go,
Ne folwen him, she sette her doun right tho,
Til she was caught and fetered in prisoun.
  This tale is seid for this conclusioun....
Unfinished.

447

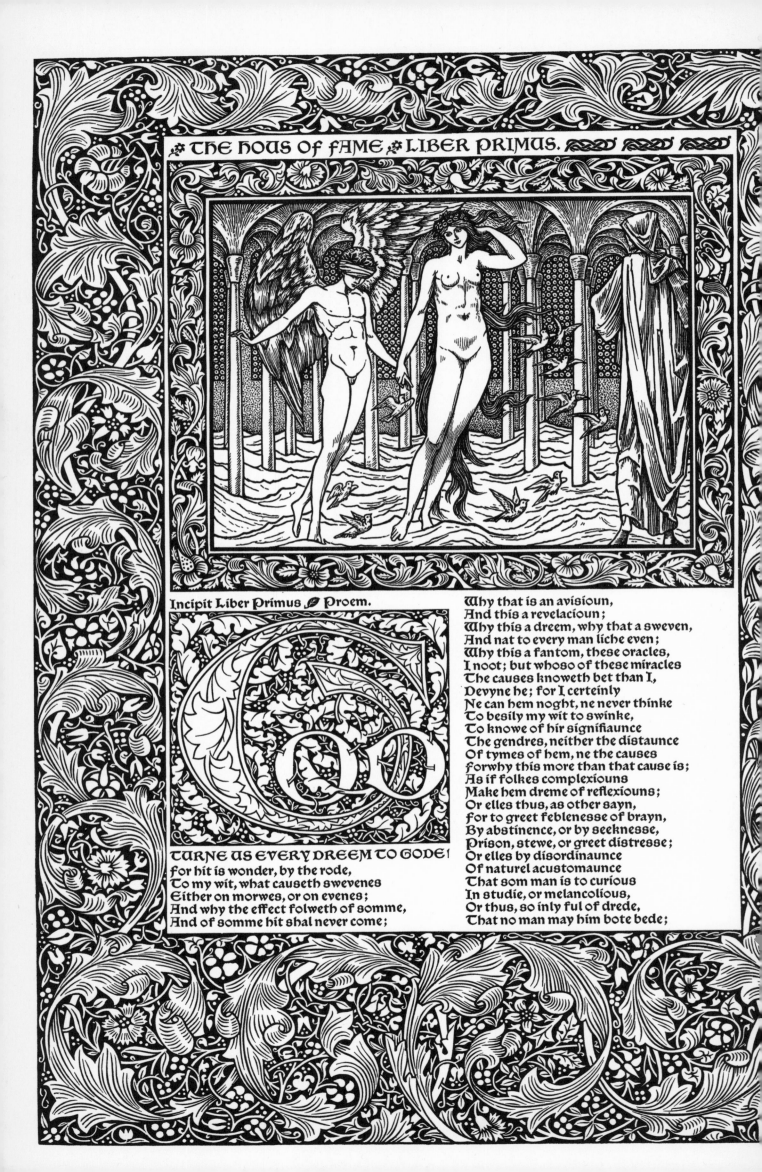

Incipit Liber Primus ❦ Proem.

TURNE US EVERY DREEM TO GODE!
For hit is wonder, by the rode,
To my wit, what causeth swevenes
Either on morwes, or on evenes;
And why the effect folweth of somme,
And of somme hit shal never come;

Why that is an avisioun,
And this a revelacioun;
Why this a dreem, why that a sweven,
And nat to every man liche even;
Why this a fantom, these oracles,
I noot; but whoso of these miracles
The causes knoweth bet than I,
Devyne he; for I certeinly
Ne can hem noght, ne never thinke
To besily my wit to swinke,
To knowe of hir signifiaunce
The gendres, neither the distaunce
Of tymes of hem, ne the causes
Forwhy this more than that cause is;
As if folkes complexiouns
Make hem dreme of reflexiouns;
Or elles thus, as other sayn,
For to greet feblenesse of brayn,
By abstinence, or by seeknesse,
Prison, stewe, or greet distresse;
Or elles by disordinaunce
Of naturel acustomaunce
That som man is to curious
In studie, or melancolious,
Or thus, so inly ful of drede,
That no man may him bote bede;

Or elles, that devocioun
Of somme, and contemplacioun
Causeth swiche dremes ofte;
Or that the cruel lyf unsofte
Which these ilke lovers leden
That hopen over muche or dreden,
That purely hir impressiouns
Causeth hem avisiouns;
Or if that spirits have the might
To make folk to dreme anight
Or if the soule, of propre kinde,
Be so parfit, as men finde,
That hit forwot that is to come,
And that hit warneth alle and somme
Of everiche of hir aventures
By avisiouns, or by figures,
But that our flesh ne hath no might
To understonden hit aright,
For hit is warned to derkly;
But why the cause is, noght wot I.
Wel worthe, of this thing, grete clerkes,
That trete of this and other werkes;
For I of noon opinioun
Nil as now make mencioun,
But only that the holy rode
Turne us every dreem to gode!
For never, sith that I was born,
Ne no man elles, me biforn,
Mette, I trowe stedfastly,
So wonderful a dreem as I
The tenthe day dide of Decembre,
The which, as I can now remembre,
I wol yow tellen every del.

The Invocation.

BUT at my ginning, trusteth
wel,
I wol make invocacioun,
With special devocioun,
Unto the god of slepe
anoon,
That dwelleth in a cave of
stoon
Upon a streem that comth
fro Lete,
That is a flood of helle unswete;
Besyde a folk men clepe Cimerie,
Ther slepeth ay this god unmerie
With his slepy thousand sones
That alway for to slepe hir wone is;
And to this god, that I of rede,
Preye I, that he wol me spede
My sweven for to telle aright,
If every dreem stonde in his might.
And he, that mover is of al
That is and was, and ever shal,
So yive hem joye that hit here
Of alle that they dreme toyere,
And for to stonden alle in grace
Of hir loves, or in what place
That hem wer levest for to stonde,
And shelde hem fro povert and shonde,
And fro unhappe and ech disese,
And sende hem al that may hem plese,
gg 1

That take hit wel, and scorne hit noght,
Ne hit misdemen in her thoght
Through malicious entencioun.
And whoso, through presumpcioun,
Or hate or scorne, or through envye,
Dispyt, or jape, or vilanye,
Misdeme hit, preye I Jesus God
That (dreme he barfoot, dreme he shod),
That every harm that any man
Hath had, sith that the world began,
Befalle him therof, or he sterve,
And graunte he mote hit ful deserve,
Lo! with swich a conclusioun
As had of his avisioun
Cresus, that was king of Lyde,
That high upon a gebet dyde!
This prayer shal he have of me;
I am no bet in charite!
Now herkneth, as I have you seyd,
What that I mette, or I abreyd.
The Dream.

OF Decembre the tenthe day,
Whan hit was night, to
slepe I lay
Right ther as I was wont
to done,
And fil on slepe wonder
sone,
As he that wery was forgo
On pilgrimage myles two
To the corseynt Leonard,
To make lythe of that was hard.
BUT as I sleep, me mette I was
Within a temple ymad of glas;
In whiche ther were mo images
Of gold, stondinge in sondry stages,
And mo riche tabernacles,
And with perre mo pinacles,
And mo curious portreytures,
And queynte maner of figures
Of olde werke, then I saw ever.
For certeynly, I niste never
Wher that I was, but wel wiste I,
Hit was of Venus redely,
The temple; for, in portreyture,
I saw anoon, right hir figure
Naked fletinge in a see.
And also on hir heed, parde,
Hir rose-garlond whyt and reed,
And hir comb to kembe hir heed,
Hir dowves, and daun Cupido,
Hir blinde sone, and Vulcano,
That in his face was ful broun.
BUT as I romed up and doun,
I fond that on a wal ther was
Thus writen, on a table of bras:
I wol now singe, if that I can,
The armes, and also the man,
That first cam, through his destinee,
Fugitif of Troye contree,
In Itaile, with ful moche pyne,
Unto the strondes of Lavyne.
And tho began the story anoon,

449

As I shal telle yow echoon.
IRST saw I the destruccioun
Of Troye, through the Greek
Sinoun,
That with his false forsweringe,
And his chere and his lesinge
Made the hors broght into Troye,
Thorgh which Troyens loste al hir joye.
And after this was grave, allas!
How Ilioun assailed was
And wonne, and king Priam yslayn,
And Polites his sone, certayn,
Dispitously, of dan Pirrus.
AND next that saw I how Venus,
Whan that she saw the castel brende,
Doun fro the hevene gan descende,
And bad hir sone Eneas flee;
And how he fledde, and how that he
Escaped was from al the pres,
And took his fader, Anchises,
And bar him on his bakke away,
Cryinge, Allas, and welaway!
The whiche Anchises in his honde
Bar the goddes of the londe,
Thilke that unbrende were.
AND I saw next, in alle this fere,
How Creusa, daun Eneas wyf,
Which that he lovede as his lyf,
And hir yonge son Julo,
And eek Ascanius also,
Fledden eek with drery chere,
That hit was pitee for to here;
And in a forest, as they wente,
At a turninge of a wente,
How Creusa was ylost, allas!
That deed, but noot I how, she was;
How he hir soughte, and how hir gost
Bad him to flee the Grekes ost,
And seyde, he moste unto Itaile,
As was his destinee, sauns faille;
That hit was pitee for to here,
Whan hir spirit gan appere,
The wordes that she to him seyde,
And for to kepe hir sone him preyde.
Ther saw I graven eek how he,
His fader eek, and his meynee,
With his shippes gan to sayle
Toward the contree of Itaile,
As streight as that they mighte go.
HER saw I thee, cruel Juno,
That art daun Jupiteres wyf,
That hast yhated, al thy lyf,
Al the Troyanisshe blood,
Renne and crye, as thou were wood,
On Eolus, the god of windes,
To blowen out, of alle kindes,
So loude, that he shulde drenche
Lord and lady, grome and wenche
Of al the Troyan nacioun,
Withoute any savacioun.
HER saw I swich tempeste aryse,
That every herte mighte agryse,
To see hit peynted on the walle.

450

HER saw I graven eek withalle,
Venus, how ye, my lady dere,
Wepinge with ful woful chere,
Prayen Jupiter an hye
To save and kepe that navye
Of the Troyan Eneas,
Sith that he hir sone was.
HER saw I Joves Venus kisse,
And graunted of the tempest lisse.
Ther saw I how the tempest stente,
And how with alle pyne he wente,
And prevely took arrivage
In the contree of Cartage;
And on the morwe, how that he
And a knight, hight Achatee,
Metten with Venus that day,
Goinge in a queynt array,
As she had ben an hunteresse,
With wind blowinge upon hir tresse;
How Eneas gan him to pleyne,
Whan that he knew hir, of his peyne;
And how his shippes dreynte were,
Or elles lost, he niste where;
How she gan him comforte tho,
And bad him to Cartage go,
And ther he shuldë his folk finde,
That in the see were left behinde.
AND, shortly of this thing to pace,
She made Eneas so in grace
Of Dido, quene of that contree,
That, shortly for to tellen, she
Becam his love, and leet him do
That that wedding longeth to.
What shulde I speke more queynte,
Or peyne me my wordes peynte,
To speke of love? hit wol not be;
I can not of that facultee.
And eek to telle the manere
How they aqueynteden in fere,
Hit were a long proces to telle,
And over long for yow to dwelle.
HER saw I grave, how Eneas
Tolde Dido every cas,
That him was tid upon the see.
AND after grave was, how she
Made of him, shortly, at oo word,
Hir lyf, hir love, hir lust, hir lord;
And dide him al the reverence,
And leyde on him al the dispence,
That any woman mighte do,
Weninge hit had al be so,
As he hir swoor; and herby demed
That he was good, for he swich semed.
Allas! what harm doth apparence,
Whan hit is fals in existence!
For he to hir a traitour was;
Wherfor she slow hirself, allas!
O, how a woman doth amis,
To love him that unknowen is!
For, by Crist, lo! thus hit fareth;
Hit is not al gold, that glareth.
For, also brouke I wel myn heed,
Ther may be under goodliheed

Kevered many a shrewed vyce;
Therfor be no wight so nyce,
To take a love only for chere,
For speche, or for frendly manere;
For this shal every woman finde
That som man, of his pure kinde,
Wol shewen outward the faireste,
Til he have caught that what him leste;
And thanne wol he causes finde,
And swere how that she is unkinde,
Or fals, or prevy, or double was.
Al this seye I by Eneas
And Dido, and hir nyce lest,
That lovede al to sone a gest;
Therfor I wol seye a proverbe,
That He that fully knoweth therbe
May saufly leye hit to his yë
Withoute dreed, this is no lye.

BUT let us speke of Eneas,
How he betrayed hir, allas!
And lefte hir ful unkindely.
So whan she saw al utterly,
That he wolde hir of trouthe
faile,
And wende fro hir to Itaile,
She gan to wringe hir hondes two.

ALLAS! quod she, what me is wo!
Allas! is every man thus trewe,
That every yere wolde have a newe,
If hit so longe tyme dure,
Or elles three, peraventure?
As thus: of oon he wolde have fame
In magnifying of his name;
Another for frendship, seith he;
And yet ther shal the thridde be,
That shal be taken for delyt,
Lo, or for singular profyt.

IN swiche wordes gan to pleyne
Dido of grete peyne,
As me mette redely;
Non other auctour alegge I.
Allas! quod she, my swete herte,
Have pitee on my sorwes smerte,
And slee me not! go noght away!
O woful Dido, wel away!
Quod she to hirselve tho.
O Eneas! what wil ye do?
O, that your love, ne your bonde,
That ye han sworn with your right honde,
Ne my cruel deeth, quod she,
May holde yow still heer with me!
O, haveth of my deeth pitee!
Ywis, my dere herte, ye
Knowen ful wel that never yit,
As fer forth as I hadde wit,
Agilte I yow in thoght ne deed.
O, have ye men swich goodliheed
In speche, and never a deel of trouthe?
Allas, that ever hadde routhe
Any woman on any man!
Now see I wel, and telle can,
We wrecched wimmen conne non art;
For certeyn, for the more part,

g g 2

Thus we be served everichone.
How sore that ye men conne grone,
Anoon, as we have yow receyved,
Certeinly we ben deceyved;
For, though your love laste a sesoun,
Wayte upon the conclusioun,
And eek how that ye determynen,
And for the more part diffynen.

O, WELAWEY that I was born!
For through yow is my name lorn,
And alle myn actes red and songe
Over al this lond, on every tonge.
O wikke fame! for ther nis
Nothing so swift, lo, as she is!
O, sooth is, every thing is wist,
Though hit be kevered with the mist.
Eek, thogh I mighte duren ever,
That I have doon, rekever I never,
That I ne shal be seyd, allas,
Yshamed be through Eneas,
And that I shal thus juged be:
Lo, right as she hath doon, now she
Wol do eftsones, hardily!
Thus seyth the peple prevely.

BUT that is doon, nis not to done;
Al hir compleynt ne al hir mone,
Certeyn, availeth hir not a stre.

AND whan she wiste sothly he
Was forth unto his shippes goon,
She in hir chambre wente anoon,
And called on hir suster Anne,
And gan hir to compleyne thanne;
And seyde, that she cause was
That she first lovede Eneas,
And thus counseilled hir therto.
But what! when this was seyd and do,
She roof hirselve to the herte,
And deyde through the wounde smerte.
But al the maner how she deyde,
And al the wordes that she seyde,
Whoso to knowe hit hath purpos,
Reed Virgile in Eneidos
Or the Epistle of Ovyde,
What that she wroot or that she dyde;
And nere hit to long to endyte,
By God, I woldë hit here wryte.

BUT, welaway! the harm, the routhe,
That hath betid for swich untrouthe,
As men may ofte in bokes rede,
And al day seen hit yet in dede,
That for to thenken hit, a tene is.

LO, Demophon, duk of Athenis,
How he forswor him ful falsly,
And trayed Phillis wikkedly,
That kinges doghter was of Trace,
And falsly gan his terme pace;
And when she wiste that he was
fals,
She heng hirself right by the hals,
For he had do hir swich untrouthe;
Lo! was not this a wo and routhe?
EEK lo! how fals and reccheles
Was to Briseida Achilles,

451

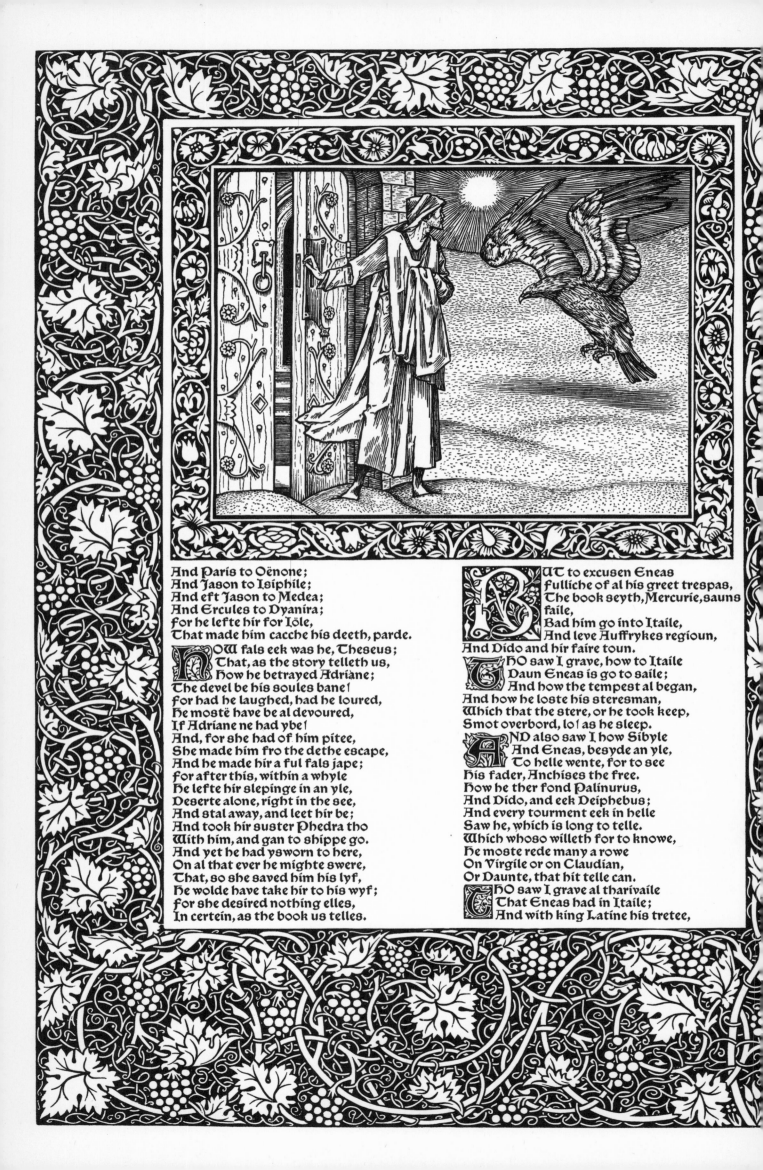

And Paris to Oënone;
And Jason to Isiphile;
And eft Jason to Medea;
And Ercules to Dyanira;
for he lefte hir for Iöle,
That made him cacche his deeth, parde.

NOW fals eek was he, Theseus;
That, as the story telleth us,
How he betrayed Adriane;
The devel be his soules bane!
for had he laughed, had he loured,
He mostë have be al devoured,
If Adriane ne had ybe!
And, for she had of him pitee,
She made him fro the dethe escape,
And he made hir a ful fals jape;
for after this, within a whyle
He lefte hir slepinge in an yle,
Deserte alone, right in the see,
And stal away, and leet hir be;
And took hir suster Phedra tho
With him, and gan to shippe go.
And yet he had ysworn to here,
On al that ever he mighte swere,
That, so she saved him his lyf,
He wolde have take hir to his wyf;
for she desired nothing elles,
In certein, as the book us telles.

BUT to excusen Eneas
fulliche of al his greet trespas,
The book seyth, Mercurie, sauns
faile,
Bad him go into Itaile,
And leve Auffrykes regioun,
And Dido and hir faire toun.

THO saw I grave, how to Itaile
Daun Eneas is go to saile;
And how the tempest al began,
And how he loste his steresman,
Which that the stere, or he took keep,
Smot overbord, los as he sleep.

AND also saw I how Sibyle
And Eneas, besyde an yle,
To helle wente, for to see
His fader, Anchises the free.
How he ther fond Palinurus,
And Dido, and eek Deiphebus;
And every tourment eek in helle
Saw he, which is long to telle.
Which whoso willeth for to knowe,
He moste rede many a rowe
On Virgile or on Claudian,
Or Daunte, that hit telle can.

THO saw I grave al tharivaile
That Eneas had in Itaile;
And with king Latine his tretee,

And alle the batailles that he
Was at himself, and eek his knightes,
Or he had al ywonne his rightes;
And how he Turnus refte his lyf,
And wan Lavyna to his wyf;
And al the mervelous signals
Of the goddes celestials;
How, maugre Juno, Eneas,
For al hir sleighte and hir compas,
Acheved al his aventure;
For Jupiter took of him cure
At the prayere of Venus;
The whiche I preye alway save us,
And us ay of our sorwes lighte!
WHAN I had seyen al this sighte
In this noble temple thus,
A, Lord! thoughte I, that madest us,
Yet saw I never swich noblesse
Of images, ne swich richesse,
As I saw graven in this chirche;
But not woot I who dide hem wirche,
Ne wher I am, ne in what contree.
But now wol I go out and see,
Right at the wiket, if I can
See owher stering any man,
That may me telle wher I am.
WHEN I out at the dores cam,
I faste aboute me beheld.
Then saw I but a large feld,

As fer as that I mighte see,
Withouten toun, or hous, or tree,
Or bush, or gras, or ered lond;
For al the feld nas but of sond
As smal as man may see yet lye
In the desert of Libye;
Ne I no maner creature,
That is yformed by nature,
Ne saw, me for to rede or wisse.
O Crist, thoughte I, that art in blisse,
Fro fantom and illusioun
Me save! and with devocioun
Myn yën to the heven I caste.
THO was I war, lo! at the laste,
That faste by the sonne, as hyë
As kenne mighte I with myn yë,
Me thoughte I saw an egle sore,
But that hit semed moche more
Then I had any egle seyn.
But this as sooth as deeth, certeyn,
Hit was of golde, and shoon so brighte,
That never saw men such a sighte,
But if the heven hadde ywonne
Al newe of golde another sonne;
So shoon the egles fethres brighte,
And somwhat dounward gan hit lighte.
Explicit Liber Primus.

THE HOUS OF FAME ❧ LIBER SECUNDUS.

Incipit Liber Secundus. ❧ Proem.

And ye, me to endyte and ryme
Helpeth, that on Parnaso dwelle
By Elicon the clere welle.
O THOUGHT, that wroot al that I mette,
And in the tresorie hit shette
Of my brayn! now shal men see
If any vertu in thee be,
To tellen al my dreem aright;
Now kythe thyn engyn and might!
The Dream.

HERKNETH, EVERY MANER MAN
That English understonde can,
And listeth of my dreem to lere;
For now at erste shul ye here
So selly an avisioun,
That Isaye, ne Scipioun,
Ne king Nabugodonosor,
Pharo, Turnus, ne Elcanor,
Ne mette swich a dreem as this!
Now faire blisful, O Cipris,
So be my favour at this tyme!

THIS egle, of which I
have yow told,
That shoon with feth-
res as of gold,
Which that so hyë gan
to sore,
I gan beholde more
and more,
To see hir beautee and
the wonder;
But never was ther dint of thonder,
Ne that thing that men calle foudre,
That smoot somtyme a tour to poudre,
And in his swifte coming brende,
That so swythe gan descende,
As this foul, whan hit behelde
That I aroume was in the felde;
And with his grimme pawes stronge,
Within his sharpe nayles longe,
Me, fleinge, at a swappe he hente,
And with his sours agayn up wente,

Me caryinge in his clawes starke
As lightly as I were a larke,
How high, I can not telle yow,
for I cam up, I niste how.
for so astonied and asweved
Was every vertu in my heved,
What with his sours and with my drede,
That al my feling gan to dede;
forwhy hit was to greet affray.

THUS I longe in his clawes lay,
Til at the laste he to me spak
In mannes vois, and seyde: Awak!
And be not so agast, for shame!
And called me tho by my name.
And, for I sholde the bet abreyde,
Me mette, Awak, to me he seyde,
Right in the same vois and stevene
That useth oon I coude nevene;
And with that vois, soth for to sayn,
My minde cam to me agayn;
for hit was goodly seyd to me,
So nas hit never wont to be.

AND herwithal I gan to stere,
And he me in his feet to bere,
Til that he felte that I had hete,
And felte eek tho myn herte bete.
And tho gan he me to disporte,
And with wordes to comforte,

And sayde twyës: Seynte Marie!
Thou art noyous for to carie,
And nothing nedeth hit, parde!
for also wis God helpe me
As thou non harm shalt have of this;
And this cas, that betid thee is,
Is for thy lore and for thy prow;
Let see! darst thou yet loke now?
Be ful assured, boldely,
I am thy frend. And therwith I
Gan for to wondren in my minde.
O God, thoughte I, that madest kinde,
Shal I non other weyes dye?
Wher Joves wol me stellifye,
Or what thing may this signifye?
I neither am Enok, ne Elye,
Ne Romulus, ne Ganymede
That was ybore up, as men rede,
To hevene with dan Jupiter,
And maad the goddes boteler.

LO! this was tho my fantasye!
But he that bar me gan espye
That I so thoghte, and seyde this:
Thou demest of thyself amis;
for Joves is not theraboute,
I dar wel putte thee out of doute,
To make of thee as yet a sterre.
But er I bere thee moche ferre,

I wol thee telle what I am,
And whider thou shalt, and why I cam
To done this, so that thou take
Good herte, and not for fere quake.
Gladly, quod I. Now wel, quod he:
First I, that in my feet have thee,
Of which thou hast a feer and wonder,
Am dwelling with the god of thonder,
Which that men callen Jupiter,
That dooth me flee ful ofte fer
To do al his comaundement.
And for this cause he hath me sent
To thee: now herke, by thy trouthe!
Certeyn, he hath of thee routhe,
That thou so longe trewely
Hast served so ententifly
His blinde nevew Cupido,
And fair Venus goddesse also,
Withoute guerdoun ever yit,
And nevertheles hast set thy wit,
Although that in thy hede ful lyte is,
To make bokes, songes, dytees,
In ryme, or elles in cadence,
As thou best canst, in reverence
Of Love, and of his servants eke,
That have his servise soght, and seke;
And peynest thee to preyse his art,
Althogh thou haddest never part;
Wherfor, also God me blesse,
Joves halt hit greet humblesse
And vertu eek, that thou wolt make
A-night ful ofte thyn heed to ake,
In thy studie so thou wrytest,
And evermo of love endytest,
In honour of him and preysinges,
And in his folkes furtheringes,
And in hir matere al devysest,
And noght him nor his folk despysest,
Although thou mayst go in the daunce
Of hem that him list not avaunce.

WHERFOR, as I seyde, ywis,
  Jupiter considereth this,
  And also, beau sir, other thinges;
That is, that thou hast no tydinges
Of Loves folk, if they be glade,
Ne of noght elles that God made;
And noght only fro fer contree
That ther no tyding comth to thee,
But of thy verray neyghebores,
That dwellen almost at thy dores,
Thou herest neither that ne this;
For whan thy labour doon al is,
And hast ymaad thy rekeninges,
In stede of reste and newe thinges,
Thou gost hoom to thy hous anoon;
And, also domb as any stoon,
Thou sittest at another boke,
Til fully daswed is thy loke,
And livest thus as an hermyte,
Although thyn abstinence is lyte.

AND therfor Joves, through his
  grace,
  Wol that I bere thee to a place,

Which that hight The Hous of Fame,
To do thee som disport and game,
In som recompensacioun
Of labour and devocioun
That thou hast had, lo! causeles,
To Cupido, the reccheles!
And thus this god, thorgh his meryte,
Wol with som maner thing thee quyte,
So that thou wolt be of good chere.
For truste wel, that thou shalt here,
When we be comen ther I seye,
Mo wonder thinges, dar I leye,
Of Loves folke mo tydinges,
Bothe soth-sawes and lesinges;
And mo loves newe begonne,
And longe yserved loves wonne,
And mo loves casuelly
That been betid, no man wot why,
But as a blind man stert an hare;
And more jolytee and fare,
Whyl that they finde love of stele,
As thinketh hem, and overal wele;
Mo discords, and mo jelousyes,
Mo murmurs, and mo novelryes,
And mo dissimulaciouns,
And feyned reparaciouns;
And mo berdes in two houres
Withoute rasour or sisoures
Ymaad, then greynes be of sondes;
And eke mo holdinge in hondes,
And also mo renovelaunces
Of olde forleten aqueyntaunces;
Mo love-dayes and acordes
Then on instruments ben cordes;
And eke of loves mo eschaunges
Than ever cornes were in graunges;
Unethe maistow trowen this?
Quod he. No, helpe me God so wis!
Quod I. No? why? quod he. For hit
Were impossible, to my wit,
Though that Fame hadde al the pyes
In al a realme, and al the spyes,
How that yet she shulde here al this,
Or they espye hit. O yis, yis!
Quod he to me, that can I preve
By resoun, worthy for to leve,
So that thou yeve thyn advertence
To understonde my sentence.

FIRST shalt thou heren wher she
  dwelleth,
  And so thyn owne book hit telleth;
Hir paleys stant, as I shal seye,
Right even in middes of the weye
Betwixen hevene, erthe, and see;
That, whatsoever in al these three
Is spoken, in privee or aperte,
The wey therto is so overte,
And stant eek in so juste a place,
That every soun mot to hit pace,
Or what so comth fro any tonge,
Be hit rouned, red, or songe,
Or spoke in seurtee or drede,
Certein, hit moste thider nede.

NOW herkne wel; forwhy I wille
Tellen thee a propre skile,
And worthy demonstracioun
In myn imagynacioun.
GEffREY, thou wost right wel this,
That every kindly thing that is,
Hath a kindly stede ther he
May best in hit conserved be;
Unto which place every thing,
Through his kindly enclyning,
Moveth for to come to,
Whan that hit is awey therfro;
As thus; lo, thou mayst al day see
That any thing that hevy be,
As stoon or leed, or thing of wighte,
And ber hit never so hye on highte,
Lat go thyn hand, hit falleth doun.
RIGHT so seye I by fyre or soun,
Or smoke, or other thinges lighte,
Alwey they seke upward on highte;
Whyl ech of hem is at his large,
Light thing up, and dounward charge.
AND for this cause mayst thou see,
That every river to the see
Enclyned is to go, by kinde.
And by these skilles, as I finde,
Hath fish dwellinge in floode and see,
And treës eek in erthe be.
Thus every thing, by this resoun,
Hath his propre mansioun,
To which hit seketh to repaire;
As ther hit shulde not apaire.
Lo, this sentence is knowen couthe
Of every philosophres mouthe,
As Aristotle and dan Platon,
And other clerkes many oon;
And to confirme my resoun,
Thou wost wel this, that speche is soun,
Or elles no man mighte hit here;
Now herkne what I wol thee lere.
SOUN is noght but air ybroken,
And every speche that is spoken,
Loud or privee, foul or fair,
In his substaunce is but air;
for as flaumbe is but lighted smoke,
Right so soun is air ybroke.
But this may be in many wyse,
Of which I wil thee two devyse,
As soun that comth of pype or harpe;
for whan a pype is blowen sharpe,
The air is twist with violence,
And rent; lo, this is my sentence;
Eek, whan men harpe-stringes smyte,
Whether hit be moche or lyte,
Lo, with the strook the air tobreketh;
Right so hit breketh whan men speketh.
Thus wost thou wel what thing is speche.
NOW hennesforth I wol thee teche,
How every speche, or noise, or soun,
Through his multiplicacioun,
Thogh hit were pyped of a mouse,
Moot nede come to fames House.
I preve hit thus, tak hede now,

By experience; for if that thou
Throwe on water now a stoon,
Wel wost thou, hit wol make anoon
A litel roundel as a cercle,
Paraventure brood as a covercle;
And right anoon thou shalt see weel,
That wheel wol cause another wheel,
And that the thridde, and so forth, brother,
Every cercle causing other,
Wyder than himselve was;
And thus, fro roundel to compas,
Ech aboute other goinge,
Caused of othres steringe,
And multiplying evermo,
Til that hit be so fer ygo
That hit at bothe brinkes be.
Althogh thou mowe hit not ysee
Above, hit goth yet alway under,
Although thou thenke hit a gret wonder.
And whoso seith of trouthe I varie,
Bid him proven the contrarie.
And right thus every word, ywis,
That loude or privee spoken is,
Moveth first an air aboute,
And of this moving, out of doute,
Another air anoon is meved,
As I have of the water preved,
That every cercle causeth other.
Right so of air, my leve brother;
Everich air in other stereth
More and more, and speche up bereth,
Or vois, or noise, or word, or soun,
Ay through multiplicacioun,
Til hit be atte Hous of fame;
Tak hit in ernest or in game.
NOW have I told, if thou have minde,
How speche or soun, of pure kinde,
Enclyned is upward to meve;
This, mayst thou fele, wel I preve.
And that the mansioun, ywis,
That every thing enclyned to is,
Hath his kindeliche stede:
Than sheweth hit, withouten drede,
That kindely the mansioun
Of every speche, of every soun,
Be hit either foul or fair,
Hath his kinde place in air.
And sin that every thing, that is
Out of his kinde place, ywis,
Moveth thider for to go
If hit aweye be therfro,
As I before have preved thee,
Hit seweth, every soun, pardee,
Moveth kindely to pace
Al up into his kindely place.
And this place of which I telle,
Ther as fame list to dwelle,
Is set amiddes of these three,
Heven, erthe, and eek the see,
As most conservatif the soun.
Than is this the conclusioun,
That every speche of every man,
As I thee telle first began,

456

Moveth up on high to pace
Kindely to fames place.
TELLE me this feithfully,
Have I not preved thus simply,
Withouten any subtiltee
Of speche, or gret prolixitee
Of termes of philosophye,
Of figures of poetrye,
Or colours of rethoryke?
Pardee, hit oghte thee to lyke;
For hard langage and hard matere
Is encombrous for to here
At ones; wost thou not wel this?
And I answerde, and seyde, Yis.
AHA! quod he, lo, so I can
Lewedly to a lewed man
Speke, and shewe him swiche skiles,
That he may shake hem by the biles,
So palpable they shulden be.
But tel me this, now pray I thee,
How thinkth thee my conclusioun?
Quod he. A good persuasioun,
Quod I, hit is; and lyk to be
Right so as thou hast preved me.
By God, quod he, and as I leve,
Thou shalt have yit, or hit be eve,
Of every word of this sentence
A preve, by experience;
And with thyn eres heren wel
Top and tail, and everydel,
That every word that spoken is
Comth into fames Hous, ywis,
As I have seyd; what wilt thou more?
And with this word upper to sore
He gan, and seyde: By Seynt Jame!
Now wil we speken al of game.
NOW farest thou? quod he to me.
Wel, quod I. Now see, quod he,
By thy trouthe, yond adoun,
Wher that thou knowest any toun,
Or hous, or any other thing.
And whan thou hast of ought knowing,
Loke that thou warne me,
And I anoon shal telle thee
How fer that thou art now therfro.
AND I adoun gan loken tho,
And beheld feldes and plaines,
And now hilles, and now mountaines,
Now valeys, and now forestes,
And now, unethes, grete bestes;
Now riveres, now citees,
Now tounes, and now grete trees,
Now shippes sailinge in the see.
BUT thus sone in a whyle he
Was flowen fro the grounde so
hyë,
That al the world, as to myn yë,
No more semed than a prikke;
Or elles was the air so thikke
That I ne mighte not discerne.
With that he spak to me as yerne,
And seyde: Seestow any toun
Or ought thou knowest yonder doun?

I SEYDE Nay. No wonder nis,
Quod he, for half so high as this
Nas Alexander Macedo;
Ne the king, dan Scipio,
That saw in dreme, at point devys,
Helle and erthe, and paradys;
Ne eek the wrecche Dedalus,
Ne his child, nyce Icarus,
That fleigh so highe that the hete
His winges malt, and he fel wete
Inmid the see, and ther he dreynte,
For whom was maked moch compleynte.
NOW turn upward, quod he, thy face,
And behold this large place,
This air; but loke thou ne be
Adrad of hem that thou shalt see;
For in this regioun, certein,
Dwelleth many a citezein,
Of which that speketh dan Plato.
These ben the eyrish bestes, lo!
AND so saw I al that meynee
Bothe goon and also flee.
Now, quod he tho, cast up
thyn yë;
See yonder, lo, the Galaxyë,
Which men clepeth the Milky Wey,
For hit is whyt: and somme, parfey,
Callen hit Watlinge Strete:
That ones was ybrent with hete,
Whan the sonnes sone, the rede,
That highte Pheton, wolde lede
Algate his fader cart, and gye.
The cart-hors gonne wel espye
That he ne coude no governaunce,
And gonne for to lepe and launce,
And beren him now up, now doun,
Til that he saw the Scorpioun,
Which that in heven a signe is yit.
And he, for ferde, loste his wit,
Of that, and leet the reynes goon
Of his hors; and they anoon
Gonne up to mounte, and doun descende
Til bothe the eyr and erthe brende;
Til Jupiter, lo, atte laste,
Him slow, and fro the carte caste.
Lo, is it not a greet mischaunce,
To lete a fole han governaunce
Of thing that he can not demeine?
AND with this word, soth for to seyne,
He gan alway upper to sore,
And gladded me ay more and more,
So feithfully to me spak he.
THO gan I loken under me,
And beheld the eyrish bestes,
Cloudes, mistes, and tempestes,
Snowes, hailes, reines, windes,
And thengendring in hir kindes,
And al the wey through whiche I cam;
O God, quod I, that made Adam,
Moche is thy might and thy noblesse!
AND tho thoughte I upon Boëce,
That writ: A thought may flee so hyë,
With fetheres of Philosophye,

457

To passen everich element;
And whan he hath so fer ywent,
Than may be seen, behind his bak,
Cloud, and al that I of spak.

THO gan I wexen in a were,
And seyde: I woot wel I am here;
But wher in body or in gost
I noot, ywis; but God, thou wost!
For more cleer entendement
Nadde he me never yit ysent.
And than thoughte I on Marcian,
And eek on Anteclaudian,
That sooth was hir descripcioun
Of al the hevenes regioun,
As fer as that I saw the preve;
Therfor I can hem now beleve.

WITH that this egle gan to crye:
Lat be, quod he, thy fantasye;
Wilt thou lere of sterres aught?
Nay, certeinly, quod I, right naught;
And why? for I am now to old.
Elles I wolde thee have told,
Quod he, the sterres names, lo,
And al the hevenes signes to,
And which they been. No fors, quod I.
Yis, pardee, quod he; wostow why?
For whan thou redest poetrye,
How goddes gonne stellifye
Brid, fish, beste, or him or here,
As the Raven, or either Bere,
Or Ariones harpe fyn,
Castor, Pollux, or Delphyn,
Or Atlantes doughtres sevene,
How alle these arn set in hevene;
For though thou have hem ofte on honde,
Yet nostow not wher that they stonde.
NO fors, quod I, hit is no nede;
I leve as wel, so God me spede,
Hem that wryte of this matere,
As though I knew hir places here;
And eek they shynen here so brighte,
Hit shulde shenden al my sighte,
To loke on hem. That may wel be,
Quod he. And so forth bar he me
A whyl, and than he gan to crye,
That never herde I thing so hye:
Now up the heed; for al is wel;
Seynt Julyan, lo, bon hostel!
See here the Hous of Fame, lo!
Maistow not heren that I do?
WHAT? quod I. The grete soun,
Quod he, that rumbleth up and doun
In Fames Hous, ful of tydinges,
Bothe of fair speche and chydinges,
And of fals and soth compouned.
Herkne wel; hit is not rouned.
Herestow not the grete swogh?
Yis, pardee, quod I, wel ynogh.
And what soun is it lyk? quod he.

Peter! lyk beting of the see,
Quod I, again the roches holowe,
Whan tempest doth the shippes
swalowe;
And lat a man stonde, out of doute,
A myle thens, and here hit route;
Or elles lyk the last humblinge
After the clappe of a thundringe,
When Joves hath the air ybete;
But hit doth me for fere swete.
Nay, dred thee not therof, quod he,
Hit is nothing wil byten thee;
Thou shalt non harm have, trewely.
AND with this word bothe he and I
As nigh the place arryved were
As men may casten with a spere.
I nistë how, but in a strete
He sette me faire on my fete,
And seyde: Walke forth a pas,
And tak thyn aventure or cas,
That thou shalt finde in Fames place.
NOW, quod I, whyl we han space
To spek, or that I go fro thee,
For the love of God, tel me,
In sooth, that wil I of thee lere,
If this noise that I here
Be, as I have herd thee tellen,
Of folk that doun in erthe dwellen,
And comth here in the same wyse
As I thee herde or this devyse;
And that ther lyves body nis
In al that hous that yonder is,
That maketh al this loude fare?
NO, quod he, by Seynte Clare,
And also wis God rede me!
But o thinge I wil warne thee
Of the which thou wolt have wonder.
Lo, to the Hous of Fame yonder
Thou wost how cometh every speche,
Hit nedeth noght thee eft to teche.
But understond now right wel this;
Whan any speche ycomen is
Up to the paleys, anon right
Hit wexeth lyk the same wight,
Which that the word in erthe spak,
Be hit clothed reed or blak;
And hath so verray his lyknesse
That spak the word, that thou wilt gesse
That hit the same body be,
Man or woman, he or she.
And is not this a wonder thing?
Yis, quod I tho, by hevene king!
And with this worde: Farwel, quod he,
And here I wol abyden thee;
And God of hevene sende thee grace,
Som good to lernen in this place.
And I of him took leve anoon,
And gan forth to the paleys goon.
Explicit liber secundus.

458

Incipit Liber Tercius ❧ Invocation.

O GOD OF SCIENCE AND OF LIGHT,
Apollo, through thy grete might,
This litel laste book thou gye!
Nat that I wilne, for maistrye,
Here art poetical be shewed;
But, for the rym is light and lewed,
Yit make hit sumwhat agreable,
Though som vers faile in a sillable;

And that I do no diligence
To shewe craft, but o sentence.
And if, divyne vertu, thou
Wilt helpe me to shewe now
That in myn hede ymarked is,
Lo, that is for to menen this,
The Hous of fame to descryve,
Thou shalt see me go, as blyve,
Unto the nexte laure I see,
And kisse hit, for hit is thy tree;
Now entreth in my breste anoon !...

The Dream.

W HAN I was fro this egle goon,
I gan beholde upon this place.
And certein, or I ferther pace,
I wol yow al the shap devyse
Of hous and site; and al the wyse
How I gan to this place aproche
That stood upon so high a roche,
Hyer stant ther noon in Spaine.
But up I clomb with alle paine,
And though to climbe hit greved me,
Yit I ententif was to see,
And for to pouren wonder lowe,
If I coude any weyes knowe
What maner stoon this roche was;

for hit was lyk a thing of glas,
But that hit shoon ful more clere;
But of what congeled matere
Hit was, I niste redely.
BUT at the laste espyed I,
And found that hit was, every deel,
A roche of yse, and not of steel.
Thoughte I: By Seynt Thomas of Kent!
This were a feble foundement
To bilden on a place hye;
He oughte him litel glorifye
That heron bilt, God so me save!
THO saw I al the half ygrave
With famous folkes names fele,
That had ybeen in mochel wele,
And hir fames wyde yblowe.
But wel unethes coude I knowe
Any lettres for to rede
Hir names by; for, out of drede,
They were almost of/thowed so,
That of the lettres oon or two
Was molte away of every name,
So unfamous was wexe hir fame;
But men seyn: What may ever laste?
THO gan I in myn herte caste,
That they were molte awey with hete,
And not awey with stormes bete.
for on that other syde I sey
Of this hille, that northward lay,
How hit was writen ful of names
Of folk that hadden grete fames
Of olde tyme, and yit they were
As fresshe as men had writen hem there
The selve day right, or that houre
That I upon hem gan to poure.
But wel I wiste what hit made;
Hit was conserved with the shade,
Al this wrytinge that I sy,
Of a castel, that stood on hy,
And stood eek on so cold a place,
That hete mighte hit not deface.
THO gan I up the hille to goon,
And fond upon the coppe a woon,
That alle the men that ben on lyve
Ne han the cunning to descryve
The beautee of that ilke place,
Ne coude casten no compace
Swich another for to make,
That mighte of beautee be his make,
Ne be so wonderliche ywrought;
That hit astonieth yit my thought,
And maketh al my wit to swinke
On this castel to bethinke.
So that the grete craft, beautee,
The cast, the curiositee
Ne can I not to yow devyse,
My wit ne may me not suffyse.
BUT natheles al the substance
I have yit in my remembrance;
forwhy me thoughte, by Seynt Gyle!
Al was of stone of beryle,
Bothe castel and the tour,
And eek the halle, and every bour,

Withouten peces or joininges.
But many subtil compassinges,
Babewinnes and pinacles,
Imageries and tabernacles,
I saw; and ful eek of windowes,
As flakes falle in grete snowes.
And eek in ech of the pinacles
Weren sondry habitacles,
In whiche stoden, al withoute,
ful the castel, al aboute,
Of alle maner of minstrales,
And gestiours, that tellen tales
Bothe of weping and of game,
Of al that longeth unto fame.
THER herde I pleyen on an harpe
That souned bothe wel and sharpe,
Orpheus ful craftely,
And on his syde, faste by,
Sat the harper Orion,
And Eacides Chiron,
And other harpers many oon,
And the Bret Glascurion;
And smale harpers with her gleës
Seten under hem in seës,
And gonne on hem upward to gape,
And countrefete hem as an ape,
Or as craft countrefeteth kinde.
THO saugh I stonden hem behinde,
Afer fro hem, al by hemselve,
Many thousand tymes twelve,
That maden loude menstralcyes
In cornemuse and shalmyes,
And many other maner pype,
That craftely begunne pype
Bothe in doucet and in rede,
That ben at festes with the brede;
And many floute and lilting/horne,
And pypes made of grene corne,
As han thise litel herde/gromes,
That kepen bestes in the bromes.
THER saugh I than Atiteris,
And of Athenes dan Pseustis,
And Marcia that lost her skin,
Bothe in face, body, and chin,
for that she wolde envyen, lo!
To pypen bet then Apollo.
Ther saugh I famous, olde and yonge,
Pypers of the Duche tonge,
To lerne love/daunces, springes,
Reyes, and these straunge thinges.
THO saugh I in another place
Stonden in a large space,
Of hem that maken blody soun
In trumpe, beme, and clarioun;
for in fight and blood/shedinge
Is used gladly clarioninge.
THER herde I trumpen Messenus,
Of whom that speketh Virgilius.
Ther herde I Joab trumpe also,
Theodomas, and other mo;
And alle that used clarion
In Cataloigne and Aragon,
That in hir tyme famous were

To lerne, saugh I trumpe there.
THER saugh I sitte in other seës,
Pleyinge upon sondry gleës,
Whiche that I cannot nevene,
Mo then sterres been in hevene,
Of whiche I nil as now not ryme,
For ese of yow, and losse of tyme:
For tyme ylost, this knowen ye,
By no way may recovered be.
THER saugh I pleyen jogelours,
Magiciens and tregetours,
And phitonesses, charmeresses,
Olde wicches, sorceresses,
That use exorsisaciouns,
And eek thise fumigaciouns;
And clerkes eek, which conne wel
Al this magyke naturel,
That craftely don hir ententes,
To make in certeyn ascendentes,
Images, lo, through which magyk
To make a man ben hool or syk.
Ther saugh I thee, queen Medea,
And Circes eke, and Calipsa;
Ther saugh I Hermes Ballenus,
Lymote, and eek Simon Magus.
Ther saugh I, and knew hem by name,
That by such art don men han fame.
Ther saugh I Colle tregetour
Upon a table of sicamour
Pleye an uncouth thing to telle;
I saugh him carien a wind-melle
Under a walsh-note shale.
WHAT shuld I make lenger tale
Of al the peple that I say,
Fro hennes into domesday?
WHAN I had al this folk beholde,
And fond me lous, and noght yholde,
And eft ymused longe whyle
Upon these walles of beryle,
That shoon ful lighter than a glas,
And made wel more than hit was
To semen, every thing, ywis,
As kinde thing of fames is;
I gan forth romen til I fond
The castel-yate on my right hond,
Which that so wel corven was
That never swich another nas;
And yit hit was by aventure
Ywrought, as often as by cure.
HIT nedeth noght yow for to tellen,
To make yow to longe dwellen,
Of this yates florisshinges,
Ne of compasses, ne of kervinges,
Ne how they hatte in masoneries,
As, corbets fulle of imageries.
But, Lord! so fair hit was to shewe,
For hit was al with gold behewe.
But in I wente, and that anoon;
Ther mette I crying many oon:
A larges, larges, hold up wel!
God save the lady of this pel,
Oure owne gentil lady Fame,
And hem that wilnen to have name

Of us! Thus herde I cryen alle,
And faste comen out of halle,
And shoken nobles and sterlinges.
And somme crouned were as kinges,
With crounes wroght ful of losenges;
And many riban, and many frenges
Were on hir clothes trewely.
THO atte laste aspyed I
That pursevauntes and heraudes,
That cryen riche folkes laudes,
Hit weren alle; and every man
Of hem, as I yow tellen can,
Had on him thrown a vesture,
Which that men clepe a cote-armure,
Enbrowded wonderliche riche,
Although they nere nought yliche.
But noght nil I, so mote I thryve,
Been aboute to discryve
Al these armes that ther weren,
That they thus on hir cotes beren,
For hit to me were impossible;
Men mighte make of hem a bible
Twenty foot thikke, as I trowe.
For certeyn, whoso coude yknowe
Mighte ther alle the armes seen
Of famous folk that han ybeen
In Auffrike, Europe, and Asye,
Sith first began the chevalrye.
O! how shulde I now telle al this?
Ne of the halle eek what nede is
To tellen yow, that every wal
Of hit, and floor, and roof and al
Was plated half a fote thikke
Of gold, and that nas nothing wikke,
But, for to prove in alle wyse,
As fyn as ducat in Venyse,
Of whiche to lyte al in my pouche is?
And they wer set as thikke of nouchis
Fulle of the fynest stones faire,
That men rede in the Lapidaire,
As greses growen in a mede;
But hit were al to longe to rede
The names; and therfore I pace.
BUT in this riche lusty place,
That Fames halle called was,
Ful moche prees of folk ther nas,
Ne crouding, for to mochil prees.
But al on hye, above a dees,
Sitte in a see imperial,
That maad was of a rubee al,
Which that a carbuncle is ycalled,
I saugh, perpetually ystalled,
A feminyne creature;
That never formed by nature
Nas swich another thing yseye.
For altherfirst, soth for to seye,
Me thoughte that she was so lyte,
That the lengthe of a cubyte
Was lenger than she semed be;
But thus sone, in a whyle, she
Hir tho so wonderliche streighte,
That with hir feet she therthe reighte,
And with hir heed she touched hevene,

461

Ther as shynen sterres sevene.
And therto eek, as to my wit,
I saugh a gretter wonder yit,
Upon hir eyen to beholde;
But certeyn I hem never tolde;
For as fele eyen hadde she
As fetheres upon foules be,
Or weren on the bestes foure,
That Goddes trone gunne honoure,
As John writ in thapocalips.
Hir heer, that oundy was and crips,
As burned gold hit shoon to see.
And sooth to tellen, also she
Had also fele upstonding eres
And tonges, as on bestes heres;
And on hir feet wexen saugh I
Partriches winges redely.
BUT, Lord! the perrie and the richesse
I saugh sitting on this goddesse!
And, Lord! the hevenish melodye
Of songes, ful of armonye,
I herde aboute her trone ysonge,
That al the paleys-walles ronge!
So song the mighty Muse, she
That cleped is Caliopee,
And hir eighte sustren eke,
That in hir face semen meke;
And evermo, eternally,
They songe of fame, as tho herde I:
Heried be thou and thy name,
Goddesse of renoun and of fame!
THO was I war, lo, atte laste,
As I myn eyen gan up caste,
That this ilke noble quene
On hir shuldres gan sustene
Bothe tharmes and the name
Of tho that hadde large fame;
Alexander, and Hercules
That with a sherte his lyf lees!
Thus fond I sitting this goddesse,
In nobley, honour, and richesse;
Of which I stinte a whyle now,
Other thing to tellen yow.
THO saugh I stonde on either syde,
Streight doun to the dores wyde,
Fro the dees, many a pileer
Of metal, that shoon not ful cleer;
But though they nere of no richesse,
Yet they were maad for greet noblesse,
And in hem greet and by sentence;
And folk of digne reverence,
Of whiche I wol yow telle fonde,
Upon the piler saugh I stonde.
ALDERFIRST, lo, ther I sigh,
Upon a piler stonde on high,
That was of lede and yren fyn,
Him of secte Saturnyn,
The Ebrayk Josephus, the olde,
That of Jewes gestes tolde;
And bar upon his shuldres hye
The fame up of the Jewerye.
And by him stoden other sevene,
Wyse and worthy for to nevene,

462

To helpen him bere up the charge,
Hit was so hevy and so large.
And for they writen of batailes,
As wel as other olde mervailes,
Therfor was, lo, this pileer,
Of which that I yow telle heer,
Of lede and yren bothe, ywis.
For yren Martes metal is,
Which that god is of bataile;
And the leed, withouten faile,
Is, lo, the metal of Saturne,
That hath ful large wheel to turne.
Tho stoden forth, on every rowe,
Of hem which that I coude knowe,
Thogh I hem noght by ordre telle,
To make yow to long to dwelle,
These, of whiche I ginne rede.
THER saugh I stonden, out of drede,
Upon an yren piler strong,
That peynted was, al endelong,
With tygres blode in every place,
The Tholosan that highte Stace,
That bar of Thebes up the fame
Upon his shuldres, and the name
Also of cruel Achilles.
And by him stood, withouten lees,
Ful wonder hye on a pileer
Of yren, he, the gret Omeer;
And with him Dares and Tytus
Before, and eek he, Lollius,
And Guido eek de Columpnis,
And English Gaufride eek, ywis;
And ech of these, as have I joye,
Was besy for to bere up Troye.
So hevy therof was the fame,
That for to bere hit was no game.
But yit I gan ful wel espye,
Betwix hem was a litel envye.
Oon seyde, Omere made lyes,
Feyninge in his poetryes,
And was to Grekes favorable;
Therfor held he hit but fable.
THO saugh I stonde on a pileer,
That was of tinned yren cleer,
That Latin poete, dan Virgyle,
That bore hath up a longe whyle
The fame of Pius Eneas.
AND next him on a piler was,
Of coper, Venus clerk, Ovyde,
That hath ysowen wonder wyde
The grete god of Loves name.
And ther he bar up wel his fame,
Upon this piler, also hye
As I might see hit with myn yë:
Forwhy this halle, of whiche I rede
Was woxe on highte, lengthe and brede,
Wel more, by a thousand del,
Than hit was erst, that saugh I wel.
THO saugh I, on a piler by,
Of yren wroght ful sternely,
The grete poete, daun Lucan,
And on his shuldres bar up than,
As highe as that I mighte see,

The fame of Julius and Pompee.
And by him stoden alle these clerkes,
That writen of Romes mighty werkes,
That, if I wolde hir names telle,
Al to longe moste I dwelle.
AND next him on a piler stood
Of soulfre, lyk as he were wood,
Dan Claudian, the soth to telle,
That bar up al the fame of helle,
Of Pluto, and of Proserpyne,
That quene is of the derke pyne.
WHAT shulde I more telle of this?
The halle was al ful, ywis,
Of hem that writen olde gestes,
As ben on treës rokes nestes;
But hit a ful confus matere
Were al the gestes for to here,
That they of write, and how they highte.
But whyl that I beheld this sighte,
I herde a noise aprochen blyve,
That ferde as been don in an hyve,
Agen her tyme of out-fleyinge;
Right swiche a maner murmuringe,
For al the world, hit semed me.
THO gan I loke aboute and see,
That ther com entring in the halle
A right gret company withalle,
And that of sondry regiouns,
Of alleskinnes condiciouns,
That dwelle in erthe under the mone,
Pore and ryche. And also sone
As they were come into the halle,
They gonne doun on kneës falle
Before this ilke noble quene,
And seyde: Graunte us, lady shene,
Ech of us, of thy grace, a bone!
And somme of hem she graunted sone,
And somme she werned wel and faire;
And somme she graunted the contraire
Of hir axing utterly.
But thus I seye yow trewely,
What hir cause was, I niste.
For this folk, ful wel I wiste,
They hadde good fame ech deserved,
Althogh they were diversly served;
Right as hir suster, dame Fortune,
Is wont to serven in comune.
NOW herkne how she gan to paye
That gonne hir of hir grace praye;
And yit, lo, al this companye
Seyden sooth, and noght a lye.
MADAME, seyden they, we be
Folk that heer besechen thee,
That thou graunte us now good
fame,
And lete our werkes han that name;
In ful recompensacioun
Of good werk, give us good renoun.
I WERNE yow hit, quod she anoon,
Ye gete of me good fame noon,
By God! and therfor go your wey.
Alas, quod they, and welaway!
Telle us, what may your cause be?

FOR me list hit noght, quod she;
No wight shal speke of yow, ywis,
Good ne harm, ne that ne this.
And with that word she gan to calle
Hir messanger, that was in halle,
And bad that he shulde faste goon,
Up peyne to be blind anoon,
For Eolus, the god of winde;
In Trace ther ye shul him finde,
And bid him bringe his clarioun,
That is ful dyvers of his soun,
And hit is cleped Clere Laude,
With which he wont is to heraude
Hem that me list ypreised be:
And also bid him how that he
Bringe his other clarioun,
That highte Sclaundre in every toun,
With which he wont is to diffame
Hem that me list, and do hem shame.
THIS messanger gan faste goon,
And found wher, in a cave of stoon,
In a contree that highte Trace,
This Eolus, with harde grace,
Held the windes in distresse,
And gan hem under him to presse,
That they gonne as beres rore,
He bond and pressed hem so sore.
THIS messanger gan faste crye:
Rys up, quod he, and faste hye,
Til that thou at my lady be;
And tak thy clarions eek with thee,
And speed thee forth. And he anon
Took to a man, that hight Triton,
His clariouns to bere tho,
And leet a certeyn wind to go,
That blew so hidously and hye,
That hit ne lefte not a skye
In al the welken longe and brood.
THIS Eolus nowher abood
Til he was come at Fames feet,
And eek the man that Triton heet;
And ther he stood, as still as stoon.
And herwithal ther com anoon
Another huge companye
Of gode folk, and gunne crye:
Lady, graunte us now good fame,
And lat our werkes han that name
Now, in honour of gentilesse,
And also God your soule blesse!
For we han wel deserved hit,
Therfor is right that we ben quit.
AS thryve I, quod she, ye shal faile,
Good werkes shal yow noght availe
To have of me good fame as now.
But wite ye what? I graunte yow,
That ye shal have a shrewed fame
And wikked loos, and worse name,
Though ye good loos have wel deserved.
Now go your wey, for ye be served;
And thou, dan Eolus, let see!
Tak forth thy trumpe anon, quod she,
That is ycleped Sclaunder light,
And blow hir loos, that every wight

Speke of hem harm and shrewednesse,
In stede of good and worthinesse.
For thou shalt trumpe al the contraire
Of that they han don wel or faire.
ALAS! thoughte I, what aventures
Han these sory creatures!
For they, amonges al the pres,
Shul thus be shamed gilteles!
But what! hit moste nedes be.
WHAT did this Eolus, but he
Tok out his blakke trumpe of bras,
That fouler than the devil was,
And gan this trumpe for to blowe,
As al the world shulde overthrowe;
That throughout every regioun
Wente this foule trumpes soun,
As swift as pelet out of gonne,
Whan fyr is in the poudre ronne.
And swiche a smoke gan out wende
Out of his foule trumpes ende,
Blak, blo, grenish, swartish reed,
As doth wher that men melte leed,
Lo, al on high fro the tuel!
And therto oo thing saugh I wel,
That, the ferther that hit ran,
The gretter wexen hit began,
As doth the river from a welle,
And hit stank as the pit of helle.

Allas, thus was hir shame yronge,
And giltelees, on every tonge.
THO com the thridde companye,
And gunne up to the dees to hye,
And doun on knees they fille anon,
And seyde: We ben everichon
Folk that han ful trewely
Deserved fame rightfully,
And praye yow, hit mot be knowe,
Right as hit is, and forth yblowe.
I graunte, quod she, for me list
That now your gode werk be wist;
And yit ye shul han better loos,
Right in dispyt of alle your foos,
Than worthy is; and that anoon:
Lat now, quod she, thy trumpe goon,
Thou Eolus, that is so blak;
And out thyn other trumpe tak
That highte Laude, and blow hit so
That through the world hir fame go
Al esely, and not to faste,
That hit be knowen atte laste.
FUL gladly, lady myn, he seyde;
And out his trumpe of golde he
brayde
Anon, and sette hit to his mouthe,
And blew hit est, and west, and southe,
And north, as loude as any thunder,

That every wight hadde of hit wonder,
So brode hit ran, or than hit stente.
And, certes, al the breeth that wente
Out of his trumpes mouthe smelde
As men a potful bawme helde
Among a basket ful of roses;
This favour dide he til her loses.
AND right with this I gan aspye,
Ther com the ferthe companye,
But certeyn they were wonder fewe,
And gonne stonden in a rewe,
And seyden: Certes, lady brighte,
We han don wel with al our mighte;
But we ne kepen have no fame.
Hyd our werkes and our name,
For Goddes love! for certes we
Han certeyn doon hit for bountee,
And for no maner other thing.
I graunte yow al your asking,
Quod she; let your werk be deed.
WITH that aboute I clew myn heed,
And saugh anoon the fifte route
That to this lady gonne loute,
And doun on knees anoon to falle;
And to hir tho besoughten alle
To hyde hir gode werkes eek,
And seyde, they yeven noght a leek
For fame, ne for swich renoun;
For they, for contemplacioun
And Goddes love, hadde ywrought;
Ne of fame wolde they nought.
WHAT? quod she, and be ye wood?
And wene ye for to do good,
And for to have of that no fame?
Have ye dispyt to have my name?
Nay, ye shul liven everichoon!
Blow thy trumpe and that anoon,
Quod she, thou Eolus, I hote,
And ring this folkes werk by note,
That al the world may of hit here.
And he gan blowe hir loos so clere
In his golden clarioun,
That through the world wente the soun,
So kenely, and eek so softe;
But atte laste hit was on-lofte.
THOO com the sexte companye,
And gonne faste on Fame crye.
Right verraily, in this manere
They seyden: Mercy, lady dere!
To telle certein, as hit is,
We han don neither that ne this,
But ydel al our lyf ybe.
But, natheles, yit preye we,
That we mowe han so good a fame,
And greet renoun and knowen name,
As they that han don noble gestes,
And acheved alle hir lestes,
As wel of love as other thing;
Al was us never broche ne ring,
Ne elles nought, from wimmen sent,
Ne ones in hir herte yment
To make us only frendly chere,
But mighte temen us on bere;
hh 1

Yit lat us to the peple seme
Swiche as the world may of us deme,
That wimmen loven us for wood.
Hit shal don us as moche good,
And to our herte as moche availe
To countrepeise ese and travaile,
As we had wonne hit with labour;
For that is dere boght honour
At regard of our grete ese.
And yit thou most us more plese;
Let us be holden eek, therto,
Worthy, wyse, and gode also,
And riche, and happy unto love.
For Goddes love, that sit above,
Though we may not the body have
Of wimmen, yet, so God yow save!
Let men glewe on us the name;
Suffyceth that we han the fame.
I GRAUNTE, quod she, by my trouthe!
Now, Eolus, withouten slouthe,
Tak out thy trumpe of gold, let see,
And blow as they han axed me,
That every man wene hem at ese,
Though they gon in ful badde lese.
This Eolus gan hit so blowe,
That through the world hit was yknowe.
THO com the seventh route anoon,
And fel on knees everichoon,
And seyde: Lady, graunte us sone
The same thing, the same bone,
That ye this nexte folk han doon.
Fy on yow, quod she, everichoon!
Ye masty swyn, ye ydel wrecches,
Ful of roten slowe tecches!
What? false theves! wher ye wolde
Be famous good, and nothing nolde
Deserve why, ne never roughte?
Men rather yow tohangen oughte!
For ye be lyk the sweynte cat,
That wolde have fish; but wostow what?
He wolde nothing wete his clowes.
Yvel thrift come on your jowes,
And eek on myn, if I hit graunte,
Or do yow favour, yow to avaunte!
Thou Eolus, thou king of Trace!
Go, blow this folk a sory grace,
Quod she, anoon; and wostow how?
As I shal telle thee right now;
Sey: These ben they that wolde honour
Have, and do noskinnes labour,
Ne do no good, and yit han laude;
And that men wende that bele Isaude
Ne coude hem noght of love werne;
And yit she that grint at a querne
Is al to good to ese hir herte.
THIS Eolus anon up sterte,
And with his blakke clarioun
He gan to blasen out a soun,
As loude as belweth wind in helle.
And eek therwith, the sooth to telle,
This soun was al so ful of japes,
As ever mowes were in apes.
And that wente al the world aboute,

That every wight gan on hem shoute,
And for to laughe as they were wode;
Such game fonde they in hir hode.

THo com another companye,
That had ydoon the traiterye,
The harm, the gretest wikkednesse
That any herte couthe gesse;
And preyed hir to han good fame,
And that she nolde hem doon no shame,
But yeve hem loos and good renoun,
And do hit blowe in clarioun.
Nay, wis! quod she, hit were a vyce;
Al be ther in me no justyce,
Me listeth not to do hit now,
Ne this nil I not graunte yow.

THo come ther lepinge in a route,
And gonne choppen al aboute
Every man upon the croune,
That al the halle gan to soune,
And seyden: Lady, lefe and dere,
We ben swich folk as ye mowe here,
To tellen al the tale aright,
We ben shrewes, every wight,
And han delyt in wikkednes,
As gode folk han in goodnes;
And joye to be knowen shrewes,
And fulle of vyce and wikked thewes;

Wherfor we preyen yow, a-rowe,
That our fame swich be knowe
In alle thing right as hit is.

I GRAUNTE hit yow, quod she, ywis.
But what art thou that seyst this tale,
That werest on thy hose a pale,
And on thy tipet swiche a belle!
Madame, quod he, sooth to telle,
I am that ilke shrewe, ywis,
That brende the temple of Isidis
In Athenes, lo, that citee.
And wherfor didest thou so? quod she.
By my thrift, quod he, madame,
I wolde fayn han had a fame,
As other folk hadde in the toun,
Althogh they were of greet renoun
For hir vertu and for hir thewes;
Thoughte I, as greet a fame han shrewes,
Thogh hit be but for shrewednesse,
As gode folk han for goodnesse;
And sith I may not have that oon,
That other nil I noght forgoon.
And for to gette of fames hyre,
The temple sette I al afyre.
Now do our loos be blowen swythe,
As wisly be thou ever blythe.
Gladly, quod she; thou Eolus,

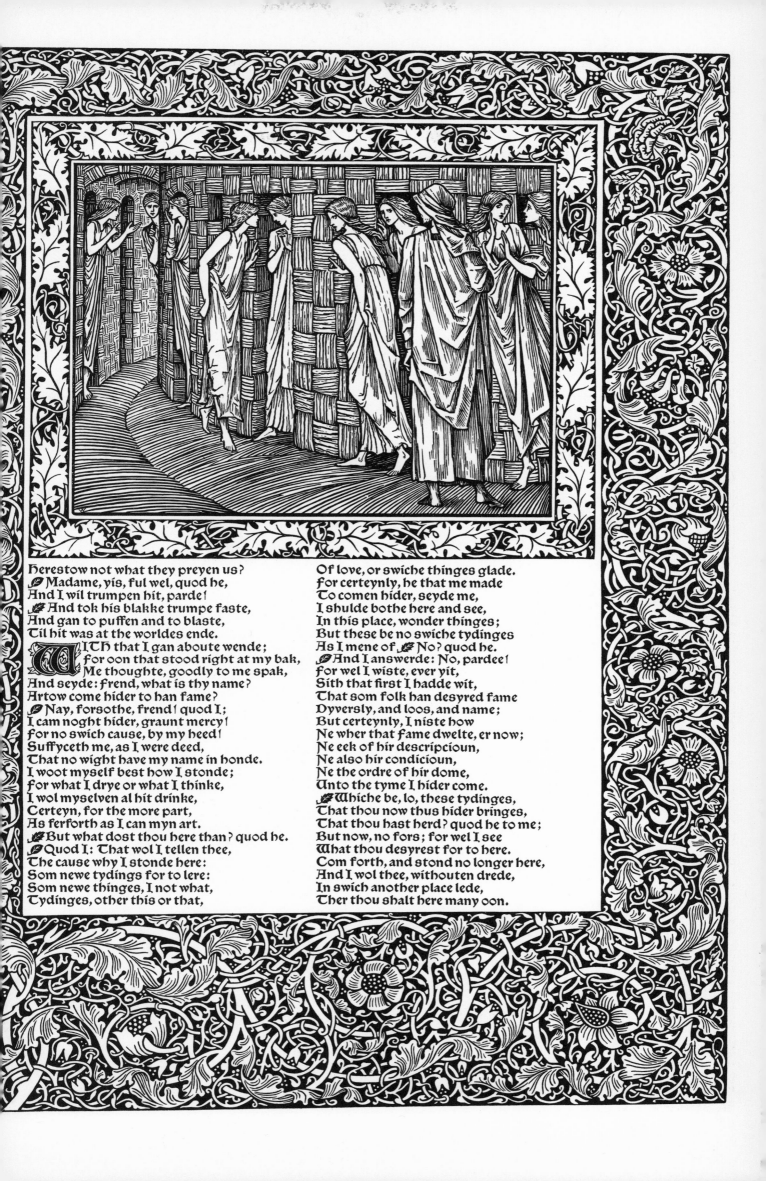

Herestow not what they preyen us?
  Madame, yis, ful wel, quod he,
And I wil trumpen hit, parde!
  And tok his blakke trumpe faste,
And gan to puffen and to blaste,
Til hit was at the worldes ende.
WITH that I gan aboute wende;
    for oon that stood right at my bak,
    Me thoughte, goodly to me spak,
And seyde: frend, what is thy name?
Artow come hider to han fame?
  Nay, forsothe, frend! quod I;
I cam noght hider, graunt mercy!
for no swich cause, by my heed!
Suffyceth me, as I were deed,
That no wight have my name in honde.
I woot myself best how I stonde;
for what I drye or what I thinke,
I wol myselven al hit drinke,
Certeyn, for the more part,
As ferforth as I can myn art.
  But what dost thou here than? quod he.
  Quod I: That wol I tellen thee,
The cause why I stonde here:
Som newe tydings for to lere:
Som newe thinges, I not what,
Tydinges, other this or that,

Of love, or swiche thinges glade.
for certeynly, he that me made
To comen hider, seyde me,
I shulde bothe here and see,
In this place, wonder thinges;
But these be no swiche tydinges
As I mene of. No? quod he.
  And I answerde: No, pardee!
for wel I wiste, ever yit,
Sith that first I hadde wit,
That som folk han desyred fame
Dyversly, and loos, and name;
But certeynly, I niste how
Ne wher that fame dwelte, er now;
Ne eek of hir descripcioun,
Ne also hir condicioun,
Ne the ordre of hir dome,
Unto the tyme I hider come.
  Whiche be, lo, these tydinges,
That thou now thus hider bringes,
That thou hast herd? quod he to me;
But now, no fors; for wel I see
What thou desyrest for to here.
Com forth, and stond no longer here,
And I wol thee, withouten drede,
In swich another place lede,
Ther thou shalt here many oon.

THO gan I forth with him to goon
Out of the castel, soth to seye.
Tho saugh I stonde in a valeye,
Under the castel, faste by,
An hous, that domus Dedali,
That Laborintus cleped is,
Nas maad so wonderliche, ywis,
Ne half so queynteliche ywrought.
And evermo, so swift as thought,
This queynte hous aboute wente,
That nevermo hit stille stente.
And therout com so greet a noise,
That, had hit stonden upon Oise,
Men mighte hit han herd esely
To Rome, I trowe sikerly.
And the noyse which that I herde,
For al the world right so hit ferde,
As doth the routing of the stoon
That from thengyn is leten goon.

AND al this hous, of whiche I rede,
Was made of twigges, falwe, rede,
And grene eek, and som weren
whyte,
Swiche as men to these cages thwyte,
Or maken of these paniers,
Or elles hottes or dossers;
That, for the swough and for the
twigges,
This hous was also ful of gigges,
And also ful eek of chirkinges,
And of many other werkinges;
And eek this hous hath of entrees
As fele as leves been on trees
In somer, whan they grene been;
And on the roof men may yit seen
A thousand holes, and wel mo,
To leten wel the soun out go.

AND by day, in every tyde,
Ben al the dores open wyde,
And by night, echoon, unshette;
Ne porter ther is non to lette
No maner tydings in to pace;
Ne never reste is in that place,
That hit nis fild ful of tydinges,
Other loude, or of whispringes;
And, over alle the houses angles,
Is ful of rouninges and of jangles
Of werre, of pees, of mariages,
Of reste, of labour of viages,
Of abood, of deeth, of lyfe,
Of love, of hate, acorde, of stryfe,
Of loos, of lore, and of winninges,
Of hele, of sekenesse, of bildinges,
Of faire windes, of tempestes,
Of qualme of folk, and eek of bestes;
Of dyvers transmutaciouns
Of estats, and eek of regiouns;
Of trust, of drede, of jelousye,
Of wit, of winninge, of folye;
Of plentee, and of greet famyne,
Of chepe, of derth, and of ruyne;
Of good or mis governement,
Of fyr, of dyvers accident.

468

AND lo, this hous, of whiche I wryte,
Siker be ye, hit nas not lyte;
For hit was sixty myle of lengthe;
Al was the timber of no strengthe,
Yet hit is founded to endure
Whyl that hit list to Aventure,
That is the moder of tydinges,
As the see of welles and springes,
And hit was shapen lyk a cage.

CERTES, quod I, in al myn age,
Ne saugh I swich a hous as this.
And as I wondred me, ywis,
Upon this hous, tho war was I
How that myn egle, faste by,
Was perched hye upon a stoon;
And I gan streighte to him goon
And seyde thus: I preye thee
That thou a whyl abyde me
For Goddes love, and let me seen
What wondres in this place been;
For yit, paraventure, I may lere
Som good theron, or sumwhat here
That leef me were, or that I wente.

PETER! that is myn entente,
Quod he to me; therfor I dwelle;
But certein, oon thing I thee telle,
That, but I bringe thee therinne,
Ne shalt thou never cunne ginne
To come into hit, out of doute,
So faste hit whirleth, lo, aboute.
But sith that Joves, of his grace,
As I have seyd, wol thee solace
Fynally with swiche thinges,
Uncouthe sightes and tydinges,
To passe with thyn hevinesse;
Suche routhe hath he of thy distresse,
That thou suffrest debonairly,
And wost thyselven utterly
Disesperat of alle blis,
Sith that fortune hath maad amis
The fruit of al thyn hertes reste
Languisshe and eek in point to breste,
That he, through his mighty meryte,
Wol do thee ese, al be hit lyte,
And yaf expres commaundement,
To whiche I am obedient,
To furthre thee with al my might,
And wisse and teche thee aright
Wher thou maist most tydinges here;
Shaltow anoon heer many oon lere.

WITH this worde he, right anoon,
Hente me up bitwene his toon,
And at a windowe in me broghte,
That in this hous was, as me thoghte,
And therwithal, me thoghte hit stente,
And nothing hit aboute wente,
And me sette in the flore adoun.
But which a congregacioun
Of folk, as I saugh rome aboute
Some within and some withoute,
Nas never seen, ne shal ben eft;
That, certes, in the world nis left
So many formed by Nature,

Ne deed so many a creature;
That wel unethe, in that place,
Hadde I oon foot-brede of space;
And every wight that I saugh there
Rouned ech in otheres ere
A newe tyding prevely,
Or elles tolde al openly
Right thus, and seyde: Nost not thou
That is betid, lo, late or now?
No, quod the other, tel me what;
And than he tolde him this and that,
And swoor therto that hit was sooth:
Thus hath he seyd, and Thus he dooth:
Thus shal hit be: Thus herde I seye:
That shal be found: That dar I leye:
That al the folk that is alyve
Ne han the cunning to discryve
The thinges that I herde there,
What aloude, and what in ere.
But al the wondermost was this:
Whan oon had herd a thing, ywis,
He com forth to another wight,
And gan him tellen, anoon-right,
The same that to him was told,
Or hit a furlong-way was old,
But gan somwhat for to eche
To this tyding in this speche
More than hit ever was.
And nat so sone departed nas
That he fro him, that he ne mette
With the thridde; and, or he lette
Any stounde, he tolde him als;
Were the tyding sooth or fals,
Yit wolde he telle hit nathelees,
And evermo with more encrees
Than hit was erst. Thus north and southe
Went every word fro mouth to mouthe,
And that encresing evermo,
As fyr is wont to quikke and go
From a sparke spronge amis,
Til al a citee brent up is.
AND, whan that was ful yspronge,
And woxen more on every tonge
Than ever hit was, hit wente anoon
Up to a windowe, out to goon;
Or, but hit mighte out ther pace,
Hit gan out crepe at som crevace,
And fleigh forth faste for the nones.
AND somtyme saugh I tho, at ones,
A lesing and a sad soth-sawe,
That gonne of aventure drawe
Out at a windowe for to pace;
And, when they metten in that place,
They were a-chekked bothe two,
And neither of hem moste out go;
For other so they gonne croude,
Til eche of hem gan cryen loude:
Lat me go first! Nay, but lat me!
And here I wol ensuren thee
With the nones that thou wolt do so,
That I shal never fro thee go,
But be thyn owne sworen brother!
We wil medle us ech with other,
That no man, be he never so wrothe,
Shal han that oon of two, but bothe
At ones, al beside his leve,
Come we a-morwe or on eve,
Be we cryed or stille yrouned.
Thus saugh I fals and sooth compouned
Togeder flee for oo tydinge.
THUS out at holes gonne wringe
Every tyding streight to fame;
And she gan yeven eche his name,
After hir disposicioun,
And yaf hem eek duracioun,
Some to wexe and wane sone,
As dooth the faire whyte mone,
And leet hem gon. Ther mighte I seen
Wenged wondres faste fleen,
Twenty thousand in a route,
As Eolus hem blew aboute.
AND, Lord! this hous, in alle tymes,
Was ful of shipmen and pilgrymes,
With scrippes bretful of lesinges,
Entremedled with tydinges,
And eek alone by hemselve.
O, many a thousand tymes twelve
Saugh I eek of these pardoneres,
Currours, and eek messangeres,
With boistes crammed ful of lyes
As ever vessel was with lyes.
And as I alther-fastest wente
Aboute, and dide al myn entente
Me for to pleye and for to lere,
And eek a tyding for to here,
That I had herd of som contree
That shal not now be told for me:
For hit no nede is, redely;
Folk can singe hit bet than I;
For al mot out, other late or rathe,
Alle the sheves in the lathe:
I herde a gret noise withalle
In a corner of the halle,
Ther men of love tydings tolde,
And I gan thiderward beholde;
For I saugh renninge every wight,
As faste as that they hadden might;
And everich cryed: What thing is that?
And som seyde: I not never what.
And whan they were alle on an hepe,
Tho behinde gonne up lepe,
And clamben up on othere faste,
And up the nose on hye caste,
And troden faste on othere heles
And stampe, as men don after eles.
ATTE laste I saugh a man,
Which that I nevene naught ne can;
But he semed for to be
A man of greet auctoritee . . . .
Unfinished.

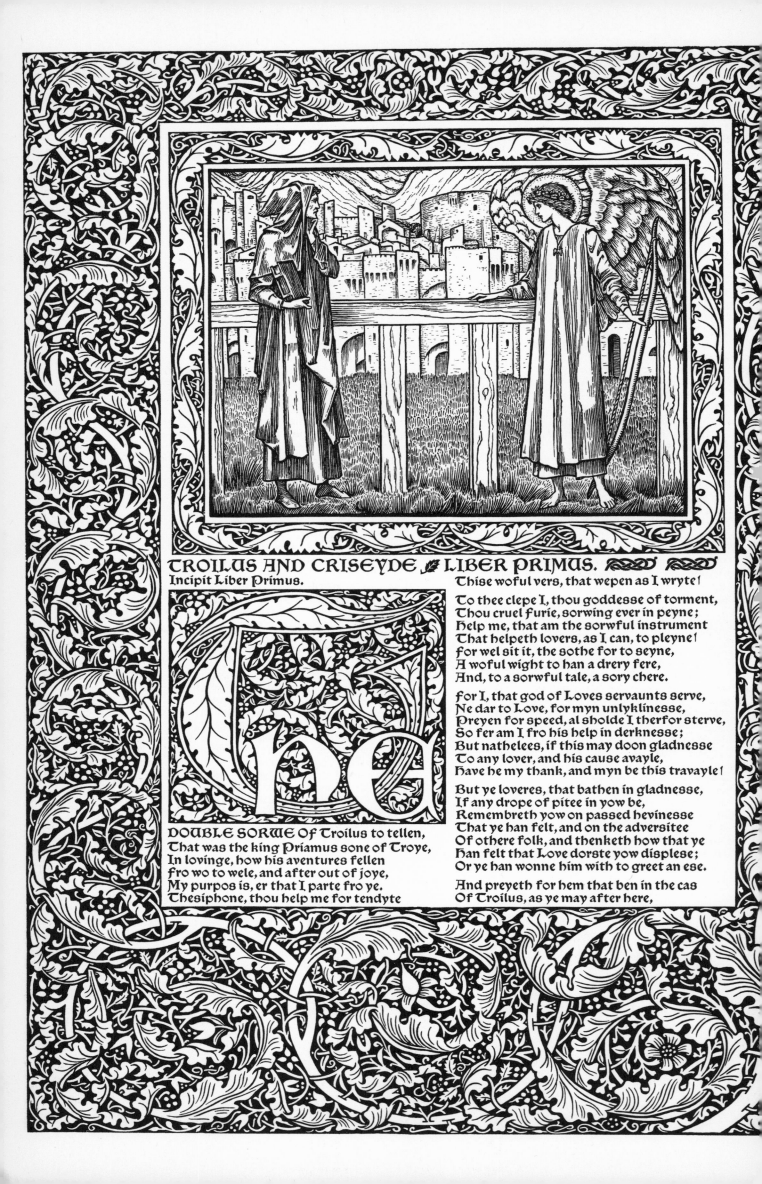

TROILUS AND CRISEYDE ❧ LIBER PRIMUS.

Incipit Liber Primus.

The **DOUBLE SORWE** Of Troilus to tellen,
That was the king Priamus sone of Troye,
In lovinge, how his aventures fellen
fro wo to wele, and after out of joye,
My purpos is, er that I parte fro ye.
Thesiphone, thou help me for tendyte

Thise woful vers, that wepen as I wryte!

To thee clepe I, thou goddesse of torment,
Thou cruel Furie, sorwing ever in peyne;
Help me, that am the sorwful instrument
That helpeth lovers, as I can, to pleyne!
for wel sit it, the sothe for to seyne,
A woful wight to han a drery fere,
And, to a sorwful tale, a sory chere.

for I, that god of Loves servaunts serve,
Ne dar to Love, for myn unlyklinesse,
Preyen for speed, al sholde I therfor sterve,
So fer am I fro his help in derknesse;
But nathelees, if this may doon gladnesse
To any lover, and his cause avayle,
have he my thank, and myn be this travayle!

But ye loveres, that bathen in gladnesse,
If any drope of pitee in yow be,
Remembreth yow on passed hevinesse
That ye han felt, and on the adversitee
Of othere folk, and thenketh how that ye
han felt that Love dorste yow displese;
Or ye han wonne him with to greet an ese.

And preyeth for hem that ben in the cas
Of Troilus, as ye may after here,

That love hem bringe in hevene to solas,
And eek for me preyeth to God so dere,
That I have might to shewe, in som manere,
Swich peyne and wo as Loves folk endure,
In Troilus unsely aventure.

And biddeth eek for hem that been despeyred
In love, that never nil recovered be,
And eek for hem that falsly been apeyred
Thorugh wikked tonges, be it he or she;
Thus biddeth God, for his benignitee,
To graunte hem sone out of this world to pace,
That been despeyred out of Loves grace.

And biddeth eek for hem that been at ese,
That God hem graunte ay good per-
severaunce,
And sende hem might hir ladies so to plese,
That it to Love be worship and plesaunce.
For so hope I my soule best avaunce,
To preye for hem that Loves servaunts be,
And wryte hir wo, and live in charitee.

And for to have of hem compassioun
As though I were hir owene brother dere.
Now herkeneth with a gode entencioun,
For now wol I gon streight to my matere,
In whiche ye may the double sorwes here

Of Troilus, in loving of Criseyde,
And how that she forsook him er she deyde.

T is wel wist, how that the
Grekes stronge
In armes with a thousand
shippes wente
To Troyewardes, and the citee
longe
Assegeden neigh ten yeer er
they stente,
And, in diverse wyse and oon
entente,
The ravisshing to wreken of
Eleyne,
By Paris doon, they wrought-
en al hir peyne.
Now fil it so, that in the toun
ther was
Dwellinge a lord of greet auc-
toritee,
A gret devyn that cleped was
Calkas,
That in science so expert was, that he
Knew wel that Troye sholde destroyed be,
By answere of his god, that highte thus,
Daun Phebus or Apollo Delphicus.

So whan this Calkas knew by calculinge,
And eek by answere of this Appollo,
That Grekes sholden swich a peple bringe,
Thorugh which that Troye moste been fordo,
He caste anoon out of the toun to go;
For wel wiste he, by sort, that Troye sholde
Destroyed been, ye, wolde whoso nolde.

For which, for to departen softely
Took purpos ful this forknowinge wyse,
And to the Grekes ost ful prively
He stal anoon; and they, in curteys wyse,
Him deden bothe worship and servyse,
In trust that he hath conning hem to rede
In every peril which that is to drede.

The noyse up roos, whan it was first aspyed,
Thorugh al the toun, and generally was spoken,
That Calkas traytor fled was, and allyed
With hem of Grece; and casten to ben wroken
On him that falsly hadde his feith so broken;
And seyden, he and al his kin at ones
Ben worthy for to brennen, fel and bones.

Now hadde Calkas left, in this meschaunce,
Al unwist of this false and wikked dede,
His doughter, which that was in gret penaunce,
For of hir lyf she was ful sore in drede,
As she that niste what was best to rede;
For bothe a widowe was she, and allone
Of any freend, to whom she dorste hir mone.

Criseyde was this lady name aright;
As to my dome, in al Troyes citee
Nas noon so fair, for passing every wight
So aungellyk was hir natyf beautee,
That lyk a thing inmortal semed she,
As doth an hevenish parfit creature,
That doun were sent in scorning of nature.

This lady, which that alday herde at ere
Hir fadres shame, his falsnesse and tresoun,
Wel nigh out of hir wit for sorwe and fere,
In widewes habit large of samit broun,
On knees she fil biforn Ector adoun;
With pitous voys, and tendrely wepinge,
His mercy bad, hirselven excusinge.

Now was this Ector pitous of nature,
And saw that she was sorwfully bigoon,
And that she was so fair a creature;
Of his goodnesse he gladed hir anoon,
And seyde: Lat your fadres treson goon
Forth with mischaunce, and ye yourself, in joye,
Dwelleth with us, whyl you good list, in Troye.

And al thonour that men may doon yow have,
As ferforth as your fader dwelled here,
Ye shul han, and your body shal men save,
As fer as I may ought enquere or here.
℘ And she him thonked with ful humble chere,
And ofter wolde, and it hadde ben his wille,
And took hir leve, and hoom, and held hir stille.

472

And in hir hous she abood with swich meynee
As to hir honour nede was to holde;
And whyl she was dwellinge in that citee,
Kepte hir estat, and bothe of yonge and olde
Ful wel beloved, and wel men of hir tolde.
But whether that she children hadde or noon,
I rede it nought; therfore I lete it goon.

The thinges fellen, as they doon of werre,
Bitwixen hem of Troye and Grekes ofte;
For som day boughten they of Troye it derre,
And eft the Grekes founden no thing softe
The folk of Troye; and thus fortune onlofte,
And under eft, gan hem to wheelen bothe
After hir cours, ay whyl they were wrothe.

But how this toun com to destruccioun
Ne falleth nought to purpos me to telle;
For it were here a long disgressioun
Fro my matere, and yow to longe dwelle.
But the Troyane gestes, as they felle,
In Omer, or in Dares, or in Dyte,
Whoso that can, may rede hem as they wryte.

But though that Grekes hem of Troye shetten,
And hir citee bisegede al aboute,
Hir olde usage wolde they not letten,
As for to honoure hir goddes ful devoute;
But aldermost in honour, out of doute,
They hadde a relik hight Palladion,
That was hir trist aboven everichon.

And so bifel, whan comen was the tyme
Of Aperil, whan clothed is the mede
With newe grene, of lusty Ver the pryme,
And swote smellen floures whyte and rede,
In sondry wyses shewed, as I rede,
The folk of Troye hir observaunces olde,
Palladiones feste for to holde.

And to the temple, in al hir beste wyse,
In general, ther wente many a wight,
To herknen of Palladion the servyse;
And namely, so many a lusty knight,
So many a lady fresh and mayden bright,
Ful wel arayed, bothe moste and leste,
Ye, bothe for the seson and the feste.

Among thise othere folk was Criseyda,
In widewes habite blak; but nathelees,
Right as our firste lettre is now an A,
In beautee first so stood she, makelees;
Hir godly looking gladede al the prees.
Nas never seyn thing to ben preysed derre,
Nor under cloude blak so bright a sterre

As was Criseyde, as folk seyde everichoon
That hir bihelden in hir blake wede;
And yet she stood ful lowe and stille alloon,
Bihinden othere folk, in litel brede,
And neigh the dore, ay under shames drede,
Simple of atyr, and debonaire of chere,
With ful assured loking and manere.

This Troilus, as he was wont to gyde
His yonge knightes, ladde hem up and doun
In thilke large temple on every syde,
Biholding ay the ladyes of the toun,
Now here, now there, for no devocioun
Hadde he to noon, to reven him his reste,
But gan to preyse and lakken whom him leste.

And in his walk ful fast he gan to wayten
If knight or squyer of his companye
Gan for to syke, or lete his eyen bayten
On any woman that he coude aspye;
He wolde smyle, and holden it folye,
And seye him thus: God wot, she slepeth softe
For love of thee, whan thou tornest ful ofte!

I have herd told, pardieux, of your livinge,
Ye lovers, and your lewede observaunces,
And which a labour folk han in winninge
Of love, and, in the keping, which doutaunces;
And whan your preye is lost, wo and penaunces;
O verrey foles! nyce and blinde be ye;
Ther nis not oon can war by other be.

And with that word he gan caste up the browe,
Ascaunces: Lo! is this nought wysly spoken?
At which the god of love gan loken rowe
Right for despyt, and shoop for to ben wroken;
He kidde anoon his bowe nas nat broken;
For sodeynly he hit him at the fulle;
And yet as proud a pekok can he pulle.

O blinde world, O blinde entencioun!
How ofte falleth al theffect contraire
Of surquidrye and foul presumpcioun;
For caught is proud, and caught is debonaire.
This Troilus is clomben on the staire,
And litel weneth that he moot descenden.
But al day fayleth thing that fooles wenden.

As proude Bayard ginneth for to skippe
Out of the wey, so priketh him his corn,
Til he a lash have of the longe whippe,
Than thenketh he: Though I praunce al biforn
First in the trays, ful fat and newe shorn,
Yet am I but an hors, and horses lawe
I moot endure, and with my feres drawe.

So ferde it by this fers and proude knight;
Though he a worthy kinges sone were,
And wende nothing hadde had swiche might
Ayens his wil that sholde his herte stere,
Yet with a look his herte wex afere,
That he, that now was most in pryde above,
Wex sodeynly most subget unto love.

Forthy ensample taketh of this man,
Ye wyse, proude, and worthy folkes alle,
To scornen Love, which that so sone can
The freedom of your hertes to him thralle;
For ever it was, and ever it shal bifalle,
That Love is he that alle thing may binde;
For may no man fordo the lawe of kinde.

That this be sooth, hath preved and doth yet;
For this trowe I ye knowen, alle or some,
Men reden not that folk han gretter wit
Than they that han be most with love ynome;
And strengest folk ben therwith overcome,
The worthiest and grettest of degree;
This was, and is, and yet men shal it see.

And trewelich it sit wel to be so;
For alderwysest han therwith ben plesed;
And they that han ben aldermost in wo,
With love han ben conforted most and esed;
And ofte it hath the cruel herte apesed,
And worthy folk maad worthier of name,
And causeth most to dreden vyce and shame.

Now sith it may not goodly be withstonde,
And is a thing so vertuous in kinde,
Refuseth not to Love for to be bonde,
Sin, as himselven list, he may yow binde.
The yerde is bet that bowen wole and winde
Than that that brest; and therfor I yow rede
To folwen him that so wel can yow lede.

But for to tellen forth in special
As of this kinges sone of which I tolde,
And leten other thing collateral,
Of him thenke I my tale for to holde,
Bothe of his joye, and of his cares colde;
And al his werk, as touching this matere,
For I it gan, I wil therto refere.

Withinne the temple he wente him forth pleyinge,
This Troilus, of every wight aboute,
On this lady and now on that lokinge,
Wherso she were of toune, or of withoute:
And upon cas bifel, that thorugh a route
His eye perced, and so depe it wente,
Til on Criseyde it smoot, and ther it stente.

And sodeynly he wex therwith astoned,
And gan hire bet biholde in thrifty wyse:
O mercy, God! thoughte he, wher hastow woned,
That art so fair and goodly to devyse?
Therwith his herte gan to sprede and ryse,
And softe sighed, lest men mighte him here,
And caughte ayein his firste pleyinge chere.

She nas not with the leste of hir stature,
But alle hir limes so wel answeringe
Weren to womanhode, that creature
Was never lasse mannish in seminge.
And eek the pure wyse of here meninge
Shewede wel, that men might in hir gesse
Honour, estat, and wommanly noblesse.

To Troilus right wonder wel withalle
Gan for to lyke hir mening and hir chere,
Which somdel deynous was, for she leet falle
Hir look a lite aside, in swich manere,
Ascaunces: What! may I not stonden here?
And after that hir loking gan she lighte,
That never thoughte him seen so good a sighte.

And of hir look in him ther gan to quiken
So greet desir, and swich affeccioun,
That in his hertes botme gan to stiken
Of hir his fixe and depe impressioun:
And though he erst hadde poured up and doun,
He was tho glad his hornes in to shrinke;
Unnethes wiste he how to loke or winke.

Lo, he that leet himselven so konninge,
And scorned hem that loves peynes dryen,
Was ful unwar that love hadde his dwellinge
Withinne the subtile stremes of hir yën;
That sodeynly him thoughte he felte dyen,
Right with hir look, the spirit in his herte;
Blessed be love, that thus can folk converte!

She, this in blak, lykinge to Troilus,
Over alle thing he stood for to biholde;
Ne his desir, ne wherfor he stood thus,
He neither chere made, ne worde tolde;
But from afer, his maner for to holde,
On other thing his look somtyme he caste,
And eft on hir, whyl that servyse laste.

And after this, not fulliche al awhaped,
Out of the temple al esiliche he wente,
Repentinge him that he hadde ever yjaped
Of loves folk, lest fully the descente
Of scorn fille on himself; but, what he mente,
Lest it were wist on any maner syde,
His wo he gan dissimulen and hyde.

Whan he was fro the temple thus departed,
He streyght anoon unto his paleys torneth,
Right with hir look thurgh-shoten and thurgh-
darted,
Al feyneth he in lust that he sojorneth;
And al his chere and speche also he borneth;
And ay, of loves servants every whyle,
Himself to wrye, at hem he gan to smyle.

And seyde: Lord, so ye live al in lest,
Ye loveres! for the conningest of yow,
That serveth most ententiflich and best,
Him tit as often harm therof as prow;
Your hyre is quit ayein, ye, God wot how!
Nought wel for wel, but scorn for good servyse;
In feith, your ordre is ruled in good wyse!

In noun-certeyn ben alle your observaunces,
But it a sely fewe poyntes be;
Ne nothing asketh so grete attendaunces
As doth your lay, and that knowe alle ye;
But that is not the worste, as mote I thee;
But, tolde I yow the worste poynt, I leve,
Al seyde I sooth, ye wolden at me greve!

But tak this, that ye loveres ofte eschuwe,
Or elles doon of good entencioun,
Ful ofte thy lady wole it misconstrue,
And deme it harm in hir opinioun;
And yet if she, for other enchesoun,
Be wrooth, than shalt thou han a groyn anoon:
Lord! wel is him that may be of yow oon!

But for al this, whan that he say his tyme,
He held his pees, non other bote him gayned;
For love bigan his fetheres so to lyme,
That wel unnethe unto his folk he feyned
That othere besye nedes him destrayned;
For wo was him, that what to doon he niste,
But bad his folk to goon wher that hem liste.

And whan that he in chaumbre was allone,
He doun upon his beddes feet him sette,
And first he gan to syke, and eft to grone,
And thoughte ay on hir so, withouten lette,
That, as he sat and wook, his spirit mette
That he hir saw a temple, and al the wyse
Right of hir loke, and gan it newe avyse.

Thus gan he make a mirour of his minde,
In which he saugh al hoolly hir figure;
And that he wel coude in his herte finde,
It was to him a right good aventure
To love swich oon, and if he dide his cure
To serven hir, yet mighte he falle in grace,
Or elles, for oon of hir servaunts pace.

Imagininge that travaille nor grame
Ne mighte, for so goodly oon, be lorn
As she, ne him for his desir ne shame,
Al were it wist, but in prys and upborn
Of alle lovers wel more than biforn;
Thus argumented he in his ginninge,
Ful unavysed of his wo cominge.

Thus took he purpos loves craft to suwe,
And thoughte he wolde werken prively,
First, to hyden his desir in muwe
From every wight yborn, al-outrely,
But he mighte ought recovered be therby;
Remembring him, that love to wyde yblowe
Yelt bittre fruyt, though swete seed be sowe.

And over al this, yet muchel more he thoughte
What for to speke, and what to holden inne,
And what to arten hir to love he soughte,
And on a song anoon-right to biginne,
And gan loude on his sorwe for to winne;
For with good hope he gan fully assente
Criseyde for to love, and nought repente.

And of his song nought only the sentence,
As writ myn autour called Lollius,
But pleynly, save our tonges difference,
I dar wel sayn, in al that Troilus
Seyde in his song; lo! every word right thus
As I shal seyn; and whoso list it here,
Lo! next this vers, he may it finden here.

Cantus Troili.

If no love is, O God, what fele I so?
And if love is, what thing and whiche
is he?
If love be good, from whennes comth
my wo?
If it be wikke, a wonder thinketh me,
Whenne every torment and adversitee

That cometh of him, may to me savory thinke;
for ay thurste I, the more that I it drinke.

And if that at myn owene lust I brenne,
fro whennes cometh my wailing and my pleynte?
If harme agree me, wherto pleyne I thenne?
I noot, ne why unwery that I feynte.
O quike deeth, o swete harm so queynte,
How may of thee in me swich quantitee,
But if that I consente that it be?

And if that I consente, I wrongfully
Compleyne, ywis; thus possed to and fro,
Al sterelees withinne a boot am I
Amid the see, bytwixen windes two,
That in contrarie stonden evermo.
Allas! what is this wonder maladye?
for hete of cold, for cold of hete, I dye.

And to the god of love thus seyde he
With pitous voys: O lord, now youres is
My spirit, which that oughte youres be.
Yow thanke I, lord, that han me brought to this;
But whether goddesse or womman, ywis,
She be, I noot, which that ye do me serve;
But as hir man I wole ay live and sterve.

Ye stonden in hire eyen mightily,
As in a place unto your vertu digne;
Wherfore, lord, if my servyse or I
May lyke yow, so beth to me benigne;
for myn estat royal here I resigne
Into hir hond, and with ful humble chere
Bicome hir man, as to my lady dere.

In him ne deyned sparen blood royal
The fyr of love, wherfro God me blesse,
Ne him forbar in no degree, for al
His vertu or his excellent prowesse;
But held him as his thral lowe in distresse,
And brende him so in sondry wyse ay newe,
That sixty tyme a day he loste his hewe.

So muche, day by day, his owene thought,
for lust to hir, gan quiken and encrese,
That every other charge he sette at nought;
forthy ful ofte, his hote fyr to cese,
To seen hir goodly look he gan to prese;
for therby to ben esed wel he wende,
And ay the ner he was, the more he brende.

for ay the ner the fyr, the hotter is,
This, trowe I, knoweth al this companye.
But were he fer or neer, I dar seye this,
By night or day, for wysdom or folye,
His herte, which that is his brestes yë,
Was ay on hir, that fairer was to sene
Than ever was Eleyne or Polixene.

Eek of the day ther passed nought an houre
That to himself a thousand tyme he seyde:
Good goodly, to whom serve I and laboure,
As I best can, now wolde God, Criseyde,

Ye wolden on me rewe er that I deyde!
My dere herte, allas! myn hele and hewe
And lyf is lost, but ye wole on me rewe.

Alle othere dredes weren from him fledde,
Bothe of the assege and his savacioun;
Ne in him desyr noon othere fownes bredde
But arguments to this conclusioun,
That she on him wolde han compassioun,
And he to be hir man, whyl he may dure;
Lo, here his lyf, and from the deeth his cure!

The sharpe shoures felle of armes preve,
That Ector or his othere bretheren diden,
Ne made him only therfore ones meve;
And yet was he, wherso men wente or riden,
founde oon the best, and lengest tyme abiden
Ther peril was, and dide eek such travayle
In armes, that to thenke it was mervayle.

But for non hate he to the Grekes hadde,
Ne also for the rescous of the toun,
Ne made him thus in armes for to madde,
But only, lo, for this conclusioun,
To lyken hir the bet for his renoun;
fro day to day in armes so he spedde,
That alle the Grekes as the deeth him dredde.

And fro this forth tho refte him love his sleep,
And made his mete his foo; and eek his sorwe
Gan multiplye, that, whoso toke keep,
It shewed in his hewe, bothe eve and morwe;
Therfor a title he gan him for to borwe
Of other syknesse, lest of him men wende
That the hote fyr of love him brende.

And seyde, he hadde a fever and ferde amis;
But how it was, certayn, can I not seye,
If that his lady understood not this,
Or feyned hir she niste, oon of the tweye;
But wel I rede that, by no maner weye,
Ne semed it as that she of him roughte,
Nor of his peyne, or whatsoever he thoughte.

But than fel to this Troilus such wo,
That he was wel neigh wood; for ay his drede
Was this, that she som wight had loved so,
That never of him she wolde have taken hede;
for whiche him thoughte he felte his herte blede.
Ne of his wo ne dorste he not biginne
To tellen it, for al this world to winne.

But whanne he hadde a space fro his care,
Thus to himself ful ofte he gan to pleyne;
He sayde: O fool, now art thou in the snare,
That whilom japedest at loves peyne;
Now artow hent, now gnaw thyn owene cheyne;
Thou were ay wont eche lovere reprehende
Of thing fro which thou canst thee nat defende.

What wole now every lover seyn of thee,
If this be wist, but ever in thyn absence
Laughen in scorn, and seyn: Lo, ther gooth he,

475

That is the man of so gret sapience,
That held us loveres leest in reverence!
Now, thonked be God, he may goon in the daunce
Of hem that Love list febly for to avaunce!

But, O thou woful Troilus, God wolde,
Sin thow most loven thurgh thy destinee,
That thow beset were on swich oon that sholde
Knowe al thy wo, al lakkede hir pitee:
But al so cold in love, towardes thee,
Thy lady is, as frost in winter mone,
And thou fordoon, as snow in fyr is sone.

God wolde I were aryved in the port
Of deeth, to which my sorwe wil me lede!
A, Lord, to me it were a greet comfort;
Then were I quit of languisshing in drede.
For by myn hidde sorwe yblowe on brede
I shal bijaped been a thousand tyme
More than that fool of whos folye men ryme.

But now help God, and ye, swete, for whom
I pleyne, ycaught, ye, never wight so faste!
O mercy, dere herte, and help me from
The deeth, for I, whyl that my lyf may laste,
More than myself wol love yow to my laste.
And with som freendly look gladeth me, swete,
Though never more thing ye me bihete!

Thise wordes and ful manye another to
He spak, and called ever in his compleynte
Hir name, for to tellen hir his wo,
Til neigh that he in salte teres dreynte.
Al was for nought, she herde nought his pleynte;
And whan that he bithoughte on that folye,
A thousand fold his wo gan multiplye.

Biwayling in his chambre thus allone,
A freend of his, that called was Pandare,
Com ones in unwar, and herde him grone,
And sey his freend in swich distresse and care:
Allas! quod he, who causeth al this fare?
O mercy, God! what unhap may this mene?
Han now thus sone Grekes maad yow lene?

Or hastow som remors of conscience,
And art now falle in som devocioun,
And waylest for thy sinne and thyn offence,
And hast for ferde caught attricioun?
God save hem that biseged han our toun,
And so can leye our jolyte on presse,
And bring our lusty folk to holinesse!

These wordes seyde he for the nones alle,
That with swich thing he mighte him angry
maken,
And with an angre don his sorwe falle,
As for the tyme, and his corage awaken;
But wel he wiste, as fer as tonges spaken,
Ther nas a man of gretter hardinesse
Than he, ne more desired worthinesse.

What cas, quod Troilus, or what aventure

Hath gyded thee to see my languisshinge,
That am refus of every creature?
But for the love of God, at my preyinge,
Go henne away, for certes, my deyinge
Wol thee disese, and I mot nedes deye;
Therfor go wey, ther is no more to seye.

But if thou wene I be thus syk for drede,
It is not so, and therfor scorne nought;
Ther is another thing I take of hede
Wel more than ought the Grekes han ywrought,
Which cause is of my deeth, for sorwe & thought.
But though that I now telle thee it ne leste,
Be thou nought wrooth, I hyde it for the beste.

This Pandare, that neigh malt for wo and
routhe,
Ful often seyde: Allas! what may this be?
Now freend, quod he, if ever love or trouthe
Hath been, or is, bitwixen thee and me,
Ne do thou never swiche a crueltee
To hyde fro thy freend so greet a care;
Wostow nought wel that it am I, Pandare?

I wole parten with thee al thy peyne,
If it be so I do thee no comfort,
As it is freendes right, sooth for to seyne,
To entreparten wo, as glad desport.
I have, and shal, for trewe or fals report,
In wrong and right yloved thee al my lyve;
Hyd not thy wo fro me, but telle it blyve.

Than gan this sorwful Troilus to syke,
And seyde him thus: God leve it be my beste
To telle it thee; for, sith it may thee lyke,
Yet wole I telle it, though myn herte breste;
And wel wot I thou mayst do me no reste.
But lest thow deme I truste not to thee,
Now herkne, freend, for thus it stant with me.

Love, ayeins the which whoso defendeth
Himselven most, him alderlest avayleth,
With desespeir so sorwfully me offendeth,
That streyght unto the deeth myn herte sayleth.
Therto desyr so brenningly me assaylleth,
That to ben slayn it were a gretter joye
To me than king of Grece been and Troye!

Suffiseth this, my fulle freend Pandare,
That I have seyd, for now wostow my wo;
And for the love of God, my colde care
So hyd it wel, I telle it never to mo;
For harmes mighte folwen, mo than two,
If it were wist; but be thou in gladnesse,
And lat me sterve, unknowe, of my distresse.

How hastow thus unkindely and longe
Hid this fro me, thou fool? quod Pandarus;
Paraunter thou might after swich oon longe,
That myn avys anoon may helpen us.
This were a wonder thing, quod Troilus,
Thou coudest never in love thyselven wisse;
How devel maystow bringen me to blisse?

Ye, Troilus, now herke, quod Pandare,
Though I be nyce; it happeth ofte so,
That oon that exces doth ful yvele fare,
By good counseyl can kepe his freend therfro.
I have myself eek seyn a blind man go
Theras he fel that coude loke wyde;
A fool may eek a wys man ofte gyde.

A whetston is no kerving instrument,
And yet it maketh sharpe kerving-tolis.
And ther thow woost that I have ought miswent,
Eschewe thou that, for swich thing to thee scole is;
Thus ofte wyse men ben war by folis.
If thou do so, thy wit is wel biwared;
By his contrarie is every thing declared.

For how might ever sweetnesse have be knowe
To him that never tasted bitternesse?
Ne no man may be inly glad, I trowe,
That never was in sorwe or som distresse;
Eek whyt by blak, by shame eek worthinesse,
Ech set by other, more for other semeth;
As men may see; and so the wyse it demeth.

Sith thus of two contraries is a lore,
I, that have in love so ofte assayed
Grevaunces, oughte conne, and wel the more
Counsayllen thee of that thou art amayed.
Eek thee ne oughte nat ben yvel apayed,
Though I desyre with thee for to bere
Thyn hevy charge; it shal the lasse dere.

I woot wel that it fareth thus by me
As to thy brother Parys an herdesse,
Which that ycleped was Oenone,
Wrot in a compleynt of hir hevinesse:
Ye say the lettre that she wroot, I gesse?
Nay, never yet, ywis, quod Troilus.
Now, quod Pandare, herkneth; it was thus:

Phebus, that first fond art of medicyne,
Quod she, and coude in every wightes care
Remede and reed, by herbes he knew fyne,
Yet to himself his conninge was ful bare;
For love hadde him so bounden in a snare,
Al for the doughter of the kinge Admete,
That al his craft ne coude his sorwe bete.

Right so fare I, unhappily for me;
I love oon best, and that me smerteth sore;
And yet, paraunter, can I rede thee,
And not myself; repreve me no more.
I have no cause, I woot wel, for to sore
As doth an hauk that listeth for to pleye,
But to thyn help yet somwhat can I seye.

And of o thing right siker maystow be,
That certayn, for to deyen in the peyne,
That I shal nevermo discoveren thee;
Ne, by my trouthe, I kepe nat restreyne
Thee fro thy love, thogh that it were Eleyne,
That is thy brotheres wyf, if ich it wiste;
Be what she be, and love hir as thee liste.

Therfore, as freend fullich in me assure,
And tel me plat what is thyn enchesoun,
And final cause of wo that ye endure;
For douteth nothing, myn entencioun
Nis nought to yow of reprehencioun
To speke as now, for no wight may bireve
A man to love, til that him list to leve.

And witeth wel, that bothe two ben vyces,
Mistrusten alle, or elles alle leve;
But wel I woot, the mene of it no vyce is,
For for to trusten sum wight is a preve
Of trouthe, and forthy wolde I fayn remeve
Thy wrong conceyte, & do thee som wight triste,
Thy wo to telle; and tel me, if thee liste.

The wyse seyth: Wo him that is allone,
For, and he falle, he hath noon help to ryse
And sith thou hast a felawe, tel thy mone;
For this nis not, certeyn, the nexte wyse
To winnen love, as techen us the wyse,
To walwe and wepe as Niobe the quene,
Whos teres yet in marbel been ysene.

Lat be thy weping and thy drerinesse,
And lat us lissen wo with other speche;
So may thy woful tyme seme lesse.
Delyte not in wo thy wo to seche,
As doon thise foles that hir sorwes eche
With sorwe, whan they han misaventure,
And listen nought to seche hem other cure.

Men seyn: To wrecche is consolacioun
To have another felawe in his peyne
That oughte wel ben our opinioun,
For, bothe thou and I, of love we pleyne;
So ful of sorwe am I, soth for to seyne,
That certeynly no more harde grace
May sitte on me, forwhy ther is no space.

If God wole thou art not agast of me,
Lest I wolde of thy lady thee bigyle,
Thow woost thyself whom that I love, pardee,
As I best can, gon sithen longe whyle.
And sith thou woost I do it for no wyle,
And sith I am he that thou tristest most,
Tel me sumwhat, sin al my wo thou woost.

Yet Troilus, for al this, no word seyde,
But longe he lay as stille as he ded were;
And after this with sykinge he abreyde,
And to Pandarus voys he lente his ere,
And up his eyen caste he, that in fere
Was Pandarus, lest that in frenesye
He sholde falle, or elles sone dye:

And cryde, Awake! ful wonderly and sharpe;
What? slombrestow as in a lytargye?
Or artow lyk an asse to the harpe,
That hereth soun, whan men the strenges plye,
But in his minde of that no melodye
May sinken, him to glade, for that he
So dul is of his bestialitee?

477

And with that Pandare of his wordes stente;
But Troilus yet him no word answerde,
Forwhy to telle nas not his entente
To never no man, for whom that he so ferde.
For it is seyd: Man maketh ofte a yerde
With which the maker is himself ybeten
In sondry maner, as thise wyse treten,

And namely, in his counseyl tellinge
That toucheth love that oughte be secree;
For of himself it wolde ynough outspringe,
But if that it the bet governed be.
Eek somtyme it is craft to seme flee
Fro thing which in effect men hunte faste;
Al this gan Troilus in his herte caste.

But nathelees, whan he had herd him crye
Awake! he gan to syke wonder sore,
And seyde: freend, though that I stille lye,
I am not deef; now pees, and cry no more;
For I have herd thy wordes and thy lore;
But suffre me my mischef to biwayle,
For thy proverbes may me nought avayle.

Nor other cure canstow noon for me.
Eek I nil not be cured, I wol deye;
What knowe I of the quene Niobe?
Lat be thyne olde ensaumples, I thee preye.
No, quod tho Pandarus, therfore I seye,
Swich is delyt of foles to biwepe
Hir wo, but seken bote they ne kepe.

Now knowe I that ther reson in thee fayleth.
But tel me, if I wiste what she were
For whom that thee al this misaunter ayleth,
Dorstestow that I tolde hir in hir ere
Thy wo, sith thou darst not thyself for fere,
And hir bisoughte on thee to han som routhe?
Why, nay, quod he, by God and by my trouthe!

What? not as bisily, quod Pandarus,
As though myn owene lyf lay on this nede?
No, certes, brother, quod this Troilus.
And why? for that thou sholdest never
spede.
Wostow that wel? Ye, that is out of drede,
Quod Troilus, for al that ever ye conne,
She nil to noon swich wrecche as I be wonne.

Quod Pandarus: Allas! what may this be,
That thou despeyred art thus causelees?
What? liveth not thy lady? benedicite!
How wostow so that thou art gracelees?
Swich yvel is not alwey botelees.
Why, put not impossible thus thy cure,
Sin thing to come is ofte in aventure.

I graunte wel that thou endurest wo
As sharp as doth he, Ticius, in helle,
Whos stomak foules tyren evermo
That highte volturis, as bokes telle.
But I may not endure that thou dwelle
In so unskilful an opinioun
That of thy wo is no curacioun.

But ones niltow, for thy coward herte,
And for thyn ire and folish wilfulnesse,
For wantrust, tellen of thy sorwes smerte,
Ne to thyn owene help do bisinesse
As muche as speke a resoun more or lesse,
But lyest as he that list of nothing recche.
What womman coude love swich a wrecche?

What may she demen other of thy deeth,
If thou thus deye, and she not why it is,
But that for fere is yolden up thy breeth,
For Grekes han biseged us, ywis?
Lord, which a thank than shaltow han of this!
Thus wol she seyn, and al the toun at ones:
The wrecche is deed, the devel have his bones!

Thou mayst allone here wepe and crye and knele;
But, love a woman that she woot it nought,
And she wol quyte that thou shalt not fele;
Unknowe, unkist, and lost that is unsought.
What! many a man hath love ful dere ybought
Twenty winter that his lady wiste,
That never yet his lady mouth he kiste.

What? shulde he therfor fallen in despeyr,
Or be recreaunt for his owene tene,
Or sleen himself, al be his lady fayr?
Nay, nay, but ever in oon be fresh and grene
To serve and love his dere hertes quene,
And thenke it is a guerdoun hir to serve
A thousand fold more than he can deserve.

And of that word took hede Troilus,
And thoughte anoon what folye he was inne,
And how that sooth him seyde Pandarus,
That for to sleen himself mighte he not winne,
But bothe doon unmanhod and a sinne,
And of his deeth his lady nought to wyte;
For of his wo, God woot, she knew ful lyte.

And with that thought he gan ful sore syke,
And seyde: Allas! what is me best to do?
To whom Pandare answerde: If thee lyke,
The best is that thou telle me thy wo;
And have my trouthe, but thou it finde so,
I be thy bote, or that it be ful longe,
To peces do me drawe, and sithen honge!

Ye, so thou seyst, quod Troilus tho, allas!
But, God wot, it is not the rather so;
Ful hard were it to helpen in this cas,
For wel finde I that fortune is my fo,
Ne alle the men that ryden conne or go
May of hir cruel wheel the harm withstonde;
For, as hir list, she pleyeth with free and bonde.

Quod Pandarus: Than blamestow fortune
For thou art wrooth, ye, now at erst I see;
Wostow nat wel that fortune is commune
To every maner wight in som degree?
And yet thou hast this comfort, lo, pardee!
That, as hir joyes moten over goon,
So mote hir sorwes passen everichoon.

For if hir wheel stinte anything to torne,
Than cessed she Fortune anoon to be:
Now, sith hir wheel by no wey may sojorne,
What wostow if hir mutabilitee
Right as thyselven list, wol doon by thee,
Or that she be not fer fro thyn helpinge?
Paraunter, thou hast cause for to singe!

And therfor wostow what I thee beseche?
Lat be thy wo and turning to the grounde;
For whoso list have helping of his leche,
To him bihoveth first unwrye his wounde.
To Cerberus in helle ay be I bounde,
Were it for my suster, al thy sorwe,
By my wil, she sholde al be thyn tomorwe.

Loke up, I seye, and tel me what she is
Anoon, that I may goon aboute thy nede;
Knowe ich hir ought? for my love, tel me this;
Than wolde I hopen rather for to spede.
⚘ Tho gan the veyne of Troilus to blede,
For he was hit, and wex al reed for shame;
⚘ A ha! quod Pandare, here biginneth game!

⚘ And with that word he gan him for to shake,
And seyde: Theef, thou shalt hir name telle.
⚘ But tho gan sely Troilus for to quake
As though men sholde han lad him into helle,
And seyde: Allas! of al my wo the welle,
Than is my swete fo called Criseyde!
⚘ And wel nigh with the word for fere he deyde.

And whan that Pandare herde hir name nevene,
Lord, he was glad, and seyde: Freend so dere,
Now fare aright, for Joves name in hevene,
Love hath biset thee wel, be of good chere;
For of good name and wysdom and manere
She hath ynough, and eek of gentilesse;
If she be fayr, thow wost thyself, I gesse.

Ne I never saw a more bountevous
Of hir estat, ne a gladder, ne of speche
A freendlier, ne a more gracious
For to do wel, ne lasse hadde nede to seche
What for to doon; and al this bet to eche,
In honour, to as fer as she may strecche,
A kinges herte semeth by hires a wrecche.

And forthy loke of good comfort thou be;
For certeinly, the firste poynt is this
Of noble corage and wel ordeynè,
A man to have pees with himself, ywis;
So oughtest thou, for nought but good it is
To loven wel, and in a worthy place;
Thee oughte not to clepe it hap, but grace.

And also thenk, and therwith glade thee,
That sith thy lady vertuous is al,
So folweth it that ther is som pitee
Amonges alle thise othere in general;
And forthy see that thou, in special,
Requere nought that is ayein hir name;
For vertue streccheth not himself to shame.

But wel is me that ever I was born,
That thou biset art in so good a place;
For by my trouthe, in love I dorste have sworn,
Thee sholde never han tid thus fayr a grace;
And wostow why? for thou were wont to chace
At love in scorn, and for despyt him calle
⚘ Seynt Idiot, lord of thise foles alle.⚘

How often hastow maad thy nice japes,
And seyd, that loves servants everichone
Of nycetee ben verray Goddes apes;
And some wolde monche hir mete alone,
Ligging abedde, and make hem for to grone;
And som, thou seydest, hadde a blaunche fevere,
And preydest God he sholde never kevere!

And some of hem toke on hem, for the colde,
More than ynough, so seydestow ful ofte;
And some han feyned ofte tyme, and tolde
How that they wake, whan they slepen softe;
And thus they wolde han brought hemself alofte,
And nathelees were under at the laste;
Thus seydestow, and japedest ful faste.

Yet seydestow, that, for the more part,
These loveres wolden speke in general,
And thoughten that it was a siker art,
For fayling, for to assayen overal.
Now may I jape of thee, if that I shal!
But nathelees, though that I sholde deye,
That thou art noon of tho, that dorste I seye.

Now beet thy brest, and sey to god of love:
Thy grace, lord! for now I me repente
If I mis spak, for now myself I love.⚘
Thus sey with al thyn herte in good entente.
⚘ Quod Troilus: A! lord! I me consente,
And pray to thee my japes thou foryive,
And I shal nevermore whyl I live.

⚘ Thow seyst wel, quod Pandare, & now I hope
That thou the goddes wraththe hast al apesed;
And sithen thou hast wepen many a drope,
And seyd swich thing wherwith thy god is plesed,
Now wolde never god but thou were esed;
And think wel, she of whom rist al thy wo
Hereafter may thy comfort been also.

For thilke ground, that bereth the wedes wikke,
Bereth eek thise holsom herbes, as ful ofte
Next the foule netle, rough and thikke,
The rose waxeth swote and smothe and softe;
And next the valey is the hil alofte;
And next the derke night the glade morwe;
And also joye is next the fyn of sorwe.

Now loke that atempre be thy brydel,
And, for the beste, ay suffre to the tyde,
Or elles al our labour is on ydel;
He hasteth wel that wysly can abyde;
Be diligent, and trewe, and ay wel hyde.
Be lusty, free, persevere in thy servyse,
And al is wel, if thou werke in this wyse.

479

But he that parted is in every place
Is nowher hool, as writen clerkes wyse;
What wonder is, though swich oon have no grace?
Eek wostow how it fareth of som servyse?
As plaunte a tre or herbe, in sondry wyse,
And on the morwe pulle it up as blyve,
No wonder is, though it may never thryve.

And sith that god of love hath thee bistowed
In place digne unto thy worthinesse,
Stond faste, for to good port hastow rowed;
And of thyself, for any hevinesse,
Hope alwey wel; for, but if drerinesse
Or over/haste our bothe labour shende,
I hope of this to maken a good ende.

And wostow why I am the lasse afered
Of this matere with my nece trete?
For this have I herd seyd of wyse ylered:
Was never man ne woman yet bigete
That was unapt to suffren loves hete
Celestial, or elles love of kinde,
Forthy som grace I hope in hir to finde.

And for to speke of hir in special,
Hir beautee to bithinken and hir youthe,
It sit hir nought to be celestial
As yet, though that hir liste bothe and couthe;
But trewely, it sete hir wel right nouthe
A worthy knight to loven and cheryce,
And but she do, I holde it for a vyce.

Wherfore I am, and wol be, ay redy
To peyne me to do yow this servyse;
For bothe yow to plese thus hope I
Herafterward; for ye beth bothe wyse,
And conne it counseyl kepe in swich a wyse,
That no man shal the wyser of it be;
And so we may be gladed alle three.

And, by my trouthe, I have right now of thee
A good conceyt in my wit, as I gesse,
And what it is, I wol now that thou see.
I thenke, sith that love, of his goodnesse,
Hath thee converted out of wikkednesse,
That thou shalt be the beste post, I leve,
Of al his lay, and most his foos togreve.

Ensample why, see now these wyse clerkes,
That erren aldermost ayein a lawe,
And ben converted from hir wikked werkes
Thorugh grace of God, that list hem to him
drawe,
Than arn they folk that han most God in awe,
And strengest/feythed been, I understonde,
And conne an errour alderbest withstonde.

Whan Troilus had herd Pandare assented
To been his help in loving of Criseyde,
Wex of his wo, as who seyth, untormented,
But hotter wex his love, and thus he seyde,
With sobre chere, although his herte pleyde:
Now blisful Venus helpe, er that I sterve,
Of thee, Pandare, I may som thank deserve.

480

But, dere frend, how shal myn wo ben lesse
Til this be doon? and goode, eek tel me this,
How wiltow seyn of me and my destresse?
Lest she be wrooth, this drede I most, ywis,
Or nil not here or trowen how it is.
Al this drede I, and eek for the manere
Of thee, hir eem, she nil no swich thing here.

Quod Pandarus: Thou hast a ful gret care
Lest that the cherl may falle out of the mone!
Why, Lord! I hate of thee thy nyce fare!
Why, entremete of that thou hast to done!
For Goddes love, I bidde thee a bone,
So lat me alone, and it shal be thy beste.
Why, freend, quod he, now do right as thee
leste.

But herke, Pandare, o word, for I nolde
That thou in me wendest so greet folye,
That to my lady I desiren sholde
That toucheth harm or any vilenye;
For dredelees, me were lever dye
Than she of me ought elles understode
But that, that mighte sounen into gode.

Tho lough this Pandare, & anoon answerde:
And I thy borw? Fy! no wight dooth but so;
I roughte nought though that she stode & herde
How that thou seyst; but farewel, I wol go.
Adieu! be glad! God spede us bothe two!
Yif me this labour and this besinesse,
And of my speed be thyn al that swetnesse.

Tho Troilus gan doun on knees to falle,
And Pandare in his armes hente faste,
And seyde: Now, fy on the Grekes alle!
Yet, pardee, God shal helpe us at the laste;
And dredelees, if that my lyf may laste,
And God toforn, lo, som of hem shal smerte;
And yet me athinketh that this avaunt me asterte!

And now, Pandare, I can no more seye,
But thou wys, thou wost, thou mayst, thou art al!
My lyf, my deeth, hool in thyn honde I leye;
Help now, quod he. Yis, by my trouthe, I shal.
God yelde thee, freend, and this in special,
Quod Troilus, that thou me recomaunde
To hir that to the deeth me may comaunde.

This Pandarus tho, desirous to serve
His fulle freend, than seyde in this manere:
Farwel, and thenk I wol thy thank deserve;
Have here my trouthe, & that thou shalt wel here.
And wente his wey, thenking on this matere,
And how he best mighte hir beseche of grace,
And finde a tyme therto, and a place.

For every wight that hath an hous to founde
Ne renneth nought the werk for to biginne
With rakel hond, but he wol byde a stounde,
And sende his hertes lyne out fro withinne
Alderfirst his purpos for to winne.
Al this Pandare in his herte thoughte,
And caste his werk ful wysly, or he wroughte.

But Troilus lay tho no lenger doun,
But up anoon upon his stede bay,
And in the feld he pleyde tho leoun;
Wo was that Greek that with him mette that day.
And in the toun his maner tho forth ay
So goodly was, and gat him so in grace,
That ech him lovede that loked on his face.

For he bicom the frendlyeste wight,
The gentileste, and eek the moste free,
The thriftieste and oon the beste knight,
That in his tyme was, or mighte be.

Dede were his japes and his crueltee,
His heighe port and his manere estraunge,
And ech of tho gan for a vertu chaunge.

Now lat us stinte of Troilus a stounde,
That fareth lyk a man that hurt is sore,
And is somdel of akinge of his wounde
Ylissed wel, but heled no del more:
And, as an esy pacient, the lore
Abit of him that gooth aboute his cure;
And thus he dryveth forth his aventure.
Explicit Liber Primus.

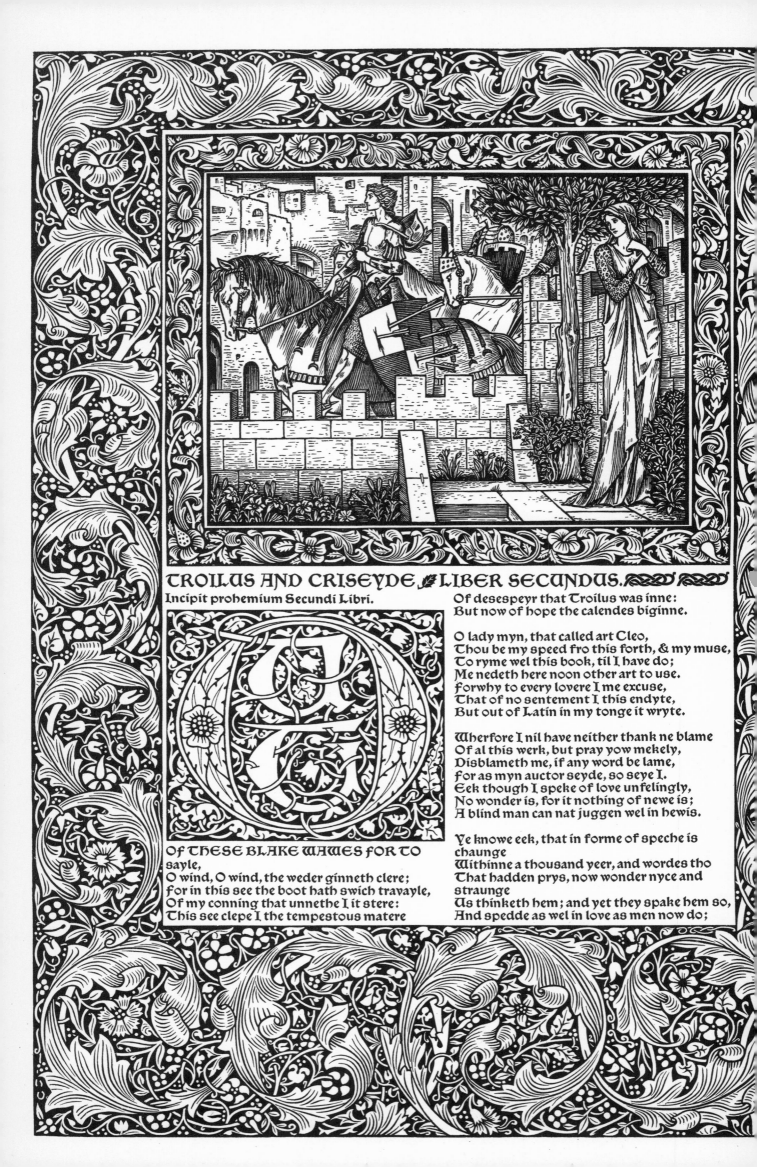

TROILUS AND CRISEYDE ❧ LIBER SECUNDUS. ❧❧

Incipit prohemium Secundi Libri.

Of desespeyr that Troilus was inne:
But now of hope the calendes biginne.

O lady myn, that called art Cleo,
Thou be my speed fro this forth, & my muse,
To ryme wel this book, til I have do;
Me nedeth here noon other art to use.
Forwhy to every lovere I me excuse,
That of no sentement I this endyte,
But out of Latin in my tonge it wryte.

Wherfore I nil have neither thank ne blame
Of al this werk, but pray yow mekely,
Disblameth me, if any word be lame,
For as myn auctor seyde, so seye I.
Eek though I speke of love unfelingly,
No wonder is, for it nothing of newe is;
A blind man can nat juggen wel in hewis.

Ye knowe eek, that in forme of speche is chaunge
Withinne a thousand yeer, and wordes tho
That hadden prys, now wonder nyce and straunge
Us thinketh hem; and yet they spake hem so,
And spedde as wel in love as men now do;

OF THESE BLAKE WAWES FOR TO sayle,
O wind, O wind, the weder ginneth clere;
For in this see the boot hath swich travayle,
Of my conning that unnethe I it stere:
This see clepe I the tempestous matere

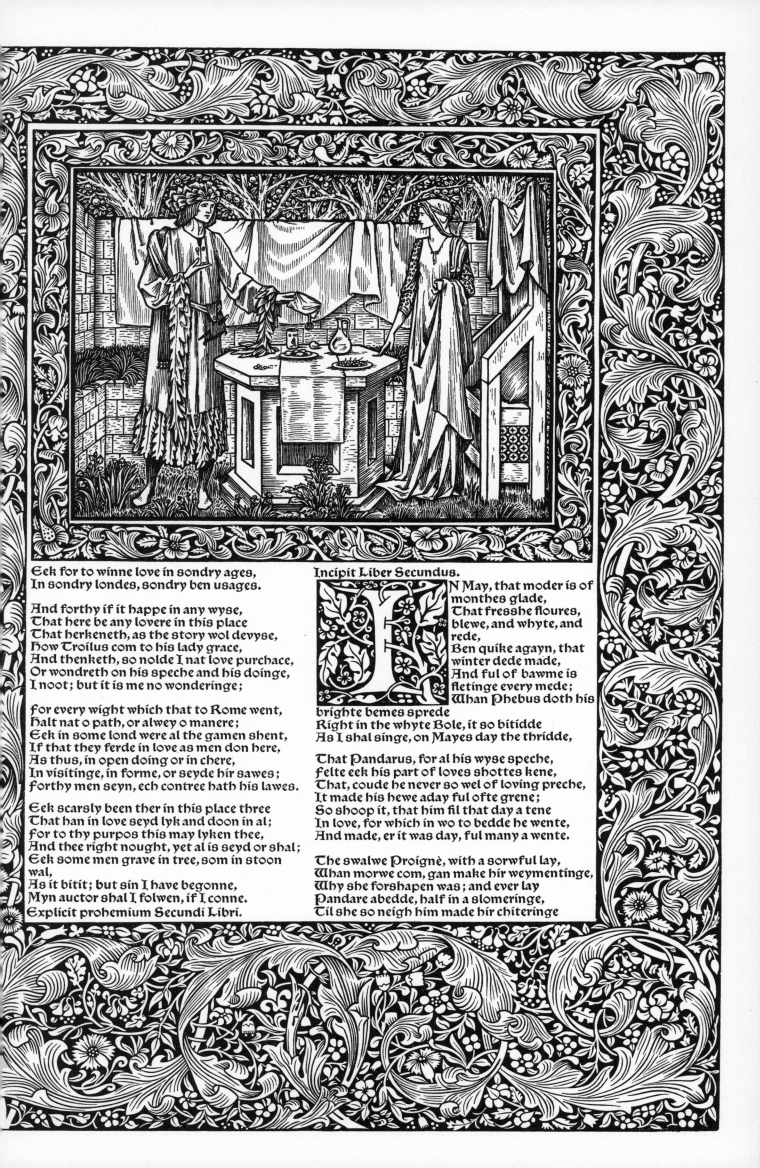

Eek for to winne love in sondry ages,
In sondry londes, sondry ben usages.

And forthy if it happe in any wyse,
That here be any lovere in this place
That herkeneth, as the story wol devyse,
How Troilus com to his lady grace,
And thenketh, so nolde I nat love purchace,
Or wondreth on his speche and his doinge,
I noot; but it is me no wonderinge;

For every wight which that to Rome went,
Halt nat o path, or alwey o manere;
Eek in some lond were al the gamen shent,
If that they ferde in love as men don here,
As thus, in open doing or in chere,
In visitinge, in forme, or seyde hir sawes;
Forthy men seyn, ech contree hath his lawes.

Eek scarsly been ther in this place three
That han in love seyd lyk and doon in al;
For to thy purpos this may lyken thee,
And thee right nought, yet al is seyd or shal;
Eek some men grave in tree, som in stoon wal,
As it bitit; but sin I have begonne,
Myn auctor shal I folwen, if I conne.
Explicit prohemium Secundi Libri.

Incipit Liber Secundus.

IN May, that moder is of monthes glade,
That fresshe floures, blewe, and whyte, and rede,
Ben quike agayn, that winter dede made,
And ful of bawme is fletinge every mede;
Whan Phebus doth his brighte bemes sprede
Right in the whyte Bole, it so bitidde
As I shal singe, on Mayes day the thridde,

That Pandarus, for al his wyse speche,
Felte eek his part of loves shottes kene,
That, coude he never so wel of loving preche,
It made his hewe aday ful ofte grene;
So shoop it, that him fil that day a tene
In love, for which in wo to bedde he wente,
And made, er it was day, ful many a wente.

The swalwe Proignè, with a sorwful lay,
Whan morwe com, gan make hir weymentinge,
Why she forshapen was; and ever lay
Pandare abedde, half in a slomeringe,
Til she so neigh him made hir chiteringe

How Tereus gan forth hir suster take,
That with the noyse of hir he gan awake;

And gan to calle, and dresse him up to ryse,
Remembringe him his erand was to done
from Troilus, and eek his greet empryse;
And caste and knew in good plyt was the mone
To doon viage, and took his wey ful sone
Unto his neces paleys ther bisyde;
Now Janus, god of entree, thou him gyde!

Whan he was come unto his neces place,
Wher is my lady? to hir folk seyde he;
And they him tolde; and he forth in gan pace,
And fond, two othere ladyes sete and she
Withinne a paved parlour; and they three
Herden a mayden reden hem the geste
Of the Sege of Thebes, whyl hem leste.

Quod Pandarus: Ma dame, God yow see,
With al your book and al the companye!
    Ey, uncle myn, welcome ywis, quod she,
And up she roos, and by the hond in hye
She took him faste, and seyde: This night thrye,
To goode mote it turne, of yow I mette!
    And with that word she doun on bench him
sette.

    Ye, nece, ye shal fare wel the bet,
If God wole, al this yeer, quod Pandarus;
But I am sory that I have yow let
To herknen of your book ye preysen thus;
for Goddes love, what seith it? tel it us.
Is it of love? O, som good ye me lere!
    Uncle, quod she, your maistresse is not here!

    With that they gonnen laughe, and tho she
seyde:
This romaunce is of Thebes, that we rede;
And we han herd how that king Laius deyde
Thurgh Edippus his sone, and al that dede;
And here we stenten at these lettres rede,
How the bisshop, as the book can telle,
Amphiorax, fil thurgh the ground to helle.

    Quod Pandarus: Al this knowe I myselve,
And al the assege of Thebes and the care;
for herof been ther maked bokes twelve:
But lat be this, and tel me how ye fare;
Do wey your barbe, and shew your face bare;
Do wey your book, rys up, and lat us daunce,
And lat us don to May som observaunce.

    A! God forbede! quod she, be ye mad?
Is that a widewes lyf, so God you save?
By God, ye maken me right sore adrad,
Ye ben so wilde, it semeth as ye rave!
It sete me wel bet ay in a cave
To bidde, and rede on holy seyntes lyves:
Lat maydens gon to daunce, and yonge wyves.

    As ever thryve I, quod this Pandarus,
Yet coude I telle a thing to doon you pleye.
    Now uncle dere, quod she, tel it us
484

for Goddes love; is than the assege aweye?
I am of Grekes so ferd that I deye.
    Nay, nay, quod he, as ever mote I thryve!
It is a thing wel bet than swiche fyve.

    Ye, holy God! quod she, what thing is that?
What? bet than swiche fyve? ey, nay, ywis!
for al this world ne can I reden what
It sholde been; som jape, I trowe, is this;
And but yourselven telle us what it is,
My wit is for to arede it al to lene;
As help me God, I noot nat what ye mene.

    And I your borow, ne never shal, for me,
This thing be told to yow, as mote I thryve!
    And why so, uncle myn? why so? quod she.
    By God, quod he, that wole I telle as blyve;
for prouder womman were ther noon onlyve,
And ye it wiste, in al the toun of Troye;
I jape nought, as ever have I joye!

    Tho gan she wondren more than biforn
A thousand fold, and doun hir eyen caste;
for never, sith the tyme that she was born,
To knowe thing desired she so faste;
And with a syk she seyde him at the laste:
Now, uncle myn, I nil yow nought displese,
Nor axen more, that may do yow disese.

    So after this, with many wordes glade,
And freendly tales, and with mery chere,
Of this and that they pleyde, and gunnen wade
In many an unkouth glad and deep matere,
As freendes doon, whan they ben met yfere;
Til she gan axen him how Ector ferde,
That was the tounes wal and Grekes yerde.

    ful wel, I thanke it God, quod Pandarus,
Save in his arm he hath a litel wounde;
And eek his fresshe brother Troilus,
The wyse worthy Ector the secounde,
In whom that every vertu list abounde,
As alle trouthe and alle gentillesse,
Wysdom, honour, fredom, and worthinesse.

    In good feith, eem, quod she, that lyketh me;
They faren wel, God save hem bothe two!
for trewely I holde it greet deyntee
A kinges sone in armes wel to do,
And been of good condiciouns therto;
for greet power and moral vertu here
Is selde yseye in o persone yfere.

    In good feith, that is sooth, quod Pandarus;
But, by my trouthe, the king hath sones tweye,
That is to mene, Ector and Troilus,
That certainly, though that I sholde deye,
They been as voyde of vyces, dar I seye,
As any men that liveth under the sonne,
Hir might is wyde yknowe, and what they conne.

Of Ector nedeth it nought for to telle;
In al this world ther nis a bettre knight
Than he, that is of worthinesse welle;

And he wel more vertu hath than might.
This knoweth many a wys and worthy wight.
The same prys of Troilus I seye,
God help me so, I knowe not swiche tweye.

By God, quod she, of Ector that is sooth;
Of Troilus the same thing trowe I;
For dredelees, men tellen that he dooth
In armes day by day so worthily,
And bereth him here at hoom so gentilly
To every wight, that al the prys hath he
Of hem that me were levest preysed be.

Ye sey right sooth, ywis, quod Pandarus;
For yesterday, whoso hadde with him been,
He might have wondred upon Troilus;
For never yet so thikke a swarm of been
Ne fleigh, as Grekes fro him gonne fleen;
And thorugh the feld, in every wightes ere,
Ther nas no cry but: Troilus is there!

Now here, now there, he hunted hem so faste,
Ther nas but Grekes blood; and Troilus,
Now hem he hurte, and hem alle doun he caste;
Ay where he wente it was arayed thus:
He was hir deeth, and sheld and lyf for us;
That as that day ther dorste noon withstonde,
Whyl that he held his blody swerd in honde.

Therto he is the freendlieste man
Of grete estat, that ever I saw my lyve;
And wher him list, best felawshipe can
To suche as him thinketh able for to thryve.
And with that word tho Pandarus, as blyve,
He took his leve, and seyde: I wol go henne.
Nay, blame have I, myn uncle, quod she thenne.

What eyleth yow to be thus wery sone,
And namelich of wommen? wol ye so?
Nay, sitteth down; by God, I have to done
With yow, to speke of wisdom er ye go.
And every wight that was aboute hem tho,
That herde that, gan fer awey to stonde,
Whyl they two hadde al that hem liste in honde.

Whan that hir tale al brought was to an ende
Of hire estat and of hir governaunce,
Quod Pandarus: Now is it tyme I wende;
But yet, I seye, aryseth, lat us daunce,
And cast your widwes habit to mischaunce:
What list yow thus yourself to disfigure,
Sith yow is tid thus fair an aventure?

A! wel bithought! for love of God, quod she,
Shal I not witen what ye mene of this?
No, this thing axeth layser, tho quod he,
And eek me wolde muche greve, ywis,
If I it tolde, and ye it toke amis.
Yet were it bet my tonge for to stille
Than seye a sooth that were ayeins your wille.

For, nece, by the goddesse Minerve,
And Juppiter, that maketh the thonder ringe,
And by the blisful Venus that I serve,

113

Ye been the womman in this world livinge,
Withoute paramours, to my witinge,
That I best love, and lothest am to greve,
And that ye witen wel yourself, I leve.

Ywis, myn uncle, quod she, grant mercy;
Your freendship have I founden ever yit;
I am to no man holden trewely
So muche as yow, and have so litel quit;
And, with the grace of God, emforth my wit,
As in my gilt I shal you never offende;
And if I have er this, I wol amende.

But, for the love of God, I yow beseche,
As ye ben he that I most love and triste,
Lat be to me your fremde maner speche,
And sey to me, your nece, what yow liste:
And with that word hir uncle anoon hir kiste,
And seyde: Gladly, leve nece dere,
Tak it for good that I shal seye yow here.

With that she gan hir eyen doun to caste,
And Pandarus to coghe gan a lyte,
And seyde: Nece, alwey, lo! to the laste,
Howso it be that som men hem delyte
With subtil art hir tales for to endyte,
Yet for al that, in hir entencioun,
Hir tale is al for som conclusioun.

And sithen thende is every tales strengthe,
And this matere is so bihovely,
What sholde I peynte or drawen it on lengthe
To yow, that been my freend so feithfully?
And with that word he gan right inwardly
Biholden hir, and loken on hir face,
And seyde: On suche a mirour goode grace!

Than thoughte he thus: If I my tale endyte
Ought hard, or make a proces any whyle,
She shal no savour han therin but lyte,
And trowe I wolde hir in my wil bigyle.
For tendre wittes wenen al be wyle
Theras they can nat pleynly understonde;
Forthy hir wit to serven wol I fonde:

And loked on hir in a besy wyse,
And she was war that he byheld hir so,
And seyde: Lord! so faste ye me avyse!
Sey ye me never er now? what sey ye, no?
Yes, yes, quod he, and bet wole er I go;
But, by my trouthe, I thoughte now if ye
Be fortunat, for now men shal it see.

For to every wight som goodly aventure
Som tyme is shape, if he it can receyven;
And if that he wol take of it no cure,
Whan that it cometh, but wilfully it weyven,
Lo, neither cas nor fortune him deceyven,
But right his verray slouthe and wrecchednesse;
And swich a wight is for to blame, I gesse.

Good aventure, O bele nece, have ye
Ful lightly founden, and ye conne it take;
And, for the love of God, and eek of me,

485

Cacche it anoon, lest aventure slake.
What sholde I lenger proces of it make?
Yif me your hond, for in this world is noon,
If that you list, a wight so wel begoon.

And sith I speke of good entencioun,
As I to yow have told wel herebiforn,
And love as wel your honour and renoun
As creature in al this world yborn;
By alle the othes that I have yow sworn,
And ye be wrooth therfore, or wene I lye,
Ne shal I never seen yow eft with yë.

Beth nought agast, ne quaketh nat; wherto?
Ne chaungeth nat for fere so your hewe;
For hardely, the werste of this is do;
And though my tale as now be to yow newe,
Yet trist alwey, ye shal me finde trewe;
And were it thing that me thoughte unsittinge,
To yow nolde I no swiche tales bringe.

🖙Now, my good eem, for Goddes love, I preye,
Quod she, com of, and tel me what it is;
For bothe I am agast what ye wol seye,
And eek me longeth it to wite, ywis.
For whether it be wel or be amis,
Sey on, lat me not in this fere dwelle;
🖙So wol I doon, now herkneth, I shal telle:

Now, nece myn, the kinges dere sone,
The goode, wyse, worthy, fresshe, and free,
Which alwey for to do wel is his wone,
The noble Troilus, so loveth thee,
That, bot ye helpe, it wol his bane be.
Lo, here is al, what sholde I more seye?
Doth what yow list, to make him live or deye.

But if ye lete him deye, I wol sterve;
Have her my trouthe, nece, I nil not lyen;
Al sholde I with this knyf my throte kerve:
🖙With that the teres braste out of his yën,
And seyde: If that ye doon us bothe dyen,
Thus giltelees, than have ye fisshed faire;
What mende ye, though that we bothe apeyre?

Allas! he which that is my lord so dere,
That trewe man, that noble gentil knight,
That nought desireth but your freendly chere,
I see him deye, ther he goth upright,
And hasteth him, with al his fulle might,
For to be slayn, if fortune wol assente;
Allas! that God yow swich a beautee sente!

If it be so that ye so cruel be,
That of his deeth yow liste nought to recche,
That is so trewe and worthy, as ye see,
No more than of a japere or a wrecche,
If ye be swich, your beautee may not strecche
To make amendes of so cruel a dede;
Avysement is good bifore the nede.

Wo worth the faire gemme vertulees!
Wo worth that herbe also that dooth no bote!
Wo worth that beautee that is routhelees!

486

Wo worth that wight that tret ech under fote!
And ye, that been of beautee crop and rote,
If therwithal in you ther be no routhe,
Than is it harm ye liven, by my trouthe!

And also thenk wel, that this is no gaude;
For me were lever, thou and I and he
Were hanged, than I sholde been his baude,
As heyghe, as men mighte on us alle ysee:
I am thyn eem, the shame were to me,
As wel as thee, if that I sholde assente,
Thorugh myn abet, that he thyn honour shente.

Now understond, for I yow nought requere
To binde yow to him thorugh no beheste,
But only that ye make him bettre chere
Than ye han doon er this, and more feste,
So that his lyf be saved, at the leste:
This al and som, and playnly our entente;
God helpe me so, I never other mente.

Lo, this request is not but skile, ywis,
Ne doute of reson, pardee, is ther noon.
I sette the worste that ye dredden this,
Men wolden wondren seen him come or goon:
And ther ayeins answere I thus anoon,
That every wight, but he be fool of kinde,
Wol deme it love of freendship in his minde.

What? who wol deme, though he see a man
To temple go, that he the images eteth?
Thenk eek how wel and wysly that he can
Governe himself, that he nothing foryeteth,
That, wher he cometh, he prys and thank him
geteth;
And eek therto, he shal come here so selde,
What fors were it though al the toun behelde?

Swich love of freendes regneth al this toun;
And wrye yow in that mantel evermo;
And, God so wis be my savacioun,
As I have seyd, your beste is to do so.
But alwey, goode nece, to stinte his wo,
So lat your daunger sucred ben a lyte,
That of his deeth ye be nought for to wyte.

🖙Criseyde, which that herde him in this wyse,
Thoughte: I shal fele what he meneth, ywis.
🖙Now, eem, quod she, what wolde ye devyse,
What is your reed I sholde doon of this?
🖙That is wel seyd, quod he, certayn, best is
That ye him love ayein for his lovinge,
As love for love is skilful guerdoninge.

Thenk eek, how elde wasteth every houre
In eche of yow a party of beautee;
And therfore, er that age thee devoure,
Go love, for, olde, ther wol no wight of thee.
Lat this proverbe a lore unto yow be;
🖙To late ywar, quod Beautee, whan it paste;🖙
And elde daunteth daunger at the laste.

The kinges fool is woned to cryen loude,
Whan that him thinketh a womman bereth hir hyë,

So longe mote ye live, and alle proude,
Til crowes feet be growe under your yë,
And sende yow thanne a mirour in to pryë
In whiche ye may see your face amorwe! *
Nece, I bidde wisshe yow no more sorwe.

* With this he stente, and caste adoun the heed,
And she bigan to breste awepe anoon.
And seyde: Allas, for wo! why nere I deed?
for of this world the feith is al agoon!
Allas! what sholden straunge to me doon,
When he, that for my beste freend I wende,
Ret me to love, and sholde it me defende?

Allas! I wolde han trusted, doutelees,
That if that I, thurgh my disaventure,
Had loved other him or Achilles,
Ector, or any mannes creature,
Ye nolde han had no mercy ne mesure
On me, but alwey had me in repreve;
This false world, allas! who may it leve?

What? is this al the joye and al the feste?
Is this your reed, is this my blisful cas?
Is this the verray mede of your beheste?
Is al this peynted proces seyd, allas!
Right for this fyn? O lady myn, Pallas!
Thou in this dredful cas for me purveye;
for so astonied am I that I deye!

* With that she gan ful sorwfully to syke;
* A! may it be no bet? quod Pandarus
By God, I shal no more com here this wyke,
And God toforn, that am mistrusted thus;
I see ful wel that ye sette lyte of us,
Or of our deeth! Allas! I woful wrecche!
Mighte he yet live, of me is nought to recche.

O cruel God, O dispitouse Marte,
O furies three of helle, on yow I crye!
So lat me never out of this hous departe,
If that I mente harm or vilanye!
But sith I see my lord mot nedes dye,
And I with him, here I me shryve, and seye
That wikkedly ye doon us bothe deye.

But sith it lyketh yow that I be deed,
By Neptunus, that god is of the see,
fro this forth shal I never eten breed
Til I myn owene herte blood may see;
for certayn, I wole deye as sone as he.
* And up he sterte, and on his wey he raughte,
Til she agayn him by the lappe caughte.

Criseyde, which that wel neigh starf for fere,
So as she was the ferfulleste wight
That mighte be, and herde eek with hir ere,
And saw the sorwful ernest of the knight,
And in his preyere eek saw noon unright,
And for the harm that mighte eek fallen more,
She gan to rewe, and dradde hir wonder sore;

And thoughte thus: Unhappes fallen thikke
Alday for love, and in swich maner cas,
ii4

As men ben cruel in hemself and wikke;
And if this man slee here himself, allas!
In my presence, it wol be no solas.
What men wolde of hit deme I can nat seye;
It nedeth me ful sleyly for to pleye.

* And with a sorwful syk she seyde thrye:
A! Lord! what me is tid a sory chaunce!
for myn estat now lyth in jupartye,
And eek myn emes lyf lyth in balaunce;
But nathelees, with Goddes governaunce,
I shal so doon, myn honour shal I kepe,
And eek his lyf * and stinte for to wepe.

* Of harmes two, the lesse is for to chese;
Yet have I lever maken him good chere
In honour, than myn emes lyf to lese;
Ye seyn, ye nothing elles me requere?
* No, wis, quod he, myn owene nece dere.
* Now wel, quod she, and I wol doon my peyne;
I shal myn herte ayeins my lust constreyne,

But that I nil not holden him in honde,
Ne love a man, ne can I not, ne may
Ayeins my wil; but elles wol I fonde,
Myn honour sauf, plese him fro day to day;
Therto nolde I nought ones have seyd nay,
But that I dredde, as in my fantasye;
But cesse cause, ay cesseth maladye.

And here I make a protestacioun,
That in this proces if ye depper go,
That certaynly, for no savacioun
Of yow, though that ye sterve bothe two,
Though al the world on o day be my fo,
Ne shal I never on him han other routhe.
* I graunte wel, quod Pandare, by my trouthe.

But may I truste wel therto, quod he,
That, of this thing that ye han hight me here,
Ye wol it holden trewly unto me?
* Ye, doutelees, quod she, myn uncle dere.
* Ne that I shal han cause in this matere,
Quod he, to pleyne, or after yow to preche?
* Why, no, pardee; what nedeth more speche?

* Tho fillen they in othere tales glade,
Til at the laste: O good eem, quod she tho,
for love of God, which that us bothe made,
Tel me how first ye wisten of his wo:
Wot noon of hit but ye? * He seyde, No.
* Can he wel speke of love? quod she, I preye,
Tel me, for I the bet me shal purveye.

* Tho Pandarus a litel gan to smyle,
And seyde: By my trouthe, I shal yow telle.
This other day, nought gon ful longe whyle,
Inwith the paleys-gardyn, by a welle,
Gan he and I wel half a day to dwelle,
Right for to speken of an ordenaunce,
How we the Grekes mighte disavaunce.

Sone after that bigonne we to lepe,
And casten with our dartes to and fro,
487

Til at the laste he seyde, he wolde slepe,
And on the gres adoun he leyde him tho;
And I after gan rome to and fro
Til that I herde, as that I welk allone,
How he bigan ful wofully to grone.

Tho gan I stalke him softely bihinde,
And sikerly, the sothe for to seyne,
As I can clepe ayein now to my minde,
Right thus to Love he gan him for to pleyne;
He seyde: Lord! have routhe upon my peyne,
Al have I been rebel in myn entente;
Now, mea culpa, lord! I me repente.

O god, that at thy disposicioun
Ledest the fyn, by juste purveyaunce,
Of every wight, my lowe confessioun
Accepte in gree, and send me swich penaunce
As lyketh thee, but from desesperaunce,
That may my goost departe awey fro thee,
Thou be my sheld, for thy benignitee.

For certes, lord, so sore hath she me wounded
That stod in blak, with loking of hir yën,
That to myn hertes botme it is ysounded,
Thorugh which I woot that I mot nedes dyen;
This is the worste, I dar me not biwryen;
And wel the hotter been the gledes rede,
That men hem wryen with asshen pale & dede.

With that he smoot his heed adoun anoon,
And gan to motre, I noot what, trewely.
And I with that gan stille awey to goon,
And leet therof as nothing wist hadde I,
And come ayein anoon and stood him by,
And seyde: Awake, ye slepen al to longe;
It semeth nat that love dooth yow longe,

That slepen so that no man may yow wake.
Who sey ever or this so dul a man?
Ye, freend, quod he, do ye your hedes ake
For love, and lat me liven as I can,
But though that he for wo was pale and wan,
Yet made he tho as fresh a contenaunce,
As though he shulde have led the newe daunce.

This passed forth, til now, this other day,
It fel that I com roming al allone
Into his chaumbre, and fond how that he lay
Upon his bed; but man so sore grone
Ne herde I never, and what that was his mone,
Ne wiste I nought; for, as I was cominge,
Al sodeynly he lefte his compleyninge.

Of which I took somwhat suspicioun,
And neer I com, and fond he wepte sore;
And God so wis be my savacioun,
As never of thing hadde I no routhe more.
For neither with engyn, ne with no lore,
Unethes mighte I fro the deeth him kepe;
That yet fele I myn herte for him wepe.

And God wot, never, sith that I was born,
Was I so bisy no man for to preche,

Ne never was to wight so depe ysworn,
Or he me tolde who mighte been his leche.
But now to yow rehersen al his speche,
Or alle his woful wordes for to soune,
Ne bid me not, but ye wol see me swowne.

But for to save his lyf, and elles nought,
And to non harm of yow, thus am I driven;
And for the love of God that us hath wrought,
Swich chere him dooth, that he and I may liven.
Now have I plat to yow myn herte schriven;
And sin ye woot that myn entente is clene,
Tak hede therof, for I non yvel mene.

And right good thrift, I pray to God, have ye,
That han swich oon ycaught withoute net;
And be ye wys, as ye ben fair to see,
Wel in the ring than is the ruby set.
Ther were never two so wel ymet,
Whan ye ben his al hool, as he is youre:
Ther mighty God yet graunte us see that houre!

Nay, therof spak I not, a, ha! quod she,
As helpe me God, ye shenden every deel!
O mercy, dere nece, anoon quod he,
Whatso I spak, I mente nought but weel,
By Mars the god, that helmed is of steel;
Now beth nought wrooth, my blood, my nece dere.
Now wel, quod she, foryeven be it here!

With this he took his leve, and hoom he wente;
And Lord, how he was glad and wel bigoon!
Criseyde aroos, no lenger she ne stente,
But straught into hir closet wente anoon,
And sette here doun as stille as any stoon,
And every word gan up and doun to winde,
That he hadde seyd, as it com hir to minde;

And wex somdel astonied in hir thought,
Right for the newe cas; but whan that she
Was ful avysed, tho fond she right nought
Of peril, why she oughte afered be.
For man may love, of possibilitee,
A womman so, his herte may tobreste,
And she nought love ayein, but if hir leste.

But as she sat allone and thoughte thus,
Thascry aroos at skarmish al withoute,
And men cryde in the strete: See, Troilus
Hath right now put to flight the Grekes route!
With that gan al hir meynee for to shoute:
A! go we see, caste up the latis wyde;
For thurgh this strete he moot to palays ryde;

For other wey is fro the yate noon
Of Dardanus, ther open is the cheyne.
With that com he and al his folk anoon
An esy pas rydinge, in routes tweyne,
Right as his happy day was, sooth to seyne,
For which, men say, may nought disturbed be
That shal bityden of necessitee.

This Troilus sat on his baye stede,
Al armed, save his heed, ful richely,

And wounded was his hors, and gan to blede,
On whiche he rood a pas, ful softely;
But swich a knightly sighte, trewely,
As was on him, was nought, withouten faile,
To loke on Mars, that god is of batayle.

So lyk a man of armes and a knight
He was to seen, fulfild of heigh prowesse;
For bothe he hadde a body and a might
To doon that thing, as wel as hardinesse;
And eek to seen him in his gere him dresse,
So fresh, so yong, so weldy semed he,
It was an heven upon him for to see.

His helm tohewen was in twenty places,
That by a tissew heng, his bak bihinde,
His sheld todasshed was with swerdes & maces,
In which men mighte many an arwe finde
That thirled hadde horn and nerf and rinde;
And ay the peple cryde: Here cometh our joye,
And, next his brother, holdere up of Troye!

For which he wex a litel reed for shame,
Whan he the peple upon him herde cryen,
That to biholde it was a noble game,
How sobreliche he caste doun his yën.
Cryseyda gan al his chere aspyen,
And leet so softe it in hir herte sinke,
That to hirself she seyde: Who yaf me drinke?

For of hir owene thought she wex al reed,
Remembringe hir right thus: Lo, this is he
Which that myn uncle swereth he moot be deed,
But I on him have mercy and pitee;
And with that thought, for pure ashamed, she
Gan in hir heed to pulle, and that as faste,
Whyl he and al the peple forby paste,

And gan to caste and rollen up and doun
Withinne hir thought his excellent prowesse,
And his estat, and also his renoun,
His wit, his shap, and eek his gentillesse;
But most hir favour was, for his distresse
Was al for hir, and thoughte it was a routhe
To sleen swich oon, if that he mente trouthe.

Now mighte som envyous jangle thus:
This was a sodeyn love, how mighte it be
That she so lightly lovede Troilus
Right for the firste sighte; ye, pardee?
Now whoso seyth so, mote he never thee!
For every thing, a ginning hath it nede
Er al be wrought, withouten any drede.

For I sey nought that she so sodeynly
Yaf him hir love, but that she gan enclyne
To lyke him first, and I have told yow why;
And after that, his manhod and his pyne
Made love withinne hir herte for to myne,
For which, by proces and by good servyse,
He gat hir love, and in no sodeyn wyse.

And also blisful Venus, wel arayed,
Sat in hir seventhe house of hevene tho,

Disposed wel, and with aspectes payed,
To helpen sely Troilus of his wo.
And, sooth to seyn, she nas nat al a fo
To Troilus in his nativitee;
God woot that wel the soner spedde he.

Now lat us stinte of Troilus a throwe,
That rydeth forth, and lat us tourne faste
Unto Criseyde, that heng hir heed ful lowe,
Theras she sat allone, and gan to caste
Wheron she wolde apoynte hir at the laste,
If it so were hir eem ne wolde cesse,
For Troilus, upon hir for to presse.

And, Lord! so she gan in hir thought argue
In this matere of which I have yow told,
And what to doon best were, and what eschue,
That plyted she ful ofte in many fold.
Now was hir herte warm, now was it cold,
And what she thoughte somwhat shal I wryte,
As to myn auctor listeth for to endyte.

She thoughte wel, that Troilus persone
She knew by sighte and eek his gentillesse,
And thus she seyde: Al were it nought to done,
To graunte him love, yet, for his worthinesse,
It were honour, with pley and with gladnesse,
In honestee, with swich a lord to dele,
For myn estat, and also for his hele.

Eek, wel wot I my kinges sone is he;
And sith he hath to see me swich delyt,
If I wolde utterly his sighte flee,
Paraunter he mighte have me in dispyt,
Thurgh which I mighte stonde in worse plyt;
Now were I wys, me hate to purchace,
Withouten nede, ther I may stonde in grace?

In every thing, I woot, ther lyth mesure.
For though a man forbede dronkenesse,
He nought forbet that every creature
Be drinkelees for alwey, as I gesse;
Eek sith I woot for me is his distresse,
I ne oughte not for that thing him despyse,
Sith it is so, he meneth in good wyse.

And eek I knowe, of longe tyme agoon,
His thewes goode, and that he is not nyce.
Ne avauntour, seyth men, certein, is he noon;
To wys is he to do so gret a vyce;
Ne als I nel him never so cheryce,
That he may make avaunt, by juste cause;
He shal me never binde in swiche a clause.

Now set a cas, the hardest is, ywis,
Men mighten deme that he loveth me:
What dishonour were it unto me, this?
May I him lette of that? why nay, pardee!
I knowe also, and alday here and see,
Men loven wommen al this toun aboute;
Be they the wers? why, nay, withouten doute.

I thenk eek how he able is for to have
Of al this noble toun the thriftieste,

To been his love, so she hir honour save;
For out and out he is the worthieste,
Save only Ector, which that is the beste.
And yet his lyf al lyth now in my cure,
But swich is love, and eek myn aventure.

Ne me to love, a wonder is it nought;
For wel wot I myself, so God me spede,
Al wolde I that noon wistë of this thought,
I am oon the fayreste, out of drede,
And goodlieste, whoso taketh hede;
And so men seyn in al the toun of Troye.
What wonder is it though he of me have joye?

I am myn owene woman, wel at ese,
I thank it God, as after myn estat;
Right yong, and stonde unteyd in lusty lese,
Withouten jalousye or swich debat;
Shal noon housbonde seyn to me, Chekmat!
For either they ben ful of jalousye,
Or maisterful, or loven novelrye.

What shal I doon? to what fyn live I thus?
Shal I nat loven, in cas if that me leste?
What, par dieux! I am nought religious!
And though that I myn herte sette at reste
Upon this knight, that is the worthieste,
And kepe alwey myn honour and my name,
By alle right, it may do me no shame.

*But right as whan the sonne shyneth brighte,
In March, that chaungeth ofte tyme his face,
And that a cloud is put with wind to flighte
Which oversprat the sonne as for a space,
A cloudy thought gan thorugh hir soule pace,
That overspradde hir brighte thoughtes alle,
So that for fere almost she gan to falle.

That thought was this: Allas! sin I am free,
Sholde I now love, and putte in jupartye
My sikernesse, and thrallen libertee?
Allas! how dorste I thenken that folye?
May I nought wel in other folk aspye
Hir dredful joye, hir constreynt, and hir peyne?
Ther loveth noon, that she nath why to pleyne.

For love is yet the moste stormy lyf,
Right of himself, that ever was bigonne;
For ever som mistrust, or nyce stryf,
Ther is in love, som cloud is over the sonne:
Therto we wrecched wommen nothing conne,
Whan us is wo, but wepe and sitte and thinke;
Our wreche is this, our owene wo to drinke.

Also these wikked tonges been so prest
To speke us harm, eek men be so untrewe,
That, right anoon as cessed is hir lest,
So cesseth love, and forth to love a newe:
But harm ydoon, is doon, whoso it rewe.
For though these men for love hem first torende,
Ful sharp biginning breketh ofte at ende.

How ofte tyme hath it yknowen be,
The treson, that to womman hath be do?
490

To what fyn is swich love, I can nat see,
Or wher bicomth it, whan it is ago;
Ther is no wight that woot, I trowe so,
Wher it bycomth; lo, no wight on it sporneth;
That erst was nothing, into nought it torneth.

How bisy, if I love, eek moste I be
To plesen hem that jangle of love, and demen,
And coye hem, that they sey non harm of me?
For though ther be no cause, yet hem semen
Al be for harm that folk hir freendes quemen;
And who may stoppen every wikked tonge,
Or soun of belles whyl that they be ronge?

*And after that, hir thought bigan to clere,
And seyde: He which that nothing undertaketh,
Nothing ne acheveth, be him looth or dere.
*And with an other thought hir herte quaketh;
Than slepeth hope, and after dreed awaketh;
Now hoot, now cold; but thus, bitwixen tweye,
She rist hir up, and went hir for to pleye.

Adoun the steyre anoon/right tho she wente
Into the gardin, with hir neces three,
And up and doun ther made many a wente,
Flexippe, she, Tharbe, and Antigone,
To pleyen, that it joye was to see;
And othere of hir wommen, a gret route,
Hir folwede in the gardin al aboute.

This yerd was large, and rayled alle the aleyes,
And shadwed wel with blosmy bowes grene,
And benched newe, and sonded alle the weyes,
In which she walketh arm in arm bitwene;
Til at the laste Antigone the shene
Gan on a Troian song to singe clere,
That it an heven was hir voys to here.

She seyde: O love, to whom I have and shal
Ben humble subgit, trewe in myn entente,
As I best can, to yow, lord, yeve ich al
For evermore, myn hertes lust to rente.
For never yet thy grace no wight sente
So blisful cause as me, my lyf to lede
In alle joye and seurtee, out of drede.

Ye, blisful god, han me so wel beset
In love, ywis, that al that bereth lyf
Imaginen ne cowde how to ben bet;
For, lord, withouten jalousye or stryf,
I love oon which that is most ententyf
To serven wel, unwery or unfeyned,
That ever was, and leest with harm distreyned.

As he that is the welle of worthinesse,
Of trouthe ground, mirour of goodliheed,
Of wit Appollo, stoon of sikernesse,
Of vertu rote, of lust findere and heed,
Thurgh which is alle sorwe fro me deed,
Ywis, I love him best, so doth he me;
Now good thrift have he, wherso that he be!

Whom sholde I thanke but yow, god of love,
Of al this blisse, in which to bathe I ginne?

And thanked be ye, lord, for that I love!
This is the righte lyf that I am inne,
To flemen alle manere vyce and sinne:
This doth me so to vertu for to entende,
That day by day I in my wil amende.

And whoso seyth that for to love is vyce,
Or thraldom, though he fele in it distresse,
He outher is envyous, or right nyce,
Or is unmighty, for his shrewednesse,
To loven; for swich maner folk, I gesse,
Defamen love, as nothing of him knowe;
They speken, but they bente never his bowe.

What is the sonne wers, of kinde righte,
Though that a man, for feblesse of his yën,
May nought endure on it to see for brighte?
Or love the wers, though wrecches on it cryen?
No wele is worth, that may no sorwe dryen.
And forthy, who that hath an heed of verre,
Fro cast of stones war him in the werre!

But I with al myn herte and al my might,
As I have seyd, wol love, unto my laste,
My dere herte, and al myn owene knight,
In which myn herte growen is so faste,
And his in me, that it shal ever laste.
Al dredde I first to love him to biginne,
Now woot I wel, ther is no peril inne.

And of hir song right with that word she
stente,
And therwithal: Now, nece, quod Criseyde,
Who made this song with so good entente?
Antigone answerde anoon, and seyde:
Ma dame, ywis, the goodlieste mayde
Of greet estat in al the toun of Troye;
And let hir lyf in most honour and joye.

Forsothe, so it semeth by hir song,
Quod tho Criseyde, and gan therwith to syke,
And seyde: Lord, is there swich blisse among
These lovers, as they conne faire endyte?
Ye, wis, quod fresh Antigone the whyte,
For alle the folk that han or been on lyve
Ne conne wel the blisse of love discryve.

But wene ye that every wrecche woot
The parfit blisse of love? why, nay, ywis;
They wenen al be love, if oon be hoot;
Do wey, do wey, they woot nothing of this!
Men mosten axe at seyntes if it is
Aught fair in hevene; why? for they conne telle;
And axen fendes, is it foul in helle.

Criseyde unto that purpos nought answerde,
But seyde: Ywis, it wol be night as faste.
But every word which that she of hir herde,
She gan to prenten in hir herte faste,
And ay gan love hir lasse for to agaste
Than it dide erst, and sinken in hir herte,
That she wex somwhat able to converte.

The dayes honour, and the hevenes yë,

The nightes fo, al this clepe I the sonne,
Gan westren faste, and dounward for to wrye,
As he that hadde his dayes cours yronne;
And whyte thinges wexen dimme and donne
For lak of light, and sterres for to appere,
That she and al hir folk in wente yfere.

So whan it lyked hir to goon to reste,
And voyded weren they that voyden oughte,
She seyde, that to slepe wel hir leste.
Hir wommen sone til hir bed hir broughte.
Whan al was hust, than lay she stille, & thoughte
Of al this thing the manere and the wyse.
Reherce it nedeth nought, for ye ben wyse.

A nightingale, upon a cedre grene,
Under the chambre-wal ther as she lay,
Ful loude sang ayein the mone shene,
Paraunter, in his briddes wyse, a lay
Of love, that made hir herte fresh and gay.
That herkned she so longe in good entente,
Til at the laste the dede sleep hir hente.

And, as she sleep, anoon-right tho hir mette,
How that an egle, fethered whyt as boon,
Under hir brest his longe clawes sette,
And out hir herte he rente, and that anoon,
And dide his herte into hir brest to goon,
Of which she nought agroos ne nothing smerte,
And forth he fleigh, with herte left for herte.

Now lat hir slepe, and we our tales holde
Of Troilus, that is to paleys riden,
Fro the scarmuch, of the whiche I tolde,
And in his chambre sit, and hath abiden
Til two or three of his messages yeden
For Pandarus, and soughten him ful faste,
Til they him founde, & broughte him at the laste.

This Pandarus com leping in at ones
And seide thus: Who hath ben wel ybete
Today with swerdes, and with slinge-stones,
But Troilus, that hath caught him an hete?
And gan to jape, and seyde: Lord, so ye swete!
But rys, and lat us soupe and go to reste;
And he answerde him: Do we as thee leste.

With al the haste goodly that they mighte,
They spedde hem fro the souper unto bedde;
And every wight out at the dore him dighte,
And wher him list upon his wey he spedde;
But Troilus, that thoughte his herte bledde
For wo, til that he herde som tydinge,
He seyde: Freend, shal I now wepe or singe?

Quod Pandarus: Ly stille, and lat me slepe,
And don thyn hood, thy nedes spedde be;
And chese, if thou wolt singe or daunce or lepe;
At shorte wordes, thow shalt trowe me.
Sire, my nece wol do wel by thee,
And love thee best, by God and by my trouthe,
But lak of pursuit make it in thy slouthe.

For thus ferforth I have thy work bigonne,

fro day to day, til this day, by the morwe,
Hir love of freendship have I to thee wonne,
And also hath she leyd hir feyth to borwe.
Algate a foot is hameled of thy sorwe.
What sholde I lenger sermon of it holde?
As ye han herd bifore, al he him tolde.

But right as floures, thorugh the colde of night
Yclosed, stoupen on hir stalkes lowe,
Redressen hem ayein the sonne bright,
And spreden on hir kinde cours by rowe;
Right so gan tho his eyen up to throwe
This Troilus, and seyde: O Venus dere,
Thy might, thy grace, yheried be it here!

And to Pandare he held up bothe his hondes,
And seyde: Lord, al thyn be that I have;
for I am hool, al brosten been my bondes;
A thousand Troians who so that me yave,
Eche after other, God so wis me save,
Ne mighte me so gladen; lo, myn herte,
It spredeth so for joye, it wol tosterte!

But Lord, how shal I doon, how shal I liven?
Whan shal I next my dere herte see?
How shal this longe tyme awey be driven,
Til that thou be ayein at hir fro me?
Thou mayst answere, Abyd, abyd, but he
That hangeth by the nekke, sooth to seyne,
In grete disese abydeth for the peyne.

Al esily, now, for the love of Marte,
Quod Pandarus, for every thing hath tyme;
So longe abyd til that the night departe;
for al so siker as thow lyst here by me,
And God toforn, I wol be there at pryme,
And for thy werk somwhat as I shal seye,
Or on som other wight this charge leye.

for pardee, God wot, I have ever yit
Ben redy thee to serve, and to this night
Have I nought fayned, but emforth my wit
Don al thy lust, and shal with al my might.
Do now as I shal seye, and fare aright;
And if thou nilt, wyte al thyself thy care,
On me is nought along thyn yvel fare.

I woot wel that thow wyser art than I
A thousand fold, but if I were as thou,
God helpe me so, as I wolde outrely,
Right of myn owene hond, wryte hir right now
A lettre, in which I wolde hir tellen how
I ferde amis, and hir beseche of routhe;
Now help thyself, and leve it not for slouthe.

And I myself shal therwith to hir goon;
And whan thou wost that I am with hir there,
Worth thou upon a courser right anoon,
Ye, hardily, right in thy beste gere,
And ryd forth by the place, as nought ne were,
And thou shalt finde us, if I may, sittinge
At som windowe, into the strete lokinge.

And if thee list, than maystow us saluwe,

492

And upon me make thy contenaunce;
But, by thy lyf, be war and faste eschuwe
To tarien ought, God shilde us fro mischaunce!
Ryd forth thy wey, and hold thy governaunce;
And we shal speke of thee somwhat, I trowe,
Whan thou art goon, to do thyne eres glowe!

Touching thy lettre, thou art wys ynough,
I woot thow nilt it digneliche endyte;
As make it with thise argumentes tough;
Ne scrivenish or craftily thou it wryte;
Beblotte it with thy teres eek a lyte;
And if thou wryte a goodly word al softe,
Though it be good, reherce it not to ofte.

for though the beste harpour upon lyve
Wolde on the beste souned joly harpe
That ever was, with alle his fingres fyve,
Touche ay o streng, or ay o werbul harpe,
Were his nayles poynted never so sharpe,
It shulde maken every wight to dulle,
To here his glee, and of his strokes fulle.

Ne jompre eek no discordaunt thing yfere,
As thus, to usen termes of phisyk;
In loves termes, hold of thy matere
The forme alwey, and do that it be lyk;
for if a peyntour wolde peynte a pyk
With asses feet, and hede it as an ape,
It cordeth nought; so nere it but a jape.

This counseyl lyked wel to Troilus;
But, as a dreedful lover, he seyde this:
Allas, my dere brother Pandarus,
I am ashamed for to wryte, ywis,
Lest of myn innocence I seyde amis,
Or that she nolde it for despyt receyve;
Thanne were I deed, ther mighte it nothing
weyve.

To that Pandare answerde: If thee lest,
Do that I seye, and lat me therwith goon;
for by that Lord that formed est and west,
I hope of it to bringe answere anoon
Right of hir hond, and if that thou nilt noon,
Lat be; and sory mote he been his lyve,
Ayeins thy lust that helpeth thee to thryve.

Quod Troilus: Depardieux, I assente;
Sin that thee list, I will aryse and wryte;
And blisful God preye ich, with good entente,
The vyage, and the lettre I shal endyte,
So spede it; and thou, Minerva, the whyte,
Yif thou me wit my lettre to devyse:
And sette him doun, and wroot right in this
wyse.

first he gan hir his righte lady calle,
His hertes lyf, his lust, his sorwes leche,
His blisse, and eek this othere termes alle,
That in swich cas these loveres alle seche;
And in ful humble wyse, as in his speche,
He gan him recomaunde unto hir grace;
To telle al how, it axeth muchel space.

And after this, ful lowly he hir prayde
To be nought wrooth, though he, of his folye,
So hardy was to hir to wryte, and seyde,
That love it made, or elles moste he dye,
And pitously gan mercy for to crye;
And after that he seyde, and ley ful loude,
Himself was litel worth, and lesse he coude;

And that she sholde han his conning excused,
That litel was, and eek he dredde hir so,
And his unworthinesse he ay acused;
And after that, than gan he telle his wo;
But that was endeles, withouten ho;
And seyde, he wolde in trouthe alwey him holde;
And radde it over, and gan the lettre folde.

And with his salte teres gan he bathe
The ruby in his signet, and it sette
Upon the wex deliverliche and rathe;
Therwith a thousand tymes, er he lette,
He kiste tho the lettre that he shette,
And seyde: Lettre, a blisful destenee
Thee shapen is, my lady shal thee see.

This Pandare took the lettre, and that by tyme
Amorwe, and to his neces paleys sterte,
And faste he swoor, that it was passed pryme,
And gan to jape, and seyde: Ywis, myn herte,
So fresh it is, although it sore smerte,
I may not slepe never a Mayes morwe;
I have a joly wo, a lusty sorwe.

Criseyde, whan that she hir uncle herde,
With dreedful herte, and desirous to here
The cause of his cominge, thus answerde:
Now by your feyth, myn uncle, quod she, dere,
What maner windes gydeth yow now here?
Tel us your joly wo and your penaunce,
How ferforth be ye put in loves daunce.

By God, quod he, I hoppe alwey bihinde!
And she to laughe, it thoughte hir herte breste.
Quod Pandarus: Loke alwey that ye finde
Game in myn hood, but herkneth, if yow leste;
Ther is right now come into toune a geste,
A Greek espye, and telleth newe thinges,
For which come I to telle yow tydinges.

Into the gardin go we, and we shal here,
Al prevely, of this a long sermoun.
With that they wenten arm in arm yfere
Into the gardin from the chaumbre doun.
And whan that he so fer was that the soun
Of that he speke, no man here mighte,
He seyde hir thus, and out the lettre plighte:

Lo, he that is al hoolly youres free
Him recomaundeth lowly to your grace,
And sent to you this lettre here by me;
Avyseth you on it, whan ye han space,
And of som goodly answere yow purchace;
Or, helpe me God, so pleynly for to seyne,
He may not longe liven for his peyne.

Ful dredfully tho gan she stonde stille,
And took it nought, but al hir humble chere
Gan for to chaunge, and seyde: Scrit ne bille,
For love of God, that toucheth swich matere,
Ne bring me noon; and also, uncle dere,
To myn estat have more reward, I preye,
Than to his lust; what sholde I more seye?

And loketh now if this be resonable,
And letteth nought, for favour ne for slouthe,
To seyn a sooth; now were it covenable
To myn estat, by God, and by your trouthe,
To taken it, or to han of him routhe,
In harming of myself or in repreve?
Ber it ayein, for him that ye on leve!

This Pandarus gan on hir for to stare,
And seyde: Now is this the grettest wonder
That ever I sey! lat be this nyce fare!
To deethe mote I smiten be with thonder,
If, for the citee which that stondeth yonder,
Wolde I a lettre unto yow bringe or take
To harm of yow; what list yow thus it make?

But thus ye faren, wel neigh alle and some,
That he that most desireth yow to serve,
Of him ye recche leest wher he bicome,
And whether that he live or elles sterve.
But for al that that ever I may deserve,
Refuse it nought, quod he, and hente hir faste,
And in hir bosom the lettre doun he thraste,

And seyde hir: Now cast it away anoon,
That folk may seen and gauren on us tweye.
Quod she: I can abyde til they be goon.
And gan to smyle, and seyde him: Eem, I preye,
Swich answere as yow list yourself purveye,
For trewely I nil no lettre wryte.
No? than wol I, quod he, so ye endyte.

Therwith she lough, and seyde: Go we dyne.
And he gan at himself to jape faste,
And seyde: Nece, I have so greet a pyne
For love, that every other day I faste;
And gan his beste japes forth to caste;
And made hir so to laughe at his folye,
That she for laughter wende for to dye.

And whan that she was comen into halle:
Now, eem, quod she, we wol go dyne anoon;
And gan some of hir women to hir calle,
And streyght into hir chaumbre gan she goon;
But of hir besinesses, this was oon
Amonges othere thinges, out of drede,
Ful prively this lettre for to rede;

Avysed word by word in every lyne,
And fond no lak, she thoughte he coude good;
And up it putte, and went hir in to dyne.
And Pandarus, that in a study stood,
Er he was war, she took him by the hood,
And seyde: Ye were caught er that ye wiste;
I vouche sauf, quod he, do what yow liste.

493

Tho wesshen they, and sette hem doun & ete;
And after noon ful sleyly Pandarus
Gan drawe him to the window next the strete,
And seyde: Nece, who hath arayed thus
The yonder hous, that stant aforyeyn us?
Which hous? quod she, and gan for to biholde,
And knew it wel, and whos it was him tolde,

And fillen forth in speche of thinges smale,
And seten in the window bothe tweye,
Whan Pandarus saw tyme unto his tale,
And saw wel that hir folk were alle aweye:
Now, nece myn, tel on, quod he, I seye,
How lyketh yow the lettre that ye woot?
Can he theron? for, by my trouthe, I noot.

Therwith al rosy hewed tho wex she,
And gan to humme, and seyde: So I trowe.
Aquyte him wel, for Goddes love, quod he;
Myself to medes wol the lettre sowe,
And held his hondes up, and sat on knowe,
Now, goode nece, be it never so lyte,
Yif me the labour, it to sowe and plyte.

Ye, for I can so wryte, quod she tho;
And eek I noot what I sholde to him seye.
Nay, nece, quod Pandare, sey not so;
Yet at the leste thanketh him, I preye,
Of his good wil, and doth him not to deye.
Now for the love of me, my nece dere,
Refuseth not at this tyme my preyere.

Depar/dieux, quod she, God leve al be wel!
God helpe me so, this is the firste lettre
That ever I wroot, ye, al or any del.
And into a closet, for to avyse hir bettre,
She wente allone, and gan hir herte unfettre
Out of disdaynes prison but a lyte;
And sette hir doun, and gan a lettre wryte,

Of which to telle in short is myn entente
Theffect, as fer as I can understonde:
She thonked him of al that he wel mente
Towardes hir, but holden him in honde
She nolde nought, ne make hirselven bonde
In love, but as his suster, him to plese,
She wolde fayn, to doon his herte an ese.

She shette it, and to Pandarus gan goon,
There as he sat and loked into strete,
And doun she sette hir by him on a stoon
Of jaspre, upon a quisshin gold ybete,
And seyde: As wisly helpe me God the grete,
I never dide a thing with more peyne
Than wryte this, to which ye me constreyne;

And took it him: he thonked hir and seyde:
God woot, of thing ful ofte looth bigonne
Cometh ende good; and nece myn, Criseyde,
That ye to him of hard now ben ywonne
Oughte he be glad, by God and yonder sonne!
forwhy men seyth: Impressiounes lighte
ful lightly been ay redy to the flighte.
494

But ye han pleyed tyraunt neigh to longe,
And hard was it your herte for to grave;
Now stint, that ye no longer on it honge,
Al wolde ye the forme of daunger save.
But hasteth yow to doon him joye have;
for trusteth wel, to longe ydoon hardnesse
Causeth despyt ful often, for distresse.

And right as they declamed this matere,
Lo, Troilus, right at the stretes ende,
Com ryding with his tenthe some yfere,
Al softely, and thiderward gan bende
Theras they sete, as was his wey to wende
To paleys/ward; and Pandare him aspyde,
And seyde: Nece, ysee who cometh here ryde!

O flee not in, he seeth us, I suppose;
Lest he may thinke that ye him eschuwe.
Nay, nay, quod she, and wex as reed as rose.
With that he gan hir humbly to saluwe,
With dreedful chere, and ofte his hewes muwe;
And up his look debonairly he caste,
And bekked on Pandare, and forth he paste.

God woot if he sat on his hors aright,
Or goodly was beseyn, that ilke day!
God woot wher he was lyk a manly knight!
What sholde I drecche, or telle of his aray?
Criseyde, which that alle these thinges say,
To telle in short, hir lyked al yfere,
His persone, his aray, his look, his chere,

His goodly manere and his gentillesse,
So wel, that never, sith that she was born,
Ne hadde she swich routhe of his distresse;
And howso she hath hard ben herbiforn,
To God hope I, she hath now caught a thorn.
She shal not pulle it out this nexte wyke;
God sende mo swich thornes on to pyke!

Pandare, which that stood hir faste by,
felte iren hoot, and he bigan to smyte,
And seyde: Nece, I pray yow hertely,
Tel me that I shal axen yow a lyte.
A womman, that were of his deeth to wyte,
Withouten his gilt, but for hir lakked routhe,
Were it wel doon? Quod she: Nay, by my trouthe!

God helpe me so, quod he, ye sey me sooth.
Ye felen wel yourself that I not lye;
Lo, yond he rit! Quod she: Ye, so he dooth.
Wel, quod Pandare, as I have told yow thrye,
Lat be your nyce shame and your folye,
And spek with him in esing of his herte;
Lat nycetee not do yow bothe smerte.

But theron was to heven and to done;
Considered al thing, it may not be;
And why, for shame; and it were eek to sone
To graunten him so greet a libertee.
for playnly hir entente, as seyde she,
Was for to love him unwist, if she mighte,
And guerdon him with nothing but with sighte.

But Pandarus thoughte: It shal not be so,
If that I may; this nyce opinioun
Shal not be holden fully yeres two.
What sholde I make of this a long sermoun?
He moste assente on that conclusioun
As for the tyme; and whan that it was eve,
And al was wel, he roos and took his leve.

And on his wey ful faste homward he spedde,
And right for joye he felte his herte daunce;
And Troilus he fond alone abedde,
That lay as dooth these loveres, in a traunce,
Bitwixen hope and derk desesperaunce.
But Pandarus, right at his incominge,
He song, as who seyth: Lo! sumwhat I bringe.

And seyde: Who is in his bed so sone
Yburied thus? It am I, freend, quod he.
Who, Troilus? nay helpe me so the mone,
Quod Pandarus, thou shalt aryse and see
A charme that was sent right now to thee,
The which can helen thee of thyn accesse,
If thou do forthwith al thy besinesse.

Ye, through the might of God! quod Troilus.
And Pandarus gan him the lettre take,
And seyde: Pardee, God hath holpen us;
Have here a light, and loke on al this blake.
But ofte gan the herte glade and quake
Of Troilus, whyl that he gan it rede,
So as the wordes yave him hope or drede.

But fynally, he took al for the beste
That she him wroot, for sumwhat he biheld
On which, him thoughte, he mighte his herte reste,
Al covered she the wordes under sheld.
Thus to the more worthy part he held,
That, what for hope and Pandarus biheste,
His grete wo foryede he at the leste.

But as we may alday ourselven see,
Through more wode or col, the more fyr;
Right so encrees of hope, of what it be,
Therwith ful ofte encreseth eek desyr;
Or, as an ook cometh of a litel spyr,
So through this lettre, which that she him sente,
Encresen gan desyr, of which he brente.

Wherfore I seye alwey, that day and night
This Troilus gan to desiren more
Than he dide erst, thurgh hope, & dide his might
To pressen on, as by Pandarus lore,
And wryten to hir of his sorwes sore
Fro day to day; he leet it not refreyde,
That by Pandare he wroot somwhat or seyde;

And dide also his othere observaunces
That to a lovere longeth in this cas;
And, after that these dees turnede on chaunces,
So was he outher glad or seyde Allas!
And held after his gestes ay his pas;
And aftir swiche answeres as he hadde,
So were his dayes sory outher gladde.

But to Pandare alwey was his recours,
And pitously gan ay til him to pleyne,
And him bisoughte of rede and som socours;
And Pandarus, that sey his wode peyne,
Wex wel neigh deed for routhe, sooth to seyne,
And bisily with al his herte caste
Som of his wo to sleen, and that as faste;

And seyde: Lord, and freend, and brother dere,
God woot that thy disese dooth me wo.
But woltow stinten al this woful chere,
And, by my trouthe, or it be dayes two,
But God toforn, yet shal I shape it so,
That thou shalt come into a certayn place,
Theras thou mayst thyself hir preye of grace.

And certainly, I noot if thou it wost,
But tho that been expert in love it seye,
It is oon of the thinges that furthereth most,
A man to have a leyser for to preye,
And siker place his wo for to biwreye;
For in good herte it moot som routhe impresse,
To here and see the giltles in distresse.

Paraunter thenkestow: though it be so
That kinde wolde doon hir to biginne
To han a maner routhe upon my wo,
Seyth Daunger: Nay, thou shalt me never winne;
So reuleth hir hir hertes goost withinne,
That, though she bende, yet she stant on rote;
What in effect is this unto my bote?

Thenk hereayeins, whan that the sturdy ook,
On which men hakketh ofte, for the nones,
Receyved hath the happy falling strook,
The grete sweigh doth it come al at ones,
As doon these rokkes or these milne-stones.
For swifter cours cometh thing that is of wighte,
Whan it descendeth, than don thinges lighte.

And reed that boweth doun for every blast,
Ful lightly, cesse wind, it wol aryse;
But so nil not an ook whan it is cast;
It nedeth me nought thee longe to forbyse.
Men shal rejoysen of a greet empryse
Acheved wel, and stant withouten doute,
Al han men been the lenger theraboute.

But, Troilus, yet tel me, if thee lest,
A thing now which that I shal axen thee;
Which is thy brother that thou lovest best
As in thy verray hertes privetee?
Ywis, my brother Deiphebus, quod he.
Now, quod Pandare, er houres twyes twelve,
He shal thee ese, unwist of it himselve.

Now lat me allone, and werken as I may,
Quod he; and to Deiphebus wente he tho
Which hadde his lord and grete freend ben ay;
Save Troilus, no man he lovede so.
To telle in short, withouten wordes mo,
Quod Pandarus: I pray yow that ye be
Freend to a cause which that toucheth me.

495

Yis, pardee, quod Deiphebus, wel thow wost,
In al that ever I may, and God tofore,
Al nere it but for man I love most,
My brother Troilus; but sey wherfore
It is; for sith that day that I was bore,
I nas, ne nevermo to been I thinke,
Ayeins a thing that mighte thee forthinke.

Pandare gan him thonke, and to him seyde:
Lo, sire, I have a lady in this toun,
That is my nece, and called is Criseyde,
Which som men wolden doon oppressioun,
And wrongfully have hir possessioun:
Wherfor I of your lordship yow biseche
To been our freend, withoute more speche.

Deiphebus him answerde: O, is not this,
That thow spekest of to me thus straungely,
Criseyda, my freend? He seyde: Yis.
Than nedeth, quod Deiphebus hardely,
Namore to speke, for trusteth wel, that I
Wol be hir champioun with spore and yerde;
I roughte nought though alle hir foos it herde.

But tel me, thou that woost al this matere,
How I might best avaylen? now lat see.
Quod Pandarus: If ye, my lord so dere,
Wolden as now don this honour to me,
To prayen hir tomorwe, lo, that she
Com unto yow hir pleyntes to devyse,
Hir adversaries wolde of hit agryse.

And if I more dorste preye as now,
And chargen yow to have so greet travayle,
To han som of your bretheren here with yow,
That mighten to hir cause bet avayle,
Than, woot I wel, she mighte never fayle
For to be holpen, what at your instaunce,
What with hir othere freendes governaunce.

Deiphebus, which that comen was, of kinde,
To al honour and bountee to consente,
Answerde: It shal be doon; and I can finde
Yet gretter help to this in myn entente.
What wolt thow seyn, if I for Eleyne sente
To speke of this? I trowe it be the beste;
For she may leden Paris as hir leste.

Of Ector, which that is my lord, my brother,
It nedeth nought to preye him freend to be;
For I have herd him, o tyme and eek other,
Speke of Criseyde swich honour, that he
May seyn no bet, swich hap to him hath she.
It nedeth nought his helpes for to crave;
He shal be swich, right as we wole him have.

Spek thou thyself also to Troilus
On my bihalve, and pray him with us dyne.
Sire, al this shal be doon, quod Pandarus;
And took his leve, and never gan to fyne,
But to his neces hous, as streght as lyne,
He com; and fond hir fro the mete aryse;
And sette him doun, and spak right in this wyse.

496

He seyde: O veray God, so have I ronne!
Lo, nece myn, see ye nought how I swete?
I noot whether ye the more thank me conne.
Be ye nought war how that fals Poliphete
Is now aboute eftsones for to plete,
And bringe on yow advocacyes newe?
I? no, quod she, and chaunged al hir hewe.

What is he more aboute, me to drecche
And doon me wrong? what shal I do, allas?
Yet of himself nothing ne wolde I recche,
Nere it for Antenor and Eneas,
That been his freendes in swich maner cas;
But, for the love of God, myn uncle dere,
No fors of that, lat him have al yfere;

Withouten that, I have ynough for us.
Nay, quod Pandare, it shal nothing be so.
For I have been right now at Deiphebus,
And Ector, and myne othere lordes mo,
And shortly maked eche of hem his fo;
That, by my thrift, he shal it never winne
For ought he can, whan that so he biginne.

And as they casten what was best to done,
Deiphebus, of his owene curtasye,
Com hir to preye, in his propre persone,
To holde him on the morwe companye
At diner, which she nolde not denye,
But goodly gan to his preyere obeye.
He thonked hir, and wente upon his weye.

Whanne this was doon, this Pandare up anoon,
To telle in short, and forth gan for to wende
To Troilus, as stille as any stoon,
And al this thing he tolde him, word and ende;
And how that he Deiphebus gan to blende;
And seyde him: Now is tyme, if that thou conne,
To bere thee wel tomorwe, and al is wonne.

Now spek, now prey, now pitously compleyne;
Lat not for nyce shame, or drede, or slouthe;
Somtyme a man mot telle his owene peyne;
Bileve it, and she shal han on thee routhe;
Thou shalt be saved by thy feyth, in trouthe.
But wel wot I, thou art now in a drede;
And what it is, I leye, I can arede.

Thow thinkest now: How sholde I doon al this?
For by my cheres mosten folk aspye,
That for hir love is that I fare amis;
Yet hadde I lever unwist for sorwe dye.
Now thenk not so, for thou dost greet folye.
For right now have I founden o manere
Of sleighte, for to coveren al thy chere.

Thow shalt gon over night, and that as blyve,
Unto Deiphebus hous, as thee to pleye,
Thy maladye awey the bet to dryve,
Forwhy thou semest syk, soth for to seye.
Sone after that, doun in thy bed thee leye,
And sey, thow mayst no lenger up endure,
And lye right there, and byde thyn aventure.

Sey that thy fever is wont thee for to take
The same tyme, and lasten til amorwe;
And lat see now how wel thou canst it make,
For, pardee, syk is he that is in sorwe.
Go now, farewel! and, Venus here to borwe,
I hope, and thou this purpos holde ferme,
Thy grace she shal fully ther conferme.

Quod Troilus: Ywis, thou nedelees
Counseylest me, that sykliche I me feyne!
For I am syk in ernest, doutelees,
So that wel neigh I sterve for the peyne.
Quod Pandarus: Thou shalt the bettre pleyne,
And hast the lasse nede to countrefete;
For him men demen hoot that men seen swete.

Lo, holde thee at thy triste cloos, and I
Shal wel the deer unto thy bowe dryve.
Therwith he took his leve al softely,
And Troilus to paleys wente blyve,
So glad ne was he never in al his lyve;
And to Pandarus reed gan al assente,
And to Deiphebus hous at night he wente.

What nedeth yow to tellen al the chere
That Deiphebus unto his brother made,
Or his accesse, or his syklych manere,
How men gan him with clothes for to lade,
Whan he was leyd, and how men wolde him glade?
But al for nought, he held forth ay the wyse
That ye han herd Pandare er this devyse.

But certeyn is, er Troilus him leyde,
Deiphebus had him prayed, over night,
To been a freend and helping to Criseyde.
God woot, that he it grauntede anon-right,
To been hir fulle freend with al his might.
But swich a nede was to preye him thenne,
As for to bidde a wood man for to renne.

The morwen com, and neighen gan the tyme
Of meel-tyd, that the faire quene Eleyne
Shoop hir to been, an houre after the pryme,
With Deiphebus, to whom she nolde feyne;
But as his suster, hoomly, sooth to seyne,
She com to diner in hir playn entente.
But God and Pandare wiste al what this mente.

Come eek Criseyde, al innocent of this,
Antigone, hir sister Tarbe also;
But flee we now prolixitee best is,
For love of God, and lat us faste go
Right to the effect, withoute tales mo,
Why al this folk assembled in this place;
And lat us of hir saluinges pace.

Gret honour dide hem Deiphebus, certeyn,
And fedde hem wel with al that mighte lyke.
But evermore: Allas! was his refreyn,
My goode brother Troilus, the syke,
Lyth yet And therwithal he gan to syke;
And after that, he peyned him to glade
Hem as he mighte, and chere good he made.

kk 1

Compleyned eek Eleyne of his syknesse
So feithfully, that pitee was to here,
And every wight gan waxen for accesse
A leche anoon, and seyde: In this manere
Men curen folk; this charme I wol yow lere.
But there sat oon, al list hir nought to teche,
That thoughte, best coude I yet been his leche.

After compleynt, him gonnen they to preyse,
As folk don yet, whan som wight hath bigonne
To preyse a man, and up with prys him reyse
A thousand fold yet hyer than the sonne:
He is, he can, that fewe lordes conne.
And Pandarus, of that they wolde afferme,
He not forgat hir preysing to conferme.

Herde al this thing Criseyde wel ynough,
And every word gan for to notifye;
For which with sobre chere hir herte lough;
For who is that ne wolde hir glorifye,
To mowen swich a knight don live or dye?
But al passe I, lest ye to longe dwelle;
For for o fyn is al that ever I telle.

The tyme com, fro diner for to ryse,
And, as hem oughte, arisen everychoon,
And gonne a while of this and that devyse.
But Pandarus brak al this speche anoon,
And seyde to Deiphebus: Wole ye goon,
If youre wille be, as I yow preyde,
To speke here of the nedes of Criseyde?

Eleyne, which that by the hond hir held,
Took first the tale, and seyde: Go we blyve;
And goodly on Criseyde she biheld,
And seyde: Joves lat him never thryve,
That dooth yow harm, & bringe him sone of lyve
And yeve me sorwe, but he shal it rewe,
If that I may, and alle folk be trewe.

Tel thou thy neces cas, quod Deiphebus
To Pandarus, for thou canst best it telle.
My lordes and my ladyes, it stant thus;
What sholde I lenger, quod he, do yow dwelle?
He rong hem out a proces lyk a belle,
Upon hir fo, that highte Poliphete,
So heynous, that men mighte on it spete.

Answerde of this ech worse of hem than other,
And Poliphete they gonnen thus to warien:
An-honged be swich oon, were he my brother;
And so he shal, for it ne may not varien.
What sholde I lenger in this tale tarien?
Pleynly, at ones, alle they hir-highten,
To been hir helpe in al that ever they mighten.

Spak than Eleyne, and seyde: Pandarus,
Woot ought my lord, my brother, this matere,
I mene, Ector? or woot it Troilus?
He seyde: Ye, but wole ye now me here?
Me thinketh this, sith Troilus is here,
It were good, if that ye wolde assente,
She tolde hirself him al this, er she wente.

For he wole have the more hir grief at herte,
By cause, lo, that she a lady is;
And, by your leve, I wol but right in sterte,
And do yow wite, and that anoon, ywis,
If that he slepe, or wole ought here of this.
And in he lepte, and seyde him in his ere:
God have thy soule, ybrought have I thy bere!

To smylen of this gan tho Troilus,
And Pandarus, withoute rekeninge,
Out wente anoon to Eleyne and Deiphebus,
And seyde hem: So there be no taryinge,
Ne more pres, he wol wel that ye bringe
Criseyda, my lady, that is here;
And as he may enduren, he wole here.

But wel ye woot, the chaumbre is but lyte,
And fewe folk may lightly make it warm;
Now loketh ye, for I wol have no wyte,
To bringe in prees that mighte doon him harm
Or him disesen, for my bettre arm,
Wher it be bet she byde til eftsones;
Now loketh ye, that knowen what to doon is.

I sey for me, best is, as I can knowe,
That no wight in ne wente but ye tweye,
But it were I, for I can, in a throwe,
Reherce hir cas, unlyk that she can seye;
And after this, she may him ones preye
To ben good lord, in short, and take hir leve;
This may not muchel of his ese him reve.

And eek, for she is straunge, he wol forbere
His ese, which that him thar nought for yow;
Eek other thing, that toucheth not to here,
He wol me telle, I woot it wel right now,
That secret is, and for the tounes prow.
And they, that nothing knewe of this entente,
Withoute more, to Troilus in they wente.

Eleyne in al hir goodly softe wyse,
Gan him saluwe, and womanly to pleye,
And seyde: Ywis, ye moste alweyes aryse!
Now fayre brother, beth al hool, I preye!
And gan hir arm right over his sholder leye,
And him with al hir wit to recomforte;
As she best coude, she gan him to disporte.

So after this quod she: We yow biseke,
My dere brother, Deiphebus, and I,
For love of God, and so doth Pandare eke,
To been good lord and freend, right hertely,
Unto Criseyde, which that certeinly
Receyveth wrong, as woot wel here Pandare,
That can hir cas wel bet than I declare.

This Pandarus gan newe his tunge affyle,
And al hir cas reherce, and that anoon;
Whan it was seyd, sone after, in a whyle,
Quod Troilus: As sone as I may goon,
I wol right fayn with al my might ben oon,
Have God my trouthe, hir cause to sustene.
Good thrift have ye, quod Eleyne the quene.

498

Quod Pandarus: And it your wille be,
That she may take hir leve, er that she go?
Or elles God forbede, tho quod he,
If that she vouche sauf for to do so.
And with that word quod Troilus: Ye two,
Deiphebus, and my suster leef and dere,
To yow have I to speke of o matere,

To been avysed by your reed the bettre:
And fond, as hap was, at his beddes heed,
The copie of a tretis and a lettre,
That Ector hadde him sent to axen reed,
If swich a man was worthy to ben deed,
Woot I nought who; but in a grisly wyse
He preyede hem anoon on it avyse.

Deiphebus gan this lettre to unfolde
In ernest greet; so dide Eleyne the quene;
And rominge outward, fast it gan biholde,
Downward a steyre, into an herber grene.
This ilke thing they redden hem bitwene;
And largely, the mountaunce of an houre,
They gonne on it to reden and to poure.

Now lat hem rede, and turne we anoon
To Pandarus, that gan ful faste prye
That al was wel, and out he gan to goon
Into the grete chambre, and that in hye,
And seyde: God save al this companye!
Com, nece myn; my lady quene Eleyne
Abydeth yow, and eek my lordes tweyne.

Rys, take with yow your nece Antigone,
Or whom yow list, or no fors, hardily;
The lasse prees, the bet; com forth with me,
And loke that ye thonke humblely
Hem alle three, and, whan ye may goodly
Your tyme ysee, taketh of hem your leve,
Lest we to longe his restes him bireve.

Al innocent of Pandarus entente,
Quod tho Criseyde: Go we, uncle dere;
And arm in arm inward with him she wente,
Avysed wel hir wordes and hir chere;
And Pandarus, in ernestful manere,
Seyde: Alle folk, for Goddes love, I preye,
Stinteth right here, and softely yow pleye.

Aviseth yow what folk ben here withinne,
And in what plyt oon is, God him amende!
And inward thus ful softely biginne;
Nece, I conjure and heighly yow defende,
On his half, which that sowle us alle sende,
And in the vertue of corounes tweyne,
Slee nought this man, that hath for yow this peyne!

Fy on the devel! thenk which oon he is,
And in what plyt he lyth; com of anoon;
Thenk al swich taried tyd, but lost it nis!
That wol ye bothe seyn, whan ye ben oon.
Secoundelich, ther yet devyneth noon
Upon yow two; com of now, if ye conne;
Whyl folk is blent, lo, al the tyme is wonne!

In titering, and pursuite, and delayes,
The folk devyne at wagginge of a stree;
And though ye wolde han after merye dayes,
Than dar ye nought, and why? for she, and she
Spak swich a word; thus loked he, and he;
Lest tyme I loste, I dar not with yow dele;
Com of therfore, and bringeth him to hele.

But now to yow, ye lovers that ben here,

Was Troilus nought in a cankedort,
That lay, and mighte whispringe of hem
here,
And thoughte: O Lord, right now renneth
my sort
fully to dye, or han anoon comfort,
And was the firste tyme he shulde hir preye
Of love; O mighty God, what shal he seye?
Explicit Secundus Liber.

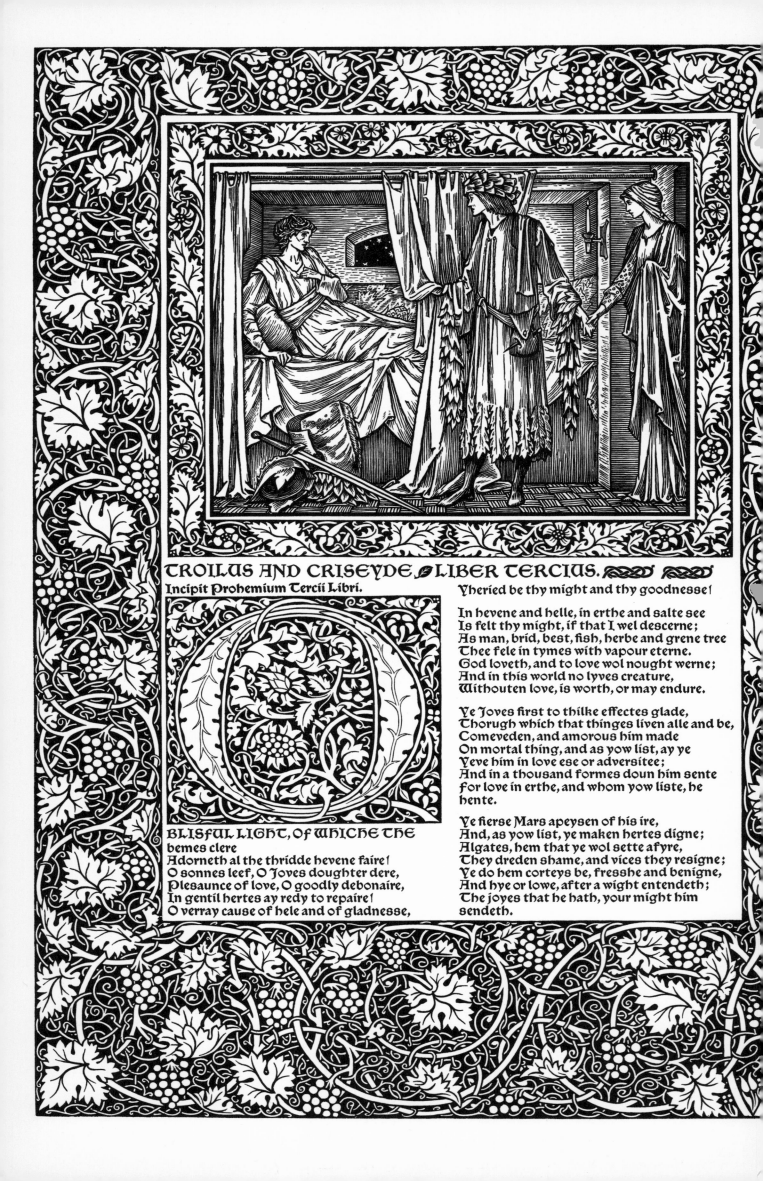

TROILUS AND CRISEYDE ♦ LIBER TERCIUS. ✿✿✿ ✿✿✿

Incipit Prohemium Tercii Libri.

Yheried be thy might and thy goodnesse!

In hevene and helle, in erthe and salte see
Is felt thy might, if that I wel descerne;
As man, brid, best, fish, herbe and grene tree
Thee fele in tymes with vapour eterne.
God loveth, and to love wol nought werne;
And in this world no lyves creature,
Withouten love, is worth, or may endure.

Ye Joves first to thilke effectes glade,
Thorough which that thinges liven alle and be,
Comeveden, and amorous him made
On mortal thing, and as yow list, ay ye
Yeve him in love ese or adversitee;
And in a thousand formes doun him sente
For love in erthe, and whom yow liste, he
hente.

Ye fierse Mars apeysen of his ire,
And, as yow list, ye maken hertes digne;
Algates, hem that ye wol sette afyre,
They dreden shame, and vices they resigne;
Ye do hem corteys be, fresshe and benigne,
And hye or lowe, after a wight entendeth;
The joyes that he hath, your might him
sendeth.

BLISFUL LIGHT, OF WHICHE THE
bemes clere
Adorneth al the thridde hevene faire!
O sonnes leef, O Joves doughter dere,
Plesaunce of love, O goodly debonaire,
In gentil hertes ay redy to repaire!
O verray cause of hele and of gladnesse,

Ye holden regne and hous in unitee;
Ye soothfast cause of frendship been also;
Ye knowe al thilke covered qualitee
Of thinges which that folk on wondren so,
Whan they can not construe how it may jo,
She loveth him, or why he loveth here;
As why this fish, and nought that, cometh to were.

Ye folk a lawe han set in universe,
And this knowe I by hem that loveres be,
That whoso stryveth with yow hath the werse:
Now, lady bright, for thy benignitee,
At reverence of hem that serven thee,
Whos clerk I am, so techeth me devyse
Som joye of that is felt in thy servyse.

Ye in my naked herte sentement
Inhelde, and do me shewe of thy swetnesse.
Caliope, thy vois be now present,
For now is nede; sestow not my destresse,
How I mot telle anon right the gladnesse
Of Troilus, to Venus heryinge?
To which gladnes, who nede hath, God him bringe!
Explicit prohemium Tercii Libri.

Incipit Liber Tercius.

AY al this mene whyle
Troilus,
Recordinge his lessoun
in this manere:
Ma fey! thought he,
thus wole I seye and thus;
Thus wole I pleyne un-
to my lady dere;
That word is good, and
this shal be my chere;
This nil I not foryeten in no wyse.
God leve him werken as he gan devyse.

And Lord, so that his herte gan to quappe,
Heringe hir come, and shorte for to syke!
And Pandarus, that ladde hir by the lappe,
Com ner, and gan in at the curtin pyke,
And seyde: God do bote on alle syke!
See, who is here yow comen to visyte;
Lo, here is she that is your deeth to wyte.

Therwith it semed as he wepte almost:
A ha, quod Troilus so rewfully,
Wher me be wo, O mighty God, thou wost!
Who is al there? I see nought trewely.
Sire, quod Criseyde, it is Pandare and I.

Ye, swete herte? allas, I may nought ryse
To knele, and do yow honour in som wyse.

And dressede him upward, and she right tho
Gan bothe here hondes softe upon him leye:
O, for the love of God, do ye not so
To me, quod she, ey! what is this to seye?
Sire, come am I to yow for causes tweye;
First, yow to thonke, and of your lordshipe eke
Continuance I wolde yow biseke.

This Troilus, that herde his lady preye
Of lordship him, wex neither quik ne deed,
Ne mighte a word for shame to it seye,
Although men sholde smyten of his heed.
But Lord, so he wex sodeinliche reed,
And sire, his lesson, that he wende conne,
To preyen hir, is thurgh his wit yronne.

Cryseyde al this aspyede wel ynough,
For she was wys, and lovede him neverthelasse,
Al nere he malapert, or made it tough,
Or was to bold, to singe a fool a masse.
But whan his shame gan somwhat to passe,
His resons, as I may my rymes holde,
I yow wol telle, as techen bokes olde.

In chaunged vois, right for his verrey drede,
Which vois eek quook, and therto his manere
Goodly abayst, and now his hewes rede,
Now pale, unto Criseyde, his lady dere,
With look doun cast and humble yolden chere,
Lo, the alderfirste word that him asterte
Was, twyes: Mercy, mercy, swete herte!

And stinte a whyl, and whan he mighte out-
bringe,
The nexte word was: God wot, for I have,
As feythfully as I have had konninge,
Ben youres, also God my sowle save;
And shal, til that I, woful wight, be grave.
And though I dar ne can unto yow pleyne,
Ywis, I suffre nought the lasse peyne.

Thus muche as now, O wommanliche wyf,
I may outbringe, and if this yow displese,
That shal I wreke upon myn owne lyf
Right sone, I trowe, and doon your herte an ese,
If with my deeth your herte I may apese.
But sin that ye han herd me somwhat seye,
Now recche I never how sone that I deye.

Therwith his manly sorwe to biholde,
It mighte han maad an herte of stoon to rewe;
And Pandare weep as he to watre wolde,
And poked ever his nece newe and newe,
And seyde: Wo bigon ben hertes trewe!
For love of God, make of this thing an ende,
Or slee us bothe at ones, er that ye wende.

I? what? quod she, by God and by my trouthe,
I noot nought what ye wilne that I seye.
I? what? quod he, that ye han on him routhe,

502

For Goddes love, and doth him nought to deye.
Now thanne thus, quod she, I wolde him
preye
To telle me the fyn of his entente;
Yet wiste I never wel what that he mente.

What that I mene, O swete herte dere?
Quod Troilus, O goodly fresshe free!
That, with the stremes of your eyen clere,
Ye wolde somtyme freendly on me see,
And thanne agreën that I may ben he,
Withoute braunche of vyce in any wyse,
In trouthe alwey to doon yow my servyse

As to my lady right and chief resort,
With al my wit and al my diligence,
And I to han, right as yow list, comfort,
Under your yerde, egal to myn offence,
As deeth, if that I breke your defence;
And that ye deigne me so muche honoure,
Me to comaunden ought in any houre.

And I to ben your verray humble trewe,
Secret, and in my paynes pacient,
And evermo desire freshly newe,
To serven, and been ylyke ay diligent,
And, with good herte, al holly your talent
Receyven wel, how sore that me smerte,
Lo, this mene I, myn owene swete herte.

Quod Pandarus: Lo, here an hard request,
And resonable, a lady for to werne!
Now, nece myn, by natal Joves fest,
Were I a god, ye sholde sterve as yerne,
That heren wel, this man wol nothing yerne
But your honour, and seen him almost sterve,
And been so looth to suffren him yow serve.

With that she gan hir eyen on him caste
Ful esily, and ful debonairly,
Avysing hir, and hyed not to faste
With never a word, but seyde him softely:
Myn honour sauf, I wol wel trewely,
And in swich forme as he can now devyse,
Receyven him fully to my servyse,

Biseching him, for Goddes love, that he
Wolde, in honour of trouthe and gentilesse,
As I wel mene, eek mene wel to me,
And myn honour, with wit and besinesse,
Ay kepe; and if I may don him gladnesse,
From hennesforth, ywis, I nil not feyne:
Now beeth al hool, no lenger ye ne pleyne.

But nathelees, this warne I yow, quod she,
A kinges sone although ye be, ywis,
Ye shul namore have soverainetee
Of me in love, than right in that cas is;
Ne I nil forbere, if that ye doon amis,
To wrathen yow; and whyl that ye me serve,
Cherycen yow right after ye deserve.

And shortly, derë herte and al my knight,

Beth glad, and draweth yow to lustinesse,
And I shal trewely, with al my might,
Your bittre tornen al into swetnesse;
If I be she that may yow do gladnesse,
For every wo ye shal recovere a blisse;
And him in armes took, and gan him kisse.

Fil Pandarus on knees, and up his yën
To hevene threw, and held his hondes hye:
Immortal god! quod he, that mayst nought dyen,
Cupide I mene, of this mayst glorifye;
And Venus, thou mayst make melodye;
Withouten hond, me semeth that in towne,
For this merveyle, I here ech belle sowne.

But ho! no more as now of this matere,
Forwhy this folk wol comen up anoon,
That han the lettre red; lo, I hem here.
But I conjure thee, Criseyde, and oon,
And two, thou Troilus, whan thow mayst goon,
That at myn hous ye been at my warninge,
For I ful wel shal shape your cominge;

And eseth ther your hertes right ynough;
And lat see which of yow shal bere the belle
To speke of love aright! therwith he lough,
For ther have ye a layser for to telle.
Quod Troilus: How longe shal I dwelle
Er this be doon? Quod he: Whan thou mayst
ryse,
This thing shal be right as I yow devyse.

With that Eleyne and also Deiphebus
Tho comen upward, right at the steyres ende;
And Lord, so than gan grone Troilus,
His brother and his suster for to blende.
Quod Pandarus: It tyme is that we wende;
Tak, nece myn, your leve at alle three,
And lat hem speke, and cometh forth with me.

She took hir leve at hem ful thriftily,
As she wel coude, and they hir reverence
Unto the fulle diden hardely,
And speken wonder wel, in hir absence,
Of hir, in preysing of hir excellence,
Hir governaunce, hir wit; and hir manere
Commendeden, it joye was to here.

Now lat hir wende unto hir owne place,
And torne we to Troilus ayein,
That gan ful lightly of the lettre passe,
That Deiphebus hadde in the gardin seyn.
And of Eleyne and him he wolde fayn
Delivered been, and seyde, that him leste
To slepe, and after tales have reste.

Eleyne him kiste, and took hir leve blyve,
Deiphebus eek, and hoom wente every wight;
And Pandarus, as faste as he may dryve,
To Troilus tho com, as lyne right;
And on a paillet, al that glade night,
By Troilus he lay, with mery chere,
To tale; and wel was hem they were yfere.

kk4

Whan every wight was voided but they two,
And alle the dores were faste yshette,
To telle in short, withoute wordes mo,
This Pandarus, withouten any lette,
Up roos, and on his beddes syde him sette,
And gan to speken in a sobre wyse
To Troilus, as I shal yow devyse.

Myn alderlevest lord, and brother dere,
God woot, and thou, that it sat me so sore,
When I thee saw so languisshing to yere,
For love, of which thy wo wex alwey more;
That I, with al my might and al my lore,
Have ever sithen doon my bisinesse
To bringe thee to joye out of distresse;

And have it brought to swich plyt as thou wost,
So that, thorugh me, thow stondest now in weye
To fare wel, I seye it for no bost,
And wostow why? for shame it is to seye,
For thee have I bigonne a gamen pleye
Which that I never doon shal eft for other,
Although he were a thousand fold my brother.

That is to seye, for thee am I bicomen,
Bitwixen game and ernest, swich a mene
As maken wommen unto men to comen;
Al sey I nought, thou wost wel what I mene.
For thee have I my nece, of vyces clene,
So fully maad thy gentilesse triste,
That al shal been right as thyselve liste.

But God, that al wot, take I to witnesse,
That never I this for coveityse wroughte,
But only for to abregge that distresse,
For which wel nygh thou deydest, as me thoughte.
But gode brother, do now as thee oughte,
For Goddes love, and keep hir out of blame,
Sin thou art wys, and save alwey hir name.

For wel thou wost, the name as yet of here
Among the peple, as who seyth, halwed is;
For that man is unbore, I dar wel swere,
That ever wiste that she dide amis.
But wo is me, that I, that cause al this,
May thenken that she is my nece dere,
And I hir eem, and traytor eek yfere!

And were it wist that I, through myn engyn,
Hadde in my nece yput this fantasye,
To do thy lust, and hoolly to be thyn,
Why, al the world upon it wolde crye,
And seye, that I the worste trecherye
Dide in this cas, that ever was bigonne,
And she forlost, and thou right nought ywonne.

Wherfore, er I wol ferther goon a pas,
Yet eft I thee biseche and fully seye,
That privetee go with us in this cas,
That is to seye, that thou us never wreye;
And be nought wrooth, though I thee ofte preye
To holden secree swich an heigh matere;
For skilful is, thow wost wel, my preyere.

503

And thenk what wo ther hath bitid er this,
For makinge of avauntes, as men rede;
And what mischaunce in this world yet ther is,
Fro day to day, right for that wikked dede;
For which these wyse clerkes that ben dede
Han ever yet proverbed to us yonge,
That firste vertu is to kepe tonge.

And, nere it that I wilne as now tabregge
Diffusioun of speche, I coude almost
A thousand olde stories thee alegge
Of wommen lost, thorugh fals and foles bost;
Proverbes canst thyself ynowe, and wost,
Ayeins that vyce, for to been a labbe,
Al seyde men sooth as often as they gabbe.

O tonge, allas! so often herebiforn
Hastow mad many a lady bright of hewe
Seyd: Welawey! the day that I was born!
And many a maydes sorwes for to newe;
And, for the more part, al is untrewe
That men of yelpe, and it were brought to preve;
Of kinde non avauntour is to leve.

Avauntour and a lyere, al is on;
As thus: I pose, a womman graunte me
Hir love, and seyth that other wol she non,
And I am sworn to holden it secree,
And after I go telle it two or three;
Ywis, I am avauntour at the leste,
And lyere, for I breke my biheste.

Now loke thanne, if they be nought to blame,
Swich maner folk; what shal I clepe hem, what,
That hem avaunte of wommen, and by name,
That never yet bihighte hem this ne that,
Ne knewe hem more than myn olde hat?
No wonder is, so God me sende hele,
Though wommen drede with us men to dele.

I sey not this for no mistrust of yow,
Ne for no wys man, but for foles nyce,
And for the harm that in the world is now,
As wel for foly ofte as for malyce;
For wel wot I, in wyse folk, that vyce
No womman drat, if she be wel avysed;
For wyse ben by foles harm chastysed.

But now to purpos; leve brother dere,
Have al this thing that I have seyd in minde,
And keep thee clos, and be now of good chere,
For at thy day thou shalt me trewe finde.
I shal thy proces sette in swich a kinde,
And God toforn, that it shall thee suffyse,
For it shal been right as thou wolt devyse.

For wel I woot, thou menest wel, parde;
Therfore I dar this fully undertake.
Thou wost eek what thy lady graunted thee,
And day is set, the chartres up to make.
Have now good night, I may no lenger wake;
And bid for me, sin thou art now in blisse,
That God me sende deeth or sone lisse.

Who mighte telle half the joye or feste
Which that the sowle of Troilus tho felte,
Heringe theffect of Pandarus biheste?
His olde wo, that made his herte swelte,
Gan tho for joye wasten and tomelte,
And al the richesse of his sykes sore
At ones fledde, he felte of hem no more.

But right so as these holtes and these hayes,
That han in winter dede been and dreye,
Revesten hem in grene, whan that May is,
Whan every lusty lyketh best to pleye:
Right in that selve wyse, sooth to seye,
Wex sodeynliche his herte ful of joye,
That gladder was ther never man in Troye.

And gan his look on Pandarus up caste
Ful sobrely, and frendly for to see,
And seyde: Freend, in Aprille the laste,
As wel thou wost, if it remembre thee,
How neigh the deeth for wo thou founde me;
And how thou didest al thy bisinesse
To knowe of me the cause of my distresse.

Thou wost how longe I it forbar to seye
To thee, that art the man that I best triste;
And peril was it noon to thee bywreye,
That wiste I wel; but tel me, if thee liste,
Sith I so looth was that thyself it wiste,
How dorste I mo tellen of this matere,
That quake now, and no wight may us here?

But natheles, by that God I thee swere,
That, as him list, may al this world governe,
And, if I lye, Achilles with his spere
Myn herte cleve, al were my lyf eterne,
As I am mortal, if I late or yerne
Wolde it biwreye, or dorste, or sholde conne,
For al the good that God made under sonne;

That rather deye I wolde, and determyne,
As thinketh me, now stokked in presoun,
In wrecchednesse, in filthe, and in vermyne,
Caytif to cruel king Agamenoun;
And this, in alle the temples of this toun,
Upon the goddes alle, I wol thee swere,
Tomorwe day, if that thee lyketh here.

And that thou hast so muche ydoon for me,
That I ne may it nevermore deserve,
This knowe I wel, al mighte I now for thee
A thousand tymes on a morwen sterve,
I can no more, but that I wol thee serve
Right as thy sclave, whiderso thou wende,
For evermore, unto my lyves ende!

But here, with al myn herte, I thee biseche,
That never in me thou deme swich folye
As I shal seyn; me thoughte, by thy speche,
That this, which thou me dost for companye,
I sholde wene it were a bauderye;
I am nought wood, al if I lewed be;
It is not so, that woot I wel, pardee.

But he that goth, for gold or for richesse,
On swich message, calle him what thee list;
And this that thou dost, calle it gentilesse,
Compassioun, and felawship, and trist;
Departe it so, for wyde/where is wist
How that there is dyversitee requered
Bitwixen thinges lyke, as I have lered.

And, that thou knowe I thenke nought ne wene
That this servyse a shame be or jape,
I have my faire suster Polixene,
Cassandre, Eleyne, or any of the frape;
Be she never so faire or wel yshape,
Tel me, which thou wilt of everichone,
To han for thyn, and lat me thanne allone.

But sin that thou hast don me this servyse,
My lyf to save, and for noon hope of mede,
So, for the love of God, this grete empryse
Parforme it out; for now is moste nede.
For high and low, withouten any drede,
I wol alwey thyne hestes alle kepe;
Have now good night, and lat us bothe slepe.

Thus held him ech with other wel apayed,
That al the world ne mighte it bet amende;
And, on the morwe, whan they were arayed,
Ech to his owene nedes gan entende.
But Troilus, though as the fyr he brende
For sharp desyr of hope and of plesaunce,
He not forgat his gode governaunce.

But in himself with manhod gan restreyne
Ech rakel dede and ech unbrydled chere,
That alle tho that liven, sooth to seyne,
Ne sholde han wist, by word or by manere,
What that he mente, as touching this matere.
From every wight as fer as is the cloude
He was, so wel dissimulen he coude.

And al the whyl which that I yow devyse,
This was his lyf; with al his fulle might,
By day he was in Martes high servyse,
This is to seyn, in armes as a knight;
And for the more part, the longe night
He lay, and thoughte how that he mighte serve
His lady best, hir thank for to deserve.

Nil I nought swerë, although he lay softe,
That in his thought he nas sumwhat disesed,
Ne that he tornede on his pilwes ofte,
And wolde of that him missed han ben sesed;
But in swich cas man is nought alwey plesed,
For ought I wot, no more than was he;
That can I deme of possibilitee.

But certeyn is, to purpos for to go,
That in this whyle, as writen is in geste,
He say his lady somtyme; and also
She with him spak, whan that she dorste or leste,
And by hir bothe avys, as was the beste,
Apoynteden ful warly in this nede,
So as they dorste, how they wolde procede.

But it was spoken in so short a wyse,
In swich awayt alwey, and in swich fere,
Lest any wyght divynen or devyse
Wolde of hem two, or to it leye an ere,
That al this world so leef to hem ne were
As that Cupido wolde hem grace sende
To maken of hir speche aright an ende.

But thilke litel that they speke or wroughte,
His wyse goost took ay of al swich hede,
It semed hir, he wiste what she thoughte
Withouten word, so that it was no nede
To bidde him ought to done, or ought forbede;
For which she thoughte that love, al come it late,
Of alle joye hadde opned hir the yate.

And shortly of this proces for to pace,
So wel his werk and wordes he bisette,
That he so ful stood in his lady grace,
That twenty thousand tymes, or she lette,
She thonked God she ever with him mette;
So coude he him governe in swich servyse,
That al the world ne mighte it bet devyse.

Forwhy she fond him so discreet in al,
So secret, and of swich obëisaunce,
That wel she felte he was to hir a wal
Of steel, and sheld from every displesaunce;
That, to ben in his gode governaunce,
So wys he was, she was no more afered,
I mene, as fer as oughte ben requered.

And Pandarus, to quike alwey the fyr,
Was ever ylyke prest and diligent;
To ese his frend was set al his desyr.
He shof ay on, he to and fro was sent;
He lettres bar whan Troilus was absent.
That never man, as in his freendes nede,
Ne bar him bet than he, withouten drede.

But now, paraunter, som man wayten wolde
That every word, or sonde, or look, or chere
Of Troilus that I rehersen sholde,
In al this whyle, unto his lady dere;
I trowe it were a long thing for to here;
Or of what wight that stant in swich disjoynte,
His wordes alle, or every look, to poynte.

For sothe, I have not herd it doon er this,
In storye noon, ne no man here, I wene;
And though I wolde I coude not, ywis;
For ther was som epistel hem bitwene,
That wolde, as seyth myn auctor, wel contene
Neigh half this book, of which him list not wryte;
How sholde I thanne a lyne of it endyte?

But to the grete effect: than sey I thus,
That stonding in concord and in quiete
Thise ilke two, Criseyde and Troilus,
As I have told, and in this tyme swete,
Save only often mighte they not mete,
Ne layser have hir speches to fulfelle,
That it befel right as I shal yow telle,

That Pandarus, that ever dide his might
Right for the fyn that I shal speke of here,
As for to bringe to his hous som night
His faire nece, and Troilus yfere,
Wheras at leyser al this heigh matere,
Touching hir love, were at the fulle upbounde,
Hadde out of doute a tyme to it founde.

For he with greet deliberacioun
Hadde every thing that herto mighte avayle
Forncast, and put in execucioun,
And neither laft for cost ne for travayle;
Come if hem lest, hem sholde nothing fayle;
And for to been in ought espyed there,
That, wiste he wel, an inpossible were.

And dredelees, it cleer was in the wind
Of every pye and every lette-game;
Now al is wel, for al the world is blind
In this matere, bothe fremed and tame.
This timber is al redy up to frame;
Us lakketh nought but that we witen wolde
A certein houre, in whiche she comen sholde.

And Troilus, that al this purveyaunce
Knew at the fulle, and waytede on it ay,
Hadde hereupon eek maad gret ordenaunce,
And founde his cause, and therto his aray,
If that he were missed, night or day,
Therwhyle he was aboute this servyse,
That he was goon to doon his sacrifyse,

And moste at swich a temple alone wake,
Answered of Appollo for to be;
And first, to seen the holy laurer quake,
Er that Apollo spak out of the tree,
To telle him next whan Grekes sholden flee,
And forthy lette him no man, God forbede,
But preye Apollo helpen in this nede.

Now is ther litel more for to done,
But Pandare up, and shortly for to seyne,
Right sone upon the chaunging of the mone,
Whan lightles is the world a night or tweyne,
And that the welken shoop him for to reyne,
He streight amorwe unto his nece wente;
Ye han wel herd the fyn of his entente.

Whan he was come, he gan anoon to pleye
As he was wont, and of himself to jape;
And fynally, he swor and gan hir seye,
By this and that, she sholde him not escape,
Ne lenger doon him after hir to gape;
But certeynly she moste, by hir leve,
Come soupen in his hous with him at eve.

At whiche she lough, and gan hir faste excuse,
And seyde: It rayneth; lo, how sholde I goon?
Lat be, quod he, ne stond not thus to muse;
This moot be doon, ye shal be ther anoon.
So at the laste herof they felle at oon,
Or elles, softe he swor hir in hir ere,
He nolde never come ther she were.

506

Sone after this, to him she gan to rowne,
And asked him if Troilus were there?
He swor hir: Nay, for he was out of towne,
And seyde: Nece, I pose that he were,
Yow thurfte never have the more fere.
For rather than men mighte him ther aspye,
Me were lever a thousand-fold to dye.

Nought list myn auctor fully to declare
What that she thoughte whan he seyde so,
That Troilus was out of town yfare,
As if he seyde therof sooth or no;
But that, withoute awayt, with him to go,
She graunted him, sith he hir that bisoughte,
And, as his nece, obeyed as hir oughte.

But nathelees, yet gan she him biseche,
Although with him to goon it was no fere,
For to be war of goosish peples speche,
That dremen thinges whiche that never were,
And wel avyse him whom he broughte there;
And seyde him: Eem, sin I mot on yow triste,
Loke al be wel, and do now as yow liste.

He swor hir: Yis, by stokkes and by stones,
And by the goddes that in hevene dwelle,
Or elles were him lever, soule and bones,
With Pluto king as depe been in helle
As Tantalus! What sholde I more telle?
Whan al was wel, he roos and took his leve,
And she to souper com, whan it was eve,

With a certayn of hir owene men,
And with hir faire nece Antigone,
And othere of hir wommen nyne or ten;
But who was glad now, who, as trowe ye,
But Troilus, that stood and mighte it see
Thurghout a litel windowe in a stewe,
Ther he bishet, sin midnight, was in mewe,

Unwist of every wight but of Pandare?
But to the poynt; now whan she was ycome
With alle joye, and alle frendes fare,
Hir eem anoon in armes hath hir nome,
And after to the souper, alle and some,
Whan tyme was, ful softe they hem sette;
God wot, ther was no deyntee for to fette.

And after souper gonnen they to ryse,
At ese wel, with hertes fresshe and glade,
And wel was him that coude best devyse
To lyken hir, or that hir laughen made.
He song; she pleyde; he tolde tale of Wade.
But at the laste, as every thing hath ende,
She took hir leve, and nedes wolde wende.

But O, fortune, executrice of wierdes,
O influences of thise hevenes hye!
Soth is, that, under God, ye ben our hierdes,
Though to us bestes been the causes wrye.
This mene I now, for she gan hoomward hye,
But execut was al bisyde hir leve,
At the goddes wil; for which she moste bleve.

The bente mone with hir hornes pale,
Saturne, and Jove, in Cancro joyned were,
That swich a rayn from hevene gan avale,
That every maner womman that was there
Hadde of that smoky reyn a verray fere;
At which Pandare tho lough, and seyde thenne:
Now were it tyme a lady to go henne!

But goode nece, if I mighte ever plese
Yow anything, than prey I yow, quod he,
To doon myn herte as now so greet an ese
As for to dwelle here al this night with me,
Forwhy this is your owene hous, pardee.
For, by my trouthe, I sey it nought agame,
To wende as now, it were to me a shame.

¶ Criseyde, whiche that coude as muche good
As half a world, tok hede of his preyere;
And sin it ron, and al was on a flood,
She thoughte, as good chep may I dwellen here,
And graunte it gladly with a freendes chere,
And have a thank, as grucche and thanne abyde;
For hoom to goon it may nought wel bityde.

¶ I wol, quod she, myn uncle leef and dere,
Sin that yow list, it skile is to be so;
I am right glad with yow to dwellen here;
I seyde but agame, I wolde go.
¶ Ywis, graunt mercy, nece! quod he tho;
Were it a game or no, soth for to telle,
Now am I glad, sin that yow list to dwelle.

¶ Thus al is wel; but tho bigan aright
The newe joye, and al the feste agayn;
But Pandarus, if goodly hadde he might,
He wolde han hyed hir to bedde fayn,
And seyde: Lord, this is an huge rayn!
This were a weder for to slepen inne;
And that I rede us sone to biginne.

And nece, woot ye wher I wol yow leye,
For that we shul not liggen fer asonder,
And for ye neither shullen, dar I seye,
Heren noise of reynes nor of thonder?
By God, right in my lyte closet yonder.
And I wol in that outer hous allone
Be wardeyn of your wommen everichone.

And in this middel chaumbre that ye see
Shul youre wommen slepen wel and softe;
And ther I seyde shal yourselve be;
And if ye liggen wel tonight, com ofte,
And careth not what weder is on-lofte.
The wyn anon, and whan so that yow leste,
So go we slepe, I trowe it be the beste.

¶ Ther nis no more, but hereafter sone,
The voydë dronke, and travers drawe anon,
Gan every wight, that hadde nought to done
More in that place, out of the chaumber gon.
And evermo so sternelich it ron,
And blew therwith so wonderliche loude,
That wel neigh no man heren other coude.

Tho Pandarus, hir eem, right as him oughte,
With women swiche as were hir most aboute,
Ful glad unto hir beddes syde hir broughte,
And toke his leve, and gan ful lowe loute,
And seyde: Here at this closet-dore withoute,
Right over-thwart, your wommen liggen alle,
That, whom yow liste of hem, ye may here calle.

¶ So whan that she was in the closet leyd,
And alle hir wommen forth by ordenaunce
Abedde weren, ther as I have seyd,
There was no more to skippen nor to traunce,
But boden go to bedde, with mischaunce,
If any wight was steringe anywhere,
And late hem slepe that abedde were.

But Pandarus, that wel coude eche a del
The olde daunce, and every poynt therinne,
Whan that he sey that alle thing was wel,
He thoughte he wolde upon his werk biginne,
And ganne the stewe-dore al softe unpinne,
And stille as stoon, withouten lenger lette,
By Troilus adoun right he him sette.

And, shortly to the poynt right for to gon,
Of al this werk he tolde him word and ende,
And seyde: Make thee redy right anon,
For thou shalt into hevene blisse wende.
¶ Now blisful Venus, thou me grace sende,
Quod Troilus, for never yet no nede
Hadde I er now, ne halvendel the drede.

¶ Quod Pandarus: Ne drede thee never a del,
For it shal been right as thou wilt desyre;
So thryve I, this night shal I make it wel,
Or casten al the gruwel in the fyre.
¶ Yit blisful Venus, this night thou me enspyre,
Quod Troilus, as wis as I thee serve,
And ever bet and bet shal, til I sterve.

And if I hadde, O Venus ful of mirthe,
Aspectes badde of Mars or of Saturne,
Or thou combust or let were in my birthe,
Thy fader prey al thilke harm disturne
Of grace, and that I glad ayein may turne,
For love of him thou lovedest in the shawe,
I mene Adoon, that with the boor was slawe.

O Jove eek, for the love of faire Europe,
The whiche in forme of bole away thou fette;
Now help, O Mars, thou with thy blody cope,
For love of Cipris, thou me nought ne lette;
O Phebus, thenk whan Dane hirselven shette
Under the bark, and laurer wex for drede,
Yet for hir love, O help now at this nede!

Mercurie, for the love of Hiersë eke,
For which Pallas was with Aglauros wrooth,
Now help, and eek Diane, I thee biseke,
That this viage be not to thee looth.
O fatal sustren, which, er any clooth
Me shapen was, my destenë me sponne,
So helpeth to this werk that is bigonne!

507

Quod Pandarus:Thou wrecched mouses herte,
Art thou agast so that she wol thee byte?
Why, don this furred cloke upon thy sherte,
And folowe me, for I wol han the wyte;
But byd, and lat me go bifore a lyte.
And with that word he gan undo a trappe,
And Troilus he broughte in by the lappe.

The sterne wind so loude gan to route
That no wight other noyse mighte here;
And they that layen at the dore withoute,
Ful sykerly they slepten alle yfere;
And Pandarus, with a ful sobre chere,
Goth to the dore anon withouten lette,
Theras they laye, and softely it shette.

And as he com ayeinward prively,
His nece awook, and asked: Who goth there?
My dere nece, quod he, it am I;
Ne wondreth not, ne have of it no fere;
And ner he com, and seyde hir in hir ere:
No word, for love of God I yow biseche;
Lat no wight ryse and heren of our speche.

What! which wey be ye comen, benedicite?
Quod she, and how thus unwist of hem alle?
Here at this secre trappe,dore, quod he.
Quod tho Criseyde: Lat me som wight calle.
Ey! God forbede that it sholde falle,
Quod Pandarus, that ye swich foly wroughte!
They mighte deme thing they never er thoughte!

It is nought good a sleping hound to wake,
Ne yeve a wight a cause to devyne;
Your wommen slepen alle, I undertake,
So that, for hem, the hous men mighte myne;
And slepen wolen til the sonne shyne.
And whan my tale al brought is to an ende,
Unwist, right as I com, so wol I wende.

Now nece myn, ye shul wel understonde,
Quod he, so as ye wommen demen alle,
That for to holde in love a man in honde,
And him hir Leef and Dere herte calle,
And maken him an howve above a calle,
I mene, as love an other in this whyle,
She doth hirself a shame, and him a gyle.

Now wherby that I telle yow al this?
Ye woot yourself, as wel as any wight,
How that your love al fully graunted is
To Troilus, the worthieste knight,
Oon of this world, and therto trouthe plyght,
That, but it were on him along, ye nolde
Him never falsen, whyl ye liven sholde.

Now stant it thus, that sith I fro yow wente,
This Troilus, right platly for to seyn,
Is thurgh a goter, by a privé wente,
Into my chaumbre come in al this reyn,
Unwist of every maner wight, certeyn,
Save of myself, as wisly have I joye,
And by that feith I shal Pryam of Troye!

And he is come in swich peyne and distresse
That, but he be al fully wood by this,
He sodeynly mot falle into wodnesse,
But if God helpe; and cause why this is,
He seyth him told is, of a freend of his,
How that ye sholde love oon that hatte Horaste,
For sorwe of which this night shalt been his laste.

Criseyde, which that al this wonder herde,
Gan sodeynly aboute hir herte colde,
And with a syk she sorwfully answerde:
Allas! I wende, whoso tales tolde,
My dere herte wolde me not holde
So lightly fals! allas! conceytes wronge,
What harm they doon, for now live I to longe!

Horaste! allas! and falsen Troilus?
I knowe him not, God helpe me so, quod she;
Allas! what wikked spirit tolde him thus?
Now certes, eem, tomorwe, and I him see,
I shal therof as ful excusen me
As ever dide womman, if him lyke;
And with that word she gan ful sore syke.

O God! quod she, so worldly selinesse,
Which clerkes callen fals felicitee,
Ymedled is with many a bitternesse!
Ful anguisshous than is, God woot, quod she,
Condicioun of veyn prosperitee;
For either joyes comen nought yfere,
Or elles no wight hath hem alwey here.

O brotel wele of mannes joye unstable!
With what wight so thou be, or how thou pleye,
Either he woot that thou, joye, art muable,
Or woot it not, it moot ben oon of tweye;
Now if he woot it not, how may he seye
That he hath verray joye and selinesse,
That is of ignoraunce ay in derknesse?

Now if he woot that joye is transitorie,
As every joye of worldly thing mot flee,
Than every tyme he that hath in memorie,
The drede of lesing maketh him that he
May in no parfit selinesse be.
And if to lese his joye he set a myte,
Than semeth it that joye is worth ful lyte.

Wherfore I wol deffyne in this matere,
That trewely, for ought I can espye,
Ther is no verray wele in this world here.
But O, thou wikked serpent jalousye,
Thou misbeleved and envious folye,
Why hastow Troilus me mad untriste,
That never yet agilte him, that I wiste?

Quod Pandarus: Thus fallen is this cas.
Why, uncle myn, quod she, who tolde him this?
Why doth my dere herte thus, allas?
Ye woot, ye nece myn, quod he, what is;
I hope al shal be wel that is amis.
For ye may quenche al this, if that yow leste,
And doth right so, for I holde it the beste.

So shal I do tomorwe, ywis, quod she,
And God toforn, so that it shal suffyse.
Tomorwe? allas, that were a fayr, quod he,
Nay, nay, it may not stonden in this wyse;
for, nece myn, thus wryten clerkes wyse,
That peril is with drecching in ydrawe;
Nay, swich abodes been nought worth an hawe.

Nece, alle thing hath tyme, I dar avowe;
for whan a chaumber afyr is, or an halle,
Wel more nede is, it sodeynly rescowe
Than to dispute, and axe amonges alle
How is this candele in the straw yfalle?
A! benedicite! for al among that fare
The harm is doon, and farewel feldefare!

And, nece myn, ne take it not agreef,
If that ye suffre him al night in this wo,
God help me so, ye hadde him never leef,
That dar I seyn, now there is but we two;
But wel I woot, that ye wol not do so;
Ye been to wys to do so gret folye,
To putte his lyf al night in jupartye.

Hadde I him never leef? By God, I wene
Ye hadde never thing so leef, quod she.
Now by my thrift, quod he, that shal be sene;
for, sin ye make this ensample of me,
If I al night wolde him in sorwe see
for al the tresour in the toun of Troye,
I bidde God, I never mote have joye!

Now loke thanne, if ye, that been his love,
Shul putte al night his lyf in jupartye
for thing of nought! Now, by that God above,
Nought only this delay comth of folye,
But of malyce, if that I shal nought lye.
What, platly, and ye suffre him in distresse,
Ye neither bountee doon ne gentilesse!

Quod tho Criseyde: Wole ye doon o thing,
And ye therwith shal stinte al his disese;
Have here, and bereth him this blewe ring,
for ther is nothing mighte him bettre plese,
Save I myself, ne more his herte apese;
And sey my dere herte, that his sorwe
Is causeles, that shal be seen tomorwe.

A ring? quod he, ye, hasel-wodes shaken!
Ye, nece myn, that ring moste han a stoon
That mighte dede men alyve maken;
And swich a ring, trowe I that ye have noon.
Discrecioun out of your heed is goon;
That fele I now, quod he, and that is routhe;
O tyme ylost, wel maystow cursen slouthe!

Wot ye not wel that noble and heigh corage
Ne sorweth not, ne stinteth eek for lyte?
But if a fool were in a jalous rage,
I nolde setten at his sorwe a myte,
But feffe him with a fewe wordes whyte
Another day, whan that I mighte him finde:
But this thing stont al in another kinde.

This is so gentil and so tendre of herte,
That with his deeth he wol his sorwes wreke;
for trusteth wel, how sore that him smerte,
He wol to yow no jalouse wordes speke.
And forthy, nece, er that his herte breke,
So spek yourself to him of this matere;
for with o word ye may his herte stere.

Now have I told what peril he is inne,
And his coming unwist to every wight;
Ne, pardee, harm may ther be noon ne sinne;
I wol myself be with yow al this night.
Ye knowe eek how it is your owne knight,
And that, by right, ye moste upon him triste,
And I al prest to fecche him whan yow liste.

This accident so pitous was to here,
And eek so lyk a sooth, at pryme face,
And Troilus hir knight to hir so dere,
His privë coming, and the siker place,
That, though that she dide him as thanne a grace,
Considered alle thinges as they stode,
No wonder is, sin she dide al for gode.

Cryseyde answerde: As wisly God at reste
My sowle bringe, as me is for him wo!
And eem, ywis, fayn wolde I doon the beste,
If that I hadde grace to do so.
But whether that ye dwelle or for him go,
I am, til God me bettre minde sende,
At dulcarnon, right at my wittes ende.

Quod Pandarus: Ye, nece, wol ye here?
Dulcarnon called is fleminge of wrecches;
It semeth hard, for wrecches wol not lere
for verray slouthe or othere wilful tecches;
This seyd by hem that be not worth two fecches.
But ye ben wys, and that we han on honde
Nis neither hard, ne skilful to withstonde.

Thanne, eem, quod she, doth herof as yow list;
But er he come I wil up first aryse;
And, for the love of God, sin al my trist
Is on yow two, and ye ben bothe wyse,
So wircheth now in so discreet a wyse,
That I honour may have, and he plesaunce;
for I am here al in your governaunce.

That is wel seyd, quod he, my nece dere,
Ther good thrift on that wyse gentil herte!
But liggeth stille, and taketh him right here,
It nedeth not no ferther for him sterte;
And ech of yow ese otheres sorwes smerte,
for love of God; and, Venus, I thee herie;
for sone hope I we shulle ben alle merie.

This Troilus ful sone on knees him sette
ful sobrely, right by hir beddes heed,
And in his beste wyse his lady grette;
But Lord, so she wex sodeynliche reed!
Ne, though men sholden smyten of hir heed,
She coude nought a word aright outbringe
So sodeynly, for his sodeyn cominge.

But Pandarus, that so wel coude fele
In every thing, to pleye anoon bigan,
And seyde: Nece, see how this lord can knele!
Now, for your trouthe, seeth this gentil man!
And with that word he for a quisshen ran,
And seyde: Kneleth now, whyl that yow leste,
Ther God your hertes bringe sone at reste!

Can I not seyn, for she bad him not ryse,
If sorwe it putte out of hir remembraunce,
Or elles if she toke it in the wyse
Of duëtee, as for his observaunce;
But wel finde I she dide him this plesaunce,
That she him kiste, although she syked sore;
And bad him sitte adoun withouten more.

Quod Pandarus: Now wol ye wel biginne;
Now doth him sitte, gode nece dere,
Upon your beddes syde al there withinne,
That ech of yow the bet may other here.
And with that word he drow him to the fere,
And took a light, and fond his contenaunce
As for to loke upon an old romaunce.

Criseyde, that was Troilus lady right,
And cleer stood on a ground of sikernesse,
Al thoughte she, hir servaunt and hir knight
Ne sholde of right non untrouthe in hir gesse,
Yet nathelees, considered his distresse,
And that love is in cause of swich folye,
Thus to him spak she of his jelousye:

Lo, herte myn, as wolde the excellence
Of love, ayeins the which that no man may,
Ne oughte eek goodly maken resistence;
And eek bycause I felte wel and say
Your grete trouthe, and servyse every day;
And that your herte al myn was, sooth to seyne,
This droof me for to rewe upon your peyne.

And your goodnesse have I founde alwey yit,
Of whiche, my dere herte and al my knight,
I thonke it yow, as fer as I have wit,
Al can I nought as muche as it were right;
And I, emforth my conninge and my might,
Have and ay shal, how sore that me smerte,
Ben to yow trewe and hool, with al myn herte;

And dredelees, that shal be founde at preve.
But, herte myn, what al this is to seyne
Shal wel be told, so that ye noght yow greve,
Though I to yow right on yourself compleyne.
For therwith mene I fynally the peyne,
That halt your herte and myn in hevinesse,
Fully to sleen, and every wrong redresse.

My goode, myn, not I forwhy ne how
That jalousye, allas! that wikked wivere,
Thus causelees is cropen into yow;
The harm of which I wolde fayn delivere!
Allas! that he, al hool, or of him slivere,
Shuld have his refut in so digne a place,
Ther Jove him sone out of your herte arace!
510

But O, thou Jove, O auctor of nature,
Is this an honour to thy deitee,
That folk ungiltif suffren here injure,
And who that giltif is, al quit goth he?
O were it leful for to pleyne on thee,
That undeserved suffrest jalousye,
And that I wolde upon thee pleyne and crye!

Eek al my wo is this, that folk now usen
To seyn right thus: Ye, jalousye is love!
And wolde a busshel venim al excusen,
For that o greyn of love is on it shove!
But that wot heighe God that sit above,
If it be lyker love, or hate, or grame;
And after that, it oughte bere his name.

But certeyn is, some maner jalousye
Is excusable more than som, ywis.
As whan cause is, and som swich fantasye
With pietee so wel repressed is,
That it unnethe dooth or seyth amis,
But goodly drinketh up al his distresse;
And that excuse I, for the gentilesse.

And som so ful of furie is and despyt,
That it sourmounteth his repressioun;
But herte myn, ye be not in that plyt,
That thanke I God, for whiche your passioun
I wol not calle it but illusioun,
Of habundaunce of love and bisy cure,
That dooth your herte this disese endure.

Of which I am right sory, but not wrooth;
But, for my devoir and your hertes reste,
Wherso yow list, by ordal or by ooth,
By sort, or in what wyse so yow leste,
For love of God, lat preve it for the beste!
And if that I be giltif, do me deye,
Allas! what mighte I more doon or seye?

With that a fewe brighte teres newe
Out of hir eyen fille, and thus she seyde:
Now God, thou wost, in thought ne dede untrewe
To Troilus was never yet Criseyde.
With that hir heed doun in the bed she leyde,
And with the shete it wreigh, and syghed sore,
And held hir pees; not o word spak she more.

But now help God to quenchen al this sorwe,
So hope I that he shal, for he best may;
For I have seyn, of a ful misty morwe
Folwen ful ofte a mery someres day;
And after winter folweth grene May.
Men seen alday, and reden eek in stories,
That after sharpe shoures been victories.

This Troilus, whan he hir wordes herde,
Have ye no care, him liste not to slepe;
For it thoughte him no strokes of a yerde
To here or seen Criseyde his lady wepe;
But wel he felte aboute his herte crepe,
For every teer which that Criseyde asterte,
The crampe of deeth, to streyne him by the herte.

And in his minde he gan the tyme acurse
That he cam there, and that he was born;
For now is wikke yturned into worse,
And al that labour he hath doon biforn,
He wende it lost, he thoughte he nas but lorn.
O Pandarus, thoughte he, allas! thy wyle
Serveth of nought, so weylawey the whyle!

And therwithal he heng adoun the heed,
And fil on knees, and sorwfully he sighte;
What mighte he seyn? he felte he nas but deed,
For wrooth was she that shulde his sorwes lighte.
But nathelees, whan that he speken mighte,
Than seyde he thus: God woot, that of this game,
Whan al is wist, than am I not to blame!

Therwith the sorwe so his herte shette,
That from his eyen fil ther not a tere,
And every spirit his vigour in knette,
So they astoned and oppressed were.
The feling of his sorwe, or of his fere,
Or of ought elles, fled was out of towne;
And doun he fel al sodeynly aswowne.

This was no litel sorwe for to see;
But al was hust, and Pandare up as faste:
O nece, pees, or we be lost, quod he,
Beth nought agast, but certeyn, at the laste,
For this or that, he into bedde him caste,
And seyde: O theef, is this a mannes herte?
And of he rente al to his bare sherte;

And seyde: Nece, but ye helpe us now,
Allas, your owne Troilus is lorn!
Ywis, so wolde I, and I wiste how,
Ful fayn, quod she; allas! that I was born!
Ye, nece, wol ye pullen out the thorn
That stiketh in his herte? quod Pandare;
Sey Al foryeve, and stint is al this fare!

Ye, that to me, quod she, ful lever were
Than al the good the sonne aboute gooth;
And therwithal she swoor him in his ere:
Ywis, my dere herte, I am nought wrooth,
Have here my trouthe and many another ooth;
Now speek to me, for it am I, Cryseyde!
But al for nought; yet mighte he not abreyde.

Therwith his pous and pawmes of his hondes
They gan to frote, and wete his temples tweyne,
And, to deliveren him from bittre bondes,
She ofte him kiste; and, shortly for to seyne,
Him to revoken she dide al hir peyne.
And at the laste, he gan his breeth to drawe,
And of his swough sone after that adawe,

And gan bet minde and reson to him take,
But wonder sore he was abayst, ywis.
And with a syk, whan he gan bet awake,
He seyde: O mercy, God, what thing is this?
Why do ye with yourselven thus amis?
Quod tho Criseyde; is this a mannes game?
What, Troilus! wol ye do thus, for shame?

And therwithal hir arm over him she leyde,
And al foryaf, and ofte tyme him keste.
He thonked hir, and to hir spak, and seyde
As fil to purpos for his herte reste.
And she to that answerde him as hir leste;
And with hir goodly wordes him disporte
She gan, and ofte his sorwes to comforte.

Quod Pandarus: For ought I can espyen,
This light nor I ne serven here of nought;
Light is not good for syke folkes yen.
But for the love of God, sin ye be brought
In thus good plyt, lat now non hevy thought
Ben hanginge in the hertes of yow tweye:
And bar the candele to the chimeneye.

Sone after this, though it no nede were,
Whan she swich othes as hir list devyse
Hadde of him take, hir thoughte tho no fere,
Ne cause eek non, to bidde him thennes ryse.
Yet lesse thing than othes may suffyse
In many a cas; for every wight, I gesse,
That loveth wel meneth but gentilesse.

But in effect she wolde wite anoon
Of what man, and eek where, and also why
He jelous was, sin ther was cause noon;
And eek the signe, that he took it by,
She bad him that to telle hir bisily,
Or elles, certeyn, she bar him on honde,
That this was doon of malis, hir to fonde.

Withouten more, shortly for to seyne,
He moste obeye unto his lady heste;
And for the lasse harm, he moste feyne.
He seyde hir, whan she was at swiche a feste
She mighte on him han loked at the leste;
Not I not what, al dere ynough a risshe,
As he that nedes moste a cause fisshe.

And she answerde: Swete, al were it so,
What harm was that, sin I non yvel mene?
For, by that God that boughte us bothe two,
In alle thinge is myn entente clene.
Swich arguments ne been not worth a bene;
Wol ye the childish jalous contrefete?
Now were it worthy that ye were ybete.

Tho Troilus gan sorwfully to syke,
Lest she be wrooth, him thoughte his herte deyde;
And seyde: Allas! upon my sorwes syke
Have mercy, swete herte myn, Cryseyde!
And if that, in tho wordes that I seyde,
Be any wrong, I wol no more trespace;
Do what yow list, I am al in your grace.

And she answerde: Of gilt misericorde!
That is to seyne, that I foryeve al this;
And evermore on this night yow recorde,
And beth wel war ye do no more amis.
Nay, dere herte myn, quod he, ywis.
And now, quod she, that I have do yow smerte,
Foryeve it me, myn owene swete herte.

511

This Troilus, with blisse of that supprysed,
Put al in Goddes hond, as he that mente
Nothing but wel; and, sodeynly avysed,
He hir in armes faste to him hente.
And Pandarus, with a ful good entente,
Leyde him to slepe, and seyde: If ye ben wyse,
Swowneth not now, lest more folk aryse.

What mighte or may the sely larke seye,
Whan that the sparhauk hath it in his foot?
I can no more, but of thise ilke tweye,
To whom this tale sucre be or soot,
Though that I tarie a yeer, somtyme I moot,
After myn auctor, tellen hir gladnesse,
As wel as I have told hir hevinesse.

Criseyde, which that felte hir thus ytake,
As writen clerkes in hir bokes olde,
Right as an aspes leef she gan to quake,
Whan she him felte hir in his armes folde.
But Troilus, al hool of cares colde,
Gan thanken tho the blisful goddes sevene;
Thus sondry peynes bringen folk to hevene.

This Troilus in armes gan hir streyne,
And seyde: O swete, as ever mote I goon,
Now be ye caught, now is ther but we tweyne;
Now yeldeth yow, for other boot is noon.
To that Criseyde answerde thus anoon:
Ne hadde I er now, my swete herte dere,
Ben yolde, ywis, I were now not here!

O! sooth is seyd, that heled for to be
As of a fevre or othere greet syknesse,
Men moste drinke, as men may often see,
Ful bittre drink; and for to han gladnesse,
Men drinken often peyne and greet distresse;
I mene it here, as for this aventure,
That thourgh a peyne hath founden al his cure.

And now swetnesse semeth more swete,
That bitternesse assayed was biforn;
For out of wo in blisse now they flete.
Non swich they felten, sith they were born;
Now is this bet, than bothe two be lorn!
For love of God, take every womman hede
To werken thus, if it comth to the nede.

Criseyde, al quit from every drede and tene,
As she that juste cause hadde him to triste,
Made him swich feste, it joye was to sene,
Whan she his trouthe and clene entente wiste.
And as aboute a tree, with many a twiste,
Bitrent and wryth the sote wode-binde,
Gan eche of hem in armes other winde.

And as the newe abaysshed nightingale,
That stinteth first whan she biginneth singe,
Whan that she hereth any herde tale,
Or in the hegges any wight steringe,
And after siker dooth hir voys outringe;
Right so Criseyde, whan hir drede stente,
Opned hir herte, and tolde him hir entente.

512

And right as he that seeth his deeth yshapen,
And deye moot, in ought that he may gesse,
And sodeynly rescous doth him escapen,
And from his deeth is brought in sikernesse,
For al this world, in swich present gladnesse
Was Troilus, and hath his lady swete;
With worse hap God lat us never mete!

Hir armes smale, hir streyghte bak and softe,
Hir sydes longe, fleshly, smothe, and whyte
He gan to stroke, and good thrift bad ful ofte
Hir snowish throte, hir brestes rounde and lyte;
Thus in this hevene he gan him to delyte,
And therwithal a thousand tyme hir kiste;
That, what to done, for joye unnethe he wiste.

Than seyde he thus: O, Love, O, Charitee,
Thy moder eek, Citherea the swete,
After thyself next heried be she,
Venus mene I, the welwilly planete;
And next that, Imeneüs, I thee grete;
For never man was to yow goddes holde
As I, which ye han brought fro cares colde.

Benigne Love, thou holy bond of thinges,
Whoso wol grace, and list thee nought honouren,
Lo, his desyr wol flee withouten winges,
For, noldestow of bountee hem socouren
That serven best and most alwey labouren,
Yet were al lost, that dar I wel seyn, certes,
But if thy grace passed our desertes.

And for thou me, that coude leest deserve
Of hem that nombred been unto thy grace,
Hast holpen, ther I lykly was to sterve,
And me bistowed in so heygh a place
That thilke boundes may no blisse pace,
I can no more, but laude and reverence
Be to thy bounte and thyn excellence!

And therwithal Criseyde anoon he kiste,
Of which, certeyn, she felte no disese.
And thus seyde he: Now wolde God I wiste,
Myn herte swete, how I yow mighte plese!
What man, quod he, was ever thus at ese
As I, on whiche the faireste and the beste
That ever I say, deyneth hir herte reste.

Here may men seen that mercy passeth right;
The experience of that is felt in me,
That am unworthy to so swete a wight.
But herte myn, of your benignitee,
So thenketh, though that I unworthy be,
Yet mot I nede amenden in som wyse,
Right thourgh the vertu of your heyghe servyse.

And for the love of God, my lady dere,
Sin God hath wrought me for I shal yow serve,
As thus I mene, that ye wol be my stere,
To do me live, if that yow liste, or sterve,
So techeth me how that I may deserve
Your thank, so that I, thurgh myn ignoraunce,
Ne do nothing that yow be displesaunce.

For certes, fresshe wommanliche wyf,
This dar I seye, that trouthe and diligence,
That shal ye finden in me al my lyf,
Ne I wol not, certeyn, breken your defence;
And if I do, present or in absence,
For love of God, lat slee me with the dede,
If that it lyke unto your womanhede.

Ywis, quod she, myn owne hertes list,
My ground of ese, and al myn herte dere,
Graunt mercy, for on that is al my trist;
But late us falle awey fro this matere;
For it suffyseth, this that seyd is here.
And at o word, withouten repentaunce,
Welcome, my knight, my pees, my suffisaunce!

Of hir delyt, or joyes oon the leste
Were impossible to my wit to seye;
But juggeth, ye that han ben at the feste
Of swich gladnesse, if that hem liste pleye!
I can no more, but thus thise ilke tweye
That night, betwixen dreed and sikernesse,
Felten in love the grete worthinesse.

O blisful night, of hem so longe ysought,
How blithe unto hem bothe two thou were!
Why ne hadde I swich on with my soule ybought,
Ye, or the leeste joye that was there?
Awey, thou foule daunger and thou fere,
And lat hem in this hevene blisse dwelle,
That is so heygh, that al ne can I telle!

But sooth is, though I can not tellen al,
As can myn auctor, of his excellence,
Yet have I seyd, and, God toforn, I shal
In every thing al hoolly his sentence.
And if that I, at loves reverence,
Have any word in eched for the beste,
Doth therwithal right as yourselven leste.

For myne wordes, here and every part,
I speke hem alle under correccioun
Of yow, that feling han in loves art,
And putte it al in your discrecioun
To encrese or maken diminucioun
Of my langage, and that I yow biseche;
But now to purpos of my rather speche.

Thise ilke two, that ben in armes laft,
So looth to hem asonder goon it were,
That ech from other wende been biraft,
Or elles, lo, this was hir moste fere,
That al this thing but nyce dremes were;
For which ful ofte ech of hem seyde: O swete,
Clippe ich yow thus, or elles I it mete?

And, Lord! so he gan goodly on hir see,
That never his look ne bleynte from hir face,
And seyde: O dere herte, may it be
That it be sooth, that ye ben in this place?
Ye, herte myn, God thank I of his grace!
Quod tho Criseyde, and therwithal him kiste,
That where his spirit was, for joye he niste.

This Troilus ful ofte hir eyen two
Gan for to kisse, and seyde: O eyen clere,
It were ye that wroughte me swich wo,
Ye humble nettes of my lady dere!
Though ther be mercy writen in your chere,
God wot, the text ful hard is, sooth, to finde,
How coude ye withouten bond me binde?

Therwith he gan hir faste in armes take,
And wel an hundred tymes gan he syke,
Nought swiche sorwful sykes as men make
For wo, or elles whan that folk ben syke,
But esy sykes, swiche as been to lyke,
That shewed his affeccioun withinne;
Of swiche sykes coude he nought bilinne.

Sone after this they speke of sondry thinges,
As fil to purpos of this aventure,
And pleyinge entrechaungeden hir ringes,
Of which I can nought tellen no scripture;
But wel I woot a broche, gold and asure,
In whiche a ruby set was lyk an herte,
Criseyde him yaf, and stak it on his sherte.

Lord! trowe ye, a coveitous, a wrecche,
That blameth love and holt of it despyt,
That, of tho pens that he can mokre and kecche,
Was ever yet y-yeve him swich delyt,
As is in love, in oo poynt, in som plyt?
Nay, doutelees, for also God me save,
So parfit joye may no nigard have!

They wol sey Yis, but Lord! so that they lye,
Tho bisy wrecches, ful of wo and drede!
They callen love a woodnesse or folye,
But it shal falle hem as I shal yow rede;
They shul forgo the whyte and eek the rede,
And live in wo, ther God yeve hem mischaunce,
And every lover in his trouthe avaunce!

As wolde God, tho wrecches, that dispyse
Servyse of love, hadde eres also longe
As hadde Myda, ful of coveityse;
And therto dronken hadde as hoot and stronge
As Crassus dide for his affectis wronge,
To techen hem that they ben in the vyce,
And loveres nought, although they holde hem nyce!

Thise ilke two, of whom that I yow seye,
Whan that hir hertes wel assured were,
Tho gonne they to speken and to pleye,
And eek rehercen how, and whanne, and where,
They knewe hem first, and every wo and fere
That passed was; but al swich hevinesse,
I thanke it God, was tourned to gladnesse.

And evermo, whan that hem fel to speke
Of any thing of swich a tyme agoon,
With kissing al that tale sholde breke,
And fallen in a newe joye anoon,
And diden al hir might, sin they were oon,
For to recoveren blisse and been at ese,
And passed wo with joye countrepeyse.

lli

513

Reson wil not that I now speke of sleep,
For it accordeth nought to my matere;
God woot, they toke of that ful litel keep,
But lest this night, that was to hem so dere,
Ne sholde in veyn escape in no manere,
It was biset in joye and bisinesse
Of al that souneth into gentilnesse.

But whan the cok, comune astrologer,
Gan on his brest to bete, and after crowe,
And Lucifer, the dayes messager,
Gan for to ryse, and out hir bemes throwe;
And estward roos, to him that coude it knowe,
Fortuna major, than anoon Criseyde,
With herte sore, to Troilus thus seyde:

Myn hertes lyf, my trist and my plesaunce,
That I was born, allas! what me is wo,
That day of us mot make desseveraunce!
For tyme it is to ryse, and hennes go,
Or elles I am lost for evermo!
O night, allas! why niltow over us hove,
As longe as whanne Almena lay by Jove?

O blake night, as folk in bokes rede,
That shapen art by God this world to hyde
At certeyn tymes with thy derke wede,
That under that men mighte in reste abyde,
Wel oughte bestes pleyne, and folk thee chyde,
That theras day with labour wolde us breste,
That thou thus fleest, & deynest us nought reste!

Thou dost, allas! to shortly thyn offyce,
Thou rakel night, ther God, makere of kinde,
Thee, for thyn hast and thyn unkinde vyce,
So faste ay to our hemispere binde,
That nevermore under the ground thou winde!
For now, for thou so hyest out of Troye,
Have I forgon thus hastily my joye!

*This Troilus, that with tho wordes felte,
As thoughte him tho, for pietous distresse,
The blody teres from his herte melte,
As he that never yet swich hevinesse
Assayed hadde, out of so greet gladnesse,
Gan therwithal Criseyde his lady dere
In armes streyne, and seyde in this manere:

O cruel day, accusour of the joye
That night and love han stole and faste ywryen,
Acursed be thy coming into Troye,
For every bore hath oon of thy bright yën!
Envyous day, what list thee so to spyen?
What hastow lost, why sekestow this place,
Ther God thy lyght so quenche, for his grace?

Allas! what han thise loveres thee agilt,
Dispitous day? thyn be the pyne of helle!
For many a lovere hastow shent, and wilt;
Thy pouring in wol nowher lete hem dwelle.
What proferestow thy light here for to selle?
Go selle it hem that smale seles graven,
We wol thee nought, us nedeth no day haven.

514

*And eek the sonne Tytan gan he chyde,
And seyde: O fool, wel may men thee dispyse,
That hast the Dawing al night by thy syde,
And suffrest hir so sone up fro thee ryse,
For to disesen loveres in this wyse.
What! hold your bed ther, thou, & eek thy Morwe!
I bidde God, so yeve yow bothe sorwe!

*Therwith ful sore he sighte, & thus he seyde:
My lady right, and of my wele or wo
The welle and rote, O goodly myn, Criseyde,
And shal I ryse, allas! and shal I go?
Now fele I that myn herte moot atwo!
For how sholde I my lyf an houre save,
Sin that with yow is al the lyf I have?

What shal I doon, for certes, I not how,
Ne whanne, allas! I shal the tyme see,
That in this plyt I may be eft with yow;
And of my lyf, God woot, how that shal be,
Sin that desyr right now so byteth me,
That I am deed anoon, but I retourne.
How sholde I longe, allas! fro yow sojourne?

But nathelees, myn owene lady bright,
Yit were it so that I wiste outrely,
That I, your humble servaunt and your knight,
Were in your herte set so fermely
As ye in myn, the which thing, trewely,
Me lever were than thise worldes tweyne,
Yet sholde I bet enduren al my peyne.

*To that Criseyde answerde right anoon,
And with a syk she seyde: O herte dere,
The game, ywis, so ferforth now is goon,
The first shal Phebus falle fro his spere,
And every egle been the dowves fere,
And every roche out of his place sterte,
Er Troilus out of Criseydes herte!

Ye be so depe inwith myn herte grave,
That, though I wolde it turne out of my thought,
As wisly verray God my soule save,
To dyen in the peyne, I coude nought!
And, for the love of God that us hath wrought,
Lat in your brayn non other fantasye
So crepe, that it cause me to dye!

And that ye me wolde han as faste in minde
As I have yow, that wolde I yow biseche;
And, if I wiste soothly that to finde,
God mighte not a poynt my joyes eche!
But, herte myn, withoute more speche,
Beth to me trewe, or elles were it routhe;
For I am thyn, by God and by my trouthe!

Beth glad forthy, and live in sikernesse;
Thus seyde I never er this, ne shal to mo;
And if to yow it were a gret gladnesse
To turne ayein, soone after that ye go,
As fayn wolde I as ye, it were so,
As wisly God myn herte bringe at reste!
*And him in armes took, and ofte keste.

Agayns his wil, sin it mot nedes be,
This Troilus up roos, and faste him cledde,
And in his armes took his lady free
An hundred tyme, and on his wey him spedde,
And with swich wordes as his herte bledde,
He seyde: farewel, my dere herte swete,
Ther God us graunte sounde and sone to mete!

To which no word for sorwe she answerde,
So sore gan his parting hir destreyne;
And Troilus unto his palays ferde,
As woo bigon as she was, sooth to seyne;
So hard him wrong of sharp desyr the peyne
For to ben eft there he was in plesaunce,
That it may never out of his remembraunce.

Retorned to his real palais, sone
He softe into his bed gan for to slinke,
To slepe longe, as he was wont to done,
But al for nought; he may wel ligge and winke,
But sleep ne may ther in his herte sinke;
Thenkinge how she, for whom desyr him brende,
A thousand/fold was worth more than he wende.

And in his thought gan up and doun to winde
Hir wordes alle, and every contenaunce,
And fermely impressen in his minde
The leste poynt that to him was plesaunce;
And verrayliche, of thilke remembraunce,
Desyr al newe him brende, and lust to brede
Gan more than erst, and yet took he non hede.

Criseyde also, right in the same wyse,
Of Troilus gan in hir herte shette
His worthinesse, his lust, his dedes wyse,
His gentilesse, and how she with him mette,
Thonkinge love he so wel hir bisette;
Desyring eft to have hir herte dere
In swich a plyt, she dorste make him chere.

Pandare, amorwe which that comen was
Unto his nece, and gan hir fayre grete,
Seyde: Al this night so reyned it, allas!
That al my drede is that ye, nece swete,
Han litel layser had to slepe and mete;
Al night, quod he, hath reyn so do me wake,
That som of us, I trowe, hir hedes ake.

And ner he com, and seyde: How stont it now
This mery morwe, nece, how can ye fare?
Criseyde answerde: Never the bet for yow,
Fox that ye been, God yeve your herte care!
God helpe me so, ye caused al this fare,
Trow I, quod she, for alle your wordes whyte;
O! whoso seeth yow knoweth yow ful lyte!

With that she gan hir face for to wrye
With the shete, and wex for shame al reed;
And Pandarus gan under for to prye,
And seyde: Nece, if that I shal ben deed,
Have here a swerd, and smyteth of myn heed.
With that his arm al sodeynly he thriste
Under hir nekke, and at the laste hir kiste.

112

I passe al that which chargeth nought to seye,
What! God foryaf his deeth, and she also
Foryaf, and with hir uncle gan to pleye,
For other cause was ther noon than so.
But of this thing right to the effect to go,
Whan tyme was, hom til hir hous she wente,
And Pandarus hath fully his entente.

Now torne we ayein to Troilus,
That resteles ful longe abedde lay,
And prevely sente after Pandarus,
To him to come in al the haste he may.
He com anoon, nought ones seyde he Nay,
And Troilus ful sobrely he grette,
And doun upon his beddes syde him sette.

This Troilus, with al the affeccioun
Of frendes love that herte may devyse,
To Pandarus on knees fil adoun,
And er that he wolde of the place aryse,
He gan him thonken in his beste wyse;
A hondred sythe he gan the tyme blesse,
That he was born to bringe him fro distresse.

He seyde: O frend, of frendes the alderbeste
That ever was, the sothe for to telle,
Thou hast in hevene ybrought my soule at reste
Fro flegiton, the fery flood of helle;
That, though I mighte a thousand tymes selle,
Upon a day, my lyf in thy servyse,
It mighte nought a mote in that suffyse.

The sonne, which that al the world may see,
Saw never yet, my lyf, that dar I leye,
So inly fair and goodly as is she,
Whos I am al, and shal, til that I deye;
And, that I thus am hires, dar I seye,
That thanked be the heighe worthinesse
Of love, and eek thy kinde bisinesse.

Thus hastow me no litel thing y/yive,
Fo which to thee obliged be for ay
My lyf, and why? for thorugh thyn help I live;
For elles deed hadde I be many a day.
And with that word doun in his bed he lay,
And Pandarus ful sobrely him herde
Til al was seyd, and thanne he him answerde:

My dere frend, if I have doon for thee
In any cas, God wot, it is me leef;
And am as glad as man may of it be,
God help me so; but tak now not agreef
That I shal seyn, be war of this myscheef,
That, thereas thou now brought art into blisse,
That thou thyself ne cause it nought to misse.

For of fortunes sharp adversitee
The worst kinde of infortune is this,
A man to have ben in prosperitee,
And it remembren, whan it passed is.
Thou art wys ynough, forthy do nought amis;
Be not to rakel, though thou sitte warme,
For if thou be, certeyn, it wol thee harme.

515

Thou art at ese, and holde thee wel therinne.
For also seur as reed is every fyr,
As greet a craft is kepe wel as winne;
Brydle alwey wel thy speche and thy desyr.
For worldly joye halt not but by a wyr;
That preveth wel, it brest alday so ofte;
Forthy nede is to werke with it softe.

Quod Troilus: I hope, and God toforn,
My dere frend, that I shal so me bere,
That in my gilt ther shal no thing be lorn,
Ne I nil not rakle as for to greven here;
It nedeth not this matere ofte tere;
For wistestow myn herte wel, Pandare,
God woot, of this thou woldest litel care.

Tho gan he telle him of his glade night.
And wherof first his herte dredde, and how,
And seyde: freend, as I am trewe knight,
And by that feyth I shal to God and yow,
I hadde it never half so hote as now;
And ay the more that desyr me byteth
To love hir best, the more it me delyteth.

I noot myself not wisly what it is;
But now I fele a newe qualitee,
Ye, al another than I dide er this.
Pandare answerde, and seyde thus, that he
That ones may in hevene blisse be,
He feleth other weyes, dar I leye,
Than thilke tyme he first herde of it seye.

This is o word for al; this Troilus
Was never ful, to speke of this matere,
And for to preysen unto Pandarus
The bountee of his righte lady dere,
And Pandarus to thanke and maken chere.
This tale ay was span newe to biginne
Til that the night departed hem atwinne.

Sone after this, for that fortune it wolde,
Icomen was the blisful tyme swete,
That Troilus was warned that he sholde,
Ther he was erst, Criseyde his lady mete;
For which he felte his herte in joye flete;
And feythfully gan alle the goddes herie;
And lat see now if that he can be merie.

And holden was the forme and al the wyse,
Of hir cominge, and eek of his also,
As it was erst, which nedeth nought devyse.
But playnly to the effect right for to go,
In joye and seurte Pandarus hem two
Abedde broughte, whan hem bothe leste,
And thus they ben in quiete and in reste.

Nought nedeth it to yow, sin they ben met,
To aske at me if that they blythe were;
For if it erst was wel, tho was it bet
A thousand fold, this nedeth not enquere.
Agon was every sorwe and every fere;
And bothe, ywis, they hadde, and so they wende,
As muche joye as herte may comprende.

516

This is no litel thing of for to seye,
This passeth every wit for to devyse;
For eche of hem gan otheres lust obeye;
Felicitee, which that thise clerkes wyse
Commenden so, ne may not here suffyse.
This joye may not writen been with inke,
This passeth al that herte may bithinke.

But cruel day, so welawey the stounde!
Gan for to aproche, as they by signes knewe,
For whiche hem thoughte felen dethes wounde;
So wo was hem, that changen gan hir hewe,
And day they gonnen to dispyse al newe,
Calling it traytour, envyous, and worse,
And bitterly the dayes light they curse.

Quod Troilus: Allas! now am I war
That Pirous and tho swifte stedes three,
Whiche that drawen forth the sonnes char,
Han goon som bypath in despyt of me;
That maketh it so sone day to be;
And, for the sonne him hasteth thus to ryse,
Ne shal I never doon him sacrifyse!

But nedes day departe moste hem sone,
And whanne hir speche doon was and hir chere,
They twinne anoon as they were wont to done,
And setten tyme of meting eft yfere;
And many a night they wroughte in this manere.
And thus Fortune a tyme ladde in joye
Criseyde, and eek this kinges sone of Troye.

In suffisaunce, in blisse, and in singinges,
This Troilus gan al his lyf to lede;
He spendeth, justeth, maketh festeyinges;
He yeveth frely ofte, and chaungeth wede,
And held aboute him alwey, out of drede,
A world of folk, as cam him wel of kinde,
The fressheste and the beste he coude fynde;

That swich a voys was of hym and a stevene
Thoroughout the world, of honour and largesse,
That it up rong unto the yate of hevene.
And, as in love, he was in swich gladnesse,
That in his herte he demede, as I gesse,
That there nis lovere in this world at ese
So wel as he, and thus gan love him plese.

The godlihede or beautee which that kinde
In any other lady hadde yset
Can not the mountaunce of a knot unbinde,
Aboute his herte, of al Criseydes net.
He was so narwe ymasked and yknet,
That it undon on any manere syde,
That nil not been, for ought that may betyde.

And by the hond ful ofte he wolde take
This Pandarus, and into gardin lede,
And swich a feste and swich a proces make
Him of Criseyde, and of hir womanhede,
And of hir beautee, that, withouten drede,
It was an hevene his wordes for to here;
And thanne he wolde singe in this manere.

Love, that of erthe and see hath governaunce,
Love, that his hestes hath in hevene hye,
Love, that with an holsom alliaunce
Halt peples joyned, as him lest hem gye,
Love, that knetteth lawe of companye,
And couples doth in vertu for to dwelle,
Bind this acord, that I have told and telle;

That that the world with feyth, which that is
stable,
Dyverseth so his stoundes concordinge,
That elements that been so discordable
Holden a bond perpetuely duringe,
That Phebus mote his rosy day forth bringe,
And that the mone hath lordship over the
nightes,
Al this doth Love; ay heried be his mightes!

That that the see, that gredy is to flowen,
Constreyneth to a certeyn ende so
His flodes, that so fersly they ne growen
To drenchen erthe and al for evermo;
And if that Love ought lete his brydel go,
Al that now loveth asonder sholde lepe,
And lost were al, that Love halt now tohepe.

So wolde God, that auctor is of kinde,
That, with his bond, Love of his vertu liste
To cerclen hertes alle, and faste binde,
That from his bond no wight the wey out wiste.
And hertes colde, hem wolde I that he twiste
To make hem love, and that hem leste ay rewe
On hertes sore, and kepe hem that ben trewe.

In alle nedes, for the tounes werre,
He was, and ay the firste in armes dight;
And certeynly, but if that bokes erre,
Save Ector, most ydrad of any wight;
And this encrees of hardinesse and might
Cam him of love, his ladies thank to winne,
That altered his spirit so withinne.

In tyme of trewe, on haukinge wolde he ryde,
Or elles hunten boor, bere, or lyoun;
The smale bestes leet he gon bisyde.

And whan that he com rydinge into toun,
Ful ofte his lady, from hir window doun,
As fresh as faucon comen out of muwe,
Ful redy was, him goodly to saluwe.

And most of love and vertu was his speche,
And in despyt hadde alle wrecchednesse;
And doutelees, no nede was him biseche
To honouren hem that hadde worthinesse,
And esen hem that weren in distresse.
And glad was he if any wight wel ferde,
That lover was, whan he it wiste or herde.

For sooth to seyn, he lost held every wight
But if he were in loves heigh servyse,
I mene folk that oughte it been of right.
And over al this, so wel coude he devyse
Of sentement, and in so unkouth wyse
Al his array, that every lover thoughte,
That al was wel, whatso he seyde or wroughte.

And though that he be come of blood royal,
Him liste of pryde at no wight for to chase;
Benigne he was to ech in general,
For which he gat him thank in every place.
Thus wolde Love, yheried be his grace,
That Pryde, Envye, Ire, and Avaryce
He gan to flee, and every other vyce.

Thou lady bright, the doughter to Dione,
Thy blinde and winged sone eek, daun Cupyde;
Ye sustren nyne eek, that by Elicone
In hil Parnaso listen for to abyde,
That ye thus fer han deyned me to gyde,
I can no more, but sin that ye wol wende,
Ye heried been for ay, withouten ende!

Thourgh yow have I seyd fully in my song
Theffect and joye of Troilus servyse,
Al be that ther was som disese among,
As to myn auctor listeth to devyse.
My thridde book now ende ich in this wyse;
And Troilus in luste and in quiete
Is with Criseyde, his owne herte swete.
Explicit Liber Tercius.

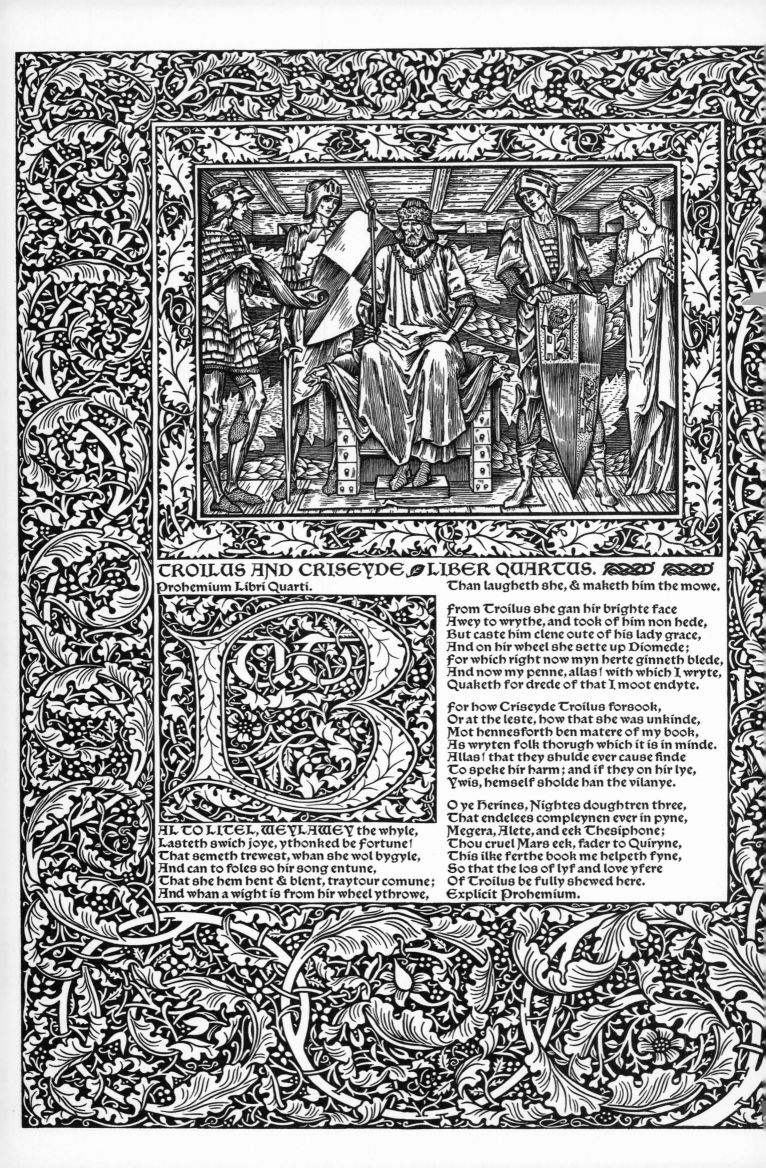

TROILUS AND CRISEYDE ❦ LIBER QUARTUS.

Prohemium Libri Quarti.

Than laugheth she, & maketh him the mowe.

from Troilus she gan hir brighte face
Awey to wrythe, and took of him non hede,
But caste him clene oute of his lady grace,
And on hir wheel she sette up Diomede;
for which right now myn herte ginneth blede,
And now my penne, allas! with which I wryte,
Quaketh for drede of that I moot endyte.

for how Criseyde Troilus forsook,
Or at the leste, how that she was unkinde,
Mot hennesforth ben matere of my book,
As wryten folk thorugh which it is in minde.
Allas! that they shulde ever cause finde
To speke hir harm; and if they on hir lye,
Ywis, hemself sholde han the vilanye.

O ye Herines, Nightes doughtren three,
That endelees compleynen ever in pyne,
Megera, Alete, and eek Thesiphone;
Thou cruel Mars eek, fader to Quiryne,
This ilke ferthe book me helpeth fyne,
So that the los of lyf and love yfere
Of Troilus be fully shewed here.
Explicit Prohemium.

AL TO LITEL, WEYLAWEY the whyle,
Lasteth swich joye, ythonked be fortune!
That semeth trewest, whan she wol bygyle,
And can to foles so hir song entune,
That she hem hent & blent, traytour comune;
And whan a wight is from hir wheel ythrowe,

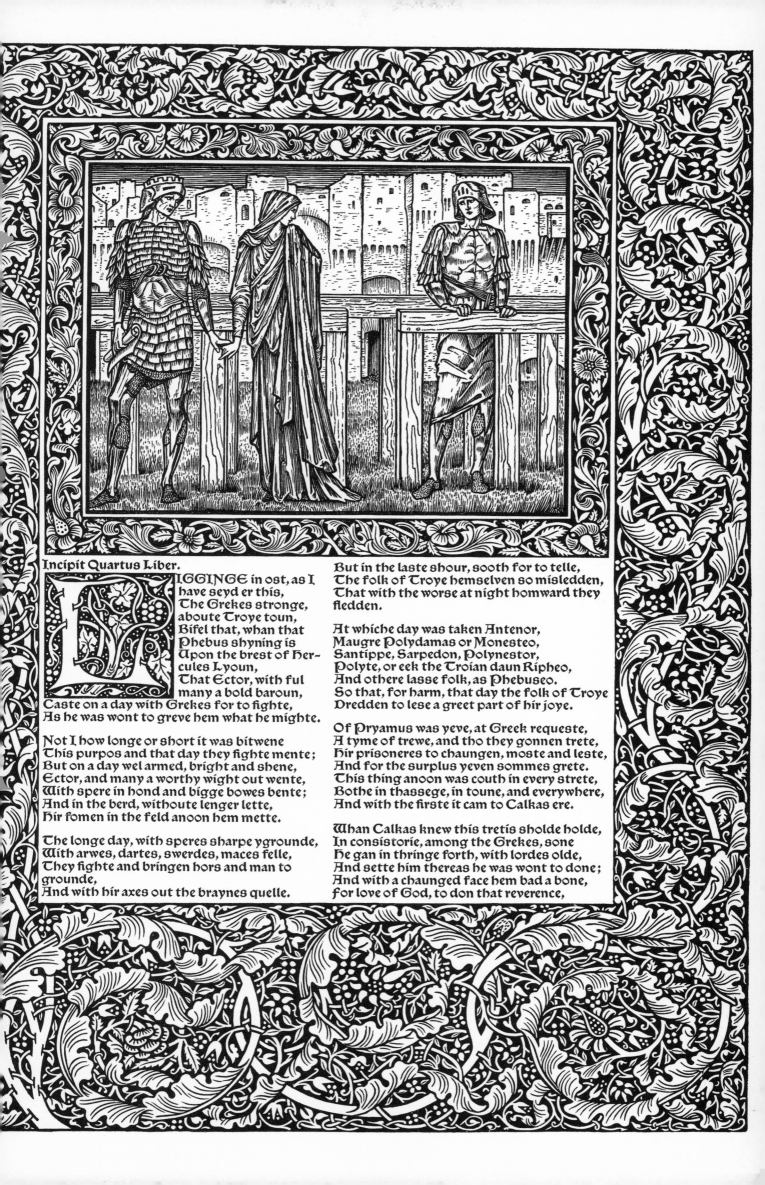

Incipit Quartus Liber.

BIGGINGE in ost, as I
have seyd er this,
The Grekes stronge,
aboute Troye toun,
Bifel that, whan that
Phebus shyning is
Upon the brest of Her-
cules Lyoun,
That Ector, with ful
many a bold baroun,
Caste on a day with Grekes for to fighte,
As he was wont to greve hem what he mighte.

Not I how longe or short it was bitwene
This purpos and that day they fighte mente;
But on a day wel armed, bright and shene,
Ector, and many a worthy wight out wente,
With spere in hond and bigge bowes bente;
And in the berd, withoute lenger lette,
Hir fomen in the feld anoon hem mette.

The longe day, with speres sharpe ygrounde,
With arwes, dartes, swerdes, maces felle,
They fighte and bringen hors and man to
grounde,
And with hir axes out the braynes quelle.

But in the laste shour, sooth for to telle,
The folk of Troye hemselven so misledden,
That with the worse at night homward they
fledden.

At whiche day was taken Antenor,
Maugre Polydamas or Monesteo,
Santippe, Sarpedon, Polynestor,
Polyte, or eek the Troian daun Ripheo,
And othere lasse folk, as Phebuseo.
So that, for harm, that day the folk of Troye
Dredden to lese a greet part of hir joye.

Of Pryamus was yeve, at Greek requeste,
A tyme of trewe, and tho they gonnen trete,
Hir prisoneres to chaungen, moste and leste,
And for the surplus yeven sommes grete.
This thing anoon was couth in every strete,
Bothe in thassege, in toune, and everywhere,
And with the firste it cam to Calkas ere.

Whan Calkas knew this tretis sholde holde,
In consistorie, among the Grekes, sone
He gan in thringe forth, with lordes olde,
And sette him thereas he was wont to done;
And with a chaunged face hem bad a bone,
For love of God, to don that reverence,

To stinte noyse, and yeve him audience.

Thanne seyde he thus: Lo! lordes myne, I was
Troian, as it is knowen out of drede;
And if that yow remembre, I am Calkas,
That alderfirst yaf comfort to your nede,
And tolde wel how that ye sholden spede.
For dredelees, thorugh yow, shal, in a stounde,
Ben Troye ybrend, and beten doun to grounde.

And in what forme, or in what maner wyse
This town to shende, and al your lust to acheve,
Ye han er this wel herd it me devyse;
This knowe ye, my lordes, as I leve.
And for the Grekes weren me so leve,
I com myself in my propre persone,
To teche in this how yow was best to done;

Havinge unto my tresour ne my rente
Right no resport, to respect of your ese.
Thus al my good I loste and to yow wente,
Wening in this you, lordes, for to plese.
But al that los ne doth me no disese.
I vouchesauf, as wisly have I joye,
For you to lese al that I have in Troye,

Save of a doughter, that I lafte, allas!
Slepinge at hoom, whanne out of Troye I sterte.
O sterne, O cruel fader that I was!
How mighte I have in that so hard an herte?
Allas! I ne hadde ybrought hir in hir sherte!
For sorwe of which I wol not live to morwe,
But if ye lordes rewe upon my sorwe.

For, by that cause I say no tyme er now
Hir to delivere, I holden have my pees;
But now or never, if that it lyke yow,
I may hir have right sone, doutelees.
O help and grace! amonges al this prees,
Rewe on this olde caitif in destresse,
Sin I through yow have al this hevinesse!

Ye have now caught and fetered in prisoun
Troians ynowe; and if your willes be,
My child with oon may have redempcioun.
Now for the love of God and of bountee,
Oon of so fele, allas! so yeve him me.
What nede were it this preyere for to werne,
Sin ye shul bothe han folk and toun as yerne?

On peril of my lyf, I shal not lye,
Appollo hath me told it feithfully;
I have eek founde it by astronomye,
By sort, and by augurie eek trewely,
And dar wel seye, the tyme is faste by,
That fyr and flaumbe on al the toun shal sprede;
And thus shal Troye turne in asshen dede.

For certeyn, Phebus and Neptunus bothe,
That makeden the walles of the toun,
Ben with the folk of Troye alwey so wrothe,
That thei wol bringe it to confusioun,
Right in despyt of king Lameadoun.

520

Bycause he nolde payen hem hir hyre,
The toun of Troye shal ben set on fyre.

Telling his tale alwey, this olde greye,
Humble in speche, and in his lokinge eke,
The salte teres from his eyën tweye
Ful faste ronnen doun by eyther cheke.
So longe he gan of socour hem byseke
That, for to hele him of his sorwes sore,
They yave him Antenor, withoute more.

But who was glad ynough but Calkas tho?
And of this thing ful sone his nedes leyde
On hem that sholden for the tretis go,
And hem for Antenor ful ofte preyde
To bringen hoom king Toas and Criseyde;
And whan Pryam his savegarde sente,
Thembassadours to Troye streyght they wente.

The cause ytold of hir cominge, the olde
Pryam the king ful sone in general
Let hereupon his parlement to holde,
Of which the effect rehersen yow I shal.
Thembassadours ben answered for fynal,
Theschaunge of prisoners and al this nede
Hem lyketh wel, and forth in they procede.

This Troilus was present in the place,
Whan axed was for Antenor Criseyde,
For which ful sone chaungen gan his face,
As he that with tho wordes wel neigh deyde.
But nathelees, he no word to it seyde,
Lest men sholde his affeccioun espye;
With mannes herte he gan his sorwes drye.

And ful of anguish and of grisly drede
Abood what lordes wolde unto it seye;
And if they wolde graunte, as God forbede,
Theschaunge of hir, than thoughte he thinges
tweye,
First, how to save hir honour, and what weye
He mighte best theschaunge of hir withstonde;
Ful faste he caste how al this mighte stonde.

Love him made al prest to doon hir byde,
And rather dye than she sholde go;
But resoun seyde him, on that other syde:
Withoute assent of hir ne do not so,
Lest for thy werk she wolde be thy fo,
And seyn, that thorugh thy medling is yblowe
Your bother love, there it was erst unknowe.

For which he gan deliberen, for the beste,
That though the lordes wolde that she wente,
He wolde late hem graunte what hem leste,
And telle his lady first what that they mente.
And whan that she had seyd him hir entente,
Therafter wolde he werken also blyve,
Though al the world ayein it wolde stryve.

Ector, which that wel the Grekes herde,
For Antenor how they wolde han Criseyde,
Gan it withstonde, and sobrely answerde:

Sires, she nis no prisoner, he seyde;
I noot on yow who that this charge leyde,
But, on my part, ye may eftsone him telle,
We usen here no wommen for to selle.

The noyse of peple upstirte thanne at ones,
As breme as blase of straw yset on fyre;
For infortune it wolde, for the nones,
They sholden hir confusioun desyre.
Ector, quod they, what goost may yow
enspyre,
This womman thus to shilde and doon us lese
Daun Antenor? a wrong wey now ye chese,

That is so wys, and eek so bold baroun,
And we han nede of folk, as men may see;
He is eek oon, the grettest of this toun;
O Ector, lat tho fantasyès be!
O king Pryam, quod they, thus seggen we,
That al our voys is to forgon Criseyde;
And to deliveren Antenor they preyde.

O Juvenal, lord! trewe is thy sentence,
That litel witen folk what is to yerne
That they ne finde in hir desyr offence;
For cloud of errour lat hem not descerne
What best is; and lo, here ensample as yerne.
This folk desiren now deliveraunce
Of Antenor, that broughte hem to mischaunce!

For he was after traytour to the toun
Of Troye; allas! they quitte him out to rathe;
O nyce world, lo, thy discrecioun!
Criseyde, which that never dide hem skathe,
Shal now no lenger in hir blisse bathe;
But Antenor, he shal com hoom to toune,
And she shal out; thus seyden here and howne.

For which delibered was by parlement,
For Antenor to yelden up Criseyde,
And it pronounced by the president,
Altheigh that Ector Nay ful ofte preyde.
And fynaly, what wight that it withseyde,
It was for nought, it moste been, and sholde;
For substaunce of the parlement it wolde.

Departed out of parlement echone,
This Troilus, withoute wordes mo,
Unto his chaumbre spedde him faste allone,
But if it were a man of his or two,
The whiche he bad out faste for to go,
Bycause he wolde slepen, as he seyde,
And hastely upon his bed him leyde.

And as in winter leves been biraft,
Eche after other, til the tree be bare,
So that ther nis but bark and braunche ylaft,
Lyth Troilus, biraft of ech welfare,
Ybounden in the blake bark of care,
Disposed wood out of his wit to breyde,
So sore him sat the chaunginge of Criseyde.

He rist him up, and every dore he shette

And windowe eek, and tho this sorweful man
Upon his beddes syde adoun him sette,
Ful lyk a deed image pale and wan;
And in his brest the heped wo bigan
Outbreste, and he to werken in this wyse
In his woodnesse, as I shal yow devyse.

Right as the wilde bole biginneth springe
Now here, now there, ydarted to the herte,
And of his deeth roreth in compleyninge,
Right so gan he aboute the chaumbre sterte,
Smyting his brest ay with his festes smerte;
His heed to the wal, his body to the grounde
Ful ofte he swapte, himselven to confounde.

His eyen two, for pitee of his herte,
Out stremeden as swifte welles tweye;
The heighe sobbes of his sorwes smerte
His speche him rafte, unnethes mighte he seye:
O deeth, allas! why niltow do me deye?
Acursed be the day which that nature
Shoop me to ben a lyves creature!

But after, whan the furie and the rage
Which that his herte twiste and faste threste,
By lengthe of tyme somwhat gan asswage,
Upon his bed he leyde him doun to reste;
But tho bigonne his teres more outbreste,
That wonder is, the body may suffyse
To half this wo, which that I yow devyse.

Than seyde he thus: Fortune! allas the whyle!
What have I doon, what have I thus agilt?
How mightestow for reuthe me bigyle?
Is ther no grace, and shal I thus be spilt?
Shal thus Criseyde awey, for that thou wilt?
Allas! how maystow in thyn herte finde
To been to me thus cruel and unkinde?

Have I thee nought honoured al my lyve,
As thou wel wost, above the goddes alle?
Why wiltow me fro joye thus depryve?
O Troilus, what may men now thee calle
But wrecche of wrecches, out of honour falle
Into miserie, in which I wol biwayle
Criseyde, allas! til that the breeth me fayle?

Allas, fortune! if that my lyf in joye
Displesed hadde unto thy foule envye,
Why ne haddestow my fader, king of Troye,
Byraft the lyf, or doon my bretheren dye,
Or slayn myself, that thus compleyne and crye,
I, combre-world, that may of nothing serve,
But ever dye, and never fully sterve?

If that Criseyde allone were me laft,
Nought roughte I whider thou woldest me
stere;
And hir, allas! than hastow me biraft.
But evermore, lo! this is thy manere,
To reve a wight that most is to him dere,
To preve in that thy gerful violence,
Thus am I lost, ther helpeth no defence!

O verray Lord of love, O God, allas!
That knowest best myn herte and al my thought,
What shal my sorwful lyf don in this cas
If I forgo that I so dere have bought?
Sin ye Criseyde and me han fully brought
Into your grace, and bothe our hertes seled,
How may ye suffre, allas! it be repeled?

What I may doon, I shal, whyl I may dure
On lyve in torment and in cruel peyne,
This infortune or this disaventure,
Allone as I was born, ywis, compleyne;
Ne never wil I seen it shyne or reyne;
But ende I wil, as Edippe, in derknesse
My sorwful lyf, and dyen in distresse.

O wery goost, that errest to and fro,
Why niltow fleen out of the wofulleste
Body, that ever mighte on grounde go?
O soule, lurkinge in this wo, unneste,
Flee forth out of myn herte, and lat it breste,
And folwe alwey Criseyde, thy lady dere;
Thy righte place is now no lenger here!

O wofulle eyen two, sin your disport
Was al to seen Criseydes eyen brighte,
What shal ye doon but, for my discomfort,
Stonden for nought, and wepen out your sighte?
Sin she is queynt, that wont was yow to lighte,
In veyn fro/this/forth have I eyen tweye
Yformed, sin your vertue is aweye.

O my Criseyde, O lady sovereyne
Of thilke woful soule that thus cryeth,
Who shal now yeven comfort to my peyne?
Allas, no wight; but when myn herte dyeth,
My spirit, which that so unto yow hyeth,
Receyve in gree, for that shal ay yow serve;
Forthy no fors is, though the body sterve.

O ye loveres, that heighe upon the wheel
Ben set of fortune, in good aventure,
God leve that ye finde ay love of steel,
And longe mot your lyf in joye endure!
But whan ye comen by my sepulture,
Remembreth that your felawe resteth there;
For I lovede eek, though I unworthy were.

O olde unholsom and mislyved man,
Calkas I mene, allas! what eyleth thee
To been a Greek, sin thou art born Troian?
O Calkas, which that wilt my bane be,
In cursed tyme was thou born for me!
As wolde blisful Jove, for his joye,
That I thee hadde, where I wolde, in Troye!

A thousand sykes, hottere than the glede,
Out of his brest ech after other wente,
Medled with pleyntes newe, his wo to fede,
For which his woful teres never stente;
And shortly, so his peynes him torente,
And wex so mat, that joye nor penaunce
He feleth noon, but lyth forth in a traunce.

Pandare, which that in the parlement
Hadde herd what every lord and burgeys seyde,
And how ful graunted was, by oon assent,
For Antenor to yelden so Criseyde,
Gan wel neigh wood out of his wit to breyde,
So that, for wo, he niste what he mente;
But in a rees to Troilus he wente.

A certeyn knight, that for the tyme kepte
The chaumbre/dore, undide it him anoon;
And Pandare, that ful tendreliche wepte,
Into the derke chaumbre, as stille as stoon,
Toward the bed gan softely to goon,
So confus, that he niste what to seye;
For verray wo his wit was neigh aweye.

And with his chere and loking al totorn,
For sorwe of this, and with his armes folden,
He stood this woful Troilus biforn,
And on his pitous face he gan biholden;
But Lord, so often gan his herte colden,
Seing his freend in wo, whos hevinesse
His herte slow, as thoughte him, for distresse.

This woful wight, this Troilus, that felte
His freend Pandare ycomen him to see,
Gan as the snow ayein the sonne melte,
For which this sorwful Pandare, of pitee,
Gan for to wepe as tendreliche as he;
And specheles thus been thise ilke tweye,
That neyther mighte o word for sorwe seye.

But at the laste this woful Troilus,
Ney deed for smert, gan bresten out to rore,
And with a sorwful noyse he seyde thus,
Among his sobbes and his sykes sore:
Lo! Pandare, I am deed, withouten more.
Hastow nought herd at parlement, he seyde,
For Antenor how lost is my Criseyde?

This Pandarus, ful deed and pale of hewe,
Ful pitously answerde and seyde: Yis!
As wisly were it fals as it is trewe,
That I have herd, and wot al how it is.
O mercy, God, who wolde have trowed this?
Who wolde have wend that, in so litel a throwe,
Fortune our joye wolde han overthrowe?

For in this world ther is no creature,
As to my doom, that ever saw ruyne
Straungere than this, thorugh cas or aventure.
But who may al eschewe or al devyne?
Swich is this world; forthy I thus defyne,
Ne trust no wight to finden in Fortune
Ay propretee; hir yeftes been comune.

But tel me this, why thou art now so mad
To sorwen thus? Why lystow in this wyse,
Sin thy desyr al holly hastow had,
So that, by right, it oughte ynow suffyse?
But I, that never felte in my servyse
A frendly chere or loking of an yë,
Lat me thus wepe and wayle, til I dye.

And over al this, as thou wel wost thyselve,
This town is ful of ladies al aboute;
And, to my doom, fairer than swiche twelve
As ever she was, shal I finde, in som route,
Ye, oon or two, withouten any doute.
Forthy be glad, myn owene dere brother,
If she be lost, we shul recovere another.

What, God forbede alwey that ech plesaunce
In o thing were, and in non other wight!
If oon can singe, another can wel daunce;
If this be goodly, she is glad and light;
And this is fayr, and that can good aright.
Ech for his vertu holden is for dere,
Bothe heroner and faucon for rivere.

And eek, as writ Zanzis, that was ful wys:
The newe love out chaceth ofte the olde;
And upon newe cas lyth newe avys.
Thenk eek, thyself to saven artow holde;
Swich fyr, by proces, shal of kinde colde.
For sin it is but casuel plesaunce,
Som cas shal putte it out of remembraunce.

For also seur as day cometh after night,
The newe love, labour or other wo,
Or elles selde seinge of a wight,
Don olde affecciouns alle overgo.
And, for thy part, thou shalt have oon of tho
To abrigge with thy bittre peynes smerte;
Absence of hir shal dryve hir out of herte.

Thise wordes seyde he for the nones alle,
To helpe his freend, lest he for sorwe deyde.
For doutelees, to doon his wo to falle,
He roughte not what unthrift that he seyde.
But Troilus, that neigh for sorwe deyde,
Tok litel hede of al that ever he mente;
Oon ere it herde, at the other out it wente:

But at the laste answerde and seyde: freend,
This lechecraft, or heled thus to be,
Were wel sitting, if that I were a feend,
To traysen hir that trewe is unto me!
I pray God, lat this consayl never ythee;
But do me rather sterve anon-right here
Er I thus do as thou me woldest lere.

She that I serve, ywis, what so thou seye,
To whom myn herte enhabit is by right,
Shal han me holly hires til that I deye.
For, Pandarus, sin I have trouthe hir hight,
I wol not been untrewe for no wight;
But as hir man I wol ay live and sterve,
And never other creature serve.

And ther thou seyst, thou shalt as faire finde
As she, lat be, make no comparisoun
To creature yformed here by kinde.
O leve Pandare, in conclusioun,
I wol not be of thyn opinioun,
Touching al this; for whiche I thee biseche,
So hold thy pees; thou sleest me with thy speche.

Thow biddest me I sholde love another
Al freshly newe, and lat Criseyde go!
It lyth not in my power, leve brother.
And though I mighte, I wolde not do so.
But canstow pleyen raket, to and fro,
Netle in, dokke out, now this, now that, Pandare?
Now foule falle hir, for thy wo that care!

Thow farest eek by me, thou Pandarus,
As he, that whan a wight is wo bigoon,
He cometh to him a pas, and seyth right thus:
Thenk not on smert, and thou shalt fele noon.
Thou most me first transmuwen in a stoon,
And reve me my passiounes alle,
Er thou so lightly do my wo to falle.

The deeth may wel out of my brest departe
The lyf, so longe may this sorwe myne;
But fro my soule shal Criseydes darte
Out nevermo; but doun with Proserpyne,
Whan I am deed, I wol go wone in pyne;
And ther I wol eternally compleyne
My wo, and how that twinned be we tweyne.

Thow hast here maad an argument, for fyn,
How that it sholde lasse peyne be
Criseyde to forgoon, for she was myn,
And live in ese and in felicitee.
Why gabbestow, that seydest thus to me
That Him is wors that is fro wele ythrowe,
Than he hadde erst non of that wele yknowe?

But tel me now, sin that thee thinketh so light
To chaungen so in love, ay to and fro,
Why hastow not don bisily thy might
To chaungen hir that doth thee al thy wo?
Why niltow lete hir fro thyn herte go?
Why niltow love another lady swete,
That may thyn herte setten in quiete?

If thou hast had in love ay yet mischaunce,
And canst it not out of thyn herte dryve,
I, that livede in lust and in plesaunce
With hir as muche as creature onlyve,
How sholde I that foryete, and that so blyve?
O where hastow ben hid so longe in muwe,
That canst so wel and formely arguwe?

Nay, nay, God wot, nought worth is al thy reed,
For which, for what that ever may bifalle,
Withouten wordes mo, I wol be deed.
O deeth, that endere art of sorwes alle,
Com now, sin I so ofte after thee calle;
For sely is that deeth, soth for to seyne,
That, ofte ycleped, cometh and endeth peyne.

Wel wot I, whyl my lyf was in quiete,
Er thou me slowe, I wolde have yeven hyre;
But now thy cominge is to me so swete,
That in this world I nothing so desyre.
O deeth, sin with this sorwe I am afyre,
Thou outher do me anoon in teres drenche,
Or with thy colde strook myn hete quenche!

Sin that thou sleest so fele in sondry wyse
Ayens hir wil, unpreyed, day and night,
Do me, at my requeste, this servyse,
Delivere now the world, so dostow right,
Of me, that am the wofulleste wight
That ever was; for tyme is that I sterve,
Sin in this world of right nought may I serve.

This Troilus in teres gan distille,
As licour out of alambyk ful faste;
And Pandarus gan holde his tunge stille,
And to the ground his eyen doun he caste.
But nathelees, thus thoughte he at the laste:
What, parde, rather than my felawe deye,
Yet shal I somwhat more unto him seye:

And seyde: Freend, sin thou hast swich distresse,
And sin thee list myn arguments to blame,
Why nilt thyselven helpen doon redresse,
And with thy manhod letten al this grame?
Go ravisshe hir ne canstow not for shame!
And outher lat hir out of toune fare,
Or hold hir stille, and leve thy nyce fare.

Artow in Troye, and hast non hardiment
To take a womman which that loveth thee,
And wolde hirselven been of thyn assent?
Now is not this a nyce vanitee?
Rys up anoon, and lat this weping be,
And kyth thou art a man, for in this houre
I wil be deed, or she shal bleven oure.

To this answerde him Troilus ful softe,
And seyde: Parde, leve brother dere,
Al this have I myself yet thought ful ofte,
And more thing than thou devysest here.
But why this thing is laft, thou shalt wel here;
And whan thou me hast yeve an audience,
Therafter mayst thou telle al thy sentence.

First, sin thou wost this toun hath al this werre
For ravisshing of wommen so by might,
It sholde not be suffred me to erre,
As it stant now, ne doon so gret unright.
I sholde han also blame of every wight,
My fadres graunt if that I so withstode,
Sin she is chaunged for the tounes goode.

I have eek thought, so it were hir assent,
To aske hir at my fader, of his grace;
Than thenke I, this were hir accusement,
Sin wel I woot I may hir not purchace.
For sin my fader, in so heigh a place
As parlement, hath hir eschaunge enseled,
He nil for me his lettre be repeled.

Yet drede I most hir herte to pertourbe
With violence, if I do swich a game;
For if I wolde it openly distourbe,
It moste been disclaundre to hir name.
And me were lever deed than hir defame,
As nolde God but if I sholde have
Hir honour lever than my lyf to save!

524

Thus am I lost, for ought that I can see;
For certeyn is, sin that I am hir knight,
I moste hir honour levere han than me
In every cas, as lovere oughte of right.
Thus am I with desyr and reson twight;
Desyr for to distourben hir me redeth,
And reson nil not, so myn herte dredeth.

Thus wepinge that he coude never cesse,
He seyde: Allas! how shal I, wrecche, fare?
For wel fele I alwey my love encresse,
And hope is lasse and lasse alwey, Pandare!
Encressen eek the causes of my care;
So welawey, why nil myn herte breste?
For, as in love, ther is but litel reste.

Pandare answerde: Freend, thou mayst, for me,
Don as thee list; but hadde ich it so hote,
And thyn estat, she sholde go with me;
Though al this toun cryede on this thing by note,
I nolde sette at al that noyse a grote.
For when men han wel cryed, than wol they roune,
A wonder last but nyne night never in toune.

Devyne not in reson ay so depe
Ne curteysly, but help thyself anoon;
Bet is that othere than thyselven wepe,
And namely, sin ye two been al oon.
Rys up, for by myn heed, she shal not goon;
And rather be in blame a lyte yfounde
Than sterve here as a gnat, withoute wounde.

It is no shame unto yow, ne no vyce
Hir to witholden, that ye loveth most.
Paraunter, she mighte holden thee for nyce
To lete hir go thus to the Grekes ost.
Thenk eek fortune, as wel thyselven wost,
Helpeth an hardy man to his empryse,
And weyveth wrecches, for hir cowardyse.

And though thy lady wolde a litel hir greve,
Thou shalt thy pees ful wel hereafter make,
But as for me, certayn, I can not leve
That she wolde it as now for yvel take.
Why sholde than for ferd thyn herte quake?
Thenk eek how Paris hath, that is thy brother,
A love; and why shaltow not have another?

And Troilus, o thing I dar thee swere,
That if Criseyde, whiche that is thy leef,
Now loveth thee as wel as thou dost here,
God helpe me so, she nil not take agreef,
Though thou do bote anoon in this mischeef.
And if she wilneth fro thee for to passe,
Thanne is she fals; so love hir wel the lasse.

Forthy tak herte, and thenk, right as a knight,
Thourgh love is broken alday every lawe.
Kyth now sumwhat thy corage and thy might,
Have mercy on thyself, for any awe.
Lat not this wrecched wo thin herte gnawe,
But manly set the world on sixe and sevene;
And, if thou deye a martir, go to hevene.

I wol myself be with thee at this dede,
Though ich and al my kin, upon a stounde,
Shulle in a strete as dogges liggen dede,
Thourgh-girt with many a wyd & blody wounde.
In every cas I wol a freend be founde.
And if thee list here sterven as a wrecche,
Adieu, the devel spede him that it recche!

This Troilus gan with tho wordes quiken,
And seyde: freend, graunt mercy, ich assente;
But certaynly thou mayst not me so priken,
Ne peyne noon ne may me so tormente,
That, for no cas, it is not myn entente,
At shorte wordes, though I dyen sholde,
To ravisshe hir, but if hirself it wolde.

Why, so mene I, quod Pandarus, al this day.
But tel me than, hastow hir wel assayed,
That sorwest thus? And he answerde: Nay.
Wherof artow, quod Pandare, than amayed,
That nost not that she wol ben yvel apayed
To ravisshe hir, sin thou hast not ben there,
But if that Jove tolde it in thyn ere?

Forthy rys up, as nought ne were, anoon,
And wash thy face, and to the king thou wende,
Or he may wondren whider thou art goon.
Thou most with wisdom him and othere blende;
Or, upon cas, he may after thee sende
Er thou be war; and shortly, brother dere,
Be glad, and lat me werke in this matere.

For I shal shape it so, that sikerly
Thou shalt this night som tyme, in som manere,
Com speke with thy lady prevely,
And by hir wordes eek, and by hir chere,
Thou shalt ful sone aparceyve and wel here
Al hir entente, and in this cas the beste;
And fare now wel, for in this point I reste.

The swifte fame, whiche that false thinges
Egal reporteth lyk the thinges trewe,
Was thourghout Troye yfled with preste winges
Fro man to man, and made this tale al newe,
How Calkas doughter, with hir brighte hewe,
At parlement, withoute wordes more,
I-graunted was in chaunge of Antenore.

The whiche tale anoon-right as Criseyde
Had herd, she which that of hir fader roughte,
As in this cas, right nought, ne whanne he deyde,
Ful bisily to Juppiter bisoughte
Yeve him mischaunce that this tretis broughte.
But shortly, lest thise tales sothe were,
She dorste at no wight asken it, for fere.

As she that hadde hir herte and al hir minde
On Troilus yset so wonder faste,
That al this world ne mighte hir love unbinde,
Ne Troilus out of hir herte caste;
She wol ben his, whyl that hir lyf may laste.
And thus she brenneth bothe in love and drede,
So that she niste what was best to rede.

But as men seen in toune, and al aboute,
That wommen usen frendes to visyte,
So to Criseyde of wommen com a route
For pitous joye, and wenden hir delyte;
And with hir tales, dere ynough a myte,
These wommen, whiche that in the cite dwelle,
They sette hem doun, and seyde as I shal telle.

Quod first that oon: I am glad, trewely,
Bycause of yow, that shal your fader see.
Another seyde: Ywis, so nam not I;
For al to litel hath she with us be.
Quod tho the thridde: I hope, ywis, that she
Shal bringen us the pees on every syde,
That, whan she gooth, almighty God hir gyde!

Tho wordes and tho wommannisshe thinges,
She herde hem right as though she thennes were;
For, God it wot, hir herte on other thing is,
Although the body sat among hem there.
Hir advertence is alwey elleswhere;
For Troilus ful faste hir soule soughte;
Withouten word, alwey on him she thoughte.

Thise wommen, that thus wenden hir to plese,
Aboute nought gonne alle hir tales spende;
Swich vanitee ne can don hir non ese,
As she that, al this mene whyle, brende
Of other passioun than that they wende,
So that she felte almost hir herte dye
For wo, and wery of that companye.

For which no lenger mighte she restreyne
Hir teres, so they gonnen up to welle,
That yeven signes of the bitter peyne
In whiche hir spirit was, and moste dwelle;
Remembring hir, fro heven unto which helle
She fallen was, sith she forgoth the sighte
Of Troilus, and sorowfully she sighte.

And thilke foles sitting hir aboute
Wenden, that she so wepte and syked sore
Bycause that she sholde out of that route
Departe, and never pleye with hem more.
And they that hadde yknowen hir of yore
Seye hir so wepe, and thoughte it kindenesse,
And eche of hem wepte eek for hir distresse;

And bisily they gonnen hir conforten
Of thing, God wot, on which she litel thoughte;
And with hir tales wenden hir disporten,
And to be glad they often hir bisoughte.
But swich an ese therwith they hir wroughte
Right as a man is esed for to fele,
For ache of heed, to clawen him on his hele!

But after al this nyce vanitee
They took hir leve, and hoom they wenten alle.
Criseyde, ful of sorweful pitee,
Into hir chaumbre up wente out of the halle,
And on hir bed she gan for deed to falle,
In purpos never thennes for to ryse;
And thus she wroughte, as I shal yow devyse.

525

Hir ounded heer, that sonnish was of hewe,
She rente, and eek hir fingres longe and smale
She wrong ful ofte, and bad God on hir rewe,
And with the deeth to doon bote on hir bale.
Hir hewe, whylom bright, that tho was pale,
Bar witnes of hir wo and hir constreynte;
And thus she spak, sobbinge, in hir compleynte:

Alas! quod she, out of this regioun
I, woful wrecche and infortuned wight,
And born in corsed constellacioun,
Mot goon, and thus departen fro my knight;
Wo worth, alas! that ilke dayes light
On which I saw him first with eyen tweyne,
That causeth me, and I him, al this peyne!

Therwith the teres from hir eyen two
Doun fille, as shour in Aperill, ful swythe;
Hir whyte brest she bet, and for the wo
After the deeth she cryed a thousand sythe,
Sin he that wont hir wo was for to lythe,
She mot forgoon; for which disaventure
She held hirself a forlost creature.

She seyde: How shal he doon, and I also?
How sholde I live, if that I from him twinne?
O dere herte eek, that I love so,
Who shal that sorwe sleen that ye ben inne?
O Calkas, fader, thyn be al this sinne!
O moder myn, that cleped were Argyve,
Wo worth that day that thou me bere on lyve!

To what fyn sholde I live and sorwen thus?
How sholde a fish withoute water dure?
What is Criseyde worth, from Troilus?
How sholde a plaunte or lyves creature
Live, withoute his kinde noriture?
For which ful oft a byword here I seye,
That, Rotelees, mot grene sone deye.

I shal don thus, sin neither swerd ne darte
Dar I non handle, for the crueltee,
That ilke day that I from yow departe,
If sorwe of that nil not my bane be,
Than shal no mete or drinke come in me
Til I my soule out of my breste unshethe;
And thus myselven wol I do to dethe.

And, Troilus, my clothes everichoon
Shul blake been, in tokeninge, herte swete,
That I am as out of this world agoon,
That wont was yow to setten in quiete;
And of myn ordre, ay til deeth me mete,
The observaunce ever, in your absence,
Shal sorwe been, compleynte, and abstinence.

Myn herte and eek the woful goost therinne
Biquethe I, with your spirit to compleyne
Eternally, for they shul never twinne.
For though in erthe ytwinned be we tweyne,
Yet in the feld of pitee, out of peyne,
That hight Elysos, shul we been yfere,
As Orpheus and Erudice his fere.

526

Thus herte myn, for Antenor, allas!
I sone shal be chaunged, as I wene.
But how shul ye don in this sorwful cas,
How shal your tendre herte this sustene?
But herte myn, foryet this sorwe and tene,
And me also; for, soothly for to seye,
So ye wel fare, I recche not to deye.

How mighte it ever yred ben or ysonge,
The pleynte that she made in hir distresse?
I noot; but, as for me, my litel tonge,
If I discreven wolde hir hevinesse,
It sholde make hir sorwe seme lesse
Than that it was, and childishly deface
Hir heigh compleynte, and therfore I it pace.

Pandare, which that sent from Troilus
Was to Criseyde, as ye han herd devyse,
That for the beste it was accorded thus,
And he ful glad to doon him that servyse,
Unto Criseyde, in a ful secree wyse,
Theras she lay in torment and in rage,
Com hir to telle al hoolly his message.

And fond that she hirselven gan to trete
Ful pitously; for with hir salte teres
Hir brest, hir face ybathed was ful wete;
The mighty tresses of hir sonnish heres,
Unbroyden, hangen al aboute hir eres;
Which yaf him verray signal of martyre
Of deeth, which that hir herte gan desyre.

Whan she him saw, she gan for sorwe anoon
Hir tery face atwixe hir armes hyde,
For which this Pandare is so wo bigoon,
That in the hous he mighte unnethe abyde,
As he that pitee felte on every syde.
For if Criseyde hadde erst compleyned sore,
Tho gan she pleyne a thousand tymes more.

And in hir aspre pleynte than she seyde:
Pandare first of joyes mo than two
Was cause causinge unto me, Criseyde,
That now transmuwed been in cruel wo.
Wher shal I seye to yow Wel come or no,
That alderfirst me broughte into servyse
Of love, allas! that endeth in swich wyse?

Endeth than love in wo? Ye, or men lyeth!
And alle worldly blisse, as thinketh me,
The ende of blisse ay sorwe it occupyeth;
And whoso troweth not that it so be,
Lat him upon me, woful wrecche, ysee,
That myself hate, and ay my birthe acorse,
Felinge alwey, fro wikke I go to worse.

Whoso me seeth, he seeth sorwe al at ones,
Peyne, torment, pleynte, wo, distresse.
Out of my woful body harm ther noon is,
As anguish, langour, cruel bitternesse,
Anoy, smert, drede, fury, and eek siknesse.
I trowe, ywis, from hevene teres reyne,
For pitee of myn aspre and cruel peyne!

And thou, my suster, ful of discomfort,
Quod Pandarus, what thenkestow to do?
Why ne hastow to thyselven som resport,
Why woltow thus thyselve, allas, fordo?
Leef al this werk and tak now hede to
That I shal seyn, and herkne, of good entente,
This, which by me thy Troilus thee sente.

Torned hir tho Criseyde, a wo makinge
So greet that it a deeth was for to see:
Allas! quod she, what wordes may ye bringe?
What wol my dere herte seyn to me,
Which that I drede nevermo to see?
Wol he have pleynte or teres, er I wende?
I have ynowe, if he therafter sende!

She was right swich to seen in hir visage
As is that wight that men on bere binde;
Hir face, lyk of Paradys the image,
Was al ychaunged in another kinde.
The pleye, the laughtre men was wont to finde
In hir, and eek hir joyes everychone,
Ben fled, and thus lyth now Criseyde allone.

Aboute hir eyen two a purpre ring
Bitrent, in sothfast tokninge of hir peyne,
That to biholde it was a dedly thing,
For which Pandare mighte not restreyne
The teres from his eyen for to reyne.
But nathelees, as he best mighte, he seyde
From Troilus thise wordes to Criseyde:

Lo, nece, I trowe ye han herd al how
The king, with othere lordes, for the beste,
Hath mad eschaunge of Antenor and yow,
That cause is of this sorwe and this unreste.
But how this cas doth Troilus moleste,
That may non erthely mannes tonge seye;
For verray wo his wit is al aweye.

For which we han so sorwed, he and I,
That into litel bothe it hadde us slawe;
But thurgh my conseil this day, fynally,
He somwhat is fro weping now withdrawe.
And semeth me that he desyreth fawe
With yow to been al night, for to devyse
Remede in this, if ther were any wyse.

This, short and pleyne, theffect of my message,
As ferforth as my wit can comprehende.
For ye, that been of torment in swich rage,
May to no long prologe as now entende;
And herupon ye may answere him sende.
And, for the love of God, my nece dere,
So leef this wo er Troilus be here.

Gret is my wo, quod she, and sighte sore,
As she that feleth dedly sharp distresse;
But yet to me his sorwe is muchel more,
That love him bet than he himself, I gesse.
Allas! for me hath he swich hevinesse?
Can he for me so pitously compleyne?
Ywis, this sorwe doubleth al my peyne.

Grevous to me, God wot, is for to twinne,
Quod she, but yet it hardere is to me
To seen that sorwe which that he is inne;
For wel wot I, it wol my bane be;
And deye I wol in certayn, tho quod she;
But bidde him come, er deeth, that thus me threteth,
Dryve out that goost, which in myn herte beteth.

Thise wordes seyd, she on hir armes two
Fil gruf, and gan to wepe pitously.
Quod Pandarus: Allas! why do ye so,
Syn wel ye wot the tyme is faste by,
That he shal come? Arys up hastely,
That he yow nat biwopen thus ne finde,
But ye wol han him wood out of his minde!

For wiste he that ye ferde in this manere,
He wolde himselve slee; and if I wende
To han this fare, he sholde not come here
For al the good that Pryam may despende.
For to what fyn he wolde anoon pretende,
That knowe I wel; and forthy yet I seye,
So leef this sorwe, or platly he wol deye.

And shapeth yow his sorwe for to abregge,
And nought encresse, leve nece swete;
Beth rather to him cause of flat than egge,
And with som wysdom ye his sorwes bete.
What helpeth it to wepen ful a strete,
Or though ye bothe in salte teres dreynte?
Bet is a tyme of cure ay than of pleynte.

I mene thus; whan I him hider bringe,
Sin ye ben wyse, and bothe of oon assent,
So shapeth how distourbe your goinge,
Or come ayen, sone after ye be went.
Wommen ben wyse in short avysement;
And lat sen how your wit shal now avayle;
And what that I may helpe, it shal not fayle.

Go, quod Criseyde, and uncle, trewely,
I shal don al my might, me to restreyne
From weping in his sight, and bisily,
Him for to glade, I shal don al my peyne,
And in myn herte seken every veyne;
If to this soor ther may be founden salve,
It shal not lakken, certain, on myn halve.

Goth Pandarus, and Troilus he soughte,
Til in a temple he fond him al allone,
As he that of his lyf no lenger roughte;
But to the pitouse goddes everichone
Ful tendrely he preyde, and made his mone,
To doon him sone out of this world to pace;
For wel he thoughte ther was non other grace.

And shortly, al the sothe for to seye,
He was so fallen in despeyr that day,
That outrely he shoop him for to deye.
For right thus was his argument alwey:
He seyde, he nas but loren, waylawey!
For al that comth, comth by necessitee;
Thus to be lorn, it is my destinee.

527

For certaynly, this wot I wel, he seyde,
That forsight of divyne purveyaunce
Hath seyn alwey me to forgon Criseyde,
Sin God seeth every thing, out of doutaunce,
And hem desponeth, thourgh his ordenaunce,
In hir merytes sothly for to be,
As they shul comen by predestinee.

But nathelees, allas! whom shal I leve?
For ther ben grete clerkes many oon,
That destinee thorugh argumentes preve;
And som men seyn that nedely ther is noon;
But that free chois is yeven us everichoon.
O, welaway! so sleye arn clerkes olde,
That I not whos opinion I may holde.

For som men seyn, if God seth al biforn,
Ne God may not deceyved ben, pardee,
Than moot it fallen, though men hadde it sworn,
That purveyaunce hath seyn bifore to be.
Wherfor I seye, that from eterne if he
Hath wist biforn our thought eek as our dede,
We have no free chois, as these clerkes rede.

For other thought nor other dede also
Might never be, but swich as purveyaunce,
Which may not ben deceyved nevermo,
Hath feled biforn, withouten ignoraunce.
For if ther mighte been a variaunce
To wrythen out fro Goddes purveyinge,
There nere no prescience of thing cominge;

But it were rather an opinioun
Uncerteyn, and no stedfast forseinge;
And certes, that were an abusioun,
That God shuld han no parfit cleer witinge
More than we men that han doutous weninge.
But swich an errour upon God to gesse
Were fals and foul, and wikked corsednesse.

Eek this is an opinioun of somme
That han hir top ful heighe and smothe yshore;
They seyn right thus, that thing is not to come
For that the prescience hath seyn bifore
That it shal come; but they seyn, that therfore
That it shal come, therfore the purveyaunce
Wot it biforn withouten ignoraunce;

And in this manere this necessitee
Retorneth in his part contrarie agayn.
For needfully bihoveth it not to be
That thilke thinges fallen in certayn
That ben purveyed; but nedely, as they seyn,
Bihoveth it that thinges, whiche that falle,
That they in certayn ben purveyed alle.

I mene as though I laboured me in this,
To enqueren which thing cause of which thing be;
As whether that the prescience of God is
The certayn cause of the necessitee
Of thinges that to comen been, pardee;
Or if necessitee of thing cominge
Be cause certeyn of the purveyinge.

528

But now ne enforce I me nat in shewinge
How the ordre of causes stant; but wel wot I,
That it bihoveth that the bifallinge
Of thinges wist biforen certeynly
Be necessarie, al seme it not therby
That prescience put falling necessaire
To thing to come, al falle it foule or faire.

For if ther sit a man yond on a see,
Than by necessitee bihoveth it
That, certes, thyn opinioun soth be,
That wenest or conjectest that he sit;
And fertherover now ayenward yit,
Lo, right so it is of the part contrarie,
As thus; now herkne, for I wol not tarie:

I seye, that if the opinioun of thee
Be sooth, for that he sit, than seye I this,
That he mot sitten by necessitee;
And thus necessitee in either is.
For in him nede of sitting is, ywis,
And in thee nede of sooth; and thus, forsothe,
Ther moot necessitee ben in yow bothe.

But thou mayst seyn, the man sit not therfore,
That thyn opinion of sitting soth is;
But rather, for the man sit ther bifore,
Therfore is thyn opinion sooth, ywis.
And I seye, though the cause of sooth of this
Comth of his sitting, yet necessitee
Is entrechaunged, bothe in him and thee.

Thus on this same wyse, out of doutaunce,
I may wel maken, as it semeth me,
My resoninge of Goddes purveyaunce,
And of the thinges that to comen be;
By whiche reson men may wel ysee,
That thilke thinges that in erthe falle,
That by necessitee they comen alle.

For although that, for thing shal come, ywis,
Therfore is it purveyed, certaynly,
Nat that it comth for it purveyed is:
Yet nathelees, bihoveth it nedfully,
That thing to come be purveyed, trewely;
Or elles, thinges that purveyed be,
That they bityden by necessitee.

And this suffyseth right ynow, certeyn,
For to destroye our free chois every del.
But now is this abusion to seyn,
That fallinge of the thinges temporel
Is cause of Goddes prescience eternel.
Now trewely, that is a fals sentence,
That thing to come sholde cause his prescience.

What mighte I wene, and I hadde swich a thought,
But that God purveyth thing that is to come
For that it is to come, and elles nought?
So mighte I wene that thinges alle and some,
That whylom been bifalle and overcome,
Ben cause of thilke sovereyn purveyaunce,
That forwot al withouten ignoraunce.

And over al this, yet seye I more herto,
That right as whan I woot ther is a thing,
Ywis, that thing mot nedefully be so;
Eek right so, whan I woot a thing coming,
So mot it come; and thus the bifalling
Of thinges that ben wist bifore the tyde,
They mowe not been eschewed on no syde.

Than seyde he thus: Almighty Jove in trone,
That wost of al this thing the soothfastnesse,
Rewe on my sorwe, or do me deye sone,
Or bring Criseyde and me fro this distresse.
And whyl he was in al this hevinesse,
Disputinge with himself in this matere,
Com Pandare in, and seyde as ye may here.

O mighty God, quod Pandarus, in trone,
Ey! who seigh ever a wys man faren so?
Why, Troilus, what thenkestow to done?
Hastow swich lust to been thyn owene fo?
What, parde, yet is not Criseyde ago!
Why lust thee so thyself fordoon for drede,
That in thyn heed thyn eyen semen dede?

Hastow not lived many a yeer biforn
Withouten hir, and ferd ful wel at ese?
Artow for hir and for non other born?
Hath kinde thee wroughte alonly hir to plese?
Lat be, and thenk right thus in thy disese,
That, in the dees right as ther fallen chaunces,
Right so in love, ther come and goon plesaunces.

And yet this is a wonder most of alle,
Why thou thus sorwest, sin thou nost not yit,
Touching hir goinge, how that it shal falle,
Ne if she can hirself distorben it.
Thou hast not yet assayed al hir wit.
A man may al by tyme his nekke bede
Whan it shal of, and sorwen at the nede.

Forthy take hede of that that I shal seye;
I have with hir yspoke and longe ybe,
So as accorded was bitwixe us tweye.
And evermo me thinketh thus, that she
Hath somwhat in hir hertes prevetee,
Wherwith she can, if I shal right arede,
Distorbe al this, of which thou art in drede.

For which my counseil is, whan it is night,
Thou to hir go, and make of this an ende;
And blisful Juno, thourgh hir grete mighte,
Shal, as I hope, hir grace unto us sende.
Myn herte seyth, Certeyn, she shal not wende,
And forthy put thyn herte a whyle in reste;
And hold this purpos, for it is the beste.

This Troilus answerde, and sighte sore:
Thou seyst right wel, and I wil do right so;
And what him liste, he seyde unto it more.
And whan that it was tyme for to go,
Ful prevely himself, withouten mo,
Unto hir com, as he was wont to done;
And how they wroughte, I shal yow telle sone.

m m I

Soth is, that whan they gonne first to mete,
So gan the peyne hir hertes for to twiste,
That neither of hem other mighte grete,
But hem in armes toke and after kiste.
The lasse wofulle of hem bothe niste
Wher that he was, ne mighte o word outbringe,
As I seyde erst, for wo and for sobbinge.

Tho woful teres that they leten falle
As bittre weren, out of teres kinde,
For peyne, as is ligne aloës or galle.
So bittre teres weep nought, as I finde,
The woful Myrra through the bark and rinde.
That in this world ther nis so hard an herte,
That nolde han rewed on hir peynes smerte.

But whan hir woful wery gostes tweyne
Retorned been theras hem oughte dwelle,
And that somwhat to wayken gan the peyne
By lengthe of pleynte, and ebben gan the welle
Of hire teres, and the herte unswelle,
With broken voys, al hoors for-shright, Criseyde
To Troilus thise ilke wordes seyde:

O Jove, I deye, and mercy I beseche!
Help, Troilus! and therwithal hir face
Upon his brest she leyde, and loste speche;
Hir woful spirit from his propre place,
Right with the word, alwey up poynt to pace.
And thus she lyth with hewes pale and grene,
That whylom fresh and fairest was to sene.

This Troilus, that on hir gan biholde,
Clepinge hir name, and she lay as for deed,
Withoute answere, and felte hir limes colde,
Hir eyen throwen upward to hir heed,
This sorwful man can now noon other reed,
But ofte tyme hir colde mouth he kiste;
Wher him was wo, God and himself it wiste!

He rist him up, and long streight he hir leyde;
For signe of lyf, for ought he can or may,
Can he noon finde in nothing on Criseyde,
For which his song ful ofte is Weylaway!
But whan he saugh that specheles she lay,
With sorwful voys, and herte of blisse al bare,
He seyde how she was fro this world yfare!

So after that he longe hadde hir compleyned,
His hondes wronge, and seyd that was to seye,
And with his teres salte hir brest bireyned,
He gan tho teris wypen of ful dreye,
And pitously gan for the soule preye,
And seyde: O Lord, that set art in thy trone,
Rewe eek on me, for I shal folwe hir sone!

She cold was and withouten sentement,
For aught he woot, for breeth ne felte he noon;
And this was him a preignant argument
That she was forth out of this world agoon;
And whan he seigh ther was non other woon,
He gan hir limes dresse in swich manere
As men don hem that shul be leyd on bere.

529

And after this, with sterne and cruel herte,
His swerd anoon out of his shethe he twighte,
Himself to sleen, how sore that him smerte,
So that his sowle hir sowle folwen mighte,
Theras the doom of Mynos wolde it dighte;
Sin love and cruel Fortune it ne wolde,
That in this world he lenger liven sholde.

Thanne seyde he thus, fulfild of heigh desdayn:
O cruel Jove, and thou, Fortune adverse,
This al and som, that falsly have ye slayn
Criseyde, and sin ye may do me no werse,
Fy on your might and werkes so diverse!
Thus cowardly ye shul me never winne;
Ther shal no deeth me fro my lady twinne.

For I this world, sin ye han slayn hir thus,
Wol lete, and folowe hir spirit lowe or hye;
Shal never lover seyn that Troilus
Dar not, for fere, with his lady dye;
For certeyn, I wol bere hir companye.
But sin ye wol not suffre us liven here,
Yet suffreth that our soules ben yfere.

And thou, citee, whiche that I leve in wo,
And thou, Pryam, and bretheren al yfere,
And thou, my moder, farewel! for I go;
And Attropos, make redy thou my bere!
And thou, Criseyde, o swete herte dere,
Receyve now my spirit! wolde he seye,
With swerd at herte, al redy for to deye.

But as God wolde, of swough therwith she
   abreyde,
And gan to syke, and Troilus she cryde;
And he answerde: Lady myn Criseyde,
Live ye yet? and leet his swerd doun glyde.
Ye, herte myn, that thanked be Cupyde!
Quod she, and therwithal she sore sighte;
And he bigan to glade hir as he mighte;

Took hir in armes two, and kiste hir ofte,
And hir to glade he dide al his entente;
For which hir goost, that flikered ay onlofte,
Into hir woful herte ayein it wente.
But at the laste, as that hir eyen glente
Asyde, anoon she gan his swerd aspye,
As it lay bare, and gan for fere crye,

And asked him, why he it hadde outdrawe?
And Troilus anoon the cause hir tolde,
And how himself therwith he wolde have slawe.
For which Criseyde upon him gan biholde,
And gan him in hir armes faste folde,
And seyde: O mercy, God, lo, which a dede!
Allas! how neigh we were bothe dede!

Thanne if I ne hadde spoken, as grace was,
Ye wolde han slayn yourself anoon? quod she.
Ye, douteless, And she answerde: Allas!
For, by that ilke Lord that made me,
I nolde a forlong wey onlyve han be,
After your deeth, to han be crowned quene
Of al the lond the sonne on shyneth shene.

But with this selve swerd, which that here is,
Myselve I wolde have slayn! quod she tho;
But ho, for we han right ynow of this,
And late us ryse and streight to bedde go,
And there lat us speken of our wo.
For, by the morter which that I see brenne,
Knowe I ful wel that day is not fer henne.

Whan they were in hir bedde, in armes folde,
Nought was it lyk tho nightes herebiforn;
For pitously ech other gan biholde,
As they that hadden al hir blisse ylorn,
Biwaylinge ay the day that they were born.
Til at the last this sorwful wight Criseyde
To Troilus these ilke wordes seyde:

Lo, herte myn, wel wot ye this, quod she,
That if a wight alwey his wo compleyne,
And seketh nought how holpen for to be,
It nis but folye and encrees of peyne;
And sin that here assembled be we tweyne
To finde bote of wo that we ben inne,
It were al tyme sone to biginne.

I am a womman, as ful wel ye woot,
And as I am avysed sodeynly,
So wol I telle yow, whyl it is hoot.
Me thinketh thus, that neither ye nor I
Oughte half this wo to make skilfully.
For there is art ynow for to redresse
That yet is mis, and sleen this hevinesse.

Sooth is, the wo, the whiche that we ben inne,
For ought I woot, for nothing elles is
But for the cause that we sholden twinne.
Considered al, ther nis no more amis.
But what is thanne a remede unto this,
But that we shape us sone for to mete?
This al and som, my dere herte swete.

Now that I shal wel bringen it aboute
To come ayein, sone after that I go,
Therof am I no maner thing in doute.
For dredeles, withinne a wouke or two,
I shal ben here; and, that it may be so
By alle right, and in a wordes fewe,
I shal yow wel an heep of weyes shewe.

For which I wol not make long sermoun,
For tyme ylost may not recovered be;
But I wol gon to my conclusioun,
And to the beste, in ought that I can see.
And, for the love of God, foryeve it me
If I speke ought ayein your hertes reste;
For trewely, I speke it for the beste;

Makinge alwey a protestacioun,
That now these wordes, whiche that I shal seye,
Nis but to shewe yow my mocioun,
To finde unto our helpe the beste weye;
And taketh it non other wyse, I preye.
For in effect whatso ye me comaunde,
That wol I doon, for that is no demaunde.

Now herkeneth this, ye han wel understonde
My going graunted is by parlement
So ferforth, that it may not be withstonde
For al this world, as by my jugement.
And sin ther helpeth noon avysement
To letten it, lat it passe out of minde;
And lat us shape a bettre wey to finde.

The sothe is, that the twinninge of us tweyne
Wol us disese and cruelliche anoye.
But him bihoveth somtyme han a peyne,
That serveth love, if that he wol have joye.
And sin I shal no ferthere out of Troye
Than I may ryde ayein on half a morwe,
It oughte lasse causen us to sorwe.

So as I shal not so ben hid in muwe,
That day by day, myn owene herte dere,
Sin wel ye woot that it is now a truwe,
Ye shul ful wel al myn estat yhere.
And er that truwe is doon, I shal ben here,
And thanne have ye bothe Antenor ywonne
And me also; beth glad now, if ye conne;

And thenk right thus: Criseyde is now agoon,
But what! she shal come hastely ayeyn,
And whanne, allas? by God, lo, right anoon,
Er dayes ten, this dar I saufly seyn.
And thanne at erste shul we been so fayn,
So as we shulle togederes ever dwelle,
That al this world ne mighte our blisse telle.

I see that ofte, theras we ben now,
That for the beste, our conseil for to hyde,
Ye speke not with me, nor I with yow
In fourtenight; ne see yow go ne ryde.
May ye not ten dayes thanne abyde,
For myn honour, in swich an aventure?
Ywis, ye mowen elles lite endure!

Ye knowe eek how that al my kin is here,
But if that onliche it my fader be;
And eek myn othere thinges alle yfere,
And nameliche, my dere herte, ye,
Whom that I nolde leven for to see
For al this world, as wyd as it hath space;
Or elles, see ich never Joves face!

Why trowe ye my fader in this wyse
Coveiteth so to see me, but for drede
Lest in this toun that folkes me dispyse
Bycause of him, for his unhappy dede?
What woot my fader what lyf that I lede?
For if he wiste in Troye how wel I fare,
As neded for my wending nought to care.

Ye seen that every day eek, more and more,
Men trete of pees; and it supposed is,
That men the quene Eleyne shal restore,
And Grekes us restore that is mis.
So though ther nere comfort noon but this,
That men purposen pees on every syde,
Ye may the bettre at ese of herte abyde.

m m 2

For if that it be pees, myn herte dere,
The nature of the pees mot nedes dryve
That men moste entrecomunen yfere,
And to and fro eek ryde and gon as blyve
Alday as thikke as been flen from an hyve;
And every wight han libertee to bleve
Wheras him list the bet, withouten leve.

And though so be that pees ther may be noon,
Yet hider, though ther never pees ne were,
I moste come; for whider sholde I goon,
Or how mischaunce sholde I dwelle there
Among tho men of armes ever in fere?
For which, as wisly God my soule rede,
I can not seen wherof ye sholden drede.

Have here another wey, if it so be
That al this thing ne may yow not suffyse.
My fader, as ye knowen wel, pardee,
Is old, and elde is ful of coveityse.
And I right now have founden al the gyse,
Withoute net, wherwith I shal him hente;
And herkeneth how, if that ye wole assente.

Lo, Troilus, men seyn that hard it is
The wolf ful, and the wether hool to have;
This is to seyn, that men ful ofte, ywis,
Mot spenden part, the remenaunt for to save.
For ay with gold men may the herte grave
Of him that set is upon coveityse;
And how I mene, I shal it yow devyse.

The moeble which that I have in this toun
Unto my fader shal I take, and seye,
That right for trust and for savacioun
It sent is from a freend of his or tweye,
The whiche freendes ferventliche him preye
To senden after more, and that in hye,
Whyl that this toun stant thus in jupartye.

And that shal been an huge quantitee,
Thus shal I seyn, but, lest it folk aspyde,
This may be sent by no wight but by me;
I shal eek shewen him, if pees bityde,
What frendes that ich have on every syde
Toward the court, to doon the wrathe pace
Of Priamus, and doon him stonde in grace.

So, what for o thing and for other, swete,
I shal him so enchaunten with my sawes,
That right in hevene his sowle is, shal he mete!
For al Appollo, or his clerkes lawes,
Or calculinge avayleth nought three hawes;
Desyr of gold shal so his sowle blende,
That, as me lyst, I shal wel make an ende.

And if he wolde ought by his sort it preve
If that I lye, in certayn I shal fonde
Distorben him, and plukke him by the sleve,
Makinge his sort, and beren him on honde,
He hath not wel the goddes understonde.
For goddes speken in amphibologyes,
And, for a sooth, they tellen twenty lyes.

531

Eek drede fond first goddes, I suppose,
Thus shal I seyn, and that his cowarde herte
Made him amis the goddes text to glose,
Whan he for ferde out of his Delphos sterte.
And but I make him sone to converte,
And doon my reed withinne a day or tweye,
I wol to yow oblige me to deye.

And treweliche, as writen wel I finde,
That al this thing was seyd of good entente;
And that hir herte trewe was and kinde
Towardes him, and spak right as she mente,
And that she starf for wo neigh, whan she wente,
And was in purpos ever to be trewe;
Thus writen they that of hir werkes knewe.

This Troilus, with herte and eres spradde,
Herde al this thing devysen to and fro;
And verraylich him semed that he hadde
The selve wit; but yet to lete hir go
His herte misforyaf him evermo.
But fynally, he gan his herte wreste
To trusten hir, and took it for the beste.

For which the grete furie of his penaunce
Was queynt with hope, and therwith hem bitwene
Bigan for joye the amorouse daunce.
And as the briddes, whan the sonne is shene,
Delyten in hir song in leves grene,
Right so the wordes that they spake yfere
Delyted hem, and made hir hertes clere.

But natheles, the wending of Criseyde,
For al this world, may nought out of his minde;
For which ful ofte he pitously hir preyde,
That of hir heste he might hir trewe finde.
And seyde hir: Certes, if ye be unkinde,
And but ye come at day set into Troye,
Ne shal I never have hele, honour, ne joye.

For also sooth as sonne uprist on morwe,
And, God! so wisly thou me, woful wrecche,
To reste bringe out of this cruel sorwe,
I wol myselven slee if that ye drecche.
But of my deeth though litel be to recche,
Yet, er that ye me cause so to smerte,
Dwel rather here, myn owene swete herte!

For trewely, myn owene lady dere,
Tho sleightes yet that I have herd yow stere
Ful shaply been to failen alle yfere.
For thus men seyn: That oon thenketh the bere,
But al another thenketh his ledere.
Your sire is wys, and seyd is, out of drede:
Men may the wyse at-renne, and not at-rede.

It is ful hard to halten unespyed
Bifore a crepul, for he can the craft;
Your fader is in sleighte as Argus yëd;
For al be that his moeble is him biraft,
His olde sleighte is yet so with him laft,
Ye shal not blende him for your womanhede,
Ne feyne aright, and that is al my drede.

532

I noot if pees shal evermo bityde;
But, pees or no, for ernest ne for game,
I woot, sin Calkas on the Grekes syde
Hath ones been, and lost so foule his name,
He dar no more come here ayein for shame;
For which that weye, for ought I can espye,
To trusten on, nis but a fantasye.

Ye shal eek seen, your fader shal yow glose
To been a wyf, and as he can wel preche,
He shal som Grek so preyse and wel alose,
That ravisshen he shal yow with his speche,
Or do yow doon by force as he shal teche.
And Troilus, of whom ye nil han routhe,
Shal causeles so sterven in his trouthe!

And over al this, your fader shal despyse
Us alle, and seyn this citee nis but lorn;
And that thassege never shal aryse,
Forwhy the Grekes han it alle sworn
Til we be slayn, and doun our walles torn.
And thus he shal you with his wordes fere,
That ay drede I, that ye wol bleve there.

Ye shul eek seen so many a lusty knight
Among the Grekes, ful of worthinesse,
And eche of hem with herte, wit, and might
To plesen yow don al his besinesse,
That ye shul dullen of the rudenesse
Of us sely Troianes, but if routhe
Remorde yow, or vertue of your trouthe.

And this to me so grevous is to thinke,
That fro my brest it wol my soule rende;
Ne dredeles, in me ther may not sinke
A good opinioun, if that ye wende;
Forwhy your faderes sleighte wol us shende.
And if ye goon, as I have told yow yore,
So thenk I nam but deed, withoute more.

For which, with humble, trewe, and pitous herte,
A thousand tymes mercy I yow preye;
So reweth on myn aspre peynes smerte,
And doth somwhat, as that I shal yow seye,
And lat us stele away bitwixe us tweye;
And thenk that folye is, whan man may chese,
For accident his substaunce ay to lese.

I mene this, that sin we mowe er day
Wel stele away, and been togider so,
What wit were it to putten in assay,
In cas ye sholden to your fader go,
If that ye mighte come ayein or no?
Thus mene I, that it were a gret folye
To putte that sikernesse in jupartye.

And vulgarly to speken of substaunce
Of tresour, may we bothe with us lede
Ynough to live in honour and plesaunce,
Til into tyme that we shul ben dede;
And thus we may eschewen al this drede.
For everich other wey ye can recorde,
Myn herte, ywis, may not therwith acorde.

And hardily, ne dredeth no poverte,
For I have kin and freendes elleswhere
That, though we comen in our bare sherte,
Us sholde neither lakke gold ne gere,
But been honoured whyl we dwelten there.
And go we anoon, for, as in myn entente,
This is the beste, if that ye wole assente.

Criseyde, with a syk, right in this wyse
Answerde: Ywis, my dere herte trewe,
We may wel stele away, as ye devyse,
And finde swiche unthrifty weyes newe;
But afterward, ful sore it wol us rewe.
And help me God so at my moste nede
As causeles ye suffren al this drede!

For thilke day that I for cherisshinge
Or drede of fader, or of other wight,
Or for estat, delyt, or for weddinge
Be fals to yow, my Troilus, my knight,
Saturnes doughter, Juno, thorugh hir might,
As wood as Athamante do me dwelle
Eternaly in Stix, the put of helle!

And this on every god celestial
I swere it yow, and eek on eche goddesse,
On every Nymphe and deite infernal,
On Satiry and Fauny more and lesse,
That halve goddes been of wildernesse;
And Attropos my threed of lyf tobreste
If I be fals; now trowe me if thow leste!

And thou, Simoys, that as an arwe clere
Thorugh Troye rennest ay downward to the see,
Ber witnesse of this word that seyd is here,
That thilke day that ich untrewe be
To Troilus, myn owene herte free,
That thou retorne bakwarde to thy welle,
And I with body and soule sinke in helle!

But that ye speke, awey thus for to go
And leten alle your freendes, God forbede,
For any womman, that ye sholden so,
And namely, sin Troye hath now swich nede
Of help; and eek of o thing taketh hede,
If this were wist, my lif laye in balaunce,
And your honour; God shilde us fro mischaunce!

And if so be that pees herafter take,
As alday happeth, after anger, game,
Why, Lord! the sorwe and wo ye wolden make,
That ye ne dorste come ayein for shame!
And er that ye juparten so your name,
Beth nought to hasty in this hote fare;
For hasty man ne wanteth never care.

What trowe ye the peple eek al aboute
Wolde of it seye? It is ful light to arede.
They wolden seye, and swere it, out of doute,
That love ne droof yow nought to doon this dede
But lust voluptuous and coward drede.
Thus were al lost, ywis, myn herte dere,
Your honour, which that now shyneth so clere.

m m 3

And also thenketh on myn honestee,
That floureth yet, how foule I sholde it shende,
And with what filthe it spotted sholde be,
If in this forme I sholde with yow wende.
Ne though I livede unto the worldes ende,
My name sholde I never ayeinward winne;
Thus were I lost, and that were routhe and sinne.

And forthy slee with reson al this hete;
Men seyn, The suffraunt overcometh, pardee;
Eek Whoso wol han leef, he leef mot lete;
Thus maketh vertue of necessitee
By pacience, and thenk that lord is he
Of fortune ay, that nought wol of hir recche;
And she ne daunteth no wight but a wrecche.

And trusteth this, that certes, herte swete,
Er Phebus suster, Lucina the shene,
The Leoun passe out of this Ariete,
I wol ben here, withouten any wene.
I mene, as helpe me Juno, hevenes quene,
The tenthe day, but if that deeth me assayle,
I wol yow seen, withouten any fayle.

And now, so this be sooth, quod Troilus,
I shal wel suffre unto the tenthe day,
Sin that I see that nede it moot be thus.
But, for the love of God, if it be may,
So lat us stele prively away;
For ever in oon, as for to live in reste,
Myn herte seyth that it wol been the beste.

O mercy, God, what lyf is this? quod she;
Allas, ye slee me thus for verray tene!
I see wel now that ye mistrusten me;
For by your wordes it is wel ysene.
Now, for the love of Cynthia the shene,
Mistrust me not thus causeles, for routhe;
Sin to be trewe I have yow plight my trouthe.

And thenketh wel, that som tyme it is wit
To spende a tyme, a tyme for to winne;
Ne, pardee, lorn am I nought fro yow yit,
Though that we been a day or two atwinne.
Dryf out the fantasyes yow withinne;
And trusteth me, and leveth eek your sorwe,
Or here my trouthe, I wol not live til morwe.

For if ye wiste how sore it doth me smerte,
Ye wolde cesse of this; for God, thou wost,
The pure spirit wepeth in myn herte,
To see yow wepen that I love most,
And that I moot gon to the Grekes ost.
Ye, nere it that I wiste remedye
To come ayein, right here I wolde dye!

But certes, I am not so nyce a wight
That I ne can imaginen a way
To come ayein that day that I have hight.
For who may holde thing that wol away?
My fader nought, for al his queynte pley.
And by my thrift, my wending out of Troye
Another day shal torne us alle to joye.

Forthy, with al myn herte I yow beseke,
If that yow list don ought for my preyere,
And for the love which that I love yow eke,
That er that I departe fro yow here,
That of so good a comfort and a chere
I may you seen, that ye may bringe at reste
Myn herte, which that is at point to breste.

And over al this, I pray yow, quod she tho,
Myn owene hertes soothfast suffisaunce,
Sin I am thyn al hool, withouten mo,
That whyl that I am absent, no plesaunce
Of othere do me fro your remembraunce.
For I am ever agast, forwhy men rede,
That Love is thing ay ful of bisy drede.

For in this world ther liveth lady noon,
If that ye were untrewe, as God defende!
That so bitraysed were or wo bigoon
As I, that alle trouthe in yow entende.
And douteles, if that ich other wende,
I nere but deed; and er ye cause finde,
For Goddes love, so beth me not unkinde.

To this answerde Troilus and seyde:
Now God, to whom ther nis no cause ywrye,
Me glade, as wis I never unto Criseyde,
Sin thilke day I saw hir first with yë,
Was fals, ne never shal til that I dye.
At shorte wordes, wel ye may me leve;
I can no more, it shal be founde at preve.

Graunt mercy, goode myn, ywis, quod she,
And blisful Venus lat me never sterve
Er I may stonde of plesaunce in degree
To quyte him wel, that so wel can deserve;
And whyl that God my wit wol me conserve,
I shal so doon, so trewe I have yow founde,
That ay honour to meward shal rebounde.

For trusteth wel, that your estat royal
Ne veyn delyt, nor only worthinesse
Of yow in werre, or torney marcial,
Ne pompe, array, nobley, or eek richesse,
Ne made me to rewe on your distresse;
But moral vertue, grounded upon trouthe,
That was the cause I first hadde on yow routhe!

Eek gentil herte and manhod that ye hadde,
And that ye hadde, as me thoughte, in despyt
Every thing that souned into badde,
As rudenesse and poeplish appetyt;
And that your reson brydled your delyt,
This made, aboven every creature,
That I was your, and shal, whyl I may dure.

And this may lengthe of yeres not fordo,
Ne remuable fortune deface;
But Juppiter, that of his might may do
The sorwful to be glad, so yeve us grace,
Er nightes ten, to meten in this place,
So that it may your herte and myn suffyse;
And fareth now wel, for tyme is that ye ryse.

And after that they longe ypleyned hadde,
And ofte ykist and streite in armes folde,
The day gan ryse, and Troilus him cladde,
And rewfulliche his lady gan biholde,
As he that felte dethes cares colde.
And to hir grace he gan him recomaunde;
Wher him was wo, this holde I no demaunde.

For mannes heed imaginen ne can,
Ne entendement considere, ne tonge telle
The cruel peynes of this sorwful man,
That passen every torment doun in helle.
For whan he saugh that she ne mighte dwelle,
Which that his soule out of his herte rente,
Withouten more, out of the chaumbre he wente.
Explicit Liber Quartus.

Incipit Liber Quintus.

PRO EME N

GAN THE FATAL DESTINEE
That Joves hath in disposicioun,
And to yow, angry Parcas, sustren three,
Committeth, to don execucioun;
for which Criseyde moste out of the town,
And Troilus shal dwelle forth in pyne
Til Lachesis his threed no lenger twyne.

THE golden-tressed
Phebus heighe onlofte
Thryës hadde alle with
his bemes shene
The snowes molte, and
Zephirus as ofte
Ybrought ayein the
tendre leves grene,
Sin that the sone of
Ecuba the quene
Bigan to love hir first, for whom his sorwe
Was al, that she departe sholde amorwe.

ful redy was at pryme Dyomede,
Criseyde unto the Grekes ost to lede,
for sorwe of which she felte hir herte blede,
As she that niste what was best to rede.
And trewely, as men in bokes rede,
Men wiste never womman han the care,
Ne was so looth out of a toun to fare.

This Troilus, withouten reed or lore,
As man that hath his joyes eek forlore,
Was waytinge on his lady evermore
As she that was the soothfast crop and more
Of al his lust, or joyes heretofore.
But Troilus, now farewel al thy joye,
for shaltow never seen hir eft in Troye!

Soth is, that whyl he bood in this manere,
He gan his wo ful manly for to hyde,
That wel unnethe it seen was in his chere;
But at the yate ther she sholde oute ryde
With certeyn folk, he hoved hir tabyde,
So wo bigoon, al wolde he nought him pleyne,

That on his hors unnethe he sat for peyne.

for ire he quook, so gan his herte gnawe,
Whan Diomede on horse gan him dresse,
And seyde unto himself this ilke sawe:
Allas, quod he, thus foul a wrecchednesse
Why suffre ich it, why nil ich it redresse?
Were it not bet at ones for to dye
Than evermore in langour thus to drye?

Why nil I make at ones riche and pore
To have ynough to done, er that she go?
Why nil I bringe al Troye upon a rore?
Why nil I sleen this Diomede also?
Why nil I rather with a man or two
Stele hir away? Why wol I this endure?
Why nil I helpen to myn owene cure?

But why he nolde doon so fel a dede,
That shal I seyn, and why him liste it spare:
He hadde in herte alwey a maner drede,
Lest that Criseyde, in rumour of this fare,
Sholde han ben slayn; lo, this was al his care.
And elles, certeyn, as I seyde yore,
He hadde it doon, withouten wordes more.

Criseyde, whan she redy was to ryde,
ful sorwfully she sighte, and seyde Allas!
But forth she moot, for ought that may bityde,
And forth she rit ful sorwfully a pas.
Ther nis non other remedie in this cas.
What wonder is though that hir sore smerte,
Whan she forgoth hir owene swete herte?

This Troilus, in wyse of curteisye,
With hauke on hond, and with an huge route
Of knightes, rood and dide hir companye,
Passinge al the valey fer withoute.
And ferther wolde han riden, out of doute,
ful fayn, and wo was him to goon so sone;
But torne he moste, and it was eek to done.

And right with that was Antenor ycome
Out of the Grekes ost, and every wight
Was of it glad, and seyde he was welcome.
And Troilus, al nere his herte light,
He peyned him with al his fulle might
Him to withholde of wepinge at the leste,
And Antenor he kiste, and made feste.

And therwithal he moste his leve take,
And caste his eye upon hir pitously,
And neer he rood, his cause for to make,
To take hir by the honde al sobrely.
And Lord! so she gan wepen tendrely!
And he ful softe and sleighly gan hir seye:
Now hold your day, and dooth me not to deye.

With that his courser torned he aboute
With face pale, and unto Diomede
No word he spak, ne noon of al his route;

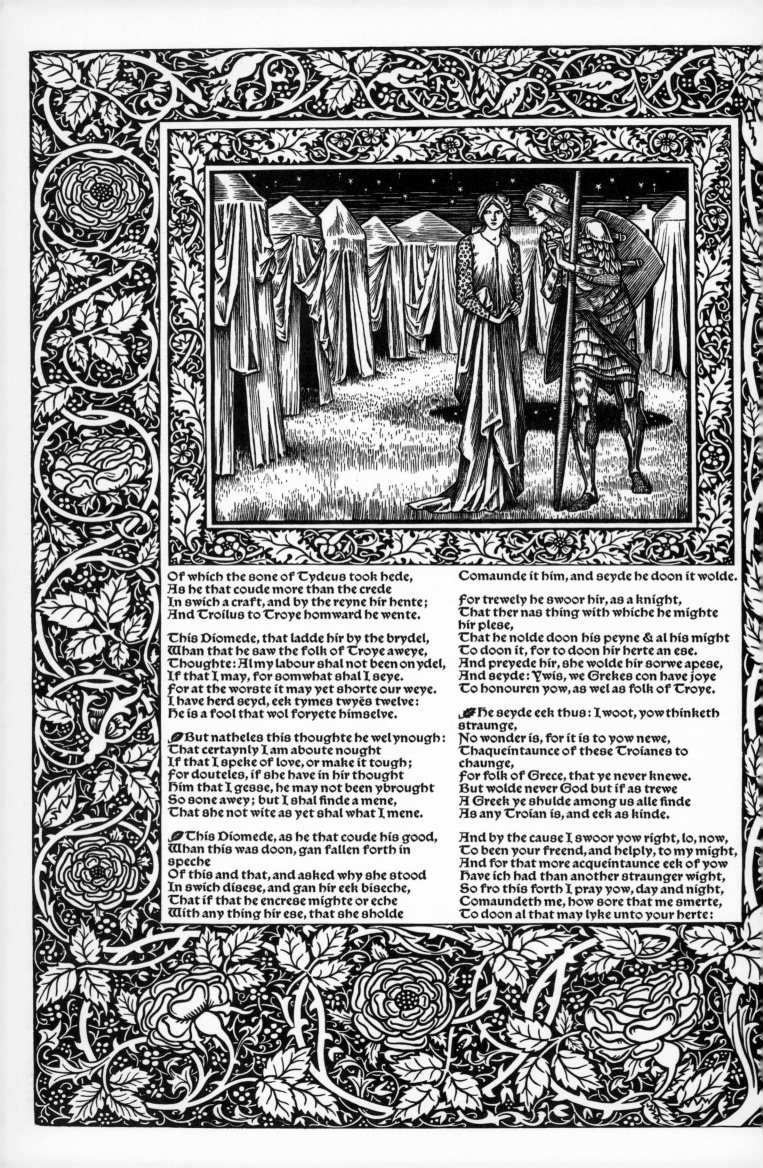

Of which the sone of Tydeus took hede,
As he that coude more than the crede
In swich a craft, and by the reyne hir hente;
And Troilus to Troye homward he wente.

This Diomede, that ladde hir by the brydel,
Whan that he saw the folk of Troye aweye,
Thoughte: Al my labour shal not been on ydel,
If that I may, for somwhat shal I seye.
For at the worste it may yet shorte our weye.
I have herd seyd, eek tymes twyës twelve:
He is a fool that wol foryete himselve.

*But natheles this thoughte he wel ynough:
That certaynly I am aboute nought
If that I speke of love, or make it tough;
For douteles, if she have in hir thought
Him that I gesse, he may not been ybrought
So sone awey; but I shal finde a mene,
That she not wite as yet shal what I mene.

*This Diomede, as he that coude his good,
Whan this was doon, gan fallen forth in speche
Of this and that, and asked why she stood
In swich disese, and gan hir eek biseche,
That if that he encrese mighte or eche
With any thing hir ese, that she sholde

Comaunde it him, and seyde he doon it wolde.

For trewely he swoor hir, as a knight,
That ther nas thing with whiche he mighte
hir plese,
That he nolde doon his peyne & al his might
To doon it, for to doon hir herte an ese.
And preyede hir, she wolde hir sorwe apese,
And seyde: Ywis, we Grekes con have joye
To honouren yow, as wel as folk of Troye.

*He seyde eek thus: I woot, yow thinketh
straunge,
No wonder is, for it is to yow newe,
Thaqueintaunce of these Troianes to
chaunge,
For folk of Grece, that ye never knewe.
But wolde never God but if as trewe
A Greek ye shulde among us alle finde
As any Troian is, and eek as kinde.

And by the cause I swoor yow right, lo, now,
To been your freend, and helply, to my might,
And for that more acqueintaunce eek of yow
Have ich had than another straunger wight,
So fro this forth I pray yow, day and night,
Comaundeth me, how sore that me smerte,
To doon al that may lyke unto your herte:

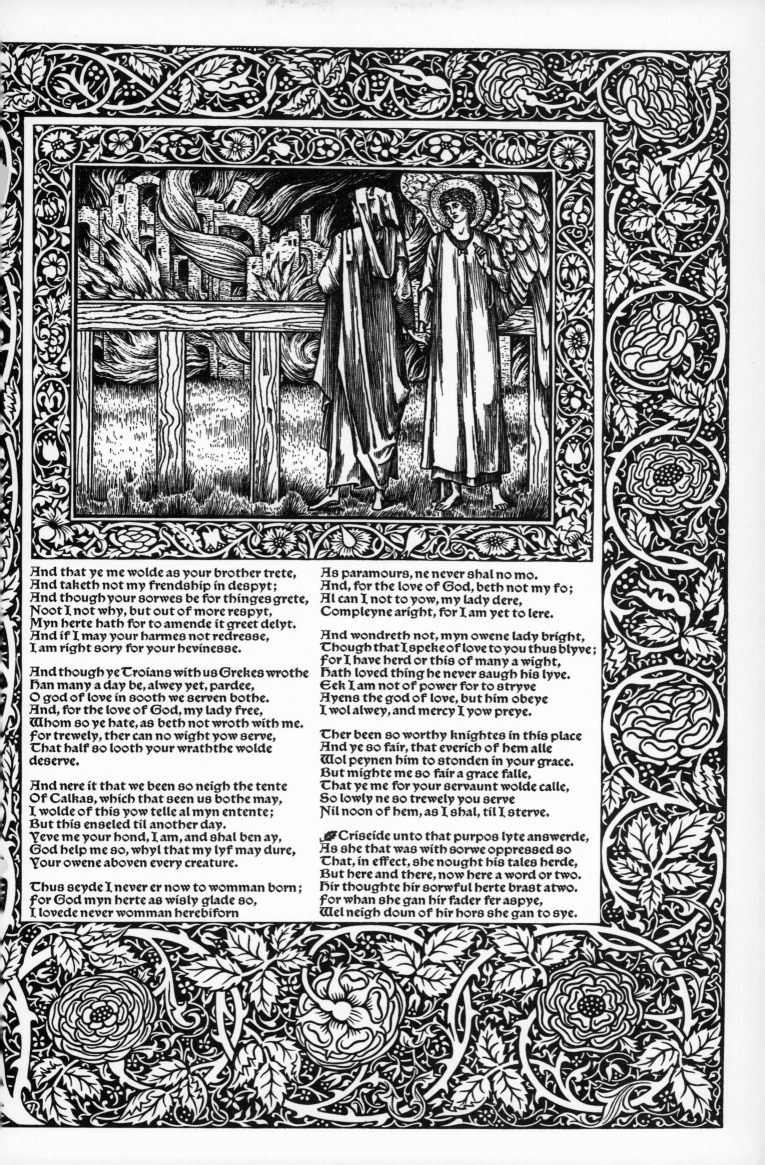

And that ye me wolde as your brother trete,
And taketh not my frendship in despyt;
And though your sorwes be for thinges grete,
Noot I not why, but out of more respyt,
Myn herte hath for to amende it greet delyt.
And if I may your harmes not redresse,
I am right sory for your hevinesse.

And though ye Troians with us Grekes wrothe
Han many a day be, alwey yet, pardee,
O god of love in sooth we serven bothe.
And, for the love of God, my lady free,
Whom so ye hate, as beth not wroth with me.
For trewely, ther can no wight yow serve,
That half so looth your wraththe wolde
deserve.

And nere it that we been so neigh the tente
Of Calkas, which that seen us bothe may,
I wolde of this yow telle al myn entente;
But this enseled til another day.
Yeve me your hond, I am, and shal ben ay,
God help me so, whyl that my lyf may dure,
Your owene aboven every creature.

Thus seyde I never er now to womman born;
For God myn herte as wisly glade so,
I lovede never womman herebiforn

As paramours, ne never shal no mo.
And, for the love of God, beth not my fo;
Al can I not to yow, my lady dere,
Compleyne aright, for I am yet to lere.

And wondreth not, myn owene lady bright,
Though that I speke of love to you thus blyve;
For I have herd or this of many a wight,
Hath loved thing he never saugh his lyve.
Eek I am not of power for to stryve
Ayens the god of love, but him obeye
I wol alwey, and mercy I yow preye.

Ther been so worthy knightes in this place
And ye so fair, that everich of hem alle
Wol peynen him to stonden in your grace.
But mighte me so fair a grace falle,
That ye me for your servaunt wolde calle,
So lowly ne so trewely you serve
Nil noon of hem, as I shal, til I sterve.

Criseide unto that purpos lyte answerde,
As she that was with sorwe oppressed so
That, in effect, she nought his tales herde,
But here and there, now here a word or two.
Hir thoughte hir sorwful herte brast atwo.
For whan she gan hir fader fer aspye,
Wel neigh doun of hir hors she gan to sye.

But natheles she thonked Diomede
Of al his travaile, and his goode chere,
And that him liste his friendship hir to bede;
And she accepteth it in good manere,
And wolde do fayn that is him leef and dere;
And trusten him she wolde, and wel she mighte,
As seyde she, and from hir hors she alighte.

Hir fader hath hir in his armes nome,
And tweynty tyme he kiste his doughter swete,
And seyde: O dere doughter myn, welcome!
She seyde eek, she was fayn with him to mete,
And stood forth mewet, mildĕ, and mansuete.
But here I leve hir with hir fader dwelle,
And forth I wol of Troilus yow telle.

To Troye is come this woful Troilus,
In sorwe aboven alle sorwes smerte,
With felon look, and face dispitous.
Tho sodeinly doun from his hors he sterte,
And thorugh his paleys, with a swollen herte,
To chambre he wente; of nothing took he hede,
Ne noon to him dar speke a word for drede.

And there his sorwes that he spared hadde
He yaf an issue large, and Deeth! he cryde;
And in his throwes frenetyk and madde
He cursed Jove, Appollo, and eek Cupyde,
He cursed Ceres, Bacus, and Cipryde,
His burthe, himself, his fate, and eek nature,
And, save his lady, every creature.

To bedde he goth, and weyleth there and torneth
In furie, as dooth he, Ixion, in helle;
And in this wyse he neigh til day sojorneth.
But tho bigan his herte a lyte unswelle
Thorugh teres which that gonnen up to welle;
And pitously he cryde upon Criseyde,
And to himself right thus he spak, and seyde:

Wher is myn owene lady lief and dere,
Wher is hir whyte brest, wher is it, where?
Wher ben hir armes and hir eyen clere,
That yesternight this tyme with me were?
Now may I wepe allone many a tere,
And graspe aboute I may, but in this place,
Save a pilowe, I finde nought tenbrace.

How shal I do? Whan shal she com ayeyn?
I noot, allas! why leet ich hir to go?
As wolde God, ich hadde as tho be sleyn!
O herte myn, Criseyde, O swete fo!
O lady myn, that I love and no mo!
To whom for evermo myn herte I dowe;
See how I deye, ye nil me not rescowe!

Who seeth yow now, my righte lode-sterre?
Who sit right now or stant in your presence?
Who can conforten now your hertes werre?
Now I am gon, whom yeve ye audience?
Who speketh for me right now in myn absence?
Allas, no wight; and that is al my care;
For wel wot I, as yvel as I ye fare.

538

How shulde I thus ten dayes ful endure,
Whan I the firste night have al this tene?
How shal she doon eek, sorwful creature?
For tendernesse, how shal she this sustene,
Swich wo for me? O pitous, pale, and grene
Shal been your fresshe wommanliche face
For langour, er ye torne unto this place.

And whan he fil in any slomeringes,
Anoon biginne he sholde for to grone,
And dremen of the dredfulleste thinges
That mighte been; as, mete he were allone
In place horrible, makinge ay his mone,
Or meten that he was amonges alle
His enemys, and in hir hondes falle.

And therwithal his body sholde sterte,
And with the stert al sodeinliche awake,
And swich a tremour fele aboute his herte,
That of the feer his body sholde quake;
And therewithal he sholde a noyse make,
And seme as though he sholde falle depe
From heighe alofte; and than he wolde wepe,

And rewen on himself so pitously,
That wonder was to here his fantasye.
Another tyme he sholde mightily
Conforte himself, and seyn it was folye,
So causeles swich drede for to drye,
And eft biginne his aspre sorwes newe,
That every man mighte on his sorwes rewe.

Who coude telle aright or ful discryve
His wo, his pleynte, his langour, and his pyne?
Nought al the men that han or been onlyve.
Thou, redere, mayst thyself ful wel devyne
That swich a wo my wit can not defyne.
On ydel for to wryte it sholde I swinke,
Whan that my wit is wery it to thinke.

On hevene yet the sterres were sene,
Although ful pale ywaxen was the mone;
And whyten gan the orisonte shene
Al estward, as it woned is to done.
And Phebus with his rosy carte sone
Gan after that to dresse him up to fare,
Whan Troilus hath sent after Pandare.

This Pandare, that of al the day biforn
Ne mighte have comen Troilus to see,
Although he on his heed it hadde ysworn,
For with the king Pryam alday was he,
So that it lay not in his libertee
Nowher to gon, but on the morwe he wente
To Troilus, whan that he for him sente.

For in his herte he coude wel devyne,
That Troilus al night for sorwe wook;
And that he wolde telle him of his pyne,
This knew he wel ynough, withoute book.
For which to chaumbre streight the wey he took,
And Troilus tho sobreliche he grette,
And on the bed ful sone he gan him sette.

My Pandarus, quod Troilus, the sorwe
Which that I drye, I may not longe endure.
I trowe I shal not liven til tomorwe;
For whiche I wolde alwey, on aventure,
To thee devysen of my sepulture
The forme, and of my moeble thou dispone
Right as thee semeth best is for to done.

But of the fyr and flaumbe funeral
In whiche my body brenne shal to glede,
And of the feste and pleyes palestral
At my vigile, I pray thee take good hede
That al be wel; and offre Mars my stede,
My swerd, myn helm, and, leve brother dere,
My sheld to Pallas yef, that shyneth clere.

The poudre in which myn herte ybrend shal torne,
That preye I thee thou take and it conserve
In a vessel, that men clepeth an urne,
Of gold, and to my lady that I serve,
For love of whom thus pitously I sterve,
So yeve it hir, and do me this plesaunce,
To preye hir kepe it for a remembraunce.

For wel I fele, by my maladye,
And by my dremes now and yore ago,
Al certeinly, that I mot nedes dye.
The owle eek, which that hight Ascaphilo,
Hath after me shright alle thise nightes two.
And, god Mercurie! of me now, woful wrecche,
The soule gyde, and, whan thee list, it fecche!

Pandare answerde, and seyde: Troilus,
My dere freend, as I have told thee yore,
That it is folye for to sorwen thus,
And causeles, for whiche I can no more.
But whoso wol not trowen reed ne lore,
I can not seen in him no remedye,
But lete him worthen with his fantasye.

But Troilus, I pray thee tel me now,
If that thou trowe, er this, that any wight
Hath loved paramours as wel as thou?
Ye, God wot, and fro many a worthy knight
Hath his lady goon a fourtenight,
And he not yet made halvendel the fare.
What nede is thee to maken al this care?

Sin day by day thou mayst thyselven see
That from his love, or elles from his wyf,
A man mot twinnen of necessitee,
Ye, though he love hir as his owene lyf;
Yet nil he with himself thus maken stryf.
For wel thow wost, my leve brother dere,
That alwey freendes may nought been yfere.

How doon this folk that seen hir loves wedded
By freendes might, as it bitit ful ofte,
And seen hem in hir spouses bed ybedded?
God woot, they take it wysly, faire and softe.
Forwhy good hope halt up hir herte onlofte,
And for they can a tyme of sorwe endure;
As tyme hem hurt, a tyme doth hem cure.

So sholdestow endure, and late slyde
The tyme, and fonde to ben glad and light.
Ten dayes nis so longe not tabyde.
And sin she thee to comen hath bihight,
She nil hir hestes breken for no wight.
For dred thee not that she nil finden weye
To come ayein, my lyf that dorste I leye.

Thy swevenes eek and al swich fantasye
Dryf out, and lat hem faren to mischaunce;
For they procede of thy malencolye,
That doth thee fele in sleep al this penaunce.
A straw for alle swevenes signifiaunce!
God helpe me so, I counte hem not a bene,
Ther woot no man aright what dremes mene.

For prestes of the temple tellen this,
That dremes been the revelaciouns
Of goddes, and as wel they telle, ywis,
That they ben infernals illusiouns;
And leches seyn, that of complexiouns
Proceden they, or fast, or glotonye.
Who woot in sooth thus what they signifye?

Eek other seyn that thorugh impressiouns,
As if a wight hath faste a thing in minde,
That therof cometh swiche avisiouns;
And othere seyn, as they in bokes finde,
That, after tymes of the yeer by kinde,
Men dreme, and that theffect goth by the mone;
But leve no dreem, for it is nought to done.

Wel worth of dremes ay thise olde wyves,
And treweliche eek augurie of thise foules;
For fere of which men wenen lese her lyves,
As ravenes qualm, or shryking of thise oules.
To trowen on it bothe fals and foul is.
Allas, allas, so noble a creature
As is a man, shal drede swich ordure!

For which with al myn herte I thee beseche,
Unto thyself that al this thou foryive;
And rys up now withoute more speche,
And lat us caste how forth may best be drive
This tyme, and eek how freshly we may live
Whan that she cometh, the which shal be right sone;
God help me so, the beste is thus to done.

Rys, lat us speke of lusty lyf in Troye
That we han lad, and forth the tyme dryve;
And eek of tyme cominge us rejoye,
That bringen shal our blisse now so blyve;
And langour of these twyës dayes fyve
We shal therwith so foryete or oppresse,
That wel unnethe it doon shal us duresse.

This toun is ful of lordes al aboute,
And trewes lasten al this mene whyle.
Go we and pleye us in som lusty route
To Sarpedon, not hennes but a myle.
And thus thou shalt the tyme wel bigyle,
And dryve it forth unto that blisful morwe,
That thou hir see, that cause is of thy sorwe.

539

Now rys, my dere brother Troilus;
For certes, it noon honour is to thee
To wepe, and in thy bed to jouken thus.
For trewely, of o thing trust to me,
If thou thus ligge a day, or two, or three,
The folk wol wene that thou, for cowardyse,
Thee feynest syk, and that thou darst not ryse.

This Troilus answerde: O brother dere,
This knowen folk that han ysuffred peyne,
That though he wepe and make sorwful chere,
That feleth harm and smert in every veyne,
No wonder is; and though I ever pleyne,
Or alwey wepe, I am nothing to blame,
Sin I have lost the cause of al my game.

But sin of fyne force I moot aryse,
I shal aryse, as sone as ever I may;
And God, to whom myn herte I sacrifyse,
So sende us hastely the tenthe day!
For was ther never fowl so fayn of May,
As I shal been, whan that she cometh in Troye,
That cause is of my torment and my joye.

But whider is thy reed, quod Troilus,
That we may pleye us best in al this toun?
By God, my conseil is, quod Pandarus,
To ryde and pleye us with king Sarpedoun.
So longe of this they speken up and doun,
Til Troilus gan at the laste assente
To ryse, and forth to Sarpedoun they wente.

This Sarpedoun, as he that honourable
Was ever his lyve, and ful of heigh prowesse,
With al that mighte yserved been on table,
That deyntee was, al coste it greet richesse,
He fedde hem day by day, that swich noblesse,
As seyden bothe the moste and eek the leste,
Was never er that day wist at any feste.

Nor in this world ther is non instrument
Delicious, through wind, or touche, or corde,
As fer as any wight hath ever ywent,
That tonge telle or herte may recorde,
That at that feste it nas wel herd acorde;
Ne of ladies eek so fayr a companye
On daunce, er tho, was never yseyn with yë.

But what avayleth this to Troilus,
That for his sorwe nothing of it roughte?
For ever in oon his herte piëtous
Ful bisily Criseyde his lady soughte.
On hir was ever al that his herte thoughte.
Now this, now that, so faste imagininge,
That glade, ywis, can him no festeyinge.

These ladies eek that at this feste been,
Sin that he saw his lady was aweye,
It was his sorwe upon hem for to seen,
Or for to here on instrumentz so pleye.
For she, that of his herte berth the keye,
Was absent, lo, this was his fantasye,
That no wight sholde make melodye.

540

Nor ther nas houre in al the day or night,
Whan he was theras no wight mighte him here,
That he ne seyde: O lufsom lady bright,
How have ye faren, sin that ye were here?
Welcome, ywis, myn owene lady dere.
But welaway, al this nas but a mase;
Fortune his howve entended bet to glase.

The lettres eek, that she of olde tyme
Hadde him ysent, he wolde allone rede,
An hundred sythe, atwixen noon and pryme;
Refiguringe hir shap, hir womanhede,
Withinne his herte, and every word and dede
That passed was, and thus he droof to an ende
The ferthe day, and seyde, he wolde wende.

And seyde: Leve brother Pandarus,
Intendestow that we shul herë bleve
Til Sarpedoun wol forth congeyen us?
Yet were it fairer that we toke our leve.
For Goddes love, lat us now sone at eve
Our leve take, and homward lat us torne;
For trewely, I nil not thus sojorne.

Pandare answerde: Be we comen hider
To fecchen fyr, and rennen hoom ayeyn?
God helpe me so, I can not tellen whider
We mighten goon, if I shal soothly seyn,
Ther any wight is of us more fayn
Than Sarpedoun; and if we hennes hye
Thus sodeinly, I holde it vilanye,

Sin that we seyden that we wolde bleve
With him a wouke; and now, thus sodeinly,
The ferthe day to take of him our leve,
He wolde wondren on it, trewely!
Lat us holde forth our purpos fermely;
And sin that ye bihighten him to byde,
Hold forward now, and after lat us ryde.

Thus Pandarus, with alle peyne and wo,
Made him to dwelle; and at the woukes ende,
Of Sarpedoun they toke hir leve tho,
And on hir wey they spedden hem to wende.
Quod Troilus: Now God me grace sende,
That I may finden, at myn hom-cominge,
Criseyde comen! and therwith gan he singe.

Ye, hasel-wode! thoughte this Pandare,
And to himself ful softely he seyde:
God woot, refreyden may this hote fare
Er Calkas sende Troilus Criseyde!
But natheles, he japed thus, and seyde,
And swor, ywis, his herte him wel bihighte,
She wolde come as sone as ever she mighte.

Whan they unto the paleys were ycomen
Of Troilus, they doun of hors alighte,
And to the chambre hir wey than han they nomen.
And into tyme that it gan to nighte,
They spaken of Criseyde the brighte.
And after this, whan that hem bothe leste,
They spedde hem fro the soper unto reste.

On morwe, as sone as day bigan to clere,
This Troilus gan of his sleep tabreyde,
And to Pandare, his owene brother dere:
For love of God, ful pitously he seyde,
As go we seen the paleys of Criseyde;
For sin we yet may have namore feste,
So lat us seen hir paleys at the leste.

And therwithal, his meyne for to blende,
A cause he fond in toune for to go,
And to Criseydes hous they gonnen wende.
But Lord! this sely Troilus was wo!
Him thoughte his sorweful herte braste atwo.
For whan he saugh hir dores sperred alle,
Wel neigh for sorwe adoun he gan to falle.

Therwith whan he was war and gan biholde
How shet was every windowe of the place,
As frost, him thoughte, his herte gan to colde;
For which with chaunged deedlich pale face,
Withouten word, he forth bigan to pace;
And, as God wolde, he gan so faste ryde,
That no wight of his contenaunce aspyde.

Than seyde he thus: O paleys desolat,
O hous, of houses whylom best yhight,
O paleys empty and disconsolat,
O thou lanterne, of which queynt is the light,
O paleys, whylom day, that now art night,
Wel oughtestow to falle, and I to dye,
Sin she is went that wont was us to gye!

O paleys, whylom croune of houses alle,
Enlumined with sonne of alle blisse!
O ring, fro which the ruby is outfalle,
O cause of wo, that cause hast been of lisse!
Yet, sin I may no bet, fayn wolde I kisse
Thy colde dores, dorste I for this route;
And farewel shryne, of which the seynt is oute!

Therwith he caste on Pandarus his yë
With chaunged face, and pitous to biholde;
And whan he mighte his tyme aright aspye,
Ay as he rood, to Pandarus he tolde
His newe sorwe, and eek his joyes olde,
So pitously and with so dede an hewe,
That every wight mighte on his sorwe rewe.

Fro thennesforth he rydeth up and doun,
And every thing com him to remembraunce
As he rood forth by places of the toun
In whiche he whylom hadde al his plesaunce.
Lo, yond saugh I myn owene lady daunce;
And in that temple, with hir eyen clere,
Me caughte first my righte lady dere.

And yonder have I herd ful lustily
My dere herte laughe, and yonder pleye
Saugh I hir ones eek ful blisfully.
And yonder ones to me gan she seye:
Now goode swete, love me wel, I preye.
And yond so goodly gan she me biholde,
That to the deeth myn herte is to hir holde.

And at that corner, in the yonder hous,
Herde I myn alderlevest lady dere
So wommanly, with voys melodious,
Singen so wel, so goodly, and so clere,
That in my soule yet me thinketh I here
The blisful soun; and, in that yonder place,
My lady first me took unto hir grace.

Thanne thoughte he thus: O blisful lord Cupyde,
Whanne I the proces have in my memorie,
How thou me hast werreyed on every syde,
Men mighte a book make of it, lyk a storie.
What nede is thee to seke on me victorie,
Sin I am thyn, and hoolly at thy wille?
What joye hastow thyn owene folk to spille?

Wel hastow, lord, ywroke on me thyn ire,
Thou mighty god, and dredful for to greve!
Now mercy, lord, thou wost wel I desire
Thy grace most, of alle lustes leve.
And live and deye I wol in thy bileve;
For which I naxe in guerdon but a bone,
That thou Criseyde ayein me sende sone.

Distreyne hir herte as faste to retorne
As thou dost myn to longen hir to see;
Than woot I wel, that she nil not sojorne.
Now, blisful lord, so cruel thou ne be
Unto the blood of Troye, I preye thee,
As Juno was unto the blood Thebane,
For which the folk of Thebes caughte hir bane.

And after this he to the yates wente
Theras Criseyde outrood a ful good paas,
And up and doun ther made he many a wente,
And to himself ful ofte he seyde: Allas!
From hennes rood my blisse and my solas!
As wolde blisful God now, for his joye,
I mighte hir seen ayein come into Troye.

And to the yonder hille I gan hir gyde,
Allas! and there I took of hir my leve!
And yond I saugh hir to hir fader ryde,
For sorwe of which myn herte shal tocleve.
And hider hoom I com whan it was eve;
And here I dwelle outcast from alle joye,
And shal, til I may seen hir eft in Troye.

And of himself imagined he ofte
To ben defet, and pale, and waxen lesse
Than he was wont, and that men seyde softe:
What may it be? who can the sothe gesse
Why Troilus hath al this hevinesse?
And al this nas but his malencolye,
That he hadde of himself swich fantasye.

Another tyme imaginen he wolde
That every wight that wente by the weye
Had of him routhe, and that they seyen sholde:
I am right sory Troilus wol deye.
And thus he droof a day yet forth or tweye.
As ye have herd, swich lyf right gan he lede,
As he that stood bitwixen hope and drede.

541

for which him lyked in his songes shewe
Thencheson of his wo, as he best mighte,
And make a song of wordes but a fewe,
Somwhat his woful herte for to lighte.
And whan he was from every mannes sighte,
With softe voys he, of his lady dere,
That was absent, gan singe as ye may here.

O sterre, of which I lost have al the light,
With herte soor wel oughte I to bewayle,
That ever derk in torment, night by night,
Toward my deeth with wind in stere I sayle;
for which the tenthe night if that I fayle
The gyding of thy bemes brighte an houre,
My ship and me Caribdis wol devoure.

This song when he thus songen hadde, sone
He fil ayein into his sykes olde;
And every night, as was his wone to done,
He stood the brighte mone to beholde,
And al his sorwe he to the mone tolde;
And seyde: Ywis, whan thou art horned newe,
I shal be glad, if al the world be trewe!

I saugh thyn hornes olde eek by the morwe,
Whan hennes rood my righte lady dere,
That cause is of my torment and my sorwe;
for whiche, O brighte Lucina the clere,
For love of God, ren faste aboute thy spere!
For whan thyn hornes newe ginne springe,
Than shal she come, that may my blisse bringe!

The day is more, and lenger every night,
Than they be wont to be, him thoughte tho;
And that the sonne wente his course unright
By lenger wey than it was wont to go;
And seyde: Ywis, me dredeth evermo,
The sonnes sone, Pheton, be onlyve,
And that his fadres cart amis he dryve.

Upon the walles faste eek wolde he walke,
And on the Grekes ost he wolde see,
And to himself right thus he wolde talke:
Lo, yonder is myn owene lady free,
Or elles yonder, ther tho tentes be!
And thennes comth this eyr, that is so sote,
That in my soule I fele it doth me bote.

And hardely this wind, that more and more
Thus stoundemele encreseth in my face,
Is of my ladyes depe sykes sore.
I preve it thus, for in non othere place
Of al this toun, save onliche in this space,
Fele I no wind that souneth so lyk peyne;
It seyth: Allas! why twinned be we tweyne?

This longe tyme he dryveth forth right thus,
Til fully passed was the nynthe night;
And ay bisyde him was this Pandarus,
That bisily dide alle his fulle might
Him to comforte, and make his herte light;
Yevinge him hope alwey, the tenthe morwe
That she shal come, and stinten al his sorwe.

542

Upon that other syde eek was Criseyde,
With wommen fewe, among the Grekes stronge;
for which ful ofte a day, Allas! she seyde,
That I was born! Wel may myn herte longe
After my deeth; for now live I to longe!
Allas! and I ne may it not amende;
for now is wors than ever yet I wende.

My fader nil for nothing do me grace
To goon ayein, for nought I can him queme;
And if so be that I my terme passe,
My Troilus shal in his herte deme
That I am fals, and so it may wel seme.
Thus shal I have unthank on every syde;
That I was born, so weylawey the tyde!

And if that I me putte in jupartye,
To stele awey by nighte, and it bifalle
That I be caught, I shal be holde a spye;
Or elles, lo, this drede I most of alle,
If in the hondes of som wrecche I falle,
I am but lost, al be myn herte trewe;
Now mighty God, thou on my sorwe rewe!

Ful pale ywaxen was hir brighte face,
Hir limes lene, as she that al the day
Stood whan she dorste, and loked on the place
Ther she was born, and ther she dwelt hadde ay.
And al the night wepinge, allas! she lay.
And thus despeired, out of alle cure,
She ladde hir lyf, this woful creature.

Ful ofte a day she sighte eek for destresse,
And in hirself she wente ay portrayinge
Of Troilus the grete worthinesse,
And alle his goodly wordes recordinge
Sin first that day hir love bigan to springe.
And thus she sette hir woful herte afyre
Thorugh remembrance of that she gan desyre.

In al this world ther nis so cruel herte
That hir hadde herd compleynen in hir sorwe,
That nolde han wopen for hir peynes smerte,
So tendrely she weep, bothe eve and morwe.
Hir nedede no teres for to borwe.
And this was yet the worste of al hir peyne,
Ther was no wight to whom she dorste hir pleyne.

Ful rewfully she loked upon Troye,
Biheld the toures heighe and eek the halles;
Allas! quod she, the plesaunce and the joye
The whiche that now al torned into galle is,
Have I had ofte withinne yonder walles!
O Troilus, what dostow now, she seyde;
Lord! whether yet thou thenke upon Criseyde?

Allas! I ne hadde trowed on your lore,
And went with yow, as ye me radde er this!
Thanne hadde I now not syked half so sore.
Who mighte have seyd, that I had doon amis
To stele awey with swich on as he is?
But al to late cometh the letuarie,
Whan men the cors unto the grave carie.

To late is now to speke of this matere;
Prudence, allas! oon of thyn eyen three
Me lakked alwey, er that I cam here;
On tyme ypassed, wel remembred me;
And present tyme eek coude I wel ysee.
But futur tyme, er I was in the snare,
Coude I not seen; that causeth now my care.

But natheles, bityde what bityde,
I shal tomorwe at night, by est or weste,
Out of this ost stele on som maner syde,
And go with Troilus wheras him leste.
This purpos wol I holde, and this is beste.
No fors of wikked tonges janglerye,
For ever on love han wrecches had envye.

For whoso wole of every word take hede,
Or rewlen him by every wightes wit,
Ne shal he never thryven, out of drede.
For that that som men blamen ever yit,
Lo, other maner folk commenden it.
And as for me, for al swich variaunce,
Felicitee clepe I my suffisaunce.

For which, withouten any wordes mo,
To Troye I wol, as for conclusioun.
But God it wot, er fully monthes two,
She was ful fer fro that entencioun.
For bothe Troilus and Troye toun
Shal knotteles throughout hir herte slyde;
For she wol take a purpos for tabyde.

This Diomede, of whom yow telle I gan,
Goth now, withinne himself ay arguinge
With al the sleighte and al that ever he can,
How he may best, with shortest taryinge,
Into his net Criseydes herte bringe.
To this entente he coude never fyne;
To fisshen hir, he leyde out hook and lyne.

But natheles, wel in his herte he thoughte,
That she nas nat withoute a love in Troye.
For never, sithen he hir thennes broughte,
Ne coude he seen her laughe or make joye.
He niste how best hir herte for tacoye.
But for to assaye, he seyde, it nought ne
greveth;
For he that nought nassayeth, nought nacheveth.

Yet seide he to himself upon a night:
Now am I not a fool, that woot wel how
Hir wo for love is of another wight,
And hereupon to goon assaye hir now?
I may wel wite, it nil not been my prow.
For wyse folk in bokes it expresse:
Men shall not wowe a wight in hevinesse.

But whoso mighte winnen swich a flour
From him, for whom she morneth night and day,
He mighte seyn, he were a conquerour.
And right anoon, as he that bold was ay,
Thoughte in his herte: Happe, how happe may,
Al sholde I deye, I wole hir herte seche;
I shal no more lesen but my speche.

This Diomede, as bokes us declare,
Was in his nedes prest and corageous;
With sterne voys and mighty limes square,
Hardy, testif, strong, and chevalrous
Of dedes, lyk his fader Tideus.
And som men seyn, he was of tunge large;
And heir he was of Calidoine and Arge.

Criseyde mene was of hir stature,
Therto of shap, of face, and eek of chere,
Ther mighte been no fairer creature.
And ofte tyme this was hir manere,
To gon ytressed with hir heres clere
Doun by hir coler at hir bak bihinde,
Which with a threde of golde she wolde binde.

And, save hir browes joyneden yfere,
Ther nas no lak, in ought I can espyen;
But for to speken of hir eyen clere,
Lo, trewely, they writen that hir syen,
That Paradys stood formed in hir yën.
And with hir riche beautee evermore
Strof love in hir, ay which of hem was more.

She sobre was, eek simple, and wys withal,
The beste ynorisshed eek that mighte be,
And goodly of hir speche in general,
Charitable, estatliche, lusty, and free;
Ne nevermo ne lakkede hir pitee;
Tendre-herted, slydinge of corage;
But trewely, I can not telle hir age.

And Troilus wel waxen was in highte,
And complet formed by proporcioun
So wel, that kinde it not amenden mighte;
Yong, fresshe, strong, and hardy as lyoun;
Trewe as steel in ech condicioun;
On of the beste enteched creature,
That is, or shal, whyl that the world may dure.

And certainly in storie it is yfounde,
That Troilus was never unto no wight,
As in his tyme, in no degree secounde
In durring don that longeth to a knight.
Al mighte a geaunt passen him of might,
His herte ay with the firste and with the beste
Stod paregal, to durre don that him leste.

But for to tellen forth of Diomede:
It fil that after, on the tenthe day,
Sin that Criseyde out of the citee yede,
This Diomede, as fresshe as braunche in May,
Come to the tente theras Calkas lay,
And feyned him with Calkas han to done;
But what he mente, I shal yow telle sone.

Criseyde, at shorte wordes for to telle,
Welcomed him, and doun by hir him sette;
And he was ethe ynough to maken dwelle.
And after this, withouten longe lette,
The spyces and the wyn men forth hem fette;
And forth they speke of this and that yfere,
As freendes doon, of which som shal ye here.

He gan first fallen of the werre in speche
Bitwixe hem and the folk of Troye toun;
And of thassege he gan hir eek byseche,
To telle him what was hir opinioun.
fro that demaunde he so descendeth doun
To asken hir, if that hir straunge thoughte
The Grekes gyse, & werkes that they wroughte?

And why hir fader tarieth so longe
To wedden hir unto som worthy wight?
Criseyde, that was in hir peynes stronge
for love of Troilus, hir owene knight,
As ferforth as she conning hadde or might,
Answerde him tho; but, as of his entente,
It semed not she wiste what he mente.

But natheles, this ilke Diomede
Gan in himself assure, and thus he seyde:
If ich aright have taken of yow hede,
Me thinketh thus, O lady myn, Criseyde,
That sin I first bond on your brydel leyde,
Whan ye out come of Troye by the morwe,
Ne coude I never seen yow but in sorwe.

Can I not seyn what may the cause be
But if for love of som Troyan it were,
The which right sore wolde athinken me
That ye, for any wight that dwelleth there,
Sholden spille a quarter of a tere,
Or pitously yourselven so bigyle;
for dredelees, it is nought worth the whyle.

The folk of Troye, as who seyth, alle and some
In preson been, as ye yourselven see;
for thennes shal not oon onlyve come
for al the gold bitwixen sonne and see.
Trusteth wel, and understondeth me,
Ther shal not oon to mercy goon onlyve,
Al were he lord of worldes twyës fyve!

Swich wreche on hem, for fecching of Eleyne,
Ther shal be take, er that we hennes wende,
That Manes, which that goddes ben of peyne,
Shal been agast that Grekes wol hem shende.
And men shul drede, unto the worldes ende,
from hennesforth to ravisshe any quene,
So cruel shal our wreche on hem be sene.

And but if Calkas lede us with ambages,
That is to seyn, with double wordes slye,
Swich as men clepe a word with two visages,
Ye shul wel knowen that I nought ne lye,
And al this thing right seen it with your yë,
And that anoon; ye nil not trowe how sone;
Now taketh heed, for it is for to done.

What wene ye your wyse fader wolde
Han yeven Antenor for yow anoon,
If he ne wiste that the citee sholde
Destroyed been? Why, nay, so mote I goon!
He knew ful wel ther shal not scapen oon
That Troyan is; and for the grete fere,
He dorste not, ye dwelte lenger there.

What wole ye more, lufsom lady dere?
Lat Troye and Troyan fro your herte pace!
Dryf out that bittre hope, and make good chere,
And clepe ayein the beautee of your face,
That ye with salte teres so deface.
for Troye is brought in swich a jupartye,
That, it to save, is now no remedye.

And thenketh wel, ye shal in Grekes finde
A more parfit love, er it be night,
Than any Troyan is, and more kinde,
And bet to serven yow wol doon his might.
And if ye vouche sauf, my lady bright,
I wol ben he to serven yow myselve,
Ye, lever than be lord of Greces twelve!

And with that word he gan to waxen reed,
And in his speche a litel wight he quook,
And caste asyde a litel wight his heed,
And stinte a whyle; and afterward awook,
And sobreliche on hir he threw his look,
And seyde: I am, al be it yow no joye,
As gentil man as any wight in Troye.

for if my fader Tydeus, he seyde,
Ylived hadde, I hadde been, er this,
Of Calidoine and Arge a king, Criseyde!
And so hope I that I shal yet, ywis.
But he was slayn, allas! the more harm is,
Unhappily at Thebes al to rathe,
Polymites and many a man to scathe.

But herte myn, sin that I am your man,
And been the ferste of whom I seche grace,
To serven you as hertely as I can,
And ever shal, whyl I to live have space,
So, er that I departe out of this place,
Ye wol me graunte, that I may tomorwe,
At bettre leyser, telle yow my sorwe.

What shold I telle his wordes that he seyde?
He spak ynow, for o day at the meste;
It preveth wel, he spak so that Criseyde
Graunted, on the morwe, at his requeste,
for to speken with him at the leste,
So that he nolde speke of swich matere;
And thus to him she seyde, as ye may here:

As she that hadde hir herte on Troilus
So faste, that ther may it noon arace;
And straungely she spak, and seyde thus:
O Diomede, I love that ilke place
Ther I was born; and Joves, for his grace,
Delivere it sone of al that doth it care!
God, for thy might, so leve it wel to fare!

That Grekes wolde hir wraththe on Troye wreke,
If that they mighte, I knowe it wel, ywis.
But it shal not bifallen as ye speke;
And God toforn, and ferther over this,
I wot my fader wys and redy is;
And that he me hath bought, as ye me tolde,
So dere, I am the more unto him holde.

That Grekes been of heigh condicioun,
I woot eek wel; but certein, men shal finde
As worthy folk withinne Troye toun,
As conning, and as parfit and as kinde,
As been bitwixen Orcades and Inde.
And that ye coude wel your lady serve,
I trowe eek wel, hir thank for to deserve.

But as to speke of love, ywis, she seyde,
I hadde a lord, to whom I wedded was,
The whos myn herte al was, til that he deyde;
And other love, as helpe me now Pallas,
Ther in myn herte nis, ne never was.
And that ye been of noble and heigh kinrede,
I have wel herd it tellen, out of drede.

And that doth me to han so gret a wonder,
That ye wol scornen any womman so.
Eek, God wot, love and I be fer asonder;
I am disposed bet, so mote I go,
Unto my deeth, to pleyne and maken wo.
What I shal after doon, I can not seye;
But trewely, as yet me list not pleye.

Myn herte is now in tribulacioun,
And ye in armes bisy, day by day.
Hereafter, whan ye wonnen han the toun,
Paraunter, thanne so it happen may,
That whan I see that I never er say,
Than wole I werke that I never wroughte!
This word to yow ynough suffysen oughte.

Tomorwe eek wol I speke with yow fayn,
So that ye touchen nought of this matere.
And whan yow list, ye may come here ayeyn;
And, er ye gon, thus muche I seye yow here:
As helpe me Pallas with hir heres clere,
If that I sholde of any Greek han routhe,
It sholde be yourselven, by my trouthe!

I sey not therfore that I wol yow love,
Ne I sey not nay, but in conclusioun,
I mene wel, by God that sit above:
And therwithal she caste hir eyen doun,
And gan to syke, and seyde: O Troye toun,
Yet bidde I God, in quiete and in reste
I may yow seen, or do myn herte breste.

But in effect, and shortly for to seye,
This Diomede al freshly newe ayeyn
Gan pressen on, and faste hir mercy preye;
And after this, the sothe for to seyn,
Hir glove he took, of which he was ful fayn.
And fynally, whan it was waxen eve,
And al was wel, he roos and took his leve.

The brighte Venus folwede and ay taughte
The wey, ther brode Phebus doun alighte;
And Cynthea hir char-hors overraughte
To whirle out of the Lyon, if she mighte;
And Signifer his candeles shewed brighte,
Whan that Criseyde unto hir bedde wente
Inwith hir fadres faire brighte tente.

n n 1

Retorning in hir soule ay up and doun
The wordes of this sodein Diomede,
His greet estat, and peril of the toun,
And that she was allone and hadde nede
Of freendes help; and thus bigan to brede
The cause why, the sothe for to telle,
That she tok fully purpos for to dwelle.

The morwe com, and goostly for to speke,
This Diomede is come unto Criseyde,
And shortly, lest that ye my tale breke,
So wel he for himselve spak and seyde,
That alle hir sykes sore adoun he leyde.
And fynally, the sothe for to seyne,
He refte hir of the grete of al hir peyne.

And after this the story telleth us,
That she him yaf the faire baye stede,
The which she ones wan of Troilus;
And eek a broche, and that was litel nede,
That Troilus was, she yaf this Diomede.
And eek, the bet from sorwe him to releve,
She made him were a pencel of hir sleve.

I finde eek in the stories elleswhere,
Whan through the body hurt was Diomede
Of Troilus, tho weep she many a tere,
Whan that she saugh his wyde woundes blede;
And that she took to kepen him good hede,
And for to hele him of his sorwes smerte.
Men seyn, I not, that she yaf him hir herte.

But trewely, the story telleth us,
Ther made never womman more wo
Than she, whan that she falsed Troilus.
She seyde: Allas! for now is clene ago
My name of trouthe in love, for evermo!
For I have falsed oon, the gentileste
That ever was, and oon the worthieste!

Allas, of me, unto the worldes ende,
Shal neither been ywriten nor ysonge
No good word, for thise bokes wol me shende.
O, rolled shal I been on many a tonge;
Throughout the world my belle shal be ronge;
And wommen most wol hate me of alle.
Allas, that swich a cas me sholde falle!

They wol seyn, in as muche as in me is,
I have hem don dishonour, weylawey!
Al be I not the firste that dide amis,
What helpeth that to do my blame awey?
But sin I see there is no bettre way,
And that to late is now for me to rewe,
To Diomede algate I wol be trewe.

But Troilus, sin I no better may,
And sin that thus departen ye and I,
Yet preye I God, so yeve yow right good day
As for the gentileste, trewely,
That ever I say, to serven feithfully,
And best can ay his lady honour kepe:
And with that word she brast anon to wepe.

545

And certes, yow ne haten shal I never,
And freendes love, that shal ye han of me,
And my good word, al mighte I liven ever.
And, trewely, I wolde sory be
For to seen yow in any adversitee.
And giltelees, I woot wel, I yow leve;
But al shal passe; and thus take I my leve.

But trewely, how longe it was bitwene,
That she forsook him for this Diomede,
Ther is non auctor telleth it, I wene.
Take every man now to his bokes hede;
He shal no terme finden, out of drede.
For though that he bigan to wowe hir sone,
Er he hir wan, yet was ther more to done.

Ne me ne list this sely womman chyde
Ferther than the story wol devyse.
Hir name, allas! is publisshed so wyde,
That for hir gilt it oughte ynow suffyse.
And if I mighte excuse hir any wyse,
For she so sory was for hir untrouthe,
Ywis, I wolde excuse hir yet for routhe.

This Troilus, as I biforn have told,
Thus dryveth forth, as wel as he hath might.
But often was his herte hoot and cold,
And namely, that ilke nynthe night,
Which on the morwe she hadde him byhight
To come ayein: God wot, ful litel reste
Hadde he that night; nothing to slepe him leste.

The laurer-crouned Phebus, with his hete,
Gan, in his course ay upward as he wente,
To warmen of the est see the wawes wete;
And Nisus doughter song with fresh entente,
Whan Troilus his Pandare after sente;
And on the walles of the toun they pleyde,
To loke if they can seen ought of Criseyde.

Til it was noon, they stoden for to see
Who that ther come; and every maner wight,
That cam fro fer, they seyden it was she,
Til that they coude knowen him aright.
Now was his herte dul, now was it light;
And thus byjaped stonden for to stare
Aboute nought, this Troilus and Pandare.

To Pandarus this Troilus tho seyde:
For ought I wot, bifor noon, sikerly,
Into this toun ne comth nought here Criseyde.
She hath ynow to done, hardily,
To winnen from hir fader, so trowe I;
Hir olde fader wol yet make hir dyne
Er that she go; God yeve his herte pyne!

Pandare answerde: It may wel be, certeyn;
And forthy lat us dyne, I thee biseche;
And after noon than mayst thou come ayeyn.
And hoom they go, withoute more speche;
And comen ayein, but longe may they seche
Er that they finde that they after cape;
Fortune hem bothe thenketh for to jape.

546

Quod Troilus: I see wel now, that she
Is taried with hir olde fader so,
That er she come, it wol neigh even be.
Com forth, I wol unto the yate go.
Thise portours been unkonninge evermo;
And I wol doon hem holden up the yate
As nought ne were, although she come late.

The day goth faste, and after that comth eve,
And yet com nought to Troilus Criseyde.
He loketh forth by hegge, by tree, by greve,
And fer his heed over the wal he leyde.
And at the laste he torned him, and seyde:
By God, I woot hir mening now, Pandare!
Almost, ywis, al newe was my care.

Now douteles, this lady can hir good;
I woot, she meneth ryden prively.
I comende hir wysdom, by myn hood!
She wol not maken peple nycely
Gaure on hir, whan she comth; but softely
By nighte into the toun she thenketh ryde.
And, dere brother, thenk not longe to abyde.

We han nought elles for to don, ywis.
And Pandarus, now woltow trowen me?
Have here my trouthe, I see hir! yond she is.
Heve up thyn eyen, man! maystow not see?
Pandare answerde: Nay, so mote I thee!
Al wrong, by God; what seystow, man, wher art?
That I see yond nis but a fare-cart.

Allas, thou seist right sooth, quod Troilus;
But hardely, it is not al for nought
That in myn herte I now rejoyse thus.
It is ayein som good I have a thought.
Noot I not how, but sin that I was wrought,
Ne felte I swich a confort, dar I seye;
She comth tonight, my lyf, that dorste I leye!

Pandare answerde: It may be wel, ynough;
And held with him of al that ever he seyde;
But in his herte he thoughte, and softe lough,
And to himself ful sobrely he seyde:
From hasel-wode, ther joly Robin pleyde,
Shal come al that that thou abydest here;
Ye, farewel al the snow of ferne yere!

The wardein of the yates gan to calle
The folk which that withoute the yates were,
And bad hem dryven in hir bestes alle,
Or al the night they moste bleven there.
And fer within the night, with many a tere,
This Troilus gan hoomward for to ryde;
For wel he seeth it helpeth nought tabyde.

But natheles, he gladded him in this;
He thoughte he misacounted hadde his day,
And seyde: I understonde have al amis.
For thilke night I last Criseyde say,
She seyde: I shal ben here, if that I may,
Er that the mone, O dere herte swete!
The Lyon passe, out of this Ariete.

for which she may yet holde al hir biheste.
⌇And on the morwe unto the yate he wente,
And up and down, by west and eek by este,
Upon the walles made he many a wente.
But al for nought; his hope alwey him blente;
For which at night, in sorwe and sykes sore
He wente him hoom, withouten any more.

This hope al clene out of his herte fledde,
He nath wheron now lenger for to honge;
But for the peyne him thoughte his herte bledde,
So were his throwes sharpe and wonder stronge.
For when he saugh that she abood so longe,
He niste what he juggen of it mighte,
Sin she hath broken that she him bihighte.

The thridde, ferthe, fifte, sixte day
After tho dayes ten, of which I tolde,
Bitwixen hope and drede his herte lay,
Yet somwhat trustinge on hir hestes olde.
But whan he saugh she nolde hir terme holde,
He can now seen non other remedye,
But for to shape him sone for to dye.

Therwith the wikked spirit, God us blesse,
Which that men clepeth wode jalousye,
Gan in him crepe, in al this hevinesse;
For which, bycause he wolde sone dye,
He ne eet ne dronk, for his malencolye,
And eek from every companye he fledde;
This was the lyf that al the tyme he ledde.

He so defet was, that no maner man
Unnethe mighte him knowe ther he wente;
So was he lene, and therto pale and wan,
And feble, that he walketh by potente;
And with his ire he thus himselven shente.
And whoso axed him wherof him smerte,
He seyde, his harm was al aboute his herte.

Pryam ful ofte, and eek his moder dere,
His bretheren and his sustren gonne him freyne
Why he so sorwful was in al his chere,
And what thing was the cause of al his peyne?
But al for nought; he nolde his cause pleyne,
But seyde, he felte a grevous maladye
Aboute his herte, and fayn he wolde dye.

So on a day he leyde him doun to slepe,
And so bifel that in his sleep him thoughte,
That in a forest faste he welk to wepe
For love of hir that him thise peynes wroughte;
And up and doun as he the forest soughte,
He mette he saugh a boor with tuskes grete,
That sleep ayein the brighte sonnes hete.

And by this boor, faste in his armes folde,
Lay kissing ay his lady bright Criseyde:
For sorwe of which, whan he it gan biholde,
And for despyt, out of his sleep he breyde,
And loude he cryde on Pandarus, and seyde:
O Pandarus, now knowe I crop and rote!
I nam but deed, ther nis non other bote!

nn2

My lady bright Criseyde hath me bitrayed,
In whom I trusted most of any wight,
She elleswhere hath now hir herte apayed;
The blisful goddes, through hir grete might,
Han in my dreem yshewed it ful right.
Thus in my dreem Criseyde I have biholde.
⌇And al this thing to Pandarus he tolde.

⌇O my Criseyde, allas! what subtiltee,
What newe lust, what beautee, what science,
What wratthe of juste cause have ye to me?
What gilt of me, what fel experience
Hath fro me raft, allas! thyn advertence?
O trust, O feyth, O depe asëuraunce,
Who hath me reft Criseyde, al my plesaunce?

Allas! why leet I you from hennes go,
For which wel neigh out of my wit I breyde?
Who shal now trowe on any othes mo?
God wot I wende, O lady bright, Criseyde,
That every word was gospel that ye seyde!
But who may bet bigylen, if him liste,
Than he on whom men weneth best to triste?

What shal I doon, my Pandarus, allas!
I fele now so sharpe a newe peyne,
Sin that ther is no remedie in this cas,
That bet were it I with myn hondes tweyne
Myselven slow, than alwey thus to pleyne.
For through my deeth my wo sholde han an ende,
Ther every day with lyf myself I shende.

⌇Pandare answerde and seyde: Allas the whyle
That I was born; have I not seyd er this,
That dremes many a maner man bigyle?
And why? for folk expounden hem amis.
How darstow seyn that fals thy lady is,
For any dreem, right for thyn owene drede?
Lat be this thought, thou canst no dremes rede.

Paraunter, ther thou dremest of this boor,
It may so be that it may signifye
Hir fader, which that old is and eek hoor,
Ayein the sonne lyth, on poynt to dye,
And she for sorwe ginneth wepe and crye,
And kisseth him, ther he lyth on the grounde;
Thus shuldestow thy dreem aright expounde.

⌇How mighte I thanne do? quod Troilus,
To knowe of this, ye, were it never so lyte?
⌇Now seystow wysly, quod this Pandarus,
My reed is this, sin thou canst wel endyte,
That hastely a lettre thou hir wryte,
Thorugh which thou shalt wel bringen it aboute,
To knowe a sooth of that thou art in doute.

And see now why; for this I dar wel seyn,
That if so is that she untrewe be,
I can not trowe that she wol wryte ayeyn.
And if she wryte, thou shalt ful sone see,
As whether she hath any libertee
To come ayein, or elles in som clause,
If she be let, she wol assigne a cause.

Thou hast not writen hir sin that she wente,
Nor she to thee, and this I dorste leye,
Ther may swich cause been in hir entente,
That hardely thou wolt thyselven seye,
That hir abood the beste is for yow tweye.
Now wryte hir thanne, and thou shalt fele sone
A sothe of al; ther is no more to done.

Acorded been to this conclusioun,
And that anoon, thise ilke lordes two;
And hastely sit Troilus adoun,
And rolleth in his herte to and fro,
How he may best discryven hir his wo.
And to Criseyde, his owene lady dere,
He wroot right thus, and seyde as ye may here.

Right fresshe flour, whos I have been and shal,
Withouten part of elleswhere servyse,
With herte, body, lyf, lust, thought, and al;
I, woful wight, in every humble wyse
That tonge telle or herte may devyse,
As ofte as matere occupyeth place,
Me recomaunde unto your noble grace.

Lyketh it yow to witen, swete herte,
As ye wel knowe how longe tyme agoon
That ye me lafte in aspre peynes smerte,
Whan that ye wente, of which yet bote noon
Have I non had, but ever wers bigoon
Fro day to day am I, and so mot dwelle,
While it yow list, of wele and wo my welle!

For which to yow, with dredful herte trewe,
I wryte, as he that sorwe dryfth to wryte,
My wo, that every houre encreseth newe,
Compleyninge as I dar or can endyte,
And that defaced is, that may ye wyte
The teres, which that fro myn eyen reyne,
That wolde speke, if that they coude, and pleyne.

Yow first biseche I, that your eyen clere
To look on this defouled ye not holde;
And over al this, that ye, my lady dere,
Wol vouchesauf this lettre to biholde.
And by the cause eek of my cares colde,
That sleeth my wit, if ought amis me asterte,
Foryeve it me, myn owene swete herte.

If any servant dorste or oughte of right
Upon his lady pitously compleyne,
Than wene I, that ich oughte be that wight,
Considered this, that ye these monthes tweyne
Han taried, ther ye seyden, sooth to seyne,
But dayes ten ye nolde in ost sojourne,
But in two monthes yet ye not retourne.

But forasmuche as me mot nedes lyke
Al that yow list, I dar not pleyne more,
But humbely with sorwful sykes syke;
Yow wryte ich myn unresty sorwes sore,
Fro day to day desyring evermore
To knowen fully, if your wil it were,
How ye han ferd and doon, whyl ye be there.

548

The whos welfare and hele eek God encresse
In honour swich, that upward in degree
It growe alwey, so that it never cesse;
Right as your herte ay can, my lady free,
Devyse, I prey to God so mote it be.
And graunte it that ye sone upon me rewe
As wisly as in al I am yow trewe.

And if yow lyketh knowen of the fare
Of me, whos wo ther may no wight discryve,
I can no more but, cheste of every care,
At wrytinge of this lettre I was onlyve,
Al redy out my woful gost to dryve;
Which I delaye, and holde him yet in honde,
Upon the sight of matere of your sonde.

Myn eyen two, in veyn with which I see,
Of sorweful teres salte arn waxen welles;
My song, in pleynte of myn adversitee;
My good, in harm; myn ese eek waxen helle is.
My joye, in wo; I can sey yow nought elles,
But turned is, for which my lyf I warie,
Everich joye or ese in his contrarie.

Which with your cominge hoom ayein to Troye
Ye may redresse, and, more a thousand sythe
Than ever ich hadde, encressen in me joye.
For was ther never herte yet so blythe
To han his lyf, as I shal been as swythe
As I yow see; and, though no maner routhe
Commeve yow, yet thinketh on your trouthe.

And if so be my gilt hath deeth deserved,
Or if you list no more upon me see,
In guerdon yet of that I have you served,
Biseche I yow, myn hertes lady free,
That hereupon ye wolden wryte me,
For love of God, my righte lode-sterre,
Ther deeth may make an ende of al my werre.

If other cause aught doth yow for to dwelle,
That with your lettre ye me recomforte;
For though to me your absence is an helle,
With pacience I wol my wo comporte.
And with your lettre of hope I wol desporte.
Now wryteth, swete, and lat me thus not pleyne;
With hope, or deeth, delivereth me fro peyne.

Ywis, myn owene dere herte trewe,
I woot that, whan ye next upon me see,
So lost have I myn hele and eek myn hewe,
Criseyde shal nought conne knowe me!
Ywis, myn hertes day, my lady free,
So thursteth ay myn herte to biholde
Your beautee, that my lyf unnethe I holde.

I sey no more, al have I for to seye
To you wel more than I telle may;
But whether that ye do me live or deye,
Yet pray I God, so yeve yow right good day.
And fareth wel, goodly fayre fresshe may,
As ye that lyf or deeth me may comaunde;
And to your trouthe ay I me recomaunde

With hele swich that, but ye yeven me
The same hele, I shal noon hele have.
In you lyth, whan yow list that it so be,
The day in which me clothen shal my grave.
In yow my lyf, in yow might for to save
Me from disese of alle peynes smerte;
And fare now wel, myn owene swete herte!
Le vostre T.

This lettre forth was sent unto Criseyde,
Of which hir answere in effect was this;
Ful pitously she wroot ayein, and seyde,
That also sone as that she might, ywis,
She wolde come, and mende al that was mis.
And fynally she wroot and seyde him thanne,
She wolde come, ye, but she niste whanne.

But in hir lettre made she swich festes,
That wonder was, & swereth she loveth him best,
Of which he fond but botmelees bihestes.
But Troilus, thou mayst now, est or west,
Pype in an ivy leef, if that thee lest;
Thus gooth the world; God shilde us fro
mischaunce,
And every wight that meneth trouthe avaunce!

Encresen gan the wo fro day to night
Of Troilus, for taryinge of Criseyde;
And lessen gan his hope and eek his might,
For which al doun he in his bed him leyde;
He ne eet, ne dronk, ne sleep, ne word he seyde,
Imagininge ay that she was unkinde;
For which wel neigh he wex out of his minde.

This dreem, of which I told have eek biforn,
May never come out of his remembraunce;
He thoughte ay wel he hadde his lady lorn,
And that Joves, of his purveyaunce,
Him shewed hadde in sleep the signifiaunce
Of hir untrouthe and his disaventure,
And that the boor was shewed him in figure.

For which he for Sibille his suster sente,
That called was Cassandre eek al aboute;
And al his dreem he tolde hir er he stente,
And hir bisoughte assoilen him the doute
Of the stronge boor, with tuskes stoute;
And fynally, withinne a litel stounde,
Cassandre him gan right thus his dreem
expounde.

She gan first smyle, and seyde: O brother dere,
If thou a sooth of this desyrest knowe,
Thou most a fewe of olde stories here,
To purpos, how that Fortune overthrowe
Hath lordes olde; through which, withinne a
throwe,
Thou wel this boor shalt knowe, & of what kinde
He comen is, as men in bokes finde.

Diane, which that wrooth was and in ire
For Grekes nolde doon hir sacrifyse,
Ne encens upon hir auter sette afyre,
nn3

She, for that Grekes gonne hir so dispyse,
Wrak hir in a wonder cruel wyse.
For with a boor as greet as oxe in stalle
She made up frete hir corn and vynes alle.

To slee this boor was al the contree reysed,
Amonges which ther com, this boor to see,
A mayde, oon of this world the best ypreysed;
And Meleagre, lord of that contree,
He lovede so this fresshe mayden free
That with his manhood, er he wolde stente,
This boor he slow, and hir the heed he sente;

Of which, as olde bokes tellen us,
Ther roos a contek and a greet envye;
And of this lord descended Tydeus
By ligne, or elles olde bokes lye;
But how this Meleagre gan to dye
Thorugh his moder, wol I yow not telle,
For al to long it were for to dwelle.

Argument of the 12 Books of Statius' Thebais.
Associat profugum Tideo primus Polimitem;
Tidea legatum docet insidiasque secundus;
Tercius Hemoniden canit et vates latitantes;
Quartus habet reges ineuntes prelia septem;
Mox furie Lenne quinto narratur et anguis;
Archimori bustum sexto ludique leguntur;
Dat Graios Thebes et vatem septimus umbris;
Octavo cecidit Tideus, spes, vita Pelasgis;
Ypomedon nono moritur cum Parthonopeo;
Fulmine percussus, decimo Capaneus superatur;
Undecimo sese perimunt per vulnera fratres;
Argivam flentem narrat duodenus et ignem.

She tolde eek how Tydeus, er she stente,
Unto the stronge citee of Thebes,
To cleyme kingdom of the citee, wente,
For his felawe, daun Polymites,
Of which the brother, daun Ethyocles,
Ful wrongfully of Thebes helde the strengthe;
This tolde she by proces, al by lengthe.

She tolde eek how Hemonides asterte,
Whan Tydeus slough fifty knightes stoute.
She tolde eek al the prophesyes by herte,
And how that sevene kinges, with hir route,
Bisegeden the citee al aboute;
And of the holy serpent, and the welle,
And of the furies, al she gan him telle.

Of Archimoris buryinge and the pleyes,
And how Amphiorax fil through the grounde,
How Tydeus was slayn, lord of Argeyes,
And how Ypomedoun in litel stounde
Was dreynt, and deed Parthonope of wounde;
And also how Cappaneus the proude
With thonder-dint was slayn, that cryde loude.

She gan eek telle him how that either brother,
Ethyocles and Polimyte also,
At a scarmyche, eche of hem slough other,
And of Argyves wepinge and hir wo;
549

And how the town was brent she tolde eek tho.
And so descendeth doun from gestes olde
To Diomede, and thus she spak and tolde.

This ilke boor bitokneth Diomede,
Tydeus sone, that doun descended is
fro Meleagre, that made the boor to blede.
And thy lady, wherso she be, ywis,
This Diomede hir herte hath, and she his.
Weep if thou wolt, or leef; for out of doute,
This Diomede is inne, and thou art oute.

Thou seyst nat sooth, quod he, thou
sorceresse,
With al thy false goost of prophesye!
Thou wenest been a greet devyneresse;
Now seestow not this fool of fantasye
Peyneth hir on ladyes for to lye?
Awey, quod he, ther Joves yeve thee sorwe!
Thou shalt be fals, paraunter, yet tomorwe!

As wel thou mightest lyen on Alceste,
That was of creatures, but men lye,
That ever weren, kindest and the beste.
for whanne hir housbonde was in jupartye
To dye himself, but if she wolde dye,
She chees for him to dye and go to helle,
And starf anoon, as us the bokes telle.

Cassandre goth, and he with cruel herte
foryat his wo, for angre of hir speche;
And from his bed al sodeinly he sterte,
As though al hool him hadde ymad a leche.
And day by day he gan enquere and seche
A sooth of this, with al his fulle cure;
And thus he dryeth forth his aventure.

fortune, whiche that permutacioun
Of thinges hath, as it is hir committed
Through purveyaunce and disposicioun
Of heighe Jove, as regnes shal ben flitted
fro folk in folk, or whan they shal ben smitted,
Gan pulle awey the fetheres brighte of Troye
fro day to day, til they ben bare of joye.

Among al this, the fyn of the parodie
Of Ector gan approchen wonder blyve;
The fate wolde his soule sholde unbodie,
And shapen hadde a mene it out to dryve;
Ayeins which fate him helpeth not to stryve;
But on a day to fighten gan he wende,
At which, allas! he caughte his lyves ende.

for which me thinketh every maner wight
That haunteth armes oughte to biwayle
The deeth of him that was so noble a knight;
for as he drough a king by thaventayle,
Unwar of this, Achilles through the mayle
And through the body gan him for to ryve;
And thus this worthy knight was brought of lyve.

for whom, as olde bokes tellen us,
Was mad swich wo, that tonge it may not telle;

And namely, the sorwe of Troilus,
That next him was of worthinesse welle.
And in this wo gan Troilus to dwelle,
That, what for sorwe, and love, and for
unreste,
ful ofte a day he bad his herte breste.

But natheles, though he gan him dispeyre,
And dradde ay that his lady was untrewe,
Yet ay on hir his herte gan repeyre.
And as these loveres doon, he soughte ay newe
To gete ayein Criseyde, bright of hewe.
And in his herte he wente hir excusinge,
That Calkas causede al hir taryinge.

And ofte tyme he was in purpos grete
Himselven lyk a pilgrim to disgyse,
To seen hir; but he may not contrefete
To been unknowen of folk that weren wyse,
Ne finde excuse aright that may suffyse,
If he among the Grekes knowen were;
for which he weep ful ofte many a tere.

To hir he wroot yet ofte tyme al newe
ful pitously, he lefte it nought for slouthe,
Biseching hir that, sin that he was trewe,
She wolde come ayein and holde hir trouthe.
for which Criseyde upon a day, for routhe,
I take it so, touchinge al this matere,
Wrot him ayein, and seyde as ye may here.

Cupydes sone, ensample of goodlihede,
O swerd of knighthod, sours of gentilesse!
How mighte a wight in torment and in drede
And helelees, yow sende as yet gladnesse?
I hertelees, I syke, I in distresse;
Sin ye with me, nor I with yow may dele,
Yow neither sende ich herte may nor hele.

Your lettres ful, the papir al ypleynted,
Conseyved hath myn hertes piëtee;
I have eek seyn with teres al depeynted
Your lettre, and how that ye requeren me
To come ayein, which yet ne may not be.
But why, lest that this lettre founden were,
No mencioun ne make I now, for fere.

Grevous to me, God woot, is your unreste,
Your haste, and that, the goddes ordenaunce,
It semeth not ye take it for the beste.
Nor other thing nis in your remembraunce,
As thinketh me, but only your plesaunce.
But beth not wrooth, and that I yow biseche;
for that I tarie, is al for wikked speche.

for I have herd wel more than I wende,
Touchinge us two, how thinges han ystonde;
Which I shal with dissimulinge amende.
And beth nought wrooth, I have eek un-
derstonde,
How ye ne doon but holden me in honde.
But now no fors, I can not in yow gesse
But alle trouthe and alle gentilesse.

Comen I wol, but yet in swich disjoynte
I stonde as now, that what yeer or what day
That this shal be, that can I not apoynte.
But in effect, I prey yow, as I may,
Of your good word and of your frendship ay.
for trewely, whyl that my lyf may dure,
As for a freend, ye may in me assure.

Yet preye I yow on yvel ye ne take,
That it is short which that I to yow wryte;
I dar not, ther I am, wel lettres make,
Ne never yet ne coude I wel endyte.
Eek greet effect men wryte in place lyte.
Thentente is al, and nought the lettres space;
And fareth now wel, God have you in his grace!
La vostre C.

This Troilus this lettre thoughte al straunge,
Whan he it saugh, and sorwefully he sighte;
Him thoughte it lyk a kalendes of chaunge;
But fynally, he ful ne trowen mighte
That she ne wolde him holden that she highte;
for with ful yvel wil list him to leve
That loveth wel, in swich cas, though him greve.

But natheles, men seyn that, at the laste,
for any thing, men shal the sothe see;
And swich a cas bitidde, and that as faste,
That Troilus wel understood that she
Nas not so kinde as that hir oughte be.
And fynally, he woot now, out of doute,
That al is lost that he hath been aboute.

Stood on a day in his malencolye
This Troilus, and in suspecioun
Of hir for whom he wende for to dye.
And so bifel, that throughout Troye toun,
As was the gyse, ybore was up and doun
A maner cote-armure, as seyth the storie,
Biforn Deiphebe, in signe of his victorie,

The whiche cote, as telleth Lollius,
Deiphebe it hadde yrent from Diomede
The same day; and whan this Troilus
It saugh, he gan to taken of it hede,
Avysing of the lengthe and of the brede,
And al the werk; but as he gan biholde,
ful sodeinly his herte gan to colde,

As he that on the coler fond withinne
A broche, that he Criseyde yaf that morwe
That she from Troye moste nedes twinne,
In remembraunce of him and of his sorwe;
And she him leyde ayein hir feyth to borwe
To kepe it ay; but now, ful wel he wiste,
His lady nas no lenger on to triste.

He gooth him hoom, and gan ful sone sende
for Pandarus; and al this newe chaunce,
And of this broche, he tolde him word and ende,
Compleyninge of hir hertes variaunce,
His longe love, his trouthe, and his penaunce;
And after deeth, withouten wordes more,
ful faste he cryde, his reste him to restore.

Than spak he thus: O lady myn Criseyde,
Wher is your feyth, and wher is your biheste?
Wher is your love, wher is your trouthe, he seyde;
Of Diomede have ye now al this feste!
Allas, I wolde have trowed at the leste,
That, sin ye nolde in trouthe to me stonde,
That ye thus nolde han holden me in honde!

Who shal now trowe on any othes mo?
Allas, I never wolde han wend, er this,
That ye, Criseyde, coude han chaunged so;
Ne, but I hadde agilt and doon amis,
So cruel wende I not your herte, ywis,
To slee me thus; allas, your name of trouthe
Is now fordoon, and that is al my routhe.

Was ther non other broche yow liste lete
To feffe with your newe love, quod he,
But thilke broche that I, with teres wete,
Yow yaf, as for a remembraunce of me?
Non other cause, allas, ne hadde ye
But for despyt, and eek for that ye mente
Aloutrely to shewen your entente!

Through which I see that clene out of your minde
Ye han me cast, and I ne can nor may,
for al this world, within myn herte finde
To unloven yow a quarter of a day!
In cursed tyme I born was, weylaway!
That ye, that doon me al this wo endure,
Yet love I best of any creature.

Now God, quod he, me sende yet the grace
That I may meten with this Diomede!
And trewely, if I have might and space,
Yet shal I make, I hope, his sydes blede.
O God, quod he, that oughtest taken hede
To fortheren trouthe, and wronges to punyce,
Why niltow doon a vengeaunce on this vyce?

O Pandare, that in dremes for to triste
Me blamed hast, and wont art ofte upbreyde,
Now maystow see thyselve, if that thee liste,
How trewe is now thy nece, bright Criseyde!
In sondry formes, God it woot, he seyde,
The goddes shewen bothe joye and tene
In slepe, and by my dreme it is now sene.

And certaynly, withoute more speche,
from hennesforth, as ferforth as I may,
Myn owene deeth in armes wol I seche;
I recche not how sone be the day!
But trewely, Criseyde, swete may,
Whom I have ay with al my might yserved,
That ye thus doon, I have it nought deserved.

This Pandarus, that alle thise thinges herde,
And wiste wel he seyde a sooth of this,
He nought a word ayein to him answerde;
for sory of his frendes sorwe he is,
And shamed, for his nece hath doon amis;
And stant, astoned of thise causes tweye,
As stille as stoon; a word ne coude he seye.

But at the laste thus he spak, and seyde:
My brother dere, I may thee do no more.
What shulde I seyn? I hate, ywis, Criseyde!
And God wot, I wol hate hir evermore!
And that thou me bisoughtest doon of yore,
Havinge unto myn honour ne my reste
Right no reward, I dide al that thee leste.

If I dide ought that mighte lyken thee,
It is me leef; and of this treson now,
God woot, that it a sorwe is unto me!
And dredelees, for hertes ese of yow,
Right fayn wolde I amende it, wiste I how.
And fro this world, almighty God I preye,
Delivere hir sone; I can no more seye.

Gret was the sorwe and pleynt of Troilus;
But forth hir cours fortune ay gan to holde.
Criseyde loveth the sone of Tydeus,
And Troilus mot wepe in cares colde.
Swich is this world; whoso it can biholde,
In eche estat is litel hertes reste;
God leve us for to take it for the beste!

In many cruel batayle, out of drede,
Of Troilus, this ilke noble knight,
As men may in thise olde bokes rede,
Was sene his knighthod and his grete might.
And dredelees, his ire, day and night,
Ful cruelly the Grekes ay aboughte;
And alwey most this Diomede he soughte.

And ofte tyme, I finde that they mette
With blody strokes and with wordes grete,
Assayinge how hir speres weren whette;
And God it woot, with many a cruel hete
Gan Troilus upon his helm to bete.
But natheles, fortune it nought ne wolde,
Of otheres hond that either deyen sholde.

And if I hadde ytaken for to wryte
The armes of this ilke worthy man,
Than wolde I of his batailles endyte.
But for that I to wryte first bigan
Of his love, I have seyd as that I can.
His worthy dedes, whoso list hem here,
Reed Dares, he can telle hem alle yfere.

Bisechinge every lady bright of hewe,
And every gentil womman, what she be,
That al be that Criseyde was untrewe,
That for that gilt she be not wrooth with me.
Ye may hir gilt in othere bokes see;
And gladlier I wol wryten, if yow leste,
Penelopeës trouthe and good Alceste.

Ne I sey not this alonly for thise men,
But most for wommen that bitraysed be
Through false folk; God yeve hem sorwe, amen!
That with hir grete wit and subtiltee
Bitrayse yow! and this commeveth me
To speke, and in effect yow alle I preye,
Beth war of men, and herkeneth what I seye!

552

Go, litel book, go litel myn tregedie,
Ther God thy maker yet, er that he dye,
So sende might to maken som comedie!
But litel book, no making thou nenvye,
But subgit be to alle poesye;
And kis the steppes, wheras thou seest pace
Virgile, Ovyde, Omer, Lucan, and Stace.

And for ther is so greet diversitee
In English and in wryting of our tonge,
So preye I God that noon miswryte thee,
Ne thee mismetre for defaute of tonge.
And red wherso thou be, or elles songe,
That thou be understonde I God beseche!
But yet to purpos of my rather speche.

The wraththe, as I began yow for to seye,
Of Troilus, the Grekes boughten dere;
For thousandes his hondes maden deye,
As he that was withouten any pere,
Save Ector, in his tyme, as I can here.
But weylaway, save only Goddes wille,
Dispitously him slough the fiers Achille.

And whan that he was slayn in this manere,
His lighte goost ful blisfully is went
Up to the holownesse of the seventh spere,
In convers letinge every element;
And ther he saugh, with ful avysement,
The erratik sterres, herkeninge armonye
With sownes fulle of hevenish melodye.

And doun from thennes faste he gan avyse
This litel spot of erthe, that with the see
Enbraced is, and fully gan despyse
This wrecched world, and held al vanitee
To respect of the pleyn felicitee
That is in hevene above; and at the laste,
Ther he was slayn, his loking doun he caste;

And in himself he lough right at the wo
Of hem that wepten for his deeth so faste;
And dampned al our werk that folweth so
The blinde lust, the which that may not laste,
And sholden al our herte on hevene caste.
And forth he wente, shortly for to telle,
Ther as Mercurie sorted him to dwelle.

Swich fyn hath, lo, this Troilus for love,
Swich fyn hath al his grete worthinesse;
Swich fyn hath his estat real above,
Swich fyn his lust, swich fyn hath his noblesse;
Swich fyn hath false worldes brotelnesse.
And thus bigan his lovinge of Criseyde,
As I have told, and in this wyse he deyde.

O yonge fresshe folkes, he or she,
In which that love up groweth with your age,
Repeyreth hoom from worldly vanitee,
And of your herte upcasteth the visage
To thilke God that after his image
Yow made, and thinketh al nis but a fayre
This world, that passeth sone as floures fayre.

And loveth him, the which that right for love
Upon a cros, our soules for to beye,
First starf, and roos, and sit in hevene above;
For he nil falsen no wight, dar I seye,
That wol his herte al hoolly on him leye.
And sin he best to love is, and most meke,
What nedeth feyned loves for to seke?

Lo here, of Payens corsed olde rytes,
Lo here, what alle hir goddes may availle;
Lo here, these wrecched worldes appetytes;
Lo here, the fyn and guerdon for travaille
Of Jove, Appollo, of Mars of swich rascaille!
Lo here, the forme of olde clerkes speche
In poetrye, if ye hir bokes seche.

O moral Gower, this book I directe

To thee, and to the philosophical Strode,
To vouchen sauf, ther nede is, to corecte,
Of your benignitees and zeles gode.
And to that sothfast Crist, that starf on
rode,
With al myn herte of mercy ever I preye;
And to the Lord right thus I speke and seye:

Thou oon, and two, and three, eterne on lyve,
That regnest ay in three and two and oon,
Uncircumscript, and al mayst circumscryve,
Us from visible and invisible foon
Defende; and to thy mercy, everichoon,
So make us, Jesus, for thy grace digne,
For love of mayde and moder thyn benigne!
Amen.
Explicit Liber Troili et Criseydis.

Kelmscott

HERE ENDS the Book of the Works of Geoffrey Chaucer, edited by F. S. Ellis; ornamented with pictures designed by Sir Edward Burne-Jones, and engraved on wood by W. H. Hooper. Printed by me William Morris at the Kelmscott Press, Upper Mall, Hammersmith, in the County of Middlesex. Finished on the 8th day of May, 1896.

The hearty thanks of the Editor and Printer are due to the Reverend Professor Skeat for kindly allowing the use of his emendations to the Ellesmere MS. of the Canterbury Tales, and also of his emended texts of Chaucer's other writings. The like thanks also the Editor and Printer give to the Delegates of the Oxford University Press for allowing them to avail themselves of Professor Skeat's permission.

554

A HISTORY OF 1000 YEARS OF
GREEK VASE PAINTING

A HISTORY OF 1000 YEARS OF

GREEK VASE PAINTING,

TEXT AND NOTES BY P. E. ARIAS

PHOTOGRAPHS BY MAX HIRMER.

HARRY N. ABRAMS, INC., *Publishers*
NEW YORK
[1962]

TRANSLATED AND REVISED BY B. SHEFTON

LIBRARY OF CONGRESS CATALOG CARD NUMBER 61–13857

CONTENTS

PREFACE

This book is intended not only for the learned reader but also for a much wider public of art lovers and our introductory essay may serve as a first guide for those new to this field, though the beauty of the plates will attract the layman no less than the expert. The descriptive catalogue and commentary following the plates attempts to interpret individual vase pictures and give other relevant comments. A selected list of bibliographical references is given after each entry.

The rich selection of representative works presented here could never have been brought together and shown by new photographs specially taken but for the generous cooperation of colleagues and the keepers of museums and other collections; our gratitude is due to them in the first instance. Their names will be found below in Professor Hirmer's introductory note as author of the photographic section of this book. One name must be particularly mentioned in gratitude, a scholar to whom the whole science of Greek archeology and particularly vase painting owes a profound debt, Sir John Beazley. His untiring efforts to identify the work and deepen our understanding of individual artists and schools has revolutionized our knowledge and appreciation of Attic vases especially. His work carried on over a lifetime with humility and patience is the foundation of our approach to the subject. Finally it is a particular pleasure to thank my fellow author, Professor Max Hirmer, for the enthusiasm, devotion, and exceptional talents, which he has brought towards the making of the pictorial documentation of the book.

We hope that this work will be useful to scholars as a collection of good photographs and to the wider public as a means to a greater awareness and love of classical art in all its beauty and harmony.

PAOLO ENRICO ARIAS

It has long been my ambition to publish a comprehensive work on the development of Greek vase painting, and with this in view more than thirty museums and other collections have been visited over a period of years to prepare new photographs taking advantage of the latest refinements of technique. We now offer this collection of plates showing works outstanding both from an artistic and an archeological point of view, spanning a period approaching a millennium. A particular feature is the series of colour plates, which faithfully reproduce the original tones; without these colour reproductions the wealth and variety of Greek vase painting could scarcely be conveyed.

Our aim is to present vases in their entirety, their combination of shape with pictorial decoration, and then to linger over details, to explore their own magic. Only thus can we appreciate the full beauty of these vases. Similar principles have been applied to the selection of the material as a whole. In the following pages we shall watch an art, highly differentiated into local styles, evolving from the beginnings to its various peaks and then entering on a decline. We shall have occasion to notice the interaction of vase painting with other arts, as well as its links with the religion and mythology of the Greek world.

My warmest thanks are due to Professor Arias for giving of his profound knowledge, whilst leaving me a free hand in the selection of works to be illustrated. It has been possible to present here some of the most outstanding Greek vase paintings owing to the generosity with which the Directors and Keepers of great collections entrusted their treasures to me for photographing. I have to thank Dr. Christos Karouzos and Mrs. Semni Karouzou-Papaspyridi, National Museum, Athens; Dr. Yannis Miliadis, Kerameikos Museum, Athens; Prof. Bernard Ashmole, British Museum, London, (and lately Oxford) and his successor, Mr. D. E. L. Haynes; MM. Jean Charbonneaux and Pierre Devambez, Musée du Louvre, Paris, M. Jean Babelon, Cabinet des Médailles, Paris; Mme. V. Ver-hoogen, Musées Royaux d'Art et d'Histoire, Brussels. Furthermore Professor Arias wishes me to thank in his name the Superintendents, Directors and Assistant Keepers of museums in Italy and the Vatican: Soprint. Renato Bartoccini, Museo Nazionale di Villa Giulia, Rome; Soprint. Luigi Bernabò Brea and Dott. Gino V. Gentili, Museo Archeologico, Syracuse; Soprint. Jole Bovio-Marconi and Dott. V. Tusa, Museo Archeologico, Palermo; Soprint. Giacomo Caputo, Museo Archeologico, Florence; Soprint. Nevio Degrassi, Museo Nazionale, Taranto; Dir. gen. Filippo Magi and Dr. Hermione Speier, Musei Vaticani, Città del Vaticano; S. Eccellenza Soprint. Amadeo Maiuri, Dott. Olga Elia and Dott. Mario Napoli, Museo Archeologico Nazionale, Naples; Dott. Mario Moretti, Museo Nazionale, Tarquinia; Dott. G. A. Mansuelli and Dott. Rosanna Pincelli, Museo Civico, Bologna; Dott. Gaetano Panazza, Museo Civico Romano, Brescia; Dir. Carlo Pietrangeli, Palazzo dei Conservatori, Rome. Last but not least I want to thank the Directors and Assistants of the German collections, Professor Hans Diepolder and Dr. Reinhard Lullies, Munich; Dr. Adolf Greifen-hagen, Berlin-Dahlem; Professor Hans Möbius and Dr. W. Schiering, Würzburg. I must also express my gratitude to Baron Hans von Schoen, Cureglia near Lugano and Cav. Athos Moretti, Bellinzona, for allowing me the freedom of their possessions. Dr. Franz Willemsen of the Archeological Institute of the University of Munich gave me much precious help and advice.

The directors of the museums in Copenhagen, Stockholm, New York and Boston as well as the German Archaeological Institute in Athens courteously provided photographs for use in this publication.

I must once again express my grateful appreciation to my collaborator Miss Julia Asen who worked with me photographing the majority of the objects and who devoted skill and understanding to this difficult and specialized task. She also was in charge of the processing and printing of the pictures and saw the plates through the press.

MAX HIRMER

In preparing this edition a number of changes and revisions inevitably suggested themselves through-out the text of the book. The introductory essay, however, has been left almost unaltered, and most of the substantial changes lie in the central portion of the commentary, much of which is entirely new. Changes in the early part and in the later sections of the commentary are less extensive, though there too entire sections are new. The captions to the plates have been revised throughout and the biblio-graphy has been extensively added to in many places.

BRIAN SHEFTON

INTRODUCTION

The study of Greek vase painting introduces us to many facets of Greek society over a period of almost a thousand years. It can be a mirror of the artistic activity, indeed the entire culture of ancient Greece, for the pictures on these vases are valuable sources for our knowledge of ancient life in the widest sense of the word, ranging from the ordinary things, such as dress or the objects in everyday use, to the understanding of Greek religion and mythology as well as details of domestic and public affairs, the theatre or athletic contests. A whole new world is thereby opened up to us.

Beyond this Greek vases are objects of art in their own right; they may be the product of craftsmen and are perhaps not to be compared in artistic merit with the highest examples of Greek art in architecture, sculpture or major painting. Yet they reach astonishing heights of achievement, such as have in their kind not been attained by subsequent ages. Thus they provide an illuminating example of how the Greek genius for form manifested itself even in objects of everyday use.

Greek vases then are important documents for the history of art, and this from their very beginning, the time of the striking series of vases from the Dipylon Cemetery which are so important for our knowledge of early Athenian culture. But not only in Attica, for the same thing can be said about the products of workshops in the rest of Greece and the Aegean islands. Our plates and commentary will make this clear by showing a selection of choice pieces ranging over some eight centuries. Here in this introduction we shall endeavour to sketch in some of the background for their appreciation and particularly to examine the value of these vases as evidence for Greek painting as a whole, which is almost entirely and irretrievably lost apart from these vase pictures. They alone can give us some idea of what has been lost. We must remember though all the time that a complete account of Greek vase painting would have to include also the more modest products of the various workshops which we for the purposes of this book have had to ignore.

From the 11th to the 8th centuries B.C. the prevailing style in Attica is called Geometric. This is not the place to discuss the origins of a style, which has given us so many interesting creations of decorative art. Looking at even the earliest products of the Geometric period we see very plainly that this art is not the outcome of a primitive stage of attainment but on the contrary that it is born of a harmoniously balanced and well developed artistic culture. The amphorae and kraters of this period with their highly organized ornamental structure are evidence of a developed and sophisticated style. One of the fascinating problems that arise in connection with this period is the emergence of human and animal figures into this decorative scheme. On the krater in the Louvre (plate 3) datable to the later-9th century B.C. we find in addition to the ordinary motives of meander and zig-zag lines two delightful little horses which despite their naive and still rather stiff forms show the beginnings of a new figure style differing from the older scheme of purely abstract decoration. Vases of this new kind span a considerable period of time, and many of the larger ones were used for burial purposes and the cult of the dead, thus encouraging the rise of more complicated figure compositions on their surface, such as the scenes of the lying-in-state (*prothesis*) of the dead. We know now from our increased knowledge of early Peloponnesian and Cretan art that the schematization of the human body

in these pictures with the strong constriction at the waist is based upon a tradition which goes back to Cretan art of the latter half of the second millenium B.C. These large funerary vases sometimes up to 1.80 m in height and serving as grave monuments are covered with human and animal figures. In addition to direct allusions to the burial we often find representations of the dance of men and women, such friezes being usually found on the neck of vases. Pictures of fights at sea with ships such as occur on a krater in New York (plate 7) are probably not generic but refer to special legends, probably the Trojan cycle, which at this time were crystalized into the various epic poems to receive their final shape during the 6th century B.C. Already during the middle of the 8th century we find the confinement of figures within a metope-like field, an idea which was successfully developed in Attic vase-painting right up to the first decades of the 5th century B.C.

Towards the end of the 8th century a change comes into the Geometric style, a change both in decoration and in the subject matter of the pictures. The amphorae decrease in size, plastic snakes (plate 9) are attached to their handles, the chariot scenes become monotonous and new decorative elements appear, derived from new sources. The Orientalizing style makes its appearance in Attica as early as anywhere, though at first its scope is limited and it does not affect the current decorative system of vases.

Whereas the Geometric style had had a certain unity throughout the Aegean world, the Orientalizing style during the 7th century B.C. underwent considerable differentiation in the various regions throughout the Greek world. Here the development of the Protocorinthian style is particularly interesting from the artistic point of view, ranging, as it does, from a series of very small vases with miniature decoration to the maturity of the Chigi Vase (plates 16, 17, IV). This is one of the masterpieces of archaic vase painting not only because of the rich variety of themes represented but also because of the artistry displayed in the arrangement of opposing lines of warriors, and the skilful rendering of individual figures, such as the flute player. The vase is also evidence of a strong sense for polychrome effects which must in some way reflect painting on surfaces other than vases.

The islands produced a variety of Orientalizing styles; on Paros (plate 25) we meet an elegance reminiscent in some ways of the Geometric style. On Naxos (plate V) new decorative and symbolic motives emerge. On Melos (plates 22, 23) painters created mythological pictures of some beauty. In Attica too a powerful style called Protoattic loves the presentation of human figures in mythological pictures often with a grotesque streak which comes out well in the new Gorgon amphora from Eleusis (plates 12, 13). If the Gorgons show a fierce and barbarous expression, other figures on the vase with their elongated proportions and linear style remind one of contemporary creations in the Cycladic islands. Looking at the Nessos amphora in Athens (plates 18–20), an Attic work towards the end of the century (and almost beyond the limits of the Protoattic style), we notice that the strength of its impact is derived from the careful study of the human form, from the intense expressiveness and the harmony of the design which have gone into the representation. Here a contrast with a non-Attic work of roughly the same period, namely the Eretrian amphora, (plate III), is instructive. There is a rich polychromy on that vase but little life. It is an interesting document of primitive art, but it is clear that from here no progress was possible. On the other hand Attic vase painting is guided onwards by a never-failing succession of artistic endeavour, unfolding a development in human figure painting which was to last several centuries. Other orientalizing workshops on Chios or Naucratis and in Rhodes (plates 26–29) never attempted anything beyond purely decorative compositions, repeating a succession of colourful but monotonous motifs, which were derived from plant and animal life

and successfully give the impression of tapestry patterns without however ever touching the problem of the human form.

An orientalizing fabric which managed at the crucial moment to escape from the danger of this monotony is the Corinthian style, though the temptation to succumb to a purely decorative tendency was particularly strong in its case. It too drew upon the common stock of Orientalizing motifs, such as the rosette, the lotus-bud and the palmette, to which was added a variety of fantastic animal- and other motifs of Assyrian origin (plates VI–VIII, 31). But it was the introduction of mythological pictures with their human actors which gave new life to Corinthian art, and this was probably due to the existence in Corinth of an important school of painting. We know very little about this school, but the names of Ekphantos and Kleanthes, to the latter of whom the origin of the linear style in painting (painting in outlines) is ascribed, have come down to us. Thus there were produced in Corinth in addition to the mass of vases decorated with rosettes and other orientalizing motifs with an occasional insertion of a human figure, also vases where the human figure is part of narrative scenes with mythological content (plates 32–34, IX–XII). We know from Pausanias of the Chest of Cypselus which stood in Olympia and was decorated with an extensive series of mythological pictures. These are the counterparts, perhaps even inspiration of figure scenes on Corinthian vases. Many themes appear repeatedly on those vases such as Herakles, the Argonauts (the funeral games in honour of Pelias), Tydeus and Ismene, the departure of Amphiaraos, Perseus and Andromeda, Theseus and the heroes of the Trojan legend. These are representative of an enormous mythological repertoire, which also influenced 6th century Attic Black-figure.

It is in the 6th century B.C. that Attica increasingly begins to dominate the art of vase painting. It is the period of the Black-figure style, a technique which had originated in Corinth. Throughout the first half of the 6th century Corinthian influence upon Attica is very noticeable as can be seen from the works of the Gorgon Painter (plates 35–37), one of the vital artists at the beginning of the 6th century B.C., and even more in the so-called Vourva-style amphorae with their orientalizing animal friezes. The climax however of Corinthian influence on Attic vase painting comes in the elaborate works of Sophilos and Kleitias (plates 39; 40–46). Particularly the François Vase by Kleitias reveals the Attic synthesis and adaptation of many Corinthian forms. If the painted metopes from the temple of Apollo at Thermon in Aetolia (now in the National Museum in Athens) are still vivid examples of Corinthian painting at the turn of the 7th and 6th centuries B.C., it is nevertheless true that Corinthian vase-painting progressively degenerated into lifeless and monotonous repetitions of motifs, whilst Attic vase-painting during the 6th century expanded into a lively figure style, welcoming experiments, tied to human feelings and keeping up with the progress in other, major arts.

The works of Lydos, the Amasis Painter, and Exekias are typical of this tendency in Attic painting. The sources from which these artists drew their repertoire are the epic poems, above all the *Iliad*, and the cycle of Dionysiac myths. These artists had the ability to isolate individual episodes and to pick out the important characters. In this the new generation of painters went beyond the achievement of Kleitias. The Amasis Painter (plates 54–57, XV) is perhaps the most conventional of the three but also the smoothest, whilst Exekias (plates 59–65, XVI–XVIII) has a sympathetic intuition for the heroic strain in his narrative, for harmony and equilibrium. He masters what had already started with Sophilos, namely the art of constructing a picture with but few figures, emphasizing the individual elements with the greatest clarity. It is interesting to compare these creations with the

contemporary achievements in Greek sculpture. Often the similarity is so striking that they seem like translations of sculptured *kouroi* into two-dimensional drawings, witness the figures of Castor and Polydeuces on the Exekias amphora in the Vatican (plate 63). We see the same dry, nervously sensitive outline, the same elegant and dynamic conception of the figure, the same reposeful profile. Exekias incidentally also painted on clay plaques, so-called *pinakes*, as we know from his cycle of funerary plaques (plates 60, 61). Though the technique is the same as in vase-painting, the composition is more extensive and varied and shows the artist reaching beyond the normal achievement of vase painters.

In addition to these great masters of the mid-6th century B.C. and later, we know of other, less prominent artists who also are in the succession of Kleitias. There are the so-called Little Masters, who decorated their products, mostly cups, in a miniature style with a delicate polychromy based upon the traditional black, white and purple (plates 47–50). Two types of cups can be distinguished above all. There are the band-cups on the one hand, where the figure frieze is confined in one long zone, the lip-cups on the other, with their decoration disposed according to different principles. Viewed against this background we can again see the superior creativeness and versatility of Exekias who in his Munich cup (plate XVI) presents us with the poetry-inspired picture of Dionysus at sea on the inside of the bowl, and scenes of combats on the outside, creating thereby a new kind of cup with new principles of decoration which became dominant in future development.

However even Attic Black-figure, had it continued, would have gone into an inevitable decline, for we can see in its latest products the increase of stereotype scenes repeated again and again without any attempt to offer new solutions even in respect of polychrome effects (plates 66–69; XIX–XXI). Even Psiax, who next to the Lysippides Painter is the most important artist working at the end of Black-figure, found no new solution, even though his work shows that he was aware of the insufficiency of the old style. The crisis of Black-figure may have been brought about, even if indirectly, by the increasing complexity of anatomical knowledge displayed in contemporary sculpture, and the tendency to reproduce details such as tendons and veins. These new developments in sculpture must have had a fertilizing influence upon vase painting and have contributed to the rise of a new technique which could trace more naturally the details of the naked human body as well as the complexities of folds and drapery. In our opinion this connection between the advance of sculpture and the technical and stylistical revolution in vase-painting of the second half of the 6th century has never been sufficiently stated.

Apart from the Attic school we know during the 6th century other styles which display completely different characteristics. We content ourselves with showing some characteristic examples of Laconian, Chalcidian and Caeretan only (plates 73, 74, XXIV; 75, 76, XXV, XXVI; 77–80, XXVII). All these fabrics however were comparatively short lived and could never compete with Attic.

We have now reached the period of Pisistratus and his sons, a period of the greatest importance in the history of 6th century Athens not only because during this period the seeds were sown of the future clash with Persia, but also because it was an unusually fertile period in every form of artistic activity, particularly in sculpture. It was then that the cult of the nude and youthful athlete began to influence every artistic endeavour, witness the friezes on the Treasury of the Siphnians and the metopes on the Athenian Treasury, both at Delphi, or the two statue bases from the Themistoclean wall in Athens. All these show a profound change in artistic taste which was also to influence vase painting. How could Black-figure with its possibilities largely exhausted accommodate this new

dynamic conception of the human body? Not by refining even further the technique of incision, for however delicate and virtuoso-like the application of the incising tool, in the last resort it destroys the solidity of the black surface, fails to infuse life and certainly does not give a sufficient sense of colouring, as can be seen by looking at the late stage of Black-figure production (plates 71, 72, XXIII).

The Andokides Painter is usually credited with the invention of the new Red-figure technique (plates 82–88, XXIX). This change involves that the figures are no longer painted in black over a red-clay background, but rather that they appear ('are reserved') in the red of the clay whilst the background area surrounding the figures is filled with black. Black lines of various intensity are then used to fill in the detail markings within the reserved area of the figure.

On a vase which combines both techniques, the 'bilingual' of plates 88, 89 and XXIX, where one side is in Black-figure the other in Red-figure, we can clearly see how the black-figured side, the work of the Lysippides Painter, contrasts in its insufficiency with the richness and novelty of the red-figured picture from the hand of the Andokides Painter, to convince any doubters of the superiority of the new style!

In the second half of the 6th century B.C. we first meet a new phenomenon, the so-called love-names, names of prominent Athenian youths inscribed on the vase followed by the word *kalos* = 'beautiful' or 'fair'. A number of these can be identified with historically known personalities such as Leagros and his son Glaukon, both of them Athenian commanders (*strategoi*) in their time, and also Euaion whom we now know from the evidence of three vases to be identical with the son of the poet Aeschylus. The usual explanation of these inscriptions is that the beauty of these youths is praised in accordance with Greek predilections, though a rival interpretation has been propounded according to which the praise is in honour of the dead*.

Early Red-figure as represented by the works of Oltos, Epiktetos or Euphronios delights in displaying the human figure in a great variety of poses. This tendency to show the most complicated postures with limbs, heads and body twisted in different directions is not merely the consequence of the painter's whim, but reflects the achievements of painting in other media particularly the work of the painter Kimon from Cleonae. We know from a passage in Pliny (*Nat. Hist.*, 35, 36) that he invented the so-called *katagrapha* or *obliquae imagines*, that is the facility to show faces in a variety of positions looking back or upwards or downwards. He distinguished the individual limbs and their movements, represented such details as veins and the individual folds of drapery. Such achievements are reflected in vase painting of the end of the 6th and beginning of the 5th centuries B.C. particularly in the works of Oltos, Euphronios and Euthymides (plates 99–104; 108–115; 116, 117). The last two were amongst the leading artists of their time, not least on account of their ability to analyze the human frame and to infuse a powerful sense of life into their pictures.

The second half of the 6th and the first half of the 5th century is the period when artists' signatures are most frequent. The potter writes *epoiesen* (= made) after his name, the painter *egrapsen* (= painted). Often the potter alone signs. There are also cases where potter and painter are the same person, as we know from double signatures, where the same person signs as potter and painter. In other cases we can only guess that potter and painter were identical, particularly so in the case of the Amasis Painter where the works which are assigned to the painter on the strength of the style of drawing also have a certain unity in the form of the pottery, a unity which has some of the characteristics

* See S. Ferri in *Rendic. Acc. Lincei* 1938.

15

found also in the paintings. An artist may also have been painter and potter, but at different stages of his career. Such was the case with Euphronios who signs as painter early in life, whilst later he puts his name as potter on vases which are certainly not *painted* by his hand. This profusion of signatures and of explanatory inscriptions on vases in the decades at the turn of the 6th and 5th centuries provides eloquent testimony both to the pride of artists, potter and painters, and to the value which was attached not only to the works of sculpture and major painting (where artists' names have come down to us through literary sources), but also to the humbler products of vase painter and potter.

During the first three decades of the 5th century we may note in particular three artists, the Brygos Painter, Douris and Makron (plates 135–143, XXXIII, XXXIV; 143–148; 132, 133). These three are cup-painters and the vases they decorated were used for religious libations and for drinking at banquets. They were decorated with mythological scenes or with pictures of Dionysiac or indeed mortal revelling, the so-called *kōmoi*, that is scenes of drinking and dancing. Their mythological pictures drew on the same traditions as that used by major painting; this included of course the epic and other poetry. At this time we cannot yet trace any influence of the fresco paintings of the period after 480 B.C.

Other painters go different paths, again without any dependence upon major painting as far as we can tell. Thus the Kleophrades Painter, the Berlin Painter, the Pan Painter and the Pistoxenos Painter all reveal to us different temperaments. The Kleophrades Painter (plates 119–128, XXX, XXXI) with his severe and grandiose figures is particularly outstanding in his Dionysiac scenes, though we must not forget the beauty he lends to the picture of the dead youth. The Berlin Painter (plates 150–157, XXXV) just as his successors Hermonax and the Achilles Painter, likes to decorate his vases with but few figures and these in isolation. He paints with sure and elegant touch exploring movement or unstable postures as well as analyzing the linear complexity of the nude. The Pan Painter (plates 160–165) stands apart from the rest harping back with his mannered style to the archaic. The Pistoxenos Painter (plates 166, 167), who worked for the potter Euphronios, excels in his polychrome masterpieces on white ground.

If at the end of the 6th century it was Kimon of Cleonae who profoundly affected the development and changes of figure drawing, now in the second quarter of the 5th century B.C. another and perhaps even greater artist brought about new changes in vase painting. He was Polygnotos from Thasos. Though his work is completely lost, we know that he was responsible for some of the most important wall paintings in Athens during the period immediately preceding Pericles. It is through vase painting alone that we can form some idea of his manner and work. He together with Mikon painted in the years between about 460 and 445 B.C. the frescoes on the walls of the Stoa Poikile (the Painted Porch) and the Anakeion (the Sanctuary of the Dioscuri). Other works by him include the decoration of the Club Room of the Cnidians in Delphi with wall paintings of the *Ilioupersis* (Sack of Troy) and the *Nekyia* (The Underworld). We possess fairly detailed descriptions of these paintings in Pausanias, who often uses the words 'above' and 'below' to indicate figures on different levels. It is precisely this arrangement of figures on different levels with the ground indicated by wavy lines which we find on the Louvre krater by the Niobid Painter (plates 173–175). But more than this; for we also see in some of the figures on the krater an attempt to express emotion by different postures and by making the figures 'talk' as it were. Pliny (*Nat. Hist.*, 35, 58) basing himself on Xenocrates reports that Polygnotos dressed his women in transparent garments and was also the first to open the mouth of

his figures, letting them reveal their teeth to give varied expressions in contrast with the more severe ancient style. Thus the Louvre krater by the Niobid Painter is representative of these innovations. Amongst other vases of the second half of the century which also show this new tendency there are the Boston pelike by the Lykaon Painter with a picture of Odysseus between Elpenor and Hermes, and the pyxis also in Boston with Odysseus and Nausicaa by Aison; both these vases are probably inspired by Polygnotan paintings. This is also the period of the elaborate battle pictures of Amazons and Greeks, a theme which we know to have been favoured by Mikon who collaborated with Polygnotos in decorating the Stoa Poikile. Anyhow, during this period of the middle and second half of the 5th century we find a whole series of vase paintings which show the influence of Polygnotos either in choice of subject or in the adoption of motifs, proving that these new inventions were accepted into the common artistic stock. Thus they are not only seen in the circle of the Niobid Painter but are taken for granted in succeeding generations. Scenes on different levels occur on vases by the Meidias Painter and Aison (plates 214–217, XLVI; 205). At the beginning of the fourth century the Suessula Painter again arranges his figures in various levels (plate 221), now in a new endeavour to create spatial relationships in depth.

A further characteristic of the works of the fresco painter Polygnotos, which is hardly ever emphasized despite the clear testimony of our literary sources, was his use of the four basic colours, black, red ochre, terra di Sinope, which gave a brilliance to the colours, and white.

Towards the end of the first half of the 5th century B.C. an increasing interest in the psychological interpretation of individual figures as well as their relationship to each other became current in many vase paintings. We particularly point to the works of the Penthesilea Painter (plates 168–171). The endeavour to bring out the *ethos* of his heroes recalls a passage in Aristotle (*Poet.* 6) where he calls the fresco painter Polygnotos a 'fine painter of character' (*ethographos*). The passionate meeting of eyes between Achilles and Penthesilea at the very moment when the hero plunges his sword into the breast of the Amazon Queen, or again the passionate fury of Apollo's revenge against Tityos, all these show the expressive power of the painter. However, he is not alone in this, there are others who could also be called Polygnotan in this sense; thus the vase painter Polygnotos and his school (including the Orpheus Painter), the Chicago Painter, the Kleophon Painter, all these are in the following of Polygnotos as *ethographos*.

The latter part of the 5th century is in turn deeply influenced by two other artists, Parrhasios and Zeuxis. Parrhasios came from Ephesus; he was an Ionian and became for Attic art what Pollaiuolo was for the Italian renaissance. He searched for a contour-line which would also suggest the volume of figures. As a well-known passage in Pliny tells us, he succeeded in indicating the outline of bodies in such a way that the boundary still suggested the existence and indeed the appearance of mass beyond the point where vision is eclipsed (*Nat. Hist.*, 35, 67–69). Parrhasios was alive to psychological situations as we know from the reports of his conversation with Socrates (Xenophon, *Memorab.*, III, 10, 1) and also from testimonies about the character of his works such as the symbolic figure of Demos (Pliny, *Nat. Hist.*, 35, 69). Since his *floruit* was about 420 B.C. it is not surprising that just during the last two decades of the 5th century we find on Attic vases an increasing interest in both the problem of the line and also in psychological analysis of human characters.

It is particularly on white-ground funerary lekythoi that we may study the so-called 'functional line', a phenomenon to which Bianchi Bandinelli has drawn attention.* Here we see figures in outline

* See R. Bianchi Bandinelli, *Storicità dell'arte classica*, Florence 1950, pp. 45 ff.

drawing, done sometimes in a black, sometimes a red pigment. Moreover the problem of polychromy has been mastered with particular sensitivity on the finest of these vases. We refer here less to the works of the Achilles Painter or his pupil, the Phiale Painter, masterpieces though they are, for their pictures are still very much conceived as a flat surface (plates 185–187, XXXVIII, XXXIX; XLI, XLII), but rather to the later period, the works of the Reed Painter, the Triglyph Painter or those belonging to Group R (plates 200, XLV). These mourning scenes with their melancholic, foreshortened figures sitting by the grave stele, show just this linear technique which suggests volume and roundness even beyond the limits of the appearance.

Another phenomenon of the last few decades of the 5th century is the mannerism of the Meidias Painter. His art is not decadent or symptomatic of a degenerative development in painting, as has so often been stated, but rather is to be understood as a last attempt, at times magnificently successful, to transfer the achievements of large scale painting of a Parrhasios or a Zeuxis to the surface of a vase. The hydriai in London and Florence (plates 214–217, XLVI) are splendid examples of this attempt. Something of the manner of Parrhasios comes through in these delicate, almost fragile figures, with their complicated and capricious play of lines, with their intense and pathetic expressiveness which even nowadays strikes a cord in beholders used to aesthetic experiences of a different order. Again the effeminate figures of Phaon or Adonis, foreshortened and disposed in the centre of the figured zone (just as Dionysus is on many 4th century Attic and Italiote vases), remind one with their melting gaze of Pliny's report of Parrhasios' figures, the elegance of their hair, the beauty of their mouth, and other elaborate and minutely executed details.

Zeuxis seems to have followed a different direction. Pliny and his sources describe him as having an affinity with Apollodoros, in fact as his successor. Zeuxis was particularly interested in the problem of perspective. As is well known, perspective in Greek painting always assumed several vanishing points and never reached the stage of central perspective. Another artist close to Apollodoros was Agatharchos from Samos who created stage sets for Aeschylus. These two artists developed in the second half of the 5th century an elaborate substructure of geometric theory for their perspective figure paintings. Thus the Meidias Painter worked not only in the tradition of Polygnotos but was also familiar with the linear problems of Parrhasios and the search after perspective effects which inspired the works of Apollodoros and Zeuxis. In the 4th century B.C. the Kerch vases (plates 223–228, XLVII) show these same interests combined with a tendency towards a central composition. Thus the London pelike with Peleus and Thetis (plate XLVII) is basically a classicistic return to a central composition, perhaps influenced by Euphranor, a classicising painter working at that time.

After the Meidias Painter there were no more important new problems to challenge vase painting. Major painting was developing in a way which removed it more and more from what was feasible in vase painting, dealing increasingly not only with the problems of figure composition but with those of colour and light. Already Apollodoros had interested himself in the problem of light and shade apart from his researches in perspective. Zeuxis continued this tendency and vase painting during the 4th century was no longer in a position to keep up with the various innovations of the Theban and Attic schools of painting. Furthermore, painting as a major art came to deal less with complex figure compositions and more with the study of individual figures in its cultivation of easel painting. With this lack of direct inspiration from major art, vase painting in the 4th century was

18

reduced to repeating old motifs in various permutations. There were vain attempts at regeneration, such as the attempts at polychromy on Kerch vases, but they could not save vase painting as a continuing vital art.

Italiote vases too are a case in point illustrating this same development (plates 230–240, XLIX–LII). Here perhaps more than anywhere else vase painters sensed the superiority of easel painting, and Asteas of Paestum (plate 240) and other vase painters may have been directly influenced by Zeuxis and his school, since Zeuxis probably came from Lucanian Heraclea.

Surveying the development of Greek vase painting as a whole, there can be no doubt that from the aesthetic point of view the most interesting periods were the 6th and 5th centuries B.C. During that time vase painting succeeded in creating lively representations of human figures both as objects in themselves and as beings moving in space. They thus created something of great importance in art.

In conclusion we must still touch upon another problem, the significance and purpose of Greek vases. Most of them have been found in graves and this has led scholars to give the scenes a funerary interpretation. At the beginning of the 19th century, when the problem of the interpretation of figure scenes came to the fore, a symbolic reading of the scenes was the fashion. Thus Otto Crusius with his romantic reconstruction of ancient Greece gave to the pictures a symbolic significance that was widely accepted by his contemporaries, despite its rejection by Goethe. But Otto Jahn in his famous preface to the catalogue of the Munich collection published in 1854 showed that the majority of pictures were mythological whilst others referred to everyday life. These views gained general acceptance and are current nowadays. However, we may still ask whether the choice of mythological pictures on Greek vases was really quite haphazard, whether these vases were really destined for common use. Were such exceptional pieces as the Niobid krater in the Louvre, the Penthesilea cup in Munich or the Meidias Painter's hydria in London with the rape of the daughters of Leucippus made to be a joy to the living alone, or were they from the beginning meant to follow them into their graves in Vulci, Orvieto or elsewhere? In other words is it possible that these famous pieces had scenes painted on them which made them particularly suitable to serve as furniture of a tomb which was conceived to be the home of the departed? These questions recently raised by Ernst Langlotz*, would be worth pursuing. Though we are not likely to return to the romantic interpretations of a Crusius, it might well be worth while with our increased knowledge of the ancient world to investigate the significance of the various mythological scenes; for not infrequently we find that vase paintings display a particular preference which can hardly be accidental. Thus there may yet be surprises in store on further investigation of the subject matter of these vases. At all events they are an eloquent testimony to the cult of the dead.

There is no other civilization of the ancient world which has left a tradition of figure painting so vivid and so creative. Nor has any other people of antiquity or indeed in later times used the surface of clay vases for pictures of such beauty or such narrative power. Thus Greek vase painting as a living testimony to a great culture is on the level with classical sculpture.

Looking at the pictures of combat between Greeks and Amazons which appear so often on Attic vases of the 5th century we can sense as it were an echo of an epigram, which, so tradition had it, was

* See in *Eine Freundesgabe* (Festschrift für Robert Boehringer), Tübingen 1957, pp. 397 ff.

composed by Simonides in honour of those who died with King Leonidas at Thermopylae in 480 B.C. (*Anthol. Pal.*, 7, 251):

"Ἄσβεστον κλέος οἵδε φίληι περὶ πατρίδι θέντες
κυάνεον θανάτου ἀμφεβάλοντο νέφος·
οὐ δὲ τεθνᾶσι θανόντες, ἐπεὶ σφ' ἀρετὴ καθύπερθεν
κυδαίνουσ' ἀνάγει δώματος ἐξ 'Αίδεω.

'Winning fame that never will fade for their dear country
they entered the dark cloud of death.
They died, but have not perished, for their bravery
sounding their glory here above leads them out of Hades.'

The meaning, then, of these vase paintings was nothing less than the knowledge that virtue and bravery bring immortality, a certainty which Plato has expressed in these words (*Phaedo*, 114 C):

καλὸν γὰρ τὸ ἆθλον καὶ ἡ ἐλπὶς μεγάλη

'Fair is the prize and the hope great'

1. Attic protogeometric amphora. 10th century B.C. Athens, Kerameikos Museum.

2. Attic early geometric amphora. First half of 9th century B.C. Athens, Kerameikos Museum.

3. Attic geometric krater with lid. Later 9th century B.C. Paris, Louvre.

4. Attic geometric amphora. Lying-in-state and lamentations. Mid-8th century B.C. Athens, National Museum.

I. Attic geometric amphora. Mid-8th century B.C. Munich.

5. Attic geometric krater. Funerary procession and lamentation. Below, procession of chariots. After middle of 8th century B.C. Athens, National Museum.

6. Attic geometric oinochoe. Hunting scene with foxes. Third quarter of 8th century B.C. Boston.

7. Attic geometric krater. Within panels, lying-in-state and lamentation. Below, naval battle.
Third quarter of 8th century B.C. New York.

8. Attic geometric kantharos. Two lions devouring a man, duel, lyre player and women. Last quarter of 8th century B.C.
Copenhagen.

9. Attic geometric amphora with lid. War chariots and file of warriors. Last quarter of 8th century B.C.
Athens, National Museum.

10. Attic amphora, geometric transitional. Chariots and animal scenes. End of 8th century B.C. London.

II. Protoattic amphora by the Analatos painter. Chariots, dance of men and women, and sphinxes. First two decades of 7th century B.C. Paris, Louvre.

12. Protoattic amphora by the Menelas Painter. Perseus and the Gorgons, animals and the blinding of Polyphemus. Circa 670–650 B.C. Eleusis

13. Detail from neck of amphora (plate 12). Blinding of Polyphemus, Eleusis.

14. Krater signed by Aristonothos. Naval battle. Mid-7th century B.C. Rome, Museo dei Conservatori.

15. Krater signed by Aristonothos. Reverse of plate 14. Blinding of Polyphemus. Rome, Museo dei Conservatori.

16. Protocorinthian olpe by the Macmillan Painter (Chigi Vase). Main friezes: hoplites going into battle; below, Judgement of Paris; riders; chariot. In narrow frieze, hunting. Circa 640 B.C. Rome, Villa Giulia.

IV. Detail from plate 16, upper frieze. Hoplites being played into battle. Rome, Villa Giulia.

17. Details from the Chigi Vase (plate 16). Middle and lower friezes. Above: lion hunt; hounds after hare. Below: riders and chariot; huntsmen in ambush. Rome, Villa Giulia.

18. Nettos Painter. Detail of Attic neck-amphora (plate 19). Gorgons. Athens, National Museum.

19. Nettos Painter. Attic neck-amphora. Medusa beheaded, her two sisters pursuing Perseus. On neck, Herakles and Nessos.
Last quarter of 7th century B.C. Athens, National Museum.

22. Melian amphora. Apollo with the Hyperborean Maidens being met by Artemis. Circa 625 B.C.
Athens, National Museum.

23. Above: detail from amphora (plate 22). Combat of two heroes in the presence of their mothers. Below: detail from a Melian amphora.
Horsemen confronting across palmette. Circa 640–630 B.C. Athens, National Museum.

24. Cycladic geometric krater with lid. Third quarter 8th century B.C. New York.

V. Cycladic (Naxian?) amphora. Second quarter of 7th century B.C. Athens, National Museum.

25. Cycladic (Parian?) amphora. Grazing stag. Circa–650 B.C. Stockholm.

26. Rhodian oinochoe. Wild goats and animal friezes. Circa 630-620 B.C. Munich.

27. Rhodian plate. Menelaus and Hector fighting over the fallen Euphorbus.
Late 7th century B.C. London.

28. Chiot chalice. Animal friezes. Last quarter 7th century B.C. Würzburg.

29. Rhodian plate. Gorgon. End of 7th or early 6th century B.C. London.

30. Fikellura amphora. Running man. Circa 540 B.C. London.

VI. Early-Corinthian amphora. Animal friezes. Last quarter of 7th century B.C. London.

VII. Early-Corinthian olpe. Snake between lions; fantastic panther birds. Circa 600 B.C. London.

VIII. Early-Corinthian alabastron. Man with wings (a Boread?).
Last quarter of 7th century B.C. Paris, Louvre.

31. Middle-Corinthian aryballos. Griffin and panthers. Early 6th century B.C. Berlin.

32. Early-Corinthian column-krater; detail of plate IX. Herakles, Iole and others in the house of Eurytos. Paris, Louvre.

IX. Early-Corinthian column-krater. Herakles in the house of Eurytos; cavalcade. End of 7th century B.C. Paris, Louvre.

X. Late-Corinthian column-krater by the Three Maidens Painter. Reverse of plate XI. Mounted horsemen; animal frieze. Circa 570–560 B.C. Vatican.

XI. Late-Corinthian column-krater by the Three Maidens Painter. Obverse of plate X.
Departure of bride and bride-groom; animal frieze. Vatican.

XII. Late-Corinthian neck-amphora. Detail of plate 33. Tydeus killing Ismene. Paris, Louvre.

33. Late-Corinthian neck-amphora. Tydeus killing Ismene. Circa 560–550 B.C. Paris, Louvre.

34. Late-Corinthian cup. Woman's head. Circa 560 B.C. Paris, Louvre.

35. Gorgon Painter. Dinos with stand. Perseus and the Gorgons. Animal friezes. Circa 600–590 B.C. Paris, Louvre.

44. Kleitias. The François Vase. Side A. Friezes on body of vase. Above: Procession of gods and goddesses to the wedding of Peleus and Thetis; Achilles pursues Troilus, the fountain house. In the middle: The two friezes continued. Below: Achilles pursues Troilus (continued), Priam being warned and a rescue party emerging from the gates of Troy. Florence.

45. Kleitias. The François Vase. Details from body of vase. Above: From side B, the return of Hephaistos into Olympus. In the middle and below: Details from the animal friezes on the lowest body zone. Lion felling bull. Lion felling stag. Griffin. Florence.

46. Kleitias. The François Vase. Outer side of handle. Above: 'Potnia Theron'. Below: Ajax carrying the body of the fallen Achilles. Florence.

47. C-Painter. Tripod kothon. Above: Judgement of Paris. Below: Birth of Athena. Circa 570 B.C. Paris, Louvre.

48. C-Painter. Top of tripod kothon (plate 47). Combats. Paris, Louvre.

XIII. Painter N. Nicosthenic neck-amphora. Satyrs and menads. Circa 530 B.C. Bellinzona, Private Collection.

XIV. Internal medallion of Lip cup (plate 49). Herakles and Triton; dance of Nereids. Tarquinia.

49. Lip cup. Chariot race. Mid 6th century B.C. The foot does not belong to the cup. Tarquinia.

50. Band cup signed by the potters Archikles and Glaukytes. Above: Hunt of the Calydonian boar. Below: Theseus and the Minotaur. Circa 540 B.C. Munich.

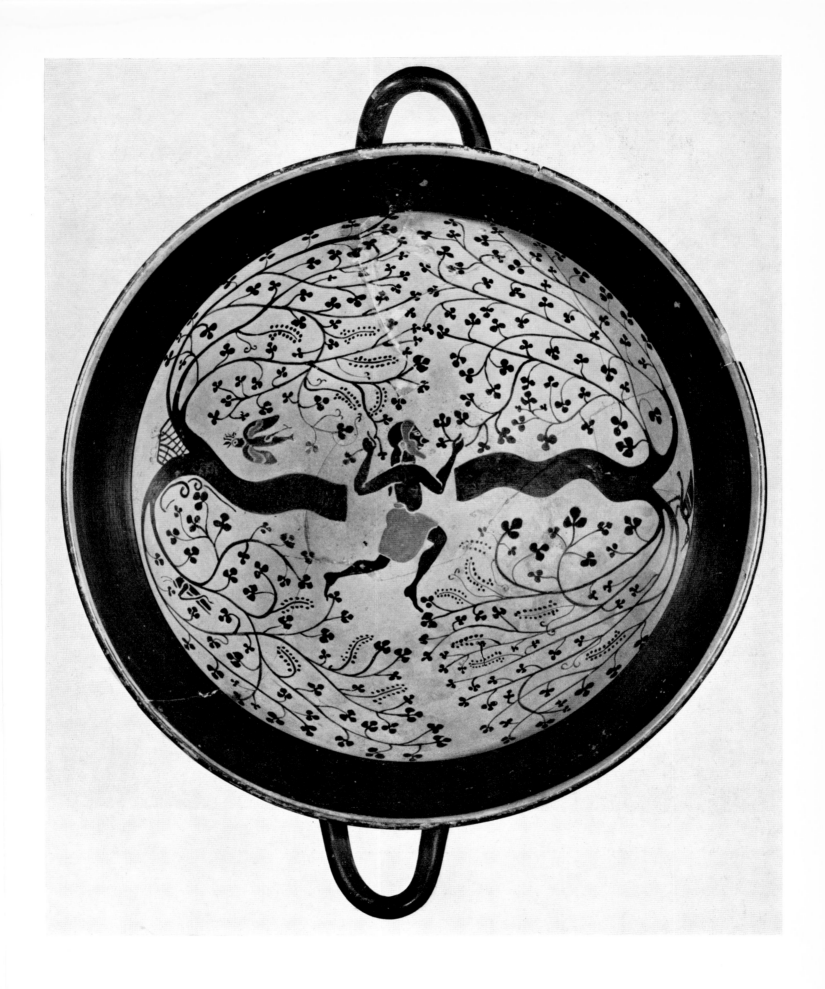

51. East Greek cup. Internal picture. Man between two trees. Mid 6th century B.C. Paris, Louvre.

54. Amasis Painter. Oinochoe. Herakles being introduced to Olympus. Mid 6th century B.C. Paris, Louvre.

55. Amasis Painter. Amphora. Satyrs treading grapes. Circa 530 B.C. Würzburg.

AΘΕΝΑΙΑ

ΑΜΑΣΙΣ ΜΕΠΟΙΕΣΕΝ

ΡΟΡΕΙΔΟΝ

222

56. Amasis Painter. Obverse of neck-amphora (plate XV). Athena and Poseidon. Circa 540 B.C.
Paris, Bibliothèque Nationale.

XV. Amasis Painter. Neck-amphora. Reverse of plate 56. Dionysus and menads. Circa 540 B.C.
Paris, Bibliothèque Nationale.

57. Amasis Painter. Detail of neck-amphora (plate XV). Dionysus and menads.
Paris, Bibliothèque Nationale.

58. Cup signed by the potter Nikosthenes. Two ships under sail. Circa 520 B.C. Paris, Louvre.

XVI. Exekias. Internal view of cup. Dionysus crossing the sea. Circa 535 B.C. Munich.

59. Exekias. Outsides of cup (plate XVI). Combats over fallen warrior, and eye decoration.

60. Exekias. Clay plaques with funerary scenes. Above, mourners proceeding to the right.
Below, lamenting inside the house. Circa 540 B.C. Berlin.

61. Exekias. Fragment from same series as plate 60.
Harnessing of two mules to a cart. Berlin.

62. Exekias. Amphora. Achilles and Ajax playing a game. 540–530 B.C. Vatican.

XVII. Exekias. Detail of amphora (plate 62). Achilles and Ajax playing a game. Vatican.

63. Exekias. Reverse of amphora (plate 62). Return of the Dioscuri, Castor and Polydeuces, to their home. Vatican.

64. Exekias. Detail of neck-amphora (plate XVIII). Achilles killing Penthesilea. London.

XVIII. Exekias. Neck-amphora. Obverse of plate 65. Achilles killing Penthesilea. Circa 530 B.C. London.

65. Exekias. Reverse of neck-amphora (plate XVIII). Dionysus and Oinopion. London.

66. Psiax. Amphora. Return home of two horsemen. Circa 520 B.C. Brescia.

67. Psiax. Detail of amphora (plate 66). Returning horsemen and their parents. Brescia.

68. Psiax. Obverse of amphora (plate 66). Herakles wrestling with the Nemean lion. Brescia.

XIX. Psiax. Detail of plate 68. Herakles and the Nemean lion. Brescia.

XX. Psiax. Detail of plate 68. Athena. Brescia.

XXI. Lysippides Painter or his manner. Hydria. Dionysus feasting; Hermes, satyrs and menads; Hephaistos arriving on the left.
Circa 530–520 B.C. London.

69. Lysippides Painter or his manner. Detail from hydria (plate XXI). Dionysus feasting with Hermes, satyrs and menads. London.

70. Rycroft Painter. Amphora. Dionysus on a donkey; two satyrs. Circa 510–500 B.C. Taranto.

71. Painter of Tarquinia RC6847. Herakles and Apollo struggling for the tripod. Circa 520 B.C. Tarquinia.

72. Leagros Group. Hydria. Death of Priam. Circa 510 B.C. Würzburg.

73. Laconian cups. Above: Hunt Painter. Boar hunt. Circa 550 B.C. Paris, Louvre. Below: Naucratis Painter.
Zeus and eagle. Circa 570–560 B.C. Paris, Louvre.

74. Laconian cup by the Arkesilas Painter. Outside view of plate XXIV. Circa 565–560 B.C.
Paris, Bibliothèque Nationale.

XXIV. Laconian cup by the Arkesilas Painter. Internal picture of cup (plate 74).
King Arkesilas supervising the weighing and storing of wool(?). Paris, Bibliothèque Nationale.

XXV. Chalcidian hydria by the Inscription Painter. Zeus attacking Typhon. Circa 550–530 B.C. Munich.

XXVI. Chalcidian krater by the Inscription Painter. Reverse of plate 75. Horsemen. Circa 540 B.C. Würzburg.

75. Chalcidian krater by the Inscription Painter. Obverse of plate XXVI. Leave taking of Hector from Andromache;
Paris and Helen. Circa 540 B.C. Würzburg.

76. Lid of Chalcidian krater by the Inscription Painter (plates XXVI and 75). Procession of boars. Würzburg.

77. Caeretan Hydria. Herakles attacking Alkyoneus. Circa 525 B.C. Vatican.

78. Detail of Caeretan hydria, plate XXVII. Eurystheus in the vat taking refuge from Cerberus. Paris, Louvre.

XXVII. Caeratan hydria. Obverse of plate 79. Herakles and Cerberus. Circa 530–525 B.C. Paris, Louvre.

79. Caeretan hydria. Reverse of plate XXVII. Two eagles and hare. Paris, Louvre.

80. Caeretan hydria. Blinding of Polyphemus. Circa 520 B.C. Rome, Villa Giulia.

XXVIII. Panathenaic amphora. Kuban Group. Athena with shield device of Tyrant Slayers.
End of 5th century B.C. London.

81. Panathenaic amphora. Kuban Group. Chariot race (reverse of vase). End of 5th century B.C. London.

86. Andokides Painter. Detail of plate 87 (reverse of amphora plate 82). Trainer. Berlin.

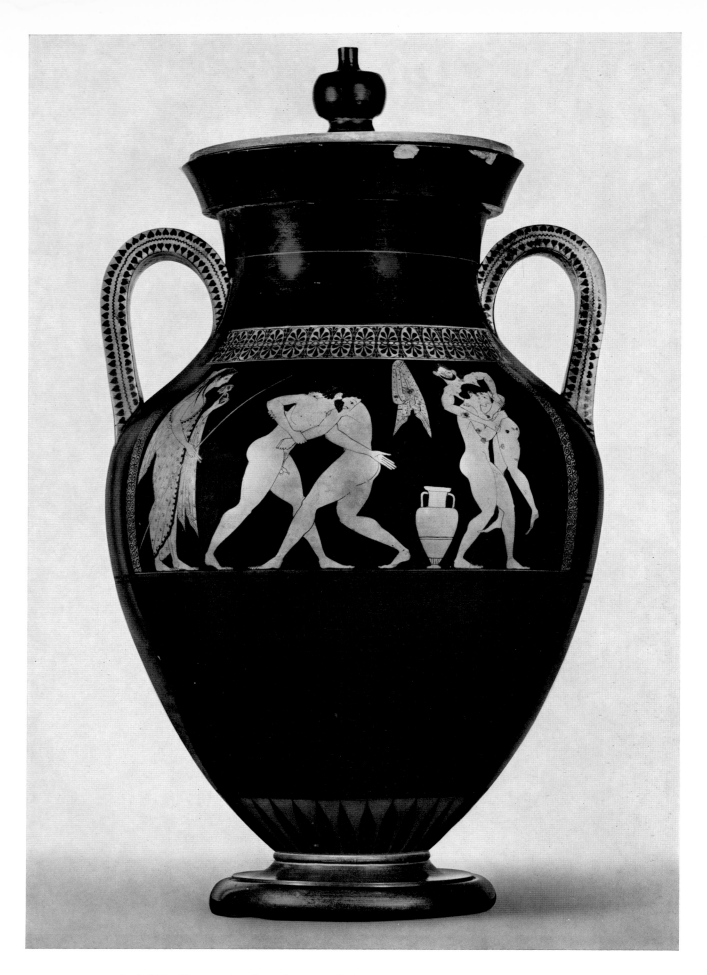

87. Andokides Painter. Amphora (reverse of plate 82). Wrestling. Circa 530–520 B.C. Berlin.

88. Andokides Painter. Amphora. Herakles and Cerberus. Circa 510 B.C. Paris, Louvre.

XXIX. Andokides Painter. Detail of plate 88. Herakles coaxing Cerberus. Paris, Louvre.

89. Lysippides Painter. Amphora (reverse of plate 88). Dionysus with satyrs and menads. Circa 510 B.C. Paris, Louvre.

90. Phintias. Amphora. Reverse of plate 91. Athletes. 510–500 B.C. Paris. Louvre.

91. Phintias. Obverse of amphora (plate 90). Tityos carrying off Leto. Apollo and Artemis to the rescue. Paris, Louvre.

92. Phintias. Amphora. Herakles and Apollo struggling for the tripod. Circa 510 B.C. Tarquinia.

93. Detail of plate 92. Herakles. Tarquinia.

94. Phintias. From obverse of plate 92. Dionysus, menad and satyr. Tarquinia.

95. Phintias. From obverse of amphora (plate 92). Above, Dionysus, satyr and menad. Below, satyr and menad. Tarquinia.

96. Epiktetos. Cup, front and reverse. Armed satyr between eyes. Circa 520 B.C. London.

97. Epiktetos. Internal medallion of cup plate 96. Horseman. London.

98. Epiktetos. Plate. Archer. Circa 520–510 B.C. London.

99. Oltos. Nicosthenic neck-amphora (front and reverse). Satyr and menad; on neck, girl adjusting sandal.
Circa 520–515 B.C. Paris, Louvre.

100. Oltos. Details from reverse of cup (plate 101 top). Dionysus mounting his chariot. Satyrs and menads. Tarquinia.

101. Oltos. Cup. Above, gods in Olympus (Athena, Zeus, Ganymede, Hestia). Below (internal medallion of cup), warrior.
Circa 515–510 B.C. Tarquinia.

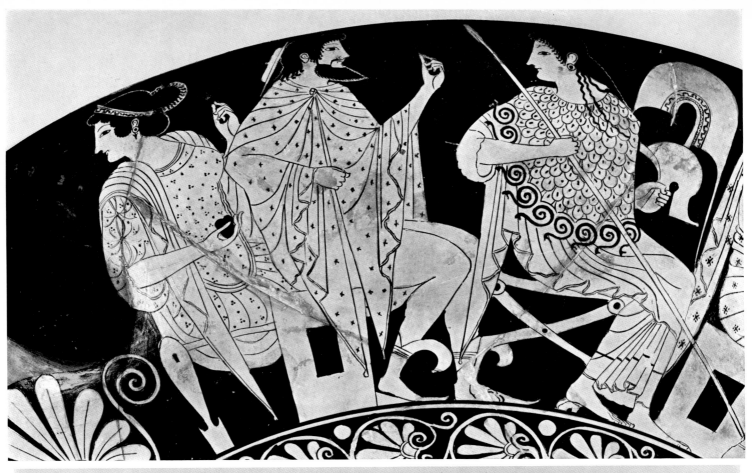

102. Oltos. Details from plate 101 top. Gods in Olympus. From left to right: Hebe, Hermes, Athena and (continued in lower picture) Zeus, Ganymede, Hestia. Tarquinia.

103. Oltos. Details from plate 101 top, continued. Above: (continued from plate 102 below) Aphrodite, Ares. Below: Head of Hebe (left); head of Hestia (right). Tarquinia.

104. Oltos. More details from cup (plate 101 top). From left to right, Hermes, Athena (above): Zeus, Ganymede (middle): Aphrodite, Ares (below). Tarquinia.

105. Smikros. Stamnos. Reverse of plate 106. Servants seeing to the wine for the feast. Circa 515–510 B.C. Brussels.

106. Smikros. From the obverse of the stamnos (plate 105). Young men wining in the company of girls. Brussels.

107. Smikros. Scene continued from plate 106. Smikros himself on the couch. Brussels.

108. Euphronios. Calyx-krater. Herakles and Antaios. Circa 510 B.C. Paris, Louvre.

109. Euphronios. Detail from plate 108. Herakles and Antaios. Paris, Louvre.

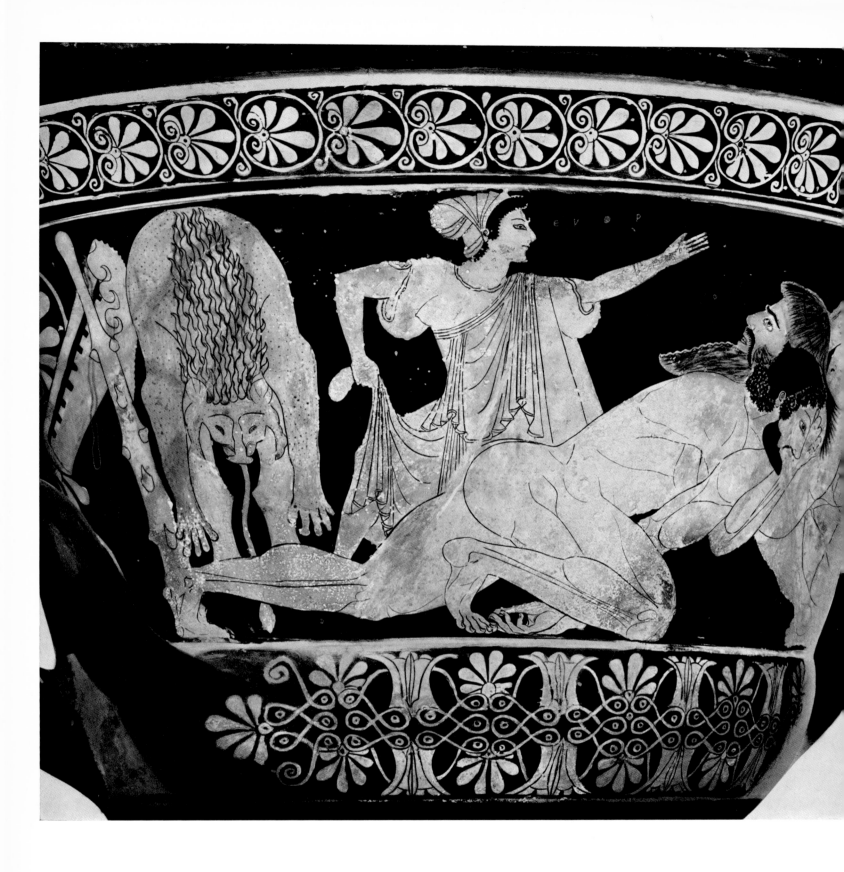

110. Euphronios. Details from calyx-krater plate 108. Herakles and Antaios. Paris, Louvre.

111. Euphronios. Scene continued from plate 110. Paris, Louvre.

112. Euphronios. Calyx-krater. Athletes. Shortly before 500 B.C. Berlin.

113. Euphronios. Volute-krater. Herakles against the Amazons. 510–500 B.C. Arezzo.

114. Euphronios. Detail from volute-krater plate 113. Telamon and a stricken Amazon. Arezzo.

115. Euphronios. Scene continued from plate 114. Herakles and Amazons. Arezzo.

116. Euthymides. Amphora. Reverse of a picture of the rape of Korone. Her companions running to the rescue.
Circa 510–500 B.C. Munich.

117. Euthymides. Amphora (reverse). Male revellers. Circa 510–500 B.C. Munich.

118. Sosias Painter. Internal medallion of cup. Achilles bandaging Patroclus. Circa 500 B.C. Berlin.

119. Kleophrades Painter. Details from calyx-krater (plates 120–121). Throwing the javelin; discus throwing. Tarquinia.

120. Kleophrades Painter. Calyx-krater. Discus thrower and trainer. Circa 500–490 B.C. Tarquinia.

121. Kleophrades Painter. Calyx-krater, reverse of plate 120. Akontist (javelin thrower) and trainer. Tarquinia.

122. Kleophrades Painter. Pointed amphora. Reverse of plate 123. Satyr and menads. On neck: Athletes.
Circa 500–490 B.C. Munich.

123. Kleophrades Painter. Pointed amphora, obverse of plate 122. Dionysus with satyrs and menads.
On neck: Athletes. Circa 500–490 B.C. Munich.

124. Kleophrades Painter. Detail from plate 122. Menad. Munich.

XXX. Kleophrades Painter. Detail from plate 123. Dionysus. Munich.

XXXI. Kleophrades Painter. Detail from plate 122, extreme left. Menad. Munich.

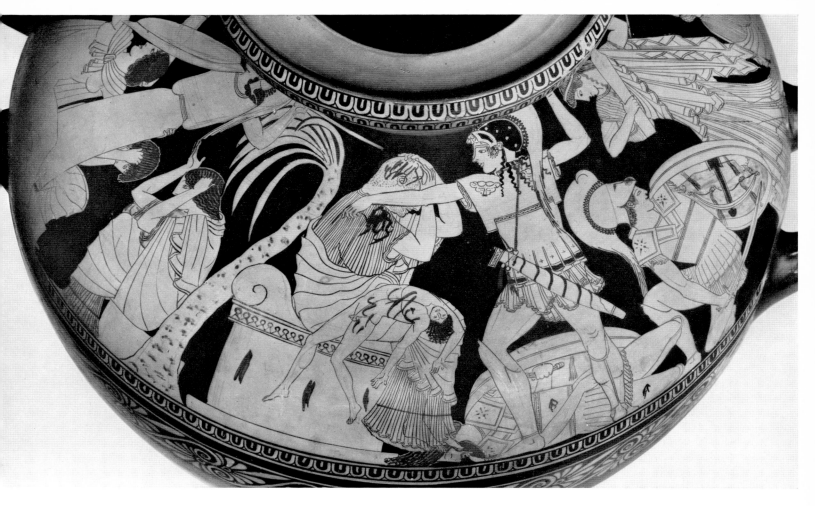

125. Kleophrades Painter. Hydria. Sack of Troy. Above, the death of Priam. Below, (joining on the left of the picture above),
Ajax raping Cassandra at the image of Athena; on the left Aeneas carrying Anchises. Circa 480 B.C. Naples.

130. Myson. Amphora, reverse of plate 131. Theseus carrying off Antiope, Queen of the Amazons. Paris, Louvre.

131. Myson. Amphora, obverse of plate 130. King Croesus on the pyre. Circa 500 B.C. Paris, Louvre.

132. Makron. Outside of cup. Revelling in progress. Circa 490 B.C. Rome, Villa Giulia.

133. Makron. Internal medallion of cup (plate 132). Dionysus. Rome, Villa Giulia.

134. Panaitios Painter. Internal picture of cup. Theseus in the realm of Amphitrite. Circa 500–490 B.C. Paris, Louvre.

XXXII. Mug in the shape of girl's head by the potter Charinos. Circa 500 B.C. Tarquinia.

135. Brygos Painter. Skyphos. Revelling. Men and girls. Circa 490 B.C. Paris, Louvre.

136. Brygos Painter. From the reverse of skyphos (plate 135). Lyre-playing reveller and girl. Paris, Louvre.

137. Brygos Painter. Skyphos. Detail from plate 135. Reveller and girl. Paris, Louvre.

138. Brygos Painter. Outside of cup. Revelling, men and girls. Circa 490 B.C. Würzburg.

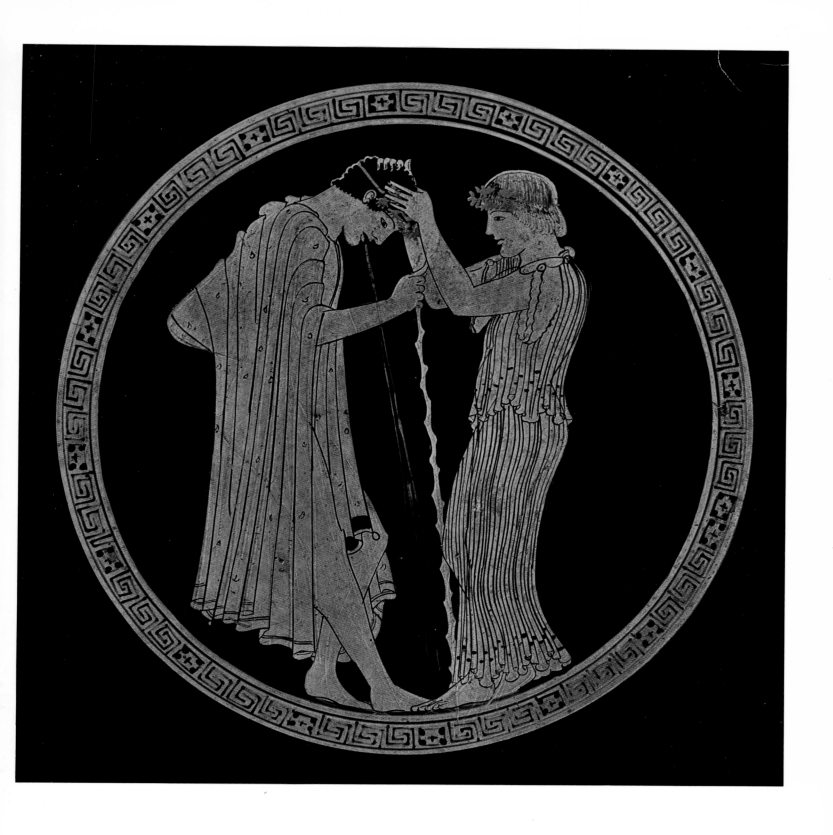

XXXIII. Brygos Painter. Internal medallion of cup (plate 138). Youth being sick and girl. Würzburg.

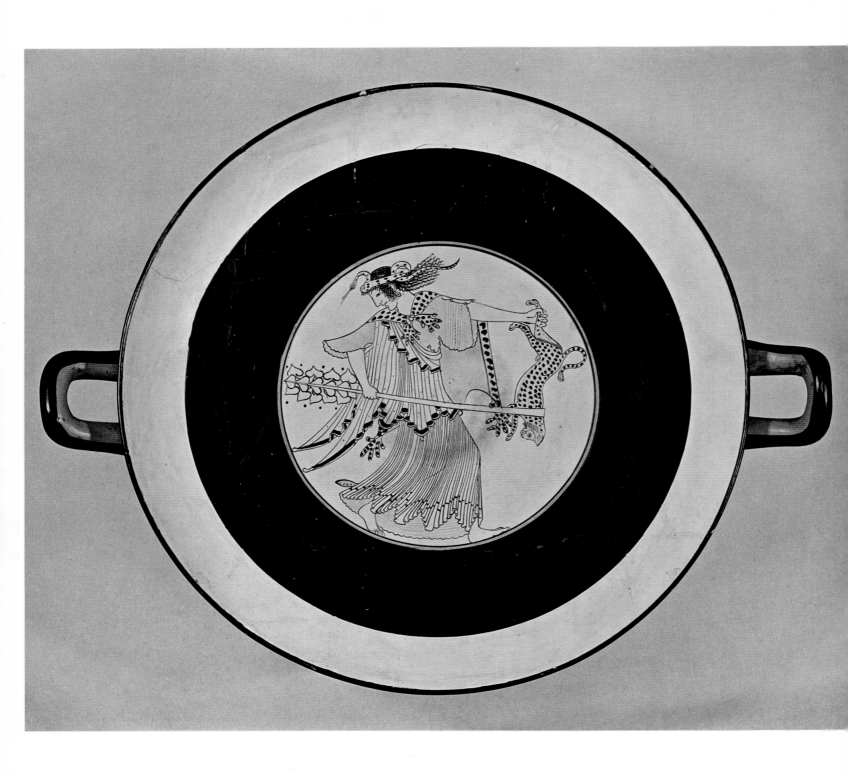

XXXIV. Brygos Painter. Internal (white-ground) picture of cup (plate 143 top). Menad. Circa 490 B.C. Munich.

139. Brygos Painter. Outside of cup. Sack of Troy. (Above, the death of Priam). Circa 490 B.C. Paris, Louvre.

140. Brygos Painter. Internal medallion of cup (plate 139). Phoinix and Briseis. Paris, Louvre.

141. Brygos Painter. Detail of plate 140. Briseis. Paris, Louvre.

142. Brygos Painter. Rhyton (dog's head). On neck, symposium. Circa 500–490 B.C. Rome, Villa Giulia.

143. Upper picture: Brygos Painter. Outside of cup, plate XXXIV. Dionysus with satyr and menads. Circa 490 B.C. Munich.
Lower picture: Douris. Cup. Peleus taming Thetis. Circa 475 B.C. or shortly after. Munich.

144. Douris. Outside of cup. Above, Menelaus against Paris. Below, Ajax against Hector. Circa. 490 B.C. Paris, Louvre.

145. Douris. Internal medallion of cup (plate 144). Eos and Memnon. Paris, Louvre.

146. Douris. Kantharos. Herakles and the Amazons. Circa 490–480 B.C. Brussels.

147. Douris. Internal picture of cup. Jason being disgorged by the dragon guarding the Golden Fleece; Athena.
Circa 480–470 B.C. Vatican.

148. Douris. Outside of cup. Above, revelling. Below, return of Hephaistos to Olympus. Circa 470 B.C.
Paris, Bibliothèque Nationale.

149. Onesimos. Internal medallion of cup. Girl preparing to wash. Circa 480 B.C. Brussels.

150. Berlin Painter. Amphora. Reverse of plate 151. The satyr Orochares holding lyre and kantharos. Berlin.

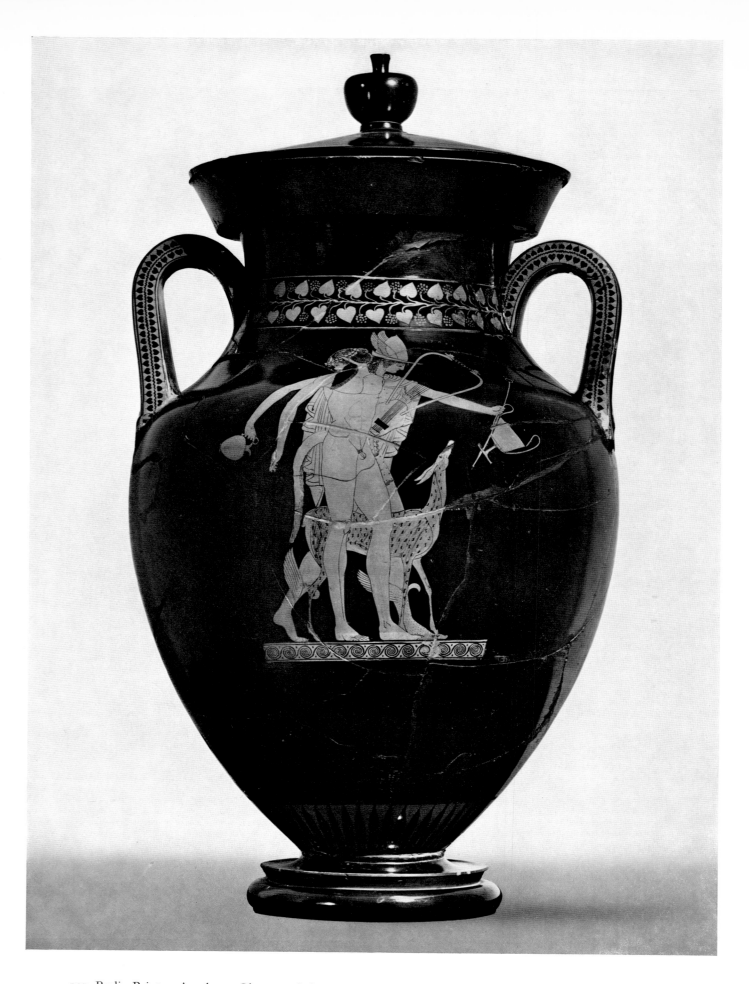

151. Berlin Painter. Amphora. Obverse of plate 150. Hermes and the satyr Oreimachos. Circa 490 B.C. Berlin.

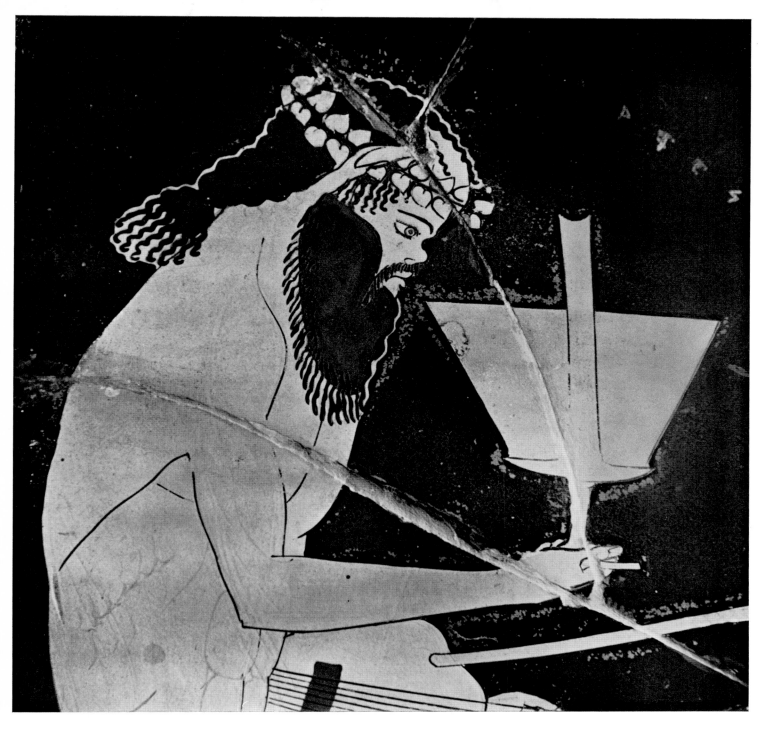

152. Berlin Painter. Detail of plate 150. The satyr Orochares. Berlin.

153. Berlin Painter. Detail of plate 151. Hermes and the satyr Oreimachos. Berlin.

154. Berlin Painter. Bell-krater. Reverse of plate XXXV. Companion of Europa. Tarquinia.

XXXV. Berlin Painter. Bell-krater. Obverse of plate 154. Europa and the bull. Circa 490 B.C. Tarquinia.

155. Berlin Painter. Detail from bell-krater (plate 157). Ganymede. Paris, Louvre.

156. Berlin Painter. Bell-krater. Obverse of plate 157. Zeus after Ganymede. Circa 490 B.C. Paris, Louvre.

157. Berlin Painter. Bell-krater. Reverse of plate 156. Ganymede. Paris, Louvre.

158. Oreithyia Painter. Pointed amphora. Reverse of plate 159. Companions of Oreithyia telling the news to her father, King Erechtheus. King Kekrops also present. Munich.

159. Oreithyia Painter. Pointed amphora. Obverse of plate 158. Boreas carrying off Oreithyia; two of her companions.
Circa 475 B.C. Munich.

164. Pan Painter. Lekythos. Young huntsman, perhaps Kephalos.
Circa 470 B.C. Boston.

165. Pan Painter. Column-krater. Revelling. Circa 460 B.C. Syracuse.

166. Pistoxenos Painter. Skyphos. Below: Obverse, Linos and Iphikles at music lesson. Above: Reverse, Herakles arriving late with his nurse Geropso. Circa 470 B.C. Schwerin.

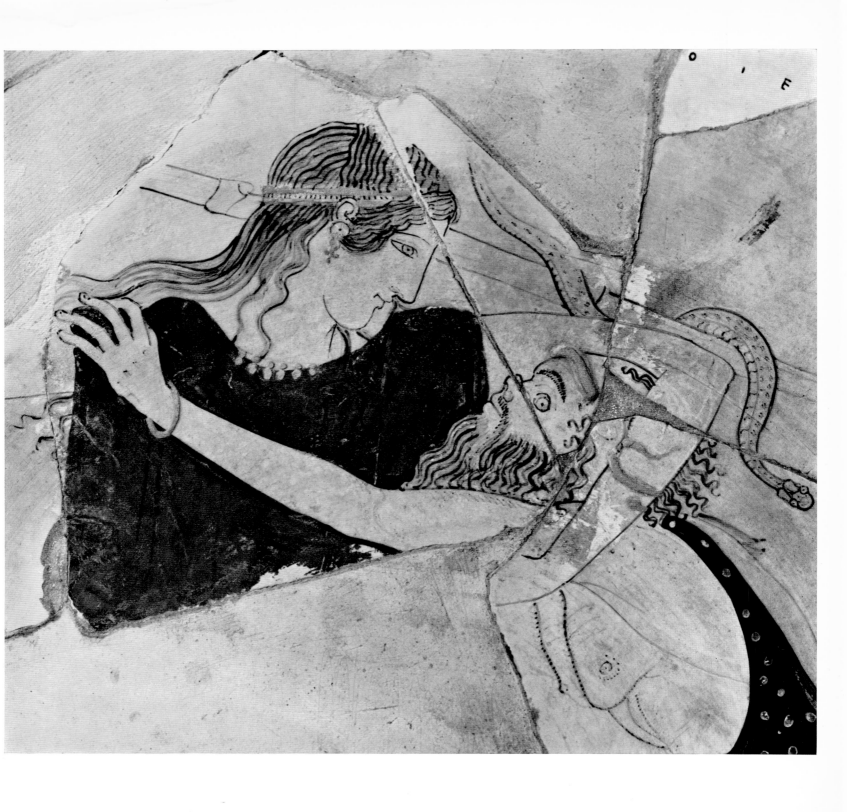

167. Pistoxenos Painter. From internal medallion of a white-ground cup. Menad defending herself against satyr. Circa 465–460 B.C. Taranto.

168. Penthesilea Painter. Internal view of cup. Greek killing Amazon, probably Achilles and Penthesilea. Circa 455 B.C. Munich.

169. Penthesilea Painter. Detail of plate 168. Achilles and Penthesilea. Munich.

170. Penthesilea Painter. Internal view of cup. Apollo killing Tityos. Circa 455 B.C. Munich.

171. Penthesilea Painter. Detail of plate 170. Apollo and Titytos. Munich.

172. Lyandros Painter. Internal view of white-ground cup. Woman, perhaps Aphrodite, being decked by Erotes.
Circa 460 B.C. Florence.

XXXVI. Lyandros Painter. Detail of plate 172. Aphrodite. Florence.

XXXVII. White-ground lekythos close to the Timocrates Painter. Mistress and maid.
Circa 460 B.C. Brussels.

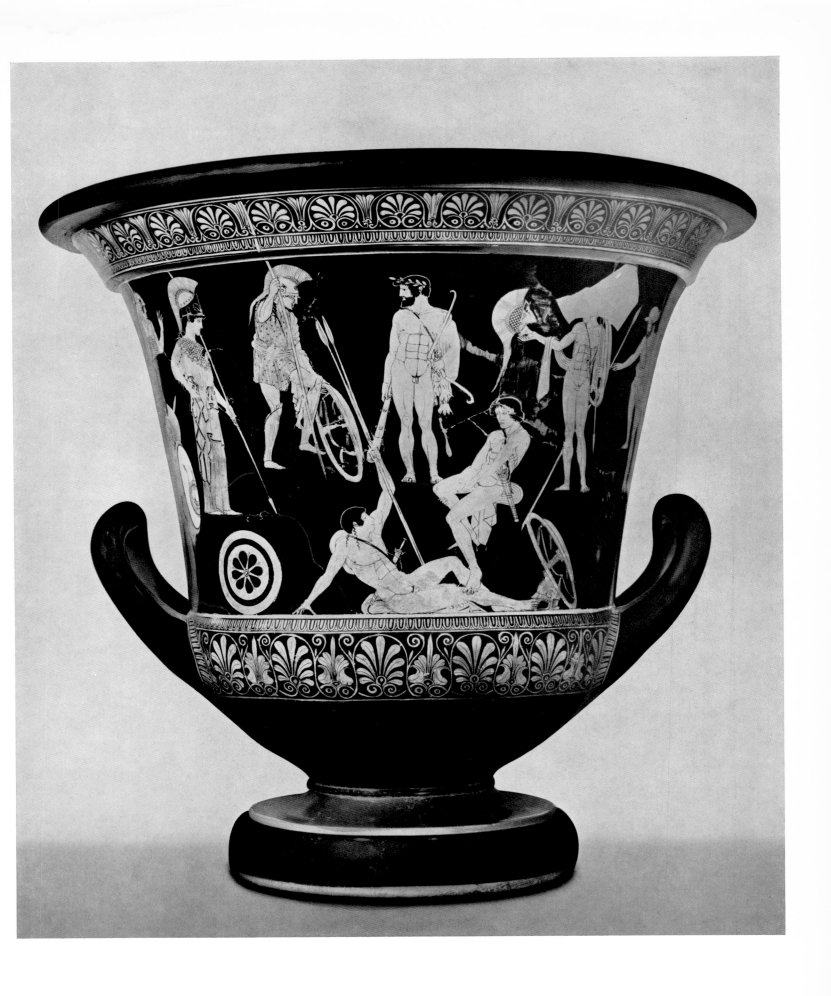

173. Niobid Painter. Calyx-krater. Obverse of plate 175. Unidentified subject, Herakles and Athena present.
Perhaps the Argonauts at Lemnos. Circa 455–450 B.C. Paris, Louvre.

174. Niobid Painter. Detail from calyx-krater (plate 173). Herakles and other heroes. Paris, Louvre.

175. Niobid Painter. Reverse of calyx-krater (plate 173.) Apollo and Artemis slaying the children of Niobe. Paris, Louvre.

176. Niobid Painter. Volute-krater. Battle of Greeks and Amazons. On neck, battle of Lapiths and Centaurs.
Circa 460 B.C. Palermo.

177. Niobid Painter. Volute-krater (plate 176) continued. Amazonomachy. On neck Centauromachy. Palermo.

180. Niobid Painter. From volute-krater, plates 176–177 (scene continued from plate 179). Amazonomachy. Palermo.

181. Niobid Painter. Reverse of volute-krater, plates 176–177. Amazonomachy continued.
On neck, Herakles at the lair of the centaur Pholos. Palermo.

182. Hermonax. Detail of stamnos (plate 183). Hephaistos. Munich.

183. Hermonax. Stamnos. The birth of Erichthonius in the presence of Athena, Hephaistos and Erotes
Circa 460 B.C. or shortly after. Munich.

184. Thanatos Painter. White-ground lekythos. Sleep and Death raising the body of a warrior.
Circa 440–435 B.C. London.

XXXVIII. Achilles Painter. White-ground lekythos. Muse on Mount Helicon. Circa 445 B.C.
Lugano, private collection.

XXXIX. Achilles Painter. White-ground lekythos. Scene of plate XXXVIII continued.
Muse playing the kithara on Mount Helicon. Lugano, private collection.

185. Achilles Painter. White-ground lekythos. Mistress and maid. Circa 445 B.C. Lugano, private collection.

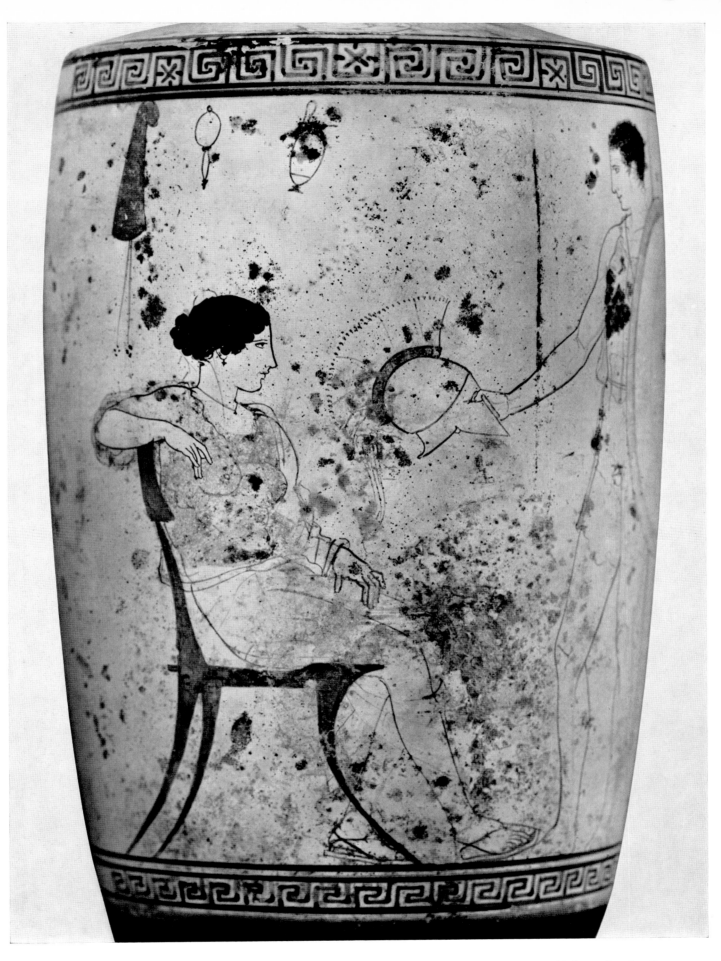

186. Achilles Painter. White-ground lekythos. Warrior's leave-taking from his wife. Circa 440 B.C. or shortly after.
Athens, National Museum.

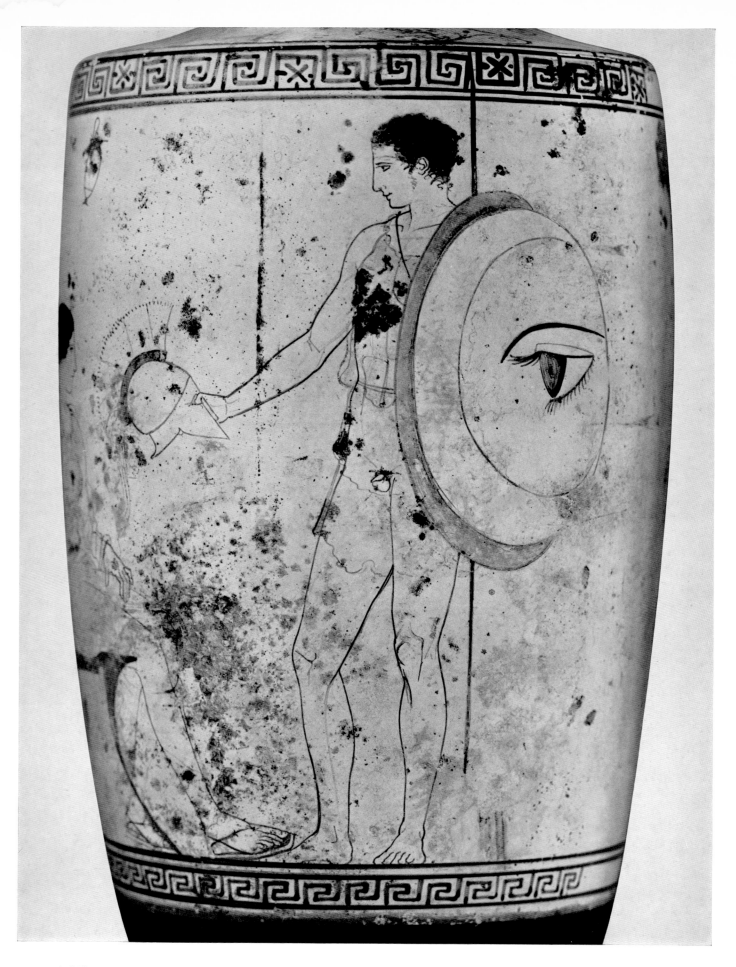

187. Achilles Painter. White-ground lekythos. Scene of plate 186 continued. Warrior's leave-taking. Athens, National Museum.

188. Achilles Painter. Amphora. Achilles. Circa 445–440 B.C. Vatican.

XL. Achilles Painter. Detail of plate 188. Achilles. Vatican.

XLI. Phiale Painter. White-ground lekythos. Hermes waiting for departing woman. Circa 440–430 B.C. Munich.

XLII. Phiale Painter. White-ground lekythos. Scene of plate XLI continued. Woman departing to the Underworld. Tomb in the background. Munich.

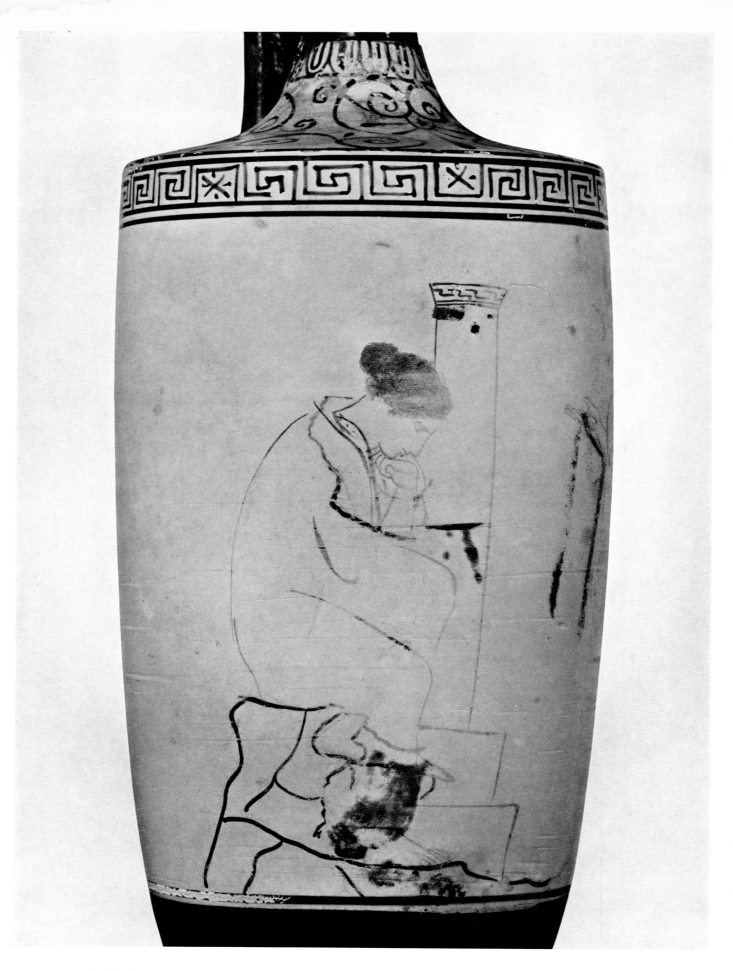

189. Phiale Painter. White-ground lekythos. Departed woman seated on the bank of the river of the dead. Her tomb in the background being visited by another woman. Circa 440–430 B.C. Munich.

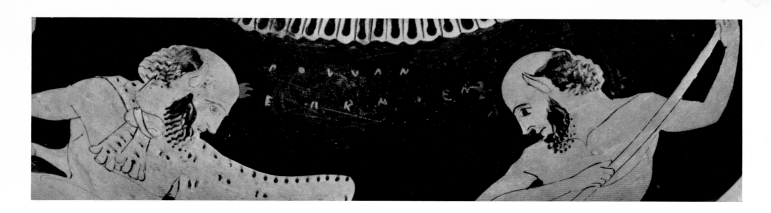

190. Polygnotos. Stamnos. Centaurs against the Lapith Kaineus. Top picture: Details of the Centaurs' heads and the painter's signature. Circa 440 B.C. Brussels.

191. Group of Polygnotos. Pelike. Greeks against mounted Amazon. Circa 440–430 B.C. Syracuse.

192. Orpheus Painter. Column-krater. Greeks against mounted Amazon. Circa 430 B.C. Syracuse.

XLIII. Phiale Painter. White-ground calyx-krater. Reverse of plate XLIV. Three Muses. Vatican.

XLIV. Phiale Painter. White-ground calyx-krater. Obverse of plate XLIII. Hermes bringing the new-born Dionysus to the nymphs and Papposilenus at Nysa. Circa 440–435 B.C. Vatican.

193. Kleophon Painter. Stamnos. Warrior's departure from home. Circa 430 B.C. Munich.

194. Kleophon Painter. Detail from stamnos (plate 193). The warrior's wife. Munich.

195. Kleophon Painter. Detail from stamnos (plate 193). Departing warrior holding libation bowl. Munich.

196. Kleophon Painter. Pelike. Return of Hephaistos to Olympus. Circa 435–430 B.C. Munich.

197. Kleophon Painter. Detail from pelike (plate 196). Satyr and menad. Munich.

198. Kleophon Painter. Detail from pelike (plate 196). Hephaistos drunk being supported by a satyr. Munich.

199. Kleophon Painter. Scene of plate 198 continued. Dionysus. Munich.

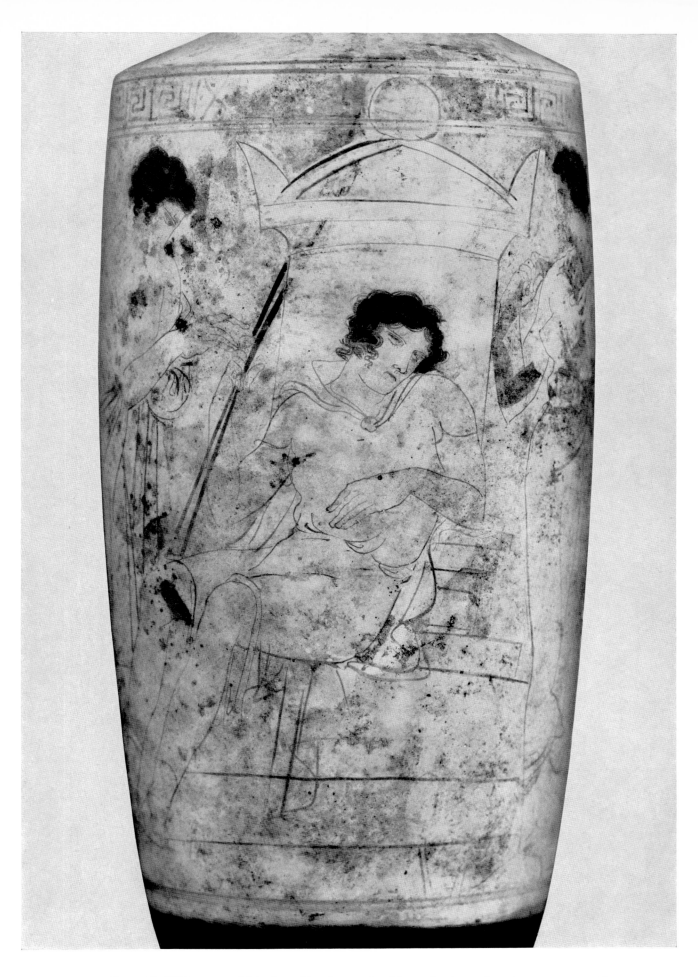

200. Group R. White-ground lekythos. Youth seated at his tomb. A youth and a woman on sides.
End of 5th century B.C. Athens, National Museum.

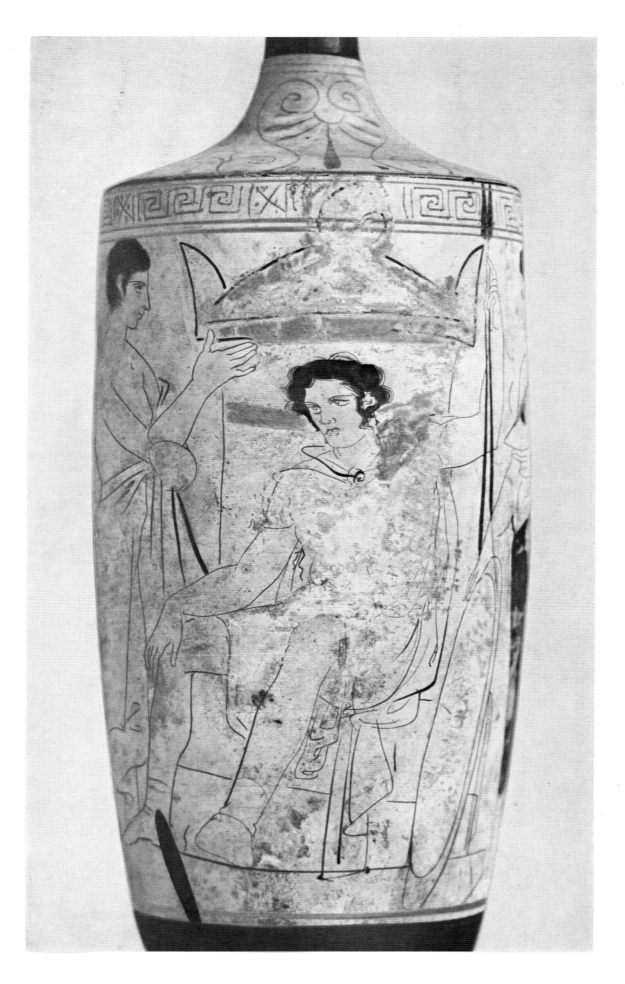

XLV. Group R. White-ground lekythos. Warrior seated at his tomb. Youth and young woman on sides.
End of 5th century B.C. Athens, National Museum.

201. Woman Painter. White-ground lekythos. Young woman seated at her tomb. Women on sides, the one on the right bringing a tray of offerings. Circa 425 B.C. Athens, National Museum.

202. Eretria Painter. Head vase (satyr's head). On neck, two Amazons. Circa 420 B.C. Naples.

203. Eretria Painter. Epinetron. Above: Alcestis in her bridal chamber. Middle picture: Aphrodite with Harmonia, Peitho, Hebe and others of her following. Below: General view of shape with the Alcestis picture showing. Near bust of woman a frieze with Peleus and Thetis. Circa 420 B.C. Athens, National Museum.

204. Shuválov Painter. Oinochoe (chous). Game of ephedrismos. Circa 425 B.C. Berlin.

205. Aison. Squat-lekythos. Theseus and other Greeks against the Amazons. Circa 420 B.C. Naples.

206. Dinos Painter. Stamnos. Obverse of plate 207. A festival of Dionysus. Menads dancing and ladling wine in front of an image of Dionysus, a stake covered with the god's mask and dress. Circa 420 B.C. Naples.

207. Dinos Painter. Stamnos. Reverse of plate 206. Menads dancing at festival of Dionysus. Naples.

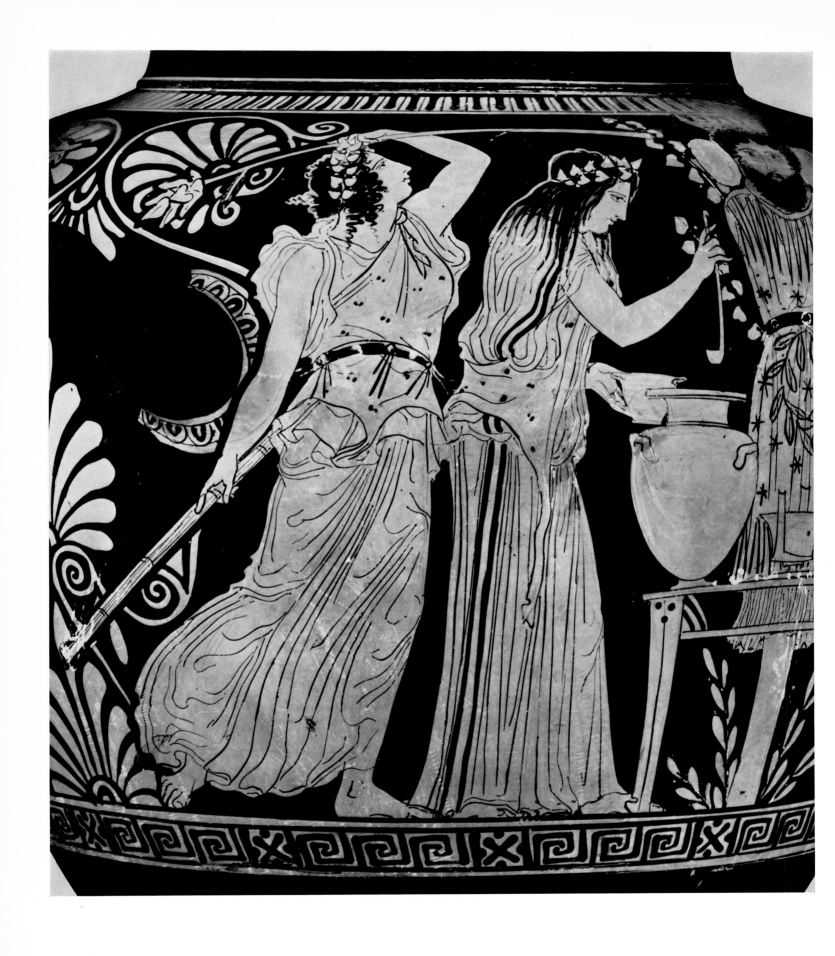

208. Dinos Painter. Detail of stamnos (plate 206). Menads, one dancing, another ladling wine.
Image of Dionysus on extreme right. Naples.

209. Dinos Painter. Scene of plate 208 continued. Menads dancing and playing the tambourine. Naples.

210. Dinos Painter. Details from stamnos (plate 207). Menads dancing and playing the flute. Naples.

211. Dinos Painter. Scene of plate 210 continued. Menads dancing and beating the tambourine. Naples.

212. Neck-amphora with twisted handles near the Meidias Painter. Hippodameia in the chariot with Pelops.
On the neck, a sphinx. Circa 410 B.C. Arezzo.

213. Near the Meidias Painter. Detail from neck-amphora (plate 212). Pelops and Hippodameia. Arezzo.

214. Meidias Painter. Hydria. In upper frieze: The Dioscuri carrying off the daughters of Leucippus in the sanctuary of Aphrodite. Lower frieze: Herakles in the garden of the Hesperides. Circa 410 B.C. London.

215. Meidias Painter. Detail from plate 214. Above, Hilaeira being carried off in the chariot by Polydeuces; the image of Aphrodite in the background. Below, Castor carrying off Eriphyle; Aphrodite seated next to her altar. Circa 410 B.C. London.

216. Meidias Painter. Hydria. Phaon in a bower with Demonassa. Nymphs and gods surrounding them.
Circa 410 B.C. Florence.

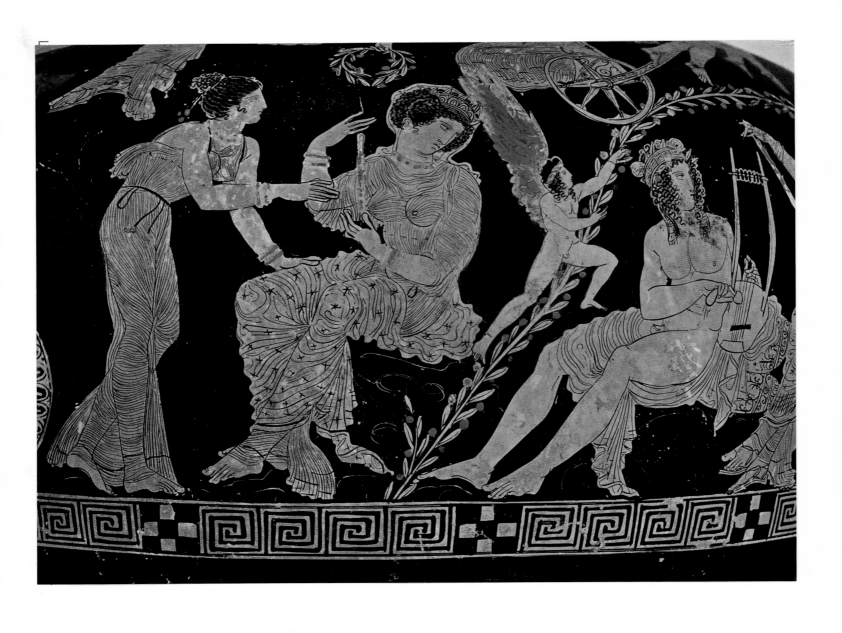

XLVI. Meidias Painter. Detail of plate 216. Phaon playing the lyre, winged Himeros in front of him.
On the left the nymphs Leura and Chrysogeneia. Florence.

217. Meidias Painter. Detail from the hydria (plate 216) upper zone. Aphrodite crossing the heavens in a chariot drawn by Himeros and Pothos; Nymphs amongst the clouds. Florence.

218. Prononomos Painter. Volute-krater. Obverse of plate 219. Dionysus, lord of the Stage, and Ariadne amidst players and characters of the Theatre; Pronomos the flute player, the poet, lyre player and the chorus men of a satyr play with Pappo-silenos; also Laomedon, Hesione and Herakles, the heroes and heroine of the play. End of the 5th century B.C. Naples.

219. Pronomos Painter. Reverse of volute-krater, (plate 218). Dionysus and Ariadne amidst
satyrs and menads. Naples.

220. Calyx-krater (fragmentary) in the manner of the Pronomos Painter. From a battle of gods and giants. On the right, above the canopy of heaven, Helios (the Sun) rising in his chariot. Below the canopy, giants piling up rocks to storm Olympus; the goddess Ge (Earth), their mother, rising out of the ground. End of 5th century B.C. Naples.

221. Suessula Painter. Neck-amphora with twisted handles. Battle of gods and giants
(reverse of a picture covering both sides of vase).
Ares and Aphrodite in the chariot. Circa 400 B.C. or shortly after. Paris, Louvre.

222. Meleager Painter. Internal picture of stemless cup. Dionysus with Ariadne. Beginning of 4th century B.C. London.

223. Calyx-krater, near the Helena Painter. Paris in front of Helen. Kerch style. Circa 370 B.C. Munich.

224. Pompe Painter. Oinochoe (chous). Dionysus and Pompe. Kerch style. Mid 4th century B.C. New York.

XLVII. Marsyas Painter. Pelike. Peleus taming Thetis, who is surprised whilst bathing. Kerch style.
Early in third quarter of 4th century B.C. London.

225. Marsyas Painter. Nuptial lebes. Bringing of gifts to the newly-wed bride. Scene continued on plates 226–228.
Kerch style. Mid-4th century B.C. Leningrad.

226. Marsyas Painter. Nuptial lebes. Bringing of gifts to the bride continued from plate 225.
Bride being decked by Erotes. Leningrad.

227. Marsyas Painter. Nuptial lebes. Scene continued from plate 226. Leningrad.

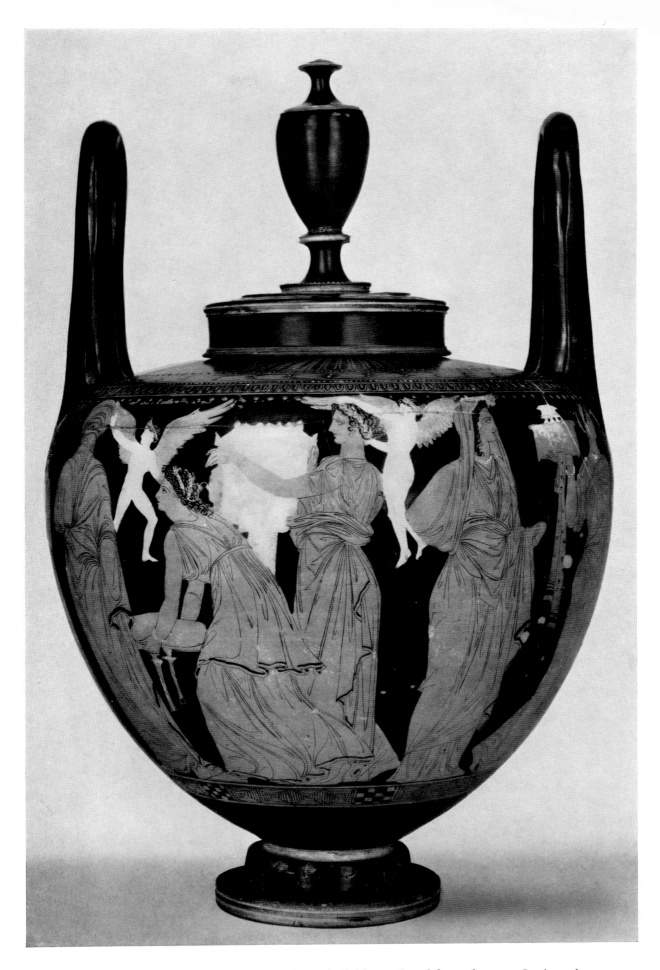

228. Marsyas Painter. Nuptial lebes. Gifts to the bride continued from plate 227. Leningrad.

XLVIII. Etruscan (Faliscan) volute-krater by the Aurora Painter. Reverse of plate 229.
Peleus taming Thetis caught bathing at a fountain. Circa 340 B.C. Rome, Villa Giulia.

229. Etruscan (Faliscan) volute-krater by the Aurora Painter. Obverse of plate XLVIII. Eos (Aurora) crossing the sea in her chariot; Kephalos, or Tithonus, with her. Circa 340 B.C. Rome, Villa Giulia.

230. Italiote volute-krater by the Karneia Painter. Obverse of plate 234. Dionysus with menads and satyr.
Circa 410 B.C. Taranto.

231. Karneia Painter. Details from Italiote volute-krater, plate 230. Menads dancing and playing the flute in front of Dionysus. Taranto.

232. Karneia Painter. Detail of plate 231. Menad playing the flute. Taranto.

233. Karneia Painter. Detail of plate 230. Satyr. Taranto.

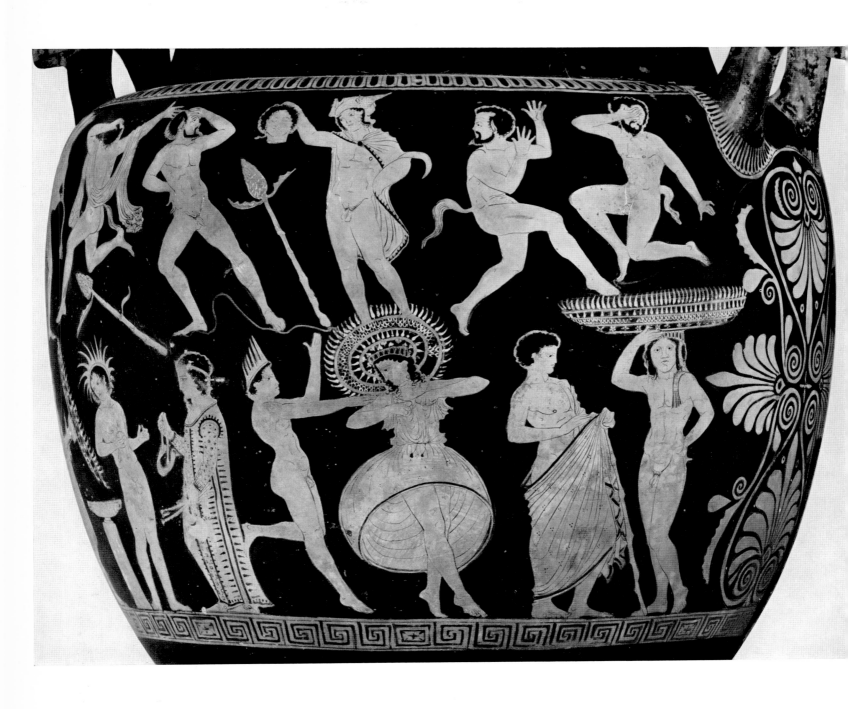

234. Italiote volute-krater by the Karneia Painter. Reverse of plate 230. Lower zone, kalathiskos-dancers at the festival of
Apollo Karneios. Upper zone, Perseus holding out the Gorgon's head amidst terrified satyrs. Circa 410 B.C. Taranto.

235. Karneia Painter. Detail of plate 234. Kalathiskos-dancing girl partnered by boy. Taranto.

236. Italiote volute-krater by the Sisyphos Painter. Obverse of plate 237. Laertes with Autolycus and Antikleia (upper frieze):
Jason's conquest of the Golden Fleece (in lower frieze). On the neck, Erotes at play. Circa 420 B.C. Munich.

237. Italiote volute-krater by the Sisyphos Painter. Reverse of plate 236. The nine Muses (upper frieze);
battle of Centaurs and Lapiths (lower frieze). On neck, horse race. Munich.

238. Early Apulian squat-lekythos. Aphrodite nursing Erotes; Helen and Paris watching two Erotes wrestling. First quarter of 4th century B.C. Taranto.

239. Early Apulian volute-krater. Orestes taking refuge at the omphalos in Delphi. Circa 370 B.C. Naples.

240. Paestan calyx-krater by Asteas. From a phlyax-play. Dancing girl performing in front of Dionysus; buffoons gloating. Circa 350 B.C. Lipari.

XLIX. Apulian calyx-krater. Pan piping, and menads dancing. Mid-4th century B.C. Lipri.

L. Apulian volute-krater with mascaroons. The sending of Triptolemos from Eleusis.
Third quarter of 4th century B.C. Vatican.

LI. Lekanis with lid by the Lipari Painter. Winged Nike and two young women.
Last quarter of 4th century B.C. Lipari.

LII. Krater with lid from Centuripe. Mistress and maids. Third century B.C. Catania, University, Institute of Classical Archaeology.

THE GEOMETRIC STYLE

The art in the Aegean area of the end of the second millennium B.C. and the beginning of the first is that of a period of profound historical change. This is equally true whether one assumes a Dorian invasion shortly before about 1000 B.C. or believes in a great invasion at about 1700 B.C. and therefore in a cultural continuity between the Mycenaean and the archaic Greek culture, a view confirmed by the recent decipherment of Linear B. There is no doubt at all about the profound change of artistic taste which took place in the period between the eleventh century and the end of the eighth. In the past the view has been held that the purely geometric system of decoration, and its primacy over figural work on vases as well as on small objects of ivory or gold, was symptomatic of an artistic decline or at any rate of a primitive and still emerging stage of Greek art. This is not the place to expound the various theories which have been held about the primitiveness or otherwise of the geometric style which even now are the object of learned discussion. It is clear that the examples we present in this book of geometric art reveal a sophisticated style and a mature feeling for the structure of the pot which have nothing in common with either lack of skill or an undeveloped sense for form.

After the fall of Mycenae which is usually put into the middle of the 12th century B.C., the Argolid lost its cultural and political hegemony, the Mycenean hill-top citadels were abandoned and life continued in smaller units of a different type corresponding to new social needs. In art too a new style arose. Already in the Sub-Mycenaean period there developed a style which abandoned the repertoire of figure decoration which had been maintained throughout the Mycenaean period, albeit in stylizations, and started using geometric motifs such as broken lines, concentric semi-circles and angular shapes.

Our appreciation of the earliest stage of this geometric style has been greatly advanced through the finds from the great Dipylon cemetery, excavated since about 1870 and now even better known through the recent researches of Kübler and Kraiker. This earliest stage is called Protogeometric and its progress from the beginning of the 10th century in Attica and elsewhere is most probably contemporary with the introduction of cremation which is to be found side by side with inhumation. The simple decoration of the protogeometric amphorae concentrated particularly on the shoulder of the vase prepares, however modestly, the system which was to become the great feature of the Attic geometric style. Certainly these vases are small fry when compared to the great kraters and amphorae of the classical Dipylon style, but in the simplicity of their decoration they already reveal the desire for harmony and the sense of structure, which is the basis of the true geometric style in Attica. From the 10th century B.C. to the beginning of the 9th the protogeometric style continues with a certain monotony showing that in Attica pottery had achieved its own character, which was presently to grow into maturity.

From the later 10th century figure decoration begins to interest vase painters, though at first only in the way of rather diffident silhouettes of animals such as horses or deer. Also, round the middle of the century we first meet the large-bowled krater on a high conical foot and the amphorae decorated with simple motifs taken over from the preceding period, which now cover the belly or the vase also.

The first phase of the geometric style, usually put from the early 9th century to the mid 9th century, produces a great variety of shapes, *amphorae, kraters, oinochoai* with trefoil mouths, *pyxides*, two-handled cups (inappropriately called *kantharoi*) and *kotylai*. The decoration in this phase of the style is limited to rectangular areas on the shoulder of the vase looking rather like metopes. In the second half of the 9th century B.C. down to the first quarter of the 8th the decoration grows more complex, invades the rest of the body of the vase and increasingly becomes peopled with living creatures. Even small ships appear

occasionally, a token of the importance the sea had during the period of the great colonizing activities in the western Mediterranean. It is however only in the third phase, from about 775 B.C. down to the end of the century that the geometric style reaches its greatest height—and rapid dissolution.

In this phase the subject of the figure decoration especially on the great amphorae is mainly funerary; these great vases are considered to have served as grave monuments and even as ossuaries. These scenes at first are part of a complicated decorative system, but progressively the interest is concentrated more and more upon the figured frieze which in due course contains scenes which may be mythological and have connections with that body of epic poetry which in just those centuries was receiving its definitive shape. In the examples shown here, which naturally represent only a small selection, we can observe the profound changes from the funerary scenes with their figures closely tied to the geometric vision to those where a more naturalistic conception appears in scenes of fighting and sea faring.

The geometric style is not confined to Attica; it is found in the Argolid, in Corinth, in Laconia, in Boeotia (where it has links with Attic Geometric as well as with the Cyclades), in Euboea, in the Cycladic Islands, in Rhodes and in Crete. The style was widely diffused in pottery and not only in pottery; but none of the other centres produced an art of such strong and harmonious character as Attica. Here by fortunate combination of circumstances and spiritual qualities there arose a style of pottery peculiarly Attic, perfect in its form and decoration which expresses most notably the ability of the Greek genius to create organic and harmonious forms and which constituted a foundation for the rise of Attic sculpture.

Bibliography; V. Desborough, *Protogeometric Pottery,* Oxford 1952—a comprehensive study. For the Dipylon style and recent excavations cf. K. Kübler and W. Kraiker, *Kerameikos, Ergebnisse der Ausgrabungen,* Berlin 1939 ff., 6 volumes to date (still in course of publication). In general see also Pfuhl, I, pp. 58–61; Matz, p. 38 ff.; Rumpf, pp. 17–23; Cook, pp. 5–13. On the birth of the geometric style and on its primitive character or otherwise see also R. Bianchi Bandinelli, *Organicità ed astrazione,* Milan 1956 and C. A. Blanc, *Dall'astrazione all' organicità,* Rome 1958 and L. Polacco, *Arte antica e astrattismo,* Venice 1959. On Attica see now Jean M. Davison, *Attic Geometric Workshops,* New Haven 1961 (with many illustrations). A broadly based study of local styles is being prepared by J. N. Coldstream. Outstanding amongst those advocating a substantially earlier dating for the classical Dipylon style (plates 4 ff.) than the one adopted here is E. Kunze, e.g. in *Götting. Gel. Anz.,* 1937, 7, pp. 289–93; *Schweitzer Festschrift* (1954) p. 58; cf. also Himmelmann-Wildschutz, in: *Gnomon,* 34, 1962, p. 80–81.

1

ATTIC PROTOGEOMETRIC AMPHORA. Athens, Kerameikos Museum, 544. From tomb 15 of the Dipylon cemetery. Light grey clay; brown glaze. Height 41.5 cms (16⁵/₁₆″); diam. of mouth 29.5 cms (11⁵/₈″).

Neck black, terminating in a thin lip with concave profile. Decoration of inside of lip consists of concentric semi-circles in units of 6, alternating with vertical lines straight and zig-zag. The rest of the decoration is confined to the shoulder and middle portions of the vase.
On shoulder six concentric semi-circles (made with a multiple brush on a compass); in between these are groups of vertical strokes in mid-field, suspended from the upper border, alternating with irregular zig-zag verticals. Below this zone there is a broad brown band between two narrow ones. On belly of vase two parallel wavy lines. On either side of the sloping handles two brush strokes terminating in a point. Then follow three parallel bands. The foot is brown.
Early decades of 10th century B.C.; belongs to an early phase of Attic Protogeometric.

Bibl.: K. Kübler – W. Kraiker, *Kerameikos I,* Berlin 1939, p. 189–90, pll. 55, 58, no. 544. Cf. also V. Desborough, *op. cit.,* pl. 4, no. 904. On the multiple brush, Boardman, in: *Antiquity,* 34, 1960, p. 85 ff.

2

ATTIC GEOMETRIC AMPHORA. Athens, Kerameikos Museum, 2146. From tomb 41 of the Dipylon cemetery.

Reconstructed from fragments, well preserved, apart from some gaps. Height 69.5 cms (27⁵/₁₆″).

High neck with taut profile and expanding lip. Neck is black except for zone reserved in clay colour and decorated with four parallel lines describing a battlement meander. Dots within the area.
On shoulder, friezes of solid triangles, cross-hatched lozenges and triangles alternatively pointing up and down. The belly of the vase between the handles (double handles joining in a rib) has an elaborately decorated zone, above and below which runs a row of triangles. The zone itself consists of hatched triangles set one above the other, a hatched key meander, hatched lozenges, chevrons and sloping lines. There are two metopes filled with six concentric circles (compass-drawn with a multiple brush) surrounding a cross reserved within a solid circle.
First half of 9th century B.C.; early geometric period. During this phase the syntactic style of decoration arises and is applied to the belly of the vase.

Bibl.: K. Kübler – W. Kraiker, *Kerameikos V,* Berlin 1954, pl. 46, p. 235 and pl. 41, pp. 57, 60, 109, 129, 135, 165, 170 etc.

3

ATTIC GEOMETRIC KRATER WITH LID. Paris, Louvre, A 514. From the Dipylon cemetery. Red clay, yellow slip; glaze is dark but in patches shades into red and yellow. Much restored and reconstructed from many fragments.

Height 57 cms (22⁷/₁₆″), diam. between handles 25.8 cms (10³/₁₆″).

Mouth and interior black. Vertical handles are decorated with horizontal lines; broken lines on handle attachment. The lid has its knob shaped like a trefoil oinochoe, with ribbon handle and decorated with black bands on its belly, a meander on its neck and a series of black dots on its lip.

On the shoulder of the krater a hatched key meander enclosed in a metope, and two small metopes next to the handles within each of which there is a small horse in silhouette. Underneath the right handle a sow between two small boars; under left handle a stag. On belly of vase, bands in light and dark, zig-zag lines, triangles, and nearer the foot of the vase black bands alternating with reserved zones.

Later 9th century B.C.

Bibl.: A. Conze, in: *S. B. Akademie*, Vienna, 1870, pl. 9, no. 1; E. Pottier, *V.A.L. I*, p. 22, A 514.

I

ATTIC GEOMETRIC AMPHORA. Munich, Museum Antiker Kleinkunst, 6080 (1250). From Attica, probably from the Dipylon cemetery. Unbroken and well preserved. Paint has fired reddish. Height 41 cms (16¹/₈″).

Shape is still early; body contracts towards the bottom; the neck is fairly squat. The handles spring from the middle of the neck and join the shoulders. Flaring lip decorated on its rim with dotted lozenges. On neck a frieze of grazing deer, zones of meanders, lozenges, big and small meanders. On shoulder band of lozenges between two of hatched triangles. Between the handle roots a frieze of lying stags with heads turned back. Below this frieze zones of meanders, lozenges, chessboard pattern, meanders, lozenges between rows of standing and pendant hatched triangles, and a row of water birds who stretch their long necks or peck the ground. Brown paint in bands covers the bottom of the vase. Narrow foot.

Attributed by some to the painter of the great Dipylon amphora (pl. 4).

Mid-8th century B.C.

Bibl.: Pfuhl, I, p. 69; Buschor, *Gr Vsm*, p. 35, fig. 18; id., *GV*, p. 12, fig. 11. P. Kahane, in: *AJA*, 44, 1940, p. 477, no. 1. G. Nottbohm, in: *Jdl*, 58, 1943, p. 17, no. 4 and p. 19. Matz I, p. 60, pl. 8. *CVA*, Munich fasc. 3 (Lullies) p. 10, pl. 106–7. D. Ohly, *Griechische Goldbleche*, pl. 27 (neck frieze). Davison, *Workshops*, p. 26; 134, no. 5 (Dipylon Master).

4

ATTIC GEOMETRIC AMPHORA. Athens, National Museum, 804. From the Dipylon cemetery. Reconstructed from many fragments. The foot is restored and should perhaps be higher. Fine yellow clay; brown glaze fired red in places. Height 1.55 m (60¹⁵/₁₆″), greatest diam. of body 74 cms (29¹/₁₆″)″.

Very close system of decoration with meander recurring eight times in its most important variants. On the neck lozenges and triangles alternate with straight lines and meanders. Three rows below the rim there is a frieze of grazing deer; again at the bottom of the neck there is another row of stags lying down and looking back. There are horizontal double handles joined in a central rib.

Between the handles there is the main scene which is framed by meanders and other geometric motifs; it is the lying-in-state of the dead body, the *prothesis*.

On the front of the vase the body of a man in long dress on a bed with high legs. His head is turned upwards, the trunk is frontal whilst all below the waist is in profile. Above him is the shroud, indicated by a hatched area. Below the bed are two skirted figures kneeling and with their hands touching their head in mourning; also two unskirted figures each sitting on a high stool. One of these touches the head with one hand only and makes a gesture with the other. To the right of the bed there are seven standing figures. The one nearest to the bed, a small child, touches it. The others make the familiar mourning gesture. On the left of the bed another group of seven mourners. The two on the extreme left hold their swords which hang by their sides, and with their free hand each touches his head. No other indications of sex, though the skirted mourners are presumably women. All figures have a long neck; nose and chin are indicated by projection of the lower face; the trunk is triangular, the waist very drawn in, the legs are slightly parted and given in profile.

On the back of the vase lamentation continued by eight persons with their hands on their heads in mourning. To the left and right here is a rosette surrounded by concentric circles within a field of meanders. The filling ornament consists of stars, rosettes, swastikas and broken lines. Under the handles there are two figures in mourning gestures whilst the field is filled with birds and lozenges.

One of the classic vases of the geometric style and amongst its most harmonious and balanced creations particularly in the relationship of form and decoration. The shape is designed to perfection; its decoration is governed by the system developed in the earlier phases of geometric.

Middle of the 8th century B.C. or a little earlier.

Bibl.: Brueckner-Pernice, in: *AM*, 18, 1893, pp. 103 ff. S. Wide, in: *Jdl*, 1899, p. 201, fig. 69. Collignon-Couve, *Cat. Vas. Ath.*, no. 200, pp. 42–3. Pfuhl I, pp. 61–3, 70, fig. 10, pl. 1. *CVA*, Athens, fasc. 1 (S. Papaspyridi), p. 8, pl. 81. Idem, *Cat. Mus. Ath.*, p. 284. Buschor, *GV*, p. 13, fig. 12. Rumpf, pp. 16–20. Dunbabin, *The Greeks and their Eastern Neighbours*, London 1957, pl. 1, 1 (detail of the *prothesis*). Similar details in: Matz, pl. 2; Lane, *Greek Pottery*, pl. 5, b; Cook, pl. 5; R. Hampe, *Gleichnisse Homers*, pl. 4, pl. 3 (back), pp. 23–26 (interpretation); *AM*, 69–70, 1954–5, Beil. 8 (large detail of two figures to left of bed). On the shroud, Marwitz, in: *Antike und Abendland*, 10, 1961 p. 77 ff. Davison, *Workshops*, p. 133, no. 1 (Dipylon Master). Female authors (Nottbohm, Davison) take the dress and the hair of the dead to mark her as woman, others do not! The only other person with hair indicated is the second mourner on the right, who touches the shroud, the widow or mother of the dead, standing next to the orphan child. The two *men* on the left may hint at the next stage, the funeral cortège, a men's task (see plate 5).

5

ATTIC GEOMETRIC KRATER. Athens, National Museum, 990. From the Dipylon cemetery. Reconstructed from large fragments. On the back there are large portions

missing. Height 1.23 m (48⁵/₁₆″), diam. of mouth 78 cms (30⁵/₈″).

The flat rim has on its outer ledge a row of brown dots. The neck is decorated with a continuous meander. Horizontal double handles, on either side of which there are two six-leaved rosettes surrounded by concentric circles within a rectangle. The figured zones reach down from the neck to beyond the middle of the vase. Below this there are dark bands, broad and narrow, and one band consisting of vertical wavy lines densely crowded together. The high conical foot has a zone of meanders.

The funeral cortège *(ekphora)*. In the centre of the figured zone is the body of a dead man lying on a bed with high, turned legs, above him the shroud with a chessboard pattern. On the left four mourners standing, the one nearest to the bed a child touching it. To the right of the bed are three swastikas and a heron, then five women mourners. Supporting the bed is a hearse drawn by two long-legged horses. To the left there are nine women in attitudes of mourning (the breasts are indicated). Immediately behind the hearse, perhaps in charge of it, a smaller figure, not a woman. To the right there are eleven figures, four of whom are of greater size, men with swords on their sides. The nearest one leads the horse by a rope. Under the handles eight women in familiar attitudes of mourning. In the lower frieze we see ten chariots with charioteers and two horses each. The charioteers hold the reins and are protected with helmet and armour (the 'double lunette' or 'figure of eight' shape may indicate a corslet or a shield).

The shape of the vase goes back to early geometric and even protogeometric times. This vase has its bottom pierced and served as grave monument and as receptacle for offerings to the dead which could thus percolate into the ground. The date of this krater is slightly later, by a decade perhaps, than the Dipylon amphora (pl. 4) and belongs to after the middle of the 8th century. The painter was particularly interested in the human figure. The face is indicated by a circle within which a dot represents the eye. The same painter probably also decorated a krater in the Nicholson Museum in Sydney which has a similar subject. We can notice a certain variety introduced into the strict symmetry of the geometric system. The figure decoration too seems to be infused with a greater freedom than the areas of geometric decoration which in any case have lost in importance. There is in particular a freshness in the rendering of the hearse and the small figures which conventionally precede the funeral procession. Another krater in New York with a similar subject is ascribed to the same hand (Metrop. Mus., 14. 130. 14).

Bibl.: O. Hirschfeld, in: *AI*, 1872, p. 142, no. 41. Id., in: *MI*, IX, pl. 39, 1; 40. 1. O. Rayet–M. Collignon, *Céramique grecque*, pl. I. Kroker, in: *Jdl*, I, 1886, p. 95. Baumeister, *Denkmäler des klass. Altertums*, Munich-Leipzig 1885–1888, III, p. 1943. Collignon–Couve, pp. 48–9, no. 214. S. Papaspyridi, *Cat. Mus. Athènes*, p. 284. Buschor, *GV*, p. 16, fig. 15. Zervos, *L'art en Grèce*, pl. 45. Kunze, in: *Festschrift Schweitzer*, p. 48, assigns six more fragments to this vase, also listed in: Davison, *Workshops*, p. 141, no. 1. (Hirschfeld Painter). For the function of these vases as grave-monuments see *AM* 18, 1893, p. 92, fig. 4; also G. Karo, *An Attic Cemetry*, Philadelphia 1943, pp. 11–12. Rumpf, *Religion d. Griechen*, fig. 177; B. Schmidt, in: *Arch. Religionswiss.* 25, 1927, p. 77; F. Poulsen, *Dipylongräber*, Leipzig 1905, pp. 18 ff.

6

ATTIC GEOMETRIC OINOCHOE. Boston, Museum of Fine Arts, 25.42. From Attica, formerly in the Schliemann Collection. Restorations. The lip is broken. Pale yellow clay, black glaze, fired unevenly. Height 23 cms (9″).

The lip has a dip in the centre but is not yet trefoil. It is decorated with groups of alternately slanting bars. On the neck lozenges and chessboard pattern. On the shoulder two rows of lozenges, dotted and hatched respectively. The handle has a cylindrical cross-section and is decorated with a snake. The figured frieze on the body shows foxes (note the bushy tail) a fawn and dogs, grouped one above the other, moving to the left. In the middle there is a male figure and there are two more males, on each side of the handle. They seem to have a whip in their hand. Swastikas as filling ornament.

Third quarter of 8th century B.C. The vase belongs to a group of representations of animal fights and war scenes which in these decades particularly interested Attic vase painters. The human figures are well developed and supple. The vase deserves more study than it has so far received.

Bibl. A. Fairbanks, *Catalogue of Greek and Etruscan Vases, Museum of Fine Arts, Boston*, Cambridge/Mass. 1928, p. 81, no. 269b, pl. 23. Hampe, *Gleichnisse Homers*, pl. 5–6. Davison, *Workshops*, p. 154, no. 3 (The Burly Workshop).

7

ATTIC GEOMETRIC KRATER. New York, Metropolitan Museum, 34.11.2. From Attica. Surface well preserved, but much restored. Gaps in several places. Height 97.5 cms (38⁵/₁₆″).

Lip curling out above neck which is decorated with a continuous key meander. Below this a narrow fillet decorated with vertical lines. On the body of the vase there are two metopes with cross within concentric circles. These metopes are enclosed by bands of meanders and chevron pattern. In the centre, again in a metope, there is a scene of the lying-in-state of the dead body *(prothesis)*. The vase bottom is pierced; see on plate 5 and bibliography.

Below this zone and separated from it by a band of pattern is the rare theme of a battle taking place both around two long ships which are beached, and on their decks. There are no rowers, as the warriors themselves man the oars. The two battles are separated by a row of warriors with 'figure of eight' shields of the Dipylon type. On deck there are single combats with the sword, also an archer drawing and a spearman hurling against an attacker charging up the prow. The boat on the other side has unfurled sails and shows one of the crew wounded. The vase has a high conical foot.

The human figures are well developed. The warriors wear a crested helmet and the special type of shield, which may have been used to depict figures of heroic legend taken from epic tradition. The subject may therefore refer to Homeric battles.

This krater cannot be dated, as some scholars have done, to the early decades of the 8th century B.C. but rather must come within the third quarter of the 8th century. It is one

of the most notable and successful examples of a picture of human events conceived strictly in accordance with geometric principles and yet rendered with freshness and spontaneity.

Bibl.: G. M. A. Richter, in: *Metr. Mus. Bull.*, 1934, pp. 169ff, fig. 1–3. J. M. Cook, in: *ABSA*, 35, 1934–35, p. 171, n. 5, p. 192, n. 4. R. S. Young, in: *Hesperia*, Suppl. II, 1939, p. 172. G. S. Kirk, in: *ABSA*, 44, 1949, p. 99, no. 6. G. M. A. Richter, *Metr. Museum of Art—Handbook of Greek Collection*, 1953, p. 25, fig. 14d. E. Kunze, in: *Festschrift Schweitzer*, p. 50, n. 11; 39. T. B. L. Webster, in: *ABSA*, 50, 1955, p. 43, n. 38. Kunze, in: *Eph. Arch.*, 1953–4, p. 168, n. 6. Marwitz, in: *Antike Kunst* 4, 1961, pp. 39ff; pll. 17–18 (full study; dates late, as here). Davison, *Workshops*, pp. 110; 112–13; 130 (dates early, as also Kunze).

8

ATTIC GEOMETRIC KANTHAROS. Copenhagen, National Museum, 727. From the Dipylon cemetry. Some gaps. Light red clay, micaceous. Brown glaze fired red in places. Height 17 cms (6⅝″).

On the outside of each handle are three zones one above the other; bird, leaf cross, bird, all with dot rosettes and other filling ornament. On the return of the handle facing the mouth are double diagonals within a rectangle, and hatched triangles.

The decoration is within a broad metope both on neck and shoulders of the vase. On the neck two ducks on either side, then two leaf crosses and in the centre a lying deer with head turned back. Underneath on the shoulder from left to right, man and woman, duel between two men, in the centre two lions devouring a man, to the right a lyre player and two women who carry water pitchers *(hydriai)*.

The other side has a similar decorative scheme. The main picture has a dance of two warriors with 'figure of eight' shields. In the centre a boxing contest, to the right high jumpers and lyre player.

Under the frieze, zone of dotted circles linked by tangents.

The subjects are mainly athletic, the presence of 'figure of eight' shields shows that the painter wanted to represent also contests in armour no longer in use (according to Miss Lorimer these shields are reflections of the armour of the Mycenaean period). The vase is certainly Attic and belongs to the last quarter of the 8th century B.C. In that period there were a number of painters with a particular interest in the human figure, an interest which had already appeared in the mature phase of the geometric. The running frieze of circles linked by tangents is an island element and places our vase in the period of the first appearance of orientalizing elements.

Bibl.: *AZ*, 1885, p. 134, pl. 8, 2. A. Furtwängler, *Kleine Schriften*, II, p. 114ff., pl. 24, 2. Perrot-Chipiez, VII, p. 180, fig. 65–6. *AM*, 1901, p. 37. *CVA*, Copenhagen, fasc. 2 (Johansen), pl. 73, 5a-b. W. Hahland in: *Corolla Curtius*, pll. 42–43. Dunbabin, *Greeks and their Eastern Neighbours*, pl. 2. Webster, in: *ABSA*, 50, 1955, p. 40, n. 19. Kunze, in: *Eph. Arch.*, 1953–4, p. 171, n. 1 (dates it early, contemporary with our plate 4). Davison, *Workshops*, p. 154, no. 3 (The Burly Painter).

9

ATTIC GEOMETRIC AMPHORA. Athens, National Museum, 894. From the Dipylon cemetery. Lid, neck and lower part of vase restored. Fair preservation; glaze has disappeared in places. Height 65 cms (25 9/16″).

The lid has its knob in shape of a pommel, and is decorated with birds and grazing deer. Plastic serpents on the rim of the vase and the base of its neck and on the side of the handles. On the neck geometric patterns; net of lozenges, meander, chessboard, broken lines, meander, zig-zag and meander. The body of the vase is more oval than the amphorae of the best period. It is again decorated with geometric friezes and two large figured zones. The upper zone has a procession of four- and two-horsed chariots; the lower zone has a file of warriors armed with two spears and round shield. All warriors in both zones wear helmets with long fluttering crests. The horses' necks and croup are more massive than in the preceding periods. The mane is unkempt. There is hastiness in the execution of both ornament and figure work, which is in pure silhouette. The gestures, however, are surprisingly vivid, and even in the bearing of the heads there is an expressiveness which is hardly found in previous pictures.

The amphora shows the fundamental changes which occurred in the geometric style after about 730 B.C. The round shields, also found in Protocorinthian pottery, indicate a change in armour connected with the rise of the hoplite system. Our vase is stylistically related to amphorae, also with plastic snakes, in the Louvre, Cleveland, and Athens. These vases of the last quarter of the 8th century come at a decisive change in Attic vase painting. The human figure increases in importance, new decorative elements are also introduced, including plastic motifs. The snakes here have chthonic significance and allude to the funerary use of the pot.

About 725 to 710 B.C., a little after the Louvre amphora mentioned above.

Bibl.: S. Wide, in: *Jdl*, 1899, p. 197, fig. 61. For the connections with the amphora Athens 897, the Cleveland amphora and the one formerly in the Vlastos Collection in Athens see J. M. Cook, in: *ABSA*, 42, 1947, pp. 139ff., with a rather low chronology. See also J. M. Cook, in: *BSA*, 35, 1934–5, p. 167. For the Louvre amphora see F. Villard, in: *Mon. Piot*, 49, 1957, pp. 17ff., fig. 1–12. On the question of armour and the introduction of hoplite shields in the second half of the 8th century see H. L. Lorimer, in: *ABSA*, 42, 1947, pp. 76ff. and id., *Homer and the Monuments*, p. 129. *EWA II*, pl. 32, top right. Davison, *Workshops*, p. 144, no. 1 (Painter of Athens 894).

10

ATTIC AMPHORA, very late geometric, transitional. London, British Museum, 1936. 10-17.1. From Attica. Restored but well preserved. The glaze has flaked in a good many places. Height 62 cms (24⅜″).

Lip has small black stripes. On the neck, bands of lozenges and triangles; then enclosed within a rectangular frame a lion seizing a fawn. On the shoulders (on both sides of vase) three fawns grazing. The body of the vase is covered with repeated bands of lozenges and sigma pattern. Round the belly is a frieze of chariots each drawn by one horse with charioteers holding a goad. Swastikas, stars and N-shaped elements serve as filling ornaments. On the handles there are

small plastic serpents. The vase is still decorated in a manner typical of late geometric, but the ornamental schemes are now used in monotonous repetition. The motif of the lion felling a fawn is typically orientalizing. Here is one of its earliest occurrences on Attic vases. Moreover, the appearance of the plastic snakes, as well as the new tautness of shape shows that the vase belongs to the transitional phase between the geometric and orientalizing periods. End of 8th century B.C.

Bibl.: *British Museum Quarterly*, XI, 1936/7, p. 56, pll. 18–19a. J. M. Cook, in: *ABSA*, 42, 1947, p. 150. Beazley, *Development*, p. 5. Davison, *Workshops*, p. 148, no. 2 (Painter of Oxford 1935. 18). R. Hampe, *Frühattischer Grabfund*, Mainz 1960, p. 79 (N-Painter, after the shape of the filling ornament, but the name is bespoke already, see our plate XIII; see also J. M. Cook, in: *JHS*, 81, 1961, p. 221).

THE ORIENTALIZING STYLE

This term is used for that period of Greek art which saw the introduction of oriental motifs not only in pottery but in every aspect of art including sculpture (particularly in terracotta and small-scale sculpture, ivories and gems). It has rightly been pointed out that even before this time oriental motifs of all kinds had appeared in vase painting and other types of art in the Aegean. It is however only now in the later 8th and particularly in the 7th century B.C. that clear evidence appears of the diffusion of a new artistic taste linked to an orientalizing world, of which Cyprus, Crete and the Ionian coast of Asia Minor formed a major part. This new artistic language, so different from the geometric with its rigid, prescribed formulas, spread throughout the Mediterranean drawing its origin from somewhere in the general area of Syria, Phoenicia and Cyprus rather than from Egypt. Whilst the geometric had a strict unity of style which had above all governed Attic pottery, the focus of all vase painting between the 10th and the 8th century, we now witness the fragmentation of style into various centres of production. Nevertheless there was a fundamental unity based upon a common stock of decorative elements. Unlike, however, the geometric which was based upon Attica, the new orientalizing style did not arise there; rather it developed in a region which was to become the greatest rival of Attica, namely Corinth. We shall often have to refer in this section to the details of Corinthian style, as it became at the crucial period the dominant influence in the Aegean. This even applies when discussing Protoattic, the orientalizing style of Attica.

Corinth became from the later part of the 8th century the great centre of distribution of a highly individual type of pottery. First of all there is 'Protocorinthian' and then 'Corinthian', both of them orientalizing styles. Vases of the 'Corinthian' style became the most widely spread export commodity in the whole Mediterranean, from Ionia to Greece, Sicily and Spain. One could say that Corinthian pottery at that time became what centuries earlier the Late Mycenaean pottery had been. We must not, however, forget that in addition to Corinth there were other centres of production; in the Cyclades, in Euboea, Crete, Rhodes, Cyprus, Ionia, Chios and Naucratis. In the Cyclades alone we have evidence so far of four centres of production, Paros, Naxos, Thera and Melos, all of them with their own characteristics. Thus it was that Corinth for all its commercial activities under the progressive rule of the Bacchiads and the Kypselids was unable to liquidate the rival centres of production, which in fact made special efforts to render their ware as individual as possible.

'Protocorinthian' vases are distinguished from 'Corinthian' by a particular finesse of drawing and by their miniature style. Protocorinthian according to modern views began early in the last quarter of the 8th century and continued into the third quarter of the next century through a period when pottery was diversified, bigger shapes were created and more complex figure compositions adopted. A characteristic of this style is the use of animal friezes, whose oriental origin is demonstrated not only by their constituents (felines, cocks, sphinxes, griffins, sirens) but also by direct comparison with Assyrian and Phoenician motifs. Corinthian vase painting was further enriched by the introduction of incision which was used side by side with plain silhouette. This use of incision created the 'Black-figure' style and came to be adopted by almost all archaic styles. Another important innovation is the use of purple and white colour which enliven the black figures which otherwise might seem monotonous. With the 6th century Corinthian vase-painting pays increasing attention to the human figure and therefore plays a vital part in the development of black-figure which in Attica reached its greatest artistic achievements. Literary sources speak of an important school of Corinthian wall painting and the attempts by various Corinthian painters of the archaic period to create new techniques. This shows that Corinthian vase painting derived inspiration

from wall paintings and decorative friezes such as covered the Chest of Cypselus. If we do not have any examples of these pictures, we can through the reflection of archaic Corinthian vase-painting still form a dim notion of their artistic importance.

Of other centres we possess some few examples of the orientalizing style of the Argolid, such as the remarkable fragment with Odysseus blinding Polyphemus. More notable is the orientalizing style of Laconia, once wrongly called Cyrenaic. It developed individual shapes such as the lakaina, and a decorative system of strong oriental flavour (lotus flowers, pomegranates, palmettes) as well as a limited but unusual repertoire such as the nymph Cyrene wrestling with a lion, episodes from the life of Herakles, and the realistic representation of wool being weighed on the famous Arkesilas cup in Paris (pl. 74 and XXIV). Laconian pottery was produced throughout the 7th century and continued down to the second half of the 6th. In other regions too, in Attica, Euboea, the Cyclades and Rhodes the orientalizing style took on individual forms.

In Attica the ornamental character of the orientalizing style, its animal friezes and floral motives, never succeeded in obliterating the inherent qualities of Attic art, its ever growing interest in the human figure. None of the other orientalizing fabrics ever succeeded in creating works of such grandeur and dramatic intensity as Protoattic. Perhaps amongst Cycladic vases we have the nearest approach to this achievement in some mythological scenes from Naxos and Melos. In any case Attica in this phase reaches great heights with its orientalizing vases, in some of which we may perhaps recognize links with Crete, whose orientalizing elements have perhaps not yet been given sufficient recognition.

Quite different again are the orientalizing fabrics of Rhodes, Cyprus and in Eastern Greece generally. They remain steeped in a decorative tradition veering sometimes towards an imitation of Corinthian (though with different motifs and a rather East Greek flavour) sometimes again towards oriental influence, particularly in the ample application of white together with freer use of colours.

The orientalizing style then with its experimental tendencies and special attention to the use of colour also provided for Attica a good schooling in its progress towards classical Black-figure ware. We shall see that in the early 6th century before the rise of classical Black-figure (represented by such masters as Lydos, the Amasis Painter, and Exekias) a good number of painters made great use of motifs and ornaments which were derived from the orientalizing style of the previous generations, suffice it here to mention Kleitias.

Bibliography: There is no comprehensive work on the orientalizing style. We must therefore confine ourselves to mentioning some fundamental studies on several of the various fabrics. For Protocorinthian and Corinthian *cf.* K. F. Johansen, *Les Vases Sicyoniens,* Copenhagen 1923; H. Payne *Necrocorinthia,* Oxford 1931. On the fragment from Argos with Odysseus and Polyphemus see P. Courbin, in: *BCH,* 79, 1955, pp. 1ff. and M. Robertson, *Greek Painting,* Geneva, 1959, p. 44. For Laconian cf. E. A. Lane, in: *ABSA,* 34, 1933-4, pp. 99ff. B. B. Shefton, in: *ABSA,* 49, 1954, p. 299ff. id., in: Dunbabin and others, *Perachora,* II. On Protoattic cf. J. M. Cook, in: *ABSA,* 35, 1934-5, p. 165ff. On Cycladic pottery cf. Ch. Dugas, *La Céramique des Cyclades,* Paris 1925; id. *Délos,* X and XVII. On Euboean cf. J. Boardman, in: *ABSA,* 47, 1952, p. 20ff. On Crete cf. J. K. Brock, *Fortetsa,* Cambridge 1957; J. Boardman, *The Cretan Collection in Oxford.* On Rhodian cf. W. Schiering, *Werkstätten orientalisierender Keramik auf Rhodos,* Berlin 1957; Cook p. 38ff. For chronological problems of the period, see Dunbabin, in: *Arch. Eph.,* 1953-4, pp. 247ff. See also R. M. Cook, in: *JHS,* 66, 1946, p. 92ff., especially on East Greek.

II

PROTOATTIC AMPHORA. Paris, Louvre CA2985. From Attica, Well preserved; some restorations. Reddish-yellow clay, surface of extremely fine texture and glossy. Plastic decorations consisting of three wavy rolls on the lip, two on handles and three at the base of the neck, are glazed in black. The black glaze has fired red in places. Height 80 cms (31$^7/_8''$); height of neck alone 35 cms (13$^3/_4''$), greatest circumference 86 cms (33$^3/_4''$).

Elongated neck widening towards the top. The shape of the lower part of the vase is also elongated. Handles are three quarters solid, but with perforations in the wall. A certain amount of incision is used for ornamental detail and figure work.

The neck has four zones. From the top downwards: two winged sphinxes; three rosettes with seven leaves each, separated by a vertical cable pattern; five human figures; long alternating curved triangles in silhouette. The sphinxes in the upper zone have a slim body, short wings, faces in outline and reserved in clay colour, wings decorated with scales, big claws. The zone with human figures on the neck shows a flute player in the centre, between two couples on either side, man and woman holdings hands, carrying branches and engaged in a dance. Same subject and decoration on the other side.

On the body of the vase below the clay rolls a zone of stepped lines. Below that pendant spiral hooks. Underneath comes the figure frieze, double spirals, then a row of leaves in silhouette, then stepped lines and bands of parallel and broken lines.

The main figure frieze has four chariots with charioteers in long chiton, each holding a goad and the reins. Their faces are alternately in outline and silhouette.

The shape which recalls late geometric amphorae should be funerary and may have served as a *loutrophoros*. The vessel belongs to the first decades of the 7th century B.C. It is Protoattic; whilst the organization of the geometric motives is geometric the individual elements are clearly orientalizing. The vase has been attributed to the Analatos Painter. The plastic clay rolls recall the plastic snakes found on amoperae of the latest geometric phase towards the end of the 8th century.

Bibl.: J. Audiat, in: *Mon. Piot*, 36, 1938, pp. 36–58, pl. 2. J. M. Cook, in: *ABSA*, 35, 1934–5, p. 173 (attribution to Analatos Painter), p. 205; idem, in: *ABSA*, 42, 1947, p. 150; also p. 142, 149 (on Analatos Painter. More on this important artist, in: R. Hampe, *Frühattischer Grabfund*, p. 77 ff.; reviewed by J. M. Cook, in: *JHS*, 81, 1961, p. 220. Davison, *Workshops*, p. 45, 51 ff.). Buschor, *GV*, p. 37, fig. 43.

III

ERETRIAN AMPHORA. Athens, National Museum, 12129. From Eretria in Euboea. Well preserved though reconstructed from many fragments. Purple is used for the women's dress and for most of the sphinx. Clay is light yellow; brown glaze. Height 75 cms (29$^1/_2$″).

The shape with its high conical foot recalls geometric kraters. The thick neck, which ends in a shallow ledge decorated with triangles (sets of three of which are in silhouette, followed by one in outline), has a group of three females in chitons (drawn in outline), and a mantle (himation) which is thrown across their shoulders and painted in purple. The two leftmost women carry branches in their hands and offer them to a female standing to their right and facing them; perhaps an offering to a goddess.

On the body of the vase there is a big sphinx whose long hair comes down her back in a great bunch and falls on her shoulders in smaller tresses. Additional decoration consists of hatched pendant triangles and scattered dot rosettes. Also a double spiral motive underneath the sphinx's body. Dot rosettes in faded white (barely visible on our plate) sprinkled all over the sphinx's body.

Underneath the handle and on the back of the vase big spiral loops which recur on all vases of this group and are typical of Eretrian.

The orientalizing nature of the decoration is clear (rosettes, palm branches, spiral complexes, loops and sphinx). The use of incision is due to Corinthian influence but the shape of these amphorae is due to Boeotian prototypes. The workshop used elements from the repertoire of various provincial centres. The loop ornament also provides a link with Cycladic whilst the sphinx recalls certain motives of Protoattic. This eclectic style has something of folk art about it

and this is one of the main reasons for the present day interest in these fringe manifestations of archaic art. Last quarter of 7th century B.C.

Bibl.: J. Boardman, in: *ABSA*, 47, 1952, p. 22 ff. and p. 27, C6; pl. 6. (women on neck interpreted as mourners). Cf. Pfuhl III, fig. 101 where a similar amphora is reproduced but with a lion instead of a sphinx.

II

BOEOTIAN AMPHORA. Athens, National Museum, 5839 (220). From near Thebes in Boeotia. Foot restored. Some flaws in the shape of the vase. Grey-yellow clay. Height 87 cms (34$^1/_8$″). Diam. of mouth 24 cms (9$^7/_{16}$″).

The two horizontal double handles recall similar handles of Attic geometric vessels. The neck widens towards the top and has an inset lip. The body of the vase is an elongated oval, the foot is conical with a slightly concave profile. One feels that the potter tried to follow an Attic model without attaining its perfection of profile. The neck is decorated with a row of dots, then a simple meander ornament, then a dotted zig-zag line. Then follows a broad zone of vertical thick zig-zag lines, a motive rather typical of Boeotian geometric.

The body of the vase is decorated in its lower third with a large black zone, above which, and supported by some narrow black bands, we have more broad vertical zig-zag lines, like those on the neck but shorter. On the foot similar wavy verticals, together with straight black verticals. The brush strokes of the verticals (straight, wavy and zig-zag) on neck, body and foot are of the same thickness.

The principal subject, as well as its counterpart on the other side of the vase, is set within a metope, a composition familiar also from Attic geometric and the Cycladic styles. Above this metope is a narrow zone of water birds; on the sides it is framed by a serpent like line enclosed within vertical lines.

The main picture shows in an interesting way the penetration of orientalizing motives into a provincial workshop. The female in the centre holds her arms outstretched, her face is heart-shaped and framed with thin tresses. She wears a curious chiton decorated with geometric motifs. Its lower part clearly shows the design of a fish. She is the 'Mistress of the Beasts' (*potnia thērōn*) whose cult spread from Assyria to Crete, Corinth, Olympia and the whole of the Aegean. She is flanked by two lions with gaping mouths and panting tongue. Above the enormous arms of the goddess two birds; to her right a bull protome. The filling ornament consists of hatched triangles, swastikas, crosses and other motifs.

The other side shows an even more bizarre picture. A great bird with wings outstretched, presumably a bird of prey, flies above a small fawn with long ears (more probably a hare?); there are other birds within this area. Other elements in the picture are a hatched leaf cross, triangles, swastikas and two continuous vertical spirals on the edge of the field. This amphora has been dated by comparison with engraved Boeotian fibulae, and with Protoattic pottery, particularly with the Analatos hydria, to about 700 B.C., but the stylistic development in Boeotia is not well established. The figured

scene which is unparalleled in its decorative arrangement shows contacts with Cycladic vases.

Bibl.: P. Wolters, in: *Eph. Arch.*, 1892, p. 613, pl. 10 and in: *Praktikà*, 1890, p. 92. Collignon-Couve, pp. 108–9, no. 462. R. Hampe, *Frühe griechische Sagenbilder in Böotien*, Athens 1936, pl. 17–18. Nilsson, *Geschichte d. griech. Religion*, Munich, 1941, p. 287ff., pl. 30, 3. Zervos, *L'art en Grèce*, pl. 55 (detail). S. Benton, in: *JHS*, 81, 1961, pl. 5, 1–2 (front and back), p. 53 (on the birds). On the date of 700 B.C., see: Hampe, *op. cit.*, p. 21 and Kunze, in: *Götting. Gel. Anz.*, 1937, 7, p. 288. The face of the goddess has a striking analogy on a relief pithos in Tenos with the 'head birth' (*AJA*, 58, 1954, p. 240; *Atti VII Congr. Int. Arch. Class. I*, p. 272, pl. 2) which is already full 7th century B.C.

12, 13

PROTOATTIC AMPHORA. Eleusis Museum. From Eleusis. It contained the skeleton of a boy about 10 years old. Clay is pale red, in places almost orange-coloured. Excellently fired. Glaze black but fired brown in streaks. Recomposed from large fragments with considerable gaps, specially in the figure of Athena and of Perseus, of whom only the lower left leg and the complete right leg are preserved. The white which covered the body and face (but not the neck) of Odysseus has largely gone. White, applied directly over the clay ground is used to fill in the faces of Odysseus' companions, the Gorgons' legs protruding from the chiton, the chiton of Medusa and the upper part of her bodice. Height 1.42 (55¹³/₁₆″), diam. 59 cms (23³/₁₆″).

The form of the handles recall those of the Analatos hydria the Kynosarges amphora and the Nessos amphora (pl. 18–20). They are related to the solid (but perforated) handles which originate at the end of the geometric period and are common in Protoattic. The fretwork of the handles consists of stars and crosses of various shapes. They are decorated with concentric circles, palmettes, and series of lines. On the outer edge of the lip stepped lines, underneath the lip a cable pattern in black and white which recurs on the shoulders under the animal scene, and again under the principal figure scene. Great variety of filling ornament; specially noteworthy are those of vegetable origin, such as the palmette between the legs of Odysseus' first companion. None of these motives are new to Protoattic, but here because of the size of the vase they are given greater emphasis. The back of the vase has on its neck linked double spirals, loops on the shoulders, and large vegetable motifs on the body which terminate in lily-like flowers. They also intrude into the figured part, where the decapitated body of Medusa lies. A cable pattern and triangles springing from the foot complete the decoration.

Figure decoration: On the neck Odysseus (painted in brown outlines and wash, originally filled in with white) one leg up, the other straining on its toes, plunges together with his companions the stake into the eye of the Cyclops, Polyphemus, who holds in his hands a double-handled cup, perhaps of metal. The figures have slender waists, their hair is tied and falls over the neck. The figure scene on the body shows the story of Perseus and Medusa. The body of Medusa lies on the left, headless amongst flowers. She wears a scaly tunic over her upper body. It opens out below, like

a himation, revealing a white peplos. Her small feet are visible. The small arms are rendered awkwardly. Nearer the centre of the picture the two sisters of Medusa, Gorgons also, pursue Perseus, who is running off with winged boots to the right. Their pursuit is halted by Athena, who interposes commandingly between hero and pursuers. She wears a closely fitting dress richly decorated with purely geometric pattern, and a himation thrown over her shoulders and decorated with simple dots. Beyond Perseus on the extreme right a bird of prey swoops down (see Benton, in: *JHS*, 81, 1961, p. 49, n. 56). The Gorgon sisters are strange figures in the extreme. Their faces have nothing human about them, but resemble the very early bronze caudrons with their lion and snake heads attached to neck and head.
Second quarter of the 7th century B.C.

Bibl.: G. E. Mylonas, *Protoattikos amphoreus tis Eleusinos*, Athens 1957, id. in: *AJA*, 62, 1958, p. 225. Robertson, pp. 40–45 (commentary and colour plates). K. Schauenburg, *Perseus*, p. 33; 121; 139; pl. 7 (complements our pictures). Main views also in: *AJA*, 59, 1956, pl. 67, 3; *BCH*, 79, 1955, p. 221, fig. 1; *EWA*, I, pl. 339; IV, pl. 167 top left. Good details in: *RIASA*, n.s. 9, 1960, pp. 153ff., figg. 36–8. The vase is an earlier work by the painter of the inscribed Berlin Menelas stand the 'Menelas Painter' therefore (though Mylonas pointlessly rechristens him the 'Polyphemos Painter'). Miss Jeffery, most recently in *Scripts*, p. 110, suggests that he was by origin an Aeginetan, because of the script and the Doric dialect used for the spelling of *Menelas*. This, however, is not the only possible explanation. The vase belongs to the important group of very early (recognizably) mythological pictures, for which see now the lists in: T. J. Dunbabin, *The Greeks and their Eastern Neighbours*, pp. 77ff. (ours is no. 16); cf. also E. Brann, in: *Antike Kunst*, 2, 1959, p. 35ff., especially n. 6; K. F. Johansen, *Ajas und Hektor*. Here are the first 'Perseus and the Gorgons', (its 'rival', the relief pithos Louvre, CA 795, Dunbabin, p. 85, no. 2, must be a good deal later. Is it much earlier than the kouroi of the Sounion Group?), the first winged boots (see Yalouris, in: *BCH*, 77, 1953, pp. 294ff.), and perhaps also the first 'blinding of Polyphemus' in Greek art, though the newly found fragment from Argos (see reference in bibl. on p. 272) is not much later. For the Aristonothos krater see plates 14–15. Ours too is the earliest Athena in Attic art; (for near-contemporary *armed* Athenas in Protocorinthian and Cretan art see *AM* 74, 1959, p. 58, n. 3). She is unaccoutred but for a spear in her hand. This lack of attributes is common to Athenas in *Attic* art (e.g. plates 35–7) before the time of the C-Painter. This may however be due to chance, see commentary on plate 47. On the very early bronze cauldrons with *lion* protomes see, Kunze: *Olympiabericht*, 2, pp. 108–9; Amandry, in: *Syria*, 35, 1958, pp. 102–3. Our Gorgon faces are pre-canonical and have no close parallels; see on plate 29. Mylonas, *Eleusis*, Princeton, 1961, p. 74–5.

14, 15

ARISTONOTHOS KRATER. Rome, Museo dei Conservatori. From Cervetri. Much restored and rather worn; the figures have disappeared in places, the handles have lost the fine slip which covers the rest of the vase. Red-brown clay, micaceous but well levigated. The inside and outside of the vase is covered with an ivory-coloured slip which sometimes has turned greenish or orange coloured. The figures are painted in grey-black. White is used for some details on the shields, helmets and ships. There is a marked difference in the glaze of the lower part of the vase and the upper; this must be due to some mishap in the firing. Height 36 cms (14³/₁₆″), diam. of mouth 32 cms (12⁵/₈″).

The shape is an oddity for its period. Comparisons have been made with the Syracuse kraters from the Fusco cemetery and recently with kraters from Ischia (the ancient Pithe-

kousa). These suggest that the shape belongs to Italy rather than mainland Greece.

A very low lip which protrudes slightly, is decorated with groups of vertical bars. Underneath the figure scene a chessboard pattern. From the foot spring solid triangles alternating with a spiked leaf on a stalk. These are joined to the triangles by an arc; on the foot are parallel bands. These decorative motifs, though they recall similar patterns in the geometric style of Greece proper, do not occur there in these combinations; on the other hand, as Schweitzer has pointed out, there is a match amongst the Syracuse kraters from the Fuseo cemetery.

Back of vase: Odysseus and four companions are in the act of pushing the stake, which they hold in both hands, into the eye of the Cyclops, Polyphemus. Behind Polyphemus is a small box or shelf which may have served as receptacle for his milk and cheeses. Above Polyphemus is the artist's signature Aristonothos, in letters which are related to the Chalcidian alphabet, as used in several of the Greek colonies in Italy and Sicily. Dotted circles serve as a filling ornament.

Front of vase: A fight between two ships; the one on the left has oars and ram, the one on the right sails. Both ships have warriors on a high deck ready to hurl their spears. The left ship has five rowers below deck. That the ship on the right is Etruscan is suggested by the shield device, of crab and cruciform stars, which are also found on Etruscan coins. On the other hand the shield devices on the second ship, the attacker, recall in their motives, whirligig, cartwheel and St. Andrews cross, ornaments on Corinthian pottery. This ship therefore should be Greek. The Etruscan ship has a look-out man up on the mast. It has the round build of a merchantman. It faces a warship.

The subject reminds one of the many sea battles on late geometric vases, which were a reflection not only of an interest in sea stories, but also of the many naval engagements which must have taken place during the colonizing era. Our krater belongs to the orientalizing period when in mainland Greece this theme had lost its popularity. In Etruscan and particularly the art of Cervetri this interest in sea faring was now very much alive. Schweitzer has shown by a series of cogent comparisons the pertinence of our vase to the Etruscan sphere. Thus we suggest Aristonothos to have been an immigrant artist from Greek Southern Italy or Sicily to Etruscan Cervetri (Caere).

Mid 7th century B.C. or slightly later.

Bibl.: Helbig-Amelung, *Führer*³ I, p. 551ff. A. Köster, *Das antike Seewesen*, Leipzig 1923, fig. 35. E. Buschor, *GV*, p. 47, fig. 53. H. L. Lorimer, in: *ABSA*, 42, 1947. p. 124ff., fig. 13. G. S. Kirk, in: *ABSA*, 44, 1949, pp. 120–121. M. Santangelo, in: *Mon. Piot*, 44, 1950, p. 12, fig. 7. Matz, pll. 161–2. B. Schweitzer, in: *RM*, 62, 1955, p. 79ff. pl. 34–5; 36; 3; 40, 1 (details). *BCH*, 79, 1955, p. 21, n. 1; fig. 13 (side view), Pfuhl, fig. 64–5. For the writing of the artist's signature *Aristonothos epoi(e)sen* = 'A. made (me)', see now Jeffery, *Scripts*, p. 239 (perhaps Cumaean). It is still perhaps the earliest known artist's signature on a Greek vase. Potter and painter are probably not yet differentiated in the term *epoiesen*, which occurs regularly in the early signatures in the 7th century B.C. Such are Kallikleas of Ithaca on a *figured* candle stick – mid 7th century? (Jeffery, *Scripts*, p. 230–1; pl. 45, 2); Pyrrhos on an *ornamented* aryballos, assigned to Euboea, which might be quite early in the century (Jeffery, *Scripts*, p. 83–4; pl. 6, 22); the missing name of the signature on late-7th century *figured* fragments in Palermo, from Selinus, of uncertain fabric (Jeffery, *Scripts*, p. 270, n. 3); Nikesermos on a *barely ornamented* Chiot chalice of the end of the 7th century (Jeffery, *Scripts*, p. 377; pl. 65, 42e). On the other hand Istrokles on a *figured* fragment from Old Smyrna of about 630 B.C. (J. M. Cook) *may* have signed *egrapsen* = 'painted' (E. Akurgal, *Kunst Anatoliens*, Berlin 1961, p. 229; 308, fig. 223). The only certain *egrapsen* signature of the 7th century and thus the first specifically *painter's* signature in the history of European art is on a Naxian *figured* fragment, see commentary on plate V, (bibl.).

For early artist's signatures see, Beazley, *Develop.*, p. 8; Jeffery, *Scripts*, p. 62. For the *Antenor* on a Protoattic fragment attributed to the Ram Jug Painter (mid 7th century) and possibly part of a signature, see now: S. Karouzou, in: *Eph. Arch.*, 1952, p. 162, fig. 25. On the relationship of potter and painter in the 7th century see also: R. Hampe, *Frühattischer Grabfund*, pp. 46–7.

16, 17, IV

PROTOCORINTHIAN OINOCHOE (CHIGI VASE). Rome, Museo Nazionale di Villa Giulia. From Formello near Veii. Formerly in the Chigi Collection. Reconstructed from many fragments; numerous gaps. Light, rather coarse clay; over the surface a slip of same colour. Polychrome decoration; dark red which in parts turns to violet and orange. Greatest height 26.2 cms (10⁵/₁₆″); greatest circumference 58 cms (22³/₁₆″); smallest circumference 27.5 cms (10¹³/₁₆″). Diam. of mouth 12 cms (4¹¹/₁₆″).

The shape is related to East Greek models. It is called an *olpe*, a type of oinochoe with round mouth and two discs attached near the upper end of the handle. The shape, which was to have a long life in Corinthian ware where it underwent various modifications, is in this particular variety typical of late Protocorinthian. The handle consists of three ribs which coalesce at both ends. On the neck, on the dark band above the upper figure frieze, again above the lower handle root, and on the handle discs there are palmettes and lotus motifs painted in white on a dark ground. On the inside of the mouth this same pattern is confined to the space between the two handle discs, the rest is decorated with eight-leaved flowers. The use of polychrome decoration is noteworthy for the combination of two techniques on one vase, that is, the application of white on a dark ground on the one hand and on the other hand black, red and warm brown colours on a light ground. The vase has a low foot ring of about 12 cms (4¹¹/₁₆″) diameter from which a row of triangular leaves rise.

There are three figure friezes and one intermediate zone. The first from the top is 5.2 cms (2″) high and is separated from the middle frieze by a brown zone with a goat hunt painted on it in faded white. This zone is 2.5 cms (1″) high. The middle frieze is 4.7 cms (1¹³/₁₆″) high and is in turn separated from the lowest frieze by three fine lines.

Upper frieze: From left to right, two soldiers, one of whom bends to fasten his greave, the other one, only just preserved, may be putting on his corslet or his helmet. On the ground are their round shields each propped against two spears planted into the soil. Then comes a line of nine warriors armed with crested helmet, corslet, big round shields and greaves. They are still sloping their spears, are therefore on the march. In front of this line we see a boy flute player,

unarmed, wearing a short brown chiton with dark red belt and having a big lock curled over his forehead. He has his face thrown backwards playing the soldiers into battle; from his right arm hangs his instrument case. He has a mouth-band across his cheeks to give him better control over his playing. Whilst not in the exact centre of the frieze this boy yet takes pride of place.

Near the actual centre we see the clash of two lines of hoplites, four against five. The actual centre, below one of the down pointing lotus ornaments on the dark band above, is formed by the crossing of the spear points, an effective means of bringing out the fierceness of the clash. The polychrome effect of the vase is enhanced by the details of the shield emblems, eagle, bull's head, gorgon mask, lion and boar protome, all standing out against the light background. The reinforcement troop on the right (out of view in plate IV) consists of seven hoplites, several of whom have their spears held level at their side, ready to raise them to their shoulders when the time comes to engage, whilst the others, thought to be still on the march, have them at the slope. Similar compositions are found on other Protocorinthian vases, such as the Macmillan aryballos in the British Museum, and one in Berlin. They show the influence of a larger pictorial conception, perhaps a wall painting. We also think of the decoration on the Chest of Cypselus of which we have a detailed description in Pausanias V, 17–19. In a different way the vase is also evidence for the transformation of tactics in the mid 7th century with the development of hoplite fighting.

Between this upper and the middle frieze is a narrow dark band on which in faded white are painted hounds after wild goats.

Middle frieze: beneath the handle the Judgement of Paris. Paris (his name is inscribed next to him in letters now partly missing: Al[exand]ros—an alternative name for Paris) wears a red chiton, Hermes is all but missing except for the tip of his herald's staff (kerykeion), Hera too is lost apart from the upper part of her diademed head, Athena (inscribed Athanaia) has survived from her neck upwards and similarly Aphrodite (inscribed Aphrod[ita]) remains only from her shoulders upwards, her right hand probably held a wreath. To the left of the 'Judgement' follows a lion hunt (plate 17 top) with five huntsmen, one of whom is being mauled by the lion, whilst his comrades attack the beast from side and front. This type of lion hunt, whilst rare in Greece, is often found in the Orient, particularly in Assyria and thus illustrates Oriental influence; to the right of the 'Judgement' four pairs of horses, one of each pair being mounted. In front of this cavalcade is a four-horse chariot (plate 17 lower picture) with a charioteer and preceded by a naked boy who leads one of the horses by a rope. The horses of the team are alternately brown and purple; the chariot cage itself is red whilst its four-spoked wheels are incised on the clay ground. Separating these two scenes of lion hunt and cavalcade there is a double-bodied, symmetrically disposed, sphinx out of whose single head grow two tendrils terminating in spirals. The sphinx is polychrome with much violet, its hair is hazel streaked with brown.

Lower frieze: The Hunt (plate 17 below). Behind the bush a huntsman with two hares already secured to his back crouches in ambush, busy restraining his hound. To the right a huntsman in the open also keeping a dog on leash (tail and rump alone preserved). Then after a gap of about 10 cms (3¹⁵/₁₆″) is another huntsman in ambush, then a hare followed by a pack of hounds (plate 17 top). Beyond a bush another chase, a vixen pursued by hounds (plate 16). Filling ornaments include rosettes with stalked petals, double spirals, crosses within an outline quatrefoil, hooked triangles etc.

Together with the Macmillan and the Berlin aryballoi, mentioned already, the Chigi Vase represents the peak of achievement of a vase painter who was particularly interested in exploring variety of colour, a predilection of Corinthian artists in general, witness the well-known statements in Pliny (N.H. 35, 15–16). The present artist also had a good eye for the spatial representation of human figures.

Late Protocorinthian; third quarter of 7th century B.C., perhaps between 645–635. A later dating to about 600 or even 590 B.C. which formerly had its supporters, is now no longer tenable. Comparison with the Thermon metopes and also with the bronze shield reliefs from Olympia clinch the higher date. By the Macmillan Painter.

Bibl.: E. Ghirardini, in: NS, 1882, p. 291ff. G. Karo, in: Antike Denkmäler des deutsch. arch. Inst., II, 1899–1901, p. 7ff., pll. 44–5. C. Robert, in: BI, 1882, p. 98. Cultrera, in: Ausonia, 8, 1913, p. 104ff. F. Johansen, Les Vases Sicyoniens, Copenhagen 1923, pp. 103, 112ff., pll. 39–40. Payne, p. 38; 96; 272, no. 39. Id., Protokorintische Vasenmalerei, Berlin 1933, pp. 14–15, pll. 27–9. CVA, Villa Giulia, fasc. 1. (Giglioli) pll. 1–4. J. L. Benson, Geschichte der korintischen Vasen, Bâle 1953, p. 18, no. 3. Dunbabin and M. Robertson, in: ABSA, 48, 1953, p. 179, no. 12. M. Robertson, Greek Painting (Skira), 1959, pp. 47–49. On the chronology see F. Villard, in: MEF, 60, 1948, p. 7ff.; Rumpf, Chalkidische Vasen, 1927, p. 148; L. Curtius, Die klass. Kunst Griechenlands, Potsdam 1938, p. 141; A. W. Byvanck, in: Mnemosyne, 13, 1947, p. 252. Benson as well as Dunbabin and Robertson have attributed the Chigi Vase to an artist who also painted the Macmillan and the Berlin aryballoi, though otherwise their lists of attributions do not coincide. For the Macmillan and Berlin aryballoi see Payne, Protokorintische Vasenmalerei, pl. 22, 1–2, 5; pl. 23, 1–3. Pfuhl, fig. 58. On the Cypselus Chest see W. von Massow, in: AM, 41, 1916, p. 1ff. On the script used for the inscription, Jeffery, Scripts, p. 264; also Lejeune, in: REA, 47, 1945, p. 102; Rumpf, p. 33 (not Corinthian; Aeginetan? or North East Peloponnese?).

18–20

ATTIC AMPHORA BY THE NETTOS PAINTER. Athens, National Museum, 1002. From the Dipylon cemetery. Reconstructed from many fragments without however spoiling the main parts of the figure scenes. Foot entirely restored. The surface of the vase is in poor condition; much of the purple and white painted over the black has gone. Purple for heads of Nessos and Herakles, also for his chiton and that of the Gorgons; in patches also on the Gorgons' faces. Height 1.22 m (47¹⁵/₁₆″).

The vase, which served as grave monument, recalls late geometric amphorae in the way its handles are solid. They are decorated in the upper register with an owl, and a swan in the lower. Meanders separate these two as well as framing the contour of the handle. On the mouth of the vase a file of geese; dot rosettes as filling ornament. Immediately

276

below the lip a running dog pattern in outline. On both sides of the neck picture rosettes flanked by vertical meander. On shoulder, palmette and lotus chain. On the body of the vase scattered amongst the figure representation are dot rosettes. Below this main picture runs a frieze of double spirals with palmettes; below these again solid triangles.

On the neck: Herakles (inscribed) on the left, the centaur Nessos (inscribed *Netos*, the archaic spelling of *Nettos*, which is the Attic form for Nessos) on the right. Herakles avenging the assault on his wife Deianeira, has leapt on the centaur's back, seized him by the hair and is about to push the sword into his side. The centaur is stretching imploring hands towards his executioner. Note the contrast between Herakles' neat moustache and the straggling beard of the centaur.

Main scene: The Gorgons' pursuit of Perseus (who is off the picture). Shown are the headless body of Medusa (below the left handle), and her two sisters who pursue Perseus, who has made off with Medusa's head across the sea which is indicated by a school of dolphins. A bird swoops down above the trunk of Medusa; compare the corresponding bird of prey on plates 12–13.

The figures of the Gorgons as indeed of Herakles, have a powerful feeling for roundness and solid form. There is much use of incision and it is the sureness of line and generous sweep of the stylizations of the Gorgons' faces which give this picture its special character.

The Nettos painter is the first great painter of Attic Black-figure. He still uses orientalizing elements for his decoration. A number of other works have been assigned to him.

Last quarter of 7th century B.C. (J. M. Cook: c. 625 B.C.).

Bibl.: *Antike Denkmäler des deutsch. arch. Inst.*, I, pl. 57, Pfuhl III. fig. 85. Matz, pll. 48–50, 231b. Beazley, *Dev.*, pp. 13–6. Id., *ABFVP*, p. 4ff. K. Kübler, *Altattische Malerei*, Tübingen, 1950, p. 27. Rumpf, p. 25. Cook, pl. 17, and pp. 68–9 (where the vase is dated to about 615 B.C.). J. M. Cook, in: *ABSA*, 35, 1934–5, p. 200–1. *RIASA*, n.s. 9, 1960, p. 170, fig. 53 (Medusa and bird). Robertson pp. 55–6 (colour).

21

ATTIC BLACK-FIGURED AMPHORA. Athens, National Museum, 221. From Attica. Reconstructed from many fragments. Figure work damaged through many cracks. Purple on face of the siren. Pale grey clay. Incision used for details of face and the wings. Height 57 cms (22⁷/₁₆″); diam. of mouth 24 cms (9³/₈″).

Broad-bellied; continuous unbroken curve between neck and body. Short handles with cylindrical section. Lip decorated with sigma pattern. A single picture spreading over neck and body; this becomes characteristic of a particular type of Attic amphora (compare pl. 38).

On top and bottom of the panel hooked triangles, pendant and standing. Within field amongst other filling ornaments rosettes in silhouette with a hole in the centre reserved in clay ground.

Front: Siren with spread wings. Incision for locks, hair ribbon, features of face and plumage. The face and hair ribbon are painted in purple.

Back: Similar siren but with wings folded.

The Corinthian influence here reveals itself in the use of purple, in the poppy-like filling ornament and in the use of incision for details. Also some fossil geometric elements, viz. the wavy lines and the battlement meander used as filling ornaments. The wing tips of the siren are straight, not curved back as in Corinthian. They recall an East Greek, or rather Rhodian type.

Whilst deeply influenced by Corinthian our vase has something of the eclectic character noticeable on a number of vases at the end of Protoattic. Close to the Nettos Painter; perhaps an early work. Datable to about 625 B.C. according to J.M. Cook's high chronology for the end of Protoattic, but according to Kübler about 600–590.

This is a forerunner of the so-called amphora type B, of which we show the following examples in this book: plates 38, 52, 53, 70, 188. The shape is an Attic creation of the end of the 7th century B.C. and goes on being produced until the third quarter of the 5th century B.C. (see commentary on plate 188). From the time of Exekias onwards, *i.e.* soon after the middle of the sixth century, type B became overshadowed by the sturdier and more elaborate type A, of which we have a good sequence in this book, the earliest being plates 62–3. For the history and importance of type A see the commentary on plates 150–153. On amphorae in general see also Beazley in *JHS* 42, p. 70; id. in: *Mon. Piot* 35, 1936, pp. 16ff.; id. in: *Antike Kunst*, 4, 1961, p. 49–50.

Bibl.: K. D. Mylonas, in: *BCH*, 5, 1881, p. 359, no. 22. J. Boehlau, in: *Jdl*, II, 1887, p. 64. L. Couve, in: *Eph. Arch.* III, 1897, p. 72. Id. in: *BCH*, 22, 1898, p. 282ff. J. M. Cook, in: *ABSA*, 35, 1934–5, p. 199. K. Kübler, *Altattische Malerei*, Tübingen 1950, p. 26. Beazley, *ABFVP*, p. 6. (Kübler's 'stretched' chronology of Protoattic is criticized by J. M. Cook, in: *Gnomon*, 23, 1951, p. 212ff.).

22, 23 above

MELIAN AMPHORA. Athens, National Museum, 3961(911) From Melos. Reconstructed from large fragments; small gaps on the shoulder, a large one on the neck. Pale yellow clay. The polychrome effect and the brown glaze have worn off in many places. Total height 95 cms (37³/₈″); height of neck 22 cms (⁵/₈″). Diam. of mouth 49 cms (19¹/₄″).

Neck high and broad in relation to rest of vase, which contracts sharply near base. Conical foot with rectangular vents. The double handles each with central rib sit horizontally on body. Dark red and violet is used for figures and decoration.

Front of vase: On neck figure scene within three metope fields divided from each other by a cross-hatched triglyph. In central metope; fight of two heroes armed with helmet, spear, corslet, greaves and shield. Between them is a set of armour, helmet, corslet and greaves. In the side metopes the mothers are watching the struggle. In the background filling ornament of spirals, flowers, circles, crosses and swastikas.

On shoulder of vase a procession of ducks, in the main panel between the handles a two-wheeled chariot drawn by four winged horses. Within the chariot Apollo, bearded and playing the seven-stringed kithara, which he keeps in his left

hand; with the right hand he holds the plectrum. Behind him, also in the chariot, two women who raise their hands in adoration. They are probably two Muses or perhaps the Hyperborean Maidens who were honoured at Delos. The main theme, however, is the epiphany of Apollo and Artemis, who comes up to meet him. In her right hand she holds a stag by its antlers. In her left she has an arrow, on her back quiver and bow. Under this panel a frieze of spirals, followed by chevrons, and finally palmettes between spiral volutes. The conical foot is decorated with a running S pattern, then metopes each filled with a woman's head drawn in outline, then a meander and finally down-pointing solid triangles.

Back of the vase: On neck spirals round two lotus flowers. On body ducks and palmettes with zig-zags and meanders. On main panel two confronting horses between which there is a female head in profile. (Photograph now in *BCH*, 84, 1960, p. 365, fig. 8).

The name 'Melian' is conventional. These vases were not certainly made in that island. They are Cycladic but where from is unknown. The filling ornament on plate 23 below and on the back of the amphora plate 22, both of which are early in the series, suggests links with the earlier so-called Ad Group.

Early in the last quarter of the 7th century B.C.

Bibl.: A. Conze, *Die Melischen Thongefässe*, pll. 3–4. E. Brunn, *Griechische Kunstgeschichte I*, fig. 107–9. Collignon-Couve, p. 120ff., no. 475. Matz, pl. 171–2. P. Pelagatti, in: *Enciclopedia dell' Arte Classica*, s.v. 'Cicladici vasi'. Pfuhl, fig. 108; Zervos, *L'art en Grèce*, pl. 56 (detail). Boardman, in: *ABSA*, 47, 1952, p. 24ff.; id, in: *ABSA*, 52, 1957, p. 18. Salviat and Weill, in: *BCH*, 84, 1960, p. 385ff.

23 below

MELIAN AMPHORA. Athens, National Museum, 3963, (912). From Melos. Pale yellow clay; brown glaze; use of dark red and violet colour. Total height 90 cms (35³/₈″). Height of neck 22 cms (8⁵/₈″).

On top of belly just below the junction of the neck a chain of alternately up- and down-pointing lotus flowers. Below the figure panel a frieze of double spirals, then a zone of linked volutes with palmettes and lattice pattern. Below the handles complex spirals with lattice work.

Front of vase: Two horsemen on either side of a quadruple palmette supported by four spirals. Each of the horsemen holds the reins of a second unmounted horse; they are clean-shaven, have long hair held up by a purple ribbon and wear a chiton also in purple, as are the horses' manes. Filling ornament consists of palmettes, rosettes, multiple zig-zags, swastikas and lozenges.

Back of vase: In central panel unmounted horses stand on either side of a big palmette volute.

Our vase strikingly demonstrates the closely interwoven system of decoration which covers the surface of the vase. The two horsemen (possibly the Dioscuri) also seem to form part of this decorative tapestry. A little earlier than the vase of plate 22 and 23 above, probably about 630 B.C.

Bibl.: Conze, *op. cit.*, pll. 1–2. Collignon-Couve, no. 474, pll. 119–20.

Pfuhl, p. 105, fig. 105; Matz, p. 265, pl. 170. P. Pelagatti, in: *Enciclopedia dell' Arte Classica* II, s.v. Cicladici Vasi, p. 591, fig. 807. Boardman, as in bibl. to pl. 22.

24

CYCLADIC GEOMETRIC KRATER. New York, Metropolitan Museum, 74.51.965. From Cyprus (Kourion?). Some restorations, but well preserved together with its lid. Height 1.15 m (45³/₁₆″).

Unusual shape, rather like a pithos; certainly not Attic. Four vertical ribbon handles decorated with grazing deer in panels, one above the other. The knob of the lid is in the shape of a hydria decorated with grazing deer and chessboard pattern. Between it and the lid proper a cylindrical junction also decorated with chessboard pattern. Chessboard pattern again on the lid.

The vase has a short straight neck, decorated with leaf crosses alternating with chessboard pattern, all in metopes. The ovoid body of the vase is covered with geometric patterns, broken meanders, lozenges, spirals and a number of panels of which the central one shows two goats heraldically placed on either side of a tree, one of them giving suck to her kid. This panel is flanked by two others each with a tethered horse and a bird between its long legs; an axe is suspended from above. Below this area, and, as it were, girding the vase, is a procession of grazing horses. Then follow bands of solid and concentric circles linked by tangents, dark bands, broad and narrow. The conical foot is covered with solid circles linked by tangents and hatched leaves.

Comparison with certain vases from Delos shows that our vase belongs to a Cycladic workshop.

Third quarter of 8th century B.C.

Bibl.: J. L. Myres, *Handbook of the Cesnola Collection*, pp. 286–7, no. 1701. R. S. Young, in: *Hesperia*, Suppl. II, 1939, pp. 85, 97, 196, no. 1. N. M. Kondoleon, in: *Arch. Ephem.*, 1945–47, p. 11ff., fig. 4. G. M. A. Richter, *Metrop. Mus.*, *Handbook of Greek Collection*, Cambridge Mass., 1953, p. 25, pl. 14c. T. J. Dunbabin, *The Greeks and their Eastern Neighbours*, p. 73, iii, no. 1 (list of early Greek vases found in the East). K. F. Johansen, *Exochi*, Copenhagen 1958, p. 146, n. 266.

V

CYCLADIC AMPHORA (? Naxos). Athens, National Museum, 11708. From Thera, tomb 7. Reconstructed from large fragments; neck in particular being damaged. Creamy slip over reddish brown clay. Height 82 cms (32¹/₄″).

The shape is an elongated oval with a high and narrow neck. Horizontal handles on shoulder, lip projecting outwards. Two thirds of the body are covered with parallel lines. On lip lozenges; followed by more lozenges on the neck; cable pattern above and below a figure zone; then lozenges again. On shoulder cable pattern, lozenges and, below the figure zone, three parallel lines followed again by cable pattern. Low conical foot.

On the neck within a panel formed by upright cables two rampant lions placed antithetically and looking back. Their heads are in outline, the rest of the body in silhouette.

Within the rest of the area filling ornament of zig-zags, crosses within a circle, lozenges. Between the lowered front legs of the lions a group of triangles and lozenges represent the three motif which is flanked by the lions. The two side panels each have a rampant lion looking back over their shoulders.

On the body the figural zone runs between the handle. The side panels have a rampant winged lion and a rampant sphinx respectively; the central panel is filled with a winged lion. The tongue protrudes from his gaping mouth revealing his fangs. A snake tail.

Mid 7th century B.C. A typical example of the 'Heraldic Group' which has been plausibly assigned to Naxos. The name is self-explanatory; the scheme of decoration is similar on all, though the animals in the metopes may vary. We can trace, and attribute to Naxos, a continuous line of workshops from about the middle of the 7th century B.C., the date of our amphora (the date in the caption is too early), to quite late in the second half of the century. Horse protomes on later Heraldic amphorae link them with the so-called Protome Group, broad-bellied neck-amphorae with protomes of lions and horses disposed with some sophistication in metopes on neck and shoulder of the vase. These come well within the second half of the 7th century. Closely connected with them is a small but important group of vases (all very fragmentary) with polychrome figure decoration, which seem to have maintained the belly handles for their amphorae; other shapes such as kraters are reported too. The best known is the inscribed amphora with Ares and Aphrodite in a chariot. These should probably come down to early in the last quarter of the century and are largely the work of one hand, an excellent artist who is the earliest one known in Greek art to have signed himself as *painter*.

Bibl.: For our amphora see H. Dragendorf, *Thera*, II, pp. 212–4, fig. 419a-b, 420a-b; Ch. Dugas, *La Céramique des Cyclades*, Paris, 1925, p. 229ff. For the various Cycladic fabrics particularly those of Paros and Naxos see Buschor, in: *AM*, 54, 1929, p. 142ff. and now Cook, p. 109ff., and p. 344. Brock, in: *ABSA*, 44, 1949, p. 74ff. See now in general also P. Pelagatti, in: *Enciclopedia dell' Arte Classica* II, p. 587ff. For the amphora (lost during the war) with Aphrodite and Ares from Naxos town see Chr. Karouzos, in: *JdI*, 52, 1937, p. 166ff., figg.; Matz, pl. 174; Buschor, *GV*, p. 55, fig. 65; Rumpf, pl. 6, 6 (on the inscription see Jeffery, *Scripts*, p. 291; for the **style cf.** also the pithos fragments from Naxos, *Atti VII Congresso Internaz. Archeol. Class.* I, p. 272, pl. 3). The fragmentary chariot amphora from Delos, Dugas, *Délos*, XVII, pl. 9, 2; pl. 70 (colour) is by the same painter. Also from Naxos town a remarkable fragment of a chariot race by the same hand (*BCH*, 85, 1961, p. 851, fig. 3) with the *painter's* signature *(egrapsen)*, but the name is lost. The date is early in the last quarter of the 7th century (compare the rather later Attic horse race, Buschor, *GV*, p. 45, fig. 52, for similarly bold overlapping). It is by a good margin the earliest preserved *painter's* signature in Greek and European art. Next in time are the early 6th century painter's signatures of Sophilos (plate 39), and Kleitias (plates 40ff.) in Athens, and Timonidas in Corinth. On early signatures see also on plates 14–15, bibl.

25

CYCLADIC AMPHORA (? Paros). Stockholm, National Museum. From an island in the Aegean. Light red clay, dark brown glaze. Well preserved and intact with only a few chips on the lower part of the vase and on the neck. Height 59 cms (23³/₁₆″); diam. at mouth 19 cms (7⁷/₁₆″).

Short neck with slightly concave profile; projecting lip. Ovoid body on conical foot, which splays out at the bottom like a plinth. The lower half of the body is dark relieved by a narrow light band. The foot is also mainly dark but has a light area within which straight and wavy lines. On the flat of the mouth groups of vertical strokes. On neck two narrow dark bands immediately below the projecting lip, then parallel lines, and series of triangles in outline, vertical wavy bands. Front of vase: On body between the handles a large metope framed on either side by eleven vertical lines, within which a long-legged grazing stag. The head, parts of the nearside legs, the hindquarters the underside of the belly and the tail are in outline. Small dark dots cover the reserved areas. The rest of the body, in turn, being black is covered with light dots. The whole is an effective way of representing the spots on the animal and gives the picture a certain lightness.

Back of vase: Two panels within each of which there are three concentric circles.

Probably Parian; descended from the Linear Island Style. Two other vases from the same workshop have been identified, one in Paris, Bibliothèque Nationale, which seems to be by the same hand, another in Leiden which is later and more remote in style. Not before 650.

Bibl.: S. Wide, in: *JdI*, XII, 1897, p. 195ff. Buschor, *G. Vsm*, p. 69, fig. 51. Rumpf, p. 31, pl. 6, 3. Matz, pl. 181 (also back). P. Pelagatti, in: *Enciclopedia dell'Arte Classica*, s.v. Cicladici Vasi. For the other vases from the same workshop see H. Payne, in: *JHS*, 46, 1926, p. 206. J. K. Brock, in: *ABSA*, 44, 1949, p. 76 and 80. Cook, p. 108. Rumpf, p. 27, n. 1. For chronology cf. J. M. Cook, in: *ABSA*, 35, 1934–5, p. 207.

26

RHODIAN OINOCHOE. Munich, Museum Antiker Kleinkunst, 449. From Rhodes. With restorations which include one of the handle discs. Some chips, but well preserved on the whole. Some modern repainting of the brown glaze. Light greenish slip. Height 32.5 cms (12³/₄″).

Trefoil mouth with discs where the handles join. Purple used for body of wild goats; their head and part of their underside are outlined, giving to the whole vase a rather light effect. On neck, cable pattern, on shoulders bars at irregular intervals; then two animal friezes separated by a zone of loops. In upper frieze grazing goat, winged griffin, a goose pecking at a central palmette and spiral ornament. Within this area rosettes, swastikas, daisies, concentric semicircles and other decorative elements. In the lower frieze seven wild goats; usual filling ornaments. Below this another zone of loops, below which again an alternation of lotus buds and flowers.

Belongs to the first phase of the Rhodian Wild Goat Style (sometimes called 'Kameiros Group'), that is some time after the middle of 7th century B.C. Another vase by the same hand, and very similar to one, is in Zurich.

C. 630–620 B.C.

Bibl.: Hackl-Sieveking, *Die Königliche Vasensammlung zu München*, Munich 1912, I, pp. 42, 43, fig. 54, 55. Rumpf, pl. 7, fig. 6. W. Schiering, *Werkstätten orientalisierender Keramik auf Rhodos*, Berlin 1957, pp. 46–8, pl. 12, 3. For the oinochoe in Zurich see H. Bloesch, *Antike Kunst in der Schweiz*, Zurich 1943, p. 37ff., pll. 9–11 and pp. 157–8. Schefold, *Meisterwerke*, Basle 1960, pl. 133, no. 77.

27

RHODIAN PLATE. London, British Museum, A749
From Kameiros, in Rhodes, much restored but nothing vital
missing. Cream coloured slip over buff clay. Black glaze.
Diluted brown glaze for two helmets on left for crests and
the chiton under the corslet. Added red for human flesh.
Incision. Diam. 38.5 cms (15$^1/_8$").

The raised lip projects outward and is decorated with dot
rosettes separated from each other by groups of four bars.
On the inside edge of the lip a row of dots and a black band
which covers the junction between the lip and the flat of the
plate. Surrounding the circular composition is a zig-zag line
between two parallel lines. The figure scene shows two
warriors fighting over the body of a third. The lower
segment of the circle consists of a cable pattern and a
series of vertical tongues in black, purple and in outline.
Between the two warriors and suspended from above is a floral
ornament consisting of a triangular chessboard pattern terminating on its sides in spirals out of which a palmette grows,
at the bottom apex a reserved circle. Two eyes and eye brows
painted with perfect naturalism on either side of this ornament give it the aspect of stylized face. The warriors
wear corslet and greaves as well as helmets. Two of the
helmets have their crest on stilts, whilst one has it attached
directly to the helmet. The inside of the shields, where
visible, are decorated with spiral volutes. The outside of the
shield carried by the right hand warrior has an eagle as
emblem. The two warriors fighting are identified by inscriptions, Menelaus (inscribed *Menelas*) on the left against Hector
(*Ektor*), whilst the fallen warrior is Euphorbos (*Euphorbos*),
the Trojan who had been the first to wound Patroclus, and
was then in turn killed and stripped by Menelaus. His body
was retrieved by Hector (*Iliad* 17, 59 ff.). Filling ornament
consists of big ten-petalled rosettes, daisies and other flowers,
a menader formed into a swastika.

This is the only important Rhodian representation of heroic
myth; also its only inscribed vase picture. It is also unique
in its polychrome technique. The script with the exception
of the *beta* is that of Argos, and it has been suggested that
an Argive prototype (bronze relief?) together with its inscription may have served as model here. The subject is not
found elsewhere, but the shield of Euphorbos happens to
have been in the Hera sanctuary near Argos, dedicated by
Menelaus (Pausan. 2, 17, 3) and may have inspired the choice!
On the other hand a similar alphabet has now been found in
the Dodecanese island of Kalymnos, and our painter may
have learnt his writing there.

Last quarter of 7th century B.C., perhaps quite late in it.

Bibl.: H. Dümmler, in: *JdI*, 6, 1891, p. 263. Studniczka, in: *JdI*, 18,
1903, p. 22. Rumpf, in: *JdI*, 48, 1933, p. 76, no. 1, below (Euphorbos
Group). K. Schefold, in: *JdI*, 67, 1942, p. 130. W. Schiering, *Werkstätten
orientalisierender Keramik auf Rhodos*, Berlin, 1957, p. 11–12, (date) 73;
104. Salviat and Weill, in: *BCH*, 85, 1961, p. 114 (shape). Cook, p. 122.
Pfuhl, fig. 117. Buschor, *GV*, p. 53, fig. 62; *EWA*, I, pl. 335 (colour).
On the inscriptions Jeffery, *Scripts*, p. 354; 153–4.

28

CHIOS: CHALICE. Würzburg, University (Martin von
Wagner) Museum, K.128. Formerly in the Feoli Collection,

therefore presumably from Vulci. Excellent state of preservation, extraordinarily light fabric. Dark grey clay,
covered with a light yellow slip; dark brown glaze. Height
15.4 cms (6"). Diam. 20.2 (7$^{15}/_{16}$").

Front of vase: On lip broken meander underneath which a
frieze of tongues above an arcading line. Underneath the
figure frieze a guilloche pattern between a tongue ornament
growing from the handle roots. Below this handle zone a
broken meander and rays springing from below.

The main representation, framed by vertical meanders,
consists of a bull and a water bird to the left of a central
ornament consisting of four spiral volutes, linked in pairs,
with palmettes and other pattern sprouting from it. To the
right a goose and a lion with raised tail and head in outline.
The body of the bull is piebald with a reserved pattern. The
underside of the lion is also reserved. Filling ornament
consists of triangles, circles, lozenges, daisies, etc.

Back of the vase: Ornament like the front but meander
under figure frieze. This frieze shows a file of wild goats, the
first of which climbs up a rock and turns back to the others.
Head and underside of belly in outline.

This chalice as well as its companion piece, Würzburg
K. 129, belongs to the middle phase of Chiot Wild Goat
style and is to be dated within the last quarter of the 7th
century B.C.

This style flourished in the second half of the 7th century
B.C., though some of its products seem to go on well into
the 6th century. The style is typically orientalizing. The
elegant polychromy with its striking use of red-brown on a
white slip, suggests close and neighbourly links with Ionia.

Bibl.: W. Helbig, *AI*, 1881, pl. R. p. 221. FR II, p. 173, 1. Prinz, *Nau-
kratis*, 18. Kinch, *Vroulia*, p. 229, no. 1. Price, *JHS*, 1924, pl. 9, 12,
p. 216. *AM*, 1920, p. 166, no. 4. Rumpf, in: *Gnomon*, I, 1925, p. 328
(dates this vase to the end of the 7th century B.C.). Langlotz, no. 128,
pl. 13. R. M. Cook, in: *ABSA*, 44, 1949, p. 155. J. Boardman, in:
ABSA, 51, 1956, p. 55 ff. Cook, p. 126 ff.

29

RHODIAN PLATE. London, British Museum, A 748.
From Kameiros in Rhodes. Restored from large fragments.
Cream slip over buff clay; glaze fired red-brown. Diam.
38.5 cms (15$^1/_8$").

The shape of the plate resembles that of the Euphorbos plate
(pl. 27). Raised lip on which eight groups of multiple bars,
purple used for wings and rosettes. Filling ornament consists
of rosettes, lozenges, swastikas and hooked triangles. By
comparison with the Euphorbos plate these ornaments are
more sparsely and more regularly distributed.

The picture shows a four-winged Gorgon as 'Mistress of
Birds', running to the right not in the usual 'knees-bent'
scheme with short dress (as on plate 18) but with straight
legs and long dress, as on the Eleusis amphora (plate 12)
where the bare striding leg comes out of the split peplos
too. The head is almost rectangular in shape; hair and beard
fall in thread-like tresses and spikes. The nose is highly
schematized and recalls the pendant motif in the middle of
the Euphorbos plate (plate 27). The mouth is immense and

oblong; ill-drawn fangs curl up from its corners. The tongue is short and in purple. Her chin is formed by two spirals meeting. She is dressed in a tightly belted peplos which is pulled out to a blouse effect above the belt; incision indicates the folds cast below. The flesh of her arms and leg, drawn in outline, is peppered with dot rosettes and other ornament (compare the similar peppering of the sphinx on plate III). Unlike most Rhodian plates the composition fills the whole of the roundel; no lower segment as on plate 27. Our Gorgon holds two geese by the neck, one in each hand. No 'Mistress of Beasts' therefore (for which see plates 11 or 46), but 'Mistress of Birds', who seems to have had her own identity though often merged with the 'Mistress of Beasts' *(Potnia thērōn)*. On Corinthian vases in particular birds invariably take the place of beasts in the hands of the winged Artemis (see Payne, p. 78; von Massow, in: *AM*, 41, 1916, p. 87). Here a Gorgon has taken the place of the usual 'Mistress of Birds', just as elsewhere she has taken over the lions of the 'Mistress of Beasts' (e.g. *Olympiabericht*, 3, pl. 33). This facet of the Gorgon is rare, though it has been argued that the Gorgon and panthers of the pediment of the Artemis temple in Corfu is to be interpreted similarly. Our Gorgon in the stylization of the face and in other ways stands aside from the main development of the type, which as Payne has shown, was taking place in Corinth, and under its influence (e.g. pl. 18). Hence also the long dress which she shares with some very early Gorgons.

The plate is not easy to date. The drawing of leg and arms and other features harp back to conventions of earlier in the last third of the 7th century B.C., but our plate is undoubtedly nearer the end of the century. It should perhaps be slightly earlier than the Euphorbos plate (plate 27).

Bibl.: J. Six, in: *JHS*, VI, 1885, pp. 275–6, pl. 59. Brunn, *Griechische Kunstgeschichte*. Fr. Studniczka, *Kyrene*, p. 153, fig. 30. C. Blinkenberg, in: *RA*, 1924, p. 274, no. 1. A. J. Frothingham, in: *AJA*, 15, 1911, p. 369 (compares the motif of the Gorgon's left leg with that of the Hittite caryatids of Eflatun Bunar). Buschor, *G Vsm*, p. 79, fig. 60. E. Niki, in: *RA*, 1933, p. 145 ff. Payne, p. 230, n. 5 (earliest 4-wings). M. P. Nilsson, *Geschichte der griechischen Religion*, Munich 1941, pp. 211, 286, p. 30, 2. T. Ph. Howe, in: *AJA*, 58, 1954, p. 213 ff. Rumpf, in: *JdI*, 48, 1933, p. 76, no. 18, below (Euphorbos Group). T. B. L. Webster, *Greek Theatre Production*, London 1956, p. 194, no. 24. W. Schiering, *Werkstätten oriental. Keramik*, pp. 103 ff. Hampe, in: *AM*, 60–1, 1935–6, p. 271. M. Robertson, in: *JHS*, 60, 1940, p. 10. E. Will, in: *RA*, 1947, I, p. 63. Webster, *Greek Art and Literature 700–530 B.C.*, p. 119, no. 93. G. Riccioni, in: *RIASA*, n.s. 9, 1960, pp. 152 ff. Kunze, in: *Olympiabericht*, 3, p. 102. Willemsen, *ibid.*, 7 (1961), pp. 187 ff. On Gorgons, see: Payne, pp. 79 ff. (p. 88 on our vase); Hampe, *Sagenbilder*, p. 58 ff.; Kunze, *Schildbänder*, pp. 65 ff.

30

FIKELLURA AMPHORA. London, British Museum, A 1311. From Kameiros in Rhodes. Fairly well preserved; some chips on the undecorated part of the vase. The low foot is partly broken. The whole vase is covered in a whitish slip. Brown glaze. Height 34 cms (13³⁄₈″). Diam. of mouth 16 cms (6¹⁄₄″).

On the flaring lip bars, on the neck a guilloche pattern in three rows; on the shoulders are pomegranates suspended from interlocking arcs. Under the handle a big floral ornament consisting of antithetically placed spirals with a

palmette springing above and below, and an ivy leaf on either side.

In mid-field a running man in full silhouette with a few details marked by reserved lines; no incision. The powerfully developed thighs are jointed to thin legs giving to the figure a quaint impression of rather hasty work. The arms are flung out in different directions; long tapering fingers. Rhodian fabric.

The Fikellura style begins about 580 B.C. and continues into the last quarter of the 6th century; it is called after a place near Kameiros in Rhodes. It is the continuation of the Rhodian orientalizing wild goat style but it may also have had a centre of production in Samos. Our amphora dates to about 540 B.C. and belongs to a group of vases decorated by one artist who has been called the Running Man Painter. Other vases by the same hand have several figures rather than a single one. Fikellura begins by using the old stock of Rhodian orientalizing of the end of the 7th century and hence only vegetable and animal motifs. The human figure comes in only towards the middle of the 6th century and always in silhouette as here. The subjects tend to be Dionysiac dancing or athletics. The style reveals a blend of various motifs partly of Rhodian origin, partly Laconian (pomegranates), partly again of generally Ionian stock. Sometimes careless, at other times almost pedantically exact in design, it reveals a certain measure of originality.

Bibl.: E. Schmidt, in: *Münchener Arch. Stud.*, p. 300, fig. 24. Buschor, *G Vsm*, fig. 62. Buschor, *GV*, fig. 105. Jacobsthal, pl. 21a. R. M. Cook, in: *ABSA*, 34, 20 (L, I), 23–4, 66, 82–4, pl. 11a. *CVA*, Brit. Mus. fasc. 8, (Cook) p. 6, pl. 4, 14 (7) 5 (1) 14 (1). Cook, p. 132 ff.

VI

CORINTHIAN AMPHORA. London, British Museum, 1914.10–30.1 From Rhodes. Well preserved, apart from mouth and neck where there are large gaps. Height 35 cms (13³⁄₄″).

On the neck a rectangular area within which a siren on the front, and a boar on the back of the vase. On the rounded shoulders a double lotus chain on the one side, on the other a siren between two sphinxes. Below this follow friezes filled with lions, panthers, boars, goats, sirens and swans. Incised rosettes are thickly strewn over the field. Rays growing from foot of vase.

Early-Corinthian; last quarter of the 7th century B.C.

Bibl.: Payne, p. 300, no. 770; pl. 23 (other side of vase).

VII

CORINTHIAN OLPE. London, British Museum, A 1352. From Kameiros in Rhodes. Well preserved. Height 29 cms (11⁷⁄₁₆″).

Round mouth; lip and neck in dark brown. White rosette on the discs attached to the upper end of the handle. Incised rosettes scattered in the figure field which consists of two superimposed zones divided from each other by a dark band which is enlivened by two purple lines. Rays spring from the foot of the vase. The upper frieze shows two confronting lions in profile and a serpent between them. Behind them a cock and a small rabbit. In the frieze below two symmetrically

arranged panther-birds with a common head in front view. These are flanked by a lion and bird respectively.

End of 7th century B.C., towards the end of Early-Corinthian.

Bibl.: Murray, in: *JHS*, II, pl. 15, 1. G. Karo, in: *Strena Helbigiana*, Leipzig 1900, p. 149. On the lower terminal date of Early Corinthian see now J. M. Cook, in: *ABSA*, 53–4, 1958–9, p. 26–7 (reviews evidence that it should be somewhat lowered—to about 590 B.C.).

VIII

CORINTHIAN ALABASTRON. Paris, Louvre, MNB 500. From Tanagra; formerly in the Rayet Collection. Mouth plate and foot damaged. Light clay; dark reddish glaze. Height 23.5 cms (9³/₁₆″). Diam. of mouth aperture 1.5 cms (⁹/₁₆″).

On the flat surface of the mouth plate there are tongues, on its side dots. Underneath a zone of vertical tongues, then a dot pattern followed by the main decorative area which shows the large figure of a winged man whose right knee touches the ground whilst his arms are flung out, as he speeds along. Purple for beard, hair, and the chiton which is bordered with zig-zag and wavy lines.

Perhaps one of the Boreads, a subject found also on other vases of this type. Between 625 and 600 B.C.; Early-Corinthian.

Bibl.: A. Merlin, *Vases Grecs Louvre*, I, pl. 15b, cf. *CVA*, Louvre fasc. 6, (Pottier) pl. 4, p. 6. Pottier, *VAL*, pl. 43 E 586, pl. 46 E 629 CN.

31

CORINTHIAN ARYBALLOS. Berlin, Staatliche Museen, F 1090. From Nola. Excellent state of preservation. Height 17.5 cms (6⁷/₈″).

Flat-bottomed. Mouth plate and shoulder decorated with tongues. Much purple used on the figures. Incised rosettes of various kinds as filling ornaments. A majestic griffin bird is flanked by a panther on each side.

Middle-Corinthian; early in the 6th century B.C.

Bibl.: Furtwängler, *Beschreibung der Vasensammlung, Berlin*, no. 1090. Payne, p. 304 no. 829.

32, IX

CORINTHIAN COLUMN-KRATER. Paris, Louvre, E 635. From Cervetri. Light yellow clay. Incrustation and damage to surface on the foot and lower parts of the vase. Under the handle the figures of Odysseus and Ajax have practically vanished. Height 46 cms (18¹/₁₆″). Diam. of mouth 47 cms (18¹/₂″).

The inner surface of mouth black. On shoulder of vase a chain of alternately up- and down-pointing lotus and palmette ornament. Two figure friezes divided from each other, by a dark band over which one purple line is running. Below the second frieze there is a broad dark band on which there are three purple lines. Rays spring from the foot which is dark, enlivened by purple lines.

The upper zone has a banqueting scene with four couches and tables occupied by the participants in the feast and their food. Inscriptions in the Corinthian alphabet, using *F (digamma)* = *w*, give their names. The subject is Herakles in the house of Eurytos. On the right Herakles with some morsel in his left hand and knife in his right, reclines on a couch. Near his feet stands Iole who turns towards her brother Iphitos, who also reclines on another couch and is in the act of taking a cup from the table placed before him. On the next couch are Eurytos (inscribed *Eyrytios*) and Didaion; on another couch again are Klytios and Toxos. Neck and faces are in purple (except in the case of Iole, the only woman present, whose head and feet are drawn in outline), beard, hair, chest and arms in black, whilst the coverlets of the couches and the cloaks (himatia) of the diners are in purple. Dogs which are tied to the couches are black except for the one under Herakles' table which is in outline. The tables are laden with food. Under the handle arch a big cauldron (dinos), an oinochoe and the bearded figure of a cook coping with a leg chop, and a servant.

On the other side of the vase a combat between pairs of hoplites fighting with spears. Under the handle root archers kneeling and preparing to draw. Under the left handle arch Diomede and Odysseus on either side of Ajax who has fallen on his sword, committing suicide.

In the lower frieze a cavalcade of eleven mounted youths. On the left handle-plate two mounted youths; on the right handle-plate a naked man piercing with his spear a hind next to a stag. On the upper rim of the mouth a file of animals, hind, lion, griffin-bird, ram, lion, lioness, swan, two sphinxes, ram, swan, two dogs, three birds in flight.

The date of this vase has been disputed. Rumpf even now maintains a date in Late-Corinthian, near the Amphiaraos krater. Payne, however, basing himself on a detailed analysis of the decoration and particularly on the style of the figure of Iole maintained a date in Early-Corinthian, i.e. the end of the 7th century B.C. The rider frieze too on our vase is earlier than those found on Late-Corinthian vases.

Bibl.: Pottier, *VAL*, I, p. 56 ff. Payne, pp. 100–3, 302 no. 780. Rumpf, p. 52, pl. 13b. *Encyclop. photograph. de l'art* ('Tel') II, 9, pll. 270–273.

X, XI

CORINTHIAN COLUMN-KRATER. Vatican, Museo Gregoriano Etrusco 126. From Cerveti. Orange red slip over clay; brilliant black glaze, diluted at times to a brown and greenish wash; use of white and purple. Reconstructed from large fragments. Height 42.5 cms (16³/₄″). Diam. with handles 20.5 cms (8″).

The inside of the neck has two purple bands at its lower end. On the upper rim of the mouth a chain of lotus-and-palmette ornament. On each handle-plate bearded gorgoneion (Gorgon's head) with an incised moustache on one of them. On shoulder, tongues alternately black and purple. Under the figure friezes a black band with four purple lines over it, then rays springing from the foot which is black, enlivened by purple lines.

Front of vase (plate XI): In the middle of the upper frieze

a chariot with a bearded charioteer and a woman beside him both standing on the platform. He holds the reins and the goad whilst the woman with her left hand moves aside the edge of the himation which covers her head and holds on to the chariot rail with her right. Facing her another woman opening her himation from the shoulder, behind her three women covered by one himation which they open up. Behind them a man with a spear resting against his shoulder. To the left of the chariot there are two groups of three women, again covered with one himation; they are separated from each other by two men, a youth with a wrap over his shoulders and an older man with a long white chiton holding an upright spear in his left hand. On the extreme right of the frieze two bearded men with spears face each other; one of them wears a long white chiton, the other a wrap over his shoulders. Then come two more figures, a woman with a himation over her shoulders and a man in white chiton. The chitons of men and women are white, except that of the middle person of the group of three females under one mantle which is purple.

Back of vase (plate X): Four mounted horsemen procede to the left, each of them is leading a second horse on their further side. They wear Corinthian helmets in purple, lowered over their face. Purple is also used for greaves.

Under the handle to the right of the main picture a siren looking back with spread wings. Feathers alternately in black and white. Under the left wing a rosette. On either side an eagle with details in purple. Under the other handle a siren to the right, in front of her a bird and a small siren looking backwards.

In the lower frieze going right round the vase, the group of panther and goat confronting is repeated five times. Purple used for the neck, underside and ribs of the animals.

The picture on the front of the vase represents the departure of bride and bridegroom. The representation of the three women under one mantle is found fairly often in archaic vase painting but disappears later. It has been shown that this group does not represent the offering of a garment to a goddess, but rather that it belongs to some essentially female cult, probably that of the two goddesses Kore and Demeter. It is here not part of an ordinary wedding, but rather signifies the mystic nuptials of one of the two goddesses. Nonetheless these representations lost by degrees their purely mythological content and became enlarged by the addition of further figures. In our view, however, some remnant of religious significance always remained, even here; besides it would be unusual to find a wedding scene in archaic times completely devoid of mythological content. Our krater is earlier than the Amphiaraos krater once in Berlin. Other vases have been attributed to the same artist, who has been called the Three Maidens Painter on account of his predilection for this group of three women. His style is somewhat cold and academic, particularly with his repetition of the group of three women; however, he uses his polychrome effects very well. The vase is Late-Corinthian and to be dated between 570 and 560 B.C.

The red slip over the Corinthian light-yellow clay becomes frequent at this period for the more elaborate Corinthian vases probably in imitation of the colour of Attic vases, whose competition now comes to be felt in Corinth.

Bibl.: E. Pinza, in: *RM*, 22, 1907, p. 151. Helbig-Amelung, *Führer*³, p. 295, no. 455. Payne, no. 1452. M. Guarducci, in: *AM*, 53, 1928, p. 151 ff. C. Albizzati, *Vasi antichi dipinti del Vaticano*, pll. 10–11. Benson, *Gesch. kor. Vas.*, p. 49 ff. no. 82, 3. Id., *AJA*, 60, 1956, p. 227. Cook, pl. 13. On the bride uncovering her face, Karouzos, in: *JdI*, 52, 1937, p. 172.

33, XII

CORINTHIAN AMPHORA. Paris, Louvre, E 640. From Cervetri. Lip partly restored; foot chipped. Height 32 cms (12⁵/₈″).

Neck and lip flare out. On inner surface of mouth black and red tongues. On outer surface of lip net of degenerate pomegranates in black, red and white. On neck three rosettes on each side of vase, consisting of a purple core and white dots. On shoulder, tongues in black and purple applied over black. Under the figure frieze again a pomegranate net. Then a black band and rays springing from the foot which is black.

Front of vase: Tydeus (this as well as the other names are inscribed in Corinthian alphabet, including the use of *koppa* = K) naked and bearded is about to kill Ismene with a big sword, painted in white. She is naked and lies uncovered down to her breasts on the couch from which Periklymenos, also naked and looking back, has just made his escape. Ismene and Periklymenos are painted in white and are outlined; the dog underneath the couch is in similar technique. On the extreme left of the picture a mounted youth, Klytos.

Back of vase: A siren with spread wings (body and face in white) between two sphinxes rendered in white. Incized rosettes in the field.

Much use of incision and of polychrome effects.

The myth depicted is unexplained though it is casually referred to in an ancient literary source. Tydeus was one of the heroes participating in the expedition of the Seven against Thebes and Ismene was presumably the daughter of Oedipus and Jocasta, but we do not know why she was killed by Tydeus, nor how Periklymenos comes into the story.

Late-Corinthian, between 560 and 550 B.C.

Bibl.: Pottier, *VAL*, I, p. 58 E 640. Payne, pp. 110–1, 327, no. 1437, pl. 40, 1–2. Rumpf, p. 51, pl. 13, 4. M. Robertson, *Greek Painting*, p. 80. See also G. C. Richards, in: *JHS*, 13, 1892, p. 286.

34

CORINTHIAN CUP. Paris, Louvre. From Etruria. Well preserved. Diam. 22.7 cms (8¹⁵/₁₆″).

The inside of the convex lip is decorated with chessboard pattern. In the centre of the bowl, surrounded by a zone of tongues alternately in black and outline, a woman's head looking to the left. Her hair comes down onto her shoulders in a wavy mass. She wears a ribbon (reserved in clay ground) on her head.

About 560 B.C. Late-Corinthian.

ATTIC BLACK-FIGURED VASES

EARLY PERIOD

The boundary between Black-figure and later Protoattic is to some extent a matter of convention depending on whether the term Black-figure is used solely to define a technique or whether it is also a matter of style. Certainly the Nessos vase (plates 18–20) is in full and unmixed Black-figure (i.e. black silhouette with incised details and the use of additional colours) and scholars like Beazley and Payne count the works of the Nettos Painter and his contemporaries as Black-figure; yet others including J. M. Cook regard the Nettos Painter as still Protoattic and put the boundary later, considering the Gorgon Painter (plates 35–7) as the first identifiable personality working in the new style. Here there is a difference in outlook, one side looking at the Nettos Painter as continuing the large scale vision of Protoattic, whilst the others regard him as inseparable from the Black-figure artists of the early 6th century.

Bibl.: Payne, p. 344ff. J. M. Cook, in: *ABSA*, 35, 1934–5, p. 201, n. 1. Beazley, *Development*, p. 12. Cook, pp. 70, 341 (who puts the boundary between the Nessos amphora and a later work in Berlin by the same painter. Much the same view seems to be implied in Kübler, *Altattische Malerei*, p. 20). E. Brann in: *Hesperia*, 30, 1961, p. 311, n. 36.

35–37

DINOS WITH STAND BY THE GORGON PAINTER. Paris, Louvre, E874. From Etruria; formerly in the Campana Collection, perhaps from Vulci? Yellowish clay. Well preserved on the whole. Much use of incision and of purple (applied over black) which, however, has in most cases vanished. No white for female flesh. Inside black. Total height 93 cms (36^1/$_2$″). Height of dinos alone 44 cms (17^5/$_{16}$″); height of stand 59 cms (23^3/$_{16}$″). Diam. of mouth 30 cms (11^{13}/$_{16}$″).

On the upper surface of the lip, palmette-and-lotus chain. On body six figure zones one above the other. The first zone shows the killing of the Gorgon Medusa by Perseus. She falls headless to the ground in the presence of Athena, unarmed and dressed in a himation, and of Hermes wearing a petasos (broad brimmed hat) and carrying the kerykeion (herald's wand). Her two sisters pursue Perseus, who has taken to flight. They have enormous wings and wear a short, sleeveless chiton and have winged boots. Perseus too wears a petasos hat, winged boots and a chiton with decorated borders and he carries his sword in the scabbard on his side. Then follows a different scene without any explicit division. We see two warriors fighting with each other, armed with helmet, corslet and shield. The right hand warrior has a bull's head, seen frontally, as shield device. Behind each of the two protagonists there is a chariot drawn by four horses with a charioteer on the platform. These latter with shield strapped to their back watch the fight. Under this main frieze there is a big double chain of palmettes and lotuses. Underneath, again, there follow four animal friezes filled with lions, panthers (one man between them in the uppermost of the friezes), boars, sirens, sphinxes,

goats and others. At the very bottom there is a whirligig, separated from the other friezes by a zone of cable pattern. On the stand which is separate from the bowl there is another palmette and lotus chain on the side of the receiving bowl, and again on the torus member of the stand. Then follow a cable pattern and three animal friezes separated from two more on the foot by another palmette-and-lotus chain. There is evidently much influence of Corinthian tradition in the animal friezes, and the floral complexes. Nonetheless there is in the various animals a certain individual character, such as is hardly ever found in Corinthian animal friezes. The painter of this dinos, the so called Gorgon Painter, stands in the succession of the painter of the Nessos amphora (plates 18–20). Indeed the Nessos Painter had also treated the subject of Perseus and the Gorgons on his Athens amphora and also on a fragmentary louterion (spouted bowl) in Berlin. However, the Gorgon Painter has expanded the narrative details of his picture and shows all the characters of the story with some loss of concentration. Our vase belongs to the first decade of the 6th century B.C.
Beazley has attributed 29 vases of various shapes to this painter. On almost all of them the subjects are under Corinthian inspiration particularly in the use of animal friezes; only one other seems to have had a mythological scene, the fragment in Louvain.

Bibl.: Pottier, *Cat.*, p. 571, E 874. Perrot-Chipiez X, pl. 2, pp. 117–8, pll. 83–4. Pfuhl I, p. 124, III, fig. 92. J. Holwerda, in: *JdI*, 1890, p. 245. *CVA*, Louvre fasc. 2 (Pottier). Beazley, *Development*, pp. 16–7 id., *ABFVP*, pp. 8–10 and no. 1. Cook, p. 71ff.

38

AMPHORA. Athens, National Museum, 903. From Velanideza in Attica. Preserved is a metope like panel with a

horse head turned to the right. The long mane is rendered alternately in black and purple.

About 600 B.C. or a little later.
This amphora belongs to a series of one-piece (type B) amphorae of which a precursor is shown on plate 21 (see commentary there). Their usual subject, within a light reserved panel let into an otherwise unrelieved black background, are a horse head, a horseman, a helmet or, exceptionally, a woman's head.

Some of these so called horse-head amphorae were used as markers over tombs. They are generally datable within the first half of the 6th century B.C., mostly in the first quarter.

Bibl.: Collignon-Couve, p. 198, no. 662. E. Loeschke, in: *AI*, 1878, p. 309; id., *JdI*, 2, 1887, p. 276. R. Hackl, in: *JdI*, 22, 1907, p. 85 ff. A. Conze, *Grabrel*, p. 4. Brueckner-Pernice, in: *AM*, 18, pp. 151 ff. Malten, in: *JdI*, 29, 1914, p. 179 ff. esp. p. 256, fig. 4. Pfuhl I, p. 246; III, fig. 200–201. Beazley, *Development*, p. 39 ff.; id., *ABFVP*, p. 15 ff., no. 5. Cf. also *CVA*, Munich, fasc. 1. (Lullies) p. 5 ff., p l. 1 and 2. Compare also Beazley, in: *Mon. Piot*, 35, 1936, p. 18, n. Diepolder, in: *Festschrift C. Weickert*, Berlin, 1955, pp. 111 ff. Cook, p. 78. Ars Antiqua, Lucerne, Sale III, 29.4.61, on item 135 (Schauenburg).

39 SOPHILOS

We have four signed vases by this artist. On three of them, including the fragment illustrated here on plate 39, he has signed as painter, on one of them, a fragment in Athens from Menidi, as potter. Another 38 vases have been attributed to him mainly through the work of Semni Karouzou and Beazley. He holds a key position in the formation of the Attic narrative and also animal frieze styles, which were influenced by but are different from Corinthian. His main work is a fragmentary dinos from the Athenian Acropolis with a representation of the wedding of Peleus and Thetis, a subject also found on the François Vase (plates 40 ff.). Some of the stylizations on the dinos such as the rendering of the chitons of Hestia, Demeter, Chariklo and Leto in several overlapping planes remind one of Corinthian vases of the same period. Also the white of female flesh and of horses is applied directly on the clay ground, the figures being outlined in purple. These too are Corinthian characteristics. The subjects on most vases by this painter are decorative friezes, particularly orientalizing animals, a good example being on an amphora found at Marathon. Nonetheless the dinos from the Acropolis and the one shown here from Pharsalos, show his taste for narrative. He has, however, none of the miniaturist's gift for concentration, which comes out so clearly in the François Vase painted by Kleitias. He is too close to the Gorgon Painter and the Corinthianising tradition; besides, as Beazley has justly pointed out, he is not a very good draughtsman. Yet he has spirit and the fragmentary pieces which have survived from his larger compositions show an acute observation of psychological reactions. His grouping together of heads (which is also found on contemporary Corinthian vases but schematised there into a meaningless formula as on plate XI) is effective, as for instance in the group of the *Nysai* on the Acropolis and the matching *Muses* on the Erskine dinoi.

A modest precursor to the much greater Kleitias, Sophilos must yet be given his due as one who aimed at a loosening of the stereotyped Corinthian influence and who sought to increase the Attic repertoire with new themes and new formulas. His activity is within the second and third decades of the 6th century B.C.

Bibliography: Payne, pp. 105–6, 200, 346. S. Karouzou, in: *AM*, 62, 1937, p. 111 ff. (she considers the Gorgon Painter and Sophilos to have been one and the same). Beazley, in: *Hesperia*, 13, p. 50 ff. id., *Development*, pp. 17–8, 107; id., *ABFVP*, p. 37 ff. Fragments from the Acropolis dinos are conveniently figured in Pfuhl, fig. 202; Buschor, *Gr. V.*, p. 102, fig. 117. On *Nysai* see Vanderpool, in: *Am. Journ. Philol.*, 74, 1953, p. 322 (a mistake for *Mousai*), supported by the new dinos and stand with Sophilos signing as painter, in the possession of the Hon. Robert Erskine, London. This important vase has an almost complete Wedding of Peleus (see also p. 293, *ad fin*). On Sophilos see also Boardman, in: *ABSA*, 53–4, 1958–9, p. 154 ff. (Smyrna nuptial lebes); Johannowsky, in: *ASAIA*, 33–4, 1955–6, p. 45 ff. (Gortyn dinos).

39

FRAGMENT OF DINOS by Sophilos. Athens, National Museum, 15499. From Pharsalos. The largest fragment is shown here. Three more fragments all of them consisting of a number of joining pieces are preserved, one of these comes from the animal frieze. Height of fragment shown here 5.2 cms (2″). The total height of the vase must have been about 30 cms (11 13/16″) and the diam. of the mouth 31 cms (12 3/16″).

On the upper surface of the lip, 3.6 cms (1 7/16″) broad, two sirens confronting, panther, goat and lion. Below the rim on the shoulder of the vase tongues alternating in black and purple. Then two figure friezes divided by a black line. The upper frieze shows four horses pulling a chariot which

is now lost. The two middle horses have black faces and purple necks. The third is black whilst the outer horse is white applied straight on the clay and outlined in purple. Between the front legs of the horses and the scene on the right there are two inscriptions from right to left, the first one is the painter's signature (*Sophilos m'egrapsen* = Sophilos painted me), the second gives the subject of the picture, the funeral games of Patroclus (= *Patrokleous athla* – misspelled; use of *koppa* for *K*).

To the right an artificial, stepped platform full of gesticulating spectators. They watch the chariot race. They wear a short chiton, black and purple; on the topmost step there is one who watched the events on the other side of the platform (now lost) but has now turned round to look at the team on the left. On the extreme right the name of Achilles is inscribed and probably refers to a figure in the middle distance, now lost. Achilles, of course, presided over the funeral games of his friend and companion.

Above the horses' backs there is the beginning of another inscription reading from right to left *Soph...*, perhaps *Soph[ilos m'epoiesen]* = Sophilos made me, a potter's signature such as is found on a fragment in Athens (from Menidi) whose style shows that it was also painted by him. Below this there are remnants of an animal frieze, a lion turning round next to a floral motif, which presumably was flanked by another lion on the left now lost. Much use of purple and incision.

The theme of the funeral games of Patroklos is taken from *Iliad*, book 23. This subject is also pictured with a great wealth of detail on the François Vase (plate 42). The representation of a wooden stand for spectators is rare in archaic vase painting. Béquignon mentions only two other examples, on a Tyrrhenian amphora in Florence and on an amphora from Kameiros now in the Bibliothèque Nationale (Cab. Méd), Paris. We are reminded in some ways of the crowds watching bull fighting on the frescoes from Minoan Knossos.

This fragment as well as other works by this painter show the influence of Corinthian.

About 580 to 570 B.C.

Bibl.: *BCH*, 55, 1931, pp. 453, 492; *ibid.*, 56, 1932, p. 98. Y. Béquignon, in: *Mon. Piot*, 33, 1933, p. 1 ff., pl. 6. S. Karouzou, in: *AM*, 62, 1937, pl. 52-3. Beazley, *Development*, pp. 18-19, 107. Rumpf, p. 39. Cook, p. 72 ff. Dilke, in: *ABSA*, 43, 1948, p. 131 (on tribune). Robertson, p. 58.

40-46 KLEITIAS AND ERGOTIMOS

Kleitias has signed five vases. On four of them a second signature is preserved, that of Ergotimos as potter; these four vases are the François Vase in Florence (where he writes 'Klitias'), a small stand in New York (where he writes 'Kletias') and two cups (where most of the name is lost). The fifth example, cup fragments in London, is too incomplete for one to tell but it probably had the second signature also. A number of other vases have been attributed to Kleitias by Beazley, none of them in any way as elaborate as the François Vase. On some, however, elements which are found as part of the ensemble on the François Vase, are repeated in isolation. For example the dance of youths and maidens which is one of the most attractive scenes in the episode of Theseus and the Minotaur on the François Vase recurs three times on fragments from the Acropolis in Athens; again the Nereids reappear on a hydria fragment from the Acropolis and the Gorgons were on a krater of which a fragment is in Moscow. Admittedly when put beside the profusion on the masterpiece in Florence these fragments do not add much to our knowledge. Yet the liveliness and neatness of design and the richness of colour of the Nereids on the hydria fragment from the Acropolis give a good idea of the original appearance of the female figures on the François Vase which unfortunately are preserved only as silhouettes, as the added colours have gone.

Kleitias follows in the stylistic line of Sophilos and also the Gorgon Painter. The design of the palmettes is identical in all three, but the animals are different; those of Kleitias being nimbler and more slender. The touch of his incision is not unlike that of Sophilos. A comparison with elaborate Corinthian vases of the period, between 570 and 560 B.C., (such as the Vatican krater pls. X, XI), shows the much greater liveliness and technical versatility of our painter. He is tied, let it be said, to Corinthian influence, which during the first half of the 6th century was still dominant, but his figures are alive and have character in a way which cannot be found even amongst the finest products of Corinthian workshops. Kleitias is a true pioneer for this time and a worthy follower of Sophilos and the Gorgon Painter.

Bibliography: In general compare the bibliography for pl. 40–46, (François Vase). In addition see Richter in: *Bull. Metropolitan Museum*, 26, 1931 pp. 289–91. For the signature of Kleitias on 'Gordion cups' cf. Beazley, in: *JHS*, 49, 1929, p. 265 ff. and M. Robertson, in: *JHS*, 71, 1951, p. 143 ff. Note that there is in Berlin a footless cup which is signed by Ergotimos as potter but which is not, to judge by the style of the painting, decorated by Kleitias, cf. Rumpf, pl. 9, 4. A. Greifenhagen, *Antike Kunstwerke*, Berlin 1960, pl. 18. The spelling of the name as Kletias (= Kleitias as written in Attic spelling), found on the stand in New York, must be the correct form, from *kleitos* = famous. The form Klitias found on the François Vase is probably due to the way the diphthong *ei* was popularly pronounced. See Milne, *Bull. Metropolitan Museum*, 26, 1931, pp. 290–1 and *ibid.* 1946–7 p. 225; also Kretschmer, *Vaseninschriften*, p. 135. For the hydria fragments from the Acropolis see Beazley, *Development*, pl. 12, 1–2.

VOLUTE KRATER (François Vase). Florence, Museo Archeologico 4209. From Chiusi (Contrada Fonte Rotella). Found in the autumn of 1845 by the painter Alessandro François about a mile north of Chiusi as a vast number of small fragments which turned up for the most part in one tumulus grave, but also, mixed up with other fragments, in a neighbouring tomb. The vase was reconstructed and restored by François, but in 1900 shattered into 638 fragments by a maniac. With the renewed restoration a fragment found subsequently to the original discovery was inserted and the whole vase apart from some unavoidable losses gained in clarity. Red clay, black glaze, use of purple and white sometimes applied over black, sometimes upon the clay directly. Unfortunately in almost all cases both the purple and the white as well as any details, such as eyes, painted in dark over the white of the women's flesh have disappeared, removed by excessive zeal in cleaning and by careless handling. Besides, the accounts show that the excavations were conducted with rather less than deliberation and meticulousness. There are numerous serious gaps in the various friezes and in the fourth one down even the fragments preserved are in poor condition. The glaze on the inside of the vase has fired red. Height 66 cms ($25^{15}/_{16}''$), diam. of mouth 57 cms ($22^3/_8''$), greatest circumference 1.81 m ($71^1/_8''$).

The size of the vase is exceptional. The proportions of the basin, large and high, recall those of Corinthian column-kraters but the addition of the volutes give it a character of its own. The volutes are probably derived from metal prototypes; note the sharply raised flanges of the handle which are more appropriate to bronze technique. The sides of the handles are decorated with a double palmette chain. Where the basin joins the neck, there is a frieze of tongues, black and purple alternately, outlined with incision. In the centre of the fifth frieze down there is a large floral complex consisting of a double palmette flanked by double lotuses out of which in turn grow volute tendrils with a palmette in the centre. On both sides of this ornament two sphinxes turn towards it, their face in white (details of the features have disappeared) and one paw raised to touch the upper volute. To the left a lion has seized a stag (pl. 45, middle, right), to the right a panther is breaking the back of a piebald bull (pl. 45, middle, left). On the corresponding place on the other side of the vase we find griffins flanking the floral motif (pl. 45, bottom) followed on either side by similar scenes of felines attacking a boar and a piebald bull. The lowest zone of the body consists of rays springing from the foot. The foot itself which is in the shape of a flattened echinus is decorated by tongue pattern above and below a figure frieze.

On the flat of the handles there is on the inner face, overlooking the basin, a picture of the two Gorgons, one on each side, with serpent hair and tongue stretched out. The apex of the handle is decorated with a double palmette-and-lotus chain. Then facing outwards there are two decorated panels, one above the other (pl. 46). On top we have the picture of the *potnia theron*, the Mistress of the Beasts, whom we have met before. She is shown in full view, her face is in profile, her wings spread and she is dressed in a peplos elaborately decorated with a square pattern enriched alternately with a dot rosette in white and with engraved crosses. She holds in her lowered arms a spotted feline (spots not showing on photograph pl. 46) and a stag by their neck. Her face and arms are outlined and covered in white applied directly on the clay. The incision is sensitive, the face is delicately featured, the pupil of the eyes is indicated by a black dot. The other handle has the same subject with some variations. The lower panel on the handles shows Ajax (inscribed) armed with corslet, helmet and greaves, raising the lifeless body of Achilles (inscribed), which he has put over his shoulders. The dead hero's hair hangs listlessly to the ground in a telling way. There is much sensitive incision. Note the long tapering fingers of both heroes.

The neck is decorated by two friezes on each side, making four subjects.

Neck, side A, upper frieze: The hunt of the Calydonian boar (pl. 42). The picture is flanked on either side by a sphinx with scaly plumage and raised paw within a field enclosed on its sides by an upright lotus-and-palmette chain and a double palmette chain. In the centre of the frieze we see an enormous boar with white tusks (not visible in the photograph) who has already killed one of the hunters, Antaios (his name is inscribed as are all the other names on this and the other friezes; we shall not mention this on each occasion), who is stretched out dead and disembowelled on the ground; similarly the hound Ormenos lies in the dust, his entrails showing through his slit belly. However, another hound, Marpsas, has jumped on the boar's back and belabours him with his fangs. Painted in white, he is hardly visible on the photograph. Facing the boar are four pairs of hunters as well as one archer, Euthymachos, who wears the characteristic cap of an archer. The huntsmen are led by Peleus and Meleager who jointly grasp a pike to meet the monster. They are followed by Melanion and Atalanta, the formidable huntress maiden. Her flesh is painted white, she wears a tucked up peplos or some kind of very short dress fastened on the shoulders with pins which are clearly visible. With them hunts the hound Methepon. Then behind the archer follow Thorax and Antandros again with a hound, painted in white and called Labros. The final pair are Aristandros and Harpylea. The huntsmen are dressed in short chiton and several of them wear animal skins as well, lion's and fawn. They are armed with spears except for Aristandros who is hurling a stone. Behind the boar there are more huntsmen coming up in pairs. This time they are joined by two archers depicted in the act of drawing, Kimmerios and Toxamis, both of them carrying quivers and wearing the characteristic peaked cap. Their arrows and those of Euthymachos on the other side have found their mark on the boar, as can be seen. Nearest to the boar and getting his teeth into his haunches is the hound Korax (= raven). Then follow the Dioscuri, Castor and Polydeuces, then Akastos and Asmetos, hunting with the hound Egertes, painted in white. Behind the archer follow Antimachos and

Simon with their hound Ebolos again in white. Finally behind the archer Toxamis, Pausileon and Kynortes bring up the rear. All the heroes with the exception of the two archers use spears, carry their swords on their sides and most of them wear animal skins over their chiton.

Neck, side A, lower frieze: Funeral games in honour of Patroclus (pl. 42). On the extreme right we see Achilles who is giving the games, holding a sceptre in his hand and standing in front of a prize for victory, a tripod. Of the leading chariot team there only remain part of the heads of the four horses and the name of the competitor, Odysseus. Then follows the team of Automedon, of whose horses hardly anything has remained; and he himself is for the most part obscured by the horses of the next team which was driven by Diomede. Diomede is quite visible holding the reins and a goad and wearing a long white sleeveless chiton, as all the other charioteers do too (as far as one can tell from what is preserved). He is followed by two more teams under each of which a prize is shown, a tripod and a cauldron respectively. No doubt there were similar prizes under the other teams, but they are lost. Damasippos and Hippothoon are the names of these last two charioteers. On the extreme left there is a pillar round which, no doubt, the chariots had to turn (compare plate 81).

Neck, side B, top frieze: Dance of the liberated Athenian youths and maidens in Crete (pl. 43). On the left a ship, probably a triacontere, with its stern (which terminates in two swan heads) pointing to land. We see the helmsman sitting in the back turning round to the land and raising his right hand in excitement. The steering oars are by his side. The mast has been lowered and is visible between the heads of the oarsmen. Altogether there are sixteen oarsmen in the preserved part of the ship. (The ship's prow terminating in a boar's head is preserved too after a large gap, and is barely visible on the top left of pl. 41.) There is great commotion amongst the crew, much gesticulation and joy and a number of them have risen and let go of their oars. Indeed one of them has jumped into the water and with rapid strokes is making for land. On land there is a dance of seven maidens and seven youths, each with their name against them: From left to right Phaidimos, Hippodamaia, Daidochos, Menestho, Eurysthenes, Koronis, Heuxistratos, Damasistrate, Antiochos, Asteria, Hernippos, Lysidike, Prokritos, Epiboia. Theseus as fifteenth leads the dance playing the lyre, whilst Phaidimos brings up the rear, or rather he hastens up to join the others. Facing Theseus on the extreme right is Ariadne holding a wreath and the famous thread rolled up into a ball. She is accompanied by her nurse (inscribed *throphos* = nurse, in an aspirate spelling).

The subject refers to the annual dispatch of the tribute of fourteen youths and maidens from Athens to King Minos of Crete for sacrifice to the Minotaur. Theseus with the help of Ariadne, the daughter of Minos, liberated the Athenians at last from this scourge by killing the Minotaur and rescuing the youths and maidens, who are here shown performing a dance of thanksgiving. This dance had for long been thought as taking place in Delos, where indeed a ritual dance associated with these events, the so called *geranos*, was regularly performed in the sanctuary of Apollo (see Plutarch, *Theseus* 21). Friis Johansen, however, has recently shown that the scene here is set in Crete immediately after the successful outcome of Theseus' quest. The ship then had been ordered to lie offshore to avoid trouble from the hostile Cretans. At an appointed time they were to approach land again to find out what had happened. Now, to their great joy they see the dance taking place on land and realize that all is well. The names of the Athenian youths are known also from later sources, the cup by Archikles and Glaukytes in Munich (pl. 50 below) and on a vase from Vulci in Leiden; they do not however correspond with the names of the François Vase. On the left of the frieze above the ship we have the end of two signatures, Ergotimos the potter and Kleitias the painter.

Neck, side B, lower frieze: Centauromachy, that is the battle between Lapiths and Centaurs (pl. 43). On the left there is a centaur throwing a rock against Theseus. Then follows a gap with only parts preserved of a fallen centaur and of another fighting against Antimachos who is also largely missing. Facing the other way towards the centre of the picture we see the centaur Hylaios, branch in hands, bearing down on Kaineus, the invulnerable Lapith whom the centaurs had to pound into the ground (see also plate 190, below). Hylaios is helped by two more centaurs, Akrios and Hasbolos (the latter with white equine body) who approach from the other side with boulders in their hands, within one of which is written [*lith*]*os* = rock, over the white. We then see the centaur Petraios, branch in arms, matched against Hoplon who fights like the other Lapiths in full armour. Then follows another centaur with two rocks in his hands, Melanchaites (?). His opponent is largely missing. Next to him another centaur called Pyrrhos is down and out of the fight. Then a very fragmentary patch in which the centaur Therandros fights against a Lapith (almost totally missing), who is also attacked from the other side by another centaur. A duel between Dryas and the centaur Oroibios ends the frieze. The centaurs have flowing hair bristling in front and long shaggy beards. They have wild but regular features.

Main body, top frieze: This goes right round the vase including the space between the handles, indeed it is thought of as continuing underneath the actual handle roots. Its subject is the wedding of Peleus with Thetis. This great wedding between mortal and immortal was one of the fateful events in Greek mythology. The gods and more besides were invited and came. Out of that union sprang Achilles whilst as a result of a quarrel during the wedding feast arose the events leading to the Judgement of Paris, the abduction of Helen and the Trojan War. Our picture shows the procession of guests arriving at the house within which Thetis is sitting whilst Peleus receives the guests outside. This house is on the extreme right of side A (pl. 40). We begin our description with the group under the handle to the left of side A (pl. 44, top left) and proceed to the right towards the house. Three Muses, Stesichore, Erato and Polymnis are seen facing to the right dressed in peploi richly decorated with squares alternately incised with crosses and

288

painted with stars. Their faces have lost all detail as so many other female faces have on this vase for the reason stated in the introductory paragraph. They move forward one next to the other, overlapping, with hands open and held out in front of them as though they made gestures to accompany their singing. In the plane this side of them there is a team of four horses two of them with their fore mane knotted into a plume. They are the two pole horses in the centre more elaborately done up than the trace horses here as on other teams in the frieze. The chariot drawn by these horses, which we know from the inscriptions on the other side of the handle to carry Ares and Aphrodite, is thought of as being covered by the handle root and therefore invisible. Similarly to the extreme right of the panel in front of the horses we see the inscriptions *Amphitrite* and ...*seidon* (misspelled). Here too the persons, that is Poseidon and Amphitrite, and the chariot carrying them are thought of as being eclipsed by the other handle root. Only their team of horses is visible emerging from under the handle root on the other side into the main frieze. One of these horses is white. On the farther side of this team there are four more Muses, Melpomene, Kleio (Clio), Euterpe and Thaleia. They are covered in one mantle whose edge is held out by Thaleia. We have met this motif before (see commentary on plates X and XI) and have noted its cult significance. The painter here has used it on this frieze again in the group of the Horai and twice more. The peploi of the four Muses are decorated with squares incized with crosses, or painted with white dot rosettes, or again covered with incised meanders. In the case of Euterpe, the peplos is just black, in order to set off the densely decorated peploi of the two companions on her either side. Then follows on the right the chariot with Zeus and Hera. Again on the further side of their horses we see two more Muses, Ourania and Kalliope, the former turned to the right, speaking and making a solemn gesture, whilst Kalliope is frontal to the spectator and plays the syrinx. Kalliope's dress is decorated in the same way as those of the other Muses but Ourania's has most elaborate embroidery in superimposed panels running from neck to foot. The main motifs are orientalizing animals and ornaments, such as lotus chain, winged horses, sphinx and also part of a chariot scene. Hera's dress in so far as it is not covered by her himation is seen to be even more elaborately embroidered but Zeus is dressed in a plain white chiton over which is thrown a himation which is dragging over his arms. He holds a short sceptre (or is it a goad?), the reins and his thunderbolt. Again the two pole horses have their mane in a top knot. The farther one of the trace horses is white.

Below the muzzle of this white horse we see the potter's signature running downwards, *Ergotimos m'epoiesen* = Ergotimos made me (plate 44, middle). Then come the three Horai, again under one mantle. The farthest of them wears another one of the elaborately embroidered dresses, the middle one is in plain purple, whilst the outer one has her dress decorated in squares filled with incised crosses alternating with painted white dot rosettes. Then comes Dionysus staggering under the load of a golden amphora, his gift to Thetis, on his shoulder. (The amphora, decorated

on the neck with two concentric circles flanked by two vertical wiggly lines on either side, and on its body with a few horizontal bands is of a type known from examples in clay, an SOS-amphora, so called after the neck ornament.) His face is frontal, gazing at the spectator (for sympathy) with his masklike bearded face of a type which is known as a common motif from a number of vases dating from the middle of the 6th century and beyond (see here pl. XXII)— long hair, big staring eyes, triangular beard. Here he is dressed in a long chiton decorated with squares alternately incised with crosses and enhanced in purple, and a white himation which he has thrown over both shoulders. The next group to the right are three women again covered by one himation which is held up in front by the furthest of the three, Demeter. The middle one is Chariklo, the wife of the centaur Chiron, whom we shall meet presently. The nearest of the trio is Hestia. Chariklo in the centre again wears a peplos with decorated squares whilst the two outer women have a simpler dress enhanced with purple vertical areas.

In front of the building in which Thetis awaits the procession we see Peleus receiving the first group of guests consisting of Iris and of Chiron, the most civilized of centaurs who had taught amongst others Peleus himself and who was to bring up his son, Achilles. He carries on his right shoulder a branch from which are suspended his quarry, two hares and a deer. Next to him on the hither side comes Iris in a short chiton leaving her legs and arms exposed as befits the swift messenger of the gods. In her right she carries a huge *kerykeion* (herald's staff). Over her dress, again decorated with squares incised with crosses or painted with dot rosettes, she wears a spotted fawn's skin. The details of her face, as those of the other women, have vanished. Between these two and Peleus we see an altar on top of which rests a kantharos. The altar itself has inscribed on it *bom[os]* = altar. Above the altar an inscription reading downwards *Klitias m'egrapsen* = Kleitias painted me. Peleus himself shakes hands with Chiron. He has long hair and a beard, is dressed in a white chiton and has a purple himation with rich borders thrown over his shoulders.

The house on the extreme right of the frieze is seen frontally. The artist has turned the building round by 90 degrees towards the spectator so as to be able to show the entrance with its half opened double door which reveals Thetis seated inside holding aside the cloak which covers her head. She herself is in profile facing not the spectator but the oncoming procession of guests. The building too should of course be facing that way but Kleitias has twisted it round to enable us to see more. The building is of great interest for its representation of architectural details as well as for the construction of the whole. The shape of the roof for instance has given rise to problems. The two side walls project as antae between which two fluted Doric columns on bases support a Doric entablature. Between the columns is visible the double door which is set into the further wall. This wall about three quarters of the way up has a number of horizontal bands in brownish colour. They are not easy to interpret; one suggestion has been beams to strengthen a structure of clay walls but they may very well be merely

ornamental, as we find a similar motif as border ornament on Etruscan wall paintings. The capitals of the columns as well as the bases are white as against the dark column shafts, possibly an indication of stone capitals and bases as against wooden pillars.

We turn to side B (plate 41) where the procession of the guests is continued. We begin from the side nearest to the handle where we started our account of this frieze and then work backwards away from the house, that is from right to left on plate 41. Nearest to the handle we have the inscriptions Ares and Aphrodite, but as stated already at the beginning, the chariot with these two divinities is thought of as being under the handle and only the horses are shown in the panel between the handle roots. We then have a chariot drawn by four horses, one of which is white. (It is worth noting that a number of the horses on this side of the frieze including the ones pulling this chariot have their tails elaborately looped at the bottom end). The upper section of this part of the frieze is lost hence the occupants of the chariot cannot be named with certainty, but Apollo is the strongest candidate, as he must have been represented in the procession. The woman next to him in the chariot may have been his sister Artemis or his mother Leto. Apollo is dressed in a long embroidered chiton over which a heavy himation with elaborate border is draped. On the farther side of the horses are the lower part of three women, usually identified as the Charites (Graces), the daughters of Zeus. The middle one has a purple dress whilst her two sisters have peploi of greater elaboration, the hither one with squares of incised crosses or painted white dot rosettes, whilst the farther one has a garment embroidered with animal panels. The next chariot team is better preserved. It holds Athena and another unnamed goddess, perhaps Artemis. Athena is unarmed and dressed simply in black; she holds the reins and a goad. Turned towards her to give welcome is a tall woman standing on the farther side of the horses; she wears a peplos and has moved her himation away from her head. She is Doris the mother of the bride and wife of Nereus who is next to her facing the same way but pointing forward to indicate the way with an expressive gesture. He is a venerable old man with long white hair, hoary beard and wrinkles on his balding forehead, and is dressed in a long white chiton with a purple himation thrown over his shoulders. The next chariot team is driven by Hermes with his mother Maia. He is in a black chiton and purple himation with some indication of folds (folds are indicated on several of the himatia, and on some of the other garments on side B even more than on side A), his long hair coming down his back is tied into a loop. In his left hand he carries a long kerykeion (herald's wand), in his right a goad. Maia's dress has stripes of meanders all the way down, she holds one side of her himation in front of her. Standing on the hither side of the horses and therefore (unlike the other groups of females in a similar position) visible for their whole length are the Moirai (Fates). There are four women, one of them being probably Themis, the mother of the three Moirai. They walk along holding hands and each overlapping a little the one by her side. Their linked hands all point downwards except the

left, outer, hand of the woman nearest to the horses. She breaks the rhythm by pointing her hand upwards and forwards. Their peploi are different each from the other and are rendered with impressive elaboration. The second one from the left is embroidered (rendered in white) with chariots drawn by winged horses, in superimposed panels separated by floral and other ornamental friezes (some of them incised and therefore discernible on the photograph pl. 41). The others of the quartet wear simpler peploi but impressive nonetheless. They are enhanced in purple and with elaborate borders; particularly the overfall over the breast is beautifully drawn with all details including the long shoulder pins. The third from the left has an elaborate chain joining the two pins across her breast. Behind this chariot follows the last team which is almost totally lost. The front part of the four horses indeed remain as well as some women's feet standing on the farther side of the horses. On the extreme upper left corner of the frieze we also have part of a bull's head and the remnant of the inscription *Okeanos*. He then, the grandfather of the bride, mounts the last chariot presumably with his wife Tethys. He was bull-headed with human features as river gods often are. The remnants of the women on the farther side of the horses mentioned just now are probably the Nereids, sisters of Thetis, who could scarcely have been absent from the wedding. They are not the only company of Okeanos as we see when we look under the handles behind Okeanos' chariot. For there we have the grotesque sight of Hephaistos bringing up the rear holding a whip and riding side saddle on a braying donkey. (The donkey's mouth is wide open.) His two feet are twisted outwards to indicate the cripple. On the farther side of the donkey we see the scaly seamonster-like coils of Triton ending in an enormous fish tail. His foreparts will have passed underneath the handle and his human face and body are to be thought as hidden by it. Hephaistos lived for long with Eurynome and Thetis, daughter and granddaughter of Okeanos, in one of the submarine caves, and not unnaturally he is shown here still in the general company of the denizens of the sea.

Main body, side A, second frieze down: The death of Troilus (pl. 44). This episode from the Trojan war was dealt with in the *Cypria*, an epic poem now lost. It became very popular in Greek art; there are representations in Corinthian as well as elsewhere including one well known Etruscan wall painting. In the centre of the frieze just where there is a large gap we see the right leg and remnants of the scabbard of Achilles who is running with long strides after a mounted youth with flowing hair, Troilus, a son of Priam. Achilles wears greaves and holds a spear of which the rear part is plainly visible; Troilus with two spears and the reins in his hands is galloping away leading a second horse by his side (in fact Achilles will catch up with him). In front of this group we have another gap but the lower part of a woman, from her waist downwards, is preserved. She too runs away, her name is given by a fragmentary inscription as Polyxena, a sister of Troilus. In the scurry of the flight she has dropped her water pot which is shown fallen on its side (against the pot is written *hydria*, the name for this kind of vessel). She had gone with Troilus to the fountain, where Achilles

290

was lying in ambush. Behind Achilles we see Athena, unarmed and richly dressed in ornamental peplos and a himation (with indications of folds). Her hair is done up in an elaborate loop at the back whilst two tresses come down her shoulder. She is encouraging Achilles. Behind her is Hermes with *kerykeion* in his hand, a *petasos* on his head and a spotted fawn skin worn over a short chiton. He has turned round towards Thetis, the mother of Achilles, who is following the chase with some agitation. Next comes a smaller female figure called Rhodia. She is a Trojan girl, a companion of Polyxena, and with both arms raised in horror, she watches the events in the centre. Her peplos is fastened on her shoulders with two pins joined by a small chain across her breast (the representation here, as elsewhere on this frieze, is more summary than on the main frieze of the wedding of Peleus). She stands on a low platform which has been explained as a watering trough for horses. On the extreme left of the frieze we have the fountain house, a building in Doric style with three fluted columns (on bases) between two antae. It is named by an inscription *krene* = fountain. Two spouts in the shape of lion's heads are seen in the background, underneath one of which stands a hydria. A Trojan youth (called *Troön* in the inscription) approaches the other spout with a hydria. Behind him comes the huge figure of Apollo bearded and draped in a himation (with indications of folds) thrown over his shoulders. His left hand is forward in a gesture of concern and annoyance. It was of course his altar which was to be desecrated by Achilles' barbarous slaughter of Troilus. The reason for this murder was an oracle that, if Troilus reached his twentieth year, Troy would never be taken. We now turn to the other end of the frieze, which is taken up by the walls of Troy, shown as regular squared blocks surmounted by battlements and piles of stones heaped in the interstices ready for use against the attacker (pl. 44, bottom). Out of a double gate issues a rescue party in a vain attempt to save Troilus. It is headed by Hector and Polites, two brothers of Troilus; one of them has a shield with a Gorgon's head emblem. Some distance away, underneath the walls is a block (inscribed *thakos* = seat) on which Priam had been sitting taking the sun. He is dressed in a white chiton and a purple himation thrown over his shoulders. He has a stubbly beard and long hair receding from an aged and wrinkled forehead. He holds a long sceptre, his left leg is drawn back whilst his left hand supports itself against the seat in an instinctive effort to rise. He is alarmed and the cause of this agitation is Antenor (one of the Trojan elders and another figure in white chiton), who has hastened towards him no doubt to tell the frightful news about Troilus.

Main body, side B, second frieze down: Return of Hephaistos (pl. 41). Though no continuous account has come down to us of this story, we can reconstruct it as the theme of what must have been an early and influential poem from the pictures which have been preserved; this has been done notably by Wilamowitz-Moellendorff. After the expulsion of Hephaistos from Olympus at the instigation of Hera, his mother, who was disgusted at having given birth to a cripple, he avenged himself by sending her a splendid throne

for a present. Once the Queen of Heaven had sat down on this throne she was unable to rise again enmeshed by finely devised and invisible bonds which Hephaistos had fitted to the throne—and none of the gods could help her. Hephaistos was sent for but would not come, not even when Ares, the god of war, was despatched to fetch him. Indeed he had to retire ignominiously, chased away by lumps of molten metal directed against him by Hephaistos. Eventually Dionysus succeeded by getting Hephaistos drunk and thus persuading him to come up and liberate Hera. The reward for Hephaistos was to be the hand of Aphrodite, the loveliest of the goddesses, whilst Dionysus was henceforth to be admitted to Olympus.

In the centre slightly to the left we see Zeus with sceptre and thunderbolt (only the upper tips of the latter are preserved). He sits on a rich throne covered with tapestries and with a back rest ending in a volute. He wears a white chiton and a himation. Behind him on a similar throne (the back rest ending in a swan's head) sits Hera, his Queen, with impatient gestures, unable to move. Her feet rest on a foot stool. A similar foot stool will have been in front of Zeus in the lost portion of the frieze. To the left stands Athena in a chiton and purple himation, with folds indicated. She turns round, no doubt to jeer at Ares who sits on a low block feeling his discomfiture. He is in full panoply his shield being decorated with a demon's face modelled almost fully in the round. Behind him Artemis coming forward with a gesture. Then follow two more figures, both male, whose lower part alone is preserved (see pl. 44, bottom picture, extreme right). The first one is generally taken to be Poseidon, dressed in the long white of the senior gods, and holding the trident whose lower end is still visible. Behind him comes the last figure in the frieze, Hermes booted as usual and dressed in a short chiton. The lower end of his kerykeion is still there.

We now turn to the right half of the frieze and look at the procession which is approaching the seat of the gods (pl. 45, top picture). Dionysus is leading an ithyphallic mule ridden by Hephaistos whip in hand and dressed in a rich chiton and himation. His two feet point in opposite directions, to indicate the cripple. His face, as some of the others on this vase, is in purple, applied over black. In front of Dionysus and between him and Zeus we see Aphrodite, her hands expressing dismay as she sees Dionysus and her future husband.

Hephaistos on his mule is followed by a band of satyrs and nymphs. The satyrs (called *silenoi* in the inscription) are ithyphallic and all have equine legs, tails and ears. The first one is bending under the load of a wine skin filled to the bursting. He is followed by another playing the flute and wearing a mouthband. Then emerging out of the break in the surface we see the remnants of a satyr with a nymph in his arms. Another nymph follows but is lost apart from her hand (against her is written *nyphai* = nymphs misspelled). Two more nymphs in richly decorated peploi bring up the rear, the last one playing the cymbals, an instrument surely heard now for the first time in Olympus.

Foot of the vase (the frieze goes right round): The battle of the Pygmies and Cranes (pl. 40), the *geranomachy* mentioned

in the *Iliad* III, 1–7. Our eye is caught by three pairs of pygmies in action against one crane each (pl. 40). The scales are even and there are casualties on both sides. The cranes peck, the pygmies use sticks with a curved end to collar and clubs to brain their adversaries (their cavalry uses sling stones). One of the pygmies is stretched dead on the ground; above him struts a crane, who however is now collared and attacked with a club by the fallen pygmy's comrade. On his right a crane is down in the dust laid low by a pygmy who himself is in dire danger of having his eye pecked out by the swift onset of another crane. However, both he and another pygmy have caught the crane's neck with the curved stick and will pull it down. To the left we have a crane collared by one pygmy and being brained by another. Further left we see three cranes facing up to a detachment of pygmy cavalry mounted on goats. The pygmies are armed with slings, and they ride over a dead pygmy who is being pecked at by one of the cranes. Even further left the battle is going in favour of the pygmies; one crane is down and being finished off by a pygmy, whilst another one has been collared by one and is being finished off with the club by another pygmy (pl. 41 extreme right). Then disappearing in a gap we see a crane pecking at a dead pygmy. We now move across to the right of the battle scene described first (pl. 40). We see there a squadron of pygmy cavalry mounted on goats with their loaded slings hanging down their sides. They are being faced by a detachment of cranes one of whom is down already. Finally a pygmy has collared a crane and is now grappling with him. On the ground below a dead pygmy. There follows another pygmy facing a crane who has disappeared in the lacuna.

The whole of this episode is treated with a light touch of parody. Ancient lore represented by Hecateus (as reported by Herodotus), Ctesias of Cnidus, Aristotle and other sources put the pygmies in Africa, near the sources of the Nile. Other authors again placed them on the shores of the Black Sea. Again it is possible that they were localized in the marshy regions of Thrace, where the cranes halted twice a year in their migrations between Scythia and Egypt.

On this vase Kleitias has celebrated above all the tale of Achilles; for he or his father Peleus are the subjects of the main frieze (the wedding of Peleus) and also of several of the others, i.e. the pursuit of Troilus, the funeral games of Patroklos and to a lesser extent the hunt of the Calydonian boar, where Peleus is one of the leading heroes. All these are placed on what can be claimed as the principal face of the vase. Finally Achilles' dead body is carried by Ajax on the handle pictures. It has also been argued that the painter wanted to give prominence to the deeds of Theseus. Certainly the dance of the Athenian youths and maidens shows him as hero, on the other hand he appears in only a very minor role in the centauromachy frieze, and we are not justified in claiming any great place for him on this vase, particularly since there is no evidence that at this time Theseus had reached the prominence in Attic art and consciousness which he had later, at the end of the 6th and during the 5th centuries. The François Vase as a compendium of mythological

representations has often been compared with the chest of Kypselos, a work of Corinthian art described to us by Pausanias. Though there is Corinthian influence on the vase, the style and conception of the narrative friezes and the characterizations are essentially Attic and tie up with the previous generation of artists such as the Gorgon Painter. We place the vase at about 570 B.C., and not later as some scholars do. Only thus does the krater acquire its special place in the development of the Attic style of the 6th century. Kleitias then is practically contemporary with Sophilos, but a much greater artist. He more than anyone else is the accomplished master of the narrative style which after all was the great achievement of Attic vase painting.

Bibl.: The best publication of the vase are the excellent drawings by Reichhold, in: FR, pll. 1–3; 11–13 with some additions; and modifications given in a supplementary page issued after the repair following upon the damage done in 1900 (FR, I, pp. 62a-b). For description and commentary see FR, I, pp. 1–14; 54–62b; Beazley, *Development*, pp. 26–37. Further bibliography: General works: Jahn, pp. CLIII–CLXII; Rayet-Collignon, pp. 86–94. H. Brunn, *Kunstgeschichte der Griechen II*, p. 676ff. Id., *Geschichte der gr. Künstler I*, p. 166ff. Pottier, *Cat. III*, p. 614ff. Walters I, p. 128. Reinach, *RV*, I, pp. 134–6. Perrot-Chipiez, X, pp. 138–78, figg. 93–110. Langlotz, *Zeitbest*, p. 11. Buschor, *G Vsm*, p. 14ff., figg. 90–1. Id., *GV*, p. 103ff., fig. 118. Hoppin *BFV*, pp. 150–5. Ducati, I, pp. 221–9, figg. 177–84. Swindler, pp. 165–6. Payne, *NC*, p. 346, n. 1. Rumpf, p. 40. Kraiker, p. 41ff., fig. 15, 2. Cook, pp. 73–4. On the inscriptions see Kretschmer, *Vaseninschriften*, p. 112ff. Klein, p. 32ff.

Monographs: E. Braun, in: *MI*, IV, 1848, pll. 54–58. A. François-E. Braun, *Le dipinture di Clizia sopra vaso chiusino di Ergotimo*, Roma 1849, p. 84. E. Gerhard, in: *AZ*, 1850, p. 257ff., pll. 23–4. Birch, in: *BI*, 1850, p. 7ff. J. Overbeck, *Galerie heroischer Bildwerke der alten Kunst*, 1853, p. 19ff., pl. 91. H. Brunn, in: *BI*, 1863, p. 188ff. *AI*, 1866, pl. G. P. Weizsäcker, in: *Rhein. Mus.*, 32, 1877, p. 28ff., 33, 1878, p. 364ff., 35, 1880, p. 350ff. H. Luckenbach, *Das Verhältnis der griech. Vasenbilder zu den Gedichten des ep. Kyklos* in: *XI Suppl. Jahrb. klass. Phil.*, 1880, p. 493ff. Reichel-Loeschke, in: *Arch. ep. Mitt.*, 1880, p. 38ff. A. Schneider, *Der troische Sagenkreis in der ält. gr. Kunst*, Leipzig 1886, pp. 25, 45–6, 84–5, 90–1, 128–158 and *passim. Wiener Vorlegeblätter*, 1888, pll. II–IV, 1 e. H. Heberdey, in: *Arch. ep. Mitt.*, XIII, p. 78ff. A. Schneider, in: *Ber. Sächs. Ges. Wissensch.*, 1891, p. 204ff. C. Smith, in: *JHS*, 1894, p. 215. Wilamowitz-Moellendorff, in: *Nachrichten der Götting. Gesellschaft*, 1895, pp. 220ff. = *Kleine Schriften*, 5, 2, pp. 5ff. W. Amelung, *Führer durch die Antiken in Florenz*, Munich 1897, n. 223, pp. 202–26. L. A. Milani, in: *Atene e Roma*, 1902, p. 705ff. Jolles, in: *JdI*, 1904, p. 27. F. Lenormant, in: *RA*, VI, 1911, p. 205ff. L. A. Milani, *Il R. Museo Archeologico di Firenze*, Florence 1912, pp. 148–9. H. Sulze, in: *Arch. Anz.* (JdI), 51, 1936, p. 26ff. K. Friis Johansen, 'Thesée et la Danse à Délos', *Kgl. Danske Videnskab. Selskab*, Ark-Kunsthist. Meddel., III, 3 (1945). P. de la Coste-Messeliere, in: *RA*, 28, 1947, pp. 145–56. Steuding s.v. *Theseus* and Waser s.v. *Pygmän*, in: Roscher. A. Minto, in: 'Atti Acc. Toscana Sc. e Lett. La Colombaria' 1952, p. 97ff. Id. in 'Anthemion–Miscell. Ant.' Florence 1955, pp. 21–40. Id., *Il vaso François* (Acc. Toscana Sc. e Lett. La Colombaria VI Studi) Florence 1960. Dugas-Flacelière, *Thesée-Images et Récits*, Paris 1958, p. 59, pll. 2–3. Rumpf, in: *Gnomon*, 25, 1953, p. 470 (adopted here; persuasive interpretation of Dionysus' amphora, comparing *Odyssey*, 24, 73ff.). *RIASA*, 1960, p. 172, fig. 58–9 (photo of handle Gorgons). M. Santangelo, *Musei e Monumenti Etruschi*, Novara 1960, pl. 44 (colour; side view). Buschor, *Meermänner* (*S.B.* Munich 1941), p. 24.ff – Important for reconstruction of tail of the wedding procession (Hephaistos, Okeanos). On page 291 here we have adopted his solution postulating the Triton, and making the bull's neck part of an otherwise human Okeanos mounting his chariot. This is a neat and possible solution. Against it, however, is the fact that the label *Triton* is not found, unlike the case of the other 'eclipsed' figures. Again, the new Erskine dinos by Sophilos (see p. 285) shows Okeanos (inscribed; again with Hephaistos) represented in the manner of Nereus as 'Old man of the Sea' with monster coils and the symbol of change (snake) and a fish in his hands; but his human head is surmounted by the river god's horn. It is thus possible that on the François Vase too the head of Okeanos is to be joined to the coils (though the restoration would be difficult), that there was no Triton, and that the couple in the last chariot is entirely lost.

These were made in the middle and the third quarter of the 6th century B.C. Two main types can be distinguished, the so-called lip cup and the band cup. The lip cup (example on plate 49 but with wrong foot, which should be more like that on plate 50) has the lip and handle zones reserved and separated by a black line just below the juncture of the lip. The lip has usually one figure or at least a compact group placed in the middle, the 'spot-light' system of decoration, the rest of the lip being left plain. The handle zone also is sparsely decorated, palmettes springing from the handles (or single figures taking their place as on plate 49) are its only ornament. However, the space between the palmettes is usually filled with letters, either signatures of the potter or painter, or an exhortation to enjoy the contents of the cup, or even series of letters without any meaning at all, their purpose being decorative only. The other variety, the band cups (example on plate 50) are quite different. Here the lip is black and the transition to the handle zone is less angular than on the lip cup. The whole impression of the cup is dark as against the rather light lip cup. The handle zone is usually well filled with figures; inscriptions used for decorative purposes are therefore less called for and signatures consequently scarcer on this type of cup. The Little-Master Cups were preceded in the second quarter of the 6th century by the so-called Siana cups (after a find spot in Rhodes) of which we do not show any example, though one of the chief painters of Siana cups, the C Painter, is represented by a work of another shape on plates 47, 48. Siana cups were made in a period of strong Corinthian influence on Attic and the C Painter in particular (C for 'Corinthianizing') is very much under its spell in the use of colour as well as in his style in general. The 'Little Masters', however, are a generation further away from this influence. They excel in fine incision and careful if rather sombre use of colour.

Of the many preserved Little-Master Cups more than 150 are signed, with some 30 different names, practically all of them potters' signatures. In a number of cases the vases signed by one potter were also painted by one hand, who may or may not have been the same person as the potter. For example we know Tleson as a potter from signatures. Nearly all his cups with figure work were decorated by one painter whom we therefore call the Tleson Painter who may or may not have been the same as Tleson. He is one of the best and was particularly attracted to the lip cup which he decorated with the greatest elegance. He has painted some beautiful central medallions in the inside of cups representing for instance two goats rampant and butting each other across a floral ornament or again, also in a central medallion, a hunter returning from the chase with his quarry and his dog (many lip cups have a central medallion, whilst band cups on the whole are plain inside). Other notable artists are the Phrynos Painter who painted a remarkable lip cup now in London with Herakles' entry into Olympus on one side and the Birth of Athena on the other, and perhaps also a lip cup in Boston with a woman's head in outline on the lip. Both these cups are signed by Phrynos the potter. Other lip cups with female heads in outline are found on a number of cups thrown by Hermogenes.

Some Little-Master cups were made by artists who normally worked on larger scale. We know for instance that the Amasis Painter (see plates 54–56) decorated a number of band cups; on the other hand a miniaturist like the Phrynos Painter is also known to have decorated an amphora though a rather small one (plate 52). Lip cups seem to come to an end about 530 B.C., band cups go on rather later into the twenties. The best period however are the decades just before and after the middle of the century.

Bibliography: On these cups in general see Pfuhl, I, p. 273 ff. Beazley, in: *JHS,* 52, 1932, pp. 167 ff. Idem, *Development,* pp. 54 ff. Idem, *ABFVP,* pp. 159 ff. Cook, pp. 79–81.

47, 48

TRIPOD KOTHON BY THE C PAINTER. Paris, Louvre, CA 616. From Thebes. Well preserved; some gaps in one of the legs. The white has largely gone from the female figures leaving a dullness on the black over which it was applied. Height 12.5 cms (4⁷/₈″). Diam. 25 cms(9³/₁₆″).

The inner wall of the mouth is decorated, starting from the bottom, with a zone of tongues alternately black and reserved, then a dot band, then a zone of reserved leaves slanting up and down. The flat top surrounding the mouth has a series of combats painted in a miniaturist's style. There is great variety of postures, broken spears, warriors down

and begging for mercy or being despatched. Shield devices are incised, amongst them are the chinless lion, ram's head, horse head as well as heads of a woman and a satyr.

The sides of the tripod legs are painted in a larger style. On one of them we see the Birth of Athena (plate 47 lower picture). Zeus bearded and in a long chiton sits on an elaborate throne, supported between the legs by an image of a squatting youth. His feet rest on a foot stool, in his right he holds a sceptre, in his left the thunder bolt. Out of his head emerges Athena, tiny, but fully armed. In front and behind him are the two goddesses assisting at the birth, the Eileithyiai, one of them soothing his head; further away are Poseidon, carrying his trident and striding away to the right, and on the left Hephaistos wearing long boots and carrying in his left hand the double axe with which he had split the skull of Zeus to bring forth Athena. His right hand is up in a gesture of satisfaction, two fingers out. On the two extremities are goddesses whom we cannot name with certainty. They are dressed in rich garments as indeed are the goddesses of birth in the centre.

On the second leg (not illustrated here) we see a four-horse chariot carrying a bearded male and next to him a woman who moves her himation away from her face in a gesture we have met before. In front of the couple three women richly dressed and offering wreaths. The subject ought to be Zeus and Hera met by the three Horai.

The third leg (plate 47 upper picture) has a Judgement of Paris, one of the earliest in Attic vase painting though we have met an earlier example on the Protocorinthian Chigi Vase (plates 16–17). Hermes with boots, petasos hat and kerykeion (herald's wand) invites the three goddesses forward, one of whom is pulling her himation away from her face in the familiar gesture. In front of Hermes is a woman carrying a wreath who can hardly be anyone but Iris, also a messenger of the gods. Paris is represented bearded and of mature years and rather frightened, indeed running away from the sudden apparition. This is the normal scheme in archaic art.

Much incision; the white is applied over black, which becomes normal practice in mature and late Black-figure. The C Painter is one of the best painters of Siana cups in the second quarter of the 6th century. He has left a great variety of subjects in his pictures, some of them of great iconographic value. Amongst his best known works, apart from this vase, are a cup with the pursuit of Troilos in New York, and a lekanis lid in Naples with the death of Priam.
C. 570 B.C.

Bibl.: Beazley, in: *Metropolitan Museum Studies V*, 1934, p. 114, no. 85. *Idem, Development*, pp. 23–4. *Idem, ABFVP*, p. 58, no. 122. C. Clairmont, *Das Parisurteil in der antiken Kunst*, Zurich, 1951, p. 28, pl. 7. One of the earliest fully armed Athenas in Attic art; also the earliest Attic picture of her birth, when she was always thought of as springing up fully armed *(Hymn. Homer.* 28,5; cf. also the divinity on the Tenos pithos—bibl. on plate 11). See Beazley, *Development*, p. 106, n. 11; Kunze, *Schildbänder*, p. 79; C. M. Bowra, *Greek Lyric Poetry²*, p. 123 (but Stesichorus cannot have invented the motif, which is earlier).

XIII

NECK-AMPHORA OF NICOSTHENIC SHAPE, SIGNED BY THE POTTER NIKOSTHENES. Bellinzona,

Private collection. No provenience known but the shape suggests that it was Cervetri. Height 59 cms (23³/₁₆"). Purple and white are applied over black. Women's flesh is white; drapery is touched with red, so are the hair and beards of the satyrs as well as details in the animal frieze.

The shape of this particular type of amphora was almost exclusively confined to the potter Nikosthenes. It imitates an Etruscan shape which goes back to a much earlier date.
On the neck dancing youths, on one side around a big krater; they wear fillets in white round their bodies or hanging from the arm. On the shoulders a fossilized animal frieze, a sphinx between two lions. The main figure frieze on the body has a procession of satyrs and menads. Under one of the handle-roots can be discerned the beginning of the potter's signature of Nikosthenes.
The vase belongs to the so-called Thiasos Group decorated by the Painter N, who specialized in decorating this particular type of amphora. See also plate 99.
C. 530 B.C.

Bibl.: Beazley, *Development*, p. 72 ff. Idem, *ABFVP*, p. 218, no. 24.

58

CUP SIGNED BY THE POTTER NIKOSTHENES. Paris, Louvre, F 123. From Vulci. Formerly in the collections of Canino, Durand, Beugnot, Hope and Rondel. Well restored. The white has flaked in places. Surface of clay is orange coloured. Height 11.5 cms (4¹/₂"). Diam. 28 cms (11").

Inside plain apart from reserved central medallion with a black dot in its centre. On the outside black line immediately below the edge of the lip; thick black band below the figure scene; outline rays below springing from the base. Purple fillet with reserved line at junction of foot. The hollow cone underneath the foot is black.
The figure scenes on the outside of the cup are practically identical on both sides. We see two ships under sail driven by the wind. They proceed side by side to the right. Their prow consists of a boar's head; their stern ends in a curved swan's head. There is a forecastle on each ship, painted in purple. A man stands watch on each. Along the sides of the boat can be seen the openings for the oars. At the back we see on both ships the helmsman controlling the steering oars. Landing ladders fixed to the stern. Next to the sails the potter's signature *Nikosthenes epoie* = Nikosthenes made (me). From the handle on the right springs a tendril on which a siren sits turning her head towards the ship. Under the handles a dolphin.
The workshop of the potter Nikosthenes employed a good number of painters. This cup is not by one of those who worked habitually for him. We cannot assign any other works to the same hand.
C. 520 B.C.

Bibl.: Th. Panofka, *Vasenbilder*, 1849, p. 23 ff. H. Brunn, *Gesch. gr. Künstler*, 1859, II, p. 718 ff., no. 4–2. J. H. Harrison, in: *JHS*, VI, 1885, p. 21, pl. 49. E. Pottier, *VAL*, p. 108, F 123. Idem, *Cat.*, p. 754 ff. Pfuhl, III, fig. 259. Beazley, in: *ABSA*, 32, 1931–32, p. 22. Bloesch, *Formen*, p. 9, *REA*, 48, 1946, p. 175, no. 4. Carpenter, in: *AJA*, 52, 1948, pl. IB. *CVA*, Louvre, fasc. 10 (Villard), pll. 95–6, p. 88 ff. Beazley, *ABFVP*, p. 231, no. 8.

LIP CUP. Tarquinia, Museo Nazionale, RC 4194. From the Monterozzi cemetery, Tarquinia. Diam. 32 cms (12⅝″), height 17 cms (6⅝″) (but this may include the foot which has been supplied by the restorer and is of quite the wrong type).

Outside on lip (both sides): A four horse chariot in full course. The two columns indicate the turning posts. Purple for the charioteer's chiton; fine incision. In the handle zone sphinxes instead of handle palmettes, and in between *XAIPEKAIΠEIIEY* (*chaire kai piei eu* = cheers and good drinking!). In the inside (plate XIV) the central picture is surrounded by a dance of seventeen maidens probably the Nereids. In the central roundel Herakles wrestling with Triton. The hero is astride the sea monster which has a human head and chest but a scaly sea serpent's body. Herakles wears the lion's skin over his head and his quiver is just visible on his back. Triton tries to break the hero's grip. The effective tondo composition is completed by five dolphins. Extremely good miniature work especially on the outside and in the frieze of the dancing Nereids. Much use of purple to enliven the picture. The scene of Herakles and Triton is very popular in the second half of the 6th century. Mid 6th century B.C.

On the form of the imperative *piei* see E. Schwyzer, *Griechische Grammatik*, I, p. 804. Beazley, in: *Eph. Arch.*, 1953–4, p. 201–2.

Bibl.: *NS*, 1880, p. 462. H. Philippart, *Collections de céramique grecque*, Brussels 1932, p. 115. Beazley, in: *JHS*, 52, 1932, p. 178, fig. 14. P. Romanelli, *Tarquinia*, p. 67. *CVA*, Tarquinia fasc. I, pl. 21, 5–6. On the subject of Herakles and Triton see Roscher, *Myth. Lex.* s.v. Triton, Tritonen; S. B. Luce, in: *AJA*, 26, 1922, p. 174ff.; cf. also H. Bloesch, *Antike Kunst in der Schweiz*, Zurich 1943, p. 46 and p. 163 ff.; also M P., Nilsson, *Geschichte der griech. Religion*, I, p. 223ff. For a hydria in Rimini with the same subject see Arias, in: *Archeologia Classica*, II, 1950, p. 119ff. Cf. in general also F. Brommer, *Herakles*, Münster 1953, pp. 7. ff Buschor, *Meermänner* (on Triton).

50

BAND CUP SIGNED BY THE POTTERS ARCHIKLES AND GLAUKYTES. Munich, Museum Antiker Kleinkunst 2243. From Vulci. Reconstructed from large fragments. Some made-up gaps on the lip. Height 18.5 cms (7¼″). Diam. 26.5 cms (10⁷⁄₁₆″). Purple used for garments, the sphinxes and for the hair and beards of males; white applied over black for female flesh and one of the dogs. Incision used for anatomical details and for decoration of the female dress. The inside of the cup has a reserved roundel at its centre. The tooled side of the base of the foot is also reserved.

Figure work is confined to the handle zone on both sides of the vase. Between the handle roots are the signatures of two potters, Archikles and Glaukytes (*Archikles m'epoiesen*, *Glaukytes m'epoiesen* = ... made me), one signature on each side. We do not know how these two artists divided their work. Next to the handles are sphinxes with their head turned round towards the centre, they take the place of handle palmettes normally found on these cups.

Side A (plate 50 lower picture): Theseus slaying the Minotaur. Theseus is unbearded, has long hair reaching down his back and is dressed in a short chiton over which he wears an animal skin with incised spots. Similar spots are all over the body of the Minotaur, whom Theseus has grasped by one of the horns and is about to pierce with his sword, the sword which the Minotaur is desperately trying to push away. There is a mass of inscriptions next to the figures all over the place, making the letters part of the decorative system. All the persons are named and some of the objects too, such as the lyre (*lyra*) which Athena holds in her hands to the left of Theseus, ready to give it to him when he leads the dance after his victory (see commentary on the François Vase, p. 287). Behind Athena follow the Athenian youths and maidens, Euanthe, Lykinos, Anthyla, Antias, Glyke, Simon (he has a beard and has been thought to be in fact Minos watching the struggle, Simon being an anagram of Minos) Enpedo. On the very left the sphinx has got its name = *sphix* (misspelled) written against it too. We now turn to the right half of the picture. Ariadne is immediately behind the Minotaur holding in her hand the ball of thread which saved Theseus; *kalē* (= beautiful) is written against her. Then follow the nurse shaking with excitement, Lykios, Eunike, Solon, Timo, Syon. In the very centre, above Theseus and the Minotaur, there is written *eutilas* whose significance is not clear (it may refer to the thread of Ariadne). Side B. The hunt of the Calydonian boar. The hunters, again named by inscriptions, are Meleager, Peleus, Melanion, Kimon. These are to the right of the boar. On top of it the dog Leukios (in white) has dug his teeth into it, but below the dog Podes or rather his severed parts lie in the dust. On the other side and facing the beast are five more hunters, Castor, Polydeuces, Mophsos (= Mopsos), Jason and Idasos. Running amongst the men on both sides are more hounds, Gorgos, Charon, Thero (a bitch) and Podargos. The huntsmen on the left are seen in chest view, those on the right from the back.

The two themes on this vase were already on the François Vase. Here they are treated rather differently. Both figures and inscriptions serve primarily decorative purposes and there is less individual variation.
C. 540 B.C.

Bibl.: Jahn, no. 333. Roscher, *Mythol. Lex.*, V, p. 692 s.v. Theseus. *FR*, III, p. 219ff., pl. 153, 1, fig. 105. Buschor, p. 126, fig. 143. Bothmer, in: *Bulletin Metropolitan Museum*, 5 (new series), 1946/7, p. 224. Beazley, *Development*, p. 55 ff. *Idem*, *ABFVP*, p. 163, no. 2. On 'double signatures' see Beazley, *Potter and Painter*, p. 26; Hampe, *Frühattischer Grabfund*, p. 47. For similarly crowded inscriptions, cf. band cup, *Auction 22; 13 May, 1961, Münzen und Medaillen*, Basle, pl. 38, no. 25.

51

EAST GREEK CUP. Paris, Louvre F 68. From Etruria, formerly in the Campana Collection. Yellowish clay with red tint. Brilliant black glaze, restored from many fragments. Height 15 cms (5⅞″), diam. 23 cms (9″).

The outside of the cup has black handles; black also the lower part of the bowl and the foot apart from a small reserved band on the tooled side of the base of the foot.

On the lip, which is reserved, there is an ivy branch with double leaves. Purple used for the hair, beard and short chiton of the men in the centre of the roundel. Purple also on the wings of the bird.

The scene which fills the inside of the cup seems to be essentially decorative. A bearded man in the centre grasps a branch from each of two trees which with their foliage (looking rather like vine with tendrils) fill the entire interior of the bowl. On the tree on his left we see a nest just where the trunk divides into branches. In it are four fledglings drawn in diluted glaze and barely visible in the photograph. Their mouths are open. Towards them flies a bird with an insect in its mouth. Amongst the foliage of this tree we also notice a grasshopper and what has been taken by some to be a snake. On top of the other tree we see a bird. The technique of the vase, which has no incision but produces a similar effect by the use of reservation, is that of Fikellura (see plate 30), and the cup may have been made therefore in Samos. It belongs to a group of rather fine cups made in Eastern Greece but influenced by Attic Little-Master cups.

Middle of 6th century B.C.

Bibl.: Pottier, VAL, p. 97, pl. 68. D. Rhomaios, in: AM, 31, 1906, p. 190. Perrot-Chipiez, X, p. 232, pl. 149. Pfuhl, I, pp. 254–5, III, p. 50, fig. 212. Jacobsthal, p. 82, no. 122, Swindler, fig. 218. Beazley, in: JHS, 52, 1932, p. 169, n. 13. Kunze, in: AM, 1934, p. 101–4. R. M. Cook, in: BSA, 34, 1933/4, p. 3. CVA, Louvre fasc. 8 (Pottier), p. 61, pl. 78, 3–5–8. Cook, p. 131. Robertson, p. 69 (below).

52
AMPHORA BY THE PHRYNOS PAINTER. Würzburg, University (Martin von Wagner) Museum, 241. Formerly

in the Feoli Collection, therefore from Etruria. Well preserved. Height 36 cms (14³/₁₆″).

The shape is squat but nicely rounded; the handles describe a wide loop. The lid with a pommel handle does not certainly belong. This one piece amphora (type B; see plate 21) is all black except for a zone just above the foot and the long but narrow figure panel. We had a similar scheme on the horse-head amphorae (plate 38). The subjects on both sides are courting scenes. Here we see the upper part of the one side, a bearded man of mature years caresses the chin of a youth. He has a white fillet hanging from his arm; a similar fillet is draped round the shoulders of the youth who also holds in his left a wreath in faded white. A spear is planted between the two. The hair of both man and youth is in purple. The hair of the youth is particularly elaborately done, tied in a bunch on its back and with two tresses down his cheek in front of his ears (this peculiarity often found in Laconian has made some scholars, quite unnecessarily, think of the youth as Spartan or philo-Spartan; but compare the Theseus on plate 50, below).

Firm use of incision for the outline of limbs and for anatomical markings. The vase is attributed to the Phrynos Painter who worked in the years following the middle of 6th century B.C. and is one of the best painters of Little-Master cups, see above p. 293.

C. 540 B.C.

Bibl.: Beazley, in: JHS, 52, 1932, p. 198. E. Langlotz, Frühgr. Bild-hauerschulen, p. 17, pl. 13 e. Idem, Vasen Würzburg, pl. 64–5, p. 44 no. 241. Buschor, G Vsm, p. 109. Beazley, Development, p. 54 ff. Idem, ABFVP, p. 169, no. 5. For the subject cf. CVA, Bibliothèque Nationale, pl. 34, 8; Beazley, Vases in Cyprus Museum, 1948, p. 6 ff. (ours is on p. 9, α 10).

THE MASTERS OF MATURE BLACK-FIGURE

53 LYDOS

We have two vases with his signature; on both he signs as painter (ho Lydos = the Lydian!). On one of the vases, however, dinos fragments in Athens from the Acropolis, there was a potter's signature too, but since the name is missing we cannot tell whether Lydos signed there as potter too. This dinos, a mature work of his middle period, is even now not worthily published, at least as far as pictures are concerned. The animal frieze on the fragments still harps back to the Corinthianizing tradition of the preceding generation of painters, whose love for decorative motives he indeed keeps up. However, the scene of animals led to sacrifice by attendants shows our painter as an innovator. Not much remains of the gigantomachy (battle of gods against giants) on this vase, but his sense for dramatic rendering comes out even in these fragments. In the wealth of his mythological repertoire, ranging from the deeds of Herakles to the destruction of Troy (pictured by him at least twice), he rivals the great masters like Exekias and the Amasis Painter. Amongst shapes decorated by him are Panathenaic amphorae (one in Halle which is very close to him in style is perhaps the earliest extant example of its type; the series continues right into the 4th century and Hellenistic times, see plates XXVIII and 81), Siana cups and funerary plaques of which some impressive fragments remain, bearded men rendering their last homage to a dead friend.

Lydos makes free use of incision and of purple which we find on armour and hair. His incision is beautifully controlled; he gives to both his humans and animals, such as horses, a new solidity and

grandeur quite different from the daintier figures of Kleitias or even the Amasis Painter. The activity of Lydos ranges from about 560 to 540 B.C. He is known to have worked for at least two potters who signed their names each on one of his works, Nikosthenes and Kolchos. Two more of his vases have been attributed to the potter Amasis whilst another amphora decorated by him has been assigned to the potter Nikosthenes. His work is closely linked with the Attic masters of the first half of the 6th century but he himself appears to have been active in the creation of a new repertoire of mythological subjects and figures. He ranks thus with the Amasis Painter and Exekias as one of the great personalities of Black-figure; in boldness he may even surpass them. He never reaches, however, the psychological insight of Exekias, or the light and mannered touch of the Amasis Painter.

Bibl.: A. Rumpf, in: Thieme-Becker, *Künstlerlexikon*, s.v. Lydos; idem, *Sakonides*, Leipzig 1937. Beazley had once called him the Painter of London B 148; and it was Miss Richter who noted that the style of this amphora (B 148) was identical with that of the Acropolis dinos signed by Lydos, cf. *Metr. Mus. Stud.*, IV, p. 169 ff. M. Robertson, in: *JHS*, 57, 1937, p. 266 ff. Beazley, *Development*, pp. 41 ff., 90 ff., Idem, *ABFVP*, p. 107 ff. Cook, pp. 82, 273, 342. The Acropolis dinos is figured in: Rumpf, *Sakonides*, pll. 18–20; also partly in: Pfuhl, III, fig. 238–40.

53

AMPHORA by Lydos. Naples, Museo Nazionale, 2770 (81292). From the Santangelo collection. Mended with some modern repainting. Much purple used on figure work. Height 58.3 cms (22¹⁵/₁₆″), diam. of mouth 24.8 cms (9¹¹/₁₆″). Type B; see plate 21.

The shape is stocky. Short handles; broad-ledged lip. Between the upper handle-roots a frieze of double palmette-and-lotus chain. Purple for core of the ornament.
In a comparatively narrow field two horsemen advance to the right. The one further away is in full panoply, helmet, corslet and a long spear of which only the lower part is visible underneath the barrel of the horse. Beside him rides his squire bare-headed with his carefully groomed hair coming down his back. He also holds a long spear in his right hand and wears a tight-fitting purple chiton with short sleeves. The horses are magnificent, the barrel and chest are particularly powerfully rendered. Long sensitive muzzle, much fine incision for mane and tail. The haunches are rendered with four incised arcs supported by purple brush strokes. Note the slender foot and toes of the squire. Behind the pair an eagle with spread wings; use of incision and purple. The scene is repeated on the other side of the vase.
Attributed to Lydos. A work of his mature phase, c. 540 B.C.

Bibl.: Heydemann, no. 2770. Beazley, in: *JHS*, 51, 1931, p. 284, pl. XIII. Richter, in: *Metr. Mus. Stud.*, IV, 1933, p. 174, no. 5, fig. 14. Beazley, in: *ABSA*, 32, 1937, pp. 8, 27, no. 62. *CVA*, Napoli fasc. I, (Adriani), pl. 6. Beazley, *ABFVP*, p. 109, no. 23. Idem in: *Mon. Piot.*, 35, 1936, p. 187.

54–57, XV THE AMASIS PAINTER

The name Amasis occurs on eight vases always as a potter's signature, i.e. *Amasis m'epoiesen* = Amasis made me. The style of their decoration shows that they were all painted by the same hand. It is of course possible that Amasis also painted these vases, but in the absence of a painter's signature we must be content to speak of the Amasis *Painter* as the man who decorated these eight amongst some ninety odd vases attributed to him altogether.

The name is of course Egyptian, recalling the king of that name who reigned in Egypt from 569 to 525 B.C. This Egyptian connection has been the subject of much learned discussion: Some think of an Egyptian origin for the painter, and he may have been born in the Greek settlement of Naucratis in the Nile delta, an important trading centre in the first half of the 6th century B.C., coming to Athens later; others again suggest that one of his parents, perhaps his mother, was Egyptian; it is also possible that he was given the name for some reason which we cannot guess—names of oriental potentates were occasionally adopted by Greeks for reasons of fashion or otherwise. The name Amasis indeed was not confined to the pharaoh but used by other Egyptians as well, hence it is hazardous to draw chronological conclusions from the date of accession of King Amasis.

The earliest works of our painter date to just after 560 B.C. Their style reminds one of the earliest Panathenaic amphorae, particularly the one in Halle which may be contemporary with the introduction of athletic contests into the Panathenaic festival, usually dated to 566 B.C. though that date is not absolutely secure. In general the activity of the Amasis Painter starts a little before that of Exekias and actually may go on a little after him.

The Amasis Painter has definite preference for certain shapes. His neck amphorae have short necks rising from broad flattened shoulders; he also likes ovoid lekythoi and the oinochoe with high handle springing from about two thirds up the body and with round or trefoil mouth; finally he decorates several types of cups some with high foot others with low. On his amphorae the figures are enclosed in a metope-like panel and they are grouped, particularly in his early period, round an imaginary centre often marked by the presence of one or two dogs.

By preference his subjects are taken from mythology, particularly from Homeric legend (Achilles and Thetis; Theseus and Peirithoos with Helena) and the exploits of Herakles (his struggle for the tripod with Apollo; his entry into Olympus, plate 54), nor are Perseus and the Gorgons forgotten, a theme which had been so dear to the preceding generations of painters. Above all, however, Dionysus and his rout appear in many of his vases, such as an amphora in Berlin and that in the Bibliothèque Nationale (plate 57). Even more remarkable are his Dionysiac vases in Würzburg (plate 55) and in a Swiss collection.

The first period of his activity produced many one-piece amphorae with short neck passing into the shoulders without any break. There the metope-like panel contains many figures in a centripetal composition round the most important character. Five or six figures crowd into the available space. Incision is limited to essential details. Of additional colour purple is used for dresses in particular, whilst white is used for women's flesh. In some cups towards the end of the first period the Amasis Painter acquired a miniaturist style with much use of white such as on the Louvre cup-skyphos with an erotic scene. Progressively he decreases the number of figures in his panels—he does maintain his liking for these metope-like compositions—and his incision becomes more extensive and extremely fine. His oinochoai are regularly decorated with three figures only and display a very sober use of colour.

The final phase of his work includes a number of neck-amphorae which show a different conception of decoration; the body of the vase is reserved, and the ornament, painted in a shiny brown glaze, spreads freely and lightly over the surface. There are few figures, two or three at the most, as in the earlier one in the Bibliothèque Nationale (plates 56, 57, XV) and the late amphorae in Boston. In these there is not only greater clarity of presentation but also a tendency to underline by means of the design certain expressive characterizations. Thus the figure of Achilles on the Boston amphora recalls through its vivid characterization the work of Exekias, which at this period undoubtedly exerted some influence on our painter, though he never loses his individuality. Thus his faces are always strongly accentuated and always maintain the same structure, which can be observed even in his earliest works, which are so close to the Heidelberg Painter, one of the artists decorating Siana cups. The gesticulations of his figures with their long and tapering fingers (which have lead to comparisons with the so-called Affecter, a painter of much less interest) become in this last phase rather restrained, though in the drawing of the fingers the finesse is maintained. To the last phase also belong a number of cups with decoration on reserved ground and several trefoil-mouthed oinochoai which reveal a certain tiredness in their repetition of commonplace motifs such as conversation scenes with seated figures.

Amongst interesting subjects we may pick out his picture of women working at the loom on a lekythos in New York, which is one of the rare archaic representations of this subject. His activity comes to an end about 520 B.C. or even later, as can be seen from a study of the kind of drapery folds represented on his latest works and also by comparison with black-figured lekythoi.

Bibliography: G. Karo, in: *JHS*, 19, 1899, p. 192 ff. E. Langlotz, *Zeitbestimmung*, p. 12 ff. Buschor, in: *FR*, III, p. 225. B. Schweitzer, in: *JdI*, 44, 1929, p. 112 ff. Beazley, in: *JHS*, 51, 1931, p. 256 ff. Haspels, *Lekythoi*, pp. 10 ff., 30. R. M. Cook, in: *JHS*, 68, 1948, p. 148. Rumpf, pp. 50–1. Pfuhl, I, p. 258 ff. Beazley, *Development*, p. 56 ff. *Idem, ABFVP*, pp. 150–8. S. Karouzou, *The Amasis Painter*, Oxford 1956. J. Boardman, in: *JHS*, 78, 1958, p. 1 ff. S. Stucchi, in: *Enc. Arte class. e orientale*, s.v. Amasis. Cook, pp. 82–3. Bothmer, in: *Antike Kunst*, 3, 1960, p. 71 ff.; idem in: *Gnomon*, 29, 1957, p. 538. W. Züchner in *Beiträge zur Klass. Altertumswissenschaft* (Festschrift B. Schweitzer, ed. R. Lullies), 1954, pp. 103 ff.

54

OINOCHOE by the Amasis Painter. Paris, Louvre F 30. From Vulci. Reconstructed from fragments but complete. The colours are well preserved. Much use of incision. Height 28 cms (11").

The subject is Herakles entering Olympus on his apotheosis, a popular subject in archaic and later art. On the left Poseidon, trident in hand watches the scene whilst in front of him Hermes, dressed in short chiton and a mantle over his shoulders, petasos on his head and kerykeion in his hand,

makes a gesture of welcome (purple used for his hat, his boots and his dress). Then follows Athena carrying a shield with a large owl incised on it. She wears a helmet and holds her spear and is leading the hero onwards. Between Athena and Hermes is the potter's signature running vertically, *Amasis m'epoiesen* = Amasis made me. Colour even more than incision is used on this vase for decorative effect, but the general impression of the picture is sober. The hero is represented without his club and lion's skin but has his sword, bow and his arrows in the quiver, which he carries on his back. He makes a gesture of expectant joy.

This shape of a trefoil-mouthed oinochoe is found with Amasis and his contemporaries and goes back to a preceding generation of potters. The figure field is on one side of the vase only, the side which would show outwards when the contents are poured with the right hand. The hither side is black apart from the usual pair of spherical reserved triangles —apotropaic? after the middle of the 6th century.

Bibl.: Beazley, *ABFVP*, p. 152, no. 29; Idem, in: *Bulletin van de Vereeniging*, 17, 1942, p. 51; Idem, *Development*, p. 58–9. S. Karouzou, *The Amasis Painter*, Oxford 1956, pp. 9–10, 32, no. 31. For reserved triangles, Jacobsthal p. 16 ('white of eyes'!; some oinochoai with nipples —*Hesperia*, 31, 1962, p. 92); earliest occurrence, *Hesperia*, 30, 1961, p. 349 (mid-7th century—E. Brann). For off-centre placing of panel, Haspels, *Lekythoi*, p. 13, n. 1.

55

AMPHORA by the Amasis Painter. Würzburg, University (Martin von Wagner) Museum. 265. From ?Vulci. Formerly in the Feoli Collection. Reconstructed. Some repainting, as in the heads of the satyrs on the left of face B and of Dionysus and his kantharos on the same side. Height 34.7 cms (13⁵/₈″).

Purple used for the hair and tails of the satyrs, for the flowers and on the himation of Dionysus; white, which has largely gone, was for female flesh (of the menads), whilst a yellowish colour was applied for the stream of wine flowing from the treading platform into the pithos. Above the foot a reserved zone filled with a zone of doubled rays. On both handles where they are anchored to the body, there is a reserved zone, filled with vertical zig-zag lines. At handle roots a palmette within a reserved patch.

Along the top of the panel a miniature frieze with five satyrs and four menads dancing around Dionysus seated with a drinking horn in his hand. Underneath, the main picture represents a vine harvest scene. On the left a satyr pours water from a hydria into a large earthenware vessel full of must. In the right part of the picture a heavily built swinish-looking satyr treads the grapes which are being shot into a sort of basket by one of his companions. The treading basket is on a trestle platform which slopes gently towards a spout, thus collecting the liquid oozing through the basket. The juice then drains into a pithos (earthenware store vessel) sunk into the ground, of which the top is visible. On the ground under the trestle a jug and further to the left a kantharos. To the extreme right a satyr plucks a bunch of grapes growing from a vine tree which extends from the right of the picture into the centre supported by two poles. Another satyr further to the left makes music with a flute to accompany the work.

Side B. The small upper frieze has five satyrs and four menads dancing. Underneath in the main picture Dionysus dancing with ivy in his left and a kantharos in his right hand, lowered to receive a taste of the new wine from a satyr who is pouring it out for him from a skin. Other satyrs make music with the flute or drink from horns. A couple of them with arms round each other as the menads on plate 57. The amphora is of type A (see plates 62–63), but is abnormal both in its general shape and its details, such as the form of the foot and the decoration of the handles. For the canonical shape see plate 62. The satyrs are given an exceptional solidity of form, more so than other figures by this painter. The indication of hairiness on the satyr's body is fairly rare.

For the scene compare another amphora also attributed to this painter in a Swiss private collection in Meggen. Our vase belongs to the mature phase about 530 B.C.

Bibl.: *JHS*, 19, 1899, p. 135, pll. 5, 6; 1914, p. 190, no. 10. Bulle, *Silene in der Kunst*, p. 16, no. 23. Walters I, p. 383, n. 2, p. 358. Buschor, *G Vsm*, p. 13, fig. 96. Pfuhl I, p. 258, III, fig. 222. Hoppin, *BFV*, p. 45, 31. Beazley, in: *ABSA*, 22, 1922, p. 32, no. 2. Kraiker, in: *JdI*, 1929, p. 114, 2. Langlotz, *Vasen in Würzburg*, no. 265, pl. 73–4. Buschor, *GV*, p. 121, fig. 139. Beazley, *Development*, pp. 59–60. Karouzou, *Amasis Painter*, pp. 14, 17–18, 29, pll. 25, 28, 29. W. Züchner in: *Beiträge...* p. 103 ff and pl. 15–18 (for lid of this vase). For the amphora in Switzerland see A. Bruckner, in: *Antike Kunst* 1958, p. 34 ., pll. 17, 19, 2; also K. Schefold, *Meisterwerke griechischer Kunst*, Basle 1960, p. 20 ff. III, 138. Hairy satyrs see Brommer, *Satyroi*, p. 53, n. 13.

56, 57, XV

NECK-AMPHORA by the Amasis Painter. Paris, Bibliothèque Nationale (Cabinet des Médailles) 222. From Vulci. Red clay but brownish surface. Some restorations. Height 33 cms (13″). Diam. of mouth 16.8 cms (6⁹/₁₆″).

The lid does not belong. The handles of the vases are three-ribbed, the belly is spreading, the low foot is in two degrees. Very fine system of palmettes and spirals under the handles from which springs an upturned lotus flower. On the surface of the lid leaves and other decoration. On neck a double lotus and palmette chain. Under the figure frieze a linked and arcaded row of lotus buds, underneath doubled rays springing from the base.

Purple applied over black. The flesh of the menads is left reserved and is outlined, a technique very rare by this time, but the flesh of Athena on the other side is rendered conventionally, white over black. There is much detailing in purple on the chitons of Dionysus and of Poseidon. Ample use of incision for details everywhere, some of it extremely fine. On the shoulders above the main figures (and barely visible in our picture) is a miniature frieze of fighting warriors engaged in duels except for a central group round one already fallen. On face A we also see a herald with a petasos on his head who sounds a trumpet, whilst another warrior runs carrying a quiver on his side; numerous shield devices.

Side A. Athena with helmet and spear and wearing the aegis over her shoulder (but also a pair of bracelets on her arms) faces Poseidon who holds his trident in front of him. Between the two is the potter's signature, *Amasis m'epoiesen* = Amasis made me. The names of the two divinities are inscribed next to their heads.

Side B. Dionysus with kantharos in his right hand, faces two menads who advance towards him with their arms round each other's shoulder. One of them wears a leopard's skin over her chiton; both carry ivy branches in one hand and a small animal in the other, the nearer one a little stag, whilst the other offers a rabbit to the god. Above the heads we have the name of the god inscribed as well as the potter's signature. Neck-amphorae encourage a composition different from those of the one-piece amphorae. Here we do not have the decoration confined to a metope-like panel, but placed freely in the field. Hence none of the crowded composition but rather few figures generously disposed. The light surface of the vase covered only sparingly with the black of the figures, and the floating lines of the ornament give to the scene as well as to the vase as a whole an airy appearance. This is also enhanced by the contract between the dark masses of the two male divinities and the lighter figures of Athena and the menads with their use of white or reservation respectively.

All this is a great change from the heaviness of the painter's earlier work. It has been suggested that this new lighter manner is due to the influence of Exekias; but we need not invoke that name, as in the last third of the 6th century a certain Ionic influence on Attic art was anyhow widespread and will surely have influenced our painter towards a greater lightness of style away from the heavier Corinthian tradition. C. 540 B.C.

Bibl.: Lenormant-De Witte, *Elite céramographique*, I, pl. 78, p. 254. W. Klein, *Meistersignaturen*, p. 43, no. 1. Kretschmer, *Griechische Vaseninschriften*, p. 74ff. G. Karo, in: *JHS*, 1899, p. 137. Perrot-Chipiez, X, p. 179, fig. 111–5. Ducati I, p. 233. figg. 191–2. Pfuhl I, p. 259ff., III, fig. 220. Buschor, *Gr Vsm*, p. 137, fig. 98, p. 139. P. Jacobsthal, *Ornamente*, pl. 35a, p. 57ff. *CVA*, Bibliothèque Nationale, fasc. I, pll. 36–7, pp. 28–9. On the shoulder frieze of warriors see R. Nierhaus, in: *JdI*, 53, 1938, p. 108, fig. 9. F. Magi, in: *ASAIA*, I–II, 1939–40, p. 67, fig. 4. S. Karouzou, *op. cit.*, pp. 18–9, pll. 31–3, p. 31, no. 22. For similar menads on an amphora now in a Swiss private collection, see A. Bruckner, in: *Antike Kunst*, 1958, p. 34ff., pl. 17, 18, 19, 3. and K. Schefold, *Meisterwerke griechischer Kunst*, p. 20ff., III, 138. Robertson, p. 63ff.

59–65, XVI–XVIII EXEKIAS

The name Exekias appears in signatures on eleven vases as potter; but on two of them as painter as well, with the formula *Exekias egrapse k'apoiese me* = Exekias painted and made me. This double signature occurs on a neck-amphora in Berlin with Herakles and the Nemean lion and on the Vatican amphora with Achilles and Ajax (plates 62, 63, XVII). The other vases with potter's signature alone, as well as some twenty others are all painted by the same hand as the amphorae in Berlin and the Vatican, though several of the potter's signatures are on vases which are almost plain, and therefore can give no real evidence as to their painter. We thus know Exekias both as potter and as painter. Amongst his earliest work we would like to place an amphora in the Louvre with Herakles and Geryon which is signed by Exekias as potter and has the love name Stesias. A comparison with other pictures of the same subject on vases attributed to the so-called Group E (a large collection mostly of amphorae which are closely related to Exekias and in fact constitute the artistic background from which he sprang but which he transcended) shows the greater maturity and organization of the Louvre amphora. Admittedly it belongs to a very early stage of Exekias' development but already we sense his ability to give a personal interpretation to his figures as well as his psychological insight into a situation. The Herakles on the Louvre amphora has a characterful face; purple and white is used for details of the beard, the lion's skin and the face. By contrast the figures in Group E vases are absolutely conventional.

The next phase of his development is exemplified by a neck-amphora in Berlin which shows on one side the popular subject of Herakles wrestling with the Nemaean lion. On the other side are the sons of Theseus, Demophon and Akamas. There is also rich ornament in the shape of several rows of floral friezes above and below the figure scene and light spiral and palmette ornament under the handles. The painter's interest in the psychological state of his figures is well shown in the figure of Iolaos standing behind Herakles and watching the struggle. In the grip of tension he clenches one fist, and grasps the wrist firmly with the other hand. Very careful and fine incision shows close attention to decorative detail without, however, falling into mannerism.

We next mention a work of his later maturity, a calyx-krater (one of the earliest known) from the North Slope of the Acropolis in Athens and now in the Agora Museum in the Stoa of Attalos. The subjects are the apotheosis of Herakles and the fight over the body of Patroclus. The bearded face of Poseidon in its nobility recalls not only the Ajax of the Vatican amphora (plate XVII) but also the same hero on an amphora in Boulogne, where he prepares for his suicide. The figures of the fighting warriors in violent movement reveal a new side of our painter, who does not often show such scenes, being more

interested in the expression of character and states of mind. The calyx-krater has the love name Onetorides, which also occurs on the Berlin neck-amphora and the amphora in the Vatican (plate 62–3). In the battle scenes on this krater the figures are not merely decorative but are the result of a passionate observation of human nature. This power, certainly, was never present in Kleitias, who though he tried to transcend them was still tied to the schemes of Corinthian art; nor did the Amasis Painter ever have this interest in human nature, for his work arose so largely out of the decorative needs of the vase, rather than a deep sympathy for the human content of his compositions.

Exekias worked during one of the most exciting periods of the 6th century B.C. during the enlightened tyranny of Pisistratus, between about 550 and the twenties of the 6th century, and his work is deeply imbued with its spirit. This is strikingly shown by comparisons which can be made between some of his figures and contemporary works of sculpture. Thus the Leda on his Vatican amphora (plate 63) has been aptly compared with the 'peplos kore' from the Acropolis and the figure of the Dioscuri have the same grace which can be found on an archaic grave stele in New York, whilst his horses recall the marble horses from the Acropolis.

Bibliography: W. Technau, *Exekias*, Leipzig 1936. B. Neutsch, in: *Ganymed*, Heidelberg 1949, p. 29 ff. B. Neutsch, in: *Marburger Jahrb. für Kunstwiss.*, XV, 1949–50, p. 43 ff. Beazley, *Attic Black-Figure, A Sketch*, London 1928, p. 17 ff., idem, *Development*, pp. 63–72. Idem, *ABFVP*, p. 143 ff. (Beazley maintains his view that the Louvre amphora with Herakles and Geryon and signed by Exekias as potter belongs to Group E and was probably not *painted* by Exekias); see also P. Clement, in: *Hesperia*, 24, 1958, p. 8 ff. Cook, pp. 83–5. For the peplos kore see R. Lullies and M. Hirmer, *Greek Sculpture*[2], London 1960, pll. 43–45; for the New York grave stele G. M. A. Richter, *Handbook of Greek Art*, p. 63, fig. 73. *EWA* V, p. 279 ff. (Paribeni).

58

For details and description see above p. 294, preceding the description of pl. 49.

59; XVI

CUP by Exekias. Munich, Museum Antiker Kleinkunst, 2044. From Vulci. Well preserved though reconstructed from numerous fragments. The inside is covered with a special red glaze called 'coral' red or 'intentional' red. This cup is the earliest occurrence of this technique. The sparkling brilliance of the red has now largely disappeared. The face of the god is damaged and the white on the sail has largely gone. Diam. 11.5 cms (4¹/₂").

Deep bowl on a squat foot. On the outside underneath the figures concentric lines and bands in black and purple. Then follow rays closely set and springing from the foot, which is separated from the bowl by a fillet. On the reserved sides of the foot plate the potter's signature of Exekias, *Exekias epoiese* = Exekias made (me).
Outside of the vase: Beside the handle roots and facing towards them two groups of three warriors each, fighting over a dead body which has been stripped and lies between them underneath the handle. One of the warriors is in the act of pulling him away. Much use of purple. Moderate but well placed incision. The other handle has a similar subject, but there the fallen warrior has not yet been stripped.
The main pictures on the outside are a pair of apotropaic eyes on each side of the vase. The eye socket is in outline, the pupils are rendered as white, purple and black circles. Between the eyes is an ornament which can be interpreted as a nose. This cup is the earliest of the so-called eye cups and will be followed by many others of similar type reaching down to the end of the 6th century B.C.

The shape is called cup type, A and we also show a late example in red-figure in plate 96.
Inside decoration: The picture fills the whole of the bowl, unlike the smaller circular medallions found for instance on some of the Little-Master cups. Painting is against a ground covered with special red which has been referred to in the opening paragraph. In the centre a ship with a mast and a broad sail. Its prow is in the shape of a stylized boar's head, its stern curves up into a swan's head. Steering oars and landing ladder are clearly visible. The mast is entwined with two vine trees, which have grown up to overshadow the ship. Within the ship itself reclines the figure of Dionysus. He holds a drinking horn in his right hand. Seven dolphins play in the sea round about the ship; four of them have a white line under their belly. Two more dolphins in white are painted on the sides of the ship. The splendid isolation of Dionysus is not only conditioned by the story but also symptomatic of Exekias' desire to isolate his figures in the decorative field in contrast to his predecessors and also contemporaries who liked crowded scenes full of action.
For a Dionysiac subject the inside of a cup is of course a most suitable place. Dionysus was the god of wine and his picture would be seen as one held the cup to drink or to pour a libation. Dionysus crossed the sea on his way to Greece and a boat (carried or on wheels) with one impersonating the god in it played a great part in certain of his ceremonies. The picture on our cup may however allude directly to the story recounted in the Homeric *Hymn to Dionysus* (VII), when he was captured by Tyrrhenian pirates. In his own time and manner the god revealed himself, vine and ivy began to grow and entangle the mast and the rest of the ship, and the pirates, having jumped overboard in terror, were turned into dolphins.
This cup brought several innovations into Black-figure; for its shape and eye-decoration it was, as we said, a pioneer

piece, but also in its use of coral red, though that technique always remained rare. We also note that the black glaze is in places applied more thickly to build up the surface. Above all, however, there is the individual ability of Exekias to infuse a tranquility into his pictures, unrivalled amongst his contemporaries.

C. 535 B.C.

Bibl.: Klein, p. 40, 7. Jahn, no. 339, p. 105. *FR*, I, p. 227 ff., pl. 42. Pfuhl, fig. 231. W. Technau, *Exekias*, pll. 5–6. Idem in: *Marb. Jahrb.*, pp. 47–8. Beazley, *Development*, p. 67 ff., 113. Idem, *ABFVP*, p. 146, no. 21. For the shape and its importance see H. Bloesch, *Formen attischer Schalen*, Berne 1940, p. 2, pl. 1. For the coral red see M. Farnsworth and H. Wiseley, in: *AJA*, 62, 1958, pp. 165 ff. with references there to some earlier work by Miss G. M. A. Richter. Dionysus is shown crossing the sea in a boat in the company of satyrs and menads on a black-figured neck-amphora in Tarquinia (see references in *JHS* 78, 1958, p. 128, n. 25). For Dionysus in the boat during ceremonial rites see Frickenhaus in: *JdI* 27, 1912, p. 75 ff; also Boardman in *JHS* 78, 1958, p. 4 ff. Buschor, in: *AM*, 1928, p. 100, n. 2, Deubner, *Attische Feste*, p. 110. Robertson, p. 71 (colour).

60, 61

PAINTED CLAY PLAQUES (PINAKES) by Exekias. Berlin, Ehemals Staatliche Museen, F1811. From Athens. Used for the decoration of a grave monument. Thickness between 2 to 3 mms (¹⁄₁₆ to ¹⁄₈″). Average height 37 cms (14⁹⁄₁₆″), average breadth 43 cms (16¹⁵⁄₁₆″).

We show fragments from this series of funerary plaques which seems to come in three sequences; scenes from the lying-in-state of a dead mother (*prothesis*); mourning by the women within the house; and the preparations for the last journey (*ekphora*).

One of the fragments (plate 60 lower picture) shows a column with capital indicating that the setting is indoors. A woman tears her face and hair with one hand and clutches her head in mourning with the other. In front of her an old man called *Ar[.]es[-* clutches his head in sorrow. The lips of both are open; they are wailing. Purple is used on the woman's dress, white for her flesh and yellow for the column. Other mourners proceeding to the right are shown on plate 60, upper picture; particularly impressive is a man turned to look full face at the spectator. On plate 61 we see the front of two mules (named *Phalios* and -]*is*) being harnessed to a cart. In front of the mules a naked attendant (*Mylios*) helps in the harnessing; behind him stands a woman (*Sime*).

C. 540 B.C.

Bibl.: *Ant. Denkmäler*, II, pll. 9–10. Pfuhl, fig. 278. Rumpf, pl. 12, 1–4, Technau, *op. cit.*, pll. 14–8. Beazley, *Development*, p. 71 ff. Idem, *ABFVP*, p. 146, nos. 22–3. A. Greifenhagen, *Antike Kunstwerke*. Berlin 1960, plates 22–3. J. Boardman, in: *ABSA*, 50, 1955, p. 63 ff., discusses the arrangement of these plaques and also the inscriptions. For the full face figures see H. Kenner, *Weinen und Lachen* (*S.B.* Vienna 1960), p. 39 ff. For the harness on plate 61 see Greifenhagen, in: *JdI*, 75, 1960, p. 84 ff.

62, 63, XVII

AMPHORA by Exekias. Rome, Vatican Museum, 344. From Vulci. Reconstructed but well preserved. Some modern repainting on side B. The clay surface between the figures is somewhat eroded. Black glaze with metallic sheen. Much of the white has vanished, thus on the corslets, the shields and on the lower borders of the greaves and on the dog. Purple is used on the satyr mask of Achilles' shield, on the chlamys of Castor, on the harness of the horse, on the peplos of Leda and for the cloak folded on the stool carried by the boy on side B. There is also a purple band on the fillet placed at the junction of foot and body of the vase. Height 61 cms (23¹⁵⁄₁₆″). This is the earliest amphora type A shown here. Type A comes into vogue at this time and soon eclipses in importance its older rival type B; see plate 21 and plates 150–153.

On the sides of the flanged handles double-leaved ivy. At the lower handle roots a palmette within reserved patch. A double lotus-and-palmette chain serves as upper border to the figure panel. Purple for palmettes and flowers. On the upper surface of the mouth Exekias' signature as painter and potter, *Exekias egrapse k'apoiese me* = Exekias painted and made me.

Side A. The scene is within a large panel which covers most of the side of the pot in its breadth and half the surface in its height. Achilles and Ajax (names inscribed in the genitive = image of …, as often) sit on a low chest or block stooping over another block which is set between them and on which they play some game of skill or chance, no doubt devised by Palamedes to while away the time between fighting during the siege of Troy. Achilles sits on the left, helmet on his head with the tail of the crest drooping forward. He like Ajax holds two spears in his hand. Both heroes wear a leather corslet and cloaks most elaborately embroidered. The most marvellously intricate and delicate incision is used on these cloaks. Achilles also wears a metal guard for his upper arm and both heroes again wear thigh guards as well as greaves. Note how the lower edge of the corslet is indicated as a hump in the outline of the cloaks. On the extreme left is Achilles' shield resting against the wall. It is decorated with a satyr's head and a snake above and a panther below. On the right the shield of Ajax is decorated with a bearded Gorgon's head and snakes above and below. Note that the shields are of the so-called Boeotian kind which seem by preference to have been used for scenes from heroic mythology (see commentary on plate 7). Ajax's helmet is suspended above the shield. The two heroes are caught in mid-play; next to Achilles is written the Greek for four, next to Ajax the Greek for three. Ajax is the loser. Two more inscriptions are in the void area. Behind Achilles on the left is the potter's signature of Exekias, on the right going down vertically behind Ajax's back we have the love name *Onetorides kalos* = Onetorides is beautiful. These love names start round about this time and remain fashionable until about the middle of the 5th century. They refer to young men prominent at the time, the Athenian aristocratic *jeunesse dorée*.

The incised detailing on this vase is almost unparalleled. On the arm guard of Achilles we see a lion's head; a feline head also on the shoulder flap of Ajax's corslet; the cloaks are decorated with stars, flowers and other motifs reminding

one of East Greek orientalizing, or perhaps the famous Milesian embroidery. It is interesting to note that the ends of the hair curls of the heroes have the glaze applied more thickly to build up a plastic mass, a technique employed later in some red-figured vases.

Side B (plate 63). The return of the Dioscuri. On the left Polydeuces (this and the other names are inscribed) is welcomed by his dog who jumps up towards him. Further towards the centre comes his mother, Leda, dressed in a peplos carrying a flower in her right and some twigs in the left. She holds them out towards Castor who is in front of her but in the act of leading his horse away. He turns round towards his mother, carrying a spear in his left. The horse is named Kylaros. On the extreme right is Tyndareos dressed in a himation and patting the horse on his muzzle. A small slave boy brings out a stool with a change of clothing on it; also an aryballos containing the oil for cleaning and anointing hangs from his wrist.

On this side too the same characteristics which were noted on the main face. Extremely detailed incision for the dress of Leda and the mane and tail of the horse. As has been noticed already in the general remarks on Exekias, both Leda and the Dioscuri have parallels in contemporary sculpture. Finally we note the psychological insight revealed in several touches, such as the dog's affectionate greeting and the human response to it, in Leda's gesture and finally again in the relationship between Tyndareos and the horse.

The love name Onetorides is found on this side again, inscribed vertically under the horse.

Both sides are perfect in their way, the affectionate family scene on the back and the solemn and rather remote scene on the front of the two heroes at play in utter concentration forgetful of reality outside. In both pictures a new humanity is infused into the world of mythology. This was the time when Pisistratus introduced the regular recitation of the Homeric poems to Athens.

The vase represents the acme of Exekias' art, both in its technical perfection and the human sympathy displayed. Beyond it Black-figure could not go.

C. 540–530 B.C.

Bibl.: *Mon. Ined.*, II, pl. 22. FR, pl. 131ff. Ducati, p. 237, fig. 193. Pfuhl, III, p. 57, fig. 229. Jacobsthal, p. 67. C. Albizzati, *Vasi antichi dipinti del Vaticano*, V, p. 127ff., pll. 40–1–2. Beazley, *Attic Black-Figure, A Sketch*, p. 18ff. Idem, *Development*, pp. 65–7. Idem, *ABFVP*, p. 145, no. 13. Rumpf, pl. 12, 5. Technau, pll. 20–1. Idem, in: *Marb. Jahrb. Kunstwiss.*, pp. 59–61. On the chronology of Exekias' amphorae see Bloesch in *JHS* 71, 1951, p. 29, n. 2. Robertson, p. 60. Kunze, *Schildbänder* p. 142 (on subject of A); Robert, *Heldensage*, p. 1126.

64, 65, XVIII

NECK-AMPHORA by Exekias. London. British Museum, B 210. From Vulci. Mended from large fragments. Modern restorations have recently been removed, leaving some gaps visible across the body and shield of the Amazon. Height 41.3 cms (16¹/₄″).

Lip, handles and foot are black; the rest is reserved in clay colour with decoration painted on it. On neck double lotus-and-palmette chain with much use of purple. On lower part of body below the main picture an arcaded chain of buds; continuous meander; rays springing from the bottom. Under handles an ornament of floating spirals of great exquisiteness.

Side A. Achilles kills the Queen of the Amazons, Penthesilea. Both names are inscribed as well as the love name *Onetorides kalos* = Onetorides is beautiful. Further, behind Achilles is Exekias' signature as potter going down vertically, *Exekias epoiese* = Exekias made. Achilles is completely armed with Corinthian helmet pulled down over his face, a metal corslet worn over a short chiton, and greaves. He carries a shield, and his sheathed sword. Purple is used extensively on the crest of his helmet also for the outlining of the engraved decoration on the corslet as well as for the edges of his greaves and details of his scabbard and his chiton. It is also used for the inside of his shield which is just visible in an early example of three-quarter view, with some of the inner attachments showing in white. The Queen of the Amazons, Penthesilea, is down already pierced by Achilles' spear. Blood gushes from the wound in her throat but she still bravely holds up her spear. Her flesh is in white applied over black, in parts the white has disappeared. She wears an elaborate helmet with a little griffin projecting above the forehead; an opening is left for her ears in the metal. She wears no corslet but an elaborately decorated short and closely fitting chiton over which hangs a leopard skin. Purple is used for her blood and for border lines on the helmet and its crest as well as for some other details, as in the case of Achilles.

In contrast to the neck-amphora London B 209 where Exekias has treated the same subject more summarily and with greater looseness of composition, here, in our picture the artist has succeeded in concentrating the two opposing figures into a single group, victor and defeated opposed and yet united. We have here something already of the psychological interpretation of the Amazonomachy, which we shall find again in the Penthesilea Painter's cup in Munich (plates 168–9). For the love name Onetorides see the commentary on plates 62–3.

Side B. Dionysus holding his kantharos and ivy branches with his son Oinopion, who holds the wine jug (oinochoe). Both names are inscribed. Behind the boy the potter's signature of Exekias. Dionysus is dressed in a long white chiton which has lightly incised folds down its length. Over it he wears a himation with folds indicated and purple stripes and dots. Oinopion is naked, with sparing but flowing incision indicating anatomical details; particulary elaborate is the incision of his hair which is worn looped up in the back.

About 530 B.C.

Bibl.: *Cat. Br. Mus.*, II, p. 138. Hoppin, *BFV*, p. 94. *CVA*, London, fasc. 4, p. 4, pl. 49, 2a–2b. W. Technau, *Exekias*, Leipzig 1936, p. 22, no. 13, pl. 25; Idem, in: *Marb. Jahrb. Kunstwiss.*, XV, 1949–50, pp. 55, 58, figg. 23, 25–7. Beazley, *ABFVP*, p. 144, no. 7. For the Amazono-machy see D. von Bothmer, *Amazons in Greek Art*, Oxford 1957, pl. 51, 1, p. 71. For love names see D. M. Robinson, *A study of Greek love-names*, Baltimore 1937, p. 161, no. 208. Handle ornament in Jacobsthal, pl. 37a.

LATER BLACK-FIGURE

66–68, XIX, XX PSIAX

He was a fertile artist at the time of transition from Black-figure to Red-figure; he worked in both techniques and was associated with at least three potters, as we know from signatures on vases assigned to him, Andokides, Menon and Hilinos. His earliest work is naturally in Black-figure (the Brescia amphora, plates 66–68, is as early as any we know) and he carried on producing works in that technique even after he had adopted Red-figure for many of his vases. He also painted a number of so-called bilinguals, that is vases where one side is in Black-figure and the other in Red-figure. His black-figure work is of course affected by the changes brought about by the new technique. We can discern two sides in him, on the one hand he draws his figures in depth and has a sense for corporeality and spatial relationship, yet on the other hand we come across works where he shows himself to be almost a miniaturist as on a neck-amphora of special type in Castle Ashby with Dionysus dancing between satyrs, drinking-horn in hand. Such Dionysiac scenes are evidently congenial to him. He experiments also in other techniques, such as white ground. We have several smallish vases by him in this technique.

On two alabastra, one in Karlsruhe, the other one in Odessa, Psiax signs as painter (his name also occurs without qualification as painter or potter on two bilingual cups which however cannot be attributed to him with certainty), but much of his work had been assembled before the pertinence of the two signed alabastra was recognized. He was then known as the Menon Painter after the potter's signature on a red-figured amphora in Philadelphia.

Our painter loves scenes with horses, as Lydos and Exekias had done before him; he also carefully shows all details of the outlandish dress affected by archers and cavalry in Athens at that time, the Scythian cap, the spotted jacket and the trousers of the archers, or the Thracian costume of the cavalry men, the fox-skin cap (alopekis), the blanket cloak and the high boots of rawhide (shown in plate 66). Such costumes are not of course confined to the paintings of Psiax, but are found in other near contemporary works by Epiktetos and the Brygos Painter, for instance, (the Scythian cap for archers is found as early as the François Vase, plate 42, upper and lower pictures). Psiax in his picture of a mounted archer on the inside of his red-figured cup in New York and on a black-figured plate in London, where he depicts an archer in full dress blowing a trumpet, shows himself an acute observer of these costumes.

Some have seen a connection between him and a rather younger man, Phintias, one of the great pioneers of Red-figure (plates 90–95), who may have been his pupil. Much of Psiax's best is in Black-figure to which he brings in his later works some of the flavour of the new Red-figure style; but it is on red-figured vases like the New York cup and one in Munich, that we find him sharing in the contemporary search for and experiments in bold postures and foreshortening. His activity can be dated between 530 and 510 B.C.

Bibliography: Early studies in: Langlotz, *Zur Zeitbestimmung der streng-rotfigurigen Vasenmalerei*, Leipzig 1920, p. 20. Pfuhl, I, pp. 287 and 414–5. Rumpf, p. 61. H. R. W. Smith, *New Aspects of the Menon Painter*, in: *Univ. of California Publ. in Classical Archaeology* ,I, no. 1, 1929. Beazley, in *JHS*, 33, 1913, p. 143 (review of Leroux's Madrid Catalogue) suggested that the Menon Painter might be Psiax, and Miss Richter in: *AJA*, 1934, pp. 547 ff. clinched the case fully. See also Zahn in: *FR*, III, p. 230 ff. on the Berlin hydria. W. H. Gross, in: *Würzburger Festgabe für Bulle*, p. 47 ff. Richter, in: *AJA*, 43, 1939, p. 645 ff. Idem, in: *AJA*, 45, 1941, p. 587, on a *kyathos* in Milan (Poldi-Pezzoli collection). Beazley, in: *AJA*, 54, 1950, p. 315 (on inscriptions on the Würzburg hydria); idem, *ARFVP*, p. 7; *ABFVP*, p. 292 ff. *Development*, pp. 78–9 and 114–5. Cook, pp. 87–8.

66–68, XIX, XX

AMPHORA by Psiax. Brescia, Museo Civico. From Vulci. Formerly in the Tosi collection. Dense black glaze. Cleaned and restored in 1948 from fragments which had been heavily overpainted. Height 58.5 cms (23″). Diam. of mouth 26.3 cms (10³/₈″). Type A; see plate 62–3.

Beautifully preserved. The two pictures are in broad panels on the otherwise black surface of the body. The sides of the handles are reserved with double-leaved ivy branch. The bottom of the body too has a reserved zone with dense rays springing from the foot. The upper frame of the panel consists of a double palmette chain with residual lotus flowers in between. Much use of purple for beards, for the fox-skin caps and boots of the youth's.

Side A. Herakles wrestles with the Nemean lion. Having got

him down on his fore legs he is now dealing with one of his rear paws, at the same time holding the underside of the beast in an iron grip. Behind him suspended from a tree are his cloak and quiver, whilst his sword and scabbard still seem to be hanging on his side. Also on the left is his companion (Iolaos?) dressed in a white short chiton and a chlamys. He holds two spears and watches the struggle intently. Behind the lion is Athena encouraging the hero, her protegé. Her flesh is in white; white also the owl which is her shield device. Much purple on her dress, shield and helmet. (Details of the wrestling in H. Bloesch, Kunst, p. 55). Side B. On the farther side of their horses stand two youths dressed in short white chiton and a chlamys buttoned over their shoulder. They wear heavy and high laced boots lined with hide which comes up over their knees. They also have fox-skin caps over their heads (for the dress see the introductory remarks on Psiax). They carry two spears each and advance towards a couple, a man seated on a stool holding a staff and a woman standing. Both of them, husband and wife, have their hands stretched forwards in greeting. The interpretation of the scene could be a generalized parting or welcoming scene or perhaps more specifically the Dioscuri, as on the Vatican amphora by Exekias (plate 63).

This little known amphora is an early work of our master. We do not see in it yet the kind of spatial composition found on the New York red-figured cup by him.
C. 520 B.C.

Bibl.: E. Gerhard, *Etruskische und Kampanische Vasenbilder*, Berlin 1843, p. 48, pl. D 1–3. E. Langlotz, *Zeitbestimmung*, p. 20. H. R. W. Smith, *New Aspects of the Menon Painter*, passim. Beazley, in: *JHS*, 51, 1931, p. 120. H. Gross, in: '*Würzburger Festgabe*'. Beazley, *ARFVP*, p. 9, no. 13 and *ABFVP*, p. 292, no. 1. M. Cagiano de Azevedo, in: *Boll. d'Arte*, 34, 1949, p. 44ff. Jacobsthal, *Greek Pins*, fig. 339.

69, XXI

HYDRIA IN THE MANNER OF THE LYSIPPIDES PAINTER. London, British Museum B 302. From Tarquinia. Reconstructed from large fragments. Slightly damaged on the lip. Height 47 cms (18⁷/₁₆″). Diam. of mouth 18 cms (7″).

Neck and handles black. On top of shoulders at junction of neck a tongue pattern in black and purple. Below this on shoulders a fight between two warriors fully armed over the body of one fallen and stripped. On both sides women showing fright. On the extreme left a fully armed warrior moves away. On the extreme right another man with spear in hand. On the main body the picture is in a panel framed on both sides by a vertical double leaved ivy branch and below by a frieze of linked lotus buds. The picture shows Dionysus reclining on a couch with his companions, satyrs and menads. On the extreme left Hephaistos approaches. Dionysus hides a wine-skin under his pillow. Its end, however, is discovered by Hermes who approaches from the right and holds a kantharos which is also being grasped by Dionysus. Hermes is accompanied by a menad who crowns Dionysus. Between the couch and the table laden with food we see an ithyphallic satyr playing the kithara with a

plectrum. On the left a satyr and a menad advance towards the god whilst on the extreme left Hephaistos raises his hand in surprise carrying a hammer over his shoulders. The couch of the god is entwined with ivy branches.

Delicate and elaborate design. The hydria is attributed by Beazley to the manner, or the workshop of the Lysippides Painter, though formerly he considered it to be a work by the painter himself. The Lysippides Painter is the author, amongst other works, of the black-figured pictures on six bilingual amphorae (one of them being figured on pl. 89) and one bilingual cup. The red-figured work on these seven vases is by the Andokides Painter (plates 82–88). Beazley considered for a long time these two artists to be one and the same; now however he has separated them making each of the two work in one technique only.
C. 530–520 B.C.

Bibl.: E. Pernice, in: *JdI*, 21, 1906, pl. 1, p. 42ff. *CVA*, *Brit. Mus.*, fasc. 6, IIIH, pll. 74, 3, 75, 3. Beazley, *Development*, p. 77, has an interesting explanation for the scene, which is that it represents part of the story of the return of Hephaistos. Dionysus finds him busy in his workshop and persuades him to be his guest; but Hephaistos first wants to wash and dress and tells Dionysus not to wait for him. When Hephaistos at last arrives in the house of Dionysus he finds that the god is already celebrating. Overcome by the splendour the simple Hephaistos raises his hand in wonder. Beazley, *ABFVP*, p. 261, no. 40. For a similar interpretation see also M. Robertson, in: *JHS*, 70, 1950, p. 25, n. 9. 'I take it that Dionysus is handing Hermes the cup to take to the lame god, for this is surely the party at which Dionysus makes Hephaistos drunk'.

70

AMPHORA BY THE RYCROFT PAINTER. Taranto, Museo Nazionale. 31. From Taranto. In perfect preservation apart from some damage on the foot. Height 49.5 cms (19⁷/₁₆″). Type B; see plate 21.

Short handles with cylindrical section. They are black as is all the vase except for the broad panel and a zone near the foot which is filled with rays springing from the base.
Side A (not shown). Dionysus crowned with vine leaves and holding a drinking horn in his left mounts a chariot drawn by four horses. He holds the reins in his right hand. By the side of the chariot a dancing menad with castanets in her hands, a satyr and in front of the horses another menad.
Side B. Dionysus riding on an ithyphallic donkey (on his way to Olympus?) accompanied by two satyrs. One of them goes ahead and turns his head back towards the god, the other brings up the rear with a full wine skin on his back and a drinking horn in his left. In the background trailing ivy branches. Note the torsion of the satyr's abdomen.
The painter of this vase tends to avoid the use of purple and is sparing with the incising tool; he shapes his figures with a certain ease and sureness of design without, however, much conviction in his lines. One realizes that he works at a time when the new technique of Red-figure is already established. Our painter is related to Psiax and is named after a collection which once contained one of his vases.
C. 510–500 B.C.

Bibl.: Beazley, *ABFVP*, p. 336ff., no. 12.

XXII

NECK-AMPHORA. Tarquinia, Museo Nazionale, RC 1804. From Tarquinia. Well preserved. Height 39.5 cms (15⁹/₁₆″). Diam. of mouth 25 cms (9¹³/₁₆″).

Black mouth, black handles and black disc foot (with some reserved bands); the rest of the vase is light. The neck ornament consists of the usual double palmette chain and residual lotus flowers with some use of purple. The shoulder, just below the junction of the neck, is lined by tongues in purple and black. Under the handles ornamental system with four palmettes, and lotus flowers. Under the figure zone a band of continuous meander; linked lotus buds; rays springing from the base. In the centre a large mask of Dionysus bearded and with locks hanging down the sides and hair descending in waves from the top of the forehead. The head is crowned with a wreath of ivy leaves alternately black and purple. The undulating hairline is reinforced with incision whilst the upper edge of the beard is emphasized by a line of purple. The god is moustached and twigs of ivy issue from the sides of his hair.

Similar picture on the other side of the vase. The amphora belongs to a group of vases with masks of Dionysos or of a satyr. They all date in the last few decades of the 6th century, one of them is decorated by Psiax, another by the Antimenes Painter, a close companion of Psiax. For the idea of the mask compare the much later stamnos in Naples, (plate 206). Assured, if rather free use of incision.

C. 530–520 B.C.

Bibl.: Beazley, *ABFVP*, p. 275, no. 5. *CVA*, Tarquinia fasc. 1, pl. 32, 4. For the theme see also Beazley, *ABFVP*, p. 205 ff. (Krokotos Group) and T. B. L. Webster, *Greek Art and Literature, 700–530 B.C.*, London 1959, p. 66. See also Wrede, in: *AM*, 53, 1928, p. 66 ff.

XXIII

HYDRIA (kalpis) IN STYLE NEAR THE NIKOXENOS PAINTER. Rome, Museo Nazionale di Villa Giulia 47457. From Cervetri. Well preserved. Height 34 cms (13³/₈″); diameter at mouth 15 cms (5⁷/₈″); greatest circumference 94 cms (37″).

The upper surface of the mouth is reserved, so are the inner sides of the handle. Figure field covering both the shoulder and body of the vase; below it two purple lines encircle the pot. The shoulders merge into the body without break in this variety of the hydria, which becomes fashionable from now onwards and is often called kalpis. The water pots shown in this picture are all of this type. Contrast the shape on plates XXI, 72.

The sides of the panel are framed with linked pomegranates whilst the top border consists of downpointing linked lotus buds. Three women drawing water at a fountain. The first one has placed a hydria on the steps of the fountain house underneath a water spout in the shape of a lion's head. The women wear a chiton with ample sleeves. The two other women carry their pots on their heads. The first one balances it on its side, the pot is therefore still empty; the second balances it upright, it might be full already. A deer is in the background sniffing. It is caressed by the third woman. Branches in the background, one of them being held by the second woman. All three women have little pads on their heads to help them carry the water pots.

The architecture of the fountain house is not quite clear. The two columns with white capitals are not put into proper relationship with the steps. Again the lion spout seen frontally should in reality be in profile set against the wall on the right as depicted on a number of vases. The convention shown here is known from other vase pictures. One has the impression that the painter has taken some model and adapted it not very successfully. The Doric architraves with their white mutules and guttae recur in a related hydria in Munich also black-figured and belonging to the Leagros Group. Compare also the representations of water spouts seen frontally and in profile on a black-figured hydria in the British Museum by the Antimenes Painter, and a little earlier than our hydria.

Our vase has been compared by Beazley with some other hydriai of the same type near the Nikoxenos Painter, an artist who also worked in Red-figure. His Black-figure oeuvre belongs to the so-called Leagros Group (see plate 72). C. 510 B.C.

Bibl.: This vase has been unpublished so far and is mentioned in: Beazley, *ABFVP*, p. 393. On fountains in the 6th century and their representations on vase paintings see B. Dunkley, in: *ABSA*, 36, 1935–6, specially 152 ff. and p. 156, fig. 5 and pl. 22a, where the comparanda mentioned in our text will be found.

71

AMPHORA BY THE PAINTER OF TARQUINIA RC 6847. Tarquinia, Museo Nazionale, RC 6847. From Tarquinia. Well preserved. Height 55 cms (21⁵/₈″). Diam. of mouth 25 cms (9¹³/₁₆″). Type A; see plate 62–3.

Handles are decorated with a double-leaved ivy branch on a reserved ground, the bottom of the vase is lightened by a reserved zone near the foot filled with rays springing from the base; also the foot in several degrees is partly reserved giving the pot a lighter appearance than is usual for this type of amphora. The panel has an upper border of a chain of double palmettes and residual lotus flowers.

Side A. Herakles naked apart from his lion's skin (which also covers his head and falls down his back) has seized the tripod of Apollo and defends its possession against the god by raising his club against him. Apollo, who has hastened up to retrieve his own, has grasped the tripod with his right and holds a bow in his left hand, a quiver hangs on his left side. A little hind has run up between the two and looks round towards Herakles. Behind Herakles stands Athena with her helmet and aegis holding a spear with her right and a flower in her left. Behind Apollo another woman, presumably his sister Artemis, who holds up her chiton with the left hand. White over black used for female flesh. Purple for the beard of Herakles and details on the tripod.

Side B. Four-horse chariot to the right with charioteer in white chiton and himation holding a goad in his hand; also a bearded man in the chariot.

Beazley has assigned to the painter of this vase a Panathenaic amphora in Athens. The style of both these vases is close to that of the Rycroft Painter. He also compares the Psiax amphora in Brescia (here plates 66–8), with which the disposition of the figures and the rendering of the hair of Athena should be compared. Contemporary with the early red-figure painters.
About 520 B.C.

Bibl.: H. Philippart, *Collections de céramique grecque*, Brussels 1932, p.113, no. 9. P. Romanelli, *Tarquinia*, p. 119. *ASAIA*, IV–V, 1924, p. 129, no. 1. *CVA*, Tarquinia fasc., 1, pl. 19, 2–3. Beazley, *ABFVP*, p. 338, no. 1. For theme Parke-Boardman in: *JHS*, 77, 1957, p. 276ff.; Bremmer, *Herakles*, p. 87, no. 7.

72

HYDRIA IN THE LEAGROS GROUP. Würzburg, University (Martin von Wagner) Museum 311. From Vulci. Formerly the Feoli Collection. Well preserved. Right handle is restored. Height 52 cms (20⁷/₁₆″).

Neck is black. On shoulder below junction of the neck a zone of tongue pattern alternately black and purple. The shoulder picture is separated from the main body by a black line. The subject of this shoulder picture is Achilles and Ajax playing a game, as on the Vatican amphora by Exekias (plate 62).

Main picture: The sides are framed by ivy branches, the bottom by enclosed down-pointing palmettes. Much incision but little use of purple which only appears on the horses and their harness, as well as for the pattern on Priam's chiton. High up in the picture the name Leagros is inscribed. It is a love name widely used towards the end of the 6th century and which also gives the name to a large and important group of vases. The subject of the picture is the destruction of Troy, the so-called *Ilioupersis*. In the centre the altar on which the aged Priam has taken refuge. He sinks back against the volute on the side of the altar. In front of him is Neoptolemos fully armed and about to pierce the old man with his spear. Priam lifts up his right in vain imploration and protest. His forehead is wrinkled, his hair and beard white. Behind Priam a standing woman with gestures of distress, behind Neoptolemos another woman with more indolent gestures. On both extremities of the field the foreparts of four horses, no doubt drawing a chariot.

The subject of the death of Priam at the hand of Neoptolemos is frequently found on vases of the Leagros Group and in several different versions. The story which does not occur in Homer will have been taken from some other epic poem, probably the *Ilioupersis* of Arctinus from Miletus.
About 510 B.C.

Bibl.: *RM*, 3, 1888, p. 108. Langlotz, *Vasen Würzburg*, no. 311, pl. 88. Klein, *Lieblingsinschriften*, p. 71, 5. Klein, *Meistersignaturen*, p. 131,5. Beazley, *Development*, pp. 84 and 115. Beazley, *ABFVP*, p. 362, no. 35. Arias, in: *RIASA*, IV, 1955, p. 104, no. 19. M. Wiencke, in: *AJA*, 58, 1954, p. 298 and pl. 59, 18.

NON-ATTIC BLACK-FIGURE APART FROM CORINTHIAN

LACONIAN VASES

Here we deal only with the appearance in the 6th century of a characteristic black-figure style under strong Corinthian influence, but with a well formed individuality. There had been vases made in Spartan territory ever since geometric times, but the pieces shown here are of the fine style developed early in the 6th century. The clay is brown, but there is usually a creamish slip on that part of the surface which is to be covered with ornament or figure painting. The style is Black-figure with much use of purple. The favourite shape is a cup on a high foot. The outside of the bowl is effectively decorated with zones of floral design including handle palmettes, whilst inside the cup we find complex pictures, not just the singletons or the Gorgon's head met on Corinthian and Attic before the middle of the century. Unlike most other styles during the first half and the middle of the 6th century the Laconian painters made not the outside, but the inside of the cup their principal surface for narrative painting. Hence the peculiar attraction of these cups; but the price paid for this choice was the failure ever to develop an effective tondo composition. One of the devices often used was to divide the circular area by a line cutting off the lower segment which is then treated as a subsidiary picture filled with floral or other ornament. On the Arkesilas cup (plate XXIV), however, the segment is made part of the main picture. Other shapes used for figure decoration are hydriai, dinoi, kraters, and aryballoi. These vases, which used to be called Cyrenaic, are now known to have been produced in Sparta from where they were widely exported to all parts of the Mediterranean, from Naucratis in the Nile delta to the island of Samos and to Etruria, as well as to Taranto and Catania in Southern Italy and Sicily. These are the main concentrations of finds, but isolated pieces have been found as far afield as Spain with quite numerous finds in Marseilles. The output of the finer pieces seems to have concentrated in three workshops, that of the Arkesilas Painter and those of his two pupils, the Naucratis and the Hunt Painters. Each of these workshops also produced pieces decorated by assistants and followers. The range of dates involved is from about 580 to 510 B.C. We illustrate one work by each of the three masters.

Bibliography: P. Mingazzini, *Vasi Castellani*, Rome 1930, p. 186, pll. 42–3 (black kraters). Beazley-Magi, *Raccolta Guglielmi*, p. 13, pll. 1, 3. Swindler, pl. 7. E. A. Lane, in: *ABSA*, 34, 1933, 34, p. 128 ff., pll. 28–48 (basic study). B. Shefton, in: *ABSA*, 49, 1954, p. 299 ff. (attributions to painters and chronology); idem in: Payne, Dunbabin and others, *Perachora* II. P. Pelagatti, in: *ASAIA*, 33–4, 1955–56, p. 7 ff. Rumpf, pp. 53–4. Cook pp. 91–100. Recent finds in Catania, *Boll. d'Arte*, 45, 1960, p. 250; 253; fig. 11; 15.

73 below

LACONIAN CUP BY THE NAUCRATIS PAINTER. Paris, Louvre, E 668. From Italy. In excellent condition. Height 13 cms (5^1/$_{16}$″). Diam. 18 cms (7″).

Purple used for beard and on chiton of Zeus and on the eagle. Outside; narrow black band on top of lip with another even narrower one immediately below; rest of lip reserved. Handle zone reserved with handle palmette (incised) springing from each handle. Rest of bowl is slipped and covered with bands (some purple), zones of rays and pomegranates; foot black.

Inside picture. The bowl is covered in a light yellow slip. It shows Zeus seated with an eagle flying towards him. He is dressed in a long chiton over which a cloak is wrapped. The cloak is elaborately decorated with zig-zag and meander pattern, some of it incised. His hair is long and falls down the whole length of his back. Two filling rosettes in the field. The picture of Zeus Lykaios known from coins of Arcadia recurs in reverse direction on a cup in Taranto by the same hand. The filling ornament is derived from Corinthian. For the decorative patterns on Zeus' cloak we may also compare contemporary Attic vases.

Ca. 570–560 B.C. One of the earlier works by the Naucratis Painter, so called after a much damaged cup in the British Museum from Naucratis.

Bibl.: Pottier, *VAL*, p. 63. *CVA*, Louvre (Pottier), fasc. 1, p. 4, pll. 3, 6; 4, 4. E. A. Lane, in: *ABSA*, 34, 1933–34, p. 166. B. Shefton, in: *ABSA*, 49, 1954, p. 304, no. 5; fig. 2. P. Pelagatti, in: *ASAIA*, 33–4, 1955–56, pp. 26–8.

LACONIAN CUP BY THE HUNT PAINTER. Paris, Louvre, E 670. From Italy. Reconstructed but in good condition. Height 12 cms (4¹¹/₁₆″); diam. 19.5 cms (7⁵/₈″).

Light yellow slip on the inside tondo. Much use of incision. On the outside edge of the lip a broad black band. Rest of lip reserved. Handle zone is reserved with an incised palmette reaching out from each handle root. On lower part of bowl, which is slipped, bands, zone of rays, bands, zone of balls (= residual pomegranates), bands. Some of the bands are in purple. Black foot.

Interior picture: Two hunters after a boar most of which is outside the picture. The scene may be an excerpt from the Calydonian boar hunt but not necessarily so. Of the two hunters one is bearded, both have raised their arms to bring down their spear. Between the legs three eagles with spread wings. In the segment formed by the black lines three fishes.

C. 550 B.C. By the Hunt Painter who in his earlier works uses the 'porthole composition' a number of times breaking off the picture where the roundel cuts it off. It is one way of dealing with the problem set by using the circle for the narrative figure field.

Bibl.: Pottier, *VAL*, p. 64. *CVA*, Louvre fasc. 1, p. 4, pll. 3, 5. E. A. Lane, in: *ABSA*, 34, 1933–34, p. 141 ff., pl. 41. B. B. Shefton, in: *ABSA*, 49, 1954, p. 306, no. 4; pl. 54b. P. Pelagatti, in: *ASAIA*, 33–4, 1955–56, p. 31.

74, XXIV

LACONIAN CUP BY THE ARKESILAS PAINTER. Paris, Bibliothèque Nationale (Cabinet des Médailles) 4899, 2707. De Ridder 189. From Vulci. Formerly in the Durand Collection. Yellow reddish clay well levigated and baked. On the inside and outside light yellow slip turning into red where lightly applied. Numerous restorations. The figures are in a brilliant black glaze with much use of purple. White also used and directly on the slip; where it is lightly applied over black, as on the two workers in the segment, the effect is bluish. Height 20 cms (7¹³/₁₆″). Diam. with handles 38 cms (14¹⁵/₁₆″).

Outside of cup: The lip is filled with pomegranate net, the handle zone with linked buds. Palmettes springing from each handle. Below this, zones of bands, rays, tongues and pomegranates. High foot with expanding foot plate. Handles and foot are black, but with seven purple bands on the upper part of the stem of the foot.

Inside: Lip has zone of linked lotus buds. The circular field is divided two thirds down by a dark line into larger and a smaller segment.

The subject whilst clear in its general intent is extremely difficult to interpret in detail.

In brief the picture seems to represent Arkesilas, king of Cyrene, watching the weighing, packing and storing of some produce, probably wool rather than silphium. Beyond this everything is problematic. Is the scene aboard a ship and the storing therefore in a hold, or on land? The sail, once white, which extends on the upper left does not decide the question, as an awning against the sun can also be put up on land. Further, though the name Arkesilas is clear enough, the meaning of the other inscriptions is not. Are some or all of them names, or exclamations in a dialect or spelling not readily understandable?

Now to details. We see on the left under an awning or sail Arkesilas (inscription next to his hat) sitting on an elaborate stool under which sits a cheetah (with collar). He wears a broad-brimmed conical hat, an elaborate petasos, ending in a flower. His long hair comes down the whole length of his back and he is bearded. He is dressed in a long white chiton with a cloak over it; he also wears elaborate shoes. Much purple on all these; some bluish effect on the hat. In his left hand he holds a budding triple headed sceptre and points forward to a man wearing a loin cloth who looks at him and is called Sophortos. Behind Arkesilas' chair a running lizard.

Sophortos stands next to a pair of large scales suspended from a beam above; around it various other men dressed in short chiton or loin cloth are busy. One carries a large net bag full of some whitish material, others are filling such a bag, whilst one more man looks to the weighing of this same white substance, which fills both scale pans. The substance used to be identified as silphium, a drug widely used in the classical world and exported from Cyrene, but wool seems more likely to judge by the picture. It is being weighed, put into containers and then stored away into a cellar or a hold indicated by the lower segment. This store room is guarded by a man at the upper left of the segment appropriately called Phylakos.

Numerous other inscriptions are placed next to people and things. We read from left to right *stathmos* = balance, written vertically upwards next to where the straps of the left weighing pan are joined to the beam. Next Irmophoros, then Sliphomachos written against a person pointing upwards on the right. The name is sometimes connected with silphium. Between the last two is written *oryxo* = (?)haul away. In the lower segment is written *maen* which has been interpreted as meaning 'packed'. Above the scales we see a crane in full flight; two other birds are perched on the beam looking downwards. A monkey too balances on this beam, whilst on the left another bird swoops down.

It has generally been thought that Arkesilas II is represented, the king of Cyrene for a very short time in the early sixties of the 6th century (569–568 B.C.), though lately Rumpf has taken the subject of the picture to be a Spartan merchant.

This, the best-known of the Laconian vases, is remarkable in the vigour of its expressive gestures, even if we cannot fully interpret them. It was of course used as an argument for the theory of a Cyrenian origin of Laconian. It is one of the latest works of the Arkesilas Painter to whom a number of other works can be attributed and who in turn was succeeded by the Naucratis and Hunt Painters.

C. 565–560 B.C.

Bibl.: *MI*, I, pl. 47A. Brunn, *Griech. Kunstgesch.*, I, p. 61. Pottier, *Catalogue Louvre*, II, pp. 380, 525. Perrot-Chipiez, IX, p. 494, pl. 20,

pp. 497, 563, 568. De Ridder, *Cat. Vases Bibl. Nat.*, p. 98, no. 189. R. Demangel, in: *Mon. Piot.*, 26, 1923, p. 70, no. 3. Pfuhl, I, p. 225 ff., III, fig. 93. FR, III, pl. 151. Buschor, *G Vsm*, p. 118 ff., fig. 86. Rumpf, p. 54. *CVA*, Bib. Nat. fasc. I, (Lambrino), pp. 17–8, pll. 20–1. Beazley, in: *JHS*, 48, 1928, p. 251 (on restorations and on the 'blue' pigment). E. A. Lane, in: *ABSA*, 34, 1933–34, p. 161 ff. B. B. Shefton, in: *ABSA*, 49, 1954, pp. 300, no. 14; 308 ff. J. Boardman, in: *ABSA*, 51, 1956, p. 61; Idem, in: *JHS*, 78, 1958, p. 9. On the inscriptions see Kretschmer, *Die griechischen Vaseninschriften*, pp. 13–15. On Arkesilas see S. Mazzarino, *Fra oriente ed occidente*, Florence 1947, pp. 150

and 313. Cook, p. 97. Miss Benton, in: *Archaeology*, 12, 1959, p. 178 ff. has an interesting interpretation of the birds. They are woodpeckers (*sliphomachos* being 'insect hunter'). The two workers on the right then look up at the birds on the beam and encourage them; *oryxo* then is an order, 'dig in', addressed to the birds. The scene according to Miss Benton is on board ship, but in a harbour, where King Arkesilas can watch the operations; the ship is infested with insects and attracts the woodpeckers, which are welcomed by the ship's company. On the name Sophortos see Beazley in *AJA*, 54, 1950, p. 310; also *Hesperia*, 12, 1943, p. 88. *EWA I*, pl. 338 (colour). Brown, *Lion*, p. 172 (on cheetah).

CHALCIDIAN VASES

There are some three hundred Chalcidian vases belonging to a black-figure fabric of which the locality of production is still not known with certainty. Favourite shapes are an amphora with short neck and round handle and a krater with characteristic handles not unlike a column-krater. The technique is black-figure on a bright red clay ground with white used for female flesh. Also purple is much used. There are many inscriptions in the so-called Chalcidian alphabet. Three views have been held about the centre of manufacture. It has been thought that they were made in Chalkis in Euboa, though not a single figured fragment has so far turned up there. Another view assigns them improbably to Cervetri (Caere) in Etruria, whilst others again place them in one of the Chalcidian colonies in the West, such as Reggio di Calabria, the ancient Rhegion, where many of them have been found.

These vases have been studied by Rumpf who has distinguished various painters and groups. They date between 550 and about 510 B.C. A wide range of myths is figured: Herakles; the Trojan war; Dionysus; and his throng; Phineus (on the well-known Würzburg cup) and much else. The animal frieze and the ornaments recall Corinthian, but Attic and later Ionian influences are also strong. According to Rumpf the style, which appears suddenly and fully grown without any known early stages, was created by the Inscription Painter, an artist of genius who influenced his colleagues and successors.

Bibliography: Pfuhl, I, p. 195 ff. A. Rumpf, *Chalkidische Vasen*, Leipzig 1927, passim. H. R. W. Smith, in: *Univ. of California Publ. in Class. Arch.*, I, 3. Berkeley, 1932, p. 85 ff. Rumpf, pp. 54–5. L. Banti, in: *Enciclopedia dell'Arte classica*, s.v. Calcidesi vasi. Cook, pp. 157–60; G. Vallet, *Rhégion et Zancle*, Paris, 1958, pp. 211 ff.; idem in: *REA*, 58, 1956, pp. 42 ff. Trendall, *Felton Vases*, Canberra 1958, p. 5 ff. (outstanding new psykter-amphora by the Inscription Painter with Homeric battle in Melbourne). On inscriptions see Jeffery, *Scripts*, p. 81 ff. On recent finds in Old Smyrna see provisionally: *ABSA*, 52, 1957, p. 12; in Catania, *Boll. d'Arte*, 45, 1960, p. 251; 254; figg. Many miniature plain Chalcidian kraters (see plate 75) and at least one such skyphos of characteristic shape with buttoned wishbone handle (Griso-Laboccetta C 1201) have turned up in Reggio. Being of local manufacture they strengthen the claim of Rhegion as place of origin for Chalcidian. Similarly the dip technique of several of the less ambitious vases (as Rumpf nos. 31, 41, 42, 153, 160–4, 168, 170, 171) is common in the local pottery of Rhegion and neighbouring sites. (cf. Rumpf, *op. cit.*, p. 128; id. in: *BPW*, 1934, p. 683).

XXV

CHALCIDIAN HYDRIA BY THE INSCRIPTION PAINTER. Munich, Museum Antiker Kleinkunst, 596. From Vulci. Mended from large fragments. Clay orange coloured; black glaze with blue metallic sheen and sometimes fired dark red. Height 46 cms ($18^{15}/_{16}$"). Diam. of mouth 17.5 cms ($6^{13}/_{16}$").

Foot is echinus-shaped. The body elongated and tapering towards the bottom. Horizontal shoulders. The handle attachments copy metal forms; note the vertical handle which even has two imitation rivets above. Much use of purple. Relief-line in shoulder ornament (*FRI*, p. 165, 167). The main figure frieze runs above a zone of stepped lines below which is an animal frieze with panthers and goats; also siren with spread wings between two panthers, and a bird with head turned back; filling rosettes. Pointed rays spring from the base. On shoulders a frieze of eleven riders galloping and dressed in a short purple chiton. At junction

of neck and shoulders tongue ornament, purple and black. Neck is black with wavy purple band above, mouth is black except for a purple upper moulding. The inner face of the neck is black with four bands in purple. The handles are black apart from the central rib which is reserved. Handle attachment discs are black with purple surround. Under the horizontal side handles two lions sitting on their haunches and lotus flowers hanging down from the ends of the handle or the side border.

Side A (not shown). In the centre there is displayed the skin of the Calydonian boar with its head cut off, which is separately resting on a table. In front of it we see Atalanta (name inscribed) dressed in a short chiton leaving her thighs and arms exposed. Her flesh is in white. She faces to the right and is about to wrestle with a man who is entirely naked and is called Maophsos in the inscription. Behind him a man dressed in a long white chiton and with a himation over his shoulders, carrying a spear. The name Peleus is written on his chiton. Two more men one of them Klytios

follow. In the left part of the picture, behind Atalanta, a man with spear followed by a pair, woman and youth, and a man. The precise mythological incident cannot be explained, but Mopsos, Atalanta and Peleus all took part in the hunt of the Calydonian boar. A wrestling contest between Mopsos and Atalanta is not otherwise known, but there was a famous one between Peleus and Atalanta at the funeral games of Pelias after the end of the expedition of the Argonauts. It is conceivable that this contest was in the artist's mind, and that he made a slip when labelling his characters, and also that he somewhat irrelevantly added Atalanta's prize of the boar's skin and head, which she had acquired years before at the Calydonian hunt.

Side B. Zeus with a purple cloak thrown over his shoulders and about to hurl the thunder bolt in his right faces Typhon, a monster with long beard, human trunk, wings, and two coiled serpent's bodies instead of legs. Purple is used for the patterning of the serpents' bodies and the wings as well as for the hair and beard of the monster. He wears a white chiton over his human upper body.

C. 550–530 B.C. and attributed to the Inscription Painter.

Bibl.: Jahn, p. 38, no. 125. FR, I, pl. 31–2, p. 161 ff., II, pp. 216, 220. III, p. 10; p. 215, 20. Buschor, *G Vsm*, p. 95. Sieveking-Hackl, I, no. 596, p. 67 ff., fig. 77, pll. 23–4. Ducati, *Ceramica Greca*, I, p. 198, fig. 156 ff., 199 ff. Rumpf, *Chalkidische Vasen*, p. 12, pll. 23–5 and pp. 47–54, 63–70, 73, 78, 89 etc. Brommer, *Vasenlisten*, p. 183 C 1. L. Banti, in: *Enc. dell'Arte classica*, s.v. Calcidesi Vasi; on the subject of Side A see also Beazley in: *AJA*, 54, 1950, p. 310, and *AJA*, 64, 1960, p. 224. On Typhon compare Buschor in *AJA*, 38, 1934, p. 31. Kunze, *Schildbänder*, p. 82 ff. The reserved middle rib of the handles is imitated by the Northampton Group amphorae, and on some Etruscan Black-figure.

75, 76, XXVI

CHALCIDIAN KRATER BY THE INSCRIPTION PAINTER. Würzburg University (Martin von Wagner) Museum 160. From Vulci. Formerly in the Feoli Collection. Excellent preservation, mended from large fragments. Height with lid 47.5 cms (18^{11}/$_{16}$''), without lid 37.9 cms (14^{15}/$_{16}$'').

Lid with knob fashioned in the shape of a small vase. The handles are stirrup-shaped rather than columns, and in their peculiar form occur also on Corinthian and Laconian kraters. The lip of the krater flares out slightly and is decorated with a dense stepped pattern. The neck is black but decorated on each side with four solid circles in purple surrounded by white dots. At the junction of neck and shoulder a tongue pattern, black and purple. Underneath the figure scene a zone of linked buds and flowers of buxom type typical of Chalcidian, then vertically sloping zig-zag lines, followed by rays springing from the base. The foot disc is black on its top surface and purple on the upper third of the side. The rest of its side is reserved. A thick fillet painted purple at junction of body and foot.

Lid (plate 76): From the centre outwards rays, then linked flowers and buds, then a circular figure frieze consisting of boars proceeding to the left. Much purple and incision. Filling rosettes.

Side A (plate 75). Leave-taking of Hector from Andromache. In centre Hector (inscribed) with Chalcidian helmet, metal corslet, greaves, shield (swooping eagle as blazon) and carrying a spear, faces to the left conversing with his wife Andromache, who dressed in a long chiton opens up to him her purple himation which covers most of her body as well as her head. The white which covered her flesh has largely gone, leaving a dull black surface. Behind her a man in short purple chiton carrying a bow in his hand and bow-case and quiver on his back. He wears winged boots, is called Paris by the inscription in front of his face, and in turn takes leave from his wife, Helena (inscribed), who however looks away from him over her shoulders. She has closed herself up in her purple himation. The white of her face is fairly well preserved. Behind Hector in the right part of the vase a youth mounted on one horse and leading another. He must be Hector's squire and is called Kebriones. Behind him an eagle in flight. The face of Hector is contoured with incision. A setting of *Iliad* 6, 344 ff.; 484 ff.

Side B (Pl. XXVI). Two youths dressed in short purple tight fitting chiton are galloping on horses. Much use of purple for details on horses and birds which are between the horses' legs, or flying in the background; one of the birds seems to be a duck, the rest are birds of prey. Under the left handle a bearded nude male running; his face is contoured with incision.

C. 540 B.C. By the Inscription Painter.

Bibl.: E. Langlotz, *Vasen Würzburg*, no. 160, pll. 24–5. Rumpf, *Chalkidische Vasen*, no. 14, pll. 31–4. Jacobsthal, p. 30, fig. 43. FR, II, pl. 101, p. 215 ff. L. Banti, in: *Enc. dell'Arte classica*, s.v. Calcidesi Vasi, Cook, fig. 36.

CAERETAN HYDRIAI

This is a group of 30 hydriai. Many, perhaps most, of which has been found in Cervetri (Caere) in Etruria. Some few have also turned in Vulci whilst one, very fragmentary, in Paris has a doubtful provenance of Naucratis, the Greek trading post in the Nile delta. (Louvre AM 1364 – see Devambez, p. 59; Hemelrijk, pp. 64; 121 – bibliography below).

These vases are all products of one single black-figure workshop though it is possible that the principal master had some assistants. There is much orientalizing ornament, such as palmettes, lotus, ivy with berries on a stalk and myrtle; also some landscape elements, such as hills, bushes with rabbits running about, and mythical creatures, such as sphinxes, griffins, and winged horses. Many of these features connect with the Ionian east. The two masterpieces of the series, both by virtue of their rich polychromy and their

outstanding liveliness, are the hydria in Vienna with Herakles and Busiris and one in the Louvre with Apollo and Tityos. But in all of them we can discern an intense desire to give character to the figures by vivid gestures and other spontaneous, if sometimes naive means. The subjects are taken from the mythological repertoire of the orientalizing period, the adventures of Herakles (but only on few examples), Eos and Kephalos, the hunt of the Calydonian boar, the blinding of Polyphemus, the rape of Europa, the theft of the cattle of Apollo by Hermes. It is interesting to note the strong correspondence between these vase pictures and the literary sources for these legends, particularly the epic and Cyclic poems.

It is possible that we deal with the work of an artist from Phocaea in Asia Minor, who emigrated to Caere, for there are well known links between that city and Ionia. The artist always remains true to his Ionian character, so much so that some think that he always remained in Ionia and exported his vases to Etruria. These hydriai are datable between 530 and 510 B.C.

Bibliography: T. B. L. Webster, in: *JHS*, 48, 1928, p. 196 ff. P. Devambez, in: *Mon. Piot.*, 41, 1946, p. 36 ff. M. Santangelo, in: *Mon Piot.*, 44, 1950, p. 1 ff. V. Kallipolitis, in: *Antiquité Classique*, 24, 1955, p. 384 ff. Rumpf, pp. 67–8. M. Santangelo, in: *Enciclopedia dell'arte classica*, s.v. Ceretane Idrie. Cook, pp. 160–1. J. M. Hemelrijk, *De Caeretaanse Hydriae*, 1956. On the literary sources see N. Plaoutine, in: *Rev. Arch.*, 18, 1941, p. 5 ff.; *idem*, in: *Rev. Etud. Grecques*, 55, 1942, p. 161 ff. See also idem, *CVA*, Louvre, fasc. 9, (text). On the inscriptions, Jeffery, *Scripts*, p. 339 (Ionic), Busiris hydria *EWA I*, pl. 362 (colour); Robertson, p. 76 (colour). J. Anderson, in: *JHS*, 75, 1955, (in Dunedin); Kallipolitis, in: *Mon. Piot.*, 48, 2; Brown, *Lion*, p. 74.

77

CAERETAN HYDRIA. Rome, Vatican Museum, 52. From Vulci. Some restorations. The figure of Herakles is damaged and has lost some details. Height 44 cms (17¹⁵/₁₆″); diam. of mouth 21 cms (8¹/₄″).

On the side of the mouth cable pattern, on the neck zig-zag lines, solid circles and a double necklace of beads and astragals holding up in the centre a bucranium (ox head) and underneath a bulla (medallion). On neck double leaved ivy with berries on stalks. Handle roots are surrounded by tongues in purple with black border. Under the figure zone palmettes in purple and black rising from volutes which are formed by the stalks of lotus flowers which alternate with the palmettes. Rays in purple, white and black spring from the foot which itself is decorated with tongues in purple and white bordered with black. The general impression is one of vivid polychromy.
Side A. On the right and reclining on the ground is the enormous figure of the giant Alkyoneus with shaggy beard and hair in purple with much incised detail. His body in black with incised anatomic details contrasts with the lighter and smaller figure of Herakles who has touches of white applied to him on his body. In his left he holds the bow, in his right he raises the club about to attack Alkyoneus. Herakles' posture recalls the archaic convention for running, one knee down, the other one up. Here the effect is slightly burlesque, intentionally as we are well past the period when this particular scheme was valid—or is it meant to show him tip-toeing? Behind Herakles we see Hermes with a hat pulled down onto his head and wearing a chiton and a himation with indications of folds. He carries his kerykeion (herald's wand) in his right.
Side B. Two pairs of athletes wrestling and boxing.
Herakles killed the giant Alkyoneus but the version here represented can only be tentatively reconstructed from some vase pictures and stray references in Pindar and other literary sources. After the giant had first beaten back Herakles and his companions, killing a number of them,

Athena ordered Hypnos (Sleep) to help, and thus enabled Herakles to kill Alkyoneus. Usually the giant is represented asleep when Herakles arrives (as on the Munich cup by Phintias, see note on p. 318). Here, however, he has woken up and is about to rise and defend himself.
Belongs to the later vases of this series. c. 525 B.C.

Bibl.: Helbig-Amelung, *Führer*, p. 300, no. 471. C. Albizzati, *Vasi antichi dipinti del Vaticano*, no. 229, pll. 19–20. T. B. L. Webster, in: *JHS*, 48, 1928, p. 196, no. 4. M. Santangelo, in: *Mon. Piot.*, 44, 1950, p. 19, fig. 10. V. Kallipolitis, in: *Antiquité Classique*, 24, 1955, p. 388, no. 22 and p. 400, n. 2. On the legend see C. Robert, *Heldensage*, II, 2, p. 564. Verdelis in: *Eph. Arch.*, 1942–4, p. 63 ff. On provenance, *CVA*, Louvre 9, p. 4.

78, 79, XXVII

CAERETAN HYDRIA. Paris, Louvre, E 701. From Cervetri. Unbroken except for the foot which is restored. Some of the purple and white has disappeared and some of the incision has been retraced in modern times. Height 43 cms (16¹⁵/₁₆″).

Use of purple and white. Some of the black has been restored on the moustache and pupil of Eurystheus, and on Cerberus and on the serpents' heads. On the neck a cross ornament terminating in double volutes and a bud. On shoulder and round the handle roots are tongues in white and purple bordered with black. Below the figure zone a frieze of palmettes and lotus flower linked by stalks ending in spirals. Black, purple and white used in the ornament. Below this rays in black, white and purple springing from the foot which itself is decorated with tongues in purple and white bordered in black. Below the side handles picture of a bush. Incised preparatory sketch.
Side A. On the left King Eurystheus, the task master of Herakles' twelve labours, bearded and long-haired has taken refuge in a pithos (storage vat). He is dressed in a black chiton over which he wears a purple cloak. His flesh is in white. He raises his hand in terror at the approach of Cerberus, the three-headed guardian dog of the Underworld, who has been brought up by Herakles from Hades at his

behest. Herakles has the dog on a leash and he raises his club. He is dressed in a purple lion's skin (with the lion's head covering his own head) which he wears over a black chiton. White applied over black for his flesh. Cerberus' three heads are black, white and purple respectively, snakes issue from his forelegs and his heads.

The motif of Eurystheus taking refuge in a pithos is common in archaic and classical art, but usually the bogy is the Erymanthian boar brought in by Herakles. Here the idea is transferred to Cerberus.

Side B. Two eagles in flight towards each other above a running hare. Purple and white used on the eagles. Incised sketch; much incision used for the plumage of the eagles.

The subject recurs on the Villa Giulia hydria 50.649, though there are some differences in detail (Kallipolitis no. 4).

About 530–525 B.C.

Bibl.: Pottier, *VAL*, pp. 66, 70 ff. Reinach, *Répertoire*, I, p. 153, no. 3. Pottier, in: *BCH*, 16, 1892, p. 254. Perrot-Chipiez, IX, 1911, p. 527. Ducati, *Ceramica Greca*, p. 184. Buschor, *G Vsm*, p. 113, fig. 81. T. B. L. Webster, in: *JHS*, 48, 1928, p. 198. Kallipolitis, in: *Antiquité Classique*, 24, 1955, p. 387, no. 10. *CVA*, Louvre 9, pl. 616–7.

80

CAERETAN HYDRIA. Rome, Museo Nazionale di Villa Giulia. From Cervetri. Mended from many fragments. Some abrasions on the figures. The foot is modern. Height 41 cms ($16^1/_8$"), diam. of mouth 21.5 cms ($8^7/_{16}$").

Inside of neck and the handles are black. The inner surface of the mouth is decorated with black tongues, the outer rim with continuous meander pattern. On neck double lotus flowers alternating with star pattern. On shoulder double ivy leaves and berries on stalks. Black tongues round the handles. Under the figure frieze black palmettes springing from volutes which are linked to lotus flowers. White used on the flowers. Rays springing from the base. Under the right handle a hare, under left handle an ape next to a shrub. Much use of incision also for contours of figures.

Side A. The blinding of Polyphemus. Three men in short chiton push forward a stake whilst a fourth directs the operation from behind, presumably Odysseus. The Cyclops is seated on the ground holding a cup in his right hand. For the story see Homer *Odyssey* IX, 319 ff.; for the Cyclops compare also the figure of Alkyoneus on plate 77.

Side B. (not shown). Herakles killing the centaur Nessos. On the left Herakles in lion's skin is about to shoot an arrow. On the other side of the picture a woman in chiton and himation runs towards him arms outstretched in agitation. Further away to the right the centaur with flowing hair and beard runs away to the right looking back.

C. 520 B.C.

This hydria is a good example of the tendency of later hydriai to avoid the flamboyant use of purple and white and to use the more sober black figure. This is presumably due to the influence of Attic vase painting.

Bibl.: This hydria together with two others also from the Banditaccia cemetery in Cervetri is published by M. Santangelo in: *Mon. Piot.*, 44, 1950, p. 1 ff. and pl. 1; 3, 1. Kallipolitis in: *Antiquité Classique*, 24, 1955, p. 388, no. 21. Santangelo, *Musei e Monumenti Etruschi*, p. 137, fig. top left.

PANATHENAIC AMPHORAE

During the greater Panathenaic festival which took place in Athens every four years the victors in the games were given amphorae filled with olive oil as prizes. The origin of this festival is lost in the mists of antiquity, but we know that the games connected with it were reorganized to include athletic contests in 566 B.C. or round about then. The shape of the prize amphorae was special and such it remained, though the proportions were elongated as time went on in accordance with general changes in taste. The latest ones known are of the 2nd century B.C.; whilst the earliest are the so-called Burgon amphora in the British Museum which has a racing cart on it (and could therefore precede the reorganization of 566 B.C.) and an amphora in Halle with a foot race. The short neck and spreading belly of these earliest vases find their parallel in a number of amphorae decorated by Lydos and his companions. The front of the Panathenaic amphorae is regularly decorated with an Athena fully armed with her spear raised aloft. In this posture she is called Athena Promachos. Presently, at the beginning of the last third of the 6th century a column is placed on her either side with a cock roosting on top. An inscription regularly put on this side says *tōn Athēnēthen athlōn* = 'I am (or 'this is') one of the prizes from Athens.' The picture on the other side of the vase is of the event for which presumably the prize was awarded, such as discus throwing, throwing the javelin, foot race, pentathlon, chariot race. A good number of such Panathenaics, but without the inscription, may have been souvenir pieces.

A traditionalism always dominated the decoration of these vases. Since they were first made during the earlier 6th century, they always maintained the black-figure technique and were in fact after the middle of the 5th century B.C. the only black-figured vases still produced in Athens, and, ironically enough, they went on being produced when Red-figure had ceased to be made altogether. Some alterations, it is true, were made in the course of time, such as a change in the direction in which Athene is striding. This occurred between 359 and 348 B.C. and henceforth Athena advances to the right and her shield device is no longer visible. It is interesting to note that whilst the figure of Athena was from the 5th century onwards always rendered in a rather conservative manner which in the 4th century turned into a definitely archaistic style, the backs of the vases depicting the contests were painted in a style contemporary to the time of production despite the traditional technique used.

Of black-figure painters Lydos is known to have decorated Panathenaics, also an artist near the Lysippides Painter, and there are a number in the Leagros Group; but also some of the best red-figure artists decorated Panathenaics such as the Kleophrades Painter, the Berlin Painter and the Achilles Painter. An example of the more elongated shape of the end of the 5th century is given on plate XXVIII (though this precise melon shape is exceptional and uncanonical), an amphora belonging to the Kuban group, so-called after the find spot in Southern Russia of one of the group, now in Leningrad. We can see here something of the contrast between the rather traditional fold system of Athena's dress on the front of the vase and the free contemporary style of the end of the 5th century B.C., or the beginning of the 4th, on the back of another vase belonging to the same group (plate 81).

For a longish period in the 4th century it became practice to add the name of the archon (the annual chief magistrate) on the vase. The earliest name is that of Hippodamas (375/4 B.C.), the latest Polemon (312/11 B.C.). One of the oddities here is that none of the archons mentioned held office during a Panathenaic year.

Bibl.: K. Peters, *Studien zu den Panathenäischen Preisamphoren*, Leipzig 1942. Idem, in: *JdI*, 57, 1942, p. 143 ff. Beazley, *ABFVP*, pp. 403–417. Idem, in: *AJA*, 1943, p. 441 ff. Idem, *Development*, pp. 88 ff., 116 ff. Cook, p. 89 ff. On the Burgon amphora see P. Corbett, in: *JHS*, 80, 1960, p. 52 ff.

XXVIII

PANATHENAIC AMPHORA. London, British Museum, B 605. From Teucheira, Cyrenaica. Well preserved, but in lower part of vase signs of faulty firing. Height 72.5 cms (28^1/$_2$").

Side A. Athena turned to the left in elaborate dress decorated with flowers and myrtle branch. Purple used for the border of the overfall. White for her flesh, details of the dress and the shield device. She has raised her spear in her right hand and carries the shield in her left. As shield device we see the group of the Tyrannicides, the statues of Harmodios and Aristogeiton by the sculptors Kritios and Nesiotes. These statues had stood in Athens since 477/6 B.C. and their use as shield emblem on this and two other Panathenaics in Hildesheim has been plausibly held to refer to the fall of the Thirty Tyrants and the reestablishment of democracy in Athens in 403 B.C. The device therefore dates these vases to 402 B.C., a Panathenaic year. On either side of Athena a column with a cock. On the left the customary inscription referred to in the introductory note.

Side B. Athlete with javelin. Another, clothed, holds a tall palm branch.

End of 5th century. Belongs to the so-called Kuban group.

Bibl.: *Cat. Br. Mus.*, B 605. Von Brauchitsch, *Die Panathenäischen Preisamphoren*, p. 49, fig. 11. Schmidt, *Archaistische Kunst*, p. 89. *CVA*, Br. Mus. (Walters) fasc. I, III H f, p. 3, pl. 11, 3, 6. Beazley, *Development*, p. 96. Idem, *ABFVP*, p. 411, no. 4. For the shield device of the Tyrannicides see the works by K. Peters, mentioned at the end of the introductory note and B. Shefton, in: *AJA*, 64, 1960, p. 178, n. 39.

81

PANATHENAIC AMPHORA, London, British Museum, B 606. From Teucheira, Cyrenaica. Excellent preservation. Height 67 cms (26^3/$_8$").

Face A (not shown). Athena turned to the left. On her lower hem a frieze of dancing girls. Star device in white as shield emblem. Columns with cock on each, as on plate XXVIII. Customary inscription for which see introductory note.

Face B. Four-horse chariot in full course turning round the post which is in white. Charioteer in white chiton with wind-blown hair. An extremely successful attempt to capture an impression of the speed of the race. The charioteer holds reins in each hand and the goad in the right.

End of 5th century: Belongs to the Kuban group.

Bibl.: *Mon. Inst.*, X, 48c and 48h, 13. Von Brauchitsch, p. 48. Pfuhl, fig. 306. Schmidt, p. 427. *CVA*, Br. Mus. fasc., I, III H f, pl. 1, 2a–2b, Beazley, *Development*, p. 96; for the subject see ibid. p. 93. Idem. *ABFVP*, p. 411, no. 3.

ATTIC RED-FIGURE

THE BEGINNINGS AND THE LATE-ARCHAIC PERIOD

82–88, XXIX THE ANDOKIDES PAINTER

This painter is called after the potter Andokides four of whose signed vases he decorated. All his work is in Red-figure though one vase, an amphora in the Louvre, with pictures of Amazons, and of women bathing is in a special technique, like Red-figure but the figures are reserved on a white slip which had been applied over the panel before the black glaze. He also decorated the red-figured sides of a number of bilingual vases, on which see our remarks in the commentary on plate 69. Altogether some twelve vases, mostly amphorae, have been assigned to him.

The Andokides Painter though closely linked to the tradition of Black-figure, clearly seeks to break new ground, largely by experiments in colour effects. His rich drapery ornaments, crosses, stars, swastikas, circles and complex meanders, indeed harp back to Black-figure (compare the Vatican amphora by Exekias, plate XVII); but he also uses purple a good deal on the ivy shoots and vine, which fill his background, and on wreaths and the flowers held in the hands of his figures. In all this he looks for colour effect, sometimes using purple on the red clay ground or next to it, thus varying the shades of red. His figures appear large and isolated against the black background; they have long and flowing hair with undulating lines. The locks are drawn with a thick and slightly raised pigment with incision to outline the hair as well as to indicate individual clusters of locks. Here too the Andokides Painter still uses a technique which is really black-figure. Peculiar to him is an extremely refined and sometimes even precious manner which we find also in some late-6th century sculpture.

The Andokides Painter is usually credited with the invention of Red-figure, and indeed we can sense the triumph of this innovation which dispenses with incision and gives birth to new decorative schemes and a new elegance. He has been called a pupil of Exekias and the quality of his line certainly links him with that great master. He also repeats some of his themes such as the game of Ajax and Achilles. However, his pictures ranging from the palaestra, the chariot race, to mythology (Herakles, Dionysus, the Amazons) show little of the profound human sympathy of an Exekias. He is much more engaged in exploiting the possibilities of his new technique. His activity is in the last third of the 6th century, particularly in its earlier years. No love names are known to occur on his vases.

Bibliography: FR II, p. 267, III, p. 75. Langlotz, *Zeitbestimmung*, p. 23. Pfuhl I, p. 286. B. Schweitzer, in: *JdI*, 44, 1929, p. 129. W. Kraiker, in: *JdI*, 44, 1929, p. 145. Beazley, in: *JHS*, 54, 1934, p. 91. W. Technau, in: *Corolla Curtius*, Stuttgart, 1937, p. 132 ff. pll. 44–7. Beazley, *ABFVP*, pp. 252–3. Idem, *ARFVP*, pp. 1–7. Idem, *Development*, p. 75 ff. H. Bloesch, in: *JHS*, 71, 1951, p. 29. E. Paribeni, in: *Enc. dell'Arte Classica*, s.v. Andokides. On the technique of Red-figure see our Introduction page 15, and also the standard works such as Miss Richter's *Survey*, pp. 29 ff., but above all the recent study by J. V. Noble in *AJA*, 64, 1960, p. 314 ff. Compare also some remarks by Beazley in *Antike Kunst*, 4, 1961, p. 53 ff. 'It is the relief line that more than anything else gives red-figure drawing its masculine precision and power: a wiry line that stands up from the surface of the vase; can be felt with the finger; and looked at closely may be seen to consist of a furrow between two ridges. The instrument, whatever it was, that produced it would not make just any sort of mark, but only certain sorts of line: straight line, simple curve, open double curve. With these the artist draws the contour or parts of it, and the major lines within the contour. The total design is made up of many shapely, patternized areas, so that one is reminded of those poems in which every line is a poem in itself.' (For relief-line in Black-figure see Beazley, *EVP*, p. 25, n. 3, and here p. 311).

The relief line was trailed from a fine, rigid nozzle through which the black glaze was forced presumably out of a bag-like container. Long, smooth, even and unspoiled lines could thus be laid down, which in their character remind one of Jackson Pollock's drip lines, untouched as they are too by the brush. They show a measure of control and spring remarkable for a trailed line. (For different account of instrument see *FR* and Winter, below)

Black glaze was also applied with the brush, thus for filling in the background; it was diluted to form various kinds of brown washes also to be applied with the brush. A short tough brush was used for some of the finer inner markings in golden-brown dilute, and the tell-tale traces of the bristles can be detected on white-ground vases, where the slip reveals them better than the ordinary red clay; see plates XXXVII–XXXIX; XLI–XLIV. (For relief line see also *FR I*, p. 146 ff.; 191–2; 229; II, p. 211. A. Winter, in: *Technische Beiträge zur Archäologie*, Mainz 1959, p. 30).

82–87

AMPHORA by the Andokides Painter. Berlin, Ehemals Staatliche Museen F2159. From Vulci. Formerly in the

Canino Collection. Well preserved. Height with lid 58.2 cms (22⅞"). Type A; see on plates 150–153.

The broad figure panel is bordered above by a chain of

double palmettes and lotus in Black-figure and on the sides by black-figured palmettes and lotus flowers. On side B the same pattern on top but on the sides a sequence of black-figured double spirals crossing each other.

Side A. Struggle for the tripod (pl. 83, detail), the same subject as on plate 71. Herakles in short chiton and lion's skin has seized the Delphic tripod with both hands. Apollo in short chiton and a wrap over his shoulder, long haired, with down growing on his cheeks, and wreathed has taken hold of one of the tripod legs to challenge Herakles' possession. On his left he carries his bow. Behind him his sister Artemis (plate 85) dressed in a long chiton and himation which comes up in a series of folds over the back of her hair. She also is wreathed and holds in her right hand a flower in red-figure (with purple petals), in her left one in black-figure. Both flowers are stylized into ornaments. On the left behind Herakles is his protectress Athena (plate 84) wearing helmet and her aegis with snakes protruding. On it is fixed the Gorgon's head, again with snakes. She also carries a spear and a shield which is shown in a sort of three-quarter view. Under the handles instead of the normal palmette we find a rabbit about to leap.

Side B (plate 87). Athletes. On the left a youth long haired and wreathed with hair outlined in incision (plate 86, detail); incision also used for indication of locks—still in black-figure technique. He has a staff in his right hand and sniffs at a flower with his left. He is presumably the trainer. In the middle a pair of wrestlers trying to throw each other. A cloak hangs on the wall aloft; a neck amphora sits on the floor. On the right another pair of wrestlers. The younger one has gripped his bearded opponent round the middle and has lifted him up bodily, whilst the other one tries to break his grip. Interesting frontal face of the bearded wrestler. The inscription, incised on the foot and visible on plate 82, is *Andokides epoiesen*, the potter's signature of Andokides. The lid belongs to the vase and has a pomegranate knob as on pl. 150–51.

Between 530 and 520 B.C. Rather mannered style.

Bibl.: A. Furtwängler, *Kat. Berlin*, 2159. FR, pl. 133, III, p. 73 ff Pfuhl, fig. 314. Beazley, *ARFVP*, p. 1, no. 1. A. Greifenhagen, *Antike Kunstwerke*, Berlin 1960, pll. 30–32. Idem: *Eine attische schwarzfigurige Vasengattung*, p. 74 (front-face of worsted wrestler).

88, (89), XXIX
AMPHORA by the Andokides Painter. Paris, Louvre, F 204.

From Vulci. Well preserved, though with some restoration. Height 58.6 cms ($23^{15}/_{16}''$). Type A, see plates 150–3.

On side of handles double-leaved ivy branch. The figure scenes are enclosed in a panel. On side A, which is red-figured, this panel is framed above by a black-figured double lotus and palmette chain, on the sides by linked pomegranates in black-figure. The lower frame is just a reserved line. Side B, which is black-figured, has no side frames at all, indeed they are not usually found on black-figured amphorae, but only the top frame of a double lotus and palmette chain.

Side A (red-figured). Herakles coaxing Cerberus. On the left Athena with helmet, spear and snake-bordered aegis. She makes a gesture of encouragement towards Herakles who is stooping over a rather docile two-headed Cerberus with snakes springing from the top end of his mane. Herakles is dressed in lion's skin and short purple chiton. He carries his quiver, whose open lid reveals the arrow tips and one end of his bow, and his sheathed sword. His club is aslant in the field. With his right he makes a soothing gesture towards the dog, in his left he holds a chain. A spreading tree with purple leaves grows in front of the house guarded by Cerberus whose dog's body has a lion's mane and a snake-headed tail.

Side B. This side in Black-figure is work by the Lysippides Painter (see above, on plate 69). Dionysus, satyrs and a menad. Dionysus in long white chiton and himation with purple stripes and ornaments holds a kantharos in front of him and sprays of ivy and vine in his left hand. In front of him a menad (or could it be Ariadne?) dressed in peplos and himation. White for her flesh. She carries an oinochoe in her right, no doubt full of wine to be poured into Dionysus' kantharos. Satyrs on left, one of them playing a kithara; satyr on right carrying a full wine skin over his shoulder. About 510 B.C.

Bibl.: *AJA*, 1896, p. 14 ff. Pottier, *VAL*, pl. 78. Perrot-Chipiez, X, p. 277. Beazley, *ABFVP*, p. 254, no. 1; Idem, *ARFVP*, p. 2, no. 6. H. Bloesch, in: *JHS*, 71, 1951, p. 30, no. 7; p. 31. The *coaxing* of Cerberus into captivity is not preserved in our literary sources, though there may be some hints of it (Apollodorus *Bibl.*, 2, 125–6; Euripides, *Herakles* 613; Diodorus 4, 24 ff.). In most pictures Herakles uses a show of force to drag Cerberus away; on some black-figured vases however (see Kunze, *Schildbänder*, p. 111, n. 1) he or his protectors, such as Hermes, humour (or spell-bind?) the animal to get the chain on. In Red-figure however this motive is very rare, recurring only on the recently found amphora by the Nikoxenos Painter in Paestum (*RIASA* 1953, p. 5, figg.), where Hermes does the coaxing.

90–95 PHINTIAS

This artist spelled his name in four different ways, Phintias, Philtias, Phintis, Phitias and signed four vases as painter. He also signed as potter on three vases, two of them without figure decoration at all (or at least not preserved) and one of them a cup painted by the Berlin Painter at the beginning of his career (see below, p. 343). Love names on his vases are Sostratos, Chairias and Megakles who may have been the son of Hippokrates, ostracised in 486 B.C. or his cousin, the son of Kleisthenes. In either case he would be a member of the great Alcmaeonid family, to which Perikles also belonged.

His vases are almost all large, amphora, volute-krater, calyx-krater, hydria and *psykter* (wine cooler). He was a pot-painter and only three out of his eleven known works are cups. His contemporaries

include Euphronios and Euthymides. The latter was a friend of his as we know from the shoulder picture on a hydria in Munich by Phintias. There, in the subsidiary picture, he shows two courtesans playing kottabos, a party game in which you propelled the dregs from your cup at a target. One of the two girls calls out 'this for you, beautiful Euthymides'.

His earliest work seems to be the cup in Munich signed by Deiniades as potter. The subject is Herakles and Alkyoneus (for the subject see the commentary on plate 77); on the other side the struggle for the tripod. His figures have massive bodies with curving lines rendered in a slightly academic style; they do not display the interest in anatomy and daring poses which we find in Euthymides and Euphronios. His repertoire contains scenes from the palaestra and the banquet, whilst mythological subjects are rarer. They include the struggle for the tripod, fighting at Troy and Theseus against the Marathonian Bull.

A comparison between the courtesans on the Munich hydria and those on the Leningrad psykter by Euphronios shows how much less happy Phintias is at foreshortening and the differentiation of gestures and movements. With his somewhat mannered style it is not surprising to find that connections exist between his latest work and the early Myson, who may have been his pupil, and who in turn was at the head of the mannerist school of red-figure vase painters in the 5th century. Phintias' activity must come between 525 and 510 B.C.

Bibliography: Beazley, in: *JHS*, 37, 1917, p. 234. Hartwig, *Meisterschalen*, p. 167 ff. FR, II, pp. 65–71, 169–70. F. Hauser, in: *JdI*, 10, 1896, p. 108 ff. Langlotz, *Zeitbestimmung*, p. 63. Pfuhl, II, p. 441 ff. Richter, *Survey*, p. 56. Beazley, *ARFVP*, pp. 21–3. Lullies-Hirmer, *Griechische Vasen der reif-archaischen Zeit*, pp. 10, 14 ff., 30, 31, pl. 9a, 10, 33–35. (Munich hydria). For the tag on the Munich hydria see Beazley, *Potter and Painter in Ancient Athens*, London 1946, p. 19.

90, 91

AMPHORA by Phintias. Paris, Louvre, G 42. From Vulci. Formerly in the Beugnot Collection. Fairly well preserved but with numerous restorations. Brilliant black. Height with lid 65 cms (25 9/16"), without lid 60 cms (23 9/16"). Diam. of mouth 25 cms (9 13/16"). Type A; see plates 150-3.

Side of handles with double ivy. The figure panel is framed on all sides; above with enclosed palmettes in Red-figure, below with black-figured palmettes, linked with double spirals, alternately pointing up and downwards. The side borders on A are red-figured palmettes pointing downwards and linked with spiral tendrils. On side B the same motif but in Black-figure. Reserved zone above foot filled with rays. Inscriptions in purple, incision for outline and details of hair. Side A. In the centre Tityos has seized the goddess Leto round her middle, has lifted her off the ground and is about to carry her off. From both sides her two children, Apollo and Artemis, come to rescue. Apollo has got hold of Tityos' elbow and his mother's arm; his bow and quiver are in the background and behind him, as though there was no use for them! On the right Artemis with bow and an arrow in her left hand. She is dressed in a chiton with a cloak over her shoulders. The long hair of both Apollo and Leto are elaborately tucked up. For the story see Homer, *Odyssey* XI 580 and Apollodorus *Bibl.* I, 23. Leto and Apollo are named in the inscriptions: also *chaire* = hail, three times in the field, and next to Artemis *aidōs* = reverence or shame, instead of her name.
Side B. Athletes. From left to right: Bearded man dressed in himation and leaning on his stick, he is perhaps an interested onlooker rather than the trainer who should have a different sort of stick. Then a naked youth holding a discus in his

left at the level of his head; another youth putting the finger of his right hand into the loop of the javelin for testing. On the extreme right a rather older athlete, bearded and naked like the rest, carries a javelin in his left. Inscriptions in purple letters, Sotinos, Sostratos, Chares; *chaire Demostrate* = hail Demostratos; also the beginning of *Sosi— — s.* Spelling is poor.
Note the right foot of the akontist (javelin thrower), which is strongly foreshortened, and also the side twist of the same athlete's body. There is also an attempt at three quarter view of the abdominal musculature and chest of the bearded man on the right.
C. 510–500 B.C.

Bibl.: E. Pernice, in: *JdI*, 1908, p. 95. Fr. Hauser, in: FR, II, p. 273, pl. 112. Hoppin, *Euthymides*, p. 125, pl. 31. Hoppin, *RFV*, II, p. 368, no. 17. Pfuhl, fig. 383. *CVA*, Louvre fasc. III, pl. 28. E. N. Gardiner, *Greek athletic sports*, fig. 123. Beazley, *Attic Vases in American Museums*, p. 29, no. 1. Beazley, *ARFVP*, p. 22, no. 1. Bloesch, in: *JHS*, 71, 1951, pp. 31 ff. K. A. Pfeiff, *Apollon*, p. 53, pl. 14b. A. Greifenhagen, in: *Jahrb. Berliner Museen*, 1, 1959, p. 19 (*aidos* refers to Artemis' virginity, compare Euripides *Hippol.* 78). For the appellation of Artemis we may also compare the near contemporary black-figured neck-amphora by the Antimenes painter in a Swiss private collection (Dr. S. Schweizer) where Artemis, in a picture of the struggle for the tripod, is called *arete* = virtue (Beazley *ABFVP*, p. 269, no. 41; K. Schefold, *Meister-werke*, Basle 1960, pl. 160, no. 149, pp. 26–7). In some places Artemis had the epithet *Eukleia* = Good Repute (see Nilsson, *Gesch. Griech. Relig. I²*, p. 493).

92–95

AMPHORA by Phintias. Tarquinia, Museo Nazionale, RC 6843. Mended from many fragments. Numerous gaps including the right lower leg of Herakles and much of the face and body of Apollo. Considerable gaps also on the other side of the vase. Height 66 cms (25 15/16"), diam. of mouth 25.5 cms (10"). Type A, see plates 150-3.

Handles with regular section; usual ivy ornament. Lip flaring outwards. Foot in two degrees. The figure panel on side A has a black-figured border; above a multiple chain of double palmettes and residual lotus flowers. The three other borders have pattern similar to that on plate 90, the Louvre amphora by the same painter. The panel borders on side B are similar except for the upper one which has red-figured enclosed palmettes. Purple used. Notable is the use of raised black (some of it in dots) for the grapes on side A and the hair curls of the Herakles on side B (plate 93, detail). Incision used for the outline of some of the hair whilst the full red-figure technique of leaving a reserved area is found for instance on the satyr's head, plate 95 lower picture.

Side A. Dionysus with menads and satyrs. In the centre Dionysus bearded and dressed in a long sleeved chiton with a himation draped over his shoulders. Parts of him are showing on the extreme left of plate 94 and on 95 upper picture. He carries a vine branch in his raised left and holds a kantharos in his lowered right. In front of him a pair, satyr and menad. The satyr carries a pair of flutes in his left and his flute case in his right, whilst the menad, dressed in chiton and himation, wearing her hair in loose curly locks but crowned with ivy (in purple), carries a thyrsus (the fennel stalk capped with a bundle of ivy); the usual attribute of menads from now. A small leopard has lept onto her shoul-

ders. Behind Dionysus again a group of satyr and menads whose heads we show on plate 95, lower picture. Notable is the frontal face of the satyr. The painter's signature of Phintias (*Phintias egrapsen*) between the legs of the satyr on plate 94, though most of the letters have disappeared now. Similarly the names of Dionysus, the satyr Simades and the menad Kissine have now all gone, but are known from earlier drawings of the vase.

Side B. Struggle for the tripod (plates 92 and 93, detail). Herakles on the left is moving away having taken the Delphic tripod of Apollo. He is preparing to defend his booty with the club against Apollo who has moved up to retrieve it. Apollo carries his bow in his left hand. Eyes are drawn dot in circle, eye lashes are tellingly indicated; Herakles' hair curls are applied in raised dots; note the down on Herakles' cheek, applied in diluted glaze. (For subject see plate 71.) The names of Apollo and Herakles are inscribed, also Phintias' signature as painter.

Close to the Munich cup with Herakles and Alkyoneus, one of the earliest works of Phintias.

C. 520–515 B.C.

Bibl.: *Mon. Inst.*, pll. 27–8. W. Helbig, in: *Boll. Inst.*, 1879, p. 85. Reinach, I, p. 223ff. FR, pl. 91; II. p. 167ff. Perrot-Chipiez, X, p. 463, fig. 264. Hoppin, *Euthymides and his Fellows*, Cambridge Mass. 1917, pl. 26. Hoppin, *RFV*, II, p. 356, no. 3. *CVA*, Tarquinia fasc. I, pl. 1. Beazley, *ARFVP*, p. 22, no. 2.

96–98 EPIKTETOS

He is almost wholly a cup painter and though one skyphos, two kantharoi and some ten plates number amongst his almost ninety known works, only one calyx-krater and one oinochoe. He worked for the potters Hischylos, Nikosthenes, Andokides, Pamphaios, Python and Pistoxenos. These are all known by their potter's signatures. He himself has also signed a good number of his works as painter.

His repertoire does not vary much. Dionysiac themes, the deeds of Theseus and Herakles are favourite mythological themes. He also likes to place one or two figures between the apotropaic eyes on the outside of his cups, athletes, archers, satyrs. His inside roundels have beautifully adapted figures of satyrs, warriors, flute players.

His favourite love name is Hipparchos, who may have been the son of Pisistratus, a *bon viveur* and a lover of the arts. If this is so, the cups with his love name ought to antedate 514 B.C., the date of his death at the hands of Harmodios and Aristogeiton, the tyrannicides. Since some of the works in question seem to be later, the Hipparchos of these inscriptions may be another member of the tyrant's family, the archon of 496–5, who was ostracised in 487 B.C.

Some of his early cups are bilingual, inside black-figured, outside red-figured. He flourished between 520 and the beginning of the 5th century. In his later years he may have felt the influence of the great painters of the end of the 6th century, such as Euthymides and the early Kleophrades Painter. Typical examples of his late style are a skyphos in London with Dionysus and satyr with donkey, and a kantharos in Odessa, with revelling in progress.

His works have a charming simplicity and economy of line, their fascination deriving from a sure grasp of outline; also a certain grace and rhythm seem to come naturally to him. As example we may quote the picture on a plate in Castle Ashby, of a youth riding a cock, the most charmingly human interpretation of a bizarre motive which goes back to Corinthian art. He is one of the greatest archaic cup painters with an unerring sense for the linear interpretation of the human figure. In his pictures of

armed soldiers, satyrs and archers we see him aware also of the possibilities offered by the exploitation of new poses and the study of depth; yet he does not explore and analyze the anatomy of the human body like Euphronios and Euthymides. For him it was the outline of the figure which mattered.

Bibliography: FR, II, p. 82 ff. Langlotz, *Zeitbestimmung*, pp. 32–4. Pfuhl, II, p. 416 ff. Beazley, in: *Pap. Br. Sch. Rome*, 11, 1929, p. 16 ff. W. Kraiker, in: *JdI*, 44, 1929, p. 141 ff. Beazley, *ARFVP*, p. 44. E. Paribeni, in: *Enc. dell' Arte classica e orientale*, s.v.

96, 97

CUP by Epiktetos. London, British Museum, E 3. Formerly in the Basseggio Collection in Rome. Mended from fragments; fairly well preserved. Height 13.5 cms (5 5/16″). Diam. 30 cms (11 13/16″).

Outside (red-figured). Palmettes next to handles. Incision used for outlining the hair of the two satyrs, purple for ivy wreaths and tails.

Between each of the two pairs of eyes an ithyphallic satyr ready for battle, but instead of offensive arms they carry a drinking horn on one side and wine jug on the other. On side A (plate 96 upper picture) the satyr moves carefully forward with his cut-out shield (pelta) on guard and the drinking horn in his right. At the height of his head the beginning of the painter's signature, viz. *Epiktetos*—to be continued on side B, *egrasphen* = Epiktetos painted (me). On this side B the satyr moves to the left, shield and jug in his right hand but with his head turned back over his left shoulder, blowing a trumpet. He wears a mouth-band. A mock picture, reminding one that satyrs do go into battle, together with Dionysus, in the Gigantomachy.

Inside picture (black-figured). A young man mounted on horseback. He carries two spears. He wears a cloak with white embattled border at the lower edge, and white spots and stripes elsewhere. The white has gone leaving however a dull surface on the black. Placed in the roundel is the potter's signature, *Hischylos epoiese* = Hischylos made.

This is an example of a red-figured eye cup, a so-called cup type A of which we had the earliest example in the Exekias cup in Munich (plate 59). The bowl and foot are sharply separated from each other and there is a fillet at their junction. Epiktetos decorated at least five or six cups for Hischylos, all of them bilinguals.

An early work of Epiktetos, c. 520 B.C.

Bibl.: *Cat. Br. Mus.*, III, p. 42, E 3. Hoppin, *RFV*, pp. 308–9, no. 7. Beazley, *ARFVP*, p. 45, no. 3. For battling satyrs see Brommer, *Satyroi*, p. 55, nn. 21; 22. Buschor, *Satyrtänze und frühes Drama*, p. 89, figs 49–50. For the inversion *egrasphen* for *egrapsen* compare also plate 98. It is common in Epiktetos' early work, (the Attic alphabet having no letter *psi*, the sound is actually rendered by *phi* and *sigma*).

98

PLATE by Epiktetos. London, British Museum, E 135. From Vulci. Excellent preservation. Diam. 19.4 cms (7 5/8″).

Archer. The strap holding the quiver, the bow and the inscriptions are in purple. A narrow reserved line frames the tondo. The archer wears Scythian costume, flappy cap, sleeved jacket and trousers. In his left he holds his bow whilst with his right he withdraws one arrow from his well-stocked quiver which is open with flap hanging down. Note how his running feet touch the circular border, giving to the whole composition something of a moving wheel effect. Inscription: *Epiktetos egraspen* (misspelled for *egrapsen*) = Epiktetos painted. Ca. 520–510 B.C.

Bibl.: Hoppin, *RFV*, I, p. 314. W. Kraiker, in: *JdI*, 44, 1929, p. 163, no. 13. Beazley, *ARFVP*, p. 50, no. 77. Robertson, p. 82 (colour).

99–104 OLTOS

He is primarily a cup painter. We have only two signatures by him, one on a cup in Berlin, the other one on a cup in Tarquinia (plates 100–104). Some hundred and ten vases are attributed to him including two neck amphorae of Nicosthenic type (see plate 99), one stamnos, one psykter and three skyphoi. The rest apart from a few plates are cups. From potters' signatures we know that he worked for Kachrylion, ?Tleson, Pamphaios, Chelis and Euxitheos. His favourite love name is Memnon. His subjects are those of other contemporary painters, particularly Euphronios and Epiktetos. The inside of his cups show warriors, archers, dancers, satyrs; the outside banquets, Dionysiac revels and athletic scenes. A third of his work though are mythological scenes with a particular stress on epic subjects. They include Theseus and the Minotaur, Theseus and Antiope, Achilles and Patroclus, Ajax leaving home, Achilles and Ajax, the young Achilles being brought to the centaur Chiron. Herakles too appears in a number of his exploits, with Eurystheus, Nessos, fighting against Kyknos or against the Nemean lion or again seizing the Delphic tripod.

His early work is so closely related with the Andokides Painter that he has been thought to have been

his pupil. There are the same ornaments on drapery, the same triangular edge folds of the himatia, the same affected hand gestures. The figures on the outside of his eye-cups and on their inside tondos too reveal an affinity with Euphronios, who seems to have influenced Oltos, particularly his more lively scenes. Though his style has not the refinement and the interest in anatomical details so typical of Euphronios, and indeed is more sketchy, the strength of some of his interlacing compositions (for instance the triangular grouping of Herakles and the Nemean lion on a cup in Bologna) does reveal an affinity with the Euphronios of the Louvre Antaios krater (plate 108). His dates range between 525 and 500 B.C.

Bibliography: Pfuhl, pp. 431-2. Beazley, in: *PBSR*, 11, 1929, p. 15-6. F. P. Johnson, in: *Art Bulletin*, 19, 1937, p. 537 ff. A. Bruhn, *Oltos and Early Red-Figure Vase Painting*, Copenhagen 1943. Beazley, *ARFVP*, pp. 34-43.

99

NICOSTHENIC NECK-AMPHORA by Oltos. Paris, Louvre, G2. From Etruria. Formerly in the Campana Collection. Restored but in good condition. Some use of purple. Height 38.5 cms (15⅛"). Diam. of mouth 15 cms (5⅞").

We have met the shape before in plate XIII. The potter, who signs himself on side B, is Pamphaios. On the upper surface of the mouth linked palmettes; on the upper flat of the handles, lotus flowers open and closed. On shoulder lotus flowers to the right. Under the handles an ornament of four enclosed palmettes and tendrils. Below the figure zone a broad black band between two narrow reserved lines. Then at bottom, reserved zone filled with rays springing from the base. Foot flaring and in two degrees. Relief lines used for anatomical details.

On the vertical sides of the handles naked youth with fillets and branches in his hands, a victorious athlete.

Side A. On neck naked girl with necklace, her hair in a sakkos, bending down to tie her sandals. In the main picture a satyr attacking a menad, though with little hope of success. The satyr has grasped her on one arm and shoulder. She carries a long branch.

Side B. On neck a naked girl with necklace, sitting on a couch doing up her sandals. In the main picture a menad with her hair in a sakkos and an animal skin over her neck and shoulders has downed a satyr who has no doubt been attacking her. She grasps him by the hair and pushes a snake towards him with the other hand. The satyr on this and the other side is wreathed in ivy done in purple. The potter's signature of Pamphaios at the level of the menad's head, *Pamphaios epoiesen.*

This vase, attributed to Oltos by Beazley, has been detached from his work proper by Miss Bruhn, who would place it with the stamnos London E437 as a work of a follower. C. 520-515 B.C.

Bibl.: *CVA*, Louvre fasc. 5 (Pottier), pl. 26. Pfuhl, pl. 104, fig. 362. Beazley, *ARFVP*, p. 34, no. 4. A. Bruhn, *Oltos*, pp. 111-12.

100-104

CUP by Oltos. Tarquinia, Museo Nazionale, RC6848. From Tarquinia. Mended from fragments but in good condition. Height 22.5 cms (8¹³⁄₁₆"). Diam. 52 cms (20⁷⁄₁₆").

The shape is elegant but the foot is thickstemmed with heavy disc foot. The cup is of type B, where the bowl and foot merge without a break; there is however a step just above the disc of the foot. Cup type B is a new shape created at this time, though some of the Amasis Painter's late cups have some similarity in their design. The *potters* Euxitheos and Kachrylion were pioneers in its early development and the new cup soon superseded type A (see on plate 59 and 96-97) as the favourite cup shape. Our plates will show a number of examples. The development of the shape was one of the great artistic achievements of the Attic potter. (For this development contrast our plate 101, top, with the two cups on plate 143.) Together with the new type of neck amphora with twisted handles (see below page 345) its creation was one of the significant innovations during the early period of Red-figure. For cup type C see plates 144-145.

Below the figure field a zone of enclosed palmettes linked with tendrils and lying on their left side. Between the handle roots there is a reserved patch. Under the handle roots a palmette with double spirals springing from its base. Inscriptions, flowers and bracelets are in purple. Under the foot an Etruscan inscription scratched into the baked clay. Such inscriptions are called graffiti.

Inside (plate 101, lower picture). Medallion framed by narrow reserved circle. A warrior moving to the left dressed in a spotted leopard's skin, sword in his right hand, and holding a shield (device is a lion in Black-figure) in his left hand. On his head is a crested Corinthian helmet, on his legs greaves. His hair comes down in short curls which we find elsewhere in the work of this painter. Round about the medallion the potter's signature *Euxitheos epoiesen.*

Outside. Side A. Assembly of the gods (plate 101, upper picture and plates 102-104). In the centre Zeus (his name and those of the others are inscribed) dressed in a sleeved and buttoned chiton and a himation spotted with dotted crosses. He holds the thunderbolt in his left and a phiale in his right which is about to be filled by his cupbearer Ganymede, who stands in front of him naked and holding an oinochoe in his right hand. Behind Ganymede, to the right and facing Zeus, is the goddess Hestia. Whilst Zeus is seated on a block she has a chair with a high back ending in a swan's head. She is dressed in chiton and himation, wears ear rings and bracelet and holds a flower in her left and a twig with foliage and some fruit. Between the legs of her chair the painter's

signature of Oltos in two lines going up from the bottom, *Oltos egrapsen* = Oltos painted. Next on the right we see Aphrodite seated rather upright on a block. She too wears sleeved chiton and a himation decorated with swastikas. Her hair is in a sakkos; she wears ear rings and a bracelet. In her raised right she carries a flower, in her left a dove. Her face is turned backwards and so is the face of her neighbour Ares, the god of war, who is seated on a stool whose feet terminate in lion's paws. He wears chiton and himation draped round his lap. He carries his Corinthian helmet in his left, putting his index and middle finger as well as his thumb into the eye holes of the helmet. In his right he holds his spear. Turning to the left part of the cup we see sitting just behind Zeus Athena wearing a long aegis, terminating in snakes, over her chiton and himation. She too sits on a stool with lion's paw feet holding her Attic type helmet in the left and her spear in her right. She has turned round towards Hermes who is sitting on a block, dressed in a spotted chlamys which is fastened at his neck. His petasos hat is tilted back over his neck and he has large boots which seem to be winged. He holds a flower in his left hand. Behind him on the left we see Hebe. She wears a diadem with embattled pattern over her hair, a spotted chiton and a himation. She carriers a flower in her left hand and a fruit in her right. She sits on a chair without back rest.

Side B (plate 100). In the centre Dionysus mounting a chariot. He holds the reins in his right hand and a kantharos in his left. His name is inscribed in letters from right to left going outwards, from his face. In front of him by the side of the horses is a satyr called Terpes who faces him playing the kithara with a plectrum which he holds in his right hand. Ahead of the horses is a menad holding a thyrsus in her right and a deer in her left. Next to her the inscription *theos* = god. A snake in the background. Behind Dionysus another menad with a leopard's skin knotted round her neck holding the thyrsus in her left and supporting a lion in her right. Behind her an ithyphallic satyr playing the flute. He is called Terpon; behind him the inscription *kalos* = beautiful.
Ca. 515–510 B.C. It can be compared with contemporary works of Euphronios, Euthymides and Phintias. The cup belongs to the best period of Oltos.

Bibl.: Hoppin, *Hand-book of Attic red-figured Vases*, II, p. 250, no. 2. *Mon. Inst.*, X, pll. 23–4. Reinach, *Répertoire*, I, p. 203. *Ann. Inst.*, 1875, p. 171. Hartwig, II, p. 71. Perrot-Chipiez, X, pp. 468–71, figg. 267–70. Pfuhl, II, p. 433 ff. *CVA*, Tarquinia fasc., I, III, I, pll. 2–3. Beazley, *ARFVP*, p. 38, no. 50. A. Bruhn, *Oltos*, p. 10 ff. For the Etruscan graffito under the foot see besides the *Corpus Inscr. Ital.*, suppl. III, 356, the article by Pallottino in *St. Etr.*, V, 1931, p. 244 ff. The graffito reads *itum turnce venel apelinas tinas cliniiaras* which means according to Pallottino 'this cup Venel Apelinas (or Atelinas) dedicated to the sons of Zeus'. For the red-figured cup type B see Bloesch, *Formen*, p. 41 ff, compare also Beazley, *Development*, p. 61–2.

105–107 SMIKROS

Smikros was a follower of Euphronios signing as painter on two stamnoi, one in London and one in Brussels (plates 105–7). His love names are Antias, Pheidiades and Eualkides who may possibly be the Eretrian boy victor at Olympia in the teens of the 6th century who died in battle in 498 B.C. at Ephesus leading the Eretrian contingent in the Ionian Revolt (Herodotus 5, 102). Though no Euphronios, the movements of his figures have life, and the scenes a certain realism. His activity is between 520 and 510 B.C. and later.

Bibliography: Gaspar, in: *Mon. Piot.*, IX, p. 15 ff. Beazley, in: *JHS*, 37, 1917, p. 236. Pfuhl I, p. 444 ff. Beazley, *ARFVP*, pp. 56–7. Rumpf, p. 75. Richter, *Survey*, pp. 56–7.

105–107

STAMNOS by Smikros. Brussels, Musées Royaux d'Art et d'Histoire, A 717. Formerly in the Campana Collection. Restored but in good condition. Under the foot a graffito in the shape of a triangle. Height 38.5 cms (15 3/16″). Diam. 39 cms (15 5/16″).

Purple and white used for details, preparatory sketch visible. Outline of hair is incised as well as some of the hair ends. At junction of shoulder and neck tongue pattern in black, then a zone of enclosed palmettes. Under the figure frieze slanting black-figured palmettes (enclosed and linked). Round about the handles ornament of five linked palmettes. At lower end of body reserved zone with black rays springing from the base.
Side A (Plates 106–7). Three youths on couches which are covered with a spread mattress and a pillow. In front of each couch a low table covered with food. Also vine leaves and grape clusters hang down from the tables. The legs of the couches are elaborately carved and decorated. The legs at the upper end terminate in volutes above. The reclining youths are wreathed and also have fillets tied round their heads. They all have cups in their left hands and each of them is busy with a girl. On the left Choro has sat down on the couch of Pheidiades and invitingly takes off her fillet (plate 106). In the middle Helike plays the flute whilst Smikros, the painter himself represented as youth, listens in rapt attention (plate 107, detail). On the right Rhode claims rather closer attention from her companion whose name is lost apart from the first two letters *Al[*— Above just below the palmette frieze the painter's signature, *Smikros egrapsen* = Smikros painted.
Side B (Plate 105). Two servants, one bearded, one not, are

busy round a big dinos on a stand (for the shape compare plate 35). Two jugs of different shapes stand on the ground. Euarches on the left has shouldered a large pointed amphora, Euelthon on the right has put his down on the floor. These pointed and undecorated amphorae were used to store and transport the wine. Here new supplies have been brought up to be poured into the dinos for mixing and consumption. Love-names: *Antias kalos*; *Eualkides kalos*. Three stamnoi have been assigned to Smikros, two pelikai and one psykter. He is a faithful imitator of Euphronios whose face contours he imitates; he also takes from him the intense gestures and movement and the passionate glance.

C. 510 B.C.

Bibl.: *Arch. Anz.*, 1865, p. 20, no. 36. Kretschmer, *Vaseninschriften* p. 172, no. 150. Klein, *Meistersignaturen*, p. 127. Pottier, *Douris*, fig. 3. Perrot-Chipiez, IX, p. 373, fig. 186, X, p. 518, figg. 291–2. FR, II, pp. 4, 10, n. 2. Langlotz, pp. 51, no. 5, 84, 114, no. 4. Ducati, *Ceramica Greca*, II, p. 296. Pfuhl, p. 444. Jacobsthal, *Ornamente*, pl. 92b. Nachod, in: *RE*, s.v. Smikros. *CVA*, Brussels fasc. 2, pp. 36–7, pll. 12–3. For the 'self-portrait' of Smikros see Beazley, *Potter and Painter*, p. 19. He is portrayed again (as a youth in a symposium) by Euphronios on a calyx-krater fragment. For his relationship with Euphronios compare the neck-amphora Louvre G 107. For the inscription on Euphronios' neck-amphora Louvre G 107 often cited in this connection see Lippold, in: *Festschrift B. Schweizer*, p. 134.

108–115 EUPHRONIOS

Euphronios was painter as well as potter. He has signed four vases as painter, ten as potter. The latter are decorated by the Panaitios Painter, Onesimos (who may be the Panaitios Painter) and the Pistoxenos Painter. All these vases are later than the ones signed by Euphronios as painter (see p. 333; 348–49). Some sixteen vases of various shapes have been attributed to him as painter, four calyx-kraters (see plates 108–112), one volute krater (plates 113–115), one stamnos, two neck-amphorae, two pelikai, one hydria, two psykters and several cups including the famous one in Munich with the mounted youth on the inside and Herakles and Geryoneus on the outside. This cup which has Euphronios' signature as painter is signed by the potter Kachrylion. He also worked for the potter Euxitheos (cf. pl. 322).

His love names are Leagros (several times), Melas, Philiades, Xenon, Smikythos. The name of Antias whom we have already met in the work of Smikros, occurs several times but without the epithet *kalos* (= beautiful). Leagros *kalos* occurs not only on eleven vases by Euphronios but on many other contemporary ones. The name no doubt refers to Leagros the son of Glaukon, member of a prominent Athenian family who later in 465 B.C. was killed in battle when general in charge of an Athenian expedition in Thrace (Herodotus 9,75; Thuc. 1,51). The decade 510 to 500 B.C. is a probable date for Leagros' youth.

The repertoire of Euphronios includes scenes from the palaestra of which we give an example on plate 112, banqueting and revelling scenes, such as can be seen on the neck of the Arezzo krater (plate 113) and also on a well-known psykter in Leningrad. Of myths he favours the story of Herakles which we have on the Louvre krater (plates 108–111) and the kylix (cup) in Munich mentioned already and also on the calyx-krater Louvre G 110, as has been shown by new fragments recently added. Only once, on another calyx-krater in the Louvre, does Dionysus occur. There is also an elaborate but fragmentary cup in Athens from the Acropolis with the wedding of Peleus and Thetis. A remarkable picture is found on a pelike in Leningrad of the first swallow in spring. This, however, is now only doubtfully ascribed to Euphronios. He may also have painted black-figured panathenaic amphorae.

In the slightly affected poses of some of his characters, dancers and athletes, some have seen a continuation of the manner of the Andokides Painter; but this would be to ignore Euphronios' much greater force and originality. One of his main characteristics is the interest in the anatomy of the human body, an interest which also appears in contemporary sculpture as on the Treasury of the Athenians in Delphi. In Euphronios this interest is most striking, for not only do we see the fluency and the sureness of outline of an Epiktetos but also the ability to draw solid bodies articulate with musculature strained or at rest and anatomical details derived from a minute and analytical observation.

Amongst those nearest to Euphronios are Phintias, Euthymides and Oltos, all with similar interest in anatomy. None of them however ever drew a group of originality as powerful as that of the Herakles and Antaios on the Louvre krater (plate 108) or attain the pure linear simplicity of the mounted youth, perhaps Leagros himself, on the inside of the Munich cup, or reproduce the ripple of folds and rustle of material as successfully as the women folk on the same Louvre krater (plates 110–111), or mirror physical pain as faithfully as the face of Antaios (plate 109). Whilst Phintias and Euthymides tend to

lose the feeling for the whole body amongst a mass of anatomical formulas, Euphronios has the peculiar gift of grasping both, the outline and its detailed structure. His painter's career is between about 515 B.C. and the end of the century. As *potter* (of cups) he goes on into the second quarter of the 5th century. His dedication as 'potter' on the Acropolis dates from then.

Bibliography: Beazley, *ARFVP*, p. 15 ff. Rumpf, p. 74. Richter, *Survey*, p. 53 ff. [Important additions have recently been made to his painter's oeuvre, especially from amongst the Campana fragments in the Louvre (Villard in: *Mon. Piot.*, 45, p. 1, 47, 35). See also Caskey-Beazley II, p. 1–2, 102; *EWA V*, col. 141 ff. (Paribeni). Or the Acropolis dedication, Raubitschek, *DAA*, no. 225].

108–111

CALYX-KRATER by Euphronios. Paris, Louvre, G 103. From Cervetri. The four purple lines on the inside of the krater have been repainted in modern times. More repainting on the figures, thus on the left, lower side of Antaios (plate 109). Modern also the foot of vase. Height 46 cms ($18^{15}/_{16}$"). Diam. at mouth 55 cms ($21^5/_8$").

The calyx expands outwards towards the top. The handles curve upwards and have a cylindrical section maintaining their thickness throughout; later these handles tend to thin out in the centre.

On a ledge beneath the rim of the mouth a zone of enclosed palmettes tilted to the right. Underneath the figure zone a festoon of double palmettes and flowers. Above the handles three linked palmettes floating upwards. Between the handle roots reserved patch. Above the base a zone of black tongues. Side A. Herakles and Antaios. Both names inscribed as well as the painter's signature *Euphronios egrapsen* (clearly visible on plate 109); the letters are in purple. Herakles is strangling the giant with a vice-like grip for which he has tensed up his body bulging with the effort. His right knee is forward whereas his left leg is straight and reaching to the rear; his thighs, buttocks and calves are swelling with power. He is seen in taut profile, whereas Antaios' frame is displayed in frontal unprotected nakedness. His head is twisted back and shows every sign of agony (teeth bared in pain, gasping for breath, pupils turned up and losing their focus). His right arm is already paralyzed with his fingers impotently twitching on the ground; his left hand is bent backwards, no doubt trying to loosen the grip. His right leg is doubled up behind his thigh. This doubling up of limbs is a favourite motif of Euphronios (we meet it again on the fallen Amazons on the Arezzo krater, plates 113–115); it is part of his interest in the torsion of the body and its spatial rendering on the surface of the vase. We also note the calculated contrast between the spruce beard and hair of Herakles (the curls applied in raised dots of glaze) and the unkempt shaggy growth on Antaios. Continuous beetling eye brows reinforce this impression. The two bodies are disposed in a triangle. On the left behind Herakles a woman in chiton and himation with her hair in a sakkos. She is plainly on Herakles' side. Finally on the left extremity we see Herakles' lion's skin suspended as well as his club and quiver. On the right behind Antaios two women with loose hair and manifest signs of distress, they presumably are the women-folk of Antaios or possibly local nymphs. (On the wrestling, E. N. Gardiner, *Athletics*, p. 220.)

Side B (not shown). A youth about to give a flute recital in front of three of his friends. The youth, called Polykles, flute in hand is stepping on a platform. He is dressed in a long sleeveless chiton which he lifts up with one hand. On either side seats on which three coevals are preparing to listen. They all hold knotted sticks in their hands. In the field *Leagros kalos* = Leagros is beautiful; one of the listeners is called Kephisodoros. On the platform is written *Me]las kalos* = Melas is beautiful.

This is one of the earliest of Euphronios' vases. The anatomical details are drawn with the finest of black lines, with diluted glaze used for shading area such as the hollows between the abdominal musculature of the body of Antaios, or again his hair and beard. His extraordinary gift for the linear representation of details of the body, such as the triangular rendering of the inguinal arch, the loving care bestowed on foot, toes and fingers, the convincing differentiation between the outside of a leg and the inside as exemplified in the contrast between the drawn up legs of Herakles and Antaios, all this and more places him amongst the most remarkable artists at the end of the 6th century. This great vase shows Euphronios in his early and most creative stage.

C. 510 B.C. To be compared with some of the sculptures from the pediment of the Apollo temple in Delphi.

Bibl.: E. Pottier, *VAL*, II, p. 154, G 103. Klein, *Euphronios*, p. 118–119. *CVA*, Louvre, III, IC, pl. 4, p. 4. Swindler, p. 156–7. A. della Seta, *Il nudo nell'arte*, Milan 1930, p. 164, fig. 70. Jacobsthal, *Ornamente*, pl. 46. Pfuhl, III, figg. 392–3. Beazley, *ARFVP*, pp. 15–6, no. 1. Rumpf, p. 74, pl. 20, 2. For a parallel contrast of Herakles and monster compare plate 20. *FR*, pl. 92; 93, 1. Robertson, p. 93 (colour).

112

CALYX-KRATER by Euphronios. Berlin, Ehemals Staatliche Museen, F 2180. From Capua. Well preserved, but some restorations. Height 35 cms ($13^3/_4$"). Diam. at mouth 44.5 cms ($17^1/_2$").

Shape like that of the Louvre krater in the preceding plates. The ornament below the rim of the mouth is a double ivy branch with berries. Below the figure frieze enclosed linked palmettes sloping sideways. Tongues above the base of the bowl. Above the handles enclosed palmettes ballooning in the space. Purple used for inscriptions, wreaths of athletes and other details such as the sling holding the aryballos on plate 112, and the oil which is sprinkled out of it.

Scenes from the palaestra and gymnasium. On plate 112 we show details from side B of a youth called Lykon, who has disrobed and is folding up his garment. On his right the hand and leg belonging to a little boy who is on the extreme right of that side and presumably attends him. On Lykon's

other side a chair with a garment thrown on it. In the space above the chair the love name Leagros (*Leagros kalos* = Leagros is beautiful). On the left Hegesias is pouring oil into his left palm from an aryballos which is suspended by a thong from his right wrist. He is anointing himself. Further left and going out of the picture on plate 112 a boy bends down to examine the raised foot of another athlete who is seen in bold back view. His name is Hippomedōn whilst the boy is called Traniōn(?). Hippomedōn keeps his balance whilst his leg is up, by supporting himself on a stick and with the other hand leaning on the head of Traniōn(?).

On side A the central group is of a discus thrower called Antiphon receiving instruction from the trainer called Hipparchos, (spelled *Hippchos*). Behind Antiphon an athlete tying himself up; a small boy is behind him attending. In the right of the picture another athlete, Polyllos, is folding his cloak, whilst a boy is bringing up his aryballos.

Slightly later than the Louvre krater. Note that the treatment of the drapery is less stylized, especially in its system of folds; also the movement of the bodies is more relaxed and true to life; finally the back view of the athlete on side B is more advanced than anything on the Antaios krater. Traces of the preparatory sketch are visible. The names of Leagros and Hipparchos and the points just mentioned above should place the vase nearer the end of the last decade of the 6th century.

Bibl.: Furtwängler, *Beschreibung Vasen Berlin*, pp. 501–3. Hoppin, *RFV*, I, p. 439, no. 6. Langlotz, *Zeitbestimmung*, pp. 45, 53, 62, 82. Pfuhl, I, p. 451, FR, III, p. 245 ff., pl. 157. Klein, *Meistersignatur*. pp. 79–80. Beazley, *ARFVP*, p. 16, no. 41. Greifenhagen, *Antike Kunstwerke*, Berlin 1960, pll. 33–35. Rumpf, p. 74.

113–115

VOLUTE KRATER by Euphronios. Arezzo, Museo Civico, 1465. From the Baccio Collection, Arezzo. Foot is modern and of wrong shape. Other restorations, which however do not detract from the scene as a whole. Height 60 cms (23⅝"). Diam. of mouth 41 cms (16⅛").

Projecting lip and ledge over a neck which curves out. The outer rim of mouth has continuous meander, whilst the ledge underneath is decorated with a festoon of double palmettes and lotus flowers. On the neck, figure frieze. At junction of shoulders and neck, frieze of tongues. On the actual handle roots small opposed palmettes in quadruple order (plate 114 top). Below the handles and covering most of the height of the figure zone opposed palmettes with a volute ornament on two sides. Below the figure zone enclosed palmettes to the right. Above the base of the body reserved zone filled with black rays.

On neck, scenes of revelling with ten young men and one older, bearded and with receding hair line. All of them are wreathed (use of purple) and wear wraps over their shoulders. In the centre a flute-player, called Xinis, turned to the left; facing him is one playing the lyre and called Teisis. Then someone dancing, hands flung forward and clasped above his head; he is called Chorithōn. Then a couple of whom one holds a jug in his right and a skyphos

(wreathed in ivy) in his left; he pours into a cup held by his companion. Neither of these two have particularly athletic figures, but rather corpulent stomachs. Finally on the left one bringing a pointed amphora wreathed with ivy. Above in the field the love inscription *Xenon kalos* = Xenon is beautiful. In the right half of the neck frieze a dancer clapping hands and facing a pot-bellied reveller, called Kaikeios, who raises a drinking horn in his right. Then an elderly man stepping out and raising a big *skyphos* (mug) to his mouth. Then a flute-player and one playing the castanets. Between them the inscription *Lysis*(?) *kalos* = Lysis(?) is beautiful. On reverse side of vase similar scene with eight dancers, some of them repeating identical motifs; also a lyre player and two flute-players, and meaningless inscriptions.

Side A, main picture. Herakles and the Amazons. In the centre Herakles advances to the right against three Amazons. He is naked apart from the lion's skin which covers his head, is knotted about his shoulders and hangs down over his left arm. He is fighting with his club (which he has swung above his head) and his bow and two arrows which he holds in front of him with his outstretched left arm. His sword in the scabbard hangs by his side. In front of his head the name Herakles is inscribed. At his feet lies a dying Amazon wounded in four places with her blood (marked in purple) gushing out. She is fully armed with Corinthian helmet, leather corslet with a black silhouette lion decorating the shoulder flap, and greaves. We note her left thigh seen frontally and her lower leg pulled back and invisible as in the case of the Antaios in the Louvre krater (plate 111). A kantharos is blazoned on her shield, her sword is in her right, but no longer used; she is about to die, as can be seen from the upward tilt of her pupil. Her name is Kydoime (the inscription is retrograde going, as is usual, in outward direction from the person named). Above the dying Kydoime the battle continues; three Amazons are taking the field against Herakles, two of them armed with spears, whilst the hither one, Teisipyle, is an archer, dressed in the familiar Scythian uniform of trousers, sleeved jacket and a characteristic horizontal pattern. She wears a Greek, Corinthian, helmet though. She is about to let go her arrow; her scabbard is by her side and with her we notice another Euphronian experiment, the swing of her body and twist of her right leg with the underside of the sole showing. The other two Amazons, dressed more conventionally in leather corslet, helmet and greaves, are called Hypsipyle and Thraso; the latter has a Gorgon's head on her shield seen in profile. On the left side of Herakles (plate 114) we see his companion Telamon about to finish off another Amazon archer who is down already and bleeding from several wounds. Her name is Toxis and she wears the Scythian flappy cap as well as the rest of the costume. To the left of Telamon the inscription *he pais* = the girl.

Note the drawing of Telamon's receding left leg (plate 114) and the disappearing lower leg of the struck Amazon beside him. Telemon's lower left leg is mistakenly drawn in back view!

Side B (not shown). Four Amazons running to the left

towards the trio which is still fighting with Herakles. Three of them are hoplites (spear, helmet, greaves, shields with scorpion, raven and kantharos as device), the fourth is an archer in Scythian uniform. Between the legs of the Amazons the inscriptions *Philliades kalos* and *Xenon kalos* = ... is beautiful. This unsigned krater which was first attributed to Euphronios by Furtwängler, has many striking similarities with the Munich cup of Herakles fighting against Geryoneus. Compare, for instance, our two Amazons fighting side by side with the three-bodied Geryoneus also striding side by side. Our Amazonomachy is a great design, and the Herakles particularly noteworthy. Here even more than in the corresponding figure of the Munich cup we see Euphronios

at work exploring the torsion of the body in the drawing of the abdominal musculature. The details are drawn in fine relief lines with diluted glaze used only for subsidiary indications. 510–500 B.C.

Bibl.: FR, II, p. 1 ff., pll. 61–2, p. 14 ff. Perrot-Chipiez, p. 441 ff. *AM*, 30, 1915, Beil. p. 388. Pfuhl, fig. 395. W. Kraiker, in: *JdI*, 44, 1930, p. 123. Beazley, *ARFVP*, p. 16, no. 5. *Mus. Helvet.*, I, 1944, p. 200, fig. 5. D. von Bothmer, *Amazons in Greek Art*, Oxford 1957, pp. 131, no. 5, 136–7, pl. 69, 3a and b. On the sword motive of Telamon see B. Shefton, in: *AJA*, 64, 1960, p. 175. The dance of Chorithon in the neck-picture seems to be the *oklasma;* see Beazley, in: *JHS*, 59, 1939, p. 31; B. Schweizer, in: *Hermes*, 71, 1936, p. 288 ff. On the shape of the vase see M. Robertson, in: *JHS*, 70, 1950, p. 23, n. 5; S. Karouzou, in: *BCH*, 79, 1955, pp. 195 ff. (development and history of shape). Beazley in: *Spina e l'Etruria Padana*, p. 52.

116, 117 EUTHYMIDES

A contemporary of Phintias with whom he has several points of contact. He too is a pot painter decorating amphorae, one psykter, one pelike, hydriai, one plate and two cups, but these last two shapes only account for three out of the eighteen works attributed to him. Like Phintias he makes his figures rather heavy. He has signed six vases often adding the name of his father, Pollias, who may have been the sculptor known from a number of signed bases found on the Athenian Acropolis. Love names on his vases are Megakles, whom we have already discussed in connection with Phintias, and Leagros; also Hestiaios who appears on a plate in Boston; this however is a workshop piece in his manner only.

On the back of an amphora in Munich with Hector arming (plate 117) there is his well known challenge to Euphronios, 'as never Euphronios could do' (*hōs oudepote Euphronios*). This is written next to three revellers (plate 117) who are particularly successful examples of foreshortening! On two of his vases, a cylinder in the Athenian Agora and a cup in Florence, there is also a potter's signature but the name is lost, so we cannot say whether it was he who signed as potter or someone else.

His favourite scenes are from the palaestra, the arming or departure of warriors and the banquet. Mythological subjects seem to interest him less, but they do occur, thus Theseus running off with Korone (or Helen?), Apollo with Leto and Artemis, Hector. It is the figures of athletes however which give him full scope for foreshortening and bold attitudes. Even if there are inconsequential renderings of perspective on his Munich amphora with Theseus and Korone there can be no doubt that the splendid figure of Helen striding along determinedly has a grandeur which is rarely reached by vase painters of this period. Again the two companions of Korone on the other side of the vase (plate 116) are creations of rare success, tripping along, as they do, with their chiton and mantle fluttering in the wind in an almost mannered elegance. Also the arming scene of Hector in Munich (the front of the vase on plate 117) has a gravity with Priam and Hekabe standing on either side, which marks Euthymides out amongst his fellow artists. In comparison with Phintias then Euthymides has the advantage in greater quality and depth of expression, also in a feeling for the volume of his figures as well as in the ability to find decorative formulas in the design of his garments and the markings of the body. However, when compared to Euphronios he must yield the palm to him.

Euthymides' activity must have been between 520/515 and 500 B.C. He is thus still one of the pioneers of the red-figure style and with his fellows experiments with formulas for the representation of new poses and views of the body. He loves the detailed rendering of the chest and the abdominal musculature and even more the decorative design of the parts round the ribs.

Bibliography: Langlotz, *Zeitbestimmung*, p. 51 ff. FR, I, p. 63 ff., 173 ff. Buschor, *GV*, p. 153 ff. Beazley, in: *JHS*, 30, 1910, p. 41 ff. Hoppin, *Euthymides and his Fellows*, Leipzig 1896. Pfuhl, I, p. 433 ff. Talcott, in: *Hesperia*, 1936, p. 59 ff. Beazley, *ARFVP*, p. 24 ff. Richter, *Survey*, p. 55 ff. Lullies and Hirmer, *Griechische Vasen*, pll. 17–31. Rumpf, pp. 73–4. On Pollias, see now Raubitschek, *Dedications from the Athenian Akropolis*, p. 522; compare also Beazley in *JHS*, 51, 1931, p. 53; Boardman in *JHS*, 76, 1956, p. 21. But the name in Euthymides' signatures is always in the genitive; it may have been Polios in the nominative! On Euthymides' challenge (plate 17) see Beazley, *Potter and Painter*, p. 20.

AMPHORA by Euthymides. Munich, Museum Antiker Kleinkunst, 2309. From Vulci, once in the Canino Collection. Excellently preserved, mended from large fragments. Height 57.5 cms (22⁵/₈″). Diam. of mouth 28.5 cms (11¼″). Type A, see pl. 150-3.

On side A the picture panel is framed above by red-figured enclosed palmettes and on the sides and below by black-figured palmettes. The lower frame has these palmettes linked and alternately pointing up- and downwards, whereas the side ones are sloping up- and downwards linked in pairs by spiral tendrils. On side B (plate 116) the top and bottom frame are the same but the sides are formed by linked black-figured pomegranates. The reserved sides of the handles are filled with double-leaved ivy and the reserved zone above the base with black pointed leaves.

Side A (not shown). Theseus naked but for a wrap is carrying off Korone whom he has lifted off the ground already. She does not seem to mind for though she tries to break his grip with one hand, she caresses his hair with the other. In the centre Helen (so inscribed) strides up energetically, gets hold of Korone's arm and makes an imperious gesture to Theseus. Behind her Peirithoos, boon companion of Theseus, brings up the rear, looking round at the bevy of girls who are following him on the other side of the vase.

Here on side B (plate 116) two girls in sleeved chiton and mantle run after Theseus and Peirithoos. They must be Korone's companions. One of them has her hair in a sakkos and is called Antiopeia; both of them wear wreaths rendered in purple. On the extreme right of the figure there is the vertical inscription *Eidon, theōmen* = I have seen, let us run. On the left a man, one would have thought the father of Korone, raises one hand in resignation, his other holds a knotted staff. Behind him is the vertical inscription, *chaire Theseus* = hail Theseus. There is a touch of irony in the spectacle of the two girls, far from running away as we might expect, towards the old man for protection and to let him know the fate of his daughter, actually race after the abductor. They too want to be carried off? For the normal scheme of abduction scenes see plates 158-9 and the commentary there; for ours compare p. 332, the abduction of Antiope.

The rape of Korone is not otherwise known and it has been suggested that the labels *Korone* and *Helene* should be switched round. This would turn the picture into the abduction of Helen by Theseus, a well-known episode.
About 510-500 B.C.

Bibl.: Jahn, no. 410, p. 141. Hoppin, *Euthymides and his Fellows*, p. 15 ff. FR, I, p. 173 ff., III, pp. 118, 244, 278. Beazley, *ARFVP*, p. 25, no. 3. Lullies and Hirmer, *Griechische Vasen*, pp. 13, 30, pl. 17-23 (for a different explanation of Korone). Also Beazley, *Development*, p. 115, n. 34.

117

AMPHORA by Euthymides. Munich, Museum Antiker Kleinkunst, 2307. From Vulci, formerly in the Canino Collection. Well preserved but some restorations on the face of Hector on side A. Height 60 cms (23⁵/₈″). Diam. of mouth 29.7 cms (11¹¹/₁₆″). Type A, see plate 150-3.

On reserved side of handles ivy branch. Figure panel on both sides is framed by red-figured enclosed palmettes above, black-figured linked buds below and black-figured linked pomegranates on the sides.

Side A (not shown). The arming of Hector in the presence of Priam and Hecuba. In the centre Hector, seen frontally but with his right leg in profile and his profile face looking down to his right side, is putting on his leather corslet. On the right his shield with satyr's head device. Then his mother Hecuba (inscribed *Hekabe*) holds his helmet and spear. On the left Priam with bald pate, stubbly beard and wrapped up in his himation, holds a knotted staff in his left, whilst his right is raised to underline some word of advice. Next to him the painter's signature, *egrapsen Euthymides ho Poliou* = Euthymides the son of Pollias painted (me).

Side B (plate 117). Three male revellers, all naked but for a wrap hanging from their bodies. They are crowned with wine leaves in purple. They dance in tipsy elation, the one on the left called Komarchos has a kantharos in his right hand, the one in the centre is shown in a successful three-quarter back-view as he swings his staff turning back to Komarchos. His name is given in an inscription between his legs, Euedemos probably misspelt for Eudemos. Finally on the right we see Teles dancing with his arms and fingers spread in consonance with the rhythm. On the extreme left of the panel behind Komarchos there is the inscription running from top to bottom, *hōs oudepote Euphronios* = as never Euphronios could do; for this see the introductory remarks on Euthymides.

Later than plate 116, the Theseus amphora, and in a more reposeful style. Between 510 and 500 B.C.

Bibl.: Jahn, no. 378, p. 123. Hoppin, *op. cit.*, p. 3. FR, I, pp. 63, 66-70, pl. 14. Beazley, *ARFVP*, p. 24, no. 1. Lullies, *op. cit.*, pll. 24-29. On kantharoi in the hands of ordinary mortals see M. Robertson, in: *JHS*, 70, 1950, p. 25; also here on plates 206-211. Robertson, p. 91-2.

118

CUP BY THE SOSIAS PAINTER. Berlin, Ehemals Staatliche Museen, F 2278. From Vulci. Much restored. Considerable gaps on the outside, particularly side A, but the inside picture is well preserved. Height 10 cms (3¹⁵/₁₆″). Diam. 32 cms (12⁵/₈″).

On the inside within the medallion but below the figures three enclosed palmettes linked by spiral tendrils. Round the disc of the foot the potter's signature *Sosias epoiesen*.

Outside of cup (not shown). Herakles entering Olympus. Side A with Zeus and Hera enthroned and other divinities is severely damaged. Side B which is better preserved shows other divinities and in its right half Herakles himself, complete with lion's skin, club and quiver raising his hand in joy shouting *Zeu phile* = dear Zeus. One of the earliest instances of gilding applied to clay occurred on the plastically raised pomegranates carried on a branch by one of the Horai, though the gilt has not survived. Underneath the handle to the right of side B the head and neck of a woman in outline

within a reserved circle, a representation of Selene, the Moon.

Inside picture (plate 118). Achilles tending the wounded Patroclus. Both heroes have their names inscribed. Achilles is kneeling on the right and putting a white bandage on the left upper arm of his friend and comrade Patroclus with extreme solicitude and tenderness. He is dressed in a transparent chiton with elaborate folds and a scale corslet, also a scale helmet of the Attic type with hinged cheek pieces which are turned up. The crest is secured by a joint, decorated with pomegranates. He wears sandals. Patroclus is seated on a shield which has a tripod as shield device. He is shown almost frontally, his left leg pressing against the tondo frame in agony. His right is doubled under his thigh, so that the shin and foot are seen frontally. Note that this is the exact counterpart to the lower leg disappearing behind the thigh which we have seen in works by Euphronios (plates 111 and 114). He is dressed and armed very much like Achilles except that he has discarded his helmet but kept on a felt scull cap which would act as a pad for the metal helmet. He grasps his left upper arm to ease the pain, his head is slightly inclined looking away from the wound, his teeth (in white) are showing, the sign of suppressed pain. Remarkable drawing of eyes which are wide open in pain or solicitude. Both heroes have side whiskers, Patroclus a moustache and short beard as well. To the left an arrow stuck in the ground, probably the arrow withdrawn from the wound. This remarkable and famous painting in its detailed drawing which even goes as far as the skin folds on the toe joints reminds one of Euphronian elaboration.

The comradeship and solicitude displayed in this picture is perhaps a commentary on the period which was the heyday of the use of love names. There is no precise allusion to any particular event in the *Iliad*.

For the relationship of Euphronios and Sosias, the potter of this cup (he may of course have been the painter too and therefore be the Sosias Painter), we note a graffito scratched on the foot of a bowl found in the Athenian Agora, *Sōsias katapygōn. E[uphron]ios phēsin ho grapsas* = Sosias is a lewd so-and-so says Euphronios the writer of this, if indeed the names refer to the ones we know. C. 500 B.C.

Bibl.: FR, III, p. 13 ff. Perrot-Chipiez, X, pp. 505–9. Pfuhl, fig. 418. Hoppin, II, p. 423. Swindler, figg. 310, 315. Buschor, *GV*, p. 149. Beazley, *ARFVP*, p. 21, no. 1. Richter, *Survey*, p. 57. Rumpf, p. 73, pl. 20, 5. Bloesch, *Formen*, p. 55–6. Greifenhagen, *Antike Kunstwerke*, pl. 56–7. For the Agora graffito see Beazley, *Potter and Painter in Ancient Athens*, London 1946, p. 20; also Milne and von Bothmer in: *Hesperia*, XXII, 1953, p. 218, with Ed. Fraenkel, in: *Glotta*, 34, 1955, pp. 42–5.

119–128, XXX, XXXI THE KLEOPHRADES PAINTER

He is one of the greatest artists of the late archaic period, that is about 500–480 B.C. The name of the potter Kleophrades occurs on a very fragmentary cup in the Cabinet des Médailles (535; 699) with Herakles and the Amazons. The signature continues with the fragmentary name *Amas—*, to be followed after an interval by another letter. The whole has been restored to mean Kleophrades made it, the son of Amasis. If the restoration is right, Kleophrades the potter would presumably be the son of the Amasis we know as the great black-figure potter. To the painter of these cup fragments, the so-called Kleophrades Painter, more than hundred vases have been assigned. We probably even know his real name, because on a late and rather weak work of his, a pelike in Berlin, we find the painter's signature of Epiktetos *(Epiktetos egrapsen)*. The most natural explanation is probably the true one, namely that the Kleophrades Painter's name is Epiktetos, and that he happens to have the same name as the cup painter Epiktetos whom we have met previously (plates 96–98). There are of course other explanations possible, such as a forged signature of the cup painter, but this is not very plausible in this instance, though there are cases on Attic vases where just this is likely to have happend. Nonetheless we still call our painter the Kleophrades Painter to avoid the more cumbersome name Epiktetos II. He decorated a variety of shapes, amphorae, neck amphorae, a pointed amphora, a rare shape (plates 122–124; for another example by a later painter see plates 158–9), black-figured Panathenaic amphorae, a loutrophoros, pelikai, a good number of calyx-kraters, volute-kraters, stamnoi, three psykters, hydriai and five cups. He likes large shapes on which he can develop his broadly conceived figures. His subjects are the usual ones for the time, many athletic scenes but also the myths of Theseus, Herakles and Dionysus. He is a pupil of Euthymides and indeed some of his early works are difficult to distinguish from those of his master. He shares with him the grandness of design and the strength of his lines, but he gives in addition to it a pathos and dramatic intensity of feeling which is unrivalled for his time. His work comes after the pioneer period and the experimental poses and daring foreshortenings or three-quarterings of a Euphronios or even a Euthymides, though not absent in his work, no longer interest him in the same way. Amongst the criteria of his style

are the brown (not black) circle-and-dot for the iris and pupil of the eye, a large, strong and often slightly aquiline nose with rounded line for the nostril, the black edging of lips, with a fossette at the corner. He is also interested in giving depth to his composition as can be seen on the London stamnos with Theseus and the Minotaur or the Vivenzio hydria in Naples (plate 125). It is, however, the powerful pathos of some of his pictures which has caused one scholar to say that here more than anywhere else can we sense something of the ethos of the great fresco paintings by Polygnotos of Thasos. The active life of our painter is from about 500 to a period beyond the eighties of the 5th century. Amongst his earlier works are the cup fragments in the Cabinet des Médailles mentioned already, the Tarquinia calyx-krater (plates 119–121) and also the pointed amphora in Munich (plates 122–4). The Vivenzio hydria in Naples (plate 125) and the Louvre loutrophoros (plates 126–8) are rather later works of his, though powerful enough. In his latest works after 480 B.C. such as the Berlin pelike, mentioned before, his strength and power seem however to have left him.

Bibliography: Hartwig, *Meisterschalen*, p. 400 ff. FR, I, p. 262 ff., II, p. 228. Beazley, in: *JHS*, 36, 1916, p. 123 ff. Pfuhl, II, p. 435 ff. Beazley, *Der Kleophrades-Maler*, Berlin 1933. G. M. A. Richter, in: *AJA*, 1936, p. 100 ff. Den Tex, in: *AM*, 62, 1937, p. 38 ff. Beazley, *ARFVP*, p. 120–9. Richter, *Survey*, pp. 66–68. Beazley, in: *Antike Kunst*, I, 1958, p. 6 ff. L. Schnitzler, in: *Opuscula Atheniensia 2*, 1955, p. 47 ff.

119–121

CALYX-KRATER by the Kleophrades Painter. Tarquinia, Museo Nazionale, RC 4196. From Tarquinia. Intact but some surface damage. Height 45 cms (17³/₄"). Diam. of mouth 48 cms (18⁷/₈").

The shape of the krater is less squat than the Euphronios krater (plate 108) but the diameter of the mouth and therefore the breadth is still somewhat bigger than the height. This will change later, see for instance plate 173, the Niobid Painter's calyx-krater in the Louvre, where the height is much greater than the breadth. Rounded lip. On the ledge underneath we have on side A a frieze of red-figured enclosed palmettes, on B a frieze of alternately up- and downpointing black-figured palmettes linked by spiral tendrils. Underneath the picture we again have distinction between A and B. On the main face A we have a T-meander, on B a simple continuous meander. Black tongues immediately above the base.
Side A (plate 120 and 119, right). A youth naked and wreathed holds a discus with both hands whilst swinging his left leg during the throw. To the right a young trainer, beardless and with his back to us, is turning to him probably to give instruction. He is dressed in a himation and holds the usual forked hazel twig, the wand of the trainer. On the right a pick stuck in the ground. It would be used to loosen the soil for jumping or wrestling. Inscription in front of the trainer, *kalos ei* = you are beautiful. Note on plate 119 right the details of draftmanship, the main outlines of chest and the lower abdomen are in the black relief line but details of the musculature between the chest and navel as well as the ribs are in a brown diluted glaze.
Side B (plate 121 and plate 119 left). A trainer with himation and two-forked twig. In front of him the inscription, *kalos ei*, as on side A. Then a frontal athlete putting his finger into the throwing loop of a javelin and steadying the tip with the other hand. Since his right foot is practically off the ground, it is evident that he is about to begin his run for the throw. Behind him a pick.

An early work of the best period of the Kleophrades Painter. C. 500–490 B.C.

Bibl.: E. N. Gardiner, *Greek Athletic Sport*, p. 324, fig. 78. E. N. Gardiner, in: *JHS*, 1907, p. 16, fig. 5. Pfuhl, III, fig. 375. Beazley, *Der Kleophrades-Maler*, Berlin 1933, p. 10, pll. 16–8. Idem, *ARFVP*, p. 123, no. 32. *CVA*, Tarquinia, fasc. I, p. 4, pl. 15. Beazley and Caskey, *Boston Vases*, II, Oxford 1954, p. 4 (for attitude of the javelin-thrower).

122–124, XXX, XXXI

POINTED AMPHORA by the Kleophrades Painter. Munich, Museum Antiker Kleinkunst, 2344. From Vulci. Formerly in the Canino Collection. Repaired in antiquity; in good condition. Height 56 cms (22").

This is a rare shape for a decorated vase though it was common for the plain pottery containers of wine and oil. It required a stand to remain upright safely. As a miniature vase in clay or glass the shape is used as scent bottle. At junction of neck and shoulders black tongues. Under the figures a so-called labyrinth meander with saltires. At the bottom, black rays rising from the base.
Side A (plate 123). Main picture. Dionysus dressed in chiton and himation with a panther's (leopard's) skin thrown over his back and knotted across his neck, is proceeding to the right but looking back behind him (plate XXX, detail). He holds an empty metal kantharos in his hand. Diluted glaze is used for the animal skin as well as for the metallic sheen of the kantharos. In his left hand the god holds a vine branch with leaves and bunches of grapes. Purple for the leaves. The grapes are outlined with incision. On either side of him are two junonesque menads carrying a thyrsus (fennel stalk crowned with an ivy-cap). They use it to ward off the attacks of satyrs, one of whom comes out from under each of the two handles. The menad on the right wears her hair in a sakkos and is using the butt end of the thyrsus to jab where it hurts; she has also taken hold of the satyr's arm; evidently the satyr is in greater danger than the menad. On the left of Dionysus a similar scene, though the satyr is in less immediate difficulties. The menad has a dappled deer

skin thrown over her dress (deer skins are also worn by all the satyrs on this vase) and in her left she holds a snake which hisses at a satyr, who has taken hold of her thyrsus and wants to lay hands on her person. She moves away haughtily looking back over her shoulders.

Side B. A lyric scene and pendant to the front of the vase. An ithyphallic satyr whose body and face are seen frontally is playing the flute. On his either side a menad in ecstacy steps away. The one on the left (plate XXXI) is fair-haired (done in dilute) purple wreathed and blue-eyed (dot within a circle). Her lips are barely parted, her walk is feathery as she muses, forgetful of the snake which has curled round her left arm. She has sloped her thyrsus. A dappled deer skin is over her dress. The other menad on the right (plate 124) is of a different mood, black-haired, curly and dark-eyed she has thrown back her head and opened her lips in a wild shout whilst she heaves herself away with her right foot which is seen frontally. In her ecstacy she almost twists the thyrsus. In front of her face is written *kalos* in front of the other menad, *kalē*, that is 'beautiful' in the masculine and feminine genders.

We have noted already the use of dilute often worked up into several shades for hair, deer skin, serpent's body and metal and also for the ripple of the folds on the chiton. Purple is used for the wreaths, the vine leaves and details of the serpent. There are traces of the preparatory sketch.

Neck pictures. Athletes. On A (plate 123) they hold javelins and discus. A discus and a pick are on the ground. On B (plate 122) again javelins. The youths on the two sides are putting their fingers into the throwing loop. The athlete in the middle is holding a discus shown head on, narrow side facing. Picks on the ground. On high between the middle and the right athletes are suspended a sponge bag and an aryballos containing oil for anointing.

An early work of his mature period and one of his masterpieces. C. 500–490 B.C.

Bibl.: Jahn, no. 408, p. 139. Beazley, *Der Kleophrades-Maler*, pp. 12, 23, no. 5, pll. 3–6. Pfuhl, fig. 379. Buschor, *G Vsm*, pp. 166 and 170. Lawler, in: *Mem. Amer. Acad. Rome*, VI, 1927, pp. 102, 106. Swindler, p. 178. Buschor, *GV*, p. 169. Beazley, *ARFVP*, p. 121, no. 5. Lullies and Hirmer, *Griechische Vasen Reifarchaischer Zeit*, p. 15 ff., pll. 36–47. *CVA*, Munich fasc. 4 (Lullies) p. 26, pl. 199. R. Lullies, *Die Spitzamphora des Kleophrades-Malers*, Bremen 1957. (On p. 18 he notes that the earliest reports mention a stand which was found with the amphora).

125

HYDRIA by the Kleophrades Painter. Naples, Museo Nazionale, 2422. From Nola. Formerly in the Vivenzio Collection. In perfect preservation. Height 42 cms (16¹/₂").

On outer ledge of mouth, above and on the side, tongues. On the neck above the figure zone a frieze of linked spirals. Below the figure zone, tongues and after a narrow interval side-sloping linked double palmettes, which encircle the middle of the pot at the level of the side handles.

The picture which covers the neck and shoulders only shows the destruction of Troy (Ilioupersis). In the middle an altar on which Priam has taken refuge (plate 125 upper picture). He is dressed in chiton and himation. His garments

and head are smeared with blood. He covers his face and clutches his head in horror. On his lap is flung the lifeless, naked, bloodstained and much pierced body of his grandson Astyanax, the son of Hector. In front of him is the huge figure of Neoptolemos, the son of Achilles, who is about to slay Priam on the very altar. Neoptolemos is seen in rear-view (note the interesting back-view of his right leg which also occurs elsewhere in this painter's work) in full panoply, Attic helmet with hair piece, leather corslet (note the lion's head decorating each shoulder piece) and greaves. His sword (not visible on plate 125 owing to the overhanging mouth of the vase), enormous and almost a butcher's knife, is no doubt the so-called *machaira* (observe its huge scabbard). At his feet is a dead Trojan, at least we take him to be a Trojan, one who had had time to snatch up a shield and put on greaves and corslet despite the surprise of the night. Note the perspective inside view of the shield, and the lower leg disappearing behind his thighs, a motif which we found in the work of Euphronios. Further to the right we see the remarkable figure of a Trojan woman who has snatched up a pestle and uses it against a Greek attacker who has to duck quickly and take cover behind his shield. Note again the perspective drawing for the inside of the shield and the foreshortened front view of his left thigh and foot. Even further to the right and no longer visible in our picture is a group known from other representations too, of Akamas and Demophon, the two sons of Theseus who were amongst the besieging Greeks, finding their grandmother Aithra. She had been taken to Troy with Helen. Aithra is seated on a low block and one of her grandsons is raising her up. On the extreme right a young girl is sitting low on the ground and mourning. Such figures are known to occur on *prothesis* scenes, of which the Kleophrades Painter did at least one (pl. 126–8). This, then, and perhaps some of the other motifs for mourning on this vase, will have come from such a background.

We turn now to the left part of the picture (plate 125, lower picture), starting again from the altar where Priam has taken refuge. Immediately behind this altar a palmtree bent by the storm of misfortune. Below it a Trojan woman mourning. Then follows the Palladium, the ancient statue of Athena, who is represented in the Promachos type, with wooden, rather archaic features, which become usual in the depicting of cult statues. At her feet on the farther side another Trojan woman cowering in fright. In the foreground we see Cassandra the prophetess daughter of Priam taking refuge at the image which she clasps with her left hand. She is naked but for a mantle knotted round her neck and she has been seized by her hair by the Lesser Ajax, the son of Oileus, no respecter of sanctuary. At Ajax's feet another slain Trojan lying on his back, bloodstained, mouth open and eyes glazed. He too is fully armed apart from his helmet. On the extreme left we see old Anchises with stubble beard and hair being hauled away by Aeneas, who staggers under the load. Beside him Ascanius, the son of Aeneas. Aeneas is shown in back view, the crest of his helmet hangs over the shield (a snake device). All three turn for a last look.

There is much that is new in the iconography of this vase,

perhaps the greatest of all extant pictures of the Ilioupersis. The mood of despair and mourning comes out with singular immediacy. Note also the fine rendering of the nude of Cassandra. One of the later works of the Kleophrades Painter but still at the height of his powers. This Ilioupersis should be compared with that of the Brygos Painter on plate 139. C. 480 B.C.

Bibl.: P. Hartwig, in: *Arch. Epig. Mitt. aus Oesterr.*, 16, 1893, p. 114. FR, pl. 34, I, pp. 122–7. C. Robert, *Bild u. Lied*, p. 66ff. Idem, *Ilioupersis des Polygnot*, p. 72. Pfuhl, fig. 378. B. Schweitzer, in: *Die Antike* ,V, 1929, pp. 242–86, especially, p. 280. C. Dugas, in: *REG*, 49, 1936, pl. 8, fig. 7. Beazley, *ARFVP*, p. 126, no. 66 (55). Beazley, *Der Kleophrades-Maler*, Berlin, 1933, p. 27, no. 55, fig. 27. G. M. A. Richter, 'The Kleophrades Painter' in: *AJA*, 40, 1936, pp. 100–15. O. M. Washburn, in: *AJA*, 22, 1918, pp. 146–53. Beazley, in: *Antike Kunst*, I, 1958, pp. 6ff., (on the shape and date). For the theme of the Ilioupersis see M. J. Wiencke, in: *AJA*, 58, 1954, p. 285ff. and P.E. Arias in: *RIASA*, IV, 1955, pp. 105–6. Beazley, in: *JHS*, 30, 1910, p. 53 ff. For the helmet of Neoptolemos with its hair-piece see on plate 146. Aeneas-Anchises, Schauenburg in: *Gymnasium*, 1960, p. 176ff.

126–128

LOUTROPHOROS by the Kleophrades Painter. Paris, Louvre, CA 453. From Attica. Some restorations and over-painting. The vase has no bottom, in order that the contents could percolate into the grave; (cf. p. 268). Height 81 cms (31⁷/₈″). Diam. of mouth 30 cms (11¹³/₁₆″).

On lip snaky line in white underneath which curving meander also in white. A wavy line also on the sides of handle, whilst their outer surface is decorated with a snake-like curve. All this in white. In white also the rosettes on the solid area between handle and neck. Beneath the neck picture enclosed linked palmettes in black-figure. At junction of neck and shoulder black tongues below which a continuous meander. For 'chthonic' snakes, see on plate 9.

Side A (plate 126). On neck two women mourning. One of them clutches her head, the other carries a loutrophoros. The main picture shows the lying in state (*prothesis*) of a young man who has died (plate 128, detail). His eyes are shut, he is wreathed and a band passes under his chin to keep his mouth closed. Round about the couch four women in gestures of mourning or busy about the dead body.

Below a subsidiary frieze in Black-figure. Horsemen raising their arms in valediction. For their costume see the introductory note on Psiax (p. 304).

Side B. On neck same subject as A but a little more restored (plate 127). On the body five young men with their right arm outstretched in mourning, palms turned upwards.

One of the later works of the painter, c. 480 B.C. or shortly after. For the purpose of the shape see on plate 129.

Bibl.: M. Collignon, in: *Mon. Piot.*, I, 1894, pp. 49–60. Ducati, *Ceramica Greca*, II, pp. 363–4. Leonard, in: *RE*, s.v. Kleophrades-Maler, p. 803 (XI, 1). W. Zschietzschmann, in: *AM*, 53, 1928, p. 45, no. 109. *CVA*, Louvre fasc. 8 (Pottier) III, Ic, pll. 56–7. Beazley, *ARFVP*, p. 122, no. 20. On chin-bands, *ABSA* 50, 1955, p. 61, n. 83. The white 'chthonic' snake-lines are also found on wedding Loutrophoroi (see on pl. 129)!

129

LOUTROPHOROS-HYDRIA BY THE PAINTER OF BOLOGNA 228. Athens, National Museum, 1170. From Pikrodaphni (Phaleron). Poor state of preservation; frag-

mentary; much of the glaze has deteriorated. Height 93 cms (36⁹/₁₆″). Diam. of mouth 32.5 cms (12¹³/₁₆″).

Shape and decoration of lip similar to plate 126. The arrangement of handles is however different, only one tall upright one from shoulder to top of neck, and two shorter ones, one on each side, rising from and returning to the shoulder. Above the main figure scene, remnants of palmettes, underneath figure scene meander with checkers.

On neck (not shown) four mourning women dressed in peplos, two of whom tear at their hair, whilst the others wear it short in mourning.

Face A. On body of vase the lying in state (*prothesis*) of a young woman. She lies on a couch, her head resting on a pillow; her long hair is encircled with the bridal crown. Her mouth is open despite the head band which passes under her chin. Behind her an old woman dressed in a peplos, her nurse surely, puts some last touches to the arrangement and array of the dead girl. The nurse wears her hair short (rendered in reddish dilute, perhaps to indicate fair or red hair), her face is haggard with cheek bones showing, and skin hanging loose under a double chin, her nose is aquiline.

To the left stands another, young woman in mourning. She is dressed in a chiton with long disarrayed hair flowing down her back and shoulder. She clutches her head and hair in mourning.

Side B (not shown). Under vertical handle a cavalcade of two riders in Thracian costume (for this see the introductory note on Psiax p. 304) to the right. Then five bearded men dressed in himation lamenting.

The motive of one of the mourning women on the neck (not shown) is particularly interesting. She stands deep in misery supporting her chin with her right arm and hand, whilst the left arm comes across the body and clasps her right near the elbow. This pose is also known from elsewhere, such as white-ground funerary lekythoi and from one of the servant girls on the Berlin skyphos by the Penelope Painter with Odysseus slaying the suitors. The posture was presumably invented by one of the great fresco painters of the time, perhaps Polygnotos of Thasos. The vase belongs to the *early-classical* period, c. 470–460 B.C.

Loutrophoroi were used on the wedding day to bring the water for the nuptial bath and ceremonies (see also plate 203, top picture). Those vases were decorated accordingly. Loutrophoroi were however also used for placing on the tombs of those who died before wedlock. Hence the decoration on this vase. The girl is shown crowned for the wedding. The water in the loutrophoros will give her in Hades what she never had in life. The vase on plates 126–8 was no doubt used on the tomb of a young man, also unwed.

Bibl.: Collignon-Couve, n. 1167. Perrot-Chipiez, X, pl. 18. Buschor, *GV*, p. 182. Idem, *Grab eines attischen Mädchens*, p. 17. Swindler, fig. 322. Beazley, *ARFVP*, p. 336, no. 11. *CVA*, Athens, Nat. Mus. fasc. 2 (Karouzou), pl. 22–3. Richter, *Survey*, p. 110. H. Kenner, *Weinen und Lachen in der griech. Kunst*, Vienna 1960, p. 34–5. Zchietzschmann, in: *AM*, 53, 1928, p. 17ff. On *prothesis* see now also Boardmann, in: *ABSA*, 50, 1955, p. 55 ff. On the dead girl's bridal crown, compare Euripides *Medea*, 980–1; also von Salis, in: *Rhein. Mus. Philol.*, 73, 1920–4, p. 212ff.; Cook, *Zeus* III, p. 394, p. 372ff. (purpose of shape).

His one preserved signature on a column-krater in Athens (from the Acropolis) shows that he was both potter and painter. Most of his fifty odd known vases are column-kraters, but there are also a number of pelikai, a red-figured amphora of Panathenaic shape, a calyx-krater in London and the Louvre amphora shown here on plates 130–1. His stock column-kraters show mostly scenes from the palaestra, the banquet and revelling; but his grander vases, calyx-krater and amphorae, have mythological subjects, such as the struggle for the tripod or, as on the Louvre amphora, the Amazonomachy and one of the rare historical pictures in Greek art, King Croesus on the pyre (another such historical picture is on the Laconian Arkesilas cup, plate XXIV). Myson seems to have been a pupil of Phintias, whose rather precious gestures he makes his own. He himself stands at the head of the mannerist school of painters, which continues to beyond the middle of the 5th century. His most notable pupil was the Pan Painter (see below p. 346). His work dates to the turn of the 6th and 5th centuries B.C. and must have gone on into the first two decades of the 5th century.

Bibliography: FR, II, p. 277. D. Levi, in: *CVA*, Florence, pl. 25. Beazley, *ARFVP*, pp. 169–72. Richter, *Survey*, pp. 71–2. Beazley, in: *AJA*, 49, 1915, p. 475. Rumpf, p. 81.

130, 131

AMPHORA (type A) by Myson. Paris, Louvre, G197. Perhaps from Vulci. Restored but in good condition. Height 58.5 cms (23″). For shape see plates 150–3.

On handles an ivy branch. No panel but the figures live unconfined on the surface of the vase. There is a lower border consisting of a meander with crosses at intervals. The length of this base line is adapted to the width of the pictures; on side A it stops short of the pyre.

Side A. For the free field system of decoration see commentary on plates 150–153. King Croesus (*Kroesos* inscribed) on a rich throne with foot stool is set on top of a lit pyre. He is bearded, dressed in a chiton, carries a sceptre in his left and makes a libation from the tilted phiale (no doubt of gold) in his right hand. The flow of the wine is indicated. He wears a wreath over his carefully groomed hair. A man dressed in a loin cloth and called Euthymos is setting light to the pyre. Note the remarkable detail of perspective by which the lowest end of throne and footstool are eclipsed by the topmost logs of the pyre. No exact parallel comes to mind for this period.

This famous vase is the earliest document (apart perhaps from the name Croesus given to a young Athenian who fell in battle some time round 530 B.C. and whose commemorative statue has been found at Anavyssos in Attica) of the fascination which Croesus, the King of Lydia of legendary wealth, exerted upon the Greeks. Not until about 30 years later do we have the earliest references in literature; in Bacchylides III, an Olympic victory ode of 468 B.C., and two years earlier, in 470 B.C., an allusion in Pindar *Pythian* I,

184. (Herodotus' account, I. 86, is half a century later.) Croesus at the time of his prosperity had made splendid gifts to Greek sanctuaries in Delphi and Ephesus. Then his fortune turned and in 547 B.C. he was utterly defeated by Cyrus of Persia. He then went on the pyre, doomed to it by the victor according to Herodotus and other sources, according to Bacchylides of his own accord. Both versions agree that rain sent by Apollo extinguished the fire, though on the final fate of Croesus they diverge again. It is clear that Myson follows the story found in Bacchylides. The king's action is not done under direct constraint, his servant (Euthymos), not a Persian, is tending to the kindling, just as in Bacchylides. On the other hand no hint of Apollo's intervention to save. He ought to have appeared on side B.

Side B (plate 130). Theseus carrying off the Amazon queen Antiope, Peirithoos bringing up the rear. Antiope is in Scythian archer's costume (see plates 98; 114), which is often worn by Amazons; she carries a battle axe. Her right arm reaches out in vain appeal towards her companions, who ought to have appeared on side A! Perithoos too turns to keep an eye on them. A more complete version of this incident by the same painter with eight Amazons and Greeks taking part is found on a psykter in the collection of Signor Mario Astarita in Naples, see von Bothmer cited below. C. 500 B.C. An early work, as all his grander vases.

Bibl.: *Mon. Inst.*, I, pll. 54–5. FR, II, p. 277ff. E. Pottier, in: *Mon Piot*, 29, 1927–8, p. 178ff. Beazley, *ARFVP*, p. 171, no. 47. Richter, *Survey*, p. 71. Rumpf, p. 81. D. von Bothmer, *Amazons in Greek Art*, Oxford 1957, pp. 125, 137, pl. 68, 5, for the psykter *ibid.*, p. 125, no. 10, pp. 129, 137. Dugas-Flacelière, *Thésée-Images et Récits*, p. 62, pl. 8. For the Anavyssos kouros see Lullies and Hirmer, *Greek Sculpture²*, London 1960, pll. 57–61; see also the caution in: G. M. A. Richter, *Kouroi²*, London 1960, p. 116. A. B. Cook, *Zeus III*, p. 518ff.

132, 133 MAKRON

About 250 vases have been attributed to Makron, almost all of them cups, though three notable skyphoi are amongst his best work. Otherwise there are just one plate, one pyxis, one aryballos and two askoi.

He signed only once, on his masterpiece, the Helen skyphos in Boston. There is a fragmentary inscription on his pyxis in Athens but we cannot be sure that it was his signature. A number of his cups and all his skyphoi are signed by the potter Hierōn. In fact all but three of the thirty odd vases signed by the potter Hierōn are decorated by Makron. Many of his cups show love scenes or pictures of Dionysiac dances, revels, drinking or the palaestra. These everyday life scenes easily account for the majority of his works, though there are notable mythological scenes by him, such as pictures of the Trojan War legends, including Briseis, Paris, and Helen, or again the Eleusinian subject of the departure of Triptolemos or yet again legends of Theseus and Herakles, or the battle of gods and giants. His favourite love name is Hippodamas, which is also used by Douris. Praxiteles occurs on a cup in Munich. Of female love names Rhodopis occurs once. (One Rhodopis was also a celebrated courtesan in the early 6th century connected with Sappho's brother Charaxos). Two more women on one cup each are acclaimed, Nauklea and Melitta. Finally on the cup in New York which names Nauklea, Antiphanes is called *kallistos* = very beautiful or the most beautiful.

At his best he can draw folds of drapery with unrivalled delicacy and also catch the ecstasy of the menads' dance, though he does not reach the impetuosity of the Brygos Painter. The balance of his compositions is often remarkable and on his masterpiece, the skyphos in Boston, he manages to give under one silhouette many figures in completely harmonious design, yet differentiated so that each comes out in its own right. His work covers the late archaic period, about 495–480 B.C. and perhaps later.

Bibliography: Hartwig, p. 270ff. FR, II, p. 129ff. Leonhard, in: *PW*, s.v. Hieron. Beazley, in: *AJA*, 1921, p. 325ff. Langlotz, *Zeitbestimmung*, pp. 85ff., 110ff. Pfuhl, I, p. 467ff. Beazley, *ARFVP*, pp. 301–15. Richter, *Survey*, pp. 81–3. Rumpf, p. 88. On Hieron, Bloesch, *Formen*, p. 91ff.; Beazley, *Potter and Painter*, p. 35.

132, 133

CUP by Makron. Rome, Museo Nazionale di Villa Giulia, 50396. From Cervetri. Castellani Collection. Mended from many fragments. Height 13 cms (5¹/₈"). Diam. 32.5 cms (12³/₄").

Reserved area between handle roots. Under handle roots on one side two linked enclosed palmettes, on the other side one tilted enclosed palmette. The inside medallion is framed by a continuous meander. The potter's signature of Hierōn is in incision on the reserved inner surface of the handle and is just visible on the lower right of plate 132, *Hierōn epoiesen.* Inside picture. Dionysus moving to the right but looking back; drinking horn in his right, thyrsus in his left. He is crowned with ivy, wears a sleeved chiton and a himation.

Outside. Scenes of revelling. Side A (plate 132, upper picture). In the middle a bearded man with lowered lyre in his right and a cup in his left hand faces a girl flute-player. Behind her another man with stick and kantharos. On the right a youth with stick and skyphos.

On B more revelling. All the males have opened out their cloaks and dance. On the left a youth is advancing on a flute girl who has stopped playing and is skipping away. On the right two men wearing sandals. One holds a drinking horn and seems to invite the flute girl into his arms, the other dances more detachedly, arms outstretched, balancing a cup which is no doubt brim full. He is bald in front. C. 490 B.C.

Bibl.: Hartwig, p. 283ff. Klein, *Meistersignaturen*, no. 10. *JdI*, 1896, p. 23, fig. 3. Perrot-Chipiez, X, p. 496ff. Hoppin, *RFV*, II, p. 84. Beazley, *ARFVP*, p. 306, no. 68.

134, 149 THE PANAITIOS PAINTER (ONESIMOS)

A cup painter, he is called after the love name which occurs on eleven of his vases. Most of his cups were made by Euphronios who signs six of them (including plate 134) as potter. These are all later than the vases signed by Euphronios as painter or indeed any other vase paintings assigned to him. It is clear therefore that Euphronios continued as potter (or indeed changed over to become a potter) after he had ceased to decorate vases. The Panaitios Painter's real name may have been Onesimos, for the vases assigned to Onesimos (see plate 149) are so close to the later style of the Panaitios Painter that it is probable that we deal with one and the same person. Here too the *potter* was Euphronios.

Some thirty-five vases, mostly cups, have been assigned to the Panaitios Painter and some sixty, all cups, to Onesimos. In addition there are about twenty cups, many of them very fine, somehow connected with the Panaitios Painter; some of these may be early work of his, whilst others belong to the circle out of which he grew. These early cups have been detached by Beazley from the Panaitios Painter himself

and assigned in part to the so-called Proto-Panaitian Group, partly collected under the heading of 'probably early work by the Panaitios Painter.' The painter's favourite love name is Panaitios, who occurs on at least eleven of his vases (a Panaitios distinguished himself at the battle of Salamis, see Herodotus VIII, 82). Others are Leagros, on a well known cup in Boston with a satyr sitting on a pointed amphora which should be an early work of the painter (Leagros was one of the great love names of about the last decade of the 6th century, see above p. 323); Athenodotos too is only known to occur on early works of the painter. (Athenodotos is on other vases associated with Leagros). The other love names in the so-called Proto-Panaitian group and therefore belonging to a rather earlier period than the developed work of our painter are Krates, Dorotheos, Kephisophon and Olympiodoros. All these have been tentatively identified with Athenians who are known later in the 5th century in some capacity or other, thus there was a Olympiodoros who distinguished himself in events preceding the battle at Plataea in 479 B.C. (Herodotus IX, 21-2). However, it would be idle to pretend that these identifications are in any way secure, unless either a father's name in the inscription gives a further clue and narrows down the field, – and this occurs very rarely and then only in the middle decades of the 5th century (see on plates XXXVII and XXXVIII, XXXIX), or a name is particularly characteristic. These love inscriptions are most frequent between the last decade or so of the 6th century B.C. and the middle of the 5th; the youths referred to seem to be drawn from the prominent strata of Athenian society and several of them are known to have attained prominence in later life. It is perhaps also interesting to note that the names most familiar to us from 5th century Athens are absent, though Euaion, the son of Aeschylus the poet, is amongst them and perhaps also Miltiades of Marathon fame. Not every name need have been young. Fans and favourites grow older together.

His favourite subjects are scenes from the palaestra, the banquet and revelling, but Dionysiac scenes are common too. Of mythological subjects the deeds of Theseus and Herakles are his prime choice.

He is an outstanding artist. Sinuous but strong lines give substance and vibrancy to his figures; he is a master of foreshortening, which he uses to fine effect on his magnificent backviews of persons bending forward, a favourite motif of his. We show here a comparatively early work in the Louvre, which reveals his quality of line, particularly in his treatment of the drapery.

His work covers the first twenty years of the 5th century.

Bibliography: FR, II, p. 110ff. Beazley, *ARFVP*, pp. 212–22. Richter, *Survey*, pp. 77–8. Rumpf, p. 85. On love names in general see Langlotz, *Zeitbestimmung*, pp. 43 ff. D. M. Robinson and E. J. Fluck, *A Study of the Greek Love-Names*, Baltimore 1937, and the review of the book by Rumpf, in: *Gnomon*, 14, 1938, pp. 449 ff. Also Rumpf, p. 48–9. Lists of love names are given in Beazley, *ABFVP* and *ARFVP*. On Euphronios, p. 350, bibl.

134

CUP by the Panaitios Painter. Paris, Louvre, G 104. From Cerytri. Much restored. Gaps in the inner tondo include much of the area behind Theseus, also parts of the face and neck of Amphitrite. Further gaps in the outside pictures.
The foot is missing. It had already broken and was repaired in antiquity as is shown by a bronze pin left in the stump. Conjectured height 7 cms (2¾"). Diam. 40 cms (15¾").

On the inside of the bowl, immediately below the lip, a frieze of enclosed down-pointing palmettes. Then a broad black band followed by the large central medallion which is bordered by a meander. A meander also underneath the figure scene on the outside of the vase.
Inside picture. The boy Theseus being greeted by Amphitrite in her realm at the bottom of the sea. His protectress Athena is present. Theseus (name inscribed) is long-haired and dressed in a short transparent chiton. His sword hangs by his side by means of a baldric. He himself is kept up in the water by Triton, bearded and with a sea serpent's body, who supports the soles of his feet. Triton, whose name is inscribed, was after all Theseus' half brother also begotten by Poseidon but born of Amphitrite. Behind Theseus are three dolphins. Together they establish the scene as being under water. Behind Theseus also the potter's signature of Euphronios, *Euphronios epoiese*. Theseus holds out his right hand towards Amphitrite (name inscribed) who sits on a throne without back support, wearing sandals and dressed in sleeved chiton and himation which comes up in stacked folds over the back of her hair. She too stretches out her hand towards Theseus, the son of her consort Poseidon by a mortal woman, Aithra. In her other hand, the left, she holds a big wreath painted in white with red leaves, which she will present to Theseus. The white has now largely vanished and is not visible in the photograph. Some of the purple strokes for the leaves can be seen however on Amphitrite's right shoulder. Between the two is Athena (name inscribed) with a long snake-lined aegis which has the Gorgon's head fixed in the centre. She wears an Attic helmet and carries a spear in her left and an owl in her right hand.
This remarkable picture in which the restless ripple of the lines seems to suggest a vision under water is the earliest

version we have of a story which is known to us through one of the dithyrambs of Bacchylides (Ode 16). It was also the subject of a fresco painting by Mikon in the sanctuary of Theseus at Athens, executed in the second quarter of the 5th century B.C. Again an elaborate vase picture of the last quarter of the 5th century by the Kadmos Painter in Bologna repeats the theme. A recently acquired cup by the Briseis Painter in New York, a little later in date than our cup, has the same subject. Theseus, so the story goes, was challenged by Minos to prove his divine paternity. This happened when Theseus accompanied the fourteen Athenian youths and maidens on their voyage to Crete to be sacrificed to the Minotaur. Minos, who had come to Athens for the selection of the victims, threw a ring into the sea in mid voyage and tauntingly invited Theseus to retrieve it if he was the son of Poseidon. Theseus jumped into the sea, was received by its denizens and brought to the house of his father. There Amphitrite receives him kindly, gives him a garment and a gleaming wreath, which had been her wedding gift from Aphrodite. Then triumphantly Theseus ascends from the depths of the sea.

Outside (not shown). On A and B there are two deeds of Theseus each. On A he throws Skiron over the precipice giving him the treatment he himself had meted out to so many previously. The metal foot bath, in which he forced wayfarers to bathe his feet is also represented. On the right Theseus beats Procrustes to death with his own hammer.

On side B Herakles wrestles with Kerkyon and in the other picture he ties up the Marathonian bull. Theseus there is shown in a particularly splendid back view stooping over the bull to apply the fetters.

There is considerable contrast between the quiet solemn scene of the inside with its rippling garment folds and the violent scenes of the struggle of nude bodies on the outside. C. 500–490 B.C.

Bibl.: *BI*, 1872, p. 190. FR, I, p. 27 ff., pl. 5 (inside medallion, commentary by Furtwängler). III, p. 117 ff., pl. 141 (outside pictures, commentary by Buschor). Pottier, *VAL*, pll. 102–4. Swindler, pl. 9, fig. 300. Beazley, *ARFVP*, p. 214, no. 10. Dugas-Flacelière, *Thésée-Images et Récits*, p. 63, pl. 9. For the subject of Theseus and Amphitrite see P. Jacobsthal, *Theseus auf dem Meeresgrunde*, Leipzig 1911. Gentili, in: *Arch. Class*, 6, 1954, p. 121–5. For the new cup in New York, *Bull. Metrop. Mus.*, 13, 1954, p. 62–3. Bloesch, *Formen*, p. 71, n. 5 (Euphronios, potter).

149

CUP by Onesimos. Brussels, Musées Royaux d'Art et d'Histoire, A889. From Chiusi. Formerly in the van Branteghem Collection. Some restorations, otherwise well preserved. Diam. 24.2 cms (9½″).

The inside picture which is the sole figure decoration of the cup is framed by a meander. We see a naked girl going to wash. Her hair is short and she carries her clothes in the left hand and a bronze bucket, no doubt filled with water, in her right. She walks towards a metal basin resting on paw feet and with side handles ending in snake's heads. Inscriptions: above the clothes: *he pais* = the girl, underneath the clothes with the writing going down vertically, *kalos* = is beautiful, but in the wrong, masculine gender; for a girl it should be *kale* which is in fact found written on the bronze bucket.

Attributed to Onesimos, an artist who continues the style of the Panaitios Painter. His name is known from one signature on a cup in the Louvre. He may in fact be the Panaitios Painter. C. 480 B.C.

Bibl.: Hartwig, p. 374, no. 14. Perrot-Chipiez, X, p. 647. Six, in: *JdI*, 1915, p. 91, fig. 12. Hoppin, *RFV*, I, p. 413. Beazley, *ARFVP*, p. 222, no. 60. *CVA*, Brussels fasc. 1, pl. 1. Robertson, *Greek Painting*, p. 105. On the motif: *RA* 1933, i. p. 154 ff. On Onesimos see also Beazley, *Potter and Painter*, London 1946, p. 36; Richter, *Survey*, p. 85.

XXXII

HEAD VASE (MUG) BY THE POTTER CHARINOS. Tarquinia, Museo Nazionale, 6845. From Tarquinia. Well preserved though mended from a number of pieces. There are some gaps. Height 21 cms (8¼″). Diam. of mouth 14 cms (5½″).

This head vase has the shape of a woman's head. At the back there is a ribbon handle reaching from the lip of the mug to the back of the head. On this handle the incised potter's signature of Charinos, *Charinos epoiese*. The white of the eye done in white slip, pupils black with incised iris; high-arched eye-brows in black; purple for lips. Incision also used to indicate strands of hair round the forehead. Her hair is in a bag which is decorated with a meander pattern on its edge, with black silhouette animals (winged horse, lion, bull, cock as well as sphinx, siren and horse), and, further towards the back, with a broad hatched zone, a band of ivy and a field of lozenges. The mouth of the vase which could be thought of as a polos crown is white-slipped and chequered with black. The vase is moulded, but the mouth made on the wheel.

The workshop of Charinos is one of the earlier producers of the so-called head vases. Some five or six of these, either Negro or woman's heads, have been attributed to the same modeller and the date is about the beginning of the 5th century. Our Tarquinia woman is one of his earliest products, eyes, cheekbones and the cast of the face are still archaic. The date may therefore go back to the very end of the 6th century B.C.

The production of head vases in Attica goes on to the end of the 5th or the beginning of the 4th centuries B.C.; for a latish example see plate 202. Head vases (human shaped, including of course gods, heroes or satyrs) always stand up, on a neck or a base, for essentially they are either mug, jug or oil bottle. They must be distinguished from the rhyton in the shape of an animal's head (such as plate 142) which is descended from the drinking horn and in its most usual variety at any rate cannot stand on its own. These in turn must be distinguished from other kinds of plastic vases such as rhyton-mouthed Amazon riders or rhyton-mouthed groups of a negro being eaten up by a crocodile, or of a pygmy pulling along a dead crane. These do stand up being plastic groups.

Bibl.: E. Reisch, in: *RM*, 1890, p. 313. Hoppin, *BFV*, p. 67. Perrot-Chipiez, X, p. 749. Klein, *Meistersignaturen*, p. 215, no. 2. Pfuhl, I, p. 289 ff., III, fig. 269. Beazley, in: *JHS*, 49, 1929, p. 43, no. 2. Philippart, *Céramique gr. en Italie*, I, p. 175. Beazley, *ARFVP*, p. 894, no. 2. *CVA*, Tarquinia fasc. II, pl. 42, 1–3.

Primarily a cup painter, he gets his name from the potter's signature *Brygos epoiesen* which is found on five of the cups decorated by him. Eight more of Brygos' potter's signatures, all on cups, are known. Some of these cups are decorated by followers of the Brygos Painter such as the Castelgiorgio and the Briseis Painters, whilst two are painted in a style which has no relation at all to that of the Brygos Painter.

Some hundred and seventy vases painted by the Brygos Painter have been identified, of which more than hundred and twenty are cups, a number of them magnificent ones. We also have seven skyphoi by him including the famous ransom of Hector in Vienna, and one in the Louvre, shown here on plates 135–7, three kantharoi, nine rhyta including one in the Villa Giulia, shown here on plate 142, a few Nolan amphorae, a good number of lekythoi, three oinochai, also a plate and a few decorated kyathoi (ladles). The Brygos Painter was much imitated and a number of artists who may claim some personality of their own, such as the Briseis Painter and the Painter of the Paris Gigantomachy, must be counted as members of his circle. Love names found on his vases are Diphilos, Philon and Alkmeon, a member perhaps of the prominent aristocratic family in Athens to which Kleisthenes and Pericles belonged. Also one woman, Nikophile.

Our painter is a master of movement often violent. His figures are drawn with precise and swinging lines as can be seen from our pictures. Even the isolated figures found on some of his skyphoi and lekythoi, for all their simplicity of posture and calmness of the scene, are stamped all of them, menads, athletes, gods, with the potentiality of rapid movement by such devices as giving the body in front view moving in one direction, whilst the head is turned round violently in profile looking back in the opposite direction (see plate XXXIV). In his latest works though, some time after 480 B.C., the fire seems to have gone out of him, his style has become tired and the exuberance gone. The drapery folds no longer have the archaic tension and life but are drawn in a riper and less spontaneous way, which makes the lines seem mannered and uninteresting. His drawing of the nude gives the essentials. Brown lines of diluted glaze are used for the deltoid and leg muscles. His noses are full, expanding slightly towards the nostrils, the chin is long and powerful.

His activity extends from about 500 to well beyond 480 B.C. Fragments of a plate painted by him, with the picture of a reveller, have been found on the Acropolis. The piece was clearly damaged during the Persian destruction of the Acropolis in 480 B.C., for the fragments are burnt and were found together with pieces of marble affected by flames and charred wood. The piece therefore helps in the construction of the chronology of early Red-figure.

Bibliography: Hartwig, p. 307 ff. Langlotz, *Zeitbestimmung*, pp. 84, 99. Pfuhl, I, p. 459 ff. Beazley, in: *Papers of Brit. School at Rome*, 11, 1929, p. 19 ff. Beazley, *ARFVP*, pp. 244–56. Rumpf, p. 86. Robertson, *Greek Painting*, pp. 106 ff.; idem in: *Brit. Mus. Quart.*, 16, 1951–2, p. 19 ff. (on his late work).

135–137

SKYPHOS by the Brygos Painter. Paris, Louvre, G 156. Preservation is indifferent. Much restoration and repainting, thus on the lower part and middle of the girl on plate 137; also gaps in a number of figures. Height 19.5 cms (7¹¹/₁₆″). Diam. of mouth 23.5 cms (9¹/₄″).

Revelling at night.
Side A (plate 135). Revelling. On the left under the handle a boy crowned with ivy, and holding a big cup in his hand. Then a bearded man discarding his cloak, and embracing a girl. He has put his right arm (with his knotted stick) over her shoulders and with his left taken hold of her left wrist (plate 137). A thick wreath of wool or straw on his head as well as a fillet. His lips are parted; he talks to her; she does not respond. Then follows another and similarly attired couple of man and girl; both he and the first man are past their first youth. The two girls wear their hair long and have a fillet tied over it. They are dressed in chiton and himation with embattled borders. Under the handle on the right a boy dressed in himation carries a cup, probably full, by its foot. In his other, left hand, he holds a lighted lamp. Behind him a tree with purple foliage.

Side B (only partially shown on plate 136). A small girl in a himation plays the flute whilst a naked youth stick in hand and cloak on his shoulders dances. He wears a wreath. In front of him a girl ties a fillet over her hair. Then a wreathed man playing the lyre, head thrown back, mouth wide open, singing (his plectrum is attached to the lyre), whilst a girl with her hair in a sakkos turns towards him (plate 136); then a tree with foliage and a small flute girl hastening forward to the right.

Anatomical detail is summary, the hair on chest and abdomen is indicated, as often by our artist. A reserved band serves as base line.

A sense of great abandon comes out in these pictures. The hair is very carefully done, particularly of the women. The dotted himation recurs often in his work; see plates 138, 141. C. 490 B.C. Work of his best period.

Bibl.: Pottier, *VAL*, III, pl. 123. Hoppin, *RFV*, I, p. 137, no. 86. Beazley, *ARFVP*, p. 259, no. 130.

138, XXXIII

CUP by the Brygos Painter. Würzburg, University (Martin von Wagner) Museum 479. From Vulci. Formerly in the Feoli Collection. Well preserved. Height 14 cms (5½″). Diam. 32.2 cms (12¹¹/₁₆″).

The potter's signature *Brygos epoiesen* = Brygos made, is visible on plate 138 lower picture on the inside of the right handle. The inscription is in black letters on the reserved inner surface of the handle.

Inside picture (plate XXXIII). The medallion within the black surface of the cup is framed by meander with enclosed crosses. The girl's hair is done in diluted glaze and is blonde; purple is used for the vine leaves tied round her head and that of the youth, also for the wine disgorged.

The youth on the left is sick during the carousal, of which more is shown on the outside. He supports himself on his knotted stick with his right, his head is supported and comforted by a girl who is dressed in sleeved chiton with overfall. Her hair is short. The boy's cloak is spotted with little circles. The preliminary sketch, drawn with a hard point before the painting, has left its traces in the picture on plate XXXIII. The picture would of course be in one's eye as one sipped from the cup.

Outside. A tilted and enclosed palmette under the handle roots on each side. The subject are revellers on the march, perhaps from one party to the next.

Side A (plate 138 upper picture). In the centre a bearded and hairy reveller has spread his cloak over his back and holds it up on both sides whilst he dances heavily to the rhythm of a flute player who himself is dressed in a cloak and wearing shoes. Behind the central dancer another one who moves forward in a dancing step, left arm stretched forward, whilst his right holds up the end of a fillet tied round his head. A food basket in the field. Finally a young lyre player. At the right end of this side of the cup two more dancers, one ripely grown, the other young, step out in a rather self-centred manner, the youth flapping back his hand.

Side B (plate 138, lower picture). On the extreme left a boy looks back at the antics of the boy on the extreme right of face A. Then follow two groups of three, each centering on a girl. On the left a bearded brute has laid hands on a girl who stands cross-legged, and has pushed his left arm over her shoulder to get hold of the handle of a full cup which she has been carefully holding by the foot. She is trying to push him aside. In front of her a youth also holds a full cup by the foot whilst in his other hand he carries a knotted stick. He looks back disapprovingly at the scene behind him. His mouth is open, and he will have expressed his feelings. On the extreme right of the picture a bearded and hairy man has turned round and pushed his hand into a girl's dress, who however continues playing the flute unconcernedly. She blows hard, her cheeks are puffed up, as can be seen. Behind her a bearded and hairy man lurches forward heavily, left arm pointing forward at the last man and threatening him with his stick to keep off the girl.

The girls in carousal scenes of this nature will have been *hetairai*, which is usually translated as courtesans.

Typical work of the Brygos Painter. C. 490 B.C.

Bibl.: Hartwig, *Meisterschalen*, pp. 371, 105, no. 7. FR, I, p. 252, pl. 50. Buschor, *G Vsm*, p. 171, fig. 122. von Lücken, in: *AM*, 1919, p. 109. Pfuhl, I, pp. 365, 389–90, figg. 421–3. Jacobsthal, *Ornamente*, p. 120, no. 212. Langlotz, *Vasen Würzb.*, no. 479, pll. 145–7. Beazley, *ARFVP*, p. 248, no. 27. Robertson, *Greek Painting*, pp. 104ff. Bloesch, pl. 22, 2.

XXXIV, 143 above

CUP by the Brygos Painter. Munich, Museum Antiker Kleinkunst, 2645. From Vulci. Formerly in the Canino Collection. Mended from fragments but well preserved. Some modern restorations and repainting. Height 14.4 cms (5⅝″). Diam. 28.5 cms (11¼″).

The inside has a narrow black band at the lip, then a broad band in white slip, then again an even broader black zone which is separated from the white-slipped central medallion by a very narrow *reserved* band, followed by a very narrow black band. Inside the medallion a dancing menad with thyrsus held horizontally, butt forward. With her left she brandishes a leopard cub holding it by one of his hind legs. Her hair is encircled by a hissing and poison spitting serpent; she wears sleeved chiton, a himation fastened over her right shoulder and passing under her left armpit. A leopard skin is tied over her neck and comes down her back with the tail just visible behind her right foot. She is moving in great agitation as can be seen by the swinging corners of her himation. She has also tossed her head violently so that her hair is still trailing behind her. She may be about to swing round altogether.

There is striking use of golden brown diluted glaze for the menad's hair, for the folds on her sleeves and the inside of the chiton visible next to her feet; also for the shading of the leopard cub and the skin worn by the menad.

The picture is in white-ground technique, using relief glaze lines and dilute as in Red-figure, but the effect is of course that the figures are drawn in outline.

Outside. Side A (plate 143 upper picture). Dionysus seated on a stool covered with a leopard skin holds kantharos and vine branch. He is surrounded by menads and a satyr. The menads dance, one of them plays the castanets, the other holds a thyrsus and a jug. The satyr in front of Dionysus wears high boots and he plays the flute. Between him and Dionysus a full wine skin, with some letters devoid of sense written on it, is suspended from above.

Side B (not shown). On right and left sides of picture menads dance in ecstasy having pulled out their sleeves over their

arms ('wing sleeves'). In the middle a menad warding off the advances of a satyr.

C. 490 B.C.

Bibl.: Jahn, p. 98. Furtwängler, in: *AM*, 1881, p. 113. FR, I, p. 249. Hartwig, p. 316. Perrot-Chipiez, X, p. 711. Hoppin, *RFV*, I, p. 134, no. 72. Beazley, *ARFVP*, p. 247, no. 14. Lullies-Hirmer, *Griechische Vasen* etc., pp. 19–20, figg. 64–9. Robertson, *Greek Painting*, pp. 107–8. *EWA* I, pl. 373 (colour). On the satyr's boots (side A), see plates 230–5, bibliography. Bloesch, Formen, pl. 23, 1.

139–141

CUP by the Brygos Painter. Paris, Louvre, G152. From Vulci. Much restored, specially at breaks. Some gaps. Height 13.5 cms (5⁵⁄₁₆″). Diam. 32.5 cms (12³⁄₄″).

Purple used for fillet of Phoinix in the inside picture. White used for hair and beard of the same Phoinix, and of Priam on the outside picture. Extensive traces of preliminary sketch. Relief line used for main anatomical indications with dilute lines for musculature especially in the legs. The circles of the shields and the rings of the tripod are incised and drawn in black, no doubt with the compass, as the pivot holes are clearly discernible in the glaze (hence they were done late in the process). Under one of the handles only, an enclosed palmette with tendrils from which springs another palmette. Under the figure frieze two small reserved bands. The inside medallion is framed by meander with crosses. Some traces of gilding on helmet and corslet of Orsimes (side B) and on the tripod. On the inner side of the handle the potter's signature *Brygos epoiesen* (plate 139 lower picture, right).

Inside picture (plates 140–1). Phoinix and Briseis. An old man is seated on a cushioned chair and holds a sceptre with his left and a phiale in his right. (This is in applied clay, over which there was gilding, now lost.) He wears chiton, a himation over it and shoes. At the level of his head, between the sword and the edge of the shield the name Phoinix, written retrograde and in very faded letters, has been read. A girl in front of him called Briseis in the inscription is pouring from a wine jug into the phiale for a libation. Note the flow of the wine indicated in purple (plate 141, detail). Her left hand is raised. She wears a sleeved chiton and a himation over it. Her long hair is tucked up in the back, she wears a diadem and ear rings. A shield with a bull as blazon hangs on the wall, so does a sheathed sword. We know Briseis from the *Iliad* as the girl who had been Achilles' share of the booty from the conquered town of Lyrnessos. She was taken from him by Agamemnon, but later restored. Phoinix was the mentor of Achilles. He is resting here in Achilles' tent, perhaps whilst the battle is raging outside.

Outside. The sack of Troy (Ilioupersis). Side A (plate 139 top picture). In the centre an altar behind which a tripod. On the altar is seated old Priam, his legs convulsively pulled up. He is white-haired; the hair at the back is rolled up over a metal circlet. His hands are stretched forward trying to protect himself against Neoptolemos who brutally approaches swinging in his right arm the body of Astyanax, the little son of Hector, holding it by one of the legs. An instant later he will club Priam to death with his grandchild's body. Neoptolemos wears an Attic crested helmet,

corslet, over which is flung a wrap, and greaves. His shield has a black lion as device. From it is suspended a leather apron of which we can see the lower extremity preserved next to Neoptolemos' left knee. (On these aprons see note on plates 176–181). A spear in the background. The names of both Priam and Neoptolemos are inscribed. To the left of the altar and tripod a young woman is being led away gently by a warrior who is called Akamas. She has turned to give a last look at the horror behind her, then picking up her dress with the left hand she will follow her captor, or is it her saviour? (The motif of picking up her dress has been commonly misread as that of her carrying a spotted fillet—rather like the one on plate XXXVII—on the supposed significance of which much nonsense has been written; but there can be no mistaking of her action; see a similar representation on the right of plate 159). We would expect the woman to be the aged Aithra (see the commentary on the Vivenzio hydria plate 125). In fact she is young and the name of Polyxena is written against her. Either the Brygos Painter has got his stories mixed up or there is here a tale about Akamas and Polyxena, one of the daughters of Priam, which we do not otherwise know of. In the usual version Polyxena is sacrificed to the shades of Achilles, soon after the destruction of Troy. But here the scene is peaceful; no scowling at the girl, no drawn sword (as in the contemporary 'Sacrifice of Iphigenia' by Douris in Palermo —see page 339—or in pictures of 'Helen Regained'), rather the escape away from the terrors at which she casts a parting glance (as Aeneas and Anchises on plate 125). Only her sacrificial name makes the scene sinister, for the action befits a rescue more than a walk to death.

On side B (plate 139 lower picture) the same scenes continued. Trojans are being slaughtered right and left, naked and unprepared as they are surprised during the night. They have swords but no protective armour whilst the attacking Greeks are fully armed. From left to right: The Greek warrior Hyperos (a snake as his shield device) is about to finish off a Trojan who is already down on his right knee whilst his left is unbalanced in the air. He is desperately trying to protect himself with his outstretched left which is wrapped in his chlamys. He has a sword still raised in fight. Both swords, that of the Trojan and of Hyperos are of the *machaira* type, slashing swords. Further in the centre the Greek Orsimes strides over a Trojan who is bleeding from wounds in his thigh and right arm and whose sword has already fallen from his right hand. He is waiting for the death blow from Orsimes. Behind the fallen Trojan, though, a woman dressed in a chiton (which is so arranged that it has an overfall and a girt *kolpos*, giving a bloused effect, with the ends of the belt hanging down from her middle) is rushing up with a pestle in her hands which she will bring down on Orsimes with an axe-like blow. Here too then as on the Kleophrades Painter's Vivenzio hydria (pl. 125) the Trojan women are the only ones to show fight. Actually on this cup the woman is called Andromache, the widow of Hector, and behind her we see a boy, naked but for a cloak over his shoulders, running away out of the picture. He surprisingly enough is called Astyanax. Here too there are

difficulties, for we would expect Astyanax to be the child on side A flung by Neoptolemos at Priam's head. We may be dealing here with a different version, or, more likely, the Brygos Painter may mistakenly have put the name of Andromache's child next to Andromache herself. Continuing the description we see in the left half of the picture another Trojan woman with her hair loose and all over the place, running away.

As to details, note the rendering of the inside of Orsimes' shield, also the daring scheme in which the fallen Trojan under the handle on the left is rendered with his right leg doubled up and the left in the air. Neither this figure nor the contracted feet of Priam on side A are particularly successful. This kind of figure was not the Brygos Painter's forte. His liking for the presentation of body hair comes out in the fallen Trojan in the centre of side B where the hair runs across the chest, abdomen, thigh, lower legs and foot. This shading in diluted glaze does not come out very well in the photograph. Another kind of shading which is lost in the photograph is at the edge of the convex part on the outsides of shields. It indicates the projection.

The sack of Troy was related in epic poems now lost, such as the *Little Ilias* and the *Ilioupersis*; also there are some references in Homer. We do not know what sources the Brygos Painter used and whether his sometimes idiosyncratic nomenclature is based on these sources or are his own invention. For instance the woman with the pestle is nameless in the Vivenzio hydria but called Andromache here; also the name Orsimes is not known from elsewhere. Some of the iconographic motifs such as Astyanax's body being used by Neoptolemos as club, though they have no literary warrant as far as we know, go back a very long way, to the time of the C-Painter (see on plates 47–8), whilst others such as the woman with the pestle may be of more recent inspiration.

An early cup by the Brygos Painter, about 490 B.C. at the latest. Together with the slightly later Vivenzio hydria (plate 125) it is the most powerful Ilioupersis representation we have, though pitched in a violent key very different from the Kleophrades Painter's interpretation.

Bibl.: FR, I, pl. 25. Pfuhl, III, figg. 419–20. Ch. Dugas, in: *REG*, 1936, pll. 4, 7. Hoppin, *RFV*, I, p. 118. Pottier, *VAL*, III, p. 183 ff. Perrot-Chipiez, X, pll. 12–3. Beazley, *ARFVP*, p. 245, no. 1. For the literary sources and the iconography of the subject see T. Tosi, in: *Studi e materiali di archeologia e numismatica*, IV, 1912, p. 39 ff. also M. J. Wiencke, in: *AJA*, 58, 1954, p. 285 ff. and P. E. Arias, in: *RIASA*, IV, n.s. 1954, p. 95 ff. Shape; *Encycloped. Photograph.* ('Tel'), III, pl. 18.

For the name Phoinix inscribed on the inside medallion see R. Hampe, in: *Corolla Curtius*, Stuttgart 1937, p. 142, n. 3. For a recent discussion of the group of Akamas and Polyxena on side A see L. Ghali-Kahil, *Les Enlèvements et le retour d'Hélène*, Paris 1955, p. 112. On the name Hyperos of one of the Greeks see Caskey-Beazley, *Attic Vase Paintings, Boston*, II, p. 73, n. 1.

142

RHYTON by the Brygos Painter. Rome, Museo Nazionale di Villa Giulia, 867. From Falerii Veteres (Celle necropolis). Well preserved but some gaps and restorations. Height 17 cms (6^{11}/$_{16}$″). Diam. of mouth 11 cms (4^5/$_{16}$″).

Two-handled, in shape of a hound's head. Black skin, purple nostrils and whiskers, white nose, white hair below reserved ears, white of eye rendered. The mouth of the vase has the representation of a drinking party. We see a bearded man reclining on a mattress and pillow having a skyphos in his left hand and castanets in his right. He is wreathed with ivy. Out of sight of plate 142 there is a young man with a lyre in his right hand and a skyphos in his left. On the wall there are a food basket, stick and perhaps a flute case (visible on the other side of the handle on plate 142). Beyond the basket, and again out of sight, a lyre player reclining on a cushion with a fillet round his head. Behind him an amphora wreathed in ivy. Inscriptions in field: *ho pais kalos* = the boy is beautiful and *kalos* = beautiful.

The painting, but of course not the modelling, has been attributed to the Brygos Painter by Savignoni and by Beazley. Between 500 and 490 B.C.

For the shape see the commentary on plate XXXII *ad finem*. These rhyta are usually in the shape of animal heads though there are even more elaborate mouldings such as a group of a crocodile and negro boy or pygmy and dead crane. The plastic vases in the shape of animal heads do not in their most usual variety at any rate stand on their own, so that when they are put down the animal head comes into its own and is upright, when the vase is taken up for a drink the head is reversed but the painted pictures come into their own. Once full it cannot be set down until it is drained sufficiently to rest on its handle.

Bibl.: E. Brizio, in: *Nuova Antologia*, 1889, p. 429. L. Savignoni, in: *Boll d'Arte*, X, p. 343. A. della Seta, *Villa Giulia*, p. 63. Hoppin, *RFV*, I, p. 140, no. 96 bis. G. Q. Giglioli, in: *Dedalo*, 1922, p. 81. *CVA*, Villa Giulia fasc. I, pl. 2, III, Ic. Beazley, *ARFVP*, p. 254, no. 141. On rhyta and their origin see now H. Hoffmann, in: *Antike Kunst*, 4, 1961, pp. 21 ff. He calls our type 'animal head cup'.

143 below–148 DOURIS

About two hundred cups have been attributed to this artist, also a number of lekythoi including a white-ground one with the rare theme of the sacrifice of Iphigenia, a well known psykter in the British Museum with satyrs having games, two kantharoi, three rhyta, a neck amphora and one aryballos. He has signed over thirty vases as painter, *Doris* (= Douris) *egrapsen*, but we also know him as potter from two signatures, one (*epoiesen*) on his aryballos in Athens and a double signature as painter and potter (*egrapsen* and *epoiesen*) on the Brussels kantharos (plate 146). Douris was of course mainly a cup painter and Bloesch has shown that nearly all his cups were made by the potter Python, who put his name on three of his

cups (without the verb *epoiesen*). Other cups painted by Douris were made by Kleophrades and Kalliades, as we know from their potter's signatures, and even by Euphronios (Bloesch), but these are exceptions.

Douris had a long career and his work can be divided into three periods. In his early period his favourite love name was Chairestratos (who however goes on into the early middle period), whilst Hippodamas becomes the favourite in his mature middle period. This Hippodamas also occurs in the work of Makron, in fact is pictured by him on a cup in Berlin, and he may be the same as the Athenian general who is named in the Athenian casualty list of the Erechtheid tribe of about 459/8 B.C. (I.G.I², 929 = Tod, *Greek, Historical Inscriptions*. I, no. 26). Another love name is Hermogenes whom some have identified with the brother of Kallias, the son of Hipponicus, though the name occurs often enough. Other love names are Aristagoras, Menon, Diogenes and Pythaios. Panaitios too occurs twice as love name and in his later period we find the name Polyphrasmon, whom some want to identify with the son of the tragic poet Phrynichus who also wrote tragedies and in 467 B.C. is known to have competed unsuccessfully against Aeschylus. (For all those identifications see the cautionary remarks in the introduction to the Panaitios Painter, p.333). Also Athenodotos occurs on an early cup by Douris. This Athenodotos is also known as love name in works by the Panaitios Painter and elswhere, in some cases together with Leagros on the same vase.

The activity of Douris extends over a long period from soon after 500 B.C. to beyond the seventies of the 5th century. His early work is influenced by the Panaitios Painter but the majority of his extant works belong to his middle period, the late nineties and eighties of the 5th century, when his style was developed and mature with a certain stately and academic conservatism of form which became more pronounced as time went on. To this period we may count the cup with Eos and Memnon (plates 144-5), the 'schoolmaster' cup in Berlin, the psykter in the British Museum. To the last phase in the 470-ies and 460-ies belongs a cup in Boston with the inside picture of satyrs attacking a menad and a fine cup in New York with the inside picture of two women putting away their clothes. Whilst the outside of these cups are decorated with conventional conversation scenes the insides are fine pictures carefully done in a rounded full style and a refined calmness, paying particular attention to details of hands or drapery. To this late period belong our plates 143, below; 147; 148.

Many of Douris' works give an animated yet somehow serene picture of feasts, drinking or Dionysiac revels with some of the same motifs recurring on different vases. Beyond this however he can also devise most striking pictures both from life such as the school scenes in Berlin and from mythology as the cup with Eos and Memnon (plates 144-5), often bringing an original and new rendering to well known mythological scenes.

His output was very large and his style developed steadily, even into the ripeness of his later years when unlike the Kleophrades Painter and for that matter the Brygos Painter, he did not lose his vitality. He had a considerable influence on other painters and pupils, and in the succeeding generation his tradition is continued by the Euaion Painter, and even by pot painters such as the Villa Giulia Painter.

Bibliography: E. Buschor, in: *JdI*, 31, 1916, p. 74ff. Pfuhl, II, p. 475ff. Beazley, in: *JHS*, 39, 1919, p. 84ff. E. Pottier, *Douris and the Painters of Greek Vases*, London 1909. Richter, *Survey*, p. 83ff. Beazley, *ARFVP*, pp. 279-94. Rumpf, pp. 86-7. Cook, p. 174. For the followers of Douris see Beazley, *ARFVP*, pp. 521ff. For the potter Python see H. Bloesch, *Formen attischer Schalen*, Berne 1940, p. 96ff. Beazley, *Potter and Painter*, p. 36.

143 above

CUP by the Brygos Painter. See p. 337 above (with plate XXXIV).

143 below

CUP by Douris. Munich, Museum Antiker Kleinkunst, 2648. From Vulci. Restored but well preserved. The left handle in our picture has the potter's signature of Hieron incised in it; but the handle is alien having been fastened with lead brackets in antiquity to replace the original one broken off. Bloesch has shown that the cup was made by the potter Python. Diam. 33 cms (13").

The outside pictures of both sides have one subject, Peleus taming the Nereid Thetis to make her his wife. In the centre of side A (shown on plate 143 lower picture) we see Peleus dressed in a short chiton wrestling with Thetis who wears chiton and himation, her hair in a sakkos. Thetis had the power of changing her shape and here the lion which claws

and bites Peleus' right upper arm signifies one of her various metamorphoses before she yielded. On both sides Nereids running away with signs of distress. Some of them carry a dolphin or other fish in their hands. On the other side five more Nereids, one of whom clasps their father Nereus by the head appealing for help.

Inside picture (not shown). Medallion framed by meander and crosses within which Herakles resting on a rock holds out a kantharos towards Athena who pours wine into it. Athena is in an informal mood, has taken off her helmet and wears a diadem. In her left hand she holds the owl, and with her arm supports a spear.

About 470 B.C. The cup belongs to his late period. The figure of Athena reminds one a little of the much later Athena Lemnia by Pheidias.

Bibl.: FR, I, pl. 24. Beazley, *ARFVP*, p. 289, no. 151. Lullies-Hirmer, *Griechische Vasen etc.*, p. 24ff., figg. 80b, 88–91. H. Bloesch, *Formen attischer Schalen*, p. 98, no. 17. pl. 27, 4.

144, 145

CUP by Douris. Paris, Louvre, G 115. From Santa Maria Capua Vetere. Mended from many fragments but otherwise well preserved apart from damage in the interior medallion. Height 12 cms (4³/₄″). Diam. 26 cms (10¹/₄″).

Interior medallion. The frame consists of the so-called Dourian meander, that is one meander unit alternating with one black-packed cross or occasionally a saltire. Note the junction of the tail with the head in an incomplete meander at the lowest point on plate 145,—a likable foible in Douris. On the outside, palmette ornament underneath and on both sides of the handles. Preparatory sketch is visible. Incision is used on details of shields and arms to complement the glaze lines. Letters in purple; brown diluted glaze for details of musculature.

The cup is of so-called type C. The foot is much squatter and thicker than that of cup type B for which see the two examples on plate 143. The stem rests on a thick flat disc foot and is joined to it by a thick fillet. Above, the stem merges into the bowl without break. Above the level of the handles the contour of the bowl changes into an offset concave lip as can be seen on plate 144. Our cup is signed by the potter Kalliades within the inside medallion (plate 145).

Inside medallion. Eos, the goddess of Dawn, stoops down to carry off the bloodstained body of her son Memnon, King of the Ethiopians, who has died at the hands of Achilles, who has also stripped him of his armour. Eos is winged, dressed in a chiton and has her hair in a sakkos. The hair curls over her forehead are indicated by raised dots of glaze. Inscriptions are: *Hermogenes kalos* = Hermogenes is beautiful, on the left behind Eos; next to it another inscription which is hard to interpret, *eenemeknerine*, which Beazley has persuasively resolved into ἤν ἐμὲ ἐνκρίνη(ι) = '(Hermogenes is fair), if he counts me in among his friends'. Above and in front of Eos' head we have her name *Eos*, then the painter's signature *Doris egrapsen*. Below Memnon's head his name *Memnon* (misspelled *Memlon*). Then the potter's signature *Kaliades epoiesen*—one *l* still standing for the doubled consonant. On him, Bloesch, *Formen*, p. 134.

Eos gathered up the body of her son from the battlefield (compare Pollux, *Onomast.*, IV, 130) and then obtained for him the boon of immortality from Zeus (Proclus, *Chrest. 2*, giving a synopsis of the lost epic poem, the *Aithiopis*). Our cup is the greatest of the pictures showing the body of Memnon being borne away by his mother. On some few pictures this office of mercy seems to be carried out instead by Death and Sleep, a motive taken over from the Sarpedon story (see plate 184).

Outside. Homeric fights. On side A (plate 144 upper picture) Menelaos (name inscribed) against Paris (the name Alexandros is inscribed retrograde from right to left, starting from his face) who is scuttling off. Menelaos strides forward, sword in hand, Attic helmet on his head and a metal corslet above a short chiton on his body. Good view of the inside of his shield. Paris (Alexander) is similarly armed except that he wears a scale corslet and carries a spear. The goddesses on either side cause some difficulty. On the left supporting Menelaos we see an unnamed goddess holding a flower, she being the only unnamed figure on the cup. Similarly Artemis, who is named in the inscription, is on Paris' side. She carries her bow in the left hand and her quiver on her shoulder. Her right hand is raised in a gesture to halt Menelaos' onrush. Why Artemis should be on Paris' side is by no means clear, even though in the *Iliad* she is pro-Trojan. She also appears as protectress of Paris on a cup by the Brygos Painter in Tarquinia, if Hampe's interpretation of the scene there is correct. The goddess behind Menelaos can hardly by Aphrodite (as she is often called but only at the cost of misreading the goddesses' actions as hindering the heroes and not helping them). The last thing Aphrodite would do, is to help Menelaos against Paris!

On side B Ajax defeating Hector. Ajax fully armed with reinforced leather corslet, helmet and greaves, advances with a spear in his right and his shield in the left. Note the interesting foreshortening. Hector (misspelled *Heklor*) is naked apart from his shield, helmet and scabbard. He reels back a wound in his left chest. He has swung his great slashing sword (machaira) forward but has missed the spear of Ajax and is in fact in mortal peril were it not that Apollo (name inscribed) hastens up from behind to intervene (sleeved chiton, himation, bow, and quiver on his back). On the left we see Athena (Atheaia) on Ajax's side. She is dressed as usual in sleeved chiton, himation worn diagonally across her breast and scale aegis. She wears her helmet and carries a spear. The oddly shaped element between Ajax's shield and the reeling Hector must be the rock which Ajax had hurled against Hector stunning him.

The episodes on the outside are taken from *Iliad* III and VII, whereas the inside picture must be inspired by the lost epic, the *Aithiopis*, which carried on the story from the end of the *Iliad*. The 'pietà' of the inside medallion is moving.

The cup comes early in Douris' middle period and should date to about 490 B.C.

Bibl.: Schneider, *Der troische Sagenkreis*, p. 145. Pottier, *VAL*, p. 954. Idem, *Douris*, pp. 44ff. H. Dümmler, in: *Berl. Phil. Wochenschrift*, XI, 1891, p. 469 = *Kleine Schriften*, III, p. 359. C. Robert, *Bild und Lied*, p. 98. Klein, *Meistersignaturen*, p. 160, no. 21. Perrot-Chipiez, X, p. 530.

fig. 299. Hartwig, p. 615. Hoppin, *RFV*, p. 244, no. 19. Pfuhl, fig. 466. Beazley, *ARFVP*, p. 285, no. 70. On the motive of Hector's sword grip see B. Shefton, in: *AJA*, 64, 1960, p. 174, n. 10. On Artemis behind Paris, see R. Hampe, in: *Corolla Curtius*, Stuttgart 1937, p. 142, n. 3. On the inscriptions of the inside medallion see Beazley, in: *AJA*, 64, 1960, p. 219, rejecting Dümmler's interpretation as an obscene tag (see earlier in this bibliography). On the misspellings on this cup see Beazley, *Potter and Painter*, p. 40, n. 1. On the subject of the inside medallion (the gathering of Memnon's body) see G. E. Lung, *Memnon*, Bonn 1912, pp. 51ff; K. Heinemann, *Thanatos*, Munich 1913, p. 64, n. 2; Pfuhl I, p. 327; E. Simon, in: *Gnomon*, 33, 1961, p. 649.

146

KANTHAROS by Douris. Brussels, Musées Royaux d'Art et d'Histoire, A 718. From the Campana Collection. Well preserved, but some restoration, especially on the shield. Height 18.2 cms (7⅛"). Diam. of mouth 15.3 cms (6").

Anatomical details in brown dilute. Purple for blood stains, the strap of Herakles' quiver and the baldrics on the Amazons. Inscriptions in purple along the lip of the vase on A, *Doris egraphsen. Doris ep[oiesen]*, the painter's and potter's signature of Douris. On B the inscription *Chairestratos kalos* = Chairestratos is beautiful.

Face A. Herakles against the Amazons. He is dressed in his usual garb, the lion's skin over his chiton. The lion's head encases the head of the hero. Herakles carries the bow in his left (the curving element above his hand and bow is the lion's tail!), the quiver is slung across the body in front and he plunges his sword into the breast of an Amazon before she had a chance to draw her own sword. On her farther side her quiver is just visible. The Amazon wears an Attic helmet with her cheek pieces pulled up. It comes down to just above the root of her nose, but the part covering the forehead is given the shape of hair curls. The other Amazons on this side have similar forehead pieces and helmets (for another example of the forehead piece see the Greek warrior on the right of plate 180, the Niobid Painter's Amazonomachy in Palermo). On the left of the dying Amazon another one approaches. Behind Herakles on the right two more Amazons aim at him, one archer who is kneeling and another one who points her spear at Herakles. She carries a shield with a lion's device and is the only one to have a corslet.

Side B (not shown). Telamon, a bearded warrior with a large shield (a goat as device), plunges his sword into the breast of an Amazon who is down. On the right another Amazon against a Greek warrior. She holds her bow in her left. On the left two more Amazons, one with shield and a spear, the other with bow and battle axe. C. 490–480 B.C. On the singular shape, Beazely, *Potter and Painter*, p. 40.

Bibl.: C. Robert, in: *RE*, s.v. Douris. Klein, *Meistersignaturen*, p. 100, no. 13. FR, II, p. 85 ff., pl. 74, 1. Hoppin, *RFV*, I, p. 233. E. Pottier, *Douris*, p. 54. Perrot-Chipiez, X, p. 543 ff. Buschor, in: *Jdl*, 1916, p. 81. Pfuhl, II, p. 478. Ducati, II, p. 308. *CVA*, Brussels fasc. I, (Mayence), p. 2, pll. 5–6. Beazley, *ARFVP*, p. 292, no. 197. D. von Bothmer, *Amazons in Greek Art*, Oxford 1957, p. 139 ff. On the helmet with the hair-shaped forehead piece see, Hauser in: *Jahreshefte Österreich. Archäol. Inst.*, 9, 1906, pp. 96 ff., who collects examples (including the Neoptolemos on our plate 125), though his identification of the forehead piece with the *tettix* is disputable. For more see B. Schröder, in: *Arch. Anz.*, 1905, p. 20. This forehead piece is a refinement occasionally found on Attic helmets with nose guard. It gives the impression of hair, where

hair might have appeared on the basic type of Attic helmet which left the forehead free (as on plate 102 top). Douris was particularly fond of showing it. For an actual example compare perhaps the Attic helmet from Macedonia, *British Museum, Guide to Greek and Roman Life Exhibition*[3], 1929, p. 75, fig. 65, which in this respect is very like the helmets on the Vienna skyphos by the Brygos Painter or the helmet of Menelaos on the Boston skyphos by Makron.

147

CUP by Douris. Rome, Vatican Museum. From Cervetri. Restored but well preserved. Height 12 cms (4¹¹⁄₁₆"). Diam. 30 cms (11¹³⁄₁₆").

Outside. Palmettes under the handles. Inside, the medallion is framed by a so-called Dourian meander, a simple meander unit alternating with a black-packed cross. Notice the suture where the starting point meets the end at about 5 o'clock of the roundel. Purple and white for the foliage in the inside picture.

Outside on both A and B (not shown) youths holding sprays in conversation with bearded men. One of the youths has in his hands a spray of unusual size which terminates in a palmette. The character of the scene is presumably amorous. Hartwig many years ago assigned a number of late Dourian cups to the painter of this cup, whom he called the Master of the Spray (*Meister mit der Ranke*) who however is none other than Douris.

Inside picture. Jason and the dragon which guards the Golden Fleece. Athena watches sympathetically whilst the dragon disgorges Jason, head first. She is dressed in sleeved chiton, himation and aegis which comes down her back, as can be seen by the snake edges. A Gorgon's head is placed in the middle of the aegis. She wears an Attic helmet decorated with a black sphinx. Note that her chiton and himation below the knees have been badly repainted in modern times. She leans against her spear which is planted with the pointed rear end (the *sauroter*) in the ground. In the background we see the tree on which the Golden Fleece hangs.

The version in which Jason was first swallowed by the guardian dragon is not otherwise known.

A late work by Douris, 480–470 B.C.

Bibl.: *Mon. Inst.*, II, pl. 35. Hartwig, p. 667 ff. Pfuhl, fig. 467. Hoppin, *RFV*, I, p. 289, no. 102. Beazley, *ARFVP*, p. 286, no. 93. For a discussion of Jason and the dragon on this cup see L. Radermacher, *Mythos und Sage bei den Griechen*[2], Vienna 1938, p. 204.

148

CUP by Douris. Paris, Bibliothèque Nationale, Cabinet des Médailles, 542. Restored with repainting in several places. Height 12 cms (4¹¹⁄₁₆"). Diam. 31 cms (12¼").

Interior medallion framed by a zone of two meander units alternating with a cross. Outside, palmettes below and on the side of the handles.

Inside medallion (not shown). Hera and Prometheus. The goddess (name inscribed) is seated on a chair with straight back. Her himation covers her head and hair which is within a sakkos. She holds her sceptre in her left and in her

right she has a phiale. In front of her stands Prometheus (inscribed *Promethes*) sceptred and with diadem.

Outside picture. Side A (plate 148 lower picture). Return of Hephaistos. In the left half of the picture we see Dionysus leading Hephaistos by the wrist. Hephaistos is dressed in a short chiton over which he wears a chlamys. His lameness is not indicated. On his head he wears a close-fitting round cap which is often worn by workmen; on his shoulders he has a large double-headed hammer. He is followed by a satyr who carries some more of the smithy's equipment, a narrow hammer on the shoulders and fur-lined bellows in his right hand with the pumping ends trailing on the ground. In the middle of the picture in front of Dionysus a splendidly successful menad whose swirl of garment shows that she has just pirouetted with her arms outstretched and hands holding castanets. Then follows a satyr, bending under the weight of a full lug-handled bell-krater. In his right he holds a drinking horn, another drinking horn is held by Dionysus. The procession is led by a flute playing satyr wearing animal skin and high boots. His instrument case hangs from his left arm.

Side B (plate 148, upper picture). Revels. A group of men and youths dance round each other perhaps to see who spills least from the brim full cups. In the middle a man and youth carrying a cup each (the cup seems to be of type C) cavort about each other. On their left two more come up to join them, one of them holding a skyphos also full, the other playing the lyre. On the right two others capering, one of them holds a stick in one hand and the cup (empty?) in the other. Late work by Douris, about 470 B.C.

Bibl.: de Ridder, *Cat. Cab. Méd. Mon. Inst.*, V, pl. 35. Reinach I, p. 141. E. Braun, in: *BI*, 1846, p. 115. Hartwig, p. 672 ff. Kretschmer, *Vaseninschriften*, p. 192. W. Eldridge, in: *AJA*, 1917, p. 43, n. 8. Hoppin, *RFV*, I, pl. 285, no. 84. Beazley, *ARFVP*, p. 287, no. 113. Idem, in: *AJA*, 64, 1960, p. 219 (on the inside medallion). For the bellows of Hephaistos compare Polion's volute-krater from Spina, Alfieri-Arias-Hirmer, *Spina*, pl. 111. For the satyr's boots (side A), see on plates 230-5, bibliography.

149

CUP by Onesimos, see p. 335 above.

150-157, XXXV THE BERLIN PAINTER

This artist, named after his great amphora in Berlin (plates 150-3), sprang out of the school of Phintias and Euthymides, the late-6th century masters of detailed analysis of the human frame and the exploration of movement and foreshortening. His earliest work is now more clearly recognized through recent research by Professor Martin Robertson who has shown that the fine cup in Athens, signed by Phintias as potter, is his work as well as two pelikai which had been grouped together as works of the Vienna Painter, who however is none other than the very early Berlin Painter. One of these two pelikai is the well known one in Vienna with the slaying of Aegisthus. Accordingly the Berlin Painter's beginnings go back into the final years of the 6th century. He had a long career and well over 200 vases have been attributed to him. In his developed phase he liked large shapes; he is a pot painter, though a few cups have now been assigned to his earliest period. Other shapes are amphorae, including red-figured amphorae of Panathenaic shape, neck-amphorae of different types including so-called Nolans of which he was one of the earliest decorators, some pelikai, all varieties of krater, calyx-, bell-, volute- and column-kraters, many stamnoi; also hydriai, oinochoai, plates and numerous lekythoi. He also is known to have painted black-figured Panathenaic amphorae. In many of his pictures he uses one figure compositions, against the black background without any frame or panel.

His mythological pictures include the Dionysiac circle, the heroes Herakles, Achilles, Penthesilea and of gods, particularly Apollo, Poseidon, Zeus and Athena. Beside these his favourites are athletes, again as isolated figures against the black background.

He very rarely indeed uses love names, and then only in his early period. Sokrates and Nikostratos occur three times altogether in his works and Krates twice, on a cup fragment in Florence and the Gorgos cup from the Athenian Agora, both being according to Robertson very early works of the painter. An oinochoe with the love-names of Alkmeon and Nikostratos has recently turned up (see *Auktion XXII* of 13.5.1961, Münzen und Medaillen. A.G. Basle, no. 164).

The bodies of his figures are taut with muscles and sinews, yet slender and long limbed. Such are the satyrs playing the lyre on an amphora of Panathenaic shape in Munich or the Herakles in the tripod struggle on an amphora of similar shape in London, or again the youth on a neck-amphora with twisted handles (E 265) also in London or again the satyr playing the flute on a stamnos in Castle Ashby. On all

343

these the markings and musculature largely painted in dilute, are closely knit and taut with implied movement. His figures are tensed even when apparently in repose. This has led some scholars to connect his style with Epiktetos. The truth, however, is that his masters were the great explorers of movement and anatomical analysis, Euthymides and Phintias.

The frame of his figures can also be compared with contemporary sculpture of the early years of the 5th century B.C. His career ranges from the latest 6th century down to the seventies of the 5th century or even later, the peak years being the first twenty years of the century. He is thus essentially a late-archaic artist; in his latest works of the seventies and beyond the tension has gone out of his figures as well as the loving care which went into his earlier paintings. Some of these very late vases may in fact be school pieces. His style with many of his characteristics of line and notation is continued in the next generation by able pupils such as Hermonax and the Providence Painter and even later towards the middle of the 5th century by the Achilles Painter.

His work may perhaps be seen as the successful incorporation of some of the formal discoveries of contemporary sculpture into the experience and tradition of vase painting.

Bibliography: Beazley, in: *JHS,* 31, 1911, p. 276 ff.; 42, 1922, p. 70 ff. Idem, in: *Pap. Brit. Sch. Rome,* 11, 1929, p. 20 ff. FR, III, p. 77 ff. Pfuhl, II p. 487 ff. FR, III, p. 255 ff. Beazley, *Der Berliner Maler,* Berlin 1930. Idem, *ARFVP,* p. 131 ff. E. Paribeni, in: *Enc. dell'Arte classica,* s.v. Beazley in: *Hesperia,* 28, 1959, p. 106. K. Peters, in: *Arch. Anz.,* 1950, p. 10 ff. n. 1–2. D. von Bothmer, in: *Dartmouth Alumni Magaz.,* June 1959. For his early work see C. M. Robertson, in: *JHS,* 70, 1950, p. 23 ff. Idem, in: *AJA,* 62, 1958, pp. 55 ff. (on the Gorgos cup from the Athenian Agora).

150–153

AMPHORA (type A) by the Berlin Painter. Berlin, Ehemals Staatliche Museen, F2160. From Vulci. Mended from many fragments. During storage in the Second World War and afterwards some fragments on the face of the satyr on side A (plate 153) have flaked off and been partially lost. Height 69 cms (27^1/$_8$″). Max. circumference 138 cms (54^5/$_{16}$″). The inside of this amphora is also lustrous black, not the diluted brownish wash usually found on the insides of this shape.

Side of handles decorated with double ivy; on the narrow between the handles a zone of double ivy and berries. As groundline for the figures there is a bar of linked spirals. The lid belonging to this vase has a pomegranate knob, as on pl. 87.

Side A (plate 151; also detail on plate 153). Hermes and the satyr Oreimachos. Two figures and a fawn in one silhouette. The satyr is in the foreground, long legged, with short and compact trunk. He holds a long lyre, the so-called barbiton, in his left, pressing it against his body and stopping the strings with his left. The right holds the plectrum which is attached to the lyre by a string, which hangs across Oreimachos' body. He looks back in the direction of his fellow satyr following on side B. On his farther side is Hermes, (name inscribed), with winged and brimmed hat, winged boots, and wearing a chlamys over a short sleeveless chiton. In his left he holds his kerykeion or herald's wand and a high-footed metal kantharos, in his right an oinochoe. Between them a spotted fawn with long delicate ears looks up. The main anatomical details are drawn in relief lines, the musculature and other details in dilute. Dilute is also used for the skin of the fawn, the hair of the satyr and of Hermes. Arms, jug, kantharos and satyr's tail reach out into the black from the compact light oblong silhouette in the middle.

Side B (plate 150). Another satyr called Orochares (note that

between the *r* and *e* at the end of the name, a mistaken *t* is struck out, as is visible on plate 152). He steps forward carefully because the kantharos held in his right hand unlike the drinking vessels held by Hermes, is brimful. With his left he presses the barbiton against his body stopping the strings with his left hand.

'Hermes and the Silens are frequently found together, the herald had often to pass through wild country, and it was as well for him to be on good terms with the savage inhabitants.'—Thus Beazley in 1911, later in his *Berliner Maler* he wrote: 'There are many vase pictures of the komos—the band of mortal revellers with lyres and wine-cups. This is the komos in a higher sphere; where the scene is Kyllene or some other remote and sacred place, and the revellers are the giver of the lyre, and the boon-companions of the god of wine himself.' More recently in his *Development of Attic Black-Figure* he has suggested a setting for the scene in the Return of Hephaistos. Hermes and the satyrs go on in advance to the house of Dionysus, whilst Hephaistos will follow presently after getting rid of the grime from his workshop (as in Iliad XVIII, 412 ff). See the commentary on plate 69 (bibliographical note).

About 490 B.C.

Two more type A amphorae are known to have been decorated by the Berlin Painter. One in the Louvre with Dionysos on one side and a satyr on the other is smaller and later than the Berlin vase, the other a recently acquired one in Basle with a magnificent Athena on one side of the vase about to pour from a jug into the kantharos of Herakles who stands on the reverse side, approaches the Berlin vase in grandeur and size. For this new amphora see H. A. Cahn in *CIBA-Blätter,* January–February 1961, and Beazley in *Antike Kunst,* 4, 1961, p. 49 ff. Bloesch, *ibid.,* 5, 1962, p. 18 ff. This is the last amphora type A to be shown in our plates, the shape which first came into prominence just after the mid-6th

344

century (see on plates 62–3) and which as a panel amphora saw much of the best work of the great pot painters of developed Black-figure and early Red-figure (plates 62–3 Exekias; 66–8 Psiax; 82–7 Andokides Painter; 88–9 Andokides and Lysippides Painters; 90–1 and 92–5 Phintias; 116, 117 Euthymides; compare also 55, Amasis Painter).

Towards the end of the 6th century B.C. the shape gets rare and the old-fashioned panel decoration was replaced by figures in free field, of which we showed an early example by Myson (plates 130–1). This free field system of decoration may have been previously developed for the neck-amphora and we possess some very successful examples by the hand of Euphronios and near him on neck-amphorae with twisted handles. There even the groundline is suppressed. Since the black-figured neck-amphora had by convention no panel (see plates XV; 65; XXII), experiments, when its shape and decoration were adapted to Red-figure by the development of the tall and narrow neck-amphora with twisted handles, might easily have led to this free field decoration. If this is so, the development of the twisted-handle neck-amphora would be one of the most important events in early Red-figure. (For late examples of the shape see plates 212 and 221).

The Berlin Painter is the most successful master of free field decoration and only he with his gift of making figures appear spot-lit in the black makes something thrilling out of this new way of decorating the amphora A. But everywhere now the accent is on the upsurge of the shape rather than its girth, fewer figures, but reaching higher. Where there is an upper border, as here, it sits higher than ever before to accommodate the new growth. For a successful spot light treatment on an amphora of type B see plate 188, the Vatican amphora by the Achilles Painter, a master in the succession of the Berlin Painter. Even the modernized decoration of the amphora A did not save it and by the middle of the 5th century B.C. the shape had gone out of production.

Bibl.: Furtwängler, Beschr. Vasen Berlin, no. 2160. Buschor, G Vsm, pp. 134, 138. Beazley, in: JHS, 31, 1911, p. 276ff.; 34, 1914, p. 185; 42, 1922, p. 70. Pfuhl, II, pp. 307, 363, 431. FR, III, pp. 255–6, pl. 159, 2, fig. 121 (R. Zahn). Beazley, Der Berliner Maler, p. 7, pll. 1–5. Beazley, ARFVP, p. 131, no. 1. Idem, Development, p. 114, n. 15. A. Greifenhagen, Antike Kunstwerke, Berlin, 1960, p. 13, pll. 36–39. See also Beazley and Bloesch, in: Antike Kunst, 4, 1961; 5, 1962 (apropos the Basle amphora referred to above). Buschor, Satyrtänze und Frühes Drama, Munich 1943, pp. 99–100, (Hermes as guest of the satyrs, a theme grown out of an earlier satyr-play for which there is other evidence, or perhaps sooner to be connected with the subject of the London psykter by Douris, see here page 339, where the satyrs seem to have taken the insignia of Hermes to make sport, no doubt after having got their guest blind drunk). For early neck-amphorae with twisted handles see Beazley, Greek Vases in Poland, pp. 13–14.

154, XXXV

BELL-KRATER by the Berlin Painter. Tarquinia, Museo Nazionale, RC7456. From Tarquinia. Some chips at the edge of the mouth. Some parts of the surface have fired red. Height 28 cms (11″). Diam. 28.5 cms (11¼″).

This type of bell-krater with sharply cornered mouth and lug handles is normal for the Berlin Painter, in fact normal for early bell-kraters, of which this one is as early as any we have. See also the krater of this type depicted on the Douris cup, plate 148 lower picture. The more usual shape of later bell-kraters is somewhat different, but no examples are shown in this book. Ours is footless, see on plate 160.

The pictures are in the free field, only supported by a bar of key meander of sufficient length to accommodate the figures.

Side A. Europa and the bull. A young woman moving to the right dressed in a sleeved chiton over which she wears a himation. She has bracelet and a diadem over her hair which is elaborately tucked up at the back. (The front curls are rendered in raised black dots.) She touches a rather magnificent bull by the horn. Both bull and the girl are off the ground. Dilute used for the folds of the chiton sleeves and for some internal folds, as well as for the hair ends at the back of the girl's head and for details on the bull including the curls above its forehead. Europa just before being carried off by Zeus in the guise of a bull.

Side B. A young woman in dress similar to Europa, though her hair comes down at her back in curls. She hastens forward in some concern no doubt in alarm at what is about to happen to Europa.

An early work by the Berlin Painter. C. 490–480 B.C.

Bibl.: Beazley, in: JHS, 31, 1911, pl. 10, 2; ibid., p. 283 on the shape. Idem, ARFVP, p. 137, no. 98. For the lug-handled shape see also H. R. W. Smith, in: CVA, San Francisco fasc. 1, text pp. 44–45 (on pl. 20, 1). Beazley, Vases in American Museums, p. 114; idem, Vases in Poland, p. 54, n. 4; Caskey-Beazley II, p. 50; cf. also CVA, Oxford, 2, on pl. 51, 3.

155–157

BELL-KRATER by the Berlin Painter. Paris, Louvre, G175. From Etruria. Restoration in patches including the right arm of Ganymede and an area going across his body; also part of his legs. Also repainting on Zeus. Height 33 cms (13″). Diam. of mouth 33 cms (13″).

The shape and decorative scheme are close to the Tarquinia krater on plate 154, also with lug handles. Under the figures a continuous key meander long enough to support the figures. Inside shiny black with a reserved line.

Side A (plate 156). Zeus wreathed, dressed in a himation and carrying his sceptre at the carry hurries after—side B (plate 157)—Ganymede who is playing with his hoop. He has long fair hair painted in dilute which comes down his back in a big bunch. (Note the end of the bunch coming into view behind his arm pit.) In his left he carries a game cock, the recognized lover's gift which no doubt he received from Zeus. Ganymede's main anatomical details are rendered in relief line (see plate 155 detail), whilst the musculature of the abdomen is done in dilute.

490–480 B.C.

Bibl.: Pottier, VAL, p. 194. Reinach, Répertoire, I, p. 335. Beazley, in: JHS, 1911, p. 284. Hoppin, RFV, I, p. 65, no. 41. Beazley, Berliner Maler, p. 137, no. 96. CVA, Louvre fasc. 2 (Pottier), p. 9, pl. 12. Beazley, ARFVP, p. 137, no. 96. M. Robertson, Greek Painting, p. 98. For the subject see H. Sichtermann, Ganymed, Berlin 1953, pp. 23 ff.; p. 77, no. 45. Idem, in: Antike Kunst, 2, 1959, pp. 10 ff.

158, 159

POINTED AMPHORA BY THE OREITHYIA PAIN-
TER Munich, Museum Antiker Kleinkunst, 2345. From
Vulci. Mended from many fragments; abrasions and damage
particularly at joins. Under the foot a graffito. Height 58 cms
($22^{13}/_{16}''$).

Mouth which is of rounded profile is black inside and outside but on the top edge has a reserved area. A reserved
fillet between mouth and neck; between neck and body
another fillet in purple. Under the figure zone meander with
checkers. Above the figure field, frieze of tongues. On neck
double palmette frieze (palmettes are alternately enclosed
and open). The palmettes on side A are more refined.
Side A (plate 159). Boreas carries off Oreithyia, the daughter
of Erechtheus, King of Athens. Boreas (the North Wind
personified) has spiky hair and beard (representing the wind),
overhanging furrowed brow, hooked nose, and is dressed
in a sleeveless short chiton and himation; he is sturdy limbed
and has put his arms round Oreithyia's waist having lifted
her off the ground. She wears a diadem and bracelet and is
dressed in a long chiton. The names of both Boreas and
Oreithyia are inscribed, as well as those of the other two
women on side A, on the left Herse, on the right Pandrosos.
These two and Aglauros on side B are daughters of Kekrops,
also King of Athens though strictly speaking of at least a
generation earlier. Here they are Oreithyia's companions.
Herse is trying to rescue Oreithyia (she wears a sakkos over
her hair, chiton and himation), whilst Pandrosos on the right
is running off though not without looking back. She wears
a diadem over her hair.
Side B (plate 158). Continuing behind Pandrosos we see on
the left of face B another girl picking up her chiton with her
left and running to the right (*kalos* = beautiful in masculine
gender is written next to her). Also looking to the right is
King Kekrops (name inscribed) who carries a sceptre and
wears his hair long. On the extreme right we see standing
frontally and akimbo King Erechtheus (name inscribed) the
father of Oreithyia and the focus of attention on side B. He
too carries sceptre and is dressed like Kekrops. Aglauros
(name inscribed), sister of the two companions of Oreithyia
on side A, has run up to him, touches his beard in supplica-
tion and tells the alarming news about his daughter.
(Aglauros wears a sakkos with patterned border over her
hair, a chiton with running dog lower edge and other pattern

just above it; also a himation with embattled borders.)
Pictures of Boreas carrying off Oreithyia to his home in
Thrace are very common in the early classical period, the
second quarter and the middle of the 5th century B.C. There
is no doubt that this popularity is connected with the help
which Boreas was thought to have given the Athenians
during the Persian war in 480 B.C. (Herodotus 7, 189). On
this the Athenians dedicated a sanctuary to Boreas. (Cf. Ars
Antiqua, Lucerne, *Auction II*, 1960, on no 161—Schauenburg.)
For the motif of the companions of the raped girl rushing
for help to her father we may compare the back of the
Euthymides amphora with the rape of Korone (plate 116)
where the irony of the situation on the front of the vase is
increased by the fact that Korone's companions are not
running towards her father on the left but towards the
abductor.
The painter has decorated another pointed amphora in
Berlin with the same subject, but without the elaboration
and thought-out motifs of this vase. It is an earlier attempt.
Furtwängler suggested that our picture (and that in Berlin)
might be influenced by Aeschylus, who produced a play,
now lost, on this subject at an unknown date, because the
face of Boreas with the spiky hair and beard reminded him
of a mask. A similar type of face occurs on the Berlin
amphora. The suggestion is however unnecessary; the early
classical period has a liking for the grotesque face in its
place, see plate 166, top picture, and the note below.
The Oreithyia Painter is called after the subject of this and
the Berlin amphora. He is one of the earliest masters of the
grandiose style in the early classical period and his work
dates to the seventies and early sixties of the 5th century.
About 475 B.C.

Bibl.: Beazley, *ARFVP*, p. 325, no. 2. *CVA*, Munich fasc. 4 (Lullies),
pp. 27-9, pl. 205. FR, II, pp. 185 ff.; pll. 94-5. Compare also H.
Diepolder, *Der Pistoxenos-Maler*, Berlin 1954, pp. 13-14. For the shape
see also Th. Lau, *Die griechischen Vasen, ihr Formen u. Dekorationssystem*,
Leipzig 1877, pl. XXIV, I, p. 31. Jahn, no. 376. See also L. Séchan, *La
tragédie grecque dans ses rapports avec la céramique*, Paris 1926, p. 138, no. 4.
For the 'masklike' face of Boreas compare the Lewis Painter's skyphos
in Naples; *JdI*, 71, 1956, p. 116, fig. 23. H. R. W. Smith, *Der Lewis-
maler*, Leipzig 1939, pl. 13,c. Here too the winged pursuer has hair
bristling like a porcupine's spines, the mark of a wind god? On the
other hand we should also compare the pelike in Berlin by a Mannerist,
where the dank, wig-like hair of the two dancers impersonating menads
is held to be due to the influence of tragic masks. (Beazley, *ARFVP*,
p. 397, no. 39; idem in *Hesperia*, 24, 1955, p. 312, pl. 87. Greifenhagen,
Kunstwerke, pl. 40-41). Similar Boreas on Acropolis 814, Kephalos
Painter.

160–165 THE PAN PAINTER

One of the great pot painters of the early classical period. He decorated kraters of various shapes, a good
number of column-kraters, two lug-handled bell-kraters, one of them shown on plates 160–162, the
other one being his name piece in Boston with the death of Actaeon as the principal picture and Pan
pursuing a shepherd boy on the other side; also two volute-kraters and one largely eroded calyx-krater.

Other shapes are two stamnoi, a good number of neck-amphorae, some loutrophoroi and pelikai, including the famous one in Athens with Herakles and Busiris, a few hydriai, a well known psykter in Munich with Idas and Marpessa, a number of lekythoi, some of them very beautiful, and even some cups, though none of them very distinguished. Add to these some nuptial lebetes and a red-figured amphora of Panathenaic shape. Altogether well over 200 pieces have been attributed to him by Beazley. No love names occur on any of his vases.

His draftmanship is often of astonishing virtuoso quality; he can master difficult themes such as the death of Actaeon on the Boston krater with the greatest sensitivity both for the dramatic content of the picture and its formal qualities. Nonetheless there is something disconcerting in the mannered archaism which he affects so often especially in the rendering of garment folds. This often veers into the precious, as for instance on the Marpessa psykter in Munich or the fragmentary death of Actaeon in Athens. On other vases however, such as the Syracuse column-krater (plate 165) his drapery folds are conceived in broader terms and more removed from mannered archaism. He is a pupil of Myson and is also in some ways connected with the 5th century mannerists referred to in the introductory note on Myson. However, to quote Beazley, 'he stands apart from them, his quality is incomparably finer; his choice of shape is not theirs, and it is doubtful if he sat for long in the same workshop as they.'

His activity ranges from about 480 to 450 B.C. His mythological interests are widespread and in some respects also harp back to an earlier period, in line with many of his stylistic peculiarities.

Bibliography: M. Robertson, in: *JHS*, 55, 1935, p. 67 ff. Beazley, *Der Pan-Maler*, Berlin 1931. Richter, *Survey*, p. 94 ff. Beazley, *ARFVP*, p. 361 ff. Rumpf, p. 83. Kraiker, *Malerei*, p. 58.

160–163

BELL-KRATER by the Pan Painter. Palermo, Museo Nazionale, V 778. From Agrigento. Damage at the foot, the rest well preserved. Height 35,6 cms (14″). Diam. of mouth 33.7 cms (13¹/₄″). Lug handles, see on plate 154. The shape has now acquired a foot; contrast plate 154, 156.
Under the mouth, zone of egg pattern. Under the figures a groundline of meander and crosses.
Side A (plate 160). Dionysus wreathed with ivy, dressed in chiton and himation, carries an empty kantharos in his left and a branch of vine and grapes in his right (the bunches are outlined with incision, see plate 163 detail). He is greeted by a menad who is dressed in chiton with a fawn skin passing from her right shoulder to under her right arm pit. Her hair is wreathed with ivy and she has a purple fillet over her hair. She carries a thyrsus (plate 162 detail).
Side B (plate 161). Two revellers. One of them is young, booted, infibulated, and naked apart from a wrap over his shoulders. He plays the flute. In front of him an older man, bearded, wreathed with ivy and holding a full cup raised aloft in his left hand; in his right he balances his stick horizontally aloft. A greyhound is between the two looking up towards the man.
About 460 B.C., a latish work.

Bibl.: Hoppin, RFV, II, p. 317, no. 40. Beazley, *ARFVP*, p. 361, no. 2. *CVA*, Palermo fasc. I Caskey-Beazley II, p. 50, p. 18, pl. 34.

164

LEKYTHOS by the Pan Painter. Boston, Museum of Fine Art, 13.198. From Gela. Neck restored. Some repainting on the left shoulder and breast of huntsman, also the drapery below his left hand. Otherwise well preserved. Height 38.7 cms (15¹/₄″).

At top of shoulders where the neck joins, a zone of egg pattern. Under the figures a groundline of key meander with saltires.

A young huntsman dressed in short chiton and chlamys, high boots and a broad-brimmed hat, the so-called petasos (note the strap to secure the hat), turns round to the right. He is well equipped carrying a sword in a scabbard, two spears (note his two fingers in the throwing loop) and a short club, the so-called lagobolon. His intention was to move to the left, but he has been stopped by some noise from behind or perhaps his hound, who is also looking back, has noticed something.

A fragmentary skyphos in Athens from the Acropolis by the same painter gives, as far as its preserved part goes, almost a replica of our picture; but there grasping hands, which touch the hunter's arm and shoulder, suggest that the subject was Kephalos pursued by Eos. The painter may have thought of Kephalos here too, which would explain the air of expectancy. Perhaps Eos was painted as a one-figure composition on a matching lekythos, (but not on the one, now also in Boston, which is said to have been found with this one). Lekythoi, as some other shapes, were often bought in pairs, and the decoration at times took account of this.
C. 470 B.C.

Bibl.: Beazley, *Vases in American Museums*, p. 114. Idem, *Der Pan-Maler*, pl. 24, 1 and 13, 2. Beazley, *ARFVP*, p. 366, no. 63. L. D. Caskey- J. D. Beazley, *Attic Vase Paintings in the Museum of Fine Arts*, II, *Boston* 1954, p. 54, no. 97, pl. 51; ibidem, p. 55, no. 99 for the lekythos said to have been found with this one.

165

COLUMN-KRATER by the Pan Painter. Syracuse, Museo Nazionale, 12781. From Randazzo. Well preserved apart from some chips on side B and some restorations. Height 41.5 cms (16³/₈″). Diam. of mouth 37 cms (14⁹/₁₆″).

Outer rim of mouth has double ivy in black. Neck has a frieze of intricately linked down-pointing buds in black, which stops near the handles. The picture on the body is framed above, at the junction of the neck, by black tongues, and on its side, by a bar of ivy in black.

Side A. Revellers, all young. In the middle one playing the flute and wearing high boots, otherwise naked apart from a wrap over his back. On the right and facing towards the player one with an empty cup in his left and a jug in his right. His stick is leaning against the wall. On the left another youth who has turned back, also towards the flute player. He is wrapped in his himation, stands akimbo with his left and has raised the stick with his right. Behind the flute-player we see a covered food basket suspended on the wall.

Side B (not shown). More revellers.

Late work by the Pan Painter, about 460 B.C. The drapery folds are loosely curving, the hair is fringed with little dots, a convention for curls. The outlines of the body have lost in sensitivity.

Bibl.: Beazley, *Der Pan-Maler*, pp. 17, 21, no. 13, pll. 29, 2; 30, 2. Idem, *ARFVP*, p. 362, no. 15.

166, 167 THE PISTOXENOS PAINTER

About twenty vases, almost all of them cups, have been attributed to this painter. He is named after his skyphos in Schwerin, plate 166, which is signed by the *potter* Pistoxenos (four more vases, but none of them decorated by our painter, bear Pistoxenos' signature as potter, the earliest of them being a skyphos by Epiktetos in London). Other potters with whom our painter collaborated were Megakles who signed a pyxis in Brussels, and Euphronios, who signed a very fragmentary white-ground cup in Berlin. On analogy with this cup the name of Euphronios has been restored on two more very fragmentary white-ground cups in Athens and Taranto (plate 167) respectively, where the remaining traces show that a potter's signature existed. The Berlin cup and its two probable companions must be amongst the latest works of the by now aged Euphronios. Love names occurring in his work are Glaukon and Lysis. Glaukon is known from a number of vases of the early classical period (see plates 167 and plate XXXVII for example), on some of which his father's name is given, Leagros, who himself had figured as love name on many vases in the last decade of the 6th century (see introduction to Euphronios, page 323). We know that Glaukon, the son of Leagros, was Athenian general for at least three or four yearly terms between 441–440 and 433–432 B.C. The youth of Glaukon, the time of his *kalos* appellation, should be between 470 and 460 B.C. approximately.

Some scholars including Hartwig, Furtwängler and Buschor have considered his work to be an early phase of the Penthesilea Painter. Beazley, however, and now also Diepolder have seen that we deal with two distinct personalities. There is indeed in some of their works an affinity of conception which comes out in the juxtaposition of faces, but whereas those of the Penthesilea Painter are linked to each other by the direction and intensity of gaze those of the Pistoxenos Painter are not, except in the Taranto cup, where in any case the heads are almost touching. More important still, whilst the Pistoxenos Painter has a smooth sometimes pretty style which links him with such artists as the Sabouroff Painter, the Penthesilea Painter belongs to a different school of early-classical artists, one which has conciously rejected daintiness and smooth finish in favour of a restless, sometimes sketchy line. Both painters occasionally use white-ground technique, the Pistoxenos Painter for his masterpieces the inside of four grand cups, the Penthesilea Painter on two pyxides and a bobbin in New York, but on none of his more than hundred preserved cups. The best known works by the Pistoxenos Painter are the white-ground cups in Berlin with Achilles and Diomede, in Athens with the death of Orpheus, in London with Aphrodite on a goose, and one in Taranto which we show here on plate 167; also the skyphos in Schwerin, plate 166. Some of these works show a pleasant originality of pictorial conception, occasionally achieving an almost classical tranquility. He likes giving his figures plenty of space; his roundels contain only one or two figures, again unlike the Penthesilea Painter.

The use of colour on these white-ground cups goes well beyond the stage of for instance the Brygos

348

Painter's menad cup in Munich (plate XXXIV) and linear design is now set off against solid areas of colouring. Another change. Though on his Berlin white-ground cup the Pistoxenos Painter still uses the black relief line for outlining his figures, he has abandoned it on the cups in London (with Aphrodite) and Taranto (plate 167) in favour of the golden brown dilute line which gives to the outlines a greater warmth. For the solid areas he uses several kinds of red, a brownish and a purplish variety. All this makes the Pistoxenos Painter one of the first decorators of vases who succeeded in creating *paintings*. This polychromy, later developed on white-ground funerary lekythoi, gave new possibilities to vase-painters, but its promise was not to be fulfilled owing to ceramic weaknesses. The white slip which was so effective a background for colouring, easily flakes off; moreover the colours known to the Greeks which could survive the kiln were limited in range and variety, and the full exploitation of the white background for a rich polychromy could only be achieved on vases where permanence of the decoration was not of primary importance, that is the funerary lekythoi discussed on pages 359ff. There a rich palette of delicate colours which could not have withstood the firing came to be applied onto the white slip *after* the pot had passed through the kiln, at the cost of course of impermanence. For other vases, however, where the requirements were more stringent, such as cups or kraters (see also plates XLIII, XLIV), the white-ground technique ceased with very few exceptions to be used soon after the middle of the century. As white-ground vases they invited comparison with the then increasing polychromy of the lekythoi, with which they could no longer compete.

The search after a pictorial method which would bring out the psychological state of persons even in tranquility by gestures and particularly by facial expression was one way of breaking through a certain sterility which was beginning to afflict vase-painting, making it into a series of perfect but soulless pictures. In this search our painter played a distinguished part. His work ranges from about 475–460 B.C.

Bibliography: Hartwig, p. 490ff. FR, I, p. 284. Buschor, *GV*, p. 182ff. Swindler, in: *AJA*, 1909, p. 143ff. Pfuhl, II, p. 528ff. H. Diepolder, *Der Penthesilea Maler*, Berlin 1936. Richter, *Survey*, p. 99. G. Gullini, in: *Arch. Class.*, 2, 1950, p. 191ff.; 3, 1951, p. 1ff. H. Diepolder, *Der Pistoxenos-Maler*, Berlin 1954. Beazley, *ARFVP*, pp. 574–8. Rumpf, pp. 88–9. Cook, p. 180. On Euphronios' career as potter see Bloesch, *Formen attischer Schalen*, p. 70ff.; Beazley, *Potter and Painter*, p. 25–6, 34–6. On white-ground technique see Beazley, *Attic White Lekythoi*, Oxford 1938, pp. 4–5. Philippard, *Les coupes attiques à fond blanc*, Brussels 1936. On the difference in character between the Pistoxenos and Penthesilea Painters see Beazley, *Greek Vases in Poland*, Oxford 1928, pp. 34–35. On the development of the Pistoxenos Painter and the sequence of his works see also M. Robertson, pp. 112ff. who differs substantially from Diepolder's views (of 1954). Beazley, *op.cit.*, p. 31–2 (on the quality of his white-grounds).

166

SKYPHOS by the Pistoxenos Painter. Schwerin, Staatliches Museum, 708. From Cervetri. Well preserved though there are some restorations. The back of the head of the old woman Geropso has been lost. Height 15 cms (5¹³/₁₆″). Diam. of mouth 18.5 cms (7¹/₄″).

Around and underneath the handle, palmette and floral ornament. Underneath the figure zone a meander with saltires encircles the vase.

Side A (plate 166 lower picture). Linos and Iphikles. On the left the white-haired sparse-bearded music master is sitting on a chair with finely swung legs and back playing the lyre. In the background a kithara, the more elaborate professional instrument, is suspended; also a bag and a cross-like object, which cannot easily be identified. Facing Linos and sitting demurely on a simpler stool is Iphikles who has come for music lessons. He too plays the lyre. Iphikles was the twin brother of Herakles born also of Alkmene, but fathered by the mortal Amphitryon, whereas Herakles was begotten of Zeus. Inscriptions: Linos (only the last letters are preserved) Iphikles, and the potter's signature: *Pistoxenos epoiesen*, in two lines (not quite *stoichedon*).

Side B (plate 166, top picture). Herakles (name inscribed) wrapped up in his himation, curly haired, big-eyed and surly looking comes to his lesson—is he late for it? He has a smart, sporty arrow-stick in his right, no lyre for him! That is being carried for him by his nurse a bent, toothless, white-haired, wrinkle-faced, hook-nosed, double-chinned and glaring-eyed hag, who follows him on a crooked stick. Her name is Geropso, as we know from the inscription. She is Thracian as can be seen by the tatooing marks on her throat, arms and feet. Trouble is brewing surely and according to the story Herakles will soon smash the schoolmaster's skull with a table leg or even the lyre itself.

Buschor following an earlier suggestion by Jahn considered the possibility that the picture was inspired by a satyr play, as the subject is known to have been dealt with in a rather later satyr play by Achaios, a contemporary of Sophocles. However, the absence of satyrs does not strengthen this suggestion, which yet is not impossible. The fact that the Thracian nurse is named might imply a literary source for the picture. Helbig and Hartwig wanted to read the name *Geropso* as *Aeropso* = falcon eye.

The cup is a masterpiece of characterization. Like goes with like on each side of the vase. There is difference in age yes, and it is well brought out reminding one of the subtle differentiation of physique in the East pediment at Olympia,

but there is an elective affinity between the demure Iphikles and the sallow, skinny schoolmaster, (even though there is a glint of potential ill-temper in the bright eye of Linos too), whilst again on the other side there is a ferocity common to Herakles and the hag. As to age, contrast Linos slumping in the chair with the straight-backed Iphikles, not to mention the convincingly rendered bent gait of Geropso.

The skyphos is an early work of the painter, about 470 B.C. or even a few years earlier.

Bibl.: W. Helbig, in: *AI*, 1871, pl. F. Reinach, *Répertoire*, I, p. 326. J. Maybaum, in: *JdI*, 27, 1912, p. 24ff. Perrot-Chipiez, X, p. 585ff. Buschor, *G Vsm*, p. 179, fig. 129. Hartwig. p. 375ff. Hoppin, *RVF*, II, p. 372. Klein, *Meistersignaturen*, p. 150, 2. Pfuhl, fig. 471. Buschor, in: FR, III, p. 272ff. H. Diepolder, *Der Penthesilea-Maler*, Leipzig 1936, pl. 4, p. 8. Idem, *Der Pistoxenos-Maler*, Berlin 1954, pll. 3–4. Beazley, *ARFVP*, p. 576, no. 16. See also E. Simon, *Geburt der Aphrodite*, Berlin 1959, p. 59 and fig. 39.

167

CUP by the Pistoxenos Painter. Taranto, Museo Nazionale. From Locri. Very fragmentary. Part of the inside medallion and a small piece of the lip of the cup have survived. Of the outside picture large parts of one side are preserved. The most important fragment measures about 18 cms (7″) across. The estimated diameter is about 30 cms (11 3/4″).

Inside picture in white-ground technique. Plate 167 gives the upper part only of the preserved portion. The medallion covering most of the inside of the cup is bordered by a narrow black band. A satyr called *Byba[x]* (letters behind his back and out of plate 167) and covered with a deer skin has made up to a menad and bends slightly forward in order to lift her dress with his right hand whilst reaching for her shoulder with his left. She is giving a good account of herself; having put her left arm over his head she grips him under his arm pit. With the other arm she swings her snake-entwined thyrsus in the air towards him.

Above, near the border, parts of the potter's signature: *ep]oiesen*, which on the analogy of the same painter's white-ground cup in Berlin, has been restored to *[Euphronios ep]oiesen*. On the left behind the menad and out of plate 167 the remnants of a love inscription in two lines *[Glauk] on [kalo]s*.

White-ground technique with ample use of additional colour. The figures are no longer outlined with relief lines, but with golden brown dilute. Dilute is also used for the hair and beard. The main strands were drawn in a dark mixture, with the general area of the hair shaded in a lighter tone. The satyr's deer skin is in dark blue (not glaze) dappled with white spots. The menad's chiton is violet red with dark fold lines. Ornaments have been rendered plastically with raised clay which was coloured in violet red or gilded. Such are the bracelets of the menad and the satyr, the menad's necklace, ear-ring and double circlet, and the satyr's head ornament. Much detailing (done in dilute) is given to the satyr whose finger nails are shown as well as his hairy arms and chest. (The shading of his arm may have been intended to suggest the roundness of the limb rather than the body hair.) He is wide eyed, bushy-browed, moustached and has a bald pate with lots of hair coming down his back. He also has the satyr's snub nose.

Outside (red-figured; not shown). Very fragmentary groups of men and women in conversation.

A developed work by the painter some time in the later sixties, a dating also suggested by the love name Glaukon, for which see the introductory note.

Bibl.: Beazley, in: *AJA*, 1941, p. 601. G. Gullini, in: *Arch. Class.*, 3, 1951, p. 1ff. H. Diepolder, *Der Pistoxenos-Maler*, pp. 5, 7ff., figg. 2 and 7, pl. 2b. Beazley, *ARFVP*, p. 575, no. 4. M. Robertson, *Greek Painting*, frontispiece and p. 114. For the restored name of the satyr Beazley (in *AJA* cited above) quotes the rare word *bybos* = big. The form is like *babax* = babbler; cf. Ch. Fränkel, *Satyr-u.-Bakchennamen*, p. 31.

168–171 THE PENTHESILEA PAINTER

He is named after his masterpiece in Munich, a cup with a picture of Achilles and Penthesilea (plates 168–9). Almost 150 vases have been attributed to him, the great majority of them being cups including the largest known cup, 72 cms [28 1/4″] across from handle to handle, which was recently found in Spina with the deeds of Theseus inside and scenes from the Trojan War outside. Other shapes are a few skyphoi including a well-known one in Boston with the rising of a goddess out of the ground, some kantharoi, a white-ground bobbin in New York with two fine roundels, which have been compared to his Munich cups and several pyxides including the well-known one in white-ground technique in New York with the Judgement of Paris, and one in Ancona, also white-ground, with the birth of Aphrodite; also one hydria has been attributed to him. His usual repertoire consists of genre scenes from the palaestra, or youths conversing, arming or with horses. These, his ordinary works, often approach hack production. Then, however, we have some outstanding paintings some of which rise to an astonishing degree above his run-of-the-mill works. The most famous one of these is the Penthesilea cup in Munich, red-figured but with additional colours (plates 168, 169). On his few white-ground works he adopts less intense colouring for solid areas than the Pistoxenos Painter, and unlike him he does not go the whole way towards using the golden brown dilute for outlines. For this and more on our painter, see also the introductory remarks on the Pistoxenos Painter, p. 348, above.

His white-ground Judgement of Paris on the pyxis in New York gives to the encounter a certain intimate children's atmosphere which indeed reflects the spirit of many of his genre pictures. Of the pictures in more heroic cast we show his two cups, pendants to each other, in Munich. They must date from the fifties of the century. His new cup with the deeds of Theseus from Spina belongs to a slightly earlier period. The style of his ordinary cups gives few anatomical details and has a restless, if easy flow of line. In his conversation scenes the relationship of the interlocutors is often very well brought out and it is out of these humbler pieces that the great encounters of the Penthesilea and the Tityos cups grew. There the contrast and relationship between the antagonists is not merely one of external positioning, but an intimate connection which comes out in everything, but particulary in the direction and intensity of their gaze.

Some have seen links between his work and wall-paintings on the one hand and the tragedy of Aeschylus and Sophocles on the other, deriving his search after expressing psychological states and relationships from wall painting and his ability to isolate highly tragic situations from the dramatists.

Love names occur scarcely, if ever, in his works or those of his followers; on the other hand the generic *ho pais kalos* = the boy is beautiful, is found often enough.

The Penthesilea Painter was much imitated in his workshop and a whole series of school pieces and works by followers have been identified, some of the latest products of his workshop reaching down beyond the third quarter of the century. A feature of the workshop was that sometimes two painters collaborated in the decoration of one cup, the division being between the inside medallion on the one hand and the outsides on the other. The Penthesilea Painter himself is not known to have collaborated in this way. His work dates from the later sixties to beyond the middle of the century.

Bibliography: Swindler, in: *AJA*, 1909, p. 243 ff.; 1915, p. 398 ff. Pfuhl, II, p. 528 ff. H. Diepolder, *Der Penthesilea-Maler*, Berlin 1936. Swindler *Ancient Painting*, p. 179 ff. Rumpf, pp. 100–1. Richter, *Survey*, p. 97 ff. Kraiker, *Malerei*, p. 69 and specially pp. 75–6. Beazley, *ARFVP*, p. 581 ff Cook, p. 180. For the new cup from Spina see Alfieri-Arias-Hirmer, *Spina*, Munich 1958, pll. 28–33, and particularly Alfieri in: *RIASA*, 8, 1959 pp. 59 ff. For 'collaboration' in his workshop, see Beazley, *Potter and Painter*, p. 29–30.

168, 169

CUP by the Penthesilea Painter. Munich, Museum Antiker Kleinkunst, 2688. From Vulci, formerly in the Canino Collection. Mended from many fragments with much repainting in places, especially across the fractures (a bad case is the upper line of the Amazon's upper arm on plate 169). The more important parts, such as the face of Achilles, have however been cleaned from repainting. Height 7.3 cms (2⁷/₈″). Diam. 43 cms (16⁷/₈″).

The technique is very unusual. The contours and musculatur were drawn in dilute, and then for the most part traced over again with the relief line. The cloak of Achilles is red turning in its lower portions into light yellow, the border pattern being grey-blue, lined with white. The interior of his shield is shaded with a reddish wash. Helmet and corslet of the left hand warrior are red-brown; his cloak is purple, applied in a micaceous slip, over which fold lines and a circle ornament are drawn in white. The jerkin of Penthesilea is light yellow; its fold lines are drawn in diluted glaze. The body of Achilles has a red wash applied over it, that of the other warrior, those of Penthesilea and the dying Amazon have a brown wash. Altogether the colour enhancement is quite exceptional for a red-figured vase.
On the outside (not shown) are scenes of youths getting ready for an armed excercise, some of them are with horses. One puts on his greaves, others have swords, spears and

helmets. Several wear chlamys (short cloak) and have a petasos (broad brimmed hat) hanging down their back. The inscription *ho pais kalos* = the boy is beautiful, is repeated several times on both sides.
Inside. The pictures on plates 168–9 should have their poise somewhat altered, so that the upper arm of the falling Amazon is horizontal and the body and cloak of the left hand warrior perpendicular. The lip of the vase has a zone of ivy and berries (done in purple and white); then comes a narrow reserved band bounding the medallion which takes up almost the entire inside area of the cup. The scene shows Achilles slaying the Amazon queen Penthesilea. Achilles is naked but for his greaves and helmet, which is of Thracian type and richly decorated with palmettes and a sphinx on his cheek piece, all painted in black. He is bearded and has long hair which comes down in cork-screw curls below his helmet. A red cloak hangs down his left shoulder covering the shield-carrying arm. With his right he plunges his sword into the breast of Penthesilea, who has lifted her right arm up, perhaps imploringly, and with her left has tried to keep off Achilles' sword arm. Their glances meet taking away something of the sternness of Achilles' expression. Penthesilea is dressed in a short sleeveless chiton and a belted jerkin-like dress. Behind Penthesilea another warrior, a Greek, also looking sternly. He wears a scale helmet of Attic type, is bearded and has a magnificent leather corslet over his short chiton. Great

care is expended over the details of the corslet, we see a lozenge pattern over the breast piece, the shoulder flaps are splendid with ends in raised clay to indicate the fastening devices. Over his left shoulder he carries a red, decorated cloak. The tail of his helmet crest comes into view below his right arm pit. In his left hand he carries a spear of which the bottom spike, the so-called sauroter, is raised in gilded clay. With sword in his right he is moving to the left, but looking back. Behind Achilles a dying Amazon, her pupils contorting, her arms clasped and her teeth bared in agony as she is bleeding to death from a wound above her right breastbone and another on her right hip. One of her legs is doubled up, the other slightly bent. She wears the sleeved and trousered Scythian dress, which is often associated with Amazons. Above it she wears a loose and belted over-dress similar to the one on Penthesilea. Her hair comes down her temples and is gathered up at her ears, quite like the hair of Penthesilea except that the ends come down loose whereas Penthesilea has her hair taken up.

This remarkable and famous cup may perhaps have been inspired by large scale painting. The psychological content can be measured by comparing it with the fine picture of the same subject by Exekias on the London neck-amphora, plate 64 and XVIII. In decorative effect the picture by Exekias is the finer, but in the intimacy of gaze and gestures the Penthesilea Painter has the advantage of the pictorial language developed in the early classical period. According to a lost epic poem, the *Aithiopis*, Achilles was so moved by Penthesilea's beauty that after killing her he surrendered her body to the Trojans for which act of love he was reviled by Thersites. Later romance made much of the love of Achilles for Penthesilea, which, it was said, was kindled at the very moment when he killed, and thus was frustrated even when it began. It is tempting to read this very situation into the meeting of the gaze on plate 169. We may, however, not be justified in this; nor indeed is the interpretation of the picture as Achilles and Penthesilea (rather than as a Greek and an Amazon) secure.

Some of the enrichment of the drawing has been referred to already. The detail picture on plate 169 shows the application of gilded clay for Penthesilea's ear ring, circlet and bracelets, also for the raised decoration of the helmet palmettes and the edges of the neck guard and other details of the helmet. The guard of the sword, the upper edge and lower end of scabbard and greaves are similarly raised. There are details in gilded clay application on the other Greek warrior and the dying Amazon on the right.

About 455 B.C.

Bibl.: Jahn, no. 370, pp. 116–7. FR, I, pp. 31 ff. (see there pp. 34–35 for Reichhold's remarks on the technique), pll. 6; 56, 1–3; also II, pp. 90–91. (Reichhold's drawing must be consulted for details of the inside picture.) Pfuhl, fig. 501. H. Diepolder, *Der Penthesilea-Maler*, p. 14, n. 32 (for description of colouring), pll. 12,2–15 (pictures of the vase after cleaning). Beazley, *ARFVP*, p. 582, no. 1. Rumpf, p. 101. Kraiker, *Malerei*, p. 85. D. von Bothmer, *Amazons in Greek Art*, Oxford 1957, pp. 147ff. (important for the interpretation) and pl. 71,4 (picture properly poised). M. Robertson, *Greek Painting* (Skira), pp. 115–6 (in colour). On the shape see Bloesch, *Formen*, pl. 30; also p. 103ff., and p. 107. *EWA*, III, pl. 355 (colour).

CUP by the Penthesilea Painter. Munich, Museum Antiker Kleinkunst, 2689. From Vulci; formerly in the Canino Collection. Mended from many fragments with many details of the drawing lost though the composition is clear enough. Under the foot of the vase a Etruscan graffito inscription of which only the word *fufluns* (= the Etruscan Dionysus) can be deciphered. Height 7 cms (2 3/4"). Diam. 40 cms (15 3/4").

On the outside (not shown), conversation scenes between boys standing and sitting, some holding a lyre. Much restored. The inscription *ho pais kalos* = the boy is beautiful, written in two lines.

Inside picture on a scale similar to the Penthesilea cup, to which it can be considered a pendant. The lip too has a frieze of ivy and berries. It is very difficult to poise the picture convincingly. Apollo should be upright, even more so than on plate 170, yet in that case the fall of Tityos' cloak would defy the laws of gravity.

Apollo killing Tityos. Apollo is wearing a rich floral wreath with applied gilded berries over his long hair which comes down the side of his cheeks and in a tail down his back. He swings his cutting sword machaira to dispatch Tityos who is already down defenceless on his knees and holding out his arms instinctively to ward off his doom. Tityos is wild eyed; his teeth are showing. He only wears a cloak over his shoulders and a purple fillet round his hair. Apollo also has a cloak over his left shoulder and carries his bow and two arrows in his left arm, which is adorned with a bracelet. He carries his scabbard on his left side, the baldric coming across his body. Behind Tityos a woman, no doubt a goddess, unveiling herself. She wears a high-belted peplos with an overfall and pulls up the skirt with her left hand. She is most naturally taken to be the mother of Tityos, the goddess Ge (Earth), who reveals herself at the moment of her son's agony, though she cannot help. A similar figure unveiling herself occurs on several black-figured vases where she is certainly Ge. It has, however, recently been suggested by Greifenhagen that the goddess here is Leto, the mother of Apollo who is being saved from Tityos (for the story see on plate 91). Above Tityos the inscription: *ho pais kalos* = the boy is beautiful, in two lines, not quite *stoichedon*.

The cup is less rich than its pendant, the Penthesilea cup, also in Munich (plates 168–9). Though applied gilding is used, the chromatic enrichment is avoided. The composition is effective, the drawing quite fine but its success only moderate; in particular the mass of Tityos is poorly differentiated from that of his mother behind him. The strength of the picture lies again in the contrast between the cold ferocity of the god and the despair in the face of Tityos. The vase must be very close in date to the Penthesilea cup.

Bibl.: Jahn, no. 402. FR, pl. 55, I, p. 279. C. M. Galt, in: *AJA*, 35, 1931, p. 388, fig. 13. H. Diepolder, *Der Penthesilea-Maler*, pll. 16–17, 1 and 18. K. A. Pfeiff, *Apollon*, Frankfurt 1943, pp. 90ff., pll. 16–17. Beazley, *ARFVP*, p. 583, no. 2. Kraiker, *Malerei*, p. 85. A. Greifenhagen, in: *Jahrbuch der Berliner Museen*, 1, 1959, pp. 5 ff.

172, XXXVI

WHITE-GROUND CUP BY THE LYANDROS PAINTER.

Florence, Museo Archeologico, 75409. From Cesa near Bettolle. Mended from many fragments. Some of the white slip is lost and with it the painting, though the central figure is reasonably well preserved. Behind Aphrodite there are three sets of rivet holes, above and below the figure of Eros. These are the traces left by an ancient repair of the cup made with bronze clamps. Height 10.8 cms (4¹/₄″). Diam. 28.5 cms (11¹/₄″); without the handles.

On outside, underneath the handles double palmette. On the sides near handles isolated ivy leaves pointing upwards.
The inside of the cup is in white-ground technique. There is a black band round the lip, then a little way down the sides two thin brown lines which are the actual border lines of the medallion, though the white slip reaches up to the black of the lip. The figure drawing uses the black relief line extensively for outlines and details such as the chiton folds. In this respect it goes with the earlier Brygos Painter cup in Munich (plate XXXIV) rather than the Taranto fragment (plate 167) where this work is done in dilute. On our cup dilute in dark concentration is used for the hair and chair legs, and in a lighter tone elsewhere in the picture. Red is used for the solid area of Aphrodite's himation and for the fillet held by one of the Erotes. Fold lines within the red himation are in dark brown. There is also a yellowish line along the edge of the himation.
Inside picture. In the centre of the roundel Aphrodite is seated on a richly decorated chair with back rest. She is holding between her hands a wreath to put on her head. She is dressed in chiton with sleeves and has a himation over her left shoulder and across her lap. Her hair which comes down long at her back is encircled with a plain diadem. The chair has carved legs with double volutes at its upper end. In front of her is a so-called thymiaterion (incense burner) standing on a high base. Behind her are the remnants of a chest decorated with various motifs including a star. Hovering about the goddess are two Erotes (winged boy genii of love who accompany Aphrodite). The one in front (whose wings pierce the border lines of the medallion) holds a fillet with which to crown the goddess. Another one approaches from behind also holding a wreath or something of the kind, though the actual object has disappeared. The scene thus should be the adornment of Aphrodite, or could it be Helen?
Outside (red-figured; not shown). On A five youths in conversation, and the love-name [L]yandr[os]. On B five more boys. One more cup in London and perhaps another one in Rome have been attributed to this painter. His work is close to that of the Pistoxenos Painter.
C. 460 B.C.

Bibl.: L. A. Milani, in: *Rend. Acc. Linc.*, II, 1893, p. 1007ff. L. Pollak, in: *RM*, 13, 1898, p. 79ff. Klein, *Lieblingsinschriften*, p. 157. H. Philippart, in: *Mon. Piot.*, 29, 1927–28, p. 108, no. 32. Idem, *Collections de céramique grecque en Italie*, I, 1932, p. 17ff. Idem, *Les coupes attiques à fond blanc*, p. 69ff. Beazley, in: *Gnomon*, 1937, p. 91. Idem, *ARFVP*, p. 569, no. 1. *CVA*, Florence, fasc. 2 (Levi), pl. 1. N. Himmelmann, *Eigenart d. Klass. Gotterbildes*, pl. 23.

XXXVII

WHITE-GROUND LEKYTHOS.

Brussels, Musées Royaux d'Art et d'Histoire, A 1019. From Eretria. Mended from many fragments but in good condition. Height 42 cms (16¹/₂″). Diam. at shoulder 14 cms (5¹/₂″).

For the general shape see plate 184. Mouth, neck, shoulders and bottom are black with red-figured floral ornament (palmettes and flowers) on shoulder. The upper three-quarters of the cylindrical body are covered with white slip which is bounded above and below by a band of meander. Below the white area two purple lines on the black. The painting is in diluted glaze. A more intense, snowy white than that used for the slip has been applied on the face, arms and hands of the two women as well as on the fringed fillet or scarf. The picture shows a mistress with long hair coming down her back; her head is decorated with a circlet in purple. She wears ear-rings, is dressed in a chiton and carries a fringed scarf. In front of her a smaller servant girl with short hair carrying a chest, probably the jewel casket. She wears a black chiton. Notice the indications of the belt and folds painted in red. In the background we see a mirror and a lekythos (oil flask). The inscriptions are *Glaukon* (below the scarf) *kalos* (next to the servant girl's head) = Glaukon is beautiful.
This lekythos is connected by Beazley with his so-called Group of Athens 1929, five lekythoi which are very likely by the hand of the Timocrates Painter, an artist of white ground lekythoi whose work is close to that of the Pistoxenos Painter. The love name Glaukon is known from a number of vases of the early classical period including some of the finest of the Pistoxenos Painter's cups (see introductory remarks on the Pistoxenos Painter p. 348).
For the uses of this white lekythos see p. 359 below, the introductory note on white-ground funerary lekythoi.
C. 460 B.C.

Bibl.: A. Fairbanks, *Athenian White Lekythoi*, II, p. 246, no. 10, pl. 33, 2. Buschor, *Attische Lekythen der Parthenonzeit*, p. 24 (on its chronological importance); fig. 11. *CVA*, Brussels fasc. 1, (Mayence) pl. 2, 5, III J b. Beazley, *ARFVP*, p. 579 below. Arias, in: *Enc. arte classica*, I, p. 873, s.v. Atene 1929 (pittore di). For Glaukon see D. M. Robinson and E. J. Fluck, *A Study of Greek Love-Names*, Baltimore 1937, p. 114, no. 104, and Richter, *Survey*, p. 93. On the 'snowy' white for the women's flesh which is also used by the Achilles Painter in his early white-ground lekythoi which are near contemporaries to this lekythos see Beazley, *Attic White Lekythoi*, pp. 13–14. On the Timocrates Painter see *ibid.*, p. 13, n. 5.

His activity ranges from about 465 B.C. to the middle of the century and he has been named after one of the subjects on his famous calyx-krater in the Louvre (plates 173-5). Here and on some of his other pictures we can trace the influence of the contemporary or slightly earlier art of the great fresco painters, Polygnotos from Thasos and Mikon the Athenian, whose works though entirely lost are known to some extent at any rate through literary descriptions and allusions. Thus we have a detailed description by Pausanias of Polygnotos' work in the House of the Knidians in Delphi, where the subjects were the Destruction of Troy (Ilioupersis) and Odysseus in the Underworld (Nekyia). In Athens itself work by Polygnotos and Mikon could be seen in the Painted Porch (Stoa Poikile), where the subjects were the Amazonomachy, Ilioupersis, the Battle of Marathon and the Battle of Oinoe, in the Sanctuary of Theseus, where the paintings included a Centauromachy, an Amazonomachy and Theseus being received by Amphitrite, and in the Sanctuary of the Dioscuri, the so-called Anakeion, where the Voyage of the Argonauts was one of the pictures. From Pausanias' description it is clear that the figures in some if not all of these paintings were arranged in various levels, such as we find on the Louvre krater and furthermore that a good number of devices and motifs were used which we also find in vase paintings of this period. Some of these will be referred to in our commentary on the Louvre krater. Again, the popularity of certain subjects at this time is very probably also due to the wall-paintings. This above all is the time of the great Amazonomachy pictures on vases, of which the Niobid Painter himself has given us at least four. On plates 176-181 we show one of his best on a volute krater found in Gela and now in the Museum of Palermo, which is here for the first time properly published in worthy photographs. Quite recently another of his Amazonomachies on a volute-krater which stylistically though not so much in its motifs, resembles the Palermo Amazonomachy, has been found in Spina and is now in the museum of Ferrara.

We sometimes speak of 'Polygnotan' when referring to the aims and achievements of early classical painting. By this we mean the new way of portraying through postures perhaps even more than gestures, moods and emotional states, particularly in the moments before and after a crisis. The East Pediment of the temple of Zeus at Olympia is a good illustration of this in sculpture; a similar language is used on the Louvre krater, especially the side with the heroes standing in the presence of Athena and Herakles. Just because the moment chosen for depicting is before or after a crisis rather than the action itself, the interpretation of such pictures in the absence of external help is often desperately difficult. For the particular motifs which reflect this atmosphere of expectancy see the commentary on the Louvre krater; suffice it here to point to the youth clasping his leg below the knee on plate 174. Though there are other vases which reflect the influence of Polygnotan wall-painting the Louvre krater has remained the classic example ever since its importance in this respect was recognized by Carl Robert soon after its discovery in 1880. Ancient writers spoke of the *ethos* of Polygnotos' figures, though the term is not used in connection with Mikon. It has been translated as 'high moral purpose'.

The Niobid Painter is not perhaps a great draftsman but in a number of his pictures something of the quality of his models gets through. A frigid detachment is noticeable in his work, which gives it something of the coldness of Olympus without its elevation. This impression is reinforced by a certain hardness of line which comes out in his preference for the black relief line even where we would have expected the softer dilute to be used, and also in his liking for the straight rather than the curved, for verticals and horizontals, in anatomical details as well as for drapery folds. All this gives to some of his figures a wooden quality which has made some, not very happily perhaps, think of the influence of sculpture!

He likes large shapes and amongst his vases, which number almost ninety, there is a preference for the volute- and calyx-krater, which are used for his monumental compositions, Amazonomachy, Centauromachy, Gigantomachy and Ilioupersis, subjects all of which are also known to have been treated by the fresco painters. He does not despise the bell-krater either but will not touch the column-

krater. There are also a few amphorae type B, one red-figured amphora of Panathenaic shape, neck-amphorae and hydriai in some number, as well as some oinochoai and pelikai. Many of these have the more usual subjects, gods, especially Apollo, and human activities. Though his own paintings show no special interest in daring foreshortening we have pictures by followers of his, such as the two Amazonomachies in New York (found together at Numana, near Ancona) by the Painter of the Woolly Satyrs and the Painter of the Berlin Hydria respectively, which are replete with foreshortening, shading and other tricks derived from wall-painting.

No love names are found in any of his works.

Bibliography: Pfuhl, II, p. 533 ff. T. B. L. Webster, *Der Niobidenmaler*, Leipzig 1935. Ch. Dugas, in: *REG*, 1937, p. 185 ff. H. R. W. Smith, in: *CVA*, San Francisco, fasc. 1, p. 39. E. Bielefeld, *Amazonomachia*, Halle 1951. D. von Bothmer, *Amazons in Greek Art*, Oxford 1957, p. 163 ff. Richter, *Survey*, p. 101. Rumpf, p. 93 ff. Cook, pp. 180, 325, 350. For the two Amazonomachies in New York by followers of the Niobid Painter, see conveniently Pfuhl, fig. 507; 506. For the lower status of the column-krater, see Beazley, in: *Spina e l'Etruria Padana*, Florence 1959, p. 51 ff.

173–175

CALYX-KRATER by the Niobid Painter. Paris, Louvre, MNC 511 (G 341). From Orvieto. Formerly in the Tyszkiewicz Collection. Mended but in good condition with some few gaps. Height 54 cms (21¼"). Diam. of mouth 55 cms (21⅝").

For the proportions of the shape see commentary on plates 119–121. On the ledge below the mouth a frieze of enclosed linked palmettes with flowers between. The handle roots below the calyx are surrounded by tongues. Below the pictures a narrow frieze of egg pattern; then palmettes alternating with flowers enclosed by lyre shaped tendrils.

Side A (plates 173 and 174). A picture of uncertain interpretation. In the centre and standing on raised terrain (indicated by purple line over the black, similar lines are used throughout the picture to indicate variations of level) is Herakles. He is naked carries his lion's skin on his left shoulder and holds his club and his bow. He is wreathed, and looks to his right at a warrior whose Thracian helmet is pulled down over his face, who wears greaves, holds a spear and a shield at rest (foreshortened inside view of shield). Behind that warrior stands Athena in chiton and overgirt himation. She wears her aegis with the Gorgon head set in it and an Attic helmet of elaborate kind which has its side parts (cheek and nose piece) hinged up. At a lower level a shield with a wheel device. Three more persons are behind Athena. On a higher level and hidden behind the rock up to his middle is a warrior with scale corslet, uncrested helmet, spear and shield. He is seen in backview, but turning round to make a gesture towards the centre. Below him a warrior with helmet, shield (snake device) and spear; he is naked apart from a chlamys buttoned up at his shoulder. He turns away out of the picture looking up. At a slightly higher level, to clear the height of the handle (and not visible on our plates) is another warrior, naked, holding a spear, and with his helmet (of pilos or Laconian type) hanging down his neck. His sheathed sword hangs down his side. He stands frontal, right hand akimbo and inclines his head (three quarter view) towards the centre. He may be one of the Dioscuri.

We now turn back to the centre of the picture (plate 174 detail). On the right side of Herakles and slightly below him we see one naked sitting on his cloak carrying his sheathed sword on his side. His face is in three quarter view with the lips fully drawn. He raises his right leg gripping it in a rocking motion just below the knee. Looking at him from below is another youth, also naked, with his hat down his back, and his sword by his side. He holds up two spears with his left and whilst reclining holds his body upright by supporting it with his right hand placed behind his back. His right foot is turned outwards. His shield and helmet repose by his feet. This pair with the carefully observed postures is amongst the most striking figures on this vase. The inspiration undoubtedly goes back to major art, wall-painting probably, which had developed these two types within the last decade or so. Thus we know from Pausanias 10, 31, 5 that Polygnotos in his Nekyia picture at Delphi showed Hector in just this posture of sitting and clasping one knee. Further up on the right we see one holding his helmet in front of him and standing frontal but looking towards the centre. He also carries shield, spear and sword. Then follows a bearded man with striking three quarter view of his face and the petasos (broad brimmed hat) which he wears over his head. He is dressed in a short transparent chiton and has a cloak worn like a scarf round him. He carries a spear and has his right leg up on a raised piece of terrain in a motif which, as we know from Pausanias (10, 30, 3), was used for Antilochos in Polygnotos' painting of the Nekyia (Underworld) in Delphi. Finally and no longer visible on our plates a horseman dismounted. His horse faces inwards towards the centre, and shows a striking, if rather pedantic three-quarter rendering of its head. The hero himself is naked, wears a pilos or Laconian type helmet, carries two spears and his sword. He might be one of the Dioscuri corresponding to the matching figure on the left.

The figures are disposed on various levels which are indicated by undulating lines. On the extreme left of plate 173 and also on plate 175 lower right we have figures which are hidden to greater or lesser extent by the terrain. Again we know that Mikon, probably in one of his Athenian frescoes, painted the hero Boutes so that he was completely hidden by a hill apart from his helmet and one eye, a figure which

became proverbial! Hence there can be no doubt that the Niobid Painter used a number of devices such as different levels and telling postures which were taken straight from wall-painting. More than that. We note that Herakles, the armed warrior on his left, the youth clasping his knee and others on this side of the vase have their mouth slightly open showing their teeth, not just in agony as we have seen before on the Antaios krater (plate 109) or even on the Penthesilea cup (plate 168) but in tranquillity. It is just this which Pliny (*nat. hist.* 35, 58) ascribes to Polygnotos: *os adaperire, dentes ostendere, voltum ab antiquo rigore variare.*

The draughtsmanship of the vase is hard and linear, largely because the relief line is used for details such as the abdominal musculature and the muscles along the ribs where we normally expect the application of dilute. Our painter has in fact used dilute for these muscles too but only for shading in support of the relief line. This linear impression is underlined by the extensive use of vertical and horizontal lines rather than curvatures in the abdominal zone of the body.

Side B (central area only shown on plate 175). Slaughter of the Niobids. Apollo and Artemis are on high in the centre of the picture shooting away with their bow and arrow. Apollo is wreathed in laurel, naked with his cloak over his left arm. He holds the bow in his outstretched left and is about to release an arrow with the right. His quiver is suspended on his left from a baldric. Behind him Artemis is withdrawing an arrow from her quiver. She has her hair in a sakkos, wears an overgirt peplos with overfall; the pins holding the peplos up on the shoulders are clearly visible. She also wears an ornament suspended on a string round her neck. Some indication of landscape by a tree in front of Apollo. Round about Niobids in flight and dying. Below the two archers we see a girl with frontal face dead with an arrow stuck in her back. She wears a diadem across her hair. A little to her right a boy is also dead with an arrow in his back. He clutches with his left the top of the rock convulsively. Another arrow has sped past him striking the ground just in front. Further up on the right at the level of Apollo another boy entirely naked is still on the run but about to collapse, with an arrow piercing his ribs. The merciless god is aiming another arrow in his direction. Behind Artemis another boy who has wrapped his cloak over his left side to shield himself, has been struck by an arrow in his breast and will collapse.

Whilst the interpretation of side B is clear enough that of side A is not. Amongst proposed interpretations we may mention that of Girard, who following up earlier suggestions by Helbig and Carl Robert considered our vase picture to show the Argonauts at Lemnos where they had settled and taken to the local womenfolk until Herakles stirred them up to proceed on their quest for the Golden Fleece. However, there are no special characteristics in our picture to clinch this interpretation. We do not even know the precise content of Mikon's picture of the Voyage of the Argonauts, which was in the Sanctuary of the Dioscuri at Athens (Pausanias 1, 18, 1). Another interpretation is that of Gardner who thought of the expiation ceremony of the Argonauts after the killing of Kyzikos, king of the Doliones

(Apollod. *Bibl.* 1, 9, 18), an explanation which incidentally has since been given to the scene on a volute-krater from Spina now in Ferrara, belonging to the School of the Niobid Painter. This vase must now take its place in any full discussion of our krater. Hauser again basing himself upon Pausanias' description (1, 15, 3) of the 'Battle of Marathon' by Mikon and Panainos in the Painted Porch and also on Pausanias' account (10, 10, 1) of the Athenian victory dedication in Delphi (of the statues of Miltiades and the Attic heroes) from the spoils of the Battle of Marathon argued that the picture shows the Athenian tribal heroes on the morrow of the battle of Marathon in the presence of Athena and Herakles in whose sanctuary the Athenian army had encamped. Of other interpretations we may mention the one by Six who places the whole scene in the Underworld, and takes the subject to be Herakles releasing Theseus from his constraint in Hades.

The vase is of exceptional importance above its artistic merits, because it provides evidence for contemporary developments in the major art of wall painting.

A latish work of the Niobid Painter, about 455–450 B.C.

Bibl.: Pottier, *VAL*, p. 227, pl. 136, G341. C. Robert, *AI*, 1882, p. 273. Idem, *Die Nekyia des Polygnot*, p. 40. Idem, *Die Marathonschlacht*, p. 61. Reinach, *Répertoire*, 1, p. 226. P. Gardner, in: *JHS*, 1889, p. 117. P. Girard, in: *REG*, 1894, p. 360. FR, II, pp. 244, 251 (Hauser). J. Six, in: *JHS*, 39, 1919, p. 130. Buschor, *G Vsm*, p. 183, fig. 127. Pfuhl, II, p. 524. Hoppin, *RFV*, II, p. 242, no. 34. T. B. L. Webster, *Niobidenmaler*, pp. 15–16, pll. 2–4. H. R. W. Smith, in: *CVA*, S. Francisco, fasc. 1, p. 38. *CVA*, Louvre fasc. 2 (Pottier). III, Id. pl. 1. Beazley, *ARFVP*, p. 419, no. 20. For the Spina volute-krater in Ferrara with the expiation ceremony, Beazley, *ARFVP*, p. 428, no. 1, see now Alfieri-Arias-Hirmer, *Spina*, pll. 42–4. For the pilos helmet worn by the Dioscuri on side A see now A. Rumpf, *Kranos Boiotiourges* (*Abhandl. Berlin Akad.*, Phil.-hist. Klasse 1943), pp. 3–5; Chr. Kardara in *ABSA*, 55, 1960, p. 150, n. 6; Diepolder, in: *Münchner Jahrbuch*, 5, 1928, p. 227 (17). Compare also K. M. T. Chrimes, *Ancient Sparta*, Manchester 1949, pp. 362 ff. For the connection of the Dioscuri with the pilos see also Furtwängler, in: Roscher, *s.v.* 'Dioskuren', col. 1172; Tod and Wace, *Catalogue of Sparta Museum*, p. 115 – referring to later material. For the sitter with knees clasped (plate 174), compare the striking precursor of the late 6th century on a cup fragment in Florence by Paseas (Cerberus Painter), Beazley, *ARFVP*, p. 56, no. 11. Cf. also the skyphos by the Triptolemos Painter, von Bothmer, *Ancient Art*, pl. 89, 247. [On interpretation of side A also Ch. Christos, in: *Eph. Arch.*, 1957 (1961), p. 168 ff. – Nekyia]. Robertson p. 124

176–181

VOLUTE-KRATER by the Niobid Painter. Palermo, Museo Nazionale, G 1283. From Gela. Excellent preservation. Height 78 cms (30⁵/₈″). Diam. of mouth 47 cms (18¹/₂″).

On sides of volute handles, linked spirals. On outer edge of lip, meander with saltires. On ledge below it chain of double palmettes and flowers and a narrow line of egg pattern below. On shoulders at junction of neck a frieze of tongues. Below the main picture a band of meander and saltires. Black rays at bottom of bowl rising from the base.

The neck picture on side A (plates 176–7) shows the battle of Centaurs and Lapiths. The Centaurs fight with branches and with rocks, some of them have an animal skin over their arm for protection. On the extreme left a Lapith plunges his sword into the back of a Centaur; then a Centaur advancing to the right with a branch. In front of him a Lapith with a

spear against a Centaur who has already collapsed but still holds his tree branch aloft. The Lapith wears a conical helmet. On the right a Lapith helmeted and carrying shield with a leather apron is advancing with his sword against a Centaur who is heaving a rock against him. Another rock is hurtling through the air near the Lapith. On side B (plate 181) we see Herakles at the lair of the Centaur Pholos in Elis whom he visited when he hunted for the Erymanthian boar. Herakles had been well received by the Centaur, but trouble started when he asked for wine and the big storage vat, which we see in the centre of the picture half buried in the ground, was opened. Attracted by the smell, the other Centaurs came and demanded their share; a fight ensued in which they were killed. Here we see the Centaurs approaching as yet polite but with tree branches in their hand.

The main picture is an Amazonomachy which goes right round the vase. The central group on side A is shown in detail on plate 179; it is that of the Greek hero killing the Amazon queen. He wears crested Thracian helmet and a metal corslet over a short chiton and greaves. His shield which has a leather apron hanging down is shown in successful three quarter view. Such aprons which must have been of leather or similar material are known from many representations especially in the first half of the 5th century. We have met one on the Ilioupersis cup by the Brygos Painter, (plate 139 upper picture). His spear has entered the shoulder of the Amazon queen who is dressed in sleeved and trousered Oriental garment above which she wears a Greek short chiton and leatherbacked scale corslet with star-adorned shoulder flaps and a Gorgon's head over her breast. On her head she has a special beret-like covering surmounted by a sphinx from which in turn rises a tall crest. Part of the neck guard is also visible above her left shoulder. Her quiver is just visible on her left side. The Amazon queen had wielded a slashing sword machaira with her right to cut the spear of her opponent, had missed and now mortally wounded has let go of her sword which is seen hurtling to the ground. Her grip on the shield is also loosening. The painter has omitted the pupils; we would expect them to be tilted upwards, as is usual with dying persons. The Amazon queen wears ear-rings, has her face in three quarter view, her lips fully rendered and indicated by shading. Shading is also used for the hair curls protruding from her helmet. Behind the Amazon queen an Amazon wearing Attic helmet and short belted chiton with sword hanging down her side, comes to the defence of her queen with her spear. Note the back view of her right leg and knee (plates 180). Behind the attacking Greek on the left of side A another Amazon (plate 178), this time again in Oriental costume (trousers—note the way they are draped—sleeves and flappy cap) on top of which she has a short chiton and corslet. She uses her sword against a Greek warrior who is attacking uphill crouching slightly and seeking cover behind his shield. He is a striking figure in his splendid cone helmet with neck guard, hinged cheek pieces and pony-tail crest, a variant of the Thracian helmet which occurs on several contemporary Attic vases. He also wears a metal corslet with the usual leather flaps skirting its bottom edge. Between him and the

Amazon is a spear which has been cut to pieces. The Amazon opposing him is modelled in some details of her posture on the Harmodius of the Tyrannicide group by Kritios and Nesiotes.

The battle continues on the other side (plate 181). We take up the story behind the warrior we just described. A mounted Amazon on the right of plate 181 hastens up. She wears the high fur-lined boots of cavalry, short chiton, corslet and helmet. In her left hand which is stretched out behind her she holds a trumpet (visible on the extreme left of plate 176). A bow lies on the ground underneath her. Then in the centre a striking group of an Amazon attacking a Greek with her battle axe, but the Greek has swiftly come up and arrested her blow by pushing up her right elbow. The Greek carries his spear in his left hand which also carries his shield. Finally on the left of side B (see detail on plate 180) we see another Greek attacking an Amazon with his sword which is swung backwards behind his head. He wears high laced shoes; his shield is blank. As a particular item of the Greek's equipment we notice the forehead piece on his helmet, for which see the commentary on plate 146. The Amazon under the handle is drawing back keeping the Greek at a distance with her spear. Apart from her spear she carries a bow and two arrows in her left. She wears shoes, a flappy cap, a sleeved garment and over it a short peplos. Across her right shoulder an accidental splash of black glaze. Behind her in the mêlée a quiver falls to the ground.

We may note the dearth of interesting shield devices on this and other vases by the Niobid Painter, a dearth which is common from now onwards. It seems to reflect contemporary mid-5th century conditions when Athenian shield devices tended to be an *alpha* (for *Athenaioi*) and those of the Spartans a *lambda* (for *Lakedaimonioi*; see Eupolis frag. 359 Kock). There may be a connection between this phenomenon and the declining use of love names, both due to social changes in contemporary Athens.

We cannot be quite sure whether the group of hero and queen is that of Achilles and Penthesilea or of Theseus and Antiope. Our krater is one of a series of grand Amazonomachy pictures of the advanced early classical period which continues into the fully classical period. It is natural to think of these battles as the Athenian Amazonomachy with Theseus as the hero, indeed several times he is named by inscriptions. The Niobid Painter and his school have painted these Amazonomachies on their large vases, especially volute kraters, but their relationship to the early classical wall-paintings of the subject in Athens, in the Sanctuary of Theseus and the Painted Porch cannot be determined with certainty. An early work by the painter, about 460 B.C. or even earlier.

Bibl.: FR, I, pp. 125, 128–9, 132. W. Klein, in: *JdI*, 33, 1918, p. 13 ff. Swindler, figg. 356, 359–60. A. Della Seta, *Italia antica*², p. 111, b. J. Bovio-Marconi, *Museo di Palermo*, pl. 49. T. B. L. Webster, *Niobidenmaler*, p. 20, no. 2. D. von Bothmer, *Amazons in Greek Art*, Oxford 1957, pp. 161, 166–7. Beazley, *ARFVP*, p. 418, no. 2. For the sword motifs of the Amazon queen and the Amazon fighting on the left of side A see Shefton, in: *AJA*, 64, 1960, p. 174, n. 10 and n. 8; pl. 49, For the disappearance of heraldry on shields see also Caskey-Beazley p. 79. For the types of Thracian helmet see B. Schröder, *JdI*, 27, 1912, pp. 317 ff. Shield aprons, Lippold in *Münchener Archäol. Studien* (1909) p. 489; P. Corbett, in: *BMQ*, 24, 1961, p. 97.

This painter's signature is preserved on ten vases, four stamnoi in Paris, Orvieto, Boston and Florence; five pelikai, in Rome, Vienna and Bellinzona; and a white cup from Brauron. He is a pot painter and a pupil of the Berlin Painter. His shapes are stamnoi, pelikai, numerous neck-amphorae, a few loutrophoroi, some hydriai, lekythoi, an important lekanis lid in Ferrara (from Spina) with a gigantomachy, some cups and an important cup-kotyle in Barcelona from Ampurias. Altogether about 110 vases have been attributed to him. He took over a number of his stylistic characteristics from his master, the Berlin Painter, especially his way of drawing the ankle and some of the subsidiary chiton folds. His eyes have an unusually alert expression.

A good few of his vases have mythological subjects, such as for instance the birth of Erichthonios on the Munich stamnos (plates 182, 183), Eos and Kephalos, Dionysiac themes, Zeus and Ganymede, Zeus and the nymph Aegina, the sphinx, the mission to Achilles, the daughters of Proetus (cup-kotyle from Ampurias). Generally he does not crowd his scenes but rather endeavours to create movement within individual figures. These have delicate outlines and swinging curving lines for garment folds and are the nearest thing in Attic painting to the style of the Ludovisi Throne (Lullies and Hirmer, *Greek Sculpture*[2], plates 134–7). His activity is between about 470 and the 450's B.C.

Bibliography: M. Pallottino, in: *Atti Acc. d'Italia*, VII, 1, 1940, F. P. Johnson, in: *AJA*, 51, 1947, p. 233 ff. Buschor, *GV*, p. 182. Beazley, *ARFVP*, pp. 317–23. Richter, *Survey*, pp. 108–9. Rumpf, p. 99. On the unpublished signed pelike in Rome, Schauenberg, *Perseus*, p. 84.

182, 183

STAMNOS by Hermonax. Munich, Museum Antiker Kleinkunst, 2413. From Vulci. Several areas (obvious in the photograph) are restored or patched up. Height 39 cms (15 3/8″). Diam. of mouth 12 cms (4 11/16″).

On the lip egg pattern. On top of shoulders near junction of neck a frieze of black tongues. Meander with dotted saltires below the figure zone. Ornament of spiral tendrils and palmettes above and below the handles. The ornament is linked to the Erotes standing next to the handles.

Side A. Birth of Erichthonios. On the right Athena with fillet round her hair whose ends are tied up in a small bag. Her aegis is converted into a napkin worn over her breast and taken up to cradle the new born child. A fringe of snakes though emerges along her back. With her left she is taking the new born baby Erichthonios from the hands of Ge, the Earth, who is seen emerging from the ground. On the left a bearded male stands by and watches, right hand akimbo, the left leaning on what should be a spear or perhaps a sceptre. Behind Athena an Eros holding a lyre with the lowered left and a flower with his raised right. On the left behind the bearded male another Eros, holding on with his right to the spiral tendril whilst his left arm is akimbo. Both Erotes stand on the spiral tendrils, the right-hand one on tip-toe and in profile, the one on the left stands frontal with his body and wings but head and feet turned in profile. The tip-toe and flat foot respectively of the pair could be due to their being thought as see-sawing on the tendrils.

Side B (not shown). In the centre Zeus, bearded and dressed in a chiton and himation, is seated on a deer-legged stool, with Gorgon's faces fore and aft at the end of the joints. He is holding a sceptre in his left and a phiale in his outstretched right. On his farther side standing frontal, but head turned to him is the tall figure of a winged woman, Iris, wrapped in her himation. Her right hand is lowered and eclipsed by the cloak of Zeus. She must be holding an oinochoe (jug). By the handle, again standing on a spiral tendril belonging to the handle ornament, is an Eros who stretches out his right hand towards Zeus and the centre whilst holding on to the tendril with his left. Behind Zeus another Eros again standing on the spiral tendril playing the lyre.

On A the subject is the Attic legend of the birth of one of the earliest kings of Athens, who was the issue of an unsuccessful assault on Athena by Hephaistos. The earth teemed with the sperm and gave birth to Erichthonios whom Athena received and secretly nurtured. The male figure on the left should therefore be Hephaistos though there is nothing to identify him as such. A. B. Cook *Zeus III* pp. 185, 221, fig. 141.

On B Zeus ministered to by Iris celebrates the event by offering a libation thus giving to the birth of the Attic king a cosmic significance (so Hauser). The Erotes on A watch in silent expectancy, though one of them holds a lyre; on B there is music, the Eros on the left plays away, whilst the one on the right stretches his hand out 'let me have a go now'; (this rather than the quaint idea that the winged boy wants to have a sip from Zeus' bowl!) A and B are thus linked.

A latish work by Hermonax, about 460 B.C. or even later.

Bibl.: Jahn, no. 345, p. 108. Th. Panofka, in: *AI*, 1829, p. 292. B. Sauer, *Theseion*, p. 58. FR, III, p. 95 ff. (Hauser). Beazley, *ARFVP*, p. 318, no. 18. E. Simon, *Opfernde Götter*, Berlin 1953, p. 92. A. Greifenhagen, *Griechische Eroten*, Berlin 1958, pp. 26 and 72, figg. 21–24. Rumpf, p. 99. Jacobsthal, *Ornamente*, p. 100. For the subject see Brommer, in: *Charites* (Langlotz Festschrift, ed. K. Schauenburg), Bonn 1957, p. 157. The interpretation of the Erotes on the spiral tendrils has given rise to much ingenious speculation and there is danger that we read more into them than is warranted. For parallels to their attitude on side A compare the figures on the *trapeza* on a white-ground lekythos in Boston, Fairbanks, *Athenian White Lekythoi*, I, pl. 6. For side B the Eros with hand outstretched finds a close match, as has been pointed out before, on the Eros perched on Aphrodite's arm on the Locrian relief, type 10–1, photograph in, R. Pagenstecher, *Eros und Psyche* (S.B. Akad. Heidelberg, Phil.-hist. Klasse, 1911, 9), pl. 1A.

White-ground, that is a white chalky slip applied over the clay, is found on Attic vases from the 6th century B.C. onwards. Thus the Andokides Painter used it in an experiment on an amphora in the Louvre at the beginning of Red-figure. More lasting is its use on cups and small vases such as pyxides, alabastra, lekythoi and oinochoai where the whole picture surface is coated with the slip. Some cup fragments in Eleusis by the so-called Eleusis Painter are striking examples at the end of the 6th century and the somewhat later Munich cup by the Brygos Painter of about 490 B.C. is shown on plate XXXIV. The ordinary red-figure linear technique was used on these vases, that is black relief line and brownish dilute, but since the figures were not surrounded by a black background they became outline design. (We ignore in this note the less important Black-figure on white ground.) In the advancing second quarter of the century white-ground technique developed by the use of a wider range of pigments for solid areas, particularly drapery or non-human objects; also increasing use was made of the warmer golden-brown dilute at the expense of the wiry black relief-line. (See for this the introduction to the Pistoxenos Painter, p. 348–49.) The Pistoxenos-, the Sabouroff- and also the Sotades Painters are amongst the most important artists in the development of this technique. Thus the Sotades Painter has left us three delicate white-ground cups with wishbone handles all from Athens and now in the British Museum, of which the most famous perhaps is the one with the girl picking apples. All three cups are painted with dilute outlines.

In the decades after the middle of the 5th century the white-ground technique came however to be almost entirely confined to funerary lekythoi. Its abandonment for other shapes such as cups or kraters must have been due to the instability of the medium as explained on page 349. On white-ground lekythoi, however, this instability mattered less, at least on those which were put into the grave or left standing at the foot of the stele (grave pillar), or were otherwise used for funerary rites.

The specialized manufacture of lekythoi for funerary purposes does not seem to have developed to any extent until towards the middle of the 5th century. At any rate earlier lekythoi, black-figured, red-figured and even white-ground, are with some well defined exceptions such as the work of the Tymbos and Inscription Painters who decorated white-ground lekythoi, in no way specially linked to the grave by the theme of their decoration. They seem (again with the exception of some specially designed by the Beldam Potter, for which see below and on plate 189) to have been used as ordinary oil flasks such as we have seen hanging on the wall in the picture on the white-ground lekythos in Brussels (plate XXXVII), which itself may not have been made specially for the tomb – it was found at Eretria in Euboea. Such vases might of course also find their way into tombs. The export of these vases, white-ground included, is fairly wide; in Sicily they seem to have been particularly popular. It is noteworthy, however, that the special groups we referred to as being more specifically tied to the grave either by their decoration or special construction (Tymbos and Inscription Painters; some by the Beldam Potter) are not on the whole found beyond the confines of Attica, or the Athenian settlement in Eretria. This may be significant as we find this same confinement to Attica and Eretria with the specialized funerary lekythoi of the Achilles Painter and his successors.

It was the Achilles Painter who gave a new status and direction to the white-ground lekythos. From now on white-grounds are funerary, though the converse is not quite true, not all funerary lekythoi are white-ground. Indeed the Achilles Painter himself decorated a few red-figured lekythoi (amongst a good number of others with ordinary mythological or life subjects) which by their picture are evidently meant for the tomb. Some of these red-figured lekythoi also have the internal oil container first devised by the Beldam Potter (see on plate 189) which shows that they were never intended for ordinary use as oil flasks; thus von Bothmer, *Ancient Art*, pl. 85, 237.

Not that the Achilles Painter's early and early-mature lekythoi have in their picture any connection with death or the grave. At the most there is on some of them a hint of their destination by pictures which are most naturally interpreted as preparations for visiting the grave side. On the ones we show (all of

them early-mature works of the painter) even this indirect hint is absent. Thus on our plate 185 the scene is that of mistress and maid; plates XXXVIII, XXXIX show the Muses on Helicon, again by the Achilles Painter. Here an other-worldly interpretation metamorphosing a dead girl into one of the Muses has been attempted. On plates 186, 187, again by the Achilles Painter, the scene is a warrior's departure. Some scholars such as Miss Richter have therefore doubted whether these early and early-mature lekythoi by the Achilles Painter were ever specifically made for the tomb. It can also be pointed out that love inscriptions occur frequently on these lekythoi with non-funerary subjects whilst they are not found on those later ones by the Achilles Painter which by the presence of a tomb or more direct allusion of subject matter point to death. Such doubts, however, cannot be upheld in face of the fact that these fine lekythoi, even the earliest of them, were found in tombs, that some of them have the internal oil container (see on plate 189) and could therefore never have been intended for ordinary use, and that, unlike the red-figured lekythoi of non-funerary import, they were on the whole not exported outside Attica or the Athenian settlement in Eretria, where these Attic funeral customs were observed. As to the presence or absence of love-names, it would surely have been ill-omened to put these names into directly sepulchral pictures though it must be owned that this does in fact happen very occasionally on a lekythos.

As time goes on the subject matter becomes more closely linked to death. We have pictures of Death and Sleep picking up the dead (plate 184), of Hermes calling for the dead (plates XLI, XLII), even Charon the ferry man waiting for his passenger and also of course friends and relatives visiting the tomb or mourning (plate 201). Towards the end of the century we have some notable lekythoi with a young warrior brooding by his tomb surrounded by a couple of friends (plates 200; XLV).

White-ground lekythoi in the first half of the 5th century had followed the same evolution in drawing technique as white-ground cups. Thus the black relief line which we find used for outlining the figures on the fine white-ground lekythoi by Douris or the Pan Painter was abandoned in favour of the line in diluted glaze, as we saw it on plate XXXVII. Additional colours not derived from glaze were increasingly used on ambitious pieces as the second quarter of the century advanced into the third. Such colours were reds of several kinds which were pretty permanent, also a matt ochre yellow, rose-red or vermilion, sky-blue matt black and light purple, all of which tend to be more or less fugitive. Good examples of lekythoi with a fairly rich palette are those by the Achilles Painter in his early mature period on plates XXXVIII, XXXIX; 185–187, and one by the Phiale Painter, plates XLI, XLII. The additional snowy white (see plate XXXVII) favoured in the second quarter of the century is abandoned by the Achilles Painter soon after about 450 B.C., though it is found occasionally later and on other shapes, as on plates XLIII, XLIV.

Some time about the middle of the century, or very soon after, the new practice came in by which the outlines were no longer drawn in golden brown dilute but in a matt colour not derived from glaze. The Sabouroff Painter adopted it as early as any, the Achilles Painter resisted it almost to the end. These outlines were usually red, sometimes black or a mixture of the two. Neither of these colours are as permanent as glaze colours. Again the colours for solid areas were towards the last quarter of the century extended in range by the addition of green and mauve, both very fugitive colours. These as well as the other matt colours were applied *after* the pot had been fired, as such pigments, unlike the ordinary glaze, the purple and the white, could not have survived the kiln (see also p. 349). The use of matt outlines was, as time went on, accompanied by certain changes in the type of draftsmanship, not paralleled in contemporary Red-figure. A sketchy, loose lined style developed which reached its fullness on the white-ground lekythoi of the last decades of the 5th century; plates 200 and XLV are amongst the finer examples. This development is not easy to account for. Since paintings were now done in mineral or vegetable colours on the fired pot, they could perhaps increasingly become the preserve of artists trained in a background and tradition different from that of vase painters using the normal technique of drawing in slip glaze over the leather-hard pot, eminently a potter's technique. It is perhaps significant that the white funerary lekythoi of the later 5th century come from specialized workshops which are not known ever to have produced Red-figure (see below).

Furthermore some differences in technique between the application of the glaze and the matt lines may

have been sympathetic to the changing character of draftsmanship. The lines in diluted glaze were evidently drawn with a rather fine, stiff brush whose bristle marks can actually be recognized on examining white-ground lekythoi in detail (see also on plates XLI, XLII). This stiff brush tended to give a certain tension to the line. Matt lines, however, when examined, show no traces of the individual bristles. This may be due to the fact that they were drawn with a different, a soft-haired springy brush applying a pigment made easy-flowing by the admixture of gum or like substance to prevent the drag on the brush which would be caused by the body of the vase being now after firing much more absorbent than before. Altogether the new practice was more akin to free painting than was the drawing with the slip glaze. The change over to the matt outline can be seen in our plate 189, a work by the Phiale Painter, a pupil of the Achilles Painter, who himself too in some of his latest work also adopted the matt line. The Phiale Painter, it must be said, also used the earlier technique, as on his masterpiece on plates XLI, XLII.

The Achilles Painter who gave direction and status to the white-ground lekythoi will be dealt with in a special introduction. His earliest white-grounds must date to about 460 B.C. and for the first ten years or so he used the snowy white we saw on plate XXXVII for his women's flesh. Another contemporary who also produced ambitious pieces is the Sabouroff Painter. Both these artists worked as much in ordinary Red-figure, touching a variety of vase-shapes, as on white-ground lekythoi. The Phiale Painter, a pupil of the Achilles Painter, is mainly a red-figure artist; but by his time already specialist lekythoi-painters had sprung up and the Bosanquet Painter, the Thanatos Painter, the Woman Painter, the Reed Painter and the Triglyph Painter decorated, as far as we can tell, only white-ground lekythoi. These latter, apart from the first two who are still close in time to the Phiale Painter, work in the technique of matt outlines only and develop a freedom of brushwork which results at times in a misty design. Also the sketchy line is used to suggest volume in figures and give an illusion of perspective, helped by colouring. In the latest lekythoi, as represented by Group R (plates 200; XLV), there is a spontaneity of design and a functional character of line which may reflect the influence of major art. The name of Parrhasios has been suggested as the innovator and renewing force in painting in the last decades of the 5th century. He is credited by ancient authors not only with having given the laws of symmetry to art but also to have reached perfection in outlining the shapes of bodies (Pliny, *Nat. hist.* 35, 10, 67–69; see for this the introductory essay, p. 17).

White-ground lekythoi cease at about the end of the 5th century B.C., though there is still a reference to a lekythos painter in Aristophanes' *Ecclesiazusae* of 391 B.C. We do not know the reason for this alteration in funerary customs. Possibly also a change had come over Greek painting which by becoming more and more easel painting, lost its contact with the craft of the vase painter and thus removed its fructifying influence. After Parrhasios problems such as blending of light and shade attracted painters, problems which could no longer be even attempted on the surface of vases.

Bibliography: On white-ground cups H. Philippart, *Les coupes attiques à fond blanc*, Brussels 1936 and Beazley's review, in: *Gnomon*, 13, 1937, pp. 289 ff. The three London cups by the Sotades Painter are in colour now in M. Robertson, *Greek Painting*, pp. 129–31. On white ground lekythoi E. Pottier, *Étude sur les lécythes blancs attiques à représentations funéraires*, Paris 1883. A. Fairbanks, *Athenian White Lekythoi*, 2 volumes, New York 1907, 1914. W. Riezler, *Weissgrundige attische Lekythen*, Munich 1914. Beazley, *Attic White Lekythoi*, London 1938. Buschor, *Attische Lekythen der Parthenonzeit*, Munich 1925; = extract from *Münchner Jahrbuch der bildenden Kunst*, 1925. Idem, *Grab eines attischen Mädchens*[2], Munich 1941 (particularly on the Achilles Painter and lekythoi of his and the immediately succeeding period; a new edition has appeared in the *Piper Bücherei*, Munich 1959, to which we refer as 'Munich 1959'). Rumpf, pp. 104–116. See also Richter, *Survey*, p. 121. On probable Athenian resettlement of Eretria after the Persian deportations in 490 B.C. see Boardman, in: *ABSA*, 47, 1952, p. 47, n. 316. For the Beldam Potter see Haspels, *Attic Black-Figured Lekythoi*, pp. 176 ff. (special design for ritual purposes with a small internal oil container). For colours applied after firing see now J. V. Noble, in: *AJA*, 64, 1960, pp. 316–317. On the matt *red* for outlines see Rumpf, in: *Gnomon*, 25, 1953, p. 469; *EWA IV*, col. 472–3.

184

WHITE-GROUND LEKYTHOS BY THE THANATOS PAINTER. London, British Museum, D 58. From Ambelokipi. Extensively restored and repainted. Height 48.8 cms (19³/₁₆″).

On shoulder below junction of neck egg, pattern, then alternating palmettes. On the side walls, above the painting, meander. Lines are done in dilute, as is also the hair. The fillets and the cloak of the warrior are red with black fold lines. The body of Hypnos is filled with a red wash.

In the centre a grave stele with the drawing of a helmet on its upper part above a frieze of egg pattern. Fillets in red on the stele and the step. On the left winged Thanatos (Death) with wild hair and beard bends to lift up the dead body of a young warrior by his legs. He is helped at the upper end of the body by Hypnos (Sleep), also winged but young, who

has picked up the warrior under the arm pits. The warrior wears a leather corslet and a wrap which hangs over his shoulder and arms.

For the Homeric motif of Sleep and Death raising the body of Sarpedon from the battle field and carrying it to his home, see *Iliad* 16, 666 ff.: 'even to the twin brethren, Sleep and Death, who shall set him speedily in the rich land of wide Lycia. There shall his brethren and his kinsfolk give him burial with mound and pillar; for this is the due of the dead'. 'On the lekythos, and others like it, the dead is a young soldier and the scene may still be thought of as the legendary story. If so it is used as the antetype of a contemporary death in battle; but it may be rather the contemporary dead who is shown as honoured like the hero; or the distinction may not be exactly made—ambiguity is a characteristic of this art. So, though the tomb is shown, they are not to be thought of as laying the body on its steps. They are rather lifting the youth from the battlefield; and that behind is the stone, the dead's due, which his family will raise above him' (M. Robertson).

On funerary lekythoi (as against earlier representations as well as Homer) Death is usually the older of the two, a notion we also find in Eukleides of Megara (later 5th century B.C.) quoted in Stobaeus, *Florileg* III, 6, 63. On this vase he is given plumage (in red) all over his body in addition to his wings, whilst Sleep is dark-coloured. Neither feature is found elsewhere on vases.

The works of this painter are based on those of the Achilles Painter. Notice the effective three quarter view of the warrior's head. Though the Thanatos Painter has been named after this vase, it is not one of his best works nor does he repeat its subject. Most of his lekythoi show mourners and the departed, mistress and maid, brother and sister on either side of the tomb expressing grief with gestures or just facing each other absorbed each in their own doing. His great strength lies in restrained and reticent simplicity which informs all his paintings. The slight swaying of the bodies of his mourning women and the hip thrown out by his standing males show him to belong already to the generation following the Achilles Painter.

440–435 B.C.

Bibl.: A. S. Murray and A. H. Smith, *White Athenian Vases in the B.M.*, London 1896, p. 21; pl. 11. *Cat. Br. Mus.*, III, p. 405, D 58. Pfuhl, fig. 535. Swindler, pl. 13C. Buschor, *GV*, p. 205. Riezler, *Lekythen*, p. 10. Beazley, *Attic White Lekythoi*, pp. 18–19. Idem, *ARFVP*, p. 808, no. 10. See also R. C. Bosanquet, in: *JHS*, 19, 1899, pp. 182–184, and for the interpretation of the subject, M. Robertson, p. 148 (quoted above). For the theme in general see Waser, in. Roscher *s.v.* 'Thanatos'; also L. Deubner, *ibid. s.v.* 'Personifikationen' col. 2111; K. Heinemann, *Thanatos*, Munich 1913, pp. 52 ff., 69 ff; Buschor in: FR, III, p. 244; idem, *Attische Lekythen*, p. 9; A. Lesky: *Alkestis, Mythos und Drama*, Vienna 1925, pp. 67 ff.; idem, in: *RE, s.v.* 'Thanatos'; Schauenburg, in: *JdI*, 73, 1958, p. 53–4. For an important new representation of two warriors raising their dead comrade from the battlefield, see now the calyx-krater in Agrigento by the Pezzino Painter (end of 6th century B.C.) P. Griffo, *Breve Guida del Museo Civico di Agrigento*, p. 26; L. von Matt, *Das antike Sizilien*, pl. 124. This and a small late black-figured neck-amphora, the 'Bourguignon amphora', by the Diosphos Painter, now in New York (Haspels, *Lekythoi*, p. 239, no. 137, and now *Bulletin Metropolitan Museum*, 1957, p. 172, fig. 5) are early examples of a non-mythological treatment of the theme. On our vase and on other white-ground lekythoi Death and Sleep have taken over the office of mercy, as in the story of Sarpedon. That the body on these representations is raised and not deposited, as the quotation from Homer might lead one to suppose, is perhaps also shown by the early Italiote bell-krater in New York by the Sarpedon Painter which shows Death and Sleep *descending* from their flight bringing the body with them home to Lycia. (Richter, *Handbook of Greek Collection, Metropolitan Museum*, New York, 1953, pl. 96, C; also M. Bieber, *History of Greek and Roman Theater²*, p. 77, fig. 283. A. W. Pickard-Cambridge, *The Theatre of Dionysus*, Oxford 1946, fig. 30).

185–188, XXXVIII–XL THE ACHILLES PAINTER

A pupil of the late Berlin Painter, this artist is called after the Vatican amphora, plates 188 and XL. Almost a hundred white-ground lekythoi have been attributed to him in addition to some ninety red-figured vases. On his key position in the development of the white-ground funerary lekythos see the notes on pages 359 ff. Of red-figured vases some twenty are lekythoi, those with mythological subjects to a large extent coming from Sicilian sites, whereas those with funerary themes and his white-grounds have for the most part been found in Attica or Eretria. Of his other red-figured work we note the Vatican amphora shown here, a fine but hopelessly overpainted pointed amphora in Paris (Cabinet des Médailles) with a Dionysiac subject, a few neck-amphorae including a well known one, again in the Cabinet des Médailles, with Euphorbos and Oedipus, many Nolan amphorae, following here in the line of the Berlin Painter, a striking though rather fragmentary calyx-krater in Ferrara (from Spina) with Theseus in an Amazonomachy, a very small sized dinos in Würzburg. A few stamnoi, oinochoai and hydriai have also been attributed to him. Amongst his few bell-kraters we note an early one in New York with an elderly warrior of well-marked facial features, reminding one of the early classical tendency for occasional gross realism. Finally a small number of black-figured Panathenaic prize amphorae have been assigned to him; here again he follows the practice of the Berlin Painter. On many of his vases ranging from large bell-krater to smallish Nolan amphorae he shows a preference for having just two figures on the principal side and one on the back of the vase. Thus we have on the main side Eos and Kephalos,

Euphorbos and Oedipus, Oedipus and the sphinx, Zeus pursuing a woman, warrior and his wife and so forth.

In his earlier work some of the Berlin Painter's formulas of anatomical analysis and rendering are still apparent, as well as his way of disposing figures. As he develops, his own exceptional capacity for combining the beauty of formal perfection with spiritual content manifests itself, as can be seen on the Achilles of the Vatican amphora and even more on his many white-ground lekythoi of his mature period. The Vatican amphora actually preserves something of the Berlin Painter's gift of spotlighting a figure against a completely black and unframed background. The Achilles Painter's main strength, in which he surpasses his contemporaries, lies in his simple and serene figures which bespeak a remarkable inner calmness and spiritual strength. His white-ground lekythoi with their womenfolk, or men departing for battle, are amongst the finest expressions of Greek sepulchral art. He shared with the Sabouroff Painter in the decoration of a loutrophoros, now in Philadelphia, the subject of which is rare for the shape (see on plate 129). Instead of the usual lying in state we have a battle scene, reminding us that our painter worked during a period of Athenian imperial expansion which must have made many inroads upon Athenian families in cost of blood; his activity falls in the fifties and forties of the 5th century B.C., beginning about 460 B.C., and going on into the thirties.

He uses a good number of love names both in his red-figured work and his early and early mature white-ground lekythoi. One of these, Diphilos, son of Melanopos, who occurs fourteen times on his early white-ground lekythoi is also known from an honorary decree found at Olympia (see for this most conveniently Robinson and Fluck, *Greek Love-Names*, pp. 98 ff.). Though he writes so great a variety of male love names on so many of his works, it remains true, as Buschor has put it, that his white-ground lekythoi draw their strength from the nobility and beauty of his women, who are shown with an exalted simplicity which makes one think of the name of Pheidias.

Bibliography: Beazley, in: *JHS*, 34, 1914, p. 149 ff.; 66, 1946, pp. 11–12. Idem, *Greek Vases in Poland*, pp. 49 ff. ('the most classical of all vase-painters'). Caskey-Beazley, *Attic Vase Paintings, Boston*, I, pp. 46–7. Richter-Hall, *Athenian Vases in the Metropolitan Museum, New York*, pp. 147 ff. Richter, *Survey*, p. 118. Rumpf, p. 103 ff. M. Cagiano de Azevedo, in: *Enc. dell'arte classica e orientale* s.v. Achille (pittore di). Cook, pp. 182–3. See also references to Buschor's and Beazley's work in the introductory note on funerary lekythoi, p. 362 above. Beazley, *Potter and Painter*, p. 32.

XXXVIII, XXXIX

WHITE-GROUND LEKYTHOS by the Achilles Painter. Lugano, Private Collection. From Attica, found in a girl's grave. Shape as plate 184. Well preserved apart from some damage on the dress of the seated Muse. Height 36.7 cms ($14^7/_{16}$"). The plates here are enlarged 5:3.

Egg pattern on shoulder below junction of neck; then palmettes (black and red petals) and tendrils. Above the picture, meanders in groups of three followed by an enclosed saltire, pendant or rising. Golden brown dilute for outline of figures.

Two Muses on Mount Helicon. On the right (plate XXXIX) we see a woman seated on a rock which is inscribed *Helikon*. She is dressed in a yellow ochre coloured chiton (with a vermilion line near the hem) and a wine-red himation (with light-brown fold lines) wrapped over her lap. A vermilion head scarf is bound elaborately round the hair. She plays a kithara (partly in pale reddish-brown) with seven strings. The outlines of the upper body are seen through the chiton. The rock lines are done in dilute. Below her feet but still on the rock, a nightingale *symphonos Mounais* (Aristophanes *Birds*, 659) 'singing together with the Muses'.

On the left (plate XXXVIII) another woman standing dressed in a sleeveless red-lined chiton and a himation of vermilion colour with black fold lines, worn over her left shoulder. She is listening to the music, her right arm is raised to the level of her hip, hand and fingers hanging down listlessly, perhaps following the beat of the music. Is she a mortal, a poet, Sappho perhaps or Corinna awaiting the goddess's inspiration, as Robertson suggests? Between the two the love inscription, written *stoichedon* in three lines: *Axiopeithes kalos Alkimachou* = Axiopeithes, the son of Alkimachos, is beautiful. About 445 B.C.

Bibl.: FR, III, p. 303 (Buschor). Beazley, *Attic White Lekythoi*, pp. 15–16, pl. 3,3. Publication of the girl's grave: Buschor, *Grab eines att. Mädchens²*, Munich 1941, pp. 35 ff. and pp. 65 ff. (Munich 1959, figg. 23–25 and frontispiece, also pp. 52 ff.). Beazley, *ARFVP*, p. 642, no. 130. Richter, *Survey*, pp. 119–120. Rumpf, p. 105, pl. 32, 7. R. Lullies, *Eine Sammlung gr. Kleinkunst*, Munich 1955, p. 36, no. 80, plate 39–41. Robertson, pp. 136–139 (colour). Jessen, in: *AA*, 1955, 292 ff. (but no hawk. I owe nightingale and Aristophanes to Miss S. Benton. Nightingale and lyre also on the white lekythos London D 69). For theme compare also the A. Painter's lekythos, *JHS*, 34, 1914, pl. 14, 1. For the stemma of Axiopeithes see Caskey-Beazley, I, p. 45, whence, Robinson and Fluck, *Greek Love-Names*, p. 79. For the *stoichedon* arrangement of the love inscriptions see R. C. Bosanquet, in: *JHS*, 16, 1896, p. 168.

185

WHITE-GROUND LEKYTHOS by the Achilles Painter. Lugano, Private Collection. From Greece. Restored but well preserved. Height 40.7 cms (16"). Enlargement of plate is 5:3.

Shoulder similar to previous vase. Above the picture a meander frieze; continuous key meander below the picture. Black or dark brown outlines in dilute.

Mistress and maid. The mistress seated on a grey brown chair with curving legs and a back rest. She wears a head scarf which once was red, a chiton of which more may once have been indicated in fugitive colour and a himation over her lap. In her hands she holds a red, now unrecognizable, object, a vase or a jewel? In front of her a servant girl (not in our picture) who holds a grey brown trinket chest in her hands. She wears a chiton which once was red. Above the chest the *stoichedon* inscription in two lines: *Hygiainon kalos* – Hygiainon is beautiful. Behind the mistress' head we see the end tapes of a head scarf suspended on the wall. There is also a jug on the wall, but out of sight in our plate.

About 445 B.C.

Bibl.: E. Buschor, *Grab eines attischen Mädchens*[2], Munich 1941, p. 48 and fig. 36 (Munich 1959, fig. 30). Beazley, *ARFVP*, p. 642, no. 129. R. Lullies, *Eine Sammlung griechischer Kleinkunst*, Munich 1955, p. 35, no. 79; pl. 38 and frontispiece.

186, 187

WHITE-GROUND LEKYTHOS by the Achilles Painter. Athens, National Museum, 1818. From Eretria. Fair state of preservation. Height 42.5 cms (16³/₄"). Diam. of mouth 4.5 cms (1³/₄"). Height of figured zone ca. 20.7 cms (8¹/₈").

On shoulder palmettes. Above figure zone, meander in groups of three followed by one enclosed saltire, pendant or rising. Below the figure zone, key meander.

A man dressed in short chiton (painted in yellow ochre) stands in front of a seated woman. He holds helmet, shield and spear in his hands. She sits at ease with her arm resting over the back of her chair. His shield has a profile eye as device. The woman wears sandals, sleeved chiton (in yellow) and himation (once dark red) over her lap, also a necklace and ear rings. In the background a red head scarf or a fillet with tapes, a mirror and a jug, all hanging on the wall set the scene in the home.

The outlines of the figures are in golden brown dilute; diluted glaze is also used for hair. The chiton of warrior and woman are yellow ochre. The crest holder of the helmet is dark-red and there is grey shading for the rim of the shield.

Exquisite drawing. The relationship of the young husband preparing to leave and his wife who stays behind is tenderly depicted.

About 440 B.C. or shortly after.

Bibl.: Collignon-Couve, *Catal. des Vases peints du Musée Nat. d'Athènes*, Paris 1902, no. 1837. W. Riezler, *Weissgrundige attische Lekythen*, Munich 1914, p. 109, pl. 36. FR, III, p. 113. Pfuhl, fig. 543. Beazley, *Attic White Lekythoi*, p. 14. Idem, *ARFVP*, p. 643, no. 135. M. Robertson, *Greek Painting*, pp. 144-5 (in colour).

188, XL

AMPHORA (type B) by the Achilles Painter. Rome, Vatican Museum. From Vulci. Poorly restored from many fragments. The girl on side B is badly damaged. Height 60 cms (23⁵/₈"). Diam. of mouth 30 cms (11³/₄").

For this type of amphora (type B) which goes back to the late 7th century and the horse amphorae, see commentary on plate 21. Actually type B goes on a little longer than the amphora type A (see on plates 150–3), but it too comes to an end before the outbreak of the Peloponnesian War (431 B.C.). This is the last one we show. For the free field decoration see the commentary on plates 150–3. Here there is a base line for the figure, which on A consists of a bar of meanders in groups of two, followed by a saltire, pendant or rising. A similar pattern on side B but with crosses not saltires.

Side A. Achilles (name inscribed) stands frontal with his head turned to the right. His right hand is akimbo, his left grasps a heavy spear just above the handling sleeve. He is dressed in a short sleeveless chiton and a leather corslet reinforced on its side with scales. The shoulder flaps are down and secured to a central Gorgon's head. A baldric across his shoulder carries his sword. Note the four securing buttons on his left side; this is where the corslet opens. A cloak hangs over his left arm. His gaze is towards side B, Briseis standing, dressed in a peplos with her hair covered by a sakkos. She holds a phiale in her left hand and a wine jug in her right. She looks to the left answering to Achilles and is about to hand him the phiale for a libation before battle.

The figure of Achilles has often been compared to the statue of the so-called Doryphoros by the Argive sculptor Polykleitos, who must have created it (it may well represent an Achilles too) about this time or a little later. Though our Achilles as yet scarcely throws out his hip, his right free leg touches the ground with the ball of his foot only, as do Polykleitos' athletes and heroes. Notice the elaborate hair arrangement of Achilles. His back hair is tied into pigtails which come round to the front where they are knotted and hidden by the front hair which is brushed on top. This hair style in one variety or another is also known from a number of famous sculptures in the first half of the 5th century ranging from the Fair-haired Boy from the Athenian Acropolis, to the bronze god from Artemisium.

About 445–440 B.C.

Bibl.: E. Gerhard, *Auserlesene Vasenbilder*, pl. 184. Beazley, in: *JHS*, 34, 1914, pp. 185–6. FR, III, pp. 293–5, pl. 167, 2, fig. 137. Ch. Dugas, *Aison*, fig. 4. Helbig-Amelung, *Führer*[3], pp. 307–8, no. 487. Beazley, *ARFVP*, p. 634, no. 1. Richter, *Survey*, p. 118. Rumpf, p. 105, pl. 32, 6. See also Beazley, in: *Mon. Piot.*, 35, 1936, p. 17, n. 6 (on the one figure decoration). *EWA*, III, pl. 358.

XLI, XLII

WHITE-GROUND LEKYTHOS BY THE PHIALE PAINTER. Munich, Museum Antiker Kleinkunst, 2797. From a tomb in Oropos, on the frontiers of Attica and Boeotia. Some restorations but well preserved. Height 36 cms (14³/₁₆"). Diam. of mouth 5 cms (1¹⁵/₁₆"). Height of picture zone ca. 15.2 cms (6"). For the internal oil container see on plate 189.

Palmettes on shoulder have petals in black, red and white. Golden brown glaze dilute for outlines of body and tomb, of garments, of cap of Hermes, and for some of the terrain lines; matt black lines for rocks and the folds of the woman's dress as well as for other details. More matt colours are used as specified below. The black dots specially concentrated on the hands and feet of the sitting Hermes are the points were the glaze collected at the beginning and end of each stroke, particularly short strokes, when the brush rested momentarily. The stiff, short brush used for applying the diluted glaze (see above page 361) will allow such pools to form, because it does not retain the fluid as easily as will a soft brush.

Hermes is sitting on the left on a rock waiting for a woman to get ready for her last journey, as she puts on her diadem (matt yellow and black). Behind her on the right a round-topped grave-stele decked with fillets. Hermes is dressed in a short sleeveless chiton which is just shown in outline and a matt red chlamys which is fastened on his shoulder. He holds his herald's staff (kerykeion) in his left, with the right he points towards the woman. He wears a so-called pilos cap, the main part of which is painted in matt red-brown, the rest in matt black lines. He sits on a rock over which he has spread a cloak. The woman facing him is dressed in a chiton with folds indicated in matt red. Over it she wears a heavy himation painted in matt brown with matt black fold lines. 'Hermes waits; the time has come; she puts the last touch to her attire, and starts to go' (Beazley). But there is no unity of place! Hermes, the guide of the souls, sits on the rocky bank of the River of the Dead; she decks herself at home; the grave stele is outside the town. Yet the meaning is plain.

The Phiale Painter, called after a red-figured phiale of his in Boston, is the outstanding pupil of the Achilles Painter 'whose tranquil style he transforms by a strong personality into something extraordinarily winsome and vivacious... he was able when the mood summoned him, to create forms of Parthenonian grandeur' (Beazley, *Greek Vases in Poland*, pp. 51 and 52). This was written a good number of years ago; more recently new discoveries and attributions by Beazley have further increased our estimate and the Phiale Painter is now seen as a major painter of his generation. Amongst his red-figure work Nolan amphorae naturally take a prominant place as one would expect of an artist in the line of the Berlin and the Achilles Painters, (on the Nolans of the Phiale Painter, see Beazley, in: *ABSA*, 30, 1928–30, pp. 109–112), but he touches a variety or shapes. On an important stamnos by him once in Castle Goluchow now in Warsaw see here on page 374.

The works shown in our photographs here are all from his white-ground oeuvre (which has recently been enriched by the fine Andromeda calyx-krater in Agrigento, see under plates XLIII–XLIV), two funerary lekythoi, amongst the finest of all extant ones, and the well-known calyx-krater in the Vatican (plates XLIII, XLIV).

440–430 B.C.

Bibl.: E. Buschor, *Attische Lekythen der Parthenonzeit*, Munich 1925, pp. 1 ff., esp. pp. 7 ff., pl. 1, 2 and plate 2. Beazley, *Attic White Lekythoi*, London, 1938, pp. 17–18, pll. 1, 2. E. Buschor, *Grab eines attischen Mädchens²*, Munich 1941, pp. 12–3. (Munich 1959, fig. 6). Beazley, *ARFVP*, p. 658, no. 101. For Hermes' pilos cap see Chr. Kardara, in: *ABSA*, 55, 1960, p. 150, n. 6. On the Phiale Painter see also, S. Karouzou, in: *AJA*, 50, 1946, p. 127. On the woman's diadem see bibl. on plate 129.

189

WHITE-GROUND LEKYTHOS BY THE PHIALE PAINTER.

Munich, Museum Antiker Kleinkunst, 2798. From Oropos, from same tomb as last vase (Munich 2797). Well preserved. Height 37 cms (14⁹/₁₆"). Height of figure zone c. 15.3 cms (6").

This lekythos as well as its companion on plates XLI, XLII has its oil container—for quite a small quantity of oil—attached at the bottom of the neck and masked by the body of the vase, which was never meant to contain anything like its full capacity. See Buschor, *Lekythen*, pp. 2–4; Haspels, *Attic Black-figured Lekythoi*, pp. 176ff.; also Beazley, in: *JHS*, 66, 1946, p. 11, notes 3 and 4. See also our introductory note on white-ground lekythoi, p. 359.

For an illustration of this container, see R. Hampe and E. Simon, *Griechisches Leben im Spiegel der Kunst*, Mainz, 1959, pl. 36; also Bothmer, *Ancient Art*, pl. 88, 239.

On shoulder, egg pattern, palmettes and tendrils. Above figure zone, meander in groups of three followed by saltire, pendant or rising. The outlines of the figures and the stele are *matt* reddish and there are no glaze lines anywhere in the figured part of the vase, though they are still used for the ornamental patterns. Other *matt* colours are a grey-brown for the hair of the two women and for the fold lines of the yellow chiton of the standing woman; black for the rock and the edge lines of the sitting woman's himation.

A woman sitting on a rock by the river of the dead in pensive posture. Just behind the rock a grave-stele (decked with matt red fillets) which is approached on the right (not on our plate) by another woman who holds a matt red fillet in her hands. The pensive woman is wrapped in her himation (reddish lines with black borders above and below, everything in matt) under which her dress emerges painted in matt red colour.

'The group of mistress and maid, or of two sisters, is complete in itself. The tomb is added. Yet one feels that the seated woman belongs to two worlds: she is the beloved mistress, or sister; she was also buried in the grave, and sits sorrowing on the rocky bank of the river of the dead. Two subjects intersect in the chief person' (Beazley).

440–430 B.C.

Bibl.: E. Buschor, *Attische Lekythen der Parthenonzeit*, pl. 1, 1 and pl. 3; pp. 1 ff., esp. pp. 10ff. Idem, *Grab eines attischen Mädchens²*, Munich 1941, pp. 66–7, figg. 53–4 (Munich 1959, fig. 45). Beazley, *Attic White Lekythoi*, p. 18; pl. 5. Idem, *ARFVP*, p. 658, no. 102. M. Robertson, *Greek Painting*, p. 152 (in colour).

XLIII, XLIV

WHITE-GROUND CALYX-KRATER BY THE PHIALE PAINTER,

see p. 367.

We have Polygnotos' signature on two stamnoi, in Brussels and London, on an amphora in Moscow and a pelike in Syracuse. He had a large number of pupils and followers. There are also two other vase painters with the same name, who, however, are old-fashioned in style, and in their work much less important than the Polygnotos we deal with here. The others are conventionally called the Lewis Painter and the Nausicaa Painter, in order to avoid confusion. The Lewis Painter signs his name Polygnotos on two skyphoi, in Baltimore and Tübingen, the Nausicaa Painter on an amphora in London.

Our Polygnotos was a productive as well as an outstanding artist. Beazley attributes to his hand about 60 vases and more than double this number to his pupils and followers. One may say that Polygnotos to a large extent dominated the production of vases between about 445 to 430 B.C.

Polygnotos differs from the Achilles Painter, an early contemporary of his, above all by the more commonplace, and perhaps broadly based character of his figures and representations, which thereby, however, lose in impact when compared with the Achilles Painter. Artistically he is successor to the Niobid Painter, who, as we saw, was strongly influenced by wall paintings; without him Polygnotos would not be what he was. Both artists as well as the Achilles Painter are strongly affected by the art of Pheidias. This is particularly the case with Polygnotos. The idealisation of the human face, the refined perfection of the drapery representations and a certain lassitude, noticeable in several of Pheidias' creations (such as the wounded Amazon or some of the heroines on the Parthenon metopes), all these are exalted by Pheidias in his earnest search for the universally human. In the case of Polygnotos, however, these same qualities all too often turn out to be a superficial veneer covering an emptiness of feeling. Thus we may contrast the powerful drama and pathos of the Penthesilea Painter's Munich cup with the almost colourless striving after the pathetic in Polygnotos' amphora in London, which also shows Achilles and Penthesilea.

The vases decorated by Polygnotos are mostly of large dimensions like those of the Niobid Painter; stamnoi are frequent. But his workshop also produced small oinochoai with boudoir scenes in a rather calligraphic style, looking like precursors of the miniaturist tendency which flourished in the mannerism of the end of the 5th century. Thus we find scenes which were popular at the end of the 5th century such as the myth of Phaon and the allegorical personifications of Pothos and Himeros. Of course there were also the common stock themes of the classical period of the 5th century, such as the Amazonomachy, the Dionysiac and Apollonian cycles, as well as scenes of musical entertainment, of encounters, of libations.

Of his close pupils and followers we may mention the Orpheus Painter (plate 192), the Peleus Painter and the Kleophon Painter (plates 193–9).

Bibliography: Pfuhl, II, pp. 542 ff. Swindler, fig. 361. E. Loewy, *Polygnot*, Vienna 1929, fig. 38. Beazley, *ARFVP*, pp. 677 ff. Richter, *Survey*, pp. 127 ff. Rumpf, p. 107. Alfieri-Arias-Hirmer, *Spina*, Munich 1958, pp. 49–56, pll. 63–81. (Polygnotos); pp. 56–58, pll. 88–97 (Peleus Painter). Cook, pp. 182 ff.

190

STAMNOS by Polygnotos. Brussels, Musées Royaux d'Art et d'Histoire, A 134. From Vulci. Formerly in the Durant Collection. Almost undamaged. Traces of preliminary sketch. Height 36 cms (14³/₁₆″), diam. of mouth 21 cms (8¹/₄″).

At edge of mouth, egg pattern; on shoulder junction, frieze of tongues. Above and below the handles palmettes with spirals. Egg pattern round handle roots.

Side A. Centauromachy. Two centaurs with purple wreaths against the invulnerable Lapith Kaineus. The left centaur has a feline's skin over his arm and with his right holds a rock. The centaur on the right is using a tree trunk to hit at Kaineus who is already half pounded into the soil. He has a Thracian helmet, a corslet, shield and short sword with which to defend himself. Above his head the inscription Kaineus. Between the heads of the centaurs the painter's signature *Polygnotos egrapsen* (note the use of the letter *psi*) = Polygnotus painted. (For story see p. 288).

Side B (not shown). A menad with thyrsus between two satyrs with drinking horn and oinochoe respectively. Early work of the painter. C. 440 B.C.

Bibl.: Klein, *Meistersignaturen*, p. 199, 2. C. Robert, in: *Mon. Inst.*, IX pl. II, p. 6. Hoppin, *RFV*, II, p. 374. *CVA*, Brussels (Mayence), fasc. 1, p. 2, pl. 7. Beazley, *ARFVP*, p. 677, no. 1.

PELIKE ASSIGNED TO THE GROUP OF POLY-GNOTOS. Syracuse, Museo Nazionale Archeologico, 9317. From Syracuse, Fusco Necropolis. Well preserved. Height 43 cms (16^{15}/$_{16}$").

On the neck between the handles, band of palmettes and lotus. Below the figure zone a meander with saltires. Under the handles two large palmettes, one above the other.
Side A. Amazonomachy. On the left a mounted Amazon with pelta shield, in Oriental costume with alopekis cap (of fox skin). In front of her a naked Greek armed with sword and shield (feline hindquarters as device) and Thracian helmet points his spear at the Amazon. Behind him (and no longer visible in the picture) a youth with pilos on his head and wearing high boots, holds his spear in his raised right arm.
Side B (not shown). A bearded person in a rich dress and with sceptre in his hand between two women who are wrapped in their garments.
Refined Polygnotan style. The work recalls the Amazono-machies on a pelike signed by Polygnotos in Syracuse and a pelike with the same subject in Palermo by the Kleophon Painter.
C. 440–430 B.C.

Bibl.: P. Orsi, in: *Not. Scav.*, 1891, p. 33 ff. *CVA*, Syracuse (Arias), fasc. 1, pl. 5, 1–2. Beazley, *ARFVP*, p. 701, no. 92.

192

COLUMN-KRATER BY THE ORPHEUS PAINTER. Syracuse, Museo Nazionale Archeologico, 37175. From Noto. Well preserved. Height 39 cms (15^{3}/$_{8}$"), diam. of mouth 38,5 cm (15^{1}/$_{8}$").

On outer rim of mouth a degenerate ivy branch and leaves. On neck, linked narrow buds. On the shoulders zone of tongues. Side frames of picture consists of degenerate ivy branch and leaves.
Side A. Amazonomachy. On the left a Greek fights sword above his head against an invisible enemy. Presumably this part is an excerpt from a larger scene. In the middle and on the right an Amazon with Oriental cap and costume on horseback riding towards two Greeks who ward her off with their long spears. One of them is naked with Corinthian helmet and shield, the other behind the tree wears pilos and himation. A pelta, the usual Amazon's shield, is on the ground below the mounted Amazon.
Side B (not figured). Two groups with men and youth.
C. 430 B.C.

Bibl.: P. Orsi, in: *Not. Scav.*, 1915, p. 211. P. E. Arias, in: *Clara Rhodos*, VIII, p. 217. Beazley, *ARFVP*, p. 703, no. 2. D. von Bothmer, *Amazons in Greek Art*, Oxford 1957, p. 177, pl. 77, 5.

XLIII, XLIV

CALYX-KRATER BY THE PHIALE PAINTER. Rome, Vatican Museum, 559. From Vulci. Well preserved. Height 35 cms (13^{3}/$_{4}$").

On ledge above, a frieze of slanting double palmettes linked by spirals. Under figure zone a meander with crosses, under-neath which another frieze of linked slanting double palmettes.
Side A. Hermes (winged hat, winged boots, kerykeion, the herald's wand) handing over the child Dionysus to the nymphs and Papposilenos in the ivied glens of Nysa. Zeus had taken the foetus of his unborn son when Semele, the mortal mother, perished and sewn him into his thigh until the time of birth arrived, and then sent the baby to be brought up to Nysa out of the way of Hera's jealousy. This is one of the earliest appearances of Papposilenos ('grand-dad satyr') in art. It may have been at this time that he was also introduced by Sophocles in his satyr play *Dionysiskos* (Nauck fragg. 174, 175) which dealt with the same story of Dionysus' childhood. Indeed the play is thought to be the inspiration behind this and a small group of other pictures dating to about this time. For Papposilenos see also plate 218. The woman behind him may be a menad rather than a local nymph as she wears a deer skin over her peplos; but as the nymphs of Nysa became the first followers of Dionysus, the proto-menads, the distinction is unreal (see *Homeric Hymns* 26 and François Vase p. 291).
Side B. Three Muses on mount Helicon, one of them seated and playing the barbiton, the long-armed lyre. For the subject compare plates XXXVIII, XXXIX.
The figure field is covered with a light yellow slip over which the purple and brown-red colours for the garments are applied. A special snowy white is used for the hair, beard and shaggy body of Papposilenos, also for the flesh of the two nymphs and the three Muses and the chiton folds on Hermes, as well as for some details on the lyre of the standing muse on side B. The outlines of the figures and the shading of the rocks are in diluted glaze. The technique then is that of the later white-ground cups (see page 349). Notable is the use of the additional snowy white well after it had been abandoned by the Achilles Painter on his white-ground lekythoi. There are other instances of the use of this additional white at this period, including white-ground lekythoi such as several by the Klügmann Painter, Beazley, *ARFVP*, p. 764.
440–435 B.C. Beazley now assigns the krater to the Phiale Painter (see on plates XLI, XLII) who also painted another important white-ground calyx-krater in Agrigento. It was found there in 1940 and has a picture of Perseus rescuing Andromeda on one side, on the other two local nymphs, one of them sceptred.

Bibl.: FR, III, p. 302 ff. (Buschor). Helbig-Amelung, *Führer*³, p. 336, no. 559. F. Brommer, *Satyrspiele*, pp. 55 ff., fig. 47; idem, *Satyroi*, p. 27 (on Papposilenos). Beazley, *ARFVP*, p. 671. Rumpf, p. 103. Robertson, *Greek Painting*, pp. 125–127. For the subject of side A see now E. Simon, in: *Antike Kunst*, 3, 1960, p. 10. For the general iconography of Dionysus at Nysa see also, H. Philippart, *L'iconographie des Bacchantes de l'Euripide*, Paris, 1930, pp. 21 ff. Metzger, *Représentations céram. IV siècle*, p. 108. For the earlier representations compare also, E. Simon, *Opfernde Götter*, p. 48; Coche de la Ferté, in: *RA*, 38, 1951, pp. 20–22. Buschor, *Grab eines attischen Mädchens*², pp. 53 ff. (Munich 1960, p. 42 ff.) on the subject of side B. See also C. Boulter, in: *AJA*, 54, 1950, p. 120, n. 2 for a list of white-ground calyx-kraters to which the new krater in Agrigento by the Phiale Painter (see above) should be added (P. Griffo, *Breve Guida del museo civico di Agrigento*, p. 29; von Matt, *Das Antike Sizilien*, pl. 123 – detail of Perseus; *Fasti Archeologici*, 12, 1959, pl. 4; *EWA*, III, pl. 366 (colour); cf. Milne, in: *AJA*, 60, 1956, p. 300. Add also fragments of a krater in Reggio di Calabria, from Locri, by the Villa Giulia Painter, with the upper part of women preserved (use of snowy white).

The name of this artist refers to his stamnos in Leningrad with the love names Megakles and Kleophon. His figures even more than those of Polygnotos express something visionary. Fluid lines for drapery, which is still full of Pheidian character, and serene idealisation of the face are peculiarly characteristic of this painter. His work is always extremely soigné, his lines are carefully drawn, unlike some of the products of the workshop of Polygnotos.

In the profundity of his psychological analysis and in the telling pathos of his parting scenes he shows himself a master unsurpassed for his period. Pheidian influence is particularly direct in his volute-krater from the Valle Pega necropolis of Spina and now in the Museum of Ferrara which shows a ritual ceremony in the presence of Apollo at Delphi. The procession of animals for the sacrifice could be taken straight from the Parthenon frieze. His pictures are all full of the harmony and emotional equilibrium of the classical period.

His shapes tend to be amphorae, kraters, stamnoi and hydriai. His activity ranges from about 435 B.C. into the late twenties of the 5th century.

Bibl.: Beazley, *ARFVP*, pp. 784ff. Richter, *Survey*, p. 143. Rumpf, p. 108. P. E. Arias, in: *Clara Rhodos*, VIII, 1936, pp. 217ff. Beazley, in: *JHS*, 59, 1939, pp. 16, 43ff. Alfieri-Arias-Hirmer, *Spina*, p. 56, pll. 82–87. P. E. Corbett, in: *Brit. Mus. Quart.*, 17, 1952, p. 73–4.

193–195

STAMNOS by the Kleophon Painter. Munich, Museum Antiker Kleinkunst, 2415. From Vulci. Well preserved. Preliminary sketch visible. Height 44 cms (17⁵/₁₆″).

On rim of mouth egg pattern; on top of shoulder, tongues. Under figure frieze, meander with saltires. Near base of body, frieze of tongues. Tongue pattern round handle roots. Above and below handles palmette ornament. Graffito on underside of foot: *TP (= rho)*.
Side A. Warrior's departure. The warrior with Attic helmet, spear, shield (with an eye as device) and carrying a sword on his side holds a phiale in his raised right hand for the parting libation. In front of him his young wife dressed in a peplos with overfall. She holds in her lowered right the oinochoe with which she had filled the phiale. Behind her an old man with white hair. Behind the warrior another woman, his mother or sister. Her hair is in a sakkos, her hand raised in a parting greeting. On the surface of the vase the words: *kalos, kale* = beautiful, in the masculine and feminine gender.
In the nobility and beauty, in the refined humanity as well in its almost dreamy tranquillity this picture is a precious reflection of the art of the Parthenon period. The warrior and his young wife radiate a humanity which is conscious of its fate.
Side B (not shown). Three youths in conversation.
There is an exact replica in Leningrad.
C. 430 B.C.

Bibl.: FR, I, pp. 190ff. Beazley, *ARFVP*, p. 784, no. 2. C. Dugas, *Aison*, fig. 12. Rumpf, p. 108, pl. 33, 8.

196–199

PELIKE by the Kleophon Painter. Munich, Museum Antiker Kleinkunst, 2361. From Gela. Well preserved. Height 46 cms (18¹/₁₆″).

Above picture, enclosed palmettes between flowers. Under figure zone, meander with saltires. Below the handles, palmette.
Side A. Return of Hephaistos into Olympus. Dionysus wears a long chiton, the ependytes above it, and a deer skin on top of it again. His himation hangs from his left arm. He is followed by Hephaistos who is drunk, crowned with ivy (like Dionysus) and dressed in short chiton. His right arm lies across the shoulders of the satyr who supports him round the hip. Hephaistos carries the blacksmith's tools, tongs and a hammer. On the right preceding Dionysus a satyr with a deer skin over his shoulder and ivy in his hair. In his left hand he carries a torch. His right hand is raised beating time to the tambourine played by a menad. Contours and the folds are loosely billowing; the gaze of the figures is inspired, Dionysus is majestic, whilst Hephaistos with his unsteady walk is lost to the world. However, the Dionysiac ecstasy is restrained by the classical tenor and form of the picture, perhaps best embodied in the great figure of the menad.
The painting is still in the later style of the Pheidian period; it is one of the most telling examples of the monumental style of the Kleophon Painter. There is much, however, which points forward to the rich style.
Side B (not shown). Two women and an old man.
C. 435–430 B.C.

Bibl.: Beazley, *ARFVP*, p. 785, no. 27. *CVA*, Munich (Lullies), 2, pl. 74, pp. 15ff.

LATE CLASSICAL TO THE END OF THE FIFTH CENTURY

200, 201, XLV LATE WHITE-GROUND FUNERARY LEKYTHOI

The pictures on these lekythoi show a changed feeling for life different from the earlier ones we saw before. An oppressive atmosphere hangs over these figures of warriors whose bodies seem heavy as though they had lost the tension and heroic elasticity of those created by the Achilles Painter. The heaviness of the last days of the Peloponnesian War rests on them, a presentiment of the bitter end of the war. For the relationship of these late lekythoi, especially of Group-R, with Parrhasios see the Introduction p. 18, also Rumpf p. 116; S. Karouzou, in: *Antike und Abendland* 5, 1956, p. 73. For the technique of matt outlines and its effect on the style see pages 360–1.

200

WHITE-GROUND LEKYTHOS OF THE GROUP OF THE REED PAINTER. Athens, National Museum, 1817. From Eretria in Euboea. The surface is damaged; some of it has flaked off. Height 49 cms (19¹/₄″). Height of figure zone 28.7 cms (11⁵/₁₆″).

Warrior with youth and young woman standing by the grave. The powerful figure of the young warrior dominates the picture which is also accentuated by the broad grave stele with its pediment and akroteria. He sits on the topmost step dressed in a chlamys. Two spears on his side. The two side figures act like a frame, a young woman who touches the edge of her himation and a youth.
Group-R, connected with the Reed Painter.
End of 5th century B.C.

Bibl.: Collignon-Couve, p. 533, no. 1669. *CVA*, Athens (Papaspyridi), pll. 16, 4–6; pl. 17, 1. W. Riezler, *Weissgrundige attische Lekythen*, Munich 1914, pl. 91. Pfuhl, fig. 552. Beazley, *ARFVP*, p. 828, no. 12. Robertson, *Greek Painting*, p. 154 (colour).

XLV

WHITE-GROUND LEKYTHOS OF THE GROUP OF THE REED PAINTER. Athens, National Museum, 1816. From Eretria in Euboea. Surface damaged. Height 48 cms (18⁷/₈″). Height of the figure frieze 30 cms (11¹³/₁₆″), diam. of cylinder 15 cms (5⁷/₈″).

Picture similar to plate 200. Here too the young warrior dominates the centre of the picture in his bulk and heaviness.

This heaviness is underlined by the broad stele in the background with pediment and akroteria. He is seated on its base holding two spears in his raised hand. The girl next to him holds his shield and passes the helmet to him. The youth on the left seems to talk to him.
Group-R, connected with the Reed Painter.
End of 5th century B.C.

Bibl.: Farmakovski, pl. 3. Collignon-Couve, p. 534, no. 1670. W. Riezler, *Weissgrundige attische Lekythen*, Munich 1914, p. 109, pl. 36. *CVA*, Athens (Papaspyridi), pl. 16, 1–3; pl. 17, 2. Beazley, *Attic White Lekythoi*, Oxford 1938, p. 10, 24, pl. IV, 2. Idem, *ARFVP*, p. 828, no. 15. Robertson, *Greek Painting*, p. 155.

201

WHITE-GROUND LEKYTHOS BY THE WOMAN PAINTER. Athens, National Museum, 1956. From Eretria in Euboea. Surface somewhat eroded. Height 39 cms (15³/₈″).

A young woman seated on the steps of a grave stele which is topped by a red acanthus ornament. In one hand she holds an alabastron, the other rests on her knee. She wears a stephane round her head. Her himation was formerly green with touches of red. In front of her a woman who stretches out a hand towards her. Behind her a girl holding a big tray with fruit. She is dressed in a short blue himation worn above a long chiton.
C. 425 B.C.

Bibl.: *JdI*, 11, 1896, p. 129. Collignon-Couve, p. 535, no. 1672. W. Riezler, *Weissgrundige attische Lekythen*, Munich 1914, pp. 3 ff., pl. 72. *CVA*, Athens (Papaspyridi), pl. 11, 4; pl. 12, 1–3. Beazley, *ARFVP*, p. 818, no. 3.

202–203 THE ERETRIA PAINTER

This painter gets his conventional name after an *epinetron* now in Athens and found in Eretria. He was active between 430 and 420 B.C., and fairly productive, as Beazley has assigned to him about 80 vases. His miniature style flourishes best on small vases, cups, oinochoai, kantharoi (one of which is signed by the potter Epigenes), rhyta as well as pyxides, small hydriai and lekythoi.

His drawing is accurate and delicate, full of sensitivity and never affected. His figures small though they are, are well differentiated in their postures and expressions of moods and emotions. A pyxis in

London shows the bride being dressed on the morning of the wedding. She is full of serenity and lost in her thoughts, whilst her maids bustle round her with an engaging grace. Another outstanding work of his in the miniature style is a lekythos in New York, unfortunately not well preserved, with three zones of decoration, red-figured above and below, white-ground (once with polychrome enhancement) in the middle. The upper zone shows a chariot scene, the lowest an Amazonomachy, whereas in the middle in the white-ground zone we see Achilles and Patroclus on one side, on the other Thetis and the Nereids bringing to Achilles the new set of armour made by Hephaistos. In its polychromy this white-ground picture probably approached the easel paintings of the end of the 5th century. However, the Eretria Painter in the poise of his figures and specially in his drapery style has still much of the spirit of Pheidias. He may be said to stand between Pheidias and Parrhasios.

Bibl.: Beazley, *ARFVP*, pp. 724 ff. Richter, *Survey*, pp. 132 ff. Rumpf, p. 109. C. Dugas, *Aison*, Paris 1930, pp. 79 ff. Alfieri-Arias-Hirmer, *Spina*, p. 59, pll. 100, 101.

202

HEAD VASE by the Eretria Painter. Naples, Museo Nazionale Archeologico, Stg., 57. From Ruvo. Fair preservation. Height 22 cms (9″).

Side A (not figured). The plastic part is a menad's head with polychrome flowers on her temples. Side B. Head of a satyr crowned with flowers.
The mouth of the vase has on each side two Amazons in Oriental dress and cap which is rendered in white.
About 420 B.C.

Bibl.: H. Heydemann, *Vasensammlungen Neapel*, p. 650, no. 57. Beazley, *ARFVP*, p. 726, no. 28.

203

EPINETRON by the Eretria Painter. Athens, National Museum, 1629. From Eretria. Well preserved. Length 29 cms (11⁷⁄₁₆″).

The epinetron (or 'onos') is in shape like a strongly curved roof tile, with the sides joining across the front. The front is often decorated with a plastically-worked bust. The epinetron is meant to fit over knee and thigh, and was used for roughening the thread after spinning. The epinetra in daily use were plain and undecorated. Such have turned up, particularly in Athens. Decorated pieces like ours are rarish but occur in both Black- and Red-figure. (*AJA*, 49, 1945, p. 488 ff).
Side A. On the right the bride Alcestis (inscribed) outside her chamber. In front of her Hippolyte, her sister-in-law, seated and playing with a bird, whilst Asterope, sister of Alcestis, leans against her. Then further to the left is a woman who has put myrtle into a loutrophoros, her name seems to be Theano. Behind her on the left is Theo stooping over two marriage vessels (nuptial lebetes) and putting sprigs into them. Another girl, Charis watches her.
Side B. On the left Aphrodite with a wreath in her hands. In front of her Eros followed by Harmonia holding a mirror in her left, Peitho, who is seated, and Kore. On the extreme right Himeros is seated offering a scent bottle (a glass amphoriskos) to Hebe, who is standing next to him.

If on side B we exchange the reference of the names Peitho and Harmonia, we have as subject another famous bride, Harmonia, to match Alcestis on side A and the reluctant Thetis on the third frieze (see Beazley, *Etruscan Vase-Painting*, p. 134, n. 1; Schweitzer, see bibl. below). *Kore* and *Peitho* should also be changed round. We would have then the bride Harmonia seated and surrounded by an attendant (Kore), and by Peitho (Persuasion) who leans over cross-legged to talk to her. Aphrodite, mother of the bride, is also at hand.
In the frieze running at right angles to the sides, we see the conquest of Thetis by Peleus in the presence of Nereus her father, and of the Nereids who are scattering in terror. A sea horse symbolizes Thetis' power of changing her shape.
From an artistic point of view, figures like Alcestis, her friends as well as Aphrodite, Peitho and Hebe are still much influenced by the art of Pheidias, despite our painter's delicate miniaturist work. But there is also more than a hint of the new style which was to find its most famous expression in the balustrade reliefs of the Nike temple on the Acropolis which were carved after the victories of Alcibiades over the Peloponnesians in 410–409 B.C. However, there is nothing yet of the art of the Meidias Painter despite the rich detailing of garments and hair on our vase. It is true enough though that the Meidias Painter is to a large extent rooted in the style of our epinetron.
In front the bust of Aphrodite.
C. 430–425 B.C.

Bibl.: *Eph. Arch.*, 1897, pl. 9 and 10. Collignon-Couve, no. 1588. U. Koehler, in: *AM*, X, 1885, p. 378, no. 5. FR, I, pp. 290 ff. Brueckner, in: *AM*, 32, 190 , pp. 94 ff. (interpretation). Pfuhl, II, pp. 570 ff.; fig. 561. FR, III, p. 148 (Buschor). Beazley, *ARFVP*, p. 726, no. 27. C. Dugas, *Aison*, Paris 1930, p. 80, fig. 14. B. Schweitzer, *Mythische Hochzeiten*, Heidelberg 1961 (special study; complete photographic coverage). On the twigs and flowers in the vessels on side A see L. Curtius, in: *AM*, 48, 1923, p. 40, n. 1; Cook, *Zeus III*, p. 388; Beazley, *EVP*, p. 191. For the pet bird compare the Adonis hydria by the Meidias Painter (see on plate 216). The motif occurs several times in his work, and is known thus or as children's delight on white (matt-painted) funerary lekythoi as well. We think inevitably of Lesbia's sparrow, a bird associated with Aphrodite (see now D. Page, *Sappho and Alcaeus*, p. 7–8). Compare also plate 223. Harmonia, though the bride of legend here, occurs as *personification* of that quality on a number of Meidian vases. On Theano, Beazley in: Proceed. Brit. Acad. 43 (1957), p. 244 ('Helenes Apaitesis').

Beazley has named this artist after an amphora with Apollo and a Muse in the Shuválov Collection of the Hermitage Museum in Leningrad. The Shuválov Painter still works in the same artistic movement as Polygnotos though in a richer style. He paints smallish vases, including oinochoai of the kind used for Dionysiac ceremonies especially during the feast of the Anthesteria. His favourite themes are pictures from the boudoir, children at play, youths in the palaestra and above all Aphrodite and Eros. Mythological pictures are rare and are so chosen that two or at most three figures cover the surface; thus Polyneikes and Eriphyle, Perseus and the Gorgon, Peleus and Thetis, Amazons, Persians and Greeks. His anatomical renderings are summary without much detail, yet his draftmanship is clear and accurate. His treatment of drapery again is summary aiming in the first instance after calligraphic effect, without however attaining the richness of the Eretria or the Meidias Painters. We can sense from his preference for scenes with women and children, the importance which the anecdotal episode is now gaining in vase painting.

The activity of the Shuválov Painter begins after 440 B.C. as is shown by an amphora in Baltimore with a parting scene between young warrior and old man. Its style recalls the Achilles Painter. At the other extreme his oinochoe in Adolfseck with Eros and women and the skyphos in the Louvre with Eros sitting on a chest which is resting on a woman's knees belong to about 420 B.C.

Bibl.: Beazley, *ARFVP*, pp. 753 ff. Idem, in: *PBSR*, XI, 1929, pp. 25 ff. Richter, *Survey*, p. 137. Alfieri-Arias-Hirmer, *Spina*, pp. 60 ff., pll. 102–107.

204

OINOCHOE ('CHOUS') by the Shuválov Painter. Berlin, Ehemals Staatliche Museen F 2417. From Nola. Excellent preservation though a few anatomical details have disappeared. Height 17.5 cms (6⁷/₈″), diam. of mouth 8 cms (3¹/₈″).

On the neck, frieze of enclosed palmettes. Under figure zone, meander with checkers. At the lower end of the handle a satyr's head in relief work with stylized beard.

A presentation of the game of *ephedrismos*, a sort of blindman's buff. A stone, the *dioros*, is set up, two players aim at it with stones or balls to knock it down. The loser (the 'donkey'), whose eyes are then covered by the hands of the winner (the 'king', whom he has to carry on his back), must grope blindfold with his feet until he finds the *dioros*. On this vase a third boy crouches by the *dioros*, which has been knocked

sideways, to watch, perhaps to divert the 'donkey'. The game is described by Pollux, *Onom.*, 9, 119. Above the players, in the field the inscription *kalos* = beautiful.

This particular type of oinochoe the 'chous' was used for the ceremonial drinking of the new wine during the second day of the festival of the Anthesteria at the beginning of spring, the end of February or early March. In accordance with hallowed custom, each person had his own jug for his personal use only. See also p. 373.

C. 425 B.C.

Bibl.: C. Robert, in: *AZ*, 37, 1879, pp. 78 ff. Idem, *Archäologische Hermeneutik*, Berlin 1919, p. 305. Deubner, in: *Die Antike*, 6, p. 175. Beazley, *ARFVP*, p. 754, no. 23. For the 'chous' in general see, G. von Hoorn, *Choes and Anthesteria*, Leyden 1951, (p. 45 and catalogue no. 315 for our vase); L. Deubner, *Attische Feste*, p. 98; also Buschor, in: FR, III, pp. 315–316 (who compares a 'chous' in the Vatican with youths getting ready for a cock-fight. Buschor, *GV*, p. 222, fig. 241). For another 'chous' with an *ephedrismos* scene, see Bothmer, *Ancient Art*, pl. 89, 233.

205 AISON

His signature appears on a cup in Madrid. He was active in the last decades of the 5th century. He still belongs to the circle round Polygnotos even though he is a late follower working in a richer style of draftmanship.

205

SQUAT-LEKYTHOS by Aison. Naples, Museo Nazionale Archeologico, RC 239. From Cumae. Mended from fragments. Some gaps in the drawing. Height 18.5 cms (7¹/₄″).

On the neck palmettes. On the shoulder egg pattern. Palmettes with volutes under the handles. Under the figure zone meander with checker.

Amazonomachy with Theseus taking his part on the side of the Greeks. The battle is ranged in several levels in the

manner of the frescoes by Polygnotus of Thasos and by Mikon. The violence of the attackers and the courage of the defenders is presented with great bravura and an admirable expertise in rendering the great variety of movement.

C. 420 B.C.

Bibl.: E. Gábrici, in: *ML*, 22, 1913, pp. 531 ff., pl. 86. Swindler, fig. 297, 327. B. Schröder, in: *JdI*, 30, 1915, p. 109. C. Dugas, *Aison*, fig. 11. Löwy, *Polygnot*, Vienna, pl. 35. Beazley, *ARFVP*, p. 799, no. 11. Bothmer, *Amazons in Greek Art*, p. 174. On early history of shape see Greifenhagen, in: *Jahrb. Berlin Mus.* 3, 1961, p. 117; cf. also Dugas, in: *BCH*, 70, 1946, pp. 172 ff.

His conventional name is derived from the dinos in Berlin which shows Dionysus reclining amongst satyrs and menads. He was formerly called the Atalante Painter after the subject of a krater in Bologna. He too is still in the wake of the Polygnotan tradition, being a pupil of the Kleophon Painter, from whom he has taken over the monumentality of his figures and the purity of their contours. However, the tranquillity which had distinguished the Kleophon Painter has now yielded place to greater excitement both in the matter of subject and in the detailed execution of line and movement. This is exemplified by the Berlin dinos with dancing satyrs and menads and other works such as the Oxford krater with Prometheus surrounded by satyrs, a subject taken no doubt from a satyr play. His mythological scenes are almost all Dionysiac, other subjects being exceptional such as the deeds of Theseus on the Oxford krater or Atalante and Hippomenes on the Bologna krater.

His activity ranges within the last quarter of the fifth century B.C. but his style shows still much of the sensitivity of the Pheidian Period with which truly he has more in common than with the mannerism of his own days. He is the last great artist of the Pheidian tradition in vase painting.

Bibl.: Beazley, *ARFVP*, pp. 789ff. Richter, *Survey*, pp. 143ff. Rumpf, p. 122. Cook, p. 184. On development and chronology see B. Philippakis, in: *Hesperia*, 21, 1952, p. 111ff.

206–211

STAMNOS by the Dinos Painter. Naples, Museo Nazionale Archeologico, 2419. From Nocera dei Pagani, found with lid and bronze ladle; formerly in the Vivenzio Colection. Excellent preservation. Height 49 cms (19¼").

On the lip egg pattern. On top of shoulder, frieze of black tongues. Under figure zone, meander with saltires.

An important detail which is bleached out in our plates is the shading broadly applied in dilute to indicate the roundness of the vessels on the table in front of the image of Dionysus, and also of the tambourine. This shading is also used to indicate the deep furrow-like folds on the dress of the menads. We know these deep furrows and the strong contrast of light and dark they bring out from sculptures in the last quarter of the 5th century B.C., the Nike of Paionios in Olympia or the reliefs from the Nike balustrade on the Acropolis, to give but two examples. This shading comes out well in the FR plates reproduced in Pfuhl fig. 582.

Side A (details 208, 209). A festival of Dionysus. Menads drawing wine and dancing around an image of Dionysus, which consists of a dummy and a mask surmounted by a crown, both fixed to a stake or a smooth tree. The dummy is dressed in chiton and an ornamental overgarment into which ivy twigs are thrust. An ornamental wreath is affixed below the belt. Two round ritual cakes, known also from other representations are placed on either side of the god's mask. In front of the image stands a sacred table which supports two stamnoi on either side of a kantharos. Furthermore fillets and bloodless offerings, such as fruits or cakes, can be seen rendered in white on this table. On the left a menad called *Dione* by the inscription (ivy wreath, loose long hair and the *nebris*, the deer skin, worn across her chiton) ladles wine out of a stamnos into the skyphos held in her left hand. The skyphos, we know from other representations, holds the wine for human consumption, whilst the kantharos on the table contains the god's own portion. The

other three menads are dancing, one called *Mainas* strikes the tambourine, whilst behind her another is in violent movement holding two burning torches of which she brandishes one behind her. The menad on the left extremity behind Dione holds the thyrsus in her raised hand and is brandishing a burning torch with her lowered right.

Side B (details on plates 210, 211). More menads. On the left one in chiton and himation playing the flute and leading the others; she is followed by *Thaleia*, who advances in stately movement holding thyrsus and a burning, down-pointing torch. Next *Choreia* has turned round suddenly (the deer's legs of the *nebris* are still swinging with the impetus) and beats the tambourine energetically towards the last menad, a remarkable figure striding along in a state of exaltation, majestically wrapped up in her himation and supporting a thyrsus. She may be thought of as the leader of the *thiasos* (sacred band).

The ceremony, whatever it was, *may* be taking place at night, but the brandishing of torches by our menads is not enough to prove it. Torches first came into the hands of menads and satyrs in the early-classical period, in the sixties of the 5th century or thereabouts; before that they are hardly ever seen in this context (a torch is held by a menad on the late-archaic neck-amphora in the Louvre, G 202, by the Eucharides Painter; a couple are used by a menad on a black-figured lekythos of the Gela Painter in Hamburg, for which see now H. Hoffmann, *Kunst des Altertums in Hamburg*, Mainz, 1961, pl. 62; compare also the two torches held by the new-born Dionysus on the Diosphos Painter's black-figured neck-amphora in the Bibliothèque Nationale, Paris, Haspels, *Lekythoi*, pp. 96–7). Torches become more frequent in the second half of the century, and by the time our stamnos was painted and later (see plates 219 and 230) the torch is almost as much part of the appurtenances of Dionysiac revels as the thyrsus or the tambourine. (The tambourine, incidentally found here in the hands of *Mainas* and *Choreia* is an innovation into these scenes of the second half of the

5th century, about 440 B.C. though there are isolated earlier examples. It was brought in from the ecstatic cult of the Asiatic goddess Cybele). No doubt where this new imagery came from. Though religious festivals in the Mediterranean then as now reached their peak in the cool after sundown and particularly so with the all-night dances of the Dionysiac revels (see Euripides, *Bacchae*, 486, 862), yet we specially find in Attic poetry again and again the image of the heights of Parnassus aglow at night with the flickering of torches, when Dionysus leads his throng at his festival celebrated at Delphi every two years (Sophocles, *Antigone*, 1126, 1153. Euripides, *Ion*, 716, 550, 1125; *Bacchae*, 306 ff.; frag. 752 – *Hypsipyle*. Aristophanes, *Clouds*, 603. Compare also Aeschylus, frag. 171 – *Xantriai*). To this festival which took place in the winter, the Athenians too sent a contingent of women, the only occasion as far as we know, when Athenian 'wild women' (menads) were in evidence in a regularly conducted festival. (See for a sober statement of what is known of this L. R. Farnell, *The Cults of the Greek States*, V, Oxford 1909, pp. 153–4).

This evocation in poetry is surely paralleled in those vase-paintings where torches are brandished; the image of the companions of Dionysus is linked to the realities of the nocturnal rites at Delphi and elsewhere. But somehow we did not think of the timeless companions of Dionysus in late-archaic art, on the Brygos Painter's cup in Munich (plates XXXIV and 143 top) or the Kleophrades Painter's pointed amphora (plates 122 ff.) or even those by the Pan Painter on his Palermo krater (plates 162–3) as performing at night or indeed on any particular occasion. They were the god's constant companions. That now they are thought of in terms of the caperings of the Thyiads at Delphi is a particularisation of their image which goes hand in hand with the 'civilizing' of the picture of the Bacchic ceremonies to which we shall refer presently.

The torches then have become attributes and must not be always taken literally as indicating night. How else could we explain their presence in the hands of menads and satyrs in pictures such as the Return of Hephaistos, where there can be no suggestion of a nocturnal procession. Yet we find the torches there, as on the Munich pelike by the Kleophon Painter (plates 196–199), the recently found volute-krater by the same painter from Spina, or again on Polion's volute-krater also from Spina (Alfieri, Arias and Hirmer, *Spina*, Munich 1958, plates 83–4 and plates 110–111). These vases are approximately contemporary with our Naples stamnos. So much in fact did torches become the property of menads that only slightly later menad-like figures representing rage and madness, such as the Furies, regularly adopt the torch from them. (Earliest mention, Aristophanes, *Plutus*, 423–5, in 388 B.C.)

Though our stamnos is not the only vase picture of this ceremony with torches, the general impression given by the pictures is that of a rite taking place during daytime, and to offset the torches there are at least two representations where a parasol is carried by one of the participating women! It is very unlikely therefore that the torches on our stamnos mean to stamp the ceremony as nocturnal.

What is taking place? This vase together with a number of others all showing what is evidently the same rite performed in honour of Dionysus in front of his mask-image have been the subject of much controversy. Are they to be connected with the Athenian winter festival of the Lenaea, celebrated in January with rites which may, as the name *Lenai* (= menads) suggests, have been orgiastic in nature but about which we know nothing at all unless we actually ascribe these pictures to this very rite—and this opinion has been defended notably by Frickenhaus, the first scholar to treat these vases systematically, and by Deubner—or do we have here, as Nilsson in particular has argued repeatedly, a representation of a ceremony we know from the statement of a fourth century B.C. Athenian writer to have taken place every year during the spring festival of the Anthesteria (Phanodemus quoted by Athenaeus, XI, p. 465 A)? During this festival which was celebrated at the very beginning of March or late February, the newly opened wine of last year's vintage was brought by the Athenians to the sanctuary of Dionysus 'in the Marshes', the Limnaion (situated probably due west of the Acropolis just south of the Areopagus hill) to be mixed there with water and consecrated to the god before it was fit for drinking. 'Anthropology has collected endless examples of such consecration of the fruits of field, orchard or vineyard, whereby the taboo is taken off the food of the community before they dare to enjoy it' (Farnell, *The Cults of the Greek States*, V, p. 215).

Our knowledge of these festivals is very sketchy and largely based upon such disconnected scraps of information as chance has preserved. The efforts of scholars to build up a coherent picture though heroic may in fact be misleading. Anyhow the vase representations if, as we must, we consider the series as a whole, do not in fact agree entirely with either of the festival ceremonies as reconstructed by modern scholarship. It is very likely that what is shown is indeed a 'consecration of wine' in front of the mask-image of Dionysus (why else should the stamnos be so prominent in so many of the pictures), yet the occasion is one for women only, women who are acting as menads, albeit peculiar menads since we do not ordinarily expect menads to make the mixing, drawing or drinking of wine their main occupation. As our plates show, menads may serve as ministers to Dionysus and bring wine (so on plates 89; 43 top), they may rather less frequently be seen holding the kantharos or skyphos on their own account, but they never make drinking their main and only business. An exception to this rule is the menad *Kraipale* on a well-known oinochoe in Boston (00.352) but the occasion there may have been specially privileged if the allusion is really to the Anthesteria; see Caskey-Beazley, II, p. 93, no. 112. Nor is there evidence that in actual life the ecstatic worshippers of Dionysus used wine as the prime inducer of excitement. In the most realistic picture of ecstacy set in actual life that we have from the fifth century B.C., the Spina volute-krater of the Group of Polygnotos (Beazley, *ARFVP*, p. 696, no. 23; Alfieri, Arias and Hirmer, *Spina*, pl. 74–81), no wine, no cup, no vessel is in evidence. Music, drums and dance are sufficient.

That the women on the vases belonging to our series are

menads is beyond cavil, though it has naturally been denied by Nilsson who has no use for menads during the celebration of the Anthesteria. For him these women are priestesses, the so called *gerairai*, who, he suggests, perform the rites on behalf of the Athenians, a view entirely unsupported by the Phanodemos quotation referred to above, perhaps even going against its meaning. Conversely the presence of menads has been one of the main arguments in favour of taking the festival represented to be the Lenaea; but why then the stress on the stamnoi and the drinking?

Our vase is the latest in the series of pictures of this rite and one of the very finest. The earliest are a number of vases at the beginning of the 5th century including numerous black-figured vases of various shapes. Outstanding, yet representative in character, amongst these early representations is the red-figured menad cup by Makron in Berlin (worthily published at last in A. Greifenhagen, *Antike Kunstwerke*, pll. 65–67) of about 485 B.C. On all these early 5th century pictures we see a stake or column decked with the mask-image of Dionysus, round which menads (with thyrsi) or women performing like menads execute ecstatic dances. No reference here to the consecration of wine, only on the Makron cup in Berlin one of the menads hugs a large skyphos, which however need have no special significance as similar motifs occur on other works by Makron. The central core of vase pictures is however formed by a remarkable group of stamnoi, all replicas or near-replicas of each other, by the Villa Giulia Painter dating between about 460–450 B.C. (nine are listed in Beazley, *ARFVP*, p. 403, to which one in the Florence market should be added, and perhaps, to judge by the description in *RA*, 1933, 1, p. 160, another in the Castello Sforzesco in Milan). These works of the Villa Giulia Painter mark a clear break with the earlier representations just as they set the tone for subsequent renderings of the subject. We now see junonesque women engaged in a stately ceremonial in a setting similar to that of our Naples stamnos. There is a sacred table placed in front of the mask-idol, on it are two stamnoi out of which wine is ladled into a skyphos by women. These women look like grave matrons, though on a number of these vases one of the women on the other side of the vase is given a thyrsus to mark her as menad. Altogether there can be no doubt about the menadic character of these women, though the painter tends to play down the orgiastic element by turning the women into matrons performing a sacred ceremony (*narthekophoroi* perhaps rather than *bacchae*, to use the contrast made by a Greek saying quoted by Plato, *Phaedo*, 69 C), which after all was the truth of the matter—a strange and significant metamorphosing of the timeless companions of the god into his human worshippers in a Greek city state. On two stamnoi indeed, one in Boston and another one in the Louvre, where none of the women are characterized as menads, the principal celebrant, the one adorned with a diadem, carries a parasol, as unmenadic an implement as can be imagined. Here as elsewhere the women dance with skyphoi in their hands. Men are never present. The Villa Giulia Painter's pupil, the Chicago Painter, has left two stamnoi with a slightly different treatment of the subject but the tone is that of his master. Similarly so with pictures by the Eupolis Painter, an older colleague of the Chicago Painter, who on two of his works stresses the offering of the brimful kantharos to the mask of Dionysus, whilst on a third the stamnos is in prominence again. Another representation, by the Phiale Painter (see here on plates XLI, XLII), on a stamnos formerly in Castle Goluchow and now in Warsaw, has infused some greatness into the picture by an original variation (see Beazley, *Greek Vases in Poland*, p. 52). The chief celebrant's baby child is brought along to the ceremonial, baby child of an Athenian matron indeed, but also baby child of a menad and so the baby is transformed into a little satyr! All these stamnoi by the Chicago, Eupolis and Phiale Painters preserve something of the calm 'civilized' stateliness which the Villa Giulia Painter had imparted to the scene. (Compare for this stately atmosphere another vase which must be related in subject, the stamnos in New York by the Menelaos Painter, Beazley, *ARFVP*, p. 667, no. 1, Richter and Hall, pl. 112; also the stamnos New York 21.88.3, Richter and Milne, *Shapes and Names*, p. 8 or again one in Hamburg by the painter of the Louvre Centauromachy, see Hoffmann, *Kunst des Altertums in Hamburg*, pll. 70, 71). On our stamnos by the Dinos Painter, the latest in the series and drawing away from the Pheidian period, this influence is waning (though the table with the stamnoi introduced by the Villa Giulia Painter survives), and something of the original character found in the late-archaic pictures at the beginning of the century reasserts itself; the menadic names given to the women underline this. All the celebrants are menads pure and simple and the orgiastic character is of the essence of the picture. Its repression just before and after the mid 5th century was primarily due to the personality of one artist, the Villa Giulia Painter.

From the time of the Villa Giulia Painter onwards the vases with this theme are all stamnoi; stamnoi are the mixing vessels from which the wine is shown being ladled into skyphoi for consumption by the women, whilst the kantharos in these pictures is reserved for the god's own portion. Skyphoi are being at times replenished from oinochoai, which incidentally are never of the so-called *chous* shape, the jug used on the second day of the Anthesteria (see on plate 204). If the occasion took place during this festival, we might have expected to see the *chous* represented; yet the oinochoe on our vases is used to replenish someone else's drinking bowl, whereas it was of the essence of the *chous* that everyone should have this own and serve himself alone. The menads for this ceremony may not have been subject to that general ordinance of the festival just as we find an oinochoe, which is not a *chous*, in the hand of the satyr who faces Kraipale on the Boston oinochoe mentioned above, where the picture has been plausibly connected with the Anthesteria.

What our stamnos then shows are menads performing a ceremony at a wine festival, probably consecrating the wine, in front of the mask-idol of Dionysus. The menads are shown engaged in an orgiastic rite which, as we saw from the mid 5th century representations, was actually performed by Athenian women. Whether the consecration is that of

the new wine mixed with water at the time of the Anthesteria we cannot say, but it is not unlikely. Some support for the Anthesteria has been claimed by Nilsson from the picture on a *chous* by the Eretria Painter in Athens (Vlastos Collection), Beazley, *ARFVP*, p. 275, no. 10; pictures in G. van Hoorn, *Choes and Anthesteria*, p. 97; fig. 38, 271; Pickard-Cambridge, *Dramatic Festivals*, fig. 17; Nilsson, *Geschichte griech. Religion*, I², pl. 38, 1; idem, *Dionysiac Mysteries*, p. 27, fig. 4. The shape of this vase certainly connects it with the Anthesteria and its picture shows the mask of Dionysus, not put up on a pillar but cradled in a ceremonial winnowing basket (*liknon*) and placed on a table. Women bring up a kantharos full of wine and a basket of bloodless offerings. But though the mask of Dionysus is there, it is not put up and there is no certainty that we deal with the same ceremony as on our stamnoi; nor do we know for certain that the mask of Dionysus was ceremonially displayed only on this one occasion.

Our series of pictures has thus not yet been unambiguously matched with any Dionysiac ceremony we know of.

About 420 B.C.

Bibl.: H. Heydemann, *Vasensammlungen Neapel*, no. 2419. FR, I, pll. 36–37, p. 193ff. (Furtwängler), *ibid.*, III, p. 28 (Hauser). Rumpf, *Religion der Griechen*, Leipzig 1926, fig. 17 and p. IV. Beazley, *ARFVP*, p. 789, no. 2. Rumpf, p. 112. For the names of the menads see, Ch. Fränkel, *Satyr- und Bakchennamen auf Vasenbildern*, Halle 1912. On the theme of th s vase and its companions, see R. Frickenhaus, *Lenäenvasen*, Berlin Winckelmannsprogramm 72, 1912, passim, esp. p. 16 there for our vase (the only adequate treatment of the vase evidence). L. Deubner, *Attische Feste*, Berlin 1932, pp. 127ff. Both Frickenhaus and Deubner argue for the Anthesteria. M. Nilsson argues for the Anthesteria in *JdI*, 31, 1916, p. 323ff. and subsequently in numerous articles cited in his *Geschichte griech. Religion* I², 1955, p. 587, n. 8 and in his *Dionysiac Mysteries*, Lund 1957, p. 28ff. (mainly on the Vlastos chous). A bibliography of the principal articles up to 1927 is given by Beazley in *CVA*, Oxford, fasc. I, text to pl. 28, 1–2. Other discussions are found in A. Pickard-Cambridge, *Dramatic Festivals of Athens*, Oxford 1953, pp. 27ff. (for the Lenaea). Coche de la Ferté, in: *RA*, 38, 1951, pp. 12ff. F. Willemsen, *Frühe Griechische Kultbilder*, Munich dissert., 1939, pp. 35 and 41–2 (suggestive remarks favouring Anthesteria). B. C. Dietrich, in: *Hermes*, 89, 1961, p. 45ff. (interesting for related ritual). K. F. Johansen, 'Eine Dithyrambosaufführung', (*Arkaeol. Kunsthist. Medd. Dan. Vid. Selsk.*, 4, no. 2, 1959), pp. 39–40. Buschor, in: *AM*, 53 1928, p. 100; Wrede, *ibid.*, pp. 81ff. (on the mask-idol; accepts the Anthesteria). R. Hampe and E. Simon, *Griechisches Leben im Spiegel der Kunst*, Mainz 1959, p. 31 (for Lenaea; the authors connect the representation on a skyphos with our ceremony without, however, very good reasons. Some skyphoi at any rate are in their subject matter connected with the Anthesteria, thus two by the Penelope Painter, the well-known one in Berlin with a woman on a swing, and one recently found, *Kunstwerke der Antike*, Auction Sale XXII of 13.5.1961, Münzen und Medaillen, A.G., Basle, pl. 59, 177). Compare also W. Otto, *Dionysos*, pp. 8off., 92ff. G. van Hoorn, *Choes and Anthesteria*, pp. 24–5. For Dionysiac religion in Athens see in addition to Farnell's *Cults of the Greek States*, cited in our text, the edition of Euripides, *Bacchae* by E. R. Dodds, Oxford 1944 and 1961, introduction, I, ii; for 'official menads' outside Athens see Farnell, *op. cit.*, V, pp. 151ff. For a list of vases

related in subject with our stamnos see above all, Frickenhaus, *op. cit.*, p. 33ff. Though additions have been made to this list since, none of them alter the picture. For such additions consult the entries in Haspels, *Lekythoi*, index *s.v.* 'Image of Dionysus' (in Black-figure) and Beazley, *ARFVP*, p. 982, *s.v.* 'Dionysus, mask and image' (in Red-figure). Not included there are a stamnos in Florence, market, by the Villa Giulia Painter, and one in Milan, Castello Sforzesco, 05238, described in *RA* 1933, 1, p. 160ff. (there also a list of vases showing the mask idol of Dionysus); also a late-archaic red-figured krater fragment in Naples, *ASAIA*, 4–5, 1921–4, pp. 130ff.

212, 213

NECK-AMPHORA with twisted handles. Arezzo, Museo Civico, 1460. From Casalta near Lucignano in the valley of the Chiana. Mended from fragments but fairly well preserved. Height 54 cms (21¹/₄").

The mouth flares out almost cup-like. The outer edge of lip has an egg pattern. On the shoulder long black tongues beneath which a zone of egg pattern. On the neck, picture of a sphinx in white. Under figure zone meander with saltires.

The picture shows Pelops (name inscribed) in his chariot with his bride Hippodameia (inscribed). He looks round towards his pursuer, King Oinomaos, the father of the bride. The race is also described in Pindar (*Ol.*, 1, 36). The chariot is pulled by the horses of Poseidon which the god had given to his favourite, and seems to make its way across the sea, which is indicated by a dolphin (extreme right of plate 212) and stippling to indicate the glitter of the waves. The journey of Pelops across the sea to which Euripides and Sophocles allude (*Orest.* 988; *Hel.* 504) may refer to a version according to which Oinomaos, the father of Hippodameia, was king of Lesbos and not of Pisa in Elis.

Hippodameia is painted in great elaboration, with billowing folds of her chiton. Her himation and her veil are decorated with small circles. On one of the bay trees a pair of doves are mating. They are sacred to Aphrodite and probably symbolic of Hippodameia's love which is also dwelled on in a fragment of Sophocles (Nauck. *Tr. gr. fr.* 430).

On side B (not shown) two girls hastening towards a man. The front of the vase (shown here) is very close to the Meidias Painter, whilst the back (side B) is in the manner of the Dinos Painter.

C. 410 B.C.

Bibl.: R. Kekulé, in: *AI*, 1864, pp. 83ff. Milchöfer, in: *JdI*, 1894, p. 64 FR, II, p. 32ff. Pfuhl, fig. 583. W. Hahland, *Vasen um Meidias*, pl. 8a. G. Becatti, *Il maestro di Olimpia*, Florence 1943, p. 37, no. 13. Beazley, *ARFVP*, p. 793. See also A. Pickard-Cambridge, *Dramatic Festivals of Athens*, p. 219.

214–217, XLVI, THE MEIDIAS PAINTER

The *potter* Meidias has signed a hydria in London (pl. 214, 215). There are four other hydriai painted in the same style, also four squat-lekythoi, two lekanai, two pyxides and one oinochoe. Many more vases have been attributed to the workshop. We do not know the name of our painter, and it is conceivable that he is the same as the potter Meidias. There is undoubtedly a close relationship between this painter and the Eretria Painter.

His favourite subjects are the myths round Aphrodite and Eros and of Dionysus. Women and their world are very prominent in all his works. They are represented doing their toilet or dancing, often with outstretched arms and heads affectedly tilted forward. His pictures often seem like magnified designs of the Eretria Painter transferred to a large scale; but they are mannered and affected. His penchant for arabesque flourishes of line, which tended to turn into purely decorative patterns, draws him away from realism. His hydriai in London and Florence (plates 214–17; XLVI) well illustrate the profound changes in style and content which took place in the painting of the last decades of the 5th century B.C. A refined and elegant conception of the human form, which in the last resort goes back to the idealisations of Pheidias, lives on in his sensitively drawn figures. He often uses perspective and foreshortening striving for new effects and new solutions to artistic problems.

There are also still links with the tradition of Polygnotus of Thasos; his interest in the rendering of spatial depth is one of them; another is the way he arranges his figures on different levels within the picture. This Polygnotan method is carried on into the fourth century B.C. and is also well known in Italiote, particularly Apulian vase-painting.

Like his other contemporaries he often uses symbolic figures, thus we have Hygieia as personification of Health, Paideia symbolizing Discipline and Breeding, and Eudaimonia Happiness. Such figures also occurred in the easel paintings of Parrhasios and Zeuxis.

His activity falls within the last two decades of the 5th century but his influence reaches well down into the 4th century. The 'Meidian manner' in respect of the rendering of space and colour was to become the basis for several groups of painters in the fourth century amongst them the Kerch vases as well as the style of the Italiote and Siciliote vase-painters.

Bibl.: Beazley, *ARFVP*, pp. 831ff. W. Hahland, *Vasen um Meidias*, Berlin 1930. Richter, *Survey*, pp. 146ff. C. Becatti, *Meidias, Un manierista antico*, Florence 1947. Rumpf, pp. 113ff.

214, 215

HYDRIA by the Meidias Painter. London, British Museum E224. Formerly in the Hamilton Collection. Restored but well preserved. Height 52.1 cms (20¹/₂").

Upper zone: the rape of the daughters of Leucippus by the Dioscuri, Castor and Polydeuces, in the sanctuary of Aphrodite. The young heroes have surprised the two sisters called here Helera (Hilaeira) and Eriphyle, whilst they gathered flowers with their companions. The picture shows in its lower reaches Aphrodite sitting next to her altar. On a higher level her archaic looking image (face and arms white, garments enhanced with raised gilding) can be seen holding a phiale in the right, the left hand also raised. On the extreme left of the picture Zeus as father of the Dioscuri is sitting on a rock holding the sceptre. The girl Agaue runs towards him whilst her companion Chryseis kneels in front of Aphrodite with flowers in her lap. To the right of Aphrodite Peitho runs off, though not without turning round to look at Eriphyle being carried off by Castor. Flowers, grass indicated by flourishes characteristic of the painter, and bay trees represent the flowery groves of Aphrodite. At a slightly higher level the actual rape is shown. On the left Polydeuces is already moving off in his chariot with Hilaeira, whilst on the right Castor is still busy carrying Eriphyle to his chariot which is held in readiness by his charioteer Chrysippos. Wavy ground lines indicate the levels of the chariot on the one hand and of Castor and Eriphyle on the other.

Lower zone. Herakles in the garden of the Hesperides. In the centre the miraculous tree which bears the golden apples, the wedding gift of Ge to Zeus and Hera. A snake is coiled round the trunk. To the left of the tree is Chrysothemis reaching for an apple; behind her Asterope; then seated Hygieia holding a sceptre in her left hand; next to her Klytios. To the right of the tree we see Lipara holding one of the apples in her left. She has turned round towards Herakles who is seated on a rock resting his arm on his club. Behind him stands his nephew Iolaos. On the other side of this zone we have eleven figures. Next to Iolaos is Hilaeira, then Medea followed by Arniope; then follow seven heroes, Philoktetes, Akamas, Hippothoon, Antiochos also Klymenos, Oineus and Demophon, the brother of Akamas. The series is closed by Chryseis who is then followed by Klytios whom we have already seen on the left of the front picture. These heroes who people the garden are drawn in part from the Argonauts (Medea, Klytios, Klymenos, Philoktetes), of whom Herakles was also one for a time, though we have no version where his quest for the golden apples was made in association with the Argonauts. More interesting and significant is the crowding in of the rest, all Attic local heroes four of whom are actually 'tribal heroes'. Herakles's quest is thus linked to Attic local patriotism, of which we have more signs on other vases of this period.

Both zones are distinguished by the grace of their figures, by the rich drawing of the garments as well as by singular finesse and wealth of linear draftmanship. There is gold enhancement in the garments.

376

About 410 B.C.

Bibl.: The bibliography up to 1896 in: C. H. Smith, *Catalogue Vases Brit. Mus.*, London 1896, III, pp. 173–177. Additional bibl. up to 1927 in: *CVA*, Brit. Mus. (H. B. Walters) III, pl. 91, p. 6. FR, I, pll. 8–9, pp. 38 ff. P. Ducati, *Midia*, pp. 96 ff., fig. 1. G. Nicole *Meidias*, p. 55, fig. 1. G. Becatti, *Meidias, Un manierista antico*, Florence 1947, p. 10, pl. 1. Beazley, *ARFVP*, p. 831, no. 1. Richter, *Survey*, pp. 146–7. Rumpf, p. 113. Buschor, *Gr. Vn.*, pp. 225 ff., figg. 250, 251. On the appearance of the Attic tribal heroes on vases of this period see Beazley in *AJA* 39, 1935, p. 487, also *ibid.* 54, 1950, p. 321; compare T. B. L. Webster, *Art and Literature in Fourth Century Athens*, London 1956, p. 14. For the garden scene see Brommer, in: *JdI*, 57, 1942, p. 116; idem *Herakles*, p. 50.

216, 217, XLVI

HYDRIA by the Meidias Painter. Florence, Museo Archeologico, 81947. From Populonia. Good state of preservation. Height 47 cms (18$\frac{1}{2}$″); diam. of mouth 16.5 ms (6$\frac{1}{2}$″).

Lip is decorated with egg pattern as on the London hydria. At lower end of neck, frieze of enclosed palmettes. Under the picture zone meander with checkers.

In the centre of the picture zone Phaon and Demonassa sit on a rock, covered with cushions. Phaon an old boatman had been transformed by Aphrodite into a beautiful youth irresistible to women with the gift of remaining so for ever as reward for having ferried her across the straits of Lesbos without taking a fare when she came to him in the guise of an old woman. Here in the picture he is seen wreathed in laurel and playing the lyre. Demonassa dressed in ample chiton and a star-embroidered himation, which she has put across her knees, passes to Phaon a golden diadem. The pair is under a canopy of laurel. The little boy Himeros with spread wings stretches out his arms towards Phaon. To the right of Demonassa is Leto looking down full of love at her son Apollo, who is sitting on a rock. To the left of Phaon the nymphs Leura (seated and holding a diadem) and Chryso-

geneia. Above them on a higher level Aphrodite in a light chariot drawn across the air by a winged Pothos and Himeros. Pothos holds a golden phiale in his left and a laurel wreath in his right, whilst Himeros carries a big incense burner in his left. To the right amongst the clouds we see the nymphs Hygieia (Health) and Eudaimonia (Happiness); to the left Pannychia (All-night Feasting) and Erosora (Spring Time).

An infinite wealth of gilded detail floods the whole picture, diadems, necklaces, bracelets, the wings of Himeros and Pothos, details of garments and laurel. All this together with a restless flow of line for garments, locks, even ground lines and stones contributes towards building up an atmosphere of almost daydreaming reverie, so typical for the Meidias Painter; it vibrates in the sweetness of his womenfolk, in his every line. From the art-historical point of view the Phaon hydria together with the Adonis hydria found in the same tomb, also in Florence, form the climax of the Meidias Painter's rich mannerism. About 410 B.C.

Bibl.: L. A. Milani, *Mon. scelti del Museo arch. di Firenze*, I, pll. 4, 5, 3. G. Nicole, *Meidias et le style fleuri dans la céramique attique*, Geneva 1908, pl. 3, 2. P. Ducati, *Midia*, Rome, 1909, p. 102. Pfuhl, fig. 594. Ducati *Ceramica Greca*, II, p. 400. C. Dugas, *Aison*, Paris 1930, p. 117. *CVA*, Florence (Levi), fasc. 2, pl. 61, 64, 65, fig. X, p. 57. G. Becatti, *Meidias, Un manierista antico*, Florence 1947, pp. 11–12, pll. V–VII. *EWA*, III, pl. 375 (part; in colour). Beazley, *ARFVP*, p. 832, no. 4. For Phaon and Demonassa see Beazley, in: *AJA*, 54, 1950, p. 320 ff. For the myth of Phaon see also FR I, p. 296, on pl. 59, a calyx-krater near the Meidias Painter showing Phaon frigidly rejecting the attention of nymphs; compare also T. B. L. Webster, *Art and Literature in Fourth Century Athens*, p. 34 (see *ibid.* pp. 40 ff. on the personification names of Aphrodite's companions; cf. also Hampe, in: *RM*, 62, 1955, p. 120 ff.; Deubner, in: Roscher, *s.v.* 'Personifikationen'). The earliest picture of Phaon seems to be on a fragment of an early classical white-ground cup in Reggio di Calabria, from Locri, *Arch. Class.* 2, 1950, pl. 53, 1–2. Pannychia (or -is) occurs as personification of nocturnal ceremonies (see p. 374), at least three more times in the work of the Meidias Painter and his circle: the Adonis hydria and Manner of Meidias Painter nos. 9; 76 (Beazley *ARFVP*).

218, 219 THE PRONOMOS PAINTER

This is the name given to the painter of the Naples volute krater (plate 218) which shows on its front a picture of the flute-player Pronomos, a performer who is known also from written records. He is connected in some ways with the Dinos Painter, yet is particularly close to the mannerism of the Meidias Painter. His picture of Dionysus and Ariadne recurs on a number of other contemporary vases which suggests that all these representations are modelled on a fresco painting of the subject dating to the end of the 5th century B.C.

218, 219

VOLUTE-KRATER by the Pronomos Painter. Naples, Museo Nazionale Archeologico, 3240. From Ruvo. Almost undamaged. Colouring fairly well preserved. Height 75 cms (29$\frac{1}{2}$″).

On outer rim of mouth egg pattern. Then on ledge below, a frieze of heart-shaped cyma pattern followed by a frieze of palmettes. On lowest zone of neck as well as on the sides

of the volutes laurel with berries. On the neck zone there are two opposed branches meeting and entwining in the centre. On the shoulder, tongues with an egg pattern underneath. Below the figure zone, meander with checkers. There is much use of additional white as on Ariadne, Himeros, Papposilenos, the masks of the actors and of Papposilenos, and elsewhere. Yellow wash for the chiton of Ariadne and Herakles' corslet. Brown dilute wash used over Ariadne's chiton and Herakles' corslet, for the ground

colouring of the furry drawers of the chorus men, for the shading of the animal skins worn by Herakles and Pappo-silenos, for the skin folds on some of the masks and for other shading. Purple is used for some of the fillets hanging from the tripods, for the edging on Ariadne's dress and the diadem and ivy leaves on the mask of Papposilenos.

The principal side, plate 218, shows the chorus of a satyr play consisting of eleven men wearing their special drawers (one of them out of sight on our plate, is dressed in an ornamental kind of chiton and a himation), and an actor impersonating Papposilenos ('grand-dad' satyr) on the upper right. We also see the poet Demetrios seated on a stool at the lower left, the lyre player Charinos standing and next to him seated on a fine chair in the centre of the lower tier, Pronomos, the flute-player, and also reformer of his instrument. He alone of all present, apart from one of the chorus men of whom more below, actually 'performs'. He is shown playing his instrument. Satyr plays were closely linked to tragedy, they were performed as the last of a series of four plays of which the first three were tragedies.

There are five figures in the upper zone which evidently do not belong to this chorus. They are Dionysus embracing Ariadne who shares his couch and three more who carry masks and wear the richly embroidered dress of tragic actors. The males in this group all wear the boots of tragedy, the up-pointed cothurnus. Of the three Herakles on the right is self-evident, in fact has his name written against him. He wears in addition to his lion's skin a corslet and he carries his club and bow, as well as his quiver. His mask shows the lion's head. The other two hold masks with an Oriental tiara and have accordingly been identified as Laomedon, the king of Troy, and his daughter Hesione, who was rescued from the sea-monster by Herakles, who was then, so the story goes, cheated of his reward. Of these three the woman at any rate with a leaf diadem in her hair and holding the mask can be no ordinary actor. We do not know of the female actors of that time, and she sits on the couch occupied by the divine couple, hardly the place for a mortal. Again winged Himeros (Desire), so called in the inscription, has come up to her with a chaplet indicating real, not mimed passion. She has been interpreted by Bulle as Paideia, the personification of the discipline of the theatre, holding here the mask of Hesione. On a relief from the Piraeus in Athens a seated figure also sharing the couch with Dionysus is called Paideia by the inscription. Buschor however (see references below) argued that the woman and indeed the other two, Herakles and Laomedon, are to be thought of as the characters themselves holding their masks and appearing, as it were, in their own roles here where the god of the festival, the heroes of the tragedy, the human dancers of the satyr chorus, the musicians and the tragic poet are all assembled in the sanctuary of Dionysus indicated by the tripods, which are placed under the handles on both sides of the picture. There is much to be said for Buschor's view of the heroic presences in the cast. Even in the nomenclature the painter has differentiated between them and the chorus men. These latter, as also the musicians and the poet, are given contemporary names of Athenian citizens (for these see below) not satyr names, whilst the divine pair, the heroic cast and Pappo-silenos are either left nameless or given their heroic or divine identity. Thus *Herakles* (not the name of an Athenian actor!), *Dionysos* and *Himeros* in the inscriptions. Moreover, in those pictures where we can compare an actor and his mask as on the recently found Ferrara bell-krater from Spina ca. 460 B.C. (*Arte Antica e Moderna* 5, 1959, pp. 37 ff., pl. 17 – G. Riccioni; T. B. L. Webster, *Monuments illustrating Tragedy and Satyr Play*, London 1962, pl. 1a) and on the well-known Gnathian bell-krater fragment, Würzburg 832, mid-4th century B.C. or just before (e.g. Pickard-Cambridge *Dramatic Festivals* fig. 34) we find not unexpectedly a studied contrast between mask and the actor's face. The opposite is the case on our krater. Herakles as person has the face and head of hair we would expect Herakles to have (though he might have been beardless at this period) and the similarity between this face and that of the mask has not been denied by even those most determined to see the portrait of an actor here. The same applies to Laomedon, a king in his own appearance, and probably also in the case of Hesione. More equivocal is the status of Papposilenos who is bearded too, whilst all the chorus men, the musicians and the poet are beardless. He evidently is a human *actor*, yet assimilated in some way to the 'heroic cast', rather than to the chorus men and the rest of the human company. (Would a beard in real life not have interfered with the mask? We would expect actors to be beardless, or at least stubble bearded only, as on the Würzburg actor fragment).

That characters can hold their masks and have other attributes of the stage and yet be no actors, but the heroes of the myth is no stranger than those numerous instances of satyrs who are *satyrs* and not chorus men even though they wear the drawers of the satyr play (see below). Thus of the list of such satyrs and Pans given by Brommer, *Satyrspiele*[2], pp. 71 ff. nos. 1–14a; 23; 150, (cf. Webster, in: *Hesperia*, 29, 1960, p. 256, n. 10), no more than six or perhaps seven, including our krater, are chorus men. The rest are satyrs in the context of a satyr play.

Fragments of another volute-krater from Taranto now in Würzburg and in a style close to that of our krater show the chorus and characters of a tragedy all carrying their masks, together with the flute player and probably the poet and a Muse; Dionysus is also present. Here even the chorus, though they carry their masks, are transfigured into the sphere of the myth; they are women, not male chorus men impersonating women.

Some details now. The members of the satyr chorus have, with two exceptions which are out of sight on plate 218, the furry drawers required to fix the satyr's tail and erect phallos. They carry their masks in their hands except for one, Nikoleos, who is shown in the lower register between the poet Demetrios and the flute-player Pronomos with mask on and doing his stuff dancing the 'sikinnis'. These masks are in most cases carried by their handling straps. They are seen in profile, front, and three-quarter views—once even from inside. Most of the chorus-men are wreathed, to indicate their present status of being in the service of the god. The actor representing Papposilenos gives a good imper-

sonation of the character we saw in reality on the Vatican krater, plate XLIV. He is dressed in a tight-fitting costume with tufts of white body hair all over, the so-called shaggy garment *(mallotos chiton)*. His mask is white-bearded and white-haired with an ornate diadem and ivy leaves over his ears. A few long teeth are showing, with big gaps between them. He carries a leopard's skin over his shoulders. He is not at his age ithyphallic.

The poet Demetrios is not, it seems, otherwise known to us except possibly as a name in a late list of dramatic poets given by Diogenes Laertius. He holds his manuscript still rolled up and tied with strings. Another roll rests against the bench. The flute-player Pronomos here in full performing dress and the central character in the picture apart from the god, is known as a bearded character from Aristophanes, *Ecclesiazusæ* (line 102 and scholiasts) performed in 391 B.C. His name also appears on other records of about this period. If we press the representation here, he may have been a younger man at the time of this picture, still beardless! Pronomos was a Theban and it could be argued that his popularity in Athens must date after the end of the Peloponnesian War and may have started in the last years of the 5th century when the restored Athenian democracy had established relations with Thebes. Hence a date at the end of the century or just after is suggested by the subject of the picture. In front of the seated Pronomos stands another musician, who must have performed during the play, Charinos holding a lyre.

All but two of the satyr chorus have their names written against them, Eunikos, Charias, Euagon, Kallias in the upper row, Nikomachos, Dorotheos, Nikoleos, Dion, Philinos below.

Bulle has pointed out that Pronomos the flute player apart from his central position in the picture also wears his full theatrical regalia which he would have had on during the performance and suggests that the vase picture is based upon a votive picture dedicated to Dionysus by Pronomos himself on the occasion of a particularly outstanding musical success during the performance of the otherwise unknown *Hesione* of Demetrios and the subsequent satyr-play. We may note it as strange that the choregus does not appear in the picture when the cast, chorus, musicians and poet do.

Side B. Dionysus and Ariadne embracing each other as they move forward surrounded by a rout of satyrs and menads in ecstasy. A tripod on the extreme right indicates the god's sanctuary. Ariadne and one of the menads carry torches. Is the scene set at night?; see the commentary on pages 372–3. Behind Dionysus an Eros hovering with cymbals in his hands. Behind him some leaves. The same group of Dionysus and Ariadne occurs on a number of other pictures, thus for instance plate 222. There must have been a common model to all these.

End of 5th century B.C. or the very beginning of the 4th.

Bibl.: *MI*, III, p. 31. H. Wieseler, *Theatergebäude*, VI, p. 2. H. Heydemann, *Vasensammlungen Neapel*, pp. 546 ff., no. 3240. A. von Salis, in: *JdI*, 25, 1910, p. 48, pl. 4. L. Séchan, *Études sur la tragédie grecque dans ses rapports avec la céramique*, Paris 1926, p. 45–46. FR, III (Buschor) pp. 132 ff., pll. 143–145, fig. 61, (the fundamental study). Buschor, *Gr. Vasen*, fig. 257. M. Bieber, *Theaterwesen*, p. 91, 94. H. Bulle, *Eine Skenographie* (94. Winckelmannsprogramm, Berlin 1934), p. 27 ff. Beazley, *ARFVP*,

p. 849, no. 1. Idem, in: *Hesperia*, 24, 1955, p. 313–314. H. Metzger, *Représentations*, pp. 115, 118 ff. Rumpf, p. 115. A. Pickard-Cambridge, *Dramatic Festivals of Athens*, Oxford 1953, p. 179–180. T. B. L. Webster, *Greek Theatre Production*, London 1956, p. 174, no. A9. Idem, *Art and Literature in Fourth Century Athens*, p. 32. F. Brommer, *Satyrspiele*[2], Berlin 1959, pp. 11; 72, no. 4. M. Bieber, *History of Greek and Roman Theater*[2], p. 10; p. 274 n. 26
(the best photographic reproduction of the vase is still in her *Theaterwesen*, pl. 48). For the chronological indications given by the flute player Pronomos see Richter, *Survey*[2], p. 142. For pictures of poets and music artists on vases see now K. Friis Johansen, 'Eine Dithyrambos-Aufführung' in *Arkaeol. Kunsthist. Medd. Dan. Vid. Selsk.* 4, no. 2 (1959), p. 11 ff. with ample references. The poet at this time was still producer and chorus trainer, the *didaskalos*. On our vase just as on the Copenhagen bell-krater published by Johansen he is shown as being under the spell of inspiration. For the roles of poet and actor at this time and the later development see also Bulle in *Festschrift James Loeb*, Munich 1930, p. 6 ff. On the evidence of this vase for the size of the satyr chorus see N. E. Collinge, in: *Proceedings Cambridge Philol. Soc.* N.S. 5, 1958–59, p. 30 ff; also ibid. p. 29 on the number of actors in the satyr play and the status of Papposilenos, who at the time of our vase was no longer leader of the satyr chorus but a full actor; cf. also A. M. Dale's edition of Euripides' *Alcestis*, Oxford 1954, p. XIX, n. 2. On the *sikinnis* danced by the chorus man Nikoleos see Beazley, *Some Attic Vases in the Cyprus Museum*, London 1947, p. 41–42; also E. M. W. Tillyard, *The Hope Vases*, Cambridge 1923, p. 80. On the oriental tiara and the costume of the theatre king see A. S. F. Gow in *JHS* 48, 1928, pp. 140, n. 30; 148, n. 44 and n. 45. The rich clothing worn by Laomedon and the others is not confined to actors but is found from time to time in mythological pictures of the end of the 5th century and beyond. On this dress see S. Karouzou, in: *JHS*, 65, 1945, p. 41; Webster, *Monuments illustr. Tragedy*, London 1962, p. 5–6; idem, *Greek Theatre Production*, p. 37 n. 1. (Webster quite inexplicably seems to deny the tiara to Laomedon's mask wanting to make it into a decorative back-strap. There are indeed *holding* straps painted in white, but they are additional to the tiara. Also *ibid.* p. 40 Webster takes the masks of Laomedon and Herakles to be yellow-white as against the dead white of Hesione's mask. However, the publications only show that the two male masks are creased with folds indicated in brown dilute, whereas the girl's mask is smooth. All seem to be equally white).

Buschor has recently defended his interpretation of the 'heroic cast' in *Studies presented to D. M. Robinson* II, pp. 90 ff. against Bulle. If his interpretation is not accepted, a name and explanation has to be found for the woman holding the mask of Hesione. She must be a muse or a nymph. On this see L. Curtius, *Pentheus* (88 Winckelmannsprogramm, Berlin 1929), p. 16 n. 1; Bulle, *Skenogr.*, pp. 28–29; idem in *Corolla L. Curtius*, Stuttgart 1937, p. 156. More crucial is the question of whether the separation of the cast, be they the heroes themselves or the actors impersonating them, from the satyr chorus is justified. Our commentary in this respect accepts Buschor's position, who takes them to be the representatives of the higher species of drama, tragedy, whilst Papposilenos and the chorus stand for the satyr play. Thus the complete dramatic tetralogy is present surrounding Dionysus as his 'music' companions (from whom 'tragedy' could hardly have been absent) to be matched on the back of the vase by Dionysus in the midst of his bacchic followers. This reading of the vase as a whole with a correspondence between front and back pictures is not the only one possible; thus another view going back to von Prott in *Schedae philol. H. Usener oblatae*, 1891, pp. 47 ff., takes the picture to be derived from a votive picture dedicated to Dionysus by one of those primarily concerned in the dramatic festival. Bulle has restated this view more cogently pointing out that the dedicator of the model would not have been the choregus, (as von Prott) but rather Pronomos himself, the flute player (see his *Skenographie* and idem in *Corolla Curtius*). If this view is accepted, the absence of 'tragedy' from the picture could be borne with equanimity (though Bulle himself accepted Buschor's view of a tragic cast). The costume of the 'cast' is tragic. It is possible though that the actors in the satyr play had at this time the same costumes, but we have no independent information on this and it is certainly dangerous to argue, as has been done, from this vase that this was so. Even the Naples mosaic from the Casa del Poeta Tragico at Pompeii, whatever its value as evidence, can only tell us about masks of the satyr play and not the rest of the costume. An Athenian would have known and been able to interpret our picture with assurance; we cannot.

The Würzburg fragments from Taranto (mentioned above in our commentary) near the Pronomos Painter (Beazley *ARFVP* p. 965) showing chorus and characters from a tragedy are published by Bulle in *Corolla Curtius* pll. 54–56 (whence Pickard-Cambridge, *Dramatic Festivals* figg. 40a–c; see ibid. p. 183 and p. 218 for Beazley's comments on some details of the interpretation); see also Buschor in *Studies Robinson* l.c. and Webster *Greek Theatre Production* pp. 40–41, who reports Möbius' impor-

tant observation that two fragments had been wrongly combined in the restoration of one of the actors. The theatre fragments seemed on examination to belong to the same vase as sherds in Würzburg and also from Taranto, with the great gigantomachy published by A. von Salis in *JdI*, 55, 1940, pp. 127–131, figg. 21–24.

For the cymbals in the hands of Eros on side B see the boy in the ecstatic picture on the Ferrara volute-krater belonging to the Group of Polygnotos, from Spina, Alfieri-Arias-Hirmer, *Spina*, pl. 80. This type is rare in vase painting as indeed cymbals are altogether. They are orgiastic implements *par excellence* found in the hands of menads as early as the François Vase (see page 292).

220

CALYX-KRATER IN THE MANNER OF THE PRONOMOS PAINTER. Naples, Museo Nazionale Archeologico, 2045. From Ruvo. Fragmentary. Estimated height of complete vase 31 cms (12¹/₄″). Diam. 38 cms (15″).

The battle of the giants against the gods. The portion shown on plate 220 shows an arched pilaster of myrtle leaves which represents the canopy of heaven. Below it on the right we see emerging from the ground Ge (Earth), the mother of the giants, looking with concern at their activity. The giants carry leopard skins and are engaged in prising great rocks from the hillside, lifting them and staggering under their weight. They are piling them up on the heights of the hill to storm the seat of the gods, an original variation of the common motif of giants hurling stones and rocks against the gods.

Beyond the canopy the gods are about to engage in battle. The time is the early morning for on the right the chariot of Helios, the Sun, is rising, whilst to the left of the canopy Selene, the Moon, riding side-saddle, is going down.

Above the Sun a chariot is visible (of Zeus?), whilst on the extreme right of our plate the back of the vase comes into view, satyrs and menads charging into battle no doubt in the following of Dionysus. The one satyr preserved intact is helmeted and armed with a spear, a menad is preparing to throw a stone; she also carries a thyrsus and is just visible on the extreme right of our plate. Also on the back of the vase and at the edge of the preserved portion are the legs of a giant half-downed already. A vine tree has sprung up ominously in front of him.

Two of the giants are named, *Enkelados* and *[Porphyr]ion*, whilst on the back the menad is called *Paidia*. On that same side the beginnings of another name are preserved, *Eu[———]*. It may belong to the charging satyr or the downed giant.

Fragmentary though the vase is, it is the most haunting picture of the gigantomachy we possess. The source of its inspiration has caused much speculation. A. von Salis in a notable study connected it with the painting of the subject known to have existed on the inner side of the shield of Pheidias' Athena Parthenos, but other suggestions have been offered, such as the embroidered battle picture on the peplos worn by the image of Athena (thus H. Walter).
C. 400 B.C.

Bibl.: FR, II, p. 195, figg. 72–75. Hoppin, *AFV*, II, p. 449, no. 2. Pfuhl, II, fig. 585. W. Hahland, *Vasen um Meidias*, pll. 9 and 10, 2. A. von Salis, in: *JdI*, 55, 1940, pp. 90 ff. F. Vian, *La guerre des géants*, p. 149. Idem, *Répert. Gigant.*, p. 85, no. 389. Beazley, *ARFVP*, p. 850, no. 1. H. Walter, in: *AM*, 69–70, 1954–55, pp. 95 ff. Rumpf, p. 111, pl. 35, 1. Photographic coverage, also of the back of the vase in *ÖJH*, 10, 1907, p. 254, 256–7, fig. 83–5 (Ducati). On the canopy of heaven, Beazley, *CVA*, Oxford 2, p. 121 (on pl. 66, 25); E. Simon in: *ÖJH* 41, 1954, p. 85; Herbig in: *SE* 24, 1955, p. 188.

221 THE SUESSULA PAINTER

His conventional name comes from four amphorae with twisted handles painted by him and found in a grave at Suessula near Naples. Three of these are now in the Metropolitan Museum in New York, the fourth in the Boston Museum of Fine Arts. Some indication of the date of his activity is given by the find of a krater fragment close to his style in the grave (in the Kerameikos cemetery) of the Spartans who fell fighting in the Piraeus in 403 B.C. during King Pausanias' expedition at the time of the Thirty Tyrants.

Though there are still connections with the Meidias Painter our painter is already rooted in the spirit of the early fourth century. His works are informed with a strong and vivid pictorial imagination. We see lively movement of men and horses, ample use of three quarter view, underlined by frequent enhancement of the drawing with applied white and yellow.

221

NECK AMPHORA with twisted handles by the Suessula Painter. Paris, Louvre, S 1677. From Melos. Perfectly preserved. Height 68 cms (26³/₄″).

Side A (not shown). Gigantomachy. Zeus, who has descended from the chariot driven by Nike, hurls his thunderbolt. Next to him Dionysus in a chariot drawn by leopards. Also

Poseidon on horseback, Athena, Apollo, Artemis and other gods as well as Herakles, all battling against the giants.
Side B. Gigantomachy continued. Ares in his chariot, which is driven by Aphrodite, aims his spear against the giant Porphyrion. Squatting on the back of one of the horses is a little Eros drawing his bow. On the upper right of the picture one of the Dioscuri raising his spear against a giant who is facing the team of Ares and is half obscured by an

uneveness in the ground. In the middle under the horse team of Ares, Kore fighting against a giant. Behind her on the extreme left Demeter. To Kore's right, the second of the Dioscuri on horseback stabbing a giant with his spear.

The picture must be modelled on some work of major art. Similar motifs recur on fragmentary kraters in Würzburg and Leipzig and on a pelike in Athens of about the same period. It is not possible, however, to connect these representations with the picture on the shield of the Athena Parthenos, because our model must be later. However, the popularity of this theme at the beginning of the fourth century may be due in the last resort to the influence of the Parthenos shield (see on plate 220).

The charming motif of a tiny Eros taking part in the battle as archer is important as it is one of the very rare cases of Eros using the bow and arrow in 5th century representations. They became his common attributes only from the mid-4th century onwards and have continued to be so until today. Eros using bow and arrow has also been restored with some probability by Praschniker on the Parthenon metope East XI (*Parthenon Studien*, p. 174, fig. 108 and p. 216, fig. 128), again in a gigantomachy. Here the date is more than a generation earlier than our amphora. Again a bronze ring with a picture of Eros drawing the bow has recently been reported found in a tomb in Epirus which is said to date from the 2nd quarter of the 5th century B.C. (*BCH* 80, 1956, p. 305).

Why the bow and arrows? In literature from the time of the early Hellenistic period onwards, such as the epigrams of Asclepiades preserved in the Palatine Anthology, we know them as the wounding shafts of desire, a notion which occurs already in a number of passages in Euripides and is stated particularly clearly in *Iphigenia in Aulis*, 550. But the image never seems to have caught on, for it is only after a very long interval that it became popular in Hellenistic literature and from then onwards. In art its popularity starts a little earlier, shortly before the middle of the 4th century B.C., as is shown by the following: Attic hydria, Kerch style, Berlin 3166 (Schefold, *Untersuchungen*, figg. 19 and 20; Metzger, *Représentations*, pl. 44, 2); engraved mirror, Paris, Louvre (Züchner, *Klappspiegel*, no. 17; Beazley-Ashmole, *Greek Sculpture and Painting*, fig. 141); some 4th century gems e.g.

Furtwängler, *Antike Gemmen*, pl. 14, 7 = Lippold *Gemmen*, pl. 26, 11; a number of South Italian vases from the late second quarter of the 4th century B.C. onwards (see e.g. the old list in Furtwängler, *Eros*, p. 71 = *Kleine Schriften* I, p. 46. As early as any is the Apulian volute-krater, Berlin F 3257, FR iii, p. 175, fig. 91). Quite probably one or more Eros statues by Praxiteles had the bow, though the evidence is not secure, and there is the Lysippan Eros stringing the bow (Lippold, *Plastik*, pl. 100, 4).

In so far as the early 5th century represented pictorially the sentiment implied by Eros the archer, the overpowering and ravaging force of Eros, it did so in the forceful imagery of Eros using the whip or even chasing the victim with a chastizing sandal (see S. Karouzou in: *Arch. Delt.*, 1927-8, pp. 106 ff. on the Asopodoros lekythos by Douris in Athens; also Greifenhagen, *Eroten*, pp. 67-8). However, this image of Eros does not seem to persist much after the late archaic period, after about 470 B.C., until at any rate it reappears changed to an archer in the more playful mood of the full 4th century B.C. Do the three 5th century examples of Eros as an archer, of which our amphora is one, bridge the gap between the early 5th century pictures of Eros as task master and the full emergence of Eros as archer? The evidence is hardly sufficient for us to tell but there seems to be no particular reason why Eros should in a gigantomachy be given bow and arrow rather than another weapon. We may take them therefore to have the same meaning as in Euripides whose references to the arrows of Eros go back at least to 431 B.C., the date of the *Medea*. It is probable then, though by no means certain, that the bow and arrow of our Eros in the gigantomachy is no accidental attribute but connected with Eros sending the shafts of desire, an image to take the place of the earlier whip or sandal.

C. 400 B.C. or shortly after.

Bibl.: FR, II, p. 193, pll. 96-97. Pfuhl, III, fig. 584. Hoppin, *RFV*, p. 450, no. 3. W. Hahland, *Studien zur Attischen Vasenmalerei*, pp. 12, 19, 74. A. B. Cook, *Zeus*, Cambridge 1914-1940, III, 1, pl. 7. Beazley, *ARFVP*, p. 852, no. 6. D. B. Thompson, in: *Hesperia*, Suppl. VIII 1949, p. 368, pl. 50, 1. F. Vian, *Répertoire des Gigantomachies figurées dans l'art grec et romain*, Paris 1951, p. 86, no. 393. H. Walter, in: *AM*, 69-70, 1954-1955, pp. 95 ff., pl. 11, 1. B. Andreae, in: *RM*, 65, 1958, pp. 33 ff. For the Würzburg fragments see also the bibliography on plates 218-9.

ATTIC VASE-PAINTING IN THE FOURTH CENTURY

The last phase and catastrophic end of the Peloponnesian War had very largely brought to a halt the export of Attic vases, and even with the economic recovery of the early 4th century the former position could not be retrieved. In particular the market in Southern Italy, the so-called Magna Graecia, was lost for good, because new centres of production had sprung up in the Greek cities there supplying their own needs of decorated vases.

As far as Attic production in the fourth century is concerned two main lines of stylistic development can be identified. One of them remains within the tradition of Pheidian art, whilst the other bases itself on the art of the Meidias Painter and the polychrome effects pursued by him. These are the Kerch Vases

so called after the locality in the Crimea, in the region of the ancient Pantikapaion, where a great many of these vases have been found.

A leading painter of the first group, which was still based on the Pheidian tradition, is the Painter of the New York Centauromachy, named after a volute-krater in New York with Theseus and the Centaurs. His style is very close to that of the Dinos Painter. Another leading artist in this line is the Meleager Painter who is characterized by a touch of ecstasy which he imparts to his figures. This quality is even more accentuated, almost exaggerated, in certain artists near the Meleager Painter, such as the Jena Painter and the Retorted Painter.

The Kerch vases (which incidentally were not only exported to the region of Crimea but also elsewhere within Greece proper and the southern shores of the Mediterranean) represent perhaps the last stage in the development of Attic Red-figure vase-painting. Though based upon the style of the Meidias Painter the figures now no longer have the clean and delicately curving outlines, nor are the inner details rendered with the close-meshed throbbing lines which we knew in the work of the great master of the Rich Style, but rather we see a multitude of short, broken, often rather harsh strokes marking out body, garments and folds. In addition to the sober red and black of the Red-figure painting there is now much enhancement in white, yellow, gilt and at times even blue and grey. Yet despite this stepping up of polychromy the general impression of these pictures is strongly plastic not only pictorial, perhaps just because of this sketchy manner of drawing, which, as Buschor points out, has a powerfully modelling effect giving substance almost in the round to two dimensional figures. The stylistic equivalents in sculpture to Kerch vases are to be found in the works of Praxiteles, the pedimental sculptures from Tegea with their play of light and shade and statues such as the Mausolus in London. Yet there was a dilemma in vase-painting consisting very largely in the contrast between the functional line of a Parrhasios with its strong hints at spatial interrelationships and the two-dimensional vision of an art essentially tied to the surface of a pot. Thus the colouring on Kerch vases, not being meant to create the illusion of mass or space, never developed into anything more than decorative enhancement. This dilemma is particularly conspicuous on Kerch vases during their acme between 360 and 320 B.C.

We must not forget in this context vases with relief decoration. Already the Meidias Painter had added plastic details and gilding to his paintings. However, the development led to even greater emphasis on relief decoration. Thus a squat lekythos in New York (28.57.9) with Telephos, the son of Herakles, and Auge in Argos, and also an oinochoe in New York (44.11.10) with Aphrodite and Erotes, are excellent examples of this art in the last decades of the fourth century. These vases were coloured with the addition of gilding, thus combining modelling with painting. Yet their popularity was limited as we can see from their rarity. They were the products of a crisis in development, as all hybrid creations are, and the same can be said about Italiote relief ware as well as the Arretine pottery of the Roman period.

Bibl.: P. Ducati, *Saggio di studio sulla ceramica attica figurata del IV secolo a.C.*, in: ML 1916. H. Metzger, *Représentations céram. IV siècle*, Paris 1953. K. Schefold, *Die Kertscher Vasen*, Berlin 1930. Idem, *Untersuchungen zu den Kertscher Vasen*, Berlin 1934.

222 THE MELEAGER PAINTER

The painter is named after the volute-krater Vienna 158 with Meleager and Atalante. He is still linked to the tradition of the vase painter Polygnotos, being particularly close to the Dinos Painter. His favourite scenes are Dionysiac, also representations of youths in the palaestra. His activity dates in the first quarter of the fourth century.

222

STEMLESS CUP by the Meleager Painter. London, British Museum, E 129. From Nola. Well preserved. Diameter 24.4 cms (9⁹/₁₆″).

Inside picture. On lip vine tendrils and leaves with bunches of grapes in gilt. The medallion is framed by meander with checkers.

The youthful Dionysus with chiton wrapped round his

shoulder and leg holds a lyre in his right embracing the girlish figure of Ariadne. Ariadne in turn clasps his body. Ariadne is richly dressed, holds a tambourine in her left hand. Behind them a winged Eros floating in the air beating the tambourine and singing.

The motif of this sensuously painted picture recurs on several vases of the late 5th and early 4th centuries, also on Italiote vases. We saw a similar group on the back of the Pronomos krater (plate 219), extended there by the addition of satyrs and menads.

Outside (not shown). On lip myrtle branch with berries. In the pictures on both sides Dionysus with menads and satyrs. Thyrsus and ornament in gilt; diadems and wreaths in violet purple.

Beginning of 4th century B.C.

Bibl.: *Cat. Br. Mus.*, III, pp. 132 ff. A. von Salis, in: *JdI*, 25, 1910, pp. 126 ff. Beazley, *ARFVP*, p. 872, no. 42. Richter, *Survey*, p. 157. H. Metzger, *Représentations céram. IV siècle*, Paris 1953, p. 115. P. E. Corbett, in: *JHS*, 80, 1960, pp. 58 ff.; pll. 4–7. H. Walter, *Vom Sinnwandel griech. Mythen*, Waldsassen, 1959, p. 15 ff.

223–8, XLVII KERCH STYLE

See introductory note on Attic Vase-Painting in the Fourth Century, page 381.

223

CALYX-KRATER NEAR THE HELENA PAINTER. Munich, Museum Antiker Kleinkunst, 2388. From Greece. Mended from fragments with numerous gaps. Otherwise well preserved. Height 28.4 cms (11 3/16″).

The shape of the krater with its expanding calyx and strongly curved handles is typical of its late stage of development. Under the figure zone, tongue pattern followed by a frieze of enclosed palmettes and lotus flowers.

Paris and Helen. In the centre of the picture we see the queenly figure of a well developed young woman with a dove in her lap. Above her a winged Eros floats in the air with a lyre in his hand. He is leading towards her a youth who having but a himation over his left arm, approaches her almost hesitantly.

The usual interpretation is that of Paris standing in front of Helen. Yet we must remember that at the turn of the first and second quarters of the 4th century there is a tendency to invest ordinary human events with, as it were, mythological gilding. The subject may therefore be no more than young man meeting young woman in love and affection. We are therefore inclined to interpret the so-called Dioscuri in this picture as ordinary youths. Similarly we may think of Aphrodite on the other side of the vase as symbolizing love rather than setting a concrete mythological situation. C. 370 B.C.

Bibl.: K. Schefold, *Untersuchungen zu den Kertscher Vasen*, Berlin 1934, p. 88, 139. H. Metzger, *Représentations céram. IV siècle*, Paris 1953, p. 48, no. 24, p. 280. H. Walter, *Vom Sinnwandel griech. Mythen*, p. 29 ff., fig. 22. Ghali-Kahil, *Enlèvement et Retour d'Hélène*, Paris 1955, pl. 22.

224

TREFOIL OINOCHOE BY THE HELENA PAINTER. New York, Metropolitan Museum, 25.190. From Attica

(Athens?). The shape is that of a *chous* (see note on pl. 204). Height 23.5 cms (9 3/16″). On neck a wreath of ivy leaves with flowers, representing the real wreath which was at the end of the festivities dedicated in the sanctuary of Dionysus (see van Hoorn, *Choes and Anthesteria*, p. 31).

On the right we see Dionysus seated on a chair with a high back, holding a thyrsus in his left; his upper body is bare, his chiton being wrapped across his legs and lap. Of truly royal appearance he turns to a female figure behind him called *Pompe* (= Procession) by the inscription. She too is of great beauty, both in posture and bodily charms which are fully displayed. She is turning towards Dionysus, holding a myrtle branch in her hand. On the left an Eros tying up his sandals ready to proceed. Between him and Pompe is a ritual basket apparently made of metal which is rendered in raised clay. Such baskets were used in sacred processions; here the allusion is probably to the Dionysiac festival of the Anthesteria, as is suggested by the 'chous' shape. We note the symbolic character of the representation. It is a development of the earlier personification met in the works of the Eretria and the Meidias Painters. Now on Kerch vases these personifications become incorporated into mythological scenes. Extremely delicate drawing enhanced with white, yellow and gilt.

Middle of the 4th century B.C.

Bibl.: Richter-Hall, *Vases in Metropolitan Museum*, no. 169, pll. 164, 177. Richter, *Survey*, p. 161. K. Schefold, *Die Kertscher Vasen*, pl. 10. O. Brendel, in: *AJA*, 49, 1945, pp. 519 ff. M. Bieber in *Hesperia*, suppl. 8, 1949, pl. 4, 1. (Her text is fantasy; see Nilsson, *Opuscul. Select.* III, p. 243 ff.). T. B. L. Webster, *Art and Literature in Fourth Century Athens*, pl. 16, p. 105 ff. (on personifications). For the ritual basket see Richter, in: *AJA*, 11, 1907, p. 422; 30, 1926, pp. 422 ff. L. Deubner, in: *JdI*, 40, 1925, p. 215; 42, 1927, p. 176. Idem, *Attische Feste*, pp. 97 ff. p. 103 (on our vase). See now the striking representation of the metal basket carried aloft on her head by the woman leading the Delphic procession on the Kleophon Painter's volute-krater from Spina, Alfieri-Arias-Hirmer, *Spina*, pl. 87 top; see also G. van Hoorn, *Choes and Anthesteria*, no. 273, fig. 23. For the basket in context of the wedding see our plates 226–7. Schefold in: Wolters-Bruns, *Kabiren-heiligtum*, Berlin 1940, p. 87, n. 2. (Helena Painter, withdrawing previous attribution to the Pompe Painter.)

This artist is so called after a pelike in Leningrad with the representation of Marsyas. He is distinguished by the splendour and poise of his figures as well as by his striking mastery of most complicated and daring foreshortening. He dates to the third quarter of the fourth century and falls within the Kerch style.

XLVII

PELIKE by the Marsyas Painter. London, British Museum, E 424. From Kameiros in Rhodes. Well preserved. Height 42.5 cms (16³/₄″).

On the lip, egg pattern. Above figure zone, two kinds of egg pattern. Under figure zone, meander with checkers. White with details in dilute for Thetis and Eros; gilt for wings of Eros and the diadem in the hair of Thetis and the hat of Peleus; turquoise blue for wings of Eros; green (and white edges) for the garment on the rock behind Thetis.

Thetis, all naked, has been surprised bathing in the sea by Peleus, who is crowned by Eros. Her green dress is laid out on a rock. Two sister Nereids run off or cower to seek modesty. The sea monster biting Peleus represents Thetis' changes of shape to evade her mortal suitor before she surrendered. On the left Aphrodite seated and without attributes but on a larger scale than the rest; by her side a companion, Peitho perhaps. The third girl, dressed and next to Thetis, may be another Nereid. Compare the more violent encounter in similar circumstances on plate XLVIII.

Side B (not shown). Dionysus between satyr and menad.

'Both shape and figures painted on it are as it were extended beyond their natural selves to proportions of Praxitelean slenderness. Starting from the bathing Thetis in the foreground there is a continuing progression into depth as figures turn and twist in a rich three-dimensional life towards the girl in backview pivoting round herself like a tendril. Yet the compositional plane still coincides with the surface of the wall of the pot. Thus the newly-found three-dimensional vase-picture is still in harmony with the flowing line of the shape and the Alexandrine baroque is still able to fuse with the fundamentals of the classical vision, nowhere more than in the mythological content of the picture. Far removed from the naive story telling of the sixth century it has yet much that is basic in common with the early classical narrative of a Douris and a Brygos Painter. Even if the artist's involvement is now less immediate, the dramatic event linking the various figures in the scene is still felt as the bond uniting the picture into one experience. It is not until this bond is dissolved in the last quarter of the century that the classical style will have died' (Buschor).

C. 340–330 B.C.

Bibl.: *Cat. Br. Mus.*, III, E 424. P. Ducati, *Saggio*, p. 13, A 3, pl. 3, 1. FR, III, pp. 332 ff., pl. 172. Rumpf, p. 133, pl. 43, 9. K. Schefold, *Die Kertscher Vasen*, pp. 122–124, 126, 129. Buschor, *Gr. Vasen*, pp. 251 ff., fig. 265. G. Lippold, *Gemäldekopien*, pll. 11, 60. H. Metzger, *Représentations céram. IV siècle*, p. 268, no. 3, pp. 273, 420. F. Brommer, *Vasenlisten zur gr. Heldensage*, Marburg-Lahn, 1956, p. 189, no. 48. Beazley, *Etruscan Vase-Painting*, p. 83. H. Walter, *Vom Sinnwandel griech. Mythen* p. 33 ff. Cook, pl. 51. On the attitude of Thetis see R. Lullies, *Die kauernde Aphrodite*, Munich 1954, p. 59.

225–228

NUPTIAL LEBES by the Marsyas Painter. Leningrad, Hermitage Museum, 15592. From Kerch, the ancient Pantikapaion. Mended from fragments but well preserved. Height 46 cms (18¹/₁₆″).

The lid has as its knob a moulded amphora without handles. It is decorated with a gilded laurel branch. On shoulder of lebes, egg pattern; immediately above figure zone a row of gilded dots. Under figure zone, meander with checkers. Much additional colour used, white and gilding.

The picture goes without break round the whole of the vase and shows the *epaulia*, the bringing of gifts to the newly married bride the morning after the wedding. In the centre (plate 226) is the young bride with bared bosom seated on a gilded chair. She is dressed in a himation (solidly painted) which is decorated with plastically raised and gilded circles. On her lap is a little Eros; other Erotes flutter about her, and throughout the whole picture. They are painted in white. A little girl eagerly offers the bride a *lekanis* (covered dish) which, so we know from other sources, contained gifts for this occasion. Standing in front of the bride is a young Athenian woman who caresses the little Eros in the lap of the bride. Behind her other gifts are being brought (plates 226, right, and 227), such as a basket similar to the one on the New York oinochoe (plate 224). Then follow two women who are taking a tapestry out of a chest. An Eros is above the one stooping down over the chest. Then we see a woman completely wrapped up in her himation leaving only her eyes free. Two servants come and offer her a chair and cushion (plate 228). Turning to the other side of the bride we see on plates 225 right, and 226, first of all a woman in rich chiton who turns round to face a queenly looking woman carrying a nuptial lebes and a small chest. Behind her are two more women carrying gifts; one of them with a chest, the other with pyxis and incense vessel. Finally a veiled woman visible on the right of plate 228. She may be a personification of chastity in accordance with the symbolizing tendencies of the period. Mid-4th century B.C.

Bibl.: K. Schefold, *Die Kertscher Vasen*, p. 16, pll. 19, 20. Idem, *Untersuchungen zu den Kertscher Vasen*, Berlin 1934, p. 30, no. 286, pl. 34, 1–2. On the *epaulia* see L. Deubner in *JdI* 15, 1900, p. 144 ff.; A. Brueckner in: *AM* 32, 1907, p. 91 ff. P. Zancani Montuoro, in: *Arch. Class.*, 12, 1960, p. 48 ff. On the woman completely wrapped up in her himation see Hampe and Simon, *Griechisches Leben im Spiegel der Kunst*, on pl. 34.

NON-ATTIC RED-FIGURE

ETRUSCAN VASE-PAINTING

Etruscan vase-painting never reached the artistic importance attained by the Italiote vases which we shall describe below. Painted vases in central Italy during the 6th century B.C. were largely influenced by the Ionian style. Such were the Caeretan Hydriai (plates 77–80, XXVII) whose production however was locally limited, and also the so-called Pontic Vases of more provincial style, followed by the work of the Micali Painter, who was influenced by late Attic Black-figure. However, the red-figured vases made in Etruria as well as those of Southern Italy indicate the existence of a local art which may claim our interest not least because of its special characteristic.

An interesting instance of how Etruscan painters literally copied a Greek vase is found on the handsome cup in the Musée Rodin in Paris reproducing the outside of the Vatican cup from Vulci with Oedipus and the Sphinx, by a follower of Douris. It must be dated about 460 B.C. Towards the end of the 5th century we can distinguish the systematic production of Etruscan Red-figure with its own technical characteristics centred in Falerii Veteres (Civita Castellana) in Faliscan territory. Some influence of Apulian and probably Lucanian vase-painting can also be detected.

The beautiful volute-krater with Eos and Kephalos (plates 229; XLVIII) is the masterpiece of this workshop but is an isolated work, as the other artists of this workshop identified by Beazley are well behind in artistic merit. Many of them figure mythological themes as well as subjects touching death and the burial of the dead. None of them have been so clearly influenced by the Greek spirit as the Aurora Painter who was probably a Greek settled in Etruria.

Bibl.: Beazley, *Etruscan Vase-Painting*, Oxford 1947. T. Dohrn, *Die schwarzfigurigen etruskischen Vasen*, Bonn 1937. C. Albizzati, *Vasi antichi dipinti del Vaticano*. For the Rodin cup see Plaoutine, in: *JHS*, 57, 1937, pl. 1; Beazley, *op. cit.* pl. 4, 1–3. It may have been made in Vulci, since its model was found there. An Etruscan later-5th century stamnos in Vich (Museo Episcopal) copies the Achilles Painter's pointed amphora in the Cab. Médailles (see page 362), also found in Vulci. The black-figure Micali Painter too may have worked there. His figures closely match 'Vulci bronzes' (see Luisa Banti, *Welt der Etrusker*, Stuttgart 1960, p. 64. Compare her pl. 57 with the M. Painter's amphora, *Kunstwerke der Antike*, Münzen und Medaillen A.G., Basle, Auction XXII, 13-5-1961, pl. 64, 195). Pontic vases too seem to have been made in Vulci, though Caere is a possibility. See also L. Banti, in: *SE*, 24, 1955, p. 179.

229, XLVIII THE AURORA PAINTER

He is called after the picture of Eos and Kephalos on the volute-krater shown here. He was easily the finest artist on Etruscan soil. Other works by him are the stamnos with women bathing and a skyphos with Apollo and Artemis (Berkeley 8.997) both of them from Falerii Veteres.

229, XLVIII

FALISCAN VOLUTE-KRATER by the Aurora Painter. Rome, Museo Nazionale di Villa Giulia, 2491. From Falerii Veteres (Civita Castellana). Well preserved but the white which covered the horses and most of the figures has largely gone. Height 59.2 cms (23¼″).

Very rich and novel decoration, mostly in Red-figure. The handles terminate in large volutes and a smaller scroll near the lip. Plastic fawn heads in pairs are attached near the handle roots underneath which are human heads painted in white. The outer edge of the lip has egg pattern followed by beads and reels. Then down pointing palmettes in white alternating with upright red-figured leaves charged with a black palmette. On neck a pattern of hooked triangles. On shoulder, frieze of tongues, then egg pattern. Under the figure zone, meander with saltires ending in lozenges. Under the handles, palmette ornament of enormous size. On neck, pictures of a bull and stag respectively being attacked by winged griffins.

Side A (plate 229). Kephalos being carried off by Eos, the goddess of Dawn. Kephalos is already in Eos' chariot which is preceded by Phosphoros, the Morning Star. Below at the bottom of the picture sea monsters on left and right, between

them a dolphin. All three indicate the sea above which the chariot of Dawn plies its course. Eos has an aureole of rays. Rosettes indicating stars are scattered over the heaven. Side B (plate XLVIII) shows Peleus wrestling with Thetis who desperately tries to keep her freedom. Above them a dove with a wreath in its beak. On the right near the upper edge a rock with two pipes coming out presumably indicating a spring where Thetis had been bathing. Two Nereids scatter in terror, one of them holding a chest in her hand

the other a mirror. A cista with two alabastra in it has been knocked over. Compare plate XLVII. C. 340 B.C.

Bibl.: L. Savignoni, in: *Boll. d'Arte*, 1916, pp. 354ff. *CVA*, Villa Giulia (Giglioli), fasc. 1, pll. 5–7. Della Seta, *Villa Giulia*, p. 75. Ducati, *Ceramica greca*, p. 468. Beazley, *Etruscan Vase Painting*, Oxford 1947, pp. 7, 80–84, pl. XX, 1. Catal. mostra arte e civ. etrusca, Milan 1955, no. 365, pp. 109ff. On the subject of side A see also K. Schauenburg in *Antike und Abendland*, 10, 1961, p. 81, n. 51; for side B. see K. Schefold in FR III, p. 334–6. M. Santangelo, *Musei e Monumenti Etruschi*, 1960, pl. 120 (side A in colour). On the aureole rays, *RE* XVII, col. 601; cf. Schauenburg, *Perseus*, p. 64ff.

ITALIOTE AND SICILIOTE VASE-PAINTING

We shall not be able to give a proper account of Italiote vase-painting until further research has been done into the question of the creative personalities who gave impetus to the rise of this art in Southern Italy and brought it to further development. In what follows we shall give some examples to show the importance which this art attained from the middle of the 5th century B.C. onwards. It was an industry which though basing itself on Attic Red-figure developed in its own way in several of the Greek cities of Southern Italy and other local centres there.

The most popular shapes in Southern Italy were the bell-krater and the volute-krater, later also the calyx-krater. Very probably the earliest painters of Italiote vases came from Greece. Thus the Sisyphos Painter in his centauromachy (plate 227) shows both in style and in motifs great similarity to the sculptured friezes from the temple of Apollo at Bassae. This of course argues his Greek origin. Similar examples could be given for a number of other painters. It was Furtwängler who first recognized the influence of Attic vase-painting on local Italiote schools. He attributed this influence to the influx of Greek settlers and artists especially of Ionian origin who came after the foundation of Thurii in 443 B.C. through Athens and, still further, after the foundation of Heraclea in 432 B.C., a colony which was a common foundation of Tarentum and Thurii on the site of the ancient Siris to act as a centre against the increasing pressure of the indigenous Lucanians against the Greek settlements in that part of Italy.

We distinguish two groups of painters. The earlier one is centred round the Amykos and the Pisticci Painters and is stylistically closely linked to Attic Red-figure. It is also the soil for the development of the style of Paestan vases and those of the rest of Lucania. This style, however, soon degenerated and by the 4th century had removed itself considerably from its Greek models. The other group begins with the Sisyphus Painter (plates 236–7) and is continued by artists such as the Tarporley Painter, the Lycurgus Painter and the Darius Painter. Whilst the first group was probably centred round Lucanian Heraclea the second was undoubtedly rooted in Tarentum possibly also Canosa di Puglia, the ancient Canusium.

In the first group there is one painter of distinction who gave status to the vase-painting of Paestum. His name is Asteas; he was active in Paestum between 360 and 330 B.C. (Paestum had been founded as a Greek colony from Sybaris in the 7th century B.C. under the name of Poseidonia). His vivid pictures show by preference scenes from the theatre and therefore claim our special interest. Besides those, we also find the amorous adventures of Zeus and Dionysiac themes. By entering as it were into the life of his own figure world he can invest it with a feeling of immediacy, humour, and the striking mimicry of an Italiote actor. He also enlivens his painting with polychrome effects. Together with Python, a personality of lesser dimension, he marks the centre of a group of painters who bring before our eyes the South Italian theatre particularly the comedy of Tarentum and Syracuse, a world which also finds reflection in the krater from Lipari (plate 240).

Turning to Apulian vases we find that their painters are fascinated by subjects taken from tragedy. From the time of the Sisyphos Painter onwards (plates 236–7) pictures gain increasingly in monumentality. The Karneia Painter who, though he belongs to the first group, was much influenced by the Tarentine style and is still quite in the Greek tradition. His krater (plate 230–5) shows how close he is in inspiration and

unleashed intensity to the Dinos Painter. One might even say that the earliest Italiote vase paintings were decisively influenced by the tradition of the vase painter Polygnotos even more than by the rich style of the Meidias Painter.

Apart from vases where pictures were inspired by the stage, there are also the *loutrophoroi*, whose function was to be taken over by the Apulian amphorae of monumental size, on which we find pictures of small *heroa*, shrines or grave chapels. These pictures undoubtedly point to the ceremonies of burial and the heroization of the dead. It has been pointed out that they probably refer to the cult of the heroized dead, indeed may have connections with Orphic ideology and cults. Moreover the mythological subjects on these vases were not selected hap-hazardly, but were also connected with the cult of ancestors, as it was practised by the Orphic sect and the Pythagoreans. Of artistic influences there is the obvious one of the great fresco paintings of Polygnotus of Thasos and Mikon of Athens, which determined the practice of arranging the figures on various levels. But apart from this there are also many motifs and elements taken from the art of the Meidias Painter and his circle. The way the garments flutter about the limbs in an almost independent life of their own, and the rich decoration on these garments, all this goes back to Meidian influence, as taken over by Italiote and especially Apulian vase-painters of the 4th century.

Another group of Italiote vases was made in Gnathia. Their decorative effect is often very striking. The main production was of small vases modelled on metal shapes, and decorated with painted volutes and tendrils in a polychrome style. They are characteristic of the decorative sense of the 4th and 3rd centuries B.C.

Vase-painting in Sicily still presents a good number of unsolved problems. Already some time ago after many Paestan vases had been found in Sicily the problem was posed how far local workshops existed in the island and could be identified. A. D. Trendall, the leading expert on Italiote vase painting, believes that there was a centre of production in Gela which was responsible for small stamnoi and pyxides with ivy decoration but without any figured representations. Another workshop seems to have been in Leontini producing polychrome vases which particularly favoured yellow and white. During the last few years a number of finds in the Lipari Isles have revealed a new centre of production there. There are lekanides which show a new kind of polychromy recalling that of Kerch vases, but fresher, richer, in fact Siciliote. Favourite colours are rose-red, light blue, yellow and green, as shown on plate LI. These colour effects are real innovations in Liparian workshops. Similar polychrome effects are also found on vases from Centuripe, the ancient Centuripae of the Sikels, in the heart of eastern Sicily. They are extraordinary products whose chronology is not yet quite determined. They are Hellenistic in an almost baroque style. Their shapes include covered vases of several varieties ranging from amphora to krater including a type of large lekanis. The painting recalls in its effects fresco work. It presumably dates from the third century B.C. and imitates a manner of painting which we know elsewhere from Pompeii and Alexandria. The subjects, like those on Italiote vases, refer to the cult of the dead. The colours are surprising in their varieties of blue, rose-red, red, yellow and gilt. They are monumental vases of sepulchral character derived from ash urns. They have large surfaces suitable for painting, which are utilized almost in the manner of wall painting. The scenes as we said refer to the funerary ceremonies and are rendered in a broadly conceived yet graceful style.

Bibl.: G. Patroni, in: *Atti. Acc. Arch. Lett.*, Naples 1897, pp. 33 ff., 113 ff. C. Albizzati, in: *Diss. Acc. Pont. Arch.*, 14, 1920, pp. 149 ff. N. R. Moon, in: *PBSR*, 11, 1929, pp. 30 ff. P. Wuilleumier, in: *RA*, 1929, pp. 185 ff. A. D. Trendall, *Frühitaliotische Vasen*, Leipzig 1938. Idem, *I vasi antichi, dipinti del Vaticano, Vasi Italioti ed Etruschi a figure rosse*, Vatican 1953–1955, I–II. Idem, *Paestan Pottery*, London 1936. Idem, in: *PBSR*, 21, 1953, pp. 160 ff. G. Libertini, *Centuripe*, Catania 1926. Idem, in: *Atti Soc. Magna Grecia*, 1932, pp. 187 ff. Richter, in: *Metropolitan Mus. Studies*, II, 2, 1930 pp. 187 ff. P. E. Arias, in: *Arch. Storico Sic. Orientale*, 50, 1954, pp. 104 ff. Summary accounts by Trendall of the development of South Italian Red-figure will be found in the following: *Handbook to the Nicholson Museum*, Sydney 1948, pp. 315–336; G. M. A. Richter, *Handbook of Greek Art*, 1958, pp. 347–353, and in *Atti del VII Congresso Internazionale di Archeologia Classica*, Rome 1961, II, pp. 117–141.

230–235

VOLUTE-KRATER BY THE KARNEIA PAINTER.
Taranto, Museo Nazionale Archeologico, 8263. From Ceglie del Campo. Excellent preservation. Height 72 cms (28⁵/₁₆″).

One of the masterpieces of Italiote vase-painting of the end of the 5th century B.C. On the sides of the volute handles, ivy in black. On the lip, egg pattern followed by palmettes enclosed by lotus flowers. Below this a tendril of ivy with

leaves in yellow. On shoulder, tongue pattern. Under figure frieze, meander with crosses. Under handles palmette ornaments with tendrils.

Side A. In the centre of the picture Dionysus young and beardless sitting on a rock. His himation is thrown over his thighs. He wears high boots (the cothurnus?) with fur lining. A scarf decorated with black palmettes is tied round his head. Leaning against his shoulder is a thyrsus with flowers. In front of him a menad dances, her head thrown back in ecstasy. She holds a thyrsus in her hands. Between the two a flute player in transparent chiton which allows her breasts and body to gleam through her dress (plates 231–2). Behind Dionysus another menad dressed in a short chiton and an animal skin thrown over her left shoulder. In her right she carries a burning torch which she holds above Dionysus, in her left a situla. On the extreme right a bearded wreathed satyr leaning against a pillar (plates 230–3). Ornaments are rendered plastically in clay; such are the pendants on the menads' necklaces and their bracelets, also belts and shoes.

Our painter was evidently brought up in the style of Attic vase-painting; however, he exaggerates the expressiveness of some of its features.

Side B (plate 234). In the centre of the upper register Perseus with winged cap and the sickle which had cut off the head of Medusa. In his right hand he carries the Gorgon's head. On his right and left four satyrs scatter in terror covering their faces. Curving lines indicate the terrain of the upper register. Thyrsi abandoned by the frightened satyrs are seen lying in the field.

In the lower register we see a ceremonial dance in honour of Apollo Karneios held during the Karneia, a Doric festival, which was celebrated towards the end of August in Sparta and its colonies of which Taranto was one. It was a vintage and harvest festival combined with ceremonies of expiation. In the centre a couple of dancers, the girl wearing a white *kalathiskos* ('basket') on her head and pirouetting; she is being partnered by a youth. On the left two young men conversing; one of them in a sleeved richly embroidered dress is the flute-player holding the flutes in his left and his mouth band *(phorbeia)* in the right hand, the other is entirely naked except for his spiky head gear. Beyond a basin a youth next to a pillar (inscribed *Karneios*) is holding a *kalathiskos*. On the right of the dancing girl a youth half covered in a cloak. Beside him another youth entirely naked except for the big *kalathiskos* on his head.

The two rows of the picture must be connected and probably show events during the Karneia festival, the *kalathiskos* dance and dramatic performances, here exemplified by a scene inspired by a satyr play.

C. 410 B.C.

The painting shows connections with the style of the Eretria and the Meidias Painters without, however, attaining their calligraphy in the rendering of drapery or bodily forms.

Bibl.: Q. Quagliati, in: *NS*, 1900, p. 504. C. Albizzati, in: *Atti Pont. Acc. Arch.*, 14, 1919, p. 212. P. Wuilleumier, in: *RA*, 1933, ii, p. 3. N. R. Moon, in: *PBSR*, XI, 1929, pp. 30ff. Oakeshott-Moon, in: *JHS*, 55, 1935, p. 231. G. E. Rizzo, *Thiasos*, Rome 1934, p. 33. A. D. Trendall, *Frühitaliotische Vasen*, Leipzig 1938, p. 24. P. Wuilleumier, *Tarente*, Paris 1939, pp. 449–450, 481, pl. 46, 3. *CVA*, Taranto (Drago), fasc. 1, pll. 4–6. On the festival of the Karneia see M. P. Nilsson, *Geschichte der griech. Religion*, I², p. 532, n. 5. Idem, *Griech. Feste von religiöser Bedeutung*, Leipzig 1906, pp. 118ff. On side B see also Beazley in: *Hesperia*, 24, 1955, pp. 315ff.; A. B. Brommer, *Satyrspiele²*, p. 74, no. 41 and especially K. Schauenburg, *Perseus*, Bonn 1960, pl. 33; pp. 99ff.; also Cook, *Zeus* III, 2, p. 996–1009, pl. 71 details (kalathiskos dancers). For the boots worn by Dionysus on side A see Charlotte Fränkel, *Satyr- und Backschennamen auf Vasenbildern*, Halle 1912, p. 37ff.; Pickard-Cambridge, *Dramatic Festivals of Athens*, p. 232ff.; Bieber, *History of the Greek and Roman Theater²*, p. 26. For the thyrsus held by Dionysus on side A, which is the simple fennel *(narthex)* with its own flowers, see Beazley in *AJA* 37, 1933, p. 400, n. 3. It occurs fairly often on Italiote vases, especially in the hands of Dionysus, sometimes as here in the same picture as the ordinary ivy crowned thyrsus. Very occasionally we find an ivy bunch added even to this flowering fennel, as on a bell-krater in Bari, *JdI* 32, 1917, p. 88, fig. 59 = Pickard-Cambridge, *Dramatic Festivals*, fig. 41. There are precursors in Etruscan black-figured vases. For the torch held by the menad on side A, see on our plates 206–211. For a colour picture of our vase see *EWA* III, pl. 376. On the stylistic placing of the vase see now Trendall, in: *Atti del VII Congresso Intern. di Archeol. Class.* II, p. 125 (Group A, Proto-Lucanian, but under strong Tarentine influence).

236, 237

VOLUTE-KRATER BY THE SISYPHOS PAINTER.

Munich, Museum Antiker Kleinkunst, 3268. From Ruvo. Fair state of preservation. Height 73 cms (28³/₄″).

On side of volute handles, ivy branch. On outer rim of lip, meander on side A; myrtle branch on side B. On ledge below, enclosed palmettes with lotus flowers. On shoulder, tongues. Between the two figure zones a frieze of egg pattern. Below the figure zones, meander with crosses.

Side A. On neck, Erotes playing. In the middle Aphrodite seated on a low stool. An Eros brings her a crown. On either side a pair of Erotes, the pair on the right are playing the game of *mora* (Greifenhagen, *Griech. Eroten*, pp. 50ff.; 78). Main picture, upper frieze. Laertes wooing Antikleia. The picture is in two sequences divided by the Ionic column. To its right the aged king Autolycus showing Laertes, the wooer of his daughter Antikleia, an ivy leaf with the name of Sisyphos written on it. Meanwhile, further to the right, his queen is with her daughter, touching her shoulder to comfort her at this critical moment. To the left of the pillar the next stage of the story is shown. Laertes together with Antikleia whom he grasps by the wrist, the formal way of taking possession of the bride. To the left of the couple four youths. Antikleia wears her bridal crown.

The myth represented is related in several versions. According to Homer Odysseus was the son of *Laertes* and Antikleia. But according to later versions known to Sophocles and Euripides Odysseus was the son of *Sisyphos*, king of Corinth and craftiest of all mortals, who had put Antikleia with child before Laertes married her. Here Autolycus informs Laertes of the position by showing the guest token of Sisyphos, which he has taken out of the large hydria where it was stored. On the right the bride is yet uncertain of the outcome; in the centre Laertes shows that he will have her nonetheless, despite the expressions of astonishment of his friends. This, the commonly accepted interpretation by the picture, is due to Furtwängler and at a further remove to Robert. It is not without its difficulties,

not the least of which is that it requires a serial sequence of pictures, with the same characters appearing several times, though this is not unparalleled in vase painting (compare von Bothmer, *Ancient Art*, on no. 243). Still Löwy's suggestion (see bibl. below) of an otherwise unknown allotment of three royal brides by their father to a number of suitors is worth noting. Sisyphos' name then has just come out of the hydria; other suitors are standing on the left. For the shape of the lot Löwy compares the Syracusan *petalismos* (an equivalent to the Athenian ostracism; names written on olive leaves).

Side A, lower frieze. Jason assaulting the dragon to get the Golden Fleece. Behind Jason Medea with her box of magic. Then follow Argonauts including the two Boreads with wings.

Side B. On the neck horse racing by mounted youths.

Main picture, upper frieze. The nine Muses indoors (as is indicated by the column on the right). In the centre three of them making music with harp, kithara and lyre.

Lower frieze. Fight of Centaurs and Lapiths.

Although the vase certainly comes from an Apulian workshop, the pictures are filled with Pheidian spirit. There may also be some harping back to Polygnotan wall-paintings. C. 420 B.C.

Bibl.: Jahn, p. 254, no. 805. FR, II, pp. 201ff., pll. 98, 99. A. D. Trendall, *Frühitaliotische Vasen*, Leipzig 1938, pp. 22, 39, no. 15, pll. 19, 20. N. R. Moon, in: *PBSR*, XI, 1929, pp. 32ff. A. D. Trendall, *Handbook to the Nicholson Museum*, Sydney 1948, p. 321. Idem, *Vasi antichi dipinte del Vaticano, Vasi italioti*, Vatican 1953, I, p. 70. P. Wuilleumier, *Tarente*, p. 449, n. 3. On the myth see Dümmler, 'Autolykos', in: *RE*; Escher, 'Antikleia', in: *RE*; Bethe, 'Sisyphos', in: *RE*. Fundamental for the interpretation C. Robert, in: *Berliner Winckelmannsprogramm*, 50, 1890, pp. 90–96. See also Löwy in: *Jahreshefte Österr. Archäol. Inst.* 24, 1929, p. 40, n. 42; L. Curtius in: *Scritti in onore di B. Nogara*, Vatican 1937, p. 116; von Salis in: *Corolla Curtius*, Stuttgart 1937, p. 165. For the 'Homeric bowl' which gave the clue to the interpretation see now also U. Hausmann, *Hellenistische Reliefbecher*, Stuttgart 1959, p. 56, no. 33 with references (pl. 44, 1–2; the jug of the potter Dionysios in Berlin). On the bridal crown worn by Antikleia see von Salis in: *Rhein. Mus. f. Philol.* 73, 1920–24, p. 207. On guest tokens, which do not as rule look like the leaf on our vase, see Daremberg and Saglio, *Dictionnaire*, s.v. hospitium, p. 295; D. L. Page on Euripides, *Medea* (ed. Oxford, 1938) p. 117, on 613; *Hesperia* 20, 1951, p. 51–2, pl. 25c (on tallies). Cook, pl. 52a.

238

EARLY-APULIAN SQUAT-LEKYTHOS. Taranto, Museo Nazionale Archeologico, 4530. From the necropolis of Taranto. Mended from large fragments. Mouth, part of the neck and handle are missing. Preservation of figure work is excellent. Height 18.5 cms (7¼″).

On shoulder below neck, egg pattern, then tongues, then egg pattern again. Under the figure zone meander with checkers. For the shape compare and contrast the earlier (and Attic) plate 205.

The picture shows a young woman presumably Aphrodite, suckling a young Eros who nestles in her lap. Further tiny Erotes emerge from a kind of Pandora's box on the floor. Behind the chest Peitho about to release a swan, the bird of Aphrodite. Behind Aphrodite a woman with a parasol, probably Helen in two minds. She holds a wreath, the prize

of victory, over two tiny Erotes wrestling with each other. Facing her a youth with a cat sitting on his arm. He should be Paris. The Eros on his side is getting the better of his opponent! She will follow *him* and leave her husband—all this the work of Aphrodite.

First quarter of fourth century. Early-Apulian. Ornate style. Another squat lekythos by the same painter, London, British Museum F107 (A. B. Cook, *Zeus*, III, pl. 15, 1) shows the boy Herakles being suckled by Hera, the only Greek (but South Italian) representation of a myth popular in Etruscan art (see Beazley, in: *JHS*, 69, 1949, p. 14), though the epigram in the *Palatine Anthology*, IX, 589 suggests that there had been other Greek representations. Evidently our painter liked this motif. Other examples of *Erotes* being suckled by *Aphrodite* are: A Greek gem in Leningrad from Kerch (Crimea) (Furtwängler, *Antike Gemmen*, pl. 13, 4 = Lippold, *Gemmen*, pl. 24, 1) still 5th century B.C.; calyx-krater Würzburg 523 by the Meleager Painter (Beazley, *ARFVP*, p. 871, no. 6) early 4th century B.C.—the group is used to fill a corner in a rather haphazard picture of a Dionysiac rout. Compare also a skyphoid pyxis in Lipari by the Lipari Painter (Bernabò Brea, *Musei e Monumenti in Sicilia*, p. 81 = p. 85 of English edition) and the Italiote nuptial lebes, Taranto 52535 (*Antike und Abendland*, 10, 1961, p. 84 and fig. 21).

The motif of babies being suckled is altogether rare in Greek art at any time. Of recently discovered examples we mention as also being the work of Greeks on Italian and Sicilian soil, the 6th century *kourotrophos* limestone statue of a woman (Leto?) suckling two babies in Syracuse (from Megara Hyblaea; L. von Matt, *Das antike Sizilien*, pl. 52; Bernabò Brea, *Musei e Monumenti in Sicilia*, p. 29 = p. 33 of English edition) and the late classical, 4th century B.C., *kourotrophos* terracotta of a woman feeding a baby from Paestum, (*AA* 1956, col. 443, fig. 155). In Attica the earliest example known to me from vase painting is the hydria Berlin F. 2395 (*AZ* 1885, pl. 15) of about 430 B.C., Alcmeon being nursed by Eriphyle. Somewhat later are the hydria fragments by the Meidias Painter in the Kerameikos Museum, Athens, (Beazley, *ARFVP*, p. 832, no. 2). The subject is uncertain. A woman (mostly lost) turned to the right suckles a baby; another with hair loose sits on the right, body turned towards the first woman but looking back over her shoulder. On a second fragment (which should probably be placed to the right of the first fragment), a woman turned left sits in pensive posture looking ahead. The third fragment shows part of the lower zone with a woman dancing wildly. The baby is wingless, and will hardly therefore be an Eros at this period. Herakles is conceivable, but there is nothing to go by. More pictures of women giving the breast to the young are: the Thracian nurse on the Italiote fragment London, British Museum E509 (photograph in FR III, p. 361, fig. 371; see also Rumpf, p. 116); a Lucanian vase *AI*, 1865, pl. E; a plastic vase, Berlin F2913. The latter two have been interpreted as showing nymphs nursing the young Dionysus. Finally we must not forget the young Hippothoon being suckled by a mare on the fragmentary early-4th century Attic oinochoe, Tübingen 1610 = Watzinger pl. 39, E180. We

have literary evidence for further examples. Pausanias 10, 25, 9, describing the Ilioupersis picture by Polygnotus in Delphi probably indicates that Astyanax was shown being suckled by his mother Andromache. From the 4th century we know that Zeuxis painted a female centaur giving suck to her young and Aristides of Thebes depicted a baby on its mother's breast as part of a scene of the sack of a city. For the whole question of the motif in Greek art Furtwängler's treatment in his *Collection Sabouroff*, on plate 71, is still of importance.

There are also geometric precursors. The child grasping the mother's breast with one hand, but not feeding, occurs twice on geometric kraters in Athens and New York, (see Kunze, *Neue Beiträge zur klassischen Altertumswissenschaft, Festschrift B. Schweitzer*, Stuttgart 1954, p. 53, n. 22, pl. 6). As to the animal world, the motif is by no means rare in geometric bronzes, and in vase painting can be seen on our plate 24.

When Erotes are being nursed by Aphrodite they are evidently thought of as children of Aphrodite and our earliest pictures of Erotes in Greek art show them (or him) wingless held in the arms of Aphrodites as her little children. These pictures are Attic black-figure and go back into the early 6th century, the best known being a plaque from the Athenian Acropolis 2526, roughly contemporary with the François Vase, (see now A. Greifenhagen, *Griechische Eroten*, Berlin 1957, p. 39, fig. 29, and p. 75). In most pictures however this relationship of Eros to Aphrodite is by no means so clear, and there were other genealogies current in mythology. Thus in Hesiod Eros is already present at the birth of Aphrodite, as one of the primeval forces and this version was familiar to Attic representations of the subject in the fifth century (see e.g. Beazley in *AJA* 45, 1941, p. 599; E. Simon, *Geburt der Aphrodite*, fig. 23–29). In that role we see him as a grown youth rather than a child.

The motif of Erotes wrestling with each other is popular in 4th century and later art, see for instance the gems Lippold, *Gemmen*, pl. 26, 2 and 3, or to keep to Tarentine work, the miniature terracotta altar, R. Pagenstecher, *Unteritalische Grabdenkmäler*, Strasbourg, 1912, pl. 18a. It goes back to the 5th century where we find the pair wrestling on two fine vases by the Washing Painter of about 430 B.C. or a little after, Beazley, *ARFVP*, p. 742ff., nos. 15 and 95. One is a pyxis in Würzburg, the other, even finer, a fragmentary nuptial lebes in Professor Buschor's possession (*AM*, 71, 1956, Beil. 115, p. 208; see also Greifenhagen, *op. cit.*, p. 43). The original mythological setting of the group escapes our knowledge. Somehow it recalls the main scene of the 'Boston Throne'.

Bibl.: P. Wuilleumier, in: *RA*, 1936, II, p. 146. C. Dugas, in: *REG*, 1938, p. 167, fig. 32. Ch. Picard, in: *Gaz. Beaux Arts*, 1937, I, p. 215, figg. 215, 216. P. Wuilleumier, *Tarente*, Paris 1939, pp. 452ff., pl. 47, 2–3. A. B. Cook, *Zeus*, III, pl. 15, 2. *Enciclopedia dell'arte classica*, III, p. 430 (H. Speier). *Italy's Life*, no. 26 (1953), p. 111 (colour). For Eros as athlete see Beazley, *Attic Vases in Cyprus Museum*, p. 47; also Bowra *GLP²* p. 293 (Eros as boxer entering lists against mortal in Anacreon). On cats in Greek art, see now W. Llewellyn Brown, *Lion*, p. 176. On 'Helen in two minds', cf. also N. Himmelmann, in: *Gnomon*, 29, 1957, p. 221.

239

EARLY-APULIAN VOLUTE-KRATER. Naples, Museo Nazionale Archeologico, 3249. From Ruvo. Well preserved including the lid. Total height including lid 90 cms (35³/₈").

Two large volute handles with double spirals and swan protomes. There is a conical lid with a cylindrical knob. Both the shape of the lid and the plastic enhancement of the handles are influenced by bronze models particularly kraters from Taranto and Locri. Large palmette ornament under handle. Well preserved yellow and white used for enhancement of ornament and the main picture. On the lid the picture is framed on sides and below by branches with leaves in white. On one side a seated Muse playing the lyre, on other side a bearded satyr all in white and other added colours. On neck of krater a frieze of enclosed palmettes and lotus flowers. On shoulder, tongues and egg pattern. Below the picture, meander with saltires and checkers.

Side A. Orestes taking refuge at the omphalos in Delphi. The sanctuary of Apollo is indicated by the three Ionic columns. Orestes embraces the omphalos, sword in his right hand. To the left Apollo, holding a bow in his left hand. He is wreathed and has a himation draped across his middle. He stretches out his right against a Fury who is black-brown with short white chiton, and a snake twisted round her arm. The Pythian priestess raises her hands in terror at the sight and hastens away dropping her key. To the left and in the centre a tripod each. On the extreme right behind the laurel tree on tip-toe and gazing the handsome figure of Artemis in transparent chiton wearing also an animal skin. She has high laced boots (as Dionysus in pl. 231), and holds two hunting spears in her left hand. Two hounds besides her. Above, two helmets and two chariot wheels are suspended, dedications in the sanctuary.

The scene shows the moment when Apollo appears in his role as avenger and puts the fury to flight. Pythia runs off in terror at the sight of the Furies (Aeschylus, *Eumenides*, 175ff.). The picture has all the colourfulness of Italiote painting, yet shows a happy harmony with Attic artistic tradition, nowhere more than in the figures of Apollo and Artemis.

Side B (not shown). Dionysus and Ariadne with Eros, menad and Papposilenos.

C. 370 B.C. Early Apulian. Ornate Style.

Bibl.: H. Heydemann, *Vasensammlungen Neapel*, p. 563, no. 3249. H. Huddilston, *Greek tragedy in the light of Vase Painting*, London 1898, p. 61, fig. 6. L. Séchan, *La tragédie grecque dans ses rapports avec la céramique*, Paris 1926, pp. 95ff. N. R. Moon, in: *PBSR*, XI, 1929, pp. 45ff. FR, III, (C. Watzinger), pp. 362ff., pl. 179–180–3.

240

PAESTAN CALYX-KRATER BY ASTEAS. Lipari, Museo Eoliano, 927. From Lipari. Well preserved, including the colours. Height 41 cms (16¹/₈").

On the lip, olive branch. The picture shows Dionysus seated on the left, wreathed in ivy and holding the thyrsus in his left hand. He is dressed in an ornate chiton and holds his

right arm across his head in surprise of what he sees in front of him, a girl acrobat standing on her hands. She is naked, her body in white with details in golden yellow. Behind her two *phlyakes* (buffoons) in their characteristic costumes. One of them gloats all over her body whilst the other surveys the scene more nonchalantly. Above, two windows with a woman wearing a white mask looking out of each. The curtain underneath the picture shows that the setting is on the stage.

About 350 B.C.

Bibl.: L. Bernabò Brea, *Musei e Monumenti in Sicilia*, Novara 1958, p. 79. Idem, *Il Castello di Lipari*, pl. XXVII. A. D. Trendall, in: *JHS*, 76, 1956, suppl., p. 48. L. Bernabò Brea, in: *Kokalos*, IV, 1958, p. 130. A. D. Trendall, *Phlyax Vases* (Institute of Classical Studies, Bulletin, Suppl. 8) London 1959, p. 37, no. 74. Bieber, *History of the Greek and Roman Theater*², Princeton, 1961, p. 144, fig. 535.

XLIX

APULIAN CALYX-KRATER. Lipari, Museo Eoliano 2241. From Lipari. Some restoration on foot; otherwise well preserved. Height 53 cms (20⁷/₈″).

Of magnificent quality. Beneath lip, branch of ivy with bright red tendrils and light green leaves. The picture itself is framed by a vine which rises from the ground on the right and grows in a canopy across the whole picture. Golden yellow bunches of grapes and a white mask of a woman with yellow head scarf hang from the vine.

On the right Pan bearded and goat-footed with shaggy thighs and a tail plays on the flute. His two small horns are yellow, the hair brown. In the centre a menad with bracelet, necklace and white diadem. She rushes up holding in her left a yellow situla, in the right a stylized thyrsus. Further to the left another menad beating the tambourine. Under the figures row of dots as ground lines. Underneath picture a broad meander.

Side B (not shown). Two youths.

The female mask with head scarf suspended from the vine recalls the so-called Gnathia Ware whilst the shape of the krater is close to those from Leontini or Caltagirone. Yet the krater should be Apulian rather than Siciliote and is to be dated to the middle of the 4th century B.C.

Bibl.: L. Bernabò Brea, in: *Kokalos*, IV, 1958, p. 130. A. D. Trendall, in: *JHS*, 77, 1957, suppl. p. 34. Idem, *Phlyax Vases*, p. 61, no. XIV. For masks on Gnathian vases see T. B. L. Webster, in: *JHS*, 71, 1951, pp. 222 ff. and particularly p. 223, no. 12, 13. Idem in *Antike Kunst* 3, 1960, p. 30 ff.

L

APULIAN VOLUTE-KRATER. Rome, Vatican Museum. From the neighbourhood of Bari. Well preserved; handles restored. Height 82 cms (32¹/₄″).

The volutes are faced with female masks recalling Gorgon's heads. Near handle roots swan protomes. Outer rim of lip has egg pattern. On neck, tendrils of ivy with yellow berries. Below this, head of Adonis with Phrygian cap between acanthus volutes out of which flowers grow. On the other

side wavy spiral motifs, laurel with berries and palmettes with figures.

Side A. In lower centre Triptolemus on his winged chariot pulled by snaky dragons. This chariot was given to him by Demeter. He is crowned with myrtle, wears his hair long to his shoulders and carries a sceptre in his left. One of the dragons is being fed by a seated female figure who wears a peplos with overfall and white shoes. The other dragon looks at a female who carries a torch, stands to the left of the chariot and proffers to Triptolemus ears of corn. She is Demeter. Behind her Hekate also carrying a burning torch painted in yellow. Hekate too is a chthonic deity. Above these earthly events Zeus watches. In front of him is Hermes possibly receiving the order to bring back Persephone. Hermes' head is wreathed, he wears winged shoes and carries the kerykeion. On the right Aphrodite with diadem, necklace and bracelets. Her hand touches her himation. On the extreme right Peitho with one leg up on a slight eminence. Side B (not shown). Several figures with gifts in front of a heroon within which there are several persons. The picture is probably inspired by a heroon in Tarentum.

C. 340 B.C., the time of the Darius krater in Naples.

Bibl.: W. Helbig, *Führer*³, I, p. 318, no. 514. C. Albizzati, in: *Diss. Pont. Acc.*, XIV, 1920, pp. 218 ff., fig. 61, 62. Pagenstecher, *Unter-italische Grabdenkmäler*, p. 94. A. D. Trendall, *Vasi antichi dipinti del Vaticano*, Vatican 1955, II, pp. 177 ff.

LI

LEKANIS BY THE LIPARI PAINTER. Lipari, Museo Eoliano. From Lipari; tomb 144. Well preserved. Diam. 15 cms (5⁷/₈″).

The handles have separately worked flanges: Handle knob has star motif with leaves in cream colour and blue. On one side of the lid (plate LI, upper picture) Nike with large wings (in blue and white with a band of chestnut brown between the two colours), and a white himation across her legs. Her body is light rose-red to grey, reserved in the clay ground. Nike is offering up a girdle, the sign of virginity, on the altar. On the other side (plate LI, lower picture), two girls with their body naked down to their legs which are covered by a chiton in white and blue. The one on the left pulls up the edge of her chiton and with her right holds a tambourine. The other carries a box with votive objects and a girdle which will no doubt also be offered up. Presumably the vase was used for bringing wedding gifts, as shown on plate 226.

Last quarter of 4th century B.C.

The Lipari Painter worked in the last quarter of the 4th century in Lipari itself. Pyxides in Lipari, in Cefalù and in Naples as well as lebetes and amphorae have been attributed to him.

Bibl.: A. D. Trendall, in: *Bull. Metrop. Mus. of Art*, 13, 1955, p. 165. Idem, *Vasi antichi dipinti del Vaticano*, Vatican 1953, I, p. 41. Idem, in: *JHS*, 76, 1956, suppl. p. 48 ff. L. Bernabò Brea, *Il Castello di Lipari*, Palermo 1958, pl. 23, 1. Idem, in: *Kokalos*, IV, 1958, p. 133. Idem, *Musei e Monumenti in Sicilia*, pl. 83 (colour) = English edition plate 87. A. D. Trendall, 'Lipari (pittore di)' in *Enciclopedia dell'arte classica*.

LII

KRATER WITH LID, CENTURIPAN WARE. Catania, University, Institute of Classical Archeology. From Centuripe. Mended from many fragments. Well preserved. Total height 56 cms (22″).

The shape combines elements of lekanis and bell-krater. Sloping handles near mouth of vase. The lid has a tubular grip with a gilded band. Picture on lid shows a sea panther between white dolphins on rose-red background. The lower border of the lid ends in a plastically rendered moulding of beads and reels. Vessels of this shape are often on a stand, which is of one piece with the body of the vase. In some cases the lid too is undetachable, being of one piece with the bowl.

The vessel itself has just below the lip plastic lion heads and flowers between white palmettes. Underneath this a frieze of light blue and rose-red rectangles followed by a plastically rendered moulding once in gilt.

The picture shows three women framed on either side by two volutes in white. The central figure is the mistress seated on a stool with large, modelled legs. She supports herself with her right arm and with her left seems to carry a mirror. She wears a blue chiton and above it a yellow stole.

To the right an attendant maid holding a parasol over the head of the mistress. To the left another maid who holds a white fan for her mistress. No picture on the back of vase These paintings were done on the *fired* pot with a wide variety of tempera colours on a chalky slip, which itself is coloured rose red.

The scene can be interpreted either as showing the deceased woman or a ritual act in front of the goddess Aphrodite. We prefer the first interpretation basing it amongst other things on comparisons with similar representations on Italiote vases.

3rd century B.C.

Bibl.: G. Libertini, in: *Atti Soc. Magna Grecia*, 1932, pp. 195 ff., pl. IV. Compare also A. D. Trendall in: *Bull. Metropol. Mus.* 13, 1955, p. 161 ff. (good account of fabric with bibliography). M. Robertson, *Greek Painting*, p. 173 and Cook, p. 211 (good summary). For the calyx of modelled acanthus leaves above the foot typical of the fabric see K. Parlasca, in: *JdI*, 70, 1955, p. 147 ff. For the parasol in Apulan pictures of ritual cf. M. Schmidt, *Der Dareiosmaler*, Münster, 1960, p. 45, n. 69.

ABBREVIATIONS

PERIODICALS

AA	Archäologischer Anzeiger (part of *JdI*)
ABSA	Annual of British School of Athens
AI	Annali dell'Instituto di Corrispondenza Archeologica
AJA	American Journal of Archaeology
AM	Mitteilungen des Deutschen Archäologischen Instituts-Athenische Abteilung
Arch. Class	Archeologia Classica
ASAIA	Annuario della Scuola Archeologica Italiana di Atene
AZ	Archäologische Zeitung
BCH	Bulletin de Corréspondance Hellénique
BI	Bullettino dell'Instituto di Corrispondenza Archeologica
BMQ	British Museum Quarterly
BPW	Berliner Philologische Wochenschrift (after 1920: Philol. Wochenschr.)
Eph. Arch.	Ephimerìs archaiologikì (now: Archaiol. Ephem.)
JdI	Jahrbuch des Deutschen Archäologischen Instituts
JHS	Journal of Hellenic Studies

MEF	Mélanges de l'Ecole Française de Rome
Mus. Helv.	Museum Helveticum
Mon. Inst.	Monumenti Inediti dell'Istituto di Corrispondenza Archeologica
ML	Monumenti antichi dei Lincei
Mon. Piot.	Monuments et Mémoires de la Fondation Eugène Piot
NS	Notizie degli Scavi
ÖJh	Jahreshefte des Österreichischen Archäologischen Institutes
PBSR	Papers of the British School at Rome
RA	Revue Archéologique
REA	Revue des Etudes Anciennes
REG	Revue des Etudes Grecques
RIASA	Rivista dell'Istituto di Archeologia e Storia dell'arte.
RM	Mitteilungen des Deutschen Archäologischen Instituts-Römische Abteilung
SE	Studi Etruschi

BOOKS

Alfieri-Arias-Hirmer	*Spina*, Munich 1958.
Baumeister	A. Baumeister, *Denkmäler des klass. Altertums*, Munich-Leipzig 1899.
Beazley, *ABFVP*	J. D. Beazley, *Attic Black-Figure Vase-Painters*, Oxford 1956.
Beazley, *ARFVP*	J. D. Beazley, *Attic Red-Figure Vase-Painters*, Oxford 1942.
Beazley, *Dev.*	J. D. Beazley, *The Development of Attic Black-Figure*, London 1951.
Beazley, *EVP*	J. D. Beazley, *Etruscan Vase-Painting*, Oxford 1947.
Bloesch, *Formen*	H. Bloesch, *Die Formen der attischen Schalen von Exekias bis zum Ende des strengen Stils*, Berne 1940.
Buschor, *G Vsm*	E. Buschor, *Griechische Vasenmalerei²*, Munich 1925.
Bloesch, *Kunst*	H. Bloesch, *Antike Kunst in der Schweiz*, Zurich 1943.
Bothmer, *Ancient Art*	D. von Bothmer, *Ancient Art from New York, Private Collections*, New York, (Metrop. Mus. Art) 1961.
Bowra, *GLP²*	C. M. Bowra, *Greek Lyric Poetry²*, Oxford 1961.
Brown, *Lion*	W. Llewellyn Brown, *The Etruscan Lion*, Oxford, 1960.
Buschor, *GV*	E. Buschor, *Griechische Vasen*, Munich 1940.
Caskey-Beazley	L. D. Caskey-J. D. Beazley, *Attic Vase Paintings in the Museum of Fine Arts, Boston*, I–II, Oxford, 1931, 1954.
Collignon-Couve	M. Collignon-J. Couve, *Catalogue des vases grecs du Musée National d'Athènes*, Paris 1902.
Cook	R. M. Cook, *Greek Painted Pottery*, London 1960.
CVA	*Corpus Vasorum Antiquorum.*
Daremberg-Saglio	Ch. Daremberg-E. Saglio (ed.), *Dictionnaire des Antiquités*, Paris 1877–1919.
Davison, *Workshops*	Jean M. Davison, *Attic Geometric Workshops* (= *Yale Classical Studies*, vol. xvi) New Haven, 1961.
Ducati	P. Ducati, *Storia della ceramica greca*, Florence 1922.

EWA	*Encyclopedia of World Art* (McGraw Hill Book Company), New York and London, 1959 – in progress.
FR	A. Furtwängler-K. Reichhold, *Griechische Vasenmalerei: Auswahl hervorragender Vasenbilder*, I–III, Munich 1904–32.
Gardiner, *Athletics*	E. N. Gardiner, *Athletics of the Ancient World*, Oxford, 1930.
Hackl-Sieveking	K. Hackl-J. Sieveking, *Die kgl. Vasensammlung zu München*, I, Munich 1912.
Hampe, *Gleichnisse*	R. Hampe, *Die Gleichnisse Homers und die Bildkunst seiner Zeit*, Tübingen 1952.
Hartwig	P. Hartwig, *Die griechischen Meisterschalen der Blütezeit des strengen rotfigurigen Stiles*, Stuttgart-Berlin 1893.
Haspels, *Lekythoi*	C. H. E. Haspels, *Attic black-figured Lekythoi*, Paris 1936.
Hoppin, *RFV*	J. C. Hoppin, *A Handbook of Attic red-figured Vases*, Cambridge, Mass., 1919, I–II.
Hoppin, *BFV*	J. C. Hoppin, *A Handbook of Greek black-figured Vases*, Paris 1924.
Jacobsthal	P. Jacobsthal, *Ornamente griechischer Vasen*, Berlin 1927.
Jahn	O. Jahn, *Beschreibung der Vasensammlung König Ludwigs in der Pinakothek zu München*, Munich 1854.
Jeffery, *Scripts*	L. H. Jeffery, *The Local Scripts of Archaic Greece*, Oxford 1961.
Johansen	K. F. Johansen, *Les vases sicyoniens*, Paris-Copenhagen 1923.
Klein	W. Klein, *Die griechische Vasen mit Meistersignaturen*, Vienna 1887.
Kraiker	W. Kraiker, *Die Malerei der Griechen*, Stuttgart 1958.
Kretschmer	P. Kretschmer, *Die griechischen Vaseninschriften*, Gütersloh 1894.
Kunze, *Schildbänder*	E. Kunze, *Archaische Schildbänder (Olympische Forschungen*, II*)*, Berlin 1950.
Langlotz, *Zeitbest.*	E. Langlotz, *Zur Zeitbestimmung der strengrotfigurigen Vasenmalerei und der gleichzeitigen Plastik*, Leipzig 1920.

Matz F. Matz, *Geschichte der griechischen Kunst*, I, Frankfurt a.M. 1950.

Payne H. Payne, *Necrocorinthia*, Oxford 1931.

Perrot-Chipiez G. Perrot-Ch. Chipiez, *Histoire de l'art dans l'antiquité*, IX–X, Paris 1911, 1914.

Pfuhl E. Pfuhl, *Malerei und Zeichnung der Griechen*, Munich 1923 (3 vol.).

Pottier, *Cat.* E. Pottier, *Catalogue des vases antiques de terre-cuite*, Paris 1896.

Pottier, *VAL* E. Pottier, *Vases antiques du Louvre*, I–III, Paris 1897–1922.

Raubitschek, *DAA* A. Raubitschek, *Dedications from the Athenian Akropolis*, Cambridge, Mass. 1949.

Rayet-Collignon O. Rayet-M. Collignon, *Histoire de la céramique grecque*, Paris 1888.

RE *Paulys Real-Encyklopädie der classischen Altertumswissenschaft*, Stuttgart 1894ff.

Reinach S. Reinach, *Répertoire des vases peints*, I–II, Paris 1899–1900.

Richter, *Survey* G. M. A. Richter, *Attic red-figured Vases – A survey*, New Haven 1946, rev. ed. 1958.

Richter, *AVM* G. M. A. Richter, *Red-figured Athenian Vases in the Metropolitan Museum of Art* (New York), New Haven 1937.

Richter, *Shapes* G. M. A. Richter-J. Milne, *Shapes and names of Athenian Vases*, New York 1935.

Robert, *Heldensage* C. Robert, *Die Griechische Heldensage*, Berlin 1920–1926.

Robertson M. Robertson, *Greek Painting*, Geneva 1995.

Roscher W. H. Roscher, *Ausführliches Lexikon der griechischen und römischen Mythologie*, Leipzig 1884–1937.

Rumpf A. Rumpf, *Malerei und Zeichnung der Griechen*, Munich 1951.

Rumpf, *Ch V* A. Rumpf, *Die chalkidischen Vasen*, Berlin-Leipzig 1927.

Swindler M. H. Swindler, *Ancient Painting*, New Haven 1931.

Walters H. B. Walters, *History of ancient pottery*, London 1905.

INDEX TO COLLECTIONS

The plates are from photographs specially taken for this work, supplemented by pictures supplied by the following: Athens, German Archæological Institute: 2, 12, 13, 203. – Berlin, Ehemals Staatliche Museen: 118. – Boston, Museum of Fine Arts: 6, 164. – Copenhagen, Ny Carlsberg Glyptotek: 8. – New York, Metropolitan Museum of Art: 7, 24. – Stockholm, National Museum: 25.

INDEX

NOTE

Ordinary numbers refer to pages; italics refer not to illustrations but to commentaries upon the illustrations.
Abbreviations: cent. = century   Geom. = Geometric   incl. = including   P. = Painter   Protogeom. = Protogeometric

upon vase-painters, 15; influence of Meidias P. upon Italiote vase-painters, 387

ducks in Greek vase-painting, in Geom., *8*; 'Melian', *22–23a*

E, Group, see *Group E*

Egypt, 271, *40–6*, 297

Eileithyiai, by C Painter, *47–8*

EKPHANTOS (Corinthian vase-painter), 13

Eleusis, 12, *12–3*, 333, 359

ELEUSIS PAINTER, 359

Elis, *176–81*, *212–3*

Elpenor, by Lykaon P., 17

emotion in Greek vase-painting, in Leagros Group, *72*; pain depicted by Euphronios, 323, *108–11*; pain depicted by Sosias P., *118*; by Kleophrades P., *122–4*, XXX–XXXI; Polygnotos of Thasos, 16–7; 354; in mid-5th cent. vase-painting, 17; by Penthesilea P., *168–9*, *170–1*; Eretria P., 369–70

Enkelados, by Pronomos P.(?), 220

Eos, on Caeretan hydriai, 312; by Douris, 340, *144–5*; Pan P.(?), *164*; Hermonax, 358; Achilles P., 362; Aurora P., 385, *229*, XLVIII

Ephesus, 17, 322, *130–1*

EPIGNES (potter), 369

EPIKTETOS, 15, 304, 319–20, *96–8*, 323, 328, 343, 348

EPIKTETOS II (Kleophrades P.), 328

epinetron, by Eretria P., 369, *203*

Erechtheid tribe, 340

Erechtheus, by Oreithyia P., *158–9*

Eretria, 12, III, 323, XXXVII, 359–60, 361, 362, *186–7*, *200*, XLV, *201*, 369, *203*

ERETRIA PAINTER, 369–70, *202–3*, *206–11*, 375–6, *224*, *230–5*

ERGOTIMOS (potter), 286, *40–6*

Erichthonius, by Hermonax, 358, *182–3*

Eriphyle, by Shuválov P., 371; Meidias P., *214–5*. See also *238*

Eros, Erotes, by Lyandros P., *172*, XXXVI; Hermonax, *182–3*; Eretria P., *203*; Shuválov P., 375; Meidias P., 376; Pronomos P., *218–9*; Suessula P., 221; in Kerch vases, 382; by Meleager P., *222*; Helena P.(?), *223*; Pompe P., *224*; Marsyas P., XLVII, *225–8*; Sisyphos P., *236–7*; in Apulian, *238*, *239*

Erskine dinos, 285, *40–6*

Erymanthian boar, *78–9*, XXVII, *176–81*

Ethiopia, *144–5*

Etruria, *14–5*, *34*, *35–7*, *51*, *52*, 308, 310, 311–2, *99*, *155–7*, *238*; Etruscan graffitti, *100–4*, *170–1*; Etruscan Red-figure, 385, *229*, XLVIII; Black-figure, *230–5*

EUAION (son of Aeschylus), 15; as love-name, 334

EUAION PAINTER, 340

EUALKIDES, love-name of Smikros, 322, *105–7*

Euboea, in Geom., 266; Orientalizing, 271–2, III, *14–5*. See also 310

EUCHARIDES PAINTER, *206–11*

EUKLEIDES OF MEGARA (Greek philosopher), *184*

Euphorbos, in Rhodian, 27; by Achilles P., *362–3*

Euphorbos plate, 27, 29

EUPHRANOR (artist), influence on Marsyas P., 18

EUPHRONIOS, 15; as painter and potter, 16, 317, 318, 320; influence on Oltos, 320–1; compared with Oltos, *100–4*; 322; imitated by Smikros, *105–7*; 323–4, *108–15*, 326, *117*, *118*, 328, *119–21*, *125*; potting for Panaitios P., 323, *134*, *150–3*, 348, 349, *167*

EUPOLIS (dramatist), *176–81*

EUPOLIS PAINTER, *206–11*

EURIPIDES (dramatist), *88–9*, XXIX, *206–11*, *212–3*, *218–9*, *221*, *236–7*

Europa, on Caeretan hydriai, 312; by Berlin P., *154*, XXXV

Eurynome, *40–6*

Eurystheus, on Caeretan hydriai, *78–9*, XXVII; by Oltos, 320

Eurytos, in Corinthian, *32*, IX

Euthymachos, by Kleitias, *40–6*

EUTHYMIDES, 15, 317–8; influence on Epiktetos, 319–20; influence on Oltos, 320; compared with Oltos, *100–4*; compared with Euphronios, 323, 326, *116–7*, 328, 343–4, *150–3*, *158–9*

EUXITHEOS (potter), 320, *100–4*, 323

EXEKIAS, 13, 14, 272, *21*, 296–7; affinity with Amasis P., 298, *55–7*, XV, 300–1, *59–65*, XVII–XVIII; chronology of, 62–3, XVII; 305, *66–8*, XIX–XX, 72, 316, *96–7*, *150–3*; compared with Penthesilea P., *168–9*

'eye-cups', by Exekias, *59*, XVI; Epiktetos, 319, *96–7*; Oltos, 321

Falerii Veteres, *142*, 385, *229*, XLVIII

fawns in Greek vase-painting, in Geom., *6*; transitional Geom., *10*; Boeotian, *11*; by Berlin P., *150–3*

Fikellura ware, *30*, *51*

Formello, near Veii, *16–7*, IV

foxes in Greek vase-painting, in Geom., *6*; Protocorinthian, *16–7*, IV

François vase, 13, 285, *39*, 286, *40–6*, *50*, 304, *238*

'functional line', 17–8, 360–1, 382

funeral games in Greek vase-painting, of Pelias (in Corinthian), 13; of Patroclus, *27*; by Sophilos, *39*; by Kleitias, *40–6*

funerary plaques, see *plaque*

funerary vases, Geom., 11–2, 268, *4*, *5*, *7*, *9*; Orientalizing, 12, *18–20*; Black-figure, *38*; Apulian grave-amphorae, 387, Siciliote vases, 387. See also *lekythes* and *loutrophoros*

Furies, *206–11*; in Apulian, *239*

Fusco Cemetery (Syracuse), *14–5*, *191*

Ganymede, by Oltos, *100–4*; Berlin P., *155–7*; Hermonax, 358

Ge, by Penthesilea P., *170–1*; Hermonax, *182–3*; Pronomos P.(?), *220*. See also *214–5*

Gela, *164*, 354, *176–81*, 359, *196–9*, 387

GELA PAINTER, *206–11*

Geometric style, origins and development, 265–6; origins of humans and animals in, 11, 265; in Attica, 11, 265–6, *1–10*, I; in the Aegean, 12; the Argolid, 266; Corinth, 266; Laconia, 266; Boeotia, 266; Cyclades, 266, *24*; Euboea, 266; Rhodes, 266; Crete, 266; transition to Orientalizing, *10*, 270. See also *238*

Geryon, by Exekias, 300

Geryoneus, by Euphronios, 323, *113–5*

Gigantomachy, by Lydos, 296; Makron, 333; Niobid P., 354; Hermonax, 358; Pronomos P.(?), *220*; Suessula P., 221. See also *96–7*

GLAUKYTES (potter), *40–6*; *50*

Gnathia ware, 385, XLIX

goats in Greek vase-painting, in Protocorinthian, *16–7*, IV; Cycladic, *24*; Wild Goat style, *26*, *28*, *30*; Corinthian, VI, X–XI; by Sophilos, *39*; Kleitias, *40–6*; Tleson P., *293*; Inscription P., XXV

Gordian cups, 286

Gorgons in Greek vase-painting, in Protoattic, 12, *12–3*; on Nettos vase, *18–20*; Rhodian, *29*; by Gorgon P., *35–7*; Kleitias, 286; Amasis P., 298; Andokides P., *82–7*; Shuválov P., 371; Karneia P., *230–5*

Gorgon amphora, 12, *12–3*

401

Kraipale, on oinochoe in Boston, *206–11*

krater, in Geom., 11, 12, 265, *3, 5, 7, 24*; Laconian, 308; Chalcidian, 310; Siciliot, 387; S. Italian—popularity of kraters in, 386; Centuripan, LII
Volute kraters: by Kleitias (François vase), *40–6*; Phintias, 317; Euphronios, 323, *113–5*; Kleophrades P., 328; Berlin P., 343; Pan P., 346–7; Niobid P., 354, *176–81*; Kleophon P., 368; Polion, *206–11*; Pronomos P., 377; *218–9*; New York Centauromachy P., 382; Meleager P., 382; Aurora P., 385, *229*, XLVIII; Karneia P., *230–5*; Sisyphos P., *236–7*; in Apulian, *239*, L
Calyx-kraters: by Exekias, 300–1; Phintias, 317; Epiktetos, 319; Euphronios, 323, *108–11, 112*; Kleophrades P., 328–29; *119–21*; Myson, 332; Berlin P., 343; Pan P., 346–7; Niobid P., 16, 17, 19, 354, *173–5*; Achilles P., 362; Phiale P., XLI–XLII, XLIII–XLIV; Pronomos P.(?), *220*; Helena P.(?), *223*; Asteas, *240*; in Apulian, XLIX
Column-kraters, in Corinthian, *32*, IX, X–XI; by Myson, 332; Berlin P., 343; Pan P., 346–7, *165*; Orpheus P., *192*
Bell-kraters: by Berlin P., 343, *154*, XXXV, *155–7*; Pan P., 346–7, *160–3*; Niobid P., 354; Achilles P., 362

KRATES, love-name of Panaitios P., 334; of Berlin P., 343

KRITIOS (sculptor), XXVIII, *176–81*

Krokotos Group, XXII

Kuban Group, 314, XXVIII, *81*

kyathos, by Brygos P., 336

Kyknos, by Oltos, 320

kylix, see *cup*

Kyllene, *150–3*

Kynosarges amphora, *12–3*

Kypselid tribe, 271

KYPSELOS, see *Cypselus*

Kyzikos, by Niobid P.(?), *173–5*

Laconian vase-painting, on Caeretan hydriai, 310; by Niobid P., *173–5*; Meidias P., *214–5*; Marsyas P., XLVII; Aurora P., *229*, XLVIII

Laomedon, by Pronomos P., *218–9*

Lapiths in vase-painting, by Kleitias, *40–6*; Niobid P., *176–81*; Polygnotos-*190*; Sisyphos P., *236–7*

LEAGROS (common love-name), of Leagros Group, *72*; of Euphronios, 323, *108–11, 112*; of Euthymides,

326; of Panaitios P., 334, 340. See also 15, 348

Leagros Group, XXIII, *72*, 314

Lebes gamikos, 283; by Pan P., 347; Marsyas P., *225–8*; depicted by Eretria P., *203*. See also *238*

Leda, by Exekias, 301, *62–3*, XVII

lekanis, lid of, by Hermonax, 358; by Meidias P., 375; Lipari P., LI; Siciliote, 387

lekythos, Ovoid: by Amasis P., 298
Red figure: by Brygos P., 336; Berlin P., 343; Pan P., 347, *164*; Hermonax, 358
White ground: 17–8, *129*, 349, XXXVII, *182–3*; by Douris, 339, *221*; Achilles P., 359–63, XXXVIII–XXXIX, *185, 186–7*; Thanatos P., *184*; Phiale P., XLI–XLII, *189*; late white-ground, 369, *200–1*, XLV; Eretria P., 369–70
Squat: by Aison, *205*; Meidias P., 375; Apulian, *238*. See also *203*

Lemnos, *173–5*

Lenaea, *206–11*

LEONIDAS (king of Sparta), 20

Leontini, 387, XLIX

Lesbos, *212–3, 216–7*, XLVI

Lesche of the Cnidians at Delphi, see *club-room*

Leto, by Sophilos, 285; Kleitias, *40–6*; Phintias, *90–1*; Euthymides, 326; Penthesilea P.(?), *170–1*; Meidias P., *216–7*, XLVI

Leukippidai, rape of, by Meidias P., 19, *214–5*

LEWIS PAINTER (Polygnotos), *158–9*, 366

Limnaion, *206–11*

Linear B, 264

Linear Island style, *25*

Linos, by Pistoxenos P., *166*

lions in vase-painting, in Geom., *8*; transitional Geom., *10*; Laconian, 272; Euboean, III; Boeotian, *11*; Cycladic, V; Chiot, *28*; Protocorinthian, *16–7*, IV; Corinthian, VI, VII, *32*, IX; Protoattic, *12–3*; by Gorgon P., *35–7*; Sophilos, *39*; Kleitias, *40–6*; Painter N, XIII; Inscription P., XXV; Douris, *143b*

Lipari, 386–7, *240*, XLIX, LI

LIPARI PAINTER, *238*, LI

lip-cups, 14, 293, XIV, *49*

Little Masters, 14, 293, *47–51, 58*, XIII

Little-Master cups, 14, 293, *47–51, 58*, XIII, *52, 59*, XVI

Locri, *167, 239*

loutrophoros, II, *126–8*; by Kleophrades

P., 328–29, *126–8*; Pan P., 347; Hermonax, 358; Achilles P. and Sabouroff P., 363; Apulian, 387; loutrophoros-hydria, *129*

LOUVRE CENTAUROMACHY PAINTER, *206–11*

love-names, in 2nd half of 6th cent., 15; of Exekias, 300–1, *62–3*, XVII, *64–5*, XVIII; Leagros Group, *72*; Phintias, 317; Epiktetos, 319; Oltos, 320; Smikros, 322; Euphronios, 323, *108–11, 112, 113–5*; Euthymides, 326, *118*; Makron, 333; Douris, 333, 340; Panaitios P., 333–4; in 1st half of 5th cent., 334; Brygos P., 336; Berlin P., 343; Pistoxenos P., 348, *167*; Timocrates P.(?), XXXVII; Achilles P., 360, 363, XXXVIII–XXXIX, *185*; Kleophon P., 368; female love-names 333, 336; *kallistos* for *kalos*, 333; decline in the use of, *176–81*

Lucania, 19, 385, 386

Ludovisi throne, 358

LYANDROS PAINTER, *172*, XXXVI

Lycia, *184*

LYCURGUS PAINTER, 386

Lydia, 296, *130–1*

LYDOS, 13, 272, 296–7, *53*, 304, 314

LYKAON PAINTER, 17

Lyrnessos, *139–41*

LYSIPPIDES PAINTER, 14, 15, *69*, XXI, 314; collaborating with Andokides P., *88–9*, XXIX, *150–3*

LYSIPPOS (sculptor), *221*

Lysis, love-name of Euphronios(?), *113–5*; of Pistoxenos P., 348

Macmillan aryballos, *16–7*, IV

Maia, by Kleitias, *40–6*

major painting, Kimon of Cleonae, 15; Parrhasios, 17–8; Zeuxis, 17–9; Apollodoros, 18; Agatharchos of Samos, 18; Euphranor, 18; Polygnotos of Thasos, 16–8, 329; Mikon, *134*; influence on Niobid P., 354, 366, *173–5*; on white-ground lekythoi painters, 361; on Aison, *205*; on Meidias P., 376; on Suessula P., *221*; on Marsyas P., XLVII, *225–8*; on Italiote, 387, *236–7, 238*

MAKRON, 16, *132–3*, 332–3, 340, *146*, *206–11*

Marathon, battle of, 334; depicted by Polygnotos of Thasos, 354; by Mikon and Panainos, *173–5*

Marathonian bull, by Phintias, 318; Panaitios P., *134*

Marpessa, by Pan P., 347

Marseilles, 308

Marsyas, by Marsyas P., 384

MARSYAS PAINTER, 384, *225–8*, XLVII

MAUSSOLLOS (satrap of Caria), 382

meander, Boeotian oriental, *11*; 'battlement' style, *21*; on drapery, by Kleitias, *40–6*; 'T' variety, by Kleophrades P., *119–21*; 'labyrinth' variety by Kleophrades P., *122–4*, XXX–XXXI; 'Dourian' meander, *144–5, 147, 148*

Medea, by Meidias P., *214–5*; Sisyphos P., *236–7*

Medusa, in Protoattic, *12–3*; by Nettos P., *18–20*; Gorgon P., *35–7*; Karneia P., *230–5*

MEGAKLES, love-name of Phintias, *317*; of Euthymides, *326*; of Kleophon P., *368*; potter, *348*

MEIDIAS (potter), *375*

MEIDIAS PAINTER, 17, 18–9, *203*, *212–3*, *214–7*, XLVI, *375–6*, *377*, *380*, *381–2*, *224*, *387*, *230–5*, *238*

MELAS, love-name of Euphronios, *323*, *108–11*

Meleager, by Kleitias, *40–6*; on Little-master cup, *50*; by Meleager P., *382*

MELEAGER PAINTER, 382, *222, 238*

MELITTA, female love-name of Makron, *333*

Melos and 'Melian' vase-painting, 12, *22–3*; in Orientalizing, *271, 272*; amphorae, *22–23a, 23b, 380*

Memnon, by Douris, *340, 144–5*

MEMNON, love-name of Oltos, *320*

menads in vase-painting, by Painter N, XIII; Amasis P., *55, 59*, XVI; Lysippides P., *69*, XXI, *88–9*, XXIX; Rycroft P., *70*; Phintias, *92–5*; Oltos, *99, 100–4*; Kleophrades P., *122–4*, XXX–XXXI; Makron, *333*; Brygos P., *336*, XXXIV, *143a*; Douris, *340, 148*; Pan P., *160–3*; Pistoxenos P., *167*; Polygnotos, *190*; Kleophon P., *196–9*; Eretria P., *202*; Dinos P., *372, 206–11*; Pronomos P., *218–9, 220*(?); Meleager, *222*; Marsyas P., XLVII; Karneia P., *230–5*; Apulian, *239*, XLIX. See also *158–9*, XLIII–XLIV

Menelaus, in Rhodian, *27*; by Douris, *144–5*. See also *12–3, 146*

MENELAOS PAINTER, *206–11*

MENELAS PAINTER, *12–3*

Menelas stand, *12–3*

MENON (potter), *304*; love-name of Douris, *340*

'MENON PAINTER' (Psiax), *304*

MICALI PAINTER, *385*

MIKON (artist), associate of Polygnotos

of Thasos, 16–7, *134, 355, 173–5, 205, 387*

Milesian embroidery, *62–3*, XVII

MILTIADES (Athenian general), *173–5*; love-name, *334*

miniature painting, Protocorinthian, 12, *271*; by Little Masters, 14, *293, 47–51, 58*, XIII, XIV, *49*; by Amasis P., *298, 55, 56–7*, XV; Psiax, *304*; late 5th cent., *366*; Eretria P., *369–70, 203*

Minos, *134*

Minotaur, on Little-master cup, *50*; by Oltos, *320*; Kleophrades P., *329*. See also *286, 134*

Moirai, by Kleitias, *40–6*

Mopsos, on Little-master cup, *50*; by Inscription P., XXV

mourning scenes in vase-painting, in Geom., *11–2, 4, 5, 7*; in Euboean, III; by Exekias, *60–1*; Kleophrades P., *125, 126–8*; Bologna 228 P., *129*; on white-ground lekythoi, 18, *360*; by Thanatos P., *184*

Muses, by Kleitias, *40–6*; Achilles P., *360*, XXXVIII–XXXIX; Phiale P., XLIII–XLIV; Shuválov P., *370*; Sisyphos P., *236–7*; in Apulian, *239*

music in vase-painting, in Geom., *8*; Protoattic, *11*; Protocorinthian, *16–7*, IV; 'Melian', *22–23a*; by Kleitias, *40–6*; Amasis P., *55*; Lysippides P., *69*, XXI, *88–9*, XXIX; Epiktetos, *319*; Oltos, *100–4*; Smikros, *105–7*; Euphronios, *108–11, 113–5*; Kleophrades P., *122–4*, XXX–XXXI; Makron, *132–3*; Brygos P., *135–7, 138*, XXXIII, XXXIV, *142, 143a*; Douris, *148*; Berlin P., *343*; Pan P., *160–3, 165*; Pistoxenos P., *166*; Hermonax, *182–3*; Achilles, XXXVIII–XXXIX; Polygnotos, *366*; Phiale P., XLIII–XLIV; Kelophon P., *196–9*; Dinos P., *206–11*; Meidias P., *216–7*, XLVI; Pronomos P., *218–9*; Meleager P., *222*; Karneia P., *230–5*; Sisyphos P., *236–7*; in Apulian, XLIX

Mycenae, 265, *271*

MYSON, 318, 332, *130–1, 150–3, 347*

mythology: for different painters' treatment of mythological themes, see individually under the various characters

Naucratis, 12, *271, 297, 308, 73b, 311*

NAUCRATIS PAINTER, 308, *73b, 74*, XXIV

NAUKLEA, female love-name of Makron, *333*

Nausicaa, by Aison, 17

NAUSICAA PAINTER (Polygnotos), 366

Naxos, 12, *5, 271, 272, 14–5*; Heraldic Group, V

Nekyia, of Polygnotos of Thasos, 16, *354, 173–5*

Nemean lion, by Exekias, *300*; Psiax, *66–8*, XIX–XX; Oltos, *320–1*

Neoptolemos, by Leagros Group, *72*; Kleophrades P., *125*; Brygos P., *139–41*. See also *146*

Nereids, by Kleitias, *286, 40–6*; on Little-master cup, *49*, XIV; by Douris, *143b*; Eretria P., *370*; *203*; Marsyas P., XLVII; Aurora P., *229*, XLVIII

Nereus, by Kleitias, *40–6*; Douris, *143b*; Eretria P., *203*

NESIOTES (sculptor), XXVIII, *176–81*

Nettos, by Nettos P., *18–20*; on Caeretan hydria, *80*; Oltos, *320*

Nettos amphora, 12, *12–3, 18–20, 284, 35–7*

NETTOS PAINTER, *18–20, 21, 284, 35–7*

NEW YORK CENTAUROMACHY PAINTER, 382

'Nicosthenic' amphorae, by Nikosthenes, XIII; Oltos, *320, 99*

Nike, temple of on Acropolis, *326, 203*; by Suessula P., *221*; Lipari P., LI

NIKESERMOS (potter), *14–5*

NIKOPHILE, female love-name of Brygos P., *336*

NIKOSTHENES (potter), XIII, *58*, 297, 319

NIKOSTRATOS, love-name of Berlin P., *343*

NIKOXENOS PAINTER, XXIII, *88–89*, XIX

Nile, 308, 311

Niobids, slaughter of, by Niobid P., *173–5*

NIOBID PAINTER, 16, 17, *119–21, 146, 354–5, 173–81*, 366

Nocera dei Pagani, *206–11*

Nola, 31, *125, 204, 222*

Nolan amphorae, by Brygos P., *336*; Achilles P., *362*; Phiale P., XLI–XLII

Noto, *192*

N PAINTER, XIII. See also *10*

Nysa, XLIII–XLIV

Nysai, by Sophilos, *285*

obliquae imagines, invention of Kimon of Cleonae, 15

Odysseus, in Argive Orientalizing, *271*; Protoattic, *12–3*; on Aristonothos krater, *14–5*; Corinthian, *32*, IX; by Kleitias, *40–6*; on Caeretan hydria, *80*; by Penelope P., *129*; Lykaon P., 17, Aison P., 17. See also *236–7*

Oedipus, by Achilles P., *362–3*; in

Etruscan, 385. See also *33*, XII
Oileus, *125*
Oineus, by Meidias P., *214–5*
oinochoe, in Geom., 265, *3, 6*; Protocorinthian, *16–7*, IV; Rhodian, *26*; by Amasis P., 298, *54*; Epiktetos, 319; Brygos P., 336; Berlin P., 343; Niobid P., 355; white-ground, 359; Achilles P., 362; Polygnotos, 366; Eretria P., 369; Shuválov P., 371; Meidias P., 375; 'chous', *204, 224* (Pompe P.); on late 5th cent. Menad vases, *206–11*
Oinoe, battle of, painted by Polygnotos of Thasos, 356
Oinomaos, in Corinthian, 13. See also *212–3*
Oinopion, son of Dionysus, by Exekias, *64–5*, XVIII
Okeanos, by Kleitias, *40–6*
olpe, in Corinthian, *16–7*, IV, VII
OLTOS, 15, 320–1, *99–104*; compared with Euphronios, 323
Olympia, 13, *11*, *16–7*, IV, 322, *166*, 354, 363
OLYMPIODOROS, love-name of Panaitios P., 334
ONESIMOS, 333; is he the Panaitios P.?, 333, *149*
ONETORIDES, love-name of Exekias, 301, *62–3*, XVII, *64–5*, XVIII
Oreimachos, by Berlin P., *150–3*
Oreithyia, by Oreithyia P., *158–9*
OREITHYIA PAINTER, *158–9*
Orestes, in Apulian, *239*
Orientalizing style, in Attica, 12, *8*, *10*, 271–2, II, *12–3*; Corinth, 13, 271–2, *16–7*, IV, VI, VII, VIII, *31, 32*, IX; Euboea, 271–2, III; Laconia, 271–2; Boeotia, *11*; Argolid, 271–2; Cyclades, 12, 271–2, V; 'Melian', *22–23a, 23b*; Linear Island style, *25*; in Rhodes, 271–2, *27, 29*; Rhodian Wild Goat style, *26*; Chios, 271–2; Chiot Wild Goat style, *28*; Fikellura, *30*; in Crete, 271–2; Cyprus, 271–2; Naucratis, 271–2; Ionia, 271–2; Aristonothos krater, *14–5*; influence on Gorgon P., 284; on Sophilos, 285; on Kleitias, *40–6*; on Exekias, *62–3*, XVII; on Caeretan hydriai, 311
Oropos, XLI–XLII, *189*
Orpheus, by Pistoxenos P., 348
ORPHEUS PAINTER, 17, 366, *192*
Orphism, 387
Orsimes, by Brygos P., *139–41*
Orvieto, 19, *173–5*

Paestum, *88–9*, XXIX, 386–7, *238*
Paideia, by Meidias P., 376; Pronomos P., *218–9*
PAIONIOS (sculptor), *206–11*
palaestra, see *athletics*
Palamedes, *62–3*, XVII
Palladium, by Kleophrades P., *125*
PAMPHAIOS (potter), 319, 320, *99*
Pan, by Pan P., 346; in Apulian, XLIX. See also *218–9*
PAN PAINTER, 16, *160–5*, 332, 346–7, 360, *206–11*
PANAINOS (artist), *173–5*
PANAITIOS, love-name of Panaitios P., 333–4; of Douris, 340
PANAITIOS PAINTER, 323, 333–4, *134*, *149*, 340
Panathenaic amphora, 314, XXVIII, *81*; by Lydos, 296; by Tarquinia RC 6847 P., *71*; Kleophrades P., 328; -shape, by Myson, 332; Berlin P., 343; -shape, by Pan P., 347; -shape, by Niobid P., 355; Achilles P., 362
Pandrosos, by Oreithyia P., *158–9*
Pantikapaion (Kerch), 382, *225–8*
Papposilenus, by Phiale P., XLIII–XLIV; Pronomos P., *218–9*; in Apulian, *239*
Paris, in Protocorinthian, *16–7*, IV; by Exekias, *40–6*; C Painter, *47–8*; Inscription P., *75–6*, XXVI; Makron, 333; Douris, *144–5*; Penthesilea P., *350–1*; Helena P.(?), *223*
PARIS GIGANTOMACHY PAINTER, 336
Parnassus, *206–11*
Paros, 12, *25*, 271
PARRHASIOS (artist), influence on 5th cent. painters, 17; on Meidias P., 18; on white-ground painters, 361, 369, 370, 376, 382
Parthenon, in Athens, XLI–XLII, 366, 368, *193–5*, 221
Patroklos, in Rhodian, *27*; by Exekias, 300; Oltos, 320; Sosias P., *118*; Eretria P., 370; funeral games of, by Sophilos, *39*; Kleitias, *40–6*
PAUSANIAS (geographer), on the Chest of Cypselus, 13, *16–7*, IV, *40–6*; on the Clubroom of the Cnidians at Delphi, 16, 354, *173–5*, *238*
PAUSANIAS (king of Sparta), 380
Peitho, by Eretria P., *203*; Meidias P., 376, *214–5*; Marsyas P.(?), XLVII; in Pompeian wall-painting, *225–8*; in Apulian, L
Peleus, by Sophilos, 285; Kleitias, *40–6*; on Little-master cup, *50*; Inscription P., XXV; Euphronios, 325; Douris,

143b; Eretria P., *203*; Shuválov P., 371; Marsyas P., 18, XLVII; Aurora P., *229*, XLVIII
PELEUS PAINTER, 364
Pelias, funeral games of, in Corinthian, 13; by Inscription P., XXV
Pelike, by Smikros, *105–7*; Euphronios, 323; Euthymides, 326; Kleophrades P., *328–30*; Myson, 332; Berlin P., 343; Pan P., 347; Niobid P., 355; Hermonax, 358; Polygnotos, 366; Polygnotan school, *191*; Kleophon P., *196–9*; Lykaon P., 17; Marsyas P., 18, 384, XLVII
Peloponnesian War, *188*, XL, 369, *203*, *218–9*, 380, 381
Pelops, in Corinthian, 13; Meidias P.(?), *212–3*
PENELOPE PAINTER, *129*, *206–11*
Penthesilea, by Exekias, *64–5*, XVIII; Berlin P., 343; Penthesilea P., 17, 350, *168–9*; Niobid P.(?), *176–81*; Polygnotos, 366
Penthesilea cup, *350–1*, *168–9*, *170–1*, 366
PENTHESILEA PAINTER, 17, *64–5*, *168–71*; affinity with Pistoxenos P., 348, 349, *350–1*, 366
Peplos kore, 299, 301
PERICLES (Athenian statesman), 16, 317, 336
Periklymenos, in Corinthian, *33*, XII
Perithoos, by Amasis P., 298; Euthymides, *116*; Myson, *130–1*
Persephone, L
Perseus, in Protoattic, *12–3*, *18–20*; by Gorgon P., *35–7*; Amasis P., 298; Phiale P., XLIII–XLIV; Shuválov P., 371; Karneia P., *230–5*
perspective, as treated in major painting, 18; by Kleophrades P., 329, *125*; Myson, *130–1*; on white-ground lekythoi, 361; by Meidias P., 376; Marsyas P., XLVII
PEZZINO PAINTER, *184*
PHANODEMUS (Athenian writer), *206–11*
Phaon, by Polygnotos, 366; Meidias P., 18, *216–7*, XLVI
Pharsalos, *39*
PHEIDIADES, love-name of Smikros, 322; of Euphronios, 323
PHEIDIAS (sculptor), influence on Niobid P., 366; on Achilles P., 363, 366; on Polygnotos, 366; on Kleophon P., 368, *196–99*; on Eretria P., 370, *203*; on Dinos P., 372, *206–11*; on Meidias P., 376; influence in 4th cent., 381–2; on Italiote, *236–7*. See also *220*

PHIALE PAINTER, 18, 360–1, XLI–XLII, *189*, XLIII–XLIV, *206–11*

PHILLIADES, love-name of Euphronios, *113–5*

Philoktetes, by Meidias P., *214–5*

PHILON, love-name of Brygos P., 336

PHINTIAS, 304, *77*, 317–8, *90–5*; compared with Oltos, *100–4*; compared with Euphronios, 323, 326, 332, 343–4, *150–3*

Phocaea, 312

Phoenicia, 271

Phoinix, by Brygos P., *139–41*

Pholos, by Niobid P., *176–81*

Phosphoros, by Aurora P., *229*, XLVIII

PHRYNICUS (dramatist), 340

PHRYNOS (potter), 293

PHRYNOS PAINTER, 293, *52*

Pikrodaphne, *129*

PINDAR (poet), *77*, *130–1*, *212–3*

Piraeus, *218–9*, 380

Pisa, *212–3*

PISISTRATUS (tyrant of Athens), 16, 301, *62–3*, XVII, 319

PISTICCI PAINTER, 386

PISTOXENOS (potter), 319, 348, *166*

PISTOXENOS PAINTER, 16, 323, 348–49, 350, *166–7*, *172*, XXXVI, XXXVII, 359

Pithekousa, *14–5*

pithos, 11, *12–3*, 24, V, *55*, *47–8*, *78–9*, XXVII

plaques, by Lydos, 296; by Exekias, 14, *60–1*. See also *238*

plastic snakes, 12, *6*, *9*, *10*, II

Plataea, battle of, 334

plates, Rhodian, 27, *29*; by Epiktetos, 319, *98*; Euthymides, 326; Makron, 332; Brygos P., 336; Berlin P., 343

PLATO (philosopher), 20, *206–11*

PLINY (Roman writer), on Kimon of Cleonae, 15; on Polygnotos of Thasos, 16–7, *173–5*; on Parrhasios, 17–8, 361

POLEMON (Athenian archon), 314

POLION, *206–11*

Polites, by Kleitias, *40–6*

POLLIAS, father of Euthymides, 326, *117*

POLLUX, JULIUS (grammarian and critic), *144–5*, *204*

polychromy, in Protocorinthian, 12, *16–7*, IV; Corinthian, X–XI, *33*, XII; Cycladic, V; Rhodian, 27, Chiot, 28; 'Melian', *22–23a*; Laconian, *73*, *74*, XXIV; Caeretan hydriai, 311, *77*; by Little Masters, 14; Psiax, 14; Pistoxenos P., 16, 348–49, *167*; Penthesilea

P., 350, *168–9*, *170–1*; white ground lekythoi, 18, 360; limitations due to firing, 349, 360–1; Achilles P., XXXVIII–XXXIX, *185*, *186–7*; Phiale P., XLI–XLII, *189*, XLIII–XLIV; Woman P., *201*; Eretria P., 370, *202*; Pronomos P., *218–9*; Meidias P., *214–7*, XLVI, 381–2; in 4th cent., 381–2, *224*, XLVII, *225–8*; Asteas, 386; Italiote, 386–7; Siciliote, 387; Apulian, *239*, XLIX; Lipari P., LI; Centuripan, LII; Kerch vases, 19

Polydeuces, see Castor and Polydeuces

POLYGNOTOS, 364, *190*, 368, 371, 372, 382, 387; Polygnotan School, *191*, *206–11*, *218–9*

POLYGNOTOS of Thasos (artist), use of 4 basic colours, 17; influence on Red-figure painters, 16–8; affinities with Kleophrades P., 329, *129*, 354, *173–5*; affinities with Meidias P., 18, 376; influence on Aison, *205*; on Italiote vases, 387, *236–7*, *238*

POLYKLEITOS (sculptor), *188*, XL

Polyneikes, by Shuválov P., *370*

Polyphemos, in Argive, 271; on Aristonothos krater, *14–5*; on Caeretan hydriai, 312, *80*

'POLYPHEMOS PAINTER', *12–3*

POLYPHRASMON, love-name of Douris, 340

Polyxena, by Kleitias, *40–6*; Brygos P., *139–41*

Pompeii, *218–9*, XLVII, *225–8*, 387

'Pontic' vases, 385

Populonia, *216–7*, XLVI

Porphyrion, by Pronomos P.(?), 220; Suessula P., *221*

Poseidon, by Kleitias, *40–6*; C Painter, *47–8*; Amasis P., *54*, *56–7*, XV; Exekias, 300; Berlin P., 343; Suessula P., *221*. See also *134*, *212–3*

Poseidonia, see *Paestum*

Pothos, by Polygnotos, 366; Meidias P., *216–7*, XLVI

potnai thērōn in Boeotian, *11*; Rhodian, *29*; by Kleitias, *40–6*

PRAXITELES, love-name of Makron, 333; (sculptor), *221*, 382, XLVII

Priam, by Kleitias, *40–6*; C Painter, *47–8*; Leagros Group, *72*; Euthymides, 326, *117*; Kleophrades P., *125*; Brygos P., *139–41*

PROCLUS (philosopher), *144–5*

Proetus, daughters of, Hermonax, 358

Prokrustes, by Panaitios P., *134*

Prometheus, by Douris, *148*; Dinos P., 372

PRONOMOS (musician), by Pronomos P., 377, *218–9*, 222(?)

PRONOMOS PAINTER, 377, *218–9*, 222

prothesis, in Geom., 11, *4*, *7*; Black-figure, *60–1*; Kleophrades P., *215*, *126–8*; Bologna 228 P., *129*

Protoattic style, 12, 271–2, II, *11*, *12–3*; chronology of, *21*, 285

Protocorinthian style, 12, *9*, 271–2, *12–3*, *16–7*, IV

Protogeometric style, in Attica, 265, 266, *1*, 268

Protome Group, V

'Proto-Panaitian Group', 334

PROVIDENCE PAINTER, 344

PSIAX, 14, *66–8*, XIX–XX, 304, *70*, XXII, *71*, *126–8*, *129*

psychology in vase-painting, 17; in Exekias, *62–3*, XVII, *64–5*, XVIII; Pistoxenos P., 349; Penthesilea P., 351, *168–9*, 354; Achilles P., *185–8*, XXXVIII–XL; Kleophon P., 368

psykter, by Inscription P., 310; Phintias, 317; Euphronios, 318, 323; Oltos, 320; Smikros, *105–7*; Euthymides, 326; Kleophrades P., 328; Myson, *130–1*; Douris, 339–40; Pan P., 347

purpose of Greek vases, 19, *122–4*, XXX–XXXI, *129*, 359

Pygmies and Cranes, battle of, by Kleitias, *40–6*; as rhyta, XXXII

PYRRHOS, *14–5*

Pythagoreanism, 387

PYTHAIOS, love-name of Douris, 340

PYTHON (potter), 317, 339, 340, *143b*; (Italiote vase-painter), 386

pyxis, in Geom., 265; by C Painter, *47–8*; Makron, 332–3; Penthesilea P., 350; white-ground, 359; by Eretria P., 369–70; Meidias P., 375; Aison, 17; in Siciliote, 387; by Lipari P., *238*; Washing P., *238*

R, Group, see *Group R*

rabbits in vase-painting, in Geom., VII; by Amasis P., *56–7*, XV; on Caeretan hydriai, 311; by Andokides P., *82–7*

RAM JUG PAINTER, *14–5*

Randazzo, *165*

REED PAINTER, 18, 359, *200*, XLV

Red-figure, *Attica:* transition from Black-figure, *66–72*, XIX–XXIII; Attic beginnings and Late-archaic period, 15–6, *82–157*, XXIX–XXXV; Attic Early Classical and Classical, *158–83*, *188*, *190–9*, XXXVI, XL; by white-ground artists, 361–2; Late Classical to end of 5th cent., 17, *202–21*,

XLVI; Attic 4th cent., *222–8*, XLVII *Non-Attic Red Figure*: Etruscan, 385, *229*, XLVIII; Italiote and Siciliote, *386–7, 230–40*, XLIX–LII

Reggio, see *Rhegion*

RETORTED PAINTER, 382

Revelry and Dionysiac themes, in Fikellura, *30*; by Kleitias, *40–6*; Amasis P., *55*; Psiax, 304; Lysippides P., *69*, XXI; Rycroft P., *70*; Andokides P., *88–9*, XXIX; Phintias, *92–5*; Epiktetos, 319; Oltos, 320; Euphronios, *113–5*; Euthymides, *117*; Kleophrades P., 16, *122–4*, XXX–XXXI; Myson, 332; Makron, 16, 333, *132–3*; Panaitios P., 334; Brygos P., 16, 336, *135–7, 138*, XXXIII, XXXIV, *143a, 142*; Douris, 16, 340, *148*; Berlin P., *150–3*; Pan P., *160–3, 165*; Achilles P., 362; Polygnotos, 366; Kleophon P., *196–9*; Dinos P., 372, *206–11*; Meidias P., 376; Meleager P., 382, *222*; Asteas, 386; Karneia P., *230–5*

Rhegion, 308

Rhodes, in Geom., 265; Orientalizing, *12–3*, 271–2, *27, 29*; influence on Attica, *21*; Wild Goat style, *26*; Fikellura, *30*. See also 293, VI

RHODOPIS, female love-name of Makron, 333

rhyton, as distinct from Head Vase, XXXII; by Brygos P., 336, *142*; Douris, 339; Eretria P., 369

RUNNING MAN PAINTER, *30*

Ruvo, 202, 208–9, 220, 236–7, 239

RYCROFT PAINTER, *70, 71*

SABOUROFF PAINTER, affinity with Pistoxenes P., 348, 359, 360, 361; collaboration with Achilles P., 363

Salamis, battle of, 334

Samos, *30*, 308

Sanctuary of Dioscuri (*Anakeion*), in Athens, 16, 354

Sanctuary of Theseus, in Athens, 354, *176–81*

Santa Maria Capua Vetere, *144–5*

SAPPHO (poetess), 323; by Achilles P.(?), XXXVIII–XXXIX

Sarpedon, *144–5; 184*

SARPEDON PAINTER, *184*

satyrs in vase-painting, by Kleitias, *40–6*; Painter N, *40–6*; Amasis P., *55, 59*, XVI; Psiax, 304; Lysippides P., *69*, XXI, *88–9*, XXIX; Phintias, *90–5*; Epiktetos, 319–20, *96–7*; Oltos, 320, *99, 100–4*; Kleophrades P., *122–4*, XXX–XXXI; Panaitios P., 334;

as Head Vases, XXXII; by Brygos P., XXXIV, *143a*; Douris, 339–40, *148*; Berlin P., 343, *150–3*; Pistoxenos P., *167*; Polygnotos, *190*; Papposilenus (by Phiale P.), XLIII–XLIV; Kleophon P., *196–9*; Eretria P., *202*; Shuválov P., *204*; Dinos P., 372; Pronomos P., *218–9*,(?) *220*; Meleager P., 222; Marsyas P., XLVII; Karneia P., *230–5*; in Apulian, *239*

satyr-plays, *166, 206–11, 218–9, 230–5*

sculpture, influenced by Geom. painting, 266; by Orientalizing, 271; compared with Ripe Black-figure, 14; influence on Black-figure, 14, 16; compared with Exekias, 301, *62–3*, XVII; with Andokides P., 316; with Euphronios, 323, *108–11*; with Berlin P., 344; Anavyssos kouros, 129–30; Athena Lemnia of Pheidias, *143b*; Temple of Zeus at Olympia, *166*, 354; Ludovisi throne, 358; Doryphoros of Polykleitos, *188*, XL; the 'Blonde Boy', *188*, XL; 'Poseidon' from Artemisium, *188*, XL; Pheidias, 366, 368; Nike of Paionios, *206–11*; Nike balustrade, *203, 206–11*; Athena Parthenos, *220, 221*; influence on vases in 4th cent., *382*, XLVII; influence of Phigaleia frieze on Sisyphos P., *386, 238*; influence of 'Vulci bronzes' on Micali P., 385

Scythia, *40–6*

Scythian archers, 304; by Epiktetos, *98*; Euphronios, *113–5*; Myson, *130–1*

Selene, by Sosias P., *118*; Pronomos P. (?), *220*

'self-portrait', by Smikros, *105–7*

Selinus, *14–5*

Semele, XLVIII–XLIV

ships in vase-painting, in Geom., 12, *7*, 265; on Aristonothos krater, *14–5*; by Kleitias, *40–6*; on Little-master cup, *58*; by Exekias, *59*, XVI; on Arkesilas cup, *74*, XXIV

SHUVÁLOV PAINTER, 370–1, *204*

Siana cups, 293; by C Painter, *47–8*; Lydos, 296; Heidelberg P., 298

Sicily, *14–5*, 308, 359, 362; Siciliote vase-painting, 376, 386–7

'sigma' pattern, in Geom., *10*; Black-figure, *21*

signatures, see *inscriptions*

SIMONIDES (poet), 20

Siphnian Treasury, at Delphi, 14

sirens in vase-painting, in Corinthian, 271, VI, X–XI, *33*, XII; Black-figure,

21; Gorgon P., *35–7*; Sophilos, *39*; on Little-master cup, *58*; Inscription P., XXV

Siris, 386

Sisyphos, *236–7*

SISYPHOS PAINTER, 386, *236–7*

Skiron, by Panaitios P., *134*

skyphos, in Chalcidian, 310; by Epiktetos, 319; Oltos, 320; Makron, 332–3; Brygos P., 336, *135–7*; Pan P., *164*; Pistoxenos P., 348, *166*; Penthesilea P., 350; Lewis P., 366; Shuválov P., 371; on late 5th cent. Menad vases, *206–11*; by Aurora P., 385

Skyros, XLVII

SMIKROS, 322, *105–7*, 323

SMIKYTHOS, love-name of Euphronios, 323

Smyrna, *14–5*, 310

SOCRATES (philosopher), 17

SOKRATES, love-name of Berlin P., 343

SOPHILOS, 13, *39*; signature, V; 285, 286

SOPHOCLES (dramatist), *166*, 351, XLIII–XLIV, *206–11, 212–3, 236–7*

SOSIAS (potter), *118*

SOSIAS PAINTER, *118*

SOSTRATOS, love-name of Phintias, 317

SOTADES PAINTER, 359, 361

Spain, 308

Sparta, 308, 380, *230–5*

sphinxes in vase-painting, in Protocorinthian, *16–7*, IV; Corinthian, 271, VI, *33*, XII; Protoattic, II, III; by Gorgon P., *35–7*; Kleitias, *40–6*; Painter N, XIII; on Little-master cups, XIV, *49, 50*; Caeretan hydriai, 311; by Hermonax, 358; Achilles P., 363; in Etruscan, 385

Spina, 350–1, 354, *173–5*, 358, 362, 368, 370, 371, *206–11, 218–9, 224*

stags in vase-painting, in Geom., *3*; 'Melian', *22–23a*; Cycladic, *25*; Corinthian, *32*, IX; by Kleitias, *40–6*; Amasis P., *56–7*, XV; Aurora P., *229*, XLVIII

stamnos, by Oltos, 320, *99*; Smikros, 322, *105–7*; Euphronios, 323; Kleophrades P., 328–29; Berlin P., 343; Pan P., 347; Hermonax, 358, *182–3*; Achilles P., 362; Phiale P., XLI–XLII; Polygnotos, 366, *190*; Kleophon P., 368, *193–5*; Dinos P., *206–11*; Villa Giulia P., *206–11*; on Menad vases in late 5th cent., *206–11*; Aurora P., 385; in Etruscan, 385; Siciliote, 387

STESIAS, love-name of Exekias, 300

STESICHORUS (poet), *47–8*